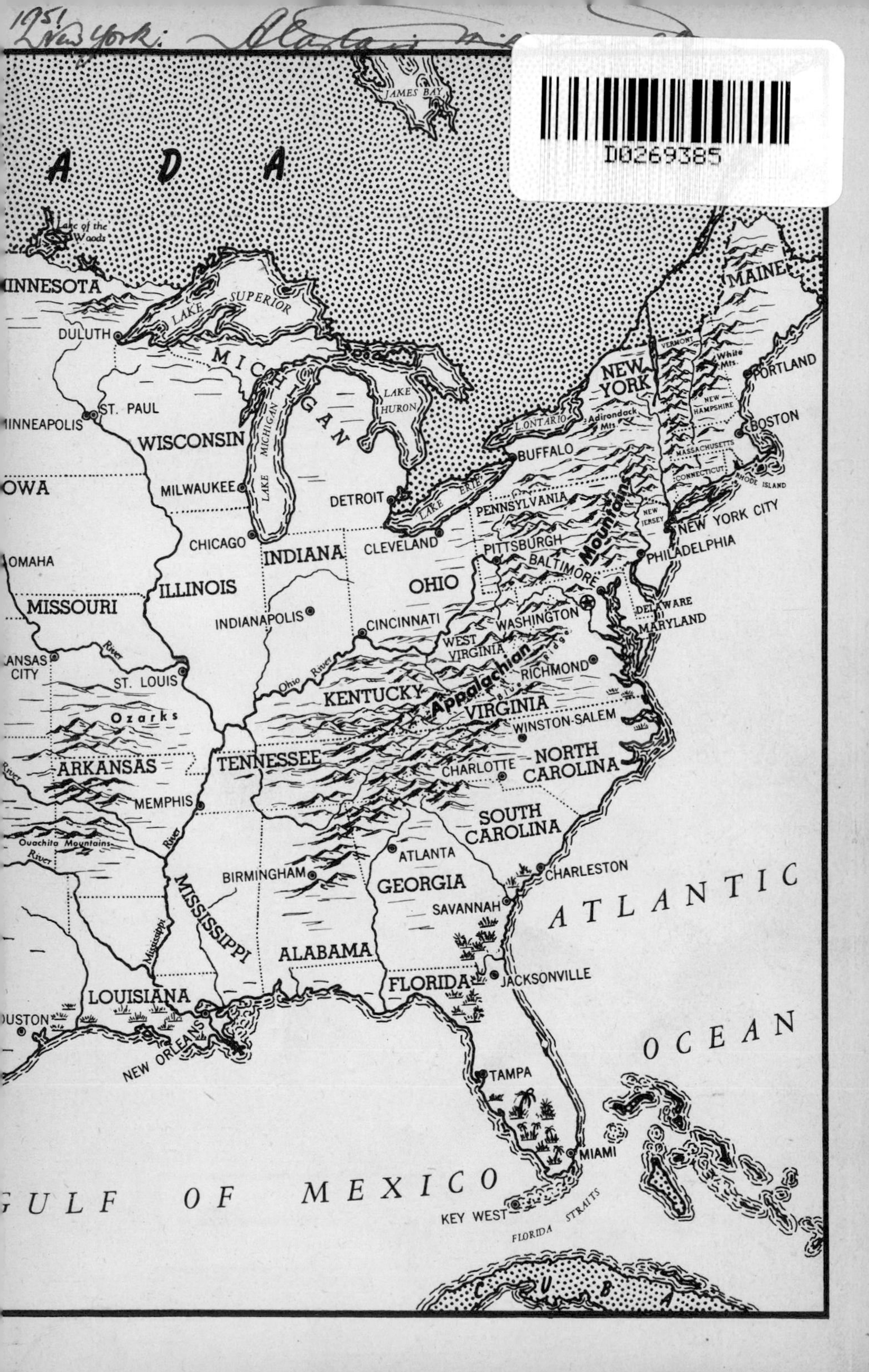
JAMES BAY
A D A
Lake of the Woods
INNESOTA
LAKE SUPERIOR
DULUTH
MICHIGAN
ST. PAUL
INNEAPOLIS
WISCONSIN
LAKE MICHIGAN
LAKE HURON
MILWAUKEE
OWA
DETROIT
LAKE ERIE
CHICAGO
INDIANA
CLEVELAND
OMAHA
ILLINOIS
OHIO
MISSOURI
INDIANAPOLIS
CINCINNATI
River
ANSAS CITY
ST. LOUIS
Ohio River
KENTUCKY
Ozarks
ARKANSAS
TENNESSEE
MEMPHIS
Ouachita Mountains
River
MISSISSIPPI
Mississippi
BIRMINGHAM
ALABAMA
ATLANTA
GEORGIA
LOUISIANA
OUSTON
NEW ORLEANS
FLORIDA
JACKSONVILLE
TAMPA
MIAMI
KEY WEST
FLORIDA STRAITS
GULF OF MEXICO
C U B A
MAINE
VERMONT
White Mts.
PORTLAND
NEW YORK
NEW HAMPSHIRE
L. ONTARIO
Adirondack Mts.
BOSTON
MASSACHUSETTS
BUFFALO
CONNECTICUT
RHODE ISLAND
PENNSYLVANIA
NEW JERSEY
NEW YORK CITY
PITTSBURGH
PHILADELPHIA
BALTIMORE
DELAWARE
MARYLAND
WASHINGTON
WEST VIRGINIA
Appalachian Mountains
Blue Ridge
RICHMOND
VIRGINIA
WINSTON-SALEM
NORTH CAROLINA
CHARLOTTE
SOUTH CAROLINA
CHARLESTON
SAVANNAH
ATLANTIC OCEAN
D0269385

Ex Libris

ALASTAIR M. DUNNETT

$8.00
11718

# *The American Guide*

# *The American Guide*

A SOURCE BOOK
AND
COMPLETE TRAVEL GUIDE
FOR
THE UNITED STATES

EDITED BY
HENRY G. ALSBERG

*Hastings House*

PUBLISHERS NEW YORK

# *Editors*

HENRY G. ALSBERG

MARY BARRETT
EDWARD DREYER
DORA THEA HETTWER
WILLIAM R. McDANIEL
WALTER McELROY
H. H. MILLER
JOSEPH MILLER
DALE L. MORGAN
MONTANA LISLE REESE
ELLEN M. ROLLINS

TYPOGRAPHY BY CARL PURINGTON ROLLINS

COPYRIGHT 1949 BY HASTINGS HOUSE

*Printed in the United States of America*

All rights reserved including the right to reproduce this book or parts thereof in any form

# PREFACE

Although work on *The American Guide* was first begun only some four and a half years ago, the idea of a guide-book for the entire United States dates back to the early days of the Federal Writers' Project of the WPA. When that organization envisaged a plan for its State Guides, a plan that was eventually carried to completion, the director and editorial staff of the project also considered the possibility of doing a national guide as the logical capstone to the whole undertaking. By the time the State Guides were well under way, first steps were taken to lay the groundwork for this final volume.

With the limitations put on the Writers' Project in 1939, however, and its termination, the scheme had to be dropped. But the plan of the one-volume guide for the whole country was not abandoned. The need for such a book seemed clear. The last all-over guide for the United States had been the Baedeker of 1910.

Several attempts were made to secure private support for this far-reaching project. Finally, after considerable discussion, Hastings House decided to back it. Although a great deal of preliminary exploration was done, neither the publisher nor the editor at the time realized the vast scope and difficulties of the undertaking. From very small beginnings the editorial staff gradually expanded, and, while its headquarters remained in New York City, editors in the various states were added as work proceeded. In addition to the independent research carried on by the editorial staff, a huge correspondence developed with governmental agencies—Federal, State and Municipal, with public and private organizations and with some thousands of individuals. More than one hundred thousand points of interest had to be checked; this was done, in part at least, by correspondence which brought in a huge amount of material. After assembly of all the data, the problem of condensation into one volume faced the editors. The first text, when completed, far exceeded the space available, and a second and after that a third process of condensation had to be carried out. Nevertheless, the selection and elimination were done always with an eye to retaining the most essential points of interest and the most colorful material. The result is presented to the public as a reasonably complete coverage, in guide-book form, of the contemporary United States.

THANKS are due the governmental agencies that have cooperated by supplying information and checking data. And equally, acknowledgments are due the many organizations—scientific, historical and antiquarian societies, universities and other educational institutions, house and garden clubs, chambers of commerce, museums, etc.—which have patiently and helpfully responded to requests for information. Thanks also are due the individuals throughout the country who cheerfully answered requests for information—concerning an old house, an historic church, a covered bridge, a scenic point of interest—often undertaking considerable local research to identify and properly describe the subject of inquiry.

In addition to the editors who have labored with the greatest devotion to bring the book to completion, other members of the staff, Floreida Bush, Rose Bussolini,

Helene Cunningham, Max de Novellis, Gorham Munson, B. B. Perry, Karl Pinner, Nedda Tichenor and Marion Ullstein, have rendered valuable service. Acknowledgment is due Miss Jeannette Eckman who painstakingly checked much of the Delaware material. Finally, the editors wish to express their appreciation of the patient understanding and constant encouragement given them throughout the duration of the work by Mr. Walter Frese, President of Hastings House. Thanks are due Mr. Bailey A. Bill, who gave his generous interest and support and Mr. Herbert P. Spencer, who with tireless patience solved the many and difficult production problems.

# HOW TO USE THE AMERICAN GUIDE

Because of limitations of space it has been necessary to employ an extremely condensed style and to make use of a comparatively large number of abbreviations, a list of which is given at the back of the book.

*The American Guide* divides the country into eight regions: New England, the Middle Atlantic States, the Lake States, the Plains States, the South, the Southwest, the Mountain States and the West Coast. Each region is described separately and is prefaced by a general essay. Within each region, with the exception of New England (where tours run through from one state into the next), each state is described by tours within that state.

Main tours follow main U.S. highways, or the more important state highways, and are identified by the highway number. They run east-west and north-south, except in the upper half of the country where there are some south-north tours. Tours generally run from state border to state border and link up with tours (and highways) in adjacent states. Mileage on main tours is indicated by figures in boldface type followed by a period (i.e., **12. 52. 89.**), and is measured to the nearest half mile. Within each section of a tour, mileage indicated is cumulative until the end of a section is reached. Towns and other points of interest on the main highways are in boldface capitals (i.e., **CENTERVILLE**). Points of interest within towns and all points not on the main highways are in boldface also, but in capital and small letters (i.e., **Long Beach**). From the main highways, side trips branch off at many points. These are indicated by the words SIDE TRIP and are set in smaller type. Side trips branching off from side trips are indented. All side-trip mileage is indicated by the superior "m" (i.e., $12^{m}$ $52^{m}$ $89^{m}$) and such mileage is also cumulative but only for the particular side trip.

The most important cities and the most important national parks, state parks, and other distinctive areas are described separately in each state section after the tours; cities are listed alphabetically. In cities and regions where there are numerous points of interest, such points are numbered. Points of interest in the vicinity of a large city are described in trips out of that city, such trips being, in general, limited to round-trip distances which may be easily covered in a day's journey.

Brief and very general information on transportation, accommodations, recreation facilities, and annual events for larger cities and towns is given (in small type).

Tour maps for each section, showing all main tours, are included, as are detailed maps of the larger cities. On the latter, points of interest are numbered to correspond to their numbers in the text.

In the text the word "see" in parentheses (see) indicates that the subject is treated elsewhere and the reader is referred to the Index, unless the reference is to a highway number. In the latter case the reader should consult that highway tour in the same state.

The Table of Contents lists the states under the regions in which they are included. The highways described in each state and the cities and areas given separate treatment are listed under that state.

# GENERAL INFORMATION

THE UNITED STATES OF AMERICA, bounded on the east by the Atlantic Ocean & on the west by the Pacific, on the north by Canada & on the south by Mexico & the Gulf of Mexico, comprises 48 States & a Federal District (which constitute the "continental" United States) &, in addition, 2 territories, Alaska & Hawaii, & a number of dependencies, including Puerto Rico & the Virgin Islands, the Panama Canal Zone, & numerous islands in the Pacific. The area of the continental United States is 3,022,367 square miles; the total area, including territories & dependencies, 3,619,000 square miles. The continental United States extends south from the 49th parallel to latitude 25°50′ (at the southernmost tip of Texas); its easternmost point is West Quoddy Head, Me. (longitude 66°57′) & its westernmost, Cape Alava, Wash. (longitude 124°44′). Its geographic center is near Lebanon, Smith County, Kansas. From east to west, its maximum distance is 2,807 miles; from north to south, 1,598 miles. The smallest of the 48 states is Rhode Island (1,214 square miles); the largest, Texas (267,339 square miles).

*Topography:* The Atlantic Coast of the continental United States is edged by a seaboard lowland & hinterland Piedmont strip, beyond which (except in the far south) rises the Appalachian Mountain system (6,000′ to 7,000′ at its highest), running north & south. The Adirondacks, a separate mountain group in northern New York, are geologically the oldest in the Western Hemisphere. West from these eastern mountains, the central plains of the Mississippi Valley sweep for 1,000 miles. North of them are the Great Lakes (Ontario, Erie, Huron, Michigan & Superior), world's biggest inland body of fresh-water; south of the plains, the low-lying, swamp-fringed Gulf Coast. The central plains rise gradually to a plateau area known as the Great Plains, bordered on the west by the lofty ranges, running north & south, of the Rocky Mountains, & through which runs the Continental Divide. West of the Rocky Mountains is the Great Basin, a high arid tableland, partly desert & traversed by numerous mountain ranges. To the west rise the Cascades & the Sierra Nevada, dominating the chain of fertile valleys which parallels the Pacific Coast. The latter is abruptly edged by a coastal range of generally lesser altitude.

The chief river of the continental U.S. is the Mississippi, draining the whole area between the Appalachians & the rockies, flowing c.2,550 miles from northern Minn. to the Gulf of Mexico. Its principal tributaries are the Ohio, flowing west from the Appalachians, & the Missouri, flowing east from the Rockies; other important tributaries, flowing eastward, are the Arkansas & the Red. The St. Lawrence, flowing from the Great Lakes to empty into the Atlantic, forms part of the country's northern border; & the Rio Grande, emptying into the Gulf of Mexico, part of its southern.

Among the chief rivers of the Atlantic Coast are the Hudson, running into New York Harbor; the Delaware, running into Delaware Bay; & the Potomac, running into Chesapeake Bay. Among those of the Pacific Coast are the Columbia in the northwest & the Colorado in the southwest. All of the rivers named (except the Arkansas, Rio Grande & Colorado) are navigable for considerable distances (the Missouri & Red by light-draft vessels only). They comprise, together with the N.Y. State Barge System, the Illinois Waterway, the San Joaquin-Sacramento River system of California & the Great Lakes, a network of inland waterways. Other important rivers include the Connecticut, Susquehanna & James on the Atlantic Coast; the Tennessee & Cumberland, which are tributaries of the Ohio; & the Tombigbee & Warrior in Alabama on the Gulf Coast. Maine has four rivers navigable inland for considerable distances. Along most of the Atlantic & Gulf Coasts extend Intracoastal Waterway, sheltered from the open sea.

Among the chief natural wonders of the continental U.S. are Niagara Falls on the N.Y.-Canada border; Mammoth Cave in Kentucky, Carlsbad Caverns in New Mexico & Wind Cave in South Dakota; Bryce & Zion Canyons in Utah, the Grand Canyon of the Colorado in Arizona, Hells Canyon of the Snake River on the Idaho-Oregon border; the geysers of Yellowstone National Park in Wyoming; Yosemite Valley in California; Crater Lake in Oregon; Mt. Lassen in California, only recently active volcano in the continental U.S.; Mt. Hood in Oregon; Mt. Rainier in Washington, with the greatest single-peak glacial system in the U.S.; Mt. Whitney & Death Valley in California, the highest & the lowest points, respectively, in the continental U.S.

*Population:* The 1940 census gave the population of the continental U.S. as 131,669,275; the estimated population, on April 30, 1947, was 143,592,000. The population density (in 1940) was 44.2 per square mile. The most populous states (1940) were, in order, New York, Pennsylvania, Illinois, Ohio & California. Since 1940 California is estimated to have risen in population to third place. Five cities have populations exceeding 1,000,000; in order of rank according to the 1940 census these were New York, Chicago, Philadelphia, Detroit & Los Angeles. Since 1940, Los Angeles is estimated to have risen to fourth place. Twelve other cities were estimated in 1948 to have populations of 500,000 or more: Cleveland, Baltimore, St. Louis, Boston, Pittsburgh, Washington, San Francisco, Milwaukee, Buffalo, New Orleans, Minneapolis & Cincinnati.

*Climate:* The range in gradations of climate, from north to south, is between north temperate & sub-tropical. At Duluth, Minn., the average January temperature is 8°, the average July temperature, 64°; at Brownsville, Texas, the average January temperature is 60°, the average July temperature, 84°. In most of the rest of the country, average temperatures range between these extremes. From east to west, wide variations occur. The highest average annual precipitation—120 inches—occurs on the coast of Oregon, at Tillamook; the lowest, in Death Valley, California, where the highest temperature ever recorded in the U.S. (134°) occurred in 1931.

*Time:* The U.S. is divided into four time zones: Eastern (which is 5 hours earlier than Greenwich time), Central, Mountain & Pacific. The use of Daylight Saving Time (1 hour in advance of Standard Time) is a matter of local option; it is used in most of the larger cities of the eastern U.S. during the summer months.

*Currency:* The monetary system of the U.S. is based on the gold standard. Its currency follows the decimal system; the basic unit, the dollar, being divisible into 100 cents. Coins in common circulation are the penny (1 cent), the nickel (5 cents), the dime (10 cents), the quarter (25 cents) & the 50-cent piece. The silver dollar is less commonly used than the paper dollar. Paper bank notes in common circulation are the $1, $2, $5, $10 & $20 bills.

*Information Sources:* Inquiries are answered & informational literature supplied by a wide variety of agencies, both governmental (Federal, State & Municipal) & private. The U.S. Travel Division of the National Park Service, U.S. Dept. of the Interior, compiles & publishes information about the recreational attractions of the country as a whole. For information about National Parks, write to park superintendents or to the Director, National Park Service, Dept. of the Interior, Washington 25, D.C. For information about National Forests, write to the Forest Service, U.S. Dept. of Agriculture, Washington 25, D.C.

Each of the 48 states maintains an agency, with headquarters at the state capital, which supplies information. State Park Commissions provide informational literature about state parks & State Highway Departments publish highway maps. Many of the larger cities support Tourist Bureaus which answer inquiries & nearly all cities of 5,000 population or more have Chambers of Commerce which publish informational literature. The American Automobile Association, with headquarters at Pennsylvania Ave. & 17th St., Washington, D.C., & branch offices in the larger cities, provides information to members. Many oil companies throughout the United States supply maps & verbal information through service stations. Public libraries are always good sources of information.

*Railroads:* The American railroad system comprises more than 225,000 miles of track in operation. The single-class system prevails in passenger travel. Sleeping accommodations on long trips (& the most comfortable accommodations on short trips) are provided by Pullman cars; the cost of Pullman accommodations adds considerably to the total rail fare. Most passenger trains carry dining cars on long trips & many also carry club cars in which beverages & refreshments are available.

*Motor Buses:* The U.S. is covered by a network of bus lines both paralleling rail lines & reaching points without rail facilities. Travel by bus is considerably cheaper than by train.

*Airlines:* More than 30 airlines operate to all parts of the U.S.

*Waterways:* During the summer months, steamer service is provided between various ports on the Atlantic Coast, the Great Lakes & the Hudson, Ohio, Mississippi & Columbia Rivers. At many points, steamers provide auto-ferry facilities. Summer cruises on the Hudson extend between New York & Albany; on the Mississippi, between St. Paul, Minn. & New Orleans, La.; on the Ohio, eastward to Cincinnati (with a branch route down the Tennessee River to Chattanooga, Tenn. & Muscle Shoals, Ala.); on the Columbia, inland to Portland. Private yachts & motorboats may use the Intracoastal Waterway along the Atlantic & Gulf Coasts & the N.Y. State Barge System between Albany & Buffalo, which links the Hudson River with the Great Lakes.

*Taxis:* Fares for taxicabs are fixed according to distance traveled, with an extra charge for carrying outside luggage.

*Highways:* The paved highway system comprises more than 3,000,000 miles, of which more than 70,000 have been built with Federal subsidies (indicated on maps & road signs with the letters "US" & a number, enclosed in a shield). Even-numbered Federal highways extend generally in an east-west direction; odd-numbered ones run north-south. State highways are also numbered, the numbers being enclosed in a circle or triangle on maps & road signs.

*Traffic Regulations:* Since speed limits are the province of the states & municipalities, they vary widely. In 23 states & the District of Columbia, the law forbids "hitchhiking" (soliciting rides), sometimes penalizing the driver as well as the hitchhiker.

Non-resident motorists are required by a few states to register or secure a permit after spending a stipulated time in the state.

## ACCOMMODATIONS

*Hotels, Auto Courts & Tourist Homes:* Most American hotels are operated on the European plan (i.e., meals are not included in the price of a room); but a few in resort areas operate on the American plan (i.e., meals as well as lodging are included in one price). The "Hotel Red Book," which gives a general list of hotels classified by state, is available at most hotels & public libraries & in all Pullman cars. Numerous auto courts or "motels" (with garage facilities as well as lodgings) & tourist homes, usually found on the outskirts of cities & towns or in recreational areas along highways, provide relatively inexpensive lodgings. Trailer camps equipped with water & electric connections & sanitary facilities are widely distributed.

*Restaurants:* Although good restaurants will be found in all the larger cities (very commonly offering French, Italian, German or other foreign cuisines), the most widely patronized eating establishments in the U.S. are the cafeteria (a self-service restaurant) & the lunch counter.

*Liquor Regulations:* In some localities, the sale of liquor is prohibited by local legislation. In a few states, liquor can be bought only in licensed shops. The sale of alcoholic beverages in bars is commonly forbidden on Sundays (or until after a prescribed hour on Sundays) & closing time at night varies.

*Accommodations for Negroes:* In the Southern States (& Okla. & Texas) Negroes are legally restricted to special hotels & restaurants, special motion picture theaters & parks & sections of railroad cars, buses & streetcars. Throughout most of the rest of the country, discrimination against Negroes is not customary; & in many states, it is forbidden by law. "Travelguide" (published by Travelguide, Inc., 1674 Broadway, New York 19, N.Y.) lists hotels, restaurants & resorts throughout the U.S., which do not practice discrimination.

*Tipping:* It is generally customary throughout the U.S. to tip a minimum of 10% for any service.

## OUTDOOR RECREATION

*National Parks:* The U.S. has 26 National Parks, in addition to 82 National Monuments & 51 other areas (battlefields, historic sites, memorials, etc.) maintained by the National Park Service of the Dept. of the Interior. Most National Parks provide accommodations ranging from campsites & cabins to luxury hotels, & in most there are grocery stores & restaurants or cafeterias. Hunting is forbidden in National Parks, though fishing is usually allowed. In most of them fires may be built only at designated campsites unless special permission is obtained.

*National Forests:* There are 160 National Forests comprising 176,000,000 acres in 36 states, administered by the Dept. of Agriculture, all of which offer picnicking, camping, hiking, motoring, fishing & hunting, & most of which also offer swimming & boating. There are some 3,800 improved campsites. Within the National Forests are 77 Wilderness Areas, each of more than 100,000 acres & accessible only by trail, in which no roads or lodging accommodations may be built; guides & saddle & pack horses are available near-by for hire on pack trips through these areas, which are permanently maintained in their natural state. The National Forests also have extensive snow trails for winter sports enthusiasts, & in some there are shelters & ski lifts as well. In both National Parks & National Forests fishing & hunting are governed by state game laws.

*Other Federal Recreational Areas:* Important recreational areas have been developed around many of the larger dams & reservoirs under government control. The Indian Reservations are often of interest for sightseeing & recreational purposes. Many of the National Wildlife Refuges provide picnicking & recreational facilities, & a few provide lodgings; fishing is permitted at some seasons, subject to state laws.

*State Parks & Forests:* Nearly 8,000,000 acres have been set aside in more than 3,300 state parks & forests, most of which provide lodging & recreational facilities.

*Trails:* There are about 150,000 miles of hiking & riding trails in the National Forests. The Appalachian Trail, crossing 8 National Forests & 2 National Parks, extends 2,050 miles from Mt. Katahdin, Me., to Mt. Oglethorpe, Ga., along the crest of the Appalachians. The Pacific Crest Trail, crossing 19 National Forests & 6 National Parks, will extend, when completed, 2,265 miles from Canada to Mexico along the crests of the Cascades, Sierra Nevada, & Pacific Coast ranges.

*Hunting & Fishing Regulations:* Laws concerning hunting & fishing vary from state to state. For information, apply to the state fish & game commissions. In some states, license fees are higher for non-residents than for residents.

*Poisonous Reptiles, Insects & Plants:* Poisonous snakes of the U.S. are the copperhead, the eastern, central & southern states; the coral snake, found in parts of the far South; the cottonmouth moccasin, which inhabits swamps & bayous in the South; & the rattlesnake, widely distributed, of which 13 varieties occur, 10 of them in the Southwest. The Gila monster is a poisonous lizard found in the Southwest. The Black Widow spider, found throughout U.S., painful & dangerous; the bites of the scorpion, tarantula & other venomous insects are painful but not dangerous. The chief poisonous plants are poison ivy & poison oak which cause annoying but not dangerous skin irritations. Ticks sometimes carry Rocky Mountain Fever.

## SPORTS & AMUSEMENTS

*Athletics:* Baseball, the national game, is played by professional as well as college teams throughout the country; the World Series, played between winning teams of the American & National Leagues for the national championship each autumn, is probably the country's chief sporting event.

Football is played mostly by college teams but also increasingly in recent years by professionals. Basketball is also a widely played college sport. The U.S. National Tennis Championships & the international Davis Cup & Wightman Cup matches are held at Forest Hills, Long Island, N.Y. Championship golf matches at various courses throughout the U.S. attract many spectators. Ski championship matches take place at leading winter sports centers. The leading intercollegiate rowing regatta occurs on the Hudson at Poughkeepsie, N.Y.; Yale & Harvard crews compete on the Thames R. at New London, Conn. Boxing & wrestling matches draw heavy attendance in the large cities.

*Horse Racing:* The chief American tracks for running races are located in the northeastern states; in Ky., Fla., La. & Ark.; in Ill. & Mich., & in Cal. They offer pari-mutuel betting facilities. Most famous of American races is the Kentucky Derby at Churchill Downs. Harness racing is also widely popular, particularly at state & county fairs. The major harness racing event is the Hambletonian at Goshen, N.Y.

*Rodeos:* The rodeo is an exhibition of cowboys' skill at roping & riding, including such feats as "bronc" (bronco) & bull riding, lassoing steers & "bulldogging" (wrestling with a steer). One of the most heavily attended is the Pendleton Round-up at Pendleton, Ore.

*State & County Fairs:* The fair, on a county-wide or state-wide scale, at which agricultural & industrial products are exhibited, races & other contests of various kinds held, & traveling carnival concessions & other amusement facilities provided, is a national institution.

*Annual Events:* Festivals, celebrations & sports events of various kinds are staged, particularly in resort centers, throughout the U.S. Among the most popular are the Tournament of Roses & East-West football games at Pasadena, Cal.; the Mummer's Parade at Philadelphia on Jan. 1; Mardi Gras at New Orleans, ending on day preceding Ash Wed.; Japanese Cherry Blossom Festival at Washington, D.C. in Ap.; Tulip Festival at Holland, Mich.; Cotton Carnival at Memphis, Tenn.; Kentucky Derby at Louisville, Ky., in May; American Passion Play at Bloomington, Ill., Palm Sun. to June 1; 500-Mile Automobile Race at Indianapolis on Memorial Day; Festival of Roses at Portland, Ore., in June; Play Festival at Central City, Colo., in July; National Air Races at Cleveland, Ohio, in Aug.; Miss America Pageant Week (beauty contest) at Atlantic City, N. J.; Pendleton Round-up at Pendleton, Ore., in early Sept.; Veiled Prophet Festival at St. Louis in early Oct.

*Public Holidays:* The following are legal holidays in all states: New Year's Day, Jan. 1; Washington's Birthday, Feb. 22; Independence Day, July 4; Labor Day, first Monday in Sept.; Armistice Day, Nov. 11; Thanksgiving Day, 4th Thurs. of Nov.; Christmas Day, Dec. 25. Lincoln's Birthday, Feb. 12, is observed in 31 states; Decoration or Memorial Day, May 30 (Confederate Memorial Day in Va.) is observed except in some of the Southern States. Columbus Day, Oct. 12, in all states except Ala., Idaho, Iowa, Me., Miss., N. Car., S. Car., S. Dak. & Tenn. Election Day, observed when general or presidential elections are held, is the first Tues. after the first Mon. in Nov. In some states, Sat., from noon to midnight, is a legal holiday; & in most, banks are closed all day Sat. Days widely observed (though not legal holidays) include Arbor Day, various dates in different states; St. Patrick's Day, Mar. 17; Army Day, Ap. 6; Mother's Day, 2nd Sun. in May; National Maritime Day, May 22; Flag Day, June 14; Father's Day, 3rd Sun. in June; Navy Day, Oct. 27.

## CULTURAL FACILITIES

*Newspapers, Periodicals & Books:* Daily newspapers are published in all the larger cities & in many small towns. The tabloid, containing more photographs & less extended news articles than the standard newspaper, is popular in the biggest cities. The range of periodicals to be found on most newsstands is very wide. Bookshops, outside the chief metropolitan areas, are somewhat thinly distributed. The price of books is higher in the U.S. than in many other countries. However, there are various series of reprint editions, comprising classic as well as current works, which may be purchased for $1.50 or less; & there are also several series of paper-bound books selling for 25¢, chiefly devoted to current popular literature but including some standard classics.

*Radio:* The U.S. has more radio-receiving sets in operation than any other country—more than 60,000,000, or a little less than one for every two people—& more transmitting stations—a total of over 1,100. The television receiver has become a popular fixture in bars, along with the "juke-box" (a coin-slot phonograph).

*Motion Pictures:* The U.S. has the highest ratio of motion picture theaters to population in the world. There are (1949) nearly 19,000 theaters with a seating capacity of nearly 11,500,000. Hollywood, Cal., is the motion-picture capital.

*Drama:* The production of stage plays is largely confined to New York City. Popular plays are usually taken on tour to the other larger cities. Summer stock companies perform at many resort centers during the summer. "Little" or non-commercial theaters are maintained in many of the larger cities.

*Music:* Most of the larger cities have symphony orchestras which present concerts between late autumn & early spring; among the most notable are those of New York, Boston, Philadelphia, Pittsburgh, Cleveland, Cincinnati, Chicago, Detroit, Minneapolis & San Francisco. The chief permanent opera companies are those of New York, Chicago & San Francisco. Important music festivals include the Bach Festival at Bethlehem, Pa., Xmas & Easter, Composers' Festival at Rochester, N.Y., in May & the Berkshire Festival at Tanglewood, Mass., in Aug. Summer concerts are given at outdoor amphitheaters in or near most of the larger cities.

*Art Museums & Galleries:* Among the most notable museums are the Metropolitan of New York, the National Gallery of Washington, D.C. & the Art Institute of Chicago. New York has also the Brooklyn Museum, the Frick Collection, Hispanic Society of America Museum, Museum of Modern Art & Whitney Museum of American Art; & Washington has the Corcoran Gallery of Art & Phillips Gallery. Other leading art museums include those of Baltimore, Boston, Buffalo, Cincinnati, Cleveland, Denver, Detroit, Indianapolis, Kansas City, Los Angeles, Manchester (N.H.), Milwaukee, Minneapolis, Montclair (N.J.), Newark, New Orleans, Omaha, Philadelphia, Pittsburgh, Pittsfield (Mass.), Richmond, St. Louis, San Diego, San Francisco, Sarasota (Fla.), Seattle, Toledo, Worcester (Mass.) & the universities of Harvard, Yale & Kansas. The chief commercial art gallery center is 57th Street & vicinity in New York City; a few other large cities have small galleries.

*Scientific & Historical Museums & Planetariums:* Leading natural history & science museums are the Smithsonian Institution in Washington, the American Museum of Natural History in New York & the Chicago Natural History Museum. Others of note are those of Buffalo, Cleveland, Denver, Los Angeles, Philadelphia, San Diego & San Francisco & the universities of Alabama, Arizona, Kansas, Oregon & Texas & Harvard & Yale universities. Outstanding museums of science & industry are in New York (Rockefeller Center) Philadelphia, & Chicago. Important historical collections are: Institute of Early American History & Culture, Williamsburg, Va.; Kansas State Historical Society, Topeka; Louisiana State Museum, New Orleans; Mariners' Museum, Hampton Roads, Va.; Minnesota Historical Society, St. Paul; Museum of the City of New York; Museum of New Mexico, Santa Fe; New Bedford (Mass.) Whaling Museum; New Hampshire Historical Society, Concord; New York Historical Society; & Woolaroc Museum near Bartlesville, Okla. The chief planetariums are the Hayden Planetarium, New York; Fels Planetarium, Philadelphia; Buhl Planetarium, Pittsburgh; Adler Planetarium, Chicago; & Griffith Observatory & Planetarium, Los Angeles.

*Educational Facilities:* The public schools common to all parts of the U.S. are the grammar school, with eight grades, & the high school, with four. In the larger population centers, kindergartens, junior high schools (comprising the 7th through 10th grades), & junior colleges (comprising the first two years of college) are often found. All the states have state universities, at which tuition fees are much lower than at the many private universities & colleges.

*House & Garden Pilgrimages:* In many localities, especially those of historic interest, conducted tours to notable houses & gardens are held, usually during May. For information, consult local or state chambers of commerce or state publicity or development commissions.

*Libraries:* Among the country's leading reference & research libraries are the Library of Congress, Washington; New York Public Library & New York Academy of Medicine Library; Army Medical Library & Folger Shakespeare Library, Washington; Newberry Library & John Crerar Library, Chicago; Henry E. Huntington Library, San Marino, Cal.; & the libraries of Duke, Harvard, Northwestern, Princeton, Columbia & Yale & the universities of Chicago, Illinois, Michigan, Minnesota, Texas & Virginia. Public circulating libraries are found in most larger population centers. To secure a borrower's card, it is usually necessary to furnish identification & proof of residence; sometimes guarantors' signatures are required.

# CONTENTS

**THE SOUTH (continued)**

# *LIST OF MAPS*

# The American Guide

# *HISTORY*

The American nation is an amalgam of many peoples & diverse institutions fused in the crucible of nearly four centuries of history. A vast continent with limitless resources & a relative handful of red-skinned aborigines was opened after the 15th century by the voyages of intrepid explorers of various western European nations. Their respective monarchs, their ecclesiastics, their commercial entrepreneurs, & their soldiers of fortune soon began, under a complex of motions, the process of rival empire-building. A New Spain poised in the Caribbean & Mexico pushed its military frontiers & its missions up into Florida, across the Rio Grande into Texas, & into the heart of California. A New France of soldiers, missionaries, & fur traders expanded from the St. Lawrence Valley into the Great Lakes area & the Mississippi Valley. A "New" England honoring the great virgin queen was planned for the heart of the eastern seaboard, only temporarily to be challenged by a New Sweden on the Delaware & a New Netherlands along the Hudson. The future of North America was from the start dependent upon an imperial rivalry that soon developed into bloody conflict, indeed, into a series of world wars. From these the British, with their superior sea power & with the equally interested colonists, were emerging triumphant just before the restless seaboard provinces began to experience how heavily the chains of empire might really burden them.

From the first, however, & especially as decade followed decade, the human pawns in the game of the empire thought largely of their own happiness and well-being. America became for them—from bond-servants under servile indenture to colonists favored by influence and fortune—increasingly a new homeland, a land of rich opportunity for all, though in different ways & to different degrees. Its utopian appeal beckoned not only across the Atlantic, which did so much to aid the western wilderness in qualifying the sanction of Old World ideas & institutions, but even across the political boundaries of European states, inviting the unprivileged, the dissenters, & the restless to seek their fortunes in the New World. Soon there developed the concept of an "American," a proud, independent freeholder whose success & destiny was in his own hands & not at the mercy of distinctions as to origin, wealth, or influence—a concept that found its best development in colonies like Pennsylvania that welcomed a motley of peoples, with diverse national origins, religious & political beliefs. Even the Puritan theocracy of the northern colonies felt among their more homogeneous population the same divisive groping —& at times the bold & defiant leadership of a Roger Williams—toward a more egalitarian concept, such as the conquest of the wilderness had often imposed upon them as a necessity.

Colonial politics increasingly turned around a hostility to & even a defiance of the efforts of vice-regal proprietors & of royal governors to maintain some semblance of imperial control by policies that commended themselves more to the privileged few than to the masses of colonial Americans. Not understanding these warnings, the home government in England, relieved of the formidable threat of its powerful French rival by the glorious Peace of Paris (1763) that followed the French & Indian War, felt that the time had come to set its empire in order, to replace a prolonged period of "salutary neglect" by a fundamental reorganization that would make more real & effective the imperial bonds, both political & economic.

A colonial patriotism promptly evinced itself, the general scope of which included the vast body of Americans, leaving in the main only the direct & indirect beneficiaries of imperial favor to champion the principles of imperial reorganization. The patriot cause found spokesmen who differed as to its extent & as to the proper measures for its defense. Some harked back to the "rights of Englishmen" that colonial charters had granted them & challenged imperial policies of taxation—"without representation"—& of enforcement as contrary to those rights; others, imbued with the doctrines of Locke & Rousseau, spoke of "natural rights" & spun fine egalitarian theories. Some were ready only for protest & petition against their grievances & made strong protestations of their loyalty to the British constitution & empire; others felt the call to action & as "Sons of Liberty" organized mass demonstrations & in due course revolutionary committees to plan concerted opposition &, if necessary, the armed defense of their "rights."

In 1774, as tension increased following various items of coercive legislation to penalize colonial opposition, a Continental Congress gathered at Philadelphia as an intercolonial agency for protest. It planned a program that reached far into the area of revolutionary activity & forced an issue between the colonies & the British government, the issue of loyalty to the one or to the other. Staunch defenders of imperial prerogative now found allies in former patriots who were not willing to become involved in the activities of revolutionary committees. Veteran radicals inclined toward drastic action found themselves supported by former conservatives who had previously regarded them with suspicion. There were many who were unwilling or unable to take either side. But when the muskets blazed at Lexington & Concord, the possibility of armed clash had become a reality & the issues in the struggle were refined to the gauge of battle. In the throes of war a nation was born. The cold logic of events shifted a struggle for a redress of grievances into a struggle for independence. The immortal words of Jefferson in the Declaration of Independence cut the Gordian knot that bound the colonies to the British crown. Their validity depended upon the ability of the new nation to win its cause, especially in the "opinions of mankind" for which a "decent respect" was so validly proclaimed. The war that was waged for six years or more was not only a rebellion that by its success became the outstanding revolution in human history. It was also a civil war in which Americans fought Americans—with strong measures of reprisal meted out by both groups & especially by the victorious patriots. But even more important, perhaps, was the fact that it became a phase of another world war, in which the former enemies of Britain took advantage of the opportunity to strike back at the proud victor of 1763 & thereby lent invaluable aid to the revolution. Equally important for the patriot cause, perhaps, was the sympathy for its ideals that came from various quarters abroad, even from the ranks of many British subjects at home, & the aid that was rendered by European idealists as well as soldiers of fortune who cast their lot in person with the revolutionary armies. The young aristocrat, the Marquis de Lafayette, symbolized the interest that many of his fellow-countrymen felt in the success of the Americans, an interest readily aroused by the presence in France of the venerable Benjamin Franklin, whose very person seemed the embodiment of American democratic ideals, even to the statesmen whose aid he sought.

The ebb & flow of fortune upon the battlefield did not seriously check important progress along political lines. In time the revolutionary Continental Congress & its agencies gave way to a new regime under the Articles of Confederation, the first national constitution, which took form as the logical consequence of the Declaration of Independence. The new government was still grounded upon the authority of the states. It lacked an effective executive branch & adequate powers in general, but it functioned much more successfully than its later repudiation has made it possible to see.

The greater vigor of state action made the substitution of revolutionary state constitutions for royal colonial charters an important phase of American democratic progress. Concepts of social revolution were whittled down to meet practical demands from more conservative quarters. But somewhat more liberal concepts of suffrage were defined & an almost complete liquidation of aristocratic institutions that stemmed from European backgrounds was achieved when patents of nobility were repudiated along with the principles of primogeniture & entail. Anglo-Saxon traditions in the liberal area lent impetus to a movement to define & to widen in a truly revolutionary spirit the areas of civil rights & liberties. Under the leadership of George Mason of Virginia & John Adams of Massachusetts bills of rights applied principles also stated in the Declaration of Independence to the field of state government & spelled out the inalienable rights of men which even this government might not trespass. Religious liberty was declared in sweeping terms beyond the capacity of the times to put into full practice. The Massachusetts Bill of Rights declared so boldly that "all men are born free & equal" that three years later the state supreme court could only interpret this as having disposed locally of the institution of Negro chattel slavery.

When at length in 1783 a new Treaty of Paris proclaimed British recognition of the new republic, peace brought new opportunities & added new problems. Its peoples renewed their push into the western wilderness; they wrestled to secure effective social & economic adjustments at home, only to find ideals & practical needs in sharp conflict; & they awaited with declining patience evidence that the central government might secure effective recognition abroad. This national government—which was not truly national—was viewed with suspicion on the one hand, & on the other was made the repository of authority over the territories across the mountains. Conflicting forces were arrayed over the effort to extend the national authority until finally in 1787 a Constitutional Convention met at Philadelphia, theoretically to revise the Articles of Confederation—which in fact it had no right to do—but actually to inaugurate the process of scrapping the first American national constitution & substituting one which might more effectively cope with the accumulating problems at home & abroad.

At Philadelphia, under the chairmanship of George Washington, fifty-five of the ablest of the nation's leaders shaped a new constitution. It enlarged the powers of the central government & extended them to include the right to lay taxes & to regulate commerce. It provided for areas of executive & judicial authority that were equally important, & balanced against each other the powers in these respective fields. It established direct relations between the individual & the central government, including direct jurisdiction over him in its proper area. It also set up safeguards against the unchecked will of the people, denying them direct participation in the choice of their officials—except in the case of members of the lower house of the Congress—& further sought to limit the danger of popular aberration by restrictions upon the powers of the state governments. In most particulars, however, a wide area of authority was still left to the states.

Fortunately the convention arranged for the ratification of its work in popularly elected state conventions. Approval was opposed by many of the former leaders in the Revolutionary cause & by others also inclined toward democratic & libertarian beliefs. Many, like George Mason, Patrick Henry & Richard Henry Lee, opposed it because of its lack of a Bill of Rights which would guarantee civil liberty & without which there would be grave danger of tyranny. It was supported by advocates of more effective federal controls, by a large group of speculators in federal securities, & by those who sought better protection of their vested interests in property. A direct popular referendum, even by the limited electorate of the day, would have promptly voted down the new Constitution. Various factors, however, including the lack of a constructive & adequate alternative & the prospect of early amendment to add the desired Bill of Rights, combined to bring about acceptance, as the state conventions successively wrestled with the problem. An important factor was the exposition & support of the document in the "Federalist" papers, written by Hamilton, Madison & Jay. Various states, moreover, formulated recommendations for a Bill of Rights to be added by amendment; as a result, ten articles were promptly acted upon & thenceforth became a part of the Constitution, constituting the charter of American civil liberties.

Soon a new government under George Washington was in operation & the genius of Alexander Hamilton, however much committed to exploitation & even to monopoly, was laying firm foundations for an experiment that originally faced more prospects of failure than of success. Hamilton & his associates outlived their usefulness once their constructive work was done but, not realizing this, overreached themselves & were effectively replaced by Thomas Jefferson & his followers.

A fairly well-defined division into party groupings had evolved even before the constitutional convention of 1787. The cleavage was fundamentally between the wealthy & the privileged, on the one hand; & the plain people, especially the yeoman farmers, on the other. The latter were strong in numbers & in leaders idealistically devoted to their cause, such as Jefferson. His party, the Republicans, now took the reins of power from the Hamiltonian Federalists (who lost strength & gradually disappeared). Jefferson's inaugural was a great text-book in American democracy & long influenced developments in that direction. Prosperity began under Washington & Hamilton, & continued under Jefferson. The latter struggled bravely to prevent a proper concern about neutral rights from drawing the United States into a world conflict that was then waging around the rivalry of Napoleon & Britain. These efforts broke down under Jefferson's successor, Madison, & the nation became involved in its first foreign war, the War of 1812.

The conflict, however lacking in genuine glory for either side, made important contributions to a genuinely American self-consciousness, self-confidence, & sense of destiny. The war was in part a consequence of an American concept of citizenship based not primarily upon birth but upon choice, and therefore open to the foreign-born by the process of naturalization. In part it arose from assuming a leading role among nations in demanding the freedom of the seas. In part it originated out of the buoyant overconfidence of fórces identified with a West that was strongly expansionist & national. It was, moreover, an important step in the process of supplementing political independence with a cutting of the economic bonds that linked us with Britain.

Returning peace brought a new optimism & sense of nationality, one that sometimes offended fastidious foreign visitors & critics. The new spirit prepared the way for new concepts of national right & duty. Statesmen nurtured by states rights concepts now talked of the need for American self-sufficiency & action in every field. They authorized a new bank monopoly with Henry Clay as important for its success as he had been for its failure five years earlier; they proclaimed the advantages of protective tariff legislation—an "American System"; they projected a great program of road & canal building at the national expense. Looking beyond national boundaries, they espoused the cause of Latin-American republics & through Monroe assumed the championship of western hemispheric interests; even the cause of revolution in Greece aroused their concern. To foreign critics of American cultural deficiencies, appropriate reply was made: "We have been busy conquering a wilderness & building a nation. But culture will come in due course."

At the grassroots, moreover, a democratic urge was fermenting. Across the Alleghanies a new & more liberal land policy had attracted new settlers by the hundreds of thousands. New states that came into being were broadening the suffrage to include all men & were discarding traditional concepts of privilege. A similar attack was soon under way in the older areas where the unenfranchised showed an increasing restlessness & zeal for organization & action. Progressive leaders joined hands with them; the combined attack overthrew or weakened the defenders of privilege who rallied (with the aid of a Chancellor Kent & a Daniel Webster) to the theory that property-holders had the real "stake in government."

American democracy was finding a new scope & a wider recognition. Its triumph came in the election of 1828 of Andrew Jackson, the symbol of the popular will &, for many, of popular rights. His election was more than a demonstration of the power of the West & of the democratizing influence of the frontier. It represented the rallying of all democratic forces, whether they originated in the American scene or in the dreams of American idealists. The battle between human rights & privilege was a complex one, particularly as it was fought in the national political arena. The issues were often clearer as they were joined in the states or in local communities. But Andrew Jackson, however much the genuineness of his democracy may have been challenged, always represented himself as the repository of the popular will charged with the duty of returning to the people the trust confided to his charge.

Jackson's presidency witnessed the crisis that developed out of the proposal of South Carolina to "nullify" tariff legislation, the benefits of which accrued especially to the industrial areas & the burdens of which fell particularly upon the planting & exporting states in which the Negro-slave system prevailed. The traditional sectional cleavage between areas that were sharing the frontier experience & the older areas along the seaboard was now subjected to an attack that threatened to realign against each other the free & the slave states. In another thirty years this new cleavage was so complete as to bring about a bloody civil war. For a long period, however, the two contrasting sectional concepts contended against each other with a resulting complex & confusing situation.

Over nullification President Jackson broke with Calhoun, its proponent, his vice-presidential associate for four years. He answered the nullification ordinance adopted by the official convention of South Carolina by issuing a strongly worded proclamation in which he announced his intention to fulfill his sworn duty to enforce the law. Congress supported the President by enacting a Force Bill but a clash was avoided when Clay sponsored a tariff revision acceptable to the nullifiers, which became known as the Compromise Tariff of 1833.

Even before the nullification crisis cleared, southern sectionalism found a new source of grievance in a strong abolition movement that came to be organized about the leadership of William L. Garrison & Theodore Weld. Whereas before 1830 antislavery activity had been non-sectional & local antislavery societies were particularly numerous in the border slave states, the new & more uncompromising attack found itself almost entirely a northern movement. The intransigency of its leaders soon caused Calhoun & his southern associates to shift their attitude from the earlier position of regarding it as a "necessary evil" to one in which it was increasingly defended as a "positive good."

The "peculiar institution" of the South had evolved as the answer dictated by circumstances to the problem of securing an adequate labor supply for the cultivation of its various staples, later, especially cotton. Whatever validity this answer might have had prior to the Jackson period was largely invalidated by its failure to offer a sound long-range solution to the problem of the Negro's place in the American scene. There was now, moreover, abundant evidence of its rapidly increasing economic unsoundness as a system of labor. Yet Southerners—preachers, educators, jurists, & others—were now busying themselves with the development of a proslavery argument that claimed for a decaying institution more virtues than it had ever before been supposed to possess. Alongside of this attitude a growing hatred of the abolitionist became a chief phenomenon in southern opinion.

Northern abolitionists also lacked a constructive practical solution to the ominous problem of race relationship. Indeed, they often concentrated their spleen upon slaveholders & southern politicians, as corrupted by the taint of slavery—upon the sinners & not the sin. Their views were often too extreme, not only for apologists for slavery, but even for sincere critics of the institution (who felt that Garrison alienated more northerners than he converted). Yet, as in the case of the southern ultras, by everlastingly hammering away at their extreme version of sectionalism, they accustomed their neighbors generally to the fact of controversy & to the general acceptance of at least a moderate version.

The regular political parties—now the Whigs & the Democrats—long successfully evaded being drawn into the sectional controversy; Democrats, northern & southern, could ponder the plight of the common man & labor for improvements in his lot, some radical & some moderate; Whigs representing the aristocratic & propertied interests of different types labored to maintain their privileges & found in the fact that they were generally men of property a restraining force. As a result of the old party tactics of evasion, the abolitionists, or some of them, felt that they should enter the field of independent political action. They organized a Liberty Party which supported the presidential candidacy of a former slaveholder, James B. Birney; they saw their vote grow from some seven thousand votes in 1840 to over five times that number in the next campaign, wherein they seemed to hold the balance of power & to seal the doom of Henry Clay's presidential aspirations as the Whig candidate.

While the slavery question had found only a minor role in American politics prior to 1844, it was henceforth to loom up as a leading issue. The proposal of the annexation of Texas seemed to most abolitionists a slaveholders' conspiracy to secure the widening of the domain of slavery. Many of the planters, however, together with Henry Clay, rejected such a program, especially at the price of international complications & of internal agitation. Expansion was to them a doubtful advantage, especially since it might weaken slavery by dispersion, as Clay had forecast in 1820. Texas was annexed as a result of an apparent mandate from the plain people, coming more from the West & from the back-country areas of the South than from the plantations of the Black Belt.

The warnings of Clay were still ringing in the ears of many of his Whig followers, when a war arose as a result of the official adoption at Washington of the doubtful claims of the new state of Texas. Soon the armies of the nation were poised to accomplish the conquest of Mexico. Bold expansionists, in the Polk administration & out, were encouraged to press their claims & some did not stop short of a desire to swallow up entirely the southern neighbor. In due course Henry Clay & his Whig following came out strongly against the acquisition of territory. His Lexington speech to that effect was supplemented by the active support, by southern as well as northern Whigs, of "no territory" resolutions introduced into Congress. Indeed, the authors of such resolutions in both houses were Georgians.

A somewhat different question was posed when David Wilmot, a Pennsylvania Democrat, introduced a proviso to an appropriation bill that slavery should never exist in any territory that might be acquired by the money that would therein be authorized. This proposal reflected a growing popular feeling in the free states that the further extension of slavery should be checked & that the Congress had the right as well as the duty to enact such a limitation. Wilmot's proposal was promptly passed by the House with its northern majority but was rejected in the Senate with the aid of northern votes—a pattern that recurred regularly in the years that followed. The proviso reflected a logical northern extreme position on the slavery question within the framework of the Constitution.

It was not long before Calhoun, self-appointed spokesman of the South, though himself an opponent of territorial acquisition at the expense of Mexico, replied in his famous "doctrine of the transmigratory function of the Constitution," that the territories were or should be deemed automatically open, without let or hindrance by Congress but as a matter of constitutional right, to the slaveholder & his slave property. To this doctrine Southerners rallied with even more unanimity than that seen in the northern acceptance of the Wilmot Proviso doctrine.

In 1820 the nation had confronted a similar issue over the Louisiana purchase territory & had settled it by drawing the Missouri Compromise Line between the domain of freedom & that of slavery along the parallel of 36° 30′. Recalling this amid the menacing aspects of the new controversy, some moderates now suggested that the proposed accession be divided by the extension of the line to the Pacific Ocean. In due course, also, Senator Lewis Cass of Michigan suggested that the question of freedom or slavery in the new territory be left to the people thereof, under a popular sovereignty principle that was an American tradition. The war came to a close before any solution was reached; the cession of New Mexico & California was made by Mexico; & a presidential campaign was at hand with the electorate divided over the territorial issue.

Antislavery Democrats & "Conscience" Whigs went to their conventions determined to force Wilmot Proviso platforms; southern champions were equally bent upon securing endorsement of the Calhoun doctrine. Both groups were rebuked by their respective parties which had to find some way in which their members could continue to work together regardless of their sectional interests. Cass was nominated by the Democrats & General Taylor, the "hero of Buena Vista" by the Whigs, though the latter had in many ways been an anti-war party. Both parties avoided platform declarations on the slavery issue. Whereupon the disappointed "Conscience" Whigs & Proviso Democrats combined with former Liberty party men & other antislavery elements to launch a "Free Soil" party & to nominate ex-president Martin Van Buren. In this race the third party held the balance of power & gave the victory to the Whig candidate, a Southerner & a slaveholder.

A baker's dozen of Free Soil members of the lower house of Congress soon held the balance of power & in delaying organization brought out in full force the hostility of the two sections & precipitated the crisis of 1850. Calhoun was trying to align his section about a desperate effort to maintain its "rights" & to restore the equilibrium of the Union, which seemed fatally threatened by the impending admission of California as a free state, breaking the now traditional tie in the Senate. Less far-sighted southern members of Congress talked privately of defending the rights & honor of their states & section, if need be, by force. Amid the confusion & conflict, Clay returned from his retirement with a series of proposals that promised to settle by compromise the outstanding issues between the two sections. As a compromise, it encountered opposition from the extremists of both sections. President Taylor, moreover, had a plan of his own & opposed that of Clay. As a result, the compromise proposal failed.

With Taylor's death, however, & a new approach, five laws were enacted which covered the ground of Clay's proposals. But the sectional storm was not calmed. Even more serious controversy was precipitated, with grave danger of disunion in at least three southern states. Never before had the forces of southern sectionalism been as determined or so strongly organized. But in the critical tests of strength, these forces lost—largely because the friends of the Union proclaimed a willingness merely to "acquiesce" in the recently enacted legislation. In due time, a weariness with agitation, a new economic prosperity, & a revival of old party ties, recalled both the friends & foes of the Union to traditional lines of political activity with the legislation of 1850 accepted as a "finality."

A president elected upon this basis had hardly congratulated the nation upon the sectional repose that prevailed when an issue arose with his endorsement which again loosed the full fury of the sectional controversy. In the name of "popular sovereignty" but for a combination of reasons that represented the full gamut of political & economic motivation, Stephen A. Douglas sponsored the Kansas-Nebraska Act; in this role he accepted the necessity of a repeal of the Missouri Compromise restriction which he himself had once hailed as "canonized in the hearts of the American people, as a sacred thing." Its repeal seemed to Southerners a belated act of justice; to Northerners it seemed a ruthless breach of trust. The Whig party split on the issue & soon disappeared. The Democratic party was officially committed to the act but could not hold its ranks in the North against a tide of protest that swept nearly every state.

Party lines had already weakened to the point that a new movement, the American or Know Nothing party, had suddenly come forward as a secret ritualistic political society & was winning sweeping local victories. A strange combination of nativist & Protestant bigotry, of reform, & of political opportunism, its chief strength lay in its promise to rid the nation of the wearisome slavery issue, a promise which it soon proved unable to fulfill. With old party allegiance thus under attack, the opponents of the Kansas-Nebraska Act felt free to defy those who supported it & to enter into fusion movements to protest its passage. Such movements arose in most northern states & soon won significant victories. More important, however, was the decision, made in the states of Wisconsin, Michigan, & Vermont, to foreswear completely old party allegiance & to organize a new Republican party, dedicated to the repeal of the Kansas-Nebraska Act & to the exclusion of slavery from the territories. This movement spread from state to state winning new victories, &, with careful planning, was launched as a national political party, whose nominee, John C. Frémont, seemed for a time to have such strong prospects of winning that southern leaders committed themselves to readiness for secession in that event.

Though the Democrats were continued in power they found only embarrassment growing out of their success. They generally rejoiced when the Dred Scott decision invalidated the Missouri Compromise & substantially upheld the Calhoun contention; Douglas, however, had reason to squirm over its implications for him & for his popular sovereignty concept. Under this principle, moreover, a struggle in Kansas led to widespread violence & even bloodshed. The proslavery forces in the territory received a support from Washington that encouraged them in methods which led successive governors to refuse to continue to be party to the process. Douglas with studied impartiality declared that under his doctrine of popular sovereignty, he did not care "whether slavery was voted up or voted down." In due course, however, he repudiated as fraudulent the local version of popular sovereignty & broke with President Buchanan on that issue. The "Little Giant" clung to his principle, modifying it or reinterpreting it to suit the needs of new situations until, his party split, the conflict between the more extreme positions of the North & the South led to bloody Civil War.

If Douglas claimed the role of a great compromiser, Lincoln stood firm for the principle on which he chose to make his appeal "to the liberal party of the world." He was fearful that the South might press any advantage it might win to the point of increasing the domain of slavery generally. His "House Divided" speech (1858), therefore, was, as he always insisted, a forecast of what might result from a head-on clash between abolitionists & proslavery forces, some of the latter proclaiming slavery to be "the normal status of the laboring man, white or black." To this Lincoln replied moderately but firmly. "Let there be no compromise on the question of extending slavery." Nominated by the Republicans he was elected in 1860 over the divided Democracy & over a new Constitutional Union Party, launched to stem the tide of sectionalism. It remained to be seen whether Southerners would swallow their disappointment & pride & acquiesce in their defeat. For a dozen years they had anticipated the triumph of the northern majority & their leaders had prepared for the event. They had protested the growing tyranny of a "Lord North" more ruthless than the British original. Increasingly concerned about the minority status, they deemed the mere fact of northern preponderance a point of grievance, however little they could do about it. They attacked their northern opponents as "Abolitionists," despite the fact that the real abolitionists were steadily losing strength & caste. Proud Southerners realized that they were becoming an important minority defending a declining social system based upon slavery; they resented the growing power of an industrial capitalism that had powerful allies in its free labor system & in the social institutions that represented a growing democratic strength.

Led by South Carolina ten southern states withdrew from the Union. Officially they claimed a constitutional right of peaceable secession but many proclaimed a right of revolution & a cause worth fighting for. Alexander H. Stephens of Georgia, a personal friend of Lincoln, fought secession in his home state, though he insisted that Lincoln's election "put the institution of nearly half of the states under the ban of public opinion & national condemnation." Unsuccessful but elected vice-president of the new Southern Confederacy, he proclaimed that its corner-stone rested "upon the great truth that the negro is not equal to the white man, & that slavery—subordination to the superior race—is his natural condition," a truth that he was willing to put to the judgment of the civilized & enlightened world.

With this challenge & with war-minded Northerners now increasingly inclined to the opinion that the issue was freedom vs. slavery, Lincoln's realistic insistence that the major problem was the preservation of the federal union, seemed increasingly to lack validity. Behind the scenes he was trying to induce loyal slaveholders to abandon this institution. His lack of success forced him to promulgate an Emancipation Proclamation (1862) which struck at disloyal slave areas but left him to ponder the problem of liquidating the institution generally by a constitutional amendment—if possible, with compensation.

The modern student of Abraham Lincoln sees in this great leader less of the "Great Emancipator" & more of the "Great Conciliator." He tried to preserve civil liberties from the stresses & strains of a conflict to suppress a "rebellion." After less than a year of hostilities he ordered released on parole all "political prisoners"—his own term. "Imbued with a reverence for the guaranteed rights of individuals," he had no sympathy with those who desired to enact sedition legislation. Bitterly denounced by the opposition forces &

their press—even as "a tyrant & usurper fit only to split rails"—he intervened in critical cases to stay the hand of military suppression. Even before his Proclamation of Amnesty of Dec. 8, 1863, he was known to favor a generous use of his pardoning power to former "rebels" & a quick & easy restoration of the southern states to their former places in the Union. Leading radical members of his party condemned this policy as one of "dictatorial usurpation"—to establish satellite states committed to his support. But Lincoln did not yield to their vengeful pleas. Amid the jubilant celebration of Lee's surrender came the tragic news of Old Abe's assassination. Lincoln was borne to a martyr's grave. But the Union was safe, even though its fate was temporarily entrusted to those who spoke the language not of charity but of vengeance—to a group whose selfishness as well as idealism Andrew Johnson lacked the tact but not the will to hold in check. The bonds of American nationalism, rewelded in the furnace of four years of fratricidal strife, were to prove strong enough to withstand the corrosive forces of a plan of reconstruction which, unlike Lincoln's, meant the rule of the sword & bayonet & which collapsed of its own weight in less than ten years.

With all its forces of destruction, the Civil War made its contribution to the material growth of the nation. The westward movement, hastened by the gold rush of the forty-niners, brought new frontiers in mining camps, upon cattle ranges & in a new plains agriculture. Transcontinental railroads soon linked the great valley with the Pacific seaboard. Industry grew by leaps & bounds, what with wartime needs & with protective tariffs. The latter started as revenue measures to help finance a war. When thereafter the balancing internal taxes were withdrawn, truckling politicians talked of the iniquities of the rebels & of the rights of the Negro; they waved the "bloody shirt" generally, to distract attention from the monstrous burden that remained upon the people generally, that the industrialist might enjoy the full measure of ill-gotten prosperity. In American politics, the war was fought for a generation or more, lest the people direct their political efforts toward a solution of the economic powers that grew apace.

On this basis the Republican Party, now increasingly subservient to the forces of the new industrialism that prospered in the "Gilded Age," perpetuated itself in power. Stalwarts who claimed to represent the canons of party orthodoxy winked at forces of corruption that fed upon the demoralization that followed the great effort to preserve the national Union. Reformers in their party who even sought to preserve & extend the essential of civic decency found themselves often on the defensive. Yet they succeeded, in alliance with opposition elements, in laying the legislative basis for civil service reform and in 1884, as "Mugwumps," cooperated in achieving the election of Grover Cleveland, the first Democratic president in twenty-four years. Recognizing the need on practical grounds for achieving a genuine reform of the tariff, he led his party in the attack upon this bulwark of privilege, only to find elements within it which resisted or blunted the effectiveness of the attack. His temporary retirement for a term was effected with the aid of Democrats who preferred local or personal success to his leadership.

In the meantime the nation experienced, after a brief interruption in the seventies, a new era of prosperity. The genius of the American people, again refreshed by an immigrant stock that supplied the brawn & in due time additional brains for an unprecedented national progress, rose to new heights.

New inventions revolutionized industry & life. A prosperous agriculture was established in the Great Plains area. Cities, old & new, grew with mushroom-like rapidity. Colorful social forces & institutions embellished the work-a-day picture of the American democracy & concealed the new growing-pains that warned of future dangers to the body politic.

The development of mass production methods was especially spectacular in the United States. By 1890, after two decades of drastic reorganization led by the textile & metal industries, large scale production became a typical aspect of American manufacturing. The pattern was so completely established that, except in new enterprises, such as those for the manufacture of automobiles, rubber products, & electrical apparatus, further plant expansion was to be achieved largely by horizontal & vertical combination. Andrew Carnegie, who had risen from a humble Scotch immigrant background to a dominant status in the manufacture of steel & iron, sincerely felt that serious responsibilities devolved upon successful enterprisers according to a "Gospel of Wealth" which he elaborated in a volume by that title (1890). But it was not so clear that, even with rising American standards of living, the benefits of the new prosperity were being evenly distributed. The entrenched power of the new industrial plutocracy became especially evident when, after the panic of 1893, wage rates declined & failed to improve materially for two decades; furthermore, a problem of unemployment, at least seasonally or cyclically—dramatized by the march of Coxey's army of protest in 1894—became a serious factor in industrial relations.

The reshaping of the pattern of American society was accentuated, if not caused, by the gradual disappearance of the American frontier & of the free lands that had long spelled opportunity. As pointed out by Frederick Jackson Turner (1893), the frontier had been a chief factor in the growth of democracy, by virtue of its promotion of a militant individualism that resented outside authority. By now, however, workers had combined in labor unions—organized nationally by crafts & in a few cases by industries—& were demanding their "rights" from employers & their associations, &, in instances, government protection from certain menaces to their interests. In due course elements chose various panaceas from a range of offerings that included paper & silver currency inflation, the "nationalism" of Edward Bellamy, the Single Tax of Henry George, & various brands of socialism.

The agricultural forces, which had in turn faced difficulties that blighted their share in the national prosperity, also became more militant in behalf of their interests. They too began to reject the traditional individualism & to favor aggressive assertion of the powers of government as an instrument of social reconstruction. Their organization, the Farmer's Alliance, & its political counterpart, the Populist Party, formulated an extensive program of governmental intervention. They demanded of legislation a contribution equivalent to the former role of free lands in maintaining the democratic ideal. Even their defeat, in 1896, in alliance with the Democrats & Bryan, did not destroy their belief that relief for distressed agriculture was a proper claim upon the nation & its government at Washington.

Issues in the new Republican administration of President McKinley were soon diverted to the field of foreign relations. Increasing American interest in the western hemisphere & especially in an isthmian canal had increasingly evidenced itself in the leadership of men like James G. Blaine. More general public concern was now aroused by incidents in the Cuban War for independence from Spain; these led to a popular demand for intervention, following the destruction of the "Maine" by an explosion in Havana harbor. Business interests & President McKinley found their reluctance over becoming embroiled with Spain subjected to the pressure of a public aroused by the talents of a "yellow" journalism that made lurid pleas in behalf of the rights & interests of suffering humanity. As a result, the nation fought a short & strategically successful war, one which established a world power status beyond anyone's capacity to doubt.

With new colonial acquisitions in the Philippines & in Puerto Rico & with the simultaneous annexation of Hawaii, which was promptly accorded territorial status, the fact of imperialism was now a reality, despite a large & nonpartisan group of anti-imperialists who idealistically protested & opposed this departure from the American democratic tradition. If they were ineffective in undoing the "wrong," they constituted a body of sentiment which influenced a development under which over the years successive stages of increasing self-government were provided for with a resulting gradual liquidation of the imperialistic factor. Strangely enough, this was paralleled in the early decades of the century by a new & expanded conception of the Monroe Doctrine which, formulated by Theodore Roosevelt, was applied by his successors, including Woodrow Wilson. This new phase of imperialism placed the republics of the Caribbean under the tutelage, if not the thumb, of the United States until it was liquidated under the "Good Neighbor" policy of the later Roosevelt, after the Hoover administration had taken significant steps in the same direction.

Lurking in the background of many of the imperialistic trends stood the sinister figure of a new finance capitalism which was to furnish many of the issues of the twentieth century. Taking more definite form under the new general incorporation act of New Jersey, vast industrial empires were built up through holding companies, back of which stood the giant power of organized finance, centering in Rockefeller & Morgan interests. For a dozen years & again in the period of Harding "normalcy" & of Coolidge prosperity, these forces exercised a powerful influence in directing or checkmating national political policy.

Made aware of their menace by the penetrating analysis of Thorstein Veblen & by the exposures of a body of crusading liberals who won the unflattering cognomen of "muckrakers," a great progressive revolt was set in motion to undo the evil. Gathering strength as it grew, it soon found a significant leadership in the colorful personality of Theodore Roosevelt, who in 1912 placed himself at the head of forces which he summoned to "march to Armageddon & battle for the Lord." But he was not to be the ideal or sole champion of the cause of "social justice," which he sometimes confounded with a concept of "substantial justice" that was highly tinged by his own personal judgment. Woodrow Wilson was borne into the presidency by the same tide & his first administration achieved important legislative gains for a concept of democracy adjusted to the new social needs of the day.

Then came American involvement in a great world conflagration despite early efforts to remain neutral & detached. At the cost of devastating attacks upon personal rights & liberty, a substantial unity was hammered out of diversity, & the economic & military resources of the nation were harnessed for a victory which it was hoped would bring, according to the idealistic pleas of the President, an end to the era of armed conflict. But peace, without acceptance of the commitment to world cooperation so imperfectly formulated at Versailles, brought only disillusionment at home & helplessness in the face of preparations abroad for a new attempt to solve the problems of national interest & international relations by new regimes of force.

Meantime the nation enjoyed the doubtful blessings of a "normalcy" that sought unsuccessfully to conceal rather than suppress exploitation as well as economic distress & the forces of political corruption as well as the will to reform. But the scandals of the Harding administration could not balk exposure. From this the reformers moved on to another crusading effort under the lead of Senator Robert M. La Follette, a devoted veteran in the Progressive Movement, albeit previously within his old party connection. High hopes were followed by discouragement over the really significant strength revealed by the new movement & it soon dissolved before the forces of the "Coolidge prosperity," which concealed its false foundations & which many Americans believed to have a guarantee of permanence.

Even the well-intentioned promises of a Herbert Hoover were dashed by the events of the Great Depression, when the nation faced the wide-spread distress that followed in the wake of successive financial & economic reverses. Time-honored palliatives & even newly conceived remedies had not checked the tide of disaster when popular opinion demanded new leadership. In due course the Democrats returned to power under Franklin D. Roosevelt. Expectations & promises of a revival of Wilsonian progressivism were scrapped during the banking crisis of 1933 for the more drastic formulae of a New Deal which was soon fighting to maintain the essentials of an enterprise system, even at the price of concessions to national authority that seemed to some to verge upon socialism or fascism. The scope of individual freedom was considerably reduced but luckily not in the area of civil liberties. Reform legislation, relief agencies in various fields, new rights for labor, & aid to distressed agriculture brought varying results in the general direction of social democracy but enough to extend the support of the New Deal & to continue it in office at the sacrifice of the anti-third term tradition.

Returning prosperity, a recession, & a new revival in the face of the threats of another World War continued the machinery & the popular support of the new regime. As a result, the nation was able to face with minor adjustments the problems that arose from its new benevolent neutrality toward the enemies of national socialism & fascism & its later participation in the struggle in which it was now a full-fledged ally. As the "arsenal of democracy," the American nation pledged & prodigally drew upon its resources for the victory that was finally won at so much cost for civilization & humanity.

On the threshold of an uncertain future, the American nation, surveying its past, can point with pride to the conquest of a wilderness, to an almost miraculous development of the limitless resources with which nature had so generously endowed it, to a persistent but spasmodic achievement of most elements in an expanding democratic ideal, & to a dominant role in a family of nations within which discord, if not conflict, may be expected to continue. That it will offer leadership in the direction of world peace & prosperity should be more than a pious hope, when the course of its history is properly appraised.

—Arthur H. Cole

# GOVERNMENT

The United States is a federation of states established by the Constitution of 1789. There are 48 states in this federal union. Recently, proposals have been under consideration to admit the territories of Hawaii & Alaska as states.

The powers of the National Government are drawn from the Constitution & all powers not given to the National Government in that document are reserved to the states. The National Government's powers are not all strictly defined in the Constitution, but are generally in the fields of foreign relations, foreign & interstate commerce, declaring & carrying on of war, taxation, currency, the posts, naturalization & bankruptcy.

The National Government is divided into 3 branches: the Legislative, the Executive, & the Judicial. The authors of the Constitution aimed by a system of checks & balances to keep these three branches separate & independent of each other & to prevent either the Legislative or Executive from attaining a preponderance of influence.

The Congress is the Legislative branch. It consists of the Senate & the House of Representatives. The Senate has 96 members—two from each state—elected by popular vote. Senatorial terms are for six years, so arranged, however, that one-third of the members retire every two years. The House at present has 435 members, also elected by popular vote, but for terms of only two years, terms which expire concurrently, so that elections to the House occur biennially. The Representatives, as members of the House are known, are apportioned on the basis of population. Hawaii, Puerto Rico & Alaska elect two delegates each to the House who, however, have no vote.

The Vice-President, elected in the same manner as the President & always of the same party, is the presiding officer of the Senate. The Vice-President succeds the President in case of the latter's death, resignation, or removal from office. The House elects its own presiding officer, the Speaker, whose authority, therefore, because he is a leader of the majority party, is greater than that of the Vice-President. The Senate must confirm the more important presidential appointments & must approve treaties with foreign nations by a two-thirds vote. The Congress initiates amendments to the Constitution.

Debate in the House is much more limited by that body's rules than is debate in the Senate. Committees in both Houses prepare legislation & therefore are very important in the operation of the Congress. Money bills originate in the House. Laws may be adopted over the presidential veto by a two-thirds majority of both Houses. The Congress alone has the power to declare war.

The President is the chief executive. He is elected every four years. Political parties nominate electors in each state pledged in advance to vote for the Presidential candidate of the party which has nominated them. Each state is entitled to a number of electors equal to the number of its Representatives in the House, plus its two Senators.

The President exercises the executive functions of the government. His nominees for the more important positions in the government must be approved by the Senate. He also nominates members of the Federal judiciary, who are also subject to Senatorial approval. The Executive negotiates treaties with foreign governments, but these treaties must be approved by a two-thirds majority of the Senate. The President has a cabinet consisting of heads of the various governmental departments: State, corresponding to foreign offices in other countries, Treasury, Defense, Justice, Post Office, Agriculture, Labor, Commerce & Interior. The Cabinet is purely advisory & cabinet officers are subject to removal by the President. There are a number of independent Bureaus & Offices not included under the jurisdiction of any of the departments. Recently, a general plan for reorganization of the executive branch has been proposed. This plan contemplates bringing many of the independent Bureaus & Offices under one or another of the departments.

The President is head of his party & as such & by reason of his position as President, has great influence on the course of legislation in the Congress. But his position is not comparable to that of the British Prime Minister. He may have to deal with a majority in the Congress belonging to the opposition party. The latter situation, in fact, because of the system of election of members of the House & Senate, has frequently developed in the middle of a presidential term. In Britain, in such a case, the ministry resigns or goes to the people. In the United States, the situation remains unresolved. The President may veto any law passed by Congress, but his veto, as already pointed out, may be overridden by a two-thirds majority in that body.

The Judiciary is entirely independent of the other two branches of the government. Federal judges are appointed for life & may not be removed except for misconduct in office. The Supreme Court, composed of nine judges, is the highest tribunal. It is largely an appeals court. In addition, there are Circuit Courts of Appeal & District Courts. Generally speaking, the jurisdiction of the Judiciary is in the field of interpretation of the Constitution, enforcement of Federal criminal laws, bankruptcy laws, admiralty & maritime matters, suits against the government, suits between the states & between citizens of different states. The most important function, historically, has been in the interpretation of the Constitution. Early in its existence, the Supreme Court decided that it had the right to declare not only a law passed by Congress, but also one enacted by a state, unconstitutional. Such decisions cannot be overridden except by an amendment to the Constitution.

THE STATES: The governmental structure of the states somewhat resembles that of the national government. The states have bicameral legislatures, an executive, known as the Governor, & an independent judiciary. The members of the higher courts, in most of the states, however, are elected by popular vote & usually for specific terms. The Governors are elective; their terms vary from two to four years. The members of the legislatures are also elected, but their terms also vary in the various states. Elections both for national & state officials, are held in November, except in Maine where state elections are held in September.

# INDIANS

In describing the Indians of the various sections of the United States at different stages in their history, some of the factors which account for their similarity amid difference can be readily accounted for, others are difficult to disentangle.

The basic physical similarity of the Indians from Alaska to Patagonia is explained by the fact that they all came originally from Asia by way of Bering Strait & the Aleutian Islands into Alaska & thence southward. They came in different waves, the earliest around 25,000 years ago, the latest probably not long before America was discovered by Europeans. Because these people all came from Asia & were therefore drawn from the same pool of Asiatic people, the so-called Mongoloid race, they tended to look alike. But since the various waves crossed into Alaska at widely separated times, there were differences among them in their physical characteristics, particularly in bodily size, shape & size of head, face & nose.

There were also differences in cultural equipment. The earliest arrivals are known to science only through their simple tools of chipped stone & bone. Chipped stone implements include points used to tip the darts propelled by a spear-thrower as well as knives & scraping tools. Despite their limited technical equipment, the early Folsom & Sandia cultures, as they are called from sites in New Mexico, were very successful big game hunters in the great Plains area. Twenty-five thousand years ago they were hunting the wooly mammoth, the giant bison, the ground sloth & the camel, all characteristic animals of the closing phases of the last ice age. Later hunters brought additional weapons such as the bola & the bow & arrow. Though there are many gaps between the early periods that archaeology reveals & the period of the coming of the Europeans, the general outline of what must have happened is reasonably clear.

After their arrival from Asia in various waves across Bering Strait, the early peoples in the Americas slowly spread southward into the vast empty spaces of the two continents. A group of people moving slowly down the Mackenzie river valley east of the Rockies into the general region of Southern Alberta, then eastward across the northern prairies reaching the wooded country around the upper Mississippi & the western Great Lakes, then in a southeastward movement following the Mississippi valley until some final settlement was reached in the Gulf states, would encounter a wide variety of physical environments. At various stages of such wanderings they would have to evolve methods of coping with the cold, barren, tundra country of northern Canada; the prairies, cold, treeless but well-stocked with large game; then later the completely different flora & fauna of the Minnesota-Wisconsin-

Illinois area, thickly forested & well-watered & providing an abundance of small game & wild vegetable foods; then the semi-tropical character of the lower Mississippi country as they neared the Gulf of Mexico. Since such a migration would be spread over many centuries, the modification of whatever basic culture they had on their arrival from Asia would be very slow. Yet the end-result would be completely different from their original culture. It would also be different from the final culture of a closely allied group who became separated from them early in their wanderings & whose movements led them into different types of country. In its final form, the culture of this second group would have little in common with that of the first except perhaps a continuing resemblance in language & in physical type.

Only on some such theory of early migrations can we explain the distribution of the various language families in North America. One of the great language families of the northern & eastern United States, the Algonkin language family, was found in the 16th century heavily concentrated in Quebec, New England & around the Great Lakes, with its "heartland" apparently between the Great Lakes & Hudson's Bay. But on the other side of the continent in northern California were living a few small, unimportant tribes (Yurok, Wiyot) who have nothing in common with the great Algonkin tribes of the east except that they spoke languages belonging to the Algonkin family. In all other respects they were typically Californian Indians.

In endeavoring to fill the gaps between the story revealed by archaeology & the situation described by the early white settlers, we have to be aware of three different factors. First, we must believe that what later became widely separated & quite distinct tribal groups were once the same people. The best evidence of such earlier unity of groups that later became distinct is the evidence of language.

Secondly, the geographical differences in the varied sections of the United States are very great, & man's dependence upon the geography, especially among hunting & wild-food-gathering peoples, is very close. The early Indians, therefore, as they moved into different sections of country, would work out ways of life suited to local conditions. For example, to provide clothing, blankets, or house coverings, skins were utilized in one region, bark in another, furs in a third. Different folklores & religions were built around the local animals, local mountains, streams, etc. People lived in densely populated fishing camps in some places, in scattered hunting groups in others. As time passed, each culture would become more or less "fixed" to the local region as it became more & more tied in with local conditions. Marked differences would appear between the cultures of the forested & open regions, between the cultures of the cold north & the warm south, or between the east & the west, between the mountains & the plains.

Thirdly, as each regional cultural pattern became more or less fixed to a particular area, one region in particular began to forge ahead of all others & to develop or "invent" many elements of a civilization of a high order. This development of the higher civilizations of the American Indian took place in Middle America somewhere in the country stretching from Peru to Mexico. As agriculture, pottery, village & town life, weaving, architecture, science, & elaborate social & political organization were developed in the Middle American centers, they tended to spread from the people who made them (the Maya, the Inca, & later the Aztec) to the more barbarous peoples on the fringes of

Middle America. Thus we discover a northward flow of ideas (not necessarily or even probably of peoples) from Mexico into the southern sections of the United States. By the time the whites arrived, two regions were noticeably affected by this northward spread of southern ideas. One was the Southwest (particularly the Pueblos of New Mexico and Arizona); the other was the Southeast. In both areas, civilizations had developed by 1500 which were much more efficient than anything that had previously existed north of the Rio Grande. The Southeast peoples in turn were passing on, in a rather crude & diminished form, some of these new ideas to the Mississippi valley & to the Atlantic seaboard. As these ideas were all diffusing from a central region in Middle America, they tended to be similar in form & hence to spread a layer of later similarity on top of the lower layers of diversity which the regional specializations had given the various areas. The coming of the whites, however, arrested this diffusion of ideas from the south into the United States before it had time to spread very widely or become firmly established. Areas well to the west & north, notably the Pacific northwest coast & the area around Hudson's Bay, had not been affected by them when Mexico fell to the Spaniards.

Working on these three bases of original movement of peoples from north to south, regional specialization & separation, & a final movement of higher ideas out of Mexico northward, the basic similarities & differences in the Indian cultures of the United States can be understood. It is most convenient to divide the cultures into five main areas for separate treatment, these being: (a) the Southwest; (b) the Southeast; (c) the Northeast; (d) the Pacific & Mountain region; (e) the Plains.

THE SOUTHWEST: Probably one of the first areas of the United States to receive the impact of the new developments from the higher centers of civilization to the south, was that region loosely called the Southwest. Prior to the appearance of the southern ideas, well before the Christian era, the Southwest had been settled by a sparse population subsisting largely by hunting & the gathering of wild seeds. Subsequent to this occupation, at least four distinctive cultures developed in the Southwest, though for only two of these do we know the main developments in any detail.

The lowland, desert region of southern Arizona is the center of development of one of these culture divisions, called the Hohokam. Perhaps around 500 B.C. this culture had already taken form under the stimulus of the introduction of agricultural practices. Pottery was manufactured early & characteristically bears red designs on a buff background. The people lived in individual houses of posts & brush, partially subterranean. We can ascribe the basic change in life—from one based on hunting game & gathering wild seeds & roots to a settled life based on farming—to the influence of the higher civilizations in Middle America; the pottery & many other items were borrowed from the same source. The Hohokam peoples constructed courts for a ritual ball game played with balls of rubber, duplicating an activity of the Mexican area. In the same category are to be placed such items as mosaic mirrors of pyrite, copper bells, stone palettes for pigment & pottery figurines.

While an evolution of culture was taking place in the lowland area of the Southwest, the peoples of the highland region were more gradually receiving the impact of the new ideas. This regional culture, called the Anasazi, is divided into Basket Maker & Pueblo phases. The earliest Basket Maker culture dates from around the time of the earliest Hohokam developments & while this group practiced agriculture, they still did not manufacture pottery. Containers consisted of baskets & soft-fibre bags. Houses must have been fragile structures since no traces of them are found. Unlike the Hohokam people to the south who used the bow & arrow, the early Basket Makers used a spear-thrower & dart. The next period of development of the Basket Makers saw additional cultural innovations. Subterranean pit-houses were constructed & possibly as a result of Hohokam stimulation pottery was developed.

Succeeding developments are known under the term Pueblo because of an innovation in the method of constructing houses, & masonry or adobe houses built above ground are now found. The bow & arrow & the use of cotton for cloth was introduced early from the Hohokam to the south. This was followed by a marked clustering of houses, often with united walls, around a subterranean ceremonial chamber known as the kiva. This structure seems to be a survival of the pit-house of the Basket Maker phase. Population groups were small & scattered until the next phase of development when large apartment house structures were built such as the noted ones in Chaco Canyon. Though the earlier Anasazi developments had lagged behind the evolution of culture in the Hohokam region, later they became sufficiently virile & expansionistic to dominate & alter the latter culture. In the latter Pueblo phase characteristic polychrome & glaze paint pottery typical of the historic pueblos was developed. At this time, a gradual restriction in the area occupied brought about a regrouping of Pueblo peoples into the towns in which they were first discovered by the Spanish explorers in 1540 & which they still occupy today.

In 1540 it is estimated that there were about 20,000 Pueblo Indians living in around 70 towns. Although they spoke several distinct languages, all were quite similar in their social customs & material culture. The Hopi in the northwest spoke a Shoshonean language while the Zuni on the western border of New Mexico can not be readily grouped with any other language type. On the Puerco River & on the Rio Grande north of Albuquerque, the Pueblos spoke a Keresan language while the other Pueblos, also largely on the Rio Grande, spoke Tanoan languages. Today these pueblo peoples live in largely the same places though a few groups have become extinct & the total population is drastically reduced.

The Southwestern Indians today still preserve many of the features gradually developed over the period sketched above. The marked regional diversity & specialized Mexican traits of the early period are largely lost, overwhelmed by the Anasazi culture. The most characteristic feature of Pueblo life is the pueblo itself which is best illustrated in its traditional form by Taos. Here the pueblo consists of a series of connected rooms of adobe, terraced to a maximum height of five stories. The outer & upper rooms are used as living quarters while interior rooms provide storage space. Associated with the pueblos are the kivas, the chambers which were formerly subterranean & entered through the roof though now in some pueblos they are often above ground. These serve as a clubhouse for the men & also as the scene of the secret portions of the religious ceremonies.

Though the Pueblos now have cattle & raise a variety of European crops, in the past they were primarily dependent upon agriculture with corn as the principal crop. Through a skilful use of irrigation or the selection of areas that took advantage of runoff water, crops were raised in extremely arid regions. They did not rely entirely upon their own technical skill to ensure good crops since their religion in large part revolves around the insurance of an adequate crop. Elaborate ritual, in fact, surrounds every crisis in the life of the individual or activities of the pueblo. The elaborate ritual, with its annual & often spectacular ceremonies, welds the pueblo into a unified body.

Each pueblo is an independent political unit & is mainly organized through religious societies & on the basis of extended groups of blood relatives. These latter groupings, called clans & moieties, consist of divisions considered to be blood kin whose function is mainly to regulate marriage & the behavior of individuals. Heads of the clan direct many of the activities in the pueblos; since these individuals are religious as well as political leaders, the government to a certain extent is theocratic.

The Pueblos excel in many arts & crafts which continue the traditions developed during the prehistoric period. Women at most of the pueblos are extremely skilful in making elaborately painted pottery. The men are adept in weaving locally raised cotton into fabrics. Formerly the Pueblos also made excellent basketry.

Though the pueblo peoples were never particularly warlike, they were forced to defend themselves from other more primitive nomadic peoples who also lived in the Southwest. The nomadic groups lived in a much closer relationship to the environment & depended to a greater extent upon the natural resources of the area, both in the form of wild game & wild plant foods. They, consequently, lived in smaller groups with less elaborate political controls.

The nomadic tribes may be divided into two linguistic stocks. One, the Athabascan, consists of the Navaho & several Apache tribes who live primarily in northern New Mexico & Arizona. The second linguistic division is the Yuman which includes the Walapai, Yavapai & Havasupai who live in the western portion of Arizona & the lower Colorado River Valley. Their customs vary widely, some, like the Navaho, having taken over many features of Pueblo life. The Navaho tend to have more permanent houses of timber & earth while the others make easily constructed shelters of branches & thatch. Though most of them practiced some agriculture, they relied to a great extent upon hunting & the gathering of wild foods. Their clothing tended to resemble more the buckskin garments of the Plains than it did the cloth materials of the Pueblos. Many crafts, such as a crude form of pottery, were borrowed but they tended to excel in basketry techniques. Despite the excellence of Navaho weaving, this technique was probably not borrowed before the Spanish period. Metal working is similarly a recently introduced craft.

Only a few groups like the Navaho & Western Apache have clans which regulate marriage & other social duties. Most of the nomadic tribes are simply organized into loose bands. The religious practices have much in common with those of the Pueblos, though the occasions on which ceremonies are held vary considerably. Healing ceremonies & puberty rites are important. The Navaho in particular have developed or borrowed more elaborate ceremonies under the control of a group of priests.

The Navaho & Apache groups illustrate quite clearly how Indian tribes readily dropped older features of their culture & adopted new ones to meet the requirements of different environments. Though they now share most of the culture of other tribes of the Southwest, linguistically their only relatives in the United States are on the Pacific coast in California. The great mass of

Athabaskan peoples live in the extreme northwest of the Canadian prairies on the so-called "Barren Grounds" & inhospitable country immediately south of the Eskimo. The Navaho & Apache must be viewed as rather recent arrivals in the southwest who despite the short time they have been there have succeeded in taking over most of the Indian way of life in that area.

THE SOUTHEAST: The Southeastern portion of the United States, the region roughly including Arkansas, Tennessee & Virginia & all states to the south, was also occupied at an early period by small groups of hunting & seed-gathering peoples. Agriculture appears to have been introduced from the tropical regions to the south, possibly prior to the other arts we associate with an advanced culture, traits such as pottery & an elaborate political & religious system. Developments in these aspects begin at a period approximately the same as the formative period of Southwestern pueblo culture. Though a few traits can be shown to be of southern origin, much of the content of the southeastern cultures may well be a local development.

The early archaeological remains are often loosely called remains of the "Mound Builders" though actually such a classification is a misnomer. The practice of building mounds is associated with many distinct peoples & the form & function of the mounds varied considerably in the 1500 years during which the trait is found. The general developments made during this period can be characterized in terms of Burial Mound & Temple Mound periods. Though the following description is based on the sequence found in the lower Mississippi Valley, the same general developments are to be found throughout the entire area & in fact through most of the adjacent Northeastern area as well.

The beginning of the Burial Mound period is marked by small villages consisting of only crude dwellings. Though making pottery & practicing agriculture, the people still relied to a considerable extent upon hunting & gathering. Burial customs varied since cremations as well as flexed & extended primary inhumations are found. The burials were placed in mounds, 10 to 15 feet in height, foreshadowing the later elaboration in this custom. In the latter part of this period, a single culture complex spread over much of the Mississippi Valley. The Marksville culture in the south, like its northern relative, the Hopewell culture, is marked by technical progress in ceramics, stone work, the utilization of copper for ornaments & tools, & a richly symbolic art & religious complex. The burial mounds were much larger, some conical forms ranging up to 25 feet in height & 150 feet in diameter. Many new types of ornaments such as copper ear-spools, head ornaments of antler & copper, as well as other forms are found. The significance of the new ornaments appears to lie in the fact that they had a limited distribution in the population as a whole suggesting that they are marks of status, the group being divided into classes. In the close of the period, we find the introduction of a new mound-building complex from the south. The new mound was designed not for use as a burial place but had the form of a truncated pyramid & was used as a platform on which a temple or chief's house was erected. Regular cemeteries rather than burial mounds came into use.

The innovation in type of mound construction that marks the beginning of the Temple Mound period reflects profound changes in social & political organization. During the preceding period, the mound clusters were ceremonial centers where the population gathered for funerals & perhaps religious ceremonies but they were not centers where large populations lived. In the Temple Mound period the villages were larger, the greatest of them combining religious & population centers. They contain groups of flat-topped mounds arranged round a central plaza & are often of impressive size since individual mounds reach a height of 80 feet. These indications of larger population centers suggest that the economy is more firmly rooted in advanced agricultural techniques. Warfare is also becoming an important factor in the latter part of the Temple Mound period, since palisaded villages were of common occurrence.

Indians of this cultural stage were seen & described by the members of the DeSoto expedition which passed through the Southeast in 1541. The Spaniards were particularly impressed by the wealth of pearls possessed by the Indians & by the fact that many groups appeared to be ruled by women. Many specific items of culture are mentioned by the explorers that had clearly spread from the tropical regions of the south. These include the use of the blow-gun, feather cloaks, & the custom of carrying a chief about in a litter. Their general descriptions suggest a high culture stage, a fact which is confirmed by later ethnographic investigations. Except for the Southwest, the most intensive agriculture in the United States was found here. The diet was supplemented by the hunting of game animals such as deer, bear, & even bison in the western portion of the territory. Fish, fowl & shellfish along the coast also varied the diet. Even cannibalism is reported on the Gulf coast of Florida.

Houses were generally rectangular with a curved roof. Branches were woven in the wall posts which then might be covered with clay. The houses are arranged to form large towns which have regular streets & are surrounded by a palisade and moat. Choctaw houses were usually round & dome-shaped, the exterior being plastered. Some Seminole houses were raised four to five feet on stilts & have an overhanging, gabled roof with partially open sides. Such houses are admirably adapted to their warm & moist habitat in Florida. Though both the Southwest & the Southeast had a similar economy & manufactured similar craft products, the differences between the two areas illustrate well the variability found between Indian cultures. Pottery, for example, was made in both regions. The pottery of the Southwest depends upon contrasting color achieved through painting techniques for its effect. Southeastern pottery emphasizes form & surface texture. Vessels were manufactured in a greater variety of shapes & surfaces were incised, engraved or modified by paddling techniques. Basketry was also found in both regions. The Southeast in its late phase lacked the elaborate coiled basketry so typical of the Southwest & concentrated instead upon twill-plaiting of strips of cane. Each area tended to develop in its own distinctive manner.

A marked contrast is to be noted in social & political organization. Clans were also widespread in the Southeast, consisting of a number of households or lineages united by blood & having a common totem. The tribe, however, is here an actual political unit having not only a common language but also a definite territory. It is usually governed by a council of chiefs representing the various clans. Beyond this, the tribes might be united in a larger confederacy. Throughout much of this region, we find few parallels to the Southwestern situation of independent villages, but rather a marked tendency toward larger political units. It is in terms of such a background that the well-known tribes of the Southeast, the Choctaw, Chickasaw, Creek & Cherokee as well as the linguistically & culturally related Iroquoian tribes of the Northeast, must be understood. The political integration that was achieved after white conquest & Indian removal to the present state of Oklahoma would probably not have been possible in the absence of similar patterns in their own culture.

THE NORTHEAST: At the opening of the historic period, the situation in the northeastern & north central part of the United States was already confused by what appears to have been a relatively recent northward & westward thrust by the Iroquoian-speaking peoples from the Southeast into Ohio, New York & particularly through the Mohawk & Hudson valleys to the Great Lakes area. It was clearly a late intrusion into what had previously been an area predominantly occupied by Algonkin-speaking peoples. The Algonkins had agriculture but were not as efficient at it nor as dependent upon it as their Iroquoian enemies. Some of the far northern Algonkins in the vicinity of Hudson's Bay were beyond the limits of cultivation & lived entirely by hunting & collecting wild vegetables. Along the east coast, however, from the Potomac northward to the St. Lawrence, in the Hudson, St. Lawrence & Ohio valleys prior to the Iroquoian expansion, & both north & south of the Great Lakes westward at least to the Chicago region, there was or had been a fairly uniform type of language & culture. Primarily hunters of deer & small forest animals, they also raised corn & beans though their gardens were only small patches of cleared land, tended by the women. Sites of villages were moved frequently according to the seasons since winter encampments differed from summer camps & also to suit the convenience of the hunters. The type of house was a dome-shaped wigwam made of bark contrasting very unfavorably with the wooden long-houses of the Iroquois. The chief method of travel was by water in dugout & birchbark canoe. Metal was of course unknown, weapons being of stone, wood or bone, & household utensils of wood or bark. Pottery was made though it was of a crude inferior type compared with other areas of North America. The Algonkins were able to make mats, bags & crude baskets but their weaving was very primitive.

The chief handicap of the Algonkins, both in their contacts with the Iroquois & with the whites, lay in the weakness of their political organization. Anthropologists distinguish a large number of so-called "tribes" making up the Algonkin family, but the tribe seldom did anything as a unit. The chiefs were usually little more than heads of villages or at the most a loose federation of villages. Petty feuds between villages even of the same tribe were not uncommon. Under such circumstances no tradition of joint action existed whereby a large war party could be organized against a common foe. The so-called "kings" mentioned in the early history of New England, such as the famous "King Philip," were nothing more than petty chieftains whose authority did not extend beyond their own small village & even there was not unquestioned. The rare occasions when it was possible to unite any considerable body of Algonkins under a single leader, as for example when Pontiac, an Ottawa, managed in 1763 to unite members of at least six different tribes under his command & lay siege to Detroit & Pittsburg at the same time, shows how difficult such a feat was. In Pontiac's case, lack of quick success led his allies to desert him, emphasizing the fact that they were allies & not in any sense under his orders.

Upon people of such a level of culture, the double pressure of the Iroquois & of the whites had disastrous results. The tribes of the Atlantic coastal region died out or were wiped out early. One or two of them, notably the Delaware, managed to retain their individuality by retreating far to the west. Starting from the valley of the Delaware at the time of the first white settlements, the Delaware reached Ohio in 1751. By 1789 they were in Missouri, in Kansas in 1835, & finally in 1867 they joined the Cherokee in Oklahoma. Other Delaware bands appear at times in Texas & in Ontario.

The Algonkin to the north, already near the fringes of possible cultivation, tended to withdraw still further, thus abandoning their incipient agriculture. In many cases, such as the Ojibway of Northern Canada, they managed to survive as hunting tribes to the present day. The Algonkin of western New York, Ohio, southern Ontario, Michigan, Indiana & Illinois, were in large part driven westward by Iroquoian pressure. Many of them, like the Sauk, Fox, Kickapoo, Miami, Illinois & Potawatomi, found a final refuge in Wisconsin behind the shelter of Lake Michigan. Others were turned by the demands of the fur trade into full-time hunters who retreated north & west as the beaver became extinct in the eastern rivers & lakes. This movement of the Algonkins toward the west was apparently not a new movement since at least one Algonkin tribe, the Menomini, was already west of Lake Michigan well before 1500, & other Algonkins such as the Blackfoot, Cheyenne & Arapaho were apparently out in the prairies before 1600. The pressures introduced by the whites merely intensified an east to west movement of the Algonkins that started centuries before.

THE PACIFIC COAST AND THE MOUNTAIN REGION: On the other side of the continent, in Washington, Oregon, & California, & extending into the mountain states of Nevada & Idaho, there existed in pre-white times other types of Indian economy. To the north around the waters of Puget Sound was the southern extension & final boundary of the very distinctive & specialized culture of the Northwest coast. This type of culture, whose centers & high points are in British Columbia, was based on two abundant products of the environment: salmon & cedar. The salmon provided abundance of food; the cedar provided a material from which could be made a variety of manufactured products. On this base was built the noted culture of the Northwest coast tribes, containing such spectacular features as the totem pole, the large multi-family wooden houses, the potlatch, a high degree of ceremonialized economics & hereditary rank. For a non-agricultural people, there was a heavy density of population in the villages along the fiords & bays. But this culture was only possible in the regions where the salmon were abundant & easily caught. Because of the decline in quantity of salmon, south of Puget Sound & east of the Cascades it thins out & disappears to be replaced throughout the rest of the Pacific & mountain areas by a much poorer type of culture.

The Indians who lived in California, Nevada, Idaho, Utah & the interior of Washington & Oregon had to exploit to the fullest all edible materials in their environment. It is an indication of the comparative poverty of the far western flora & fauna that the staple food of many of these Indians was the wild acorn. From this unpromising source, a type of bread was produced by pounding the acorns into a fine meal, then soaking the meal repeatedly to remove the bitter qualities, followed by a final drying of the paste. In addition to preparing this acorn bread, they hunted deer & small game in the mountains & gathered whatever seeds, roots, bulbs & wild fruit & vegetables the local environment provided. The acorns which were the main source of food in central California were replaced almost entirely in western Washington & Idaho by bulbous roots roasted & eaten or roasted & pounded into a mush which was then made into bread. In Utah the main staple was the seed of a different tree, the pinyon. Despite these regional variations there was one constant feature throughout the wild-seed area, an emphasis upon food storage, unusual among primitive gatherers. This was perhaps the combined result of rather sparse food supply & dependence upon vegetable resources. Vegetable foods when suitably treated can be more readily stored & kept in good condition than animal food.

With the exception of their techniques for storing food, these gatherers lived at a comparatively low level of culture. They were loosely organized in small settlements & were unwarlike. They usually went barefoot, wore little clothing & apart from very good basketry did not develop much in the way of higher cultural features. In this they offer a marked contrast with their neighbors of the Southwest. Pueblo elements affected the California area slightly & then only the extreme southern portion of the state.

The whole Pacific & mountain area is best described as a low level cultural area based on root & seed gathering. It existed in a static & unchanging way between the two higher level areas of Northwest & Southwest, but was not noticeably affected by either of these. In essentials the same way of life was followed by all the Indians who lived in the mountains & on the plateau. It is only when the Continental Divide is crossed & we are among the foothill peoples on the prairie side of the mountains that noticeably new features enter. These are, of course, prairie or buffalo-hunting features seeping into the mountain regions from the eastward.

THE PLAINS: Lying between the forested regions of the Northeast & Southeast & the mountains of the west is the enormous area of the American plains. After the coming of the white man, most of the spectacular events of Indian history took place in this area which quickly became the buffalo hunting ground of the Indian on horseback, the country of the feathered war-bonnet, the tipi, Sitting Bull & Custer's Last Stand. All these things were the results of the coming of the whites & particularly of the arrival of the horse. Introduced by the Spaniards in the far south, the horse was quickly taken over by the Indians from Texas to the Canadian border.

Before the coming of the horse, which reached the Lower Missouri before 1680, the Upper Missouri by 1740, & the Saskatchewan by 1750, the Plains were scantily populated. Indians traveling & hunting on foot could not make a dependable living from the constantly moving buffalo herds since these could travel much faster than foot-hunters. Buffalo-hunting, therefore, was but an occasional & seasonal activity. Most of the tribes who became famous as buffalo-hunting tribes after they acquired horses—such as the Cheyenne, the Blackfoot, the Arapaho, the Comanche—did not live on the Plains at all in the pre-European period, or if they did, obtained their living from other sources than the buffalo. Such peoples tended to cling to the fringes of the woodlands like the Dakota tribes who were still in Minnesota on the Upper Mississippi when the French began to arrive in that region. Here their economy was the forest-hunting & rudimentary farming of the Northeast similar to that of the Algonkin peoples east of them in Wisconsin & Michigan. Occasionally hunting parties penetrated on foot out into the open plains but it was a raid, not an attempt at permanent settlement. On the other side, the Comanche in the Wyoming foothills & valleys & the Blackfoot further north in the foothills of western Montana also made occasional forays on foot into the open plains. The horse revolutionized the way of life of all these tribes around the fringes by drawing them into the central plains as permanent dwellers. It was now possible to establish themselves as full-time hunters of the buffalo & to abandon farming. A host of other cultural changes followed as results of the basic change in economy. The conical tipi, clothing, tent-covers & receptacles of rawhide, the feathered headdress, the ordered camp-circle, skilful horsemanship, emphasis on bravery & prestige derived from bravery, the development of war-leaders, high mobility & unsettled tribal boundaries—all these & many other features of Plains culture are among the immediate results of the move into the plains. When we add to the horse, the acquisition of the gun & the iron kettle introduced by the early traders, it is clear that the hunters of the plains underwent an expansionist period of cultural efflorescence with a new environment to exploit & new tools with which to exploit it. So for a short period, approximately between 1650 and 1850, there was a new & impressive type of Indian culture developing west of the Mississippi. The depletion of the buffalo herds & the remorseless westward surge of white settlement finally snuffed it out.

Both archaeology & early history show that some agricultural settlements existed in prehistoric days well out from the forest areas on the east & the foothill areas on the west. The best-known of these are the Mandan-Hidatsa villages on the upper Missouri in North Dakota. These Indians continued to farm & keep to their permanent villages even after the horse appeared and the plains around them became full of buffalo-hunting tribes. They are called the "village Indians" & referred to in terms of high admiration for their stage of culture by all the early explorers of the northern prairies. Some of the French suggest that they had seen nothing so civilized since they had left the Iroquoian villages far to the east. The archaeological evidence of more extensive agricultural settlements west of the Mississippi in prehistoric times, particularly on the bigger river systems, does not necessarily contradict the basic notion of the plains being relatively empty before the coming of the horse. The agricultural settlements were restricted to the more important drainage systems, less favorable areas becoming depopulated during the periodic droughts which struck the plains. With the exception of the Mandan-Hidatsa groups & the Pawnee, however, none of these agricultural peoples was able to withstand the attraction of the horse or to continue their old way of life into the historic period.

THE INDIAN AT THE PRESENT TIME: The story of the Indian in the past few hundred years has been a sad one. Estimates of the population at the time of the coming of the whites are difficult to make, but around one million for the whole of the United States is a reasonable figure. The present Indian population is less than half that figure, being under 400,000 for those people reckoned by law as being Indians. This does not include that considerable number of Americans with Indian blood, often a high proportion of Indian blood, who have become absorbed into the general population & are indistinguishable from other Americans.

Regional differences continue to be noticeable even in the way different areas were affected by the white conquest. In the northeast & southeast most of the Indians were completely wiped out, or driven into other areas, though some, perhaps many in certain sections, were assimilated into the white population. In the Pacific, Mountain & Plains regions, they have survived physically, but not as functioning societies. In those regions all the picturesque tribal & cultural differences have been reduced to a monotonous, pathetic uniformity called "reservation Indians" who present the same depressing features whether they speak of themselves as Blackfoot, Sioux, Klamath, or Ojibway. Only in the southwest have Indian groups managed to preserve their way of life, relatively unchanged. The Pueblo Indians alone, of the 600 or more distinct Indian societies in the United States before 1500, have been successful in resisting the extinction, assimilation or pauperization which have affected all other tribes.

THE INDIAN OF THE HISTORIC PERIOD: To a considerable extent, the discovery of America by Western Europe & the intrusion of Europeans into the New World produced effects comparable to those of the earlier invasions of Asiatics across Bering Strait. The contact of the two peoples led to an exchange of many culture traits, a blending of the two physical types, & the development of a new mode of life. This process operated most fully in Mexico & South America where the Indian & White cultures met on an almost equal plane of development & only to a lesser extent in the United States proper. In the higher centers of Indian civilization which were the centers of greatest population density, the impact of conquest was most easily absorbed & the large population was able to survive decimation & then rebuilt itself into a significant, & potentially dominant, element of the population. In the United States the effect of contact was also dependent in part upon the cultural stage & population density of the particular Indian group, but whereas Latin America in general had to deal with the Indian policy of but a single nation, the Indians of what later became the United States & Canada were affected by the policies & rivalries of many different nations & were later subjected to the vacillating policies of our own government. The story of the Indian in the historic period can therefore be best treated in terms of the national groups with whom they came in contact.

The early exploration & tentative attempts at colonization probably had limited effects on the Indian. Norse settlement in Greenland & visits to the northern section of the continent did not materially change their culture. The earliest Spanish penetration, however, aside from the frankly exploratory voyages & expeditions like DeSoto's entrada through the Southeast, was largely motivated by a desire to change the Indian culture. Spain sincerely hoped to convert the Indians to Christianity & to improve their condition by teaching them the mode of life of western Europe. In the United States, the impact of Spanish policy was first strongly felt by the Pueblo Indians of the Southwest.

After an initial exploratory trip by a Franciscan friar, Marcos de Niza, the Southwest was entered in force by the Spaniards in 1540 with an expedition under Francisco Coronado. Though militarily successful in conquering the pueblos, the expedition returned to Mexico the following year. Only intermittent contacts followed this until in 1598 Juan de Oñate was allowed to colonize the country. The important pueblos submitted to his party & the occupation resulted in most of the villages being provided with churches & missionaries by 1630. The Indians, however, resented both the harsh civil control & the activities of the missionaries & planned a concerted rebellion in 1680 which forced the withdrawal of the Spaniards. Bitter fighting took place under the leadership of several governors until Don Diego de Vargas finally achieved general control of the region around 1692. Though the rebellion was unsuccessful in its objective, it did bring about less harsh treatment & greater tolerance in religious practices. The Pueblos were, therefore, able to continue life in their own villages with but little change.

The penetration into California began somewhat later. The earliest major influences were those of the Jesuits on the peninsula of Lower California. In 1765 the Franciscans replaced the Jesuits & within four years had expanded into what is now the United States. By 1823 missions had been built as far northward as San Francisco, twenty-three mission villages being under their control. The Indians of California lived primarily by hunting wild animals & gathering plant foods rather than in the agricultural patterns of the Southwest. The effect of the missions, aside from grouping them into villages, was to turn the Indians into agriculturalists & acquaint them with varied forms of domesticated animals. During their early periods the missions were relatively prosperous, producing food surpluses which permitted an expanding population. However, beginning around 1800 there was an increasing governmental interference with the program of the missionaries & even a deliberate attempt to create disaffection among the Indians toward the paternalistic policy of the missions. The varied opposition to the early missionary policy was successful in securing a tremendous decline in population & the segregation of the remaining groups on barren reservations.

A similar expansion of missions into the Southeast also resulted in an early success which was later thwarted by conflicting European policies. In the Southeast the earliest expeditions of De Soto & De Narvaez were not able to achieve complete subjugation of the Indians. The first Dominican missionaries who sailed to Florida in 1549, unarmed & without soldiers, were also unsuccessful. Mission activity was therefore impossible until De Aviles conquered Florida in 1565, using persuasion as much as force. Jesuit activity in Florida began in the same year & was paralleled by Franciscans who arrived in 1592. The region was rapidly converted to Christianity & the Indians settled in villages around the mission churches. The area had been broadly conceived as an experiment to determine what success could be achieved in the acculturation of the Indian without the constant pressure of military force. As a result, only a small garrison of Spanish soldiers was maintained at St. Augustine. No European immigration was permitted since the region was to be a land of Christian Indians & the general success of the experiment was such that the prosperity of the Florida missions around 1680 seems comparable to those of California in the eighteenth century. At this time slave raiding activity of the Creek, Cherokee, & Yuchi instigated by the English caused a withdrawal from the Georgia region. These raids were eventually extended into Florida proper, the major blow being struck by an expedition led by Colonel Moore of Carolina in 1704 during the war between England & Spain which resulted in the sacking of Apalatchee. By 1745 all mission villages established by Spain in Florida were abandoned.

Of the various contacts in the north & east, those of the French were perhaps the least harmful to Indian life & culture. The early French in Quebec were less land-hungry than the English or the Dutch further south, for their concern was almost exclusively with the fur-trade or with Catholic missionary activity. Since the Indian economy of most of this region at the time of their arrival was still substantially a hunting one with minor reliance upon agriculture, the French desire for furs had the effect of halting the elementary agricultural trend among the Algonkins & redirecting Indian energy into hunting & trapping. They had no wish to dispossess the Indian of his land but on the contrary their policy was to encourage the Indian to become "still more Indian," provided, of course, that he brought his furs to the French trading posts. The French officials strove therefore to preserve tribal life & to protect the Indian territory from invasion by land-hungry white farmers & from molestation by other Indians likely to interfere with the hunting. The geography of the northeast was peculiarly suited to the carrying out of such a policy. Because of the extensive network of waterways leading from the mouth of the St. Lawrence into the heart of the continent, French explorers, traders & priests had penetrated by canoe to Lake Superior, Wisconsin & the Upper Mississippi before the English in Virginia had moved more than a few miles inland from the coast. Furs from Minnesota were being marketed in Quebec City at a time when the Dutch had only reached Albany. This extensive travel & trade by canoe was, of course, an Indian pattern which the French adopted & improved.

As with the Spaniards, so with the French the presence of the priests did something to humanize still further the white contacts with the Indians. The absorption of the government in the fur-trade promoted a rather paternalistic policy, & the extensive use of "coureurs de bois" as middlemen in the trade led to easy intermarriage between the two races. But above all, the readiness of the Jesuits & the Oblates to live as the Indians lived, to learn their languages & to treat them as "equals in the sight of God" was the main factor.

Of course, the French were no more altruistic than any other 17th century colonizers. But the story of French-Indian contacts has a more attractive atmosphere than we find in other areas or in later periods. There is good evidence, for example, that Champlain could have concluded a satisfactory alliance with the Iroquois & thus relieved the French traders & their Algonkin & Huron proteges of their most constant & deadly problem had he been willing to outbid the Dutch at Albany in the amount of guns & liquor that he would supply as the price of alliance. His refusal was at least partly dictated by his own strong views (shared by his home government & his priests) on the evil effects of liquor upon native life. However mixed their motives, the French should be given credit for having made some effort to soften the impact of European culture upon Indian life.

Unlike the expansion of Spain & France after the very early explorations, the early colonizing activity of the remaining north European countries was largely in the hands of business corporations. After the destruction of the Roanoke Colony in North Carolina, private commercial companies took over the privileges to exploit North America. The region south of the Delaware was under the control of the Virginia Company which founded Jamestown, the first permanent colony of English in America. To the north, the Plymouth Company, later reorganized, began the settlement of New England. The general pattern, so far as the English were concerned, was to permit the colonies to be built up by private organizations who had absolute powers in their territory & who established the basic policy toward the Indian. The charters were later revoked & Crown colonies established.

Dutch companies similarly began operations nearly as early as the English, a trading post having been established on Manhattan Island as early as 1598 & a permanent trading post in 1614. The Dutch, having no legal right to land on the East coast through rights of discovery, are probably responsible for the establishment of the policy of purchasing lands from the Indians. The famed purchase of Manhattan Island for the equivalent of $24 may thus have been a gambit in a game for higher stakes designed to give the Dutch a legal foothold in America. The English, however, refused to accept the claims of the Dutch, driving them out in 1664.

To the English on the coast, trade with the Indians was not of great importance, nor were Indians seriously considered as an important labor source. To the south, in the Virginia colony, indentured white labor was first important & later Negro slave labor. Until 1622 the English in Virginia lived in relative peace with the Indians, their chiefs being recognized as independent monarchs. However, in this year a massacre of the colonists planned by the Indians was discovered, & was followed by guerrilla warfare lasting 12 years. Though in 1634 peace was reestablished, the Indians were now considered a definite nuisance. The English colony at Plymouth had less trouble with the Indians since a large portion of them had been killed off by smallpox prior to the arrival of the Pilgrims. Like the colonists in Virginia, the various New England settlements treated the Indian tribes as sovereign nations & continued the Dutch policy of purchasing land from the Indians though the titles were not valid unless also granted by the state. Despite land purchases, friction inevitably developed & led to the Indian Wars of 1637-1644, a pattern repeated many times on the frontier. The war was followed by the initiation of a new policy, the segregation of Indians on reservations.

The early reservations grew almost imperceptibly out of the increasing reluctance of the colonists to recognize the Indian title to land unless expressly conferred by the whites. After the wars of 1637-1644, the beaten tribes were assigned land by the colonial government to which it was hoped they would confine themselves. After a short period of experiment, it was found expedient to make such lands inalienable since otherwise the Indians under the influence of liquor would sell their land to unscrupulous settlers for next to nothing. In this haphazard way the reservation system came into existence, one of the earliest examples of such a policy being the establishment of the remaining Pequots on a reservation in Connecticut after the Pequot War of 1637. Such a system gradually became general throughout the colonies, each making its own improvisations in Indian policy.

However as settlement spread into the hinterland & the British & French Empires began to clash in the country beyond the Alleghenies, Indian affairs came to assume national & international importance. Indian alliances played a vital role in the war with the French of 1756-1763, & it was as a measure necessitated by the war that the British crown was led on the outbreak of war to take over the direct control of Indian affairs throughout the colonies. General Braddock appointed two Indian agents, one for the north & one for the south & while these agents were subject to the military command during the period of hostilities, after 1763 they became civil appointees under the immediate control of the Crown. It was under this agency system that the patchwork Indian administration was made definite & relatively uniform throughout the original thirteen colonies.

After the formation of the United States the new Federal government adopted the Indian policy & machinery of the mother-country & organized an Indian Department to perform for the new nation the functions that had been performed by the two Indian agents of the British era. From then on treaties were made between the Indian groups & the United States government.

The reservation system, stated in its simplest terms, had come into being as a means of settling Indians on lands that the whites did not want, & of persuading or coercing them into remaining on those lands. But on any long-term view such a policy was hopelessly short-sighted. Lands the whites did not want today, they always wanted tomorrow. Areas which, like the Ohio country, were cheerfully ceded in perpetuity to the Indians as "Indian country" or "the western reserve" by one generation would become very attractive to homesteaders in the next. As the tide of colonization flowed irresistibly westward, the Ohio country, the North West, the Louisiana Purchase, & the country beyond the Mississippi which had been solid blocks of Indian population were broken into, settled, alienated to white ownership. These formerly tribal areas became shrinking islands of Indian land surrounded by territory belonging to the United States government.

The forced migration of the Southeastern tribes (Chickasaws, Choctaws, Creeks & Cherokees) to Oklahoma, effected between 1820 & 1840, removed the last big concentration of Indians from the east & thus by 1842 only unimportant reservations remained in the eastern United States. The "Indian country" by this time was the western plains from the Mississippi to the mountains which now contained not only its pre-Columbian inhabitants, but the survivors of hundreds of eastern tribes who had been driven back into it. Into this area the tide of westward expansion still flowed, especially after the gold discovery in California in 1849. The eastern story of warfare, massacre, treaties made & treaties broken on both sides, reservations, forced removals, shrinking reservations & further removals of Indians is repeated in the western regions during the last half of the nineteenth century.

The basic difficulty was never really solved. Treaties were made with defeated Indian tribes & lands were allotted to them as if they were sovereign powers, yet the government by such improvisations as the appointment of agents, the giving of presents at treaty-makings which later turned into annual payments & so-called "treaty money," & other extensions of bureaucratic usages into the nominally "sovereign" Indian areas, tended to reduce the Indians to the status of "wards" of the Federal authority. This anomaly became particularly pronounced as the Indian wars of the 19th century drew to a close, and as early as 1871 it was the subject of legislation by Congress. In that year an Act laid down that treaty-making with the Indians—any Indians—was hereby declared ended. The Supreme Court, however, when the matter came before it in the case of Lone Wolf vs. Hitchcock, held that Congress had no power to abrogate existing treaties, of which there were by this time hundreds, but that "henceforth" the Indians were to be treated as "wards" of the United States, to be dealt with by congressional enactment. Such attempts to legislate the matter only sharpened the anomalies & in 1873 we find the Commissioner of Indian Affairs complaining to the President in his annual report of the "anomalous relation of the Indian tribes to the government, which requires that they be treated as sovereign powers & as wards at one & the same time."

By this time everybody was heartily sick of the Indian problem & most thinking people were deeply ashamed of the "century of dishonor" in Indian-American relations that was drawing to a close. The Dawes Act of 1887 & the Burke Act of 1906 reflected this disgust & a determination to find the quickest basis for a permanent solution. The whole continent from Atlantic to Pacific was now a white man's country & with the Civil War over, America was a nation. The surviving Indian reservations were archaic hang-overs. The "melting-pot" philosophy of American nationhood was becoming popular & to leave the Indians—the oldest Americans—outside the melting pot was clearly illogical. Hence the new philosophy of Indian administration inaugurated by the Dawes Act. To bring the Indian into normal American life two steps had to be taken. The communally-owned land of the reservations had to be broken up into individual holdings, & the Indian had to be helped to accept ordinary American citizenship with its obligations as well as its privileges. The difficulty was of course the familiar one—how to prevent the Indian with an individual holding of land from being swindled out of it by a white man, & how to make him an ordinary American citizen if paternalistic legislation to prevent him being swindled was continued or new legislation for the "protection" of the Indian was enacted. The best way, it was thought, to assimilate the Indian into normal life was to leave him to "sink or swim," just like any other section of the population. But in practice it was hard for well-wishers of the Indian to watch with a clear conscience while he proceeded to sink, as he too often did, in the unfamiliar atmosphere of private property, individual responsibility, & rugged capitalism that he was thrown into. The legal citizenship tangle was finally resolved by an Act of Congress of 1924 which conferred automatic citizenship on all Indians who had not already acquired it by various previous acts conferring it in special cases. The question of Indians voting was left (as it still is) to the qualification requirements of the various states.

The "quick assimilation to ordinary Americanism" policy, of which the Acts of 1887, 1906 & 1924 were highlights, was probably the only possible policy for the United States government in the circumstances that had been created by the history of the previous three hundred years, & by & large it was not unsuccessful. Like all "sink or swim" policies it can be severely criticized as heartless or praised as realistic & economical. The dimensions & acuteness of the Indian problem were at least reasonably reduced between 1887 & 1930 by the individual allotment policy & the aim of quick assimilation. However, it is not surprising that a policy aimed at fitting many thousands of primitive people of varied cultures into the complicated, highly competitive American culture in the shortest possible time should produce a large number of abuses and deplorable incidents. The period between the Dawes Act & the 1930's witnessed a fairly large number of flagrant cases of exploitation & victimization of Indians, especially when some of the worthless areas ceded to them in the 19th century proved to be sources of mineral wealth. By the beginning of the New Deal enough indefensible abuses of the allotment system had occurred to give friends of the Indians powerful arguments against the policy of rapid assimilation or at least against the way that policy was being administered. A "New Deal for Indians" was therefore one of the basic innovations of President Roosevelt's regime. Under Harold Ickes as Secretary of the Interior, & John Collier as Indian Commissioner, the allotment system of the Dawes Act was abolished & a new policy was embodied in the Indian Reorganization Act of 1934 (known as the Wheeler-Howard Act). Under the new policy, Indian groups were encouraged by the Federal Government to become self-sufficient corporate units within the American economy. Instead of promoting the gradual extinction of the reservation lands by the process of individual ownership, Indian holdings were added to by repurchases by the department, for collective Indian use, of land previously alienated by individual Indian owners. In general, it would appear as if the Ickes-Collier policy of building up corporate Indian units & encouraging tribes to become business corporations, was a necessary & desirable antidote to the too-rapid individualization & assimilation of the previous policy. This was especially true in the Southwest where the imperviousness of the Pueblos & the Navaho to white ideas had presented a soil very unfavorable to rapid assimilation.

In the last few years there is evidence that the aims & objectives of the earlier period are likely to be revised & that fairly rapid liquidation of the Indian problem, as far as Federal control & supervision is concerned, is being contemplated as a Federal policy. In February, 1947, the Senate Committee on Civil Service received from the Acting Commissioner of the Office of Indian Affairs a program for the gradual withdrawal of Federal control over Indian affairs. This program, presented in response to a request by the Committee for some such scheme, envisaged the final withdrawal of the Federal government from the supervision of some ten Indian groups at "an early date"; withdrawal from supervision of some ten to twenty other groups within the next five to ten years; & classified all the remaining Indian areas or tribes together in a third group which would "remain a Federal responsibility for ten to twenty-five years longer, depending upon the strength or weakness of any Federal or other program to make them self-sufficient."

This report, visualizing the extinction of the Indian problem within the next twenty-five years, was presented to a Committee of the 80th Congress. What action the 81st Congress will take upon it remains to be seen.

—D. A. Baerreis and C. W. M. Hart

# LABOR

If we take a bird's-eye view of American labor history, we shall see that not until just after the Civil War was there any movement of consequence toward the organization of labor. The Knights of Labor, formed in 1869, for a time promised to become the spearhead of an active labor movement. But without sufficient organization, the Knights of Labor tried to spread over too much territory, political as well as industrial, & the promise did not materialize.

The American Federation of Labor, founded in 1881, eventually became the dominant force in organized labor in the United States from the last decade of the 19th century until around 1933. Agitation by the workers for organization was amazingly slow compared with the tremendous growth of American industry. It was only after 1933, rising from the greatest industrial & financial depression that this country has known, that labor grew strong & became an influence in public affairs. The great growth both in membership of existing unions & in the increase in number of industries with which labor engaged in collective bargaining, was due first to the protective labor measures growing out of New Deal legislation.

The greatest increase was due, undoubtedly, to the Congress of Industrial Organizations which succeeded on industrial lines in organizing industries which previously had had little or no organization. Millions of new members, particularly in the basic industries, were thus secured.

It is a far cry from this bird's-eye view back to 1633, when the Massachusetts Bay Colony passed a statute that denied workers the right to receive more than two shillings per diem when they were paying their own board & 14 pence a day when board was furnished. This statute provided fines for employers & employees who transgressed its provisions.

Later, employers were exempted from penalties for violation. The workers continued to be fined. In 1636 this statute was repealed & another enacted, which gave the town authorities jurisdiction to fix wages. In 1640, when prices collapsed, the Colonial legislature ruled that wages must be reduced to correspond with reduced prices.

When the Declaration of Independence was proclaimed, the workers were in a pitiable condition. John Bache McMaster, in his "History of the People of the United States," shows that wages in the colonies were about seven shillings a week—a little less than two dollars. McMaster said, "On such a pittance it was only by the strictest economy that a mechanic kept his children from starvation & himself from jail."

During the Colonial period, the position of a wage worker was that of an inferior. Exceptions were few. Suffrage laws, before the Constitution was adopted, prevented a majority of wage-workers from having any political influence. The right of franchise involved a property qualification that could not possibly be claimed by many workers. This qualification held in some states until 1842 when Rhode Island, the last state to keep the law on its books, abolished it, following "Dorr's Rebellion." Daniel Webster, Chancellor Kent & others openly opposed universal suffrage. This attitude on the part of various political leaders explains what happened to groups of workers when they joined together in the early days. They had no chance to defeat elected officials who used the powers of government to punish the worker for union activity.

In 1802 the sailors in New York, who had been receiving $10 a month, struck for $14. The strike was broken by violence on the part of constables & the leader was jailed. This struggle is sometimes cited as the first strike in America. Then came the strike of the shoemakers in Philadelphia in 1806. The courts entered this struggle & the shoemakers were indicted for combining to raise their wages.

Between 1800 & the beginning of the 1830's, in spite of the attitude of the public authorities, there is a record of over a score of attempts by the workers to organize. At the time of Andrew Jackson's inauguration some workers had secured the suffrage & at least a minority determined to use political as well as industrial action.

However, on the other side, we have the employers gathered together in firms or corporations enabling them more effectively to act against labor organization. Many hurdles were put in the way of the workers. In some instances, they were made to sign contracts agreeing not to join a union. Sometimes this provision went so far as to make them forfeit wages if they disobeyed. In an attempt to overcome this opposition, the Workingmen's Party of New York was organized in 1829. The Workingmen's Party was called the "Infidel Ticket." The public was warned that the rights of "property, religion & order" were in jeopardy & that the Workingmen's Party was a "mob" that "threatened the foundations of society." In view of this abuse, it is remarkable that even one of their candidates was elected to office. The majority of the press urged the legislature to unseat him.

During & immediately following this period, over twoscore labor papers had been established. They demanded changes in the industrial, political & social setups. The lives of these publications were short. This flareup of the Workingmen's Party was the first attempt by the workers to act on the political field. But by 1837 this activity was blanketed by a depression & it was not until the end of the Civil War that similar stirrings were again noted.

Following the two Jackson Administrations (1829-1836), the attempts to organize were almost negligible. There was one exception. A number of workers in an industry sometimes described as "the art preservative of all arts"—the printing industry—were organized in 1852 into the International Typographical Union, often called the "grandfather of organized labor in the United States."

It is interesting that between the Jackson Administration & the beginning of the Civil War, Abraham Lincoln, in December 1847, dealing with the protective tariff agitation of that period, had something to say about labor not paralleled by any public man of his generation. He said: ". . . if we except the light & the air of heaven, no good thing has been or can be enjoyed by us without having first cost labor. And inasmuch as most good things are produced by labor, it follows that all such things of right belong to those whose labor has produced them. But it has so happened, in all ages of the world, that some have labored, & others have without labor enjoyed a large proportion of the fruits. This is wrong & should not continue. To secure to each laborer the whole product of his labor or as nearly as possible, is a worthy object of any good government."

At Hartford, Conn., in March 1860, commenting on a current shoemakers' strike, Lincoln is quoted as having said that he "thanked God that we have a system of labor where there can be a strike. Whatever the pressure there is a point where the workmen may stop."

During the Civil War period there was very little organizational activity. But in 1863 one group, the locomotive engineers, founded the Brotherhood of the Footboards. Adopting the present name of the International Brotherhood of Locomotive Engineers in 1864, they eventually became one of the most thoroughly integrated unions in the United States.

During the Grant Administration in 1869, the Noble Order of the Knights of Labor—at first a secret society—was formed. Much has been made of the fact that they adopted secrecy. To use their own words, the reason was that "no spy of the boss can find his way to the lodge room to betray his fellows." In the 1880's, when their membership increased to almost a million, they felt that secrecy was no longer necessary.

In 1881, alongside the Knights, the American Federation of Labor was founded under the leadership of Samuel Gompers. Based on the craft philosophy, growing out of the predominant industrial structure, the American Federation of Labor fitted into the picture. Unions of the various crafts were formed, affiliating with the A.F. of L., which was practically a confederation of crafts with local autonomy. The membership of the Federation grew until it reached nearly the million mark at the end of the 19th century. 1881 was also the date when the carpenters organized. They affiliated with the A.F. of L. in the very early days & became a powerful influence in that body on account of their large membership.

Along with the formation of the A.F. of L. came an independent movement of railway workers. The operating sections of the great transportation system have had great influence on both the industrial & political life of the country. With the exception of the Locomotive Engineers, already mentioned, they developed largely as a direct result of the great railway strike of 1877. While the Order of Railway Conductors was organized in 1868, this name was not adopted until 1878, after the railway strike.

In short contrast to the method followed in collective bargaining by other unions in the United States, the railroad brotherhoods negotiate according to procedure prescribed by the Railway Labor Act, passed in 1926 & considered at that time to be the most perfect labor management act ever passed by the Congress. This did not prevent the railroad strike of 1946 which, while it tied up railroad transportation from one end of the country to the other, was of short duration, lasting only about 48 hours.

During the last quarter of the 19th century the labor movement went through three major struggles in which there was violence & conflict with the public authorities as well as with private police hired by the employers.

The first was the railroad strike of 1877 when Pennsylvania troops were ordered out & the Battle of the Round House took place in Pittsburgh with resulting loss of lives & destruction of property.

In 1894 the American Railway Union, formed in an attempt to organize all railroad workers into one big union, led by Eugene V. Debs, struck in Illinois against the Pullman Company. This company, which built, owned & operated the sleeping & parlor cars on almost all the railroads of the country, was charged with paying pittance wages. It was supported in this strike by the Railway Managers' Association. Violence broke out & since railroad mail cars were involved in the stoppage of transportation, Federal troops were used. Debs was jailed for disobeying a court injunction.

This strike widened the use of injunctions. Out of it arose an issue which was only partially settled after nearly 40 years of agitation & resulted in the Norris-LaGuardia anti-injunction legislation. But later, due to the Taft-Hartley Act, use of injunctions again became an issue. There was practically no public sympathy with these strikers in 1894 since the general press blamed the strikers for the upheaval. However, a commission appointed by President Cleveland to investigate the violence which had rocked Chicago found that the greater part of the guilt lay with the railway managers whose private police had set fire to railroad cars & then cut the fire department hoses. This strike practically ended the American Railway Union.

The older railroad unions grew in membership & it was not until 1920 that any further notable strike took place. This time the railroad unions were divided in their support of the workers. Violence was not much in evidence but Attorney General Daugherty secured an injunction against the strikers from a Federal Court. This, in a few years, was a great factor in securing anti-injunction legislation from Congress.

In 1892 the steel mills at Homestead, Pa., saw more violence. Here a fierce & bloody battle was fought on the banks of the muddy Monongahela River. There was little destruction of property. The fight was between the private Pinkerton detective army hired by Carnegie, Frick & Schwab & the steel workers. The strike was broken, union membership fell off & the union became almost moribund.

The slow growth of the labor movement compared with the giant strides in industry during the first third of the 20th century is easily grasped after examining the figures dealing with factory production. Between 1900 & 1920, with greatly increased production, there was also an increase in factory workers, though not in proportion to the increase in production.

However, in 1930, while production increased there was a decrease in the number of factory workers. Labor-saving devices had developed to such an extent that the number of jobs had decreased.

At that time the labor movement, dominated by the American Federation of Labor, had been based on craft production & not on mass production. This latter production method enabled the manufacturers to employ fewer workers & to make use of semi-skilled & unskilled people where previously they had been compelled to rely mainly on workmen trained in a particular craft.

Until about 1935 those in control of the A.F. of L. largely failed to meet the problems which craft unionism posed—particularly in the basic industries whose structures demanded industrial unionism, which is a combination of all workers in a plant, skilled, semi-skilled & unskilled, in one organization, in order to engage effectively in collective bargaining. Here we find one reason for the decrease in union membership in 1930 compared with the increase in population since the 1920 census. New Deal legislation has materially changed the point of view of the A.F. of L. as has the formation of the Congress of Industrial Organizations.

Another factor in the decrease of union membership was the intensive & organized effort of the employers directed against the labor movement from 1920 to 1930. This movement was directed primarily against the closed shop & was called the "American Plan." No story of the labor movement in the 20th century can ignore the first attempt to meet the labor problems which came with mass production. The Industrial Workers of the World, known as the IWW, tried to meet this new situation but were bitterly opposed not only by the employers but by most of the organized labor movement of the day.

The IWW was not very active in the factory system but did most of its work in the mining & lumber industries in the western part of the country. It was in reality a frontier organization & encountered much of the violence that our general frontier history has recorded. In most of the states where the IWW operated, the corporations controlled the political powers & their opposition resulted in violence, even in killing. Finally, in 1919, a number of the active members of the organization were charged with interfering with the conduct of World War I & the Espionage Law was invoked against them. To many people the jail terms to which members of the IWW were sentenced seemed inhuman. A few years later they were all released.

The only considerable factory labor struggles in which the IWW was involved occurred in the great woolen mills at Lawrence, Mass., in 1912 & in Paterson, N.J., in 1913 among the workers in the silk industry. The low standard of living among the workers in Lawrence, largely of foreign birth or extraction, caused an almost spontaneous walk-out from the mills. The existing textile union failed to function & leadership was taken over almost entirely by the IWW. The strike became very violent & a congressional investigation was ordered. It was proved that the management paid agents to set off a bomb & then attempted to blame the outrage on the strikers. Two IWW strike leaders, Ettor & Giovannitti, were charged with murder. After a dramatic trial they were found not guilty. This strike was lost & not until some 25 years later, when the C.I.O. Textile Union appeared on the scene, were the Lawrence workers organized.

The Paterson strike in 1913 was very bitter & New York reporters dramatized it highly. The strikers were helped by a group of liberals living in New York, who staged a pageant in the old Madison Square Garden to arouse public sympathy for the underpaid workers. This strike was also lost & was about the last attempt of the IWW organization to function in the highly industrialized sections of the country. As a factor in the general labor movement, the IWW has long ceased to have any influence.

Now let us glance at the rise of several great unions in key industries, beginning with the struggle in the steel industry. In the period covering the election of Woodrow Wilson & the start of World War I, there were two violent outbreaks in the steel industry. One took place at the great Edgar Thompson plant of the U.S. Steel Corporation in western Pennsylvania & the other in Colorado where the Rockefeller-dominated Colorado Fuel & Iron Company was located.

In the Pennsylvania plant the private police of the U.S. Steel Corporation came into a conflict with the steel workers & the militia was called ou . In Colorado, at a tent colony in Ludlow which housed some striking workers &

their families, there was a massacre of men, women & children. This massacre was undoubtedly the reason for the appointment in 1913 by President Wilson of a Commission on Industrial Relations which traveled from coast to coast, holding hearings to investigate the relationship between employers & employees.

A short time after this commission completed its work & before an opportunity for remedial legislation was possible, the United States entered World War I. The employers, needing every available worker to fulfill their government contracts, ceased militant opposition to labor organization. But in 1919, after the war, the steel corporations came to a head-on collision with their employees. Some twenty A.F. of L. affiliated unions endeavored to organize the steel workers who struck. But their treasury was low & the strike was broken.

In 1935 the Committee for Industrial Organization entered the picture & in 1937 the Steelworkers Organizing Committee was formed. This later became the United Steelworkers of America which absorbed the little that was left of the steelworkers' organization of Homestead days.

In 1937, at South Chicago, a great battle broke out between the steelworkers & the Republic Steel Corporation. Men were killed & maimed by the Chicago police & indignation was aroused over the slaughter. This attitude on the part of the public may have been responsible two years later for the agreement by the Republic Steel Corporation & other large steel corporations to follow the lead of the U.S. Steel Corporation, which had earlier in the year entered into contractual relations with their workers, to bargain through the Congress of Industrial Organizations. Through the same labor channels the smaller steel corporations also entered into contracts with their employees. The United Steelworkers is nearly a million strong today & has collective bargaining agreements with the great majority of the steel corporations.

The miners have always bulked large in the history of the American labor movement. Although mining of coal is an extra-hazardous occupation, the workers in that industry had been so poorly paid that their living conditions were pitiable. In 1902, led by John Mitchel, the hard coal (anthracite) miners struck. Since for household purposes hard coal was more used than any other, President Theodore Roosevelt felt compelled to intervene. A settlement was reached which to some extent improved the conditions of the miners.

In the next thirty years there were many conflicts between miners & owners, particularly in the soft coal (bituminous) districts where a majority of the men were employed. At the end of the Hoover Administration, the miners' organization was in desperate straits, financially & industrially. With the passage of the National Industrial Recovery Act in 1933, its Section 7a, which protected the workers in their organizing activities, was grasped by the president of the United Mine Workers as a life-saving opportunity to increase membership in the union, which had fallen to a new low, with a corresponding low treasury.

In 1936, by a seeming miracle, 600,000 miners were enrolled in the United Mine Workers, all debts were paid & Lewis, their leader, became the head of the Committee for Industrial Organization, which later changed its name to Congress of Industrial Organizations.

Lewis fell out with the C.I.O., which he had had a large part in forming; the miners withdrew from that organization & reaffiliated with A.F. of L., from which they had been expelled. In a short time, the miners withdrew from the A.F. of L. & then had no affiliation with either the Congress of Industrial Organizations or the American Federation of Labor. The wages & working conditions of the miners, after they took advantage of the labor laws passed in the Roosevelt Administration, have greatly improved. Not only have yearly earnings advanced but in recent settlements with employers social welfare measures, including pensions, have been included in their contracts.

Although there are about 1,250,000 workers employed in the production of textiles, from the beginning of the century to 1937 the attempts to organize them were not very successful. What little organization was accomplished was in the Northern states. When the organizers turned to the South, they met with the most bitter opposition. Not only were the manufacturers opposed to them but the political setup favored the owners of the textile mills. In the 1920's & early 1930's opposition to organizing activities in the industry took on a most violent character. Memory of what happened in Gastonia, N.C., where the workers were beaten up, are still most vivid in the minds of the oldest textile workers.

A great change came with the formation by the Committee for Industrial Organization of the Textile Workers Organizing Committee in 1937. The number of members grew so rapidly that in 1939 the Textile Workers Union of America was launched & today nearly half a million textile workers have collective bargaining agreements with the employers. Previous to the formation of this union, the textile workers who had been organized were affiliated with the A. F. of L. Some of these workers are still with the Federation.

After 1937 & the appearance on the labor stage of this new union of textile workers, the entire picture changed. While opposition from southern political & industrial groups is still in evidence, their power has been curtailed & there are now about 100,000 organized textile workers in the South who, through the Textile Workers Union of America, have bargaining contracts with their employers. In the North the majority of textile workers are members of the Textile Workers Union of America.

The workers in the needle trades were organized in large numbers before World War I. It is paradoxical that the unions in the needle trades which emerged from sweatshop conditions in the men's & boys' clothing & the dress industries were the first two unions to pioneer for arbitration between employees & employers in order to prevent strikes. These unions were the Amalgamated Clothing Workers of America & the International Ladies' Garment Workers Union. Today each of these unions has a membership of about 375,000.

This arbitration activity began at almost the same time in both unions, when they were much smaller than at present. In the case of the Amalgamated, it grew out of the Hart, Schaffner & Marx strike in 1910, which was settled in 1911. This settlement provided for "impartial machinery" to adjust daily differences arising between management & employees. This machinery, which has since been used in other clothing markets, has functioned in the Hart, Schaffner & Marx factories for nearly forty years without a strike.

At about the same period in New York, the International Ladies' Garment Workers in an agreement arranged for a "protocol" between employers & employees in an attempt to end strikes which had been occurring in their industry. The late Justice Brandeis, who about 1909 had given up a very lucrative law practice to devote his time & talent to acting as what was practically an advocate for the common good, had much to do with the "protocol" plan.

Both of these attempts drew a great deal of attention to arbitration rather than strikes. As the years went on, impartial arbitration machinery was adoped in some other trades. The leaders in the clothing industries were now bent on securing benefits other than just better wages & working conditions. They became active in furthering general social legislation in both federal & state fields.

The Amalgamated, having tried & failed to secure legislation to provide funds for the workers during unemployment periods, instituted as a laboratory test an unemployment insurance fund in Chicago, through agreement with the employers. When this experiment proved successful in Chicago, it was instituted in other markets & was abrogated only when national unemployment insurance took its place in the Roosevelt Administration.

The attempts by the International Ladies' Garment Workers to improve living conditions of their workers were for a time interfered with by the activity of the followers, in this country, of the Russian dictatorship. They had formed in the needle trades a Trade Union Educational League & almost succeeded in bankrupting the ILGWU. The leaders of this union, however, succeeded in thoroughly rehabilitating it in the New Deal days & the union again became active in promoting social legislation.

It is convenient to mention here a technique used by the workers in an industrial struggle, known as the "sit-down" strike which had its birth in 1935 in the great rubber works at Akron, Ohio. The workers, instead of putting a picket line around a plant, stayed inside without working, in some instances for a number of days. The sit-down strike of the rubber workers lasted only a short time & therefore aroused little public attention. Not until sit-down strikes took place in the Flint, Mich., & other plants of the General Motors Corporation in 1936 did this strike technique become an issue & provoke discussion throughout the country. Management called upon the state authorities in Michigan to evict the auto workers for violating laws protecting private property. Governor Murphy of Michigan refused to order out troops on the ground that violence would result.

The long & bitter controversy was resolved only after the dominant management in the automobile industry—except the Ford Motor Co.—agreed to negotiate with their employees organized under the Congress of Industrial Organizations. After violence by company police at the River Rouge, Mich., plant, the Ford Motor Co. followed the example of other companies in the automobile industry & entered into collective bargaining contracts with the automobile union affiliated with the C.I.O.

We come now to an intertwined story, the story of the New Deal & the rise of Congress of Industrial Organizations (C.I.O.). It can be asserted that out of the New Deal of the Roosevelt administrations a new labor movement emerged. While on paper the workers always had had a right to organize, employers were free to fire them for union activity. Many employers used this power & that was undoubtedly the prime reason for the slow growth of the labor movement previous to the New Deal labor & social legislation.

The forerunner of the changed attitude of the government toward labor can be found in a statement in the Norris-LaGuardia anti-injunction legislation which said that the workers' rights to self-organization & collective bargaining were the public policy of the United States. Later, in conformity with this policy, Section 7a was put into the National Industrial Recovery Act of 1933, to protect workers from discharge for organizing activity. This Act was found to be unconstitutional by the Supreme Court. The National Labor Relations Act, passed in 1935, which was declared constitutional by the same court, included in its provisions one similar to Section 7a, but even more specific. It provided that workers should be protected from discharge for union activity & in addition provided that if workers had been so discharged, they must be reinstated & paid for time lost. This explains the great increases in union membership after 1936.

It is obvious that the democratic process has been largely extended from the political to the industrial field, with the result that in 1949 we find nearly 16,000,000 organized workers as compared with less than three million in 1933. At present, there are upwards of eight million workers affiliated with the A.F. of L.; over six million with the C.I.O. & nearly two million members of independent unions—that is, those not affiliated with either of the two great divisions of organized labor.

Frances Perkins, for over twelve years Secretary of Labor & previously engaged in activities having to do with the relations between employees & employers, has said "the National Labor Relations Board became extremely important in the labor history of the United States. Undoubtedly big-scale unionization of labor was made possible under its protection."

In 1937, President Roosevelt decided to press for legislation setting a minimum hourly wage & a maximum hour work week. The Fair Labor Standards Act actually grew out of a decision of the Supreme Court, which sustained the power of Congress to regulate labor conditions in manufacturing industries in interstate commerce. Since the minimum wage was put at forty cents an hour & the maximum work hours a week at forty, the Act came to be known as the forty-forty bill. Other clauses in the bill prohibited labor by youngsters under sixteen years of age in industries engaged in interstate commerce & the employment of children between the ages of sixteen & eighteen in extra-hazardous occupations was forbidden.

There was bitter opposition to the Act by a bi-partisan combination in Congress & it was not until 1938 that it was finally passed with a twenty-five cent hourly minimum to be raised to forty cents within seven years. However, a provision for industry hearings was included & this resulted in the forty cent minimum being reached long before 1945.

Now for the story of the origin & rise of the C.I.O. In 1935, eight unions affiliated with the A.F. of L., after having failed to secure action in the Federation's convention that year toward organizing the unorganized on the basis of whole industries in place of crafts, formed the Committee for Industrial Organization, while still affiliated with the A.F. of L.

By the middle of 1936, four more unions joined this Committee. The twelve unions thus joined were the United Mine Workers of America; the International Typographical Union; International Union of Mine, Mill & Smelter Workers; Oil Field, Gas Well & Refinery Workers of America; United Textile Workers of America; International Ladies' Garment Workers; Hatters, Cap & Millinery Workers; Amalgamated Clothing Workers of America; the

Federation of Flat Glass Workers; United Automobile Workers; United Rubber Workers & the Amalgamated Association of Iron, Steel & Tin Workers. This Committee became very active in organizing but was told that it must stop this activity or be expelled from the Federation. In September, 1936, ten of the unions were expelled. Only two out of the twelve—the International Typographical Union & the United Hatters, Cap & Millinery Workers—were exempted from expulsion. Some time later the International Ladies' Garment Workers, which had been expelled with the other unions, reaffiliated with the A.F. of L.

In its drive for organization the Congress of Industrial Organizations was successful in many fields where previously little along that line had been attempted. This was true of the maritime industry. In 1937 a group of workers, formerly affiliated with the A.F. of L. International Seamen's Union, withdrew from the Federation & formed the National Maritime Union of America affiliated with the C.I.O. This Union, engaged in the water transportation industry, is very militant & contracts with the owners of vessels, as well as wages paid, are in sharp contrast to those that existed prior to their C.I.O. affiliation. It is apparent that two great factors have been responsible for the upsurge in the labor movement in the United States. First, the passage of the National Industrial Recovery Act in 1933 with its Section 7a which protected the workers engaged in organization & thereafter passage of the National Labor Relations Act. Then in 1937 came the Congress of Industrial Organizations which took advantage of Section 7a to organize the great unorganized industries along industrial instead of craft lines, in sharp contrast to the craft system of the American Federation of Labor.

The last ten years of the labor movement record drastic changes in the attitude of almost all of the unions on both the political & industrial fronts. They aim for a continuing improvement in the general social conditions of the workers—more life insurance & assurance against certain economic hazards have been introduced into their programs. Some of the unions have introduced pensions to add to the small amount provided by the government. Many contracts with employers embody provisions for health insurance, with hospitalization & maternity insurance, vacations with pay & other stipulations which a few years ago would have been looked upon as impractical. Today, in a large portion of industry they are a reality.

Many workers feel that the progress they have made since 1936 is largely due to the part they have played in politics. They blame the recession of 1946, when legislation was enacted which they claim was opposed to their interests, on their failure to be as active in politics as they had been formerly.

The spokesmen for the A.F. of L. & C.I.O. & the unions unaffiliated with either claimed that the legislation against labor enacted in the 80th Congress was directly responsible for the defeat of the Republicans who had been in control. They claimed that the vote of organized labor & of the farmer put Truman, in the 1948 elections, in the presidential chair & the Democrats in control of the Congress.

The principal legislation to which they objected was the Taft-Hartley Act. Both the A.F. of L. & the C.I.O. claim that this Act was deliberately aimed at crippling the provisions of the National Labor Relations Act. They went further & charged the Republican-controlled 80th Congress with having failed to further general social legislation.

There is no labor press in the country—that is, periodicals & papers owned by labor & intended for general circulation, presenting labor's case to the people. There is an inside labor press with some millions of circulation going to the members of the various unions, supported out of union treasuries & used to keep the administration of unions in contact with their members. At the last count there were about 181 of these papers.

In the last thirty years there has been a continuous growth in educational activities within the labor movement. In the last fifteen years, it has been accelerating. Beginning as a movement directed primarily to post union members on problems facing them as workers, the educational activities have widened until they touch not only on problems arising from our general social structure but in many cases extending to the general cultural field. Study classes are run often in cooperation with the large general educational institutions in the country. Not only is special literature printed for members but books of a general cultural character are bought in large lots & distributed to members at cost. Some of our educational authorities have hailed the workers' educational movement as a great step towards a continual widening of the democratic process in the U. S.

Labor in the U.S. has been on the march. The story of its march can be best summed up in the statistical comparisons listed below. They are statistics eloquent of progress in labor organization.

The 1900 census showed 76 million population & a little over one million union members—one union member to every 76 persons.

In 1910 population was 92 million with a little over two million union members—one to every 46 persons.

The 1920 census figures were 105 million & over five million union members—one to every 21 persons.

In 1930 the population was 123 million & union membership 3,392,000—one to every 35 persons. This was before the full effect of the depression was felt. By 1933 union membership was just a little over two million.

The 1940 census showed 132 million & eight & a half million union members—one to every 16 persons.

The estimated population in 1948 was 145 million & as the last estimate of union membership showed something over 15 million, there was now one union member to every nine persons.

—CHARLES ERVIN

# ARCHITECTURE

Americans, pre- & post-Columbian, have bequeathed to us in their buildings a rich & vivid record of their lives & times. To even the casual tourist, these buildings can dramatically unfold the enthralling American story of struggle & progress. To the serious traveler, they are tangible & indispensable interpreters of our predecessors' abilities & aspirations. For in America, no less than in Europe & the Orient, architecture forms a sure & revealing index to the dynamic course of successive civilizations.

A building discloses many facts about its builder. Its functional arrangement indicates the owner's mode of life & ability to satisfy his needs for shelter. The materials demonstrate what resources he commanded. The structure itself reveals what technical skills his architect & builder mustered to ensure a feasible & safe construction. And, finally, the building's appearance within & without displays unequivocally with what taste & discrimination owner & architect solved their complex problem.

In emphasizing the place of buildings in history we must remember, of course, that buildings were not built for the sake of history, but were dynamic & complete solutions of urgent needs at the moment of their construction. They were meant to be used & enjoyed in their own right. Too often, of course, the effects of time, neglect, or alteration make it difficult to recapture the true character of the original design. Many authentic structures have been irretrievably mutilated by well-intentioned but ignorant "restoration," but fortunately today the aims & technique of good preservation are becoming better understood & more widely applied.

Most historic buildings were intended to be seen as parts of village or city landscapes, but the continual rebuilding characteristic of normal American communities makes the preservation of any extended group of buildings extremely rare. It is possible, however, to obtain a feeling of civic context from early views of American towns usually displayed in local history museums or illustrated in history picture books.

PRE-COLUMBIAN ARCHITECTURE: The dwellings of the American Indians reveal the power of primitive techniques over stringent limitations imposed by a wide range of environments. Cumulative discoveries suggest that nomadic Paleo-Indians came from northeastern Asia to North America via Alaska in a long succession of migratory waves at the end of the last glaciation around 20,000 B.C. The earliest men thus far identified, the Folsom & the Cochise, of around 10,000 B.C., were apparently simple food gatherers & hunters. No dwellings have been found, but camp hearths have been uncovered. Perhaps these primitive Americans erected temporary shelters of brush or with a sapling frame covered by skins, bark, or mats.

The hunting, food gathering men of the Archaic Period built tiny settlements of pit-houses, roughly circular, with a shallow excavation roofed by a rough log framing supported on log posts & with walls and roof fashioned of convenient materials—earth, adobe, interwoven saplings with or without mud plaster, skins, bark, brush, or even matting. Remains of these pits with their central hearths—the smoke escaped through a hole in the roof—have been found in New York state, Washington, the Great Plains, & the Southwest. For foraging & the chase, temporary brush windscreens & moveable tents were adopted. These still survive in the Pai Ute wickiup & the plainsman's tepee.

With the advent of agriculture, perhaps around 500 A.D., population increased & permanent village life became feasible. In the eastern woodland, the sapling-framed, bark-covered wigwams were now built above ground. Palisaded walls defended the group. In the Southwest, however, timber was scarcer & soon rough stone masonry was used to construct long rows of apartment units likewise above ground. The pit-house of the Southwest was conserved in the *kiva,* a subterranean ceremonial hall.

The elaboration of agriculture in succeeding centuries fostered the slow maturing of two great cultural traditions whose most spectacular achievement was an impressive architecture. The Pueblo civilization of Arizona & New Mexico, evolved directly from the archaic Basket-Makers, came to full flower between 1050 & 1300, & constructed dramatic stone-walled, multi-storied, terraced apartments, housing whole towns. Though most of the easily accessible pueblos now remaining post-date the Pueblo Rebellion of 1680, the now ruined Pueblo Bonita in Chaco Canyon 60 miles northeast of Gallup, New Mexico, dates from about 1050, the famed Cliff Palace of Mesa Verde in southwest Colorado is of approximately the same antiquity, & Oraibi, some 80 miles northeast of Flagstaff, Ariz., has been continuously occupied since about 1150. In addition to the tiered suites for dwelling, large kivas for esoteric rites & spacious plazas for ceremonial dances indicate an enlightened concern for communal amenities.

The other great tradition arose along the majestic valleys of the Middle West. Beginning around 500 with the Adena culture of Ohio & adjoining states to the south, there appear conical burial mounds 10 to 70 feet high, & defensive earthworks. From 900 to 1300 the succeeding Hopewell culture of the same area greatly elaborated both burial mounds & vast systems of earthworks defining ceremonial centers. Fort Ancient, 25 miles northeast of Cincinnati, stretches a mile along the Little Miami river & includes an enclosed oval plaza 1500 feet long & a 600 foot long axial road leading to an elevated circular platform 500 feet in diameter. The mound system at Newark, Ohio, is even more extensive. Such works imply a sophisticated sense of design in the grand manner & a highly developed social organization capable of marshaling a vast force of labor.

The culmination of Hopewell stimulus came following 1300 in the Temple Mound Civilization of the Greater Mississippi area. From Arkansas to Georgia, & from Alabama to Illinois, along the fertile valleys there blossomed myriad village states whose capitals presented imposing civic groups of temple mounds & plazas. The Cahokia site at East Saint Louis, Ill., once boasted a huge complex made up of numerous villages & about 300 mounds, the central pyramid being 100 feet high & 710 by 1080 feet at the base, the largest in the United States. The Etowah pyramid at Cartersville, Ga., stands 70 feet high & 380 feet square at its base. A winding ramp leads to the top platform from which one clearly sees the vast rectangular plaza marked by moats. The village itself extended 3000 feet along the river & 1500 feet inland. Other groups at Moundville, Ala., Macon, Ga., and Newburgh, Ind., likewise witness the energy & ambition in architecture & city planning of these primitive cultures.

SEVENTEENTH CENTURY COLONIAL: With the arrival of European explorers & colonists in the sixteenth & seventeenth centuries, these native architectural traditions were soon eclipsed. Spaniard, Frenchman, Hollander, & Englishman strove to create in the new world a reflection of his native land, but inevitably new conditions, local materials, & limited resources sired mutations. Thereby American colonial buildings possess unique & peculiar character in their own right.

Spaniards founded Saint Augustine, Fla., in 1565, but it long remained an unpretentious outpost. Its fine four-bastioned Fort San Marcos, built of gray *coquina,* begun in 1672, was not completed until 1756. In the Southwest the first Spanish settlement & church were established in the Chama river valley of New Mexico in 1598. In 1609 Santa Fe was founded & the Governor's Palace was built. The flat-roofed, stuccoed adobe structure still faces the colonial plaza. Franciscan & Jesuit promptly organized Indian workmen to build missions & churches, but extant examples in the Southwest, Texas, & California date almost entirely from the eighteenth century. In New Mexico the church of San Miguel at Santa Fe, & those at Acoma, Laguna, & Zia give some hint of this meager, static, frontier style. That at Ranchos de Taos, late eighteenth century, forms a picturesque grouping. Texas' historic Alamo, built about 1744 as the chapel of the mission of San Antonio do Valero in San Antonio, illustrates the introduction & translation of Spanish Baroque into colonial terms. In California the beautiful Mission at Santa Barbara, built in 1786, shows the delayed penetration of the style along the Pacific Coast.

The opening of the seventeenth century saw the colonizing of the Atlantic seaboard by England, Holland, & Sweden. In Virginia the first buildings within the tiny stockade at Jamestown in 1607 were timber frames covered with wattle-&-daub & roofed with thatch. Fire & decay demanded almost continuous replacement, but gradually fire-resistant brick & tiles were substituted. Recent excavations have revealed foundations of small town houses with plans directly derived from contemporary late medieval English practice. The only remaining structure at Jamestown is the original brick tower & foundations of the parish church completed in 1647. Its tiny buttressed plan came straight from late Gothic English models.

Fortunately the full flavor of this American medieval style is preserved in several Virginia buildings. Adam Thoroughgood's story-and-a-half brick country house, built about 1640 northeast of Norfolk, exhibits the unsymmetrical, one-room-deep "hall-&-parlor" plan, both the big freestanding & the embedded T-shaped chimney types, & the typical steep-pitched roof; but the original leaded casements are gone. The finest seventeenth-century house is "Bacon's Castle," built by Arthur Allen in 1655 northwest of Smithfield, with projecting vestibule & stairhall forming a cross-shaped plan. Its massive end chimneys rise to three detached square flues silhouetted against Jacobean gables decorated with quadrants & steps. Finally, St. Luke's church, east of Smithfield, probably completed in 1682, presents a Gothic plan with tower & nave, Gothic brick traceried windows, & medieval stepped gables. Parallel development occurred in Maryland. At St. Mary's, the capital, the brick State House is now rebuilt in its 1676 form. Resurrection Manor, built in the 1660's facing the Patuxent River southeast of Hollywood, is a typical brick cottage of the period & region. At Makepeace, built in 1663 near Crisfield on the Eastern Shore, the story-&-a-half gable ends are decorated with elaborate patterning in brick. Beside these brick constructions, a more humble, wood-framed, unpainted clapboard tradition continued.

Seventeenth century building in Massachusetts likewise sprang from English medieval models. The crude "wigwams" of the first years, now seen in reconstruction in Salem's Pioneer Village, & the palisaded cabins at Plymouth were soon replaced with timber-framed houses covered with clapboards. Single room cottages with lofts & large end-wall chimneys grew with accumulating prosperity & progeny into two-room two-story dwellings with massive central chimneys. The Hathaway House at Salem illustrates this process. With the addition of a rear lean-to the typical "salt-box" house was achieved. The Boardman house, built in 1651 at Saugus, exemplifies the full form with overhang, pilastered chimney, small windows, & long unbroken roof. The Parson Capen house, 1683, at Topsfield, has "drops" decorating the overhang. Many other examples could be cited. The "Old Ship" Meeting House at Hingham, erected in 1681 & enlarged with eighteenth century galleries, is a simple, timber-framed representative of early Nw England religious architecture. The Peter Tufts House, 1680, at Medford, is a rare instance of brick in the early period. From Massachusetts this timber style spread to Rhode Island & Connecticut & achieved charming local variations.

The picturesque seventeenth century Dutch architecture of New Amsterdam & the Hudson valley is now known solely from old prints. Only the Dutch town plans preserved on the southern tip of Manhattan & in the old central sections of Beverwyck (Albany), Wiltwyck (Kingston), & Schenectady recall the thrifty merchants of the day. A number of Dutch farmhouses still remain, but most have suffered alteration. A few, such as the sadly neglected Jan Breese house built south of Rensselaer in 1723, show the Dutch version of the colonial story-and-a-half cottage with steeply pitched gables & wrought iron beam anchors borrowed from Dutch town dwellings. The octagonal Dutch Reformed churches have all disappeared.

Although the brief life of Swedish colonization in northern Delaware left slight architectural effect, it did introduce the Scandinavian system of building with notched horizontal logs. The Mortonson House in Prospect Park, Philadelphia, consists of a one-room log cabin built in 1654, which, with an additional unit of 1698 separated by an open, roofed passage, formed an early instance of the "breezeway" or "dog-trot" dwelling. So appropriate was this system for the forested frontier that it quickly spread throughout the colonies. It was also used for blockhouses, as in the Garrison House built about 1675 at Dover, New Hampshire.

GEORGIAN COLONIAL: During the latter part of the seventeenth century, & increasing during the eighteenth, the American medieval style gave way to the new English vogue for an architecture inspired from Renaissance Italy.

At first a few decorative pilasters taken from London handbooks, quoins, & cornices were applied to designs continuing former plans & gables, as in the Winslow House, 1699, at Marshfield, Mass. Gradually the central-hall, deep plans & the even-corniced massing of the new fashion became better understood.

The first Virginian phase of this change is brilliantly witnessed at Williamsburg, to which the Virginia capital was transferred in 1699. In the College of William and Mary, begun in 1695, the original walls still display the sober, stately design attributed to the royal architect, Christopher Wren. The Governor's Palace, built in 1706-20 & now faithfully reconstructed, may likewise have come from Wren's office. Its restrained orderliness is enriched by the plastic Palladian grouping of office & kitchen forming a forecourt of great dignity. Although the interior was elegantly fitted, the exterior has little ornament & depends for effect on its gracious proportions, its color, & its fine craftmanship. The dependencies preserve the form of seventeenth century small houses. The restored Capitol of 1705, the Powder Magazine, the original Second Bruton Parish Church, & many other structures, original & reconstructed, combine to present a unique full-scale museum of an early eighteenth century Virginia community.

Influenced by Williamsburg, the great plantation owners were stimulated to rehouse themselves in elegant country palaces. Some, like Stratford, north of Montross, built by Thomas Lee about 1725, adopted a Jacobean H-plan with baroque massed chimneys & finely rendered Renaissance interiors. Others, like Westover built by William Byrd II about 1730, display more ornate details. As the elaboration of the English Georgian progressed, handbooks & immigrant architects matured Georgian Colonial design into an elegant & acclimated style. The Palladian five-part grouping of "flankers" & "hyphens" around the dominant central block became the accepted pattern. Mount Airy, east of Warsaw, built in 1758 by John Tayloe possibly from plans by John Ariss, was one of the finest expressions & unique in employing stone. The most famed example is, of course, Mount Vernon, enlarged by Washington in 1757-59 from a simple cottage & completed in 1787. Here the high Georgian formalism was translated into wood, cut to represent stonework, but its gracious dignity matches its historical importance.

The other southern colonies paralleled this Georgian development with almost equal brilliance. In Maryland the great country places, Tulip Hill, 1743, near Owensville, Mount Clair, 1754, in Baltimore, Montpelier, about 1770, near Laurel, & Hampton, 1783-90, near Towson, display the elegance of the proprietors. The galaxy of fine town mansions in Annapolis, the Brice House, 1740, the Chase House, 1769-74, & the superlative Hammond-Harwood House, 1770-74, is no less sophisticated. In South Carolina the plantation homes of Hampton, 1735, on the Santee southwest of Georgetown, & Drayton Hall, 1738, northwest of Charleston, are but the most famous of a large group. At Middleton Place, near Drayton, the majestic gardens designed in 1740 convey a unique impression of the aristocratic settings of these country palaces. In Charleston itself, the town houses of Miles Brewton, about 1765, John Stuart, 1772, & many others, illustrate the adaptation of the style to local variations of plan.

New England Georgian grew in similar stages, but regional conditions fostered more compact solutions. Yankee profits came from shipping rather than crops; consequently town houses predominated. Renaissance decoration appeared in the 1690's, but full use of the new fashion came somewhat later. The full academic repertoire is displayed in the Vassall ("Longfellow") House, built in 1759 at Cambridge, Mass. The Jeremiah Lee House, 1768, at Marblehead is another superb design both within & without.

English rule in New York gradually affected Dutch tastes. The DePeyster House, 1750, at Beacon adopted Georgian forms. In 1749 Sir William Johnson built his frontier home at Fort Johnson with Georgian symmetry & clarity & imported London paneling, hardware, & fittings. Albany's Schuyler Mansion, 1762, represents the climaxing mid-century phase. The Robert Morris (Jumel) House, 1765, New York, is especially interesting for its "colossal" two-story portico, unique before the Revolution.

Along the Delaware, Newcastle is a veritable Georgian museum. In Philadelphia the early houses such as Penn's House, 1682, now moved to Fairmount Park, reflect the smaller Restoration town dwellings of London; Cedar Grove, 1721 & later, preserves a certain Quaker spareness despite its Georgian trim; & Mount Pleasant, 1761, shows the elaborations & refinements of the full style.

Eighteenth century builders did not confine themselves to domestic construction. Civic, mercantile, & religious buildings still standing round out our view of colonial life. The Old State House built in 1739 at Newport, R.I., shows in name & design the influence of house forms. Boston's Old State House, 1748, achieves more public character. Pennsylvania's State House (Independence Hall), 1732-35, illustrates not only domestic scale, but likewise the five-part Palladian grouping of the large plantation houses. Charleston's Exchange, 1767-71, displays a more accomplished public character. Educational building is represented by Harvard's Massachusetts Hall, 1720, & the Redwood Library built in 1750 by Peter Harrison at Newport, R.I. The Bethesda Orphanage, founded in 1740 south of Savannah by George Whitfield, retains its group of Georgian buildings. Colonial town planning, a much neglected field of study, may be seen at Philadelphia, 1682, Annapolis, 1695, Williamsburg, 1699, Savannah, 1733, & in New England villages.

The Atlantic seaboard is especially rich in its heritage of eighteenth century churches. The simple meeting houses, such as Boston's "Old South," 1729, grew to monumental elaboration in the Baptist Church, 1763-66, at Providence. The same process appeared in more liturgical faiths, as shown by the contrast of the tiny country chapel, as Washington's Pohick Church, 1769-72, in Fairfax County, Va., with a fully developed city establishment like Christ Church, Philadelphia, built 1727-54, King's Chapel, 1749, Boston, St. Michael's, Charleston, 1752-61, & St. Paul's, New York, 1764-66. The steeples of these structures, based on models by Wren & Gibbs, were the most prominent features of colonial skylines.

Alongside of this Georgian Colonial architecture, other non-English immigrants introduced equally interesting buildings. The Flemish farmers of northern New Jersey & Rockland County, N. Y., brought their native "flying gutters" which, combined with gambrel roofs, produced the sweeping overhangs of their picturesque "Dutch Colonial" homes. The German Palatines introduced their stone constructions into the Schoharie valley of New York & the Shenandoah of Virginia. Huguenots built charming cottages at New Paltz, N. Y., & influenced design in southwest Virginia & at Charleston. The massive decorated barns of the Mennonite "Pennsylvania Dutch" give special character to southeastern Pennsylvania. At Ephrata, Trappe, Bethlehem, & Winston-Salem, Germanic religious groups added to the architectural melting pot.

Across the Appalachians, Frenchmen in the early eighteenth century held a line of outposts along the Great Lakes & down the Mississippi. At Fort Niagara, N. Y., the stone Castle, 1726, masqueraded as a manor house to disguise its purpose from the Indians. Fort Ticonderoga, N. Y., portrays French military design of 1755. In the Illinois territory at Cahokia, the first settlement founded in 1698, & at Ste Genevieve, settled about 1750, only buildings of the end of the century remain, but they exhibit the typical French palisaded & post-on-sill methods of construction. The foundations of the Fort de Chartres, built 1753-58 near Prairie du Rocher, Ill., prove this stronghold to have been the most formidable in the valley. The original half-timbered French buildings at New Orleans were soon replaced by eighteenth century stuccoed-brick construction, but even these, as at St. Louis, have succumbed to fire and progress.

THE FEDERAL PERIOD: 1790-1830: Although the Revolution established American political independence, American architecture continued to draw inspiration from European models. Antique & Palladian Italy found her most fervent enthusiast in the statesman & amateur architect, Thomas Jefferson, who had designed his own home, Monticello, just before the war, & had planned houses for many friends. At Richmond the State Capitol was built from 1789-98 from his design based on a Roman temple. French taste influenced the fine porticoed mansion, The Hill, south of Hudson, N. Y., built about 1796 by Henry Walter Livingstone shortly after his diplomatic tour in Paris. Likewise New York's fine City Hall, 1803-14, built by John McComb but designed by the French military engineer, Joseph Mangin, reflects Parisian models. The attenuated style of Robert Adam & his London colleagues bore strongest in New England, as in the Tontine Crescent, a speculative row of town houses built in Boston by Charles Bulfinch in 1793.

All these influences impinged upon the new capital at Washington. Major L'Enfant laid out the city in a noble pattern of streets combining ideas suggested by the gardens at Versailles & by Wren's plan for London. The Capitol building itself was designed by Dr. William Thornton with Georgian wings flanking a Roman rotunda. James Hoban leaned heavily on Palladian Georgian precedents for his presidential palace, the White House. Despite diverse sources, these architects created a truly American setting capable of growing to maturity with the young republic. The Octagon, built by John Tayloe in 1798-1800, exhibits Thornton's domestic manner.

Cotton supplemented tobacco as the staple of the South & society there continued predominantly agricultural. Characteristic of post-war plantation houses were the superb Carroll house, Homewood, 1798-1800, in Baltimore, Hayes, 1801, at Edenton, N. C., & Bremo, 1815-19, near Bremo Bluff, Va. Many smaller farmhouses in the southern Piedmont reflected the motives of their pretentious cousins. Trade brought new impetus to urban centers & prosperity fostered increased building. At Charleston, the Joseph Manigault House, about 1790, & the Nathaniel Russell House, about 1811, at Savannah, the Richardson-Owens House (1816) & the Scarborough House attributed to the

English architect, John Jay, & at Richmond, the John Wickham House (1815; now the Valentine Museum) by Robert Mills, attest this urban affluence.

In northern states commerce & industry gradually dominated economic life. Samuel Slater's modest timber spinning mill built in 1793 at Pawtucket, R. I., was the first to harness American water power to textile processes. From it stemmed the countless textile mills lining New England streams. Around them neat rows of workers' cottages formed bucolic mill villages; Fiskeville, R. I., is a charming example. As mills grew larger, trim mill towns developed at power sites. On textile & other industries, & especially on shipping, the great ports of Boston, Salem, New York, New Bedford, Philadelphia, & Baltimore waxed rich. Their waterfronts still preserve a few of the merchants' warehouses.

Salem reflects, par excellence, the impact of commerce on architecture. The merchants' counting houses, their comfortable mansions, & the associated community buildings witness their owners' profitable enterprises. Samuel McIntire, architect & carver, effectively exploited these opportunities, as in the Pierce-Nichols House, 1782, & the Gardner-Pingree House, 1810. Bulfinch ornamented Boston with similar monuments. The Massachusetts State House, 1795-1808, the old Courthouse (now the City Hall), 1810, the General Hospital, 1816-21, New North Church (now St. Stephen's), 1807, & numerous houses such as the third Otis House, 1806, on Beacon Street display Bulfinch's creative interpretation of English precedent. His church at Lancaster, 1810-13, is a consummate masterpiece. Gore Place, built 1804-06 at Waltham, possibly from London drawn plans, is a rare New England example of the five-part country house in the Adam manner.

Through the handbooks issued by Asher Benjamin & carried by pioneers to the new frontier, the Yankee style spread west over upstate New York & beyond into Ohio's Western Reserve. At Albany the Academy (now the City Education Office), 1816, & at Clinton the Hamilton College Chapel, 1828, illustrate Philip Hooker's conservation of the Georgian-Adam manner. Villages such as Rensselaerville, southwest of Albany, serve as museums in which to observe its charming cumulative effectiveness. From Virginia, the Federal style passed to Kentucky, as seen at Federal Hill, the Stephen Foster home built in 1795 at Bardstown, & at Liberty Hall, 1796, at Frankfort.

Around 1800 a new phase of European design, the neo-classic style of Soane in England, Percier in France, & Schinkel in Germany, began to exert influence in America, chiefly through the agency of Benjamin H. Latrobe & his pupils, Robert Mills & William Strickland. Arriving in 1796 at Norfolk, Latrobe was already an accomplished professional architect. In 1798 he settled in Philadephia & built the waterworks & his first masterpiece, the epoch-making Bank of Pennsylvania, long since destroyed, with its broad monumental wall surfaces, Grecian portico, & brick domed hall. His Catholic Cathedral, built 1806-21 at Baltimore, introduced a monumental spaciousness new to America. In 1803 he took over the building of the U. S. Capitol & later restored it after the British fire. The old Senate chamber (later the Supreme Court room) & the House of Representatives (now the Statuary Hall) still possess, despite loss of their original furnishings, true architectural grandeur.

French neo-classicism is apparent in the monumental grouping of Union College, Schenectady, planned in 1813 by the Bourbon refugee, Joseph Jacques Ramée. The oldest buildings there have a sober gravity in interesting contrast to Jefferson's Palladian "academic village," the University of Virginia, 1817-26, at Charlottesville.

Latrobe's pupils, Mills & Strickland, steadily developed the new manner. Mills, a native of Charleston, S. C., had studied with Hoban & Jefferson, but his five years with Latrobe were the most formative in his architectural training. Entering independent practice, in 1808 he built the County Gaol, still standing at Burlington, N. J. In 1809 he added the connecting fireproof galleries to Independence Hall. At Richmond, his Monumental Church, commemorating the theater catastrophe of 1811, has a severe, almost abstract, classicism. His Washington Column, 1815-29, at Baltimore, was the first American design of truly Roman scale & majesty. Mill's interest in masonry vaulted buildings, the only fireproof system before the skyscraper, is displayed in Charleston's County Record Office, 1823.

THE GREEK REVIVAL: 1817-1850: Both Latrobe & Mills had on occasion employed decorative details inspired by Greek, rather than Roman, architecture. Since the rediscovery of Greek art in the mid-eighteenth century, European interest had mounted. As revolution & war tended to alienate America from England & France, Greece gradually replaced them, as well as Italy, as architectural arbiters. The full force of Greek inspiration was first felt in the remarkable second Bank of the United States (later the Customs House), built at Philadelphia, 1817-24, & designed by William Strickland. The competition program had been dominated by the president, Nicholas Biddle, who a decade before had seen at first hand the ruins at Athens. It called for "a chaste imitation of Grecian architecture, in its simplest & least expensive form." Full eight-columned Greek Doric pedimented porticoes, front & rear, establish the marble temple's theme; but within the splendid Roman barrel vaulted public hall & groin-vaulted offices reveal Strickland's debt to Latrobe & his fearless eclecticism.

Strickland's Bank caused an immediate sensation. St. Paul's Church, built in 1819 at Boston by Alexander Parris, has an Ionic portico. John Haviland, just arrived from England via St. Petersburg, Alexander I's neo-classic capital, used an Ionic portico for the First Presbyterian Church, 1820, & the Deaf & Dumb Asylum, 1824, in Philadelphia. But when the full majesty of the Bank was finally realized, Greek architecture came to dominate the American scene for two decades, replacing the brick & wood domestic scale of earlier structures with monumental ideals born of noble pedimented porticoes & the cool, broad surfaces of stone masonry. Despite their admiration for the columned temple form, most architects went far beyond mere copies. When funds permitted, construction was continually improved, especially in resistance to fire. And the variety of new compositional effects proves the imagination & ingenuity of their designers.

Boston's Quincy Market, 1825, a million dollar granite project by Parris, & the Providence, R. I., Arcade, 1828, by Bucklin & Warren, exemplify the expanding commerce of the period. Naval hospitals—Strickland's at Philadelphia, 1827-48, & Haviland's at Portsmouth, Va., 1827-30—indicate the invasion of governmental types. New York's Customs House (later the Sub-Treasury & now a museum), 1833-42, was the early work of Ithiel Town & A. J. Davis, who joined to form the country's first partnership firm. Exchanges —Strickland's in Philadelphia, 1832-34, & New York's, 1836-42, by Isaiah

Rogers—display monumental elegance. One of the most imposing & least known Greek revival structures is the Insane Asylum at Utica, New York, built 1839-42, with its 48-foot limestone columns & 550-foot five-part facade. In Washington, Mills built his splendid Treasury Building, 1836-43, & the Patent Office, 1836-40, with equal grandeur. Perhaps the most Grecian & ambitious of all is Girard College, 1833-47, with its full Corinthian peristyle & vaulted classrooms, a masterpiece by Strickland's pupil, Thomas Ustick Walter.

The Grecian taste quickly spread from metropolitan centers. On large provincial projects, local architects would often seek the aid of nationally known designers. Thus, Town & Davis collaborated with David Patton on the Capitol at Raleigh, N. C., 1833-40. Occasionally an easterner migrated to a burgeoning new town, as did Strickland when he moved to Nashville, Tenn., to build his elegant Capitol, 1850-55. Some westerners, on the other hand, went east to learn their trade. Gideon Shryock studied under Strickland & on his return showered his native Kentucky with a galaxy of public & private constructions, such as the Old Capitol at Frankfort, 1828-29, Morrison Hall at Transylvania College in Lexington, 1831-34, the Jefferson County Court House at Louisville, 1835-39, and many others. Sometimes the designer had contact with the style only by illustrated books & consequently produced works of charming naivete & hybridism. Gaineswood, the General Whitfield house at Demopolis, Ala., 1842-49, combines Greek details with Soane-like Roman rooms. Dunleith at Natchez, 1847, is a gracious masterpiece of attenuated Doric.

New Orleans abounds in excellent examples of the style. Strickland's U. S. Mint, 1835, is noteworthy, & the Pontalba blocks, 1849, by James Gallier, Sr., nobly frame Jackson Square. Mobile, likewise, boasts its Grecian Cathedral, 1830-50, the Barton Academy, 1836, by James & Charles Dakin, who also designed the handsome Presbyterian Church on Government Street.

Space permits only the briefest selection of the myriad Greek Revival houses that dot the highways & towns east of the Great Plains. Berry Hill, about 1838, near South Boston, Va., was the Parthenon plantation home of James Cole Bruce. Beverwyck, the Van Rensselaer manor house, 1840-43, north of Rensselaer, N. Y., still attests the magnificence created by Frederic Diaper. Rose Hill, about 1835, overlooking Seneca Lake opposite Geneva, N. Y., is an impressive example. The Reed House at Erie is the finest in Pennsylvania. The Ward House, 1859, Georgetown, Ky., is equally pretentious. The Governor's Mansion at Milledgeville, Ga., the President's House, University of Alabama, 1840, at Tuscaloosa, the Belo House, Winston-Salem, 1849, the elegant Governor's Mansion, 1842, Jackson, Miss., by William Nichols, & Oak Alley near Donaldsville, La., show the extension & acclimation of the style in the deep south. Ornamental details of doors & windows, together with diminutive porticoes, inspired by fashionable handbooks, were widely used for middle class homes & farmhouses.

Paralleling the invocation of Greek & Roman antiquity, a reawakening interest in medieval life & art fostered a romantic reaction that manifested itself in Gothic & Romanesque architectural revivals. Actually "Georgian" Gothic was often used in late eighteenth century England, but American examples, such as New York's second Trinity Church, 1788, are all destroyed. The chapel of St. Mary's Seminary, built in 1807 at Baltimore by the French refugee, Maximilian Godefroi, is a naive but charming neo-Gothic confection. English "castellated" Gothic inspired Haviland's epoch-making Eastern State Penitentiary, 1821-35, which initiated an era of reform in prison planning. In 1838 Town & Davis used a smoother baronial version for Lyndhurst, the Paulding mansion at Tarrytown. Davis' First Congregational Church, 1836, at New Bedford is Gothic in powerful rusticated granite. Davis, too, furnished Gothic cottage designs for A. J. Downing's "The Architecture of Country Houses," 1850, which inspired numerous examples throughout the country. Others sent to Davis for plans, as did Francis Key Hunt for his mansion, Loudoun, 1850, at Lexington, Ky. Pratt's "Castle," built about 1845 at Richmond, Va., is an exotic fantasy of medieval details. The Old State Capitol, 1847-49 (rebuilt in 1882) at Baton Rouge, La., designed by Dakin, is an extraordinary Gothic design within & without.

A closer archaeological use of Gothic was introduced by the English-trained architect, Richard Upjohn. His third Trinity Church, 1839-46, in New York still proves his skill despite crowding skyscrapers, & brought him numerous commissions, such as St. Paul's, Buffalo. Poorer parishes used his stock plans for charming "board-&-batten" chapels, as St. Paul's, Kinderhook, N. Y. James Renwick, Jr., shared this desire for correctness, illustrated in Grace Church, 1843-46, & St. Patrick's Cathedral, 1853-79, both in New York City. An effective Gothic composition reflecting Rhenish influence is Young & Angell's Mormon Temple begun in 1853 at Salt Lake City.

An amusing episode concerns experiments in acclimating ancient Egyptian architecture to the American scene. Haviland's Tombs, the New York jail, 1838, has long since disappeared, but Egyptian Hall built in 1854 by Thomas S. Stewart, a Philadelphia architect, to house the Medical College of Virginia in Richmond still stands. At Essex, Conn., the Baptist Church, 1846, translated Egyptian forms into Yankee clapboards. The most famous Egyptian motif, the obelisk, was used by Solomon Willard as early as 1825 for the Bunker Hill Monument at Charlestown, but Mills far surpassed it in his masterpiece, the majestic Washington Monument, 1836-84. It is interesting to note that these obelisks, though originally Egyptian, came down to us via Rome & thus harmonized with the neo-classic spirit of the age.

The twenties, thirties, & forties also saw rapid development in commercial & industrial building although the few examples now standing are hidden & neglected. Mill towns like Lowell, Massachusetts, exhibit in microcosm the same cycles of fashion both in its textile factories & workers' housing. The standard blocks of Greek revival stores have been largely replaced or so remodeled as to be unrecognizable; but here and there one remains with its rhythmic granite piers & austere fenestration. Galena, Ill., still treasures its Market House built in 1845 by Henry J. Stouffer. The growth of the railroads is represented by the castellated Gothic Boston & Maine depot built at Salem, Mass. in 1847, & the superb Thomas Viaduct built of granite in 1835 nine miles south of Baltimore & still carrying the Baltimore & Ohio main line over the Patapsco River. Another magnificent neo-classic engineering monument is the fourteen arch aqueduct built in 1841 to carry the Erie Canal across Schoharie Creek, near Fort Hunter, N. Y. Its clean vigorous stonework compares most favorably with the finest contemporary structures in Britain. Also of architectural interest are the military fortresses of the period, such as Ft. Pulaski, east of Savannah, 1829-47.

THE MIDDLE YEARS: 1850-1886: It has long been fashionable to smile indulgently at cultural manifestations of mid-nineteenth-century America. The rapid expansion of industry, commerce, & speculation & the discovery of western gold created rampant prosperity in the early fifties that enriched an ever broadening market for luxury & ostentation. Though some classic revival designs continued to be built, they were more effulgent in character, as for example the wings of the United States Capitol added by Walter in 1851-67, or the Customhouse at Norfolk, 1857, or the overripe Grecian Bellamy mansion, 1859, built by Rufus Bunnell at Wilmington, N. C.

The new generation drew its principal inspiration from Victoria's England & the Second Empire of Napoleon III. The Italian Renaissance style via France via England & the mansarded baroque straight from Paris dominated larger projects. Venetian Gothic via Ruskin & Britain lent its polychromatic masonry to churches, schools, & other structures. And the Italian "villa" style via England, popularized by handbooks by Downing, Vaux, & many others, produced in town & country those pretentious "arks" so ridiculed today.

These European influences reached America in various ways. Native American architects learned the new fashions either by travel or through the new illustrated architectural journals. European trained men brought the latest modes with them when they emigrated. Vaux & Withers from England & a host of Germans have left their mark. In 1845 Richard Morris Hunt was the first American architectural student at the Ecole des Beaux-Arts in Paris. Two years after his return in 1857 he began to instruct pupils according to the Ecole system. One of these students, William R. Ware, settled in Boston & organized a two-year course for his own pupils. In 1865 Ware was made director of the first U. S. architectural school, a unit of the Massachusetts Institute of Technology, & classes opened in 1868. In 1870 architectural instruction was inaugurated at the University of Illinois, & there, in March, 1873, Nathan Clifford Ricker received the first American degree in architecture. Cornell in 1871, Syracuse in 1873, & Columbia in 1880 followed. At M.I.T., French influence was strong; at Illinois there was direct inspiration from Berlin's Bauakademie; at Cornell English influence was important.

Despite this stylistic heterodoxy, there underlay considerable architectural unity. Beneath the demand for multiplicity & ornamental eclecticism, architects continued to compose their buildings' elements in formal Palladian or picturesque romantic groupings. But the deepest continuity is found in the steady progress made in evolving suitable plans to accommodate new functional requirements, in the gradual refinement of iron-framed structural systems, & in applying scientific resources to the problems of heating, sanitation, lighting, & vertical transportation. Although all these problems had received earlier solution in England, American genius for gadgetry & industrial production contributed much of the essential development basic to present-day modern architecture.

The Houghwout Department Store, built in 1857 by J. P. Gaynor, architect, on the northeast corner of Broadway & Broome, New York, is an overlooked but important monument. The tiers of Renaissance arcades—one to a story—have a genuine beauty, & exterior walls are entirely of cast iron. Inside, the store installed the first regular passenger elevator in America. Haviland had built a cast-iron bank facade in 1830 & one-story cast iron store fronts had been common since the mid-thirties; but it remained for James Bogardus to popularize it so that it became the dominant type of commercial construction up through the eighties. Mercer & Greene Streets, New York, are lined with cast-iron-fronted warehouses, & three miles of iron fronts still remain below Canal Street. Almost every American city—even Honolulu—has similar structures shipped from eastern foundries. So safe, strong, & cheap was the material that it was used by Walter to line the House & Senate Halls of the Capitol, & for the marvelously fine new dome with which he capped that building.

The middle years witnessed remarkable urban expansion which in turn fostered the first steps toward the amelioration of city life. Office buildings began their upward climb especially in the early eighties in Chicago's Loop where masonry fireproofing of the metal skeleton, thin exterior curtain walls supported on the frame, & secure foundations to carry the stupendous loads were brought to practical solution. Progress has destroyed the key examples, such as Burnham & Root's Montauk Building, 1881-82, & the Home Insurance Company's Building, 1883-85, by Jenny & Mundie. The first American apartment house, the Stuyvesant, built by Hunt in 1869, still stands at 138 East 18th Street in New York. The fight against tenement slums, provoked by unbelievable squalor, began in 1867 with the first Tenement House Law. For those who could afford to commute, suburban towns like Garden City, Long Island, and Riverside, Ill., both laid out in 1869, gave escape from civic cacophony. The rise of the park movement—Central Park in New York, 1858-70, Druid Hill Park in Baltimore, 1860, Lincoln Park in Chicago, 1864—recaptured a fragment of space & greenery from the grasp of greedy speculators. Cities were becoming at once the symbol of dynamic opportunity & of almost hopeless degradation.

Despite continual rebuilding of growing cities, a few of the significant constructions of the period still stand. The mansarded Second Empire style first appeared in Boston's City Hall, 1861-65, by Gridley Bryant & Arthur Gilman. The finest example, however, is the State, War, & Navy Building, 1871-87, by A. B. Mullet, west of the White House in Washington. Near-by is James Renwick's old Corcoran Art Gallery (now the Court of Claims), 1874. Another most conspicuous masterpiece is the Philadelphia City Hall, built 1874-87, by John McArthur. Across the country, post offices such as the old one at Cincinnati, 1874-89, also by Mullet, courthouses such as at Lafayette, Ind., 1881-84, business blocks such as the lavish cast iron Powers Building built in 1870 at Rochester, N. Y., by Andrew Jackson Warner, & numerous hotels spread the style.

The earlier Gothic trend continued throughout the middle years. The finest example of the Victorian phase preached by Ruskin is Harvard's Memorial Hall, a colossal polychromatic essay by Ware & Van Brunt, 1871-74. The Connecticut Capitol at Hartford, 1873-78, by Richard M. Upjohn, son of Richard Upjohn of Trinity Church, is likewise Victorian Gothic. Vaux & Withers also used it in 1866-72 for the Hudson River State Hospital, north of Poughkeepsie. Numerous churches still exhibit it, though most of their sparkle is subdued with grime.

Along with the upper-crust, Europe-inspired high styles favored by the more knowing training architects, the great mass of ordinary buildings was designed by men schooled only as carpenters or masons. Despite their limitations, these men possessed little reticence & culled from important monuments, handbooks, or other available resources what stimulus they could for fancy & effect. Often the result was sheer malevolent ugliness, but much of it has the authentic interest of a sort of folk architecture, joining bits of detail from many sources to form new concoctions which, though naive, possess a certain freshness & vitality. Dr. Kenneth Conant groups these buildings into an "Americanese" style. Their interest & importance have too long been overlooked.

For those who can see, almost all towns and cities retain in their older business districts a fascinating collection of "Americanese" commercial blocks that ring every conceivable change of material & motive. The jigsaw bracketed cornices & lavish tortured ornament of the residences of the period show an ingenuity & ambition that cannot be denied. The camp meeting cottages at Round Lake, north of Albany, N. Y., form a miniature museum of "Americanese." The sheer gorgeousness of Longwood, or Nutt's Folly, a Natchez "Persian" villa designed by Samuel Sloan of Philadelphia & built 1858-64, has hardly ever been matched. Similar fantasy pervades the unbelievable Grand Union Hotel, 1872, at Saratoga Springs.

Most architects of the middle years so preferred to crowd their designs with a multiplicity of motives joined to produce a nervous, broken mass that they lost the majesty of scale & lucid unity that had distinguished neo-classic taste. They sought exciting, dynamic effects, but too often attained only a frustrating pettiness. The rediscovery of true architectural monumentality was accomplished largely through the genius of Henry Hobson Richardson.

While a student at the Ecole, Richardson had admired the powerful, vigorous masonry of the French & Spanish Romanesque. To these he fused the tremendous, heavy arches & twinkling foliate ornament of Syrian fifth century churches just then made known by publication; but from these inspirations he evolved a personal expression of great breadth. His early masterpiece, Trinity Church, Copley Square, Boston, built 1872-77, had an immediate & wholesome effect & brought him the largest practice of the decade. Steadily he refined his taste, sloughed off extraneous complexities, & achieved the most effective masonry & massing in American history. Sever Hall (1878-80) & Austin Hall (1881-83), both at Harvard, exemplified his institutional work. His finest remaining structure is the Allegheny County Courthouse & Jail, 1884-87, at Pittsburgh, but it was the Marshall Field Wholesale Store in Chicago, begun in 1885 a year before his death, that turned the course of taste back to severe block masses & restrained detail. Its demolition robbed us of one of the great buildings of all time. A similar compactness of mass characterizes his domestic work, whether in stone, as the Glessner House, 1800 Prairie Avenue, Chicago, built 1886, or in wood shingles, as the Stoughton House, Mason & Brattle Streets, Cambridge, Massachusetts, 1882-84, or the Potter House, 1886, in St. Louis.

Richardson's colleagues were quick to adopt the superficial aspects of his style and their buildings still dot the country. Every college has at least one Romanesque example, while Romanesque churches, city halls, public schools, libraries, & banks are still familiar landmarks. The industrial town, Pullman, Ill., is a complete Romanesque community designed by S. S. Beman. At their best, these structures attain a certain powerful dignity; at their worst, they have only clumsy stolidity.

THE TURNING POINT: 1886-1918: Commercial vigor, industrial productivity, vast continental resources, & a rapidly growing population demanded a more mature architecture as a setting for the new imperial spirit of the nineties. In scope & ambition America was a unit, but in method and mode of expression she was still a melting pot.

Burgeoning Chicago, less inhibited by foreign influence than the east, enjoyed a decade & a half of exciting leadership. Pressure for space within its restricted Loop forced architects to solve ever higher structures. The Monadnock Office Building, 53 W. Jackson Boulevard, built 1889-91 by Burnham & Root, shows the new severity inspired by Richardson & was the last of the skyscrapers to use exterior masonry piers as actual supports. In contrast, the Tacoma Building, La Salle & Madison Streets, 1887-88, by Holabird & Roche, reveals the lightness, openness, & glass area permitted by adoption of metal skeleton construction.

It remained, however, for Louis Sullivan with his partner, Dankmar Adler, to transmute these new techniques into an integrated aesthetic composition. Strongly stimulated by Richardson's Marshall Field Store, Sullivan immediately reoriented his own manner, as shown in the magnificent Auditorium Building (now Roosevelt College), Michigan Avenue & Congress Street, 1886-90. In the Wainwright Office Building in St. Louis, 1890-91, & in the Prudential Building, 1894-95, in Buffalo, he achieved the first full & mature aesthetic exploitation of skyscraper verticality. Sullivan's genius for decoration enriched all his work.

In the east the new monumentalism evolved differently. There the leaders had usually attended the Ecole des Beaux-Arts & had absorbed the beauty of historic models. McKim, Mead, & White began as followers of Richardson, but in the Villard Houses, Madison & 50th, New York, built 1883-85, they turned to the restrained grandeur of the Italian Renaissance. Their Boston Public Library, 1887-93, was "the first American building of which a Medici prince could be proud." Carrere & Hastings drew on the Spanish Renaissance for their luxurious fantasy, the Ponce de Leon Hotel, 1887, at St. Augustine. R. M. Hunt outdid them all in his palatial French Renaissance "Biltmore," built in 1890-95 at Asheville, N. C., for George Washington Vanderbilt. But in George B. Post's World Building, 1889-90, opposite New York's City Hall, the basic difficulty of translating old forms to new uses is all too evident.

Eastern influence acutely undermined Chicago experimentation when McKim, Hunt, & the others were called in by Daniel H. Burnham to design Chicago's World's Columbian Exposition in 1893. Sullivan's Transportation Building was the sole representative of the Chicago group. Dramatic vistas everywhere led to exhibition sheds costumed in classic, Renaissance, or baroque plaster shells. Charles B. Atwood's neo-classic Fine Arts Building (now the Rosenwald Science Museum) still proves the impact projected by the monumental white ensemble. Overawed visitors returned home to demand a rash of neo-classic civic monuments.

One result of the fair was a lively interest in the rediscovery of L'Enfant's design for Washington. In 1901 Burnham & McKim pushed through its re-adoption & began the clearing of extraneous nineteenth century accretions, including a railroad station directly on the Mall. McKim refurbished the White House; Burnham built the Union Station as a triumphal gateway to the city.

Other cities followed suit with Burnham's Chicago plan, 1907, outdoing the rest both in grandiosity & farseeing vision.

The neo-classicists produced many effective designs, such as McKim's group at Columbia University, 1895 on, his Pennsylvania Railroad Station, 1906-10, & his Municipal Office Building, 1908-10, all in New York. The Lincoln Memorial, 1911-22, by Henry Bacon, is perhaps the epitome of this cycle, at once beautiful in form & exasperating in logic. The Georgian & Colonial revivals which paralleled the neo-classic trend likewise stifled more vigorous & progressive architectural thought, and their formulae repeated ad infinitum tend to hide some excellent examples.

Medieval influences continued all through the period & closer study produced buildings increasingly correct in design & execution. All Saints' Church, Dorchester, Mass., 1892, by Ralph Adams Cram is an early example. Cram, Goodhue, & Ferguson used Gothic most effectively in the reconstruction of the Military Academy at West Point from 1903 on. And Goodhue, with his master touch, created his lovely Gothic tour-de-force in St. Thomas' Church, New York, 1906-11. Gothic verticality expressed the record-breaking height of Cass Gilbert's Woolworth Building, New York, 1911-13.

But there were those who believed that American architecture could not fulfill its own destiny in terms of historic models, however skillfully they were translated. It was from the second generation of the Chicago group that the progressive leaders came, & the most famous & influential genius was Frank Lloyd Wright. From 1887 to 1893 Wright served his apprenticeship under Sullivan at his peak, & to his own penchant for individualistic experimentation added his master's courage & facility. The Winslow House, Auvergne Place, River Forest, Ill., 1893, exhibits his early work, while the Larkin Company's Administration Building, 680 Seneca Street, Buffalo, 1904, & the Martin House, 125 Jewett Parkway, Buffalo, 1904, display the mature expression of space & materials that antedates similar trends both here & in Europe. The Unity Church, Oak Park, Ill., 1906, is an early masterpiece in concrete. Among his finest, most imaginative works are the Robie House, 5757 Woodlawn Avenue, Chicago, 1909, & the Coonley House, 300 Scottswood Road, Riverside, 1908.

Sullivan, after his split with Adler in 1895, never regained his former momentum. The Carson, Pirie, Scott department store, Chicago, 1899-1904, retained his superb decorative touch; but thenceforth only a few small banks, such as at Grinnell, Iowa, 1914, marked the tragic years. Other members of the Chicago group, notably Purcell, Feick, & Elmslie, continued the Sullivan trend, as in the Merchants' Bank, Winona, Minnesota, 1912. A contemporary, but independent, evolution was pioneered in California by Bernard Maybeck & by Greene & Greene.

Almost unnoticed by architects were certain problems that would create strong influences in the future. Industrial & utilitarian structures slowly attracted major talent. The flight of the textile industry to southern states provided unusual opportunities for improved mill design & for the inclusion of amenities in operatives' housing. In Detroit Albert Kahn applied high architectural skill to the growing needs of the automotive industry. Urban congestion began to call for new techniques of amelioration, as in the New York Zoning Ordinance of 1916, and the construction of the garden suburb, Forest

Hills, begun in 1911. During World War I the creation of new industrial towns such as Yorkship Village (now Fairview) near Camden, N. J., gave valuable training for future leaders in low-cost public housing.

BETWEEN TWO WARS: 1918-1941: The cessation of building during World War I created the record boom of the gilded twenties, of which the most conspicuous feature was the speculative reconstruction of metropolitan commercial centers led by Manhattan and Chicago. The skyscraper was the symbol of the age & its economic preoccupations. Experts refined their plans to obtain the last square inch of rentable area. Engineers calculated their steel skeletons & elevators to exploit maximum capacity. And designers sought to make each tower dominate its neighbors by some special "treatment."

The fabulous Chicago Tribune Tower competition of 1922 drew over 400 aspirants who ransacked history & ideas to tempt the jury. The lucky winners, Raymond Hood & J. M. Howells, skillfully wrapped their very practical plans in an aurora of Flamboyant Gothic. Many, including Sullivan, regretted that the prize did not go to the runner-up, an admirable translation of the Woolworth scheme entered by the Finnish architect, Eliel Saarinen. Saarinen settled in Detroit & in the years following created a potent center of Scandinavian influence in the superb group of buildings forming the Cranbrook Academy at Bloomfield Hills.

Hood, himself, restlessly continued to experiment with other "treatments," in the black & gold of the American Radiator Building, the vertical stripes of the Daily News Building, & the horizontal banding of the McGraw-Hill Building, all in New York. Despite their inconclusive air, they were vastly superior to the strained ornamentalism of the usual current solutions.

These tentative essays in pure abstract design did not penetrate the institutional or residential fields. Churches had to be in a "religious style," surcharged with Gothic emotion, or "correct" as in Cram's nave at St. John the Divine's Cathedral, or "adapted" in the auditorium-&-skyscraper complex of the Riverside Church, both in New York, or with Colonial placidity as in Hobart Upjohn's First Presbyterian Church in Fayetteville, N. C. Colleges preferred Georgian, as in Harvard's house groups overlooking the Charles, or Oxfordian Gothic as at the University of Chicago, Princeton, & Duke. Houses ranged the gamut of high & provincial styles from Normandy half-timber deep in the heart of Texas to acres of cunning Cape Cod cottages in every urban subdivision. In Florida Addison Mizner with irresistible showmanship purveyed a curious variety of bastard Spanish villas complete with phony manufactured antiques. The best work of the period, as in the buildings of Frank Forster, Harry T. Lindeberg, or Delano & Aldrich, had the genuine charm of fine detail & craftsmanship; the worst was a theatrical travesty of honest architecture.

The more progressive traditionalists tended toward a stripping away of reminiscent detail. Goodhue in his Nebraska State Capitol, 1922-25, attained a sort of personal & sculptural classicism, richly restrained & powerful. His Los Angeles Public Library, 1925-26, moved further toward abstract classicism. Paul Philippe Cret illustrated the same process, from his cool Renaissance Detroit Art Museum, 1925, to his famed "modern classic" Folger Shakespearean Library in Washington, 1932. The same contrast appears between the magnificent traditional Missouri State Capitol, 1917-24, by Tracy &

Swartwout, & its modernized counterpart at Salem, Oregon, by Francis Keally & Trowbridge & Livingston.

It was Wright, however, who stood alone against these conservative conceptions. His most famous work, the Imperial Hotel in Tokyo, 1917-22, is important both for subtle amalgamation of native & Wrightian forms & for the ingenious structural precautions which successfully withstood earthquake damage. His American projects of this period, located chiefly in California, attest his preoccupation with textured concrete block. The Millard House (1923), 645 Prospect Crescent, Pasadena, the Ennis House (1924), 2607 Glendower Road, Los Angeles, & the Jones House (1929), 3700 Birmingham Road, Tulsa, are typical of his magical exploitation of materials, forms, & sites. His own home, Taliesin, at Spring Green, Wisconsin, rebuilt after the fire of 1925, has become a mecca for architects & students from all over the world, & his influence has also been felt increasingly in the work of younger men.

The four great monuments of the boom period, all completed after its collapse, symbolize the technical & social milieu. The first, the Empire State Building, New York, 1930-31, by Shreve, Lamb, & Harmon, not only holds the record for height, but in its construction & erection illustrated the unprecedented organizational proficiency achieved by American builders. At Rockefeller Center the heterogeneity of isolated skyscrapers, the bane of metropolitan landscapes, was skillfully resolved by welding the complex group into a dramatic & profitable unity basic to civic order. Third, the Cincinnati Union Station, opened in 1933, proved that logic of plan & form can be beautifully expressed without extraneous reminiscence & can be effectively integrated into the community pattern as well. The fourth is the community itself, planned for humane living, as exemplified by the epoch-making town of Radburn, N. J. Here the integration of open green space, forthright housing, commercial center, & school into an harmonious & logical neighborhood plan revealed new & exciting vistas.

The great depression influenced & was influenced by a faltering demand for new construction. Strenuous national measures centered on its revival. Widespread rebuilding of governmental facilities not only primed the economy, but often resulted in designs of excellent quality, such as the Washington Airport Terminal & many post offices throughout the country. Liberal assistance to semi-public institutions, especially educational, produced many schools & college buildings, but too often the standard of quality was both ultra-conservative & uninspired. In public housing, however, considerable strides were made in replacing slums with good quality shelter. The challenge of Radburn was answered with special felicity in the magnificently planned suburban town of Greenbelt, developed by the Resettlement Administration northeast of Washington. Relief projects among architectural personnel set up the Historic American Buildings Survey which recorded 6,389 irreplaceable historic structures in 23,765 measured drawings & 25,357 photographs, an invaluable archive for architectural scholars.

American architectural design during the thirties continued its eclecticism, but limited funds tended to enforce a healthy simplification of reminiscent detail, producing abstractions of Georgian, Classic, & Gothic that gained new breadth. At the same time, however, there came increasing interest in European post-war developments, especially in the work of the so-called International School led by Gropius in Germany & LeCorbusier in France. This work differed sharply from the ornamental modern of the Austrian theatrical designer, Joseph Urban, as displayed in his Ziegfeld Theater, New York, 1926, or his fantastic Hutton House, Palm Beach, 1927, or from the romantic modern of Saarinen at Cranbrook. In general, it aimed to restrict itself to an exploitation of characteristic new materials functionally disposed, & assembled to produce new aesthetic effects of plane-defined space. At first derided by conservatives as "packing box and gas pipe design," its impact raised profound questioning of principles previously thought to be immutable.

First awareness of these exciting developments was obtained from journals & books, but was soon reinforced by a potent stream of European architects. From 1925 on, the work of the Viennese architect, Richard Neutra, of Los Angeles, was of increasing interest. His house for Dr. Lovell, 1929, Los Angeles, was one of the first statements of the new creed in America. During the past two decades he has created a large number of significant structures in the new idiom. More authoritative leadership came with the arrival of the former directors of the German Bauhaus. In 1936 Walter Gropius became head of Harvard's architectural school, & soon after Ludwig Miës van der Rohe began direction of the architectural department of the Illinois Institute of Technology. Although the primary efforts of both have been the training of student architects, the practical effect of which is already apparent, they have also built a number of instructive buildings. Gropius' own house & its neighbors at Lincoln, Mass., already seem comfortably acclimated. Miës' austere campus at Illinois Tech is slowly taking form to prove the elegance & subtlety of his style. All these contributions are provocative, stimulating, & significant additions to the American architectural scene.

American achievement in the "International Style" began slowly but steadily gained momentum. Howe & Lescaze broke successfully with former "skyscraper treatments" & produced in the Philadelphia Savings Fund Society's building, 1932-33, a clean-cut expressive design. Philip Goodwin & Edward Stone, aided by sympathetic clients, erected a beacon for modernism in their Museum of Modern Art, New York, 1935. Chicago's Century of Progress exposition, 1933-34, helped to some extent & New York's World of Tomorrow, 1939-40, to a greater degree, to win public acceptance to new forms.

Nevertheless it was still the American master, Wright, who steadily dominated the thirties, not alone by executed buildings, but also by exciting, imaginative, & astounding projects. The Kaufmann House, Falling Water, at Bear Run, Penn., 1936, is an amazing masterpiece of glass, stone, & concrete, intimately interwoven with the stream & ledges of the dramatic site. The Administration Building of the Johnson Company at Racine, Wisconsin, 1936-39, solves a usually routine problem with extraordinary inventiveness. His own winter headquarters, Taliesin West, 1938, near Phoenix, on Maricopa Mesa, & the Florida Southern College group at Lakeland, 1940, set in a lush orange grove, are linked by the same uncommon touch.

WORLD WAR II AND AFTER: Preparation for & prosecution of total conflict presented prodigious demands for buildings. New industrial plants at Willow Run, Fort Worth, Wichita, & elsewhere set records for size & speed of erection. Industrial housing, much of it temporary, sheltered armies of factory personnel. Vast training camps, each a complex city, took form in incredibly short time.

Return to peace found deficits in every kind of building space & a tremendous pent-up urge to satisfy them. Despite shortages of materials and labor, despite abrupt inflation, peak demands persisted & presented American architects with challenging opportunities. In almost all types of buildings, public acceptance of the contemporary manner has been notable. Only in houses, churches, & schools is there some lingering nostalgia for traditional emotional values.

Widespread commercial construction exploiting dramatic modernism for its sales-inducing novelty has led the way. Foley's Department Store, Houston, Texas, is an outstanding & effective example. The coordinated shopping center also helps mold public taste. Modern movie palaces, modern factories, modern sports centers, all indoctrinate their users.

The question is, "What kind and quality of modern architecture shall we have?" A survey of recent work conveys the impression that within its doctrines an amazing scope & variety is pregnant with multitudinous possibilities. America is asserting her traditional felicity in absorbing many strains & is transmuting them into a rich vocabulary & grammar capable of a full expression of her varied regions & problems.

The roster of American architects now producing significant work is far too long to list here. Many old established firms continue to turn out buildings of high quality. Holabird & Root of Chicago, for example, designed Washington's luxurious Hotel Statler. The Saarinens, father & son, created the beautiful Kleinhans Auditorium in Buffalo & what is perhaps the finest modern church in America, the Congregational Church, Columbus, Indiana. Igor Polivitzski's Shelburne Hotel, Miami Beach, is a brilliant essay in the contemporary manner. Pietro Belluschi of Portland, Oregon, is breaking new paths in his advanced designs. Alden Dow of Albion, Mich., has created many buildings of outstanding character, & Burnham Hoyt, in his Red Rock Theater at Denver, won a unique effectiveness from its intriguing site. Unfortunately the mere mention of such a limited group does severe injustice to many others.

It has been amply indicated that the American grand tour, if undertaken with alertness & appreciation, can pay rich rewards of beauty & deeper understanding of our common culture. The tangibility & human associations of our buildings, past and present, make them invaluable foci around which to form our feeling for the stream of American history. Their immediacy gives us symbols of social & cultural goals that are basic to a dynamic, evolving civilization. These sticks & stones sum up the American story, centuries in the making, & can give us the foundation on which to erect a future consonant with our honorable past. —TURPIN C. BANNISTER

# ART

Up to the latter part of the 19th century there was no painting or sculpture that could, strictly speaking, be called American. The work of the professional artists who came to America or were born here tended to be a provincial variation of the styles of Europe. American personalities, objects & scenes appeared in their canvasses, but they were not American in the sense of a native way of seeing & creating. On the other hand, the decorations & designs produced by non-professionals, by artisans & handicraftsmen, though they had an indigenous flavor, were improvisations too random & sporadic to result in an artistic tradition.

In the Colonies, a handful of Englishmen, one or two Dutchmen & Frenchmen who had been trained abroad, & a few native craftsmen who had picked up the knack by studying the occasional paintings or engravings to be seen in the better homes, did portraits "on the side," either as a hobby or as a way of earning extra money. It was only after several of the settlements had grown quite large and prosperous that a small number of artists were able to support themselves through commissions. These men painted portraits in the English style: usually three-quarter views of a stiffly posed lady or gentleman whose face, not too melting to begin with (considering the hard life in the Colonies & necessary toughness of spirit), is given added severity by the rigorous linear treatment of contemporary British draftsmanship. The sitter wears his or her best clothes, of course, & the artist exhibits his skill by reproducing its every careful fold, surface sheen and textile pattern. John Singleton Copley was the best of these Colonial painters.

Along with this portrait art addressed to the Colonial worthies came the shop & inn signs, coach decorations, ships' figureheads, weathervanes, gravestone & wood carvings, lawn figures & hitching posts, glassware & other "practical" art turned out for the delectation of the general public. American sculpture was for a long time restricted to the carving shops. William Rush, the first to achieve a memorable reputation, made figureheads as well as portrait busts. Connected in spirit with this workmanlike art were the portrait "limnings" popular on the farms as well as in the towns. These were in the main the work of self-taught painters, anonymous to us, who wandered about the settlements with a stock of portraits all finished except for the head. The customer selected the one he liked best &, for a price sometimes as low as a night's lodging & a few meals, the artist filled in the face. Some of these portraits have come to be valued as "primitives" because of their rich color, clean design, fancifulness & insight into character.

Winning the Revolutionary War brought a feeling for history & new public buildings for artists to decorate. Benjamin West, an expatriate from the

Colonies, had set up in London a school which came to be known as "the American School." West taught that painting should tell a noble story, religious or historical. Almost all the early Republican painters received some of their training in West's school or accepted its influence, & hopes among them were high that they would soon have the opportunity to introduce the most exalted images among their rather earth-bound compatriots. Congress, however, proved less generous with commissions than had been expected, &, to make matters more irritating, imported French artists & an Italian or two to decorate the new capitol in Washington. Instead of heroes, the Americans for the most part either had to go on painting portraits of merchants & their wives or give up the profession & go into something else. Turning out literally thousands of portraits, Thomas Sully & Chester Harding achieved enormous popularity. Malbone & Fraser were much admired for their miniatures.

The new sense of history did manage to express itself to some extent. John Trumbull, who had served in the Revolutionary army, did full length portraits of Washington, Hamilton & Jay, & such significant scenes, now familiar through prints to every schoolboy, as "The Battle of Bunker Hill," "The Surrender of Cornwallis," "The Signing of the Declaration of Independence." Numerous portraits of George Washington, often bearing little resemblance to one another, were executed by his contemporaries. The most celebrated is the Athenaeum portrait by Gilbert Stuart, perhaps the best painter of the country's early decades. Though Stuart studied under West, his work has a softer tone & more subtle modeling than that of the West School. Another portraitist of Washington was Charles Willson Peale, father of the painters Rembrandt & Raphaelle Peale. The career of the elder Peale, like those of the artist-inventors Robert Fulton & S. F. B. Morse, reveals the extent to which, even after the Revolution, painting often tended to be less than a full-time occupation; besides being an artist, Peale was a craftsman, an entrepreneur, a soldier, a naturalist, & lectured & ran a museum of natural curiosities.

With the opening of new territories to settlers, Americans became increasingly interested in what their country looked like—& genre painting & landscapes soon rivaled portraiture in popularity. George Caleb Bingham, "the Missouri artist," Henry Inman, William Sidney Mount, & Eastman Johnson were outstanding among those who depicted life in the towns, the backwoods, on the Mississippi. They worked in the painstaking manner of the Düsseldorf School in Germany at which several of the group studied. Paintings & drawings of this type, having generally the quality of a photograph whose maker is indifferent to light & shadows, are still being produced. They are popular with the neighbors & with art editors of American family magazines for the stories they tell of Thanksgiving at home, rowing with one's girl on a lake, a Negro playing a guitar in front of a shack.

With genre & landscape as their subjects, painters began to set up their easels outdoors. The Hudson River School of landscape painters began with Thomas Cole, who worked directly from nature in the Hudson River Valley. It soon came to include landscapists who traveled many miles from New York. The Hudson River painters sought primarily to convey visual information & feelings about nature; problems of structure, composition, color values bothered them very little. Their panoramas might be pastorals like Kensett's, or they might be filled with the melodrama of mountain peaks, waterfalls and icebergs like those of Church & Bierstadt. Americans of the period did not object to thin paint quality, clutterings of detail, lack of esthetic order, so long as they were shown the place "the way it looks." In the paintings of Moran you could see the Rocky Mountains; in those of Church, Niagara Falls or a tropical daybreak—these painters were a huge success & brought amazing prices.

To this impulse to get a record made of nature & people belongs the work of George Catlin, who spent years among the Indians creating his valued gallery of portraits & customs, & John James Audubon, who followed unfamiliar birds across the slopes of Kentucky & the marshes of the Mississippi to compile his famous "Birds of America." In Audubon's bird "portraits," fresh in color & drawn with striking precision & originality of conception, the desire to know & picture the new American land resulted in an art of great power & authenticity. Almost wholly self-taught, Audubon achieved a personal mode that was a mixture of the techniques of the folk craftsmen, the scientist & the "fine" artist. Though born in France, he is perhaps the first genuine American artist, in that his style as well as his subjects were born out of American experience.

Apart from some strong creations by the woodcarvers, carpenters and stonecutters, William Rush, John Frazee, Samuel McIntire, Hezekiah Augur & Clark Mills, who made America's first equestrian statue, nothing much was done in American sculpture before the Civil War. As West attracted the painters, the neo-classical school of Thorwaldsen & Canova in Italy drew most American students of sculpture. In the imitations of Greek & Roman figures by Greenough, Crawford & Powers it is difficult to detect a trace of anything either personal or American; though Powers succeeded better in his earlier realistic mood.

With the industrialization that came after the Civil War, the United States begins to have an art of its own. Some Americans trained after European models were no longer satisfied merely to inject native subject matter into pictures mechanically imitative; each sought to build a style & manner belonging to himself & to his way of responding to his world. With Thomas Eakins & Winslow Homer a new realism replaced the fussy decor of the Hudson River landscapists & Düsseldorf genre painters. With Albert Pinkham Ryder a new passionateness contrasts with the sentimentality & melodrama of the classicists & the scenarists of mountains & rivers. Henceforth, American artists in portraying the life about them were to go past "what it looks like" to "what it is"—or with a fidelity just as devoted they were to turn from appearances & strive to transmit to canvas or stone their deepest inner harmonies & anguish.

Thomas Eakins had the best art schooling available in his day; he studied at the Ecole des Beaux Arts & with Leon Bonnet, & he was familiar with the realists of France & Spain. Unlike his predecessors, & of course many who have followed him, his goal was not to produce a painting in the manner of the most prominent European movement but to understand & picture the experiences most meaningful to him. These experiences were for the main part composed of prosaic & raw elements. The grace and charm of a Degas or a Pissarro were hardly to be found in the streets and entertainments of his contemporary America. Eakins painted portraits of determined men, violent sports, surgeons performing operations in clinics. He painted them with the concentration & respect for fact of one who knew he was beholding the most serious aspects of a new kind of social life. With him American realism left behind the slick surfaces of Düsseldorf reporting.

Winslow Homer, partly self taught, also ventured to subordinate Art to reporting and thus achieved authentic artistic qualities. Engraver & illustrator as well as painter, he covered the Civil War for "Harper's Weekly" & later turned up with his sketch pad in many parts of the world. His watercolors & oils caught with candid-camera accuracy & verve the movements of the sea on the coast of Maine, of sailors in oilskins, of Negroes & palm trees in the South.

Advanced twentieth-century tastes, emphasizing imagination & passion in art, find little interest in the American artists of the past century. "Primitives" like the limners, the homespun Pennsylvanians Hicks & Pickett, the print-makers Currier & Ives, the ultra-realist Harnett, the carvers of black boys & eagles for steamships, these arouse excitement today, largely through associations with the *douanier* Rousseau & the surrealists. But of genuine painters of inwardness we have few in that period, except for Albert Ryder. Ryder foreshadows the modern "night mind" in art that refuses to regard visible environment as the final human reality. One might say that the lonely Ryder was too literal, even to the point of crudeness, in his intuition of art as dreaming, for he invariably "naturalizes" his visions by setting them in darkness & moonlight, unlike, say, Miró, who transforms his night images into bright-colored & distinct linear shapes. With Ryder night & night-feeling turns into blue-black & silver masses of jagged clouds, sea & shore, with faint green glimmerings of ghostly horsemen, ships & distances, conveying by suggestion themes drawn from Shakespeare, the Bible, folklore or personal fantasy. Strongly religious & ascetic, Ryder belongs among those painters who work slowly, repaint much & shun as if it came from the devil any temptation to please an audience. The modern eccentric & primitive Eilshemius belongs to the Ryder tradition of strong individualism.

By the last quarter of the nineteenth century, England and Germany were finished as influences in American art, except for the brief turn to the Munich School exemplified by Chase & Duveneck. All the broad movements were now to come from France. American landscapists learned atmosphere & harmony from the Barbizon painters, as Sargent learned dash & virtuosity from Manet. Beginning with formless panoramas à la Hudson River, George Inness & Homer Martin progressed with the aid of French examples towards landscape as mood in the manner of Millet & Corot. Martin even reached as far as the Impressionists, the next major derivation. Hassam, Glackens, Twachtman, Weir & dozens of others now caused American streets, buildings & fields to shimmer with the interweaving tones & strokes of pure color of the French *plein air*. In American Impressionism, Art with its formulae was once more asserting itself against direct experience & the result was a quick transformation into academicism.

The absorption of European styles had by now, however, been speeded up & was taking place on a more sophisticated level than formerly. It was the time of Henry Adams & Henry James, of Hunt & La Farge's admiration for the Italian Rennaissance, reflected in their murals, of the founding of the great Morgan, Frick & Havemeyer collections, of the establishment of museums & art schools of cosmopolitan stature. By the turn of the century Americans like Whistler, with his adaptations of Japanese prints, & Mary Cassatt, a ranking follower of Degas, could count among the vanguard in European art. American sculpture had advanced in self-consciousness from the pioneering ruggedness of Henry Kirke Brown & his pupil John Q. A. Ward to the "musical" plasticity of Homer St. Gaudens, followed by such ambitious monument makers as MacMonnies & Barnard.

Each new surge of vitality had, of course, to make its way against the obstacles presented by "the Academy," operating under various names. Ryder, Eakins, Inness, Wyant, Martin, Hunt & La Farge had had to join together in exhibitions, in order to overcome official indifference. A generation later it was the turn of the "Henri Group" to run the gauntlet of the enemies of novelty & originality. Most of the artists grouped around Robert Henri, & the artists who followed their trend, had ideas that went beyond a strict concern with art—they talked about the labor movement, Henry George, Bellamy's "nationalism," Nietzsche, Tolstoy. They sketched bathing beaches, city rooftops, poolrooms, restaurants, racetracks, prizefights, circuses, panhandlers, children jumping rope. They had a sense of the American idiom which prevailed over their technical borrowings from abroad, which by now had reached a rich variety. This realistic movement, which contained its strain of romanticism, also brought a revival in political & social cartooning, recalling Thomas Nast's earlier Tweed Ring assaults, & a stimulation of lithography, wood engraving & other graphic arts, as well as of photography as an art medium.

In the same year (1908) that the Henri Group of realistic depicters of social life held their first exhibition under the title of "The Eight," & were greeted with contempt & acrimony on the part of newspaper editorials & art critics, Alfred Stieglitz, later famous as a photographer, brought together at his "291" gallery in New York the European experimentalists who have come to represent what is called "modernism" in art—Cézanne, Matisse, Picasso, Braque & others. In the same rooms Stieglitz exhibited advanced Americans like Marin, Hartley, Weber.

Modernism & realism were later to find themselves opposed, at times rancorously antagonistic. But their early appearance in America was arm in arm at the epoch-making "Armoury Show" held in New York in 1913. While the realists had turned toward the streets, the bars, the political meetings, the modernists drew upon the "pure forms" of mathematics & the machine, upon dreams & deliberately inspired fantasies, upon the art of savages, ancient civilizations, children, lunatics. In its simplest definition, the opposition between realistic & "abstract" art is the opposition between a picture that represents an external object accessible to the eye & one that constitutes a sign that relates itself primarily to the mind & spirit. If Cubism, Futurism & Surrealism often caused American artists to deny that their visible surroundings were important in themselves, it made them more sensitive to such artistic factors as architectural balance, rhythm, hue; & it opened their understanding to design as conceived by peoples belonging to different cultures & by individuals in extreme psychological states.

In sculpture as well as in painting the new eclecticism drew on discoveries in archaeology, on new industrial materials & devices, on the creations of the Negro, Indian & other art traditions far removed from our own. Both in connection with building decoration & in pieces for independent exhibition, American sculpture has come to include every shade of conception from the most literalist nudes & portrait busts to works totally abstract. Mural painting, which saw an enormous expansion in the 1930's under the sponsorship of the Federal government, shows a similar range, from the most prosaic picturizations of historical & allegorical themes to the distorted shapes & color masses of the neo-realists & experimentalists.

Today a typical overall show of American art impresses one chiefly by its tremendous variety in feeling, craftmanship & derivation. Bland pictures of oil-wells & big-city storefronts hang by the side of symbolist declamations, surrealist outcries, stone-age sign language, shapes formed out of spontaneous gestures, patterns composed of lines & relations infinitely calculated. Paintings of the American scene, such as Charles Sheeler's lighthouses, Grant Wood's small-town types, Thomas Benton's writhing protagonists of regional history & folklore, John Steuart Curry's convulsive prairies, Georgia O'Keefe's enameled flowers & objects, have become almost as familiar to Americans as Manhattan's skyline or the Grand Cànyon. Older formalists like Stuart Davis & Milton Avery have also achieved a large measure of acceptance. On the other hand, the public continues to be treated in the press to periodic assaults on the "excesses" of such younger non-descriptive painters as William Baziotes, William de Kooning, Ashille Gorki (recently deceased), Jackson Pollack, Markis Rotko, Robert Motherwell, Max Spivac, & Adolf Gottlieb.

If the most advanced American art often seems to express personal withdrawal & forlornness, the general rule in contemporary American painting & sculpture no doubt is: a style for every taste & cultural background. With the vastly enlarged attendance at museums & galleries, with the progress made recently in the techniques of reproduction, & with the policy of an increasing number of popular magazines & even commercial advertisers of making color prints for mass distribution, there seems reason to suppose that some kind of art plays a part in the life of practically every American.

—Harold Rosenberg

# LITERATURE

Early American writing is a thin branch of the literature of seventeenth century England, but with the important difference that the major concerns of those who settled the colonies were overwhelmingly religious. It is a literature largely given over to such matters as the relationship of church & state, the absolute sovereignty of God, Biblical infallibility—a narrow religiosity the effects of which can still be felt in some contemporary writing, still tirelessly engaged in reacting against its distant influence. While the idea of human damnation & the vision of life as evil have produced some of the masterpieces of world literature, the authoritarian & dogmatic Calvinism of early New England, which stamped on almost every activity of mankind the mark of the devil, was scarcely hospitable to the production of works of art. It made room for pamphleteering, sermons, & for authorities on sin—for the fierce scolding of Cotton Mather, the remarkable & frequently brilliant sermons of Jonathan Edwards, most famous of Calvinism's champions, & for the vigorous & rebellious opponent of theocracy, Roger Williams.

While the earliest writers emphasized the ways of God to the exclusion of almost all other ways, their followers were increasingly devoted to the life of reason. Untouched by his Calvinist upbringing & frequently celebrated as the country's earliest figure of urbanity and cosmopolitanism, Benjamin Franklin was such a devotee, & one who excelled as a diplomat, politician, & economist as well as a writer. His *Autobiography* is still widely read. Franklin is perhaps the most important individual to span the period leading up to the Revolutionary War, a period most notable for its politics, oratory, & pamphleteering. Thomas Paine, with his *Common Sense,* made a reputation as a fiery advocate of American Independence. Patriotic versifiers were busily at work; best remembered are Philip Freneau, the first American poet of talent, who brought bitter satire to the national cause, & Joel Barlow. The towering reputation of Thomas Jefferson is in part due to his writings, among them the Declaration of Independence, as well as to his statemanship.

It was not, however, until the early nineteenth century that the country produced a writer of outstanding imaginative gifts. Washington Irving's *Knickerbocker History of New York* has been called "the first American book that stood solidly on its own feet." Irving, representative of a new & aristocratic generation that celebrated elegance, romanticism & the picturesque, though a man poorly equipped for understanding either himself or his world—of expansion, middle-class revolution & industrial change—left, in *Rip Van Winkle, The Legend of Sleepy Hollow,* & the *Knickerbocker History,* still popular records of his flight into the legendary. It was a flight that was to be repeated by numerous writers that followed. Stimulated by the success of Scott's

Waverly novels, James Fenimore Cooper discovered the Indian & served up the romantic myth of the American hinterland, employing devices of suspense that in their crudity foreshadowed the effects of Pearl White & the Lone Ranger. "Every time a Cooper person is in peril, and absolute silence is worth four dollars a minute," wrote Mark Twain, "he is sure to step on a dry twig." Nathaniel Hawthorne, saturated in the allegorical, in irony, & with a deep sense of evil, dramatized the Puritan tragedy as his forerunners had been unable to do. For it was only when Calvinism had begun to decline as a controlling force, apparently, that it could be put to creative use. It was Calvinism's appeal as a great fact of imagination, rather than its religiosity, that drew Hawthorne to brood on it for a lifetime & to produce four masterly novels, *The Scarlet Letter, The House of the Seven Gables, The Blithedale Romance,* & *The Marble Faun.* But to the critics who have assessed American writers on the basis of extroversion and "involvement," Hawthorne is "a romancer of the twilight instead of the human heart," and "the extreme & finest expression of refined alienation from reality." Herman Melville, one of the most lacerated & savagely honest figures in our literature, has encountered similar treatment. In the author of *Moby Dick,* such critics have been tireless in pointing out, there is too much hatred of life, too much meaningless suffering, too much escapism, symbolism, obscurity, bombast, Shakespearean rhetoric, too much awareness of human evil, too much that is inchoate & sordid, too much of doom & fatality. In recent years Melville & Hawthorne have come to be recognized as two of America's greatest novelists, & both have claimed wider audiences than ever before.

Melville's total disgust for the materialism & emptiness of his own time limited his public in his own lifetime in a way that the vigorously critical but serenely transcendental views of Ralph Waldo Emerson, however deeply they judged American realities, could never do. Though he was devoid of a tragic sense, there is an austerity & craftmanship that set Emerson apart from all the rest of the New England literary men of his time, except for Thoreau, whose arch-individualism, anarchism, & espousal of creativity single him out to many as the most modern of Nineteenth Century writers. And while Thoreau was turning his back on the values of his countrymen, & while Edgar Allan Poe was creating new artistic values of his own & living out one of the most tragic of all among the many tragic lives of American artists, Walt Whitman, a walking anthology of affirmation & celebration, appeared to chant the inexhaustible glories of Democracy. No two figures could be less alike than Poe & Whitman, & they stand today as archetypes of many less important writers who followed. While Poe wrestled with his private & heartsick nightmares, marked by a pre-existentialist intensity & by guilt-ridden suffering, Whitman married extroversion to blank verse, drawing the citizens of the entire continent to him in his vision of the bright tomorrows promised by liberty, equality & fraternity. With Whitman, the remnants of Calvinism fray out to nothing. Never before had the doctrine of the perfectibility of man enjoyed so assured & robust a celebrant.

Poles apart from Whitman & unknown to her own time, representing a sort of provincialism of the self, was Emily Dickinson, in whose verse emerged the finest voice & one of the most strongly defined personalities of the century. For the first time, the country had produced a writer who was completely an artist, capable of the purest communication of sensation & perception, one beyond the dominion of either ideas or rhetoric, & secure in the dominion of poetic ultimates.

While her reputation has steadily increased, an overhauling in taste has been less kind to five poets once strongly established & significant to their contemporaries—Oliver Wendell Holmes, John Greenleaf Whittier, James Russell Lowell, Henry Wadsworth Longfellow, & William Cullen Bryant. Today, the rather tame & Bostonian wit of Holmes, the Abolitionist fervor & idealism of Lowell, the impassioned democratic faith of Bryant, the old-fashioned Quakerism of Whittier, & the placid sentimentality of Longfellow have all merged in a general blur that obscures their individual works & personalities.

Noteworthy, if for no other reason than because of his position as the foremost Southern poet of the period, is Sidney Lanier, who attempted to blend music & language in his writings. Other Southern writers of the time include the scholarly & cultivated Hugh Legaré, the vigorous & prolific romantic novelist, William Gilmore Simms, Augustus Longstreet, an early exponent of frontier humor, & John P. Kennedy, a neglected novelist who was influenced by his friend, Washington Irving.

Meanwhile, other novelists were discovering the great world of fact. Mark Twain, chief ornament of a long humorist tradition, offered his vision of the frontier, progressing in a score of books from the sparkling wit of *Innocents Abroad* to his masterpiece, *Huckleberry Finn,* to the disenchanted satire of his last years. Harriet Beecher Stowe pioneered in the propaganda novel with *Uncle Tom's Cabin.* William Dean Howells devoted himself to the novel of manners, Bret Harte to the mining camps, Joel Chandler Harris to Georgia plantation life, George W. Cable to romance in the Old South, Ambrose Bierce to impressive themes of the savage & the sardonic, Sara Orne Jewett to the New England past. Though Henry Adams' anonymous novel of Washington politics, *Democracy,* reveals a novelistic talent, it is in his autobiography, *The Education of Henry Adams,* his letters, & *Mont-Saint-Michel and Chartres,* a study of the nature of history through the meaning of the Middle Ages, that he is acclaimed today as one of the most distinguished minds of his time. With a greater awareness & sharper insight into the multiplicity of industrial society than any of his contemporaries, & with an unrivaled skepticism & wit, Adams never faltered in his search for the permanent & genuine. His description of his life as a failure is one of the major ironies in the records of self-evaluation.

From 1876 to his death in 1916, Henry James relieved fiction of its commitments to parochialism, crudity & topicality by the publication of a succession of unmatched novels & stories, among them some of the few flawless works in American literature. In James' hands, fiction was charged with an artistry that could take its place with the fiction of France & England & Russia. The lesson of Henry James—at least the lesson of structure & tone—has been largely ignored by later generations of American novelists, whose adherence to the cult of raw material & autobiography has been noteworthy. In Edith Wharton, however, James had a devoted pupil &, in several of her best books, a brilliant one.

James was widely unread. The novelists who dominated the early years of the twentieth century found no easier an acceptance. But their difficulties lay in their outspoken insistence on a world of fact that post-Victorian sensibilities preferred to ignore. Their novels might have been the result of an outline drawn up to emphasize everything that their predecessors had left out, & to re-emphasize everything that those predecessors had touched on but lightly—the grossness of the physical world, sexuality, the corruption & debasement of a business society, the social consequences of the profit motive, the suffering of the poor—all accompanied by an onslaught against smugness, puritanism, & sentimentality. Most of the American naturalists, whose efforts were accompanied by the exposés of the "muckrakers" of business & politics—Lincoln Steffens, Ida Tarbell, Ray Stannard Baker among them, were to see America as a pigeonhole stuffed with problems. Robert Herrick rooted into feminism, the academic situation, labor. Upton Sinclair dealt with legal injustice, coal mining, the meatpackers, international politics. Jack London explored the Alaskan frontier, the South Seas, and socialism. Frank Norris, deeply marinated in French naturalism, concerned himself with the city & the wheatfields. E. W. Howe, Hamlin Garland, & Henry B. Fuller proclaimed, in their novels, the first literary movement of the Middle West. Stephen Crane, a finer artist than any of these men, was a naturalist saved by poetry; his novels & stories of suffering & poverty are shot through with imagistic flashes & a feeling for texture none of his colleagues remotely apprehended.

The story of Theodore Dreiser's difficulties in launching his first novel, *Sister Carrie,* with his publishers burying copies of it in the basement, is frequently told to emphasize the hostility engendered by the new Naturalism. To the inheritors of the genteel tradition, it seemed a literature spawned in the basement, if not the sewer. With Dreiser, Naturalism was set forth in a style a moving-van might have conceived. "He is," Ludwig Lewisohn has said, "the worst writer of his eminence in the entire history of literature." Tasteless, brooding, sluggish, plodding, measuring life to a mechanistic pattern, Dreiser is nevertheless evaluated as one of the greatest of American novelists, & *Sister Carrie, Jennie Gerhardt, An American Tragedy,* & the Cowperwood novels retain whatever vitality they may have because Dreiser builds a broad, real, varied, doomed & haunting world.

If Dreiser was limited by a simple-mindedness of outlook & devoid of the remotest sensitivity to verbal effects, Sherwood Anderson could surpass him in the ultimate of limitations. Anderson's whole life was a floundering, for neither as a man nor as an artist, as he frequently confessed, could he ever make up his mind what it was that he wanted. While Dreiser, like a person engaged in pushing a rhinoceros into a phone booth, somehow incredibly approached a degree of success in his endeavor, Anderson was a man stripped of all aims except for longing & deflection. His accomplishment, if that it can be called, was in the struggle of a baffled & inarticulate man to find something to say about all the ineffable torments & yearnings that possessed him. When this was his proclaimed theme, as it is in a number of his stories, he made his only estimable statements. Anderson had a vision of the frustrations & longings of the simple & the dispossessed, but to a later generation it seemed, in its wispiness & endless questioning, rather the vision of a sleepwalker than of an artist.

The most ambitious workman of the period, Sinclair Lewis, summoned up, in a cycle of novels, a vision of American life unmatched in its variety of themes & characters. With the energy of a Zola, Lewis descended upon the small towns, the business men, on science, the ministry, education, politics, hotel management, feminism, Fascism, Communism, like an assured marksman picking off his enemies one by one. His weapon was satire, & through a fantastic exaggeration of the banalities of small talk he created a parody of realism that mocked the provincialism & narrowness & intolerance that were his special targets. While Lewis pursued his quarries through fiction, Henry Louis Mencken went after the same game as an essayist & critic. Both men were convinced that American society was politically corrupt, morally hypocritical, & in general a desert of mediocrity & idiocy. It was a climate in which Mencken basked with a limitless satisfaction and delight. Beginning as a Nietzschean individualist, Mencken became a sort of muckraker of the Right, lashing out with equal vigor at gentility, prohibition, censorship, bigotry, academicism, prudery, & whatever else seemed to require the touch of his truncheon. Mencken's goal was laughter & exposure; he was quite without remedies except for the remedy of being H. L. Mencken or a disciple of Mencken—a member of an *elite* who regarded life as a ridiculous joke to be enjoyed to the utmost. That it was a satire without heart became clear to the disciples of his liberation only slowly; with the Depression & the replacement among the intelligentsia of Mencken by Marx, his approval of slavery, war, & political reaction made certain his decline. Mencken's reputation today rests largely on his scholarship—on his life-long work, *The American Language.*

Mencken's influence in the Twenties, however, cannot be overestimated. Not only was he indefatigable as a gadfly, but also as a press agent who promoted such talents as Dreiser & Lewis. Two of his other major enthusiasms were James Branch Cabell, author of *Jurgen* & a score of novels that contrast the tediousness of existence with the solaces of escape into a romantic dreamworld; and Joseph Hergesheimer, whose elegant & decorative novels, though not inferior to Cabell's, are little heard of today.

Never had there been so many writers heralded as "significant." Never, indeed, had there been so many writers. And never had there been such machinery of publicity & aggrandizement to serve them. The era of the best-seller & the book clubs was firmly entrenched as Elinor Wylie upheld the tradition of elegance & fragility, Carl Van Vechten took over the field of urbanity & sophistication, & Ben Hecht assumed bizarre attitudes of cynicism & violence. Ring Lardner, with a sharper ear than Sinclair Lewis's & with a sense of scorn & disenchantment Lewis never reached, impaled an assortment of middle-class figures upon a well-sharpened spear. Playwrights like Eugene O'Neill, George Kelly, Sidney Howard brought fresh material & viewpoints to the theatre. Willa Cather went back to the theme of the defeat of the pioneer to create a more substantial & enduring kind of novel. Booth Tarkington, Ruth Suckow, Josephine Herbst, Ellen Glasgow, Dorothy Canfield explored the life of the middle class. It was during this period, too, that Negro writers, for the first time, were widely published & finding readers, although there had been such forerunners as Paul Laurence Dunbar; among the best known today are James Weldon Johnson, Langston Hughes, Richard Wright, Countee Cullen, & Claude McKay.

As early as 1912, a whole new school of poetry had begun to make its appearance. Robinson Jeffers, Vachel Lindsay, Amy Lowell, Sara Teasdale, Ezra Pound, Edna St. Vincent Millay published their early work. Two Middle-westerners, Carl Sandburg, later to become the most formidable of Abraham Lincoln's biographers, & Edgar Lee Masters, were mining American speech for a realistic & altogether native poetry previously staked out by Whitman.

Edwin Arlington Robinson, who had brought out his first book in 1896 without creating a ripple of interest, began to be read, along with Robert Frost, whose first appearance pre-dated Robinson's. The founding of *Poetry: A Magazine of Verse,* by Harriet Monroe, ushered in a period of unprecedented activity in verse. If the new poets displayed a diversity of aims & techniques that make hazardous any generalizations about them as a group, on one point they were united—in a deep hostility to almost the complete body of earlier American poetry, & particularly to such classroom perennials as Bryant, Holmes, & Longfellow.

In the forefront of the attack was an American poet self-exiled in Europe. As an instigator & enthusiast of the new poetry, Ezra Pound brought an unflagging energy & imagination that erupted in a stream of manifestoes, movements, theories, programs & magazines, as well as in a body of poems to whose example every poet of consequence who followed him owes a debt. From the beginning Pound was to insist on precision & clarity in writing, on the use of "the *exact* words, not the merely decorative words." He called for new rhythms based on the language of common expression to produce poetry "that is hard & clear, never blurred or indefinite." Out of such doctrine as this came the school of Imagism, whose early ornaments included John Gould Fletcher, Amy Lowell, & H. D., & a later movement, Objectivism, numbering as its chief & most gifted practitioner Pound's friend, William Carlos Williams, equally talented as both short story writer and poet.

Along with another American abroad, T. S. Eliot, Pound was engaged in discovering & reassessing the literature of the past. If American writing is today animated by a wider & more discriminating appreciation of world literature than previously, it is largely because of the work of Pound & Eliot—their fresh evaluations of classical & Oriental poetry, of Dante & his predecessors, Elizabethan & Jacobean playwrights & poets, of Baudelaire, Laforgue, Rimbaud & Corbière. Through their criticism, Pound & Eliot were not only to widen the cultural vistas of American writers, but to set forth in their own poetry a whole new range of effects. This they accomplished through an eclectic use of fragments & styles taken from the very literature they were engaged in re-evaluating. Indeed, one of the touchstones of poetic modernism is its revelation of the modern world through the device of an infinitely sophisticated fragmentation that results in a more subtle, complex, & shifting view of the world's meaning. By far the most authoritative & influential poems of our time, Eliot's *The Waste Land* & Pound's still unfinished *Cantos,* first made use of this method, a use that is still unrivaled.

While Mencken's criticism was most widely read, and Eliot's & Pound's the most influential in a subterranean way, the critical competition had never before included such a variety of antagonists. There were the Humanists, led by Paul Elmer More & Irving Babbitt, counseling a stern classicism & hostility to modernism; Van Wyck Brooks, whose early sober & searching reexamination of American literature has given way to an emphasis on the recollection of its history; Edmund Wilson, whose vigor, intelligence, & breadth of interests have saved him from the relative obscurity of many of his critical contemporaries; Vernon Louis Parrington, widely known for his lengthy study of American literature, *Main Currents in American Thought.* In recent years a group of critics who share a concern with the close analytical study of poetry, among them Allen Tate, R. P. Blackmur, Yvor Winters, John

Crowe Ransom, & Cleanth Brooks, have been influential. A list of recent critics of importance would be incomplete without mentioning at least the names of Randolph Bourne, Ludwig Lewisohn, Mark Van Doren, Joseph Wood Krutch, Newton Arvin, & Kenneth Burke.

The growing revolution in language & taste in the twentieth century not only animated such contemporary poets as Wallace Stevens, Marianne Moore, Conrad Aiken, E. E. Cummings (whose prose books, *The Enormous Room* & *Eimi* rank among the more brilliant products of the period), Allen Tate, John Crowe Ransom, Hart Crane, W. C. Williams, Archibald MacLeish & still younger poets, but spread to the novelists of the post-World War I generation —Ernest Hemingway, John Dos Passos, William Faulkner, F. Scott Fitzgerald.

These four, perhaps the most celebrated members of "the lost generation," as Gertrude Stein memorably baptized them, emerged from their years of war service with a highly articulate bitterness & disillusionment that was to color everything they wrote. In general more cultivated & intense than the novelists that had just preceded them, they were also better craftsmen, post-graduates from the universities of European experimentalism. From Pound, from the influential Gertrude Stein, an American expatriate in France whose insistently repetitive & rhythmic style provided her countrymen with many an uneasy & baffled moment, Hemingway discovered how to use & discipline the monotonous patterns of American speech to create a bare & chiseled precision of statement. Exploring a wide geography of experience—his boyhood in the Middle West, a series of wars, the Spain of bullfights & cafés, the Paris of expatriates, the worlds of big-game hunters, prize-fighters, rum-runners & gangsters—Hemingway's stories & novels are documents of violent action & chaotic uncertainties, where annihilation is everywhere & only the values of stoicism, courage & personal integrity are meaningful.

Hemingway's *The Sun Also Rises* & *A Farewell to Arms* were instantly successful. Dos Passos, Faulkner, & Fitzgerald made their first appearances on the literary scene with personalities less fully defined & with styles still flawed & unmatured. Dos Passos' *Three Soldiers,* one of the first of many novels to express a radical criticism of the first World War, was followed by a series of related novels that dealt ambitiously with no less than twentieth century American society as a whole. Impelled by the techniques of James Joyce's *Ulysses* (which was more discussed & celebrated than influential), as much as by the theories of such French novelists as Jules Romains, who portrayed a civilization through the lives of individuals drawn from all social classes, Dos Passos produced his massive trilogy, *U.S.A.* Covering an enormously diversified world & the lives of hundreds of representative people, the book is interlarded with three recurrent technical devices—*collages* of newspaper headlines, current slang & popular songs, to give rapid summations of a period's tone & sentiment; staccato & frequently ironic sketches of the lives of representative Americans like Henry Ford & Woodrow Wilson; & passages of subjective & poetic observation that contrast with the behavioristic presentation of the characters in the main narrative. Sympathetic to the political Left (though his growing disrelish for the orthodoxies of the official Communists makes itself felt in the closing sections of the book), Dos Passos pledged his most profound allegiances to the outcasts, rebels & dispossessed of American society, & centered his satirical sights on such figures as profiteers, opportunists, advertising men & politicians.

While Dos Passos' commitments to broad documentation & expansion led to a lack of thickness in the lives of his characters, William Faulkner's attachments, geographically narrow, centering almost exclusively on one small county in Mississippi, have led to precisely that thickness & body & particularity of individual human experience that Dos Passos lacks. Though Faulkner's county is inconsiderable in terms of mileage, it has yielded as many satisfactions as recent American literature can offer, so densely has Faulkner populated it with his doomed & haunted characters, & so thoroughly has he explored it, to the last cabin & plantation house. For Faulkner is engaged in writing no less than a vast history of Southern experience, from the middle of the eighteenth century to the present day. Even in a period like our own, when themes of violence, confusion & decay are obsessive & omnipresent, Faulkner has pursued such themes with a particular intensity. Yet with all his concern for mutilation, incest, rape, insanity, extremes of pain, & violent death—concerns so sensationally conceived in *Sanctuary*—there is much love & pity in Faulkner, & a sense of humor not unlike that of Mark Twain. His lack of a wide audience is more likely due, not to his material, but to his lack of conventional continuity, & to a rhetoric that is often overblown & frequently meaningless.

Scott Fitzgerald, who died in 1941, had a leaner talent but a more novelistic one. Like Hemingway, he was to become a legendary & symbolic figure; while the author of *Men Without Women* summed up the world of Byronic adventure, Paris in the Twenties, the tough-tender literary man, Fitzgerald came to stand for the Jazz Age, wild parties on fancy Long Island estates, the middle-aged crackups of permanent collegians. Both stand for a good deal else. There is a real tragedy in Fitzgerald's career, & much that is merely trashy—the considerable hack-work he wrote for popular magazines (though not all of that is by any means contemptible)—and much that is immature. What remains most notably is *The Great Gatsby,* a definitive statement of the Twenties legend—the loaded and overdecorated facade of ostentation & wealth behind which the average man's dream of superiority goes on, and *Tender Is the Night,* an equally definitive picture of the frayed-out lives & smashed careers toward which the world of the Twenties pointed.

The crash of 1929 ushered in a period more notable for its meetings, manifestoes & controversies than for its creativity. And in a world where the question of where one's next meal was coming from assumed a towering importance, this is not to be wondered at. Hundreds of writers gravitated to the political Left, dominated by the Communist Party. Its rigid formulas for writing had a withering effect that can still be felt. Probably the most durable talents to develop during the period were James T. Farrell, whose trilogy, *Studs Lonigan,* carried on the Dreiser tradition; Kenneth Fearing, whose trenchantly satirical poems of urban life seemed a last extreme gasp of protest against Whitmanian optimism; & Nathanael West, a satirical novelist of uncommon originality. Thomas Wolfe established himself with a series of defiantly autobiographical novels, & Erskine Caldwell emerged with his studies of depravity & fantastic behavior among the back roads of the South.

The post-Depression years were notable for an atmosphere of creative debility; fewer new writers of originality appeared; & only a handful of the older writers, most of them poets, seemed able to push ahead to maturity. Those who were sensitive to the lineaments of dead ends & turning-points could detect, in a growing nostalgia for the 1920's, a symptom of the times. This nostalgia, far from confining itself to the recent past, reached back ever further; & one of the major publishing phenomena of recent years has been literary revivalism on a major scale. Henry James, Melville, Hawthorne, Scott Fitzgerald are only a few of the writers who have been rescued, in these cases, from obscurity, the classroom, or misinterpretation. It is probably not by chance that many of the novelists who figured in this revival were men preoccupied with form, for it was precisely a lack of this preoccupation, indeed an indifference or imperviousness to the problem of form, that had characterized so much of recent American fiction. There were some notable exceptions—in the stories of Katherine Anne Porter & some of her younger feminine disciples, in Allen Tate's novel, *The Fathers,* in Djuna Barnes' *Nightwood,* in Hemingway's earlier books, in Glenway Wescott, Willa Cather, Thornton Wilder, John O'Hara.

It was to the example of Henry James that a good many of these novelists aspired. And it was James, more than any other figure in American literature, who represented a significant break in its history. His expatriation, his profound & inflexible concept of the task of the writer, his mastery of form, his skepticism & irony, his international attitude, his highly conscious use of the methods of such Europeans as Flaubert, Balzac, & Turgenev, all combined to set him apart from the men of letters who had preceded him. It is possible that his revival, along with that of Melville, Hawthorne, Henry Adams & a number of other earlier writers, is as significant as any literary activities of the last few years.

—WELDON KEES

# MUSIC

## I

Perhaps the chief distinction between folk music & popular music is that the first is created by the people themselves, almost anonymously, while popular music is largely written music, usually limited to the diatonic scale taught most of us in grade school. H. E. Krehbiel once wrote that popular music was written for the people whereas folk music was created by them in melodies sacred & secular & to work & play rhythms—hoeing songs of work gangs & hoedowns for dancing, songs of cattle trail & of camp fire.

Since folk music is a product of many creators & perpetuators, there are often many versions of the same song. "Careless Love," as sung in the mountains, where its theme was pregnancy, differed from "Careless Love" in New Orleans bordellos, where it was a love blues. The famous "Red River Valley" (Texas border) was also the music for "The Mohawk Valley" (New York).

The popular song, whatever its source, is traceable to one specific set of notes on paper. But by its very nature popular music draws heavily upon folk music, sometimes merely fitting new words to an old tune, as with "Yankee Doodle." At its worst, popular song, like radio soap opera, tends to stoop to sentiment, rather than rise to it. And while that amorphous body of music called hillbilly is the outstanding offender in this respect, genuine folk music in such sad & sinister themes as "Pretty Polly" lends a robust treatment that turns a sob song into a saga.

In its first stage of growth, popular song owed most to the British Isles, though native composers included William Billings who wrote "Chester," popular song of the American Revolution. In general, a native trend was first discernible in words more often than in music. American types to poke fun at (such as the country bumpkin) made an early appearance but an impressive number of songs were patriotic & political as different sets of lyrics were adapted to an identical melody. The English glee "To Anacreon" served both in support of Jefferson & of Hamilton when they represented opposed political forces. This tune had several sets of words before Francis Scott Key wrote his impassioned verses for what was to become our national anthem.

Meanwhile population was on the increase & growing urban centers nurtured popular song even while frontiersmen broke the path westward through the wilderness, their lives closer to folk music than those of city dwellers. Their songs, like their axes, blazed the trail for Forty-niners & railroad workers, & for such heroes of humor in homespun as "The Arkansas Traveler."

The minstrels cradled popular song from 1840 to about 1870 much as vaudeville was to do later on. Plantation rhythms & melodies, as well as dance forms, testified to the contribution of the Negro to this phase of popular music & slave songs such as "Jim Crow" were changed only slightly as they were added to the repertoire of the burnt cork trail. Thus an urban popular music, for the minstrels were essentially that, also had roots in early American folk music.

In 1845 a minstrel troupe, playing in Stephen Collins Foster's native Pittsburgh, added his "Oh, Susanah" to their program, & before it became the theme song of the Forty-niners, Foster had become a songwriter. Fearing for his musical reputation, his first songs for Christy's Minstrels appeared under the name of Edwin P. Christy. Later on he asked that "Swanee River" and others of his famous compositions carry his own name; the popularity of the music had convinced him that to be tagged "an Ethiopian Composer" was no longer a dishonor.

In 1861 Bryant's Minstrels advertised a "grand Tin-Pan-O-Ni-On Pot Pourri" but the term Tin Pan Alley as a nickname for the realm of popular song, did not take hold until toward the close of the century. By this time the bulk of musical activity, scattered in many cities previously, had channeled into New York's brownstone byways. And moving up from the Bowery to East 14th Street in this era Tony Pastor's was to song pluggers & performers what the Palace was to be in the 1920's.

A potato famine in Ireland in the 1840's, revolutionary uprisings in Europe during the same period, and religious persecution, all served to swell migration to America. Thus, in the 1860's & 1870's Tin Pin Alley was introduced to jigs, reels & Irish ballads as there developed a productive linking up of one country's music to another. Harrigan & Hart played Tony Pastor's, & Harrigan & Braham wrote "The Mulligan Guards." Later in the century the German-American population of the midwest was represented in popular song by such names as Harry Von Tilzer ("Wait 'Til the Sun Shines, Nelly") & Paul Dresser ("On the Banks of the Wabash").

The post-Civil War period produced hundreds of songs, many of which are still familiar—"The Bowery," "Silver Threads among the Gold," "Daisy Bell," etc. By 1900 vaudeville, musical comedy & revues had pushed minstrelsy toward obscurity. Irish-American tradition persisted into the 20th century as George M. Cohan wrote such hits as "Give My Regards to Broadway," "Mary Is a Grand Old Name" and "Over There." During the same era, while some writers ground out tawdry dialect & "Coon" songs, Dublin-born Victor Herbert wrote light operettas, setting the pace for such talented writers of a later period as Sigmund Romberg & Jerome Kern.

It was an era when the Gibson Girl & the flirtatious femininity of "The Merry Widow" set the style for the stage. In 1907, the year of the first "Ziegfeld Follies," Irving Berlin was already writing songs. In show music the pattern then was either musical comedy or operetta but in the 1920's these influences were fused & another, that of jazz, added (Jerome Kern, George Gershwin). Progression from then on was steady, many of the songs being written for Hollywood but a substantial bit of the progress being contributed by stage shows. Finally, with the Rodgers-Hammerstein production "Oklahoma," ballet & Broadway mingled happily in a book that combined sophistication & home-grown humor.

Except for the borrowings of minstrel writers, the spirituals had not in themselves a direct influence upon popular song. Groups from Fisk (1871) &, later, Hampton Institute, literally "built up" Negro colleges by way of concert tours. At first treated as curiosities of the Chautauqua belt, their music came to be as popular as Moody & Sankey.

Meanwhile, the more primitive spirituals survived, & still do, amongst congregations often too poor to buy hymn books. These simply constructed, recitative-type spirituals are perhaps as close to old Afro-American spirituals as any in folk music. Theirs are the rhythms of slave songs & the weird harmonies of plantation hollers. The primitive spirituals, as one might expect, are close to folk blues & probably preceded the latter as a direct influence. With the blues, free rhythmic accent led to jazz syncopation, & blues harmony to a band style roughly polyphonous, that had its beginnings chiefly in New Orleans in the last century.

Ragtime was contemporaneous with—but, so far as is known, did not precede—early jazz. It was based upon the playing of pianists who roved from city to city, whose boast it was they could play everything "from opera to blues." Thus, in creating by ear (improvising), the rag pianists showed their indebtedness to folk music but their music was also related to the popular music of the day & was published in written form at least as early as the 1890's in St. Louis.

In contrast to early ragtime, which was a keyboard style, early jazz was a band style &, of course, a vocal style. The origin of jazz as an instrumental style might be best explained by the fact that the musicians, inspired by blues, played by ear. They experimented with instruments quite as naturally as they improvised upon melodies & the plunger mute is still called that, after the bathroom plunger that inspired it! Thus the style grew out of the blues.

Almost all early jazz musicians doubled in brass band work, playing marches for Lodge parades & the Negro bands playing oldtime hymns for funerals. At night, to make a living, they played in cabarets where patrons liked the music to be as roughhouse as the places. New Orleans' Storyville, as the Red Light district was called, offered early jazzmen an opportunity to play pretty much as they liked, as did the saloons of St. Louis the rag pianists.

As jazz bands ventured further afield, jazz began to be heard on a broad scale—soon records & radio helped—& its styles & stars became nationally &, finally, internationally famous. In widespread parts of the world jazz clubs were formed & in France during World War II Zazous, jazz fans who dressed like Apache zoot-suiters, were active in the Underground. In 1948 a controversy over the merits of Dixieland versus the new Bop style was taken quite as seriously in Prague as it was in New York.

Hundreds of men & bands have contributed to the development of jazz from the time when Jelly Roll Morton first played his blues piano to the recent occasion when Stan Kenton gave a Bop concert at Carnegie Hall. Somewhat distinguishable in early jazz, Negro & white styles are less so today, especially since most of the better known jazzmen—Goodman, Louis Armstrong, Jack Teagarden, et al.—often play in mixed groups. Early jazz bands based their orchestral style on the small band & though other leaders preceded him in the use of large orchestras, Duke Ellington may be taken as the outstanding user of jazz style in big band work.

In contrast to ragtime, publication of early jazz was rare until about 1910 when W. C. Handy published "Memphis Blues." Jelly Roll Morton created many of his own numbers years before he published them. Such men as James P. Johnson & Fats Waller wrote show tunes growing directly out of jazz & it is interesting to note that before 1920 these composers, George Gershwin, & others, "cut" piano rolls & often worked on shows together. While maintaining its own identity & developing its styles, jazz was also contributing to the development of popular music as a whole. —Charles Edward Smith

## II

America's importance in musical culture has emerged in the last half century, particularly in the last thirty years, with the growth of the American school of composition. American musical history is therefore a history of "modern" music; it parallels in time & character the contemporary art movement in Europe, & its scope includes every aspect of the European development. In addition, American music has assimilated various ingredients, especially in the rhythmic sphere, from vernacular expressions at home, so that the impressive literature of music these years have amassed has an unmistakably "American" sound in spite of immensely varied methods & idioms.

An outstanding feature of the musical evolution has been the remarkable power of leadership in some of the composers. Such men as Aaron Copland, Roger Sessions, Virgil Thomson, Henry Cowell & others have been enlightened & tireless workers on behalf of composers & their problems; they have created publishing & performance possibilities, & have fostered the generation coming after them. Before World War I Arthur Farwell was a prominent agitator for the publication of new compositions.

The 1920's & '30's gave us the Composer's Guild, founded by Edgar Varese & Carlos Salzedo, & augmented by Carl Ruggles, Dane Rudhyar, Charles Ives, Colin McPhee, Henry Cowell & a host of others. Those years saw the founding of the League of Composers & the appearance of the magazine, "Modern Music," the eighty-nine issues of which are already a collectors' item & form a unique commentary & documentation of the whole period. They brought the Copland-Sessions concerts in New York, & the Friends & Enemies of Modern Music in Hartford over which Virgil Thomson presided as musical adviser. Sessions organised the American Chapter of the International Society for Contemporary Music. These years also saw the Guggenheim & other Foundations set up funds for Fellowships & Awards for the creative men to come. In the exciting 1920's one heard on the American Scene the clash & bang of all brands of the new music; the numerous opposing camps seemingly shared one common denominator, maximum dissonance!

America's late romantic Edward MacDowell had given way to the impressionism of Charles Griffes & later to the massive chromatic block dissonances of the superbly gifted amateur Charles Ives, so that the transition to the formidable orchestral masterpieces of Carl Ruggles, & the rugged percussive piano music of Dane Rudhyar & Leo Ornstein that followed, evoked increased excitement rather than surprise. Edgar Varese produced his astonishing sound pieces, "Ironisation" & "Hyperprism," for massed percussion orchestras that included klaxon horns, telephone bells, cigar boxes & milk bottles, expounding an esthetic somewhere between Dada & movie noise-track or sound-collage. He established a tradition for percussion experiment that has been a more or less continuous factor in American musical life ever since,

& which has its latest exponent in John Cage who charms audiences everywhere with the magic understatement in percussion of his "prepared piano."

Henry Cowell's dissonance & chromaticism were evolved around percussion & keyboard experiment, & his works embodying the "tone cluster" (large blocks of piano notes depressed by fist, elbow or whole forearm!) caused hissing & rioting in the concert halls of Europe. George Antheil too, one of the more terrible of infants of the twenties, achieved a similar distinction in Berlin in 1922 at the premier of his symphony, "Zingareska," a work that was among the first to employ, in symphonic form, the jazz esthetic & its rhythmic frenzy.

Dissonance was approached from every angle, as was shown by Sessions & Riegger with the atonally contrapuntal, & Antheil & the early Copland of the "Piano Concerto" with a super-syncopated jazz cacophony that utilized a recruit or two, such as Gershwin, from the vernacular world. Finally two main camps—Atonalism, employing the chromatic, & Neo-classicism, employing the diatonic elements—began to form on either side of a widening gap. The hubbub mounted & mounted to a point of maximum dissonance, & then the storm's climax was suddenly quieted by the still small voice of Virgil Thomson, whose Dada opera, "Four Saints in Three Acts," reversed the trend (as had Sauguet's ballet "La Chatte" in Paris by similar means) from the ultimate in dissonant overstatement to a miracle of consonant understatement & melodious diatonic calm. The fashionable modernist world was stunned, & the indignation that rocked musical circles rumbles still, especially in the academic world, & is provoked from time to time by the composer's no less brilliant & witty utterances as critic of the "New York Herald Tribune."

Copland & Thomson blazed the trail to Paris & Nadia Boulanger, & an overwhelming number of younger musicians have followed the path to her door in the Rue Ballu. As a result, the American school is on the whole basically French in method, though Schoenberg, Krenek & others are still a bulwark of atonalist theory & the twelve tone system is also vigorously explored all over the country.

But the movement in France, interrupted by war, seemed to come westward en masse, & the musical revolution—like the People's Revolution of an earlier France—brought forth its most vital descendants in America. That the principles of the French school are so sturdily manifest seems to indicate some affinity between it & American expression, for just before, during & after World War II, almost every teaching & composing figure of note from Europe's musical movements has come here. They have come, seen, conquered & been conquered in turn by the richness of the field & the vitality & good fellowship that abounds. A few have returned home; most have stayed here to become part of the life of America, & of the extensive organization for the instruction of the young.

This organization is continent-wide & has distributed both the foreign & native composer-celebrities throughout the country in schools & universities. Darius Milhaud is at Mills College, California, Hindemith at Yale, Martinu at Princeton, Rieti & Nicholas Nabokoff at the Peabody Institute in Philadelphia. Schoenberg was for ten years at the University of California at Los Angeles & has now retired, his place being taken by Roger Sessions & Ernest Bloch. Stravinski roams the country conducting his works, new & old, & resides when at home on the West Coast. Nadia Boulanger's stronghold when she is in the country is Cambridge & Walter Piston, as Director of Music at Harvard, upholds, both in his scores & in his precepts, the same tradition as she.

Roy Harris held forth for many years at Colorado College to multitudes of enthusiastic students & followers, & now does likewise at the State Agricultural College at Logan, Utah. At Rochester there is Howard Hanson, & if he himself harbors in his musical style a nostalgia for the twilight of the romantic gods, he nonetheless turns out from the Eastman School a sturdy group of apprentices of every inclination.

At Columbia University one finds Douglas Moore, Otto Leuning, Elliot Carter & others, who represent among them everything from polished neo-classicism to "American Homespun." At New York University there are Philip James & Marion Bauer, while the largest publishing house, G. Schirmer, & the largest music school, the Juilliard School, are both headed by the thirty-nine year old composer & administrator, William Schuman.

A middle generation, David Diamond, Paul Bowles, Alexei Haieff, Lucas Foss, Alan Hovhaness, William Bergsma, Peter Mennin, Norman Dello Joio & others of varying trends, ages & degrees of recognition produce their annual output of new music & get it played.

The scholastic & concert worlds are not the whole story. The conducting field has claimed one of the brighter composers, Leonard Bernstein, & the theatre—especially the ballet in latter years—has repeatedly claimed the best among the creative minds, as such scores as Copland's "Rodeo," "Billy the Kid," & "Appalachian Spring," Bernstein's "Fancy Free," Samuel Barber's "Medea," & Schuman's "Undertow" have demonstrated. There is an impressive list of operas too, though a lack of anything like a permanent home for experimental opera cramps production except in isolated instances. Virgil Thomson's "Four Saints in Three Acts" & "The Mother of Us All" to Gertrude Stein's libretti undoubtedly rate as classics, while Gian Carlo Mennotti's "The Telephone" & "The Medium," Douglas Moore's "The Devil and Daniel Webster," Otto Leuning's "Evangeline" & Randall Thompson's "Solomon & Balkis," Marc Blitzstein's "The Cradle Will Rock," to name only a few, present many shapes & kinds of modern operatic experiment.

The documentary film & incidental music for theatre productions have also called forth the leading contemporary composers, Blitzstein, Copland, & Thomson being outstanding in the former, Paul Bowles in the latter. There is, too, a semi-vernacular theatre movement subscribed to by Marc Blitzstein, Gerome Morross, Lehman Engel, Henry Brant & others, & if it sometimes falls into an esthetic category of "hybrid corn," taking the clichés of both worlds & losing much of the strength & vitality of either, it has nevertheless been a vital factor in narrowing the gap between the "serious" musical field & Broadway, between art & entertainment, & it has done much toward preparing the way for straight ballet & straight opera in its modern form for the greater public.

The United States' entry into the war signaled the curtain up on the final phase of America's musical coming-of-age. At Boston, New York, Philadelphia, Cleveland, Chicago, Kansas City—everywhere where there is an orchestra & a conductor with an enthusiasm for "first performances," the young Americans are being heard, premiered side by side with the "first performances" of current work by Europe's advance guard composers, both those resident here & those still in their native lands. —P. Glanville Hicks

# NEW ENGLAND

## CONNECTICUT — RHODE ISLAND
## MASSACHUSETTS — VERMONT
## NEW HAMPSHIRE — MAINE

### A FEW NOTES ON NEW ENGLAND

New England is, perhaps, the section of the United States most homogeneous in social & economic make-up. To use Bernard De Voto's phrase, it is the only part of the country that is "finished," that has reached "stability in its conditions of life." Usually the New England character is summed up as consisting, in varying proportions, of frugality, individualism, hardness, industriousness, eccentricity, &, with generous exceptions, conservatism. It is strange that these characteristics should have persisted despite the fact that during the last hundred years the racial elements of the population have been so completely transformed through emigration of native New Englanders & influx of newcomers from all quarters of the globe. Today, in Connecticut, Massachusetts, Rhode Island & the industrialized parts of New Hampshire, "foreign" elements generally outnumber descendants of the 17th & 18th century inhabitants. It should, however, be added that in finance, industry, commerce & even politics, the original stock has maintained its influential status fairly well despite its proportionate decrease in number.

Perhaps New England's homogeneity has been determined as much by its topography as by the character of its first settlers. New England is an isolated region, isolated by mountain ranges on the west, where it borders on New York, & by mountains & great forests to the north & east. It is a wedge thrust deep into Canada which encircles it on the north & east. Long Island Sound & the Atlantic cut it off on the south. There were in this compact wedge no good avenues of communication with the rest of the country, save by sea. Most of the chief rivers, the Housatonic, the Connecticut, the Merrimac, the Kennebec & the Penobscot, drain from the north into the sound or ocean. And there were no broad valleys by which early settlers could easily pass westward. The rivers, themselves, were not navigable except for short distances & this made land communication arduous.

New England was slowly & painfully settled by land-hungry pioneers pushing gradually into western Connecticut, north into New Hampshire & Vermont, & east into Maine. The land, itself, except for limited areas, as in the Connecticut Valley, was hilly & not very productive. This made for a small farm economy. Since the pioneer farmer was poor & had little surplus to exchange for imported articles, it also made for a self-sufficient economy. The New Englander of the interior produced everything he & his family used, right on the farm. Thus a hardy, independent yeoman class grew up which naturally rebelled against interference by a government three thousand miles away, & enthusiastically supported the Revolutionary cause. This economy also fostered a skilled class of handicraftsmen ready to fill the factories of the industrial era. Necessity fostered ingenuity, & the Yankee's proverbial inventiveness made New England the Nation's workshop.

The population of the seacoast was likewise largely determined in its development by environment. Most of the shoreline is rock-bound & picturesque, reaching a climax in Maine, whose deep inlets & rocky, wooded islands rival in beauty those of Norway. The coast, also, has many good harbors. It was natural, therefore, that New Englanders should take to the sea, especially as the hinterland had little but a hard, pioneering life to offer. And the abundant forests provided timber for ships. Boston launched its tiny "Blessing of the Bay" soon after the first settlement, &, from that time on, through the period when clippers whitened the seven seas, &

until the Civil War, New England dominated American coastal trade & foreign commerce. Her ports sent out the greatest whaling fleets which only declined when petroleum replaced sperm oil. Fish were abundant off-shore. Cape Cod was given its name by a sea Captain who anchored there & whose crew caught huge quantities of Massachusetts' "sacred" fish. The near-by Grand Banks added to the fishing opportunities. Yankee ingenuity discovered that salting would preserve cod, & so the way was opened for export. Down to our own times, fishing & fish processing have been among the region's chief sources of employment.

The great importance of commerce & shipping, which competed with British trade, especially in the West Indies, was one of the chief causes of the conflict with England. New England's agricultural surplus, small as it was, also competed with the home country's farmers. This was important, since England in the late 18th century was still predominantly agricultural. It was different in the Southern states which had tobacco & other non-competitive crops to send overseas. Encroachments on colonial freedoms by Britain, therefore, eventually found the merchants & the farmers, groups whose interests otherwise were not identical, united against the home country.

There was a good deal of early trouble with the Indians. The coastal regions of Massachusetts, Rhode Island & Connecticut for the most part disposed of their aborigines in the Pequot war of 1637 & King Philip's war of 1675. But New England's topographical isolation protected her against the worst ravages of the 18th century wars, which ended in the expulsion of the French. Maine & the frontiers were the chief sufferers during these conflicts.

New England has no coal or other fuel, except wood. But the falls & rapids of its rivers, a hindrance to navigation, turned the wheels of early mills, as today they provide electric power for great factories. The Revolution & War of 1812 forced New Englanders, while their sea-born commerce was choked off, to turn to manufacture. The need for arms & munitions encouraged them in this direction. Eli Whitney invented the cotton gin, others invented envelope-making machines, hooks & eyes, machinery for shoe & clock making, &, above all, the use of interchangeable & standardized parts. Capital accumulated in commerce was invested in industry. The wealthy merchant, Moses Brown of Providence, financed Samuel Slater in setting up the first thread mill in Pawtucket. Slater had worked in an English mill. Not being able to smuggle out drawings of it, he memorized the construction of the new spinning loom invented by Arkwright, a loom which he reproduced. Out of this small beginning grew the great textile factories.

The English Civil War & Revolution, with Oliver Cromwell's government in sympathy with Calvinist New England, gave the latter almost complete independence. Then came the comparatively brief interlude of the Stuarts between 1660 & 1688, & the attempt to deprive New England, as well as New York & New Jersey, of autonomy. Massachusetts & New Hampshire lost their charters at this time; Connecticut & Rhode Island managed to keep theirs despite Stuart Gov. Andros' attempt to annul them. After the revolution of 1688, the sympathetic government of William & Mary somewhat trimmed away the autonomy of Massachusetts & New Hampshire. But all four New England colonies, despite frequent clashes with their Governors, managed to keep government largely in the hands of their legislatures. Indeed, the conflict with the Crown was held more or less in abeyance until 1763, since both the colonies & the home government had to concentrate on efforts in the common cause against the French.

By 1763, with a population approaching 3,000,000, the colonies were able to embark on the struggle for independence with considerable prospects of success. Most of the measures by Parliament, from the Writs of Assistance & the Sugar Act, to the Townshend Acts & the Tea Act, were directed against New England much more than any of the other colonies. Britain considered New England the center of disaffection. Nevertheless, there was a considerable Tory & Loyalist element, which, however, being unorganized, could offer little coherent resistance to the patriots who resorted to violence to suppress the dissidents. The Tories were roughly handled, & the Loyalists, who tried to remain politically inactive, fared scarcely better.

During the Revolution, New England's topography again stood her in good stead. The most important battles were fought outside her territory. However, the first outbreak came in Massachusetts, with the Boston Massacre, followed by the clashes at Lexington & Bunker Hill. Then came the siege & capture of Boston, under Washington. Although the British considered New England the chief nest of rebellion, they now abandoned the region for more strategic objectives, & concentrated much of their effort on New York & the Hudson River Valley, hoping to split the colonies & isolate New England which was to be subdued later at their leisure. Only part of Rhode Island remained in British hands & part of Maine, then largely, except for the southwestern towns, still a wilderness. Otherwise New England suffered mostly from harrying expeditions launched by the British navy against coastal towns, & in the destruction of its sea-born trade.

In the period between the coming of the Pilgrims in 1620 & the end of the Revolution in 1781, a struggle in the domestic field had been going on intermittently between the masses & their rulers. New England's first settlements were made by refugees from the autocracy of the Anglican Church, & for many years the influx continued to consist of these same elements. The early settlers set up their own despotic theocracy, being no more in favor of religious tolerance than their English oppressors. The church, composed of the clergy & church members (rigidly restricted) became the government, governing according to Mosiac law. The mass of the people had no votes. Dissenters, especially Quakers, Baptists & such libertarians as Roger Williams, were persecuted & banished. The theocracy regulated not only property rights & the population's relations to the state, but private life as well by the notorious "blue laws." Rhode Island was of course the shining exception. Here Roger Williams proclaimed a policy of complete religious tolerance & separation of church & state. But it is well not to imagine an all too pervasive austerity. We have early 18th century accounts that describe considerable drinking and joviality even in that center of Puritan godliness, Boston. The hysteria of witch-baiting that swept New England in the late 17th century, centering around Salem, must be regarded as a terrible but temporary return to an earlier pattern, at the very time when a greater liberalism was beginning to make itself felt. Also "The Great Awakening" of the middle of the 18th century, led by Jonathan Edwards, might be regarded as a reaction to the trend toward libertarianism.

The struggle of the disenfranchised took on a dual character. First came the demand for a widening of church membership which automatically would give a larger number of orthodox Calvinists the right to vote. In Massachusetts & New Hampshire, by 1684, under pressure of the Stuart Governors, intolerance & "bible" government had been considerably curtailed. By the first part of the 18th century, toleration of non-Calvinist sects was becoming more general, & admission of their members to the franchise gradually followed.

The conflict now shifted to a new plane. The masses, who were disenfranchised because the right to vote was restricted by property qualifications, began to assert themselves. The Revolutionary leaders had been prodigal of slogans proclaiming the equality of man & his natural rights. But in domestic affairs, even rabble rousers like Samuel Adams, proved themselves to be extreme conservatives. The discontent increased after the revolution, due to the prevailing economic chaos, when many small farmers found themselves bankrupt & imprisoned for debt, & it culminated in Shay's Rebellion. Finally, in 1820, the Massachusetts constitution greatly extended the suffrage; the other New England states took similar action, with the exception of Rhode Island, where it required Dorr's rebellion of the 1840's to bring about this reform. In Maine, which peaceably separated from Massachusetts, of which it had been a part till 1820, the new constitution also granted a widened suffrage. Vermont, which acquired independence by rebellion against New York & became the 14th state in 1791, provided for complete religious freedom & manhood suffrage from the very beginning. However, universal white manhood suffrage was not attained in all the New England states till the mid-1840's.

The basis of New England government was the township, whose town meeting controlled all local affairs & sent representatives to the central legislative body. The county was a much later development & to this day has fewer functions. The legislatures of the New England Colonies were at first composed of "General Courts" in which centered both legislative & executive authority. To Councils, usually chosen by members of the General Courts, was delegated much authority in both fields. But finally executive functions were given to the Governor, & legislatures eventually became bicameral, as they are today. Unusual features have been the surviving Governors' Councils which to a certain extent share executive authority with the governor in Massachusetts, New Hampshire & Maine.

After the Revolution, because of its fortunate position, New England was able to take advantage of the difficulties of the British merchant marine during the Napoleonic wars & capture much of the carrying trade. Then came the interlude of Jefferson's Embargo Act & "Mr. Madison's War" of 1812 which killed off legitimate shipping but gave profitable opportunities for privateering, smuggling & even trading with the enemy, the latter a traditional practice inherited from the French-Indian War. With peace, commerce resumed its upward course. New England captured most of the coastal trade of the country, & branched out into whaling & the China trade & built most of the nation's ships. It was not until construction of the Erie Canal, the railroads, & steamboats, that New England's glorious maritime era came to an end. With the 19th century came the industrial revolution & New England was prepared to profit to the fullest extent by use of the new labor-saving machinery, much of which, in fact, she had invented.

But some of the factors that favored industrialization also favored emigration. The poor farmers moved on into western New York & Pennsylvania, & eventually, with building of the Erie Canal, into the Northwest Territory. Ohio was largely populated by New Englanders. The California gold rush took additional thousands, & Kansas, in the struggle between free-soilers & slavers, attracted a large New England contingent, including John Brown who led the Kansas free soil forces. The places of those who trekked westward were taken by an influx from abroad, first the Irish, driven out by the famine, then people from Northern Europe, & finally from all quarters of the globe. These newcomers, as well as many natives, filled the factories. Conditions of work, were, as in other regions, deplorable by present-day standards. Hours were up to 13 daily, for a mere pittance. Housing & living conditions were unbelievably bad. Labor organizations began to make themselves felt early. But the courts & the community generally viewed strikes as subversive. Nevertheless, several walkouts had occurred by the 1830's. Ten hour laws were eventually adopted; factory conditions were gradually ameliorated. Conditions of women's work were regulated & child labor restricted. The Danbury (Conn.) Hatter's strike of 1902 was declared in restraint of trade under the provisions of the Sherman Anti-trust law & made history insofar as it led to enactment of national legislation exempting unions from operation of the law. In Massachusetts took place long-drawn out strikes at Lynn in the shoe industry, & at Lawrence in the textile mills, the latter—because the leaders were accused of planting dynamite &, after trial, acquitted—having nationwide repercussions. New Hampshire had bitter strikes in its textile & paper mills.

Schools were provided for in the 1630's & 40's & laws were passed making it obligatory upon the towns to establish them. But the schools that were built were pretty primitive & the poorly paid teachers often equally so. It was not until the middle of the 19th century that the public school system was reorganized. Horace Mann of Massachusetts was the movement's leader & his influence became national. The states began to subsidize & supervise local primary education. Meanwhile, before their establishment by public funds, the place of high schools in the first three-quarters of the 19th century was taken by the "academy." These schools were by no means patronized only by the rich. Many of New England's leaders in their youth managed to work their way through the local academy, which, in fact, was the center of culture in the small New England community. Interest in higher education dated from the decade after the Pilgrims arrived with founding of Harvard at Cambridge.

Just as there was a movement to bring democracy into government, so there was a revolt in the early 19th century against the established (Congregational) church. Already the deism of Franklin & other national leaders had begun to undermine the old faith & encourage a trend away from strict orthodoxy. The new sect, which largely succeeded in displacing the old, was called Unitarianism & dispensed with the stern doctrines of predestination, original sin & the Calvinist conception of heaven & hell and eternal damnation. King's Chapel, in Boston, was the first conquest of the libertarians, late in the 18th century. Soon, under leadership of William Ellery Channing & others, Harvard College & a great many churches were taken over, so that Protestant New England thereafter assumed a decidedly Unitarian complexion.

Together with the religious revolt came the burgeoning of other liberal movements. New England became a hothouse for "strange isms." Transcendentalism, a sort of platonism somewhat transformed en route through Germany to America, was expounded rather turgidly by the intellectuals. The woman's rights, the prohibition & international peace movements were born & flourished abundantly. Experiments in communal living stirred nationwide interest, due to the fact that, under leadership of Bronson Alcott, the greatest figures in American literature took part in the Brook Farm experiment.

Abolition of slavery, however, led by the redoubtable William Lloyd Garrison, was the most important of the radical movements. There had been plenty of agitation for solution of the slavery problem before, even in some of the southern states. But Garrison's movement for the first time brought a sectional character into the controversy which aligned the free-soil North against the slave South. Even today historians are at odds on the question of whether the fury & bitterness of his propaganda brought about this alignment or merely hastened it. The "rich & well-born" looked with disapproval on the movement; they did business with the South—cotton for manufactured goods—& they deprecated anything that would interfere with business. For once the masses were with them. It was not till the late forties & early fifties that the tide turned & New England became generally abolitionist.

Almost contemporaneous with the liberation of the human spirit in the field of politics & religion was New England's great literary flowering in the 19th century. The 17th & 18th centuries had produced little of real significance although sermons & religious tracts were in great demand. Probably the most important book brought out in New England before the 19th century was Noah Webster's great dictionary. The 19th century was a period of great historians—Bancroft, Prescott, Palfrey, Parkman, Fiske; of eminent philosophers—Emerson, Thoreau, Channing, Pierce, William James; of poets—Whittier, Longfellow, Lowell, Holmes, Emily Dickinson; of novelists—Hawthorne, Melville, Stowe, Henry James, Jewett; of essayists, critics & preachers—Emerson, Parker, Channing, Beecher, Charles Eliot Norton, Wendell Philips, & a host of others. The graphic & plastic arts flowered less exuberantly, although such eminent artists as Samuel Morse, F. K. Church, James McNeil Whistler, Winslow Homer, William Morris Hunt, Albert Ryder, John La Farge, Edwin Abbey & John Singer Sargent, either were natives or contributed to the decoration of New England's buildings. Perhaps the earlier period of the 18th century produced a greater crop of eminent painters—John Smibert, born in Scotland, who, however, painted portraits in New England, Robert Feke, Ralph Earle, who although born in Long Island, lived in Newport, Copley, Benjamin West, Gilbert Stuart, John Trumbull, Edward Malbone, miniaturist, & a score of others.

Architecture also reached its height in the 18th century, & the first half of the 19th, as well as the handicrafts—silver-working, wood-carving, furniture & glass. The wealthy merchants of Providence, Newport, Boston, Portsmouth & other cities had the money to pay for noble mansions & fine paintings & furnishings to fill them with. Peter Harrison designed King's Chapel in Boston & some of the finest buildings in Newport & Providence; Ithiel Town, Trinity & Center Churches in New Haven; David Hoadley, the United Church in New Haven; Charles Bulfinch, the Massachusetts State House & many of Boston's finest residences; Samuel McIntyre, some of the loveliest mansions of Salem. This list includes only a few of New England's early architects. However, much of the architecture of the 17th & 18th centuries, as illustrated in farm houses, city dwellings, courthouses & churches, remains anonymous.

In the 20th century, New England has experienced somewhat of an economic crisis. It could scarcely have hoped permanently to keep its industrial predominance in competion with other regions with greater natural resources & raw materials & cheaper labor. New England's industrial salvation in the face of competition from other parts of the country has been due to the fact that its industry is tremendously varied. Exhaustion of forest wealth has pretty nearly ended export of lumber, but what remains is used for papermaking. The great cotton textile industry has been hard hit by competition of the southern states which have cheap labor & power. It is authoritatively stated that the wage difference between the South & New England was alone sufficient, although there were other factors, to account for the extensive migration of cotton mills. Lowell, Lawrence, Fall River, New Bedford & other textile towns were ruined by the flight of their chief industry in the twenties

& thirties; & the migration is still going on. The extent of the decline of the industry can be gauged by the fact that in 1905 there were 14,000,000 cotton spindles in New England & in 1938 only 4,780,000. Fairly successful efforts have been made to fill the deserted textile mills with new industries.

Today New England is a region of highly diversified industries. Insurance at Hartford is a multi-billion dollar business, employing some 15,000 white collar workers. Boston is still the country's largest fish & fish handling center. Both World Wars brought tremendous booms. New England executed more than 9 per cent of all World War II contracts—amounting to some $16,000,000,000. The region produces more than $5,000,000,000 worth of goods annually; Massachusetts, one-half of this total & Connecticut more than 25 per cent.

Originally New England was covered by vast forests. Four-fifths of Maine is still forest land, the largest ratio of any state. And millions of acres throughout the region have been & are still going back to woodland, as farms are being abandoned. Unfortunately, most of these tracts are worthless from the lumberman's point of view. Today, New England has to import some 80 per cent of its lumber. Farming has continuously declined in importance. Of a 40,000,000 acre area, some 15,000,000 are in farm & pasture, but a great percentage of this has been abandoned.

Recreation has become one of New England's chief industries, bringing in more than $500,000,000 annually. The region offers a heightened attraction to the tourist, old villages, with their charming village greens, simple white churches & fine old houses, set in picturesque coastal or mountain scenery.

New England's cities are still important cultural centers, with their great institutions of higher learning, professional & technical schools, outstanding museums, famous publishing houses. The "Atlantic Monthly," of the glorious days of Boston's literary predominance, still survives, although that landmark of an earlier type of newspaper, the "Boston Transcript," has disappeared. "The Christian Science Monitor" is published here. Boston with its celebrated symphony orchestra has become an important music center. Lyme, Provincetown, Gloucester, Marblehead, Peterborough have interesting summer art & literary colonies.

## US 1—NEW ENGLAND

**NEW YORK CITY (NE) to FORT KENT, ME. 855. US1**

Via: Bridgeport, New Haven, New London, Conn.; Newport, Providence, R.I.; Boston, Newburyport, Mass.; Portsmouth, N.H.; Biddeford, Portland, Brunswick, Bath, Belfast, Bangor, Calais, Houlton, Presque Isle, Me. N.Y., N.H. & H. RR. parallels route fairly closely to Boston; B. & Me. RR., from Boston to Portland, Me. Central RR. & Bangor & Aroostook RR. for remaining secs. Bus Lines to Calais, Me., & bus conn. at Houlton, Me. Accoms.: Limited beyond Houlton.

Route runs along Long Island Sound on Conn. border; then skirts R.I. shore line to Providence; thence proceeds (NE) cross-country to Boston & N.H. Line; through N.H. & Me. along Atlantic Coast to Calais at E. end of Me. Here hy. turns (N) & follows Canadian Boundary to Van Buren, Me., then (W) to Ft. Kent. US1 to Portsmouth is heavily traveled. In Conn., R.I. & N.H. it runs through hist. & scenically int. regions; in Me., along magnificent coast line & through some of finest scenery in the East; from Calais to Kent, through little-populated country (excellent h.&f.).

**Sec. 1: From Geo. WASHINGTON BRIDGE to NORWALK. CONN. 37.**
(see N.Y.C. I)

**Sec. 2: NORWALK, CONN. to NEW HAVEN, CONN. 32.**

**0. NORWALK** (see N.Y.C. I). **3.5. WESTPORT** (resort), an old shipping town. Washington stopped over to rest (1775) under the great elm, still standing, on Grounds of Christ Ch., on his way to take command of the Army in Boston. In Jr. High Sch. Auditorium, murals by John Curry. On US1 in W. part of town, **Congr. Ch.** (1832). Beaches & summer colonies on L. I. Sound. In near-by **Weston,** on St.57, is fine **Congr. Ch.** (1830). **7.5.** Mon. on **SITE OF GREAT SWAMP FIGHT** (1637), last conflict of Pequot War (see Hist.).

**9. FAIRFIELD** (sett. 1639)

Town merges into Bridgeport & is considerable industrial center. However, the old sec. has been preserved much as it was a hundred yrs. ago. During Rev., city was burnt by Brit. Gen. Tryon, but some early houses survived. Capt. S. Smedly fought & captured Brit. ship "Cyrus" offshore here, 1777. Fairfield only in 1946 abandoned the old town meeting & adopted a representative type of mun. gov. PTS. OF INT.: Township boasts upward of 80 pre-Rev. Hs.: (1) Cor. Unquowa & New Post Rds., **Fairfield Mem. Lib.** (O) houses Fairfield Hist. Soc.; coll. of rare hist. documents, & other items. (2) On Green, **Town Hall** (O.1794.rest.). (3) 573 New Post Rd. (S) of Old Post Rd., **Isaac Hull H.** (1799.fine exter.& inter.). (4) 19 Beach Rd. **Tucker H.** (1766) was saved by a Negro servant when town was burnt. (5) 33 Beach Rd., **Justin Hobart H.** (1776), in which town meetings & courts were held till 1785. (6) 37 Beach Rd., **Nathan Bulkeley H.** (pre-Rev.), which Brit. used as mess hall. (7) at SW. cor. of Green, **Sun Tavern** (1780.fine exter.& inter.). Washington supposed to have spent night here (1789). (8) Old Post Rd., just (W) of St. Paul's Ch., **Fairfield Academy** (1804), occupied by D.A.R. (9) Old Post Rd., cor. of Penfield Rd., **Thaddeus Burr H.** (1790.fine exter.& inter.), with fine garden. Dorothy Quincy & John Hancock were married here (1775). (10) 570 Old Post Rd., **Rowland H.** (pre-1769). The small son of the family is said to have warned of Brit. arrival, having seen it from church steeple. H. is said to have been spared by intercession of Brit. officer who had once been entertained here. (11) 405 Old Post Rd., **William Silliman H.** (1786-91). (See below.) (12) (NE) Cor. Benson & Old Post Rds., **Gen. Elijah Abel H.** (1780); later a tavern. (13) Mill Plain Rd., (N) of Redfield Rd., **Aug. Jennings H.** (1760.adds.). (14) Bronson Rd. in vicinity of Oak Lawn Cemetery, **David Ogden H.** (1705). Three of Ogden's sons served in Rev. (15) At NW. cor. Barlow & Round Hill Rds., **Isaac Jennings H.** (c.1780); later a tavern. (16) 546 N. Benson Rd., **"Uncle Ben" Wakeman's H.** (1800.fine exter.& inter.) was noted for its owner's hospitality & as rendezvous for Conn. peddlers traveling country roads. (17) Holland Hill, N. side of Jennings Rd., **Gen. Gold Selleck Silliman H.** (1746). The General was taken prisoner with his son Wm. by the Brit., but, by his presence of mind, saved the silver of the First Ch., left in his care. (18) On Holland Hill, N. side of Jennings Rd. cor. of Black Rock Rd., **Rbt. Silliman H.** (late 17th or early 18th cent.int.inter.); birthpl. of Gen. Silliman; old barns, smoke house, slave quarters. (19) In Fairfield are bldgs. (Coll.Goth.) of recently (1947) est. **Fairfield Univ.** (Cath.), which evolved out of Fairfield Preparatory College. (20) **Fairfield Beach** (bath.boat.f.). (21) On Unquowa Rd., **Bird Sanctuary** (O).

SIDE TRIP: On Bronson Rd., c.4m from city, **Greenfield Hill,** an old village with a pleasant Green & number of attractive old Hs. It is part of Fairfield township. In Old Cemetery are buried Rev. soldiers. On (W) side of Hillside Rd., facing Old Greenfield Rd., **Hubbell H.** (1751), where Timothy Dwight started his academy before being called to Yale. On Bronson Rd. (W) side, at (S) end of Green, **Rufus Blakeman H.** (1822). Dr. Blakeman, an abolitionist, had a secret room for Underground Railroad. On (W) side of Banks North Rd. (N) of Cross Hy., **Banks H.** (pre-Rev.). Nathan Banks walked 28 "Redcoat" prisoners all the way from Fairfield to Hartford.

**14. BRIDGEPORT** (sett.1639)

Info.: C. of C., Stratfield Hotel. (Excursion steamers from Battery Pl., N.Y.C., in summer).

On Pequonnock R. & L. I. Sound, Bridgeport is an industrial city; turning out a variety of products—airplanes, machinery, chemicals, textiles, typewriters, plastics, rubber goods. During World War II, its factories won more Army-Navy E awards per capita than any other U.S. city. Bridgeport has distinction of being one of few Amer. cities that has had a Socialist adm. for a long succession of years. Like other coastal towns, Bridgeport did its share of privateering during Rev. & Napoleonic Wars. Elias Howe, co-inventor of new type of sewing machine, put up a factory in the city in 1863. During Civil War, town became veritable arsenal, turning out materiel for Fed. armies. Although Bethel, Conn., was his birthpl., Bridgeport was home of P. T. Barnum, famous circus impresario. PTS. OF INT.: (1) Larger plants (O.appl.). (2) 500 N. Avenue, **Pixlee Tavern** (1700), where Washington is supposed to have stayed on his way (1775) to Boston. (3) 956 North Ave., **Tom Thumb H.;** P. T. Barnum's prize exhibit, the midget Gen. Tom Thumb, lived here with his midget wife. (4) On Dewey St., **Mt. Grove Cemetery,** where are buried the great showman, P. T. Barnum, & Tom Thumb. (5) Inters. Park & Fairfield Aves., **Nath. Wheeler Fountain,** by Gutzon Borglum. (6) 925 Broad St., **Pub. Lib.** (O); also Hist. Mus. (7) 202 State St., **City Hall** (1854.Gr.Rev.remod.). (8) Cor. Main & Gilbert Sts., on top floor of Board of Education Bldg., **P. T. Barnum**

# NEW ENGLAND I

CANADA
MAINE
NEW HAMPSHIRE
VERMONT
NEW YORK
ATLANTIC
White Mountains
Green Mts.
Mt. Washington
Mt. Mansfield
Rangeley Lakes
Lake Champlain
L. Memphremagog
L. George
L. Winnepesaukee
Kennebec
Androscoggin
Connecticut
Salmon Falls
Winooski
Augusta
Waterville
Lewiston
Auburn
Wiscasset
Bath
Brunswick
PORTLAND
Old Orchard
Biddeford
Saco
Sanford
Stratton
Rangeley
South Arm
Errol
Berlin
St. Johnsbury
Woodsville
Rochester
Dover
Laconia
Danbury
West Lebanon
Lebanon
Claremont
Charleston
Newport
St. Albans
Jeffersonville
Stowe
Waterbury
Montpelier
Barre
Burlington
Vergennes
Warren
Hancock
White River Jct.
Rutland
Springfield
Manchester
Middlebury
Chimney Point
Rouses Point
Plattsburg
Glens Falls
1
2
3
4
5
7
10
14
16
26
27
28
100
103
201
202
302

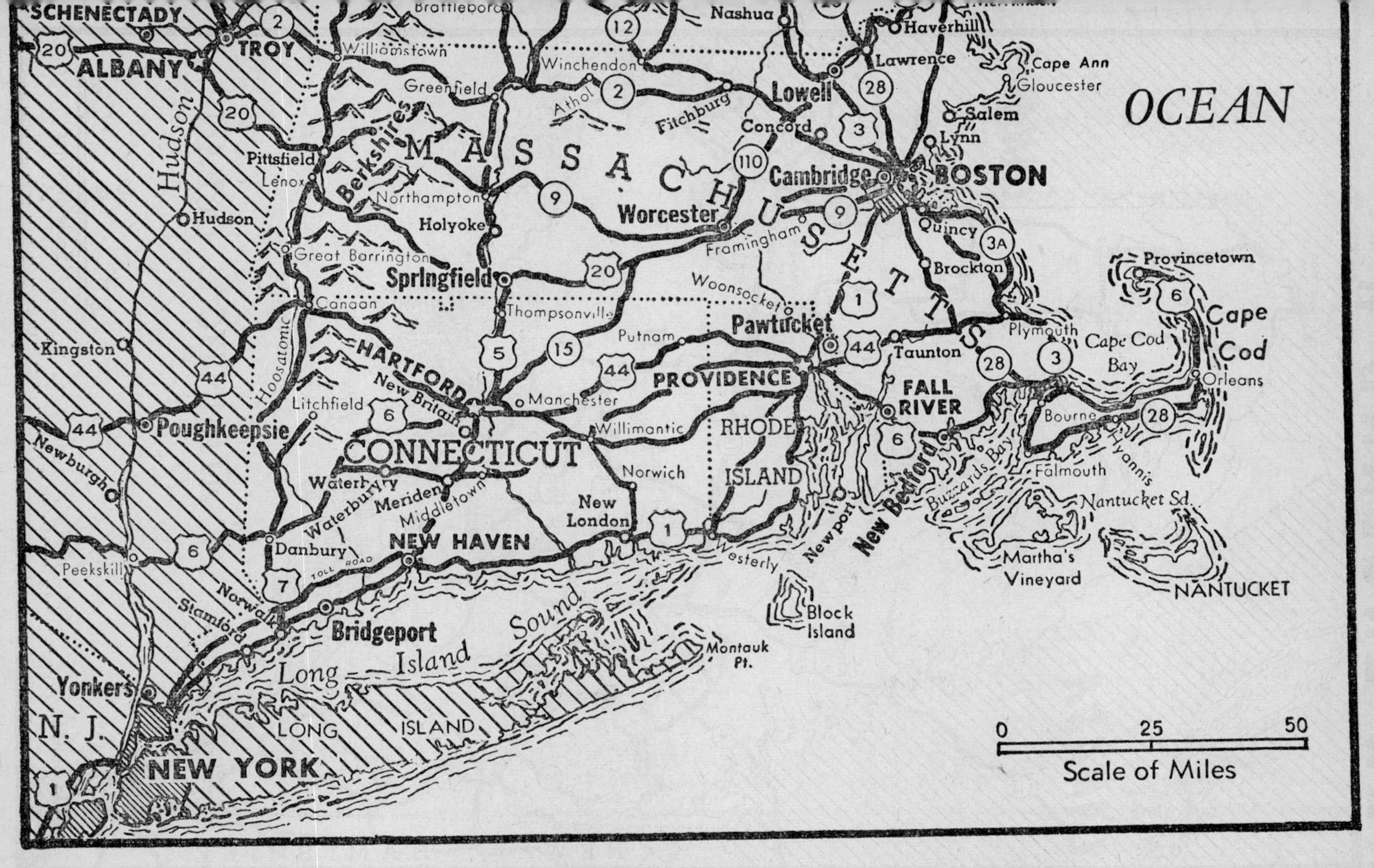

OCEAN
Cape Ann
Gloucester
Salem
Lynn
BOSTON
Haverhill
Lawrence
Nashua
Lowell
Concord
Cambridge
Quincy
Brockton
Plymouth
Cape Cod Bay
Provincetown
Cape Cod
Orleans
Hyannis
Bourne
Falmouth
Nantucket Sd.
NANTUCKET
Martha's Vineyard
Buzzards Bay
New Bedford
FALL RIVER
Taunton
Pawtucket
PROVIDENCE
RHODE ISLAND
Newport
Block Island
Westerly
Montauk Pt.
Woonsocket
Framingham
Worcester
Fitchburg
Winchendon
Athol
MASSACHUSETTS
Brattleboro
Greenfield
Williamstown
Northampton
Holyoke
Springfield
Thompsonville
Putnam
Manchester
Willimantic
Norwich
New London
HARTFORD
New Britain
CONNECTICUT
Middletown
Meriden
Waterbury
NEW HAVEN
Litchfield
Canaan
Great Barrington
Berkshires
Pittsfield
Lenox
SCHENECTADY
TROY
ALBANY
Hudson
Hudson
Hoosatonic
Poughkeepsie
Kingston
Newburgh
Peekskill
Danbury
TOLL ROAD
Norwalk
Stamford
Bridgeport
Long Island Sound
LONG ISLAND
Yonkers
NEW YORK
N. J.
0 25 50
Scale of Miles

# NEW ENGLAND II

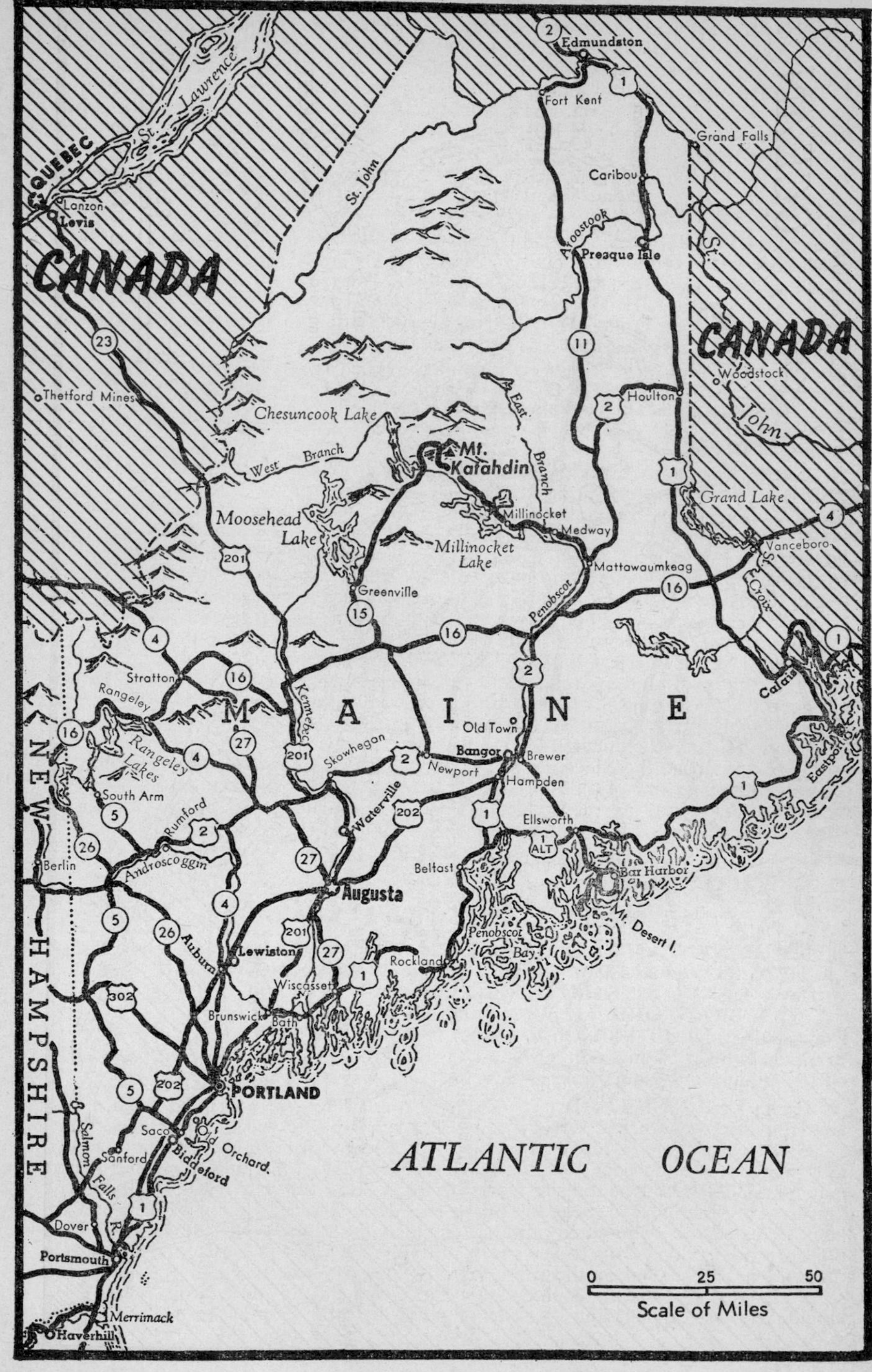

**Mus.** (O.Mon.Fri.aft.). (9) In Seaside Pk., on L. I. Sound, **Statue of Elias Howe, Jr.,** inventor of sewing machine (see Va. & Ga.) & **Statue of Barnum.** Near Pk. is **Court Marina** (Vict.), former residence of Barnum, now owned by Bridgeport Univ. (est. 1947) which evolved out of Junior College of Conn. (10) On Noble Ave., **Beardsley Pk.** (234 as.recr.) on W. bank of Pequonnock R. Zoo. Near Bridgeport is **Pleasure Beach Pk.** (pic.bath.recr.), on L. I. Sound near large amusement center. In Bridgeport is **J.** with St.58.

SIDE TRIP: Take St.58 (N) out of Bridgeport. At 17m **Gen. Putnam Mem. Campgrounds,** Conn.'s Valley Forge, where Putnam's troops wintered in 1778-79. **Mus.** (O.summer) has relics found on grounds. Reprods. of log cabins of soldiers.

**17.5. STRATFORD** (sett. 1639), although an industrial center, has preserved fairly intact part of the old town & boasts of some 60 Hs. antedating 1800. On Main St., **David Judson H.** (O.sm.fee.1723.int.inter.rest.), occupied by Stratford Hist. Soc. Other old bldgs. are **Dr. Wm. S. Johnson H.** (1779), former home of signer of the Constitution & **Gen. Walker H.** (1723). Behind Christ Ch. is **Oldest Burying Ground** dating from 1727. In Stratford is **J.** with St.8.

SIDE TRIP: (N) on St.8. At 12m, **J.** with Rd. crossing (R) Naugatuck R. to **Ansonia;** copper & brass products. 37½ Elm St., **Humphreys H.** (1698.rebuilt), birthpl. of David Humphreys, Rev. Gen. Opp. is **Episc. Burying Ground** (1737). 35 Jewett St., **Mansfield H.** (O.sm.fee.1747-48) was occupied by Rich. Mansfield, first Episc. Rector of Derby. At 15m, **Naugatuck R. Falls.**

**21.** J. with Rd. which leads (R) short distance into **Milford** (sett. 1639), resort on Wepawaug R. with a charming Green. Bath. at the Gulf, L. I. Sound. Town was sett. by refugees from religious persecution under Charles I. Site was purchased for usual commodities considered desirable by Inds.—coats, blankets, kettles, hatchets, shoes, knives & mirrors. Capt. Kidd, pirate, is supposed to have visited town in 1699 but, reportedly, behaved in peaceable manner. During late 17th & 18th cents., Milford became a busy ship building & trading, as well as oystering, center. At outbreak of Rev., there were conflicts bet. Tories & patriots, but town's majority supported patriot cause. Among 17th & 18th cent. bldgs. of considerable int. are: (1) W. River St., **First Congr. Ch.** (1832.supposedly by Hoadley), one of finest examples of early 19th cent. church architecture in Conn. (2) 46 W. River St., **Clark Tavern** (supposedly 1660.remod.), where Washington breakfasted &, to his chagrin, without a silver spoon. (3) W. Main St., **Plymouth Ch.** (1834.Gr.Rev.). (4) 32-34 High St., **Eels-Stow H.** (O.wks.Sun.aft.1669.adds.int.exter.& inter.rest.), owned by Milford Hist. Soc. (5) Broad St., **Stockade H.** (17th cent.). (6) 27 North St., **Buckingham H.** (1640.adds.alters.), one of oldest in vic. (7) Prospect St., **Old Burying Ground** (1675). Other old Hs. of int. are on W. Main, North, Gulf & Broad Sts. & on Governor's Lane & on the Post Rd. (8) Handsome **Town Hall** (1915.Fed.Class.).

At **29.5.** J. with St.122 on (W) outskirts of New Haven.

**32. NEW HAVEN** (see).

## Sec. 3: NEW HAVEN to OLD SAYBROOK. 33.

**0. NEW HAVEN. 3.5. EAST HAVEN.** Cor. Main & High Sts., **Old Stone Congr. Ch.** (1774.inter.rebuilt.1850). On Hemingway Ave., **Elnathan Street H.** (1810.fine Gr.Rev.). **4. SALTONSTALL L.,** where is old mill. **5.5.** J. with US1 Alt. US1 cont. (R) to **6.7. BRANFORD.** 112 W. Main St., **Nath. Harrison H.** (c.1685). On Green, **Branford Academy** (1820). On E. Main St., **Sam. Frisbie H.** (1792). In near-by **N. Branford** is lovely Congr. Ch. (1813). In Branford is J. with St.143, which branches off (R) along picturesque shore of Sound to Guilford (see below).

At **15.** on US1, **GUILFORD** (sett. 1639), a beautifully preserved old village, first known as Menunkatucket, sett. by colonists from New Haven led by Henry Whitfield. They had come as religious refugees from Eng. & on the way to New Haven, they signed a solemn pact pledging themselves to work faithfully together in their new home. They bought the site from Mohegan Inds. for mirrors, shoes, hatchets, knives. At Sachem Head, near the town, the Mohegans, led by Uncas & with Brit. help, defeated the Pequots & captured & killed the latter's Sachem. During Rev., Guilford men raided Brit. forces successfully at Sag Harbor & repelled attacks on their town, 1777. One of the most famous citizens was Abraham Baldwin, who served in Rev. as chaplain & later moved to Georgia (see). At Constitutional Convention, he cast the deciding vote for adoption of Conn. Compromise for organization of the U.S. Senate. Also from Guilford were Fitz-Greene Halleck, the poet, & Wm. H. H. Murray, the writer known as "Adirondack" Murray because he publicized the Adirondack region. Guilford Township, incl. N. Guilford, Nortontown & other villages, claims upward of 150 Hs. built bet. 1639 & 1810 & 6 beautiful early 19th cent. Chs. In Guilford town itself, on Fair St., are 13 Hs. dating from 18th cent. On State St. are Sam. Hill H. (1699), Capt. Nath. Bradley H. (c.1665), & Henry Kingsnorth H. (1646), & 18 Hs. dating from 18th cent. Other Sts. on which are a number of int. old Hs. are Water, Whitfield, Boston, Union, River, Church, Broad, Park & York Sts. Some fine old Hs. are found in the West Side district, on Long Hill Rd., at Moose Hill, at Mulberry Farm, at Leete's Island, Sachem's Head, Nut Plains, Clapboard Hill, Goose Lane. Many also (mostly 18th cent.) in N. Guilford & Nortontown. Notable in Guilford are: **First Congr. Ch.** (1830) on Green; **Christ Episc. Ch.** (1838); **Meth. Ch.** (1830) & **Third Congr. Ch.** (1844). In N. Guilford, off St.77 (N): **St. John's Ch.** (Episc.1812) & **Congr. Ch.** (1814). Hs. in Guilford (O) to visitors: **Whitfield H.** (O.except Mon.N.O.in Nov.1639.rest.) on Whitfield St., supposedly oldest stone H. in New England, now St. Mus. On Boston St., **Hyland H.** (O.June-Oct.except Sun.sm.fee.1660); antique furnishings. **20. MADISON,** another old town, with some 60 Hs. dating, for the most part, from 18th cent. Around Green are **Congr. Ch.** (1838.lovely Gr.Rev.), whose early silver is on exhibit; **Nath. Allis H.** (O.Sun.aft.summer.sm.fee.1739), which has period furniture & exhibit of antiques; home of Madison Hist. Soc. Here lived C. S. Bushnell who financed bldg. of the "Monitor" (see Norfolk, Va.). In **N. Madison,** reached by St.79 (N) is a charming **Congr. Ch.** (1837). (S) of Madison is **Hammonassett St. Pk.** (bath.camp. recr.), on L. I. Sound. In **Hammonassett** is Cemetery (1658). Near Madison, **West Cemetery** (1691). **24. CLINTON.** Near Church Green, is **Stanton H.** (O.wks.aft. 1789); Mus. with coll. of antiques & reprod. of old Stanton Store. On Green is Mon. comm. early classes in school which eventually became Yale College.

SIDE TRIP: (L) 2.5m on Queenstown Rd. to J. with Cow Hill Rd. **Little Red Schoolh.** (O.appl.1800); coll. of odd antique items.

**25.** J. with St.145 on which (R) is **Grove Beach** (bath.boat.). **28. WESTBROOK. David Bushnell H.** (O.1678-79.rest.). Mus. has parts of "Turtle," submarine with which Bushnell tried to blow up Brit. frigate in N.Y. harbor. **33. OLD SAYBROOK** (sett. 1635), on Conn. R. Town suffered from Ind. raids during Pequot War. Here Yale College was founded (1710). Here also was promulgated the Saybrook Platform (1708) regulating government of Conn.'s Congr. churches for nearly a century. Near here David Bushnell built his submarine. On Old Boston Post Rd., near Main St., **Acton Lib.** (O), with coll. of relics. On Main St., **Congr. Ch.** (1839).

### Sec. 4: OLD SAYBROOK, CONN. to R.I. LINE. 36.

Via: (Old Lyme), East Lyme, New London, Groton, Mystic, Stonington.

**0. OLD SAYBROOK. 3.** J. with St.156 which leads (R) directly into **Old Lyme,** former shipping, shipbuilding & fishing town, with lovely Green & many early houses. Now an artists' colony & resort. On Lyme St., **Congr. Ch.,** a replica of earlier one destroyed by fire (1907); one of loveliest in New England. Near-by is Parsonage (late 18th cent.). On Boston Post Rd., **Lyme Art Gallery** (exhibits.summer). On Shore Rd., **Duck R. Cemetery,** one of oldest in state. At Post Rd. & Sill Lane, **Peck Tavern** (late 17th cent.). Lyme St. & Beckwith Lane, **Moses Noyes H.** (early 18th cent.). Shore Rd., **McCurdy H.** (18th cent.). Lyme St., **Capt. John Sill H.** (1818.attrib.to Belcher.int.exter.& inter.). On Post Rd., near Lyme Art Gallery is **Wm. Noyes H.** (O.except Mon.,June-Aug.1817.by Belcher.fine inter.& exter.), also called Florence Griswold H. Here, in 1900, was founded Lyme Art Assoc. Panels were painted for Miss Griswold by noted Amer. artists & the house itself has been favorite subject for painters.

SIDE TRIP: St.156 cont. along picturesque coast. At 9m (R) **Thos. Lee H.** (O.special days & appl.sm.fee.c.1660.rest.), a notable bldg. with fine inter., furnished in period; coll. of relics. Adj. is **Little Red Schoolh.** (1734). Both owned by East Lyme Hist. Soc. St.156 cont. through Niantic to rejoin US1 (W) of New London.

**19. NEW LONDON** (sett. 1646)

Info.: C. of C. at 18½ Meridian St. Airport: through conns. Annual Yale-Harvard crew races (late June). Yachting regattas. Ocean Beach offers bath. & other facils. Steamers (autos) daily in summer to Fisher's I., Block I. (see Newport) & points on L.I.

The city, on Thames R., was founded by John Winthrop & settlers from Mass. Colony in 1646 & early became shipping & shipbuilding center, engaging in West Indies & transatlantic trade. During Rev. it sent out maritime expeditions against Brit. & was set afire by Brit. under Benedict Arnold's direction (1781). In 1784, first New England whalers set out from here for southern waters & thereafter it became a great whaling port. In 19th cent., many swift clipper ships were built in New London yards. Today city is a considerable port & industrial beehive. Most important industry is Electric Boat Co., in Groton (see below) across the R., largest submarine shipyard in world.

PTS. OF INT.: (1) Mill St., **Old Town Mill** (O.1650.rebuilt). (2) Bank St., **U.S. Customh.** (1833). (3) William St. & Mohegan Ave., **Lyman Allyn Mus.** (O.wks.except Mon.;Sun.aft.Class.by Chas.A.Pratt); colls. of art, furniture, handicraft, antiques; loan exhibits. (4) Mohegan Ave., **U.S. Coast Guard Academy** (O.wks.), much expanded during World War I & II; number of students has quadrupled. (5) Mohegan Ave., **Conn. College** (women), on spacious campus; Arboretum; Palmer Lib. (O. 1933.adds.) has rare documents, books & other items, some on exhibit in Palmer Mem. Room. (6) State St., **County Cth.** (O.1784.rest.) where "peace ball" was held (1815) with Brit. as well as Amer. officers attending. (7) SE. cor. Huntington & Broad Sts., **Jedediah Hunting H.** (c.1796). Huntington & State Sts., **Pub. Lib.** (O.by Richardson.fine example). (8) Huntington & Richards Sts., **Nathan Hale School** (O.wks.rest.), where Hale taught (1774-75). Near-by is "ancientest burying ground" (1653). (9) 11 Blinman St., **Shaw Mansion** (O.sm.fee.1756.remod.); period furnishings & Washington's room kept intact; occupied by New London Cty. Hist. Soc. On grounds is **Whalemen's Mem.** (10) 77 Thurman St., **Shepherd's Tent** (c.1839). (11) 11 Hempstead St., **Hempstead H.** (O.1678 & 18th.cent.adds.); maintained by Antiquarian & Landmarks Soc., Inc. (12) Inters. of Hempstead, Jay & Coit Sts., **Huguenot H.** (O.c.1751), supposed to have been built by Huguenot refugees; now a tea-room. (13) Foot of Ocean Ave., **Ocean Beach** (recr.bath.). (14) In Williams Pk., **Statue of Nathan Hale,** duplicate of one by MacMonnies, in N.Y. City. (15) Near Bulkeley School, **Winthrop Mon.,** by Bela L. Pratt. (16) In Gardner Cemetery, **Grave of Rich. Mansfield,** celebrated actor. (17) On East St., **U.S. Coast Guard Training Base** almost conceals, with its many new structures & those of other navy organizations, old **Ft. Trumbull** (O.appl.) & **Old Powder H.** (1775), used during Rev. (18) Off Howard St., on Pequot Ave., **New London Lighth.** (O.1760.rebuilt.1801). Fisher's I. (resort) off-shore, belongs to N.Y. St. Only recently the I.'s inhabitants voted again to remain under N.Y. jurisdiction.

SIDE TRIPS: (A) **Groton** (sett.1649). Cross Thames R. by Groton-New London Bridge (1943. 1⅛$^m$ long, with a clearance of 135′ above river; construction cost $6,000,000). Groton was once a part of New London & in old days a fishing, shipping & shipbuilding center. After New London was burnt by Benedict Arnold, Brit. attacked Groton (1781). At Ft. Griswold in Groton Heights occurred heroic stand of company of militia against several Brit. regiments. When fort finally surrendered, the patriot garrison was massacred. PTS. OF INT.: 108 Thames St., **Mother Bailey H.** (1782), home of Mother Anna Bailey, famous because, during attack by Brit. fleet (1813), she sent her red petticoat to be used as gun wadding by the hard-pressed garrison. On Fort St., **Ft. Griswold,** where militia made brave stand. Near-by, **Groton Mon.** (O.sm.fee) comm. event. Fine view. Adj., **Monument H.** (O); relics of battle. Just (N) of Mon., **Bill Mem. Lib.;** notable coll. of butterflies & sword of Col. Ledgewood, massacred when fort surrendered. At foot of hill below Ft. Griswold, **Ebenezer Avery H.** (pre-Rev.) where wounded in battle were brought. In Groton is J. with St.12, which at 2$^m$ (N) of Groton, passes **U.S. Navy Atlantic Submarine Base** (O.appl.) & continues (N) 14$^m$ to **Norwich,** paralleling Side Trip (C).

(B) Cross Thames R. to Groton & then R. I. Line by St.84 (E). This is a somewhat shorter but less int. route to Providence, R. I. It passes through old town of **Center Groton.** At 7$^m$ is **Old Mystic,** another hist. village on Mystic R., once a shipping town. St.84 reaches R. I. Line at 13.5$^m$, less than 2$^m$ from **Hopkinton** (see).

(C) St.32 (N). At 2$^m$ **U.S. Coast Guard Academy** & just beyond it, **Conn. College** (for both, see New London). 9$^m$ **Mohegan Village. Tantaquidgeon Lodge** (O); built by descendants of Tantaquidgeon, one of Uncas' followers, contains Ind. material. Near-by, **Congr. Ch.** (1831). Ind. Arbor Festival held here Aug. 9.5$^m$ J. with marked Rd.

(R) 1.5$^m$ to **Site of Ft. Shantok St. Pk.** (177 as.pic.camp.bath.), where Uncas was besieged by Narragansett Inds. (1645). Mon. comm. Lt. Thos. Leffingwell, who brought supplies for relief of garrison.

14$^m$ **Norwich** (sett. c.1659). (Info.: C. of C., Peck Lib., for pts. of int.) Founded by settlers from Saybrook on land acquired from Uncas by Thos. Leffingwell. The "Battle of the

Great Plains," 1643, in which Uncas defeated Narragansett Inds., was fought near city. Samson Occum, famous Ind. preacher & missionary to Inds., who helped found Dartmouth College was born near-by. Norwich became important shipbuilding center & port since it is located on the Thames at J. of Yantic & Shetucket Rs. In late 18th cent., industry developed & continued to expand during 19th cent. Pistols & rifles were among chief products. Today, city is one of industrial centers of state, producing textiles, thermos bottles, shoes, clothing, machinery. PTS. OF INT.: (1) Broadway & Chelsea Parade, **Slater Mem.** (O.wks.Sun.aft.) on grounds of Norwich Free Academy (est.1854.). Notable coll. of rare books & documents, art, Oriental & Ind. material; loan exhibits. (2) On Green, Chelsea Parade, **Boulder** comm. S. C. Reid, naval hero of War of 1812. He is alleged to have been designer of present Amer. flag. (3) 42 Rockwell St., **Old Rockwell H.** (O.Mon.-Fri.;Sun.aft.). Gen. A. P. Rockwell served in Civil War. (4) Sachem & Washington Sts., **Uncas Mon.,** comm. Uncas, friend of early settlers; Ind. gravestones. (5) NE. cor. Washington St. & Arnold Pl., **Site of Birthpl. of Benedict Arnold.** On Washington, Town, E. Town & Elm Sts., are a number of int. old Hs., among which are: (6) 328 Washington St., **Reynolds H.** (1659.alts.). (7) 344 Washington St., **Leffingwell Inn** (2nd half 17th cent.adds.), owned by Thos. Leffingwell (see above). Washington stopped here for dinner. (8) 34 E. Town St., **Sam Huntington H.** Gov. Huntington was signer of Decl. of Ind. Also on E. Town St., is fine **Congr. Ch.** (1801). (9) On Cemetery Lane, **Old Burial Ground** (1699). (10) On Lee Ave., **Post Gager Burial Ground** (1661), (11) 112 W. Town St., **Adams Tavern** (2nd half 18th cent.), still a tavern; once owned by ancestor of Grover Cleveland. Norwich is at J. with St.12 & St.165.

(1) Take St.12 (N) out of Norwich. At $4^m$, **Miantonomo Mon.,** comm. Narragansett sachem executed near this spot after his defeat at "Great Plains" by Uncas, chief of the Mohegans.

(2) Take St.165 (E) from Norwich. At $13.5^m$ **Voluntown,** J. with St.95. Here is **Robbins Tavern** (O), another inn Washington patronized. Take St.95 (N) (L) here c.$0.5^m$ to J. with Rd. running (L) to For. Rangers hqs. in **Pachaug St. For.** (21,675 as. pic.bath.trls.).

(D) St.85 (NW). At $8^m$ is **New London Reservoir.** At $13^m$ Salem (sett. 1700), with fine **Old Ch. & Town Hall.** At $18.5^m$ is J. with Rd. leading (L) past **Hayward L.** (resort) to **Devil's Hopyard St. Pk.** at $4.5^m$. Fine Chapman's Falls (pic.). $20^m$ **Colchester,** in which & in vic. are many fine old bldgs.: **Congr. Ch.** (O.c.1841); **Old Bacon Academy** (O) where John Adams once taught. Adj. is old **Cemetery.** Near the Green, **Foote H.** (O.1703) & several other int. old Hs. About $7^m$ from Colchester, on St.16 is old **Comstock Covered Bridge** (adj.pic.). At Colchester is J. with St.2 which cont. (NW) to Hartford (see). At $3^m$ (E) of Colchester on St.2 is **State Hy. Pk.** (pic.).

**27. MYSTIC,** formerly shipbuilding & shipping center. Fastest clipper ship was built here. Near Mystic, on St.169, is **Marine Hist. Mus.** (O); notable coll. of clipper ship models. Berthed at dock is 100-yr.-old whaler, **"Chas. W. Morgan,"** which earned its owner $2,000,000. Town is summer art colony & has **Mystic Art Gallery** (O.sm.fee); exhibits contemporary Amer. art. Seaport of Mystic is being rest. as it was more than 100 yrs. ago. Waterfront or near it is being paved with cobblestones & a blacksmith shop, a little stone bank of 1833 to be used as a merchant's countingh. & a spar shed & seaport store have been built, as has **Mallory Mem. Bldg.** (O. summer). The early 19th cent. **Greenman H.** has been rest. **N.Y. Yacht Club** bldg. (O), containing int. furnishings & relics, has been moved from Oyster Bay, N.Y. to grounds of Marine Hist. Soc. **31.5.** US1 now passes just (N) of **Stonington.**

SIDE TRIP: (R) here into **Stonington** (1649), early shipbuilding & shipping center. Town was attacked during Rev. & War of 1812 by Brit. PTS. OF INT.: (Town has many fine old houses.) SE cor. Main & Elm Sts., **Congr. Ch.** (1829.Gr.Rev.). SE cor. Main & Grand Sts., **Jos. Smith H.** (c.1800). On Grand St. (L), **Sam. Denison H.** (c.1811). Cor. Main & Wall Sts., **Amos Palmer H.** (1787), boyhood home of Whistler, Amer. artist. 16 Mason St., **Old Stone Customh.** (1823), now tenement. 35 Water St., **Elkanah Cobb H.** (1760). End of Water St., **Old Lighth.** (O) contains relics & is home of Stonington Hist. Soc.

**36.** Cross **CONN.-R.I. LINE** (Pawcatuck R.) here into Westerly.

## Sec. 5: WESTERLY, R.I., to PROVIDENCE, R.I. 55.

**0. WESTERLY** (sett. 1661) on Pawcatuck R.; shipbuilding & shipping port in 18th & 19th cents. Today it is an industrial city, producing textiles & granite, & market town for numerous near-by resorts. On Broad St., **Westerly Mem. Lib.** (O); Mus. & Art Gallery. 120 Main St., **Pawcatuck Seventh Day Baptist Ch.** (O.appl.). 196 Main St., **Lucy Carpenter H.** (early 18th cent.remod.). 12 Margin St., **Capt. Card H.** (1750). 124 Granite St., **Babcock H.** (middle 18th cent.). On Granite St., **Smith Granite Quarry** (O) produces the much sought-after Westerly granite.

SIDE TRIP: (S) $5^m$ on Watch Hill Rd. to **Watch Hill;** fine views & access to beaches (f. boat.bath.) & **Watch Hill Lighth.** (O). From village, Fort Rd. leads (R) $1.5^m$ to **Napatree Pt.**

In Westerly is J. with St.3, a shorter route to Providence.

ALT. ROUTE: (NE) $39^m$ to Providence on St.3 (Via: Ashaway, Hope Valley, Crompton & Cranston.)

$4.5^m$ **Ashaway. First Seventh Day Baptist Ch.** (1835). At $7^m$ **Hopkinton,** named for Gov. Stephen Hopkins. Town has some int. Colonial Hs. **Second Seventh Day Baptist Ch.** (late 18th cent.alt.). Near Hopkinton is **Ashaway Grove** (pic.). At $11^m$ **Hope Valley** which has some int. 18th & early 19th cent. dwellings. $12^m$ **Wyoming** (sett.1758). J. with St.138. Near this J. (L) is **Dawley Tavern** (O.1800). In Wyoming also is J. with Old Nooseneck Rd., which branches (N) to **Arcadia For. Pk. Reserv.** (pic.bath.). $13^m$ **Six Principle Bapt. Ch.** (early 18th cent.), near which are old cemeteries with quaint inscriptions. $16.5^m$ **Dawley Mem. Pk.** (pic.camp.trlrs.). At $18^m$ is J. with Ten Rod Rd. (St.165).

(L) $7^m$ on Rd. to 3,000-a. **Beach Pond Reserv.** (pic.camp.cabins.trlrs.bath.); Wild Life Sanctuary. Ten Rod Rd. makes J. with Conn. St.138. to Voluntown (see).

$19^m$ J. with St.102, which leads (SE) $11.5^m$ to **Wickford.** $26.5^m$ St.3 forks.

(N) $2.5^m$ on St.3A to **Anthony.** (E) on State St. a short distance to **Nath. Greene H.** (O.aft.Wed.Sat.& Sun.1770.rest.), home of general who, after Washington, was perhaps most important military figure in Revolution (see Hist. & Savannah, Ga.). At $7.5^m$ St.3A rejoins St.3.

$28^m$ on St.3, **Tioga L.** (resort). $38^m$ **Cranston** (sett.1638), an important iron-manufacturing center during Col. times because of near-by iron-ore bogs, today an industrial town, producing textiles & textile machinery. Large plants (O.appl.). 1538 Plainfield St., **Fenner H.** (c.1677). Cranston St. & Dyer Ave., **Sprague Mansion** (1800.adds.). 219 Phoenix Ave., **Caleb Arnold Tavern** (1775). 109 Wilbur Ave., **Edw. Searle H.** (1671.adds.). 229 Wilbur Ave., **Friends Meetingh.** (1729). In W. sec. of city, **Meshanticut Pk. & L.** (pic.bath.boat. f.sports.facils.). At $39^m$, St.3 makes J. with US1, on outskirts of Providence (see).

Main tour cont. from Westerly on US1. At frequent intervals, Rds. branch off (R) to coastal resorts. At **2. OLD WHIPPING POST FARM** where public whipping used to take place. **7. MON. TO GEN. STANTON,** Rev. officer, & **Wilcox Tavern** (O. summer.c.1730.rest.), Stanton's birthpl.

SIDE TRIP: (L) $1^m$ on Rd. here to **Burlingame St. Reserv.** (pic.bath.boat.f.). Near-by is **Kimball Bird Sanctuary.**

**11. KING TOM FARM** (O.summer.appl.). Tablet on old chimney shows reprod. of orig. house (mid.-18th cent.). **Coronation Rock,** where Narragansett Inds. crowned their chiefs, is on farm. **12. CHARLESTOWN.** Here 2 corn-meal grinding mills, over 200 yrs. old, still function. Near Charlestown is **Fort Neck Lot Pk.** around what used to be thought the remains of Ind. fortress, now believed to be site of Dutch fort. Near Charlestown is old **Ind. Burial Ground,** state reserv. On Charlestown Beach Rd. (S) is **Charlestown Beach** (resort).

SIDE TRIP: (N) $6^m$ from Charlestown on St.2 to Marker on **Site of Great Swamp Fight** (1675) when Narragansett Ind. village was destroyed. For other pts. on St.2, see Providence).

**16.** (R) here $2^m$ to **Moonstone Beach,** resort. **17.5.** (R) here on Matunuck Pt. Rd. to **Matunuck Beach,** summer resort. **19.** (L) here less than $1^m$ to **Oliver Hazard Perry H.** (O.summer.fee.early 18th cent.rest.), where lived hero of L. Erie battle (see N.Y. & Ohio) & Adm. M. C. Perry, who opened up Japan; relics. **21. WAKEFIELD,** 17th cent. town, now an industrial center. On old Kingston Rd., (W) of High St., is **Rodman H.,** one of several claimed to be birthpl. of Commodore Perry. **22. J.** with Kingston Rd.

SIDE TRIP: Take latter (L) $1.5^m$ to **Peace Dale,** where is **Mus. of Primitive Culture** (O. morn.) with good coll. Ind. relics. Rd. cont. to **Old Kingston,** home of R. I. College (see Providence).

**24. NARRAGANSETT,** famous summer resort on Atlantic Ocean. Many hotels & other accoms., exclusive clubs & many beaches. Narragansett Pier is noted for its fine bathh. & other recr. facils. Handsome bldg., with towers, spans. hy. In vic. is **Ft. Nath. Greene,** U.S. Army Post.

SIDE TRIP: From Narragansett, $5.5^m$ to **Pt. Judith** on the ocean. Lighth.; fine view. On way to it, Rd. passes Pentaquanscott Pk. & Beach, Scarborough Beach St. Reserv. & Sand Hill Cove Reserv. (all pub.bath.).

**28.** J. with St.138 to Kingston (see Providence). **28.5. J.** with Rd.

SIDE TRIP: (R) half-mile on this Rd. to **Franklin Perry H.,** which was ferry terminal in 18th cent. for Coanticut Is. & Newport. (L) c.$1^m$ from Perry H. to **Hannah Robinson H.** (early 18th cent.int.inter.), home of Hannah Robinson, who in Rev. period was heroine of romance with French officer with whom she eloped & by whom she was finally deserted. Occupied by Lafayette for a time.

**30.5.** J. with Hammond Mill Rd. (well marked).

SIDE TRIP: (L) on this Rd. to **Gilbert Stuart H.** (O.summer.sm.fee.1751.rest.), birthpl. of famous Amer. painter who did many portraits of Washington; exhibits. Near-by is Snuff & Grist Mill, put up by Stuart's father.

**31.** J. with Rd. leading (R) to **Jamestown Bridge** to Coanticut Is., from which ferry to Newport (see). **34. WICKFORD** (sett. c.1709). Charming old town, center of N. Kingstown Township. Claims to have more fine 18th cent. houses than any other New England town. Just (S) of Wickford, on US1, is **South Cty. Barn Mus.** (O.sm. fee). (W) of town center, on W. Main St., **Old Town H.** (1807). (W) of Bridge St., **Stephen Cooper H.** (1728). 64 Main St., **Immanuel Case H.** (1786). About half-mile (E) of Town Hall, **Poplar Pt. & Old Lighth.** (1831). On Main St., **St. Paul's ("Old Narragansett") Ch.** (O.summer.appl.at Wickford H.). This very lovely old Ch. (1707) was moved here in 1800. Main & Fountain Sts., **Old Narragansett Bank H.** (1786. remod.). Pleasant St., (N) of Main St., **John Updyke H.** (1745). About 1m from Main St., **St. Lobster Hatchery,** where 1,500,000 lobsters are released annually. (W) of Wickford is **Richard Smith Grove** (pic.) & **Gooseneck Spring Hatchery** (trout). (NE) are **Quonset Pt.** & **Quonset Pt. Air Base.** "Quonset Hut" derives from this place where this type of bldg. was first used. In Wickford is J. with St.102. **35.5.** Marker on **Roger Williams Trading Post Site** (L) where R.I. founder traded with Inds. (R) **Site of Smith's Ft.** (1639) on what is today known as Cocumcussock Farm. Just beyond on a hill (R) is **Richard Smith H.** (late 17th cent.), home of early settler. Tablet marks graves of men killed by Inds. in Great Swamp Fight (1675). **39.5. SPRING BROOK FARM** (Old Coggeshell H.early 18th cent.).

**41. EAST GREENWICH** (sett. early 17th cent.). Today this old town, like others in R.I., is industrialized, with textiles & fish products in front rank. PTS. OF INT.: (1) Main & Division Sts., **Varnum Mem. Armory** (O.info.late 19th cent.), home of Varnum Continentals; military & naval mus. (2) Main St., **Kent County Cth.** (1750. good Col.inter.remod.), where convention met (1842) to frame St. Constitution. (3) Also on Main St., **Meth. Ch.** (1833.adds.). (4) King & Water Sts., **Second Jail** (1804.adds.), still in use. (5) Pierce & Armory Sts., **Armory of Kentish Guards** (est. 1774). Among early houses are: (6) Division & West Sts., **Windmill Cottage** (early 19th cent.), which Longfellow acquired for his friend, Geo. Washington Greene. Warwick & Division Sts., very fine **Gov. Wm. Greene H.** (late 17th cent.adds.), where Gen. Nath. Greene was married (1774). Greene, as is well known, was born a Quaker & had severe struggle with his conscience when he took up arms in Rev. He was expelled from Society of Friends. (7) 294 Main St., **First Brick H.** (1767). (8) 57 Pierce St., **Gen. Jas. Mitchell Varnum H. & Mus.** (O.1773.fine exter.& inter. adds.), where Gens. Lafayette, Rochambeau & Sullivan met during Rev. Washington was guest here. Furnished in period; coll. of photographs of old Hs. in town & vic.; hist. items. (9) 28 King St., **Capt. Thos. Arnold H.** (1735). (10) At SW. cor. Division & Pierce Sts., **Eldridge H.** (2nd half 18th cent.). (11) Pierce & Court Sts., **Old Dr. Peter Turner H.** (12) Pierce & Division Sts., **Capt. John Congdon H.** (1711). (13) About 2m (E) of town on Howland Rd., off Division St., **Clement Weaver H.** (1679). At inters. of these 2 hys. is **Marker** to comm. attempt by Tories (1774) to burn down the town.

SIDE TRIPS: (A) On Potowomut Rd., 1m to **Elizabeth Spring,** where Roger Williams stopped & which he named for wife of his friend, John Winthrop.
(B) Take Old Forge Rd. 1m to **Site of Old Forge & Gen. Nath. Greene Birthpl.** (see above). Cont. on Ives St. to **Goddard Mem. Pk.** (470 as.recr.).

**44. APPONAUG,** mun. center of city of **WARWICK;** sett. (1643) by Sam. Gorton & other dissenters from stern rule of Mass. Puritans & from the more tolerant jurisdiction of Providence colonists. Mass. took over Gorton's settlement by force & condemned him to death; sentence commuted to banishment. He returned under protection of Earl of Warwick, for whom he named colony. Settlement was destroyed by Inds. during King Philip's War. Warwick became center of textile industry. Within limits are many beaches as well as fresh-water ponds. (Take **St.117** & then West Shore Rd. past or near, shore pts. & several fine beach resorts.)

**45. GORTON POND** (R) (boat.f.). **50.** Outskirts of **CRANSTON.** J. with US1 Alt.

SIDE TRIP: (R) on US1 Alt. to picturesque **Pawtuxet** on Pawtuxet R. (boat.f.). Near village are following Reserves (pub.boat.f.): Pawtuxet R., Edgewood Beach & Stillhouse Cove. From Pawtuxet take Narragansett Pky. (S) to **Gaspee Pt.,** where (1772) Brit. ship "Gaspee" went aground & was burnt by Amer. Patriots (see Providence).

**55. PROVIDENCE** (see).

### Sec. 6: From PROVIDENCE, R.I., to MASS. LINE. 5.5.
(for this sec. see Providence)

### Sec. 7: From R.I.-MASS. LINE to BOSTON. 36.

**7.5.** Js. N. Washington St. & St.1A, alt. route to Boston.

SIDE TRIPS: (A) On N. Wash. St. (L), **North Attleboro,** 1m, an industrial town. At 224 S. Washington St., **N. Attleboro Hist. Soc.** (Old Hatch H. O.summer). Orig. sign, "Steam Boat Hotel, I. Hatch," is in Society's possession; adj., **Hist. Mus.**

(B) Alt. route on St.1A to J. with US1 near Dedham, 21m. At 1m **Plainville;** int. old village. At 16.5m **Norwood,** another industrial town; home also of Plimpton Press (O) & Norwood Press (O). **Norwood Mem. Mun. Bldg.** has lofty tower & fine chimes. Walpole & Beacon Sts., **Morrill Mem. Lib.,** on whose grounds is stone comm. Capt. Aaron Guild, who took part in Battle of Lexington. 93 Day St., **Day H.** (O.appl.c.1860.remod.); antiques, genealogical charts & other hist. material. **Ebenezer Dean Homestead** (c.1700) & **Guild Homestead** (1794) are well-preserved. At 21m **Dedham** (see below). J. with US1.

**19.5.** J. with Moose Hill R., which runs (R) to **Moose Hill Bird Sanctuary;** fine view from Tower. **27. DEDHAM** (sett. 1635) is an industrial town & practically a suburb of Boston; scene of Sacco-Vanzetti trial. PTS. OF INT.: (1) 612 High St., **Dedham Hist. Soc.** (1887), on site of first P. O. (est.1795); very int. coll. of antiques & other items. (2) **Norfolk County Cth.** (1827), where trial (1918) of Sacco & Vanzetti took place. (3) Tablet on County Registry Bldg. marks **Site of Woodward Tavern,** where met Convention (1774) that eventually (in Milton) adopted Suffolk Resolves, which "lighted the match that kindled the mighty conflagration" of the Amer. Rev. Also Tablet marking **Birthpl. of Fisher Ames,** conservative politician of 18th & early 19th cents. & author of Lucius Brutus papers. (4) 511 East St., **Fairbanks H.** (O.Ap.-Nov.oldest part built 1636.well-preserved); antique items. (5) On Green are: **First Ch.** (orig.1638.present bldg.1762.remod.1819). (6) Near-by, Tablet on **Site of Ames School** (orig.1644-45). (7) **Base of Pillar of Liberty** (1766), erected by Sons of Liberty to comm. Wm. Pitt "who saved America from impending slavery." (8) High St., **Allin Mem. Ch.** (1819). (9) **Community (Haven) H.** (O.1795-99). (10) On hill off Ames St., **Powder H.** (1766). (11) 74 Church St., **Horace Mann's Office,** where famous educator practiced law in early 19th cent. (12) East St., **Avery Oak,** 80′ high & 16′ in circumference; standing when first settlers arrived. (13) Inters. Bridge & High Sts., **Training Field,** rendezvous for militia during King Philip's War. (17) Village St., **Burial Ground,** dating from 1636. (18) Court St., tablet comm. **French Army's Encampment** (1782). (19) East & Washington Sts., **Mother Brook,** 1st Canal in Amer. (1639), conn. Charles R. & East Brook. Just beyond Dedham, St.1A merges with US1.

**36. BOSTON** (see).

### Sec. 8: From BOSTON, MASS. to N.H. LINE. 42.

(St.1A (see Boston Trip IV) is much more attractive route to Portsmouth, N.H., giving access to coast resorts & int. old towns.)

**0.** At Commonwealth Ave. & Cottage Farm Bridge. US1 now passes through **CAMBRIDGE,** skirts **SOMERVILLE** at **3.5.** (L) here on Somerville Ave. into Somerville, suburb of Boston & industrial city on Mystic R., with pop. of more than 100,000. Has meat packing & paper products plants. Ford Assembly Plant (O.appl.). First Nat. Stores has its chief office in city. PTS. OF INT.: In Nathan Tufts Pk., facing Powder H. Sq., **Old Powder H.** (c.1703), built first as a gristmill; here stored powder seized by Brit. Gen. Gaige, 1774. 78 Sycamore St., **Oliver Tufts H.** (18th cent.), occupied by Amer. officers during Rev. On Munroe St., **Prospect Hill Tower,** where stood Rev. fort. Here Brit. captured at Battle of Saratoga were held prisoner. Near-by, **Tablet,** recording that here was flown 1st Amer. flag. On Washington St., near its J. with Sumner St., **Marker** comm. Jas. Miller, killed here by Brit. after Battle of Lexington. On Highland Ave. & Walnut St., **Central Hill Pk.** Here are **Civil War Mon.** by A. Lukeman & **Sp. War Mon.** by R. Porter. Near-by **Pub. Lib.** (O.wks.) in which is reprod. of Parthenon frieze. On Sumner St., near Belmont St.,

**St. Catherine's Ch.** (Cath.by Maginnis & Walsh), notable bldg. **Tufts College** is on College Ave. at city line, in adj. Medford (see).

US1 now crosses **EVERETT,** Boston industrial suburb. 88 Waverly St., Milburn coll. of Hawthorneiana (O.to qualified persons). At **6.** is J. with St.1A (see). At **9.,** J. with Salem St.

SIDE TRIP: Take latter (L) into **Malden.** On Malden Sq., **Malden Pub. Lib.** (O.fine example of Richardson's Romanes.); int. art coll. 145 Main St., **Parsonage H.** (1724). Near-by, **Bell Rock Mem. Pk.,** in which is replica of small fort. 51 Appleton St., **Greene H.** (1648).

At **11.** J. with Main St.

SIDE TRIP: Take latter (R) into **Saugus.** On Central St. is **Ironworks H.** (O.1643.many adds.rest.very int.inter.); owned by town; 17th cent. furnishing. Opp. is **Site of Forge** operated in 17th cent.

**12.5.** J. with Lynn Fells Pky.

SIDE TRIP: (L) c.1$^{m}$ on Pky. to Howard St., in Saugus. At No. 7 is **"Scotch" Boardman H.** (O.appl.sm.fee.1651.int.inter.); named for Scotch prisoners taken at Battle of Dunbar by Cromwell & imprisoned here.

US1 now skirts **BREAKHEART RESERV.** (recr.). At **15. SUNTAUG L.** US1 now passes **PURITAN LAWN MEM. PK.** At **24.,** J. with St.97.

SIDE TRIP: Take latter (L) short distance to **Topsfield.** Howlett St. near Common, **Parson Capen H.** (O.wks.in summer.1683.fine inter.), notable example of Col. architecture; period furnishings. **Pub. Lib.** has murals by H. Kellogg. At 1$^{m}$ **Pine Grove Cemetery** (1663). At 5.5$^{m}$ **Boxford.** On Green is pleasant old **First Congr. Ch.** Cor. Elm & Topsfield Rd., **Holyoke-French H.** (O.Sun.aft.sm.fee.1760.rest.1940), primitive portraits & antiques.

**32. DUMMER ACADEMY** (campus O.bldgs.on appl.est.1762). Finest bldg. is **Gov. Dummer Mansion** (1715). At **36.5.** J. with St.1A, near Newburyport (see Boston). Route now crosses Merrimack R. **39. SALISBURY** (c.1638). On Green, **Boulder** marking spot where Maj. Rbt. Pike halted whipping of Quaker women from Dover. J. with St.1A leading (R) past **Old Burying Ground** (1639) to **Salisbury Beach** (bath. recr.) at 2$^{m}$. **42. N.H. LINE.**

### Sec. 9: From MASS.-N.H. LINE to N.H.-ME. LINE. 15.

**3.** Charming **HAMPTON FALLS** village. **Old Wellwood Inn** (R), now a shop. On Lafayette Rd. (US1), **Elmfield** (O.appl.18th cent.), with orig. furnishings. Whittier spent many summers here & died in this house (1892). **Gov. Weare H.** (1735.very fine Col.), on Exeter Rd. near town sq. Mon. comm. Gov. Weare is in Sq.

SIDE TRIP: (L) 5$^{m}$ on Kensington Rd. to **Falls River.** Here is **Dodge H.** (1787) & near-by, **Chapel of the Little Gate** (O), tiny Episc. church, orig. an ice house.

At **5.** (L), **HAUNTED H.** (1769.fine Georg.), also known as Gov. Jon. Moulton H.; celebrated by Whittier in "The New Wife and the Old." Near-by are **Meetingh. Green Pk.** & **Log Cabin** (O.special days & hrs.), reprod. of orig. Meetingh. (L) is **Tuck Mem. H.** (O.special days); hist. relics. Short distance further on US1 is **HAMPTON** (sett.17th cent.), typical New England village. Hampton & Dover are two towns where Quakers were whipped & otherwise persecuted. **10. RYE.** J. with St.1A (see Trips out of Boston).

**15. PORTSMOUTH** (see). US1 crosses Piscataqua R. over Portsmouth-Kittery Bridge into Maine.

### Sec. 10: From PORTSMOUTH, N.H. to PORTLAND, ME. 50.

Autoists in a hurry may take Super Highway (toll 50¢ for passenger autos), from Portsmouth to Portland.

US1 runs fairly close to shore, with frequent Rds. branching off to ocean resorts & coastal towns.

**0. PORTSMOUTH-KITTERY BRIDGE.** Short distance beyond is J. with Rd.

SIDE TRIP: Take this Rd. (R) to **Kittery,** old shipbuilding town & birthpl. of Gen. Wm. Whipple, signer of Decl. of Ind. Near-by on Badger I., the "Ranger," Paul Jones' ship was launched (1777). **Portsmouth Navy Yard** (O) is on I. in harbor; scene of Russo-Jap. Peace Conference (1905); Mus. of Sp. War trophies; also parts of submarine "Squalus," sunk in 1939, raised & renamed "Sailfish" which vanquished many Jap. ships; also German and Amer. submarines (O.appl.). Near Kittery is U.S. Army **Ft. Foster.** At 2$^{m}$ **Congr. Ch.** (1729. alts.), oldest Ch. in Me. In graveyard, Celia Thaxter, poet (see Portsmouth), is buried. Opp. is **Lady Pepperell H.** (O.2nd half 18th cent.fine Georg.); home of wife of Sir Wm. Pepperell, who took part in capture of Louisburg, 1745 (see Hist.). Near-by is **Sparhawk H.**

(1742.int.exter.inter.), home of Mary Sparhawk, who induced Brit. to spare Portsmouth (see). At 2.5m, in **Ft. McClary Mem. Pk.** (pic.bath.), are (R) remains of Ft. McClary (1690. rebuilt.19th cent.). **Block H.** (1812). Ft. was named for Andrew McClary, who fell at Bunker Hill. At 3m **Kittery Point Village,** an old settlement. Pepperell H. (late 17th cent.) home of Wm.'s father. At 8m **Sewall's Bridge.** The orig. bridge on this site was first pile draw bridge (1761) in U.S. Rd. cont. to J. with St.1A, which leads (R) to **York** (sett. 1630); named originally Agamenticus. **Old Gaol** (O.wks.sm.fee.1653); coll. of antiques. Lovely **Ch.** (middle 18th cent.) & old cemetery. On York St., **Jefferd's Tavern** (O.wks.May-Labor Day. 1750); moved from Wells in 1939. St.1A cont. along **York Harbor** (resort) & **York Beach** (resort) to J. with US1, main tour, at Cape Neddick.

**11. CAPE NEDDICK,** J. with St.1A & side Rd., which latter runs (R) along shore, passing over **Bald Head Cliff** high above the sea to **Ogunquit** on US1.

**15. OGUNQUIT** (resort) was chosen by Gorges (see) for his hqs. There is a big summer art colony here. **18.5. OLD CONGR. CH.** (remod.1936). US1 cont. to **MOODY.** (From here Rd. runs (R) along coast via **Wells Beach** (resort) to **Wells,** at J. with US1 again). At **19.** on US1 is **STORER GARRISON H.** where 15 soldiers withstood (1692) siege by 500 Fr. & Inds. **20. WELLS.** At **22.** is J. with St.9.

SIDE TRIP: (R) 3m on St.9 to **Kennebunk Beach** (resort) & (E) to **Kennebunkport** (resort), in which are some fine old Hs. & beautiful **Congr. Ch.** (1784), on Temple St. The late Booth Tarkington had studio here in old bldg. (O) on wharf & old sailing ship (O). Hy. forks in Kennebunkport. St.9A runs (W) to **Kennebunk** (see below), while St.9 leads along shore past **Cape Porpoise** to **Goose Rocks** (Beachwood), artists' colony. Watercolor Gallery (summer exhibits). St.9 cont. (N) to **Fortune Rocks** (resort) near **Biddeford Pool** (resort). Here it turns (W) to J. with US1 in Biddeford.

**25. KENNEBUNK** (sett.1650), resort. In 1947 for. fires swept through vic. of Kennebunk, Kennebunkport & Biddeford destroying many bldgs. **First Parish Unitarian Ch.** (1774.19th cent.alts.). On Storer St. **Storer H.** (post-Rev.), birthpl. of Kenneth Roberts, author. **Lafayette Elm,** huge tree under which Lafayette received townsfolk in 1825. On Main St., **Five Elms** which, legend maintains, were planted on day Lexington battle was fought. Among numerous old mansions are **Nathaniel Frost H.** & **Bourne H.** (1850). (R) 1m on St.35 is **Wedding Cake H.** (c.1825), with most unusual Vict. trimmings. **33. BIDDEFORD** (sett.c.1630), on W. bank of Saco R.; an industrial town with textile mills & other mfg. plants (O). **34. SACO** (sett. c.1629), on E. bank of Saco R. 375 Main St., **York Institute;** colls. of antiques, art, Ind. relics. 271 Main St., **Cyrus King H.** (1807), now rectory of Cath. Ch. In Saco is J. with St.5 & St.9. (R) on St.9 are good beaches & summer resorts, incl. famous **Old Orchard Beach** (amusements).

SIDE TRIP: From **Saco** to **South Arm** (Richardson L.). 126m St.5.

Via: Waterboro Center, Cornish, Hiram, Fryeburg, Lovell Village, Center Lovell. B. & Me. RR. in Saco, Bethel, Newry & Andover. Hiram to Fryeburg, Me. Central RR.; Bethel, Grand Trunk RR. (to Shelburne, N.H.). Bus: Hiram to Fryeburg.

This route traverses pleasant lake & mountain country along Saco R. Valley, at Lovell Village & Center Lovell passes by beautiful Kezar L. N. of Kezar L. to Bethel, it skirts Me. sec. of White Mt. Nat. For. From Bethel St.5 runs (NE) to Rumford Pt. where it turns (N) through fine wilderness area to terminus at Richardson L., one of the Rangeley chain. At 14m J. with St.4-US202, running (SW) to Portsmouth. At 33.5m **Cornish.** J. with St.25 running (W) into L. Winnepesaukee Reg. of N.H. 54m **Fryeburg** at J. with US302 leading (W) to Conway in heart of White Mts. At 91m **Bethel.** J. with US2 (see) & St.26 (see). At 103.5m **Rumford Pt.** Here St.5 turns (N) to **South Arm** (Richardson L.) at 126m.

**43. OAK HILL.** J. with St.207.

SIDE TRIP: (R) on St.207 past **Hunnewell H.** (1684.rest.) to **Scarboro** where is **Parson Lancaster H.** (1766). St.207 cont. past **Higgins Beach** (resort) & **Massacre Pond** where, in 1713, Richard Hunnewell & followers were trapped by Inds. Farther on is marker on spot where Chief Mogg Heigon was killed (see Whittier's "Mogg Megone") & a half-mile beyond, **Prout's Neck** (sett.1633), resort.

**50. PORTLAND** (see).

## Sec. 11: PORTLAND to BRUNSWICK, ME. 29.

**0. PORTLAND.** US1 cont. along Casco Bay, with its 365 Is. **13. YARMOUTH** (sett. 1635), shipbuilding town, now devoted to fisheries & handling of fish products. In vic. are **Old Academy, Old Bapt. Ch.** (1796) & **Ind. Burial Ground** (early 1700's). **19. FREEPORT.** In **Old Tavern** (1779), it is claimed, an agreement was signed with Mass., 1820, est. Maine as a separate state. **29. BRUNSWICK** (RR. & Bus Stas. on Maine St. Airport. Info. C. of C.), on Androscoggin R., was first sett. (1628) by Thos.

Purchase; city was known in early days as Pejepscot. In 1714, the Pejepscot Proprietors received grant of land incl. site of Brunswick. New settlement was destroyed by Inds. in 1690 & again in 1722. In Brunswick, Harriet Beecher Stowe wrote "The Pearl of Orr's Island" (see below) & "Uncle Tom's Cabin." Formerly a lumber-exporting & shipbuilding center, town today has pulp, paper, rayon, cloth, canning & other industries, but is best known as home of Bowdoin College. One of its famous citizens was Sam. Melcher, architect who designed many of New England's finest old bldgs. As in many New England towns, population is largely from French-Canadian stock. PTS. OF INT.: (1) Union & Oak Sts., **Gilman Mansion** (O.appl.sm.fee.1789.by Melcher.remod.1840.fine inter.& exter.); period furnishings & relics. (2) 25 Federal St., **Emmons H.** (1814.alts.), home of Longfellow while professor at Bowdoin College. (3) 27 Federal St., **Old Gov. Dunlap H.** (4) 12 School St., **Pejepscot Hist. Mus.** (O.wks.July-Aug.); hist. colls. (5) 63 Federal St., **Harriet Beecher Stowe H.** (O.1806.remod.1941) where author wrote "Uncle Tom's Cabin." (6) 75 Federal St., **Rundlett-Chandler H.** (1806.by Melcher.very fine).

SIDE TRIPS: (A) Take Maine St. (S). At 7m is **Mem. Boulder,** comm. landing at Mare's Point of first round-the-world flight (1924).

(B) St.123 down Harpswell Peninsula, c.13m. PTS. OF INT.: **Old Town H.** (1788). **Elijah Kellogg Ch.** (1843). Kellogg, author of popular boys' books, was minister here. S. is **Eagle I.,** summer home of the late Adm. Rbt. Peary, discoverer of N. Pole.

(C) St.24 makes round trip to **Bailey I.** 28m, crosses Great I. on which is **Candy's Harbor** (resort); then to **Orr's I.** In Orr's Village is **Pearl of Orr H.,** home figuring in Mrs. Stowe's "Pearl of Orr's Island." Route crosses to Bailey I. (summer resort); steamers from here to Portland touch at several Is. on route to Casco Bay. **Ragged Is.** can be seen here; owned by Edna St. Vincent Millay.

(D) US201 (N) to **Canadian Border.** 70.5m

Via: Topsham, Gardiner, Hallowell, Augusta, Winslow, Waterville, Fairfield, Norridgewock, Madison, Solon, Bingham, The Forks, Jackman Sta. & Moose R.

Route follows Kennebec R. for c.128m to The Forks, when route branches off through lake & for. reg. (good h.f.canoe).

1m **Topsham,** 26 Elm St., **Aldrich H.** (1800.by Sam Melcher.very fine). 21.5m **Peacock Tavern** (c.1790), still hotel. 25.5m **Gardiner,** boyhood home of poet, Edwin A. Robinson. 30m **Hallowell.** Old Powder H., Vaughan Mansion & Worster H. (O.1832), famous hotel. 31.5m **Augusta** (see below), Js. with US202, St.9, St.27 (running NW. to Belgrade Ls.) & other main routes. 42.5m **Vassalboro.** Grove Academy (est.1840) on whose campus is **Wild Life Sanctuary.** 50.5m **Winslow,** paper mfg. town. At J. of Kennebec & Sebasticook Rs., Lithgow St., **Lithgow H.** (late 18th cent.). On Sebasticook R., **Block H.** (O.1754) remains of Ft. Halifax. View of **Ticonic Falls.** 51.5m **Waterville** (sett.c.1754.RR.bus.airport.accoms.), on Kennebec R. at Ticonic Falls, which provide power for cotton & woolen mills, paper factories, was shipping center until coming of RRs. PTS. OF INT.: College Ave., **Colby College** (founded 1813). On Old Campus are **Mem. Hall** (1869.Norman.by A.R.Estey), **South College** (1821), **Champlin Hall** (1836.by Thos.Utter), **Coburn Hall** (1872), **North College** (1822). On Mayflower Hill is New Campus (600 as.), with mod. (Amer.Col.) bldgs., to which college is in process of transferring. **Miller Lib.,** focal point, has E. A. Robinson, Henry James & Book Arts colls. 64 Silver St., **Redington Mus.** (O.wks.except Mon.1814. Col.); hist. & archeology colls. Main St., **Old Ind. Burial Ground.** 61.5m **Goodwill Farm** (O.wks.); Mus. This is a privately endowed school for deserving boys & girls. 69m J. with US2 (see) & St.147 just S. of Skowhegan (see US2). St.147 is a shorter alternate to Solon (see below). 75m **Norridgewock** (see US2). J. with US2. 80.5m **Father Rasles Mon.** comm. Jesuit missionary who founded 1st school (1696) on Kennebunk R. He was tarred & feathered by Brit. during sack of Norridgewock (1724). 81m **Old Pt.** (pic.camp.). 87.5m **North Anson.** From bridge across Carrabasset R., view of falls. 95.5m **Solon.** In vic. is **Caratunk Falls.** Short distance from Falls is marker comm. spot where Benedict Arnold's expedition to Canada passed (1775). 104m **Bingham.** J. with St.16, near point where Wyman Dam impounds Kennebunk R. **Old Ch.** (1836). 113.5m **Tablet** comm. Arnold expedition into Canada. 128m **The Forks.** Here Kennebunk & Dead Rs. join (see canoe trips). In vic. (R) c.5m are **Moxy L. & Falls.** 137.5m Trl. to summit of Coburn Mt. (3,718′). 142.5m **Parlin L.** (trout & salmon f.resort). 154.5m **Jackman Sta.** Here is Junction with St.15 (R) to Rockwood on Moosehead L. (see) 32m. 157m **Moose R.** in lumbering reg. One hotel, Holden Tavern (1842). 170.5m **Canadian Line** 93m (S) of Quebec, Canada.

## Sec. 12: From BRUNSWICK to THOMASTON, ME. 50.

**0. BRUNSWICK. 8. BATH** (sett.c.1660), on Kennebec R.; formerly great shipbuilding center. The "Virginia," claimed to be 1st vessel built (1607) in America, was constructed at near-by Popham, & many clipper ships came from Bath Yards. Here was built "The Ranger," American Cup defender. On Front St., **Bath Iron**

**Works** (O.appl.), shipyard, very active during both World Wars. **Davenport Mem. Bldg.;** Mus. has maritime exhibits. On Whiskeag Rd., **Residence** (1805) **of Wm. King,** first Gov. of Maine. On Washington St., **Peterson H.** (1770). In Winnegance, suburb of Bath, is **Old Lumber Mill** operated until recently by tides.

SIDE TRIP: On St.209, 216 & 217 (S) to **Ft. Popham,** 46m round trip. St.209 runs along Peninsula, with good views of the sea. At 7m **Phippsburg** (sett.1737). **James McCobb H.** (1774.int.inter.). Other pts. of int. on routes: **Sabasco & Small Pt.** (resorts). At 16.5m **Ft. Baldwin** (O). Here was site of settlement made by Sir Geo. Popham (1607). At 17m **Popham Beach.** Ft. Popham (O.1861) & Ft. Popham Light. Seguin I. Lighth. (O) on Seguin I.

**9.5. WOOLWICH** (sett.1638), first known as Nequasset.

SIDE TRIP: St.127 (S) to Georgetown & Five Islands & return, 25m. This picturesque route crosses several Is. with fine view of Kennebec R. & Sheepscot Bay. **Five Islands** (resort) with good beach.

**11.** (L) **NEQUASSET MEETINGH.** (1757). **19. WISCASSET** (sett.17th cent.). Charming old town, originally known as Pownalborough. On a specific day in Aug., all hist. houses are open (fee) for benefit of Pub. Lib. It was Capt. Sam. Clough, a native, who plotted to rescue Marie Antoinette & bring her to America (see N. Edgecomb below). Failing this, he brought back some of the Queen's possessions. Talleyrand is supposed to have visited town on trip to U.S. David Robinson made 1st ice cream in America here, served to Gen. Lafayette (1825). Among handsome old bldgs.: On Common, **Lincoln County Cth.** (1824), oldest functioning in Me.; Daniel Webster practiced law here. **Town Lib.** (O.wks.aft.early 19th cent.); curios, old fire apparatus & other exhibits. On High St., **Lee-Payson-Smith H.** (early 19th cent.fine example). High & Lee Sts., **Abiel Wood H.** (1812). At Main & Fort Sts., **Nickels-Sortwell H.** (1807). E. end of High St., **Tucker Mansion** (1807.adds.), alleged copy of Dunbar Castle, Scotland. **Meetingh.** (1909) is charming reprod. of one destroyed by fire (1907); has rare Paul Revere bell. Wiscasset is at J. with St.218 & St.27.

SIDE TRIPS: (A) St.218 (L) 7m to **Alna Meetingh.** (1789.O.appl.int.inter.). At 10m **Head Tide,** birthpl. of E. A. Robinson, poet.

(B) Unnumbered Rds. & St.127 to **Newagen** & return, 39m. Take Rd. (R) at c.1m (E) of bridge at Wiscasset. About 0.5m from J. is J. with unimproved Rd. (R) on latter to **Fort Edgecomb** (grounds O.c.1809); int. Block H.; fine view. At 1m, in North Edgecomb Village, **Marie Antoinette H.** (O.appl.1774), built by Capt. Decker on Squaw I. Later it was owned by Capt. Clough (see Wiscasset above). At 1.5m J. with St.27, on which route cont. (S) to **Edgecomb** (sett.1774) & **Boothbay** (sett.1630.resort), where is ancient **Meetingh.** & cemetery. Near-by is **E. Boothbay,** where is century-old Tide Mill. Route cont. to **Boothbay Harbor** (resort); steamers to Squirrel & Monhegan Is. Info. Bur. in Town Hall. Between Monhegan I. & Pemaquid Pt. occurred (1813) naval battle bet. Amer. "Enterprise" & Brit. "Boxer." Route cont. to **Southport** (resort), steamers to Boothbay, Bath & Newagen, where is Tablet comm. visit (1623) by Christopher Levitt, founder of Portland.

(C) On St.27 (NW) to **Stratton, Me.** 109m.

Via: Pittston, Randolph, Gardiner, Hallowell, Augusta, Belgrade, Farmington, Kingfield & Bigelow. Me. Central RR. & bus conns. to Farmington. Js. with main tours in Augusta, near New Sharon, & at Stratton with St.4 which runs to Rangeley Ls.

Route runs along Kennebec R., past Belgrade L. & then along Carrabassett R. through wilderness country. At 10.5m J. with St.128; (L) here 3m to **Powneborough Cth.** (1761), where Tories were tried during Rev. 24m **Augusta** (see below). 35m Belgrade. 36 m J. with St.11 (E) along Belgrade Ls. to Waterville (see). 42m **Belgrade Ls.** (resort) a beautiful chain of Ls. (trout, salmon, bass). 95m **Carrabassett,** on R. of same name. At 101.5m **Bigelow,** near which is Bigelow Game Reserv. (no h.). 109m **Stratton,** J. with St.16-St.4.

**26.5. NEWCASTLE** (sett.17th cent.) still has many well-preserved early houses.

SIDE TRIP: (L) here 2.5m is **Kavanaugh H.** (1803.fine example). At 3m **St. Patrick's Ch.** (Cath.1803-08); very old Fr. altar & painting seized during Mex. War.

**27. DAMARISCOTTA,** named for Chief Damorin who was also known as Chief Robin Hood. In vic. are **Capt. Wm. Vaughan & Cottrell** (1803) **Hs.** J. with St.129.

SIDE TRIP: On St.129, 130 & 132 (S) down Peninsula & back to J. with US1. 56m via Christmas Cove & Waldoboro. (S) 3m on St.129 is J. with St.130, which Side Trip follows (S).

St.129 cont. (S) 3m to **Walpole.** Old Ch. (1772.services in summer); then to **South Bristol & Christmas Cove,** summer resorts.

At 10.5m **Pemaquid.** Old Cemetery. Rd. (R) from Pemaquid leads to excellent **Pemaquid Beach.** Here are Replica of Ft. Wm. Henry (O.1692) with relics; Old Cemetery; Dunbar H. built in 1720. St.130 cont. to **New Harbor** (resort) at 13m. This was home of Chief Samoset, who had learned words "Welcome, Englishmen" with which he greeted Pilgrims at Plymouth. Pemaquid Pt. Lighth. Take St.32 (NE) from New Harbor past **Round Pond,** to J. with US1 at 56m.

**36.5.** J. with St.220, just (N) of Waldoboro (see below).

SIDE TRIP: (S) on St.220 into **Waldoboro,** sett. by Germans (1748), on Monadnock R. First Amer. 3- & 5-masted schooners built here. **Lutheran Ch.** (1795). **Old German Cemetery** (1750). **Col. Isaac Reed Mansion; Old Shipyards.** St.220 cont. (S) to charming village of **Friendship** (sett.1743), then turns (NE) across peninsula to J. with US1 near S. Warren.

At c.**44.** US1 turns (SE) to **SOUTH WARREN.** At **49.** J. with Rd., the peninsular route (see above). In vic. are **Knox St. Arboretum & Academy of Arts & Sciences;** zoological, botanical, mineral & Ind. colls. **50. THOMASTON** (sett.c.1730), on St. George's R. Steamers to coastal pts. **Weymouth Boulder** marks first landing of Capt. George Weymouth (1605). Thomaston claims New England's largest cement works. About 1m beyond, on US1, is **Montpelier** (O.summer.fee.1928), reprod. of home (1793) of Gen. Henry Knox, hero of Bunker Hill; many Knox items & furnishings.

SIDE TRIP: (S) on St.131 to Port Clyde. 31m round trip. Route runs down Peninsula, along St. George's R. At **Port Clyde,** steamer conn. with coastal pts. & Is.

## Sec. 13: From THOMASTON to BELFAST. 31.

**0. THOMASTON. 4.5. ROCKLAND** (resort). Info.: C. of C. Steamers to North Haven, Vinalhaven & Deer I. in Penobscot Bay (see Orland below). Rockland boasts it ships out more lime than any other U.S. port, also great quantities of fish. Its lobsters are famous. Navy tests new ships offshore. 200 Broadway, **Birthpl. of Edna St. Vincent Millay,** the poet, & **Farnsworth Lib. & Art Mus.** (O); colls. incl. paintings, art objects & glassware. Adj. is old **Farnsworth Homestead** (O), where lived Lucy Farnsworth, who endowed Mus. Rockland is at J. with St.17. On St.17. (S) is **Owl's Head Lighth.** (O.1826). Fine view from cliff. **10.5. ROCKPORT** (resort). Alpine Gardens & Amesbury Hill. **12. CAMDEN** (resort), surrounded by picturesque hills. **Bok Amphitheater** (concerts). **Camden Hills St. Pk.** (pic.camp.trlr.). Near-by (W) is **Megunticook L.** Mun. bath. beach. at **Bayview Beach.** (L) 1m on St.137 is trl. to **Mt. Battie;** fine view. (St.137 cont. to Lincolnville Center, whose **Meetingh.** is one of oldest in state.) **17.5. LINCOLNVILLE** (resort) Ferry to Islesboro I. **31. BELFAST** (sett.1770), on Penobscot Bay. Has Info. Bur. **City Pk.** (trlr. camp.pool); boat to Islesboro. 30 Church St., **White H.** (1825). 130 Main St., **Clay H.** (1825). 137 High St., **Field H.** (1807). Also on High St., **Blaisdell Mansion** (supposedly from designs by Christopher Wren); **Sexton H.** (1779); **Old Bishop & Williamson Hs.; Jeremiah Evans H.** (1827); former home of Adm. Wm. V. Pratt (1812). On Poor Mill Rd., **Jos. Miller Tavern.** On High St., (N) of town, **Otis H.** (1800).

## Sec. 14: From BELFAST to BANGOR. 35.

**0. BELFAST. 6. SEARSPORT.** Near close of 19th cent., one-tenth of all Amer. ships were commanded by Searsport captains, & in that century, 2121 ships were built here. **Penobscot Marine Mus.** (O) hist. material concerning Me. shipping. At c.**10. STOCKTON SPRINGS,** J. with US1 Alt.

SIDE TRIP: US1 Alt., short-cut to Ellsworth (see below). At 8m across Penobscot R. (toll bridge) is **Bucksport.** In cemetery "Witch's Curse" is a mark on a gravestone attributed to a curse put by a condemned woman on Col. Jas. Buck for whom town was named. Fish Hatchery at Craig Brook. **Jed Prouty Tavern** (1804). **Congr. Ch.** (1848). From here US1 Alt. cuts across neck of a ragged peninsula. 9m **Orland,** J. with St.175, US1 Alt. cont. to **Ellsworth** at 27m.

Take St.175 (S) from Orland on a beautiful coastal trip. At c.12m on St.175 is J. with St.166; (S) on St.166 to **Castine** (sett.1626), resort named for Baron Vincent de St. Castin, who married daughter of Ind. chief. Baron Castin took part in conflicts with the Brit. The town changed hands several times during Fr. & Ind. War. During Rev., it was occupied by Brit. Among beautiful old bldgs. are: **Old Meetingh.** (1790); **Old Courth.** (1800), now Lib. On Perkins St., **Wilson Mus.** (O.wks.). Cor. Main & Court Sts., **Blake H.** (O.1797.add.1857); orig. furnishings. Amer. **Ft. Madison** (O.1812) & **Ft. George** (O.1814), latter built by Brit. Boats from Castine to Belfast & Islesboro.

From Castine return via St.166 & St.199 to J. with St.175 (S) on St.175 to Sargentville. J. with St.172. Take St.172 (S) 5m across New Bridge to **Deer Isle.** At Stonington, on I., **Eastern Penobscot Archive Mus.** (O) with Penobscot Bay area material. Return by St.172 to J. with St.175, then (E) on St.172 to **Blue Hill,** home of Ethelbert Nevin, composer. **Congr. Ch.** (1772). Cont. through **Surry** to **Ellsworth** (see below). J. with US1.

**14.5.** on US1, **PROSPECT.** (R) here on St.174 is old **Ft. Knox St. Reserv.** (1846), built of massive granite. **21.5. WINTERPORT.** In Congr. ch. is Paul Revere Bell

(1832). **Blaisdell H.** (1786), attributed to Christopher Wren, & several other fine old mansions. **Dorothy Dix Mem. Pk.**

**30.5. HAMPDEN,** captured by Brit. in War of 1812. J. with US202.

SIDE TRIP: (W) on US202. At 42.5m **China** on China L. 45m **Friends Meetingh.** (alts.). 49m **S. China** (J. with St.3). 60m **Augusta** (Me. Central RR., bus conns.accoms.). Augusta (sett.1629), lies on both sides of the Kennebec R. It is the St. Capital as well as industrial center (cotton, shoes, pulp, paper). Business sec. is for most part on W. side of R. which supplies water for Augusta's industries. John Alden (see Longfellow's "Courtship of Miles Standish") shared command in 1634 of 1st settlement with John Howland, also one of orig. Mayflower immigrants. During 1st half of 19th cent., city was important shipping center. In 1832 it became St. Capital. PTS. OF INT.: (1) On Bowman St., **Ft. Western** (O.summer. fee.1754.rest.& furnished in period); coll. of items from Southwest. (2) Near-by is **Boulder** with tablet comm. passage of Benedict Arnold expedition to Canada, 1775. (3) SW. cor. Stone & Cony Sts., **Reuel Williams H.** (O.appl.c.1810.Fed.); portraits, old furnishings, hist. relics. (4) N. of bridge, **Kennebec Dam** (1837). (5) NW. cor. Capitol & State Sts., **Blaine H.** (O.wks.except Sat.2-4.executive mansion.1830.remod.). (6) Capitol & State Sts., **State H.** (O.1829-32.wings & dome added 1911); Mus. with hist. relics. (7) Capitol & Union Sts., **State Pk.** (8) 81 Green St., **Stump of the Jacataqua Oak,** named for an Ind. princess. (9) State & Court Sts., **Kennebec Cty. Jail** (pre-1835). (10) Winthrop & State Sts., **Lithgow Lib.** (1895.Romanes.Ren.by J.Neal & A.Hopkins.int.stained glass windows); material on New England. (11) On Western Ave., **St. Mary's Ch.** (Cath.1927.Norman Goth.very fine). (12) On Western Ave., **Ganeston Pk.** (O.pedestrians only). In Augusta are Js. with main hys. Near Augusta, **Hallowell** (c.1754), Me.'s smallest incorporated city, with near-by granite quarries & number of int. bldgs. incl.: **First Bapt. Ch.** with steeple copied from Sir Christopher Wren; **Hubbard Lib.,** with hist. mus.; **Page H.** (early 1800s) & **Vaughan H.** (1796). 65m **Manchester,** formerly known as The Forks. 66.5m entrance to **Island Pk.** on Cobbosseecontee L. (recr.amusements.launch trips). 71m **Winthrop** (1765) at Ls. Maranacook & Annabessacook. 89m (On Rd. 2m here (R) is **Gulf Is. Dam** on Androscoggin R.). 91.5m **Lewiston** (sett.1770) & **Auburn** (sett.1786) are twin cities, situated on opp. sides of Androscoggin R. at Lewiston Falls. Lewiston is textile manufacturing town & Auburn makes shoes. Cities are connected by bridges. (Me. Central RR. & busses serve both cities. Accoms.). In Lewiston: **Textile Plants** (O.appl.) are for the most part on Canal St. On Campus Ave., **Bates College** (1864.coed.). On campus are the Chapel (1912.Coll.Goth.); oldest bldg., Hawthorne Hall (1856) on College St., Carnegie Sci. Bldg. with Stanton Mus. & fine ornithological & geological colls. & Coram Lib., with colls. hist. documents. From campus, path runs to summit of **Mt. David.** From N. Bridge, view of Lewiston Falls & Dam, supplying water power. In Auburn: **Androscoggin County Cth.**; murals, hist. relics. **Goff Hill,** fine views. At Auburn is J. with St.4 (see). From Auburn route cont. on St.11 (R) (NW) from US202. 108m **Tripp L.** (bath.pic.recr.). 122m St.11 joins with US302 to **Naples** (see Portland) at 123m. US302 cont. to N.H.

**35. BANGOR** (sett. 1769).

Exchange & Washington Sts., RR. Union Sta. Bus. conns. at Bangor House & Union (bus) Sta. Airport (NW) 3m on Cooper Rd. Info.: Maine Publicity Bur., on Post Office Sq., & C. of C. at 23 Franklin St. Accoms.: All types. Symphony House. Art exhibits at Pub. lib., 145 Harlow St. Fish. in Salmon Pool & in many Ls. within radius of 50m.

Bangor, formerly known as Kenduskeag, is located at head of navigation on Penobscot R., at point where Kenduskeag Stream bisects city to join the R. In 1604, Champlain sailed up Penobscot to Falls (near present Salmon Pool), but not till 1769 was 1st permanent settlement made, by Jacob Buswell. When inc. in 1791, town received its present name after "Bangor," favorite hymn of its 1st pastor, Seth Noble. City was occupied by Brit. during War of 1812. From 1830's on, Bangor's growth depended on lumber snaked down from the backwoods, driven over falls, & worked up by local sawmills. Shipbuilding & shipping became corollary to lumbering, & Bangor built vessels for lumber trade & became a great port. In those days lumbermen & sailors turned the city into a "wide-open" town, not unlike some lumber towns of Pac. Northwest, of more recent date. Bangor still depends on lumber, pulp, woodworking & shipping for much of its employment; also center of important hydroelectric system. It is starting point for vacationists headed for Moosehead & Ls. farther (N), for Mt. Katahdin, & also for coastal resorts. **Dow Field,** near Bangor, is Air Force military base where newest jet-propelled planes are stationed. PTS. OF INT.: (1) 5th St., **Hannibal Hamlin H.** (O.appl.), home of Vice Pres. under Lincoln. (2) **Hamlin Statue** (by Chas.E.Tefft) is in Kenduskeag Pky., where also is (3) **Tablet** comm. Champlain's visit (Sept. 1604), & cannon taken from Amer. ship lost offshore (1779). (4) 145 Harlow St., **Pub. Lib.** (O); Bangor Hist. Soc. Mus. (O.wks.). (5) 166 Union St., **Symphony H.** (c.1833.attrib.to Rich.Upjohn), home of Bangor Symphony Soc. (6) Cor. Union & Hammond Sts., **Union Theological Seminary** (O. Congr.est.1814), originally known as Maine Charity School. (7) 117 Court St., **Jos. Garland H.** (1830.attrib.to Rich.Upjohn). (8) In Davenport Pk., at Main St., **U.S. Battleship Maine Mon.** (9) 157 Broadway, **Boutelle H.** (1834.attrib.to Bulfinch). (10) State St., **Grotto Cascades Pk.,** illuminated. (11) Harlow St., **Pierce Mem.** (by Tefft), vivid portrayal in bronze of lumbermen & river drivers. (12) In Norumbego Pky., along Kenduskeag Stream, is **Veterans Mem.** (by Tefft). (13) In Summit Pk., **Observatory.** Bangor is at J. with US2, St.9 (in Brewer) & St.15 which runs (NE) to Moosehead L. (see). [US2 (see) (N) $8^m$ to Orono, once called Stillwater, seat of Un. of Maine.]

## Sec. 15: From BANGOR to ELLSWORTH. 26.5.

**0. BANGOR.** Across R. is **Brewer,** industrial suburb, where, at State & Main Sts., is **Old Chillicote H.** (antique shop). 80 Chamberlain St., **Joshua Chamberlain H.,** home of famous Civil War General. **12. LUCERNE-IN-MAINE,** resort on shores of beautiful Philips L. **26.5. ELLSWORTH** (Info.Bur.), on Union R.; much damaged by for. fire of 1947. Is known as Gateway to Mt. Desert I. On State St., handsome **Congr. Ch.** (1812). **Tisdale H.** (O.pre-1812), now Pub. Lib. on W. Main St., **Black Mansion** (O.May-Nov.fee); family relics, painting, antiques. (N) is **Graham L.** (good f.). In Ellsworth US1 Alt. rejoins main tour. Also J. with St.3, which runs (S) to Bar Harbor.

SIDE TRIP: (S) on St.3 & St.102 to Mt. Desert I., $80^m$ round trip. Via: Bar Harbor & Acadia Nat. Pk. One of most beautiful & exciting tours in Maine. Accoms.: In Bar Harbor & other towns. Bridge across Narrows to **Mt. Desert I.** St.3 skirts (N) & (E) shore. At $14^m$ **Salisbury Cove,** with view of lively Frenchman's Harbor. **Mt. Desert I. Biological Lab.** (O.on special days). $20^m$ **Bar Harbor,** fashionable resort. Cars for rent. Info. Bur. at West St. Bath. beach. Boat trips to various Is. Hqs. of Acadia Nat. Pk. at Main St. & Park Rd. (guide & lecture serv. on hikes & sea-trips. Auto caravans. Fireside programs. Pub. campgrounds near Bar Harbor & Seawall).

Mt. Desert I. was discovered by Champlain, 1604. In 1688, Louis XIV gave Island to Sieur de La Mothe Cadillac, later founder of Detroit (see Mich.) & Gov. of Louisiana. In 1713, it was ceded to England. First settlement, c.1759. Mass. gave Mt. Desert I. to Sir Francis Bernard, last Brit. Gov. &, although his property was confiscated, the State gave half of I. to his son after Rev. Other half was given to Cadillac's granddaughter whose grave is at Hull's Cove. Both owners sold their shares, & I. became fashionable summer colony after Civil War. **Acadia Nat. Pk.** (est.1916), wildlife sanctuary comprising 15,000 as., is one of most beautiful tracts in Eastern U.S. It centers around **Mt. Cadillac** (1,532′). On Oct. 17, 1947, the I. was swept by disastrous fire that destroyed bldgs. & improvements valued at 8 to 10 million dollars. Some 17,000 as. of for. land were burnt over.

Harbor St. (R) to Mt. Cadillac Dr. At $1.5^m$ is **Entrance to Acadia Nat. Pk.** (R) $2.5^m$ here on Rd. to beautiful Eagle L., Jordan Pond & Seal Harbor (see below). At $6.5^m$ **Summit of Mt. Cadillac** with magnificent views of sea, seacoast, & Mt. Katahdin.

Cont. (S) on St.3. At $21.5^m$ is J. with Rd. which leads (L) along ocean; magnificent view. At $22^m$ entrance to **Site of Jackson Mem. Cancer Lab.** (destroyed by 1947 fire; being rebuilt). Near-by is Pub. Camp Site. At $22.5^m$ (R) to Nat. Pk. Hqs. Bldg. (Info.). Near Sieur de Monts Springs, named for 17th cent. Can. Gov., is **Mus.** (O) with stone age Ind. coll. At c.$28.5^m$ **Seal Harbor** where is summer home of John D. Rockefeller, Jr. $29.5^m$ **Asticou.** Thuya Lodge (O) has Lib. & Mus. $32.5^m$ **Northeast Harbor.** Boat here to Little Cranberry I. on which at **Islesford** is Sawtelle Mus. (O.summer); colls. of prints, documents & relics of region. Tour cont. (N) on Sargeant Dr. along Cliffs. At $40^m$ **Somesville** (Mt. Desert Village). Take (W) arm of St.102, (S) here, along Somes Dam, past Echo L. (R) to **Tremont** $54^m$, at SW. tip of I. Rd. leads (E) here to Seawall Pub. Campgrounds (pic.cabins). St.102 now swings (W) & then (N) along W. side of I. to J. near **Narrows Bridge** (see above) at $71^m$ with St.3. Latter leads (R) to Bar Harbor, (L) back to **Ellsworth** at $80^m$.

## Sec. 16: From ELLSWORTH to CALAIS. 127.

US1 now affords magnificent views of heavily fringed coast & Mt. Desert I.

**0. ELLSWORTH. 9.5. HANCOCK,** resort. **19.5. WEST GOULDSBORO.** J. with St.186.

SIDE TRIP: For fine coastal loop alternate trip, take St.186 (R), $18^m$. Via: **Winter Harbor** (resort), **Grindstone Neck** (resort), **Schoodic Pt.,** part of Acadia Nat. Pk., & **Prospect Harbor** (resort) to J. with US1 in Gouldsboro.

**22.5. GOULDSBORO,** resort, J. with St.186. US1 now enters blueberry country. **39. CHERRYFIELD,** blueberry-packing town. **45. HARRINGTON,** in heart of blueberry country. In old days, 52 sea captains lived in this famous seafaring town.

In vic. are more than 40 trout streams. **50. COLUMBIA FALLS,** another blueberry town. **Ruggles H.** (by Aaron Sherman.rest.) is outstanding example of Col. architecture; fine wood-carving in inter. by English handicraftsman. Fine **Maude Bucknam H.** (1820) &, across from it, the **Old Lippincott H.** Beyond Columbia Falls is J. with St.187 (scenic shore route, via old seacoast towns, to J. with US1, near Jonesboro). **59. JONESBORO.** Hannah Weston, a native, earned fame by carrying ammunition through forest to Machias & so helped win Battle of Machias Bay (see below). **67.5. MACHIAS,** on river of same name running through gorge in the town, was first a trading post (1633) operated by Rich Vines, later destroyed by Inds.; 1st permanent sett. in 1763. Town prospered by privateering. Bellamy, the pirate, made it his hqs. in 18th cent. Active shipbuilding center in old days. 1st Liberty Pole to proclaim U.S. independence was raised in the township. **Burnham Tavern** (O.summer.wks.sm.fee.1770); Rev. relics. **70.5.** J. with St.92, route (R) to **Machiasport,** old shipping & fishing village. Offshore here occurred 1st naval clash of Rev. (June 12,1775) when Machias patriots, attacking in small boats, captured Brit. "Margaretta." Earthworks of old **Ft. Machias.**

**71.5. EAST MACHIAS,** on E. Machias R. **Washington Academy,** est. 1792. **Sturdevant Mem. Lib.** (O); relics & hist. painting. **75. GARDEN L. 77.5. INDIAN L.** f.boat.). **84.5. WHITING,** J. with St.189.

SIDE TRIP: St.189 (NE) to Lubec & return, total of c.22m. **Lubec,** most easterly town in U.S., sardine & fish center. **Chaloner Inn** (Cleaves Tavern.1804) & **Old Golden Ball Inn** (pre-Rev.). **Comstock H.** & several other int. old homes. Ferry to **Treat's I.,** where beginnings of Passamaquoddy Project (see below) may be seen. Ferry to **Campobello I.** (f.) where late Pres. Roosevelt had summer home.

**92.5. DENNYSVILLE,** Excellent fishing in Danny's R. Salmon Pool in village. Lincoln H. (1786), where Rev. Gen. Lincoln lived. **Kilby H.** (O.Col.); stone age coll.

**99. WEST PEMBROKE,** in hunting & fishing region, incl. **Meddybemps L. 100. PEMBROKE** (sett.1770), on Pennamaqun R. **Old Iron Works** (1828), which used bog iron. Today town is center of blueberry & sardine industries. A few miles beyond is J. with Rd.

SIDE TRIP: Unnumbered Rd. & St.190, alternate route to Perry 15m, via Quoddy Village & Eastport. (R) on Rd. to J. with St. 190. (R) on St.190 to **Quoddy Village** where is Exhibit Bldg. with model of Passamaquoddy Project to harness the tides running 28′, for hydroelectric power. Project was halted due to cutting off of funds by Congress. A scheme to use the 130-odd bldgs. as center of industrial development, with displaced persons from Europe as workers, never materialized. St.190 cont. to **Eastport** (sett.1780), fishing & fish-packing center. Return by St.190 to J. with US1 at **Perry.**

**106.5. PERRY,** on Boyden R. Good salmon trout & deep-sea fishing in vic. J. with St.190 (see above). **108.5. MARKER** at spot midway bet. Equator & North Pole. **127. CALAIS** (sett.1779), a former shipbuilding center. On Can. border & on St. Croix R., Calais is a beautiful old town, its streets shaded by giant trees. Near-by is excellent bathing beach. Starting pt. for hunting & fishing trips. Internat. Bridge over St. Croix R. to St. Stephen. Boat conns. for St. Andrews, Grand Manan & Is. of Passamaquoddy Bay.

## Sec. 17: CALAIS to FORT KENT. 215.

US1 passes (N) through Aroostook Cty., which figured in boundary dispute with Brit. settled by Webster-Ashburton Treaty of 1842. Before treaty was signed, some clashes between Maine men & Canadians occurred known as the "Bloodless Aroostook War." Most towns in this great potato-growing reg. have potato starch factories. From Van Buren, route follows Can. border to Ft. Kent.

**0. CALAIS. 21. PRINCETON** (sett.1815.h.f.guides). Near-by are Big & Grand Falls Ls. At Princeton begins Grand L.-Machias Water Canoe Trip. **23.5.** J. with Rd. to **Dana Ind. Reserv.,** on Big L. **36. TOPSFIELD** (h.f.). J. with St.16 which runs (NE) to **Vanceboro** from which starts trip through Ls. along Can. border. (W) on St.16 lies Musquash L. **44. BROOKTON** (resort), on Jackson Brook L. (W) c.1.5m is **Baskahegan L.** (f.). At **56.** on US1 is **DANFORTH** (Ls.in vic.f.), a lumber town along East Grand L. **ORIENT** at **69.5.,** is at N end of Grand Lakes-Spednic L. Chain on Can. border. **91.5. HOULTON** (sett. 1807)

Through RR. & bus conns. Airport. Starting point for fishing & hunting expeditions; guides. Fish. & bath. in Nickerson & Carry Ls. Hotel accoms. Track for harness racing. Old Home Wk. in summer. Info.: C. of C.

Houlton, on Meduxnekeag R., tributary of great St. John R., is seat of Aroostook Cty. & market center for potato growers. In 1779 southern half of township was granted to Salem (Mass.) Academy, & northern half to Williams College (Mass.). In 1804 Jos. Houlton & Associates purchased the Academy half & in 1807 made 1st settlement here. Town was active in "Aroostook War." Houlton has immense potato warehouses & claims to be potato-starch capital of nation. PTS. OF INT.: **Starch Plants** (O). 22 North St., **Black Hawk Tavern** (1815.int.inter.). 98 Court St., **Peabody H.** (c.1826). On High St., **Ricker Classical Institute** (1847). Main St., 2nd floor of Cty. Bldg., **Aroostook Hist. Mus.** Route to Gaspé, Quebec, starts from Houlton.

**104.5. MONTICELLO** (f.in near-by L.). **Fish & Game Pk.** on Meduxnekeag R. **137. PRESQUE ISLE** (Info. Bur.in C. of C.), on Aroostook R., in center of one of best potato-growing regions in U.S. An acre produces 300 to 400 bushels. N. Maine Fair (July-Aug.) is visited by Aroostook people from miles around; harness racing. **Mon.** on Fair Grounds comm. famous race horse, John Braden, born in the county. In summer, Potato Blossom Festival. Near city is **Univ. of Maine Experimental Farm.** S. is **Quoggy Joe Mt.** (1,213′) in Aroostook St. Pk. (430 as.pic.camp.bath.winter sports). **150. CARIBOU** was sett. by soldiers from "Bloodless Aroostook War," 1839. Airport. Good fishing in near-by streams. Town has huge potato-storing warehouses, & ships out some 4,000 carloads annually. In good yrs. farmers earn large incomes & spend their money freely, buy expensive autos & television sets; but good yrs. are frequently followed by poor ones, when Aroostook people have to pull in their belts. Workers come from long distances to help garner crop. At annual Sportsman Show (Feb.-Mar.), chief event is Ski Marathon from Bangor. **Nylander Mus.** (O); nat. hist. coll. **172. VAN BUREN** on St. John R. spanned at this point by bridge to St. Leonard, New Brunswick. Town is peopled largely by descendants of settlers driven out of Nova Scotia (1775). Annual Potato Festival (July). Five Is. in the river form natural piers for construction of booms that hold thousands of logs in spring drive. **203. FRENCHVILLE,** J. with St.162, route (L) to **St. Agatha** (guides. accoms.) on Long L. (f.), starting pt. for canoe trip on Fish R. Chain of Lakes.

**215. FORT KENT,** also on St. John R., is N. terminus of US1. It was settled by Acadians (see Longfellow's "Evangeline"). On Main St., **Ft. Kent** (1841) & **Blockh.** (O), planned as defense during "Aroostook War." Ft. Kent has access to Allagash & Upper St. John Reg. (good f.) & is terminus of Allagash R. canoe trips. **Internat. Bridge** to St. Clair, N.B., J. with St.11.

SIDE TRIP: St.11 (S) to **Mattawamkeag,** J. with US2 (see) 144m.

Via: Wallagrass, Eagle L., Portage, Ashland, Patten, Sherman & Medway. Rd. not very good but traverses sparsely populated for. region with good h. & f. & numerous pub. camp sites. Sportsmen's accoms.

# US 6—NEW ENGLAND

**PROVINCETOWN, MASS. (W) to PEEKSKILL, N.Y. 281. US6**

Via: Orleans, Wareham, Fairhaven, New Bedford & Fall River in Mass.; Providence in R.I.; Danielson, Willimantic, South Manchester, Hartford, Bristol, Plymouth, Thomastown, Watertown, Southbury, Newtown & Danbury in Conn.; Brewster in N.Y.

## Sec. 1: PROVINCETOWN to J. with St.28 near Bourne. 65.

(For this sec. see Cape Cod Tour.)

## Sec. 2: J. with St.28 to MASS.-R.I. LINE. 49.

To **WAREHAM** at **7.,** US6 skirts (N) of Buzzards Bay. **12. HOLMES MEM. WOODS** (camp.). **17.5. MATTAPOISETT R.** Here is **Herring Weir,** int. in spring because of "herring run." **22. FAIRHAVEN** (sett.2nd half 17th cent.), once important whaling & shipping center. On Main St., **Fairhaven Academy** (O.appl.late 18th cent.); schoolroom preserved in orig. state. 199 Main St., **Capt. Thos. Bennett H.** (O.wks.;Sun.appl.sm.fee.1810). 6 Cherry St., **Coggeshall Mem. Bldg.** (O.wks.Sun. aft.); art & antiques. **33. NEW BEDFORD** (sett. 1st half 17th cent.).

Steamers to Martha's Vineyard, Nantucket & N.Y. City. Accoms.: All types. Info.: C. of C. & New Bedford Auto Club. Mun. bath. beach.

New Bedford, once the leading shipping & whaling port of the country, took active part in maritime warfare against Brit. during Rev. & was occupied & partially burnt by them, 1778. Now mfg. center, 3rd largest in value of products, in state, produces canned foods, textiles, clothing. Pop., like that of other New England coast towns, has become a mixture of English, Fr., Portuguese, Poles, Armenians, Germans, Ital. PTS. OF INT.: (1) Bet. William & Market Sts., **Pub. Lib.** (O.1850); Quaker & whaling material. (2) Near Lib., **Whaleman Mon.** by Bela Pratt. (3) **Old Dartmouth Hist. Soc. & Bourne Whaling Mus.** (O.wks.sm.fee); ship models, whaling relics, log books. (4) Across the way is **Seamen's Bethel** (O) which figures in Melville's "Moby Dick." (5) N. 2nd St., **U.S. Custom H.** (1st half 19th cent.). (6) **Acushnet Pk.** (O.amusement resort.bath.). (7) In **Buttonwood Pk.,** Barnard Mon.

**36. FALL RIVER** (sett. 2nd half 17th cent.). Info.: C. of C. Accoms.: All types. Town was formerly most important cotton textile mfg. city in U.S. With migration of mills to South (1921) production was cut in half. Textiles have since made a recovery (now employing 17,000 workers) & some 160 plants, mfg. variety of products incl. rubber & plastics, have been attracted. PTS. OF INT.: (1) N. Main St., **City Hall** with Tablet comm. site of clash bet. patriots & Brit., 1778. (2) **Pub. Lib.** (O); coll. of minerals. (3) 451 Rock St., **Fall River Hist. Soc.** (O.Mon.-Fri.& Sat.aft.); paintings & hist. material. (4) June St., **Old Church H.** (2nd half 18th cent.), oldest in town, was home of active Tory during Rev. (5) Eastern Ave. & St. Joseph St., **Notre Dame Ch.;** ceiling painting of "The Last Supper" by Cremonini.

**40.5.** J. with Rd. (R) 0.5$^{m}$ to **Swansea.** Cor. Fall River Ave. & Short St., **Martin H.** (O.June-Nov.1.sm.fee.1728); antique furnishings, portraits, etc. **49. MASS.-R.I. LINE,** a few miles from Providence.

### Sec. 3: MASS.-R.I. LINE (Fall River) to R.I.-CONN. LINE (Danielson). 25.

(For this sec. see Providence, R.I.)

### Sec. 4: R.I.-CONN. LINE to HARTFORD, Conn. 52.

**1.5. S. KILLINGLY. Congr. Ch.** (1837). **4. DANIELSON,** textile mill town. **Old Congr. Ch.** (recent steeple & spire). J. with St.12. (Take latter (N) here 3.5$^{m}$ to **Attawangun.** J. with Rd. (L) 1$^{m}$ to **Wildwood Pk.** (pic.boat.bath.) on Alexander L.). **7.5.** J. with Rd.

SIDE TRIP: Short distance (R) to **Trinity Ch.** (Episc.1771), erected by prominent Tory, Godfrey Malbone, in opposition to Congr. Ch. put up by Israel Putnam & friends. At 1$^{m}$ **Putnam Elms** (18th cent.adds.), home of Gen. Putnam's son, who married Malbone's daughter.

**8.5. BROOKLYN** (sett. early 18th cent.). At Green, **Unit. Ch.** (1771) & near-by, **Congr. Ch.** (1832). In vic., equestrian **Statue of Gen. Israel Putnam** by K. Gerhardt. In cemetery is Putnam's Grave, marked by a stone copied from orig. one now in Hartford's State H. There are several int. old Hs. **14.5. HAMPTON,** charming old village. **Congr. Ch.** (1840). Main St., **Moseley H.** (late 18th cent.). (E) outskirts of town, **Cleveland H.** (1831). **19. BUTTONBALL BROOK ST. PK.** (135 as.pic.trls.). Just (W) of Pk. on US6 is **Sherman's Corner.** J. with St.91.

SIDE TRIPS: (A) Take latter (R) 1.5$^{m}$. Here take Rd. (L) into **Chaplin.** On Main St., **Congr. Ch.** (1814). Several int. early 19th cent. Hs.

(B) At 5.5$^{m}$ on St.91 is J. with Rd. Take latter (R) into **Nathaniel Lyon St. Pk.** (216 as.pic.). **Site of Birthpl.** of **Nath. Lyon,** Union Gen. who fell in the Civil War. St.91 cont. to J. with US44 (see) in Phoenixville at 8$^{m}$.

**25.** J. with St.14 (see US6 Alt.). **26. WILLIMANTIC,** known as the "Thread City," at J. with Willimantic & Natchaug Rs., produces silk, cotton & rayon thread, clothing, foundry products. **Amer. Thread Co.** (O.appl.). Willimantic St., **Teachers College.** US6 shortly crosses Willimantic R. At **30.** J. with US6 Alt. (see). **36. ANDOVER** (sett.early 18th cent.); some fine old Hs. **38.** J. with Rd. Less than 0.5$^{m}$ (R) is **Hendee H.,** oldest in township. **41. BOLTON NOTCH.** J. with US44. (For stretch bet. Bolton Notch & Hartford see Hartford.) **52. HARTFORD.**

### Sec. 5: HARTFORD, CONN. to CONN.-N.Y. LINE. 63.

**11.** J. with St.10 running (N) to Farmington (see Hartford Trip III). **17.** US6 here circles (N) of outskirts of **BRISTOL** (sett. 1727), one of earliest clock-making towns & still important in this line, although it manufactures other products too. On Maple St., **First Congr. Ch.** (1832.Gr.Rev.); congregation org. 1747. Among int. old Hs. on Maple St. is No. 100, **Lewis H.** (O.appl.1801). Near city are **Rockwell** (recr.) & **Page** (recr.bath.) **Pks. 20. TERRYVILLE,** named for Eli Terry, famous 19th cent.

clockmaker. **Congr. Ch.** (O.appl.1st half 19th cent.); orig. Terry clock with wooden works. Opp. is **Pub. Lib.** with orig. Terry Mantle Clock. Near Ch. is **Eli Terry H.** **22. PLYMOUTH,** also former clock-making town. At Green, **Congr. Ch.** (1st half 19th cent.) has another old Terry Clock. **23. THOMASTON,** named for Seth Thomas, another well-known clockmaker. **Congr. Ch.** (1845). **24. BLACK ROCK ST. PK.** (713 as.pic.trls.). **29. WATERTOWN,** industrial center that has preserved a pleasant Green, near which are some int. old Hs. **36. N. WOODBURY. North Ch.** (Congr.early 19th cent.int.exter.& inter.). **37. WOODBURY** (sett.1672), charming old village. On Hollow Rd. (W) of Main St., **Glebe H.** (O.wks.Sun.aft.c.1690. remod.1740-45.rest.); antique furniture, documents, pictures. Also on Hollow Rd., **Jabez Bacon H.** (1762.rest.very fine). **First Congr. Ch.** (early 19th cent.good example). **St. Paul's Ch.** (Episc.late 18th cent.alts.) one of earliest of this sect in state. Adj., **Old Rectory.** (S) end of Green. **Masonic Hqs.** (King Solomon's Temple) (1839.Gr. Rev.). **37.5.** J. with US6 Alt. (see). At **39.** J. with St.67 to **Roxbury** (see US7). Here is **Col. Mosely H.** (early 19th cent.fine example). **41. SOUTHBURY** (sett.1673), int. old bldgs., located chiefly on main street: **Congr. Ch.** (1844); **Congr. Ch. Parsonage** (early 19th cent.); **Meth. Ch.** (1841); **Bullet Hill School** (2nd half 18th cent.). US6 now shortly passes Zoar L. **48. NEWTOWN. Congr. Ch.** (org.1714.bldg.early 19th cent.).

**58. DANBURY** (sett.1684), home of Gen. David Wooster, Rev. patriot mortally wounded in skirmish with Brit., 1777. City is summer resort but also famous hat-making center notable in labor hist. because of Danbury Hatters' Case in which members of local union were held liable for damage to their employer because of their strike & boycott against him. Their action was held violation of Sherman Anti-Trust Law, eventually amended to exempt unions (see Labor). PTS. OF INT.: (1) 71 Main St., **County Cth.** (O.wks.); antiques & hist. relics. (2) 254 Main St., **Danbury Pub. Lib.** (O) with Children's Room; murals by C. A. Federer. (3) 43 Main St., **Old St. John's Homestead** (O.1776.rest.) houses Hist. Mus. & Art Center. (4) 342 Main St., **Col. Jos. P. Cooke H.** (1770.adds.) owned by Amerigo Vespucci Soc. (5) 384 Main St., **Asa Hodge H.** (c.1695), oldest in town. (6) On Ellsworth Ave., **Wooster Cemetery** in which is Grave of Gen. Wooster. (7) W. Wooster St., **Old Town Cemetery** (late 18th cent.). (8) W. Wooster St., **Sycamore Tree,** reputedly more than 3 cents. old. (9) **Hat-Making Plants** may be visited on appl. About 1$^{m}$ (W) of town are **Danbury Fair Grounds** where one of most visited New England fairs is held Sept.-Oct. As many as 35,000 people attend. Here can be seen typical old county fair with conventional agric. exhibits, handicraft articles, oddities & freak items. Recently harness racing has been abandoned in favor of midget auto races. There are all sorts of Coney Island amusements & usually a circus. Near Danbury is **White Turkey Inn** (O.1760) & a number of recr. areas, nearest of which is (S) **Wooster Mt. St. Pk.** (see US7). J. with US7 (see).

**63.** US6 reaches N.Y. State Line.

**Sec. 5: CONN.-N.Y. LINE to PEEKSKILL. 27.**

**2.** J. with St.121; take latter to **PEACH L.** (resort). **4. BREWSTER** (resort). J. with St.22. **9. CARMEL** (resort) on charming Glendale L. **14.5. MAHOPAC** (resort.boat. bath.accoms.) on Mahopac L. **23. MOHEGAN** (resort.boat.bath.f.) on Mohegan L.

**27. PEEKSKILL.** J. with US9 (see).

## CAPE COD TOUR—NEW ENGLAND

### I. CAPE COD LOOP TOUR. 128. St.28 & US6

There are 3 main approaches to Cape Cod: US6 (see) at Cape Cod Canal; St.28 (see) from Boston; & St.3 & St.3A (see) from Boston. All have Js. at Bourne. RR. to Yarmouth & then back after June 10. Before June 10, bus from Providence. From Yarmouth, bus to Provincetown.

Cape Cod is a 62$^{m}$ fishhook jutting into the Atlantic from Buzzards Bay. Its "hook" points N. & bends back (W) to make Cape Cod Bay. The Atlantic with Martha's Vineyard & Nantucket Is. in the offing, pounds the Cape's S. & E. shores. Except for its W. base, which extends for almost 20$^{m}$ from Cape Cod Canal to Falmouth in the S., the Cape is narrow, from 6$^{m}$ at its widest to a mere mile at its upper end. Pine woods, salt marshes, small Ls. & some hills at the "hook" end characterize its topography. Both along the "Bayside" & the "Back" (ocean) side are strung picturesque old fishing villages, culminating in Provincetown, crowded into the "2-street wide" barb of the "hook."

In 1602, Capt. Gosnold, when his crew caught great quantities of cod offshore, bestowed the name of Cape Cod, & for several centuries thereafter, fishing was chief means of subsistence. Recently Cape Cod people have turned to the tourist industry for a livelihood. Several hundred thousand visitors arrive each summer attracted by local color, the charm of the Cape landscape, the beaches & the excellent fishing & sailing on both Bay & ocean. Provincetown has a special attraction. Here the new Amer. theater was born & here have dwelt or still dwell many well-known writers & artists. Provincetown might be called the Latin Quarter of the Cape.

### Sec. 1: BOURNE to ORLEANS. 63. St.28

**11. WEST FALMOUTH** with **Old Quaker Meetingh. & Burial Ground.** In vic., off side Rd., is **Bowman Rainbow Roof H.** (c.1685.adds.) whose roof resembles ship's bottom. This type of house is known as a ship's bottom roof H. **15. FALMOUTH** (sett.2nd half 17th cent.resort), in its heyday, a great whaling town & home port of 148 sea captains. On **Green,** dating from mid-18th cent., militia trained during Rev. In 1779, Brit. fleet attacked but little damage resulted. In 1814, Brit. ship "Nimrod" bombarded town when it refused to surrender its artillery: 2 brass cannon. In late 18th cent., conservative Falmouth voted against inoculation for smallpox. PTS. OF INT.: At Green, **Congr. Ch.** (1796) with an old Revere bell. Receipt of payment, signed by Paul Revere, is in Falmouth National Bank. At "Head of the Green" are several old houses. Capt. Jenkins who refused to surrender "the Artillery," had his home near Green. Palmer Ave., at Green, **Falmouth Hist. Soc.** (O.Tues.-Fri.aft.Sat. 10-2.sm.fee.1790); costumes, furnishings, relics of whaling ships & War of 1812.

SIDE TRIP: Take Woods Hole Rd. (R) 3.5m to **Fay Rose Gardens** (O.appl.). Here Michel Walsh originated the Rambler Rose (1893). Roses do marvelously well on the Cape. At 4m, **Woods Hole.** On Main St., **Oceanographic Institute** (1930) & **Marine Biological Lab.** (1888). Both study all branches of oceanography & offer courses. Marine Biological Lab. has **Mus.;** coll. local fauna & flora. Main & West Sts., **U.S. Fisheries Sta.** (est.1876) does research & conservation. Bldg. has aquarium (O) & exhibit (O) showing methods & progress of oceanographic research. There is also a fish hatchery.

From Falmouth to Orleans are frequent beaches (bath.facils.) reached by Rds. running (R) off St.28.

**25.5.** J. with unimproved Rd. leading (L) short distance to **Old Ind. Ch.** (O.1684. remod.rest.). Here Rev. Rich. Bourne carried on work with Mashpee Inds. Near-by, **Ind. Burial Ground. 36.** J. with E. Main St. leading (R) into **HYANNIS** (resort). **Colonial Candle Co.** (O) makes hand-dipped candles.

**46. JOHNSON JUNCTION.** Here is J. with St.24.

SIDE TRIP: Take latter (L) into **Harwich** (sett. 2nd half 17th cent.) not pronounced "Harrich" as in Eng. town for which it was named, located in cranberry-growing district. **Old Ch.** (1834). **Brooks Lib.** (O.Sat.aft.) with coll. statuettes by John Rogers. **Old Powder H.** (1770), a barn used during Rev.

**53. CHATHAM** (resort), once a fishing, shipping & whaling town. Fishing is still important. At **Monomoy Shoals** off Chatham, the "Mayflower's" navigators encountered difficulties & changed course back to Provincetown. The many wrecks at the Shoals caused some inhabitants to be suspected of "moon cussing"—using false lights to lure vessels. **Congr. Ch.** (O.1830) has murals by Alice Stallknecht Wight: "Christ Preaching to the Multitudes" & "The Last Supper." On Stage Harbor Rd., **Jos. Atwood H.** (O.Wed.& Fri.aft.July-Aug.1752), famous sea captain's house, said to be oldest in town; furniture & relics. Just beyond Atwood H., **Old Wind Mill** (1794) & near it, **Coast Guard Sta. 53.5.** J. with Chatham Shore Dr.

SIDE TRIP: Take latter (R) to **Chatham Lighth.** (O) & **Mack Mon.** comm. Capt. Mack who perished when his barge, "Wadena," was wrecked on shoals.

**59.5.** St.28 passes **KENRICK H.** (built soon after Rev.), one of the finest examples extant of the Cape Cod Cottage. Kenrick, noted sea captain who wandered all over the Pacific, was accidentally killed by a salute fired by a Brit. ship from a gun which the crew did not know was loaded. **63. ORLEANS,** J. with US6 (see below).

### Sec. 2: ORLEANS to PROVINCETOWN. 28. US6

(For this sec. see Sec. 3 (below) which begins at Provincetown.)

**Sec. 3: PROVINCETOWN to J. with St.28. 65.**
(Occasional side Rds. branch off (R) to shore pts.)

**0. PROVINCETOWN**

Boats in summer from Boston. Busses make conn. with N.Y., N.H. & H. RR. at Yarmouth. Accoms.: All types. Numerous bath. beaches. Deep-sea fish. Sail. & fish. boats at Town Wharf.

Provincetown, squeezed in bet. the ocean & Cape Cod Bay, is nearly 4 miles long & only 2 streets wide—Commercial & Bradford Sts. run the length of the town. Here the Pilgrims 1st landed, Nov. 11, 1620 & stopped over some 5 wks. before going on to Plymouth. Settlement early became a whaling port & had a large fishing fleet that sailed to the "Banks." The glories of those times have passed, but today fishing is a chief source of income for descendants of orig. settlers, Portuguese from the Azores & Lisbon, & "bravas," a mixture of Portuguese & Africans, mostly from Cape Verde Is. The other chief source is the tourist. Town triples its pop. during summer. Provincetown was birthpl. of modern Amer. theater. In 1915, Geo. Cram Cook, Eugene O'Neill, John Reed, Susan Glaspell, Max Eastman, Edna St. Vincent Millay, Mary Heaton Vorse & others started the Provincetown Theater. Later the group moved to New York's MacDougal St., where they revolutionized Amer. drama. Artists also were attracted by the beautiful shore line & picturesque fishing fleet. Today town is a summer art center & summer home of well-known writers & artists. It is also a mecca for those who like superb seashore recreation combined with bohemianism of an art & literary colony. The Town Crier still goes his rounds here, ringing his bell & making announcements. PTS. OF INT.: (1) On Commercial St., No. 612A, **Bissell H.,** where Provincetown Players had beginning; No. 577, **House** where Eugene O'Neill lodged. Near-by, **Little Ch. of St. Mary of the Harbor** (Episc.), ornamented with work of Portuguese craftsmen. No. 517, **Figurehead H.,** notable for figurehead of woman found by a Cape Cod captain in Indian Ocean. No. 473, **H. of Comdr. Don. B. MacMillan,** member of Peary's expedition to N. Pole. No. 468, **Provincetown Art Assoc.** (O.exhibits in summer). (2) **Town Wharf & Monument Dock,** where Boston steamers berth, social center, picturesque with fishing boats & fishing activities. (3) On Commercial St., is **Town Hall** with mural by Ross Moffett & art & hist. coll. (4) On Ryder St. near Town Hall, **Tablet** comm. Mayflower Compact & **Compact Mem.** by Cyrus F. Dallin. The "Compact," signed at Provincetown by Pilgrims, established general outlines of gov. of colony. (5) Bradford St. near Ryder St. has another Mayflower Mem. **Tablet** comm. 5 Mayflower immigrants who died on voyage over. (6) Off Bradford St., **Pilgrim Mon.** (O.Mar.-Nov.sm.fee), 252′, fine view. (7) 230 Commercial St., **Hist. Mus.** (O.June-Oct.sm.fee), art, Ind. & maritime items, Sandwich glass & Arctic Coll. of Comdr. Macmillan. (8) Winthrop St., **Cemetery** (1723) in which is Tablet to Gov. Bradford's wife, Dorothy, drowned during Pilgrims' sojourn at Provincetown. (9) 15 Tremont St., **"Norse Wall H.,"** built on a wall conjectured to have been constructed by Norsemen with stones they brought as ballast. (10) Commercial St. & Beach Hy., Tablet marking **Site of Landing of Pilgrims.** (11) 72 Commercial St., **Nickerson H.** (shop), allegedly oldest in town. (12) **Woodend Lighth. & Long Point Lighth.,** fine view. (13) Race Pt. **Coast Guard Sta.** (O). (14) **Universalist & Meth. Churches** are decorated with frescoes. (15) **Fish Freezing Plants,** worth visit.

**6.5. NORTH TRURO.** Take Rd. (L) here 1.5$^{m}$ to Cape Cod (Highland) **Lighth.** (O.1797); magnificent view. On US6, (N) of Truro, is Hill of Churches. Here is **Bell Meetingh.** (1827) with Paul Revere bell. Another Ch. (1726) once stood near-by, removed, it now serves as studio near beach. **10.5. TRURO** (sett.1700.resort), once whaling & shipping port. **15. WELLFLEET** (sett.early 18th cent.) once a whaling & fishing village. Near here in 1717, pirate Sam. Bellamy's ship the "Whidah" went on the rocks & upward of 101 buccaneers were drowned. **Mem. Hall** (early 19th cent.). **25. EASTHAM** (sett.1st half 17th cent.) was founded by Thos. Prence & others from Plymouth & 1st known as Nauset. On Samoset Rd., **Old Windmill** (O.c.1793.rest.). On same Rd., **Prince Hurd H.** (O.appl.1st half 18th cent.). **28. ORLEANS** (sett.late 17th cent.), old seafaring town. In 1814 Brit. ship, "Newcastle," raided town, burnt some of its shipping & captured rest. On Skaket Rd. (L) is **Capt. Linnel H.** (mid-19th cent.); Linnell was commander of fast clipper ship, "Flying Mist." **29.5. HIGGINS TAVERN** (1829), adj. to a garage. Here Thoreau stopped overnight. **Kenrick H.** (see St.28 above). At 2$^{m}$ from J. of Tonset

& E. Orleans Rds., **J. Crosby H.** (early 18th cent.). On H. is tablet comm. Joshua Crosby, who fought on the "Constitution" in the battle with the "Guerrière" (1812). **31. NICKERSON ST. PK.** (cabins.camp.f.). **34. BREWSTER** (sett.mid-17th cent.), named for a Plymouth preacher. **First Parish Ch.** (O.1844) on site of one built before 1700. At rear, old cemetery in which 51 stones are on graves of men who lost their lives at sea. **Capt. Elijah Cobb H.** (O.July & Aug.;1800.Georg.) has captain's walk & now houses Cape Cod music center. When Capt. Cobb's ship was sequestered in a Fr. port during Fr. Rev., he went to Paris & interviewed Robespierre to get ship released. **36.5.** Two **DILLINGHAM Hs.** (late 17th cent.), built by 2 Quakers.

**40.5. DENNIS** (sett.1st half 17th cent.), named for Rev. Josiah Dennis. Here many of fastest clipper ships were built. Movie theater has **Murals** by Rockwell Kent & Jo Mielzener. **Dennis Playh.**, one of best-known summer stock theaters in East. In **S. DENNIS** is **Congr. Ch.** with murals by Edwin Blashfield. **44.5. YARMOUTH** (sett.1st half 17th cent.), where some 50 sea captains had homes. Yarmouth issued its own Decl. of Ind. several wks. before more famous Philadelphia Decl. In **YARMOUTH PORT,** cor. King's Hy. & Thatcher Lane, **Col. John Thatcher H.** (O.wks.summer.sm.fee); period furniture. Also on King's Hy., **Winslow Crocker H.** (O.appl.18th cent.); period furniture. In **S. Yarmouth** is old **Quaker Meetingh. 48. BARNSTABLE** (sett.1st half 17th cent.) another old seafaring town. **Sturgis Lib.** (O.1644), part of which was built by Rev. Lothrop, town's 1st preacher. **49.5. SACRAMENT ROCK** where tablet reads: "Here the settlers received their first sacrament & held their first town meeting." **52.5. W. BARNSTABLE.** About 1$^{m}$ (R) from town's center is **Congr. Ch.** (1717), one of oldest in U.S. **59.5. SANDWICH** (sett. 1st half 17th cent.), famous for Sandwich glass formerly manufactured here, is a beautiful town with a number of houses more than 2 centuries old. At Green, cor. Grove & Canal Sts., **Sandwich Hist. Mus.** (O.Wed.aft.summer.sm.fee); hist. relics & Sandwich glass. Grove & Main Sts., beautiful **Congr. Ch.** (O.appl.). On School St., **Hoxie H.** (O.sm.fee.c.1637). It is said Rev. R. Cotton built house as parsonage out of proceeds of whales stranded in harbor, which he claimed as his perquisites. Main St., **Old Daniel Webster Inn,** former stagecoach stopover, with room in which Webster stayed. Near Town Hall, **Old Mill Shop,** formerly a gristmill. **62.** US6 here crosses Cape Cod Canal at **SAGAMORE.** J. with St.3 (see). At **65.,** J. with St.28 (see above), with which US6 unites to point near Wareham.

## CONN. ST. 14, US 6 AND US 6A—NEW ENGLAND

**PROVIDENCE, R.I. (W) to J. with US6 S. of WOODBURY, CONN. 119. St.14, US6 & US6A**

Via: Central Village, Plainfield, Canterbury, Scotland, Windham, Willimantic, Columbia, E. Hampton, Portland, Middletown, Meriden & Waterbury.

This route is a more southerly alternate to US6 bet. Providence & Willimantic, Conn. & bet. Willimantic & J. with US6, near Woodbury, Conn.

### Sec. 1: PROVIDENCE, R.I. to R.I.-CONN. LINE. 28.

This sec. more or less parallels US6 (see Providence Trip IV).

### Sec. 2: R.I.-CONN. LINE to J. with US6 (E) of Willimantic. 28. St.14

**0. CONN. LINE. 7. CENTRAL VILLAGE. 10. PLAINFIELD,** a mill town. Near the Green: lovely Congr. Ch. (early 19th cent.). **Plainfield Academy,** one of whose bldgs. dates from early 19th cent. (by Ithiel Town), & several sturdy old 18th cent. Hs. J. with St.12 which runs (S) to Norwich (see New London). **15. CANTERBURY. First Congr. Ch.** (O.early 19th cent.). **Elisha Payne H.** (O.appl.early 19th cent.) where Prudence Crandall had a school to which she admitted a Negro girl. As a result, she was forced to flee from an indignant mob. **18. WESTMINSTER, Congr. Ch.** (O.2nd half 18th cent.). **21. SCOTLAND** (sett.1700). On St.14 here, is **Huntington H.** (O.appl.early 18th cent.), birthpl. of Sam. Huntington, signer of Decl. of Ind. **25. WINDHAM,** which boasts 42 pre-Rev. bldgs. Near the Green are some int. Hs. (O.appl.). (1) On S. side of Green (to be moved 1949, above the Green) is **Old Apothecary Shop & Doctor's Office** (O). (2) S. of Green, **Pub. Lib.** (O.wks.1832), formerly a bank; antiques & relics, incl. figure carved out of wood by Brit. prisoners during Rev. (3) Near Lib., **David Young H.** (2nd half 17th cent.). (4) Near-by, **St.**

**Paul's Ch.** (early 19th cent.). (5) E. of Green, **Old Elderkin & Dyer Hs.** (6) N. of Green, near a church, is a fine **Gr. Rev. H.** (7) SW. of it is **Webb H.** (O.vacant.18th cent.). (8) N. of Green, **Old Jail** (vacant) & (N) of it, 2 fine old Hs. & to the (R) on St.14, **Frog Pond,** where during Fr.-Ind. wars the frogs made such a din that everybody thought the enemy had arrived. **28.** J. with US6 (E) of Willimantic.

**Sec. 3: J. with US6 to pt. where US6A branches off (SW). 4. (see US6).**

**Sec. 4: Point where US6A branches off (SW) from US6 to J. with US6 S. of Woodbury. 59. US6A**

**2. COLUMBIA.** Main St., **Old Congr. & Old Schoolh.** ("Moore's Charity School"). Opp., **Saxton B. Little Lib.** (O); hist. relics, documents & painting of Sam Occum, one of Wheelock's Ind. converts (see Norwich). **Old Congr. Ch. & Old Schoolh. Wheelock H.** (early 18th cent.), where Eleazer Wheelock had school for Inds. Wheelock finally moved institution to Hanover, N.H. & from it evolved Dartmouth College. **Old Inn** (middle 18th cent.).

SIDE TRIPS: (A) Take St.87 (R) from Columbia 1m & then (L) to **Columbia L.** (boat.f. bath.).

(B) Take St.87 (L) 7m to **Lebanon,** at time of Rev., 6th largest town in Conn. & hqs. of powerful Trumbull family when Jon. Trumbull was Gov. of Colony. He was so indispensable in planning aid for Continental Army that Washington used to say: "We must consult Brother Jonathan," & the term "Brother Jonathan" became a byword. Lebanon was center of Rev. activities. Fr. troops came here, 1781. PTS. OF INT.: (1) **Jon. Trumbull H.** (1769), home of 2nd Gov. of that name. (2) **War Office** (O.sm.fee.1727). Here 1st Trumbull directed his activities & Washington, Lafayette, Rochambeau & Franklin held conferences. (3) **Gov. Trumbull H.** (O.Thurs.Sat.1740), built by 1st Gov.; now Mus. (4) St.87 & Colchester Rd., **Redwoods** (1704.remod.later in 18th cent.), where 1st Gov. Trumbull was born. Here Fr. staff had hqs. (5) **First Congr. Ch.** (1804.remod.), designed by artist, John Trumbull, son of Gov. While in London, during Rev., John was jailed as spy. (6) At S. end of Common, **Welles H.** (1712.alts.), birthpl. of Wm. Williams, signer of Decl. of Ind. (7) Opp., **Buckingham Hs.** (respectively c.1735 & 1804). One of them was birthpl. of Wm. Buckingham, Gov. during Civil War. (8) Cor. St.202, **Wm. Williams H.** (early 18th cent.). (9) Goshen Rd. has several int. Hs. incl.: **Clark H.** (1708), home of Col. Jas. Clark, hero of Bunker Hill. (10) St.207 (L) (E) from Lebanon, 1m, **Cemetery** where the three Govs. Trumbull, Wm. Williams & Rev. soldiers are buried. At 15m St.87 joins St.32 4m from Norwich (see New London).

**7. HEBRON. St. Peter's Ch.** (1st quarter 19th cent.inter.rest.1935-42). Adj., **Brick Mansion** (O.appl.1816) built by Gov. Peters; occupied by some of his collateral descendants. **12. Marlboro** (sett.early 18th cent.). **Congr. Ch.** (early 19th cent.). **Tavern** (O.1st half 18th cent.). US6A now passes Pocotopaug L. **17. E. HAMPTON.** (R) from E. Hampton a short distance is **Sears Pk.** (pic.bath.boat.). **19.5. Cobalt,** named for cobalt mine in vic.

SIDE TRIP: Take St.151 (L) here 0.5m to Middle Haddam, with Labor Day Fair featuring horse show visited by thousands on Haddam Neck. **Christ Ch.** (Episc. 1798.tower added 1840). Cont. on St.151 to **Hurd St. Pk.** (pic.boat.bath.trls.); fine views of Mt. Tom. Part of park once owned by Jesse Hurd, shipbuilder & merchant. Hy. cont. to J., near E. Haddam, with St.82 (see New Haven).

**25. PORTLAND,** on Conn. R., 18th cent. shipbuilding town, has several old Hs.: **Philip Gildersleeve & Geo. Lewis Hs.,** former homes of early shipbuilders; **Sam. Hall H.,** one of finest in town; **Warner H.** (early 18th cent.); sold by heirs of Deliverance Warner to Capt. Diggins; impressive **Portland Brownstone Quarries,** nearby, were worked as early as 1667. **26. MIDDLETOWN** (see Hartford Trip VII), home of Wesleyan Univ. **31. BLACK POND ST. PK.** (f). **34. MERIDEN** (see Hartford Trip VI). US6A now passes **HANGING HILLS & HUBBARD PK.** (see Hartford Trip VI). **42.5. HITCHCOCK L.**

**48. WATERBURY** (sett.c.1674).

Through bus & RR. conn. Swim. in city pks. Mun. golf course. Accoms. Info.: C. of C. & Conn. Motor Club, both at 7 Field St.

Waterbury, on Naugatuck R. (W) of Mad R., was 1st known as Mattatuck. Present Green was a swamp near which 1st settlers, from Farmington, built homes. During Queen Anne's War, Inds. made several attacks. 1st school est. 1689, its teacher being an unusually well-educated carpenter named Jeremiah Peck. Town early voted to support Continental Congress in struggle with mother country. Fr. army passed through city on its way to & from Yorktown. 1st water mill providing power

for industry rather than grain was built in 1802, & marked town's beginning as industrial center. Jas. Harrison, who built mill, was a clockmaker. Another early industry was making of buttons. Out of these beginnings grew today's great button & clockmaking plants. Waterbury Clock Co. was maker of famous "dollar" Ingersoll watch, of which, 5,000,000 were produced in one year. In 2nd half of 19th cent., the brass industry was founded & Waterbury has been called "brass center of the country." Amer. Brass Co. & Chase Co. are connected with nationwide copper & brass concerns. Scoville Co. is independent. Waterbury produces vast variety of other goods. The 8 largest plants employ some 23,000. PTS. OF INT.: (1) Central Green, **Mem. Fountain** for horses & dogs. Near-by, site of 1st permanent settlement. (2) W. end of Green, **Civil War Mon.** (3) N. side of Green, **Ch. of Immaculate Conception** (1928.Ren.by Maginnis & Walsh). (4) **First Congr. Ch.** (5) **Second Congr. Ch.** (6) W. of Green, **St. John's Ch.** (Episc.Vict.Goth.). (7) 119 W. Main St., **Mattatuck Hist. Soc.** (O.wks.); lib., Colonial industrial appliances & curiosities, Vict. furnishings, Ind. relics, Children's Mus. (8) Grand near Field St., **Mun. Bldg.** (by Cass Gilbert). (9) Grand St., **Chase Brass & Copper Co. Offices** (1917.by Cass Gilbert). (10) Cor. Grand & High Sts., **Amer. Brass Co. Offices.** (11) 267 Grand St., **Bronson Lib.** with Statue of Benj. Franklin by Paul Bartlett. (12) Grand & Meadow Sts., **Union Station** (by McKim, Mead & White). (13) Freight St., **Amer. Brass Co. Plant.** (14) Across R., via Freight St. Bridge, **Pilgrim Mem.** (by H. MacNeil). (15) E. Main St., **Scoville Co. Plant.** (16) E. Main & Silver Sts. is large **Hamilton Pk.** (recr.). (17) On S. Main St., **Waterbury Clock Co.**
Here is J. with St.8.

**59.** US6A makes J. with US6, c.0.5$^{m}$ (S) of Woodbury.

## US 44—NEW ENGLAND

### PLYMOUTH, MASS. (W) to KERHONKSEN, N.Y. 239. US44

Via: (Mass.) Middleborough & Taunton; (Conn.) Putnam, Pomfret, S. Manchester, Hartford, Winsted, Norfolk, Salisbury & Lakeville; (N.Y.) Millerton, Amenia & Millbrook.

#### Sec. 1.: PLYMOUTH to MASS.-R.I. LINE. 40.

**0. PLYMOUTH**

Accoms.: All types in summer. 18$^{m}$ of salt water beaches. Pub. camps.: Nelson St., Mun. camp grounds, Ind. Reserv. & Miles Standish St. For. F. in fresh water ponds in vic.; salt water f. at St. Pier & Manomet near Coast Guard Sta.; facils. Info. booth at Depot Green & at C. of C. Each Fri. in Aug., pageant of "The Pilgrim's Progress."

Plymouth, site of 1st permanent Eng. settlement in America, is today a bustling industrial community & a lively summer resort that has preserved many of its early hist. bldgs. The "Mayflower," with 102 religious refugees, landed at Plymouth Rock on Dec. 21, 1620. Colonists had already signed the Mayflower Compact at Provincetown (see) where they had stopped for over 5 weeks. The compact set a pattern of theocratic gov. that was to prevail throughout New England. That unregenerate libertarian, Thos. Morton, set up his settlement at "Merrymount," near Quincy, & thither tried to transfer a bit of "Merry England." Especially scandalous to the Pilgrims was the heathenish celebration of the Maypole. Miles Standish was sent to arrest Morton, who was then sent back to England but returned once more only to be suppressed again. In 1639, Nov. 28th was appointed as day of Thanksgiving, origin of our Thanksgiving Day custom. No other holidays were kept unless one were to consider the austere Sabbath as such. When some of the colony's later arrivals refused to work on Christmas Day, the Gov. took away their farm tools saying that it was against conscience they should play at games while others worked. Plymouth in the 18th & 19th cents. became an important fishing, shipping & whaling port. Industries developed at the same time, among them, ropemaking factories. One of these is still functioning: Plymouth Cordage Co., reputedly largest plant of its kind in the world.

PTS. OF INT.: (1) Court St., **Mem. Hall,** comm. those who fought in Amer. Wars. (2) 126 Water St., **Antiquarian H.** (O.summer.1809.add.1830.sm.fee); furniture, china, costumes, toys of early 19th cent. (3) Court & Chilton Sts., **Pilgrim Hall** (O. wks.Sun.aft.Ap.-Nov.1824.Gr.Rev.); relics of 1st settlers—Peregrine White (1st

Pilgrim child born in colony) & Fuller cradles; chairs of Elder Brewster & Gov. Carver; Miles Standish sword; & paintings: "Landing of Pilgrims" by H. Sargent, "Departure (of Pilgrims) from Delft Haven" by Chas. Lucy, "Embarkation" by R. F. Weir, "Mayflower, Plymouth Harbor" by W. F. Halsall. (4) Court St., **Tabitha Plasket H.** (18th cent.). (5) North St., **Pub. Lib.** with linden trees planted 1760. (6) North & Winslow Sts., **Mayflower Hist. Soc. H.** (O.exc.Mon.June-Oct.1754.alt.), built by grandson of Gov. Ed. Winslow of the "Mayflower"; Queen Anne & early Chippendale furniture. (7) Water St., **Plymouth Rock** where Mayflower Pilgrims are said to have landed. It is said that in 1741 Elder Thos. Furnace, at age of 95, came in a great tizzy to protest building of wharf over rock. It is also claimed rock has been moved several times, & that it was split in two in Rev. days when zealous patriots moved it to Town Square as base for a Liberty Pole. In 1880 the 2 halves were reunited, the story goes, at orig. location here. (8) Water & North Sts., **Pilgrim Mother Statue Fountain.** (9) Carver St., **Cole's Hill,** with Mem. Sarcophagus containing bones of early settlers, & Mon. to Massasoit, Ind. chief who aided Pilgrims. Fine view. (10) Leyden & Carver Sts., **Sites of First Hs.** (11) Near-by, **Brewster Gardens,** named for Wm. Brewster, ruling elder of 1st Pilgrim ch. Here is Ship Anne Mem. & Pilgrim Spring.

(12) At Town Sq. are several Chs. & **Plymouth Town H.** (1749) oldest still functioning gov. bldg. in U.S. Near-by is site of homes of Miles Standish & John Alden. (13) Spring & Summer Sts., **Sparrow H.** (O.sm.fee.rest.), housing Plymouth Potteries; old-fashioned garden. (14) Beyond Town Sq., **Burial Hill;** graves of Pilgrims. Site of old Fort. Reprod. of old Powder H. Here is held Pilgrim's Progress Service (Fri.afts.in Aug.). (15) Sandwich & Water Sts., **John Howland H.** (O.June-Nov.sm. fee.1666.rest.1941), early window glass & relics. (16) 119 Sandwich St., **Wm. Harlow H.** (O.July-Labor Day.sm.fee.1677.rest.1921). Many beams of this H. are from Fort on Burial Hill; early furnishings & demonstrations of 17th cent. handicraft industries. (17) 8 Winter St., **Kendall Holmes H.** (O.wks.Sun.aft.Apr.-Dec.sm.fee. 1666); antique furniture & int. inter. (18) **Nat. Mon. to the Forefathers** (1888) is said to be largest granite mon. in world, rising 81′ above hill. On main pedestal is figure of Faith. At base are seated figures—Morality, Law, Education & Freedom. There are smaller symbolic figures & scenes from Pilgrim hist. (19) In N. Plymouth on St.3 c.3$^{m}$ is **Crowe H.** (1664). (20) To (SW) of Plymouth is **Miles Standish St. For.** (camp.cabins.pic.trlrs.bath.f.). Other pts. of int. in vic.: Major Lever H., Bradford H., Grave of Miles Standish, John Alden H., Miles Standish Mon., Deborah Sampson H., etc. In Plymouth is J. with St.3 (see).

Replicas of several of the original thatched houses of 1621 are being erected.

**8. NORTH CARVER** (sett.2nd half 17th cent.). J. with St.58, leading (R) 2.5$^{m}$ to **Plympton** (sett.2nd half 17th cent.). On Elm St. (L) from village, **Deborah Sampson H.** Deborah fought in Rev. disguised as a man. **17.5.** J. with St.28 (see). **25. TAUNTON.** (Accoms.: All types. Info.: C. of C. & Auto Club of R.I., Taunton Div.) Taunton, sett. 1st half 17th cent., preceded Boston in declaring for Amer. independence & early became important shipbuilding center & one of New England's main ports. Industry developed during 19th cent. Stoves were one of chief products & have remained so. The city also manufactures silverware, cotton textiles, machinery, etc. At Central Green is **Gen. Cobb Boulder,** comm. conflict here during Shays's Rebellion. White St. & Somerset Ave., **King Philip's Oak,** supposedly 400 yrs. old. 66 Church Green, **Old Col. Hist. Soc.** (O.Mon.-Fri.sm.fee.1853.by Rich. Upjohn) in former Bristol Academy; hist. relics. Summer St., **Statue of Rbt. Treat Payne,** native & signer of Decl. of Ind. Also allegedly largest Glove Factory in U.S.

**32. ANAWAN ROCK,** short distance (L) from hy. Here Anawan, King Philip's follower, surrendered in 1676. **33.5. OLD ANAWAN H.,** still an inn.

**40. MASS.-R.I. LINE** (E. Providence).

### Sec. 2: MASS.-R.I. LINE to R.I.-CONN. LINE. 24.

(For this stretch of Rd. see Providence.)

### Sec. 3: R.I.-CONN. LINE to HARTFORD. 52.

**6. PUTNAM,** small industrial city whose industries early developed by use of power from near-by Cargill Falls. Today it manufactures chiefly textiles. From Putnam c.0.5$^{m}$ is **Quinebaug Pine St. Pk.** (trls.). In Putnam is J. with St.12, which cont. (S) to Norwich (see).

**6.5.** Beautiful **CARGILL FALLS. 10. POMFRET** (sett.late 17th cent.), a residential community. **Pomfret Sch.** has modern Col. bldgs. **Norman Chapel** (mod.Goth.). **Congr. Ch.** (1832.Gr.Rev.). **Grosvenor Inn** (1st half 18th cent.adds.). **Col. Grosvenor H.** (late 18th cent.alts.); houses Rectory School for Boys; & several other int. old Hs. **13.5.** J. with Rd.

SIDE TRIP: Take latter (L) 2m in **Mashamoquet St. Pk.** (628 as.pic.bath.trls.). Marked trl. leads to **Israel Putnam's Wolf Den** where Rev. hero had famous encounter with the she-wolf.

**14.5. ABINGTON. Pub. Lib.** (O); rare items. **Congr. Ch.** (middle 18th cent.alts.).

**23. WARRENVILLE,** with int. 18th cent. houses, especially **Palmer Tavern** (int. inter.). (For stretch of Rd. from Warrenville to **HARTFORD** at **52.,** see Hartford).

### Sec. 4: HARTFORD to CONN.-N.Y. LINE. 56.

For stretch of Rd. from Hartford to & incl. **NEW HARTFORD** at **19.** see Hartford. **20.5.** J. with St.181 which leads (N) to **Pleasant Valley,** near which are **Amer. Legion St. For.** (camp.pic.f.) & **People's St. For.** (pic.recr.), & cont. along Barkhamsted Reservoir. **25. WINSTED** (sett.2nd half 18th cent.). Once clockmaking town, now manufactures great variety of articles, incl. clocks, pins, hardware. 1st condensed milk (1857) in U.S. was made here. **Highland L.** encircled by a drive to (SW) of city is recr. area. 225 Prospect St., **Sol. Rockwell H.** (O.wks.aft.exc.Mon.June-Oct.;1815. Gr.Rev.); furniture, portraits. **35. NORFOLK,** summer residential community, beautifully situated in hill country. At Green, **Jos. Battell Mem. Fountain** (designed by St. Gaudens; executed by Stanford White), comm. one of town's prominent merchants. **Congr. Ch.** (early 19th cent.remod.). **Battell Homestead** (18th cent.). Near-by, **Music Shed;** choral concerts in June. Several int. old houses in vic. **Haystack Mt.** (1,680') **St. Pk.** (287 as.pic.boat.trls.winter sports) is short distance (N) of town. Fine view from tower. From just (N) of Norfolk, St.49 runs (N) to **Campbell Falls St. Pk.** (102 as.) at boundary bet. Conn. & Mass. These are among finest falls in either state. **40. EAST CANAAN. Congr. Ch.** (early 19th cent.fine example). **43. CANAAN. 45. HOUSATONIC R.,** J. with Rd. at bridge. Take this Rd. (R) 1m to **Twin Lakes** (resort). **50. SALISBURY** (sett. early 18th cent.) a charming old village which, because of near-by iron mine, early became iron-foundry town. Until recently, town was without street lights. When movement was started to install electricity on main street a woman of the opposition said: "Seems to me that if I were being chased by a stranger, I'd rather it were dark." **Scoville Lib.** (O.est.1803) was 1st tax supported lib. in U.S.; int. coll. books & relics. Impressive **Congr. Ch.** (late 18th cent.). **Old Town Hall, Old Town Jail,** & other int. old houses.

SIDE TRIPS: (A) Take Rd. (R) 2m to top of **Mt. Riga** (2,000'), skiing.
(B) On another side Rd. 2m (NW) is Bear Mt. (2,355'), highest in state.
(C) Take St.41 (R) crossing Sage's Ravine (see US7).

**52. LAKEVILLE** (resort), where Ethan Allen, Rev. hero, had forge which cast cannon for Continental Army. Here is another J. with St.41.

SIDE TRIP: Take latter (L) past Wononscopomuc L. where is **Hotchkiss Sch. for Boys.** At 8m **Sharon,** home of Benj. B. Hotchkiss who invented new type of explosive shell. Several fine old houses. **Congr & Episc. Chs.** both 1st quarter 19th cent.

**56. CONN.-N.Y. LINE.**

### Sec. 5: CONN.-N.Y. LINE to KERHONKSEN. 67. (see N.Y.).

## US 20—NEW ENGLAND

### BOSTON, MASS. (W) to ALBANY, N.Y. 185. US20

Via: Waltham, Watertown, (Weston), Wayland, (S.Sudbury), Marlborough, Northborough, (Worcester), (Auburn), (Sturbridge), Brimfield, Springfield, Westfield, Huntington, Chester, Lenox & Pittsfield, Mass.; New Lebanon & Nassau, N.Y.

This is 1st part of a cross-continental tour to W. Coast. Bet. Boston & Worcester, it passes through or near a number of cities or towns, most of them industrial, all of considerable hist. int. In the W. reg., tour crosses the Berkshire Mts.

### Sec. 1: BOSTON to MARLBOROUGH. 26. (for this sec. see Boston VI).

### Sec. 2: MARLBOROUGH to J. with St.12 on outskirts of WORCESTER. 22.

**0. MARLBOROUGH** (sett.1657). 227 Main St., Hqs. for Amer. Legion, in which is **John Brown Bell,** taken from Harpers Ferry (1861). To (NE) of city, **Marlborough St. For.** (R) from Marlborough on St.85 is **Fort Meadow Reservoir** (recr.), & (L) on St.85 **Sudbury Reservoir. 1. WILLIAMS INN CLUB** (1662), burned by Inds. but rebuilt during Rev. US20 now passes **WILLIAM L. 3.5. MON. & GRAVE OF MARY GOODNOW,** killed by Inds., early 18th cent. **6. NORTHBOROUGH** (sett. 2nd half 17th cent.). On Green, **Congr. Ch.** (early 19th cent.). **7.** J. with Rd., shortcut to Worcester.

SIDE TRIP: (R) 2.5m on this Rd. to **Artemas Ward H.** (O), home of Rev. Gen. Ward, now owned by Harvard Univ. Furnished with relics of Ward family. Near-by, **Dean Pk.** (bath.). At 4m, **Shrewsbury** (sett.early 18th cent.). **Howe Mem. Lib.;** coll. of Ward family material. Rd. cont. to J. with St.9 just (E) of Worcester (see Mass.St.9).

**9** J. with St.9 (see Worcester). **22.** J. with St.12. Off St.12 (S) of J., near Oxford, is **Oxford St. For.** (recr.).

### Sec. 3: J. with St.12 to SPRINGFIELD. 44.

**12.5.** J. with St.15.

SIDE TRIP: (L) short distance on St.15 & then (L) on St.131 to **Sturbridge** (sett.early 18th cent.). **Josiah Howe Lib.** (O.Wed.aft.,Sat.aft.& eve.); coll. of Ind. relics. In Sturbridge has been reproduced an 18th cent. New England town on a 500-a. tract (pic.). Of 23 bldgs. —shops, mills, & houses—18 have exhibs. & demonstrations of handicraft. Half of the bldgs. were moved here, intact, from orig. sites. Remainder are copies or adaptations of old structures elsewhere. More important bldgs. (O.daily exc.Mon.June-Sept.fee.group rates.handicraft articles for sale): **Gun Shop & Fire Arms Mus., Woodworking Tool H., Amer. Optical Shop, Cabinet Shop, Finishing Shop, Miner Grant Store** (country store), **Dennison School** (toy coll.), **Old Stephen Fitch H.** (pre-1737), **Shoe Shop, Inn & General Mus., Gebhard Barn** (1800.old vehicles & implements), **Sol. Richardson H.** (c.1748), **Cheney Saw Mill, Wright Grist Mill, Blacksmith Shop.** On Mechanic St., **Amer. Optical Co.** (O. appl.). St.131 cont. to J. with St.12 (N) of Putnam, Conn. (see US44).

**14.5. FISKDALE. Shrine of St. Anne,** with Stations of the Cross on **hill. 19.5.** J. with Rd., which leads (L) 5.5m to **Holland Reservoir** (pic.recr.).

**20. BRIMFIELD** (sett.early 18th cent.). Lovely **Old Ch.** "on the hill" J. with St.19.

SIDE TRIP: Take St.19 (L) here via Wales, near which is Wales Pond, through W. sec. of 3,050-a. **Brimfield St. For.** (bath.hik.f.). In For. are several Ls. Trls. to Mts. Tom, Wachusett, & Waddanquadnuck, on which is **"Steerage Rock",** old Ind. lookout. St.19 cont. to J. with St.32, at **Stafford Springs,** Conn.

**44. SPRINGFIELD**

RR. Sta.: At Lyman & Liberty Sts., near Main St., Union Sta. Bus Term. on Bridge St., near Main St. At Westfield, Barnes Airport; through conns. Accoms. all types. Info.: 134 Chestnut St., C. of C.; 140 Chestnut St., Auto Club of Springfield. Springfield Symphony Orchestra & other concerts in Civic Aud. Plays in Court Sq. Theater. Bath. at municipal bath. beach. Sports events at Eastern States Exposition Coliseum. In 3rd wk. of Sept., Eastern States Exposition.

Springfield (sett.1636), on (E) bank of Conn. R., is industrial capital of western Mass., founded by Wm. Pynchon, who resigned as treasurer of Mass. Colony, to move with some comrades to then frontier country of Conn. R. Valley. A tract at site of Springfield was bought from Agawam Inds. & settlement consequently became known as Agawam. In 1651 there developed a witchcraft scare when Hugh Parsons & his wife were tried for bewitching their own child. Hugh was convicted, but verdict was set aside. Wm. Pynchon himself, in 1650, was condemned for heresy because of his book, "The Meritorious Price of Our Redemption," which was burned on Boston Common. Disgruntled, he sailed for England never to return. During King Philip's War the town was almost entirely destroyed but was soon rebuilt. During Rev. its factories, powered by Mill R., produced weapons for army that defeated Burgoyne. In 1786 Shays's rebels attacked the Arsenal in order to secure arms, but were repulsed. When Fed. Govt., in 1794, est. its Armory & Water Shops (Forge) at Springfield, city received strong impulse toward industrial development. Before the Civil War, John Brown of Harpers Ferry fame (see Harpers Ferry) & a partner operated a warehouse in town, but he had already become involved in abolitionist movement & devoted much time to stimulating local antislavery sentiment. Springfield became a sta. on Underground Railway & Frederick Douglass, Negro agitator for his race's freedom, received a warm welcome. During Civil War Springfield turned out great quantities of arms for Union forces, & a considerable boom developed. Since then industrial expansion has continued; annual production of factories today is valued at more than $200,-000,000. Population has shown same shift in racial make-up as that of other New England industrial towns. "Foreign elements"—people of Fr.-Canadian, Scotch, Swedish, Ital., Polish, Jewish, German & Irish derivation—far outnumber descendants of orig. New Englanders. City is a considerable cultural center, with several institutions of higher learning, outstanding art & scientific museums, Symphony Orchestra, & little theater group. Pk. system comprises upward of 2,000 as. Recently city celebrated centenary of publication of Webster's Dictionary by a local house which is still in business.

PTS. OF INT.: (1) At Court Sq., **Springfield Mun. Group** (1913.by Pell & Corbett); twin bldgs., in one of which is Civic Auditorium, the other being Admin. Bldg. Bet. them is **Campanile** (O.Mon.-Fri.;Sat.morn.exc.July-Aug.), 300', with carillon of 12 bells; illuminated at night; fine view. (2) Across from Mun. Group., **First Ch. of Christ** (Congr.1819.by Isaac Damon). Surmounting steeple is a rooster brought from London (1750). (3) **Hampton County Cth.** (1874.late Goth.by H.H.Richardson. remod.). Adj. is Hall of Records (1907). (4) Cemetery Ave., **Springfield Cemetery;** bronze relief (by Saint-Gaudens) of Dr. J.G. Holland, author, editor of "Springfield Republican," one of New England's most important dailies. Among many old graves is that of Mary Pynchon Holyoke, daughter of Wm. Pynchon (see above). (5) Maple & High Sts., **South Ch.** (Congr.1875); fine stained-glass windows. (6) State & Chestnut Sts., **Merrick Pk.,** in which is **"The Puritan"** (by Saint-Gaudens), statue of Deacon S. Chapin, early settler. (7) Chestnut St., at entrance of driveway into Mus. Quadrangle, is **Christ Ch. Cathedral** (Episc.O.1876); carvings by Kirchmayer & by Alois Lang, nephew of the late Anton Lang, the "Christ" of Oberammergau Passion Play; window by John La Farge, "Mary & Magdala at the Tomb of Christ." (8) **Mus. Quadrangle: City Lib.** (O.wks.& Sun.aft.1912.Ital.Ren.by E.L. Tilton). **Smith Art Gallery** (O.Tues.-Sat.aft.Sun.aft.exc.July-Aug.Mon.by appl.1896. Ital. Ren. by Renwick,Aspinwall & Renwick,& W.T. Owen); outstanding colls. of jade, bronzes, paintings, lacquer, porcelain, cloisonée, embroidery & ancient armor. **Mus. of Nat. Hist.** (O.by Tilton & Githens). **Wm. Pynchon Bldg.** (O.1927.Georg.Col. by M.H.Westhoff), houses Conn. Valley Hist. Soc. & Americana coll. **Mus. of Fine Arts** (O.1933.by Tilton & Githens); coll. of prints & water colors & art lib. (9) Further along on State St. is **Ch. of the Unity** (Unit.Universalist.Ital.Goth.by H.H. Richardson); Louis Tiffany windows designed by La Farge & other noted artists. (10) On State St., **U.S. Armory & Arsenal** (O.appl.at Adm.Bldg., Federal St.1794); **Arms Mus.** (O.Mon.-Fri.). (11) At edge of Benton Lawn, cor. Federal & State Sts., **Brownstone Mon.,** comm. Jos. Worth's escape (1763) from a blizzard. (12) Benton Lawn, bet. Federal St. & St. James Ave., Boulder & Tablet marking **Site of Shays's Attack** on Armory. (13) State St., **Indian Motorcycle Factory** (O). (14) State & Amaron Sts., **Amer. Internat. College** (Georg.Col.coed.), founded at Lowell, 1885, as Fr.-Protestant College; nonsectarian. (15) Blunt Pk. Dr., **Blunt Pk.** (pic.recr.). (16) Wilbraham Rd., **Massasoit L.** (bath.boat.), created by dam built to provide power for the shops of Armory. (17) Also on Wilbraham Rd., **Springfield College Camp** on Massasoit L. **Pueblo of Seven Fires** (belonging to College), named for its huge fireplaces, has murals by Ind. artists. (18) Alden St., near Wilbraham Ave., **Springfield College** (Goth.). Offers B.S. & M. of Ed. degrees, & trains social workers in leadership of recr. activities. (19) on Hickory St., **Water Shops of U.S. Armory** (1794). (20) Sumner Ave., & Oakland St., **Trinity Ch.** (Meth.Goth.by Allen & Collins). In 100' tower, carillon of 61 bells. Sanctuary has 24 stained-glass mem. windows. A huge Good Will Batik depicts "The Adoration of the Wise Men." (21) Sumner Ave., **Forest Pk.** (pic.sports facils.). **Zoo** (O). Fossil footprints of dinosaurs found near Holyoke. **Trailside Nat. Hist. Mus.** (O). Rose garden. (22) Near-by is **Pecousic Villa** (O), former home of E. H. Barney, skate manufacturer, who donated part of For. Pk.; now industrial **Mus.** (23) At NE. limits, **Westover Field** (O.appl.), great Army Air Base. (24) **Northeastern Univ.;** evening courses in business, law & engineering.

TRIPS OUT OF SPRINGFIELD. I. On US20 (see below) are **West Springfield & Westfield.** II. (N) on US5 are **Holyoke & Northampton,** home of Smith College (see US5). III. (N) also are int. old towns of **Hadley** (see St.9) & **Hatfield** (see US5). IV. In **Longmeadow,** (S) of Springfield, is former home of Eleazar Williams, who claimed to be "Lost Dauphin."

(see US5). V. St.116 (N) to **Amherst.** 4m **Chicopee,** an industrial city. **City Hall** (Ital.Goth. by Chas.E.Parker). Front & Grape Sts., **Ames H.** (O.1844); coll. of hist. relics. 93 Church St., **Birthpl. of Ed. Bellamy,** author of "Looking Backward." **College of Our Lady of the Elms** (Cath.). 13.5m **South Hadley** (sett.2nd half 17th cent.). On Woodbridge St., **Skinner Mus.** (O.Wed.& Sun.aft.), in old Ch. (1846) moved here from Prescott; coll. early Amer. furniture, pewter, glass, farm implements, Ind. relics & South Sea Is. items. Adj., an old New England cottage & old country schoolh. In carriage shed, coll. of Old Amer. Vehicles. **Mt. Holyoke College** (est.1836.campus 600 as.), founded by Mary Lyon. **Clinton Mem. Chapel** (Goth.). **Dwight Art Mem.** (O); colls. incl. Louise Rogers Jowett Gallery of old & mod. masters. **Wollaston Mem. Lib.** (O); Treasure Room has coll. of Americana. Take St.63 & then Mt. Holyoke Rd. to **Joseph Allen Skinner St. Pk.** (375 as.), in which is **Mt. Holyoke** (995'). **Summit H.,** reached by Rd., has on its registry many famous names: Jerome Bonaparte, Longfellow, Abr. Lincoln, et al. Through foot of Mt. (pic.) runs "Pass of Thermopylae," rock-bound gorge. Cable car from Halfway H. to Summit H. Int. volcanic formations in Pk. 23m **Amherst** (see Mass.St.9). J. with St.9.

## Sec. 4: SPRINGFIELD to CONN.-N.Y. LINE. 64.

**2. WEST SPRINGFIELD** (sett.2nd half 17th cent.), industrial suburb. The Common was drill ground for Brit. soldiers under command of Gen. Amherst during Fr.-Ind. War & by Burgoyne's army on his retreat from Canada & later by Shays's insurgents. Town boasts that it was birthpl. of largest work horse on record—which founded famous Morgan strain. The old **White Ch.** is now Masonic Temple. Also standing is old **First Ch.** (Congr.). 70 Park St., **Day H.** (O.May 30-Oct.1 sm.fee.1754.rest.1943), owned by Ramapogue Hist. Soc.; antique furnishings, Col. relics. Near-by are Eastern States Agric. & Industrial Exposition Grounds (Exposition,3rd wk.in Sept.). At 2m from town **Storrowton** (O.June-Oct.fee.), another reprod. of early N.E. town. Accoms. Old-fashioned dancing Fri. eve. Handicrafts articles for sale. 11 original bldgs. of Col., pre-Rev. & early 18th cent. periods incl.: **Potter Mansion** (1760), **Country Store & Tavern** (late 19th cent.), **Meetingh.** (1834), **Philips H.** (1767), **Blacksmith Shop** (1750), **Town H.** (1822), **Little Red Schoolh.** At West Springfield is J. with St.5A (see US5). At **4.** on US20 is entrance to **Mittineaque Pk.** (pic.recr.). **9. WESTFIELD** (sett.2nd half 17th cent.), a busy factory town. Cor. Elm & Court Sts. on the Green, **Westfield Athenaeum** (O.Pub.Lib.); incl. Smith Hist. Mus., with coll. of antique furnishings, & Jasper Rand Art Mus., with coll. of Amer. Art. Court St., **St. Teachers College,** housed in handsome bldg., founded (1839) at Barre & moved to Westfield (1884); claims to be 2nd-oldest teacher-training institution in U.S. **Grandmother's Garden** (O) of flowers.

**14. TEKOA PK.** (pic.recr.), with view of Mt. of same name. **15. WORONOCO.** J. with St.23, leading (W) to J. with US7 near Great Barrington.

**21. HUNTINGTON.** (N) is **Huntington St. For. 23. BOULDER PK.** (pic.camp.bath. sm.fee), part of Chester-Blandford St. For. **25.** J. with Rd. that leads (L) 1m to impressive **Sanderson Brook Falls** (St.Reserv.). **28. CHESTER** (sett.2nd half 18th cent.). **Hamilton Mem. Lib.** (O); mineral coll. Near Chester is **Mt. Gobble** (1,600') reached by Rd. & trl. **32.** Eastern J. with St.8.

SIDE TRIP: Take St.8 (N) 2m to **Becket Center.** Old **Ch.** (late 18th cent.). At 5m take Rd. (L) into **October St. For.** (14,189 as.pic.camp.winter sports). **Schermerhorn Gorge & Felton L.** Several mt. peaks are reached by trl.

**35.** Summit of route (2,100';pic.camp.tower O.sm.fee). **38. W. BECKET.** Here is western J. with St.8. Near J. **Shaw Pond** (pic.camp.resort).

SIDE TRIP: St.8 runs (S) past **Tolland St. For.** (2,948 as.pic.camp.trl.to summit of Mt. Tolland) to **Winsted,** Conn. (see US44).

US20 now passes **GREENWATER POND. 45. EAST LEE.** J. with St.102.

SIDE TRIP: Take latter (W) through Amer. Legion Pk. At 2.5m **South Lee** to S. of which lies **Beartown St. For.** (7,990 as.pic.camp.winter sports); fine view from **Mt. Wilcox** (2,150'; pic.facils.on Benedict Pond). At 3.5m **J.** with US7 in **Stockbridge** (see US7).

**45. LEE** (sett.mid-18th cent.). Handsome **Congr. Ch.** (mid-19th cent.); old frescoes. At Orchard St., entrance to Ferncliff hill, where is **Peter's Cave,** in which Peter Wilcox, refugee, after Shays's Rebellion, is supposed to have hidden. Paper Mills (O. appl.) in Lee, S. Lee & at Goose Pond. **49. LENOX.** J. with US7 (see) with which US20 unites to **PITTSFIELD** (see US7 for this stretch) at **56.** Here US20 branches (W) & crosses Taconic Range, with fine views. **62. SUMMIT H.** (1,480'). Tower (view). **64. MASS.-N.Y. LINE.**

### Sec. 5. MASS.-N.Y. LINE to ALBANY, N.Y. 29.

US20 now passes some Shaker bldgs. Here was est. (1785) **MT. LEBANON SHAKER SETTLEMENTS,** one of earliest of sect in U.S. In 1947 some of last members of this community migrated to Hancock, Mass., leaving only a few here. **2.** J. with N.Y. St.22 (see). **3. NEW LEBANON,** birthpl. of Sam. Tilden, who smashed N.Y. city's Tweed Ring & lost to Hayes in disputed 1876 Pres. election. US20 passes **SHRINE OF OUR LADY OF LOURDES** (O.May-Nov.). **5.5. LEBANON VALLEY** winter sports area. **21.** US20 unites with US9 (see). **24.** J. with US4 (see). **29. ALBANY** (see US9).

## MASS. ST. 9—NEW ENGLAND

**BOSTON to J. with US7 (N) of Pittsfield. 139. St.9.**

Via: Brookline, (Needham), Wellesley, (Natick), Framingham Center, (Westborough), Worcester, Leicester, Spencer, (N. Brookfield), Brookfield, Ware, Amherst, Northhampton, Dalton & Pittsfield.

### Sec. 1. BOSTON to FRAMINGHAM. 19.

(For this sec., see Boston Trip VI)

### Sec. 2. FRAMINGHAM to WORCESTER. 20.

**0. FRAMINGHAM** (see Boston Trip VI). At **9.** J. with Rd. which leads (R) half-mile to **Chauncey L.** (pic.boat.bath.f.). **17. L. QUINSIGAMOND,** on which is **White City Pk.** (amusements.recr.fee).

**20. WORCESTER,** (sett.1673).

Accoms. all types. Boat. & bath. at Quinsigamond L. Concerts, lectures, in Mem. Auditorium. Info.: C. of C. & Bancroft Auto Club, in Sheraton Hotel.

Worcester, first known as Quinsigamond, is both an industrial city & an old-time cultural center. Among its noted citizens was Geo. Bancroft, historian & diplomat. Today it has 6 institutions of higher learning, excellent libs. & several outstanding museums. The tract which incl. Worcester's site was orig. purchased from Inds. by Dan. Gookin for £12, 2 coats & 4 yds. of cloth. Early settlers were forced to abandon their homes during King Philip's War. Ind. troubles cont. until early 18th cent., witness kidnapping of Sam. Lenorson (see below) & murder of Mrs. Sargent & kidnapping of her children. But by middle of cent. the town had settled down to peaceful expansion. John Adams, who taught school in Worcester (1755-58), recorded that he found it a pleasant & congenial place. At outbreak of Rev. Worcester was divided bet. Patriots & Tories, most of latter belonging to wealthy class; but Patriots gained the upper hand. In 1774 they forced Timothy Paine, Royal Mandamus Counselor, to read his resignation in public with his hat off. The 110 men the town sent to Concord arrived after the Brit. retreat but later took part in Battle of Bunker Hill. Following Rev., general hard times culminated in Shays's Rebellion, during course of which the local Cth. was besieged; it was only through the determination of Judge Artemas Ward that the rebels were stopped. The courts, which imprisoned bankrupt farmers for debt, were chief objective of the rebels. One of their marching songs ran: "Put green boughs in your hat & renew the old cause. Stop the courts in each county & bully the laws."

Worcester early turned abolitionist. In 1819 a meeting voted to condemn admission of Missouri as slave state. City became important sta. on Underground Railroad & U.S. Marshalls attempting to seize runaway slaves were prevented by local mobs. The Free Soil Party evolved out of a meeting held in Worcester (1848). In 1850, a Woman's Rights Convention initiated Women's Suffrage movement. Meanwhile town's industries steadily expanded. With completion of Blackstone Canal, industrial growth began in earnest. Worcester was already a considerable commercial center. The local stagecoach tycoon, Twichell, owned 200 horses & had stagecoaches on all the Rds. Rivers of the vic. were harnessed to furnish power. Ichabod Washburn, blacksmith, & his friend, Goddard, started wiremaking, which today is carried on by the great Amer. Steel & Wire Co. plants. Envelope manufacture began in 1840 & expanded rapidly when Dr. Russell L. Hawes, of Worcester, invented 1st envelope-making machine (1853). The great U.S. Envelope Co. plant has evolved from these early beginnings. City now has more than 500 factories producing a great variety of articles.

PTS. OF INT.: (1) Main St., **City Hall** (Ital.Ren.by Richard,Howland & Hunt), with 205′ campanile, on site of Old South Ch. The clock, made by Abel Stowell, early Worcester clockmaker, which used to hang in tower, is now in use at Coes Wrench Co. Plant. (2) 39 Salisbury St., **Worcester Hist. Soc.** (O.wks.aft.exc.Mon.); hist. & other colls. (3) 55 Salisbury St., **Worcester Art Mus.** (O.wks.Sun.aft.); notable coll. of paintings of various schools, especially fine examples of modern Fr. & Amer. (4) Salisbury St., **Mun. War Mem. Bldg.** (O.1933.by Briggs & Hirons). (5) State & Harvard Sts., **Natural Hist. Soc.** (O); among exhibs. are mastodon bones found at Northborough. (6) 61 Harvard St., **Salisbury H.** (O.Sat.a.m.1835) houses Amer. Red Cross. (7) 6 Mass. Ave., **Trumbull H.** (formerly Cth.), which Shays's Rebels tried to storm. (8) Off Mass. Ave., **Bancroft Tower;** good view. (9) W. Boylston St., **John Woodman Higgins Armory** (O.Mon.-Fri.); notable coll. of antique armor & items connected with steel industry. (10) Grove & Faraday Sts., **Industrial Mus.** of Amer. Steel & Wire Co. (O.Mon.-Fri.). (11) Elm & Chestnut Sts., **Worcester Horticultural Soc.** (O.summer on special days); flower shows.

(12) On Mt. St. James, c.2$^{m}$ from city center, **Holy Cross College** (O.est.1843), on 163-a. campus; under direction of Jesuit Order. **Fenwick Hall,** named for College's founder, Bishop B.J. Fenwick, is oldest on campus; has 2 lofty towers. **O'Kane Hall,** student center, also has impressive tower. **Dinand Lib.** (Ital.Ren.) has Mus. (O) in (W) wing, containing hist. material & coll. of Jesuitana. **St. Joseph's Mem. Chapel** (Class.) is imposing bldg. with great columned portico. (13) 140 Lincoln St., **Timothy Paine H.** (O.appl.see above); hqs. of D.A.R. (14) Lincoln St., Green Hill Pk. in which is **Birthpl. of Andrew H. Green** (see NYC.). (15) Main St., c.1.5$^{m}$ from City Center, **Clark Univ.** (est.1887), which has both undergrad. & grad. depts. In 1942 the Woman's College was est. Lib. has exhibs. of art from coll. of its founder, & 8 stained-glass windows by J. Reynolds, Jr. (16) 486 Chandler St., **Worcester St. Teachers College** (coed.). (17) Highland St., Elm Pk. in which is **Kennedy Mem.** (by Maurice Sterne). (18) On Salisbury St., **Worcester Polytechnic Institute,** on whose grounds is reprod. of **Norse Mill** (see Newport, R.I.). (19) Salisbury St., **Amer. Antiquarian Soc.** (O.Mon.-Fri.); notable coll. of Americana, & rare mss. (20) Park Dr., **Davis Tower,** comm. exploits of Sam. Lenorson, who was kidnapped by Inds. & escaped with a fellow captive, Mrs. Hannah Dustin (see). They killed 10 Inds. before escaping. (21) 81 Providence St., **Worcester Academy** (Bapt.). (22) Adj. to New Union Sta. is **Old Union Sta.** (1875.by Ware & Van Brunt,architects of Harvard's Mem.Hall), a quaint Vict. Goth. relic.

TRIPS OUT OF WORCESTER. I. From Worcester (S) on St.12. 10.5$^{m}$ J. with country Rd. On latter 1$^{m}$ (R) to **Birthpl. of Clara Barton** (O.appl.), now home for diabetics. Clara Barton was founder of Red Cross & a heroic nurse during Civil War. At 12$^{m}$ **Grave of Clara Barton,** marked by Red Cross. 13.5$^{m}$ **Oxford** (sett.late 17th cent.), textile town. Near Town Hall is **Universalist Ch.** (late 18th cent.alts.), one of 1st in st. From Oxford (L) 3$^{m}$ is **Oxford St. For.** (28 as.). St.12 cont. (S) to Conn. Line 20$^{m}$.

II. St.12 (N). 13$^{m}$ **Sterling,** at one time noted for chairs it made. Ebenezer Buttrick began producing standardized dress patterns here. On Redstone Hill Rd. (R) from Sterling, 1.5$^{m}$, is **Mary Sawyer H.** (O.appl.), allegedly home of Mary celebrated in "Mary Had a Little Lamb." **Schoolh.** where lamb came to school is now in S. Sudbury, near Wayside Inn (see Boston Trip VI). 20$^{m}$ **Leominster,** industrial town. In Pub. Lib. is **Mus.** (O); int. coll. rare books & Col. relics. On Common, **Ind. Mortar** for crushing cornmeal. St.12 cont. (N) & (NE) to N.H. Line, SE. of Keene (see N.H. St.10-12).

III. St.122 (NW). 8$^{m}$ J. with St.31 leading (R) 5$^{m}$ to **Holden.** At 13$^{m}$ **Princeton.** In **Goodnow Mem. Bldg.** (O) is Mus. with rare items & antiques. Rd. runs (L) from Princeton into **Mt. Wachusett St. Reserv.** (pic.trls.) 5$^{m}$ to summit of **Mt. Wachusett** (2,018′).

At 14$^{m}$ on St.122 is (W) J. with St.122A. On latter (R) 2$^{m}$ to **Putnam H.** (O.aft.sm.fee), home of Gen. Rufus Putnam, Rev. patriot who played part in settlement of NW. territory (see Ohio). In vic. is **Rufus Putnam Mem. Pk.**

IV. St.122 (SE) to R.I. Line. At 15$^{m}$ J. with Rd. Take latter (R) 1.5$^{m}$ to **Whitinsville** & then (R) on Sutton Rd. to **Purgatory Chasm St. Pk.** At 23$^{m}$ **Millville,** near which is **Chestnut Hill Meetingh.** (2nd half 18th cent.; inter. preserved much in orig. state). At 26$^{m}$ St.122 crosses R.I. Line (15$^{m}$ from Providence).

V. St.110 (NE) (see).

## Sec. 3: WORCESTER to AMHERST. 49.

**12.5. SPENCER.** On Pleasant St., **Sugden Lib.** (O.wks.aft.& eve.), coll. hist. material & Ind. relics. Take Maple St. (L) 1$^{m}$ then (R) c.2$^{m}$ into **Howe Mem. Pk.** (pic.f.), named for inventor of improved sewing machine, born here (see Va.). **16. E. BROOKFIELD** on Lashaway L. (boat.bath.f.pic.). **18.** J. with Rd. leading (L) here to **Quabaug L.** (camp.f.bath.boat). **19. BROOKFIELD** (sett.2nd half 17th cent.). **Merrick Lib.** (O.wks.aft.) has hist. relics. **Brookfield Inn** (2nd half 17th cent.), still hotel. **30.5. WARE CENTER. Meeting H.** (O.appl.at Gould Tavern), fine 19th cent. example. Second H. beyond church, going toward Belchertown (see below) is **Gould Tavern** (18th cent.), now a residence. **34.5.** J. with Rd. (R) to great Quabbin Reservoir. **39.5.** J. with US202 leading (L) short distance to **Belchertown. Stone H.** (O.one wk.day.sm.fee.1st half 19th cent.); antiques.

**49. AMHERST** (sett.early 18th cent.) Accoms. & Info.: Lord Jeffrey Inn. Town, named for Lord Amherst of Fr.-Ind. War fame, was scene of conflict during Shays's Rebellion. Among notable natives or residents were Noah Webster, Henry Ward Beecher; Helen Hunt Jackson & the poets Emily Dickinson, Eugene Field & Robert Frost. Amherst has 2 outstanding educational institutions—Amherst College & Univ. of Mass. In near-by Northampton is Smith College & in S. Hadley, Holyoke College.

PTS. OF INT. (1) 280 Main St., **Home of Emily Dickinson** (1813) built by poet's grandfather, one of Amherst College's founders. Her grave is in near-by West Cemetery. (2) Near-by, **The Evergreens** (O.appl.late 18th cent.in part), home of Martha Dickinson Bianchi, poet, novelist, biographer of Emily, her aunt; Emily's lib. & some of her belongings. (3) Amity St., **Jones Lib.** (O.by Putnam & Cox), in Conn. valley style of architecture; on 2nd fl., coll. of works of Amherst authors; throughout bldg. are paintings & bronzes donated by family of late W. A. Burnett. (4) NW. cor. Amity St. & Lincoln Ave., **Eugene Field H.** (1838), where poet spent his early boyhood. He refers in his poems to "The old New England homestead far away." (5) Amity & N. Prospect Sts., **Strong H.** (O.Tues.& Fri.aft.May-Oct.also appl.1744); coll. of local material, incl. piano at which Eugene Field took lessons. Henry Ward Beecher lived here when freshman at Amherst. Hqs. of Amherst Hist. Soc. (6) Cor. (NE) Amity St. & Sunset Ave., **Boltwood H.** (1745.fine example of period.) (7) 43 Sunset Ave., **Home of Robert Frost,** where poet lived while professor at Amherst. (8) 249 Pleasant St., former **Home of Helen Hunt Jackson,** author of "Ramona" (see Cal.). (9) SE. cor. Main & East Sts., **Dickinson-Baggs Tavern** (c.1770) known formerly for its "excellent flip & toddy." (10) 18 S. East St., facing Common, **Noah Dickinson H.** (c.1754), home of Lt. Noah Dickinson, who threatened Shays's looting rebels. (11) Town Common (E), **Lord Jeffrey Inn** (mod.Col.); pre-Rev. & Rev. relics, old furniture. (12) Pleasant St., **Amherst College** (est.1821), which evolved out of old Amherst Academy, founded 1812, 1st known as "Collegiate Charitable Institution," a Congr. seminary for "indigent young men of piety & talents." In Chapel Row, **S. College Hall** (O.1821.Col.), **N. College Hall** (O.1822-23) **& Johnson Chapel** (O.1826), named for farmer who left 1st bequest to college. At cor. of Northampton Rd., **College Hall** (1829), originally town meetingh. **In Converse Mem. Lib.** (O.1917) is the **Study of Clyde Fitch,** Amer. dramatist, with his lib. & furnishings, also, **Treasure Room,** in which is outstanding Wordsworth coll. **Dept. of Fine Arts** contains Amer. paintings & sculpture. There are also **Zoological Mus. & Geological Mus.** Pratt Butterfly Coll. & Hitchcock Coll. of Minerals, in Geology Bldg. (13) N. Pleasant St., **Univ. of Mass.** (est.1863.coed.), founded as an agric. land grant college. In 1947 state legislature gave it rank of univ. **Goodell Lib.** (O.mod.Georg.Col.), named for a former president. In **Fernald Hall** is Mus. with science exhibs., incl. int. insect coll. Dept. of Floriculture has colls. of tropical & native plants. There is also an int. Veterinary Mus. On campus, Stockbridge Rd., is **Stockbridge H.** (O.1728), used as faculty club; oldest in town. In 1867 it was 1st studio of sculptor, D. C. French, whose father was Pres. of the College. Near Abigail Adams Hall, **The Homestead** (O. c.1762.rest.), used by Dept. of Home Economics. In Amherst is J. with St.116, which runs (S) to Springfield (for S. Hadley, Holyoke & Chicopee, on this hy., see Springfield) & (N) & (NW) to Adams (see).

### Sec. 4: AMHERST to J. with US7. 51.

**5. HADLEY** (sett.1659). Here in 1683, Mary Webster was sentenced for witchcraft; though hanged, she survived to die a natural death. On Middle St., fine **First Congr. Ch.** (O.Wed.Sat.Sun.aft.1782); antiques. On West St., Stone marking **Site of John Russell H.** where regicides, Whalley & Goffe (see New Haven), took refuge. One of them is said to have been buried in cellar of H. & the other in near-by lot. Also on West St., **Porter H.** (O.appl.early 18th cent.). Here is J. with St.63 going (R) 2m to **Porter-Phelps-Huntington H.** (O.exc.winter.appl.1753.adds.recently rest.). **7.5. NORTHAMPTON** (see US5). J. with US5. **16. WILLIAMSBURG.** J. with St.143.

SIDE TRIP: On St.143 (L) 8.5m to **West Chesterfield.** About 1m (L) here is fine **Chesterfield Gorge.** 13m **Worthington Corners.** Take St.112 (L) here 5.5m to **South Worthington.** On Conwell Rd., near-by, is **"Eagle's Nest"** (O.July-Sept.sm.fee.1790), former home of Rev. Russell H. Conwell, founder of Temple Univ., Phila. Barn contains replicas of drawing & dining rooms of his Broad St. (Phila.) residence. St.143 cont. from S. Worthington to pt. near Dalton (see below).

**21. OLD WHALE INN** (O.int.inter.). Inquire here for directions to near-by **Packard Falls** & **Devil's Den Chasm.** Also for Rd. to **"Daughters of the Rev. St. For."** (1237 as.camp.f.bath.); pic. areas on Highland L. & Twining Brook, from which path runs up Moore's Hill. **29.** J. with Rd. leading (R) 1.5m to **Bryant Homestead** (O.Mon.Wed. Fri.aft.June-Sept.sm.fee.pre-1794.Dutch Col.), where poet Wm. C. Bryant lived; old household furniture. **33.5. WEST CUMMINGTON.** [Take Rd. (R) here 3m & then (R) c.3.5m into **Windsor St. For.** (1,616 as.bath.). Rd. leads to Windsor Jambs, fine gorge from which & through the Dells, a brook rushes in picturesque cascades.] **43.5.** J. with Rd. leading (L) 0.5m to **Wahconah Brook Falls. 46.5.** J. with St.8 (S) to Becket (see US20). **47. DALTON.** Here is **Crane Mus.** (O) with Rag Room of Stone Mill (1844) & hist. exhibits of paper industry since 1801. Crane Co. makes paper used in U.S. bank notes & paper money for many countries. **51. J.** with US7 (see), (N) of Pittsfield.

## MASS. ST. 2, N.Y. ST. 2—NEW ENGLAND

**BOSTON to TROY, N. Y. 172. MASS. St.2 & N.Y. St.2**

Via: Cambridge, Arlington, Lexington, Concord, Littleton, Ayer, Fitchburg, Westminster, Gardner, Athol, Greenfield, Shelburne, Charlemont, Florida, North Adams & Williamstown.

This route, known as the Mohawk Trail, runs through hist. area of Concord & Lexington & eventually climbs into the Berkshires, fine scenic & vacation reg.

**Sec. 1: BOSTON to J. with Cambridge Turnpike** (Concord). **17.**

(For this sec., see Boston Trip III.)

**Sec. 2: From J. with Cambridge Turnpike to FITCHBURG. 30.**

**8.5. MAGOG L.** (pic.f.recr.). **12. LITTLETON CENTER. Reuben Hoar Lib.** (O); antiques. **Old Tory H.** (O.appl.sm.fee), home of Tory active before Rev. Less than 1m (E) of Littleton Center is **Littleton Common** & J. of St.2 with St.119.

SIDE TRIP: Take St.119 (NW) at J. 7m **Groton** near which is famous boys' prep. school (founded 1883) with many handsome bldgs. One of its founders was Phillips Brooks, famous liberal preacher. Among graduates was Franklin D. Roosevelt. In center of town, **First Parish Meetingh.** (Unit.1755), typical Col. Ch. On Main St., opp. Town Hall, **Gov. Boutwell H.** (O.appl.1851.remod.very int.); hist. relics & old furniture. Hollis St., **Old Burying Ground** (c.1678); Grave of Capt. Job Shattuck, Rev. patriot. 13.5m **Townsend Harbor.** On Lunenberg Rd. are: **Spaulding's Gristmill** (O.c.1840), stands at river; antique household & farm implements; **Spaulding Cooperage Shop** (O.summer.c.1845); **Conant H.** (O.appl.c.1730). 17m **West Townsend. Old Tavern** (O.1774). 20m **Willard Brook St. For.** (1,431 as. pic.camp.hik.f.Danon Pond & Trap's Falls). 22m **Ashby. First Parish Ch.** (1809). 25m **Watatic Pond,** at foot of **Watatic Mt.** (1,847′); reached by trls.; ski slopes. On summit is cairn. Ind. legend said that anyone who reached summit & did not add stone would have forever unhappiness. St.119 crosses into N.H. at 28m & cont. to J. in N.H. with US202 & conts. to **Fitzwilliam** (see Keene, N.H.) & **Winchester** (see N.H. St.10-12).

**16.** J. with St.110 (see). **17. AYER. Pub. Lib.;** Ind. relics, etc. **30. FITCHBURG** (sett.1730), industrial town on Nashua R., which furnished power for early mills. Some 110 plants produce textiles, machine tools, rayons, & bicycles. City is located in lovely mountain country. Mt. Wachusett lies (SW), as does **Leominster St. For.** (see Worcester). **Coggshall Pk.** (recr.) has annual speed skating competition & ice carnival on Mirror L. 50 Grove St., **Fitchburg Hist. Soc.** (O.Sun.-Thurs.aft.); rare items. Merriman Pkwy., **Fitchburg Art Center** (O.wks.exc.Mon.& Sun.aft.closed 3 summer months); antique furniture; arts & crafts exhibits. Pearl St., **St. Teachers College** (O). **Simonds Saw & Steel Co.** (O.wks.) is notable as one of 1st windowless factories in U.S. In Fitchburg is J. with St.12 (see Worcester).

**Sec. 3: FITCHBURG to GREENFIELD. 49.**

**7. WESTMINSTER** (sett.1737), J. with St.140 (to Worcester). **11. SOUTH GARDNER.** (R) here on St.68 into **Gardner,** which early became home of chairmaking industry. Here Boston rocker was invented. **Crystal L.** (bath.). **19.** J. with US202 (N) to **Winchendon,** toy-making town, & to Peterborough, N. H. (see). **26. ATHOL.** Take Royalston Rd. (R) here 5m to **Doane's Falls. 33.** J. with Rd. (L) into **Wendell** near which is **Wendell St. For.** (6,356 as.). **40.5.,** St.2A (L) here to Green Pond (recr.). **42.** St.2 crosses Conn. R. **44.5. OLD RED H.** (O.1736) now tea room. **49. GREENFIELD.** Church & Union Sts., **Greenfield Hist. Soc.** (O); exhibits. Federal & High Sts., **St. James Ch.** (Episc.1st half 19th cent.). Main & High Sts., **Potter H.** (Gr.Rev.). J. with US5 (see).

**Sec. 4: GREENFIELD to MASS.-N.Y. LINE. 50.**

**3.5. SHELBURNE SUMMIT** with tower (O.sm.fee.pic.), fine view. **11. SHELBURNE FALLS,** through which runs picturesque Deerfield R. (see Deerfield). Here are **Salmon Falls. 12.** J. with St.112, leading (L) 3.5m to **Buckland. Lyon H.** (O.1818) where Mary Lyon, who est. Mt. Holyoke College, conducted a school. **Baron Rudduck H.** (late 18th cent.). **20. WARNER H.,** boyhood home of Chas. Dudley Warner, author who wrote entertainingly about his boyhood here. **22.5.** Hy. crosses **MOHAWK TRL. ST. FOR.** (5,746 as.pic.camp.bath.h.f.trls.bridle paths.cabins). **26.** J. with Black Brook Rd., leading (L) 2m into **Savoy Mt. St. For.** (10,641 as.pic.camp. trls.bath.f.) & at 2.5m to **Tannery Falls Pk.** (pic.cabins). **29.5. FLORIDA** (sett.1783. 2,180′), good starting point for **Monroe St. For.** (4,237 as.). **31.** Whitcomb Summit (2,110′). Trl. starts here (R) for **Moore's Summit.** Rd. now descends sharply with many turns, & calls for careful driving. **37.5.** Side Rd. (L) leads to Windsor Pond (f.boat.bath.). **38. NORTH ADAMS** (sett.1737), textile mill town. Fort Mass. was built here in 1745 to guard against Fr. & Ind. raids; was wiped out next year & rebuilt (see below). Hoosac Tunnel ends in town. At N. Adams is J. with St.8.

SIDE TRIPS: (A) Take St.8 (N). At 1.5m is J. with Rd. (L) to marble **Natural Bridge** described by Hawthorne.

(B) Take St.8 (S) to **Adams** 6m, industrial town producing textiles, leather, paper, lime & marble, with Blue L. in vic. Friend & Maple Sts., **Friends Meetingh.** (late 18th cent.). On Orchard St. (St.116), **Eleazer Brown H.** (O.summer;1778); antiques; fine view. On East Rd., at Four Corners, **Susan B. Anthony Birthpl.** (O.c.1815); birth room furnished in Quaker style. Here was born leader of the women's rights movement. 8.5m **Cheshire Harbor** where is trl. to summit of Mt. Greylock, highest Mt. in state (3,505′). 11m **Cheshire** (sett. 1660). **Cole H.** (O.tearoom.c.1804.int.inter.). **Cheshire Reservoir** (f.).

**39.5.** J. with Notch Rd. (L) to **Mt. Greylock** (see US7). **40.5. Replica of Old Fort Mass.** (O.summer;see above). **43. WILLIAMSTOWN** (see US7). **MASS.-N.Y. LINE** at **50.**

**Sec. 5: MASS.-N.Y. LINE to TROY. 26. St.2.**

St.2 passes **PETERSBURG MT. TOWER** (O.sm.fee), just (W) of N.Y. St. Line, skirts Petersburg Mt. to **PETERSBURG** at **5.,** J. with N.Y. St.22 (see). **11. GRAFTON** (resort); Ls. in vic. **26. TROY** (see).

## MASS. ST. 110—NEW ENGLAND

**WORCESTER, MASS. (NE) to SEABROOKE, N.H. 78. St.110**

Via: W. Boylston, Clinton, (Lancaster), (Bolton), Harvard, Littleton, (Westford), Chelmsford, Lowell, Lawrence, Haverhill, Merrimack, (Amesbury).

A fairly direct route to N.H., this avoids congested Boston area. It circles (W) of Wachusett Reservoir & traverses industrial cities of Lowell, Lawrence, Haverhill & finally crosses through Whittier's country.

**Sec. 1: WORCESTER to CLINTON. 16.**

St.110 circles around W. shore of Wachusett Reservoir.

**Sec. 2: From CLINTON to LOWELL. 29.**

**3.5.** J. with St.117.

SIDE TRIP: Take St.117 (L) here. At 2m is Rd. Fork. Take Rd. (L) here 3m into **Lancaster** (sett.1643). **Old Meetingh.** (O.early 19th cent.by Bulfinch.very fine). From Lancaster c.1m, **Thayer Bird Mus.** (O.Mon.Wed.Sat.summer).

At **5. OLD MARSHALL PLACE** (O); overnight guests. **7.5.** J. with "Fruitlands" Rd.

SIDE TRIP: Take latter (L) 1$^{m}$ to **Fruitlands** (rest.) & **Wayside Mus.** (both O.May 25-Oct.1.sm.fee). Fruitlands was site of Bronson Alcott's short-lived experiment in communal living, known as New Eden & is now **Transcendentalist Mus.**; relics of the movement & fine coll. of landscapes of Hudson R. school. Louisa M. Alcott describes her father's adventure in "Transcendental Wild Oats." **Shaker H.** (O.as above), home of Mother Ann Lee, founder of "Society of Shakers" in Amer.; int. exhibs. **Indian Mus.** (O.as above).

**8.5. HARVARD VILLAGE. Pub. Lib.** (O.wks.aft.); lib. dating from late 18th cent. On Old Littleton Rd. (R) is Harvard Observ. (O) (see Cambridge). Fine view. **17.5. LITTLETON.** Js. with St.2 & St.119 (see St.2). **20.5.** J. with Boston Rd. **25. CHELMSFORD** (sett.1633) with several int. old Hs., incl. **Fiske H.** (1790) with lovely fanlight door. Near Common, **Unit. Ch.** (O.1st half 18th cent.). **29. LOWELL** (see US3) near which is J. with US3.

### Sec. 3: LOWELL to SEABROOKE, N.H. 33.

**9.5.** J. with St.28. **10.5. LAWRENCE** (see St.28). J. with St.28 (S) to Andover (see Boston VII). **19. HAVERHILL** (sett.1640) on Merrimack R., once shipping & ship-bldg. town, today industrial; chief products: shoes & shoe accessories. PTS. OF INT.: (1) Green & Main Sts., **Statue comm. Hannah Dustin** who, abducted by Inds., escaped with 10 of kidnappers' scalps at her belt (1697) (see Worcester). (2) 240 Water St., **The Buttonwoods** (O.Tues.Thurs.Sat.aft.;Sun.appl.1814); Ind. material, period furniture, Hannah Dustin relics. (3) Also at 240 Water St., **Rev. John Ward H.** (O.as above.pre-1645.remod.); complete 17th cent. furnishings. (4) Summer St., **Haverhill Pub. Lib.** (O.wks.Sun.aft.Nov.-Ap.); Whittier relics & 1st editions. (5) Groveland & Water Sts., **Spiller H.** (late 17th cent.). Mill & Saltonstall Sts., **Ayer H.** (17th cent.). (6) On Kenoza Ave. is **Winnikenni Reserv. & Kenoza L.** (recr.). (7) Cor. Salem St. (St.125), **Kimball Tavern** (O.late 17th cent.). (8) Near-by, facing the Common, lovely **First Ch.** (Congr.1st half 19th cent.).

**22.5. WHITTIER'S BIRTHPL.** (O.exc.Mon.sm.fee.1688); furnished as in poet's time. Used by him as setting for "Snowbound." Near-by, **Whittier Family Mon. 23.5.** J. with Rd. On this Rd. (R) 1.5$^{m}$, No. 29, is **Birthpl. of Mary Ingalls**, who figures in Whittier's "The Countess." **25. MERRIMAC** (sett.1638). On St.110, **Sawyer H.** (O.1st half 18th cent.); antiques. **Old Pilgrim Ch.** (Congr.int.inter.). In vic. is **L. Attitash,** beloved of Whittier. **29. UNION CEMETERY,** where Whittier is buried. Just beyond Cemetery, St.110 makes J. with Main St.

SIDE TRIPS: (A) Take latter (R) here. No. 259, **Macy-Colby H.** (O.Wed.aft.summer. 1650), which figures in Whittier's poem, "The Exile." Furnished as typical pioneer home. No. 277, **Old Bagley H.** (O.sm.fee), in which Mary Baker Eddy lived.

(B) Take Main St. (L) past reprod. of **Old Well** (see Whittier's "The Captain's Well") & **Statue of Doughboy** by Leonard Kraske, to **Amesbury** (sett.1654), center of witchcraft hysteria (1693). 86 Friend St., **Whittier H.** (O.wks.pre-1836.Remod.) where poet lived for 56 yrs. & wrote many of his poems. Greenleaf St., **Friends Meetingh.** (1851) with Whittier's pew.

**30.5.** J. with Elm St. running (L) c.0.5$^{m}$ to **Rocky Hill Meetingh.** (O.late 18th cent. fine exter.& inter.). **33. MASS.-N.H. LINE** a short distance from **SEABROOKE, N.H.** (see US1).

## N.H. ST. 101, & ST. 9, VT. ST. 9, N.Y. ST. 7—NEW ENGLAND

**PORTSMOUTH, N.H., to TROY, N.Y., 192. St.101 & St.9, Vt. St.9, N.Y. St.7**

Via: In N.H.: Exeter, Epping, (Raymond), Manchester, Milford, Wilton, Peterborough, Dublin, Marlborough, & Keene; in Vt.: Brattleboro, Wilmington, Searsburg, Woodford, & Bennington; Hoosic, N.Y. (J. with N.Y. 22). B. & M. RR. parallels route to Manchester. Bus transportation from Peterborough to Bennington. Accoms. in larger centers.

Most southerly tour across N.H. & Vt., this route passes through country of hist. int., with many old Hs. & considerable scenic beauty, especially the Grand Monadnock reg. in N.H.

### Sec. 1: PORTSMOUTH, N.H., to MANCHESTER, N.H. 47. St.101

**0. PORTSMOUTH.** J. with US1. **28.** Eastern J. with St.107, with which route unites for short distance. (For tours & pts. of int. this sec., see Portsmouth Trip I). **29.**

Western J. with St.107, which runs (N) 3$^{m}$ to J. with Pawtuckaway Reserv. Rd. (R) on latter into **Pawtuckaway Reserv.** (recr.). Cont. on side Rd. At 4.5$^{m}$ J. with trl. (R) 0.5$^{m}$ to summit of **Mt. Pawtuckaway.** Int. Pawtuckaway Boulders. At **36.** on St.101 is **Candia Four Corners,** where is old **Charming Fare Inn.** [Rd. leads (R) 0.5$^{m}$ here to **Candia Hill Village. Fitts Mus.** (O.Sat.2-5), in ancient house; coll. of relics.]

**c.43. MASSABESIC L.,** near J. with St.121.

SIDE TRIP: Take latter (L) along E. side of L. to **Auburn** with some int. old bldgs. at 4$^{m}$. 8.5$^{m}$ **Chester,** with group of early Georg. Col. Hs. (1720-85). From Chester take St.121A. At 15$^{m}$ turn (L) on country Rd. 0.5$^{m}$ to **Sandown Meeting H.** (O.2nd half 18th cent.spireless.orig.inter.& exter.).

**47. MANCHESTER.** J. with US3 (see).

### Sec. 2: MANCHESTER to N.H.-VT. LINE. 74.

**5. BEDFORD** (sett.1st half 18th cent.). Fine **Old Town Hall** (Fed.). **Old Woodbury Mansion** (R). **Presb. Ch.** (1832.int.inter.). Canal St. at Amoskeag Bridge, **Home of Gen. John Stark** (O) (see Manchester, N.H.). From Bedford, country Rd. leads (R) 3.5$^{m}$ to **Birthpl. of Horace Greeley** (see N.Y.C.). **12.5.** J. with Rd. leading (L) to **Baboosic L.** (resort) at 2.5$^{m}$. **13. AMHERST** (sett.1st half 18th cent.). On Common, **Mem. to Horace Greeley.** In Cth. here (no longer standing) Dan. Webster tried his 1st case in 1805. E. of Common, **Cth.** (1825.Georg.) & **Old Cemetery.** At Common, **Rbt. Means H.** (late 18th cent.), where Franklin Pierce married Jane Means Appleton. In town center, **Brick H.** (early 19th cent.). Opp., **Cabinet Office,** where "Farmer's Cabinet," founded 1802, was 1st published (now published in Milford).

**16. MILFORD** (c.1738), mill town. Here John Shepard built mill at Souhegan R. in 1741. Now granite-quarrying, lumber & textile center. At Union Sq., **First Meetingh.** (c.1785) now houses Odd Fellows Soc. Clock & Paul Revere Bell removed to Town Hall. Elm & Union Sts., old **Lullwood** (O.aft.one wkday), hqs. of Milford Hist. & Genealogical Soc. To be demolished to make way for Pub. Lib. **Livermore Mansion** (O.1842.int.exter.), now Community H. **21. WILTON.** J. with St.31 (see Peterborough below). **28.5.** J. with country Rd. leading (R) 1.5$^{m}$ to **Gen. Miller St. Pk.** (named for Rev.Gen.), on Pack Monadnock Mt. (2,257';fine views). **30.5. WILSON TAVERN** (R) (late 18th cent.fine exter.& inter.). **31.5.** (R) **BLEAK H.** (O. c.1770-90.Georg.Col.remod.late 19th cent.), ten-room guest house. **33. PETERBOROUGH** (sett.1749), named for Earl of Peterborough, beautiful old town at confluence of Nubanusit & Contoocook Rs., in Monadnock reg. (winter sports facils. RR. & bus conns. Accoms.). Grove & Main Sts., **Town H.** is modern copy of Boston's Faneuil Hall. On Grove St. also is **Hist. Soc. Bldg.** (O); Americana. At Main & Summer Sts., **Unit. Ch.** (by Bulfinch.notable example). On Elm St., **Goyette Mus. of Americana** (O.summer.fee); int. coll. of antiques. On MacDowell Rd. (N) 1$^{m}$ is **MacDowell Colony** for musicians, writers & other artists (June-Oct.). **Grave of Edw. MacDowell,** famous Amer. composer. **Hillcrest,** his former home. **Log Cabin** (MacDowell's studio). **The Eaves** (mid-19th cent.). **Lib.** (all O.wks.). Near city is **Peterborough Pool St. Reserv.** (bath.no pic.). In Peterborough is **J.** with US202.

SIDE TRIPS: (A) (N) on US202. At 7$^{m}$, **Hancock** (sett.1764), semingly little touched by time. Accoms. **Congr. Ch.** (1st quarter 19th cent.Class.Rev.). Main St., **Hist. Bldg.** (O.summer.c.1810); coll. of paintings & other antiques. On St.123, **John Hancock H.** (O.late 18th cent.), for more than 150 yrs. an inn; unique wall paintings by anonymous itinerant artist. 11$^{m}$ **Bennington,** from which along Contoocook riverbanks are paper mills & other factory bldgs., to **Antrim** at 12$^{m}$. At c.19$^{m}$ hy. crosses fine **Stone Bridge** (18th cent.). At 20$^{m}$ St.9 makes J. with US202 (see) (W) of **Hillsborough** (See Concord, Side Trip, US4).

(B) US202 (S). At 6.5$^{m}$ **East Jaffrey,** good mt. views. (L) from E. Jaffrey 1.5$^{m}$ is **Contoocook L.** In E. Jaffrey is J. with St.124.

Take latter (W). At 2.5$^{m}$, **Jaffrey** (resort.wintersports & carnival on Grand Monadnock). **Meetingh.** (early 19th cent.now the Town Hall) & **Old Cemetery.** To (S) lies charming Gilmore Pond reached by country Rd. Just (W) of Jaffrey is J. with country Rd. [Take latter (R) past **Wier-Buckley H.** (probably most ancient in township) to **The Ark** (early 19th cent.adds.hotel) at 1.5$^{m}$. Take Rd. (L) here 1$^{m}$ into **Monadnock St. Reserv.** (pic. trls. accoms. summer & winter sports) & then trl. to **Summit of Grand Monadnock** (3,166').]. At 5.5$^{m}$ on St.124 J. with Toll Rd. which take (R) 1$^{m}$ to **Halfway H.,** from which trl. runs to **Summit of Grand Monadnock.** St.124 cont. to J. with St.101 at **Marlboro** (see below).

US202 cont. (S) through lake reg. At 12$^{m}$ **Rindge. Congr. Ch.** (1796;alts.). J. with St.119 which runs (SE) to **Townsend,** Mass. (see Mass. St.2). 15.5$^{m}$, **Monomonac L.** at **N.H.-Mass. Line** c.4$^{m}$ from Winchendon, Mass., toy-making center.

(C) About 1m (E) of Peterborough on St.101 is J. with St.123 which take (SE). At 2.5m **Sharon.** (NE) is seen **Temple Mt.** (2,081'). **Laws H.** (O.appl.1800) houses part of Sharon Arts Center. St.123 cont. through wild mt. scenery to J. with St.31 at **Greenville.** St.123 cont. (SE) to **West Townsend,** Mass. (see Mass. St.2). St.31 turns (NE) to **Wilton** (see above).

**40. DUBLIN** (sett.mid-18th cent.resort). Fine view across beautiful **Dublin L.** of **Grand Monadnock;** in this L. are found unique type of trout. Take Rd. from Dublin (L) 1m to Pumpelly Trl. to summit of Monadnock, 4.5m. **53. KEENE.** J. with St.10 (see). From Keene, route follows St.9 (W). For St.9 (E), see Concord, Side Trip US4. **61.5.** (R) here on dirt Rd. to **Chesterfield Gorge. 65. SPOFFORD L.** (resort.accoms.). **66. CHESTERFIELD.** Among early Bldgs. are **Stone Town Hall** & **Stone Store. 74.** Bridge across Conn. R. to Vt.

### Sec. 2: N.H.-VT. LINE to VT.-N.Y. LINE. 45. St.9

**0. BRATTLEBORO** (see US5) at J. with US5. **2.5. W. BRATTLEBORO. Hayes Tavern** (1791.porch add.), built by Pres. Rutherford B. Hayes' grandfather. **10.5.** J. with Rd. leading (L) to **Marlboro,** scene of battle with Inds., June 26, 1748. **15.5. MARLBORO TAVERN** (hotel.fine view). Trl. leads (R) here 0.5m to **Mt. Olga Fire Lookout Tower. 17.5.** J. with Rd. leading (R) 1.5m to **Raponda L.** (recr.). **19.** J. with St.8.

SIDE TRIP: Take latter (L) 5.5m to **Jacksonville.** At 9m, **Sadawaga Pond** (recr.), with floating I., which broke from shore & lodged in new position. 10m J. with dirt Rd. leading (R) 1.5m to **Harriman Dam,** said to be world's highest earth dam, impounding **L. Whitingham,** largest in Vt. St.8 cont. to **N. Adams,** Mass. (see Mass. St.2).

**20. WILMINGTON. Bapt. Ch.** (1st half 19th cent.). **21. L. WHITINGHAM** (see above). **27. SEARSBURG** (1,760'), mt. town. [Take Rd. (R) to beautiful **Somerset Reservoir** 9m.] **34.5. WOODFORD** (2,215'), with highest elevation of any Vt. village, dominated by rugged mts. **41. BENNINGTON** at J. with US7 (see) & short distance beyond, **Old Bennington** (see US7). **45. VT.-N.Y. LINE** with view (S) of **Mt. Anthony** (2,345').

### Sec. 3: VT.-N.Y. LINE to TROY. 26. St.7

**3. HOOSIC. 14.5. TOMHANNOCK RESERVOIR,** Troy water supply. **26. TROY** (see N.Y. St.7).

## US 4—NEW ENGLAND

### PORTSMOUTH, N.H. (W) to WHITEHALL, N.Y. 179. US4

Via: In N.H.: Durham, Northwood, (Rochester), Epsom, Concord, Boscawen, Andover, Canaan Village, W. Lebanon. In Vt.: White R. Junction, Woodstock, Bridgewater, Sherburne, Rutland, Castleton Corners, Fair Haven.

RR. parallels route from Concord to W. Lebanon, N.H. RR. & bus conns. at White R. Junction, Rutland, Vt. & Whitehall, N.Y. Accoms.: At all larger centers; tourist camps bet. Concord, N.H. & Fairhaven, Vt.

Route passes through some of N.H.'s fine old towns & then winds (NW) through rugged mt. scenery into Vt., where it enters several charming cities & crosses southern Green Mts. Its terminus in Whitehall, N.Y. is near L. Champlain & beautiful L. George.

### Sec. 1: PORTSMOUTH to CONCORD, N.H. 45.

For stretch to Northwood, incl. Rochester on US202, see Portsmouth II. **23. NORTHWOOD. 33. EPSOM** (sett.pre-1743). In near-by Epsom Center is **John Tucke H.** (2nd half 18th cent.), home of 1st minister; adj. is **Early Cemetery** & opp., **First Parsonage** (2nd half 18th cent.). **Webster Pk.** (pic.swim.). **Old Covered Bridge** at Short Falls.

**45. CONCORD** (1726), state capital.

RR. & bus conns. Airport. Good accoms. Info.: Booth at State House & N.H. Auto Assoc. in Eagle Hotel. Winter sports at Russell's Pond. Bear Brook St. Pk., well-developed, is 11m (SE) off St.28.

On Merrimack R., Concord is financial as well as political center of N.H. In vic. are large apple orchards & noted Concord granite quarries. First St. Constitutional Convention was held in Concord, 1778, but St. Capital moved about to 8 different cities & it was not till 1808 that it finally came to rest in Concord. Concord men fought in Fr.-Ind. wars & under Gen. John Stark in Rev. & were among 1st Civil War volunteers. PTS. OF INT.: (1) Near Main St., **State H.** (O.wks.1819.remod. 1866.annex 1911), surmounted by lofty dome supposed to be modelled on that of Hotel des Invalides in Paris. Dome is topped by an eagle. In 1864, Manchester offered to build a St. Capitol, but it was decided to remain at Concord & remodel the existing bldg. In Plaza are statues of Pres. Pierce, Dan. Webster, John P. Hale, Gen. John Stark & his son, Caleb. Inter. of Bldg.: **Hall of Flags. Senate Chamber** has notable murals by Barry Faulkner, representing N.H. scenes. **Representatives' Hall.** Hist. portraits in corridors & special chambers. At rear of State H., **Statue of Commodore Perkins,** by D. C. French. (2) 20 Park St., **State Lib.** (O.wks. 19th cent. Romanes.). (3) State & Park Sts., **Hist. Soc. Bldg.** (O.wks.1912.by Guy Lowell). Hist. sculpture above entrance by D. C. French; noteworthy paintings, portraits & colls. On N. Main St. are: (4) **Franklin Pierce H.** (O.summer.wks.1826.Georg.Col.remod.), now Mus. of Hist. Soc. Here Pierce had his law office. (5) **Home of First Minister** (1734.later adds.), Rev. Timothy Walker. (6) **Eagle Hotel,** said to be "The Pelican" of Winston Churchill's novels. (7) 243 Pleasant St., **Pleasant View,** home for old people belonging to Christian Science sect. On this spot stood Mary B. Eddy's home. (8) Int. are **Granite Quarries** in vic. (9) 5$^m$ (S) at Bow, **Birthpl. of Mary Baker Eddy.** Near Bow is **Bow Mill,** oldest in state. For pts. of int. in vic. on US202 (see below) & on US3 (see).

SIDE TRIP: US202 & St.9 (SW) to Keene. 1.5$^m$ **Pleasant View Home** (see above). Across hy. is **Bradley Mon.,** comm. massacre of whites by Inds. (1746). 2.5$^m$ beautiful bldgs. & grounds of **St. Paul's School** (Episc.boys), est. 1856 with nonsect. student body. In front of **Sheldon Lib.** is statue of Amer. soldier (by Bela Pratt). **Sheldon Hall;** Natural Hist. coll. 6.5$^m$ **Morse Tavern,** former stagecoach inn. 7$^m$ **Birthpl. of Grace Fletcher,** wife of Dan. Webster. [Rd. leads (L) here 4$^m$ to J. with Rd. on which turn (R) 1.5$^m$ to **Stark Family Burying Ground & Stark Mansion,** Gen. John Stark's home. Gen. Stark is buried at Manchester, N.H. (see).] 8$^m$ **Hopkinton** (sett.1st half 18th cent.). Of special int. are **Long Mem. Lib.:** coll. antique items; **Congr. Ch.** (late 18th cent.) & **St. Andrew's Ch.** (early 19th cent.); on South Rd., **Ella Kimball H.** (1791); adj., **J. H. George H.** (c.1791); **Lerned H.** (late 18th cent.). Hopkinton Fair, early Sept. 17$^m$ **Henniker** (c.1760). Ski tow operated by Henniker Inn. **New England College. Tucker Lib.** (O) with Ind. relics. Take St.114 (L) 0.5$^m$ & then (R) on country Rd. to **Ocean-Born Mary H.** (O.sm.fee) at 3$^m$. H. so-named because Mary Wallace was born on shipboard during a pirate raid.

(1) St.114 leading (NW & N) 18$^m$ to J. with St.11, several miles (E) of L. Sunapee (see). Int. route in summer resort reg. among Ls. & Mts.

(2) On St.114 (S) to Manchester. At 8$^m$ **Weare,** orig. Quaker settlement. In vic. is **Quaker Meeting H.** (late 18th cent.), & **Mt. William Pond** (f.) & **Clough Reserv.** (pic.). 18$^m$ **Goffstown,** pleasant village on Piscataquog R. (SW) from Goffstown, 6$^m$ on St.13 is **New Boston,** where in Wason Mem. Lib. is famous **Molly Stark Cannon** that has figured in 3 wars. 19$^m$ **Shirley Hall Sta.** (L) here 2.5$^m$ to RR. up Uncanoonuc Mt.). 27$^m$ **Manchester** (see US3).

24$^m$ **Hillsborough** on US202. **Community H.** in which is Hist. Room; coll. of miscellaneous items. (R) from Hillsborough on School St. 4$^m$ is **Hillsborough Center,** which has some int. old Hs. In Hillsborough is J. with St.9 on which side trip cont. (SW). For US202 to Peterborough (see). 26$^m$ (on St.9) J. with St.31, on which NW. (R) a short distance is **Franklin Pierce Homstead** (O.wks.except Sat.), state hist. shrine. 39$^m$ **Munsonville,** on Munson L. (resort). 53$^m$ **Keene** (see N.H. St.10). J. with St.101, St.10 & St.12. St.9 cont. (W) to Vt. Line near Brattleboro, Vt. J. with US5 (see).

## Sec. 2: CONCORD to N.H.-VT. LINE. 64.

In Concord US4 unites with US3. **9. BOSCAWEN.** (For this stretch of Rd. see US3.) US4 swings (L) to J. with St.11 at **22.** On St.11 (E) 9$^m$ is **Franklin,** at J. with US3 (see). For a few miles (W) US4 & St.11 unite. **23. ANDOVER,** home of **Proctor Academy,** for boys, founded in 1848 (Unit.). A short distance (S) is **Bradley L.** (resort). **25. POTTER PLACE.** (W) J. with St.11.

SIDE TRIP: (W) on St.11, which follows Sugar R. At 3$^m$ J. with Rd. (S) 2.5$^m$ to trl. up **Mt. Kearsarge** (2,937′) in **Wilmot Site St. Pk.** (pic.camp.recr.). 4.5$^m$ **Elkins,** on Pleasant L. At 7$^m$ J. with St.114 which runs (S) to **Wadleigh St. Pk.** (pic.swim.sports facils.on lake). 9$^m$ **New London,** seat of **Colby Jr. College for Women.** Several beautiful old bldgs. 12$^m$ **Little Sunapee L.** 13.5$^m$ **Georges Mills** on (N) shore of L. Sunapee. **Collins Clock Mus.** (O. sm.fee) with more than 200 old timepieces. 17.5$^m$ **Sunapee** (summer & winter sports.9$^m$ long L.Sunapee.f.boat.many resorts). To (S) are Sunapee Mts. **Newport** at 23$^m$, J. with St.10 (see). 35$^m$ **W. Claremont.** J. with St.12A (see). At 37$^m$ **J.** with US5 (see) in Vt. at **Ascutney.**

At **26.** on US4, Rd. leads (R) to **Ragged Mt. Fish & Game Club** (no parking without permit). From here trl. runs to summits of **Ragged Mts.,** highest 2,225′. US4 winds through beautiful reg. of many ponds, in sight of magnificent peaks. **46.5. CANAAN** (sett.2nd half 18th cent.winter sports.accoms.). [(1) About 2^m^ (NW) is **Canaan Street,** on Canaan L. Village consists of tree-lined avenue of summer homes & quaint early bldgs., incl. old spired **Col. Ch.** (2) (R) on St.118 & then (R) on country Rd. 2.5^m^ from Canaan to **Orange,** where dirt Rd. enters **Cardigan St. Reserv.** (c.4,000 as.pic. facils.); trls. to **Mt. Cardigan** (3,121′) & other peaks.] From Canaan, US4 turns (W). **54. ENFIELD,** small industrial town on Mascoma R. near Mascoma L. (Accoms.). S. 2^m^ is former Shaker Village, now used by **La Salette Seminary** (Cath.). **56. MASCOMA** (resort) on Mascoma L. **60. LEBANON.** At J. with St.10 (see). **64. W. LEBANON.** J. with St.12A & St.10 (see); hy. crosses bridge here to **WHITE RIVER JUNCTION,** Vt. (see US5).

### Sec. 3: N.H.-VERMONT LINE to WHITEHALL. 70.

**0. WHITE RIVER JUNCTION.** J. with US5 (see) & N. of city is J. with St.14. (For Side Trip on St.14 to Barre, see US5.) US4 starts directly (W), then curves across **Quechee Gorge** over lofty bridge, with superb view of rocky chasm & Ottaquechee R. below. Hy. follows R.'s course.

**14. WOODSTOCK** (sett.1768, summer & winter sports, resort).

Bus conns. with Rutland & White R. Junction & RR. conns. from these pts. Accoms. Ski meets.

Woodstock is one of St.'s most charming villages, known for its Col. houses & early churches with Paul Revere bells. **Birthpl. of Hiram Powers,** whose "Greek Slave" is in Corcoran Gallery, Wash, D.C. PTS. OF INT.: (1) **Norman Williams Pub. Lib.** (1885.Richardson-Romanes.); Vermontiana & Williams Japanese Art colls. (2) Adj. is **Windsor County Cth.** (1855.Georg.Col.). (3) Elm St., **Old White Meetingh.** (2nd Congr.Ch.1808.rest.); fine steeple & Revere bell. 2 other fine old Chs. dating from 1st half 19th cent. (4) Elm St., **Johnson H.** (early 19th cent.Georg. Col.). (5) At Pub. Sq., inc. in White Cupboard Inn is **Hutchinson H.** (1794). (6) Opp. Woodstock Inn. **Bailey H.** (1st quarter 19th cent.fine Georg.) (7) Elm St., **Dana H.** (early 19th cent.), now Woodstock Hist. Soc. Bldg.

US4 cont. along Ottaquechee R. **20. BRIDGEWATER.** Here are woolen mills of Vermont Native Industries (products for sale). **22. BRIDGEWATER CORNERS,** mountain-enclosed. J. with St.100A.

SIDE TRIP: (S) 17^m^ on St.100A & St.100 to **Ludlow.** 6^m^ **Plymouth,** where Pres. Coolidge was born, took oath of office & is buried. On either side of hy. are secs. of **Calvin Coolidge St. For.** (pic.trls.ski trls.). Near-by is **Coolidge farm.** 7^m^ **Plymouth Union.** J. with St.100, which runs past lovely Amherst, Echo & Rescue Ls. St.100 cont. (S) to **Ludlow** (see US5) 17^m^, where Calvin Coolidge went to high school. At J. with St.103 (see US5).

**32. SHERBURNE.** J. with St.100, with which US4 unites to **34.** at (SE) tip of **GREEN MT. NAT. FOR.** (f.h.pic.camp.swim.winter sports). US4 cont. (W) along S. border of Nat. For., while St.100 turns (N). [Off St.100 (N) from J. is **Gifford Woods St. For. Pk.** (pic.camp.trls.). For special pts. of int. on St.100 (N) see Side Trips off US7.] **35. SHERBURNE PASS** (2,190′) where Long Trl. crosses hy. [(1) (S) is **Long Trl. Lodge** (meals.rooms.cabins) & 2.5^m^ (S) on trl. (by side trl.) is **Pico Peak** (3,961′) & short distance (S) of it (by side trl.) is **Killington Peak** (4,241′). (2) Just (N) of hy. on Long Trl. is **Deer Leap Lodge.**] **46. RUTLAND.** J. with US7. (see). **50. W. RUTLAND,** in midst of some of country's finest marble deposits. Bet. 400,000 & 600,000 cu. ft. of marble are quarried here annually. In **Proctor** (N) (4^m^ on St.3) is **Marble Exhibit.** US4 now crosses Taconic Range. **54. CASTLETON,** where Ethan Allen completed plans for attack on Ft. Ticonderoga. Several Col. Hs. designed by Thos. R. Dake. **Federated Ch.** (1st half 19th cent.). Graceful **Cole H.** (1st half 19th cent.by Dake). **56. CASTLETON CORNERS.** J. with St.30. In the distance may be seen Adirondack Mts. On St.30 (N) is **L. Bomoseen** (resort). (For St.30 see US7). **59. FAIR HAVEN,** attractive community in slate belt. On S. Main St. **Zenas Ellis H.;** was fugitive slave depot of Underground RR. Near Common is **Maj. Gilbert H.** (1806.Georg.), antique shop. Matthew Lyon, citizen of Fair Haven, cast deciding vote in House of Representatives that elected Jefferson to Presidency, 1801. **62. POULTNEY R.** boundary bet. Vt. & N.Y. US4 cont. across R. to **WHITEHALL, N.Y.** (see N.Y. St.22) at **70.**

# US 2—NEW ENGLAND

## HOULTON, ME. to ROUSES POINT, N.Y. 470. US2

Via: Island Falls, Mattawamkeag, West Enfield, Milford, Orono, Bangor, Newport, Skowhegan, New Sharon, Farmington, Wilton, Rumford & Bethel in Me.; Shelburne, Gorham, Jefferson & Lancaster in N.H.; Lunenburg, St. Johnsbury, Montpelier, Middlesex, Waterbury, Richmond, Burlington, Grand Isle (across Sand Bar Bridge) in Vt. & (across toll bridge) into Rouses Pt., N.Y., (S) of Montreal, Canada.

RR. parallels route from Houlton, Me. to Island Falls, Me. & from Mattawamkeag, Me. to Newport, Me. & from Bethel, Me. to Gorham, N.H. RR. conns. at Lancaster, N.H. RR. easily accessible or parallels route from Lancaster to W. Danville, Vt., & from Marshfield, Vt. to Rouses Pt., N.Y.

US2 begins in Aroostook Cty., known for potatoes, then turns (S) through reg. of Ls. & Rs. in view of Mt. Katahdin, & along Penobscot R. to Bangor. From Bangor, hy. runs (W) through sparsely settled country, conns. with routes to Moosehead & Rangeley Ls. US2 cont. in N.H. along Androscoggin R. & then through White Mts. to Lancaster on Conn. R. In Vt., the route lies through heart of Green Mts., giving access to Mt. Mansfield. From Burlington it crosses bridge to traverse (S-N) islands in L. Champlain, then (W) to Rouses Pt., N.Y., on main route from N.Y.C. to Montreal. US2 makes J. with most (N-S) tours.

### Sec. 1: HOULTON, ME. to ME.-N.H. LINE. 279.

**0. HOULTON.** J. with US1 (see). **28. ISLAND FALLS** near Mattawamkeag & Pleasant Ls. (camp.f.). **65. MATTAWAMKEAG** (RR.). Here US4 unites with St.11.

SIDE TRIP: (W) on St.11, St.157 & Private Rd. (O) to Greenville at 106m

Via: Medway, Millinocket, Baxter St. Pk. (Mt. Katahdin), Ripogenus Dam & Kodakjo. RR. at Mattawamkeag, Millinocket, Greenville. Limited accoms. & considerable distances bet. gas stations. Permit to cross Ripogenus Dam obtainable at Gt. Northern Paper Co., Bangor; Spruce Wood Office Millinocket; or Company Shop, Greenville Junction.

Route traverses almost uninhabited forest reg., past number of Ls. to Mt. Katahdin, highest in state.

0m **Mattawamkeag.** 11m **Medway,** where E. & W. branches of Penobscot R. meet. J. with St.157 on which cont. 23.5m **Millinocket** (Info. Bureau), in reg. of many Ls. (Info. Bureau, summer). **Gt. Northern Paper Co.,** one of world's largest producers of newsprint. Permit is required from Company to cross Ripogenus Dam (see below). From here hy. is unnumbered &, although passable, is not good. 30.5m **Millinocket L.** (summer resort.pub.camp site) & **Black Mt.** 44m **Katahdin St. Game Preserve** (no h.), which incl. **Baxter St. Pk.** (127,000 as.camps on trls. & ponds). In pk. are **Mt. Katahdin** (5,267′), highest in state, **N. Brother** (4,143′), **S. Brother** (3,951′) & **Fort** (3,861′). Preserve covers 144 sq. miles with numerous brooks, ponds & trls. (guides advisable). 48.5m **Baxter Camp.** Here begins 5-mile Hunt Trl. (pub.camp sites) to Baxter Peak (summit of Mt. Katahdin) & N. terminus of Appalachian Trl. (2,054 miles to Mt. Oglethorpe, Ga.) (For trls. in Pk., see Maine Sec. of publication on Appalachian Trl. by Appalachian Mt. Club). 70.5m **Ripogenus Dam** across river gorge. 71m Private Rd. (O.untreated gravel) of Gt. Northern Paper Co. 74.5m Route passes S. arms of **Chesuncook** & **Caribou Ls.** (pub.camp sites) & then S. end of **Ragged L.** View of **Spencer Mt.** (3,035′). 92.5m **Kokadjo** (Boarding H. & filling sta.). 99m **Lilly Bay,** on Moosehead L. (hotel & filling sta.). 106m **Greenville,** J. with St.15 (see below).

US2 follows Penobscot R. for many miles (S). **79. LINCOLN** (pub.camp site), near **Mattanawcook L.** (f.resort). **90.5. WEST ENFIELD,** near **Cold Stream L. 114.5. MILFORD.** US2 swings (W) across arm of Penobscot R. to **OLD TOWN,** made famous by the **Old Town Canoe Co.** (O). On **Indian I.** (rowboat ferry) is Penobscot Ind. Reserv. (O) where live last of great tribe of Abnaki. **120.5. ORONO,** pleasant college town. **Univ. of Maine** (opened 1868) has beautiful 200-a. campus. Of special int. are College of Agric. bldgs. & univ. farms & forest. **Fernald Hall** (1870), oldest bldg. **Coburn Hall** (1888); extensive biological colls. & herbarium. In **Lib.** (1947) is Art Coll. **128.5. BANGOR** (see US1). J. with US1. US2 swings (W) from Penobscot R. **156.5. NEWPORT,** on L. Sebasticook (recr.resort). J. with St.7 which unites here with St.11.

SIDE TRIP: To Rockwood. St.7 & St.15. Via: Corinna, Dexter, Dover-Foxcroft, Greenville, (Moosehead L.). Accoms. Me. Cent. RR. at Newport. Bangor & Aroostook RR. at Dover-Foxcroft. Can. Pac. & B. & A. RRs. at Greenville. Bus conns at Newport & at Greenville.

0m **Newport.** St.7 passes L. Sebasticook. 15m **Dexter** on L. Wassookeag. 28m **Dover-Foxcroft.** Cont. (L) here on St.15, which joins with St.16 to Abbot Village. At c.36m **Guilford** (sett.1806). In vic. (R) (N) on St.150 is **Sebec L.** (accoms.), also **Boarstone Mt.** 39m **Abbot**

**Village.** Tour turns (N) here on St.15. 47.5m **Monson** (good trout f.in vic.camp sites); large slate quarry. 62m **Greenville,** center for Moosehead L. reg. (f.h.canoe). RR. & bus conns., airport. Accoms. should be reserved; guides. Steamer on Moosehead L. touches chief pts. of int.

**Moosehead L.,** largest in Me., has shore line of c.350 miles. Width varies from 1 to 20 miles, alt. is 1,028'. Stocked with trout, salmon & togue. Out of heart of L. rises precipitous Kineo Mt. Along S. shore are Baker, Big & Little Squaw Mts. Among larger islands are Deer & Sugar Is. In Greenville is J. with Private Rd. (see Side Trip from Mattawamkeag above). Hy. follows W. side of L. 66m **Hotel** & camps (guides) near **Big Squaw Mt.** (3,267'). 70m **St. Fish Hatchery** (extensive salmon breeding). 86m **Rockwood.** Across narrow neck of L. is **Mt. Kineo** (1,806'), with hotel at base. From Rockwood, St.15 swings (W) by **Brassua L.** & **Long Pond** to **Jackman Sta.** & J. with US201 (see US1, Brunswick, Me.). A private Rd. cont. (NW) from Rockwood to **Canadian Line** (5m from St. Zacharie, Canada).

**172.5. CANAAN.** In vic., **David Nason H.** (1807). **181.5. SKOWHEGAN,** rural shipping pt. & mfg. center on Kennebec R. Name in Ind. means "place to watch," referring to salmon at R. falls. Accoms. Landing field. **History H.** (O.rest.) on Elm St. At Weston St., **Arnold Boulder,** on spot where Benedict Arnold camped, 1775, during expedition to Quebec. **Coburn Pk.,** overlooking "Great Eddy" R. gorge. In Skowhegan is J. with St.147 & US201.

SIDE TRIP: Take St.147 (N) 5m to **Lakewood,** summer resort on L. Wesserunsett. Leading summer theater. 15m **Solon** (see) at J. with US201 (see US1, Brunswick, Me.).

**186.5. NORRIDGEWOCK** (see US1, Brunswick, Me.). Here US201 turns (N) to Rangeley Ls. while main tour cont. (W) on US2. **199.5. NEW SHARON.** J. with St.27 (S) to **Belgrade Ls. Chain** (resort). **208.5. FARMINGTON,** seat of St. Normal School. Trade center & starting pt. for trips to Rangeley Ls. & Deer R. regs. East J. with St.4 (see Me. St.100-St.4 out of Portland, Me.), route to Rangeley Ls. (Near Farmington is birthpl. of Lillian Nordica for which see Me. St.100-St.4 out of Portland, Me.). **217. WILTON,** near Wilson L. & stream (recr.). West J. with St.4. **239. RUMFORD** (winter sports) at Falls of Androscoggin R. in heart of lake reg. **Oxford Paper Mills** (O.appl.), one of largest in U.S. **257. NEWRY,** J. with St.26 (see). **263. BETHEL** on Androscoggin R.; famous old **Bethel Inn.** J. with St.5 (another route to Rangeley Ls.; see Saco, Me., US1). **273.5. GILEAD** on N. edge of **White Mt. Nat. For.** (pic.camp.). Most of White Mt. Nat. For. lies in N.H. Just W. of Gilead, take St.113 (S) past **Gilead For. Camp** (pic.camp.) to **N. Chatham** & the Rd. (R) through scenically fine **Evans Notch** to **S. Chatham** (see N.Conway, N.H. & Fryeburg, Me.). **279. ME.-N.H. LINE.**

### Sec. 2: ME.-N.H. LINE to N.H.-VT. LINE. 37.

Route, paralleling Androscoggin R. & crossing White Mt. area, has great scenic int. **3.5. SHELBURNE,** on edge of White Mt. Nat. For. Splendid views of **Mt. Washington** (6,288') & other peaks. At **9.** a fine stopping pt. is **LEAD MINE BRIDGE.** Just beyond, on US2, is **GORHAM,** J. with St.16 (see White Mt. Tour). Popular resort in guarded valley among loftiest peaks of Presidential Range; at N. entrance to scenic **Pinkham Notch,** from which trls. lead to Mt. Washington & other peaks. At c.11m off hy. (N) is **Moose Brook St. Pk.** (f.pic.camp.bath.recr.bldg.). As US2 climbs Gorham Hill, the **Crescent Range** appears (N) & **Mt. Madison** (5,380') & **Mt. Adams** (5,805') to S. **15. RANDOLPH,** resort; accoms. of various types. Trl. over highest of Presidential Range from here. **19. BOWMAN,** from which trls. lead (L) to **Mts. Washington & Jefferson. 22. JEFFERSON HIGHLAND,** a small cluster of houses. **23.** J. with St.115.

SIDE TRIP: Take latter (S) 1.5m to J. with Jefferson Notch Rd. which leads (L) & then (S) through magnificent scenery to J. with Mt. Washington Rd. near **Bretton Woods** (see US302 sec. of White Mt. Tour). St.115 cont. (SW) to **Carroll,** J. with US3, (N) of Twin Mt. (see White Mt. Tour) at 10m.

**27. JEFFERSON,** in resort reg.; accoms. Panoramic views. Trl. (R) to **Starr King** (3,913'); **34. LANCASTER** (see US5). J. with US3 (see White Mt. Tour). At **37.** US2 crosses Conn. R. by one of St.'s many rustic covered bridges.

### Sec. 3: N.H.-VT. LINE to MONTPELIER, VT. 64.

**0.5.** J. with St.102 (see Newport, Vt. Side Trip A). **5.5. LUNENBURG** (sett.1768). N. to **Neal Pond** (trout). **12. MILES POND.** US2 crosses Moose R. which runs (N) through excellent f. & h. area. **18.5. CONCORD,** near Shadow & Miles Ls. Sam

Hall, a local schoolteacher, claimed to be inventor of the blackboard. **27. ST. JOHNSBURY** (see US5). J. with US5 & Side Trip A from Newport, Vt. **34. DANVILLE** (sett.late 18th cent.), named for Fr. Admiral D'Anville; birthpl. of Thaddeus Stevens, abolitionist & instigator of impeachment of Pres. Johnson. **Town Hall** (early 19th cent.rebuilt). **Elm H.** & other early 19th cent. Hs. **37. WEST DANVILLE,** at Joe's Pond. J. with St.15.

SIDE TRIP: (NW) to Jeffersonville, via Hardwick & Morrisville. Through mts. & past small rural villages. 10m J. with St.12 (see Newport, Vt., Side Trip B). 13m **Hardwick,** J. with St.12B (see Newport, Vt., Side Trip B). 27m just N. of Morrisville (see Waterbury below), J. with St.100 (see Newport, Side Trip C) & (S) to J. with US2, main tour, at Waterbury. At 45m **Jeffersonville,** J. with St.108 which is route (S) to Mt. Mansfield reg. For St.108 & balance of St.15 to Winooski, see Waterbury below.

From W. Danville, US2 angles SW. At **c.49. MARSHFIELD.** Rd. (SE) here to **Groton St. For.** (15,000 as.hqs.at New Discovery.f.pic.camp.summer & winter sports), incl. Groton & other Ls. **57. EAST MONTPELIER** on Winooski R. Troops were mustered here for march to Battle of Plattsburg, 1814. **Quaker Burying Ground.** J. with St.12.

SIDE TRIP: At 3m (N) on St.12 is **North Montpelier.** At 5m J. with side Rd. [Take latter (L) to **Calais. Kent Tavern & Country Store Farmer's Mus.** (O.1837); old farm implements, etc.] St.12 cont. (N) to Hardwick (see Newport Trip C).

**64. MONTPELIER** (sett.c.1788), state capital.

Central Vt. & Montpelier & Wells River RRs. Bus conn. Airport in near-by Berlin. Accoms.: Various kinds.

City is beautifully situated on Winooski (Ind. "Onion") & N. Branch Rs. Birthpl. of Admiral George Dewey. Important insurance & granite-quarrying center. Good f. in vic. PTS. OF INT.: On State St.: (1) **Capitol** (1836.Gr.Rev.by Ammi B.Young. rest.1850's), a noble bldg. of local granite. Statue of "Ceres" on dome, by L. J. Mead. In lobby are hist. portraits. Representatives Hall & especially the Senate Chamber are very beautiful. (2) **Supreme Court Bldg.** housing State Lib. & other depts. & **Hist. Soc. Mus.,** with fine genealogical, hist. & nat. hist. colls. (3) No. 89, **Wood Art Gallery;** of special int. are paintings by Thos. Waterman Wood, one of the founders, & other Vt. artists. (4) **Washington County Cth.** (1st half 19th cent.). (5) No. 159, **Wright H.** (early 19th cent.). (6) **Dewey H.** where famous Admiral was born, 1837. (7) Northfield St., **Athenwood** (O), former home of painter, T. W. Wood. (8) 91 Elm St., **Davis H.** (late 18th cent.), oldest frame house in city; only part of orig. still standing. (9) On Seminary Hill, **Vermont Jr. College.** (10) (N) 5m on Worcester Rd., **Wrightville Dam,** flood control project; earth dam 1,500′ long. Montpelier is at J. with St.12 & US302.

SIDE TRIPS: (A) 7m (SE) on US302 to **Barre.** The vic. of Barre leads world in production of granite for monuments. It is also a center for winter sports & f. & h. PTS. OF INT.: (1) **Granite Sheds,** along valley, where cutting & polishing are done. (2) **Nat. Mus. of Memorial Art** (O); models, photographs & sculptures. (3) On Plaza, **Rbt. Burns Mem. Statue** (designed by J.Massey Rhind;carved by Sam.Novellie of Barre). (3) In City Pk., **Youth Victorious,** World War I Mem. (4) 188 S. Main St., **Paddock H.** (early 19th cent. Georg.), fine example. (5) 145 N. Main St., **Wheelock H.** (1st quarter 19th cent.). (6) 431 N. Main St., **Twing H.** (1st half 19th cent.). In residential S. Barre is (7) **Denison Smith H.** (early 19th cent.). For best view of granite quarries, follow Rd. leading (E) from St.14 at S. city limits to Websterville & Graniteville. (For US302 to Wells River, see Side Trip from US5.) From Barre, St.14 runs (S) to White River Junction (see US5).

(B) (S) on St.12 to Randolph. At 10m **Northfield,** seat of Norwich Univ. (est.1819), one of oldest military schools in country. Many of its graduates, incl. Admiral Dewey, attained outstanding positions. Northfield has Winter Carnival. 11m **Northfield Center;** here hy. forks with St.12A running (W & S) through Roxbury & Roxbury St. For. & uniting with St.12 in Randolph. St.12 cont. (S) from Northfield through **Northfield Gulf** at 17m. (E) is **Allis St. For. Pk.** (pic.camp.). Branching off hy., Rd. leads (E) short distance to summit of **Bear Hill** (2,000′). 26m **Randolph,** cheerful industrial village, on Cent. Vt. RR. Handsome **Congr. Ch.**

(E) 3.5m to **Randolph Center.** Among early 19th cent. Hs., the **Parrish H.** is notable as former home of Salmon P. Chase, Chief Justice of U.S. Supreme Ct. It was to Randolph Center that Justin Morgan brought colt that was to become famous as 1st of Morgan breed. Once considered for St. capital, Randolph Center is now known for Vt. State School of Agric.

From Randolph, St.12 cont. (S) to **Woodstock** (see US4) at 52m.

### Sec. 4: MONTPELIER to ROUSES POINT, N.Y. 90.

**0. MONTPELIER. 12. WATERBURY,** on Winooski R. in mt. reg. **Congr. Ch.** (1st quarter 19th cent.). One of earliest houses is **Carpenter H.** (early 19th cent.). The **Waterbury Inn** dates back to Civil War period. **Waterbury Pub. Lib.;** Mus. In Waterbury, St.100 leaves US2 & turns directly N. For St.100A & St.100 (S) from Montpelier, see US7, Side Trip from New Haven Junction to Warren.

SIDE TRIP: To Winooski (J. with US7) 56m St.100, St.108 & St.15 (Via: Stowe, Smuggler's Notch, Jeffersonville, Cambridge, Underhill Flats, Jericho & Essex Junction.) This tour circles Mt. Mansfield reg., highest in St. St.100 leads (N) in full view of Green Mts. on either side. 10m **Stowe** (ski jump.accoms.daily bus for Mt.Mansfield Hotel), summer & winter resort & starting pt. for **Mt. Mansfield** (4,393′). **Green Mt. Inn** is more than 100 yrs. old. Tour cont. (L) on St.108. At 15.5m, J. with Mt. Mansfield Toll Rd.

Take Toll Rd. (L) 4.5m to **Mt. Mansfield Hotel** near summit. Seen from distance, especially from the E., the long ridge resembles a man's face turned skyward. Most of Mt. Mansfield reg. is in **Mt. Mansfield St. For.** (pic.shelters.camp.ski trls.). Long Trl. runs along the ridge, crossing four of its peaks, known respectively (S-N) as the **Forehead** (3,900′), **Nose** (4,062′), **Chin** (4,393′) & **Adam's Apple.** At the Chin is little **L. of the Clouds.** Trl. runs to **Cave of the Winds,** which has ice throughout yr. (For trls. in the region, see "The Long Trail," published by Green Mt. Club, Rutland, 50¢). View on clear days from the Chin, Mansfield's summit, is superb. To the (W) may be seen steamers on L. Champlain & further off, the Adirondacks. To (E) lie White Mts. & (S) Mt. Killington, 2nd highest in state. Far (N) is Mt. Royal, at Montreal.

At 16m on St.108, **Smuggler's Notch** (accoms.ski.), narrow defile through which goods were formerly smuggled into Canada. At 27m **Jeffersonville,** J. with St.15 on which tour cont. (W) to **Cambridge** at 30m, on the Lamoille R. Cont. on St.15 turning sharply (S) circling (W) of Mt. Mansfield. At 41m **Underhill Flats,** J. with Rd. (E) 3m on latter to **Underhill Center.**

Rds. run respectively from here to **Stevensville** (resort) from which trl. leads to **Mt. Mansfield** summit & to **Halfway H.,** from which trls. also lead to summit of Mt. Mansfield.

St.15 now turns (W) to **Winooski** (see US7) at 56m near Burlington.

**14.** US2 has J. with Rd. (2.5m N. is **Waterbury Dam,** large flood-control project.) Route cont. along Winooski R. to **BOLTON** at **20.;** view of Camel's Hump. Here hy. crosses Long Trl., running (S) to **Camel's Hump** (4,083′) & (N) to **Mt. Mansfield. 39. BURLINGTON** (see US7); ferries to Ft. Kent & Douglas, N.Y. Here US2 unites with US7 (N) 9.5m from Burlington (for this stretch of Rd. see US7) & then turns (W) along Lamoille R. **52.5. SAND BAR ST. FOR. PK.** (f.boat.bathh.pic.camp.).

**54. SAND BAR BRIDGE** to Grand Isle, in L. Champlain. Among the Is. of the L., Benedict Arnold maneuvered his fleet, preparatory to conflict with Brit. fleet in Valcour Bay (see US7). **57. SOUTH HERO,** 1st stop on Grand Isle; **Old Stone Inn** (1st quarter 19th cent.). The "Hero" towns were named for Ethan Allen & his brother, Ira. At **59.** St.F3 leads (NW) to Plattsburg Ferry. **62. GRAND ISLE,** resort. Just N. of village is **Log Cabin** (O.1783) owned by Vt. Hist. Soc. At **66.** bridge with fine view of L. & Is. **70. NORTH HERO,** on I. of same name. **Cth.** (1st quarter 19th cent.). Just N. is **City Bay** (swim.). **75. ISLE LA MOTTE STA.,** J. with St.129 leading (L) to **Isle La Motte Village,** supposedly 1st settlement (1666) in Vt. (R) 2m from this village is **Shrine of St. Anne. 81.** J. with St.104 which returns (E) to **Swanton, Vt.** (see US7). **85. ALBURG. 89.** Here take toll bridge to **ROUSES POINT, N.Y.** (see US9) at **90.**

## US 7—NEW ENGLAND

### NORWALK, CONN. (N) to CANADIAN BORDER (Montreal). 312. US7

Via: Conn.: Danbury, Kent & Canaan; Mass.: Sheffield, Great Barrington, Stockbridge, Lenox, Pittsfield & Williamstown; Vt.: Bennington, Manchester, Rutland, Middlebury, Vergennes, Burlington, St. Albans (Rouse's Pt., N.Y.), (Montreal, Canada). Through RR. & bus conns. Accoms.: All types, especially in summer.

This Tour makes J. with chief New England cross-state tours, & traverses some of fine scenic regions of New England—Housatonic Valley, Berkshire & Green Mts. & L. Champlain. It is known as the Ethan Allen Hy. because it passes through the Green Mts., where Ethan Allen & his Green Mt. Boys fought for independence of Vt. from N. Y. domination & at same time put down Tory opposition during Rev. & in 1775 launched their successful attack on Ft. Ticonderoga.

## Sec. 1: NORWALK, CONN. to CONN.-MASS. LINE. 77.

For trls. along this route see Conn. Walk Book, pub. by Conn. For. & Pk. Assoc., 839 Chapel St., New Haven.

**1.** J. with Rd. (Take latter (L) 2m to **Silvermine. Silvermine Artists Guild** (O.summer. art exhibits), on Parry Ave. 3.5m **Old Buttery Sawmill** (17th cent.), still functioning). **6. WILTON. Congr. Ch.** (1790.rest.fine exter.inter.). **Old Town Hall,** now garden center; once housed Wilton Academy (1832). **Old Wilton Academy** (1820), is adj. **10.5.** J. with St.53.

SIDE TRIP: Take latter (R) traversing country which Mark Twain loved & in which he had his home (no longer standing). At 4.5m, **Mark Twain Lib.** (O.Mon.Wed.Fri.& Sat.aft.), founded by Twain, in which are his own books.

**16.** J. with St.35.

SIDE TRIP: Take latter (L) 3m to **Ridgefield.** Tablets on Main St. comm. Battle of Ridgefield bet. Benedict Arnold's militia & Brit. Gen. Tryon's troops. Several int. old Hs., incl. old **Keeler Tavern** (1760) now occupied by Mrs. Cass Gilbert, widow of Amer. architect.

US7 now skirts Wooster Mt., named for Gen. Wooster who commanded patriot forces which attempted to block Brit. Gen. Tryon's troops here. **18.5. WOOSTER ST. PK.** (pic.). **22. DANBURY** (see US44). J. with US44 (see) & St.37.

SIDE TRIP: Take latter (NW) around **Candlewood L.** (resort). At 6m **New Fairfield,** Rd. leads (R) 4m to **Squantz Pond St. Pk.** (19 as.pic.trls.). At 20m, St.37 rejoins US7.

**36.5.** J. with St.25 near New Milford.

SIDE TRIP: Take St.25 (R) short distance into **New Milford** (sett.early 18th cent.). Roger Sherman (see New Haven) had his cobbler shop here (1743). On Main St., **Congr. Ch.** (1833).

**50. KENT,** art colony. Some int. old Hs. **54. KENT FALLS ST. PK.** (275 as.pic. trls.fine views). In pk. are some lovely waterfalls. **58.5. CORNWALL BRIDGE.** J. with St.4.

SIDE TRIPS: (A) Take latter (R) here. 4m to **Cornwall. Congr. Ch.** (1841.Gr.Rev.). S. of village, primeval **Cathedral Pines.** 5.5m **Mohawk St. Pk.,** in which is **Mohawk Mt.** (1,570'); fine view from outlook tower. 10m **Goshen. Old Congr. Ch.** 11m. Handsome **Birdseye Norton H.** (early 19th cent.). J. with Pother Rd. leading (L) 1m to site of **Birthpl. of John Brown** (see Harpers Ferry). 18m **Torrington,** industrial city with brass hardware & needles among most important products. 1st brass kettles in U.S. were made here. J. with St.25. Take latter (R). 24m **Litchfield** (sett.1720). Swim. at Sandy Beach on **Bantam L.** Litchfield is one of most beautifully preserved New England towns. Suffered from Ind. raids, 1772. At outbreak of Rev. sent contingent to Bunker Hill & during Rev. became center in which military stores were kept & arms factories est. Litchfield disputes with Williamsburg honor of having 1st law sch. in U.S., that of Tapping Reeve, where Benedict Arnold was student. Among noted graduates was John C. Calhoun, ardent Jeffersonian when Litchfield was as ardently Federalist. Reeve expressed disapproval of Jeffersonian principles in the "Litchfield Monitor" in terms so violent that he narrowly escaped going to jail. Ethan Allen was born in the town, as were Harriet Beecher Stowe & Henry Ward Beecher.

PTS. OF INT.: On or near East St.: (1) Facing Green, **Congr. Ch.** (1829.by Levi Newell. rest.fine portico. steeple reconstructed.inter.reproduces much of orig.). (2) Near-by, **Phelps Tavern** (1787). (3) On S. side of East St., **Chas. Bennett H.** (1814.furnished in period). (4) At cor. of East & South Sts. **Litchfield Pub. Lib.** (O.wks.); displays of old textiles; Lib. bldg. houses **Hist. Mus. of Litchfield Hist. Soc.** (O); coll. of 9,000 items incl.: portraits by Ralph Earl, painted before 1800, miniatures by Anson Dickinson, antique furnishings. (5) At Green, on East St., near foot of North St., **Collins H.** (1782); (6) adj., **Apothecary Shop** (1781), still a shop. (7) NE. cor. East & North Sts., **Corner H.** (early 19th cent.). Adj. is **Ben. Talmadge H.** (1775). (8) Near-by at J. of North & West Sts., **Cty. Jail** (c.1812) in front of which is whipping post elm—15' in circumference. Malefactors, it is said, were manacled to it & whipped. (9) Just above jail on North St., **Old Bank Bldg.** (1816).
(10) On South St.: **Hanks H.** (1780) built by Ben Hanks, clockmaker, used by him as home & workshop. (11) **Abbey H.** (1832.Gr.Rev.very fine example of period). (12) On South St., at Wolcott St., **Oliver Wolcott, Sr. H.** (1753.adds.19th cent.). Wolcott was Gov. of Conn. as were his father & his son; was signer of Decl. of Ind. It was in garden of this H. that the leaden statue of George III, hauled by oxen from Bowling Green, N.Y.C., was melted down into bullets. (13) Near-by is **Tapping Reeve H.** (1774) & **Law School** (1784.rest.1930), (both O.wks.Sun.aft.June-Nov.); orig. furniture, incl. 2 chairs once owned by Gov. Wolcott. Reeve married Sally Burr, Aaron Burr's sister. (14) South St., **Ephraim Kirby H.** (1773). Gen. Kirby fought in Rev. & compiled 1st law reports published in U.S. (15) SW. cor. South St. below Wolcott St., **Oliver Wolcott, Jr. H.** (1799.alts.), built by son of 1st Oliver, & also Gov. of Conn.; (16) On Old South Rd. at High St., **Ethan Allen H.** Here it is be-

lieved Ethan Allen (see Vt.) was born. (17) Also on South St., **Seymour H.** (1784.adds.), now Episc. Rectory. (18) On North St.: **Julius Deming H.** (1793, one of finest in town, built by Wm. Spratt, Scot, who designed a number of Hs. in Conn. Deming was prosperous merchant engaged in China trade. (19) SW. cor. North & Prospect Sts., **Lynde Lord H.** (1771); Lynde Lord was High Sheriff of Litchfield Cty. (20) There is another **Lord H.** (1785. rest.); has a huge side doorstep stone, dragged from Salisbury by 12 pairs of oxen. (21) Near-by, **Sheldon Tavern** (1760) has been carefully preserved in its orig. state. Washington stopped over here. At c.2m S. of Litchfield are **White Woods Bird Sanctuary** (trls.).

(B) From **Cornwall Bridge** to **Gt. Barrington.** 35m St.4, St.41, US44, St.41. This side trip traverses one of scenically fine regs. in southern Berkshires. Take St.4 (L) out of Cornwall Bridge. At 8m old village of **Sharon.** At 16m **Lakeville** & J. with US44. Take US44 (R) to charming old town of **Salisbury.** At 18m J. with St.41. Cont. on latter (N). St.41 from here is known as Undermountain Rd. At 23m **Mass. Line. Sage's Ravine,** into which trl. branches off. 23.5m (Trl. (L) here to beautiful Bear Rock Falls & Plantan Pond). 24.5m Take trl. here to Race Brook Falls. 31m J. with **Mt. Everett Reserv.** This Rd. runs (L) into the Reserv.; gives access to trl. to **Profile Rock** (fine view); to a Rd. to **Bash-Bish Falls Reserv.** (pic.) (see N.Y. St.22), where is **Bash-Bish Falls & Gorge,** one of most beautiful in Berkshires; to Rd. running up slopes of **Mt. Everett** (2624′) to **Guilder Pond,** one of highest in state, from which trl. runs to top of the mt. 31.5m **South Egremont** (sett.1730), named for Earl of Egremont, Brit. Secy. of State during Rev. Old **Egremont Tavern** (O.1730.rest. 1931); **Mt. Everett Inn** (O.1780.rest.); both still hotels. **Old Grist Mill** (O.1790. rest.). 35m J. with US7, just (S) of Great Barrington (see below).

**58.5. HOUSATONIC MEADOW PK.** (1,060 as.pic.) on Housatonic R. **61.5.** Here US7 crosses through **Housatonic St. For.** (8,528 as.pic.trls.). **69. SOUTH CANAAN. Congr. Ch.** (1802). **76. CANAAN,** another fine old village. J. with US44. **77. CONN.-MASS. LINE.**

## Sec. 2: CONN.-MASS. LINE to PITTSFIELD. 31.

**0.5. RED MILL** (O) in operation, 200 yrs.; still owned by orig. Dunham family. **5. SHEFFIELD** (sett.c.1725), charming old town within sight of **Mt. Everett.** It is recorded that in order to promote zeal in bldg. 1st Ch. here (1735), town set up free beer & passed around rum. Geo. Francis Root, who wrote "Tramp, Tramp, Tramp, the Boys are Marching" & other popular songs, was a native. **6. SHEFFIELD PLAIN.** Within 0.5m of village are 2 ancient Covered Bridges. **10. GREAT BARRINGTON** (sett.early 18th cent.resort.winter sports. Fair in Sept.). Although Great Barrington sent contingent to Boston after Battle of Lexington, it was nevertheless, something of a Tory hotbed. Prominent loyalist was David Ingersoll, who finally was banished, 1778, & his property confiscated. Humbler townspeople took part in Shays's Rebellion, kidnapped local judges, captured the jail & released debtors. Wm. Cullen Bryant practiced law, became town clerk & made his home here. Ward McAllister of the "400" (see Newport, R.I.) used to hunt in vic. During an expedition his party shot almost 2,000 birds in 1 week. 362 Main St., **Wm. Cullen Bryant H.** (O.May-Nov.c.1759), home of poet who, in one of his poems, recorded his distaste for drudgery of practicing law. Tablet in front of **Town Hall** comm. site of 1st armed resistance to Brit. rule, July 16, 1774, when the local people seized the cth. US7 now climbs to **MON. MT. RESERV. & SQUAW PEAK** (fine view). **18. STOCKBRIDGE** (sett.1736.resort.skiing), fashionable summer colony located in fine mt. sec. John Sergeant became resident missionary & worked among Inds. who, however, were finally pushed off their land & forced to seek refuge in the Oneida Reserv. in N.Y. Jon. Edwards later was pastor here. In early 19th cent. Dan. Webster, Van Buren & other notables put up at Red Lion Inn & Stockbridge Hotel. Later, Dudley Field, Wm. Ellery Sedgwick & other notables were summer residents & more recently, Dan. C. French, sculptor & the late Owen Johnson, writer. At Common, **First Congr. Ch.** (1824); **Town Hall** (mod.) which is on site of spot where Shays's rebels imprisoned some of town's wealthy citizens; **Field Chime Tower** comm. Rev. Dudley Field; near-by, **Jon. Edwards Mon.**; near Common, **Old Cemetery** in which are buried Cyrus W. Field, who financed laying of Transatlantic Cable, Jos. Choate, famous lawyer, John Sergeant & John Konkopot, Chief Sachem. At J. with St.102, famous **Red Lion Inn** on site of orig. (1774); notable Plumb Coll. of antiques. Opp., **St. Paul's Ch.** (Episc.by McKim); baptistry by St. Gaudens, windows by La Farge. (W) on St.102, **Mission H.** (O.May-Nov.sm.fee.1739), built by John Sergeant; here Jon. Edwards preached & wrote his "An Inquiry into Freedom of the Will." Mission H. & adj. bldgs. are restorations of Col. bldgs. In Mission H. is notable coll. of Amer. antiques, Ind. Room, Weaving Room, etc.; Old Fashioned Garden. Take Rd. (R) from Stockbridge 0.5$^m$ to **Ice Glen,** fine bit of scenery. 1.5$^m$ (E) on St.102 is **South Lee. Merrill Tavern** (O.May-Nov.appl.c.1760.adds.); antique furnishings. In W. Stockbridge Center (NW) on St.102 is a lovely **Congr. Ch.** (1788).

**24.** J. with US20. **25. LENOX** (sett.c.1750.resort.skiing), known originally as Yokuntown, after local Ind. sachem, later named for Chas. Lenox, Duke of Richmond, favorable to Amer. Colonies. Lenox has since middle of 19th cent. been fashionable summer colony where Harrimans, Stuyvesants, Vanderbilts & other wealthy families built summer homes. This town was a Tory hotbed during Rev. Gideon Smith, prominent local loyalist, was hung up by the patriots until he agreed to swear adherence to patriot cause. **The Curtis Hotel** (1834) was famous hostelry. Fanny Kemble (see Ga.), actress & author, stopped over there for a time. It is told of her that she rebuked a man at the hotel desk; "You should remove your hat. Gentlemen always remove their hats in my presence." "But I am not a gentleman," the man replied. "I'm a butcher." **Lenox Lib.** (O.summer.Gr.Rev.1816), was formerly the Cth.; rare books. On Laurel L., **The Mount,** home of late Edith Wharton, noted author. [Take St.183 (L). At 1.5$^m$, entrance to Tanglewood, where Hawthorne had his cottage (now, 1949, being rebuilt), where he worked on "The House of Seven Gables" & some of his short stories. It was at this time that his close friendship developed with Herman Melville, who was living at Pittsfield (see below) & who was working on "Moby Dick." Here in summer musical events take place incl. concerts by Boston Symphony Orchestra. At 3$^m$ is entrance to **L. Mahkeenac** ("Stockbridge Bowl".boat.swim.f.).] Just (N) of Lenox, on US7, is **THE CH. ON THE HILL** (1805.attrib.Bulfinch); very fine example. **27.** J. with New Lenox Rd. [Take latter (R) 2$^m$, then (L) into **October Mt. St. For.** (14,189 as.recr.skiing) **Schermerhorn Gorge** is its finest bit of scenery.]

**31. PITTSFIELD.**

## Sec. 3: PITTSFIELD to MASS.-VT. LINE. 24.

**0. PITTSFIELD** (sett.1743) is an industrial town &, because of its beautiful location in the Berkshires, center for vacationists. Gen. Electric Co. has 1 of its largest plants here & there are textile, silk thread & paper factories. Town named for Wm. Pitt, popular before Rev. because of his defense of colonists' rights. Site of town was part of tract bought by Col. Jacob Wendell, great grandfather of Oliver Wendell Holmes. Early settlers were harassed by Inds. At outbreak of Rev., despite considerable Tory sentiment, town supported Patriot cause & sent contingent to Boston after Lexington & another to take part in Battle of Bennington.

PTS. OF INT.: (1) **City Hall Pk.** in which is Sun Dial, marking spot where for 267 yrs. stood **The Old Elm.** The redoubtable Lucretia Williams saved the tree once by literally interposing her body bet. it & woodman's ax. However, tree, struck by lightning, eventually, had to be taken down. (2) SE. cor. East St. & Wendell Ave., **Peace Party H.** (1776.alts.), so-called because of memorable celebration held in it after signing of Treaty of Paris (1783). (3) 44 Bank Row, **Berkshire Athenaeum** (O.wks.); Lib. & art objects. (4) 39 South St., **Berkshire Mus. of Natural Hist. & Art** (O.wks.except Mon.Sun.aft.), sculptures, paintings & Egyptiana; art coll., incl. works by Rubens, Van Dyck, Reynolds, Copley & Stuart; among curiosities exhibited are sledge used by Peary in discovery of N. Pole, Hawthorne's desk & Holmes' "One Horse Shay." (5) Cor. North St. & Maplewood Ave., **Bulfinch Ch.** (1793). (6) Near J. of Elm & William Sts., **Brattle H.** (O.fee.1762) oldest in Pittsfield; furnished with antiques. (7) Near-by, at 847 Elm St., **Old Wells Tavern,** former stagecoach stop. (8) On Holmes Rd., near its J. with Pomeroy Ave., **Holmesdale** where Holmes lived & wrote, & **Old Wind Mill.** (9) On Holmes Rd., further along, is **Arrowhead,** where Melville wrote "Moby Dick" & other works; fine view of Mt. Greylock. (10) On East St., **Gen. Electric Plant** (O.appl.). (11) On South Mt. Rd., **Walton Wild Acre Sanctuary** (O.pic.sm.fee). (12) On South St. is **Broad Hall,** now Pittsfield Country Club, where Longfellow once stayed. (13) Off South St. (US7 & US20) is South Mt. Here is **South Mt. Music Colony** on Coolidge estate. (14) On Hancock Rd., off US7, is **Pontoosuc L. Pk.** (pic.bath.boat.f.). (15) NW. of Pittsfield on Lakeway Dr. is **Onota L.** (Ind. "Lake of the White Deer"), one of 6 within city's boundaries. (16) On Shamrock Blvd., **Pittsfield St. For.** (3,854 as.camp.pic.f.bath.trls.ski runs). In For. are **Lulu Cascades & Berry Pond** (2,150′; pic.) highest in Mass.; fine view. In For. is **Radium Springs Cave** (Marble), 3rd largest in Mass. **Trailside Mus.** (O.summer).

At **4.5.** on US7, J. with Rd. (L) to **Pontoosuc L. & Pk.** (see above). **6. LANESBORO. 7.** J. with Rockwell Rd.

SIDE TRIP: Take latter (L) to summit of **Mt. Greylock** (3,505′), highest in Mass., 10m. Rd. affords many fine views; makes J. with trls., incl. Appalachian Trl., to various scenic pts. of int. (Consult Mass. Sec. of New England Appalachian Trl., published by the Appalachian Mt. Club). 7.5m J. with Rd. Take latter (L) 2.5m to **Stony Ledge** from which magnificent view. 10m, **Thunderbolt Ski Run,** & just a little further along, **Mt. Greylock Summit,** with Mem. Tower & Lodge (O). Fine view.

**8.5. ST. TOURIST PK.** (pic.camp.f.). **11.5. RED BAT CAVERN** (O). **13. NIGHT HILL** (night skiing). **19.** J. with St.2 (see). **22. WILLIAMSTOWN** (sett.1749), encircled by higher Berkshires, summer resort as well as home of Williams College. Town, named for Col. Ephraim Williams (see below), suffered from Ind. raids in Fr.-Ind. War. During Rev., Benedict Arnold stopped here to obtain volunteers & provisions. Town was base for campaign which ended in patriot victory at Bennington.

PTS. OF INT.: Cor. Simonds St. & N. Hoosac Rd., **Old Well Sweep H.** (1770) where for a time lived Col. Simonds of Rev. fame. Opp., **River Bend Tavern** (1765) where beans & bread were cooked in the huge cellar oven for soldiers hurrying to Bennington. On St.2 c. 0.5m (E) toward North Adams, is **Green River Mansion** (1770-77), home of Col. Smedley, where bread was also baked for Rev. troops. At J. of St.2 & US7, Boulder on **Site of Blockh.** (1756). On Buckley St., c.0.5m from J. of St.2 & US7, near Hemlock Brook Bridge, is **Proprietors H.** (1753) where 1st town meeting was held. On St.2, **Williams College,** founded 1790 with money bequeathed by Col. Ephraim Williams who was killed in Fr.-Ind. War (1755), £1200 proceeds of the Williamstown Lottery, & voluntary contributions. Among prominent graduates have been William Cullen Bryant & Jas. A. Garfield. College has number of handsome bldgs., some of which were designed by Cram & Ferguson. Oldest bldg., **West College** (1791). In **Thompson Mem. Chapel** (1905.Goth.) is grave of Col. Ephraim Williams. **Stetson Hall** houses Lib. in which is A. C. Chapin Lib. of rare books, among whose int. items are 4 Shakespeare folios, Columbus' letter disclosing discovery of America & Bishop Cramner's Bible. **Lawrence Hall** (O.wks.Sun.aft.Georg.) houses Mus. with outstanding art coll. incl. early Amer. furniture, Ren. & mod. drawings, mediaeval, renaissance & mod. paintings, a predominantly mod. coll. of prints, Etruscan, Mayan & Peruvian pottery, Egyptian, Assyrian, hellenistic, mediaeval & mod. sculpture. **Haystack Mon.** comm. spot where several students met to pray for est. of foreign missions. A sudden storm drove them to take shelter in haystack. Adj. to **President's H.,** on Main St., charming **Congr. Ch.** Back of Chapin Hall, **Van Rensselaer H.,** former home of Dutch patroon who promoted bldg. of Erie Canal & founded Rensselaer Polytechnic Institute in Troy, N.Y. Many trls. run from Williamstown to scenic points of int. in near-by high Berkshires incl. trl. to summit of Mt. Greylock. (Consult "Appalachian Trl. Book," New England Sec. published by Appalachian Mt. Club.)

**24. MASS.-VT. LINE.**

## Sec. 4: MASS.-VT. LINE to RUTLAND. 68.

For Long (Appalachian) Trl. in Vt., see "Guide Book of Long Trail" pub. by Green Mountain Club, Rutland, Vt. **2.5. POWNAL** (sett.1766). N. Pownal, on St.346, was **birthpl. of Jim Fiske,** Jay Gould's high-flying partner (see N.Y.C.). **3. OAK GROVE SEMINARY,** where Jas. A. Garfield & Chester A. Arthur taught school. **5. POWNAL CENTER. Union Ch.** (1789). Dan. Dean, who furnished part of lumber to build Ch., offered prize of $10 for 1st bride married here. Died in 1811 & offer expired. 1st wedding held in Ch. in 100 yrs. was in Dec. 1947.

**11. BENNINGTON** (sett.1761). Info.: C. of C. For Long Trl., Office of W. Holden, 100 South St.

Old Bennington is resort & hist. town. New Bennington is industrial, with plants producing yarns, underwear, knitting machines, plastics, woolen textiles, brushes, furniture, leather. Bennington, named for Gov. Benning Wentworth (see Portsmouth, N.H.) was center of Green Mt. Boys' revolt against claims over Vt. At the Catamount Tavern they planned capture of Ft. Ticonderoga (1775). Near city took place Battle of Bennington (1777) which led to Burgoyne's defeat, later, at Saratoga. Bennington was birthpl. of J. F. Winston, builder of the "Monitor" (see Newport,

Va.). The Long Trl. crosses St.9 (E) of Bennington. It runs (N) to Glastonbury Mt. (3,764′). PTS. OF INT.: (1) On Main St., **Hist. Mus.** (O.sm.fee); hist. relics (incl. Bennington battle flag) & pottery. (2) On W. Main St., **Old Jedediah Dewey, Jr. H.** (3) 208 Pleasant St. (in New Bennington), **Norton-Fenton H.** (1838), named for famous pottery-makers, Chris. Fenton & John Norton. (4) On Monument Ave. are: At Green, **Old Burying Ground** with graves of soldiers who fell in Battle of Bennington & of Vt. notables; **Congr. Ch.** (O.wks.aft.est.1672.bldg.1804.by Lavius Fillmore), one of finest in state; **Jedediah Dewey, Sr. H.** (2nd half 18th cent.alts.), home of famous preacher; **Walloomsac Inn** (O.1766), oldest in st., but greatly alt.; **Site of Catamount Inn,** on which is figure of a catamount; **Tichenor Mansion** (late 18th cent.), located behind Walloomsac Inn, was home of early Gov. Isaac Tichenor; **Academy Lib.** (O.Mon.Thurs.aft.early 19th cent.); **Marker** on site of home of 1st settler, Sam. Robinson; **Gen. David Robinson H.** (1795.Georg.). Robinson fought in Battle of Bennington; **Statue of Seth Warner,** comrade of Allen & hero of Battle of Hubbardton & Bennington. There is a marker on **Site of Ethan Allen's H.**; another marker is on site of **H.** where Wm. Lloyd Garrison printed "Journal of the Times" early in 19th cent. On Hill, **Bennington Battle Mon.** (O.sm.fee) 306′, from whose top fine view. (5) (L) from Warner Statue, take Rd. for trip around Bennington battlefield which extends into N.Y. For description see N.Y. St.22. To N. of city is **Vt. Soldiers' H.** (O) which has Hunt's famous fountain throwing world's highest jet (196′).

**13.** J. with St.67A.

SIDE TRIP: Take latter (L). At **1.5m J.** with marked Rd. which take (R) to **Bennington College for Women** (est.1928). Campus 400 as., arranged in style of New England village. College is noted for pioneer work in mod. educational methods. Important feature is community government conducted by members of student body & faculty jointly.

**16. SOUTH SHAFTSBURY. Cole Hall** (1st half 19th cent.). At S. end of village is **Rbt. Frost H.** (1769), former home of poet. At N. end of village, **Monroe-Hawkins H.** (early 19th cent.Georg.by Lavius Fillmore.fine exter.& inter.). **17.5. SHAFTSBURY CENTER. Gov. Galusha H.** (Col.attrib.to Lavius Fillmore). Galusha fought in Rev. **26. ARLINGTON** (sett.1763), charming mountain resort. Ethan Allen & his comrade, Remember Baker, & Thos. Chittenden, Vt.'s 1st Gov., once lived here. **St. James Ch.** (1830) in whose cemetery is grave of Martha Brownson, Allen's 1st wife. Dorothy Canfield Fisher, author, has her home here. **Martha Canfield Lib.** (O.wks.) was orig. home of Canfields. **29. ETHAN ALLEN TAVERN** (O.summer & skiing season), now hotel. Here Ethan & Ira Allen had hqs. **30.5.** J. with Toll Rd. Take latter (L) to **Mt. Equinox** (3,816′); magnificent view. **35. MANCHESTER** (resort.winter sports), with view of **Mt. Equinox** (SW) & of **Mt. Aeolus** (3,135′) to (N). Town was center of Ira Allen's activities against Tories. Many fine old Hs. Pavements of dazzling white marble. **Burr & Burton Seminary** (est.1829); art exhibits & flower shows. **36. MANCHESTER CENTER** (resort), another fine old village. **Old Tavern** (late 18th cent.), now rooming H. & antique shop. J. with St.11 & St.30.

SIDE TRIPS: (A) St.30 to Middlebury (see below). Via: Dorset, Poultney, Castleton Corners, Bomoseen, Hubbardton, Sudbury, Whiting & Cornwall. Runs through picturesque, sparsely populated country, punctuated by small towns in which are int. old bldgs. It passes by St. Catherine, Bomoseen, Twin, & Hortonia Ls. (resorts). 6.5m **Dorset.** In Cephas Kent Tavern (no longer standing) on July 24, 1776 met the 1st Constitutional Convention to org. Vt. "as a free & independent state." **Dorset Inn** (O.1791). **Dorset Mem. Lib.** (O.1790). 8.5m **E. Rupert.** Take Rd. (L) to Rupert at 6m. Here Rupert Harmon (1785) had exclusive concession to make pennies for sovereign republic of Vt. **Old Congr. Ch.** 47m on St.30. **Hubbardton.** (R) here 6m is **Site of Battle of Hubbardton,** marked by Mon., where Seth Warner fought rearguard action, making possible victory at Bennington. 70m **Middlebury** (see below).

(B) St.11 to Springfield (see US5). Via: Manchester Depot, Peru, Londonderry, Simondsville & Chester. This route passes through scenically fine southern Green Mts. & some charming villages. 6m J. with Long Trl. near J. with St.30 (see US5). Trl. runs (N) here to **Bromley Mt.** (3,260′;skiing). 16m **Londonderry. Pub. Lib.** (formerly Universalist Chapel), charming little bldg. Near village, lovely **Lowell L.** (2,500′) & **Glebe Mt. J.** with St.8.

Take latter (L) 5.5m to **Weston,** which is in process (1949) of restoration. At Common, **Farrar-Mansur H.** (O.wks.Sun.aft.1787.rest.), now community center; antique furnishings typical of an old tavern, & murals by contemporary Amer. painters. Also at Common, **Ross H.** (O.appl.1830). **Spaulding-Taylor H.** (O.appl.1795 & 1832); antiques.

**Wilder Homestead** (1827.alts.). On Landgrove Rd., **Gilmore H.** (O.appl. 1797), birthpl. of Jos. Gilmore, Civil War Gov. of N.H. **Weston Playh.** (19th cent.Gr.Rev.). 30m **Chester** (see US5). 38m **Springfield** (see US5).

**48. DANBY** (sett.1765), founded by Quakers, is near Mt. Tabor (3,584′) & is famous for its marble quarries (O) which are c.1m (W) of village. One of chief local industries is picking of ferns, which are cold-storaged & sold in winter to florists. **55.** J. with Rd. [(R) here 2m & then trl. 0.5m to fine cliffs known as **White Rocks.** Path conts. to **Ice Caves** under the cliffs & makes J. with Long Trl.] **57. WALLINGFORD. Paul Harris H.** (O.1818), boyhood home of founder of Rotary Internat. **Old True Temper Inn** (O.Col.) in front of which is **Boy & Boot Fountain. Old Stone Shop** (O), where were 1st made steel hay forks; now gift shop. Chief industry is **True Temper Fork Factory** (O).

**68. RUTLAND.**

Accoms.: All types. Info.: C. of C.; for Long Trl., Hqs. of Green Mt. Club, in Mead Bldg.

City (sett.1770), on Otter Creek, is center of marble area; has many industries, turning out maple sugar utensils, wood products, machinery, clothing, medical products, monuments, marble, etc. It is also vacation & skiing center. Thirty ponds in vic. City was birthpl. of John Deere, inventor of steel plow. Rutland's 1st newspaper was est. 1792 by Anthony Haswell. Another eminent native was Rev. Sam. Williams, historian & scholar. PTS. OF INT.: (1) Court & Center St., **Pub. Lib.** (O.wks. Sun.aft.1856.by Ammi B.Young.rest.); Vermont material. (2) In Main St. Pk., **Statue of Green Mountain Boy.** (3) 27 S. Main St., **Pond H.** (early 19th cent.), home of Sol. Foot, Civil War Senator. (4) On Main St., in vic. of Pk. (see above), **Kilburn H.** (late 18th cent.alts.). (5) Cor. Main & Madison Sts., **Morse H.** (Georg.alts.). (6) 64 N. Main St., **Temple H.** (1812.Georg.). (7) No. 1 Aiken St., **Old Aiken H.** Near-by is old **Congr. Ch.** (1st half 19th cent.). (8) On West St.: **Fed. Bldg.** (1933.Class.) with murals by Stephen Belaski. (9) **Ripley Mill** where marble-cutting is done. (10) **Evergreen Cemetery** in which are many old graves, incl. that of Col. Jas. Mead, early settler. (11) Near Cemetery, **Gookin H.** (late 18th cent.). (12) On Dorr Rd., **The Maples,** in which many of the great literary figures of the 19th cent. were entertained. (13) **Rutland Jr. College** (est.1941) has 100-a. campus & fine bldgs. Near city are **Rutland (Mead's) Falls** which can be seen off US4. In Rutland is J. with US4 (see). On US4, to W., is **W. Rutland** where are great marble quarries & cutting sheds. 10m (E) on US4 is **Sherburne Pass,** J. with Long Trl. which runs (S) here past **Pico Peak** (3,967′;ski lift) & **Killington Peak** (4,241′), 2nd highest in state.

## Sec. 5: RUTLAND to BURLINGTON. 68.

**7. PITTSFORD MILLS.** J. with Rd. Take latter (L) 4.5m to **Proctor** (see Proctorsville), marble center. Here is **Vt. Marble Co.,** where cutting may be observed, as well as company's marble exhibit (O.summer). Beautiful **Sutherland Falls. 8.5. PITTSFORD,** whose citizens aided in capture of Ft. Ticonderoga. **Old Cemetery** (1774). On Main St., **Drake Homestead** (early 19th cent.), birthpl. of Pres. Fillmore's mother. **16. BRANDON,** burnt by Inds., 1777. **Birthpl. of Stephen A. Douglas** (O) (see Ill.); adj., **Bapt. Ch.** & near-by **Congr. Ch.;** both built 1st half of 19th cent. From bridge over Neshobe R., view of Neshobe Falls. [From Brandon, St.115 runs (E) through **Brandon Gap,** passing **Mt. Horrid** (3,120′) near J. with Long Trl., at 9m. At 15m **Rochester** (resort).] **23. SALISBURY** (sett.1774), another center of Green Mt. Boys' activities. **Mon.** to Mrs. Story, widow of 1st settler, Amos Story. She braved Ind. attacks & perils of Rev. conflicts. Near-by, **St. Fish Hatchery** (O). J. with Rd.

SIDE TRIP: Take latter (R) to beautiful **L. Dunmore** (resort), at 1.5m. Two trls. run to **Mt. Moosalamoo** (2,659′), one of which, Cascade Trl. passes fine **Dana Falls** (pic.). On Mt. is **Ethan Allen Cave.** At (N) end of L. is **St. For. Pk.** (pic.bath.).

**29.** J. with Rd.

SIDE TRIP: Take latter (L) 1m & then (L) again to **Shard Villa** (O.Tues.Fri.aft.Vict.), quaint Vict. furnishings; frescoes by Silvio Pezzoli; built by Columbus Smith who made fortune winning Amer. claims to Eng. inheritances. He named H. in honor of his 1st case, claim to fortune left by Frances Mary Shard.

**30.** J. with St.125.

SIDE TRIP: Take St.125 (E). At 7m **Bread Loaf,** seat of Summer School of Eng. & Writers' Conference of Middlebury College (during sessions accoms.are very limited). Trls. radiate into Green Mts. from here. Skiing on Burnt Hill & near Pleiad L. For info. as to trls., inquire Bread Loaf Inn. In Middlebury Gap, to (E) of Inn, J. with Long Trl.

(1) (N) on latter through **Battell St. Pk.** 6.5m to **Bread Loaf Mt.** (3,823'). (2) (S) on Long Trl. 0.5m to beautiful **Pleiad L.** (2,140') & **Pleiad L. Camp** (camp).

At 17m **Hancock** (skiing).

**33. MIDDLEBURY** (sett.1773), summer & winter resort. Accoms.: All types. Middlebury straddles Otter Creek on slope of Chipman Hill. **Mun. Pk.** (NE) on an eminence, from which panoramic view. During Rev. townsmen had to evacuate settlement because of raid by enemy. In 1800 when town consisted of only 30 log cabins surrounded by wilderness, Middlebury College was founded. Since those days, aside from marble-working, Middlebury has been chiefly a college town. Among notable citizens was Jeremiah Hall, inventor of circular saw. PTS. OF INT.: N. of Common, fine **Congr. Ch.** (early 19th cent.; after design by Ben. Asher). On Main St., **Sheldon Art Mus.** (O.wks.May-Nov.except Tues.Sun.aft.sm.fee.1829); art, antiques & items illustrating early New England life. On Court St., **Wainwright H.** (1807.Fed.), former home of Gamaliel Painter, one of Middlebury College's founders. Cor. Main & Seymour Sts., **Community H.** (O.wks.except Mon.Sun.aft. 1815). On Washington St., **Old Jail** (1810), now residence. **Middlebury College** & affiliated Women's College are located on hill with fine view. Summer session at Bread Loaf (see above). College was founded by Gamaliel Painter, who was a miller, some lawyers & doctors, & Timothy Dwight, Yale Pres., who spent one night at Middlebury helping outline plans for proposed institution. Among its many bldgs., of int. are: **Mead Mem. Chapel** (1917) which is a New England meetingh. type of bldg.; **Adm. Bldg.** (formerly Old Chapel.1836); **Painter Hall** (1815.remod.), oldest bldg. & fine example of period; **Egbert Starr Lib.** (Class.1900 & 1908): extensive lib., Middleburyana, local hist. items, etc.; **Chateau** (1925), inspired by Pavillion Henri IV at Fontainbleau, perhaps oldest Maison Francaise in U.S., for students studying French; **Warner Science Hall,** in which is Nat. Hist. Mus.: fossils of Vt. & Champlain Valley & flora of reg., etc. In Middlebury is J. with Rd. via Weybridge to Vergennes. [Take this Rd. (L) 2m to **U. S. Morgan Horse Farm** (O). Mon. to the Morgan Horse (see Randolph Center).]

**33.5. CHIPMAN HILL** (skiing.see above). **36.5. BROOKSVILLE. Dog Team Tavern** built by Sir Rich. Grenfell, well-known for welfare work in Labrador. Adj. **Old Ch.** (O); Labrador handicrafts articles, which, however, because both Tavern & Ch. have passed out of hands of Grenfell Mission, are to be removed. **41. NEW HAVEN JUNCTION.** J. with St.17.

SIDE TRIP: (A) Take St.17 (E). 6m **Bristol. Old Bristol Inn.** (Bus to Lincoln). Just (E) of Bristol on St.17 is huge boulder (R) on which has been carved "Lord's Prayer." 10.5m **Lincoln.** Rd. now climbs through fine Lincoln Gap (2,424'). 15m J. with Long Trl. Trl. runs (N) to **Mt. Abraham** (4,052'), **Mt. Lincoln** (4,013') & **Mt. Ellen** (4,135').

19m **Warren.** J. with St.100.

(1) Take latter (S) through fine gorge & across natural bridge into Mad R.'s **Granville Gulf** at 4.5m & cont. through Gulf past fine waterfalls to **Hancock** (see above) at 16m. (2) Take St.100 (N) from Warren. At 5.5m, **Irasville.** Here side Rd. runs (W) to **Mad R. Glen,** skiing area. Ski lift to summit of **Gen. Stark Mt.** (3,585') & J. with Long Trl.

(B) Take St.17 (W) (L) from New Haven Junction. 8m **Addison** (sett.early 18th cent.). Fine view from near-by Smoke Mt. 14.5m **W. Addison. Gen. John Strong H.** (O.1783-94. int.inter.). 16m **Chimney Pt. & Champlain Bridge** (Toll) to Crown Pt., N.Y. (worth visit. see N.Y. St.22). At Chimney Pt. there was early settlement destroyed by Inds. (1760). Ruins still visible. **Barnes H.** (O), formerly inn; int. hist. relics.

**46. VERGENNES** (sett.1766), named for Count Vergennes, foreign minister of Louis XVI, is on Otter Creek, where Macdonough's Fleet, which later defeated Brit. in Battle of Plattsburg, was built. Main St., **Gen. Sam. Strong H.** (O.summer.1793. Col.), whose owner fought in War of 1812. **U. S. Arsenal** (1828), now occupied by school. **Mon. to Macdonough.** Short distance (NW) of Vergennes is **Basin Harbor** (resort). Fine view of Adirondacks. **49. ROKEBY** (O.May-Nov.late 18th cent.), once sta. of Underground Railroad. Antiques & pictures collected by Vt. author, Rowland E. Robinson. **53.** J. with Rd. Take latter (R) 1.5m to **Mt. Philo St. For. Pk.** (camp.pic.); fine view. **56. CHARLOTTE** on US7. **Congr. Ch.** (est.1792.bldg.1848-50.Gr.Rev.) Take Rd. (L) here short distance to Ferry across L. Champlain to Essex, N. Y.; this side Rd. also reaches lake resorts of Cedar Beach & Thompson Pt. **61.**

**SHELBURNE** on US7. Take Rd. (L) here $1^m$ to Webb Estate (grounds O.appl.) on L. Champlain. **Hist. Mus.** (O).

**68. BURLINGTON** (sett.1773).

Airport.Ferries to Ft. Kent & Port Douglas, N. Y. Steamer trips on L. Champlain. Accoms.: All types. Mun. Tourist Camp $2.5^m$ (N) of city. Info.: C. of C. on Main St. Bath. at North Beach.

Burlington, largest city in Vt., is located on L. Champlain, with splendid views of Adirondacks. City is important industrial & commercial town as well as starting pt. for vacationists. Ethan & Ira Allen were large landowners in vic. Many Burlington men joined Allen's forces. During War of 1812, city saw considerable military & naval operations. An attack by Brit. fleet was repulsed, June, 1813. City owes its prosperity to L. Champlain & canal that conns. with Hudson R. 1st canal built 1823. In 20th cent. it was deepened & improved. City is home of Univ. of Vt.
PTS. OF INT.: (1) At Main & Church Sts., **City Hall** (Georg.by McKim,Mead & White). (2) Pearl & Battery Sts., **Battery Pk.** where, 1813, guns repelled Brit. fleet. (3) Pearl St. & Elmwood Ave., **Unit. Ch.** (1816.attrib.to Peter Banner.probably under supervision of Bullfinch.very fine). (4) Elmwood Ave., **Elmwood Ave. Cemetery,** where are buried Ethan Allen's wife, Rev. soldiers & many notables. (5) S. Winooski Ave. & Buell St., **First Ch.** (Congr.1842.Gr.Rev.). (6) Colchester Ave., **Greenmount Cemetery,** in which are graves of Ethan Allen, Rev. soldiers & Vt. notables. (7) 411 Main St., **Grassemount** (O.1804.Georg.). (8) St. Paul St., **St. Paul's Ch.** (Episc.1832. Vict.Goth.adds.). (9) **Univ. of Vt.** campus occupies c.175 as. on a hill reached by Main St. The constitution of the Independent Republic of Vt. declared that a state univ. be established. Ira Allen was particularly interested in project, offered £4,000 in 1789 toward founding the institution, but Assembly rejected offer. 1st general assembly, after Vt. joined Union in 1781, chartered Univ. & Ira Allen was made member of the Corp. College, however, did not begin to graduate students until 1804. Univ. benefited under various Fed. land grants by est. a College of Agric. College of Medicine was founded in 1804. In addition there is a College of Arts & Sciences. All male students of Freshmen & Sophomore classes must take military training. Univ. has extension courses throughout St. **Old College** consists of 3 bldgs. which were connected together several yrs. after they were built (1825-30) & consists of the Old Mill (1823), South, whose cornerstone was laid by Lafayette, & Middle Colleges. Fine view from tower. **Medical College Bldg.** contains Medical Mus. **Mabel Louis Southwick Mem. Bldg.** is Women's Center (1935.by McKim,Mead & White). **Rbt. Hull Fleming Mus.** (O.wks.Sun.aft.1931,by McKim,Mead & White); exhibits of art, natural hist., archeology, Ind. relics, oriental material, old Vt. furniture & furnishings. **Ira Chapel** (1927.by McKim,Mead & White) has fine tower. **Billings Lib.** (O.wks.Sun.aft.of academic yr.by H.H.Richardson), one of finest of this architect's bldgs.; outstanding coll. of Vt. material & portraits, incl. one of Ira Allen. **Williams Science Hall** (1896); notable botanical coll. **Ethan Allen Pk.,** c.$2.5^m$ N. of city, incl. part of Ethan Allen's orig. farm. Fine view from tower comm. Allen.
At Battery Pk. is J. with Lake Shore Dr. which runs (N) along L. Champlain to Mallett's Bay (resort.amusements) & rejoins US7 at $10^m$. In Burlington is J. with US2 (see), which unites northward from Burlington with US7. For side tour to Mt. Mansfield, see US2.

## Sec. 6: BURLINGTON to U.S.-CANADIAN LINE. 44.

This sec. runs fairly close to L. Champlain with fine views. **2. WINOOSKI,** industrial city, supplied with power from Winooski R. dam; fine view from bridge in city. **St. Michael's College** (Cath.) for men. On outskirts is **Ft. Ethan Allen,** military hqs. of state. J. with St.15, circling Mt. Mansfield (see US2). **9.** Here J. with US2 (see) which branches off (L). **22.5. GEORGIA CENTER,** another fine old village, where was born Gardiner Colton, who, it is claimed, invented elec. locomotive. Handsome **Town Hall** (1800). **24. MON.** on site of **BIRTHPL. OF GEN. G. J. STANNARD,** whose troops broke Pickett's charge at Gettysburg. **29. ST. ALBANS** (sett.late 18th cent.), is also on L. Champlain. Township was named by Charles II for his son, Duke of St. Albans. City, sett. by Jesse Weldon, c.1788, is shipping pt. for dairy products of reg. On Oct. 19, 1864, Confederates staged a raid here, killed 1 man & decamped to Canada with $200,000 stolen from local banks. In 1866, the Finians (Irish patriots) here organized an expedition to attack Canada; attempt fizzled out miserably. Lawrence Brainerd, who convened 1st Republican Convention in Pittsburgh (1856), Chester A. Arthur, 21st Pres. of U.S., Rbt. Le Tourneau, whose machines revolutionized the moving of earth, & John G. Saxe, best known Vt. poet, were natives of Franklin Cty., in which St. Albans is located. Warren R. Austin, U.S. representative at U.N., was once mayor of city. Near-by are **St. Albans Bay** & **Great Back Bay** (summer resorts.f.& bath.).Not far from city is a pub. bath. beach. A Dr. runs along lake shore for 20[m] affording fine views. From For. Service area (pic.) on **Bellevue Hill** (E) of city, panoramic view. Maiden Lane, **St. Albans Free Lib.** (O); Sen. Greene's Coll. of Vt. hist. material. **37. SWANTON,** in early days scene of border troubles & smuggling operations. Several int. old bldgs. **Mon.** on **Site** of **Jesuit Chapel** (c.1700). Fish. at Maquam Bay. J. with St.104 which branches off (W) across L. Champlain to J. with US2 (see) near Alburg. **41. HIGHGATE SPRINGS** (resort) on Missisquoi Bay. In vic., Highgate falls & gorge of Missisquoi R. **44. CANADIAN BORDER.** On Canadian side, fashionable **Lafayette Manoir** (resort).

## US 5—NEW ENGLAND

**NEW HAVEN, CONN. (N) to DERBY LINE, VT.** (Sherbrooke, Can.). **311.5.**

Via: (Wallingford), Meriden, Berlin, Hartford, S. Windsor, Enfield in Conn.; Longmeadow, Springfield, Holyoke, Northampton, (Hatfield), Deerfield, Greenfield, Bernardston in Mass.; Brattleboro, Bellows Falls, Windsor, White River Junction, Norwich, Newbury, St. Johnsbury, Lyndonville, Barton, Orleans & Newport in Vt. RR. & bus conns. throughout. This route follows Conn. R. & only turns away in Northern Vt.

### Sec. 1: NEW HAVEN to MERIDEN. 20. (see New Haven Trip I.)

### Sec. 2: MERIDEN to HARTFORD. 19. (see Hartford Trip VI.)

### Sec. 3: HARTFORD to CONN.-MASS. LINE. 20.

**0. HARTFORD.** US5 crosses Conn. R. & runs along E. side of R. **1.5. E. HARTFORD** (see Hartford). **2.5.** J. with Rd. Tour cont. on latter (L) straight ahead. (For John Fitch Mon., see Hartford.) **5.5. S. WINDSOR,** whose chief industry is handling of tobacco grown in vic. On Main St., from S. Windsor to E. Windsor Hill (see below), is series of int. old Hs. **6. CONGR. CH.** (1802). **7.** (R) **SITE OF JON. EDWARDS BIRTHPL.** A short distance (N) on hy. is **Mem. Gateway** to cemetery in which parents of this famous divine are buried. **8. E. WINDSOR HILL.** (R) Handsome **Watson-Bancroft H.** (1785.Col.), with old farm bldgs. J. with US5 on which tour cont. Hy. now passes through tobacco growing countryside. **17. ENFIELD.** On Mem. Boulder on **Site of Jon. Edwards Ch.** is inscription reading: "In this Meeting House on July 8, 1741, during 'The Great Awakening,' Jonathan Edwards preached his celebrated sermon 'Sinners in the hands of an angry God.'" **Town Hall** (1775.Gr.Rev.). **Congr. Ch.** (est.1683.bldg.1849.Gr.Rev.). **20. CONN.-MASS. LINE.**

### Sec. 4: CONN.-MASS. LINE to NORTHAMPTON. 23.

**2.5. LONGMEADOW** (sett.2nd half 17th cent.). 697 Longmeadow St., **Storr's Parsonage** (O.summer); coll. of Col. antiques; houses Longmeadow Hist. Soc. 674 Longmeadow St., **Eleazer Williams H.** (18th cent.), where Eleazer Williams lived; supposed to be Lost Dauphin, son of Louis XVI (see Green Bay, Wis.). **5. SPRINGFIELD** (see US20). US5 now crosses Conn. R. again. **6.5. W. SPRINGFIELD** (see US20).

**15. HOLYOKE** (sett.mid-18th cent.), known as the "paper city" for its chief industry. Int. plants are Whitney Paper Co. & Skinner Silk Co. Power for factories comes from **Holyoke Dam,** best seen from Prospect Pk. At 335 Maple St., handsome **Pub. Lib.** (Class.); Mus. (O.wks.); outstanding hist. coll., Ind. & war relics & paintings, incl. Ital., Fr., Dutch & Amer. schools. At Appleton & Maple Sts., lovely **Skinner Mem. Chapel** (O.Goth.). Cabot & Pine St., **Wistariahurst** (O.Fri.aft.tickets at Skinner Silk Co. office); Belle Skinner Coll. of Musical Instruments, which are played for visitors by attending musician. **Mt. Tom** (1,214′) in Mt. Tom Pk. (O), is reached from US5 at a pt. several miles (N) of town. Dinosaur tracks in Pk. Beyond Pk. 2[m] (N) on US5 is **Mt. Tom St. Reserv.** (pic.). **23. NORTHAMPTON** (sett.1654). Beautiful residential, but also industrial, city. Home of Smith College for Women. Here Jon. Edwards had pastorate in 1700's until he removed to Stockbridge, & from here he inspired the "Great Awakening." City took prominent part in Shays's Rebellion, 1786. PTS. OF INT.: (1) Bridge St., in Masonic Temple, **Calvin Coolidge Law Office.** (2) 58 Bridge St., **Cornet Parsons H.** (O.1658.remod.c.1806); int. coll. of antique furnishings & other items. (3) 46 Bridge St., **Isaac Damon H.** (O.Wed.aft.summer.appl. at Parsons H.1813.remod.1825), built by Isaac Damon, famous New England architect & bridge builder; has Damon's drawing instruments, models of his bridges, musical items & Jenny Lind coll. (4) Court St., **Wiggins Tavern** (1786) & **Northampton Hotel.** In rear is **Country Store** (c.1797), moved from North New Salem, reconstructed & opened to public (1947). Tavern is Mus. of Americana, incl. famous coll. of Currier & Ives prints, household & other utensils. Store is stocked with early-day merchandise; Civil War barber shop. (5) Main St., **Mem. Hall** (O.Wed.Sat.) houses Northampton Hist. Soc. (6) On Round Hill Rd., **Clark School for the Deaf** (O.appl.) where Mrs. Calvin Coolidge taught before her marriage. (7) West St., **Forbes Lib.** (O.wks.Sun.aft.); has portraits of Pres. & Mrs. Coolidge & coll. of miniatures. (8) On street (R) from High St., **The Beeches,** home of Calvin Coolidge, where he died. (9) 21 Massasoit St., **1st Coolidge home.** (10) On Prospect St., **Capen H.** (O.during academic yr.1825.remod.1883) is owned by Smith College & is dormitory of Capen School. (11) On Main St., **Old Smith College Campus** (est.1871). College was founded by Sophia Smith, of Hatfield, who wrote in her will: "It is my opinion that by the higher . . . education of women what are called 'their wrongs' will be reduced, their wages adjusted, their weight of influence in reforming the evils of society will greatly increase . . . their power for good will be incredibly enlarged." Campus extends on both sides of Conn. R., which has been dammed to create Paradise Pond. **Grecourt Gates** (1924), ent. from Main St., replica of those of Château at Grecourt, France, comm. work of Smith College Relief Unit during & after World War I. Beyond is towered **College Hall** (Coll.Goth.). On rear wall is Tablet, with bas-relief by Alice Wright, comm. a beloved night watchman. On Elm St., **Tryon Art Gallery** (O.wks.Sun.aft.1926); canvasses by Amer. landscape painter D. W. Tryon & other exhibits. Near-by is **Dewey H.** (O.1827.remod.). Also on Elm St., **Hillyer Art Gallery;** Amer. art coll. & auditorium. 109 Elm St., **Sessions H.** (O.acad. yr.), built by Lt. Jon. Hunt, whose daughter married Rev. Gen. Seth Pomeroy; secret stairway supposedly was used by Gen. Burgoyne. In Students' Bldg. is **Theater Workshop** & small theater where student plays are presented. Northampton is at J. with St.9 & St.10.

## Sec. 5: NORTHAMPTON to MASS.-VT. LINE. 32.

**4. WEST HATFIELD.** J. with Rd.

SIDE TRIP: (R) on latter 2$^{m}$ to **Hatfield** (sett.1661) which suffered from Ind. attacks 1675-77. Many settlers were taken captive to Canada. In 1677-78, Ben. Waite & Stephen Jennings paddled to Quebec to ransom their kidnapped families. **Old Ch.** (1844.by Isaac Damon). 75 Main St., **H. of Sophia Smith** (O.c.1790), owned by Smith College.

**12. S. DEERFIELD,** scene of Bloody Brook Massacre, 1675 (see Deerfield below). J. with St.116.

SIDE TRIP: St.116 (W) to Adams in the Berkshires (see St.2). Route runs through sparsely populated hill country bet. St.2 & St.9. 6.5$^{m}$ **Conway.** On Elm St., **Marshall Field Mem. Lib.** (O); hist. coll. At 7$^{m}$, J. with Rd. [Take latter (L) to fine Covered Bridge across South R.] At 12$^{m}$ J. with Rd. [Take latter (L) 2.5$^{m}$ to lovely **Chapel Falls.**] 13.5$^{m}$ **Ashfield. Town Hall** (1814); formerly Ch., with fine steeple.

**17. DEERFIELD** (sett.1673). In 1704, Deerfield was practically wiped out by Ind. raid. Town's mile-long street is lined with lovely old Hs. & ancient elms. PTS. OF INT.: (1) SE. cor. of Common, **Frary H.** (oldest portion 1689), built by Sam. Frary, who was massacred by Inds. Became a tavern, in barroom of which Benedict Arnold is supposed to have closed deal for 15,000 lbs. of beef for his troops. (2) On Old Deerfield St.: **The Old Manse** (Willard H.O.1694.Georg.Col.rest.1768); antique items & old wall-paper; named for Sam. Willard, early Unit. minister, & was home of Rich. Hildreth, early Amer. historian. It is recorded that 3 daughters of the house were married here in identical blue-gray silk gowns & pink bonnets. (3) **Ch.** (1824. attrib.to Isaac Damon). (4) **Indian H.** (O.wks.exc.Tues.Sun.aft.sm.fee.1929), reprod. of John Sheldon's Ind. H. (1698); furnished in period; coll. of antique items & paintings by native artists. (5) To rear is **Old Bloody Brook Tavern** (O.1700), moved from S. Deerfield (see above) where massacre of Capt. Lothrop & 85 men occurred (1675).

All were buried in a common grave. (6) **Bardwell-Stebbins-Abercrombie H.** (1714), once home of best broom-maker in Conn. valley. (7) On Albany Rd., **Deerfield Academy** (est.1797) & (8) **John Williams H.** (O.appl.Academy.1707). Rev. Williams was kidnapped by Inds. & taken to Canada, but survived to write "The Redeemed Captive." H. has secret stairway & witch's cross on door & windows, as protection against evil spirits, finest doorway in Deerfield. (9) On Memorial St., **Mem. Hall** (O. wks.Sun.aft.1798), now Mus. (10) **Ephraim Williams H.** (O.appl.Academy.1760.add. 1794), built by J. P. Bull, gunsmith & armorer in Col. Ephraim Williams' regiment (see Williamstown). (11) **Nims H.** (O.appl.Academy.1710).

**20. GREENFIELD.** J. with St.2 (see). **26. BERNARDSTON.** J. with St.10 (see N.H. St.10 & 12). **32. MASS.-VT. LINE.**

### Sec. 6: MASS.-VT. LINE to BELLOWS FALLS. 33.

In Vt. through RR. parallels route. Through bus conns. From Brattleboro to Barnet, numerous bridges across Conn. R. to pts. in N.H.

**9. BRATTLEBORO** (sett.c.1753). (Accoms.: All types. Info.: C. of C. & Booth on Main St.). Busy commercial & industrial city, at J. of West & Conn. Rs. Manufactures autos, rugs, optical instruments, textiles, furniture, wooden heels & sports goods. Birthpl. of Amer. painter, Wm. Morris Hunt, & his brother, architect Rich. Morris Hunt (see Newport, R.I.), of W. R. Mead, of McKim, Mead & White, architects, & his brother, Larkin Mead, sculptor.

PTS. OF INT.: 200 Main St., **Pub. Lib.** (O.wks.); coll. of early Amer. antiques & art, incl. canvas by Hunt. On Main St., Center Ch. (Congr.1842), & also **All Souls Ch.** (Goth.) in which is copy of Mead's "Recording Angel," which, as a young man, he first modeled in snow. In **Town Hall** is Summer Theater. W. of Cedar St., **Brattleboro Outing Club & Ski Jump.** On St.9 (see) is **Hogback Mt.,** ski area.

SIDE TRIP: St.30 (NW) to J. with St.11, E. of Manchester (see US7). This picturesque route is a diagonal link with US7. At 6$^{m}$, **W. Dummerston,** which, in 1774, protested against Brit. encroachment on Amer. liberty. Near-by is **Black Mt.** of solid blue-white granite. **Quarries** (O). On **Furnace Brook** are fine cascades. 12.5$^{m}$ **Newfane,** site of early battle with Inds. Eugene Field, whose grandfather was early settler, spent boyhood days here. **County Cth.** (1825), one of finest in Vt. **Congr. Ch.** (1839). **Newfane Inn** (late 18th cent.); still hotel. **Union Hall** (1832). (N) 6$^{m}$ from Newfane is **Brookline. Round Schoolh.** (1822) was built by Dr. John Wilson, believed to have been Capt. Thunderbolt, highwayman, wanted for murder in Eng. 17$^{m}$ **Townshend.** Father of Pres. Taft was born here. **Congr. Ch.** (late 18th cent.). 19$^{m}$ J. with Rd. (L) into **Townshend St. For.** (pic.trls.); trl. to **Bald Mt.** (2,000';skiing). 27$^{m}$ **Jamaica. Bapt. Ch.** (early 19th cent.). Near Jamaica are **Hamilton Falls** (124') & **Ball Mt.** (1,745'). St.30 cont. to J. with St.11, at 42.5$^{m}$.

**12.5.** J. with Rd. [Take latter (L) 2$^{m}$ to **Naulahka,** where Rudyard Kipling lived. He married Caroline Balestier, a Vt. woman. Eventually he had differences with his neighbors & moved away.] **27.5. WESTMINSTER** (sett.1734). In 1774-75, when rival claims of N.Y., N.H. & Vt. were being fought out, several conventions were held here. When N.Y. authorities tried to hold court in town, fight resulted in which 1 man was killed & 3 mortally injured. Ethan Allen married his 2nd wife, Fanny Buckman, in this town. **Community H.** (Westminster Institute.1923) has Mus. of Vt. hist. material. Marker on **Site of Old Cth. 33. BELLOWS FALLS** (sett.early 18th cent.) at Great Falls of Conn. R., facing Mt. Kilburne, N.H. In mid-19th cent., a canal was built around Falls to accom. river traffic. Hetty Green, eccentric millionairess & once thought to be richest woman in the world, had her home here. Today, city & vic. are paper-making district. 65 Westminster St., **Rockingham Pub. Lib.** (O); has coll. of hist. relics & paintings. [In Bellows Falls is J. with St.121 leading (L) 4.5$^{m}$ to **Saxton's River. Vt. Academy for Boys.** At 13$^{m}$, **Grafton. The Tavern** (O.summer.1835;remod.1865). To SW., **Grafton St. For.** (pic.camps.).]

### Sec. 7: BELLOWS FALLS to WHITE RIVER JUNCTION. 43.5.

**3.5.** J. with St.103.

SIDE TRIP: From J. with US5 to J. with US7, S. of Rutland, 44. St.103. Via Rockingham, Chester, Ludlow, Cuttingsville & E. Clarendon. This tour links US5 & US7 following Williams & Black Rs. & then crossing high mt. reg. & finally descending into valley (W) of Green Mts. At 2$^{m}$ **Rockingham village. Rockingham Meetingh.** (O.1787.Col.rest.1906.

int.exter.& inter.) is a splendidly preserved example of the period. It is characteristic of a certain type of northern New England architecture in having no steeple. Special services in Aug. 9m **Chester,** charming old village. (Ski.trl.ski jump.ski tow.). **Bapt. Ch.** (1st half 19th cent.). **Congr. Ch.** (1st half 19th cent.). 9.5m **Chester Depot,** which also has some fine old bldgs. **Universalist Ch.** (1st half 19th cent.). St.103 now threads its way through fine **Proctorville Gulf** passing (L) **Proctor-Piper St. For.** (1,500 as.pic.trls.). 22m **Fletcher Farms** (late 18th cent.), arts & crafts summer school & meetingplace for discussion of various social problems. 24m **Ludlow** on Black R. **Black R. Academy,** where Calvin Coolidge went to school. **Home of J. G. Sargent,** Attorney Gen. in Coolidge's cabinet. St.103 now passes (L) **Okemo St. For. Pk.** (4,400 as.skiing.pic.trls.). Rd. almost to summit of **Okemo Mt.** (3,372'). 26m J. with St.100 (see US4). 42m J. with Long Trl. Take latter (L) (S) distance to impressive **Clarendon Gorge.** 44m **Pierce's Corner.** J. with US7.

**11.** is J. with St.11. **12. CHESHIRE TOLL BRIDGE** across Conn. R. near Charlestown, N.H.

SIDE TRIP: Take St.11 from J. with US5 near Cheshire Toll Bridge 4m to **Springfield** on Black R.; machine tool mfg. plants (most of them O.). 1st settlement was at Eureka, a few miles (N) of city. The orig. grantees, among other duties, had to pay 1 ear of corn on Dec. 1 annually to the grantor. However, Black R. Falls called by Inds. "Comtu" (great noise) lured settlers to site of present city to use water power of the Falls. Town is center for amateur telescope makers who have local assoc. which corresponds with like-minded hobbyists throughout the country. On Main St., **Congr. Ch.** (1st half 19th cent.alts.). On Park St. **Holt H.** (early 19th cent.). On Summer Hill Ave., **Old Chimney H.** (Col.). From Falls Bridge, fine view of **Black R. Gorge.** Side Trip conts. (N) from Springfield on St.10 to **Reading** (Felchville) near which are stones comm. spot where Mrs. Johnson, kidnapped by Inds. in Charlestown, N. H., gave birth to a daughter. From Reading, St.106 cont. N. to Woodstock (see US4).

**14. GEN. LEWIS MORRIS H.** (late 18th cent.fine example). **21. WEATHERSFIELD BOW.** Wm. Jarvis, Consul to Portugal, imported the 1st merino sheep to America & pastured them on his land here. **23. WILGUS ST. FOR.** (pic.trls.). **24. ASCUTNEYVILLE,** from which view of Mt. Ascutney (see below). **29. WINDSOR;** manufactures machinery, castings, rubber goods. Here in 1777 was adopted Constitution of Vt. as an independent state. Town was birthpl. of V. L. Rice who invented roller process of making flour. On Main St., **Old South Ch.** (1798.by Asher Benjamin) & **Green H.** (1791), now Masonic Lodge. Other int. Hs. on N. Main St. are: **Harriet Lane H.** (1804.attrib.to Asher Benjamin), now a shop; **Old Constitution H.** (O.c.1772), in which st. constitution was adopted; coll. of hist. relics, mss., old furniture. **Vt. St. Prison & House of Correction** (O.exc.Sat.aft.& Sun.). **Concord Toll Bridge** (c.1866), longest covered bridge in Vt.

SIDE TRIP: Take Rd. (L) & then (S) to **Mt. Ascutney** (3,320') in **Ascutney St. For. Pk.** (pic.camp.trls.ski runs); Rd. runs nearly to summit.

**34. HARTLAND** (sett.1763). **Summer-Steele H.** (early 19th cent.Georg.alts.); antique shop. Near village is **Hartland Community Fair Horse Show Grounds** (Aug).

**40. N. HARTLAND,** at falls of Conn. & Ottaquechee Rs., where Rogers' Rangers, on their retreat from Canada (1759) were stranded. **43.5. WHITE RIVER JUNCTION,** a RR. center. J. with US4. On White R. is J. with St.14.

SIDE TRIP: From White R. Junction to Barre. St.14. This Rd. runs through Williamstown Gulf, following White R. & its branch. 13m **Sharon,** on White R. is another mt. enclosed village. **Old Congr. Ch.** & **Old Town Hall** are both charming. J. with Rd. [Take latter (R) 4m to **Downer St. For.** (pic.f.).] 17m J. with Rd. [Take latter (R) 2m to **Jos. Smith Mon.** on site of birthpl. of Mormon prophet (see Carthage, Ill.) **Guest H.** (O) contains coll. of relics).] 18m J. with St.110.

(1) Just (S) across the R. from this pt. is **S. Royalton,** where is **Mon. to Hannah Handy,** whose daring saved her children from Ind. Massacre, 1780.

(2) Take St.110 (N) 5.5m to **Tunbridge.** Hilarious "World's Fair" in Sept., featuring harness races, stock exhibits., etc.

20m **Royalton. Granite Mon.** comm. burning of village in 1780. **Old Bowman H. Old Meth. Meetingh.** (Old Academy Bldg.) **Congr. Ch.** & **Episc. Ch.** (all early 19th cent.). Royalton Academy was a famous institution in its day & many of its graduates figured importantly in national hist. **Old Lyman H.** (late 18th cent.). 25.5m **E. Bethel. Old Bapt. Ch. Hexagonal School H.,** still in use. (Both 1st half 19th cent.). 27m **S. Randolph. Antique Shop** (O.late 18th cent.). 37m **E. Brookfield.** J. with Rd. [Take latter (L) & bear (L) to **Brookfield** at 2.5m. **Sunset L.,** noted for unique floating bridge. (W) c.2.5m of Brookfield is **Allis St. For. Pk.** (pic.camp.). Rd. runs to summit of **Bear Hill.** Fine view.] St.14 now traverses scenically fine Williamstown Gulf. 41.5m **Ainsworth St. For. Pk.** 45m **Williamstown. Mon.** to Thos. Davenport, inventor of electric motor. **Old Congr. Ch.** 48.5m J. with Rd. leading (R) 2m to **Graniteville** with impressive views of quarries (see Barre). 51m **Barre** (see US2).

## Sec. 8: WHITE RIVER JUNCTION to ST. JOHNSBURY. 66.

**17. E. THETFORD.** J. with Rd.

SIDE TRIP: 2.5m (L) to **Thetford Hill. Congr. Ch.** (late 18th cent.), reputedly oldest in state. At 3.5m **Abenaki L.** (recr.).

**22.5. ELY.** J. with Rd. which leads (L) 2.5m to **Fairlee L.** (recr.). **27.5. FAIRLEE** (resort); has several fine old Hs. Birthpl. of Sam. Morey who claimed to have invented steamboat in 1793, long before Fulton. (L) to **Morey L.** (resort), where Morey in despair at failure to win recognition, sank his steamboat. **32. BRADFORD** (sett. early 18th cent.), at pt. where Waits R. joins Conn. R. Town was birthpl. of Adm. Chas. E. Clark who brought the battleship "Oregon" around the Horn in time to take part in Battle of Santiago de Cuba in Sp. Amer. War. Several int. old Hs. **39.5. S. NEWBURY.** Here is beautiful **Ox-Bow Cemetery. 40.5. NEWBURY.** Ox-Bow Antique Shop in home of Rev. hero, Jacob Bayley, to whom there is a Mon. in town. **Congr. Ch.** (1794). Several other int. old bldgs. **45.5. WELLS RIVER** (sett. 2nd half 18th cent.), on R. of same name near its J. with Conn. R.; was founded by Gen. Jacob Bayley (see above). **Congr. Ch.** (late 18th cent.). J. with US302.

SIDE TRIP: Take US302 (W) from Wells River. 10m **Groton,** on Wells R., lumber & granite center. 11m J. with dirt Rd.

Take latter (R) 1.5m to **Ricker Mills,** old sawmill on Lund Pond. Beyond extends **Groton St. For.** (15,300 as.camp.pic.trlrs.swim.f.h.ski trls.), with 3 mt. pks. & 6 ponds. Rd. winds uphill to summit of **Owl's Head,** 3m.

Cont. (W) from J. (above) on US302 past **Wm. Scott Mem.** (L) comm. Vt. Civil War soldier condemned to death for sleeping on sentry duty but pardoned by Lincoln & later killed in action. 26.5m **E. Barre Dam** on branch of Winooski R., of earth, 1,410′ long. 27m **E. Barre,** at J. with St.110, running (S) to J. with St.14 (see above). From J. with St.110, US302 cont. (NW) to **Barre** at 30m & at 35m J. with US2 (E) of Montpelier 2m.

**56.5. BARNET** (sett.1770), at Stevens Falls. [(L) 4.5m to **W. Barnet,** near **Harvey Pond** (resort). **Old Covenanters Ch.,** only remaining Ch. of this sect in state.] **59. E. BARNET,** near J. of Passumpsic & Conn. Rs. [2.5m (R) here to **Great Fifteen-Mile Falls Dam** (O), across Conn. R., which generates 300,000 h.p., greatest E. of Niagara.] Route now leaves Conn. R. & follows Passumpsic R.

**66. ST. JOHNSBURY** (Through RR. & bus conns. Mun. airport. Accoms.: All types. Info. Booth & C. of C.) is located at confluence of the Passumpsic, Moose & Sleeper's Rs. Last was originally known as the West branch but was given present name when Thos. Todd, surveyor employed by Jon. Arnold, was found asleep on the riverbank. Arnold, who had represented R.I. in the Continental Congress, was the orig. settler, 1787. He had received a large grant covering the present city site. The town was literally hacked out of the forest & till the late 1820's remained an isolated cross Rds. connected with outside world only by post-riders. Stagecoaches came no closer than Haverhill, N.H. The 1st boom began with manufacture of platform scales invented by Thaddeus Fairbanks, who because of his invention was made Knight of the Imperial Order by the Austrian Emperor & Comdr. of Nishan el Iftihar by the King of Siam. Soon after est. of the Fairbanks Plant, Geo. Cary, who had been traveling to sell groceries, began making maple sugar products. He started his business by persuading a customer to use maple instead of cane sugar for cementing together & flavoring plug tobacco. From these small beginnings, the business developed a $2,000,000 annual output & has made the city the Maple Capital of the World. John G. Saxe, Vt. poet, celebrated maple sugar as one of Vt.'s 4 famous products:

> Men, women, maple sugar & horses;
> The first are strong, the latter fleet,
> The second & third are exceedingly sweet
> And all are uncommonly hard to beat.

The RR. came in 1850 & industries thereafter multiplied—flour milling, farm implements, knife blades, iron foundries. One of the most curious early products was hoop-skirts—until they went out of fashion. Today the city's plants turn out—in addition to platform scales & maple sugar—flour, furniture, farm implements, bowling pins, etc.

PTS. OF INT.: On Main St.: **Civil War Statue** by Vt. sculptor Larkin Mead; **Mus. of Nat. Sciences** (O.1891.Richardson.Romanes.); **Athenaeum Lib. & Mus.** (O); art coll.; **Old South Congr. Ch.** (mid-19th cent.); **Paddock Mansion** (1820). At cor. Main & Winter Sts., **A. G. Chadwick H.** (1845). On Central St., **Meth. Ch.,** with Tiffany window. The bell in the orig. church on the site was used to sound alarms for fires in key of E, which clashed so with other church bells tuned in the key of F, that something had to be done to resolve the discord. Portland St., **Cary Maple Sugar Co.** (O). Central Ave., **Fairbanks Co.** (O). At Four Cors., **Century H.** (late 18th cent.). Eastern Ave., **Octagon H.** (middle 19th cent.). Old Gov. E. Fairbanks H. which became **Maple Grove Inn.** 3$^{m}$ distant, in St. Johnsbury Center, is **First Congr. Ch.** (1804), 5 of whose members were appointed to keep dogs out on Sundays. At Emerson Falls, W. of town, Gov. Fish Hatchery, where 2,000,000 trout are raised annually. In St. Johnsbury is J. with US2.

SIDE TRIP: Take US2 (E) & then turn (S) on St.18 to **Lower Waterford** on Fifteen-Mile Falls. (R) from Waterford several miles is the great Fifteen-Mile Dam (O.see above).

## Sec. 9: ST. JOHNSBURY to DERBY LINE. 55.

Route cont. along Passumpsic R. **9. LYNDONVILLE.** On Depot St., **Cobleigh Pub. Lib.;** various colls. On Elm St., **St. Peter's Ch.** (Episc.by Henry Vaughan). **9.5. J.** with St.114.

SIDE TRIP: (N) (R) on St.114 to Canadian Border (S.of Sherbrooke, Can.). This route passes through wild & unsettled country & by several fine Ls. At 5.5$^{m}$ **E. Burke. White Schoolh.** (O.1817); hist. coll. (R) from E. Burke, 5$^{m}$ to **Burke Mt. Reserv.** (17,000 as.pic. camp.). Toll Rd. 3$^{m}$ to **Summit** (3,267′). For balance of St.114 (N), see Newport Trip A.

**17. W. BURKE.** Take Rd. 2$^{m}$ (R) here to **Burke Hollow;** where are several old Hs. & **Union Meeting H.** (O.1st quarter 19th cent.very int.). In W. Burke is J. with St.5A.

SIDE TRIP: St.5A & St.105 to **Derby.** An easterly alternate route through primitive country of fors. & Ls. (good f.). At 11.5$^{m}$, **Willoughby L.,** (bath.boat.f.in L.& near-by brooks), dominated by **Mts. Pisgah** (2,654′) & **Hor** (1,592′). At 19$^{m}$ is J. with St.105, on which trip cont. (L) to **Derby Center,** where is J. with Main Tour, US5, at 26$^{m}$.

**22. WILLOUGHBY ST. FOR. 25.5. WILLOUGHBY,** center for winter sports, on Crystal L. where is **Pageant Pk.** (recr.camp.winter sports). In Pk., trl. to **May Falls.**

**30. BARTON.** Orleans Cty. Fair (Aug.) is held in **Roaring Brook Pk.** Route follows Barton R. **35.5. ORLEANS.** [L. here to **Brownington,** birthpl. of Stephen P. Joselyn, noted Ind. fighter; at 3$^{m}$ **Old Stone H.** (O.fee.1828); coll. of antiques.] US5 now follows Black R. of the North, trout stream. **47. NEWPORT** (sett.1793), resort. Through RR. & bus conns.; steamer for L. trips. Town is on **L. Memphremagog** (bath.boat.f.) 30$^{m}$ long & 4$^{m}$ wide; popular starting pt. for Canada. View of **Mt. Owl's Head** (3,360′). Rogers' Rangers made this first stop on their retreat, 1759, after raid on St. Francis in Canada (see above). On Main St., **Goodrich Mem. Lib.** (O); exhibits.

SIDE TRIPS: (A) Loop Tour from Newport to St. Johnsbury & return, 171. US5, St.111, St.114, St.102, US2, US5. Via: Derby Center, Morgan, (Island Pond), Norton, Canaan, Bloomfield, Maidstone, Guildhall, Lunenburgh. St. Johnsbury, Lyndonville, West Burke, Barton, Orleans, Coventry.

Tour circles sparsely populated NE. cor. of Vt., a forested & mountainous reg. (good f.& h.), bordering upper Conn. R. At 5$^{m}$ on US5, **Derby Center,** just (S) of which route turns (SE) (L) on St.111. 12$^{m}$ **Morgan,** on Seymour L. (f.) in hill-encircled valley. At 24$^{m}$ J. with St.114, which route follows (N) over "Roller Coaster Rd." 33$^{m}$ **Norton Pond** (f.). (E) is **Gore Mt.** (3,300′). 40$^{m}$ **Norton Mills,** near Canadian border. RR. Customh. St.114 cont. (E) along border, past **Averill. Great Averill L.** (accoms.) & near-by **Little Averill Pond** & **Wallis L.** (good f.). 54$^{m}$ **Canaan.** Customh. Good fish. & hunt. in vic. J. with St.102, which trip takes (S) along Conn. R. At c.62$^{m}$, (R) **Monadnock Mt.** (3,140′). At 83$^{m}$ J. with Rd. (R) to beautiful **Maidstone L.** (pic.boat.swim.). 92$^{m}$ **Guildhall** (sett.2nd half 18th cent.). **Old Town Hall** & **County Cth.** 98$^{m}$ J. with US2, which route follows (W) to **St. Johnsbury.** 124$^{m}$ (see US2 for this stretch). J. with US5, return route to Newport, (see US5) 171$^{m}$. (B) Loop Tour from Newport to Hardwick & return, 79. US5, St.12, St.15, St.12B, US5. Via: Coventry, Orleans, Barton, Glover, Greensboro Bend, Hardwick, Craftsbury, Albany, Irasburg. Tour follows US5 to **Barton,** 16$^{m}$. (For this stretch see US5.) In Barton is J. with St.12 which tour follows (S). 22.5$^{m}$ J. with Rd. (W) to **Shadow L.** (resort). Hy. now passes several ponds. 32.5$^{m}$ **Greensboro Bend.** [Take Rd. (NW) here 3$^{m}$ to **Greensboro** (resort) on Caspian L., in unusually beautiful setting of wooded hills.] St.12 follows course of Lamoille R. At 37$^{m}$ J. with St.15, with which St.12 unites for a few miles (W). 40$^{m}$ **Hardwick,** another of st.'s "granite" towns. On Main & Church Sts., **Mem. Bldg.** of Vt. granite & marble, comm. soldiers of Rev. & Civil Wars. Route now turns (N) from Hardwick on St.12B, passing Hardwick L. At 52$^{m}$ **Craftsbury,** named for Rev. Col. Ebenezer Crafts, orig.

grantee. Birthpl. of Fanny (Burnham) Kilgore, said to be 1st woman admitted to practice law in U.S. At 53.5m **Craftsbury Common,** charming village. **Congr. Ch.** (1st quarter 19th cent.). **Old Covenanter Ch.,** now part of Craftsbury Academy. Just (N) off hy. (R) are **Little & Great Homer Ponds.** St.12B winds along Black R. to **Coventry** (see above) & near J. with US5 at 72m which leads back to **Newport,** 79m. (For this stretch, see US5.)

C. Newport to Morrisville. St.105, St.100, St.15 & St.100.

This tour closely parallels the northern Green Mts. & Long Trl. & makes J. with St.15 near Morrisville. 0m **Newport.** Take St.105 (W) to J. with St.100 at 4m. Tour cont. (S) on St.100. 13m **Westfield.** J. with country Rd.*

Take latter (R) 5m to **Jay** & then Rd. (L). At c.7m, steep trl. runs c.2m to **Jay Peak** (3,861′); magnificent view. Both to (S) & (N) are pub. camps on the Long Trl.

24.5m charming **Eden L.** (L) 41m **Hyde Pk.** J. with St.15, which tour follows (SE) to eastern J. with St.100 at 43m. Tour cont. (S) on St.100 to **Morrisville** at 44m. Here is Rd. leading (L) 4.5m to **Elmore St. For. Pk.** (pic.bath.facils.boat.f.trls.). St.100 cont. (S) to **Stowe** (see Waterbury, US2).

US5 now climbs past **DERBY POND. 55. DERBY LINE. LEGION PK.,** at frontier, is Internat. World War I Mem.

## MASS. ST. 10, N.H. ST. 10 & 12 & US 302—NEW ENGLAND

**BERNARDSTON, MASS. (N) to TWIN MOUNTAIN, N.H. 167. Mass. St.10, N.H. St.10, St.12 & US302**

Via: Northfield, Mass.; Winchester, Keene, Walpole, Charlestown, Claremont, Plainfield, W. Lebanon, Hanover, Lyme, Haverhill, Woodsville Junction, Bath & Littleton in N.H. On side trip, St.10 from Keene to W. Lebanon, via Newport & Lebanon. RR. parallels route from Keene to Claremont. From Claremont to Woodsville, RR. runs along W. side of Conn. R. in Vt. & is easily accessible. From Woodsville to Littleton, RR. parallels route. RR. conn. at Twin Mt. Bus conns. at chief centers. Accoms.: At short intervals.

N. of Keene, route clings close to Conn. R. along W. border of N.H., paralleling US5 on Vt. side; linked by good Rds. with other tours. There are bridges to Vt. & J. with US5 at numerous pts.

### Sec. 1: BERNARDSTON, MASS. to KEENE, N.H. 24. St.10

**0. BERNARDSTON** (see). J. with US5. **3.5. MT. HERMON SCHOOL FOR BOYS** (whose parents could not afford to give them educational opportunities) founded 1881 by Dwight L. Moody. Hy. crosses Conn. R. **6. NORTHFIELD** (1714) one of most attractive old towns & birthpl. of D. L. Moody, famous evangelist & founder of Bible Institute in Chicago. St.10 follows Main St. under arching elms. Accoms. Info. at Northfield Inn. This little town has a few int. old Hs. **Dwight L. Moody H.** (O). N. of town on St.10 is **Northfield School for Girls,** founded by Rev. Moody for girls without means for higher education. On grounds are birthpl. of the founder & graves of Mr. & Mrs. Moody. **8.** St.10 crosses **MASS.-N.H. LINE. 14. WINCHESTER** (1733) on Ashuelot R. This was a frontier town in 18th cent. & consequently suffered from Ind. raids. **Nelson Bird Mus.** (O). J. with St.119.

SIDE TRIPS: (A) On St.119 (E) 14m to **Fitzwilliam** (see below).

(B) St.119 (W) & (NW) 13m along Ashuelot R. to Brattleboro, Vt. 2m **Ashuelot,** where is picturesque Covered Bridge. Near-by is **Harvard For.** with primeval hemlock & pine. 6m **Hinsdale** (1742), nicely situated mfg. village. 9m **Squire Hinsdale H.,** built by owner of 1st grist mill. 13m **Brattleboro,** Vt. at J. with US5 & St.9 (see); on latter return trip may be made to Keene & J. with main tour.

From Winchester, St.10 cont. (N) along Ashuelot R. **21.5. WEST SWANZEY; Grave of Denman Thompson,** author of "The Old Homestead," the orig. of which still stands in Swanzey (E.2m across old covered bridge). **24. KEENE,** a wood-working town. Accoms. On Drumalock Hill is 1,000′ ski tow. Summer Theater & Spring Music Festival. On Central Sq., **First Congr. Ch.** (1786.Georg.remod.). **Teachers College** (1901.Georg.bldgs.), one of largest in New England. Among college bldgs. are **Hale Adm. Bldg.** (1860.beautiful inter.) & **President's H.,** formerly Miss Fiske's Seminary (1814). **N.H. Arts & Crafts Shop. Robin Hood Pk.;** fine view from tower. Keene is at J. with St.101, St.12 & St.9.

SIDE TRIPS: (A) 53m (NE) on St.9 to **Concord** at J. with US3, US4 & US202 (see US4, Concord for this trip).

(B) 19m (W) on St.9 to **N.H.-Vt. Line** (N) of Brattleboro (see N.H. St.101 & St.9).

(C) (SE) on St.12. Popular route through Monadnock Reg. Trls. & Rds. lead to mt. slopes & peaks & to Mt. Monadnock St. Reserv. At 9.5m **Troy,** at J. with St.124, the route to E. Jaffrey through popular winter & summer sports area giving access to Grand Monadnock (see US202). Accoms. at various centers. 13m **Fitzwilliam** (sett.2nd half 18th cent.). Accoms. Lovely **Congr. Ch.** (1817) & several int. old Hs. A half-mile from town is **Rodman Gallery** (O.summer); good coll. of Mod. art. 3m (W) is **Rhododendron St. Reserv.** At 20m is **N.H.-Mass. Line** (Winchendon, Mass.).

## Sec. 2: KEENE to WEST LEBANON. 68. St.12

Main tour cont. from Keene on St.12.

SIDE TRIP: Alt. route: St.10 (N) to J. with St.12 at W. Lebanon. 64. Alt. to St.12. Via: Gilsum, Marlow, E. Lempster, Newport, Grantham, Lebanon.
At 14m is J. with St.123, which leads (E) past **Pitcher Mt.** (2,153′). At 15m **Marlow,** near North J. with St.123 (see Main Tour below). At 31m just S of Mill Village is J. with St.31, which leads (SE) (R) 4.5m & then (L) 1m to **Pillsbury St. Reserv.** (no f.h.;pic.& camp.at May Pond). 3,005-a. wilderness incl. several ponds; game sanctuary. 36m **Newport** (1766), mfg. town on Sugar R. in lovely L. Sunapee dist. Accoms. Here Sarah J. Hale wrote "Mary Had a Little Lamb." **Old South Ch.** (Congr.1822.rest.1937), considered beautiful Col. type. On Main St., **The Lafayette,** now apt. bldg., named for famous Fr. general entertained here (1825). **Ski Club trls.; Pine Needle Ski Jump.** J. with St.11 (E) (see US4) to L. Sunapee. At 59m, J. with US4. [E. a few miles on US4 is **L. Mascoma** (see US4).] US4 unites with St.10 (W) along Mascoma R. to **Lebanon,** mfg. center & excellent summer & winter sports country. Accoms. At 64m in **West Lebanon** is J. with St.12A. From this pt. (N) St.10 becomes main tour (see below).

From Keene St.12, main tour angles (NW) ascending gradually. **7. EAST WESTMORELAND.** In highest part of Westmoreland (S. on St.63) is **Park Hill,** a cluster of Col. Hs. around hilltop. Notable **Ch.** (2nd half 18th cent.Class.Rev.adds.1827). **18. WALPOLE** (sett.1749), a distinguished old town. **Allen H., Bellows H. & Rowe-Bradley H.** (all 2nd half 18th cent.). **Knapp H.** & **Old Colony Inn;** old Fr. wallpaper. (Both Hs. date from 1st quarter 19th cent.). **19.** (L) **BELLOWS MANSION** (2nd half 18th cent.). **21.** J. with St.123.

SIDE TRIP: (R) on St.123 to **Alstead** (sett.late 18th cent.) at 5m, past old Covered Bridge (L). Here some of N.H.'s earliest paper mills were est. Handsome **Shedd-Porter Mem. Lib.** (O.Mon.Wed.Fri.& Sat.). St.123 returns (SE) to J. with St.10 at **Marlow** (see alt. route above). About 1m beyond Alstead is **Vilas Pool** (O.summer), beautiful pic. & recr. area on Cold R. St.123A branches (NE) near this pt. to **South Acworth.** (L) on country Rd. is **Acworth** with lovely **Ch.** & **Button Mus.** (O). St.123A cont. (NE) to J. with St.10 (see alt. route above). Cont. from Alstead on St.12A (W) to J. with St.12 at S. Charlestown.

**27. SOUTH CHARLESTOWN.** Here St.12A provides alt. route (S) to Keene. **31. CHARLESTOWN,** where once stood a ft. which was besieged by Fr. & Inds. (1744). Fine Col. Hs. line town's elm-shaded streets. **Marker** on Site of H. from which Mary Johnson was kidnapped by Inds. (1754) (see Felchville, Vt.). **43. CLAREMONT.** Accoms., tourist & sports facils. Largest town in Dartmouth-L. Sunapee area. Important industries along Sugar R. whose swift current powered early mills. On Broad St. are **Soldiers' Mon.** (by Martin Milmore) & **Fiske Free Lib.** (O.wks.); art, natural hist. & antique colls. Notable among town's old Hs. are a number in S. Col. style, incl. 4 on Central St., now owned by St. Mary's Ch. (Cath.) & one at 5 Central St. & one on Broad St. At J. with St.11 (E) 15.5m on latter to L. Sunapee reg. (For this sec. of St.11, see Potter Place, US4.) St.12 unites (W) with St.103 from Claremont to Conn. R. where St.103 crosses bridge to Ascutneyville, Vt. (see). Main tour cont. (N) here on St.12A.

**51. BIRTHPL. OF SALMON P. CHASE,** Pres. Lincoln's Secy. of Treasury & Chief Justice of U.S. Supreme Court. Just beyond are **Wellman H.** (2nd half 18th cent.), **Old Weld H.** opp. **Trinity Ch.** (1809). In cemetery, graves of Rev. soldiers. At c.**52.** J. with Rd. (L) to **Old Covered Bridge** (sm.toll) across Conn. R. to Windsor, Vt. (see), one of finest covered bridges in New England. **54.5.** Marked Rd. leads (R) to **Saint-Gaudens Mem.** (O.May 30-Oct.15.sm.fee), on former estate of noted Amer. sculptor who attracted art & literary colony to Cornish & vic. Here are his former home (orig.furnishings) & studios, with replicas of his work. By pool in garden is "Pan" by Saint-Gaudens. At the small Temple is altar above ashes of Mr. & Mrs. Saint-Gaudens. St.12A curves along Blow-Me-Down Pond. **68. WEST LEBANON.** J. with US4 (see) & St.10 (see alt. route, above). From here main tour follows St.10 (N).

## Sec. 3: WEST LEBANON to WOODSVILLE. 42. St.10.

### 5. HANOVER

RR. conns. at Norwich, Vt. & White R. Junction, Vt. Ledyard Bridge on Tuck Dr. to Wilder, Vt. (see US5). Lebanon Airport, (S) c.5$^m$, for Dartmouth Airways, conn. with through lines. Accoms. Info.: 33 Main St., Hanover Inn & N.H. Auto Assoc. Trl. info.: Dartmouth Outing Club. Outstanding winter sports facils. Winter Carnival (Feb.).

The village of Hanover, overlooking Conn. R., has its main interest in Dartmouth College, founded 1769 for Inds. (see Columbia, Conn. US6 Alt.). Dan. Webster, in the Dartmouth College Case (1818) defended his alma mater against hostile action of the st. legislature & Chief Justice Marshall's epoch-making decision guaranteed survival of the private college & the inviolability of charters. Dartmouth is traditionally an undergrad., liberal arts college with associated medical, engineering & business schools. PTS. OF INT.: **Dartmouth College** (guide at Hanover Inn): Most bldgs. on **College Green** are Col. in style. Notable are (1) **Baker Mem. Lib.** (1927-28. Col.by Jens F.Larsen.beautiful inter.); in Tower Rm. is part of orig. college lib. & other rare books. In Reserve Rm. are the famous **Murals** (1932-34) illustrating Aztec mythology & development of Amer. civilization by José Clemente Orozco, Mex. artist. (2) **Carpenter Fine Arts Bldg.** (1929); art & archaeology colls. & lib. (3) **Sanborn English H.** (1929.beautiful inter.& exter.), in which is Sanborn Mem. Rm., reprod. of Prof. E. D. Sanborn's study. (4) **Parkhurst Hall** (1911), adm. bldg. (5) College St., **Webster Hall** (1901) with auditorium for academic occasions; coll. of Webster portraits. (6) Near-by, **Dartmouth Row,** nucleus of the Old College, incl. Dartmouth Hall, reconstruction of orig. bldg. (1784), twice wrecked by fire (last reconstructed 1936), **Wentworth** & **Thornton Halls** (1829) & **Reed Hall** (1840). (7) **Wilson Mus.** (O.Mon.-Fri.academic year.otherwise appl.). (8) In College Pk. are **Shattuck Observ.** (1854); **Medical Bldg.** (1811); **Bartlett Tower** (fine view). (9) College St., **Ch. of Christ** (1935.early N.E.). (10) **Rollins Chapel.** Of unusual int. are: (11) **Dick's H.,** infirmary, which has a lib. consisting of books inscribed by each donor to E. K. Hall who gave the building. The volume "Have Faith in Massachusetts" bears this inscription by Calvin Coolidge: "To Edward K. Hall in recollection of his son & my son, who have the privilege by the grace of God to be boys through all eternity." (12) **Tuck School of Business Adm.** (13) **Cummings Mem.,** Thayer School of Engineering. (14) **Mem. Field,** near Gymnasium. (15) On Occom Pond, **Outing Club H.,** one of hqs. of the Dartmouth Outing Club which maintains trls., ski trls. & cabins & shelters & is host at winter carnival. (16) The Dartmouth **Ledyard Canoe Club** is named for the son of Dartmouth, who in 1773 paddled from Hanover down the Conn. R. in a dugout. Dartmouth College owns 27,000 as. of undeveloped land at N. tip of N.H.

Across Conn. R. in Norwich, Vt. is J. with US5 (see). **16.5.** on St.10, **LYME** (sett. 2nd half 18th cent.). Accoms. **Congr. Ch.** (early 19th cent.). **22. ORFORD,** where Sam. Morley built & operated a steamboat in 1793. Attractive old Hs. J. with St.25A, running E. 7$^m$ to **Mt. Cube Hotel** & trl. up Cube Mt. (2,911′), & at 15$^m$ **Wentworth** (see Plymouth, White Mt. Tour). **28. PIERMONT.** A country Rd. follows (E) from here past **Tarleton L.** (clubh.recr.facils.), to **Warren** (see Plymouth, White Mt. Tour). **33. HAVERHILL.** On or near Common are **Haverhill Academy** (early 19th cent.); **Cth.** (1st half 19th cent.), now Alumni Hall; **Haverhill Lib.; Col. Johnston H.** (2nd half 18th cent.) & **Green Door Inn** (O.late 18th cent.), an old stagecoach stop. Just N. of town on St.10 is **Montgomery H.** (late 18th cent.) which now houses a concern manufacturing "Koch recorders" (O.appl.). **34.** J. with St.25 leading (SE) through Oliverian Notch (see Plymouth, White Mt. Tour). **38. NORTH HAVERHILL,** with good view of **Black Mt.** (2,836′). **42. WOODSVILLE JUNCTION.** J. with US302, which turns (W) through near-by **Woodsville** & over bridge to Wells R., Vt. (see). St.10 unites (E) with US302 & main tour cont. over this hy.

## Sec.4: WOODSVILLE JUNCTION to TWIN MOUNTAIN. 33. US302.

**4.** J. with St.112, which follows Wild Ammonoosuc R. (SE) through picturesque Lost R. reg. of White Mt. Nat. For. to J. with US3 (see N. Woodstock, N.H.). **5. BATH** (1765), on Ammonoosuc R. Long **Covered Bridge** (1st half 19th cent.). Near Common are **Brick Store** & **Stone H.** (both 1st half 19th cent.). **Colonial Inn,** called sometimes "Payson's Folly" because it cost so much to build in early 19th cent. **6. UPPER BATH,** also has many Hs. of early Col. & early 19th cent. periods. **10.**

**LISBON**, extending among hills on Ammonoosuc R. Winter sports center. Accoms. Woodworking industries. About $1^m$ beyond on US302 is **Cobleigh Tavern** (O.mid-18th cent.), one of oldest Hs. in reg.; an early **Blockh.** is incorporated in bldgs.; adj. is ancient **Barn. 12.** J. with St.117. A country Rd. leads (L) here to lovely **Ogontz L.** St.117 leads (R) to **Franconia** (see Echo L., White Mt. Tour). Hy. cont. along R. to **LITTLETON, 20.** at edge of White Mts. Resort & winter sports center. Good accoms. J. with St.18 & St.116.

SIDE TRIPS: (A) On St.18 (NW) c.$6^m$ to J. with Rd. (L) to **Partridge L.,** resort. At $8^m$ J. with St.135 running (SW) along **Fifteen Mile Falls** of Conn. R. (see St. Johnsbury, Vt.). St.18 cont. to J. with US2, E. of St. Johnsbury, Vt.
(B) On St.116 (E). At c.$6^m$ is Rd. (L) to **Forest L. St. Pk.** (pic.swim.bathh.); trls. into Dalton Mts. $12^m$ **Whitefield,** J. with US3 (see White Mt. Tour).

**22.5.** on US302 is (E) J. with St.18 which leads (S) $13^m$ to **Echo L.** (see White Mt. Tour). **25. BETHLEHEM STREET,** all-yr. resort. Excellent accoms. RR. & bus conns. From here Mt. Agassiz Rd. (toll.auto July-Oct.) leads (S) to summit of **Mt. Agassiz** (2,394′). **33. TWIN MOUNTAIN.** J. with US3 (see White Mt. Tour).

## MASS. ST. 28 (N)—NEW ENGLAND

**BOSTON, MASS. (N) to MANCHESTER, N.H. St.28. 56.**

Via: In Mass.: (Somerville), (Medford), Stoneham, Reading, (Wakefield), Andover, Lawrence, Methuen. In N.H.: Salem Depot, Derry, N. Londonderry. B.& M. RR. & bus lines parallel route. Good accoms.

**Sec. 1: BOSTON to SHAWSHEEN. 26.** (see Boston for this sec.).

**Sec. 2: SHAWSHEEN to MANCHESTER. 30.**

**3. LAWRENCE,** woolen & worsted center deriving power from Bodwell's Falls on Merrimack R. RR. & bus conns. Mun. Airport, through conns. In 1912 town was scene of great strike in which I.W.W. & its leaders, Haywood, Ettor & Giovanitti, were involved; strike resulted in Congressional investigation. 33 Haverhill St., **Bodwell H.** (early 18th cent.), only relic of early settlement. **Lawrence Print Works,** one of largest in world; **Wood Worsted Mills,** largest in world (neither O.). Great stone **Lawrence Dam** (1845-48). At N. edge is **METHUEN** (sett.1st half 18th cent.). **Nevins Mem. Lib.** In vic. is **Vacation Farm for Horses** (O). **5.5. MASS.-N.H. LINE. 9. SALEM DEPOT.** Near-by is **Rockingham Pk.;** summer horse races. **11. CANOBIE LAKE** near L. of same name (amusements.facils.). At **17.** hy. forks, Bypass 28 running (N), skirting Manchester, to J. with US3. Tour follows St.28 through **DERRY, 18.5.,** on Beaver Brook, originally, as name implies, sett. by Scotch-Irish, shoemaking village in charming setting of hills & meadows near Beaver L. (resort). **25. WHITE'S TAVERN** (early 19th cent.int.exter.). At **26.** hy. forks again, St.28A by-passing, & St.28 entering **MANCHESTER** (see White Mt. Tour), largest city in N.H. at **30.** J. with US3 & St.101. St.28 cont. (N) united with US3 to Suncook where it swings away (NE). (See White Mt. Tour.)

## MASS. ST. 28 (S)—NEW ENGLAND

**BOSTON (S) to BOURNE (Cape Cod). 62. St.28**

Via: Milton, Randolph, Avon, Brockton, W. Bridgewater, Bridgewater & Buzzards Bay. St.28 is shortest route from Boston to Cape Cod.

**Sec. 1: BOSTON to J. with St.128. 14.**

(For this sec. see Boston Trip II.)

**Sec. 2: J. with St.128 to BOURNE. 48.**

**3. RANDOLPH,** named for Peyton Randolph, 1st president of Continental Congress. Union & S. Main Sts., **Town Hall** (early 19th cent.Class.Rev.). N. of Town Hall, **Old Bass H.** (pre-1810). Further (N), at N. Main near West St., **Old Jon. Belcher H.** (O); period furniture. S. Main St., near Maple St., **Birthpl.** (c.1840) of Mary Wilkins Freeman, author of New England stories. Take street (L) $2^m$ to **Holbrook.** 324 N. Franklin St., **Nath. Belcher H.** (1754), home of Rev. patriot & tavern for Rev. soldiers. Union St. near Cedar Hill Rd., **Bernard H.** (1746); Union St., opp. Dalton Rd., **Jordan H.** (1763). **9. BROCKTON,** great shoe manufacturing center.

815 Belmont St., **Bryant H.** (O.appl.), where Wm. Cullen Bryant wrote early poems. White Ave. & Main St., **Pub. Lib.** (O); important Copeland Coll. of Amer. paintings. 82 Perkins Ave., **Walk-Over Shoe Co.** (O.appl.). 133 Spark St., **Douglas Shoe Co.** (O.appl.). **14. WEST BRIDGEWATER** (sett.mid-17th cent.). 162 Harvard St., **Bridgewater Hist. Soc.** (O.appl.); rare books & documents incl. deed to 1st settlers by Massasoit, Ind. Sachem who welcomed Pilgrims when they landed (appl.at local bank). 58 South St., **Judge Baylies H.,** where Bryant studied law. On River St., **Keith H.** (1680) built by 1st settlers for Jos. Keith, 1st pastor. Local Pk. (pic.). **17. BRIDGEWATER** (sett.mid-17th cent.). School St., **Unit. Ch.** (1845) with fine steeple. Opp., **Bridgewater Teachers College.** At Common, **Washburn H.** (early 18th cent. rest.), home of a stubborn Tory. On High St., **Deacon Jos. Alden H.** (early 18th cent.) built by descendant of John & Priscilla Alden. **23.** J. with US44 (see). **42.** J. with US6 (see) with which St.28 unites for several miles. **46. BUZZARDS BAY. 47.5.** Handsome bridge (by Cram & Ferguson) spanning Cape Cod Canal.
A project for a canal at this point was broached as early as 1676. Waterway connecting Buzzards with Mass. Bay would shorten route from L.I. Sound to Boston & also avoid perils of circumnavigating the Cape. (Bet. 1900 & 1920 there were 974 wrecks in Cape Cod waters). In 1909, Aug. Belmont started building a canal & in 1918, Fed. Gov. took over & completed the waterway. Total cost was c.$40,000,000.
St.28 branches off (S) here, crossing bridge to **BOURNE** (sett.1st half 17th cent.) at **48.** Named for Jon. Bourne, descendant of Richard Bourne who did missionary work among Mashpee Inds. Largely due to Bourne's influence, these Inds. refused to join King Philip in his uprising. Near Shore Rd., **Aptuxet Trading Post** (O.exc. Mon.Ap.-Nov.1) is a reprod. of Plymouth Colony's 1st trading post (1627); hist. relics & reprod. of furnishings of Pilgrim period. (For St.28 beyond this point, see Cape Cod.)

## US 1, MASS. ST. 3, ST. 3A, & US 6—NEW ENGLAND

**BOSTON (S) to J. with St.28 near BOURNE at Cape Cod Canal. 65. US1, St.3, St.3A & US6**

Via: Quincy, Weymouth, (Norwell), (Hanover Center), (Pembroke), Hingham, Nantasket, Cohasset, Scituate, Marshfield, (Duxbury), Kingston, & Plymouth.

Tour skirts picturesque "South Shore," passing hist. fishing & shipping towns with int. old bldgs, & many beaches & harbors (swim.yacht.f.facils.). Tour makes J. with US6, which runs along N. shore of Cape Cod, at Sagamore Bridge, & with St.28 which runs along S. shore of Cape from near Bourne (see Cape Cod tour).

### Sec. 1: BOSTON to QUINCY. 10. US1.

(For this sec. see US1 & Boston Trip II.)

### Sec. 2: QUINCY to J. of St.3A & St.3 near KINGSTON. 31.

**1.** J. of St.3A & St.3.

SIDE TRIPS: Take St.3 (R) here. At 3m from Quincy is **Weymouth** (see Boston Trip II). At 11m, J. with St.123 at **Assinippi.** Cor. Main St. & Jacob's Lane, **Jacob's Farmh.** (O.Mon. Thurs.c.1726.adds.); fire apparatus dating from 1760 to early 1900's.

(1) Take St.123 (L) here 3m to **Norwell** (sett.1634), famous for "North River" ships it built. **Kent Mem. Bldg.** (O.2nd half 17th cent.); Hist. Soc. & hist. materials. River & Wall Sts., **Old First Parish Ch.** (Unit.). Stetson Rd., off River St., old **"Cornet" Rbt. Stetson H.,** former home of high official of Plymouth colony. On St.123, Main St. near Second Herring Brook, **Bryant-Cushman H.** (1698). At Oak & High Sts., **Early Shoe Shop.**

(2) Take St.123 (R) 7m to **Abington** (sett.c.1668), an industrial town. On St.18, bet. Elm & Niles Sts., **Congr. Ch.** (1849). St.18, near Elm St., **Cth.-Masonic Hall,** formerly 2nd Meetingh. **Island Grove Pk.** (pic.); here is boulder on spot where Wm. Lloyd Garrison & other abolitionists, 1846-65, held mass meetings. Also **Mem. Arch** comm. Soldiers & Sailors of Civil War.

At 13.5m J. with St.139.

Take latter (R) c.1.5m to **Hanover Center** (sett.1st half 17th cent.). Near the Green, **"Drummer" Sam Stetson H.** (O.wks.Sun.appl.sm.fee.c.1694.adds.1716) with Briggs Mem. Room.

Just S. of last J. on St.3 is **Quaker Meetingh.** (O.summer on certain occasions.1706.rest.). At 23m on St.3 is J. with St.3A.

**6.** from Quincy on St.3A, J. with North St.

SIDE TRIP: (R) here to **Hingham** (sett.1633), once important fishing town. PTS. OF INT.: (1) On Main St., **Old Ship Ch.** (Unit.1681) said to be oldest functioning Ch. in state. Its name derives from fact that lookout for ships was kept in steeple. (2) Adj., **Hingham Cemetery,** incl. grave of Rev. Gen. Lincoln. (3) 19 Lincoln St., **Old Ordinary** (O.wks.aft.Ap.19-Nov.1.sm.fee.c.1650); antique furnishings. Fine example of wayside inn. (4) North & Lincoln Sts., **Third Congr. (New North) Ch.** (O.appl.1807.by Bulfinch). (5) North & Lincoln Sts., **Ben. Lincoln H.** (1667), occupied by Rev. Ben. Lincoln, alleged ancestor of the President. Gen. Lincoln received Cornwallis' sword at surrender at Yorktown. (6) North St. & Fearing Rd., **Cushing H.** (18th cent.). (7) On Main St., beyond Hingham Center, St.128, **Rainbow Roof H.** (c.1690) so called because of unusual roof lines (see Cape Cod Tour).

Just beyond last J., St.3A makes J. with Summer St.

SIDE TRIP: Take latter (L) to **Nantasket Beach** (bath.recr.excursion boats from Boston). In **Hull,** near end of Nantasket Peninsula, are several int. houses incl.: On Main St., near Natasco Ave., **First Rectory** (1644) now Town Lib.

**9.5.** J. with Rd.

SIDE TRIP: Here (L) 1.5m to **Cohasset** (sett.1690), formerly famous cod & mackerel fishing port. Name is contraction of Ind. "Quonohassit." Elm & S. Main Sts., **Hist. H.** (O.Wed. Fri.Sat.aft.June-Aug.;1810); hist. items. N. Main St. & Highland Ave., **First Parish Meetingh.** (1747); very fine. On S. Main St., **St. Stephen's Ch.** (Episc.Goth.by Cram, Ferguson & Goodhue); fine windows & 50-bell carillon. At **Landing Cove,** c.1m from town's center, at Border St., on harbor, **Marker** on spot where Capt. John Smith landed in 1614. Jerusalem Dr. along rockbound shore is scenically int.

**13.5.** J. with First Parish Rd.

SIDE TRIP: Take latter (L) here 2.5m into **Scituate** (inc.1636), old seafaring & shipbuilding town, now summer resort. On First Parish Rd. at High School, **Cudworth H.** (O.wks.July 1-Labor Day.1729); hist. relics. Barker Rd., Scituate Harbor, **Garrison Inn** (1634) now Hatherly Inn. Old Oaken Bucket Rd., **Home of "Old Oaken Bucket" & Well,** comm. by Longfellow. **Old Mill** near J. of St.3A & Country Way.

**20. MARSHFIELD** (sett.1st half 17th cent.). Caswell & Webster Sts., **Winslow H.** (O.June 15-Sept.15.sm.fee.1699.remod.1756); **Dan. Webster Room.** (At c.2.5m from town, on Webster St., Winslow Burying Ground with **Grave of Dan. Webster.**) **26.5.** J. with St.14 leading (L) short distance to **Duxbury** (sett.1st quarter 17th cent.), founded by John Alden & others of Plymouth Colony; old seafaring town. Alden St., near RR. sta., **John Alden H.** (O.1653) built by John Alden, 3rd son of John & Priscilla Alden; antique furnishings. On Standish St., **Alex. Standish H.** (O.when owner is in residence.1666.remod.1946) built by son of Miles Standish; panelling, pewter. Chestnut St., **Old Burying Ground** where are buried Miles Standish & his 2 daughters. (John Alden is supposed to be buried here also). On Crescent St., **Standish Mon.** (O) 130'; fine view. **31.** J. with St.3 on which tour cont. (S).

### Sec. 3: J. with St.3A to J. with St.28, near Bourne. 24.

**1. KINGSTON,** sett. early 17th cent. by colonists who came to Plymouth on 1st ships from England, 1620. Main St., **First Congr. Ch.** (Unit.early 18th cent.). Landing Rd. near St.3 & St.3A, **Maj. John Bradford H.** (O.wks.July 1-Labor Day.Sun. appl.sm.fee.1674.remod.1720.rest.1921), furnished in style of Pilgrim home. Brewster Rd., near inters. of St.3 & St.3A, **Brewster H.** (O.wks.June-Oct.sm.fee.1690), built by son of Gov. Bradford; period furnishings, family relics. St.3 now skirts shore to **PLYMOUTH** (see US44) at **5.** & cont. to J. with US6 at **SAGAMORE BRIDGE** spanning Cape Cod Canal, at **21.** From this point take US6 (R) to J. with St.28 near Bourne at **24.**

## WHITE MOUNTAIN TOUR—NEW ENGLAND

**From BOSTON, Mass., through Franconia Notch, Crawford Notch, (Pinkham Notch) & return via N. Conway & Conway to PORTSMOUTH, N.H. 308. US3, US302, St.16A & St.16**

Via: in Mass.: Cambridge, Arlington, (Woburn), Burlington, Billerica, Lowell, (Tewkesbury), Tyngsborough; in N.H.: Nashua, Merrimack, Manchester, Suncook, Concord, Boscawen, Franklin, Laconia, L. Winnipesaukee, The Wiers, Meredith, Holderness, Ashland, Plymouth, Woodstock, N. Woodstock, Franconia Notch, Twin Mountain, Fabyan, Bretton Woods, Crawford Notch, Bartlett, Glen, Intervale, N. Conway, Conway, Chocorua, W. Ossipee, Ossipee, Center Ossipee, Sanbornville, Milton,

Rochester & Dover. Good accoms. at chief resort pts. RR. parallels route from Boston to Plymouth & from Twin Mountain to Portsmouth. Bus conns. throughout.

This route, with its side trips, takes in the high spots of the L. Winnipesaukee & White Mt. regs. L. Winnipesaukee circuit is made by a side trip from The Wiers. A side trip out of Glen, on St.16 (N), takes in Pinkham Notch. Otherwise chief pts. of int. lie along the main route or on short side trips from it.

### Sec. 1: BOSTON to MASS.-N.H. LINE. 36. US3

**0. BOSTON. 4.5. CAMBRIDGE,** at Harvard Univ. **8. ARLINGTON** (see Boston Trip III for this sec.). **11.5.** J. with St.128.

SIDE TRIP: On St.128 (R) c.2$^{m}$ to **Woburn** (1640). On Pleasant St., **Winn Mem. Lib.,** one of H. H. Richardson's bldgs.; in tower, "Antique Kitchen" (O.wks.); mineral & ornithological colls.; Statue of Count Rumford (see below). Park & Center Sts., **Old Burying Ground** (1642); graves of ancestors of Presidents Pierce & Garfield. 90 Elm St., **Count Rumford's Birthpl.** (O.wks.1714), born Ben. Thompson (1753-1814), scientist & administrator; made Count of Holy Roman Empire; antiques & portrait of the Count.

**15.5. BURLINGTON. Old Marion Tavern** (O). **18. PINEHURST PK.** (recr.). **23.** on Chelmsford Rd. (L) a short distance, **Manning Manse** (late 17th cent.O.tearoom). **25. LOWELL** (sett.1653), at confluence of Concord & Merrimack Rs., owes its industrial position to water power of the Merrimack. Formerly great textile mfg. center, now has diversified industries. PTS. OF INT.: (1) 243 Worthen St., **Birthpl. of J. M. Whistler,** Amer. artist (O.except Mon.1824), now home of Art Assoc. (2) Jefferson & Lewis Sts., **Greek Orthodox Ch.** (Byzantine). (3) Colonial Ave. & Moody St., **Lowell Textile Institute;** exhibit (O). (4) 275 Pawtucket St., **Spaulding H.** (2nd half 18th cent.rest.). (5) 850 Broadway, **Lowell St. Teachers College.** (6) In Lincoln Sq., **Lincoln Mem.** (by Bela Pratt). **36. MASS.-N.H. LINE.**

### Sec. 2: MASS.-N.H. LINE to CONCORD. 42. US3

**4. NASHUA** (Info. C. of C.), 1st settlement in southern N.H., was chartered 1673 as Dunstable & renamed 1842; suffered from Ind. attacks, 1675-1725. Town was abandoned during King Philip's War. A canal around the falls permitted shipping to reach town. City is located near confluence of Merrimack R. & Nashua R. which bisects it. Water power helps make Nashua 2nd city of N.H. Nashua produces a variety of products; plants employ c. 12,500. PTS. OF INT.: On Main St.: (1) No. 120, **Old Town Hall** (1843). (2) No. 182, **Arts & Crafts Shop;** classes; articles for sale. (3) No. 341, **Amer. Shearer Co.** (O.appl.). In rear is **Bird Meeting H.** (1746), now used by plant. (4) No. 322, **Marsh Tavern** (early 19th cent.). (5) Main & Lock Sts., **Pub. Lib.;** has Charter granted town of Dunstable by George II; art exhibits. (6) 1 Abbott Sq., **Colonial H.** (early 19th cent.fine example.int.inter.). (7) Concord & Manchester Sts., **Christian Science Ch.,** former home of Rev. Gen. John Stark (see Manchester). (8) 27½ Concord St., **H.** (1st half 18th cent.), supposed to have been haunted. (9) On Ferry Rd., **Proctor Animal Cemetery** (1929). (10) Broad St., **U.S. Fish Hatchery.** (11) Many of city's factories may be visited. Consult C. of C.

SIDE TRIP: On St.111 (E) 1.5$^{m}$ to **Hudson,** seat of Revier College for Women (Cath). At 3$^{m}$ is **Benson Wild Animal Farm** (O.yr.round to sunset.sm.fee.pic.amusements), circus & carnival.

**10.5. HORSESHOE POND** (pic.). **12. MERRIMACK** [At 6$^{m}$ (L) is **Baboosic L.,** resort.] Near Merrimack are **Atherton Falls. 20. BEDFORD GROVE** (resort.pic.). **23. MANCHESTER** (sett.1722) (Mun.Airport.Accoms.Winter carnival.Info. C. of C.). Industrial development of St.'s largest city & commercial center was due to Amoskeag Falls on Merrimack R. & the Amoskeag Mfg. Co. (1810), largest cotton-textile concern in world until it went bankrupt in 1935. Other companies now occupy the huge plant which city has taken over & subleased. Gen. J. Stark, hero of Bennington, was a native & led N.H.'s men in both Fr.-Ind. & Rev. Wars.

PTS. OF INT.: (1) Pine & Amherst Sts., **Manchester Hist. Assoc.** (O.Tues.Thurs. Sat.aft.); extensive hist., Ind., portrait & print colls. & hist. lib.; especially notable are **John Rogers Groups** (terra cotta) showing early Amer. life in miniature. (2) 405 Pine St., **Carpenter Mem. Lib.** (Ital.Ren.by E.L.Tilton), founded in late 18th cent. (3) Pine & Concord Sts., **Institute of Arts** (O.wks.), courses in literature & arts; exhibits of handicrafts. (4) 52 Concord St., **Canado-Américaine Bldg.,** with noteworthy lib. on French in Amer. (5) Orange & Beech Sts., **Currier Art Gallery**

(1927.by Tilden & Githens); Ital. mosaics, by Salvatore Lascari; Fountain by Harriet Frishmuth. In (1st fl.) Gallery, showing Col. furniture, notable glass & pewter, is the famous **French Wallpaper** from Vaughan H. in Thetford, Vt. In arcade & on 2nd fl. are colls. of paintings, prints & etchings. (6) Canal St. at Amoskeag Bridge, **Home of Gen. John Stark** (see above). (7) In Derryfield Pk., **Observatory,** fine view. (8) In Stark Pk., **Grave of Gen. Stark.** Near Manchester is **Crystal L.** (swim.). (9) Just outside city is **St. Anselm's College,** of Benedictine Order (est.in N.H.1889). (10) On St.101, 4$^{m}$ (E) **Massabesic L.** Manchester is at J. with St.114 (see US4), St.101 & St.28, which last unites with US3 to **Suncook** (short distance (W) of US3) at **34.**

SIDE TRIP: St.28 runs (NE) from Suncook through pleasant country of streams & ponds to **Alton Bay** on L. Winnipesaukee at 32$^{m}$ & cont. along E. side of L. to **Wolfeborough.** St.109 circles lake (N) from this pt. to J. with St.25 at **Moultonborough** & from there St.25 follows along L. to J. with US3 at **Meredith** (see below). St.28 cont. (NE) through **Ossipee** to J. with St.16 (S) of Center Ossipee (see below).

**42. CONCORD** (see US4). J. with US202 (see US4) & with US4, with which US3 unites for c.10$^{m}$.

## Sec. 3: CONCORD to PLYMOUTH. 60. US3

**6. PENACOOK. Washington Hotel,** century-old inn. On island in Merrimack R. is **Mon. to Hannah Dustin** (see Worcester, Mass.). **9. BOSCAWEN** (sett.c.1733). On Main St., **Tablet** marks Site of Dan. Webster's Law Office; near-by, **Webster Homestead** (1805).

SIDE TRIP: (R) 8.5$^{m}$ on Rd. through Canterbury, to **Shaker Village** (Main bldg.late 18th cent.), home of sect founded by "Mother" Ann Lee, & named for the "shaking" in religious ecstasy. 11$^{m}$ **Worsted Ch.** (1839), decorated with int. worsted embroideries.

**9.5.** US4 branches (NW) here. **15.5.** (R) **WEBSTER PLACE** (O) where Dan. Webster lived as a boy; surrounded by bldgs. of **N.H. Orphans' Home. 17.5.** Rd. leads (L) here c.3$^{m}$ to **Dan. Webster's Birthpl.** (O.summer.c.1762-65); relics & antiques. **19. FRANKLIN** (sett.2nd half 18th cent.), at meeting of Pemigewassett & Winnipesaukee Rs., which form the Merrimack & furnish water power for paper, textile & other mills. In **Mortar Lot** is granite block used by Inds. for grinding corn. **Congr. Ch.** (early 19th cent.rest.), in which is Dan. Webster's pew. On grounds, **Bust of Webster** (by D.C.French & his daughter). Near Franklin is Hogback Ski-track. J. with St.11 which leads (W) past **Webster L.** at 2.5$^{m}$ to L. Sunapee reg. (see US4).

SIDE TRIP: On US3A (N) to **W. Plymouth.** 26$^{m}$. Scenic & shorter alt. route follows Pemigewasset R., on which at 10.5$^{m}$ is **Profile Falls.** At 12$^{m}$ **Bristol,** center for recr. area. 15$^{m}$ **Newfound L.** (f.h.beaches.winter sports), mountain-enclosed. 17$^{m}$ **Bridgewater** (accoms.); music & drama colony in summer. 21$^{m}$ **E. Hebron & Hebron** (where is early 19th cent. Ch.) are at N. end of L. (pic.camp.cabins.inns). 26$^{m}$ **W. Plymouth,** J. with St.25 which leads (E) to Plymouth & J. with US3 (see below).

**22. TILTON** (1768). **Tilton School & Jr. College.** (R. short distance to Tilton Arch, reprod. of Arch of Titus, Rome, Italy, comm. Tilton family.) Hy. now crosses **WINNISQUAM L.** At **29. LACONIA,** bet. Winnisquam & Winnipesaukee Ls., industrial, trade & recr. center. (Airport.Accoms.). Church & Main Sts., **Gale Mem. Lib.;** E. P. Jewell Ind. Coll. 10 Gilford Ave., **Jewett Homestead** (1780). Steamer trips on L. Winnipesaukee, largest in N.H.

SIDE TRIP: On St.11A (E) 4$^{m}$ to **Gilford** (accoms.facils.winter sports). Rd. runs from here into Belknap Mts. (recr.area.winter sports.facils.). Chair Tramway.

**32. LAKEPORT. A. L. Drake Ind. Coll.** (O) at 40 Prospect St. **35. THE WEIRS,** popular center for Lakes Reg. on 22$^{m}$-long L. Winnipesaukee. **Endicott Rock Pk.** (beach.bathh.). Steamer tours of Is. & resorts; speedboats from Board Walk. J. with St.11B running SE. along L. to Alton Bay (see above). US3 now runs close to Winnipesaukee L., with fine views. **40. MEREDITH,** bet. L. Winnipesaukee & L. Waukewan, with hills in background. J. with St.25 (see above). Hy. cont. through lovely mt. & lake country to **SQUAM L.;** many resorts in vic. **48. HOLDERNESS,** bet. Little Squam & Squam Ls., with views of lofty peaks. **Trinity Ch.** (late 18th cent.) was built by Sam. Livermore, N.H. chief justice, 2nd oldest Episc. Ch. in state. **60. PLYMOUTH** (sett.1764), sports center in Baker R. valley (skiing). Juckins Hill & Frontenac Ski Development near-by. **Pub. Lib.** was formerly Cth., where Webster tried his 1st jury case. **Plymouth Normal School,** outgrowth of pioneer Academy (1808).

SIDE TRIP: Take St.25 (W) from Plymouth. 4m **W. Plymouth,** J. with US3A (see above). 5.5m **Polar Caverns** (O.sm.fee); worth a visit. 7.5m **Rumney Depot.** [Take Rd. (R) here 5m to **Stinson L.** with view of high peaks.] 20m **Warren. Morse Mus.** (O.summer); allegedly world's largest shoe coll. From near Warren a Rd. runs (R) to trl. to summit of **Mt. Moosilauke** (4,810'); finest view in White Mts. J. with Appalachian Trl. 23m **Glencliff** at S. end of Oliverian Notch. 32m J. with St.10 (see) N. of Haverhill.

## Sec. 4: PLYMOUTH to TWIN MOUNTAIN. 46. US3

US3 conts. (N) through fine scenery of the Pemigewasset Valley & Franconia Notch. **17. WOODSTOCK** & **22. N. WOODSTOCK,** summer resorts. Near latter (L) is **Fay Reserv.** (recr.) J. with St.112.

SIDE TRIP: St.112 (W) & (NW) to J. with US302, E. of Woodsville at 17m. Picturesque route through **Kinsman Notch.** At c.2m J. with St.118.

Take latter (L). At c.8m J. with Rd. (R) to **Ravine Cabin** from which trl. runs to summit of **Moosilauke Mt.** (see Hanover). St.118 cont. to **Warren** (see above) at c.13m.

At 5.5m **Lost River Reserv.** Here are **Glacial Caverns** (O.sm.fee). Just beyond, on St.112, trl. runs (L) to **Mt. Moosilauke.** Another trl. runs (R) to **Mt. Kinsman** (4,363') & **Mt. Cannon** (Profile) (see below). 17m J. with US302, E. of Woodsville (see St.10-12-US302).

**27. INDIAN HEAD** (tourist camp at foot of mt.). US3 from here on is the only hy. through beautiful **Franconia Notch** (accoms.at various centers). At S. end is **Franconia Notch Reserv. 28.5. FLUME GORGE** (tea house), with fine mt. view. Trls. lead along & across deep narrow chasm to head of Flume & over **AVALANCHE FALLS.** At **c.29.** (L) on US3 is **WHITEHOUSE BRIDGE.** Trl. leads (L) to **Cascades.** Liberty Spring Trl. leads (R) to Mt. Liberty (4,460'). **31.5. LAFAYETTE CAMPGROUND** (facils.); trl. (L) 1.5m to beautiful **Lonesome L.,** where is Appalachian Club cabin (O.summer). **33.** Above Profile L. towers **PROFILE MT.** (Cannon Mt. 1,500' above L.), from side of which the stern Old Man of the Mountain surveys the valley, inspiration of Hawthorne's "Great Stone Face." From parking place, short distance beyond, is best view. Trls. to summit & to **Eagle L.** & **Mt. Lafayette. 35.** Rd. (L) here short distance to **Cannon Mt. Aerial Tramway** (takes passengers up c.2,000' to top of mt.). On Cannon Mt. is **Richard Taft Ski Run.** Just beyond this pt. on US3 is **Eagle Cliff** & lovely **Echo L. 35.5.** J. with St.18 which runs through fine scenic reg. to J. with US302 E. of Bethlehem Street (see St.10-12-US302) at 10m. **41.5. GALE R. CAMP** (facils.), from which trl. leads (R) to **Mt. Garfield** (4,488'). Hy. now swings (NE) to important summer resort of **TWIN MOUNTAIN** at **46.** Splendid views of **Mt. Washington** (6,288') & other peaks of Presidential Range. J. with US302 which main tour now follows (SE). For US302 (W) from Twin Mountain, see St.10-12-US302.

SIDE TRIP: From Twin Mountain (N) to **Third Connecticut L.** by US3. At 9m **Whitefield** (accoms.resort). J. with St.116 which leads (S) 3m. Here take country Rd. (R) 2m to **For. Lake St. Pk.** (recr. winter sports). At 15m on US3, take Rd. (E) here to **Mt. Prospect St. Pk.** (pic.bldgs.). Mt. ski tow. 18m **Lancaster,** at meeting of Israel & Conn. Rs. Accoms. Some int. old Hs. **Mon.** comm. pioneers. At N. end of town are **Fair Grounds.** J. with US2. Bridge across Conn. R. (see Newport, Vt., Trips).

55m **Colebrook,** farm & tourist center (accoms.). J. with St.26 which leads (E) along Mohawk R. through scenically fine **Dixville Notch** to J. with St.16 (see below & Me. St.26). US3 swings (E) with Conn. R. 74m **Pittsburg,** at (W) end of **L. Francis.** Hy. winds (NE) through wild country past **First & Second Conn. Ls.** (on latter is Camp Idlewild) & then **Conn. Ls. St. Reserv.** (pic.camp stay limited;swim.f.) near **Third Conn. L.** Just beyond Third Conn. L. at 97m is **Canadian Boundary,** 4m S. of Chartierville, Canada.

## Sec. 5: TWIN MOUNTAIN to GLEN. 30. US302

**0. TWIN MOUNTAIN. 2.5. ZEALAND FOR. CAMP. 3. LOWER AMMONOOSUC FALLS. 5. FABYAN** (resort). **6. BRETTON WOODS** (resort), scene July 1944 of U.N. Monetary & Financial Conference which developed Internat. Monetary Fund & Internat. Bank for Reconstruction & Development. Here is **MT. PLEASANT H.**

SIDE TRIP: Take Rd. (R) here 1m to **Mt. Washington Hotel;** fine view. At 2.5m **Upper Ammonoosuc Falls.** 4m **Marsh-Field** (cabins.&restaurant), sta. of **Mt. Washington Cog Railway** (July 1-Oct.12), 1st of kind in world, which climbs 3.5m to summit of **Mt. Washington,** highest peak in White Mts., affording magnificent view. (Summit also reached by Mt. Washington Automobile Rd. from J. with St.16 at Glen House, see below). At summit are **Summit H.** (room.meals) & **Tip Top H.** (bunks).

**9. CRAWFORD H.** (hotel.swim.boat.sports facils.). (1) Here take Carriage Rd. (L) (on foot or by burro) to **Ledge of Mt. Willard** (marvelous view). (2) Take Crawford Bridle Path (R) here 8$^m$ to **Summit of Mt. Washington. 10.** N. end of **CRAWFORD NOTCH.** Splendid view. Just beyond, on US302, are **Flume & Silver Cascades. 12. WILLEY CAMPS.** Here occurred in 1826 destructive avalanche described in Hawthorne's "The Ambitious Guest." **15.5.** J. with Trl. (R) 1.5$^m$ to **Arethusa Falls,** highest in N.H. **22.** View of **Mt. Parker,** near Sawyer Rock For. Camp. Next, hy. affords view of **Mt. Carrigain** (4,647'). **24. BARTLETT** (resort. winter sports), with views of mts.

SIDE TRIP: From Bartlett, Bear Notch Rd. runs (R) around **Bear Mt.** (ski-trl.) 9$^m$ to **J.** with Swift River Rd. which runs (E) to J. with St.16 near Conway (see).

**30. GLEN.** J. with St.16 on which main tour cont. (S).

SIDE TRIP: St.16 (N) to Errol. Chief feature of this side trip is scenically fine Pinkham Notch. 1.5$^m$ **Goodrich Falls.** 3$^m$ **Jackson,** resort & ski center (slopes.trls.lift.jump.skating rink); fine scenery; accessible to pts. in Pinkham & Crawford Notches. Hy. now enters **Pinkham Notch.** 12$^m$ Parking here for **Glen Ellis Falls,** reached by marked path (R), short distance; among most beautiful in N.H. 13$^m$ **Pinkham Notch Camp** (lodging.meals), ski trl. center.

From Pinkham Notch Camp take Tuckerman Ravine Trl. short distance (L) to beautiful **Crystal Cascade.** 2$^m$ **Hermit L.,** overshadowed by high cliffs. Just beyond is entrance to scenically notable **Tuckerman Ravine,** mighty glacial cirque. 2.5$^m$ **Snow Arch,** formed by piled-up snow, one of most spectacular sights in White Mts.

14.5$^m$ Path leads (R) here short distance to **Thompson's Falls.** View of the Ravine. 16$^m$ **Glen House** (hotel), with impressive view of Presidential Range. J. with Mt. Washington Automobile (Toll) Rd. 8$^m$ to **Summit** (see above). 17$^m$ **Dolly Copp For. Camp** (pic.shelters. camp.swim.). Fine view. Js. with trls. to mt. pts. 24$^m$ **Gorham,** at confluence of Androscoggin & Peabody Rs. RR. & bus conns. Accoms. Summer & winter resort (ski trls.jump.tow). Surrounded by impressive mts., Gorham is one of best starting pts. for excursions into Presidential Range. Union St. leads (L) to marked trl. 2.7$^m$ long, to **Pine Mt.** (2,440';fine view). In Gorham is J. with US2 (see).

Route now follows Androscoggin R. 31$^m$ **Berlin** at J. of Dead & Androscoggin Rs., with pulp & paper mills. RR. & bus conn. Accoms. Near town are ski tow, shelters & jump & ski & hik. trls. to near-by mts. 58$^m$ **Errol,** at J. with St.26 [see Me. St.26 for St.26 (NE).] St.26 turns (W) from Errol through fine Dixville Notch to J. with US3 at Colebrook (see above). St.16 cont. (NE) around **Rangeley Ls.** to **Rangeley** (see Maine St.100-St.4).

## Sec. 6: GLEN to PORTSMOUTH. 94. St.16.

**0. GLEN** (RR. conn.). **4. INTERVALE,** in narrow valley dominated by Presidential Range (NW), at J. with trl. to **Mt. Bartlett,** 1$^m$ & **Mt. Pequawket,** 3.5$^m$. **6. N. CONWAY,** yr.-round resort (accoms.) on Saco R. Fine view of Presidential Range. **Skimobile-Tramway** takes skiers in winter, sightseers in summer, to top of **Cranmore Mt.** (fine view). Rds. & trls. run to many scenic pts. of int.: **Echo L. St. Pk.** (pic.swim.); **Cathedral Ledge St. Reserv.; Thompson Falls & Diana's Baths.**

SIDE TRIP: Take Rd. (N) from N. Conway 1.5$^m$ to **Kearsarge Village** (hotel).
(1) Kearsarge Trl. leads 3$^m$ to summit of **Mt. Pequawket.** Splendid view.
(2) Rd. from Kearsarge cont. (E) to **S. Chatham** & from there (N) through fine **Evans Notch** to J. with US2 (see Fryeburg, Me.).

**8.** South J. with US302 which runs (E) from here to Fryeburg, Me. (see) & from there to Portland, Me. (see). **11. CONWAY** (sett.1764-66) at J. of Saco & Swift Rs., yr.-round resort (summer theater. ski trls. & jump) with fine views of Mt. Chocorua, Sandwich Range & Mt. Washington.

SIDE TRIP: Take Swift R. Rd. (R) along scenic Swift R. past several For. Camps to mt. hamlet of **Passaconaway** (accoms.), near **Passaconaway For. Camp** & near J. with Bear Mt. Rd. (see Bartlett above). Trl. branches off Swift R. Rd. up **Mt. Passaconaway** (4,060').

**16. WHITE LEDGE FOR. CAMP. 19. PEQUAWKET,** J. with Piper Trl. leading (R) 4$^m$ (2 camps) to summit of **Mt. Chocorua** (3,475'), named for Ind. chief; magnificent view. St.16 now passes **Chocorua L. 23. CHOCORUA,** near mt. of same name (see above). J. with St.113. (E. on latter is **Silver L.**).

SIDE TRIP: Take St.113 (W) 4$^m$ to **Tamworth,** on Swift R. From Tamworth (R) 2$^m$ to **Hemenway St. Reserv.** (2,000 as.camp.tower lookout). Rd. cont. to **Chinook Kennels** (fee), at 5.5$^m$ with sledge dogs & exhibit of sledging equipment. Rear Adm. Rich. E. Byrd's Antarctic expedition dogs were trained here.

**26. WHITE L. ST. PK.** (258 as.pic.camp.trls.swim.bathh.f.). **27. W. OSSIPEE,** on Whittier R. Near here poet Whittier spent summers & wrote. North J. with St.25

(see Suncook, US3 above). **28.5.** J. with paved Rd. leading (L) 0.5$^{m}$ to **Ossipee L.** (swim.f.seaplane bases). **33. CENTER OSSIPEE,** South J. with St.25 which runs (E) & then (SE) to Portland, Me.
**37.** Here is J. with St.28 (see above) near Ossipee (S. of J.). **49. SANBORNVILLE,** scene of fight bet. Capt. John Lovewell & Inds. in 1725, at end of **Lovell L. 60. MILTON,** still mill town. **70. ROCHESTER.** J. with US202 (For towns & pts. of int. from Rochester to Portsmouth, see Portsmouth Trip I). **94. PORTSMOUTH.**

## ME. ST. 26—NEW ENGLAND

**PORTLAND (NW) to ME.-N.H. LINE** (Errol, N.H.). **100. St.26**

Via: Gray, Sabbathday, Poland, (Norway), S. Paris, Bethel, Newry & Upton.

This route runs through scenically mountainous, river & lake country culminating in Grafton Notch & Umbagog L. of the Rangeley Chain.

**Sec. 1: PORTLAND to J. with St.11. 33.**

(For this sec., see Portland Trip I).

**Sec. 2: J. with St.11 to ME.-N.H. LINE. 67.**

**12.** J. with St.117 which leads (L) short distance to **Norway** (resort), on **Pennesseewassee L.** In vic. is **Little Pennesseewassee L. Norway L.** is a few miles (W). **13.5. SOUTH PARIS** on Little Androscoggin R. **15.** J. with Rd. which leads (R) 1.5$^{m}$ to **Paris Hill. Old Stone Jail** (1st quarter 19th cent.). **Birthpl. of Hannibal Hamlin** (see Portland). **Hubbard H.** (1806) & several other int. old Hs. **Bapt. Ch.** (early 19th cent.). **19.5. SNOW FALLS** of Little Androscoggin R. **22. MAINE MINERAL STORE;** mineral coll. **29.5. BRYANT POND. 33. LOCKE'S MILLS.** In vic., **North, South & Round Ponds.** On a side Rd. (W) 3$^{m}$ are **Greenwood Ice Caves. 38.5. BETHEL.** J. with US2 (see). **45. NEWRY** (see US2). **50. NORTH NEWRY,** on Bear R. along which are many fine cascades. **54.5. SCREW ANGUS FALLS. 57.** Impressive **GRAFTON NOTCH.** To W., **Old Speck Mt.** (4,250'), after Mt. Katahdin, highest pt. in state. To (NE), **Bald Mt.** (4,080'). **58.** J. with Appalachian Trl. **65. UPTON,** at Umbagog L., one of Rangeley Chain (guides avail.). **Bragg H.** (1838). **67. ME.-N.H. LINE,** c.7.5$^{m}$ (E) of Errol, N.H. St.26 in N.H. traverses scenically fine Dixville Notch. (See White Mt. Tour.)

## THE APPALACHIAN TRAIL

For detailed information, guide books & maps, etc., covering the trail, apply to the Appalachian Trail Conference, Washington, D.C. This organization & its allied bodies have available at reasonable cost publications which will enable the hiker easily to follow any section of the trail.
**THE APPALACHIAN TRAIL** extends from Mt. Katahdin, Me., to Mt. Oglethorpe, Ga., a distance of some 2,050 miles. It traverses 14 states, is well marked throughout & offers camping facilities & shelters at reasonably frequent intervals. It crosses through 8 National Forests & several National Parks. Starting in Maine at Mt. Katahdin (5,267'), it crosses some of the highest peaks of the Appalachians: Mt. Washington (6,288') in New Hampshire, &, if its branch, the Long Trail, be included, Mt. Mansfield (4,393') in Vermont, & Greylock (3,505') highest in Massachusetts. After crossing through New York, Pennsylvania & Maryland, it climbs the Blue Ridge, paralleling the Skyline Drive of Shenandoah National Park, & the Blue Ridge Parkway all the way to Great Smokies National Park. The greatest height it climbs to is Clingman's Dome (6,641') in the Great Smokies.
**NEW ENGLAND SECTION.** The trail starts from New York St.22 at Webatuck, & crosses from there into Connecticut, where it runs NE. & N. along mountain ranges, reaching its greatest altitude, at Bear Mt. (2,355'), highest in Connecticut, near the state line, which it crosses, via beautiful Sage's Ravine. In Massachusetts, it climbs along the Taconic Mts. & over Mt. Everett (2,624') &, in the N. sec. of the state, Mt. Greylock, & then crosses into Vermont, where it is known as the Long Trail & travels along the ridges of the Green Mountains for 100 miles to Sherburne Pass. Here the Long Trail branches off (N) & climbs eventually to the summit of Mt. Mansfield & continues (NE) to Jay Peak (3,861') & the Canadian Line.

At Sherburne Pass, the Appalachian Trail proper turns (E) across Vermont, into New Hampshire near Hanover, & continues passing Mt. Moosilauke (4,810'), through Crawford Notch & over the Presidential Range, culminating in Mt. Washington, to Gorham, New Hampshire, from where it crosses the Maine line to Grafton Notch. From there, Old Speck (4,150') is easily reached. The trail continues over Baldpate (3,996') in Maine.

From here it traverses a wilderness of forests, mountains, rivers & lakes. Some of the outstanding scenic points of interest are: the Rangeley Lakes, Sugarloaf (4,237′), third highest in Maine, Moosehead Lake (accessible from trail by road), White Cap (3,707′) with fine view & Mt. Katahdin, highest in the state, where the trail ends.

US7 parallels the trail fairly closely in Connecticut & Massachusetts & less closely to the (W) in Vermont, to Sherburne Pass. It parallels the Long Trail from that point (N) to New Heaven Junction. Vermont St.100 parallels the Long Trail on the (E) all the way from Ludlow, Vt., to Newport, Vt. Numerous highways cross the trail in Connecticut & Massachusetts. In Vermont, East-West highways cross it at frequent intervals, connecting US7 & St.100. In New Hampshire, the trail is accessible from numerous main highways. In its W. section in Maine, the trail is accessible at frequent intervals by main highways coming up from the S. In its middle Maine section, one main highway running from Bangor to Greenville, on Moosehead Lake, crosses the trail at Blanchard & Monson. Otherwise, in the middle & E. Maine sections, only a few secondary roads reach the trail.

# BOSTON

RR. Stas.: 120 Causeway St., North Sta. for B. & M. RR.; Rutland, Cent. Vermont & Can. Pacific; at Summer St. & Atlantic Ave., South Sta. for N.Y., N.H. & H.; 145 Dartmouth St., Back Bay Sta. for N.Y., N.H. & H.; Trinity Place Sta. for B. & A. Through bus conns. to all parts of U.S. & Canada. Airport in E. Boston, via Summer Tunnel. Sightseeing tours from Copley Plaza & Statler hotels: around Boston & Cambridge; to Lexington, Concord & Cambridge; along South Shore, via hist. Quincy to Plymouth; along North Shore to Gloucester & Rockport, Marblehead & Salem. Boat trips: around Charles R. basin from the Esplanade, near Hatch Mem. Shell; Harbor trips: by Airport Speed Ferry; at Rowe Wharf, excursion trips to Nantasket (pub.amusements). Steamers from Foster's Wharf (370 Atlantic Ave.) to Provincetown. Pub. bath. beaches along shore front: (N) Revere Beach, Winthrop, Lynn, Nahant, Swampscott, etc.; (S) Columbus Pk., Savin Hill Beach (Dorchester), Quincy Shore Dr. (near Quincy), Hough's Neck (near Quincy & Weymouth), Nantasket, etc. Recr. facils. in various metropolitan Pk. areas: (S) Jamaica Pond, Stony Brook & Blue Hills Reservs., & Franklin Pk.; (W) Charles R. Reserv., Mystic R. Reserv. & Mystic Ls., etc. (N) & (NE) Middlesex Fells, Breakhart Reserv., Lynn Woods, etc. Amusement resort at Revere Beach. Baseball: Braves' Field (Cambridge). Amer. League Field at Brookline Ave. near Kenmore Sq. Running races at Suffolk Downs Race Track (summer & fall seasons), reached by Sumner Tunnel. Intercollegiate sports at Harvard Stadium (Cambridge). Sports events at Boston Garden near North Sta. Four theaters at which plays, musicals, etc., are given. Burlesque house. Symphony concerts at Symphony Hall & during summer at Hatch Mem. Shell, on Esplanade. Accoms.: All types. Flower shows, in Horticultural Hall at Mass. & Huntington Aves. Info.: C. of C., 80 Federal St.; New England Council, Statler Bldg., 20 Providence St.

Boston (sett.1630) is still called "the hub of the universe" by its C. of C., using phrase coined by Oliver Wendell Holmes, who also intimated that the flowers of the metropolitan area inclined from all sides in direction of Boston Common, hub of the hub. Bostonians consider Boston, in any event, as the hub of "their" universe, & standard of measurement of things & values. Wall Street they speak of as N.Y.'s State Street & they take the slow milk train home from megalopolis rather than spend a night away from their own tight little metropolis. But not so little either. Boston is, at any rate, the hub of New England. It is financial capital of a highly industrialized region, one of country's greatest ports, a mighty industrial beehive, world's greatest center for shoes & leather, country's greatest fishing, fish-packing & distributing port, its greatest woolen market, focus from which are disseminated products of New England's cotton spindles, ¼ of all spindles whirling busily in the 48 states, & last but not least, a cultural center, perhaps 2nd only to New York.

City proper has about 750,000 inhabitants, but metropolitan district with its great adj. suburbs has some 2,500,000. The "old town" is crowded into E. end of the crooked finger that juts out into Boston Harbor. This quasi-peninsula is bounded by Charles R. on the N., & a Channel on the S., bet. it & S. Boston. Beacon Hill rises to a small hump (c.300′) in the NE. Within this small area are concentrated city's chief financial & business institutions, largely around State Street, & its two chief RR. stas., as well as most of town's hist. pts. With a natural instinct for conservation, Bostonians have managed to preserve against encroachments of builders & city planners alike, their chief hist. landmarks as living & visual proof that here was born American freedom & independence. They have even managed to keep intact many private houses of the Bulfinch period & some of their finest old churches.

And much of what has been added in the 19th & 20th cents. has been in harmony with the great architectural tradition. Sometimes the instinct toward conservation takes a slightly whimsical turn, as when Beacon Hill fights for & wins right to keep brick sidewalks against the intrusion of concrete.

Boston now includes some 40 former suburbs, not counting independent municipalities. There remains still a small fashionable residential area for Boston's socially elite on Beacon Hill & in sec. to N. & S. of Commonwealth Ave. Poorer districts are largely to E. & S. of city center. Subways enable vast majority of pop. to live at some distance from its jobs. Traffic problem is perhaps even more troublesome than N.Y.'s, although a partial solution has been had by putting streetcars underground until they reach a comparatively uncongested dist. near Copley Square.

With City's vast expansion in 19th cent. came a radical change in racial make-up. Influx from abroad which arrived to fill new factories & do heavy manual work, brought people from all over the globe, while a considerable part of the "natives" trekked west. Earlier newcomers were mostly Irish, some of them refugees from famine. Henry Adams in his autobiography tells how antipathy bet. old & newer elements led to day-long battles bet. Latin School boys & Irish youngsters. The Irish went into politics in a big way, although "native" stock still figures prominently enough in the Hoars, Cabots, Lodges & Saltonstalls, who became governors, senators, congressmen. Financial control, however, of banks, utility companies, & industrial enterprises has remained to a greater extent in hands of "old" Boston families. But Boston is by no means an Irish city: in fact, the combined groups of other stocks far outnumber the Irish—French Canadians, Italians, Jews from various European countries, Greeks, Armenians & even some Chinese. Once you have left the city's center, you are apt to find yourself among foreign accents. Nevertheless, Boston has preserved a distinct flavor of old New England, especially in the downtown sec. Sensible zoning laws have kept the Boston skyline reasonably low & uniform. Visitors from abroad are apt to remark that Boston is most "European" of our cities.

Like other New England cities, Boston, in early 19th cent., as a port, became one of casualties of Erie Canal, which lured shipping away to N.Y. More recently, building of Cape Cod Canal has somewhat compensated for the earlier disadvantage. Railway rate discrimination resulted from competition of Erie Canal, & this even today is cause of complaint.

Boston's cultural advantages are many: Harvard Univ., Mass. Institute of Technology, Boston Univ. & near-by Tufts, outstanding art galleries, an opera season, the Boston Symphony, the Lowell Institute lectures, a public lib. architecturally far surpassing New York's & of equal quality in contents, a number of country's great publishing houses. The Metropolitan District is notable for pks. & pkwys. with which central city has been ringed. Full advantage has been taken of various Rs.—the Charles, the Mystic, etc., that debouch into Boston Harbor & Mass. Bay. The seacoast has been similarly reclaimed for recr. purposes.

Boston's history is largely that of New England. Although Norsemen, Champlain & the Dutch are said to have visited Boston harbor, & Capt. John Smith left us a map of it, & Miles Standish explored it for the Pilgrim Fathers, no actual settlement was made until late 1620's. Colonists had already est. themselves on outer fringes at Medford, Weymouth, Quincy, Hull, Dorchester, & on some of the harbor's Is. But the 1st settler is usually conceded to have been William Blackstone, former Anglican clergyman who put up log cabin on Shawmut (Beacon Hill). In 1630 he persuaded Gov. Winthrop, who had already migrated with a company to marshy neighborhood of Charlestown, to remove to site of present-day city. Blackstone recommended particularly excellent spring near his house. On September 17, 1630, Winthrop with an augmented band of colonists passed over to the "Hill."

Settlement soon became capital of Mass. Bay Colony, governed by a theocracy which rigidly dictated to citizens in matters of religious dogma & private conduct. Dissenters were persecuted. Roger Williams & his Quaker followers were driven out, as were Anabaptists and Antinomians (latter led by indomitable Anne Hutchinson). When Quakers returned, they were severely punished. In 1659-60, 3 men & 1 woman were executed on Common for thus offending. Nevertheless, culture & education (if orthodox) were valued by Puritans. In 1635 General Court est. 1st free school in Boston & about same time set up Harvard University in near-by Cambridge.

Never much of a farming community, city from beginning prospered greatly as port & trading center. Immigration to New England funnelled through Boston harbor. In 1631, Boston-built vessel, the tiny "Blessing of the Bay," was launched, & from then on shipbuilding continued as important industry down to Civil War era. After Stuart restoration, in 1660, Boston, which had actively sympathized with the Cromwell Regime, became scene of monarchical reprisals. In 1684, Court of Chancery sitting in Town H. (on site of which now stands old State H.), voided orig. colonial charter. Presiding Chief Justice Dudley declared when citizens invoked their rights under Magna Carta, that "they must not expect the laws of England to follow them to the ends of the earth." Governor Andros, sent by James II, est. virtual dictatorship. He attempted to break down religious & political monopoly of Puritans by widening the franchise & establishing right of free worship. He had Anglican services celebrated, to community's great scandal, in Old South Church & ordered building of King's Chapel, to be dedicated to Anglican worship.

Boston put on a curtain-raiser to witchcraft hysteria in 1688, but when epidemic broke out in full force in 1692, suffered perhaps less from its ravages than other towns, largely because sinister accusations finally were leveled at wife of Governor Phipps, who, naturally enough, thereupon bore down on witchbaiters. But at one time at least 100 persons were in jail, charged with illicit supernatural activities. By this time, Boston's population had grown to 7,000. City's trade boomed mightily with development of Rum-Slave-Molasses Traffic: rum to Africa in exchange for slaves, slaves to W. Indies in exchange for sugar & molasses & molasses & sugar back to Boston to be distilled into rum. By 1666, 300 ships, mostly Boston-owned, plied out of port. Gradually commerce became diversified; ships sailed to the Canaries, Azores, & Europe. Bet. 1714 & 1717 some 1,267 vessels cleared from Boston. During the 18th cent. wars, that ended in expulsion of the Fr. from N. America, struggle against the Crown never actually came to a head, because colonists were cooperating with home country in common effort.

When peace finally came, struggle with Crown was renewed & Boston became stage on which revolutionary drama reached its climax. In old State H., Jas. Otis, in 1761, made his great oratorical attack upon the Writs of Assistance, &, sitting in Boston, the General Court, after passage of Stamp Act, issued call for 1st Continental Congress. In 1775, Brit. ships & troops arrived in Boston Harbor to enforce obedience to Townshend Acts. On March 5th occurred Boston Massacre, port was closed & General Gage, accompanied by a fleet, occupied city. In rapid succession came Battle of Lexington, provoked by dispatch of soldiers from Boston across Charles R. to seize patriot arms stored in Concord, Battle of Bunker Hill, Siege of Boston under Washington's direction, & Brit. evacuation. Rev. left Boston with its pop. reduced from 25,000 to 10,000, its commerce ruined. But recovery was rapid.

During troubles that followed French Rev., Boston ships successfully evaded Brit. fleets & traded with continental ports. But Jefferson's Embargo Act, & then Mr. Madison's War (as War of 1812 was known), threw city back into stagnation. That war became so unpopular that in 1814, General Court, sitting in Boston, issued call for a New England Convention, later held at Hartford, to consider secession from Union. With War's end, commercial expansion resumed. In 1790, 1st ship to ply in the China trade, sailed from harbor. City's commerce now covered seven seas. Among chief exports was salt cod, of which 1,000,000 quintals were sent abroad annually. Its merchants largely monopolized Amer. coastwise trade. With development of clipper ships, Boston commerce reached its apex. But already city's primacy was being challenged by the Erie Canal, & the RRs. & the steamship gave N.Y. & ports to the (S) great advantage. But Boston's growth continued. Industrial age made New England nation's workshop & Boston became great mfg. center. Prosperity of 19th cent. brought a great literary & cultural flowering which centered in Boston. And this was accompanied by a religious revolution. As early as 1787, Rev. Jas. Freeman swung King's Chapel congregation to the new faith. Eventually Unit. liberalism captured Harvard Univ. & many of Boston's churches. Perhaps most memorable social & political phenomenon of mid-19th cent. was antislavery movement, launched in 1830's by a New Englander, Wm. Lloyd Garrison, who made Boston, for a time, his propaganda hqs. By both the "rich & wellborn" & the masses, Abolitionists were considered subversive radicals. Mob erected a gallows before Garrison's house at 23 Brighton Street as warning; later they hauled him out of the office of his abolitionist "Liberator" & would have lynched him had not Mayor intervened & smuggled him away to city jail. As late as 1842, Boston mob rioted to prevent liberation of a fugitive slave. By mid-1850's the tide had turned. In 1854 a mob, led by Thos. Wentworth Higginson (later to become a prosperous banker & highly respected citizen) rioted, this time in an attempt to **liberate** a fugitive slave.

In those days, Boston must have seemed to rest of country much as Los Angeles appears today, the breeding place of isms & crack-pot ideas: Brook Farm, a communal experiment in Utopia, Thoreau refusing to pay his poll tax, Transcendentalism, prohibition, women's suffrage. Women played great rôle on the local scene. Margaret Fuller was figure of national importance, & Louisa M. Alcott no less so. Amy Lowell & Mrs. Jack Gardner later kept up tradition of feminine importance. During Civil War, Boston loyally supported Lincoln & the Union. The 1st blood shed in conflict was Boston blood, when Mass. Sixth was attacked by mob as it was passing through Baltimore in 1861. A Boston man, Col. Rbt. Gould Shaw led 1st Negro regiment to fight with Fed. armies. Although city had draft riots (1863), its Civil War record was outstanding. Out of a 178,000 pop., 26,175 served in Union armies. City's liberal tradition was carried on after Spanish War by arch-conservative, Senator Hoar, who organized Anti-Imperialist League to oppose America's annexation of Philippines. Although movement failed of its immediate objective, it had considerable influence on Amer. policy resulting in ultimate independence of islands. Boston has, perhaps unjustly, in recent years, been accused of turning away from its liberal past. Actually, Boston never was more liberal than rest of the country, except maybe during Rev. era. The tradition of the "rich & well-born" has continued here as elsewhere almost from the beginning. Liberals have always been in minority & have had to fight to get their principles into action. Old families, whose prominence dates for most part from later 18th & the 19th cents. when they became wealthy through foreign commerce, industry, Calumet copper & so forth, are naturally conservative & "exclusive." Because they have managed to hang onto their wealth, they are probably more exclusive than N.Y. society.

Various political items—police strike which rode Coolidge into Vice Presidency, the Sacco & Vanzetti case & others—are cited by liberals to back their assertion that Boston is not a liberal town. The Watch & Ward Society with its index expurgatorius, is another item. Works by Whitman, Wells, Lewis, Dos Passos, Anderson, Dreiser, Hemingway & others have been banned from local bookshops. But this sort of morality as opposed to literary quality was practiced even before the Society began its sedulous watch. "The Boston Transcript" (now deceased) maligned Poe & when he died, carefully failed to mention fact that he was born in Boston. Some plays have been banned as salacious; but there is a flourishing burlesque theater. Rejection of MacMonnies' "Bacchante" because of her nudity, & acceptance of the statue by less squeamish N.Y., will be recalled. On the other hand, there are Faneuil & Ford Halls, dedicated expressly to free speech, & Boston Common where one may air any ism he fancies without interference by police. Boston, all in all, is as liberal as the average American city, &, in many respects, more efficiently administered than most.

PTS. OF INT.: For convenience, the city has been divided into 3 secs.: Sec. 1 incls. all pts. of int. E. of an arc drawn from N. to S., starting at the North Sta., passing just W. of the State H., then E. of the Common, to South Sta.; Sec. 2 incls. all pts. of int. W. of Sec. 1 & up to Exeter St., in the Back Bay dist.; Sec. 3 incls. all pts. of int. W. of Exeter St. Secs. 1 & 2 are better traveled on foot. Sec. 3 can be covered by auto, or take Huntington Ave. streetcar at Boylston St. subway sta. & get off at Christian Science Ch.

**Sec. 1:** (1) On Beacon St., facing (NE) sec. of Boston Common, is the **State H.** (O. wks.1795.by Chas. Bulfinch). This is one of finest Bulfinch bldgs., marred, however, by add. of 2 later wings. It is topped by a gilded dome & has handsome columned portico. In Ent. Hall, portraits of Mass. govs. & hist. murals. In Hall of Flags, st.'s regimental flags. In Hall of Representatives hangs the "Sacred Cod," st. emblem. (2) On Beacon St., facing State H., **St. Gaudens Mon.,** comm. Col. Rbt. Gould Shaw leading his Negro regiment during Civil War. Architectural setting by Chas. F. McKim. (3) 10½ Beacon St., **Boston Athenaeum** (O.appl.c.1847.by Ed. C. Cabot), contains splendid lib. & colls. of hist. documents, mss., etc. Nucleus of coll. was Geo. Washington's private lib., purchased after his death. (4) Cor. Tremont & Park Sts., ("Brimstone Corner") **Park Street Ch.** (Congr.1809.Gr.Rev.

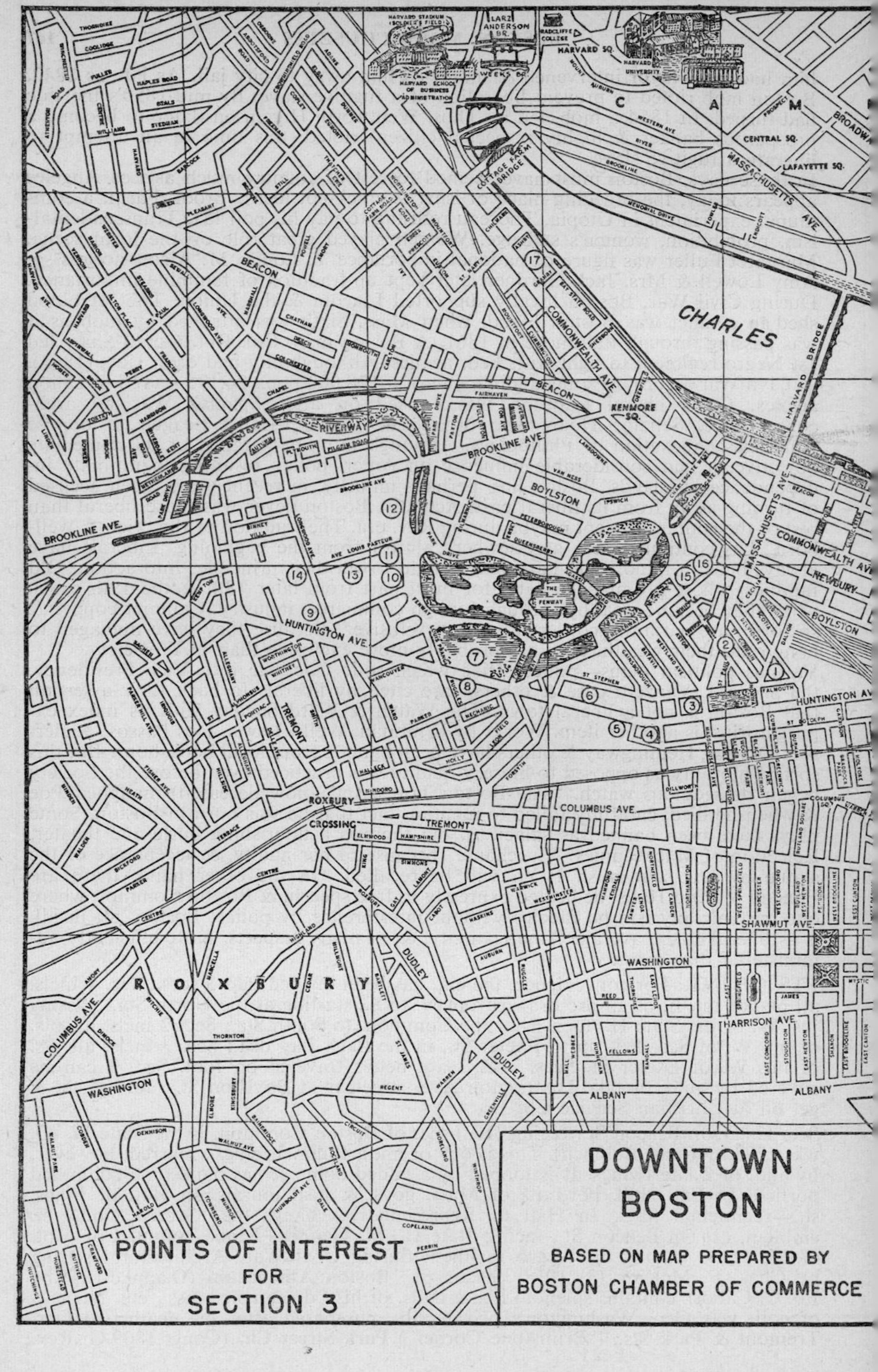
DOWNTOWN
BOSTON
BASED ON MAP PREPARED BY
BOSTON CHAMBER OF COMMERCE
POINTS OF INTEREST
FOR
SECTION 3
CHARLES
C A M
ROXBURY
HARVARD STADIUM (SOLDIER'S FIELD)
LARZ ANDERSON BR.
RADCLIFFE COLLEGE
HARVARD SQ.
HARVARD UNIVERSITY
HARVARD SCHOOL OF BUSINESS ADMINISTRATION
WEEKS BR.
COTTAGE FARM BRIDGE
CENTRAL SQ.
LAFAYETTE SQ.
MASSACHUSETTS AVE.
HARVARD BRIDGE
BROADWAY
MEMORIAL DRIVE
BEACON
COMMONWEALTH AVE.
KENMORE SQ.
BROOKLINE AVE.
RIVERWAY
BOYLSTON
THE FENWAY
HUNTINGTON AVE.
TREMONT
NEWBURY
COLUMBUS AVE.
ROXBURY CROSSING
SHAWMUT AVE.
WASHINGTON
HARRISON AVE.
ALBANY
DUDLEY
CENTRE
WASHINGTON
COLUMBUS AVE.
ST STEPHEN
WESTLAND AVE.
AVE. LOUIS PASTEUR
1
2
3
4
5
6
7
8
9
10
11
12
13
14
15
16
17

INMAN SQ.
C A M B R I D G E
Drawn to Scale
MECHANIC SQ.
KENDALL SQ.
MASSACHUSETTS INSTITUTE OF TECHNOLOGY
NORTHERN ARTERY
WASHINGTON
CAMBRIDGE
SULLIVAN SQ.
SOMERVILLE
SOMERVILLE AVE.
RUTHERFORD AVE.
MAIN
BRIDGE
LECHMERE SQ.
C H A R L E S T O W N
Not Drawn to Scale
THOMPSON SQ.
BUNKER HILL MON.
CHARLESTOWN AVE.
COMMERCIAL
CHARLES RIVER DAM
CITY SQ.
CHELSEA
NAVY YARD
RIVER
LONGFELLOW BRIDGE
CHARLES
CAMBRIDGE
EMBANKMENT RD.
NASHUA
CAUSEWAY
NORTH STATION
BEACON
COMMONWEALTH AVE.
NEWBURY
COPLEY SQ.
PUBLIC GARDEN
BOSTON COMMON
BEACON
JOY
PARK
HANOVER
FRIEND
CANAL
CROSS
NORTH
SALEM
COMMERCIAL
PARK SQ.
BOYLSTON
TREMONT
WINTER
STUART
COLUMBUS AVE.
BERKELEY
CLARENDON
ARLINGTON
WASHINGTON
BEDFORD
CHAUNCY
SUMMER
FRANKLIN
DEVONSHIRE
FEDERAL
MILK
CONGRESS
STATE
BROAD
INDIA
ATLANTIC AVE.
KNEELAND
LINCOLN
SHAWMUT AVE.
HARRISON AVE.
ALBANY
SOUTH STATION
ATLANTIC AVE.
BROADWAY
DORCHESTER AVE.
BOSTON
HARBOR
CHANNEL
FORT POINT
S O U T H
B O S T O N
NORTHERN
CONGRESS
SUMMER
COMMONWEALTH PIER
N
1 2 3 4 5 6 7 8 9 10 11 12 13 14 15 16 17 18 19 20 21 22 23 24 25 26 27 28 29 30 31 32 33 34 35 36 37 38 39 40 41 42 43 44 45 46 47 48 49 50 51 52 53 54 55 56 57 58 59 60 61
LEGEND
15 ... POINTS OF INTEREST
SCALE IN FEET
0 1000 2000 3000 4000
POINTS OF INTEREST FOR SECTIONS 1 & 2

by Peter Banner). Here Henry Ward Beecher preached his fiery sermons. (5) Around the cor., on Tremont St., **Old Granary Burial Ground** in which are graves of John Hancock, Sam. Adams, Rbt. T. Paine, signers of Decl. of Ind.; Paul Revere, Peter Faneuil (donor of Faneuil Hall, see below); parents of Ben. Franklin; victims of the Boston Massacre; & "Mother" Goose, claimed by some to be author of famous children's rhymes. (6) 82 Tremont St., **Tremont Temple** (Bapt.), founded 1839, famous place of worship. (7) Cor. Tremont & School Sts., **Kings Chapel** (Unit.O. Mon.-Fri.Sat.morn.1749.by Peter Harrison, see Providence & Newport.fine inter.). Bldg. is on site of earlier Ch. (1686) which was 1st Episc. place of worship in America. In 1787 Kings Chapel was taken over by Unitarians. (8) Adj. is **Burial Ground** (O.1630), in which are graves of Gov. Winthrop, Rev. John Cotton, Mary Chilton, believed to be 1st woman to step ashore from the "Mayflower." (9) Cor. School & Washington Sts., bldg. in which formerly was **Old Corner Bookstore** (1712), patronized by Emerson, Hawthorne & other literary lights. One of the late proprietors led fight against censorship of books. (10) 60 School St., Parker H., on whose wall is tablet marking **Site of Latin Sch.** (1635) alleged to be 1st in U.S. (see Sec.3, below). The original Parker H. on this site was popular with Harvard students & once, when a stranger inquired his way to the Univ., a wit replied, "Look in the bar of the Parker H." (11) Cor. Washington & Milk Sts., **Old South Meeting H.** (O.exc.Sun.sm.fee.1729.by Rbt. Twelve). Here Rev. history was made. Jas. Otis, Sam. Adams, Jos. Warren & John Hancock held forth here, & from here Boston Tea Party set out. It is still used for public meetings. During Rev., Brit. turned it into riding academy. Contains considerable coll. of hist. relics. (12) Near-by, at 17 Milk St., is **Site of Birthpl. of Ben. Franklin,** whose bust decorates bldg. front. (13) At Milk & Congress Sts., **U.S. P.O.** (by Cram & Ferguson). (14) 30 State St., **Site of Boston Massacre** (see intro.above). (15) At Washington & State Sts., **Old State H.** (O.Mon.-Fri.Sat.morn.1713.rest.), noteworthy bldg.; coll. hist. items, incl. last cocked hat worn in Boston. Bldg. stands on site of hist. Old Town Hall, where Provincial Legislatures & Courts met. From balcony, Decl. of Ind. was proclaimed. In 1895 it was proposed to pull the Old State H. down. This aroused considerable protest. A Chicago visitor remarked: "And do I understand that Massachusetts people are going to permit the destruction of this Capitol? If they do, all I have to say is just give us people in Chicago a chance & we will buy it and we will move it piece by piece as we did the Libbey Prison, and we will put it up in our city as the very choicest relic there." Tablets on S. & N. sides of Old State H. comm. hist. events. Near-by, in the old days, stood pillory, whipping posts & stocks.

(16) At 17 Court St., **Tablet** marking site of shop where Ben. Franklin worked as apprentice in printing trade. (17) 175 Washington St., **Tablet** marking site of Paul Revere's Goldsmith Shop. (18) At N. Market St. & Dock Sq., **Faneuil Hall** (pronounced Fun′-el), known as "Cradle of Liberty" (O.Mon.-Fri.Sat.morn.Sun.aft.1742. From design by John Smibert,painter,see Newport). In 1761, orig. bldg. was destroyed by fire, but rebuilt soon after. It was enlarged by Bulfinch & 3rd story added, 1805. On Tower is grasshopper weathervane, by Drowne, who figures in Hawthorne's "Drowne's Wooden Image"; coll. portraits & paintings, incl. G. P. A. Headley's of "Webster's Reply to Hayne." Faneuil Hall was gift of Peter Faneuil, descendant of Huguenot refugees from vic. of LaRochelle, France. One record of him says that "his cellar was bursting with good wine, arrack, cheshire & gloucester cheeses . . . & he died owner of 8 bldgs. . . . with many vessels & parts of vessels." Hall is dedicated to free speech & free meeting. Today practically any group may use bldg. In it, probably, Boston Tea Party was hatched. Protest meetings against the Stamp Act & other Rev. demonstrations took place here & later anti-abolitionist & abolitionist gatherings. On an upper fl. are Hqs. of The Ancient & Honorable Artillery Co. (O.wks.;Sat.morn.) which has Military Mus. This org. dates from 1638 & still takes part, in its ancient costumes, in parades. (19) Adj. to Hall, is **Quincy Market** (1826.Class.Rev.by Alex. Parris). (20) Near-by, at N. Market St., **Durgin & Park Restaurant,** famous old eating place. At 41 Union St., **Union Oyster H.,** another famous old restaurant. (21) 9 Ashburton Pl., **N.E. Hist. Genealogical Soc.** (O.wks.exc.Sat.); important lib. & coll. of int. items incl. Atkinson-Lancaster Coll. of antique furnishings & materials gathered in East India trade, etc. (22) At 19 North Sq., **Paul Revere H.** (O.wks.exc.Mon.,Sun.aft.sm.fee.c.1676.rest.); old furniture, furnishings, old fireplaces, old Eng. scenic wallpaper, relics. Supposedly oldest frame house in Boston. Paul Revere was descended from Huguenot

family named Rivoire. Became famous gold- & silversmith & manufacturer of church bells, many of which still hang in New England churches. He supplied coppering for dome of State H. & various equipment for "USS Constitution." Most remembered for famous ride at time of Battle of Lexington. (23) 187 Salem St., **Old North (Christ.) Ch.** (Episc.1723.by Wm. Price, in style of Sir Chris. Wren. Steeple by Bulfinch.1808.int.inter.). From belfry of Old North, on Ap. 17, 1775, lanterns were hung signalling to Paul Revere: "The British are coming." (24) Charles & Hill Sts., opp. Old North, **Copp's Burying Ground,** in which are buried eminent Puritan divines Cotton & Increase Mather, Edmund Hart, builder of the "Constitution" ("Old Ironsides") & Rbt. Newman, who signalled to Paul Revere from tower of Old North. (25) 409 Commerce St., at end of Hanover St. on waterfront, **Constitution Wharf** (O.1797) where "Constitution" was launched. Along waterfront are some good sea-food restaurants. (26) N. State St., off Atlantic Ave., **U.S. Customs H.** (O.1847.Class.Rev.by Ami R.Young & Isaiah Rogers.490′ tower.by Peabody & Stearns.1915.over orig.dome.elevator.fine view). (27) 344 Atlantic Ave., **Rowe's Wharf,** where in 1680 Gov. Andros was seized. (28) At (NE) cor. of Atlantic Ave. & Pearl St., Griffin Wharf, **Site of Boston Tea Party,** Dec. 16, 1773, marked by tablet on wall of bldg. at Atlantic Ave. (29) 140 Federal St., **U.S. Shoe Machinery Corp.,** in which is Shoe Mus. (O.wks.). (30) 60 Congress St., **Marker** on site where Wm. Lloyd Garrison in 1831 began publication of "The Liberator." It was from his office here that he was dragged out by proslavery mob & narrowly escaped lynching. (31) Cor. Washington & Boylston St., marker on **Site of Liberty Tree,** set up by Rev. patriots.

**Sec. 2:** (32) 45 Beacon St., **Wadsworth H.** (1807.Fed.by Bulfinch). (33) 40 Beacon St., **Women's City Club** (O.appl.1818. attrib.to Bulfinch). (34) 141 Cambridge St., **Harrison Gray Otis H.** (O.wks.Sat.a.m.sm.fee.1795.attrib.to Bulfinch.rest.). Hqs. of Soc. for the Protection of New England Antiquities. Contains period furnishings, costumes, glass, ceramics. (35) On Cambridge St., near-by, **Old West Ch.** (1806.by Asher Benjamin), now branch pub. lib. (36) Allen St. & Charles R. Embankment, **Mass. General Hospital** (main bldg.by Charles Bulfinch). Here anesthesia was 1st used in an operation; Oliver Wendell Holmes, Sr., while staff member, published important paper on "Contagiousness of Puerperal Fever"; & R. H. Fitch invented operation for appendix. (37) 85 Mt. Vernon St., **Sears H.** (1800.by Bulfinch). (38) 59 Mt. Vernon St., **Thos. Bailey Aldrich H.,** home of the author. (39) 13 Chestnut St., **Home of Julia Ward Howe,** (attri.to Bulfinch), author of "Battle Hymn of the Republic" & later, of John S. Sargent, Amer. painter. (40) 29A Chestnut St., **Home of Edwin Booth,** America's most famous actor, & brother of John Wilkes Booth who assassinated Lincoln. (41) Cor. Charles & Mt. Vernon Sts., **Charles Street Ch.** (1807.Fed.by Asher Benjamin). (42) to (W) is Esplanade with Hatch Mem. Shell (summer concerts). (43) Take Charles St. (S) to **Pub. Gardens.** In Pub. Gardens is **George R. White Fountain,** by D. C. French. Across Pub. Gardens on (S side are several more Mems., in Boylston St. Mall: **Wendell Phillips Mon.** (by D. C. French comm. famous Boston clergyman); **Kosciuszko Mon.** (by A.R. Kitson). Kosciuszko volunteered to serve in Amer. Rev. Army. After Rev. he was killed fighting in Polish rebellion against Russia. He is comm. in Campbell's lines: "And Freedom shrieked when Kosciuszko fell"; **Charles Sumner Mon.** (by Thos. Ball). Sumner was Civil War Sen. from Mass. At Arlington & Boylston Sts., **Wm. Ellery Channing Statue.** Channing, friend of Emerson, & himself a philosopher, was one of leaders in Unit. revolt against Congr. Ch. (44) **Boylston St. Sta.** of subway which runs underground to Huntington Ave. (see Sec.3). (45) Boylston & Arlington Sts., **Arlington Street Ch.** (O.Ren.) has some fine Tiffany windows & tablets comm. Wm. Ellery Channing & other notables. (46) **Crispus Attucks Mon.** Attucks was Negro & one of those killed in Boston Massacre.

(47) **The Boston Common** was orig. bought by Gov. Winthrop as pasture for cows & as training field. Here stood pillory & stocks in which offenders were placed for punishment. Here also Quakers & other dissenters were punished & "witches" executed. It was gathering place for protests against Brit. tyranny before Rev. & used as parade ground for Brit. & Amer. troops. Brit. started from here to Lexington & Bunker Hill. It has always been used as forum for free public discussion & the right to use it thus was recently definitely confirmed. (48) In Common is **Cemetery** in which are buried Gilbert Stuart, portrait painter, & some Rev. soldiers. (49) On Tremont & Winter Sts., **St. Paul's Cathedral** (1819-20.Class.Rev.by Alex.

Parris & Sol.Willard). Dan. Webster was pew holder. (50) In the Mall, Commonwealth Ave. near Berkeley St., is **Statue of Alex. Hamilton** by Wm. Rimmer. (51) 115 Commonwealth Ave., **St. Botolph's Club,** (N.O.) one of most exclusive in Boston. Named for St. Botolph's Ch., Boston, Eng. Has some int. relics of Brit. city for which Amer. Boston was named. Also has occasional art exhibits (O.appl.). (52) Cor. Berkeley & Marlboro Sts., at Park St. Subway Sta., **First Ch.** (Unit.) in Boston, est. 1630, has statue of Gov. Winthrop, its founder, by R.R. Greenough & tablets & statues comm. various Col. worthies. (53) Proceed (W) on Commonwealth Ave. to Clarendon St., **First Bapt. Ch.** (Romanes.early H.H. Richardson), with frieze on tower by Bartholdi, sculptor of Statue of Liberty. (54) Further (W) on Commonwealth Ave., is **Statue of Wm. Lloyd Garrison,** abolitionist, by Olin Warner. (55) 138 Newbury St., **Institute of Modern Arts** (O.wks.exc.Mon.;Sun.aft.); loan exhibits, lectures, concerts. (56) 645 Boylston St., on Copley Sq., **Old South Ch.** (1875), with 246′ campanile (rebuilt 1940). Orig. tower, soon after it was built, began to lean. When asked why, a wit replied: "I don't know, but if I did, I would take some myself." Copley Sq. was named for John Singleton Copley, 18th cent. Amer. portrait painter, & is largely filled-in land. In building the old Westminster Hotel, on the Sq., 6,000 piles had to be driven for the foundation. (57) on (E) side of Sq. is **Boston Pub. Lib.** (Ital.Ren.by McKim,Mead & White). In arches above entrance, panels by St. Gaudens; reliefs on bronze doors, by D. C. French; above inter. stairway, fine mural by Puvis de Chavannes, only one in U.S. by this artist. In Main Reading Room are murals depicting "The Quest of the Holy Grail," by Edwin Abbey. Lib. also contains int. court inspired by Palazzo della Cancellario in Rome, J. S. Sargent's murals "The Triumph of Religion," & important colls. of rare books, documents, incunabula, etc. (58) On Copley Sq. also is **Trinity Ch.** (O.Episc.1877. Romanes.). One of H.H. Richardson's finest bldgs., it was also erected on filled-in land & 4,500 piles had to be driven as support. Some of windows were designed by Burne-Jones. (59) On Huntington Ave., adj. to Ch., St. Gaudens' **Statue of Phillips Brooks & Christ.** (60) At Washington & Malden Sts., **Cathedral of the Holy Cross** (Early Goth.), probably largest Cath. Ch. in New England. (61) 136 Harrison Ave., new home of **Tufts College Medical & Dental Sch.,** occupied fall of 1948.

**Sec. 3:** For this sec. take Huntington Ave. street car at Boylston St. Subway Sta. & get off at the Christian Science Ch. (1) **Christian Science Ch.** consists of two churches, the Mother Ch. (1894), around which is built the Main Ch. (1904.Ital.Ren.very ornate). Main Ch. has huge nave, topped by 108′ dome. (2) Near Ch. is **Christian Science Publishing H.** (O), where "Christian Science Monitor" is published; richly equipped & decorated inter. with "mapparium" in a spherical room whose walls of colored glass are a map of the world. Near-by is Horticultural Hall (Flower show). (3) At Huntington & Mass. Aves., **Symphony Hall** (1900.by McKim, Mead & White). Casadesus coll. of ancient musical instruments is accessible during concerts by Boston Symphony Orchestra. (4) Proceed (W) on Huntington Ave. At cor. Gainsborough St., **New England Conservatory of Music,** (O) founded 1867. In lobby, Statue of Beethoven, by Crawford. Int. coll. of musical instruments. (5) 360 Huntington Ave., **Northeastern Univ.** (coed.) with colleges of Liberal Arts, Engineering & Bus. Admin., an adult education program at Lincoln Tech. Institute, & Law Sch. at 47 Mt. Vernon St. (6) Cor. Opera Place & Huntington Ave., **Boston Opera H.** with limited winter opera season. (7) At 465 Huntington Ave., **Mus. of Fine Arts** (O. wks.exc.Mon.Sun.aft.). At entrance to bldg., statue: "Appeal to the Great Spirit" by Cyrus Dallin. Mus. contains outstanding art colls.: Egyptian, Greek, Roman & Near Eastern, Ind., Chinese & Japanese art, paintings of European & Amer. schools incl. works by Bellini, Titian, Van der Weyden, Dürer, Rubens, Poussin, Rembrandt, Ruisdael, El Greco, Velasquez, Watteau, Tiepolo, Gainsborough, Stuart, Copley, Sully, Corot, Delacroix, Millet, Courbet, Degas, Monet, Renoir, Gauguin, Van Gogh, Whistler, Sargent. Spaulding coll. incl. import mod. Fr. canvasses by Degas, Pissaro, Monet, Utrillo, Van Gogh, Gauguin, Cézanne. Int. also are period rooms, colls. of decorative & minor arts, & E. D. McCormick coll. of costumes & embroideries. Mus. has fine lib., lectures, concerts. In courtyard is Replica of MacMonnies' "Bacchante." Orig. (now in N.Y. Metropolitan Mus.) was rejected because its nudity shocked Boston. (8) 550 Huntington Ave., **Wentworth Institute** (O.Sept.-May.exc.Sat.Sun.), founded by Arvid Wentworth, himself a mechanic at one time, gives training in the "Mechanical Arts." (9) Huntington Ave. & Worthington St., **Mass. College of Pharmacy.** (10) 280 The Fenway, **Isabella S. Gardner Mus.**

(O.Tues.Thurs.Sat.sm.fee;Sun.aft.free;closed Aug.& hols.1902 by Edwin H.Sears). Bldg. is in Ital. style & contains notable coll. of art & art objects. Ital. Schools particularly well represented. Among these canvasses are some by Botticelli, Raphael, Pinturicchio, Fra Angelico, Bellini, Mantegna, Tiepolo, Veronese, Titian, Tintoretto, Giorgione, Bronzino, Masaccio, Correggio, etc. There are a bust by Cellini, terra cottas by Della Robbia, & works by Rembrandt, Van Dyck, Vermeer, Rubens, Velasquez. Concerts. Motion pictures. (11) 300 The Fenway, **Simmons College**, pioneer in giving women business training. (12) 400 The Fenway, **Emmanuel College** (Cath.for women). (13) Louis Pasteur Ave. off The Fenway, is **Boston Pub. Latin School** (est.1635.see above), oldest of this type still functioning in U.S. (14) At Longwood & Louis Pasteur Aves., **Harvard Medical-Dental-Public Health Schools.** Medical School founded 1782 (present bldgs.1906.mod.Class.of white marble by Rutan, Shepley & Coolidge). (15) Return to The Fenway. At No.8, **Boston Medical Lib.** (O). (16) 1154 Boylston St., **Mass. Hist. Soc.** (O.Wed.aft.); outstanding colls. of hist. documents, mss., relics. (17) Commonwealth Ave. & Granby St., fronting on Charles R., is new campus of **Boston Univ.** (est.1869.coed.). This is main campus but many departments are in different secs. of city. Univ. has Liberal Arts College, professional schools, etc.

## TRIPS OUT OF BOSTON

### I. (NW) of BOSTON, just across Charles R. to CAMBRIDGE

Cambridge (reached by subway from Park St.), founded by Gov. Winthrop, 1630, as "New Town" & chosen capital of Mass. Bay Colony. A few wealthy colonists built homes around what is now Harvard Sq. When Harvard College was founded, 1636, town's name was changed to Cambridge, thought more appropriate for an academic center. Settlement was a strict Puritan theocracy, sharply repressing dissident elements—Baptists, Anabaptists, Quakers—which generally sprouted in New England scene. A Synod, meeting in Cambridge in the 1640's, adopted "Cambridge Platform" establishing dominance of the church in the state & over the individual. Before Rev., Cambridge took part in demonstrations against the Brit. encroachments on colonial liberties. On Ap. 19, 1775 Brit. troops marched through town to Lexington. Cambridge citizens took part in battle & later sent 1000 men to Bunker Hill. Washington assumed formal command of Continental Army & made hqs. here during Siege of Boston. In 19th cent. Cambridge developed as cultural center of New England whither poets, philosophers, scholars & scientists gravitated: Oliver Wendell Holmes, Margaret Fuller, Longfellow, Geo. Tichnor, Jas. Russell Lowell, Agassiz, Francis Parkman, Wm. Prescott, John Fiske, Charles Eliot Norton, Wm. James & many others. In 1879, Radcliffe College for women was founded & in 1916, Mass. Institute of Technology moved to outskirts of city on splendid new campus facing Charles R. Meanwhile, an industrial Cambridge & suburb of Boston developed alongside academic city. In 1948 local plants produced more than $255,000,000 worth of goods annually. Majority of pop. either work in these plants or in offices or crowd into the subway daily to jobs in Boston.

PTS. OF INT.: A good starting point for touring Cambridge is Harvard Sq. (Subway Sta.) which is bounded on one side by Harvard Univ. Yard. Brattle St. runs (NW) from Harvard Sq. & has many fine old houses, which caused it to be called Tory Row, incl.: (1) 42 Brattle St., **Brattle H.** (O.Mon.-Fri.c.1735.alts.int.inter.), once home of Margaret Fuller & one of finest mansions in Cambridge; owned by Cambridge Social Union. (2) Cor. of Brattle & Story Sts., Marker on **Site of Village Smithy,** celebrated in Longfellow's "The Village Blacksmith" & near-by, at 56 Brattle St., Cock Horse Tea-room (O), home of the "Village Blacksmith." (3) 105 Brattle St., **Craigie-Longfellow H.** (O.aft.exc.Mon.,June-Nov.;Wed.Sat.& Sun.aft. Nov.-June.1759.adds.) was built by Tory Major John Vassal, who left on eve. of Rev. H. was confiscated, & Washington made hqs. in it. Later Dr. Craigie lived here & Longfellow roomed here when he first taught at Harvard, & finally acquired H. as his lifetime home. Contains furniture, pictures, books, mss. Near-by is **Longfellow Pk.** in which is Mon. by D. C. French. 175 Brattle St., **Fayerweather H.** (c.1760), once housed a private school attended by Jas. Russell Lowell. (4) Cor. Mason & Gardens Sts., **Radcliffe College** (women), with undergrad & grad. schools, founded 1879 largely through efforts of Arthur Gilman with cooperation of Harvard's faculty & named for Ann Radcliffe, 1st woman to endow a scholarship at Harvard; 1st president was Mrs. Louis Agassiz. College became closely associated with Harvard, with its faculty drawn entirely from it. In 1943 it became integral part of Harvard Univ. Bldgs. are in Col. & Georg. styles. Fay H. (1807) is oldest & contains admin. offices. In Founder's H., 1st classes were conducted (1879). (5) Beyond Radcliffe College on Brattle St., is **Episc. Theological Seminary** which cooperates with Harvard Divinity Sch. Take Mason St. to Garden St., which runs along the Common. (6) Here is Marker on **Site of Washington Elm** under which Washington took command of Continental Army (1775); elm collapsed of old age, 1923. In Common is wooden-wheeled cannon hauled from Ft. Ticonderoga to help break Siege of Boston. (7) **Geo. Washington Mem. Gate** at Common.

(8) Opposite (S) end of Common, on Garden St., **Christ Ch.** (1760.by Peter Harrison, see Newport & Providence.fine inter.), oldest Ch. in Cambridge. Because of congregation's Tory sympathies, Patriots melted down organ pipes for bullets. Ch. was later rest. Washington's pew is preserved here. (9) In adj. **Old Burying Ground** (O. 1636) are buried Cambridge men killed during Brit. retreat from Lexington, & Dexter Pratt, "the Village Blacksmith." (10) On Mass. Ave. at Church St., **First Ch.** (Unit.org.1633.built 1833) where Harvard Univ. commencements once took place. (11) On Linden St., **Apthorpe H.** (1760), home of 1st minister of Christ Ch. (see above). (12) At Boylston & South Sts., **Hicks H.** (O.appl.1762), used as Army office by Washington & Putnam. (13) 5 Jarvis St., **Children's Mus.** (O.schooldays). (14) Cor. Mt. Auburn & Elmwood Ave., **Elmwood (Lowell) H.**, (1767), built by Thos. Oliver, last of Col. Deputy Govs. Used as hospital after Battle of Bunker Hill. Birthpl. & Home of Jas. Russell Lowell, distinguished poet, critic & Harvard professor. (15) **Mt. Auburn Cemetery** (O) with graves of notables incl. Longfellow, Lowell, Holmes, Mary Baker Eddy, Julia Ward Howe, Chas. Sumner, Edwin Booth, Charlotte Cushman, Ed. Everett, Wm. Ellery Channing, Louis Agassiz, Phillips Brooks, Francis Parkman & Chas. W. Eliot (perhaps best known of Harvard's Presidents). (16) 60 Garden St., **Harvard Observatory** (O.appl.). Has 400,000 glass photos of the sky—considered largest stellar lib. (17) Cor. of Garden & Linnaean Sts., **Harvard Botanic Garden** (O.exc.Sun.). Here is Gray Herbarium (O.Mon.-Fri. Sat.morn.), with over 1,000,000 sheets of plant specimens. (18) 21 Linnaean St., **Cooper-Frost-Austin H.** (O.Thurs.aft.sm.fee.c.1657), one of oldest in Cambridge. (19) Cor. Broadway & Trowbridge St., **Pub. Lib.** (O.Romanes.), contains copies of famous paintings; also murals.

(20) **Harvard Univ.,** founded 1636 (entrance on Mass. Ave.), is oldest Univ. in country; named for Rev. John Harvard of Charleston, Puritan clergyman who, in 1638, bequeathed his lib. & half his estate (approx. £779) to found college. Univ.'s activities cover many fields—an undergrad. college, professional & grad. schools, etc. Radcliffe College (see above) is part of the Univ. **The Yard,** at Harvard Sq., is oldest part of campus, for which overseers purchased an "eighth-acre house lot & one-acre cowyard behind it." Hence name. To (S) extending to Charles R., are a number of dormitories supervised by resident faculty. On (S) side of R., facing them, are School of Business Administration (by McKim,Mead & White), Central bldg. is Baker Lib. Near-by are Soldiers Field & Harvard Stadium. The Law School is on Mass. Ave., N. of the Yard as are the Physical, Chemical & Biological Labs., Engineering & Divinity Schools, the University, Germanic & Semitic Museums & the Institute of Geographic Exploration. Fogg Art Mus. is E. of Yard, on Quincy St. The Medical, Dental & Pub. Health Schools are located in Back Bay Boston (see). For Arnold Arboretum, see Boston Trip V. Also outside Cambridge are Univ. Observatories located in Blue Hills Reserv. (see Boston Trip V); at Oak Ridge Sta. (see Harvard, Mass.); at Mazelsport (South Africa); & at Climax, Colo. Harvard For. (2,287 as.) is located at Petersham, Mass. for practical study in forestry.

**The Yard:** 1341 Mass. Ave., opp. Holyoke St., **Wadsworth H.** (O.wks.exc.June through Sept.when closed Sat.1727.adds.1783.1810). Here Harvard Presidents lived for 123 yrs. Geo. Washington had hqs. here in July 1775. Facing Mass. Ave., **Widener Mem. Lib.** (O.wks.exc.Sat.in summer.1915.by H. Trumbauer); coll. of rare books, incl. a Gutenberg Bible, Shakespeare Folios, a single volume saved from John Harvard's Lib., & dept. of Printing & Graphic Arts. In halls & Treasure Room rare items are exhibited. There is also a reconstruction of John Harvard's Lib. Above stairway, Murals by John S. Sargent. Geo. Edw. Woodberry Poetry Room, comm. poet & critic, contains Amy Lowell Lib., incl. unique Keats coll. In front of Lib. is **Chinese Student Mem.**, presented by Chinese alumni. Noteworthy old bldgs. in Yard are: **Univ. Hall** (1815.by Bulfinch), with many portraits, incl. a Copley, & **Statue of John Harvard** by D. C. French, in front. W. of Univ. Hall is **Mass. Hall** (1720.remod.& rest.1924). To N. of latter is **Harvard Hall** (1766.Georg. adds.1842.1870). And beyond it, **Hollis & Stoughton Halls** (1763), used by Continental Army in Rev. & **Holworthy Hall** (1812). Charming little **Holden Chapel** (1744.reconst. several times) in (NW) part of the Yard. E. of it, & N. of Univ. Hall, **Appleton (Mem.) Chapel** comm. Harvard men who died in World War I (O.1932.by Coolidge, Shepley, Bulfinch & Abbott), contains Mem. Room, with figures by J. Coletti & sculpture by Malvina Hoffman. E. of Mem. Chapel is **Robinson Hall** (1901.by McKim, Mead & White), housing Schools of Arch., Regional Planning & Landscape Arch. to (S) of latter, **Sever Hall** (Romanes.by Richardson). Its style clashes with architecture of other Yard bldgs. Cor. Mass. Ave. & Quincy St., **Dana-Palmer H.** (1820) once home of Rich. Henry Dana, author of "Two Years Before the Mast."

Other Harvard pts. of int.: At Quincy & Harvard Sts., **Harvard Union** (1901.by McKim, Mead & White), freshman center. On Quincy St. opp. Sever Hall, **Fogg Mus. of Art** (O.wks.Sun.aft.closed summer Sat.aft.& Sun.; 1895.by Chas.A.Coolidge & H.R. Shepley), contains outstanding coll. of classical sculpture, Greek vases, oriental sculpture, paintings, bronzes & pottery; Romanesque sculpture; Ital., Sp., Fr. & Flemish paintings; watercolors & prints. In triangle formed by Quincy, Cambridge & Kirkland Sts., **Mem. Hall** (1870.Vict.Goth.), comm. Harvard men who fell in Civil War, has some fine mem. windows. Contains Sanders Theater & concert hall. Cor. of Kirkland St. & Divinity Ave., (L) is **Germanic Mus.** (O.wks.Sun.aft.). Houses important colls. of Germanic sculpture, paintings, & decorative arts from 15th to 20th cents. In courtyard is reprod. of Brunswick Lion (1166). (N) on same side of Divinity Ave. is **University Mus.** (O.wks.Sun.aft.). Incl. Museums of Comparative Zoology, Botany, Mineralogy, Geology & Peabody Mus. of Archeology & Ethnology. Important among exhibits is Ware Coll. of Glass Models of Plants ("The Glass Flowers"). These marvellous examples of glass handicraft were executed by Leopold & Rudolph Blaschka from 1887 to 1924. Mus. also contains coll. of Fluorescent Minerals. Opp. on Divinity Ave., **Semitic Mus.** (O.wks.Sun.aft.), devoted to Near Eastern Archeology. Oldest map in the world is exhibited in Assyrian Room. Just S. of Semitic Mus., **Institute of Geographical Exploration** (O.Mon.-Fri.Sat. morn.). N. of Semitic Mus. are **Biological Labs.** (O.exc.Sat.Sun.by Henry Shepley), fine example of modern design. Frieze by Kath. Lane. By same artist, rhinoceros & carving on doors. N. of Semitic Mus., is **Harvard Divinity Sch.** which dates from founding of college. School is free from denominational control & is affiliated with various other Schools of religion & divinity. Mass. Ave. & Jarvis St., **Harvard Law Sch.** (est.1815). Law Lib. is one of most complete in U.S. In Main Reading Room are portraits of notables incl. one of Isaac Royal, early teacher, by Rbt. Feke (1741). Another int. bldg. is Garnett H. (c.1830).

(21) Mass. Ave. on N. bank of Charles R., **Mass. Institute of Technology** (1861. coed. moved to present site 1916) gives combination training in undergraduate work & various branches of Science, Engineering, Architecture, Business Admin., etc. It also has a grad. school. Institute conducts evening courses in Lowell Institute Sch. An elementary military training course is obligatory for male students. Bldgs. class. in style. In various depts. are many int. exhibits: in Lib. (Bldg. No.10), ceramics; in Naval Arch. Dept. (Bldg.No.5), very int. Nautical Mus.; in Bldg. No. 33, Aeronautical Lab.; in Bldg. No. 44, great Cyclotron; & next to it Bldg. No. 46, Nuclear Research; in Bldg. No. 6, apparatus for Spectroscopy. Another bldg. worth a visit is Paper Mus. At SE. end of campus, is Walker Mem., center of student activities, with Mural by E. Blashfield. W. of Mass. Ave. is athletic field & parade ground.

**II. From downtown BOSTON across Charlestown Bridge to CHARLESTOWN**

Charlestown was settled c.1630. PTS. OF INT.: (1) **U.S. Navy Yard** (O), with U.S. Frigate, "Constitution" ("Old Ironsides") which may be visited, & berthed modern warships. (2) Near Navy Yard is **Bunker Hill Mon.** (O.sm.fee), 220′ (1825-42). Hill on which Mon. stands was actually Breed's Hill. (3) At Mon.'s foot, **Statue of Col. Wm. Prescott** by W.W. Storey. (4) **Mus.** (O) with coll. concerning Battle of Bunker Hill. 2 of Dan. Webster's celebrated speeches were made here: at laying of corner-

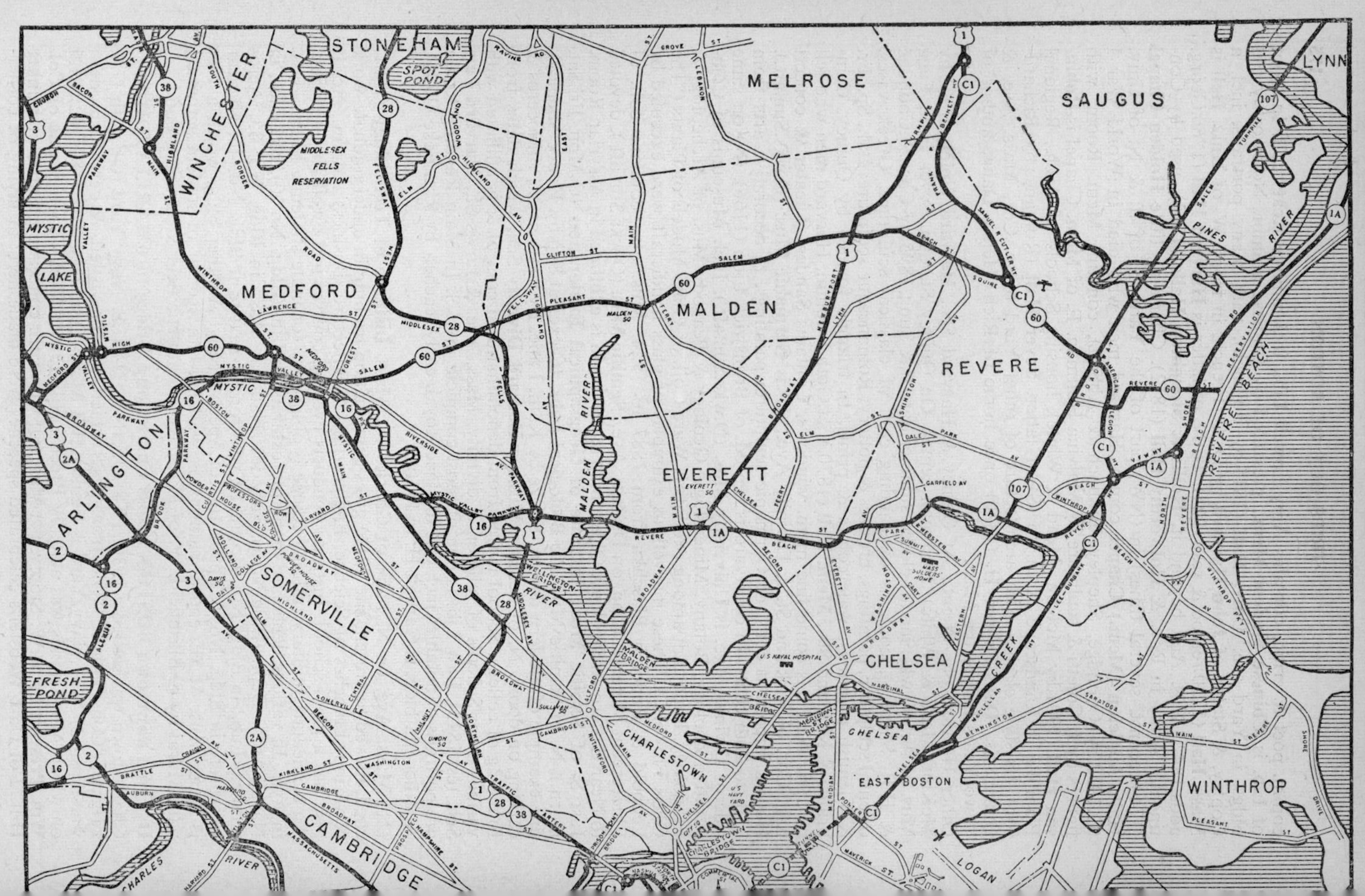

STONEHAM
MELROSE
SAUGUS
LYNN
WINCHESTER
MIDDLESEX FELLS RESERVATION
SPOT POND
MEDFORD
MALDEN
REVERE
EVERETT
ARLINGTON
SOMERVILLE
CHELSEA
CHARLESTOWN
EAST BOSTON
WINTHROP
CAMBRIDGE
LOGAN
MYSTIC LAKE
FRESH POND
PINES RIVER
REVERE BEACH
MALDEN RIVER
MYSTIC RIVER
CHARLES RIVER
CHELSEA CREEK

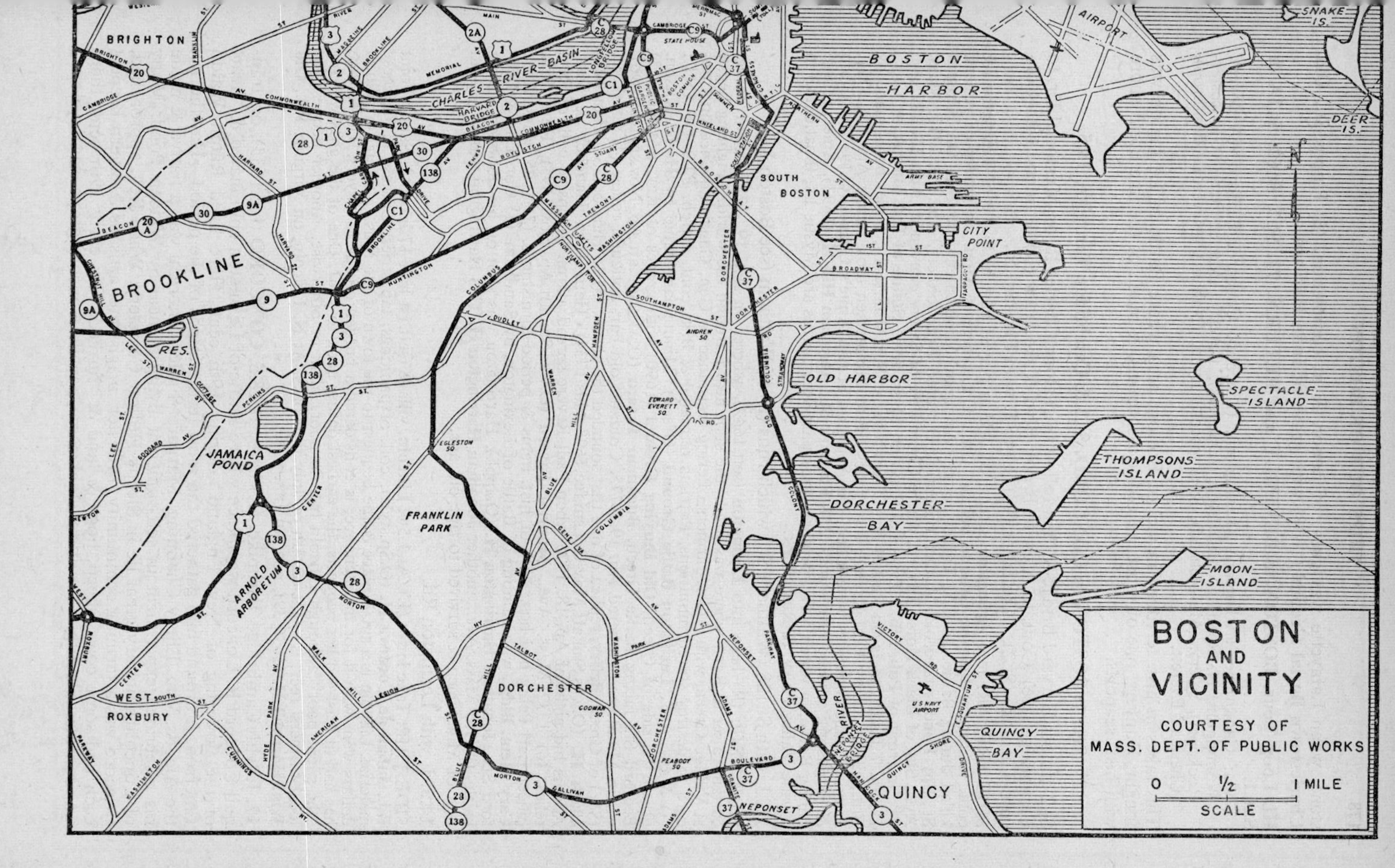
BOSTON
AND
VICINITY
COURTESY OF
MASS. DEPT. OF PUBLIC WORKS
0
1/2
1 MILE
SCALE
BOSTON
HARBOR
AIRPORT
SNAKE IS.
DEER IS.
BRIGHTON
BROOKLINE
CHARLES RIVER BASIN
HARVARD BRIDGE
LONGFELLOW BRIDGE
STATE HOUSE
SOUTH BOSTON
CITY POINT
ARMY BASE
OLD HARBOR
SPECTACLE ISLAND
THOMPSONS ISLAND
DORCHESTER BAY
MOON ISLAND
JAMAICA POND
RES.
FRANKLIN PARK
ARNOLD ARBORETUM
EGLESTON SQ.
ANDREW SQ.
EDWARD EVERETT SQ.
DORCHESTER
CODMAN SQ.
PEABODY SQ.
WEST ROXBURY
NEPONSET
NEPONSET RIVER
QUINCY
QUINCY BAY
U.S. NAVY AIRPORT

stone, when Lafayette was guest of honor, & at completion. (5) Phipps St., **Old Charlestown Burial Ground** (1638) with grave of John Harvard.

**III. Loop Tour. BOSTON to BEVERLY and RETURN. 71. St.2, St.62, St.1A & St.C1.**

Via: Cambridge, (Arlington), (Lexington), (Lincoln), Concord, Bedford, (Andover), Wilmington, N. Reading, Middleton, (Danvers), Beverly, (Manchester), (Gloucester-Rockport), Salem, (Marblehead), Swampscott, Lynn, (Nahant), (Revere), (Winthrop), (Chelsea), Everett.

This takes in hist. territory in vic. of Boston; area where Battle of Lexington was fought; Danvers, one of most int. old Mass. towns, & much of the fine north shore with hist. seaports.

**Sec. 1: BOSTON to CONCORD. St.2 & Cambridge Turnpike. 18.5.**

St.2 crosses Harvard Bridge & then follows (L) along Charles R. on Memorial Dr. to Cambridge (see). Cont. to Alewife Brook Blvd. Take latter (R) to inters. with Concord Turnpike (St.2). Take latter (W) (L) to J. with Pleasant St.

SIDE TRIP: (R) into **Arlington** (sett.1630), which played part in Battle of Lexington, & cont. to ancient **Burying Ground** behind Unit. Ch., where is **Mon.** on graves of Amers. killed during Battle. At Ch., **Tablet** comm. Arlington Minutemen's exploits. On Pleasant St., **Spy Pond,** where old Mother Batherick captured Brit. soldiers, Apr. 19, 1775. Mass. Ave., **Site of Black Horse Tavern,** where Committee of Safety convened, Apr. 18, 1775. In Pk., in front of **Pub. Lib.** (O.wks.Ital.Ren.) on Mass. Ave., **Statue of Ind. Hunter** by C. E. Dallin. 7 Jason St., **Jason Russell H.** (O.Ap.-Nov.exc.Sun.Mon.1680); bullet holes made by Brit.; silverware by Paul Revere; hist. relics. Here Minutemen took refuge Apr. 19, 1775. Jason & some comrades were killed. On Appleton St., **St. Anne's Chapel** (O.1916.by Cram & Ferguson); antique furnishings. 338 Pleasant St., **Abraham Hill H.** (1693), Amer. refuge during Battle, in which 5 Hill brothers took part. Recr. areas are Mystic Ls. (boat.bath.) in Mystic Valley Pkwy. & Russell Pk.

**12.** J. with St.128 (Waltham St.) which runs (L) to Waltham (see Boston VI).

SIDE TRIP: (R) here into **Lexington** (sett.1642), where, on Ap. 19, 1775 began battle, curtain-raiser to Rev., where was fired "the shot heard around the world." Fighting began at Village Green, with Amer. farmers offering resistance to Gen. Gage's advance on Concord to destroy stored munitions. Patriots retreated & Brit. cont. march. PTS. OF INT.: (1) Mass. Ave., **Lexington Battle Ground** (Green). Minuteman Statue by H. H. Kitson. (2) on N. side of Green, **Old Burying Ground** (1690) with graves of Rev. notables. (3) Bedford St., facing Battle Green, **Buckman Tavern** (O.wks.Sun.aft.Ap.-Nov.sm.fee.1690), where Minutemen gathered Ap. 19, 1775. Contains old bar, antiques, relics. (4) Clark St. (SW) of Green, **Belfry,** replica of one that sounded the alarm. (5) 35 Hancock St., **Hancock-Clark H.** (O.wks.Sun.aft.May-Oct.sm.fee.1698.adds.1734). Here John Hancock & Sam. Adams hid night of Ap. 18, 1775 when Paul Revere spread alarm. Extensive coll. of Rev. relics. (6) 1332 Mass. Ave., **Munroe Tavern** (O.wks.Sun.aft.Ap.-Nov.1695). Here Brit. officer Earl Percy had hqs.; coll. of hist. items & period furnishings. (7) 1605 Mass. Ave., **Cary Mem. Bldg.,** with painting of Battle of Lexington, by Sandham. (8) Cor. Elm & Bedford Sts., **Jonathan Harrington H.** (O.appl.). Harrington was shot on his doorstep during battle. (9) 955 Mass. Ave., another **Jonathan Harrington H.** This Harrington was 17-yr.-old fifer of Minutemen & survived to ripe old age.

**14.5.** J. with Lexington Rd.

SIDE TRIP: Take latter (L). At 1.5m, **Lincoln,** village (sett.1st half 17th cent.). Sandy Point Rd., **Julian de Cordova H.** (O.Sp.style); coll. of paintings, tapestries, Chinese & Japanese material. Lincoln is a small place & the bequest to the town of the Mus., although a million dollars went with it for maintenance, is considered a burden on the taxpayers. The village has had at least 4 other bequests, the earliest dating back to 1761. One of the gifts was for "the silent poor" although Lincoln has no poor, silent or otherwise. Another bequest for local farmers' recr. is spent on 4th of July fireworks. At N. Lincoln, on Virginia Rd., **Old Wm. Hartwell H.** (1636-39), now an Inn.

**17.** J. with Cambridge Turnpike. (R) here, at **18.5. CONCORD** (inc.1635), on tranquil Concord R. Concord was place where Battle of Lexington culminated & "heart of the flowering of New England" during 19th cent. Here lived Ralph Waldo Emerson, & around him gathered the most fertile minds of the period—Hawthorne, the Alcotts, Wm. Ellery Channing, Margaret Fuller. Thoreau was a native & made his celebrated experiment in self-sufficient living at near-by Walden Pond. Many of Concord's literary great lie in Sleepy Hollow Cemetery. When Rev. approached, Concord was a farming community. Minister, magistrate, artisans & tavern keepers each had some cows, sheep, hogs & land & "farmed." By early 19th cent. there was considerable mfg.—furniture, clock cases, pencils. Concord grape was developed here, although no longer grown commercially in its birthpl. In 1774, Concord was meeting place of Provincial Congress. Delegates authorized training of Minutemen "for defense only," & collection of munitions & stores. This "stock pile" Brit. Gen. Gage wanted to capture, & his attempt precipitated battle. Warning of Brit. approach from Lexington was brought to Concord by Wm. Prescott, who had been riding with Paul Revere, but escaped capture. Brit. took Concord & occupied both North & South Bridges, the Minutemen having withdrawn across R. Finally Concord men, re-enforced by arrivals from near-by towns, approached & Brit. withdrew across North Bridge, where shots were exchanged. Brit. now began retreat & Patriots followed to Merriam's Corner. Here, with re-enforcements, full scale pursuit ensued, Amers. shooting from behind walls, houses & barns, until Brit. retreat became disorderly rout.

PTS. OF INT.: (1) Concord (Mon.) Sq., **Civil War Mem.** Two boulders comm. respectively Sp. War & World War I soldiers. (2) Bedford St., **Sleepy Hollow Cemetery,** where lie Emerson, Hawthorne, Thoreau, Wm. Ellery Channing & the Alcotts. (3) 11 Concord Sq., **Colonial Inn.** (O.oldest part 1770). (4) 36 Monument St., **Bullet-Hole H.,** where Elisha Jones stored supplies for Minutemen. Orig. part of H. built by John Smedlay, 1st settler. Bullet from bullet-hole made by Brit. in door is exhibited. Near-by on Monument St., **Old Manse** (O.wks.Ap.-Nov.exc.Mon.Sun. aft.sm.fee). Books, furnishings, unchanged since Hawthorne lived here. (See his "Mosses from an Old Manse"). Emerson's grandfather who built the H. watched battle from a window. End of Mon. St. is **Battleground** at North Bridge. "The Minuteman," by D. C. French. At dedication, Pres. Grant climbed off platform, when it showed signs of collapsing, & sat among the ladies. Louisa Alcott thought he looked so bored she wanted to offer him a big, black cigar. Tablet marking graves of Brit. troops is inscribed with verses by Lowell. (5) At Sq. (No. 2 Lexington Rd.), **Wright Tavern** (O.exc.Mon.1747), hqs. of Brit. Col. Smith & Maj. Pitcairn, Ap. 19, 1775, has old bar & Rev. relics. (6) On Main St., **Pub. Lib.** (O) has Statue of Emerson by D. C. French & coll. of hist. & other items. (7) 75 Main St., **Thoreau-Alcott H.,** where Thoreau died. (8) On Lexington Rd.: **Hill Burying Ground** (L), 1677. Headstones of magistrates & ministers have particularly lengthy epitaphs & that of John Jack, Negro slave, who died before Rev., is famous. (9) **First Parish Ch.** (rebuilt 1901 after fire), on site of earlier Ch. where Provincial Congress met (1774). (10) No. 15, **Concord Art Assoc.** (O.Ap.-Oct.pre-1753.art exhibits summer), built by John Ball, goldsmith; coll. of hist. items. (11) No. 27, **Old Reuben Brown H.** (O). At inters. of Lexington Rd. & Cambridge Turnpike. (12) **Emerson H.** (R) (O.Ap.-Dec.sm.fee.1828), Emerson's home, 1835 until death. Furnishings of Emerson's time, portraits & his lib. Same intersection (L) (13) **Antiquarian H.** (O.wks.exc. Mon.Sun.aft.Ap.-Nov.sm.fee.1929). Important coll. of antique furnishings, contents of Emerson's study, Thoreau coll., incl. Thoreau hut furniture, hist. relics, Paul Revere's lanterns, diorama of Concord fight. On Lexington Rd., (14) **Sch. of Philosophy** (L), where Bronson Alcott pontificated. Just beyond (15) **Orchard H.** (L) (O. wks.exc.Mon.Sun.aft.Ap.-Nov.sm.fee.1650 & 1730), home of Alcotts, preserved as at that time. Here Louisa wrote "Little Women." Beyond (L) is (16) **Wayside** (O. May-Oct.sm.fee.pre-1717.remod.1845), home at various times of Hawthorne (who wrote here "Tanglewood Tales" & "Marble Faun" as well as of Louisa M. Alcott & Margaret Sydney, author of "The Five Little Peppers." Int. exhibits. Further along on Lexington Rd. (17) **Grapevine Cottage** (O.summer.12-8:30), with antiques & grapevine grown from orig. planted by Ephraim Wales Bull, who never profited from grapes he developed. Cont. on Lexington Rd., Merriam's Cor. where Lexington Rd. becomes St.2A. Cont. on St.2A to J. with Bedford St. At c.1.5$^{m}$ (E) of J. is pt. where Paul Revere was taken prisoner. Here is tablet on spot where Patriot pursuit intensified (see above).

SIDE TRIP: (S) from Concord on Walden St. (St.126) to Walden Pond St. Reserv. (bath. boat.f.trls.). Cairn on **Site of Thoreau's Cabin** built by his own hands. He has described his experiment in solitary living here in "Walden." Cont. on St.126 to Wayland. Near-by is Longfellow's **Wayside Inn & Red Schoolh.** of "Mary had a little lamb" fame in S. Sudbury (see Boston VI).

### Sec. 2: CONCORD to BEVERLY. 32.5. St.62

**0. CONCORD. 18.** J. with St.28 which leads (N) c.5$^{m}$ **Andover,** home of Phillips Andover Academy (see Boston Trip VII). **27.5.** J. with US1. Here is **Birthpl. of**

**Israel Putnam** (O.1648.adds.1760 & later), famous Rev. Gen. Marker states that Jos. Putnam, son of orig. builder, opposed Salem witchcraft trials. Gen. Putnam's boyhood room has relics & wall paper dating 1800. H. occupied by 10th generation of Putnam descendants (1948). **30.** J. with Conant St.

SIDE TRIP: (R) here to **Danvers,** figuring in witchcraft hysteria (1688-92) (see Salem). PTS. OF INT.: (1) 11 Page St., **Page H.** (O.Mon.Wed.& Sat.aft.Ap.-Nov.appl.sm.fee), Hist. Soc. hqs., with coll. of portraits, antiques. (2) 149 Pine St., **Rebecca Nurse H.** (O.wks.summer.or appl.1678), where lived Rebecca Nurse, old woman hanged as witch. Int. 17th cent. rooms. (3) Near new Town Hall, **Peabody Institute,** founded by Geo. Peabody, London banker, who also endowed Peabody Institute in Baltimore, left legacies for education in South, etc. (4) 171 Holten St., **Holten H.** (1670), hqs. of D.A.R. (5) Center St., Marker on **Site of Salem Ch.** Ministers' children launched witchcraft hysteria by tales about Old Tituba (see Salem). (6) 166 High St. (in Danversport), **Sam. Fowler H.** (O.summer.sm.fee.1810); antiques, early wall paper. (7) 42 Summer St., **Jas. Putnam H.** (O.1680.remod.1715), home of Jas. Putnam, prominent 18th cent. lawyer; now an Inn. (8) Also on Summer St., **Oak Knoll** (O), once home of Whittier, now home for aged.

**32.5. BEVERLY** (see Boston Trip IV).

### Sec. 3: BEVERLY to BOSTON. 20. (see Boston Trip IV).

## IV. BOSTON to PORTSMOUTH, N.H. 69. St.C1, St.1A & US1 in Mass. & St.1A in N.H. (Alt. to US1)

Via: (Marblehead), Salem, Beverly, (Gloucester & Rockport), Wenham, Hamilton, Ipswich, Newburyport & Salisbury in Mass., & Newcastle in N.H.

This is more interesting route than US1, since it skirts North Shore, famous resort area, & frequented N.H. shore region, & passes through or near number of hist. towns.

### Sec. 1: BOSTON to MASS.-N.H. LINE. 47.

Take Sumner Tunnel & then St.C1 past Suffolk Downs Race Track to J. with Winthrop Ave.

SIDE TRIP: (R) here c.1.5m to **Winthrop** (sett.1635). At 40 Shirley St., is **Winthrop H.** (O.certain wks.in aft.1637) where Deane Winthrop, son of the Gov., lived. Pictures, relics & records of Winthrop family. About 1.5m from Winthrop is **Great Head,** with fine view. Cont. to Pt. Shirley (f.) which has a few int. old Hs.

Cont. on St.C1 to J. with St.1A. Take St.1A (R) here to **Revere** (sett.c.1636) & Revere Beach, Mass.'s Coney Island. Route now cont. on St.1A along the shore across Gen. Edwards Mem. Bridge to **LYNN** at **c.12.** (sett.1629) whose great shoe industry developed from early Col. beginnings. 12 Broad St., **Mary Baker Eddy H.** (O.wks.) where Christian Science leader is said to have written "Science & Health." 125 Green St., **Hyde-Mills H.** (O.one aft.wk.1838), home of Hist. Soc; hist. materials, antique furnishings & early shoe shop. On Western Ave., **Lydia Pinkham Med. Co.** (O.appl.). In **High Rock Pk.,** Tower with fine view. Lynnfield St., **Lynn Woods Pk.** (2,000 as.). Near Lynn, Lynn Beach (recr.amusements).

SIDE TRIPS: (A) Turn (R) in Lynn to Lynn Shore Dr., & (S) on it & Nahant Rd. to **Nahant** (resort) on rocky peninsula jutting out into ocean. Fine views. Steamers to Boston. (B) Turn (L) on Lynn Shore Rd., to Swampscott (see below). From Swampscott, St.129 runs (NE) along shore to Marblehead (see below) & J. with St.1A in Salem (see below). This is scenically int. alternate to St.1A bet. Swampscott & Salem.

Cont. on St.1A to **SWAMPSCOTT** at **c.13.** (resort), once port of a considerable fishing fleet. 23 Paradise Rd., **Mary Baker Eddy H.** (O.wks.morn.Sun.aft.sm.fee) where Mary Baker Eddy began her healing career. 99 Paradise St., **Humphrey H.** (O.17th cent.int.inter.), coll. of relics.

At **c.18.** is **SALEM** (sett.1629), which derives from Hebrew word "Shalom," for peace. Roger Conant & company migrated to site in 1626 from Cape Ann. When Gov. Endicott arrived, a few yrs. later, disagreements arose & earlier group moved away to what today is Beverly. Salem was noted for religious intolerance. Roger Williams & his Quakers were persecuted & driven out. The witchcraft hysteria that swept much of early New England had its center at Salem (1692). It all began when some young girls were seized with delusions brought on by tales told them by a West Indian slave-girl servant, Tituba, who was convicted of witchcraft, with several other old women, on the strength of youngsters' accusations. In 18th cent., Salem's ships earned large profits in West Indies & China trade. Privateering, especially during Rev., brought added wealth. But Embargo Act & War of 1812 nearly ended

Salem's foreign commerce; moreover, city's harbor was not deep enough to accommodate largest vessels. Growth of industry made up for loss of shipping. From the beginning, handicrafts contributed to local prosperity. Shoemaking began in 1629, with importation of an Eng. cobbler. Old Salem furniture is prized today by collectors. Textile mills were est. early in 19th cent. Leather-tanning was one of 1st industries. City's plants now produce some $57,000,000 worth of goods annually. Hawthorne, born in Salem, lived there as Surveyor of Port for several yrs. gathering material for his "Scarlet Letter," "House of the Seven Gables" & "Dr. Grimshaw's Secret." Also born in Salem was outstanding Amer. architect of late 18th & early 19th cents., Sam. McIntire, designer of city's finest structures.

PTS. OF INT.: (1) On Essex St.: 71, **Narbonne H.** (mid-17th cent.very fine); 128, **Pingree H.** (O.wks.fee.1804.by McIntire.int.inter.): furnishings of Salem merchant's home of period; 132, **Essex Institute** (O.wks.) with Ward China Lib. & colls. of paintings, antiques & hist. material. Adj., **John Ward H.** (O.wks.May 1-Nov.1.1684). 17th & 18th cent. furnishings & early 19th cent. apothecary shop. Also on grounds, reprod. of **Lye Shoe Shop** (O), with equipment of early 19th cent. shoe-maker. Also on Essex St., **Peabody Mus.** (O.wks.Sun.aft.); nat. hist., ethnology, maritime items, ships' models, paintings of Chinese ports & portraits of East India merchants. Old Town Sq. & Essex St., **Town H.** (1816) on Site of 1st Town Hall where 1st Provincial Congress met. Here stood Hawthorne's old "Town Pump." Near-by on Washington St., **City Hall** in which is Ind. deed to town site. Cor. Essex & North Sts., **Witch H.** (O.sm.fee.rest.pre-1662), home of Judge Corwin, witchcraft judge. Near Witchcraft H., on Summer St., **Old Nath. Bowditch H.** (being rest.in 1948). 318 Essex St., **Ropes Mem.** (O.wks.exc.Mon.sm.fee.1719.very fine); china, glassware, antique furniture, portraits, etc.; 339 Essex St., **Salem Athenaeum** (O.by invit.only); rare books. 384 Essex St., **East India H.** (O.1706.by McIntire.int.inter.); chimney has so-called "Tory Hideout." Cor. Daniels St., **Stephen Daniels H.** (O.sm.fee.1667.wing added 1756. rest.1940); period furnishings.

(2) On Chestnut St., are number of beautiful houses, mostly of Fed. period, some by McIntire. Cor. Cambridge & Chestnut Sts., **Hamilton Hall** (1805.by McIntire.alts.), famous Assembly Hall. 18, **Hawthorne H.,** where writer lived while Surveyor of the Port (1846). (3) Cor. Pickering & Broad Sts., **Pickering H.** (alt.), said to be oldest in Salem City. (4) On Federal St., number of fine old houses, incl.: No. 4, **Old House** (O.fee.1684), incorporates frame & timber of old jail in which persons accused of witchcraft were imprisoned. Contains relics of old jail. 142, **Cook-Oliver H.** (1804. by McIntire). 138, **Assembly Hall** (1782.by McIntire.alts.). Here Washington & Lafayette were entertained. 80, **Pierce-Nichols H.** (O.certain days.aft.fee.1782.by McIntire); period furnishings. Further along on Federal St. is the Courth. in which are kept witch pins & many documents of the witchcraft hysteria. (5) **Salem Common** (Washington Sq.), est. after great fire, 1714, & used as militia training ground. In Sq., **Statue of Rbt. Conant,** city's founder, by H. H. Kitson. (6) On Mall St., H. occupied by Hawthorne for 3 yrs. & where he wrote "The Scarlet Letter." (7) 54 Turner St., **House of the Seven Gables** (O.wks.Sun.aft.fee.1668.rest.) which is said to have figured in Hawthorne's novel; antiques, furnishings, secret stairway, etc. On grounds, **Hathaway H.** (O.fee incl.main H.1682); two 17th cent. rooms & furniture. On grounds, **Retire Beckwith H.** (O.1652), now tearoom; antiques.

(8) Derby Wharf & Derby St., **Salem Maritime Nat. Hist. Site,** est. 1938 by Fed. Govt. which incl.: 168 Derby St., **Rich. Derby H.** (O.sm.fee.1761.int.inter.), probably oldest brick H. in Salem, built by Capt. Rich. Derby whose ships sailed to Russia, Cape of Good Hope & Canton; antique furnishings & family portraits. 178 Derby St., **Custom H.** (O.1819.Fed.). Here Hawthorne had office (1846); Hawthorne relics. Near Custom H., **Derby Wharf,** begun by Capt. Derby (1762). Here privateers were fitted out during Rev. Near-by, **Central Wharf** (1791-92), built by Simon Forrester, privateer Capt. **Old Forrester Warehouse,** owned by Capt. Forrester. Near Derby H. is **Hawkes H.** (O.c.1780.by McIntire), home of Capt. Ben. Hawkes, shipbuilder & merchant. Also "Rum Shop" (O.c.1800). (9) 48 Bridge St., **Thos. Woodbridge H.** (lower floor O.c.1810.by McIntire.rest.). (10) Hawthorne Blvd., **Hawthorne Mon.,** by Bela Pratt. (11) Charter St., bet. Central & Liberty Sts., **Charter St. Burying Ground** where Gov. Bradstreet, Rich. More, who came over on Mayflower, & other notables are buried. (12) Near-by, on same side of St., is **Grimshaw H.,** figuring in Hawthorne's "Dr. Grimshaw's Secret." (13) 27 Union St., **Hawthorne's Birthpl.** (1692); author was born here 1804. (14) Congress St., **Pequot H.** (O.reprod.of mid-

17th cent.H.). (15) On Harbor, Forest River Pk., in which is **Pioneer Village** (O.June 15-Nov.11.sm.fee), reprod. of Salem when first sett. Among reprods. is **Ruck H.,** oldest bldg. Salem records give account of.

SIDE TRIPS: (A) From Salem take St.129 (R) (E) c.5m to **Marblehead** (sett.1629). (Resort. bath.beaches.yacht.f.). Accoms.: All types, summer. Info.: C. of C. & Rotary Club. Marblehead is situated on a fine, rocky peninsula. Marblehead Neck is connected with main peninsula by narrow strip of land noted for its precipitous shores. 1st arrivals were Eng. fishermen. During Rev., shipping was tied up by Brit., but privateering flourished. Marblehead disputes with Machiasport, Me., claim of having captured 1st enemy ship in Rev. War of 1812 pretty much ended town's foreign commerce. During that conflict "USS Constitution" took refuge here under guns of old Ft. Sewall. PTS. OF INT.: (1) Washington Sq., **Abbot Hall** (O) has Willard's famous painting "Spirit of '76." (2) On Washington St. are number of fine old Hs., incl.: 161, **Jeremiah Lee Mansion** (O.wks.Ap.-Dec.;Sun. aft.July-Oct.sm.fee.1768), owned by Marblehead Hist. Soc.; antique furnishings, hand-painted wall paper. **Old Town H.** (O.1727). 44, **Elbridge Gerry H.,** birthpl. of E. Gerry, signer of Decl. of Ind. & Vice-Pres. of U.S. during War of 1812. **Old North Ch.** (O.1824. Col.Georg.). Cor. Washington & Summer Sts., **St. Michael's Ch.** (O.Episc.1714). (3) 8 Hooper St., **King Hooper H.** (O.aft.exc.Mon.sm.fee.1745); period furniture, panelling; home of Marblehead Arts Assoc. (4) Orne St., **Old Brig** (c.1720), birthpl. of Moll Pitcher, celebrated in Whittier's "Witch of Wenham." Also on Orne St., **Old Burial Hill** with gravestones dating from 1638. (5) 7 Franklin St., **Parson Barnard H.** (pre-1716). (6) Front St., **Ft. Sewall** (O.early 18th cent.) in Seaside Pk. (7) 82 Front St., **Old Tavern** (1680). (8) 11 Glover St., **Glover's H.** (1762), home of Gen. John Glover (see Beverly, below).

(B) Take Boston St. (NE) out of Salem to **Peabody,** old leather mfg. center. 35 Washington St., **Gideon Foster H.** (O.summer,certain aft.& appl.c.1800); antique furnishings & houses Peabody Hist. Soc. Here also is **Peabody Institute,** founded by bequest of Geo. Peabody, London philanthropist (see above).

At **c.20.** on St.1A is **BEVERLY,** sett. c.1626 by Roger Conant & his company after leaving Salem. Men of Beverly & Marblehead, under command of Gen. John Glover, helped ferry Washington across Delaware. After Rev., town became important shipping center. Beverly claims several important "firsts": 1st ship of U.S. Navy, "The Hannah," sailed out of Beverly (1775) from America's 1st Navy Yard; 1st cotton mill in U.S. (1788); oldest drugstore (1796); 1st Britannia Ware (1808); & 1st Sunday Sch. in New England (1810). Among distinguished citizens were Nathan Dane, who presented in Congress "Ordinance of 1787" which abolished slavery in Northwest Territory, & Geo. Edward Woodberry, poet, critic & philosopher.

PTS. OF INT.: On Cabot St., are **First Ch.** (1656) & at No. 117, **Cabot H.** (O.wks. July & Aug.Sat.morn.1788), built by John Cabot; documents, portraits, furniture. 39 Hale St., **Hale H.** (O.wks.exc.Mon.& Sun.June 15-Sept.15.; 1694), built by Rev. John Hale; Nathan Hale's fire brigade bucket, antiques. 448 Cabot St., **John Balch H.** (O.wks.appl.1638); Col. furnishings. Conant St., in N. Beverly, **Second Ch.** (1714). Inters. of St.62 & US1, **U.S. Shoe Machinery Co.** (O.appl.), largest of its type in world. Mingo Hill & Beach, named for Robin Mingo, Negro servant, whose master promised him freedom if ever the tide ran so low that one could walk dry-shod to Aunt Becky's Ledge. This happened & Mingo was free. St.1A has J. with St.127 c.0.5m S. of Beverly.

SIDE TRIP: Take latter (R) along shore front past public beach. At 4m **Pride's Crossing,** named for John Pride, nephew of the regicide. 4.5m **Beverly Farms,** former home of Oliver Wendell Holmes & his son, late Chief Justice of Supreme Court. 7m, **Manchester** (sett. c.1626). **Ch.** (1809). 12 Union St., **Trask H.** (O.one aft.a wk.July-Aug.or appl.c.1830.rest.). 15m **Gloucester** (sett.1623.resort). **Rockport** (sett.1690.resort).

Info.: In Gloucester, Info. Booth, summer. In Rockport, Bd. of Trade. Accoms.: All types, summer; limited, winter. (bath.beaches.yacht harbors.f.boat.) End of May or in June, 4-day fiesta in honor of Our Lady of Good Voyage & blessing of fishing fleet. In Aug., Mem. service at Fishermen's Mon. & casting of flowers on Annisquam R.

Both towns are on rocky, picturesque Cape Ann: Gloucester at lower end with good harbor in which are several islands; Rockport at New Harbor, crowded with fishing boats & yachts. Cape Ann has become a notable summer art colony. Gloucester has always been a great fishing town, & its fleets have for several hundred yrs. fished the treacherous Grand Banks on which, it is claimed, more than 8,000 of her fishermen have lost their lives. The old Yankee fishermen have been reinforced in recent years by Portuguese, mostly from the Azores. Gloucester today is still one of the great fishing towns of the East coast.

PTS. OF INT.: In Gloucester: (1) Legion Sq., **Amer. Legion Mem.** (former Town Hall), in front of which stands Statue of Jeanne d'Arc, by A. V. Hyatt. Orig. in Paris. (2) **Universalist Ch.** (1806) on site of 1st Ch. of this denomination in Amer. (3) 49 Middle St., **Sargent-Murray-Gilman-Hough H.** (O.wks.July & Aug.sm.fee.1768.fine panelling); shells, old furniture & portraits. (4) 27 Pleasant St., **Cape Ann Hist. Assoc. H.** (O. June 15-Sept.

sm.fee.c.1805); maritime, marine & antique items. Near-by, Y.M.C.A. is on Site of the Old Whipping Post. (5) On Esplanade (Western Ave.), **Mon. comm. Gloucester Fisherman,** by L. Kraske. (6) On Prospect St., **Ch. of Our Lady of Good Voyage** from which starts procession for blessing of fishing fleet. (7) On St.127, bet. Gloucester & Rockport, **Jas. Babson Cooperage Shop** (O.Sat.aft.July & Aug.;1659), furnished as it was orig. Ebenezer, one of James's 10 children, was object of suspicion because he protected "witches" during witchcraft hysteria (1692). (8) On Washington St., to (N) of Gloucester, **Ellery H.** (1704). (9) Further (N) on Washington St., in Riverdale, is **Riggs H.** (O.appl.fee.log cabin sec.1638. main sec.1700), oldest in Gloucester; first schoolh., old household equipment. (10) 197 E. Main St., **North Shore Arts Assoc.** (O.wks.summer.Sun.aft.art exhibits).
(11) Further along on E. Main St., take Rocky Neck Ave. (R) to **Rocky Neck,** in E. Gloucester, where is an art colony & Gloucester School of the Little Theater. Cont. on E. Main St., & then on E. Point Rd. (12) 59 E. Point Rd., **Gloucester Soc. of Artists** (O. wks.summer.Sun.aft.exhibits). Rd. cont. to E. Point, where is (13) **Lighth.** & (14) **Mother Ann,** int. Rock formation. Near here also is (15) **Beauport** (O.wks.Sun.aft.fee.1907), a great mansion with 56 rooms furnished in period styles. (16) On Western Ave., **Stage Fort Pk.** Tablet comm. 1st settlement. (17) Off shore in Gloucester Harbor, are **Five & Ten Pound Is.** bought from Inds. for 5 & 10 pounds respectively. (18) Off Hesperus Ave., (S) of Gloucester, **Rafe's Chasm,** deep cleft through which sea roars continually. Fine view here of Kettle Is., off shore; also of Norman's Woe, reef comm. by Longfellow in his "Wreck of the Hesperus." (19) On Hesperus Ave., near-by, **"Castle" of John Hays Hammond** (O.summer.wks.a.m.fee); art, antiques. (20) In Gloucester are Frank E. Davis Fish Co. (O) & Gorton-Pew Fish Co. (O). In 1623 latter shipped 1st cargo of fish to Spain. (21) In W. Gloucester, **Haskell H.** (c.1652).

PTS. OF INT.: In Rockport: (1) On Main St., **Rockport Art Assoc.** (O.summer.exhibits) in old tavern (1770). (2) Dock Sq. (25 Main St.), **Ebenezer Pool H.** (1805.very fine). (3) Cor. Main & School Sts., **First Congr. Ch.** (1803), known as "The Old Sloop." (4) On Main St., Marker comm. **Site of 1st Settler's H.** (5) Beach St., **Old Burying Ground.** (6) Granite St., at Pigeon Cove, **Old Castle** (O.Sat.& Sun.aft.;1715). (7) Pigeon Hill St., **Paper H.** (O.summer.sm.fee.1922). 100,000 copies of newspapers were used in construction of this H. & its furniture. (8) Off Granite St., near Pigeon Cove, **Old Witch H.** (O.appl.1670.adds.) where a group of refugees from witchcraft hysteria hid. (9) Near Halibut Point, off St.127, is **Gott H.** (O.appl.1702). (10) Near-by is **Pub. Reserv. & Beach.**

In Beverly is J. with St.62 (see Boston Trip III). **23.5.** Wenham L. comm. in Whittier's "Witch of Wenham," & just beyond it, **WENHAM** (sett.1635). On Green, handsome **First Ch.** (1843.int.inter.rest.). **Claflin-Richards H.** (O.wks.aft.summer;Sun. appl.); doll coll., old shoe shop & barn with old implements. (R) on Larch Rd. a short distance is **Lowe-Pickering H.** (O.appl.pre-1680). Linden trees near-by are said to have been planted by Alex. Hamilton. **26. HAMILTON** (sett.1638). Here are a number of fine old bldgs. **29.5.,** J. with St.121.

SIDE TRIP: Take latter (R) 4.5m **Essex** (sett.1634), with some fine old Hs. **Old Congr. Ch.** & **Old Shipyards,** still functioning. On Western Ave., **Old Malt H.** (O), now a hooked-rug. shop.

**30. IPSWICH** (sett.1635), 1st known as Agawam; old fishing town famous during last 300 yrs. for succulent clams. Furniture carved here by Dennis family has achieved fame among collectors. Town was home of colonial poet, Anne Bradstreet & Nath. Ward, author of "The Cobbler of Agawam." PTS. OF INT.: (1) On S. Green, **Waters Mem.,** marking militia training ground, & **South Ch.** (1748). (2) 53 S. Main St., **Whipple H.** (O.1640.adds.1670-1700); documents, 17th & 18th cent. furniture. (3) 6 Water St., **Preston-Foster H.** (O.sm.fee.1640). (4) Cor. Linebrook Rd. & Kimball Ave., **Hart H.** (O.1640), now an inn; antiques. (5) On N. (Meetinghouse) Green, **Congr. Ch.** (1847), on site of older one where Whitefield preached so eloquently that the Devil listened, perched on Ch. roof &, when angered by sermon, jumped down & left his footprint on near-by rock. (6) On Green, **Tablet** comm. resistance (1687) by townspeople to Gov. Andros. (7) 41 Turkey Shore Rd., **Emerson-Howard H.** (O.sm.fee.c.1648); period furnishings. (8) **Choate Bridge** (1764) spanning Ipswich R. (9) **Old Wade H.,** int. because here lived Pomp, Negro servant, hanged for murder. (10) High & N. Main Sts., **Old Burial Ground.** Hawthorne records in his diary that he "always counted the buttons of Rev. Rogers' gown" on latter's monument. There are a number of other int. old houses here. Boats to Plum I. Ipswich Beach (swim.).

**34. ROWLEY,** old shipbuilding & shipping town. On Main St., **Platts-Bradstreet H.** (O.appl.); relics, old shoe shop, Eng. garden. On Bradford St. (St.133), **Chaplin-Clarke-Williams H.** (O.appl.sm.fee.c.1671). **40.5. NEWBURY.** On St.1A, near S. Green, **Jackman-Willett H.** (O.appl.1696); relics. 33 High Rd., **Short H.** (O.wks.

summer;Sun.appl.sm.fee.1733); antiques. 14 High St., **Coffin H.** (O.aft.3 days wkly. sm.fee.c.1651.adds.); period furnishings. 4-6 High Rd., **Swett-Ilsley H.** (O.Mar. through Christmas exc.Sat.& Mon.pre-1670); old woodwork, tap-room.

**42. NEWBURYPORT** (sett.1635) on Merrimack R., once important shipping & fishing town; built some of fastest clipper ships. Today, busy industrial center. PTS. OF INT.: Among old bldgs. are: (1) Pleasant St., **Ch. of First Religious Soc.** (O.1801). (2) Fed. & School Sts., **Old South Ch.** (O.1756.alt.) where Whitefield preached. (3) 164 High St., **Pettingell-Fowler H.** (O.wks.June-Sept.aft.sm.fee); Hist. Soc., relics, portraits, ship models. (4) High & Market Sts., **St. Paul's Ch.** (Episc.O.). (5) High St., **Old Hill Burying Ground.** (6) 94 State St., **Tracy H.** (O.1771); pub. lib., 18th cent. furniture & Gilbert Stuart portrait. (7) 28 Green St., **Bradbury-Spaulding H.** (O.appl.& 3 days wkly.sm.fee.c.1788-91); antique furniture, paintings, doll coll. (8) Aubin St., **Old County Jail** (1744).

SIDE TRIP: Take St.113 (W) to **West Newbury** c.6m. On Indian Hill St., **Ind. Hill Farm** (O.wks.summer.fee.1830.adds.); 37 completely furnished rooms, old outbuildings.

In Newburyport is J. with US1. Cont. on latter (NE) to **SALISBURY** at **44.5.** (For this stretch see US1, sec. 8). In Salisbury is J. with St.1A which cont. (R) to **MASS.-N.H. LINE** at **47.**

### Sec. 2: MASS.-N.H. LINE to PORTSMOUTH. 22.

St.1A in N.H. passes through or near a series of fine resort & beaches. **4.5. GREAT BOAR'S HEAD,** rocky promontory, described by Whittier in "The Tent on the Beach." **15. ODIORNE'S PT.,** where David Thompson made 1st N.H. settlement (see Portsmouth). **16.5. SEAVEY HOMESTEAD** (1730), now tearoom. **17.** J. with St.1B on which this tour cont.

SIDE TRIP: St.1A (R) here 1m, then (L) on Little Harbor Rd. 1m to **Benning Wentworth Mansion** (O.appl.oldest sec.1695) built by unpopular N.H. Gov. of pre-Rev. period (see Portsmouth); palatial structure with int. inter., especially fine Council Chamber.

Cont. on St.1B (L). **20. NEW CASTLE,** charming old village (chartered 1693) on an island at entrance to Portsmouth Harbor. **Meetingh.** (O.appl.1828). Rev. Lucius Alden, descendant of John Alden, preached here. **Ft. Constitution** (captured 1774 from Brit.), now a ruin. From New Castle, St.1B crosses bridges linking island to mainland. Fine views. **22. PORTSMOUTH.**

### V. Loop Tour (S. of Boston) to WEYMOUTH & RETURN. c.30. St.3, St.128, St.28, US1, Arbor Pkwy. & Jamaica Way

Via: South Boston, Dorchester, Quincy, Weymouth, Milton Center & Roxbury

Take Summer St. (SE) from South Station & cont. on L St. to J. with Broadway which leads (L) to Farragut Rd. where is **Boston Aquarium** (O). [Off Broadway (L), on Gardner Way, is **Fort Independence** (grounds O.1801) in Castle I. Pk. jutting out into sea. Fine views.] Cont. (W) on Broadway.

SIDE TRIP: Off Broadway is **Telegraph Hill** in Thomas Pk., on which is Mon. comm. battery trained from here on Brit. during Rev. This is in Dorchester Hts. PTS. OF INT.: in **Dorchester** incl.: Dorchester & Mercer Sts., **St. Augustine's Chapel** (O.appl.1819) & old Graveyard. In Richardson Pk. at J. of Pond & E. Cottage Sts., **Blake H.** (O.1648). At Everett Sq., **Statue of Edw. Everett,** statesman & orator, by W. W. Story. Everett made chief address at dedication of Gettysburg Battlefield, Nov. 1, 1863, a speech which lasted two hours. Lincoln was merely asked to make a few remarks, which turned out to be his "Gettysburg Address." Tablet at Sq. marks **Site of Everett's Birthpl.** Boston St. & Willow Court, **Clapp H.** (O.c.1635) built by Roger Clapp who came from Eng. on the "Mary & John" (1630); now Hist. Soc. Hqs. On grounds is another old H. (O.1806) & outbuildings with old farm implements, vehicles. 31 Shirley St. (in adj. **Roxbury**), **Shirley-Eustis H.** (1748.very fine), home of 18th cent. Gov. Wm. Shirley. On Ashmont St., **All Saints Ch.** (1894.Goth.by Ralph Adams Cram.).

Cont. on Broadway (W) to J. with Dorchester St. & cont. (L) on it to J. with St.C37. (L) (S) here (Columbia Rd. & Old Colony Pkwy.), along shore front, past **Columbus Pk.** (bath.beach), on Dorchester Bay, to J. with St.3, which take (L) to J. with Southern Artery, as St.3 is called at this point. Take Rd. (R) here into Quincy.

**10. QUINCY** (sett. 1625).

First sett. by Thos. Morton at Merrymount. Morton, because of his hostility to Puritanism & encouragement of "heathenish practices," such as riotous celebration of May Day, but also because of his competition with Plymouth for Ind. trade, was arrested by Miles Standish. First sentenced to death, he was finally dispatched to

Eng. On his return he was again arrested & sent back. Quincy is notable as home of 4 generations of the most famous Amer. family, the Adamses. John Hancock, Rev. patriot, was also a native. John Adams, 1st Vice-Pres. & 2nd Pres. of U.S., was born (Oct. 19, 1785) & lived here, when not at seat of govt., with his wife, Abigail, whose letters give an amusing picture of the period. His son, John Q. Adams, 6th Pres., was also born in Quincy. After serving one term as Pres. & being defeated for a 2nd, he was elected to House of Representatives. Here he braved the majority by his insistence that the House receive petitions of abolitionists. When a very old man, he won out. The petitions were finally accepted. Charles Francis Adams, of the next generation, was U.S. minister to Britain during Civil War. He contributed greatly toward keeping Britain from openly siding with Confeds. Perhaps the 2 most distinguished of the 4 sons of Charles Francis were Henry & Brooks. Henry was author of the much-read "Mont-Saint-Michel & Chartres," a re-interpretation of the Middle Ages, & "The Education of Henry Adams," which has become a classic among Amer. autobiographies. Brooks wrote "Law of Civilization & Decay" which anticipated much that has been written since on same subject. Quincy today is a lively commercial town. Shipbuilding & granite-quarrying are among most important industries. The old Yankee pop. that John Quincy Adams so long represented in Congress, has been swamped by influx from abroad that has changed racial make-up of most New England cities.

PTS. OF INT.: (1) 135 Adams St., **Adams Mansion Nat. Hist. Site** (O.exc.Mon.sm. fee.guides) est. by Fed. Gov., 1946. Hqs., 135 Adams St., Quincy. Here is **Adams Mansion** (O.exc.Mon.sm.fee.guides.1731.adds.), named by John Adams "Peacefield." Oldest part built 1731, by Maj. Leonard Vassall. Bought by Adams, 1787. He added a sec. Other adds. were made by John Quincy & Charles Francis. Brooks Adams, who died 1927, was last of family to occupy it. Site also incl. lib., garden, stables, furnishings, portraits, relics. (2) 129 Franklin St., **John Adams Birthpl.** (O. sm.fee.rest.1896.int.inter.); old Adams cradle, belongings of John & Abigail Adams. (3) 131 Franklin St., **John Quincy Adams Birthpl.** (O.Apr.1-Nov.1.sm.fee.1663.rest. 1896); china, furnishings, John Q.'s law office. (4) Hancock Ave. & Butler Rd., **Dorothy Quincy H.** (O.Apr.19-Nov.1.sm.fee.1639-1700.remod.1706) built by Wm. Coddington, a founder of R.I. (see); & birthpl. of Dorothy Quincy, wife of John Hancock; antique furniture. (5) 1226 Hancock St., **Ch. of the Presidents** (1828.by Alex.Parris), so-called because both John & John Q. Adams were members; Old Cemetery (1666) where Quincys & Adamses are buried. (6) **Crane Mem. Lib.** (O.by H.H.Richardson.very fine). (7) 20 Muirhead St., **Josiah Quincy H.** (O.wks.sm.fee. 1770). (8) **Granite Quarry.** (9) In Merrymount Pk., **Mon.** to John & John Q. Adams, by B. W. Saville. (10) **Fore R. Shipyards** of Bethlehem Steel Co.

From Quincy take Washington St. (SE to J. with St.3, on which tour cont. Here is J. with St.3A (see). Continue on St.3, to **WEYMOUTH** (sett.1630), at **c.13.5.** on Fore R. Good pub. bath. beaches at Hough's Neck & Nantasket Beach. Weymouth's most important industries are shoes & granite. PTS. OF INT.: Cor. Norton & North Sts., **Abigail Adams Birthpl.** (O.1740.rest.). 75 Commercial St., **Sam. Arnold H.** (c.1803). On Columbian Sq., **Fogg Lib.** (O.wks.exc.Wed.aft.); Weymouth Hist. Soc. coll. 1284 Washington St., **Old Toll H.** (c.1800), 1st house built of Weymouth seam-faced granite. From Weymouth, take Union St. (R) to J. with Franklin St. at 16m & take latter (R) to J. with St.128 at 17m.

SIDE TRIP: From J. take St.128 (R) 2m to **Braintree** (sett.1st half 17th cent.), 1st known as Mt. Wollaston, after Capt. Wollaston, companion of Thos. Morton (see Quincy above). City is today industrial with shoes, paper & oil among chief products. In this city occurred the 1920 payroll robbery of which Sacco & Vanzetti were accused (see Dedham). On Washington St. bet. Taylor & Central Sts., **Town Hall** in which is kept orig. deed (1665) from Inds. granting site of city to settlers. 766 Washington St., **French H.** (1695) on land continuously owned by same family since founding of colony.

Main tour cont. (L) (W) on St.128 through **BLUE HILLS RESERV.** (recr.f.boat. several Ls.), where is Harvard's **Blue Hill Observatory**, to J. with St.28 at **18.5.** Take latter (R) (N) here. At **22.** St.28 reaches **MILTON CENTER** (sett.1636) on Neponset R.; industrial city. On Canton Ave., **Milton Pub. Lib.** (O), hist. material, prints, paintings. On Center St. & Randolph Ave., **Milton Academy** (est.1807). Near-by, cemetery where Wendell Phillips is buried. In field, off Brush Hill Rd. near Fairmount Ave., **Rbt. Tucker H.** (pre-1681), oldest in Milton. 38 Adams St., in Lower Mills, is **Vose H.** (1773) where in 1774 were adopted the Suffolk Resolutions (see Dedham). 215 Adams St., **Reprod. of A. Lincoln Birthpl.** (O.appl.); hist. relics. 362 Adams St., **Nathan Babcock H.** (1753). 401 Adams St., **Gov. Belcher H.** (O. appl.1776.rest.); old gardens. Gov. Belcher assisted in founding Princeton Univ. Canton Ave., near Thacher St., **"Little Ch."** for children only, adj. First Parish Ch. Cont. (N) on St.28 to J. with St.138 (Blue Hill Ave.) with which St.28 now unites, at **23.5.** At **25.** J. with St.3 with which St.28 now unites (L) & cont.

SIDE TRIP: N. of J., c.1$^{m}$ on Blue Hill Ave., to **Franklin Field** (sports facils.). Blue Hill Ave. cont. (N) along E. side of **Franklin Pk.** (Zoo).

Cont. (L) on St.3-28 (Morton St.), along SW. side of Franklin Pk. to beautiful **FOREST HILLS CEMETERY.** Gen. Jos. Warren (killed at Bunker Hill), Wm. Lloyd Garrison, the great abolitionist, & Ed. Everett Hale, author of "The Man Without a Country," are buried here. Mon. on Grave of M. Milmore by D. C. French. Cont. on Arbor Way, past **Arnold Arboretum** (O.no autos.guidebooks avail.), with one of finest botanical gardens in U.S. Herbarium in Adm. Bldg., to J. at 27$^{m}$ with Center St. & US1 with which latter St.3-28 unite (N).

SIDE TRIPS: (A) From J. (S) (L) on Center St. (US1). At cor. of St. Theresa Ave. is **Roxbury Latin School** (1645), founded by Rev. John Eliot (known as Apostle to Inds.) as a free school, one of oldest schools in U.S. On Baker St., **Brook Farm** (O) now **Martin Luther Orphanage,** where in mid-19th cent. was est. one of most famous communal settlements, of which Emerson, Alcott, Hawthorne, Margaret Fuller & other notables were members. Main bldg. was burned in 1847. Hawthorne used Brook Farm as background for his "Blithedale Romance."
(B) Take Center St. (R) to J. with South St. At 12 South St. (Whitcomb Sq.) is **Loring-Greenough H.** (O.1758.very fine exter.& inter.); coll. card cases. 60 Burroughs St., in Jamaica Plain, **Children's Mus.** (O.wks.exc.Mon.Sun.aft.).

Cont. (N) on US1 (Jamaica Way) past **JAMAICA POND RESERV.** (restaurant. boat.f.by permit) to J. with Perkins St.

SIDE TRIP: Take latter (R) & then Center St. into **Roxbury.** At Eliot Sq., **First Ch.** (O. special days.1804) has orig. chair of John Eliot. At 183 Roxbury St., **Dillaway-Thomas H.** (O.Apr.1-Oct.1.Wed.aft.1750.int.inter.). At Warren Sq., **Statue of Gen. Jos. Warren** (see above) by Paul Bartlett. At Washington & Eustis Sts., **Eliot Burying Ground** (c.1630) with grave of John Eliot.

Cont. along Jamaica Way to J. with Huntington Ave. in Boston at **30.**

**VI. Loop Tour, BOSTON to WAYLAND & RETURN. 38. US20, St.126 & St.9**
Via: Watertown, (Newton), Waltham, (Weston), Wayland, (Sudbury), (Framingham Center), (Framingham), (Natick), (Wellesley), (Needham), Brookline.

This route incl. some industrial towns, in which are important pts. of int., hist. old towns incl. S. Sudbury with Longfellow's Wayside Inn & the Little Red Schoolhouse, & college town of Wellesley.

Take Beacon St. (W) from State H., then Commonwealth Ave., & then Brighton Ave., across Charles R. **6. WATERTOWN** (sett.1630), on Charles R., busy factory city & suburb. Development was early aided by power from R. A native son, B. R. Curtis, rendered dissenting opinion in the Dred Scott case as Assoc. Justice of U.S. Supreme Court. Later, in Congress, he cast deciding vote for Pres. Johnson's acquittal at latter's impeachment trial. PTS. OF INT.: (1) 562 Main St., **Abr. Browne, Jr., H.** (O.wks.aft.sm.fee.oldest sec.1690.adds.1720.rest.); 17th & 18th cent. rooms; & (2) **Rich. Derby's Barn** (O.appl.by McIntire); old vehicles. (3) Arsenal St., **U.S. Arsenal,** est. 1816. (4) On Riverside St., **Perkins Institute & Mass. Sch. for Blind** (O.wks.), founded 1829. Dr. S. G. Howe, whose wife was Julia Ward Howe (author of "Battle Hymn of the Republic"), was 1st director. Mus. (O.wks.Sat.morn.); nat. hist. coll. & material used in teaching blind. (5) On Charles R. Rd., **Statue of Sir R. Saltonstall,** one of 1st settlers (by H. H. Kitson).

SIDE TRIP: Take Galen St. (L) into **Newton** (sett.1639), suburb of Boston. John Eliot, apostle of the Inds., was 1st minister in the town. PTS. OF INT.: (1) Magnolia St., **Eliot Mem.** (2) At Chestnut Hill, **Boston College** (Cath.) with handsome Coll. Goth. bldgs. (3) At 400 Beacon St. also at Chestnut Hill, **Mary Baker Eddy H.** (O.wks.aft.appl.Boston Ch.). Mrs. Eddy lived here 1908-10. (4) In Newton Center, 1181 Center St., **Smith H.,** former home of Francis Smith, author of "America." (5) On Institution Ave., **Andover Newton Theological Seminary.** (6) In Oak Hill, on Homer St., **City Hall & War Mem.** In Mem. are miniature wax groups depicting major events in Amer. hist. (7) In Newton Lower Falls, at 2349 Washington St., **Baury H.** (O.1750), now hqs. of Lucy Jackson Chapter of D.A.R. (8) Near-by is a charming **Ch.** (O.1814). (9) In W. Newton is **First Unit. Ch.** (O. Goth.by Cram & Ferguson). (10) **Charles R. Reserv.** (bath.beach.recr.facils.) extends from near Newton Upper Falls to Boston.

**9. WALTHAM** (sett.1634). Info.: C. of C. Concerts, lectures at Hovey Mem. Institute. Waltham, on Charles R., has 154 plants turning out variety of products, with watches best-known. "Firsts" incl.: 1st factory (est.1813) where all operations from raw cotton to finished cloth were performed under 1 roof; & 1st manufacture of crayon pencils; here kerosene was 1st refined & made available for household use; clocks were here 1st successfully manufactured (1845) by machinery. Board of Education has est. unique school of watchmaking in cooperation with Waltham Watch Co. Prominent citizens incl.: Gov. Chris. Gore & Sam. Livermore, Rev. patriots (latter figures in Kenneth Roberts' "Northwest Passage"); Civil War Gen. Nath. P. Banks; Dan. H. Burnham, architect, known as father of the skyscraper. Ralph Waldo Emerson once taught at Waltham's Ripley School & Geo. K. Gissing taught Eng. at local high school.

PTS. OF INT.: (1) On Gore St., near Main, **Gov. Gore H.** (O.sm.fee.1802-04.very fine); period furniture. (2) On Crescent St., **Waltham Watch Co.** (O); coll. rare watches. Here watches were 1st manufactured by machine on system of interchangeable parts. (3) On South St., **Brandeis Univ.** (non-sectarian.founded 1947) which took over 100-a. campus & bldgs. of former Middlesex College. Name comm. late Louis D. Brandeis, noted liberal & Assoc. Justice of U.S. Supreme Court. Univ. was "founded in behalf of the nation's Jews" but is entirely non-sectarian. The "Castle" with 22″ thick walls, battlements & towers, affords fine views. (4) 735 Main St., **Pub. Lib.** (O.wks.); coll. concerning Amer. artist, Chas. Woodbury. (5) At Trapelo Rd., **Walter E. Fernald Sch.** (O.special days) for feeble-minded. (6) On Lyman St., **Theo. Lyman H.** (1798.attrib.to Sam.McIntire.adds.), once home of Theo. Lyman who served on Gen. Meade's staff during Civil War, wrote book, "Meade's Headquarters." **12.** J. with Wellesley St. & Old Upper Boston Post Rd.

SIDE TRIPS: (A) Take Wellesley St. (L) here. At 1.5m **Regis College** (Cath.) for women, on beautiful campus.

(B) Take Old Boston Post Rd. (R) into **Weston** (sett.1st half 17th cent.). **Weston Pub. Lib.** (O.aft.) with coll. of Japanese art. Cor. Concord & Boston Rds. (R), **Artemas Ward H.** (1785) (see Worcester). 662 Boston Post Rd., **Elisha Jones H.** (1781), where Tories met during Rev. About 1.5m from Weston on Concord Rd. is **Weston College** (Cath.1922. Jesuit Order), beautifully situated on hill. Grants Dr. of Divinity degrees. Seismological Observatory (O.appl.)

**16. WAYLAND** (sett.1st half 17th cent.). **Unit. Ch.** (1815). J. with St.126 on which Loop Tour cont. (S).

SIDE TRIPS: (A) On Old Sudbury Rd., (R) c.1m, **Lydia Child H.** (O.appl.); home of abolitionist, associate of Wm. Lloyd Garrison.

(B) At 2.5m (W) of Wayland, on US20, is J. with Concord Rd.
Take latter (R) short distance to **Goodnow Lib.** (O); rare items. On Concord Rd., c.0.5m from J., is **Goulding H.** (O.c.1690.rest.); old furnishings, woodwork. At 1.5m **Sudbury.** Handsome old **Adam Howe H.**

(C) At 5m (W) of Wayland, on US20, is J. with Old Boston Post Rd.
Take latter (R) c.0.5m to **The Wayside Inn** (O.sm.fee.1686.rest.adds.) in S. Sudbury; celebrated by Longfellow & now owned by Henry Ford. Washington, Lafayette & Dan. Webster put up at Inn, built by Sam. Howe. Ezekiel Howe led company of Sudbury men in the Battle of Concord. Inn has period furnishings, a parlor where Longfellow's "travelers sat," several bedrooms, incl. Longfellow's, Lafayette's. In **Coach H.** is Gov. Eustis' Coach, in which Lafayette & Dan. Webster rode to laying of cornerstone of Bunker Hill Mon. In **Longfellow Mem. Garden** is bust of poet. Less than 0.5m from Inn is **Redstone Sch.,** claimed (but disputed) to be school of "Mary Had a Little Lamb" fame. Also near are charming **Martha-Mary Chapel** (1940) built of timber leveled by 1937 hurricane & an ancient **Grist Mill.**

**21.** On St.126 is J. with St.9 on which main trip cont. (E).

SIDE TRIP: (W) on St.9 c.0.5m to **Framingham Center.** On Vernon St., **Hist. & Nat. Hist. Soc.** (O.Sat.aft.summer). On Maynard Rd., **Framingham St. Teachers College,** founded 1839, one of 1st teachers training schools.

**23.5.** is J. with St.27.

SIDE TRIP: Take latter (R) into **Natick,** home of Henry Wilson, famous as "The Cobbler of Natick," abolitionist & U.S. Vice-Pres. (1873-75). On Common he is comm. by a **Stone.** Take Union St. into S. Natick. **Natick Hist. & Lib. Soc.** (O.2 days wkly.aft.); hist. material. Stone on **Site of Ch.** where John Eliot preached to Inds. On Pleasant St., **Stowe H.** (1816), boyhood home of Prof. Calvin Stowe, husband of Harriet Beecher Stowe, author of "Uncle Tom's Cabin." Tablet marking **Grave of Takwambait,** one of Eliot's converts.

**28. WELLESLEY HILLS,** where is Stone Clock Tower. Take Washington St. (St.16) here (R) into **Wellesley** (sett.1660), in hilly countryside. Charles R., Waban L. & Morse Pond provide recr. facils. Town was named for Sam. Welles, early settler. Wellesley men fought at Lexington. Town is important educational center & home of Wellesley College. It is claimed that Dr. W. T. G. Morton, 1st user of ether & anesthetic, was resident (1846) when he made discovery. Another resident was Gamaliel Bradford, biographer. PTS. OF INT.: (1) Washington St. & Pond Rd., **Welles H.** (c.1770), home of Sam. Welles. (2) Also on Washington St., **Hunnewell Gardens.** (3) Next to City Lib. is stone comm. **Site of W. T. G. Morton H.** (4) On Wellesley Sq., is a charming **Ch.** (1918), 4th on the site. (5) On Central St., **Wellesley College** (women.guides.chartered 1870); campus borders on Waban L. In 1914, main bldg., College Hall, burned. Since then, many new bldgs. have been erected, for most part in Coll. Goth. manner. Especially noteworthy are **Hetty H. R. Green Hall,** in which are murals by Albert Herter; **Farnsworth Art Mus.** (O.Mon.-Fri.aft.) with fine coll. paintings, sculpture, art objects; **Claflin Hall** in whose main room are carvings illustrating "Alice in Wonderland"; **Alumnae Hall** (1925.by Cram & Ferguson). (6) On Wellesley Ave. is **Babson Institute** for business training; **Coleman Bldg.** (O.wks.Sat.Sun.hols.aft.summer) has huge relief map of U.S. which required half a generation to construct.

**36.5. BROOKLINE** (sett.1638), fashionable Boston residential suburb. Known orig. as "Muddy River." Home of poetess, Amy Lowell, whose idiosyncrasies of dress & of smoking black cigars, aroused comment. PTS. OF INT.: (1) 347 Harvard St., **Edw. Devotion H.** (O.Sat.aft.& on appl.sm.fee.1680); orig. furniture. (2) 361 Washington St., **Pub. Lib.** (O.wks.Sat.aft.& eve.1910.by R.C.Sturgis); coll. of paintings. (3) 1773 Beacon St., **All Saints Ch.** (1926.Goth.by Cram,Goodhue & Ferguson). Fine rose window by C. J. Connick, who did windows in N.Y.'s Cathedral of St. John the Divine. (4) 120 Seaver St., **Longyear Foundation** (O.wks.exc.hols.aft.), coll. of Mary Baker Eddy material. (5) On Netherlands St., **Netherlands H.** (copy of 16th cent. Dutch Town Hall). (6) 1341 Beacon St., **Brookline Trust Co.;** E. B. Dane coll. of tapestries (incl. 4 Gobelin tapestries). (7) 215 Warren St., **Davis-Cabot Goddard H.** (1730.int.inter.). (8) 235 Goddard Ave., **Goddard H.** (1732.18th cent.adds.). **38.** Huntington Ave. (Boston).

## VII. BOSTON to METHUEN. 29. St.28 (N)

Via: (Somerville), (Medford), Stoneham, Reading, & Andover.

This is first sec., running through Boston's suburban area, of St.28. Follow US1 (see US1, Sec. 12) from Boston. At **6.5.** St.28 branches off (L) from US1. At **c.7.** J. with Salem St.

SIDE TRIP: Take latter (L) into **Medford** (sett.c.1630), on Mystic R., famous in old days for its rum & clipper ships. PTS. OF INT.: (1) 121 High St., **Medford Pub. Lib.,** formerly Thatcher Magoun H. (O.wks.1835); rare items. (2) 15 George St., **Usher Royall H.** (O.aft. summer.exc.Mon.& Fri.sm.fee.1637.adds.1690 & 1732.very fine); period furnishings. (3) 350 Riverside Ave., **Peter Tufts H.** (O.sm.fee.c.1678); superb oak beams, early staircase. Said to be oldest brick house in Amer. (4) 57 High St., **Andrew Hall H.** (1703) where Paul Revere made 1st stop on his ride. (5) At Grove & High Sts., **Board** marking Paul Revere's route. Here returning Minute Men were served food & chocolate "but no tea." (6) Off S. Border Rd., **Lawrence Observatory;** tower, fine view. (7) Salem St., **Old Burial Ground** (1705). (8) On Bradley Rd., **Old Garrison H.** (9) **Major Wade H.** (1685). (10) On Bradbury Ave., **Old Wellington H.** (1634). (11) On College St., **Tufts College** (coed.) on fine campus with some 75 bldgs. College named for Chas. Tufts who gave hill on which it stands. When asked by a friend what he was going to do with the hill, he said, "I will set a light on it." There is an undergrad. school, grad. school of Arts & Sciences & Schs. of Engineering, Religion, Law & Diplomacy. Tufts Medical Sch. & Dental College are in Boston. Affiliated is **Jackson College for Women. Goddard Chapel** has fine tower, mem. windows, busts. **Barnum Mus.** (O.wks.Sat.morn.); P. T. Barnum's curiosities incl. Jumbo, largest elephant ever in captivity. Adj. campus is a **Rev. Powder H.**

St.28 now crosses Middlesex Fells Reserv. in which are several lakes & a zoo. **12. STONEHAM** (sett.1645).

SIDE TRIP: Take Franklin St. (R) from Stoneham 3m into **Melrose.** 253 Upham St., **Phineas Upham H.** (O.appl.1703.rest.1914); period inter. Near Melrose is **Mt. Hood Pk. & Observatory;** fine view.

**15. READING.** 99 Washington St., **Parker Tavern** (O.Sun.aft.summer); period furnishings. On Common is **Ch.,** reprod. of Boston's Old South Ch.

SIDE TRIP: Take St.129 (R) along Quannapowitt L., (recr.) into **Wakefield** (sett.1639). **Bebe Mem. Lib.** (by Cram & Ferguson). On Quannapowitt L., at Church St., **Col. Jas. Hartshorne H.** (O.1681.adds.18th cent.rest.); antiques, int. garden. Near Wakefield are **Hart's Hill** & **Wakesaw Reserves.** (recr.).

**19.** J. with St.62 (see Boston loop tour I). **21.5.** J. with St.125 leading (R) to **Harold Parker St. For.** (260 as.camp.bath.pic.hik.h.f.); several lakes.

**25. ANDOVER** (sett.c.1642). PTS. OF INT.: (1) **Phillips Andover Academy,** founded 1778. Claims to be oldest boys' boarding sch. in U.S. Org. by Sam. & John Phillips (latter also founded Phillips Exeter Acad. in Exeter, N.H.). Sch. has about 150 bldgs.; most of modern ones are in Col. Georg. style, by well-known architects like Guy Lowell, Chas. A. Pratt, & Perry, Shaw & Hepburn. Graduates incl.: Sam. F. B. Morse, inventor of the telegraph; Oliver Wendell Holmes, who celebrated sch. in poem, "The School Boy" & Henry L. Stimpson, U.S. Sec. of War & State. On campus are: **Pearson Hall** (1818.by Bulfinch.remod.1922) which was orig. sch. chapel; **Cochran Ch.** (1932.Georg.); **Bulfinch Hall** (1818.designed by Bulfinch), described by Holmes in his poem; **Addison Gallery of Amer. Art** (O.wks.Sun.aft.1931) with notable coll. of Amer. paintings of Col., 19th cent., & contemporary periods, & Amer. ship models, Col. furnishings, & loan exhibits. **Holmes Lib.;** rare books, hist items. On Chapel Ave., **Andover Inn** (O.1930), old portraits, prints & furniture. Phillips & Main Sts., **Archeology Bldg.** (O.wks.Sun.aft.), material on Amer. Inds., etc. **Mem. Tower** (1923) with fine carillon. Near-by is **Armillary Sphere** by Paul Manship. 80 Bartlett St., **Stowe H.** (1828.remod.), residence of Harriet Beecher Stowe, buried in **Chapel Cemetery** near-by. 6 School St., **Samaritan H.,** where Mrs. Stowe also lived. Charming **Moncrieff Cochran** (Bird) **Sanctuary** (90 as.). (2) 189 Main St., **Phelps H.** (supposedly by Bulfinch). (3) 97 Main St., **Deacon Amos Blanchard H.** (O.aft.appl.1819.int.inter.); period furniture & Staffordshire glass; Hqs. of Hist. Soc. (4) 147 Main St., **America H.,** home of Sam. F. Smith who wrote words of the song, "America." (5) **Abbot Academy** (girls.est.1829). On campus are **John Esther Art Gallery, & Abbot Hall** (1829). (6) 70 Elm St., **Isaac Abbot Tavern** (c.1680). (7) At Andover St. & Argilla Rd., **Ben. Abbot H.** (1685). (8) 2 Chestnut St., **Kneeland-Marland Cottage** (1786), where Rev. patriot, John Kneeland, made welcoming address to Lafayette (1825). (9) 210 Main St., **Newman H.** (1811), where Holmes lived as student & which he described in his "The School Boy." At Andover is J. with St.110.

SIDE TRIP: At 11$^{m}$ (R) (NE) on St.110 is **Haverill** in the Whittier country (see St.110).

**26. SHAWSHEEN** village. [Take St.133 (R) here 2$^{m}$ into N. Andover, with some fine old Hs. 153 Academy Rd., **North Andover Hist. Soc. Cottage** (O.1796); pewter, early textiles, appliances, laces, gowns, etc. Also the **Bradstreet H.** (1667)]. **29. METHUEN.** (For Lawrence, near-by, see St.28.)

## HARTFORD

Through RR., plane & bus conns. Accoms.: all types. Info.: C. of C. in Old State H.; Auto Club of Hartford. Golf: 2 mun. & 6 private courses. Boat. on Conn. R. Concerts, operas & plays at Bushnell Mem. Hall. Hartford Rose Festival at Elizabeth Pk., June.

Hartford, on (W) bank of Conn. R., is st.'s capital, largest city & business & financial center. Once it was also a busy port, but shipping eventually moved to more favorably situated towns. Insurance is chief industry today. Underwriting started here before end of 18th cent. in fire & marine lines. Life underwriting & casualty insurance developed in next cent. Insurance companies now employ some 15,000 workers & have aggregate assets of c.$3,000,000,000. Several insurance companies' skyscrapers are visible at a great distance emphasizing, visually, importance of these enterprises. Hartford & its metropolitan area also constitute an important industrial dist. Here took place early experiments in interchangeability of parts that laid foundations of mod. Amer. industry. The Columbia bicycle was 1st built & pneumatic tires were 1st produced here. Among many important plants of city & of E. Hartford are: Pratt & Whitney—airplane engines, Hamilton Standard Co.—propellers, Colt's Firearms Co.—maxim silencers, Fuller Brush Co., & 2 of country's largest typewriter plants—Royal & Underwood.

Hartford started as Dutch trading post, 1623, & fort was built, 1633. In 1636, Thos. Hooker & a group of settlers arrived from Newton (Cambridge, Mass.). The Fundamental Orders, one of 1st Amer. documents to proclaim principle of government "by the people," was adopted 1639. The Dutch were finally expelled, 1654. Settlement became capital in 1665, when Hartford & New Haven Colonies were consolidated, but New Haven alternated with Hartford in this role until 1875. In 1662, Charles II granted a charter providing for considerable autonomy. When, later, Gov. Andros made an attempt to get possession of this document, citizens removed & hid it in the "Charter Oak" until the hated Gov. was driven out. Hartford Hist. Soc. has a piece of orig. parchment. Among Hartford's citizens were many literary lights—Mark Twain, Harriet Beecher Stowe & Chas. Dudley Warner, to name only a few. There are a number of institutions of higher learning, outstanding art museums, an excellent pub. lib.; Pk. system is unusually extensive (2,700 as.).

PTS. OF INT.: (1) Capitol Hill, **St. Capitol** (O.1878.by Rich. Upjohn). Lofty dome (fine view) is surmounted by statue: "Genius of Conn.", by R. Rogers. On 1st floor corridor: battle flags, relics, orig. gravestone from grave of Gen. Israel Putnam (see Brooklyn, Conn.). On 2nd floor: chair of the President of the Senate is carved of wood from the "Charter Oak." (2) On **Capitol Grounds** & (3) in **Bushnell Pk.** adj., are several Mons. & statues, incl. "The Andersonville Prison Boy," by Bela Pratt, comm. Union troops who perished in Confed. prisons. (4) Opp. Capitol, **State lib.** (O); documents, hist. material. In W. Wing, Supreme Court Rm.; Albert Herter's mural, "Signing of the Colonial Orders." In S. Wing, Mem. Hall; relics, incl. a duplicate of the Chas. II Charter, Gilbert Stuart's "George Washington" & a numismatic coll. (5) Washington St. & Capitol Ave., equestrian **Statue of Lafayette,** reprod. of orig. by Paul Bartlett in Paris. (6) 95 Washington St., **County Bldg.** (Mod.by Paul Cret & Smith & Bassette); murals by J. R. L. Hubert. (7) 166 Capitol Ave., **Bushnell Mem. Hall** (by H.Corbett); concerts & operas. (8) 307 Main St., **South Ch.** (Congr. 1827.George.). (9) Charter Oak Ave. & Charter Oak Pl., **Charter Oak Mem.** comm. spot where stood oak in which charter was hidden, Oct. 31, 1687. (10) 675 Main St., **Center (First) Ch.** (1807); old stained-glass windows. (11) Adj., on Gold St., **Burial Ground** (1640), oldest in Hartford. (12) Bet. Main & Prospect Sts., near river, a group of bldgs. (O.wks.): **Morgan Mem. Lib.** (1910.by B.W.Morris); **Colt Mem.; Wadsworth Athenaeum** (1842.by Ithiel Town); & **Avery Mem.** In Wadsworth Athenaeum is Hartford Pub. Lib.; unusual coll. rare books, incunabula, etc. On 2nd floor, Conn. Hist. Soc.; rare publications, remnant of "Charter," & other hist. items. In Morgan, Colt & Avery Mems. are: museum containing J. P. Morgan's antiques & bronzes; coll. of paintings, incl. examples of some of greatest masters, from 1490 to date; Wallace Nutting Coll. early Amer. furniture; period rooms, 18th & 19th cents.; tapestry, arms & armor, early Central & South Amer. art. Hartford Sch. of Art is located here. (13) 38 Prospect St., **Hunt Mem.** (O.Georg.by McKim, Mead & White); medical lib. (14) 26 Grove St., **Travelers Insurance Bldg.** Tower (O.wks.by Donn Barber) is 527′ high; searchlight. (15) Main St. & Central Row, **Old State H.** (O.wks.1796.Fed.by Bulfinch.adds.); beautiful example of period. Senate & House chambers, Supreme Court Room & Sec. of State's office are noteworthy. (16) 955 Main St., **Christ Ch. Cathedral** (Episc.1829.Goth.Rev.). (17) 73 Forest St., **Harriet Beecher Stowe H.,** home of author of "Uncle Tom's Cabin." (18) 57 Forest St., **Chas. Dudley Warner H.** Here lived editor & novelist, co-author with Mark Twain of "The Gilded Age." (19) 351 Farmington Ave., **Mark Twain H. & Mem. Lib.** (O.wks.). House was built by Twain. Mem. Room has bust, relics. One wing somewhat resembles pilot house to remind Twain of river-boat days. (20) Grand Ave. & Elizabeth St., **Hartford Seminary Foundation.** Most of the bldgs. are Goth. Seminary represents a union of 3 religious schools. Case Mem. Lib. (O). in Avery Hall; outstanding coll. of theological material. (21) 915 Prospect Ave., **Elizabeth Pk.** (100 as.); famous rose garden. (22) Cor. Main & Elizabeth Sts., **Kenney Mem. Tower** (Goth.). (23) 256 Blue Hills Ave., **St. Justin's Ch.** (Cath.by Whitin & McMann). (24) Main St., **Kenney Pk.** (694 as.sports facils.). (25) Park St., **Pope Pk.** (recr.swim.). (26) Broad & Summit Sts., **Trinity College** (est.1823.campus 80 as.) orig. occupied Capitol Hill. In center of campus is statue of Bishop Brownell, College's founder. Bldgs. are Goth. Oldest, dating from late 1870's & early 1880's & designed by Wm. Burgess, were probably 1st college bldgs. in Coll. Goth. style in U.S. **Chapel** (1933.Goth.by Frohman, Robb & Little) is finest of group. In Boardman Hall is Mus. of Nat. Hist. (27)

Wethersfield Ave. near Conn. R., **Colt Pk.** (174 as.) with Mem. to Sam Colt, arms manufacturer. (28) Two int. old Hs. are: 91 Lafayette St., **Timothy Steele H.** (1715) reputedly oldest in city; 396 Main St., **Butler McCook H.** (1782). (29) In addition to institutions of higher learning mentioned above, Hartford has: **Hartford College of Law & Insurance** of the Univ. of Conn.; **La Sallette Missionary College; Hillyer College; St. Joseph College** (for women). (30) Most of the bldgs. of the insurance companies, located in vic. of the St. Capitol, either near Main St. or near Asylum St. are of architectural int.

## TRIPS OUT OF HARTFORD

### I. HARTFORD to BOLTON NOTCH. 13. US6 (E).

**1.** (E) of Hartford on US6 is **EAST HARTFORD,** industrial suburb specializing in airplane engines & parts. On Main St., **Congr. Ch.** (1836), **Town Hall** (1833), & **Center Burying Ground** (1711) with graves of Rev. patriots. At Green, on Pitkin St., **Pitkin H.** (18th cent.). On Silver Lane are several int. old Hs. On a smaller Green, c.0.5m from city's center, on Silver Lane, **Rochambeau Boulder** where Fr. army camped. On King St., c.3m from city's center, off US5, is **Mon. Comm. John Fitch** who constructed a steam-driven boat long before Fulton & had it operating on Delaware R. (see New Jersey & Va.). **7.5. SOUTH MANCHESTER.** Large **Cheney Bros. Mills** (silk). **13. BOLTON NOTCH** (see below).

### II. HARTFORD to MANSFIELD CORNERS. 22.5. US44 (E).

US44 & US6 parallel each other through same towns & for part of distance to Bolton Notch at **13.,** then unite. Just before US44 reaches Bolton Notch, is J. with Rd.

SIDE TRIP: Take latter (R) short distance to **Bolton Notch,** fine bit of scenery.

**16.5.** on US44, **COVENTRY.** Here is J. with St.31.

SIDE TRIP: Take latter (R) (SE) 6m to **South Coventry.** (NW) of S. Coventry, c.1.5m on St.31, are **Root H.** (1st half 18th cent.) & **Ripley H.** (late 18th cent.). On Main St., **Bidwell H.** (1st quarter 19th cent.) & two old **Chs.** A short distance (R) from town's center is **Nathan Hale Cemetery** in which are buried members of Hale family & Asa Wright, who served with Nathan Hale. About 1m (L) from town is **Huntington H.** (1763) where Nathan Hale studied with Rev. Dr. Huntington.

Take Rd. (R) from Huntington H. 2.5m & then (L) 1m, to **Birthpl. of Nathan Hale** (O.Sun.appl.mid.-18th cent.rest.); some original items of Nathan Hale's day. Hale was hanged as a spy during Rev. by Brit. & at execution said, "I only regret that I have but one life to lose for my country." (see Halesite, N.Y.).

St.31 cont. from S. Coventry to J. with St.32 which later turns (S) to J. with US6 just (W) of Willimantic.

Cont. from Coventry on US44. **22.5. MANSFIELD CORNERS,** J. with St.195.

SIDE TRIP: Take latter (R). 1.5m **Conn. State Univ.,** founded originally as Storrs Agricultural School, a land-grant college, in 1881. Campus proper comprises c.110 as.; c.1600 additional as. are owned by College, incl. farm for practical education in agric. College of Pharmacy, in New Haven; School of Law & Insurance, in Hartford; additional educational facils. in other cities of St. Worth a visit is **Crombie Beach Mem. Coll.** (O) of c.75 paintings. Cont. on St.195. 5.5m **Mansfield Center.** Fine old Congr. Ch. **Old Cemetery,** with graves of Inds. Just (N) of town, on St.195, **Eleazar Williams H.** (early 18th cent.), oldest in township.

### III. HARTFORD to FARMINGTON. 13. US6 (W), St.10.

**11.** On US6, J. with St.10. Take St.10 (R) (N) to **FARMINGTON** (sett.1st half 17th cent.), which developed a variety of industries in late 18th & early 19th cents.—glass, hats, textiles, etc., but today is merely market town for vic. There are many fine old Hs., evidence of former commercial prosperity. PTS. OF INT.: (1) Main St. & Farmington Ave., **Rochambeau Mon.** comm. halt here of Fr. army (1781). (2) 37 High St., **Stanley-Whitman H.** (Farmington Mus.). (O.Tues.Wed.all yr.&Fri. Sat.winter.sm.fee.c.1660.rest.1934); notable for unusual overhang & small windows; antique furnishings, relics; int. herb garden. (3) On Main St., **Congr. Ch.** (1771), designed by Jas. Woodruff, architect of many of town's old Hs. (4) On Main St. are at least a dozen fine old Hs. (5) On Main St., **Old Cemetery** (1685). (6) On Maple St., **Riverside Cemetery** with Mon. comm. Tunxi Inds. & grave of Foone, one of the Negroes of the "Amisted." The case of the "Amisted," slave ship whose human cargo mutinied to win freedom, is famous in Amer. legal hist. John Quincy Adams finally won the "cargo's" freedom in U.S. Supreme Ct. (7) School St., **Barney Mem. Lib.** (O); exhibits. (8) Mill Lane, **Old Grist Mill** (late 18th cent.) still grinding corn meal. (9) On Farmington Ave., **Elm Tree Inn** (O.17th cent.-late 18th cent.adds.). High St. also has int. old Hs.

**IV. HARTFORD to NEW HARTFORD. 19. US44** (W).

**4.** W. of Hartford is J. with Rd.

SIDE TRIP: Take latter (L) 1.5$^{m}$ into **W. Hartford.** 227 Main St., **Birthpl. of Noah Webster** (late 17th cent.adds.), author of earliest & best-known Amer. dictionary.

**8.** J. with US202-St.10. At J. **Old Farms Inn** (2nd half 18th cent.) & **Phelps Tavern** (late 18th cent.), now apartment H. **9. AVON** (sett.1738) **with Congr. Ch.** (1st quarter 19th cent.by D.Hoadley.alts.).

SIDE TRIP: (N) 5$^{m}$ on US202-St.10 to **Simsbury** (sett. 1st half 17th cent.). **Congr. Ch.** (1st half 19th cent.Gr.Rev.). 11$^{m}$ **Granby** (sett.1664); also has several noteworthy old Hs. J. with St.20. Take latter (E). At 14$^{m}$ J. with Rd. leading (L) 1$^{m}$ to **Newgate Prison** (O.1773. sm.fee), showing cruel penal methods of Rev. times. At 15$^{m}$ on St.20 **E. Granby.** Early 19th cent. **Congr. Ch.** & fine old Hs. in vic. In E. Granby, take St.187 (S) (R) to J. with St.9 at 19.5$^{m}$ & then St.9 (S) through **N. Bloomfield. St. Andrews Ch.** (Episc.18th cent.) & **Bloomfield** at 25$^{m}$. 2 fine old churches. 30$^{m}$ **Hartford.**

**19. NEW HARTFORD. Congr. Ch.** (1828) & **Parsonage** (1838).

**V. EAST HARTFORD to COLCHESTER. 22.5. St.2** (SE).

**0. EAST HARTFORD** (see Trip I). **4.5. WELLES CORNER. Sam. Welles H.** (late 18th cent.alt.) where once lived Gideon Welles, Lincoln's Sec. of Navy. J. with St.17.

SIDE TRIP: Take latter (R) short distance to **Glastonbury** (sett.1650), suburb of Hartford. In city & vic., mostly on St.17, are number of fine old 18th cent. Hs. At 1.5$^{m}$, (SE) of center of city, on St.17 (R), **Kimberly H.** (1st half 18th cent.). During 19th cent., here lived 5 Kimberly sisters who are said to have drawn 1st antislavery petition, presented to Congress by John Quincy Adams. (See Quincy, Mass.) The Kimberlys were ardent suffragettes after Civil War, refusing to pay taxes as long as they did not have the right to vote. St.17 cont. to **South Glastonbury** in which are several int. old Hs. & **Rattlesnake Hunt Club,** whose annual snake hunt used to be featured in the "N.Y. Sun." At 9$^{m}$ on St.17 is **Gildersleeve**, on Conn. R., formerly shipbuilding town. **Congr. Ch.** (1850). 11$^{m}$ J. at Portland with US6A (see).

**8. LANE'S TOWER** (O). Fine view. **9.5.** on St.2 is J. with Rd. leading (R) to **Meshomasic St. For.** (7,226 as.pic.recr.). **14. MARLBORO,** J. with US6A (see). **22.5. COLCHESTER.** Here is J. with St.85 to New London. (For Colchester & St.85 see New London.)

**VI. Loop Tour. HARTFORD & ENVIRONS. 38. US5, St.71 & St.175.**

Via: Berlin, Meriden, Kensington, Newington Center.

**11.5.** (S) of Hartford on US5 is **BERLIN.** Manufacturing town since mid-18th cent., orig. specialized in tin utensils sold all over country by Yankee pedlers. Town was birthpl. of Emma H. Willard, pioneer in women's education. Robbins St., **Congr. Ch.** (late 18th cent.) near which is ancient oak dating from town's early days. **Worthington Academy** (late 18th cent.). **Fuller Tavern** (2nd half 18th cent.). **18. MERIDEN** (sett.2nd half 17th cent.). Sports facils. in city pks. Pub. beaches at Baldwin's & Beaver Ponds. Swim. & boat. at Hubbard Pk. Accoms. all types.

Meriden is known as the "silver city" because here in early 19th cent. began production of silver & silverplate ware. Today, International Silver Co., several of whose plants are in Meriden, is greatest manufacturer in this field. But Meriden has never been a 1-industry town. In 1849, there were 34 plants making Brittania ware, combs, cutlery, bone buttons, spring balances & harness trimmings. Today 100 factories employ c.15,000, turning out silver & silverplate ware, ball bearings, lamps, electric fixtures, printing presses & household electrical equipment. Community Forum attracts well-known lecturers & a Civic Music Assoc. provides concerts. PTS. OF INT.: (1) E. Main & Broad Sts., **Center Ch.** (Congr.1831); columned portico & charming belfry. (2) Adj., **Bapt. Ch.** (1847); columned portico but simple steeple, characteristic of New England village Chs. (3) 48 State St., **International Silver Co.** (O.appl.). (4) 35 Center St., **St. Rose's Ch.** (Cath.), one of town's handsome mod. Chs. (5) There are a number of int. 18th cent. Hs.: 75 Curtis St., **Ben. Curtis H.** (late 18th cent.); Curtis & Ann Sts., **Berry H.** (1743); (SW) cor. Hall & Gale Aves., **Plumb H.** (1st half 18th cent.); Westfield Rd., **Hough H.** (1st half 18th cent.); 425 W. Main St., **Andrews H.** (18th cent.). (6) On US5, 0.5$^m$ (S) of Meriden, at 677 Colony St., Old **1711 Inn** (O), where delegates of the Inter.-Amer. Conference were entertained in 1944. (7) 2$^m$ (S) of Meriden, **Hubbard Pk.** (12,000 as.pic.trls.). Here is Mirror L. overshadowed by twin peaks of the Hanging Hills—W. Peak (1,007′) & E. Peak on which is Castle Craig; fine view. Both peaks reached by hys.

At a point slightly (W) of Meriden, take St.71 (N). **27. KENSINGTON** (sett.late 17th cent.). **Congr. Ch.** (2nd half 18th cent.) In village, near Ch., & on Christian Lane, are several 18th cent. Hs. Cont. on St.71 to J. with St.175 on (E) edge of New Britain at **28.5.** Turn (W) here into **NEW BRITAIN** (sett.late 17th cent.). Known as country's hardware center, its development dates from early 19th cent. It has always produced a great variety of products. Today some 100 plants employing 31,000 turn out hardware, household appliances, ball bearings, knit goods, clothing. An extensive pk. system incl. Stanley Quarter Pk. (swim.golf) & Willow Brook Pk. (swim.). New Britain was birthpl. of Elihu Burritt who, while working as a blacksmith, educated himself & finally became founder of, in its day, much-discussed organization for promotion of universal brotherhood. PTS. OF INT.: W. Main St. & High St., **Pub. Lib.** (O) with New Britain Institute Mus. (O.aft.); natural hist., Amer. hist. exhibits & various curios. 56 Lexington St., **Art Mus.** (O); canvasses of Amer. painters. In Pk., **World War Mem.** Stanley St., **St. Teachers College** (Goth. bldgs.). Elm St., **Mon. Comm. Elihu Burritt.** 161 S. Main St., **St. Trade School.** On Mill St., **Willow Brook Pk.** with Spanish-Amer. War Mem. Tour now cont. on St.175 via Newington Center to **HARTFORD. 38.**

## VII. HARTFORD to MIDDLETOWN. 15. St.9 (S).

3. from Hartford on St.9 is J. with Hartford Ave. Take latter (L) to **Wethersfield** (sett.1634) on (W) side of Conn. R. Town early profited by its location & engaged in shipbuilding & foreign commerce. In 19th cent. considerable industrial development took place. Both shipping & industry have departed almost altogether, & today, town is suburb of Hartford. PTS. OF INT.: On Main St. many of the older bldgs. have been preserved, incl.: cor. Marsh St., **Congr. Ch.** (2nd half of 18th cent.alts.); adj. **Cemetery,** dating from 1698. On both sides of Main St., especially bet. Center & Church Sts., a number of 18th cent. Hs. No. 211, **Webb H.** (O.wks.Sun.aft.sm. fee.1678.adds.1752.rest.1916); antique furnishings. Here Washington & Rochambeau met to plan Yorktown campaign. Washington's room has been kept intact. No. 203, **Silas Deane H.** (pre-Rev.), home of founder of Amer. Navy. No. 196, **Hist. Soc.** (O), in school bldg.; hist. relics. No. 133, **Wright H.** (late 18th cent.), once school for girls. Mary Lyon, founder of Mt. Holyoke College, was pupil. No. 150, **Town Hall** (1801), once an Academy. On Broad St.: the Green. Here is **Wethersfield Elm,** dating from middle of 18th cent. 138 Broad St., **Skaats H.** (early 18th cent.). No. 249, **Williams H.** (late 17th cent.); fine example. State St., **State Prison** (1st half 19th cent.). In Chapel is mural by Genevieve Cowles.

**8.5.** on St.9 **ROCKY HILL,** once a booming river town. **Congr. Ch.** is fine early 19th cent. example. There are a number of int. old Hs. 69 Main St., **Duke of Cumberland Inn** (1767.Georg.), especially noteworthy. **13. CROMWELL** (sett.1st half 17th cent.), also formerly prosperous shipbuilding town. **First Congr. Ch.** (est.1715. built 1840). Here one minister rebuked the less honest members of the congregation as follows: "O Lord, some of us are so righteous, we would not shave ourselves on Sunday, but we would shave our neighbors on Monday." On Pleasant & Main Sts. are int. 17th & 18th cent. Hs.

**15. MIDDLETOWN** (sett.1650), on W. bank of Conn. R., was 1st known as Mattabeset, after local Ind. sachem. One of town's 17th cent. preachers, Sam. Stow, left a legacy which, with other bequests, formed basis of the Donation Fund, still used for city school district. In 1668 First Congr. Ch. was organized & Cotton Mather called it "the candlestick" which illumined the whole colony. Shipbuilding & the "three-corner trade"—slaves, sugar, rum—brought great prosperity. The town's Main St. was lined with shops of saddlers, hatters, apothecaries & silversmiths, rope-walks, taverns, slave markets, & churches. By 1756, Middletown was Conn.'s largest city. It played an active part in Rev. & Conn. General Assembly & Council of Committee of Safety met here, 1766-67. Local lead mine supplied Continental army with bullets. Prominent citizens incl.: Silas Hosmer, who signed Articles of Confederation; Col. John Meigs, who commanded raid on Sag Harbor, & fought at Stony Pt.; Major Gen. Sam Parson, who was a judge at court-martial of Maj. André; Commodore MacDonough, who fought at L. Champlain (1812); Rich. Alsop, one of the "Hartford wits," known as the "millionaire poet" because he inherited West Indies trade fortune; & Henry Clay Work, author of "Marching Through Georgia" & "Father, dear father, come home with me now." Because of Brit. interference with shipping during Rev. & War of 1812 & because of shift of commerce to more favored ports, Middletown turned to industry—mfg. of paper, powder, arms. Today it turns out a great variety of products, but is perhaps best-known as home of Wesleyan Univ.

PTS. OF INT.: (1) Main & Court Sts., **Middlesex Cty. Hist. Soc.** (O.1st & 3rd Fri. monthly); early Amer. material. (2) 151 Main St., **Sam. Mather H.** (early 19th cent.). (3) College St., **Christian Science Ch.** (early 19th cent.Gr.Rev.). (4) St. John Sq., **Riverside Cemetery** with grave of Commodore MacDonough. (5) High St., **Wesleyan Univ.,** founded 1831 on Site of the Academy of Capt. Partridge. Bldgs. of note: **South College** (1824), one of "Academy" bldgs.; **Mem. Chapel** (1871) comm. Wesleyan men who fell in Civil War; & windows to those who died in World Wars I & II as well. **Rich Hall;** theater & portraits. **Fisk Hall;** mathematical models. **Olin Lib.** (O.wks.Sun.aft.Ren.by Henry Bacon). Contains Hallock Room, coll. of Americana; Davison Art Rooms, art exhibits; Henry Bacon Room, relics of the architect of the Lincoln Mem. in Washington, D.C.; Wesleyan Memorabilia Room; & Gov. Winthrop Chair, dating from 1661. **Judd Hall** (O.special aft.); natural hist. & ethnographic coll. High St., **Alsop H.** (1836-38, owned by Univ.) is partly Gr.Rev. but shows Mediterranean influence. Frescoes, decorating exter. & inter. in Pompeian manner, believed to be by Brumidi, decorator of Capitol in Washington, D.C. High St., opp. Alsop H., **Russell H.** (1828.Gr.Rev.by Ithiel Town), a notable bldg. & mon. to wealth & culture produced by New England maritime commerce. It now houses Honors College.

**VIII. HARTFORD to CONN.-MASS. LINE. 21. US5A** (N).

This route follows W. bank of Conn. R. to Springfield, Mass., via Windsor & Windsor Locks.

**2.5. WILSON VILLAGE. Barber H.** (late 18th cent.), birthpl. of J. W. Barber, well-known Amer. historian. **6. WINDSOR** (sett.1633), located on W. side of Conn. R. in a tobacco growing region. Town has preserved some of its charm as early settlement, despite fact that it is practically a suburb of Hartford. Dutch had already built a ft. on present site, when 1st settlers from Plymouth Colony arrived, but were finally evicted. Oliver Ellsworth, signer of Decl. of Ind. & Chief Justice of U.S. Supreme Court, was a native, as was Gov. Roger Wolcott. PTS. OF INT.: (1) At Palisado Green are **Ship Mon.** to orig. settlers by E. B. L. Batchelder, & other mems. (2) 96 Palisado Ave., **Walter Fyler H.** (O.appl.1st half 17th cent.adds.18th cent.). (3) Also on Palisado Ave., **First Congr. Ch.** (1794.Gr.Rev.adds.). (4) To rear of Ch., **Palisado Cemetery,** dating from 1644. Among graves of notables are those of Oliver Ellsworth & Gov. Roger Wolcott. (5) 778 Palisado Ave., **Ellsworth Homestead** (O. wks.exc.Wed.;Sun.aft.May-Dec.1740), home of Chief Justice Oliver Ellsworth. A notable bldg. with colonial heirlooms, etc. Washington & Adams visited here. (6) On Palisado Ave., a number of other 18th & early 19th cent. Hs. (7) Broad St. Green, **World War I Mem.** & near-by, several old Hs. (8) Broad St. Green, **Windsor Pub. Lib.** (Oliver Mather H.) (O.wks.1777.alts.19th cent.). (9) Island Rd., **Loomis Institute,** school for boys. On campus, **Jos. Loomis H.** (mid-17th cent.adds.18th cent.). Loomis was a 1st settler. (10) Poquonock Ave. & East St., **Wareham Grist Mill** (O. 1649), supposedly oldest grist mill in state. (11) 35 Elm St., **John Moore H.** (1664), oldest in town. (12) At Cook Hill is **St. Tobacco & Vegetable Field Sub-Station** (O). In Windsor is J. with St.75.

US5A cont. to **WINDSOR LOCKS** at 14. Here a canal was built around Conn. R. rapids to permit passage of shipping. Hy. cont. past several ancient Hs. **21. CONN.-MASS. LINE,** 5m from Springfield, Mass. (see US20).

# NEW HAVEN

Union Sta., Union Ave. Airport: through conns. Accoms.: All types. Info.: C. of C., 152 Temple St. One theater for current plays. Sports: At Yale Bowl. Swim.: Lighthouse Pk.

**NEW HAVEN** (sett.1638) is located at the triangle where West, Mill & Quinnipiac Rs. empty into New Haven Harbor, itself an arm of Long I. Sound. East & West Rocks, precipitous outcroppings, flank the city on either side. The beautiful Green, Yale's elm-shaded campus, the elm-shaded streets temper one's 1st impression of the town as a congested industrial center within whose metropolitan area are crowded almost 19% of the plants of Conn. Descendants of the orig. English are greatly outnumbered by elements of more recent foreign derivation—Italians, Poles, Jews, Greeks, Armenians, & other groups. New Haven, like Hartford, is a leading cultural center. It is home of Yale Univ., which, however, dominates New Haven's life perhaps less than Harvard does that of Cambridge. There are also several other institutions of higher learning. The Univ. Fine Arts Mus. is one of the most important in the country. Peabody Mus. has outstanding nat. hist. colls. The city was 1st sett. by Rev. John Davenport & the retired merchant, Theophilus Eaton, both of London, accompanied by a group of colonists migrating to Boston because of religious persecution. They sett. on land owned by Quinnipiac Inds., which they purchased for price of some coats, knives, hatchets & other inexpensive articles. The new colony was at first known as Quinnipiac.

Like other Conn. & Mass. settlements, New Haven's constitution, adopted 1639, placed all power in the hands of the church, whose voting membership was strictly limited. Under this regime, the famous "blue laws" were passed, fixing severe penalties for breaches of the Puritan code & attempting strictly to regulate the private lives of the colonists. So many offences were listed that, as one historian puts it, "It is a wonder one pair of stocks on Market Place (today's Green) was enough." This theocracy, like that of Mass., was guilty of considerable persecution of Quakers. But apparently New Haven did not succumb to the general witchcraft hysteria that swept New England. It is recorded that one Elizabeth Godman had become suspected of evil supernatural powers. She was accused of turning a barrel of beer sour, of producing a fatal disease among chickens & of causing an enemy, Mistress Bishop, to bring forth a stillborn child. Elizabeth was tried, but acquitted. In 1664 New Haven was inc. into the Colony of Conn. under a more liberal charter. In 1677 the citizen's rights were further extended. Thereafter the settlement's slow evolution toward a broader democracy & religious tolerance followed the pattern of New England generally. In 1666 Wm. Goffe & Ed. Whalley, regicides, arrived & were concealed by Rev. Davenport until they found refuge elsewhere. Col. John Dixwell, another of the judges who sentenced Charles I to be beheaded, came several yrs. later & managed to circulate freely under an assumed name, although regarded with suspicion by royal Gov. Andros. During Rev., city was temporarily occupied by Brit. Although they did some looting, they refrained from setting fire to the town for fear of destroying houses of their Tory supporters. They soon had to retreat when menaced by gathering patriot forces. On May 19, 1780, came "The Dark Day," comm. by Whittier, when everyone, incl. the legislature which stayed in solemn session, awaited Coming of the Judgment Day.

In 1784, the town was inc. as a city, & its 1st mayor was Roger Sherman, Rev. patriot who played a chief role in getting Conn. to ratify the Constitution. From 1701 to 1785, the city was one of state's capitals, Hartford being the other. In the early 19th cent. the city became an important center for shipping. In 1850's it was center of an abolitionist movement & during Civil War, staunchly backed Union cause with money, arms & men. New Haven boasts that it was birthpl. of a large amount of Yankee inventiveness: Eli Whitney invented cotton gin & founded Whitney Arms Co. (later taken over by Winchester Repeating Arms Co.), where he employed principle of standardized parts & division of labor; Eli Whitney Blake invented first stone-crusher; Chauncey Jones founded a clock company (now New Haven Clock Co.), which employed use of standardized metal parts; Thomas Sanford invented phosphorus match; Sam. Morse, inventor of telegraph, was a graduate of Yale. Some of the more important plants in the city are: New Haven Clock Co. (founded 1817); Sargent's, one of world's largest manufacturers of hardware; Winchester Repeating Arms Co., which has branched into manufacture of auto & airplane radiators, ice & roller skates, dies, & other articles.

PTS. OF INT.: (Yale Univ. is described as a unit in Pt. 30). (1) On Green: **Trinity Ch.** (Episc.1814.Goth.Rev.by Ithiel Town & David Hoadley); **Center Ch.** (1815. Georg.by Ithiel Town.fine exter.& inter.). It has a window showing Davenport preaching at landing of 1st settlers & comm. tablets. Crypt contains number of old gravestones & graves of notables. Behind Ch. is Mon. comm. John Dixwell. Tablets on rear wall comm. two other regicides, Ed. Whalley & Wm. Goffe (see above). **United Ch.** (1813-15.Georg.Col.by David Hoadley.very fine exter.& inter.). Within are tablets comm. various notables. (2) On Elm St.: No. 35, **John Cook H.** (O.1807), now home of Visiting Nurses Assoc. (NE) cor. Temple & Elm Sts., **Ives Mem. Lib.** (O.wks.1911.Mod.Class.by Cass Gilbert). (NW) cor. Temple & Elm Sts., **Gov. Ingersoll H.** (1830.Gr.Rev.), houses Yale Univ. Press. No. 149, **Pierpont H.** (1767), occupied by Yale Faculty Club. No. 155, **Bushnell H.** (1800.Fed.), houses Yale Graduates Club. No. 175, **Tory Tavern** (latter part of 18th cent.), was used before Rev. as Tory hqs., now houses Yale Elihu Club. (3) On College St.: (NE) cor. Elm & College Sts., **First Meth. Ch.** (1854.Gr.Rev.). No. 123, **Elizabethan Club of Yale** (c.1815.Gr.Rev.style); fine coll. of Elizabethana. (4) 275 Orange St., **Bowditch H.** (O.c.1800.by Hoadley), in which Eli Whitney, of cotton gin fame, worked & died. Now children's bldg. (5) On Trumbull St.: No. 58, **Wier H.** (c.1810). No. 87, **Silliman H.** (1807), former home of Prof. Ben. Silliman, famous scientist in his day & teacher of Sam. Morse. (6) On George St., **Bishop H.** (1815), which was moved here from Elm St. (7) 114 Whitney Ave., **New Haven Colony Hist. Soc.** (O.1930.Georg.by J.F.& H.S.Kelley); coll. of antiques, paintings.

(8) No. 4 Hillhouse Ave., **Ithiel Town H.,** former home of architect of post-Rev. period who designed many New Haven bldgs. (9) On Grove St., **Grove St. Cemetery,** in which are graves of Noah Webster (of dictionary fame), Eli Whitney & J. W. Gibbs, famous physicist, etc. (10) College & George Sts., **Tablet** comm. site of 1st landing of settlers. (11) On wall of 1032 Chapel St., **Marker** comm. site of home of Roger Sherman, signer of all four "founding documents": Decl. of Ind., Articles of Association, Articles of Confederation & Federal Constitution. He was also 1st mayor of New Haven. (12) At crossing of Broadway & Elm Sts., **Christ Ch.** (1895. Goth.by Henry Vaughn). (13) 86 Broadway, **Hull H.** (c.1812.by Hoadley), now rectory. (14) At inters. of Chapel St. & Derby Ave., **Monitor Sq.**, in which is **Bushnell Mon.** (by H.Adams), comm. C. S. Bushnell, builder of the "Monitor," designed by John Ericsson, which ended menace of the "Merrimac" (see Norfolk, Va.). (15) 700 Prospect St., **St. Albertus Magnus College** (Cath.), with spacious grounds & handsome bldgs. (16) On Orange St., **East Rock Pk.** (sports.recr.), with fine outlook. (17) On Derby Ave., Yale Field. **Yale Bowl** (by Chas.A.Ferry), seating c.75,000. **Walter Camp Mem. Gateway** (by Chas.A.Ferry), comm. famous Yale graduate authority on sports. **Coxe Mem. Gymnasium.** (18) 986 Forest Rd., **Hopkins Grammar School,** founded (17th cent.) by Davenport, with help of Gov. Ed. Hopkins, is one of oldest schools in U.S. (19) On Forest Rd., **Edgewood** (now school), former home of Donald G. Mitchell, who, under pen name of "Ik Marvel" wrote once popular "Reveries of a Bachelor," "Dream Life," etc. One of his books was about his home—"My Farm at Edgewood."

(20) On Blake St., **West Rock Pk.** Here is Judge's Cave, where Whalley & Goffe are supposed to have hidden from vengeance of Charles II. (21) 789 Howard Ave., **New Haven Hospital,** which cooperates with Yale Sch. of Medicine. (22) On Davenport Ave., **Institute of Human Relations & Sterling Hall of Medicine,** both conn. with Yale Univ. & New Haven Hospital. The Institute of Human Relations is devoted to research in field of human behavior—problems of motivation, processes of learning & influences of social environment on development of personality. (23) Inters. of Davenport & Congress Aves., **Defenders' Mon.** comm. New Haven men & Yale students who fought Brit. attack upon city. (24) On Chapel St., **Edgewood Pk.** (sports facils.recr.). (25) On (N) outskirts, at Whitney Ave. & Armory St., reached by US10A, **Old Whitney Model Barn** (supposedly 1816). May be merely replica of orig. (26) From City Center (S) $2^m$ is **Ft. Hale Pk.** (bath.), site of Ft. Hale, which resisted Brit. in 1779 & kept their fleet out of harbor in War of 1812. (27) 325 Lighthouse Rd., **Pardee-Morris H.** (O.wks.exc.Mon.;Sun.aft.1680-85.reb.after being burnt by Brit.1779.later adds.18th cent.inter.); now hist. mus.; herb garden. (28) From City Center (S) $4^m$, **Lighth. Pt. Pk.** Mun. bath. beach. **Old Lighth.** (O.appl.1840) & new Lighth. (29) **Ft. Wooster Pk.,** where militia fought Brit. during latter's raid.

(30) **Yale Univ.** (guides avail.). John Davenport planned founding of college, but his dream was not realized until 1701, after his death. Yale first functioned in Killingworth. Its founders were all Harvard alumni. In 1707 the college was moved to Saybrook & in 1716 ended its migrations by coming to New Haven. It had been endowed with £562/12s. by Elihu Yale, grandson of one of John Davenport's orig. colonists, & a prosperous merchant. Bishop Berkeley gave the college his R.I. farm & lib. (see Newport, R.I.). In 1810 the "Medical Institute" was est. & soon after, the Schools of Divinity & Law. Out of the work of Silliman, Loomis & Dana grew Sheffield Scientific School (1861). Today, besides the college & professional schools already listed, the Univ. comprises a number of grad. schools & other depts. College students live in 10 residential colleges of c.200 individuals each. Although an important source of income to the city, there were times when relations bet. Univ. & municipality were "uneasy," due to tax exemption of Univ. properties. In the old days, there was considerable antagonism bet. students & "towners." The former used to choose a "Bully" to lead them against the latter. In ensuing encounters the students sometimes came off second-best. It is recorded that, while the "gowns" were bathing off the Long Wharf, oystermen, longshore roustabouts & wharf "rats" attacked with considerable effect. In 1854, students, besieged by "towners" in S. College, had to be rescued by police. Medical students suspected of "body-snatching" were threatened by mobs. Today, of course, Univ. has become well integrated into city's cultural life.

Here are listed only a few of the many noteworthy Univ. bldgs. On Elm St.: **Old Campus,** notable for fine elms. **Conn. Hall** (1752), oldest bldg. **Statue of Nathan Hale** (by Bela Pratt), who lived here as student. **Dwight Hall** (1842-46.remod.1931. by C.Z.Klauder), in which is Dwight Mem. Chapel, with fine window. Bldg. comm. Timothy Dwight & his grandson of same name, both Yale presidents. Bldgs. on Old Campus of more recent date are Vict.Goth., Coll.-Goth. & Goth. in style. **Battell Chapel** (Vict.Goth. by Russell Sturges, Jr.). Bounded by Elm, High, York & Chapel Sts., **Mem. Quadrangle** (Mod.Goth.by Jas.Gamble Rogers). **Harkness Tower,** more than 220′ high, designed after tower in Wrexham, Wales, where Elihu Yale is buried. On High St., **Jonathan Edwards Coll.** (1889.Goth.by Rogers), named for Yale graduate & famous divine. Here is **Statue of Slave Boy,** said to have been property of Elihu Yale. Cor. Chapel & High Sts., **Gallery of Fine Arts** (O.sm.fee), founded by Col. John Trumbull (1831), to house coll. of portraits & his paintings of Amer. Rev.; antiquities from Egypt, Babylon, Greece & Rome, incl. objects from Univ.'s excavations in Mesopotamia; Near & Far Eastern Art; European Art of Middle Ages & Ren.; Americana; & modern paintings. On York St., facing New Quadrangle, **University Theater** (O.academic yr.), where Prof. G. P. Baker, who taught Eugene O'Neill, conducted drama courses. On York St., **Davenport College** (1889.Goth.by Rogers), affiliated with Yale Univ. Named for Davenport, joint founder with Eaton of New Haven. On High St., **Sterling Mem. Lib.** (1931.Goth.by Rogers); notable coll. of rare books & other items, incl. Gutenberg Bible & Bay Psalm Book, 1st book printed in Amer. Colonies; Yale Memorabilia Room; coll. of Books in Yale Lib. in 1742. Adj. to Lib., **Sterling Law Bldgs.** (1889.by Rogers). Near-by, **Sterling Power H.** (by C.Z.Klauder). On Tower Pkwy., **Payne Whitney Gymnasium** (O.academic yr. Goth.), in which is Trophy Room. Cor. College & Grove Sts., **Bicentennial Bldgs.** Hewitt Quadrangle (1901-02.all but one bldg.by Carrère & Hastings). In Mem. Hall, a circular bldg., are tablets comm. Yale men who died in U.S. wars & Coll. of "Autographed Letters & Portraits of Eminent Yale Men." (S) of Univ. Hall, one of the Quadrangle Bldgs. is **Alumni War Mem. Colonnade,** comm. Yale men who fell in World War I. On College & Grove Sts., **Sheffield Scientific School** (by Chas.C. Haight). **Sterling Mem. Tower** (1892.by C.C.Zantzinger). Cor. Whitney Ave. & Sachem St., **Peabody Mus.** (O.Goth.by C.Z.Klauder); notable coll. of nat. hist. exhibits. On Prospect St., **Sterling Divinity Quadrangle** (1895.Georg.Col.by Wm.A. Delano). Inter. of Marquand Chapel resembles early Puritan Ch. At Prospect & Sachem Sts., **Berkeley Divinity School** (est.1854) affiliated with Yale Univ.

(31) **Industrial Plants** (O.appl.). (32) **S. New England Telephone Co. & Union & New Haven Trust Co.** & other handsome skyscrapers, facing the Green. (33) **County Cth. & U.S. Post Office** (both Class.), facing the Green. (34) Educational institutions, in addition to those mentioned: **Arnold College of Hygiene & Physical Education; Conn. College of Pharmacy; The Women's College.** For walking trips in

vic., see "Connecticut Walk Book" (50¢), pub. by Conn. For. & Pk. Assoc., 839 Chapel St., New Haven. (35) **Savin Rock** (amusements), on Sound, is c.5$^{m}$ (SW). Marker on Site of Gen. Tryon's Landing (1779).

## TRIPS OUT OF NEW HAVEN

### I. Loop Tour to SOUTHINGTON & return. 49. St.10 Alt., St.10, St.120, US6A & US5

Via: Whitneyville, Centerville, Mt. Carmel Center, Ives Corner, Cheshire, Plantsville, Southington, Meriden, Wallingford & North Haven.

Take US10 Alt. (N) from New Haven. At **2.** suburban **WHITNEYVILLE. Eli Whitney Barn** (see above). **6. CENTERVILLE. Grace Ch.** (Episc.1810.attrib.to Hoadley). J. with St.10 which tour follows. **7.5. MT. CARMEL CENTER.** Fine **Congr. Ch.** (1840.Gr.Rev.). **Sherman H.** (2nd half 18th cent.).

SIDE TRIP: Near Mt. Carmel is **Sleeping Giant St. Pk.** (1,071 as.pic.trls.). Trl. to Outlook Tower. **Dickerman H.** (1770), near Admin. Bldg. (R) to Clark's Pond (pic.).

**11. IVES CORNERS.** (Rd. (L) here to Brooksvale at 1$^{m}$. At 1.5$^{m}$ go (L) to J. with Quinnipiac Trl., at 2.5$^{m}$, to fine Roaring Brook Falls). **13. CHESHIRE;** Cheshire Academy (O.appl.), some of whose bldgs. date from 18th cent. **Abijah Beach Tavern** (1814) & **Hitchcock H.** (1788), both now part of Academy. At Green, **Cong. Ch.** (O.1826). **19.5. PLANTSVILLE.** On S. Main St., handsome **Nath. Lewis H.** (early 19th cent.) & **Old Dr. Skilton H. 20. SOUTHINGTON. Pub. Lib.** in which is Sylvia Bradley Mus. (O.aft.& eve.exc.Sat.Sun.& hols.); coll. of antiques & hist. relics. **Congr. Ch.** (1828.Gr.Rev.). Near Green, **Root H.** (early 18th cent.remod.). On outskirts of Southington on St.10 is **Curtis Robinson H.** (latter 18th cent.), notable old mansion.

SIDE TRIP: 2$^{m}$ (N) of Southington on St.10 is **Powers Quonset Hut Auto Mus.** (O.sm.fee), with coll. of ancient autos. At 3.5$^{m}$ J. with Rd. [Take latter (L) to Resort (pic.f.bath.b.) on Compounce L.]

In Southington is J. with St.120 on which loop tour conts. (SE) to J. with US6A, at **24.** (E) here on US6A past **Hubbard Pk.** to **MERIDEN** (see Hartford Trip VI) at **29.** In Meriden is J. with US5 on which tour conts. (S). **37.** J. with street into **WALLINGFORD,** silverware center. Wallingford Hist. Soc. in **Parsons H.** (O.1770); hist. colls. Famous (Boys) **Choate School,** whose Lib., Infirmary & Chapel, latter in old New England style, are by Ralph Adams Cram. Winter Sports Bldg. **Caleb Atwater H.** (1774). **Carrington H.,** where lived Rev. Gen. Carrington & a house dating from 1690 are both owned by Sch. 538 N. Main St., **Nehemiah Royce H.** (O. June-Sept.sm.fee.1672). Mus. of antique items. **38. Wharton Brook St. Pk.** (pic.).

**41. NORTH HAVEN.** At Green, **St. John's Ch.** (1835.Goth.Rev.) & **Parsonage** (1761). **49. NEW HAVEN.**

### II. From NEW HAVEN to OLD SAYBROOK. 38. St.80, St.9.

Via: N. Branford, (N. Guilford), N. Madison, Deep River, (East Haddam), (Haddam), (Higganum), (Middletown), & (Essex).

This tour is longer, but int. alternate for US1 to Old Saybrook. St.80 passes through **N. BRANFORD** (see Branford) to J. with St.77, at **c.11.5.** (Take St.77 (L) here short distance to **N. Guilford**—see Guilford). St.80 then passes **Shelley Ls. 17.5. N. MADISON** (see Madison). At **19.** is picturesque cleft of Hammonassett R. **20.** J. with Kelsey Dr. [Take latter (L) to **Cockaponset St. For.** (14,550 as.pic.rds.& trls.] **21.** J. with St.81.

SIDE TRIP: (L) on St.81 short distance to **Killingsworth,** where are **Ely H.** (O.appl.1782) & **Barnelee H.** (O.appl.1752), outstanding examples of period, & lovely **Congr. Ch.** (1817. rest.).

**24.5. MENUNKETESUCK L.** & St. Pk. (pic.). **30. DEEP RIVER.** J. with St.9. on which Tour cont. (SE).

SIDE TRIP: Take St.9 (N) to **Tylerville,** at c.6$^{m}$. J. with St.82.

(R) on St.82 across Conn. R. to **East Haddam.** In **St. Stephen's Ch.** is bell dated 1815, taken by Napoleon during Spanish wars. At Cemetery above river, **Schoolh.** where Nathan Hale taught (operated by D.A.R.).

At 9.5$^{m}$, **Haddam,** straddling Conn. R. **Congr. Ch.** (1847). **Town Hall** (O.1839). 11$^{m}$ **Higganum,** an old shipping town. **Congr. Ch.** (1845). **Hubbard H.** (early 19th cent.).

Take St.81 (L) here. At 1$^{m}$, **Witch-Hazel Distilleries,** worth a visit. At 2.5$^{m}$, **Ponset.** (E) is extensive **Cockaponset St. Pk.** (pic.hiking).

12m **Seven Falls St. Hy. Pk.** (pic.). 19m **Middletown** (see Hartford, Trip VII), seat of Wesleyan Univ.

**33.5.** J. with Rd.

SIDE TRIP: (L) 0.5m to **Pratt Smithy** (est.1678), still operated by orig. family (1948). At 1m, **Essex** (sett.1690), where warships were built during Rev. & War of 1812, when town was attacked by Brit. 48 Main St., **Ye Old Griswold Inn** (O.1776), still a hostelry & said to be 1st 3-story house in Conn. **Capt. Lewis H.** (c.1760), opp. Inn. **Hayden Tavern** (1776), now clubh. Other int. old Hs.

**37.5. OLD SAYBROOK** (see US1).

# NEWPORT

RR. conns. at Providence, Kingston & Fall River. Bus Terminal, head of Washington Sq. Ferry to Jamestown & Conanticut I. (see below). Yacht Races (Aug.), N.Y. Yacht Club Cruise & other yachting events. Internat. Tennis Matches, at Casino (Aug.). Bath. at several beaches. Sailboats for hire & deep-sea fish. In Casino, 194 Bellevue Ave., stock-company productions, concerts. Info.: C. of C., in Old Brick Market, Washington Sq.; Auto Club of R.I., 2 Meetinghouse St.

Perhaps Newport's fame as summer capital of high society during Gilded Age has somewhat obscured its other claims to interest; its fine beaches & its charm as an old New England town dotted with unusually beautiful hist. bldgs. Period of greatest social glories extended from 1880's through Gilded Age & into early 1920's. The real decline set in with 1929 crash & long depression that followed. Yet Newport's career as a fashionable resort is by no means over. Some of the sprawling palaces have been sold; one at least has been acquired as a museum, in which the less well-to-do may now learn how the upper stratum lived; one now houses a college; others have been closed. But the boom following World War II shows signs of a comeback, & places left empty by the older rich are being taken over by newcomers. Up to the Civil War, Southern planters came to spend their summers here; after that the Boston invasion developed, & then arrived Philadelphia's & Wall Street's tycoons. The fact that Newport is a great naval base has not been one of its least attractions to the socially minded. Townsfolk are by no means eager to become part of high society & content themselves with "wringing" a living out of Bellevue Ave. & Ocean Dr.

Newport is situated on (S) arm of R.I. & is flanked on 3 sides by a fine rockbound coast. Bellevue Ave. & Ocean Dr. are lined with great mansions. Old Newport clusters around Washington Sq., formerly known as The Parade, & off Thames & other downtown streets. Great naval installations, at the Landing & on near-by Goat, Coaster's & other Is., provide a contingent of officers & enlisted personnel. Conanticut I. blocks off the bay to the (W).

City was founded in 1639 by Wm. Coddington & John Clarke, leading a small group of religious dissenters from Mass. Colony's strict orthodoxy. Guided by Roger Williams, they came down the bay in canoes. The 1st settlers evinced a certain Yankee shrewdness in offering a coat with brass buttons to a friendly Ind., who strung the buttons on a string around his neck &, in no time, had their swamp-clearing job done. Major event of early 18th cent. was arrival of Dean (later Bishop) Berkeley, famous Brit. philosopher, who came to America to found a University in Bermuda. He built himself a house in Middletown's vicinity, called Whitehall, where he & his wife stayed 3 years, waiting vainly for a grant of £20,000 promised by Sir Rbt. Walpole. While waiting, he helped organize the Philosophical Soc. which stimulated Newport's intellectual life & eventually aided in founding of Redwood Lib. Berkeley finally returned to Britain. In cemetery of Trinity Ch. is grave of his infant daughter, Lucy, who was born & died at Whitehall. Ch. still has the organ he gave it, & Whitehall is still standing. Newport became a center of rum-molasses-slave trade. Pirates interfering with this legitimate commerce were run down, caught & hanged. During wars with France, privateering reaped mighty profits. Godfrey Malbone, who operated a fleet of "corsairs," was one of wealthiest citizens & established tradition of lavish entertainment. It is said that, during a banquet, his princely mansion caught fire. He thereupon had his slaves move the tables onto the lawn, where he & his guests watched the fireworks while dining sumptuously.

By middle of 18th cent., Newport's pop. had risen to 12,000 & it had a considerable number of industries, among which 22 rum distilleries figured prominently. The city rivalled Providence, Boston & New York in commercial importance. During 17th & 18th cent. its cosmopolitan character was enhanced by influx of Portuguese & Sp. Jews, who were well received, as had been all religious refugees. Some of these had been Marranos (Jews forced to profess Christianity). In their new homes they could openly practice their own faith but, so deep was the old habit, Jewish women settlers in Newport still counted their beads while repeating Hebrew prayers. Prosperous citizens lived in splendid style, with handsome city & country mansions & hosts of servants. It was recorded with some astonishment that one rich burgher moved to his country estate, taking "only" 25 servants. Many houses were designed by Peter Harrison, who came from Eng. with Berkeley. Richard Munday was another prominent architect. Art flourished. John Smibert, another gift to America by Berkeley, Cosmo Alexander, with whom Gilbert Stuart studied, & Robert Feke were popular portraitists. Edward G. Malbone, born in Newport, 1777, is perhaps the most celebrated painter of miniatures America has produced.

Period of commercial greatness was abruptly halted by the Rev. Brit. occupied city from 1777 into fall of 1779 & did tremendous damage. Although French fleet entered port in 1778, it was forced to retire & did not return till 1780, when it slipped by enemy ships in the fog. In Newport, Washington & Rochambeau planned Yorktown campaign. After Rev., the town was in ruins. Count de Rochefoucault-Leancourt, in 1798, described it as "cette ville triste et basse." During late 18th & early 19th cents., troubles with both French & Brit. (culminating in War of 1812) & the suppression of slave trade completed city's commercial decline. But already Newport had begun its career as a resort. In late 18th cent., Southern planters came & built fine mansions, a few of which are still standing. One Southerner continued tradition of extravagance, which was to make city famous, when he ornamented his doors with solid silver fixtures &, it is said, used molasses to make mortar for his house. Ward McAllister, in "Society in Newport as I Found It," says: "At that time Newport was really a southern colony."

After Civil War, when Newport still alternated with Providence as St. capital, the Bostonians began to arrive, among them a large nucleus of intellectuals, the Julia Ward Howes, Raphael Pumpelly, Charlotte Cushman, famous actress, & Wm. Ellery Channing, a native. Mrs. Elliott, daughter of Julia Ward Howe, tells in "This Was My Newport," that she remembers Channing walking under the oaks composing his sermons, his head protected against sun by his wife's bonnet. Thos. Wentworth Higginson, a visitor both summer & winter, commemorated Newport in his "Old Port" sketches. Edith Wharton, known before her marriage as Pussie Jones, lived in town with her parents. Wm. Morris Hunt, painter, established himself at "The Hilltop." Here his brother, Richard M., joined him & became architect of many great mansions. He "found Newport a town of wooden houses and left it one of marble palaces." John La Farge, who came to study with Hunt, later designed windows for Channing Mem. Ch. Howard Gardner Cushing, another artist, was a native of the city, & Washington Allston, famous painter in his day, was a visitor.

In late 19th cent., the New York invasion was on in full force. Mrs. Astor, who, at suggestion of Ward McAllister, created the exclusive "400" (the number she could crowd into her New York ballroom), gave resplendent dinners served on gold service. On these occasions, she wore her fabulous pearl necklace which, when appraised after her death, proved to have a small number of artificial pearls. The complicated cotillion was the popular dance. Bathing & croquet, in which the men joined them, were the ladies' main "sports." Between five p.m. & sundown, the élite turned out in barouches & drove slowly about town. Mrs. August Belmont's equipage was drawn by 4 horses, 2 mounted by postillions in resplendent liveries. It was the incredible period when Mr. Astor seriously remarked: "A man who has a million dollars is as well off as if he were rich." Mrs. Stuyvesant Fish eventually became social arbiter. Harry Lehr, her chief social adviser, earned nickname of "King" Lehr at one of Mrs. Fish's banquets given in honor of Russian Grand Duke Boris. When the "pièce de résistance" failed to turn up, Lehr masqueraded as the Czar of Russia & received the serious homage of the guests. Fred Garetson was somewhat disapproved of, because, although belonging to exclusive set, he opened up a fashionable grocery store to make money out of the cliff-dwellers. Oliver Belmont had such a passion for horses that he turned the ground floor of his mansion into a stable, & two stuffed equines were exhibited in his "salon." His horses had morning, afternoon & evening clothes. One hostess gilded trees on her grounds & hung them with golden fruits. The Bradley-Martins gave a famous ball at which guests appeared in gorgeous, jewel-encrusted costumes. O. Belmont came in full coat of mail, under whose weight he collapsed. Harry Lehr's monkey dinner & the banquet whose guests of honor were a hundred dogs gave rise to public censure.

Today the note of extravagance has disappeared, but there is still a pervading atmosphere of wealth & luxury. International tennis matches draw a fashionable crowd to the Casino; Bailey's Beach is still center of exclusive society; & New York Yacht Club cruises & regattas still bring luxurious private yachts & set off series of dinners & dances. Meanwhile, Newport continues to attract many visitors who want merely to enjoy its recr. resources & view its hist. bldgs. Recently, the Preservation Society has undertaken a campaign for restoration of hist. landmarks.

PTS. OF INT.: (1) **Washington Sq.,** center of old city. **Statue of Commodore Perry,** hero of Battle of L. Erie. 127 Thomas St., **Old Brick Market H.** (O.1762.by Peter Harrison, who designed King's Chapel, Boston), the old City Hall; built by funds raised by lottery; now Newport C. of C. Has paintings of Old Newport by Helena Sturtevant. **Old Colony H.** (O.sm.fee.1738.Georg.by Richard Munday.very fine exter.& inter.); served as Capitol; wrecked by Brit. during Rev. Geo. Washington was entertained here. (2) Cor. Washington Sq. & Duke St., **Rivera H.** (2nd half 18th cent.); Portuguese Jew, Abram Rivera, owner, was forced, due to shipping losses, to make an assignment to his creditors. Years later he invited them to a banquet at which each creditor found a check for full amount due. (3) At Broadway is imposing **City Hall,** facetiously described as combination of "occidental & accidental." (4) 5 Charles St., **Pitts Head Tavern** (O.pre-1744) was home of Ebenezer Flagg, business associate of Henry Collins, patron of the arts, the "Lorenzo de Medici of R.I." Hqs. of Preservation Soc. (5) 76 Bridge St., **Townsend Shop** (O.early 18th cent. rest.) was originally joiner's (carpenter) shop; now occupied by Restorations, Inc. (6) 17 Broadway, **Wanton-Lyman-Hazard H.** (O.appl.sm.fee.18th cent.fine exter.& inter. rest.panelling), was owned by Jos. Wanton, Col. Gov. who was deposed & his property confiscated because of opposition to Patriots. Philosophical Soc. occasionally met here. Now owned by Newport Hist. Soc. (7) 46 Clarke St., **Vernon H.** (O.wks. early 18th cent.adds.1758.Georg.), once occupied by Rochambeau (1780-81); unusual frescoes in Chinese style. (8) 23 Clarke St., **Newport Artillery Co.** (O.appl.) houses one of oldest military orgs. in U.S. (1741); hist. relics & portraits of Washington. (9) 15 Clarke St., **Central Congr. Ch.** (1733), damaged during Brit. occupation. (10) Spring & Church Sts., **Trinity (Episc.) Ch.** (O.appl.c.1725.by Rich.Munday), one of finest New England Col. Chs. Bell (recast) dates from 1709. Inter. is in orig. state. Although Patriots stripped Ch. of Royal insignia, they left the crowns on both steeple & organ. Washington attended services here. In cemetery are buried Adm. de Ternay & Berkeley's infant daughter, Lucy. (11) 30 Spring St., **John Clarke Mem. Ch.** (1846), org. by Rev. John Clarke, one of Newport's founders. (12) 228 Spring St., **Maudsley H.** (O.sm.fee c.1758.Georg.very fine exter.& inter.). From here Caleb Gardner set out to pilot Fr. fleet past Brit. blockade, through fog, into Newport harbor. (13) 62 W. Broadway, **Cemetery,** in which John Clarke is buried. (14) 155 Broadway, **Rochambeau Mon.,** replica of one in France, by F. Hamer. (15) 30 Marlborough St., **Friends Meetingh.** (oldest part 1690), one of earliest Quaker Chs. in country; now Community Center. (16) Marlborough St., **Jon. Nichols H.** (1st half 18th cent.). (17) Also on Marlborough St., **St. Paul's Ch.** (Meth.1806-07). (18) 50 Farewell St., **Governor's Cemetery,** where are graves of early settlers. (19) 24 Warner St., **Common Ground Cemetery** (dating from c.1660). (20) 30 Warner St., **Island Cemetery, in** which are Mons. to comm. O. H. Perry & M. C. Perry. (21) 72 Touro St., (Temple Jeshuat Israel) **Touro Synagogue** (O.1763.by Peter Harrison), recently est. as Nat. Hist. Site; hist. & other relics. Woodwork of inter. beautifully hand-carved. Columns represent 12 tribes of Israel. From domed ceiling hang 5 large candelabra, one of which is said to have been brought from Spain. Balcony was for women worshippers. Portrait of Abr. Touro, brother of Judah (see below), by Gilbert Stuart in Synagogue Annex. Underground passage from beneath desk was possibly intended as hiding place from persecution, fear of which Newport Jews could not quite discard. Isaac Touro came from Jamaica to Newport in 1760 as Rabbi. In 1780, St. Assembly met here, & in 1790 Washington visited Synagogue & then wrote famous statement on religious freedom, ending: "Happily, the government of the United States which gives to bigotry no sanction, to persecution no assistance, requires only that they who live under its protection should demean themselves as good citizens, in giving it on all occasions their effectual support." (22) Opp. Synagogue, **Sheffield H.** (Gr.Rev.), Jewish Comm. Center. (23) 82 Touro St., **Newport Hist. Soc. & Seventh Day Bapt. Ch.** (O.1729); in Mus. among other items are Ida Lewis' lifeboat (see Ida Lewis Yacht Club below) & records of Colony which were dumped into New York Harbor during Rev. & fished out again later. Ch. is notable for "wineglass" pulpit, fine stairs, original panelling. Clock made by Wm. Claggett (1731) is still ticking. (24) 2 Bellevue Ave., **Jewish Cemetery,** dating from c.1677. (25) Bellevue Ave., & Mill St., **Redwood Lib.** (O.wks.reading room for members only.1748.by Peter Harrison.rest.), founded by donation of Quaker, Abr. Redwood. Henry Collins gave his "Bowling Green" for site, & £5,000 was raised by contributions. Among rare items is portrait of Judah Touro. (26) 76 Bellevue Ave., **Art Assoc.** (O.wks.); exhib. (summer) & art classes. Next to Art Assoc., **Cushing Mem. Bldg.** has paintings by H. G. Cushing. (27) Bellevue Ave., at Mill St., **Touro Pk.,** named for donor, Judah Touro, son of 1st rabbi. Touro, philanthropist (see New Orleans), furnished money to complete Bunker Hill Mon. & was also a benefactor of Boston's Mass. Gen. Hospital. (28) N. of Pk., bet. Mill & Pelham Sts., on Bellevue Ave., **Old Stone Mill,** which has aroused much speculation. According to some, it was built by Vikings who visited coast under Eric the Red, in 12th cent. Another theory is that it was built by Benedict Arnold (not the traitor, but an early R.I. Gov.) during 17th Cent. Excavations are being conducted to discover origin of bldg. (29) E. side of Pk., **Statue of M. C. Perry,** who "opened up" Japan. At W. side, **Statue of Wm. Ellery Channing,** famous Unitarian minister, born in Newport. (30) 142 Mill St., **Tillinghast H.** (1760.fine exter.& inter.), which entertained many celebrities. (31) On Washington St., notable H. is No. 24, **Hunter H.** (O.pre-1730), now owned by Preservation Soc. Once occupied by Deputy Gov. Jos. Wanton (see above) & confiscated because of his Tory activities. Hqs. of French Adm. de Ternay who died here, 1780. (32) **National Portuguese Mus.** in the old Mallory H.; colls. of paintings, carved wood & ivory & brass work. (33) Bet. Girard & Hillside Aves., **Miantonomi Pk.** (pic.recr.), where it is said Ind. Chief had his seat. Old Brit. earthworks. Tower on Hill comm. Newport's war heroes. (34) Thames St. & Jamestown Ferry dock, **Gov. Landing. U.S. Torpedo Sta. Mem.** From here can be seen **Goat I.,** on which is Navy Torpedo Sta. It is claimed 1st torpedo was constructed at Newport & 1st submarine was tested in harbor. (35) On Coaster's Harbor I. is **U.S. Naval Training Base** (O.no cameras), reached by causeway from 3rd St. Here at Naval War College officers are trained in higher strategy. "USS Constellation" (1794) is here. (36) **Cliff Walk,** footpath from Easton's Beach & Bath Rd., skirting fine, rockbound shore 4$^{m}$ to Bailey's Beach. In sharp conflict with estate owners concerning right of way, townspeople won out, & today public can get glimpses of great Hs. in beautifully landscaped grounds. (37) Another walk from Easton's Beach skirts shoreline of Easton's Pt., past "Purgatory," Second Beach, & Hanging Rocks, to Third Beach.

## TRIPS OUT OF NEWPORT

### I. Loop Tour. Ten Mile Ocean Drive.

Tour starts on Bellevue Ave., at inters. with Bath Rd., & passes **Newport Casino,** 194 Bellevue Ave. Across Ave. is **Stone Villa,** built by Jas. Gordon Bennett, owner of N.Y. "Herald." He became voluntary exile & managed paper from abroad by cable. At Dixon St., **The Elms,** huge Berwind Mansion. At inters. of Bellevue Ave. with Narragansett Ave., take latter (L) to inters. with Ochre Pt. Ave.; turn (R) on Ochre Pt. Ave. At **0.5.** from inters. is (L) **OCHRE COURT, a** 50-room villa, recently presented by Goelets to Cath. Diocese of Providence, to house Salve Regina College, R.I.'s 1st Cath. women's college. At **c.1.** (L) **THE BREAKERS** (O.fee.by Rich.M.Hunt), $3,000,000 Vanderbilt mansion, now owned by Preservation Soc. At inters. of Ochre Pt. Ave. & Ruggles Ave., turn (R) on latter, past great houses. Then turn (L) on Bellevue Ave. At **1.5.** (L) **MARBLE H.** (by Rich.M.Hunt), one of Newport's most luxurious estates. At end of Bellevue Ave., turn (R) on Ocean Dr. At **2.5. BAILEY'S BEACH** (N.O.), exclusive resort. A little beyond is **CROSSWAYS** (R), famous Stuyvesant Fish Mansion. At **6.5.** take Ridge Rd. (L) & then Harrison Rd. (L). Near inters. of Harrison & Moorland Rds. is (L) one of oldest Hs. on the I. **7.5.** J. of Harrison Rd. with Ft. Adams Rd., which leads (L) to **FT. ADAMS,** built c.1824, on site of one built in 1799. Present Ft. dates from late 19th cent. Harrison Rd. now passes (R) Arthur Curtiss James Mansion (Med.style). At **8.** turn (L) here on Halidon Ave. & then (R) on Wellington Ave. Just beyond inters. is **IDA LEWIS YACHT CLUB** (L), which occupies old Lighth. where Ida Lewis was keeper, becoming legendary figure. Tour passes **KING PK.** (L), in which is **Rochambeau Mem.** Turn (L) on Thames St., to Washington Sq. at **10.**

## II. CONANICUT ISLAND. 20.

Via Ferry from Mill St. Construction of Bridge from Newport to Jamestown, Conanicut I., has been contracted for (1948). Conanicut I. is conn. with mainland by Jamestown-Saunderstown Bridge, near which is J. with US1. Recr. facils. (bath.h.f.). Info.: Board of Trade, Narragansett Ave., Jamestown.

Conanicut, whose chief town is Jamestown, is some 9$^{m}$ long & from 1$^{m}$ to 2$^{m}$ wide. Was refuge of Quakers in early days; occupied by Brit., 1776-79; now largely a resort.

Tour of I. follows Rd. (N) along E. side & return along W. side.

**0. JAMESTOWN. 2.** J. with North Ferry Rd. (Eldred Ave.); on latter (E) is **Site of 1-Gun Battery,** which John Eldred, single-handed, trained on Brit. ships during Rev. **4.5. PAINE H.** (c.1700), also known as Cajacet, was home of buccaneer Capt. Thos. Paine, whom Kidd visited. **6.** J. with North Rd., on which tour turns (S) **8. OLD SCHOOLH.** (1803). Just beyond is J. with Carr's Lane. Short distance (L) to **Nicholas Carr H.** (O. appl. 1778); int. old furnishings). **8.5.** J. with Cemetery Lane.

SIDE TRIP: (R) on Lane is **Friends' Burying Ground,** in which are many Quaker gravestones. At end of Lane is old **Ebenezer Slocum H.**

On North Rd., just beyond J. with Lane, is **OLD TOWN HALL.**

**9.5. OLD WINDMILL** (O.1787), still grinding flour. A little farther on is **Friends' Meetingh.** (1765). Rd. now passes **Sheffield Pond & Mackerel Cove** (pub.bath. pavilion sm.fee). Cont. (S) to (SW) tip of I. where is **Beaver Tail Light;** fine view. Take Rds. (R) here along shore back to Jamestown, **20.**

## III. BLOCK ISLAND

Steamer daily, mid-May to mid-Oct.; daily exc. Sun., rest of yr. Steamers also daily from Providence, Pt. Judith, R. I., & New London, Conn. Airplane serv. in summer, daily; rest of yr., Sun. only. Accoms.: All types, summer. Swim. at Crescent & other beaches. Sea fish. & fish. in many fresh-water Ls. Boat. equipment avail. Hik. & bridle paths. Info.: C. of C., in Village.

Block I. lies in Atlantic Ocean bet. Pt. Judith & Montauk Pt., L.I. Excellent climate, cool in summer & mild in winter, as compared with mainland. Besides many ocean beaches, has 365 fresh-water Ls. & Great Salt Pond. High cliffs add picturesqueness to shore line. Besides tourist business, fishing is chief industry. 1st Englishman to land, as far as is known, was John Oldham, who arrived 1636 & was slain by Inds. Early settlers (1661) suffered from Ind. attacks. Other difficulties came from raids of Fr. privateers during late 17th & early 18th cent. During Rev. it became haven of refugees from mainland, many of them criminal; islanders had difficulty coping with them. Brit. raided I. During War of 1812, pop. profited by trading with the enemy. There was no good harbor until 1778, when Old Harbor was built, picturesque today with its fishing fleet. Later, in 1880, New Harbor was constructed, capable of giving shelter to entire Atlantic fleet.

PTS. OF INT.: (1) On Center Rd., in Block I. village, **Town Hall** (1814). On Ocean Ave., **Tercentenary Mon., & New Harbor Coast Guard Sta.** (O): fine view from Tower. (N) of village, **Crescent Beach** (bath.facils.). At Grove Pt., extreme N. tip of **I., is Settlers' Rock,** comm. landing of 1st settlers, whose names are engraved on plaque. On Beacon Hill Rd., c.1$^{m}$ from village, is **Mem. to Block I. Mariners** (O. sm.fee).

Trip around S. part of I. begins on Spring St., which turns into Mohegan Trail, (S) from town; then passes **SOUTHEAST PT. LIGHT,** whose Tower (O) is c.200′ above sea; follows along **CLAY (Mohegan) CLIFFS,** some 150′ above sea; scenically situated golf course (O.fee). On Coonemus Rd., some 5$^{m}$ from town, marker on **PALATINE GRAVES** (L), probably site of Ind. burial ground. Here are interred bodies of 16 persons who, in 18th cent., survived wreck of "The Palatine." The crew had mutinied & deserted, leaving passengers to perish. See Whittier's poem, "The Palatine Light." From Coonemus Rd., West Side Rd. leads (R) past several lovely ponds & **FREE WILL (Bapt.) CH.** (1820). Return past Mem. to Block I. Mariners to village, c.**8.**

**IV. Loop Tour of I. of RHODE ISLAND ENVIRONS. 24. St.138-St.114, St.138, & Boyd Lane & return on St.114**

Take St.138-St.114 (N) out of Newport. At **c.1.5.** (R) **DUDLEY PLACE** (2nd half 18th cent.), where lived Chas. Dudley, Collector of Customs who fled Colony because of Tory sympathies. At **2.5.** St.138 branches (R) from St.114. Tour cont. on St.138 into **MIDDLETOWN TOWNSHIP,** which suffered from Brit. equally with Newport during Rev. **3.5.** J. with Acquidneck Ave.

SIDE TRIP: Take latter (R) 1m to J. with Green End Ave.

(L) 0.5m on Green End Ave. to (L) **Honeyman H.** (1742), home of Rev. Jas. Honeyman, minister of Trinity Ch., in Newport, who abruptly ended his sermon, when he heard Dean Berkeley's ship was just landing, dismissed the congregation, & hurried off to greet the distinguished visitor. Just beyond Honeyman H. is **Whitehall** (O.summer.sm. fee.17th cent.remod.by Dean Berkeley.1729.rest.int.exter.& inter.), which was for 3 yrs. Berkeley's home; now owned by Yale Univ. Exhibits.

Cont. on Acquidneck Ave. to J. with Purgatory Rd. Take latter (L) to J. with Tuckermann Ave., on which (R) a few rods is "Purgatory," deep cleft in rocks up which tides rush. Cont. on Purgatory Rd. to J. with Paradise Rd. [(L) on Paradise Rd. a short distance is Easton Farm, where is **Grave of Mary Williams,** daughter of Roger Williams.] Purgatory Rd. soon changes to Hanging Rock Rd., near which is **Second Beach** (bath.no facils.). Hanging Rock Rd. passes **Hanging Rocks,** one of Berkeley's favorite haunts, & makes J. with Third Beach Rd. to (R) **Third Beach** (bath.no facils.). Footpath from here to Newport.

At **9.** on St.138, (L) **QUAKER MEETINGH.** (early 18th cent.), with old cemetery. **9.5. PORTSMOUTH** (sett. 1638), where Coddington & Clarke 1st est. themselves before moving on to Newport. In vic. was fought Battle of R.I., after which, although Brit. had been driven back, the Amers. retreated to Tiverton (see below). At c.**11.5.** is J. with Boyd Lane, on which tour cont. (L).

SIDE TRIP: (E) c.1.5m on St.138 & across Sakonnet R. on Stone Bridge to **Tiverton** (sett. late 17th cent.), which was a base for Amer. forces while Brit. held R.I. From here Maj. Talbot & small company set out & captured Brit. ship "Pigot" stationed in Sakonnet R. St.138 cont. past several int. Hs. to Mass. Line, (S) of Fall River (see US6). In Tiverton is also J. with St.126.

Take latter S. along Sakonnet R.; fine views. At 8.5m **Amesa Gray H.** (c.1684). At 10m is J. with another Rd., which runs (R) short distance to **Pabodie H.** (late 17th cent.), where lived Eliz. Alden Pabodie, daughter of John and Priscilla Alden. 13m **Sakonnet Pt.** (resort), on ocean.

Loop tour cont. on Boyd Lane (NW) to J. with St.114, near Mt. Hope Toll Bridge (see Providence). Turn (S) on St.114. At c.**14.5. LEHIGH HILL PK.** (pic.) & short distance beyond, **OLD GRIST MILL** (1812.rest.1929). **16.5. BOYD'S MILL** (1810), still grinding Johnny-cake meal. **18. LAWTON'S VALLEY** (pic.). Just (S), **Redwood H.,** country estate of Abr. Redwood (see Newport above). At c.**19. (L), OVERING H.** (early 19th cent.), where Col. W. Barton & his company surprised & captured Brit. Gen. Rich. Prescott in daring raid, July 9, 1777. At **21.5.** is J. with St.138, with which St.114 unites to Newport, **24.**

# PORTLAND

Through RR., air & bus conns. Accoms.: All types. Sight-seeing tours through city to Cape Elizabeth. Boat tours of Casco Bay Is. & coastal points. F. in bay & to (N) in Sebago & other lakes. Pub. beach: Eastern Promenade & at Willard Beach. Info.: Bureau at 3 St. Johns St., & C. of C.

Portland (largest city in Me.), on beautiful Casco Bay, famous for 365 islands, many of which are well-known summer resorts, is located on a peninsula, bounded by Casco Bay, Fore R. & Back Bay. Western & Eastern Promenades & Baxter Blvd. afford views of waterfront & deep-water harbor which has made it st.'s principal port. Portland is tourist center for Casco Bay, Maine coastal reg. & Ls. to (N). 1st settlement of any duration (1663) by Geo. Cleaves & Rich. Tucker. Cleaves, appointed Deputy Gov. by Sir Ferdinando Gorges, proprietor of Me. & most of N. H. (see Portsmouth), had his jurisdiction disputed. Lengthy litigation resulted concerning title to vast territory of what now is Maine. In 1652, Mass. colony acquired control. In 1676 & again in 1690, Inds. wiped out settlement which was re-established 1716. Falmouth, as Portland was then known, developed rapidly as port of export & import in West Indies trade. During Rev., city was almost entirely destroyed by Brit.

(Oct. 16, 1775). Afterwards it again boomed as shipping center. Portland became St. capital (1828) but in 1832 capital was moved to Augusta. Before Civil War it developed considerable antislavery sentiment & provided large contingents to Civil War armies. Shortly after Confed. surrender, city (July 4, 1866) was almost completely wiped out by fire. But catastrophe only temporarily retarded Portland's growth. Its exports today incl. pulpwood, fish, potatoes, newsprint. It has some manufacturing establishments; chief local industry is fishing & shipping of fish products.

PTS. OF INT.: (1) State & Pine Sts., **Longfellow Sq.,** with Mon. to Henry Wadsworth Longfellow, city's most illustrious citizen. (2) On Congress St., **Mon. Sq.,** with Mon. to Civil War heroes by Frank Simmons. Originally Market Sq., where stood Old Military Hall & the 18th cent. Jail. Mon. Sq. remains one of city's busiest centers. (3) 487 Congress St., **Wadsworth-Longfellow H.** (O.wks.summer.sm.fee. 1785-86.3rd story added 1815), built by Gen. Peleg Wadsworth; relics of the Wadsworths & Longfellows; old garden. Here Longfellow spent boyhood years. (4) To rear is **Mus. of Maine Hist. Soc.** (O.wks.Sat.a.m.); hist. & Ind. material; lib. In vic. are many fine old Hs. (5) 103 High St., **L. D. M. Sweat Art Mus.** (O.wks.exc.Mon. Sun.aft.); paintings by Gilbert Stuart, Sargent, Homer & other 19th cent. artists; 16th cent. Belgian tapestries; Mex. & Ind. potteries; sculptures by Frank Simmons & Paul Akers' "The Dead Pearl Diver"; exhibits. (6) To rear is **Sweat Mansion** (O. same as Mus.1800.fine post-Col.example.from designs by Parris). (7) 97 Spring St., **School of Fine & Applied Art,** conducted in connection with Sweat Mus. (8) Other old Hs. on High St. incl.: 116 High St., **Cumberland Club H.** (1800.from sketches by Parris). SW. cor. High & Danforth Sts., **Storer-Mussey H.** (O.fine Fed.exter.& inter.), part of Children's Hosp. (9) On State St., int. bldgs. incl.: 51 State St., **Dole H.** (Churchill H.) (1801.by Parris); 137 State St., **St. Luke's Cathedral** (1855.Goth.by Henry Vaughan,rose window & reredos carved by Kirschmeyer). In Codman Mem. Chapel is "Madonna & Child" by John LaFarge; 162 State St., **Portland Club** (Shepley H.) (1805.from designs by Parris.fine post-Col.); 166 State St., **Mellen-Fessenden H.** (O.1807), now Cath. Chapel, was home of Secy. of Treas. under Lincoln, Wm. P. Fessenden. (10) 24 Elm St., **Soc. of Nat. Hist.** (O.wks.aft.); lib., Nat. Hist. material, Ind. relics. (11) 435 Congress St., **First Parish Ch.** (O.Unit.1825). (12) 380 Congress St., **City Hall & Mun. Auditorium** (O.1809-12.by Carrère & Hastings,& Stevens & Stevens), on site of orig. Cth. (1782-1816). Auditorium (summer concerts) has one of largest pipe organs in world. (13) Cor. Federal & Pearl Sts., **Cumberland County Cth.** (O.wks.1906-07.by Geo.Burnham). Opp. is Fed. Cth. (14) On Congress St., **Second Parish Ch.,** where Elijah Kellogg preached (see Harpswell). (15) Just beyond, **Lincoln Pk.,** created after 1866 fire.

(16) 12 Franklin St., **Birthpl. of N. P. Willis,** the poet, & sister, Sara, known by her pen name, Fanny Fern. (17) 307 Congress St., **Cathedral of the Immaculate Conception** (Cath.1869.French Goth.fine exter.& inter.), seat of the Me. diocese; notable Stations of the Cross & fine stained glass windows. (18) On Congress St., further along, is **Eastern Cemetery** (250 yrs. old). Here is buried Commodore Preble, who, in command of the "Constitution" as his flagship, defeated Barbary pirates, 1803. Here also are graves of Brit. & Amer. sea captains killed in Battle off Monhegan Is. (1813) (see Boothbay Harbor). (19) 161 Fore St. cor. Hancock St., **Birthpl. of Longfellow** (O.summer.fee.1784). (20) 15 Hancock St., **Birthpl. of Thos. B. Reed,** for yrs. speaker of U.S. House of Rep. & famous for ironical quips. (21) 714 Congress St., **Neal Dow H.** (1824), owner was author of Me.'s prohibition law. (22) Opp., at 717, is his **Birthpl.** (1800); eventually to become a Mus. (23) At J. with Fore St. & Eastern Promenade, **Ft. Allen Pk.;** fine view of Casco Bay, site of old fts. (24) Off Eastern Promenade, **Pub. Bath. Beach.** (25) End of Congress St., at Eastern Promenade, 2.2$^{m}$ from city center is **Mon. to Cleaves & Tucker,** city's founders. (26) Inters. of North & Congress Sts., **Portland Observ.** (O.sm.fee.1807); fine view. (27) On North St., **Ft. Summer Pk.,** on site of old fort. Cont. on Baxter Blvd. past **Baxter Mem.** (28) At 85 Bedford St., **Deering Mansion** (O.1804), once a sea captain's home; period furniture & relics. (29) At Deering Ave., **Deering Oaks Pk.,** site of successful stand by Major Ben. Church (see Bristol, R.I.), & company against Inds., 1689. Next yr. occurred massacre at Ft. Loyal & its destruction. (30) 32-38 Thomas St., **Williston Congr. Ch.,** where was born Christian Endeavor Soc. (31) On Western Promenade, **Thos. B. Reed Mon. & Western Cemetery,** with Longfellow family tomb, & grave

of Elijah Kellogg (see above). (32) On Westbrook St., in Stroudwater W. of city 3m is **Tate H.** (O.appl.1755.rest.fine inter.). (33) No. 2 Waldo St., in Stroudwater, **Old Means H.** (fine inter.).

## TRIPS OUT OF PORTLAND, MAINE

### I. LOOP TOUR to SEBAGO LAKE AREA. 79. St.26, St.11, US302

Via: W. Falmouth, Gray, Sabbathday Village, Poland, Tripp L., Naples, S. Casco, Raymond, N. Windham.

This Loop Tour gives access to Sebago L. vacation area & int. old towns.

**0. PORTLAND. 7. WEST FALMOUTH,** on Piscataqua R., near Highland L. **11.5. WEST CUMBERLAND.** Near-by, Forest L. & Little Duck Pond. **17. GRAY** (sett.1750), was nearly destroyed by Inds. during Fr. & Ind. Wars. **20.5. DRY MILLS.** 1m (R), **St. Fish Hatcheries** (O), one of largest trout hatcheries in U.S. Adj., **St. Game Farm** having pheasants & other game birds. J. with St.4 (see). **25.5. SABBATHDAY LAKE VILLAGE** (resort) near Royal R. & Sabbathday Pond, originally a Shaker settlement (est.1793), one of few still active (see Shakers). **26.5.** several old **Shaker Bldgs. 28. POLAND SPRING** (resort); famous bottled water. **State of Maine Bldg.;** exhibits. **29.5. Middle Range Pond** (boat.bath.f.). **33.** (S) J. with St.11 on which tour cont. (SW). **34.5. Tripp L.** (boat.bath.pic.resort). **48. NAPLES** (boat.bath.f.resort), on Bay of Naples, Sebago L., Long L. & Songo & Crooked Rs. Near-by, Trickery & Brandy Ponds. Naples is heart of Sebago L. recr. area (see below). Boat. trip on Songo R. View of Mt. Washington, N.H. J. with US302, which tour now follows (SE).

SIDE TRIP: Take US302 (NW). At 1.5m **The Manor** (late 18th cent.int.exter.& inter.now hotel). 8.5m **Bridgton** (sett.1770.resort.winter sports) on **Highland L.** (boat.bath.f.). **Enoch Perley H.** (1776). **Walter Hawkins H.** (2nd half 18th cent.). Pub. camp site.

Take St.117 (R) 3.5m to N. Bridgton on Long L. (resort). **Bridgton Academy for Boys** (est.early 19th cent.) has mus.; coll. Ind. material, antiques & other items. Near Bridgton are Moose & Wood Ponds & a pub. camp site.

14m **Moose Pond.** 25m **Fryeburg** (sett.1762.summer & winter resort) is one of Me.'s most charming towns. It is claimed Capt. John Smith visited the vic. in 1614. **Fryeburg Academy** (est.1791) where Dan. Webster taught school (1802). **Congr. Ch.** (1775).

From Fryeburg St.113 runs (N) through E. sec. of White Mt. Nat. For. through fine scenery, via Evans Notch, to J. with US2 at **Gilead,** near which is **Gilead For. Camp.** St.113 makes J. near **N. Chatham** with Rd. running (S) to **S. Chatham** & then (W) **Kearsarge Village** (see N. Conway, N.H.).

At Fryeburg is J. with St.5. At 28m on US302 is **Me.-N.H. Line** (see White Mountains Tour).

**54.5. SOUTH CASCO,** on Sebago L.

SIDE TRIP: Take Rd. (R) from S. Casco. At 0.5m (R) **Manning H.** (early 19th cent.int. inter.); home of Hawthorne's uncle, Capt. Dingley. Near Manning H., (L) **Murch H.** (late 18th cent.) & old **Windmill.** On other side of Dingley Brook, c.0.5m (L), is **Hawthorne H.** (O.June-Sept.1812) where young Nathaniel lived with his mother. At 4.5m **Pulpit Rock & Frye's Leap Cliff** named for Capt. Frye who is said to have leaped into lake to escape Inds. Under Cliff, Hawthorne is said to have begun "The Scarlet Letter."

**57.5. RAYMOND** (resort) on E. shore of Sebago L. (f.). Near-by are Panther, Crescent & Raymond Ponds. Boat trip (summer) through lake (see Naples above). **Fish Hatchery** for land-locked salmon. Old Hs. incl.: **Morton & Hayden Hs.** (both 2nd half 18th cent.). In vic., **Fitch H.** (1828) & old **Dyer & Brown Homesteads. 63. N. WINDHAM,** charming old town, gateway to Sebago-Long Ls. reg. Dam built on Presumpscot R. by settlers interfering with salmon coming up-river to spawn, provoked 6-yr. war with Inds. **79. PORTLAND.**

### II. LOOP TOUR TO STANDISH. 72. St.25, St.35, St.114 & US302

Via: Westbrook, Gorham, Standish, Sebago L. Village, Naples, S. Casco.

**0. PORTLAND. 6. WESTBROOK,** a mill town, & birthpl. of B. P. Akers, sculptor, & Rudy Vallee, radio artist. **Dana Warp Mills** (O.cotton). Near-by, **Bean H.** (1805). **Haskell Silk Mills** (O.1805), & c.1m from town, **S. D. Warren Co.** paper mills (O). **10.5. GORHAM** (sett.early 18th cent.). Near-by, **Ft. Hill** (view) on site of ft. (1745). **Congr. Ch.** (1797). Near-by on South St., **Baxter Mus.** (O.aft.certain wks.summer. 1808); Amer. wars & Ind. relics. Near-by, **Gorham Normal School.** 120 Fort Hill

Rd., **McClellan H.** (1773). On Main St., **Smith H.** & **Crockett H.** (both 2nd half 18th cent.). J. with St.4 (see Portland Trip III). **17.5. STANDISH** (sett.c.1750), near Watchic & Bonny Eagle Ls.; named for Miles Standish (see Plymouth, Mass.). **Unit. Ch.** (1806). **Marrett H.** (late 18th cent.). In Standish, St.35 (R) to **Sebago L. Village** at **19.5.** (see Portland Trip I), & from there take St.114 (L) circling W. shore of Sebago L. to **NAPLES** at **42.** (see Portland Trip I). For US302 (NW) to Fryeburg on N.H. Line, see Portland Trip I. In Naples, take US302 (S) to **PORTLAND** at **72.** (For this stretch of Rd., see Portland Trip I.)

**III. PORTLAND to CANADIAN BORDER** (S. of Megantic, Que.). **172. St.100, St.4**

Via: Gray, Auburn, Turner, Farmington, Rangeley, Stratton & Eustis. Conns. with Maine Central RR. in Auburn, Livermore Falls & Farmington. Bus conns. all way to Rangeley. Accoms. to Rangeley; limited beyond.

This route travels through some int. old villages to Rangeley Ls. region. Then through a wild for. section where, however, there are camp. facils.

**0. PORTLAND. 17. GRAY** (sett.1762) (See Portland Trip I). J. with St.4 & St.26. Tour cont. on St.4. **34. AUBURN** (see). **37. Auburn L.** (boat.f.no bath.). **45. TURNER. Old Town H.** (1831). Bear Mt. (fine view). Pleasant Ponds. **52.** (L) here on St.219 to **Bear Pond Park** (resort.boat.in summer) & **Little Bear Pond. 63. Livermore Falls. Internat. Paper Co.** (O). **71. WILTON,** J. with US2 (see). Wilson Pond & stream. **79. FARMINGTON** (see US2). J. with US2 & St.27 (see). On Rangeley Rd. 2.3$^{m}$ is **Birthpl.** of famous, Maine-born opera star, **Lillian Nordica** (O.sm.fee.1840;Nordica relics). **92. STRONG,** where in 1854, Me. Republican Party was born. **124. RANGELEY** (info.bureau) on Rangeley L. (1,500';good h.f.accoms. guides.canoe trip on Rangeley Chain of Ls.). This is one of Me.'s scenic chain of Ls. consisting of Rangeley, Upper & Lower Richardson, Mooselookmeguntic, Cupsuptic, & Umbagog Ls.

SIDE TRIP: From **Rangeley** to **Errol, N.H.** 44$^{m}$ St.16. Via: Oquossoc & Wilson's Mills. Pub. camp sites along Ls. This route circles N. bet. the Ls. At 9$^{m}$, **Haines Landing,** where steamboats leave for other parts of L. Mooselookmeguntic. From here St.16 becomes a gravel surfaced Rd. It passes Cupsuptic & Upper Richardson Ls. At 28$^{m}$, **Wilson's Mills,** where paved Rd. resumes. 44$^{m}$ **Errol, N.H.**

**142.5. STRATTON.** From here canoe trip to Rockwood on Moosehead L. (see). J. with St.27 (see Wiscasset, Me.). **143.5.** At N. end of Cathedral Pines grove here, Site of Benedict Arnold's encampment on expedition to Canada, 1775. **145.** A dirt Rd. leads (L) here 2$^{m}$ to **Eustis Ridge,** fine view of Mts., highest being **Sugar Loaf** (4,237'). **148.5. EUSTIS,** near frontier. St.4 now passes several camp sites. **172. ARNOLD POND,** at Amer.-Canadian border, 12$^{m}$ S. of Megantic, Que.

**IV. PORTLAND, ME. to ME.-N.H. LINE** (7.5$^{m}$ E. of Errol, N.H.). **100. St.26**

Via: Gray, Sabbathday, Poland, (Norway), S. Paris. Bethel, Newry & Upton.

This route runs through scenically mountainous, river & L. country culminating in Grafton Notch & Umbagog L. of the Rangeley Chain. Cont. to Errol, N.H., near Dixville Notch, White Mts. (see).

**Sec. 1: PORTLAND to J. with St.11. 33.** (For this sec. see Portland Trip I.)

**Sec. 2: J. with St.11 to N.H. LINE. 67.**

At **11.5.** J. with St.117 leading (L) on latter short distance to Norway (resort), on Pennesseewassee L. In vic., Little Pennesseewassee L. & Norway L., a few miles W. **13.5. S. PARIS** on Little Androscoggin R. **15.** J. with Rd.

SIDE TRIP: Take latter (R) 1.5$^{m}$ to **Paris Hill. Old Stone Jail** (1st quarter 19th cent.). **Birthpl. of Hannibal Hamlin** (see Portland). **Hubbard H.** (1806) & several other int. old Hs. **Bapt. Ch.** (early 19th cent.).

**19.5. Snow Falls** of Little Androscoggin R. **22. Maine Mineral Store;** mineral coll. **29. Bryant Pond. 33. Lock's Mills.** In vic., North, South & Round Ponds. On a side Rd. (W) 3$^{m}$ are Greenwood Ice Caves. **38.5. BETHEL,** J. with US2 (see). **45. NEWRY** (see US2). **49.5. N. NEWRY,** hemmed in by peaks of Blue Mt. Range, on Bear R. along which are many fine cascades. **54.5. Screw Augur Falls. 57. Grafton Notch.** To W., Old Speck Mt. (4,250'), after Mt. Katahdin, highest pt. in state; to (NE), Baldpate Mt. (4,080'). **58.** J. with Appalachian Trl. (see). **65. UPTON,** at Umbagog L., one of Rangeley Chain (guides avail.). **Bragg H.** (1838). **67. ME.-N.H. LINE,** c.7.5$^{m}$ (E) of Errol, N.H. (see White Mountain Tour).

## PORTSMOUTH

RR. Sta.: Vaughan & Deer Sts., B.& Me.RR. Market Sq., Bus Sta. N. Bow St., Steamers to Isles of Shoals (June-Sept.). Near-by ocean beaches (see US1). Resorts & recr. facils. on Great Bay. Excellent f. in Ocean & inland waters. Info.: C. of C., 50 Daniels St. Accoms.: All types. Boat trips to Isles of Shoals (wk.summer).

Portsmouth (sett.1623) was formerly one of America's busiest ports & shipbuilding centers. Its crowded harbor reported, even early in 18th cent., as many as 16 vessels in foreign trade leaving or coming on 1 day. Hundreds of boats comprised its fishing fleet. Old Pepperell, father of Sir William, conqueror of Louisburg, who came to N.H. with bare hands & native shrewdness as his only assets, owned 100 boats in Grand Banks fisheries. Shipyards on Badger's I. & elsewhere in vic. resounded with hammer & saw. Ropewalks were populous with workmen twisting hawsers for vessels sliding down the ways. Great pines from the backwoods were snaked through the forest & arduously chivied around Salmon Falls into the harbor, to be trimmed down to size for the Brit. Navy. Until N. H. began supplying them, Britain, as Pepys noted, feared for her sea supremacy because of lack of good sticks for her ships. During the Rev. & War of 1812, her men-o'-war, because she no longer could get good masts, had to be equipped with patched ones, which often collapsed under stress of bad weather. This business of lumber for masts led to clashes between local people & Brit. commissioners, who marked the most desirable trees with the "Broad Arrow" for the navy. Local lumbermen were apt to disregard the sacred mark & sell designated trees to the highest bidder. During Fr.-Ind. wars, Rev. & War of 1812, Portsmouth prospered. Her shipping suffered from Brit. men-o'-war & French privateers, it is true. While the "cold war" with France was being waged in late 1790's & early 19th cent., so many of her ships were captured by the Fr. that it was currently said, "Yankees are cheap in Guadaloupe," whither the prizes were taken. But Portsmouth's own privateers did very well &, in fact, became big business. They netted rich dividends for their owners. 10 of them brought in some 400 ships. During Rev., the cargo of the "Prince George," destined for Brit. Gen. Gage in Boston, was captured by a Portsmouth ship & supplied Washington with much-needed material. The famous "Fox," out of Portsmouth, during "Mr. Madison's War," was nicknamed the "million dollar privateer." On one voyage alone, she showed a profit of $328,731. From 1840's until after Civil War, Portsmouth built some of fastest clippers, whose great mainsails whitened the seas from Australia & China to the Mediterranean.

The days of Portsmouth's glory have departed, but evidences of early wealth & luxury are many mansions built by merchants & ship captains along her often narrow & tortuous streets. Portsmouth has a number of industries, but biggest source of income is U.S. Navy Yard on Seavey's I., employing 5,300 men (1948). Besides the Navy Yard & the business its personnel provides, sometimes on the boisterous side, the most important revenue comes from tourists. Portsmouth is a central point for vacationists headed for N.H. & Main coast resorts, the White Mts. & Vermont. Portsmouth is situated on W. bank of Piscataqua R., several miles from the R's. mouth, & is bounded (N) by North Mill Pond, in old days site of shipbuilding & ropewalk activities, & (S) by South Mill Pond. Badger's & other Is. dot the estuary of the river, & (S) are the hist. Isles of Shoals, out in the Atlantic. W. of the city is Great Bay, an arm of the Piscataqua which has become a favorite summer resort. The vic. was explored & mapped by Capt. John Smith, working for Sir Ferdinando Gorges, before Smith took to colonizing Jamestown, Va. But even prior to that, the excellent fishing grounds off the Piscataqua & Isles of Shoals attracted fishermen from Europe, who, however, made no permanent settlements. Gorges & his partner, John Mason, acquired a vast concession of land from the Plymouth Council, & in 1623 they granted Scotch David Thompson a tract near Portsmouth. Thompson & his companions built their homes at Odiorne's Pt.

Portsmouth, together with Dover, Hampton & Exeter, grew rapidly, shipbuilding on Badger's I. being an early industry. In 18th cent., the city became capital of Colony of N. H., which King Charles II had separated from Mass., & up to 1800, Portsmouth achieved its greatest prosperity. It played a prominent part in the Fr.-Ind. wars. Wm. Pepperell, one of its citizens, commanded the land forces in the successful siege of Louisburg (1745). When conflict with Brit. crown began, Portsmouth did its share in resisting Brit. encroachments. After passage of Stamp Act, city went into mourning. Bells tolled, flags were flown at half-mast, & the N. H. "Gazette" appeared with black borders. Tea & Tories were expedited to Halifax, probably the origin of the expression "Go to Halifax." In 1774 Paul Revere galloped posthaste to Portsmouth to warn of Brit. approach. Immediately the Sons of Liberty set out for near-by Ft. William & Mary, whose commander made but a show of resistance, firing cannon to points where no blood was likely to be shed & then, honor having been satisfied, surrendered. Gov. John Wentworth, graduate of Harvard, sponsor of Dartmouth's founding & shrewd administrator, could not make head against the Patriots. When Capt. Fenton, unpopular port collector, took refuge in Wentworth's house, the Sons of Liberty trained a cannon on the building, & the Gov. had to give Fenton up. Wentworth finally fled to England, returned to the Isle of Shoals & made his final exit to the Tory haven of Halifax. It was with the warship "Ranger," built at Portsmouth during Rev., that Jones made his hist. raid on Brit. commerce in the Irish Sea & burnt shipping at White Haven. When, in 1775, the Brit. fleet threatened to sack the city, it is said that pretty Mary Sparhawk, of Kittery, persuaded the commander to sail away to Portland (then Falmouth), where he did a thorough job of destruction, burning more than 400 houses. During the Rev. & War of 1812, Portsmouth's pockets were filled by her privateers, but its pre-eminence as a port was nearing its end. The short prosperity induced by the clipper shipbuilding period could not revive past glories. Its shipyards declined after the Civil War, with the coming of steam as motive power. The st. capital had long before been moved to Concord.

While never a center where the arts flourished generously as in Newport, R.I., nevertheless Portsmouth counts a number of literary lights. Best known are Daniel Webster (born in Salisbury, N.H.), who had a house in the city; Celia Thaxter, poet, daughter of lighth. keeper on one of Isles of Shoals; & Thos. Bailey Aldrich, poet & editor of "Atlantic Monthly." Aldrich's "An Old Town by the Sea" gives pleasant portrait of Portsmouth in 1870's, & in "Story of a Bad Boy" he tells of boyhood pranks, notably burning of old stagecoach in Market Sq.

PTS. OF INT.: (1) At Market Sq., Pleasant & Congress Sts., **North Ch.** (1712.rebuilt. 1854). (2) 143 Pleasant St., **Gov. Langdon H.** (O.fee.1784.notable exter.& inter.), former home of Gov. John Langdon, Rev. leader & Signer of Constitution. It was at session of the new state's legislature that Langdon made his famous declaration dedicating all his property to Patriot cause & concluding with: "If we succeed in defending our firesides and homes, I may be remunerated; if we do not then the property will be of no value to me." (3) 134 Pleasant St., **South Parish Parsonage** (O.appl.1749.Georg.Col.); period furniture; original stables. (4) 179 Pleasant St., **Mark Wentworth H.** (fine Georg.Col.). (5) 214 Pleasant St., **Jacob Wendell H.** (O. appl.1789); orig. door fittings, antique furnishings. (6) Pleasant & Edward Sts., **Haven Pk.,** in which is equestrian **Statue of Gen. Porter** (by J.E.Kelley). Here is **Site of Parry H.** whose owner, E. Parry, was forced by patriots to ship consignment of tea to Halifax. (7) 34 Livermore St., **Gen. Fitz-John Porter H.** (1735). (8) Livermore St., **Dr. Nath. Parker H.** (Col.), with fine doorway. Parker was pastor of S. Church, 1808-33. (9) Pleasant & Wentworth Sts., **Wentworth Home for Aged People;** right wing was part of Gov. John Wentworth's H. (1769). (10) 444 Pleasant St., **Rollins H.** (c.1800). (11) 51 Hunking St., **Lear H.** (O.fee;c.1740.Georg.Col.), home of Tobias Lear, Washington's secy. & tutor of his 2 step-children. (12) 141 Mechanic St., **Wentworth-Gardiner H.** (O.wks.May-Nov.sm.fee.1760.rest.fine exter.& inter.). (13) Mechanic & Marcy Sts., **Point of Graves,** cemetery dating from 1671. (14) 151 Marcy St., **Site of Liberty Pole** put up in 1766 by Sons of Liberty. (15) 429 Court St., a dilapidated bldg., part of which is all that remains of **Old State H.** (16) Court & Atkinson Sts., **Pitt Tavern** (pre-Rev.), originally "The Earl of Halifax Tavern," Tory meetingplace. Sons of Liberty pulled down sign & made proprietor put up one in honor of the beloved Pitt.

(17) 386 Court St., **Thos. Bailey Aldrich H.** (O.wks.& Sun.aft.summer.sm.fee.c.1790), furnished as described in "Story of a Bad Boy." (18) Court & Washington Sts., **Chase H.** (O.appl.1730), now a shop. (19) 9 Market Sq., **The Athenaeum** (O.appl.1803.late Georg.fine exter.); colls. incl. models of clipper ships, hist. documents, relics. (20) 154 Congress St., **Cutter H.** (1750.Georg.Col.) where Pres. Monroe was entertained. (21) Middle & Islington Sts., **Pub. Lib.** (1809.Georg.Col.supposedly by Bulfinch. remod.). (22) 2 Islington St., **Buckminster H.** (1720), has a captain's walk; now funeral home. (23) 180 Middle St., **Larkin H.** (1815.supposedly by Bulfinch). (24)

152 Middle St., **Langley Boardman H.** (1805). (25) **Haymarket Sq.** Here, Sept. 12, 1765, Geo. Meserve, Royal Stamp Agent, Lord Bute, author of the Stamp Act, & the Devil were burnt in effigy. (26) At Haymarket Sq., **Pierce H.** (1800), a square wooden mansion; orig. garden. (27) Middle & State Sts., **John Paul Jones H.** (O.summer.sm.fee.1758); hist. relics. Here John Paul Jones boarded with the widow Purcell, in 1777, while waiting to take command of the "Ranger." The story goes that a group of young girls org. a quilting party at which they tore up their petticoats to make a Stars & Stripes flag for Jones' ship, the 1st Stars & Stripes to be seen in European ports. (28) N. cor. State & Chestnut Sts., **Whipple H.** (prior to 1752), home of Wm. Whipple, Col. collector of the port. (29) NW. cor. State & Fleet Sts., **Whitcomb H.** (pre-Rev.), where lived Molly Pitman, who rejected Gov. Benning Wentworth's marriage proposal. Wentworth then contracted a romantic marriage with Martha Hilton, his housekeeper. To the Whitcomb H., as Aldrich tells us in "Story of a Bad Boy," the youngsters came to eat ice cream after burning stagecoach. He says that, thereafter, the "ringleader" regularly celebrated the anniversary of this daring deed by consuming a dish of ice cream in the parlor of the H. (30) SW. cor. State & Fleet Sts., **Old Spence H.,** once home of Harriet Spence, mother of Jas. Russell Lowell. (31) NE. cor. State & Fleet Sts. (321 State St.), **Davenport H.** (O. appl.1758.Georg.Col.fine inter.).

(32) State & Church Sts., **South Parish Ch.** (1824-26.Gr.Rev.). Congr. was org. 1714. Paul Revere bell. (33) 130 Court St., **Old Folsom Slater H.** (rest.), now business bldg. (34) State St., **Episc. Chapel** (1832.Gr.Rev.), now parish H. (35) NE. cor. Chapel & Daniels St., **Warner H.** (O.wks.summer.sm.fee.1718), oldest brick H. in city. It is said Franklin installed lightning rod here. Has int. early murals. (36) Chapel St., **St. John's Ch.** (O.appl.at rectory.1807.fine inter.int.murals); has rare "Vinegar Bible" printed 1717; old furnishings & portraits; communion service presented by Queen Caroline. Church bell was captured at Louisburg, 1745. In **Graveyard** are buried several Col. Govs. (37) 51 Market St., **Moffet-Ladd H.** (O.summer.fee.1763.fine exter.& inter.); antique furnishings. (38) 25 Deer St., **Deer Tavern** (1705). (39) 63 Deer St., **Home for Aged Women** (O.appl.18th cent.). (40) 93 Deer St., **Old Rice H.** where in 1814 was held a "calico party" when lady guests helped themselves to calico captured by Capt. Rice's privateers. (41) 107 Deer St., H. with **Old State H. Balcony,** from which Decl. of Ind. was read in 1776. (42) Northwest St., just off St.4, **Richard Jackson H.** (O.summer.sm.fee.1664.adds.int.inter.). (43) Vaughan St. & Raite's Court, **H.** (marked by tablet), part of which was famous **Assembly H.,** where balls were held in post-Rev. era. (44) 50 Daniels St., **Site of Birthpl. of Celia Thaxter** (now C. of C. Bldg.) whose most popular poems are in "Among the Isles of Shoals." (45) On Seavey's I. off Kittery, Me., **Portsmouth Navy Yard** (O.appl.); est. 1794 (see US1, Sec. 10). During World War II, some 20,000 were employed at yard which is still constructing submarines. (46) 364 Middle St., 1m W. of city center, **Old Rundlet-May H.** In vic. are **Cutt H.** (see Portsmouth Trip II); town of **New Castle** (see Boston Trip IV); the **Benning Wentworth Mansion** (see Boston Trip IV); **Proprietors' Burying Ground; Isles of Shoals** incl. White I. on which is former **Home of Celia Thaxter,** near Lighth.

## TRIPS OUT OF PORTSMOUTH

### I. LOOP TOUR to RAYMOND & RETURN. c.60. St.101, St.111, St.107

Via: Exeter, Kingston, Raymond & return via Epping.

**13.5. EXETER** (sett.1638). Town, on Exeter R. (swim.), was 1st sett. by John Wheelwright, a college mate of Oliver Cromwell. To middle of 19th cent., it was prosperous shipbuilding center & port. Like other towns in N. H. & Me., it was scene of riots against king's surveyor when he tried to appropriate best for. trees for Brit. Navy. City was st. capital for a time during Rev. when Portsmouth was considered too exposed. Here, in 1776, N.H. declared its independence several months before Philadelphia Decl. Today Exeter is chiefly notable as home of famous Phillips Exeter Academy (for boys). PTS. OF INT.: (1) Water & Front Sts., **Bandstand** (1913 by Henry Bacon, architect of Lincoln Mem., Washington, D.C.). (2) NW. cor. Water & Front Sts., **Town Hall** (1855). (3) Front & Elm Sts., **Nath. Gilman H.** (O.18th cent. rest.). On Front St. are several fine 18th & early 19th cent. Hs. & (4) **Congr. Ch.** (late 18th cent.int.facade). (5) Water & Clifford Sts., **Gilman-Clifford H.** (O.appl.

1650-58), also called Garrison H., allegedly one of oldest in state. Dan. Webster boarded here when a student at Exeter. On High St. also are several handsome old Hs. (6) Water & Gov. Sts., **Cincinnati Hall** or Gilman-Ladd H. (O.Thurs.aft.& appl. caretaker.1721.adds.1775.fine inter.), owned by N. H. Soc. of Cincinnati. Here lived Nicholas Gilman, Signer of Const., & here was housed St. Treasury during Rev.; coll. of portraits, old furnishings, hist. relics. (7) Water & Spring Sts., **Folsom Tavern** (2nd half 18th cent.Georg.Col.rest.). (8) 11 Cass St., **Birthpl. of Lewis Cass** (1740), 1st Gov. of Mich. Territory (see Mich.) & U.S. Secy. of State & War. On Park & Winter Sts. are several int. old Hs. (9) Front & Pine Sts., **Soldiers' Mem.** (by Dan.C.French). (10) On Front St., **Phillips Exeter Academy,** founded 1781 by John Phillips (see Andover, Mass.). Among noted students were Dan. Webster, Lewis Cass, Ed. Everett, Geo. Bancroft (historian), Geo. Ed. Woodberry, poet & critic, Rbt. T. Lincoln, & Booth Tarkington. In **Yard** are some of oldest bldgs. Several of the handsome modern structures are by Ralph Adams Cram. Oldest bldg. is **Dean's H.** (1783.rest.by Cram). **Principal's H.** dates from 1811. (11) 72 Front St., **Birthpl. of Ed. Tuck** (1750), benefactor of Dartmouth U.

**19.** J. with St.111 on which Loop Tour cont. (L). **25. KINGSTON. Bartlett H.** (2nd half 18th cent.remod.Gr.Rev.), home of Josiah Bartlett, Signer of Decl. of Ind. Near Kingston is **Kingston L. St. Reserv.** (bath.boat.f.). In Kingston is J. with St.107, on which tour cont. (NW). At **28.** on St.107 is J. with Rd.

SIDE TRIP: Take latter (L) 3m past old cemetery. Just beyond on same Rd. (R) is **Danville Meeting H.** (O.appl.1760.int.inter.& exter.), notable because it is one of few churches in N. H. without a steeple.

At **28.5.** (R) **Fremont Meeting H.** (O.during Aug.services.1800.int.inter.& exter.), also without a steeple. St.107 shortly passes through **FREMONT & RAYMOND** (sett.early 18th cent.) to J. with St.101 at **34.** from Portsmouth. Cont. (E) on St.101. At **39.** is **EPPING** (sett.1741), formerly an important industrial town. Cont. (E) on St.101 to **PORTSMOUTH, c.60.**

## II. LOOP TOUR to DURHAM & RETURN. 60. St.16, US202 & US4

Via: Dover, Rochester, Northwood.

Take St.16 (N) out of Portsmouth. **0.5.** J. with Northwest Ave., on which is (R) **Rich. Jackson H.** (O.see Portsmouth). **1. Cutt H.** (early 19th cent.). Near here Mrs. Ursula Cutt was killed by Inds., 1694. **4.5.** J. with St.151.

SIDE TRIP: (L) 1.5m on St.151 to **Newington** (1670). **Meetingh.** (1st half 18th cent.). **Old Parsonage** (late 17th cent.) with Paul Revere Bell.

**5.** on St.16 **SULLIVAN TOLL BRIDGE,** named in honor of Gen. John Sullivan (see below) across Great Bay. At N. end of Bridge is J. with US4 (see below & US4).

**7. QUAKER BURYING GROUND** (17th cent.). **11. DOVER** (sett.c.1723), at falls of Cocheco R., which supplies power for city's industries, largely cotton goods & machinery. Town was devastated by Inds., 1689. Shipping once came up R., making city something of a port, & logs were here shaped into masts for Brit. Navy. Many Quakers settled in vic. of Dover in 17th cent., & were grimly persecuted (see Salisbury, Mass.).

PTS. OF INT.: (1) Hale & Locust Sts., **Lafayette H.** (early 19th cent.fine inter.), now Parish H. of St. Thomas' Episc. Ch. (2) 107 Locust St., **Lincoln H.** (1st half 19th cent.), where Lincoln stayed over (1860). (3) On Silver St. & on Central Ave. are a number of fine old Hs. (4) On Central Ave. is **Pine Hill Cemetery,** oldest in township. (5) Also on Central Ave. is **Friends Meetingh.** (2nd half 18th cent.), which Whittier often attended. (6) 182-192 Central Ave., **Woodman Institute** (O.wks.aft. lectures), which occupies 3 old Hs.: at 182 Central Ave., **Woodman H.** (1818), containing Nat. Hist. Coll.; **Old Fort** made of logs & containing pioneer furnishings; & at 192 Central Ave., **Hale H.** (1813). (7) 448 Central Ave., **Tablet** on business bldg. comm. Cocheco massacre (1689). Major Rich. Waldron who took prisoner 400 peaceful Inds. & thereby aroused Ind. hostility, was massacred here. The massacre spread to entire settlement. (8) 35 2nd St., **Osgood H.** (O.1st half 19th cent.); int. primitive murals. (9) 604 Central Ave., old H. occupied by **First Ch. of Christ Scientist** (Gr.Rev.remod.). (10) On Portland Ave., **Cocheco Burying Ground** (L) in which Major Waldron is buried. (11) 138 Portland Ave., **Guppy H.** (late 17th cent.). (12) 7 Varney St., **Varney-Ham H.** (late 17th cent.). (13) **Garrison Hill,** by path from Varney St., affords fine view. Near Dover is **Bellamy Pk.** (bath.).

**11.5.** St.4 (Portland Ave.) branches off (NE) from St.16.

SIDE TRIP: Take St.4 (R) past **Wentworth Manor** (O.summer.parts date from 17th cent. fine inter.). At 3m in **Rollinsford** are **Philpot H.** (17th cent.) & an old inn, former home of Chas. Doe, Chief Justice of N.H. 4m **Salmon Falls.** Great pine masts were sent down here in what was probably 1st log drive in U.S. Cont. on St.4 into Maine. **South Berwick** at 4.5m. NE. cor. Main & Portland Sts., **Sarah Orne Jewett H.** (O.summer.sm.fee.1774.fine portico.int.exter.&inter.), birthpl. of author whose novels depicting New England life are among earliest Amer. realist fiction. Her novel, "Deephaven," is said to have used Dover as its setting. H. contains old furniture, Jewett relics & mss. Near-by, on Portland Ave., is **Eastman Community H.** (O) where the author also lived. On Academy St. (E) 0.5m is **Berwick Academy,** one of oldest in Me. **Old Cemetery** (1728). On Walnut Hill, **Warren Garrison H.** (mid-18th cent.), former home of Gladys H. Carroll, author of "As the Earth Turns."

(R) 2m on Academy St. is **Hamilton H.** (late 18th cent.), one of several ancient Hs. at this point.

At 16m on St.4, **Bauneg Beg. Pond.** 25.5m Alfred (1784) named for Alfred the Great. At J. here with St.111, **Whipping Tree** where criminals were flogged. At Kennebunk & Main Sts., **Cth.;** documents date from 1635. Near Green, **Holmes H.** (O.1802). John Holmes was one of commissioners who negotiated Webster-Ashburton Treaty (1842). Another int. old bldg. is **Crooked H.** In vic. are several lakes. 28m **Shaker Pond. Institute of Notre Dame** (O), formerly Shaker Settlement, with old bldgs. restored. 34m **East Waterboro,** J. with St.5 (see). 41.5m **Bar Mills.** (R) on Rd. 1.5m along E. bank of Saco R. to **Salmon Falls.** (R) from Bridge, in village of Hollis, **Quillcote** (early 19th cent.), former home of Kate Douglas Wiggin. 49m **Gorham, Me.** J. with St.25 (see Portland Trip II). St.4 cont. (NE) in Me. almost to Canadian Border (see Portland, Trip III).

**13.** J. with St.16A, which tour follows (R).

**16.** on St.16A, **SOMERSWORTH,** an industrial town. **Jos. Wentworth H.** (18th cent.).

**18.** J. with St.16 which tour follows (N).

**22.5.** on St.16, is **Dame H.** (O.summer.sm.fee.1758.int.inter.). Near here occurred massacre of settlers by Inds. (1746). **24. ROCHESTER** (sett.1728), an industrial town, on Cocheco R.; suffered from Ind. attacks as late as 1746. It was once important stagecoach stop on Rd. to upper part of St. On Central Sq., **Parson Main Mon.** comm. Rev. Amos Main, much revered by the Inds. S. Main St., **Congr. Ch.** (18th & 1st half 19th cents.); **Pub. Lib.** (O); rare books & various colls. In Rochester is J. with US202A on which Loop Tour cont. (S). **37. NORTHWOOD,** a pleasant old New England town. Near-by are Bow, Harvey, Northwood & other Ls. In Northwood is J. with US4 on which Loop Tour cont. (SE). About 1m from Northwood (E) on US4, is J. with St.152.

SIDE TRIP: (SE) on St.152 to **Nottingham Sq.,** around whose Green are located some fine old bldgs. Mon. near Common honors Rev. patriots. Stone on **Site of Ind. Raid** (1747) & another on **Site of Early Blockh. Site of Dearborn H.** where lived Henry Dearborn who led militia to Boston after Battle of Lexington. (SW) of Nottingham Sq., c.4m on Rd. branching (R) from St.152, is **Pawtuckaway Pond St. Reserv.**

**47.** J. with St.155 which leads (S) 4.5m to **Lee. C. S. Cortland Estate** & **Old Friends' Schoolh.** (both O) of which Whittier wrote in "The Birches of Lee." **50. DURHAM** (sett.1633) suffered during King Philip's War & was practically destroyed by Inds. in 1694. One of its most famous citizens was Gen. John Sullivan, in command during Battle of R.I., & leader of an expedition in N.Y. & Pa. which ended menace of the Iroquois during Rev. After taking part in many battles Gen. Sullivan died of wounds received at Yorktown. On (S) side of Oyster R., on which town is located, is **Gen. John Sullivan H.** (1716); his grave is in cemetery at rear. In Durham is **Univ. of N. H.,** coed.; founded in 1866 as land-grant college & branch of Dartmouth. In 1890, St. Legislature established it as independent institution to meet terms of will of Benj. Thompson, who left $800,000 for establishment of a college on his land in Durham. 1st class was graduated in 1892 "from a cow barn." Univ. owns some 2,300-as. of which campus comprises about 170 as. Undergraduate Dept., granting B.A. & B.S. degrees; College of Agric., Univ. Farm & Fors.; College of Technology. Univ. also grants professional degrees in mechanical, electrical & civil engineering & has extension service covering state. From Durham, return on US4 to **PORTSMOUTH** at **60.**

# PROVIDENCE

N.Y., N.H. & H. RR. Sta. at Exchange Place. Bus Sta. on Fountain St. bet. Eddy & Mathewson Sts. Airport S. of city. Steamers to N.Y.C. at Point St. Bridge; to Newport & Block I.; excursion trips. Info.: C. of C., 75 Fountain St.; Auto Club of R.I., 50 Fountain St. Concerts at Metropolitan Theater. Sports at Infantry Hall, 144 S. Main St. & in Auditorium, 111 N. Main St.; outdoor sports at Brown Univ. field. Beaches on Narragansett Bay. Harness racing at Roger Williams Pk. (Pawtucket) & Lincoln Downs, on St.146 (NW). Golf in city pk. & private clubs.

Providence is at J. of Woonasquatucket & Moshassuck Rs., which join to make Providence R., which in turn loses itself in upper Narragansett Bay. City is built on 3 hills, & most important pts. of int. are clustered around Prospect St. or College Hill. The crowded lower city occupies dist. around downtown Westminster St. Most financial institutions are located E. of Dorrance St. & shopping dist. W. of it. Providence, st. capital, was settled in 1636 by Roger Williams & his followers seeking refuge from Mass. religious persecution. Williams dedicated the new settlement to "persons distressed for conscience" & named it "in commemoration of God's Providence." He was beloved by Inds., who gave him the name of "Netop" (Friend). Shortly after arrival, Williams procured deed from Narragansett Inds. for land chosen for settlement, & relations with them were friendly until King Philip's War, 1676.

Development of Providence followed along lines typical of New England coastal settlements on the "Fall Line," where water power was available. Very soon its economy shifted from agric. to shipbuilding & commerce. As at Newport, rum, molasses, slaves & privateering brought wealth to its citizens. With approach of Rev., Providence proved as active in resistance to Brit. as Boston. It had its own "Tea party" in 1772 & on May 4, 1776, at the Old State H., the independence of R.I. was proclaimed 2 months before the Philadelphia Declaration. During Rev., city furnished men, money & supplies but, unlike Newport, it escaped miseries of Brit. occupation. Providence built its own navy during Rev., Abr. Whipple being its 1st chief & R.I. urged Government to found a navy. When this was done, Esek Hopkins, Providence citizen, became first Comdr. in Chief. Three quarters of the officers of the new ships were R.I. men.

With first decades of 19th cent. came typical shift to industry, but Jabez Gorham had already founded the shop which is today Gorham Silver Co. The machine age, here chiefly in textile mills, transformed Providence & brought great influx of immigrants to man new machines. City today is important mfg. center, especially of textiles, jewelry, metals & rubber goods. With growth of Brown Univ., Providence became a considerable cultural center. The theater had developed in the 18th cent., despite a prohibiting law passed in 1762. It is recorded that despite law "The School for Scandal" was produced in the Colony (old State) H. The law was repealed in 1792. The Players, a dramatic group which now has repertory theater of its own, was founded early in 20th cent. In mid-19th cent. occurred Poe's famous romance with Mrs. Sarah Whitman, herself a poet of some reputation. A considerable group of artists made their homes in Providence in 19th & early 20th cents., among them the Hoppin brothers, one of whom (Thos.) designed the window of the Four Apostles in New York's Trinity Church. Others were E. L. Peckham, Thos. Robinson, Marcus Waterman, Geo. Whittaker, J. F. Weir & Chas. Hemingway. A group of resident artists founded the Art Club. R.I. School of Design, founded in 1878, has developed into an important influence in national cultural life, with its museum & unusual educational facilities.

PTS. OF INT.: (1) On Exchange Place, **City Hall** (1878) over whose main entrance is bust of Roger Williams; handsome **Industrial Trust Bldg.**, skyscraper (416'); **Federal Bldg.**, with new Parcel Post Bldg. In pk. & Mall are several Mons. incl. **Bajnotti Fountain.** (2) In Memorial Sq., **World War I Mem.** (by Paul Cret); granite shaft (115'), topped by figure of "Peace." (3) N. Main St., bet. Waterman & Thomas Sts., **First Bapt. Meetingh.** (O.1775.by Jos.Brown int.exter.& inter.), one of finest in New England. Steeple supposedly inspired by plans of Jas. Gibbs, architect of St. Martin's-in-the-Fields, London. The bell, several times recast, originally bore a famous inscription dedicating bldg. to freedom of conscience. The city pays the sexton $125 a yr. to toll the bell 3 times daily. (4) Opp. Ch., **R.I. School of Design** occupying block through to Market Sq. Jewelry Bldg. is devoted to jewelry, silver, & other handicrafts; Metcalf Mem. Bldg. (see below) to textiles. (S) is Auditorium,

School gives training in arts, handicrafts & design; exhibits & art lectures. (5) 11 Thomas St., **Providence Art Club** (O.wks.Sun.aft.1787 & 1793); also houses Prov. Water Color Club; permanent & temporary exhibs. (6) 9 Thomas St., **Deacon Ed. Taylor H.** (c.1790.fine inter.), home of Community School of Music. (7) 7 Thomas St., **Fleur de Lys Bldg.** (1886.17th cent.Norman & Breton mod.), studios; constructed by Sidney R. Burleigh, painter, & his artist friends. Unique designs in wood & stucco are work of Burleigh. (8) Waterman & N. Main Sts., at street car tunnel, tablet on **Site of Town H.** where Roger Williams presided (1644-47). (9) 118 N. Main St., **Jos. Russell H.** (1772-73), home of wealthy East India merchant. (10) 21 Meeting St., **"Shakespeare's Head" H.** (1763), where John Carter, apprentice to Ben. Franklin, & publisher of "Providence Gazette & Country Journal," lived; it is supposed to have been Underground Railway Sta. (11) 24 Meeting St., **Brick Schoolh.** (1769), temporary home of Brown Univ. (1770) & later school for Negroes. (12) Meeting & N. Main Sts., **Friends Meetingh.** (earlier structure on site.1723. erected 1844-5). A member, Moses Brown, backed Sam Slater (see Pawtucket) in est. 1st Amer. textile mill. Brown financed Friends School, now at Hope St. & Lloyd Ave. (13) 155 N. Main St., **Old State H.,** (1762.some disfiguring adds.), also known as Colony H., which till 1901 housed Gen. Assembly (now at Cth.). Tablet comm. Act declaring R.I. independent republic (May 4, 1776). Decl. of Ind. was proclaimed from balcony. (14) 42 N. Court St., **Sam Bridgham H.** (c.1790.19th cent. adds.), home of 1st mayor.

(15) In little Pk. on N. Main St., **Roger Williams Spring.** (16) On H. opp. at cor. Howland St., tablet marks **Site of Roger Williams' H.** (17) 271 N. Main St., **St. John's Cathedral** (Episc.est.1720.built 1810.by J.H.Greene), on ground donated by French Huguenot refugee, Gabriel Bernon, whose grave is in crypt. In **Cemetery** (O. appl.) are graves of R.I. notables. (18) A mile (N) on N. Main St., in North Burial Ground, **Grave of Roger Williams;** earth was brought from orig. burial place (see below); graves of French soldiers (1780-82). (19) Opp. at cor. Rochambeau Ave., **Morris Homestead** (1750). Near-by is **Marker** comm. French encampment (1781-82). (20) 83 Benefit St., **Whitman H.** (c.1790). According to legend, Poe fell in love with Sarah Whitman when he saw her picking roses by moonlight, & wrote for her his "Helen" & "Annabel Lee." Their betrothal was broken in 1848 because of his excessive drinking (see Richmond, Va.). Benefit St., originally Back St., derived present name from fact that it was built "for the benefit of all." (21) 109 Benefit St., **Sullivan Dorr H.** (1810.by Greene), supposed to have been inspired by Pope's Twickenham Villa. T. W. Dorr, Sullivan's son, was leader of Dorr's Rebellion (1842) aimed at widening of franchise. (22) To rear of Dorr H. is **Roger Williams' First Grave** (1683), marked by broken column. (23) 176 Benefit St., **Old Arsenal** (1840), former home of hist. Providence Marine Corps of Artillery. (24) 224 Benefit St., **R.I. School of Design Mus.** (O.wks.Sun.aft.). In Colonial House is famous Pendleton Coll. of paintings, old furnishings, utensils of Rev. period. Mus. of Art, mostly in new Radeke Bldg., has outstanding colls. incl. more than 40,000 items. (25) 235 Benefit St., **R.I. College of Pharmacy.** (26) 314 Benefit St., **Burnside H.** (c.1850), once residence of Gen. A. E. Burnside (see Bristol). When Gen. Grant was entertained here, he announced he would make no speech but, being pressed to say "just a few words," he arose, bowed silently & said "I won't."

(27) 42 College St., **Truman Beckwith H.** (1820.Georg.Col.very fine.by Greene) houses Handicraft Club; period furnishings. (28) Opp. cor. College St., **Providence Athenaeum** (O.wks.1838) est. in 1753 as Lib., one of oldest in U.S. Has Reynolds & Van Dyke canvasses & famous miniature, "The Hours," by Malbone. In large book coll. is copy of "American Review," Dec. 1847, in which is anonymous "Ulalume" on which Poe wrote his name for Mrs. Whitman. Bldg. was scene of courtship of Poe & Sarah. (29) Cor. Hopkins & Benefit Sts., **Stephen Hopkins H.** (O.Tues.& Thurs.aft.c.1743), home of Signer of Decl. of Ind. who exclaimed, as he signed, "My hand trembles but my heart does not." H. has bed in which Washington slept after evacuation of Boston (1776). (30) Benefit & Benevolent Sts., **First Congr. Ch.** (Unit.1816.by Greene. very fine). Was called "2-horse church" because many members had 2-horse spans to their carriages. In steeple is largest bell cast by Paul Revere & Son. (31) 12 Benevolent St., **Crawford Allen H.** (1820.by Greene), very fine brick example. (32) 68 Waterman St., former **Cabinet of R.I. Hist. Soc.** (1844. adds.1890), now part of Univ. (33) 72 Waterman St., **Ed. Dexter H.** (1796) moved here from George St. (34) 64 Angell St., **Benson H.** (1796.Georg.Col.), home of

merchant in S. Amer. & China trade. (35) Cor. Prospect & Meeting Sts., **First Ch. of Christ Scientist** (1913.by Hoppin & Ely); impressive dome. On this site beacons were set up to warn of Ind. attack &, later, of Brit. approach. (36) At Prospect Terrace, **Roger Williams Mem. Mon.** (37) Cushing St., bet. Brown & Thayer Sts., **Pembroke College** of Brown Univ. (see below). (38) 21 Brown St., **Annmary Brown Mem.** (O.Tues.-Fri.1907.Class.by Norman Isham); fine bronze doors. Lib. has early portraits, printed items, heirlooms & Civil War relics. (39) 66 Power St., **Thos. Poynton Ives H.** (c.1811.Georg.Col.very fine), former home of member of firm, Brown & Ives, whose ships sailed to chief ports of the world. (40) 52 Power St., **John Brown H.** (O.wks.Tues.eve.Sun.aft.1786,int.exter.& inter.), designed by Jos. Brown for his brother; one of finest examples of Georg. Col. John Quincy Adams described it as one of most magnificent in America. Now home of **R.I. Hist. Soc.**; coll. of R.I. material, portrait gallery & Mus. of Ind., Col. & early Fed. relics, incl. Roger Williams' compass-sundial. John Brown was leader of Gaspee plot (see below) & first to send a ship from Providence to East Indies. (41) 357 Benefit St., **Jos. Nightingale H.** (c.1792.very fine), also referred to as John Carter Brown H., one of largest Col. frame Hs. extant. (42) 66 Williams St., **Edw. Carrington H.** (O. aft.exc.Mon.1812.early Republican), owned by R.I. School of Design; Col. furnishings & rare items brought from Orient by ships of Ed. Carrington; original wall paper. (43) 154 Power St., **Elisha Dyer H.** (1818.by Greene), architect Greene's home & later of two Elisha Dyers, both Govs. (44) At end of Power St., **Roger Williams Rock Mon.** in Pk. facing Seekonk R., down which Williams paddled his canoe looking for site for settlement. (45) 209 Williams St., home of Gaspee Chapter, D.A.R., part of which is **Gaspee Room,** originally part of Sabin Tavern (formerly on S.Main St.), where plot to burn Brit. ship, "Gaspee," was hatched. Ship which grounded at Gaspee Pt., was burnt by patriots, June 1772. (46) 77-79 Hope St., **Old Friends Meetingh.** (1723), moved from Constitution Hill. (47) 400 Benefit St., **Tillinghast Burial Ground;** graves of family of Pardon Tillinghast, early settler who became Bapt. minister & built 1st church at his own expense "in the shape of a haycap, with the fireplace in the middle, the smoke escaping from a hole in the roof." (48) 53 Transit St., **"Lightning Splitter H.,"** with steep roof like that of medieval H. Transit St. was so named because transit of Venus was observed here, 1769, by Jos. Brown, Stephen Hopkins & Jabez Bowen. (49) 403 S. Main St., **Dolphin H.** (c.1770), built by Jos. Tillinghast & supposed to have been sailors' tavern.

(50) 312 S. Main St., **De Fersen H.,** named for its owner, Axel de Fersen, Swedish nobleman, aide-de-camp of Rochambeau & reputed lover of Marie Antoinette. He drove the coach in which Fr. royal family made ill-fated attempt to escape. (51) Cor. Power & Main Sts., **Talma Theater** (1833), built as a Ch., used as morgue during Civil War, & later as theater; now Boys' Club. (52) At Cor. of S. Main & Planet Sts., **Site of Sabin Tavern** (c.1763) where Gaspee plot was hatched. (53) 112-14 S. Main St., **Cooke H.** (c.1825.by Greene). (54) 50 S. Main St., **Jos. Brown H.** (1774). One of Rochambeau's officers, it is said, rode up the stairs but couldn't negotiate the down trip. Now occupied by old business house of Brown & Ives (see above). From 1801 to 1929 was occupied by Providence Bank, oldest in New England. (55) Hopkins & Main St., on Market Sq., **Prov. County Cth.** (1933.early Republican.by Jackson, Robinson & Adams). (56) Opp. is **Helen A. R. Metcalf Bldg.** (1937) of R.I. Sch. of Design, harmonizing in architecture with **Cth.** In bldg. is part of **Franklin H.,** famous stagecoach tavern. (57) **Market Sq.,** on Main St. at College St., political & commercial gathering place in Col. days; known then as The Parade. On March 2, 1775, a crowd here consigned to flames Lord North's speech & 300 pounds of imported tea. **Market H.** (1774.rest.) was built by proceeds of a lottery. Lower floor was used as market; upper floor for banquets. (58) 130 Westminster St., **The Arcade** (1827-28.Gr.Rev.) was a forerunner of modern department stores. Its monolithic columns, largest in Amer., with exception of some in Cathedral of St. John the Divine, N.Y.C., were dragged from quarries by 15 yoke of oxen. (59) Westminster & Matthewson Sts., **Grace Ch.** (Episc.1846.Vict.Goth.by Rich. Upjohn) & 300 Weybosset St., **Beneficent Ch.** (Congr.est.1744.erected 1808-09. remod.1836), known as "Round Top" because of its dome. (60) Washington & Empire Sts., **Pub. Lib.** (1900.Ital.Ren.). (61) Bounded by Francis, Gaspee & Smith Sts. is **Capitol** (O.1901.early Republican.by McKim, Mead & White), white Georgia marble. Dome (235′) is claimed to be 2nd only to St. Peter's in Rome, in size, & is topped by statue, "The Independent Man." Entrance flanked by statues of Nath.

Greene & Oliver H. Perry. Reception room has portrait of Washington by Gilbert Stuart, & of Nath. Greene & O. H. Perry by Gari Melchers. In Gov.'s office & corridors are portraits of R.I. Govs. In office of Secy. of State is orig. parchment charter granted by Charles II (1663). Opp. Capitol, on Smith St., is **State Office Bldg.** (62) Hayes St. off Francis St., **R.I. College of Education.** (63) 1240 Smith St., **Brigham Young H.,** Mormon shrine where was born Brigham Young's wife, Mary Ann Angell. (64) Admiral St., near Hopkins Pk., **Esek Hopkins H.** (O.1756). Tablet comm. 1st Comdr. in Chief of Amer. Navy. (65) (S) from city center, c.3$^{m}$, **Roger Williams Pk.** (450 as. boat.recr.facils.). In natural amphitheater on one of Ls. is **Benedict Mem.** (Class. colonnade) for outdoor concerts & plays. **Mus. of Nat. Hist.** (O), zoo (O) with int. Monkey I. Near Elmwood Ave. entrance, **Betsy Williams Cottage** (O.sm.fee.1773) former home of descendant of Roger Williams; antique furnishings. (66) Near J. of Elmwood & Reservoir Aves., **Gorham Mfg. Co.** (O.guides), famous silversmith firm. (67) Eaton St. & River Ave., **Providence College** (Cath.), liberal arts; founded 1917.

(68) On College Hill, at Prospect, Waterman & George Sts., **Brown Univ.,** chartered in 1764 & moved from Warren, R.I. in 1770; includes Pembroke College for Women (see above). Brown, like Jefferson's Univ. of Va., was dedicated to religious freedom. Its charter declared that "into this Liberal & Catholic Institution shall never be admitted any Religious Tests but on the Contrary all the Members thereof shall forever enjoy full free absolute debate & uninterrupted Liberty of Conscience." On Prospect St., **Van Wickle Mem. Gates.** Noteworthy bldgs. incl.: **Carrie Tower** (1904.by Guy Lowell); **Hope College** (1828); **Manning Hall** (1835.by Jas.Bucklin. Gr.Rev.); **Univ. Hall** (1770.by Jos.Brown rest.), the oldest bldg. It was much damaged by military occupation during Rev. & students have done their share of mischief also. It was recorded that "the entries resound nightly with crashing bottles & the hoarse rumbling of wood & stones," during undergrad. revels. After middle of 19th cent., considerable alterations were made &, in 1880, bldg. was rehabilitated & considerably changed. In 1905, a complete restoration was undertaken; furnished in period. In President's Office are old Grandfather Clock & a desk that belonged to Jas. Manning, 1st president. In Faculty & Corporation Meeting Room is tapestry ordered by Queen Anne for Duke of Marlborough's Blenheim Castle, & a handsome Gobelin. **R.I. Hall** (1840.remod.1940); Geological Mus. Cor. Prospect & College Sts., **John Hay Lib.** comm. John Hay, graduate, later Secy. of State under McKinley & Theo. Roosevelt; notable coll. of rare items incl. R.I. material & McClellan Coll. of Lincoln Mss. On George St., **John Carter Brown Lib.** (1904.Mod.Class.by Shepley,Rutan & Coolidge); notable coll. of Americana based on coll. formed by Brown in 19th cent. Reading Room is constructed & furnished as "gentleman's library." In **Rogers Hall** (1872) on Middle Campus, is Herbarium with 100,000 specimens. 68 Waterman St., the 100-yr.-old **R.I. Hist. Soc. Cabinet** (see above). At 85 Waterman St., **Faunce H.** (O), student center; theater & art gallery. **Arnold Biological Lab.** (O), at 91 Waterman St., has excellent lib. **Pembroke College** has separate campus. Entrance at 172 Meeting St. Chartered in 1892; named for Roger Williams' college at Cambridge in Eng. **Brown Univ. Stadium** & **Aldrich Field** are located on Elmgrove Ave., 1.5$^{m}$ from campus.

## TRIPS OUT OF PROVIDENCE

### I. PROVIDENCE to Mt. Hope Bridge to the ISLAND OF RHODE I. (Newport).

**26. Barrington Pky., St.103, St.114**

Via: Barrington & Bristol

Barrington Pky. from E. end of Washington Bridge follows (S) along Narragansett Bay (pic. parking & bridle paths en route. permits for pic. at St. House Annex.). At c.**2.**, route cont. on St.103. **3.5.** J. with Bullock's Pt. Ave., which leads (R) 1.5$^{m}$ to **Crescent Pk.** (amusements.bath.) **5.5.** J. with Washington Rd.

SIDE TRIP: Take latter (R) short distance to **Haines Mem. Pk.** (trlr.camp.pic.bath.). Washington Rd. cont. to **Nayatt Pt.** & then turns (E) through handsome estates to J. with Rd. (N) to Barrington (see below).

**6.** St.103 makes J. with St.114 on which tour cont. **7. BARRINGTON** (sett.1677), once part of Mass. Colony; today a resort center with some industry. **Barrington Beach** (pub.bath.) near-by. An early settler was Obadiah Holmes who founded one of 1st Bapt. Chs. of Mass. here (1649). Town is named for Lord Barrington, advocate of religious freedom. It suffered from Brit. during Rev. On **Nockum Hill** is tablet marking spot where stood Bapt. Ch. built by Holmes. (N) of Barrington, c.0.5$^m$ on St.114, is **Prince's Hill Cemetery** (R) dating from 1728. A few miles (S) on Rumstick Rd. is **Rumstick Pt.,** on Narragansett Bay, fashionable resort. **8.** a poor Rd. runs (R) to **Tyler's Cemetery,** dating from late 17th cent. **9. WARREN** (sett. 1632). Brit. occupation (1778) did considerable damage. Lafayette made town his hqs. following Battle of R.I. It became a whaling port, shipbuilding & textile-mill center; more recently shell fish have become important item. A number of houses on Water & Main Sts. date from 18th & early 19th cents. In 1764, Brown Univ. was founded here with Rector of Ch. as 1st Pres.On Baker St., **Narragansett Fire H.,** in which is one of oldest fire engines extant, dating from late 18th cent. Also on Baker St., **Massasoit's Spring,** walled-in; marker comm. Massasoit, Ind. Chief who befriended Pilgrims. Main St., **Haile Lib.** (O.wks.exc.Thurs.); Mus. of hist. relics. Water St., **Burr's Hill Pk.** (pic.beach.sports.facils.). **10.5. N. BURIAL GROUND** (R) dating from late 17th cent. **12.** J. with Rd. [Take Rd. (E) into Colt Dr., which circles Bay to Bristol.]

**14. BRISTOL** (sett.1672), on arm of Narragansett Bay. At Mt. Hope, near-by, King Philip made his hqs. & plotted to destroy white settlements. Town suffered from his depredations at the war's beginning (1675), but he was forced shortly to flee vic. In Col. times, like other ports, Bristol prospered on rum, molasses & slave trade. It was burned & looted by Brit. during Rev. (1778). During War of 1812, it was center for privateers & until mid-19th cent. built ships & sent them to all quarters of the globe. Today it has a number of industries, particularly textiles & fishing. Herreshoff Shipyard is famous for having turned out several winners of Atlantic Cup Races. Population is characteristic racial potpourri of New England ports.

PTS. OF INT.: (1) Cor. (SE) Court & Hope Sts., **Burnside Mem. Bldg.** (O.1883), comm. Civil War Gen. A. E. Burnside, whose style in whiskers became popular. He became St. Gov. & U.S. Senator. (2) 341 Hope St., **Howe-Churchill-Diman H.** (1809.Fed.), former home of Capt. Benj. Churchill, famous privateer during War of 1812. (3) Wardwell & Hope Sts., **Rogers Free Lib.** (O.handsome inter.). (4) Also Hope & Wardwell Sts., **Linden Place** (1810.Class.alts.), owned by the De Wolfe family, one of whose females was mother of famous comedian, De Wolfe-Hopper. Other handsome dwellings on Hope St. are: (5) Cor. (NE) Hope & State Sts., **Bradford H.** (late 18th cent.Georg.Col.); (6) 617 Hope St., **John Collins H.** (1st half 19th cent.Gr.Rev.); (7) No. 620, **Collins H.** (late 18th cent.Georg.Col.); (8) No. 736, **Borden H.** (late 18th cent.). (9) No. 814, **Bosworth H.** (late 17th cent.adds.); (10) No. 956, **Reynolds H.** (late 17th cent.), where Lafayette stopped in 1778. (11) State St., near High St., **St. Armory** houses Bristol Train of Artillery, est. 1794. (12) High & Court Sts., **Bristol County Cth.** (early 19th cent.Fed.), where general assembly sometimes met. (13) 86 State St., **Russell Warren H.** (early 19th cent.). (14) Metacom Ave. (R) is **Mt. Hope Farm** (O.appl.). Here was King Philip's settlement & here is pile of rocks he used as seat when he addressed his followers. **King Philip Mus.** (O. appl.) contains notable Ind. coll. Near-by is marker on spot where King Philip was killed by troops of Capt. Benj. Church. (N) is **King Philip's Spring.** (15) On Farm is **Sen. Bradford H.** (2nd half 18th cent.Georg.Col.), home of Deputy Gov. of State & U.S. Sen. (16) Hope & Burnside Sts., **Herreshoff Mfg. Co.** (O.appl.) founded by John B. Herreshoff, who, though blind from youth, designed a number of successful Defenders of Amer. Cup. (17) **Prudence I.** off Bristol can be reached by ferry. (18) **Twin Paddocks Polo Field** of Bristol Polo Club (matches Sun.June-Sept.) (19) **Bristol Beach** (pub.pic.).

**15.** on St.114 is **MT. HOPE BRIDGE** (toll) to R.I. Cost $4,000,000; alleged to be longest spanned bridge in New England. Towers 284′ high; has 135′ clearance over mean high water. St.114 cont. (S) to **26. NEWPORT** (see).

## II. PROVIDENCE (NW) to CONN. LINE. 22. US44

From S. Main St. take Smith St., past St. Capitol. **4. CENTERDALE,** industrial suburb, in N. Providence. On Angell Ave., **Epenetus Angell H.** (1st half 18th cent.). 138 Smithfield Rd., **Capt. Olney H.** (1805.int.inter.), former home of Rev. officer. Just W. of Centerdale, is J. of US44 & St.104 (see Providence Trip IX). **4.5.** J. with Geo. Waterman Rd.

SIDE TRIP: (L) c.1.5m on this Rd. to **Irons-Clemence H.** (R) (O.appl.late 17th cent.int. exter.& inter.).

US44 passes (L) **WATERMAN RESERVOIR** (bath.pic.camp.f.). **14.5.** South J. with St.102. At inters. are **ACOTE HILL & DORR MON.** On this hill, Thos. W. Dorr stationed his men in his rebellion (1842) to broaden franchise & gain other political advantages for the masses. **15. CHEPACHET,** North J. with St.102 which branches off (N).

SIDE TRIPS: (A) Take St.102 (N) via Mapleville & Oakland. At 4m is J. with Sweet's Hill Rd.

Take latter (L) through Sweet's Hill to **Harrisville,** a mill town, at 2m; several int. old Hs. Cont. to **Pascoag,** at 4m, another mill town, near **Pascoag Reservoir** (f.boat.). In village is fine **Old Bapt. Ch.** (1st half 19th cent.Gr.Rev.). Cont. to **Bridgeton,** at 5m in whose vic. are also fine old Hs. Near-by is harness racing track. Cont. from Bridgeton on Wallum L. Rd. past **Wilson Reservoir** (f.boat.) & (R) to **Wallum L.** (f.boat.), at 9m. Near-by is **Wallum L. St. Sanatorium.**

At 6m on St.102, **Glendale.** Herring Pond Rd. leads (L) here, 1.5m, to **Spring L.-Herring Pond** (bath.f.pic.). St.102 cont. (N) to J. with Rd. to **Uxbridge,** Mass., (S) of Worcester.

US44 cont. past **GEO. WASHINGTON MEM. FOR.** (ponds.trls.pic.camp), **20.** Just beyond, on US44 is (R) **OLD TAVERN** (O.1810). **22. R.I.-CONN. LINE,** (E) of Putnam, Conn. (see US44.).

**III. PROVIDENCE** (near St. Capitol) **to PAWTUCKET. 4. US1** (NE)

Pawtucket is a crowded industrial center, situated near confluence of Ten Mile, Moshassuck & Blackstone Rs., at Pawtucket Falls; water power for mill wheels accounts for Pawtucket's industrial development. It early became center for making tools & other articles. Rev. drew upon Pawtucket's facils. for manufacture of war material. Toward end of 18th cent., Sam. Slater, who had acquired knowledge in Eng. of Arkwright's spinning machine, was financed by Moses Brown (see above) in setting up cotton thread mill. This was beginning of Amer. textile manufacture which was to make Pawtucket & other R.I. & Mass. towns beehives of industry. Another of city's claims to fame is building of a crude steamboat by David Wilkinson & Elijah Ormsbee, whose design gave Rbt. Fulton some ideas for his steamboat. Like most other R.I. towns, Pawtucket has pop. of mixed foreign stock, Fr.-Canadian, Irish, Ital., Polish, Portuguese. PTS. OF INT.: (1) Roosevelt & Slater Aves., **Old Slater Mill** (O.several eves.a wk.) replica orig. mill (1793); has parts of Slater's machinery & other relics. Plans are being made (1948) by a committee, incl. Slater's great-grandson, to build mus. to illustrate hist. of textile industry. (2) Cor. (SW) Summer & High Sts., **First Bapt. Ch.** (est.1792.built 1842.fine exter.& inter. adds.). (3) On Summer St. near-by, is **Deborah Cook Sayles Pub. Lib.** (O.Class.by Cram,Goodhue & Ferguson). (4) 586 Pawtucket Ave. (US1), **Old Pidge Tavern** (O. appl.supposedly 1640.int.inter.), in which are many hist. relics. Lafayette lived in Tavern during Rev. & came back again on his triumphant tour of 1824-25. (5) **Slater Pk.** (pic.sports facils.); Zoo. Here is **Doggett H.** (O.summer.sm.fee.supposedly 1644.int.exter.& inter.rest.); hist. relics. (6) Roosevelt Ave., **City Hall** (O.wks.Sat. a.m.1936.by John F.O'Malley), handsome bldg. with rich inter. Notable Chs. are: Broadway & Walcott Sts., **Pawtucket Ch.** (Congr.1868); 50 Park Pl., **St. Paul's Ch.** (Episc.1902.Goth.); Grace & Pine Sts., **Ch. of the Immaculate Conception** (Cath. 1887.Goth.), with fine windows; Slater St., **Ch. of St. John the Baptist** (Cath.1927. Ren.), with ceiling panels by J. Dessauliers. On Newport Ave., **Narragansett Pk.** (running races spring & summer).

At **5.5.** US1 crosses **R.I.-MASS. LINE,** SW. of Attleboro.

**IV. PROVIDENCE to CONN. LINE, 20. US6** (W).

At **2.5.** from (R) Broad St. is **Gov. King H.** (early 18th cent.adds.), former home of Gov. S. W. King who suppressed Dorr Rebellion. At **4.5.** is J. with Atwood Ave. (L) 2m on Ave. to **Thornton** (Johnston Township), where "powwow" (O) of descendants of Algonquin Inds. is held Labor Day, on Col. Tillinghast's estate. **9.** US6 passes through **NORTH SCITUATE,** industrial town, & crosses **Scituate Reservoir.** At **10., CAPT. RICH. RHODES H.** (late 18th cent.fine inter.), now police barracks. Near here (L) is **Ezek Hopkins Grove** (pic.). At **20.,** US6 crosses **CONN. LINE** (see Conn. Sec. US6).

**V. PROVIDENCE to J. with St.138. 24. St.3 & St.2 (S)**

Follow Elmwood Ave. (S) to J. with Reservoir Ave., which becomes St.3. **1.5. CRANSTON** (see US1). At **c.9.,** St.2 over which tour branches off (SW). At **11.5.** is

J. with Middle Rd. (R) 0.5$^m$ on this Rd., past **Rocky Hill Grove** (pic.), to (L) **Spencer H.** (early 18th cent.). Just beyond (L) is **Old Brown Bread H.** (early 18th cent.), explanations of whose name are fanciful but none authenticated. At **16.** is J. with St.102. Just (N) of J. is **South County Barn Mus.** (O). Also (N), off St.2, (R) **Stony Brook Grove** (pic.) & (L) **Matantuck Grove** (pic.). At **20.5.** (R) **BASOQUTOGAUG GROVE** (pic.) & S. of it, **Quanatumpic Grove** (pic.). **21.**, J. with St.138.

SIDE TRIP: (L) 3$^m$ on St.138 to **Kingston** (sett.1700), originally known as Little Rest. At cor. College Rd. & St.138 is **Old Cth.** (O.Wed.aft.Sat.eve.1775), now Pub. Lib. Here General Assembly met during Rev. Also on St. 138 are **Kingston Inn** (O.2nd half 18th cent.), with orig. inter.; **Congr. Ch.** (1820); **Post Office** (2nd half 18th cent.); & **John T. Nichols H.** (O.appl.1802.remod.1933), now owned by South Cty. Art Assoc. A number of 18th & early 19th cent. bldgs. in town. On College Rd., is **R.I. State College** (coed.), land-grant college est. 1888 as Agric. School & Experiment Sta. In 1892 it was set up by St. Legislature as R.I. College of Agric. & Mechanic Arts. Now has Schools of Agric., Business Admin., Engineering, Home Economics & Arts & Sciences; extension courses. At entrance to campus is **Mem. Gate.** College has 50-a. farmland for Agric. Experiment Sta. (hqs. in Taft Laboratory Bldg.), which has done excellent work in discovering cause of "blackhead," which threatened extermination of nation's turkeys; in development of hardier strains of alfalfa; & in testing antidotes to Dutch Elm disease, destroyer of New England's most beautiful elms. **Watson H.** (c.1790.rest.) on Watson Farm, site of orig. Agric. School; now nursery school of Sch. of Home Economics.

St.2. cont. (S) to **CHARLESTOWN** (see), an alt. route for US1 & St.3.

**VI. PROVIDENCE to J. with St.146. 6.5. Great Road & Breakneck Hill Rd.** Out of Providence (N) on Smithfield Ave. which becomes Great Rd. **3.** J. with Parker St. (L) 0.5$^m$ on latter is **Mathurin Ballou H.** (1710). **4.5.**, J. of Great Rd. with River Rd. (L) here is **Friends Meetingh.** (O.appl.1703 & 1743) in **Saylesville.** A short distance beyond on Great Rd., is (R) **Eleazer Arnold Tavern,** the Old Stone Chimney H. (O.wks.appl.sm.fee.1687.adds.rest.), one of best-preserved old Hs. in R.I.; has largest fireplace in St. **5.** Here at further end of Moshassuck R. Bridge is J. with Breakneck Hill Rd. Cont. on Breakneck Rd. Short distance beyond Bridge is J. with Quinsnicket Rd.

SIDE TRIP: Take latter (L) into **Lincoln Woods Reserv.** (pic.camp.log shelters.hik.& bridle trls.recr.& sports facils.), with **Olney Pond. Pulpit Rock,** off Granite Lodge Rd., is supposed to have been gathering place for King Philip's bands. **Comstock H.** (1743) is on Barney's Pond.

**6.5.** J. with St.146 (see Providence VIII below).

**VII. PROVIDENCE to EAST PROVIDENCE & RUMFORD US 44 (E), St.114** Cross Washington Bridge & take US44 (E) to J. with St.114 in heart of **EAST PROVIDENCE** (sett.c.1642), a suburb, originally known as Sekonk, considerable manufacturing center. E. Providence suffered from Inds., during King Philip's War. A short distance (N) on St.114 is suburban Rumford. On Roger Williams Ave. is **Site of Roger Williams Tree,** where Williams had his home before moving to Providence. Off St.114, on Bishop Ave., **Bishop H.** (mid-18th cent. handsome exter.). Cor. Newman Ave. & St.114, **Newman Ch.** (1810;very fine), near site of orig. bldg. where Sam. Newman, a refugee from religious persecution under Charles I., preached. 9 Newman Ave., **Rumford Chem. Works** (O) manufactures baking powder, special types of flour & yeast products.

**VIII. PROVIDENCE to R.I.-MASS. LINE. 17. St.146 (NW)**

**6.** J. with Breakneck Hill Rd. (see Trip VI). **14. UNION VILLAGE** whose most prominent citizen was Peleg Arnold, Rev. officer, member of Continental Congress & Chief Justice of R.I. On Woonsocket Hill Rd., **Peleg Arnold Tavern** (17th cent.), 1st H. built in vic.; a tavern during Rev. owned by Peleg Arnold & served as patriots' meeting place & depository of arms. In Union Cemetery, **Grave of Peleg Arnold.** **17. R.I.-MASS. LINE,** (S) of Worcester.

**IX. Loop Tour. PROVIDENCE to ENVIRONS. c.33. St.104, St.11, St.114, US44.**

Via: Greystone, Esmond, Georgiaville, Woonsocket, Grant Mills, Diamond Hill, Valley Falls, Central Falls, Pawtucket, Rumford & East Providence.

**J.** of St.104 (Farnum Pike) with US44 c.4$^m$ (W) of Providence. Near this J. is J. with Mineral Spring Ave. [About 1$^m$ (E) on latter to J. with Rd., which runs (N) to **Peter Randall Reserv.** (pic.trls.), in N. Providence.] Take St.104 (N) from J. with US44. At **1.5.** J. with Esmond St., (R) into **Esmond,** where are Esmond Mills; Ex hibit Room (O). Opp. is **Post Office** (1813), formerly textile mill. **Major Wm. Smith**

**H.** (O.appl.early 17th cent.). **2.5. GEORGIAVILLE,** on lake. St.104 cont. past **STILLWATER RESERVOIR** (L). **4.5.** J. with Rd. (which leads (E) short distance to Washington Hy.pic. Grove). **12. WOONSOCKET** (sett.c.1662), 3rd largest city in R.I., textile mill town; also machinery & other manufactures. Pop. largely Fr.-Canadian. City is on Blackstone R. near R.I.-Mass. Line, at Woonsocket Falls, which furnish power for mills. PTS. OF INT.: On Court Sq., **Cth.,** in front of which is **Mon.** (by Allen Newman) comm. Woonsocket citizens who fought in Spanish & Philippine wars. Main St., **City Hall & Harris Institute Lib.** (O). NW. cor. Coe & Providence Sts., **Arnold H.** (early 18th cent.). NE. cor. Providence & E. Orchard Sts., **Willing Vose H.** (18th cent.). The city has some fine modern churches. Near Pulaski Sq., on St.122, **St. Michael's Ch.** (Ukrainian Orthodox), with bulbous steeples. City has c.122 as. of parks incl. **Barry Mem. Field,** on Smithfield Rd., (sports facils.). From Woonsocket, St.122 & St.146 run (NW) to Worcester, Mass. Take Wrentham Rd. (St.11) out of Woonsocket (E). At **c.15.** J. with W. Wrentham Rd.

SIDE TRIP: Take Rd. (R) to J. with Ballou Meetingh. Rd. (R) on latter short distance to **Ballou Meetingh.** (1740), preserved in original state, perfect example of early meetinghs.

**17.5. GRANT'S MILLS.** J. with St.114 on which Loop Tour cont. (S). At **18.5.** is **DIAMOND HILL FOR. PK. RESERV.** (recr.ski runs). **24. VALLEY FALLS,** an old textile town whose pop. is largely Fr.-Canadian or of recent European ancestry. At J. of Mill & Broad Sts., **Catholic Oak,** where Jas. C. Richmond preached in middle of 19th cent. to people of all denominations. In front of Ann & Hope Mill, **Wm. Blackstone Mon.,** not far from place where Wm. Blackstone, 1st settler & friend of Roger Williams, is buried. **26.5. CENTRAL FALLS,** an old industrial town on Blackstone R. On High St., across from Waypost Stadium, **Marker** at spot where Capt. Pierce's company was decimated by Inds. during King Philip's War. On Broad St., **Jenks Pk.;** tower has fine view. St.114 cont. through Pawtucket (see Trip III) & Rumford (see Trip VII) to E. Providence (see Trip VII). **Here is J. with US44,** which leads across Seekonk R. back into **PROVIDENCE at c.33.**

## *NOTE*

The editors sincerely regret the omission from *The American Guide* of the paragraphs on Nantucket and Martha's Vineyard, Mass. They are hereby supplied and may be inserted after page 220.

**H.** (O.appl. early 17th cent.). **2.5. GEORGIAVILLE,** on lake. St.104 cont. past **STILLWATER RESERVOIR** (L). **4.5.** J. with Rd. (which leads (E) short distance to Washington Hy.pic. Grove). **12. WOONSOCKET** (sett.c.1662), 3rd largest city in R.I., textile mill town; also machinery & other manufactures. Pop. largely Fr.-Canadian. City is on Blackstone R. near R.I.-Mass. Line, at Woonsocket Falls, which furnish power for mills. PTS. OF INT.: On Court Sq., **Cth.,** in front of which is **Mon.** (by Allen Newman) comm. Woonsocket citizens who fought in Spanish & Philippine wars. Main St., **City Hall & Harris Institute Lib.** (O). NW. cor. Coe & Providence Sts., **Arnold H.** (early 18th cent.). NE. cor. Providence & E. Orchard Sts., **Willing Vose H.** (18th cent.). The city has some fine modern churches. Near Pulaski Sq., on St.122, **St. Michael's Ch.** (Ukrainian Orthodox), with bulbous steeples. City has c.122 as. of parks incl. **Barry Mem. Field,** on Smithfield Rd., (sports facils.). From Woonsocket, St.122 & St.146 run (NW) to Worcester, Mass. Take Wrentham Rd. (St.11) out of Woonsocket (E). At **c.15.** J. with W. Wrentham Rd.

SIDE TRIP: Take Rd. (R) to J. with Ballou Meetingh. Rd. (R) on latter short distance to **Ballou Meetingh.** (1740), preserved in original state, perfect example of early meetinghs.

**17.5. GRANT'S MILLS.** J. with St.114 on which Loop Tour cont. (S). At **18.5.** is **DIAMOND HILL FOR. PK. RESERV.** (recr.ski runs). **24. VALLEY FALLS,** an old textile town whose pop. is largely Fr.-Canadian or of recent European ancestry. At J. of Mill & Broad Sts., **Catholic Oak,** where Jas. C. Richmond preached in middle of 19th cent. to people of all denominations. In front of Ann & Hope Mill, **Wm. Blackstone Mon.,** not far from place where Wm. Blackstone, 1st settler & friend of Roger Williams, is buried. **26.5. CENTRAL FALLS,** an old industrial town on Blackstone R. On High St., across from Waypost Stadium, **Marker** at spot where Capt. Pierce's company was decimated by Inds. during King Philip's War. On Broad St., **Jenks Pk.;** tower has fine view. St.114 cont. through Pawtucket (see Trip III) & Rumford (see Trip VII) to E. Providence (see Trip VII). Here is J. with US44, which leads across Seekonk R. back into **PROVIDENCE** at **c.33.**

## MARTHA'S VINEYARD & NANTUCKET

Steamer from New Bedford, stopping at Woods Hole, has limited auto space; make reservs. in advance; 2 hrs. to Martha's Vineyard; 5 hrs. to Nantucket. Plane serv. (summer) to Martha's Vineyard from New Bedford; to Nantucket from New York & Boston. Good trans. facils. on both Is. Boat., yacht., f., bath. Nantucket Annual Regatta. Accoms.: All types (summer).

**MARTHA'S VINEYARD** lies S. of elbow of Cape Cod, across Martha's Vineyard Sound. I. is pyramid-shaped with apex pointing (N) toward Woods Hole. It is c.20$^{m}$ long (E-W) & c.9$^{m}$ wide (N-S). Vineyard Haven Harbor cuts V into apex, whose tips, East & West Chop, are crowned by lighths. Oak Bluffs, where boat lands, is on E. side of V & Vineyard Haven on W. side. Edgartown lies to (S), facing landlocked bay & Chippaquiddick I. (good beaches), accessible by ferry. Pyramid's base is indented by "Great Ponds" cut off from ocean by sand pits. Land rises toward SW. end of I. to majestic multi-colored clay cliffs of Gay Head. Martha's Vineyard, supposed to have been visited by Norsemen, 1000 A.D., was put on map by Capt. Gosnold, 1602, who probably named it for his daughter, Martha. Shakespeare's inspiration for enchanted Isle of "The Tempest" is alleged to have come from accounts of Gosnold's visit. Thos. Mayhew, Sr. sett. I. 1642, establishing strict Presb. regime. His son, Thos. Mayhew, Jr., became missionary to Inds., & it was due to his work that they refused to join in King Philip's War. Martha's Vineyard boasts it started whaling industry, early settlers learning whale hunting from Inds. Vineyard whalers eventually sailed to SW. Pacific & Arctic. Life on I. assumed the more free & easy manners of a bustling seaport. Testimony to this trend is furnished by an inscription on a still extant tombstone:

> Here lies the body of our beloved Charlotte
> Born a virgin, died a harlot.
> For 16 yrs. she preserved her virginity
> Which is a very good record for this vicinity.

Joseph Allen, in his "Tales & Trails of Martha's Vineyard," tells a story about a woman who, when questioned concerning her baby, born two yrs. after her hus-

band had sailed on whaling ship, complacently remarked: "Why yes, John has written me several times since he went away," & another about a father who, when upraided because his son had seduced a local girl, remarked: "Nathan is a most careless cuss. Just this morning he busted a hoe handle on me."
The not unusual character of a local banker, Ichabod Norton, was plaintively celebrated by an apparently disappointed heir with the following tombstone inscription:

Here lies old twelve & a half per cent.
The more he had, the less he spent.
The more he had, the more he craved.
Oh! Lord, can Ichabod be saved.

During Rev., although many of its men fought with patriots, I. decided to declare itself neutral, to avoid blockade. Nevertheless, Brit. raided & plundered it in 1778. Famous natives of I. were Capt. Geo. Claghorn, designer of U.S. Frigate, "The Constitution," & Jon. Mayhew, founder of Unitarianism. Among noted visitors were Stephen Decatur, Dan. Webster, who came to escape hay fever, Chas. Sumner, Pres. U.S. Grant & Lillian Nordica, operatic star & Vineyard descendant, who gave a concert & grand reception at Oak Bluffs.
I. is popular resort, because of mild climate, lovely scenery, quaint old towns & recreat. facils. Artists come to paint old harbors crowded with fishing craft.

PTS. OF INT.: (1) **OAK BLUFFS** where boat lands. Founded as Meth. Camp Meeting Ground. **Meth. Tabernacle.** At near-by Farm Neck, **Norton H.** (1752) well-preserved. **E. Chop Lighth.** (fine view). (2) Across harbor is **VINEYARD HAVEN** (sett.1660) first known as Holme's Hole. Was raided by Brit. during Rev. **Mon.** comm. local girls who blew up Liberty Pole to prevent its being used by Brit. as spar for vessel. Town suffered from disastrous fire, 1883. On Main St., **Historical H.** (O); hist. items. **W. Chop Lighth.** (Fine view). To (W) **Ind. Hill** (fine view). (3) **EDGARTOWN,** c.5$^{m}$ (S) of Oak Bluffs, oldest settlement, formerly busy whaling port, with whale oil & candle factories. Town was named for Edgar, son of James II. Many fine old Hs. On Cooke St.: **Cooke H.** (O.1766) owned by Duke Cty. Hist. Soc.—antiques & whaling items; **Old Cemetery** on whose tombstones are curious inscriptions. Lovely **Congr. Ch.** (1828). **Meth. Ch.** (1843.Gr.Rev.). First Meth. on I. was John Saunders, refugee Negro slave. **Pub. Lib.** (O); art exhibits. **The Vineyard Gazette Bldg.,** celebrated by H.B. Hough in his "The Country Editor." (W) of Edgartown lies extensive **St. For.** On old W. Tisbury Rd., (W) of town, is rock with **Tablet** comm. leave-taking from Inds. by Thos. Mayhew, Jr. when he sailed for England. His ship with all aboard was lost. Some of stones dropped by Inds. here in his memory & which formed a cairn are still to be seen. (4) **W. TISBURY,** where for a time lived Capt. Ben. Church, conqueror of King Philip. **H. of Josiah Standish,** son of Miles Standish. Here also lived Betty Alden Peabodie, daughter of John & Priscilla Alden. (5) **N. TISBURY,** with charming old village **Ch.** (6) **CHILMARK VILLAGE.** Lovely old **Ch.** Capt. Claghorn, designer of "The Constitution" & Jon. Mayhew, founder of Unitarianism, were natives. (7) At Menemsha Pond & Vineyard Sound, at SW. end of I. is **MENEMSHA,** most picturesque & most painted village of I. On hill above pond is marker on supposed graves of Norsemen who, according to Scandinavian sagas, massacred each other here. (8) **GAY HEAD,** at extreme SW. end of I., whose multi-colored cliffs rise high above Vineyard Sound. (Boats avail.for viewing cliffs). **Ind. Reserv.** & **Lighth.** (1799.Reb.1859). Near Lighth., concealed by undergrowth, is only **Headstone,** on grave of Silas Paul, with inscription in Ind. language. Inds. fought in Rev. One, Anthony Jeremiah, is mentioned by John Paul Jones as having acquitted himself bravely in battle with Brit. ship, "Serapis." **Ind. Community Center,** on which is tablet comm. fact that in World War I, this village sent a larger percentage of men to the war than any other in Mass. **Ind. Chapel.** Pottery, made by Inds., of colored clay from cliffs is for sale. (9) N. of Menemsha, on North Rd., leading back to Vineyard Haven, is **Peaked Hill** (300'.Fine view), highest on I.

**NANTUCKET** to (E) of Martha's Vineyard, across Muskegat Channel, is c.15$^{m}$ long (E-W) & 3$^{m}$ wide (N-S). Inds. named it Nanticut, "Far Away Land," & Canopache, "Place of Peace"; far-voyaging sea captains called it "The Little Gray Lady." First settlement, by religious refugees from N. Mass., was known as Sherburne. They purchased most of I. from Thos. Mayhew, Sr. for £30 & two beaver hats. There developed a long feud bet. Mayhew's group & opposition faction as to control, a feud which resulted in Peter Folger, Ben. Franklin's grandfather, going to jail for 2 yrs. because he refused to give up a "record book" which might have established Mayhew's claims. Inds. were friendly; they refused advances of King Philip & gave shelter to one of his tribesmen who had fled from Philip's vengeance. Inds., who were notably kind to their children, had a comparatively harmless but effective method for punishing them. They steeped bayberry root in water & squirted fluid by mouth up the children's noses. Inds. taught whites to hunt whales. But "pale-face" civilization proved too much for them. The last man on I. with Ind. blood died 1854. Nantucket suffered during Rev., when it was pillaged, & War of 1812, when it was blockaded & its ships captured by Brit. Like Martha's Vineyard, it made vain attempt to remain neutral. Nantucket ships carried the tea which provoked the Boston Tea Party. Town became greatest whaling port & it was here that Melville laid opening scenes of his "Moby Dick." Harbor being blocked by a sand bar so that larger vessels couldn't enter it, ingenuous Nantucketers built what they called "Camels," a sort of floating drydock, to get ships in over the harbor "hump." During late 17th cent., Quakers drifted in from mainland & I. became ⅔ Quaker. They opposed practice of "black-birding" (slave trade) & hid runaway slaves from the U.S. Marshall. Lucretia Mott, Quaker, was a pioneer abolitionist.

Among I.'s prominent citizens was Abiah Folger Franklin, Ben.'s mother; Maria Mitchell, woman astronomer, who discovered a comet which was named for her, & received international honors; & R.H. Macy, who founded famous dept. store in N.Y. With discovery of petroleum, demand for whale oil for illumination declined & ended Nantucket's maritime importance. In 1846 Nantucket town was devastated by fire. Nevertheless, many fine old Hs. survive. After Civil War, tourist industry developed. Autos were banned in the town until 1918, when Clinton Folger, mail carrier, broke ban. He acquired a car, had it drawn from dock to town's limits by horses & then turned on the gas & chugged away to Siasconset.

PTS. OF INT.: (1) On approaching I., **Lighth.** (1901) on Brant Pt., on site of one built in 1746. (2) At Pier, **Art Gallery** (O); exhibits by contemporary artists. (3) Just off Pier, **Whaling Mus.** (O.sm.fee.1947); whaling items; was once sperm candle factory & wareh. (4) At lower end of Main St., on which are some of finest old Hs., **Rotch Wareh.** (1772). Wm. Rotch's ships carried Boston Tea Party tea. (5) Near-by, on the Square, **Pacific Bank** (1818), where whaling captains deposited their gains. (6) **South Tower** (Unit.Ch.1809) whose golden dome dominates town. Has old bell brought from Portugal, 1715. (7) On Academy Hill, **North Ch.** (Congr.1834.Goth.); vestry dates from 1711. (8) On Summer St., **Bapt. Ch.** (1841), has fine spire. (9) **Meth. Ch.** (1840.Gr.Rev.). (10) **Pub. Lib.** formerly the "Athenaeum" (1847.Gr.Rev.). (11) On Sunset Hill, **Jethro Coffin H.** (O.sm.fee. 1686), oldest on I., a wedding present to Jethro Coffin & Mary Gardner, his bride. (12) Madaket Rd., **Fountain,** comm. Abiah Folger Franklin, Ben.'s mother. (13) At No. 1 Vestal St., **Maria Mitchell Birthpl.** (O.wks.sm.fee.1790), with adj. observatory (O). (14) On Prospect St. at (S) edge of town, **Old Mill** (O.sm.fee. 1746), still grinds corn meal. (15) Cor. of Moore's Lane, **Friends' Meetingh.** (O. 1838). Adj., **Nantucket Hist. Soc.** (O.sm.fee). (16) **Coffin School** (1852), founded & endowed by Brit. Admiral Sir Isaac Coffin, 1827. (17) **Old Jail,** with heavily handwrought iron bars on windows. (18) At Old N. Wharf, **The Wharf Rats Club,** whose pennant Admiral Byrd took to the Antarctic. (19) Near town, **Elihu Coleman H.** (1722).

**SIASCONSET VILLAGE,** colloquially known as 'Sconset, on high bluffs, to E. of Nantucket town, has some ancient cottages. The moors in vic. are lovely with purple heather. (L) from village path runs along cliffs to **Sankaty Lighth.** from which magnificent view. Rd. leads from 'Sconset to **Altar Rock** (102′), highest on I.; fine view.

# MIDDLE ATLANTIC STATES

## NEW YORK — NEW JERSEY
## PENNSYLVANIA — DELAWARE — MARYLAND
## WASHINGTON, D.C. — WEST VIRGINIA

The five states of this region include within their boundaries the richest section of the country. They have nearly 27,000,000 of the country's estimated 145,000,000 population. They account for about 75% of the nation's foreign commerce & nearly one-third of its manufactured products. New York City is the country's financial center, with Philadelphia, Baltimore & Pittsburgh runners-up. Although so highly industrialized, the region's farms produce a large part of the food its population consumes.

Unlike New England, this region has neither geographic, historic nor economic unity. Its boundaries, the St. Lawrence & Lake Erie on the North, Virginia on the South, New England & the Atlantic on the East & Lake Erie, Ohio & the Ohio River on the West, do not include, by any means, a homogeneous area. There is no common mountain system. The Allegheny Plateau, starting in southern N. Y., extends through the center of Pennsylvania & Maryland & almost monopolizes West Virginia. New York has its own two groups of mountains, the 5,000′ high Adirondacks in the North, & the Catskills, not far from New York City, running to 4,000′, in the South. New Jersey, except for its northwestern section, is comparatively flat, while Delaware is altogether so. There is no common river system, although the Delaware, rising in New York, is the boundary bet. New Jersey, on the one hand, & Pennsylvania & Delaware on the other. Few of the rivers are navigable. The Hudson takes deep draft ships from New York City to Troy. But her canals give New York a man-made system of waterways connecting with Lakes Champlain, Ontario & Erie. The only navigable river of Pennsylvania, aside from the Delaware, which is navigable from Trenton, N.J. to the Ocean, is the Ohio, formed at Pittsburgh by the junction of the Monongahela & Allegheny Rivers. New Jersey & Delaware have most of the ocean frontage of the region. But through small windows on the Atlantic at New York City, on the Delaware at Philadelphia, & on the Chesapeake at Baltimore, pours a great part of the country's commerce.

New York is roughly triangular in shape, with the broad side of the triangle backed up against the mountain ranges of Connecticut, Massachusetts & Vermont. The apex of the triangle is at Buffalo, between Lakes Ontario & Erie. The valleys of the Hudson & Mohawk cut a right angle through the state.

Pennsylvania is almost rectangular, with a small opening toward the Atlantic at Philadelphia, & another in the west, on Lake Erie. Through this last pours Minnesota iron ore to feed the insatiable furnaces of Pittsburgh.

New Jersey, sausage-like in shape, is almost islanded by waterways—the Atlantic & Hudson R. on the Northeast and East & the Delaware R. & Bay on the West & South. Tiny Delaware, second smallest state in the Union, fronts on the Delaware River, where is located its only metropolis, Wilmington, Delaware Bay & the Atlantic. Maryland is a long, narrow state, extending from Chesapeake Bay westward between Virginia & West Virginia on the South & Pennsylvania on the North. Like Pennsylvania, it is split in two by the Allegheny Plateau. The eastern section, around Chesapeake Bay, resembles in topography & in historic & economic development, Virginia's Tidewater region. West Virginia is really an extension of the Allegheny Plateau, with only its Eastern Panhandle, that has topographic affinities with neighboring Virginia, & its Ohio plain in the West, flat & cultivatable.

New York's development has centered around its two great valleys—of the Hudson & the Mohawk—which provide the only sea-level route from the Atlantic to the West & early gave the state a favored position in the country's transportation. The building of the Erie Canal in the early 19th century clinched this quasi-monopoly & made New York the Empire State. New York City, at the east end of the route, became the logical outlet for commerce between the seaboard & the West. Along this sea-level route grew up a chain of great cities in the Mohawk Valley, with Albany at the eastern & Buffalo on Lake Erie at the western end of the chain. The state's industries developed because of favorable transportation conditions & consequent population concentration. It has few natural resources; the principal ones are electric power & salt. One-fifth of the nation's salt comes from N. Y.'s deposits. It was inevitable that there would be few mass-production industries based on use of raw materials, but mostly those industries to which skilled labor applies "finishing" processes. The state produces a vast miscellany of articles: garments in New York City, although the latter's 33,000 factories turn out an infinite variety of other products as well; textiles & men's shirts in Troy; glass at Corning; shoes at Binghamton; underwear in the Utica area; gloves at Johnstown & Gloversville; in Schenectady, electrical equipment & locomotives; in Rochester, cameras & photographic films; in Syracuse, chemicals, electrical equipment & china; in Yonkers, carpets & elevators; in Buffalo, steel, airplanes & chemicals; in the Hudson River Valley, bricks. The world's greatest aluminum-wire factory is at Massena.

Pennsylvania, on the other hand, is a heavy industry state, its output based on coal, oil & natural gas. The state produces annually some 60,000,000 tons of anthracite coal in its eastern section & some 150,000,000 tons of bituminous coal in the western. Pittsburgh is one of the world's greatest steel centers, although it also is a great plate glass producer. Around the basic raw material of coal has grown up a vast agglomeration of industries which make the state, after New York, the chief producer of manufactured goods in the country.

New Jersey complains that it is too often regarded as merely the corridor between New York City & Philadelphia. But what a corridor!—lined for most of its extent by industrial plants. Like New York, the state has few natural resources & its industries have developed largely because it is the link between two great population centers. In northern New Jersey is an agglomeration of large cities, usually considered part of New York's metropolitan area. And around them are grouped huge plants—oil & sugar refineries, paint factories, auto assembly plants, a great sewing machine plant & smelting works. Trenton, further south, produces the country's best wire cable & some of its finest pottery. Camden, a suburb of Philadelphia, has some 350 plants.

Maryland has plenty of bituminous coal, & this raw material has fed the factories of Baltimore. West Virginia is the youngest of the five states industrially. Coal was discovered there comparatively recently; the state's coal reserves are estimated to be the greatest in the country. The state now is one of the chief producers of this raw material. West Virginia is the country's greatest manufacturer of glass; it has great steel mills in the Wheeling area; it produces basic chemicals in the Kanawha Valley.

Delaware is distinguished from the other states of the region by the fact that it has very few industries of any kind. But Wilmington may be said to be the "corporation capital" of the nation. Due to favorable laws, many of the country's most important corporations have established their headquarters here. Although the state has no plants making explosives, several of the biggest explosive manufacturing companies have offices in the city. The Du Pont de Nemours Company is the mightiest of the corporations located in the state, which is therefore sometimes referred to as the "Du Pont Empire." This company has no factories in Delaware, but controls a vast network of industries—chemicals, nylons, plastics, lucite, explosives, automobiles—with plants located throughout the country.

The history of the five states is as miscellaneous as their topography & economics. New York & northern New Jersey were settled in 1626 by the Dutch. The Swedes settled in southern New Jersey, at what is now Gloucester Point, in 1638, & established claims to parts of Delaware. The Swedes were ousted by the Dutch, who in turn, in 1664, were ousted by the British.

New York thereafter received a charter from James II which gave a certain degree of popular representation in a provincial legislature, & aside from conflicts that developed between the royally appointed governors & the legislature, conflicts characteristic of the history of all the provinces, continued normally enough till the revolution.

But New Jersey had a checkered & stormy career. Owing to the fact that grants by James II overlapped, giving control of the state both to the New York governor & to Lord Carteret, confusion resulted & there were conflicts over land titles. Later New Jersey was split into two sections, East & West, which had separate governments under separate proprietors. The western section for a time fell into the hands of William Penn & his Quakers. It was not till 1702 that all of New Jersey was united under the rule of the royal government of New York & not till 1738 that New Jersey was set up as a separate colony under its own governor & with a constitution that guaranteed a considerable amount of self-government to its legislature.

Delaware was included in William Penn's grant of 1681, & started out as part of Pennsylvania; but after 1701, it split off & set up as an independent province with a legislature & governor of its own.

Pennsylvania was granted to William Penn in 1681, & was settled the same year by Penn's deputy & cousin, William Markham. From the beginning, due to Penn's liberal views, the settlers enjoyed considerable self-government. Various constitutions, culminating in the Charter of Privileges of 1701, assured local autonomy which included the right of all freemen to vote for members of the legislature. This Charter remained in force until the Revolution.

Maryland was settled by Catholic Lord Baltimore, who received a grant of land from Charles I, which included most of the state. The first settlers, 50% of whom were Catholics, landed in 1634. Almost from the beginning, an elected assembly exercised initiative in passing laws, an initiative which Lord Baltimore eventually sanctioned. The period of the English Revolution which climaxed in the execution of Charles I, brought trouble to the Catholic colony. Papists & adherents of the Anglican church were both outlawed. But with restoration of Charles II, the ban was lifted.

The people of New Jersey, Pennsylvania & Maryland early struggled to get rid of the proprietors—the original grantees—who did little for the provinces except draw revenues from them & cloud land titles. The proprietors were considered mere "rent chargers." Through popular pressure, the government of these colonies was shifted to the Crown & the property rights of the proprietors whittled down to invisibility.

Although there were great divergencies in the religious sects which had predominating influence in New York, Pennsylvania, New Jersey, Delaware & Maryland, nevertheless, all four provinces early adopted policies of pretty complete religious toleration. In this they differed fundamentally from New England.

West Virginia was until the Civil War the frontier of Virginia, but early developed a regional character quite different from that of the Old Dominion. Except for the Eastern Panhandle, its economy was that of the small farm, settled not by cavalier elements, as was Tidewater Virginia, but by sturdy pioneers of the yeoman class. There was no demand for slave labor, & so, quite naturally, as time went on, West Virginia turned against slave-holding, & was prepared for the eventual split with the mother state at the outbreak of the Civil War.

Both New Jersey & Delaware, because of their isolation, suffered scarcely at all during the Indian wars, which, however, involved the other three states, especially during the French-Indian War of 1755-63 that resulted in expulsion of the French from Canada. Preliminary to this conflict was George Washington's trip to the western frontier at the instance of Gov. Dinwiddie of Virginia, to inform the French who had forts there, of British claims to the region. In 1754, Washington, in command of colonial militia, was defeated by the French at Great Meadows & had to surrender Fort Necessity to them. This was the beginning of the war. In 1755 occurred Braddock's ill-fated expedition to Fort Duquesne, on Pittsburgh's present site, & the resulting Indian raids on American settlements which terrorized the colonists as far east as the Shenandoah Valley. With the capture of Fort Duquesne by the British, the Indian threat was for the time being ended. But trouble flared up again in 1763 with Pontiac's rebellion which was finally put down by Col. H. Bouquet, who defeated the Indian Confederacy of Six Nations at the bloody battle of Bushy Run, near present-day Pittsburgh. Bouquet followed up his victory with an incursion into Ohio which broke the power of the Indians for good.

Before & during the Revolution, the four provinces, & West Virginia as part of Virginia, generally backed the patriot cause. Delaware & Maryland were less inclined to a separation from the old country than Pennsylvania, which under Franklin's leadership led in the revolt. Philadelphia, however, was a Tory hotbed, &

West Virginia's Eastern Panhandle also suffered from the Tory threat, energetically suppressed by Gen. David Morgan.

The fighting during the Revolution was largely concentrated in New York, where some 92 of the war's 308 battles took place, in New Jersey & eastern Pennsylvania. New York figured so heavily in the conflict because of the British plan to split the colonies in two by occupying the Mohawk & Hudson River Valleys. Bourgoyne was to move south from Canada while Howe was to move north to join him, via the Hudson River. But Bourgoyne's defeat at Saratoga, Howe's failure to cooperate, & finally Clinton's failure to capture West Point, aborted the plan. Washington after his defeat on Long Island retreated from New York into northern New Jersey. His victory at Trenton stemmed the British advance, but he could not prevent the British from occupying Philadelphia, which, like New York, they held until toward the war's end. Delaware & Maryland saw little of the fighting. But Wilmington was occupied by the British.

The Six Nations (five until the inclusion of the Tuscaroras) sided with the British & caused terrible havoc by their raids in Central New York & Pennsylvania. Finally, the Clinton-Sullivan expedition of 1779 ended this menace.

The region experienced only two civil disturbances during the period that followed the Revolution. There was no uprising of poor farmers & debtors similar to that of Shays in Massachusetts. But Pennsylvania had its "Whiskey Insurrection" of 1791, when the western frontier counties rebelled against imposition of an excise tax on distilled spirits, an insurrection that was ended by arrival of Federal troops. In 1798 there was another short-lived uprising in the same state, known as the "Hot Water Rebellion" because the rebels poured boiling water from windows on assessors seeking to levy an unpopular tax imposed by Congress.

New York's rural troubles were delayed until toward 1838, when anti-rent agitation swept the Hudson River counties. This revolt was directed against the proprietors of the huge estates which had been established by the Dutch under the "patroon" system. But the controversy was resolved eventually by legislation & popular pressure. The "patroons" finally were compelled to break up & sell their great holdings.

After the Revolution came development of transportation to the west by building of turnpikes, of which the National Turnpike from Cumberland, Md., to Wheeling, W. Va., the James River turnpike, which ran through southern West Virginia, & the roads through the Mohawk Valley were perhaps the most important. Through these highways poured land-hungry settlers from the eastern sections of the region, from New England & finally from Europe. The early 19th century was the era of canal building, when all the states constructed waterways to promote communications to the west. The most important of these, the most used, & the only one to survive the competition of the railroads was the Erie Canal, which, as New York's Barge Canal, still carries some 2,000,000 tons of freight annually.

The only one of the five states to have figured as a battlefield during the Civil War was West Virginia, with exception of Confederate incursions, halted at Antietam, in Maryland, & at Gettysburg, in Pennsylvania, & several minor raiding operations by Confederate cavalry. Opposing armies criss-crossed West Virginia & it became a minor field of operations. Some of its towns changed hands as much as twenty times.

Maryland, a southern state in its economy & social structure, was prevented by its location between Washington, D.C., & Pennsylvania, from joining the Confederacy. Delaware was split in its sympathies. Many of Delaware's men went to join the Confederate armies.

After the Civil War, both New York & Philadelphia became financial centers for exploitation of the West. Jay Cook was the financier of western railroads, until the crash of 1873. New York's Jay Gould & Vanderbilt fought battles for control of great railroad systems. The Union Pacific was largely built through the efforts of German-born Henry Villard.

New York, New Jersey, Maryland & Pennsylvania had their era of post-Civil-War corrupt politics. The great corporations, especially the great railroad companies, interfered to control state legislatures & prevent regulatory measures. In Pennsylvania the great industrial concerns more or less controlled government. New York State was divided between democratic Tammany Hall, which bossed New York City, & the Republican machine for many years dominated by Tom Platt, which manipulated the state legislature. With election of Theodore Roosevelt to the governorship, an era of reform set in, continued by subsequent governors—Charles Evans Hughes, Alfred E. Smith & Herbert Lehman. The corruption of New York City's government, interrupted periodically by reform waves, seems finally to have been cleaned up during the late F. LaGuardia's administrations.

New Jersey, like New York, was divided between the democratic machine which controlled most of the northern tier cities, under the dictatorship of Frank Hague, & the Republicans which had the rest of the state. The reform movement really began with election of Woodrow Wilson as Governor under whose administration laws were passed to curb corporations & monopolies. The recent defeat of Frank Hague's candidate for mayor of Jersey City has given hope of a general clean-up of municipal government in the northern part of the state.

Pennsylvania has, except for short intervals, usually been Republican, including Philadelphia, which has shown a long record of corrupt local government. The state was controlled by political "machines" in the late 19th & early 20th centuries. The bosses reflected the wishes of the great corporations, the Pennsylvania Railroad & the great coal & steel interests. Because it was the center of coal mining & the steel industry, Pennsylvania has had a long record of labor conflicts, worst of which was the Homestead strike of coal miners in 1892 at Connellsville which resulted in killings & the shooting of Henry C. Frick by the anarchist, Alexander Berkman. Election of Gifford Pinchot in 1922 as governor gave the state an interval of healthy reform. After the depression of 1929, the state had a democratic interlude but reverted to the Republican standard again in 1938's gubernatorial election.

Maryland after the Civil War, like New York, New Jersey & Pennsylvania, suffered from domination of a corrupt machine & of its chief railroad, the Baltimore & Ohio. The state has had its reform movements, in the late 19th & the first quarter of the 20th century.

West Virginia, as already noted, set up as a separate state at the outbreak of the Civil War. Nevertheless, from 1871 to 1897 the state was consistently democratic. Then there was an overturn & the state thereafter joined the Republican column for some 30 years. The great depression of the 1930's brought the democrats back into power.

Delaware is as conservative as one would be led to expect, seeing that it is the headquarters of great corporations. In politics, the state after the Civil War was consistently democratic until the late 1880's, when, largely because of the energetic and well-financed leadership of financial tycoon J. Edward Addicks, it joined the Republican column. The state reverted to the Democrats during the great depression.

In southern New Jersey, in Maryland & Delaware, there is considerable discrimination against Negroes although liberal elements have made continuing efforts to give the Negro equal opportunity in education & employment. A "white supremacy" movement in Maryland failed of its objective, to deprive the Negro of his franchise.

The region can boast of its predominance in various cultural activities. New York City is the nation's cultural center. But Philadelphia, with its great University, its museums, public libraries, & an outstanding symphony orchestra, easily preserves a sturdy cultural independence. Baltimore is distinguished by its world-famous Johns Hopkins University. But culture flowers not merely in the greatest cities, but in the smaller ones as well—in Pittsburgh, with a great university & distinguished technical institute, in Rochester with an outstanding music school, in Newark which has one of the best smaller museums in the country. The measure of the region's educational resources is given by the statistics of Pennsylvania which show that this state has more colleges & universities than any other.

A list of writers & artists who have done their chief work in the Middle Atlantic States would have to include a great number who have come from other parts of the country & exclude some who, though born in the region, belong by temperament or emigration elsewhere. Washington Irving is part of mid-19th century New York. James Fenimore Cooper, though born in New Jersey, belongs to the lore of the New York colonial frontier. Walt Whitman, born on Long Island, & Stephen Crane, of Newark, N.J., are identified—the one with the magnificence & the other with the slums—of the metropolis. Edith Wharton, both by birth & by much of her material, is authentically New York. But Henry James, born in Manhattan, was neither by temperament nor habitat a New Yorker. Nor was Herman Melville, also a Manhattanite. Tom Paine, who saw the light of day in England, sparked the Revolution with his "Common Sense" & "The American Crisis" from Pennsylvania. McGuffey was born in Pennsylvania, but early migrated to Ohio where he turned out his popular grade school "readers." Gertrude Stein, also born in the Keystone State, was educated elsewhere & invented her peculiar literary style in Paris, France. Robinson Jeffers, born in Pittsburgh, belongs to the West Coast.

The genteel tradition in literature centered largely in New York, with many of its exponents coming from other parts of the country. Stanford White, a New Yorker, translated it very successfully into architecture, while Edward MacDowell put it to music.

Primitive painters flourished in the region as they did in New England. Albert Hicks, of New Hope, Pa., in his oft-repeated "The Peaceable Kingdom," put a Delaware River background to his charming canvas. Anonymous, itinerant artists celebrated the Hudson Valley's landscapes, farmhouses & people. Grandma Moses, of upstate New York, has brought the primitive school down to her own day. The prints of Currier & Ives have portrayed the lush greens of the Hudson Highlands better than the Hudson River School, which was founded by Thomas Cole, a Britisher, & Asher B. Duran, a New Jerseyite. What has been glibly termed "American Barbizon," was headed by George Innes, born in Newburgh, N.Y. But Homer, Martin, Wyant & others of the school were natives of other parts of the country. Thomas Eakins was Pennsylvania-born, as was George Luks. But Robert Henri, often bracketed with Luks, was from Ohio. George Bellows, who worked mostly in New York, was Ohio-born, too. John Sloan comes from Lock Haven, Pa., but has been painting New York scenes most of his life. The contemporary non-objective painters who center in New York, come from all over the country, & one of the best of them was born in the Caucasus.

Stephen Foster, born in Lawrenceville, a suburb of Pittsburgh, Pa., in his songs celebrated the plantation Negro's nostalgia, although he himself crossed the Mason & Dixon line only once in his lifetime. Victor Herbert, composer of light opera, was Irish-born, German-trained & lived in New York during his creative period. George Gershwin, an East Side boy, tried to bridge the gap between jazz & "classic" music in his "Rhapsody in Blue." Tin Pan Alley draws its composers from all over the country. Composers of "classic" music also center in the metropolis.

O. Henry (Wm.S.Porter), born in North Carolina, is best known for his stories about the metropolis' "four million" & "Bagdad on the Subway." Randolph Bourne (New Jersey), F. Scott Fitzgerald (Minnesota), John Reed (Oregon), Dos Passos (Chicago), Edna St. Vincent Millay (Maine), Max Eastman (N.Y.State), E. E. Cummings (Mass.) & Lewis Mumford (N.Y.State), all more or less have had their period of greatest literary development in New York. Hart Crane (Ohio) is forever linked to the metropolis by his "The Bridge." Theodore Dreiser, after writing his earlier novels in Chicago, came to New York & used a New York murder case as the basis for his "The American Tragedy." But Henry L. Mencken has, from Baltimore, Md., for more than a generation, influenced American thought & criticism.

The theater has for more than a hundred years been almost a New York monopoly. Clyde Fitch was the late 19th century's exponent of the genteel tradition in the drama. Augustus Thomas, born in St. Louis, Mo., brought regional melodrama to Broadway. David Belasco came from San Francisco to capture New York audiences with his lavish sets. The dawn of the realistic school arrived with "Salvation Nell," a play about a prostitute, by Edw. Sheldon, & Eugene Walter's "The Easiest Way." After World War I, a host of new dramatists poured through the gap breached to Broadway by Eugene O'Neill, the Provincetown Playhouse & the Theater Guild. More recent is the development of indigenous American ballet in New York. After "Oklahoma's" success, this new form of ballet invaded Broadway's "musicals."

With all their concentration of industry, finance & commerce, great stretches of these mid-Atlantic states are thinly populated. This is especially true of central Pennsylvania, western Maryland & most of West Virginia & sections of south New York. More than half of these areas are not even farmed & are reverting to forest land. In recent years, both New York & Pennsylvania have been active in reclaiming & reforesting millions of acres. New York has reserved more than 2,000,000 acres in its Adirondack Park & some 500,000 in its Catskill Park. In addition, several million acres of submarginal land are being bought & reforested. Pennsylvania has followed a somewhat similar policy in purchase of cut-over acreage. Moreover, a large section of northwest Pennsylvania is preserved within the Alleghany National Forest. At least half of West Virginia lies within national forests, a small part within George Washington & the rest within Monongahela National Forest. Inside this area & the numerous state parks lies most of the state's finest scenery. Eventually, by reforestation of publicly-owned lands, the Middle Atlantic States may again be able to supply their own lumber requirements. In this connection, it is well to note that New York, in 1871, led the country in production of lumber, & Pennsylvania came a close second. Unfortunately, the magnificent hemlock forests of the Catskills, which were cut to supply bark for leather tanning, can probably never be reestablished. In any case, these vast forest areas afford immense recreational resources for the crowded city populations, resources which are richly supplemented by the ocean front resorts extending from Long Island's eastern tip to Cape Charles in Virginia.

# MIDDLE ATLANTIC STATES

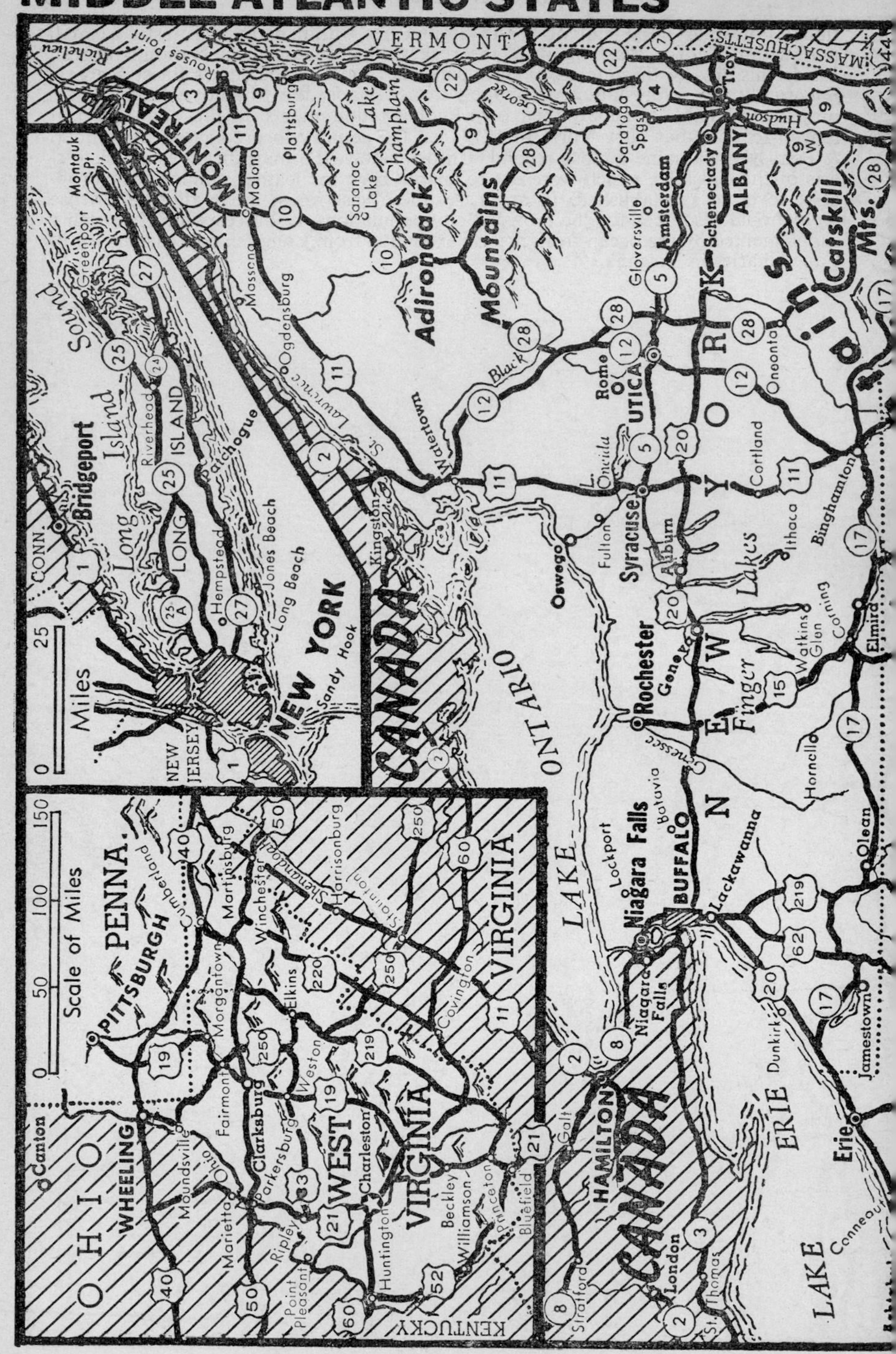

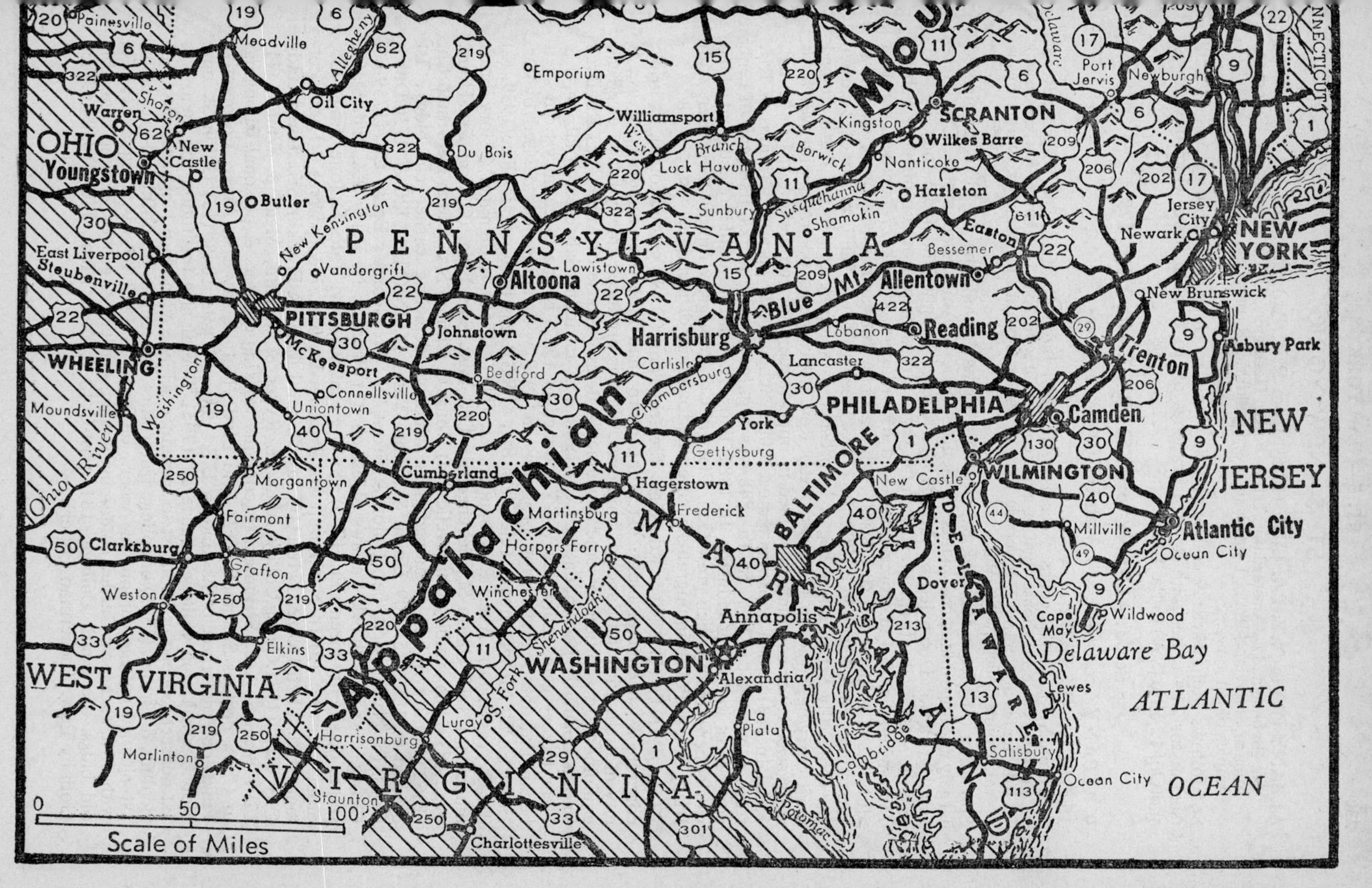

PENNSYLVANIA
NEW JERSEY
NEW YORK
OHIO
WEST VIRGINIA
VIRGINIA
MARYLAND
DELAWARE
Appalachian
Blue Mt.
ATLANTIC OCEAN
Delaware Bay
PITTSBURGH
PHILADELPHIA
BALTIMORE
WASHINGTON
WILMINGTON
WHEELING
SCRANTON
Harrisburg
Allentown
Reading
Trenton
Camden
Atlantic City
Altoona
Johnstown
Youngstown
Wilkes Barre
Hazleton
Williamsport
Lock Haven
Sunbury
Shamokin
Kingston
Berwick
Nanticoke
Easton
Bessemer
Lebanon
Lancaster
York
Gettysburg
Carlisle
Chambersburg
Hagerstown
Frederick
Cumberland
Martinsburg
Harpers Ferry
Winchester
Annapolis
Alexandria
La Plata
Cambridge
Salisbury
Ocean City
Dover
Lewes
Cape May
Wildwood
Millville
New Castle
New Brunswick
Asbury Park
Newark
Jersey City
Port Jervis
Newburgh
Emporium
Du Bois
Oil City
Meadville
Painesville
Warren
Sharon
New Castle
Butler
New Kensington
Vandergrift
Lewistown
Bedford
McKeesport
Connellsville
Uniontown
Washington
Moundsville
East Liverpool
Steubenville
Morgantown
Fairmont
Clarksburg
Grafton
Weston
Elkins
Marlinton
Harrisonburg
Staunton
Luray
Charlottesville
Susquehanna
Allegheny
West Branch
Ohio River
Shenandoah
S. Fork
Potomac
Delaware
CONNECTICUT
0
50
100
Scale of Miles

# ST. 5—NEW YORK

**ALBANY (W) to N.Y.-PA. LINE** (17.5$^m$ from Erie, Pa.). **314. St.5**

Via: Schenectady, Amsterdam, Little Falls, Herkimer, Utica, Canastota, Syracuse, Auburn, Batavia, Buffalo, Lackawanna & Dunkirk. RR. parallels entire route. Accoms.: Ample, of all types.

St.5 follows Mohawk R. & course of Erie Canal to Utica. At Auburn it joins US20 (see) & for 71$^m$ unites with it, then branches off to Buffalo from which it follows shore of L. Erie (SW) to Pa. Line.

### Sec. 1: ALBANY to WESTERN J. with US20. 179.

**0. ALBANY** (see US20), at J. with US20.

**15.5. SCHENECTADY**

Through RR. & bus conns. Accoms.: All types. Info.: C. of C., 246 State St. Road shows at Civic Playhouse; golf at mun. course, Oregon Ave. bet. Union St. & Consaul Rd.; tennis at Central & Riverside Pks.; swim. at Central Pk. Mohawk Drama Festival, Union College, July-Aug.

Spreading (SE) from Mohawk R., city that "lights & hauls the world" is dominated largely by huge industrial plants of Gen. Electric & Amer. Locomotive Cos. Here small group of Dutch led by Arendt Van Curler bought land from Inds. in 1661 & built stockaded settlement. Community was almost wiped out on night of Feb. 8, 1690 when Fr. & Ind. force massacred 69 villagers & took 27 captives, burning all but 2 of settlement's 80 houses. Although new ft. was built, recovery was slow. First Eng. settlers arrived c.1700. In 1705 Queen's Ft. was built on site of 2 earlier fts. Gradually Schenectady began to prosper as shipping center for flat-bottomed craft carrying cargo up Mohawk. After Rev. it prospered on trade with westward emigrants. River commerce declined in importance after completion of Erie Canal, 1825. In 1831, when pop. was almost 9,000, Schenectady became terminus of RR. from Albany, 1st in N.Y. St. In 1848 was org. locomotive works, until end of cent. city's most important industry. In 1886 Thos. A. Edison installed electric machine works here, from which grew Gen. Electric Co. Pop. grew rapidly thereafter, with Irish, Ital. & Polish immigrants accounting for much of increase.

PTS. OF INT.: (1) 1 River Rd., **Gen. Electric Plant** (O.wks.guided tours), its brick, concrete & sheetmetal bldgs. extending more than mile over hundreds of as., is city in itself, with thousands of employes. Here is produced chiefly heavy electrical equipment, in addition to some consumer articles. "House of Magic," as Research Lab. is popularly known, dating from 1900, was 1st industrial research lab. in U.S. Near factory gate, radio **Sta. WGY,** opened in 1922, is one of country's oldest; it began broadcasting television programs in 1928 with equipment devised by Dr. Ernst F. W. Alexanderson. Television **Sta. WRGB** has been on air since 1939. (2) 43-45 Washington Ave., **Rbt. Sanders H.** (N.O.c.1750) is dignified 3-story brick mansion. (3) 13 Union St., **Schenectady Cty. Hist. Soc. Bldg.** (O.Mon.-Fri.,Thurs. eve.; 1839) has exhibit of hist. relics. (4) Union & Church Sts., **Dutch Reformed Ch.** (1862.Goth.Rev.) has 4 stained-glass windows depicting earlier ch. bldgs., 1st erected in 1682. (5) 109 Union St., **Abr. Yates H.** (N.O.bet.1720 & 1730.Dutch Col.). (6) N. Ferry St. bet. Union & Front Sts., **St. George's Episc. Ch.** (1759-66. Georg.Col.) is Mohawk Valley's oldest ch. (7) Front & N. Ferry Sts., **Ind. Statue** stands on site of Queen's Ft. (1705). (8) 17 Front St., **Gov. Yates H.** (one wing 1735, other later.alt.). (9) 14 N. Church St., **Brouwer-Rosa H.** incorporates 3 Dutch cottages (oldest bet. 1690 & 1710). (10) Jay St. bet. Liberty & Franklin Sts., **Schenectady City Hall** (1931.Georg.Col.by John M. Ryder & McKim, Mead & White). (11) 1297 Wendell Ave., **Steinmetz H.** contains working quarters & personal belongings of Chas. Proteus Steinmetz. (12) Erie Blvd., Nott & Jay Sts., **Amer. Locomotive Plant,** one of largest of its kind in U.S., dates back to 1848. (13) Union St. opp. Nott Terr., **Union College** (chartered 1795), liberal arts institution for men, was 1st nonsect. college in U.S., 1st to introduce science & modern languages into curriculum, & birthpl. (1825) of college fraternities. It occupies beautiful 100-a. campus, 1st planned college campus in Amer., designed in 1813 by Jos. Jacques Ramée, with 27-a. **Jackson's Garden** containing sunken gardens & groves. Among venerable old bldgs. are **South College** (1814.post-Col.) & **Nott Mem. Lib.** (1858-76.Vict. Goth.by Edw. Tuckerman Potter).

SIDE TRIPS: (A) Take St.7 (R) from Schenectady 7m to **Knolls Atomic Power Lab.,** opened 1948 at cost of $20,000,000 as 1 of 4 principal research centers of Atomic Energy Commission.

(B) Take St.5S (L) from Schenectady, along south bank of Mohawk River; this is alt. route to Utica. At 6.5m is **Jan Mabie H.** (early 18th cent. Dutch Col.). 16.5m **Amsterdam** (see below). 22.5m **Auriesville,** where is **Shrine of Our Lady of Martyrs** comm. Jesuit martyrs, Father Isaac Jogues, Bros. René Goupil & Jean Lalande & 5 priests who were massacred by Inds. & in 1925 canonized as 1st N. Amer. Saints of Cath. Ch. Here also is **Kateri's Grotto** with **Statue of Kateri Tekakwitha** ("Lily of the Mohawks"), sainted Ind. convert. 38m **Canajoharie** (Ind.,"pot that cleans itself") sett. c.1730. Large hole worn out by waters of cr. at entrance to Canajoharie Gorge, (S) of town, gave rise to name. On Moyer St., **Van Alstyne H.** (O.appl.1749) containing coll. of hist. material concerning Mohawk Valley. On Church St., **Canajoharie Lib. & Art Gallery** (O.wks.Sat.& Sun.p.m.; 1924 by Tilton & Githons) containing paintings, among them some by Winslow Homer. 41.5m **Fort Plain.** On Main St., **Paris-Bleeker H.** (O.1786) containing Ind. & Col. material. 51.5m **Indian Castle Ch.** on bluff (L), site of one of Mohawk "castles." Here Sir Wm. Johnson built Ft. Hendrick. 54m **Herkimer Estate** (pic.) on which is old **Herkimer H.** (O.sm.fee. 1764.alt.1848) containing Col. & Rev. material. Near-by is **Obelisk** comm. Gen Nicholas Herkimer. 61m **Ft. Herkimer Reformed Dutch Ch.** (begun c.1730), where refugees found shelter from marauding Inds. & Tories in 1778. 64m **Mohawk,** where are several fine old houses. 66m **Ilion,** site of **Remington Arms Plant** which grew out of orig. industry est. here by Remingtons, early settlers. Here & in **Russell Pk.** are exhibits of guns. Ilion is also site of **Remington-Rand Plant,** mfg. typewriters & office equipment. 68m **Frankfort,** industrial community mfg. tools & machinery, where in 1843 wooden matches were 1st made in U.S. 78m **Utica** (see below) at J. with St.5.

At Schenectady St.5 crosses to N. bank of Mohawk R., to **SCOTIA, 16.5.,** whose 1st settler, Alex. Lindsey Glen, came from Scotland. (W) of Bridge is **Glen-Sanders H.** (1658.1713.fine old inter.) built by Glen's son, Johannes. (W) on Mohawk Ave. is **Abr. Glen H.** (O.2-9.c.1730.Dutch Col.later adds.) in which is Scotia Pub. Lib. **31.5. AMSTERDAM,** sett. c.1783, is an industrial city, one of whose chief industries is carpet-making. 57 Lyon St., **Mohawk Carpet Mills** (O.guides) & 37 Prospect St., **Bigelow Sanford Carpet Mills** (O.guides) are worth visit. W. Main St., **Guy Pk.** (O.wks.Sun.p.m.sm.fee.1766 later adds.), now mus. of Ind. & hist. relics, was built by Sir Wm. Johnson for his nephew, Guy Johnson, who married Wm.'s daughter Mary. Back of H. is **Lock No. 11** of **Barge Canal. 34.5.** Village of **FT. JOHNSON,** in which is **Ft. Johnson** (O.exc.Sun.& hols.1749.fine inter.), 3rd Mohawk Valley home of Sir Wm. Johnson, containing Ind. & Col. relics. **39.5. VISSCHER-DE-GRAFF H.** (1795.remod.in 1870's). **42.** J. with Rd. leading (R) 0.5m to fork & (R) to **Butler H.** (1742.saltbox) 1m, home of famous Tory family of Butler who led Tory Ind. expeditions during Rev. against patriots. Beyond latter J. is **FONDA,** glove mfg. center & tourist starting pt. for S. Adirondacks, sett. early in 18th cent. Railroad St., **Montgomery County Cth.** (1836.Gr.Rev.).

SIDE TRIP: Take St.148 (R) from Fonda 3.5m to **Johnstown,** sett.1762, glove mfg. center, named for founder Sir Wm. Johnson. N. Williams St., **Fulton County Cth.** (1772), built by Johnson. In cemetery of St. John's Episc. Ch. on N. Market St., **Grave of Sir Wm. Johnson.** Montgomery & S. Berry Sts., **Cty. Jail** (1772). W. Green St., **Drumm H.** (1763). S. Williams & Montgomery Sts., **Burke's Inn** (1793) now owned by D.A.R.

From Johnstown take St.29 (L) 0.5m to **Johnson Hall** (O.sm.fee.c.1761.Georg.Col.int. inter.), Johnson's last home. It was taken over by N.Y. St. when John Johnson, Sir Wm.'s son, became Tory leader.

St.148 cont. to **Gloversville,** 8m, another glove-making center. Industry dates back to c.1760, when Johnson sett. some English glovemakers here.

**49. THE NOSES,** 2 high rocks on R. from whose summits, fine views. **54.5. PALATINE BRIDGE,** sett. 1723. Here is **Ft. Frey** (L) (1739) on site of an earlier ft. Near-by is **Frey H.** (1808.Fed.).

SIDE TRIP: Take St.10 (R) from Palatine Bridge c.3.5m to **Stone Arabia.** Here are **Luth. Ch.** (1792) & **Dutch Reformed Ch.** (1788). Facing it is **Col. John Brown Mon.** comm. commander of Amer. forces in battle of Stone Arabia, 1780, against Sir John Johnson's raiders.

**60. FT. WAGNER** (R) (1750), erected by Peter Wagner. **61. PALATINE CH.** (L) (1770), spared by agreement of both parties during Rev. **62.5. FT. KLOCK** (1750), where in 1780 refugees took shelter during Battle of Klock's Field near-by bet. patriots & Sir J. Johnson's marauders. **64. ST. JOHNSVILLE,** sett. 1775, in which are some fine old hs. **72.5.** J. with Rd. leading (L) 0.5m to beautiful **Little Falls Gorge** & at 1m **Talequega Pk.** where is highest lock on Barge Canal. **75. LITTLE FALLS,** old Erie Canal boom town which once shipped Herkimer Cty. cheese, becoming country's biggest cheese market; now center for diversified mfg. industries. **81. HERKIMER,** sett. 1725, industrial, shipping & dairy farming center. On Park Ave., in Myers Pk., is **Statue of Gen. Nicholas Herkimer** (by Burr Miller), patriot leader during Rev. Main & Court Sts., **Jail** (1834); **Dutch Reformed Ch.** (1834); **Herkimer County Hist. Soc. Bldg.,** containing hist. coll.; & **Herkimer County Cth.** (1875), on site of early ft.

**98.5. UTICA**

Through RR. & bus conns. Accoms.: All types. Info.: C. of C., 8 Elizabeth St. Golf & tennis at Roscoe Conkling Pk.

Spreading over flat country from both banks of Mohawk R., Utica is trading & industrial center, among whose chief products are knit goods, cotton cloth, heating & ventilating apparatus, paper containers, & radio parts. It has large Ital., Polish & Irish colonies—& one of largest Welsh colonies in U.S. Settlement dates from 1773, when several families of Palatine German descent arrived. Community was wiped out by Ind.-Tory raid in 1776 but rebuilt after Rev. It became trading center, conn. with Schenectady by boat & with Albany by stagecoach, & in 1798 was inc. as village. Erie Canal brought new settlers & new industries after 1825. By 1832, when city was chartered, it had grist mill, pottery, iron foundry, plow factory, engine & boiler works. Textile industry, now city's leading one, dates back to late 1840's.

PTS. OF INT.: (1) John & Bleecker Sts., **St. John's Cath. Ch.** (1869.Romanes.). (2) Genesee & Pearl Sts., **Utica City Hall** (1852-53.Ital.-Lombard Romanes.by Rich.Upjohn). (3) Genesee & Elizabeth Sts., **Grace Ch.** (Episc.1856-60.Eng.Goth. by Rich.Upjohn; entrance tower 1870 by Rich.M.Upjohn;spire 1933 by Hobart B. Upjohn). (4) John & Elizabeth Sts. & Park Ave., **Oneida Hist. Soc. Bldg.** (1896. Flemish Goth.by Rich.Morris Hunt) houses curios, paintings, books & mss. dealing with Oneida Cty. (5) Rutger St. opp. John St., **Rutger B. Miller H.** (N.O.1820-30. post-Col.by Philip Hooker). (6) 312-16 Genesee St., **Munson-Williams-Proctor Institute** (O.wks.), housed in former brick Vict. mansions of Frederick T. & Thos. R. Proctor, incl. art sch. & exhibition gallery with coll. of heirlooms & paintings. (7) 303 Genesee St. & Parkway, **Baron Von Steuben Statue** (1914.by J. Otto Schwizer). (8) Oneida St. & Parkway, **Roscoe Conkling Pk.** (golf.recr.facils.) with Zoo on hilltop. (9) Oneida St. at Ballantyne Brae, in **Forest Hill Cemetery** is **Sacred Stone of Oneida Inds.** (10) Court St. bet. York & Whitesboro Sts., **Utica St. Hospital,** opened 1843, 1st N.Y. St. institution for insane; this is one of most notable examples of Gr. Rev. architecture in U.S. (by Capt.Wm.Clarke).

SIDE TRIPS: (A) Take St.12 (R) from Utica. At 17$^m$ is J. with St.46A. Take latter (L) 3.5$^m$ to **Steuben Mem. Pk.** (pic.), comprising part of 16,000-a. tract granted by N.Y. St. in 1786 to Baron Von Steuben, who trained Rev. troops. Here are **Gen. Von Steuben's Grave** & **Reproduction of Von Steuben Cabin** with early furniture.

**Alder Creek,** 25$^m$, is at J. with St.28 (see Adirondack St. Pk.). Now St.12 cont. to **Boonville,** 32$^m$, dairying center. 56.5$^m$, **Lowville** is shipping center for farm products with huge coldstorage plant. 84$^m$ **Watertown** (see US11), at J. with US11 (see).

(B) Take St.69 (R) from Utica. At 2.5$^m$ is **Yorkville.** W. Oriskany & Whitesboro Sts., **Inman H.** (1792), where Henry Inman, famous Amer. portraitist & landscapist, was born. 9$^m$ **Oriskany Battlefield Mon.** (R). Here on Aug. 4, 1777, was fought sanguinary battle bet. patriots led by Gen. N. Herkimer who were ambushed by Tory-Ind. force; Herkimer was killed but finally patriots forced enemy to retreat. 14$^m$ **Rome,** once busy Erie Canal town, is now industrial city dominated by copper & brass mills; it processes substantial share of all copper mined in U.S. Here Brit. est. fortifications in 1725 & in 1758 built Ft. Stanwix but abandoned it in 1760. Town of Rome, 1st known as Lynchville, dates from 1786, when Dominick Lynch bought land & sold lots. Dominick, Willett, Liberty & Spring Sts. bound **Site of Ft. Stanwix,** which Amers. occupied in 1776 & held for 3 wks. in Aug. 1777 against Brit. siege, during which Amer. flag is supposed to have been raised for 1st time in battle. Seneca St., **Revere Copper & Brass Works,** with world's biggest copper rolling mill. N. Washington & Elm Sts., **Jervis Lib.** (O.wks.), occupying former home of Erie Canal engineer & RR. builder John B. Jervis, contains painting (by Edw.P.Buyck) depicting siege of Ft. Stanwix.

**107.5.** J. with St.233.

SIDE TRIP: Take latter (L) 2.5$^m$ to J. with St.412 & turn (R) on this to **Hamilton College** 3$^m$, founded 1792 by missionary Samuel Kirkland as sch. for Inds. & Whites. **Buttrick Hall** (1812.rest.) is oldest bldg.; **Chapel** (1828.alt.1897.Fed.by Phil. Hooker) is finest architecturally. Others incl. **North College** (1842.Fed.), **Root Hall of Science** (1897 by Carrère & Hastings), **Biology-Geology Bldg.** (1925.Coll.Goth.) which houses natural hist. colls.

**117. VERNON,** where is **Ch. of Christ** (1821.Georg.Goth.). At **SHERRILL, 120.,** are **Oneida Ltd. Factories** (O.appl.), mfg. plated silverware. Sherrill Rd. leads (L) $1^m$ to **Oneida Ltd. Adm. Bldg.** (Tudor Goth.), near which is **The Mansion** (1860), 1st large community center of Perfectionists, famous Oneida Colony, founded in 1848 by J. H. Noyes. Sect's beliefs about relation of sexes, birth control & experiments in eugenics provoked bitter attacks. In 1881, due to internal dissension, community was disbanded & property was distributed among its members. Oneida Ltd. was then org. by former members of sect to manufacture plated silverware. At **125.** is J. with Rd. leading (R) $1.5^m$ to Oneida, industrial community which grew up around early hostelry, Railroad H., run by townsite owner Sands Higginbotham, whose home, **Cottage Lake,** Main St. is now **Madison Cty. Hist. Soc. Hqs. 128.5. CANASTOTA,** famous Erie Canal town in which are many old hs. & which is center of onion-growing region. On St.5 is **Roberts H.** (N.O.1820). **135.5 CHITTENANGO,** where are **Presb. Ch.** (1828.Georg.Goth.), **Episc. Ch.** (1865.Victorian Goth.) & **Baptist Ch.** (c.1868.2nd Empire frame). At **139.** is J. with St.290 leading (R) $2.5^m$ to **Green Ls. St. Pk.** (pic.cabins.recr.bath.golf.clubh.). **143.5. FAYETTEVILLE,** in which are some fine hs. of 1st half of 19th cent. 109 Academy St., **Grover Cleveland H.** (N.O.), where Pres. lived as boy.

## 152.5 SYRACUSE

Through RR., bus & plane conns. Accoms.: All types. Info.: C. of C., 351 S. Warren St. Dramatic productions at Civic Playh.; baseball at Mun. Stadium; swim. & tennis at city pks.; golf at Burnet & Sunnycrest Pks. & several private courses. N.Y. St. Fair, Aug.-Sept.

At mouth of Onondaga Valley, Syracuse stretches from flatlands along shore of Onondaga L. over 6 hills—an important mfg. & commercial center with well-developed educational, cultural & recr. facils. Once known as "Salt City" for its leading industry, today it has remarkably diversified economy, producing many manufactured articles.

Although 1st white settlers came c.1788 or 1789 to take land granted to soldiers of Rev. which formerly had been Ind. terr., Syracuse village had pop. of only c.500 when inc. in 1825. Salt springs along Onondaga L. made it 1st place in U.S. where salt for commercial purposes was obtained from other than sea water. Completion of Erie Canal in 1825 & advent of 1st RRs. in 1838 & 1839 boomed pop. Salt industry, all important during early yrs., reached production of 8,000,000 bushels by Civil War; but decline began in 1890's & by 1900 salt production had virtually ceased. Other industries developed after Civil War: pottery & steel (1871), plow manufacture (1876), typewriter production (1887), die-casting (1894), automobile manufacture (1902). Meanwhile cultural facils. were developed: 1st high sch. (1868), 1st pub. hospital (1870), Syracuse Univ. (1871), 1st pub. park (1886).

PTS. OF INT.: (1) W. Genesee & S. Clinton Sts., **Jerry Rescue Bldg.** (1830), formerly police sta., was site in 1851 of rescue by Dr. Samuel J. May, Gerrit Smith & other abolitionists of fugitive slave "Jerry" or Wm. Henry, who had been arrested under Fugitive Slave Act for extradition to N. Carolina. (2) 201 E. Genesee St., **St. Tower Office Bldg.** (tower O.) is city's tallest. (3) 311 Montgomery St., **Onondaga Hist. Assoc. Bldg.** (O.wks.Sat.a.m.) houses portraits & documents dealing with Onondaga Cty. (4) 335 Montgomery St., **Syracuse Pub. Lib.** (1902.Baroque Rev.by Jas. A. Randall), has colls. of old mss. & early printing & Walt Whitman coll. (5) 401 James St., **Mus. of Fine Arts** (O.wks.Sun.p.m.), 1st mus. in U.S. to form permanent coll. devoted entirely to Amer. paintings, also contains porcelains & curios, Whistler etchings & Japanese prints, paintings by masters. (6) 607 James St., **Leavenworth Mansion** (1842.Gr.Rev.). (7) 321 S. Wilbur Ave., **Burnet Pk.** (135 as.recr.facils.) contains gardens & zoo. (8) Foot of Univ. Pl., **Thornden Pk.** (76 as.swim.tennis.playgrounds) contains **Mills Rose Garden,** with more than 7,000 varieties & natural amphitheater. (9) 736 Irving Ave., **Syracuse Medical Center,** consisting of 4 hospitals & **Syracuse Univ. Medical Sch.** (est.1834) in harmonizing Georg. style. (10) Irving Ave. & Univ. Pl., **Yates Castle** (1851.Norman by Jas.Renwick), former mansion of C. Tyler Longworth, houses Syracuse Univ. Sch. of Journalism. (11) Univ. Pl., **Syracuse Univ.,** coed. & nonsect., opened 1871, commanding view of city from hilltop campus with numerous bldgs. devoted to its 15 colleges & schs., is one of 25 largest U.S. universities. Oldest of bldgs. is **Hall of Languages** (1873). Facing "Old Oval," heart of campus, is **Lib.** (1905.Fr.Ren.). Most architecturally notable bldg. is **Hendricks Chapel** (neo-Class.by Dwight Jas.Baum). **Lyman Hall** houses

Mus. of Natural Sciences. **John Crouse College** (1889.Romanes.by A.Russell) houses College of Fine Arts. **Archbold Stadium,** huge natural amphitheater accoms. football games. Adj. is **N.Y. St. College of Forestry.** (12) Just outside Syracuse, **Gen. Electric Electronics Pk.,** completed in late 1940's at cost of $20,000,000, covers campus-like site of more than 155 as. with over 1,000,000 sq. ft. of floor area in bldgs. of advanced design devoted to electronics research, engineering, mfg., power, employee welfare, education & adm. Syracuse is at J. with US11 (see).

SIDE TRIPS: (A) Take St.57 (R) from Syracuse. Along E. shore of Onondaga L. from N. city limits for distance of 6m extends **Onondaga Pky.** (fresh & salt water bath.boat. baseball.playgrounds.bridle path), in which are **Danforth Salt Pool** (bathh.), 700' long; **LeMoyne Salt Springs,** discovered 1654 by Jesuit missionary Father Simon LeMoyne; reprod. of **Ft. Ste Marie de Gannentaha,** stockaded settlement built by Fr. in 1656 but soon abandoned, with hist. relics & reprods. of early furniture; **Hiawatha Mon.** on site of founding of Iroquois Confederacy under leadership of Hiawatha & Dekanawidah; & **Salt Mus.,** constructed around last surviving vat house & chimney of salt fields reserv. est. by N.Y. St. in 1797, containing old salt-making machinery & photographs. St.57 cont. to **Liverpool,** 5m, industrial center. **Fulton,** 25m, is mfg. city producing food products, woolen goods, cardboard containers & other articles. **Pathfinder I.,** in Oswego R. (L), 26.5m, is said to be locale of fight bet. Iroquois Inds. & hero of Jas. Fenimore Cooper's "The Pathfinder." At 28m is **Battle I. St. Pk.** (L), where in 1758 Col. John Bradstreet defeated attempted ambush by Fr. & Inds. **Oswego** (see US11), 36.5m, is at J. with US104, running (E) to conn. with US11 (see) & (W) to conn. with US15 (see) at Rochester (see US15).

(B) Take St. Fair Blvd. (R) from Syracuse 4m to **N.Y. St. Fair Grounds** (fair Aug. or Sept.) with Coliseum & many exhibition bldgs. Fair is visited by more than 200,000 people.

(C) Take Milton Ave. (R) from Syracuse 2m to huge **Solvay Plant,** which produces soda.

St.5 cont. to **AUBURN** (see US20), **179.,** at J. with US20 (see), with which St.5 unites for 71.5m to c.1m beyond **Avon.** (For this part of route, see US20).

## Sec. 2: WESTERN J. with US20 to BUFFALO. 64.

At **LE ROY, 13.5.,** are **Le Roy Mansion** (before 1812.post-Col.) & **Jello Plant. 23.5. BATAVIA,** sett. 1801, named for Dutch republic of which site's proprietors were natives, is an industrial town. In **Old Batavia Cemetery** on Harvester Ave. is buried city's founder, Jos. Ellicott. Main St., **Genesee County Cth.** (1841.Gr.Rev.). E. Main St., **Richmond Mansion** (Gr.Rev.). Main & Bank Sts., **Carey Mansion** (1817.Gr. Rev.). W. Main St., **Holland Land Office Mus.** (O.summer afts.sm.fee.1804.Class. Rev.) was built by Jos. Ellicott. It contains old furniture, relics, documents, etc. This bldg. was office of huge Holland Purchase (3,300,000 as.) bought by some Dutch investors in 1793 from Rbt. Morris. Ellicott was their representative. At **40.** is J. with St.93, leading (R) 2m to Akron, where St.267 turns (R) 3.5m to **Tonawanda Ind. Reserv.,** home of group of Seneca Inds., on which is **Community H.** (1939) built on lines of Iroquois long house. **53.5. WILLIAMSDALE** where are **Dream I. Pk.** (pic. bath.recr.) & on Glenn Ave., **Glenn Pk.,** commercial amusement resort.

### 64. BUFFALO

Through RR., bus & plane conns. Piers at S. end Main St. & E. end Erie St. at Buffalo R. for Great Ls. boats. Accoms.: Plentiful & varied. Info.: C. of C., 283 Main St. Dramatic productions at The Playhouse & Erlanger Theater; baseball at Offerman Stadium; golf at Cazenovia Grove, Cleveland, Delaware, & South Pks.; tennis at mun. courts in city pks.; swim. at Cazenovia, Houghton & Riverside Pks. & at Mass. Ave. & Lawrence Pl.

Buffalo, bordering E. end of L. Erie & Niagara R., busy inland port & 2nd largest city in N.Y. St., is one of nation's biggest RR. centers & one of its 8 largest industrial centers. It is famous as flour-milling city & center of one of world's largest electrochemical & electrometallurgical production areas, with huge blast furnaces, rubber plants, wallboard factories, dye & linseed-crushing plants. From Niagara Sq., near L. front, broad blvds. radiate diagonally in all directions except (W). On E. Side, where extend far-reaching RR. yards & factory sites of industrial area, dwell Polish & German colonies who comprise large proportion of pop. Most of Buffalo's large Ital. colony live along waterfront; its Hungarians, in Black Rock; its Negroes, around Jesse Clipper Square.

First vessel built by white men to sail upper Great Ls., La Salle's "Griffin," departed on her maiden voyage from site of Buffalo in 1679. At mouth of Buffalo Cr. 1st white settlement was est. by Fr. in 1758, but Brit. destroyed it following yr. Until after Rev., Seneca Inds. retained lands here. Site was mapped in 1799 by Jos. Ellicott, who offered lots for sale in 1803-04, modelling city plan after that of

Washington, D.C. During War of 1812, in Dec. 1813, Brit. burned settlement, but it was rebuilt; Gen. Jacob Brown based his hqs. here, directing Amer. troops in capture of Ft. Erie. At Buffalo in 1819 was constructed 1st steamboat on Great Ls., "Walk-on-the-Water." Buffalo was chosen over rival community of Black Rock, $2^m$ (N), as terminus for Erie Canal, & rapidly forged ahead after 1825 as shipping & trans. center, with many warehouses & hotels. By 1832, when it was inc., pop. was 12,000. Manufacturing was soon introduced: foundry, steam engine plant, iron works were all built before 1840. During & after Civil War city became important grain & livestock market as RRs. converged here to make it leading trans. center. After 1873 Pennsylvania coal was brought by rail & L. Superior iron ore by boat to provide basis for big-scale metal industry. Irish & German immigrants poured in to provide labor. Buffalo quickly became modern metropolis: street railways were laid, sewers & water & gas mains installed, streets paved & lighted. Luxurious hotels & ornate post-Civil War mansions were erected. Buffalo in 1901 staged Pan-Amer. Exposition, at which Pres. Wm. McKinley was assassinated. Following turn of century, development of hydroelectric power from Niagara Falls began era of tremendous industrial expansion. Blast furnaces, grain elevators, shipping terminals were built. During World War I manufacture of dyes & airplanes was undertaken. Industrial expansion has since continued, with ever-ramifying diversity of industries: among biggest of recent additions have been plants mfg. car heaters, buses, telephone switchboard equipment, & electric motors.

PTS. OF INT. DOWNTOWN: (1) Niagara Sq., **McKinley Mon.** (1907.Fr.Ren.by Carrère & Hastings,architects,& A.Phimister Proctor,sculptor). (2) Niagara Sq. W., **Buffalo City Hall** (1932.by John J.Wade), with 32-story tower flanked by 14-story wings, has wall paintings depicting local hist. (by Wm.de Leftwich Dodge) in lobby & corridors. (3) Franklin St. bet. N. Eagle & Church Sts., **Erie Cty. Hall** (1872.Ital. Ren.by A.J.Warner). (4) Church & Pearl Sts., **Prudential Bldg.** (1894.by Louis Sullivan), 12 stories, notable example of Sullivan's work. (5) Shelton Sq. W., **St. Paul's Episc. Cathedral** (mid-19th cent.Goth.Rev.by Rich.Upjohn). (6) Niagara Sq. at Genesee, Franklin, & Court Sts., **N. Y. St. Bldg.** (1928-31.neo-Class.by Wm.E. Haugaard, Edw.B.Green & Sons,& A.Hart Hopkins) has ceiling paintings of early Buffalo scenes (by Wm. Andrew Mackay & Louis J.Borgo). (7) Franklin & Court Sts., **U. S. Cth.** (1936.neo-Class.). (8) Broadway & Clinton Sts., **Buffalo Pub. Lib.** (1886.Romanes.Rev.by C.L.W.Eidlitz). (9) 511 Michigan Ave., **Michigan Ave. Bapt. Ch.,** where services have been held since 1845, houses Buffalo's oldest Negro congregation; it was sta. on Underground RR. before Civil War. (10) Washington, Genesee & Huron Sts., **Electric Bldg.** (1912.by Esenwein & Johnson) is notable for tower 327′ high topped by lantern from which searchlights play at night. (11) Main & Genesee Sts., **Buffalo Savings Bank** (1899.neo-Class.by Edw.B.Green.enlarged 1933) has impressive murals depicting early Buffalo.

MIDTOWN: (12) 383 Franklin St., **Grosvenor Lib.** (O.wks.Sun.p.m.) has one of country's biggest reference colls., c.300,000 vols. (13) Main & Goodell Sts., **Buffalo Courier Express Bldg.** (1930.Mod.by Monks & Johnson) has mural by Chas. Bigelow & Ernest Davenport & observation gallery overlooking press room. (14) 473 Delaware Ave., **Mark Twain H.** (N.O.) was residence, for c.2 years after his marriage in 1870, of Sam. L. Clemens & his bride, while Clemens (Mark Twain) served as co-editor of Buffalo "Express." (15) Delaware Ave. & W. Utica St., **St. Joseph's Cathedral** (1914.Ital.Goth.by Aristides Leonori), cathedral ch. of Buffalo Cath. diocese.

NORTH: (16) Porter & Busti Aves., **The Front,** 50-a. pk. on L. shore, in which are **Statue of Oliver Hazard Perry** (1915.by Chas.H.Neihaus) comm. hero of Battle of L. Erie & **The Castle** (1837.Goth.Rev.by Col.Jas.McKay), now Girl Scouts hqs. (17) N. end The Front, **Peace Bridge** (1927) to Ft. Erie, Ontario, whose completion marked end of cent. of peace bet. U.S. & Canada. (18) Delaware & Delavan Aves., **Forest Lawn Cemetery,** in which are **Red Jacket Mon.** to famous Seneca chief & **Millard Fillmore Mon.** (19) Lincoln Pky., **Delaware Pk.** (350 as.), laid out by Fred. Law Olmsted, 1870. In pk. is **Albright Art Gallery** (O.Tues.through Sat., Sun. & Mon. p.m.1905.neo-Class.by Green & Wicks), named for donor John Jos. Albright, which houses permanent coll. of paintings by Gilbert Stuart, Bellows, Inness, Burchfield, Speicher & others & sculpture by Bourdelle, Brancusi, Despiau, Epstein, Maillol, Noguchi & others. Also in pk. is **Buffalo Hist. Mus.** (O.wks.Sun.p.m.1901. neo-Class.by Geo.Cary.adds.1927), built for Pan-Amer. Exposition, with Ind. &

pioneer relics. Pk. also contains **Zoological Gardens** (1938.by WPA). (20) 1300 Elmwood Ave., **Buffalo St. Teachers' Coll.** (1928-30.post-Col.), est. 1872. (21) 400 Forest Ave., **Buffalo St. Hospital** (1871-81.Romanes.& Vict.Goth.) comprises group of bldgs. designed by famous architect H.H. Richardson on 90-a. site landscaped by Fred. Law Olmsted. (22) Middle of Fordham Dr. bet. Elmwood Ave. & Lincoln Pky., **Site of Assassination of Pres. McKinley,** Sept. 6, 1901, by anarchist Leon F. Czolgosz, is marked by bronze tablet set in boulder. (23) 1150 Amherst St., **Goodrich (Amherst) H.** (1823-31.late Georg.Col.), whose construction was begun by Jos. Ellicott, orig. surveyor of Buffalo's site. (24) 125 Jewett Pky., **Martin H.** (1904), notable example of work of architect Frank Lloyd Wright; in rear, at 118 Summit Ave., is **Barton H.,** also by Wright. (25) Main St. & Eastwood Pl., **St. Vincent de Paul Ch.** (Cath.1926.Byzantine.by Thomas,Parry & McMullen), richly ornamented. (26) Main St. & Jefferson Ave., **Canisius College** (1911.neo-Class.), Jesuit institution. (27) Main St. at Niagara Falls Blvd., **Univ. of Buffalo,** with neo-Class. bldgs. on landscaped hill slope, was chartered in 1846, but only Medical Sch. operated until addition of other schs. & colleges from 1886 on; instruction in arts & sciences began in 1913. **Lockwood Mem. Lib.** (1935.by Green & James), houses Thos. B. Lockwood's colls. of books, mss., & coins & notable Modern Poetry Room. Chief among older bldgs. on campus is **Edmund Hayes Hall,** orig. built as Erie Cty. Almshouse. New bldgs. incl. **Clark Mem. Gymnasium** (1938) & **Engineering Bldg.** (1946). At W. end of campus is **Bookstore,** reprod. of pioneer Holland Land Office Mus. at Batavia (see).

EAST: (28) Fillmore Ave. & Best St., **Humboldt Pk.** (65 as.), arboretum containing **Niagara Frontier Rose Garden & City Greenh.** where annual chrysanthemum show is held. At NW. cor. of pk. is **Buffalo Mus. of Science** (O.wks.Sun.p.m.7-10 evenings bet.Oct.& Ap.astronomical observatory O.Fri.eves.1921.neo-Class.by Esenwein & Johnson), which offers scientific exhibits. (29) Lindbergh Dr., Curtiss & Lovejoy Sts., **N. Y. Central Terminal** (1929.neo-Class.by Felheimer & Wagner), with 17-story tower. (30) 1000-1200 William St., **E. Buffalo Stockyards,** biggest (E) of Chicago. (31) 45 Ideal St., **SS. Peter & Paul Russian Orthodox Ch.** (1933.mod.Byzantine.by Jos.Fronszak).

SOUTH: (32) 680 Seneca St., **Larkin Bldg.** (1904-05), notable example of office bldg. design by Frank Lloyd Wright. (33) 475 Abbott Rd., **Republic Steel Plant,** 3rd largest U.S. steel producer & world's largest alloy & special steels producer. (34) Extending (E) & (W) from S. end of Michigan Ave., **Buffalo Harbor,** terminus of N.Y. St. Barge Canal & Great Ls. shipping port, handling grain, limestone, iron ore & many other types of cargo, with one of world's longest breakwaters (22,603′).

SIDE TRIP: Take River Rd. (R) from Buffalo to Js. at 9$^{m}$ with St.324, on which route cont. (L), & St.266.

Take St.266 (R) 3.5$^{m}$ to **Tonawanda & N. Tonawanda,** adj. industrial communities with large Polish, Ital., & German colonies.

Cont. (L) on St.324 across Niagara R. by S. Grand I. Bridge to J. with South Pky. Take latter (L) 2$^{m}$ to **Beaver I. St. Pk.** (bathh.restaurants.pic.), handsomely equipped beach resort with boardwalk, game areas, & wooded pic. grounds.

St.324 cont. across Grand I. to **Buckhorn I. St. Pk.** (pic.trls.), haven for migratory birds & water fowl. Hy. crosses Niagara R. by N. Grand I. Bridge. 21$^{m}$, **Niagara Falls,** resort & industrial city on Niagara (Ind. "Thunderer of Waters") R. where it roars over precipice in world-famous cataract which draws more than 1,500,000 visitors—many of them, according to tradition, honeymooners—every year. Falls were visited by Father Louis Hennepin in 1678. Fr. built 2 fts. here in 1745 & 1750 to protect canoe portage around cataract but burned them when Brit. invaded in 1759. Brit. erected Ft. Schlosser. In 1805 or 1806 Augustus Porter purchased land around falls & built grist mill, around which grew settlement named Manchester; but latter was burned by Brit. in 1813. At Porter's urging, canal around falls was built 1852-62. Hydroelectric development began in 1880's; today Niagara generates more than 450,000 h.p. serving pop. of more than 2,500,000 in W. & central N.Y. St. & powering wide diversity of industrial plants. Among latter in city of Niagara Falls are factories producing flour, paper, abrasives, machinery & foundry materials.

Along R. front for more than 1$^{m}$ stretches **N.Y. St. Niagara Reserv.** (412 as.), within which are several observation pts., Is., & St. pks. **Prospect Pt.,** at edge of cataract, affords excellent view of **American Falls** (157′ high, c.1,000′ wide), over which passes 6% of flow, & Canadian Falls (c.2,500′wide), over which passes 94%, separated by Goat I.; both are veiled in rainbows & clouds of mist, & at night are lit by colored floodlights. From Prospect Pt. elevator (sm.fee) descends to foot of falls. **Hennepin Pt.** provides another view from 187′ cliff. Bridge crosses to **Goat I.** on which is 70-a. pk. (pic.); here elevator descends to

**Cave of the Winds** (guides.fee) at foot of Amer. falls, & here bridges lead to **Luna I.** & **Three Sister Is.** & handrailed walk leads to Terrapin Pt. Riverway opp. Prospect Pt., **Niagara Falls Mus.** (fee) contains, among more than 700,000 articles on exhibit, barrels in which various daredevils have gone over falls. End of Hydraulic Canal, **Niagara Falls Power Plant** (O.wks.guides), world's 1st, dating back to 1890, contains some of biggest generators ever built. Niagara Rapids Blvd. near College Ave., **Whirlpool St. Pk.**, commanding view of pothole whirlpool, 1,754' wide. N. city limit on US104, **Devil's Hole St. Pk.** (pic.lookout spots) commands view of gorge, cavern, & lower rapids. Near-by is **Niagara Univ.**, Cath. liberal arts institution, founded 1856. Niagara Falls is at J. with US104 (see US15), running (E) to Rochester (see US15) at J. with US15.

### Sec. 3: BUFFALO to N.Y.-PA. LINE. 71.

St.5 runs (SW) from Buffalo close to L. Erie. **5. LACKAWANNA,** industrial town in which is huge **Bethlehem Steel Plant.** Cor. Ridge Rd. & Pk. Ave., **Basilica of Our Lady of Victory,** capped by great dome & flanked by tall elaborately carved towers. **42. DUNKIRK,** industrial city producing boilers, radiators, machinery, silk & other articles. **43. PT. GRATIOT PK.** on L. Erie. (pic.bath.) **50. L. ERIE ST. PK.** (O.May-Labor Day.pic.recr.camp.). **71. N.Y.-PA. LINE.**

## US 20—NEW YORK

**N.Y.-MASS. LINE** (8$^{m}$ from Pittsfield, Mass.) **(W) to N.Y.-PA. LINE** (19$^{m}$ from Erie, Pa.) **387.5. US20**

Via: Albany, Richfield Springs, Cazenovia, Skaneateles, Auburn, Seneca Falls, Geneva, Canandaigua, Avon, Lancaster, Depew, (Buffalo), Silver Cr., Fredonia. RRs. parallel parts of route. Accoms.: Ample.

US20 is one of most travelled routes through central N.Y. & across Ohio & Indiana to Chicago. Its chief scenic features in N.Y. are Finger Ls. which it passes in long stretch bet. Skaneateles & Avon.

### Sec. 1: N.Y.-MASS. LINE to ALBANY. 29.

**0. N.Y.-MASS. LINE,** just (W) of which US20 passes remnants (L) of **Mt. Lebanon Shaker Settlement** (est.1785). **3. NEW LEBANON,** at J. with St.22. At W. edge is **Shrine of Our Lady of Lourdes** (O.May-Nov.).

SIDE TRIP: Take St.22 (R) 1$^{m}$ to **Lebanon Springs,** once famous spa. 18$^{m}$ **Berlin,** noted for its production of lollipop sticks & roses. 22.5$^{m}$ **Petersburg.**
32$^{m}$ S. J. with St.7 running (E) to J. with US7 at Bennington, Vt. 37$^{m}$ **Hoosick Falls.** 39$^{m}$ J. with St.67.

Take latter (R) 1$^{m}$ to **Walloomsac,** where marker comm. 2nd engagement of Battle of Bennington. At 2.5$^{m}$ is entrance to **Bennington Battlefield St. Pk.** (171 as.), where on Aug. 16, 1777, Gen. John Stark's Amer. force repelled Brit. expedition attempting to capture stores at Bennington.

59.5$^{m}$ **Salem.** On E. Broadway, **Larmon H.** (now mortuary; 1790.Georg.Col.fine example). On W. Broadway, **United Presb. Ch.** (1797.New Eng.type). 76$^{m}$, **Granville,** sett. 1781, is slate quarrying center. 89$^{m}$ J. with US4 (see).

**16. NASSAU,** where are **Rensselaer Cty. Fair Grounds. 20.5.** J. with US9 (see) with which US20 unites to Albany. **23.5.** J. with US4 (see). **28.5.** US20-9 crosses **PARKER DUNN MEM. BRIDGE** (1933) over Hudson, whose elevating center span is heaviest in country.

**29. ALBANY**

Through RR., bus & plane conns. Accoms.: Plentiful, of all types. Info.: Tourist & Convention Bureau, C. of C., 74 Chapel St. Baseball at Hawkins Stadium; swim. at Lincoln Pk. & other pools; boat. at Washington Pk., golf at Mun. Golf Course, New Scotland Ave. & Whitehall Rd.; tennis at city pks.

Capital of N.Y. St., Albany is situated along West side of Hudson R. at its confluence with N.Y.'s low-level valleys & barge canal system, followed by chief hys. & RRs., & thus is one of country's largest postal & rail transfer pts. & busy trading & distributing center. From wharves, RR. yards & factories at R.'s edge, city climbs steep slopes, crowned by Capitol & other St. bldgs., & spreads out over rolling terrain. Chartered in 1686, Albany is oldest continuously existing settlement in U.S. Here in 1614, at pt. where Henry Hudson had brought his "Half Moon" 5 yrs. earlier, Ind. fur trading post of Ft. Nassau was est. by Hendrick Christiansen & maintained for several yrs. Ft. Orange was built by 1st permanent settlers, 18 families arriving in 1624, who were mostly Walloons from Holland. Tract along both sides of R. extending (N) & (S) was purchased from Inds. in 1630 by Kiliaen Van Rensselaer & partners, who est. patroonship of Rensselaerswyck & sent colonists of various nationalities. Dutch W. India Co. soon claimed jurisdiction, sending as director-gen. Peter Stuyvesant, who in 1652 laid out village called Beverwyck around Ft. Orange; but Van Rensselaers resisted & relinquished claim to village only in 1685, following conversion of their patroon to Eng. manor after Eng. had est. rule over New Amsterdam (New York City). City was chartered following yr. & granted control of fur trade in terr. to (N), (E) & (W). It became key pt. for defense of Colonial frontier against Fr. & Inds., escaping attack by alliance with Iroquois. Here in 1754 was held 1st Colonial Congress, called by Brit. Lords of Trade, at which Benj. Franklin presented Plan of Union. After outbreak of Rev. in 1775, Albany became goal of Brit. campaign of 1777, but was saved by Burgoyne's defeat at Saratoga.

After Rev., main stream of travel to newly opened lands in central & W. N.Y. St. poured through Albany, which rapidly developed as trading & industrial center. In 1797 it was made St. capital. In 1807 Rbt. Fulton's "Clermont," 1st steamboat to make regular trips, arrived from N.Y.C. Erie Canal was opened in 1825, joining waters of Great Ls. with those of Atlantic here. Within 5 yrs., 500 sailing ships & 15,000 canal boats were docking here annually. Mohawk & Hudson RR. was opened to Schenectady in 1831. As terminal for log drives down Hudson, Albany developed into huge lumber center by Civil War, with nearly 4,000 sawmills in vic. Following curtailment of lumber supply, it developed diversified mfg. Construction of Barge Canal after 1900 revived water-borne commerce; in 1932, opening of Port of Albany made it maritime center.

PTS. OF INT.: (1) Capitol Pk., Eagle & State Sts., **St. Capitol** (O.Mon.-Fri.9-4.also Sat.& Sun.10-4.bet.Mem.Day & Labor Day.guides;1867-98), is massive 5-story granite edifice on hilltop with peaked tile & slate roofs & jutting dormers, balustrades, & chimneys, orig. designed by Thos. W. Fuller in Ital. Ren. style but modified by Henry H. Richardson to incorporate Romanes. & by Leopold Eidlitz to incorporate Goth. elements, & finally completed with modifications by Isaac G. Perry. Most often compared to huge Fr. chateau, it is one of country's most celebrated examples of inter. stone architecture; inter. has large central court, spacious corridors & pub. chambers, & profusion of stairways, stone arches & marble columns, practically defying modernization. Monumental stone staircase at E. entrance (one of largest exter. stairways ever built, extending 166′ forward from bldg. with steps 100′ wide at bottom) leads directly to **Flag Rm.** on 2nd fl., containing military mementoes & flags, Lincoln relics & Brady Civil War photographs. At SE. cor. of 2nd fl. is mahogany-wainscoted **Executive Chamber,** with portraits of Lafayette, Washington, & Govs. of N.Y. On 3rd fl. are marble-columned & onyx-paneled **Senate Chamber** & Goth.-style **Assembly Chamber,** both reached by notable Goth.-styled staircase. W. inter. stairway, known as **"Million Dollar Staircase,"** which took 5½ yrs. to build, is noted for sculptured heads of many famous Amers. incl. in ornamentation. On grounds (E) of Capitol is heroic equestrian **Gen. Philip Sheridan Statue** (by J.Q.A.Ward & Dan.Chester French); Sheridan was native of Albany. (2) (W) of Capitol Pk., Swan & State Sts., **N.Y. St. Office Bldg.** (O.wks.Sat. & Sun.June-Sept.1930.Mod.), 32 stories in setback design, is topped by tower providing fine view. (3) (N) of Capitol Pk., Washington Ave. bet. Hawk & Swan Sts., **N.Y. St. Education Bldg.** (1912.neo-Class.by Palmer,Hornbostel & Jones), contains on 2nd fl., **N.Y. St. Lib.** (O.8:30-6.wks.incl.Sat.), with outstanding colls of N.Y. St. hist. & rare early Amer. books & mss., & on top fl. **N.Y. St. Mus.** (O.9-5 wks. incl.Sat. & Sun.& hols.July 4-Labor Day), with colls. of fossils (incl.one of country's largest colls.of invertebrate fossils) & dioramas of Iroquois Inds. (4) 125 Washington Ave., **Albany Institute of Hist. & Art.** (O.10-5 wks.Sun.2-5), founded 1791, contains Amer., Eng. & Dutch paintings & period furniture. (5) Elk & Swan Sts., **Cathedral of All Saints** (Episc.Eng.Goth.by Rbt.W.Gibson), begun 1884 but still unfinished, contains stone carvings, stained-glass windows & Belgian-imported oak stalls carved in 17th cent. (6) Elk & Hawk Sts., adj. **Lafayette & Academy Pks.** comprise single tract of green on which stands **Jos. Henry Mem.** (1815.post-Col.by Philip Hooker. remod.1935), with Ionic pilaster & Class. cupola, now occupied by Albany Dept. of Education, which formerly housed Albany Academy, where Jos. Henry invented electromagnet in 1829; in front of bldg. is statue of Henry. (7) Eagle & Columbia Sts., **Albany County Cth.** (1916.Neo-Class.). (8) Eagle & Pine Sts., **N.Y. St. Court**

**of Appeals Bldg.** (1835-43.Gr Rev.by Henry Rector), of white Sing Sing marble with Ionic portico; in rear add. is Appellate Courtroom designed by H. H. Richardson. (9) Eagle St. & Maiden Lane, **City Hall** (1882.Fr.Romanes.by H.H.Richardson), dominated by tower housing carillon of 60 bells. (10) In front of City Hall, **Schuyler Mon.** (by J.Massey Rhind), comm. commander of N. frontier defenses, 1775-77, Philip Schuyler. (11) State & Lodge Sts., **St. Peter's Episc. Ch.** (1859.Goth.Rev.by Rich.Upjohn), housing congregation org. in 1716, contains beneath vestibule fl. grave of Lord Howe, killed at Ticonderoga, 1758. (12) 9 Ten Broeck Pl., **Ten Broeck Mansion** (late 18th cent.), former home of Mayor Abr. Ten Broeck. (13) Ten Broeck St. bet. 1st & 2nd Sts., **St. Joseph's Cath. Ch.** (1860.Goth.Rev.). (14) N. Pearl & Orange Sts., **First Dutch Reformed Ch.** (1797-99.by Philip Hooker.alt.& adds.1858), home of 2nd oldest Prot. Ch. congregation in Amer. (org.1642), contains old pulpit, hour glass, Bible & communion service brought from Holland in 1656. (15) N. Pearl St. & Clinton Ave., **John V. L. Pruyn Lib.** (O.wks.Sun.aft.1901. Dutch Ren.by Marcus T.Reynolds) has richly ornamented inter., with imported Dutch 17th cent. fireplace tiles. (16) Broadway & Maiden Lane, **Fed. Bldg.** (P.O.) (1936.Mod.Class.by Gander,Gander & Gander). (17) Broadway at foot of State St., **Plaza** contains tablet marking **Site of Staat Huys** (State H.), where Benj. Franklin presented 1st plan of Col. union, 1754. (18) Facing Plaza, **Delaware & Hudson Bldg.** (1918.Flemish Goth.by Marcus T.Reynolds). (19) Hudson R., S. end Church St., **Port of Albany,** opened 1932, with extensive dock facils., has world's biggest single-unit grain elevator. (20) Clinton & Schuyler Sts., **Schuyler Mansion** (O.10-12, 1.30-5.sm.fee.1762.Georg.Col.vestibule add.after 1800), home of Philip Schuyler, now St.-owned mus., contains Col. furnishings & hist. relics; here Eliz. Schuyler was married to Alex. Hamilton. (21) Eagle & Elm Sts., **St. Executive Mansion** (Civil War Period) is red brick edifice in landscaped grounds. (22) Eagle St. & Madison Ave., **Cathedral of the Immaculate Conception** (1852.Goth.Rev.). (23) Eagle St. & Park Ave., **Lincoln Pk.** (swim.bathh.athletic facils.winter sports), Albany's 2nd largest. (24) State & Willett Sts., **Washington Pk.** (boat.tennis.playgrounds). (25) Western Ave. & Robin St., **N.Y. St. College for Teachers.** (26) 629 Madison Ave., **Convent of the Holy Names,** founded 1884, private Cath. prep. sch. for girls. (27) New Scotland & Holland Aves., **Albany Law Sch.** (1928.Tudor Goth.), founded 1851. (28) 106 New Scotland Ave., **Albany College of Pharmacy** (mod.Georg.est. 1881 & part of Union Univ.), contains reconstructed **O. B. Troop Drugstore,** which operated in Schoharie in 1800. (29) New Scotland Ave. bet. Myrtle & S. Lake Aves., **Albany Hospital** (1849) & **Albany Medical College.** (30) Academy Rd. & Hackett Blvd., **Albany Academy** (1931.mod.Georg.by Marcus T.Reynolds), boys' prep. sch. org. in 1813. (31) S. Lake Ave. N. of New Scotland Ave., **Dudley Observatory** (O. 8-10 p.m.), founded 1846 & part of Union Univ., has refracting telescope; here 37 constellations have been discovered. (32) Ontario & Yates Sts., **Vincentian Institute Bldg.** contains **Chapel of Our Lady of Lourdes,** replica orig. grotto in France. (33) Madison Ave. & Partridge St., **College of St. Rose,** girls' sch. chartered 1924. Albany is at Js. with US9W (see) & St.5 (see).

SIDE TRIP: Take St.43 (L) from Albany 15.5m to J. with St.85.

Turn (L) on latter to **Rensselaerville,** 10m, sett. in late 18th cent., containing notable array of post-Col. & Gr. Rev. architecture.

At 19.5m is J. with St.157A.

Take latter (R) 4.5m to **John Boyd Thacher Pk.** (920 as.pic.trls.), at edge of picturesque & geologically notable **Helderberg Cliffs.** Near pk. entrance is **Hailes Cave,** c. 2,800′ long.

20.5m **Picher's Mill** (c.1800), still in use. 23.5m **Berne,** sett. c. 1750 by German Palatines, where in 1845 **Luth. Ch.,** still standing, housed 1st anti-rent meeting protesting feudal inequities in land tenure.

Take Rd. (R) from Berne 5m to **Knox,** near which is very int. **Knox Cave** (fee) with 6 levels, extending 165′ down through limestone strata.

31.5m **Stone H.** (1775) from which local patriots repulsed Tory-Ind. raiders during Rev. 34m **Mann Tavern** (pre-Rev.). Just beyond is J. with St.30 (see below).

## Sec. 2: ALBANY to AUBURN. 160.

In **GUILDERLAND, 9.5.,** is **Case Tavern** (R) (1799). At **20.5.** is J. with unimproved Rd. leading (L) 0.3m to **North H.** (1784-86.Georg.Col.), built by Wm. North, aide to Baron Von Steuben during Rev., & **Duane-Featherstonhaugh H.** (c.1816.Georg.Col. fine example.) At **DUANESBURG, 22.,** named for Jas. Duane, member of Continental Congress, is J. with St.7.

SIDE TRIP: Take latter (L). At 3.5m is **Quaker Street,** with **Friends Meeting H.** (1790). At 10.5m is J. with St.30.

Take latter (L) through Schoharie Valley, where German Palatines sett. 7 villages in 1712-13 & during Rev. built 3 fts. against Ind. raids under Tory leadership. Worst of latter was Johnson-Brant raid of Oct. 17, 1870, which left trail of dead & burning homesteads throughout valley. **Schoharie,** 3m, has many Col. & post-Rev. Hs. At N. edge is **Lower Ft.** (1772), with square stone tower, now mus. with pioneer relics. At SW. edge, **Johannes Ingold H.** (1795.post-Col.). **Middleburg,** 8.5m, founded 1712, oldest town in valley, has **Dutch Reformed Ch.** (1786.post-Col.brick). **Blenheim Bridge** (1855), 21m, 228′ long, is world's longest one-span covered bridge. At 24m (L) is **Lansing Manor H. Grand Gorge** (see Catskill Mts.) is at J. with St.23 (see Catskill Mts.), 32.5m.

14m Village of **Howes Cave,** with cement plant. At 15m is J. with Rd. leading (R) 1.5m to fork, where Rd. turns (R) 0.5m to **Howe Caverns** (fee), chain of caves equipped with elevator & elec. lights. 20m **Cobleskill,** which manufactures pancake flour & refrigerators, site of St.-maintained **Cobleskill Agric. Sch.** 23.5m **Site of Cobleskill Battle,** which took place in 1778 when Jos. Brant, leading Ind.-Tory raid, ambushed Amer. force here. 57.5m **Oneonta,** on Susquehanna R., crowded by encircling hills, has RR. shops & sm. factories. Here in 1883 was org. Brotherhood of RR. Brakemen, nucleus of today's Brotherhood of RR. Trainmen. On West St. is **Hartwick College** (1928), directed by Luth. Ch. & on State St. **Oneonta St. Normal Sch.** (1889). Oneonta is at Js. with St.23 & St.28 (see Catskill St. Park). At 59.5m is J. with St.23.

Take latter (R) 1m to J. with St.205; cont. straight ahead on latter to J. at 5m with marked Rd. & turn (L) here, then (R), & then (R) again to **Gilbert L. St. Pk.** (1,569 as. bath.pic.recr.trls.camp.cabins), 9m, with 40-a. L., in Lawrence Hills.

St.7 follows Susquehanna R. to **Unadilla,** 75.5m, which manufactures silos & farm machinery, across R. (L) from which is **Sidney,** with magneto mfg. plant. 85.5m **Bainbridge** has dairy products plants. 91.5m **Afton.** In this vic. Jos. Smith, leader of the Mormons, proselytized. Here is J. with St.41, leading (L) 1m to **Afton Fair Grounds,** where is **Mormon H.,** in which lived Emma Hale, Jos. Smith's 1st wife.

**Binghamton** (see US11), 120.5m, is at Js. with US11 (see) & St.17 (see).

At **23.** is **CHRIST EPISC. CH.** (1789-93.int.inter.), oldest unaltered Episc. Ch. in N.Y. St. **49. SHARON SPRINGS** (health resort) where are medicinal white sulphur springs. **57. CHERRY VALLEY** (sett.1740). **Mon.** in cemetery comm. victims massacred by raiding Tories & Inds. in Nov. 1778. At **64.** is J. with St.80.

SIDE TRIPS: (A) Take latter (R) 4.5m to **Van Hornesville,** birthpl. of former Gen. Electric Co. head, Owen D. Young, who has rest. several Hs. & old **Grist Mill** (1791), donated pk. & sch. His mansion is located here.

(B) Take latter (L) along Otsego L. to **Cooperstown,** 11m, at S. end, founded soon after 1785 by Wm. Cooper, father of Jas. Fenimore Cooper, who spent his boyhood & later wrote "The Deerslayer" & other books here. Main St. opp. Fair St., **Cooper Grounds,** pk. on site of Cooper H., in which are **Statue** of Jas. Fenimore Cooper (by V.Salvatore) & **Fenimore H.,** central hqs. of N.Y. St. Hist. Soc. (O.sm.fee), which contains colls. of life-masks, busts by John H. I. Brower made in early 19th cent., paintings, Cooper family relics, & material concerning central N.Y. Opp. is **Farmers Mus.,** with notable coll. of pioneer agric. implements. Adj. is **Christ Ch.** (Episc.1810) & in its cemetery is **Grave of J. F. Cooper. Nat. Baseball Hall of Fame Mus.** (O.summer.sm.fee) contains material conn. with baseball, incl. bronze plaques in "Hall of Fame" honoring retired players. Main St. (W) of Pioneer St., **Doubleday Field,** where modern baseball was 1st played in 1839 under Abner Doubleday's direction. Lake St. bet. Fair & Pioneer Sts., **Lake Front Pk.,** containing **"Indian Hunter,"** statue by J. Q. A. Ward.

**70.5. RICHFIELD SPRINGS** (health resort.accoms.), where are Great White Sulphur Springs.

At **BOUCKVILLE, 102.5.,** is J. with St.12B.

SIDE TRIP: Take latter (L) 5m to **Hamilton,** inc. in 1816, home of **Colgate Univ.** (chartered 1819). Bldgs. on 125-a. campus incl. **West Hall** (1827) & **East Hall** (1834). On Broad St., **Jonathan Olmstead H.,** where in 1817 was org. Bapt. Educ. Soc., which est. Colgate.

**107.5. MORRISVILLE,** seat of **St. School of Agric.,** est. 1910. **119. CAZENOVIA,** on L. of same name, sett. 1793 & named for Theophile Cazenove of Philadelphia, gen. agent of Holland Land Co. Among many notable old Hs. are **Linklaen H.** (1825) & **Lorenzo H.** (1807.Georg.). Seminary St., **Cazenovia Seminary & Jr. College,** founded 1824 by Meth. Ch., whose **Chapel** (1810.post-Col.) was orig. part of local cth.

SIDE TRIP: Take St.13 (R) 4m to **Chittenango Falls St. Pk.** (pic.) in which is fine waterfall 136′ high & gorge. St.13 cont. to J. with St.5, 9m.

**128.5. POMPEY,** hist. town in process of restoration, birthpl. of many prominent New Yorkers incl. W.G. Fargo, partner in famous Wells Fargo & Co. express business. On **Village Green** are a number of early 19th cent. houses incl. fine **Presb.**

**Ch.** (1817-19) & **Birthpl. of Horatio Seymour,** running mate of Gen. U.S. Grant in campaign of 1868.

SIDE TRIP: Take St.91 (R) here 7m to **Jamesville** & then take St.173 (L) to **Clark St. Reservation** (225 as.pic.), 8m. In pk. is fine L. enclosed by cliffs.

At **134.5.** is J. with US11 (see). **153.5. SKANEATELES,** sett. 1792, at head of Skaneateles L., one of Finger Ls. group. Town was a center of anti-slavery activities before Civil War, carried on by Gerrit Smith; & sta. of Underground RR. Here also was located one of many mid-19th cent. experiments in communal living. It was founded by John Anderson Collins but lasted only 2 years. **160. AUBURN,** at head of Owasco L., another of Finger Ls. group, is farm trading & mfg. center, producing rope, shoes, carpets, Diesel engines & farm machinery. Sett. in 1793, it soon acquired mills & in 1817 became site of St. prison & in 1821 of theological seminary. During 1840's, when it was home of Wm. H. Seward, it had hopes of becoming St. capital.

PTS. OF INT.: South St. near Genesee St., **Mem. City Hall** (1930.Georg.Col. by Coolidge, Shepley, Bulfinch & Abbott). 203 Genesee St., **Cayuga Mus. of Hist. & Art** (O.Mon.Wed.Fri.Sun.aft.1836.Gr.Rev.), occupying mansion built by John Seymour, has coll. of Ind. artifacts, Col. implements, books & documents, & art objects. 33 South St., **Seward Mansion** (1816.post Col.) was home of Wm. H. Seward, U.S. Sen. & Lincoln's Secy. of St. 19 Fort St., **Fort Hill Cemetery** contains **Grave of Wm. H. Seward & Logan Mem.** to famous early Ind. orator & peacemaker. 133 State St., **Auburn St. Prison** (N.O.) dates back to 1816; here was built in 1820's 1st cell-block, which became model for Amer. prison architecture. Auburn prisoners were used to build Sing Sing.

SIDE TRIPS: (A) Take St.38 (L) from Auburn along W. side of Wasco L. to **Enna Jettick Pk.** (O.Decoration Day-Labor Day.bath.boat.f.pic.amusements), 2.5m. At 19.5m is **Fillmore Glen St. Pk.** (857 as.pic.bath.camp.hik.) in which are fine glen & int. flora. At **Groton,** 28m, is **L. C. Smith & Corona Typewriters, Inc. Plant.** At 35m on St.38, **George Jr. Republic,** self-governing community for boys & girls, founded in 1894 by W.R. George, with 580-a. farm which accoms. c.120 youngsters, who have their own legislative, executive & judicial bodies. St.38 cont. to **Oswego** (see St.17) at 71m where is J. with St.17 (see).

(B) Take St.34 (L) from Auburn 1.5m to **Home of Harriet Tubman** (L), former sta. of Underground RR. H. Tubman was an ex-slave, active in aiding Negroes to escape from South before Civil War. St.34 cont. (S) along Cayuga L. to **Ithaca** (see US11), 38m.

### Sec. 3: AUBURN, N.Y. to WESTERN J. with St.5. 71.5.

US20 unites with St.5 (W) from Auburn. At **10.5.** is J. with St.90.

SIDE TRIP: Take latter (L) along E. side of **Cayuga L.,** 40m long & 2m wide, longest of Finger Ls. At 13.5m is **Levanna,** where once stood prehist. Ind. village & where stone carvings were found. Here are reprods. of Algonquin villages of c.900 A.D. At 15.5m **Aurora,** home of **Wells College,** for women, founded (1886) by Henry Wells of Wells-Fargo Express Co.

US20 now crosses Seneca R. on **RENÉ MENARD MEM. BRIDGE, 11.,** comm. Father René Menard, 17th cent. Fr. missionary to Cayuga Inds. At **13.,** is J. with St.89.

SIDE TRIP: Take latter (L) 3.5m to **Cayuga St. Pk.** (188 as.bath.f.camp.).

**16. SENECA FALLS,** at falls of same name, source of power for industrial development, home in mid-19th cent. of Aurelia Jenks Bloomer & Eliz. Cady Stanton, & notable center of women's rights agitation. Fall & Mynderse Sts., former **Wesleyan Meth. Episc. Ch.,** now auto sales shop, was site in 1848 of earliest suffrage convention. At W. edge of town, **Gould Pump Works,** country's largest of its type. **20. WATERLOO.** Near Lafayette Pk. is **Patriarch Elm,** 20′ in circum. & supposed to be more than 300 yrs. old. **23.5.** J. with St.96A.

SIDE TRIP: Take latter (L) 2.5m to **Rose Hill** (c.1835.Gr.Rev.), with fine portico, cupola & porches, overlooking Seneca L.

**27. GENEVA** (sett.c.1784), at head of L. Geneva in center of fruit-growing reg., is site of Geneva Outboard Regatta in July & also an industrial & commercial center. Main St., **Hobart College,** est. 1822, gives courses in liberal arts & sciences; oldest bldgs. are **Geneva Hall & Trinity Hall** (Class.Rev.) & **Chapel** (1858-62.Goth.Rev.by Rich.Upjohn). Adj. is **Wm. Smith College for Women,** est. in 1906, on whose campus is **Blackwell H.** (1861-63.by Rich.Upjohn). Castle & New Sts., **N.Y. St. Agric. Experiment Sta.** Castle St., **Burial Mound** of former Ind. village. 518-30 Main St., **Trinity Episc. Ch.** (begun 1841) modeled somewhat on Trinity Ch., N.Y.C.

SIDE TRIP: Take St.14 (L) from Geneva along W. shore of Seneca L. At 14m is J. with St.54, on which route turns (R) through grape-growing reg. to **Penn Yann,** 19m, with wineries, canneries & mills, at head of Keuka L. St.54 cont. along E. shore of L. At 23.5m is J. with Keuka Rd., leading (L) 0.5m to **Keuka College** for women, inc. in 1888. **Hammondsport,** 41m, at S. end of L., is N.Y. St.'s chief champagne-making center. It also claims to be "Cradle of Amer. Aviation," having been birthpl. of Glenn Hammond Curtiss, who built some of earliest planes here with help of Dr. Alex. Graham Bell, Lieut. Thos. Selfridge, & others. **Pleasant Valley Winery,** 44m, org. 1860, has one of oldest champagne cellars in U.S.; it holds U.S. Winery License No. 1. St.54 cont. to **Bath** (see US15), 48.5m, at J. with US15 (see).

US20 skirts Canandaigua L. to **CANANDAIGUA, 44.,** sett. 1789 on what was formerly huge tract purchased by Oliver Phelps & Nath. Gorham from Mass. in late 18th cent. PTS. OF INT.: (1) 55 North St., **Ontario Cty. Hist. Soc. & Wood Lib. Bldg.** (O.wks.mod.Georg.Col.) in which are hist. documents & life mask of Abr. Lincoln. (2) Main St., **Ontario County Cth.** (1858.Gr.Rev.); on grounds, boulder comm. **Pickering Treaty** of 1794 with Inds. (3) 2 Main St., **City Hall** (1824.late Fed.) with handsome portico & belfry. (4) 58 Main St., **First Congr. Ch.** (1812); fine portico & facade. (5) 210 Main St., **Gen. Peter B. Porter H.** (c.1800), built by War of 1812 hero who was Secy. of War under John Quincy Adams. (6) 295 Main St., **Gideon Granger H.** (1814.Fed.), supposedly built after designs by Thos. Jefferson; Granger was Postmaster Gen. during Jefferson & Madison administrations. (7) 50 Gibson St., **Carr H.** (1826.Fed.).

SIDE TRIP: Take St.21 (R) from Canandaigua 7.5m to **Manchester,** RR. center. At 9.5m (R) is **Hill Cumorah,** Mormon Mt. Sinai, where in 1823 Jos. Smith unearthed gold plates which were source of "Book of Mormon." At foot of hill is **Moroni Hqs. Bldg.** (1936. Mayan) & on summit is **Mormon Mon.** (1935), pedestal supporting figure of Angel Moroni. At 12m is J. with Rd. leading (L) 2m to **Jos. Smith Farm,** furnished with antiques, where Jos. Smith lived bet. ages of 10 & 21. **Palmyra** (see St.5) 14.5m, is at J. with St.31, which runs (E) to conn. with St.5 (see) & (W) to **Rochester** (see US15).

At **49.5.** is J. with US20A.

SIDE TRIP: Take US20A (L). At 10.5m is **Honeoye** on Honeoye L., summer resort. **Sullivan Mon.** comm. Sullivan-Clinton Expedition of 1779 against Iroquois, who supported Brit. during Rev. **Pitts' Mansion** (R) built (1821) by Gideon Pitts, whose daughter married Frederick Douglass, famous Negro anti-slavery agitator. At **Livonia,** 20.5m, is J. with US15 (see), with which US20A unites to **Lakeville,** 22.5m. At 29.5m **Geneseo,** trading center for Genesee Valley, to which Jas. & Wm. W. Wadsworth emigrated in 1790. Here annually is held Genesee Valley Hunt (Oct. & Nov.) with member of Wadsworth family as master of hounds; kennels are at E. edge of village. At 32.5m is **Boyd-Parker Shrine,** comm. 2 scouts of Sullivan-Clinton Expedition captured in 1779 by Inds. & massacred at Torture Tree here. At 34m is J. with St.36, leading (R) 5m to **Retsoff Salt Mine** (O), one of largest in U.S., where rock salt is mined, & (L) 4m to **Mt. Morris,** near **Genesee R. Dam,** more than 1,000′ long & 246′, one of biggest in East. At 36.5m is J. with St.39.

Take latter (L) through **Perry,** 4.5m, with knitting mills & tank factory, to **Castile,** 11m, from which route turns (L) into **Letchworth St. Pk.** (pic.camp.trls.), large area extending along scenic deep gorge, with waterfalls, of Genesee R. (sometimes known as "Grand Canyon of the East"), named for land donor & Buffalo manufacturer Wm. Pryor Letchworth. In pk. are **Letchworth Mus.,** containing lib. & pioneer heirlooms; **Seneca Council H.** of logs, typical of Iroquois construction, moved here from Canada; **Mary Jemison Statue,** comm. white woman captured by Inds. at 15 who spent rest of her life as Ind. wife & mother, & **Log Cabin** she built for her daughter. **Inspiration Pt. Overlook** affords fine view.

At 48.5m is **Warsaw,** mfg. center, where on Perry Ave. is **Gates H.** (1824) which was sta. of Underground RR. while occupied by Seth M. Gates, anti-slavery advocate. 74m **E. Aurora** which has toy mfg. plant. Here Elbert C. Hubbard est. in 1890's his **Roycroft Shops** (Eng. Goth.stone & timber) on S. Grove St. & here published his "Philistines" & "A Message to Garcia." 81m **Orchard Pk.,** at J. with St.277 leading (L) 3m to **Chestnut Ridge Pk.** (recr. hik.camp.) which is a game refuge. At 85.5m is western J. with US20.

**68. E. AVON,** at J. with US15 (see). **70. AVON,** canning & dairy products center, with annual horse show. **71.5.** Western J. with St.5 (see) which branches (R) to Buffalo.

### Sec. 4: (W) J. with St.5 to N.Y.-PA. LINE. 127.

US20 cuts across level farmlands. **38. ALDEN** has sanatoriums which draw health-seekers attracted by black water baths discovered here in 1896.

**42. TOWN LINE,** which in 1861 attempted to join Confed. States in secession from Union. **47.5. LANCASTER,** residential suburb of Buffalo, with **Como L. Pk.** (recr.

boat.pic.). At **49. DEPEW,** industrial suburb, US20 turns (S) bypassing **Buffalo** (see St.5). **62.** Western J. with US20A (see above). At **81.5.** US20 passes border of **Cattaraugus Ind. Reserv.** (1,680 as.O.), inhabited by Seneca Inds. who hold Ind. Fair in fall & winter & spring festivals & sell souvenirs. At **83.5.** is J. with Rd. leading (L) 6$^{m}$ to **Thomas Ind. School** (O.Mon.Wed.& Fri.aft.). **85.** J. with St.5 (see), which unites with US20 for 3$^{m}$. **87.5. SILVER CREEK** stands at N. end of Chautauqua grape-growing reg. extending 55$^{m}$ along L. **99.5. FREDONIA,** center of grape-growing area, with grape juice and conserve plants & wineries; it is said to have had 1st gas street lights in world, & here was org. one of 1st units of Women's Christian Temperance Union.

SIDE TRIP: Take St.60 (L) from Fredonia 8$^{m}$ to **Cassadaga,** & turn (R) here to **Lilly Dale** (pic.), spiritualist camp with hotels & cottages on Middle & Upper Cassadaga Ls. In **Forest Temple** spiritualist conferences are held in summer. Near-by is **Hydeville Cottage** (O.fee) moved here from Hydeville, where Fox Sisters 1st discovered spirit world manifestations in 1849. Seances take place frequently.

**107. BROCTON,** where in fall is held grape festival with much pomp comm. acclimatization of grape culture begun in Chautauqua Cty. c.1815 by Elijah Fay. Near city, on L. Erie Shore, Thos. L. Harris maintained (1867-83) his Brotherhood of the New Life sect. **116. WESTFIELD,** where Dr. Thos. B. Welch, who worked out method of manufacturing unfermented grape juice, est. Welch Grapejuice Co. in 1890's. **Welch Plant** (O) is largest of kind in world. Here is J. with St.17 (see).

**127. N.Y.-PA. LINE.**

## US 6—NEW YORK

**N.Y.-CONN. LINE** (6.5$^{m}$ from Danbury) **(W) to PORT JERVIS. 80. US6**
Via: Brewster & Peekskill. Accoms.: All types.

US6 crosses summer vacation area of lower Taconic Mts., takes Bear Mt. Bridge over Hudson R., & cuts through farm sec. to Port Jervis.
**2.** J. with St.121, leading (L) 2$^{m}$ to **Peach L.** (bath.boat.f.recr.) At E. edge of **BREWSTER, 4.,** farmers' trade center & summer resort, is J. with St.22, running (S) to New York City (see New York Trip II).

SIDE TRIP: Take St.22 (R). 13$^{m}$ J. with St.341 (Quaker Hill Rd.), leading (L) 5.5$^{m}$ to **Oblong Meetingh.** (1764), built by Quakers, where 1st protest against slavery in America is said to have been made. 14$^{m}$ **Pawling,** sett. c.1740, has many luxurious country homes. 20.5$^{m}$ (L) **Jackson Wing Inn** (c.1806). 37$^{m}$ **Amenia.**
46$^{m}$ **Millerton,** at (N) J. with US44, which runs (E) to Canaan, Conn. 59.5$^{m}$ **Copake Falls,** formerly center for iron ore mining reg., now summer resort.
Take St.344 (R) 1$^{m}$ into **Taconic St. Pk.** (6,000 as.inn.camp.cabins.pic.bath.f.hik.winter sports). In pk. are ruins of old iron works & at its S. end is **Rudd Pond.** Trls. & Rds. lead to fine **Bash Bish Falls & Glen** & other pts. of int.
65$^{m}$ **Hillsdale** (accoms), where is J. with St.23.
Take St.23 (L) 4.5$^{m}$ to **Craryville.** Take Rd. (L) here 3$^{m}$ to **Copake L.** (resort). At 13$^{m}$ on St.23, **Claverack.** Here are several fine old Hs. **Old Hudson County Cth.** (1786; Georg.Col.). At 16.5$^{m}$ is **Hudson** (see US9) at J. with US9 (see).
88$^{m}$ **New Lebanon,** birthpl. of Sam. Tilden, at J. with US20 (see).

On shore of L. Glenida is **CARMEL, 9.,** & on shore of L. Mahopac, **MAHOPAC, 14.5.** At **20.5.** is J. with Taconic St. Pky.

SIDE TRIPS: (A) Take latter, which is handsomely landscaped scenic blvd. bypassing cross-Rds. & towns, (L) 11$^{m}$ to J. with St.100 (see N.Y. Trip II).
(B) Take Taconic St. Pky. (R), traversing wooded hills for distance of 27$^{m}$ to J. with St.55, which runs 8$^{m}$ (W) to J. with US9 (see) at Poughkeepsie. This route is eventually to be extended (N) along whole length of Taconic Mt. range.

Just beyond J. with Taconic St. Pky. on US6 is **Shrub Oak,** whose old Hs. incl. **Hart H.** (c.1770), now local lib. **MOHEGAN, 23.,** on L. of same name, is vacation center. **26.5. PEEKSKILL** (see N.Y. Trip III) is at J. with US9 (see). US6 cont. to **BEAR MT. BRIDGE** (toll) across Hudson R., 2,257′ long, at whose W. approach, **32.,** are J. with US9W (see) & E. entrance to Bear Mt. Sec. of **Palisades Interstate Pk.** (see N.Y.Trip IV). US6 cont. through pk. **33.5.** J. with Perkins Mem. Dr., leading (L) 2.5$^{m}$ to summit of **Bear Mt.** (1,314′) & cont. to J. at 4.5$^{m}$ with 7 Ls. Dr. **35.** J. with 7 Ls. Dr., leading (L) into Harriman Sec. of **Palisades Interstate Pk.** (36,093 as. bath.boat.f.camp.), heavily wooded, with 35 Ls. **47. MONROE,** at J. with St.17 (see) which unites with US6 for 16$^{m}$.

**57.5.** J. with St.207, leading (R) short distance into **Goshen,** sett. in early 18th cent., famous for its annual trotting races, with **Good Time Track** (Grand circuit meets 2nd or 3rd wk.in Aug.) & **Harriman Track** (races in late July). Goshen's int. old bldgs. incl., on lower Main St., **Orange County Cth.** (1845.remod.1895) &, on Church St. **St. James Episc. Ch.** (1855.mod.Goth.by Rich.Upjohn). On Main St. opp. Sarah Wells Trl., **Ben Tustin** & **Isaac Jointer Hs.** are both of Dutch type. **63.** W. J. with St.17 (see). **80. PORT JERVIS,** sett. c.1698, on Delaware R. at pt. where N.Y., N.J. & Penn. meet, is RR. & glass-making center. Village was destroyed by Jos. Brant's Tory-Ind. band in 1779 but resettled some yrs. later. It grew in importance when D. & H. Canal, built in 1826, passed through it & was named for canal's chief engineer, John B. Jervis. 127 Main St., **Martinus Decker Ft.** (1793) incorporates part of H. which sheltered refugees from 1779 raid. Delaware R. is **N.Y.-PA. LINE.** J. with US209 (see Delaware River Tour).

## ST. 17—NEW YORK

**NEW YORK CITY (W) to WESTFIELD. 438. N.J.St.17 & N.Y.St.17**

Via: Middletown, Monticello, Liberty, Binghamton, Owego, Elmira, Corning, Wellsville, Olean, Salamanca & Jamestown. Erie RR. parallels most of route. Accoms.: All types.

This route runs diagonally across northeastern N.J. & then turns (W) to follow winding & tortuous course fairly close to southern N.Y. Line.

### Sec. 1: NEW YORK CITY to BINGHAMTON. 190.

**0. NEW YORK CITY.** Take Geo. Washington Bridge across Hudson & cont. (W) on N.J. St.4 to J. with N.J.St.17 at **16.** Turn (R) on N.J.St.17 to N.J.-N.Y. Line at **32. 34.5. SLOATSBURG,** where is **Slot H.** (R) (early 19th cent.Gr.Rev.). From Sloatsburg, Stony Brook Dr. branches off (R) into Harriman sec. of **Palisades Interstate Pk.** (see US6). **37.5. TUXEDO,** where is entrance to **Tuxedo Pk.** (O.July 4), beautiful private reservation in which many N.Y. millionaires have built their homes. At **40.** is J. with St.210, leading (R) into Harriman Sec. of Palisades Interstate Pk. (see US6). **44. ARDEN,** near which on private Rd. is **Arden** (O.appl.), great estate of RR. magnate E. H. Harriman, with huge **Harriman Mansion** (Fr.Ren.). **50.** J. with US6 (see), with which St.17 unites for 16$^m$ (see US6 for this stretch). **68. MIDDLETOWN,** industrial center. **78.5. Old DELAWARE & HUDSON CANAL,** completed in 1828 from Holmesdale, Pa. to Kingston (see US9W) & abandoned in 1899. Rd. now runs through much-frequented vacationist area, reg. of Shawangunk & lower Catskill Mts. **79.5. WURTSBORO,** in summer resort sec. Here is J. with US209 (see US9W) running (NE) to J. with US9W at Kingston. At **92., MONTICELLO** (resort accoms.) is J. with St.42, leading (L) 6.5$^m$ to **Merriwold Pk.** (private resort), where is **Sho-Fu-Den** (fee.restaurant), replica of palace of Japanese emperors. **104. LIBERTY** (all-yr.resort; ski trls.toboggan slides.water sports). At **LIVINGSTON MANOR** (summer resort;accoms.), **113.,** is J. with Johnson Hill Rd. leading (R) c.5$^m$ to **Beaverskill St. Pub. Campsite** (pic.bath.swim.camp). **133.5. E. BRANCH** at J. with St.30.

SIDE TRIP: Take St.30 (R) 15$^m$ to Pepacton Dam, backing up 11$^m$-long reservoir to supplement N.Y.C. water system. St.30 cont. to J. with St.28 (see Catskill St. Pk.) at 38$^m$.

St.17 now follows E. Branch of Delaware R. through resort area to **DEPOSIT** (resort) at **159.**

**190. BINGHAMTON**

Through RR. & bus conns. Accoms.: All types. Info.: C. of C., 66 Chenango St. Golf at Ely Pk.; tennis at Ross & recr. pks.

At confluence of Susquehanna & Chenango Rs., Binghamton is prosperous industrial city. Site was purchased in 1786 by Philadelphia merchant Wm. Bingham. Industrial development followed completion of Chenango Canal, conn. with Erie Canal at Utica, in 1837 & advents of Erie RR. in 1848 & Del., Lackawanna & W. RR. in 1851. City's 1st important industry was cigar-making, which made it country's 2nd most important tobacco center, but this declined after 1890; & manufacture of shoes, begun in 1854, took 1st place, attracting thousands of immigrant workers & resulting in construction of factories, tanneries, & rubber mills. PTS. OF INT.: (1) 78 Exchange St., **Binghamton Pub. Lib.** contains small Mus. of Fine Arts with paintings, sculpture, prints & Ind. artifacts. (2) Washington & Henry Sts., **Christ Ch.** (Episc.1855.by Rich.Upjohn,Sr.) houses city's oldest congregation. (3) Park Ave. & Morgan Rd., **Ross Pk.** (pic.tennis), wooded tract of more than 100 as. with deer pk. & zoo. (4) 16 Susquehanna St., **Endicott-Johnson Plant** (O.wks.appl.guides) manufactures shoes. (5) 40 Charles St., Gen. Aniline & Film Corp. **Ansco Division Plant** (N.O.) is country's 2nd oldest & 2nd largest producer of photographic supplies. (6) St. Hospital Hill, E. edge of city, **Binghamton St. Hospital,** founded 1854, cares for mentally ill. Binghamton is at J. with US11 (see).

## Sec. 2: BINGHAMTON to WESTFIELD. 248.

**0. BINGHAMTON** is at J. with St.17C, alt. route (W) to Owego.

SIDE TRIP: Take latter (R) along N. bank of Susquehanna R. through **Johnson City,** 2m, & **Endicott,** 7.5m, which have grown up around shoe factories of Endicott-Johnson Corp. Company has provided workers' homes on time-payment plan & instituted profit-sharing system. At Endicott is also **Internat. Business Machines Corp. Plant.** St.17C cont. to **Owego** (see below) at 23m.

St.17 follows S. bank of Susquehanna R. (W) from Binghamton to **OWEGO,** 22.5m, RR. & shoe mfg. center in site of Ind. village of Ah-Wa-Ga, at J. with St.96.

SIDE TRIP: Take St.96 (R) from Owego 29m to **Ithaca,** college town at S. end of Cayuga L., spreading over plain & up hillsides. Site, 1st sett. in 1788-89, was later acquired by Simeon De Witt, N.Y. St. Surveyor-Gen., who gave settlement its present name. Town's development has chiefly followed founding at end of Civil War, with $500,000 donated by Ezra Cornell & land grant from Fed. Gov. under Morrill Act, of Cornell Univ. Court & N. Tioga Sts., **Tompkins County Cth.** (1931.mod.Class.) houses hqs. & exhibit chambers of De Witt Hist. Soc. of Tompkins Cty., with coll. of Ind., Col. & other relics. 120 E. Buffalo St., **Ithaca College,** founded as conservatory of music in 1892. On L. shore, **Stewart Pk.** (swim.bathh.pic.athletic facils.) contains zoo & bird sanctuaries. From impressive hilltop site (entrances on Stewart, College & Thurston Aves. & Eddy St.), overlooking Cayuga L. & adj. valleys, soar towers above elm-shaded, terraced campus of **Cornell Univ.,** chartered in 1865 & opened in 1868, consisting of privately endowed colleges & schs. of architecture, arts & sciences, bus. & pub. administration, education, engineering, law, medicine, nursing, nutrition, hotel adm. & grad. study & N.Y. St.-supported colleges of agric., home economics, & veterinary medicine & sch. of industrial & labor relations. Among older bldgs. are **Morrill** (1866-68), **White** (1869), & **McGraw** (1872) **Halls** (all Fr.Ren.); **Lib. Bldg.** (1891. Romanes.by Wm.H.Miller) & adj. **Clock Tower,** 173′ high; **Sage College** (1873-74.Vict. Goth.by Rev.Chas.Babcock) & **Sage Chapel** (1874.Vict.Goth.by Rev.Chas.Babcock). Among more impressive newer bldgs. are **Myron Taylor Hall** (1932.Eng.Coll.Goth.), housing Law Sch.; **Willard Straight Hall** (1925.Eng.Coll.Goth.), student union & social center; **Men's Dormitories & War Mem.** (Eng.Coll.Goth.); **Goldwin Smith Hall** (1904-06), housing College of Arts & Sciences; & **Balch Halls** (1929.Ren.), containing women's dormitories. At outlet of Beebe L., bordering campus, is **Hydraulic Lab.** & across Fall Cr., below Beebe L. is 100′ **Suspension Bridge.** New **Lab. for Nuclear Studies** contains 300,000,000 electron-volt synchrotron.

Take St.13 (L) from Ithaca 2.5m to **Buttermilk Falls St. Pk.** (595 as.camp.cabins.bath. hik.), traversed by Buttermilk Cr., dropping 500′ in series of picturesque cascades. St.13 cont. to **Robt. H. Treman (Enfield Glen) St. Pk.** (823 as.supplies.camp.) at 4.5m, with fine gorge, 3m long, in which are 12 waterfalls.

At 39m **Taughannock Falls St. Pk.** (535 as.camp.pic.swim.baseball.bowling), which is traversed by deep gorge running into Cayuga L. Taughannock Falls drop 215′. 55m **Ovid** at J. with St.96A. Cont. on latter (L) from Ovid, past **Sampson College,** one of 3 N.Y. St. emergency colleges for veterans, utilizing facilities of Sampson Naval Training Sta. on E. shore of Seneca L. At **Geneva** (see US20), 75m, is J. with US20.

St.17 cont. (W) from Owego to **WAVERLY, 41.,** contiguous to Sayre, Pa., where RR. shops give employment. At **55.** is J. with Rd. leading (R) 1m to **NEWTON BATTLEFIELD RESERV.,** where in Aug. 1779 Sullivan-Clinton Expedition slew dozen Inds. in skirmish.

**58. ELMIRA**

Through RR. & bus conns. Accoms.: All types. Info.: C. of C., E. Church & State Sts. Swim. at mun. pool, Brand Pk.; golf at Mark Twain Pk.; tennis at several mun. courts. Nat. Glider Meet, Harris Field, 2 wks. ending c.July 4.

Spreading over hill-fringed broad valley from both banks of Chemung R., Elmira is mfg. center sett. in 1780's which 1st developed as lumber center following completion of Chemung Canal to Seneca L. in 1832. Community adopted name of early settler Nathan Teall's daughter, Elmira. After advent of Erie RR. in 1849, woolen & lumber mills multiplied. During 1860's iron industry became important with est.

of rolling mills & furnaces. Elmira also became important shipping pt. for dairy products. Today it produces variety of articles. PTS. OF INT.: 235 Lake St., **Arnot Art Gallery,** housed in Gr. Rev. mansion of donor Mathias Arnot, has paintings of Flemish, Dutch, German & Fr. schools. College Ave. at Park Pl., **Elmira College** for women, founded 1855. N. end David St., **Woodlawn Cemetery,** contains **Grave of Sam. Langhorne Clemens** (Mark Twain), who married daughter of Elmira businessman in 1870 & thereafter spent many summers here. Adj. is **Woodlawn Nat. Cemetery,** containing graves of nearly 3,000 Confed. soldiers who died in prison camp maintained here during Civil War, along with those of soldiers from time of Fr. & Ind. Wars, transferred from other cemeteries. Off East Hill Rd., c.0.5$^{m}$ beyond city limits, Quarry Farm, where is **Mark Twain Study,** built as replica of Miss. steamboat pilot house, where during summers bet. 1874 & 1903 Twain wrote parts of many of his books.

SIDE TRIPS: (A) Take St.14 (R) 19.5$^{m}$ to **Montour Falls,** industrial town mfg. electric hoists, with beautiful **Chequaga Falls** (156′) & 7 picturesque glens in vic. At 22.5$^{m}$ **Watkins Glen St. Pk.** (540 as.pic.bath.hik.camp.cabins) at town & spa of **Watkins Glen.** This is finest of Finger Ls. pks., traversed by deep gorge with 200′ cliffs. St.14 cont. (N) along W. shore of Seneca L. At 26$^{m}$ is J. with Rd. leading (R) 0.5$^{m}$ to **Internat. Salt Plant** (O.wks.), where salt is made by evaporation of brine from wells. 45.5$^{m}$, **Dresden,** where is **Robt. G. Ingersoll Birthpl.** (O.summer;c.1800), now mus. containing Ingersoll Memorabilia. St.14 cont. to **Geneva** (see US20) at J. with US20 (see), 59$^{m}$.
(B) Take St.17E (L) from Madison Ave. in Elmira 5.5$^{m}$ to J. with Harris Field Rd., leading (R) 1.5$^{m}$ to **Harris Field** where in July Nat. Glider Meet is held.

**76.5. CORNING,** on Chemung R., named for Erastus Corning, who promoted sale of real estate & bldg. of RR. here. **Corning Glass Works** (show rooms O.plant by appl.) manufactures vast variety of glass products for industrial, scientific & domestic uses. It produces fine Steuben Glass. On Public Sq. is **Observatory Mus.** (O.8:30-10 p.m.), erected to shelter 200″ lens made for Mt. Palomar Observatory. This lens was imperfect when cast & 2nd one had to be manufactured. **78.5. PAINTED POST,** industrial town at J. with US15 (see), which unites with St.17 for 4$^{m}$. St.17 now enters N.Y. St. oil field, opened before 1870 but not fully developed until 1880's.

**131. WELLSVILLE,** sett. in 1795, was named for pioneer settler Gardiner Wells, & not for oil wells which now dot environs. **164. OLEAN** is RR. & oil center. **171. ALLEGANY IND. RESERV.** (30,000 as., where still live some Seneca & Cayuga Inds. **182.5. SALAMANCA,** farmer's market & all-yr. resort. At **188.5.** is J. leading (L) 1$^{m}$ into **Allegany St. Pk.** (65,000 as.cabins.camp.pic.hik.& bridle trls.swim.f.ski-ing), well-wooded tract with many streams. Allegheny Mts. in pk. range from 1,500′ to 2,000′. **220. JAMESTOWN,** at SE. end of Chautauqua L., some of whose earliest settlers were furniture makers, is now leading furniture-making center. Before Civil War many Swedish immigrants, most of them cabinetmakers, sett. here; today pop. is largely Swedish by birth or descent. Jamestown also manufactures machinery, tools & textiles. On S. Main St., **Fenton Mem. Pk.** in which is **Statue of Reuben E. Fenton,** one of founders of Republican Party in N.Y. State. In pk. is large **Fenton Mansion.**

SIDE TRIP: Take St.17J (L) from Jamestown along Chautauqua L. 17$^{m}$ to **Chautauqua** (resort.hotels.apts.boat.recr.), center of movement begun by John Heyl Vincent & Louis Miller, which developed great network of entertainment, lectures, music, etc., that covered entire country. First Chautauqua session was in 1874. 21$^{m}$ **Mayville,** at J. with St.17.

St.17 follows E. shore of L. to **MAYVILLE, 242.** & cont. to **WESTFIELD, 248.,** where is J. with US20 (see).

## US 4—NEW YORK

**N.Y.-VT. LINE** (2$^{m}$ from Fair Haven, Vt.) **(S) to J. with US20. 84. US4**

Via: Whitehall, Hudson Falls, Ft. Edward, Schuylerville, Saratoga Nat. Hist. Pk., Mechanicville, Waterford & Troy. RRs. accessible entire route. Accoms.: All types.

US4 follows Champlain branch of Barge Canal & Hudson R. In 1777 Brit. Gen. John Burgoyne followed this route (S) in his ambitious attempt to link forces with Sir Geo. Clinton coming up from N.Y. City.

**0. N.Y.-VT. LINE. 6. WHITEHALL,** sett. 1759, RR.& mill town, known as birthpl. of Amer. Navy because here ships were built for Battle of Valcour I. on L. Champlain (1776). **17.5. FT. ANN,** site of Col. ft., where in July 1777 occurred skirmish known as Battle of Ft. Ann. **27. HUDSON FALLS** (sett.c.1760), pulp & paper-making center. It was burned by Brit. in 1780. **29. FT. EDWARD,** another paper-making center. Here on strategic portage bet. L. Champlain & Hudson was built Ft. Edward, captured by Burgoyne in 1777. **40.5.** US4 here crosses Hudson R. **42. MARSHALL H.** (pre-Rev.). **42.5. SCHUYLERVILLE** (sett.1689), before Rev. known as Saratoga, was wiped out by Inds. in 1745 & after Rev. was named for Gen. Phil. Schuyler, commanding gen. of Amer. forces until Gen. Horatio Gates took over. On Ferry St. is **Field of Grounded Arms,** where Brit. laid down weapons when they surrendered. On McCoine Ave. is **Saratoga Mon.** (O.sm.fee), 155′ high, on hill top, with statues of Gens. Gates & Schuyler & Col. Morgan in niches around its base & 4th niche, planned for Benedict Arnold's statue, empty. In Mon. is room containing relics, statues & plaques pertaining to Rev. **43.5.** J. with Rd. leading (L) short distance to **Schuyler H.** (L), built by Gen. Schuyler after destruction of his 1st H. here by Brit. in 1777.

**50.5. SARATOGA BATTLEFIELD NAT. HIST. PK.** Here was fought decisive conflict bet. Brit. & Continentals. Battle began on Sept. 19, 1777, Benedict Arnold leading attack. Later, on Oct. 7, Arnold led Amers. against Hessians, whose defeat forced Brit. to withdraw. Burgoyne delayed his retreat unduly & his forces were surrounded. On Oct. 17 he surrendered. PTS. OF INT.: **Blockh.** (replica of one of Rev. period) in which are battle relics. Near it is **H.** in which Col. Morgan & other commanders had their quarters. Also near-by are reprods. of **Arnold's Hqs. & Powder Magazine** (rest.). Other pts. of int. incl. **Mon. to Gen. T. Kosciusko,** Polish volunteer who directed fortification of Amer. positions; **Cemetery** with graves of soldiers who fell in battle; mon. on **Grave of Unknown Soldier of Rev.** (1938); **Great Redoubt,** where Hessians were defeated; **Freeman's Farm,** center of bloody fighting; **Arnold Mon.,** at spot where Arnold was wounded, whose inscription records his rank & achievements but not his name. **59.5. MECHANICVILLE,** RR., paper-making & apparel-mfg. city. **68. WATERFORD.** Here Champlain Canal branches (N) from Erie sec. of Barge Canal System. Here US4 crosses Hudson R.

SIDE TRIP: St.32 runs (S) from Waterford along W. side of Hudson. At 2m **Cohoes** (sett. 1665), industrial center. On Van Schaick St., **Van Schaick H.** (O.1735.Georg.Col.), built by son of 1st settler, Gassen Gerritse Van Schaick. Cohoes Falls, once mighty cataract, has greatly dwindled because of diversion of water for canal & industrial purposes. 5.5m, **Watervliet,** industrial city. S. Broadway, **U.S. Govt. Arsenal** (est.1813) has manufactured guns for all Amer. wars; during World War II it turned out antiaircraft guns & battleship ordnance. On 1st St. near S. edge of city, **Schuyler Homestead** (N.O.1666.slight alts.), gambrel-roofed Holland brick structure, once home of Philip Schuyler. At 8m, **Albany Rural Cemetery** (R) in which are graves of Peter Gansevoort, Gen. Schuyler, & Pres. Chester A. Arthur. At 12.5m **Albany** (see US20) at J. with US20.

**74. TROY.**

Through RR. & bus conns. Accoms.: Hotels & tourist homes. Info.: C. of C., 43 4th St. Swim. at Prospect Pk.; golf at Frear Pk.; tennis at city pks.

Strung out for 8m along E. side of Hudson R. is shipping terminal opp. mouth of Mohawk R., Troy is terminus of Barge Canal, an important commercial & educational center, an industrial city with variety of plants. Until late 18th cent. site was incl. in patroonship of Kiliaen Van Rensselaer, tended by Dutch tenant farmers. Town site was laid out in 1786 on land owned by Jacob D. Vanderheyden. Manufacture of brick was begun at same time & dam & flume built on Poestenkill, running through town, to operate paper mill. By 1806 pop. exceeded 3,000. During War of 1812, Sam. Wilson's habit of stamping with initials "U.S." beef supplied to soldiers quartered near-by gave rise to famous nickname "Uncle Sam." During 1820's Troy became important iron-mfg. center with est. of bell foundry & stove plate works. Opening of Erie & Champlain Canals brought it barge commerce. Coach shops opened by Chas. Veasie & Orsamus Eaton turned, after completion of Schenectady & Troy RR., to making RR. passenger cars. Introduction of detachable collar for men's shirts by housewife Mrs. Hannah Lord Montague in 1825 was followed by beginnings of Troy's still important collar & shirt-making industry. Civil War spurred growth of iron & collar industries. With introduction following Civil War of Bessemer steel process by Horatio Winslow at his company's works, Troy became steel center of U.S. until Andrew Carnegie est. his mills at Pittsburgh. Today its chief products incl. valves & fire hydrants, surveying & engineering instruments, women's wear—& of course collars & shirts. PTS. OF INT.: (1) 405 2nd Ave.,

**Wendell-Lansing H.** (N.O.c.1750.early Georg.Col.), of Holland brick, with thick riverside stone wall. (2) E. end 101st St., **Oakwood Cemetery,** with **Sam. Wilson Mon.** to Troy brickmaker & slaughterhouse owner who was orig. "Uncle Sam," **Russell Sage Mon.** to local commercial leader & Congressman, & **Robt. Ross Mon.** to man martyred in 1894 while defending purity of ballot at city election in incident that led to passage of new election laws in N.Y. St. (3) 433-71 River St., **Cluett, Peabody & Co. Plant** (O.wks.guides), world's largest shirt factory, has **Collar Mus.** exhibiting collars from 1st "Troy Made" to latest. (4) Sage Ave. bet. 8th & 15th Sts., **Rensselaer Polytechnic Institute** (est.1824), oldest continuously existing college of engineering in any English-speaking country, was founded by Stephen Van Rensselaer. Bldgs. in Eng. Georg. style rise from steep hillside, approached by monumental stone stairway. (5) 8th St. bet. Sage & College Aves., **St. Joseph's Seminary,** occupying seminary bldg. (1856.Romanes.Rev.with Goth.towers) & chapel (1933.Eng. Goth.). (6) Pawling & Elm Grove Aves., **Emma Willard Sch.,** one of oldest girls' college prep. schs. in U.S., dates back to 1821, when Emma Willard arrived in Troy to open Troy Female Seminary; bldgs. in Eng. Coll. Goth. style rise from landscaped hilltop. (7) Ferry & 2nd Sts., **Russell Sage College,** women's college org. 1916 with endowment by Mrs. Russell Sage; occupying former bldgs. of Emma Willard Sch. (8) 59 2nd St., **Betsy Hart H.** (N.O.1827.fine Georg.Col.), built by merchant & RR. magnate Rich. P. Hart, whose wife was said in 1886, when she died, to have been richest woman in U.S. (9) Congress & 1st Sts., **First Presb. Ch.** (1836.Gr.Rev.) houses Troy's oldest congregation, org. 1791. (10) 3rd St. bet. Congress & State Sts., **First Bapt. Ch.** (1846.Gr.Rev.). (11) 3rd & State Sts., **St. Paul's Episc. Ch.** (1827.Eng. Goth.), Troy's oldest ch.

US4 cont. (S) along E. bank of Hudson to Js. with US20 (see) & US9 (see) at **84.**

# US 9—NEW YORK

## NEW YORK CITY (N) to CANADIAN BORDER. 336.5. US9

Via: Yonkers, Tarrytown, Ossining, Peekskill, Poughkeepsie, Hudson, Rensselaer, Albany, Saratoga Springs, Glens Falls, L. George, Keeseville, Plattsburg, Rouses Pt. RRs. parallel route. Good accoms. of all types.

US9 runs along E. bank of Hudson, affording magnificent views of Palisades, Hudson Highlands & Catskill Mts. After leaving Albany, US9 crosses E. sec. of Adirondack St. Pk. In its northernmost sec., it skirts L. Champlain.

### Sec. 1: NEW YORK to ALBANY. 145.5.

For towns & pts. of int. on or near US9 bet. **NEW YORK, 0., & PEEKSKILL, 40.,** inc. latter, see N.Y. Trip III. Peekskill is at J. with US6 (see). **51.5.** J. with St.301, leading (R) 4m to 3,400-a. **Clarence Fahnestock Mem. Pk.** (camp.hik.boat.f.).

**58. CAPT. CORNELIUS R. VAN WYCK H.** (R) (O.appl.c.1785), Gen. Israel Putnam's hqs. during Rev. Just (N) of it is **Cornelius C. Van Wyck H.** (R) (c.1786). **59. FISHKILL VILLAGE** (sett.c.1700) on Fishkill Cr. Here are **Jas. Gibbon H.** (1811) & **Ye Olde Fishkill Inn** (1820.alts.). Across street from latter is **First Reformed Dutch Ch.** (1731 & 1785.inter.remod.), during Rev. used as prison. **Trinity Ch.** (Episc.c.1769.inter.alt.). In adj. cemetery are buried Brit. soldiers killed in Rev. & some Col. notables. **Obadiah Bowne H.** (1818.fine inter.).

SIDE TRIP: Take St.52 (L) from Fishkill Village 5m to **Beacon,** sett.c.1663, incorporating towns of Matteawan & Fishkill Landing. Ferry runs to Newburgh. South Ave. close to Rd., **Depeyster H.** (c.1743.Col.), now used as storeh. Van Nydeck & Teller Aves., **Brett-Teller H.** (1709.later adds.Col.fine exter.& inter.), built on orig. Rombout Manor (28,000 as.). Sargent Ave., **Wodenethe** (1825.alt.1853.grounds O.to public.fine gardens) belongs to Craig House Sanitarium. From Beacon runs Mt. Beacon Incline RR. (May 1-Oct.15) to **Mt. Top Resort.** Trl. cont. to **Summit** (1,602′) commanding fine view.

(1) St.9D turns (L) from Beacon to **Cold Springs,** 8m, & **Garrison,** c.11.5m on R. shore. Ferry runs from Garrison to West Point. St.9D cont. (S) to J. with US6 (see), 16.5m.

(2) Take St.9D (R) from Beacon. At 8m **Wappingers Falls.** On Main St. (L) **Mesier H.** (1741 & 1750), built by Matthew Mesier, tea merchant against whose profiteering in tea during Rev. housewives of town rebelled. Fine falls of Wappinger Cr. give town its name. At 9m is J. with US9.

**70. POUGHKEEPSIE**

Through RR. & bus conns. Ferry to Highland. Hudson R. Day Line makes stops (May-Oct.). Accoms. of all types. Info.: C. of C., 57 Market St.

Poughkeepsie, on high ground above Hudson, bisected by Fallkill Cr., is an industrial & shipping center of some importance although better known as home of Vassar College & Intercollegiate Regatta which takes place in Hudson here in June. City was 1st sett. in 1683. Poughkeepsie derives its name from Ind. expression Upping Ipis Ing ("covered lodge by the little water place"). In 1777, after burning of Kingston by Brit., it became temporary St. Capital. In 1788 N.Y. St. Convention ratified Constitution here. PTS. OF INT.: (1) Market & Main St., **Dutchess County Cth.** (1905) on site of former cth. in which Fed. Constitution was ratified. (2) Main & Washington Sts., **City Hall** (1831.adds.inter.alt.). (3) Vassar St. & Lafayette Pl., **Vassar Bros. Institute** (O.1-5), containing small mus. of natural hist. (4) 28 Market St., **Nelson H.** (1875.remod.) is hotel; inn has been maintained on this site ever since 1777. (5) 17 Market St., **Smith Bros. Restaurant,** est. by grandfather of Smith Bros. & still in hands of his descendants. (6) N. Clinton St., **College Hill Pk.** at highest pt. of city, from which fine views. Here is bust of W. W. Smith, one of Smith Bros. (7) White & Main Sts., **Clear Everitt H.** (O.wks.1783;Dutch Col.int.inter.& exter.fee) is D.A.R. hqs. & mus. of antique furnishings. (8) 635 Main St., **Glebe H.** (1767.int. exter.& inter.), formerly rectory of Episc. Ch. (9) At foot of Mill St., **St. Peter's Ch.** (1851 & 1853.adds.), 1st Cath. Ch. in Dutchess Cty. (10) 52 S. Hamilton St., **Old Ladies' Home** (1836), which formerly housed Dutchess Cty. Academy. (11) 134 N. Hamilton St., **Smith Bros. Plant,** manufacturers of famous coughdrops, founded by W. W. Smith & A. Smith, bearded "Trade Mark" of advertisement. (12) In environs, at Cedar Ave., **Kimlin Cider Mill** (O.exc.Mon.), containing int. coll. of hist. relics. (13) On Raymond Ave. is **Vassar College for Women,** founded in 1861 by Poughkeepsie brewer, Matthew Vassar, offering courses in liberal arts & sciences. On campus (950 as.) are some 30 bldgs., outdoor theater & Shakespeare garden in which grow all flowers mentioned by poet. **Taylor Hall** houses Art Dept. & contains an excellent sm. art coll. **Chapel** (1904.Norman Eng.) has some fine stained-glass windows. In Poughkeepsie is J. with US44, running (W) across Hudson via Mid-Hudson Bridge to J. with US9W (see) at Highland.

**74.5. JAS. R. ROOSEVELT ESTATE,** formerly home of F. D. Roosevelt's half-brother (H.dates from 1833 & 1835;alt.). Just beyond is **FRANKLIN D. ROOSEVELT MEM.** (O.exc.Mon.10-5), adm. by Nat. Pk. Serv., comprising birthpl. of former Pres., where he spent his boyhood yrs. House (O.1826.alt.adds.) was built by his father, Jas. Roosevelt, & was bequeathed by former Pres. to people of U.S. Inter. has been preserved as it was when occupied by Pres. (NE) of home is **Grave of F. D. Roosevelt,** simple marble slab, enclosed by 100-yr. old hemlock hedge. (NE) of Grave is **F. D. Roosevelt Lib.** (O), built by former Pres. in 1941, which contains books, mss., documents & hist. material, as well as pictures, models, art objects, etc. **76.5. HYDE PK.** Although exceedingly popular, F. D. Roosevelt was never able to carry his home town for Democratic ticket. Just beyond Hyde Pk. on US9 is entrance to former estate (O) of Fred. W. Vanderbilt, now owned by U.S. Gov., on which is **Vanderbilt Mansion** (O.exc.Mon.), great Ren. structure built in 1895—an enlarged copy of Petit Trianon—furnished in most luxurious manner of "gilded age." Mrs. Roosevelt, in one of her published columns, reports that Mrs. Vanderbilt "had a passion for bows & used to decorate every bathroom with bows tied around everything in sight" & that she used black satin sheets on her bed as foil to her fair complexion & her beautiful pearls. **77. ST. JAMES EPISC. CH.** (R) (1844.Eng.Goth.int. inter.), of which Pres. Roosevelt was member. **80. MARGARET LEWIS NORRIE ST. PK.** (camp.cabins.recr.restaurant) extending down to Hudson. **82.** J. with paved Rd. leading (L) c.1$^m$ to **Ogden Mills & Ruth Livingston Mills Mem. St. Pk.,** donated to St. by heirs of Ogden Mills, who was Secy. of Treasury in 1932. Mansion on grounds (c.1832.O.11-5 exc.Mon.sm.fee), orig. built by Morgan Lewis, son of Francis Lewis, signer of Decl. of Ind., who married Gertrude, sister of Chancellor Livingston, was transformed by Stanford White in 1895 as magnificent Fr. Ren. dwelling with luxuriant inter. & furnishings. **86.5. RHINEBECK,** located on vast tract of land patented by Henry Beekman, 1697. Here are **Ch. of the Messiah** (Episc. 1897.by Stanford White) & **Beekman Arms** (1700,1769,1865 & later adds.int.inter.), said to be oldest hotel in U.S. **U.S. Post Office** (1939) is reproduction of old H. built c.1700. In village also is **Reformed Dutch Ch.** (1808). (NE) of village, **Dutchess Cty. Fair Grounds** (Sept.trotting races).

SIDE TRIP: Take St.308 (L) from Rhinebeck, past **Kip H.** (mid-18th cent.), to **Rhinecliff,** from which ferry runs to Kingston.

**89.** J. with St.9-G.

SIDE TRIP: Take latter (L). At 2.5m **Rokeby** (1812.later adds.), built by Gen. John Armstrong, Secy. of War during conflict of 1812. At 6.5m is J. with paved Rd.

Take latter (L) 0.7m to **Bard College.** Formerly was branch of Columbia Univ. At c.1m entrance to **Blithewood,** estate of Gen. Armstrong. Present Georg. mansion was built in 1899. At c.1.5m **Montgomery Pl.** (1804), built by widow of Gen. Montgomery; latter was 2nd in command of 1775 expedition to Canada. At c.2m is **Quinn H.** (early 18th cent.).

At 9m is J. with paved Rd.

Take latter (L) 1m to **Tivoli.** On Flora St. is **Callander H.** (1794.Gr.verandah add. later).

At 10.5m is J. with paved Rd.

Take latter (L) 1.5m to **Clermont** (O.appl.c.1778;much alt.fine inter.), built by Margaret B. Livingston. Rbt. Fulton's steamboat "Clermont," financed by one of Livingston family, was named for this estate.

At 20m is J. with dirt Rd.

Take latter (L) 0.5m to **Oak Hill** (fine inter.), built by John Livingston.

25.5m **Hudson** (see below) at J. with US9.

**89.5. OLD STONE CH.** (1730.later adds.). **92. RED HOOK,** sett. 1713-1727. **92.5. MARTIN HOMESTEAD** (1732.fine inter.). **94.5.** J. with Rd. leading (R) short distance to **Upper Red Hook,** where is **Thomas H.** (R), Gen. Israel Putnam's hqs. in 1797. **96.5.** J. with Rd. leading (L) 0.8m to **Redder Homestead** (c.1720.fine inter.). **101.** J. with paved Rd.

SIDE TRIPS: (A) Take latter (L) 1.5m to J. with dirt Rd.

Take latter (L) 0.5m to entrance lane of **The Hermitage** (pre-Rev.), built by Col. Peter R. Livingston. At c.2m on dirt Rd. is **Teviotdale** (c.1773.Georg.Col.), another Livingston H.

(B) Take paved Rd. (R) from J. on US9 (see above) 0.5m to **Brock Livingston H.** (Dutch Col.). At c.1.5m is J. with Rd. on which route turns (R) to **Callander H.** (1773.Dutch Col.), 2m, another Livingston H.

**107.** J. with St.9H.

SIDE TRIP: Take latter (R). Just beyond J. with US9 is J. with St.82.

Take St.82 (R) 6m to **L. Taghkanic St. Pk.** (camp.cottages.f.hik.ski trls.).

Cont. (N) on St.9H c.14.5m to **Lindenwald** (1797.rebuilt 1849 by Rbt.Upjohn), home of Martin Van Buren. At 15.5m **Ichabod Crane Sch.** on site of orig. sch. that figures in Washington Irving's stories. Near-by is **Van Alen H.** (1737), where Helen Van Alen lived, who supposedly was orig. of Irving's Katrina Van Tassel in "The Legend of Sleepy Hollow." 18.5m J. of St.9H with US9.

**107.5. THE HILL** (c.1796.Class.Rev.int.inter.), built by Henry Walter Livingston, most lavish of Livingston family Hs. **112.5. HUDSON,** an industrial center, sett. c.1783 by New Englanders. NW. cor. of Partition & 2nd Sts., **Collier H.** (now Ch.; Gr.Rev.). 451 Warren St., **First Reformed Ch.** (Gr.Rev.). 215 Warren St., **Gen. Worth Hotel** (Gr.Rev.). Here is J. with St.9G. **114. TURTLE H.** (L) (1800-18), with fine columned portico. **117.5. MACY H.** (R) (1816). **125. KINDERHOOK,** early Dutch settlement. Main St., **H. of Hist.** (1810-19;fine exter.), now hqs. of Columbia Cty. Hist. Soc., containing early furniture, dolls, & hist. documents & relics. Sylvester Lane, **St. Paul's Episc. Ch.** (Goth.Rev.by Rich.Upjohn). **Grave of Martin Van Buren** is in village cemetery. **137.** J. with US20 (see), which unites with US9 to Albany. **141.** J. with US4 (see). **144.5. RENSSELAER,** suburb of Albany. Washington Ave., **Beverwyck** (c.1840-43;Gr.Rev.fine inter.), which belonged to Stephen Van Rensselaer, one of famous patroon family, now monastery & training sch. of Order of St. Francis. Riverside St., **Ft. Crailo** (O.fee.1704.adds.1762.rest.int. inter.). Inter. is preserved in orig. state. Dr. Rich. Shuckburgh, Brit. Army surgeon, in 1758 composed here words of "Yankee Doodle," adopted as popular song during Rev. St.9J leads (L) from Rensselaer to **Jan Bries H.** (1723), 3.5m, & **Van Rensselaer-Genêt H.** (1742), 4m.

**145.5. ALBANY** (see US20), at J. with US20 (see).

## Sec. 2: ALBANY to GLENS FALLS. 51.

**6.** J. with St.155.

SIDE TRIP: Take latter (L) to **Albany Airport,** 2.5m, adj. to which is **Ann Lee Home** for aged of Albany Cty. on site purchased from United Soc. of Shakers, named for Ann Lee, who led 8 converts to Amer. in 1774 & sett. here. Shakers adhered to celibacy, spiritualism, community of property, refusal to bear arms or take oaths & became famous for beautiful handicrafts. Just (W) of Ann Lee Home is **Shaker Cemetery,** with **Grave of Ann Lee.** At 3.5m are several red brick bldgs. of **Shaker Settlement.**

At **12.5.** US9 crosses Mohawk R. **16. CLIFTON PK.**, where is **Stevens' Tavern** (L) (c.1800). At **26.** is J. with St.9P, curving (R) around E. shore of **Saratoga L.** (summer resort), past **White Sulphur Spring,** 3.5$^{m}$, to **Saratoga Springs** (see below), 12$^{m}$, where it rejoins US9. **32.5. SARATOGA SPRINGS,** nationally known for hotels, race-track, & mineral springs, booms in summer, swollen with visitors. This was favorite hunting ground for Mohawk & Oneida Inds., who knew it as Saraghoga ("place of swift water"). Sir Wm. Johnson was carried on stretcher by Mohawk braves in 1767 to take springs' medicinal waters. Gideon Putnam in 1802 cleared timber around Congress Spring & built Union Hotel. In 1824, U.S. Hotel was opened & in 1832 N.Y. St.'s 2nd RR. was laid here from Schenectady. Saratoga Springs soon became N.'s chief sporting & social center of mid-19th cent. Opera H. & racetrack were built in 1865, Casino in 1870. Saratoga's racing, dancing, gambling made it gayest place in Amer.—& one of best in which to marry off eligible daughters. After 1890 commercial exploitation threatened Saratoga's continuance as spa, until N.Y. St. began in 1910 program of conservation which has resulted in development of St.-owned Saratoga Spa (see below).

PTS. OF INT.: (1) High Rock Ave. opp. Rock St., **High Rock Spring,** known to Inds. as "Medicine Spring of the Great Spirit," was 1st of springs discovered by white men. (2) Putnam & Spring Sts., **St. Drink Hall** (sm.adm.fee,free water). (3) Broadway & Washington St., **Grand Union Hotel** (oldest sec.1802.enlarged & remod.1872), mansard-roofed & turreted, with 3-story piazza & inter. courtyard, evolved from Gideon Putnam's orig. hostelry. (4) Broadway & Spring St., **Congress Pk.** (c.10 as.). contains **Spencer Trask Mem. Fountain** (by Dan.Chester French) & **Katina Trask Peabody Mem.,** granite stairway. Trask was retired banker who pioneered development of Saratoga Spa, as did Geo. Foster Peabody, whom his widow married. In center of pk. is red brick **Casino** (O.Aug.1870), opened as Saratoga Club by John Morrissey, which Rich. Canfield bought & renovated in 1894 as lavish gambling palace; it was closed in 1907. (5) Circular & Spring Sts., **Skidmore College** (inc.1922), for women, named for patroness Lucy Skidmore Scribner, with more than 2 dozen bldgs. on 10-a. campus. (6) Union & East Aves., **Saratoga Race Track** (races in Aug.), with grandstand & 45-a. landscaped pk. (7) Union Ave. (SE) of race track, **Yaddo,** handsomely landscaped estate sett. by Jacobus Barhyte in 1784 & later acquired by Mr. & Mrs. Spencer Trask, who left it & their Norman style mansion to Corporation of Yaddo, which since 1926 has conducted artists' colony here.

SIDE TRIP: Take St.50 (L) from Saratoga 1.5$^{m}$ to **Saratoga Spa** (O.all yr.), owned & operated by N.Y. St., comprising woodland area of 1,200 as. laced with bridle trls., footpaths & Rds. leading to 163 mineral springs along Geyser Brook. At center of reserv. is landscaped 140-a. tract with **Hall of Springs** (O.May through Nov.), where natural carbonated waters are served; **Spa Recr. Center** (swim.golf.tennis); **Roosevelt, Washington, & Lincoln Bathhs.** (baths & related treatments for heart & circulatory disorders, arthritis, neuritis & other ailments); **Simon Baruch Research Institute; U.S. Veterans' Facility; Gideon Putnam Hotel,** summer theater, & bottling plant. Waters of spa contain salines & alkalines & are naturally carbonated.

St.50 cont. (S) through **Ballston Spa,** 6.5$^{m}$, once fashionable spa, now industrial center with tanneries & knitting mills, to **Scotia** (see St.5) at J. with St.5 (see), 22$^{m}$.

**40. WILTON,** at J. with Rd. leading (L) 1.5$^{m}$ to **Mt. McGregor Sanitarium.** Here is **Gen. Grant Cottage** (O.sm.fee), where Gen. U. S. Grant died in 1885. **51. GLENS FALLS,** industrial city mfg. paper & chemicals, garments, & machinery, whose progress has been furthered by water power developed at Falls of Hudson R. here (60′ high). First mills were built in 1788. Beneath bridge over Hudson is **Cooper's Cave,** at foot of falls, scene of episode in Jas. Fenimore Cooper's "Last of the Mohicans." At Glens Falls is J. with St.32B, running (E) 3$^{m}$ to conn. with US4 (see) at **Hudson Falls.**

### Sec. 3: GLENS FALLS to J. with St.373. 102.5.

For this sec. of US9, see Adirondack St. Pk.

### Sec. 4: J. with St.373 to CANADIAN BORDER. 37.5.

**0. J.** with St.373, leading (R) 2.5$^{m}$ to **Port Kent,** on L. Champlain, where ferry crosses to Burlington, Vt., at J. with US7. Just (N) of J. with St.373 is N. boundary of **Adirondack St. Pk.** (see). **12. PLATTSBURG,** at pt. where Saranac R. enters L. Champlain. Here in 1814 was fought Battle of Plattsburg & just off shore, on L. Champlain, occurred Battle of L. Champlain bet. Brit. & Amer. fleets. S. River St., **Macdonough Mem.** (by John R.Pope), 135′ obelisk comm. Macdonough's victory in latter conflict. 17 Cumberland Ave., **Kent-Delord H.** (O.fee;remod.c.1810) containing hist. documents & antique furnishings. On L. shore, (S) of Saranac R., **Champlain College,** N.Y. St. institution est. for veterans at end of World War II, in former U.S. Army Barracks, whose oldest bldgs. date back to 1838. At Plattsburg is J. with St.3-365.

SIDE TRIP: Take latter (L). At 9.5m is J. with St.374, on which side route turns (R). (For St.3-365, running (SW), see Adirondack St. Pk.) St.374 runs to **Dannemora,** 14.5m, so named for city in Sweden, where convicts from Auburn St. Prison were brought during mid-19th cent. to work iron deposits. It is now site of **Clinton St. Prison.** St.374 cont. to **Chazy L.** (f.), 20.5m. At 23.5m is J. with trl. leading to summit of **Lyon Mt.** (3,830′). At 28m is iron mining town of **Lyon Mt.** 37m **Lower Chateaugay L.** (bath.boat.f.hunt.). **Chateaugay** (see US11), 45m, is at J. with US11 (see).

At **13.5.** is J. with Rd. leading (R) 0.5m to **Cumberland Beach** (bath.) off which Battle of L. Champlain was fought. At **26., COLONIAL H.** (O.May-Nov.sm.fee.1824) containing antique furnishings & hist. relics. **36. ROUSES PT.** Here Toll Bridge crosses L. providing access to J. with US2 to Alburg, Vt. **37.5. CANADIAN BORDER.**

## US 9W—NEW YORK

### N.Y. to ALBANY. 151. US9W

Via: Newburgh, Highland, Kingston & Catskill. W. Shore Div., N.Y. Central RR. parallels entire route. Accoms.: All types.

This route following W. side of Hudson R. is scenically fine. For pts. of int. & towns on or near US9W bet. **NEW YORK** at **0.**, & J. with US6 (see) at **46.**, see N.Y. Trip IV. **51.** J. with paved hy.

SIDE TRIP: Take latter (R) 2m to **U.S. Military Academy** at **West Pt.** (accoms.& guides at Thayer-West Pt.Inn;info.from military police at N.& S.gates & on grounds), oldest U.S. military post now in use, 1st occupied by troops Jan. 20, 1778. It comprises tract of 15,085 as. overlooking Hudson R.; its bldgs. (chiefly Goth.in style) rise in terraces up steep sides of Storm King Mt. Academy was opened July 4, 1802, but had hard struggle for some yrs., lacking funds, until Maj. (later Col.) Sylvanus Thayer, "Father of the Military Academy," became supt. in 1817 & instituted thoroughgoing reorganization. Cadet Corps, whose maximum strength was increased to 2,496 in 1942, is filled with appointees nominated by elected Fed. officials, honor grads. of honor military schs., sons of deceased war veterans & Congressional Medal winners & enlisted members of Army & Nat. Guard. Curriculum is mainly academic, leading to B.S. degree, though all cadets receive basic military instruction & rigorous physical training. June Wk., when diplomas & 2nd Lt.'s commissions are presented, is celebrated with colorful graduation parade.

PTS. OF INT.: (1) Mills Rd., **Michie Stadium,** football field, seats 26,000. (2) Mills Rd., **Ft. Putnam** (1778.rest.1807-10) rises from Mt. Independence. (3) Mills Rd., **Cadet Chapel** (1910.neo-Goth.by Cram,Goodhue & Ferguson), cruciform, with high buttressed tower, is West Pt.'s most impressive bldg. (4) Mills & Wash. Rds., **Chapel of the Most Holy Trinity** (Cath.1910). (5) Delafield Rd., **Gymnasium** (1908). (6) Jefferson & Wash. Rds., **Supt.'s Quarters** (c.1820). (7) Jefferson Rd., **Washington Hall** (1925-29.by Gehron & Ross) is cadets' mess hall. (8) Thayer Rd., **Grant Hall** (Tudor Goth.) is cadets' reception hall. (9) Thayer Rd., **Cadet Hospital** (1924.Goth.by Arnold W.Brunner). (10) Thayer Rd., **Adm. Bldg.** (1904.Goth.by Cram,Goodhue & Ferguson), battlemented granite structure with 160′ tower-keep, contains **Ordnance Mus.** (11) Jefferson & Cullum Rds., **Lib.** (Goth.1841), with coll. of paintings incl. Gilbert Stuart portrait of Washington. (12) Cullum Rd., **Riding Hall** (1911.by Cram,Goodhue & Ferguson) with vast arena for riding classes, indoor polo & drills. (13) **Bachelors' Bldg.,** (14) **Cullum Mem. Hall** & (15) **Officers' Club,** all on Cullum Rd., are in neo-Class. style, designed by McKim, Mead & White. (16) Cullum Rd., **Kosciusko Mon.** (1828) comm. Polish soldier who helped plan West Pt. fortifications during Rev. (17) **Flirtation Walk** scales cliff from R. shore. (18) End of Flirtation Walk, **Battle Mon.** (by Stanford White); near-by are some links from 1,700′ chain strung across Hudson from West Pt. during Rev. to block Brit. ships, & around base of mon. are captured cannon from major Amer. wars. (19) Cullum & Wash. Rds., **Washington Mon.** (20) Wash. Rd., **Old Post Chapel** (1837.rebuilt 1911.Class.Rev.), at entrance to **West Pt. Cemetery,** where Maj. Thayer & Gens. Scott & Custer are buried.

St.218 (Storm King Hy.) cont. (N) at considerable alt. above Hudson, with magnificent view of "Narrows," around Storm King Mt. It descends to **Cornwall-on-Hudson** at 7m.

**63. NEWBURGH** (sett.1709), whose streets run steeply downhill to R., is an industrial & tourist center. In Headquarters Pk. on Washington St. is **Hasbrouck H.** (O. wks.1725.adds.1749 & 1770), which was Washington's hqs., 1782 & 1783. Bldg. contains hist. paintings, engravings, furniture & relics. In Pk. are also **Mus.** (O.wks.) containing hist. relics & **Tower of Victory** comm. disbanding of Continental Army, Oct. 1783. SW. cor. Grand & 2nd Sts., **St. George Episc. Ch.** (1819.Gr.Rev.). NW.

cor. Grand & 1st Sts., **Associate Reformed Ch.** (1789 & 1821). Carpenter Ave., **Downing Pk.,** whose **Observ. Tower** affords fine view.

SIDE TRIP: Take St.32 (L) from Newburgh 2.5m to **Site of the Last Cantonment,** where Continental Army waited after surrender of Cornwallis, 1781, final signing of peace in 1783. At 4m is J. with Rd.

Take latter (R) 1m to **Temple Hill,** on which is **Temple Hill Mon.,** put up by Masons. Here in Mar. 1783, Washington read famous "Law & Order" speech urging soldiers to refrain from violence.

Just beyond last J., St.32 makes J. with St.45.

Take latter (R) 0.5m to **Gen. Knox Hqs.** (O.1734.1754.1782.int.inter.), occupied by Gen. Knox during "Last Cantonment."

**71.5.** (R) **COL. LOUIS DuBOIS H.** (c.1757). **78.5. HIGHLAND,** near W. end of Mid-Hudson Bridge to Poughkeepsie; here are Js. with St.299 & with US44 running (E) to conn. with St.22 (see US6).

SIDE TRIPS: (A) Take St.299 (L) 7m to **New Paltz** (mt.resort.accoms.recr.bath.), sett. c.1777 by Fr. Huguenots, emigrants from Rheinish Pfalz, some of whose descendants still live in vic. Near Front St., **Jean Hasbrouck H.** (1712), now maintained as mem. by 2 hist. societies. Near it, **Dan. DuBois H.** (1705.adds.1835), now tearoom. Near latter, **Bevier-Elting H.** (1699.adds.c.1735) & **Abr. Hasbrouck H.** (late 17th & early 18th cent.; fine example.int.inter.& exter.) & **Dutch Reformed Ch.** (1839.Gr.Rev.), founded 1683 as Fr. Prot. H. of worship.

(B) Take US44 (L) 21m to beautiful **L. Minnewaska** (O.Mem.Day-2nd wk.Oct.;accoms. recr.many fine trls.). 27m **Kerhonkson,** center for Shawangunk Mts. resorts (accoms.), at J. with US209 on which route cont. (L) to **Ellenville** (accoms.2 pub.bath.beaches.hik.trls. h.f.) at 35m on Ulster L., center of much-frequented vacation area, with many near-by resorts. US209 cont. to **Wurtsboro** (see St.17), 47m at J. with St.17 (see).

**85. WEST PARK.** Here is **John Burroughs Home** (1873.burned 1947.rebuilt), designed by author himself. Near-by is his **Bark Study.** Rd. leads (L) 1m to **Slabsides,** built by Burroughs to escape importunities of sightseers, which contains some orig. furnishings. US9W now runs near Hudson with view of Catskills (W). **94. KINGSTON,** at pt. where Rondout Cr. flows into Hudson. Town was sett. by Dutch in 1653 & played considerable role during Rev. St. Gov. met in Cth. in 1777 & there & in Senate H. was adopted St.'s earliest constitution. Brit. captured town & burned it in Oct. 1777. Delaware & Hudson Canal, which ran from Kingston into Pa., & river shipping accounted for much of city's prosperity during middle of 19th cent. PTS. OF INT.: (1) Clinton Ave. & N. Front & Fair Sts., **Senate H. & Mus.** (O.10:30-4:30.sm.fee.1676.Dutch Col.int.inter.), where St.'s legislature met in 1777, contains paintings & hist. relics. (2) Wall, Main & Fair Sts., **Dutch Reformed Ch.** (1852.Class. Rev.). (3) In adj. cemetery, **Grave of Geo. Clinton,** N.Y.'s 1st Gov. (4) Wall St., **Ulster County Cth.** (1818), on site of earlier bldg. where 1st constitution of St. was adopted in 1777. (5) N. Front & Green Sts., **Hoffman H.** (hqs. of Salvation Army; O.wks.;c.1660.later adds.) was one of few bldgs. to survive fire of 1777. (6) Wall St. opp. Franklin St., **Van Steenbergh H.** (N.O.;pre-Rev.adds.) in Rev. era was an inn. (7) 88 Maiden Lane, **Conrad Elmendorf Tavern** (N.O.1725) where Rev. Council of Safety met in Oct. 1777. (8) SW. cor. Crown & John Sts., **Old Kingston Academy** (O.appl.pre-Rev.), now newspaper office. (9) Crown & Green Sts., **D.A.R. Hqs.** occupy stone Tappan H. (pre-Rev.). **106. SAUGERTIES,** at confluence of Esopus Cr. & Hudson R., has many handsome old homes. 119 Main St., **Dubois Kiersteds H.** (N.O.;1727). **116.5.** J. with St.23A, running (W) into Catskills (see Catskill St. Pk.). **118. CATSKILL,** at mouth of Catskill Cr., derived its name from wildcats in fors. of vic. It was noted during Prohibition for its apple jack & Prohibition racketeers, who carried on operations here. On Spring St., **Thomas Cole H.** (1814), home of most famous of Hudson R. School of painters.

SIDE TRIP: Take St.385 (R) along R. 5m to **Athens.** Washington St., **Jan Van Loon H.** (1706). N. end of town, **Albertus Van Loon H.** (1706). At 11.5m **Coxsackie** (supposedly Ind. for "owl hoot"). In this town was issued in Jan. 1775, "Decl. of Ind." which antedated that of Continental Congress by more than a yr. At 13m, St.385 makes J. with US9W.

At **118.5.** on US9W is entrance (R) to **RIP VAN WINKLE BRIDGE,** which crosses to E. shore of Hudson R. **127. ST. VOCATIONAL INSTITUTION FOR BOYS,** which gives vocational training to delinquent youngsters. Opp. institution is **Bronck H.** (O.June-Nov.;1663 & 1738.int.exter.& inter.), built by Pieter Bronck, for whom borough of the Bronx in N.Y.C. was named. Behind H. is **Stepmother's H.** (1800), built for daughters of later Bronck who couldn't get along with their stepmother. **151. ALBANY** (see US20) at Js. with US20 (see) & US9 (see).

# US 11—NEW YORK

**ROUSES PT. (S) to N.Y.-PA. LINE** (8$^{m}$ from New Milford, Pa.). **327. US11**
Via: Malone, Potsdam, Watertown, Syracuse, Cortland, & Binghamton. RRs. parallel route. Through bus conns.

US11 follows huge arc S. of N.Y.-Canada line (SW) to Watertown near L. Ontario, then turns directly (S) past W. end of Oneida L. & through Syracuse across middle of St. to Binghamton. From its N. sec., Rds. branch off into Adirondacks (see Adirondack St. Pk.). From Watertown, Thousand Islands reg. is easily accessible.

**Sec. 1: ROUSES PT. to WATERTOWN. 168.**

**0. ROUSES PT.**, at Js. with US9 (see) & US2 (see Vt.). **42. CHATEAUGAY,** sett. by Fr. Canadians in 1796. Here is J. with St.374 (see US9), which runs (SW) to J. with St.3 9$^{m}$ (W) from Plattsburg at J. with US9 (see). **55.5. MALONE** (sett.1802) is sm. industrial city on Salmon R. Pop. is largely Fr. Canadian. Here is J. with St.10, leading (S) into Adirondacks (see Adirondack St. Pk.).

SIDE TRIP: Take St.37 (R) from Malone. This is alt. route to US11, running close to St. Lawrence R. 20$^{m}$, **St. Regis Ind. Reserv.** extending into Canada & inhabited by approx. 3,000 Inds. 25$^{m}$, **Hogansburg** has **Trading Post** exhibiting Ind. handicrafts. 28$^{m}$ **Rooseveltown,** from which Internat. Bridge (toll) crosses to Cornwall, Canada. 37.5$^{m}$, **Massena,** formerly watering resort, popular for its mineral springs, is now dairy products & industrial center, powered by electricity generated by Grass R. Canal. Massena Works of **Aluminum Co. of America** (O.appl.) is one of world's largest aluminum producers. At 52.5$^{m}$ is J. with Rd. leading (R) to Waddington-Morrisburg Ferry (toll). At 73.5$^{m}$ is J. with Rd. leading (R) 0.5$^{m}$ to **St. Lawrence Fish Hatchery** (O.summers). 75$^{m}$ **Ogdensburg,** which grew up around **Ft. La Presentation** (1749) at confluence of St. Lawrence & Oswegatchie Rs., with deep-water port, has milk products, silk & clothing & other plants run by hydroelectric power. Town is largely inhabited by people of Fr.-Canadian origin; Canada Day is chief annual event. From Ogdensburg in 1837 was launched an attack by Canadians & Amers. in abortive attempt to win Canada's independence. Washington & State Sts., **Remington Art Mem.** (O.1809) containing art works & relics of Fred. Remington. **Pub. Lib.** contains coll. of Ind. artifacts. East River St., **Maple Cty. Mill** (1797.int.inter.). On outskirts, **Judge J. Fine H.** with old barn used as ft. in War of 1812. Near-by, **Vanden Heuvel H.** (1830). 86$^{m}$ **Morristown** (resort.fish.), near beginning of Thousand Islands. 108.5$^{m}$ **Redwood** (resort.accoms.), bet. Butterfield & Mud Ls., is at J. with St.26B, running (R) to J. with St.26 which cont. to Alexandria Bay (see below). St.37 cont. to **Watertown** (see below), 134$^{m}$, at J. with US11.

**97. POTSDAM** (accoms.camp.recr.) on Raquette R., is tourist, educational, & dairying center dating back to 1804. Here are **Potsdam St. Normal Sch.** & **Thos. S. Clarkson Mem. College of Technology.** St.56 leads (L) 5$^{m}$ from Potsdam to impressive **Hannawa Falls** (85') of Raquette R. **108. CANTON** (accoms.), at Grass & Little Rs., where is St.-operated **St. Lawrence Univ.** (chartered 1856.coed.). On Miner St., **Remington H.** (N.O.), birthpl. of Fred. Remington, well-known Amer. painter of Western subjects. **131. GOUVERNEUR,** trading center of lead, talc, & zinc mining district, where is **Gouverneur Morris H.** (1809), in which Morris, who had been Minister to France, sett. toward end of his life. At **143.5.** is J. with Rd. leading (R) 6$^{m}$ to **Oxbow** on Oswegatchie R. Here Jos. Bonaparte built **Benton H.** (1838) & lived for short time with his mistress, Annette Savage, & their daughter, Caroline. **158. EVANS MILLS.**

SIDE TRIP: Take Rd. (L) from Evans Mills 3$^{m}$ to **Leraysville,** where turn (R) on dirt Rd. to **LeRay H.** (O.appl.1806-08.Fr.Ren.), 3.5$^{m}$, built by Fr. nobleman James LeRay de Chaumont.

**168. WATERTOWN,** pt. of departure for Thousand Islands resorts & L. Ontario, is industrial center dating back to 1800, when 1st settlers came to utilize power resources of Black River Falls. 228 Washington St., **Jefferson Cty. Hist. Bldg.** houses Ind. & pioneer relics. Watertown is at Js. with St.37 (see above) & St.12 (see St.5), which runs (SE) to J. with St.5 at Utica.

SIDE TRIPS: (A) Take St.12 (R) from Watertown 21.5$^{m}$ to **Clayton,** on St. Lawrence R., port & RR. terminal & gateway to Thousand Islands Reg., nationally famous as recr. center, attracting crowds of summer vacationists. More than 1,700 islands dot broad expanse of St. Lawrence R. here, where it merges with L. Ontario. State pks., sm. fishing villages & numerous bays & inlets are meccas for boating, bathing & fishing enthusiasts. Well stocked waters incl. black bass, muskellunge, perch, pike, pickerel & other species. Facils. for golf, tennis, dancing & other sports are available. From Clayton boats are avail. to **Canoe Pt. & Picnic Pt. St. Pks.** (camp.boat.bath.pic.f.) on Grindstone Is. Ferry (toll) crosses St. Lawrence to Gananoque, Can.

Take St.12E (L) from Clayton. At 3m **Bartlett's Pt. St. Campsite.** 9m, **Cedar Pt. St. Pk.** (camp.bath.f.dancing). 11m **Burnham Pt. St. Pk.** (camp.bath.boat.pic.). 15m **Cape St. Vincent** (resort.good f.accoms.) where many Fr. Napoleonic emigrés sett. At 21.5m is J. with Long Pt. Rd. leading (R) 7.5m to gravel Rd. which turns 1.5m (L) to **Long Pt. St. Pk.** (camp.boat.bath.pic.f.), on Chaumont Bay of L. Ontario. At 41m St.12E reaches Watertown.

St.12 cont. (R) from Clayton to **Grass Pt. St. Pk.,** 27m. At 29m is **Internat. Bridge** (toll) crossing via Wells & Hill Is. to Rockport, Canada. From bridge Rds. run to **Dewolf Pt. St. Pk.** (camp.boat.bath.pic.) & **Watterson Pt. St. Pk.** (bath.pic.) on Wells I. 33.5m **Alexandria Bay** (accoms.all types.motorboat tours on R. through Is.). From Alexandria Bay, **Mary I. & Cedar I. St. Pks.** (camp.boat.bath.pic.f.) can be reached by boat. Visible on Heart I. is turreted, castellated **Boldt Castle,** abandoned, built by hotel magnate Geo. C. Boldt for his wife. Rd. cont. from Alexandria Bay 10m along R. to **Kring Pt. St. Pk.** (camp.boat.bath. pic.f.), jutting out into St. Lawrence.

(B) Take St.3 (R) from Watertown. At 9m is J. with Sacketts Harbor Rd. leading (R) 1.5m to **Sacketts Harbor** (accoms.pub.bath.beaches.pic.boat.f.), sett. 1801, on Black R. Bay of L. Ontario. Here is **Madison Barracks,** U.S. Army Post at which Gen. U.S. Grant was stationed 1843-49. Main St., **Old Union Hotel** (1817), containing coll. of Ind. & War of 1812 relics, & **Augustus Sackett H.** (L) (1801). N. end Main St., **Sacketts Harbor Battlefield** where was fought Battle of Sacketts Harbor in July, 1812, when 1 Amer. ship & land force of farmers repulsed 5 Brit. battleships. 40m **Port Ontario,** where is **Selkirk Shores St. Pk.** (camp.cabins.pic.f.). 48m **Mexico** at J. with US104, which tour now follows (R).

Take Rd. (R) from Mexico 5.5m to **Spy St. Pk.** in Little Salmon R., burial place of Silas Towne, Amer. spy who warned patriots at Ft. Stanwix of approach of Brit. in 1777.

63.5m **Oswego,** easternmost Great Ls. port & Barge Canal terminal, at mouth of Oswego R., grew up around ft. built here in 1722, captured by Fr. in 1756 but recaptured in 1759 by Brit., who held it until 1796. It soon became important shipping center. Here in 1841 was built "Vandalia," 1st steamboat with screw propeller. E. side Oswego R., **U.S. Military Reserv.,** with pentagonal old **Ft. Ontario** (1755). Oneida & W. 1st Sts., **Pontiac Boulder,** comm. council held in Oswego in 1766 by Sir Wm. Johnson & Chief Pontiac which resulted in cession of Great Ls. reg. to Gr. Britain. Oswego Harbor with its extensive terminal facils. is well worth visit. 24 W. 2nd St., **Cooper H.** (N.O.) where Jas. F. Cooper lived while serving in Oswego as midshipman. Geo. Washington Blvd., **Oswego St. Normal School** (1866). Oswego is at J. with St.57 (see St.5), running (S) to J. with St.5 (see) at Syracuse.

US104 cont. (W) along L. Ontario. At 85m is J. with St.104A leading (R) 5.5m to J. with Rd. which turns (L) to **Fairhaven Beach St. Pk.** (816 as.pic.swim.) at 7.5m. US104 now runs through orchard reg.; apples are chief crop. At 97.5m is **Resort,** vacation pt. on Sodus Bay, in which grows profusely Amer. lotus. Rochester (see US15), 137.5m, is at J. with US15.

### Sec. 2: WATERTOWN to N.Y.-PA. LINE. 159.

US11 now cuts (S) across L. Ontario plain through several sm. towns & past E. end of Oneida L. to **SYRACUSE** (see St.5) at J. with St.5, **69.5.** At **75.** is J. with St.11A.

SIDE TRIP: Take latter (R) 1m to **Onondaga Ind. Reserv.,** whose self-governing inhabitants hold festivals in June, Aug. & Oct. At 2m is **Onondaga Council H.** Near-by is **Grave of Handsome Lake,** famous 19th cent. Ind. prophet.

**81.5. LAFAYETTE** & J. with US20 (see). **101. HOMER,** which was home of "David Harum" in E. N. Westcott's novel of same name, who in real life was David Hannum, kindly but astute Yankee trader. In town is **Homer Art Gallery** (O), in Homer Academy. **104. CORTLAND,** with large Ital. colony, has several factories. At **127.5.** is J. with St.79.

SIDE TRIP: Take latter (L) 12.5m to J. with St.369 & turn (R) on latter to **Chenango Valley St. Pk.** (928 as.camp.cabins.pic.boat.bath.f.hik.riding.golf.athletic facils.) at 15m.

**146.5. BINGHAMTON** (see St.17), at J. with St.17 (see). US11 cont. (S) to **N.Y.-PA. LINE, 159.**

## US 15—NEW YORK

### ROCHESTER (S) to N.Y.-PA. LINE. 102.5. US15

Via: Bath & Painted Post. RRs. parallel parts of route.

US15 crosses rural reg. of western N.Y. St.

**0. ROCHESTER**

Through RR., bus & plane conns. Ferry to Ontario; steamship serv. to L. Ontario & St. Lawrence R. pts. Accoms.: Ample. Info.: C. of C., 55 St. Paul St. Rd. shows at Masonic Temple, local productions at Community Playh.; baseball at Red Wing Stadium; boxing & wrestling at Sports Arena, Edgerton Pk.; golf at Genesee Valley & Durand-Eastman Pks.; tennis at most city pks.; swim. at Genesee Valley, Seneca, Ontario Beach & Durand-Eastman Pks. Annual Events: Easter Flower Show, Highland Pk.; Music Festival, Eastman Theater, Ap.; Lilac Display, Highland Pk., May or June; Rochester Symphony Orchestra season, Oct.-Ap.

Third largest city in N.Y. St., Rochester is important mfg. center with many specialized industries but lacks usual grimy factory-town atmosphere: its plants, mostly clean & modern-looking & set in park-like grounds, are dispersed throughout city. Rochester is notable for handsome floral displays in gardens & pks. & shaded residential areas; home of Eastman Sch. of Music, it is as well known for its musical as for its industrial activities & offers wide variety of other cultural & educational facils. City spreads more than $12^m$ along banks of Genesee R., which is bordered by many pks. & (N) of downtown sec., which it bisects, R. flows through scenic gorge to L. Ontario. Rochester is world's leading center for manufacture of photographic equipment & notable producer of men's clothing & accessories; it also leads in production of optical goods, dental & medical equipment, & other articles.

First settler was Ebenezer ("Indian") Allen, who built grist mill & sawmill at upper falls of Genesee in 1789. Col. Nath. Rochester, with 2 other Md. gentlemen, Col. Wm. Fitzhugh & Maj. Chas. Carroll, bought Allen's 100-a. tract in 1803 & 8 yrs. later, Rochester offered lots for sale. Opening of Erie Canal in 1824 provided transportation for flour ground in many mills along Genesee. By 1834, when Rochester was inc. as city, it was famous as "Flour City." Later nursery industry rose to worldwide fame: "Flour City" became "Flower City." By 1850 Rochester was city of 40,000. Among famous residents were Fox Sisters, pioneer spiritualists; Frederick Douglass, who edited "North Star"; Susan B. Anthony, advocate of women's rights. After Civil War, shoe & clothing industries rapidly developed mass-production methods. At same time, specialized industries mfg. thermometers, optical goods & gear-cutting machines developed; in 1880 Geo. Eastman began production of photographic dry plates & in 1888, of Kodaks. Industrial prosperity led to civic beautification. Eventually city put forth 2 long fingers to shore of L. Ontario, where harbor with piers & terminal facils. was developed.

PTS. OF INT.: (1) Fitzhugh & Broad Sts., **City Hall** (1875.Vict.Goth.by A.J.Warner). (2) 17 S. Fitzhugh St., **St. Luke's Ch.** (Episc.1824.Goth.) is city's oldest ch. (3) 55 Plymouth Ave. S., **Rochester Institute of Technology** is trade sch. grown out of merger of Athenaeum (est.1829) & Mechanics' Institute (est.1885). (4) Its Sch. of Arts, around cor. at Washington & Spring Sts., occupies **Bevier Mem. Hall** (1910. by Claude F.Bragdon) on site of Col. Nath. Rochester's home. (5) 37 S. Washington St., **4th Ch. of Christ Scientist** occupies former Jonathan Child H. (1837.Gr.Rev.), built by city's 1st mayor. (6) Plymouth Ave. S. & Troup St., **Fox Sisters' H.** (post. Col.) was occupied after 1848 by founders of modern spiritualism, who conducted seances here. (7) Plymouth Ave. S. & Troup St., **Plymouth Ave. Spiritualist Ch.** (1853.Vict.Goth.) is mother ch. of modern spiritualism. (8) S. Fitzhugh & Troup Sts., **Campbell-Whittlesey H.** (O.Tues.& Thurs.& Sun.p.m.1835.outstanding Gr.Rev.), built for wealthy miller Benj. Campbell, is authentically furnished & preserved as typical early Rochester home. (9) 115 South Ave., **Rundel Lib.** (O.Tues.-Sat.9-9.1936. Mod.Class.by Gordon & Kaelber & Leonard A.Wassdorp), named for patron Morton W. Rundel, is Rochester's pub. lib.; it presents current art exhibits on 2nd fl. gallery (O.12 p.m.-9 p.m.wks.). (10) Central Ave. & St. Paul St., **Frederick Douglass Mon.** (1899.by Sidney W.Edwards). (11) Central Ave. bet. Joseph Ave. & Clinton Ave. N., **N.Y. Central RR. Sta.** (1914.Mod.neo-Class.by Claude F.Bragdon), architecturally notable. (12) State & Platt Sts., **Kodak Tower** (1913.Mod.Fr.Ren.), 19 stories, is hqs. of Eastman-Kodak organization. (13) 635 St. Paul St., **Bausch & Lomb Optical Plant** (O.wks.), largest of its type in U.S. (14) St. Paul & Bausch Sts., **Lomb Mem.** (1930.by Walter Cassebeer & Lewis Brew), granite shaft 48′ high, comm. Capt. Henry Lomb. (15) Adj. is **Bausch Mem. Bridge,** with 945′ steel cantilever span, at whose approaches are bronze tablets comm. John Jacob Bausch.

(16) 485 East Ave., **Rochester Hist. Soc. Mus.** (O.wks.Sat.a.m.) exhibits materials pertaining to Rochester & vic. (17) Backus St. & Phelps Ave., **Edgerton Pk.** (63 as. winter athletics). (18) Lake & Driving Pk. Aves., **Maplewood Pk.** (145 as.pic.ice skating in winter), on W. bank of Genesee. (19) Lake Ave. & Ridge Rd. W., **Kodak Pk.** (O.wks.conducted tours), chief Rochester plant of Eastman Kodak Co., city in itself with more than 80 bldgs. At entrance is **Eastman Mem.,** plaza with pedestal on which is urn containing ashes of Geo. Eastman. (20) Ridge Rd. & Genesee R., **Veterans' Mem. Bridge** (1931.by Gehron & Ross), city's longest, 981′, praised for classic architecture. (21) 2260 Lake Ave., **St. Bernard's Theological Seminary** (Cath. est.1893) occupies group of red sandstone Goth. bldgs. (22) Foot of Lighthouse St. near Lake Ave., **Old Charlotte Lighth.** (1822). (23) Foot of Lake Ave., **Ontario**

**Beach Pk.** (swim.pic.playgrounds), with sandy beach on L. Ontario. (24) W. bank of Genesee R. at L. front, **Port of Rochester,** with 1,200′ dock & passenger & freight terminal. (25) Lake Shore Blvd., **Durand-Eastman Pk.** (506 as.swim.f.pic.golf), on L. Ontario, has zoo & several sm. Ls. (26) 3000 Ridge Rd. E., **Ward's Natural Science Establishment** (O.wks.), with minerals, fossils & other natural science specimens. (27) Monroe & Highland Aves., **Cobbs Hill Pk.,** with large reservoir, on hill 636′ high with Lookout Tower (telescope). (28) 4245 East Ave., **Nazareth College** (Cath.), women's institution. (29) 900 East Ave., **Geo. Eastman H.** (1906.Georg.Col.), built by Geo. Eastman, now instruction & demonstration center covering photography from beginnings to latest developments, with Eastman colls. of photographs & paintings, conducted jointly by Eastman Kodak Co. & Univ. of Rochester. Adj. is **Dryden Theater.** (30) 657 East Ave., **Rochester Mus. of Arts & Sciences** (O.Tues.-Sat.Sun. p.m.), with Ind., natural science, geological, Americana & early Rochester exhibits & hist. dioramas. (31) Prince St. & Univ. Ave., **Prince St. Campus** (27 as.) of **Univ. of Rochester** is occupied by College for Women. Univ. of Rochester, one of half dozen most heavily endowed univs. in U.S., was founded in 1850; it comprises 6 colleges & schs. giving courses in arts & sciences, medicine & dentistry, music, engineering, optics & nursing. Among bldgs. on Prince St. Campus are **Mem. Art Gallery** (O.Tues.-Sat.;Sun.& Mon.p.m.1913.Ital.Ren.); **Cutler Union** (1933.Eng.Coll. Goth.); & **Anderson Hall** (1861). (32) 800 Main St. E., **Rochester Dental Dispensary,** est. & endowed by Geo. Eastman in 1916. (33) Gibbs St. & Main St. E., **Eastman Sch. of Music** of Univ. of Rochester (1922.Mod.Ital.Ren.by Gordon & Kaelber & McKim,Mead & White), nationally outstanding, occupies bldg. in which are Eastman Theater, Kilbourn Hall & Art Gallery. (34) 46 Swan St., **Sibley Musical Lib.** of Univ. of Rochester, occupies only bldg. in U.S. devoted exclusively to musical literature. (35) River Blvd. & Elmwood Ave., **River Campus of Univ. of Rochester** on bluff overlooking Genesee, opened in 1930, is occupied by College for Men. Its Georg. style bldgs. incl. **Rush-Rhees Lib.,** with 186′ tower; **John J. Bausch-Henry Lomb Mem. Lab.** for study of applied optics; **Chester Dewey Bldg.,** in which is **Mus. of Nat. Hist.,** with botanical & geological colls.; **Harkness Hall,** 1st naval science bldg. erected outside U.S. Naval Academy at Annapolis; **Henry Alvah Strong Auditorium; Engineering Bldg.; Industrial X-Ray Lab.,** with 1,000,000-volt machine. Here also are large cyclotron & associated lab. for atomic research. (36) 260 Crittenden Blvd., **Sch. of Medicine & Dentistry** of Univ. of Rochester, combined with Strong Mem. & Mun. Hospitals & Sch. of Nursing. (37) S. Goodman St. & Highland Ave., **Colgate-Rochester Divinity Sch.,** operated by Bapt. Education Soc., with group of Eng. Goth. bldgs. on hilltop campus. (38) Reservoir & South Aves., **Highland Pk.** (108 as.), notable for displays of flowers in greenhouses & conservatories, especially lilac display in May. (39) 791 Mt. Hope Ave., **Mt. Hope Cemetery** contains graves of Col. Nath. Rochester, Frederick Douglass & Susan B. Anthony. (40) Elmwood Ave. & River Blvd., **Genesee Valley Pk.** (640 as.boat.pic.golf.sports), where Genesee R., Red Cr. & Barge Canal converge.

SIDE TRIP: Take US104 (W) from Rochester. At 17$^m$ is J. with St.19.

(1) Take latter (R) 6$^m$ to J. with St.360, on which turn (L) 2$^m$ to J. with St.215, & turn (R) on latter to **Hamlin Beach St. Pk.** (600 as.bath.pic.) on L. Ontario.

(2) Take St.19 (L) 1$^m$ to **Brockport,** nursery & cannery center, with **Brockport St. Normal Sch.,** opened 1841.

At 31.5$^m$ is J. with St.98, leading (L) 3$^m$ to **Albion,** with vegetable canning & freezing plant, where is **Pullman Mem. Universalist Ch.,** Main St. & E. Park Ave., on site of home of Geo. Pullman, cabinetmaker here 1848-55, who in 1858 built 1st RR. passenger cars of type known by his name. At 42.5$^m$ on US104 is J. with St.63 leading (L) 4$^m$ to **Medina,** industrial community with iron foundries & **H. J. Heinz Plant** canning many of "57" varieties. At 59.5$^m$ is J. with St.78, leading (L) 4$^m$ to **Lockport,** milling center & industrial city on Barge Canal. **Canal Bridge,** 452′ wide, affords view of 2 locks which raise & lower barges 60′, replacing set of 10 locks on old Erie Canal. US104 cont. past **Tuscarora Ind. Reserv.** (c.6,300 as.), 77$^m$, where inhabitants receive some aid from Fed. Gov. but are self-governing. 78.5$^m$ **Lewiston** on Niagara R., sett. c.1796. Settlement was wiped out by Brit. in War of 1812. On Center St., **Frontier H.** (1824.adds.c.1830) where Jas. Fenimore Cooper is supposed to have written "The Spy." From Lewiston, bridge crosses to Ontario, Canada.

Take St.18F (R) from Lewiston via **Youngstown** to **Ft. Niagara** (O.sm.fee.1725.adds. 1756.rest.1934) 7$^m$, last of several fts. built by Fr. at this strategic pt. commanding entrances to L. Ontario & L. Erie. It was attacked & taken by Brit. under Sir Wm. Johnson in 1759 & again in War of 1812. On grounds are various mons.; **Castle** (1725.int. inter.), where during Rev., when Wm. Butler & his followers & Ind. allies made their hqs. here, Amer. scalps, for which Brit. offered bounty, were brought; **Poisoned Well,** supposed to be haunted by headless Frenchmen; & **Bakeshop,** built by Fr. & rebuilt (1759) by Brit.

US104 cont. to **Niagara Falls** (see St.5), 84.5m, at J. with St.324 conn. with St.5 at Buffalo (see St.5).

From Rochester, US15 runs (S) to J. with US20 (see) at **18.** & J. with US20A (see US20) at **23.5.;** it unites with latter to **LIVONIA, 26.** At **46.5.** is **WAYLAND,** center of potato-growing reg., with vegetable canneries.

SIDE TRIP: Take St.63 (R) from Wayland 6.5m to **Dansville,** nursery & industrial community, from which St.36 runs (S) 3m to **Stony Brook St. Pk.** (560 as.) with many waterfalls in rocky gorge.

**63.5. AVOCA** turns out various woodworkers' products. Saddlery, knit goods & ladders are produced at **BATH, 71.,** founded 1793. Bath is at J. with St.54 (see US20) running (NE) to J. with St.14, which conn. with US20 (see). At **PAINTED POST** (see St.17), **90.,** is J. with St.17 (see), with which US15 unites for 4m. US15 cont. (S) to **N.Y.-PA. LINE** at **102.5.**

## ADIRONDACK STATE PARK

RRs.: N.Y. Central RR. (N) from Utica gives access to Raquette, Tupper & Upper Saranac Ls. & other pts. on W. side of pk. Delaware & Hudson RR. runs (N) from Saratoga Springs to L. George Village & to North Cr., in SE. sec. of pk., & along L. Champlain bet. Ticonderoga & Plattsburg on E. side of Pk. Hys.: US9 (see) running (N) from Saratoga Springs through E. Adirondacks, via Schroon L. & Elizabethtown conn. with St. routes leading across pk. Accoms.: All types at larger resort centers & on most of larger Ls. 25 large pub. campsites (free.no cabins. permits good for 2 wks. but may be renewed). No permit required outside pub. campsites for camping 3 days or less in 1 place; permits for longer stays available from for. rangers. Shelters have been erected along trls. & on many Ls. Info. on trls. & canoe routes may be obtained at hotels.

Adirondack St. Pk., est. in 1892, gradually has been expanded to more than 4,600,-000 as., of which c.2,150,000 are actually owned by St. Fires & lumbering have destroyed all but few patches of 1st-growth timber; but 2nd-growth trees, in some districts 100 yrs. old, provide fine forest cover. Adirondack Mts., irregular mass of tumbled peaks & deep gorges, belong to upper Laurentian system of Canada, oldest known strata of earth's crust. Pk. extends from Ls. George & Champlain in E. to Black R. Valley in W. & from line roughly 40m below Canadian border & St. Lawrence R. in N. to line roughly 15m above Mohawk R. in S. There are more than 5,000 Ls., over 1,000 of considerable size. Mts. Marcy & McIntyre reach 5,000′ & 46 other peaks run to 4,000′ or higher. Adirondacks have 2 watersheds: one draining (S) into tributaries of Hudson, other draining (N) into tributaries of St. Lawrence & L. Champlain.

Adirondack (Ind., "Bark Eaters") was name derisively applied to branch of Algonquin tribe because during winter they found themselves forced to resort for food to bark of trees; but reg. itself was never permanently occupied by Inds. First white settler appears to have been Wm. Gilliland who est. himself in 1765 on Bouquet R. near L. Champlain. After 1800 exploitation of iron deposits was begun. Especially during 2nd half of 19th cent. lumber companies attacked magnificent fors. of Adirondacks with ruthless energy. Vacation possibilities of Adirondacks were 1st discovered by Amer. painter, Wm. S. Gifford, who spent some time at Saranac L. & then persuaded several Boston intellectuals to accompany him on expedition into mts. Adirondack Club was organized following yr., with Emerson, Agassiz, Lowell & John Holmes as members; & in 1858 Wm. J. Stillman bought Ampersand L. as home for it. Keene Valley became center for considerable group of artists. Saranac became famous in medical science when Dr. Edw. Livingston Trudeau was carried there on stretcher apparently dying of tuberculosis. He recovered & est. lab. & sanatorium. Since those early days Adirondacks have become one of great vacation resorts of E. & most of pop. lives off vacationists (summer & winter).

### PARK TOURS

**I: GLENS FALLS (N) to J. with St.373. 102.5. US9**

**0. GLENS FALLS** (see US9). **6. WILLIAMS MON.,** comm. Col. Ephraim Williams, killed here in skirmish preceding Battle of L. George in 1755. **7.5.** J. with St.9K.

SIDE TRIP: Take latter (L) past **L. Vanare** (swim.boat.f.riding), 7.5m, & **L. Forest,** 9.5m, on shores of which are dude ranches, to **L. Luzerne** (all-yr.resort.ski trls.), 10m. Here route turns (L) on paved Rd. to **Conklingville Dam,** 16.5m, impounding 27m-long **Sacandaga Reservoir** (boat.swim.f.). Cont. along NW. shore of reservoir to **Edinburg,** 33.5m, where route turns (R) again to **Northville** (resort.accoms.swim.), 38.5m, on reservoir at J. with St.30, running (S) 24m to Amsterdam (see St.5) at J. with St.5. Turn (R) on St.30 & follow Sacandaga R. (N) to **Sacandaga Pub. Campsite,** c.53m. St.30 cont. (N) to J. at 61m with St.8, running (NE) to J. with St.28 (see Pk. Tour III).

**8. FT. GAGE PK.** on site of Ft. Gage, which figured in Fr. & Ind. Wars. **8.5.** Entrance to **L. GEORGE BATTLEGROUND PK.** (camp.) marked by **Mon.** with statues of King Hendrick, Mohawk chief, & Sir Wm. Johnson. Battle took place Sept. 1755. Colonials, after heavy fighting, defeated Fr. In Pk. are **Father Isaac Jogues Mon.** (by Chas.Keck), comm. Jesuit martyr who worked as missionary among Five Nations, & **Ruins of Ft. George,** built by Gen. Amherst in 1759. **9. L. GEORGE VILLAGE** (resort.winter sports near-by), at S. end of beautiful 32m-long L. of same name, along whose shores bet. this pt. & Ticonderoga (see Pk. Tour II) at N. end are many camps, resorts & summer residences (bus & steamer serv.from L.George Village to Ticonderoga). Here is Ft. Wm. Henry Hotel, on whose grounds are **Ruins of Ft. Wm. Henry,** erected by Sir Wm. Johnson & captured by Montcalm in 1758. Trl. runs up **Prospect Mt.** (2,027′) from Montcalm St. Ls. George & Champlain, because they afforded best passage from Canada to Hudson R., were for almost a century scene of struggle for possession of N. America bet. Brit. & Fr. In 1646 Jesuit missionary Father Jogues, martyred by Inds., discovered L. & called it Lac du Saint Sacrement. Sir Wm. Johnson renamed it L. George. Fr. built fts. at Crown Pt. & then at Ticonderoga, around which conflict raged. First Fr. expedition was led by Frontenac in 1693. In 1745 Fr. again came down Ls. & captured Ft. Edward & Saratoga. In 1755 Sir Wm. Johnson defeated Fr. Gen. Dieskau in engagement near present village of L. George, in which Col. Ephraim Williams & Chief Hendrick were killed. He then built, at foot of L., Ft. Wm. Henry which in 1757 Fr. commander Vaudreuil unsuccessfully attacked but which later Montcalm captured & destroyed. During this period Rbt. Rogers & his rangers operated in guerrilla fashion against Inds. & Fr. In 1758 Abercrombie set out to capture Ft. Ticonderoga, but failed; in 1759 Lord Amherst with 11,000 troops succeeded. During Rev., Crown Pt. & Ticonderoga changed hands several times. Ticonderoga was captured by Amers. under Ethan Allen. Crown Pt. was captured by Seth Warner. Not long after, however, Burgoyne on his advance to make J. with Clinton in Hudson Valley, recaptured both fts.

**10.** J. with St.9N (see Pk. Tour II). **16. WARRENSBURG,** sett. 1804. **28. CHESTERTOWN.** US9 now passes through reg. of many Ls., circling round one of largest, **Loon L.,** to **POTTERSVILLE, 36.5.,** near which are **Adirondack Natural Stone Bridge & Caves. 38.5. EAGLE POINT ST. CAMPSITE** (R) on **Schroon L.** whose W. shore US9 now skirts, with fine views, especially of **Pharo Mt.** (2,557′). **45.5. SCHROON L. VILLAGE** (resort), center of recr. area. **48.5.** J. with St.73, picturesque route running (E) through village of **Severance** & past beautiful **Paradox L.,** where is Pub. Campsite, & **Eagle L.** to Ticonderoga (see Pk. Tour II), 19m, at J. with St.9W (see Pk. Tour II). **52.5. SCHROON R.,** at J. with Rd.

SIDE TRIP: Take latter (L) through **Blue Ridge,** 5m. At c.10m take poor dirt Rd. (R) to **Clear Pond** at c.14m & **Elk L.** at c.15m. These are 2 of most beautiful Ls. in Adirondacks.

**61.5. SHARP BRIDGE PUB. CAMPSITE. 65.5. UNDERWOOD,** fine starting pt. for trips to near-by Ls. (good f.). **66.5.** J. with St.86A (see Pk. Tour IV). **77. ELIZABETHTOWN,** mt.-enclosed summer resort. Here in **Essex County Cth.** is painting of trial of John Brown. After he was hanged, his body was laid out in bldg. on its way to burial at N. Elba (see Pk. Tour IV). **92.5. POKE-O-MOONSHINE PUB. CAMPSITE** (O.May 30-Labor Day). Its name derives from illicit liquor distilling & running during Prohibition era. From here trl. runs to summit of **Poke-O-Moonshine Mt.** (2,162′). **100. KEESEVILLE,** sett. 1806 by John Keese. **102.** Bridge over **AUSABLE CHASM.** Here are fine **Rainbow Falls** & entrance to **Chasm** (O.May-Oct.foot & boat tour.fee), one of scenic high pts. of N.Y. St. & well worth visiting. **102.5.** J. with St.373, which runs (E) 2m to **Port Kent** on L. Champlain, whence ferry runs to Burlington, Vt., at J. with US7. US9 now leaves Adirondack St. Pk.

**II: J. with US9** (1m from L. George Village) **(N) to J. with US9** (5m from Keeseville). **86. St.9W, St.22**

**0.** J. with US9 (1$^{m}$ N. of L. George Village). **2. HEARTHSTONE PUB. CAMPSITE.** St.9W follows W. shore of L. George which provides good black bass & lake-trout fishing, past many fine resorts & summer residences. At **9.5. BOLTON LANDING** (resort.accoms.recr.camp.outfits & boats for rent), best. pt. for trips to St.-owned Is., of which there are 155, more than half of them suitable for camping (secure free permits from for. ranger's hqs.). **21.5. SABBATH DAY PT.** (resort. recr.) at foot of **Catamount Mt.** (2,304′) (L). **23.5. SILVER BAY. 27. HAGUE. 36. TICONDEROGA,** flanked by Ls. George & Champlain, is tourist & pencil & paper mfg. center. Montcalm St. & Moses Circle, **N.Y. St. Hist. Assoc. Hqs. H.** is replica of John Hancock H. in Boston & contains period furniture, paintings, prints, rare mss., hist. relics, etc. 159 Montcalm St., **Black Watch Mem. Lib.** comm. Royal Highlanders who fell at Battle of Ticonderoga, 1758. Montcalm St. at Moses Circle, **Liberty Mon.** (by Chas.Keck). In Ticonderoga is J. with St.347, leading (R) 1.5$^{m}$ to grounds of **Ft. Ticonderoga** (O.May-Nov.fee), which is under private restoration. Fort was built in 1755 by Fr. & withstood attack in 1758 by Brit. During Rev. it was captured May 1775 in surprise attack by Ethan Allen & his Green Mt. Boys & recaptured by Burgoyne in 1777. In ft. is mus. containing hist. documents, paintings, etc., & on grounds are various mons. From St.347 ferry crosses L. Champlain to Larrabees Pt., Vt. St.9W, now combined with St.22, cont. (N) to J. at **48.** with St.8.

SIDE TRIP: Take latter (R) 3.5$^{m}$ to entrance to **Crown Pt. Reserv.** (camp.) on L. Champlain. Here is log reprod. of **Fr. Trading Post.** St.8 now passes ruins of **Light Infantry Post & Champlain Mem. Lighth.** comm. Champlain, L.'s discoverer, with low relief, "La France," by Rodin. At 4$^{m}$ is **L. Champlain Bridge** (toll) crossing to Chimney Pt., Vt. Just beyond bridge are ruins of **Ft. St. Frederic,** built by Fr. in 1731 but destroyed by them when Gen. Amherst approached in 1759. Near ft. is **Mus.** (O.summer) containing coll. of hist. Ind. material. Just beyond are ruins of **Ft. Crown Pt.,** built in 1759 by Gen. Amherst. Remains of 2 barracks have been kept fairly intact. Ethan Allen captured ft. during Rev.

St.9N-22 now runs close to L. shore. **51. PORT HENRY,** refining point for iron ore mines in vic. & winter smelt fishing center. **61. WESTPORT** where St.9N turns (W) to J. with US9 at Elizabethtown (see Pk. Tour I). **73. ESSEX,** tourist center (ferry to Charlotte, Vt.). St.22 cont. close to L. front into **WILLSBORO, 78.,** & then turns inland to J. with US9 (see Pk. Tour I) at **86.**

**III. J. with US9 (W) to J. with St.12. 109. St.28**

**0.** J. with US9 (see Pk. Tour I). Take St.28 (L) **5.** to **THE GLEN** (resort). **10. WEVERTOWN,** at J. with St.8.

SIDE TRIP: Take latter (L) 1.5$^{m}$ to **Johnsburg,** just (W) of which is J. with dirt Rd. running (L) 8$^{m}$ to **Garnet L.** (accoms.). 23$^{m}$ J. with St.30 (see Pk. Tour I). 34$^{m}$ **Speculator** (accoms.5 trls.with camp.& winter sports facils.) on **Pleasant L.,** from which run trls. to **Speculator Mt.** (2,973′) & **Hamilton Mt.** (3,250′). Here is J. with St.10 which unites (S) with St.8 for 9$^{m}$.

Take St.10 (N) here, unpaved (inquire locally about Rd. conditions) past **Lewey L.** & **Lewey L. Pub. Campsite** (boat.f.h.) & then along (W) shore of **Ind. L.** to **Sabael,** named for Quebec Ind., Benedict Sabael, who married Dutch woman & sett. here in 1765. At 27$^{m}$ is **Ind. L. Village,** at J. with St.28 (see below).

St.8 cont. bet. Pleasant L. & **Sacandaga L.** (excellent bass f.), past **Moffitt Beach Pub. Campsite** on NE. shore of latter, to **L. Pleasant** (resort.accoms.guides), 38$^{m}$. It skirts **Oxbow L.** to southern J. with St.10.

Take latter (L) through **Higgins Bay** (resort) & along W. branch of Sacandaga R. to **Stink Ls.,** from which it cont. past **Pine, Canada, W. Caroga & E. Caroga Ls.** At latter is **Caroga L. Pub. Campsite.** St.10 cont. across boundary of Adirondack St. Pk. to J. with St.5 (see) at 48$^{m}$.

48.5$^{m}$ **Piseco** (resort.accoms.) on L. of same name, from which lead trls. to **T Lake Falls** & other pts. At 51$^{m}$ is **Poplar Pt. Pub. Campsite** on shore of Piseco L. At 52.5$^{m}$ is J. with trl. leading (L) to **Panther Mt.** (2,718′). **Pt. Comfort Pub. Campsite,** 54$^{m}$, is near S. end of Piseco L. St.8 cont. (W) to **Utica** (see St.5) at J. with St.5 (see), 98$^{m}$.

At **15.5.** on St.28, **NORTH CR.** (all yr.resort.accoms.1 pub.bath.beach.trls.f.Del.& Hudson RR.) on upper reaches of Hudson R.

SIDE TRIP: Take St.28N (R) from North Cr. 7.5$^{m}$ to **Minerva** (resort.accoms.2 pub.bath. beaches.good h.& f.trls.guides.skiing), on Minerva L. St.28N cont. (N) past **Balfour L.** to J. at 21.5$^{m}$ with St.73.

Take St.73 (R) 2$^{m}$ to **Tahawus,** where Rd. leads (L) past **Sanford L.** to starting pt. at 7$^{m}$ of trl. to summit of **Mt. Marcy** (5,344′), highest pt. in N.Y. St. Rd. cont. to **Henderson L.**

St.28N cont. past several sm. Ls. At 30$^{m}$, trl. (L) to summit of **Mt. Goodenow** (2,693′). 40.5$^{m}$ **Long L.,** at J. with St.10-365 (see below).

From North Cr., St.28 cont. (W) to J. at **20.** with fine scenic Rd. (L) up Gore Mt. to **Barton Garnet Mine,** 5m, where trl. runs to lean-to of **Gore Mt.** (3,585′) **Ski Club** (ski tow). **20.5. NORTH RIVER,** at J. with Rd. leading (L) 5m to **Thirteenth L.** (good f.& h.). **34. IND. L. VILLAGE** (accoms.of all types.pub.bath.beach.through buses), from which many int. trls. lead, at J. with St.10 (see above), which unites (W) with St.28 to Blue Mt. L. Route soon crosses **Cedar R.** (fine h.& f.). **44.5. BLUE Mt. L.** (resort.accoms.through bus conn. good starting pt. for canoe trips through streams & Ls. in vic.). Trl. runs from village to summit of **Blue Mt.** (3,808′). At Blue Mt. L. is J. with St.10-365.

SIDE TRIP: Take latter (R) 11m to **Long L. Village** (accoms.through bus conn.) on **Long L.,** narrow body of water, mt.-enclosed, 14m long, affording fine view of higher Adirondacks. From Long L., Blue Mt. Trl. runs (N) to J. with red-marked trl. which leads (R) to Mt. Marcy. St.10-365 bridges Long L. & then turns (NW). 13.5m **Eaton L.** (L) on which is **Eaton L. Pub. Campsite.** From shore opp. campsite, trl. ascends 2m to **Owl's Head Mt.** (lean-to.fine view from tower). 20m J. with unimproved Rd. leading (L) past **Little Tupper & Round Ls.** to **Sabattis** on **Long Pond** in fine L. reg. (good h.& f.). St.10 cont. (N) to **Tupper L.,** along whose E. shore it runs to **Tupper L. Village** (see Pk. Tour V), 33m, at J. with St.3 (see Pk. Tour V).

From Blue Mt. L., St.28 unites with St.365 past **EAGLE & UTOWANA Ls.** to **RAQUETTE L.** At **54.5.** is **Golden Beach St. Pub. Campsite.** Name of L. derives from the fact that in May 1776, Sir Wm. Johnson's party in flight from Johnstown Castle found it necessary because of melting snow to abandon snow shoes (raquettes) here. At **58.5.** is J. with Rd. leading (R) to **Raquette L. Village** (resort. accoms.bus conns.boat trips). **62. EIGHT L. PUB. CAMPSITE** on L. of same name (good f.). St.28 now passes **SEVENTH L., 65. 69. INLET** (resort.accoms.pub.bath. beach.many int.trls.). St.28 runs along (N) shore of Ls. from Inlet. **71. EAGLE BAY** (resort.accoms.) on Fourth L., from which Rd. leads (R) past **Moss & Darts Ls.** to **Big Moose L.,** 5.5m. **76.** J. with trl. leading (R) to **RONDAXE MT. 80.5. OLD FORGE** (resort.accoms.bus conn.) is near head of First L. & is starting pt. for canoe trips. St.28 now passes several small Ls. en route to **ALDER CREEK, 109.** Here is J. with St.12 (see St.5) running (S) to J. with St.5 at Utica & (N) to J. with US11 (see) at Watertown.

**IV. J. with US9 to J. with St.3. 37. St.86A & St.86**

**0.** St.86 branches (L) from US9 (see Pk. Tour I). **3.** Beautiful cliff-enclosed **CHAPEL POND. 5.5.** J. with Rd. leading (L) 0.5m to **St. Huberts Inn,** owned by Ausable L. & Mt. Club, from which trl. leads (S) to **AUSABLE Ls.,** incl. in 28,000-a. tract owned by club. **LOWER L.** is 2m-long gorge walled-in by mts. rising several thousand ft. **UPPER L.** affords magnificent views of **Gothics Range & Haystack Mt.** Inlet is particularly fine, dotted with noble 1st-growth pines through which vistas of Fujiyama-like Haystack appear. Long before Ausable Ls. became private reserve, upper Ausable was one of favorite haunts of famous Amer. artists: Geo. Innes, Homer Martin & others spent summers in Keene Valley & made excursions to upper L. where they had camps. **8.5. KEENE VALLEY** (resort.accoms.pub.bath.beach. many int.trls.with camp.facils.good h.& f.through bus conn.). Among int. trls. to scenic pts. leading from Keene Valley is Johns Brook Trl. which runs 9.5m to summit of **Mt. Marcy** (see). **14. KEENE** (resort.accoms.). St.86 now passes **CASCADE Ls.,** long & narrow, to whose shores rocky mts. descend. **24. MT. VON HOEVENBERG BOBSLED RUN,** built 1930 for Olympic games. **24.5.** J. with Rd. leading (L) 5m to **Adirondack Lodge** on **Heart L.,** built by Henry Von Hoevenberg, starting pt. of Ind. Pass trl., which leads (S) through **IND. PASS,** ravine with walls 1,000′ high bet. **Wallface Mt.** (3,860′) & **Mt. MacIntyre** (5,112′), to summit of **MT. MARCY** (5,344′) at 18.5m. From Ind. Pass Trl. branch trls to **L. Henderson & Mt. MacIntyre. 25. INTERVALES** (Olympic) **SKI JUMP. 25.5.** J. with Rd. leading (L) 0.5m to **John Brown's Farm** (O) & **Grave;** on grounds is **Statue of John Brown.** Brown sett. here with family in 1849 & after his execution following Harper's Ferry raid 10 yrs. later, was buried here. **27.5.** J. with St.86, on which route cont. (L).

SIDE TRIP: Take St.86 (R) along W. branch of Ausable R. through fine High Falls Gorge of Wilmington Notch. At 9m is **Wilmington Notch Pub. Campsite** (L). 12m **Wilmington** (resort.accoms.pub.bath.beach.trls.) at J. with Whiteface Hy.

Take latter (L) 5m to summit of **Whiteface Mt.** (4,872′).

St.86 cont. to **Jay** (resort.accoms.pub.bath.beach.trls.), 17m, on E. branch of Ausable R. Here is J. with St.9N which runs (N) along Ausable R. via **Ausable Forks** to Keeseville, 34m, at J. with US9 (see Pk. Tour I).

**28. L. PLACID** (all yr.resort.accoms.1 pub.bath.beach.winter sports.steamship excursions around L.100m of trls.with open lean-tos for camp.RR.& bus conn.), near L. of same name & Mirror L., among finest Ls. in mts. Village is built on W. shore of Mirror L. On opp. side is **L. Placid Club** (clubh.&cottages O.only for members & guests). L. Placid itself is c.5.5m long with several large Is. Whiteface Mt. dominates it from (N). On Main St., **Olympic Arena** (ice skating June 15-Labor Day). **33.5. MEADOW BROOK PUB. CAMPSITE.** St.86 now passes **Will Rogers Mem. Sanatorium** (L), built by Nat. Variety Artists Club but open to all actors who suffer from tuberculosis. **37. SARANAC L.** (see Pk. Tour V) at J. with St.3.

**V. PLATTSBURG (W) to WATERTOWN. 175. St.3**

**0.** St.3 branches (W) from US9 (see) at **PLATTSBURG. 9.** J. with St.374 (see US9) which runs (R) to J. with US11 (see). **35.** J. with St.99 leading (R) 3.5m to **Loon L. P.O.** (boat.bath.f.riding.golf.tennis) on L. of same name. **50. TRUDEAU SANATORIUM,** est.1885 by Dr. E. L. Trudeau, 1st outdoor tuberculosis sanatorium in America. On grounds are Dr. Trudeau's orig. cottage & **Statue of Trudeau** (by Gutzon Borglum). **51.5. SARANAC L.** (resort city.accoms.all types.symphony concerts in summer at Town Hall.boat excursions.RR.conn.many trls.with camp.facils.good h.& f.), known as "Little City in the Adirondacks," is situated on Flower L., near Lower, Middle & Upper Saranac & Kiwassa Ls. 7 Church St., **Saranac Lab. for the Study of Tuberculosis,** est. 1894 by Dr. E. D. Trudeau, 1st of its kind in America. On Stevenson Lane, **Stevenson Mem. Cottage** (O.sm.fee), where Rbt. L. Stevenson spent winter of 1887-88 as patient of Dr. Trudeau. 122 Beaver St., **Saranac L. Curling Clubh.,** where contests in Scotland's nat. game are held, has fine skating rink. St.3 follows SE. shore of Lower & Middle Saranac Ls. At **60.5.** is trl. leading (L) 3m to summit of **Ampersand Mt.** (3,865') overlooking Ampersand L. At **67.** is J. with St.10.

SIDE TRIP: Take latter (R) along W. shore of Upper Saranac L. At 5.5m is **Fish Cr. Pond Pub. Campsite** (good f.;boats for rent near-by.supplies), with 4m of shore front on Fish Cr. & Square Ponds. Boat trips may be taken through dozen Ls. & return. St.10 cont. along N. shore of Upper Saranac L. At 8.5m is J. with Rd. leading (R) here short distance to **Saranac Inn,** noted Adirondacks hostelry. 12.5m **L. Clear J.,** near Clear L. (accoms.int.trls.boats. RR.& bus conn.). St.10 cont. past **Upper St. Regis L.** to **Upper St. Regis L. Landing** at 17.5m, good starting point for canoe trips, & past **Lower St. Regis L.** to J. at 20m with St.192 leading (L) short distance to **Paul Smiths** (accoms.golf.bath.boats) & (R) 4m to **Gabriels** (accoms.) near Lucrezia L. St.10 now follows E. branch of St. Regis R. to **Meacham L. Pub. Campsite** at 30.5m & through **Duane Center** at 38.5m & past **Duane & Titus Ls.** to **Malone** (see US11), 54m, at J. with US11.

At **72.** on St.3 is **TUPPER L.,** industrial & resort city (accoms.h.f.skiing), at J. with St.10-365 which runs (S) to Blue Mt. L. at J. with St.28 (see Pk. Tour III). **97.5.** J. with Rd. leading (L) to **Cranberry L. Pub. Campsite** from which radiate many int. trls. **98. CRANBERRY L. VILLAGE** (resort.accoms.good f.& h.). St.3 passes **Star L.** (resort.accoms.2 pub.bath.beaches & trls.through bus conn.). **147. NATURAL BRIDGE VILLAGE** on Ind. R., named for limestone formation (trip by boat through caves;sm.fee). **156.5. CARTHAGE,** paper mfg. center. St.3 now follows Black R. through smaller paper-making towns to **WATERTOWN** (see US11), **175.,** at J. with US11.

**VI. CANOE TRIPS**

Unrivalled opportunities for boating & canoeing are offered by L. reg. of Adirondacks. Chain of Ls. & streams extends from SW. to NE. through heart of Adirondack forest. Most popular canoe trip is from **Old Forge** in Herkimer Cty., at ft. of Fulton Chain of Ls., through various Ls. & upper reaches of **Raquette R.** to **Tupper L., Saranac Inn, Paul Smiths** or **Saranac L.** Most int. trip is from **Old Forge** to **Loon L.,** somewhat more than 100m.

## CATSKILL STATE PARK

**CATSKILL ST. PK.**

Catskill St. Pk. (576,120 as.), created 1904, comprises Catskill Mts., southern N.Y. St.'s chief recr. reg., covering area (W) of Hudson R. extending c.50m from Kingston N. to Catskill. It reaches to within roughly 6m of Hudson R. & extends (W) c.60m. Although Catskill Mts. are usually considered part of Appalachian range, they differ in geologic formation & conformation, being characterized not by long ridges but by an unorganized group of flat-topped mts. separated from each other by narrow precipitous valleys through which steep brooks tumble, often in fine cataracts. They have few natural Ls. but many fine crs. which afford excellent fishing. There are 3 watersheds: central, draining into Esopus Cr., which cuts across heart of reg. from W. to E. & flows into Hudson R., its course interrupted by large & beautiful Ashokan Reservoir; N., for most part draining into Schoharie Cr., which in turn flows into Mohawk R.; & W. & S., draining into Del. R. There is very little first-growth timber left: most of it hardwood, with some hemlock, spruce & balsam at higher altitudes. Catskill Mts. are not notable for magnificence of scenery although view from cliff edge at Catskill Mt. H. can compare with any in U.S. Being so near to N.Y. City, they are crowded in summer with vacationists, who fill hundreds of hotels & other tourist facils. Inds. knew reg. as Onteora ("land of the sky") but Dutch who settled along Hudson called it Kaatskill, which means Wildcat Cr., since forests harbored many wildcats, sought by trappers for their fur. First industrial boom in Catskill reg. came with rise of tanning industry.

Most of Catskill reg. lies within St. Pk., of whose area c.230,000 as. are St.-owned. St. fire patrols & game wardens protect fors. against fires & destruction of fauna. Large network of trls. has been laid out & is maintained with clear markings by St. Conserv. Comm. Log lean-to shelters have been built at intervals along most trls. There are 4 pub. campsites: North L. & Devil's Tombstone (see Pk. Tour II); Woodland Valley (see Pk. Tour I); Beaverkill (see St.17). (Camping permits are issued for 2 wks. & may be renewed for an additional 2 wks.) Camping elsewhere in Catskill St. Pk. requires no permit but is restricted to 3 days.

## PARK TOURS

### I: KINGSTON (W) to MARGARETVILLE. 49. St.28

**0. KINGSTON** (see US9W) at J. with US9W. Take St.28 (W). St.28 skirts N. shore of 12m-long **Ashokan Reservoir** with fine view of **High Peak** (3,075′). At **8.5.** is J. with St.375.

SIDE TRIP: Take latter (R) 3m to **Woodstock,** famous artist colony, where summer art exhibitions are held & there are art schs.

**25.5. PHOENICIA** (Accoms.: All types; 4 pub. bath. beaches) on Esopus Cr. is much-frequented Catskill resort & hik. center. **27.** J. with Rd.

SIDE TRIP: Take latter (L) c.5m to **Woodland Valley Pub. Campsite,** where trl. leads to summit of **Slide Mt.** (4,204′).

**32.5. SHANDAKEN** (accoms.), vacation center in area of many resorts. **35.** J. with Rd.

SIDE TRIP: Take latter (L) 8m to J. with Slide Mt. Rd., leading (L) to summit of **Slide Mt.,** 10.5m, & ski trl.

**38. PINE HILL** (accoms.pub.bath.beach) on Funcrest L., from which many trls. radiate. **42.5. FLEISCHMANNS** (accoms.) is on Switzerland L.; 40 well-kept trls. (camp.facils.) radiate to various pts. of int. **49. MARGARETVILLE** (accoms.) is mt. village on Delaware R. near W. boundary of Catskill St. Pk. Near-by is **Balsam L.,** reached by trl. which cont. for c.16m with st.-built shelters along it. Margaretville is at J. with St.30, running (SW) to J. with St.17 (see) at 38m & (NE) to J. with St.23 (see below), 19m, at **Grand Gorge** (see Pk. Tour II), from which it cont. (N) to J. with US20 (see).

### II: J. with US9W (1m S. of Catskill) (W) to J. with St.23. 37. St.23A

J. with US9W (see). Take St.23A (W). At **10.** is **PALENVILLE** (accoms.), where Rip Van Winkle is supposed to have lived.

SIDE TRIP: Take Rd. (R) here 3m to J. with trl. leading (L) up **Catskill Mt.** 1m to ruins of Rip Van Winkle Boarding H. at edge of **Sleepy Hollow,** where, according to Washington Irving, Rip Van Winkle slept for 20 years.

St.23A cont. up precipitous Kaaterskill Clove & enters Catskill St. Pk. at **11. HAINES FALLS** (accoms.private & pub.bath.beaches) is resort. Trls. on which are numerous campsites radiate from here.

SIDE TRIP: Take Rd. (R) from Haines Falls 3m to **North L. Pub. Campsite,** near entrance to **Catskill Mt. H.** (sm.fee;1823), which stands near edge of high cliff (magnificent view).

**17.5. TANNERSVILLE** (accoms.) on L. Rip Van Winkle. **19.5.** J. with St.214.

SIDE TRIP: Take latter (L) 8m to **Devil's Tombstone St. Campsite** in scenic **Stony Clove.** Near camp is J. with trl. running to **Hunter** (4,025′), **Twin & Ind. Head Mts.**

**21.5.** J. with Rd. leading (L) 0.5$^{m}$ to **Colonel's Chair** (3,100'), so-called because of mt.'s peculiar formation. From here trls. run to high Catskill peaks. Just beyond last J. is **Hunter** (accoms.pub.bath.beaches.hik.hunt.) near Dolan's L. & Schoharie Cr. from which radiate 15 fine hik. trls. **37.** J. with St.23 (see Pk. Tour III).

**III: CATSKILL (W) to STAMFORD. 49. St.23**

**0. CATSKILL** (see US9W) at J. with US9W. Take St.23 (W). At **3.** is **LEEDS** (accoms.pub.bath.beaches), from which radiate several good trls. (camp.facils.). **10. CAIRO** (accoms.bath.beaches) is on Mills L. & Catskill Cr. **13.5. ACRA. 19. PT. LOOKOUT** (2,400') from whose tower is fine view (sm.fee). At **19.5.** is **E. WINDHAM** (resort), perched on height commanding fine view. St.23 now cont. through fine mt. scenery to **WINDHAM** (accoms.2 pub.bath.beaches), **24.5.,** on Silver L. near Caves Mt. (3,035'), from which radiate some int. trls. **36.** J. with St.23A (see above). Just beyond is **PRATTSVILLE** (accoms.2 bath.beaches) near Gilboa Reservoir & Schoharie Cr. In village is **Pratt's Rocks Pk.** (pic.), given by Zadock Pratt, who built village & displayed peculiar sense of humor by driving out one 4th of July bundled in furs. **41. GRAND GORGE,** at J. with St.30 (see US20), which runs (N) to conn. with US20 (see).

SIDE TRIP: Take St.30 (L) 6$^{m}$ to J. with Old Clump Mt. Rd. Take latter (R) 0.8$^{m}$ to J. with country Rd. leading (L) short distance to **Old Stone Schoolh.** where naturalist-writer John Burroughs & RR. tycoon Jay Gould were classmates. Old Clump Mt. Rd. cont. uphill to **Woodchuck Lodge,** 2$^{m}$, where Burroughs lived in later years. **Grave of John Burroughs,** in pasture (R) at 2.3$^{m}$ is marked by boulder. At 2.5$^{m}$ is **Ancestral Home** where he lived as boy. St.30 cont. to **Margaretville** (see Pk. Tour I), c.20$^{m}$, at J. with St.28 (see Pk. Tour I).

St.23 cont. (W) to **STAMFORD,** 49., biggest & most luxurious resort in Catskills at ft. of **Mt. Utsayantha** (3,213'), up which trl. runs. Mt. was named for Mohawk princess who killed herself because tribal laws forbade her to marry Sioux. There is marker on her grave.

# LONG ISLAND

## LONG ISLAND

Long I. extends from N.Y. Harbor & East R. (E) to Montauk Pt., bounded (N) by Long I. Sound & (S) by Atlantic Ocean. It is c.127$^{m}$ long &, at its widest, c.20$^{m}$ wide. Narrow strips of beach, pierced at several pts. by channels into ocean, extend along its (S) side from Brooklyn to Southampton, sheltering Jamaica, Great South, Moriches, Quogue & Shinnecock Bays, which afford excellent yachting & fishing. Peconic Bay & Gardiner Bay split E. end of I. into 2 arms somewhat resembling lobster's claw, bet. which are Shelter & Gardiners Is. Long I.'s N. shore bet. East R. & Port Jefferson, indented by well protected, deep harbors, is hilly & picturesque, occasionally dropping off in abrupt sand cliffs. Rest of I., except Montauk Peninsula, its SE. arm, which is hilly & boulder-strewn, is mostly flat plain. Western sec. of I. is, of course, part of N.Y. City, but even adj. Nassau Cty. is crowded with suburbs. Both N. & S. shores are vacation areas. Beaches are swamped by millions during summer, particularly those on S. shore, cooled by breezes off ocean. N. shore has attracted many of N.Y.'s millionaires who have built mansions on large estates.

L.I.'s W. half was sett. by Dutch & its E. half by New Englanders. E. half remained under jurisdiction of Conn. until 1664, when Brit. added it to N.Y. In 1672 Dutch recaptured New Amsterdam & Long I. but Brit. soon recovered them. Many Quakers sett. on L.I.; they were persecuted by both Dutch & Brit. During most of Rev., L.I. remained in possession of Brit. after defeat in Battle of Long I. (1776) forced Washington to abandon Brooklyn & cross over to N.Y.City. When Brit. evacuated N.Y. in 1783, they had to abandon L.I. as well.

Island's economic life, except for brief interlude of whaling, has been chiefly based on fishing & agric.—among its products are fish fertilizer, oysters, clams, potatoes, ducks, & truck garden crops. In addition to industrial plants of Brooklyn, Queens & Nassau Cty., L.I. has sm. shipyards & aircraft plants which boomed during World War II. But L.I.'s chief mainstay is vacation trade: it offers facils. for every type of sport & recr.

Western half of L.I. has fine network of St.Pkys., mostly created since 1924 under energetic direction of Rbt. Moses. These pkys. permit motorists to escape traffic delays & to reach St. Pks., many of which are located on N. & S. shores, with fine boat., bath. & recr. facils. Northern St. Pky. runs (E) from J. with Grand Central Pky. at Alley Pond Pk. (see New York City, Brooklyn & Queens) & Southern St. Pky. runs (E) from J. with Shore Pky. near Internat. Airport (see New York City, Brooklyn & Queens).

**I. QUEENSBORO BRIDGE to J. with St.25. 73. St.25A**

0. Cross Queensboro Bridge & take Northern Blvd., which traverses Flushing Meadows, site of 1939 World's Fair & temporary home of UN. At **12.** is J. with Bayview Ave. leading (L) into Great Neck Peninsula, taken up largely by fine residential suburbs & private estates. **13.5. MANHASSET.** Here is 23-a. pk. recently donated by John Hay Whitney in which is Pleasant L. Shelter Rock Rd., old **Friends Meeting H.** (1810). 2931 N. Hempstead Turnpike, **Onderdonk H.** (1836. Gr.Rev.).

SIDE TRIP: Take Plandome Rd. (L) from Manhasset to **Plandome,** where is **Plandome Mill** (N.O.1673) on Leeds Pond. At 3.5m is **Port Washington** on Manhasset Bay. At 5m **Sands Pt.,** facing Sound on Hempstead Bay in vic. pre-empted by large estates. Off Sands Pt. is islet with lighth., known as **Execution Rock,** where condemned criminals used to be chained at low water mark & left to mercy of rising tide.

Four-lane viaduct carries St.25A over head of Hempstead Harbor, bypassing **Roslyn, 16.** Bryant Ave., **Cedarmere** (N.O.1787), former home of Wm. Cullen Bryant, who is buried in Roslyn Cemetery. Main St., **Roslyn Grist Mill** (mus.& tearoom.1701). On pond across way is rest. **Grist Mill** (1744) which used to make paper.

SIDE TRIP: Take Bryant Ave. (L) from Roslyn along E. shore of Hempstead Bay, through **Sea Cliff,** 3.5m, to **Glen Cove,** 5.5m, once surrounded by more than 100 estates, incl. those of J. P.Morgan, G. D. Pratt & Chas. Pratt, many of them now abandoned. Near-by are millionaires' **Piping Rock Club,** known for polo matches & fox hunts, & **Webb Institute of Naval Architecture & Marine Engineering** (7 bldgs.28 as.), on former H. L. Pratt estate; Webb Institute moved from its Bronx campus in 1946. Forest Rd. cont. (E) from Glen Cove to 8m, **Locust Valley,** where is **John Underhill Mon.** on Feeke's Lane. 12.5m **Oyster Bay.** Dutchman De Vries in 1639 discovered excellence of oysters here. 25 W. Main St., **Raynham Hall** (O.sm.fee.1740), with hist. relics, where Sally & Audrey Townsend entertained Brit. officers during Rev., among them Maj. André, who was stationed here & became devoted to Sally. On pane of his bedrm. window are still to be seen inscriptions to the girls he scratched there. Sally discovered he was plotting against patriots & sent word to her brother Rbt., one of Washington's spies. Her info. helped to bring about his arrest & hanging & forestall Benedict Arnold's intended betrayal of West Pt. Also on W. Main St. is **Asiapum** (N.O.1705), built by Wm. Wright & owned by 7 generations of descendants until sold in 1948. (W) of village is **Council Rock** where Geo. Fox preached in 1762. On Chicken Valley Rd., **Planting Fields,** 410-a. estate of Wm. Robertson Coe, with 65-rm. Elizabethan Mansion & notable gardens with many horticultural rarities; estate was donated to L.I. Agric. & Tech. Inst. in 1948. At 14m cemetery, in which is **Grave of Theo. Roosevelt,** adj. to **Roosevelt Bird Sanctuary.** On bay is **Roosevelt Mem. Pk.** At **Cove Neck,** 14.5m, **Sagamore Hill** (N.O.), home of Theo. Roosevelt. Short distance beyond, side Rd. rejoins St.25A.

**26. ST. FISH HATCHERY** (L). **27. COLD SPRING HARBOR,** former whaling town on charming bay of same name, with large estates in vic. Near RR. sta. is **Eastern Military Academy,** occupying 80-rm. Fr. chateau built by financier Otto Kahn. **29. HUNTINGTON,** sett. in mid-17th cent., which extends down to Huntington Harbor. E. Main St. & Sabbathday Path, **Presb. Ch.** (1784.Georg.Col.), 3rd edifice on this site. High St. & N.Y. Ave., **Hist. Mus.,** containing hist. relics. Spring St. & St.25A, **Heckscher Mus.** (O.wks.except Thurs.Sun.p.m.apply curator) containing sm. art coll. & relics. W. Main St. & W. Neck Ave., **John F. Wood H.** (1750. adds.). N.Y. Ave. leads (L) 1.5m to **Hale's Mon.** on spot where Nathan Hale is believed to have been arrested by Brit. in 1776. **34.5. NORTHPORT,** on Huntington Harbor, now resort town, formerly shipbuilding center. **40.5. SUNKEN MEADOW ST. PK.** (520 as.bathhs.refreshments.pic.). St.25A now turns (S) to J. at **45.** with St.25 (see L.I. Tour II) with which it unites to **SMITHTOWN BRANCH, 46.5.,** on Nissoquogue R., navigable by sm. boats to L.I. Sound. Here is **First Presb. Ch.** (1827) on site of earlier edifice in which Joshua Hart preached sermon attacking Brit. occupation troops, for which he was arrested & bound to Negro slave. When Brit. officer asked, "How do you like your company," he replied, "Better than yours." From Smithtown Branch, St.25A branches (NE) to **STONY BROOK, 52.,** on Stony Brook Harbor, which since 1940 has been rest. by self-supporting project to its orig. appearance with creation of village green & rest. of bldgs. to styles of late 18th & early 19th cents. Shopping center is dominated by Fed.-style **Post Office.**

Old Fireh. is now **Suffolk Mus.** with large coll. of paintings, incl. many by Mount family, natives of Stony Brook, whose most int. member was Wm. Sidney Mount. NE. cor. St.25A & Gould Rd., **Mount H.** **Three Village Inn** occupies former home of shipbuilder Jonas Smith (1750). Just outside village is **Great Oak,** one of biggest (E) of Miss. R. On Mill Rd. is **Grist Mill** (1699.rebuilt 1756), still functioning. At **53.5.** is J. with Quaker Path.

SIDE TRIP: Take latter (L) 1m to **Setauket,** charming Old New-England-type village (1651) on Setauket Harbor. Here is **Caroline Ch.** (1729) to which Queen Caroline donated ch. silver which Brit. soldiers stole during Rev. Here also is **Presb. Ch.** (1714.rebuilt 1811) where guns were mounted & horses stabled during skirmish near village, bet. Brit. & patriots in 1777. In near-by **E. Setauket** is **Brewster H.** (supposedly 1665.in disrepair) on Main St. & in near-by **Old Field South** is **Old Field Lighth.**

**56.5. PORT JEFFERSON,** formerly port of call for China clippers & busy shipbldg. town. Ferry runs from here to Bridgeport, Conn. Near-by are Mt. Sinai, on which is old **Mt. Sinai Ch.**, & Miller Pl., on Rd. running toward Sound, where are old **Miller Pl. Academy** & **Millard's H.** (oldest portion c.1750.int.inter.). **69.5. WILDWOOD ST. PK.** (395 as.pic.camp.) on L.I. Sound. **73.** J. with St.25 (see L.I. Tour II).

## II. QUEENSBORO BRIDGE to ORIENT POINT. 105. St.25

St.25 is known as Jericho Turnpike in its W. sec. **0. QUEENSBORO BRIDGE. 17.5. MINEOLA.** St.25 passes through **OLD WESTBURY, 20.5.,** & **WESTBURY, 21.5.,** where on School St. is int. **Children's Mus.,** in Wheatley Hills District, reg. of handsome estates, & skirts **Bostwick Polo Field, 22.5. 23. JERICHO,** near which Brit. built, during Rev., strangely named Ft. Nonsense, is at J. with hy. leading (R) 1.5m to **Hicksville,** sett. 1648, where is **Quaker Meeting H.** (1781). **32.5.** J. with St.110, leading (R) 0.5m to **Birthpl. of Walt Whitman** (O.12-6.sm.fee;1810). At **44.** is J. with St.25A (see L.I. Tour I). **62.** J. with Rd. leading (R) 1.5m to **Brookhaven Nat. Lab.** for atomic energy research & experimentation. **73. RIVERHEAD,** on Peconic R., which flows into near-by Peconic Bay, is picturesque old town, with some fishpacking & freezing plants. Griffin Ave., **Suffolk Cty. Bldgs.** (O.wks.Mod. Georg.). W. Main St., **Suffolk Cty. Hist. Soc.** (O.1-5.1925.Georg.Col.) containing hist. relics among which is John Hurlburt's stars & stripes flag, alleged to have been flown 6 mos. before Betsy Ross flag. St.25 now runs along N. arm of eastern Long I. **82. MATTITUCK,** famous for its oysters. **91. SOUTHOLD,** sett. 1614, fine old New England type town. On Peconic Bay water front is **Founders' Pk.** where 1st settlers debarked. **95.5. GREENPORT** (resort.accoms.boats), formerly whaling town, now oystering, scalloping, fishing & vacation center. Local shipyard experienced boom during World War II. Main St., **Clark H.** (1812), formerly an inn famous for seafood, now Police Sta. Next to Presb. Ch., former **Townsend Manor** (1803.Gr.Rev.).

SIDE TRIP: Take ferry across Peconic Bay from Greenport to **Shelter I.** (resort), sett. c.1652 by Nath. Sylvester & other Quakers, fleeing persecution in New England. Just beyond ferry landing is **Shelter I. Heights,** fashionable summer colony. On St.114, c.1m from ferry landing, is **Quaker Mon.** On I. is **Sylvester Manor,** orig. acquired by Nath. Sylvester, with fine **Manor H.** (N.O.1835) & fine old **Windmill,** moved in 1775 from Southold by barge across Peconic Bay & then by oxen. From S. side of I., ferry runs to North Haven, from which St.114 cont. to **Sag Harbor** (see L.I. Tour III).

**105. ORIENT BEACH ST. PK.** (342 as.pic.bath.surf f.) at tip of N. arm of I. Just beyond is **Orient Pt. Inn** (1810.remod.), famous hostelry at which Webster, Cleveland, Cooper & Whitman were guests. From Orient Pt. ferry runs to New London, Conn.

## III. MANHATTAN BRIDGE to MONTAUK PT. 127.5. St.27

**18. VALLEY STREAM,** near which is **Valley Stream St. Pk.** (107 as.pic.). **20. LYNBROOK,** sett. before Rev.

SIDE TRIP: Take Broadway (R) from Lynbrook to **Lawrence,** 4m, where on Broadway is **Rock Hall** (N.O.1767.beautiful Georg.Col.). Side route cont. on Rockaway Beach Blvd. along Rockaway Peninsula, resort area bet. ocean & Jamaica Bay, on which there are fine boardwalk, pub. pk. on ocean front, & **Jacob Riis Pk.** (O.May 30-Labor Day.sm.fee for bathh.restaurant.sports facils.). At W. tip of peninsula is **Ft. Tilden.** W. end of peninsula is conn. by bridge with Borough of Queens.

**21. ROCKVILLE CENTRE.**

SIDE TRIPS: (A) Take Long Beach Rd. (R) here across Great South Bay 6m to **Long Beach** (resort.fine boardwalk.accoms.surf & still water bath.f.recr.), on one of outer beach strip islands.

(B) Take hy. (L) from Rockville Center 2m to J. with Rd.

Take latter (L) 0.5m to **Hempstead St. Pk.** (903 as.pic.sports facils.bridle trls.dancing. amusements.restaurant.polo field).

Main side route cont. to **Hempstead,** 3.5m, sett. 1644. Front St., **St. George's Prot. Episc. Ch.** (1822), with an older weathervane showing holes made by Brit. bullets during Rev. 120 Prospect St., **Rectory** (1793.Dutch Col.), where E. H. Harriman, RR. tycoon, was born. Fulton Ave. near Washington St., **Presb. Ch.** (founded 1644.built 1846.Eng.Goth.& Georg. Col.). Fulton Ave., **Hofstra Mem. College** (bldgs.Mod.Class.by Aymar Embury II) with 59-a. campus. 5m, **Garden City,** exclusive residential suburb, laid out by A. T. Stewart, founder of A. T. Stewart's Dept. Store in N.Y.City, now John Wanamaker's. Cathedral Ave., beautiful **Cathedral of the Incarnation** (Eng.Goth.), seat of Episc. diocese of L.I., in lovely 90-a. pk. Near Garden City are **Mitchel Field** (airport), hqs. of Air Defense Command, & **Roosevelt Field,** named for Quentin, son of Theo. Roosevelt, killed while flying in World War I. Near-by also is **Roosevelt Raceway** (trotting races in summer).

(C) Take St.27A (Merrick Rd.) from Rockville Center paralleling St.27 for 29m nearer Great S. Bay, which passes through **Freeport** (see below) at 4m. At 10m is **Massepequa** (resort), on Great S. Bay, where is **Tryon Hall** (1770.Georg.Col.). At 12.5m **Carman H.** (N.O. part of bldg.1776.rest.Gr.Rev.). Rd. cont. to **Amityville** (also on Great S. Bay), 13m; some fine old houses. **Babylon,** 18.5m, yachting & bulb-growing center. Ferries run from Babylon to cottage settlements & beaches on **Fire I. & Fire I. St. Pk.** (800 as.pic.bath.surf f.). 21m **Sagtikos Manor** (late 18th cent.mod.adds.). 23.5m **Bay Shore,** on widest part of Great S. Bay. 26m, **Islip,** sett. 1697. 28m Entrance to **Heckscher St. Pk.** (1,508 as.pic.bridle & hik. trls.bath.). 29m, J. with St.27.

On St.27 at **24.5., FREEPORT,** near Great S. Bay, commercial & sm. industrial center, largely dependent, however, on vacationists. Randall Ave. & N. Main St., **Jacob Bedell H.** (N.O.1795.Col.). **25.5.** J. with Meadowbrook St. Pky. (toll), running (S) over causeway 5m to **Jones Beach St. Pk.** (2,413 as.fine bath.facils.boat.playgrounds & kindergarten.sports.concerts & entertainment.fireworks at marine stadium.dancing), one of finest oceanfront pks. in country, located on one of outer strip Is. bet. Great S. Bay & Atlantic Ocean. **26.5. MERRICK.** Beyond **WANTAGH, 32.5.,** is **Frank Buck's Zoo** (fee). At **38.** is J. with Belmont Ave. leading (L) 1.5m to **Belmont L. St. Pk.** (348 as.boat.pic.trls.refreshments). **40.5. BAY SHORE** (see above). **43.5. ISLIP** (see above). 46.5. J. with St.27A (see above). St.27 cont. along shore of Great S. Bay. **51. SAYVILLE,** "Blue Pt." oyster-packing center, from which ferry runs to Cherry Grove on Fire I. **56. PATCHOGUE** is one of largest S. shore resorts (accoms.boat trips). St.27 now passes through **CENTER MORICHES, 68., E. MORICHES, 70. & EASTPORT, 73.,** all on Moriches Bay. **77. WESTHAMPTON** (resort.accoms.), on upper end of Shinnecock Bay at J. with Rd. leading (R) 1.5m to **Westhampton Beach. 86. HAMPTON BAYS,** supply center, on Shinnecock Canal, conn. Shinnecock & Peconic Bays. St.27 now passes low mound-like Shinnecock Hills, purplish with heather. **92.5. SHINNECOCK IND. RESERV.** (R). **94.5. SOUTHAMPTON,** sett. 1640 by colonists from Mass., is fashionable summer resort & residence town near ocean. Near village green is **Old Mill** (1810.rest.after hurricane), dragged here from orig. site by ox team in 1814. Main St., old **Hollyhocks H.** (1662). 23 Job's Lane, **Parrish Mem. Art. Mus.,** with coll. of sculpture & paintings. Dune Rd., near Agawam L., **St. Andrew's-Dunes Ch.** (est.1879), built around former lifesaving sta. & incorporating materials from various ancient Eng. ch. bldgs. N. Sea Rd. leads (L) from Southampton 4.5m to **Conscience Pt.,** landing place of 1st settlers, marked by plaque on boulder. At **WATER MILL, 97.5.** is **Mill** (O.wks.1644), now shop & tearoom, thought to be oldest surviving bldg. on L.I. **100.5. BRIDGEHAMPTON,** sett. 1660, resort near ocean & sm. bay. Sag Harbor Rd. & St.27, **Wick's Tavern** (N.O.1686). On estate, not far from Civil War Mon., is an **Old Mill.**

SIDE TRIP: Take Sag Harbor Rd. (L) 4m to **Sag Harbor,** on Peconic Bay, formerly famous whaling town. Jas. F. Cooper obtained material here for his sea novels. Hist. bldgs. incl. **Customs H. & P.O.** (before 1790.rest.) 1st Customh. in N.Y. St.; **Hannibal French H.** (c. 1800.rest.); former **Ben. Huntting H.** (1846.fine Gr.Rev.by Minard Lafever), now whaling mus. Madison St., **Whalers' Ch.** (1843-44.by Minard Lafever) lost its steeple, shaped like sailor's spy glass, during 1938 hurricane. In Oakland Cemetery is **Whalers' Mon.** (1856). Side route cont. by St.114 to ferry at 7.5m which runs to **Shelter I.** (see L.I. Tour I).

**106.5. EAST HAMPTON,** sett. 1649, is N. England type village. On village green is **Home of John Howard Payne** (O.c.1660.saltbox.int.inter.), who wrote "Home Sweet Home," containing relics, with **Old Windmill** (1774), also containing hist. relics, in rear. Adj. is **Mulford Farm** (20 as.), maintained by East Hampton Hist.

Soc., planted with trees, shrubs & flowers available in 17th cent., on which are 3-story saltbox **Farmh.** (1683), **Barn,** & several outbldgs.; this was once home of Sam Mulford, who went to London to protest to King against tax imposed by Gov. of N.Y. St. on whaling industry. On Main St. are **Clinton Academy** (1784), now East Hampton Hist. Soc. Mus.; **East Hampton Free Lib.** (designed after one in Maidstone, Eng.), containing outstanding Pennypacker Coll. (18,000 items) of L.I. material & relics; **Guild Hall** (1931.Georg.Col.by Aymar Embury II) with auditorium & art gallery, comm. actor John Drew. In **Old Burying Ground** are some int. old graves. Beyond RR. bridge is **Dominy H.,** reputedly 250 yrs. old (in bad repair). **109.5. AMAGANSETT,** sett. 1650, resort & fishing village near ocean, formerly lively whaling center. In vic. are some old Dutch windmills. St.27 now runs along Montauk Peninsula bet. Gardiners Bay & ocean, through hilly, wooded boulder-strewn country. **116.5. HITHER HILLS ST. PK.** (1,755 as.ocean bath.camp.surf f.) with fine beaches & high sand cliffs. In Gardiners Bay, opp. Pk., is **Gardiners I.,** 3,300 as., bought by Lion Gardiner in 1639 from Inds. "for 1 bbl. of rum, some blankets, a gun & a large black dog." **121.5. MONTAUK,** resort & fishing village (boat.bath.) on Fort Pond Bay, an important rum-running port during Prohibition. **127.5. MONTAUK ST. PK.** (158 as.pic.surf bath.restaurant), with fine views of ocean, at tip of S. arm of L.I. This fine, cliff-bound site has been celebrated by many poets, among them Walt Whitman, whose tribute was his magnificent "Montauk Point." On pt. are **Lighth.** (O.except Sun.1796) & **Old Windmill** (1763).

# NEW YORK CITY

## NEW YORK CITY

RR. Stas.: 42nd St. bet. Vanderbilt & Lexington Aves., Grand Central Terminal; 7th Ave. bet. 31st & 33d St., Pennsylvania Sta. which also accommodates the Long Island R.R.; ticket service for all RR.'s avail. at City Ticket Offices, 17 John St., 4 W. 33rd St., & 3 W. 47th St. Baltimore & Ohio, 122 E. 42nd St. (bus conns. from Rockefeller Center & Columbus Circle in Manhattan to main terminal in Hoboken, N.J.); Delaware, Lackawanna & Western RR., 500 5th Ave. (Ferry conn. at Christopher & Barclay Sts. to Hoboken terminal as well as from Hudson & Manhattan Tubes); Erie RR. (Bus conn. from 11 Rockefeller Plaza & Hudson & Manhattan Tubes to Jersey City, N.J.); Jersey Central, foot of Liberty St. (Ferry conn. to Jersey City, N.J.). Local service to Hoboken & Jersey City, N.J. also by Hudson & Manhattan Tubes, from Hudson Terminal Bldg., 30 & 50 Church St., & 33d St. & Herald Sq. Through Bus Conns.: Dixie Bus Center, 241 W. 42nd St.; Hotel Astor Bus Terminal, 220 W. 45th St.; Pa. Motor Coach Terminal, 242 W. 34th St.; All Amer. Bus Depot, 246 W. 42nd St.; Capitol Greyhound Terminal, 245 W. 50th St.; Consolidated Bus Terminal, 203 W. 41st St.; Midtown Bus Terminal, 143 W. 43d St.; bus conns. also to Jersey suburbs from many of these stas. (All bus terminals will be consolidated by 1950 into the Port Authority Bus Terminal at 40th-41st Sts., bet. 8th & 9th Aves.). Air Trans.: Main offices at Airlines Terminal Bldg., Park Ave. & 42nd St., opp. Grand Central Terminal. Airports at La Guardia Field & Internat. Airport, both in Queens (by way of Midtown Tunnel & Expressways); Newark Airport in Newark, N.J. SS. Lines: U.S. Passport Agency at Subtreasury Bldg., Wall & Broad Sts., & Internat. Bldg., 5th Ave. & 51st St. See Shipping News sec. of newspapers for time of arrival & departure of ships as well as pier locations. Transatlantic Docks extend from 44th to 57th Sts. on North R. Applications for landing stages for priv. boats can be made to Dept. of Marine Aviation, Pier A, Room 29. Sightseeing Tours: Guided tours around Manhattan by bus, mostly from Times Sq. Area (see Classified Telephone Directory under "Sightseeing"). Ferry boats to Staten I. from South Ferry Terminal, Battery Pk.; to Edgewater, N.J. from W. 130th St.; to Weehawken, N.J. by way of Cortlandt St. Ferry; Electric Ferry from Brooklyn to Staten I. Boat trips: Hudson R. Day Line, W. 42nd St. Pier, runs boats to Albany & other points along Hudson R.; Sutton Line from Battery & at W. 42nd St. Piers, runs lines to Bear Mt., also operates Moonlight Cruises during summer; Meseck Steamboat Co., Battery Pk., has trips to Rye Beach & Bridgeport, Conn.; SS Sandy Hook, Pier 10, has trips to Atlantic Highlands (bus conns. to Jersey shore resorts); Circle Line, at W. 42nd St. Pier, 3½ hr. cruise around Manhattan (has office in Concourse of Rockefeller Center); from Battery to Statue of Liberty on Bedloe I., sailings every hr. from 9-5; Ferry to Governor's I. from South Ferry, sailings every 15 min. Local Trans.: Subways & Elevated RRs. to all points in Manhattan & the boroughs (except Richmond, which has its own lines). Ample bus servs. Vehicular Tunnels: Lincoln Tunnel from W. 39th St. conn. with Weehawken, N.J.; Holland Tunnel, from Canal St. to Jersey City, N.J.; Queens Midtown Tunnel, from E. 37th St. to Long I. City; Brooklyn Battery Tunnel will conn. Battery Pk. dist. with Brooklyn by 1950 (toll for each tunnel: autos 50¢). A number of bridges conn. several of the boroughs & New Jersey: (1) Triborough Bridge, from 125th & 2nd Ave., or 122nd St. & East R. Drive in Manhattan; in Queens at 29th St. & 25th Ave.; in the Bronx at Southern Blvd. &

Cypress Ave. (2) Bronx-Whitestone Bridge, foot of Ferris Ave., from Old Ferry Point, the Bronx, to Whitestone, Queens. (3) Geo. Washington Bridge over Hudson R. from 179th St. & Riverside Dr. to Northern N.J. (4) Queensboro Bridge, from 59th St., has an elevator to Welfare I. on route to Queensborough Plaza, Queens. Bridges from Manhattan to Brooklyn: (1) Brooklyn Bridge, from Park Row to Sands & Washington Sts. (2) Manhattan Bridge from Canal St. & Bowery to Nassau St. & Flatbush Ave. (3) Williamsburg Bridge from Delancey & Clinton Sts. to Broadway. Amusements: Concentration of legitimate & motion picture theaters, concert halls & night clubs found in Times Sq. area, from 42nd St. to 59th St., bet. 5th & 8th Aves. Hotel Accoms.: All kinds, mostly in sec. from 42nd St. to 59th St., bet. 8th & Lexington Aves. Shopping Centers: In Manhattan, 14th St.; Herald Sq. area; & 5th Ave. from 34th to 57th Sts. In Brooklyn, at Fulton St. Restaurants: Chief restaurant dist. in same area as hotels. Foreign restaurants incl.: Armenian, bet. 25th & 29th St. in vic. of Lexington Ave.; German, Czech & Hungarian, in Yorkville dist.; Italian, in Greenwich Village & elsewhere; Spanish, on 14th St. (W) of 7th Ave.; although Chinese restaurants are concentrated in Chinatown, many are found in other parts of city. Art: In addition to Public Mus. (see Pts. of Int.) there are commercial art galleries (O) in the 5th Ave. & 57th St. areas & in Greenwich Village. Music: Symphony & other concerts at Carnegie Hall, Civic Center Theater, Town Hall, Times Hall, Brooklyn Academy; Lewisohn Stadium & city pks. in summer. NBC & CBS Broadcasting Stas. offer large variety of programs (tickets avail. by mail well in advance). Jazz orchestras in Greenwich Village. Many skyscrapers have Observ. Towers (O.fee.see Pts. of Int.). Amusement Pks.: At Coney I.; Palisades Amusement Pk., N.J. (reached by W. 130th St. Ferry); Rockaways' Playland, at Rockaway Beach, Queens. Bath. Facils.: Numerous beaches incl. Coney I., Brooklyn; Jacob Riis Pk., Queens; Jones Beach, Wantagh, Long I.; Long Beach, Long I.; South Beach, Staten I.; Orchard Beach, Pelham Bay Pk., the Bronx; Rockaway Beach, Queens. Camp. fish. & hik. facils. at Palisades Interstate & Bear Mt. Pks.; for info., apply State Pk. Commission, 80 Centre St., Manhattan. City Pks. in all the Boroughs offer large variety of recr. facils. Info. as to walking & hik. tours can be found in "N.Y. Walk Book" (published by Dodd, Mead), out of print, but obtainable at N.Y. Pub. Lib. Hik. maps are published by Hammond & Co., 1 E. 43d St. Sports: 8th Ave. & 50th St., Madison Sq. Garden; Baker Field of Columbia Univ. at 218th St. & Broadway; Randall's I. Stadium; Yankee Stadium at 161st & River Ave. (Bronx); Polo Grounds (N.Y. Giants) at 155th St.; Ebbets Field (Brooklyn Dodgers) at Bedford Ave. & Sullivan Pl. Internat. Tennis Matches at Forest Hills (Queens); Running races at Aqueduct, Jamaica & Belmont Pks. (Queens); trotting races at Roosevelt Raceways, near Mineola, L. I. Info. Centers: Police Dept. Info. Booth, Broadway & 43d St.; Daily News Info. Bureau, 220 E. 42nd St.; Esso Info. Serv., Esso Bldg., Rockefeller Center; N.Y. Convention & Visitors Bureau, 500 Park Ave.; U. S. Travel Bureau, 45 Broadway. Out of town newspapers can be bought at newsstand just (N) of Times Bldg. bet. 42nd & 43d St. & Broadway.

The New York Metropolitan area, according to the Port of New York Authority, includes some 1,500 square miles. Within this region live more than 13,000,000 people, & in it is concentrated a large percentage of the country's commerce, finance, business & industry.

A considerable part of the area is water—bays & rivers—& these have made New York's fortune, since first & foremost it has always been a port. The Lower Bay lies beyond the city to the south; it is the approach to The Narrows through which commerce pours into the Upper Bay, the real harbor. Staten Island's green shores slope down to the water's edge at The Narrows. As a ship proceeds through the Narrows & into Ambrose Channel, the towers of Manhattan & Brooklyn float up out of the haze. The harbor has no outstanding natural feature. Yet, it is one of the world's most impressive because of its man-made grandeur: bridges & skyscrapers, dense water-borne traffic & crowded factory stacks. As the ship continues up the harbor, pancake-like Governor's Island is on your right & the Statue of Liberty, on your left, & beyond, the brick buildings on Ellis Island, where the "homeless, the tempest-tossed," taken to Liberty's bosom, used to be penned up before they were allowed to land. The web of the East River bridges tangles in the further distance. When vessels enter the North River, the only striking natural feature of the New York landscape, the serrated Palisades, much defaced at their lower end by factories, advertisements & other structures, come into view. To the west lie Hoboken & Jersey City, which are at the upper edge of the vast New Jersey agglomeration of industrial cities, with a population of nearly 3,000,000. The almost solid wall of skyscrapers at the southern end of Manhattan confronts steamers as they turn in to dock & intermittent clusters of towers string along the island's backbone northward.

Manhattan Island is the city's hub, flanked on the west by the North River, which isn't north at all & is called the Hudson from about 72nd Street on, & on the east, by the East River. Brooklyn, which faces Manhattan, across the East River, with nearly 3,000,000 inhabitants, is the most populous borough of the five that constitute Greater New York. It was settled not long after Manhattan, & until incorporated into the greater city, was an independent municipality, & even up to today has preserved a considerable social & cultural independence. The East River, around the "100" streets, splits, & one branch spreads into ever-widening bays until it becomes Long Island Sound, & another branch becomes the Harlem River, connected by a ship-canal with the Hudson. East & North of Harlem River lies the large residential Borough of the Bronx which has some of the city's finest parks & parkways.

The East River has a string of islands paralleling the shore from the fifties to the hundreds. Most of them are covered with city institutions; but Randall's Island, which the Triborough Bridge uses as a footstool, is being turned into a playground.

Manhattan is long & narrow, nowhere more than 2½ miles wide & from 10 to 12 miles in length. In recent years the city has been doing what was still possible to reclaim its water front from commerce. The island is circled by highways; the west-side elevated highway takes autoists above miles of docks & warehouses & continues along beautifully parked Riverside Drive to the city's northern boundary. The East River front has been partially redeemed by construction of Franklin D. Roosevelt Drive which will be continued on both sides of the Harlem River. In Brooklyn there have been similar water-front boulevards built to skirt the harbor & reach the ocean front, which is today largely devoted to parks & public beaches.

New York is a city of bridges, & they, & the skyscrapers, are its most impressive man-made scenery. Six bridges cross the East River. George Washington Bridge, which was, until San Francisco built its Golden Gate span, the world's greatest suspension bridge, connects northern Manhattan with New Jersey. Three magnificent spans connect orphaned Staten Island with the Jersey mainland. Drawbridges swing up & down over Newtown Creek, a little estuary of the East River in Queensboro, which carries more commerce than the Mississippi; other great bridges are those crossing Jamaica Bay & Rockaway Inlet & Hendrick Hudson Bridge over the Harlem Ship Canal.

City planners have advocated tunnels, more economical of space than bridges. Manhattan is linked to the Jersey mainland by four sets of tubes, Holland & Lincoln tunnels for vehicles, the Pennsylvania & Hudson-Manhattan tubes for passenger traffic. The Midtown tunnel, under East River, connects the borough of Queens with Manhattan, & the Battery tunnel, connecting the south end of Manhattan with Brooklyn, is nearing completion.

The bridges & tunnels have been built to break the enclosing chain of rivers & bays which cramped & crowded Manhattan into an unbearable congestion. For the same reason, the network of subways was constructed. There are 239 miles of these underground thoroughfares, running from the city's northern limits to all the boroughs. You can travel at least 40 miles from 242nd Street, near the Yonkers line, to Coney Island & the Rockaways, without ever doubling back on your route. The railway lines pour a horde of a half million commuters into the city daily & the problem of getting people to & from their jobs has by no means been solved. The chief impasse is created by traffic that has to converge into Manhattan. Had the city been properly zoned from the start, factories would have been pushed to the periphery.

The lower East Side, a run-down slum district—during the depression most of the old tenements were half empty—is being rehabilitated with model housing. The whole water front from 23rd Street up into the 60's is being transformed by construction of hospitals & medical centers & the great buildings of the United Nations. The area to the west is being reclaimed for fashionable residence. The West Side all the way up to about 70th Street, is still, where not impinged upon by factories & warehouses, somewhat of a slum area, which, however, has been ameliorated by the improvement of Greenwich Village, the Chelsea district & new housing.

Central Park splits residential Manhattan in two, socially as well as physically. An east side address establishes social position, while a west side location indicates social mediocrity. Yet the middle west side is one of the pleasantest parts of Manhattan; it has Central Park bounding it on the East, & Riverside Drive, with its wonderful view of the Hudson & the Palisades, on the West.

Harlem, which used to be confined to the lowland between the heights & Harlem River, has spread out mightily. It has climbed the "hill" of the heights, which is Harlem's Fifth Avenue, and has seeped southward till it has reached below 100th Street on the west & east sides. The shopping & amusement center of Harlem is 125th Street. Lenox & Seventh Avenues, running north from it, are dotted with restaurants, churches of unusual sects & some night clubs, of which, however, the most interesting are to be found on the dark side streets. But Harlem no longer can contain the city's Negro population which has spilled over into Queens, Brooklyn & northern New Jersey.

Fifth Avenue, from 34th Street to 57th is the chief Manhattan shopping district, together with the side streets & Madison & Lexington Avenues to the East, with, however, the exception of Herald Square at 34th Street, around which clusters a group of great department stores. Wanamaker's still clings to its downtown location at Broadway & Astor Place.

Fourteenth Street is the cheaper, popular shopping center. Women's dress shops line its southern side, although the big department store of Hearn's is located here too. Klein's great emporium, where you snatch garments, male or female, from crowded racks by a unique self-service system, stares at you as you come east to Union Square, which was formerly New York's chief open-air forum. The burlesque & variety houses, chief among which was Tony Pastor's, have vanished from the street east of 4th Avenue. And the old Academy of Music has been replaced by the tower of the Consolidated Edison Company, with its illuminated bird-cage pergola. Old Tammany Hall, which was the organization's home during the days of Croker, Murphy & greatest corruption, has disappeared from the north side of the street near 3rd Avenue.

The amusement section of Manhattan runs from 41st Street along Broadway & the side streets, all the way into the low 50's. Times Square is at the district's center & subways converging under the Square engulf & disgorge more passengers than any other station. A good time to visit the Square is around 11 p.m., when theaters & movies let out, & the millions of electric bulbs, in all colors, turn night into day. Along Broadway are strung the movie palaces. Theaters are on the side streets. New York still remains the theatrical center of the U.S. Mayor LaGuardia suppressed burlesque.

Night Clubs line 52nd Street between 6th & 5th Avenues, but are also scattered pretty much everywhere in the east fifties. Madison Square Garden is on 8th Avenue & 50th Street. Sports events, conventions, the circus & political meetings jam the Garden's great auditorium. Manhattan, the Bronx & Brooklyn have out-door sports arenas—Polo Grounds, of the N.Y. Giants at 155th Street, where they have had to hang curtains at the back to prevent cliff-sitters from getting a free view of baseball games, the Yankee Stadium, in the Bronx, Ebbet's Field in Brooklyn. There is a great municipal stadium on Randall's Island.

There are at least four race-tracks in the Metropolitan area. But most of the enthusiasts place bets in local bars haunted by bookmakers who operate outside the law, which permits betting only at the tracks.

Music centers around West 57th Street, with Carnegie Hall as its nub. Behind Carnegie on 55th Street is the municipally-owned Center Theater, where cheap seats for opera, plays, concerts & ballet attract crowds. Brooklyn has its own music center at its Academy of Music. The Lewisohn Stadium, on Morningside Heights, presents open-air concerts, opera & ballet during the summer, against competition of airplane propellers overhead, & free concerts are given in Central Park, Manhattan & Prospect Park, Brooklyn. The grimy Metropolitan Opera House occupies a square block on Broadway between 39th & 40th Streets. Tin Pan Alley is not a street but a business, producing upward of $5,000,000 worth of popular music annually, a business which has followed the northward migration of the theater. Hollywood robs Tin Pan Alley of much of its best talent, at least seasonally, but New York is still the place where popular music is published.

Commercial art galleries are to be found in the Fifth Avenue shopping district & especially on 57th Street. But 8th Street has a string of them too. You can spend profitable days roaming these galleries which meet every artistic preference.

Finance, lawyers, architects, engineers & insurance companies all used to be crowded into the Wall Street district, within sound of Trinity's chimes. But in recent years many great concerns have moved to the Grand Central Terminal area. The two stock exchanges, however, keep the brokerage firms nailed to Wall Street.

The best second-hand book neighborhood is below 14th Street on 4th Avenue. Jewelry has moved up to 47th Street. The wholesale flower marts string along Sixth Avenue from 30th to near 23rd Streets. Garments, furs & allied products are turned out in the huge loft buildings in the district from 38th Street to about 26th & from 7th to 8th Avenues & at the noon hour, sidewalks are almost impassable with thousands of garment workers. The wholesale food district, which feeds New York's hungry maw, stretches along the west side from 14th Street downtown. It is worthwhile visiting it in the early morning hours, to watch the unloading of crates of fresh vegetables & fruits. Washington Market on the west side, & Fulton Fish Market, on the lower east side are also worth a visit.

Greenwich Village used to be New York's Left Bank. It still has night clubs & jazz joints & some flavor of Bohemia. Eighth Street is the Village's Main Street, from 6th Avenue to University Place, & has several exotic bars. Experimental theatre groups sprout in the Village at odd intervals.

The old Jewish East Side has been to a large extent emptied by the subways. There are many Jews left there, but Poles & other nationalities have moved in. Orchard Street is an interesting sidewalk shopping neighborhood. With the building of great new housing projects, the district will be completely transformed. There is still the old Italian quarter south of Washington Square to Mott Street, where fiestas are celebrated. Chinatown is still comparatively intact, although a number of the old rookeries have been pulled down & modern apartments put up. There are Chinese movies, a Chinese theater, restaurants, shops displaying exotic Chinese foods, joss houses. Yorktown, centering around East 86th Street, is still German. Puerto Ricans inhabit southern Harlem, but they have spread around town & many of them live in the lower west side, where Spanish has become almost the predominant language. The old Syrian quarter, west of Wall Street, has been almost altogether wiped out by building of the west side highway & approaches to the Battery tunnel. Hoboken, across the river in Jersey, is still German, & its saloons & restaurants provide good drinks & food. The water front life there is more interesting than in Manhattan.

This is a polyglot city. It has the world's greatest Jewish & Irish communities; it is probably the third largest Italian town; the greatest Negro & Puerto Rican city. Nationalities of every variety have crowded into it. There are 500,000 of Irish derivation, 123,000 Hungarians, 54,000 Greeks, 31,000 Turks, 33,000 Lithuanians, 9,000 Latvians, upward of 1,000 Bulgars. New York has easily digested this influx from abroad. But you can still hear every language under the sun on the streets & in the subways see people reading German, Greek, Yiddish, Armenian, Czech, Spanish & Italian newspapers. And you can eat in any language. Most anyone you may meet on the street comes from a foreign land or is of recent foreign extraction, or from another part of the U.S. The native New Yorker is a rare bird.

There is still discrimination against Negroes, but, largely due to the late Mayor LaGuardia's efforts, discrimination in its grosser forms has vanished. The time is past when a bartender could, with insulting impunity, break the glass in which a Negro patron had been served a drink.

New York is a city perennially in transition. That is why it has so few historic landmarks & fine old buildings. Most of Fifth Avenue's old mansions have vanished, even north of 59th Street, where tall apartments are replacing them. Washington Square, which had the last solid rows of aristocratic old New York houses, has already been rebuilt on its west side, & now New York University, unfortunately, is going to tear down many of the old houses on the south side, to make room for a law school. Most of Stanford White's charming buildings have disappeared, including old Madison Square Garden. Patchin Place, haunt of famous writers & poets, still hides away, off 6th Avenue, as if it hopes to escape destruction by remaining inconspicuous. And here & there you will find a few houses with fine grillwork balconies that remind of New Orleans.

Architecturally New York is something of a hodgepodge. It has the handsomest skyscrapers in the world. The New York Telephone Building at West Street is one of the finest. The Woolworth Building, at City Hall Park, is an outstanding adaptation of Gothic to the skyscraper form. And both these buildings have this advantage:

they can be seen from street level to top. Many of the city's skyscrapers are so hemmed in by other structures, as in the case of the beautiful Shelton Hotel, that you cannot really see them. The skyscrapers make their best showing as vistas—seen from harbor, rivers & bridges. The downtown towers loom beautifully at the end of Sixth Avenue's extension. The view from Central Park to the South is also magnificent.

The zoning law of some decades ago belatedly recognized the fact that something had to be done to keep some fresh air & some light continually filtering into New York's canyons. The result has been a sort of Babylonian effect, skyscrapers consisting of huge block masses retreating in a series of "set-backs" skyward. Sometimes a building's owners & architects chose to take their set-backs in one bite, near a building's base, & then you have a tower, pure & simple, as in the Empire State Building, whose gleaming lightness disguises the fact that it is the world's tallest structure. Rockefeller Center, however, is the one successful effort to create a coordinated skyscraper group. But aside from Rockefeller Center, the "Plaza" at 59th Street & Central Park is the only public square in Manhattan that makes a completely consolidated & dignified impression.

New Yorkers, in the old days, boasted that their city, surrounded by rivers, bays & ocean on all sides, was one of the country's finest summer resorts. But for the vast majority, the waters immediately around Manhattan are taboo. Even outlying beaches are badly contaminated. Tardily enough, the New York area's municipalities have begun to build great plants to render innocuous the sewage that pours into the surrounding waters. But even under present conditions, millions, on days when the thermometer reaches the 90's, flock to the beaches. Along the ocean front, the temperature averages at last ten degrees less than in Manhattan.

New York is more than merely polyglot. It is, in an unofficial way, the capital of the country, & increasingly, of the world. Location of the United Nations within its boundaries is perhaps more a corollary to, than an endowment of, greatness. The city is the world's greatest port & financial center & the country's greatest industrial beehive, &, as a consequence, the center of the country's cultural life, & increasingly, as European creative artists come to America, the world's cultural center.

It has always been primarily a trading post. The Dutch West Indies Company founded it as such, &, from its first settlement, when Peter Minuit landed with his company of settlers in 1626 & drove a shrewd bargain with the Indians for the purchase of Manhattan for 60 gilders ($24), trade has been the chief occupation. It is recorded that in 1635 the settlement already was exporting some $53,000 worth of pelts. The island was comparatively fertile & for some years tobacco was grown & exported. But agriculture has not played a great part in the region's development. The land within fifty miles of Manhattan is not very productive. It was as an outlet for the richer agricultural lands of the upper Hudson & the Mohawk Valleys, & later, of the West, that New York developed as a great port. New Amsterdam, as the Dutch called Manhattan, was not a religious refugee settlement, like the New England colonies. An easy religious tolerance characterized the Dutch regime, the notable exception being the persecution of Bowne & the Quaker congregation in Flushing.

The town early acquired a reputation for unpuritanical dissipation & lawlessness. Its streets were lined with grog shops, & drunkenness was prevalent. Tipsy Indians were coralled & held until sober, to find out who had sold them liquor. Laws & ordinances were generally disregarded, to the annoyance of stump-legged Gov. Peter Stuyvesant, who was in constant conflict with his unruly subjects. Already the settlement was cosmopolitan in character, composed of all nationalities, including many Negroes. There is a record of five Negroes sentenced to hang for a murder. Economically minded authorities decided to string up only one of them, a huge specimen whose weight broke the rope, & who was then also set free.

Representative government was slow in developing, although Stuyvesant tried out a sort of advisory body, elected by the burghers, which he later sought to abolish, & this was a source of trouble with his subjects. Stuyvesant had one victory: his annexation of the Swedish settlement on the Delaware. But when the British fleet arrived in 1664, he was in no position to put up a fight, since Fort Amsterdam was in poor state of repair because the home government had been parsimonious in allotment of funds to make it defendable. So New Amsterdam became New

York, & although it was recaptured by the Dutch in 1673 & held for more than a year, it was returned to the British in exchange for Java, considered a much more valuable asset.

Under the Stuarts, the colony received rather more liberal treatment than New England. Full religious freedom was given all sects. Governor Dongan, at James II's suggestion, gave the city a municipal charter with right of election of aldermen by citizens. During the interregnum after the overthrow of James II, New York had a strange political episode, when Jacob Leisler seized the government & held it until ousted by the Governor appointed by William III, who had Leisler tried for treason & executed.

In 1734 the city had its one great pre-Revolution, Civil Liberties battle, when a German immigrant, John Peter Zenger, editor of the "New York Weekly Journal," which had attacked the British for their arbitrary rule, was arrested & prosecuted for criminal libel. Popular opinion was with Zenger & he was acquitted.

When, at the end of the French-Indian wars, in 1763, the struggle with the Crown became acute, New York backed New England & after Lexington & Bunker Hill, patriot bands seized the city government & proceeded against Tories & Loyalists. But with Washington's defeat on Long Island & his retreat to New Jersey, the British took possession & held the city for seven years.

New York's boom began after 1812, & was largely the child of the Erie Canal & the steamboat & railroad age, which gave the city almost a monopoly of transportation to the west. Its history of the 19th & 20th centuries has been one of stupendous expansion, only temporarily interrupted by economic depressions & the Civil War, which is notable chiefly in New York's history for the terrible draft riots, when the Negro population was the chief sufferer. The riots had to be put down by Federal troops & the casualties are estimated by some historians to have run to over 2,000.

The city's growth continued despite an unbelievably corrupt & expensive municipal government that lasted into the 20th century, interrupted only by short-lived reform waves. The corrupt boss, Fernando Wood, ruled the city in the 1850's. Boss Tweed's dictatorship covered the late 60's & early 70's until he was brought to book, largely by the courage of the "New York Times'" editors. The Tammany Hall regime was next, exposed & thrown out through the Parkhurst & Lexow Committee exposé of the 1890's. Not even the creation of Greater New York in 1898 by annexation of Brooklyn, Queens & Staten Island (the Bronx had already been annexed) & the election of a reform mayor of the greater city & the succeeding reform administrations, ended Tammany Hall's power. From 1918 to 1934 this organization controlled New York into the "high, wide & handsome" administration of "Gentleman Jimmy" Walker, which ended with the latter's hasty resignation under fire. Hitherto corrupt government had always managed to creep back after every interlude of reform. But with Fiorello LaGuardia's election as Mayor in November, 1933, & his reelection, crooked politics seemed to have been permanently routed. With the help of Federal funds, during the great depression, LaGuardia took care of the needy as no district boss had ever been able to do by the hand-out method, & initiated great projects for the city's improvement that Tammany Hall could never rival as a means of giving employment. With building of boulevards, creation of parks, welfare centers, playgrounds, wiping out of slums & erection of new housing, pulling down of the disfiguring elevated structures, & other improvements, he left New York an infinitely better place to live in.

New York is by no means the United States, as eager westerners will hasten to inform you when accusing New Yorkers of bounding the world by the Hudson on the west. On the other hand, the mental attitudes of New Yorkers are cosmopolitan. They are curiously lacking in local patriotism. Yet the power of New York over its inhabitants is insidious, chaining them by its infinite variety. People go away to live elsewhere, but they usually return if they can.

Manhattan is not all of New York. Most of the 13,000,000 people that inhabit the vast metropolitan ant-hill, live outside of Manhattan, which has less than 2,000,000 population—3,000,000 in Brooklyn, 1,500,000 in the Bronx, 1,500,-000 in Queens, 174,000 in Richmond, 3,000,000 in New Jersey, & the balance in Westchester County, Nassau County & Connecticut. New Yorkers work & live much as Americans do everywhere. This is a city of homes, of one & two-family dwellings, & small apartment houses, often garden-enclosed, a place where you can raise a family as successfully as in any other American city. A majority of New Yorkers only visit Manhattan's hectic amusement centers occasionally; they mostly stay in their own neighborhoods, take in the local movie & attend the local churches & social centers. Indeed, the greater city is really made up of small communities with an independent cultural & social life of their own. It is a vast congregation of almost self-sufficient towns, clustered peacefully around hectic, towered Manhattan.

## POINTS OF INTEREST IN NEW YORK CITY

LOWER MANHATTAN: From the Battery to 14th St. This is only sec. of Manhattan in which streets do not follow rigid gridiron pattern, but rather the unplanned hys. of old city. (1) At tip of Manhattan, **Battery Pk.,** overlooking harbor, in area devoted to commerce & finance. Pk. is undergoing changes which will incl. an underpass linking West Side & East R. hys. & the Brooklyn-Battery Tunnel. At N. of Battery Pk., entrance & exit of 10,500′ long Brooklyn-Battery (vehicular) Tunnel, under N.Y. harbor to Brooklyn-Queens Expressway & Gowannis Pky., links in Belt Pky. System (see Brooklyn & Queens), consists of 2 tubes, with 31′ outside diam. Cost $77,000,000. The **Barge Office,** where thousands of immigrants once arrived, is being eliminated. Here will be erected the Mun. **Battery Garage** to accom. motorists using expressways. Here also is semi-circular **Ft. Clinton,** built in 1808 as part of city's fortifications. It later became great social center. Jenny Lind sang here under management of P. T. Barnum; finally became city **Aquarium.** When present improvements in Battery Pk. were made, Ft. Clinton was scheduled for demolition, but this has been held up by plan to preserve bldg. as Nat. Mon. **Statue of Giovanni da Verrazano,** Florentine navigator who supposedly entered harbor 1524. **South Ferry Terminal;** ferries to St. George, Staten I. & Governor's I., latter only a short distance S. from Battery Pk. (2) Ferry from Pier A at W. end of Pk. to **Bedloe's I.** (boats every hr.9-9.fare 70¢). **Liberty Enlightening the World,** by Fr. sculptor, F. A. Bartholdi, mounted on 142′ pedestal, which, in turn, rests on star-shaped base, erected in 1811 as part of city's fortification. Statue is 151′ high & weighs 225 tons. Total height from sea level to tip of torch, 330′. Figure holds torch in upraised right hand & tablet of Decl. of Ind. in left. Circular stairway of 168 steps leads to statue's crown. Statue was gift of Fr. people & dedicated 1886. (3) Ferry at Barge Office to **Ellis I.** (pass essential.official business only). **Main bldg.** has administration bureau, dormitories, etc., incl. kindergarten & mural by WPA artists. More than 1,000,000 immigrants used to pass through here annually; with restriction of immigration, influx has dropped to a trickle. (4) Ferry at S. Ferry Terminal (no charge. guided tour) to **Governor's I.;** island's name derives from fact that in late 17th cent., it was assigned to use of Col. Govs. **Ft. Jay** (1794). Other pts. of int. are: **Castle Williams** (1811) & **S. Battery** (1812). Polo field (games.summer.fee). (5) At foot of Broadway, is Bowling Green Pk. part of Dutch Marcktveldt (market); bronze **Statue of Abraham de Peyster** (1896), one-time city mayor. Here stood **Statue of Geo. III,** which was pulled down by Patriots at outbreak of Rev. (see Litchfield,Conn.). (6) Facing Bowling Green, **Customs H.** (1907.neo-Class.by Cass Gilbert). Bldg. occupies site of Ft. Amsterdam, where stood gov.'s house built for Peter Stuyvesant. Present bldg. has group of sculptures representing Four of the Continents & with another group of 12 dedicated to commercial centers of the world. (7) Bet. Beaver & Stone Sts., E. of Bowling Green, is huge red brick **Produce Exchange** (by Geo. Post). In its great hall, trading in produce-grain, cotton, etc., takes place. (8) Cor. Pearl & Broad Sts., **Fraunces Tavern** (O.1719.Georg.Col.) where Washington bade farewell to his officers. Hqs. of Sons of Rev. Ground floor is restaurant. Mus.; exhibits of Rev. relics. Paintings by J. W. Dunsmore in small hist. lib. on 4th fl. (9) 90 West St., **West St. Bldg.** (1905.Fr.Goth.by Cass Gilbert), & 75 West St. houses **N.Y. Post Home News,** formerly the Evening Post founded by Alex. Hamilton (1801). Wm. Cullen Bryant was editor. (10) 107 West St., **Watch Mus.** (O). (11) 30-50 Church St., **Twin Hudson Terminal Bldgs.;** sta. of Hudson-Manhattan Tubes to N.J. (12) At Vesey & Fulton Sts. on West St., **Washington Wholesale & Produce Market,** where concentrated food shipments are routed throughout N.Y. area. **Washington Retail Market.** (13) 155 Cedar St. bet. Washington & West Sts., **Ch. of St. Nicholas** (1820.Gr.Orthodox); holds ceremony on Day of Epiphany called Blessing of Waters, at which time Archbishop hurls wooden cross into water; swimmers vie with one another to retrieve prize from icy North R. (14) Bet. Church St.

to W. Broadway & Vesey to Barclay Sts., **Fed. Office Bldg.** (15) 140 West St., **N. Y. Telephone Co.** (by R.Walker), one of city's most imposing skyscrapers.

(16) South St., the water front street on East R.; at 25 South St., **Seamen's Ch. Institute of N.Y.;** figure of Sir Galahad stands guard over entrance. Institute (1834) provides lodging & meals at moderate rates & has merchant marine sch., oldest surviving of its kind in N.Y. Recently added, mural depicting invasion of Normandy (by E.Jas.Fitzgerald). (17) Cor. Wall & South Sts., **120 Wall St.,** skyscraper on site of Murray's Wharf where Washington landed on way to Fed. Hall for inauguration as Pres. (1789). (18) 70 Pine St., **Sixty Walltower** (Cities Serv.Bldg.), one of tallest in city (observ.O.wks.sm.fee). (19) 118 Cedar St., **Ye Olde Chop H.,** in its 147th yr., first to introduce chincoteague clams & oysters, small soft-shell crab. (20) 77 Cedar St., bet. Nassau & Broadway, **N. Y. Clearing H.** (1896), clearing millions in checks & drafts daily. (21) 33 Liberty St., **Fed. Reserve Bank of N.Y.** (1924.Ital.Ren.); its walls are more than 4′ thick; has 5 stories below street level; its subterreanean vaults are sealed by doors weighing c.90 tons. (22) 55 Wall St., **Nat. City Bank** (1842.adds.1907 by McKim,Mead & White) was chartered 1812 as outgrowth of first Bank of U.S. est. Phila., 1791. Part of bldg. is the old customh. (23) 48 Wall St., skyscraper of **Bank of N.Y. & Trust Co.,** est. 1784 by Alex. Hamilton. (24) 40 Wall St., **Bank of the Manhattan Co.,** (observ.tower O.) city's 2nd oldest bank, org. as water company by Aaron Burr (1799). (25) Cor. Wall & Nassau Sts., **Sub-Treasury Bldg.** (1842.Gr.Rev.by Ithiel Town & A.J.Davie), on site of old Fed. Hall, where Stamp Act Congress (1765) & Continental Congress (1785) met; here Washington took oath as Pres. of U.S.; spot above steps where he stood is marked by **Statue of Washington** (by J.Q.A.Ward). Houses various Fed. offices, incl. Passport Bureau. **Mus.** (O); relics of Geo. Washington; paintings of early city. (26) 23 Wall St., **J. P. Morgan Bldg.,** houses famous banking company; still bears slight scars of mysterious explosion in 1920 of dynamite being trucked through town. (27) 14 Wall St., is 39-story **Banker's Trust Co.** (28) At Wall, New & Broad Sts., **N.Y. Stock Exchange** (1903.adds.1923.by Geo.Post), owned & administered by some 1,375 member brokers, was developed in 1792 by group of 24. Sculptures of pediment above columns of facade are exceptionally fine. Trading is on floor of great hall, thence communicated by telegraph & cable to other markets (O.wks.10-3. guided tour). Hectic days of trading have passed, in part due to the limits set on margins by the Securities & Exchange Commission. During panic of 1869 (Black Friday), in battle for control of N. Pac. RR. bet. E. H. Harriman & J. P. Morgan in 1901, & in 1929 crash, trading on the floor reached madhouse proportions. (29) Wall St. & Broadway, brownstone **Trinity Ch.** (org.1697.1846.Goth.Rev.by Rich. Upjohn), est. on land granted by Queen Anne (1705), is one of world's wealthiest Episc. parishes & at one time owned a considerable part of S. Manhattan I. The land occupied by Ch. & cemetery is estimated to be worth $25,000,000. Main entrance doors in low relief, by Rich. M. Hunt, Karl Bitter & J. M. Rhind; & on (S) door, by G. M. Niehaus. Altar decorated by sculptures. Stained glass windows are very beautiful. Among notables buried in churchyard are Alex. Hamilton, Rbt. Fulton, inventor of steamboat, Albert Gallatin, Secy. of Treas. under Jefferson & Capt. Jas. Lawrence, killed during fight with Brit. ship "Shannon" (1813). Also Martyrs' Mon. to Amers. who perished in infamous Brit. prison hulks in N.Y. harbor during Rev. (30) Directly behind Trinity Ch., **N.Y. Curb Exchange,** 2nd largest securities market in nation. Curb once conducted transactions in open street.

Return to South St. (31) Covering 6 city blocks, at Fulton & South Sts., **Fulton Market** (1821), largest wholesale fish market on Atlantic Coast. (32) Cor. Fulton & South Sts., **Sweet's,** restaurant est. about a century ago. (33) 131 William St., cor. Fulton St., **Site of Birthpl. of Washington Irving.** (34) 149 Broadway, **Singer Bldg.** (by E.Flagg), 41-story tower. (35) 44 John St., **Old John St. Meth. Ch.** (1841.Fed.), mother Ch. of sect. in U.S. Contains relics, incl. clock from John Wesley. (36) On Broadway bet. Vesey & Fulton Sts., **St. Paul's Chapel of Trinity Parish,** oldest Ch. bldg. in Manhattan (1764), designed by McBean, pupil of Jas. Gibbs, architect of St. Martin's-in-the-Fields (London). On N. side of inter., arms of U.S. mark Geo. Washington's pew, & opp. on (S) side is pew of Gov. Clinton. (37) Broadway & Park Pl., **Woolworth Bldg.** (1913.Goth.detail.Cass Gilbert), represents adaptation of Gothic to skyscraper form. (38) Bounded by Broadway on W., Park Row on E. & Chambers St. on N., triangular **City Hall Pk.,** where Decl. of Ind. was read in 1776 in presence of Pres. Washington. At N. side of Pk. is **City Hall** (1811.Post-Col.Jos.

Mangin & John McComb), surmounted by a charming cupola topped by statue of **Justice** (by J.Dixey). Houses offices of Mayor & City Council; Gov. suite converted to Mus. (O.Mon.-Fri.,Sat.noon); hist. furniture & paintings. MacMonnies' **Statue of Nathan Hale** is W. of City Hall, while **Figure of Benj. Franklin** (by Plassman) is E. of it. Facing City Hall, brazenly nude **Civic Virtue** (also by MacMonnies). (39) Back of City Hall, on Chambers St., **City Court Bldg.** (1861-72) reminder of notorious Tweed Ring graft at cost of c.12 millions. (40) At Chambers & Centre Sts., **Hall of Records,** in ornate Ren. style, with lavish marble inter. lobby. (41) Park Row is E. boundary of the Park, once publishing center for city's great newspapers ("Newspaper Row"). **Pulitzer Bldg.,** with gilded dome formerly housing the old N.Y. World. Old Tribune Bldg. with a slender tower & old N.Y. Times Bldg. are still standing. This sec. earlier was N.Y.'s Rialto, where Barnum had one of his first museums, destroyed by fire, & famous actors appeared. At 126 Nassau St., near cor. of Beekman St., stood boarding house run by mother of Mary Rogers, victim of famous murder case of 1841 which Poe used as basis of his "Mystery of Marie Roget." (42) **Brooklyn Bridge** (1883) from Park Row (E) of City Hall, crosses East R. to Sands & Washington Sts., Brooklyn. Designed by John Roebling (1867) who died, leaving work to his son, W. A. Roebling, who in turn, directed erection of bridge from his bed although partially paralyzed from "caisson disease." Its buttressed & arched towers are constructed entirely of granite. Cost was $21,000,000. At Manhattan approach of Bridge is **Plaque,** comm. site of 1st Pres. Mansion (see below). (43) Straddling Chambers St. (E) of Hall of Records, skyscraper **Mun. Bldg.** (by McKim,Mead & White), with radio sta. WNYC. Bldg. is surmounted by heroic figure of "Civic Fame" (by Adolph A.Weinman). (44) N. of Mun. Bldg. is **Civic Center** (Foley Sq.). Here are: **U.S. Courth.** (1936.Cass Gilbert) with high central tower, capped by pointed gold-leaf pinnacle. Here in 1948-49 took place the much publicized sedition trial of 11 Communist Party leaders. **The Supreme Court** (1912. neo-Class.Guy Lowell), an hexagonal bldg.; fine law lib. On N. side of Sq., **N.Y. State Office Bldg.** (Mod.Class.). (45) N. of Foley Sq. bet. Centre & Lafayette Sts., handsome new **Criminal Courts Bldg.** (1941.by C.B.Meyer), replacing gloomy landmark of the old "Tombs" & Criminal Courts Bldg.; site has been made into parking lot. (46) Behind Supreme Court Bldg. in little Columbus Pk., is **Statue of Columbus.** Here was Five Points, once city's most notorious slums, demolished largely through efforts of Jacob Riis, campaigner for many civic improvements. (47) To (E) is **Chinatown,** hqs. for city's 30,000 Chinese. Stores here offer great variety of exotic foodstuffs & Chinese merchandise; excellent restaurants; still some joss houses. **Chinese Theater** & Movie houses. (For guided tours to Chinatown, from Times Sq. & pts. N. on Broadway see Classified telephone directory). Traditional New Year & Feast of the Moon are celebrated here to accompaniment of large dragon parades. At E. edge of Chinatown is **Chatham Sq.,** shadowed by elevated structure, where in 18th cent. city fathers decreed "horses for sale might be cantered." (48) Sq. is at center of **Bowery,** mostly pawnshops, saloons, flop houses & small retail shops. (49) Cor. Mott & Prince Sts., int. old **St. Patrick's Cathedral** (1866) & **Cemetery,** abandoned when new Ch. was built on 5th Ave. (50) No. 6 Chatham Sq., **Olliffe Pharmacy,** claiming to be oldest drugstore in Amer. (51) E. Broadway runs (NE) from Chatham Sq. to **Seward Park,** heart of the old Jewish dist. Here, facing Pk., are offices of great Jewish dailies. (52) Canal St. & Bowery, entrance to **Manhattan Bridge** (1909), through arch & colonnade inspired by Portes St. Denis & St. Martin in Paris & Bernini colonnade of St. Peter's in Rome. (53) In Lower East Side, 4 blocks (E) of City Hall at 11 Peck Slip, abandoned bldg., reputedly **Oldest H. in Manhattan** (1725). (54) In shadow of Brooklyn Bridge on Cherry St., formerly stood **House** in which the late Gov. Alfred E. Smith was born. Here are **Gov. Smith Hs.,** state financed for low-income families. (55) 8-10 Cherry St., site of **First Presidential Mansion,** occupied by Geo. Washington from Ap.23, 1789 to Feb. 23, 1790.

(56) 265 Henry St., **Henry St. Settlement** (1893) founded by Lillian Wald; has had world-wide attention for work done to procure better housing, recr. & education facils. in slums of Lower East Side. (57) 466 Grant St., **Playhouse** of Henry St. Settlement (former "Neighborhood Playhouse"); together with Provincetown Playh., had profound influence on development of mod. Amer. drama. (58) 504 Grant St., bet. Columbia & Sheriff Sts., **Amalgamated Dwellings,** built by Amalgamated Clothing Workers of Amer. (59) Bet. Gouverneur & Jackson Sts. on Madison,

**Vladeck City,** large low-cost housing development. (60) At Pier 41, near Gouverneur St., N.Y.'s first commercial **Helicopter Base.** (61) Stretching for several blocks above & below Delancey St., **Orchard St. Pushcart Market.** (62) On New Bowery, bet. James & Oliver Sts., oldest **Jewish Cemetery** in Manhattan (1682). (63) Delancey St. (Jacob Schiff Blvd.) runs into **Williamsburg Bridge** (1903) which carries more than 50,000 vehicles daily to Brooklyn. (64) On Ave. A & 3rd St., 3 blocks (E) of Bowery, **First Houses,** 1st project of N.Y.City Housing Authority (1935), built by WPA labor, using old materials. (65) Running (N) along Franklin D. Roosevelt Dr. to 23rd St. are a series of low & medium-cost housing developments sponsored by city & private enterprise; **Lillian Wald & Jacob Riis Hs.** along Ave. D; **Peter Cooper Village** & **Stuyvesant Town,** built by Metropolitan Life Insurance Co., bet. 1st Ave. & the River. Controversy arose when the company ruled to exclude Negroes. (66) At 240 Centre St., bet. Grand & Broome Sts., **N. Y. Police Hqs.,** hqs. for 5 boroughs, with 3 short wave stations & various police bureaus, plus academy for training rookie cops; **Mus. & Rogues Gallery;** coll. of firearms. On 2nd Ave. from Houston to 14th St., **Jewish Rialto,** with Jewish theaters & restaurants. (67) 2nd Ave. & E. 10th St., **St. Mark's in the Bouwerie** (1660 & rebuilt 1799), dates to time when Peter Stuyvesant built chapel on his farm here. In graveyard are buried Stuyvesant & Commodore M. Perry. Here in 1878 occurred the body-snatching of A. T. Stewart, founder of dept. store, now Wanamaker's (see); body was held for ransom, returned 2 yrs. later. (68) At 29 E. 4th St., **Old Merchants H.** (Mus.O.wks.sm.fee.1830.Gr.Rev.). (69) Bet. Broadway & Lafayette, **John Wanamaker** (Dept.Store). Orig. store erected by A. T. Stewart (see above); free concerts. (70) At inters. of Bowery, Third Ave., Fourth Ave. & Lafayette St., **Cooper Union Sq. Statue of Peter Cooper** (by A. Saint-Gaudens,once student at the Institute). Here is **Cooper Union,** est. 1859 by Peter Cooper as forum for free speech. H. W. Beecher, Wm. C. Bryant, & Pres. Lincoln spoke here. Union offers students courses in engineering & related technical subjects, secy. training, architecture & art. **Mus. for Arts of Decoration** (O). (71) E. of 3rd Ave. at 15 E. 7th St., **McSorley's Old Ale H.** (1854), perhaps only city bar where women are not served; on its walls are many mementoes of old New York. (72) E. 10th St., bet. Aves. A & B, **Tompkins Sq. Pk.,** with **Mon.** comm. loss sustained by dist. when the excursion steamer, Gen. Slocum loaded with women & children, caught fire & sank (1904).

GREENWICH VILLAGE: (73) At foot of 5th Ave., bounded by Waverly Pl. on (N), W. 4th St. on (S), MacDougal St. on (W) & University Pl. on (E) **Washington Sq. Washington Arch** (by Stanford White), is 5th Ave. approach to the Sq., comm. inauguration of Geo. Washington, decorated by statues of Pres. Washington. N. side of Sq. (Waverly Pl.), with exception of a few gaps where houses have been demolished, has finest row of 19th cent. Gr. Rev. residences in city. In Washington Sq. was potters field & neighborhood of disorderly houses. **Rhinelander H.** at (NE) cor. of 5th Ave. was designed by Rich. Upjohn. From 5th Ave. to University Pl., **Washington Mews,** fashionable group of converted stables in semi-secluded cobblestone lane. N.Y. Univ.'s bldgs. cover the Sq.'s E., University Pl. side. At 100 Washington Sq. (E) is **Mus. of Living Art** (O); coll. of modern art. At 61 Washington Sq. (S) (4th St.) is "Genius Row" where well-known writers & artists lived; purchased by N.Y. Univ. as site for Law School. At W. cor. of Thompson St. (4th St.), **Judson Mem. Ch.** (Bapt.by Stanford White), with stained glass windows by John LaFarge. Thompson & Sullivan Sts. running (S) from the Sq. into the Ital. quarter to Bleecker St. have some good Ital. restaurants. Along Bleecker St. from 7th to 6th Aves. are many Ital. food shops with sidewalk displays. On (W) side, MacDougal St. bet. 4th & 3rd Sts., is apartment house in which has been incorporated the **Provincetown Playh.,** birthpl. of mod. Amer. drama. (74) ½ block (N) of Washington Sq., blind **MacDougal Alley,** small lane of old mews made into studios; has city's only gas street lamps & is privately owned. In spring & autumn Washington Sq. open-air art exhibition is held. (75) 8th St. & 5th Ave., **Hotel Brevoort** (1854), recently closed; was famous gathering place of writers & artists. Sidewalk café & ground floor restaurant still operating. (76) NW. cor. 10th St. & 5th Ave., **Ch. of the Ascension** (1841.Episc.Eng.Goth.Rich.Upjohn.alts.1888 by Stanford White). John La Farge's mural **Ascension** (behind altar) considered his finest work. (77) On SE. cor. 5th Ave. & 9th St., **Bronze Tablet** on No. 21 5th Ave., comm. occupancy by Mark Twain (1904-08) & Washington Irving. (78) 52 W. 10th St., **MacMonnies Studio,** where La Farge, Winslow Homer & MacMonnies lived & worked. (79)

47-5th Ave., **Salmagundi Club;** members are artists & sympathetic "amateurs of art" who hold summer show from May to Oct. (80) Opp., bet. 11th & 12th Sts., **First Presb. Ch.** (mid-19th cent.Goth.by J.C.Wells).

(81) 10th St. & Broadway, **Grace Ch.** (Episc.mid-19th cent.by Jas.Renwick). Noted for stained glass windows (46 in all). (82) At 10 W. 8th St., **Whitney Mus. of Amer. Art.** (O.wks.1-5.1931), exhibits well-known works of living Amer. artists; has permanent art coll. To occupy new bldg. to be built in garden at Mus. of Mod. Art. (83) At W. 10th St. & 6th Ave. (or Ave. of Americas) **House of Detention for Women** (Mod.1932) & **Jefferson Market Court** (1876.Vict.Goth.by Withers & Vaux), (84) From W. 10th St. & from 6th Ave., **Patchin Place & Milligan Place;** housed at one time many famous writers & actors. (85) 11th St. (E) of 6th Ave., tiny **Sp.-Portuguese Jewish Cemetery** (1805.closed 1829). (86) 11th St. & Waverly Pl., **St. John's-in-the-Village** (1846), where Henry Ward Beecher preached. (87) 66 W. 12th St., **New School for Social Research** (1931.mod.by Jos.Urban) founded by Jas. Harvey Robinson & Chas. A. Beard; affords education in political & social sciences & psychology. It org. (1934) "Univ. in Exile" of refugee teachers from Nazi Germany. Auditorium is particularly interesting. Murals by T. H. Benton & Camilo Egas; frescoes by Orozco. (88) Inters. 7th Ave. & W. 4th St., **Sheridan Sq.,** focal pt. for tourist night life. At SW. cor. Christopher St. & 7th Ave., in front of store, is inscription on pavement dedicating tiny triangle to public use; title to same being in question. (89) 27 Barrow St., **Greenwich H.** (Georg.Col.1921); important for social & educational activities. (90) 59 Grove St., **Plaque,** comm. site where Tom Paine died (1809). (91) Hudson & Grove Sts., charming **St. Luke's Chapel** (1822) with wooden figure of St. Christopher brought from S. Amer. probably 17th cent.; richly decorated inter. (92) At bend of Barrow & Commerce Sts., **Cherry Lane Theater,** converted barn; now repertory theater most of yr. (93) 287-303 W. 10th St., **Plaque** indicating site of New Gate Prison dating from Rev. times to 1828, when prison was moved to Sing Sing. (94) S. of Greenwich Village, beginning at Watts St., bet. Hudson & Varick Sts., entrance to **Holland Tunnel** (toll 50¢); cost 50 million dollars. Consists of 2 tubes, one of which was damaged in May, 1949, when a chemical truck exploded en route. (95) At Canal & Varick Sts., **Plaza** at exit of Holland Tunnel, at J. of Varick St. & Ave. of the Americas. (96) 501 Broadway, near Broome St., **Francis Bannerman & Sons,** makers of firearms since 1865; coll. of military arms & war relics (O.Mon.-Fri.free). (97) Bet. Spring & W. Houston Sts., Greenwich & Washington Sts., **N.Y. Union Motor Truck Terminal,** now under construction. In area lying bet. W. Broadway & West Side Hy., (S) of the new Motor Truck Terminal Bldg., is large wholesale & retail market, supply center for Greater New York area. Worth a visit from midnight on.

MIDDLE WEST SIDE: Bounded by 14th St. on (S) & 59th St. on (N); from West Side Hy. to Broadway at center of Manhattan.

(98) 14th St. large shopping dist. with popular priced retail stores (see Intro.). (99) 14th St., bet. 7th & 8th Aves., **Sp. Ch. of Our Lady of Guadalupe.** On this block are several Sp. restaurants & int. shops selling Sp. foods. (100) Bet. 8th & 9th Aves., at 15th & 16th Sts., **Port Authority Commerce Bldg.,** in which also is **Union RR. Freight Terminal.** N.Y. Port of Authority (est.1921), has constructed network of tunnels & bridges that link Manhattan & Staten I. with N.J. mainland; developed & constructed vital land, sea, air & freight terminals. (101) 6th Ave. & 20th St., **Ch. of the Holy Communion** (Episc.1846) had 1st boy choir in Amer. (102) Bet. 20th & 21st Sts., 9th & 10th Aves., **Gen. Theological Seminary** (Episc.). (103) 191-10th Ave., **Ch. of Guardian Angel** (1930.Cath.Romanes.by J.V.VanPelt), called Seamen's Institute. (104) 23rd St. & 8th Ave., **RKO** (movie) **Theater,** originally Pike's Opera H., where Jas. Fiske, Jay Gould's partner in stock manipulations, lay in state after he had been shot in quarrel over his mistress, Josie Mansfield. (105) 21st St., near 6th Ave., old **Cemetery of Sp. & Portuguese Synagogue.**

(106) 15 W. 25th St., **Serbian Orthodox Cathedral of St. Sava** (1850), with fine stained glass windows & murals by R. Richardson. Services are usually in Old Slavonic. (107) At 27th & 28th Sts., bet. 9th & 10th Aves., **Chelsea Pk.,** named from village which occupied vic. c.1831. (108) 436 W. 27th St., **Hudson Guild** (1905), social agency whose model tenement at 441 W. 28th St. helped focus attention on need for low-rent housing. (109) Bet. 32nd & 35th Sts., inters. Broadway & 6th Ave., **Herald & Greeley Sqs.,** formerly city's Rialto; now center of shopping dist. incl. huge dept. stores of Macy's, Gimbel's & Saks. **Statue of Horace Greeley**

NEW YORK CITY
MANHATTAN
Battery Park to 14th St.
Points of Interest 65
0 1/4 1/2 3/4 1 Mile
SCALE
HUDSON RIVER
EAST RIVER
BROOKLYN
HOLLAND TUNNEL
WEST 14TH ST.
EAST 14TH ST.
WILLIAMSBURG BRIDGE
MANHATTAN BRIDGE
BROOKLYN BRIDGE
FRANKLIN D. ROOSEVELT DRIVE
SARA DELANO ROOSEVELT PARKWAY
BROADWAY
BOWERY
CANAL
HOUSTON
SPRING ST.
BROOME
GRAND
CHAMBERS
FULTON
BATTERY PL.
SOUTH
WEST

NEW YORK CITY
MANHATTAN
14th St. to 59th St.
Points of Interest
SCALE
0 1/4 1/2 3/4 1 Mile
CENTRAL PARK
EAST RIVER
QUEENS-MIDTOWN TUNNEL
QUEENSBORO BRIDGE

(by A.Doyle) in Greeley Sq. **Statue of Wm. E. Dodge** (by J.Q.A.Ward) in Herald Sq. At N. side of Herald Sq. stands great clock, flanked by 2 figures of workers with hammers with which they strike the hours, used to be on old Herald Bldg., where Jas. Gordon Bennett's famous daily was published; part of bldg. is still standing on 35th St. (N) of Sq. (110) A little further up, bet. 25th & 30th Sts., & Broadway & 6th Ave., is the **Fur Dist.,** with its approx. 2,000 shops, employing c.15,000 workers. This along with garment dist. (see below) combines to make clothing manufacturing N.Y.'s leading industry. (111) Bet. 34th & 40th Sts., from Broadway to 9th Ave., **Garment Dist.,** center from which thousands of women's ready-to-wear clothes are trundled along sts. in go-carts & loaded into huge moving vans. (112) Bet. 31st & 32nd Sts., 7th & 8th Aves., **Pennsylvania Sta.** (1910.Romanes.Class.McKim,Mead & White). Vast hall is copy of Tepidarium of Roman bath. L.I. RR. has terminal on lower level. Greyhound bus terminal adj. (113) **Hotel New Yorker** (by Sugerman & Berger), bet. 34th & 35th Sts. on 8th Ave., 2nd tallest hotel in city. (114) Across from rear of Pennsylvania Sta., on 8th Ave., **New York Gen. P.O.** (Class.by McKim,Mead & White), largest in country; (115) Broadway & 39th St., **Metropolitan Opera H.** (1883), one of world's leading opera houses; drabness of exter. belies ornate gold & red inter. with its "diamond horseshoe" of boxes. (116) 39th St. & 10th Ave., entrance to **Lincoln Tunnel,** 2 tubes conn. with Weehawken, N.J. (toll 50¢). (117) **Port Authority Union Bus Terminal,** now being built on blocks from 40th-41st Sts., & from 8th-9th Aves.; largest in world; will serve more than 60,000 bus commuters & handle the 2,500 inter-city buses. (118) 330 W. 42nd St., **McGraw-Hill Bldg.** (1930. by Raymond Hood), notable for its blue-green terra cotta exter. (119) 42nd St. & Broadway, **Times Bldg.** (Tower), at Times Sq. Broadway, 7th Ave. & side sts. are heavily lined with motion picture palaces, restaurants, legitimate theaters & night clubs. Although most "Times" offices have moved to 43rd St., weather observ. on tower still in use. (120) 42nd St. & 7th Ave., **Info. Booth,** maintained by Police Dept. (121) 43rd-44th Sts. on W. side of Broadway, **Paramount Bldg.** (35 stories), with huge clock. (122) 44th-45th Sts. on W. side of Sq., famous **Astor Hotel.** Orig. Astor H. at which Thackeray, Dickens & other notables stopped, faced City Hall Pk. (123) 43rd St. bet. 6th Ave. & Times Sq., **Town Hall** (1921.Georg.Col.), famous concert hall.

(124) At 43rd St. the theater dist. begins, the heart of which is **Shubert Alley,** bet. 44th & 45th Sts. (W) of Broadway. (125) Broadway & 47th Sts., **Palace Theater,** formerly well-known vaudeville house; has recently revived vaudeville programs. (126) Opp. Palace Theater in Sq., **Statue of Father Duffy** of famed "Fighting 69th." (127) 49th St. & 8th Ave., **Madison Sq. Garden,** sports arena & hqs. for mass meetings, seats 18,903. Among annual events are 6-Day Bicycle Races, Winter Sports Show, Skating Carnival, N.Y. Police & Firemen's Shows & the Circus. (128) From 44th St. to 57th St., bordering West Side Hy. & North R. are the **Transatlantic Docks,** largest terminal in world; concentration of docks especially designed to handle luxurious ships of Queen Mary calibre. (129) 342 W. 53rd St., **Ch. of St. Benedict the Moor,** in area first sett. by Negroes working on Croton Aqueduct (1840-42); formerly this dist. was Negro slum known as San Juan Hill. Bet. 5th & Ave. of Americas, on 52nd St., night club dist. (130) On 53rd St. bet. 5th & 6th Aves., **Mus. of Mod. Art** (sm.fee); has mod. Amer. & foreign painting, sculpture & graphic art; special exhibitions changed frequently; lectures. Strikingly Mod. bldg. by Edw. D. Stone & Philip L. Goodwin; one of Mus.'s treasures is famous "Guernica" by Pablo Picasso; film showings in auditorium (daily.3 & 5:30.tickets at desk). (131) Near 53rd St. on 6th Ave., **Ziegfeld Theater** (by Jos.Urban) built by late Florenz Ziegfeld for his "Follies"; in lounge, coll. of paintings on the Arts by Salvador Dali. (132) 57th & 7th Ave., **Carnegie Hall** (1891.Ital.Ren.by Wm.B. Tuthill.redecorated 1949), for symphony & concert recitals. On 57th St. from 7th Ave. to Lexington, incl. 5th Ave. & some of side sts. of vic., many famous commercial art galleries (no fees at most). Back of Carnegie Hall, bet. 54th & 55th Sts., **Center Theater,** municipally owned, where opera, drama & ballet is presented at popular prices.

(133) At 59th & Broadway, **Columbus Circle,** with **Statue of Columbus** (1894.Gaetano Russo), on column decorated with bronze ship prows; at base of pillar is sculptured figure. The Circle is now used as outdoor forum. **Merchants Gate,** at entrance to Central Pk. **Maine Mem.** (1912.Attilio Piccirilli), comm. those who lost lives on battleship "Maine."

MIDDLE EAST SIDE: (134) **Union Sq.,** bet. 14th & 17th Sts., 4th Ave. & Broadway, open-air forum since Civil War. Has long been gathering place for jobless & labor demonstrations. In its vic. are located many of N.Y.'s radical & progressive groups & labor organizations. In pk. are number of Mons.; **Equestrian Statue of Washington** (H.K.Brown.base by J.Q.A.Ward) near S. end of pk. facing 14th St. **Statue of Lincoln** (by Brown). **Liberty Pole** (1924) in center of sq., comm. Decl. of Ind. At 15th St. & Union Sq. (W), **Amalgamated Bank,** operated by Amalgamated Clothing Workers Union of America. (135) At NE. cor. of Sq., 100 E. 17th St., **Roosevelt Auditorium,** formerly Tammany Hall, now hqs. for Local 91 of Internat. Ladies Garment Workers. Facing E. side of Pk., **Klein Clothing Store,** outlet for women's apparel in self service style. (136) At 14th & Irving Pl., **Consolidated Edison Co.,** skyscraper on site of famous old Academy of Music opera house. (137) To (E) of Union Sq., bet. 15th & 16th St., divided by 2nd Ave., **Stuyvesant Sq.,** part of Peter Stuyvesant farm. Bordering Pk. & to (E) are several large hospitals. (138) At Rutherford Pl. on W. side of Sq., lovely **Friends Meeting H.** (1860.Fed.). Adj., **Friends Seminary.** (139) NE. cor. of 16th St., brownstone **St. George's Ch.** (mid-19th cent.by Blesch & Eidlitz). J. P. Morgan, Sr., was warden; Ch. is sometimes known as "Morgan's Ch."

(140) Next to St. George's Chapel, **St. Dunstan's H.,** rest house & hqs. for Old Caths., monastic sect; valuable coll. incl. Ital. Bible of 14th cent. & statue of St. Francis. (141) At 138 E. 27th St., **Theater** (free) operated by Basil Davenport since 1915; repertory of the classics. (142) Bet. 20th & 21st Sts., extending on both sides of Lexington Ave., is **Gramercy Pk.** (private). In Pk., bronze **Statue of Booth** as Hamlet (Edmond T.Quinn). 14 Gramercy Pk. S., **Nat. Arts Club.** At No. 16, **The Players,** actors' club founded 1888 by Edwin Booth, (remod.by Stanford White). (143) 144 E. 20th St., **Friends' Meeting H.** (mid-19th cent.) houses one of oldest active Quaker groups. (144) At 28 E. 20th St., **Roosevelt H.,** birthpl. of Theo. Roosevelt (O.wks.); coll. of mementoes of former Pres. (145) 4th Ave. & 21st St., **Calvary Ch.** (1836. Episc.). Members of Roosevelt, Astor & Vanderbilt families have attended this Ch. (146) At 9 Lexington Ave., just (N) of Gramercy Pk., **Home of Peter Cooper** (see above). (147) 137 E. 22nd St., handsome **Children's Court Bldg.,** incl. Domestic Relations Court. (148) SE. cor. of 23rd St. & Lexington Ave., **School of Civic Adm. & Business of City College of N.Y.,** one of 4 mun. colleges (see Upper Manhattan). (149) Bet. Madison & 5th Aves., from E. 23rd to 26th Sts., **Madison Sq. Pk.,** named for Pres. Madison. There are int. mons. in park. **Farragut Statue** (1881.by A.Saint-Gaudens;base by White); (W) of Pk., **Mem. to Gen. Wm. J. Worth,** Mex. War hero buried beneath shaft. At top of lofty flagpole on 5th Ave., **Eternal Light,** comm. AEF of World War I. (150) Inters. Broadway & 5th Ave. at 23rd St., **Flatiron Bldg.** (D.H.Burnham & Co.1902), one of earliest skyscrapers. This is reputedly windiest cor. in Manhattan. (151) Bet. 23rd & 24th Sts. & Madison Ave., **Metropolitan Life Insurance Bldg.** skyscraper (1908.LeBrun & Sons); has clock in tower 26½′ in diameter which has 4 chimes sounding measures of Handel every quarter-hour. Bet. 24th & 25th Sts. is recently erected skyscraper annex. (152) At N. cor. 25th St. & Madison Ave., **Bldg. of Appellate Div. of Supreme Court** (1900.by Jas.Brown Lord); above roof are statuary groups. Inter. is lavishly decorated. (153) From 26th to 27th Sts., from Madison Ave. to 4th Ave., **N.Y. Life Insurance Bldg.** (Goth.by Cass Gilbert). Here formerly stood "old" Madison Sq. Garden, designed by Stanford White, with fine, moorish-inspired tower topped by St. Gaudens' great nude figure of Diana. In this bldg. White was shot by Harry K. Thaw, Pittsburgh multimillionaire, in quarrel over famous beauty of the day. At Thaw's trial his attorney developed novel theory that his client couldn't be held responsible for his act, because at the time he had been victim of a "brainstorm." From 25th to 29th Sts., on Lexington Ave. & side sts., district of Armenian restaurants. (154) At 1 E. 29th St., **Ch. of the Transfiguration** (Episc.1870), known as "Little Ch. Around the Corner," popular for wedding ceremonies. (155) SE. cor. 34th & Park Ave., **Armory of 71st Nat. Guard Regiment,** with tower inspired by town hall in Siena, Italy. (156) Opp. on SW. cor., handsome **Vanderbilt Hotel** (by Warren & Wetmore). (157) At 231 Madison Ave., **J. P. Morgan Home. Morgan Lib.** (O.wks.1913.Ital.Ren.McKim,Mead & White) is at 33 E. 36th St., among most luxuriously appointed priv. museums in world, with valuable coll. of books & mss., sculpture & paintings, prints, objets d'art.

(158) **Empire State Bldg.** (1931.Mod.by Shreve,Lamb,Harmon.) is tallest structure in world, 1,250′ high. Rises in almost unbroken line from a base that covers c.2 as.

Atop shaft at 86th fl. is 200′ Observ. Tower (fee). Tower, due to wind-pressures, has considerable sway. Several yrs. ago aeroplane crashed into bldg., tearing out part of the walls. (159) NE. cor. of 5th Ave., bet. 34th & 35th Sts., is monumental **B. Altman Dept. Store.** (160) Opp., with ent. on 34th St., is **McCreery's Dept. Store.** (161) 409 5th Ave., **Textron Company Store** (Ital.Ren.by McKim,Mead & White). (162) At 36th St., opp. Tiffany's, **Russeks,** designed for the Gorham Co. by same firm as Tiffany's; this is one of 5th Ave.'s finest bldgs. (163) 38th & 5th Ave., **Franklin Simon's,** with new trend in dept. store architecture. (164) NW. cor. of 38th St. & 5th Ave., **Lord & Taylor's** (by Starrett & Van Vleck). (165) NW. cor. 39th St., **S. H. Kress & Co.** (int. Mod.). (166) SE. cor. of 40th St., **Arnold Constable & Co.,** one of oldest N.Y. dept. stores. (167) Bet. 41st & 42nd Sts., white marble **N.Y. Pub. Lib.** (1911.Neo-Class.by Carrère & Hastings) with more than 6,000,000 items in reference coll. Flanking 5th Ave. entrance are statues of couchant lions, by E. C. Potter. On either side of columned entrance are statues by Fred. MacMonnies. Above entrance, sculptured figures by Paul W. Bartlett. Bldg.'s architect, Carrère, always wanted to make alterations of the 5th Ave. front & his widow left funds for this purpose. Rear elevation of the Lib., facing Bryant Pk., is perhaps most impressive. Lib. developed from consolidation of Astor & Lenox libs. & Tilden Trust (1895); lib. has c.million & one-half books avail. through its Circulation Dept. & 51 branches & sub-branches throughout city. Has great colls. of Americana, of priceless incunabula, rare editions, mss., etc. On top fl. is coll. of paintings, incl. some by Gilbert Stuart & other early Amer. artists. Also exhibits of prints, etc. There is a great main reading room on the same fl., always crowded with research workers & students. (168) **Bryant Pk.,** behind N.Y. Pub. Lib., on site of Potter's Field & World Fair of 1853, as well as Crystal Palace, destroyed by fire, 1856. Was Croton Reservoir Pk.; later, Pk. named for poet Wm. C. Bryant. Outdoor "reading room" in summer with music piped from lib. record room.

(169) Opp. on 40th St., at No. 40 W., amazingly ornate **Amer. Radiator Bldg.** (by Raymond Hood). (170) At inters. of 42nd & 5th Ave., **500 Fifth Ave.,** 699′ high, by architects of Empire St. Bldg. (171) SE. cor. Fifth Ave., at No. 551, the **French Building,** ungainly 38-story skyscraper. (172) Turning E. on 42nd St., at No. 60, **Lincoln Bldg.,** 53-story skyscraper. (173) Next to Lincoln Bldg. is **Airline Terminal** (mod.-functional). (174) Opp. is **Grand Central Sta.** (1913.by Warren,Wetmore,Reed & Stem) for N.Y. Central & N.Y., N.H. & H. RRs. Double-deck RR. yard extends under Park Ave. to pt. near 59th St. Bldg.'s S. facade is surmounted by statuary group 48′ high (by Jules Coutan) & has 13′ diameter clock. Main concourse done in marble, with illuminated ceiling representing star-constellations. Directly (N) bet. 45th & 46th Sts., **N.Y. Central Bldg.,** overlooking Park Ave., with strangely ornate tower. (175) 110 E. 42nd St., **Bowery Savings Bank Bldg.** (1923.by York & Sawyer), great banking hall with lavish finish; cast-bronze doors by Wm. H. Jackson & Co. (176) 122 E. 42nd St., **Chanin Skyscraper** (1929.by Sloan & Robertson.observ.tower. fee). (177) 42nd & Lexington, **Commodore Hotel,** largest of Grand Central area's hotels. (178) 42nd & Lexington Ave., **Chrysler Bldg.** (1929.by Wm.Van Allen.Mod. Observ.Rm.O.wks.9-6.fee), world's 2nd tallest (1,048′), chiefly because of addition of slender steel spire. Notable is the contrast of color & line in tower & the basket pattern of stone in lower portion; lobby finished in African marble. (179) At 220 E. 42nd St., **Daily News Bldg.** (by Howells & Hood), one of city's most distinctive skyscrapers. Television Tower (WPIX), one of N.Y.'s 1st TV stas., has been added. (Guided tour of bldg. & plant.) Int. exhibits in entrance lobbies. The Daily News, a tabloid, was founded by Jos. M. Patterson, who had been co-editor of the Chicago Tribune; he wanted vehicle for his then liberal opinions. Supported the late Franklin D. Roosevelt until c.1939, when he began to oppose the New Deal & turned isolationist. Newspaper has largest circulation in U.S. (180) At 420 Lexington Ave., **Graybar Bldg.** (1927.Sloan & Robertson), huge office structure containing many advertising agencies. (181) At 485 Madison Ave., **Hqs. & Studios of Columbia Broadcasting System.** (182) At 49 E. 52nd St., additional studios of CBS, in handsome functional bldg. (by Fellheim & Wagner). (183) Bet. 46th & 47th Sts. on Lexington Ave., **Grand Central Palace** (by Warren & Wetmore); annual auto, flower, motorboat, industrial exhibits. (184) At Lexington Ave. & 49th St., **Shelton Hotel** (by H.L.Harmon), one of city's handsomest tall bldgs.

(185) At 48th St. & 5th Ave., **Collegiate Ch. of St. Nicholas** (1872.Goth.by W.W. Smith), oldest congregation in Manhattan (1628). Has marked pew of Theo. Roose-

velt & "Liberty Bell," 1st to be rung after reading of Decl. of Ind.; to be razed to make way for new Mass. Mutual Life Insurance Co. (186) 49th & 50th Sts. on 5th Ave., **Saks Fifth Ave.,** dept. store. (187) Bet. 5th & 6th Aves. & 48th to 51st Sts., **Rockefeller Center** (Guided Tours:9-9.fee), largest privately-owned business & entertainment center in world; about 80% built on land belonging to Columbia Univ., to which it will revert ultimately together with bldgs. 5th Ave. front buildings are: **Maison Francaise, Brit. Empire Bldg., Pallazza d'Italia, International Bldg.,** all embellished with int. sculptures. On 51st St. facing Plaza, recently completed **Esso Bldg.** Facing Rockefeller Plaza: **Time & Life Bldg.,** housing Time & Life Magazines; opp. is **Holland H.** The **RCA Bldg.** faces sunken plaza; to (N), **Associated Press Bldg.** On Ave. of the Americas: **Center Theater & Radio City Music Hall (RKO Bldg.).** Center has considerable landscaped area incl. promenade off 5th Ave. to sunken plaza, & formal gardens on roofs of many bldgs. There are a number of sculptures at different points, incl. those by Lee Lawrie ("Atlas" on 5th Ave. side), Carl Milles, Isamu Noguchi & Paul Manship ("Prometheus" in Sunken Plaza). Bldgs. are lavishly decorated by murals. On Ave. of Americas entrance of RCA Bldg. are murals by Jose M. Sert, covering murals by Diego Rivera which were disapproved of by the Center's owners. RCA Bldg. is tallest of the group & houses NBC Radio & Television Studios (daily tour.fee). At Ave. of Americas ent. of RCA Bldg., **Mus. of Science & Industry** (O.wks.sm.fee). At 40 W. 49th St., **RCA Exhibition Hall** (O.wks.); radio electronics display. At 50th & Ave. of Americas, **Radio City Music Hall,** largest movie house in world; has famous precision corps of Rockettes, & presents huge ballets. At 49th St. & Ave. of Americas, **Center Theatre,** world's largest indoor ice theater. (188) Bet. 50th-51st St., facing 5th Ave., **Saint Patrick's Cathedral** (1818-95.Goth.Rev.by Jas.Renwick.inspired by Cathedral of Cologne), with 45 of some 70 stained-glass windows from studios of Nicholas Lorin at Chartres & Henry Ely at Nantes; statuary incl. the 14 Stations of the Cross, by Peter J. H. Cuypers (Holland), a statue of St. Francis (reprod.of one by Giovanni Dupre at Assisi), & a Pieta by Wm. O. Partridge. High altar & white marble pulpit by Renwick. Behind apse are Lady Chapel & 2 smaller chapels by Chas. T. Mathews. New rose window (by Chas.J.Connick Assoc.). (189) E. side of Madison Ave., bet. 50th & 51st Sts., **Henry Villard H.** (1885.Ital.Ren.by McKim,Mead & White). Henry Villard was builder of Union Pac. RR. H. was later home of Whitelaw Reid, Ambassador to England. Now houses offices of Cath. Archdiocese.

(190) Bet. 49th & 50th Sts., Park & Lexington, **Waldorf-Astoria,** skyscraper hotel (by Schultze & Weaver), formerly located on site of Empire State Tower. The old hotel was a celebrated hostelry & its Peacock Alley famous in N.Y.'s social annals. Present bldg. is lavishly decorated & has number of fine murals, incl. those in the Sert Room by Jose M. Sert, Sp. artist. (191) On E. side of Park Ave., bet. 50th-51st Sts., **St. Bartholomew's Ch.** (Episc.1930.Byzantine.by Bertram G. Goodhue.Portico.Fr.Romanes.by McKim,Mead & White). Three bronze doors have fine low-reliefs by Andrew O'Connor. Over entrance doors, high relief frieze of biblical scenes. Inter. is richly decorated. Ch. is effectively backed by the huge **Gen. Electric Co. Bldg.** on Lexington Ave. (192) 370 Park Ave., **Racquet & Tennis Club** (1918.Ital.Ren.by McKim,Mead & White). (193) 645 5th Ave., **Best & Co.** (mod.), women's dept. store. (194) At NW. cor. 53rd St. & 5th Ave., **St. Thomas Ch.** (Episc. 1913.Goth.by Cram,Goodhue & Ferguson); statuary in great reredos over altar by Lee Lawrie. (195) NW. cor. of 5th Ave. & 51st St., new **Crowell-Collier** skyscraper harmonizing with Rockefeller Center group. (196) NW. cor. 54th St., **Univ. Club** (1900.Ital.style.by McKim,Mead & White); renaissance frescoes; murals by H. Siddons Mowbray. (197) NE. cor. 56th St., **Bonwit Teller,** exclusive women's store. (198) 57th St. & Park Ave., **Ritz Towers Hotel** (by Emory Roth & Carrère & Hastings), 42 stories high. In neighborhood of 57th St., near Pk., several new noteworthy constructions incl. Universal Pictures Bldg., composition of glass & horizontal stripes. (199) From 58th-60th Sts., the **Grand Army Plaza** serves as impressive forecourt for stately hotels surrounding it. In Plaza is **Pulitzer Mem. Fountain** (by Karl Bitter;architects:Carrère & Hastings). At Central Pk. entrance is **Equestrian Statue of Gen. Wm. T. Sherman** (by A.Saint-Gaudens), with figure of Victory. Bldgs. around Plaza complete an harmonious design: **Plaza Hotel** (Fr.Ren.by Henry J. Hardenbergh); 5th Ave. & 59th St., **Sherry-Netherland Tower** (by Schultze & Weaver); **Savoy-Plaza Hotel** (by McKim,Mead & White); & a charming bldg., at S. side of Plaza, designed by Eli Kahn. At 5th Ave. & 61st St., **Hotel Pierre** (by

Schultze & Weaver). At SE. cor. Central Pk. S. & Ave. of Americas, **N.Y. Athletic Club** (by York & Sawyer), one of most exclusive men's clubs.

MIDTOWN EAST SIDE: 3rd Ave. Elevated—sole remaining elevated through Manhattan, serves East Side. From 40th St. to 60's, fine antique shops & restaurants. (200) 1st Ave. to East R. from 26th to 30th Sts., **Bellevue Hospital** (new bldgs.by McKim,Mead & White), is one of oldest general hospitals in U.S., affiliated with 3 univs.: Columbia, Cornell & N.Y. New bldgs. have done much to remedy overcrowding. Plan is under way to build, in conn. with N.Y. Univ., a Clinic & rehabilitation Medical Center in the 4-block area (N) of present bldgs. (201) **Queens Midtown Tunnel,** with entrance bet. 36th & 37th Sts., off 2nd Ave., extends 7,750′ to Borden Ave. in L.I. City. On Plaza will shortly be erected the new Air Lines Terminal, conn. with Expressway to LaGuardia Airport. (202) Occupying area bet. 42nd St. & 48th St., bet. 1st Ave. & East R. Dr., **United Nations** (see Flushing Meadows Pk., Queens borough, temporary hqs.). Site was donated in 1946 by John D. Rockefeller, Jr. Project will consist of 3 mutually integrated elements, with large auditorium for sessions of Gen. Assembly, a Conference Area incl. 3 main conference rooms conn. to **Secretariat;** the 1st unit now being erected. **Lib.,** with capacity for 325,000 books, erected by City of N.Y. in 1947, is to be integrated into group. The city of N.Y. plans to make suitable approaches from side streets & avenues. (203) SE. cor. of 1st Ave. & 46th St., **Tablet,** comm. execution of Nathan Hale (1776), supposed to have occurred near here. (204) At 48th St. on (S) to 59th St. on (N); from 1st Ave. (E) to East R., **Beekman Pl. & Sutton Pl.,** fashionable dist. in brownstone decades of last century, but later became slum area; was reclaimed in 20's, at which time the 26-story **Beekman Tower Hotel** (1928.John Mead Howells) was built. **One Beekman Pl.** is a huge apartment bldg. with terrace gardens facing R. Bet. E. 52nd & 53rd Sts., **River H.** (by Bottomley,Wagner & White), 26-story bldg. rising from R. shore, near area dramatized in Sidney Kingsley's play "Dead End." At 124 E. 59th St., **N.Y. Cancer Institute** (main bldgs.on Welfare I.:see). (205) 59th St. here leads to entrance of **Queensboro Bridge** at 2nd Ave., crossing Welfare I. to L.I. City.

UPPER MANHATTAN: (206) From 59th St., bet. 5th & 8th Aves. to Cathedral Pky. (110th St.), **Central Pk.** (recr.facils.playgrs.boat.hik.bridle paths.zoo). Built in the 1850's at instance of Ferdinand Wood, corrupt N.Y. boss, to give jobs to unemployed. Will have new recr. center at 59th St. incl. artificial ice-rink & restaurant. **Zoo** (O.wks.) at East Dr. & 5th Ave. Entrance of 72nd St. & 5th Ave., **The Mall** (summer concerts in charmingly designed Shell). Pk. has several Ls., incl. **Conservatory L.** (boat.), a toy yacht lake. Behind Metropolitan Mus. of Art (81st St.& 5th Ave.see below), **"Cleopatra's Needle"** (quarried by Thothmes III in 1600 B.C.; brought over in 1880). Bet. 103rd & 105th Sts., **Conservatory Gardens,** seasonal exhibits; hot houses (O). At 110th St., **Blockh.,** erected during War of 1812. On W. side of Pk. at 67th St., **Tavern on the Green** (restaurant). (W) of Reservoir, **Equestrian Statue of Simon Bolivar,** S.Amer. patriot (by S.Farnum).

EAST OF CENTRAL PK. (207) At 1 E. 65th St., **Temple Emanu-El** (O.9-5:30. guide.1929.Romanes.by Kohn,Butler & Stein), richly decorated inter.; has Ark which contains scrolls of Biblical law placed in mosaic sanctuary. (208) Bet. 68th & 69th Sts., from Park to Lexington Aves., **Hunter College** (est.1870.adds.1936.1939.by Shreve,Lamb,Harmon,Harrison & Fouilhoux), mun. women's college; has branch campus in Bronx (see). Has acquired former home of Sarah D. Roosevelt (47 E. 65th St.) for community center of all faiths. Teacher's training & undergraduate courses in arts & sciences. (209) At 1 E. 70th St., **Frick Mus.** (O.wks.free.1914.Louis XVI.by Carrère & Hastings), one-time residence of steel industrialist, Henry C. Frick; outstanding coll. of paintings & other art objects; chamber music series & lectures. (210) Bet. 80th & 84th Sts. on 5th Ave., **Metropolitan Mus. of Art** (O.wks. 10-5.1880.Class.by Vaux & Mould;Hunt & Son;McKim,Mead & White), one of great mus. of world; Egyptian Coll., one of best outside Cairo, Egypt; coll. of Far East Art (Cesnola Coll.); great coll. of armor & musical instruments; Bache Coll. of pre-18th cent. paintings; the J. P. Morgan Coll. is one of most comprehensive of European decorative arts from Gallo-Roman to 19th cent.; sculpture of all periods; more than 2,300 oils & other paintings; Amer. wing incl. decorative arts & reprods. of early Amer. rooms; int. Costume Institute & large Print Room. Frick Mus. (see above) & Cloisters (see below) maintained by Mus. (211) At 1071 5th Ave. (near 90th St.), **Mus. of Non-Objective Painting** (O.wks.free); exhibitions changed frequently. (212)

SE. cor. 103rd St. & 5th Ave., **N.Y. Academy of Medicine,** centralizing agency for undergraduate medical education. Has lib. 2nd only in size to Army Medical Lib. in Washington, D.C. (213) 92nd St. & 5th Ave., **Jewish Mus.;** exhibits paintings & murals on Jewish life & tradition; coll. of ceremonial objects. (214) Bet. 103rd & 104th Sts. on 5th Ave., **Mus. of City of N.Y.** (Georg.Coll.by Jos.Friedlander.O.wks.), showing chronological development of various phases of N.Y. life; memorabilia of Geo. Washington & Alex. Hamilton. (215) Bet. 99th & 101st Sts., **Mt. Sinai Hospital.** (216) Bet. 104th & 105th Sts., on 5th Ave., **Hecksher Foundation for Children & N.Y. Soc. for the Prevention of Cruelty to Children;** Children's Theater. (217) From 76th St. to 96th St.; from Lexington Ave. to East R., **Yorkville,** with heavy pop. of German descent, intermingled with Czechs, Slovaks, Hungarians; foreign restaurants. Hqs. of Nazi Bund before World War II. (218) On East R., paralleling Yorkville, is **Welfare I.** (O.only to visitors of patients;ferry from ft. of 78th St.); located on I. are **Cancer Institute, Welfare Hospital for Chronic Diseases & N.Y. City Hospital,** among other institutions. Queensboro Bridge (see above) has pier on I. (219) Near 66th St. on Lexington Ave., **Ch. of St. Vincent Ferrer** (1917.Goth.by Bertram G.Goodhue); sculpture by Lee Lawrie. (220) Overlooking East R. bet. 64th & 68th Sts., **Rockefeller Institute for Medical Research,** developed by Dr. Simon Flexner, financed by J. D. Rockefeller, Jr.; one of world's outstanding medical research institutions. (221) Bet. 67th & 68th Sts., York & First Aves., **Mem. Hospital for Treatment of Cancer** (mod.by Jas.G.Rogers & Henry C.Pelton), one of greatest cancer research centers; combines teaching, research & practice of medicine & surgery. (222) Bet. 68th & 71st Sts., York & Marie Curie Aves., **N.Y. Hospital & Cornell Univ. Medical College** (1933.mod.Goth.by Coolidge,Shepley,Bulfinch,Abbot), newest of Manhattan's medical centers. Since 1927, N.Y. Hospital has become assoc. with Cornell Medical College. (223) From 84th St. along East R. Dr. to E. 89th St., **Carl Schurz Pk.,** in which is **Gracie Mansion** (1799), built by Archibald Gracie; now official home of Mayor of N.Y. (224) Above 96th St. begins **Harlem;** covers a considerable area in N. Manhattan. It has in recent yrs. pushed down into the 90's on both sides of Central Pk. & on up to Washington Heights in (N). (Sugar Hill, Harlem's Park Ave. dist., runs west of 8th Ave. from c.138th to 155th St.) Older sec. of Harlem lies below Morningside & St. Nicholas Parks & extends (E) to Harlem & East Rs. 125th St. leads to entrance of Triborough Bridge (see Bronx) and is Harlem's busiest thoroughfare. Harlem has been undergoing drastic transformation with erection of several extensive housing projects which are wiping out old & terribly overcrowded slums. Near 8th Ave. & 125th St. is **Apollo Theatre;** weekly programs, featuring some of best vaudeville entertainers. Lenox & 7th Aves. are at the heart of Harlem; with restaurants, churches of exotic sects & night clubs; many of latter are also located on side sts. Franklin D. Roosevelt Dr., now ending at 125th St., will extend eventually along Harlem R. to 181st St., joining Harlem R. Dr. At 103rd St. & the Dr., a footbridge is being built to Ward's I. (see Bronx). (225) At 155th St. on 8th Ave., **Polo Grounds,** home of N.Y. Giants; seating capacity of c.60,000.

WEST SIDE DIST., bounded by 59th St. on (S), Central Pk. on (E), Riverside Dr. on (W) & extending to Henry Hudson Bridge at N. end of Manhattan I.: (226) From 72nd St. **Riverside Dr.** cont. along W. bank of Hudson R., c.7$^{m}$ to Dyckman St., with excellent views of Hudson R., Palisades & Geo. Washington Bridge. Rd. parallels Henry Hudson Pky., which from 72nd St. is built over N.Y. Central RR. tracks; in reclaimed area are playgrounds. Along Dr. are tall apts., & a number of Mons. (227) Central Pk. W. & 70th St., **Congregation Shearith Israel** (1897.Ital.Ren.by Bruner & Tryon), oldest surviving Jewish congregation in America, founded 1655 by Sp. & Portuguese Jews who fled Inquisition. (228) Central Pk. W., bet. 76th & 77th Sts., **N.Y. Hist. Soc.** (O.wks.1804.by York & Sawyer.adds.by Walker & Gillette); Amer. portrait gallery; Ital. Ren. paintings; Audubon drawings. (229) Bet. 77th & 81st Sts., Columbus Ave. & Central Pk. W., **Amer. Mus. of Nat. Hist.** (O.wks.), with especially int. exhibits of life-like habitat groupings of animals of Africa & N. America; outstanding gem coll., incl. "Star of India," largest cut sapphire in world. Extensive ethnological displays; coll. of fossil vertebrates, incl. dinosaur eggs. **Hayden Planetarium** (O), entrance on 81st St. facing Central Pk.; lecturers operate control board in "Theatre of the Sky" for reproducing light images, projected on overhead screen, of all visible stars; monthly change of program. Mus. plans to est. a bird sanctuary on Great Gull I. (Borough of Queens). On Central Park W. is heroic equestrian statue of Theodore Roosevelt. (230) SW. cor. 66th St. & Columbus Ave., **Ch. of St. Paul the Apostle,** rich inter. with sculptures by famous artists. (231) At 103rd St. & Riverside Dr., **Master Institute of United Arts** (1921.by H.W.Corbett & Sugerman & Berger); has rare Tibetan mss. & mus. of mod. art; is educational & art training center. (232) At 106th St., where West End Ave. terminates in Broadway, Pk. with **Fountain in Mem. of Isidor & Ida Straus** (by A.Lukeman), who died in Titanic disaster. (233) Amsterdam Ave. & W. 112th Sts., **Cathedral of St. John the Divine** (Episc.Goth.Heins & LaFarge;Ralph A.Cram); now two-thirds finished; has been in construction for 50 yrs.; will be largest Goth. cathedral in world, seating 40,000; 601′ long & 146′ wide; the W. front is to have 2 towers 266½′ high, & there is to be a central tower more than 400′ in height; cost is to be c.30 millions, of which 20 million has already been spent. (234) At 114th St. & Morningside Dr., **Ch. of Notre Dame of Lourdes** (Cath.O.7-9.1915.Romanes.); practically the entire ch. was imported from France, together with Carrara marble & altars; one of finest examples of Ital. Ren. churches in Amer.

(235) From 114th-121st Sts., from Broadway to Amsterdam Ave., **Columbia Univ.,** located on site of Battle of Harlem Heights (1776). 2nd wealthiest Univ. in country, it has 3rd largest Univ. lib. & 4th largest law library. Included among Univ. depts. are **Barnard College** for women, facing Broadway bet. 116th & 119th Sts.; **Teachers' College** on 120th St. bet. Broadway & Amsterdam Ave.; **Columbia Presb. Medical Center** with Medical & Dental Schools (see below); & undergraduate college & various professional schools; from 17 different schools & colleges bet. 6,000 & 8,000 students are graduated annually. In the South Quadrangle facing 114th St. is the **Nicholas Murray Butler Lib.,** with Harkness Academic Theater; facing 116th St. is **Sch. of Journalism.** The easterly group of bldgs. bounded by Amsterdam Ave. & Morningside Drive, bet. W. 116th & W. 117th Sts., incl. the **President's H.,** the **Men's Faculty Club; Brander Matthews Hall** (with Brander Matthews Theater) & **East Hall** with Sch. of Painting & Sculpture. On the N. side of W. 117th St. are the following: **Maison Francaise, Deutsches Haus, Russian Institute, Casa Hispanica** & **Casa Italiana.** Directly opp., extending from 116th to 120th Sts., is Upper Quadrangle; in it among other bldgs. are the charming **St. Paul's Chapel, Philosophy Hall, Low Mem. Lib.,** a million-dollar structure given the Univ. by Seth Low, who was 1st Pres. after Univ. moved to present site; in front of Lib. is **Statue of Alma Mater** by D. C. French. (N) of Lib. is **Univ. Hall** with Gymnasium. Columbia Univ. was founded as King's College in 1754 by grant from Geo. I & was orig. located on land deeded by Trinity Ch. along Broadway opp. Park Row. At outbreak of Rev. Dr. Myles Cooper, fanatic Tory, was Pres.; he escaped on May 10, 1775 while Alex. Hamilton, a pupil 17 yrs. old, delayed the mob with a patriotic harangue on the College steps. John Jay, Rbt. Livingston & Gouverneur Morris were also students. During Rev. College was occupied by Brit. In 1857 the College was moved to 49th St. & Madison Ave., thence to its present location on Morningside Heights, in 1897. Today Univ. is under administration of Dwight D. Eisenhower, 13th Pres. The Univ. maintains several camps: Barnard College Camp, near Ossining, N.Y.; Camp Columbia for Engineering, near Litchfield, Conn.; Nevis (manor house built for son of Alex. Hamilton), near Irvington-on-Hudson, used by Dept. of Physics; Sch. of Tropical Medicine at Univ. of Puerto Rico; & Yale-Columbia Southern Station at Univ. of Witwatersrand at Johannesburg, Union of South Africa. (236) From 120th to 122nd Sts. & from Claremont Ave., (E) to Broadway, **Union Theological Seminary** (Episc.1910.by Allen & Collens), block of imposing Goth. bldgs. (237) Bet. 122nd & 123rd Sts. on Broadway, **Jewish Theological Seminary of Amer.** (Col. Georg.by Wm.Gehron); large lib. & mus.; teachers' institute & college of Jewish studies. (238) 120-130 Claremont Ave., **Juilliard Sch. of Music** (1920); has fine Concert Hall where operas & concerts are presented during winter. (239) At 120th St., Riverside Dr. circles **Grant's Tomb** (O.wks.9-5.1897.by J.H.Duncan). Over entrance are carved Grant's words: "Let us have peace." Inter. is reminiscent of Napoleon's tomb in the Invalides at Paris, France. Twin sarcophagi with remains of Gen. & Mrs. Grant are in crypt. (240) At N. end of oval where stands Grant's Tomb is **Claremont Inn** (1783). (241) South of Inn on Dr., **Grave of St. Claire Pollock,** with stone urn "Erected to Memory of an Amiable Child" (July 15, 1797). (242) Riverside Dr. & 122nd St., **Riverside Ch.** (O.wks.9-5.1921-31.by Allen,Pelton,Collens.inspired by Cathedral of Chartres), long assoc. with Rev. Harry Emerson Fosdick,

prominent as leader in social reforms. Ch. has 28-story tower in which is Laura Spelman Rockefeller Mem. Carillon of 72 bells; has clubrooms, nurseries, lib., theater & gymnasium. (243) Facing Riverside Ch. to (N) is **Internat. H.** (1924), mostly for foreign students doing academic research. (244) From 136th to 140th Sts., along Amsterdam Ave. in Washington Heights, **Main Center of City College of N.Y.** (Eng. Goth.founded 1849), one of 4 units of City College which has c.70,000 students; free to residents of city; has branches at Lexington Ave. & 23rd St. (see above) & in Bronx, Brooklyn & Queens (see). **Lewisohn Stadium;** summer symphony concerts, opera & ballet; seats c.15,000. (245) At 287 Convent Ave., (N) of 141st St., **Hamilton Grange** (O.wks.10-5.post-Col.by McComb), erected by Alex. Hamilton as summer home; Mus. has wealth of Hamiltoniana; Statue of Alex. Hamilton (by Wm.O. Partridge). (246) Bet. Riverside Dr. & Amsterdam Ave., from 153rd to 155th Sts., **Trinity Ch. Cemetery,** largest in Manhattan; here are buried members of many hist. N.Y. families; also has grave of Alfred Tennyson Dickens, son of novelist, Madame Jumel (see below), Clement C. Moore (see Chelsea Pk.) & John J. Audubon. (247) On SE. cor. of Broadway & 155th St., **Chapel of the Intercession** (1915.Amer.Goth. by Bertram G.Goodhue). High altar has stones from Holy Land & places of early Christian worship. (248) Broadway at 156th St. are: (A) **Mus. of Amer. Ind.** (O.wks. Heye Foundation); coll. of material concerning Amer. aborigines, particularly those of Mex., Guatemala & Peru. (B) **Amer. Geographical Soc.** (O); this organization has sponsored number of arctic, antarctic & other explorations. (C) **Hispanic Soc. of America** (O); important coll. of Sp. paintings; equestrian **Statue of El Cid** (by Anna H.Huntington), in court; large lib. with 1st editions & orig. mss. pertaining to Sp. & Portuguese culture. (D) **Amer. Numismatic Soc.** (O); exhibitions of U.S. & hist. coins. (E) **Amer. Academy of Arts & Letters,** Mus. (O) has memorabilia of members, among whom were W. Dean Howells, A. Saint-Gaudens, Sam. Clemens & Edw. MacDowell. (249) In Roger Morris Pk., bet. 160th & 162nd Sts., above Edgecombe Ave., is **Jumel Mansion** (O.wks.1765.Col.Georg.by Roger Morris); used as hqs. by Washington; also occupied by Aaron Burr who married Madame Jumel. (250) Along Broadway from 165th to 168th Sts., **Columbia Presb. Medical Center** (1928.by Jas. Gamble Rogers); incl. Presb. Hospital, Neurological Institute & Institute of Ophthalmology. (251) 187th St. & Amsterdam Ave., **Rabbi Isaac Elchanan Theological Seminary & Yeshiva;** Hebrew training for Orthodox Rabbinate. (252) Fort Washington Ave. & 179th St., entrance to **Geo. Washington Bridge** (1931.by Cass Gilbert); 3,500′ river span, 248′ above high water; cost 80 millions; 15,484,000 vehicles cross bridge yearly. (253) Off Riverside Dr. near Fort Washington Ave. is S. entrance to **Fort Tryon Pk.** & Site of Ft. which figured in fighting when Washington retreated to N.J. Observ. terrace overlooking Hudson R. In N. part of Pk. are **The Cloisters,** branch of Metropolitan Mus.; reprod. of medieval monastery; has important coll. of Medieval Art, incl. 15th cent. tapestry of "Hunt of the Unicorn," to which was added recently the medieval tapestry treasure, "Nine Heroes," painstakingly pieced together from fragments. (254) At 204th St. & Broadway, **Dyckman H.** (Mus.O.wks. 1748.Dutch Col.), only 18th cent. farmh. in Manhattan. (255) (W) of Dyckman H. at Payson Ave., entrance to **Inwood Hill Pk.,** once site of Algonquin Ind. settlement. Pk. is traversed by Henry Hudson Dr. to entrance of **Henry Hudson Bridge** (by Madigan-Hyland), spanning Harlem Ship Canal. (256) Adj. to Inwood Hill Pk., **Isham Pk.** Both pks. face Spuyten Duyvil Creek; old Isham Mansion on summit of hill. (257) Bet. 218th St., Broadway & Harlem R., Columbia Univ.'s **Baker Field;** sports stadium & boath. (258) **High & Washington Bridges,** both graceful spans, conn. the northern heights of Manhattan with Bronx across Harlem R. respectively at 178th & 182nd Sts.

BROOKLYN & QUEENS extend from East R. in (N) to Atlantic Oceans on (S) & from the Narrows on (W) to Nassau Cty. Line on (E). A Belt Blvd. system roughly circles water fronts of both boroughs, & pkys. criss-cross them linking the larger pks. Jamaica Bay on S. edge of area is separated from ocean by Rockaway Peninsula. Bay has been redeemed by dredging & filling & will be one of city's greatest recr. areas. Sewage disposal plants will make both the NE. Queens water front & Jamaica Bay avail. to bathers. Many fine pks. have been created in both boroughs in recent yrs. Coney I. & the Rockaways have splendid pub. bath. beaches. The 3 rapid transit systems & Long Island RR. serve the area. Throughout both Brooklyn & Queens many new pub. housing projects have been built & many more are in construction.

The metropolitan reg.'s greatest airports are located (S) of East R.: LaGuardia, Internat. & Floyd Bennett fields.

Brooklyn has an area of 88.8 sq. miles & takes in all of Kings Cty. It has upward of 2,800,000 pop. & a large slice of the shipping & industry of the metropolitan reg. Its street system is something of an unplanned maze, based upon hys. of the many villages that were brought together into the original city of Brooklyn. Despite its industrial & commercial activity, the borough is still largely residential—"a city of homes." Due to fact that it had independent mun. existence for so long, it has developed a cultural pattern of its own—colleges, univs., technical schools, museums, a music center, a symphony orchestra, a great pub. lib. & a great shopping center.

First settlement in 1637, by Dutch, was known as Breuckelin, after Holland town. In 1834 Brooklyn was incorporated as a city & in 1898 became part of Greater N.Y., whose 1st mayor, Seth Low, was a Brooklynite.

Queens is largest of the 5 boroughs, with area of 126.6 sq. miles. Its boundary with Brooklyn takes off at shipping-jammed Newtown Cr. & then runs (S) in an irregular line to Rockaway Inlet, outlet of Jamaica Bay. E. boundary is Nassau Cty. line; runs from Little Neck harbor, once famous for clams, (S) past Jamaica Bay to Atlantic Beach, on the ocean. Queens in pt. of development is youngest of boroughs (Staten I. never having boomed at all). With construction of Queensborough Bridge, L.I. RR., tubes, subways, Midtown Vehicular Tunnel & Whitestone Bridge, its wide spaces have been thrown open to Manhattan's overflow. Its pop., still expanding rapidly, is today c.1,500,000. Concurrent with pop. growth has been industrial development, mostly in Long Island City, of which Queensborough Bridge Plaza is the focal pt. Jamaica is the transfer pt. of the Long Island RR. where passengers are distributed to other boroughs & the S. shore. Queens is predominantly residential. Formerly rows of one & two family houses were the characteristic dwelling type, but in recent yrs. there have been great pub. & private apartment developments. Queens is most rural of the boroughs, with 139 farms, as opposed to Brooklyn's 41. First settlement took place at Maspeth (1642) & soon after at Flushing (Vliessingen), where in 1660's occurred persecution of Quakers by Peter Stuyvesant (see Intro. to N.Y.C.). Together with rest of L.I., Queens suffered from encroachments of New Englanders. During Rev., Tory sentiment was rampant. Both Queens & Brooklyn were occupied by Brit. after Battle of L.I.

PTS. OF INT.—DOWNTOWN BROOKLYN: Much of vic. around Brooklyn Bridge has already been cleared of slums & much is shortly to be cleared with development of new Civic Center (see below). Sand St. running NE. from Bridge & sts. branching off it are famous as sailors' hangout. (1) Flushing & Cumberland Aves., entrance to **U.S. (N.Y.) Navy Yard** (O.appl.); Fulton's steamboat was built here (1814). At East R., **Commandant's H.** (early 19th cent.). **Old Submarine** (1864) which proved impractical. **Pillar** comm. Amer. sailors killed at Canton, China (1856). Navy Hospital has been shut down after 100 yrs. of service. (2) In Williamsburg Bridge Plaza, **Statue of Geo. Washington,** by H. M. Shrady. (3) In Monitor Pk., **Monitor Mem.,** by A. di Fillipi. Monitor was built & launched near here (see Norfolk, Va.). (4) On 170 Fulton St., **Tablet,** comm. fact that Walt Whitman set up "Leaves of Grass" in printing shop here. Brooklyn Heights, to (W) of Bridge, was formerly aristocratic quarter, has fine view of harbor & several large hotels & apartment bldgs. (5) Orange St. near Henry St., **Plymouth Ch.** (1849.by J.C.Wells), where Henry Ward Beecher auctioned off a fugitive slave girl as part of his anti-slavery propaganda. Many abolitionists held forth here. Adj., **Plymouth Institute** (Ch. center). In Mem. Pk., **Statue of Henry Ward Beecher,** by G. Borglum. (6) Pierrepont & Clinton Sts., **Long Island Hist. Soc.** (O.exc.Sun.& hols.); int. coll. of Long I. material, rare mss. (7) Clinton & Henry Sts., **Ch. of the Holy Trinity** (Episc.mid-19th cent.Goth.by M.Lefèvre). (8) Henry & Remsen Sts., **Ch. of the Pilgrims** (mid-19th cent.by Rich.Upjohn). (9) Hicks St. & Grace Court, **Grace Ch.** (mid-19th cent.Goth. by Rich.Upjohn). (10) 131 Clinton St., **St. Ann's Ch.** (Episc.post-Civil War.by Renwick & Sands), known as Mother of Brooklyn Chs.

FULTON ST. DIST.: This is the political, shopping, cultural & amusement center. New Civic Center is planned at S. Parkes Cadman Plaza (named for Brooklyn clergyman famous for his radio sermons); will be bounded by Fulton, Jay, Washington & Sands Sts., & will run to Borough Hall. A new Supreme Ct. Bldg., Welfare Center, Fed. Bldgs., Housing Development & War Mem. are to be built in Center. (11) At inters. of Fulton, Joralemon & Court Sts., **Borough Hall** (Class.1849.cupola is later add.) accoms. borough offices. (12) In Pk., **Statue of Henry Ward Beecher,** by J. Q. A. Ward. In vic. are **Supreme Ct. & Hall of Records.** (13) 112 Schermerhorn St., **Friends Meetingh.** & school which was scheduled for demolition to make room for new jail, but has been reprieved. (14) On Henry St., **L.I. Medical College of Medicine** which plans new center at Clarkson St., opp. Kings Cty. Hospital. (15) 185 Livingston St., **Polytechnic Institute.** (16) 96 Schermerhorn St., **St. John's Univ.** (see below). (17) Jay St. & Cathedral Pl., **St. James Pro-Cathedral** (Cath.1822). (18) Adams & Johnson Sts., **Brooklyn Daily Eagle,** on whose editorial staff Walt Whitman served until forced off because of anti-slavery opinions. (19) Myrtle Ave. & Cumberland St., **Ft. Greene Pk. Martyr's Mon.** (by Stanford White), comm. Rev. patriots who perished in Brit. prison hulks anchored in N.Y. harbor during Rev. In near-by crypt are buried their remains. (20) Ashland Pl., **Brooklyn Academy of Music,** for opera, concerts, lectures & other cultural activities, under sponsorship of Brooklyn Institute of Arts & Sciences. (21) Atlantic & Flushing Aves., **Long I. RR. Sta.** (22) On Hanson Pl., **Williamsburg Bank Bldg.,** tallest skyscraper in Brooklyn. (23) 215 Ryerson Pl., near DeKalb Ave., **Pratt Institute,** est. 1887 by Chas. Pratt, Standard Oil partner; has group of architecturally int. bldgs. Gives training in sciences, engineering, technical branches & fine arts. Opp., **Pratt Lib.,** one of 1st free libs. in city. (24) 75 Lewis Ave., at Willoughby Ave., **St. John's Univ.,** uptown & main branch (est.1870); arts & sciences college & graduate schools. (25) In Fulton Pk., at Stuyvesant Ave., **Statue of Rbt. Fulton.** (26) 1313 Bedford Ave., **Medical Soc. of Kings Cty. & Brooklyn Academy of Medicine.** (27) In Grant Sq., at Bergen St. & Bedford Ave., **Statue of Gen. U. S. Grant** (by Wm.O.Partridge). (28) Eastern Pky. & Flatbush Ave., **Grand Army Plaza,** at entrance to Prospect Pk. Soldiers & Sailors Mem., by J. Duncan, surmounted by quadriga, by F. MacMonnies. Decorated by figures of U. S. Grant & Lincoln by W. R. O'Donovan & T. Eakins. In front of Arch is Bailey Fountain with sculptured figures. In vic. of Plaza was Brooklyn's "Gold Coast" where stood the houses of mid-19th cent. wealthy.

(29) **Prospect Pk.** comprises 526 as. It is smaller than Central Pk., but perhaps more attractive because of natural features. The Pk. has various recr. facils. & several Ls. On Flatbush Ave. is **Vale of Cashmere,** noted for its rhododendron, & the **Zoo** (O). Near Zoo is **Lefferts Mansion** (O.1777.Dutch Col.) & also **Battle Pass,** where Patriots tried to hold the Brit. during Rev. Near Mansion, at Empire Blvd. entrance, is **The Toll H.,** which was at boundary of village of Flatbush. There is a **Music Grove,** at which summer band concerts are given. On the Prospect (W) side of Pk. is **Litchfield Mansion** (O.1855) once center of Brooklyn social life. Beyond the Long Meadow is old **Quaker Cemetery.** On Prospect Hill is **Mem.,** comm. Md. regiment that fought Brit. here during Rev. Fine view. At various pk. entrances & throughout pk. are sculptures by well-known artists. (30) Eastern Pky. & Flatbush Ave., **Brooklyn Pub. Lib.** (1939.by Githens & Kelly) which cost some $5,000,000. (31) Eastern Pky. & Washington St., **Brooklyn Mus.** (O.wks.Sun.& hols.1-5.by McKim, Mead & White), contains outstanding art colls. illustrating cultural hist. of Amer., Europe, Africa & Orient. Mus. has a fine print coll. & paintings of various periods & various schools incl. moderns. Educational services. Concerts Sun. 1:30 p.m. (32) Near Mus. is **Brooklyn Botanical Garden** (O) with 50 as. of beautiful gardens, especially the Japanese Niwa. In the Systematic Sec. can be observed progression of plants from simpler to more complex forms. In court of **Lab. Bldg.** (by McKim,Mead & White) are sculptures of various famous scientists. (33) At Brooklyn Ave. & Park Pl., **Children's Mus.** (O.wks.Sun.p.m.), first of its kind, lectures, films are shown. (34) Bedford Ave. & Sullivan Pl., **Ebbets Field,** home of Brooklyn "Dodgers" baseball team. Seats more than 30,000. (35) Flatbush & Church Aves., lovely **Flatbush Reformed Ch.** (1796) on site of earlier Chs. (36) Flatbush & Church Aves., **Erasmus High School,** founded 1787, said to be 1st secondary sch. chartered by N.Y. State. **Orig. bldg.** (1787) surrounded by modern school structures, was erected with funds, part of which were contributed by Alex. Hamilton & Aaron Burr; rest. as a Mus. (37) Bedford Ave. & Ave. H., **Brooklyn College** (1937.Georg.by Randolph Evans), beautifully landscaped 42-a. tract; one of 4 mun. colleges. (38) 150 Amersfort Pl., **Faculty Club** in the Old Ditmas H. (1827). (39) 1128 E. 34th St., **Coe H.** (1793). (40) Kings Hy. & E. 22nd St., **Bennett Homestead** (1766) is an old Dutch farmh.

BELT PKY. TOUR: This Tour circles both boroughs along or near waterfront for most of its extent. Take Gowanus Pky. in S. Brooklyn near entrance to Brooklyn-

Battery Tunnel at Henry St. Pky. passes several great port installations: (41) **Atlantic Basin,** at end of Pioneer St.; (42) **Erie Basin & Port Authority Grain Terminal,** at foot of Columbia St., on Gowanus Bay; (43) **St. Barge Canal Terminal,** at foot of Henry St.; (44) **Bush Terminal** (O.appl.at 45th St.), one of largest terminal installations in the world, lies bet. 28th & 50th Sts.; (45) **N.Y. Port of Embarkation & Army Supply Base,** at foot of 58th St. (46) Near the Narrows, **Ft. Hamilton Pk.,** in which is Dover Patrol Mon., comm. U.S. Navy's part in World War I. (47) At Ft. Hamilton Pky. & 99th St., **St. John's Ch.** (1834). (48) **Ft. Hamilton** (O.1831), one of city's chain of defenses. In Reserv. is recently erected skyscraper **Veterans Hospital,** of mod. functional design; 4,000 piles had to be driven to support bldg. On an I. off Ft. Hamilton, is **Ft. Lafayette** (1822) which during World Wars I & II was used as an arsenal. Plans are on foot to restore it as a pub. mon. (49) Bet. 7th Ave. & 14th Ave., **Dyker Beach Pk.** (recr.facils.). (50) 18th Ave. & 83rd St., **New Utrecht Reformed Ch.** (org.1677.bldg.1828). (51) Belt Pky. System now reaches **Coney I.** (O.May 30-mid-Sept.), accessible by BMT, boats from 42nd St. & Battery Pk. Ocean Pky. from S. end of Prospect Pk. is most direct auto route. Coney I. is greatest amusement resort in the country & during summer, especially on scorching days, is jammed by more than 1,000,000 people. There are a long boardwalk, ample parking areas & municipally-owned bath. facils. The boardwalk, the Bowery & Surf Ave. are lined with shops, restaurants & amusement places. Luna & Steeplechase Pks. are the chief amusement centers. It is planned to build a great Oceanarium at Coney I. to replace the aquarium formerly at Battery Pk., Manhattan (see). Brighton Beach is to E. of Coney I. At E. end of Coney I. peninsula is **U.S. Maritime Service Training Sta.** From Coney I. cont. on Bay Shore Pky. to Marine Pk., on Jamaica Bay. (52) W. of Pk. is **Sheepshead Bay,** an arm of Jamaica Bay. This used to be frequented summer resort, now center of fishing fleet for visitors. (53) **Marine Pk.** on Jamaica Bay (2,000 as.recr.sports facils.) was mostly marsh, but has been dredged & filled to make lagoon, island, boat basin, etc. (54) Adj. is **Floyd Bennett Field,** large airport named for aviator who flew Byrd to N. Pole. (55) **Marine Pky. Bridge** crosses Rockaway Inlet by 3 spans to Rockaway Peninsula (see below). Bridge is c.4,000′ in length; cost $6,000,000. (56) Ave. U bet. E. 63rd & 64th Sts., **Schenck-Crooke H.** (1656.Dutch-Col.). Cont. on Shore Pky. to J. with Remsen Ave. & take latter (L). (57) Remsen & Foster Aves., huge new **Brooklyn Terminal Market.** Cont. on Shore Pky. from J. with Remsen Ave. along Jamaica Bay to J. with Cross Bay Blvd. (58) Near here to N., on Rockaway Blvd., is **Aquaduct Race Track** (running races spring & summer).

SIDE TRIP: Take Cross Bay Blvd. (S) here past **Howard Beach** (recr.bath.) & **Hamilton Beach** (recr.bath.) across Jamaica Bay & its Is. to Rockaway Beach Blvd. on **Rockaway Peninsula.** Fine boardwalk extends for several miles along ocean. Turn (W) along Peninsula to pub. bath. beach of **Jacob Riis Pk.** (O.summer.ample parking). Adj. to Pk. is **Ft. Tilden** at W. end of Peninsula, one of N.Y.'s defense works.

Cont. from J. with Cross Bay Blvd. on Southern St. Pky. to (59) **Internat. Airport,** built by New York Port Authority at cost of $200,000,000, with 7 runways, 9,500′ in length handling 1,000 flights daily, chiefly long-distance & internat. (60) Baisley Blvd. bet. 165th & 169th Sts., **Jamaica Race Track** (running races spring & summer).

SIDE TRIP: Take Rockaway Blvd. & other hys. (S) across E. Rockaway Inlet to **Atlantic Beach** (resort) on ocean. Turn (E) here to **Long Beach,** popular seaside resort (see Long I. Tour III).

Cont. from Internat. Airport on Southern St. Pky. to J. with Cross Island Pky. Take latter (N) past (61) **Belmont Race Track** (running races spring & summer), bet. Hempstead Turnpike (St.24) & Jericho Turnpike (St.25). Cont. (N) on Cross Island Pky. to J. with Grand Central Pky. (see below). (62) Near here is **Creedmore St. Hospital** for mental cases, with extensive grounds & many bldgs.

SIDE TRIP: Take Grand Central Pky. (R) to (63) **L. Success,** just beyond city line, temporary home of United Nations Secretariat & Security Council pending completion of permanent quarters in Manhattan.

Cross Island Pky. cont. (N) through (64) **Alley Pond Pk.** (c.500 as.bird sanctuary). It then runs along Little Neck Bay to (65) **Ft. Totten** (O), one of city's chain of fortifications, on peninsula jutting out into Bay, & cont. through Little Neck Bay Pk. to Queens terminus of Whitestone Bridge (see Bronx). Here take Whitestone Pky. (S) into Flushing, where formerly Wm. Prince had his **Linnaen** (botanical) **Gardens,** much admired by Geo. Washington. (66) Main St. bet. 38th & 39th

Aves., **St. George's Ch.** (Episc.est.1702.Bldg.mid-19th cent.by Rich.Upjohn). One of 1st wardens was Francis Lewis, signer of Decl. of Ind. Recently Ch. offered bldg. as special place of worship for delegates of United Nations. (67) Northern Blvd., facing Linden Pl., **Quaker Meetingh.** (1696). (68) Bowne St., near 37th Ave., **Bowne H.** (1661), home of John Bowne (see Intro.to N.Y.C.). (69) 138-28 Northern Blvd., **John Aspinwall H.** (1760), where Brit. officers lived during Rev. (70) 40-25 155th St., **Wm. K. Murray H.** (1775). Murray Hill in Manhattan was named for family owning this H. (71) 50th Ave., bet. Hollis Court & Blvd. & Fresh Meadow Rd., **Lawrence H.** (c.1743). (72) N. Hempstead Turnpike & Kissena Blvd., **Kissena Pk.,** with L. & fine coll. of trees & shrubs. (73) S. of Pk., on Kissena Blvd., **Queens College,** one of 4 mun. colleges (see Manhattan).

(74) Whitestone Pky. & Central Pky. **Flushing Meadow Pk.** (1,216 as.), site of World's Fair of 1939, mostly reclaimed marshland. Here, in one of Fair bldgs., United Nations Gen. Assembly has hqs. (adm. to pub. sessions by card) until the home in Manhattan is completed. Part of Pk. is devoted to **Queens Botanical Gardens.** Cont. on Grand Central Pky. from Flushing Meadows Pk. (NE) along Flushing Bay to (75) **LaGuardia (Mun.) Airport,** which has capacity for 350 flights daily & has handled up to 700. Most of Field, largely built with WPA labor, was redeemed from marshland & has had to be protected against flooding by dikes. Terrace of Restaurant affords view of airport activities.

Cont. on Grand Central Pky. from airport. (76) Shore Blvd., overlooking East R.; bet. 20th & 21st Aves., **Jacob Rapalye H.** (1749). (77) Hy. now passes huge plant of **Consolidated Edison Co.** (R) & cont. under (78) **N.Y. Connecting Bridge,** link bet. N.Y., N.H. & H. RR. & Pennsylvania RR., making through travel from New England to South possible without transfer in Manhattan. (79) At Queens entrance to **Triborough Bridge** (see Bronx) is **Astoria Pk.** (bath.recr.) along water front.

MIDDLE QUEENS: This part of borough has probably more cemeteries than any sec. of city. Most of them lie S. of Queens Blvd. & extend to Jamaica. In Long I. City sec., of which entrance to Midtown Tunnel & Queensborough Bridge are focal pts., is factory dist. served by Long I. RR.'s Sunnyside yards. (80) **Queensborough Bridge Plaza,** shadowed by elevated structures, is Queensborough Bridge terminus, from which Queens Blvd. (E) runs to Jamaica. (81) 53rd St. & 11th Ave., **Terminal Market,** covering 13 as. where 500,000 lbs. of poultry are handled daily. (82) Tennis Pl. & Burns St., **West Side Tennis Club,** where are played internat. & nat. tennis matches. (83) **Forest Pk.** (538 as.), through which runs Interborough Pky. (84) Jamaica Ave. & 153rd St., **King Mansion** (O.special days.mid-18th cent.), home of Rufus King, one of authors of Constitution. (85) 164th St. near Jamaica Ave., **First Presb. Ch.** (org.1662.bldg.1813).

THE BRONX, 54.5 square miles in area, population c. 1,400,000, is bounded on South by East River, on North by Westchester County, & extends from Harlem River on West to Long Island Sound on East. Along water front, of over 80 miles, much of which is used for shipping, warehouses & industry, are a number of large parks. One of these, Pelham Bay Park, on Eastchester Bay, is connected by parkway with Bronx Park which in turn is connected by a boulevard with Van Cortlandt Park. These three recreational areas are the largest of the many in the borough. The Bronx is connected with Queens by Bronx-Whitestone & Triborough Bridges; with Manhattan by a number of spans across the Harlem, with Henry Hudson Bridge in North perhaps the most beautiful. Hutchinson River Parkway avoids the dense traffic of US1, from Bronx-Whitestone Bridge to New Haven, Connecticut. Bronx River & Saw Mill River Parkways run North to connect with the state parkways in Westchester County.

The borough is named for John Bronk, first settler (c.1641). New Englanders pushed in early, as they did on Long Island, trespassing on Dutch territory. Indians gave settlers a good deal of trouble. Anne Hutchinson, who fled from religious persecution in Massachusetts, settled in the eastern section of the borough near a little stream, later named Hutchinson River, in her honor, only to perish at the hands of the Indians. Ancestors of Lewis Morris, signer of the Dec. of Ind. & Gouverneur Morris settled in that part of the borough which took their name, Morrisania.

The Bronx has had a pretty uneventful history. It played scarcely any role at all in the Revolution, & never figured prominently in any of the great political crises of the nation. It was a pleasant rural county whose population, industry & commerce developed at a leisurely gait until the late 19th Cent. Certainly there was no local inspiration for the gloomy phantasmagories of "Ulalume" which Poe wrote while living in Fordham, in 1846. Sections of what is now the Bronx were annexed by New York City in 1874 & 1895. Finally, in 1898 the entire area became a borough of Greater New York. Till the beginning of the 20th Cent. the Bronx was still comparatively inaccessible to Manhattanites. The only rapid transit was afforded by the railroads. Within memory of living Manhattanites, even to get to near-by Morrisania, you had to take a rickety, horse-drawn street car across the Harlem, from Madison Avenue. But in 1904 the first subway was completed & since then the exodus from Manhattan has flowed in in torrents. Today two lines, the Interborough & the Independent, reach most parts of the borough. The IRT cannily stops short of Yonkers some twenty blocks. Yonkersites, although their city crowds right down to the Bronx at 242nd Street, have to take a trolley to the subway terminus. That is the price they pay for municipal independence.

PTS. OF INT.: (1) **Triborough Bridge** (toll.1936) joins Queens, Manhattan & the Bronx. The approach from Manhattan is 125th St.; from Queens, at Astoria; & from the Bronx, bet. 132nd & 134th Sts. The $60,000,000 suspension bridge, c.3.5$^{m}$ long, is 2nd longest in world. It consists of an intricate network of 4 bridges over water & 12 over land. On Randall's I. (where the 3 arms meet) is pk. & recr. area around **Triborough Stadium,** seating c.30,000, equipped with one of world's largest movable outdoor stages; used for athletic & musical events. **Ward's I.** to be converted to recr. area & conn. by foot bridges to Randall's I. (N) & to Franklin D. Roosevelt Dr. in Manhattan at 103rd St.; now has ramp from Triborough Bridge. (2) Cont. from Triborough Bridge to Grand Concourse then, to Exterior St., starting at 149th St., **Bronx Terminal Market** (1918-25.adds.1935); vast wholesale fruit & vegetable warehouses & refrigerating plants. (3) Bet. E. 157th & 161st Sts. at River Ave., **Yankee Stadium** (1922), largest baseball pk. in U.S. In center field of "the house that Ruth built," plaques comm. Yankee notables: Miller Huggins, Col. Ruppert, Lou Gehrig & "Babe" Ruth. (4) On Grand Concourse, bet. 158th & 161st Sts., **Bronx Cty. Bldg.** (1934.by Freedlander & Hausle), simple 10-story civic center; cost $8,000,000. (5) Grand Concourse, bet. E. 161st & 164th Sts., **Joyce Kilmer Pk.,** comm. World War I poet, with Lorelei Fountain (1893.by Ernst Herter), with relief of Heinrich Heine, German poet. (6) Beginning at W. 180th St. at University Ave., Univ. Heights Campus (men) of **New York Univ.** (see Manhattan) where are: **Hall of Fame** (1900.by Stanford White); portrait busts & tablets comm. famous Americans; 7 may be elected to the Hall every 5 yrs.; choices are from among those dead 25 or more yrs. **Gould Mem. Lib.** (1895-1900.by Stanford White), in style of Roman Pantheon, of terra cotta brick specially made in Staten I. Lib. has fine stained glass windows, auditorium; Main Doors are Mem. to Stanford White by his fellow artists.

(7) Fordham Rd. & 3rd Ave., **Fordham Univ.** (1841.coed in certain schools.oldest bldg.1838). On campus are **Duane Lib.** with coll. of paintings & old volumes; **Seismograph Bldg.** (O.appl.1924), where work is conducted with U.S. Coast & Geodetic Survey. (8) Grand Concourse & 192nd St., **Poe Pk.** with **Poe Cottage** (O) where poet lived & worked in poverty, 1846-49. Here he wrote "Annabel Lee" for his young wife who died here, & "Ulalume." (9) Bet. Jerome Pk. Reservoir & Paul Ave., **Hunter College,** Bronx Center (see Manhattan) for freshmen & sophomores; campus has many sports fields; **Rock Garden,** planned to place rocks here from each State; 4 imposing structures. Campus was taken over as WAVE training center, 1943-45. (10) Bet. B'way & Jerome Ave., **Van Cortlandt Pk.** (c.1,130 as. sports & recr.facils.golf.playgrounds.boat.roller & ice-skating.foot & bridle trls.), orig. had been Ind. hunting grounds. In Pk., **Van Cortlandt H.** (O.1748.Georg.adds.), built by Frederick, son of Jacobus Van Cortlandt, mayor of N.Y.C. 1710-19. Has coll. of early documents & relics, Dutch & Col. furnishings. (11) Independence Ave. & W. 227th St., **Henry Hudson Mem.** (c.1912-38); on 100′ column is statue (by Karl Bitter) of explorer shown facing R. he was 1st to navigate. (12) 242nd St. & Spuyten Duyvil Pky., **Manhattan College** (Cath.founded as academy 1849.Georg. Col.) attained status as college, 1863. (13) At Hudson R. & W. 261st St., **College of Mount St. Vincent** (Cath.women). (14) E. 233 St. & Webster Ave., **Woodlawn Cemetery** (org.1863.400 as.), site of Rev. battle; graves of many Amer. notables incl. Jay Gould, Jos. Pulitzer, Herman Melville & Adm. David G. Farragut. (15) At S. 3rd & S. Columbus Aves. (in Westchester), **St. Paul's Ch.** (Episc.1765), of

with over 30 Georg.-style bldgs. on 383-a. site equipped with gymnasium, swimming pool, theater, chapel, etc. On grounds is **Boscabel** (1792.Fed.rest.), one of finest mansions of its time, built by Staats Morris Dyckman. **41.5. PEEKSKILL,** farmers' trading center with plant mfg. yeasts & alcohol, was 1st sett. in 1665 by Jan Peek. Center of town, **Chauncey M. Depew Pk.** with **Statue** of RR. attorney & U.S. Senator, & **Wm. Nelson Law Office** (rest.), moved here from orig. site, where Depew studied law. South St. E. of Wash. St., **1st Presb. Ch.** (1846.Gr.Rev.). Oregon Rd. leads (R) $2^m$ to **Van Cortlandtville,** where are **Upper Van Cortlandt Manor H.** (pre-Rev.), now boys' school, & **St. Peter's Ch.** (1767), built by Van Cortlandt family. At S. edge of town, off Welcher Ave., is **Blue Mt. Reserv.** (1,586 as.pic.hik.riding. lodge.refreshments), forest tract with trls. & bridle paths. Peekskill is at J. with US6 (see), running (W) across Bear Mt. Bridge to J. with US9W (see Trip IV) at entrance to Bear Mt.-Harriman Sec. of Palisades Interst. Pk.

**IV. US9W (N) to BEAR MT.-HARRIMAN ST. PK. 46.**

**0.** from Columbus Circle, follow Broadway (N), across Geo. Washington Bridge (toll) to J. with US9W, & follow latter (R) along crest of Palisades with fine views of N.Y. City. At **14.5.** is J. with Closter Dock Rd., leading (R) down Palisades to R. shore, where trl. leads (R) short distance to **Huyler-Dock H.** (O.Sun.p.m.c.1740) & (L) short distance to **Cornwallis Hqs.** (N.O.1750.rest.1934), where Brit. Gen. on Nov. 20, 1776 watched his army ferried across Hudson to attack Ft. Lee. At **18.5.** is **N.Y.-N.J. LINE. 19.5. TALLMAN MT. SEC.** (R) of **Palisades Interst. Pk.** (recr. facils.) **20.** J. with paved Rd. leading (L) $1.5^m$ to **Tappan,** where is **De Windt H.** (O.1700), now Masonic Shrine, which was hqs. of Geo. Washington in 1780 & in 1783. Here also are **Seventy-six H.** (O.1755), now inn containing hist. relics, where Maj. André was imprisoned after negotiating surrender of West Pt. with Benedict Arnold. **Dutch Reformed Ch.** (1835.Gr.Rev.& Fed.), on site of earlier ch. in which André was tried; & **André Hill,** where he was hanged, Oct. 2, 1780. **21 PIERMONT,** with mile-long Erie RR. pier. **25.5 NYACK,** on Hudson R., where are good pic. & bath. spots. On Piermont Ave., in S. Nyack., **Michael Cornelison H.** (1770.later adds.). On Broadway in Upper Nyack, **Old Stone Ch.** (c.1813). **36.5. HAVERSTRAW,** notable for manufacture of brick. Riverside Ave. leads (R) $0.5^m$ to **Red Stone Dock Campsite** in Palisades Interst. Pk. **37.** N.Y. St. **RECONSTRUCTION HOME** (L) for children, on site of Treason H. where André & Arnold met to negotiate surrender of West Pt. At **38.** is J. with Rd. leading (R) $0.5^m$ to **Stony Pt. Battlefield Reserv.** where Gen. "Mad" Anthony Wayne on July 6, 1779 defeated Brit. Here is **Stony Pt. Mus.** (0) containing hist. relics; fine view across Hudson. **46.** Entrance to **BEAR MT.-HARRIMAN SEC. OF PALISADES INTERST. PK.** (inn & lodges.restaurant.cafeteria.pic.dancing.amusements.swim.pool.rowing.horses & bridle paths.sports facils.winter sports). Regular steamer serv. from N.Y. City. On Nature Trl. are 5 mus. bldgs. containing natural hist. colls. There is also zoo with animals found wild, now or formerly, in pk. Good hiking trls. leading to scenic pts. Earthworks of Ft. Clinton, which guarded Hudson Highlands during Rev., have been preserved. Perkins Mem. Dr. runs to summit of **Bear Mt.** (1,314'); fine view. Just N. of entrance to pk. is J. with US6 (see). US9W (see) cont. (N) along Hudson.

# US 46—NEW JERSEY

**N.J.-N.Y. LINE** (at Geo. Washington Bridge) **(W) to DEL. R.** (across from Portland, Pa.). **73.5. US46**

Via: (Hackensack), Ridgefield Pk., Paterson, Totowa, Dover, Kenvil, (L. Hopatcong), Netcong, Hackettstown, Buttzville, Delaware. Good Rd. Accoms.: All types.

US46 crosses N.J.'s N. Mt. & L. sec. to Del. R. $c.12^m$ (S) from Del. Water Gap. It crosses Del. R. to J. with US611, part of Del. R. Tour (see Pa.). US611 runs (NW) to make J. with US209 (see), a main through tour.

**0. N.J. Side of Geo. Washington Bridge** (other entrance to this route is Holland Tunnel & then US46 united with US1).

SIDE TRIPS: (A) Take Skyline Drive (S) $c.3^m$ to **Palisades Amusement Pk.** (at N.J. end of 125th St. Ferry from N.Y.C.).

(B) From Bridge (R) on hard-surfaced Rd. to J. with Henry Hudson Dr., running along the base of the Palisades & the Hudson R. (more scenic than the present plateau drive above). Work has begun (1949) on $12^m$ upper drive which will feature a Palisades Pky.,

27-a. bird sanctuary, arboretum & dam. At J. with Hudson Dr. is Yonkers-Alpine Ferry. Here is **Cornwallis' Hqs.** (stone sec.1750.adds.), where Cornwallis waited while his army of 5,000 was ferried across river to Ft. Lee (see US1). **Huyler Dock H.** (N.O.), former trading sta. & stage-line terminal.

At **7.** is J. with St.17.

SIDE TRIP: (N) on St.17 to Polifly Rd. & then a short distance to **Hackensack,** a residential & industrial city, built on flats adj. Hackensack R. Chief manufactures are bricks, cement, wallpaper, haberdashery & slippers. It was sett. by Dutch in 1647 as New Barbadoes, a name which was not officially changed until 1922. Village was plundered by Brit. & Hessians in 1780. Majority of its pop. was pro-slavery at Civil War's outbreak & the Union flag was burned at the Green. Today many of its citizens commute to N.Y.C. PTS. OF INT.: (1) S. end of Main St., **The Green,** camping ground during Rev. of both Amer. & Brit troops. (2) **Ch. on the Green** (1st Dutch Reformed.1691.rebuilt 1728.alts.1869). (3) NE. cor. Main St. & Washington Pl., **Mansion H.** (1751), where Washington was quartered. (4) Opp. Green, **Bergen County Cth.** (1912.neo-Class.by J. Riley Gordon). (5) 274 Main St., **Pub. Lib.;** hist. coll., Ind. relics. (6) 450 River St., **Terhune H.** (1670.adds.). (7) 249 Polifly Rd., **Hopper H.** (1816-18).

**12.5. PASSAIC** (Route skirts Clifton (L), suburb of Passaic)

Through RR. & bus conns. Accoms.: All types. Info.: Traffic Bureau, 336 Passaic St. Swim.: Pulaski Pk.

Passaic, on Passaic R., is busy textile town. Main St. is shopping center; to (W) are residential districts climbing heights & to (E) extends poorer "Dundee Section" toward R. Pop. is largely of recent foreign derivation—Poles, Itals., Russians, Slovakians, Hungarians, who have preserved old folkways. Passaic, sett. by Dutch 1678, changed hands several times during Rev. In 19th cent. it developed as textile center. Botany Mills, turning out woolens, was est. 1819; plants mfg. handkerchiefs, garments, rubber articles followed. Most serious labor conflict came in 1926 with strike at Botany Mills, resulting in clashes with police over right to hold public meetings. Norman Thomas was arrested when making an address from fork of a tree. 125 Lexington Ave., **Van Schott H.** (Dutch Col.alt.& remod.1899), orig. parsonage of Old Dutch Reformed Ch. Gregory Ave. & Prospect St., **Armory Pk.** with Burial Vault constructed as morgue c.1690. NE. cor. of Monroe & 3rd Sts., **SS. Peter & Paul's Russian Orthodox Greek Cath. Ch.** (1911), built with money donated by Czar, is in style of Moscow Chs.

**13.5. PATERSON**

Through RR. & bus conns. Accoms.: All types. Info.: Alexander Hamilton Hotel, Market & Church Sts. Swim.: Barbour's Pond, Garret Mt. Reserv., S. end of New St. (free).

Paterson is built on high ground above falls of Passaic R. which has furnished power from beginning for city's industries. R. gorge has been largely preserved by pk. & further downstream is another recr. area. Stretch bet., however, is lined with factories. Business dist. centers around Main, Broadway & Market Sts.; best residential sec. is on E. Side. Paterson, sett. by Dutch in 1679, for more than a century had very slow development. Then, in 1791, Alex. Hamilton helped found Soc. for Establishment of Useful Manufactures which selected Great Falls of Passaic R. for site of industrial center. L'Enfant, planner of Washington, D.C., was hired to build system of raceways & city was named for current Gov. of N. J. Earliest industry was cotton spinning. Morris Canal, completed in 1831 & conn. city with Pa. coal fields, & RRs., arriving soon after, stimulated expansion. Textile (silk & cotton) mills & dyeing plants are chief industries, but many other plants have been est. incl. Wright Aeronautical Corp. In 1836 occurred fire which destroyed some 500 bldgs. Paterson has been labor trouble spot since early times. First conflict occurred in 1828 in textile mill. The 1910 strike, which led to a "lock-out" by employers, won support of radicals from N.Y. Despite great demonstration, strikers were defeated. It was claimed that strike led to exodus from city by industries. Strike of 1933, however, proved successful.

PTS. OF INT.: (1) On Valley Rd. at Lackawanna RR. bridge, **Garret Mt. Reserv.** (570 as.pic.hik.trls.), hill top pk., fine views. Here is **Lambert Castle** (1892); coll. of Passaic Cty. Hist. Soc. (O.Sat.Sun.afts.& Wed.Thurs.Fri.); prints, antiques & relics. Near-by is **Observatory Tower.** (2) 268 Summer St. **Paterson Mus.** (O.wks. 1-5.Sat.10-5.free); Ind. relics, hist. & nat. hist. colls. Here is 1st submarine built in 1878 by John P. Holland. (3) SE. cor. of Broadway & Auburn St., **Danforth Mem. Lib.** (O.wks.Class.by Henry Bacon). (4) SE. cor. of Ward & Hamilton Sts., **Passaic**

**Cty. Adm. Bldg.** (1898.Flemish). (5) In **East Side Pk.**, overlooking Passaic Pk., are Gen. Pulaski & Soldiers Mons. (6) On R. above falls is **West Side Pk.** (canoes.rowboats). Here is "Fenian Ram," J. P. Holland's successful submarine, launched in 1881. It was not until 1893 that Gov. awarded contract for a submarine, & not until 1900 that Navy Dept. accepted the "Holland." (7) On Market St., **City Hall** (by John M.Carrere). (8) 11 Van Houten St., **Family Shops** (O.appl.), where silk is woven under a family shop-system. (9) NW. cor. Mill & Van Houten St., **Old Gun Mill** (O.appl.1836) built by Sam. Colt, inventor of Colt revolver, who manufactured weapons here. (10) At **Passaic Falls** are hydroelectric & steam plants in gorge of Passaic R. A foot bridge spans the falls. (11) 1120 E. 19th St., **Wright Aeronautical Plant** (group tours on appl.).

**20.5. FAIRFIELD REFORMED CH.** (1804.steeple added later). **27. TROY HILLS** (has cattle & horse show in Sept.). **31.** J. with side Rd. (R) here short distance to **Mountain Lakes,** suburban development with 8 artificial Ls. **32. L. ARROWHEAD. 32.5. DENVILLE** on **Indian L.** (resort). **37. DOVER.** In vic., **Picatinny Arsenal** where will be gov. rocket research development. **41.5. KENVIL. Hercules Powder Co.,** "America's oldest continuously operated dynamite plant." **43.5.** J. with side Rd. (R) here 1.5m to S. end of **L. Hopatcong,** famous resort (accoms.amusements) with largest inland body of water in N.J. **48.5. BUDD L.** (resort). **54. MUSCONETCONG DAM** (swim.). **54.5.** J. with side Rd. leading (L) c.1.5m to **N.J. St. Fish Hatchery** (O). **55. HACKETTSTOWN. 66. BUTTZVILLE,** where is **Island Park.** (pic.boat.f.in Pequest R.). S. of Buttzville on St.30 is **Oxford** at 2m. (R) here a short distance, **Meth. Ch.,** formerly an old Grist Mill (1750). Near-by on hill (R) of the Fork is **Shippen Mansion** (N.O.1754.fine Georg.), built by owners of old blast furnace once located here. **68.5.** J. with side Rd. leading (L) 2m to **Belvidere** (see Del. R. Tour, Pa.). **69.** Hy. now follows Del. R. **73.5.** Bridge (free) across Del. R. to Pa. At bridge is J. with St.8.

SIDE TRIP: Take St.8 (N) here 9.5m to J. with side Rd.

Take latter (R) here 6m to **Hope,** sett. by Moravian colonists in 1774, but abandoned after smallpox epidemic in 1808. Many fine old stone hs. **Moravian Ch.** (R) has been remodeled as a bank. The **Old Mill** (1768) is still functioning but with modern equipment. (S) is **Jenny Jump St. For.** (camp.pic.h.).

At 14m on St.8 is J. with side Rd.

Take latter (R) c.2m to **Johnsonburg.** In town's center **Van Ness H.** (stone.pre-1781). (L) a short distance, **Christian Ch. Cemetery** with grave of Jos. Thomas, minister, known as the "white pilgrim" because he wore white raiment, whitewashed boots, & rode a white horse.

## ST. S-24 & ST. 24—NEW JERSEY

**ELIZABETH, N.J.** (across Holland Tunnel from N.Y.) **(W) to PHILLIPSBURG, N.J.** (across Del. R. from Easton, Pa.). **63.5. St.S-24, St.24**

Via: Union, Springfield, (Millburn), (Summit), Chatham, Madison, Morristown, Mendham, (Hackettstown), Washington. Good Rd. Accoms.: All types.

This tour avoids industrial towns & developments & in 1st sec. traverses reg. of large estates & commuters' homes. At Easton it makes J. with US22 (see), a main cross-country route. (W) of Morristown it climbs into int. mountain country.

**0. ELIZABETH** (see US1). **3.5. UNION,** small business town. On Chester St., **Presb. Ch.** (1782), built after orig. parsonage & most of village was burnt by Brit. Graves of Hessians in cemetery. **6. SPRINGFIELD,** a center of fighting, June 23, 1781. **First Presb. Ch.** (R) whose Chaplain, Jas. Caldwell, threw to patriot troops Watts' hymnbooks to be used as gun wadding, shouting "Give 'em Watts, give 'em Watts, boys." 231 S. Springfield Ave., **Swain H.** (1744). St.S-24 now becomes St.24 on which cont.

SIDE TRIP: (R) from Springfield 1m to **Millburn** surrounded by lakes & fine residences. 40 Main St., **Vaux Hall** was home of Caldwell (see above). (N) of Millburn is **South Mt. Reserv.** (2,000 as. good f.in R.trls.winter sports). Here is **Washington Rock** at head of Crest Dr. Plaque states that Gen. Washington in summer of 1780 here watched conflict bet. Brit. & Amer. troops. Trl. leads to **Hemlock Falls.**

**7.** J. with side Rd.

SIDE TRIP: (L) here 4m to **Summit,** residential suburb climbing First Watchung Mt. Tablet at Hobart Ave. marks **Site of Old Sow,** small cannon used as alarm gun to warn Washington of Brit. approach.

**10.5. CHATHAM.** (E) of business center, **Day's Tavern** (R) where Washington stopped. (W) of town (R) **Elm Tree Inn** (1811). **12.5. BOTTLE HILL TAVERN** (1812), so-called because it is said a bottle was used as its sign board. **13. MADISON. Mun. Bldg.** (int.inter.), donated by Mrs. Marcellus Dodge, niece of John D. Rockefeller. Ridgedale Ave., **Sayre H.** (c.1745) was "Mad Anthony" Wayne's hqs. for time during Rev. On outskirts of town, **Drew Univ.,** a theological seminary. Here are **Mead Hall** (1836.fine S.Col.), **Rose Mem. Lib.** (1938) with coll. of rare mss., & **Statue of Francis Asbury,** 1st Amer. Meth. bishop. **15. COLLEGE OF ST. ELIZABETH** for women (Cath.) on hill. **17.5. MORRISTOWN** (see US202). **25. MENDHAM.** At town's center **Black Horse Inn** (R) & **Phoenix H.** (L), both dating to Col. times. **26. RALSTON** has oldest still-functioning U.S. P.O. (1775), a post office since 1792 (int.inter.). Adj. is **Ralston H.** (1771). **27. LOUGHLIN MILL** (O) which has been making cider since Col. times. **30.5. CHESTER.** On Main St., **Chester H.** (1812.hotel). **32.5.** (L) here on good Rd. 1m to **Hacklebarney St. Pk.** Fine Black R. gorge (trls.pic.f.). **35.5. LONG VALLEY,** 18th cent. German settlement. **Long Valley Inn** (1787.remod.1922) is still functioning. Near-by (L) is **Old Ford H.** (1774), another alleged "Washington slept here" house. **37.** Summit of **SCHOOLEYS MT.** (1,073';fine view). **40.5.** J. with St.S-24 which leads straight ahead 0.5m to **Hackettstown.** Main route cont. (SW) on St.24. **43.5.** A side Rd. leads (R) here 1.5m to **Rockport** where is **St. Game Farm. 51. WASHINGTON,** which was a stop-over on old Morris Canal. (R) c.2m from Washington is **Consumers' Research Plant** (O.wks.), a much publicized org. advising through its publications on quality of food & merchandise. F. J. Schlink, a director, was co-author with Arthur Kallet, of muckraking book, "100,000,000 Guinea Pigs." **51.5.** J. with side Rd. leading (R) 1.5m to **Brass Castle,** named for an early settler, Jacob Brass, good f. here & in **Roaring Brook Falls.** A Rd. climbs up **Scott Mt.** (fine views). **63.5. PHILLIPSBURG,** small industrial city on hills above Del. R. Mfg. companies incl. Warren Foundry & Pipe Corp & Ingersoll-Rand Co. mfg. pneumatic tools.

## US 22—NEW JERSEY

**NEWARK, N.J.** (across Holland Tunnel from N.Y.C.) **(W) to PHILLIPSBURG** (across Del. R. from Easton, Pa.). **59. US22**

Via: Hillside, Union, Scotch Plains, (Fanwood), (Westfield), N. Plainfield, (Plainfield & Dunellen), Bound Brook, Somerville, Lebanon, Bloomsbury. Good but much traveled Rd. Accoms.: All types.

Take Holland Tunnel from N.Y.C. & US1 to Newark, then US22 (R). US22 traverses 1st an industrial area & then a mt. reg. to Del. R. Good fishing in streams of mt. sec. Hy. passes number of fine old stone Col. Hs.

**5.5. UNION** (see St.S-24). **7.5. RAHWAY R.** (good f.). **Rahway R. Pky.** extends on both sides of stream. **10. MOUNTAINSIDE.** Here is **Echo L. Pk.** (pic.boat.f.). **10.5.** J. with New Providence Rd.

SIDE TRIPS: (A) Take latter (L) 1m to **Sip Manor H.** (Dutch Col.), occupied by Lord Cornwallis during Rev.

(B) Take New Providence Rd. (R) 1.5m to **Watchung** (Ind.: "high hill") **Reserv.** (1,962 as. pic.fee for camp.bridlepaths & hik.trls.). At 2.5m **Surprise L.** (resort.boat.f.).

**13. SCOTCH PLAINS** has **Bapt. Ch.** founded 1847 & on Front St., **Olde Historic Inn** (1737). J. with side Rd.

SIDE TRIP: Take latter (L) a few miles to **Fanwood** on St.28. On Martine Ave., **Spence H.** (1774).

(1) From Fanwood (L) on Terrill Rd. 2m to **Frazee H.** (R) at J. with Raritan Rd. where Betty Frazee refused to bake bread for Cornwallis' troops.

(2) From Fanwood (E) c.2m on St.28 to **Westfield.** On Broad St. & Mountain Ave., **Presb. Ch.** where Jas. Morgan, murderer of Jas. Caldwell, was tried & sentenced & later hanged on Gallows Hill. Broad St. & Springfield Ave., **Ind. Burial Ground.** 819 E. Broad St., **Scudder H.** (Georg.Col.), hqs. of Amer. Gen. Wm. Alexander during Rev.

Side trip cont. on St.28 W. 3m to **Plainfield.** Watchung Ave., **Quaker Meeting H.** (O.appl. 1788). 950 Cedar Brook Rd., **Martine H.** (1717.adds.) where banker-poet E. C. Stedman spent childhood. W. Front St. & Washington Ave., **Washington Hqs.** (O.1746.Dutch Col.), occupied by Hist. Soc. In **Cedar Brook Pk.** are Shakespeare, Iris & Orchard Gardens. At 6m is **Dunellen.** (L) here c.1m to **New Market.** Because of controversies bet. local Bapts. as to whether Sabbath should be observed on Sat. or Sun., Amer. Rev. soldiers called it Squabbletown. On New Market Rd., **Vail Mansion** (1814.Gr.Rev.), built by Duncan Phyfe, famous furniture maker, for daughter Eliza Vail.

**19.** J. with side Rd. (R) here up steep grade 1$^{m}$ to **Washington Rock St. Pk.** (pic. restaurant) where is rock from which Washington observed Brit. maneuvers. **26. SOMERVILLE** (see US206). **31. NORTH BRANCH.** (R) here a short distance is **Jacob Ten Eyck H.** (1725.rebuilt c.1795.fine Col.) whose great fireplace is set with tiles illustrating Scriptural passages. **36.** J. with side Rd. leading (R) 3.5$^{m}$ to **Oldwick** with **Zion Luth. Ch. 41. STAGE COACH INN** (N.O.c.1770.int.inter.). **42. CLINTON.** On S. Branch of Raritan R. (f.) is **Old Mill** (rebuilt 1836). **Clinton H.** (c.1740), formerly a stagecoach stop. **45. PERRYVILLE.** Here (L) is **Brick H.** (1812), former tavern.

SIDE TRIP: Take Rd. (R) across Mulhockaway Cr. 1$^{m}$ to **Van Syckles Cor. Van Syckles Tavern** (1763). Jos. Bonaparte stayed here on trips from Bordentown.

**52. BLOOMSBURY** straddling Musconetcong R. **53.5.** (R) **OLD GREENWICH PRESB. CH.** (1835). Congregation est. 1740. **55. STILL VALLEY.** On Belvidere Rd., **St. James Luth. Ch.** (1854). **59. PHILLIPSBURG** (see St.24).

## US 1—NEW JERSEY

**GEORGE WASHINGTON BRIDGE** (at New York, N.Y.) **(SW) to TRENTON, N.J. 65. US1**

Via: Fort Lee, Fairview, North Bergen, Jersey City, (Newark), Elizabeth, Linden, (New Brunswick). Superhy. of 4 or 6 lanes throughout. Accoms.: In cities.

US1, highspeed route bypassing large cities, is more notable for gas stas. & advertisements than for scenic or hist. int. St.27 (see below) is more pleasant & less traveled alt. bet. Elizabeth & Trenton. N. Sec. of route is crowded with industrial developments & suburbs of N.Y.C. Further (S) there is comparatively little industry & countryside is particularly fine. Tourist in hurry to get to Trenton may use Holland Tunnel (instead of bridge), which is reached from West Side elevated hy. in Manhattan & brings him almost directly to Pulaski Skyway (see below).

**0.** US1 crosses **GEO. WASHINGTON BRIDGE** (see N.Y.C. toll) into N.J. On bridge are parking spaces (fine views). At N. J. end is J. with US9-W (see N.Y.). **1.5. FT. LEE.** Here on hts. of Palisades, Washington had ft. from which he observed (Nov.1776) surrender of Ft. Washington across R. & as result was forced to abandon Ft. Lee. **3.** J. with US46 (see). **Sam. Wright H.** (1790.Dutch Col.). **5. FAIRVIEW** (L) with **Internat. Fireworks Co.** which manufactures display fireworks for use in civic celebrations. **8.** J. with Bergen Pike.

SIDE TRIPS: Take latter (L) 1.5$^{m}$ to J. with Hudson Blvd. E.

(1) On Hudson Blvd. E. (R) again to Lincoln Tunnel (toll) to N.Y. (see). At Jersey side of Tunnel, a short distance (S) is **Hoboken.**

Through RR. & bus conns. Lincoln Tunnel direct conn. with N.Y.C. Accoms.: All types. Info.: C. of C., Newark St.; Lackawanna Terminal, Hudson Pl. (day & night).

Hoboken, which extends (S) to Jersey City, is crowded bet. Hudson R. & lower Palisades. An industrial center, it impresses visitors chiefly as lively port. River St., along waterfront, is lined by saloons, cheap hotels, sailors' boarding houses & resorts, & faces entrances to piers from which great ocean liners sail to foreign ports. Hoboken has Germanic background, as the old wisecrack, "Hoboken where only German is spoken," indicates. There are many restaurants offering good food & excellent beer, & dance halls frequented by a German clientele. Sett. by Dutch in 1640, when it was known as Hobocan Hackingh ("land of the tobacco pipe"), it suffered Ind. attacks largely provoked by Dutch aggression.

Col. John Stevens, investor & financier, was modern city's real founder. He bought land on which a good part of present city stands & auctioned off lots in N.Y.C. Hoboken became famous as suburban resort for New Yorkers. John Jacob Astor built a home & Wm. Cullen Bryant & Martin Van Buren vacationed there. General public was attracted by beer gardens & other amusements. City jumped into nation-wide notoriety when Edgar Allan Poe wrote "Mystery of Marie Roget" which was really concerned with murder of Mary Rogers, a N.Y. shopgirl whose body was found in R. near entrance of Sybil's Cave, on River Walk. In 1867, Edwin, son of Col. John Stevens, carrying out his father's idea bequeathed $650,000 for bldg. & endowment of Stevens Institute, an outstanding engineering college. During Prohibition Hoboken became mecca once more for New Yorkers. This time they were in search of good beer. Christopher Morley, Cleon Throckmorton & associates took advantage of opportunity offered by thirsty influx & opened 2 theatres which presented Victorian-period melodrama for benefit of sophisticated New Yorkers.

PTS. OF INT.: (1) On Castle Pt., **Stevens Institute** (1871) maintains summer engineering camp at Johnsonburg. Most of campus bldgs. are O. wks. incl.: 5th St. near Hudson

St., **Adm. Bldg.,** known as "Old Stone Mill," orig. home of Institute. SE. Cor. Hudson & 6th Sts., **Lib. Bldg.** (O.appl.) containing Leonardo da Vinci coll. of more than 1,000 items. On Castle Pt., **Stevens Castle,** home of John C. Stevens, now dormitory (fine view). SE. River & 6th Sts., **Navy Bldg.** with mus. (O.afts.Wed.& on appl.); exhibits of development of mechanical locomotion. (2) 42 2nd St., **Hof Brau Haus,** famous for German food & good beer. (3) 1203 Washington St., **Hetty Green H.,** apartment house, once home of eccentric millionairess. At one time she received a summons because she failed to pay Hoboken $2.00 dog-tax. Refusing to pay, she fled to Manhattan & only returned after her daughter had paid tax.

(2) On Hudson Blvd. E. (L) 2m to **Site of Hamilton-Burr Duel;** marker in small pk. at edge of palisades. Here on same spot where his son Philip had been killed in duel 3 yrs. earlier, Alex. Hamilton was mortally wounded by Aaron Burr, July 11, 1804. 200 yds. (S) on Hamilton Ave. is **Alex. Hamilton Mon.**

US1 now passes through N. sec. of Jersey City. (SW) is **Laurel Hill,** one of several outcroppings on flat Jersey Meadows. **11.5.** At traffic circle is **Entrance to Pulaski Skyway.** Straight ahead on concrete hy. to Newark Ave. (L) on latter to Hudson Blvd. (R) on latter to Jersey City.

## 12. JERSEY CITY

Through RR. & bus conns. Accoms.: All types. Info.: C. of C., 921 Bergen Ave.; Auto Club of Hudson Cty., 2330 Hudson Blvd.

Jersey City occupies peninsula bet. Hackensack & Hudson (North) Rs. Although an important industrial & shipping center in its own right a large number of its citizens commute to N. Y. At Journal Sq., the city's heart, are terminals for buses & interurban lines & the amusement dist. Hudson Blvd. extending from Union City (N) cuts through Sq. (S) to Bayonne, an adj. industrial city (especially oil refining). S. sec. of blvd. is lined with fine residences & apartment houses. Dutch made 1st sett. c.1629 &, largely as a result of colonists' aggression, there were bloody conflicts with Inds. lasting till 1660. In 1664 Brit. came into possession. On Aug. 18, 1779 Brit. ft. at Paulus Hook was captured in surprise night attack by forces under command of Major (Lighthorse Harry) Lee. Before Civil War, city became a sta. on Underground Railroad. Slaves were smuggled, hidden in Erie Canal boats. Because of its location on Upper N.Y. Bay & because it is on main route to Phila., Jersey City early developed commercial importance. In 1812 Rbt. Lewis Fulton built & put into service a steam ferry connecting with N.Y. Soon main line RRs. est. their terminals in city & industries which have since multiplied & expanded greatly followed. In 20th cent. city benefited by construction of tube & tunnel links with N.Y.: Hudson Tubes, completed in 1910, which bring commuters to heart of Manhattan, & Holland & Lincoln vehicular tubes. From Bayonne, at Hudson Cty. Blvd. & W. 7th St., is Bayonne Bridge (toll); designed by Othman H. Ammann & Leon Moisseiff (former also designed Geo. Washington Bridge); construction cost $16,000,000. Bridge is 150′ above high water across Kill Van Kull to Staten I. The arch of the bridge has a span of 1,675′, one of longest in world. On Communipaw water front on July 30, 1916, during World War I, occurred the Black Tom Explosion which cost $20,000,000 damage & shook entire met. area. Cause of explosion has never been discovered. Jersey City today is integral part of great met. industrial & port area & is terminal for number of main-line RRs. & port of passenger & freighter lines.

Jersey City politics have been noted for being on occasion unconventional & corrupt, including stuffing of ballot boxes, letting of crooked mun. contracts for improvements, etc. In recent years & up to 1947, when he retired in favor of his nephew, Frank Hague was city's colorful mayor. The opposition maintains that during his incumbency per capita cost of government was highest of any city in N.J. It was during Hague's regime that the widely publicized conflict bet. union organizers & sympathizers & police occurred. After a long drawn out legal battle, courts finally affirmed right to distribute leaflets, display placards & hold meetings in public places. An outstanding achievement of Hague's administration was creation of city's fine Medical Center & special Bureau for Juvenile Delinquency. Both have done notable work. In spring 1949 Hague political machine met severe defeat.

PTS. OF INT.: (1) SW. Highland & Bergen Ave., **Old Bergen Ch.** (1842). Cemented into front wall bet. doorways are stones from the 2 previous chs. with inscription: "1680 W-Day." "Kerk Gebouwt Het Yaer 1680. Bowt in Het Yaer 1773." (2) 298 Academy St., **Van Wagenen H.** (late 19th cent.), occupied by descendants of Dutch family that received in 1650 a share of land from Kill Van Kull to Weehawken, ceded by Inds. to Peter Stuyvesant. Lafayette entertained Washington at dinner (1779) here under large apple tree. (3) NE. cor. of Bergen Sq., **Statue of Peter Stuyvesant** (by Massey Rhind). (4) 105 Hudson St., huge **Colgate-Palmolive-Peet Plant,** est. 1806. Colgate Clock, in tower with dial 50′ in diameter & minute hand that weighs 2,200 lbs., can be seen from pts. on N. Y. harbor & Hudson R. (5) 83 Wayne St. **Ionic H.** (N.O.early 19th cent.int.inter.alts.) is now social center of adj. St. Matthew's Ch. (6) Jersey Ave. & Montgomery St., **Pub. Lib.** (O.wks.1901. Ital. Ren.by Bright & Bacon); Otto Goetzke gem coll.; Allen coll. of household furnishings & wearing apparel of 19th cent. & McGill coin coll. (7) Baldwin Ave. at Montgomery St., **Medical Center** by John T. Rowland, skyscraper with 1,800 beds & incl. Margaret Hague Maternity Center. (8) West end Belmont Ave., **Lincoln Pk.,** 287 as., developed for various sports; large lake, & statue of Lincoln by J. E. Fraser. US1 cont. (S) from Jersey City on Pulaski Skyway, named for Polish emigré who lost life in Amer. Rev. Hy. is 3.5$^{m}$ long & rises 145′ above Hackensack & Passaic Rs. Cost $21,000,000. Views of Jersey City &, beyond, Newark's tall bldgs. **17.5.** Traffic circle with Rd. leading (L) to **Newark Airport** (see Newark). **18.5.** J. with St.21 & US22 (see). As hy. cont. (S) Bayonne Bridge (L) conn. Bayonne, & Staten Island, & Goethal's Bridge conn. Elizabeth & Staten I., are visible.

**22.5. ELIZABETH**

Through RR. & bus conns. Accoms.: All types. Info.: C. of C. at Winfield Scott Hotel, N. Broad St.

Elizabeth, adj. to Newark on (N), is in heart of great northern N. J. industrial area & extends (E) to Arthur Kill opp. Staten I., with which it is conn. by Goethal's Bridge (toll) as well as by ferry. Elizabeth R., which in old days was crowded with shipping, & Rahway R. cut through city (NE) from the Kill. Elizabeth is oldest Eng. settlement in St. In 1664, 3 Long Islanders bought land bet. Raritan R. & Newark Bay from Inds. & c.1 yr. later Gov. Philip Carteret picked site on this tract for future provincial capital, named in honor of wife of his cousin, Sir Geo. Carteret, one of N. J. Proprietors. In 1686 seat of gov. was moved to Perth Amboy. Elizabeth, however, continued to thrive & became important shipbuilding & industrial town. It suffered severely during Rev. from Brit. raids. Both Alex. Hamilton & Aaron Burr went to school here &, in 19th cent., Admiral Wm. F. Halsey, Jr., of World War II fame, was born here. In 1830's port of Staten I. Sound was developed & this, together with coming of RRs., assured steady expansion. Elizabeth in this period was noted for shell fish, & rivalry bet. fishermen of "downtown" shore front & "uptown" dist. often led to brawls. Singer Sewing Machine Co., 1st great industry, 1873, was soon followed by host of others. Plants employing upwards of 50,000 people produce c.$150,000,000 worth of manufactures annually: oil refineries, machine tools, steel & cast iron machinery, hardware, chemicals, clothing. PTS. OF INT.: Some 23 structures of hist. int. in city are marked by plaques. (1) 61 Broad St., **St. John's Ch.** (Episc.1860.Vict.Goth.). (2) On Broad St., (S) of Caldwell Pl., site of **First Presb. Ch.** destroyed by fire 1947 & in process of being rebuilt. The 1st Ch. (c.1668) also served as gen. assembly; 2nd (1724) was destroyed by Brit. in 1780 & rebuilt soon after. One of pastors was Jonathan Dickinson, 1st Pres. of College of N.J., now Princeton, & 1st classes met in bldg., no longer extant, on grounds of ch. (3) Cor. Broad St. & Rahway Ave., **Union County Cth.** (1903 by Ackerman & Ross). In Annex, a 15-story tower, is Union Cty. Hist. Soc. Room (O. Wed.afts.Sat.a.m.); coll. of portraits, hist. relics. (4) SW. cor. Broad St. & Rahway Ave., **Pub. Lib.** (O.Ital.Ren.by E.L.Tilden) on site of several early taverns. (5) In Scott Pk. is **Gen. Winfield Scott Shaft,** recently completed. At 1104 E. Jersey St., opp. the pk. is **Site of Old Scott Homestead.** (6) 1073 E. Jersey St., **Boudinot H.** (O. rest.), home of Elias Boudinot, Pres. of Continental Congress. He delivered eulogy over body of Pastor Jas. Caldwell (see St.S-24). (7) 1046 E. Jersey St., **Belcher H.** (pre-1742.Gr.Rev.fine inter.& exter.), home of Jonathan Belcher, Gov. of provinces & one of supporters of plan for a College of N.J. (8) 1045 E. Jersey St., **Nath. Bonnell H.** (pre-1682). (9) 21 Westfield Ave., **Williamson H.** (1808). (10) 556 Morris Ave., **Crane H.** (pre-Rev.N.Eng.Col.). (11) 408 Rahway Ave., **Old Chateau** (c.1760), confiscated during Rev. because owner, the Cavalier Jouet, was Tory. (12) Union Square, **Statue of Minuteman** by Carl Conrads, comm. resistance to Brit. invaders, June 7, 1780 at this spot. (13) 633 Pearl St., **St. John's Parsonage** (1696.enlarged 1765.largely rebuilt 1817). (14) Several of the city's plants are open to visitors: **Amer. Type Founders Plant,** 200 Elmora Ave. (O.group tours,written appl.); SE.

end Trumbull St., **Singer Sewing Machine Plant** (O.group tours,written appl.), employing 7,000 workers; 116 Livingston St., **N. J. Pretzel Plant** (O.wks.), employing mostly deaf mutes.

SIDE TRIP: From Elizabeth (S) to Trenton. 43m St.27 & US206. Via: Rahway, Menlo Pk., Metuchen, (Stelton), Highland Pk., New Brunswick & Princeton. Adequate accoms.

St.27 follows S. Elmore Ave. branching (SW) & shortly passes **Warinanco Pk.** (stadium. boat.pic.skating), named for Lenni Lenape Ind. chief. 3.5m **Rahway,** industrial city known during Rev. as Spanktown because of local physician's habit of spanking his wife. 265 Hamilton St., **Art Center.** At 4m hy. crosses Rahway R. which has a pky. on both shores. A little further along hy. passes **Old Presb. Cemetery** (R) with grave of Abr. Clark, signer of Decl. of Ind. & delegate to Continental Congress. 9m **Menlo Pk.,** with **Site of Edison's Laboratory** marked by boulder behind which is Mem. Tower topped by huge lightbulb. Within tower is a perpetual light. Tower marks spot where 1st incandescent bulb was made. Edison's workshop & many relics have been removed by Henry Ford to mus. in Dearborn, Mich. (see). It is claimed that Edison also worked in wooden shack directly behind Mem. Eventually he moved his lab. (1887) to West Orange, N. J. (see). 11m **Metuchen.** Here are **Allan H.** (1740), Woodbridge Ave., **First Presb. Ch.** (1793.rest.), & Middlesex Ave., **Franklin Civic H.** (O), early schoolh. & meeting place of Rev. Committee of Safety. At 14.5m is J. with surfaced Rd.

Take latter (R) here through Stelton to **N. Stelton** at 2m, formerly home of **Fellowship Co-operative Community,** known for Ferrer Sch. (now called the Stelton Modern Sch.), which was outstanding in leadership in new experimental educational methods. Teachers have incl. Manuel Komroff, Will Durant & Rockwell Kent.

16.5m J. with St.S-28.

Take latter (R). At 1m is **Mercer H.** (1784.Col.). At 1.5m (L) **Ross Hall** (1793) & at 2.5m **Low H.** (1741.fine Georg.Col.). Hy. cont. past Rutgers Univ. Stadium & at 5.5m **Field H.** (1743). Near-by is **Ind. Burial Ground.** At 8m is **Bound Brook** & J. with St.28.

17m **NEW BRUNSWICK**

Through RR. & bus conns. Good accoms. Info.: C. of C., Woodrow Wilson Hotel, George St. & Livingston Ave.; Auto Club of Central N. J., Roger Smith Hotel.

New Brunswick, on Raritan R., is industrial & educational center. Founded in 1681 by company of immigrants from Long I., it was named for King George I, "Duke of Brunswick." In 18th cent. it became center of rich agric. dist. & many mills sprang up on streams in vic. Vessels coming up R. crowded the water-front. In 1774 Provincial Congress met here & elected delegates to Continental Congress, although town, due to its occupation by Brit. in 1759, had developed a good deal of Tory sentiment. Washington & his defeated army reached New Brunswick, Nov. 28, 1776, but had to continue withdrawal in face of Brit. forces which now occupied town. He returned after Battle of Monmouth & it was from New Brunswick that he ordered march (S) which resulted in Brit. surrender at Yorktown. In early 19th cent. New Brunswick continued to be important port, due to location on R. & building of Del. & Raritan Canal. Competition by RRs. resulted in decline of shipping but in 2nd half of 19th cent. town's industrial importance grew steadily. 20th cent. witnessed est. of plants turning out pharmaceutical products, followed later by factories producing automobile parts, aircraft, chemicals, rugs, clothing. In 1929 New Brunswick made headlines with Hall-Mills murder case which resulted in acquittal of Mrs. Hall & 2 of her brothers who were accused of murdering Rev. W. Hall & Elinor Mills, choir singer in his ch. The mystery of this murder has never been solved. In 1949 a lab. was est. here by U.S. Atomic Energy Commission as "bureau of standards" for chemicals & special materials used in national atomic energy program.

PTS. OF INT.: (1) **Rutgers Univ.** (most of bldgs.O.) was founded as Queens College in 1766 to prepare ministers for Dutch Reformed Ch. The ch. relinquished control in 1864 & New Brunswick Theological Seminary became separate institution. In 1917 Rutgers College became st. institution. Within a yr. N.J. College for Women was affiliated with it & in 1924 it became Rutgers Univ. Univ. also incl. N. J. College of Agric., Sch. of Education, N. J. College for Women, N. J. College of Pharmacy (at Newark), Univ. Exten. Div. & Univ. College which conducts evening courses in Newark & New Brunswick. To be completed (1951), **Inst. of Microbiology,** founded by Dr. Selman A. Waksman, discoverer of streptomycin. Univ. has several campuses. On Queens campus are oldest bldgs. In SE. part of city is N. J. College for Women & directly (S) of it, Farm of N. J. College of Agric. & Experiment Sta. Univ. bldgs. incl.: Hamilton St. bet. George & College Aves., **Queens Bldg.** (1825.post-Col.by Jas.McComb.architect of N.Y.City Hall). (E) of Queens Bldg., **Kirkpatrick Chapel** (1872.Fr.Goth.) with 90 portraits of Univ. notables. Among painters were Thos. Sully & John Vanderlyn. There are fine mem. windows. (W) of Queens Bldg., **Geological Hall** (O.wks.); coll. of Ind. relics, minerals & some fossils. SW. cor. Hamilton & George Sts., **Schanck Observatory** (N.O.1865), modeled after Temple of Winds in Athens. Hamilton St. & College Ave., **Voorhees Lib.** (O); coll. of hist. relics, early Col. drawing & paintings & coin coll. Near lib. is **N.J. Hall** (O.appl.) which contains 25,000 specimens of seed plants & oysters. 536 George St., **Ceramics Bldg.** (O.appl.Georg.Col.); ceramic exhibits & technique of manufacturing ceramics. George St. & Nichol Ave., **N. J.**

**St. College of Agric. & Experiment Sta.**, adj. Experimental Farm. (2) Neilson St. bet. Bayard & Patterson Sts., **Dutch Reformed Ch.** (1812). In graveyard are buried Rev. soldiers & New Brunswick notables. (3) 17 Seminary Place, **New Brunswick Theological Seminary.** Suydam Hall (O.wks.afts.); biblical coll. of relief maps, coins of early Christian era & other items. (4) Opp. Seminary, **Statue of William the Silent** (duplicate from orig. plaster model of Lodewyk Royer). (5) N. end College Ave., **Buccleuch Pk.** in which is **White H.** (O.afts.Sun.& hols.May 30-Labor Day.1729.Georg.Col.); hand-painted panels, Col. furnishings. (6) 17 Codwise Ave., **Joyce Kilmer Birthpl.** (O.wks.10-10.free); relics of poet. (7) 60 Livingstone Ave., **Guest H.** (O.appl.Pub.Lib.1760.Col.); coll. of lace & shawls. In this house, Thos. Paine hid from Brit. during Rev.

23.5m **Franklin Pk.** & **Dutch Reformed Ch.** (est.1710); pastor was a founder of Rutgers Univ. 30m **Kingston,** sett. 1700, an int. old town & birthpl. of Jos. Hewes, signer of Decl. of Ind. From here, Washington & his armies eluded Brit. under Cornwallis, Jan. 3, 1777, immediately after Battle of Princeton by turning (N) instead of proceeding to New Brunswick. At 30.5m, on W. side of Millstone R., J. with surfaced Rd.

(R) on latter 2m to **Rocky Hill.** Here at **Berrien H.** (O.wks.exc.Mon.10-6;Sun.2-4.sm.fee. 1730), Washington had hqs. Aug.-Nov. 1783, while Congress met in Princeton to draft peace terms with England; hist. furniture & relics.

At J. (see above) is old Kingston Flour Mill (L). Behind mill is dam which forms **Carnegie L.** Across L. are bldgs. of **St. Joseph's College** (Cath.). 32m **Castle Howard Farm** (1685.mod. O.). 33m **Princeton** (see US206). St.27 joins US206 to **Trenton** at 43m (for this sec. see US206).

US1 cont. (S) from Elizabeth past storage plants of Standard Oil Co. **25.5. LINDEN** in which is **Wheeler Pk.** (recr.). Among industries is **Gen. Motors Assembly Plant** (O.group tours wks.). **33.5. ROOSEVELT PK.** (192 as.) **35.5.** J. with side Rd.

SIDE TRIP: Take latter (L) 3.5m to **Piscataway** where is **St. James Ch.** (Episc.1837), reprod. of earlier ch. destroyed by a tornado.

**39.** US1 crosses Raritan R. & passes campus of **N.J. College for Women** (R). **40.** Traffic Circle & J. with St.S-28.

SIDE TRIP: Take latter (E) to **Old Bridge** at 7m.

(R) from Old Bridge to **Helmetta,** 5m where is **Geo. W. Helme Plant** (O.only by permit from N.Y.office), one of world's largest snuff factories, turning out some 40 million lbs. of snuff a yr.

St.S-28 cont. (SE) past **L. Lefferts** (recr.f.) to **Matawan** at 14m.

US1 cont. past grounds of **N.J. ST. COLLEGE OF AGRIC.** at **41.** (see New Brunswick above). Hy. now passes **Rockefeller Institute for Medical Research** (N.O.) which conducts investigations & health reforms throughout world. **55.5.** J. with side Rd. (L) here short distance to **Walker Gordon Farm.** (O), int. for modern dairy methods. **65. TRENTON** (see). US1 cont. through N. part of Trenton & crosses Del. R. Bridge 3m further on to Morrisville, Pa.

## US 30--NEW JERSEY

**ATLANTIC CITY, N.J. (W) to CAMDEN, N.J.** (across R. from Philadelphia). **56. US30**

Via: Absecon, Egg Harbor City, Magnolia, Berlin, (Clementon), Lindenwold, (Laurel Springs), Lawnside, Haddon, Haddon Hts., Audubon, Oaklyn, Collingswood. Accoms.: All types. Excellent Rd.

US30 traverses some rich farm areas &, at its terminus, suburbs of Camden.

**0. ATLANTIC CITY**

Through RR., air & bus conns. Accoms.: All types. Info.: C. of C.; Shore Motor Club, 130 S. Virginia Ave. Recr. facils. of all kinds (swim.f.boat.golf.horseback riding on beach.ice skate. ice hockey). Amusement centers. Horse racing at Atlantic City Race Track. Easter Parade & Sunrise Service; Auerbach Cup Motor Boat Race, May 30; Flower Show, June; Nat. Mothboat Races, Aug.; Showman's Variety Jubilee & Festival of Floats incl. "Miss America Contest," Sept.; Festival of Lights, Christmas.

Atlantic City, occupying Absecon (Ind. "place of swans") I., a series of sand dunes 10m long & less than 1m wide, is one of most popular yr.-round seaside resorts in U.S., entertaining annually bet. 13,000,000 & 16,000,000 visitors. An island waste in 1852 when the Camden & Atlantic RR. was begun, the young city blossomed into fame when 1st boardwalk, conceived by Jacob Keim (because he did not like guests tracking sand into his hotel) & Alex. Boardman, was completed June 26, 1870. The invention of the rolling chair (1884) soon produced the wicker double & triple chairs in which guests are wheeled about and in 1895 the picture postcard from Germany was naturalized in Atlantic City. The present boardwalk, the 5th, dates from 1896. It is a steel & concrete structure covered with planks laid in herringbone pattern; 60′ wide, it was extended until it was almost 8m long. The hurricane of 1944 damaged secs. of it, however, which were delayed in being repaired due to war shortages. From the boardwalk, whose neon lights give it appearance of a Broadway by the sea, 5 giant ocean piers, lined with every conceivable kind of amusement device (one advertises "16 hrs. of continuous entertainment"), jut out into the water. The beach which extends some 8m is avail. (free) for swimming, fishing & horseback riding. On the land side, boardwalk is paralleled by Pacific & Atlantic Aves. lined with palatial hotels that face the ocean & shops that sell everything from Paris gowns to salt water taffy. During World War II the army took over all hotels for basic training center, making Atlantic City its most expensive camp.

PTS. OF INT.: On Boardwalk: (1) Georgia & Mississippi Aves., **Convention Hall** (1929.guides.sm.fee), said to be largest of its kind in world with auditorium seating 41,000 & pipe organ of 32,000 pipes. Also meeting rooms & ballroom; facils. for basketball, football, ice hockey, boxing, horse shows, theatricals & concerts. (2) Arkansas Ave., **Hamid's Million Dollar Pier** (1,900′; closed from Labor Day through winter.single fee.amusements.bath.), named by Capt. J. L. Young in 1906 when cost of still incomplete pier had reached $1,000,000. (3) Tennessee Ave., **Central Pier,** once city's longest pier (2,700′) it has been three-times destroyed by fire; now one-third of orig. length. Commercial exhibits. (4) Pennsylvania Ave., **Steeplechase Pier,** juvenile attractions (fees), f. & yachting. Orig. 800′ long (1890), it was rebuilt after 1932 fire to 1,500′. (5) Virginia Ave., **Steel Pier** (single fee.2,000′), variety of attractions, incl. water carnival, zoo, theaters, ballroom, & radio studio. (6) New Jersey Ave., **Garden Pier,** youngest pier, of Sp. architecture; features sporting & theatrical events. Off the Boardwalk: (7) Pacific & Rhode Island Aves., **Absecon Lighth.** (N.O. 167′.1854). (8) Albany & Ventnor Aves., **World War Mem.** (Class. by Carrere & Hastings). Within is mon., "Liberty in Distress," a reprod. by F. W. MacMonnies of his work at Varredes, France, comm. 1st battle of the Marne.

**7. ABSECON.** J. with US9 (see). **18. EGG HARBOR CITY,** winemaking & grape juice center surrounded by vineyards. J. with Green Bank Rd.

SIDE TRIP: Take latter (N) 3m to **Franklin D. Roosevelt Pk.** (recr.bath.). Rd. cont. bet. 2 lakes (f.). At 4m dirt Rd. leads here 0.5m to **Gloucester L.** (R). At 6m on Green Bank Rd. is **Weekstown** where hy. turns (R) skirting **Green Bank St. For.** (O.daylight hrs.1,833 as.; bath.pic.h.f.). At 11.5m (R) **Richards Mansion** (rest.). Rd. now traverses Jersey Pine reg., still inhabited by segregated group of people known as "the Pineys." It is said that some of ancestors of group deserted their Col. villages as protest against rigid religious rules & that its numbers were augmented by Tory renegades & deserters from Brit. army during Rev. The Pineys in the old days had a reputation for lawlessness & lived in great squalor. Construction of Rds. through the Pines has broken down some of barriers bet. the Pineys & surrounding pop. At 12m is **Pleasant Mills** & (R) **Meth. Ch.** (1808). In cemetery Rev. soldiers were buried, incl. Jos. Johnson who claimed to have fired 1st shot at Bunker Hill. (L) a short distance is **Kate Aylesford H.** (1763) on shore of L. In Col. times Joe Mulliner, a sort of local Robin Hood, kidnapped Honoré Read, pretty daughter of owner of H. & said to be heroine of Chas. Peterson's novel "Kate Aylesford." Kidnapping took place during a party given in 1781, in revenge for Joe's not having been invited. Joe returned Honoré that night, was soon caught, tried & executed. Both he & Honoré refused to say anything about kidnapping.

**29.5.** J. (R) with US206 (see). **32. ELM,** on whose S. outskirts (L) is **Silver Fox Farm** (O.May-Dec.). **35. GRAPE EXCHANGE,** where grapes are sold each autumn for winemaking. **39.** Hy. crosses Mechescatatauxin Cr. with adj. **Atco L.** (resort). **41.** J. with St. S-41.

SIDE TRIP: Take latter (R) 6m to **Kresson L.** (bath.fee).

Just beyond J. with St.S-41 is J. with surfaced Rd. (L) here short distance to **Peacock Dahlia Farm.**

**46.5.** J. with surfaced Rd. leading 0.5m to **Laurel Springs** where during spring of 1875 Walt Whitman stayed with friends at **Stafford H.** (O.appl.) on Maple Ave. **47.5. STRATFORD.** Here (L) is **White Horse Inn** (18th cent.int.inter.) which still has orig. sign. **50.5. LAWNSIDE,** only Negro-owned & Negro-governed borough in N.J. Founded before Civil War, it expanded during 1850-60 when neighboring Quakers were operating Underground Railroad. **52. HADDON HEIGHTS.** In Haddon Heights Nat. Pk. Area. (35 as.) is **Glover Mansion** (O.c.1705.Col.remod.). **54.5. COLLINGSWOOD,** sett. in 1682 by Quakers. Near L. on Eldridge Ave. is **Friends**

**Burial Ground.** Adj. is **Sloan Burial Ground,** est. 1790 after disagreement among Quakers. Also on Eldridge Ave. is **Thackara H.** (O.aft.1754). **55.** Traffic Circle & J. with US130 (see). **56. CAMDEN AIRPORT TRAFFIC CIRCLE.** Hy. cont. 4$^{m}$ through Camden to Del. R. bridge which crosses to Phila.

## US 40—NEW JERSEY

**ATLANTIC CITY, N.J. (W) to PENNSVILLE, N.J.** (across R. from New Castle, Del.). **68. US40**

Via: Pleasantville, Mays Landing, Malaga, Woodstown. Accoms.: All types. Excellent Rd.

At Soldiers Mon. in **Atlantic City** at **0.,** US40 has J. with Ventnor Ave. leading (L) 1$^{m}$ to **Ventnor** (fashionable resort). Casting tournaments on fishing pier. **12.5. McKEE CITY** & J. with US322.

SIDE TRIP: McKee City to Bridgeport. 48.5$^{m}$ US322. Take US322 (R) from McKee City. At 10$^{m}$ is J. with side Rd.

Take latter (R) 0.5$^{m}$ to **Weymouth,** where is site of old iron works, which inhabitants claim produced cannon for Washington's army. Here is **Weymouth Meeting H.** (1805).

25$^{m}$ J. with St.42.

Take latter (R) 6.5$^{m}$ to **Grenloch** on a L. (boat.f.swim.). Near-by is **Mother of the Savior Seminary** on grounds of what was once Weber's Buffalo Farm. The old Monkey H. has been converted into an unusual chapel.

39$^{m}$ **Mullica Hill.** 43$^{m}$ J. with old King's Hy. built in 1681. L. on latter 1$^{m}$ is **Swedesboro,** one of earliest Swedish settlements in N.J. **Trinity Ch.** (Episc.former Luth.1784) still uses communion silver bought in 1730.

48.5$^{m}$ **Bridgeport.** Further on c.1.5$^{m}$ is **Ferry** to Chester, Pa.

**17.5. MAYS LANDING.** Here is **Sunshine Pk.,** home of nudist colony. **18. L. LENAPE** (resort.f.recr.). **39. IONA L.** (f.). **46.** (L) **MAYHEW H.** (1792.Col.). **55. WOODSTOWN,** sett. by Quakers in early 1700's. Many int. Col. Hs. **Quaker Meeting H.** (1784). Opp. is **Friends Infirmary,** still in use after more than century. 158 N. Main St., **Stony Harris' Sales Co. Office** where auctions of misc. articles brought in by farmers are held. **58. SHARPTOWN.**

SIDE TRIP: (R) here at Ice-Cream Plant, on narrow Rd. 2$^{m}$ is **Seven Stars Tavern.** Legend says it was visited by pre-Rev. pirate, Bluebeard, & that Tory spy was hanged from attic window. At W. side of main entrance is sm. window through which travelers on horseback were served. (R) from tavern is **Oliphant's Mill** functioning for more than century. Farm houses in vic. almost all date back to Rev. Near top of Oliphant's Hill is **Moravian Ch.** (1786).

**68. N.J.-DEL. LINE** at Pennsville. US40 cont. via New Castle to Wilmington & Baltimore (see).

## ST. 23—NEW JERSEY

**NEWARK, N.J.** (across Holland Tunnel from N.Y.) **(N) to HIGH POINT PK., N.J.** (c.1$^{m}$ from Port Jervis, N.Y.). **64.5. St.23**

Via: Montclair, Mountain View, Pompton Plains, Butler, Franklin, Hamburg, Sussex. Good Rd. Accoms.: All types.

St.23 cuts across NW. sec. of N.J. through reg. of mts., valleys & sm. Ls. & gives access to summer resort at Greenwood L. At N. terminus is High Pt. Pk., highest spot in N.J. Tour cont. to Port Jervis & from there autoist may take tour of most int. part of scenically fine Del. R. (see Del. R. Tour, Pa.).

**3. BLOOMFIELD** (see Newark).

**5.5. MONTCLAIR** (see Newark). **12.5. MOUNTAIN VIEW.** In vic., **Preakness Valley Pk.** with **Dey Mansion** (O.sm.fee), Washington's hqs. **19. POMPTON PLAINS. 19.5.** J. with surfaced Rd.

SIDE TRIP: Take this Rd. (R) which shortly passes near **Pompton Ls.** (resort). At 5$^{m}$ **Wanaque Reservoir** (Ind.: "place of the sassafras") which supplies northern N.J. cities. It has appearance of lovely mountain lake. 5.5$^{m}$ **Midvale.** J. with side Rd.

Take latter (L) 3$^{m}$ to **Nature Friend's Camp** (recr.swim.) run by labor org.

12$^{m}$ J. with surfaced Rd.

Take latter (R) here 0.5$^{m}$ to **Ringwood Manor** (grounds O.fee for parking & pic. 269 as.), owned by N.J. & formerly seat of prominent Hewitt family. Bldg. was erected c.1765 & partly burned during Rev. (extensive Vict. adds.). Relics incl. 25 links from chain stretched across Hudson R. to halt Brit. fleet. Washington frequently visited manor & was here June 20, 1781, during mutiny of some soldiers whose ringleaders were captured & shot. He also celebrated here decl. of peace.

12.5m **Ringwood,** where extensive ironworks were erected to use iron deposits in vic. Rbt. Erskine, friend of Washington, developed industry & supplied Amer. army during Rev. Cannon used in War of 1812 & weapons used in Civil War were cast here. Peter Cooper, famous philanthropist (see N.Y.C.) cont. operation of works & later Abr. S. Hewitt, one-time mayor of N.Y., headed them. They were finally closed in 1931. Behind Ringwood Pub. Sch. is entrance to old Ringwood mines, the work of which was mostly done by "Jackson Whites" whose very mixed ancestry has been traced back to shipload of women shanghaied by Brit. for their troops during Rev. Eventually women were turned loose but, being ostracized everywhere, took refuge in Jersey Mts. with a group of Tuscarora Inds. & were joined by Hessians, renegade slaves, outlawed whites, etc. Today Jackson Whites live in the fors. Nudist colony in vic. 17.5m J. with side Rd.

Take latter (R) 1m to **Greenwood L.** & cont. along shore across N.Y. Line to **Village of Greenwood L.** (resort.f.boat.accoms.recr.). Steep Mts. enclose the lovely 7m body of water.

20m **W. Milford** on **Pine Cliff L.** Here is **W. Milford Presb. Ch.** (1807.rebuilt 1815).

**37.5. STOCKHOLM.** Here is **Rock Lodge Nudist Camp. 42.5. FRANKLIN,** center of N.J. zinc mining industry. **Jewish Synagogue** was orig. Bapt. edifice & later used by Meths. & Presb. **45. HAMBURG.** Just (N) of RR., **Haines Mansion** (Dutch Col.), now a tea-room. At 0.5m (L) on St.31 is **Thos. Lawrence H.** (R), on site of former home built by Thos. Lawrence for his son-in-law Louis Morris, signer of Decl. of Ind.; heirlooms & relics. **51. SUSSEX. 53.5.** A stone & frame H. (beginning of 18th cent.) in front of which is totem pole. H. was attacked in 1781 by Jos. Brant, Ind. chief & his band. **59.5. HIGH PT. PK.** (12,000 as.; bath.boat.camp.lodge with accoms.inn.winter sports.pic.). In Pk. is **Marcia L.** at whose S. end is bear pit & reindeer paddock. A Rd. runs to **High Pt.** (1,800′) on which is **War Mem.** 235′ high with fine views—highest pt. in N.J. **64.5. N.J.-N.Y. LINE.** (See Port Jervis & Del. R. Tour.)

## US 1, US 9, ST. 35, ST. 36, ST. 4N, ST. 37—NEW JERSEY

**NEW YORK, N.Y., (W. & S.) to CAPE MAY CITY, N.J. 163. US1, US9, St.35, St.36, St.4N, St.37**

Via: Woodbridge, Perth Amboy, South Amboy, Red Bank, Eatontown, Neptune City, Avon by the Sea, Belmar, Brielle, Pt. Pleasant, Seaside Hts., (Toms R.), Manahawkin, Tuckerton, Cape May City.

This route follows closely N.J. coastline passing through or near practically all coastal resorts down to Cape May, southeasternmost pt. of N.J. Tour starts in N.Y. at Holland Tunnel through which it crosses to US1 in N.J. & follows US1 to Rahway Cloverleaf (see US1) where US9 branches off (L).

**O. RAHWAY CLOVERLEAF. 3.** J. with paved Rd. leading (L) to Outerbridge Crossing to **Staten I.**

**4. PERTH AMBOY**

Through RR. & bus conns. Ferry: Foot of Smith St. for Tottenville, Staten I. Bridges: Outerbridge Crossing to Staten I. (toll). Victory Bridge to S. Amboy & shore points. Accoms.: All types. Info.: Pub. Lib., 196 Jefferson St. Swim.: 2 beaches, Water St. Boat.: Boat Basin, foot of Water St.

Perth Amboy is industrial city at mouth of Raritan R. & on Raritan Bay, arm of Upper N. Y. Bay. To (W), across Arthur Kill, is Staten I. City, sett. 1651 by Staten I. Dutchman, Augustine Herman, had its pop. augmented by arrival (1684) of some Scots, fleeing religious persecution. Derivation of name is two-fold; Perth from Scotch settlers; Amboy, corruption of Ind. word "Ompoge" (large level piece of ground). Settlement became capital of province of E. New Jersey, 1686. At beginning of Rev., town was pro-Tory, but in June 1776, patriots took over & arrested Gov. Wm. Franklin. In same yr. Brit. retaliated by taking Rich. Stockton, signer of Decl. of Ind. During Rev., Perth Amboy changed hands several times. In early 19th cent., town became fashionable resort, but with arrival of RR. & increased shipping it began development as industrial center & port. Before Civil War it was important sta. on Underground Railroad. After John Brown's execution, his body was brought to Eagleswood, home of Rebecca Springfield, ardent Abolitionist, from where it was transported to N. Elba, N.Y. (see). Some 100 factories incl. plants producing ceramics from clay of vic., smelters, etc.

PTS. OF INT.: (1) 149 Kearny Ave., **The Westminster** (1768-70.rebuilt 1815), occupied by last Royal Gov. of province, Wm. Franklin, when he was arrested (1776) by colonists. Gen. Mercer, one of Washington's aides, had hqs. here July 1776. (2) In

Hayes Pk., SE. end of Catalpa Ave., **Kearny H.** (1780.rest.1938), moved to pk. from High St. & converted into mus. (3) In front of City Hall, **Statue of Geo. Washington** (Nils Nillson Alling). (4) In City Hall Sq., **Surveyor General's Office** (O.Wed.fee. 1860's), sm. brick bldg. Here are held semi-annual meetings of General Proprietors of E. Division of N.J. With W. Division it is survival of early Col. times. Its chief asset today is ownership of any new land appearing in N.J. Some yrs. ago Shrewsbury R. created a new I. to which corp. claimed title. (5) Rector & Gordon Sts., **St. Peter's Episc. Ch.** (1853.congregation dates to c.1698), on foundations of earlier ch. Within are pews of orig. Ch. & in cemetery are graves of early settlers. (6) Convery Pl. (N) of Smith Pl., **Old Stone H.,** now roadhouse, formerly used as studio by Amer. landscape painter, Geo. Inness. (7) 59 Buckingham Ave., **Atlantic Terra Cotta Plant** (O.for group tours on written appl.) (8) S. end Elm St., **Raritan Copper Works** (O.for group tours on written appl.). (9) **Outerbridge Crossing** (toll) from E. end Grove St. to Tottenville, Staten I., built & operated by Port of N. Y. Authority, with truss spans of 2,100′ in length & clearance of 135′. (10) **Sadowski Pky.** (boardwalk, bath.beach & recr.center) honoring Jos. Sadowski, killed in action in World War II & awarded Congressional Medal of Honor.

**7. SOUTH AMBOY,** RR. & shipping center. **7.5.** J. with St.35 on which main tour cont.

SIDE TRIP: From J. with St.35 to a pt. 1m (N) of Toms R. (J. with St.37). **36m US9.** Via: (Matawan), Freehold, Lakewood.

At 10m is J. with St.4 Alt.

Take latter (L) 5m to **Matawan,** residential community with many fine old houses. 94 Main St., **Burrowes Mansion** (1723;restaurant), home of John Burrowes, captured by Brit. during Rev. There are still bullet holes on landing to attic. On Main St. also, **First Presb. Ch.** with tower designed by Stanford White. On Mill Rd., **Hawkins H.** (1700. Dutch Col.). In Matawan is J. with St.34.

At 8.5m (S) on St.34 is J. with Side Rd. Take latter (L) 2.5m to **Phalanx,** famous mid-19th cent. experiment in communal living. Horace Greeley was Vice-Pres., & Albert Brisbane, father of late Arthur Brisbane, Hearst editor, one of its organizers in 1843. The late Alexander Woollcott was born here & in his "Letters," speaks of his memories of the community with great affection. Advocating women's rights, advanced educational methods & theories concerning wages & profit-sharing, the community achieved considerable notoriety. Fire in 1854 destroyed mills in which members had worked & shared profits. Only the old Hotel still stands in disrepair. At 10m (R) on St.34 is **Colt's Neck Inn** (1717), hqs. of Rumson Hunt Club. Here Washington is supposed to have stayed during Rev. At 15m is J. with St. 33. Take latter (L) here 3m to **Hamilton.** Here is **Old Tavern** (c.1740.Col.) where Tory spies were trapped during Rev.

At 20m on St.34 is J. with side Rd. Take latter (R) 2m to **Deserted Village of Allaire,** during 1st half of 19th cent. an important iron-producing town. Center of new (in progress, 1949) **Allaire St. Pk.**

At 10.5m on St.4 Alt. is **Freneau,** named for Philip Freneau, Rev. poet & journalist. Near-by is **Freneau Farm** (L) with Freneau's Print Shop & grave. At 17m is **Freehold** (Accoms.:Limited. Info.:Mun. Bldg., W. Main St.; Pub.Lib., E. Main St. Trotting Races:Freehold Race Track, Park Ave. & W. Main St.). Market center for farms of vic. & home of small industries, town was 1st settled c.1650. In 1715 its pop. was expanded by arrival of group of Scots from New Aberdeen (now Matawan) who fled Eng. because of religious persecution. In June 1778 town was occupied by Sir Wm. Clinton's army & was scene of skirmishing during Battle of Monmouth (see below). PTS. OF INT.: (1) Main & Court Sts., **Cth.** (1874.remod.1930.Georg.Col.). (2) In Monmouth Pk., **Monmouth Battle Mon.** (3) 70 Court St., **Monmouth Cty. Hist. Assoc. Mus.** (O.wks.exc. Mon.;Sun.aft.free); reprod. of Georg. Col. bldg. by J. Hallam Conover; hist. relics & lib. (4) 33 Throckmorton St., **St. Peter's Episc. Ch.** (1683.much alt.), built orig. by Quakers at Topanemus & later removed to Freehold & taken over by Episc.; used as hospital by Brit. during Battle of Monmouth. (5) NW. cor. of Park Ave. & W. Main St., **Freehold Race Track** (trotting races in summer). (6) 150 W. Main St., **Hankinson H.** (1755.int. exter.& inter.). Clinton & staff occupied H. night before Battle of Monmouth. (7) **A. & H. Karagheusian Carpet Factory** (O.appl.) where some of finest modern rugs are made.

Take Cty.22, (W) from Freehold, following Throckmorton St. 1.5m **Molly Pitcher's Well** (L) bet. RR. & hy. (marked). Molly, wife of an artilleryman, carried water to Amer. soldiers during Battle of Monmouth. They called out, as she approached, "Here comes Molly & her pitcher," later shortened to Molly Pitcher. When her husband, John Casper Haye, was wounded, she seized the swab & sponged the gun, keeping up fire for rest of day. He recovered & Molly remained with army for duration & was commissioned by Washington as a sergeant. At 3m **Monmouth Battlefield,** extending (W) to **Old Tennent Ch.** (O.1751). In adj. cemetery men who fell in battle are buried. Here on June 28, 1778, Brit. Gen. Clinton's army repulsed an attack by Amer. Gen. Chas. Lee's forces sent ahead to halt Brit. Washington bringing up main army ended retreat & repulsed Brit. It was during battle that Washington reprimanded Lee for incompetence, swearing "until the leaves shook on the trees."

At 26m on US9 **Lakewood,** in early 19th cent. iron smelting center using bog iron deposits. After Civil War it became a fashionable resort. Around L. Carasaljo beautiful homes were built by the Astors, Vanderbilts & Rockefellers. **Georgian Court College for Women** now occupies former Geo. J. Gould estate & **Ocean Cty. Pk.** (O), the former Rockefeller estate. In 1948 Clarence Booth began construction of underground concrete **"Atom-Bomb Proof" H.** in Lakewood.

On Rd. (R) 11m to **Cassville,** blueberry & cranberry vic. (R) from village is **Rova Farms,** community of Russian emigrees under direction of Russian Consolidated Mutual Aid Soc. of Amer.; **Chapel** & **Central Bldg.** int.

At 30m is **Seven Stars Tavern** (remod.), so-named because guests could count 7 stars through a hole in roof. At 36m is J. with St.37, just 1m (N) of Toms R. From here US9 becomes the main tour.

Take St.37 (R) 7m to **Lakehurst** near which is **U.S. Naval Sta.** (O) where are giant hangars for lighter-than-air craft. Here in 1937 the German Zeppelin, "Hindenburg," was destroyed by fire. Sta. is also training pt. for carrier pigeons. In SW. cor. of reserv. is **Cathedral of the Air.**

Main tour cont. from J. of US9 with St.35 & follows St.35 to **MECHANICSVILLE** at **13.5.** & J. with St.36 which now becomes main tour hy.

SIDE TRIP: From Mechanicsville to J. with St.34. 27m St.35. Via: (Middletown), Red Bank, Shrewsbury, Eatontown & Neptune City.

At 4.5m is J. with side Rd. leading (R) 0.5m to **Middletown.** Here is **Rainbow Inn** (late 17th cent.rest.), pre-Rev. stagecoach stop. On Kings Hy., opp. RR. bridge, **Marlpit Hall** (O.Tues. Sat.Sun.sm.fee.c.1684.Dutch Col.int.exter.& inter.), mus. maintained by Monmouth Cty. Hist. Soc. Near-by is **Christ Ch.** (1836), still supported by pirate gold left to this Ch. & another at Shrewsbury by Wm. Leeds, aide to Capt. Kidd. Also on Kings Hy., **Bapt. Ch.** (1832) & at new Monmouth Rd., **Rich. Hartshorne H.** (1670). Wm. Penn & Geo. Fox were entertained here by Hartshorne, a Quaker. At 6m is J. with side Rd.

Take latter (L) 3m to **Chapel Hill** where are a number of fine old Col. Hs. On Kings Hy. near-by is **Chapel Hill Lighth.** (O.with 1,000,000 candlepower light).

At 8.5m is **Red Bank,** center for ice boating in winter & boating & yachting in summer. At 11m is **Shrewsbury** (sett.1664). Sycamore Ave., **Post Office,** built in middle of street. NW. cor. Broad St. & Sycamore Ave., **Allen H.** (1667). In vic. were conflicts bet. Brit. & Continental troops. SE. cor. of Broad St. & Sycamore Ave., **Christ Episc. Ch.** (1769.Georg.Col.). This is other Ch. to which Wm. Leeds (see above) bequeathed part of his estate. His body rests near N. side of tower. In Ch. entry is displayed orig. charter from King Geo. II. On lectern is one of few known copies of the "Vinegar Bible," printed in 1717 at Oxford, Eng., & so-called from misprint of word "vinegar" for "vineyard" in heading of Luke XX. NE. cor. of the Cross Rds., **Friends Meeting H.** (N.O.1816). At 16.5m J. with Deal Rd. leading (R) to **Cold Ind. Spring L.** (bath.pic.tourist cabins). St.35 now cont. near seashore resorts, **Avon by the Sea, Shark R. Inlet, Belmar** & **Brielle** on Manasquan R. (sailboats can sail up R. for several miles & rowboats can proceed further to Allaire St. Pk.) to J. with St.34 at 27m.

**17.5.** J. with side Rd. leading (L) 1m to **Keansburg** (bath.f.boat.amusements). **23. ATLANTIC HIGHLANDS** on Sandy Hook Bay. Take First Ave. (L) 0.5m to Bay View Ave., known as Scenic Drive. Take latter (R) along shore front with fine views of N.Y.C., Long I. & the Atlantic to Navesink Highlands. Here Dr. rejoins St.36. **28.5. HIGHLAND BEACH** & J. with side Rd. which leads (L) a short dist. to **Sandy Hook** (O.appl.at Ft.Hancock) which juts 5m into sea. **Ft. Hancock** at tip of Hook is part of system of fortifications around N.Y. harbor. Here is **Lighth.** (1763), oldest in service in Western Hemisphere. During Rev., patriots tried unsuccessfully to destroy it to mislead Brit. shipping. St.36 ends at Highland Beach & tour now cont. (S) on Ocean Blvd. At **31.5.** J. with Rumson Rd. which leads (R) across Shrewsbury R. to Rumson, center of luxurious estates. Main tour cont. past a number of seaside resorts—**SEABRIGHT, LOW MOOR, MONMOUTH BEACH**—to **LONG BRANCH** at **33.5.,** hist. seaside resort dating from 1788 &, at its height during Gilded Age of the 19th cent., frequented by many notables: Lily Langtry, Diamond Jim Brady, Lillian Russell, Jim Fiske, Jay Gould's partner. Architecture is flamboyantly Vict. On Broadway is **Statue of Pres. Garfield** who died here after he was shot in 1881. 991 Ocean Ave., **Grant's H.,** where Pres. Grant stayed. At **Elberon Hotel,** Presidents Hayes & Harrison vacationed & Woodrow Wilson lived at **Shadow Lawn.** Main hy. cont. through more resorts—**WEST END, ELBERON, DEAL** & **ALLENHURST** on Deal L.—to **ASBURY PK.** at **42.,** developed by Jas. A. Bradley as great summer resort. The long boardwalk has restaurants, fishing pier, amusement concessions, shops. There are golf courses, bridle paths, night polo, boxing, etc. At **43.** is **OCEAN GROVE,** founded in 1869 for Meth. camp meetings & developed as a resort. Its bldgs. are largely of Grant & Vict. periods. Vehicular traffic is forbidden from midnight Sat. to midnight Sun. & during that time only pedestrians may enter or leave. Bathing is also not permitted on Sun. At head of Pilgrim's Pathway is **Auditorium** which, like Solomon's Temple, was built without use of nails. Near-by is clay **Model of the City of Jerusalem.** During last of Aug. a great revival meeting is held. The hy. cont. past more resort towns, **BRADLEY BEACH, AVON BY THE SEA, BELMAR, SPRING L.,** to **SEA GIRT** at **48.** where Jersey Nat. Guard trains. **St. Military Encampment** (O), on shore of Stockton L. named for Commodore Stockton who figured in capture of Cal. Near main entrance is **Gov.'s Residence,** known as the Little White House. At **VILLA PK., 49.,** Ocean Blvd. has J. with St.4N on which tour cont. past **MANASQUAN** on Manasquan R. to **BRIELLE, 50.** In Brielle is J. with St.35 on which tour cont. to **PT. PLEASANT, 53.** Here is J. with St.37 which becomes main tour.

SIDE TRIP: Pt. Pleasant (W) to J. with US130 (2.5m from Camden). 60m St.35 & St.40. Via: Laurelton, Lakehurst, Medford & Marlton. Accoms.: At both terminals; scarcer en route.

5m **Laurelton** & J. with St.40 on which tour cont. At 16m **Lakehurst** (see). 33m **Lebanon St. For.** (21,550 as.;cabins.campsites.pic.bath.h.). At 42m J. with Rd. leading (R) a short distance to **Red Lion,** where is **Red Lion Inn** (1710.Col.). Here lived Frank Peck, known as the "water wizard" because he was reputed to discover water with a divining rod. 46m **Medford.** On Main St., **Orthodox Friends Meeting H.** (1814). 46.5m J. with Rd. leading (L) c.3m to **Pine L.,** one of 5 Taunton Ls. (resorts). 56.5m J. with Old Kings Hy.

Take latter (L) 2m to **Haddonfield,** founded early 1700's by Quaker girl, Elizabeth Haddon, who proposed to John Estaugh, Quaker missionary when he had not courage to do so. Longfellow tells story in "Tales of a Wayside Inn." On cor. NE. Wood Lane & Marion Ave., a brick **H.** (1845.Gr.Rev.) occupies site of Elizabeth's orig. log cabin. In garden is orig. Stillhouse, built by Elizabeth who manufactured medicinal whiskey for Inds. 233 Kings Hy. E., **Ind. King Inn** (O.exc.Sun.1750); Col. furnishings & relics. N.J.'s 1st Legislature met here 1777 after being driven from Trenton by Brit. 258 Kings Hy. E., **Old Guardh.** where prisoners were kept by Council of Safety during Rev.

60m J. with US130.

From Pt. Pleasant St.37 runs along a strip of land which separates Barnegat Bay from ocean, passing a number of seaside resorts enroute. **SEASIDE HEIGHTS** at **63.**

SIDE TRIP: Take Rd. (L) straight ahead here 1.5m to **Seaside Pk.** (S) of which are 8m of splendid beaches & dunes extending to Barnegat Inlet of Barnegat Bay.

St.37 at Seaside Heights turns (R) & crosses Barnegat Bay on bridge to **Pelican I.** & from there to mainland & cont. to J. with US9 c.1m (N) of Toms River at **70.** Main tour now follows US9. At **71.** US9 reaches **TOMS RIVER,** named for its discoverer (1673), Capt. Wm. Tom. Town is famous for clam chowder. On town sq., **Ocean H.** (O.1787.alt.). On Washington St., **Ocean County Cth.** (O.wks.1850.Gr.Rev.). In Toms River (1782) occurred conflict bet. Amer. forces under Capt. Joshua Huddy & Brit. Huddy, forced to surrender, was hanged without a trial in retaliation for killing of a Loyalist prisoner by patriots. Town was burnt by Brit. **79. MURRAY GROVE has Potter Meeting H.** (1770.rebuilt 1841.int.inter.), birthpl. of Universalist Ch. in Amer. **80. ST. GAME FARM** (O.appl.where pheasants & wild ducks are bred). Warden's home dates from 1784. **80.5. FORKED RIVER,** home of Rev. Gen. John Lacey. Here is **Fork River H.,** overnight-stopping place of Capt. Huddy (see above). **84. WARETOWN,** named for Abr. Waeir, leader of the Rogerenes sect, some of whose members, after having been driven from Conn., sett. here c.1737. The Rogerenes opposed any Sabbath-Day observances. **87.5. BARNEGAT** (Dutch "Barendegat," breaker's inlet), today a resort. In Rev. times it was shipbuilding & salt-manufacturing center & earlier a haunt of pirates. **93. MANAHAWKIN** on Manahawkin L. **Old Bapt. Ch.** (R) (1758.much alt.). In Manahawkin is J. with St. S-40.

SIDE TRIP: Take St. S-40 (SE) from Manahawkin, passing **Pub. Hunt. & Fish. Grounds** (L) on Manahawkin Bay & crossing drawbridge to Cedar Bonnet I. in the bay & from there to **Ship Bottom** at 6m, the strip separating bay from ocean.

(1) From Ship Bottom a Rd. runs (N) along sand strip passing a number of resorts to **Barnegat City** at 8.5m at S. side of Barnegat Inlet. This fishing village was sett. largely by Scands. & was celebrated by F. Hopkinson Smith in "The Tides of Barnegat."

(2) From Ship Bottom a good Rd. runs (S) along sand strip passing a number of seaside resorts to **Holgate** at 9m.

US9 cont. (S) from Manahawkin & in its course all the way down to Cape May City makes J. with side Rds. branching off to resorts on ocean front. **101.** J. with side Rd.

SIDE TRIP: Take latter here a short distance (L) to **Ellen Leeds Bartlett H.** (1699). At 2.5m is **Hummock** (R), one of largest shell piles left by Inds. along Atlantic coast.

**107.** J. with side Rd.

SIDE TRIP: Take latter (R) here 2.5m to **Bass River St. For.** (9,270 as.;deer & duck h.f. pic.).

At **112.5.**, **MON.** to patriots who fell in Battle of Chestnut Neck. Battle was fought by a Brit. expeditionary force which wanted to destroy nests of Jersey privateers in this reg., against natives who were not trained troops. **120.** J. with US30 (see). **123.** J. with US40 (see). **128.5. OCEAN CITY COUNTRY** (golf) **CLUB** (18 holes;fee).

SIDE TRIP: Take Rd. (L) 0.5m to **Somers Pt.** where at cor. of May's Landing Rd. & Shore Rd. is **Somers Mansion** (O.free.late 1700;Col.). Near-by is site, marked by a tablet, of **Birthpl. of Rich. Somers,** who commanded the "Intrepid," a vessel loaded with explosives for destruction of enemy fleet at Tripoli in 1804. The "Intrepid" was blown to pieces by the Turks. Somers & 12 others were killed. At 3m **Ocean City,** resort & a bone-dry community.

**138. SEAVILLE. Old Cedar Meeting H.** (1716). Hy. cont. through or near a number of resorts to **CAPE MAY CTH.** at **150.** Here is the old **Cth.** (1851) next to a new one in which is a hist. mus. (O.wks.). **156. RIO GRANDE.** J. with St. S-49.

SIDE TRIP: Take latter (L) to **Wildwood** 3m, resort & port of call for N. Atlantic fish fleet. The 5m ocean front has several resorts.

**163. CAPE MAY CITY,** famous resort. Architecture is of Grant & Vict. periods. When Henry Clay stopped here in summer of 1847 his women admirers mobbed him on beach & snipped off some of his locks for souvenirs. Among other notables who came were Horace Greeley & Presidents Lincoln, Grant, Pierce, Buchanan & Harrison. Cape May was named for Cornelius Jacobsen Mey who sailed past this pt. in 1623. Town was frequented by Brit. men-of-war & pirates in search of fresh water at near-by Lilly Pond. Capt. Kidd is said to have visited pond & cached some of his treasure near it.

# US 202 & ST. 29—NEW JERSEY

**HAVERSTRAW, N.Y., (SW) to TRENTON, N.J. 116. US202 & St.29**

Via: Suffern, N.Y., Pompton, Mountain View, Boonton, Morris Plains, Morristown, Bernardsville & Lambertville. Lackawanna RR. accessible in N. sec. & Penn. RR. from Lambertville to Trenton. Accoms.: All types. Good Rd.

This route starts at Palisades of Hudson R., crosses Ramapo Mts. & cuts across N.J. through varied countryside of considerable hist. int. To a great extent it avoids congestion of N.Y. suburban area & thickly populated N.J. industrial reg.

## Sec. 1: HAVERSTRAW to N.Y.-N.J. LINE. 13.

**0. HAVERSTRAW,** a brick & cement mfg. town. **11. SUFFERN,** suburb of N.Y.C., has summer theater. **13. JERSEY LINE.** At 1m beyond is J. with St.17.

SIDE TRIP: Take latter (S). At 9m **Hohokus** (R). On Franklin Turnpike at Waldwick Borough line, **The Hermitage** where Washington visited (1778) & Aaron Burr courted Theodosia Provost. At 11.5m (R) **Paramus** in celery growing reg. At 13.5m is J. with St.4. (L) here 2m & then (L) again to **Bergenfield** where is **Old South Presb. Ch.** (1799). In vic. near **River Edge** is **Baron von Steuben H.** (O.wks.1757.Dutch Col.), now home of Bergen Cty. Hist. Soc.; coll. of Col. furniture, glass, Ind. relics.

## Sec. 2: N.Y.-N.J. LINE to TRENTON, N.J. 103.

Just (S) of N.Y. Line is J. with Franklin Turnpike.

SIDE TRIP: Take latter (L) 0.5m to **Winter H.** (O.Dutch Col.c.1790), now a tavern, believed to be the "House with nobody in it" about which Joyce Kilmer wrote. At c.1m is **Mahwah.** On hill is **Joyce Kilmer's White Cottage,** where it is said he wrote poem, "Trees."

**2. STONE H.** (R), a Col. dwelling. **8. OAKLAND. Borough Hall** (Georg.) is reprod. of Ch. of the Ponds erected here 1829. Adj. is present **Ch. of Ponds** (1921), a Dutch Reformed Ch., 4th Ch. of Congregation dating from 1710. **10.5. POMPTON LS.** (R) across bridge here & then (R) on Perrin Ave. c.0.5m to **Bier's Training Camp** where noted prizefighters have trained. **12. COLFAX SCHUYLER H.** (1697) which

birthpl. of Wm. Bainbridge, Commander of "Constitution"; also Rev. hqs. of Gen. Howe. (10) Witherspoon & Wiggins Sts., **Princeton Cemetery** (oldest mon.1761), graves of Aaron Burr, Grover Cleveland, Paul Tulane & members of Col. Assembly & Continental Congress. (11) Chestnut St., **Westminster Choir Sch.** (1934.Georg. Col.). (12) **Rockefeller Institute for Medical Research.** (13) SW. 1.5$^{m}$ from center of town is **Princeton Battlefield Pk.,** on site of common grave of fallen Brit. & Amer. soldiers.

**78.** (L) **DRUMTHWACKET** (grounds O.1832.Col.). **78.5. THOS. OLDEN H.** (1696) where Washington reviewed troops on march to Trenton, Dec. 1776. **81.5. CHERRY GROVE** (R) at cor. Carter Rd., was occupied by Brit. Dec. 1776. **82. LAWRENCEVILLE,** home of famous **Lawrenceville Sch. for Boys** (est.1810. Georg.). (L) **Lawrenceville Presb. Ch.** (c.1716). Here Hessians in 1776 compelled an Amer. militiaman to preach sermon. Opp., **Golding H.,** formerly tavern where Lord Cornwallis stopped, Dec. 1776. **88.5. TRENTON** (see). **92.5. WHITE HORSE.** (L) **White Horse Tavern,** named for white horse owned by Washington. Beyond village on US206 is bridge crossing Crosswicks Cr. Here in June 1778 Col. troops defeated Brit. detachment. **96. BORDENTOWN** (see US130). **98.** J. with St.S-39.

SIDE TRIP: Take latter (L) to **Wrightstown** c.9$^{m}$. Here is **Camp** (or Ft.) **Dix,** military reserv. where many thousands of recruits were quartered during both World Wars.

(1) Take Rd. (L) from Wrightstown 2.5$^{m}$ to **Cookstown. Meth. Ch.** (R) (1847). **Hendrickson Mill** (L) (1732) is still grinding grain. SE. cor. Main St. & Brinteltown Rd., handsome old **Cookstone H.,** now a bar. At 4.5$^{m}$ is **New Egypt,** so-called because when his secy., Jos. Curtis, returned with grain for army from the New Egypt reg., Washington exclaimed: "Joseph has been in Egypt & gotten the corn." Near village is **Oakford L.** (recr.).

(2) Take Rd. (R) from Wrightstown 6.5$^{m}$ to **Pemberton,** fine old town, sett. by Quakers prior 1690. On Main St., **Gristmill** (R), still functioning. SE. cor. Hanover & Elizabeth Sts., **Old Pemberton Inn** (Pa. Dutch). Just beyond Pemberton is huge **Cranberry Packing Shed** (L) where cranberries are readied for market. Berrypickers arrive each yr. & live in tents, cabins & shelters around edges of bogs.

**99.5. MANSFIELD** has an old **Friends Meeting H.** (R). **101. COLUMBUS** has many int. old hs. incl. (R) **Columbus Inn** (1812) & at 32 Main St., **Prince Murat H.,** home of son of King of the 2 Sicilies (see Bordentown). **106.** (L) here short distance on dirt Rd. to **John Woolston H.** (1710.adds.c.1800.Col.). **107.5. EWANSVILLE** (resort). **108.** J. with St.38.

SIDE TRIP: Take latter (R) 2.5$^{m}$ to J. with side Rd. leading (R) 2$^{m}$ to **Mt. Holly** (Accoms.: All types. Info.: P.O. Washington St. Swim.: Mill Dam Pk.; Rancocas Cr.). Named for near-by Mt. Holly, town was sett. by Quakers in 1676 & occupied at various times by Brit. during Rev. Rancocas Cr. cuts across town which is center of agric. area & of some sm. industries. PTS. OF INT.: (1) Main St., **County Bldgs.** incl. Cth. (1796.fine Georg.Col.), Surrogate's Office & Adm. Bldg. (1807). (2) 77 Main St., **Friends Meeting H.** (O.appl. 1775.adds.1850.int.inter.). Benches have marks made by butcher knives of commissary workers during Brit. occupation. (3) 35 Brainerd St., **Brainerd Sch.** (1759) where Rev. John Brainerd taught. He preached so violently against Brit. that they burnt down his Ch. (4) 211 Mill St., **Stephen Girard H.** (much alt.), home of famous merchant who in beginning of career kept shop in basement. Later he moved to Phila., became prosperous, helped finance War of 1812 & founded Stephen Girard College (see Phila.). (5) 99 Branch St., **John Woolman Mem. Bldg.** (O.exc.Tues.Mar.-Oct.1771) was built for his daughter by noted Quaker Woolman, one of 1st to espouse Abolitionist cause. His "Journal" was 2nd book selected by Chas. W. Eliot for Harvard Classics. (6) 15 Pine St., **Relief Fire Co. H.,** home of one of oldest active volunteer companies in U.S., est. 1752; int. relics & orig. engine shelter. (7) N. end of High St., **Mt. Holly Pk.** (path to summit; fine view).
At 3$^{m}$ on St.38 is J. with side Rd. leading (L) 1.5$^{m}$ to **Lumberton.** On Main St., **Lumberton Hotel** (c.1790) & **Meth. Ch.** (1812), moved here from Church St. where Bishop Asbury, noted Meth. divine, preached in 1813.

**110.** (R) here on good Rd. 0.5$^{m}$ to **Vincentown** with some charming 19th cent. hs. **124. ATSION,** at Atsion L., was once iron mfg. center. **131.5.** Outskirts of **HAMMONTON.**

# NEWARK

## NEWARK

Through RR., plane & bus conns. Accoms.: All kinds. Info.: C. of C. Golf: Weequahic Pk. Boat., fish., riding: Weequahic & Branch Brook Pks.

Newark is a whole metropolitan dist. in itself embedded in S. part of much larger metropolitan reg. of N.Y.C. It has, therefore, a double character as business, industrial & cultural capital of northern N.J. & as super-suburb of Manhattan. Newark with its adj. cities boasts pop. upward of 700,000. To (E) lie the great Hackensack meadows, gradually being reclaimed from marshland for industrial use. In remaining semicircle around city are strung a series of suburbs, chief among which are Maplewood, the Oranges, Bloomfield & Montclair. Elizabeth crowds into Newark. Located on Passaic R. where latter debouches into Newark Bay, an arm of N.Y. waterfront, Newark is crisscrossed by RRs. & through hys. It is also an important shipping center. Were Newark anywhere else but in shadow of its mighty neighbor it would be counted among first dozen of Amer. cities. Inters. of Broad & Market Sts., known as "the 4 Corners," is heart of downtown Newark. Market St. is shopping center. Broad St. with pks. at both ends is main business thoroughfare, notable for tall bldgs. which rival in design Manhattan's skyscrapers. Bank St. is lined with older business structures. Newark is one of country's leading mfg. centers. Industries are along riverfront where are located factories turning out practically every kind of product, incl. leather goods, paints, liquors, jewelry, cosmetics, electrical equipment. Newark was founded in 1666 by Capt. Rbt. Treat's company of colonists from New Haven & followed, in its early days, under leadership of the Puritan Congregational Ch., the New England theocratic pattern. Despite influx of more broadminded Eng. settlers, during most of 18th cent. it was a distinctly Puritan town. During Rev., the Brit., finding some Tory sympathizers, had an encampment near-by, but Washington, relying on aid from patriots, made town a base of operation. Some fighting took place at Springfield, then a part of Newark. After Rev., Talleyrand, then a refugee, lived in Newark & Thos. Moore, the Irish poet, paid city a visit. Washington Irving's "Salmagundi" papers were inspired by hospitality he enjoyed here at Kemble Mansion. Early in 19th cent. banking & insurance companies were est. Bldg. of Morris Canal & development of RRs. increased town's importance as shipping center. Successive Wars, 1812, 1860, brought with them boom periods. Scientific discoveries, after Civil War—invention of Hyatt's celluloid & Edison's electric light bulb—led to est. of new industries. World War I & II induced another boom & business of city was improved by Fed. Gov.'s development of Port Newark, a great terminal water front development. City has boasted as among its citizens such celebrities as Stephen Crane, author of "The Red Badge of Courage," Mary Mapes Dodge, author of "Hans Brinker: or the Silver Skates," Edmund Clarence Stedman, Rich. Watson Gilder, & John Cotton Dana.

PTS. OF INT.: (1) 820 Broad St., **First Presb. Ch.** (1787-91.Georg.Col.) is successor of orig. Puritan Ch. In 1719 it became Presb. (2) 744 Broad St., **Nat. Newark Bldg.** (1931), by John H. & Wilson C. Ely (35 stories). On mezzanine are 10 murals by J. Monroe Hewlett & Chas. Gulbrandsen. (3) NW. end of **Military Pk.** is **Trinity Episc. Ch.** (1743.rebuilt c.1809.later adds.). According to popular belief, ch. was founded as result of Col. Josiah Ogden breaking with older First Presb. Ch. over his right to gather wheat on Sabbath. Also in pk.: Mem. by Gutzon Borglum entitled "The Wars of America"; a tall Liberty Pole on site of another erected in 1793; Statue of Philip Kearney of Civil War fame; & bronze statue of Msgr. Hobart Doane. (4) 40 Rector St., **Newark Colleges of Rutgers Univ.,** formerly Univ. of Newark which was created in 1935 by merger of a number of pub. institutions of higher learning. (5) 540 Broad St., **N.J. Bell Tel. Bldg.** (20 stories.1929.by Voorhees, Gmelin & Walker). (6) N. end of Broad St., **Washington Pk.,** with a number of Mons.: Bridge Mem. by G. Borglum, Statue of Geo. Washington by J. Massey Rhind, Christopher Columbus Mon. by Ciocchetti, & statue of Seth Boyden, inventor of processes for making patent leather, malleable cast iron, etc., by Karl Gerhardt. (7) 49 Washington St., **Newark Mus.** (O.afts.& Wed.& Thurs.eves.), covers fields of the arts & sciences. Adj. is Mus. Addition Bldg. housing Junior Mus. & Lending Dept. Mus. has changing displays of fine & decorative arts, industrial design & processes, hist. & education. In rear is **Thos. L. Raymond Walled Garden** with coll. of botanical specimens. Behind garden is **Old Stone Schoolh.** (1784), Newark's oldest school bldg. (8) Washington & James Sts., **Second Presb. Ch.** (Mod.Goth.int.stained glass windows). (9) 5 Washington St., **Newark Pub. Lib.** (Ren.est.1888) which under leadership of J. C. Dana has taken prominent part in development of Newark's cultural activities. (10) 407 Broad St., **John Plume H.** (c. 1710.alts.Dutch Col.), now rectory of adj. **Prot. Episc. Ch.** (1849). Mistress Ann Van Wagenen Plume, during Rev., is said to have driven Hessian soldiers out of her parlor where she found them chopping wood, & later she is reported to have locked a Hessian in her icehouse. In 19th cent., Rev. Hannibal Goodwin developed a flexible photofilm in rectory which made possible the motion picture. (11) 230 Broadway, **N.J. Hist. Soc. Bldg.** (O.Tues.-Sat.exc.Aug.mod.Georg.Col.); lib. of rare early mss.; portraits by Gilbert Stuart. (12) Clifton & 6th Aves., **Sacred Heart Cathedral** (Fr.Goth.) with 2 lofty towers. (13) (W) of Clifton Ave., **Branch Brook Pk.** (recr.facils.). (14) 215 1st St., **Newark Academy** (1930.mod.Georg.Col.), est. 1774, one of city's oldest private schs. (15) High St. & 13th Ave., **Essex Cty. Hall of Records** (1927 by Guilbert & Betelle) at whose entrance are statues depicting purchase of Newark's site from Lenni Lenape Inds. (16) Springfield Ave. & Market St., **Essex County Cth.** (1906.Ren.by Cass Gilbert); painting by Frank D. Millet, portraying rebuke administered in 1774 by foreman of Grand Jury to last Prov. Chief Justice anent grievances of colonists & painting by Howard Pyle depicting "The Landing of Philip Carteret." On grounds, **Statue of Abr. Lincoln** by G. Borglum, considered perhaps finest portrait statue of Great Emancipator. (17) 131 Market St., **Bamberger Dept. Store,** one of largest retail shopping emporiums in U.S. (18) Raymond Plaza W., **Pa. RR. Sta.** (1935.neo-Class.McKim,Mead & White). Waiting Room is decorated by plaques showing Hist. of Transportation. (19) Broad & Green Sts., **City Hall** (1906.Fr.Ren.by Mowbray,Uffinger & Ely). (20) On Federal Sq., **Fed. Bldg.** (1936.neo-Class.by Lehman & Totten). (21) At Broad St., **Lincoln Pk.** & at Washington St. & Clinton Ave., **Clinton Pk.** In latter is reprod. of Verrochio's Colleono. In Lincoln Pk., Mem. Flag Pole comm. World War I, by Chas. Niehaus. (22) 1-117 Somerset St., **Douglass & Harrison Apts.,** a pub. housing project (1933-35) exclusively for Negroes; named for Fred. Douglass, famous Negro Abolitionist & Rich. Dana Harrison, who took part of "De Lawd" in "The Green Pastures." (23) Bet. Meeker Ave. & City Line, **Weequahic Pk.** (recr.facils.boat.f.). (24) 439-51 Frelinghuysen Ave., **Magnus Harmonica Corp.,** manufactures plastic harmonicas.

**THE ORANGES & MAPLEWOOD, BLOOMFIELD & MONTCLAIR**

These cities are suburbs of Newark. Maplewood & the Oranges, directly (W), Bloomfield (N) & Montclair (NE), a little further away. The Oranges & Maplewood, although separate municipalities, constitute a fairly homogeneous community of nearly 240,000 people, for most part belonging to better-to-do class. These cities have, generally speaking, excellent schs., libs., health, recr. facils. & programs.

**EAST ORANGE: Mun. Center** (Ital.Ren.). Springdale Ave. & Prospect St., **Upsala College** (Swedish Luth.). 139 Glenwood Ave., **College of Physical Education & Hygiene. ORANGE,** founded 1678, is sm. industrial town. **WEST ORANGE** has a few factories but is notable for fine estates in **Llewellyn Pk.** (O.only to visitors of residents), home of Colgates, Edisons & Gen. Geo. B. McClellan, Gov. of N.J. after Civil War. 51 Lakeside Ave., **Edison Plant** (O.appl.). Inventor moved here from Menlo Pk. (see) in 1887 & perfected his moving picture machine, phonograph & storage battery. **Edison's Lab.** (O.wks.) has Edison relics. **SOUTH ORANGE** is beautifully situated. Estates of wealthy citizens climb slopes of First Watchung Mts. **Seton Hall College** (1856.Cath.). **MAPLEWOOD** lies (S) of S. Orange. 425 Ridgewood Ave., **Timothy Ball H.** (Col.1743.alt.1775 & 1919). Washington, related to Ball, visited here.

**BLOOMFIELD,** both residential & industrial, was named in honor of Rev. Gen. Jos. Bloomfield, later Gov. Randolph Bourne, leader of new literary movement at time of World War I, was born here. Broad St. & Belleville Ave., **Old First Presb. Ch.** on Green. Facing Green, **Bloomfield College & Seminary** (Presb.1810). 409 Franklin St., **Davis H.** (1676). Davis family came from England with Rbt. Treat (see Newark).

**MONTCLAIR,** sett. c.1666, is picturesquely located. Its residences climb "the Mt." An early settler was a Crane from whom Stephen Crane was descended. City, orig. part of Bloomfield, seceded when Bloomfield refused to cooperate in building RR. bet. Jersey City & N.Y. St. Line. 128 N. Mt. Ave., **Egbert H.** (1786), built by former Hessian soldier. 369 Claremont Ave., **Slave H.,** willed by Gen. Nath. Crane (1831) to former slave. 128 N. Mt. Ave., a **Stone H.** (1786); boxwood bush on lawn planted in 1833. 471 Valley Rd., a red **Sandstone Cottage** (1685). 612 Upper Mt. Ave., **Speer Farm H.** (rest.pre-1720). Bloomfield Ave. & S. Mt. Ave., **Montclair Art Mus.;** mostly loan exhibits. Geo. Innes, great Amer. landscape painter, was resident of city. On High Sch. grounds, **Garden Theater,** in natural amphitheater (summer performances). On Undercliff Rd., **Eagle Rock Pk.** (664';fine view), used by Washington as observation post. Baldwin St., **Lucey H.,** reprod. of sm. Ital. country villa; used as a settlement house. Also of int. are: **Presb. Mem. Iris Garden; War Mem.;** & **St. Peter Claver Chapel** (Mod.). In **CALDWELL** c.2.5$^m$ from Montclair, at 1 Bloomfield Ave., **Grover Cleveland Birthpl.** (O.exc.Mon.sm.fee); papers & relics.

## TRENTON

**TRENTON**

Through RR. & bus conns. Accoms.: All types. Info.: C. of C. & Dept. of Economic Development, State H. Golf: Sunnybrae course, 4$^m$ (SE) on US130, 18 holes, greens fee. Sat., Sun. & holidays. Baseball: Dunn Field, Brunswick Ave., home of Trenton Senators, N.Y.-Pa. League. State Fair, last wk. in Sept.; Feast of Lights, religious festival in Ital. colony, 2nd Sat. & Sun. in Sept.

Trenton, at head of navigation on Del. R., is bisected by Assunpink Cr., site of a Rev. battle. Business & shopping center is largely concentrated along State St. & intersecting Warren & Broad Sts. Industrial dist. lies chiefly to (S) & (E) & bordering it are poorer neighborhoods. To (W) is the better residential area. Although politics is important local industry, factories are main source of employment. Trenton is producer of a world famous pottery. It also has wire-rope & cable-making plants & cigar factories. Trenton ranks 4th in N.J. as industrial producer. First sett. by an Englishman, Mahlon Stacy, Jr., its real founder was Wm. Trent, Phila. merchant who built a stone mill at "The Falls." His residence, Bloomsbury Court, still stands. Town's 1st chief burgess, Dr. Thos. Cadwalader, was a noted physician of his day & an advocate of inoculation for smallpox. In 1750 he contributed a considerable fund toward founding of N.J.'s 1st pub. lib. in Trenton. On Dec. 26, 1776, Washington crossed ice-clogged Del. R. & made a surprise attack, after their Christmas celebration, on Hessians in Trenton. Attack was completely successful & Amer. troops re-crossed to Pa. shore. Washington crossed back again a few days later & on Jan. 2, 1777, occurred 2nd Battle of Trenton or the Battle of the Assunpink. Brit. were repulsed by Washington, who finding himself in a dangerous situation, executed a retreat during night. Campfires were kept burning to make Brit. believe that Continental Army was still occupying the hts. Cornwallis pursued Amer. troops & on Jan. 3, took place Battle of Princeton, during course of which Brit. were again repulsed. Trenton was chosen St. capital in 1790 & with development of water-power at falls & construction of Del. & Raritan Canal & of RRs., industry advanced actively. In 1848, John Roebling moved his factory here. Pottery industry, which began in Col. times, cont. to thrive until today reg. is one of most important pottery producing dists. of U.S. During both World Wars, Trenton's business boomed & its importance as a port grew with deepening of Del. R. channel in 1932.

PTS. OF INT.: (1) 121 W. State St., **State H.** (O.wks.). Orig. bldg. dating from c.1792 is incorporated in present structure (1889); portraits, coll. of Civil War flags. (2) Opp. Taylor's Pl., **St. Capitol Annex** (O.wks.by J.O.Hunt & Hugh A.Kelley) houses St. Depts. & courts, St. Lib. & St. Mus. (O.wks.& Sun.aft.). Latter has exhibits of natural resources, archeology & fauna of N.J. (3) S. Willow St., opp. W. Front., **Old Barracks** (O.wks.sm.fee.1758-59.Georg.Col.), built orig. to house Col. troops during Fr. & Ind. War. Brit. & Amer. troops were quartered here during Rev.; colls. of Col. furniture, continental currency. On lawn is elm grown from root of Cambridge tree under which Washington took command of Continental Army (see Cambridge). (4) NE. cor. S. Willow & Lafayette Sts., **Old Masonic Lodge H.** (O.wks.Sun.aft.1793.Georg.Col.), one of oldest Masonic houses (N) of Mason & Dixon Line; coll. of relics. Meeting room is furnished as it was in Col. times. Adj. is new **Masonic Temple** (1928.neo-classic by H.A.Hill & E.G.Gollner). (5) S. Willow St., **Soldiers & Sailors War Mem. Bldg.** (O.Mon.-Fri.1931-32.Ren.by W.A.Klemann & Louis S.Kaplan). (6) On Mem. Dr. bordering Del. R. **Mahlon Stacy Pk.** (7) In pk., **Douglass H.** (N.O.) where Washington & staff planned retreat to Princeton after Battle of Assunpink. Bldg. was removed from orig. site & restored. (8) 18 W. State St., **Hotel Sterling,** part of which in early 1800's was used as Gov.'s mansion. (9) 114 E. State St., **First Presb. Ch.** (1841). In cemetery many Rev. notables are buried. (10) Cor. E. Hanover & Montgomery Sts., **Old Friends Meeting H.** (1739). In cemetery Geo. Clymer, signer of Decl. of Ind., is buried. (11) 140 N. Warren St., **St.**

**Michaels Prot. Episc. Ch.** (1819.adds.handsome post-Col.). In cemetery is grave of Pauline Joseph Ann Holton, child of Jos. Bonaparte & Annette Savage. (12) Inters. of N. Warren St., N. Broad St., Brunswick, Pennington & Princeton Aves., **Battle Mon.,** surmounted by statue of Washington, designed by John Duncan, marks spot where Washington's artillery opened fire Dec. 26, 1776. Observatory on top offers fine view (O.wks.& Hols.sm.fee). (13) 539 S. Warren St., **Bloomsbury Court** (Wm. Trent H.), oldest H. (O.wks.sm.fee.c.1719.Georg.Col.rest.) in city. Inter. is kept as when H. was 1st built. During Rev. owner, Lt. Col. John Cox, gave lavish entertainments here to officers of Continental Army. (14) NE. cor. John Fitch Way & Ferry St., **John Fitch Mem.** Fitch built a boat propelled by steam engine as early as 1786 & his packet operated on reg. schedule bet. pts. on Del. R. (15) 640 S. Broad St., **J. A. Roebling Sons Plant** (O.appl.) which produces wire-rope & cable for bridges. Roebling supplied cables for Brooklyn Bridge. (see N.Y.C.). (16) (S) of Lalor St. bet. Bunting & Reeger Aves., **Bow Hill** (c.1785). Here lived Annette Savage, mistress of Jos. Bonaparte, former King of Spain. The ex-king is said to have fallen in love with Annette when she sold him suspenders across counter of her mother's store in Phila. Trenton society ostracized her & after death of their young daughter, Bonaparte took her to his estate in N. Adirondacks of N.Y. He abandoned her when he returned to France after Rev. of 1830. Annette married again &, it is said, resumed storekeeping at Watertown. (17) 50 Meade St., **Lennox Potteries** (O.wks.) shows fine displays of its products. (18) 315 E. State St., **Mun. Bldg.** (O.1911.neo-classic by S.Roberts). In Council Chamber is mural by Everett Shinn. (19) Parkside Ave., **Cadwalader Pk.** has a sm. zoo & an out-door theatre.

## US 6—PENNSYLVANIA

**PA.-N.J. LINE** (at Matamoras, Pa.) **(W) to PA.-OHIO LINE** (at Pennine, Pa.) **426. US6**

Via: Scranton, Towanda, Wellsboro, Smethport, Warren, Union City, Cambridge Springs, Meadville, (Erie).

US6 traverses the northern part of St. from Del. R. to Ohio Line, passing en route industrial sec., mts. & fors.

### Sec. 1: MATAMORAS to SCRANTON. 74.

At **0.5. MATAMORAS** on the Del., opp. Port Jervis, N. Y. Near here is **Tri-State Rock** where Pa., N.Y. & N.J. meet. At **8.** is **MILFORD** (see Del. R. Tour). At **28.5.** J. with St. 402.

SIDE TRIP: St.402 runs (S) past **Peck's Pond St. For. Area** (f.boat.pic.) near which is **High Knob Lookout** (2,162′) & **Porters L.** (resort), through fine mt. & lake reg. of the Poconos to J. with US209 at **Marshall's Cr.** & cont. to **Stroudsburg.**

At **31.** is J. with St.507.

SIDE TRIP: St.507 runs (SW along shore of **Wallenpaupack L.** through fine mt. & lake reg. via **Newfoundland & Gouldsboro,** near **Gouldsboro Lake,** to J. with US611. At 2m (S) of J. with US6, St.507 makes J. with St.390 which runs through **Promised Land St. Pk.** & some of finest parts of Pocono reg.

**42. HONESDALE,** named for Philip Hone, distinguished N.Y. citizen, mayor of city & official of Del. & Hudson Canal Co. 810 Main St., **Wayne Cty. Hist. Soc. Bldg.** (O.Tues.& Thurs.aft.July-Aug.also on appl.); coll. of coal-mining relics. 9th & Church Sts., Stourbridge Lion Mon., comm. "Stourbridge Lion" 1st Amer. locomotive, making run, Aug. 8, 1829. J. with St.90.

SIDE TRIP: St.90 runs (N) 1m & then St.670 leads to **Bethany.** Wayne & Sugar Sts., **David Wilmot H.** (c.1832). Wilmot was author of famous so-called "proviso" offered as amendment in 1846 to a money bill intended to effect a settlement with Mexico after Mex. War. Proviso, which prohibited slavery in terr. ceded by Mex., failed of adoption.

At **57. CARBONDALE,** anthracite coal mining city on Lackawanna R. At **74. SCRANTON** (see US11).

### Sec. 2: SCRANTON to TOWANDA. 67.

US6 together with US309 travel (NW) passing **CLARKS SUMMIT** (1,240′) at **5.** J. with US11 (see). At **15. L. WINOLA. 36. MESHOPPEN,** settled 1st half 18th cent.; was stagecoach stop. At **52. WYALUSING,** sett. mid-18th cent. **56. RUMMERFIELD.** Here is J. with side Rd.

SIDE TRIP: On this Rd. (L) 2.5$^m$ to **Standing Stone Village;** then cont. (L). At 3$^m$ turn (R) a short distance to J. with St.187 & then (L) on latter 2$^m$. Then (L) again to **Mon.** on site of Fr. Asylum & foundations of "La Grande Maison." On this site refugees from Jacobin Terror sett., 1793, among whom were Louis Philippe, eventually Fr. King, & Talleyrand & Count de Lainscourt. A number of fine houses were built here. Some settlers remained but most returned to France when Napoleon permitted.

**67. TOWANDA** was boyhood home of Stephen C. Foster. Here is J. with US220 (see).

## Sec. 3: TOWANDA to WARREN. 184.

At **21.5. J.** with St.14 which runs (N) to Elmira, N.Y. & (S) to Trout Run & J. with US15. St.14 passes through picturesque mt. & for. reg. (good h.& f.) interspersed with dairy farms & grazing land. **22. TROY,** dairy farm center. **40. MANSFIELD** (resort center). **Mansfield St. Teachers College. 51. WELLSBORO,** (resort) small industrial town. Here is J. with St.660.

SIDE TRIP: On St.660 (L) 11$^m$ to **Leonard Harrison St. For. Pk.** (pic.camp.). Near-by is Lookout Rock with view of Pine Cr. Gorge, cliff-enclosed, 800′ deep, 50$^m$ long. Water falls & good trls.

**64. ANSONIA.** (S) of Ansonia, 6$^m$ is **Colton Pt. St. Pk.** (pic.fine views). **75. GALETON,** starting pt. for **Black For. Recr. Area** to (S), in which are several camps, good hunt. & fish. **97. SWEDEN VALLEY.** J. with St.44.

SIDE TRIP: On St.44 (L) 0.5$^m$ to inters. Rd. leads (R) here to **Coudersport Ice Mine** (O). Cont. on St.44. At 10.5$^m$ **Cherry Springs Pub. Camp.** (pic.). At 17$^m$ **Mt. Brodhead** (2,480′). 26$^m$ **Oleona,** where Ole Bull, famous Norweg. violinist, in 1850's, bought land & founded colony of fellow countrymen. He soon became involved in litigation over title to this tract. All the money he could earn was frittered away in lawsuits &, at times, Bull had even difficulty keeping his violin out of the law's clutches. In 1856-7, colonists moved to Wis. & with them Ole Bull (see Wis.). 27.5$^m$ **Ole Bull St. Pk.** (pic.camp.). Trl. runs 0.5$^m$ to ruins of **Bull's Castle.** Fine view. From Ole Bull St. Pk., St.44 cont. (S) through fine mt. & St. For. country to J. with US220 near Jersey shore on W. branch of Susquehanna R. At Ole Bull St. Pk. is J. with St.144 running to J. with St.120 (see) at **Renovo.**

**101. COUDERSPORT** (resort) on Allegheny R. has several Gr.-Rev. period Hs. On Main St., **Boulder** comm. David Zeisberger, early Moravian missionary to Inds. **111. ROULETTE,** named for early settler, Jean Roulette. **119. PORT ALLEGHENY,** on Allegheny R., lumber center during period when logs were floated downstream all the way to Pittsburgh; today, small industrial city. Beyond the Allegheny begins oil & natural gas reg. At **153.** J. with US219 which unites with US6 to **Kane** (see).

SIDE TRIP: US219 runs (N) here to **Limestone, N.Y.** (see), along E. edge of Allegheny Nat. For. It traverses fine mt. country, which boomed since 1870's through discovery of oil & natural gas. At about 8.5$^m$ (N) of J. of US219 & US6 is **Kennedy Spring Pic. Area,** in fine Nat. For. 16.5$^m$ **Bradford,** center of oil reg. The discovery of black gold in 1879 rocketed land values. At Bradford is J. with St.46. Take latter (L) into **N.Y. Allegheny St. Pk.** (65,000 as.camp.cabins.hik.swim.boat.). Entrance to Pk. is from **Red House** on N.Y. St.17 (see).

**154. KANE** (2,013′), summer & winter resort town, on edge of Allegheny Nat. For. At 230 Clay St., **Kane Manor Inn** (O); coll. of paintings by E. K. Kane, explorer; also orig. letters, hist. relics. At Kane are Js. with US219, running (S), skirting **Allegheny Nat. For.** & paralleling Clarion R. to J. with US322 at **Grampian,** & St.68 which cuts across SW. cor. of Nat. For. Here is J. with St.68 & US219.

SIDE TRIP: (A) On St.68 (SW) to **Pigeon** at 20$^m$. Here Rd. leads (L) to **Kelly Pines Camp.-Pic. Area** on Wolf Run Cr. At 24.5$^m$ **Marienville,** which flourished until lumber was stripped from near-by fors. J. with side Rd.

Take Rd. (S) from Marienville 6$^m$ to **Loleta Recr. Area** (camp.pic.) on **Millstone Cr.**

36$^m$ **Leeper**

Take St.36 (SE) here 6$^m$ to **Cook For. St. Pk.** (6,085 as.cabins.camp.Cook For.Inn. horses.swim.trls.good f.) which borders on Clarion R. & contains largest stand of 1st growth pine & hemlock in St. **Pt. Seneca Observ. Tower** affords splendid views. 12$^m$ (E) of Cook For. St. Pk. is **Clear Cr. St. Pk.** (cabins.camp. pic.swim.). Pk. is reached by cont. on St.36 to J. with St.949. Take latter (N) to Pk.

75$^m$ **The Narrows,** great loop of Allegheny R. Fine view. 117$^m$ **Harmony,** site of 1st settlement of Harmony Soc. (see). A number of orig. bldgs. are still standing. Near-by Cemetery, where members of Soc. are buried.

(B) Just off US219 at c.7$^m$ (S) of Kane is **Twin Lakes Recr. Area** (ample facils.bath.pic.). At 8$^m$ is **Wilcox** on little L. in Allegheny Nat. For. **Elk Tannery** (O) where process of extracting tanning fluid from hemlock bark may be observed. At 23m **Ridgeway,** small industrial city. J. with St.120 which runs (W) through most picturesque part of Allegheny Mt. reg. to J. with US220 (see). 67m **Grampian.** Here is J. with US322.

**159. LUDLOW.** Here **Olmsted Gardens** are a riot of color in spring. **174. CLARENDON,** oil town. **178.** J. with side Rd.

SIDE TRIP: On this Rd. (R) past huge glacial rocks to 10.5m. Here take Rd. (R) 16m to **Cornplanter Ind. Village,** where the half-breed, Cornplanter, Seneca chief, lived. After having helped Fr. defeat Braddock, during Rev. he aided Brit., switching finally to Amer. side, after Ft. Stanwix agreement (see N.Y.) & was rewarded by grant of land here. He lived to ripe old age of 96. The Seneca Inds. here have considerable autonomy. There is **Ch. & Mission** 21m from J. above & not far away is **Mon.** on Chief's grave in cemetery. In Feb. occurs celebration comm. Chief Cornplanter.

**184. WARREN,** oil town but with variety of industries. Warren Cty. Courth. (early 19th cent.) J. with US62, which runs (N) to Rd. conn. for Jamestown on beautiful Chautauqua L. & Chautauqua (see N.Y.). In Warren also is J. with St.69 & St.337.

SIDE TRIPS: (A) On St.69 (R) c.2m from Warren is **Morrison Run Pic. Area** (often overcrowded) & at c.5m, **Allegheny Pic. Camp. Area** (facils.) on Allegheny R.
(B) On St.337, from Warren c.11m is **Sandstone Pic. Area** (good facils.). Cont. from there on unnumbered Rd. (L) to **Hearts Content Camp. Pic. Area** (facils.). At 14m adj. to **Hearts Content Natural Area.** View from **Fire Tower** (c.3,100'); grove of magnificent 1st growth timber.

## Sec. 4: WARREN to PA.-OHIO LINE. 101.

Warren on Allegheny R., laid out c.1795, is now oil refining center, also hqs. for Cornplanter St. For. & Allegheny Nat. For. (good f. in near-by streams). Geo. Washington Pk. in vic. (60 as.pic.). At Warren is J. with US62.

SIDE TRIPS: (A) On this Rd. (N) hy. leads to **N.Y. Line** where there is J. with Jamestown & Chautauqua L. Rds.
(B) On US62 (S) 22m is J. with St.127. (R) here is **Tidioute** (sett.1790) which orig. was site of settlement of the Harmony Soc. With discovery of oil, town experienced short-lived boom. At 36m **Tionesta** (sett.1790) where long before its exploitation, David Zeisberger found oil & used it for medicinal purposes & lamps. **St. Fish Hatchery** here. Tionesta Rd. runs (W) into **Allegheny Nat. For.** At 62m **Oil City.**

At **7.** is **IRVINE** which has some fine stone Gr. Rev. bldgs. Hy. now passes **CORRY,** industrial city at **32.5.** At **33.5.** is St. Fish (trout) Hatchery. At **43. UNION CITY,** typical mill town noted for its output of coke, steel, glass & iron. Here is J. with St.8.

SIDE TRIP: On St.8 (SE) 22m to **Woodlawn Cemetery** in which is **Drake Mem.,** comm. **E. L. Drake,** 1st to drill for oil. 23m **Titusville,** near which Drake drilled 1st oil well in 1858. City almost at once experienced a tremendous boom. Oil is principal, although not only industry.
(L) from Titusville c.1m is **Drake Well Mem. Pk.** Orig. well is at Pk. entrance & near it is stone picturing 1st derrick. **Drake Mem. Mus.** (O.aft.) contains Drake relics & documents.
36m **Rouseville,** oil town, where Henry Rouse discovered oil. **Penzoil Refinery** (O.workdays) where manufacture of oil products may be observed. 39m **Oil City,** at confluence of Oil Cr. & Allegheny R. After discovery of oil (1860), land values in vic. rose sky high, & Oil Cr. became for. of oil wells. Vic. also produces large amounts of natural gas. 45m **Franklin,** located where Allegheny R. & Fr. Cr. join. Geo. Washington came to Ft. Machault, here, while on his mission for Gov. Dinwiddie to persuade Fr. to evacuate the reg. When Brit. after their victory in Fr.-Ind. War took possession, they built Ft. Venango, near where Fr. ft. had been & it, like Ft. Presque Isle, was destroyed during Pontiac rebellion. With discovery of great oil deposit at Franklin, town boomed. Today it produces not only oil but other products as well.

On main hy., US6 at **52.** is J. with US19.

SIDE TRIP: On this Rd. (N) 5m to **Waterford,** on LeBoeuf Cr., **Washington Mon.** comm. Washington's unsuccessful mission to get Fr. to evacuate reg., 1753 (see Erie). Opp. Mon., **Ruins of Ft. Le Boeuf,** one of series (Fts.Presque Isle.Machault.etc.) erected by Fr. At High & First Sts., **Eagle Hotel** (prior 1826.Fed.int.exter.-inter.); coll. of relics found on site of Ft. Le Boeuf. At 19m is **Erie.**

### ERIE

Through air, rail & bus conns. Ferry runs to Waterworks Pk. Usual accoms. Info.: C. of C., Penn Bldg., Erie Motor Club, Lawrence Hotel. Bathing: Beaches in Presque Isle Peninsula St. Pk., Waterhouse Pk. (recr.), Stony Jetty Beach Pk.; also Waldameer Beach.

Erie is chief L. Erie port bet. Buffalo & Cleveland, & Pa.'s only lake port. Its harbor is busy with shipping except in winter when it is icebound. Erie Canal, terminating at Buffalo, N.Y., from day of its construction contributed to Erie's importance as a trans. center. Erie-Pittsburgh Canal, built in 1840's, supplemented facils. afforded by N.Y. waterway, until main rail lines arrived. Coal, iron ore, wheat, lumber & oil constitute some of more important raw materials. Erie is also center for Gt. Lakes fishing fleets & handles large part of fresh water catch of country. There are number of industrial establishments. Among the important ones are—steam boiler engines, elec. locomotives, oil well supplies, & stove plants. Early Fr. explorers found Ind. tribe they named the Erie in vic. of site of present city. The Erie, however, were exterminated c.1654 by the Seneca. In 1753 Fr. built fort, known as Presque Isle, here. In same yr. Geo. Washington was sent by Gov. Dinwiddie, of Va., to order Fr. to withdraw. He interviewed Comdr. of Presque Isle. Despite lavish hospitality offered him, he accomplished little. After end of Fr. & Ind. Wars & expulsion of Fr., Ft. Presque Isle, which had been abandoned, was rebuilt by Brit. Col. Bouquet, but was destroyed by Inds. during Pontiac's rebellion. There was considerable trouble with Inds. until Gen. Wayne crushed them at Battle of Fallen Timbers, 1794. First perm. Amer. settlement occurred next yr. During War of 1812 Oliver Hazard Perry's fleet was built at Erie. Two of ships were so large they had to be lifted over harbor's sandbar to get them out. On Sept. 10, 1813, Perry's fleet decisively defeated Brit. in Battle of L. Erie, off Sandusky, Ohio.

City's pop. is a conglomerate of nationalities. Earliest considerable immigration was Pa. Dutch (Germans), followed by flood of people that came in through the Erie Canal. After Civil War tide of immigration cont. & during 1st quarter of 19th cent. bulk of the Italians, Poles & Russians arrived. However, German element is still largest.

PTS. OF INT.: 130 W. 6th St., **Erie Cty. Cth.** (1855 & 1829.Class.). 126 W. 9th St., **St. Luke's Evang. Ch.** (Luth.1844.Gr.Rev.). Cor. W. 6th & Peach Sts., **Erie Club Bldg.** (mid-19th cent.Gr.Rev.). In inter. are hist. murals by Ed. A. Trumbull. Cor. S. Park Row & French St., **Pub. Lib.** (O.wks.Sun.& hols.aft.); small art gallery & hist. mus. 407 State St., **Old Customsh.** (O.Mon.-Fri.Gr.Rev.). 416 State St., **Horace Greeley Boarding H.** where Greeley lived while working as printer on Erie Gazette (now business est.). 417 State St., **Woodruff Residence** (1st half 19th cent.Gr.Rev.), now business house. SE. cor. 2nd & French Sts., **Perry Bldg.** (O.early 19th cent. rebuilt.), where Perry lived while Amer. fleet was being built. At foot of Ash St., **Wayne Mem.,** where stood Amer. Ft. Presque Isle. Here is reprod. of **Blockh.** in which "mad" Anthony Wayne died. Wayne's body was removed for burial to Wayne near Phila. 1809. Near-by is **Pa. Soldiers & Sailors Home** (O.conducted tours). Ft. of Chestnut St., is **St. Fish Hatchery & Aquarium** (O) which hatches fish for stocking L. Erie & inland waters. W. 6th St., **Gridley Pk.** in which is mem. to Capt. Chas. Bernard Gridley, who commanded the Olympia at Manila Bay & to whom Adm. Dewey gave the famous order, "You may fire when ready, Gridley." At W. 8th St., **Villa Maria College & Academy** (Cath.). 501 E. 38th St., **Mercyhurst College** (Cath.Coll.Goth.) for women. Pub. Steamboat Landing at ft. of State St. is worth visiting. In vic. are good fish restaurants & near here fish. steamers come in & unload their cargoes. Worth a visit also is **Hammermill Paper Mill** (O.workdays) at Hess Ave. where process of paper pulp mfg. & papermaking may be observed.

About 2m from Erie, via St.5 & then St.832 is **Presque Isle Peninsula St. Pk.** (bath.facils. pic.f.). Pk. is on Presque Isle. The "Niagara" which took part in Battle of L. Erie & to which Perry transferred after his own ship the "Lawrence" had been badly raked by Brit. fire, is anchored here. At 8m is **Waterworks Pk. Reserv. & Waterworks Beach** (pic.bath.). Hy. passes **Fox Pond,** wild fowl preserve, & old **Presque Isle Lighth.,** also Beach No. 3 (pic. bath.). It then reaches **Crystal Pt. Pk.** Here is **Perry Mon.** Near-by is "Wolverine" earliest U.S. ironclad vessel. Hy. returns to Erie by way of St.832 & St.5.

US6 turns (S) & reaches **MEADVILLE** at **73.** (sett.1788 by David Mead). City of varied industries. Plant of **Amer. Brake Shoe Co.,** largest brass & bronze foundry & machine shop in U.S. At Randolph & Terrace Sts., **David Mead H.** (late 18th cent.) After fighting in Rev. on patriot side, he migrated here from Sunbury. Town is home of **Allegheny College** (founded 1815). On campus is **Bentley Hall,** (mid 19th cent.). In **Reis Lib.** is coll. of letters by hist. notables. At **81.** J. with US322. (R) is **Conneaut L. Pk.** (boat.f.). US6 now runs (NW), passing **Pymatuning Recr. Area** (17,000 as.). Here is **L. Pymatuning** (waterfowl refuge;pic.swim.boat.f.) **Reservoir & Dam** (2,700'). At **101.** hy. crosses **OHIO LINE.**

# US 22—PENNSYLVANIA

**PA.-N.J. LINE** (at Phillipsburg, N.J.) **(W) to PA.-W.VA. LINE** (5m from Wierton, W.Va.). **345. US22**

Via: Easton, Bethlehem, Allentown, Harrisburg, Lewistown, Ebensburg, Pittsburgh.

US22 crosses the St. through rich farm country of Pa. Germans & passes over the Appalachian Mt. ridges until it reaches the industrial Pittsburgh reg.

## Sec. 1: PA.-N.J. LINE to HARRISBURG. 100.

At **0.5.** is **EASTON,** located at confluence of Lehigh & Del. Rs. & Bushkill Cr. City was founded c.1752, after Del. Inds. had been expropriated as result of the "Walking Purchase" (1737). After Rev. town grew into flour milling center. Bldg. of Lehigh & Morris Canals proved most important stimulus to growth, until arrival of RRs. Easton became important as coal port, & because of near-by iron ore it soon was important industrially. Today its plants produce a large variety of products. PTS. OF INT.: **Lafayette College** (chartered 1826), pioneer institution offering courses in technology. Campus is on hill above town. South College (1834) oldest bldg. In **Markle Mining Engineering Hall** (Col.) is **Geology Mus.** (O.Mon.-Fri.). **Colton Chapel** (late 18th cent.by Carrère & Hastings). New bldgs. incl.: **Hall of Internat. Affairs & Engineering Bldg.** In the **Circle** at Northampton & 3rd Sts., is **Marker** on spot where 1st Cth. (1765) stood, near which, in Col. times were pillory & whipping post. In vic. of Circle are: 31 N. 3rd St., **First Reformed Ch.** (1776. remod.) containing items of hist. int. At Church & Sitgrave Sts., **Schoolh.** (1778. Georg.Col.). NE. cor. 4th & Ferry Sts., **Parsons H.** (1757.Georg.-Col.int.inter.) was once home of Geo. Taylor, a signer of Decl. of Ind., & now is Chapter H. of D.A.R. At SW. cor. 4th & Ferry Sts., **Mixsell H.** (O.appl.1833), hqs. of Northampton Hist. & Genealogical Soc.; lib. & mus. with hist. & Ind. material. On Church St., **Easton Pub. Lib.** (O.wks.) in old stone house (1778) which has on exhibit a flag displaying stars & stripes of the United Colonies, which was carried by our troops in 1814 & is alleged to be the orig. flag of 1776. Helen Keller has her home in Easton. [For pts. (S) of Easton see Philadelphia.] Here is J. with St.45.

SIDE TRIP: On St.45 (R) 5.5m to **Nazareth,** picturesque old Moravian town. Chestnut & N. Broad Sts., **Whitefield H.** (O.appl.Col.1740-55) was begun by Geo. Whitefield, famous Meth. evangelist, but was completed by Moravian settlers. Adj. is **Gray H.** (1740.log & stone), alleged to be earliest Pa. structure built by Moravians. Center & Green Sts., **Nazareth Hall** (1754.Georg.-Col.), formerly a school.

### 11.5. BETHLEHEM

RR., plane & bus conns. Good accoms. Info.: C. of C., 452 Main St. & Lehigh Motor Club, 528 N. New St. Annual Events: Moravian Dawn Service, Easter; Bach Festival, usually 3rd week in May.

Bethlehem straddles Lehigh R. It was sett. 1740 by German Moravians, migrating from Savannah. Part of Bethlehem (N) of R. is old town; part (S) of R. is industrial sec. Lehigh Univ. & S. Bethlehem lie on near-by hill. City's real expansion began with building of Lehigh Canal & in 1860's Bethlehem Steel Corp. was est. here. Despite fact that it is an industrial town, Bethlehem has remained music center the Moravians made it in 18th cent. It is home of famous Bach Choir founded by Dr. J. F. Wolle in 1882. PTS. OF INT.: Most of following, except Lehigh Univ., are in N. Bethlehem. (1) Cor. Main & W. Church Sts., **Central Moravian Ch.** (1803-06.Georg.Col.) where since its erection a Moravian Choir has sung at Easter service. Christmas Eve vigils are held here in great solemnity. (2) 38 W. Church St., **Schnitz Haus** (O.appl.1749.log construction); takes its name from festivity of "schnitz-making" (preparing dried apples) in which both men & women were allowed to take part. (3) Cor. W. Church St. & Heckewelder Pl., **Moravian Group,** bldgs. The **Gemein** (community) **Haus** (O.appl.1741.log.int.inter.& exter.) where married couples lived. **Old Chapel** (O.appl.1751). **Bell H.** (c.1745) was used as Seminary for Women, until College & Seminary were built. The **Sisters H.** (1742.adds. 1752 & 1773) was 1st used as a Brothers H. Separate Hs. were built for unmarried brethren & sisters, respectively. (4) 429 Heckewelder Pl., **Ind. Village H.** (pre-1760) is only remaining dwelling of Ind. settlement. (5) Near Heckewelder Pl., **Moravian Cemetery** (dating from 1742). Here Moravian trombone choir performs at Easter Sunrise. (6) At 53 Church St., **Widows' H.** (c.1768), so named because Moravian pastors' widows live here. (7) 57 E. Broad St., **Central Fire H.,** with ancient fire engines. (8) 560-64 Main St., **Sun Inn** (c.1758.add.1816.alt.) entertained many notables, incl. Washington, Franklin, John Hancock & Lafayette. (9) Main & Church Sts., **Moravian Seminary & College for Women** (est.in Germantown 1742). (10) Main St. & Elizabeth Ave., **Moravian College & Theological Seminary** (O.during academic period), est. 1807 in Nazareth. **Harvey Mem. Lib** has Francis Coll. of U.S. Presidential signatures. (11) S. New St. & Packer Ave., **Lehigh Univ.** in S. Bethlehem, founded 1866 by Asa Packer who, though he started life on canal boats of the Lehigh Canal, amassed considerable fortune & was able to give $500,000 plus land to the college. Campus has more than 20 large bldgs. & several recent ones. In **Packer Mem. Chapel** (Goth.by H.Hutton) is held world-famous Bach Festival (May). Recital is ushered in by trombone playing from tower; climax is playing of Bach Mass in B Minor. (12) Abutting the Univ. campus is **Sayre Pk.** in which is arboretum, with specimens of Pa. trees. Rd. leads to top of Washington Rock, so-called because it looks like 1st President's profile (fine view). Here is J. with Shoenerville Rd.

SIDE TRIP: On this Rd. (N) from Bethlehem 6.5$^m$ to **Northampton.** On Hokendauqua Cr. is **Old Log Ft.** (1739).

### 17. ALLENTOWN

RR., plane & bus conns. Ample accoms. Info.: C. of C., 515 Hamilton St. & Lehigh Valley Motor Club, 14 S. 7th St. Annual Event: Allentown Fair in Sept.

Allentown is situated on Lehigh R. Allentown reg. was 1st sett. c.1723, but city itself was not platted till 1762. In 1799 it was one of centers of Fries Rebellion against taxation. Lehigh Canal (1829) brought prosperity here too & est. of iron & steel mills. In late 19th cent. city became important silk-textile mfg. center. Soon cotton mills followed. Old Pa. Dutch element still predominates & some dailies are still in Pa. Dutch. PTS. OF INT.: At 24th & Chew Sts., **Muhlenberg** (Luth.) **College,** named for pastor, H. Melchior Muhlenberg, founder of Lutheranism in Phila. (see Phila. VI). Here is **Cedar Crest** (Evangelical) **College for Women.** Bet. Union & Walnut Sts., on 4th St., **Allen Pk.,** in which is **Trout Hall** (O.Wed.& Sat.aft.1770. Georg.Col.) built by Jas. Allen, city's father. H. got its name from excellent trout fish. in early days in near-by streams. **Lehigh Cty. Hist. Soc.** has its quarters in bldg. SE. cor. Church & Hamilton Sts., **Zion Reformed Ch.** (O.1888.Vict.Goth.) is on site of earlier Ch. in which Liberty Bell, from Independence Hall, Phila., was hidden after Brit. occupied Phila. In its tower hangs Allentowners' own "Liberty Bell." At 28th & Linden Sts., are 4 as. of **Rose Gardens.** At Allentown is J. with US222 running to Reading (see).

**21. TREXLER MEM. PK.** in which is **Spring H.** (1794). **25.5.** A good Rd. runs (R) here 0.5$^m$ to **Lehigh Community Pk.** (recr.). **45.5. HAMBURG** (sett.1779) on Schuylkill R. Here is J. with US122 which leads in 17$^m$ to Reading.

### READING

RR., plane & bus conns. Good accoms. Info.: C. of C., 7 N. 6th St. & Reading Auto Club, 5th & Washington Sts. Annual Events: Easter Dawn Service & Ascension Day Ceremonies (40 days after Easter).

Reading, located on Schuylkill R., was sett. in 1733 by 2 members of the family of Wm. Penn. Soon German immigrants arrived & now city is center of Pa.-Dutch country. During Rev., Germans here as elsewhere joined patriots & furnished weapons for Continental Army. This reg. was among 1st in Amer. to produce iron. Town benefitted by canals built in 1st quarter of 19th cent. & arrival of RRs. Today Reading is important mfg. center, with more than 700 plants, incl. hosiery mills, knitted wares & alloy steel. German influence in Reading has always been strong. As at Bethlehem, development of music as part of life of the people was one of chief German contributions. Reading Choral Society presents works of great composers especially Bach. PTS. OF INT.: At NW. cor. Parkside Dr. & Westside Rd., **Reading Pub. Mus. & Art Gallery** (O.wks.Sun. & hols.aft.Ital.Ren.) is located in pk. Contains natural hist., archaeological & other exhibits & excellent art coll. SW. cor. Spring St. & Center Ave., **Berks Cty. Hist. Soc.** (O.wks.Sun.aft.); lib. containing rare mss. & colls. of Bibles, old Pa. Dutch furnishings, handicraft articles, goods turned by early local forges, old fire-engine & fire-fighting paraphernalia & other relics. NW. cor. Washington & 6th Sts., **Holy Trinity Ch.** (Luth.1793.Georg.Col.adds.). On Mt. Penn, **The Pagoda** (O) on Skyline Blvd., 17-story bldg. reached by steps from Penn's Commons Pk. in which are several Mons. At Union & 13th Sts., **Albright College,** (orig.college founded in 1859 in Meyerstown;bldgs.Georg.Col.). In Reading is J. with US422 & US122.

SIDE TRIPS: (A) On US422 (SE) 6m to J. with Rd. leading (R) to **Lincoln Homestead** (1733) built by Mordecai Lincoln, Abraham's ancestor. At 7m **Baumstown.** Here is J. with St.82 running (R) 1m to **Birdsboro.** At Main & Mill Sts., **Bird Mansion** (1751), now YMCA. Here Jas. Wilson, signer of Decl. of Ind., lived. In Birdsboro is J. with St.83.

On this Rd. (S) 5m to **Hopewell Village Nat. Hist. Site** (214 as.), set aside to preserve one of the finest examples of Amer. 18th cent. iron-making villages. Wm. Bird, Englishman, built 1st forge in 1740 & later constructed the Hopewell Forge (1744.rest.) which turned out weapons for Continental Army. Near-by is **Hopewell Manor H.** Gradual rest. of entire village is contemplated by Nat. Pk. Serv. (guides are now furnished.pic. facils.avail.in Fr.Cr.Recr.Area).

At Baumstown is also J. with Rd. (L) 1.5m.

On this Rd. (L) 1.5m & again (L) c.0.5m to **Dan. Boone Birthpl.** (R) (c.1730.adds.1779. rest.by St.); at 5m is **Grandfather Boone's Homestead;** Dan. lived here until he was 16 yrs. old, when he emigrated to N.C. In vic. is **Exeter Friends Meetingh.** (1730) where services are still held in June. In near-by Cemetery members of Lincoln & Boone families are buried.

11m **Douglasville.** (L) **Molatten Ch.** (1801). Here is J. with St.662.

On this Rd. (L) 3m to J. with good Rd. leading 1.5m (L) over covered bridge to **Rutter Mansion** (1720). Near-by is **Pine Forge Office** (1725).

16m **Pottstown,** located at J. of Schuylkill R. & Manatawny Cr., industrial town which owed its 1st big development to canal system; from early days, iron producing center. Cor. Chestnut & Hanover Sts., **Old Brick Ch.** (1796). On Cr., **Mill Park Hotel** (1752) was owned by John Potts for whom town is named. 26m **Trappe** (see Phila. VI).

(B) On US122 23m (N) of Reading is J. with St.895 leading (W) c.5m to **Hawk Mt.,** Bird Sanctuary on Rittatinny Ridge, one of few existing sanctuaries for birds of prey. 32m **Schuylkill Haven** (sett.1748) was boomed by arrival of Schuylkill Canal (1825), stretches of which can still be used by light-draft boats. (N) of city. 36m (N) is Pottsville (sett.c.1780). Inds. killed off 1st inhabitants & next settlement was by John Pott, early in 19th cent.; coal-mining town. Pottsville was one of Molly Maguires' hqs., a labor org. which in the 1860's & 70's attained power in coal mining reg. Franklin B. Gowen, prominent Pa. attorney who had directed fortunes of Phila. & Reading RR. Co. for yrs., initiated movement against Molly Maguires, who had interfered with his management of coal-mining industry. Six Molly Maguires were tried & sentenced at Pottsville, 1877, to be hanged. With the Pottsville trial the Molly Maguires lost their influence in labor movement.

(C) On US222 (N) 13.5m J. with improved Rd. Take latter (L) 3.5m & then (L) a short distance to **Crystal Cave** (O.fee), one of most visited of St.'s many caverns.

At **49.** on US22 is a 4,000-a. **Indoor Miniature Amer. Village** (O). Near-by **Old Ind. Ft.** (L) antedates 1809. At **70. FREDERICKSBURG. 81. INDIANTOWN GAP MILITARY RESERV.** (18,000 as.), training grounds for Nat. Guardsmen. At **100. HARRISBURG** (see).

### Sec. 2: HARRISBURG to W.VA.-PA. LINE. 245.

At **6. ROCKVILLE.** Here is **Ft. Hunter Mus.** (O.1814), on site of old Ft. Hunter (1756); 19th cent. antiques. **Rockville Bridge,** claimed to be longest stone-arched bridge in world carries 4 P. RR. tracks across Susquehanna R., 3,808′. At **17. AMITY HALL** (O.May-Oct.c.1810) contains old household articles & old prints. At **33.** is **MILLERSTOWN.** Here is J. with St.17.

SIDE TRIP: On this Rd. (SW) to J. with St.274 which continues into **Hemlock St. For. Pk.**

At **54.** are fine **LEWISTOWN NARROWS** of Juniata R. **60. LEWISTOWN** (sett. c.1790) at one time boisterous lumbermen's hangout. Pa. Canal brought prosperity to town. Today Amer. Viccose Plant is town's chief source of employment. At **95. HUNTINGDON** (sett.c.1767) on Juniata R., bears name of Countess of Huntingdon, heavy contributor to support of Univ. of Pa. of which Dr. Wm. Smith, founder of city, was provost. At Penn & 3rd Sts., **Standing Stone Mon.** comm. Ind. settlement. At 409 Penn St., **Scott H.** (O.1810.alts.), now a pub. bldg. contains coll. of hist. & other relics. **Juniata College** (est.1876.non-sect.) was founded by Dunker Sect. Its dormitories are reminiscent of Cloister at Ephrata (see). Near Huntingdon is J. with St.545 which runs (N) & from which **Greenwood Furnace & Whipple Dam St. For. Pks.** are accessible. At **101. LINCOLN CAVES** (O.fee). Here is J. with St.45 from which **Coleraine For. St. Pk.** is accessible. **123. HOLLIDAYSBURG** (sett.1768) which became important as E. terminus of Portage RR. (1834) which carried passengers & freight over mts. from E. & W. terminals of Pa. Canal. Highest pt. of RR. was nearly 4,000′ above sea-level. RR. cars (& later canal boats) were hauled on wooden rails by cable. Eventually locomotives were used. At Hollidaysburg US22 unites with US220 (see) to Duncansville. **Col. John Vipond H.** (1790. adds.). **125. DUNCANSVILLE** which in old days had forge & produced iron, suburb of Altoona (see). **142. EBENSBURG** (est.c.1800) was sett. by Welsh emigrants. Here is J. with US219.

SIDE TRIP: On this Rd. (S) 17m to **Johnstown.**

RR., plane, & bus conns. Good accoms. Info.: Motor Club, 200 Main St.

Johnstown (founded 1800) is at confluence of Little Conemaugh R. & Stoney Creek which combine in Conemaugh R. City is narrowly enclosed by mt. ridges. (NW) 2m on St.403 is **Conemaugh Gap,** one of finest clefts through Pa. mt. ridges. To (S) 15m (off St.53) is **Quemahoning Reservoir,** one of largest in St. With finding of iron ore & then of coal, Johnstown became great iron & steel producing center. Today it is hub of one of world's greatest coal-mining & steel mfg. regs. Large plant of **Bethlehem Steel Co.** (O.appl.) is worth visit. There are a number of other steel plants as well as factories, turning out a variety of other products. General pub. remembers Johnstown chiefly because of disastrous flood of 1889, when dam of S. Fork of the Conemaugh gave way & a mighty tidal wave of water overwhelmed the city, drowning more than 2,200 people. Johnstown had always suffered because of floods even from earliest times & after the disaster of 1889 there were other occurrences, particularly the disaster of 1936 in which 25 persons drowned. Since then extensive flood control work, completed in 1943, has secured it against repetition of this kind of disaster. Vine & Union Sts., **Cambria Inclined Plane,** which carries cars & passengers up 502′ to **Westmont** (fine view from summit). In Westmont is **Grand View Cemetery** where victims of great flood are buried.

At **214.** is **PITTSBURGH** (see). From Pittsburgh US22 runs directly (W) to **W.VA. LINE** at **245.**

## US 30—PENNSYLVANIA

**PA.-N.J. LINE** (at Camden, N.J.) **(W) to PA.-W.VA. LINE** (3m from Chester, W.Va.). **333. US30**

Via: Lancaster, York, Gettysburg, Chambersburg, Bedford, Greensburg, Pittsburgh.

US30 (Lincoln Hy.) traverses S. part of St. through rich farmlands, fruit-growing areas, Alleghenies & steel reg. around Pittsburgh.

### Sec. 1: PA.-N.J. LINE to GETTYSBURG. 123.

Hy. crosses N.J. Line at **0.**, passes through **Philadelphia** & reaches **DOWNINGTON** at **33.** (For. sec. bet. Phila. & Downington, see Phila. VII). **40. COATESVILLE.** Here is world's largest steel plate-rolling mill. Ruins of old **Laurel Iron Works,** 6m down Brandywine R., are still standing. Here iron plates for "Monitor" were made. Coatesville was 1st sett. in 1714, & Brandywine Iron Works were founded here in 1810. At **51.** is J. with St.41.

SIDE TRIP: On this Rd. (L) 3m to **Christiana,** where mon. comm. bloody fight in 1851 bet. Marylander who wanted to recapture run-away slave under Fugitive Slave Law, & the local people. Thaddeus Stevens defended latter when they were tried for treason & secured their acquittal.

**66. LANCASTER.**

RR., plane, & bus conns. Accoms.: All kinds. Info.: C. of C., 45 E. Orange St.; Stevens House & A.A.A., W. King & Prince Sts.

Lancaster (sett. prior 1721) is center for SE. part of St., rich farming reg., still largely Pa. Dutch. (Geo. Gibson, Englishman, set up an inn & brewery here in 1721 & inn became new town's focal pt.) During Fr. & Ind. war (1755), Franklin arrived to procure supplies for Braddock's ill-fated expedition. Town was noted in that early day for long-barrelled rifle, later known as "Kentucky rifle," which achieved great reputation for accuracy. Continental Congress, fleeing from Phila., which was occupied by Brit., held meeting in Cth. After Rev., city became iron-producing center & after Civil War expansion cont. until today city has more than 200 industrial plants. It is home of Radio Corp. of Amer., Hamilton Watch Co., & Armstrong Cork Co. (O). Lancaster Cty. leads all counties in U.S. in production of tobacco. (E) of city are large barns in which tobacco is dried.

PTS. OF INT.: (1) Penn Sq., at W. King St., **Old City Hall** (1795.Georg.Col.restor.). (2) Bet. N. Market & King Sts., **Farmers' Market** (O.Tues.& Fri.aft.;Wed.& Sat., all day) where Pa. Dutch exhibit food products for sale. (3) 44 E. Orange St., **First Reformed Ch.** (1854), on site of earlier Ch., contains carvings by Anton Lang of Oberammergau. (4) 33 N. Duke St., former **G. Muhlenberg H.** (1772), home of botanist & pastor of Trinity Luth. Ch. He was son of Melchior, famous during Rev. as "fighting pastor" (see Woodstock, Va.). (5) S. Duke & E. Mifflin Sts., **Evangelical Luth. Ch. of the Holy Trinity** (c.1760.Georg.Col.tower 1785-94). Contains birth

certificate of Barbara Fritchie. (6) 45 S. Queen St., plaque on bldg. marking **Site of Thaddeus Stevens H.,** where he lived at time of his death. Stevens was bitter enemy of South & backed most vindictive "reconstruction" laws in Congress. He also became Pres. Johnson's implacable enemy & pushed his impeachment by Congress. (7) N. Duke & E. Orange St., **St. James Ch.** (Episc.1820). (8) College Ave., **Franklin & Marshall College** resulted from merger in 1853 of Franklin College (founded 1787) & Marshall College (founded 1836 at Mercersberg). (9) College Ave. & W. James St., **Theological Seminary of Reformed Ch.** (10) 511 S. Queen St., **Woodward Hill Cemetery,** where Pres. Jas. Buchanan is buried. (11) E. King St., **Thaddeus Stevens Industrial Sch.** (1906 campus 21.as.) was est. pursuant to Thaddeus Stevens' will, with State aid; provides for orphans & deserving boys education in Eng. & also teaches mechanical trades. On Penn. Sq., Mon. comm. former **Cth.** where Continental Congress met (1777). 307 Duke St., **Lancaster Cty. Hist. Soc.** (O.fee). In **Schreiner's Cemetery,** (12) W. Chestnut & N. Mulberry Sts., Thad. Stevens is buried. His headstone reads: "I repose in this quiet & secluded spot, not from any natural preference for solitude, but finding other cemeteries limited by charter rules as to race, I have chosen this, that I might illustrate in my death the principles which I advocated through a long life—'Equality of man before his creator.'"
At Lancaster is J. with US222.

SIDE TRIPS: (A) US222 (NE) runs through reg. of Mennonite farms whose owners will not raise tobacco because it is against their religious belief, although it is best-paying crop. At 4.5m **Landis Valley Mus.** (O), containing coll. of antiques incl. some Conestoga wagons, type of vehicle used for hauling freight in N.Y. & Pa. before RRs. arrived. Wagon's name derives from Conestoga Valley of Lancaster Cty., where it seems to have been built in mid-18th cent. It was ancestor of prairie schooner. At 7m **Oregon.** Here is **Oregon Hotel,** sta. for stage-coaches in early days. 14m **Ephrata** (see Harrisburg II).
(B) US222 (SW) 6m intersects St.741 which runs (L) 1m to **Lampeter.** Here is **W. Lampeter Vocational Sch.,** whose erection in 1909 gave rise to controversy bet. Amish & authorities, controversy which recurred when new schoolhouse in E. Lampeter was built (1937). Amish clung to little, local one-room schools, fearing effect of more mod. educational methods in new establishments. Amish eventually won out. 24.5m **Birthpl. of Robt. Fulton** (O), generally given credit for inventing steamboat. 27m **Wakefield** (sett. by the Friends). **Penn Hill Meetingh.** (1823.Congr. est.1758) & old **Quaker Cemetery.**
(C) On St.340 (Church St.) 1m (NW) is **Wheatland** (O.wks.aft.sm.fee), home of Jas. Buchanan, politician, Secy. of St., Minister to Gt. Brit., whose career was distinguished until he was elected Pres. 1856. His vacillating attitude, some historians maintain, encouraged Southern states to open rebellion.
(D) Take S. Duke St. (S) across Conestoga Cr. & at further end of bridge, turn (R) 2.5m to **Rockford** (late 18th cent.), home of Gen. Edw. Hand, who joined Sullivan's expedition against Iroquois (see N.Y.).

At **77. COLUMBIA** (sett.1726), on Susquehanna R., was sett. by Quaker missionary to Inds. Town, during period 1840-1870 handled much of lumber floated down R. from mt. fors. At end of Cherry St., **Wright Mansion** (1726.Georg.Col.) was home of 1st settler. Here is J. with St.441.

SIDE TRIPS: (A) On this Rd. (NW) along R. through **Marietta.** At 5m is J. with St.241 leading to **Maytown,** 1.5m. In vic. are **Donegal Ch.** (Presb.c.1740.Col.) & **Witness Oak,** where Col. A Lowrey of Continental Army, before Battle of Brandywine, compelled Ch.'s Tory pastor, McFarquhar, to salute Rev.
(B) On St.441 (SE) 4m along the R. through **Washington Boro,** to **Safe Harbor Hydro-elec. Plant** (O) & **Lake** (fish.), created by dam. Ind. petroglyphs are found bet. Washington Boro & Safe Harbor.

**89. WRIGHTSVILLE,** farthest NE. pt. of Confed. advance (see Gettysburg).

**94. YORK**

RR., plane & bus conns. Accoms.: All types. Info.: C. of C., Schmidt Bldg., Keystone Auto Club & White Rose Motor Club (AAA).

York, an industrial town & center for rich agric. reg., straddles Codorus Cr. It was laid out c.1741 by order of Wm. Penn's sons. Most of early settlers were German immigrants & lesser contingent of Scotch-Irish. During period, Sept. 1777-June 1778, little city became hqs. of Continental Gov. Franklin transferred his press here from Phila. & printed money & documents put out by Continental Congress. Nearby forges turned out munitions for patriot troops. During Civil War city was taken in raid by Gen. Jubal Early. But within few days occurred Battle of Gettysburg which ended Confed. threat.

PTS. OF INT.: (1) Market & George Sts., **Continental Sq.** Here stood Cth. in which Continental Congress met (1777-78). (2) NE. cor. George St. & Sq., **Site of McClean**

H., which served as Treasury of Gov. while Continental Congress had its seat in York. (3) 225 E. Market St., **Hqs. of Hist. Soc. of York Cty.** (O.Mon.-Fri.;Sat.morn.); hist. documents. (4) In pavement at No. 157-59 W. Market St., **Tablet** comm. H. where Lafayette toasted Washington. This put an end to conspiracy to remove him & to substitute Gen. Gates in command of Continental Army. (5) NW. cor. Beaver St. & Gas Alley, **St. John's Ch.** (Episc.1766.adds.) in whose tower hangs bell which rang out tidings of Decl. of Ind. Ch. contains hist. relics. In its graveyard are buried Rev. notables. (6) Phila. St. & Park Alley, **Friends Meetingh.** (1765.adds.1766 & 1780). (7) Market & Queen Sts., **First Presb. Ch.** (1789.1860) in whose graveyard lies Jas. Smith, Signer of Decl. of Ind. (8) Newberry St., **Farquhar Pk.,** in which is **Model of Orig. Cth.** (9) Carlisle Ave., **York Cty. Fair Grounds.** (10) **Penn Common** was dominated by descendants of Wm. Penn.

**123. GETTYSBURG.** (For Pts. of Int. in Gettysburg see Harrisburg V.)

## Sec. 2: GETTYSBURG to W.VA. LINE. 210.

At **8. CASHTOWN TAVERN** (1797). At **12.** is J. with St.234 leading (N) to **Conewago Mission** (Jesuit 1730) & **Mon. to Mary Jemison,** captured here by Inds., 1750. Her adopted Ind. name was Dehkewamis (beautiful girl). After her Ind. husband died she married another, Hiakato, & bore him 6 children. At **14.5. CALEDONIA ST. FOR. PK.** (camp.pic.swim.golf). Hy. passes pk.'s golf course. In pk. are **Blacksmith Shop** & **Ruins of Thaddeus Stevens Iron Furnace** (1837). **CALEDONIA** at **15.** St.233 leads (N) to **Pine Grove Furnace St. For. Pk.** From Caledonia St.233 (S) to **Mont Alto St. For. Pk.** (pic.). At **25. CHAMBERSBURG** (see US11). At **27.** is J. with St.995. This leads (S) to **Baker Cavern** (O.fee). At **32.5.** J. with St.416.

SIDE TRIP: On this Rd. (S) 8m to **Mercersburg** (sett.c.1729), situated in picturesque mt. area. Town was important center of Underground RR. **Mercersburg Academy** was est. here in 1836 as Marshall College.

**37. FT. LOUDON** (est.1795) on E. Fork of Conococheague Cr. near Tuscarora Mt. Town was named for Earl of Loudoun, who headed Brit. & Col. troops. In early days Ft. Loudon was frontier settlement which had to stand off Inds. who were constantly supplied with weapons by Phila. firms. In 1765 some of local people, tired of having their enemies thus armed, resorted to old trick later used by Tea Party raiders & disguised themselves as Inds. They held up & confiscated consignment of weapons from Sideling Hill. Under leadership of Jas. Smith, local people attacked & captured the fort. St.75 runs (N) from Ft. Loudon to **Cowan's Gap St. For. Pk.** & then past other St. For. Pks. (see US22). **41. TUSCARORA SUMMIT** (2,123') in **Tuscarora St. For. 45 McCONNELLSBURG** (est.1786), founded by McConnell Bros., was an outpost often attacked by Inds. In 1757, troop of Colonials were wiped out here. J. with St.16.

SIDE TRIP: On St.16 (S) 6m to **Jas. Buchanan St. For. Mon.** (camp.), place in which Buchanan was born. Birthpl. is marked by mon. Place was called "Stony Batter."

**64.5. JUNIATA CROSSING** on Juniata R., renowned in song & story. **Old Tavern** (1818). **80. BEDFORD.** J. with US220 (see). Near Bedford, **Mineral Springs** (resort since 1796) & **Bedford Springs Hotel** (temporarily in gov. service). Hotel has fine for. reserve of its own with bridle paths & trls. In 1757 Ft. Bedford was erected here & same Smith who captured Ft. Loudon made surprise attack on ft. & captured it, setting free settlers who had destroyed weapons which were being sent to Inds. Site can be identified by marker on Pitt St. 123 Pitt St. **Espy H.** (pre-Rev.adds.), Washington's hqs. during Whiskey Rebellion (now bakery). 113 Pitt St., **Krichbaum H.** (hotel.log construction), said to be oldest bldg. in town. **89. SCHELLSBURG** (1808) named for Schell family. **Western Hotel** (1796). **Old White Union Log Ch.** (1806). **115. JENNERSTOWN,** named for Dr. Jenner, who developed vaccination for smallpox. In vic., **Laurel Hill Summit** (2,684'). **133. LIGONIER** (see Pittsburgh I). **182. PITTSBURGH** (see). **210. PA.-W. VA. LINE.** (For sec. bet. Ligonier & W.Va. Line see Pittsburgh).

# US 40—PENNSYLVANIA

**PA.-MD. LINE** (35m from Cumberland, Md.) **(NW) to PA.-W. VA. LINE** (16m from Wheeling, W.Va.) **80. US40**

Via: Addison, Farmington, Uniontown, Brownsville, Centerville, Washington, West Alexander. Accoms. all along route.

US40, the National Rd., follows the trl. broken by Christopher Gist from Cumberland, Md., the route (for part of the way) that Gist & Geo. Washington took in Dec., 1754 (see Pittsburgh Trip VI) & later taken by Braddock's ill-fated expedition to capture Fort Duquesne. The National Rd. was authorized in 1806. By 1818 the Pa. sec. was completed. It followed the Washington-Braddock Rd. From then on until the 1870's it was a stagecoach route & freight hy., followed by thousands of pioneers in white-covered Conestoga wagons, a military pike at times & road of tourists, peddlers, politicians, actors & preachers.

**3. ADDISON,** in midst of rolling, brightly checkered farmlands. **Toll H.** (1835), which passed the wide-wheeled wagons free but charged the "land admirals" for their jaunty coaches. Among the best stagecoach lines bet. Cumberland & Wheeling was "The Good Intent." **5. WASHINGTON-BRADDOCK RD. MARKER.** At **SOMERFIELD,** at **6.5.,** is triple-spanned **Great Crossings Stone Bridge** across the Youghiogheny R., built in 1818, & the beginning of the village. Route enters some of the rich, dark fors. for which Pa. is noted. **17. FARMINGTON.** Off hy. (W) beyond village is **Ft. Necessity St. Hist. Pk.,** more than 300 as. around **Ft. Necessity Nat. Battlefield Site,** where Battle of Great Meadows took place on July 3, 1754. Here Washington & small force were defeated by larger company of Fr. & Inds. in 1st battle in Amer. of Seven Years War. **Washington's Palisade Ft.** (reconst.). **Mt. Washington Tavern** (1816), St. Mus. (O). **Gen. Braddock's Grave,** marked by mon. (1913). Early in 1755 Gen. Edw. Braddock (see) had been put in charge of Brit. troops in Amer. & set out to capture Ft. Duquesne (Pittsburgh). En route his expedition was ambushed. In skirmish with Fr. & Inds. near here on July 9, 1755, Braddock was shot. He was buried here & Geo. Washington read the burial service. In 1804 road workers found skeleton & military buttons which they buried under a great oak, which for yrs. had simple board marked "Braddock's Grave." At **23.** on Mt. Summit is **SUMMIT HOTEL** (good summer sports facils.). **28.5. UNIONTOWN** (founded 1769), among rugged Allegheny foothills, is one of W. Pa.'s bituminous coal centers. It is birthpl. of Geo. C. Marshall, Chief of Staff in World War II. The old town with its narrow, winding streets is noted for production of coke, steel, glass & iron. At Js. with St.51, which runs (NW) to Pittsburgh, & with US119.

SIDE TRIPS: (A) On US119 (N) 19.5m to Scottdale. 6.5m J. with private Dr. (R) to **Site of Christopher Gist Plantation,** where Braddock's army encamped in 1755. Farther along Dr. is **Meason H.** (1802.Georg.Col.by Adam Wilson). 12.5m **Connellsville,** industrial & B. & O. RR. center on Youghiogheny R. **Anchor Hocking Glass Corp. Plant.** J. with Rd. leading (N) c.3m to **Broad Ford,** which has been in the business of making whiskey since Col. days. **A. Overholt Distillery** (N.O.), est. by Abr. Overholt c.1800. 19.5m **Scottdale.** J. with St.819, which leads (E) 1m to **Historical H.** (O.1838), now Mus.; & adj. to it, **Birthpl. of H. C. Frick** (see). Frick's fine art coll. is at Frick Mus., in New York (see). In **Old Overholt Mill** (O) opp. are Ind. relics.

(B) On US119 (SW) 17m to Pa.-W.Va. Line (6m from Morgantown, W.Va.). 9m **Smithfield** (sett.1799). J. with St.266, which runs (W) 6m to **New Geneva,** named for Geneva, Switzerland, birthpl. of Albert Gallatin, Secy. of Treas. to Jefferson & Madison. **Friendship H.** (O.sm.fee.1789.adds.1823), Gallatin's charming L-shaped H.; period furnishings. Hy. cont. through good meadowlands to Pa.-W.Va. Line at 17m.

**40.5. BROWNSVILLE,** (founded 1785) on Monongahela R., a popular stop in 1840's. Before that it was a ship-bldg. center, sending the hist. "Comet" (1813) & the "Enterprise" up the Rs. **Brownsville Iron Bridge** (1836-39). **St. Peter's Ch.** (Cath. 1845.Goth.). Brownsville is at J. with St.88, which follows Monongahela R. bet. Pittsburgh & W. Va. Line. **46. CENTERVILLE. 48.5. MADONNA OF THE TRL. MON. 61.5.** J. with US19, which unites with US40 into Washington. **64. WASHINGTON** (sett.1781.RR.& bus conns.good accoms.& recr.facils.), important mfg. center, especially of glassware; seat of Washington & Jefferson College & Washington Seminary (girls). Town, on site of Delaware Ind. village, Catfish's Camp, became a busy stop for coaches & wagoners. Here were made drivers' whips with rawhide centers & silken cracker. Also, it was in a Washington tobacco shop that Geo. Black, in the 1820's, invented a cheap cigar later known as a Conestoga & then simply "stogie." Black's grandson moved the flourishing business to Wheeling, W.Va., where M.M. Marsh had already started making stogies on a big scale. **Washington & Jefferson College,** formed by union of 3 early schs. (see Pittsburgh Trip III), is an accredited, sm. liberal arts college. **Admin. Bldg.** (part in 1793.wings 1816). **Old Main** (c.1836.adds.1847 & 1850). **Mem. Lib.,** a gift of Benj. Franklin. At 49 E. Maiden St., **LeMoyne H.** (1812.Gr.Rev.Washington Cty.Hist.Soc.Mus.), former home of Dr. F.J. LeMoyne, anti-slavery leader & vice-pres. candidate. At 173 S. Main St., **David Bradford H.** (1787), now a shop. Bradford & others involved in Whiskey Rebellion often met here. Near town is **McGuffey Mon.,** erected by Henry Ford, who had birthpl. of Wm. H. McGuffey, early teacher, removed from here to Greenfield Amer. Village, Dearborn, Mich. Washington is at J. with US19.

SIDE TRIP: On US19 (S) 20m to Waynesburg. 10m **Amity** (sett.1797), a tiny village in whose cemetery is **Grave of Solomon Spaulding,** author of "The Manuscript Found," said to be the basis of "Book of Mormon." 22m **Waynesburg** (sett.1796), rural center & seat of **Waynesburg College** (coed.est.1849). **Hanna Hall** (1851), orig. bldg.

US40 cont. (W) through oil & coal reg. & then rolling farms. In **W. ALEXANDER,** at **79.5.,** is **Lafayette Inn** (1783), where Lafayette stopped in 1824. **80. PA.-WEST VA. LINE.**

## US 11—PENNSYLVANIA

**PA.-N.Y. LINE** (15m from Binghamton, N.Y.) **(S) to PA.-MD. LINE** (6m from Parkton, N.Y.) **254. US11**

Via: Scranton, Pittston, Northumberland, Selinsgrove, Harrisburg, Carlisle, Chambersburg.

### Sec. 1: N. Y. LINE to NORTHUMBERLAND. 130.

US11 runs through the N. anthracite reg., through farm & dairy country, & for c.125m follows the Susquehanna & its N. Branch to Md. Line.

At **9. NEW MILFORD,** a sleepy hamlet. J. with US106.

At **48. SCRANTON**

RR., plane & bus conns. Accoms.: All types. Info.: C. of C., 426 Mulberry St.

Scranton, a coal mining & industrial city on Lackawanna R., lies a few miles (NW) of that stream's J. with E. branch of the Susquehanna. Town was named for Scranton Bros. who founded iron works here. First settlement was made in middle of 18th cent. but after the "Wyoming massacre" (see Forty Fort), settlers fled & did not return for many yrs. In 2nd half of 19th cent. considerable iron & steel industry developed due to near-by iron-ore deposits & large coal mines of the reg. Today city is world's leader in anthracite coal production & leading industrial center producing, besides iron & steel, a great variety of other manufactures.

PTS. OF INT.: In Cth. Sq., **Lackawanna County Cth.** & a number of mons. One is to John Mitchell, labor leader & an early pres. of U.M.W. SE. cor. of Vine St. & Washington Ave., **Albright Mem. Pub. Lib.** (O.wks.1893.Fr.Ren.by Green & Wicks). 319 Wyoming Ave., **Univ. of Scranton** (Cath.1887) conducted by Christian Brothers. 1001 Wyoming Ave., **Internat. Correspondence Schools** (O.tours.Coll.Goth.) is home of famous correspondence courses which are carried on not only throughout U.S., but throughout the world. 420 Washington Ave., **Masonic Temple & Scottish Rite Cathedral** (O.wks.by R. M. Hood) with tall tower & large auditorium. 2300 Adams Ave., **Marywood College** (Cath.est.1915) for women. In **Liberal Arts Bldg.** (mod.Georg.) are murals of religious subjects by Gonippo Raggi. On Jefferson Ave., **Del., Lackawanna RR. Sta.** by Edward Langley & Kenneth Murchison. Walls of inter. have a number of mosaics. On Arthur Ave., **E. Scranton Nay Aug Pk.** incl. zoo, **L. Lincoln** (swim.); conservatory; mus. (O) & **Nay Aug Falls.** There is also **Everhart Mus. of Natural Science & Art** (O.wks.exc.Mon.). At entrance, portrait statue of Dr. Isaiah F. Everhart, donor of mus., which contains extensive zoological colls.; model of a mine; coll. of paintings & objets d'art & Ind. relics & fossils. On S. side of Mus. is a stone comm. Ebenezer Slocum & Frances Slocum taken prisoner by Inds. when they raided Wilkes-Barre, 1788. (E) of Mus. is **Brooks Coal Mine** (O). 3000 N. Main Ave., **Marvine Colliery** (O.conducted tours) where process of coal mining on large scale can be observed. In West Scranton is **Baker Colliery** (O.wks.appl.at Lackawanna Motor Club, 429 Wyoming Ave.). Coal mining processes may be observed.

US11 cont. along river. At **61.** is **PITTSTON,** coal-mining center. At Main & Parsonage Sts., **Site of Ft. Pittston. Log Ft.** was built in 1776. Overlooking city is impressive **Dial Rock** by which, it is alleged, inhabitants used to tell time. At **64. WYOMING,** small industrial town, is site of Battle of Wyoming (July,1778) when force of Inds. & Loyalists led by Butler (see N.Y.) defeated patriot force coming up from Forty Fort. 8th & Susquehanna Sts., **Queen Esther's Rock** where so-called

White Ind. Queen massacred patriot prisoners. Wyoming Ave. & Schulde Lane, **Wyoming Mon.** where dead of the battle were buried. **67. FORTY FORT** on outskirts of Wilkes-Barre. At Fort & River Sts. is **Site of Forty Fort,** marked by a stone. Its name derives from 1st 40 settlers in valley. Here survivors of Wyoming Battle & settlers took refuge. Although the Ft. was surrendered on condition that inhabitants should be spared c.300 of them, incl. women & children, were massacred. River St. & Wyoming Ave., **Forty Fort Meetingh.** (O.appl.1807.rest.) was built after camp meeting at which Bishop Asbury preached. Opp., beautiful **Borough Bldg.** (O). Valley was scene of controversy bet. Conn. & Pa. for its possession, known as Pennamite Yankee War.

US11 cont. through coal-mining reg. **68. KINGSTON,** industrial & mining center & suburb of Wilkes-Barre across E. Branch of the Susquehanna. Across R. from Kingston is **WILKES-BARRE,** 2nd largest anthracite coal-mining center. In Pub. Sq. is **Mon.** on site of Ft. Wilkes-Barre, 1778. City is starting pt. for vacationists to hunt., fish. & winter sports regs. of the Poconos in vic. In the River Common are sites of **Fts. Wyoming & Durkee.** Marker is on spot where Gen. John Sullivan organized his punitive expedition against the Iroquois, 1779 (see N.Y.). On R. is **Wilkes-Barre Mun. Conservatory** (O.wks.& Sun.a.m.). 71 S. Franklin St., **Osterhout Free Lib.** (O). 69 S. Franklin St., **Wyoming Hist. & Geolog. Soc. Bldg.** containing extensive lib. 78 S. Franklin St., **Mus.** in which are colls. of antiques & hist. relics. SW. cor. River & North Sts., **Luzerne County Cth.** in which are int. murals. N. Penn Ave. & Scott St., site of **Slocum H.,** now playground, comm. Frances Slocum who in 1778, at 5 yrs., was kidnapped by Inds., one of whom she later married. When found many yrs. later she refused to leave her Ind. relatives & friends. N. River St., **Dorrance Colliery** (O.for men.conducted tours). From city the mine which has been afire for three quarters of a cent., can be seen.

**72. PLYMOUTH,** anthracite town. US11 cont. along W. branch of Susquehanna R. through coal-mining town. At **109. BLOOMSBURG** on Fishing Cr., dominated by Spectator Bluff, where among other things is mousetrap factory which has adapted as its motto "The world has made a beaten path to our factory doors," an epigram popularly attributed to Emerson.

**119. DANVILLE,** also industrial town. At Mill & Bloom Sts., **Montgomery H.** (1777.Georg.Col.). **130. NORTHUMBERLAND,** located at pt. where E. & W. branches of the Susquehanna join. North Way & Hanover St., **Jos. Priestley H.** (18th cent.Georg.Col.). Here lived famous Brit. scientist, refugee because of his religious beliefs from 1794 to 1804, the yr. he died. **Mus.** in which are Priestley relics. In Northumberland is J. with US15 (For pts. of int. bet. Northumberland & Williamsport see US220). On Penn Cr. is **Mon.** on Site of Penn Creek Massacre (1775) where settlers were slain by Inds. after Braddock was defeated. (S) of Northumberland, $7^m$ on US11-15 is **Selinsgrove** (see below). Here is J. with St.14.

SIDE TRIP: (S) on St.14 $1^m$, is **Shikellemy Mon.** to Chief of the Six Nations. Just (S) of Mon. on St.14 is site of **Ft. Augusta** (1756) near orig. Ind. village of Shamokin, built as defense against Fr. & Inds. Chiefs of Six Nations, who wanted protection against raids by their Ind. enemies, allies of the Fr., asked colonial authorities to erect the ft. at this strategic pt., the confluence of E. & W. branches of the Susquehanna. During Rev. the ft. proved both a refuge for those fleeing from Ind. raids by Iroquois, & as a base of supplies & men for Gen. Sullivan's expedition (1779) which ended Iroquois menace (see N.Y.). Ft. site is now St. Pk. Here also is Northumberland Cty. hist. bldg., **Hunter Mansion** (1852), containing exhibits from Ft. Augusta. $2^m$ (S) on St.14 is **Sunbury** (sett.1772), site of several former Ind. villages. **Mon. to Chief Shikellemy.** At Sunbury Edison is supposed to have started 1st elec. lighting plant in world.

### Sec. 2: NORTHUMBERLAND to MD. LINE. 124.

At **7.** is **SELINSGROVE,** seat of **Susquehanna** (Luth.) **Univ.** (1858). At 121 Market St. **Gov. Simon Snyder's Mansion.** (1816.Georg.Col.) In R. opp. is **Isle of Que** ("tail"), alluvial strip owned by Chief Shikellemy. **39. AMITY HALL** (see Harrisburg Trip). **56. HARRISBURG** (see). At **73.** US11 crosses Pa. Turnpike, highspeed Rd. whose cost was $70,000,000, which runs without any grade crossing from near Harrisburg to Pittsburgh.

At **75. CARLISLE**

RR. & bus conns. Accoms.: All types. Info.: C. of C., 18 S. Hanover St. Good hunt. & fish. in surrounding mt. reg.

Carlisle (sett.1720) at N. end of Cumberland Valley is traversed by LeTorts Spring Run Cr.; busy industrial center & home of Dickinson College. First settler was Frenchman named Le Torts. Carlisle, during Fr.-Ind. Wars, became supply center for expeditions against French. Was Washington's Hqs. during Whiskey Rebellion. Before Civil War it was an active sta. on Underground RR. & during that war in 1863 J. E. B. Stuart's forces made an abortive attack on town, but soon withdrew in order to aid Lee in Battle of Gettysburg.

PTS. OF INT.: (1) **Public Sq.** at Hanover St. around which are located a number of public bldgs. There is a legend that Regina, daughter of some German settler who had been kidnapped by the Inds. & who was released in 1764 was brought here to rejoin her family. She failed to recognize them, until her mother sang an old lullaby with which she had rocked Regina to sleep as a baby. Washington arrived here on his way to suppress the Whiskey Uprising, & still later here occurred riots against attempts to enforce Fugitive Slave Law. Around Sq.: **First Presb. Ch.** (est.1734. built 1750-60). Carlisle's own Decl. of Independence was read in Church, May 23, 1776; **St. George Ch.** (Episc.1825.Goth.) occupies site of Old Whipping Post & Pillory. **Cumberland Cth.** (1845-6.Gr.Rev.fine exter.& inter.). (2) (S) of Sq. on South St. bet. Hanover & Bedford Sts., **Cemetery** in which is **Molly Pitcher's Grave** (for Molly Pitcher, see Monmouth Battlefield & Freehold, N.J.). (3) Near Sq. at 4 N. Hanover St., **Blaine H.** (1794), home of Col. Ephraim Blaine, Commissary Gen. of Continental Army, who spent his entire fortune procuring supplies for Valley Forge encampment. (4) SE. cor. N. Pitt St. & Dickinson Ave., **Hamilton Hist. Lib.** (O.aft. & eves.Thurs.& Fri.), containing coll. of Col. furnishings & utensils, Ind. & other relics, rare mss. & books. (5) 120 W. Dickinson Ave., **Office of Harrisburg Telegraph,** formerly Thos. Butler's Gun Shop. Butler's 5 sons were noted during Rev. as "Fighting Butlers." (6) **J. H. Bosler Mem. Lib.** (O.wks.aft.& eve.) containing some rare items. (7) On W. Louther St., **Dickinson College** (O.est.1783) which evolved out of Grammar School est. 1773 by Thos. Penn. College founder was famous physician, Benj. Rush, & was named for John Dickinson, who was 1st Pres. of College Board of Trustees, & famous Rev. pamphleteer, author of "Letters of a Farmer in Pa." By his refusal to sign Decl. of Ind., he lost considerable prestige. Nevertheless, he sat in Constitutional Convention & was influential in securing compromise as to State representation which finally was accepted. On campus, **"Old West" Hall** (1804 by B. J. Latrobe, architect of Capitol in Washington, D.C.) is outstanding early bldg. In **Tome Scientific Bldg.** is Jos. Priestley Coll. (8) Cor. College & South Sts., **Dickinson Law School** (1917.Georg.Col.) is an independent institution. (9) In NE. sec. of city on LeTort's Spring Run is **U.S. Army Medical Field Service Sch.,** on site of old army post where Hessians were imprisoned after Battle of Trenton. Old barracks were burnt by Stuart's men. **Old Hessian Guard H.** (c.1777) built by Hessian prisoners is still standing. Carlisle Ind. Sch. whose teams made football history was located here for 40 yrs. Army Field Service Sch. gave medical courses to military personnel. 1920-46. At **84.** J. with St.233.

SIDE TRIP: On St.233 (S) here to Pine Grove near which in **Pine Grove Furnace St. For. Pk.** (cabins.camp.pic.bath.) in Fuller L. reg. Near-by is site of **Old Iron Furnace.** St.233 cont. to J. with US30 (see) at Caledonia.

At **95. SHIPPENSBURG** (est.1730). On King St. are some fine old houses. 352 King St., **Cth.** (1750). This is home of St. Teachers' College. **108. CHAMBERSBURG** on Conococheague R. in Cumberland Valley is center for considerable orchard sec. Town was burned in 1864 by Confed. troops, allegedly as revenge for Sherman's Raid in Shenandoah Valley. 225 King St., **John Brown's Hqs.** (For J. Brown see Osawatomi, Kansas, & History). Brown came to Chambersburg in 1859 & there made preparations for his ill-fated Harper's Ferry Raid (see Harper's Ferry, Va.). At N. 2nd St., **Birthpl. of Jas. Buchanan** (O.cabin), removed from Mercersburg. In Chambersburg is J. with US30 (see). At **124.** Hy. crosses **MD. LINE.**

## US 220—PENNSYLVANIA

**PA.-N.Y. LINE** (0.5$^{m}$ from Waverly, N.Y. **(SW) to PA.-MD. LINE** (10$^{m}$ from Cumberland, Md.). **248. US220**

Via: Towanda, Muncy, Williamsport, Lock Haven, Altoona, Hollidaysburg, Bedford.

US220 follows creeks & Rs. & touches branches of Susquehanna R. in its course along Allegheny Mts.

## Sec. 1: PA.-N.Y. LINE to WILLIAMSPORT. 87.

US220 (S) of Waverly, N.Y., is at J. with unimproved Rd. leading (L) 0.5$^{m}$ to Spanish Hill. Earthworks here have been variously ascribed to early expeditions of Vikings, Sp. & Fr. **Brulé Mon.** comm. Etienne Brulé (see Ohio), who visited spot in 1615 (fine views;camp.pic.). **3.5. ATHENS,** at confluence of Chemung & Susquehanna Rs., so named because its location resembles that of Greek city. 724 Main St., **Tioga Pt. Mus.** (O), geologic & Ind. exhibits. Ind. town was destroyed in 1778 by patriot forces to avenge massacre of Wyoming (see). Bet. **4.** & **6.** are **QUEEN ESTHER FLATS** (L). Here stood castle of Queen Esther, known as "White Queen" of Seneca, who perpetrated massacre. At **19. TOWANDA** (see US6). At **49. LAPORTE** (resort.1,965′) on wide plateau. Here in 1853 Adventists est. Celestial Community, experiment in communal living. Here is J. with St.42 leading (R) to **Eagles Mere** at 5.5$^{m}$ (resort.recr.f.boat.swim.). Near Eagle's Mere is **Ticklish Rock.** At **69. HUGHESVILLE.** Here is J. with St.14.

SIDE TRIP: On this Rd. (S) 4.5$^{m}$ to **Muncy.** Near-by is **Site of Ft. Brady** (1777), abandoned when Brit. & Ind. allies invaded reg. To (S) 2.5$^{m}$ is John Brady's burial place in **Hall's Cemetery.** Brady was noted Ind. fighter during Rev. & was killed by Inds. soon after he built Ft.

### 87. WILLIAMSPORT

Air, RR. & bus. conns. Airport at Montoursville. Accoms.: All types. Camp. incl. facils. for trlrs. in Mem. Pk. Info.: Brown Lib., 19 E. 4th St. Bath.: Mt. Beach & Mun. Beach. In vic. are good R. & Crs. for fish.; there is also good hunting.

At spot where Williamsport now stands, on W. branch of Susquehanna R., was an Ind. settlement called French Margaret's Town after part-Ind. daughter of Mme. Montour, who was also of mixed blood. Town was finally named Williamsport because Wm. Russell kept his boat here for crossing the R. Williamsport became center for lumbering operations of reg. After fors. were stripped, town became mfg. center.

PTS. OF INT.: 119 E. 4th St., **Jas. W. Brown Pub. Lib.** (O.wks.;1907;Ren.) contains fine lib. of hist. documents & coll. of paintings of Hudson R. School. N. side of Freedom Rd., **Negro Slavery Refuge** (1638.logs concealed by clapboards) was noted sta. of Underground RR. W. 4th & Cemetery Sts., **Calvary Ch.** (Meth.1923.Goth.), on site where early settlers were attacked in 1778 by Inds. Largest of Williamsport's great industrial plants (O.wks.conducted tours) is **Aviation Mfg. Co.;** others incl. **Bethlehem Steel Corp., Armour Leather Co., Lycoming Mfg. Corp.** 858 W. 4th St., **Lycoming Cty. Hist. Soc.** (O.Sun.); Ind. material. To (E) 12$^{m}$ is **Friends Meetingh.** (1799.in continual use).

At Williamsport is J. with US15.

SIDE TRIP: On this Rd. (S) 8$^{m}$ to **Site of Ft. Freeland** where large number of pop. was massacred by Brit. & Inds. (1779). Just (S) is **Warrior Run Ch.** (1835). At 28$^{m}$ **Lewisburg** (1785), anglicized name of German colonist, Ludwig (Lewis) Doerr. Although an industrial center it is chiefly college town, home of **Bucknell U.** (est.1846.coed.) on 300-a. campus. Here is J. with St.45.

On this Rd. (W) 9.5$^{m}$ **Mifflinburg,** named for Thos. Mifflin, 1st gov. of St. under its post-Rev. constitution. In vic. on St.95 near Foresthill is **Halfway St. For. Pk.** (pic.swim.). At 15.5$^{m}$ on St.45 is **Hartleton.** At 19.5$^{m}$ is J. with St.235 leading to **McConnell's Narrows St. Pk.** (swim.canoeing.f.). St.45 now traverses **Bald Eagle St. Pk.** (pic.camp.f.hunt.); **Joyce Kilmer St. For. Mon.** (L), fine grove of old trees, comm. poet-author of "Trees"; & **Voneida St. For. Pk.** (pic.recr.). 26$^{m}$ **Woodward.** Here is **Woodward Cave** (O.May-Nov.fee). 39.5$^{m}$ **Spring Mills.** Here side Rd. leads (R) 4$^{m}$ to **Penn's Cave** (O.fee.motorboat), only all-water cavern in Amer., near Centre Hall. Legend has it that one Boger, a Frenchman, eloped with Ind. girl & was caught in this cave by her brother & starved to death here. In vic. unimproved country Rd. runs to **Veiled Lady Cave,** which gets its name from legend about white maiden who waited, veiled, for her Ind. lover who never arrived, until she froze to death.

60.5$^{m}$ **State College,** home of **Pa. St. College** (est. 1855. c.2,000 as. 80 bldgs.). **"Old Main"** (1859.rebuilt 1931. Georg. Col.) with mural by Henry Van Poor. In **Mineral Industries Bldg.** is mus. containing minerals & art colls. J. with US322. From here St.45 skirts **Logan St. For.** (camp.pic.). 69$^{m}$ is **Martha Furnace,** at J. with US220.

## Sec. 2: WILLIAMSPORT to PA.-MD. LINE. 161.

US220 follows (W) branch of Susquehanna R., crosses Blue Ridge Mts. with access to several St. For. Pks., & winds through Bald Eagle Mt. reg. of Susquehanna. **14.5. JERSEY SHORE** (sett.1785) was founded by N.J. colonists. **16.5. PINE CR.**

which runs (N) through beautiful **Pine Cr. Gorge** (see US6) can be reached from here by St.44, St.893 & St.660.

**26.5. LOCK HAVEN,** small industrial town located at pt. where Susquehanna turns (NW). Here is J. with St.120.

SIDE TRIP: St.120 (NW) follows W. branch of Susquehanna to its confluence with Sinnemahoning Cr. & then latter, picturesque mt. stream, through mt. reg. covered with good second-growth, grown up since magnificent primeval fors. were destroyed by ruthless lumbering operations of 19th cent. St. For. lands flank St.120 to (N) & (S) & many St. Pks. are easily accessible from it. Reg. affords good hunt. & fish. W. branch of Susquehanna formerly carried great rafts & booms of pine logs cut in mt. fors. Later bark of first-growth hemlocks (hemlocks were not good for lumber) was used for tanning leather. Today synthetic chemicals have largely displaced hemlock "liquor." At 28m is **Renova,** mt.-enclosed. In vic. on St.145 & St.455 are Ole Bull St. Pk. & Cherry Springs St. Pk. At 31m **Westport.** From here Rd. runs (NW) to **Kettle Cr. St. Pk.** (pic.swim.). At 56m **Driftwood.** Mon. here comm. local men, who, during Civil War, drifted downstream on rafts, picking up recruits en route, to Harrisburg where they volunteered for service, becoming famous Pa. Bucktail Brigade. Near Driftwood is J. with St.555 leading (SW) to **Tyler.** (SW) from Tyler 4m is **Parker Dam St. For. Pk.** (cabins.pic.swim.). Cont. on St.555 to **Weedville** & there take St.255 (L) to **Penfield** & then St.153 (S) to **S. B. Elliott St. For. Pk.** (cabins.pic.). 72m **Emporium.** From here St.155 leads (N) 5.5m to **Sizerville** & then (R) 0.5m to **Sizerville St. For.** (camp.pic.recr.;hunt.prohibited). 92m **St. Mary's,** whose citizens are mostly Catholics, descendants of group that sought refuge here from "Know-Nothing" Catholic witch hunts of 1840's. 102m **Ridgeway** & J. with US219 (S).

**57. MILESBURG,** on site of Ind. village of Chief Bald Eagle, killed by Capt. Sam Brady. Here is J. with St.545.

SIDE TRIP: On this Rd. (S) c.3m to **Bellefonte** (sett.c.1769), mt.-enclosed town, birthpl. of Geo. Gray Barnard, sculptor. 113 N. Allegheny St., site of **Jas. Harris H.** (1795.remod. 1828) where Talleyrand, refugee from Fr. terror, was guest. 27 N. Allegheny St., **Linn H.** (1810). Spring & Bishop Sts., **Brockerhoff H.** (1813).

At **63.** is J. with St.504 leading (R) c.8m to **Black Moshannon St. Pk.** (cabins. swim.boat.f.pic.) on lake. **74. PORT MATILDA.**

**89. TYRONE,** sett.1850 by N. Ireland emigrants. (L) **Logan Spring,** comm. John Logan, son of Shikellemy & bro. of Jas. Logan. **109. ALTOONA,** an "industrial black diamond" in mt. setting. Its important scenic attraction is world famous **Horseshoe Curve** to (W). Founded in 1849 by Pennsylvania RR., world's largest RR., which still is Altoona's chief employer. Pa. RR. made town the base of operations in pioneer work of building 1st RR. over Alleghenies. Although Diesel engines are fast replacing steam locomotives, roundh. & locomotive testing plant are still world's largest. PTS. OF INT.: **Pa. RR. Sta.** is built on site of old Logan H. where in 1862 Northern Governors pledged their aid to Lincoln in Civil War. Baker Mansion, near 36th St., houses **Blair Cty. Hist. Soc.** (O.appl.Gr.Reviv.1840); was home of early iron master, Elias Baker. On St.193 c.5m (W) of Altoona, **Blair City Mem. Hy.** leads to parking place from which both sides of Horseshoe Curve may be seen. Especially fine at night. **141. BEDFORD** (see US30), beautifully located in foothills of Alleghenies. **161. PA.-MD. LINE.**

## DELAWARE RIVER TOUR

**MATAMORAS, PA.** (across River from Port Jervis, N.Y.). **(S) to MORRISVILLE, PA.** (across R. from Trenton, N.J.). **131. US209 & US611. Unnumbered Rd. US46 & Pa.St.32**

Via: Milford, Dingmans Ferry, Archbald, Stroudsburg, Del. Water Gap, Portland; Columbia & Belvidere, N.J.; Easton, New Hope & Washington Crossing; (Washington Crossing & Trenton, N.J.)

This tour follows Del. R. traversing its most picturesque portion, incl. scenically fine Del. Water Gap. By means of side trips, over bridges or with ferries, the N.J. side can be reached.

### Sec. 1: MATAMORAS (S) to PORTLAND. 78. US209 & US611

US209-US6 here (S) cross Del. R. which is crowded bet. mts. on way to **MILFORD** at **8.5.** At Broad & Sarah Sts. is **Tom Quick Mon.** to a 1st settler killed by Inds. in 1755. Quick's son thereafter devoted himself to avenging his father & slaughtering Inds. US209 cont. (S). **17.5. DINGMANS FERRY** (small resort). Dutch Reformed Ch. (mid-19th cent.). From village a bridge (fee) runs across the R. replacing old ferry started by Andrew Dingman in 1750.

SIDE TRIPS: (A) Bridge crosses to **Dingmans Ferry, N.J.** (small resort). Just (E) of bridge is J. with Old Mine Rd. leading (R) through Flat Brook Valley to **Wallpack Center** at 5m. Just beyond town (R) is **Wallpack Inn** (N.O.1750.remod.). At 8m fine waterfall (R). At 13m turn (L) sharply to **Rosecrans Ferry** (est.1856;no serv.in winter) which runs to Pa. & J. with US209.
(B) From Dingmans Ferry, Pa. Rd. leads 1.5m (R) & then (L) to **George W. Child St. For. Pk.** (recr.bath.camp.f.).
(C) Just (S) of Dingmans Ferry a side Rd. leads (R) 0.5m & then (R) again to **Silver Thread Falls** (fee). Near-by is lofty **Dingmans Falls.**

On US209 at **30., BUSHKILL.** Side Rd. (R) here c.2m leads to J. with path running to **Bushkill Falls** (pic.recr.restaurant). **34.5. MIDDLE SMITHFIELD PRESB. CH.** At **43. STROUDSBURG,** small industrial town founded c.1776. NW. cor. 9th & Main St., **Strouds Mansion** (O.appl.janitor.1795). At Stroudsburg is J. with US611.

SIDE TRIP: (NW) on US611, 10m, to **Wiscasset L.** (pic.swim.boat.). At 10.5m **Ye Olde Swift Water Inn** (1778.adds.). 13.5m **Mt. Pocono** in heart of Pocono Vacation Area (skiing.hik.f.horse show in summer).

(1) Tunnel Knob Scenic Dr. runs from **Pocono** c.1m to **Tunnel Knob** (fine view of Del. Water Gap in distance).
(2) St.615 (R) from Pocono to J. with St.90 leading (L) to **Cresco** (resort.accoms.hik.f. skiing). Cont. on St.90 (N) to J. with St.390. Take latter (R) c.2m to J. with unimproved Rd. Take latter (L) 0.5m to fine **Buck Hills Falls.** Cont. on St.390 through resort area, past **Canadensis** (resort) which lies a little (L) of main hy., to **Sky-Top** (resort.hik.f. winter sports). Here is lake & Sky-Top Lodge. Cont. to **Promised Land St. Pk.** (cabins. camp.boat.f.) on Laura L. at c.13m (N) of Canadensis. Still further (N) on for. Rd. is **Bruce L. St. Mon.** (500 as.), in which are 2 Ls. For. is Wilderness Mon. for preservation of rare native botanical specimens.
(3) In Mt. Pocono is J. with St.940 leading (W) through fine mt. & L. resort reg., past Pocono Summit & Stillwater Ls., Lutherland, Pocono Pines, Pocono L. (resorts) to Blakeslee Corners at 14m, where is J. with St.115 which runs (N) through h. & f. reg. to Wilkes-Barre.

22m (S) of Blakeslee Corners, on St.115, is **Saylorsburg** (resort) on Saylorsburg L. & at 28m, Wind Gap village, near which is Wind Gap, a gorge in the Blue Mts. St.115 cont. (S) to J. with St.209.

On St.940 cont. (SW) from **Blakeslee** to **Eastside** & J. with side Rd. which take (SE) to **Hickory Run** (camp.swim.hik.f.).

Tour cont. from Stroudsburg (S) on US611. **49. DEL. WATER GAP** (resort). **50.** Here Del. R. makes deep & picturesque cut through 1,635′ Kittatinny Mts., a gorge which it is claimed was gouged out by R. in pre-hist. times when Mt. was being pushed upward by subterranean forces. **53. PORTLAND** on R. Just (S) of town are large **Cement Works** (O.appl.). Here is covered bridge (fee) crossing Del. R. to Columbia, N.J. (Take Rd. (N) along Del. R. 3m to New Jersey view of Del. Water Gap. Fine views.) Main route cont. from Columbia on unnumbered Rd. along R. (S) to J. with US46 on which cont. (S) past **Delaware** village, to J. with paved Rd. at **62.** Here take unnumbered Rd. (R) to **BELVIDERE** at **64.5.** on R. Here cross bridge to J. with unnumbered Rd. on Pa. side & follow it (S) to J. with US611 at **c.70.** Cont. along R. on US611 to **EASTON** at **78.**

### Sec. 2: EASTON, PA., to MORRISVILLE (across R. from Trenton, N.J.). 53. US611 & St.32.

**0. EASTON** (see US22). Hy. runs along old **Del. Division Canal.** At **12. KINTNERSVILLE,** founded 1789. Here is J. with St.32.
Route now follows Del. R. on Pa. St.32. Just (SE) of Kintnersville are the river narrows, enclosed by high cliffs. At **27.5. PT. PLEASANT.** Near here is **Ralph Stover St. Pk.** (pic.swim.cabins). Still following Del. R., St.32 reaches **NEW HOPE** at **36.** (For pts. of int. in New Hope & rest of tour to **MORRISVILLE** at **53.** see Phila. II).

## HARRISBURG

RR., plane & bus conns. Accoms.: All types. Info.: C. of C., Market Square Bldg.; Keystone Auto Club, 402 N. 3rd St.; Motor Club of Harrisburg, 101 Market St.

Harrisburg, the state's Capital, is situated on E. shore of Susquehanna R. which is esplanade, back of which on heights overlooking the R. is Front St., a fine residential sec. Capitol Hill is reached by viaduct coming in from (E). To (S) is industrial area, Market St. City was first sett. c.1712 by John Harris for whom city was named & its early inhabitants were Germans & Scotch-Irish. After Civil War immigration originating in many countries of Europe began. Town benefited greatly from bldg.

of canals conn. the Susquehanna with the Delaware. Coal & iron in vic. made city an industrial center.

PTS. OF INT.: (1) At State & 3rd Sts., **Capitol** (O.conducted tours.1906.Ital.Ren. by J.M.Huston) has lofty dome. At entrance statuary by Geo. Gray Barnard, "Burden of Life, & Labor & Brotherhood." In Dome's inter. are murals by Edwin A. Abbey (who did murals in Boston Pub. Lib.). On 2nd fl. **Senate Chamber** with hist. murals by Violet Oakley; **Chamber of House of Representatives,** with mural & ceiling painting by Edwin A. Abbey; **Gov.'s Rm.** with murals by Violet Oakley about Soc. of Friends & Wm. Penn. To (S) of Capitol, **Pa. State Mus.** (O.conducted tours. Ital.Ren.1894.by J.T.Windrim) contains archeological & hist. relics & coll. of hist. documents & mss. of Pa. writers & composers. Other bldgs. of group are: **Education Bldg.** (O.Class.by Gehron & Ross) in which, besides state offices, are **St. Lib. & Archives** & fine **Auditorium,** whose ceiling glows with lights representing star groups (in manner of Grand Central Sta. in N.Y.C.); **N. & S. Office Bldgs.** (Ital.Ren.) & **Finance Bldg.** (Class.). (2) On Front St. (N. to S.) are: At NE. cor. South St., **Maclay Mansion** (1791.remod.1909) was built by Wm. Maclay, son-in-law of John Harris II, son of 1st John Harris. On Front St., **St. Stephen's Parish H.** (1840.Gr. Rev.) has fine chapel with carved panelling. At 9 S. Front St., **Dauphin Cty. Hist. Soc.** (O.aft.) contains hist. & Ind. relics & old maps. At Front & Washington Sts., **Harris Mansion** (O.1766.Georg.Col.) was built by John Harris & is oldest structure in city. On Front St., (E) of Mansion, **Harris Pk.,** extending along R. At Washington St. is **Grave of John Harris.** Legend has it that Harris was captured by Inds. & whipped by them, but was rescued by friendly tribesmen. (3) Running (E) from Capitol is **Soldiers & Sailors Mem. Bridge** (1930.Gehron & Ross) with 2 high columns, surmounted by Amer. eagles.

## TRIPS OUT OF HARRISBURG

### I. HARRISBURG (NE) to INDIANTOWN GAP. 19. US22

Take US22 (NE) 19m to J. with side Rd. In Vic. (L) is **Indiantown Gap Military Reserv.** (18,000 as.), training grounds for Nat. Guardsmen.

### II. HARRISBURG (E) to EPHRATA. 40. US322

At **2.5.** is J. with side Rd.

SIDE TRIP: On this Rd. (L) 0.5m to **Paxtang.** At Paxtang Ave. & Sharon St., **Paxton Ch.** (Presb.1740.adds.rest.). Holes in walls were used to observe possible approach of Inds. In cemetery, graves of John Harris II (see above) & soldiers killed during Ind. War & Rev. In 1763 local people org. body of Rangers as protection against Inds. Rangers took offensive & launched brutal drive to exterminate all Inds., which was only stopped short of Phila. by Quaker intervention.

At **10. HUMMELSTOWN.** Here is J. with US422.

SIDE TRIP: Take Hanover St. (R) here c.0.5m to **Ind. Echo Cave** (O.fee) where Amos Wilson lived as hermit for many years. He had failed by seconds to save his sister from the hangman, arriving just too late with pardon. There are some Wilson relics in cave.

At **32.5. BRICKERVILLE,** where Baron Heinrich Wilhelm Stiegel, famous colonial glass manufacturer, lived toward end of his life. Here is J. with St.501.

SIDE TRIP: On this Rd. (S) 5m to **Lititz** (sett.by Moravians 1757), became center for manufacture of pianos & organs & in 19th cent. was known for its pretzels, which it still makes. In graveyard of **Moravian Ch.** on E. Main St., is buried John A. Sutter (see Cal.) Rd. (R) from Lititz runs to **Manheim** 11m (est.1762) where Baron Stiegel built his glass factories. Stiegel glass became famous in 18th cent. & examples of it are in many mus. & are much sought by collectors. He became bankrupt in 1774 & was forced to earn a living teaching at the **Luth. Ch.** (Hazel & E. High Sts.) now occupied by later structure. His H. stands in **Town Square.**

### 40. EPHRATA

Reached by Reading RR. & Reading Transportation Co. Accoms.: All types. Info.: Ephrata Review; & The Ensign. Swim., Ephrata Pk. Pool (fee). Good hunt. & fish. in vic. Farm Show in Oct.

Ephrata is best known as center of German Seventh-Day Adventists, founded by Johann Konrad Beissel. He disagreed with orig. group & founded his own. This sect was organized as a monastic body. Celibacy was advocated; although marriage bet. members was permitted, by marriage they ceased to be members. Nevertheless they were housed in small dwellings near-by. Members of the order lived in cells, worked hard & wore special white garments. All property was communal. Sat. was observed as Sabbath & on Sun. at a communal meal, the Lord's Supper was observed. Ephrata (the old Biblical name for Bethlehem) was an important cultural center. Its presses, 3rd in U.S., turned out tracts & 1st book on musical harmony in America. During Rev. it even printed Continental money. Choral singing of sacred music was a special feature of Ephrata life. There was a music school & a school to teach Goth. script writing. Music mss., rivalling in beauty those of the middle ages, were turned out in considerable numbers. Sect was pacifist, but aided patriots during Rev., after Brandywine, by caring for wounded & sick soldiers. Because married couples were eventually excluded entirely & there were few proselytes, the order grew smaller. In 1934, Soc. was dissolved. At W. edge of town, **The Cloisters** (O.sm.fee.conducted tours), group of 4 bldgs. & 5 cottages & outbldgs., now property of Pa. Hist. Commission. The **Saal** (1741), built without using any metal—only wooden pegs—contains refectory & kitchen; on walls are hand-painted mottos in German. **Sharon H.** has cells where the sisters lived; also old furnishings. The **Almonry,** from which aid to needy persons was dispensed. The **Academy** (1830), which was a high school. In cemetery, to (S) of Academy, are buried Beissel & other leaders. At (W), **Mt. Zion Cemetery,** where Rev. soldiers & the sisters who took care of them are buried.

### III. HARRISBURG (NE) to READING. 54. US422

At **13.5., HERSHEY,** & **Hershey Chocolate Corp. Plant** (O.wks.) which employs some 4,000 people. **Hershey Pk.** (1,000 as.concerts.pic.zoo). Town is owned by M. S. Hershey who has provided many recr. facils. for his employees. SW. cor. Derry & Mansion Rds., **Session H.** of **Derry Presb. Ch.** (1732.log.clapboarded). **21.5. ANNVILLE** (sett.1762). **Lebanon Valley College** (1866), est. by Ch. of the United Brethren, has a well-attended Conservatory of Music. **41.5. CONRAD WEISER ST. MEM. PK.** In Pk., **Conrad Weiser H.** (1751.rest.) contains coll. of relics & documents. Weiser, a Ger. immigrant, sett. here in early 18th cent. He was famous Ind. negotiator & it is claimed he brought Iroquois over to Brit. side. **44.5. ROBESONIA.** Here is J. with Church St. leading (R) c.0.5$^{m}$ & then (L) again c.0.5$^{m}$ to **Geo. Ege Mansion** (1809). Behind H. are ruins of **Robesonia Furnace. 52. WYOMISSING,** small industrial city. On Van Reed Rd., **Glen-Gery Shale Brick Co.** (O.wks.) where process of brick making may be observed. This factory is one of largest of its kind in U.S. On W. bank of Schuylkill R., **Wyomissing Industries** (O. work days;conducted tours) is one of most important plants turning out textile machinery & hosiery. US422 reaches **READING** at **54.**

### IV. HARRISBURG (SE) to LANCASTER. 37.5. US230

At **10.** on US230 is J. with good Rd. leading (R) here 0.5$^{m}$ to **Middletown Air Depot** (416 as.), sta. for military aviation. At **10.5. MIDDLETOWN,** industrial city which had one of country's earliest steel plants. Town grew considerably when it became J. pt. for Pa. & Union Canals, early in 19th cent. (N) of Center Sq., **St. Peter's Lutheran Ch.** (1767.adds.alts.). **18.5. ELIZABETHTOWN** (sett.c.1732). SW. cor. Market & Hummelstown Sts., **Black Bear Tavern** (1735.much alt.) was set up by Capt. John Harris, 1st settler. S. Market St., **St. Peter's Ch.** (Cath.1799). **Elizabethtown College** (founded 1899 by Ch. of the Brethren.coed.). **37.5. LANCASTER** (see US30).

### V. HARRISBURG (SW) to GETTYSBURG. 38. US15

US15 crosses toll bridge (sm.fee) from Harrisburg to **LEMOYNE** at **1.5.**

### 38.5. GETTYSBURG

RR. & bus conns. Accoms.: Limited. Info.: C. of C. & Gettysburg Motor Club, both on Center Square.

Gettysburg, scene of decisive battle which put a stop to Lee's attempt to invade the North & ended, once & for all, Confederacy's hope of final victory. Lee made his daring advance after defeating Hooker at Chancellorsville in May, 1863. Gettysburg was a 3-day battle, one of bloodiest of war. Confed. army had 75,000 men & Union army c.84,000. Lee advanced from Fredericksburg, Va., through the Blue Ridge, & moved (N) with Ridge protecting his flank. Hooker took Army of Potomac (N) along a valley, paralleling to (E) Lee's advance. Ewell, one of Lee's generals, had gone ahead with his forces & taken Carlisle, but was recalled, since Lee had changed his plan. By July 1, both Union & Confed. advance forces had reached Gettysburg. Meanwhile, Meade replaced Hooker as Comdr. of Army of Potomac. Fed. troops retreated to Cemetery Hill to (S) of town, from which Cemetery Ridge extends (S) to Round Top. Another ridge runs (SE) to Culp's Hill & then (S) to Spangler's Spring. Paralleling Cemetery Ridge is Seminary Ridge occupied by Lee. By July 2, Union line curved from Round Top along Cemetery Ridge, over Cemetery Hill to Spangler's Spring, c.3m in length. In the aft., Confed. forces attacked but were unable to dislodge Union troops. During 3rd day the 2 armies exchanged heavy artillery fire. When Fed. batteries ceased fire, Lee mistakenly assumed that his guns had silenced them & ordered Pickett to charge up Cemetery Ridge. Charge was repulsed by murderous fire of Union guns. J. E. B. Stuart's cavalry made equally abortive attempt on rear of Fed. positions. Meade failed to follow up his success & Lee escaped with his battered forces, despite attempts by Meade's cavalry to hamper retreat. Battle was one of bloodiest of war. Pickett's command was almost completely wiped out. Battle was further notable because artillery engagement was perhaps heaviest known up to that time. It is said more than 31,000 cannon shot were fired.

Battlefield has been made into a Nat. Military Pk. (2,394 as.guides avail.). It was while dedicating part of battlefield as Nat. cemetery, that Lincoln delivered his Gettysburg Address, following Edw. Everett's 2-hour oratorical fling. Newspapers of the day reported Everett's speech at great length & merely noted that the Pres. also made a few remarks. Pk. has many mons. & mems., some by famous sculptors.

PTS. OF INT.: (1) On Baltimore Rd., **Soldiers Nat. Cemetery** in which is Soldiers Mon. & Lincoln Speech Mem. (2) At Hancock Ave. & Taneytown Rd., **Meade's Hqs.** until he had to abandon it because of heavy bombardment by Confed. artillery. Near-by, statue of Meade. (3) On Hancock Ave., (S) of Meade Ave., **Bronze Book** on stone pedestal marks Bloody Angle, where some of goriest fighting took place & where Pickett's charge was finally turned back. (4) Hancock & Pleasonton Aves., **Pa. Mon.** comm. c.34,000 natives of St. who fought at Gettysburg. (5) Near-by, **Statue of Father Wm. Corby** of Fighting Irish battalion. (6) On Sykes Ave., **Little Round Top,** which barely escaped capture by Confed. troops during 2nd day of battle. (7) On W. Confederate Ave., **Statue of Lee.** (8) N. Confederate Ave., **Eternal Light Peace Mon.** (P.P.Cret) on which a flame is kept burning constantly. (9) Baltimore St., near Nat. Cemetery, **Jenny Wade H.,** where Jenny Wade was killed during the fighting; contains Mus. (mementos). At Gettysburg is J. with St.116.

SIDE TRIP: On this Rd. (SW) 6.5m is **Hanover,** where occurred a battle during Civil War bet. Gen. J.E.B. Stuart's cavalry & Union troops, which blocked Stuart's joining Lee at Gettysburg until after that battle had been raging for a day. At Hanover are **Hanover Shoe Farms** (O), famous stud farm for breeding trotting horses. From it came Dean Hanover & other winning trotters.

### VI. HARRISBURG (W) to CARLISLE. 8. US11

(For sec. bet. Harrisburg & Carlisle see US11.)

### VII. HARRISBURG (N) to AMITY. 23.5. US22

At **6.** (N) on **US22, ROCKVILLE,** (N) of which is **Ft. Hunter Mus.** (O.May-Oct. 1785 & 1814) on site of Ft. Hunter (1756). Contains coll. of early furnishings. At **17. AMITY HALL.** At **23.5. AMITY.** Here J. with St.34, near Newport leading (S) through Newport & New Bloomfield.

## PHILADELPHIA

**PHILADELPHIA**

RR. Stas.: Pa. RR., Broad & Market Sts., Broad St. Sta.; 30th & Market St., Thirtieth St. Sta.; 16th St. & Pennsylvania Blvd., Suburban Sta.; Broad St. & Glendale Ave., N. Phila. Sta. B. & O. RR., Chestnut & 24th Sts. Reading Ry. Terminal, Market & 12th Sts.; N. Broad St. Sta., Broad & Huntingdon Sts. Filbert & 13th Sts., Union Bus Terminal. Sightseeing & charter bus serv. Phila. Internat. Airport (SW) 7m. Ferries: Market St. Wharf, Pa.-Reading Seashore Lines. Passenger Steamship Piers: Market St., Wilson Line, for Chester, Pa. & Wilmington, Del.; South St., Ericsson Line, for Baltimore, Md. Accoms.: All types, incl. tourist camps in vic. Excellent recr. & sports facils. in many pks., incl. Woodside Amusement Pk., in Fairmount Pk., League I. Pk., Willow Grove & others in vic.; Pa. Athletic Club, Municipal & Temple Univ. stadia & Univ. of Pa.'s Franklin Field; mun. golf courses, tennis courts, swim. pools & beaches. Symphony Orchestra & other concerts at Academy of Music, Municipal Stadium, Robin Hood Dell (summer), Irvine Auditorium of Univ. of Pa., Convention Hall. Stage plays & motion pictures in numerous theaters; little theater groups; Hedgerow Theater (see Trip VIII below), night clubs, especially in larger hotels & restaurants. Annual Events: Mummers Parade (Jan.1), Poor Richard Celebration (Jan.17); Bok Award Presentation & Nat. Home Show (Feb.); Flower Show (Mar.); Ship of Flowers launching (May 30); Flower Mart in Rittenhouse Sq. (May); Wissahickon Day meet & Hist. Pageant at Old Swedes Ch. (June); Independence Sq. Celebration & People's Regatta (July 4); Lafayette Day, at Independence Hall (Sept.6); Columbus Day Celebration in Fairmount Pk.; Kennel Club Show (Nov.or Dec.); Assembly Ball (early Dec.); Sounding of Liberty Bell (New Year's Eve). Sansom & 17th Sts., C. of C. & Convention & Tourist Bureau.

Philadelphia, birthpl. of the U.S. as a nation, is now one of its largest cities & important ocean-shipping ports—about 100$^{m}$ inland on the Delaware R. The Central City extends across the neck of land bet. this river & the Schuylkill & is still dominated by the benign figure of Wm. Penn above City Hall at Market & Broad Sts. Across the Delaware is N.J. with Camden, Walt Whitman's home, at the end of the fine Delaware R. Bridge. Across town, at end of Market St., & on Schuylkill R., is the Penn. RR.'s Thirtieth St. Sta. Geometrically regular streets extend (N) & (S) from the Central City, lined by solid blocks of relatively low buildings & row houses, mostly brick, & the city has expanded (W) across the Schuylkill. Breaking the monotonous pattern are impressive avenues cutting diagonally from (N) & (W) to heart of the shopping & business district. In Kensington & farther to (NE) are large textile mills & other establishments that make Philadelphia a ranking industrial center & a leader in the textile field. To the (S), where the Schuylkill enters the Delaware, are League I. Pk., the Philadelphia Naval Base & large oil refineries. In environs are some of the country's most beautiful suburbs, homes of the many wealthy families that more or less control civic affairs, & within the 135-sq.-mile area of the city proper are formerly independent & distinctive communities, such as Germantown, Chestnut Hill & Oak Lane.

The Central City, in plan, is almost as Penn designed it. His High St., now Market St., & the long straight sweep of Broad St. intersect at Penn Sq., orig. Center Sq., relocated (as was Broad St.) in 1733 a little (W) of center. In the middle of each of the 4 quarters of the city is one of Penn's Parks: Franklin Sq. at Delaware R. Bridge, Washington Sq. & Rittenhouse Sq., (S) of Market St., & Logan Circle on the new Pky. Just (NE) of Franklin Sq. is Independence Sq., around which are Independence Hall, Congress Hall & other hist. shrines. Here, (E) of Broad & a few blocks (N) & (S) of Market St., is old Phila. Around beautiful Rittenhouse Sq. (in the SW. quarter), with its pleasant landscaping & notable sculptures, are tall apartment hotels, Holy Trinity Ch., & the imposing Penn Athletic Club & Curtis Institute. In the center of the city, the bronze statue of the Quaker founder towers above the City of Brotherly Love, but not far below is the very modern Phila. Saving Fund Soc. Bldg., opposing its sheer verticality to the bulky mid-Vict. City Hall with its innumerable, frequently charming or amusing ornaments. A few other skyscrapers, mostly trust company bldgs., rise above the ponderous early structures of the central area, but Phila., well-located & generously planned, has no great need for skyscrapers. Across the Schuylkill & (S) of Market St. is the Univ. of Pa. campus. The Benjamin Franklin Pky., a recent development, leads (NW) from City Hall to the Pa. Academy of Art, a great Ionic temple on a hill overlooking the Schuylkill. Off the Pky., around Logan Circle, are the Rodin Mus., the Cath. Cathedral, Franklin Institute & the Free Lib., all outstanding structures. Beyond the Mus., on either side of the R. & threaded by the Wissahickon, is Fairmount Pk., one of the largest city pks. in the U.S. & still the "Green Countrie" that attracted Wm. Penn.

It is not easy to know Philadelphia. It has been compared to Boston, but the resemblance is superficial. Its alleys, such as present Camac St., cutting the unusually large blocks (Penn planned to give each house a "street" frontage), are said to give a likeness to London. But on the surface & beneath it, Phila. is one of the few genuinely individual Amer. cities & notoriously indifferent to the opinion of the non-resident. It has long been known as a city of homes, but not in the same way as civic-minded Cleveland. The "Chinese Wall" on Market St. is a social as well as material reality. Phila. is a Republican stronghold, & Quakers & Episcopalians are still probably the strongest religious groups. The Blue Laws have not quite faded out, but the tradition of tolerance is still strong. The hist. city has long been a cultural as well as mfg. center of the nation, & the inroads of industrialization leave it fundamentally unchanged. For many yrs. it was a favored city among Negroes, who now make up about 12% of the total pop., living in S. Phila. & (N) of the

Central City. Since World War II, strong racial prejudice has led to rioting & mob violence. There are large Ital., German, Russian & other European communities, & a large, often politically important, Irish element. Phila.'s long-established Jewish community is outstanding in philanthropy & cultural developments, & the Quakers founded Bryn Mawr, Haverford, Swarthmore & other notable institutions besides their own Select Schools. Beyond these sometimes conflicting influences, another clue to Phila. lies with the membership of the Union League, the Philadelphia, & other exclusive clubs. The Dec. Assembly Ball maintains this aristocratic & conservative tradition, while the joyous Mummers Parade on New Year's Day, open to the millions, is also a traditional part of Phila. life.

A leisurely stroll through the city is very rewarding. Here around Rittenhouse Sq., on Clinton & Delancey Sts., in charming out-of-the-way corners, may be found almost every type of architecture adopted or developed in the country. Here also are exotic flowerings—Oriental, Italianate & wildly eclectic combinations. One should be on the watch, too, for the extraordinary gargoyles & curlicues embellishing both modest house & august office building—as characteristic of the city as Phila. ice cream, pepper pot & scrapple. Of almost inexhaustible interest also are the waterfront wharves, boat crews on the Schuylkill, the many museums & galleries, chs. & other bldgs. preserved in 18th-cent. simplicity, artistic Camac St., picturesque foreign neighborhoods, quiet streets lined with trees planted long ago, some rare ones introduced by John Bartram, the noted botanist. In the vic. are numerous inns of great charm, & Fairmount Pk. & the banks of the Wissahickon are a naturalist's paradise.

While the site of Phila. was still unbroken wilderness, there were Dutch, Swedish & Finnish settlements along the Delaware. The area came into Eng. control in 1667, was retaken by the Dutch in 1673 but returned to England again a yr. later. Only a few Eng. settlers came before 1680. Then, in 1681, Charles II made a grant to Wm. Penn to settle certain claims due to Penn's father, & the high-minded Quaker began his Holy Experiment. Capt. Thos. Holme surveyed the site, & Penn & his Quaker colonists arrived in the autumn of 1682. Penn had labored lovingly on his Frame of Gov. & a plan for the great city he believed he was founding. It was his idea to name the E.-W. streets after trees & flowers instead of the hist. personages chosen by Holme. Within a yr., hundreds of houses were built, & the Quakers soon est. a lucrative trade with the other Colonies & the Caribbean Is. They were not yet committed to simple attire & plain living, but their life, while lavish & gay enough, was never "rude or riotous." They were early interested in founding schools & in the development of science, especially medicine. In 1683, Francis Daniel Pastorius founded Germantown. The following yr., Penn returned to England & became involved in personal troubles & family affairs. The proprietorship was removed from him in 1692 & restored in 1694. He returned to America in 1699 but only for 2 yrs., for in 1701 he again sailed for England to fight for the autonomy of his Province. He died in 1718, at the age of 74, after several yrs. of illness.

The next great event in Phila. was the arrival of the poor young printer, Benj. Franklin. The numberless interests & practical inventions of Franklin are all part of local hist. His "Poor Richard's Almanac" was read by almost every citizen from the time it appeared in 1732 until Franklin went to London as Colonial agent. Deeply interested in civic welfare, Franklin est. the debating Junto Club, the Amer. Philosophic Soc. & a circulating lib. He also helped found the Pa. Hospital & the Academy which became the Univ. of Pa. His influence relaxed the Quaker dominance; & with the arrival of thousands of Scotch-Irish & German immigrants, dancing, fencing & theatrical entertainments became part of Phila. life. But Franklin took up the Quaker cause in the demand that Pa. be made a royal province.

When the Stamp Act was passed in 1765, Franklin was not in favor of open resistance, but in the "Buy American" boycott campaign, he suggested whiskey be used for punch & toddy instead of British rum. Repeal of the tax law was celebrated by bonfires & punch parties. The Townshend Act followed quickly, & the boycott was renewed. Colonial industry & trade had become a threat to the mother country, & Phila.'s share in this commerce was a large one. When the ship "Polly" arrived loaded with tea, the Phila. citizenry demanded that it be sent back. In May, 1774, Paul Revere brought the news that the Boston harbor was closed. On June 18, a meeting in the St. House discussed calling a "Continental Congress," & a preliminary st. conference met in Carpenters' Hall, on July 15. The First Continental Congress convened in Carpenters' Hall on Sept. 5, a body of "the ablest & wealthiest men in America" incl. many Tories who, presumably, sent information to the Brit. Some historians note, however, the strongly democratic element, symbolized in the choice of a guild hall rather than the St. House as meeting place. The Suffolk Resolves were adopted, & nonimportation & nonconsumption agreements drawn up. Phila. Tories, as elsewhere, were aghast at the results of the Congress, but the idea of union had been planted in the minds of the Colonists. The Second Continental Congress met in May, 1775, right after the clash at Lexington (Ap.19). Franklin gave up his policy of reconciliation, realizing that the time for temporizing was ended, & in July he drew up the "Articles of Confederation & Perpetual Union." Thos. Paine, who had been recommended to Franklin, arrived from Europe & published anonymously his "Common Sense," which swept the Colonies into open revolution, striking as it did at the roots of the monarchic form of gov. itself. The Decl. of Ind. was drafted by Thos. Jefferson & accepted by the Congress on July 4, 1776, & the bell in the St. House became the Liberty Bell.

The forces of Sir Wm. Howe had seized Staten I. on July 3rd, & Phila. began immediate preparations for war. Two Philadelphians, Franklin & Rbt. Morris, did more than any other single individuals to finance the Rev. Another Philadelphian, Haym Salomon, of Portuguese Jewish parentage, sacrificed his fortune to aid the patriot cause. The group of Quakers who broke away to participate in the Rev. were led by Sam. Wetherill & known as Free Quakers. After Washington was defeated at Brandywine, Howe's forces marched into Phila., Sept. 26, 1777, & the Battle of Germantown took place the following month. Washington & his ragged soldiery spent the winter at Valley Forge, while the Brit. enjoyed a fairly festive period in Phila., which did not lack for Tory men & women to entertain them. Howe withdrew from the city in the spring, & the important military campaigns thereafter were in the S. & W. In spite of, even partly because of, the war, Phila. gained in pop., banks were est., transportation improved & commerce & industry expanded. The Articles of Confederation were submitted to the Fed. Convention (May-Sept., 1787) in Independence Hall, & the Constitution of the U.S. was adopted June 21, 1788.

Philadelphia was St. capital until 1799 & nat. capital from 1775 until 1800, except for a short period in 1789 when New York was the seat of gov. Washington was frequently seen in the theaters, in Holy Trinity, at receptions or driving in his elegant coach. Philip Freneau est. in Phila. his political paper attacking Hamiltonian Federalism. In 1793, a fever epidemic swept the city, causing more than 5,000 deaths. The work of Dr. Benj. Rush, who had est. the 1st Amer. dispensary in 1786, & the aid of the banker, Stephen Girard, saved countless hundreds more. The Arsenal was built in 1800, & the Navy Yard opened in 1801. Museums & academies were being founded, Girard's bank & the Pa. Co. for Insurance were org. Rbt. Morris was in debtors' prison (1798-1801) after bankruptcy due to speculation in western lands. After the War of 1812, which involved a number of engagements on the Delaware R., Phila. looked to the opening W. for a market, & canals & RRs. were built. The city was a nat. center of the arts & sciences, & educational developments kept pace with the commercial.

In May, 1838, anti-abolitionist mobs gathered at Cherry & 6th St. corner & destroyed Pennsylvania Hall, about to be dedicated to the abolition of slavery; & in the 1840's followers of the "Know Nothing" movement wrecked Cath. schools & Chs. The Quakers were influential in bringing the town to the support of the cause of abolition in 1860. Jay Cooke, who had created a banking house in 1861, became "financier of the Civil War" & the leading banker in the U.S. for many yrs. thereafter. The citizenry responded vigorously to Lincoln's call for men. Nearly 85,000 came to Independence Hall, on Ap. 22, 1865, to file past his bier. A financial panic followed the failure of Cooke's & other banking houses in 1873, but in 1876 the Centennial Exposition opened in Fairmount Pk., & in the same yr. John Wanamaker's Grand Depot was opened near City Hall. In 1900 the Republican Convention was held in Phila., & the 1st costumed Mummers paraded Market St. Jan. 1, 1901.

As in other cities, the early 20th cent. was marked by a great inflow of immigrants & of Negroes from the southern states. At the same time, wealthier residents followed the Main Line of the Penn. RR. into the beautiful countryside. The city's powerful & corrupt political machine had been functioning for some yrs. &, in

1902, the Phila. Rapid Transit Co. was founded. Boies Penrose, J. P. McNichol & the Vare brothers were probably the best-known figures in city politics. World War I created enormous industrial expansion, marked by one serious disaster, an explosion at Eddystone Ammunition Works, near Chester, resulting in more than 100 deaths. After the war, many of the great public bldgs. arose, & Leopold Stokowski brought the Phila. Orchestra before the country. The depression turned the city towards Franklin D. Roosevelt, who was renominated at the Democratic Convention there in 1936 & reelected with the help of a large plurality in this normally Republican city. In World War II, Phila. again played an impressive part in manning the services & in producing the materials for war. During recent yrs. the slow & cautious but not at all sleepy city has continued to develop its cultural institutions & eminent social service organizations in direct ratio with its great industrial development. According to a recent plan, extensive changes will make it what it potentially is, one of the country's beautiful, but still different, cities. A better water supply is promised, slums are being cleared away, the "Chinese Wall" will be torn down, the Pennsylvania Turnpike extended, & a proper mall built at Independence Sq. (now open by U.S. Dist. Court ruling to meetings other than those of patriotic assemblies). Another enterprise in keeping with the spirit of the city's name & its founder's dream is the new Chapel of the Four Chaplains on Grace Bapt. Temple premises, a chapel with a Prot. pulpit, Jewish tabernacle & Cath. altar. Its completion is now in charge of Dr. Daniel A. Poling, whose son was one of the 4 chaplains who went down with a torpedoed troopship in 1943, after giving up their lifebelts to other men.

PTS. OF INT.—Independence Sq. Vic.: (1) Chestnut St., bet. 5th & 6th Sts., **Independence Hall.** (O.guide serv.on appl.1732-41.Georg.Col.after plans by Andrew Hamilton), put up as provincial capitol, where Assembly of the Province convened. In May 1775, the 2nd Continental Congress met here, & on July 2, 1776, after nearly a month's secret debate, the Decl. of Ind. was adopted unanimously. Final vote was postponed to allow time for Caesar Rodney to arrive from Dover & break deadlock of Del. delegation. John Hancock, Speaker, & Secy. Thompson did not sign the Declaration until July 4. On July 8, the document was made pub. & Liberty Bell rang out in celebration. The Constitutional Convention also met in Ind. Hall, completing its work there on Sept. 17, 1787. **Liberty Bell** (on 1st fl. corridor) was removed when Brit. took Phila. (1777). While tolling for the funeral of Chief Justice John Marshall (1835), a serious crack developed, but bet. 1835 & 1917, the bell was sent around the country for exhibition a number of times. On 1st fl. also are Judicial Chamber of Provincial Supreme Court & Declaration Chamber, with some of furniture used by Signers. On 2nd fl. is **Nat. Portrait Gallery,** with Benj. West's "Penn's Treaty with the Inds." & portraits of Washington by E. Pine & Jas. & Rembrandt Peale. **Col. Mus.,** in N. wing, contains costume, china, pottery & glassware colls. (2) SE. cor. 6th & Chestnut Sts., **Congress Hall** (O.wks.1789.rest.), built to house Phila. Cty. Court. U.S. Congress met here 1790-1800 & here Washington delivered "Farewell Address." In **House of Representatives Chamber** (1st fl.) are hist. exhibits; also in Senate Chamber (2nd fl.), incl. wooden statue of Washington. **U.S. Coin Room** (2nd fl.). Other Rev. period colls. incl. pewter, furniture & surgical instruments. (3) SW. cor. 5th & Chestnut Sts., **Old City Hall** (O.wks.1791), where Supreme Ct. held 1st sessions, while Phila. was nat. capital; has coll. of equipment used by fire depts. & an unusual early Quaker exhibit. In vestibule is sec. of the elm in whose shade Wm. Penn, according to legend, treated with the Inds. (4) 104 S. 5th St., **Amer. Philosophical Soc.** (O.wks.closed Sat.June-Sept.1787), home of soc. founded by Benj. Franklin in 1743 as outgrowth of his earlier Junto Club (1727); has had among members 12 Presidents (incl.Washington). Bldg. houses colls. of priceless mss., incl. orig. draft of Decl. of Ind.; portraits & statuary, incl. portrait of Washington by Gilbert Stuart; hist. relics & large coll. of Franklin material. Society's **Scientific Lib.,** outstanding in U.S., is now in Drexel Bldg., opp. in Room 223. (5) Chestnut St., bet. 5th & 4th Sts., **Old Custom H.** (1824.Gr.Rev.by Benj.H. Latrobe,architect of Nat.Capitol), now a nat. mon. **Statue of Rbt. Morris,** financial genius of the Rev., stands in front of bldg. (6) 320 Chestnut St., **Carpenters' Hall** (O.wks.1770-92) where 1st Continental Congress met in 1774. It is home of Carpenters' Co. of Phila. (est.1790.successor to Soc.of Carpenters). Brit., during Rev., occupied it as barracks, & the 1st Bank of the U.S. was set up here (1791). In hist. coll. are a Gilbert Stuart portrait of Washington & an early painting of Patrick

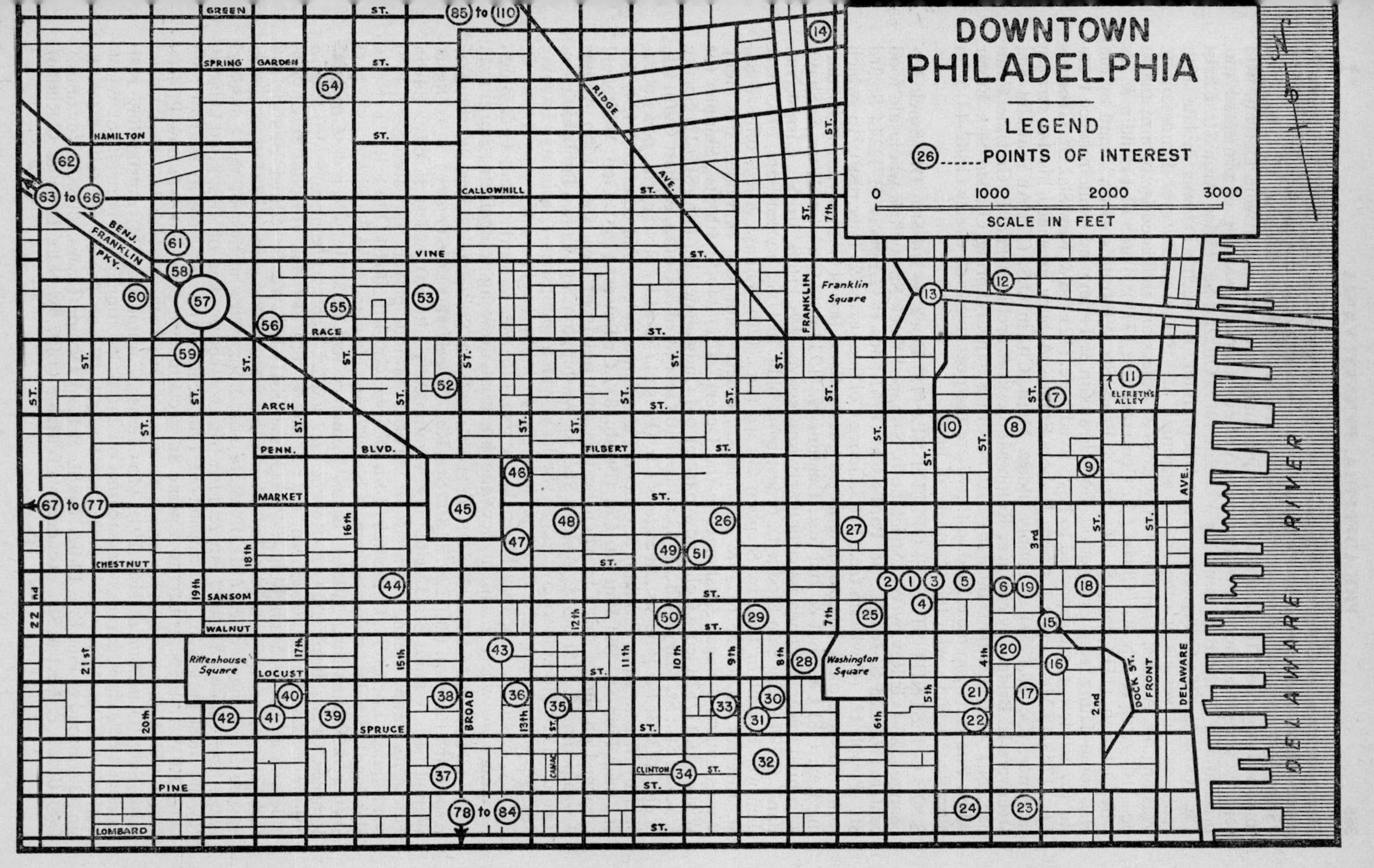
DOWNTOWN
PHILADELPHIA
LEGEND
26 ...... POINTS OF INTEREST
0 1000 2000 3000
SCALE IN FEET
DELAWARE RIVER
GREEN ST.
SPRING GARDEN ST.
HAMILTON ST.
CALLOWHILL ST.
VINE ST.
RACE ST.
ARCH ST.
PENN. BLVD.
FILBERT ST.
MARKET ST.
CHESTNUT ST.
SANSOM ST.
WALNUT ST.
LOCUST ST.
SPRUCE ST.
CLINTON ST.
PINE ST.
LOMBARD ST.
RIDGE AVE.
BENJ. FRANKLIN PKY.
FRANKLIN ST.
DELAWARE AVE.
FRONT ST.
DOCK ST.
2nd ST.
3rd ST.
4th ST.
5th ST.
6th ST.
7th ST.
8th ST.
9th ST.
10th ST.
11th ST.
12th ST.
13th ST.
BROAD ST.
15th ST.
16th ST.
17th ST.
18th ST.
19th ST.
20th ST.
21st ST.
22nd ST.
CAMAC
Franklin Square
Washington Square
Rittenhouse Square
ELFRETH'S ALLEY
85 to 110
63 to 66
67 to 77
78 to 84

Henry before the Congress. (7) 239 Arch St., **Betsy Ross H.** (c.1700), supposedly place where the Quaker seamstress, under Washington's direction, made the 1st "Stars & Stripes." (8) Arch St. bet. 4th & 3rd Sts., **Friends' Meeting H.** (1804), set in pleasant garden. In grounds are buried many notables, incl. Lydia Darrah, who sent Washington (then in Whitemarsh Valley) a timely warning of projected surprise attack by the Brit. (see Trip V below). (9) On 2nd St., (S) of Arch St., **Christ Ch.** (O.Episc.1754.Georg.-Col.rest.est.1695). Inter. is much as it was in late 18th cent.; sacred vessels & other relics among Ch.'s treasures. Pews of Penn family, Washington, Adams, Franklin, Betsy Ross & others are indicated by bronze markers. (10) Arch & 5th Sts., **Christ Ch. Cemetery** (est.1719); **Tomb of Franklin** & his wife Deborah. (11) Cherry St. bet. 2nd & Front Sts., **"Elfreth's Alley,"** lined by old Hs., some dating from Col. period. Both Franklin & Talleyrand, while refugee from the French terror, are supposed to have lived here. (12) 4th & New Sts., **St. George's Ch.** (1763-69.Meth.Episc.), where Bishop Francis Asbury preached his 1st sermon in Amer. (Oct.28,1771). Probably oldest Meth. Ch. in U.S. (13) At Franklin Sq., **Delaware R. Bridge** (by engineer Ralph Modjeski & architect Paul P. Cret), to Camden, N.J. Cost $37,000,000. (14) 530 N. 7th St. (near Spring Garden St.), **Edgar Allan Poe H.** (O.sm.fee.c.1830.rest.), where the poet lived in poverty (1842-44) with his wife, Virginia, who fell seriously ill here.

S. OF CHESTNUT ST. & E. OF 7TH ST.: (15) Dock & 3rd Sts., **Old Stock Exchange** (1834.Gr.Rev.by Wm.Strickland). S-shaped Dock St. is city's wholesale food center. (16) 225 S. 3rd St., **St. Paul's Ch.** (1761.adds.1832.Episc.). (17) 244 S. 3rd St., **Powel H.** (O.wks.sm.fee.c.1765.Georg.Col.fine exter.& inter.rest.), to which came Washington & other distinguished guests. Sam. Powel was mayor of city during Rev. (18) Chestnut & 2nd Sts., **Custom H.** (1933.mod.Class.by Ritter & Shay), with high tower. Rotunda is particularly impressive. (19) 116 S. 3rd St., **Girard Nat. Bank.** (1794-97.by Sam.Blodgett), oldest bank bldg. in U.S.; housed Bank of U.S. & then was bought in 1812 by Stephen Girard (see). (20) Willings Alley, off 3rd St., **St. Joseph's Ch.** (1733.1821 & 1838.adds.), oldest Cath. Ch. in Phila.; has Benj. West's canvas, "Hagar & Ishmael in the Desert." (21) 240 S. 4th Sts., **Shippen** (or Wistar) **H.** (1752.Georg.Col.), now part of old Cadwalader H., adj. (S). (22) Spruce & S. 4th Sts., **St. Mary's Ch.** (1763.adds.1810.Georg.Col.& Goth.), earliest Cath. Ch. in city. (23) 3rd & Pine Sts., **St Peter's Ch.** (Episc.1758-61.by Rbt.Smith); pews occupied by Washington, Franklin & others; Palladian window. Old cemetery. (24) 4th St., near Pine St., **Old Pine St. Ch.** (Presb.1837.Gr.Rev.est.1768). Geo. Whitefield preached on site of this Ch. when he was shut out from local Chs. John Adams worshiped here. (25) 6th & Walnut Sts., at Washington Sq., **Curtis Publishing Co.** (O.tours.1910.Mod.Georg.by Edgar Seiler), which publishes "Saturday Evening Post" & other widely circulated periodicals. In lobby is glass mosaic by Louis C. Tiffany, based on design by Maxfield Parrish. (26) 9th & Market Sts., **Fed. Bldg.,** covering spot where Franklin flew the kite that drew lightning from the clouds.

S. OF CHESTNUT ST. & W. OF 7TH ST.: (27) 7th St. below Market St., **Atwater Kent Mus.** (O.free). (28) 225 S. 8th St., **Rbt. Morris H.** (1786.Georg.). (29) 9th & Walnut Sts., **Walnut St. Theater** (1809.completely altered), oldest in city. Edwin Forrest, Edmund Kean, Edwin Booth & other famous players appeared here. (30) 8th St., near Locust St., **Cathedral of St. George** (Gr.Orthodox.1822.Gr.Rev.by John Haviland). Similar to **First Presb. Ch.** (1820.by Haviland), on S. side of Sq. (31) Spruce & Darien Sts., **Mikveh Israel Cemetery** (est.1783), in which is **Grave of Rebecca Gratz,** inspiration of Rebecca in Walter Scott's "Ivanhoe"; also **Haym Salomon Marker,** for Rev. hero. (32) Spruce & 8th Sts., **Pa. Hospital** (est.1751), oldest in city. Old Main Bldg. (1755.Class.adds.1929). West's "Christ Healing the Sick" is in office. On Pine St. side is **Wm. Penn Statue** (18th cent.). (33) 9th St. above Spruce St., **Bonaparte H.** (1812), where Jos. Bonaparte, brother of the Emperor, lived. (34) **Clinton St.,** bet. 9th & 11th Sts., is lined by fine old Hs. (Fed.) dating for the most part from 2nd quarter of 19th cent. (35) From Pine to Walnut Sts., bet. 12th & 13th Sts., is narrow **Camac St.,** reclaimed in early 1900's & now Phila.'s Greenwich Village, center for artists & writers. (36) Locust & 13th Sts., **Hqs. of Pa. Hist. Soc.** (O.exc.Sun.& Hols.1910.Mod.Georg.), founded 1824; outstanding coll. of documents, mss. & rare books. Mus., on 2nd fl. Paintings, incl. portraits of Washington by Gilbert Stuart & Rembrandt Peale & Wilson Peale's portrait of Franklin. (37) Broad & Pine Sts., **Phila. Textile Sch. of Design** (O.wks.1826.Gr.Rev.adds.). (38) Broad & Locust Sts., **Academy of Music** (1857.by N.Le Brun & C.Runge), center of city's cultural life for nearly a century. Here the greatest musical artists have performed, & orators, publicists & statesmen have held forth. Phila. Symphony Orchestra gives its concerts in Academy's great auditorium. (39) 1614 Latimer St., **Print Club** (O.wks.lectures.art exhibits), org. in 1916, probably 1st of kind in U.S. (40) 1726 Locust St., **Curtis Institute of Music.** (O.wks.), famous sch. est. by Mrs. Edw. W. Bok, in 1924. (41) 251 S. 18th St., on Rittenhouse Sq., **Phila. Art Alliance** (O.est.1915); exhibits leading contemporary artists & sponsors activities in various arts. Permanent coll. (42) On S. Rittenhouse Sq., **Eastern Bapt. Theological Seminary** (founded 1925). (43) 1318-1322 Walnut St., **Rosenbach Galleries** (O.wks.exc.Sat.in summer); objets d'art, paintings, prints, rare books & mss. (44) Sansom & 15th Sts., **Central-Penn. Nat. Bank** (1929.Mod.Class.by Davis,Dunlap & Barney.fine exter.& inter.).

CITY HALL AREA: (45) Broad & Market Sts., around Penn Sq., **City Hall** (Vict. Fr.Ren.by J.J.McArthur,Jr.) is a huge structure topped by 500′ **Tower** (O.wks.), which in turn is topped by 37′ **Statue of Wm. Penn** (1894.by Alex.M.Calder). Bldg., still tallest in the city, cost in excess of $24,000,000. Exter. sculptural detail has fascinating variety, & some city offices are lavishly ornate in Class. manner. Just N., at Filbert & Broad Sts., is **Masonic Temple** (1868. by J. H. Windrim. O. wks. free. except July-August. guides at certain hrs.), in which the rooms reproduce Moorish, Egyptian, Ionic, Norman & other architectural styles; hist. relics. (46) Juniper & Filbert Sts., **City Hall Annex** (1927.Ital.Ren.by Philip H.Johnston). (47) Market & 13th Sts., **Wanamaker Dept. Store** (Ital.Ren.by Dan.Burnham). In Grand Court is a great organ (hourly recitals). (48) 12th & Market Sts., **Phila. Saving Fund Soc. Bldg.** (1932.by Howe & Lescaze), a 38-story bldg. in modern functional style, 2nd in height to City Hall. **Observ.** (O.wks.sm.fee). (49) 16 S. 10th St., **Mercantile Lib.** (O.wks.est.1821). (50) 10th St., bet. Walnut & Sansom Sts., **Jefferson Medical College** (est.1825). (51) 10th & Chestnut, **Fed. Reserve Bank of Phila.** (mod.Class. by P.P.Cret.fine exter.& inter.). (52) Broad & Cherry Sts., **Pa. Academy of Fine Arts** (O.exc.Mon.1876.by Furness & Evans); incorporated in 1806; has fine arts sch. & permanent coll. (incl.works by Gilbert Stuart & the Peales) & presents annual exhibitions of contemporary art. (53) Broad St., (N) of Race St., **Hahnemann Hospital & Medical College** (1927-28.Goth.est.1848), houses oldest homeopathic educational institution in U.S. (54) Spring Garden St., bet. 16th & 17th Sts., **U.S. Mint** (O.wks. 1901); 1st mint est. in U.S. (1792). All coinage operations may be observed. (55) 1604 Summer St., near Franklin Pky., **D'Ascenzio Studio & Glass Works** (O.wks.), where stained-glass windows have been made for many Amer. Chs.

BENJ. FRANKLIN PKY. AREA (NW) from City Hall: (56) Race & 18th Sts., **Cathedral of SS. Peter & Paul** (c.1864.Ital.Ren.Cath.), seat of Phila. archdiocese. (57) Bet. 18th & 20th Sts., **Logan Sq. Fountain** (by A.S.Calder with Wilson,Eyre & McIlvaine,architects), representing 3 Rs. of Phila. (58) Facing Sq. at Vine St., **Shakespeare Mon.** (by same artist & architects). (59) 19th & Race Sts., **Academy of Natural Sciences** (O), had its inception in group meeting at a Market St. coffee house in 1812. Among exhibits in its many outstanding colls. are **Skeletons of Hadrosaurus** (duck-billed dinosaur), one found in N.J. c.1858 & another recently unearthed. At entrance is **Statue of Jos. Leidy** (1907.by Sam.Murray), eminent scientist once assoc. with Univ. of Pa. (60) 20th & Winter Sts., **Benj. Franklin Mem. & Franklin Institute** (O.exc.Mon.& certain Hols.sm.fee). The 1st show held by Institute was in Old Carpenter's Hall (see above) in 1824. Special halls are devoted to exhibits connected with various sciences & industries, incl. Franklin Printing Shop (reprod.). In 20th St. entrance is Robot Man who greets visitors. **Franklin Mem. Chamber** is reminiscent of Pantheon at Rome. **Fels Planetarium** (demonstration & lectures daily exc.Mon.1934.est.1824) is reached from Winter St. entrance. (61) Vine & 19th Sts., **Free Lib. of Phila.** (1927.Fr.Ren.); more than 2,000,000 books; colls. of Oriental mss., fine prints, Braille books; recently acquired W. M. Elkins' outstanding Americana Coll. (62) Pky. & 22nd St., **Rodin Mus.** (O.free. 1929.Fr.Ren.by P.P.Cret & J.Greber). Jules Mastbaum Coll. incl. sculptures, watercolors, paintings & drawings by Rodin. (63) Spring Garden St. & Pky., **Phila. Mus. of Art.** (O.free.1928.Mod.Class.by Zantzinger & Borie & H.Trumbauer), on hill overlooking Schuylkill R., at Fairmount Pk. In front of 25th St. is **Washington Mon.**, equestrian statue (by R.Siemering), & near-by, **Ericsson Fountain** (by Trumbauer, Borie & Zantzinger), comm. builder of "Monitor." The vast bldg. is approached by

99 steps leading to forecourt, from which a shorter flight rises to main entrance. Mus. (est.1876), one of finest in U.S., has colls. illustrating hist. of art for 2,000 yrs. & incl. some of world's greatest paintings. Amer. sec. ranges from Col. art to that of Marin, O'Keeffe & other contemporary artists. Especially notable are Geo. Grey Barnard coll. of medieval sculpture; Elkins colls. of French, Eng. & Amer. works; the John G. Johnson coll. incl. masterpieces of 1st rank; A. E. Gallatin coll. incl. Picasso & Leger; & Anna H. Wilstach colls. of European & Amer. paintings. Among architectural units are Romanes. Cloister (11th cent.), Fr. Goth. Chapel (14th cent.) & elements of early Ital. palaces, Chinese & Hindu temple inters. (64) Behind Mus., **Ital. Sea Horse Fountain** (1928.by Di Fausto); & (65) **Fairmount Pk. Aquarium** (O) in old waterworks bldgs. (Class.Rev.).

(66) **Fairmount Pk.** (3,845-a.area pic.shelters.facils.) extends (N) from Mus. of Art on both sides of Schuylkill R. & Wissahickon Cr. Along the charming driveways are many Mons. & Col. Hs. PTS. OF INT. W. SIDE OF SCHUYLKILL (S. to N.): **Solitude** (1785.int.inter.), erected by Wm. Penn's grandson, John Penn. **Phila Zoological Gardens** (O.sm.fee). Adm. offices are in Penrose Zoological Research Lab. (1903). On Lansdowne Dr. (L), **Letitia Street H.** (O.sm.fee.pre-1715.Georg.Col. rest.int.inter.), overlooking the R.; moved to pk. in 1883. Short distance further on Dr., **Sweetbrier Mansion** (O.exc.Sun.sm.fee.1797.Georg.Col.rest.), furnished in period. Beyond, on fork (R), **Cedar Grove Mansion** (O.sm.fee.1721.Georg.Col.), home of the Morris family; period furnishings. On fork (L) **Smith Mem. Arch**, with statues & busts by well-known sculptors, incl. Dan. C. French & Chas. Grafly. On N. Concourse, **Mem. Hall** (O.Vict.), built for Centennial Exposition of 1876; houses coll. of paintings & ceramics. Opp. Mem. Hall is **Welsh Mem. Fountain.** At end of Dr. is **Roman Cath. Centennial Fountain** (by Herman Kirn). On Lansdowne Dr., (S) of Belmont Ave., **Japanese Gardens & Pagoda.** Belmont Dr., (E) of Belmont Ave., **Horticultural Hall** (O), built for 1876 Centennial Exposition in style of Crystal Palace, London. E. SIDE OF SCHUYLKILL R. (N. to S.): At entrance to Pk., Dauphin & 33rd Sts., **Woodford Mansion** (O.exc.Sun.sm.fee.c.1742.adds.1756. Georg.Col.rest.), furnished with beautiful 18th cent. pieces. Near-by is **Strawberry Mansion** (O.sm.fee.1798.Gr.Rev.rest.), built by Fed. Judge Wm. Lewis, friend of Washington; furnished in period. (N) of York entrance to Pk., **Robin Hood Dell:** concerts (mid-June to mid-Aug.). On winding Rd. from entrance (S) to E. River Dr., near Reservoir, **Mt. Pleasant Mansion** (O.sm.fee.1761.Georg.Col.beautiful exter.& inter.). Benedict Arnold bought the H. in 1779 & lived here with his wife, Peggy Shippen, dispensing lavish hospitality he could ill afford. On same drive are: **Rockland Mansion** (1810), **Ormiston Mansion** (1798) & **Randolph Mansion** (1748), home of noted early Amer. surgeon, Dr. P. S. Physick. Below E. end of Girard Ave. Bridge, **Grant's Cabin** (from City Point, Va.), used during siege of Richmond. J. of Sedgley & E. River Drs., **Lincoln Mon.** (1871.by Randolph Rogers). On E. River Dr., (N) of Fairmount Ave. is **Boathouse Row** of Phila. rowing clubs whose members have won internat. contests. Opp. is **Statue of the Puritan** (by Saint-Gaudens).

WEST PHILADELPHIA: (67) 34th & Curie Ave., **Convention Hall** (1931.Ital.Ren. by Philip Johnson) seating 13,000; scene of large sports events, concerts, dog shows, political meetings. Near-by **Commercial Mus.** (O.free) has world-wide exhibits. (68) 34th St. below Spruce St., **Phila. Gen. Hospital** (org.1732). (69) Chestnut & 32nd St., **Drexel Institute of Technology** (est.1891) gives training in engineering, home economics, business administration; work-study plan. **Lib.** (O.wks.) contains coll. of rare mss. Mus. has objets d'art & hist. relics. In **Randall Hall** is art coll., incl. good representation of Fr. Barbizon & 19th cent. German schools. (70) Bet. 32nd & 38th Sts. & Walnut & Pine Sts., Campus of **Univ. of Pa.** (est.1740), with more than 180 bldgs. Franklin & a group of distinguished citizens, 10 of whom were signers of the Decl. of Ind., est. the Phila. Academy in early charity sch. bldgs. Due to alleged Tory sympathies of its trustees, the Academy's charter was taken away but revived in 1789, under present name. PTS. OF INT. ON CAMPUS: On Woodland Ave., **College Hall** (1871.Vict.Goth.by Thos.W.Richards), in which is **Mus. of Geology** (O.wks.). Spruce & 34th Sts., **Irvine Auditorium** (1926.by Trumbauer.Fr.Goth.). Walnut & 34th Sts., **Randal Morgan Lab. of Physics** (1873.Ital.Ren.) with Mus. of scientific relics. Bet. Spruce & Walnut Sts., the **Lib.** (1889.Goth.by Furness & Evans) with, in addition to great book coll., an outstanding coll. of Franklin material & many rare documents & volumes. **Stadium**, in Franklin Field, seats 73,000. Spruce &

33rd Sts., **Univ. Mus.** (O.wks.exc.Mon.1897.by Wilson Eyre.Romanes.); outstanding archaeological & ethnological colls. On Woodland Ave., at 36th St., **Wistar Institute of Anatomy & Biology,** named for Dr. Casper Wistar (as was also the flowering vine). Hamilton Walk & Woodland Ave., **Botanical Gardens,** with Greenhs. where rare plants are bred. In **Zoological Bldg.** (O.sm.fee) is Vivarium for lizards & other amphibians & herbarium. 40th & Spruce Sts., **Thos. H. Evans Institute** (1914.Fr. Goth.). **Mus.** (O.wks.).

(71) University & Woodland Aves., in **Woodland Cemetery** is **Woodlands** (1770. Georg.Col.), a beautiful H. facing Schuylkill R. (72) Kingsessing Ave. & 43rd St., **Phila. College of Pharmacy** (founded 1821), oldest in U.S. **Mus.** (O.Mon.-Fri.) has botanical coll., large lib. & reprod. of old pharmacy. (73) 54th St. & Eastwich Ave., **Bartram's Gardens** (O), started in 1728 by John Bartram, appointed Amer. Botanist to King George III. Two boxwoods planted by him are still flourishing. **Bartram H.** (O.c.1731), furnished in period. (74) 68th St. near Woodland Ave., **St. James Ch.** (founded 1760.Georg.Col.), early Swedish Ch. (75) 73rd St. & Woodland Ave., **Blue Bell Tavern,** where Washington was guest on his trips bet. Phila. & Mt. Vernon. (76) Gray's Ferry Ave. & Bainbridge St., **Naval Home** (est.1830), for retired & disabled officers. On grounds is **Figurehead** of the "Franklin," (1815), a portrait bust of Franklin. Assembly Hall is decorated with old weapons & ships' models. (77) Gray's Ferry & Washington Aves., **Schuylkill Arsenal** (1800). Powder Magazine dates from 1799 & Luddington Hall from 1800. In 1803 the Arsenal helped equip Lewis & Clark Expedition (see).

SOUTH PHILADELPHIA: (78) On Swanson St., below Christian St. near water front, **Gloria Dei Ch.** or "Old Swedes" Ch. (O.1700). The Swedes held 1st services on Tinicum I. & later in blockh. at Wicaco (1666-71). Much of inter. is orig. incl. Swedish baptismal font dating from 1550; stones in aisle mark graves of 3 early pastors. In cemetery is tombstone dating from 1708. (79) 711 Catherine St., **Graphic Sketch Club** (O.wks.free); conducts art courses. In Sanctuary (of early Ch. of the Evangelists) are religious art works & murals by well-known artists & fine altar piece. (80) 721 S. 10th St., **Arthur H.,** home of T. S. Arthur, a temperance crusader & author of "Ten Nights in a Barroom." (81) Broad & Carpenter Sts., **Lib. Co. of Phila.** (O.wks.1870.Gr.Rev.), started by Franklin & his Junto Club in 1731; said to be oldest circulating lib. in U.S. Large coll. incl. books owned by Penn, Washington, Jefferson & other famous persons; also Jas. Logan's Col. lib. Bldg. (Ridgeway Lib.) was gift of Dr. Jas. Rush. (82) S. end of Broad St., **Phila. Navy Yard** (O), est. in 1876 to succeed old Navy Yard at Federal St., where warships of War of 1812 were built. Present yard was outfitting & repair & training base during both World Wars; large dry docks; aircraft factory. **Dewey's Flagship,** the "Olympia," which fought at Manila in 1898, is docked here. (83) 19th St. & Pattison Ave., **John Morton Mem. Mus.** of Amer. Swedish Hist. Soc. Mus. (O) in Sesqui-Centennial (1926); material relating to Swedish civilization & culture. Morton, of Swedish extraction, was a Signer of Decl. of Ind. (84) On Delaware R. & Magazine Lane, **Ft. Mifflin** (O.appl.to U.S.Engineering Dept.,Custom H.1771), now a nat. mon. Ft. was captured by Brit. during the Rev.

N. PHILADELPHIA: (85) Corinthian & Girard Aves., **Girard College** (est.1848), endowed through $6,000,000 bequest from Stephen Girard (see), today said to be worth $87,000,000. College is for orphan boys from 6 to 16 yrs. old. Founder stipulated that there should be no sectarian teaching & clergymen were barred. Girard, born a Cath., seems to have been a deist, influenced by Voltaire & writers of the Encyclopedist group. **Founder's Hall** (Gr.Rev.by Thos.U.Walter). (86) Broad & Master Sts., **Moore Institute** (for women) of Art, Science & Industry, founded in 1844 as Sch. of Design for Women. (87) Montgomery Ave. & Broad St., **Temple Univ.** (Bapt.), founded in 1884 by Dr. Russell H. Conwell; incl. Theological Seminary (1893) & various professional schs. Newer bldgs. are for the most part Coll. Goth. **Conwell Hall** (1925) is center of Tower group. (88) Broad St., just below York St., **Dropsie College** (1911.Ital.Ren.by Tachau.est.1907); offers courses to graduate students in Hebrew & cognate learning. (89) Near-by is **Gratz College** (1909.Gr.Rev.est.1895), also for students of Hebrew subjects. (90) 17th St. & Montgomery Ave., **Wagner Free Institute of Science.** Mus. of nat. hist. & science.

GERMANTOWN: This suburb has the charm of age & spacious gardens around graceful early Hs. It was here that Washington met defeat at Brit. hands on Oct. 3,

1777. PTS. OF INT.: (91) 18th & Cortland St., **Stenton** (O.wks.free.1728.Georg. Col.fine exter.& inter.). Washington stopped here after Brandywine, & during Germantown Battle, Brit. Gen. Howe made it his hqs. (92) On Negley's Hill (L), (N) of Wayne J., **Loudoun** (post.Rev.Col.). (93) At Logan St. (R) & Germantown Ave., **Lower Burial Ground** (1708). (94) 5109 Germantown Ave., **Kunders H.,** on site of home of orig. settler, Thos. Kunders. (95) No. 5140, **Gilbert Stuart H.,** where artist painted portraits of Washington. (96) No. 5214, **Germantown Hist. Soc.** (O.wks.p.m. 1772.rest.), hist. lib. & mus.; portraits by Chas. W. Peale. (97) No. 5267, **Grumblethorpe** (1744.adds.1808), built by John Wistar. Here Sally Wistar wrote her gossipy diary of Brit. occupation days. (98) No. 5275-77, **Watson H.,** where Thos. Jefferson lived in 1793 during fever epidemic in Phila. (99) No. 5442, **Morris H.** (1772.fine exter.& inter.), to be made a nat. mem. Pres. Washington came here during yellow fever epidemic of 1793. (100) Greene St. & School Lane, **Germantown Academy** (est.1760), used as hospital by Brit. (101) Just (N) of High St. (R), **Green Tree Inn** (c.1748.Col.), now parsonage of First Ch. (Meth.). (102) Germantown Ave. & Walnut Lane, **Wyck** (oldest sec.1690), still in possession of descendants of orig. owners. (103) Just (N) of Herman St., **Germantown Mennonite Ch.** (1770), with orig. furnishings. (104) Germantown Ave. & Washington Lane, **Johnson H.** (1768.Col.); orig. furniture. During the battle, fighting took place in the garden. (105) Just (N) of Washington Lane, **Concord Schoolh.** (1775.Col.). **Upper Burial Ground** (1716). (106) Bet. Johnson & Cliveden Sts., **Chew Mansion** (O.appl.c.1761.Georg.Col.). Major André stayed here. The Brit. barricaded themselves in the H. during the battle, & Washington ordered it taken. Although door was destroyed by cannon fire, Amers. failed in the attack. Chew H. is a very fine example of Col. period, & inter. is beautiful. (107) Opp. Chew Mansion, **Upsala** (1798-1801), a beautiful H. in Fed. style, inside & out. (108) To the (N) is **Billmeyer H.** (1727). (109) Montana St., **First Ch. of the Brethren** (c.1770.much remod.) of the Dunker sect. Ch. was in middle of the battle, & Brit. soldiers used sheets of Christian Sauer's **Bible** as musket wadding. (110) N. Western & Stenton Aves., **Morris Arboretum** (O.free); used by Univ. of Pa. Within are rare shrubs & flowers; several early bldgs.

## TRIPS OUT OF PHILADELPHIA

### I. PHILADELPHIA to CAMDEN, N.J. (see), across Delaware R.

### II. PHILADELPHIA (NE) to MORRISVILLE. 30. US1

**16.** J. with Red Lion Rd.

SIDE TRIP: On Red Lion Rd. (W) 3.5m to J. with St.232; on St.232 (N) less than a mile to **Bryn Athyn.** On hill is **Bryn Athyn Cathedral** (O.April-Nov.1919.Goth.Cram & Ferguson), Swedenborgian hqs. in U.S. Lofty Tower is central unit of fine group of bldgs.

**30. MORRISVILLE,** sm. rural center on Del. R., opp. Trenton, N.J. (see), is named for Rbt. Morris, who raised funds to finance the Rev. Legion Ave. & Clymer St., **Summerseat** (c.1770.rest.), once owned by Morris & later by Geo. Clymer, a signer of both Decl. of Ind. & Constitution; now part of Rbt. Morris High Sch. Washington had hqs. here before Battle of Trenton (1776). In Morrisville is J. with St.32, which follows R. (NW) to **Easton** (see).

SIDE TRIP: On St.32 (NW) 17m to New Hope. 4.5m **Yardley** (sett.1682). 9.5m **Washington Crossing St. Pk.** (pic.camp.bathh.teah.trls.), ded. to Washington & the 2,400 men who crossed R. on Christmas night, 1776. (Bridge conn. with similar st. pk. area in N.J.) In pk. area is **Washington Crossing** village. Here also are **Ferry H.** (rest.mus.); **New Hope,** Washington's hqs.; **Bowman's Hill Observ. Tower** (125′), comm. Battle of Trenton; **St. Wild Flower Preserve** &, at 13.5m, **Thompson-Neely H.** (O.1702) & **Gristmill.** St.32 cont. along R. past **Roosevelt St. Pk.** bet. R. & **Delaware Division Canal** (1830's). Towpath & some locks are preserved; summer cottages. 17m **New Hope,** in ideal setting for artists' colony (est.1900); here is Bucks Cty. Playh. Along canal is **Union Paper Mill** (O.appl.est.18th cent.). In New Hope is J. with St.232, a direct route back to Philadelphia; also J. with St.202.

On St.202 (SW) 4m is **Lahaska.** Just outside the village is **Buckingham Friends Meetingh.** (O.1768.Georg.Col.), still in use. **Catalpa Inn** (c.1750), now an antique shop. **Buttonwood Inn** (1760), on York Rd., is still open for business.

On St.232 (S) c.7m to J. with St.413; (E) on St.413 a short distance is **Wrightstown;** a marker here shows where Thos. Penn's 3 picked men began the "Walking Purchase," 1737; supposedly, according to terms of agreement with Inds. (1686), the proprietors would receive as much land as walkers could cover in a day and a half. Edw. Marshall walked 65m in the time allowed. Thus the Inds. were tricked out of a great deal of land.

## III. PHILADELPHIA (NE) to MORRISVILLE. 28.5. US13

**10.5. RED LION INN** (1730.remod.). **11.** Village of **ANDALUSIA.** Just (S) is Rd. (R) to **Andalusia** (c.1794 & 1832), Biddle estate at one time owned by Nicholas Biddle, who supported Bank of the U.S. against Andrew Jackson. **19.** J. with Rd. (R) to **Bristol.** Wood & Market Sts., **Friends Meetingh.** (c.1714). Mill & Radcliffe Sts., **Delaware H.** (1765.adds.), orig. George II Inn. Signboard with King's picture was shot up by patriots. **23.5. TULLYTOWN** named for John Tully, who ran **Black Horse Tavern** (1794). **Christian Ch.** (1824).

SIDE TRIP: On good Rd. (R) to **Pennsbury Manor St. Pk.** (40 as.). In Pk. are reprods. (1939) of orig. **Manor H.** (c.1683) overlooking the Delaware, the brew H., office bldg. & stable. Manor H. is fitted with period furnishings. Gardens are landscaped in late 17th-cent. manner. In 1682 a tract on the Delaware was purchased as seat for the Proprietor, & Penn ordered the bldgs. to be erected. But he had little pleasure out of his new manor, since he was forced to return to England in 1684. He returned in 1699 but had to leave once more in 1701. Hospitality at Pennsbury was lavish, as is shown by records of the vast quantities of food consumed. Inds. were among the guests, & nearly a score of treaties were signed at the Manor.

**28.5. MORRISVILLE** (see Trip II above).

## IV. PHILADELPHIA (N) to DOYLESTOWN. 26.5. US611

US611 leads into Bucks Cty., known for its fertile countryside, Col. Hs. & artists' colony. **2.5. JENKINTOWN,** one of several attractive suburbs. In vic. on Jenkintown Rd. is **Orthodox Friends Meetingh.** (1836). A short distance away is **Abingdon Friends Meetingh.** (1786) which was taken over by the Hicksites in 1827 after split with Orthodox Friends. **Beaver College** (est.1853), one of oldest Pa. colleges for women, is on West Ave., about a half-mile from town. **13.5. WILLOW GROVE PK.** (recr.facils.pic.amusements). Near-by is **Fountain Hotel** (1717). J. with St.263.

SIDE TRIP: On St.263 (N) c.3m to **Hatboro** (sett.1701), whose name derives from early hat-making industry. On York Rd. are **Crooked Billet Tavern, Crooked Billet Mon.,** on site of encounter bet. Brit. & patriots; & **Union Lib.** (est.1755).

**16.5. HORSHAM FRIENDS MEETINGH.** (1803.meeting est.1716) & **Graveyard** (1719). At c.**19.** J. with County Line Rd., on which a short distance (L) is J. with Keith Valley Rd. to **Keith H.** (c.1718.fine exter.& inter.), built by Sir Wm. Keith, Lieut.-Gov. of the Colony, who entertained lavishly until deprived of his position by the Proprietors. Soon after (c.1721) Keith returned to England, fell on hard times & eventually died in a debtor's prison. **20. NESHAMINY.** J. with St.132.

SIDE TRIP: On St.132 (E) 3m to J. with St.263. Here is **John Fitch Mon.,** comm. man who built & operated (on Del. R.) the 1st steamboat bet. Phila. & Burlington, N.J.

**21.5.** J. with Rd. leading along cr. (R) 2m through summer resort reg. to **Neshaminy Ch.** (Presb.1743.adds.) in grove of oaks, centuries old. **26.5. DOYLESTOWN** (sett. 1735), fine old town. Pine & Ashland Sts., **Bucks Cty. Hist. Soc. Mus.** (O.wks.Sun. p.m.Ap.-Nov.1916.Georg.Col.), founded by Dr. Henry C. Mercer, archaeologist; extensive exhibit of articles used by Amers. prior to 1820. On E. Court St. are **Fonthill,** former home of Dr. Mercer, & **Pottery Works** (O.primitive Mexican.). Main & State Sts., is **Fountain H.** (part in 1748). On St.202 (W) 1m is **National Agric. College,** founded as Nat. Farm Sch. & Jr. College in 1848; beautiful campus. **27.5. CROSS KEYS INN** (1758). **28.5. WATER WHEEL INN** (1714.adds.), orig. water-wheel in cellar. (For other pts.of int.in vic., see Trip VI below).

## V. PHILADELPHIA (NW) to QUAKERTOWN. 41. US309

**12.5.** About a half-mile (N) from Phila. City line, **WHEEL PUMP INN** (L), patronized by Brit. during occupation. **15.** (R) **HOPE LODGE** (1723.fine Georg.Col.). **16. FT. WASHINGTON ST. PK.,** 360-a. extension of Fairmount Pk. around **Site of Ft. Washington.** In **Ft. Washington** village is **Clifton H.** (O), a Col. inn. Near-by, **Mill** (1717) worked for the Continental Army. J. with St.731.

SIDE TRIP: On St.731 (R) to **Van Rensselaer Property** covering place where Washington's staff conferred before Battle of Germantown. Further along is **Emlen H.,** Washington's Hqs., where (1777) he received warning through Lydia Darrah (see) that Brit. officers intended surprise attack. As a result, the Brit. failed.

Hy. cont. through Whitemarsh valley. **19. AMBLER,** off hy. (W). **Ambler H.** (c.1715). Ambler was a main supply depot for Continental Army at Valley Forge (see Trip VI below). **20.5. SPRING HOUSE,** a small village. **41. QUAKERTOWN,** founded by the Friends in 1715. This was hqs. of abortive uprising led by John Fries in 1798 to resist levy of taxes by Nat. Gov., intended to raise funds for threatened war with France. Fries was caught but eventually pardoned. US309 cont. (N) to Allentown (see).

## VI. PHILADELPHIA (NW) to POTTSTOWN. 39. US422.

Via: Norristown & Valley Forge Pk. St.23 is a direct route to Valley Forge, 24. **1.5. LAFAYETTE TENT MEM.** where Lafayette's command camped in May, 1778, & narrowly escaped capture by Brit. Along hy. are several early meetinghs. **19. NORRISTOWN** (RR. & bus conns. Accoms. & recr. facils.). Norristown (sett. c.1712), on Schuylkill R., is mfg. center & seat of St. Hospital (mental); hqs. of Valley Forge St. Pk. (see below). 18 E. Penn St., **Montgomery Cty. Hist. Soc.** (O.wks.); hist. colls. & exhibits, especially of Pa. material & Rev. & Civil War periods. J. with US202.

SIDE TRIPS: (A) US202 & St.83 (NW) c.8m to Valley Forge Pk. 1m **Bridgeport,** industrial center on Schuylkill R. J. with St.123, which runs (L) a half-mile to **Old Swede Ford,** where Washington's army of 11,000 crossed the R. 4m **King of Prussia Inn** (1709), whose signboard is said to be by Gilbert Stuart; orig. features in int. inter. J. with St.23, which trip follows (W). 7m J. with St.83, which becomes route into pk. a short distance (S). **Valley Forge Pk.** (pic.grove & tourist camp.observ.tower.info.from guards in pk.all sites clearly marked), more than 2,000 as. of Winter Encampment of Washington's Continental Army Dec. 19, 1777 to June 19, 1778. Here Baron Von Steuben began, in Feb., 1778, drilling & reorganizing the army that had endured with fortitude the winter's cold, starvation & sickness. When they arrived, Washington wrote that nearly 3,000 were almost without clothing or otherwise unfit for duty. The area has become a great hist. site dedicated to the human struggle for freedom. Tour usually begins at **Washington's Hqs.** (O.rest.c.1768). Near-by is **Stable,** now a mus. Special pts. of int. (W) of Gulph Rd. are: **New Jersey St. Mon.** in a dogwood grove; **Mt. Joy Observ. Tower** (500′); **Ft. Washington Nat. Mem. Arch** (by Paul Cret), **Gen. Wayne Statue** (by H.K.Bush-Brown) & **Baron Von Steuben Statue.** Across Gulph Rd. around the **Grand Parade** are: **Old Schoolh.** (c.1705), **Ft. Mordecai Moore** (rest.), **Washington Mem. Chapel** (O) & **Mus. of Valley Forge Hist. Soc.** (O). On the grounds are scattered **Soldier's Huts,** the **Pennsylvania Column** & Mass., Maine & other st. mons. In Upper Dublin near Valley Forge was the famous **Three Tuns Inn,** also used by Washington. It was destroyed by fire in March 1949.
(B) US202 (N & E) 24m to **Buckingham.** At 7.5m **Wm. Penn Inn** (1714.adds.), still in operation. Just beyond is **Gwynnedd Friends Meetingh.** (1823). Burial ground dates from the 18th cent. 14.5m **Chalfont,** where Tamenend, patron saint of N.Y.'s Tammany Hall, is said to be buried, although grave has never been found. The Del. Chief sold land to Wm. Penn, & Pa. patriotic groups took his name in Rev. days. 19.5m **Doylestown** (see Trip IV above). 24m **Buckingham** (sett.1702). **Gen. Greene Inn,** fine Col. bldg. with well-preserved dining room; hqs. of Gen. Nathanael Greene during Rev.

US422 cont. (NW) from Norristown. **21. JEFFERSONVILLE INN** (c.1800), a famous old hostelry. Here John Fries (see Trip V above) & his followers were tried. J. with St.363.

SIDE TRIPS: (A) On Trooper Rd. (R) 1.5m to J. with Germantown Pike. **Norriton Presb. Ch.** (1735) & graveyard.
(B) On St.363 (L) 1m to Egypt Rd. which leads (R) 1.5m to **Audubon.** In vic. is **Mill Grove Farm,** once estate of J.J. Audubon, ornithologist, most noted for his beautiful & faithful drawings & watercolors of Amer. birds. H. contains coll. of mounted birds & examples of Audubon's work. St.363 cont. (W) to **Port Kennedy** & **Valley Forge Pk.** (see above).

**26.5. COLLEGEVILLE,** seat of **Ursinus College** (est.c.1868.coed.), named for German scholar. J. with St.29, on which a few miles (N) is **Eastern St. Penitentiary.** Alex. Berkman, who was confined here for 14 yrs. for attempted killing of H.C. Frick, wrote "Prison Memoirs of an Anarchist", an exposé that brought about some reforms in prison system. **27.5. TRAPPE AUGUSTUS CH.** (Luth.1743.int. exter.-inter.), oldest Luth. ch. kept in its orig. state in the U.S. It was built by Dr. Heinrich Melchior Muhlenberg, who is buried in graveyard. Also buried here is his son, Peter, who ended a sermon in Rev. days in his ch. at Woodstock, Va. (see Va. US11) with the ringing cry: ". . . a time to preach & a time to fight . . ." Then he flung back his robes to show uniform of Cont. Army. US422 cont. (NW) to **POTTSTOWN** (see), at **39.**

## VII. PHILADELPHIA (W) to DOWNINGTOWN. 33. US30

**7.** J. with City Line Ave.

SIDE TRIP: On City Line Ave. (R) 1m, then about a half mile on Lancaster Rd. to Rd. leading (L) to **Barnes Foundation,** chartered educational institution in study of art; founded in 1922 by $10,000,000 gift of the late Albert C. Barnes. The **Gallery** (O. to enrolled students) has many examples of various countries & periods & of greatest modern French masters.

Just beyond J. (above) is **SEMINARY OF ST. CHARLES BORROMEO** (Cath.est. 1871.Ital.Ren.). **9.5. ARDMORE,** a large & wealthy suburb.

SIDE TRIP: On Anderson Ave. (R) a short distance is J. with Montgomery Ave., which leads (R) to **Old Merion Meetingh.** (c.1682), which still has peg on which Wm. Penn hung his hat. Near-by (L) is **Gen. Wayne Inn** (1704).

**10. HAVERFORD COLLEGE** (est.by Quakers,1833). **Founders Hall** (1833) is oldest bldg. & **Observatory** (1852), earliest in Pa. **11. BRYN MAWR,** home of **Bryn Mawr College** (est. by Quakers 1880), for women; non-sect. The Tudor-Goth. bldgs., vine-covered, are grouped on large attractive campus. **M. Carey Thomas Lib.** (1907). **13. VILLANOVA COLLEGE** (est.1842.Cath.). Among the many bldgs. on 160-a. campus, **Alumni Hall** is one of the oldest. In **Lib.** is coll. of incunabula & illum. mss. **15.5. WAYNE.** J. with St.252.

SIDE TRIP: On St.252 (L) 2.5$^m$ to good Rd. leading a half-mile to **St. David's Ch.** (1715. Georg.Col.Episc.), built by Welsh immigrants. Ch. was subject of Longfellow's "Old St. David's at Radnor". Tomb of Gen. "Mad" Anth. Wayne (see) in graveyard (1st burial at Erie, Pa.).

**21.** J. with Rd., on which (L) a half-mile is **Waynesborough** (1724.Georg.Col.), birthpl. of Gen. Wayne. **21.5. PAOLI,** named for Pasquale Paoli, who led revolt to achieve Corsican independence in mid-18th cent. J. with US202 (see Trip VI above).

SIDE TRIP: On US202 (SW) 5$^m$ to **Goshen Friends Meetingh.** (1855.est.1756). Cemetery. 9.5$^m$ **West Chester.** J. with US322 (see Trip IX).

**22.** Rd. here leads (L) 1$^m$ to **Malvern.** On Warren Ave. is **St. Joseph's-in-the-Hills,** Cath. Laymen's Retreat (est.1922). **Paoli Mem. Ground,** where (Sept.20,1777) Wayne's Command, after withdrawal from Brandywine Cr., was badly mauled by Brit. **33. DOWNINGTOWN,** a pleasant little town, consciously Col. in atmosphere; several small industries. J. with US322 (see Trip IX below).

## VIII. PHILADELPHIA (SW) to PA.-MD. LINE. 54. US1

**6. LANSDOWNE,** residential community. **7.5. CLIFTON HEIGHTS;** textile mills. In vic. are **Lower Swedish Cabin** (1650.log) & **Upper Swedish Cabin** (1729 or earlier. log & adds.). **9.5.** From here Saxer Ave. runs (R) 1$^m$ to Springfield Rd. About 1$^m$ (L) on this Rd. is **Springfield Meetingh.** (1851). This congregation, after lengthy debate, permitted a member, Benj. West, to go on with his art studies. **11. SWARTHMORE,** home of **Swarthmore College** (est.1864 by Religious Soc. of Friends, now coed. non-sect.). Campus, on picturesque Crum Cr., has many bldgs. in Tudor-Goth. style. **Bartol Lab.,** a Franklin Institute (see Phila.) bldg., housed atomic research during World War II, & Swarthmore is expanding research work in psychology. **Benj. West H.** (1724.rest.), where famous artist was born, is now residence of Dean of Women. **13.** J. with St.252.

SIDE TRIP: On St.252 (L) 1$^m$ to Mill Rd.; (R) on Mill Rd. 1.5$^m$, then (R) on Rose Valley Rd. to **Hedgerow Theater,** started in 1923 by Jasper Deeter, former member of N.Y.'s Provincetown Playh. Here repertory of classic & new plays is presented the yr. around by group of actors who also work around the place, build sets & make costumes.

**13.5. MEDIA. Providence Meetingh.** (1684). **21. CONCORDSVILLE.** J. with US322 (see Trip IX below). **Concord Friends Meetingh.** (1788). **25. CHADDS FORD,** on Brandywine Cr., where Washington's army was defeated (Sept.11,1777) by the Brit., who were then able to move on to Phila. **Percy Chandler H.** (1776.Col.). **Chadds Ford Inn** (1737), put up by John Chadd, who also operated ferry. J. with St.100.

SIDE TRIP: On St.100 (R) a short distance to **Chadd's H.,** John Chadd's home. In vic. are numerous sites of Rev. War battles. At 4.5$^m$, on Dilworth Lane, is **Birmingham Friends Meetingh.** (1736). Graveyard has Lafayette Pulaski Mon. Close by is **Octagonal Schoolh.** (1753), which changed hands several times during fighting.

**28. KENNETT MEETINGH.** (c.1737), where 1st encounter in battle occurred. **30.** J. with Rd. leading (R) to **Longwood Gardens** (see Wilmington III). **32. KENNETT SQ.,** birthpl. of Bayard Taylor, writer of travel books. **45. LINCOLN UNIV.,** Negro sch. founded in 1854 by Presb. Ch. & renamed for Pres. Lincoln in 1866; oldest Negro college in U.S. **54. PA.-MD. LINE** at **SYLMAR.**

## IX. PHILADELPHIA (SW) to CHESTER. 21. US13

Trip starts from Broad St. inters., by-passing central city area. **12. LANSDOWNE.** J. with US1 (see Trip VIII above). **13.5. DARBY** (sett. by Quakers 1682). Main St.

not far from 10th St., **Darby Friends Meetingh.** (1805). Near Main St., on Chester Pike, **Darby Volunteer Fire Co.** (est. 1775), fire-fighting apparatus. **Darby Lib. Co. Bldg.** (O. est.1743). **15.5. GLENOLDEN. Sharp & Dohme Biological Laboratory** (O. wks.to specially qualified visitors), very large producers of vaccines & antitoxins. **17.** J. with St.420 (Lincoln Ave.).

SIDE TRIP: On St.420 (L) a half-mile to **Morton H.** (log secs.1654 & 1698; stone sec. 1806), birthpl. of John Morton, who cast deciding vote for adoption of Decl. of Ind. Across Darby Cr. is **Essington,** site of 1st settlement on Pa. soil. Swedish officer, Johann Printz, came with group from St. Christina (see Wilmington, Del.) in 1643. Town was destroyed by explosion of powder in 1645, & then rebuilt, but today only old jail remains. Under auspices of Penn. Hist. Com., work of uncovering buried relics has begun (now in Amer.-Swedish Hist. Mus., Phila.).

**19. EDDYSTONE,** scene of disastrous explosion at Eddystone Ammunition Corp., Apr. 10, 1917. Cause of disaster was never discovered. A half-mile beyond Eddystone is **Baldwin Locomotive Works** (O. to men at all times;usually to women only when factory is not working). Company was founded in 1828 by Matthias Baldwin in Phila. & moved here about 1907. On grounds is **Hendrickson H.,** built during Swedish period.

**21. CHESTER** (RR. & bus conns. Good accoms. & recr. facils. Info.: C. of C. & Keystone Auto. Club), large industrial city on Delaware R., founded by the Swedes in 1644, taken by the Dutch in 1655, by the Brit. 1664, & retaken by the Dutch in 1673, but ceded by treaty to the Brit. less than a yr. later. The town became capital of Penn's govt. in 1681, though Penn himself did not arrive till 1682. Favorably located, it had early boom as a port but suffered from the Brit. blockade during Rev. "Mad" Anth. Wayne made the city his hqs. early in 1776, & Washington stopped over for the night after the Brandywine disaster. The Brit. occupied the city in Sept. 1777. After the Civil War, Chester developed rapidly both as a port & industrial center & during both World Wars expanded greatly. It has large shipbldg., steel, elec. & other mfg. plants.

PTS. OF INT.: (1) Market St., bet. 4th & 5th Sts., **Colonial Cth.** (O. wks.1724.Georg. Col.), still in use. Courtroom has been restored to orig. appearance. Hqs. of Del. Co. Hist. Soc. (2) Opp. Cth., **Washington H.** (1747.Georg.Col.) Inter. except 1st fl. is preserved as it was when the old inn (still functioning) had Washington for guest after Brandywine. (3) 3rd St., near Welsh St., **St. Paul Ch.** (Episc.1850.Goth.), now Union Gospel Mission. (4) Near-by, **St. Paul's Cemetery,** in which is **Grave of John Morton** (see above). (5) Market St. (S) of 3rd St., **Friends Meetingh.,** (1736. Georg.Col.), now a Gospel Tabernacle. (6) Front & Market Sts., **Steamboat Hotel Site** (1765); window was broken by Brit. shell. (7) Front & Penn Sts., **Penn Mem. Stone,** on site of landing of Penn (1682). Catercorner is marker on **Site of Essex H.,** built for Gov. Printz' daughter. It was occupied by Rbt. Wade in 1682, & Penn spent night here on his arrival. (7) Penn & 3rd Sts. **Black Bear Tavern** (1700). (8) Edgemont Ave., **Deshong Pk.,** in which is **Deshong Mem. Art Gallery** (O. Wed.Sat.Sun. & Hols.; 1914.Ital.Ren. by Frazer & Roberts); unusual ivory & Oriental colls. (9) (S) of Pk., on Edgemont Ave., **Ch. of St. Michael the Archangel** (Cath.1874.Roman Goth.). (10) Upland & Seminary Aves., **Crozer Theol. Seminary (Bapt.). Bucknell Library** (O.wks.) has fine coll. of Greek papyri, & **Lib. of Amer. Bapt. Hist. Assn.** (O. to qual. researchers). (11) Melrose Ave. & 14th St., **Penn. Military College** (est.1821 in Wilmington, Del. & removed here in 1868); one of the ranking military schs. (12) On Race St., in Upland, about a mile beyond town, **Caleb Pusey H.** (1683). Pusey had earliest mill in the province, in partnership with Penn.
Chester is at J. with US322. US13 cont. into Del. (see).

SIDE TRIP: US322 (W & N) to **Downingtown.** 11$^{m}$ **Concordville,** so named by its Quaker settlers (17th cent.) in the hope of peace & concord, a hope soon disappointed by Ind. forays. Many of its citizens today are employed in the mushroom industry. **Friends Meetingh.** (c.1788). 18.5$^{m}$ **West Chester,** an industrial town. Here "The Jeffersonian," a newspaper sympathetic to the Confed. cause, was suppressed by a mob & its plant destroyed during Civil War. On High St., are stone bldgs. of **W. Chester St. Teachers College. Lib.** has coll. of art, old documents & natural hist. J. with St.162.

On St.162 (L) 3.5$^{m}$ via **Copestown** (fine old bridge) to **Marshalltown, Marshall H.** (1773), built by Humphrey Marshall, stone mason, &, by avocation, botanist. He was cousin of the famous John Bartram.

25.5$^{m}$ **Dowingtown** (see Trip VII above).

# PITTSBURGH

## PITTSBURGH

RR. stas.: Liberty Ave. & Grant St., Pa. RR. Union Sta.; Water near Smithfield St. Bridge, B. & O. RR. Sta.; Bus Sta., 1010 Liberty Ave., for Greyhound & other lines. The Allegheny County Airport. Good accoms. Recr. facils. in Riverview, Highland, Schenley, North & South, & Frick Pks., Kennywood & West View (amusement) Pks. Symphony Orchestra. Civic Light Opera. Playhouse. Events at univs. & colleges. Glass Manufacturers' Show (Jan.); Allegheny Cty. Fair (Sept.); Exhibition "Painting in the U.S." at Carnegie Institute (Oct.); also folk festivals, flower shows & industrial exhibits. Info.: C. of C., 7th Ave. & Smithfield St.

Pittsburgh (sett.1758), the St.'s 2nd largest city, has its downtown dist., the Golden Triangle, at hist. Pittsburgh Point, where the Monongahela & Allegheny Rs. form the Ohio. From here Inds., fur traders, explorers, missionaries, soldiers & pioneers started down the great route of travel into the western wilderness. Today the Pt. is crowded with manufacturing plants that receive & ship, on the 3 great Rs., millions of tons of coal, steel, cork, glass & variety of other raw materials & manufactured goods. Pittsburgh is one of world's great steel cities, with 20 or more subsidiaries of Carnegie-Illinois within its metropolitan area, which spreads out widely along R. banks. It is also world's leading aluminum center & internationally known as home of Westinghouse Electric & H. J. Heinz companies. Smoke from the many factories mingles with river fog to make the characteristic atmosphere of Pittsburgh, lying heavy over the city most of the time, but in early morning, pleasantly veiling the streets & houses at different levels among the hills, giving them an unreal mirage-like appearance to anyone in valley below. At night its numerous furnaces flame into magnificence & are a special attraction from the air. In 1947, Pittsburgh began its billion-dollar plan, financed by Mellon foundations & other groups, to rehabilitate the 4-cty. community. A main project, for which $4,000,000 have been given, is development of Point Pk. & Penn-Lincoln Pky. at the famous "point." Program incls. Graduate Sch. of Health, to be built for Univ. of Pittsburgh by A. W. Mellon Educational & Charitable Trust & to function particularly as basic research institute in occupational & industrial hygiene. East of Golden Triangle, dominated by "Cathedral of Learning" of Univ. of Pittsburgh, are bldgs. of Carnegie Institute of Technology, Carnegie Institute & Lib., Mellon Institute, the Hist. Soc. & Schenley Pk., largest in city. The finer residential sec. is along Fifth Ave. & Beachwood Blvd. A large German pop. lives on the N. side while the S. side has a mixture of E. Europeans & Irish steelworkers. Negroes are crowded into the Hill District, which they share with neighborhood groups of many nationalities.

The only remaining pre-Rev. bldg., hist. old Blockh. on Penn Ave., near the "point," was built in 1754 by Va. troops, who surrendered it on demand of the Fr. In 1758 they evacuated & burned the Ft. before arrival of Brit. Ft. Pitt was then erected by Brit. & was named for Wm. Pitt, Prime Minister of Eng., who had been very friendly to the colonies. The Pontiac insurrection greatly retarded the settlement of the reg., but after the Rev. & the opening of the N.W. Terr., it became an important trading center. Seven out of nine representatives from Pittsburgh voted against the adoption of the Fed. Constitution believing that it favored business interests more than those of plain people & artisans for whom Jefferson was spokesman. The village around Ft. Pitt was incorporated as a borough in 1794 & after 1795, when Anthony Wayne subdued the Inds., the growth of the new city was assured. It was incorporated in 1816. In 1st quarter of 19th cent., its famous industries were founded & soon the "Steel City" emerged. Pittsburgh's great banking institutions & clearing houses make it a financial center of U.S., while the tremendous tonnage of its river ports is more than treble that of Suez & Panama canals combined.

PTS. OF INT. GOLDEN TRIANGLE: The Golden Triangle (downtown) extends (E) from fork of the Allegheny (N) & Monongahela (S). (1) **Pittsburgh Pt.,** from which the pioneers started (W) on the Ohio. On either side a bridge spans influent Rs. (2) 25 Penn Ave., **Ft. Pitt Blockh.** (1764.O.wks.), built by Col. Henry Bouquet, Ft. Pitt commandant. Bouquet also built Ft. Presque Isle at Erie (see US6) & led expedition that defeated Pontiac's Confed. at Battle of Bushy Run, in 1763 (see Pittsburgh Trip I). (3) 425 Penn Ave., **Schoenberger H.** (pre-1830.Gr.Rev.), now occupied by the Pittsburgh Club; early paintings & period furnishings. (4) 320 6th Ave., **First Presb. Ch.** (1905.Goth.by T.Chandler.est.1784). (5) 6th Ave. at Wood

St., **Trinity Episc. Ch.** (1871-72.Goth.by Upjohn & Lloyd); lofty tower & spire. In Cemetery are graves of early pioneers & soldiers of Ft. Pitt garrison & of Chief Red Pole (d.1796). (6) 620 Smithfield St., **German Evangelical Ch.** (1927.by Henry Hornbostel.est.1782. (7) Grant St. & 7th Ave. (NW). **Gulf Refining Co. Bldg.** (tower O.wks.1932.by Trowbridge, Livingstone & E.P.Mellon), highest structure in city. (8) Grant St. & 7th Ave. (SW), **Koppers Bldg.** (Mod.by Anderson, Probst & White); handsome lobby. (9) Liberty Ave. & Grant St., **Union Sta. Plaza** (1902.by D.H. Burnham.wait.rm.Ital.Ren.). (10) 717 Grant St., **Fed. Reserve Bank** (1931.Neo-Class.by Walker & Weeks). Murals in lobby by Curtis Shaw. (11) 5th Ave. & Smithfield St., in Kaufmann's Dept. Store, **Murals** by Boardman Robinson (1930), awarded gold medal by Architectural League of N.Y. (12) Grant & Diamond Sts., **Allegheny County Cth. & Jail** (1888.by H.H.Richardson), example of architect's Romanesque style, with turreted tower & massive arches. (13) 5th Ave. & Grant St., **Frick Bldg.** (1904.Mod.Class.by Burnham & Co.); fine window in lobby by John La Farge. This 20-story bldg. was put up by H.C. Frick (see), assoc. of Andrew Carnegie who was commonly blamed for violence during Homestead steel strike in 1892 (see Pittsburgh Trip II). (14) 330 Grant St., **Grant Bldg.** (Mod.by H. Hornbostel.observ.deck. O.sm.fee), home of KDKA, which claims to be pioneer broadcasting station. Bldg. is 40 stories high & has 5 stories below ground. (15) Bluff St. near Colbert St., **Duquesne Univ.** (coed.nonsect.est.1878 by Congregation of the Holy Ghost), on fine campus overlooking Pittsburgh Pt.; confers degrees in liberal arts & sciences & various professional branches & music; affiliate of Cath. Univ. of Amer.

PTS. OF INT. (E) & (NE) OF GOLDEN TRIANGLE: (16) Bigelow Blvd. & 5th Ave., **Univ. of Pittsburgh,** which developed from sch. founded in 1787 near the ft. & chartered as Western Univ. of Pa. in 1819. It has become one of the largest municipal univs. & incl. among its 17 schs. the colleges of pharmacy, medicine & dentistry which had been independently est. Main bldg., on impressive quadrangle, is **Cathedral of Learning** (by C.Z.Klauder), a 42-story shaft of Bedford stone with Goth. detail. The beautiful vaulted Commons Rm. is 4 stories high. The lower floors have rms. dedicated to Pittsburgh's nationality groups & others comm. hist. of city & state. Near cathedral is **Heinz Mem. Chapel** (Goth. by Klauder). The greater campus is extensive & nicely landscaped. **Pitt's Stadium,** seating 70,000. (17) Forbes St. & Bigelow Blvd., **Stephen Collins Foster Mem. Bldg.** (O.wks.1937.Goth.by C.Z. Klauder) comm. famous composer of "My Old Kentucky Home," who was born in Lawrenceville, now part of Pittsburgh, July 4, 1826. Murals in auditorium are descriptive of Foster's songs. **Foster Hall Coll.** (O.wks.). (18) Bigelow Blvd. & O'Hara St., **Soldiers & Sailors Mem. Hall** (O.by H.Hornbostel), comm. Civil War veterans. Lib. has coll. of war relics. (19) Bigelow & Parkman Blvds., **Hist. Soc. of Western Pa.** (O.wks.), colls. of firearms, furnishings, pottery. (20) 4400 Fifth Ave., **Mellon Institute** (O.appl.1937.Neo-class. by Johnson & Cocken), devoted to industrial research. Bldg. is a gift of Andrew W. Mellon, former Secy. of Treas., born in Pittsburgh, & Rich. B. Mellon, his brother. Funds for particular researches in some 60 fields are provided by sponsors who become owners of the processes they finance. Institute was orig. part of Univ. of Pittsburgh. (21) Entrance on Forbes St., **Schenley Pk.** (422 as.recr.facils.), cut by 5th Ave.; **Geo. Westinghouse Mem.** (by D.C.French, sculptor, & H.Hornbostel, architect) comm. inventor of the air-brake; **Phipps Conservatory** (NW), gift of H.C. Phipps, partner of Carnegie, is largest in city & has many exotic rarities. (22) Near Schenley Pk. & Boundary St., **Carnegie Institute of Technology,** on extensive campus, est. & endowed by Andrew Carnegie in 1905. Institute offers courses in fine arts, engineering, & other professional fields. College of Fine Arts is noted for its drama dept. & experimental theatre; **Margaret Morrison Carnegie College** (women) & **Carnegie Lib. Sch.** are incl. in Institute. (23) Forbes & Bellfield Sts., **Carnegie Institute & Lib.** (1895.Ren.by Longfellow, Alden & Harlow). **Dept. of Fine Arts & Mus.** (1907.by Alden & Harlow). At Forbes St. entrances are sculptures by J. Massey Rhind. Beyond E. Forbes St. entrance are **Great Hall** (mural of J.W.Alexander); **Hall of Sculpture,** with frieze copied from the Parthenon; **Art Galleries** on 2nd & 3rd floors; **Hall of Architecture,** which has reprods. in miniature of famous architectural mons. & other colls.; & **Mus.,** with exhibits in ethnology, natural science & useful arts. In galleries are extensive art colls., & here also is held (Oct.) the annual exhibition "Painting in the U.S." (since 1940). W. entrance, **Music Hall** (concerts wkly.,exc.summer). **Carnegie** (city) **Lib.** is in main bldg. (24) 40th & Butler Sts., **Allegheny Arsenal** (orig.bldgs.1813-15 by

Benj.Latrobe.Goth.Rev.), used during all major wars. On Stanton Hts. Golf Course, **Croghan H.** (O.1835.Gr.Rev.by Jefferson & Latrobe.adds.), built for Wm. Croghan, Jr., son of Amer. patriot Gen. Wm. Croghan & Mary Clark, sister of Geo. R. Clark (see).

PTS. OF INT. SOUTH PITTSBURGH: (25) Blvd. of the Allies & Horace St., **Liberty Bridge,** across the Monongahela & conn. with Liberty Tunnels that pierce Mt. Washington. (26) 2709 E. Carson St., **Jones & Laughlin Steel Corp. Plant** (O. appl.), along R. opp. 2nd Ave. plant.

PTS. OF INT. NORTH PITTSBURGH: 1062 Progress St., **H. J. Heinz Co. Plant,** where "57 Varieties" are put out. **Sharpsburg H.** was home of orig. Henry J. Heinz, where he started bottling horseradish. Auditorium is devoted to social uses of employees. **Sarah Heinz H.,** workers' community center. (28) Lincoln & Allegheny Aves., **Logan Community H.** (c.1843.Gr.Rev.adds.). (29) Perrysville Ave. & Watson Blvd., in **Riverview Pk.** (315 as.) is **Allegheny Observatory** (O.Ap.-Nov.1912), where lectures & cinemas illustrate movements of the stars. Here S. P. Langley, 1891, tried out his 1st flying machine (see Hampton, Virginia). (30) 3 Holt St., **Brashear Mus.** (O.sm.fee), former home of John A. Brashear, a famous maker of astronomical lenses who is supposed to have made 1st telescope. (31) Federal & W. Ohio Sts., **Buhl Planetarium & Institute of Popular Science;** illustrated lectures on astronomical events (sm.fee); exhibits (O.free). (32) Some 12$^{m}$ (S) from Pittsburgh in **South Pk.** are **Wild Life Mus.** (O.summer) of native animals & birds & **Old Stone Manse** (O. summer.guides.1772).

## TRIPS OUT OF PITTSBURGH

### I. PITTSBURGH (SE) to LIGONIER. 48. US30

US30 runs through the steel country of the Monongahela Valley. **7.5. WILKINSBURG** (sett. 1780. RR. & bus conns. accoms. & recr. facils. info. & touring bureau at Penn Lincoln Hotel). This large attractive residential suburb developed as center of many 19th-cent. manorial estates. J. with US22 (see). **11.5. EAST PITTSBURGH,** industrialized town in hilly Turtle Cr. valley. **Westinghouse Electric & Mfg. Co.** (O. tours). Hy. crosses Turtle Cr. **13.5. EAST MCKEESPORT,** home of many steel workers. Rd. leads (S) to McKeesport (see Trip II below). **21. IRWIN,** a miners' village. **Scull H.** (1794) was home of John Scull, who had a printing press brought over the Alleghenies in 1786 & founded the Pittsburgh "Gazette." J. with **Pa. Turnpike** (see US30). **25.** J. with Rd. leading (N) 1$^{m}$ to **Jeannette,** glass-making center, near which, (NW) off St.180, is **Bushy Run Battlefield St. Hist. Pk.** (pic. mus.). Here, in 1763, Col. Henry Bouquet defeated the Inds. of Pontiac's Conspiracy (see) & then went on to relieve Ft. Pitt. **Site of Flourbag Ft.,** on rim of valley, where wounded Brit. lay behind the flour intended for the besieged ft. **Lenni-Lenape Longh.** (reprod.). **30. GREENSBURG** (sett. 1785), important industrial center; named for Rev. Gen. Nath. Greene. In St. Clair Pk. is **St. Clair Mon.** marking graves of Gen. Arthur St. Clair & his wife. During Fr. & Ind. Wars, the Eng. nobleman, St. Clair, took part at Louisburg & Quebec but, in the Rev., took sides with the Patriots. He became Gov. of the NW. Terr. (see) &, believing in gov. control, opposed Ohio's statehood, but unsuccessfully. In Greensburg is J. with US119, which extends (S) through coal country to W. Va. Line (see US40). US30 cont. through wooded reg. broken by rich farmlands. **48. LIGONIER,** trade center for rural & summer resort area. Near here Col. Bouquet built Ft. Ligonier, in 1758, near an Ind. village.

### II. PITTSBURGH (S) to J. with St.88. c.35. St.837.

This hy., winding with the Monongahela R., is one of several routes running (S) to J. with main E-W hys. (St.88 cont. the river road to J. with US40). The area is crowded with metal-working, glass, steel & other industrial plants. **7.5. HOMESTEAD,** a smog-darkened town around busy steel plants. Here occurred the bitterly contested strike at the Homestead Works of Andrew Carnegie's steel corp. in 1892. H. C. Frick, plant mgr., had Pinkerton men brought in on river barges, &, on July 5, an armed battle between these men & strikers resulted in death of 10 men & wounding of many more. On July 10, the gov. sent members of the Pa. Nat. Guard, under whose protection plant was reopened & strike broken. It was because of this conflict that Alex. Berkman, then 19, came from N.Y. & made his terrorist attempt on Frick's life (see Phila. VI). **Carnegie-Ill. Steel Co. Plant,** in Munhall, one of largest. **11.5. DUQUESNE,** another fairly large steel town, with large foreign-born & Negro pop. Name is that of the Fr. ft. later to be named Ft. Pitt. Across the R. is **McKeesport,** (sett.1794), a large & heavily industrialized town in midst of coal & natural gas reg. Along the R. are huge stainless steel, tin plate & other mills. **19. CLAIRTON** is also home of a great Carnegie-Ill. steel plant. **21. WEST ELIZABETH. 21.5.** J. with St.51, which makes a direct return route (NW) to Pittsburgh & cont. (S) from the J. to **Uniontown** (see US40). St.837 winds (S) with the R. through **MONONGAHELA,** then (E) to **DONORA,** both important industrial towns. Hy. turns directly (W) again from Donora. **35.** J. with St.88, which cont. (S) as the river road to the W. Va. Line (see US40). (From the J., St.88 is another alternate return route to Pittsburgh.)

**III. PITTSBURG (SW) to WASHINGTON. 28. St.519 & US19.**

Both St.519 & US19 are routes through coal & steel country, uniting near J. with US40 (see). **7. CARNEGIE,** founded in 1894 & named for Andrew Carnegie, who later gave town the handsome **Free Lib.,** the community center. **18. MORGANZA,** a pleasant village named for farm of Col. Geo. Morgan, Ind. agent during Rev. & land speculator. While agent at Ft. Pitt, Morgan org. Indiana Co. to develop lands ceded by Inds., but Va. successfully contested this action. Later (1790's) he became interested in exploitation of Sp. territory in the SW. but gave up scheme & retired to his property here. It is believed he informed Pres. Jefferson of Burr's plan for a SW. empire. **Pa. Training Sch.,** reformatory for boys & girls conducted on cottage plan, somewhat similar to Children's Village in N. Y. **20. CANONSBURG** (sett. 1773), industrial town on Chartier's Cr. At Central & E. College Sts. is **Log Cabin Academy** (1780), said to be 1st Latin school (W) of Alleghenies. College founded here in 1802 became part of Washington & Jefferson College, in Washington (see US40). **Roberts H.** (part in 1804). Here St.519 turns (E). At **22.** is J. with US19 over which trip cont. (SW). **28. WASHINGTON** (see US40). US19 cont. to W. Va. Line.

**IV. PITTSBURGH (NW) to PA.-OHIO LINE** (3$^{m}$ from E. Liverpool, O.). **43. St.51, St.930 & St.68.**

Trip follows Ohio R. along the (W) & then (N) shore (paralleled roughly by RRs.). **4. MCKEES ROCKS,** fairly large industrial suburb near site of Ohio Land Co. post; named for 1st settler, Alex. McKee (1743). **11.5. CORAOPOLIS** (sett. c.1760). At **c.13** is J. with St.930, which trip follows straight ahead along the R. (St.51 becomes nearly parallel inland route to Rochester.) **21. ALIQUIPPA,** steel town of some size. **Jones & Laughlin Steel Co. Plant** is largest of several mills. **27. MONACA** (sett.1813). In 1832 the site was bought by members of Harmony Society who had split off from Rappite colony at Ambridge (see Trip V below). Village has glass, steel & other plants. J. with St.51 & St.68, which leads (E) across Ohio R. to **ROCHESTER** (see Trip V below). Trip turns (W) from Rochester on St.68 across Beaver R. to **BRIDGEWATER,** at **28.5.,** & then cont. (W) along N. shore of Ohio R. **29.6. BEAVER,** attractive town on low bluff; home town of Matthew S. Quay, Repub. party boss in late 19th cent. & U.S. Senator (1887-1904). Quay was influential in nat. & st. politics for many yrs., & party machine under his leadership was accused of considerable corruption. **34.5. MONTGOMERY I. DAM,** which forms L. 18$^{m}$ long. **39.5. MIDLAND,** industrial center with large foreign-born pop. working in steel mills, foundries, shipyards & RR. shops. **43. PA.-OHIO LINE.**

**V. PITTSBURGH (NW) to NEW CASTLE. 54. St.88 & St.18.**

This trip parallels Ohio R.'s E. bank to Rochester & there crosses to W. side of Beaver R. on St.18. St.88 is a pleasant route through small attractive riverside suburbs. **14.5. EDGEWORTH.** On Beaver Rd. is **Birthpl. of Ethelbert Nevin,** song writer who composed "The Rosary". **18.5. AMBRIDGE,** formerly called Economy Town, has large structural steel plant & other industries. This was 3rd home of the religious communal Harmony Society, est. at Harmony, Pa. (see below) in 1805 by Geo. Rapp, who came from Württenberg, Germany. The Rappites, or Harmonists, moved from this profitable colony to the banks of the Wabash R., where they est. New Harmony, Ind. (see). Then in 1825 they returned to Pa. & sett. permanently on 25,000 as. at Economy. A few yrs. later (1832), Bernard Müller who opposed doctrine of celibacy, with some 250 seceding members, withdrew to Monaca (see above). After Rapp's death in 1847, the colony declined. In 1906 its property was taken over by the St. Among Harmony bldgs. still standing (guide on appl.to Harmony Soc.Hist.Assoc.) are several **Hs.** (N.O.); the **Great H.,** Rapp's home;

**Music Hall, Wine Cellar & Carpenter Shop. 28. ROCHESTER** (sett.1799), residential community on site of Logan Town, which was home of the great Mingo chief, Jas. Logan (see). J. with St.51, which cont. (NW) to Ohio Line; with St.18, on which trip cont. (N); & with St.68, which leads (SW) to Ohio Line (see Trip IV above).

SIDE TRIP: On St.68 (NE) 14m to **Harmony.** At 13m **Zelienople** (sett.1802), resort on Connoquenessing Cr. Baroñ Dettmar Basse plotted the site in 1802 & named it for his daughter Zelie. Later he sold thousands of as. to the Harmony Society, who founded **Harmony,** at 14m. Several colony Hs. are standing, & near-by (SE) is **Harmony Graveyard,** where more than 100 Rappites are buried in unmarked graves. US19 (see Trip VI below) unites with St.68 bet. the 2 villages.

**30.5. NEW BRIGHTON** (sett.1789), a clay-products & steel center. **Merrick Free Art Gallery** (O.wks.) has early paintings & nat. hist. coll. Here trip crosses Beaver R. **32.5. BEAVER FALLS,** (good accoms.), plotted in 1806; trade & industrial center. On College Hill is **Geneva College,** founded in 1872 by Presb. Ch.; coed. lib. arts. college. **54. NEW CASTLE** (RR.& bus.conns.Good accoms.Info.:C. of C. & Motor Club). This important industrial center is at meeting of the Beaver, Mahoning & Shenango Rs., in area rich in coal, clay, limestone & sandstone. In S. sec of town is Polish community. On Court St., **Lawrence County Cth.** (1852.Gr.Rev.). At 305 N. Jefferson St., **White Homestead** (1840), once a sta. on Underground Railroad. J. with US422 & US224, alt. routes to Ohio Line. St.18 cont. (N) to J. with US6 (see) near L. Erie.

SIDE TRIP: On US422 (W) 13m to **Pa.-Ohio Line.** On the way hy. passes **Ten-Sided H.** (O.1863) at 11m, & **New Bedford** at c.11.5m. On St.278 (NE) c.3m from New Bedford is **Twelve-Sided H.** (1860).

**VI. PITTSBURGH (N) to MERCER. 59. US19.**

US19, beyond the industrial area, crosses long-sett. country where there are many Col. & frontier landmarks. **8.5. PERRYSVILLE** (sett.1794). Near edge of Pittsburgh area, hy. crosses sweep of low hills. **16.5. WARRENDALE,** in oil reg., though many wells are not now in operation. **27.5. ZELIENOPLE. 28.5. HARMONY,** at J. with St.68 (see Trip V above).

SIDE TRIP: On St.68 (E) 4.5m to **Evans City** (sett.1796), in setting of rolling hills. 7m **Washington Mon.** comm. spot where young Maj. Geo. Washington narrowly escaped being killed by a suspicious Ind., in Dec. 1753. Washington, with the frontiersman C. Gist, was returning from trip into Ohio wilderness, where he had tried to persuade Fr. to evacuate their frontier posts. 18m **Butler** (sett.1803.accoms.cottages. RR.& bus conns.), on rolling land once property of Rbt. Morris, banker. City is named for Rich. Butler, an officer in Rev. who was killed later during St. Clair's expedition against Inds. in 1791. Among important industries are Amer. Bantam Car Co., Amer. Rolling Mill Co. & Pullman-Standard Car Mfg. Co. Glass, cement & oil are other leading products. J. with US422, which leads (W) to J. with US19, the main trip.

**38.5. PORTERSVILLE.** J. with US422, which runs (W) 14m to **New Castle** (see Trip V above) & (E) 15m to **Butler. 45.5. HARLANSBURG** (sett.1797). J. with St.108, on which (W) a short distance is **Jordan St. Game Farm.**

SIDE TRIP: On St.108 (E) 7m to **Slippery Rock,** seat of **St. Teachers College.** At J. with St.68, which leads (N) c.7m through Wolf Cr. valley to **Grove City** (sett.1798). **Grove City College** (est. 1876) confers degrees in lib. arts & sciences. Newer bldgs. are Coll. Goth. in style, on upper campus.

US19 cont. (N) from Harlansburg. **59. MERCER** (sett.1803), on Neshannock Cr., is a quiet borough named for Rev. Gen. Hugh Mercer, who was killed in Battle of Princeton. J. with St.62.

SIDE TRIP: On St.62 (W) 15m to **Sharon** on Pa.-Ohio Line (NE. of Youngstown, O.), a prosperous steel town of the Shenango Valley; has large **Westinghouse Eelectric & Mfg. Co. Plant.**

**VII. PITTSBURGH (NE) to KITTANNING. 46. St.28.**

Route follows Allegheny R. through busy industrial area. **6. ETNA,** whose appropriate name is frequently noted, is small borough around furnaces & steel mills. **SHARPSBURG, ASPINWALL, & HARMARVILLE** are part of this chain of industrial towns. **13. HARMARVILLE** is a mining town with residential **Oakmont** across the R. **17. SPRINGDALE** is largely residential. Hy. follows bend in R. (N). At **19.** is bridge to **New Kensington,** aluminum-producing center since 1892. **Aluminum Co. of Amer. Plant** (O). Almost surrounded by the town is **Arnold,** glass-making center. **22. CREIGHTON,** another glass center. **23. BRACKENRIDGE** spreads out along the R., with many steel, coke & glass plants. Just beyond **NATRONA HTS.,** residential, & **NATRONA,** with large Polish community, route enters farm country of which **FREEPORT,** at **32.,** is a trade center. Hy. swings away from R. for a few miles through orchards & farmlands, then curves back to **KITTANNING** (sett.1796) at **46.** Town is leading brick center; on site of Ind. village of the same name which was destroyed by Col. John Armstrong during Fr. & Ind. wars (1756). **Site of Chief Jacobs H.** is now covered by the Alexander Hotel. **Armstrong County Cth.** (1860, late Gr. Rev.). Kittanning is at J. with US422 & St.66.

SIDE TRIP: On St.66 (S) 3.5m to **Ford City,** named for John B. Ford who est. the now important plate-glass industry here in 1887. **Pittsburgh Plate Glass Co. Plant** (O. on appl.) is probably largest in the world. Farther (S) off St.66 is **Crooked Cr. Dam.**

## US 13—DELAWARE

**DEL.-PA. LINE** (3m from Chester, Pa.) **(S) to DELMAR. 105. US13**

Via: Claymont, (Arden), Wilmington, Smyrna, Dover, Harrington, Seaford & Laurel. RRs. parallel route & main bus lines traverse it. Accoms.: All types; few tourist or trlr. camps.

US13, most direct route to Norfolk, Va. & therefore heavily traveled, runs along Delaware R. to Wilmington & then (S) through industrial suburban sec. & farming reg. In lower Del., it traverses flat, sandy, pine-wooded & truck raising sec. Along its path are some noted hist. bldgs. & int. old towns.

### Sec. 1: DEL.-PA. LINE to DOVER. 53.5.

For pts. of int. & towns on or near US13 bet. **DEL.-PA. LINE, 0., & WILMINGTON, 8.,** & bet. Wilmington & **ST. GEORGES, 23.5.,** see Wilmington Trips I & VI. US13 now crosses **Chesapeake & Del. Canal,** which to certain extent follows old Chesapeake & Del. Canal, completed in early 19th cent., largely with Irish immigrant labor, but since deepened to 27′ & now important link in Atlantic Intercoastal Waterway. **28. MACDONOUGH,** birthpl. of Commodore Thos. Macdonough, who defeated Brit. fleet at Plattsburg, L. Champlain, Sept. 1814. **Macdonough H.** (N.O.) near which is family graveyard. Macdonough himself, however, is buried at Middletown, Conn. **29.5. DRAWYERS PRESB. CH.** (O.during Sun.services.3 p.m.June. July.Aug.;c.1773.fine Georg.Col.), one of Del.'s most int. On Old Drawyers Sun. (1st in June), Ch. & grounds are filled with pilgrims coming to listen to addresses. **30.5. ODESSA,** lying somewhat to one side of main Rd., in old days was known as Cantwell's Bridge for toll bridge over Appoquinimink Cr. It became important market town & transshipment pt. for wares sent down creek to Del. Bay, but was bypassed by Del. RR. c.1855 & lost much of its importance. S. side of Main St., near 2nd St., **Dan. Wilson Mansion** (O.Tues.& Sat.c.1769.Georg.Col.fine exter.& inter.), containing **Mary Corbit Warner Mus. & Corbit Lib.** Mus. has coll. of family heirlooms & antiques. SW. cor. Main & 2nd Sts., **Castle William** (N.O.1773.very fine Georg. Col.adds.handsome exter.& inter.) was built by Quaker Corbit family who made fortune out of tanning & then out of peach orchards. NE. cor. Main & 2nd Sts., former **Odessa Hotel** (N.O.1822.rest.), once favorite resort for teamsters & traveling salesmen, sometimes had license revoked because of noise & drunkenness. NE. cor Main & 4th Sts., **Old Pub. School** (1844.adds.). S. side of Main St. (W) of US13, **Friends Meeting H.** (N.O.1783), once served as sta. on Underground Railroad.

SIDE TRIPS: (A) Take Main St. (L) from Odessa to **Fairview** (L) (N.O.1773.Georg.Col.) at 1.5m. Short distance farther, **Duncan Beard H.** (R) (N.O.c.1767.poor repair), built by Scottish clockmaker who turned out some of finest grandfather clocks in Amer.

(B) Take St.4 (R) from Odessa to **Middletown,** 3m, formerly tavern stop on old Rd. to head of navigation at Odessa. W. side of Broad St. near Crawford St., **Middletown Academy** (1826.poor repair). W. side of Broad St., near Green St., **Town Hall,** hqs. of oldest Masonic Lodge in Del., org. at Cantwell's Bridge, c.1765.

Take St.71 (L) from Middletown 1m to **Old St. Anne's Episc. Ch.** (annual service 3rd Sun. in June 10:30 & 3.O.appl.1768), one of finest old chs. in Del. with orig. pews & slave gallery; ivy on walls has grown from plants imported from England by Bishop Doane. Near Ch. is **"Old St. Anne's Oak,"** believed to be 300 yrs. old.

St.4 cont. (W) to **Cochran Grange** (N.O.1845), home of John P. Cochran, Gov. of Del., 1875-79.

**35.5. UNION M. E. CH.** (O.appl.1848), in whose graveyard is **Mon. to Bishop Levi Scott,** one of most noted Meths. of Del. **41.5.** J. with concrete Rd. leading (L) 1m to

J. with gravel Rd. which turns (R) c.0.5$^{m}$ to **Clearfield Farm** (N.O.c.1755). Capt. Wm. Clark, son of H.'s builder, fought at Battle of Monmouth & grandson was Gov. of Del., 1817-20. **42.5. SMYRNA** (R) was orig. known as Duck Cr. Cross Roads. Gen. Assembly, turned out of Cth. at Dover when repairs had to be made, met here & resolved to make this village St. capital, but later repealed resolution. Smyrna was important shipping center in 1850's due to landing on Duck Cr. only 1$^{m}$ away but lost chance to grow by forbidding RR. to come through. S. side of Commerce St. bet. US13 & Main St., **Enoch Spruance H.** (N.O.pre-1791.adds.), which once contained only bank in town, has int. antique furnishings. Across street is **Abraham Pierce H.** (N.O.mid-18th cent.). W. side of Main St., (N) of Mt. Vernon St., **Lockwood H.** (N.O.), said to have been used as barracks during War of 1812. E. side of Main St., (N) of Mt. Vernon St., old **Cummins H.** (N.O.early 19th cent.) was built by John Cummins, rich grain merchant. Next door (N) is **Presley Spruance H.** (dating from same period).

SIDE TRIP: Take St.6 (R) from Smyrna 1$^{m}$ to J. with St.300.

Take latter (L). At 2.5$^{m}$, small **White H.** (N.O.18th cent.), former tavern where Aunt Betsey offered refreshments to teamsters headed for Smyrna Landing (see above). At 4.5$^{m}$ **Bryn Zion Bapt. Ch.** (1771.adds.). In village of **Kenton,** 5.5$^{m}$, at E. cor. of J. with St.42, **Prettyman H.** (N.O.c.1775), & on SE. side of St.300 just (SW) of J., former **Kenton Hotel** (1809), now store. At 7$^{m}$ **Downs H.** (N.O.1773.porch & cornice adds. Georg.Col.). 10.5$^{m}$ J. with dirt lane leading (R) 0.5$^{m}$ to **Clark H.** (center sec.18th cent.), from which lane leads (L) 0.5$^{m}$ to bluff which is said to be **Site of Cheney Clow's Ft.** Clow was rabid Tory before & during Rev. & refused to take oath of allegiance after it. When sheriff's posse in 1782 came to arrest him, he took refuge in woods but finally surrendered; he was tried for treason & acquitted, but indicted again for having shot one of members of posse & finally convicted & hanged.

At 3$^{m}$, on St.6, **Hoffecker H.** (N.O.pre-Rev.). At 5.5$^{m}$ J. with dirt lane leading (R) 0.5$^{m}$ to **Airy Mount** (N.O.brick sec.c.1733). At 9$^{m}$, St.6 crosses **Del.-Md. Line.**

**43. ST. WELFARE HOME** (visiting hrs.1-4 Sun.& Wed.Mod.Col.) for aged people, which has replaced almshouses in 3 Del. counties. Short distance (S) is **Belmont Hall** (N.O.wings supposedly 1684.main sec.1753), whose main sec. was built by Thos. Collins, Pres. of Del. State, 1786-89; Collins with his own means org. & helped finance brigade of militia during Rev. **43.5. WOODLAWN** (N.O.Col.front sec.add. 1860). **46.5. GARRISON'S L.** (boats at near-by farms). **51.5. ST. COLLEGE FOR COLORED STUDENTS,** supported by Fed. & St. appropriations aided by gifts from P. S. du Pont, with 2 depts.: college (only one for Negroes in Del.) & high sch. **52.** J. with US113 leading (L) 1.5$^{m}$ to **Lebanon,** ghost village, formerly busy shipbuilding & shipping center, near which are beds of lotus lilies (in bloom July 20-Aug.20;inquire at Lebanon for boats) related to an Egyptian species. **52.5. SILVER L.**

**53.5. DOVER,** capital of Del., borders on St. Jones Cr. & Silver L. It is market center for surrounding agric. reg., with some industrial establishments. Legislature meets here biennially. Wm. Penn ordered that Dover be laid out as cty. seat c.1684, but town grew only very slowly up to Rev. At time of final vote on Decl. of Ind., tie was broken by Caesar Rodney, who made his home in vic.; summoned by special messenger to return to Phila., he rode 86$^{m}$, without stopping, to cast deciding vote for Del. Upon news of signing of Decl. of Ind., patriots took portrait of King George III out of Cth. & burned it on Green. Dover became St. capital on May 12, 1777, succeeding New Castle, & convention here on Dec. 7, 1787 ratified Constitution, making Del. 1st state to do so. Dover was predominantly pro-Union before Civil War & Fed. troops disarmed some young secessionists of town. During 20th cent., Dover has grown considerably due particularly to development of industry but still more due to fact that many great corporations have taken out Del. charters, which are issued at Dover, where also fees & franchise taxes are collected. City in 1924 was conn. with Wilmington by superb Du Pont Blvd. On both sides of St. Jones Cr. is 35-a. pk.; R. itself has been widened to form handsome L.

PTS. OF INT.: (1) At J. of State St. & Bank Lane, **The Green,** in which is **Mon.** comm. final review in 1780 of Del. regiment prior to its marching (S) to take part in Yorktown campaign. Elms here were planted in 1849. (2) E. side of the Green. **State H.** (O.wks.,Sat.a.m.Georg.Col.1792.E.wing 1836.remod.1874.adds. 1895-97.remod.& S.wing add.1910). Plans have been made to remove wings & rest. bldg. to its orig. appearance. Tablets on rotunda walls of 1st & 2nd stairs comm.

distinguished Delawareans. Paintings by Del. artist, Stanley M. Arthurs, hang in St. Law Lib. on 1st fl. & in rooms of St. Lib. Commission on 2nd fl. In St. Archives Commission vaults in basement are hist. documents & silver service of old battleship "Delaware." (3) (E) of the Green, **Legislative Hall** (O.wks.Sat.a.m.1933.Georg. Col.by E.W.Martin), containing House & Senate Chambers & Gov.'s suite; in latter hang Sully's portraits of Commodore Thos. Macdonough, hero of Battle of L. Champlain, & Commodore Jacob Jones, War of 1812 hero—both Delawareans. (4) SE. cor. of the Green & State St., **Kent County Cth.** (O.wks.Sat.a.m.Georg.Col.) occupies site of 1694 Cth. & of King George Tavern. (5) **No. 49 The Green** (N.O.) is supposed to be one of earliest bldgs. in city. (6) N. side of the Green, **Ridgely H.** (N.O.1728 & 1764), former home of Col. John Parke, father of Thos. Parke of Rev. fame & author of some note in his day. (7) 419 S. State St., **Loockerman H.** (N.O. 1742.int.inter.& antique furnishings). (8) (SE) of South & Water Sts., **Christ Ch.** (1707-34.rest.1785.tower 1876.remod.1913). (9) SW. cor. Water & New Sts., **Kent Cty. Jail** (O.appl.) with whipping post in yard, where whippings still take place. (10) King's Hy. & Penn. Ave., **Woodburn** (N.O.c.1790.fine Georg.exter.fine inter.), containing some rare furnishings. (11) SW. cor. Governor's Ave. & North St., **Presb. Cemetery,** in which are buried Del. notables. Adj. is **Old Presb. Ch.** (no longer used. 1790), built on site of former log Meeting H. (12) Plaza, (E) of State St., **Post Office** (O.wks.1933.Col.), in which are 5 murals by Wm. D. White.

SIDE TRIP: Take St.8 (R) from Dover to J. with Rd., 4m, leading (L) 1m to **Rosedale Cheese Plant** (O.appl.) where 200-lb. cheeses are made from milk produced on farms of Amish Mennonites of this sec.

## Sec. 2: DOVER to DELMAR. 51.5.

**3.5. CAMDEN,** laid out in 1783 by Dan. Mifflin, a Quaker. N. entrance to village, **Cooper H.** (N.O.1782.int.inter.) is supposed to have been sta. on Underground Railroad, where fugitive Negroes were concealed in sm. room above kitchen. Almost opp., **Dan. Mifflin H.** (N.O.c.1796). Warner Mifflin, brother of Dan., was among 1st Amers. to free slaves unconditionally. On Commerce St., **Friends Meeting H.** (O. appl.meeting 1st Sun.every month 10:30.c.1805).

SIDE TRIP: Take St.10 (R) from Camden 8m to **Petersburg Site** (28,000 as.), timbered tract purchased by U.S. Resettlement Adm. 1935-36, with Rds., pic. sites & fireplaces.

**17.5. HARRINGTON,** sm. industrial town. **21. THARP H.** (c.1835), built by Wm. Tharp, Gov. of Del. 1847-51, on N. outskirts of village of **FARMINGTON. 25.5. GREENWOOD,** at J. with St.16.

SIDE TRIPS: (A) Take latter (L) 1m to J. with St.36.

Take latter (L) 1m to **Amish Sch.** (private), where primly dressed children of German Amish farmers attend.

St.16 cont. (E) to **Ellendale,** 8.5m, in **Ellendale Swamp & For.** (pic.&camp site 1m S.) & to **Milton** (see Coast Tour), 16m, & J. with St.14 (see Coast Tour), 18.5m.

(B) Take St.16 (R) from Greenwood to **Todd's Ch.** (Meth.1858.Gr.Rev.), 5.5m.

**29.5.** J. with Rd. running (L) 6m to **Redden St. For.** (pic.). **30. BRIDGEVILLE,** center of large orchard & truck garden reg. **31.** J. with Rd. leading (L) 3m to **Townsend Apple Orchard,** largest in reg. with 60,000 trees (picking season,Aug.-Oct.). **33.5.** J. with St.18.

SIDE TRIP: Take latter (L) to **Georgetown,** 12m, typical S. county cth. town, made cty. seat in 1792 & named for Geo. Mitchell, one of commissioners in charge of bldg. cth. & jail. SE. cor. Sq. & E. Market St., **Sussex County Cth.** (1839.portico & tower 1914). SW. cor. Market & Race Sts., **Cth. Annex** (1835.rebuilt & adds.1866). W. side of S. Bedford St., orig. **Cth.** (1793), shingled with cypress, moved to present site 1837. SW. cor. Sq. & W. Market St., **Brick Hotel** (1836.wing add.1936). NW. cor. W. Market & Front Sts., **The Judge** (N.O.c.1810), shingled with cypress, occupied successively by various judges. There are other int. old Hs. in town. E. side of N. Bedford St., **Archaeological Coll.** (O.appl.) of Ind. material. St.18 cont. (E) to **Lewes Beach** (see Coast Tour), 28m.

**35. HEARN'S MILL POND** (boat.f.). **36.5. LAWRENCE,** frame mansion (N.O.c. 1840). **37.** J. with St.20.

SIDE TRIP: Take latter (R) 5.5m to **Reliance,** on Del.-Md. Line, where A. Hill Smith H. (N.O.) stands on **Site of Joe Johnson's Tavern,** hqs. during 1st quarter of 19th cent. of Lucretia (Patty) Cannon, noted kidnapper of free Negroes, tavern hostess & amateur wrestler. Mrs. Cannon used to sell kidnapped free Negroes to slavers lying in Nanticoke R. at Cannon's Ferry or at Sharptown, Md., just across St. line. She kept Negroes chained in her attic or in woods behind tavern. Latter's position on St. line at J. of 3 counties enabled

Patty & her son-in-law, Joe Johnson, to escape sheriffs who came to arrest them. Patty is also supposed to have murdered slave dealers & robbed them while they slept at her place. At Reliance is J. with Rd. leading (L) to **Nanticoke R.,** 9.5m, opp. **Woodland,** formerly Cannon's Ferry. Just above ferry slip is **Cannon Hall** (N.O.c.1820). **Cannon's Ferry** (free. blow horn) connects with Woodland, whence Rd. runs to J. with US13 just (N) of Laurel (see below).

**37.5. SEAFORD,** at head of navigation on Nanticoke R., is home port of considerable oyster fleet operating in Chesapeake Bay & site of E. I. du Pont de Nemours & Co. **Nylon Plant.** Seaford was sett. in 1799 & for time was important shipbuilding center. E. side Front St., bet. King & Poplar Sts., **St. Luke's Ch.** (Episc.Sun.service 11.O.appl.1843).

SIDE TRIP: Take Dulaney Mills Rd. (R) from Seaford 1.5m to **Fairview** (O.c.1849), formerly occupied by Dulaney family. (W) of H. are slave quarter & other old bldgs. It was Dulaney's custom to manumit, after some yrs., his slaves & give each family a cabin & some land.

**42. DELMARVA CAMP** (1st 2 wks.in Aug.hotel & tent accoms.), largest Meth. tent camp-meeting place in Del., with tabernacle where services are broadcast every evening. **44. LAUREL,** at head of navigation on Broad Cr., which flows into Nanticoke R., was laid out in 1802 & is center of truck garden area, with some industries. 8th St., near Central Ave., **Auction Block** (9-4 daily), where auctions are held of farm products. Delaware Ave., in N. Laurel, **Collins H.,** home of Nath. Mitchell, Gov. of Del., 1805-08. N. edge of Laurel, **Records Pond** (f.boats). **51.5. DELMAR,** trading & shipping center, which grew up following advent of RR. in 1859. It is bisected by **DEL.-MD. LINE.**

## COAST TOUR—DELAWARE

**NEW CASTLE (S) to BETHANY BEACH. 104. Unnumbered Rds., St.9, US113 & St.14**

Via: Delaware City, Port Penn, Leipsic, Little Creek, Milford & Rehoboth. Accoms. in towns.

This route crosses sparsely populated coastal reg. of fields, marshes, creeks & Rs. & in its S. sec. traverses reg. of seaside resorts.

### Sec. 1.: NEW CASTLE to MILFORD. 65. Unnumbered Rds., St.9 & US113

**0. NEW CASTLE.**

RR. & through bus conns. Ferry: Foot of Chestnut St. to Pennsgrove, N.J. (autos, frequent serv.). Info.: Amstel H., 4th & Delaware Sts. "A Day in Old New Castle," 3rd Sat. May.

New Castle, on Delaware R., is one of best preserved & loveliest old cities on Atlantic seaboard, rivalling Williamsburg & Savannah in antiquarian & architectural interest. On plantations in vic., Swedes, Finns, & Dutch were sett. in 1651 when Peter Stuyvesant, Dutch Gov. of New Amsterdam, arrived. Ft. & blockh. were still in Swedish hands when Stuyvesant sailed away. New Swedish gov., Capt. Johann Classon Rising, arrived in 1654 with reinforcements. However, in 1655 Dutch returned & took over Swedish Ft. Casimir. Finally, in Sept., 1664, Sir Rbt. Carr arrived with 2 frigates & took over for Brit., & in 1664, town's name was changed from New Amatel to New Castle. Except for short interval, when Dutch recaptured town (1673), New Castle remained Brit. until Rev. In Nov. 1682, Wm. Penn was given possession under powers granted by Duke of York. New Castle now became & remained seat of "Lower Counties" of Pa. till 1776. One of Penn's Lt. Govs., Col. Chas. Gookin, is said to have been short tempered. When justices of New Castle failed to carry out his wishes, he "sent for one of the judges & kicked him," later offering as his excuse that "his physician knew he had a weak head." In 1747 citizens were thrown into panic by arrival of Sp. privateer, commanded by Vincent Lopez, but drove it off with brisk bombardment. Though threatened by Brit. ships during Rev., New Castle escaped unscathed. In Sept. 1776, convention of counties met at New Castle & proclaimed "The Delaware State" & soon St. leg. convened here. Capital, however, was removed because of threat of Brit. in Wilmington. After Rev., New Castle became main sta. on hy. to Washington & busy port at head of navigation on Delaware, but later declined after building of RRs. & development of Wilmington as shipping & industrial center. City has body of Trustees of the Common, drawing income from Town Common (some 1,068 as. dating back to Dutch grant) which they use for city's benefit. Another body of Trustees controls pub. bldgs. on Green.

PTS. OF INT.: **The Green,** bounded by Delaware, Market, Harmony & 3rd Sts., was orig. pub. sq. laid out by Stuyvesant, on which stood blockh. for protection against Ind. or other attacks. Today it is divided in 2 secs., Cth. Sq. & Market Sq., separated by Market St. (1) N. side Delaware St., on Green, **Old Cth.** Central portion (early Georg.) is supposed to have been built in 1704. E. wing was begun before 1698. In 1845 W. wing was added. (2) Market St. adj. to Old Cth., **Old Sheriff's H.** (N.O. 1858). (3) Facing Market St., bet. Delaware & Harmony Sts. on Green, **Old Arsenal** (O.Mon.-Fri.Sat.a.m.1809.adds.& alts.1852.rest.& remod.1936). (4) On Green, at Market & Harmony Sts., **Immanuel Ch.** (Episc.O.1703-10.tower & spire.add.& alts. 1820-22), housing congregation org. in 1689. It has some fine old silver, shown on Old New Castle Day. In Ch. yard, dating from 1707, are graves of many Del. notables, incl. that of Geo. Read, signer of Decl. of Ind. & Constitution. (5) NW. cor. Green, **Old Academy** (O.appl.Rector of Immanuel Ch.1798-1811), founded shortly after Rev., which cont. until 1852. (6) NW. cor. Delaware & 2nd Sts., **Old Town Hall** (O.wks.,Sat.a.m.1823). (7) Opp. Green, **New Castle & Frenchtown Mon.,** built of stone "sleepers" used to hold down tracks of New Castle & Frenchtown RR. (8) 2nd St., bet. Delaware & Harmony Sts., **Old Presb. Ch.** (O.1707.cupola add.c.1800). (9) 3d St., bet. Harmony & Delaware Sts., facing Green, **Old Dutch H.** (probably late 17th cent.), now owned by Del. Soc. for Preservation of Antiquities. (10) 18 E. 3d St., **Gemmil H.** (O.only on Old New Castle Day.1801.fine exter.inter.). (11) 16 E. 3d Sts., **Rodney H.** (O.only on Old New Castle Day.1831) contains notable coll. of Delawareana & portrait of Geo. Read, by Gilbert Stuart; another of Geo. Ross the elder, 1st rector of Immanuel Ch., by Hesselius; & another of Geo. Ross the younger, by Ben. West. (12) 2 E. 3d St., **Kensey Johns H.** (O.only on Old New Castle Day.1789-90.fine exter. & inter.). (13) NE. cor. Delaware & 4th St., **Kensey Johns Jr. H.** (O.occasionally on Old New Castle Day. 1823). (14) N. cor. 4th & Delaware Sts., **Amstel H.** (O.wks.sm. fee.fine exter.& inter.supposedly 1706 & c.1730) houses Mus. of New Castle Hist. Soc. On windowpane in 2nd story are scratched lines:

Around her head ye angels constant vigil keep,
And guard fair innocence her balmy sleep.

Mus. coll. includes rare antique items & some old portraits.

(15) 400 Delaware St., **Sen. Nicholas Van Dyke H.** (O.only on Old New Castle Day. 1799). (16) 300 Delaware St., **Kensey Johns Van Dyke H.** (O.only on Old New Castle Day.1820.fine inter.). (17) 216 Delaware St., **Booth H.** (O.only on Old New Castle Day.c.1795.adds.), home of Chief Justice Jas. Booth, Jr., who waited here till juries arrived at verdict & crossed over to Cth. in dressing gown & slippers to hear it. (18) 210 Delaware St., **Gilpin H.** (N.O.remod.), one of town's oldest bldgs., was for many yrs. tavern. Edw. Gilpin, Chief Justice, lived here 1857-76. (19) N. side of Delaware St., **Cloud's Row,** series of orig. 3½-story, narrow brick Hs., severe in style, built 1804. (20) 202 Delaware St., **Delaware H.** (N.O.), orig. tavern during Rev. (21) 110 Delaware St., **Colby H.** (O.only on Old New Castle Day.rear part 1675. front, early 1700's.rest.1936). (22) End of Strand, **Van Leuvenigh H.** (O.only on Old New Castle Day.1732), now stuccoed. (23) NE. cor. Strand & Delaware St., **Old Jefferson Hotel** (N.O.) was an 18th & 19th cent. hostelry in which shipping & naval firm of Riddle & Bird had offices. (24) 4 Strand, **Old Farmers Bank** (O.only on Old New Castle Day.1845). (25) 6 Strand, **Gunning Bedford H.** (O.only on Old New Castle Day.c.1730), once occupied by Rev. soldier & Del. Gov., Gunning Bedford. (26) 8 Strand, **McIntyre H.** (O.only on Old New Castle Day.c.1690.fine exter. & inter.) (27) N. Side Packet Alley, on Strand, bet. Delaware & Harmony Sts., **Old Stage Tavern** (1824). (28) NW. side of Strand, bet. Harmony & Delaware Sts., **Read H.** (O.only on New Old Castle Day.1797-1801.fine exter.& inter.Georg.Col.), built by son of Geo. Read, signer of Decl. of Ind., one of city's loveliest Hs. (29) Cor. Strand & Harmony Sts., **Immanuel Parish H.** (O.appl.;O. Old New Castle Day.c. 1801.Georg.Col.). (30) E. side of Strand, **Aull Hs.** (Nos. 49-51, c.1750; Nos. 53-55, c.1775). (31) W. edge of New Castle, near Wm. Penn Sch., **The Hermitage,** partly (it is believed) c.1700 & c.1747 (main H.1818, fine inter.) (32) Near 8th St., at Washington RR. crossing, **New Castle & Frenchtown Ticket Box,** in use since 1832. (33) Near Ticket Box, **Stonum** (c.1775.alts.) which belonged to Geo. Read (see above). (34) (R) from River Rd., c. 0.5$^m$ from Ferry, old **Glebe H.** on open tract of

land, typical New Castle brick H. (35) At 1.5$^{m}$ from ferry, (L) from River Rd., **Bothhurst** (early 18th cent.add.1842.early Col.& Eng.Goth.), hidden by grove of oaks.

**2.** J. with Rd. leading (L) short distance to **Deemer's Beach** (bath.amusements). **7. LEXINGTON** (N.O.c.1847), built by Maj. Philip Reybold, "Peach King" of his day because of his great peach orchards. **9.5. DELAWARE CITY,** with picturesque water front, once important port of call, today sleepy old fishing town. Foot of Clinton St., **Battery Pk.,** entrance to old **Chesapeake & Del. Canal;** here is one of old locks. RR.'s competition stifled commerce; new canal, completed in 1927 & deepened later, bypassed town. NW. cor. Adams & Williams St., **Maxwell H.** (N.O.c.1850), built by steamboat captain who put lookout box on roof. Just (S) of town on main hy. is entrance to **Del. Health Center,** formerly Ft. du Pont, hqs. for harbor defences of Del. R. & Bay, with 65 bldgs. & 322 as. of grounds, turned over to St. by Fed. Gov. in 1947; it provides hospital accoms. for c.500 persons. Reached by boat from here, **Ft. Delaware,** on Pea Patch I., is great granite pentagon encircled by moat. During Civil War some 12,000 Confed. prisoners were confined here under incredibly crowded & terrible conditions; mortality was high, as many as 331 dying in one month of cholera. **11.** N. bank of Chesapeake & Del. Canal. **JOHN REYBOLD FARMH.,** where M. I. Pupin, famous Serbian-born scientist, renowned for his inventions in connection with X-rays & telephonic electrical devices, spent his earlier yrs. as farm hand, as described in his "From Immigrant to Inventor." **14.5. AUGUSTINE BEACH** (resort). **16.5.** J. with Rd. leading (L) to **Bayview Beach** (resort). **18.5. LONG I. FARM** (N.O.), where until 1936 lived Mrs. Catherine Fox, known as "The Muskrat Queen," because she employed trappers to catch muskrats (10,000 in one winter) on her 1,000 as. of marsh property. **24.5. HUGUENOT H.** (N.O.1711. early Col.), built by Elias Naudain, son of Huguenot refugee. **26. TAYLOR'S BRIDGE,** near which is 135′-high **Reedy I. Range Lighthouse,** at J. with Rd. leading (L) (straight ahead) 2.5$^{m}$ to **Liston H.** (N.O.1739.alt.). **34.5.** J. with St.6.

SIDE TRIPS: (A) Take St.6 (L) 3$^{m}$ to **Woodland Beach** (f.resort), just (S) of which is **Bombay Hook Migratory Waterfowl Refuge** (14,000 as.).
(B) Take St.6 (R) to **Smyrna** (see US13), 8$^{m}$.

**38.** J. with St.9, on which this tour cont. **39.5. LEIPSIC,** on edge of great marsh, is f. & oystering town; muskrat meat, snapper turtle soup, fish & oysters & wild duck are food staples here. Place was successively known as Fast Landing, Vienna & finally Leipsic, for German city renowned as a fur mart, probably because of local abundance of muskrats. Until coming of RR., it was lively shipping center & port. **41.5. WHEEL OF FORTUNE** (N.O.pre-Rev.fine inter.). **42.5. PLEASANTON ABBEY** (N.O.c.1750), built by Henry Stevens, ardent Tory during Rev. **44.5. OCTAGONAL H.** (1836), former schoolh. **46.5.** J. with Rd. leading (L) 3$^{m}$ to **Port Mahon** on Del. Bay, good starting pt. for fishing. Del. oyster fleet operates off shore in May & June. **47. LITTLE CREEK** (accoms.bait & tackle), oystering town which derives chief income from "parties" of city fishermen. **47.5.** Just (S) of Creek bridge is J. with Rd. leading (R) 0.5$^{m}$ to **Cherbourg** (N.O.one sec.c.1715.Georg.Col.), once home of Gov. C. P. Comegys (1837-41). **51.5.** J. with Kitt Hummock Rd. leading (R) c.0.5$^{m}$ to **Kingston-Upon-Hull,** home of father of John Dickinson, who, though Rev. patriot, refused to sign Decl. of Ind.; this is one of finest of reg.'s plantation Hs. Short distance beyond last J. is J. with US113, which tour now follows (S). **53. ST. JONES CREEK,** crossed by drawbridge, at S. end of which is J. with Rd. leading (R) 1.5$^{m}$ to **Magnolia,** where on E. side of Main St., (N) of inters., is **Matthew Lowber H.** (1774.add.1855). **56. JEHU REED H.** (N.O.1771.rebuilt late 19th cent. in Vict.style), at J. with Bowers Beach Rd.

SIDE TRIP: Take latter (L) to J. with Rd., 2$^{m}$.

Take latter (L) 1.5$^{m}$ to **King Crab Plant** (O.appl.) where King (horse-shoe) crabs are transformed into fertilizer.

At 3$^{m}$ **Bowers Beach** (f.resort). "Big Thurs." (2nd in Aug.) is great oystering festival, despite custom of not eating oysters till Sept. 1. "Big Sat." (1st after Big Thurs.) is Negro oyster festival, when beach is turned over to Negroes.

**57. BARRATT'S CHAPEL** (O.services every other Sun.2 p.m.1780), known as cradle of Methodism in Del. Here, Nov. 1784, Sacrament of the Lord's Supper was 1st administered in America by authorized Meth. preachers. Methodism, much persecuted elsewhere, found freedom of worship in Del. in Col. times. **58.5. FREDERICA,** formerly Johnnycake Landing, on Murderkill, was another shipping & shipbuilding town until RRs. came. Hy. bypasses town, which is noted for its oysters & fish cuisine. W. side of Market St., (N) of Main St., **Lowber H.** (N.O.pre-1750.poor repair).

SIDE TRIP: Take St.12 (R) from Frederica to J. with Harrington Rd., 0.5m.
Take latter (L) 3.5m, then turn (L) on side Rd. to **Mordington** (N.O.1777.Georg.fine inter.), 4m, fine old Del. plantation h.
Cont. on St.12 to J. with Rd., 1.5m.
Take latter (R) to old **Bonwell H.** (N.O.) 3m, on Andrews L., branch of Murderkill. H. was built by Quaker, one Bonwell, who is said to have killed Negro boy in fit of anger. His white neighbors, when he died, refused to bury him, & Negroes, fearing his ghost might walk, buried him.

**64.5.** J. with St.14, which this route now follows (L), at N. edge of Milford. **65. MILFORD** [Take St.14 (W) to center of town], on both sides of Mispillion R., is important trading & industrial center, laid out in 1787, after plantations in vic. had already been est. Milford early began shipbuilding & shipping of grain & other products. Coming of RRs. did not halt expansion. PTS. OF INT.: (1) 501 W. Front St., N. Milford, **Parson Thorne H.** (N.O.c.1785). (2) SW. cor. 3rd & Church Sts., **Christ Ch.** (Episc.O.appl.1791-1835.inter.remod. & tower add.1866). (3) North & 3rd Sts., **Old Meth. Cemetery.** (4) W. side N. Walnut St., **Odd Fellows Cemetery,** in which is buried Col. Ben. Potter Hynson, who wrote lyrics of "Our Delaware," Del.'s official song. (5) SW. cor. N. Walnut & 2nd Sts., **Torbert H.** (N.O.c.1825.adds.), orig. tavern; here lived Maj. Gen. A. T. A. Torbert, who, ignoring pleas of slave-holding relatives & friends, fought on Union side in Civil War. (6) Facing Plaza, S. Milford, **Causey Mansion** (N.O.1763.adds.1855.Gr.Rev.) with slave quarters in garden.

## Sec. 2: MILFORD to BETHANY BEACH. 39. St.14

**1.5.** J. with St.36, which runs (E) past **Ft. Saulsbury** (N.O.), 5.5m, to **Cedar Beach,** 6m. **6.5.** J. with improved Rd. leading (L) 3.5m to **Slaughter Beach** (resort) on Del. Bay, which also has its "Big Thurs." (2nd in Aug.) like Bowers (see above). **13.** Js. with St.16 & Broadkill Beach Rd.

SIDE TRIPS: (A) Take St.16 (R) 2.5m to **Milton,** former shipbuilding & shipping town on Broadkill Cr. In N. Milton is **Conwell's Boxwood Nursery,** with fine specimens of old box-woods of great age. E. side of Union St., N. Milton, **Gov. Hazzard H.** (N.O. c.1790), former home of David Hazzard, Del. Gov. 1830-33. E. side Chestnut St., N. Milton, **Peter Parker H.** (N.O. c.1835).
(B) Take Broadkill Beach Rd. (L) 4m to **Broadkill Beach** (resort.bath.f.), just (N) of entrance to Lewes & Rehoboth Canal (see below).

**14. CONWELL H.** (N.O.18th cent.), sheathed in bald-cypress shingles, probably from trees in Great Pocomoke Swamp. **17. OVERBROOK,** in whose vic. fox-hunters with packs of hounds range eagerly. **18. RED MILL POND** (f.boats). **20.** J. with St.18.

SIDE TRIP: Take latter (R) 0.5m to **Belltown,** all-Negro town where, in last cent., Voodoo rites used to be performed until leader of sect, Arnsy Moll, on his deathbed, ordered his followers to exorcise "devil" by lashing him with whips, which they did. At 4.5m on St.18 is J. with Rd.
Take latter (L) 0.5m to **Martin H.** (N.O. late 17th or early 18th cent.Col.).
12.5m, **Georgetown** (see US13).

**20.5. WESCOAT'S CORNER,** where is **Rhodes Shankland H.** (N.O.c.1767), at E. J. with St.18.

SIDE TRIP: Take latter (L) to **Lewes,** 2m, near mouth of Del. Bay & Cape Henlopen, famous as home of Del. Bay & River pilots for nearly 300 yrs. Lewes was sett. in 1631 by Dutch & named Swanendael. Soon after, Inds. attacked; only 1 man escaped. In 1658 place was fortified against Brit. encroachment, but Brit. took it over in 1664 & destroyed or seized property of newly arrived group of Mennonite settlers. During Wm. Penn's time name of Lewes was finally adopted, & Penn had settlement laid out. Brit. warships bombarded it during War of 1812, but it replied with its own guns. Cape Henlopen ocean front has been scene of many shipwrecks, but building of Del. Breakwater & completion of outer Harbor of Refuge has reduced dangers to shipping. Lewes has become one of most frequented resorts for ocean fishermen.
PTS. OF INT.: 1) S. cor. Savannah Rd. & King's Hy., **Zwaaenendael H.** (Mus.O.wks.in summer, otherwise by appl.1931.by E.W.Martin) is small scale adaptation of part of ancient Town Hall at Hoorn, Holland, where Capt. David Pietersen de Vries, who led 1st settlers of 1631, was born. Mus. contains relics, antiques, documents. (2) King's Hy., opp. Zwaanendael H., **David Hall H.** (N.O.), former home of D. Hall (Gov.1802-05). (3)

E. side of King's Hy., bet. Franklin & Washington Sts., **Lewes Presb. Ch.** (1832.remod.). (4) W. side King's Hy., (N) of Madison St., **Bride-&-Groom Trees,** 2 giant sycamores supposedly planted c.1812 by Margaret Coleman to comm. her proposed marriage. (5) **Mem. Pk.,** on site of one of defense batteries of War of 1812, contains some old guns which were used to return Brit. fire. (6) W. cor. Front & Bank Sts., **David Rowland H.** (O.appl. pre-1797), sheathed with cypress shingles. (7) W. cor. 2nd & Market Sts., **St. Peter's Episc. Ch.** (1858.Goth.), est. 1706. (8) S. cor. 2nd & Knitting Sts., **Holt H.** (N.O.allegedly pre-1685) was one of earliest inns. (9) 231 2nd St., **Dan. Rodney H.** (N.O. c.1800) was home of Dan. Rodney, Gov. of Del. (1814-17) & relative of Caesar Rodney, Rev. hero. (10) N. cor. 3rd & Knitting Sts., **Register H.** (N.O.c.1790). (11) 112 W. 4th St., residence of Ben S. Albertson, containing **Coll. of Firearms** (O.appl.). (12) Near beginning of Pilot Town Rd., **Orton H.** (N.O. allegedly c.1700). (13) At 0.5$^m$ on Pilot Town Rd., **Wm. Russell H.** (N.O. c.1790). (14) Short distance beyond Russell H., **Fountain of Youth** (R), for more than 250 yrs. believed to be youth-restoring or preserving especially if its waters were drunk out of righthanded conch-shell. (15) Opp. is **Thos. Maull H.** (N.O.c.1750), where Jerome Bonaparte & his Amer. bride "Betsy" Patterson were given shelter after their ship had been wrecked off Lewes. (16) At a little less than 1$^m$ on Pilot Town Rd., **Schellenger H.** (c.1750). (17) At 1$^m$, **Fisher's Paradise** (N.O.c.1725.) (18) At little more than 1$^m$, **De Vries Mon.** (R) on what is supposed to have been site of Ft. built by Dutch after landing in 1631. St.18. cont. (W) to **Lewes Beach** (resort.salt-water.f.bath.), 2.5$^m$. At E. entrance to Lewes Beach is J. with Cape Henlopen Dr. which runs (R) along shore front 2.5$^m$ to Cape Henlopen.

At **22.5.** is J. with St.24.

SIDE TRIP: Take latter (R) through **"Down Sockum"** reg. (named for local family, Sockum), in which live farmers called "Moors" but sometimes also Inds. or Negroes. Before Rev. an Irishwoman of vic. had children by Negro slave, who intermarried with Nanticoke Inds. Today there are separate schs. for Inds., Moors, Negroes & whites. In 1922 Nanticoke Ind. Assoc. was formed of those who insisted on Ind. ancestry. At 9.5$^m$ **Harmon Sch.,** also known as Moor Sch., at Js. with unmarked Rd. & St.5.

(1) Take unmarked Rd. (R) 1.5$^m$ to J. with 2nd Rd. leading (R) short distance to trl. which turns (R) c.0.5$^m$ to **Grave of Lydia Clark,** said to have been last of "Aborigines"; she was descendant of Irish ancestress of Moors (see above).

(2) Take St.5. (L) to **Oak Orchard,** 2$^m$, & **Riverdale Pk.,** 2.5$^m$, resorts on Indian R. Bay. At latter is **Mon. to Lydia Clark** (see above).

At 10$^m$ **Nanticoke Ind. Sch.,** which "Moors" are not permitted to attend. Just beyond sch. is J. with side Rd. leading (L) 1$^m$ to **Rosedale Beach** (resort & amusement pk. for Negroes), where public baptisms occasionally take place. 15$^m$ **Millsboro,** on Ind. R., quiet hamlet frequented by "Moors," Negroes & whites. At 19$^m$ J. with Rd. leading (R) 1$^m$ to **Carey's Campground** (Meth.for whites; week or longer in Aug.), founded prior to 1830. 25$^m$ **Gumboro.**

Take Rd. (L) here 1$^m$ into great **Pocomoc Swamp,** formerly rich in great cedars. Fire has destroyed much of old timber.

27.5$^m$ **Md. Line.**

**24.5.** J. with private dirt lane leading (R) 1$^m$ to **Marsh Family Cemetery,** typical of private plantation graveyards in lower Del., & one of largest. There are more than 125 graves, earliest dating back to 1769. **26. REHOBOTH,** resort on Atlantic Ocean. Lewes & Rehoboth Canal circles (W) of town. Its biblical name was given by Eng. settlers who came to vic. before 1675. In 1872 Methodists developed tract of land here & town became great camp-meeting center; but it soon developed as general seaside resort. Today it is often referred to as "Delaware's Summer Capital." Crowds from Washington & Baltimore pour in over summer weekends. **The Homestead** (N.O.c.1742.rest.fine inter.), at Henlopen Acres, is set in lovely garden in which are anchors & other maritime relics.St.14, crossing **Silver L.,** now runs along narrow strip bet. bay & ocean & passes number of resorts to **NAT. GUARD CAMPGROUND** at **38.** & **BETHANY BEACH** (resort) at **39.** Latter had its beginnings in est. on its site of summer activities of Christian Missionary Soc. of Md., which completed its **Tabernacle,** (R) on St.14, here in 1901.

SIDE TRIP: Take St.26 (R) from Bethany Beach to J. with Rd., 2$^m$.

Take latter (L) 3.5$^m$ to J. with 2nd Rd. leading (L) to **Assowam Site** of U.S. Dept. of Agric. on Miller Cr. & Little Assowam Bay. At 7.5$^m$ is **Strawberry Recr. Area** (shelter, bathhs.f.crabbing).

Cont. St.26 to c.10.5$^m$ **Prince George's Chapel** (Episc.O.appl.Harvest Home Service 1st Sun. Oct. 1757.orig.inter.preserved). At 11$^m$ is J. with Rd. leading (L) 1$^m$ to **A.M.E. Antioch Campground** (Negro camp-meetings Sat. before 2nd Sun. in Aug., lasting 8 days). Just (W) of last J., St.26. reaches **Dagsboro,** pleasant old village, named in 1785 for Gen. John Dagsworthy, who fought in Fr. Ind. Wars. On W. edge of Dagsboro is J. with US113.

Take US113 (S) here 2$^m$ to Frankford. J. with Rd. leading (L) 5$^m$ to **Blackwater Presb.**

**Ch.** (services 2nd Sun. Oct.; 1767), whose 1st minister, Chas. Tennent was a son of the Tennent who taught at Old Log College, later Princeton Univ. Cont. on US113. At 6m **Shelbyville,** where is **Auction Block** (May-June) with lively auction sales of vegetables. 6.5m **Del.-Md. Line.**

At 18.5m J. with St.24 on which side trip cont. (L). At 25m J. with Rd. (L) 1m to **Trappe Pond Site** (pic.boat.bath.f.). At 28.5m J. with Rd. leading (R) 0.5m to **Christ Ch.** (Episc.O. Sun.May & 3rd Sun.Sept.;1771) which has int. inter. & old silver. 39m **Md. Line.**

## US 40—DELAWARE

**NEW CASTLE (W) to DEL.-MD. LINE** (3m from Elkton, Md.). **11. US40**

US40 cuts across Del.'s narrow N. sec. **0. NEW CASTLE** (see Coast Tour), at terminal of ferry from Pennsville, N.J. **2.5.** J. with US13 (see), with which US40 briefly unites. **11. DEL.-MD. LINE.**

## WILMINGTON

### WILMINGTON

Through RR. & bus conns. Ferries to Penns Grove, N.J.; steamboats to Chester & Phila., Pa. Accoms.: All types. Info.: C. of C., 6th & Market Sts.; Del. Motor Club (AAA), 10th & Market Sts. Road shows & concerts at The Playhouse, 10th & Market Sts.; local productions at Wilmington Drama League Theater, Lea Blvd. & Market St.; boating on Brandywine Cr. in vic. of Church St. Bridge; swim. at mun. pools; golf at mun. course, Rock Manor. Annual Events: Horse Show, May; Flower Market, May; Old Swedes Anniversary, Trinity Sun.

Wilmington is situated on W. bank of Del. R., bet. Brandywine Cr. & Christina R. Latter brings deep-draft vessels into city's center & is lined with piers & industrial establishments. On its S. bank near Del. R. is modern marine terminal. Rodney Sq. is city's business focal pt., from which radiate Market St. & parallel thoroughfares running (NE) to (SW) &, in NE. sec., streets extend diagonally toward Rockford Pk. at N. city limit. Brandywine Cr., to (NE) of Rodney Sq., is lined by pkys. along both its shores. Bancroft Pky., broad, parked blvd., extends along W. side of city from Union Pk. Gardens & more thickly populated Woodlawn "flats" to most exclusive residential sec. in S. Pop. of Wilmington is of various origins, basis being early Swedish, Dutch & Eng. settlers, reinforced during 18th & 19th cents. by waves of newcomers from other parts of country & from Europe. Negroes constitute 10% of citizenry. On last Sun. in Aug., "Big Quarterly," Negro religious festival which attracts visitors from all the Middle Atlantic states, is colorfully celebrated.

Wilmington was 1st sett. by Swedes in 1638, when Peter Minuit landed with his company at The Rocks & built Ft. Christina, named for Sweden's fantastic Queen. In 1655, Dutch captured Ft. Christina, but withdrew their troops almost immediately. Then in 1664, Brit. took over in name of James, Duke of York (later James II). Wm. Penn later became proprietor of colony, arriving in 1682. Settlement had for short time been known as Willingtown, named for Thos. Willing, who was connected with laying out & plotting it. But in 1739, after granting of its new charter, name was changed to Wilmington in honor of Penn's friend, Earl of Wilmington. Much of Del. R. commerce was diverted from New Castle (S) to Wilmington, which also became an active center for smugglers & busy slave mart. During Rev., city was predominantly patriotic. In May 1776, naval battle was fought off mouth of Christina Cr. bet. Brit. & Amers. Old Ft. Christina was rehabilitated for town's defense & to prevent Brit. from coming up Del. R. Washington arrived with his army in 1777 & made his hqs. in town. But on Sept. 13, 1777, Brit. in surprise raid captured Dr. John McKinley, 1st pres. of Del. St. under its new constitution. After Battle of Brandywine, they occupied Wilmington.

Within few yrs. after Rev., city experienced considerable growth in commerce & pop. City's 1st cotton mill, built in last yrs. of 18th cent., was soon sold to E. I. du Pont, who est. in it powder mill (1802). By 1812, pop. has almost quadrupled & shipping was booming. Wilmington was also becoming important social & cultural center. Soon after 1812, 1st steam packet service operated bet. Wilmington & Phila. Bet. 1835 & 1845, whaling fleet made city its home port. Wilmington, despite its early slave-dealings, was generally antislavery & became important sta. on Underground Railroad, whose activities were directed by noted Quaker abolitionist, Thos. Garrett. City's industries & shipping experienced great expansion during two World Wars. Building of Marine Terminal on Del. R. after World War I considerably increased port's facils. Wilmington is hqs. & site of research laboratories of E. I. du Pont de Nemours & Co. & Atlas & Hercules Powder Cos., largest chemical mfg. enterprises in world; it has c.285 industries in all, among which are large shipyards & RR. shops & world's largest braided rubber hose & cotton dyeing & finishing plants; it is world's center of vulcanized fibre & glazed kid & morocco leather manufacture. Many national corporations, favored by St.'s tax & corporation laws, have est. their main offices in city, with result that there is unusually large percentage of "white collar" workers.

PTS. OF INT. DOWNTOWN: (1) **Rodney Sq.** (1½ as.) has been landscaped as sunken garden. On Market St. side, **Caesar Rodney Equestrian Statue,** by Jas. Kelly, comm. signing of Decl. of Ind., & **Drinking Fountain,** comm. Wm. Poole, descendant of early Quaker family. (2) **Pub. Bldg.** (O.wks.Sat.a.m.1915.neo-class.by Palmer & Hornbostel & J.D.Thompson) of City of Wilmington & Cty. of New Castle, in which are city & cty. offices. (3) **Wilmington Pub. Lib.** (O.wks.1923.neo-Class.by A.M. Githens & E.L.Tilton) has rich coll. of Delawareana. It traces its history back to 1754. In E. gallery are Wilmington Soc. of Fine Arts Galleries (O.aft.wks.7:30-9:30 p.m.Mon.) containing coll. of works by Del. & other Amer. artists, incl. special coll. of works by Howard Pyle, illustrator. Pyle was born in Del. of Quaker ancestry. (4) W. side Rodney Sq., **Du Pont Bldg. & Nemours Bldg.** (on Orange St.), which house offices of E. I. du Pont de Nemours & Co. Du Pont Bldg. (Ital.Ren.13 stories) contains 1,500 offices. Hotel du Pont & The Playhouse, Wilmington's chief theater. Nemours Bldg. is 15 stories (Mod.functional by F.A.Godley). Modern company dates from reorganization of its affiliates in 1902 under leadership of A. V. du Pont, great-grandson of founder, E. I. du Pont. In 1912 it was ordered dissolved by Fed. courts as being in restraint of trade under Sherman Anti-Trust Act, but was permitted to retain its monopoly of manufacture of smokeless powder. During World War I it built world's largest smokeless powder plant at Nashville, Tenn. During postwar decades du Ponts have branched out into great variety of industries: Gen. Motors, rayon & cellophane plants, chemicals, etc. Today theirs is one of great industrial empires of Amer. (5) N. side of Rodney Sq., **U. S. Post Office, Cth. & Custom H.** (1937.by E.W.Martin,G.M.Whiteside II,Robinson,Stanhope & Manning & Walker & Gillette). On 2nd fl. is Fed. Court, in which are portraits of earlier Dist. Judges & mural by Albert Pels, depicting landing of Swedes in 1638. (6) NW. cor. 11th & Market Sts., **First Central Ch.** (Presb.O.wks.1930.Georg.Col.by Brown & Whiteside). (7) NE. cor. 9th & Market Sts., **Del. Trust Bldg.** (Ren.by Dennison & Hirons.15 stories). (8) **Wilmington Savings Fund Bldg.** (Class.) on whose inter. wall is mural by N. C. Wyeth, "The Apotheosis of the Family."

(S) OF RODNEY SQ.: (9) SW. cor. 8th & Shipley Sts., **St. Andrews Ch.** (Episc.1840). (10) 701-703 West St., **Woodward Hs.** (N.O.1745 & 1760); No.703 has part of platform on which Thos. Jefferson stood when reading Decl. of Ind. (11) SE. cor. 6th & West Sts., **St. Peter's Pro-Cathedral** (1816.adds.1832), 1st Cath. Ch. est. in Wilmington. (12) 512 N. Market St., **Old Town Hall** (O.wks.Sat.a.m.1798.Georg.Col.) was designed by Peter Baudry, early Fr. settler. Many notable ceremonies took place here: processions to comm. death of Washington, banquet for Thos. Jefferson, dinner in 1824 for Lafayette. Bldg. was purchased by Del. Hist. Soc. in 1917 & later repaired. It contains (13) **Coll.** of valuable & int. curios. (14) NE. cor. 4th & King Sts., **Dr. Simms H.** (N.O.c.1820), where Dr. John Simms est. his apothecary shop, 2nd in Wilmington, 1840. (15) SE. cor. 3rd & Market Sts., **Sign of the Ship Tavern** (now shop), pre-Rev. inn. (16) SE. cor. 3rd & Walnut Sts., **Asbury Meth. Ch.,** dedicated by Bishop Francis Asbury, 1789. (17) 303 West St., **Washington's Hqs.** (N.O.front later add.), used just prior to Battle of the Brandywine. (18) West St., **Friends' Meeting H.** (O.for services.1816). Adj. is burial ground where John Dickinson, abolitionist Thos. Garrett & other Quaker notables are buried. (19) SE. cor. 7th & Church Sts., **Old Swedes (Holy Trinity) Ch.** (O.appl.sexton.1699.later adds.rest.1899) was orig. plain stone bldg. to which in 1750 an arched porch was added & in 1802, tower & belfry. Bldg. was erected through efforts of Rev. Eric Bjorck, who came from Sweden in 1697; his portrait hangs in vestry. Vicarage & gateway were built in 1855; parish house, in 1893. In channel at E. end of Ch. is marble altar which incloses orig. altar. On N. side is old pulpit (1698); on S. side, old baptistry. In cemetery, dating from shortly after 1638, it is said there have been 15,000 burials. (20) Foot of E. 7th St., **Site of Ft. Christina,** at The Rocks, where Minuit's company landed in Mar. 1638. This is now St. Pk. Here is Mon. bearing representation of "Kalmar

Nyckel" (Key of Kalmar), one of Minuit's ships. (21) On embankment, S. side of Christina R., near Del. R., **Alrichs H.** (17th cent.) on land bought by Peter Alrichs from Inds. in 1633. (22) **Marine Terminal** (O.appl.at office.1923), on S. bank of Christina R. near its J. with Del. R. (23) New Castle Ave. & F St., **Eden Pk.**

N. OF RODNEY SQ.: (24) 1203-1205 Market St., **John Marot Twin Hs.** (N.O.fine early 19th cent.). (25) Market St. bet. 13th & 14th Sts., **Price Hs.** (N.O.1825-35.Col. with Gr.Rev.motifs). (26) 1310 King St., **Jacob Starr H.** (N.O.c.1806). (27) Park Dr. at West St., **Col. Dames H.** (N.O.1740.Dutch-Col.), orig. 1st Presb. Ch., removed here in 1919. (28) N. Market St. at 16th St., **Brandywine Bridge,** crossing Brandywine Cr., whose name derives from Finn, Andrew Brandwyn, also spelled Brandwine & Brainwinde, who before 1670 had parcel of land near here. (29) **Brandywine Village,** (N) of Cr., oldest & picturesque sec. of Wilmington, was built on land granted to Jacob Vandever, Dutch settler; owned by John Dickinson. (30) **Mills** which furnished flour to Amer. Army during Rev. were located on Cr. in this vic. They were operated by Jos. Tattnall & his son-in-law, Thomas Lea. (31) At 1801 N. Market St., **Derickson H.** (N.O.c.1771) derives its name from Jacob Derickson, descendant of early Swedish settler. (32) 1803 N. Market St., **Jos. Tattnall H.** (N.O. 1770 alt.), built by Jos. Tattnall, Eng. Quaker who entertained Washington & Lafayette here. (33) 1807 N. Market St., **Edw. Tattnall H.** (N.O.c.1790), built by Jos. & given to his son, Edw. Tattnall, on latter's marriage. (34) 1901 N. Market St., **William Lea H.** (N.O.post-Col.). (35) 1905 N. Market St., **Wm. Smith H.** (N.O.post-Col.), built by Wm. Smith, cordwainer (shoemaker). (36) SW. cor. Concord Ave. & N. Market St., **Cathedral Ch. of St. John** (Episc.O.wks.Sun.7:30 a.m.-5 p.m.1853. Eng.Goth.) stands on site of old Green Tree Inn, notorious tavern. In Chapel of the Holy Innocents is Titian's "Farnese Investiture" (37) 5 Vandever Ave., **Old Brandywine Academy** (O.wks.afts.& eves.), founded in 1798 as boys' sch., now clubh. for Del. Assoc. of Police.

W. & NW. SECS.: (38) 10th St. & Park Pl., **Cool Spring Pk.,** containing **Mus. of the Soc. of Nat. Hist.** (O.Tues.Thurs.Fri.afts.June-Sept.), with coll. of flora & fauna & minerals. (39) On H. Fletcher Brown estate, best viewed from Franklin St. bet. 10th & 11th Sts., 250-yr.-old **Rodney Oak.** (40) SW. cor. 9th & Broom Sts., **Tilton H.** (N.O.1802), now occupied by Univ. Club. (41) 9th & Clayton Sts., **Rodney Reservoir,** with **Observ. Tower** (O) from which fine view. (42) Delaware Ave. & W. 14th St., **Soldiers & Sailors Mon.,** comm. Del.'s soldiers who fell in Civil War. (43) N. side of Delaware Ave., bet. Madison & Adams Sts., & extending to Brandywine Pk. Dr., **Wilmington & Brandywine Cemetery** (1843), where are buried many prominent Delawareans. (44) Washington St., **Washington Mem. Bridge** (1922.by Vance W. Torbet,arch.& Ben.H.Davis,engineer), comm. Del.'s soldiers in World War I. At N. end is **Todd Mem.** surmounted by figure of Victory. (45) NE. end of Van Buren St. Bridge, **Josephine Garden,** in which is **Josephine Mem. Fountain** (reprod.of Tribola Fountain in Florence,Italy), erected to comm. his wife by Gen. J. E. Smith. Near-by on Monkey Hill are small Zoo & Baynard Field (sports facils.). (46) Lovering Ave. near Broom St., **Site of Encampment of Continental Army** (1777), identified by marker. (47) Lovering Ave. & Union St., **Del. Academy of Medicine** (O.wks. Sat.10-12.1816.Fed.fine exter.& inter.), removed to its present location in 1931. Bldg. is used by Medical Soc. of Del., founded 1789, 3rd oldest medical soc. in U.S., & by New Castle Cty. Medical Soc. & Del. St. Dental Soc. On 2nd fl., exhibits of early dental instruments. (48) Park Dr. near Woodlawn Ave., **Del. Art Center,** which has coll. of paintings, incl. very comprehensive representation of pre-Raphaelite canvasses by Rossetti, Ford Madox Brown, Burne-Jones, Millais, Watts. (49) Woodlawn Ave., bet. Shallcross & Lovering Aves., **Statue of Thos. F. Bayard** (by Effie Stillman), several times U.S. Sen., Pres. Cleveland's Secy. of St., & later named by him as Amer. Ambassador to Brit. (50) Tower Rd. (N) of 19th St., **Rockford Tower** (O) from whose top fine views. (51) (S) of Tower, **Statue of Admiral S. F. du Pont,** who was commodore of squadron at capture of Port Royal, S.C., during Civil War.

SW. SEC.: (52) Sycamore Ave., **Canby Pk.** (pic.swim.bridle paths.trls.tennis). (53) 809 S. Broom St., **Banning H.** (N.O.early 19th cent.stucco added later.fine inter.), now rectory of St. Elizabeth's (Cath.) Ch. (54) Maryland Ave., near Broom St., fine old **Latimeria Mansion** (O.appl.1815.some Gr.Rev.features.fine inter.), built after designs by E. I. du Pont & long occupied by Miss Mary R. Latimer, who died at age of 95 in 1929.

# TRIPS OUT OF WILMINGTON

## I. WILMINGTON (NE) to DEL.-PA. LINE. 8. US13

**2.5.** J. with Rd. leading (R) 1.5m to **U.S. Lighth. Depot** (O.appl.), which is supply & repair base for Del. coastal reg. **3.** J. with Lore Ave. leading (R) to Wilmington suburb of **Hillcrest;** at 102 Lore Ave., **Jos. Wigglesworth Archaeological Coll.** (O. appl.) containing 40,000 specimens of Ind. artifacts. Short distance (N) of last J., just (S) of St. Hy. Police Sta., is **Tussey H.** (N.O.1765). **3.5. WM. DU PONT ESTATE** (N.O.). **5.5.** J. with Grubb's Rd.

SIDE TRIP: Take latter (L) 2m to **Arden,** founded by group of single taxers, socialists & liberals. Among more famous residents have been author Upton Sinclair, sculptor Frank Stephens & radical publicist Scott Nearing. Town achieved headlines when, in 1911, 11 members of community, incl. Upton Sinclair, were jailed overnight under 1793 blue law for "gaming" on Sabbath (they had been playing baseball, except Sinclair, who had played tennis); threats to invoke same law against members of a Wilmington country club, among whom were court officials & judges accustomed to playing golf on Sundays, relegated it to oblivion once more. Residents of Arden & adj. community, Ardentown, possess their land under leaseholds & holding system that follows as much as possible single-tax system proposed by Henry George. Both communities have developed handicraft enterprises, credit union & various guilds. PTS. OF INT.: (1) **Village Green** on which is held annual Town Fair. (2) **The Homestead** (N.O.1909), built by Frank Stephens, town's real founder. (3) Adj. is **Woodland Theater** (open-air) where formerly Shakespearean plays & meetings were held. (4) Woodland Lane & Theater Path, **Upton Sinclair H.,** now used as an inn. (5) Miller's Rd. & Milky Way, **Weavers' Plant,** where hand-weaving is carried on. (6) **Guild Hall** (O.a.m.) on Hy. & Clubhouse Path, hqs. of community. (7) Adj. is **Moonlight Theater** (open-air), where plays are given. (8) Grubb's Rd., opp. The Sweep (Rd.), old **Grubb's Burying Ground,** dating back to 1760. (9) Miller's Rd. near Mall, in Ardentown, **Robin Hood Theater,** where, in summer, professional actors present plays. Beyond Arden, c.0.5m on Grubb's Rd., **Grubb Homestead** (N.O.c.1682 & 1760.int.inter.& furnishings); 1st H. was built of logs & became kitchen wing of later structure. Near H. are Slave Quarter & old Stone Barn.

**6.5. CLAYMONT,** Wilmington suburb. **7.5. ROBINSON H.** (stone part c.1723), now tea room, was inn on hy. to Phila. where Washington stayed in Aug., 1777, while waiting to learn destination of Brit. army, which had landed at head of Elk R., Md. Adj. is **Stone Blockh.** (O.appl.allegedly 1654), captured by Inds. in 1671, by Brit. in 1777, & recaptured by "Light Horse Harry" Lee in 1778. **8. DEL.-PA. LINE.**

## II. WILMINGTON (N) to DEL.-PA. LINE. 6.5. US202

**2.** J. with Augustine Cut-Off, leading (L) 0.5m to **Friends Sch.** (O.Georg.Col.), private nonsect. coed. sch. founded in 1748; it is oldest educational institution in Del. Present bldg. is modern. Short distance (N) from above J. on US202, **Blue Ball Tavern** (N.O.pre-1800), formerly well-known inn, at J. with Rockland Rd. Latter leads (L) 0.5m to **Nemours** (1908.Fr.-Chateau by Carrère & Hastings), former estate of Alfred I. du Pont, now hospital. Grounds, colonnade, fountains & statuary suggest Gardens of Versailles. Carillon Tower (210'.elevator) affords splendid view; Mr. du Pont is buried in crypt of tower. Close to tower is grave of Yip, mongrel dog who survived his master only few days. At **2.5. LOMBARDY** (N.O.), purchased in 1793 by Gunning Bedford, Jr., signer of Constitution. At **5.5.** J. with Naaman's Rd.

SIDE TRIP: Take latter (R) to J. with St.261 at 2.5m & turn (L) on this to **Chester-Bethel M.E. Ch.** (1799) at 3m.

**6.5. DEL.-PA. LINE.**

## III. WILMINGTON (NW) to LONGWOOD. 12.5. St.52

At **2. GOODSTAY** & at **2.5. ST. AMOUR,** both estates belonging to members of du Pont family. Latter is at J. with Rising Sun Lane.

SIDE TRIP: Take Rising Sun Lane (R) 0.5m to **Experimental Sta. of E. I. du Pont de Nemours & Co.** (N.O.), birthpl. of nylon, country's largest & one of world's largest chemical research labs., to which $30,000,000 expansion was made beginning in 1948. Adj. is **Du Pont Country Club** for employees. Rising Sun Lane cont. to **Old Upper Hagley Yard,** 1m, where, in old days, du Ponts carried on powder making. Founder of family's fortunes, E. I. du Pont, learned art of powder-manufacture in labs. of famous Fr. chemist, Lavoisier. By 1804, he had est. industry on Brandywine Cr. Powder manufacture cont. here until disastrous explosion in 1915, which killed 30 people & broke windowpanes as far away as Wilmington. In vic. are **Old Woolen Mill** & a few other old bldgs.

Beyond J. with Rising Sun Lane are 2 more du Pont estates. **3.** J. with St.100 (Montchanin Rd.).

SIDE TRIP: Take latter (R). At 1m J. with Buck Rd.

Take latter (R) here 0.5m to **du Pont Family Cemetery,** overlooking Brandywine Cr. & site of old powder mills. Pierre Samuel du Pont, E. I.'s father, is buried here as well as later members of family. Just beyond cemetery is entrance (L) to **Eleutherian Mills** (N.O.1802-03.2 wings add.1843), built by E. I. du Pont, furnished in early Amer. style, with coll. of early Amer. prints & lithographs. (SW) of H. is **Orig. Office Bldg.** (1802) & near-by is old **Coal H.,** where charcoal was made. Below latter is early 18th cent. H. where E. I. du Pont & family spent winter of 1802-03 while larger H. was being built. At 1m on Buck Rd. is **Christ Ch. Christiana Hundred** (Episc.services Sun.at 11.1856.Goth.), where du Ponts have worshiped.

At 3.5m on St.100 is **Granogue** (N.O.), another du Pont estate. At 4m is J. with Beaver Valley Rd.

Take latter (R) 1.5m to **Smith's Bridge** (1839) one of few remaining covered bridges in Del. still in use.

**3.** J. with Barley Mill Rd.

SIDE TRIP: Take latter (L) 0.5m & turn (R) at fork to **Edgar M. Hooper Reservoir Dam,** 2.5m; dam is 135′ high & 970′ long & encloses artificial L.

**4.5. DOGWOOD** (N.O.), another du Pont estate. Just beyond is J. with St.82.

SIDE TRIP: Take latter (L) 0.5m to J. with private lane.

Take latter (L) to **Valley Garden** (O.exc.Sat.& Sun.Ap.& May), estate of Mrs. Ellen C. du Pont Wheelwright, beautifully landscaped & one of show places of Wilmington reg.

1m **Walnut Green Sch.** (1780.add.1918). 3.5m old **Covered Bridge** (closed to traffic). 5m **Yorklin** (sett.1684), where is **Helme Snuff Plant** (N.O.), built by John Garrett in late 18th cent., which still does thriving business.

Just beyond Dogwood is **Chevannes** (N.O.Fr.-Norman), another du Pont mansion. **5. WINTERTHUR** (N.O.), estate of Henry F. du Pont, U.S. Sen. 1906-17. H. is Georg.Col., decorated in various Amer. styles, with coll. of paintings & antiques. **5.5.** Hist. **BRANDYWINE CH.** (Presb.founded 1721.present bldg.1856), at J. with Old Kennett Rd.

SIDE TRIP: Take latter (L) past **Dauneport** (N.O.), another du Pont estate, & at 1m, take Owl's Nest Rd. (R) to **Owl's Nest** (N.O.Eng.-Tudor), another du Pont estate, at 1m.

**6.5.** J. with Rd.

SIDE TRIP: Take latter (R) 1m to old **Friends Center Meeting H.** (1796.service last Sun.of each month). Opp. is **Centerville Schoolh.** (N.O.pre-1818).

**8. DEL.-PA. LINE.** Here is old **Stone Line H. 8.5.** Another du Pont mansion (L) on hill. **12. LONGWOOD MEETING H.** (1856), where each yr. meetings have been held to discuss national topics. Name derives from wood where fugitive slaves hid. At **12.5.** pub. entrance for **LONGWOOD** (O.wks.fee for charity on 1st & 3rd Sun. of each month.free organ recital on Sun.3-5), estate of Pierre S. du Pont, with fine gardens and a conservatory housing large pipe organ, fountains playing under colored lights & open-air theater. Near estate is **Mon. to Hannah Freeman** (1730-1802), last of Lenni-Lenape Inds. of reg.

## IV. WILMINGTON (W) to DEL.-PA. LINE. 9. St.48 & St.41

Take St.48 (W) to J. with St.41, **7.**, & turn (R) on latter. At **9.** is J. with Valley Rd.

SIDE TRIP: Take latter (R) 0.5m to Rd. fork.

(1) Turn (R) here 0.5m to **Hockessin Friends Meeting H.** (Sun.meetings at 10.1738. adds.1745), commanding fine view. Across Rd. old **Cemetery,** in which is magnificent boxwood.

(2) Turn (L) at fork 0.5m to stone H. containing **Archaeological Coll.** (O.appl.) of Ind. artifacts.

**10. DEL.-PA. LINE.**

## V. WILMINGTON (SW) to DEL.-MD. LINE. 15.5. St.2

**3.5. PRICE'S CORNER** at J. of 3 Rds.

SIDE TRIP: Take 3rd Rd. (R) 0.5m to **New Castle Cty. Workh.** (O.Mon.& Wed.p.m.Sat. 9-4). At 1.5m **Greenbank Gristmill** (1790 & 1812) is still functioning, using water power of Red Clay Cr.

Just beyond Price's Corner, on St.2, is whitewashed **Log H.** (now roadside market. allegedly 17th cent.). **4.** J. with St.41.

SIDE TRIP: Take latter (L) 1.5m to **Newport,** on Christina R. NW. cor. James & Market Sts., former **Inn** (18th cent.). Adj., old **Double H.** (N.O.). SE. cor. Market & John Sts., **Myers (Parkin) H.** (18th cent.). W. side of John St., (S) of Market Sts., **Galloway H.** (c.1730).

At 6. is J. with St.7.

SIDE TRIP: Take latter (L) to **Stanton,** 1m, known as late as 1768 by name of Cuckoldstown. SE. cor. of main inters., **Brick H.** (N.O.) was tavern as late as 1797. E. side of Old Mill Rd., **Tattnall (Byrnes) H.** (N.O.c.1750.Dutch-Col.). On St.7 (R), **Marshall H.,** where Washington & his staff, it is said, were interrupted at breakfast by sound of Brit. cannon. At 2m **Boyce H.** (N.O.pre-1775). 4.5m **Christiana,** on Christina Cr. in 18th cent. was lively port; it has some interesting old bldgs. At 5m **Lewden H.** (N.O.1770.add.1815. recently rest.Georg.-Col.fine inter.). 8.5m **Red Lion,** where is former **Red Lion Inn** (N.O. post-Rev.).

**7.5. ST. JAMES CH.** (Episc.O.appl.Sun.service 11.1820.belfry later.Gr.Rev.int.inter), where cemetery dates back to 1726. **8. DELAWARE PK.** (running & steeplechase races one month in summer). **10.5. WHITE CLAY CH.** (Presb.Sun.services 11.1855), at J. with Rd.

SIDE TRIPS: (A) Take latter (R) up Polly Drummond Hill to **Gray H.** (late 18th cent.rest. fine old inter.).
(B) Take Rd. (L) 0.5m to old **England Manor H. & Mill** (H.1747.beautiful Col.fine exter. & inter.;Mill supposedly c.1747). Mill is still functioning, now with modern machinery.

**12.5.** J. with Chapel St. leading (R) to **Covered Bridge** at 0.5m, just beyond which is **Curtis Paper Plant** (O.appl.), dating back to 1798; across Rd. from latter is old **S. Minot Curtis H.** (N.O.). **13. NEWARK** by middle of 18th cent. had become crossroads stopover with number of inns & tavern. Newark Academy, est. in New London, Pa., 1743, after being moved from there to Md., finally was set up in Newark, 1767. For a time it became part of Del. College, but after 1859, when latter closed for lack of funds, it cont. as separate institution until 1898. Del. College reopened in 1870, financed by Fed. Land Grant, & in 1921 it united with Women's College, est. in 1914, to become Univ. of Del. PTS. OF INT.: **Univ. of Del. Campus,** bisecting town, with Del. College for Men & Women's College housed in separate group bldgs., former consisting of 3 schs.: Arts & Sciences, Agric. & Engineering & latter also of 3: Arts & Sciences, Education & Home Economics. Grad. courses are offered in Engineering & other fields. Among noteworthy bldgs. are: **Old College** (1834. adds.), built with money raised by lottery; **Elliott Hall** (late 18th cent.Georg.Col.fine inter.); **Mem. Lib.** (O.wks.aft.eves.&Sun.during academic yr.1924.mod.Georg.Col.); **Mitchell Hall** (mod.Georg.Col.) with auditorium equipped for dramatic performances. SE. cor. Main & Academy Sts., **Academy of Newark Bldgs.,** in one of which is town lib. On Old Oak Rd., **Oaklands,** built by Rathmell Wilson, who was acting Pres. of Del. College, 1859-70. College Ave. & Pa. RR., **Chrysler Corp. Del. Parts Plant** (O.appl.) completed 1948, with 16 as. of bldgs., serving dealers in 14 states.

SIDE TRIPS: (A) Take St.896 (R) from Newark 3.5m to **Del.-Pa. Line,** where side Rd. leads (R) 0.1m to **Mon.** on site of marker set by Mason & Dixon in 1765 in their survey to est. Pa.-Md.'s boundary line; marker was used later to locate Mason-Dixon line under Mo. Compromise.
(B) Take St.896 (L) 2.5m to J. with Rd. leading (R) 0.2m to **Welsh Bapt. Ch.** (O.appl. meetings 3rd Sun.in month.1746), whose congregation was org. c.1701 by group of Primitive Bapts. who in that yr. emigrated to Amer. At 3.5m is **Cooch H.** (N.O.1760.upper story added 1865), columns of whose side-porch were cut from old ships' masts. Here is mon. comm. site of only military fight of Rev. on Del. soil, **Skirmish of Cooch's Bridge,** Sept. 3, 1777.
(R) here 1m & then (R) again to **Iron Hill** (334′), highest pt. in Del. where iron was formerly mined.
11m **J.** with St.71 on which side trip cont. (S). 18m **Middletown** which has a few int. old bldgs.
Take St.4 (R) here 1m to **Cochran Grange** (1845.Gr.Rev.).
19m Old **St. Anne's Ch.** (Episc.O.appl.1768), one of finest old chs. in Del. 23m J. with US13 (see).

St.2 cont. (SW) from Newark to **DEL.-MD. LINE, 15.5.,** short distance beyond which lane leads (L) to **Tangent Stone** placed by Mason & Dixon in 1765 at inters. of Del., Md. & Pa. boundaries.

## VI. WILMINGTON (S) to ST. GEORGES. 15.5. US13

**2. OLD HOOK FARM** (N.O.oldest sec.c.1660.wing 1763.other adds.1860), built on land owned by Peter Jacquet, vice-director of Dutch Colony, on S. shore of Del. R. **3. FARNHURST,** at J. with hy. leading (L) 2m to **Del. Mem. Bridge** (toll) across Del. R., 4-lane span with vertical clearance of 175′, whose construction, at cost of $40,000,000, was begun late in 1948. **3.5.** J. with Landers Lane leading (L) 0.5m to **Stanwyck** (N.O.1820.Fr.Ren.), built by Huguenot Immigrants. **4. DEL. ST. HOSPITAL** for mentally ill. **6.5.** J. with US40 (see). **9.5. BUENA VISTA** (N.O.1846.

later adds.), built by J. M. Clayton, Chief Justice of Del., U.S. Sen. & Secy. of St. under Zachary Taylor. H. has many fine paintings, incl. one of Queen Elizabeth by Nicholas Hilliard & several by Gilbert Stuart. **14. DAMASCUS** (N.O.c.1790) built by Jesse Higgins, author of pamphlet entitled "Samson Against the Philistines" (1804) advocating arbitration as substitute for lawsuits; Del. lawyers bought up whole edition, which, however, was republished. **14.5. LINDEN HILL** (N.O.), birthpl. of Anthony Higgins, U.S. Sen. & defense counsel in case of Neal vs. Del. which est. principle that Negro accused of crime had right to trial by "jury of his peers"; on this case U.S. Supreme Court based decision ordering new trial for "Scottsboro Boys" in 1935. **15.5. ST. GEORGES,** bisected by Del. & Chesapeake Canal, was in 18th cent. important stop on King's Hy. Broad St., N. St. Georges, **Sutton H.** (N.O.1802.fine inter.).

# WASHINGTON, D.C.

## WASHINGTON, D.C.

Gen. Info.: Board of Trade, Greater Nat. Capital Committee in lobby of Evening Star Bldg., 11th & Pennsylvania Ave. RR. Sta.: Union Sta., Massachusetts & Delaware Aves. NE. for Atlantic Coast Line RR., B. & O. RR., C. & O. RR., Norfolk & Western RR.; Pennsylvania RR.; Richmond, Fredericksburg & Potomac RR.; Seaboard RR. & Southern RR. Buses: Greyhound Terminal, 12th & New York Ave. NW.; Trailways Bus Depot, 1201 New York Ave. NW. Air: Washington Nat. Airport, Mt. Vernon Hy. 3.5m NW. Steamship Pier: Norfolk & Washington Steamboat Co., 1427 H St. NW., to Norfolk (carries automobiles). Sightseeing Buses: Gray Line Terminal, 1315 New York Ave. NW. Tours of city & environs start from Union Sta. & central pts. in downtown sec. River Excursions: Potomac R. Line, 7th St. & Main Ave. SW., & Wilson Line Inc., 7th St. Wharves, SW. Accoms.: All types in city & vic. Street Arrangement: Washington is divided into 4 secs. (NW., NE., SW. & SE.) by N. Capitol, E. Capitol & S. Capitol Sts. N-S Sts. are numbered; E-W Sts. are lettered (omitting J St. & ending with W St.). "Second Alphabet" Sts. composed of 2-syllable names follow & after that "Third Alphabet" Sts. Diagonal avenues are named for States. Concert Halls: Constitution Hall, 18th & D Sts. NW., & Coolidge Music Auditorium, Lib. of Congress. Art Galleries & Museums (see Pts. of Int.). Recreation: Excellent recr. facils. in city's pks. Football: Griffith Stadium, 7th & Florida Ave. NW., & on Cath. Univ. campus. Polo: In W. Potomac Pk. (May 1 to Oct.). Swimming: Many pub. pools for Negroes & for whites. Indoor sports events at the Uline Arena, 3rd & M Sts. NE. Annual Events: Inauguration of Pres. (every 4th yr.on Jan.20). Cherry Blossom Festival (no fixed date;usually end of Mar.or beginning of Ap.). Christmas Eve.: Lighting of the community tree in ellipse by the Pres.

Within the District of Columbia, whose area of c.70 square miles is today almost entirely occupied by the City of Washington, live about 800,000 people, & in suburban Virginia & Maryland, some 300,000 more. The lives of this million largely revolve around the District's two major industries—government & politics. During World War I the population grew enormously. With the great depression of the '30's, government activities expanded once more & they continued to expand, with World War II & the boom in government functions during the postwar period.

The rectangle of the District pushes northeast into Maryland; its southwestern side, however, has a natural boundary on the Potomac facing Virginia. At the southeast angle of the District, the Potomac & Anacostia Rivers meet. The Anacostia branches off north here through the eastern section of the city.

The broad Mall is the great axis around or near which are grouped most of the public bldgs. It runs from Lincoln Memorial, at Memorial Bridge on the Potomac, northeast to Capitol Hill, imposingly crowned by the domed Capitol. Not quite halfway between Lincoln Memorial & the Capitol, on a little eminence, rises the mighty obelisk of the Washington Monument. Here is a transverse axis, from which the White House can be seen across the Ellipse on the one hand & the gleaming white temple of the Jefferson Memorial, across the Tidal Basin, on the other.

Major Pierre Charles L'Enfant, the original planner of the city, laid it out in conventional gridiron pattern; but on the "grid" he imposed a series of diagonal avenues, & this addition has given Washington a number of charming "circles" & vistas at points where streets & avenues meet.

The L'Enfant Plan was considerably obscured by the city's growth during the 19th century. It was in the early 1900's that the Federal Government made a determined effort to return to the spirit, if not the letter, of the original layout. The result has been impressive. The Mall was cleared of unsightly obstructions. The majestic vista from the Potomac to Capitol Hill was restored. Capitol Hill itself was developed with the Senate & House Office Bldgs. & the Supreme Court Bldg., the latter erected approximately on the site which L'Enfant had intended for it. A magnificent plaza was cleared to connect the Capitol grounds with the great Union Station. Both sides of the Potomac have been reclaimed for parks & parkways. The lowlands along the Anacostia River have been filled in & parked. Rock Creek has been reclaimed as a park extending through the heart of the city. Only old Tiber Creek, which flowed through the Mall from Capitol Hill westward & which L'Enfant planned to use for a "cascade & a grand fountain," has disappeared entirely. Washington has a great many trees; it is said to have more of them than any other American city. In the spring, when the magnolias are in bloom, the capital is at its best.

Most of the great public bldgs. have been concentrated in a comparatively small area at the city's south end, between Pennsylvania Avenue & the south side of the Mall. The greatest concentration is in the so-called Triangle between Pennsylvania & Constitution Avenues, where are located 12 huge structures. The result has been a serious traffic problem for which no solution has as yet been worked out.

The styles of the public bldgs. reflect the various periods in which they were erected. The charming White House belongs to the late 18th century. To the west of it the old State Department Bldg. illustrates the least attractive developments of post-Civil War architecture. The Treasury, to the East, is beautiful Greek Revival. The Capitol, magnificently placed on Capitol Hill, from which its lofty dome dominates the Mall, is Roman classic, in the Jefferson-Palladian vein. The Senate & House Office Bldgs., near-by, are restrained modern-classic, inspired by French models. The Supreme Court is a huge, white marble temple. The Union Station was inspired by Beaux Arts trends made popular by the Chicago World's Fair of 1893. The Folger Library, by Paul Cret, is one of the most successful modern bldgs. in the city. The Triangle Bldgs., planned in the 1920's, have been characterized as Italian palaces. Their colonnaded façade on Constitution Avenue is truly formidable.

More recent government structures have tended toward modern functional. The Department of Interior & the War Department (now occupied by the State Department) Bldgs. are good examples. The recently erected National (Mellon) Gallery, on the Mall, although simple in design, is a reversion to classic influences. The Jefferson Memorial is a classic temple reminiscent of Jefferson's rotunda at the University of Virginia. The Lincoln Memorial was inspired by the Parthenon.

It is in its private dwellings, mostly in Georgetown & Alexandria, Va., just outside the District, that is to be found Washington's most charming architecture, mostly of the 18th century.

One of the pressing issues that confronted Congress after ratification of the Federal Constitution, was the location of the national capital. This became a matter of bargaining between the Northern & Southern states. In return for an agreement to pass Hamilton's Assumption Bill, by which to assume the debts incurred by each state during the Revolution were to be validated, the Northerners agreed on a location in the South. In 1791 a site on the Potomac, ten miles square, situated partly in Maryland & partly in Virginia, was chosen. Maryland & Virginia ceded the necessary territory. Washington selected Major L'Enfant, French engineer, to draw up a plan for the projected capital. Washington, himself, with the help of Jefferson & Madison, selected designs for most of the public bldgs. Unfortunately, L'Enfant's proposals were considered too grandiose by more "practical" men. He became hopelessly embroiled in controversies, & Washington finally had to dismiss him.

When President Adams moved into the half-finished President's House in 1800, the capital was still in embryo. His wife Abigail complained "we have not the least fence, yard or other conveniences without, & the great unfinished audience-room (East Room) I make a drying-room of to hang the clothes in." Jefferson's occupancy of the President's House brought a new & refreshing informality to government functions. He eschewed as much as possible formal & lavish entertainment. Dolly Madison, wife of his Secretary of State, acted as his hostess, since he himself was a widower, & from then on & during Madison's Presidency, she was the acknowledged queen of Capital society.

In August, 1814, after the Battle of Bladensburg, a British force under Gen. Ross & Adm. Cockburn entered Washington at twilight & burned the partially finished Capitol, the President's House & some other public bldgs. Dolly Madison succeeded in smuggling out the Declaration of Independence & the Gilbert Stuart portrait of

Washington. To hide the slightly charred timbers above the solid stone base, the President's House, when rebuilt, was painted white; hence its present name.
During Monroe's administration, public receptions were sumptuous & always in great state. But Andrew Jackson's hurly-burly inauguration ended the aristocratic era & brought a crowd of rowdy pioneer followers into the District. The capital's matrons, led by Mrs. Calhoun, established a social boycott against the wife of the Secretary of War, John H. Eaton. Mrs. Eaton had been Peggy O'Neale, daughter of a tavern keeper. It is said Calhoun lost his chance at the Presidency because of Jackson's anger at Mrs. Calhoun. Foreigners of the 1830's & 40's were not greatly impressed by the capital. Charles Dickens called it a "monument raised to a deceased project." The city streets were still ill-lit &, in rainy weather, bogged in mud. Houses were few & far between.
In 1846, Alexandria, which had been part of the District, was returned to Virginia at the request of that state. During Polk's term, Washington became an important station on the Underground Railway. An unsuccessful slave-running incident of 1848 caused a great stir in the capital. In 1854 "Know Nothings" brazenly raided & seized the half-finished Washington Monument & in their frenzy of anti-Catholicism & xenophobia destroyed one of the stones contributed to the monument by the Pope. John Brown's raid on Harpers Ferry in 1859, only 65 miles away, greatly aggravated the slavery issue in Washington, where Southern sympathizers were strong. With election of Abraham Lincoln in 1860, the "irrepressible conflict" became inevitable, although Lincoln himself hoped for peace & compromise. He ended his inaugural address with the words: ". . . we are not enemies but friends, we must not be enemies. Though passion may have strained, it must not break, our bonds of affection." Fort Sumter fell April 13, 1861, & War between the States followed. Federal troops poured into the city & Confederate forces were massed about 30 miles southwest. A few hours after the Battle of Bull Run, the wounded began to arrive & from then on Washington became the center of military activities. Franklin Park, during the war, was filled with tents & military equipment. Before the end of 1861 more than 150,000 soldiers were encamped in or near the city. It was a returning group of these weary foot soldiers, singing "John Brown's body lies a-mouldering in his grave," that inspired Julia Ward Howe to write the words of her "Battle Hymn of the Republic" at the Willard Hotel.
After the Battle of Bull Run in 1861, the Confederates might have taken the almost defenseless city, & in 1864, Gen. Early's command reached Silver Springs, now a northern suburb, but failed to invade the capital. A few days after Gen. Lee's surrender, the city was stunned by news of Lincoln's assassination at Ford's Theater. Vice-President Johnson, who succeeded Lincoln & sought to carry out his plan to conciliate the South, came into conflict with the Northern radicals, led by the implacable Thaddeus Stephens. He was impeached & finally acquitted by a margin of only one vote. Grant's administrations marked the beginning of the post-Civil War era of graft & lavish display, temporarily interrupted by the "Black Friday" panic of 1869 & the Credit Mobilier scandals. But the Grant administrations brought great civic improvements. In 1871 Congress gave the District a territorial form of government, which, under leadership of Alexander Shepherd, practically rebuilt the city. The drive for great public works ended rather abruptly with the panic of 1873. In 1878 the "organic act" was passed by which the District became a municipal corporation managed by three commissioners appointed by the President. The citizens were given no participation in the city government. This commission form of government has continued to the present day.
Theodore Roosevelt's administration, following the assassination of McKinley in 1901, introduced an era in a way reminiscent of Jackson's time. William Allen White wrote: "He filled the White House with all sorts & conditions of men: Western bull-whackers, city prize fighters, explorers, rich men, poor men, an occasional black man, editors, writers; . . . He talked state secrets . . . so that reporters could hear."
Wilson's first administration ushered in an era of reform legislation. His second administration, during World War I, brought a flood of military activities, but his long illness & the bitter opposition in Congress to his foreign policy & to the League of Nations created, a "social-political atmosphere . . . of bleak & chill austerity." The Wilson era was followed by the high, wide & handsome days of political scandals under Harding. The most notable achievement of the Coolidge administration, as far as Washington was concerned, was the inauguration of the huge Federal Triangle

development. Hoover's incumbency was marked by the great depression & the march into Washington of the "bonus army" of unemployed veterans, culminating in a clash with Federal troops.

Franklin D. Roosevelt's first term ushered in the "New Deal" relief & works projects & many of the "alphabet" agencies had their hqs. in Washington. His long incumbency saw the completion of the Federal Triangle & erection of many new government structures, mightiest of which is the Pentagon.

Soon after Pearl Harbor the capital emerged as an armed camp. With Roosevelt's death in 1945, Washington witnessed one of the most impressive funeral marches in the nation's history. Vice-Pres. Truman succeeded to the Presidency & his 2nd term election in 1948 upset all the predictions of the public opinion polls. Truman's "Plain Deal" continues many of the New Deal's reform policies inaugurated by Roosevelt. In 1949 the Trumans moved to Blair House so that the White House could undergo much needed repairs.

During World War II the city became once more a military beehive & a world capital. It has remained the center of international politics ever since.

From the beginning of the Republic, Congress has been, on the whole, a liberal patron of the arts. The relationship between government & art has been largely impersonal & financial. Art contracted for by the government has been conservative, following, always at a considerable distance, the fluctuations of American taste.

After the Republic's founding, the government concentrated its art program on embellishment of the Capitol. Italian artists & followers of Benjamin West's school contributed murals & canvasses, & America's early sculptors, statues. Mark Twain's quip describing the Capitol as containing a "delirium tremens of art" somewhat overstates the case against the 300 or more paintings & sculptures scattered throughout the bldg. During the 19th century, some excellent monuments were designed for the city by H. K. Brown, J. Q. A. Ward & others. After the World's Fair of 1893, came a great flowering of American art, which found an outlet in the many sculptures & murals by the newer American school in the Congressional Library Bldg. After that came a whole series of impressive monuments, of which the colossal "Lincoln" by D. C. French in the Lincoln Memorial is perhaps best known. In the 1930's the Section of Fine Arts of the Public Buildings Administration, through anonymous competitions, practically eliminated politics from awards for works of art for embellishment of government bldgs. The WPA between 1935 & 1940 contributed its quota of art.

Washington has a number of outstanding museums—the Corcoran Gallery, the National Collection of Fine Arts of the Smithsonian Institute, the Phillips Memorial Gallery, with one of the finest collections in the country of modern paintings, supplemented by outstanding examples of older masters, the Freer Gallery of Oriental Art & most important of all the National Gallery with its outstanding collection of European & early American masters.

Few men of letters & no literary movements have been born in Washington. Whitman lived there during part of the Civil War & had a government job until 1873. During this period he wrote "When Lilacs Last in the Dooryard Bloomed" & "Captain, My Captain" commemorating Lincoln. John Burroughs was attracted to Washington by his admiration for Whitman & lived in the District from 1863 to 1872. Henry Adams, after Whitman the city's most distinguished literary resident, spent the greater part of his adult life there. His friend, John Hay, who made his literary debut with "Pike County Ballads," collaborated with John G. Nicolay on the monumental "Abraham Lincoln." An older historian who made his home in Washington was George Bancroft. Other prominent long-time literary residents were F. H. Burnett, author of "Little Lord Fauntleroy," Thomas Nelson Page & Elinor Wylie.

Washington is the seat of George Washington University, Catholic University of America, Georgetown University, American University & other institutions of higher learning for whites. For Negroes there is Howard University, supported by Congressional appropriations, Miner Teachers College & Frelinghuysen University.

Washington is the journalistic nerve center of the country. More than 300 newspapers & press associations, domestic & foreign, maintain bureaus & special correspondents in the capital. It was President Wilson who inaugurated the practice of holding regular conferences with the entire corps of correspondents. The late Franklin D. Roosevelt was noted for the "wide open" character of these meetings.

The population of the District is almost altogether native-born, with Negroes about 27 per cent of the total. In recent years, there has been a drive by liberals to diminish discrimination against Negroes, who are now segregated in separate schools, excluded from "white" hotels, restaurants, movie houses & residential areas, & are discriminated against in the matter of employment, even in the government. The poorest part of the Negro population lives in crowded "alleys" which it is hoped will soon be razed & replaced by decent, low-cost housing. The tuberculosis & infant mortality rates are disproportionally high among the Negroes. On the other hand, public school facilities for Negroes are in just proportion to their percentage of the population & Negro teachers' salaries are on the same scale as those of white teachers.

PTS. OF INT.: CAPITOL HILL: (1) **U.S. Capitol** (O.9-4:30 exc.Sun.&hols.guides; 1793-1865 by Latrobe & Bulfinch.dome 285′ from plaza, modeled after St.Peter's, Rome); bldg. is flanked by 2 wings in which Senate & House of Representatives meet respectively. In the Rotunda funeral rites of many notables have been held. Bldg. contains paintings & sculpture by Amer. & European artists. In Statuary Hall are life-sized bronze & marble statues of noted Amers. (2) (SW) of Capitol, **U.S. Botanic Garden** (O.wks.Sat.to noon). Its $1,000,000 conservatory & colls. rival any in world. Well-known Bartholdi Fountain is (S) of garden. (3) N.J. Ave. & E St. SE., **Capitol Power Plant** (1910). (4) Cor. of Independence & N.J. Aves., **House Office Bldg.,** on S. side of Capitol (O.1906 by Carrère & Hastings). Pedestrian subway leads from this bldg. to Capitol. (5) **Lib. of Congress** (O.Mon.-Sat.9 a.m.to 10 p.m.Sun.11:30-10 p.m.), housed in 2 massive bldgs. (E) of Capitol: Main Bldg., gray sandstone Ital. Ren. 1889-97 by Washington architects, & white marble Annex (1939) harmonizing with near-by Folger Lib. & Supreme Court Bldg. The low dome, grand stairway & Neptune Fountain are notable. Lib. contains more than 6,000,000 books besides mss. & records. The orig. Decl. of Ind. & the Constitution are exhibited here. In Coolidge Auditorium famous chamber music is played on lib.'s own Stradivari instruments. (N) of Annex is (6) **Folger Shakespeare Lib.** (O. wks.9-5 exc.Wed.;mod.Class.1932.by Paul P.Cret), housing one of greatest colls. of Shakespeariana, incl. famous Vincent Folio & reprod. of Elizabethan theater. Brenda Putnam's statue of Puck faces the Capitol from a small formal garden. (7) Cor. E. Capitol & 1st St. NE., **Supreme Court Bldg.** (O.wks.9-4:30;Sat.9-12.guides. 1935 by Cass Gilbert), glittering white marble temple, with monumental entrance & Corinthian columns. Huge allegorical figures by Jas. E. Fraser; 9 pediment figures by Rbt. Aitken. **Mem. Hall** (O.Mon.when Court is in session). Elaborate Courtroom is where Supreme Court, the tribunal of last resort on Fed. laws, convenes. (8) Cor. 1st & B Sts. NE., **Senate Office Bldg.** (O.1906.adds.by Wyeth & Sullivan) on N. side of Capitol. Below rotunda of bldg. is terminus of subway with sm. electric cars shuttling bet. it & Capitol. (9) **Union Sta.** (1907.Rom.Class.by Dan H.Burnham), monumental facade of white Vt. marble based on 3 great triumphal arches. Concourse is designed to accommodate great crowds during Presidential inaugurations & other important events. Opp. is **Columbus Mem. Fountain** by Lorado Taft with figures representing Old & New Worlds. (10) Cor. N. Capitol & Mass. Ave., **City P.O.** (1914.remod.1933 by Dan.H.Burnham.white Ital.marble) harmonizes with Union Sta. (11) N. Capitol & G Sts., **Gov. Printing Office** (10-3. wks.conducted tours at Bldg. No. 3). Massive red brick structure is largest printing plant in the world. (12) Constitution Ave. bet. 4th & 7th Sts., **Nat. Gallery of Art** (O.wks.Sun.2-10;1941.Class.by John R. Pope), one of finest & most Mod. mus. in world. Contains famous Kress & Mellon colls. of Ital. art, unsurpassed in Amer., covering Ital. painting & sculpture from 13th to 18th cent. Gallery & nucleus of exhibits were gift of Andrew Mellon, Secy. of Treasury (1921-23). Many of its Flemish, German, Dutch, Sp., Fr., Brit. and early Amer. paintings have never before been open to public. Recently some important Whistler & Sargent paintings have been acquired. Chester Dale's coll. plus many other treasures, ancient & medieval, make it a mecca not only for all art lovers but for all who visit Washington.

(E) OF ELLIPSE & (N) OF MALL: Here is Fed. Triangle consisting of group of 12 massive Gov. bldgs.: (13) Pa. & Constitution Aves., bet. 6th & 7th Sts., **Apex Bldg.,** housing **Fed. Trade Commission,** is at apex of Fed. Triangle (O.wks.Sat.till noon.1938 by Chicago architects). (14) Constitution Ave. bet. 7th & 9th Sts., **Nat. Archives** (O.wks.Sat.till noon.by John Russell Pope.completed 1935.pure Class. with Corinthian columns). Here German & Jap surrender papers are exhibited. (15)

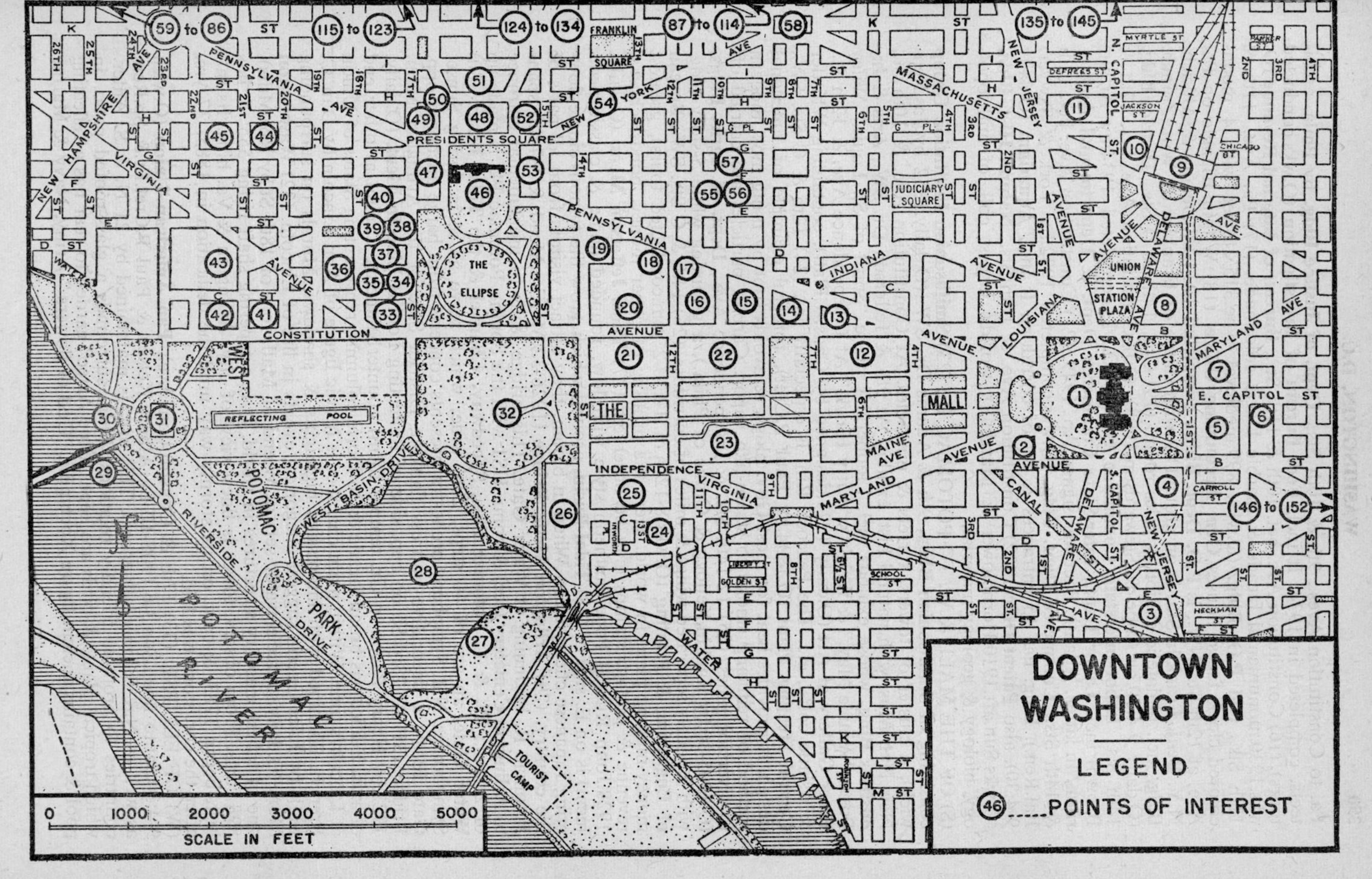
DOWNTOWN WASHINGTON
LEGEND
46 ....POINTS OF INTEREST
0 1000 2000 3000 4000 5000
SCALE IN FEET
POTOMAC RIVER
THE MALL
THE ELLIPSE
PRESIDENTS SQUARE
UNION STATION PLAZA
JUDICIARY SQUARE
FRANKLIN SQUARE
REFLECTING POOL
TOURIST CAMP
WEST POTOMAC PARK
CONSTITUTION AVENUE
INDEPENDENCE AVENUE
PENNSYLVANIA AVE
MASSACHUSETTS AVE
WEST BASIN DRIVE
RIVERSIDE DRIVE

Pa. to Constitution Aves., 9th & 10th Sts., **Dept. of Justice Bldg.** by Phila. architects, completed in 1934. It incl. **Fed. Bureau of Investigation** (O.wks.conducted tours). (16) Constitution Ave. bet. 10th & 11th Sts., **Bureau of Internal Revenue** (O.wks.1930.monumental facade & marble Doric colonnade. (17) Pa. Ave., 11th & 12th Sts., **Old P.O. Bldg.** (O.wks.1899.medieval type.315′ tower with 4 moon-colored clock faces) houses **Gen. Accounting Office.** (18) Within triangle on Pa. Ave. at 12th St., NW., is **P.O. Dept. Bldg.,** completed 1934 by Delano & Aldrich, N.Y. **Benj. Franklin Sta.** is on ground fl. with statue of Franklin by Wm. Zorach. Bldg. incl. philatelic exhibit & sales room. (19) Cor. 14th & D Sts., **District Bldg.** (O.daily 9-4:30.by Cope & Stewardson.1908). (20) Constitution Ave. bet. 12th & 14th Sts., **Labor-Interstate Commerce Group** (O.wks.completed 1934.by Arthur Brown) incl. **Labor Dept., Inter-State Commerce Dept.** & **Departmental Auditorium.** In latter, Atlantic Pact was signed Ap. 1949. (21) Constitution Ave. bet. 12th & 14th Sts., **Commerce Dept. Bldg.** (O.wks.completed 1932.by York & Sawyer. Ital.Ren.). Bldg. has 15 entrances & 8m of corridors. It incl. **Aquarium** (O.daily 9-4:30), also **Patent Office.** (22) Constitution Ave. & 10th Sts., **Natural Hist. Bldg.** (O.wks.Sun.aft.1910.Hornblower & Marshall), world's largest coll. of anthropology, biology & geology material.

(S) OF THE MALL & W. TO POTOMAC R.: (23) **Smithsonian Institution Group** consisting of **Smithsonian Bldg.,** 9th & Adams Dr. SW. (O.daily.1852 by Jas.Renwick), a cluster of towers, turrets & pinnacles. At Constitution Ave. & 10th St., **New Nat. Mus.** with natural hist. exhibit. At 9th & Jefferson Dr. SW., **Arts & Industries Bldg.** whose exhibits incl. Lindbergh's plane "Spirit of St. Louis," Wiley Post's "Winnie May," & Wright's "Kitty Hawk." At Independence Ave. & 12th St., **Freer Gallery of Art** (O.daily 1923.designed by Chas.A.Platt), containing Whistler & Asiatic colls., etc. The Peacock Rm. is especially int. (24) 12th & C Sts. SW., **Central Heating Plant** (O.1934.by Paul P.Cret), forceful example of functional design. It provides heat for most Gov. bldgs. & avoids soot by using most modern method of reducing smoke to steam-like vapor. Carbon particles are carried off to diversion pipes. (25) 12-14th Sts. & Independence Ave., **Dept. of Agric. Bldgs.** (O.1905-30.by Rankin,Kellogg & Crane of Phila.), a gleaming white 5-story bldg. with 2 widely separated wings & miles of corridors. (26) 14th & C Sts. SW., **Bureau of Engraving & Printing** (O.wks.8-12 a.m.,12:30-2 p.m.conducted tours), greatest money-making plant in world. Here the printing of paper money, bonds, checks, revenue & postage stamps may be observed. (27) **Thos. Jefferson Mem.** (O.daily. 1928.John Russell Pope.Pantheon style with low, rounded dome & classic pediment) is on E. side of (28) **Tidal Basin,** around which grow the famous single-flowering Japanese cherry trees. When in bloom, they attract visitors from all parts of the country. (29) **Arlington Mem. Bridge** (1926-32.McKim,Mead & White) spans Potomac R. beginning at Water Gate. This bridge leads to monumental entrance to **Arlington Cemetery** (see) & conn. US1 with the South. Potomac Pk. is made up of 2 secs.: **W. & E. Potomac Pks., Speedway, Channel** & the **Tidal Basin.** (30) **Water Gate,** an arc of 40 steps, 206′ wide, which serve as seats during Sunset Symphonies. Nat. Symphony orchestra presents concerts from barge anchored opp. Gate forms a decorative buttress flanking District Side of the Arlington Mem. Bridge. (31) At 23rd St. on opp. side of Reflecting Pool is **Lincoln Mem.** (O.daily. 1922.by Henry Bacon in Gr. temple form) counterbalancing Capital at other end of axis. Edifice has broad facade & 36 Doric columns, representing States of Union at Lincoln's time. Within main chamber is heroic figure of Abr. Lincoln by Dan. C. French, illumined with impressive highlights & shadows. Murals on surrounding walls by Jules Guerin suggest allegorical events in life of Lincoln. (32) **Washington Mon.** (O.daily.sm.fee.elevator serv.at W.end of Mall, foot of 18th St.by Rbt.Mills), one of tallest masonry structures in world. It is a tapering shaft rising 555′ & has 898 steps. From observ. tower is finest view of city, Arlington & Va. hills. Its int. hist. began 1783, & cont. on its stormy way until the dedication in 1885, 37 yrs. after the cor. stone was laid.

(W) OF ELLIPSE: (33) 17th & Constitution Ave., **Pan American Union** (O.wks. 9-4:30.Sat.to noon.Sun.3-6.1908-10 by Albert Kelsey & Paul P.Cret.Fr.& Sp.Ren. as well as N.& S.Amer.influences). This org. is maintained by 21 N. & S. Amer. countries to promote friendly relations. Bldg. surrounds a glass-roofed patio, in which tropical plants & birds are kept. "Blue Aztec" garden to rear has a reflecting pool & contains ancient figure Xochipilli, "God of flowers " Army, Navy & Marine bands conduct summer concerts here. (34) 17th, 18th, C & D Sts., **D.A.R. Bldgs.,** Nat. Soc. of Daughters of Amer. Rev., incl. **Mem. Continental Hall** (facing 17th St.) with auditorium & mus. (guides). (35) **Constitution Hall,** entrance on 18th St. Its fine auditorium, seating 4,000, is used for most of Washington's concerts, indoor pageants & festivals. **Lib.** has more than 20,000 vols. of hist. & genealogy (avail.for research). (36) 18th & C Sts., **Dept. of Inter., South Bldg.** Bet. it & **North Bldg.** is **Rawlins Pk.,** with a shallow wading pool. (37) 17th, 18th, D & E Sts., **Amer. Red Cross Bldg.** (O.wks.Sun.1-4:30;1913-17 by Trowbridge & Livingstone. neo-Class.with Corinthian portico). Near it is mem. bldg. dedicated to Women of World War I. (38) 17th St. bet. N.Y. Ave. & E St., **Corcoran Gallery of Art** (O. Mon.12-4:30;Tues.-Sat.9-4:30;Sun.& hols.2-5;free;1879.by Ernest Flagg). Entrance is flanked by bronze lions cast by Canova. Corcoran colls. record chronologically development of Amer. art. Gallery also has examples of Fr. & Dutch schools; ancient to mod. sculpture, rugs, tapestries & pottery. (39) SE. cor. N.Y. Ave. & 18th St., **Girl Scouts' Little H.** (O.wks.). Inter. designed after birthpl. (L.I.) of John H. Payne, author of "Home Sweet Home." (40) NE. cor. N.Y. Ave. & 18th St., **Octagon H.** (O.fine Georg.1800.by Wm.Thornton) is actually hexagonal despite its name. The house, built for Col. John Tayloe, wealthy planter friend of Washington, has an int. hist. with Dolly Madison, Aaron Burr & most of the day's notables figuring in it. Treaty of Ghent was signed here Christmas Eve, 1814. For yrs. it was the favorite haunted house in the D.C. Since 1902 it is hqs. of Amer. Institute of Architects. (41) 20th & Constitution Ave., **Fed. Reserve Bldg.** (O.1937 by Paul P.Cret). (42) 21st & Constitution Ave., **Nat. Academy of Sciences** (O.1924.by Bert G.Goodhue). (43) 21st & C Sts., **New State Dept. Bldg.** (1941.by Underwood & Foster). (44) 20th & G Sts., **Washington College of Law,** founded 1896 by Ellen Mussey & Emma Gillett, primarily to admit women students which at that time were not admitted to any other local law sch. except one est. for Negroes. Men now outnumber women students. (45) **Geo. Washington Univ.,** bldgs. mainly clustered in vic. of 20th & G Sts. Univ. (1819) embraces 13 colleges & in addition to its day & evening classes has late aft. courses to enable Gov. employees to attend. At 700—20th St. is the Sch. of Gov. in which outstanding executives of Fed. Gov. serve as lecturers. It also has a Foreign Service branch.

THE WHITE HOUSE, WASHINGTON SQ. & DOWNTOWN: (46) 1600 Pa. Ave., **The White House** (designed 1792 by Jas.Hoban on site designated by Maj. L'Enfant in his orig. plan for the Fed.City), oldest pub. bldg. in Washington. Its simplicity & purity of line, as well as its charm & dignity, have gained it praise from artists & critics alike. Main approach is through the N. Grounds. S. facade faces the "Presidential Ellipse"; clustered trees & thickets hide the "President's Walk." Executive offices flank the White House proper, running (E & W). Galleries conn. with main bldg. & both conform with it in design & color. Lower fl. of White House & East Room or "Great Hall" in ordinary times are open Tues. through Sat. till noon. On W. side are the hist. Red, Blue & Green Rooms. White H. & Grounds were closed in 1949 for necessary repairs. (47) 17th St. & Pa. Ave. NW., **Old State Dept. Bldg.** (O.wks.c.1870.by A.D.Mullet.Fr.neo-Class.& baroque). Its baroque features have earned it the nickname "squirrel cage." Although the bldg. has 2m of corridors, the expanding business of State Dept. necessitated its taking over the new bldg. on Va. Ave. (48) **Lafayette Sq.,** directly (N) of White H., is a landscaped rectangle with fascinating array of native & exotic trees & shrubs. It contains the equestrian statue of Andrew Jackson by Clark Mills; also statues of Lafayette, Rochambeau, von Steuben & Kosciusko. (49) 1651 Pa. Ave., **Blair H.** (1810.late Georg.Ionic portico & Class.cornice) now temporary "White House" while Presidential residence is being repaired. Before that it was used as a guest house for distinguished visitors from other countries. House is associated with many great Amers.: Lincoln, Jackson, Van Buren, Lee, Jefferson Davis, etc. (50) **Jackson Pl.** on which is located at No. 722, **Brookings Institution** (O.appl.1931.mod.Class.), leading nonprofit corp. devoted to research & training in economics & gov. At SW. cor. of Jackson Pl. & H St., **Decatur H.** (1819.by Benj.H.Latrobe.Georg.design), home of Commodore Stephen Decatur, scene of many grand receptions & gay parties. Its owner was killed in duel with Jas. Barron. (51) H St. from Jackson Pl. to Madison Pl., on N. side of which is located at cor. of Conn. Ave. & H St., **U.S. Chamber of Commerce** (O.wks.1925). On NW. cor. of 16th & H Sts., **Hay-Adams H.,** on site of double house built in 1885 for John Hay, Secy. of St., & Henry

Adams, historian, who wrote "The Education of Henry Adams" here. Notable visitors incl. architect Richardson, sculptor Saint-Gaudens, & painter John La Farge. NE. cor. of 16th & H Sts., **St. John's Episc. Ch.** (1816.Fed.by Benj.Latrobe. alts.by Jas.Renwick), known as "Ch. of Presidents." Pew 54 is set aside for the Pres. Dolly Madison was baptized & confirmed here. At Vermont Ave. & H St. NW., **Veterans Adm. Bldg.** (O.1918). (52) **Madison Pl.,** on which are located at SE. cor. of H St. & Madison Pl., **Cosmos Club** (1818). In 1836 Dolly Madison acquired this house from her brother-in-law & from it she ruled Washington society until 1849. At 21 Madison Pl., **Tayloe-Cameron H.** (1828 by Ben Tayloe). It was known as "Little White House" while occupied by Mark Hanna during McKinley Adm. (53) 15th St. & Pa. Ave., just (E) of White H., **U.S. Treasury Bldg.** (O.1838-42.Gr. Rev.by Rbt.Mills & T.U.Walter.). (N) of main bldg. is **Annex** (1919 by Cass Gilbert). (54) N.Y. Ave. & 13th St., hist. **N.Y. Ave. Presb. Ch.** (founded 1803.Class.Rev. with a graceful tower & lofty steeple), another "ch. of presidents" & an outstanding landmark of downtown reg. (55) 516 10th St., **Petersen H.** (O.sm.fee). Here Ap. 15, 1865, Lincoln died. He had been carried wounded from the theater across the street, the night before. (56) 10th St. bet. E & F Sts. NW., **Ford's Theater,** in which on night of Ap. 14, 1865, Lincoln was shot by J. Wilkes Booth. Little is left of orig. inter.; now incl. a mus. (O.sm.fee) containing Lincoln relics. (57) 10th St. bet. F & G Sts., **St. Patrick's Ch.,** oldest Cath. parish in D.C. (present bldg.1872.Tudor). (58) 7th & N.Y. Aves., **Pub. Lib. of D.C.** (1903.neo-Class.).

GEORGETOWN: Hist. Georgetown, once a separate town, is now an integral & altogether charming part of the city, lying along N. bank of the Potomac, (W) of Rock Cr. Old warehouses stand side by side with Georg. mansions & townhouses; Negro shacks still lean against mod. & new apartments. From 1775-1850 Georgetown was a busy seaport with some of finest Amer. gun factories & flour mills. A fleet of locally-owned ships carried internat. trade in tobacco. By 1791 it was perhaps the greatest tobacco market in the country. Building of the Potomac Canal & the Chesapeake & Ohio Canal made it possible to carry $10,000,000 worth of freight. Steam navigation & the necessity for deeper channels, as well as the RRs., destroyed Georgetown's chances of becoming a great commercial metropolis, & gradually the old town was absorbed by the new Fed. city. (59) 1623 28th St., **Evermay** (18th cent.Georg.manor house). Sam. Davidson bought the property & built the house. He was an eccentric bachelor who wanted to live alone. To accomplish this, he inserted an item into the newspaper advising people "to avoid Evermay as they would a den of devils or rattlesnakes." (60) 2715 Q St., **Dumbarton H.** (O.1780 & 1795), hqs. of Nat. Soc. of Colonial Dames of Amer., has been in hands of many noted Amer. families. Around 1805 Latrobe designed its front portico. When H. was moved to its present location, its orig. architectural composition was changed. Now Colonial Dames have rest. interior with authentic Col. pieces. Many orig. portraits incl. some by Peale & Stuart are exhibited here. (61) 1647 30th St., **Dunbarton** (1784.by Thos.Beall.Mansard roof added later). Beall's son was captured by John Brown at Harper's Ferry & held hostage until released to troops under Gen. Lee. (62) 30th & R Sts., **Oak Hill Cemetery** (est.1848). Here is buried John H. Payne, author of "Home, Sweet Home" (see Ga.). He died as U.S. consul in Tunis, but his body was brought back here. Here also is grave of Peggy O'Neale, tavern keeper's daughter who married John H. Eaton, Secy. of War under Jackson, & Minister to Spain. Her spectacular career divided Washington society. (63) 3101 R St., **Dumbarton Oaks,** one of largest late Georg. estates. Until 1940, it was home of Rbt. Woods Bliss, Ambassador to Argentina, noted art collector & manufacturer of "Castoria." (Grounds O.Ap.-Oct.Sat.& Sun.). Estate was given to Harvard Univ. for Research Lib. Contains one of world's finest colls. of Byzantine art & hist. (Mus.O.9-4.wks.exc.Mon.& hols.). Here took place in 1944 the Conversations among representatives of U.S., Gt. Brit., Russia & China, that resulted in 1st draft of United Nations' Charter. (64) 1644 31st St., **Tudor Pl.** (1794.by Francis Loundes.early Fed.). Was bought by Martha Parke Custis with money left her by Geo. Washington, her stepfather. "Temple" porch of S. entrance is especially fine. The exter. details were skillfully handled by Thornton. Tudor Pl. still houses notable coll. of Washington family relics., incl. seed pearl dress of Martha Washington. (65) 3124 Q St., **Bowie H.** (1800.late Georg.), built by Geo. Bowie, godson of Geo. Washington & inventor of Bowie knife. (66) O & Potomac Sts., **St. John's Ch.** (1807-09.oldest Episc.Ch.in D.C.). (67) 3123 Dumbarton Ave.,

**Foxall-McKenney H.** (c.1800.Fed.), built by Henry Foxall for his daughter. (68) 3033 N St., **Beall Mansion** (mid-18th cent.wings added). (69) 2823 N St., **Adm. Weaver H.** (pre-Rev.adds.later). (70) 2812 N St., **Susan Wheeler Decatur H.** (Fed.), home of Stephen Decatur's widow. She withdrew here after the duel which killed her husband. (71) 3014 N St., **Dunlop-Lincoln H.** (1799-1800 by John Laird with pillared portico). Lincoln's eldest son, Rbt. Todd, bought the house & lived in it until 1926 (O.Garden Club's showplace). (72) 3051 M St. NW., **Washington's Engineering Hqs.** (1764.by Chris.Lehman), where, according to tradition, Washington & L'Enfant planned the Fed. city. (73) 1238 31st St., **Congress St. Ch.** (Meth.1830). (74) 1066 Wisconsin Ave., **Vigilant Firehouse.** Its company was org. 1817. (S) of firehouse is sm. granite obelisk comm. building of C. & O. Canal. (75) **Key Mem. Bridge** (1823) replaces old Aqueduct Bridge & crosses Potomac R. into Va. (76) 3508 Prospect St., **Morris H.** (pre-1800 by John Templeman.rest.). (77) 3400 Prospect St., **Stoddert H.** (1789) built by Ben. Stoddert, 1st Secy. of Navy (Ital.gate & early Amer. doorway have been added). (78) 3425 Prospect St., **Worthington-Kearney H.** (1799.by John Thompson), home of Dr. Chas. Worthington, physician during War of 1812. (79) 3525 N St., **Convent of Mercy** (Cath.1787-92.old facade & belfry). Was built as Trinity Ch., 1st Cath. Ch. in D.C. (80) 3322 O St., **Bodisco H.** (Fed.), cream-colored brick & massive proportions (O.during Garden Wk.). Here in 1840 took place the wedding of Baron Alex. de Bodisco, Russian envoy to U.S., & Harriet Williams of Georgetown. (81) 1430 33rd St., **Yellow H.** (pre-1733), oldest H. in Georgetown, but gives little evidence of its age. It is 2½ stories, yellow painted-brick bldg. with exceptionally int. inter. Several of its doors are traditional Col. "witch doors" (O.sometimes on garden tours). (82) 1524 33rd St., **Yellow Tavern** (Flemish), bright red with white trim, built during Georgetown's commercial importance. (83) 1537 35th St., **Volta Bureau,** hqs. for Amer. Assoc. to Promote Teaching of Speech to Deaf & a clearing house for scientific info. & medical aids. Helen Keller, 1893, turned 1st sod for present structure. Bureau was est. by Alex. G. Bell, 1880, with money he received as prize for inventing the telephone. This prize was created by Napoleon I in honor of Count Volta, Ital. inventor of electric battery. Bell, while teaching his father's method of "visible speech" in Boston, married a deaf pupil, Mabel Hubbard, who later founded Nat. Geographic Soc. Near-by is the Alex. Melville Bell home, now used as garage. Behind house are **Converted Slave Quarters,** picturesque cottages with many-paned windows. (84) 3406 R St., **Mackall-Worthington H.** (1800.by Leonard Mackall.gray painted brick & white balcony). (85) 1500 35th St., **Convent of Visitation of Holy Mary. Chapel of Sacred Heart** was erected 1821. In 1939, ruins of Burleith, home of Henry Threlkeld, built 1716, were unearthed. It had been burnt shortly after the Rev. The Convent was founded 1799. Chapel contains gifts of Chas. X of France. (86) **Georgetown Univ.** (Coll. Goth.) is oldest Cath. college in U.S., founded 1787 by John Carroll, 1st Amer. bishop. Since 1885 it has been directed by the Jesuits. At 37th & O Sts. are Adm. offices & Foreign Serv. Sch. Univ. owns many works of art & hist. relics. It also has a Reliquary of Saints & a Liturgical Mus. Its Lib. contains orig. script of Samuel Clemens' (Mark Twain) "Tom Sawyer." The **Astronomical Observ.,** founded 1843 by Rev. J. Curley, S.J., & **Seismological Observ.,** founded by Rev. F. Tondorf, S.J., have attained nation-wide recognition. Its Foreign Serv. Sch. was 1st in country devoted entirely to this field.

MASSACHUSETTS AVE.—DISTRICT LINE TO THOMAS CIRCLE: (87) 1 block before inters. of Wisc. & Mass. Aves. is unfinished **Cathedral of SS. Peter & Paul,** also known as Washington Cathedral (O.guides), seat of Prot. Episc. Diocese in Washington; it is an excellent example of pure Goth. 1908. Inter. embodies the lightness & grace of Eng. Goth. When completed, it will be among 10 largest ecclesiastic bldgs. in world. The completed chapels contain tombs of Woodrow Wilson, Adm. Geo. Dewey & Frank Kellogg. **Cathedral's Close,** beautifully landscaped, is open from 8-6. Noteworthy among the completed secs. are **Chapel of Resurrection** (Norman), **Nave Crypts** (2 of longest crypt corridors in world) & the **Apse,** the only departure from Eng. Goth. in Cathedral. (88) At 34th & Mass. Ave., **Naval Observatory** (O.Mon.-Fri.9-4.conducted tours 10 & 2 only; apply Chief Clerk's office for pass 6 wks. in advance). It is the official Gov. establishment to collect data for navigational astronomy, the determination of Standard Time & repair of navigation instruments. (89) 3100 Mass. Ave. is **Brit. Embassy,** characteristically Eng. style. (90) 2514 Mass. Ave., former **Japanese Embassy** (designed by Delano & Aldrich); now occupied by Far Eastern Commission. (91) 2445 Mass. Ave., **Venezuelan Embassy.** (92) 2419 Mass. Ave., former home of Mary Roberts Rinehart. (93) 2340 S St., **Woodrow Wilson H.** (94) 2330 S St., **Textile Mus.** of the D.C. (O.free Mon.Wed.& Fri.), contains tapestries from 4th to 18th cents., Egyptian, Ind. & pre-Columbian. (95) 2301 Decatur Pl., **Egyptian Embassy.** (96) 2247 R St. NW., **Swedish Embassy.** (97) At 23rd & Q Sts., **Q Street Bridge** passes over Rock Cr. At each end are bronze bison by A. P. Proctor. (98) 2362 Mass. Ave., **Greek Embassy.** (99) 2342 Mass. Ave., **Belgian Mil. Attache's H.** (100) At 1600 21st St., **Phillips Mem. Gallery** (O.Oct.-June.free). Incorporated by Duncan Phillips (1918) & housed in his former home. It contains largest coll. of Daumiers in world, incl. "The Uprising." Also has fine examples of El Greco, Van Gogh, Cezanne, Picasso, Braque, Matisse & Rouault. At 2118 is former **Residence of Lars Anderson,** & nat. hqs. of Soc. of the Cincinnati, an order founded 1783 by Rev. Army officers. (101) No. 2020, former **Walsh Mansion,** girlhood home of Evalyn Walsh "Hope Diamond" McLean; now used by the Red Cross. (102) **Dupont Circle** is at inters. of 5 important thoroughfares: Mass., Conn., N.H. Aves. & 19th & P Sts. Fountain, by D. C. French, has been dismantled while the underpass is being built. At cor. of Conn. Ave. & 19th St. is **DuPont Theater** (motion picture house for whites & Negroes). (103) No. 1600 N.H. Ave., **Argentine Embassy.** (104) At 1521 N.H. Ave., **Nicaraguan Embassy.** (105) At 18th & Church Sts. is **St. Thomas Ch.** (Episc.), where Pres. & Mrs. Roosevelt worshipped. (106) 1746 Mass. Ave., **Canadian Embassy.** (107) At cor. Conn. Ave. & N St. is **Ch. of the Covenant** (1st Presb.1889), notable for tall square tower & open arches. Jas. G. Blaine & Benj. Harrison attended here. (108) On cor. of Rhode Island Ave., is **Longfellow Bldg.** (1940.Mod.by Lescaze,N.Y.). (109) At 1725 Rhode Island Ave., **St. Matthew's Cathedral** (Cath.1893.by Grant LaFarge.Class.). In contrast to its simple but imposing exter., the inter. has an air of sumptuousness, with an ornate vaulted ceiling & walls of polychrome mosaics. (110) At 1736 Mass. Ave. is **Chilean Embassy.** (111) 1320 Mass. Ave., **Peruvian Embassy.** (112) At 1500 Rhode Island Ave. (just around cor.), **Bell-Morton H.** (1889) occupied by Alex. G. Bell, Benj. Harrison, Elihu Root, Ogden Mills, etc. (113) At 1439 Mass. Ave., former **German Embassy.** (114) At 14th St. NW. is **Nat. City Christian Ch.** (1930.by John Russell Pope).

CONN. AVE.-DUPONT CIRCLE TO DISTRICT LINE: (115) 1520 20th St., **Colombian Embassy.** (116) At 2111 Florida Ave., **Friends Meeting H.** (1930.Walter Price, Phila.). (117) At Columbia Rd. stands bronze **Equestrian Statue of Gen. Geo. B. McClellan** (1907.by Fred. MacMonnies). (118) **Calvert St. Bridge** (1935.by Paul P.Cret). Just beyond bridge are 2 large hotels, Shoreham & Wardman Pk. (119) 1535 18th St., **Panamanian Embassy.** (120) At 3000 Cathedral Ave. is **Woodley,** Georg. manor house & 250-a. estate of Phil. B. Key, uncle of Francis Scott Key. (121) At Upton St., **Nat. Bureau of Standards** (N.O) is country's authority on measurements & world's largest testing lab. & institution of scientific research. **Chevy Chase Circle** is at D.C. Line. (122) At 3000 Conn. Ave. is **Nat. Zoo** (O). (123) **Rock Cr. Pk.,** an 1,800-a. area within D.C., was set aside by Congress in 1890. It extends (N) from the Zoo to 4$^{m}$ beyond Md. Line. Most of it is undisturbed woodland with a profusion of wildflowers, shrubs & trees. Tastefully improved by the building of foot bridges, pic. sites & especially by good Rds. which run along the creek. At several places the cr. can be forded by both autos & horses. Pk. has 10$^{m}$ of bridle paths & is a welcome refuge to riders & strollers alike, especially during Washington's hot summers.

16TH ST. (NW) FROM ROCK CR. PK. TO L ST.: (124) At Park Rd. is **Shrine of Sacred Heart** (Cath.1921-22.by Murphy & Olmstead of Washington) with elaborate symbolism & rich inter. Opp., Statue of Cardinal Gibbons. At inters. of Harvard St., Columbia Rd. & 16th St. are 3 of the city's most impressive churches: (125) **Nat. Mem. Bapt. Ch.** (1933.by Egerton Swartwout, N.Y.) with massive tower; (126) **Washington Chapel** of Ch. of Latter Day Saints (1933.by Young & Hanson, Salt Lake City), noteworthy for its perfect acoustics; (127) **All Souls' Unitarian Ch.** (1924.after St.Martin's in the Fields.by Coolidge & Shattuck.London). Congregation was org. 1877 & had as members Presidents J.Q. Adams, Millard Fillmore & Taft; also Senators Webster, Sumner & Calhoun. Edw. E. Hale, Ralph W. Emerson & Wm. E. Channing preached from its pulpit. (128) At 2800 16th St., is **Scottish**

**Rite Temple,** hqs. of D.C. Masons (1940.by Porter,Lockie & Chatelaine,Washington). (129) **Statue of Joan of Arc,** copy of orig. by Paul Dubois at Rheims, stands on the upper terrace of **Meridian Pk.** (130) bet. Fla. Ave., & Euclid St., landscaped with long promenades & a mall, in Fr. manner. Outstanding feature is the lavish use of water in fountains & cascades of Ital. inspiration. (131) NW. cor. at S St., **Universalist Nat. Mem. Ch.** (1930.by Allen & Collins,Boston). (132) Diagonally opp. at SE cor. of 16th & S Sts., **House of the Temple** (O.wks.1815.by J.R.Pope & Elliot Woods), hqs. of Freemasonry. Exter. developed from design of Tomb of Mausolus of Halicarnassus (7th wonder of ancient world). (133) On NE. cor. of 16th & M Sts., **Nat. Education Assoc. Bldg.** (134) At L & 16th Sts., **Embassy of U.S.S.R.** At M St. is **Hqs. of Nat. Geographic Soc.** (O.Mon.-Fri.).

NE. WASHINGTON: (135) 6th St. bet. W & Fairmont Sts. NW., **Howard Univ.,** (1867) largest & most completely developed Negro univ., nat. & internat. in scope. (136) (N) of Capitol, 3m on Rock Cr. Rd., **Soldiers' Home** (1852-91). (137) Mich. Ave. & Franklin St. NE., **Trinity College** (Cath.1897), outstanding girls' college. **Chapel of Notre Dame** (1924.Class.by Maginnis & Walsh) received the AIA award for ecclesiastical architecture. (138) (N) of Mich. Ave. & 4th St. NE., **Nat. Shrine of the Immaculate Conception,** which when completed will be largest Cath. bldg. in W. Hemisphere. Shrine is designed as basilica, Rom. & Byzantine. N. & S. crypts & basement are thus far completed. Shrine stands within grounds of (139) **Catholic Univ.,** at Mich. & Brookland Aves., foremost Cath. univ. in U.S. (Grad. schools O.to women). (140) (N) of Soldiers' Home on Rock Cr. Church Rd. is **Rock Cr. Cemetery,** oldest cemetery in D.C. Graves date from 1719. St. Paul's Ch. within grounds was founded 1712. Noted mems. are figure on grave of Mrs. Henry Adams by Augustus Saint-Gaudens, Gutzon Borglum's "Rabboni," & Jas. E. Fraser's "Journey Through Life." In Brightwood Area are remains of **Ft. Stevens,** where Gen. Early & Confed. troops were turned back from Capital, 1864. Half mile (NE) of Ft. Stevens is (141) **Battleground Nat. Cemetery** (O). Here are buried Union soldiers who fell at Ft., July 12, 1864. In vic. (NW) is **Army Med. Center,** incl. **Walter Reed Gen. Hospital** (142) 14th & Quincy Sts. **Franciscan Monastery,** on Mount St.Sepulchre (O.8-5.guides), is the Commissariat of the Holy Land. Ch. is designed like a Cal. mission surrounded by a Rosary portico. Here also is reprod. of Chapel of Portiuncula near Assisi, Italy, where St. Francis founded his order. Its rose garden is especially lovely in June. On lower level of grounds is a grotto of Lourdes. The Ch. (Byzantine & Ital.Ren.) was designed by Aristides Leonori of Rome on a tract orig. belonging to Lord Baltimore. Inter. of Ch. contains replicas of the holy places in Jerusalem, Bethlehem & Rome, such as Shrine of Holy Sepulchre, Greek altar on Mt. Calvary, the Anointing Stone, Catacombs & the Crypt of Bethlehem. (143) Just beyond D.C. Line on Bladensburg Rd. (US1 & US50) is **Ft. Lincoln Cemetery** (O.8 a.m.to sunset), laid out on site of hist. Battle of Bladensburg during War of 1812 & of Ft. Lincoln. (144) From Bladensburg Rd. to Anacostia R. is **Nat. Arboretum** with 32 types of soil permitting growth of many trees not indigenous to D.C. (145) To (W) of Arboretum on Bladensburg Rd., **Mt. Olivet Cemetery** (O.sunrise to sunset.1852.Cath.). Here are buried Jas. Hoban, designer of White H., & Mary Surratt, hanged for complicity in Lincoln's assassination.

SE. WASHINGTON: (146) Lincoln Sq., **Emancipation Mon.** (1870.by Thos.Ball), paid for by freed slaves. (147) 18th & E Sts., SE. **Congressional Cemetery** (1807), temporary burying ground for Congressmen & diplomats. John Philip Sousa, the March King, was a native of Washington & is buried here. (148) (E) of Anacostia R. is **Anacostia Pk.** (recr.facils.). In its NE. sec. are the **Kenilworth Aquatic Gardens** with 40 pools of water lilies, lotus, iris & sub-aquatics. Entire pk. is a wildlife sanctuary. (149) Bet. S. Capitol & Nicholas Sts. SE. is **St. Elizabeth's Hospital** (grounds O.), internationally known for its work in mental diseases. Est. by Congress, 1855, it has become largest Fed. institution of this kind in U.S. It is known for its medical & psychiatric staff, as well as for its excellent mod. equipment. (150) 8th & I Sts. SE., **Marine Barracks** (O), hqs. of Marine Corps in Washington. **Commandant's H.** (1805). Captured flags of Amer. Wars on display. (151) 8th & M Sts. SE., **Navy Yard** (O.guides), outstanding center of ordnance design & experimentation. Entrance Gate, Commandant's residence & the Yard Capt.'s house were designed by Latrobe (1801-5). **Mus.** contains most comprehensive coll. of rifles used by Navy & other hist. relics. (152) 4th & P Sts. SW., **Army War College** (O.87 as.) fronting Washington Channel. Present bldg. designed by McKim, Mead & White

(1903). **Lib.** is largest in military science in world. In center of parade ground is **U.S. Penitentiary** where July 7, 1865, 4 prisoners accused of complicity in Lincoln's assassination, incl. Mary Surratt & John Wilkes Booth, were hanged.

## TRIPS OUT OF WASHINGTON

### I. WASHINGTON (S) to MOUNT VERNON. c.15. Mt. Vernon Mem. Hy.

This hy. leaves SW. end of Mem. Bridge, skirts the Potomac, turns (L) at end of Bridge, opp. **Court of Honor of Arlington Cemetery,** traversing **Columbia I.** & passes **Navy & Marine Mem.** (seven sea-gulls in flight, rising from a foaming wave) by E. B. del Piatti at SE. end of island. To (R) of hy. is **Pentagon Bldg.** (Nat. Defense Bldg.) housing the Nat. Mil. Establishment, combined Army, Navy & Air Forces. It is largest office bldg. in world, with 5 sides, 5 floors & 5 rings. It contains every convenience for its 30,000 employees—P.O., restaurants, theatres & stores. Hy. then passes **Nat. Airport,** built on filled-in land dredged from river. **Terminal Bldg.,** by Howard Cheney, with most mod. appurtenances for handling passengers & baggage. At **4.5.** from Mem. Bridge is **ALEXANDRIA** (see Washington II). At **15. MOUNT VERNON** (O.wks.Sun.aft.sm.fee.1743.Georg.Col.rest.enlarged 1759 & 1775.outbldgs.were added by Washington.busses from Washington.sightseeing tours.boats make round-trip leaving 7th St. Wharves in Washington.).

Little Hunting Plantation, on which Mt. Vernon stands, was part of 5,000-a. tract patented (1674) by Nicholas Spencer & John Washington, George's great-grandfather. Part of Plantation (2,500 as.) came into possession of John's son, Lawrence, & finally into that of Augustine, George's father, who erected (1735) a H., which was destroyed by fire (1739). Lawrence, George's brother, built a home here (1743) & called it Mt. Vernon in honor of his old commander, Admiral Vernon. Rich. Blackburn of Rippon Lodge planned bldg. somewhat on lines of Belvoir, Col. Fairfax's H., which Blackburn had also designed. After death of Lawrence & his daughter, estate passed to George, who brought in 2,500 as. of the Spencer tract, & eventually expanded his holdings to 8,000 as. Despite this great tract which was pretty intensively cultivated, set income derived from it netted only $2,700 annually. In 1759, Washington moved in with his bride, Martha Dandridge Custis. The Rev. & the 2 terms as Pres. interrupted Washington's residence on "plantation," which he was ambitious to make a model of its kind. He wanted to be known as "first farmer of the country." In 1797, he returned for good & died here in 1799. Estate was eventually purchased (1856) by Mt. Vernon Ladies' Assoc., which has restored H., outbuildings & grounds, with much of orig. furnishings. H. is on bluff, its colonnaded portico overlooking the Potomac & has at either side, in the rear, numerous dependencies.

PTS. OF INT.: (1) **Banquet Hall** has marble mantel, allegedly by Canova; Gobelin rug, supposedly gift of Louis XVI; portrait of Washington by Gilbert Stuart; some orig. furnishings. Washington dispensed lavish hospitality. The Gen. is reported to have referred to Mt. Vernon as "a well-resorted tavern." (2) **West Parlor,** with some orig. engravings & furnishings. (3) **Music Room,** fitted out by Nelly Custis. Washington admitted, "I can neither sing nor raise a single note on any instrument." Nelly's harpsichord, her music books & some furnishings of Washington's time; portrait of Nelly attributed to Trumbull. (4) **Central Hall.** Key to Bastille, presented by Lafayette, & some orig. furnishings. (5) **Family Dining Room.** Nelly Custis' high-back chair. (6) Downstairs Bedroom with some orig. pieces. (7) **Washington Study.** Two maps & a few books are all that remain of his lib., greater part having been purchased by Athenaeum in Boston (see Boston,Mass.). Other origs. are: 2 thermometer-barometers, desk & chair, mahogany bookcase, globe, gun cane, riding crop, & spectacles. Round table supposed to have belonged to Rbt. E. Lee. Portrait of Lawrence Washington, attributed to Wollaston. (8) **Butler's Pantry;** some orig. silver, etc., & others typical of period. (9) On 2nd floor, 5 bed chambers, incl. **Nelly Custis Room,** where she & her husband, Lawrence Lewis, lived until Woodlawn (see) was completed. Cradle was that of her eldest child. Lafayette Room contains bed in which he slept. Small Guest Room, supposed to have been occupied by Geo. Washington Parke Custis, Nelly's brother. (10) Six small bedrooms on 3rd floor. **Washington Room** contains bed in which he died. Also his own trunk & other orig. pieces. Martha Washington Room with some originals. (11) **Dependencies: Gardener's H. & Store H. Spinning H.,** equipped with orig. spinning

& weaving machinery. **Mus.** (1928) reprod. of slave quarters, contains coll. of Washingtoniana, incl. orig. clay bust by Houdon, only one of Washington made from life, Washington's military sash & his sword, which he bequeathed to his nephews with injunction, "Not to unsheathe them for the purpose of shedding blood except it be in self-defense or in defense of their country & its rights; & in the latter case, keep them unsheathed & to prefer falling with them in their hands, to the relinquishing thereof." **Schoolh.,** where Nelly & her brother went to school. **Kitchen,** furnished in period. **Butler's H., Dairy, "Smoake H."** (Washington's spelling), **Wash H., Coach H.** (reconstructed), which contains coach of period made by Washington's coach-maker, **Brick Barn** (1782), where "Nelson," horse which carried Washington during Rev., was stabled. Garden has been rest. as Washington laid it out. (12) Down the walk, **Tomb** contains simple sarcophagi of Geo. & Martha Washington. Both he & his wife orig. were buried in family vault on slope overlooking river, built 1745 by Washington for his brother, Lawrence. In 1831, after a discharged servant had broken into the old tomb & attempted to steal Washington's skull, John Augustine Washington built present tomb. In 1837 it was completed & the sarcophagi of Geo. & Martha Washington were moved into it. In 1855, the doors were locked & the key thrown into the Potomac. In such veneration is this spot held that every U.S. Navy ship passing it lowers its flag at half-mast, the bell is tolled & the crew stands at attention.

St.235 leads (W) from Mt. Vernon, c.3$^{m}$ to **Washington's Grist Mill** (reconstructed), put up by George's father, Augustine, rest. by George. Also **Miller's H.** (reconstructed). While visiting the mill, Washington is supposed to have caught pneumonia from which he died. St.235 cont. to J. with US1.

## II. WASHINGTON (S) to ALEXANDRIA, Va. c.5.US1.

Hy. crosses 14th St. Bridge at **c.5.** & reaches **ALEXANDRIA.**

RR. & bus conns. Busses to Washington & Mt. Vernon. Accoms.: All types. Info.: C. of C., 103 N. Albert St. Boats for hire, Prince & Duke Sts., Potomac R. House & Garden Tours (fee) in spring. Occasional tours of hist. landmarks. Inquire at C. of C.

Alexandria (sett.c.1731), located on Potomac R., was named for John Alexander who in 1680 bought the land on which city stands. Alexandria became important port during 18th cent., & business, financial & social center of NE. Va. Taverns sprang up in considerable number. There were balls, fairs & horse races. Wealthy planters & merchants, as well as the Washingtons, Lees, Masons, Custises, Fairfaxes, frequented the town, often building elaborate town Hs. Geo. Washington, who helped survey Alexandria's streets in 1749, had a H. here at which he stopped when in from Mount Vernon. Braddock, with colonial contingent commanded by Washington, started out from Alexandria on his ill-fated expedition to Ft. Duquesne. During period leading up to Rev., Washington & Geo. Mason led in adoption of resolutions condemning Brit. encroachments. With est. of Washington, D.C., as Nat. Capital, Alexandria became part of Dist. of Columbia, but, in 1846, was ceded again to Va. When, in 1863, during Civil War, W. Va. broke away from Va., it became capital of "Restored Gov. of Va." (see W. Va.). Old Alexandria lies principally bet. Washington St. & the Potomac. King St., a business thoroughfare, divides town, running from (W) to (E). Many of old Sts. are named for Brit. royalty or Amer. notables. Old Col. & Fed. style Hs. often have charming gardens which can be glimpsed from the streets.

PTS. OF INT.: Tour starts at Washington & Prince Sts., at Confed. Mon. (1) SE. cor. Columbus & Cameron Sts., **Christ Ch.** (O.wks.sm.fee.1767-73.services Sun.). Tower & cupola probably 1818 Georg. (fine exter.inter.). Designed after plans by Jas. Wren (supposedly descendant of Sir Christopher Wren). Washington & Lee attended services here. Ch. has Washington family Bible & vestry book with Washington's signature. (2) At 429 N. Washington St., **Fendall H.** (pre-1791). Here Edmund J. Lee wrote Congressional Resolution declaring Washington: "First in war, first in peace, & first in the hearts of his countrymen." (3) 609 Oronoco St., **Hallowell H.** (c.1793), where Benj. Hallowell opened a sch. at which Robt. E. Lee prepared for West Pt. (4) Adj., 607 Oronoco St., **Rbt. E. Lee H.** (pre-1795.Georg.) where, after death of "Light-horse Harry" Lee, his widow lived with her children, one of whom was Rbt. E. Lee. (5) 428 N .Washington St., **Edmund J. Lee H.** (1799). (6) 220 N. Washington St., **Lloyd H.** (1793), one of largest & perhaps finest Fed. style Hs. in town. Here Lee was notified of his appointment to command Army of

N. Va. (7) 611 Cameron St., **H. of "Light-horse Harry" Lee.** (8) 607 Cameron St., **Lord Fairfax H.** (1816), where 9th Lord Fairfax lived. (9) In 500 block of Cameron St., **Site of Geo. Washington's H.,** marked by tablet. (10) On Cameron St., bet. Royal & Fairfax Sts., **City Hall** (Market H.1817.destroyed by fire & rebuilt after Civil War.adds.). (11) 132 Royal St., opp. City Hall, **Gadsby's Tavern** (O.wks.Sun. aft.sm.fee.1752 & 1792.int.inter.rest.) consists of 2 bldgs. Earlier one, City Tavern (rest.in Georg.style). Geo. Mason drew up his "Fairfax Cty. Resolves" here, 1775, famous statement of human rights. From tavern's steps, Washington after Rev. reviewed his troops for last time. (12) NE. cor. Fairfax & Cameron Sts., **Wise's Tavern** (O), where Washington stopped on way to his 1st inauguration; now Ann Lee Mem. Home. (13) 133 N. Fairfax St., **Bank of Alexandria** (est.1792), 1st in Va. Washington was depositor. (14) To rear of Bank, at 121 N. Fairfax St., **Carlyle H.** (O.wks.sm.fee.1752.Col.Georg.alt.), built by John Carlyle, Scotch merchant, one of Alexandria's founders. Here Braddock planned his expedition to Ft. Duquesne, rejecting Washington's advice. In 1785, delegates of Va. & Md. met here, a meeting which led to Constitutional Convention in Philadelphia (1787). (15) NE. cor. King & Fairfax Sts., **Ramsay H.** (1749.Georg.Col.), oldest in city, built by an Irish immigrant, Wm. Ramsay; recently partly destroyed by fire, but is to be restored. (16) 207 Prince St., **Geo. Wm. Fairfax H.** (1752.rest.), built by Col. Fairfax, supervisor of Lord Fairfax's domains. (17) 209 Prince St., **Dick H.,** home of Dr. E. C. Dick, consultant during Washington's last illness.

(18) SE. cor. Pitt & King Sts., **Marshall H.,** where, during Civil War, Lt. Ellsworth was shot by the inn-keeper (H. was tavern at that time) for pulling down Confed. flag. Ellsworth is supposed to have been 1st casualty of Civil War. (19) 317 King St., **Alexandria Gazette Bldg.,** (est.1784.mod.), oldest continuously published newspaper in U.S. (20) 107 S. Fairfax St., **Leadbeater's Apothecary Shop** (O.est.1792. rest.), operated until 1933, & then set aside as landmark. Contains coll. of relics & account books bearing names of Washingtons, Lees, Custises, etc. (21) 212 S. Fairfax St., **Brown H.** (c.1775), home of Dr. Wm. Brown, 1st Surgeon-Gen. of Continental Armies & one of Washington's physicians. (22) 210 Duke St., **Craik H.** (c.1790), home of Dr. Jas. Craik, Scotchman, who served Washington as physician from time of battle of Great Meadows to Yorktown & attended him before his death. (23) 208 Duke St., **Coryell H.,** ("flounder" type), home of Geo. Coryell, who ferried Washington across the Delaware on Christmas Eve, 1776. (24) 321 S. Fairfax St., **Old Presb. Meeting H.** (1774.rebuilt 1836.Georg.Col.fine exter.inter.), furnishings partly orig. In Graveyard, graves of notables, patriots & Unknown Soldier of Rev. (25) 301 S. St. Asaph St., **Lafayette H.,** (1795), lent by its owner, Mrs. Lawrason, to Lafayette during his farewell visit to U.S. (26) At Washington & Prince Sts., **Old Lyceum** (c.1825.fine exter.) where many famous traveling lecturers held forth. (27) Washington & Wolfe Sts., **Alexandria Academy** (1785) which Washington endowed with $1,000 worth of Alexandria Bank stock. Rbt. E. Lee was exemplary scholar here. (28) At head of King St. (Shooters Hill), **Geo. Washington Masonic Nat. Mem. Temple** (O.1932.by H.W.Corbett,inspired by ziggurat temples of antiquity) is 400′ high; contains Amphitheater, Assembly Room, Lodge Rooms & Replica Lodge, exact duplicate of one where Washington's lodge met after his death. In Geo. Washington Mem. Hall will shortly be installed a 17′ bronze statue of Washington. Murals will portray story of his life. Replica Room contains coll. of Washingtoniana. Fine view from top of bldg.

At Alexandria is J. with St.236.

SIDE TRIP: On this Rd. (W) c.9$^{m}$ to J. with Cty.650 leading (S) from here to **Oak Hill** (O.garden.wks.c.1730), said to be oldest H. in Fairfax Cty. At c.14$^{m}$ **Fairfax.** Handsome old **Cth.** (1800); wills of Geo. & Martha Washington. **Mon.** comm. J. Q. Marr, alleged to be 1st Confed. soldier killed in action. **Episc. Rectory,** also known as Mosby-Stoughton (Gurnell) H. (O.appl.). Here, March 8, 1863, Fed. Gen. E. H. Stoughton was surprised & taken by Col. J. S. Mosby's guerillas. St. 236 cont. (W) to J. with US29-211 (see US29) at c.15$^{m}$ from Alexandria.

## III. WASHINGTON (SW) to ARLINGTON HOUSE & CEMETERY via Arlington Mem. Bridge.

Hy. over Arlington Mem. Bridge leads directly to **Gate of Arlington Nat. Cemetery.** (Bus service to gate.). At Gate (R) to **Arlington H.,** "Lee Mansion," (O.sm.fee. post-1812.remod.1830.rest.), perched on hill overlooking Nat. Cemetery with Washington in the distance, on estate orig. part of 6,000-a. tract acquired by Alexander family for 6 hogsheads of tobacco. John Parke Custis, Geo. Washington's stepson, bought 1,100 as. of tract & called it Arlington. Geo. Washington Parke Custis, the grandson, built the H. His only child, Mary, who inherited it, married Rbt. E. Lee. In this H., Lee, when offered command of Fed. armies, penned his letter to Secy. of War, Ap. 20, 1861, resigning his commission. To his friend, Winfield Scott, he wrote: "I can anticipate no greater calamity than the dissolution of the Union. . . . Still a union that can only be maintained by swords & bayonets has no charm for me— If the Union is dissolved—I shall return to my native state &, save in defence, will draw my sword no more." H. has been rest. & dependencies either rest. or reconstructed. Little of H.'s old furnishings could be recovered; with few exceptions, furnishings are copies of origs. or genuine period pieces reproducing general appearance of inter. as it was when Lees occupied H. Mansion is impressive both by its situation & because of its noble proportions. The huge columns of the portico are monumental. Inter. is spacious & dignified.

**Arlington Nat. Cemetery** (O), reached by Dr. on (L) of Mem. Gate entrance (see above). This most noted of Nat. burial grounds covers 409 as. Interment reserved principally for officers & enlisted men of armed services. However, 1st man buried here was a Confed. prisoner who died in a local hospital. In old parts of cemetery, 3,802 refugee Negroes, who had attached themselves to Fed. armies at Civil War's beginning, were buried. (E) & (S) of Arlington H., **Tomb of Gen. Philip H. Sheridan,** famous Union cavalry leader. Near flagstaff, **Tomb of Adm. David D. Porter,** naval officer of Mex. & Civil Wars. **Grave of Pierre L'Enfant,** planner of city of Washington. Down slope, toward Mem. Gate, are **Graves of Rbt. Todd Lincoln & Wm. H. Taft.** Farther (S) of Arlington H. is Mon. on **Grave of Gen. Geo. H. Crook,** with low-relief showing surrender of Chief Geronimo. On high ground, just (S) of Mansion, is **Temple of Fame.** (W) of it, **Mon. to Unknown Dead of Civil War** on grave containing bodies of 2,111 unidentified soldiers. Farther (W) is **Old Amphitheater,** formerly used for Mem. Day services. On McPherson Ave. is **Field of the Dead.** Here are buried thousands killed in Civil War. Near-by are **Graves of Geo. Washington Parke Custis & Mary Custis,** builders of Lee Mansion. In Jackson Circle, **Mon. to Confed. Dead,** by Sir Moses Ezekiel.

(E) of Jackson Circle is **Sp.-Amer. War Mem. & Mem. to "Rough Riders."** On higher ground, **Mast of USS Maine,** with conning tower still intact. (W) of McPherson Ave., (S) of Jackson Circle, graves of World War I dead. Far to (SE) beyond Ft. McPherson earthworks, **Graves of Wm. Jennings Bryan & Rbt. E. Peary,** discoverer of N. Pole. (NE) of Maine Mem., **Arlington Mem. Amphitheater** (1915-20 by Carrère & Hastings), seating 4,000, in style of Gr. & Rom. theaters; incl. trophy room in which is St.-Gaudens' figure of "Victory" & chapel. (E) of Amphitheater, on terrace, is **Tomb of Unknown Soldier** (1931), by T. H. Jones, sculptor, & L. Rich, architect, cut from single block of marble, 16′ long, 11′ high & 9′ wide. Front panel of Tomb is carved with symbolic figures of "Victory through Valor Attaining Peace." On rear panel is inscription: "Here rests in honored glory an American Soldier known only to God." This Tomb is Mem. to all Amer. soldiers & sailors who fell in World War I.

**IV. WASHINGTON (NW) to GREAT FALLS. Va. Approach. c.13.5.**

Trip starts at Key Bridge. Follow from there Canal Rd. to **Chain Bridge.** First bridge here was built 1797. Above bridge are **Little Falls,** head of navigation—on the "fall line." (f.no license). It was to get around these rapids that Potomac Canal was built. **Palisades Pk.** is bet. Canal & R. Cross Chain Bridge (L). Turn (R) on St.123 toward **Great Falls. 6. LANGLEY** (suburb). Here J. with side Rd. leading (L) out of Langley, $1^{m}$, to **Entrance** (L) **of Salona, Smoot H.,** (1801), which gave temporary shelter to President Jas. Madison & his wife, Dolly, on their flight from Washington when the White H. was burned by Brit. Dolly arrived, bringing, among other precious items, Gilbert's portrait of Washington & the orig. Decl. of Ind. From lawn they watched Washington burn. Cont. from Langley on Cty.604. At **12.** Sign to Great Falls Pk. Take Rd. (R) here. At **13.5., GREAT FALLS ST. PK.** (O.parking.sm.fee.restaurant.dancing.pic.). Falls of Potomac R. are most impressive after spring & fall rains. On grounds are remains of one of Washington's mills. At S. end of Pk., 4 of old Potomac Canal locks still extant.

# US 40—MARYLAND

**MD.-DEL. LINE** (13.5$^{m}$ from New Castle, Del.) **(W) to MD.-PA. LINE** (29$^{m}$ from Uniontown, Pa.). **225. US40**

Via: Elkton, Baltimore, Frederick, Hagerstown & Cumberland. RRs. parallel route to Cumberland. Accoms.: Plentiful.

US40 skirts Chesapeake Bay to Baltimore, then cuts (NW) along pioneer line of travel to Ohio Valley. Sec. W. of Cumberland was country's 1st nationally improved hy.

## Sec. 1: MD.-DEL. LINE to BALTIMORE. 53.

**0. MD.-DEL. LINE. 2.5. ELKTON,** known as Friendship in 1681 and afterwards renamed Head of Elk, which at beginning of 19th cent. was one of America's chief wheat markets & today manufactures flour. Elkton is at J. with US213 (see). At **8.** is J. with St.272.

SIDE TRIP: Take latter (L) to **North East,** 0.5$^{m}$, a busy trade center of fertile farming. S. Main St., **St. Mary Anne's Ch.** (Episc.1742.tower & cupola added 1904). W. of Main St. on old US40, **Bryson H.** (1740.frame & covered log construction). W. end of bridge across Northeast Cr., **Green Hill** (c.1780). St.272 cont., passing through 650-a. **Elk Neck St. Pk.,** 9.5$^{m}$, to **Turkey Pt. Lighth.** (1834), on one of high bluffs which form pk.'s S. shore line.

**16. PERRYVILLE,** where mouth of Susquehanna R. enters Bay, depending on RR. repair shops, few industrial plants & veterans' hospital, is J. with US222, conn. with US1 (see). Crossing **SUSQUEHANNA R., 16.5.,** US40 enters **HAVRE DE GRACE** (pronounced "haverdegrass"), **17.5.,** sett. 1658. On Concord Pt. is **Havre de Grace Lighth.** (1827). 226 W. Washington St., **Rodgers H.** (1774.later rest.store front added on street floor recently). At end of Susquehanna Bridge, **Ferry H.** (1760.stucco finish.adds.later), now an Amer. Legion Mem. H. **19. HAVRE DE GRACE RACE-TRACK,** opened in 1912. **19.5. ABERDEEN,** residential settlement housing industrial workers. At Aberdeen is J. with St.22.

SIDE TRIPS: (A) Take latter (R) to **Tudor Hall** (1822) 9$^{m}$, once home of actor Junius Brutus Booth & birthpl. of his actor sons, Edwin & John Wilkes Booth. St.22 cont. to J. with US1 (see) at **Belair,** 12$^{m}$.

(B) Take St.22 (L) to **Aberdeen Proving Grounds,** 3$^{m}$, beside Chesapeake Bay, Fed. reserv. on which military weapons & materials are tested.

For pts. of int. & towns on or near US40 bet. Aberdeen & Baltimore, see Baltimore Trip I. **53. BALTIMORE,** at J. with US1 (see).

## Sec. 2: BALTIMORE to MD.-PA. LINE. 172.

For pts. of int. & towns on or near US1 bet. Baltimore & J. with St.96, see Baltimore Trip V. At **26.** is J. with St.96, leading (L) 3$^{m}$ to J. with macadamized Rd. which turns (R) to entrance to **Oakdale** (1838.richly panelled inter.ancestral portraits), former home of Edwin Warfield, Gov. of Md. (1904-08).

**46.5. FREDERICK,** at heart of Monocacy Valley, is commercial & industrial center of wide area of Md.'s Piedmont sec. with canneries & shipping terminals & various mfg. plants. Town site, laid out in 1745 by Dan. Dulany on part of 30,000-a. tract known as Tasker's Chance for its 1st owner, Benj. Tasker, was sett. by Rhenish Germans from Pa., led by John Thos. Schley. Named presumably for Fred. Calvert, 6th Lord Baltimore, it grew into prosperous stopping place on main route bet. Pa. & Va. & afterward on route leading through Cumberland over Alleghany Mts. Here Gen. Braddock paused in 1755 to outfit his expedition against Fr. & Inds. at Ft. Duquesne. Inc. in 1817, Frederick by 1860 had pop. of more than 8,000, having become center for surrounding agricultural reg. Occupied by forces of Gens. Rbt. E. Lee & Stonewall Jackson in 1862 & again by Gen. Jubal Early's Confed. detachment in 1864, Frederick received & helped care for wounded after battles of South Mountain & Antietam & of Monocacy. Its growth into an industrial center followed Civil War.

PTS. OF INT.: (1) Record & Church Sts., **Frederick County Cth.,** built during Civil War when 2nd cth. on this site burned. (2) Record & Council Sts., **C. Burr Artz Free Lib.** (1936), has documents signed by Geo. Washington, Thos. Jefferson & John Jay. (3) **Winchester Hall** (1843-44.Class.Rev.) is occupied by cty. offices. (4) Near inters. of US40 & US340, **Hist. Soc. of Frederick Cty. Hqs., Mus. & Lib.** occupies

Georg. brick dwelling (1807); handsome col. inter. contains large coll. of hist. relics, incl. Belt-Tyler Mem. Coll. of heirlooms. In vic. of Court Sq. are (5) **Potts H.** (1818), (6) **Ross H.** (c.1814), (7) **Mathias H.** (1816) & (8) **Spite H.** (1814). (9) 127 W. Church St., **Sappington H.** (c.1830). (10) 111 Record St., **Johnson H.** (c.1810-20). (11) 113 Record St., **Winebrenner H.** (c.1815-20). (12) NW. edge of town, **Hood College,** women's college (est.1893). (13) On grounds of **Md. St. School for the Deaf,** 242 S. Market St., are gray stone **Frederick Barracks** (1777), which house coll. of minerals & Ind. relics.

Among Frederick's more notable Chs. are (14) octagonal-spired **Trinity Chapel** (1763.cupola 1797,steeple 1807), W. Church St. near Market St.; (15) 2nd St. & Chapel Alley, cruciform open-towered **St. John's Ch.** (Cath.under construction from 1800 on); (16) Church St. bet. Market St. & Middle Alley, twin-spired **Evangelical Luth. Ch.** (c.1753.facade & spires added 1854.Goth.Rev.); (17) 9-13 W. Church St., porticoed & twin-towered **Evangelical Reformed Ch.** (1848.Gr.Rev.). (18) S. end of Market St., **Mt. Olivet Cemetery,** with bronze **Francis Scott Key Mon.** (1898), near its entrance. Contains graves of Key & his wife; of Thos. Johnson, Md.'s 1st gov.; & of Barbara Fritchie, who is comm. by granite **Barbara Fritchie Mon.** (19) 154 W. Patrick St., **Barbara Fritchie H.** (fee), is reprod. of H. in which heroine of John G. Whittier's poem, who may or may not have flaunted Union flag in face of Gen. Stonewall Jackson & his Confed. troops, lived with her husband, glovemaker John Caspar Fritchie; contains some of her clothing & belongings. (20) 123 S. Bentz St., **Roger Brooke Taney H.** (1815.fee), was residence of one-time Chief Justice of U.S. (1777-1864), best known as author of Dred Scott decision.

Frederick is at J. with US15 (see).

SIDE TRIPS: (A) Take St.73 (R) from Frederick to 8,000-a. **Frederick City Mun. For.** surrounding 77,000,000 gal. mt. reservoir.

(B) Take US340 (L) from Frederick to **Prospect Hall** (c.1732), 1.5m, in which lived Benj. Tasker Dulany, aide to Geo. Washington. At 12.5m is J. with stone Rd.

(R) here 2.5m to **Thos. Sim Lee H.** (1775). Lee, member of Continental Congress, served 2 terms as gov. of Md.

**Mt. O'Donnell** (1819), c.12.5m, was home of Francis Thomas, Congressman from Md. in 1830's & afterward gov. At 14m is J. with St.17.

(R) here 4.5m to asphalt-paved Rd. & (L) 1m on this to **War Correspondents Mem.,** bizarre-looking stone arch with a sculptured figure of Orpheus in niche, designed & erected (1896) by Civil War correspondent & novelist, Geo. Alfred Townsend. Names of 157 Civil War correspondents & artists appear on tablets. In 1946, it was rededicated & names of correspondents in later wars added.

At 19m is J. with paved Rd., on which route turns (R) 4m to gravel Rd.; (R) 0.5m on this is **John Brown H.,** farmh. near Potomac R. which John Brown in June 1859 rented as base of operations for his raid on Harpers Ferry.

**49.5.** J. with US40 Alt., leading (R) 4m to **Gambrill St. Pk.** (pic.hik.riding), 1,088 as. of mt. wilderness, straddling High Knob (1,600′) on Catoctin Mt.

**51.5. BRADDOCK HEIGHTS,** resort on summit of Catoctin Mt., has lodging & amusement facils. **53.5. MIDDLETOWN,** rural trade center sett. in 18th cent. US40 scales **SOUTH MT.,** where on Sept. 14, 1862, Gen. Geo. B. McClellan's Fed. troops defeated Gen. D. H. Hill's & Gen. Longstreet's Confeds. in Battle of South Mt. At **58.5.** is J. with Zittlestown Rd. leading (R) 1.5m to **Washington Mon. St. Pk.** (pic.), where on July 4, 1827, citizens of Boonsboro (see below) erected in 1 day mound honoring Geo. Washington. **60.5. BOONSBORO,** sett. 1774, is quiet farmer's town. Main St., **Rose Hill** (1814) & 2 blocks (R) from Main & St. Paul Sts., **Weldon** (c.1741), both settings for David Belasco's play, "The Heart of Maryland."

SIDE TRIPS: (A) Take St.66 (R) from Boonsboro 6.5m to **Mt. Aetna Caverns** (fee.parking. pic.), Md.'s largest limestone caverns, lighted for distance of 650′.

(B) Take St.34 (L) 5.5m to J. with asphalt-paved Richardson Ave.: (R) on this 1m to observ. tower commanding view of 182-a. **Antietam Nat. Battlefield Site,** where bloodiest battle of Civil War, with more than 23,000 casualties, took place Sept. 17, 1862. Area, though cultivated by farmers, is a Nat. pk. St.34 cont. to Nat. Pk. Serv. office, 6m, in which are mus. & lib., at entrance to **Antietam Nat. Cemetery,** containing 4,823 graves. 6.5m **Sharpsburg,** farmers' trade center, still containing some of stone & log houses built at time of its founding in 1763, figured so prominently in Battle of Antietam that Southerners called battle by its name.

(L) from Sharpsburg on Harpers Ferry Rd. is **Antietam,** 3m, where now-ruined iron works cast cannon & cannon balls during Rev.

St.34 cont. past **Site of Lee's Hqs.,** 7.5m, to **Mt. Airy** (c.1800), 8m, plain brick mansion used as hospital after Battle of Antietam, which Pres. Lincoln visited. 9.5m **Ferry Hill** (1813), is brick mansion in which Gen. W. H. F. Lee, son of Rbt. E. Lee, injured at Antietam, was cared for. At 10m St.34 crosses **Md.-W. Va. Line** on S. end of bridge across Potomac to Shepherdstown, W. Va.

At **61.5.** is J. with St.68, leading (L) 3.5m to 3-arched limestone **Delemere Bridge** (1833) across Antietam Cr., at W. end of which is entrance to **Delemere** (c.1776). **72.5. HAGERSTOWN,** Md.'s 3rd largest city, has up-to-date-looking bus. dist., but older secs. retain charm of past. Hagerstown trades with farmers & dairymen & handles their products; its factories turn out shoes, organs, airplanes, furniture & other products. On this site in 1737, Jonathan Hager sett. & built log house. Other settlers followed until in 1762 town was laid out. During Civil War, Hagerstown, having voted against secession, prospered through supplying food to Union forces. Advent of RRs. during next 2 decades helped promote prosperity. After 1890, pop. jumped suddenly ahead as Hagerstown's development into modern commercial & industrial center got underway.

PTS. OF INT.: (1) N. of City Pk., **Hager H.** (1739), built by Hagerstown's founder, Jonathan Hager. (2) Hager Pk., Frederick & Hager Sts., **Hager Mill** (1791), little changed, having orig. water wheel. (3) Potomac & Church Sts., **Zion Reformed Ch.** (1774.much altered), which Jonathan Hager helped build (he was killed in his saw-mill while dressing logs for it), & in whose graveyard he is buried. (4) 201 W. Washington St., **Mt. Prospect** (1789), built by Nath. Rochester, Rev. Army Col., proprietor of nail factory & Hagerstown's 1st banker, who later founded city of Rochester, N.Y. (5) 921 The Terrace, **Oak Hill** (Vict.Goth.) was home of Wm. T. Hamilton, Congressman, Senator, & Gov.; in its driveway stands Hagerstown's one-time slave block. (6) Potomac St. & North Ave., **Cannon Pk.,** contains cannon cast in France (1757), captured by Sp. from Napoleon's forces & sent to Ft. Morro in Cuba, where it was taken by Amers. in Battle of Santiago (1898). (7) **City Pk.** (50 as.baseball. tennis.playground.bandstand.zoo), is area of natural woodland with L., springs & streams. (8) In City Pk. is **Washington Cty. Mus. of Fine Arts** (opened 1931); has works by Gutzon Borglum, Gustave Courbet, Andre Dèrain, Paul Gauguin, Auguste Rodin & others. (9) 21 Summit Ave., **Washington Cty. Free Lib.** (est.1901), one of nation's 1st cty. libs. (10) Potomac St. & William Lane, **Rose Hill Cemetery,** in which are graves of 5,000 Confed. soldiers killed at Antietam & South Mt., contains **Confed. Mon.** (1877) & **Kennedy Mon.** (1919), erected by Md. Jews to honor Thos. Kennedy, buried beneath it, for his campaign for legislation granting civil rights to Jews, which he won in 1826. (11) 9 N. Potomac, **Gruber Almanac Co.,** publishers of "Hagers-Town Town & Country Almanack" (founded 1797). (12) 403 N. Prospect St., **M. P. Möller Organ Works,** founded by Mathias Peter Möller (1880), one of largest factories of its kind in world. (13) Pennsylvania Ave. & Park Lane, **Fairchild Aircraft Corp. Plant,** (founded 1926).

SIDE TRIPS: (A) Take St.64 (R) from Hagerstown to J. with Pangborn Blvd., c.1.5m. (R) here to **Pangborn Corp. Plant,** world's biggest factory of steel treating & sandblasting facing **Pangborn Pk.**

St.64 cont. to J. with St.62, 4m; turn (L) here to **The Hive** (1790), 5m, built by Rev. War veteran, Col. Wm. Fitzhugh.

(B) Take St.65 (L) from Hagerstown to **Rockland** (1808), 7.5m, 24-room brick mansion built by Col. Frisby Tilghman on his 10,000-a. estate.

US40 passes over modern concrete bridge, **79.5.,** paralleling **Old Conocheague Bridge** (1819). At 82.5. is J. with macadam Rd. leading (R) 0.5m to **Stafford Hall** (1832). **84. CLEARSPRING,** rural trading center, named for large spring.

SIDE TRIPS: (A) Take macadam Rd. (R) from Clearspring 2m to **Montpelier** (c.1770).
(B) Take macadam Ft. Frederick Rd. (L) from Clearspring 4.5m to **Jacques H.** (c.1766), in front of which is log cabin (c.1755). Ft. Frederick Rd. cont. to J. with macadam Rd. 6m. (L) on this 0.5m to 188-a. **Ft. Frederick St. Pk.** (camp.pic.), extending S. to Potomac R. Pk. surrounds **Ft. Frederick** (1756.rest.), square edifice built of stone with bastions at corners of its heavy, 17′ high walls, named for Fred. Calvert, 6th Lord Baltimore. Erected as defense against Fr. & Ind. raids, it was never attacked. Union forces used it during Civil War to guard Baltimore & Ohio Ry.

Ft. Frederick Rd. turns to J. with US40 at 8.5m.

**99.5. HANCOCK,** which depends on sand mines & fruit orchards in vic., stands at Md.'s narrowest point, known as Maryland's Neck, less than 2m wide. **101. FLINT H.,** of stucco-covered log construction, was residence of Ind. trader, "Old Mr. Flint," who several times received Geo. Washington here as visitor. US40 scales **SIDELING HILL MT.** (1,595′), whose summit at **106.5.** commands wide view of Potomac &

Hagerstown & Shenandoah valleys, cuts through N. extremity of 16,888-a. **Green Ridge St. For.** (pic.camp.hik.h.f.), then climbs to top of **MARTIN MT.** (1,675′), **128.5.**

**137.5. CUMBERLAND,** Md.'s 2nd largest city, is bustling industrial center, with RR. yards & factories, on Potomac R. at its confluence with Will's Cr. Both Rs. sometimes overflow. Cumberland has suffered heavily from floods, & up-to-dateness of bus. dist. is partly due to repairing flood damage. Tires, tin plate & steel, glass & artificial silk are important Cumberland products; city also draws trade from wide rural area.

Will's Cr. was named for Indian Will, who was living on site when 1st white settlers came. Ohio Co., org. by Va. planters & Brit. merchants to develop half-million-a. tract of land N. of Ohio R., built storehouse & trading post here in 1750. When Fr. began to advance S. to block this penetration of their territory, Gov. Dinwiddie of Va. sent young Geo. Washington to inform them their advance would be resisted. In 1754 Washington met at Will's Cr. Capt. Wm. Trent & proceeded (W), only to be defeated by Fr. & their Ind. allies in engagement at Ft. Necessity. Coming back to Will's Cr., he started building here Ft. Mt. Pleasant, renamed Ft. Cumberland in 1755 in honor of George III's 3rd son. Here, in Ap. 1755 arrived Gen. Edw. Braddock with regular troops from England. After campaign ending in disastrous defeat by Fr. & death of Braddock himself, some of his force of 2,000 straggled back to Ft. Cumberland. Ind. raids soon began forcing so many border settlers to seek refuge at Ft. that Washington, who had been appointed commander of post, found it difficult by spring of 1756 to care for them all. Attack on ft. itself, however, did not materialize. Here, in 1785, Thos. Beall of Samuel laid out settlement 1st named Washington Town & 2 yrs. later renamed Cumberland.

After commencement in 1811 of work on Nat. Rd. from seaboard to Ohio country, 1st built with Fed. funds, Cumberland throve on trade with travelers. When Baltimore & Ohio RR. was built, 1st train arriving in 1842, it became division pt. & later shipping pt. for Alleghany coal mined in vic. To orig. settlers, mostly of Brit. or Ger. descent, were added immigrants from E. Europe, Slavs & Magyars, who came to help man Cumberland's industries. As bus. bldgs., industrial plants & RR. yards spread over riverside lowlands, residences began to climb steep overlooking hillsides.

PTS. OF INT.: (1) At confluence of Will's Cr. & Potomac R., in **Riverside Pk.,** Green & Water Sts., stands **Log Cabin** supposedly used by Geo. Washington during Fr. & Ind. War, moved here from its orig. location on site of Alleghany County Cth. Here too is granite **Thomas Cresap Mon.,** honoring one of early Md.'s most noted Ind. traders. (2) Riverside Pk. lies S. of probable site of Ft. Cumberland, whose parade ground is now **Prospect Sq.,** Washington & Johnson Sts. (3) 118 Green St., **Dent H.** (18th cent.), where Cumberland's 1st white child, Frederick Dent, was born in 1786. (4) 512 Dunbar Dr., **Rose Hill** (1801.adds.). (5) Fayette St. bet. Johnson & Smallwood Sts., **Sts. Peter & Paul Cath. Ch.** (1818.later remod.). (6) Cumberland's chief industrial establishments are **Baltimore & Ohio RR. Shops,** Virginia Ave. & Queen St., this RR.'s 3rd largest. (7) Foot of Kelly Blvd., **Kelly-Springfield Tire Co. Plant,** best-equipped plant of its kind in world at time of its completion in 1920.

SIDE TRIPS: Take US220 (L) from Cumberland. 5.5m **Celanese Corp. of America Plant,** employing thousands of workers, normally produces artificial silk but is equipped during wartime to produce ammunition. US220 skirts Dan's Mt. (R), 2,000′ high in places, named for pioneer Dan. Cresap, whose sons settled before Amer. Rev. in **Cresaptown,** 12.5m. 27m, **McCool.** 27.5m, US220 crosses **Md.-W. Va. Line** on bridge across Potomac.

(B) Take St.51 (L) from Cumberland. 15.5m **Oldtown,** strung along single street bet. W. Md. RR. tracks & weed-overgrown channel of former Chesapeake & Ohio Canal, dates from soon after 1741 when 1st white settler, Col. Thos. Cresap, arrived. Here is stone, gabled **Michael Cresap H.** (c.1765.brick adds.1780), residence of Cresap's youngest son, famous Ind. fighter.

US40 passes through **Cumberland Narrows,** natural gorge in **Will's Mt.,** which has limestone cliff more than 1,000′ high. At **144.** is hexagonal, frame **TOLL H.** (c.1833). **146. ECKHART MINES.** Bituminous coal mines which have been operated on big scale in vic. since 1830's. Trading center of this mountainous coal-mining reg. is **FROSTBURG, 150.**

SIDE TRIP: Take St.36 (L) going through several industrial towns: 5.5m **Midland,** which has shirt factory & several coal companies; 8.5m **Lonaconing,** depending on coal mining &

silk manufacturing; & 17m **Westernport,** another coal mining community at head of navigation on Potomac R., with pulp & paper mills in vic.

**159.5. STONE H. INN** (1818), was for third of century favorite stopping place on Nat. Rd. At **160.** is J. with dirt & gravel Rd. leading (L) 3m to 17,000-a. **Savage R. St. For.** (log cabins.camp.pic.bath.boat.hik.riding.f.h.winter sports). **162. STANTON'S MILL** (1797.rebuilt 1856.enlarged 1900), saw long service as saw & grist mill. Just beyond is **Old Castleman R. Bridge** (1816), visible (R) from modern hy. bridge, said to have been largest of its kind in U.S. at time of construction. **166. NEGRO MT.** (2,908′), highest pt. on US40 within Md., was named for Negro member of band led by Col. Thos. Cresap who in battle with Inds. during Fr. & Ind. War was killed & buried here. At summit of **KEYSER'S RIDGE** (2,881′), **168.5.** is western J. with US219.

SIDE TRIP: Take latter (L). At 17m is J. with improved Rd. leading (L) 0.5m to **Drane H.** (pre-1800). US219 cont. to **Deep Creek L.,** 13.5m, formed by power company dam, along whose shores are several resort settlements. At 21m is J. with St.38, leading (L) 11m to entrance to 4,000-a. **Potomac St. For.** (camp.pic.hik.f.hunt.). US219 cont. to **Oakland,** 26.5m, trading center for farmers & resort colonists of vic. est. in 1851. At 35.5m is J. with US50 (see). At 38.5m is **Md.-W.Va. Line.**

US40 crosses **MD.-PA. LINE** at **172.**

# US 50—MARYLAND

**ANNAPOLIS, MD. (W) to BLADENSBURG, MD.** (7.5m from Washington, D.C.). **27.5. US50**

Accoms.: Limited.

Known as Defense Hy. because it conns. U.S. Naval Academy & National Capital, this sec. of US50 was built in 1926. Terrain is hilly & wooded.

**0. ANNAPOLIS,** near mouth of Severn R. on Chesapeake Bay, is known as "Ancient City"; it is Md.'s capital & site of U.S. Naval Academy. Town also depends on tourist & farmers' trade, seafood-packing & boatbuilding industries. Its quaint old streets, even today, will hardly permit automobile traffic; it remains quiet & dignified settlement of stately old bldgs. First settlers were Puritans, arriving in 1648 from Va., who, few years later, heartened by news of Puritan successes in England, set about trying to take over provincial government. In 1655 Gov. Wm. Stone dispatched navel expedition to put them down, which they successfully resisted; but after Restoration in England, their power waned. Community, at 1st named Anne Arundel Town, for 2nd Lord Baltimore's wife, grew slowly until 2nd royal gov., Sir Francis Nicholson, decided to remove capital here from St. Mary's. Assembly gathered in house of Edw. Dorsey for 1st meeting in new capital on Feb. 28, 1695. Renamed for Princess Anne, later Queen of England, Annapolis was intelligently laid out with streets radiating from State Circle. Soon it became lively social center, noted for dancing, drinking & gaming. Earlier frame bldgs. were gradually replaced by stately residences & public bldgs. with fine formal gardens. During Rev., mouth of Severn R. was fortified &, safe from attack, Annapolis sat out war, often entertaining troops as they passed through. Here new Congress of U.S. met from Nov. 26, 1783, to June 3, 1784. Annapolis, gradually outrivalled in prosperity by Baltimore after Rev., remained St. capital; &, when in 1850, Ft. Severn, built on Windmill Pt. to protect city against Brit. naval attack during War of 1812, was converted into U.S. Naval Academy, future prosperity was assured.

PTS. OF INT.: (1) Plain brick, white-domed **State H.** (1772-93), in State Circle, housing legislative chambers & gov.'s & adjutant general's offices, replaces 2 earlier St. capitols built on this site, 1st in 1697 & 2nd in 1706. The very interesting **Old Senate Chamber,** of Georg. Col. design, was one in which Congress of U.S. met (1783-84) to receive Geo. Washington's resignation as commander-in-chief & to ratify the Treaty of Paris; it contains 2 portraits by Chas. Willson Peale. Opp. is **Old Hall of Delegates,** with retiring room containing hist. flags. Capitol's W. extension (1905), conn. to old bldg. by Corinthian portico, contains present-day legislative chambers, both in Ital. Ren. style. (2) S. of State H. is the cross-shaped **Old Treasury** (c.1695) (occupied by the Annapolis C. of C.). (3) Bet. State & Church Circles, **Government H.** (1866.remod.1936) is Gov.'s residence. (4) Opp. is **Court of Appeals Bldg.** (1900), which houses St. Lib. (5) College Ave. & Bladen St., **St. Office Bldg.** (1939), in neo-Georg. style. (6) Church Circle & Franklin St., **Anne**

**Arundel County Cth.** (1824.enlarged 1892 & 1925), with domed cupola and arched veranda entry. (7) Church Circle & Franklin St., former Reynolds Tavern (1737), notable for brickwork & portico, houses **Pub. Lib. of Annapolis & Anne Arundel Cty.** (8) Church Circle & Northwest St., **Post Office** (1910), in late Georg. style. (9) Duke of Gloucester & Market Sts., **City Hall** incorporates 3 walls of Annapolis' onetime chief social center, Assembly Rooms, built here in 1764. (10) 170 Duke of Gloucester St., **Forensic Club** (pre-Rev.) once had Geo. Washington among its members. (11) 162 Conduit St., **Masonic Temple** (1770.adds.). (12) Church Circle, **St. Anne's Ch.** (1859), is 3rd on site since est. of St. Anne's or Middle Neck Parish in 1692. (13) Duke of Gloucester & Chestnut Sts., on grounds of **St. Mary's Ch.** (1860) stands **Carroll Mansion** (1735), birthpl. of Chas. Carroll of Carrollton, containing Annapolis' 1st Cath. chapel, now House of Second Novitiate. (14) State Circle & North St., **Calvary Meth. Ch.** (1923) is handsome modern edifice of Georg. Col. design.

(15) College Ave., **St. John's College** (chartered 1784) was successor to King William's Sch., est. in 1696. St. John's College, nonsectarian for men, attracted wide attention by adoption in 1937 of new curriculum based entirely on study of 100 great books. **McDowell Hall,** built orig. (beginning 1745) as residence for Gov. of Md., burned in 1909 & was rebuilt. **Woodward Hall** contains lib., which incl. about 400 books from coll. imported in 1696 by Thos. Bray for Md.'s 1st pub. lib. **Liberty Tree,** a tulip poplar, is so named for Rev. meetings held under it. College infirmary occupies **Pinkney H.** (1750), 5 St. John St., birthpl. of Wm. Pinkney, who became U.S. Attorney General in 1811. **Reverdy Johnson H.** (1750), on campus, once home of U.S. Senator & Attorney General, is now faculty residence; & **Carroll H.** (pre-1718), 139 Market St., is now college pres.'s residence. (16) 22 Maryland Ave., **Chase-Lloyd H.** (1769-74.late Georg.Col.upper stories of portico added recently), with impressive central pavilion, fine portico & Ionic pillared entrance is notable for rich ornament of inter., marble mantels, paneled doorways & impressive staircase; its construction was begun by Sam. Chase, signer of Decl. of Ind., & completed by Edw. Lloyd IV, Gov. of Md.

(17) Opp. Chase-Lloyd H. is **Hammond-Harwood H.** (1774.Georg.), now mus., with 2-bay central sec. flanked by 2-story wings; has inter. woodwork even more richly carved than that of Chase-Lloyd H; built by Matthias Hammond. It has been called finest example of Georg. architecture in Amer. (18) College Ave. & King George St., **Ogle H.** (1742.later adds.), was former residence of Sam. Ogle, provincial gov. (19) Randall Court, **Bordley-Randall H.** (1732.adds.). (20) Prince George & East Sts., **Brice H.** (1760). (21) Oldest part of Carvel Hall Hotel, 192 Prince George St., was **Wm. Paca H.** (1763), birthpl. of signer of Decl. of Ind. (22) 120 Duke of Gloucester St., **Ridout H.** (c.1750). (23) 130 Prince George St., **Sands H.,** oldest frame house in Annapolis (c.1680.rear wing added later). (24) 211 Prince George St., **Dorsey H.** (2-story part c.1685; 3-story part added after Civil War), built by Edw. Dorsey, ranking officer of provincial militia, served as Gov. Francis Nicholson's residence (1694-1709) & as provincial assembly's meeting place in 1695 & again in 1704. (25) 195 Prince George St., **Jennings H.** (1685), was bought from its probable 1st owner, Edmund Jennings, by Annapolis' 1st mayor, Amos Garrett. (26) 4 Shipwright St., **Scott H.** (1765) is described in Winston Churchill's novel, "Carvel Hall"; it is now convent. (27) 124 Charles St., **Jonas Green H.** (c.1680), said to be oldest house in Annapolis, was once residence of Jonas Green, publisher of "Maryland Gazette," Md.'s 2nd newspaper. Other old houses incl.: (28) Acton Pl. & Franklin St., **Acton** (c.1745); (29) 112 Duke of Gloucester St., **Slayton H.** (pre-1786); (30) 23 State Circle, **Brooksby-Shaw H.** (1720), now Elks Club; (31) 160 Prince George St., **Aunt Lucy's Bake Shop** (1716).

(32) **U.S. Naval Academy** (O.9-7; no pic.no smoking in bldgs.no photographs of inter.no automobiles except Sun. 7-12 p.m.), main entrance at Maryland Ave. & Hanover St., is housed in impressive group of Fr. Ren. bldgs. scattered over 80-a. tract along Severn R. & larger area N. of College Cr. It was opened Oct. 10, 1845, under superintendency of Franklin Buchanan, later top admiral of Confed. Navy. During Civil War school was removed to Newport, R.I., & Annapolis campus became military hospital & camp. It was reopened in 1865 with revised curriculum. After Sp.-Amer. War, curriculum was again revised & new bldgs were built. Candidates for admission to Academy must meet rigid physical specifications; after graduation, they receive commissions as ensigns. June Week, when commissions are

awarded, is Academy's chief yrly. event, whose climax comes when midshipmen toss their caps high into air following exercises. Just inside bronze grilles of Maryland Ave. Gate to The Yard is **Naval Academy Mus.,** which has coll. of battle relics, ship models, paintings, arms & other mementoes. On Lovers' Lane, where midshipmen promenade with guests, are **Herndon Mon. & Okinawa Bell. Naval Academy Chapel,** (R) from the gate on Blake Road, has crypt containing sarcophagus which holds ashes of John Paul Jones, buried in Paris in 1792 & moved here in 1906. **Dahlgren Hall,** which houses ordnance & gunnery offices, used for drill & "hops". Behind it are **Thompson Stadium,** scene of Navy's home football games, & **Farragut Field,** where parades & drills are staged. **Bancroft Hall,** (L) of Dahlgren Hall, is huge, U-shaped dormitory, at whose entrance stands bronze copy of USS "Delaware's" figurehead, representing Delaware chief, Tamenend, which midshipmen have renamed **Tecumseh;** within is Mem. Hall containing, among other naval relics, Perry's flag with its motto, "Don't give up the ship." **MacDonough Hall** (gymnasium), named for victor in Battle of Lake Champlain (Sept.11,1814), has mounted over its running track model of steam vessel "Antietam." Depts. of languages & seamanship navigation are housed in **Luce Hall.** Adj. it lie **Dewey Basin** & **Santee Basin,** accommodating vessels belonging to Academy. **Mexican Mon.** stands in middle of The Yard. Across The Yard, opp. Bancroft Hall, are **Mahan Hall,** containing auditorium decorated with captured flags & lib., at whose entrance is **Macedonian Mon.,** & to (R) & (L) of Mahan Hall, **Maury Hall,** housing depts. of Eng., hist., gov. & mathematics, & **Sampson Hall,** housing depts. of electrical engineering. Behind Mahan Hall is marine engineering bldg., **Isherwood Hall.** (S) of Isherwood Hall is **Worden Field,** where infantry & boat drills are held. Bet. mus. & dispensary bldg. is **Tripoli Mon.** On other side of Dorsey Cr. are **Naval Academy Cemetery, U.S. Naval Hospital,** athletic fields & officers' quarters.

SIDE TRIPS: (A) Take St.2 (R) from Annapolis 2m to J. with St.648, (R) on this 0.8m, then (R) 4m on St. Margaret's Rd. & (R) 1m on dirt Rd. is **Whitehall** (c.1766), former residence of Horatio Sharpe, gov. of province.

(B) Take St.2 (L) from Annapolis to **All Hallows Ch.** (1727), 8m, whose most noted parson was Mason Locke Weems, author of the apocryphal story of Washington & the cherry tree.

(L) from All Hallows Ch. 1.2m on dirt Rd. is **South River Club,** housed in gabled white frame bldg., which may be oldest active social club in U.S., having been org. in 1722 or before.

At 14m is J. with St.255.

(L) here 3m, then (L) 0.5m on macadam Rd. is **Tulip Hill** (1745.rest.).

**St. James Ch.** (1765), 18.5m, has in its graveyard Md.'s most ancient tombstones, those of Christopher Birckhead & wife, dated 1666.

US50 runs (W) from Annapolis. At **3.5.** is **THREE MILE OAK,** blackened tree stump embedded in concrete, on site where delegation from Annapolis met Gen. Geo. Washington on his journey there to resign his commission. **12.5.** J. with US301 (see). **13.5.** J. with dirt Rd. leading (L) short distance to brick **Whitemarsh Ch.** (1856. foundations 1742). Here, in 1st church on this site, Father John Carroll was nominated 1st bishop of Cath. Ch. in Amer. **14.** J. with asphalt & gravel Rd. leading (R) 1m to **Bowie Race Track,** which has 1-mile course, grandstand seating 14,500, clubh. & stables. **BELAIR, 15.,** at end of ave. lined with tulip trees, is 5-part brick mansion (main sec.1742.wings after 1900), built for Gov. Sam. Ogle. **16.5.** J. with dirt Rd. leading (L) 1.5m to oak-shaded, stucco-coated brick **Fairview** (c.1785). **19.** J. with dirt Rd. leading (R) short distance to brick **Marietta** (c.1736). **25.5.** J. with Landover Rd., leading (L) 1.5m to Georg. Col. brick **Beall's Pleasure** (c.1795). **27.5. BLADENSBURG,** named for Gov. Sir Thomas Bladen & established 1742, is now chiefly settlement of commuters to Washington. End of River Rd., **Bostwick H.** (1746). Bladensburg is at J. with US1 (see).

## US 13—MARYLAND

**DELMAR, MD.** (7m from Laurel, Del.) **(S) to MD.-VA. LINE** (22.5m from Accomac, Va.). **40.5. US13**

Via: Salisbury, Princess Anne & Pocomoke City. RR. parallels route. Accoms.: In larger towns.

US13 cuts across S. part of Md.'s Eastern Shore. **0. DEL.-MD. LINE** bisects town of **DELMAR,** rural trade center which grew up after founding of RR. repair shops here in 1859. **7. SALISBURY,** Eastern Shore's largest town & Md.'s 2nd largest port. The town lies on Wicomico R. and is a fast-growing city, untypical of Eastern Shore towns. Laid out in 1732, it had become in late 18th cent. thriving settlement. After RR. reached it in 1860, it became shipping pt. for farm products. Among industries are an iron foundry, brickyard & shipyard, several garment factories & woodworking mills, canneries, ice plants & meat-packing houses. Only old residence of note which escaped 2 fires in 19th cent. is **Poplar Hill Mansion** (1795), head of Poplar Hill Ave. In Salisbury is J. with St.349.

SIDE TRIP: Take latter (R) short distance to J. with Anderson Rd.

Turn (L) on this 2m to entrance lane to **Pemberton Hall** (1741.int.paneling).

At 6.5m on St.349 is J. with St.352, on which route turns (L) to J. with Whitehaven Rd. at end of pavement, 4.5m; (R) here to fork at 5m, then (L) (straight ahead) from fork to **Green Hill Episcopal Ch.** (1773), 5.5m.

**20. PRINCESS ANNE,** at head of once-navigable Manokin R., dates back to 1733. (N) of bridge on US13 (Somerset Ave.), **Manokin Presb. Ch.** (walls 1765.tower added after 1865), houses congregation org. about 1686. US13 bet. Broad & Prince William Sts., **Washington Hotel** (1744). One of most impressive houses on Eastern Shore is **Beckford** (1776.Georg.), opp. W. end of Washington Ave. at Beckford Ave. W. end of Prince William St., **Teackle Mansion** (1801). E. end of Prince William St., **East Glen** (1795), large Adam-style H. Antioch St., **E. Herrman Cohn H.** (1800). In Princess Anne is J. with St.363.

SIDE TRIP: Take latter (R) 5.5m to J. with asphalt Rd.; (L) on this 1m to dirt Rd., then (L) 0.5m to **Almodington,** overlooking Manokin R., large brick house (early 18th cent.), whose living-room woodwork was purchased by N.Y.'s Metropolitan Mus. of Art.

**23. BEVERLY OF SOMERSET** (1786-96.Georg.fine Adam-style woodwork, stairway & central hall arch), one of Md.'s most impressive houses, was home of wealthy plantation owner Nehemiah King II (1755-1802). King family, friends of Napoleon Bonaparte's brother Jerome (who married Elizabeth Patterson of Baltimore), were involved in scheme to rescue Napoleon from St. Helena & hide him here at Beverly; Napoleon died before plan could be carried out. **25.** J. with St.413.

SIDE TRIP: Take latter (R) 3.5m to **Kingston Hall** (18th cent. veranda & cupola added later). At 4.5m on St.413 is J. with concrete-paved Rd.

Take latter (R) 2.5m to **Greenwood** (pre-Rev.fine stairways & paneling).

At 6m on St.413 is J. with concrete-paved Rd.

Take latter (L) 3m to **Rehoboth Presb. Ch.,** oldest continuously used Presb. house of worship in U.S., erected (1705-06.windows & furnishings later replaced) by founder of this denomination in Amer., Rev. Francis Makemie, Irish immigrant of 1683.

17m **Crisfield,** facing Tangier Sound from W. terminus of St.413, styles itself "Sea Food Capital of the Country." Fish, crabs & oysters are brought in from lower Chesapeake Bay by hundreds of fishing craft. Sedate, tree-shaded upper part of town stands on tracts surveyed in 1663; but Crisfield's real growth dates from advent in 1868 of RR., for one of whose promoters, John W. Crisfield, it was renamed. Crisfield also builds & repairs boats; manufactures fishermen's gear, packing cases & clothing & other articles; & cans fruits & vegetables.

Turn (E) 1m from Crisfield on Main St. to J. with shell Rd.; (L) on this 1.5m to **Makepeace** (1663.early-Virginia type.fine exter.brickwork & inter.paneling), one of best preserved of its type on Delmarva Peninsula.

**35. POCOMOKE CITY** is an agric. shipping center whose hist. goes back to the beginning of 18th cent.

SIDE TRIP: From Pocomoke City (R) 5m on 4th St. to J. with dirt Rd. & (R) 6m on this to **Beverly of Worcester** (c.1774.service wings & portico later).

**40.5. MD.-VA. LINE.**

## EASTERN SHORE TOUR (US213)

### ELKTON, MD. (S) to OCEAN CITY, MD. 152.5. US213, US50

Via: Chesapeake City, Chestertown, Easton, Cambridge & Salisbury. Branches of Pa. RR. serve reg. Accoms.: In larger towns, limited elsewhere.

US213 traverses Md.'s Eastern Shore, fertile, low-lying reg., deeply indented by inlets & R. estuaries of Chesapeake Bay, where farmers & fishermen still live & work as did their forefathers 3 centuries ago.

US213 branches (S) from US40 (see) in **ELKTON, 0.** (see US40). **6. CHESAPEAKE CITY** stands at Maryland end of Chesapeake & Delaware Canal (opened 1829), 14m-long, toll-free route, converted from lock canal to sea-level course by

Fed. Gov. in 1927. **11. BOHEMIA MANOR,** comprises part of estate acquired after 1662 by Bohemian-born Augustine Herman, E. Shore's most important man in his time. His grave is near present manor house, erected by Delaware's U.S. Senator Thos. F. Bayard. At **13.** is **LITTLE BOHEMIA** (1743-45.Georg.fine exter.& inter. details). **30.** J. with St.292.

SIDE TRIP: Take latter (R) to two-&-a-half story brick **Runnymede** (1692), 0.5$^{m}$, & just beyond, **Shepherd's Delight** (c.1682.int.inter.paneling & carving, hand-hewn rafters). 4$^{m}$ **Betterton,** on Chesapeake Bay, is popular summer resort.

**36.5. CHESTERTOWN,** with mellow brick hs. overlooking wide Chester R., personifies unhurried graciousness of E. Shore living. Kent County Cth. was built on site in 1698. N. end of Washington Ave., **Washington College,** 1st college chartered in Md., was visited in 1784, 2 yrs. after Rev. Wm. Smith had founded it, by Geo. Washington, who gave handsomely to its endowment & served as member of its Board of Visitors & Governors. 101 S. Front (Water) St., former **Chestertown Custom H.** orig. a storehouse (1694) by Ringgolds, early merchants. High & Cross Sts., **Emmanuel Prot. Episc. Ch.** (1768.Vict.embellishments later), housed meeting in 1780 which chose for its new name & title the Protestant Episcopal Church of America, distinct from its Mother Church in Eng. 231-35 High St., **Eliason Bldg.** (c.1750), was formerly White Swan Tavern. 532 W. High St., **Palmer H.** was built by Capt. Palmer of salvaged ship's timbers & stone brought into port as ballast. 100 E. High St., **Wickes H.** (pre-Rev.hand-carved woodwork). 108-110 E. High St., **Wm. Barroll H.** (1735). 110 N. Front (Water) St., **Meteer H.** (1780). 115 N. Front (Water) St., **Perkins H.** has well kept sward. High & Front Sts., **Widehall** (1732-62) has unusually fine hanging staircase. 100 S. Front (Water) St., **Abbey,** or Ringgold-Pearce H. (1735.rest.), whose orig. drawing room paneling, now faithfully reproduced, was taken to Baltimore Mus.

SIDE TRIPS: (A) Take St.289 (R) from Chestertown 2$^{m}$ to J. with St.664. (L) on this to country lane, 2.5$^{m}$; (L) on this to clapboarded, gambrel-roofed **Godlington Manor.**

(B) Take St.20 (R) from Chestertown to J. with St.298 at rural trading center of **Fairlee,** 7$^{m}$; (R) here to dirt Rd., 0.3$^{m}$, & (L) on this to **Big Fairlee** (c.1674.orig.paneling,mantels, & int.woodwork & doors). At 8.5$^{m}$ on St.20 is J. with St.21 & with dirt Rd.

(1)Take dirt Rd. (L) to ivy-covered masonry **St. Paul's Ch.** (1713.vestry h. 1766), one of Md.'s oldest continuously used churches.

(2) Take St.21 (L) to Chesapeake Bay resort of **Tolchester Beach** (bath.f.amusements), 4$^{m}$, reached by auto ferry from Baltimore during summer.

At 11$^{m}$ on St.20 is J. with St.445, leading (R) 0.3$^{m}$ to **Hinchingham** (1774.notable inter. paneling & cabinetwork).

**43.5.** Rural trading center of **CHURCH HILL** is site of brick **St. Luke's Prot. Episc. Ch.** (1731.rest.1881;notable for curved roof & arched windows). **45.** J. with dirt Rd. leading (R) 2$^{m}$ to **Kennersley** (1704.rest.fine inter.woodwork.14′ ceilings). At **45.5.** is J. with dirt Rd. leading (R) 4.5$^{m}$ to **Readbourne** (1734.fine stairway & fireplace), built from plans which Lord Baltimore is said to have helped prepare. **53. CENTERVILLE** was laid out in 1792. S. Liberty St., **St. Paul's Prot. Episc. Ch.** has sacred vessels presented by Queen Anne. Railroad Ave. & Banjo Lane, **Yellow Brick H.** W. side of Commerce St., S. of Water St., **Palmer H.**

At **53.5.** is J. with St.18.

SIDE TRIP: Take latter (R) to J. with dirt Rd., 2.7$^{m}$.

(R) here 2$^{m}$ to **Walnut Grove** (1681-85.gambrel-roofed sec. later), perhaps oldest house in Queen Annes Cty.

St.18 cont. to **Reed's Creek H.** (1776.notable entrance.hand-hewn floors & paneled walls), 2.8$^{m}$. At 3.2$^{m}$ is J. with Rd. leading to Tilghman Neck, on which route turns (R) to fork, 4.3$^{m}$; (L) here to half-story **Blakeford** (oldest secs.late 17th & early 18th cent.), 5.5$^{m}$. Box gardens are Md. showplace.

Rural trading center of **WYE MILLS, 60.5.** Here is **Wye Oak,** one of largest oaks in U.S., 95′ high with branches spreading 165′, thought to be 4 centuries old. **Old Wye Ch.** (1722.rest.1948), is seat of one of Md.'s 1st parishes. Wye Mills is at J. with US50, which tour now follows (S).

SIDE TRIP: Take US50 (R) from Wye Mills to J. with dirt Rd., 1.5$^{m}$.

(L) on this 1$^{m}$ to **Cloverfields** (c.1730.notable for vitreous-coated brick of exter. & fine woodwork of inter.), overlooking Wye R.

US50 cont. to J. at 3.5$^{m}$.

(L) here 4.3$^{m}$ to **Wye Plantation.** Its mansion (1747), overlooking Wye R., was home of Wm. Paca, signer of Decl. of Ind. & twice Gov. of Md., whose tomb is in family graveyard.

US50 cont. to **Bloomingdale** (central sec.1792.SE.wing earlier.older bldg. is miller's H. 1698), 3.7m, one of Queen Annes Cty.'s most distinguished Georg. mansions. Two-story hexagonal portico is only one of kind in Md. St.404 bridges Kent Narrows, 12m, to Kent I., 1st sett. place in Md. At 16m, **Stevensville** is J. with St.18, leading (R) 4m to **Love Pt.** (bath. f.accoms.), summer resort. Here ferry boat conns. to Baltimore. At 18.5m is J. with St.33. [Here US50 turns (R) 0.4m to **Matapeake,** terminus of ferry line from Annapolis.] Cont. straight ahead on St.33 to J. with dirt Rd., 23m.

(R) on this 3m to **Kent Ft. Manor** (c.1640.one-&-a-half-story bldg., weatherboarded), one of Md.'s beautiful old Hs. It was one of bldgs. erected soon after Wm. Claiborne's orig. trading post on 1st sett. site within Md. burned in 1638.

St.33 cont. to ferry to Claiborne, 24.5m.

At **66.5.** is J. with St.565 (old US213).

SIDE TRIP: Take latter (R) to J. with Tunis Mills Rd., 1.5m, on which trip cont. (W).

(R) on this is **Gross' Coate** (oldest sec.1755-60), 4m, big brick H. owned successively by 6 generations of Tilghman family. It has several portraits by Chas. Willson Peale, painted here during visit in 1790.

Tunis Mills Rd. cont. to J. with dirt Rd. at 6m.

(R) on this 1m to **Wye H.,** one of Md.'s finest Hs., 5-part frame mansion with classic portico (1770-92.fine exter.& inter.details), built by Continental Congress delegate Edw. Lloyd. It stands in one of most beautiful formal gardens laid out in Col. America. Facing bowling green, **Orangery** (pre-1770.late Col., with Fr.Ren.influence).

At 7.5m on Tunis Mills Rd. is J. with asphalt-paved Rd.

(R) on this 0.5m to dirt Rd. & (R) here to **Hope H.** (main unit 1784), 1.5m, one of Md.'s most int., standing in boxwood gardens. Design of its pavilions is unusual in Md.

At **69.5.** is J. with dirt Rd.

SIDE TRIP: Take latter (R) to 2nd dirt Rd., 1m; (R) here to 3rd Rd., 1.5m; (L) here to **Myrtle Grove** (frame wing 1734.main brick sec.1789), 2m.

At **72.5.** is J. with St.331.

SIDE TRIPS: (A) Take this (L) to **Troth's Fortune** (c.1676).

(B) Take St.331 (R) to **Easton,** 1m, trading center for farmers & plantation owners, with canneries, garment factory & lumber mill; tearooms & antique shops serving station wagon set; & many spacious Hs. amid tree-shaded lawns. Easton grew out of Quaker community which sett. here around **Third Haven Meeting H.** (O.appl.to porter on the grounds), S. end of Washington St., a simple frame bldg. set amidst massive oaks, beneath one of which Wm. Penn once held meeting. It is one of oldest frame Chs. in country (1682-83). Washington & Dover Sts., **Talbot County Cth.** (1794.Vict.embellishments later). Aurora & Goldsborough Sts., **Foxley Hall** (1794). Dover & Harrison Sts., **Bullitt or Chamberlain H.** (c.1790).

(1) Straight ahead from Easton on St.33 to gravel Rd., 2m, leading (L) 0.7m to **Ratcliffe Manor** (1749.Georg.Col.) with one of Md.'s finest boxwood gardens. 11m on St.33, **St. Michaels,** onetime shipbuilding center on narrow neck bet. Miles R. & Broad Creek, now summer resort. 13m **West Martingham** (c.1670), shingled frame bldg. 16m J. with gravel Rd. leading (R) 0.3m to **Rich Neck Manor** (18th cent.), former home of Matthew Tilghman, delegate to Continental Congress, pres. of Md. Constitutional Convention. At 16.5m on St.33 is **Claiborne,** terminus of ferry from Kent I. (see above).

(2) Take St.565 (L) from Easton to J. with St.333, 0.7m, & cont. (R) on this. At 6.8m is J. with gravel Rd. leading (R) 2.3m to **Otwell** (gambrel-roofed secs.1670.other gabled secs. later; carved inter. is very fine). St.333 cont. to gravel Rd. at 8.7m leading (L) 0.3m to **Combesbury,** which has 3-story main sec. (1740) notable for patterning of its brick. At 9.5m is **Plinhimmon** (c.1736.frame wing later). 10.5m **Oxford,** overlooking Choptank R., dates back to 1668. Today it depends on f. fleet & tourist business.

**85.5. PERRY FARM H.** (c.1687), overlooking Choptank R., was once an inn. **Gov. Emerson C. Harrington Bridge** (1935) across Choptank is Md.'s longest concrete bridge (8,737'). **87.5. CAMBRIDGE,** E. Shore's 2nd largest town, has yacht basin crowded with pleasure craft & commercial harbor with crab, oyster & f. vessels. Cambridge is seafood & vegetable packing center; it also has shipyards, fertilizer plant & flour, textile & lumber mills. Two of its chief streets, High & Poplar, retain names given when town was laid out in 1686. It had become prosperous settlement by middle of 18th cent., where lawyers, country officials & tobacco planters built mansions overlooking R. Despite its industrialization, Cambridge remains city of gardens & shaded streets with many fine homes. Spring, High & Court Place, **Dorchester Cth.** (1853) is 3rd on site; 1st was built in 1687. High & Spring Sts., 1st ch. to occupy site of **Christ Prot. Episc. Ch.,** was built 1695; in churchyard are buried many Rev. heroes. N. end of Maryland Ave., **La Grange** (c.1760). Hambrook Blvd., **Glasgow** (1760). Gay & Spring Sts., **Hill** or **Wallace Mansion.** 217 High St., **Sycamore Cottage,** built by Dan. & Mary Maynadier, who fled to America after failure of Scottish Rebellion of 1715. High & Glasgow Sts., **Jordan H.** (Georg.fine inter. paneling,mantels & stairway,antique furnishings).

SIDE TRIPS: (A) Take St.343 (R) from Cambridge to asphalt-paved Rd., 2.2$^{m}$.

(R) on this is **Horn's Point,** 1.5$^{m}$, estate of U.S. Senator & industrialist Coleman du Pont (1863-1930), overlooking Choptank R.

St.343 cont. to T-shaped frame **Spocot** (S.sec.built soon after 1662). 5.7$^{m}$. At 6.2$^{m}$ is J. with gravel Rd.

(R) on this 1.6$^{m}$ to **Pokety Lodge,** estate of automobile manufacturer Walter P. Chrysler beside Choptank R.

(B) Take St.16 (R) from Cambridge to J. with St.335 (Hooper I. Rd.), 6.3$^{m}$. (R) on this 1$^{m}$ to **Old Trinity Prot. Episc. Ch.** (pre-1680.rest.1850).

US50 turns (SW) from Cambridge to **VIENNA, 103.5.,** est. as port at head of navigation on Nanticoke R. in 1706. **120.5. SALISBURY** (see US13) is at J. with US13 (see). US50 crosses **POCOMOKE R., 136.5.,** twisting through **Great Pocomoke Swamp,** which extends N. & S., great expanse of peat & buried cedar & cypress logs which remained wilderness until mid-19th cent. **144.5. BERLIN** is surrounded by some of country's largest apple & peach orchards. It has nurseries, barrel & clothing factories & chicken-dressing plant. Although Berlin's name probably derives from that of Col. Wm. Stevens' estate, Burleigh, patented in 1677, it did not grow into town until early 19th cent. Along narrow, crooked, tree-shaded streets are number of early 19th cent. white weatherboarded residences. Main St. N. of Burley, **Burleigh Cottage** (1834). Main St. S. of Burley, **Burleigh Manor** (early 19th cent.). In what is now a peach orchard, E. of Decatur St., is sign marking **Site of Birthpl. of Stephen Decatur.**

SIDE TRIPS: (A) Take US113 (L) from Berlin to **St. Martin's Prot. Episc. Ch.** (1756-59. orig.pews, gallery & chancel), 5.5$^{m}$.

(B) Take US113 (R) to **Snow Hill,** 16$^{m}$, quiet, easygoing town of white Hs. in gardens, at edge of cypress-swamp-bordered Pocomoke R., founded in 1686 on part of Col. Wm. Stevens' tract which was named Snow Hill for London suburb. Market & Church Sts., **All Hallows Ch.** (Episc.1756) has on display Bible presented by Queen Anne. Federal St. N. of Morris St., **Boxhaul** (oldest part late 18th cent.).

(C) Take St.376 (R) from Berlin 4.5$^{m}$ to woods lane leading straight ahead to **Fassitt H.** (early 18th cent.), whose brickwork with interlacing glaze patterns has been termed by some authorities most int. in Md. of its time.

US213 cont. to **148.5., GLEN RIDDLE FARM,** racehorse breeder & trainer Sam. D. Riddle's 1,500-a. estate; War Admiral, famous Kentucky Derby Winner, trained & now a stud here. **152.5. OCEAN CITY,** Md.'s biggest seaside resort, strings along narrow, sandy Barrier Reef, approached by bridge from mainland across Sinepuxent Bay. It has bath. beach, 2$^{m}$ boardwalk & amusement zone, & dozens of oceanfront hotels, cottages & apartment houses. Summer pop. reaches as high as 30,000: vacationers, convention delegates, big-game fishermen. Channel bass, tuna & marlin of great size are caught 20$^{m}$ to 30$^{m}$ offshore.

## US 1—MARYLAND

**MD.-PA. LINE** (22.5$^{m}$ from Kennett Square, Pa.) **(S) to MD.-D.C. LINE** (5.5$^{m}$ from Washington, D.C.). **82. US1**

Via: Belair, Baltimore, & Laurel. RRs. parallel route. Accoms.: All kinds plentiful.

US1 is heavily traveled main hy. affording few scenic views.

### Sec. 1: MD.-PA. LINE to BALTIMORE. 49.5.

**1.5.** J. with St.273.

SIDE TRIP: Take latter (L) to **Calvert,** 2.5$^{m}$, founded 1701, where is **E. Nottingham Friends Meeting H.** (additions 1724, stone 1751). **Blue Ball Tavern** (est.c.1710), 5.5$^{m}$.

**3. RISING SUN,** farmers' trading center.

SIDE TRIP: Take St.276 (L) from Rising Sun to J. with St.269, 1.5$^{m}$; (R) on this 1$^{m}$ are **W. Nottingham Academy** (c.1741) & **W. Nottingham Presb. Ch.** (1800).

Thought to be over 500 yrs. old, **LAFAYETTE OAK, 6.,** marks site where Lafayette & his soldiers camped Ap. 12, 1781. At **9.** are Js. with US222 (which unites with US1 for 0.5$^{m}$) & St.338.

SIDE TRIPS: (A) Take US222 (R) short distance to **Success** (1734.stone add.1849).

(B) St.338 (L) 0.5$^{m}$, **Octorara,** once home of P. S. Physick, father of Amer. surgery.

At **9.5.** US222 branches (S) from US1.

SIDE TRIP: Take US222 (L) to **Port Deposit,** 6m, on narrow shelf by R. at base of 200′ cliffs, founded in 1812. **Jacob Tome Institute** (opened 1894), Main St., housed in big brick Washington Hall & 3 adj. granite bldgs., was founded with Jacob Tome's endowment of more than $5,000,000 as early manual training sch.

**10. CONOWINGO DAM** (1927.105′ high, 4,648′ long), top of which is roadbed for US1 across Susquehanna R., impounds 14m-long **Conowingo L.** At **13.** is J. with St.162, leading (L) 2m to stone **Rigbie H.** (1731.enlarged 1750.notable stairway & paneling), where occurred mutiny among Washington's troops quelled by execution of leader. **26. BELAIR,** seat of Harford Cty. since 1782, is trading center of rich farming area. Bond St. one block (R) of Main St., **Country Club Inn** (oldest part 1718.chief addition 1790) contains old furnishings & relics. Belair is at J. with St.22 (see US40). For pts. of int. on or near US1 bet. Belair & **BALTIMORE, 49.5.,** see Baltimore Trip II. Baltimore is at J. with US40 (see).

### Sec. 2: BALTIMORE to MD.-D.C. LINE. 32.5.

For pts. of int. & towns on or near US1 bet. Baltimore & **MUIRKIRK, 23.5.,** see Baltimore Trip VI. **26.** J. with concrete-paved Rd. leading (L) 0.5m to **Nat. Agric. Research Center,** maintained by U.S. Dept. of Agric., 14,000-a. experimental farm. Once 1st sta. on stagecoach route from Washington to Baltimore, 17-room **RHODES TAVERN, 27.,** is still operating. **29.** J. with concrete-paved Rd.

SIDE TRIP: Take latter (L) to Edmonson Rd., 1.5m; (L) here to **Greenbelt,** 3.5m, model village low-cost housing project built by Resettlement Adm. (1935-38).

**29.5.** Bldgs. of **UNIV. OF MD.** (Georg.Col.) overlook US1 from knolls. Univ. is product of merger in 1920 of 2 institutions: Baltimore's Univ. of Md. (chartered 1812) & Md. St. College of Agric. (founded here 1856). Md. Agric. Experimental Sta. has done notable work in plant & tree experimentation in orchard & vineyard, spreading over a large portion of its hilly campus. **31. RIVERDALE,** suburb of Washington, D.C. On Arthur Ave., 2 blocks from Madison, is stuccoed brick **Calvert Mansion** (c.1750.Georg.Col.); cannon in garden supposedly one from "Ark," boat which brought early settlers to Chesapeake Bay. **31.5. HYATTSVILLE,** Washington suburb. **32.5. BLADENSBURG** (see US50). J. with US50, which here unites with US1. Near edge of town is **MD.-D.C. LINE.**

## US 301—MARYLAND

**BALTIMORE, MD. (S) to MD.-VA. LINE** (32m from Bowling Green, Va.) **75.5. US301**

Via: Upper Marlboro & La Plata. RRs. parallel route. Accoms.: In larger towns.

US301, cutting through S. Md., is most direct route bet. Baltimore & Richmond. For pts. of int. bet. Baltimore & J. at **23.5.** with US50, see Baltimore Trip VII. US301 unites with US50 for 0.5m & at **24.5.** branches S. At **30.5.** is J. with St.214.

SIDE TRIP: Take latter (L) 2.5m to J. with dirt Rd.
Turn (L) on this 2m to **St. Barnabas Ch.** (1774.early Georg.Col.belfry added 1930).
At 5.5m on St.214 is J. with St.202.
Turn (L) on this 1.5m to brick, hip-roofed **Mt. Lubentia** (pre-1770).

US301 cont. (S) to J. with St.4, **35.5.**; (L) 1m attractive brick, hip-roofed **Compton Bassett** (1789) overlooking Patuxent R. **37. UPPER MARLBORO,** trading center for tobacco-farming reg., founded in 1706. Opp. cth. is **Marlboro H.** (c.1732.Georg. Col.). US301 cont. to J. at **42.5.** with dirt Rd. leading (R) 1m to **Dower H.** (1660. rest.1931). Garden was designed by Maj. Pierre Charles L'Enfant, who laid out Washington, D.C. At **47.5.** are Js. with St.381 & St.5 (latter unites S. with US301 for 6m).

SIDE TRIPS: (A) Take St.381 (L) 0.5m to J. with asphalt Rd. leading (R) 0.5m to 3,510-a. **Cedarville St. For.** (camp.pic.hik.). St.381 cont. 6m to J. with asphalt Rd. leading (L) 0.5m to **St. Paul's Prot. Episc. Ch.** (1733.gabled roof.Mod.), where Thos. John Claggett, 1st Episc. bishop in U.S., was once rector.

(B) Take St.5 (R) 1m to J. with asphalt Rd.; turn (L) on this to J. with St.224. 6m.
(1) Take St.224 (L) 3.5m to J. with dirt Rd.; (R) here 0.5m is brick **Christ Ch.** (1698. rebuilt 1831).

(2) Take St.224 (R) 9.5m to J. with St.549, (L) here 3m is **Ft. Washington,** overlooking Potomac R. Present structure, replacing an older one, was designed by Maj. L'Enfant after War of 1812. Entrance is over drawbridge across moat. There are storehouses, barracks & officers' quarters bordering parade ground & subterranean chambers & galleries beneath. St.224 cont. (N) from J. with St.549 to early Georg. **Harmony Hall** (1723), 10m, **St. John's Ch.** (1723), with preserved pew of Washington, 10.5m.

**53.5. WALDORF,** at (S) J. with St.5.

SIDE TRIP: Take latter (L) 11m to tobacco growers' trading center of **Hughesville,** at J. with St.231.

Turn (L) 7m on this to once-important tobacco shipping pt. of **Benedict,** founded in 1683, where ferry crosses Patuxent R. From E. bank St.231 cont. (E) across country to **Prince Frederick,** 12.5m, seat of Calvert Cty. since 1723; at J. with St.2, on which trip cont. (R) to J. of St.266 at 25m; (R) 2m to Rd., (L) 0.5m & (R) 1m, to **Preston-on-Patuxent** (1650), where Rich. Preston, commissioner appointed by Oliver Cromwell, est. seat of gov. in 1653 & maintained it for yr. At 27m on St.2 is **Middleham Chapel** (1748), whose bell is said to be 3rd oldest on Atlantic Coast. Just beyond is J. with dirt Rd. leading (R) 0.5m to **Great Eltonhead Manor H.** (c.1750). St.2 cont. to **Solomons** (boats.fish.equipment), 35m, at mouth of Patuxent R. on island approached by causeway from mainland, which has yacht & boat-building industry & big fish. fleet.

St.5 cont. (S) from J. with St.231, to **Charlotte Hall,** 15m, early health resort near medicinal spring; now Amish settlement. **Briscoe H.** (c.1699). **Old White H.** (1803). 18.5m **Mechanicsville.** At 18.5m is J. with St.235.

Take latter (L) 2.5m to **Cremona** (1819.rest.). At 10m on St.235 is J. with macadam Rd. leading (L) 2m to **Sotterley** (Georg.Col.oldest part 1730.rest.), facing Patuxent R. St.235 cont. to J. at 14m with gravel Rd. leading (R) 2m to twin-towered **St. Andrew's Ch.** (1767). At 15m is J. with dirt Rd.; (L) on this 1m, then (R) short distance on another dirt Rd. & (L) 1m on 3rd dirt Rd. is gable-roofed **Kingston** (1670), with end chimneys typical of its period. At 19m on St.235 is **Patuxent U.S. Naval Air Test Center,** 7,000-a. airfield on which Navy aviation equipment, incl. planes, guns, bombs, torpedoes, radar & television devices, is tested.

At 31.5m on St.5 is J. with St.243 leading (R) 4.5m to frame **St. Francis Xavier Ch.** (1767. rest.). 32.5m **Leonardtown,** at head of an estuary of Potomac R., laid out in 1708, has been trading in tobacco for more than 2 centuries. Here are **Tudor Hall** (1780.Georg.) & **St. Marys Beacon Office** (1704). At 34m is J. with St.244 leading (R) 2m to **Mulberry Fields** (1760-1770.Georg.Col.), overlooking Potomac. At 40m is J. with St.249.

Turn (R) here 3m to J. with macadamized Rd.; (R) here 0.5m is **St. George's Ch.** (1750). St.249 cont. 3.5m to J. with St.251; (L) here 3m is gambrel-roofed, telescope-style **Porto Bello** (1740).

46.5m **St. Mary's City,** maintained by St. & cooperating organizations, was 1st settled place in Md. Here in 1634 Leonard Calvert led his company ashore from "Ark" & "Dove" to build ft. & lay out town, which served as Md.'s capital until 1694. **St. Marys Stateh.** (1934) is replica of orig. (1676). Bricks salvaged from the latter helped to build **Trinity Prot. Episc. Ch.** (1829), in whose churchyard is **Leonard Calvert Mon.,** marking site where Calvert's company assembled to hear read charter establishing their settlement; to rear of ch. is **Copley Vault,** holding ashes of Md.'s 1st royal gov., Sir Leonard Copley. At 53.5m is J. with dirt Rd. leading (R) 0.5m to brick **Clockers Fancy** (pre-1700). 52m **St. Inigoes,** at J. with dirt Rd.

Take latter (R) to 2nd dirt Rd. at 1.5m & turn (R) on this 1m to **Cross Manor** (1643. much altered), Md.'s oldest brick bldg.

St.5 ends at **Pt. Lookout,** 61.5m, where lighth. (1830) stands at mouth of Potomac R.

**62. LA PLATA,** on US301, seat of Charles Cty., est. after RR. reached this pt. in 1868, is at J. with St.6.

SIDE TRIP: Take latter (R) from La Plata 0.5m to clapboarded, double-chimneyed **La Grange** (1758); notable for arched doorways. At 2m is J. with St.327; route turns (R).

Take latter (L) short distance to ghost town of **Port Tobacco,** seat of Charles Cty. from 1658 to 1895 & once Md.'s chief port on Potomac. Here is **Chimney H.** (1767).

State 327 turns (R) to **Rose Hill** (1730) 3m, former home of Dr. Gustavus Brown, one of Geo. Washington's physicians. At 4m is crescent-shaped **Habre de Venture** (1742), former home of Decl. of Ind. signer Thos. Stone, architecturally notable. At 4.5m is J. with St.225. Route turns (L) on this. At 9m is **Araby** (1685-1715). St.225 cont. to **Indian Head U.S. Naval Reserv.,** 15m, est. in 1892, where powder is manufactured & naval ordnance tested.

**67. BEL ALTON** is at J. with macadamized Rd. leading (R) 2m to **St. Ignatius Cath. Ch.** (1789) & **St. Thomas Manor H.** (1741). At **71.** is J. with St.234.

SIDE TRIP: Take latter (L) 12.5m to old village of **Chaptico.** Turn (R) here on St.237 short distance to **Christ Ch.** (c.1736), designed by architect of St. Paul's in London, Christopher Wren. On St.237 at 14m is **Deep Falls** (c.1745). At 15.5m is J. with dirt Rd. leading (L) 1.5m to **Bachelor's Hope** (17th cent.). At 17m is J. with St.242.

Turn (R) on this 4.5m to J. with St.239; (R) here 1.5m is brick & stone **Ocean Hall** (c.1684).

**73.5. NEWBURG,** at Js. with St.230 & St.3.

SIDE TRIPS: (A) Take St.230 (L) 4m to village of **Mt. Victoria,** at J. with dirt Rd. leading (L) 0.5m to brick, telescope-style **Hard Bargain** (pre-Rev.). At 5m on St.230 is brick, 2-story **West Hatten** (1790).
(B) Take St.3 (L) 1m to **Mt. Republic** (1792).

At **75.5.** US301 bridges **POTOMAC R. to MD.-VA. LINE,** which follows R.'s SW. shore.

## US 15—MARYLAND

**MD.-PA. LINE** (9m from Gettysburg, Pa.) **(S) to PT. OF ROCKS, MD. 43.5. US15**
Via: Emmitsburg, Thurmont & Frederick. RR. parallels route. Accoms.: Plentiful.

US15 skirts E. side of Blue Ridge Mts., traversing Monocacy Valley. **1.5. EMMITSBURG,** sett. 1834. **2.5. ST. JOSEPH'S COLLEGE** (founded 1809), Cath. women's institution, was est. by Elizabeth Bayley Seton (1774-1821), founder & Mother Superior of Sisters of Charity at Emmitsburg; her log cabin is still preserved & she is buried here. **4. MT. ST. MARY'S COLLEGE** (founded 1808) is country's 2nd oldest Cath. College. **11.5. THURMONT,** 1st sett. in middle of 18th cent., supports thriving goldfish-raising industry. US15 skirts 12,000-a. **Catoctin Recr. Area** (pic. camp.swim.), under development by Nat. Pk. Service, covering slopes of Catoctin Mt., which runs from Md.-Pa. Line to Potomac R., 1,000′ to 1,600′ high, bordered by Monocacy Valley (E) & Middletown Valley (W). **14.5. CATOCTIN,** which still has several ancient log Hs., was site of Catoctin Furnace (opened 1774); iron sides for Monitor produced here. **18. LEWISTOWN FISH HATCHERY,** largest in Md., breeds bass & brook trout. **20.5. PETER KEMP H.** (18th cent.). **23.5. RICHFIELDS** was home of Rear Adm. Winfield Scott Schley, hero of battle of Santiago in Sp.-Amer. War. **24.5. ROSE HILL MANOR** (1770), built by Md.'s 1st gov., Thomas Johnson. **27. FREDERICK** (see US40) is at J. with US40 (see). **28.** J. with US240.

SIDE TRIP: Take US240 (L) 1m to **Monocacy Nat. Military Pk.,** covering ground where on July 9, 1864, Gen. Jubal Early's 15,000-strong Confed. detachment decisively defeated smaller Union force under Gen. Lew Wallace in Battle of the Monocacy. **Confed., N.J., Pa., & Vt. Mons.** comm. actions of various infantry groups which took part in fighting. 24m **U.S. Coast & Geodetic Observatory,** on Observatory Hill in milling & trading town of **Gaithersburg,** is 1 of 5 in world founded in 1899 by International Geodetic Assoc. to record shifting of earth's poles & consequent shifting of latitudes. 29.5m **Rockville,** seat since 1777 of Montgomery Cty.

Turn (R) from Rockville 5m to J. with St.190 (Falls Rd.) & (L) on this to Conduit Rd., 8.5m; (R) here to **Great Falls Pk.,** 10m, commanding fine view of cataracts of Potomac. Pk. preserves part of an iron foundry & walls of mill, both once owned by Geo. Washington; sec. of Chesapeake & Ohio Canal used for boating.

US240 cont. through Washington suburb of **Bethesda,** 37.5m, where is streamlined modern **Naval Medical Center,** & across Md.-D.C. Line. 44.5m, **Washington** (see) is at Js. with US1 (see) & US50 (see).

US15 cont. to **PT. OF ROCKS, 43.** At S. end of Pt. of Rocks Bridge over Potomac is **MD.-VA. LINE, 43.5.**

## US 11—MARYLAND

**MD.-PA. LINE** (16m from Chambersburg, Pa.) **(S) to MD.-W. VA. LINE** (13m from Martinsburg, W. Va.). **12.5. US11**
Via: Hagerstown. RR. parallels route. Accoms.: Ample.

US11 traverses rich, fruit-growing Hagerstown Valley. **5.5. HAGERSTOWN** (see US40) is at J. with US40 (see). **10. TAMMANY,** named for Ind. chief, is two-and-a-half-story brick mansion. **11. SPRINGFIELD** (central part 1750, wings later), stone & brick mansion. **11.5. WILLIAMSPORT,** laid out in 1786 at pt. where early trls. crossed, aspired to be capital of U.S. & Geo. Washington visited it in 1790 to investigate its claims. It lost out because Gt. Falls of Potomac prevented navigation to this pt. Today it produces brick & limestone, silk & leather, brooms & electric power. Toll bridge over Potomac carries US11 across **MD.-W. VA. LINE, 12.5.**

# BALTIMORE

## BALTIMORE

RR. Stas.: B. & O. RR.—Mt. Royal Ave. & Cathedral St., Mt. Royal Sta.; 311 W. Camden St., Camden Sta. N. Charles & Lanvale Sts., Pa. RR. Sta. 217 W. Baltimore St., Bus Sta. for Greyhound & Peninsula lines. Municipal Airport & seaplane terminal; other airports in vic. Ferries: Pier 5, Light St., for Love Pt. Ferry to Eastern Shore; Pier 16, Light St., for Tolchester Ferry to Eastern Shore. Accoms.: All types plentiful; more than 100 hotels; auto & trlr. camps on outskirts. Info.: A.A.A., Mt. Royal Ave. & Cathedral St.; Baltimore Assoc. of Commerce, 404 St. Paul St. Recr. Facils.: Many motion picture houses, 1 burlesque & 3 legitimate theaters; Lyric Theater & Peabody Conservatory of Music for concerts; horse racing at Pimlico; golf at Clifton Pk. Mun. Golf Course & many private courses; tennis at mun. courts in city pks.; swim. at Clifton, Druid Hill & Patterson Pks. & at Lakewood Pool (26th & Charles Sts.) & Meadowbrook Pool (Falls Rd. & Kelley Ave.); riding in Druid Hill Pk.; yachting at Md. Yacht Club, Broening Pk., Hanover St. Bridge. Annual Events: 2nd Bachelors' Cotillion, 1st Mon., Jan.; Md. Day Celebration, Mar. 25; Md. Artists' Exhibition, Baltimore Mus. of Art, Ap. 1-30; Md. House & Garden Pilgrimage, late Ap., early May; Flower Mart, Mt. Vernon Pl., early May; Pimlico Spring Race Meet, May 2-14; Old Defenders' Day Celebration, Sept. 12; Baltimore Live Stock Show, Union Stockyards, Oct.; Pimlico Fall Race Meet, Nov. 1-15; 1st Bachelor's Cotillion, 1st Mon. Dec.

Baltimore, the "Free State" 's metropolis & foreign & domestic port on Chesapeake Bay is seldom described as an "historic city." It is, however, an 18th century town & during the Rev. was one of Gen. Washington's dependable supply bases &, for a few months, the nation's capital. From the rich 19th century are the well-known rows of similar houses with their little white stoops of stone or wood, the narrow, twisted streets (some still paved with cobblestones), sedate Vict. mansions with wrought-iron handrails & vestibules, bronze mons. & gaslights. In some sections, especially in colorful Italian neighborhoods & wherever the old genial Germanic influence is still found, Baltimore has pleasant, easygoing overlay of distinctly Old Country feeling. But this is only part of the picture, for although Baltimore has the self-composure & rather leisurely pace of a Southern City, it is still a great modern metropolis. Turning out a bewildering diversity of products: ships, fertilizer, canned goods, straw hats, bottle caps, etc., it is rated 6th largest port & nation's 11th biggest industrial center. Reminders of Baltimore's proud past are stately mansions which overlook fountains & tree-dotted grass plots of Mt. Vernon & Washington Places on edge of downtown bus. sec. & its fashionable Charles St. shopping dist., where Baltimoreans make leisurely purchases to accompaniment of friendly gossip. Tradition's hold is manifested, too, in such social institutions as Bachelors' Cotillion, at which for more than 150 yrs. daughters of socially elect have made debuts. It is evidenced in city's reputation for good cooking, distinguished by such delicacies as terrapin, beaten biscuits & Chincoteague oysters. But Baltimore has also colorful variety of any great modern industrial city. It has its up-to-date traffic-congested bus. dist. & its foreign quarters: Little Italy, S. of Pratt St. & E. of Jones Falls, & Polish quarter, centering around St. Stanislaus Kostka Ch.; in other scattered communities are thousands of Baltimoreans of Russian, German, Brit., Irish & other European ancestry. More than 250,000 Negroes have a lively business district & amusement centers in NW. sec. along Pennsylvania Ave. Some distance away from downtown & facing Fort McHenry across Patapsco River is the changeless waterfront area, around S. Broadway, with seamen's taverns, fish markets & ropemakers' lofts.

Baltimore largely owes its metropolitan importance to its location at head of wide estuary of Patapsco R., dozen miles inland from Chesapeake Bay, which provides sheltered harbor for shipping. On tip of peninsula in estuary, later known as Whetstone Neck, tract was patented to Chas. Gorsuch, Quaker; & to N., on W. side of Jones Falls, David Jones acquired land in June, 1661. Other settlers followed, among them Chas. & Dan. Carroll, who patented 1,000 as. in 1696. By 1726, tiny settlement had grown up on E. bank of Falls. Three ys. later landholders to N., who wanted port from which to ship tobacco, persuaded provincial assembly to est. town. Laid out on 60-a. tract in shape of arrowhead, W. of Jones Falls at end of Patapsco R.'s Northwest Branch, town was named for Lord Baltimore's seat in Ireland. New settlement was slow to grow, however, & it had rival in Jones Town, already est. hamlet on E. bank of Falls. Rivalry bet. 2 communities, soon conn. by causeway &

bridge, lasted until 1745, when they were united by act of assembly into 1 town. Baltimore Town was, by middle of 18th cent., settlement of c.200 persons housed in some 2 doz. dwellings, straggling along crooked Sts., with ch. & couple of taverns. In 1755, some 40 Acadians, from the village of Grand Pre, found harbor here. First school was est. in 1766 & 1st newspaper, 4 yrs. later.

By 1768, when town was made cty. seat & cth. built, pop. had increased to 3,000 or 4,000. It increased further, 5 yrs. later, when assembly inc. within boundaries 80 as. stretching S., incl. settlement at Fell's Pt., where Wm. Fell had built wharf, shipyard & warehouse. In 1775, when news of engagements at Lexington & Concord arrived, Baltimore was already drilling soldiers & manning the famous privateers. Congress, driven out of Philadelphia by the Brit., had temporary quarters here, Dec., 1776, to March, 1777, & it was during this period Washington was given plenary powers. Baltimore furnished Continental Army with supplies, men & equipment. It got busy building vessels of every kind for Md.'s naval force, which patroled Chesapeake Bay. Bet. 1777 & 1783 Baltimore's shipyards launched almost 250 vessels, which fought & captured Brit. ships on all the seven seas. After Rev., Baltimore bottoms in growing numbers carried grain & other foodstuffs to European ports & came back loaded with manufactured goods. Baltimore's pop., 6,700 in 1776, grew within succeeding third of century to 45,000. New Sts. were opened, new bldgs. erected. War of 1812 provoked new outburst of belligerent patriotism. Fleet of more than 40 privateers set out to harry Britain's merchant marine. Neglected Ft. McHenry was put in shape again, & the Star Spangled Banner Flag, with its 15 stars & 15 bars, was raised above it. The capture & burning of Washington was followed by landing of Brit. Army at North Pt. & approach up Patapsco of Brit. fleet & it fell to defenders of Ft. McHenry to fight them off in engagement which inspired writing by Francis Scott Key of "The Star Spangled Banner."

City went on growing. Soon much of its prosperity was founded on flour, milled in & around city & shipped in Baltimore vessels. Clippers also began transporting Negroes from Africa. Baltimore became one of South's chief slave marts. Trade with newly settled West began to bring in profits, as wagons crossed mts. by way of Cumberland Rd. to unload foodstuffs & load Baltimore manufactures. Soon Baltimore's enterprising merchants conceived new means of capturing western market—Baltimore & Ohio RR., chartered Feb. 28, 1827, 1st pub. passenger RR. in U.S.; in 1830 the engine "Tom Thumb" demonstrated the locomotive power of steam & this was the beginning of the Amer. Railroad era. Meanwhile, growth of trade & industry was paralleled by growth of labor organization. By 1834, Baltimore was one of best organized cities in America.

Baltimore had expanded by mid-century into busy, brawling metropolis. It acquired notoriety for violence of its own fraud-ridden politics, until citizen's reform movement forced clean-up in 1860. Civil War divided Baltimore into opposing factions; & here occurred 1st bloodshed of Civil War. On Ap. 19, 1861, as 6th Mass. Regiment, on its way to Washington, was crossing town from one RR. sta. to another, a mob attacked them, & 15 people were killed & several wounded. At once Fed. Gov. put all Md. under military rule. Baltimore soon found itself surrounded by fts. Throughout war it served Union forces as supply center.

War's disruption of trade left city with reconversion problem. Economic depression of 1873 was setback. When B. & O. RR. workers struck in 1877 against wage cuts, Fed. troops were called out in W. Va. for 1st time in U.S. to break strike. However, Baltimore's industry & commerce went on growing. Manufacture of chemical fertilizers—an industry developed following Baltimore's importation in 1824 of 1st guano ever brought to U.S.—became important. Baltimore, drawing on Chesapeake Bay's huge oyster beds, became world's chief oyster packing center. Clothing factories & iron & steel works were est. City's shipyards, famous since days of Baltimore clippers, cont. to hum. New RRs.—Pa., W. Md., Md. & Pa.—brought new business. During latter yrs. of 19th cent. many of Baltimore's most noted cultural institutions evolved: Walters Art Gallery (1858); Peabody Conservatory (1868, 1st endowed music sch. in U.S.); Lyric Theater (1892); Johns Hopkins Univ. (1876) & Goucher College (1888); Johns Hopkins Hospital (1889) & Johns Hopkins Medical School (1893).

"Great fire" of Feb. 1904 devastated the downtown section, erasing all landmarks of Old Baltimore. This area was once enclosed (c.1750) by wooden wall with gates to E. & W. Modern structures of varying style replace the 1,000 bldgs. that were burned. World War I gave Baltimore industrial impetus. Metallurgical & chemical plants, shipyards & oil refineries, clothing factories, whiskey distilleries & meat- & seafood-packing plants all helped to swell volume of manufactures. Baltimore became site of world's biggest spice factory & copper refinery & biggest producers of bottle caps & portable electric tools; also, site of one of country's biggest whiskey industries & one of Atlantic seaboard's biggest sugar refineries. World War II saw still further expansion. Diversity of Baltimore's products—steel, copper & magnesium, ships & airplanes, electrical apparatus & radio—has cont. to multiply.

PTS. OF INT. DOWNTOWN: (1) E. Fayette & St. Paul Sts., **Baltimore City Cth.** (1899.Fr.Ren.) murals depicting notable events in Md. hist. by John La Farge, Blashfield, Chas. Y. Turner (former director of Md. Inst. of Art) & others. (2) E. Fayette & Calvert Sts., **Battle Mon.**, comm. Battle of North Pt., Sept. 12-14, 1814. (3) E. Fayette & Calvert Sts., **U.S. P.O. & Fed. Bldg.** (neo-Class.). (4) E. Fayette & Holliday Sts., **City Hall,** of 2nd Empire design. (5) 226 N. Holliday St., **Municipal Mus.** (O.Tues.-Sat.11-5,Sun.1:30-5:30.1813.rest.1930.early Republic style), was opened 1814 by Rembrandt Peale, artist son of early Amer. painter Chas. Willson Peale. The mus., as then advertised, was lit by "Gas Lights—Without Oil, Tallow, Wick or Smoke"—one of the first bldgs. in the U.S. (Baltimore sts. were lighted in 1816). Mus. contains canvasses by him & his father, as well as hist. prints & models & paintings of ships incl. the graceful Baltimore Clippers. (6) E. Fayette & Gay Sts., **World War Mem.** (O.10-4.1921-25.neo-Class.) comm. Md.'s World War I dead; it contains war trophies. (7) E. Fayette & Front Sts., **Shot Tower** (1828), down which melted lead was poured; said to be oldest remaining in U.S. (8) E. Lombard & Front Sts., **Carroll H.** (O.1823.brick.notable for exter.inter.trim), built for Mary & Rich. Caton, daughter & son-in-law of Chas. Carroll of Carrollton, & was Carroll's home several years before he died here in 1832. (9) E. Pratt & Albemarle Sts., **Flag H.** (O.10-5.wks.free.1793) is one in which Mrs. Mary Pickersgill made flag, 30′ by 42′, with 15 stars & 15 stripes to fly over Ft. McHenry, the banner hailed by Francis Key in "the dawn's early light," Sept. 14, 1814. Mus. contains relics, furnishings, documents, & pictures dating from period of War of 1812. (10) 103 S. Gay St., **U.S. Appraisers' Stores Bldg.** (1932.mod.Class.). (11) W. Lombard & Gay Sts., **U.S. Customs H.,** ornamented with Ionic colonnades. (12) Baltimore & Light Sts., **Baltimore Trust Bldg.,** 34 stories high, is city's tallest bldg. (13) Greene St. bet. Lombard & Redwood Sts., **Univ. of Md.** (see US1) **Sch. of Medicine. Schs. of Pharmacy** (1841) **& Dentistry** (1882), **Hospital, & Sch. of Law** (est.1813) are housed in 4 brick bldgs., together with Frank C. Bressler Research Lab. & Davidge Hall (containing medical & law libs.). (14) W. Lombard St. & Fremont Ave., **St. Paul's Cemetery** (O.c.1692), contains graves of many pioneers. (15) In **Westminster Graveyard,** W. Fayette & Greene Sts., is **Grave of Edgar Allan Poe.** Poe died here in 1849 after being kidnapped by hoodlums during election campaign & dragged from poll to poll to vote. Westminster Graveyard contains also graves of Baltimore's 1st mayor, Jas. Calhoun, & Washington's Secy. of War, Col. Jas. McHenry.

(16) Lexington St. bet. Pearl & Eutaw Sts., **Lexington Market,** operated since 1803, on land given by Col. John Eager Howard, Rev. hero. (17) 24 W. Saratoga St., **St. Paul's Rectory** (1791.late Georg.) was built with money raised by lottery. Across St. is **St. Paul's Prot. Episc. Ch.** (1856), 4th on this site; its parish was org. in 1692. (18) Cathedral & Mulberry Sts., **Cathedral of the Assumption of the Blessed Virgin Mary** (1806-21) was nation's 1st Cath. cathedral. Cruciform, with low dome, its Ionic portico flanked by dome-topped sq. towers, it was designed by Henry Latrobe. In crypt under main altar are buried 6 of prelates who have made cathedral their seat, incl. U.S.' 1st Cath. Bishop (later Archbishop), John Carroll (1735-1815); Jas. Cardinal Gibbons (1834-1921), 1st Amer. Cardinal. (19) Cathedral & Franklin Sts., **Enoch Pratt Free Lib.,** outstanding lib. system, with c.900,000 vols. in fine bldg. (1933.neo-Class.), was founded with gift of more than $1,000,000 & $50,000 annuity by ironware merchant Enoch Pratt. Edgar Allan Poe Room contains many of poet's letters & mss. In Md. Room are early records, pictures & engravings, & Hester Dorsey Richardson Coll. of Md. coats of arms. **Md. Academy of Sciences** (O.wks. 9-4:45.Thurs.7-10 p.m.free), 3rd floor, Enoch Pratt Free Lib., founded in 1797, conducts research & presents public lectures. Astronomical observ. is O. to public Thurs. eves. (20) Druid Hill Ave. & Paca St., **St. Mary's Seminary** (1806-08.Goth. Rev.) is one of earliest examples of its type of architecture in U.S. (21) 606-628 N. Calvert St., **Waterloo Row** (1815), 1st built of Baltimore's row houses, was designed

by Rbt. Mills who also designed Washington Mon. (see below). (22) Monument St. & Park Ave., **Md. Hist. Soc. Hqs.** (O.Mon.-Fri.9-5.Sat.9-4), housed in former residence of Enoch Pratt. Contains large coll. of books, letters & mss.; paintings & engravings; furniture, lace, jewelry, glass & silverware. Bonaparte Room contains relics of Bonaparte family, left by former Elizabeth Patterson, heiress who married Napoleon's youngest brother, Jerome. (23) N. Charles & Centre Sts., **Walters Art Gallery** (O.11-5.wks.2-5.Sun.free), white marble, Corinthian-pilastered bldg. of Ital. Ren. design, was built by RR. magnate & art collector Henry Walters to house coll. acquired over 8 decades by him & his father, Wm. Thompson Walters; at his death in 1931 he bequeathed it to city, together with his Gr. Rev. mansion, to rear of mus. at 5 W. Mt. Vernon Place. It has notable colls. of Egyptian, Etruscan, Gr. & Rom., Chinese, Persian & Mesopotamian, & European painting, sculpture & art objects. (24) From **Washington Mon.** (O.8-6;sm.fee) radiate **Mount Vernon Pl.** on Monument St. & **Washington Pl.** on Charles St., which form tree-dotted, grass- & shrub-covered sanctuary adorned with fountains & statues, overlooked by stately old residences. Here each spring is held Flower Mart. **Mon.** (1815-29), 204′ Doric column capped by observ. with dome supporting 16′ statue of Geo. Washington (Henrico Caucici, sculptor), was 1st mon. to country's 1st pres. to be begun. (25) E. Mt. Vernon Pl., **Peabody Institute** (O.wks.9-5.1868) is marble Ital. Ren. bldg., housing lib., art gallery & conservatory of music. It was founded with gift of $1,400,000 from Geo. Peabody. Conservatory of Music is nationally famous.

PTS. OF INT. EAST BALTIMORE: (26) Gay & Ensor Sts., **Number Six Fire Engine H.** (1853), with 103′ bell tower, was home of Fed. (later renamed Independent) Fire Co., org. in 1799; it was bought by city when paid fire dept. was org. in 1858. (27) Monument, Gay & Aisquith Sts., **Wells-McComas Mon.** is marble obelisk (1871) comm. 2 heroes of War of 1812. (28) Fayette & Aisquith Sts., **Friends Meeting H.** (1781). (29) Baltimore & Aisquith Sts., **McKim Free Sch.,** opened in 1822, is a beautiful example of Fr. Rev. architecture; details of the façade copied from Temple of Theseus in Athens. (30) Eastern & Patterson Park Aves., **Patterson Pk.** (boat.swim.recr.facils.casino.conservatory & music pavilion), occupies land donated to city in 1827 by Wm. Dorcas Patterson. Here is **Rogers Bastion,** line of breastworks overlooking harbor, where Baltimore's defenders held back Brit. Sept. 14, 1814; & near it is **Star Spangled Banner Mon.** (1914). On pk.'s highest point is **Pagoda** (fine view).

(31) Broadway & Monument Sts., **Johns Hopkins Hospital & Medical Sch.,** world-famous for its advances in medicine, was opened in 1889. Its 25 bldgs. spread over 12 city blocks. **Welch Lib.** contains John Singer Sargent's group portrait, "Four Doctors," of men who est. the medical sch. in 1893: Dr. Wm. Halsted, Dr. Howard A. Kelly, Dr. Wm. Osler, & Dr. Wm. Welch. (32) North Ave. & Bond St., **Columbus Mon.,** 1st to honor Christopher Columbus in W. Hemisphere, is brick obelisk dedicated Oct. 12, 1792. (33) Harford Rd. & The Alameda, **Clifton Pk.** (golf.tennis.swim. athletic fields) is 263-a. tract of land formerly owned by Johns Hopkins, in which stands former Hopkins summer residence, **Clifton Mansion H.** (Ital.Ren.structure with 6-story observ.tower). (34) Harford Rd., **Herring Run Pk.** (swim.pic.camp.model yacht basin.practice golf course) is 572-a. tract with forested secs.

PTS. OF INT. NORTH BALTIMORE: (35) Hoffman & Bolton Sts., **5th Regiment Armory,** block-square fort-like edifice of rough stone (1901.rebuilt 1934). (36) Lanvale St. & Eutaw Pl., **Francis Scott Key Mon.** (1911), comm. the author of U.S. nat. anthem. (37) Mt. Royal Ave. & Cathedral St., **Maryland Line Mon.** (1901) is Ionic shaft, topped by Goddess of Liberty, comm. Md. fighters in Amer. Rev. (38) 1300 W. Mt. Royal Ave., **Maryland Institute** (O.Mon.-Fri.10-5.Sat.9-1.Sun.2:30-5) founded in 1826 as industrial sch., to whose curriculum were added in 1850 courses that developed into present school of art & design. In big white marble bldg. is coll. incl. several bronzes & other works by Antoine Barye. (39) Greenmount & Oliver Sts., **Greenmount Cemetery,** founded 1838, contains graves of Sidney Lanier, poet; Junius Booth, actor; John Wilkes Booth, actor & assassin of Abr. Lincoln; Betsy Patterson Bonaparte, wife of Napoleon's youngest brother; Albert Cabell Ritchie, 4 times elected gov.; & Johns Hopkins, wealthy Baltimore merchant & founder of Johns Hopkins Univ. **Gate H. & Chapel** are of note for their Goth. design (Rbt. Carey Long, Jr., architect). (40) St. Paul & 22nd Sts., **First Meth. Ch.,** of rough gray granite with portico, circular bay & 165′ tower, is example of work of architect Stanford White in Romanes. style. (41) St. Paul & 23rd Sts., group of more than 20 Romanes. bldgs., gray granite with red tile roofs, built for high-ranking **Goucher College** (see Trip III below), are also work of Stanford White. As new college bldgs. are completed on the new Towson Campus, these are gradually being converted to other uses. (42) Charles & 29th Sts., **Samuel Smith Mon.,** of bronze, honors one of Baltimore's defenders against Brit. in 1814. (43) 29th St. bet. Maryland Ave. & Oak St., **Poe Mon.** is bronze statue (Moses J. Ezekiel,sculptor). (44) Remington Ave. & Wyman's Park Dr., **U.S. Marine Hospital** (1936.mod.Georg.Col.) is notable for functional architecture & modernity of facils. (45) 31st St. & Art Museum Dr., **Baltimore Mus. of Art** (O.wks.exc.Mon.11-6.also Fri.8-11 p.m.Sun. 2-6.free), mun. owned, occupies handsome neo-Class. edifice (opened 1929;John Russell Pope,architect). Among painters represented are: Botticelli, Raphael, Tintoretto, Titian, Veronese, Hals, Rembrandt, Rubens, Van Dyck, Gainsborough, Corot, Daumier, Millet. Of note are Antioch Pavement Mosaics, dated 300-500 A.D.; graphic arts coll. of 65,000 prints; coll. of oriental ceramics & bronzes. Amer. Wing contains 3 rooms paneled with woodwork from Md. Col. houses; beautiful furnishings, textiles, ceramics, glassware & silverware of Col. period.

(46) 34th & Charles Sts., **Johns Hopkins Univ.** (O.9-4.guide serv.), housed on 100 as. of lawn & woodland in group of white-trimmed red-brick bldgs. (Mod.Georg.), is internationally noted for scientific work. Founded with bequest of $7,000,000 from merchant Johns Hopkins, it opened in 1876. Bldgs. have been designed to harmonize with **Homewood,** a mansion built (1802, recently rest.) by Chas. Carroll for his son, which stands on campus on tree-wooded knoll; in this is univ. president's office. **Gilman Hall** contains statue of Johns Hopkins (Herman D.A.Henning,sculptor); Gilman Mem. Room holding books, mss. & other relics of Dr. Daniel Coit Gilman, 1st pres.; Archaeological Mus. of relics from Greece & Rome; & main univ. lib. E. of campus are **Johns Hopkins Mem. Mon.** (1934.Hans Schuler,sculptor) & **Univ. Bapt. Ch.** (1927.Ital.Ren.Palladian style.John Russell Pope,architect). (47) University Pkwy. & Charles St., **Confed. Women's Mon.** (1913.J.Maxwell Miller,sculptor) comm. in bronze Confed. cause. (48) 39th & Charles Sts., **Loyola College** is Jesuit college of arts & sciences for men, housed in group of Goth.-style gray stone bldgs. (49) In Venable Park, E. 33rd St., **Baltimore Mun. Stadium,** Md.'s biggest arena for athletic events, accommodating 70,000. (50) 33rd St. & Loch Rd., **Baltimore City College,** founded in 1839 as Male High Sch., occupies gray stone Goth.-style structure with impressive tower. (51) Mt. Royal Terrace & Park Ave., **Druid Hill Pk.** (boat.swim.tennis.athletic fields.baseball.football.bridle paths.pic.conservatory.bandstand), one of largest natural pks. within city limits in country, is tract W. of Jones Falls, partly landscaped to resemble English private pks., opened in 1860. On hilltop in center is **Mansion H.** (O), Georg.-style residence of pk. site's former owner, Nicholas Rogers. **Maryland H.** (O), built for Md. exhibit at Philadelphia Centennial Exposition (1876) & afterward dismantled & rebuilt here, contains natural history exhibits. Among other pts. of int. are **Zoo, Aquarium, Mem. Grove** & **Living Tulip Catalog; Martin Luther Statue** & **Repeal Statue,** comm. repeal of 18th Amendment; **& Columbus Mon., Wm. Wallace Mon.,** & **Union Soldiers & Sailors Mon.** (52) Belvedere & Park Heights Aves., **Pimlico Racecourse,** est. 1830; operated by Md. Jockey Club which enrolled Andrew Jackson among its members; one of first tracks to adopt pari-mutuel betting; Preakness Race run in May has heavy winner's purse.

PTS. OF INT. WEST BALTIMORE: (53) 203 Amity St., **Edgar Allan Poe H.** is place where Poe was married; he had 2nd book of poems published before entering West Point in 1830, whence he was expelled (1831) for failing roll call. (54) E. Pratt St. bet. Poppleton & Schroeder Sts., **Mount Clare Sta.,** 1st RR. passenger & freight terminal (1830) built in U.S., stands near B. & O. RR. shops. From it, on Aug. 28, 1830, 1st Amer.-made steam locomotive, the "Tom Thumb," constructed by Peter Cooper, began maiden trial run. Here also, on May 24, 1844, was received world's 1st telegraph message: "What hath God wrought," dispatched by Sam. F. B. Morse from Washington, D.C. (55) Washington Blvd. & Carey St., **Carroll Pk.** (wading pool.golf.athletic fields.bandstand) covers land once owned by father of Chas. Carroll, barrister, surrounding **Mt. Clare,** one of finest hs. in state. (57) 3445 Frederick Ave., **Loudon Pk. Nat. Cemetery** holds graves of more than 6,000 members of armed forces, many dating back to Civil War.

PTS. OF INT. SOUTH BALTIMORE: (58) Camden & Howard Sts., **Camden Sta.,** chief B. & O. RR. depot, was said to be world's largest at time of its construction

(1852). (59) 124 W. Conway St., **Otterbein United Brethren Ch.,** Mother Ch. of United Brethren in Christ, is an austerely plain brick bldg. (1785) with belfry-topped sq. tower, named for Phillip Wm. Otterbein, who founded this denomination in 1789. (60) Conway & Charles Sts., **St. Tobacco Warehouse** is hip-roofed brick 4-story structure (1846) piled high with hogsheads of tobacco from all over Md. (61) Key Hy. & Covington St., **Fed. Hill Pk.,** commanding fine view, occupies site of observ. tower built in 1797 by Baltimore's Maritime Exchange to sight incoming ships. (62) Ostend & Howard Sts., **Bailey's Roundh.** (O.Mon.-Fri.9-3.Sat.9-12) houses coll. of models, illustrating development of steam transportation on land, incl. models of famous early locomotives. (63) Foot of Fort Ave. at tip of Whetstone Pt. bet. Northwest & Middle Branches of Patapsco R., **Ft. McHenry Nat. Mon. & Hist. Shrine** (O.7-5:30.sm.fee), encompasses fortress whose successful defense against Brit., Sept. 13-14, 1814, inspired writing of national anthem. Whetstone Pt. was 1st fortified in 1776 with crude mud-&-log structure, replaced after 1790 by present star-shaped, moat-surrounded ft. with 20′-high brick walls & detached bastion with drawbridge protecting sally port. Ft. was named for Col. Jas. McHenry of Baltimore, Secy. of War (1796-1800). Two fleets of Brit. warships convoying 7,000 troops opened fire morning of Sept. 14, 1814 & kept firing all day & into night. When, in middle of night, Brit. attempted to land troops, ft.'s defense force of 1,000 swamped landing boats with heavy fire. On Brit. sloop "Minden," Francis Scott Key, who had boarded to negotiate release of Amer. hostage Dr. Wm. Beanes, was overjoyed when dawn came to see U.S. flag still flying over ft.; "The Star Spangled Banner" was his tribute. Ft. McHenry during Civil War was prison for pro-Confed. city & St. officials. It served as infantry post until 1900, was converted to hospital use during World War I, & was made Nat. Mon. in 1925. At Fort Ave. entrance is **Francis Scott Key Mon.** (Chas. H. Niehaus, sculptor). Inside, across parade grounds, runs Rd. bordered by plaques & oak trees, one of each for each St. of Union. There are 5 bldgs., 2 of which served as officers' quarters, 2 as barracks, 1 as powder magazine. In Bldg. D is E. Berkeley Bowie Coll. of Weapons; in Bldg. E, Maritime Coll. of shipbuilders' tools & pictures of warships & model of ft. as it was in 1814.

## TRIPS OUT OF BALTIMORE

**I. US40 (NE)** to J. with Edgewood Rd. **20.5. CIVIC CENTER, 0.** Take US40 (E. Fayette St., which leads into Pulaski Hy.). **4.** J. with St.151 (North Point Rd.).

SIDE TRIP: Take latter (R). In vic. of truck farm settlement of **North Pt.** is site where on Sept. 12, 1814, 3,100 Md. militia defeated 5,000 Brit. troops in Battle of North Pt. At 8$^{m}$ is J. with St.20 (Ft. Howard Rd.).

Take St.20 (R) 2$^{m}$ to **Ft. Howard** (est.1900), Baltimore's chief coast artillery defense, named for Col. John Eager Howard, hero of Battle of Cowpens in Amer. Rev.

At 11$^{m}$ is **Bethlehem Steel Co. Sparrows Pt. Plant,** largest tidewater steel plant in U.S. covering more than 2,000 as. & employing as many as 20,000, which does much of Md.'s shipbuilding.

**10.5.** J. with Middle River Rd. leading (R) 2.5$^{m}$ to **Glenn L. Martin Co. Plant,** one of East's biggest aircraft manufacturers. **20.5.** J. with Edgewood Rd., leading (R) 2$^{m}$ to **Edgewood Arsenal,** U.S. Army chemical warfare sta., where gases for military use are developed.

**II. US1 (NE) to BELAIR. 23.5.** From Civic Center, **0.,** take St. Paul St. (N) & turn (E) on E. North Ave., leading into Belair Rd. (US1). **13.** J. with marked dirt Rd., leading (R) 0.5$^{m}$ to **Perry Hall Mansion** (c.1750.rebuilt.1824). **16.** At **KINGSVILLE INN** (oldest part 1753.adds.in early 1800's; orig.paneling), Washington & Lafayette may or may not have been guests, as local legend says. From Kingsville Inn macadam Rd. leads (L) 2$^{m}$ to **Jerusalem Mills** (1772.adds.later), still operated, built by Quaker settler David Lee. **16.5. HOODOO MARKER,** rough 9′-high stone shaft believed to have been erected 17th cent.; hexed to constrain removal. **23.5. BELAIR** (see US1).

**III. US111 (N) to HEREFORD FARM. 20.5.** From Civic Center, **0.,** take St. Paul St. (N), turn (E) on E. North Ave. & (N) on York Rd. (US111). **7.5. TOWSON,** founded (1750) by Ezekiel Towson & seat since 1854 of Baltimore Cty., is site of **Md. St. Teachers College** (est.1866), housed in group of Tudor Goth. red brick bldgs. near S. limits.

SIDE TRIPS: (A) Turn (R) from Towson on Joppa Rd. Beyond E. limits is **Goucher College,** occupying group of modern bldgs. on 421-a. site, to which it began removing in 1940's from Baltimore campus. Opened in 1888 as Woman's College of Baltimore, it was renamed in 1914 for Dr. John F. Goucher, Meth. minister, donor of land for campus & college pres. (1890-1907). At 2m is J. with Loch Raven Blvd. Take Loch Raven Rd. (L) to Cromwell Bridge Rd., 2.5m; (R) on this to Cromwell Bridge Rd., 4.5m; (L) here to **Loch Raven Dam,** 7.5m, built in 1922, 75′ high & 650′ wide, damming 10m-long L. which supplies Baltimore's water.

(B) Take St.146 (Dulany Valley Rd.) (R) from Towson 1m to **Hampton** (1783-90.Georg. Col.), stuccoed stone mansion with pedimented portico & domed cupola. Built by Capt. Chas. Ridgely, Rev. officer & 1 of framers of Md.'s constitution, it was one of most magnificent houses of its period, 158′ long, with 40 as. of terraced gardens. In late 1940's it was transferred by builder's great-great-grandnephew, John Ridgely, to Nat. Pk. Service for maintenance as Nat. Mon.

**13.7. COCKEYSVILLE** is farmers' trading & marble quarrying center. **20.5. HEREFORD FARM** is site of **Grand Nat. Steeplechase Course,** one of the most difficult in the country; races held 3rd Sat. in April in competition for duplicate Astor Gold Cup; race 3m long, with 18 fences & 2 water courses. Road leads (L) 0.3m to **Hereford H.** 3-part telescope H. (2-story central sec.1714.kitchens added).

**IV. US140 (NW) to WESTMINSTER. 30.** From Civic Center, **0.,** take St. Paul St. (N), turn (W) on W. North Ave., then (NW) on Reisterstown Rd. (US140). **3.** J. with St.129 (Park Heights Ave.).

SIDE TRIP: Take St.129 (R) 13.5m to J. with Caves Rd.

(L) here 0.5m to **Stemmer H.** (1805), two-&-a-half-story brick mansion.

At 17m is J. with Tufton Ave.

(R) on this to J. with Belmont Rd., 0.8m; (R) on this at 0.3m is two-&-a-half-story brick **Belmont** (1780) & at 0.5m is **Sagamore Farms,** Alfred Gwynne Vanderbilt's horse-breeding & training stables. At 1m on Tufton Ave. is 4m **Md. Hunt Cup Course,** site of annual steeplechase (4th Sat. in Ap.).

At 18m on St.129 is **Montmorency** (c.1760), stone & stucco mansion with Ital. garden. St.129 rejoins US140 at Reisterstown (see below), 21.5m.

**9. PIKESVILLE** was sett. in late 18th cent. & named later for Brig. Gen. Pike of N.J., discoverer of Pike's Peak (see Colo.). (R), c.9m is **Druid Ridge Cemetery,** with **Monument to Queen Victoria,** probably only mon. in America to England. **10.5. GREY ROCK** (c.1700.remod.1890) was birthpl. of Rev. War hero John Eager Howard, Gov. of Md. (1788-91) & U.S. Senator (1796-1803). **18. REISTERSTOWN** was founded in 1785 on the land settled by Jacob Reister and his children before the completion of the stagecoach road from Baltimore to Gettysburg. Opp. Post Office on Main St., **Chatsworth** (c.1770). Main St. & Cockey's Mill Rd., **Polly Reister H.** (1779). Opp. latter, on Main St., **Yellow Tavern** (c.1804). Cockey's Mill Rd. 2 blocks (L) from Main St., former **Franklin Academy** (est.1820,now garage), Baltimore Cty.'s 1st pub. sch. **30. WESTMINSTER,** quiet, well-to-do community, was founded in 1764. Court St., 1 block (R) from Main St., **Carroll County Cth.** (1836) is of note for its Gr. Rev. design. 208 E. Main St., **Carroll Cty. Hist. Soc. Home** (1807) occupies town's oldest bldg. On Main St. is **Western Md. College** (Meth.est.1860) on rolling, wooded campus.

**V. US40 (W) to WAVERLY. 17.5.**

**0.** From Civic Center follow US40 (W). **7. CATONSVILLE,** residential suburb, named for Richard Caton, son-in-law of Chas. Carroll of Carrollton, is site of **St. Charles College** (est.1830), on Maiden's Choice Lane, preparatory sch. for candidates for Cath. priesthood; **Mount de Sales Academy** (est.1852), Nunnery Lane & Edmonson Ave., Cath. girls' sch.; John Wilkes Booth was student at sch. on site. **Prot. Epis. Ch.** (1844.Goth.), St. Timothy's Lane. **10.5. ELLICOTT CITY,** with houses clustering around many mills, scaling stony slopes of Tiber Cr. At E. end of Patapsco Bridge on **Site of Ellicotts' Mills,** is the **Doughnut Corp of Amer. Plant** (O.Tues.& Thurs.), where Patapsco Flour was turned out until destruction of Mill (1868) in flood. Across Rd. from Plant are three houses of the Ellicott clan, all built before 1800. On Main St., (W) of Bridge is **Patapsco Hotel;** & 2 doors (W) of hotel is **Town Hall,** the first 4 floors with hillside cellars. Facing Cth. Lane on Capitoline Hill, **Howard County Cth.** Institute Rd. at top of hill, former **Patapsco Female Institute** (est.c.1829.Gr.Rev.).

**14.5.** J. with macadam Rd. leading (L) 1m to **Burleigh Manor** (1760.Georg.Col.), among finest old Md. mansions & equal to any Col. inter. in its paneling & carving. **16.** J. with Carroll Lane, leading (L) 0.7$^{m}$ to entrance to 300′-long **Doughoregan Manor** (c.1727.front portico with chamber above added later, chapel in N. ell several times remodelled), center of estate once comprising 13,000 as. This was home of Charles Carroll of Carrollton (1737-1832), said to have been wealthiest man in U.S. at time of his death, & also last surviving signer of Decl. of Ind.

**16.5.** J. with gravel Folly Quarters Rd.

SIDE TRIP: Take latter (L) to J. with Rolling Rd., 3.3$^{m}$.
(R) on this to **Novitiate of the Franciscan Fathers** (1930), modelled after Convent of St. Francis in Assisi, Italy; Recr. Hall of Convent is housed in the **Folly Quarters Mansion** (1832), built for Charles Carroll's daughter, at cost of c.$100,000. At 5$^{m}$ is entrance to ivy-clad **Glenelg Manor** (early 19th cent.Goth.Rev.), with crenellated tower, behind which are older H. (c.1700.remod.) & other bldgs.

**17.5.** J. with dirt Rd. leading (R) 1.4$^{m}$ to stone **Waverly** (c.1750), once home of Gov. George Howard, who is said to have dreamed of owning 1,000 slaves but never did because death kept preventing total from rising above 999.

**VI. US1 (S) to MUIRKIRK. 23.**

**0.** From Civic Center take W. Fayette St. (W) & turn (S) on Monroe St. (US1). **6.5. HALETHORPE,** where first air meet in U.S. was held (1910); & also Fair celebrating centennial of B. & O. RR. (1929). Exhibits were moved to Baltimore Bailey Roundh. (see above). **7.5. RELAY** was so named because relay of horses used to be attached to B. & O. RR. cars at this pt. to finish journey to Ellicott Mills.

SIDE TRIP: Take River Rd. (R) 0.3$^{m}$ to **Thomas Viaduct;** made of stone; early became new wonder of Atlantic seaboard; although c. century old, still supports trains at full speed. 1$^{m}$ **Patapsco St. Pk.** (bath.boat.pic.camp.) is hilly, wooded tract of more than 1,000 as. along Patapsco R. gorge. On R. bank at 5.8$^{m}$ stand ruins of **Patapsco Factory** (1820), wrecked by successive floods, & **Patapsco H.** (1812.remod.), once residence of factory's owner, Edw. Gray. River Rd. cont. to J. with US40 in **Ellicott City** (see Trip V), 6.2$^{m}$.

**8.5. ELKRIDGE** is farmers' trading center whose history goes back to Col. times. **9.8.** J. with St.103 leading (R) 1$^{m}$ to 2nd paved Rd.; (L) here to **Belmont** (1783), 2$^{m}$, which stands amid fine old gardens full of lilacs & boxwood. **19. LAUREL RACE TRACK** (est.1712), one of finest in country; scene of racing season lasting one month in fall, usually in Oct. **20. LAUREL,** so named for mt. laurel covering hill back of town, grew up on land granted late in 17th cent. to Richard Snowden, one of Oliver Cromwell's officers. Mining of iron ore & milling of flour were early 19th cent. industries, later abandoned.

SIDE TRIP: Take St.197 (L) from Laurel 2$^{m}$ to **Montpelier** (begun c.1750), brick mansion on knoll with semi-octagonal wings, notable for hand-carved woodwork of inter., where Geo. Washington was often guest. At 9$^{m}$ is **Bowie Race Track** (O.1914), 1$^{m}$ long, with grandstand seating 14,500; pari-mutuel betting.

**22.** J. with dirt Rd. leading (L) 0.3$^{m}$ to **Oakland** (1798), mansion with terraced garden commanding sweeping view. **23. MUIRKIRK,** named after Muirkirk, Scotland, by early Scot settlers who began iron industry, supplied by ore from near-by hills; **Charcoal Ovens** of mid-18th cent. origin remain.

**VII. US301 (S) to J. with US50.**

**0.** From Civic Center, take W. Fayette St. (W), turn (S) on Paca St., (SW) on Washington Blvd., (S) on Russell St., leading into Annapolis Rd. (US301). **10. GLEN-BURNIE,** so named for John Glenn, owner of an estate here in 1880's, is quiet suburban place. **16.5.** J. with St.178.

SIDE TRIP: Turn (L) on this 2$^{m}$ to **Rising Sun Inn** (c.1753), maintained as inn by D.A.R. At 4.5$^{m}$ is **Belvoir** (1730.alts.), built by Francis Scott Key's great grandfather, John Ross. At 8.5$^{m}$ is J. with US50 (see).

**18.** J. with St.180 leading (R) 4$^{m}$ to **Ft. Geo. G. Meade** (est.1917), is large Army reserv. **21.** J. with dirt Rd. leading (L) 0.8$^{m}$ to **White Hall** (c.1761.frame wing & porches added after 1812), birthpl. of Johns Hopkins, founder of Johns Hopkins Univ. **23.5.** J. with US50 (see).

(Federated Garden Clubs of Md., Sheraton-Belvedere Hotel, Baltimore, publishes an annual book giving detailed information on the most important houses open during House & Garden Pilgrimage, late April & early May.

# US 50—WEST VIRGINIA

**W.VA.-VA. LINE** (20$^{m}$ from Winchester, Va.) **(W) to W.VA.-OHIO LINE** (1$^{m}$ beyond Parkersburg, W. Va.). **218. US50**

Via: Romney, Burlington, Redhouse, Aurora, Pruntytown, Bridgeport, Clarksburg & Parkersburg.

Hy. traverses rugged, mountainous N. part of St. & then descends through a coal, gas & oil reg. to Ohio R. This route, in Col. times, was followed by early pioneers; in 1786 the St. of Va. planned a Rd. along it which was finally completed in 1838 & was known as Northwest Turnpike. Primitive settlements along Turnpike boomed & taverns sprang up along its course for accom. of immigrants, drivers of Conestoga wagons loaded with freight & passengers of fast stage coaches.

## Sec. 1: W.VA.-VA. LINE to REDHOUSE, MD. 79.

**4. CAPON BRIDGE,** on Cacapon R. Ft. Edwards was built in vic. c.1750; in 1756 a force under Washington's command was badly defeated near here by Inds. **19.** J. with St.45 (N) to **Cacapon St. Pk.** (see E.Panhandle). **28. ROMNEY** (sett.c.1738), 1st known as Pearsall's Flats, was part of Lord Fairfax's vast holdings & settlers were forced to pay him rent or buy outright. During Rev., under Gen. Dan. Morgan's leadership, patriots suppressed Tories. One great benefit derived by the Romney reg. from Rev. was confiscation of Lord Fairfax's lands. At Civil War's outbreak, local people favored South. During this conflict, town changed hands, it is claimed, more than 56 times. "Stonewall" Jackson at one time attempted to resign from Confed. Army because he had been ordered to give up town which he considered of great strategic importance. PTS. OF INT.: Cor. Grafton & Main Sts., **Brady H.** (O.c.1800.log.clapboarded) now houses Pub. Assistance Dept. Near-by, **Wirgman Bldg.** (c.1825). On Gravel Lane, **Mytinger H.** (c.1770), oldest in Romney. In Romney is J. with St.28.

SIDE TRIP: (N) on St.28 past **Hanging Rock,** 300′ cliff above hy., 14$^{m}$ to **Ft. Ashby** (sett. c.1735), where is **Ft.** (O.log.rest.) built under Washington's supervision. St.28 cont. to Cumberland, Md. (see).

US50 threads through walled-in Mechanicsburg Gap. **34.5.** E. J. with US220 (see Nat.For.Reg.). **39. BURLINGTON. Old Homestead Tavern** (c.1785.rebuilt). **43.** J. with Rd. which leads (L) 4$^{m}$ to **Doll's Gap; Mon.** on site claimed as birthpl. of Nancy Hanks, Lincoln's mother. **44.** J. with Rd. leading (L) 3$^{m}$ to **Antioch** where are **Antioch Woolen Mills** (pre-1789) still grinding flour & spinning woolens. **44.5.** Old log cabin on Knobley Mt., known as Faneuil Hall of W.Va. (see Boston), because of resolutions passed here (1861) against secession. **46.** W. J. with US220. **64.5. MARKER** at boundary set by George III in treaty with Six Nations, beyond which settlers were forbidden to advance. At **69.** US50 enters Md. **73. BACKBONE MT.** (3,800′), highest pt. in Md. **79. REDHOUSE, Md.** Here is **Reed H.,** old tavern. In town is J. with US219, which leads (N) to Savage R., Swallow Falls, Potomac St. Fors., Deep Cr. L. (resort) & other scenic pts. (see Md.).

## Sec. 2: REDHOUSE, MD. to CLARKSBURG, W.VA. 58.

**4. YOUGHIOGHENY PK.** (cabins). **6.5. AURORA** (resort) on **Cheat Mt.** (3,803′). US50 now drops rapidly, skirting deep cleft of Cheat R. which is crossed at **14.** Near this pt. long **Covered Bridge** (1835). **37.5. BLUEVILLE,** birthpl. of Ann Jarvis, originator of Mother's Day. Just (S) on US119 here, is **Grafton,** market town for coal & farm dist., in narrow Tygarts R. Valley. In **Nat. Cemetery** (only one in W.Va.) is **Mon.** on grave of 1st Union soldier killed in Civil War.

SIDE TRIP: Take Park Rd. (R) here 3$^{m}$ to **Tygarts R. Dam & Reserv.,** flood control project. Dam is 1,900′ long & 219′ high. **City Pk.** near Tygarts L. (boat.pic.swim.f.).

**58. CLARKSBURG**

B. & O. RR. Bus Terminal, N. 4th St. Air conn. Info.: C. of C., 214 Court St. Accoms.: All types.

Clarksburg (sett.1764), criss-crossed by low hills, clusters around confluence of Elk Cr. & W. Fork of Monongahela R. City was named for Geo. Rogers Clark (see). It was "Stonewall" Jackson's birthpl. Today city is business & industrial center of reg. producing over 12,000,000 tons of coal annually. Fighting took place around city during Civil War; trenches on near-by hills can still be traced. PTS. OF INT.: 328 W. Main St., Plaque marking site of **Birthpl. of "Stonewall" Jackson** (see). E. Pike St., **Jackson Cemetery,** where some of Jackson family are buried, incl. Mary Payne Jackson, sister of Dolly Madison & Mrs. Mary Coles Payne, her mother. 463 W. Main St., **Nathan Goff H.** (1840), home of Nath. Goff, Repub. candidate (1876) for gov.; election was contested, voting frauds were uncovered & A. B. Fleming, one of opposition candidates, was declared elected. 521 W. Main St., **Duncan H.** (pre-1800.adds.), said to be oldest in city. On Lee Ave., near Boring Lane, **Lee H.** (1835.Gr.Rev.). **Lowndes Pk.** (fine view) is reached by S. 2nd St. W. Fork R. & Harvey St., **Akro Agate Co.** (O.appl.) manufactures toy marbles & other glass articles.

### Sec. 3: CLARKSBURG to W.VA.-OHIO LINE. 81.

**14. SALEM,** sett. 1790 by Seventh Day Baptists from Salem, N.J. Main St., **Salem College** (inc.1890;coed.) founded by Seventh Day Baptists. W.Va. Industrial Home for Girls (reformatory). **16. KIWANIS GORGE PK.** (O.appl.). **42. PENNSBORO** has Ritchie Cty. Fair (early Sept.). **Webster H.** (1807) was tavern for over a century. **47. ELLENBORO.** J. with St.16.

SIDE TRIP: (S) 17.5m on St.16 to **Smithville.** J. with St.47 which leads (W) 7m to **MacFarland.** Here are unique, solid petroleum deposits, which, like coal, have to be dug out of veins & become liquid only by application of heat.

**81. PARKERSBURG**

Through air, bus & RR. conns. Accoms.: All types. Info.: Auto Club & Board of Commerce. Golf. swim., boat., & f.

Parkersburg (sett.c.1785) crowds to the "Point" at confluence of Ohio & Little Kanawha Rs.; is a center for farm dist., shipping & industrial town (reg.is rich in coal, gas & oil) with some 125 plants. City was home of Johnson Nelson Camden, U.S. Sen. & oil magnate who 1st fought Standard Oil, then sold out to them, engaged in political battle with Theo. Roosevelt over RR. rebates practice. Across Ohio R. is Bridgeport, reached by toll bridge. PTS. OF INT.: The Point, where were 1st settlements (in sm. Murphy Pk.), is now the city's heart. (1) Cor. Court Sq. & 3rd St., **Stratford Hotel** (1812.remod.). (2) On a hill, **Nemesis Pk.** (O.summer), where Ft. Boreman was built (1863) as defense against Confed. invasion. (3) 1131 7th St., **Oakland** (grounds O.;1843.Georg.Col.) has beautiful gardens. (4) Across Little Kanawha R. on Central Ave., near George St., **Tavenner H.** (1800). Col. H. Phelps, orig. owner, was ordered to capture Aaron Burr & Harmon Blennerhasset (see Ohio) but both escaped. (5) Park Ave., near 17th St., **City Pk.** (recr.bath.sports facils. dancing.pic.). (6) In Pk., **Centennial Cabin Mus.** (1804.removed from orig.location); contains pioneer relics. (7) Stadium Dr. & Dudley Ave., **Central Jr. High Sch.** in which is Stahl Relic Coll. (O.sch.hrs.); many items were unearthed at Blennerhasset I. (8) **Ames Baldwin Wyo. Co.** (O) has made shovels since 1774. (9) **Parkersburg Rig & Reel Co.** (O); equipment for exploitation of oil. What is claimed to be largest rayon factory in world, the **Amer. Viscose Corp.,** is located in Parkersburg.

SIDE TRIPS: (A) c.1m (S) of city is **Blennerhasset I.** (see Ohio). Round trip tours leave at Ohio R. & 2nd St. (No recr.activities or pic.permitted on I.).

(B) At pt. where Lubeck & Marrtown Rds. meet, 2.5m (SW) of city, **W. H. Bickle Estate** (gardens.zoo & stables.O.appl.pic.facils.) with stables in which are kept blooded racing & show horses. At race track, harness racing & horse shows, spring & fall.

## US 33—WEST VIRGINIA

**W.VA.-VA. LINE** (c.25m from Harrisonburg, Va.) **(W) to W.VA.-OHIO LINE** (c.2m from Pomeroy, Ohio). **253. US33**

Via: Elkins, Buckhannon, Weston, Spencer, Ripley & Mason.

In W.Va., US33 is called the Blue & Gray Trl. because of fighting along it during Civil War. It cuts through central part of St., crossing rugged mt. reg. & dropping to Ohio Valley.

### Sec. 1: W.VA.-VA. LINE to ELKINS. 80.

(For this sec. of hy. through Geo. Washington & Monongahela Nat. For., see Nat.For.Reg.Tours).

**80. ELKINS**

Through RR., bus & air conns. Monongahela Nat. For. Hqs. Accoms.: All types. Info.: C. of C.

On a wide curve of Tygarts Valley R. bet. Cheat & Rich Mts. & near Monongahela Nat. For., it was 1st known as Leadsville, rechristened in honor of Sen. S. T. Elkins in 1890. The Sen. made headlines when Theo. Roosevelt bitterly attacked him for opposing expansion of authority of the I.C.C. The chief annual event is the Mt. St. For. Festival, on Davis & Elkins College Campus, featuring tilting tournaments, woodsmen's competitions & horse show. **Mun. Pk.** in which is a fine grove of ancient trees. **Davis & Elkins College** (132 as.est.1904.Presb.coed.), located on lovely hilltop; has several virgin stands of timber; occupies land formerly belonging to H. G. Davis (see) & Sen. Elkins. **Graceland Hall,** the Senator's mansion, is now a dormitory. Mus. to house a coll. of Ind. relics & antiques, gift of Susan D. Elkins, is planned. On W. edge of city, **Blue Grass Pk. Laurel Hill Battlefield.** (For other pts. of int. in vic., see Nat.For.Reg.)

**Sec. 2: ELKINS to WESTON. 46.**

**28. BUCKHANNON** (sett.1770) was laid out (1815) by Col. Edw. Jackson, grandfather of "Stonewall" Jackson; it changed hands several times, like many other W.Va. towns, during Civil War. **W.Va. Wesleyan College** (est.1890.Meth.coed.). In town is J. with St.20.

SIDE TRIP: (S) c.10$^{m}$ on St.20 to **St. Game Farm** (O.;325 as.) on French Cr. At c.30$^{m}$, J. with Rd.

Take latter (L) here c.1$^{m}$ to **Holly R. St. Pk.** (7,320 as.pic.bath.playground.trout f. cabins). Pk. is noted for profusion of its wildflowers, especially rhododendron, & abundance of game. Trls. radiate to various parts of Pk.

**46. WESTON** (sett.1784). A newspaper was published here by occupying Feds. entitled "The Ohio Seventh," whose motto read: "We come to protect, not to invade." **Weston St. Hospital** (O.1859) is said to be largest hand-cut stone edifice in U.S. Near Weston is an old **covered bridge** (pre-Civil War).

**Sec. 3: WESTON to MASON. 127.**

**27. GLENVILLE,** on Little Kanawha R., overlooking charming hill country. **Glenville St. Teachers College** (coed.). **68. SPENCER,** whose hilly sts. are crowded on week-ends with herders driving in cattle & sheep, is in oil dist. **93. RIPLEY** (sett. 1768). **97. EVANS FAIRGROUNDS** where is held Jackson Cty. Fair (Aug.). **127 MASON,** with toll bridge to Pomeroy, Ohio.

## US 60—WEST VIRGINIA

**W.VA.-VA. LINE** (22$^{m}$ from Covington, Va.) **(W) to W.VA.-KY. LINE** (9$^{m}$ from Catlettsburg, Ky.). **177. US60**

Via: White Sulphur Springs, Lewisburg, Gauley Bridge, Charleston & Huntington.

Late in the 18th & early 19th cents., Virginia, at Washington's prompting, officially sanctioned construction of a toll Rd., closely following present-day US60, from Richmond to the Ohio. Improved later so as to permit stagecoach travel, it became known as James R. & Kanawha Turnpike. (See alt. tour on St.3 & St.10.)

**Sec. 1: W.VA.-VA. LINE to GAULEY BRIDGE. 81.**

**3.5.** J. with unpaved Rd. leading (R) short distance to site of Battle of White Sulphur Springs (1863) in which, after bloody fighting, Fed. troops were defeated by the Confeds. **4.5. WHITE SULPHUR SPRINGS,** one of the oldest spas in U.S. First authenticated guest coming for the cure arrived in 1778, although local legend has it that in 1772 a woman, crippled with rheumatism, bathed in improvised tub, a hollow tree trunk, filled with heated water from the springs, & was completely cured. **White Sulphur Springs Hotel** (1854), known as "the Old White," has some 350 rooms & rivaled in mid-19th cent. magnificence the huge caravanseries of Saratoga. The resort became a pt. of departure for grand tours of near-by watering places: Warm, Red Sulphur, Sweet, Blue Sulphur, Green Sulphur Springs, etc. At c.**5. ESTATE OF GREENBRIER HOTEL** & Cottages (6,500 as.RR.conns.) with golf courses & other sports facils., 200$^{m}$ of trls. & a bath Dept. for therapeutic treatments. At outbreak of World War II, hotel housed 1,100 Germans, Italians & Japanese belonging to diplomatic staffs, who were interned until they could be sent home. Near hotel are old **Spring H.** (1835) & "rows" of cottages, many of them dating back to early 19th cent. "Wolf Row" was given over to exclusive occupancy of bachelors, Paradise Row, to honeymooners; latter's cottages are fine examples of architecture of period. Still standing is **President's Cottage** (with coll.of memorabilia), served as summer "White House" for Chief Executives from Andrew Jackson to Woodrow Wilson. **Lee Cottage,** preserved as it was during Rbt. E. Lee's occupancy (1867-69), was a center for his efforts to reconcile N. & S. in post-war era. At **5.** is J. with Rd. to Blue Bend Pk. (see For.Reg.Tours). **9.** J. with unpaved Rd. running 1.5$^{m}$ (S) to **Greenbrier St. For.** (5,004 as.bass f.cabins). **15. LEWISBURG** (sett.c.1751), named for Andrew Lewis who built Ft. Savannah here (1755), later known as Ft. Union. The settlement suffered severely in the Fr.-Ind. War, but during Lord Dunmore's War, sent a contingent to take part in Battle of Pt. Pleasant (1774). **Old Stone Ch.** (1796) in which are orig. pews, pulpit & slave balcony. **Gen. Lewis Inn** (c.1800.adds) on whose grounds stands Lewis Oak, which still bears Lewis' survey mark "L." **Greenbrier Jr. College for Women** (est.c.1808); on campus, **President's H.** (1812.remod.), was formerly Frazier Tavern. **John Wesley Ch.** (Meth.pre-Civil War), now used by Negro congregation. In town is J. with US219.

SIDE TRIP: 2$^{m}$ (S) is **Greenbrier Valley Fair Grounds** where is Aug. fair (harness races. horseshow.sports events). It is said that Lee's horse, Traveller, was a prize-winner at this fair. 9$^{m}$ J. with Rd. (L) to **Organ Cave;** during Civil War, powder was manufactured here (some orig. utensils on exhibit). (US219 cont. to Princeton at 65$^{m}$ where is South J. of hy.)

**18. MORLUNDA ESTATE** (1800.adds.); on grounds, old slave quarters. **22.** J. with paved Rd.

SIDE TRIP: (N) 6$^{m}$ to **Site of Ft. Donnally;** Shawnee attack (1778) to avenge death of Chief Cornstalk failed because of warning brought by Philip Hammond & John Pryor who were disguised as Inds. to evade capture. They had been made up by Cornstalk's sister, Nonhelema, friend of the settlers.

**47. RAINELLE,** dominated by Big Sewell Mt. **Meadow R. Lumber Co.** (O.appl.), one of largest hardwood lumber mills. **48.** J. with unpaved Rd. leading (R) short distance to Big Sewell Mt. (3,170′) where Lee camped (1861) & according to legend, obtained Traveller, the horse he rode throughout Civil War. **57.** J. with US19-St.41 to Babcock St. Pk. (see Nat.For.Reg.). **72. ANSTED** (sett.1790), a coal town. In Westlake Cemetery, grave of "Stonewall" Jackson's mother. **Old Halfway H.** (Rev. remod.1810) was occupied by Fed. troops during Civil War. **73.5. HAWKS NEST ST. PK.** (48 as.pic.restaurant) whose chief feature is precipitous Hawk Nest Rock, affording fine view of New R. Canyon & dam. Above parking area, **Mus.,** with coll. of old weapons & Ind. relics. **80.** Mouth of **HAWKS NEST TUNNEL** (3$^{m}$) which burrows through mts., diverting R. for hydroelectric power. **81. GAULEY BRIDGE,** in mountain-enclosed valley, at pt. where Gauley & New Rs. join & become Great Kanawha R. Here is site of battle in which Gen. Rosecrans defeated Confeds. (1861). **Miller Tavern,** Fed. Hqs. during Civil War, where Wm. McKinley & Rutherford B. Hayes were stationed.

## Sec. 2: GAULEY BRIDGE to CHARLESTON. 36.

**1.5. GLEN FERRIS** (sett.1812). From a rock above Kanawha Falls here, Reuben Van Bibber is supposed to have leaped into the pool below, to escape Inds. **18.5. CEDAR GROVE** (sett.1773), on Kelly's Cr. Industry today depends on coal, was formerly a busy shipbuilding center. From it, immigrants headed (W), took boat down Kanawha R. to the Ohio. On outskirts, **Little Brick Ch.** (1853.alts.adds.orig. fittings) built by Wm. Tempkins, Malden salt tycoon, is 2nd on site, 1st having been erected by town's founder, Wm. Morris. Across Kelly's Cr., opp. Ch., site of old **Ft. Kelly.** [Take unpaved Rd. (R) here 10$^{m}$ to **Mt. Desert Fire Tower.** Fine view.] **26. BELLE.** Du Pont de Nemours Factory (L) which produces, among other coal derivatives, nylons. **30. LEVI,** where is marker on site of Burning Spring, a gas well on land patented by Washington to obtain title to the well. Later, a salt well was sunk near-by; pressure from released gas drove the brine spouting high into the sky. **31. MALDEN,** formerly salt production center. Booker T. Washington, Negro leader, while employed here in the salt works & coal mines taught himself to read. **32. REED,** now a cross-roads village, once salt-making center. Brine obtained from shallow wells, as early as 1797, was boiled down into salt. **33.5. SNOW HILL.** Dan. Boone Cave (R) hideout of famous scout. Across R. was his cabin. **36. CHARLESTON** (see).

### Sec. 3: CHARLESTON to W.VA.-KY. LINE. 60.

**4. S. CHARLESTON** with large chemical plants here & on Blaine I. **Staunton Pk.** is prehist. Ind. Burial Mound, in which skeletons & artifacts have been found. **U.S. Naval Ordnance Plant** (O.wks.). **11.5. RIVERLAWN** (1832.adds.), old turnpike inn, contains some of orig. furnishings. **32. MILTON. Blenko Glass Co.** (O), known for handmade glassware. From here came windows for N.Y.C.'s Cathedral of St. John the Divine, replacements for destroyed stained glass in Rheims Cathedral & products used in Williamsburg's restoration.

**52. HUNTINGTON**

Through RR., bus & air conns. Summer & fall steamer-cruises from Pt. Pleasant to Cincinnati. Accoms.: All types. Info.: C. of C., First Huntington Nat. Bank Bldg.; Huntington Auto Club, Frederick Hotel.

Village of Guyandotte boomed with completion of James R. & Kanawha Turnpike (1830). Huntington was laid out on former Holderby's Landing (sett.1796), near-by, when Collis P. Huntington built C. & O. Terminal (1870) here. Industry has been attracted by favorable trans. facils. & abundant natural gas, coal & oil. In 1948 city boasted 162 plants producing some 420 different products. The unruly Ohio has repeatedly inundated city, but in recent yrs. flood control works have been built by U.S. Army engineers. PTS. OF INT.: 5th Ave., **Gov. Sq.**, in or near which are located **Gov. Bldg., Cabell County Cth.** & **City Bldg.** 16th St., E., **Marshall College** (founded 1837.25 as.coed), was named for U.S. Chief Justice. At W. entrance of campus is bust of Marshall. One of handsomest bldgs. is **Morrow Lib.** (1930.Col.-Georg.); murals by Marion Vest Fors. Exhibits on 1st fl. of Mus. **Mun. Market Bldg.** Tobacco auctions (winter) at which 7,250,000 lbs. are sold. In SW. sec. of city on Mem. Pky., near 12th St., is **Mem. Arch,** copy of Paris Arc de Triomphe, comm. W.Va. veterans of World War I. In SE. sec. on 13th Ave. near 12th St. E., straddling Four Pole Cr., is **Ritter Pk.** with Caldwell Mem., small Greek Temple; fine view. Pk. has lovely rose garden in which is a natural amphitheater. The **Flood Wall** constructed by the Army is 11$^{m}$ long. In town are **Internat. Nickel Co. Plant** (O.appl. guides) & great **Chesapeake & Ohio Shops** (O.appl.) where RR. equipment is repaired & reconditioned. For Pt. Pleasant & other near-by pts. see Trips out of Charleston. Tour cont. on US60. **56. CAMDEN PK.** (amusements). Hy. passes **Dreamland Pool** (O.summer.sm.fee). **60.** Toll bridge at **W.VA.-KY. LINE.**

## ST. 3 & ST. 10—WEST VIRGINIA

**W.VA.-VA. LINE** (55$^{m}$ from Roanoke, Va.) **(W) to HUNTINGTON. 210. St.3 & St.10**

Via: Union, Alderson, Hinton, Beckley, Whitesville & West Hamlin.

Route proceeds through picturesque countryside into the most recently exploited coal, oil & gas reg. of W.Va., &, (W) of Hamlin, follows the Guyandot R. valley through industrialized area to the Ohio. This is an alt. tour for US60 (see).

### Sec. 1: W.VA.-VA. LINE to HINTON. 61. St.3

**1. SWEETSPRINGS,** former spa dating back to 1792, its fashionable apogee was in 1830's with building of a great hotel in Georg. Col. style (from Thos. Jefferson's designs), now St.-owned Home for Aged Men & Women. Opp. are springs, visited by notables such as Calhoun, Clay & Fillmore; near-by is home of Maj. W. Royall, Rev. hero, chiefly remembered for his marriage to Ann Newport, whose mother had been brought to his home as a servant. Ann Newport Royall, who had been kidnapped when a child by Inds., became famous in Washington, D.C., as 1st woman muckraking journalist. **10. GAP MILLS,** birthpl. of Andrew Summers Rowan, who took the famous "Message to Garcia," during Sp.-Amer. War. At c.**17.5.** is J. with unpaved Rd. (R) running c.0.5$^{m}$ to **Rehoboth Ch.** (1786.log), where Bishop Asbury often preached. **20. UNION.** Here is J. with US219.

SIDE TRIP: (S) 2$^{m}$ on US219 to **Salt Sulphur Springs.** Old Col. Bldgs. (1820).

**21.5. ELMWOOD H.** (early 19th cent.). At **52.** St.3 overpasses 2 RR. tunnels. Here John Henry is said to have performed his legendary feat of outspeeding a steam-driven drill. **61. HINTON** (founded 1831). The town's chief source of income is from C. & O. RR. maintenance shops. (E) of town on St.3, is bath. & pic. beach & another in town itself. In Hinton is J. with St.20.

SIDE TRIP: St.20 (S) circling **Bluestone Reservoir,** artificial lake which is normally c.8.5m long, but in times of heavy flood will be backed up the New R. for 36m into Va. This project has been carried out to alleviate flood conditions of W.Va. tributaries of the Ohio. The dam is 2,061′ long & 165′ av. height above New R.'s bed.

### Sec. 2: HINTON to HUNTINGTON. 149. St.3 & St.10

**15. SHADY SPRING.** J. with US19-21. At **16.** J. with side Rd.

SIDE TRIP: (N) 11m to **Grandview St. Pk.** (52 as.), on cliff c.1,000′ above gorge of the great bend of New R.

Tour cont. on US19-21 to **BECKLEY** at **23.,** sett. 1838, center of coal reg. producing 12,000,000 tons of "smokeless coal" annually. **Gen. A. Beckley Mon.; Soldiers & Sailors Mem. Bldg.** (auditorium), comm. men of World War I. In town is J. with St.3 on which tour cont. to **RACINE** at **81.** Here is **Mon.** comm. 1st finding of coal in W.Va. (1742). Tour now cuts (SW) 14m on US119 to J. with St.3 at **95. W. HAMLIN, 127.,** where is J. with St.10 which cont. to **149. HUNTINGTON** (see US60).

## US 52—WEST VIRGINIA

**W.VA.-VA. LINE** (42m from Wytheville, Va.) **(W) & (N) to HUNTINGTON. 186. US52**

Via: Bluefield, Welch, Williamson & Wayne.

US52 crosses the Alleghenies & circles along the S. boundary of W.Va. through a coal & industrial area. The sec. along Tug Fork R. was the scene of Ind. fighting & lively brawls in frontier days.

### Sec. 1: W.VA.-VA. LINE to WILLIAMSON. 106.

**0. W.VA.-VA. LINE** is on crest of East R. Mt. **4. BLUEFIELD** (sett.1777) advertises its mild summer climate by dispensing free lemonade when temp. climbs above 91°, a rarity. It is business center of Pocahontas "smokeless" coal reg. Here was cabin of Andrew Davidson, 1st settler. In 1791 Inds. killed his children & captured his wife who, sold to Canadians, was ransomed by him. In City Pk., **Davidson H.** (1811) built by Joseph, Andrew's son. **Bluefield St. Teachers College** (1895.coed. Negro). [About 5m (S) of Bluefield, in Pocahontas, Va., is exhibition mine through which tourists may drive & see every mining operation without leaving their cars.]

**11. PINNACLE ROCK ST. PK.** (32 as.), spur of Flat Top Mt.; long view. **54. IAEGER. 55.** J. with Rd. to **Panther Cr. St. For. & Game Refuge** (7,724 as.). At c.**82** is **HORSE PEN CR.** near J. with US119. Near-by is **Marker** where Bolling Baker, who married Aracoma, Chief Cornstalk's daughter, hid horses stolen from settlers. Here is J. with US119.

SIDE TRIP: (N) 5m on US119 to **Hatfield Cemetery** (O.appl.); statue & grave of "Devil Anse" Hatfield. Anse became notorious as chief of his W.Va. clan in the feud with McCoys of Pike Cty., Ky. The feud is said to have begun when Johnse Hatfield eloped with Randall McCoy's daughter, & later returned her & her illegitimate child to her family. The feud, begun in early 19th cent., long survived those who were responsible for it & did not end until the late 1890's, after much violence, bloodshed & litigation during which the authorities of W.Va. & Ky. repeatedly obstructed justice by taking sides. At 18m on US119 is **Logan,** coal & lumber center. 425 Main St., **Mon.** on grave of Aracoma. She brought her renegade husband, Bolling Baker, here & was killed (1780) during fight bet. Inds. & settlers. Thos. Dunn English, author of "Alice Ben Bolt," was mayor (1852-57) & Jack Dempsey, heavyweight champ, worked in near-by mine. US119 cont. to Charleston (see).

US119 unites with US52 to **106., WILLIAMSON.** Center of important coal area, it is on Tug Fork of the Big Sandy, almost on Ky. Line, which derives name from Maj. Andrew Lewis' expedition (1756), reduced to boiling down boot thongs ("tugs") for food. Cor. Courth. Sq., **Coal H.,** whose walls are made of coal.

### Sec. 2: WILLIAMSON to HUNTINGTON. 80.

**38. MISSOURI BRANCH,** J. with gravel Rd.

SIDE TRIP: (E) 4m to **Cabwaylingo St. For.** (6,321 as.pic.trls.swim.f.cabins).

US52 now follows Twelvepole Cr. which was measured as "12 poles across." **62. WAYNE,** named for Gen. "Mad Anthony" Wayne (see Ohio). **80. HUNTINGTON** (see US60) where US52 cont. over toll bridge to Ironton, Ohio.

# US 19, ST. 39, ST. 16 & US 21—WEST VIRGINIA

**W.VA.-PA. LINE** (18$^{m}$ from Waynesburg, Pa.) **(S) to BLUEFIELD. 280. US19, St.39, St.16 & US 21**

Via: Morgantown, Fairmont, Clarksburg, Weston, Summersville & Princeton.

US19 is a N.-S. route from Erie, Pa. to St. Petersburg, Fla. In W. Va. it is known as Stonewall Jackson Hy. The route crosses the busy N. coal-fields of the St., then plunges into the little populated, for. central reg. & finally emerges into S. coal fields at the Va. Line.

## Sec. 1: W.VA.-PA. LINE to CLARKSBURG. 53. US19

**10. WESTOVER,** suburb of **MORGANTOWN** (sett.1767) which spreads along hills, on farther side of the Monongahela R. Center of productive agric. reg. & rich coal field; one of its plants turned out famous "Monongahela Rye" brand of whiskey. Discovery of oil in vic. brought a pipe-line. Morgantown Ordnance Works produce great quantities of chemicals for munitions. W. Va. Univ. is in Morgantown & despite industrial developments, city has air of college town. First attempt to settle Morgantown dist. (1758) was frustrated by Inds. who massacred Thos. Decker & his followers. In 1767 a son of Morgan Morgan tried again. This time the pioneers built not only houses, but also a ft. In 1783 Washington canvassed the feasibility of a route from Va. to the West. Immigration in last part of the 18th cent. was heavy, since city had become a starting pt. for the trip down-river to the Ohio. In early 19th cent. the local people successfully opposed bldg. of a RR. through their town. Later they reversed themselves, but did not get the B. & O. until 1886. PTS. OF INT.: (1) High St., **Monongahela Cth.** (O.wks.); Earlier Cth. (1846) had statue of Patrick Henry (now in Morgantown High Sch.) surmounting its dome. (2) SW. cor. Pleasant & High Sts., **McCleery H.** (1790.now a store) was built by Col. W. McCleery whose wife, Isabella Stockton, when a child, had been kidnapped by Inds. (3) 128 Wagner Rd., **Willey H.** (1838.fine portico). Willey opposed secession & became Sen. from Restored Gov. of Va., and later, from the new state of West Va. (4) 7th St., **Seneca Glass Plant** (O.appl.). (5) Valley St. & University Ave., on Observatory Hill, **entrance to W. Va. Univ.** Aside from regular univ. courses, summer courses are offered mine officials & others conn. with coal industry, with particular emphasis on accident-prevention. Its Agric. College is a forestry branch, with practical studies in Monongahela Nat. For., & several experimental farms. In Science Hall, **Biology Mus. Mountaineer Field Stadium** (1924) seats 32,000. **Lib.** (1931.Georg.Col.) has copy of "Christian Panoply" by Bishop Rich. Watson, 1st book pub. in W. Va. (1791). **Dorsey Knob** (1,438′) to (SW) of city, reached by auto or foot, affords fine panoramic view. In Morgantown are Js. with US119 & St.7.

SIDE TRIPS: (A) 3.5$^{m}$ (E) on US119 to **Easton,** site of Ft. Pierpont (1769) erected by John Pierpont, Rev. patriot. In town is J. with St.73.

Take latter 3.5$^{m}$ (E) to **Cheat L.** (recr.). Hy. crosses L., which is overshadowed by 1,000′ heights of Cheat R. Gorge. At E. end of bridge are 2 millstones marking **Birthpl. of Adam Ice,** who, it is claimed, was 1st white child born in W.Va. At 5.5$^{m}$, **Coopers Rock St. For.** (13,000 as.recr.pic.f.deer & other game h.in season); outstanding feature is **Cheat R. Canyon.** Name of For. derives, according to legend, from a cooper who, while a fugitive from justice, hid out in reg. for several yrs., earning his keep by making barrels & tubs. Until 1868 area was a center of iron smelting; here are ruins of **Davis** (1779) & **Henry Clay Furnaces** (latter in excellent condition). In For. also is **"Rock City,"** accessible by trl. which for 10$^{m}$ leads through huge, rock-tilted ledges.

(B) St.7 (NW) 11.5$^{m}$ to **Dolls Run** where occurred massacre of 18 settlers (1778) by Inds. 14$^{m}$ **Mon.** comm. Eliz. Bozarth, who defended her home against Inds., killing 3.

(C) St.7 (E) 15$^{m}$ to **Mason Town.** Here is unimproved Rd. leading 6$^{m}$ (R) to **Cornwell Cave** (O.sm.fee.guides). 18$^{m}$ **Reedsville** where St.92 cont. (S).

Take St.92 here 2$^{m}$ to **Arthurdale,** founded by Gov. for resettlement & rehabilitation of indigent families. Project is managed on cooperative plan. **Arthurdale Inn** (O), furnished by village handicraft workers.

35$^{m}$ **Terra Alta** (2,559′) where is Rd. (L) leading 2$^{m}$ to **Terra Alta L.** where are located camps of various cultural & educational institutions.

Tour cont. (S) on US19 to **25. RIVESVILLE. David Morgan Mon.,** near which Morgan had his cabin.

**28. FAIRMONT** (sett.1793).

RR., Bus & Air conns. Accoms.: Various types. Info.: C. of C., 207 Adams St.; Morin Cty. Auto Assoc. in Fairmont Hotel. Golf at White Day Golf Course (sm.fee); pool in S. Side Pk.

The Tygarts Valley & W. Fork Rs. join not far away & become Monongahela R. which flows through city. Being mining center, its prosperity has fluctuated with demand for coal. The city has large number of industrial establishments—one of the largest fluorescent tube plants, the **Fairmont Aluminum Co.** (O), the **Owens-Illinois Bottle Co.** (O) & sm. plants turning out fine, hand-blown glassware, also a plant producing coke & a variety of coal by-products. PTS. OF INT.: Adams St., **Marion County Cth.** (1897.Class.), stands on site of an older Cth. (1842) whose demolition for more modern structure gave rise to spirited controversy. NE. cor. Washington & Jefferson Sts., **Gov. Fleming H.** (1842) on site of 1st H. in city. Fairmont Ave. bet. 9th & 12th Sts., **Fairmont Farms** (gardens O.) on which is fine Sp.-mission-style mansion. Grounds are beautifully landscaped. The Farms has bred famous show horses. Locust Ave., **Fairmont St. College** (70 as.est.1865.coed.). On Pleasant Valley Rd., c.2$^{m}$ from city, **Reservoir Pk.** (pic.recr.). **32.5.** J. with Rd. leading (L) 0.5$^{m}$ to **Monongah.** Here occurred (1907) one of worst disasters in U.S. coal-mining hist., killing more than 350 miners. **42.5. SHINNSTON** (sett.1733) which voted for Lincoln (1860) & pushed for separation of W. Va. from Va. **53. CLARKSBURG** (see US50).

### Sec. 2: CLARKSBURG to WESTON. 26.

**16.5. JANE LEW** (sett.1835) whose name is a shortening of Jane Lewis. Her son, Lewis Maxwell, plotted the town. **West's Ft.** (c.1770) was destroyed by Inds. (1779).

SIDE TRIP: Take Rd. (R) here 2.5$^{m}$ & then (L) on Rd. 5$^{m}$ to **Jackson's Mill** (O.1837) where "Stonewall" Jackson lived as youth (1830-42). He worked on his grandfather's farm, educated himself, studying by light of a primitive pine-knot torch; he hired out to work on the new turnpike being put through; finally obtained appointment to West Point. Near-by, **McWhorter Cabin** (late 18th cent.), moved from Jane Lew at marked site of old Jackson H. A **4-H Camp** is now located on the farm (swim.sm.fee).

**26. WESTON** (see US33).

### Sec. 3: WESTON to SUMMERSVILLE. 82.

**8. ROANOKE. 31.5. BULLTOWN,** famous in early hist. for massacre by Jesse Hughes, noted Ind. fighter, & his friends, of all inhabitants of a Del. village in vic., as revenge for their alleged killing of Stroud family at Camden-on-Gauley. The Strouds were probably killed by some Shawnee. **66.** J. with Rd. running (R) 2$^{m}$ to **Mon.** on grave of Henry Young, who, rather than surrender, fought single-handed, until mortally wounded, against Gen. Rosecrans' Fed. Troops (1861). **82. SUMMERSVILLE** (sett.1824). Here Nancy Hart, Confed. spy, was jailed after being captured by Fed. troops, but escaped by seducing a guard & then killing him with his own pistol. Here is J. with St.39 on which tour cont. (W).

### Sec. 4: SUMMERSVILLE to GAULEY BRIDGE. 31. St.39 & St.16.

Cont. on St.39 (W) from Summersville, through **Haunted Valley,** so-called because of belief it is haunted by a Fed. soldier & his dog, both of whom died & were buried in the valley. **5.5.** J. with Rd. leading (L) 6$^{m}$ to **Carnifex Ferry Battleground St. Pk.,** where Gen. Rosecrans' forces fought a drawn battle (1861) with Confeds. Graves & trenches still extant. **26. BELVA.** Cont. (S) on St.39-16 to **31. GAULEY BRIDGE** (see US60)

### Sec. 5: GAULEY BRIDGE to BLUEFIELD. 88. US21-60 & US21-19.

At Gauley Bridge take US21-60. At **c.5.** cont. (S) on US21 past **Honey Cr. Falls,** & bet. Gauley & Sewell Mts., to **FAYETTEVILLE** (sett.1818) at **13. 36. SKELTON.** [Take Rd. (R) here to **Beckley.** (see St.3-10).] **37.** US21 & US19 are joined on which tour cont. (S). **37.5.** J. with Rd. leading (L) here 12$^{m}$ to **Grandview St. Pk.** (see St.3-10). **53.5. FLAT TOP.** Here numerous descendants of early settlers (Lillys), as well as tourists, gather annually at Lilly Family Reunion Grounds (O.mid-Aug.). At **c.74. SHAWNEE L.** (swim.sm.fee), resort. Here Mitchell Clay, nephew of Henry Clay, sett. (1775). A **Stone** at L. marks graves of his 2 children, killed by Inds. **78. PRINCETON** (sett.1826) was razed by retreating Confeds. In 1874 the 1st St. Bank was visited by Jesse James' brother, Frank, who looked it over & decided it was not worth robbing. Walker & Main Sts., **Mercer County Cth.** (1931.Mod.Class.); sculptured frieze depicting Cty.'s economic life. Main St., **Soldiers & Sailors Mem. Bldg.** (1931.Mod.Class.). **88. BLUEFIELD** (see US52).

## THE EASTERN PANHANDLE

Area is a triangle, wedged in extreme (NE) part of W.Va., projecting bet. Md. & Va. Main approach hys. are US40 (see Md.) from Hagerstown, Md. on the (N); US50 (see) on the (S); US11 & US522 cross the Panhandle from (N) to (S); US340 cuts across its (SE) cor. Potomac R. almost circles Panhandle on (E), (N) & (W). Reg. is hist. most int. Because of its location bordering Md. & Va. & adj. to Shenandoah Valley, it was sett. fairly early & saw considerable fighting during Fr.-Ind. Wars; also had active part in Rev. & later; to a certain extent pro-slavery & was on side of seceding states. Harper's Ferry, on E. edge across which Fed. & Confed. armies fought, was site of John Brown's raid. After Gettysburg, Lee escaped through Panhandle into Va. Despite ravages of war, many old Hs. & landmarks have survived, notable among which are those built by Geo. Washington's numerous kin. The E. Panhandle is treated out of Charles Town & Martinsburg, from which Rds. radiate to important landmarks.

### CHARLES TOWN

RR. & bus conns. Good accoms. & recr. facils. Spring & Fall Race Meets (pari-mutuel) of Charles Town Jockey Club; Horse Show (Aug.).

Charles Town, center of fertile agric. reg., is one of the most charming old towns in E. Panhandle. About 1770 Col. Chas. Washington, Geo.'s youngest brother, acquired title to land on which present city stands. Subsequently, when town was est., it was named for him & many of the streets bear Christian names of Washington clan members. PTS. OF INT.: (1) George & Washington Sts., **Jefferson County Cth.** (1836.adds.); tablet on cor. of bldg. comm. Chas. Washington; scene of John Brown's trial, whose attitude throughout trial was to ignore attempts by his attorneys to set up defense of hereditary insanity, while reiterating his belief that slavery was an infamous institution & his justification of violence against it. Another treason trial was held here in 1921 when several hundred miners were indicted; 3 leaders were convicted & sentenced to long terms. (2) **Chas. Washington Hall** (Market Bldg.), on site of old market built 1805, which at one time was P. O. inaugurating rural free delivery (1896). (3) W. Liberty St., **Tiffin H.** (pre-1790) where E. Tiffin, Ohio Gov., practiced medicine, 1789-96. (4) S. end Mordington Lane, **Mordington** (N.O.1774.remod.1833), home of Chas. Washington. Small structure behind house was old kitchen; near-by, **Slave H.** In grove (E) of main house is **Tablet** marking supposed graves of Chas. (d.1796), wife Mildred & their 2 grandchildren. (5) S. Samuel St., **Site of John Brown Gallows.** When Brown was brought out to be hanged, over 1,500 troops, under command of "Stonewall" Jackson were massed around gallows. In the ranks was John Wilkes Booth, who assassinated Lincoln. Brown remarked: "I had no idea that Gov. Wise considered my execution so important." (6) E. Congress St., **Zion Ch.** (1852.Episc.). In cemetery are buried members of Washington family. Tombstone erected (1788) by Lafayette in memory of child of his friend, Cmdr. Walter Brooks. (7) E. Washington St., **Presb. Ch.** (1853. Gr.Rev.) in whose vestibule hangs deed of 1787, by Chas. Washington & wife, donating site on which 1st ch. was built. (8) SE. cor. E. Washington St., **Crane H.** (pre-1800), home of Battaile Muse, who managed Washington's business affairs. House later bought by Ferdinando Fairfax, who was Lord Fairfax before becoming Amer. citizen. (9) About 1$^{m}$ (E) from town on US340, **Charles Town Race Track;** races & horse shows held since 1786, except during Civil War.

### TRIPS OUT OF CHARLES TOWN

**I. CHARLES TOWN (SW) to SUMMIT POINT. 6. Summit Pt. Rd.**

At **2.** on Summit Pt. Rd. **BRADDOCK'S WELL** (R) dug in 1755 by Braddock's soldiers. **2.5. CLAYMONT COURT** (1820 & c.1840.Georg.Col.) built by Bushrod Washington, grandnephew of Geo. In late 19th-cent., Frank Stockton, author of "Rudder Grange" & other humorous novels, lived here. **5.5. WHITE HOUSE TAVERN** (1742 & 1800), popular early 19th cent. inn. **6. SUMMIT PT.,** site of Civil War skirmish.

**II. CHARLES TOWN to KEARNEYSVILLE. 15. St.51 & St.48**

Take St.51 (W) to **c.1., ALTONA (DAVENPORT) FARM** (c.1793.Fed.), orig. owned by Lawrence Washington & later bought by Col. A. Davenport who built present elaborate mansion around old bldg. **2.**, (R) **RUINS OF ST. GEORGE'S CHAPEL** (1769) in which members of Washington family worshipped. Not far from Ruins is **Piedmont** (1730 & 1780); old portraits & early 19th-cent. wallpapers.

**3.5. HAREWOOD** (c.1770), most widely known Washington home in this sec. Geo. Washington supposedly designed house for his brother Samuel. In this house Dolly Payne Todd married Jas. Madison (1794). In 1825 Lafayette was entertained here, & later, Louis Philippe & his 2 brothers. **6.5.** J. with Rd. (R) which becomes St.48 & on which tour cont. to **LEETOWN** at **c.10.5.** Here is **Prato Rio** (O.pre-1775), home of Gen. Chas. Lee, somewhat of an eccentric, who was suspended from his command by Washington after Battle of Monmouth (see). Ground fl. of house had no partitions. Lee chalked off space into 4 quarters: in one he kept his books, in another his bed, in a 3rd his saddles & guns & in 4th his kitchen equipment. Here Lee hobnobbed with 2 other unsuccessful Rev. generals, Horatio Gates & Adam Stephen.

**14.** J. with Rd.

SIDE TRIP: Take latter (L) 0.5m to entrance to **Traveler's Rest** (O.pre-1763), home of Gen. Horatio Gates, hero of Battle of Saratoga, rival of Washington for command of Continental Armies, but later suspended from his command after his defeat by Cornwallis.

**15. KEARNEYSVILLE.**

**III. CHARLES TOWN (NE) to HARPERS FERRY. 8. US340**

At **3. RION HALL** (c.1836), home of Judge D. B. Lucas, author & poet, who served in Confed. Army; when his friend, John Y. Beall, was accused of being a spy, he managed to get through Fed. lines to N.Y., where he defended Beall. **3.5.** J. with unimproved Rd.

SIDE TRIP: Take latter (L) 1m here to **Beall Air** (pre-1800.adds.), home of Col. Lewis Washington, kidnapped & held hostage by John Brown's followers on night of Harpers Ferry raid. Brown took from Washington the sword Frederick the Great had given Geo. Washington, & was wearing it when taken.

**8. HARPERS FERRY** (accoms.) at Md. Line, located at pt. where Md., Va. & W.Va. come together & Shenandoah & Potomac Rs., flowing through cliff-enclosed gaps, meet. On night of Oct. 16, 1859, John Brown & 22 followers marched into Harpers Ferry & took possession of old Gov. armory. The little band withstood siege all next day against local militia; finally Lt. Col. Rbt. E. Lee arrived with 90 marines & captured Brown & 6 of his company. Two of Brown's sons were killed together with a number of the raiders, & several escaped. PTS. OF INT.: (1) Marked by white-painted flagstones, site of **Armory** seized by Brown & band. (2) At B. & O. Depot, **John Brown Mon.,** on site of **Engine H.** in which Brown & companions made last stand. (3) **Harpers Ferry Nat. Mon.** (c.1,500 as.), incl. hilltops in the vic. where Civil War battle bet. "Stonewall" Jackson's forces & Fed. garrison occurred, Sept. 1862. Garrison, consisting of some 12,500, surrendered & Jackson hastened to join Lee at Battle of Antietam (see). Many Fed. trenches are preserved. Stone steps, carved in solid rock (1810) lead to Pub. Walk. (4) At Stone Steps is **Harper H.** (1780), built by Rbt. Harper, 1st settler. (5) Near-by, on Pub. Walk, is **Cath. Ch.** (1830.Goth.alt.), only Ch. in town which cont. services through Civil War. (6) On slope to one side of & above Cath. Ch. are ruins of **St. John's Ch.** (Episc.), occupied as guardh. & hospital during Civil War. (7) On Cliff St. (no autos), **Jefferson Rock,** named for Thos. Jefferson who came here (1801) & later described the view in his "Notes on Virginia." (8) On Fillmore St., **Odd Fellows Lodge** (est.1833), oldest in St. Lincoln stayed here when he came to meet Gen. McClellan in 1862. (9) On same St., **Storer College** for Negroes (est.1869.coed.). On campus, **John Brown's Ft.** (O.appl.),with **Old Engine H.** (see above); **Mus.** (O.appl.coll.hist.relics). (10) On Washington St., **Lutheran Ch.** (1850), used as Fed. hospital & stable during Civil War. **Wilson H.** (O.post-1828), home of E. W. Wilson, Gov. of St. (1885-90) at time of a disputed gubernatorial election. (11) In Shenandoah R., **Herrs I.,** where government had some rifle works, branch of old armory.

**IV. CHARLES TOWN (SW) to W.VA.-VA LINE. 7. US340**

At **1.** (L) **CASSILIS** (c.1835), where many notables were entertained incl. Washington Irving & W. M. Thackeray, who may have found material here used in his "The Virginians." **1.5.** J. with unimproved Rd.

SIDE TRIP: On Rd. leading (L) 1m to **Washington's Cave** (O.fee), visited by Washington, when, as a boy of 17, he made surveying trip for Lord Fairfax. He is supposed to have revisited Cave (1754) with soldiers under his command. Cave has been used since by Masonic Order.

A short distance beyond last J. (on US340) is another J. which leads (L) 1.5m to **Blakely** (1820.rest.), home of John Augustine Washington; near-by, Braddock's forces camped on march to Ft. Duquesne (see Pittsburgh). **5.5. RIPPON,** beyond which US340 crosses **W.VA.-VA. LINE** at **7.**

## V. CHARLES TOWN (NW) & (S) to J. with US50. 80. St.9 & St.29

**7.5.** on St.9 (NW) to **KEARNEYSVILLE.** Here is J. with St.48.

SIDE TRIP: On St.48 (R) at 4.5m is **Mon. to Berkeley Riflemen** who marched some 600m to join Washington at Boston (1775). Cont. (NE) on St.48 to **Shepherdstown** at 5m. Ferry (autos) across Potomac; limited accoms. Sett.1762 by Thos. Shepherd as Mecklenberg; name derived from German settlement near-by. Many int. old Hs. In 1790 Geo. Washington seriously considered locating nat. capital at this pt. Jas. Rumsey demonstrated his steamboat (1787), priority of which was disputed by John Fitch (see Trenton, N.J.). During Civil War, number of battles were fought in vic.; most important was Antietam (see Md.). PTS. OF INT.: (1) On German St., **Shepherd St. Teachers College** (1872), with **McMurran Hall** & **Home Econ. Cottage** (log) on site of Ft. Shepherd built during Fr.-Ind. Wars, once believed to be haunted by ghost of Geo. Yontz, who supposedly murdered former occupant. **Rumsey Hall,** former old hotel & tavern, is miniature farm now conducted for demonstration purposes. (2) On High St., **Shepherdstown Flour Mill** erected 1734-62; still in operation, mill has 40′ water-wheel & produces old-fashioned flour & burr-ground corn meal. (3) On High St. near Mill, **House** (empty,c.1727), probably oldest in St., although this is disputed. (4) On Mill St., **Rumsey St. Pk.,** with **Rumsey Mon.** comm. steamboat invention. (5) On German St. near Mill, **Billmeyer H.** (1791), formerly tavern where John Fitch stayed, supposedly to spy on Rumsey's invention. (6) German & King Sts., **Sheetz H.,** formerly tavern, occupied once by Wm. Sheetz who made rifle parts for Armory at Harpers Ferry. (7) Church & High Sts., **Episc. Ch.** (now Negro.18th cent.adds.1842). Peter Muhlenberg of "There is a time to preach & a time to fight" fame (see Woodstock, Va., & Pa.), was minister until he took service in Continental Army. (8) On German St. near Duke St., **Harrington H.** (Rev.period), was Entler Tavern, used in Civil War by troops of both sides. (9) On New St., **Shepherd's Cemetery,** graves of Thos. Shepherd & family. (10) SW. cor. King & New Sts., **Old Grove H.,** once tavern which incurred displeasure of town authorities because it carried on in disorderly fashion on Sundays. On Shepherd Turnpike c.0.5m (N) of town on hilltop, **Bellevue.** Near-by is spring where band of Inds., legend says, buried one of their enemies alive & it is the beating of his heart which sends out water of spring in spurts.

At **8.5.** on St.9 is **W. VA. UNIV. EXPERIMENTAL FARM** (R) where work is done in developing fruit culture. **15. MARTINSBURG** (see). **21.** on St.9 is **HEDGESVILLE.** Here, in fine old grove, stands **Mt. Zion Ch.** (Episc.1817). **23. FOOSE'S LAWN** (O.c.1740.adds.1800), formerly inn where Geo. Washington waited (1769) while contents of his trunk, having spilled into near-by creek, were being dried out. **40. BERKELEY SPRINGS** (accoms.: all types; info.: Pk. View Inn or Washington Hotel). Orig. known as Bath, this is one of oldest spas in U.S., situated on Warm Springs Run & surrounded by picturesque hills. Inds. used waters medicinally before 1st settlers arrived (c.1740). Geo. Washington made the springs widely known. In 1756 Lord Fairfax granted land on which springs are located on condition they be "forever free to the public." Here Rumsey showed off his newly invented "mechanical" boat to Washington & other notables. PTS. OF INT.: (1) **Berkeley Springs St. Pk. & Sanitarium** with 3 principal medicinal springs & bathhs.; **Old Hot Springs Bath** (O.c.100 yrs.old); the **Fairfax Bathtub** built by Lord Fairfax. (2) Near Pk. on hilltop is **The Castle** (1887-88.Norman). (3) At edge of Pk. (L) is **Washington Elm** (20′ circum.), planted by 1st Pres. as Marker when surveying Lord Fairfax's gift. (4) Cor. Washington & Warren Sts., **Strother H.** (1850), where D. H. Strother (Porte Craven) lived & wrote many of his stories. In Berkeley is J. with US522.

SIDE TRIP: (S) on US522 10m to **Cacapon St. Pk.** (5,812 as.pic.cabins.lodge.camp.facils. swim.recr.f.trls.hik.bicycle & bridle trls). Washington in 1769 rode out with his wife to get view (4 states & bend of Potomac) from mountain-top. (The pk. may also be approached from Winchester, Va., by Va. St.7.)

**62.** J. with St.29. Tour cont. (S) on latter. At **67.5. CACAPON FORKS.** J. with St.45.

SIDE TRIP: Take Rd. (L) c.0.5m to J., then (R) 1m on unimproved Rd. & then (L), 1.5m, to **Caudy's Castle,** rocky mass towering over Cacapon R. some 600′. Trl. up rock. Here Caudy & other settlers caught raiding Inds. by surprise & pushed them over rock's edge.

Tour cont. from **Cacapon Forks** on St.45 (R) to J. with US50 (see) at **80.**

### MARTINSBURG

Accoms.: Ample. Info.: C. of C. B. & O. RR., bus & air conns.

Founded by German & English settlers (1732), city was laid out by Rev. Gen. Adam Stephen & named for relative of Lord Fairfax, Col. T. B. Martin, who served under Washington. During 1873 depression, universal work stoppage occurred in protest against wage reductions. After several clashes, Fed. troops were sent in. PTS. OF INT.: (1) At Public Sq., **Berkeley County Cth.** (1856. Romanes.); record room with Book of Commissions containing documents bearing signatures of all Va. Govs. & of Geo. Washington, Patrick Henry & other notables. (2) King & Spring Sts., **Whitmore Lemen H.** (O) incorporates walls of ft. (1774). (3) Across street is **King's Daughters Hospital,** orig. old jail. (4) On Queen St., **Boydville H.** (c.1812), one of Panhandle's finest. On grounds, **Mon. to Gen. Stephen.** (5) Cor. Burke & Queen Sts., **Everett H.** (log covered with plaster; 1784-96), where both Gens. Jackson & Sheridan had hqs. (6) Cor. Water & John Sts., **Martin H.** (O.appl.1779-1803.fine inter.). (7) On Tuscarora Rd. c.3m is **Tuscarora Ch.** (c.1740.Presb.), parts of orig. walls incorporated in bldgs.; in entry, wooden pegs for worshippers to hang guns.

### TRIPS OUT OF MARTINSBURG

**I. MARTINSBURG (N) to MAIDSTONE-ON-POTOMAC. 12.5. US11**

**1.5. MARKER ON SITE OF FT. NEALLY,** where Inds. massacred garrison & kidnapped women & children (1756). **8.5. FALLING WATERS,** so-called because Potomac R. cascades at this pt. Here Lee's army, during withdrawal after Gettysburg, repelled Fed. attack & managed to escape across R. **11.5. POTOMAC CAMP MEETING GROUNDS** (July & Aug.). **12.5.** (R) **MAIDSTONE-ON-POTOMAC** (1744), home of Evan Watkins who had a ferry across R. at this pt. Beyond H., toll bridge across to Hancock, Md.

**II. MARTINSBURG (S) to W.VA.-VA. LINE. 13. US11**

**10. BUNKER HILL** (sett.1726-32 by Morgan Morgan), reputedly earliest place sett. in St. To (E) of village, **Mon.** on site of Morgan's orig. log cabin. A short distance from which on a secondary Rd. (R) is **Christ Ch.** (1853) site of orig. Ch. (1740) built by Morgan & early settlers. Morgan, one of St.'s earliest settlers & builder of 1st Rd. (from Winchester, Va. to his home here) is buried here. **12.5. PETTIGREW MON.** (R) comm. Confed. Gen. J. J. Pettigrew who died at Boyd H. **13. W.VA.-VA. LINE.**

## NATIONAL FOREST REGIONS

W.Va.'s finest vacation area lies within the 750,000 as. of Monongahela Nat. For., extending along the Va. line from E. Panhandle to White Sulphur Springs. To the (E) is Geo. Washington Nat. For., mostly in Va. (see) but with a narrow finger thrusting into W.Va.'s 3 NE. counties. Although none of the peaks reaches more than 4,800′, the reg. is of great scenic interest—deep gorges, swift-flowing streams, waterfalls, steep cliffs & weird caverns. Little original forest cover remains, but reforestation & conservation have encouraged a good 2nd growth. Game is abundant & fishing, excellent. Of special interest are primitive communities in back-country dists. where overshot water-wheels still grind out corn meal & early folk-ways have managed to survive.

The reg.'s hy. boundaries are: US50 (N); US220 (E); US60 (S); US219 & St.15 (W). Also, US33 & US250, main E-W hys. cross reg. St.55, St.28 & St.39 give access to reg. at many pts. Jefferson Nat. For. lies (S) along W.Va.-Va. Line, entirely in Va. (see). The 3 Nat. Fors. have been intensively developed; hundreds of miles of for., Rds., trls. & recr. areas (ample pic.camp facils.) have been constructed. For info. & campfire permit on Monongahela Nat. For.: Supervisor, Elkins, W.Va. or For. Rangers at Parsons, Durbin, Petersburg, Marlinton & Richwood. For info. & campfire permit for Geo. Washington Nat. For.: Supervisor, Harrisonburg or Dist. For. Rangers at Edinburg, Bridgewater, Staunton, Buena Vista & Covington (all in Va.). For Jefferson Nat. For. see Va.

## REGIONAL TOUR 1

**W.VA.-VA. LINE** (5m from Gore, Va.) **(S) & (W) to MOOREFIELD. 49. St.259 & St.55**

**6.5.** on St.259 is **YELLOW SPRING. 12.5.** J. with Rd. leading 3m to **Capon Springs.** Here is old resort; women's wider bathh. entrance for hoop skirts of ante bellum days. **21. WARDENSVILLE** (near-by in Geo. Washington Nat. For. is **Half Moon Fire Tower**;fine view), J. with St.55 which cont. (W) with St.259.

SIDE TRIP: (L) on Main St. & cont. on unimproved Rd. along Trout Run 5m to **Blue Sea Gap.** Beyond Gap, hidden by trees, is **Devil's Garden,** high precipice with fine view.

**31. BAKER,** J. of St.259 with St.55 on which tour cont.

SIDE TRIP: (S) 7m on St.259 to **Lost River.** Here is trl. leading (L) to Lost R. which cascades into a pool here. 13m **Mathias,** J. with Rd. to **Lost R. St. Pk.** (3,841 as.recr.swim.trls. cabin). Sulphur spring in Pk. Area developed as resort by Lee family. **Lee Cabin** (early 19th cent.) built by "Light Horse Harry" Lee, of Rev. fame, father of Rbt. E. Lee. In vic. is **Gooseberry Mt.** (3,265′). St.259 to Geo. Washington Nat. For. in Va.

St.55 cont. from Baker to **49. MOOREFIELD.** Here is **Old Stone Inn** (1788), now tourist H. Here is J. with S. Branch Mt. Rd. leading 14m to **Lost R. St. Pk.** (see above). In Moorefield is J. with US220.

SIDE TRIP: (N) short distance on US220 to **Willow Hall** (1818). Built by Capt. D. R. McNeill whose son, Hanson, is known for daring S. Branch Valley raids with his Rangers during Civil War. 5m **Old Fields** with Mt. Pleasant Mansion (1832.Class.Rev.); hist. relics incl. great kettle which Washington is said to have used (1756) for making powder. Rd. here leads (R) 2m to the **Trough,** deep gorge on S. Branch of Potomac, visited by Washington in 1748.

## REGIONAL TOUR 2

**MOOREFIELD (S) to W.VA.-VA. LINE** (c.8m from Monterey, Va.). **58. US220**

**13. PETERSBURG** (sett.1745 by Germans); annual Tri-County Fair (Sept.) features medieval riding tournaments. In town is J. with St.42.

SIDE TRIP: (N) 19m on St.42 to **Scherr** & near-by **Greenland Gap** whose cliffs rise 1,000′ from valley.

Cont. (S) on US220 through Petersboro Gap. **30.** J. with Rd., 1m from hamlet of Upper Tract.

SIDE TRIP: (N) on Rd. through impressive gorge, past **Eagle & High Rocks** at 4.5m. 6m **Smoke Hole,** back country village, has trl. to **N. Fork Mt.** (3,715′). Near-by is **Smoke Hole For. Camp.** (pic.swim.camp.).

**43. FRANKLIN** (sett.1769), near J. with US33 (see Reg.Tour 4). **47.5. THORN SPRING PK.** (pic.camp.swim.). US220 cont. past **Sandy Ridge** (3,208′) & **Front Rock** (2,256′) to **W.VA.-VA. LINE** at **58.**

## REGIONAL TOUR 3

**PETERSBURG (W) to THORNWOOD. 55. St.28-4**

(W) on St.28-4 to **c.10. SMOKE HOLE CAVERNS** (electrically lit). Cont. on hy. past Castle & Champ Rocks to **MOUTH OF SENECA** at **22.** Here St.28 joins to US33 & cont. (S). At **c.22.5.** is **SENECA ROCK** (1,000′ above hy.), reached by trl. **29. RIVERTON.** Here is J. with side Rd.

SIDE TRIP: (L) on Rd. into Germany Valley with view of **Spruce Knob** (4,860′). 2m Marker on **Site of Hinkle's Ft.** (1761). 3.5m **Seneca Caverns** (sm.fee.electrically lit).

**31.** J. with Rd. (R) leading 9m to **Red Lick Run's Cascades & Ravine.** Here is trl. (R) to Spruce Knob, highest pt. in W.Va. **32. JUDY GAP.** J. with St.28 on which tour cont. (S) past **Allegheny Mt.** (4,017′) to **THORNWOOD** at **55.** For pts. (S) of US250, see Reg. Tour 7.

## REGIONAL TOUR 4

**W.VA.-VA. LINE** (c.25m from Harrisonburg, Va.) **to ELKINS. 80. US33**

**11. OAK FLAT;** marker comm. Ft. Seybert where Inds. massacred whites (1759); ft. site is some miles away on side Rd. (R). **34. JUDY GAP** (see Reg. Tour 3). **44.**

**MOUTH OF SENECA.** Here US33 turns (W). **51.5.** Fine view of **Seneca Cr. Gorge. 53.5. SUMMIT OF ALLEGHENY FRONT** (3,293′). **56. HARMAN.** Here is J. with St.32 leading (NW) c.15$^{m}$ to **Blackwater Falls St. Pk.** (trout f.free guides). **66. ALPENA GAP.** Here is E. J. to Stuart Dr., a loop hy. which passes **Shaver For. Camp** (facils.) on Shaver Cr.; **Bickle Knob Fire Tower & Bickle Pic. Area** (facils.). At 7.5$^{m}$ Dr. passes **Bear Heaven Pic. Area** & at 10$^{m}$ returns to US33 at **Alpena Nat. For. Pic. Area. 80. ELKINS** (see).

## REGIONAL TOUR 5

**ELKINS (N) to THOMAS. 35. US219**

(N) from Elkins on US219 to **20. PARSONS** where is **Battle of Corrick's Ford Mon.** comm. conflict (1861). **24.5.** J. with Rd. leading 1.5$^{m}$ to **Backbone Mt.** (3,800′). Fire tower offers wide view. **35. THOMAS,** coal town on Blackwater R. Here is J. with St.32.

SIDE TRIP: 4$^{m}$ (S) on St.32 to Rd. leading a few hundred yards to **Blackwater Falls St. Pk.**

## REGIONAL TOUR 6

**ELKINS (S) to LEWISBURG. 103. US219**

**7. BEVERLY,** where 1st settlers were wiped out by Inds.; later comers were protected by ft. built near present town site. [At c.5$^{m}$ (W) from town, Gen. McClellan defeated Confed. force (1861) at **Rich Mt.**] **16. MILL CR.** [22$^{m}$ (W) of town is paved Rd. to unique Swiss village, **Helvetia,** in which customs & language of Alps homeland are kept alive.] **17. HUTTONSVILLE. 24.** J. with marked Rd. leading c.4$^{m}$ to **Kumbrabow St. For.** (9,423 as.trout f.), one of wildest for. reservs. in St. Skyline Dr., crosses mt. tops & cont. to pic. grounds near Falls of Mill Cr. US219 cont. (S) past **Cheat Mt.** (3,803′), **Middle, Valley & Red Lick Mts.** to **EDRAY** at **59.;** near-by is **Trout Hatchery. 63.5. OLD TOLL H.** (1852.restaurant). J. with St.28 (see Reg. Tour 3). **64.** J. with St.39.

SIDE TRIP: (E) 7$^{m}$ to **Huntersville,** where is J. with Rd. leading (N) c.11$^{m}$ to **Seneca St. For.** (11,050 as.swim.trls.winter sports); cabins on L. & Greenbrier R. Fine view from fire lookouts incl. **Michael Fire Tower** (3,652′). In Huntersville is J. with Rd. leading (S) c.10$^{m}$ to **Watoga St. Pk.** (10,050 as.pic.trls.restaurant.horses.boat.swim.); small L. & arboretum (440 as.); plentiful wild life.

**71. MILL PT.** Here on Stamping Cr. is **McNeel Mill** (c.1868); water wheel still in use. In Mill Pt. is J. with St.39.

SIDE TRIP: (W) c.10$^{m}$ on St.39 is **Cranberry Glades,** weird misplaced arctic tundra swamp, probably all that is left of an ancient lake, is on mt. top (3,375′) where grow several varieties of cranberry, sphagnum moss, wildflowers & orchids.

At **c.71.5.** is Rd. leading to ferry (free) across Greenbrier R. to **Watoga St. Pk. 77. DROOP MT. BATTLEFIELD ST. PK.** (pic.trls.cabins) where Gen. Averell routed Confeds. under Gen. J. Echols in 1863. At **93. FRANKFORD. Ludington H.** (plaster over log) dates from hamlet's earliest days. Just (S) of town is J. with Rd.

SIDE TRIP: (E) on this Rd. at c.10$^{m}$ is **Entrance to Blue Bend Recr. Area** (Info. at White Sulphur Springs.camp.pic.facils.), on Blue Bend of Anthony Cr. Area has network of trls. incl. 37$^{m}$ loop trip from Lewisburg via Frankford to White Sulphur Springs; fine views of Gunpowder Ridge & Hopkins Mt. Lookout Tower.

**103. LEWISBURG** (see).

## REGIONAL TOUR 7

**W.VA.-VA. LINE** (near Monterey, Va.) **(NW) to BELINGTON. 63. US250**

Monterey, Va. is fine starting pt. for near-by peaks in Geo. Washington Nat. For. **0.** US250 crosses **W.VA.-VA. LINE** at crestline of Alleghenies. At **7.5. THORNWOOD.** E. J. with St.28 (see Reg. Tour 3). **12. FRANK,** with Pocahontas Tanning Plant (O). **13. DURBIN,** with Greenbrier Ranger Sta. of Monongahela Nat. For. Near-by is **Gaudineer Pic. Area. 32. HUTTONSVILLE.** At **c.42. TYGARTS VALLEY HOMESTEADS,** one of 3 such U.S. projects in W.Va. (est.1933); large community enterprise, for social & industrial development of reg. **48. ELKINS** (see). **51.** on US250 is **DAVID REGER FOSSIL TREE PK.** Part of 50$^{m}$ area of fossilized trees from 3 to 5 hundred million yrs. old, appear here at foot of cliff. **63. BELINGTON. J.** with Rd. leading c.2$^{m}$ to **Laurel Hill,** site of Fed. Gen. McClellan's victory.

# CHARLESTON

## CHARLESTON

C. & O. RR., S. Side Bridge; B. & O., N.Y. Central & Va. RR. at Broad St. Through bus & air conns. Seaplane for short flights in city at Kanawha R. Accoms.: All types. Golf courses (sm.fee), boating & canoeing at Kanawha City Levee; Info.: Southern W. Va. Auto Club, Ruffner Hotel, 822 Kanawha Blvd.; C. of C., 1 Capitol St. Occasional plays at Shrine Mosque; concerts at Mason Sch. of Music & Fine Arts.

Due to great coal, natural gas, oil & salt brine resources of Kanawha Valley, the St. capital is an important industrial town. The business dist. is crowded down to the water front by the narrow R. valley. The Kanawha is spanned by a number of bridges—one at W. end of town in the industrial area, one at E. end where are located the city's main recr. facils. & one crossing R. from town's heart to the S. suburbs. Kanawha Blvd. connects all three. The beginnings of the city (sett.c.1789) date from the bldg. of Ft. Lee by Col. Geo. Clendenin, who named the settlement Charles Town, in honor of his father; was shortened to present name by usage. Dan. Boone built a cabin across the R. & stayed 7 yrs., serving as member of Va. Assembly & Lt.-Col. of Militia. Ft. Lee was besieged (1788) by Inds.; siege is celebrated because of "Mad Ann" Bailey's legendary exploit. According to legend, when Ft. Lee was in dire straits for powder, the famous woman scout rode $100^{m}$ to Ft. Savannah & brought back sufficient ammunition. By 1804 Charleston had been put into communication with the E. by completion of the James R. & Kanawha Turnpike (US60) & became a pt. of transshipment. Later the salt industry boomed, only to decline due to competition by richer deposits elsewhere. But arrival of the RR., improvement by Fed. Gov. of navigation on Kanawha R., discovery of minerals used in industry have assured city's position as a metropolis of W. Va. In the 1870's Charleston waged bitter contest with Wheeling for honor of becoming the St. capital. Wheeling had been center of gov. ever since establishment of W.Va. as a separate St. during the Civil War. But in 1870 the 1st Democratic administration was elected & the St. capital moved to Charleston. After heated contest, St. legislature submitted the issue to popular vote. Charleston rolled up an enormous vote & was proclaimed St. capital in 1885.

PTS. OF INT.: (1) E. Kanawha St., **St. Capitol** (guides.1932.Ital.Ren.by Cass Gilbert). In the spacious grounds are "Stonewall" Jackson **Mon.,** by Moses Ezekiel; **Pioneer Mon.,** by Rimfire Hamrick; & **Mon.** comm. W.Va. soldiers in Civil War. The Capitol's 300′ gilded dome may be ascended (guides). Senate & House Chambers each have elaborate chandelier composed of 10,000 separate pieces of rock crystal. St. Mus. is housed in the basement; coll. of hist. relics & other exhibits. (2) Opp. is **Gov.'s Mansion** (1925.post-Rev.by W.F.Martens). (3) Also opp. the Capitol is new campus of **Morris-Harvey College** (Meth.22 as.est.1888), moved from Barboursville. (4) E. Kanawha Blvd., **Kanawha Riflemen's Mem. Pk.,** formerly cemetery. Two gravestones of the pioneer Ruffner family are still extant; also **Mon.** to Kanawha Riflemen comm. men who fought for the Confed. cause. (5) Further (E) on E. Kanawha Blvd. are markers on **Site of Ft. Lee,** one of which comm. Ann Bailey's famous ride & Fleming Cobb who also brought ammunition to the beleaguered ft. (6) SE. cor. Hale & Lee Sts., **Pub. Lib.** which was annex of old St. House, destroyed by fire in 1921. (7) Patrick St., **Market,** well worth a visit. (8) 1308 Quarrier St., **Mason College of Music & Fine Arts** (est.1906); chamber music & other concerts during season. (9) Virginia & Broad Sts., **First Presb. Ch.,** copy of Ch. designed by Stanford White, formerly in N.Y. (now torn down). (10) **Libbey-Owens-Ford Glass Co.** world's greatest producer of flat-glass, & (11) opp., **Owens-Illinois Bottle Co.** (O), one of world's greatest bottle makers. (12) Patrick St. Bridge, **Kelly Axe & Tool Factory** (O.appl.) one of world's largest axe factories.

## TRIPS OUT OF CHARLESTON

(For Pts. of Int. on US60, (E) & (W) of Charleston, see US60.)

### I. CHARLESTON (NW) to PT. PLEASANT. 57. US35

**57. PT. PLEASANT,** on ht. bet. Kanawha & Ohio Rs. In **Tu-Endie-Wei Pk.,** Mon. on site of Battle (1774) during Lord Dunmore's War (see) where Col. militia under Lewis defeated Inds. under Cornstalk. Also here is grave of "Mad Ann" Bailey (see). **Mansion H.** (1797.log), earliest in vic., is now mus. Near-by **Celeron Mon.,** comm.

unearthing of plate left by Peter J. Celeron in 1749 which claimed Ohio reg. for France. At R.'s edge, **Mon.** comm. Rev. Ft. Randolph where (1776) Chief Cornstalk & his son, coming on peace mission, were executed to avenge killing of settler. Chief's grave is in front of bullet scarred **Mason County Cth.**

**II. CHARLESTON (N) to SUTTON. 88. US119-St.4**

US119 & St.4 are joined to Clendenin. **7.5. MON.** comm. Simon Kenton, famous scout who fled to frontier, mistakenly convinced that he had killed a man in a brawl over a woman. He was a friend of Dan. Boone, whose life he is supposed to have saved. **25. QUEENS SHOALS.**

SIDE TRIP: Here is Rd. across a bridge to **Mullens Farm** at 7.5m where is the **Golden Delicious Apple Tree,** still bearing fruit, grafts from which have distributed this fine apple variety throughout the country.

St.4 cont. along Elk R. through a natural gas reg., to **SUTTON** (J. there with US19) at **88.** For sec. of US21 (N) of Charleston, see US50.

# WHEELING, WEST VIRGINIA

**WHEELING**

Pa. & Wheeling & L. Erie RRs., 11th & Water Sts. B. & O. RR., 1700 Market St. Buses: Through lines terminal, 16th & Market Sts.; Consolidated Bus Depot, 11th & Chapline Sts. Airport on W. side of Ohio R. Accoms.: All types. Info.: Ohio Valley Board of Trade, Board of Trade Bldg. Horse racing at Wheeling Downs (pari-mutuel, spring & fall).

This W.Va. metropolis (sett.1769), at center of the N. Panhandle, a narrow wedge thrust bet. Ohio & Pa., extends along E. bank of Ohio; Wheeling Cr. cuts through town to debouch into the Ohio. Pop., of mixed derivation, keeps up many old customs & religious festivals such as Feast of Our Lady of Flowers (Aug.15) & Blessing of Foods on Holy Saturday, both at St. Ladislaus Ch. A busy river port, city's industrial hist. dates from early 19th cent. City's name is claimed to have originated with Inds. who called it Wheeling ("skull") because they had decapitated white settlers & hung their skulls on posts near present site of city. Zane family, ancestors of novelist Zane Grey, were 1st settlers. Wheeling became focal pt. of movement to separate 40 western counties from Va. Convention which set up "The Restored Gov. of Va." met here, 1861. Later, city was capital of the St., a distinction finally lost to Charleston (see). In 1936, Wheeling suffered damaging Ohio R. & Wheeling Cr. floods. From Wheeling, US40 crosses Suspension Bridge (1856) to Wheeling I. which Ebenezer Zane (early settler) is said to have bought from Inds. for barrel of whiskey. PTS. OF INT.: (1) Chapline St., **City-Cty. Bldg.** (1876.Romanes.by J.S.Fairfax) formerly St. Capitol; on grounds, Civil War & Trades & Labor Mons. & Paxton Fountain, with 2 statuary groups. (2) SE. cor. Eoff & 13th Sts., **St. Joseph's Cathedral** (Cath.Romanes.by F.Aretz), seat of Wheeling Diocese; inter. of dome is decorated with frescoes; fine stained-glass windows. (3) 1526 Market St., **Customh.** (c.1854.Gr.Rev.); Constitutional Convention sat in rooms now occupied by Fed. Court (2nd fl.). (4) NE. cor. 12th & Market Sts., **Washington Hall** (1853.alt.) where Wheeling Convention met (1861). (5) Main St., bet. 11th & Ohio Sts., **Marker on Site of Ft. Henry** (1774) used during Lord Dunmore's War & later renamed to honor Patrick Henry; unsuccessfully attacked by Inds. & Brit., final attack (Sept.11-13, 1782) is claimed as last battle of Amer. Rev., during which Betty Zane made daring trip to bring ammunition. (6) Market St., **M. Marsh & Sons Stogie Factory** (O. appl.). These cigars 1st became popular among drivers of Conestoga wagons & were orig. known as Conestogas. (7) SE. cor. Market & 21st Sts., **Pub. Lib.** (1910. Mod.Class.); **Bennett Mem. Mus.** (O.wks.); coll. of firearms, costumes & musical instruments. (8) Market & 22nd Sts., **Lower Market** (O.Sat.1855); worth visit. (9) Water St., bet. 39th & 41st Sts., **Bloch Bros. Tobacco Factory** (O.wks.) where chewing tobacco is manufactured.

## TRIPS OUT OF WHEELING

**I. WHEELING (N & E) to W.VA.-PA. LINE. c.16. US40**

On Mt. Wood Rd. to Wheeling Hill, **MT. WOOD CEMETERY,** where is **Mon.** on grave of Dr. S. P. Hullihen, 1st to specialize in oral surgery & inventor of new techniques. On **HILL** is **Marker** where Maj. S. McCulloch made his daring leap over the cliff into Wheeling Cr. to escape pursuing Inds. Beyond Hill, on US40, is **THE MINGO,** bronze statue comm. Ind. tribe. On peninsula made by loop of Wheeling Cr. is **Wetzel's Cave** where noted Ind. scout, Lewis Wetzel, trapped Inds. who had been luring settlers to this spot by imitating wild turkey call. Wetzel's fierce hatred of Inds. dated from early youth when he was kidnapped by Inds. who scalped his father & mother. Also on Peninsula is **Linsly Institute.** Statue of **Aviator** by A. Lukeman. At **c.4.5., MUN. PK.** (150 as.pic.swim.sports facils.zoo.golf). At entrance of Pk., **Madonna of the Trail,** comm. pioneer women. **5.5. OLD STONE H.** (c.1820), former stage-coach tavern. Near-by is **Old Stone Mill** (c.1826), still in use. Just beyond, **Mon. Place** (O.1798.fine exter.& inter.rest.) owned by Masonic Order; furnished in period styles; built by Moses Shepherd, on site of Ft. Shepherd. Room occupied by Henry Clay & ballroom furnished as they were orig. when Lafayette, Calhoun, Jackson & other notables were visitors. US40 crosses **W.VA.-PA. LINE** at **c.16.**

## II. WHEELING (N) to WEST LIBERTY. c.10. US40 & St.88

From city's center, follow US40. **2. VANCE MEM. CH.** Here is J. with St.88 on which trip cont. At **c.3.** is J. with Greggsville Rd. which leads (L) to **Washington Farms** (O). In addition to large, modern mansion, there is smaller H. (c.1817) built by Lawrence A. Washington, nephew of 1st Pres. **5. OGLEBAY PK.** (765 as.restaurant.outdoor theater.accoms.swim.pic.riding.tennis.archery.hik.golf). Under Oglebay Institute are conducted varied cultural & educational activities. Here are held Panhandle Autumn Festival & Reg. 4H Fair. In Pk. is **Mansion H.** (O.c.1835); period furnishings & hist. items & other exhibits; sm. fee incl. visit to Mansion H. & near-by **Carriage H.** which has Frontier Travel Gallery & exhibits of local flora & fauna. **Wheeling Garden Center** (O); horticultural displays, **Arboretum Trial Gardens & Greenhouses.** Just beyond Pk., off St.88 on high sch. grounds, **Site of Ft. Van Meter** (1774). It was while in command of this ft. that Maj. Sam. McCulloch (see) was ambushed (1782) by Inds. who, according to legend, cut out his heart & ate it, believing that thus they would acquire his courage & cunning. At **c.10., W. LIBERTY** (org.1777), home of **W. Liberty St. College** (est.1838). In cemetery is **Grave** of Ind. fighter, Sam. Brady (see).

## III. WHEELING (N) to J. with US30. 46. St.2

St.2 runs parallel to Ohio R. & Ohio St.7 (see Ohio R. Tour, O.). **11. POWER,** where is **Windsor Co. Plant. 12. BEECH BOTTOM,** with 2 large plants of Wheeling Steel Corp. where mfg. processes may be observed. **15.5.** J. with St.67.

SIDE TRIP: (E) 6$^{m}$ to **Bethany. Bethany College** (1,000 as.), chartered 1840, was founded by Alex. Campbell, leader of Disciples of Christ. It is claimed that here Prof. A. E. Dolbear perfected parts of telephone as used by Bell. Near-by is orig. Campbell Homestead & old Schoolh. **Brush Run Meetingh.** (O.appl.1811), where Campbell preached.

**29. WEIRTON,** home of Weir Steel Plants, largest Co. in "Little Steel"; steel corp. provides pub. servs. & dominates town's life; workers own their homes. Nat. Steel Corp., as aggregation of Weir plants in a number of states is called, has had considerable labor trouble. When U.S. Steel ("Big Steel") met workers' demands, Little Steel held out. Long strike settled by the NLRB resulted in CIO recognition as bargaining agent. Festival of Nations (Labor Day). **35. NEW CUMBERLAND. 37.** J. with St.66 leading 1$^{m}$ to **Hartford's Mill** (1795), said to be 1st in St. to have made gunpowder. Just beyond Mill is site of **Logan Massacre** (1774) when Mingo Chief Logan's sister & others were killed. This was prelude to Lord Dunmore's War (see Ft. Henry) after which Logan sent his famous speech (see Ohio US50). At **c.40., PUGHTOWN,** J. with Rd. to **Tomlinson Run St. Pk.** (1,350 as.pic.boat.swim.f.recr.). **46.** J. with US30. [2$^{m}$ (W) on US30 is toll bridge to E. Liverpool, Ohio.]

## IV. WHEELING (S) to MOUNDSVILLE. 14. US250

**4.5. BENWOOD,** coal & steel town. In 1924 occurred terrible disaster in which 119 miners were killed by explosion. US250 passes through picturesque Narrows of the Ohio. **14. MOUNDSVILLE,** named for Grave Cr. Mound located here, one of the largest (conical) in the country (at 9th St. near Tomlinson Ave.). Tomlinson Ave., **Mun. Playground** (sm.fee.swim.sports facils.pic.); open-air arena for community sings & concerts. Fostoria Ave., **Camp Meeting Grounds** (Aug.); religious gatherings have been held here since 1787. Here US250 has J. with St.2, picturesque hy. which cont. (S) paralleling Ohio R. (see Ohio R. Tour, Ohio).

# THE LAKE STATES

## OHIO — ILLINOIS — INDIANA
## MICHIGAN — WISCONSIN — MINNESOTA

Under the Ordinance of 1787, the country around the Great Ls., north & west of the Ohio R., was organized as the Northwest Territory of the new United States; & eventually it was divided into the states of Ohio (1803), Indiana (1816), Illinois (1818), Michigan (1837), Wisconsin (1848) & Minnesota (1858). These six lake states are part of the "valley of democracy" in which the pioneers saw a chance to "better their condition" on the vast fertile prairies, & where, at first, the menace of Indian savagery & the hazards of wilderness living made for equality & close-knit human relations. The Ohio country became a testing ground for the declared ideals of the new democracy.

In the present century, the lake states are a vital part of the Middle West, the place, as John Gunther describes it, where "industry & agriculture both reach their highest American development & coalesce." Commercial & financial interests link them with the Atlantic seaboard, while for ancestry they look both South & East, a great proportion looking East beyond Ellis Island. (Henry Ford, whose impact here was immeasurable, was the son of an Irish immigrant father & a Pennsylvania Dutch mother.)

The area is a geographic unit, bordered on the north by Canada, Lake Superior & Lake Huron & separated south & west from the rest of the country by the Mississippi & Ohio rivers. Ohio is bordered on the east by West Virginia & Pennsylvania, & the Red River, for a considerable distance, separates Wisconsin from the Dakotas. In Minnesota alone there are 10,000 inland lakes, 7,000 in Wisconsin, more than 6,000 in Michigan, & each of the southerly states has its attractive lake districts. Three great river systems originate in Minnesota: the Red River, flowing north to Hudson Bay; the Minnesota & St. Croix, which join the Mississippi; & the St. Louis, a part of the St. Lawrence system by way of the Great Lakes. Illinois shares seven distinct basins, including the Lake Michigan basin, the important Inland Waterway along the Illinois, the Wabash, the Mississippi, the Ohio, the Rock & the Kaskaskia. An important factor in Michigan's great lumbering industry were its glacier-made rivers, including the famous Saginaw, shortest river in the state, with the largest basin. The Detroit, broadest Michigan river, & the St. Clair, at Port Huron, are arched by international bridges to Windsor & Sarnia, Ontario.

The altitude throughout is generally low, ranging from the lowest point at Cairo, Ill. (279′ above sea level) to the Porcupine Mountains at the west end of Michigan's Upper Peninsula (2,023′). Upper Minnesota, Wisconsin & Michigan reach altitudes between 1,600′ & 2,000′, but the southern part of these states is rolling, highly arable land suited to farms & pastures. Most of Indiana is level or gently rolling except in the south, where are the lovely Brown County hills. Ohio is more varied, with its central plain bordered on the east by the rugged foothills of the Alleghenies & on the south by fairly high & broken terrain. Illinois, preeminently the Prairie State, nevertheless has an unglaciated northwest corner & a projection of the Ozark range (reaching 1,000′) in the south.

The climate varies widely. Minnesota extends into a more northerly latitude than Maine, & Cairo, Ill., is farther south than Richmond, Va. In the main, however, the lake states have hot summers & cold winters, brief springtimes & long colorful autumns. Abundant snowfall in the north makes this excellent skiing & winter sports country, with many a snowbound village along the highways in the long winters.

The states are all fairly symmetrical in shape except Michigan, whose two peninsulars are separated by the Straits of Mackinac. The Lower Peninsula resembles a mitten with a well-defined thumb & ragged top, while the Upper has been compared to the Indians' "Great Hare" leaping the lakes. Isle Royale, in Lake Superior about 50m off the mainland of Michigan, is the largest of the lake islands. Best known among the smaller islands are those in L. Erie, including Put-in-Bay; in Lake Huron, historic Mackinac Island & the jewel-like Les Cheneaux; & in Lake Michigan, the Beaver Island archipelago.

A striking feature of this region is the distribution of population. Minnesota & Michigan have the largest primitive areas in national & state forests of any states east of the Mississippi, but wilderness gives way farther south to one of the most populous areas in the country. More than three-fifths of Ohio's population is urban. Thirteen of the fifty largest centers in the U.S. are in the lake states, including Chicago, Detroit & Cleveland. Illinois & Ohio, in state population, rank just below New York & Pennsylvania. Duluth-Superior & Toledo, the leading lakeports, are surpassed only by New York, among all U.S. ports, in amount of tonnage shipped.

In few regions has geologic history played so large a part in human affairs, & in few other places is this history so clearly visible as it is around Lake Superior. Here the untrained eye can see the progressive architecture of the earth, beginning with exposures of the granite core of the planet, inactive for more than a million years. (One such exposure is at Jasper Peak, Minn.; others occur in Michigan's Upper Peninsula & in Wisconsin.) Through eons of mountain building, volcanic action & inundation by prehistoric seas, the richest iron & copper deposits in the world were laid down around Lake Superior. Highlands of Alpine height once loomed over & around what is now the lake's basin. Molten rock was gradually erupted, & the sinking highland became a rocky bowl, to be filled later by retreating glaciers with clear icy water.

Immense ice sheets, coming late in geologic time, advanced & retreated over the lake states, forming the Great Lakes (the world's largest body of fresh water) & creating the attractive contours & thousands of inland lakes & rivers that make this region one of the great vacation areas of the country. The glaciers also were largely responsible for the dense forest coverage & fertile prairies. This combination of immense natural resources & magnificent waterways made inevitable the later history of commercial development & industrialization.

Early man found the region well suited to his needs, & scattered throughout are some of the finest existing works of the prehistoric moundbuilders. Here occur the notable effigy mounds, particularly in Wisconsin & Ohio. The finding of a fossil skeleton of a young girl (later known as "Minnesota Man") indicates even earlier occupation, perhaps some twenty thousand years ago.

In historic times, one of the largest Indian settlements in the United States area was found in the region around the "Soo" in Michigan & Canada. The white man encountered Indians on all the great waterways, & the earliest settlements were around Christian missions. Illinois, Indiana & Ohio made a thorough job of dispossession, & only in Minnesota is there now any sizable Indian group (more than 30,000). There are scattered settlements in Michigan & Wisconsin, & in the general population are many descendants of full-blooded & French-Indian ancestors.

Unless it is true that Norsemen, in 1362, left their record on the Kensington Rune Stone (see Minnesota), the first recorded white man in the region, so far as is known, was Étienne Brulé, who came to Georgian Bay on Lake Huron c.1612 & guided Le Caron, one of Champlain's four Recollet friars, into the western wilderness. In 1615 Champlain, accompanied by Brulé, looked upon Lake Huron, the "Mer Douce." Jean Nicolet, in 1634, crossed the Straits of Mackinac & entered Wisconsin country, the first European to appear in the Mississippi valley.

After him came the "coureurs de bois" to push the profitable fur trade for Louis XIV, King of France. By this time Jesuit fathers had replaced the Gray Friars who had originally invited the "Black Gowns" to share their wilderness labors. The Recollet fathers were no longer permitted at the mission in Quebec. Radisson & Groseilliers left a record (1660) of their voyage from the meeting place of three great lakes, then across Lake Superior & into Minnesota country. The Jesuits had preached to the Ojibway at the Soo in 1641, & here Père Jacques Marquette, in 1668, founded the first permanent white settlement in the Northwest.

On a fine June morning in 1671, St. Lusson, in an elaborate ceremony before assembled Indians, took formal possession of the Soo & Lakes Huron & Superior in the name of his "most redoubtable monarch." In 1671, also, Marquette established a mission at Michilimackinac (at present St. Ignace), around which developed one of the most important fur-trading posts. Two years later, Marquette, with the fur trader, Louis Joliet, explored the Mississippi to the mouth of the Arkansas River & entered the country of the agreeable Illinois Indians.

Fired by the imagination of the greatest of the French explorers, Sieur de La Salle, Louis XIV envisaged a rich empire in New France, & his Governor in Canada, Comte de Frontenac, backed La Salle's expeditions into Illinois country & down the Mississippi. Cahokia (in Illinois) was founded by French fur traders in 1699, the first permanent white settlement in the Mississippi valley. (The anniversary was celebrated there in May, 1949.) Detroit was founded by Cadillac in 1701. Soon a chain of French trading posts linked Quebec with the Great Lakes & Louisiana, named by La Salle, & around the posts the Jesuits "ruled savage hordes with a mild, parental sway" (Parkman). The French people were not eager to immigrate, the Huguenots were not permitted in New France, & the settlements consequently were never very large. The fur trade was the dominant interest, but many "ribbon" farms stretched away from the riverfronts, & life in the French villages was comfortable & gay.

In 1749 Céleron de Blainville (sometimes written Bienville) made his grandiose voyage on the Ohio River, stopping to plant a lead plate at each established landing, thus officially claiming for France the lush Ohio country. This gesture helped to precipitate the French & Indian War, an integral part of the struggle for empire waged between the British & French until 1815. By the Treaty of Paris, 1763, the French ceded New France to the British.

With the end of the French empire in America, the English colonists began to move westward toward a new frontier, although the British Government forbade private purchase of western lands & the granting of patents or warranting of surveys by the colonies. The burden of expense involved in enforcing imperial rule over this vast territory inevitably led to extra taxation & increased the tension between colonies & mother country.

The Ohio Land Company had been formed in Virginia, & at the beginning of the Revolution frontiersmen had pushed into Kentucky country. They were constantly menaced by hostile Indians, the allies of the British. George Rogers Clark's heroic & successful campaign gained the Northwest Territory for the patriots, giving the new nation a basis for claiming the area. While Washington faced the British in the East, Clark, with his Kentucky Big Knives, took the key posts of Kaskaskia & Vincennes & dreamed of an attack on Detroit. The British moved their fort at the Straits in Michigan to Mackinac Island, & even after the Treaty of Paris (1783), they held their northern posts, with the aid of Indian allies. However, in August, 1794, Gen Anthony Wayne won the Battle of Fallen Timbers (Ohio) & in 1796 raised the U.S. flag in Detroit.

The Ordinance of 1787, under which the Northwest Territory was organized, had profound & far-reaching effects. It forbade slavery & enfranchised all men who fulfilled age, residence & land-ownership requirements. The Ordinance also allowed for purchases of large tracts of land by organizations such as the new Ohio Company, founded by Rev. Manasseh Cutler & a group of Massachusetts veterans. All land grants contained the "section sixteen" allotment set aside to aid public schools. Several of the original states claimed western lands, but these claims were relinquished to the Federal Government, with certain reservations: The Virginia Military Reserve & the Connecticut Western Reserve were granted by these states to their citizens who had suffered losses during the Revolution.

The Ohio Company's first settlers, led by Gen. Rufus Putnam, finished their long journey from Ipswich, Mass., in the spring of 1788 & founded Marietta, on the Ohio River. The seat of government for the Territory was established here in 1789. The Scioto Land Company, a group from Pennsylvania & New Jersey, took up land farther west & founded Cincinnati; &, in 1796, Moses Cleaveland led his New England settlers into the Western Reserve. In 1800 the area was divided, & Vincennes became first capital of the new territory of Indiana, which was subdivided five years later into Indiana & Michigan (Lower Peninsula) territories. Land offices built of boards & canvas appeared here & there in the wilderness, but settlement was slow until after the War of 1812, which was wholeheartedly supported by the western settlers.

The frontiersmen hated the British who intrigued with the Indians against them, & they blamed British command of the seas for the economic depression that had followed the first peak of agricultural prosperity. Also in many minds was a dream of conquering Canada. Both Mackinac & Detroit fell again into the hands of the British, & the Northwest Territory was temporarily in British control. Then Oliver H. Perry won a decisive victory at Put-in-Bay, on Lake Erie, Sept. 10, 1813, Detroit was recaptured, & Wm. H. Harrison defeated the British in the Battle of the Thames, in Canada. Thereafter the scene of battle shifted from the Northwest. Peace was declared in December, 1814, & soon an army of settlers followed the trail of buffalo & deer, Indian, priest & trader into the forests & prairies.

The constitutions of the new western states were very liberal, enfranchising, in most cases, all men of proper voting age. A more liberal land policy met the demands of the West, & soon the Cumberland Road (now US40) from Maryland was literally crowded with the carts & wagons of families from the Eastern states. The Ohio River was a main artery, & thousands of southern settlers moved across it into the rich Ohio country. The era of canal building started here after the opening of New York's Erie Canal (1817-25). The West had become a major force in national politics by 1828 when Andrew Jackson, the Indian fighter & son of the frontier, was elected President by the "common man" in the East & the farmers in the West.

As highways were built & river commerce grew, many foreign born joined the westward march, moving on into Illinois & Indiana. Indian uprisings were still not infrequent, the most serious being that of Black Hawk, in Illinois, & the Sioux uprising, as late as 1862, in Minnesota. But, on the whole, growth was rapid in the southern tier. Michigan was passed over by the first wave of immigration, having been reported a morass of unhealthful swampland, but after the survey made by Gov. Lewis Cass, settlers began to come in from New England & New York.

Ahead of the settler went the railroad, the "builder of cities," as J. J. Hill, the great promoter, called the lines of steel rail vanishing into the forests. Pioneer towns grew up along the canals & at railroad junctions & the early log cabins were rapidly being replaced by houses of frame, brick & stone. The first major panic occurred in 1837, & in the depression years that followed, the pioneer sought a further frontier in the Oregon country.

The industrial revolution was already under way when Virginia-born William H. Harrison, then a resident of Ohio, became President in 1840. Harrison died when he had been in office scarcely a month, & John Tyler, an independent Democrat, succeeded to the office. Whig ascendancy was at an end, & with it a political era. In the new era the lake states, with their complementary resources in coal & iron, agricultural & forest products, & with their matchless water routes & growing network of railroads, played a large part in industrializing & urbanizing American life.

The Northwest as a whole was opposed to slavery, an increasingly urgent problem. Innumerable small towns had their Underground Railway Station for the Negro fleeing to Canada, & the abolition movement was probably stronger in this area than in any other part of the country, for both economic & humane reasons. The declining Whig party was finally destroyed, & the Democratic party split, by the anti-slavery issue. The demand for a new party dedicated to the struggle against further extension of slavery was met by the organization of the Republican party at Jackson, Mich., in July, 1854.

In October of that year, the new party won the state election in Ohio. Abraham Lincoln's challenge to the "little Giant," Stephen A. Douglas, led to the series of debates in Illinois that made Lincoln a national figure &, through Douglas' formulation of the Freeport Doctrine, created a fatal split in the Democratic party. During the Civil War, thousands from the lake states joined the Union Army, & Ohio alone furnished more than fifty high-ranking officers. Led by Clement L. Vallandigham, of Ohio, there was also bitter opposition to the war, but on the whole abolitionist & nationalist fervor swept the Northwest.

After the war began the great & reckless exploitation of natural resources. The magnificent forest coverages were rapidly plundered, particularly in Michigan & Wisconsin. Mining of iron & copper was pursued on a grand scale, & industrial development, motorized by Detroit & fed by the giant iron & steel, rubber & coal cities, overwhelmed the pioneer economy. In the heyday of prosperity, American life was dominated by powerful industrial monopolies, financial interests & railroad magnates, grown rich on huge grants of land made recklessly by the Government during the settlement of the West. Political corruption was the order of the day. An outstanding figure of the Gilded Age was Marcus A. Hanna, Cleveland capitalist & politician, who dominated American political life until his death in 1904. He was instrumental in the election of President McKinley & was the directing force in the Republican party for many years.

With industrial development the movement for organization of labor grew stronger. One of the most interesting early manifestations of the fight against monopoly was the the Granger Movement, national in scope but centered in the Middle West. It began after the Civil War, & angry farmers in local Granges discussed their grievances, particularly against railroad monopolies. So strong was the influence that many laws restricting common carriers were called Granger Laws.

The Knights of Labor, organized in 1869, reached a peak in 1886, the year in which the American Federation of Labor was organized by various craft unions. The Knights, like the modern CIO, were committed to the idea of industrial union regardless of craft. On May 4, 1886, occurred the May Day riot & bombing at Haymarket Square, in Chicago. The Knights had backed the demonstration but had no hand in the bombing, it is believed. Several leaders were arrested but later pardoned by Gov. John P. Altgeld, a great defender of civil liberties. Capitalism continued its policies of blacklisting, lockout, "yellow-dog" contracts & refusal to arbitrate. The Homestead Steel Strike in Pennsylvania, in 1892, resulted in bitter opposition to organized labor in one of the lake states' major industries for more than forty years. Following the panic of 1893, Jacob S. Coxey, of Massillon, O., led his army of jobless workers to Washington to demand work relief.

The Pullman Strike, one of the most significant in labor history, began at Pullman, Ill., May 11, 1894. The American Railway Union, which had been created by Eugene V. Debs, of Terre Haute, Ind., voted a sympathetic strike & soon twenty-seven states were involved. The Federal Government stepped in, over the protest of Gov. Altgeld, with a "blanket injunction" to break the strike. Debs & other leaders were arrested & imprisoned. For nearly a half-century afterward, organized labor fought the use of an injunction in industrial strife.

Another important labor development was the organization of the Industrial Workers of the World in Chicago, in 1905, led by Debs, Wm. D. Haywood & Daniel De Leon. In recent labor history, the chief battles of the Committee for Industrial Organization (CIO) were fought out, naturally enough, in this industrial area. The UAW is one of the world's largest unions, & John L. Lewis has a strong following in the coal-mining states.

The lake states, with the rest of the Middle West, continue to be a powerful force in politics. Ohio ranks with Virginia as the mother of Presidents, having sent seven native sons (as against Virginia's eight) to the White House, & an eighth, Wm. H. Harrison, who, though born in Virginia, was a resident of Ohio. In general the shift from liberal to conservative has been a steady one, but this is a deceptive generalization, as extremes meet in the Middle West. Eugene Debs was as typical of Indiana as was D. C. Stephenson, organizer for the Ku Klux Klan. Wisconsin's political history is unique in its fifty-year development of the "Wisconsin Idea," begun by Rbt. Marion La Follette in 1890. Backed by a strong Socialist vote in Milwaukee, many liberal reforms were inaugurated, including regulation of railroads, direct primaries, unemployment compensation & direct election of Senators.

Today all six states rank high in industry & agriculture. Ohio ranks third industrially in the nation, while Michigan is first in manufacture of automobiles & parts, chemicals & pharmaceuticals & various other products. Illinois is third in all manufactured goods. Indiana also takes high place, & Wisconsin is the leader in cheese, milk & malt products & second in construction machinery. Minnesota's industry is based on argriculture, with Minneapolis second only to Buffalo as a flour-milling center. In Ohio, 82 per cent of the area is farm land, in Wisconsin 60 per cent, the latter state pasturing more dairy cows than any other state. Minnesota shares the Red River valley wheat area, & Michigan ranks second in beans, plums & cherries. In mining, one of the great sources of wealth, Minnesota produces about 60 per cent of all iron ore mined in the United States, & Michigan ranks second, Wisconsin fourth. Michigan's noted Keweenaw Peninsula mines give it fourth rank in copper, while Iillinois, Ohio & Indiana are all great soft-coal producers. Indiana limestone & sandstone from Ohio are used throughout the country.

Forest products are still important, especially in Minnesota & in Wisconsin, which produces a large proportion of the country's fur pelts, but the most important use of the forest areas is recreational. Sports & recreation create a billion-dollar industry in the lake states, all of which have well-developed state-park systems. Millions of acres in Minnesota, Michigan & Wisconsin are in national & state forests, most of them fronting on the Great Lakes & including myriads of small lakes & fishing streams. Michigan has the greatest inland fisheries in the world. In the wake of the vacationer & the automobile, miles of splendid highways have unrolled, with resorts of all kinds along the routes. The dunelands on Lake Michigan are remarkably beautiful, with flowers & other vegetation of more than a thousand species, incl. desert & arctic.

The tradition of tolerance in religion is still strong in the Old Northwest. Ohio is noted for the number of religious, socialistic & Utopian communities established there, & the other states are not far behind. It is said that Indiana now has more Quakers than Pennsylvania. On the other hand, racial prejudice has broken forth in the metropolitan centers with great & destructive violence, & for many years the Ku Klux Klan dominated Indiana politics. As in the rest of the country, the two world wars brought industrial achievement & labor organization to a peak &, at the same time, let loose a wave of destructive passions & prejudices. A large proportion of the population in these states is foreign-born or descended from the foreign born, & the Negro population has grown too rapidly for easy adjustment.

The Ordinance of 1787 specified that "Religion, morality & knowledge being necessary to good government & the happiness of Mankind, schools & the means of education shall forever be encouraged," & cultural facilities were developed from the start. Ohio is second only to Pennsylvania in the number of its colleges, & among the several large state universities are some of the leading institutions in the nation. Not only do Chicago, Toledo & other cities have great municipal universities, but there are hundreds of fine church-sponsored colleges. Among smaller schools are such individual colleges as Kenyon & Antioch, in Ohio. Chicago is planning an immense Art Center on the lakefront where final & specialized training in all the arts will be given, the training usually sought in the East. The larger cities have ranking symphony orchestras, art museums & little theater groups. In the last-named, Cleveland has long been outstanding. The Middle West is one of the most advanced regions in adult education, vocational training, public library administration & in work with special groups of children.

In architecture, the lake states have made creative contributions of a high order through the work of Daniel Burnham, Louis Sullivan, Frank Lloyd Wright, Albert Kahn & Eliel Saarinen, the Finnish architect now at Cranbrook Academy of Art, near Detroit. The influence of the structural engineer is increasingly apparent in all types of building. Cleveland's Lakefront Mall with fine civic buildings is a model of gracious planning, & St. Paul's City Hall & Plaza are notable. The array of power plants, factory buildings, foundries, docks & railroad trackage, characteristic of all the industrial centers, are the inspiration of much modern painting & sculpture.

Artistic development at first was a by-product of pioneer life. Painting of furniture, tavern signs, cigar-store Indians & figureheads for boats & barges gave the early artists an excuse for invention. In some sections pottery, weaving & other folk arts flourished, especially with increased European immigration. Portraitists & landscape painters were in greater demand as the region prospered. One of the most successful nineteenth-century painters was George Catlin, who traveled over the Midwest for his gallery of Indian types. An unusual art product was the elaborate panorama, usually a battle scene, done by German-trained painters in Milwaukee in the 1880's. Another important nineteenth-century artist was Thos. Cole, of Ohio, who taught himself to paint the hills & river near his home & became one of the founders of the Hudson River School.

Among other better-known Ohio painters are John Twachtman, Frank Duveneck, George Bellows, Rbt. Henri & Chas. Burchfield.

The Hoosier School in Indiana was developed under J. Otis Adams, John E. Bundy & other local artists. Within the present century several Michigan artists have gained national recognition, including Gari Melchers, Zoltan Sepeshy (Carnegie prize winner in 1947), & Sarkis Sarkisien. John Steuart Curry, of Wisconsin, is ranked among the fine regional artists. In sculpture Carl Milles, the Swedish artist at Cranbrook, Mich., is outstanding, while during the first quarter of the century, one of the most popular sculptors was Lorado Taft, of Illinois. Characteristic of the area is the impulse toward art education provided by splendid art galleries & centers, such as those in Toledo, Chicago, Cleveland & Detroit, where may be seen the Rivera murals on Detroit industry.

In music, the outstanding creative contribution is Chicago jazz, but the Old Northwest had music from the beginning, especially the song & ballad. In the Gardner Chickering collection, "Ballads & Songs of Southern Michigan" (1939), tribute is paid to the inestimable service of the lumber camps "in preserving & distributing all manner of folk music. . . ." Singing societies were among the first cultural organizations, & the country dance was a musical occasion. The tradition lives in famous choral organizations, such as the choir of the College of St. Olaf in Northfield, Minn., & the Westminster (Presb.) Choir in Dayton, Ohio.

The greatest transforming influence from folk to formal music was the coming of thousands of European immigrants, particularly Germans (with their "Saengerbund" & "Maennerchor") & the music-loving Italians. The many Negro people in all the states form a strong element in revival of the Spiritual, in jazz & in leading orchestral & choral groups. Theodore Thomas, who came from Germany as a child, is the great name in orchestral development in the Middle West. In 1859, he toured the region with an operatic company &, on the night of the fire of 1871, he conducted an orchestral concert in Chicago, where he organized the Chicago Orchestra twenty years later.

The earliest writings in the region were the "Journals" of Father Marquette & the "Jesuit Relations," a priceless record of New France written in squalid Indian camps, based in part on tales told by the "coureurs de bois." Other early works too seldom read are Black Hawk's "Autobiography" & George Rogers Clark's account of his expedition, included in M.M. Quaife's "The Capture of Old Vincennes." In recent times Quaife, Walter Havighurst, Harlan Hatcher & other Midwestern writers have contributed eloquently to the epic of the Great Lakes. While not strictly creative literature, the writings of Abraham Lincoln, Carl Schurz, John Muir & Thorstein Veblen should be noted.

The lake states have produced a large number of the country's popular fiction writers, including George Barr McCutcheon of Graustark fame; Zane Grey, Jas. O. Curwood, Lew Wallace, Augusta Evans Wilson, Rex Beach, Stewart Edward White, Edna Ferber, Booth Tarkington, Louis Bromfield & Wm. Sydney Porter (O. Henry).

The most significant figure, perhaps, is Theodore Dreiser, who was rooted in the region & wrote honestly & powerfully about it. Other great regional writers are Sinclair Lewis, winner of the Nobel Prize, James T. Farrell & Richard Wright. Earlier than these were Indiana's Edward Eggleston, one of the first realists of the frontier; Hamlin Garland, who struck a new note in American literature with his simple statements about "Main Travelled Roads"; Frank Norris, who portrayed the Chicago wheat exchange in "The Pit"; & Wm. Dean Howells, friend of Garland & critic of the frontier. Of a different order were Ring Lardner & George Ade, acute observers of the world around them. Of more recent writers, the late F. Scott Fitzgerald probably had the strongest talent & a genuine message, & Sherwood Anderson has been a potent influence on younger writers.

Chicago was the focus of the literary renascence that followed the establishment there of the magazine "Poetry" by Harriet Monroe, in 1912. Local poets associated with the movement were Carl Sandburg, great interpreter of Lincoln, Edgar Lee Masters & Vachel Lindsay, all of whose work stemmed directly from their native prairie. Other nationally known poets of the region are Paul Laurence Dunbar, Wm. Vaughn Moody, Jas. Whitcomb Riley, the Hoosier poet, Paul Engle & Hart Crane, who carried from his native Ohio a strong consciousness of his American background & faith in democracy.

# LAKE STATES 1

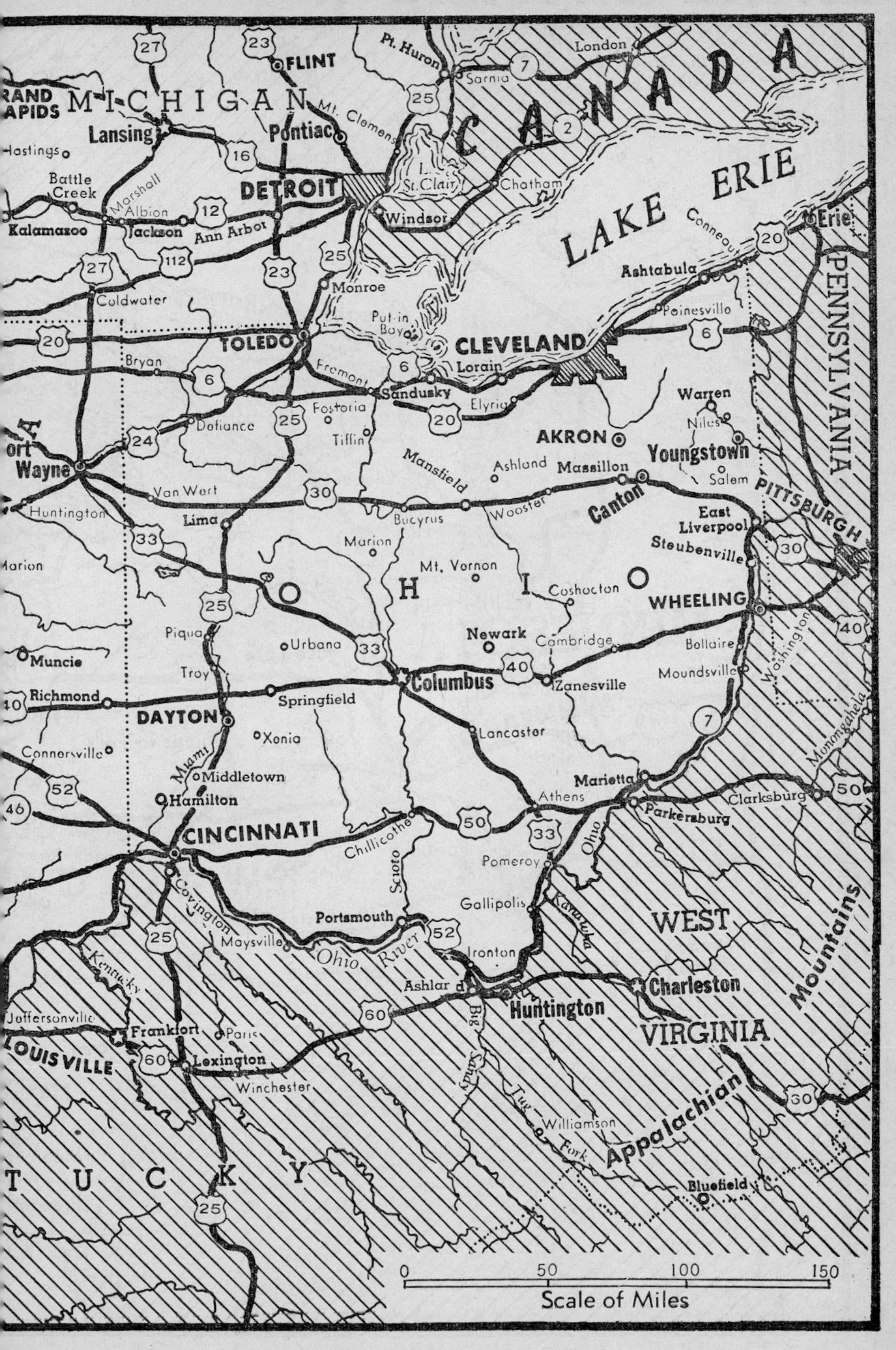

MICHIGAN
CANADA
LAKE ERIE
OHIO
PENNSYLVANIA
WEST VIRGINIA
Appalachian Mountains
FLINT
Lansing
Pontiac
DETROIT
TOLEDO
CLEVELAND
AKRON
Youngstown
Canton
PITTSBURGH
WHEELING
Columbus
DAYTON
CINCINNATI
LOUISVILLE
Lexington
Frankfort
Huntington
Charleston
Fort Wayne
Ohio River
Scale of Miles
0
50
100
150

# LAKE STATES II

Scale of Miles
0 50 100 150 200
LAKE SUPERIOR
Isle Royale
Port Arthur
Copper Harbor
Hancock
Huron Mts.
Marquette
Ishpeming
Munising
Sault Ste Marie
Blind River
North Chan.
St. Ignace
Str. of Mackinac
Manistique
Iron River
Iron Mountain
Eagle River
Rhinelander
Antigo
Menominee
Marinette
Shawano
Escanaba
Green Bay
Sturgeon Bay
Two Rivers
Manitowoc
Appleton
Oshkosh
Fond du Lac
Sheboygan
Beaver Dam
Watertown
Waukesha
MILWAUKEE
Racine
Kenosha
Waukegan
Highland Pk.
Evanston
CHICAGO
Beloit
Rockford
INOIS
LAKE MICHIGAN
Grand Traverse Bay
Petoskey
Cheboygan
Alpena
Gaylord
Traverse City
Tawas City
LAKE HURON
Saginaw Bay
Port Austin
Harbor Beach
Ludington
Midland
Mt. Pleasant
Bay City
Saginaw
Alma
Muskegon
Grand Rapids
Flint
Pt. Huron
Pontiac
Ann Arbor
Lansing
Holland
DETROIT
Windsor
Kalamazoo
Jackson
Benton Harbor
Niles
Coldwater
Toledo
L. ERIE
INDIANA
OHIO
CANADA
MICHIGAN
WISCONSIN

# OHIO RIVER TOUR—OHIO

**OHIO-PA. LINE** (at E. Liverpool, Ohio) **(S) & (W) to OHIO-IND. LINE.** (10$^{m}$ from Cedar Grove, Ind.). **426. St.7, US52.** (See also Ind. & Ky.).

Via: Steubenville, Martins Ferry, Powhatan Point, Marietta, Belpre, Pomeroy, Gallipolis, Ironton, Portsmouth, Aberdeen, Point Pleasant, Cincinnati, Harrison.

Tour follows route that Céleron de Blainville took by water in June, 1749, in what Ohio's Harlan Hatcher calls "most diverting episode in the bloody realism of all our early Ohio history." With 250 men in birchbark canoes, Céleron made his "courtly gesture," burying, with fanfare, a small lead plate at mouth of each important creek or river, thus renewing Louis XIV's possession of the wilderness. Shortly afterward (1750-51), Christopher Gist made a similar journey, but overland, for Ohio Land Co. It is possible La Salle saw "La Belle Riviére" in 1669. Inds., traders, trappers & missionaries floated down the broad, winding stream. For 50 yrs. it carried cargo & settlers in flatboats & broadhorn three-masters & keelboats, until, in 1811, the sky-blue "New Orleans" steamed up to the Cincinnati Landing, 1st steamboat on any Amer. inland waterway. Then came the "Comet," the "Vesuvius," & the famous double-decked "Washington." By 1830, promenade decks were spacious, & the cabins, halls & saloons were luxurious. The wealthy passengers enjoyed elegant barrooms & gaming cabins or danced to orchestral music. Besides the colorful passenger packets, there were floating libraries & stores & elaborate showboats. Hundreds of packets wore out, sank, blew up, or were burned in a single year. Their bells may be heard today in rivertown schools & churches. The big ships carried big cargoes, & roustabouts & crew were a lusty tribe, hard-working & fearless; singing & brawling in port towns at the end of day. Mike Fink, "Paul Bunyan of the Ohio country," was greatest of early boatmen. The Ohio was also a military road from the beginning of the white man's time.

Often the river has risen in fury & devastated the cities it fostered—1832, 1857, 1883, 1884, 1890, 1913, 1936, 1937. Over & over the cities have buried their dead & rebuilt their waterfronts. At last the great Muskingum & Miami Conservancy Dam projects were created. Today, with its many bridges, locks & dams, the R. meanders placidly through miles of "sweet scenery" (Mrs. Trollope, 1832), carrying more tonnage than ever before on spreading shoals of barges. The beauty of river & shore is unchanged, & beyond rise the ranging, forested hills.

## Sec. 1: PA. LINE to MARIETTA. 131. St.7

**0. EAST LIVERPOOL,** noted for pottery & porcelain. **4. WELLSVILLE,** small brick & pottery center. **8. YELLOW CREEK,** where Logan, the Mingo chief, had his home. Across R. is spot where members of his family were massacred in 1774. On both sides of R., the steel empire extends for many miles. Slag piles stretch along the hys., & rows of workers' houses crowd the towns. At night the sky is immensely beautiful with flares outlining a jumble of smokestacks, furnaces, bridges, rolling mills & loading docks.

**25. STEUBENVILLE**

Through RR. & bus conns. Good accoms. Market St. Bridge & Ft. Steuben Bridge to Weirton, W. Va.

This steel & coal-mining center, also known for pottery & glass, claims to be pioneer city of Ohio valley because a little settlement, La Belle, probably survived burning of Ft. Steuben in 1790. The fort, named for Prussian officer who aided Washington, was erected in 1786, thus antedating Marietta (see below). PTS. OF INT.: High & Adams Sts., **Site of Ft. Steuben.** 524 Market St., **Birthpl. of E. M. Stanton.** 301 Market St., **Jefferson County Cth.** (1871) & **Edwin M. Stanton Mon. Industrial Plants** (O.appl.) incl. Wheeling Steel Corp., Weirton Steel Co., Steubenville Coal & Mining Co. (1856), Steubenville Pottery, & Ohio Valley Clay Co.

**48. MARTINS FERRY,** where steel & coal meet to make an industrial town on site of 1st permanent settlement in Ohio (before 1785), on Ind. land. In Walnut Grove Cemetery, **Betty Zane Mon.,** comm. heroine of Ft. Henry (see); & **Tomb of Ebenezer Zane. 50. BRIDGEPORT,** platted by Zane in 1806. US250 & US40 (Zane's Trace & Nat. Rd.) enter here from W. Va.

**131. MARIETTA**

R. Stas. on 2nd St. for B. & O. & Pa. Bus Terminal in Postal Telegraph Office, 2nd St. Airport: (E) 2$^{m}$ on US50. Good accoms. & recr. facils.

Marietta is an enchanting city at meeting of Muskingum & Ohio Rs. Shady streets climb the hills & graceful bridges conn. E. & W. Marietta & carry US21 over the Ohio to Parkersburg, W. Va. Modern Marietta, seat of Marietta College, is the prosperous, but still peaceful, shipping pt. & trade center for large farm area; with various industries based on oil, sandstone & other natural resources. The 1st organized town in N.W. Terr. was started Ap. 7, 1788, when Gen. Rufus Putnam & 48 pioneers landed the "Union Galley" below Ft. Harmar & were towed up the Muskingum. During N.W. Terr. Celebration, 150 yrs. later, the long journey from Ipswich, Mass., was re-enacted by 48 men, who traveled with ox-teams & Conestoga wagons to Yougiogheny R. in Pa.; then in flatboats down the Ohio to Marietta, arriving Ap. 7, 1938. The colony, named after Marie Antoinette, was successful from the start. From this port were launched hundreds of sailing vessels & steamboats, incl. the "John Farnum," which carried corn to starving Ireland in 1847. In 1940's the shipyards turned out landing craft. From the days of the Coonskin Lib. (in St. Hist. Mus., Columbus), paid for with pelts in 1804, Marietta has been a center of cultural life.

PTS. OF INT.: (1) **Landing Place** of Putnam's party. (2) In Muskingum Pk., **"Start Westward" Mem.** (1938.Borglum), on spot where Gen. St. Clair inaugurated Terr. gov. (3) 326 Front St., **Meigs H.** (1803.remod.), home of Return Jonathan Meigs, 4th Ohio Gov. (4) Cor. Washington & 2nd Sts., **Campus Martius Mem. Mus.** (O), incl. **Rufus Putnam H.** (rest.). **River Mus.** (1941). (5) Warren St., **Moundbuilders' "Sacra Via"** from temple square, on 5th St., to Muskingum R. (6) 5th & Scammel Sts., **Mound Cemetery** (1788), enclosing Conus Mound (30'). (7) Putnam & 4th Sts., **Marietta College**, high-ranking coed. college, chartered in 1835 but developed from Muskingum Academy (1797); **Lib.** has Stimson Americana & Slack Hist. Colls. (8) At Muskingum R. mouth, **French Mon.**, gift of France (1938).

### Sec. 2: MARIETTA to CHESAPEAKE. 110. St.7

St.7 travels a narrowing valley on Ohio side. **13. BELPRE** (see US50). Along curving shores on both sides are favorite stopping-places for shanty-boaters. For hundreds of miles, these ark-like boats drift on the slow-flowing river, getting fuel & food from the banks.

Near Belpre (S) is **Capt. Jonathan Stone H.** (1799). **14.5. ROCKLAND CH.** J. with dirt Rd. leading to Rockland Cemetery from which may be seen **Blennerhassett I.** Harman Blennerhassett, Irish aristocrat, eloped from Isle of Man with his niece, Margaret Agnew &, to escape social ostracism, came to New York &, in 1797, to Marietta. Ohio society was delighted by the beautiful & talented Margaret & her scholarly husband, who bought the willow-fringed isle & created a "terrestrial paradise" around his gleaming white mansion. In 1805, Aaron Burr visited here & interested the imaginative Irishman in his Western empire. Blennerhassett mortgaged his home & resources & began to build a fleet of boats on Muskingum R. When Pres. Jefferson proclaimed Burr's enterprise unlawful, Blennerhassett escaped to a rendezvous with Burr at mouth of Cumberland R. & was joined later by his family. He was caught & taken to Richmond for trial but, after Burr's acquittal, released. Meanwhile, militiamen had ravaged the house & grounds. Floods swept over it the next spring &, in 1811, the ruins burned to the ground. Blennerhassett died on Isle of Guernsey in 1831. Margaret came to America to plead with Congress for an indemnity. She died in poverty, at 75 Greenwich St., N.Y., in 1842. **21. LITTLE HOCKING.** Just (S) is J. with St.124.

SIDE TRIP: Loop tour of Meigs Cty. Peninsula. 56. St.124, St.338. This beautiful route must be driven carefully, as landslides from eroded cliffs sometimes clutter Rd. From steep bluffs may be seen broad bends of the river, bright pastures & cultivated fields against backdrop of hills. Several river dams are along the way. 5m **Hockingport,** on **Site of Ft. Gower** (1779), from which Dunsmore departed for Pickaway Plains. 17.5m **Site of Washington's Camp,** 1770. Gen. Washington later gained title to thousands of as. 21.5m near Portland, **Buffington I. Mem. St. Pk.** (facils.). Here Morgan, Confed. raider, attempted to cross R. with 2,500 men. Nearly surrounded by soldiers & gunboats, Morgan & half his forces escaped. 25m J. with St.338, on which river trip cont. past small villages. 45m **Racine.** (N) here on St.124 again to **Pomeroy,** 56m, J. with US33 (see) & St.7, the main tour.

St.7 runs inland through highland country & across Hocking R. **41. CHESTER.** On hilltop is **Old Meigs County Cth. 50. POMEROY,** in center of mining area circling great Pomeroy Bend. Floods have battered the long water front, but newer Pomeroy is rising on the slopes. **52. MIDDLEPORT.** Drowned by 1937 flood, the town moved back among the hills. **66. KANAUGA.** Here the Gt. Kanawha R. pours into the Ohio. Silver Bridge to **PT. PLEASANT,** W. Va. (see). J. with US35 (from Charleston, W. Va.). **70. GALLIPOLIS,** 3rd oldest Ohio settlement, named by "French Five Hundred" in 1790; boyhood home of late O. O. McIntyre & birthpl. of his wife. Late in 1788, Joel Barlow & Wm. Playfair, agents of Scioto Land Co., went to Paris brandishing a map & description of a perfect land. After fall of Bastille, it was easy to sell 150,000 as. in a country where, they said, candles & custard grew on trees, 80-lb. catfish swam the rivers; cotton, tobacco & wheat produced abundant crops, while hogs fattened on wilderness pastures. A group of 500 Parisian hairdressers, craftsmen, jewellers, gourmets, gilders, watch & carriage-makers arrived at Alexandria, Va., in May, 1790. Their tract proved to be on Ohio Land Co.'s lands, but Scioto Land Co. brought them down the Ohio. A town of 80 cabins, with slight protection against Inds., had been prepared by Rufus Putnam, of Ohio Land Co. Here the French were abandoned to their fate, & Scioto Co. went into bankruptcy. The bitter winters annihilated large numbers through hunger, massacre, exposure & cholera. In 1795, the Gov. set aside the Fr. Grant in Scioto Cty. for a few survivors. Gallipolis became important river town after settlement by Virginians & New Englanders.

PTS. OF INT.: 431 1st Ave., **"Le Magasin d'Habecourt"** (N.O.1794), by 1st postmaster, a friend of Napoleon; **French Garden** (O). 434 1st Ave., **Our House** (O.1819. sm.fee.restaurant), famous hostelry; period furnishings; **Mus.** 74 Court St., **O. O. McIntyre's H.** 76 State St., **Gatewood,** Mrs. O. O. McIntyre's H. (O.appl.remod.). **81. CHAMBERSBURG.** U.S. Gov. Locks & Dam (1938); largest roller-type dam in world. **105.5. PROCTORVILLE,** where Rome Beauty apple was grown in 1816. **110. CHESAPEAKE.** J. with US52, on which tour cont.

### Sec. 3: CHESAPEAKE to IND. LINE. 185. US52

US52 runs (W) through orchards & wastelands, rocky hills & fertile bottoms. **5.5. BURLINGTON,** founded in 1817 by Rev. Plymdale (Bapt.) for his freed slaves. **8. SOUTH POINT,** at W. Va.-Ky. Line. Here US52 traverses industrial reg. that extends into 3 states (numerous bridges). **19. IRONTON,** founded by ironmaster, John Campbell, in 1848, was important iron town until Youngstown reg. developed. (N) $8^m$ is **Vesuvius Recr. Area** (camp.boat.swim.f.h.), a unit of Wayne Nat. For. (see). **48.5. PORTSMOUTH,** once a canal port, iron & RR. center, now makes shoes, stoves & other products. In Mound Pk. is prehist. **Horseshoe Mound.** US52 crosses Scioto R. & runs along high ground away from flood plain. **50.** J. with St.73.

SIDE TRIP: St.73 (N) $2^m$ to **Tremper Mound.** At $12^m$ is J. with St.371 to **Shawnee St. For.** (f.camp.facils.), densely forested tract of 37,000 as.

**56. FRIENDSHIP.** J. with St.125, which leads (NW) $4^m$ to Roosevelt Game Preserve & **Roosevelt L. Pk.** (f.hunt.boat.camp.facils.). **91. MANCHESTER,** Ohio's 4th oldest town, founded in 1791 by Nath. Massie. **111. RIPLEY,** another contented river town until 1937 flood washed away its attractive riverfront. **RANKIN H.** (sm.fee), said to have sheltered Eliza after her flight across the ice. **141. MOSCOW,** one of 1st Underground Railroad Stas. **144.** US52 passes **Gen. Grant's Birthpl. 165. CINCINNATI** (see). **185. HARRISON,** at Ohio-Ind. Line.

## US 6—OHIO

**PA. LINE** ($13^m$ from Conneaut Lake, Pa.) **(W) to IND. LINE** ($3.5^m$ from Butler, Ind.). **249. US6**

Via: Andover, Chardon, Cleveland, Lorain, Sandusky, Fremont, Bowling Green, Napoleon, Bryan. Good accoms. RR. bus & airline conns., pic., camp sites & resorts along route.

### Sec. 1: PA. LINE to SANDUSKY. 131.

**3.** Hy. turns (S) with St.7 to **10. ANDOVER,** tourist & trade center.

SIDE TRIPS: (A) On St.85 (E) $2^m$ to **Pymatuning Reservoir** (f.h.boat.winter sports.pic. camp.trlrs.); U-shaped 18,000-a. lake, created by inundating immense marshland, stretching for miles along state line, larger part in Pa. (see).

(B) On St.7 (S) $11^m$ to **Kinsman** (1799); birthpl. of Clarence Darrow. N. of Pub. Sq., **Darrow Octagon H.,** birthpl. of noted criminal lawyer, advocate of civil liberty.

**27.** Softly rolling country is cut by Grand R., which winds (N) to lake. **34. MONTVILLE. 44. CHARDON,** maple-sugar center. This is ideal farm country. **62. EUCLID. 72. CLEVELAND** (see). **85. BAY VILLAGE.** Huntington Pk. (bathh.). At 27715 Lake Rd., **Cahoon H.** (O.1816); early furniture. **90.5. AVON L.** stretches along shore for miles, & hy. follows sometimes serene, often furious, Erie waters.

**100. LORAIN,** on Black R. Harbor, one of best on Gt. Ls. R. is deep enough to float the big steamers that have come down the ways since 1893 from shipbuilding plant on E. bank. Lorain is industrial home-owned city, with good schools, playgrounds, beaches & pks. After tornado in 1924, which brought death to 70 persons & caused $25,000,000 damage, ruined city was rebuilt & replanted; thousands of lilacs, flower of French Lorraine, now fill air with fragrance during Lilac Festival (May). Settlement made by Moravians in 1787 was soon discouraged by Delaware Inds. A trading post was est. in 1807, & shipbuilding began in 1819. Lorain promised to become a metropolis, with natural harbor & possibility of RR. & canal, but canal went to Cleveland & RR. to Elyria. A second boom came late in cent. with est. of U.S.Steel Plant in S. Lorain.

PTS. OF INT.: (1) **Lorain Light** (reached by boat). (2) **Lake View Pk.;** playgrounds, beaches & notable rose gardens. (3) **Nat. Tube Co. Plant,** largest in world. (4) **Amer. Shipbuilding Plant.** (5) **Thew Shovel Co. Plant.** (6) Large commercial **fisheries.** J. with St.58 (which leads (S) 3.5$^{m}$ to J. with Rd. to **Amherst,** in sandstone-quarry reg.).

**103.5. Ship-to-shore Radio Telephone Sta.,** a short distance off hy. The level sandy beaches reach out from wooded shoreline to shallow lake (cottages.tourist camps. amusement pks.&resort centers). Vermilion R. forks on L. in series of lagoons where cruisers anchor. **110. VERMILION** (sett.1808), resort town & fishing center (camps. cottages.beaches) on red-clay soil that once made ceremonial paint for the Ottawa.

**121. HURON,** on Huron R., was important wheat-shipping point in early 19th cent. In 1878, Wheeling & L. Erie RR. Docks gave town new life; one of largest electrically operated coal dumpers on the Ls.

SIDE TRIP: (S) 6$^{m}$ on St.299 to **Milan,** birthpl. of Thos. A. Edison. Was prosperous shipping center until RR. era put end to its hopes. Around village square are houses with handsome porticos & doorways, built in 1820's. Cor. Central & Front Sts. is 2-story, red-brick house where Edison lived until he was 7.

**129. CEDAR PT. CHAUSSÉE** (sm.fee), leading (N) up narrow peninsula to **Cedar Point** (see below), summer resort since 1882 (steamer, RR. or ferry from Sandusky).

**131. SANDUSKY**

Through RR. & bus serv. Good accoms. Many pks. & sports facils. Info.: C. of C., Hotel Rieger Bldg.

Sandusky, at mouth of Sandusky Bay, is one of loveliest of Ohio cities. Bay is almost completely enclosed bet. mainland & Marblehead Peninsula, conn. by Sandusky Bay Bridge. On L. Erie's most spacious harbor, the port ranks among 10 largest on Gt. Ls. & is 2nd largest shipper of coal. Mechanical loaders are busy night & day pouring millions of tons into holds of lake steamers. Excursion boats puff out from the piers to Cedar Pt. & island resorts. E. of piers are markets & wineries that make Sandusky an outstanding fresh-water fish. & wine center. Ivy-colored, blue-limestone (local) churches & houses add to city's charm. In 17th cent., Iroquoian tribes were in "San-doos-tee" (cool water) area, in which they had annihilated the Erie & Neutral nations. White settlement began after Commodore Perry's victory at Put-in-Bay (see below), & Irish & German settlers followed the founding New Englanders. In cholera epidemic, 1849, nearly 400 died. Sandusky was strategic stop on Underground Railroad.

PTS. OF INT.: **Battery Pk.** (recr.facils.). **Pa. RR. Coal Dock** (3,500′ long). **Wineries** (O.appl.): On Water St., the blue limestone bldgs. of Dorn Co. (est.1869) & Engels & Krudwig Co. 1702 Campbell St., Meier's Wine Cellars. 1422 Clinton St., M. Hommel Co. (est.1878); pleasant taproom. 301 Putnam St., Nat. Distillers Products Corp. **Fisheries:** Lay Bros., Bickley & Port & others.

TRIPS OUT OF SANDUSKY

I. Kelleys I., Middle Bass I., Gibraltar I., S. Bass I. (Put-in-Bay), N. Bass I.

Recr. facils. Accoms. on Kelleys & S. Bass Is. Neuman Boat Line makes daily trips (May 10-Labor Day).

Mapped by Fr. geographers in 17th cent., the archipelago was not sett. until 1830's. These 20 isles of dreamlike beauty were ceded to Gt. Brit. by Fr. in 1765; in 1783,

U.S. received big Kelleys I., Bass I., Gibraltar I., & 6 smaller Is. Canada owns Pelee, the largest of all, Middle I., Harbor I. & the Hen & Chicken & Sister groups. Is. are in one of finest fresh-water fishing areas in country, although pollution from industrial centers has almost destroyed herring & whitefish. In winter, whole villages of shanties in rainbow colors move from one ice sheet to another, as men, women & children join in ice fishing.

Steamer passes close to **Cedar Point** with its luxurious Breakers Hotel (beaches. dance terraces.amusement & pic.grounds); then moves (N) some distance offshore from rugged Marblehead Peninsula to **Kelleys I.,** 9$^{m}$. Datus & Irad Kelley, in 1830's, bought the I. & started settlement. Quarrying limestone & cutting the red cedar were chief industries. In 1851 the Kelleys built 1st wine cellar on western L. Erie. **Glacial Grooves** in St. Pk. (N) 1.5$^{m}$ from dock; smoothly polished fluting in limestone. **Inscription Rock,** on (S) shore, bears petroglyphs probably made by artist of lost Erie tribe.

Steamer passes Ballast I. (NW) 10$^{m}$ from Kelleys I., to **Bass I.,** where pickerel, perch, carp, sheepshead & sauger far outnumber once plentiful bass & herring. **Middle Bass I.** (f.boat.recr.facils.) is given over to vineyards. **Lonz Winery** (1884); lovely clubh.

**South Bass I.** (Put-in-Bay), is very popular resort (boats from Ohio cities & Detroit; auto ferry to Marblehead.all kinds of accoms.& recr.facils.planes & boats). Interlake Yacht Regatta (Aug.). It is also a wine island. In harbor is **Gibraltar I.,** Jay Cooke's summer home from 1865 to 1905. Ohio St. Univ. acquired the rocky islet in 1925. **F. T. Stone Laboratory** (O.appl.) for study of fishery problems. At (E) end are **Jay Cooke Mansion,** now dormitory, & **Site of Perry's Lookout.** On South Bass I. is Internat. Peace Mem. Mon., incl. **Perry Mem.,** comm. victory in Battle of L. Erie, Sept. 9, 1813. This massive, fluted Doric column of Milford granite (352′) was erected by 9 states & Fed. Gov. (1912-15). Above observ. platform is penthouse with navigation lights &, still higher, a lighted bronze urn. Beneath rotunda are buried 3 Amer. & 3 Brit. officers. Perry, Mammoth & Crystal **Caves. North Bass I.,** not a steamer stop, may be reached by speedboat from Put-in-Bay; vineyard area since 1853.

II. Loop Tour of Marblehead Peninsula. 30. St.2, Bay Shore Rd., St.163, St.2.

Via: Danbury, Johnson's I., Marblehead, Lakeside, Catawba I., Port Clinton. RR. & bus. Resorts; all kinds of accoms.; churches.

This vacationland is also famous peach-raising country. St.2 crosses Sandusky Bay Bridge to J. with Bay Shore Rd. At 6$^{m}$ **Wilson Boat Landing** (f.boats). From here trips are made to 300-a. **Johnson's I.** (O), Civil War prison camp, where 10,000 Confed. officers were confined. In **Confed. Cemetery** are 206 marked graves (numbered list at Sandusky C. of C.). Bay Shore Rd. parallels rim of peninsula to **Marblehead,** 9.5$^{m}$, resort & quarrying center. **Marblehead Light** (O.1-3) is one of oldest in Ohio (1821) & one of most graceful on Ls. Tour cont. (W) on St.163. 10.5$^{m}$ **Lakeside,** "Chautauqua of the Great Lakes" (hotel & cafeteria.sm.fee for camp.). 16.5$^{m}$ J. with St.53 (E.Rd.& W.Rd.), which loops around beautiful Catawba Peninsula orchards. Return may be made on St.2.

## Sec. 2: SANDUSKY to IND. LINE. 118.

**0. SANDUSKY. 3.5. VENICE,** resort. **Mill** (1833) still in operation. **6. J.** with St.269.

SIDE TRIP: (S) 2.5$^{m}$ on St.269 is mysterious **Castalia Blue Hole** (sm.fee), named for Apollonian spring in Greece. Looking into crystal-clear pool, one sees pictures of castled cities & shining mts. Fish cannot live in the oxygenless water.

**24. FREMONT,** site of Ft. Stephenson & home of Pres. Hayes. **J.** with US20 (see). In rolling countryside (W) are hundreds of derricks raised in 1890's when oil gushed from Kirkbride & other wells. Lime-making is important industry. **54. BOWLING GREEN,** seat of Wood Cty., leading cattle & tomato-producing area. Big oil wells in late 19th cent. brought glass & other factories, & ornate Vict. mansions rose. After wells ceased to flow, town became rural center. Then, in 1914, H. J. Heinz Co. built large plant here, & **Bowling Green St. Univ.** was est. (1916). Notable **Lib.** (1927), **Airport, Arboretum.** J. with US25-US68 (see US25). **79. NAPOLEON. J.** with US24.

SIDE TRIP: (SW) along US24, the old canal follows Maumee R. At 4$^{m}$, **Girty's I.,** where Simon Girty, scout for Brit., visited his brother's post. The winter before Battle of Fallen

Timbers, Girty traveled among Ind. villages on the Maumee, planning their strategy. 14m **Independence St. Pk.** (facils.camp.f.swim.). 18m **Defiance. Ft. Defiance Mon.** on site of Fortress built in 1794 as challenge to "hostile Inds. of the West." Chief Pontiac's birthpl. is believed to be on opp. bank. **Defiance College** (Congr.) erected 1st bldg. in 1884-85; includes Christian Divinity School.

Beyond Napoleon, US6 crosses monotonous country, once part of great Black Swamp. **103. BRYAN,** last Ohio town of any size on route. **118. IND. LINE.**

## US 20—OHIO

**OHIO-PENN. LINE** (28m from Erie, Penn.) **(W) to OHIO-IND. LINE** (10m from South Bend). **257. US20**

Via: Conneaut, Painesville, Cleveland, Norwalk, Fremont, Perrysburg, (Toledo), Fayette. Through RR., bus & airline conns. Accoms.: Good throughout.

US20 runs inland from L. Erie along border of Western Reserve, crosses Cleveland waterfront, swerves (S) to Norwalk, then (NW) bypassing Toledo & (W) to state line.

### Sec. 1: PENN. LINE to NORWALK. 128.

**2. CONNEAUT** (sett.1796), whose natural harbor makes it 1st of series of ore ports & important station for coal & steel. Commercial fishing. At **c.7.5. Eaton H.** (O. summer.1800); beautiful Class. pillars. **15. ASHTABULA** (sett.1798), a leading ore & coal port & busy mfg. center at mouth of Ashtabula R. By 1830's it was typical village of New Englanders &, later, a favored Underground Railroad sta. A resolution in "Ashtabula Sentinel," Dec. 21, 1850, cursed Fugitive Slave Law as designed "to strip us of our humanity . . . and herd us with bloodhounds and men-stealers." **Hubbard Homestead** (O), once haven for runaway slaves; now community house. Lake Shore & Walnut Beach Pks. (good beaches).

**26. GENEVA,** sett.1805. (5m (N) on St.534 is **Geneva on the Lake,** resort). **30.** J. with Cty. Rd. to **UNIONVILLE,** where slaves found refuge in **New England H.** (O), a tavern since 1805. Throughout Western Reserve are white picket fences, taverns, churches & houses of New England origin. **42. PAINESVILLE.** In delightful **MENTOR, 49.** is **Lawnfield** (O.sm.fee.1832), rambling Vict. mansion of Pres. J. A. Garfield. **60. EUCLID.** US20 unites with US6 to become Euclid Ave. into **CLEVELAND, 71.** At **106. OBERLIN,** with noted college (see Cleveland for pts. of int. bet. Painesville & Oberlin). **128. NORWALK,** with outstanding Class. Rev. architecture. On Case & W. Main Sts., **Firelands Mus.** (O.Fri.Sat.aft.). On W. Main St. also are **Martin H.** (1831), **Fulstow H.** (1834) & **Boalt H.** (1848). At 6 S. Church St., **Stewart H.** (1833).

### Sec. 2: NORWALK to IND. LINE. 129.

For many miles, route lies among orchards, truck gardens & checkered fields of rye, corn, barley & sugar beets. **13. BELLEVUE.** Off St.18 (S) are **Seneca Caverns** (sm.fee).

SIDE TRIP: St.101 (SW) 20.5m to **Tiffin,** seat of **Heidelberg College,** founded in 1850 by Reformed Church in U. S. **Founders Hall. Kellers Cottage.**

**20. CLYDE,** said to be Sherwood Anderson's "Winesburg." Anderson, born in Camden, spent much of childhood here. **24.** J. with St.19 (5m (S) to **Green Springs,** resort). **28. FREMONT,** a good-sized city spreading out over rounded hills along Sandusky R.; canning & beet sugar center. Wyandot villages occupying site were destroyed by Brit., who set up outpost here in 1782. During War of 1812, George Croghan, 21-year-old leader of 150 Amer. soldiers, defended Ft. Stephenson against attack of 700 Inds. & Brit. by maneuvering his single cannon from place to place.

PTS. OF INT.: Birchard Lib. Pk., **Site of Ft. Stephenson.** At NW. cor. is **Grave of Maj. Croghan** & near-by is "Old Betsy," his famous cannon. J. of Hayes & Buckland Aves., **Hayes State Mem.,** incl. "Spiegel Grove," estate of Pres. Rutherford B. Hayes. **Hayes H.** (N.O.1859.Vict.Goth.). Within grounds also is **Hayes Mausoleum** (O. 1913); lib. & mus.

**57.5. PERRYSBURG,** an old & pretty town named for hero of Put-in-Bay. On Front St. are: **Sparford H.** (1822.remod.), **Lamb H.** (1830's); orig. woodwork & furnishings. **Hollister H.** (1823), once showplace of Maumee Valley. Short distance (SW), **Ft. Meigs St. Pk.** (facils.); remains of "Gibraltar of the Northwest" (1813). In Cemetery lie Amer. soldiers killed in Dudley Massacre (see Maumee below). **J.**

with US25 (see) & other main routes. Across broad Maumee R. is residential **Maumee,** on site of Fr. Can. fort (1680). In 1794, Brit. built Ft. Miami & name of city is corruption of Miami. Bronze plaque marks spot where Col. Dudley & his Kentuckians, on way to relieve Ft. Meigs, were ambushed by Brit. soldiers from Ft. Miami. E. Wayne St. & River Rd., **Hoffman's Inn** (1828). At J. Detroit Ave. & US24, **Knaggs H.** (1825), built for Gen. Wayne's interpreter.

SIDE TRIPS: (A) On US24 (SW) 3m to Fallen Timbers Mon. At 1m, in Side-Cut Pk., are limestone walls & weatherbeaten locks of Miami & Erie Canal, begun in 1825. At c.3m, **Fallen Timbers St. Mon.** (facils.), where "Mad" Anthony Wayne defeated (1794) Miami, Shawnee, & other Ind. allies of Brit. The Inds., led by 70 Canadian rangers, had entrenched themselves behind great trees uprooted by hurricane. Battle was decisive in struggle for control of Northwest. US24 rises to bluffs along R. Near J. with Farnsworth Rd. is **Columbia H.** (O.1818), antique shop. Beyond are **Indianola I.,** resort (camp.), & along canal, **Thurston St. Pk.** (bath.camp.shelterh.).
(B) US24 (N) to Toledo, 10m.

## TOLEDO

Union (RR.) Depot, foot of Knapp St.; Penn. RR., 1220 Summit St. 420 Jefferson Ave., Greyhound Bus Depot. Hanley & Moline Rds. (SE) 7m, Mun. Airport. Foot of Madison Ave. for Gt. Ls. steamers. Good accoms. Ft. Miami Race Track. Sport & recr. facils. Concerts at Mus. of Art. Show of Contemp. Amer. Art (summer). Info.: C. of C., in Commodore Perry Hotel.

Toledo spreads for 15 miles along both sides of Maumee R., which flows (NE) into Maumee Bay, inlet of L. Erie. City is 2nd only to Duluth-Superior as Great Ls.' port & ranks 3rd in tonnage among U.S. ports; world leader in shipping of soft coal, also ranking RR. center. W. & E. Toledo are conn. by high-level Anthony Wayne Bridge & 6 other bridges. On riverfront is Site of Ft. Industry, built by Anthony Wayne (1794), prophetically named beginning for a city of more than 650 different enterprises, producer or distributor of coal, iron & steel, glass, chemicals, petroleum, automobiles, machine tools, furnaces & processed foods. Whole Maumee valley was fought over by Brit. & Amer. forces (Anthony Wayne Trl.). Toledo was inc. in 1837, at conclusion of bloodless Toledo War (see Mich.). From a settlement in a swamp, the port grew rapidly after Wabash & Erie Canal to Cincinnati. Gas & petroleum fields (S) brought oil-refining, then glass. With development of Libbey-Owens-Ford Co., Toledo became the "Glass Capital." Pop. is more than 90% native born, but its inheritance is unusually cosmopolitan. Large German, Polish, Can., Hungarian, Eng. & Irish groups have characteristic churches, restaurants & festivals. Nearly 21,000 Negroes live in neighborhood of Brand Whitlock Homes & other areas. Mun. gov. is founded on traditions of "Golden Rule" Jones & 4-term Brand Whitlock. Oldest newspaper is "Toledo Blade."

PTS. OF INT.: (1) Collingwood Ave. & Islington St., **Queen of the Holy Rosary Cathedral** (1931.Sp.Ren.by Wm.R.Perry), one of America's beautiful cathedrals, said to be its 1st in Plateresque style. Rich in stained glass, frescoes, colored marbles, incl. gifts from Spain. (2) W. Bancroft St., **Univ. of Toledo** occupies spacious campus & fine modern bldgs. Founded in 1872, Toledo became one of 1st mun. universities in U.S. in 1884, now one of largest. **Univ. Hall** (Tudor Goth.). (3) Shadowlawn Dr., **Zoological Pk. & Mus. of Nat. Hist.** (1931.Sp.). (4) 2249 Monroe St., **Mus. of Art** (O); central bldg. of white marble (1901.1926.Ionic facade); School of Design & Peristyle (concert hall) in wings (1933); founded & richly endowed by Edward Drummond Libbey; one of finest glass colls. in world. **"Christ at Gethsemane,"** by El Greco. (5) Superior & Cherry Sts., **St. Francis de Sales (Cath.) Cathedral** (1861. Goth.). (6) Madison Ave. & Ontario St., **Pub. Lib.** (1890.early Norman). (7) **C. & O. Coal & Ore Docks,** on Presque Isle; 2.5m of piers, 40 miles of trackage, room for 15 lake boats. (8) **Industrial Plants** (tours on appl.); **Libbey Glass, Electric Auto-Lite, Toledo Scale, Willys-Overland, Woolson Spice.**

US20 forks in Maumee. Main tour cont. (N) along edge of Toledo suburbs, then (W) to state line. (US20 Alt. runs directly (W) to Montpelier, then (N) to rejoin US20). **68.** Beyond **OTTAWA HILLS** (W) is reg. of "oak openings," where groves of ancient trees are broken by patches of bog & fine yellow sand. Cooper called his novel of pioneer Mich. "Oak Openings" because these sun-filled breaks in the wilderness were characteristic of Old N.W. **103. FAYETTE,** shipping pt. for grain & livestock. Hy. winds over hilly wooded country. **119.** US20 Alt. rejoins main tour. **129. IND. LINE.**

# US 30—OHIO

**OHIO-W. VA. LINE** (1m from Chester, W. Va.) **(W) to OHIO-IND. LINE** (20m from Ft. Wayne, Ind.). **252. US30, US30S.**

Via: E. Liverpool, Lisbon, Canton, (Akron), Massillon, (Schoenbrunn), Wooster, Mansfield, Galion, Marion, Kenton, Lima, Delphos, Van Wert. Through RRs. & busses. Airports at Canton (Akron), Mansfield, Marion & Lima. Alternate route on US30 & US30N (see below). US224 is direct route some miles (N) of US30.

US30, the Lincoln Hy., crosses Chester Bridge at meeting pt. of 3 states, then winds through hills rich in coal, down eroded gullies & among dark fors. Large industrial centers at frequent intervals.

## Sec. 1: W. VA. LINE to MARION. 152.

**0. E. LIVERPOOL,** leading pottery center in U.S. Jas. Bennett, of Staffordshire, Eng., began pottery here in 1838 & peddled his teapots & tableware along Ohio R. Modern potteries produce porcelains exquisitely designed & colored & other plants make pottery supplies & clay novelties. **Hall China Co.** (tours). In Carnegie Lib., **Hist. Assoc. Mus.** (O.wks.); Pottery Coll. incl. Bennett's wheel. J. with St.7 (see Ohio R. Tour). **17. LISBON,** another ceramics center. Birthpl. of Marcus A. Hanna & Clement L. Vallandigham, Copperhead leader. Hanna was one of most powerful figures in 1880's & one of first to exemplify frankly the tie-up bet. big business & gov. **20.** J. with St.172, which runs (NW) to **Guilford L. St. Pk.** (f.boat.swim.camp. facils.). **26.** Along here is entrance to **Sandy & Beaver Canal** (1834-45) to Bolivar (S) of Canton. Many cut-stone locks in good condition. **47.5. E. CANTON** (1805). Glazed brick is chief product. **Wack Tavern** (O.1836).

### 53. CANTON

Market & 9th Sts., Pa. RR. Sta. 402-2nd St., Union Bus Terminal. Akron-Canton Airport, (N) 10m off St.8. Good accoms. Recr. facils. & golf courses in numerous pks. Meyers L. Pk. (bus.pic.bath.recr.facils.). Concerts by several music assocs. Info.: 428 Market Ave., C. of C.

Canton (sett.1806), home of Pres. McKinley, is one of Ohio's 8 largest cities & center of many industries, with world's largest plants making roller bearings (Timken), paving bricks, rubber gloves & electric cleaners. Steel in various forms is a leading product. Town itself is informal with air of neatness due in part to Swiss & German watchmakers who came in late 19th cent. In 1898, Henry H. Timken, carriage manufacturer, developed his patent for roller bearings. In Canton, in 1918, Eugene V. Debs made speech that led to his arrest. PTS. OF INT.: (1) In Westlawn Cemetery, **McKinley Tomb** (by Harold V. Magonigle). Within mausoleum are buried Pres. & Mrs. McKinley & 2 daughters. (2) Market Ave. & 8th St., **Site of McKinley H.,** now occupied by Mercy Hospital. (3) Cleveland Ave. & 4th St., **First Christian Ch.,** 2nd largest church congr. in U.S. (4) 1717 Market Ave., **Art. Mus.;** McKinley Coll. (5) 521 Tuscarawas St., **Timken Vocational High Sch.** (6) Industrial plants incl. **Timken Roller Bearing Co.** (O.appl.) & **Republic Steel Corp.** J. with US62 & St.8.

SIDE TRIPS: (A) On US62 (NE) 18m is **Alliance,** mfg. & RR. center on Mahoning R.; seat of **Mt. Union College** (Meth.Episc.), once attended by Presidents Garfield & McKinley; high-ranking school, founded in 1846. **Morgan Engineering Co.** (O.appl.), one of largest producers of cranes & rolling-mill machinery.

(B) On US62 (SW) 32m to MILLERSBURG. Hy. winds through lovely valley bet. Tuscarawas R. & Killbuck Cr., dotted with prosperous Amish settlements.

(C) On St.8 (N) 23m to Akron (1825).

### AKRON

Union RR. Sta., 245 E. Market St. Bus Terminal, N. Main St. at Federal St. Mun. Airport (S) 5.5m. Good accoms. Numerous golf courses & other recr. facils. in large pks. Rubber Bowl (stadium). Derby Downs. Portage Ls. near-by. Symphony orchestra. Concerts, lectures & other events at Univ. Info.: 228 Ohio Bldg., C. of C. Annual Soapbox Derby (Aug.).

Akron, Ohio's 5th city & rubber capital of the world, has nervous tempo of all industrial centers that have grown big within very few years. Added to this is an enthusiasm—pervasive as the smell of rubber—for technological research. The Univ. takes vital part in city's material development. The main street follows Ohio Canal to Little Cuyahoga R., which winds across town, & (N) the Great Cuyahoga rushes through a rocky gorge, arched by High Level Bridge to Cuyahoga Falls. Akron, named for its "high place" on watershed bet. Gt. Ls. & Miss. R., was laid out as canal town in 1825 by Gen. Simon Perkins, & in 1850's John Brown, the "angry man of God," was Perkins' partner in the wool business. A cereal mill (now Quaker Oats) was built in 1865. In 1870, the rubber industry began in Dr. Benj. Franklin Goodrich's plant. As automobiles rolled out of Detroit on their rubber tires, Akron began to boom & the "Rubber Rush" brought thousands of workers. During World War I, facils. were developed for building big dirigibles & balloons. In 1935-36, sit-down strikes involved the 3 giant rubber companies. During 1940's many millions were spent on modern research labs., & engineering college of Univ. took outstanding position. To offset factory routine, Akron has good pub. school & pk. system, Pub. Lib., Art Institute, Symphony Orchestra, the Rubber Bowl & Derby Downs.

PTS. OF INT.: (1) **B. F. Goodrich Rubber Co.,** Akron's oldest factory. (2) **Goodyear Tire & Rubber Co.** (3) **Firestone Tire & Rubber Co.** (4) **Gen. Tire & Rubber Co.** (5) **Quaker Oats Co.,** on site of old mill, 1853. Tours on appl. in above plants. (6) Goodyear Blvd. & E. Market St., **Goodyear Industrial Institute,** for employees & families. (7) Near Municipal Airport, **Goodyear Air Dock** (N.O.), where "Macon" & "Akron" were built. (8) **Firestone Research Lab.** (O.appl.1945.by Walker,Foley & Smith), the $2,000,000 rubber institute. (9) High & Market Sts., **Pub. Lib.** (1904. Gr.Rev.by F.O.Weary). (10) Mill & N. Main Sts., **Central Tower** (1931.set-back.by Walker & Weeks), tallest bldg. (11) 299 S. Broadway, **Old Stone Sch.** (1840's). (12) Cor. Copley & Diagonal Rds., **John Brown H.** (c.1825), bequeathed to Summit Cty. Hist. Soc. by Mrs. C. E. Perkins. (13) Cor. Copley Rd. & S. Portage Path, **Perkins Mus.,** formerly Perkins Mansion (1831). (14) **Univ. of Akron,** coed., fully accredited. Buchtel College (Universalist), now College of Liberal Arts, was founded in 1870 & named for its benefactor, J. R. Buchtel; given to city in 1913. **Buchtel Hall** (Gr. Rev.); **Carl F. Kolbe Hall,** housing Bierce Lib. (O). Phillips Art Coll. is in **Phillips Hall.** Near Mun. Airport, **Guggenheim Airship Institute** (O.appl.1932), part of engineering college. (15) On Manchester Rd., **Baptist Temple** (ded. 1949), unique modern edifice costing $1,000,000. Unusual features in this theater-like bldg. are soundproof "Babyland" & floodlighted River Jordan baptistery.

**60.5. MASSILLON,** industrial city at entrance to Muskingum Conservancy Dist. (14 dams). The wife of Jas. Duncan, one of founders, named town for Fr. bishop who opened funeral oration on Louis XIV with famous sentence, "Dieu seul est grand." PTS. OF INT.: **Union Drawn Steel Division,** of Republic. Lincoln Way & E. 2nd St., **Jas. Duncan H.** (1830), housing Pub. Lib. & Baldwin Mus. North Ave. & 2nd St., **Home of Jacob S. Coxey,** leader of famous "march in boots" in 1894. Coxey was arrested for walking on the grass & his "Army" dispersed, but Massillon made him mayor in 1932 in honor of his prophetic plan for Fed. work relief. Massillon is at J. with US21.

SIDE TRIP: US21, St.16 (S) 40$^{m}$ to **Gnadenhutten.** Tour of Ft. Laurens, Zoar Village & Schoenbrunn St. Mems. At 13.5$^{m}$ is J. with St.212.

(E) 6$^{m}$ on St.212 to **Bolivar,** from which Rd. leads (E) to **Bolivar Dam. Ft. Laurens St. Mem.,** (S) of village, on site of only Amer. fort in Ohio during Rev.; built in 1778 & named for Henry Laurens of S. Carolina. At 9$^{m}$ **Zoar Village St. Mem.** 11.5$^{m}$ **Zoarsville.** In 1817-18, German Separatists came into Tuscarawas Valley & est. communal corporation which lasted until 1898; named by leader, Jos. Bimeler, for city to which Lot fled from Sodom. Among low, picket-fenced cottages are log cabins & other orig. bldgs. **Mem. Mus.** (O.Ap.-Nov.sm.fee), palatial home of founder. **Zoar Garden** illustrates New Jerusalem.

22$^{m}$ **Dover,** once German settlement at collector's port on canal, now busy coal, iron & steel center. **Werther Mus.** (O.sm.fee); handcarved models of locomotives & steel mills. 24$^{m}$ **New Philadelphia** (1809), in midst of hist. Moravian country. **Schoenbrunn Village St. Mem.** (O.camp.pic.) covers site of village est. by Moravian missionaries in 1772. Schoolh., Ch. & 13 cabins rebuilt & furnished. In this luxuriant valley, David Zeisberger & other leaders built villages for Christianized Delaware Inds. In 1777 the village was abandoned because of Brit. hostility & unfriendly Inds. who later destroyed it. 40$^{m}$ **Gnadenhutten Mon.** A simple shaft marks Site of Massacre, in 1782, of 90 or more Christian Delaware Inds. by Amer. soldiers under Col. David Williamson. The Delaware brethren, who were never armed, had been sent, with their leaders, to "Captives Town" near Upper Sandusky (see below). Allowed to return to their villages for provisions, they were attacked by Pa. militia who were scouting for marauding Inds.

US30, (W) of Massillon, crosses one of most fertile counties in U.S. Pure-bred horses & herds of sheep & cattle graze in rich pastures along shady creeks. St. Agric. Exper. Sta. has 1,000-a. farm. **82.5. WOOSTER,** scene of big Cty. Fair. **College of Wooster**

(Presb.), founded in 1870, grants A.B. degree in arts & music. Bldgs. (Coll.Goth.) are attractive modern structures. **100. HAYESVILLE.**

**114. MANSFIELD**

Through RR. & bus conns. Mun. Airport. Good accoms. & recr. facils. Info.: C. of C. Mansfield is important industrial city & trade center for wide area. Around red-brick Cth. & Pub. Sq. are smart shops & modern office bldgs., & streets lead off from pleasant residential secs. to some of state's finest farmlands. According to tradition, Johnny Appleseed saved town from Ind. raiders during War of 1812 by running to Mt. Vernon to give alarm. John Sherman, brother of Civil War general & best known for Anti-Trust Act, practiced law here in 1840's. Louis Bromfield used his native town as scene of early novels & celebrated Richland Cty. with nostalgic fervor in "The Farm." PTS. OF INT.: 200 E. 5th St., **Westinghouse Electric & Mfg. Co.** (O). (2) W. Park Ave., in South Pk., **Pioneer Blockh.** (1814). In Middle Pk., **Johnny Appleseed Mon.** In center of city, **Soldiers & Sailors Mem. H.;** Mem. Mus. (O). US30 forks in Mansfield (see Alternate Tour below).

US30S runs down through dense fors. & undulating farmlands to valley of Little Scioto R. **129. GALION,** sett. by Pa. Germans in 1830's. **Galion Iron Works. 126. IBERIA,** once Underground Railroad Sta. Pres. Harding attended Ohio Central College (closed) here. **142. CALEDONIA.** On South St. is Harding's boyhood home. **152. MARION,** the town most closely associated with Pres. Harding. Here he edited the "Star" & carried on "front porch campaign" & here he & Mrs. Harding are buried. Marion is widely known for steam, electric & diesel shovels & other large-scale digging machinery. On W. Center St. is **Marion Steel Shovel Co.** (O.appl.), & on N. Greenwood St., the orig. **Huber Mfg. Co.** (O.appl.). At 380 Mt. Vernon St., **Harding H.** (O.sm.fee); some orig. furnishings. On US23, (S) side of town, **Harding Mem.** (1931.by Henry Hornbustle & Eric F. Wood). Long formal approach leads to circular structure with Doric colonnade, enclosing open court & tombs of Pres. & Mrs. Harding.

### Sec. 2: MARION to IND. LINE. 100. US30, US30S.

**0. MARION.** US30 speeds (W) through farm country broken by few towns. **26.5. KENTON,** named for scout of Boone & Geo. Rogers Clark. **Kenton Hardware Factory** (O.appl.) makes more iron & steel toys than any other U.S. plant. Beyond Kenton the Scioto Marsh (25,000 as.) begins, noted for vast onion beds, potato & truck fields. **38.5.** J. with St.69, which leads (N) 2.5$^{m}$ to **Ada,** seat of **Ohio Northern Univ.,** founded in 1871 as normal sch.; has colleges of arts, law, pharmacy & engineering. **55. LIMA** (fine recr.facils. in Mun. & Faurot City pks.). Oil pipes from Tex. & Okla. flow into big refinery S. of town. Other important industries (O.appl.) are **Lima Locomotive Works; Superior Body Co.,** makers of school busses; **Diesel-Wemmer-Gilbert Corp.,** large cigar factory; & **Westinghouse Electric & Mfg. Co.** In Mem. Hall is **Allen Cty. Hist. Mus.;** excellent pioneer coll.

At **c.65. Leslie Peltier's Observatory** (O) has modern telescope presented by Harvard Univ. Peltier's Comet was discovered by the brilliant amateur in 1936. **71. DELPHOS,** canning & honey center. Here the 2 branches of US30 reunite. Old Miami & Erie Canal, which once made Delphos a larger city than Lima, is utilized by local factories. Digging the canal was hazardous job, & German, Norweg. & Irish diggers died by hundreds of "canal chills" & cholera or in fights & accidents. **85. VAN WERT** should be visited in June when its famous peonies bloom. **100. IND. LINE**

### ALTERNATE TOUR. W. VA. LINE to IND. LINE. 241. US30, US30N

Via: Mansfield, Bucyrus, Upper Sandusky, Delphos.

**0. W. VA. LINE.** Tour is on US30 to **MANSFIELD, 114.** At **120.5.** J. with Rd. to **Doolittle H.** (c.2$^{m}$ NW.), famous link on Underground Railroad. Hy. crosses watershed to **CRESTLINE, 126.5. 139. BUCYRUS,** another town making roadbuilding & farm machinery; also copper kettles & clay products. **Bucyrus Copper Kettle Works** (O.appl.).

**156. UPPER SANDUSKY,** overlooking broad valley, where Wyandot Inds. lived until removed beyond Miss. R., 1843. Cty. is named for these Inds. who fought for their homes & cornfields. On almost every Rd. is marked site comm. the bloody hist. It was here to Captives Town that the Christian Delaware were brought from their Moravian villages in 1782 (see above). PTS. OF INT.: On plateau, S. 4th St.,

**Wyandot Cemetery.** Near-by is **Wyandot Mission** (rebuilt in 1889) on Site of 1st Meth. Episc. mission in Ohio (1821). **John Stewart Mon.** comm. 1st Meth. missionary, a mulatto. Wyandot & Spring Sts., in County Cth., **Wyandot Cty. Hist. & Archeol. Soc. Mus.** (O).

**176. WILLIAMSTOWN,** on route of Gen. Hull's march to Detroit in 1812. On US68 (N) c.10$^{m}$ is granite **Hull's Trl. Mon. 212. DELPHOS,** where US30N & US30S reunite. **241. IND. LINE.**

# US 40—OHIO

**OHIO-W. VA. LINE** (1$^{m}$ from Wheeling, W. Va.) **(NW) to OHIO-IND. LINE** (4$^{m}$ from Richmond, Ind.). **232. US40**

Via: Bridgeport, Morristown, Fairview, Cambridge, Zanesville, Hebron, Columbus, Springfield, Lewisburg. Accoms.: Excellent. RR., bus & airplane conns.

US40 follows Zane's Trace & Nat. Rd., over which an endless cavalcade streamed westward—white-hooded wagons carrying thousands of emigrants. Stone bridges over which they crossed broad streams are still standing, as are many taverns that sprang up in wake of the roadbuilders. The restless, cheerful spirit of the pioneers sings in the names of coaches & taverns. Pocahontas, Gentle Annie, Henry Clay & Rough & Ready were gaily colored Concord coaches, & favorite taverns were the Buck, Golden Ram, Orange Tree, the Hope & Anchor.

## Sec. 1: W. VA. LINE to COLUMBUS. 127.

US40 enters state over **Belmont Bridge** across Ohio R., then crosses rich coal reg. & timbered ridges & flat farmlands of Muskingum R. valley. **0. BRIDGEPORT** (1808), New England settlement. J. with US250 & St.7 (see Ohio R. Tour).

SIDE TRIP: On US250 (NW) 23$^{m}$ to Cadiz. At 11$^{m}$ is J. with St.150.

(E) 4$^{m}$ on St.150 is **Mt. Pleasant,** sett. by Quakers. 1st Abolitionist newspaper, "The Philanthropist" was published here in 1817, & Abolitionist Convention assembled in 1837. **Ohio Yearly Meeting H.** (O.appl.1816.Class.Rev.).

23$^{m}$ **Cadiz,** center of rich coal, gas & oil area; also known for Delaware sheep & shorthorn cattle. (N) c.12$^{m}$ from Cadiz is **Custer Mon.** (facils.) in **New Rumley,** birthpl. of Gen. Geo. A. Custer (see).

US40 runs for more than 70$^{m}$ through richest coal country, climbing steeply graded slopes & traversing narrow valleys. Eroded ravines lead off into somewhat desolate country, & along route are mining villages, with row upon row of similar houses, piles of slack & mounds of earth. **10. ST. CLAIRSVILLE** (1804), seat of most productive coal cty. but not a miners' town. **Lundy H.,** in which Quaker Benj. Lundy founded Union Humane Soc., 1815. **20. MORRISTOWN** (1802), once toll sta. on Nat. Rd. The many-chimneyed red-brick houses with pitched roofs are exactly like their Pa. prototypes. Other early stagecoach stops are **HENDRYSBURG, 25. & FAIRVIEW, 29.5.** In contrast are the numerous small mines cut into the hills along hy. & (S) the great shaft mines of Belmont & Guernsey Ctys. **34.5. MIDDLEBOURNE,** tourist stop since 1820's. **Hayes Tavern,** now Locust Lodge (O), was built by Greenberry Penn & is still operated by descendant of Wm. Penn. From Middlebourne (W) 2$^{m}$ is one of S-bridges used in numerous places, probably to avoid cutting down some huge tree in path of Nat. Rd. **41.** in **OLD WASHINGTON,** are 2 excellent examples of commodious stagecoach taverns. **Colonial Inn** (O.1805) had 20 rooms, floored in oak with woodwork of walnut & rosewood. **Pine Tree Inn** (O). **49. CAMBRIDGE,** dairying & livestock center; on high ridge beyond strip-mining area. Cth. & many downtown bldgs. are nearly as old as Nat. Rd., but there are also plastics & other modern plants &, a short distance (N), beautiful **Fetcher Hospital. Cambridge Glass Co.** (O.appl.), turns out hundreds of handblown pieces.

**58. NEW CONCORD,** literally created by Zane's Trace & a college town from its beginning. **Muskingum College** (founded 1836), coed., has beautiful hilly campus. Opp. entrance is log cabin **Birthpl. of Wm. Rainey Harper** (1856-1906), graduate of Muskingum & for 15 yrs. pres. of Chicago Univ. (see). A mile beyond Cambridge is another S-bridge (1828).

**73. ZANESVILLE** (1797)

Market & 2nd Sts., B. & O. & Penn. RR. Sta. N. 5th St. near Market St., Union Bus Terminal. Accoms.: Good. Mun. Stadium. Info.: 45 N. 5th St., C. of C.

This hist. city at meeting of Muskingum & Licking Rs. is noted for its faience & ceramic tile dishes, bowls, vases & art objects. Y Bridge, at foot of Main St., uniting 3 secs. of city, is 3rd on this site since 1814 & 1 of 3 in the world. Pottery-making began in early 1800's & early Zanesville goblets & pitchers are collectors' items. In 1769, Ebenezer Zane, with his 2 brothers, founded Wheeling. Then, during Rev. War, Col. Zane was practically in charge of defense of Ft. Henry (see). In 1797-98, with permission of Congress, Zane hacked the Trace from his Wheeling empire to Maysville, Ky., a narrow road walled by fors. & ribbed by roots of ancient trees, dusty in summer & muddy in spring. By 1830, more than 70 taverns had opened along route. In payment, Zane received tracts at 3 important river crossings (Zanesville, Lancaster & Chillicothe). The Muskingum site was given to Jonathan Zane & John McIntire, who created Zanesville, even had it designated St. capital (1810-12).

PTS. OF INT.: (1) Lexington Ave. & Pershing Rd., **Mosaic Tile Co. Plant,** probably largest in world. (2) Ceramic Ave., **Weller Pottery.** (3) Linden Ave., **Roseville Pottery.** At Maple & Adair Aves., (4) **Art Institute** (O.wks.); Muskingum Cty. Pioneer & Hist. Soc. exhibits. (5) 705 Converse Ave., **Birthpl. of Zane Grey,** great-great-grandson of Ebenezer Zane. (6) Woodlawn Ave. & Washington St., **Oldest H.** (1804.adds.). (7) 113 Jefferson St., **Robbins H.** (1809), academy, Underground Railroad sta. & home of Elizabeth Robbins, novelist.

SIDE TRIP: On US22 (SW) 21m to Somerset. At 5m, **Five Mile H.** (1830), 17-room stone tavern. 15m **Sego.** 21m **Somerset.** About 0.5m from village, on St.13, is **Phil Sheridan's Boyhood H.**

US40 crosses central plain, fertile whether rolling or level. **78. Headley Inn** (O. summer), serving travelers as it did when Usual Headley built 1st unit of speckled sandstone. **86.** J. with St.668, which leads (N) 3m to **Flint Ridge Mem. St. Pk.** (camp. facils.), where Inds. chipped jasper & chalcedony. **127. COLUMBUS** (see), state capital.

## Sec. 2: COLUMBUS to IND. LINE. 105.

### 0. COLUMBUS

### 43. SPRINGFIELD

Washington St., N.Y.C. RR. Sta.: Limestone & Union Sts., Penn. RR. Sta. Greyhound & other bus lines. Mun. Airport (S) 6m bet. US68 & St.72. Good accoms. & recr. facils. Info.: E. Columbia St., Auto. Club.

Springfield, in Mad R. valley, Ohio's 9th city, seat of Wittenberg College, is industrial & trade center for rich farm territory; home of Crowell-Collier Publishing Co. It is known also for its many roses. Narrow streets & massive 19th cent. brick & stone bldgs. give older part a somber, crowded appearance, but downtown bldgs. & fine homes on the slopes indicate a prosperous modern town. In (SW) sec. are the homes, mostly nondescript, of large Negro pop. Chief manufactures are diesel & gas engines, agric. & other heavy machinery, motor trucks & auto parts; extensive nurseries. In 1798, the Kentuckian, Jas. Demint, built cabin on Buck Cr. In 1830's, Springfield was terminus of Nat. Pike, the jumping-off place into the wilderness. Crowell-Collier is development of "Farm & Fireside," house organ of P. P. Mast's Cultivator Plant in 1870's. At that time, Springfield was also concerned with Wm. Whiteley's Champion binder & reaper (taken over by Internat. Harvester Co.).

PTS. OF INT.: (1) **Wittenberg College,** on slope overlooking city; founded in 1845 by Luth. Ch.; coed. school of standing. (2) E. High St., **St. Raphael Ch.;** windows designed by Mayer of Munich. (3) E. High & Spring Sts., **Arder Pub. Lib.** (1890. Richardson Romanes.). (4) Limestone & North Sts., **Covenant** (Presb.) **Ch.** (1917. Goth.by Geo.D.Savage). (5) W. High St., **Crowell-Collier Plant** (O.guides), one of largest publishing plants in world. (6) Lagonda Ave. & Buck Cr., **Internat. Harvester Co.** (tours). (7) **Columbia St. Cemetery** (pioneers). (8) E. High St. & Greenmount Ave., **Westcott H.** (1905;Frank Lloyd Wright). (9) On Masonic Home grounds, **Madonna of the Trl. Mon.**

SIDE TRIPS: (A) On US68 (N) 24m to W. Liberty, via Urbana. At 5m **Hunt Tavern** (1830), on site of Simon Kenton's home in 1803. At 14m **Urbana** (1805), a quiet country town with sm. industries. PTS. OF INT.: (1) **Urbana Univ.,** coed., founded by Ch. of the New Jerusalem in 1850; coll. of Swedenborgian literature. (2) At E. limits, **Oakdale Cemetery,** where Simon Kenton, Ind. fighter, is buried. **J. Q. A. Ward Mon.,** reprod. of sculptor's own "The Ind. Fighter." (3) In Mon. Sq., **J. Q. A. Ward's Soldiers' Mon.** (4) 510 S. Main St., **Brand Whitlock H.,** birthpl. of novelist who became Toledo's reform mayor

& U.S. Minister to Belgium. (6) **McDargh Mus.** (O.appl.); hist. colls. At 24m, **W. Liberty.** On St.275 (W) of town is **Site of Mac-O-Chee Town,** Shawnee village destroyed in 1786. Beyond on country Rd. is **Mac-O-Chee Chateau** (O.sm.fee.1864); hist. coll. Farther (E) on St.275 is J. with St.287, which leads to **Mac-O-Chee Castle** (O.sm.fee.facils.), built by Col. Don Piatt, whose newspaper, "Washington Capitol," attacked Credit Mobilier & other political scandals.

(B) On US68 (S) 10m from Springfield to **Yellow Springs,** seat of Antioch College, nationally known for cooperative work-study plan. Founded in 1853 by Horace Mann, Antioch was pioneer in admitting students regardless of color, creed or sex. **Horace Mann Lib.** on site of Mann's home. **Fels Research Institute Bldg.** (1947), gift of Sam. S. Fels, of Phila., for "Study of Man." **Mann Mon. in Bryan For. St. Pk.** (f.camp.facils.). From Yellow Springs, (S) 14.5m on US68, **Oldtown,** on **Site of Old Chillicothe,** Shawnee settlement where Dan. Boone was adopted into tribe. 18m **Xenia,** rural trading center with large Negro pop.

(NE) 3m on US42 is **Wilberforce,** Negro cultural center & seat of **Wilberforce Univ.,** named for Eng. abolitionist; founded in 1856 by Meth. Episc. Ch. Purchased, 1863, by African M. E. Ch., it is now ranking coed. school offering normal, theological & industrial courses. At 8m is **Cedarville,** home of **Cedarville College** & Theological Seminary of Reformed Presb. Ch.; founded in 1887.

**49.** J. with St.369

SIDE TRIP: On St.369 (S) 2.5m to **Geo. Rogers Clark Mem. St. Pk.** (f.facils.no camp.), where Clark defeated the Shawnee, Aug., 1780. In (SW) sec. is **Clark Mon.**

**63.5. TAYLORSVILLE DAM,** built on Miami R. after 1913 flood. **66.5. VANDALIA,** home of Amer. Trap-shooting Assoc. Grand Amer. Meet (Aug.). J. with US25 (see) to Dayton. US40 crosses Stillwater R. over **Englewood Dam,** largest in Miami Dist. (4,700′ x 725′ x 125′); large pk. (camp.pic.shelter). **74. ENGLEWOOD,** Mennonite & Dunkard village. **87. LEWISBURG,** (S) 1m from hy.; trading center in orchard belt. **105. IND LINE.**

## US 50—OHIO

**OHIO-W. VA. LINE** (Parkersburg, W. Va.) **(W) to OHIO-IND. LINE** (4m from Richmond, Ind.) **213. US50**

Via: Belpre, Little Hocking, Guysville, Athens, Albany, McArthur, Chillicothe, Bainbridge, Hillsboro, Fayetteville, Cincinnati. RR., bus & airplane conns. & good accoms. in larger towns. Route crosses Hocking R. valley, Wayne Nat. For. & hilly (SW) country.

### Sec. 1: W. VA. LINE to CHILLICOTHE. 97.

US50 crosses Parkersburg-Belpre Bridge. **0. BELPRE,** in lush orchard country; sett. by Rev. War veterans from Marietta (1789). J. with St.7 (see Ohio R. Tour), with which US50 unites for short distance. Near Belpre is **Jonathan Stone H.** (1799). **2. ROCKLAND.** Trips to Blennerhasset I. (see Ohio R. Tour). **3.5. Putnam H.** (1800); "witch" doors with cross-shaped panels. **8. LITTLE HOCKING.** US50 turns from Ohio R. & in **COOLVILLE, 16.5.,** crosses the Hocking. **38. ATHENS,** situated on hills along R.; trade center & home of some 5,000 students. **Ohio Univ.,** 1st land-grant college in U.S. (inc.1802). When Gen. Rufus Putnam org. Ohio. Co. in 1787, he recommended to Congress that 4 townships be set aside for univ., but he could not bring surveying crew until after Treaty of Greenville. Athens was laid out in 1799, & with it the univ. campus. **Mem. Elms,** honoring Wm. Holmes McGuffey, Pres. of Univ. (1839-43) & compiler of "McGuffey Readers." **Cutler Hall** (1817.by Benj.Corp.), oldest college bldg. in N.W. Terr. J. with US33 (see) & St.56.

SIDE TRIP: On St.56 (W) 10m to J. with St.356, route (S) into **Waterloo St. For.** (camp. facils.). 14m J. with St.278, route (S) to **Zaleski St. For.** (f.swim.boat.pic.camp.).

US50 cont. through sparsely settled hill country, from which the once important salt works & iron furnaces are long gone. Scattered homes on barren slopes or along rocky ravines are poor & way of life is primitive.

**97. CHILLICOTHE**

Main & Sugar Sts., Union RR. Sta. 42 E. Main St., Union Bus Terminal. Accoms. Golf & other recr. facils. Numerous pub. for. pks. in vic. Info.: 15 W. Second St., C. of C.

Chillicothe, 1st capital of Northwest & of Ohio, was perhaps also capital city of prehist. people who built mounds on which it stands. Sett. 1796, it is now important farm market & industrial center, situated bet. Scioto R. & Paint Cr., with Mt. Logan standing sentinel to the N. The aristocratic tradition lingers, & along the main streets are many elegant Gr. Rev. mansions. In 1782, Nath. Massie surveyed site, but settlement was not begun until 1796. Chillicothe became capital of N.W. Terr. in 1800 & st. capital in 1803 (1803-10 & 1812-16). Paper-making, still a leading industry, began in 1812. City has fine Carnegie Lib. & good schools, incl. 2 high schools for Negro pop. PTS. OF INT.: (1) Paint & Main Sts., **Ross County Cth.** (1855.mod.Gr.Rev.by E.Collins); **Site of 1st Capitol** at rear. (2) 45 W. 5th St., **Ross Cty. Hist. Mus.** (O). (3) Paint St. bet. 5th & 6th Sts., **Pub. Lib.** (1907), directed for many yrs. by Burton Stevenson, founded of Amer. Lib. in Paris. (4) Mulberry & 4th Sts., **Ind. Burying Ground;** pioneer graves also. (5) E. Main St., **Gen. St. Clair's Hqs.** (1798). (6) Arch & High Sts., **Site of Cross Keys Tavern** (1797). (7) In **Grandview Cemetery,** S. Paint St., are graves of Nath. Massie & early governors. (8) At S. end of Main St., **Mead Corp. Plant** (O.appl.), home office of very large paper co.; 16 plants. (9) Off Eastern Ave., **Chillicothe Paper Co. Plant** (O.appl.), makers of quality papers. (10) McArthur St., S. of 7th St., **U. S. Shoe Corp. Plant** (O.appl.). (11) At W. end of Allen Ave., **Adena** (1798.probably by Latrobe), estate of Thos. Worthington, Ohio Gov. (1814-18) & U. S. Sen. Adena Mound, which stood on estate, disclosed carved ornaments & woven fabrics.

SIDE TRIPS: (A) US23 (N) 12m. At 3.5m **Mt. Logan,** over which Wm. Creighton, Ohio Secy. of State & Gov. Tiffin saw one morning in 1803 "the rising sun of a new state" (as on Ohio seal). 4m **Hopetown** (moundbuilder) **Works.** At 12m J. with St.361, which leads (E) 1m to **Logan Elm St. Pk.,** around immense tree where Logan, Mingo chief, made celebrated speech of reproach in 1774, after massacre on Ohio R. near Yellow Creek (see Ohio R. Tour & Wheeling, W. Va., Trip III).

(B) US23 (S) 9m to 9,000-a. **Scioto Trl. St. Pk.** (f.camp.pic.all facils.). 22.5m **Waverly. J.** with St.112, Towpath Rd. past **L. White St. Pk.;** summer resort.

(C) St.104 (NW) 1.5m to U.S. Industrial Reformatory & U.S. Veterans Hospital. (N) of reformatory is **Mound City Pk.** (camp.facils.); 23 mounds somewhat restored.

### Sec. 2: CHILLICOTHE to IND. LINE. 116.

US50 winds bet. high ranging hills; then along Paint Cr., where Inds. came for colored clays. Reg. is often called Valley of the Kings, because of prehist. earthworks. More than 350 mounds were found in Ross Cty. alone. At **c.5. HOPEWELL MOUNDS,** 1st mapped in 1820. **17. SEIP MOUND ST. PK.** (facils.); mound (250′ x 150′ x 30′) was central tumulus of large group. **21. BAINBRIDGE.** In backwoods around & beyond are shacks & dingy settlements of the hill people. Just (W) of town is J. with St.41.

SIDE TRIP: On St.41 (S) 21m to Locust Grove. At c.12m **Ft. Hill St. Mem.** (camp.facils.); 1,000 forested as., around one of best-preserved prehist. fts. in state. 21m **Locust Spring.** J. with St.73; (W) 4m on St.73 to **Serpent Mound,** largest & most fascinating effigy mound in America.

US50 enters **ROCKY FORK GORGE** on Paint Cr. At **c.26., SEVEN CAVES** (illuminated), along trl. notable for diversity of flora. **38. HILLSBORO** (1807), livestock trading center. **55. FAYETTEVILLE,** J. with US68.

SIDE TRIP: On US68 (N) 20m to **Wilmington,** seat of Wilmington College & urban center of rich dairy & farming area. **Clinton County Cth.** (Class.Rev.) is one of most pleasing of Ohio's fine cths. **Wilmington College,** Quaker institution inc. in 1875 on site of Franklin College (1866); coed.; nonsectarian student body.

**94. CINCINNATI** (see). Hy. crosses city & follows Ohio R. (W). **116. IND. LINE.**

## US 25—OHIO

**MICH. LINE** (51m from Detroit) (S) **to KY. LINE** (at Cincinnati). **211. US25**

Via: Toledo, Maumee, Perrysburg, Bowling Green, Findlay, Bluffton, Lima, Wapakoneta, Piqua, Troy, Dayton, Miamisburg, Sharonville. Through RR. & bus conns. & good accoms. all along route. US23 & US24 also enter here from Mich. & US68 begins route roughly parallel to US25.

US25, the Dixie Hy., runs (N-S) across W. Ohio, first enters Maumee R. valley, made famous by Gens. Wm. Harrison & Anthony Wayne; now has internat. reputation for concentration of industry.

### Sec. 1: MICH. LINE to PIQUA. 130.

**3.5.** US25 unites with US24. **4. TOLEDO** (see). **14. MAUMEE** (see). J. with US20 (see). Across Maumee R. is **PERRYSBURG.** US25 unites with US68. **27. BOWLING GREEN,** seat of Bowling Green St. Univ. J. with US6 (see). (for this sec. see Toledo). Beyond Bowling Green is oil country, & wells are scattered around this excellent farming area. **41. N. BALTIMORE** (short distance W. of hy.) & **43. VAN BUREN** were once oil centers. **51. FINDLAY** (1821). Industrial & oil center; seat of Findlay College. Town grew up with oil boom in late 19th cent. Has large foundries, refineries & clay-products plants. In 1860's D. R. Locke, editor of "Findlay Jeffersonian" & later of "Toledo Blade," had nat. audience for his letters of "Petroleum Vesuvius Nasby," a stupid Copperhead whose arguments made Confederacy appear ridiculous. **Findlay College**, small but first-rate coed. school, & **Winebrenner Graduate Sch. of Divinity** (Churches of God) have campus in E. sec. US25 & US68 separate here.

SIDE TRIP: On US68 (S) to Bellefontaine 48m. At 4m **Hull's Trl. Mon.**, comm. march of Ohio militia in 1812. 27m **Kenton,** prosperous town on Scioto R. J. with US30S (see). 48m **Bellefontaine,** on highest land in Ohio; seat of Logan Cty., leading producer of alfalfa & rye. Off St.275 (E) 7m are **Zane Caverns** (1 hr.tour). J. with US33, route to **Ind. L. St. Pk.** (f.h.boat.camp.facils.). Scattered oil pumps, tanks & refineries shine in the fields (SW) of Findlay.

**69. BLUFFTON,** est. by Mennonite & Swiss settlers in 1833. **Bluffton College** (1900) is Mennonite school, coed. & accredited. **75. BEAVERDAM.** J. with US30N (see).

**84. LIMA** (see US30). US25 crosses Ottawa R. **97. WAPAKONETA,** on Auglaize R. J. with US33 & St. 198.

SIDE TRIP: On US33 (W) 11m to **St. Marys,** once known as Girty's Town, main supply depot in Ind. Wars, being end of portage from Ft. Laramie (S). By treaty signed here, 1818, the Wyandot, Shawnee & Ottawa gave up large tracts for settlement. From St. Marys, St.29 runs along (N) edge of **Grand L.** (St. Marys), largest inland L. in Ohio. Near **Celina,** at (NW) cor., is **Grand L. St. Pk.** (f.h.camp.resorts).

(S) 9.5m on US127 from Celina to J. with St.119; (W) 8m on St.119 to **Ft. Recovery St. Pk.** (camp.facils.), on site of Gen. St. Clair's defeat in 1791 & Gen. Wayne's return in 1793. Stockade (reprod.).

At **117.** on US25 is **SIDNEY,** named for Eng. poet. On Ohio & Court Sts., is a Louis Sullivan **Bank Bldg., 130. PIQUA,** industrial town on Great Miami R.; known widely for knitted wear & textiles. Long before Piqua became canal port, it was meeting place for Ind. tribes, particularly beloved by the Shawnee, small independent tribe originating in Florida, near Suwanee R. Tecumseh, the Shooting Star, perhaps greatest among hist. Inds., was born here in 1768. About 1752, the French destroyed Miami village of Pickawillany & built Ft. Piqua, (N) 3m from present town. Around ft. the Shawnee had their villages of Upper & Lower Piqua. Lower Piqua was destroyed by Geo. Rogers Clark in 1780 & again by Simon Kenton in 1782. Near Piqua is **Pickawillany Mon.**

## Sec. 2: PIQUA to KY. LINE. 81.

US25 follows Miami R. & route of M. & E. Canal through fertile valley. **19. VANDALIA.** J. with US40 (see).

### 28. DAYTON

Ludlow & 6th Sts., Union RR. sta. 145 W. 4th St., Greyhound Bus Sta. Mun. Airport (N) 10m at Vandalia. Accoms.: good. Sports facils. Theaters (stage & screen). Montgomery Cty. Fair (Sept.). Shows at Art Institute. Folk festivals. Info.: C. of C., in Biltmore Hotel.

Dayton, Ohio's 6th big city, home of Wright Brothers & Paul Laurence Dunbar, poet, is also home of cash register & city manager plan, of Air Material Command & Miami Conservancy Project. It is nat. aviation center & noted for diversity of its other industries. It is also a beautiful city in a beautiful setting. City plan allows a spacious downtown dist. in loop of the Miami, & throughout city are riverside pks., drives & many bridges. There is a minimum of smoke & noise, since there is no "factory dist." & because plants are mainly of light-industry type.

Site of Dayton was happy hunting ground for Inds. for many yrs. Then it was crossed by frontiersmen & soldiers & desperate bands of the dispossessed. In 1793 Jonathan Dayton purchased land here, & town was inc. in 1805. In 1840 some 70,000 crowded to the little town (6,000 pop.) to hail "Tippecanoe and Tyler too!" In 1879 the citizens laughed at James Ritty's "mechanical money drawer"; but in 1884 **John** Patterson took it over & brought precision workmen to his "daylight factory." **Wilbur** & Orville Wright were working on their flying machine near close of cent., & Barney Oldfield's racing career began. Chas. F. Kettering opened the laboratories that became Delco. In 1913 flood, approx. 400 died & damage rose above $100,000,000. Dayton's answer was Miami Conservancy Dist., est. in 1915, at cost of $31,-

000,000. Indirectly, flood brought the city manager plan, adopted to meet crisis. During 2 world wars, Dayton became nat. aviation center.

PTS. OF INT.: (1) Main & 3rd Sts., **Old Courth.** (1850.Class.Rev.by Howard Daniels). (2) 405 W. Riverview Ave., **Art Institute** (1930.Ital.Ren.by Edw.B. Green); gift of Mrs. Harrie G. Carnell; designed after triple-arched casino of Villa Farnese. Of special note are Chinese Temple, Ital. & Goth. chapels, Mrs. Carnell's Oriental Coll. & Coll. of Wright Brothers' Medals. (3) 208 W. 1st St., **Westminster First Presb. Ch.** (org.1799.bldg.1926.Goth.by Schenck & Williams), home of Westminster Choir. (4) 215 E. 3rd St., **Pub. Lib. & Mus.; McKinley Mon.** (ded.1910), presented by school children. (5) In Van Cleve Pk. is log **Newcom Tavern** (1796), city's oldest H.; pioneer coll. (6) 219 N. Summit St., **Dunbar H. St. Mem.** (O.1873), home of Paul Laurence Dunbar (1872-1906), whose "Lyrics of Lowly Life" (1896) was widely acclaimed. The poetic boy, son of former slaves, worked in Dayton elevator. (7) **Univ. of Dayton** (Cath.), coed., lib. arts & engineering colleges; founded in 1850. **Immaculate Conception Chapel.** (8) Patterson Blvd., **Deeds Carillon;** 32 bells in fine tower. (9) In Woodland Cemetery, **Graves of Wright Brothers, Col. Robt. Patterson, & Dunbar.** (10) **Industrial Plants:** 300 Taylor St., **Frigidaire** (O); **National Cash Register** (tours); **McCall Corp.,** publishers. (11) On St.4 (NE) $4^m$ is **Wright Field,** hqs. of Army Material Command, in conjunction with **Patterson Field,** c.$8^m$, & **Clinton Cty. Army Airfield;** probably world's greatest aeronautical center. From Wright Field (N) to **Wright Mem.**

**38.5. MIAMISBURG,** laid out by Pa. settlers in 1818. Has foundries, paper mills & cordage factories. 3 early tobacco warehouses still stand. A little farther on, (W) of hy., is **Miamisburg Mound** (pic.lookout), largest in state. **44.5. FRANKLIN** (1796), once busy canal port; known now for paper mills & **Eldridge Entertainment H.** (O), distributors of plays & songs.

SIDE TRIP: On St.73 (SW) $5^m$ to **Middletown,** fair-sized paper-making & tobacco center. Here, in July, 1825, Gov. DeWitt Clinton, of N. Y., & Gov. Jeremiah Morrow, of Ohio, turned spadeful of earth inaugurating construction of M. & E. Canal. Curtis St., **Amer. Rolling Mill Co.** (O.appl.). Central Ave. **Lorillard Tobacco Co.** (O.appl.).

**49.** on US25, **Poland-China Hog Mon.,** marble mem. to breed developed by Shakers.

**54. MONROE.** J. with St.63, which leads (E) $5^m$ to **Shaker Village** (1805-1913). **80. CINCINNATI** (see), which spreads (S) to Ohio R., **81. KY. LINE.**

## US 33—OHIO

**OHIO-W. VA. LINE** ($1^m$ from Mason, W. Va.) **(NW) to IND. LINE** ($9^m$ from Decatur, Ind.). **228. US33**

Via: Pomeroy, Athens, Nelsonville, Logan, Lancaster, Lithopolis, Columbus, Dublin, Marysville, Indian Lake, Wapakoneta, St. Marys, Willshire. RR. & bus conns. & good accoms. in larger towns; resorts in recr. areas & camp sites in nat. for. & St. pks. Scenic tour crossing Hocking R. valley, secs. of Wayne Nat. For., only one in state, the popular Ind. L. recr. area & hist. country along W. boundary.

### Sec. 1: W. VA. LINE to COLUMBUS. 102. US33.

**0. POMEROY,** across Pomeroy-Mason Bridge from W. Va. J. with St.7 (Ohio R. Tour). In the hill country, fox hunting is popular, & customs brought from Brit. Isles & New England survive along with johnny cake, cherry bounce & sassafras tea. US33 passes wooded ravines & hilltop orchards, an occasional coal mine.

**27. ATHENS** (see US50) bet. two units of **Wayne Nat. For.** US33 follows Hocking R. into **Wayne Nat. For.** (hqs. in Columbus), covering c. 1,500,000 as. noted for autumn coloring of its hardwoods. Before Civil War, Ohio was leading hardwood state. Then, in 1870's, rich deposits of iron ore were discovered & more fors. vanished to keep furnaces burning. Ohio lost all but fraction of primeval covering. Once the fors. were cut down, rich topsoil was washed by rains & swept along flooding rivers. Fed. Gov. is carrying out large-scale projects in reforestation & conservation of wildlife. (For.camps.pic.trls.). **42. NELSONVILLE.** Just (N) are developed pic. & camp. areas within nat. for. (f.h.). **54. LOGAN,** center of celebrated Hocking Pk. area. J. with St.75 (which leads (E) $12^m$ to **Straitsville Mine Fire,** where coal has smouldered since 1884). **Hocking Pks.** (pic.camp.shelters) owe their caves, cliffs & tunnels to rock formation composed largely of mineral quartz, which resists erosion while upper & lower layers of shale are gradually worn away. Thus fantastic grottoes, caverns & natural bridges have been created.

SIDE TRIP: On St.664 (SW) 11m to J. with St.374, which leads to noted **Old Man's Cave St. Pk.** (camp.facils.), named for hermit who lived beneath rocky ledge a cent. ago. Cascading creek follows deep gorge that runs through 1,400-a. pk. **Cedar Falls** is in grove of evergreens. Another waterfall tumbles down cliffs of **Ash Cave,** whose walls are covered with rare flowers & fern. A few miles (N) on St.374 is **Conkles Hollow,** rocky canyon covered with hardwoods. **Rockhouse** (N) of S. Bloomingville on St.374, is natural cathedral with pillars of colored stone, probably once a moundbuilders' shelter. St.374 cont. (N) through 300-a. **Cantwell Cliffs St. Pk.,** popular with picnickers & nature lovers & famous for rhododendron; St.374 rejoins US3 near **Rockbridge.**

US33 cont. (NW) from Logan. **73. LANCASTER. 88.5. CANAL WINCHESTER. 99.5. BEXLEY. 102. COLUMBUS** (see Columbus for this sec.).

**Sec. 2: COLUMBUS to IND. LINE. 126. US33**

**0. COLUMBUS.** Hy. winds along Gt. Scioto R. through recr. area created by Griggs & O'Shaughnessy dams, part of Columbus water system. Near **DUBLIN, 13.,** is J. with St.257 (which runs (N) past **Leatherlips Mon.** (1888), comm. Wyandot chieftain; the bridge & reservoir of **O'Shaughnessy Dam; Columbus Zoo). 30. MARYSVILLE,** charming town sett. in 1816; home of Otway Curry, who wrote "The Log Cabin Song" for Wm. H. Harrison's campaign. **49. ZANESFIELD,** sett. in 1819 on the land of Isaac Zane, who was adopted into Wyandot tribe. He married White Crane, daughter of Chief Tarhe, & remained in Ind. village for 40 yrs. Zane, friend of the settlers, was at signing of Greenville Treaty, 1795. **Zane-Kenton Mon.** In **Ebenezer Zane H.** (1805) was held 1st M.E. Quarterly Conference in N.W. Terr. (1819). Near Zanesfield is **Site of Wapatomica,** Shawnee town where Simon Kenton was saved from massacre by Simon Girty, 1778, before Girty threw in his lot with Brit. **56. BELLEFONTAINE** (see) near highest land in Ohio. **70. IND. L. ST. PK.** (f.h.camp.facils.boat.), around 11,000-a. L.; summer resort; centers also at **Russells Point** & **Lakeview.** In **Manary Blockh. Mus.,** Lakeview, is exhibit of pre-Rev. andirons, tintypes, printed cottons. **89. WAPAKONETA** (see). J. with US25 (see). US33 swings (N) & follows roughly the St. Marys R. to **IND. LINE.** at **126.**

# CINCINNATI

## CINCINNATI

Union RR. Terminal, Lincoln Pk. Dr. & Dalton Ave. Bus Depots: Greyhound, E. 5th & Sycamore Sts. Trailways, 123 E. Court St. Greater Cincinnati Airport, across R. in Ky. Foot of Broadway for "Island Queen" to Coney I. (daily Mem. Day to Labor Day). Foot of Main St., Greene Line Steamers for Miss. R. cruises. Excellent accoms. & recr. facils. Good theaters, symphony orchestra, art & other museums. Summer opera at Zoo. Annual Events: Good Friday Pilgrimage, Biennial May Music Festival (odd yrs.), Exhibit of Amer. Art (Oct.). Info.: C. of C., 4th & Race Sts.

Cincinnati, 2nd largest city, is still "a queen among cities" as Longfellow named it, & Cincinnatians are "courteous & agreeable" as Dickens found them in 1842. City rises on low terraces dominated by Carew Tower & Union Central Bldg., & then its suburbs spread back & high among the hills. Price Hill & Mt. Adams face each other across the Basin. Shut off from N. Ohio by rugged ranges, Cincinnati has always looked to the S., while Ohio R. has linked it with E. & W. So, today, it is cultural & econ. center for immense area. Nationally known centers of music, art & education have grown up here—Univ. of Cincinnati, Xavier Univ., Our Lady of Cincinnati & Hebrew Union colleges; Symphony Orchestra & outstanding Art. Mus. Industrial products incl. soap, radios, watches, plastics, playing cards & machine tools; also meat-packing plants, steel works & breweries. Kroger Stores & Fleischmann's Yeast began here. Once victim of boss rule, Cincinnati later won title of "best governed city."

In 1786, Benj. Stites, a trader, crossed from Ky. in pursuit of Ind. horse thieves. Impressed by the country, he carried E. a glowing report to Congressman J. C. Symmes, who promptly purchased 2,000,000 as. of land bet. Little & Big Miami Rs. In 1788, Stites & some Ky. settlers founded Columbia, & another group settled Losantiville downstream. In 1789 Symmes founded N. Bend. Terr. Gov. Art. St. Clair came to Ft. Washington, at Losantiville, in 1790, & changed name of village to Cincinnati, in honor of society org. by Continental Army officers. After War of 1812, town boomed with river commerce, becoming shipbuilding center & focus of westward immigration. With completion of Miami & Erie Canal, its flour mills, meatpacking plants & distilleries flourished. In 1830's liberal Germans came & made famous the Over-the-Rhine sec. of Vine St. After potato famine in 1848, hundreds of Irish joined Cincinnati's native-born Virginians, New Englanders & Kentuckians. Before Civil War, Cincinnati was a metropolis. During Gilded Age, Geo. Cox became city's boss, & vice flourished for nearly 40 yrs. Cth. Riot of 1884 grew out of public anger against political corruption. Finally in 1925, the reform charter group brought in a clean election & city manager system. During the yrs. that followed, Cincinnati was transformed. Now, city planners are at work on slum-clearance, riverfront development & over-all street pattern that will link scattered communities.

PTS. OF INT. DOWNTOWN: (1) Front St., **Pub. Landing,** granite-paved area where settlers landed. Greene Line Wharf for modern "Delta Queen" & "Gordon C. Greene," last of the packets (leaves St. Louis, Mo.). Coney I. Wharf (see Trip I below). Front St., in great days of river trade, was lined with hotels, stores, restaurants & saloons. Secs. of it, known as the Levee, Rat Row & Sausage Row, were notorious. (2) Pearl St., (N) 2 blocks, is still the marketplace, with famous **Pearl St. Growers Market** (1816). (3) 3rd & Walnut Sts., **United Bank Bldg.** (Richardson Romanes.). (4) 3rd & Vine Sts., **Site of Burnet H.** (1850), 340-room hotel. (5) 411 E. 3rd St., **Site of Mrs. Trollope's Bazaar** (1828), the fancy-goods establishment run by mother of Anthony Trollope. Mrs. Trollope deplored the natives' uncouth manners, while they ignored her trinkets, marked up for profit from retail price she had paid. In 1830, Mrs. Trollope left in disdain & wrote caustic "Domestic Manners of the Americans." (6) 414 E. 3rd St., **Audubon H.,** where artist-scientist worked at taxidermy. (7) 3rd St. bet. Ludlow & Broadway, **Ft. Washington Mon.** (8) 429 E. 3rd St., **Daniel Drake H.,** home of great doctor, teacher, writer (1785-1852); founder of Medical College (1817) & several schools, hospitals & libs. (9) In Fountain Sq. (1870), **Tyler Davidson Fountain** (1871.by Von Kreling of Nuremberg). (10) 5th & Vine Sts., **Carew Tower** (1930.by Walter Ahlschlager), city's tallest skyscraper. (11) E. of Sq., **Federal Bldg.** (1939.Mod.). (12) W. of Sq., **Union Central Bldg.** (1917.by Cass Gilbert). (13) 629 Vine St., **Pub. Lib.** (1865.by Jas.McLaughlin). (14) 6th St. from Vine to Race Sts., **Terrace Plaza Hotel** (1948.Mod.by Skidmore, Owings & Merrill); lobby of 8th floor, above windowless shopping & business center; restaurant on top of bldg. with **Joan Miro Mural,** sculpture by Alex. Calder & Saul Steinberg's cartoon mural. (15) Vine & 6th Sts., **Palace Hotel** & other bldgs. surviving from 1880's. (16) Plum & W. 8th Sts., **Old Cathedral of St. Peter in Chains** (1845.Gr.Rev.by Henry Walter); named for its painting by Murillo. (17) 309 W. Court St., **Lloyd Lib.** (O), noted lib. of medicine & pharmaceutics; adj. is Lloyd Bros. Plant. (18) Central Pky. & Walnut St., **Industrial Mus.** (O.wks.), of Ohio Mechanics Institute (1829). (19) Elm & Grant Sts., **Hamilton Cty. Mem. Bldg.** (1908); large hist. coll. (20) Lincoln Pk. Dr., **Lincoln Court** (1942), one of several projects for concentrated Negro pop. (21) Lincoln Pk. Dr. (W) end, **Union Terminal** (1933.by E.D. Tyler), considered one of world's most beautiful RR. stas.

PTS. OF INT. E. & NE.: (22) In Lytle Pk., **Statue of Abraham Lincoln** (1917.by Geo.Grey Barnard), considered a masterpiece. (23) 318 Pike St., **Taft Mus.** (O.1820. Gr.Rev.probably by Latrobe), housing Chas. Taft Coll. of noted paintings; also coll. of Frank Duveneck, city's 19th cent. teacher-painter. Taft H. is considered one of finest remaining examples of Adams style. (24) **Mt. Adams,** reached by Scenic Incline Ry. Good Friday Pilgrimage begins at Columbia Ave. below & proceeds up slope to **Ch. of Immaculate Conception & Our Lady of Lourdes Grotto.** Near-by are **Rockwood Potteries** (tours). By Ida St. Bridge, **Pilgrim Ch.** (Presb.1887), built by Prots. & Caths. (25) Columbia Pky. (NE) from Mt. Adams, **Eden Pk.** On wooded hilltop is **Art Mus.;** main bldg. (1886.Romanes.by J.McLaughlin); wings around open court (1907-38.Gr.Rev. & one Romanes.); Mary M. Emery Old Masters, Duveneck oils, Shelt Coll. of Ancient Egyptian Art, & Hanna Coll. In Eden Pk. also are **Art Academy & Krohn Conserv.** (O). (26) On Time Hill (NE) from downtown, **Gruen Watch Co.** (O). (27) Oak & Winslow Sts., **Ch. of the New Jerusalem** (Swedenborgian); window by Burne-Jones. (28) Gilbert & Foraker Aves., **Lyman Beecher Homestead,** in Walnut Hills Negro dist. Here, in her father's house, Harriet Beecher Stowe met abolitionists. (29) Edgecliff Rd. at Francis Lane, **Our Lady of Cincinnati,** Cath. college for women. (30) Madison Rd. & Dexter Pl., **Institutum Divi Thomae**

(O.appl.), (Cath.) center of research; est. 1935. (31) Victory Pky., **Xavier Univ.** (Jesuit.1831), in symmetrical group of bldgs. (1920-29.Tudor Goth.).
(32) **Walnut Hills,** residential suburbs. Among many mansions are **Holabird Luedeking Castle** (1833), **Longworth Estate, Shipley H.** (1875), **The Pines** (1827). (33) **Oakley Factory Colony,** begun in 1907 when **Cin. Machine Tool Co.** was est. (34) **Avondale,** long-est. & attractive Jewish settlement. At N. Crescent Ave., **Isaac M. Wise Temple Center.** Lexington Ave., **Avondale Synagogue** (1926.Class.Rev.by Oscar Schwartz). (35) Eden Ave., **Univ. of Cin. College of Medicine;** lib. has coll. of Dr. Drake's (see above) books & instruments. (36) Oak St. & Burnet Ave., **Conserv. of Music,** founded by Clara Bauer in 1867.

PTS. OF INT. W. & NW.: (37) **Price Hill,** hilltop suburb, reached by incline. Among fine churches, schools & houses are many early mansions. (38) Along Mill Cr. (E) are several industrial communities around large plants: On Colerain Ave., **Crosley Radio Corp. Main Plant;** Display Room (O) & **Lodge & Shipley Machine Tool Co.,** one of city's largest. On Spring Grove Ave., **E. Kahn's Sons,** large meat-packing plant, **Cin. Union Stock Yard Co.** (tours on appl.), huge livestock exchange opened in 1873 & **Proctor & Gamble Co.** (1837), Ivorydale (tours Tues.& Thurs.). In **Hartwell,** most northerly suburb, **Nat. Distillers Products Corp.** (O.appl.). (39) **Hebrew Union College,** bet. Riddle Rd. & Dixmyth Ave., oldest & most celebrated Jewish theological school in U. S.; founded in 1875 by Rabbi Isaac M. Wise; cooperates with Univ. of Cin. Expansion program (1948) incl. School of Sacred Music in N.Y.C. **Bernheim Lib.** (O); art coll. (40) **Univ. of Cincinnati,** at S. end of Burnet Woods; one of oldest (1870) & largest mun. colleges in U. S. Incl. early Cin. College & Medical College (1819), Cin. Astronomical Soc. (1842) & McMicken Univ. (1869). **McMicken Hall** (1895), **Hanna Hall** (1896). **Cunningham Hall** (1899). (41) At Lafayette Circle, **Abbe Meteorological Observatory,** named for Cleveland Abbe, who started nation's 1st weather serv. in Cincinati in 1869.

## TRIPS OUT OF CINCINNATI (see also Ky.).

**I. US52 (S) to GRANT MEM. ST. PK. 32.** Via: Coney I., Pt. Pleasant.
Route follows Kellogg Ave. (E) along Ohio R. **15. CONEY I. AMUSEMENT PK.** (Mem.Day to Labor Day.pic.swim.ballroom.playfields). **River Downs Race Track. Lumpkin** (mun.) **Airport,** near **Mt. Washington,** suburb. **25. NEW RICHMOND** (1816), rebuilt after every flood. Beautiful esplanade. **32. PT. PLEASANT,** birthpl. of Pres. Grant. **Grant Mem. St. Pk.** (pic.facils.) surrounds **Grant H. Mus.** (O.rest.) & **Grant Mem. Ch.**

**II. US50 (E) to FAYETTEVILLE. 43.** Via: Mariemont, Plainville, Milford. Follow Madison Rd. (NE), which becomes Wooster Pike in **Madisonville, 13. MARIEMONT,** created in 1822 on Little Miami R. as ideal Eng. village. **Mariemont Inn.** At 5801 Wooster Pike, **Eliphalet Ferris H.** (1813.Georg.Col.rest.). Adj. Mariemont is **Plainville,** summer resort.

**18. TERRACE PARK,** residential. **John Robinson H.,** on estate of great circus man.

**43. FAYETTEVILLE,** largely Cath. community. **St. Aloysius Academy** (1850).

III. **US50 (W) to IND. LINE, 19.** Via: Addyston, North Bend, Cleves.
US50 offers view of shantyboats along shore, occasionally a Greene Line packet or tremendous barge fleet. **11.5. ADDYSTON** (1871). **14.5. NORTH BEND,** one of orig. settlements (1789). **Site of Benj. Harrison's Birthpl.** & long-time home of Pres. W. H. Harrison, his grandfather. **Wm. H. Harrison Mem. St. Pk.** (facils.) overlooks R. & passing steamboats salute man buried beneath **Harrison Mem. Shaft. 19. IND. LINE.**

IV. **US22, St.350 (N) to FT. ANCIENT ST. PK. 44.** Via: Norwood, Silverton, Montgomery, Hopkinsville, Morrow, (Lebanon).
Follow Montgomery Rd. (NE). **5. NORWOOD,** a separate city, heavily industrialized, partly because of favorable tax rate. Many fine 19th cent. Hs. At Main & Moeller Aves., **Mount St. Mary's Seminary of the West.** Large industrial plants (mostly N.O.) are: **Allis-Chalmers, U. S. Playing Card Co., Globe-Wernicke, Amer. Laundry Machinery Co. & Kemper Thomas Co. 11. SILVERTON** (1804). Hy. leaves plateau & crosses R. near **HOPKINSVILLE, 26.** J. with St.48.

SIDE TRIP: On St.48 (N) 7.5m to **Lebanon.** Only remaining one of its famous taverns is **The Golden Lamb** (1815). On sign beneath the lamb are names of Dickens, Henry Clay & other distinguished guests. Here, in 1871, C. L. Vallandingham, Copperhead leader, killed himself accidentally while re-enacting a supposed murder in order to get facts to clear his client. Near Lebanon is Shaker Village, on St.63.

**38.** J. with St.350, over which trip cont. (W). **44. FT. ANCIENT ST. PK.** (pic.camp. concessions), around largest prehist. fortification in **U.S. Moundbuilder Mus.** (sm. fee).

**V. US127 (N) 23. to HAMILTON.**

**HAMILTON** (1791)

Through RR. & bus conns. Commercial airports. Good accoms. Recr. facils. in numerous pks. Le Sourdsville L. Amusement Pk. (N).

City on site of ft. built by Gen. St. Clair in 1791-92 is now important industrial center, nationally known for machine tools, safes & stoves. Wm. Dean Howells spent boyhood here. W. of Miami R. are older Hs., with grilled balconies, mingling with fine modern homes. Around site of ft. (E) is mixed area, with large pop. of factory workers. **Soldiers, Sailors, & Pioneers Mem.** (O); large hist. coll. Across from it is **Site of Ft. Hamilton.** One of world's largest makers of machine tools is **General Machinery Corp.**

**VI. US27 (NW) to IND. LINE. 47.** Via: Oxford.

**16.** J. with US50 (see), which links US27 & US127. Just beyond J., route crosses Gt. Miami R. & swings (N) through **Millville & McGonigle. 41. OXFORD,** seat of Miami Univ. & Western College; college town since 1809, when the fors. were cleared away for the univ. Hy. runs near border of rolling campus of Western Univ. (O.1825). Facing campus is **Lewis Place,** president's house. W. H. McGuffey compiled his 1st "Eclectic Reader" while pres. at Miami, & Pres. Benj. Harrison was in class of 1852. Oxford College for Women, which became part of Univ. in 1928, was started by J. W. Scott, father of Mrs. Benj. Harrison. PTS. OF INT.: **Beta Theta Pi Campanile** (1939), with Westminster bells. **Stoddard Hall,** one of orig. bldgs. Century-old **Simpson H. Alumni Lib. & McGuffey Mem. Mus.** On High St., **Caroline S. Harrison Mem. Bldg.** (1849.Queen Anne); Oak & Spring Sts., **W. H. McGuffey H. Western College For Women** (Presb.1853) was modelled after Mt. Holyoke. **Alumnae Hall** has Heath Chime. **Helen Peabody Hall** (1871) is named for great early teacher, pupil of Mary Lyon. At **47.** US27 crosses **IND. LINE** at **COLLEGE CORNER.**

# CLEVELAND

**CLEVELAND**

RR. Stas.: Pub. Sq., Union Terminal; W. 6th St. & Front Ave., Penn. RR.: Superior Ave. near W. 9th St., Erie RR. Superior Ave. & E. 9th St., Greyhound Bus Terminal. Erieside Dr. (SW) 8m, Mun. Airport. Riverside Ave., D. & C. Navigation Co. Dock. Accoms.: All types. Auditoriums & theaters incl. Pub. Auditorium, Playhouse Sq., The Play House & Severance Hall (Orchestra). Mun. Stadium & recr. facils. in 10,000-a. Pk. System. Annual Events: May Show (Ap.-June), Mus. of Art; Garden Tours (May-June), Garden Center at E. Blvd. & Euclid Ave.; Nat. Air Races (Labor Day week end); Home & Flower Show (Mar.). Info.: 400 Union Commerce Bldg., C. of C.

Cleveland, largest city in Ohio & 6th largest in U.S., is greatest L. Erie port & one of world's greatest iron & steel centers, extending nearly 30 miles along shore. Through center of city is wide valley of Cuyahoga R., & here on the Flats are steel mills, oil refineries, factories & lumber yards. Commercial & residential dists. rise on either side on higher level of old lakebed. On the Heights & in Chagrin valley are suburbs of notable beauty, incl. romantic Gates Mills, with Hunt Club & Polo Field. From High Level Bridge, the city plan is seen to be simple & orderly, with all aves. leading to Pub. Sq., above which rises the Terminal Tower, tallest bldg. in U.S. outside of N.Y.C. More than half the people are of foreign birth or parentage, representing nearly 50 nationalities. Most of the Negro citizens (8 per cent of total) live around edge of downtown dist., where housing projects are replacing slums. Chief industries are shipping & processing of iron & steel & manufacture of machine tools, automotive & aviation parts, textiles, electrical products & chemicals. Cleveland has always been model of civic enterprise, with excellent Welfare Federation & Community Fund. Townsend Plan has hqs. here. Western Reserve Univ., Case Institute of Technology, John Carroll Univ., Penn College & Ursuline College for Women are outstanding institutions, & Cleveland's Symphony Orchestra & Play House are nationally known. 1st white settlement at mouth of Cuyahoga R. was trading post, est. in 1747 by the Irishman, Geo. Croghan, 1st Brit. agent in area. When N.W. Terr. was org. (1787), Conn. was allowed to keep part of land held by grant from Charles II, from Pa. Line (W) to the "South Sea." This Western Reserve, extending 120 miles, was bought & surveyed by Conn. Land Co., led by Gen. Moses Cleaveland. The Firelands, 500,000 as., about 50 miles (W), were reserved by Conn. to repay citizens for damage during Rev. Instructed to found "a capital town," Cleaveland laid out 2 main streets (Superior & Ontario) as broad as they are today. The 49 settlers endured winter of 1796 & then forsook their capital by the frozen lake. When the "Walk-in-the-Water" steamed into L. Erie in 1818, Cleveland was smallest of 14 towns in Western Reserve. Then, in 1832, the Ohio & Erie Canal was completed with Cleveland as terminal, & in 1836 the city inc. with 5,000 citizens. Mid-century, the RRs. brought 1st loads of L. Superior ore & of bituminous coal from the E.

Cleveland was already a big city when Rockefeller & Hanna families settled here. In Civil War period, it was a vital sta. on Underground Railroad. Then came tremendous development. J. D. Rockefeller org. Standard Oil in 1870; Mark Hanna made fortune in coal & shipping, & Jephtha H. Wade in the telegraph & real estate. White Mfg. Co. made sewing machines; Sherwin Williams Paint & Otis Steel (1st open hearth) were est. Charles F. Brush lighted Pub. Sq. with carbon arc lamps; & America's 1st electric streetcars appeared in the "Forest City" (1884). Cleveland's wealthy men began to look around. J. H. Wade gave land for 1st city pk. The Opera House & "The Plain Dealer" were founded. Through series of consolidations, the industrial giants of era created some of America's notorious trusts in Cleveland. Mark Hanna, maker of Presidents, met opposition at last in Thos. L. Johnson, who was fought by Hanna but held office of mayor for 5 terms. Under him & his successor, Newton D. Baker, city politics were given a thorough cleaning. Labor, in 1880's, had fought through several widespread strikes to official recognition. Cleveland Fed. of Labor was org. in 1910. During World War I, Cleveland profited financially & in return gave 1st Red Cross unit & 1st Community Chest to the country. The Symphony Orchestra was org. in 1918, & Mus. of Art built in 1916. The Van Sweringen brothers created their famous empire, developing beautiful Shaker Heights, acquiring Nickel Plate RR. & building Terminal Tower group & Union Sta. before their financial structure collapsed. The pop. had completely changed with expanding labor market & because of this, Cleveland's interest in art, music & drama was intensified, & its Play House & Gilpin Players, a Negro theater, became nationally famous.

PTS. OF INT.: (1) **High Level Bridge** (1918), largest of its kind in world. (2) St. Clair Ave. at W. 9th St., **Site of Cleaveland's Landing.** (3) W. 6th St. & Frankfort Ave., **Weddell H.** (1854); Lincoln Room (O). (4) In 10-a. Pub. Sq.: **Moses Cleaveland Statue** (1887.G.C.Hamilton), **Tom L. Johnson Statue** (1915.H.N.Matzen). (5) **Terminal Tower Group,** adj. Pub. Sq., **The Tower Bldg.** (1930), modern structure with turreted tower (O.sm.fee), is $119,000,000 mon. to the Van Sweringens. (6) (W) of Pub. Sq., **Cleveland College,** downtown center of Western Reserve Univ. (see below), housed in Newton D. Baker Mem. Bldg. (7) **Lakeside Mall,** civic center planned with aid of the late Dan. Burnham, J. M. Carrere & other architects. Incl. are 4 bldgs. by Walker & Weeks: **Pub. Lib.** (1925.Fr.Ren.), **Fed. Reserve Bank** (1922.Ital.Ren.), **Board of Education Bldg.** (Fr.& Ital.Ren.) & **Stadium** (1931). Others in group are **Fed. Bldg.** (1910) & **Cuyahoga County Cth.** (Fr.Ren.by A.W. Brunner); **Auditorium** (1922.Ital.Ren.by Betz & MacDowell) & **City Hall** (1916. Ren.by J.M.Dyer). (8) **Ore Dock,** with Hulitt type unloading machines. (9) Euclid Ave. & E. 22nd St., **Trinity Cathedral** (Episc.1907.Perpendicular Goth.by C.F. Schweinfurth); congregation est. in 1816. (10) 2712 Euclid Ave., **Mus. of Nat. Hist.** (O), housed in Leonard Hanna Mansion (Gr.Rev.). (11) 6709 Euclid Ave., **Dunham Tavern** (sm.fee). (12) 2040 E. 86th St., **Play House** (Romanes.by C.L.Small), home of 2 experimental theaters. (13) 10915 East Blvd., **Western Reserve Hist. Mus.** (O. free); records of Conn. Land Co. (14) East Blvd. & Fairmount Rd., **Baldwin Reservoir** (1925), one of largest covered reservoirs in world (136,000,000 gals.).

(15) Euclid Ave. (E) of E. 107th St. is elm-shaded **Univ. Circle,** with **Hanna Statue** (1907.by Saint-Gaudens) & **Louis Kossuth Statue** (by And.Toth). (16) **Case Institute of Technology,** founded by Leonard Case, Jr., 1877. **Mus. of Geology** (O.appl.). On Taylor Rd., (E) 4$^{m}$ from campus, is **Warner-Swasey Observ.** (1919). (17) **Western Reserve Univ.,** founded in 1826 & moved to Cleveland in 1882. Besides Cleveland College, downtown, Univ. incl. undergraduate Flora Stone Mather (women) &

Adelbert (men) colleges, a graduate & 8 professional schools. **Amasa Stone Chapel** (Eng.Goth.) of Adelbert College, comm. philanthropist. (18) **Univ. Hospitals,** on Adelbert Rd. (19) Euclid Ave. & East Blvd., **Severance Hall** (1930.Fr.& Eng.Ren. by Walker & Weeks), home of Symphony Orchestra. (20) In 75-a. Wade Pk., white marble **Mus. of Art** (1916.Gr.Ionic.by Hubbell & Benes). Rodin's **"Man of Age of Bronze"** in rotunda. Colls. of Medieval & Byzantine, early Ital. & later European art, incl. **"Portrait of Isabella Brandt"** by Rubens. (21) Rockefeller Pk., **29 Cultural Gardens** of nationality groups, dedicated to internat. peace. Eng. Garden is modeled after Shakespeare Garden; in Hebrew Garden are cedars of Lebanon; while Ital. Garden is patterned formally around Ren. fountain & German Garden has **Unterberg Marble Fountain** from Salzburg. (22) 12316 Euclid Ave., in Lake View Cemetery, **Garfield Mon.** (1890.by Geo.Keller), tomb of Pres. Jas. A. Garfield. Also **Rockefeller Monolith.**

## TRIPS OUT OF CLEVELAND.

### I. US20 (E) to PAINESVILLE. 30.5.

Via: E. Cleveland, Euclid, Willoughby, Mentor, (Kirtland). Lake Shore Blvd. (St.283) is pleasant alternate route.

US20, Iroquois warpath against the Erie, follows Euclid Ave., street of the "robber barons," past Case-Western Reserve campus & Rockefeller's former estate. **8.5.** On outskirts of **E. Cleveland,** 3rd largest suburb, is **Nela Pk.,** research lab. of Gen. Electric. **Lighting Institute Bldg.** (usually O.). At 21320 Euclid Ave. is **Shrine of Our Lady of Lourdes** (O.outdoor serv.May-Dec.). **13.5. EUCLID** (sett.1798), suburb with lakeside residential sec. **24. MENTOR** (see). At 1059 Mentor Ave., **Garfield H.** (O).

SIDE TRIP: On St.306 (S) 3.5m to **Kirtland.** On Ap. 6, 1830, Jos. Smith org. Ch. of Jesus Christ of Latter Day Saints. He set out for Mo. but stopped instead at Mentor & gained many converts, among them Brigham Young, who became leader when Smith was killed in Nauvoo (see Ill.). Local attacks on Mormon doctrine & financial difficulties brought an end to Kirtland. **Kirtland Temple** (O), massive stone structure built by the Mormons, incl. Young, each man giving a day a wk.

**30.5 PAINESVILLE** (see), overlooking Grand R.; seat of L. Erie College, noted also for elegant early houses. At 106 E. Washington St. is **Gillette H.,** marked by corbelled chimneys above balustraded roof. 792 Mentor Ave., **Rider Tavern** (O.1818). **Lake Erie College** (women), with 50-a. wooded campus, was opened at Willoughby in 1847, with faculty chosen by Mt. Holyoke's Mary Lyon.

### II. US20 (S) to OBERLIN. 37.5. Via: Lakewood, Rocky River, Elyria.

US20 dips (S) through wealthy suburbs to the Firelands, distinguished by villages that might be in Conn. **5. LAKELAND,** Cleveland's largest suburb, mainly residential. **8.5. ROCKY RIVER,** on plateau along Black R. **28. ELYRIA** (1817). In Black R. Gorge, **Cascade Pk.** (pic.). East Ave. & 2nd St., **Octagonal H.,** popular style in early 1800's. E. River & Broad Sts., **Gates Mem. Hospital,** known for work with crippled children. **37.5. OBERLIN,** founded simultaneously with its famous college in 1833 by Rev. John J. Shipherd & Philo P. Stewart as colony pledged to "plainest living & highest thinking." One of Ohio's richest schools, **Oberlin College** keeps its democratic tradition, 1st coed. college in U.S. & 1st to admit Negroes; active in abolitionist movement. Incl. Conservatory of Music & Grad. School of Theology (non-sectarian). At 64 E. College St., **Hall H.,** where C. M. Hall worked on process that revolutionized aluminum industry. The Halls bequeathed to Oberlin $15,000,-000 ($23,000,000 endowment by 1948). **Allen Mem. Hospital** (1925) & **Allen Art Mem. Bldg.** honor Dr. Dudley P. Allen & son. **Theological Quadrangle** (1931), gift of J. D. Rockefeller, Jr. & Mrs. D. W. James. J. with St.58, hy. (N) to Lorain (see).

SIDE TRIP: (S) 9m on St.58 is **Wellington,** typical Firelands town. In 1858, fugitive slave was taken from U.S. marshal by party of townspeople & students, & resultant Oberlin-Wellington Rescue Case excited the nation. The rescue party, defended by Salmon P. Chase & other notable lawyers, was finally freed. At 9.5m is **Greenwood Cemetery,** burial place of A. M. Willard, painter of **"Spirit of '76"** & of Otis Pratt (1845-1921), whose "Landscape Discovery" decayed with him, according to his epitaph, "for want of Free Schools or Art supported by our Gov."

### III. US422 (SE) to YOUNGSTOWN. 67.

Via: Cleveland Heights, Univ. Heights, Shaker Heights, Chagrin Falls, (Taborville), Warren, (Niles), Girard.

After crossing some suburbs, US422 becomes direct route to steel empire & coal country, **CLEVELAND HEIGHTS** is composed of several communities. In **UNIV.**

**HEIGHTS** just N. of hy. is **John Carroll Univ.** (Jesuit), founded in 1886. In 1935, Univ. moved into new bldgs. (Coll.Goth.) on 50-a. campus. **9. SHAKER HEIGHTS,** restricted suburb developed by Van Sweringens on site of 19th cent. community of celibate Shakers. **18. Chagrin Falls** & winding Chagrin R. are said to carry name given by Moses Cleaveland when he found his party was not following the Cuyahoga R. At **25.** J. with Rd. to **Taborville** (S.c.4m), a village of Czechoslovak families founded c.1925.

SIDE TRIP: (S) 5m on St.700 is **Hiram College** (coed.), in pastoral setting; founded in 1850 by Disciples of Christ. Pres. Garfield was valedictorian in 1853.

At **38.** on US422 is J. with St.282, which leads (S) 2m to **Nelson Ledges St. Pk.** (pic. camp.facils.). **52.5. WARREN,** important steel city. Settled by Conn. Land Co. in 1798, it remained a small quiet city & maker of lamps for America until 1910. After est. of Trumbull Steel Co. (1914), more than 17,000 persons of foreign birth or descent were drawn to Warren's labor market. **57.5** J. with St.46.

SIDE TRIP: (S) 2m on St.46 to **McKinley Birthpl. Mem.** (O.1917.mod.Doric), at **Niles,** another steel city. In Court of Honor is **Statue of McKinley.**

**62. GIRARD,** sett. in 1800 & named for Phila. philanthropist, is part of steel & iron area.

## 67. YOUNGSTOWN

Through RR., bus & airline conns. Good accoms. & recr. facils. Theaters incl. The Playhouse. Annual Art Show & folk festivals. Info.: Auto Club at Ohio Hotel.

Youngstown (sett.1798) is center of steel domain extending through Shenango & Mahoning valleys & producing a sixth of nation's pig iron & an eighth of its steel. Bet. the Pub. Sq. & downtown sec. & Mahoning R. are RR. tracks & industrial plants. More exclusive residential sec. is (SW) along Mill Cr., withdrawn among the hills. Youngstown is a milltown, geared to production of steel, though the more unsightly scars have been cleared away. Pop. is largely working people, more than 50 per cent of foreign birth or descent. An iron smelter was set up by James & Dan. Heaton in 1802 in Yellow Creek (now Struthers), & 1st coal mine was opened in the valley in 1826. After Pa.-Ohio Canal was constructed, Youngstown became Mahoning Cty.'s seat & center of trade. In 1892, Union Iron & Steel Co. came to Mahoning R. & modern industry began in earnest, filling the town with mills & furnaces. In 1937, Youngstown was scene of one of "little steel" strikes. PTS. OF INT.: (1) In Pub. Sq., **Soldiers Mon.** (1870), granite shaft (47'). (2) Below Pub. Sq., **Mahoning County Cth.** (Ital.Ren.by Chas.Owsley); murals by E. H. Blashfield. (3) At 524 Wick Ave., **Butler Art Institute** (Ital.Ren.1919.by McKim,Meade & White). (4) At Mahoning Ave. Bridge, **Mill Cr. Pk.** (pic.); 1,400 as. of natural beauty (boat.). **Lanterman Mill** (1845-46), on site of 1st gristmill, has **Nat. Hist. Mus.** (O). **Pioneer Pavilion** (1821). (5) Cor. 5th & Park Aves., **Stambaugh Auditorium** (1925.by Helmle & Corbett). (6) At Market St. Bridge, **United Engineering Co.** (O.appl.). (7) **Republic Steel Co.** (N.O.). (8) Center St. Bridge, **Youngstown Sheet & Tube Co.** (O.appl.). (9) 410 Wick Ave., **Youngstown College,** coed., lib. arts, accredited; began as Y.M.C.A.'s Youngstown Assoc. School in 1888. Around **Main Bldg.** (1931.Tudor) are Dana Sch. of Music, Sch. of Business & Wm. Rayen Sch. of Engineering.

## IV. St.14 (SE) to RAVENNA. 46.

Via: Garfield Heights, Bedford, Twinsburg, Streetsboro, (Kent). Crosses densely populated area to J. with Pa. St.51 route to Pittsburgh.

**GARFIELD HEIGHTS, 8.5., MAPLE HEIGHTS & BEDFORD, 12.,** merge into each other. In **STREETSBORO, 26.,** is **Singletary H.** (1828), once a tavern. **29. L. ROCKWELL** (no f.), Akron's 800-a. reservoir. **46. RAVENNA** (sett.1799), is small mfg. city on watershed bet. Cuyahoga & Mahoning Rs., near Akron's L. dist. J. with St.5.

SIDE TRIP: (W) 5m on St.5 is **Kent,** on Cuyahoga R. at edge of Akron. **Walcott Lilac Gardens** (O). **Kent St. Univ.** (coed.) began as normal sch. & became univ. in 1935; incl. graduate sch. & colleges of lib. arts, education & business administration.

## V. US21 (S) to MASSILLON. 55.

Via: Cuyahoga Heights, Independence, Brecksville, Richfield, Copley, Barberton, Canal Fulton, Crystal Spring. St.8 is more leisurely route & passes Cuyahoga Falls.

US21 takes direct route across level country by-passing Akron & winding with Tuscarawas R. At **14. BRECKSVILLE,** pleasant town spreading for miles around the

Green. **Congr. Ch.** (1844). At J. with St.82 is **Brecksville Inn** (O). **16. FURNACE RUN RESERV.** (pic.recr.facils.); 400 as. of virgin for. **20. RICHFIELD CEMETERY,** where are buried children of John Brown, who lived in **RICHFIELD, 20.5.,** before beginning struggle to free Amer. slaves. **37.5. MONTROSE,** J. with St.18.

SIDE TRIP: (SE) 8m in St.18 to center of **Akron** (see), passing Univ. of Akron campus. **Barberton,** adj. Akron, is home of Diamond Match Co. (org.1889) & was planned as model industrial town by Ohio Columbus Barber. On O. C. Barber's 3,000-a. farm, blooded stock lived in luxurious stables, & the farmhouse, with marble halls, was furnished with elegance. At 2nd St. & Robinson Ave., **Diamond Match Co.** Norton Ave. & Wooster Rd., **Chief Hopocan Statue,** comm. Ind. leader who tried for 20 yrs. to bring peace, then started campaign of terror that lasted from 1775 until Greenville Treaty, 1795.

**52.5. CRYSTAL SPRINGS.** Treaty of Ft. McIntosh Boulder marks E. border of country granted to Shawnee, 1785. **55. MASSILLON** (see), coal-shipping & steel center. J. with US30 (see).

VI. **US42 (SW)** to **LAFAYETTE. 35.**

Via: Berea, Parma Heights, Middleburgh Heights, Brunswick, Medina.

**14.** Here Bagley Rd. runs (W) into **Berea,** a city of quarries, furnishing building stones & grindstones since its settlement (1827). Streets meander through town to triangular green & campus of **Baldwin-Wallace College.** Modern dormitories & observatory stand among ivy-colored sandstone halls. College was gift of John Baldwin (1845), 1st settler, to N. Ohio Meth. Conference. **Kulas Musical Arts Bldg.** houses excellent Conservatory. **29.5. MEDINA. 35. LAFAYETTE. Chippewa L. Pk.** (accoms.bath.recr.facils.).

# COLUMBUS

## COLUMBUS

E. High St., Union RR. Sta. E. Town St. bet. High & 3rd Sts., Union Bus Sta. Airport, (E) at Port Columbus. Excellent accoms. & recr. facils. Theaters (stage & screen); concerts; plays, lectures at univs. & colleges. Info.: 30 E. Broad St., C. of C. Farmers' Wk. (Feb.); St. Fair (Aug.-Sept.); Ohio Watercolor Show.

Capital & 3rd largest city, Columbus is important educational, industrial & commercial, as well as political center & convention city. Spreads over 40 sq. miles in fertile valley of Scioto & Olentangy Rs. The beautiful Civic Center rises on great bend of the Scioto & illuminated tip of Leveque-Lincoln Tower can be seen miles away. Outstanding institutions are Ohio State, Franklin & Capital Univs., St. Mary of the Springs & St. Charles Barromeo colleges; Gallery of Fine Arts, Philharmonic Symphony & Battelle Mem. Institute.

In 1812, the Legislature decided to build a statehouse & penitentiary "on the high bank east of the Scioto R. directly opp. town of Franklinton." As site for a permanent capital, a syndicate had offered a chunk of wilderness in which it would raise a capitol. Franklinton had put in a bid, but the syndicate won, & town was named for the great navigator, on Feb. 22, 1813. Mills, breweries & other industries began to flourish, but the settlement was endangered by cholera & fever until swamps were cleared. A feeder to Ohio & Erie Canal (1831) & the Nat. Rd. (1833) soon made the capital a busy shipping & trans. center. By 1900, industry was well advanced, & Columbus, founded on U.S. Military Lands, had become what it still is, a military concentration pt. Civic Center was built along the riverbank following destructive flood of 1913. Pop. is more than 96 per cent native-born, of whom some 11 per cent are Negro. Hanford & Urbancrest (S.4m) are attractive Negro suburbs.

PTS. OF INT.: (1) **St. Capitol** (1839-61), built by convict & private labor, is splendid example of Doric style, its massive simplicity adorned by fine colonnades. **McKinley Mem.** (1906.by H.A.McNeil). "These Are My Jewels" Mon. (1893.by Levi T.Scofield), with bronze figures of Presidents Grant, Garfield & Hayes, Gens. Sherman & Sheridan, Salmon P. Chase & Edwin M. Stanton. (2) **Civic Center Group,** on Scioto R. **City Hall** (1928-36.Class.) covers central block. **Leveque-Lincoln Tower** (1927. by C. Howard Crane). **Dept. of St. Bldg.** (1933.mod.Class.). (3) W. Spring St., **St. Penitentiary** (orig.units in 1830's); overcrowded & antiquated. In fire of 1930, more than 300 lives were lost. (4) Cleveland Ave. & Buckingham St., **Ft. Hayes** (O), hqs. of 5th Service Command, U.S. Army; military post since 1863. (Columbus Gen. Depot of U.S. Army, on James Rd.). (5) 280 E. Broad St., **Franklin Cty. Mem. Hall** (1904.by F.L.Packard), civic auditorium. (6) Grant Ave. & State St., **Pub. Lib.** (1906. Fr. Ren. by A.R.Ross). (7) 480 E. Broad St., **Gallery of Fine Arts** (Ital.Ren.1931.by

Richards, McCarty & Bulford); frieze by Rbt. Aitkin. Exhibits incl. Howald Coll. of mod. Fr. paintings, Schumacher Coll., work of Geo. Bellows, Columbus artist, & fine Glass Coll. (8) Sullivant Ave., bet. Powell Ave. & Binns Blvd., **Camp Chase Confed. Cemetery** (1879). (9) 505 King Ave., **Battelle Mem. Institute** (1929-37), nonprofit research lab. founded by Mrs. A. N. Battelle & son. (10) **Ohio St. Univ.,** one of country's largest. Its 1,400 as. incl. main campus, Olentangy playgrounds & Univ. farms. Est. in 1873 as Ohio Agric. & Mech. College, the univ. now grants degrees from 10 colleges, grad. & special schools. **Orton Hall** (1893.Richardson Romanes.by F.L.Packard). **Univ. Hall,** oldest bldg. **Pomerene Hall** (Tudor), women's social center. **Univ. Lib.** (1912.Fr.Ren.by Allen & Collins); Lib. & Mus. of **State Arch. & Hist. Soc.** (O.1913.1936), valuable exhibits of moundbuilder relics & reprods.; "Coonskin Lib." (see Marietta). (11) Sunbury Rd., **St. Mary of the Springs,** women's academy & college, est. in Somerset, 1830, by Sisters of Dominican Order (Cath.); wooded campus in residential area. **St. Albert Hall** houses Institutum Divi Thomae Research Unit (see Cincinnati). (12) In Bexley, **Capital Univ.** (Luth.), coed. lib. arts college founded in Canton, 1830. Especially pleasing are **Schenk Divinity Hall & Mees Hall** (music), in Tudor Goth. & **Science Bldg.** (1947-48). (13) 6m (N) on Riverside Dr. (US33), **Griggs Dam** (1908) & **Riverside Pk.** (f.boat.pic.) & (14) **O'Shaughnessy Dam** (1925), one of beauty spots of central Ohio (boat.f.). Just beyond is **Mun. Zoo.** (15) From E. Broad St. (N) on James Rd., **Port Columbus Airport** & **Curtis-Wright Corp. Plant** (O.appl.).

## TRIPS OUT OF COLUMBUS

**I. (E) on US40 & (N) on St.13 to NEWARK. 38.**

Via: Bexley, Reynoldsburg, Kirkersville, Hebron, Jacksontown. (St.16 is direct alternate route.)

**3.5. BEXLEY.** US40 follows route over which stagecoach drivers piloted their "mountain ships." Sunken milestones & weathered stone taverns are occasional reminders. **17. ETNA,** near Licking Cr. where Johnny Appleseed made his 1st planting (W) of Ohio R. For 40 yrs., he roamed the wilderness, distributing Swedenborgian literature & handfuls of appleseeds. Thinly dressed & barefoot, carrying his deerskin pack in all weathers, Johnny Appleseed became the "Saint of the Northwest Territory." In 1840's, the planter of orchards at last ". . . laid him down sweetly & slept through the night . . . there by the doors of old Ft. Wayne . . ." (Vachel Lindsay). Beyond **KIRKERSVILLE, 25.,** is J. with St.37.

SIDE TRIP: (N) 8m on St.37 to **Granville,** college town resembling Mass. town for which it was named in 1806. Granville Literary & Theological Institute (founded 1831 by Bapt. Ch.but chartered as nonsectarian) became **Denison Univ.** in 1856; ranking coed. school. At 313 E. Broadway is **Buxton Tavern** (1812); hotel, restaurant.

**27. HEBRON.** J. with St.79, alternate route along Licking R. to Newark. **31. JACKSONTOWN.** Trip turns (N) here on St.13, passing **Dawes Arboretum** (O). **38. NEWARK,** in valley bet. forks of river. Licking Cty. was center of great community of moundbuilders, & in Newark are celebrated Hopewell Mounds. Newark is home of many skilled artisans required by glass works & other precision-type industries. PTS. OF INT.: (1) Near Cth. Sq., **Bank Bldg.** by Louis Sullivan. (2) **Newark Stove Co.,** one of world's largest makers of stoves. (3) **Pharis Tire & Rubber Co.** (4) **A. H. Heisey Co.,** known for cut-glass. (5) **Holophane Co.,** makers of fine glassware (above plants O.appl.). (6) **Octagon St. Mem.,** enclosing most elaborate of Hopewell earthworks. **Octagon Mound** (50 as.) is conn. with **Circle Mound** (20 as.) by parallel mounds 300′ long & 60′ apart. A small circular mound (SE) with elevation (view of whole area) was possibly seat of tribal dignitaries. Archaeologists believe this mound system covered 2 sq. miles with avenues leading to other mounds & to (7) **Mound Builders St. Mem.** (facils.). In center of **Great Circle,** 12′ high & 1,200′ in diam. is **Eagle Mound,** one of Ohio's few effigy mounds.

**II. (SE) on US33 to LANCASTER. 30.**

US33 unites with US40 to **Bexley,** then swings (S) to **Canal Winchester,** rural center. Rd. leads (S) c.3m to **Lithopolis,** village of 300 pop. which received (1946) bequest of $2,500,000 from Mabel Wagnalls Jones, composer & writer, daughter of A. A. Wagnalls, publisher, who was born in Lithopolis. In **Wagnalls Mem.** are rare books, art coll., auditorium. Endowment provides for scholarships. **30. LANCASTER,** birthpl. of Gen. Wm. T. Sherman. At 162 E. Main St., **Mumaugh Mem.** (O.c.1817. Gr.Rev.), somewhat similar to Taft H. in Cincinnati (see); period furnishings. 163

E. Main St., **Ewing H.** (early 1800's), home of Thos. Ewing, U.S. Secy. of Treas. & adoptive father of Gen. Sherman. (3) 137 E. Main St., **Birthpl. of Gen. Sherman** (1811). (4) Broad & Wheeling Sts., **Reeves H.** (1833.Georg.). (5) **Anchor-Hocking Glass Co. Plant** (O.appl.).

III. **(S) on US23** to **CIRCLEVILLE. 26.** Via: Shadeville & S. Bloomfield.
US23 runs along E. side of Scioto R. (St.104 parallels route on W. side), following willow-fringed embankment & old towpaths. At **13.** the old O. & E. Canal bed is close to Rd. **26. CIRCLEVILLE,** built in early 1800's on circular plan within remains of octagonal moundbuilders' fort. The 1st cth. was octagonal, but burned in 1841 & townspeople replotted their city. **Pub. Lib.;** in Mem. Hall is reprod. of Circleville Ft. Pumpkin Show (Oct.). At J. with US22 & St.56.

SIDE TRIP: (SE) 8m on St.56 to **Leistville.** J. with St.159. (NE) 4m on St.159 to **Tarlton Cross Mound St. Mem.** (pic.facils.), famous cross-shaped earthwork. At 28m is vantage pt. to view Pickaway Plains, an "opening" in wilderness where the Shawnee lived for half century. Here was Cornstalk Town, named for chieftain who led Inds. in Lord Dunsmore's War.

IV. **(W) on US40** to **LAFAYETTE. 22.**
Beyond W. suburbs, US40 runs past pleasant towns, some of whose houses & taverns were built when Nat. Rd. was new. **22. LAFAYETTE.** Still a favored inn is **Red Brick Tavern** (O.1837).

V. **(N) on US23** to **MARION. 44.** Via: Worthington & Delaware.
US23 follows N. High St., past State Univ. **11. WORTHINGTON** (1803), whose village green & churches reflect New England origin. **St. John's Ch.** (Episc.1831. tower rest.). Opp. is **Presb. Ch.** (1816.remod.), where Rev. Thos. Woodrow, grandfather of Pres. Wilson, was pastor. At 778 High St., **Griswold H.** (1811). **13.** Copper-domed tower of **PONTIFICAL COLLEGE JOSEPHINUM** (O.appl.) overlooks 100-a. grounds along Olentangy R. The bldgs. (1931.Fr.Ren.) house seminary under papal jurisdiction. At **18.** Rd. leads (W) 2m to **Olentangy Caverns** (O.sm.fee). **20. PERKINS OBSERV.** (O) of Ohio Wesleyan Univ. **24. DELAWARE** (1806), trading center for farming & livestock area, seat of Ohio Wesleyan Univ. Mingo & Delaware Inds. had villages here near sulphur springs. **Delaware County Cth.** (1936.Georg.). E. William St. bet. Sandusky & Union Sts., Mon. on **Site of Pres. Hayes' Birthpl.** On rolling land along R. is **Ohio Wesleyan Univ.,** campus. Est. in 1841 by Meth. Episc. Ch. **Elliot Hall** (1835), formerly Mansion H., became 1st univ. bldg. **43. HARDING MEM.** (O). **44. MARION,** home of Pres. Harding (see US30).

VI. **ST.3, US36 & ST.229** to **GAMBIER** (Kenyon Univ.). **52.** Via: Westerville & Mount Vernon. St.3 (Cleveland Ave.) leads (N) from Broad St. **13. WESTERVILLE,** originally a Quaker town, home of Anti-Saloon League (1909) & seat of **Otterbein College** (coed.,lib.arts,accredited), founded & supported by United Brethren. **22.** At **SUNBURY** route turns (NE) on US36. **47. MOUNT VERNON,** distinguished for fine trees & Class. Rev. & Georg. houses. Leading products are cellophane, engines & bridge spans. Birthpl. of Daniel Decatur Emmett, author of "Dixie" & "Old Dan Tucker." **Knox County Cth.** (Class.Rev.). **Curtis-Devin H.** (1824-36.Class.Rev.). J. with St.229, which leads (E) 5m to **Gambier,** home of **Kenyon Coll.** This men's school, est. in 1824 by Prot. Episc. church, carries on Eng. school tradition. Students live in college pk., a wooded tract high above Kokosing R. President Hayes, S. P. Chase & E. M. Stanton were Kenyon men. Assoc. with college is Bexley Divinity School.

## US 20—INDIANA

**IND.-OHIO LINE (W) to IND.-ILL. LINE** (Chicago limits). **152. US20**
Via: Angola, La Grange, (Elkhart), South Bend, New Carlisle, Rolling Prairie, Michigan City, Gary, Hammond, E. Chicago, Whiting.

US20 takes straight path (W), avoiding large centers. From gently rolling NE. sec., with many streams (f.) & Ls., it crosses farmland & mint-growing mucklands of St. Joseph Cty. At end of route, hy. by-passes Michigan City & threads way through highly industrialized Calumet (see).

**10. ANGOLA,** resort center. **Tri-State College** offers 2-yr. courses in engineering, commerce & music; high school graduation not required. In vic. are several large Ls. (resort & recr.facils.excellent f.bath.boat.), incl. James L., L. George, & Crooked, Golden, Clear & Hamilton Ls. J. with US27 (see).

SIDE TRIP: (N) $5^m$ on US27 to **Pokagon St. Pk.** (sm.fee.f.boat.bath.winter sports), popular resort area bordering L. James & Snow L. **Potawatomi Inn** (O.yr.around). Buffalo, elk & deer are corraled. Simon Pokagon, last Potawatomi chief, wrote "Queen of the Woods" & other tales about So. Bend reg. where he was born.

**26.** J. with St.3

SIDE TRIP: On St.3 (S) $9^m$ to **Kendallville,** shipping pt. for onions, celery & other truck crops of Noble Cty. Known for its fishing waters.

**32. LA GRANGE,** named by founders (1836) for Lafayette's country estate; trade center for dairy farmers. J. with St.9.

SIDE TRIPS: (A) On St.9 (S) $11^m$ to **Rome City,** on Sylvan L., former home of Gene Stratton Porter. On site of canal-diggers' camp &, according to legend, named by the Irish who fought for better quarters & were told the proverb about "living as the Romans do." Thereafter, their huddle of shacks became "Rome." **Gene Stratton Porter St. Mem.** (see also Ft. Wayne Trip II), cabin (O) in Wildflower Woods where Mrs. Porter lived from 1914 until 1923, just before her removal to Cal. & her accidental death.
(B) On St.9 (N) $5.5^m$ to **Howe.** At edge of village is **Howe School** (mil.), est. in 1884; bldgs. in Eng. Coll. style.

**41.5.** J. with St.5, which leads (N) $2^m$ to **Shipshewana,** Amish trading center, United Brethren Camp, on L. Shipshewana. **Chief Shipshewana Mem.** comm. Ind. who returned from Kansas to die beside crescent-shaped for. L. US20 crosses range of hills of glacial origin & sweeps down into St. Joseph R. valley.

**63. ELKHART** (sett.1832)

Through RR. & bus conns. Good accoms. & recr. facils.

Elkhart, famous for band instrument factories, was named by Inds. for heart-shaped island at meeting of St. Joseph & Elkhart Rs., where several trls. converged. City was chosen by Mich. Southern Ry. for its shops in 1850. Elkhart, though highly industrial, is attractive town with 10 bridges & several fine pks. At 1000 E. Beardsley Ave., **C. G. Conn Band Instrument Co.** (O), est. in 1875 by Capt. C. G. Conn, Civil War veteran & cornetist. 117 Franklin St., **Miles Labs.** (O), est. in 1884 by Dr. Franklin Miles; best-known product is Alka-Seltzer. 518 W. Franklin St., **Ambrose Bierce H.** (remod.), where writer lived early part of life (born near Pomeroy, O.) & to which he returned to write "What I Saw of Shiloh." J. with US33.

SIDE TRIP: US33 (SE) $11^m$ to Mennonite town of **Goshen,** seat of Goshen College. Elkhart Cty. was largely settled (1841-43) by Amish & the less rigidly disciplined Mennonites. The black-bonneted Amish women & the men in broad-brimmed black hats are among world's best farmers. **Goshen College,** one of few Mennonite colleges in U.S., founded in 1894; courses in theology, liberal arts & teacher training.

**74.** N. border of **MISHAWAKA** (on US33), fair-sized town on St. Joseph R. **U.S. Rubber Co.'s** Woolen & Rubber Mfg. plant & several large heavy-machinery, steel & meat-packing plants. **Gun Club Preserve** (trap-shooting.camp.facils.). In SW. sec. are neat gardens & homes of some 6,000 Belgians who came here after World War I.

**78. SOUTH BEND** (sett.1820)

Main line RR. conns. St. Joseph Cty. Airport, served by 3 major lines. Good accoms.; also in near-by Mich. & Ind. resorts. Musical, athletic & other events at Univ. & college. Polish, Hungarian & other festivals. Info.: Assoc. of Com., Main St. & Washington Ave.

South Bend, named for wide loop of St. Joseph R., which crosses town, is seat of Notre Dame Univ. & industrial & trade center for large area in Mich. & Ind. Studebaker, Bendix, Singer, Oliver Co. & other major plants are worldwide distributors. City has virtually no slums & is well-equipped with pks. & playgrounds, schools & other cultural facils. In 1675 Père Marquette preached to the Inds. near site & La Salle met here in 1681 with chiefs of Miami & Illinois. Pierre Navarre est. Amer. Fur Co. post in 1820, & Notre Dame was founded 22 yrs. later. Along N. Shore Dr. & other shady sts. are mansions of that early period. PTS. OF INT.: (1) In Leeper Pk., **Pierre Navarre Cabin** (1821). (2) 112 S. Lafayette Blvd., **Old Cth.** (1855), housing N. Ind. Hist. Soc. **Mus.** (O). (3) Bet. US20 & M.C. RR., **Bendix Products Division** (O.guides), a city in itself. (4) Prairie Ave. (S) of M.C. RR., **Studebaker Corp.** (O. guides); Clement & Henry Studebaker began, in 1852, with wagon-making shop. **Mus. of Trans.** (O.Mon.-Fri.). (5) Portage Ave., in Highland Cemetery, **Grave of Knute Rockne.** Here also is **Council Oak,** under which La Salle met with Inds. (6) In SW. sec., **St. Mary's College** (women), on large campus; founded by Cath. order in 1855. **Loretto Chapel.** (7) In NE. sec., **Univ. of Notre Dame** (tours), on one of world's largest campuses, with golden-domed **Adm. Bldg.** (1879.neo-Goth.) in center. One of most important Cath. schools for men, founded in 1842; hqs. of Order of the Holy Cross. Widely known because of Knute Rockne, who came here in 1910. PTS. OF INT.: (1) **Rockne Stadium.** (2) **Our Lady of the Sacred Heart Ch.** (Goth.); 17th cent. baroque altar, windows by Fr. Carmelite nuns, & Gregori murals. (3) **Badin Log Chapel,** replica of one built in 1830 for Father Stephen Badin, 1st priest ordained in U.S. (4) **Wightman Mem. Art Gallery,** in Univ.; large art coll.; S. Amer. Lib. & Dante Coll. J. with US31 (see).

**91.5. NEW CARLISLE,** a leading market town. **Studebaker Proving Grounds** (O. appl.) in vic. **108.5.** US20 unites with US35 & passes SE. tip of **MICHIGAN CITY** (cloverleaf crossing), **112.,** largest resort center in Ind. (through RR. & bus conns. good accoms.& recr.facils.mun.airport). Town, founded in 1832, was once a great lakeport, & harbor is one of oldest on Ls. PTS. OF INT.: (1) End of Franklin St., **Washington Pk.** (amusements.recr.facils.pic.bathh.); "Singing Sand Beach"; Zoo; Observ. Tower. **Mich. City Harbor;** Yacht Basin & Club. (2) **Old Lighth.** (1856). (3) On US12 (E) 1.5$^{m}$ **Internat. Friendship Gardens** (O.after May 9) representing 60 nations, moved into valley of Trail Cr. from Century of Progress Exposition. Music Festival & "Gay Nineties Celebration" at Gardens Theaters.

SIDE TRIPS: (A) US12 (W) is route through dunelands. 5$^{m}$ **Beverly Shores.** 10$^{m}$ J. with St.49 which leads (N) to **Indiana Dunes St. Pk.** (hotel.cottages.pic.camp.store); 2,200 as. of woodlands & dunes, some covered with trees & flowers, others bare & desolate, shifting with the wind. At **Big Blowout,** bowl-shaped cut in line of dunes, is "graveyard," where dead trees stick up through sea of sand. **Ogden Dunes** (f.boat.bath.skiing).

(B) US35 (SE) 12$^{m}$ to **La Porte.** 10$^{m}$ **Pine L.** (f.boat.), 1st of 7 Ls. in & around **La Porte,** busy resort & mfg. center. (through RR. & bus conns. & airport. accoms.). For the Fr. it was "the door" to for. & prairie. Among large plants are **Allis-Chalmers** & various woolen mills & garment factories. **Fox Mem. Pk.,** on Clear L. In Cth. is **La Porte Cty. Hist. Soc.** (O.Tues.). **Fish Hatchery.**

**120. FURNESSVILLE,** where **Furness H.** (1856) is still occupied by members of pioneer family. US20 unites with US12 across lakeside edge of Calumet (see). **152. IND.-ILL. LINE** (SE. of Chicago).

## US 30—INDIANA

**IND.-OHIO LINE** (15$^{m}$ from Van Wert, O.) **(NW) to IND.-ILL. LINE** (7$^{m}$ from Chicago Hts.). **156. US30**

Via: New Haven, Fort Wayne, Columbia City, Warsaw, Bourbon, Plymouth, Valparaiso, Dyer. Pa. RR. parallels route. Accoms.: All types. Resorts & recr. areas easily accessible. US6 is alternate route, avoiding larger centers.

US30 is diagonal path from one industrial area to another across what was once open prairie, now covered with large, fertile farms. It was the kingdom of Little Turtle, chief of Miami Confederacy, who defeated Gen. Harmar at Post Miami (now Ft. Wayne) & was himself defeated at Battle of Fallen Timbers (see).

**8. BESANCON.** The white Ch. (Cath.) & trim cemetery are souvenirs of Fr. attempts to settle st.'s E. border. **20. FORT WAYNE** (see). J. with US24 (see), US27 (see), & US33 (see). **41. COLUMBIA CITY,** birthpl. of Lloyd Douglas, minister & religious novelist; & of Ralph F. Gates, "grass-roots Gov."; home for many yrs. of Vice Pres. Thos. R. Marshall. **54.** J. with St.13.

SIDE TRIP: On St.13 (N) 14$^{m}$ to **Syracuse,** resort center on L. Wawasee, largest in Ind. **Wawasee Fish Hatchery.**

**62. WARSAW,** seat of Kosciusko Cty., sprinkled with Ls., incl. Winona (S), & Tippecanoe (N), source of Tippecanoe R., which US30 crosses just beyond town. **88. PLYMOUTH,** shipping center. **Centennial Pk.** (camp.). **105. HAMLET** (tourist accoms.). J. with US35, route (N) to Michigan City (see).

SIDE TRIP: On US35 (S) to **Tippecanoe R. St. Pk.** 5$^{m}$ J. with St.8, leading (W) a few miles to **Kankakee Game Preserve** (pic.) on Kankakee R., link in Gt. Ls.-Miss. R. route in early days. La Salle portaged from St. Joseph R. to the Kankakee, 1879, & then downriver to the Illinois. Surrounding country was vast glacial bog, the Kankakee Swamp, of which more than 2,300 as. have been acquired by st.; noted for quail, pheasant & sm. game. 12$^{m}$ **Bass L.** (camp.trlrs.cottages.hotel); large **St. Fish Hatchery** (O) on NE. shore. **Bass L. Beach St. Pk.** (sm.fee.f.camp.pic.bath.restaurant). 17$^{m}$ **Tippecanoe R. St. Pk.** (sm.fee.pic.group camp), 6,340 as. turned over to state by Nat. Pk. Serv. in 1943.

**110.** US30 crosses Kankakee R. **121. WANATAH.** J. with St.43.

SIDE TRIP: On St.43 (S) 8m to **Lacrosse.** J. with St.8, which passes (W) **Pinney-Purdue Experimental Farm.** 19m on St.43, **Jasper-Pulaski St. Game Preserve** (pic.), nearly 5,000 as. of marsh where quail, pheasant, raccoon, fish & waterfowl are propagated.

US30 crosses highest ridge of glacial moraine in N. Ind. **131. VALPARAISO,** seat of **Valparaiso Univ. & Valparaiso Tech. Inst.** Founded in 1859 as Meth. coed. college, Univ. is now probably largest coed. Luth. school. Shortly after Civil War, it was closed for a time, then reopened by Henry Baker Brown, who made it "the poor man's Harvard." After Brown's death & World War I, it was sold to Luth. church. **Indiana Steel Co.** (O), largest producer of magnets in U.S. **Sauk Trl. Crossing** is indicated by marker on **Pub. Lib.** lawn. On St.49 (N) 4m is **Flint L.,** on which are **Blackhawk Beach** (f.bath.boat.) & **Hillcrest Pk.** & Golf Course (O). **145.** J. with St.55, which runs (N) 1m to **Merrillville,** stopping pt. for Gold Rush travelers in 1849. US30 enters Calumet (see). **153.** J. with US41 (see). **156. DYER** still has **State Line H.** (O), tavern built in 1838. **IND.-ILL. LINE.**

## US 24—INDIANA

**IND.-OHIO LINE** (3.5m from Antwerp, O.) **(W) to IND.-ILL. LINE** (12m from Watseka). **156. US24**

Via: New Haven, Ft. Wayne, Roanoke, Huntington, Lagro, Wabash, Peru, Logansport, Burnettsville, Monticello, Remington, Kentland. Route is paralleled by Wabash & Pa. RRs. Accoms.

US24 cont. (SW) along Maumee R. to Fort Wayne, then runs along beside Little Wabash & Wabash Rs. on route of Wabash & Erie Canal (see). Leaving this picturesque valley, it crosses one of richest farm areas of Midwest. Near st. line are locks of canal that helped develop, then in early 1840's impoverished, the state. **12. Gronauer H.** (1860); near-by is barn where barge mules were stabled. **14. NEW HAVEN.** Here US24 unites with US30. **20. FORT WAYNE** (see). J. with US27 (see), US30 (see) & US33 (see). **35. ROANOKE,** where Roanoke Class. Academy was founded by F. S. Reefy, in 1861, when st. had few secondary schools; nucleus of Manchester College (see). **45. HUNTINGTON,** busy center of grain & lime-producing reg. on Little Wabash R.; seat of Huntington College. Jefferson St. Bridge is possibly unique in U.S., carrying a business block out into the R. Overlooking R. are **La Fontaine Hotel** (1923) & imposing **Huntington County Cth.** City was built on Miami site ("place of flints"), home of Chief La Fontaine. In NE. sec. is campus of **Huntington College,** founded by Ch. of the United Brethren at Hartsville in 1850 & moved to present site in 1897; liberal arts, music, business & theology. At E. Park Dr. & Warren St., publishing house of **"Sunday Visitor"** & other Cath. periodicals. At W. limits is **Mem. Pk.,** with Sunken & Shakespeare Gardens. J. with US224 (alt. route to Ohio Line) & St.5.

SIDE TRIPS: (A) On St.5 (NW) 1m to **Monastery of St. Felix,** of strict Capuchin Order. At 1.5m, in Mt. Calvary Cemetery, is **Grave of La Fontaine,** Miami chief.

(B) On St.9 (SW) 26m to **Marion,** RR. & farm center, with many industries; seat of Marion College. 1st sett. in 1826 & named for Gen. Francis Marion (see), the "Swamp Fox" of Rev. War. Marion boomed in 1860's with discovery of natural gas & oil. In Aug. 1930, a mob hanged 2 Negroes from tree in **Cth. Sq.** In Matter Pk. (pic.swim.zoo) is **Octogenarian Mus.;** coll. of pioneer books, furniture, clothing. **Marion College** is Wesleyan Meth. teacher-training school (est.1890). Just S. of city is one of largest U.S. veterans' hospitals.

On US24 (W) a mile or so is **Grave of L. P. Milligan** (1812-99), prominent leader of Knights of the Golden Circle, Southern sympathizers in middle states during Civil War (c.50,000 in Ind.), later known as Sons of Liberty. Beyond Huntington, on hilltop overlooking the Little Wabash is **Victory Noll Training Sch.** (Cath.), founded in 1925 for education of women missionaries in U.S. **47. Fork of the Rivers,** where Miami signed treaty in 1840 giving up their Indiana lands. Miami village was burned by Harrison's men after siege of Ft. Wayne, in 1812, not long after death of peace-loving Little Turtle, but it was rebuilt & survived until 1840. Near-by is former homestead of Chief La Fontaine. **50.5. Stone Aqueduct.** In **LAGRO, 58.,** the canal comes vividly to life, with main street running along its edge & several locks in good condition. **Keller H.** (1840), once one of finest taverns on canal. On St.524 (S) 2m is **Salamonie R. St. For.** (pic.f.h.). **62.** J. with St.13.

SIDE TRIP: On St.13 (N) 12m, along C.C.C. & St.L. RR., to **N. Manchester** in lovely **Eel R.** valley; seat of **Manchester College** (Ch. of the Brethren), founded in near-by Roanoke in 1869; accredited liberal arts college. Along the shady streets are homes of many Dunkers, German religious sect who came to Pa. in early 18th cent. On campus is **Chief Pierish's Cabin.** Potawatomi chief, buried beneath floor, was a signer of Treaty of Paradise Springs (see below). **Zion Luth. Ch.** (1846), where Lloyd Douglas (see) was pastor (1903-05). **Peabody Mem. Home** (Presb.) for aged of any denomination. N. Manchester is birthpl. of Thos. R. Marshall, Gov. & U.S. Vice Pres.

**64. WABASH.** In **Cth.** are displayed carbon lamps used to light dome, Mar. 31, 1880, in one of 1st cities in world to be lighted by electricity. In **Cth. Sq.** is massive bronze **Lincoln of the People,** by Chas. Keck. Not far off is **Site of Paradise Springs Treaty,** 1826, which opened valley to settlement. **79. PERU** (through RR. & bus conns. good accoms. & recr. facils.), still "Circus City"; birthpl. of Cole Porter. Ben Wallace started circus here in 1884, & Peru has been winter hqs. for large shows ever since. **Lib. Annex Mus.** has fine coll. incl. carved Circus Parade, Ind., pioneer & other relics. **Bearss Hotel** (O.1837.remod.). **Cth. Mus.;** cradles, spinning wheels, vehicles, firearms. **Frances Slocum Trl.**

SIDE TRIP: (S) on Frances Slocum Trl. (marked) along Wabash & Mississinewa Rs. 2.5$^{m}$ **Site of Osage Village,** where Tecumseh lighted Council Fire, 1812. Across bridge are **Circus Winter Quarters.** Short distance (S), Rd. leads to **Grave of Francis Godfroy,** last chief of Miami. Next on Trl. is **Home of Cole Porter** & near it, "The Old Fashioned Garden" of one of his popular lyrics. In limestone cliffs along R. are **Seven Pillars,** cut symmetrically by nature. 7.5$^{m}$ **Peoria,** village in midst of exceptionally fertile valley. Trl. leads through **Mississinewa R. St. For. Pk.** incl. St. Pk. (pic.). About a mile from Peoria are **Home & Grave of Frances Slocum** (1773-1847), the White Rose of the Miami, known as Maconaquah (Young Bear). The child was stolen from her Pa. family in 1778 by Delaware Inds., then adopted by the Miami. She roved the wilderness with them & married a young chieftain. After nearly 60 yrs. of search, her brother & sister found her in 1837. The lonely woman had told her story to Geo. Ewing, trader, when he visited the valley. Maconoquah wished to remain with her children & grandchildren, & Congress, persuaded by John Quincy Adams, gave her tract of land to be held in perpetuity by her descendants. About half-way to Marion is **Somerset,** on site of Ind. village, theme of Riley's "Among the Hills of Somerset." **Jalapa** is near former home of another Indiana-born poet, Joaquin Miller. At c.22$^{m}$ is **Mississinewa Battlefield,** where Miami made their last major stand, Dec. 18, 1812. Trl. merges with St.15.

**94. LOGANSPORT** (through RR. & bus conns. good accoms. & recr. facils.), sett. in 1829, when a wolf scalp was worth a dollar bounty, now attractive industrial & trade center at meeting of Eel & Wabash Rs. Site was popular trading post for Inds. & pioneers, & W. & E. canal promoted early growth. Home of Kenesaw Mountain Landis, judge & former baseball commissioner; also birthpl. of Walker Whiteside & home of Clarence (Richard) Bennett, actors. On Biddle's I. is **Biddle H.** (1833), built for Gen. John Tipton, who had charge of Potawatomi removal from Indiana over "trail of death," in 1838. Early Hs. still standing incl. **Home of G. N. Fitch,** orig. owner of **Fitch's Glen** on the Wabash (pic.). In City Bldg. is **Cass Cty. Hist. Soc. Mus.** (O.Fri.& Sat.). J. with US35, the "Mich. Rd.," & St.25, on which is **St. Hospital** for mentally ill. **103. L. CICOTT** breaks sleepy landscape of farms & hazy woodlots. **116. MONTICELLO,** resort town bet. **Ls. Shafer & Freeman** (good accoms.f.boat.swim.), formed by dams on Tippecanoe R. **137. REMINGTON.** J. with St.53.

SIDE TRIP: On St.53 (N) c.11$^{m}$ to **St. Joseph Jr. College,** Cath. sch. for men, est.1891. At 12$^{m}$ **Rensselaer,** seat of agric. Jasper Cty.

**152. KENTLAND,** birthpl. of Geo. Ade, celebrated humorist & playwright, whose "Fables in Slang" is one of earliest & finest records of common Amer. speech. **George Ade H. J.** with US41 (see). **156. ETTNER, on IND.-ILL. LINE.**

## US 40—INDIANA

**IND.-OHIO LINE** (15$^{m}$ from Lewisburg, Ohio) **(W) to IND.-ILL. LINE** (9$^{m}$ from Marshall, Ill). **153. US40**

Via: Richmond, Cambridge City, Knightstown, Greenfield, Indianapolis, Plainfield, Stilesville, Harmony, Brazil, Terre Haute. Good accoms. in larger towns. Route paralleled by Penn. RR.

US40, wagon Rd. of 1840's, crosses undulating plain of cent. Ind. On either side dairy farms, pastures, corn & wheat fields roll away to wooded horizons. Midway on route is st.'s capital & largest city. From Indianapolis, scenery is varied by rugged coal-bearing hills, thick fors. & level prairie.

**4. RICHMOND** (through RR. & bus conns. airport. accoms. & recr. facils.). In & around city are Hs. dating back to early settlers, the soldiers of Geo. Rogers Clark. Later, one of 1st Quaker communities in Ind. made its home in Richmond, & Earlham College was est. Abolitionist sentiment was very strong. Town grew rapidly after Nat. Rd. was cut & is now center of rich trade area & a leading distributor of many products, particularly roses, lawn mowers, machine tools, pianos & phonograph records. PTS. OF INT.: (1) At A & 7th Sts., **Site of Henry Clay's Address,** in 1842, after which the Friends petitioned him to free his own slaves. (2) A & N. 9th Sts., in Morton High Sch., **Pub. Art Gallery,** one of oldest art assocs. in state. J. E. Bundy & Wm. T. Eyden, among best-known Hoosier landscape painters, were leading members. (3) 11th St., **Friends' Meetingh.** (1865); **Wayne Cty. Hist. Mus.** (O.free) has pioneer kitchen. (4) At W. limits, **Earlham College,** founded by Soc. of Friends in 1847 & early devoted to scientific research. **Mus.** has 1st natural hist. coll. made in Ind. & **Observatory** was 1st in St. Modern laboratories. (5) On US40, **"Madonna of the Trail" Mon.** (6) Easthaven Ave., **Joseph H. Hill Co.** (O) where "Better Times" rose was developed (1931-34). Other large plants: Crosley Corp., Starr Piano Co., F. & N. Lawn Mower Co., Nat. Automatic Tool Co. & Internat. Harvester Co. J. with US27 & US35.

SIDE TRIPS: (A) On US27 (N) c.9m to **Fountain City,** where Levi Coffin's store was a main depot for Underground RR. It is said that not one of 2,000 slaves who passed through his door was ever recaptured. Coffin org. a Freedman's Aid Soc. in London, 1864, & was delegate to Internat. Antislavery Conference in Paris, 1867. **Levi Coffin H.**
(B) On US35 (NW) 39m to **Muncie.**

## MUNCIE

High St., 600 block, N.Y.C. RR. Sta.; Vine & Wysor Sts., C. & O. Sta.; Race & Madison Sts., Pa. RR. 410 Mulberry St., Ind. RR. Bus Sta. Mun. Airport (N) 2m. Good accoms. & recr. facils. Civic & Children's Theaters. Many business & fraternal orgs.

From settlement around RR. sta., Muncie became peaceful rural center & college town, & then highly industrialized city with considerable interest in the arts. Because it seemed to them a typical Amer. town, Rbt. & Helen Lynd chose Muncie for "Middletown." White R. moves in succession of broad loops across N. sec., & along the drive are large pks. & residential areas. Cth. & business dist. are (S) of R. &, a short distance beyond, the RR. tracks cross middle of city. Farther (S) are many industrial plants, surrounded by homes of workmen. Munseytown, platted in 1827, named for Munsee Inds., was inc. as Muncie in 1847. Gas was discovered in 1870's & during 20-yr. boom, more than 40 factories were built. Then gas supply suddenly ended, but town had gained a sizable pop., mainly native white (as it is today) & several large companies had become solidly established. Most important is Ball Bros., known throughout U.S. for their glass fruit jars. To this family, Muncie owes its Ball Mem. Hosp. & various gifts to Ball Teachers College. City has numerous musical & dramatic clubs & choral groups & valuable art coll.

PTS. OF INT.: Bet. McKinley Ave. & Riverside Dr., **Ball St. Teachers College.** In 1917, the St. accepted from Ball family the gift of defunct Muncie Normal Institute bldgs. & 70-a. campus for a division of Ind. St. Normal School (see Terre Haute). In 1929 the Muncie school became separate institution under present name, offering degrees in education & nursing. **Adm. Bldg.,** overhung with ivy, is part of orig. gift. **Lib. & Assembly Hall** (1927) & modern **Science Hall** (1924) are important units, but most beautiful structure on 150-a. campus is **Arts Bldg.** (1935), with one of best galleries in Ind. **Sculpture Hall** has work by Paul Manship & other Amer. & European artists. Paintings range from early Dutch & Ital. to Childe Hassam & contemporary Amer. Frank C. Ball Coll. & Ital. Ren. Coll. are notable. **Beneficence Mem.** to Ball family (1937.by Dan.C.French & Rich.H.Dana, architect). (2) 2400 University Ave., **Ball Mem. Hospital** (1929.Tudor Goth.), gift of Ball Bros. Foundation. (3) Along Wheeling Ave., **Delaware Cty. Fairgrounds.** (4) Bet. Crane & Walnut Sts., N. of Minnetrista Blvd., **Ind. Village Site.** Near-by is **Cemetery of the Munsee.** (5) Broadway, (N) of R., **McCullough Pk.** (pic.playfields.zoo), city's largest. INDUSTRIAL PTS. OF INT.: (6) Macedonia Ave. & 9th St., **Ball Bros. Plant** (O), where home-canning jars, bottles, glasses & rubber rings are made, along with modern aluminum pressure cookers. The Ball holdings are widespread, & family is st.'s most munificent benefactor. Co. was among last of major plants to sign C.I.O. contracts. (7) 5th & Elliott Sts., **Delco-Remy Corp.** (O) & (8) at 1200 W. 8th St., **Muncie Products Corp.** (O); auto accessories & parts. (9) Seymour St. bet. Hackley & Blaine Sts.,

**Warner-Gear-Division,** Borg-Warner Corp. (O). (10) Macedonia Ave., S. of 8th St., **Owens-Illinois Glass Co.;** glass bldg. blocks & insulators.

**10.5. CENTERVILLE;** good examples of 19th cent. blue-gray brick Hs. **O. P. Morton H.** (1842) was home of Civil War Gov. At 323 E. Main St., **Geo. W. Julian H.** (O.1846.remod.), former home of U.S. Congressman (1849-51, 1860-71) who introduced woman-suffrage bill in 1868 & was leader of Free Soil party. At 4th & Main Sts., **John Nixon Coll.** (O.appl.) of early Indiana paintings, books, almanacs. **20. CAMBRIDGE CITY,** once depot on Whitewater Canal (see US52); canal bed can be seen along Main St. **Vinton H.** (O.1847), tavern since canal days. **21. DUBLIN. The Maples** (1825), now store & inn. **33.5. DUNREITH.** J. with St.3.

SIDE TRIP: On St.3 (N) 3m to **Spiceland,** sett. in 1828 by Carolina Quakers who est. **Spiceland Academy** (1834), influential for three-quarters of a cent.; now occupied by pub. sch. Charles A. Beard, co-author with his wife, Mary Beard, of "The Rise of American Civilization," has paid tribute to his teachers at the Academy. 11m, **New Castle.** Near-by (NE) is **Wilbur Wright Birthpl.**

**37.5. KNIGHTSTOWN,** on Big Blue R., birthpl. of Chas. Beard. **44. CLEVELAND,** where Eastern Indiana Holiness Assoc. convenes (June & Sept.). **51. GREENFIELD,** birthpl. of Jas. Whitcomb Riley. The "Old Swimmin' Hole" is preserved in **Jas. Whitcomb Riley Pk.,** & in front of Cth. is **Statue of Riley,** gift of school children. **Riley Homestead** (1850.sm.fee.tearoom.mus.) incl., as its kitchen, the log cabin where Hoosier poet was born, Oct. 7, 1849. Currier & Ives prints, Vict. furniture & Riley memorabilia. As a young man Riley painted signs, sold Bibles & shoes & traveled with medicine shows, but always writing verse. He became columnist on "Anderson Democrat" &, later, staff member of "Indianapolis Journal." **52. Eli Lilly Co.,** biological laboratories. **55. PHILADELPHIA.** About a mile (S) is **Annie Gray H.,** home of "Little Orphant Annie." **72. INDIANAPOLIS** (see). **86. PLAINFIELD** (see Indianapolis Trip IV for this sec. of route). **114. PUTNAMVILLE.** Near town (S) is **St. Farm** for short-term prisoners. Entering coal-mining country, US40 crosses **Ten O'Clock Line,** at **122.,** est. as N. boundary of white settlement by Treaty of Ft. Wayne (1809). Gov. Harrison purchased from Ind. chiefs, for $10,000 & small annuity, the fertile 3,000,000 as. bet. Wabash & White Rs. Stretch of hy. overhung by ancient sycamores runs past **McKinley Tavern** (1834). **129. BRAZIL,** on edge of rich coal & clay deposits, has several large brick, tile & other clay products plants. **Clay Cty. Hist. Soc. Mus.** (O) is in Pub. Lib. In Forest Pk., at S. limits, **Mem. Log Cabin** (O).

**146. TERRE HAUTE**

Union RR. Sta., Spruce & 9th Sts.; Big Four RR. Sta., 7th & Tippecanoe Sts.; Union Bus Terminal, Cherry & 6th Sts. At 7th St. & Davis Ave., Paul Cox Field, airport (no sched. serv.). Good accoms. & recr. facils.

Terre Haute, on high plateau along Wabash R., commercial, cultural & banking center for large mining & agric. area, is Indiana's most exciting city with gaudiest & wildest past. Also it was home of some of st.'s most notable men & women, incl. Eugene Debs, Theodore Dreiser, Paul Dresser, Rose Melville, who created "Sis Hopkins" role, Lyman Abbott, Dan. Voorhees, Gilbert Wilson, painter, & Max Eastman, founder of "The Masses," whose "Enjoyment of Living" (1948) relates to his Ind. boyhood. Predominantly a coal town, city also has brick & tile, paint & varnish, canned goods & other industries. Seat of Ind. St. Teachers College, Rose Polytechnic Institute & St. Mary-of-the-Woods College (in vic.). U.S. Penitentiary is (S) 3m on St.63, a model prison farm (1939-40). In 1811 Gen. Harrison built Ft. Harrison on Wabash R.; town was platted in 1816. With flatboats & steamboats arriving at the landing, frequently the terminal, the little town grew rapidly. In 1838, the Nat. Rd. was completed to Terre Haute, & in 1849 the W. & E. Canal, soon to be lined with factories, mills, foundries & tanneries. Coal mines were developed to feed the locomotives, & Vigo Cty. became a leader in coal production.

Labor in Terre Haute has always been an active element, 1st under Knights of Labor & then through United Mine Workers. One of most publicized strikes began in July, 1935, in behalf of employees of a stamping company. It developed into effective general strike (3rd in U.S.) when company imported professional strikebreakers & ignored warnings of some 50 A. F. of L. unions. Gov. Paul V. McNutt sent in the militia, pickets were dispersed & strike was soon called off, but the ban was not lifted until Feb. 1936. (1) 451 N. 8th St., **H. of Eugene V. Debs,** Socialist leader;

fought against bitter opposition for many social principles later embodied in nat. legislation. Debs, born in 1855, was a locomotive fireman at 16 &, in 1880, secy.-treas. of Brotherhood of Locomotive Firemen & editor of its newspaper. In 1893 he org. & was made pres. of Amer. Ry. Union, the 1st industrial, rather than craft, union. In 1895 he was a leader in famous Pullman Strike & served his 1st prison sentence. On basis of Social Democratic party, which Debs founded in 1898, the Socialist Party of U.S. was org. in Indianapolis in 1900, with Debs as U.S. Pres. candidate. In 1904, 1908, 1912, & 1920, he was again candidate, polling nearly a million votes in last election, although serving 10-yr. sentence in Fed. prison. Because of speech in Canton, O., early in 1918, protesting Gov. prosecutions for sedition, he had been convicted under Espionage Act. In Oct. 1921, Pres. Harding had him released, without citizenship. He died in 1926. Martin (in "Indiana") calls him "most effective of the many protestants who have raged through Indiana history." (2) Bet. Mulberry & Chestnut Sts., **Ind. St. Teachers College,** high-ranking institution founded in 1870, supported by city & st., has many modern bldgs. on large campus. (3) 3rd St. & Wabash Ave., **Vigo County Cth.,** in which hangs bell bequeathed by Col. Francis Vigo, who gave financial backing to Geo. Rogers Clark's operations. (4) 115 Walnut St., **Dresser H.,** where were born Theodore Dreiser (see Literature), important Amer. novelist, & Paul (Dresser), his brother, author of "On the Banks of the Wabash." (5) In Highland Cemetery, at E. limits, is **Grave of Dan. Voorhees,** the "tall sycamore of the Wabash"; U.S. Senator & eloquent orator, who defended John Brown & John E. Cook, after Harper's Ferry raid. (6) End of E. Ohio Ave., **Deming Pk.** (pic.zoo), Terre Haute's largest & most scenic recr. area. (7) Bet. 2nd & 3rd Sts., on Ohio St., **Mem. Hall** (O.wks.); military coll. (8) At W. limits, **Rose Polytechnic Institute,** founded as engineering college for men, in 1874. J. with US150, St.46 (see) & US41 (see).

SIDE TRIPS: (A) On US150 (N) 6.5$^{m}$ to **St. Mary-of-the-Woods College** (Cath.) for girls. The handsome bldgs. (Ital.Ren.) are grouped on one of loveliest campuses in St. Girls work in farm, dairy & other self-supporting projects.

(B) On US41 (N) 2.5$^{m}$ along Wabash R. to **Site of Ft. Harrison** (1811), occupied by country club. From here Gen. Harrison marched to Battle of Tippecanoe (see). At 4.5$^{m}$ is **N. Terre Haute,** mining center.

US40 crosses Wabash R. Along either side are stretches of **Dresser Mem. Pk. 148.5. W. TERRE HAUTE. 153. IND.-ILL. LINE.**

## US 52—INDIANA

**OHIO LINE** (Harrison, Ohio, 21$^{m}$ from Cincinnati) **(NW) to IND.-ILL. LINE** (3$^{m}$ from Sheldon, Ill.). **198. US52**

Via: W. Harrison, Brookville, Metamora, Rushville, Morristown, New Palestine, Indianapolis, Lebanon, Lafayette, (Oxford), Fowler, Earl Park, Kentland, Effner. Hotels in cities; accoms.: At intervals.

US52 is scenic route through valleys where settlement began & where st.'s hist. was largely shaped. It crosses Ind. diagonally from southern highlands, cut by long Whitewater R., then through Indianapolis & farmlands of Wabash valley to prairies on W. border.

**0. WEST HARRISON** was laid out in 1813, but **Oldest H.,** State St. & Broadway, was built before 1812. Confed. cavalry leader Morgan (see) made last stop in Ind. in **American Hotel,** on Harrison Ave. The Confed. raiders were still fighting, although Battle of Gettysburg ended a few days before they brought Ind. its only Civil War experience.

SIDE TRIP: On country Rd. (route of Morgan's men) 8.5$^{m}$ (W) to **Dover,** Irish & German Cath. settlement. **St. Paul's Ch.** (1837) is in **New Alsace,** 12$^{m}$, oldest Cath. parish in Ind.

Tour follows Whitewater R., along whose banks are traces of Whitewater Canal, part of Internal Improvement Program that bankrupted st. in 1838. Work began again in 1842 &, although floods rose above the steep walls, the canal was a lifeline for settlers until coming of Whitewater Valley RR., 1865. **3.** J. with St.46 (see). **8. NEW TRENTON,** where Thos. Manwarring used steps of **Manwarring Tavern** (1810) as pulpit on Sundays. At c.**16. LITTLE CEDAR BAPT. CH.** (1812) one of oldest Bapt. churches in Miss. valley; property of Brookville Hist. Soc. **19. BROOK-**

**VILLE,** platted in 1808, was center of most thickly settled reg., & many early political leaders came from here. It is birthpl. of Lew Wallace (see), author of "Ben Hur." End of 8th St., **Hermitage** (1817), former home of J. Otis Adams (1851-1927), Hoosier artist. In 700 block on Main St. are **Pioneer Hardware Store & Gen. Hanna H.** (1818). At 210 E. 10th St., **Governor Ray H.** (1825). Extending (W) for miles along restored tow path is **Whitewater Canal St. Mem.** (pic.), comm. valley's importance in early settlement. **Whitewater Canal Aqueduct** (1848) spans Duck Creek at **METAMORA, 27.** At **29.** J. with St.229.

SIDE TRIP: On St.229 (S) 14m to **Oldenburg,** outstanding Cath. center, sett. by German people in 1837. **Ch. of the Holy Family, Convent of the Immaculate Conception,** mother house of sisters of St. Francis, & **Oldenburg Franciscan Monastery.** A mile from town is **Shrine of the Sorrowful Mother,** housing Alsatian "Pieta" carved before Fr. Rev.

**31.** J. with St.121, which follows (N) the sinuous W. fork of the Whitewater.

SIDE TRIP: On St.121 (N) to **Connersville.** 5m **Laurel,** sett. in booming canal days. **Stone barn,** on Washington St., site of Canal Basin. Other early bldgs. are **Laurel Jail, General Store, & Whitehall Tavern.** On Laurel Hill is high **Ind. Mound.** 16m **Elmhurst,** an estate, with magnificent beeches & elms, on edge of **Connersville,** industrial city making refrigerator cabinets, blowers, pumps, machine tools, caskets & precision parts. City was founded in 1813 by John Conner who was raised by Inds.; later guide for Gen. Harrison & member of St. Legislature. **Canal Co. Office** (Gr.Rev.).

**47. RUSHVILLE,** founded in 1822 by Dr. Wm. B. Laughlin, of Phila., who named town for Benj. Rush, signer of Decl. of Ind. At 805 N. Main St., **Watson H.,** former home of Jas. E. Watson, whose "As I Knew Them" (1936) is story of 35 yrs. in Congress. **89. INDIANAPOLIS** (see). Beyond metropolitan area (see Indianapolis for this sec.), US52 enters farmlands set about with groves of beech, oak & cedar. **116. LEBANON. Boone County Cth.** has 3-story monolithic pillars of limestone.

**150. LAFAYETTE;** & across Wabash R., **W. LAFAYETTE,** seat of Purdue Univ. (At limits, US52 By-pass follows Concord R.)

RR. Stas.: Ferry St. & Sheridan Rd., Wabash RR.; Alabama & 2nd Sts., Big Four & Nickel Plate RRs.; North & 5th Sts., Monon RR. & Bus. Sta. Commercial airports. Good accoms.; recr. facils. in various pks. Purdue Hall of Music (O). Tippecanoe Cty. Fair. Info.: Ferry & 4th Sts., C. of C.

Lafayette is center of rich dairying, livestock & farming reg.; manufactures electrical appliances, automotive tools & many other products. Town was founded in 1825 & named for Fr. Gen. then being welcomed in U.S. PTS. OF INT.: (1) 909 South St., **Tippecanoe Cty. Hist. Mus.** (O). (2) Main & Scott Sts., **Columbian Pk.** (pic.ample playfields); large zoo. (3) On bank of R., **Tippecanoe County Cth.** (1882), with **Statue of La Fayette,** by Lorado Taft. (4) Industrial plants incl.: **Ross Gear & Tool Co., Aluminum Co. of Amer., Ralston Purina Co. Mills.**

SIDE TRIP: On US52 By-pass & St.43 (N) c.6m to J. with Rd. (E) to **Battleground.** Near village is **Tippecanoe Battlefield St. Mem.** (pic.facils.) on site of battle between Gen. Harrison's forces & Inds. under White Cloud, the Prophet, brother of Tecumseh, on Nov. 7, 1811. Tippecanoe & Wabash Sts., **Site of Prophet's Town,** est. in 1808. Alcohol was prohibited, & cornfields were carefully tended. Tecumseh's plan for Ind. confederacy to deal with the whites alarmed Gen. Harrison. At conference in Vincennes, Tecumseh suggested truce while he conferred with tribes & with Pres. Madison, but, after Tecumseh departed, Harrison led about 1,000 men to encamp near Prophet's Town. Without Tecumseh to counsel him, the Prophet launched attack. Battle was indecisive & increased Ind. hostility, but power of Tecumseh & the Prophet in Northwest was broken.

Across Main St. Bridge from Lafayette is **W. LAFAYETTE, 152.,** home of **Purdue Univ.,** land-grant institution est. in 1869 with gift of land & funds from John Purdue & others. Univ. ranks high among agric. & engineering schools, & holdings incl. nearly 6,500 as. **Heavilon Hall** (1895), with clock tower. **Univ. Hall** (1877); grave of John Purdue near-by. **Mem. Union Bldg.** (1924-39). **Purdue Hall** (1873), where are rooms once occupied by George Ade, Booth Tarkington & other famous alumni. **Hall of Music** (1939-40). In Mech. Eng. Bldg. is **Railway Mus.** On Northwestern Ave., **Ross-Ade Stadium** (1924). In W. sec., **Seneca** (1946) & **Chippewa** (1947) **Dormitories. Purdue Airport** (large & modern). On South R. Rd. (S) c.4m is **Site of Ft. Ouiatenon** (pic.cottages), built by Fr. under La Salle, c.1720, & taken over by Brit. at end of Fr. & Ind. War, 1763. Ind. villages around it were destroyed in 1791.

**185.** US52 unites with US41 (see) to **194. KENTLAND** (see). J. with US24, which unites with US52 to **IND.-ILL. LINE,** at **ETTNER, 198.**

## ST. 46—INDIANA

**J. WITH US52** (3m from W. Harrison, at Ohio Line) **(W) to TERRE HAUTE. 168. St.46**

Via: Batesville, Greensburg, Columbus, Gnaw Bone, Nashville, Bloomington, Spencer, Riley. Accoms. in larger centers; camp sites.

Midway on route is Indiana's scenic reg. in Brown, Monroe & Owen Counties, with many as. reserved in St. Fors. & Pks. St.46 crosses Whitewater Cr. & cont. directly (W). At **8.** J. with St.1, cross-state (N-S) route along E. border. **24. BATESVILLE,** attractive settlement of German & other craftsmen employed in large furniture factories. **39. GREENSBURG,** at J. of Penn. & C.C.C. & St.L. RRs.; in natural gas belt. A curiosity of town is **Tree on Cth. Tower.** J. with St.29 (see Indianapolis Trip III). **67. COLUMBUS.** J. with US31 (see). **82. GNAW BONE,** crossroads village in beautiful, sparsely settled wilderness. Some farming is done between the hills, & tourist trade is good. **84.** Rd., across creek, to **Brown Cty. St. Pk.** (f.h.swim.lodge. cottages.camp.recr.facils.guides), largest & most scenic in st., covering 16,700 as. (incl. game preserve). Miles of trls. & drives around Ls., over ridges & through deep-cut valleys. Many artists have painted these woods in autumn color or in early spring. **Archery Area, Wildlife Exhibit, Game Sanctuary, Observ. Tower.** Along one of highest ridges is Swallow Trl. Lafe Bud Trl. leads up **Weedpatch Hill** (airport & fire tower). Pk. is mem. to Frank McKinney (Kin) Hubbard (1868-1930), whose "Abe Martin," rustic philosopher of Brown Cty., is comm. by **Abe Martin Lodge,** near entrance.

**87. NASHVILLE,** among Cumberland Hills, is favorite tourist stop well-known for colony of Hoosier artists. **Art Gallery** (sm.fee), exhibits work of Brown Cty. Art Assoc. **Log Jail** (1837). **Brown Cty. Mus.** (sm.fee). Near Cth., **Liars' Bench** on lawn. **95. BELMONT.** Rd. leads (N) to Ault & Yellowwood Ls. in **Yellowwood St. For.** (free.f.h.pic.shelterh.), 20,000 as. **St. Fish Hatchery** (O). Adj. is **Hoosier Nat. For.** (f.h.camp.pic.); hqs. at Bedford (see US50). The 500,000-a. purchase unit extends (S) from Bloomington (see below) to Ohio R. Among the jumbled hills are limestone caves, quarries & mineral springs. Sawmills & factories are being developed in eroded areas. Few camp sites, but hotels & cabins easily accessible in near-by towns. Short way (S) from Belmont is **T. C. Steele St. Mem.** (sm.fee), former estate of Theo. C. Steele (1847-1926), dean of Hoosier painters. **Hilltop Studio** (O): landscapes & other paintings. **Trailside Mus.** (O). **101.5.** J. with Rd. to **Ind. Univ. Astronom. Observ.**

**106. BLOOMINGTON** (1815), seat of Indiana Univ.; more than 20 limestone quarries & mills in vic. In business dist. around limestone **Monroe County Cth.** (1908) may be heard the genuine Hoosier dialect. **Indiana Univ.,** one of oldest in this part of country, was founded as Indiana Seminary in 1820, became a college in 1828 & st. univ. in 1852; coed. since 1867. Degrees are conferred in College of Arts & Sciences & Schools of Education, Medicine (in Indianapolis), Law, Dentistry (in Indianapolis), Business, Music & Health. Univ. was one of sponsors of study on human sex behavior in charge of Alfred C. Kinsey, Prof. of Zoology. Among famous alumni are Theodore Dreiser, Wendell Willkie, Hoagy Carmichael & Paul V. McNutt. Older bldgs., mostly of limestone, form part of quadrangle facing Indiana Ave.; N. are **Lib.** (1907.remod.1942); **Student Hall** (1906), **Maxwell Hall** (1890), Law School; & **Owen Hall** (1884). On E. side **Wylie** (1900), **Kirkwood** (1894) & **Science Halls** (1902). **Biology & Swain Halls** form S. side, while modern **Adm. Bldg.** (1936) completes quadrangle (W). **Kirkwood Observ.** (1900). **Mem. Union Bldg.** (1932). **Art Center** (1941). **Mem. Stadium.** In neighborhood are **Howe H.** (1834), **Wylie H.** (O. 1835) & **Hinkle H.** (O.appl.).

**113. ELLETTSVILLE.** Some of Indiana's finest quarries in vic. **121. McCORMICK'S CR. ST. PK.** (sm.fee.hotels.cabins.camp.pic.trls.guides.swim.f.recr.facils.). Creek cuts bet. limestone walls to White R. Among beech & pine groves are group camps, **Log Cabin** (1810) & **Mus.** (free). **123. SPENCER,** in rich limestone & agric. area, is birthpl. of Wm. Vaughn Moody (1869-1910), author of "The Great Divide." Here also was home of Wm. Herschell (1873-1939), who wrote "Ain't God Good to Indiana?" **Log Courth.** (1820). **138. BOWLING GREEN** (1825). Old Settlers Reunion in the fall. St.46 crosses Eel R., dear to the Delaware Inds. for the abundant "snakefish." **157. RILEY.** Near here are stretches of W. & E. Canal & Canal Reservoir. **168. TERRE HAUTE** (see). J. with US40 (see) & US41 (see).

## US 50—INDIANA

**IND.-OHIO LINE** (18$^{m}$ from Cincinnati, Ohio) **(W) to IND.-ILL. LINE** (8$^{m}$ from Lawrenceville, Ill.). **173. US50**

Via: Lawrenceburg, Aurora, Versailles, N. Vernon, Seymour, Brownstown, Bedford, Shoals, Washington, Vincennes. Paralleled roughly by B. & O. RR. US150 is alternate route, uniting with US50 about midway.

US50 enters characteristic Hoosier country. Hillsides in spring bloom with lupine, violets & flowering shrubs, & in hazy Indian summer, goldenrod, wild aster & gentian border the roadsides. Along center of route, limestone cliffs rise from placid farmlands. Reforestation & recr. projects, incl. units of Hoosier Nat. For., occupy thousands of as. of worn-out land. Bet. forks of White R. is fertile valley producing st.'s major crop—corn; around Vincennes are spreading peach & apple orchards.

**0.** Stone marker (1838) on Ohio-Ind. Line. **3.5. GREENDALE.** Aroma of fermenting mash for whiskey has been familiar here for more than 100 yrs. On Brown St., (R) from intersec. with US50, is **Old Quaker Plant** (O.appl.tours), on site of 1st distillery (1809). **James Walsh & Co. Distillery** (O.appl.tours). **J. E. Seagram Plant** (O. appl.tours), largest in city. **5. LAWRENCEBURG** (sett.1801). Ferry. Scattered through town are evidences of its hist. as popular port in steamboat days. Flood of 1937 destroyed thousands of homes behind city's broken levee. In **Beecher Presb. Ch.**, the 24-yr.-old Henry Ward Beecher had his 1st pastorate in 1837. **Vance-Tousey H.** (O.wks.1818) was one of finest mansions along R. **9. AURORA.** Many fine Hs. here also belong to the past. Favorite landing for shantyboaters, who divide their days between hill & river. J. with St.56 (see Ohio R. Tour). **20. DILLSBORO,** mineral spa. **30. VERSAILLES ST. PK.** (f.camp.group camp.pic.riding); nearly 5,400-as. acquired from Nat. Pk. Serv. in 1943. Pub. hunting ground for archers. Semi-annual field trials for hunting dogs (horses for rent) has made pk. widely known for its excellent running grounds. At **VERSAILLES** the big event is Pumpkin Show & Farmers' Fair (Oct.). Aluminum spire of ultra-modern **Tyson Temple** (1937) rises above 19th cent. Hs. & modest business bldgs. **Morgan Raid Marker,** on Ripley County Cth. (1852) lawn, tells of hasty looting by Confed. soldiers in 1863.

**53. NORTH VERNON,** platted in 1834; RR. center. On St.7 (S) is small but lovely **Muscatatuck St. Pk.** (cottages.pic.f.). **Muscatatuck Inn. 65.** J. with US31 (see). **68. SEYMOUR,** modern factory & RR. town. **Swope Mem. Art Gallery** (O.wks.). **78. BROWNSTOWN** (sett.1816), typical Hoosier farm town. J. with St.39 & St.135.

SIDE TRIPS: (A) On St.39 (SE) 2$^{m}$ to **Jackson Cty. St. For.** (f.pic.).

(B) On St.135 (SW) 3.5$^{m}$ to **Ft. Vallonia** (1805). Near-by (S) is large **Driftwood St. Fish Hatchery** (O).

**104. BEDFORD,** attractive city with many stone Hs. & neat streets; center of St.'s limestone industry. Bedford stone was used in Empire State & many other notable bldgs. **Indiana Limestone Corp. Mills & Quarries** (O.appl.). On St.158 (W) is **Moses Fell Annex Farm** (O.guides) of Purdue Univ. (see). J. with St.54, which leads (NW) 6$^{m}$ to **Avoca St. Fish Hatchery** (O). In Bedford are Hqs. of **Hoosier Nat. For. Purchase Unit** (see). US50 unites with St.37 beyond **White R. Bridge, 107.,** then winds gradually (W) through rocky country & thick hardwood fors.

SIDE TRIP: On St.37 (S) 6$^{m}$ from bridge to **Mitchell;** (E) on St.60 to **Spring Mill St. Pk.** (sm.fee.f.swim.boat.hotels.cottages.camp.pic.), where is authentic restoration of Spring Mill Village, founded in 1815 in hidden valley. Other features are 100 as. of virgin timber; **Donaldson's Cave** (boat trips), through which winds underground R. famous for its blind fish; **Twin Caves** (boat trips). **Spring Mill Village** began with gristmill & limestone quarry opened by Sam. Jackson, ensign under Perry at Put-in-Bay (see Ohio). The properties changed hands several times but, by 1850, an elegant village & stagecoach stop surrounded a great gristmill built in 1816-17. Ox-drawn wagon fleets traveled to distant markets, & barges floated lumber, flour & whiskey down to faraway New Orleans. When the RRs. shied away from the rock-walled valley, the village began to decline. Meanwhile George Donaldson, eccentric Scotsman, had bought a cave & some land extending across valley's only outlet, & he wanted his retreat left in its natural state. Spring Mill died & weeds & grass were rank in the streets when Donaldson went home to Scotland to die (1897). A few yrs. later, Dr. Carl H. Eigenmann, Indiana Univ., discovered in Donaldson's Cave the rare blind fish he had sought in many parts of the world. His "Cave Vertebrates of

America" (1909) incl. study of these "dim-eyed" fish. When St. Pk. system was begun in 1920's under Col. Richard Lieber, Lawrence Cty. offered the Donaldson tract. Col. Lieber found that Lehigh Portland Cement Co. owned the crumbling ruins in the valley but would give site to the St. if he would fulfill his dream of a restoration. Spring Village was brought completely to life. The gristmill, with orig. burrs & stones & wheels, was rebuilt. Big logs pass under the saw in the slash mill, pioneer Hs. stand in gray-walled gardens, & along main street are still-house, tavern, hat & cobbler shops, loom house & pottery plant.

**124. MARTIN CTY. ST. FOR.** (pic.motor rd.), replanted with pine by CCC. Beyond, in rocky valley of White R., the Knights of the Golden Circle brooded over dreams of a southwestern empire; & during prohibition era, moonshiners & racketeers sheltered in the hills. **128. SHOALS.** J. with US150, which unites with US50 to state line. A short distance from Shoals (N) are the fantastic **Jug Rock** (pic.) & **McBrides Bluffs,** characteristic formations of Indiana's highlands. Along White R. are numerous caves, crystal springs & small waterfalls. Bet. forks of White R. are thousands of fertile as., incl. farms of the industrious Amish. **152. WASHINGTON,** on site of Ft. Flora (1805). **Van Trees H.** (1843.Gr.Rev.) has Doric columns handcarved from tree trunks. **172.5. VINCENNES** (see), in the orchard country of Wabash Valley. **173.** US50 crosses Lincoln Mem. Bridge at **ILL.-IND. LINE.**

# US 41—INDIANA

**IND.-ILL. LINE** (Chicago) **(S) to KY. LINE** (6$^{m}$ from Henderson, Ky.). **288. US41**
Via: Hammond, Highland, Sumava Resorts, Morocco, Kentland, Earl Park, Boswell, Attica, Rockville, (Clinton), Terre Haute, Sullivan, Busseron, Vincennes, Princeton, Evansville. RR. & bus conns. & accoms. at larger centers & resorts.

US41, heavily traveled route from L. Superior to Fla., enters Ind. at (S) limits of Chicago & crosses industrial Calumet (see). In belt of dark rich soil beyond, every acre seems to be truck farm or garden spot. US41 then runs along W. side of state, in Wabash valley for many miles.

### Sec. 1: IND.-ILL. LINE to TERRE HAUTE. 173.

**6.5. HAMMOND** (see Calumet). **10.5. MUNSTER,** at edge of sandy ridge that once shored L. Mich. Hy. beyond town is lined with fruit stalls, markets, gas stations & lunch stands. **12.5. HIGHLAND,** settled largely by Dutch truck farmers. **17.** J. with US30 (see). **22.** J. with St.8.

SIDE TRIP: On St.8 (E) 6$^{m}$ to **Crown Point,** seat of industrial Lake Cty.; founded in 1834. In 1934 John Dillinger escaped from **Lake Cty. Jail.**

**26.** Short distance (E) of hy., **Cedar L.** (hotel.cabins.boats). **37.** Edge of great **Kankakee Marsh** (see US30). US41 crosses Kankakee R. **41. SUMAVA RESORTS** extend for mile or more along R., & for many miles small villages dot the farm country. **69. KENTLAND,** J. with US24 (see). **75. Earl Park,** spacious little town canopied by maples. US41 speeds through thinly settled country along route of Gen. Harrison's army on way to Tippecanoe (see). **88. BOSWELL.** Few towns or tourist stops for many miles. **106.5.** J. with St.28, which leads (S) 1$^{m}$ to **Williamsport,** founded in 1828. **Stone Tavern,** on Old Town Hill, is reminder of once busy port on spur of W. & E. Canal. **Fall Creek** drops over high sandstone ledge & follows rocky gorge to Wabash R. **107.5.** J. with Rd. along Wabash.

US41 crosses Wabash R. to **ATTICA, 108.5.,** farm & mfg. town on site of Potawatomi village. Early home of Dr. John Evans (1814-97), influential in founding Northwestern Univ. in Evanston, Ill. (named in his honor), & Colorado Seminary, which became Univ. of Denver. In 1862, Evans was appointed Terr. Gov. of Colorado. **Harrison Steel Castings Co.** (O.appl.). Along Wabash (SW) are **Portland Arch & Bear Cr. Canyon. 121.5. STERLING.** J. with St.34; (W) of J. on St.34 is **Veedersburg,** brick-making center.

SIDE TRIPS: (A) On St.34 (W) 7$^{m}$ to **Covington,** early rivertown. Most widely known citizen was Edw. A. Hannegan, considered Dan. Webster's rival in eloquence. At 5th & Jefferson Sts. is **Hannegan H.** At 8th & Crocker Sts., **Home of Lew Wallace** (see below), during term as prosecuting attorney for Fountain Cty. The Ohio-born Hannegan (1807-59), a man of dynamic charm & violent impulse, became U.S. Senator in 1842 & was appointed Minister to Prussia in 1849. Recalled, he entered race for nomination as Demo-

cratic candidate for Presidency. In violent quarrel after heavy drinking, Hannegan killed his brother-in-law &, although exonerated, never recovered from the shock. Lew Wallace, who presented weak case against his friend, had to leave Covington.
(B) On St.34 (E) 21m to **Crawfordsville,** sometimes called the Hoosier Athens because it is seat of Wabash College & former home of Maurice Thompson, Lew Wallace, & Meredith Nicholson. In residential sec. are fine houses on pleasant streets, while business dist. is crowded with brick bldgs. of a mfg. & trade center. Pike St. & Wallace Ave., **Lew Wallace Study** (O.wks.), a square, porticoed tower. Wallace, best known as author of "Ben Hur," was Civil War Gen., Terr. Gov. of New Mex. & Minister to Turkey. 205 S. Walnut St., **Home of Meredith Nicholson,** diplomat & distinguished writer. Besides his romantic novels, Nicholson wrote "The Hoosiers," "The Poet," a life of Riley & other nonfiction. Maurice Thompson, who spent most of his life here, is widely known for "Alice of Old Vincennes." In beautiful **Henry S. Lane H.** (O.wks.sm.fee.Georg.) is **Montgomery Cty. Hist. Soc. Mus.** Col. Lane was 1st nat. chairman of Republican party. **Wabash College** (Presb.), nonsect. liberal arts college for men, founded in 1832. **Forest Hall** (1832), orig. bldg. Modern bldgs. are **Pioneer Mem. Chapel, Yandes Lib., Goodrich Hall.** Vice-Pres. Thos. Marshall, Gov. J.P. Goodrich & Lew Wallace attended Wabash.

**138.5.** J. with St.47.

SIDE TRIP: On St.47 (E) 1.5m to **Turkey Run St. Pk.** (sm.fee.hotels.cottages.camp.f.boat. swim.archery & other sport facils.), with virgin timber stands & rocky gorge of Sugar Creek; unusual diversity of vegetation & wildlife, 50m of trls. & bridle paths.

At c.**141. Hadley Mon.,** to Alfred & Rhoda Hadley, Quakers active in Underground RR. **147. ROCKVILLE,** quiet home of many retired farmers. J. with US36, which runs (W) 17m, past **Dana,** birthpl. of Ernie Pyle, to Ill. Line. In country (SW) from Rockville, grim little coal towns surround the numerous shaft mines. **158. CLINTON,** (W) of hy. on St.163, founded in 1829, is the largest center. **168. NORTH TERRE HAUTE,** coal-mining town. Settlement grew up around Marble Mill (1816), the ruins of which still stand. **173. TERRE HAUTE** (see). J. with US40 (see), St.46. (see), & US150, with which US41 unites.

## Sec. 2: TERRE HAUTE to KY. LINE. 115.

The gently rolling country is fine for cantaloupe & other fruits. **0. TERRE HAUTE. 18.** J. with St.48.

SIDE TRIP: On St.48 (E) through country wasted by strip-mining to **Shakamak St. Pk.** (sm.fee.cottages.camp.group camp.f.swim.boat.). Wildlife exhibit of deer, buffalo, elk & waterfowl. **Coal Mine** (O).

**SHELBURN,** just (S) of J., is fairly large mining town. 1st coal mine in reg. was sunk here in 1868. **27. SULLIVAN,** scene in 1925 of one of state's worst mining disasters, when gas explosion trapped 55 men. Home town of Will Harrison Hays, motion picture executive, who loves this "valley of democracy." **28.** J. with St.54 (E). **29.** J. with St.54 (W).

SIDE TRIP: On St.54 (W) 9m to **Merom Bluffs,** highest on the Wabash, named for L. where Joshua fought the Canaanite kings. Near Merom (E) are traces of prehist. mounds.

**33. CARLISLE,** sett. early in 19th cent.; for many yrs. an active mining center. In Cemetery are buried "Handy" Handley, who crossed the Delaware with Gen. Washington, & Jas. L. Scott, 1st chief justice in Ind. Terr. **U.S. Center of Pop.** (1940) is (SE) c.2m from Carlisle. **39. OAKTOWN,** center of oil & gas reg. & shipping pt. for fruits. In vic. is **Shaker Prairie,** where communal sect lived for 70 yrs.

### 58. VINCENNES

Washington & Wabash Aves., Union RR. Sta. 429 Main St., Bus Terminal. Good accoms. & recr. facils. Info.: C. of C., in City Hall.

Vincennes, once capital of Northwest Terr. & (for a few months) of Louisiana Purchase as well, is full of the whole Amer. past. It is built on site of Chippecoke, capital city of Ind. tribe, & in encircling hills are mounds of prehist. Americans. Bet. pylons of Lincoln Mem. Bridge, a hy., (US50), runs (W) to Lincoln country & the Great West. Clark's taking of Brit. Ft. Sackville at Vincennes in 1779 was a decisive victory, & Gen. Harrison was hero of later battles that won the Ind. lands. Vincennes is also a modern industrial city & market for wide area incl. Knox Cty., which is 2nd in st. in diversified agriculture, 1st in peach & apple orchards & in acreage in cantaloupes, watermelons & wheat & a leader in production of coal.
In late 17th cent., a trading post was est. on riverbank. In 1732, François Morgane de Vincennes was in command of Fr. fort on this site, & his name was given to settle-

ment in 1736, the yr. in which he was burned at the stake by the Chickasaw. After 1763 post became Ft. Sackville, one of principal Brit. forts. In summer of 1778, Geo. Rogers Clark sent Father Gibault from Kaskaskia (see Ill.) to persuade the Creole villagers at Vincennes to take Amer. side. When Gen. Hamilton, Brit. "hair buyer" from Detroit, took over the ft., a wealthy Ital. trader, Francis Vigo, took the news to Clark & gave financial support to attacking expedition. Ft. Sackville was surrendered Feb. 25, 1779. Neither Father Gibault nor Vigo was ever properly rewarded by Gov. The Fr. & Creole (Fr.-Ind.) settlers of Vincennes were a gay & carefree people. Then in 1840's, a thrifty German Cath. colony built up the "Dutch Flats" & gradually beyond the R. (N) became characteristically Amer. with community of mixed stock. Probably best way to see Vincennes is to start with Mem. Bridge, within a half-mile radius of which are all hist. sites of vanished "Frenchtown." Beyond business dist. are residential areas bordered by exclusive Burnett Heights & (E) & (N) by homes of working people.

PTS. OF INT.: (1) Clark Mem. Plaza stretches along waterfront & over **Site of Ft. Sackville.** Foot of Barnett St. is **Geo. Rogers Clark Mem.** (O) to "Conquest of the West," erected in 1931-33, by Fed. Gov. at cost of $3,000,000. Granite terraces ascend from wide plaza to circular colonnaded temple (Doric). Murals (by Ezra Winter). **Statue of Clark** (by Hermon MacNeil). (2) **Lincoln Mem. Bridge** (1931), part of Lincoln Nat. Mem. Hy. from Hodgenville, Ky., to Springfield, Ill. (see), at pt. where Lincoln family crossed in 1830. (3) E. of bridge is granite **Statue of Francis Vigo** (by John Angell). (4) 2nd & Church Sts., **St. Francis Xavier Cathedral** (O.sm. fee.1825-26.Romanes.). Bell from 1st log chapel (c.1702.recast). Father Simon Bruté de Rémur, 1st bishop of Vincennes Diocese (now Indianapolis), is buried beneath altar. (5) On Cathedral grounds, **French Cemetery,** where Inds., missionaries, soldiers, Fr. & Amer. settlers are buried in unmarked graves. (6) Adj. to Cathedral, **Old Cathedral Lib.** (1843); parish records from 1749 & Father Bruté's lib. (7) Church St., opp. Cathedral, **Statue of Father Pierre Gibault** (by Albin Polasek). (8) 2nd St. bet. Church & Barnett Sts., **Chapel of St. Clare's Convent,** founded in 1824; predecessor of St. Rose Academy (1843.now at 5th & Seminary Sts.). (9) 2nd & Barnett Sts., site (supposed) of **Home of "Alice of Old Vincennes,"** who raised Amer. flag over Ft. Sackville. (10) 10th St., in Greenlawn Cemetery, **Grave of Francis Vigo.** (11) 5th & Busseron Sts., **Vincennes Univ.** coed. jr. college; founded in 1806. (12) In Harrison Pk., **First Terr. Capitol** (c.1800.rest.O.sm.fee), used until capital was moved to Corydon (see) in 1813. (13) Park & Scott Sts., the **Wm. H. Harrison Mansion** (1803-04.O.sm.fee.); 1st burnt-brick bldg. W. of Alleghenies; orig. & period furnishings. (14) 111 N. 2nd St., **Ellis H.** (1830), now Harmony Club; built of hand-quarried local stone. (15) 214 NW. 2nd St., **Pub. Mus.** (O.free); Ind., pioneer & art colls.; concerts, exhibits. INDUSTRIAL PTS. OF INT. (O.appl.): (16) Washington Ave., **Brown Shoe Co.** (17) 537 Willow St., **Blackford Window Glass Co.** (18) 1312 Chestnut St., **Tip-Top Creamery Co.,** one of largest in state. (19) 703 State St., **Vincennes Packing Corp.,** canners of "Alice of Old Vincennes" brand.

IN ENVIRONS: (20) **Indian Mounds,** some of largest in Ind. **Sugar Loaf Mound,** about ¾-mile (E) on St.61, is most picturesque. (21) **Clark's March** on Vincennes (marked route), terminating $9^m$ (S). At $7^m$ is Rd. to **Clark's Ferry** (sm.fee) to St. Francisville, Ill., where Clark & his men crossed. J. with US50-US150 (see US50).
US41 passes **KNOX CTY. EXPER. FIELD** of Purdue Univ. **83. PRINCETON,** largest of several shipping centers in cantaloupe & fruit reg. Lincoln brought wood to the mill here in 1827. **112. EVANSVILLE** (see Ohio R. Tour). **115.** US41 crosses Ohio R., **IND.-KY. LINE.**

## US 31—INDIANA

**IND.-MICH. LINE** ($5^m$ from Niles, Mich.) **(S) to IND.-KY. LINE** (Louisville, Ky.). **262. US31**

Via: South Bend, Plymouth, Rochester, Peru, Kokomo, Westfield, Indianapolis, Franklin, Columbus, Seymour, Uniontown, Scottsburg, Jeffersonville. Through RR. & bus conns. & accoms. at short intervals. Paralleled by main line RRs.

US31, one of most heavily traveled (N-S) routes, begins in Ind. in resort area near L. Mich. & crosses several of st.'s largest centers.

## Sec. 1: IND.-MICH. LINE to INDIANAPOLIS. 145.

Route begins in fruit & truck-garden area, also one of chief mint-growing reg. of U.S. (Mich. & Ind.). Peppermint was introduced from Europe in 19th cent. &, since 1900, U.S. has produced much of world's supply. Plant grows a foot or two high before harvesting. Then the cut mint is sent to distilleries in Lake & St. Joseph counties.

**6. SOUTH BEND.** J. with US20 (see). **17. LAKEVILLE,** resort. **22.** J. with US6 (see). **29. PLYMOUTH.** J. with US30 (see). **Lake of the Woods,** in hardwood for. **Bass L.** & numerous other Ls. in vic. (f.boat.cottages.resort facils.). **28.** J. with St.10.

SIDE TRIP: On St.10 (W) 10m to **Culver Military Academy** (est.1894), well-known boys' school on banks of L. Maxinkuckee (good f.), 2nd largest in Ind. **Culver** is resort town.

US31 crosses **Tippecanoe R.** near spot where Potawatomi signed treaties giving up their lands. **49. ROCHESTER,** resort town. **Cole Bros. Circus Winter Hqs.** On 11th St., **Friends Meetingh.,** now Wayne Cty. Hist. Soc. Mus. (O). On neighboring L. Manitou (f.recr.facils.hotels.cabins) is **Fed. Fish Hatchery** (O). **67. EEL R.,** long associated with Little Turtle & the Miami. **72. PERU.** J. with US24 (see).

**93. KOKOMO** (est.1844).

Through RR. & bus conns. Municipal Airport, for Delta airlines. Ample accoms. & recr. facils. Info.: C. of C., in Courtland Hotel.

Kokomo was home of Elwood Haynes, inventor, & Elmer Apperson, builder, of 1st mechanically successful "horseless carriage," in 1893-94. Town is vigorous & civic-minded industrial center, producing steel, automobile parts & accessories, china, stoves & radios. In Pioneer Cemetery is **Mon. to Makokomo,** Miami Chief. On Main St., (S) of Wildcat Cr., **Machine Shop** where pioneer gas automobile was built. J. with US35, which leads (SE) 3m to **Elwood Haynes Mon.,** on spot where test run began. **108.** J. with St.28.

SIDE TRIP: On St.28 (E) 14m to **Elwood,** market center for leading tomato reg. Birthpl. of the late Wendell L. Willkie, Pres. candidate (1940) & author of "One World." At 23m **Alexandria,** center of rock-wool industry. **Johns-Manville Co. Plant** (O.appl.), 1st producer of rock-wool insulation.

**125. WESTFIELD,** noted Underground RR. sta. (7m (E) on St.32 is **Noblesville,** sett. in 1823. Tourist Pk. & Camp). **145. INDIANAPOLIS** (see). J. with US52 (see), US40 (see) & US36.

## Sec. 2: INDIANAPOLIS to KY. LINE. 117.

**0. INDIANAPOLIS** (see Indianapolis Trip IV for next 40 miles). **40.** US31 forks, main tour by-passing Columbus, while US31A crosses downtown sec. **43. COLUMBUS.** (Through RR. & bus conns. accoms.golf & other recr. facils.) In 1820, Gen. John Tipton, hero of Ind. wars, built cabin in bottomlands of White R. He offered land for cty. seat to be named for him, but the commission decided to forget "Tiptonia," & the founder departed from the swamps. When site was drained, many large industries gravitated to Columbus, incl. radio, automobile accessories, diesel engine plants & tanneries. In Courth. is **Bartholomew Cty. Hist. Soc. Mus.** (O). Lafayette Ave. & 5th St., **Sunken Gardens** (O), on estate of Wm. G. Irwin. On 5th St. also is **Tabernacle Christ. Ch.** (O), said to be only one in **U.S. Chimes Tower.**

SIDE TRIP: On US31A (S) 23m to **Seymour,** industrial town bet. White & Muscatatuck Rs. (pic.camp sites). **Swope Mem. Art Gallery** (O). US31A ends here. J. with US50 (see). On US50 (E) 3m to J. with US31, main tour.

**63.** J. with US50 (see). **84. SCOTTSBURG.** J. with St.56 (see Ohio R. Tour). Near **UNDERWOOD, 90.,** is **Pigeon Roost Mem.,** on grave of settlers killed by Shawnee in 1812. **92.5. CLARK ST. FOR.** (f.h.pic.camp.), in Clark's Grant (see Ohio R. Tour). Very large area with several artificial Ls. & for. nursery. Cone-shaped eroded "Knobs" are characteristic of reg. Tower on **Grand View Knob** (1,020'). **94.** J. with St.160, which runs (NW) through St. For. **108.5. SELLERSBURG.** Here hy. forks; US31W runs (SW) into **New Albany,** & main tour cont. straight (S). **116. JEFFERSONVILLE,** bordering Ohio R., **IND.-KY. LINE,** at **117.** (see Ohio R. Tour for both cities).

# OHIO RIVER TOUR—INDIANA

**IND.-OHIO LINE** (21$^m$ from Cincinnati, O.) **(W)** to **IND.-ILL. LINE** (7$^m$ from Crossville, Ill.). **263. US50, St.56, St.156, St.62, St.66** (see also Ohio & Ky.).

Via: Aurora, Rising Sun, Vevay, Madison, Charlestown, Jeffersonville, New Albany, Corydon, Leavenworth, Dale, Boonville, Evansville, Mt. Vernon, New Harmony.

## Sec. 1: OHIO LINE to NEW ALBANY. 116. US50, St.56, St.156, St.62

Tour follows 1st channel of migration into the West. Shores are lined with old towns & landings, & ferries at intervals unite Ind. with Ohio & Ky. rivertowns. In some places, valley is spread with orchards & farmlands; at other pts., hy. follows rocky bluffs along shore.

US50 (see) crosses st. line a few miles (N) of R. into area long known for its distilleries. **9. AURORA.** Shantyboaters, fishermen & houseboats make lively stir up & down R. (ferry to Petersburg, O.). J. with St.56, on which tour cont. (S) along R., then cuts across rugged country. **11. LAUGHERY CR.,** where **Col. Lochry Mon.** marks site of Ind. massacre in 1781. **17. RISING SUN** (ferry.airport), founded in 1814. **Ohio County Cth.** (1845). **20.** Tour turns on St.156, close to shore where long stretches are broken only by river signals & clumps of willows & sycamores. **48. VEVAY.** Early Hs. & sites are marked by Hist. Soc. of Switzerland Cty. which was sett. at end of 18th cent. by Swiss immigrants who named city after Vevey on L. of Geneva. Became prosperous steamboat town, known for excellent wine. **Birthpl. of Edw. Eggleston** (1837-1902), whose "Hoosier School Master" is one of earliest creative treatments of pioneer material. **Swiss Inn** (1823). Near County Cth. is **Carnegie Lib.,** housing Clementi piano brought from London in 1717. Once a week Mary Wright, in court dress & jewels, played for settlers in her father's cabin. From Vevay, tour turns (W) on St.56 again, shadowed by cliffs. **68.5. MADISON** (sett.1805), seat of tobacco-raising Jefferson Cty., has Southern flavor, particularly in antebellum Hs. near river front. Around Central & West Sts. are large tobacco warehouses, & shipyards from 1830's stand along R. Madison then was largest city in Ind. (2,000 pop.). PTS. OF INT.: (1) 1st St. bet. Elm & Vine Sts., **J. F. D. Lanier St. Mem.** (O.sm.fee.1840-44.Gr.Rev.), masterpiece of architect-builder, Francis Costigan. Orig. furnishings. Lanier financed Indiana's part in Civil War & later saved st. from bankruptcy. (2) Poplar & 2nd Sts., NW. cor., **Sullivan H.** (1818.Class.Rev.). (3) 1st & Poplar Sts., **Shrewsbury H.** (1846.by Costigan); spiral stairway. (4) 1st & Jefferson Sts., **Paul H.** (1809), oldest brick bldg. (5) 2nd & Madison Sts., **Madison Hotel** (O.1849.by Costigan). (6) 2nd & Poplar Sts. SW. cor., **Schofield H.** (1817.S.Col.). (7) **Madison Lib.,** founded 1811. **70.5. CLIFTY FALLS ST. PK.** (sm.fee.camp.pic.hotels.guides.sport facils.). Clifty Creek & Little Clifty Creek fall from ledge to ledge before dropping into boulder-strewn canyon. **Clifty Inn,** with fine view over R. **74. HANOVER,** just (S) of hy.; seat of Ind.'s oldest private college, **Hanover College** (Presb.coed.), founded in 1827. On campus, 400′ above R., are new (1947) Georg. Col. bldgs. incl. **Classic Hall; Auditorium; Science Hall,** housing laboratory science depts. in which Hanover was a pioneer. **Thos. A. Hendricks Lib.,** comm. U.S. Vice Pres., class of 1841.

From Hanover, tour follows St.62 (S) & (W) while St.56 roughly parallels route of US50 (see).

SIDE TRIP: On St.56 (W) to Salem. At 16$^m$ **Scottsburg,** J. with US31 (see). 24$^m$ where **The Knobs** begin, rounded tree-covered hills running (S) to Ohio R. 45$^m$ **Salem** (sett.1814), cheerful Quaker town on many hills. **Birthpl. of John Hay** (1838-1905), statesman & writer, Secy. of State, Brit. Ambassador. **Morgan Raid Marker.** 48$^m$ Rd. leads (S) to **Beck's Mills** (1809); **Hist. Mus.**

St.62 swings (S), no longer in sight of R. In Indiana's southern hills, the pop. is widely scattered, & life in some secs. is as primitive as when Lincoln family settled there. **97. CHARLESTOWN,** small town bridging present & past. At outskirts are **E. I. Du Pont de Nemours & Co.,** smokeless powder factory, & **Goodyear Tire & Rubber Co.;** while at N. edge of town is **1st Meth. Ch. in Ind.** (1807) &, in cemetery near-by, **Grave of Jon. Jennings,** 1st Ind. Gov. **110. JEFFERSONVILLE** (bridge to Louisville, Ky.), one of oldest towns in st.; founded in 1786 by Geo. Rogers Clark & platted in 1802 by Wm. H. Harrison, with advice of Thos. Jefferson. **Howard Shipyards** (closed), on Front St., built many Mississippi packets

& steamers. In 1937, Jeffersonville was probably most seriously damaged of all the flooded rivertowns. At 10th St. & Meigs Ave., **U.S. Quartermaster Depot,** one of largest in country. On Clark Blvd., **Oldest St. Prison** in Ind. (1821.remod.). Across Mun. Bridge is **CLARKSVILLE,** founded by Clark in 1784 on part of 150,000-a. grant made by Va. Rest of grant was divided among his men. The settlements languished & Clark died, poor & discredited by his country, in 1818. J. with US31 (see).

**116. NEW ALBANY**

E. Market & Cavell Sts., Chi. Ind. St. L. RR. Sta.; Vincennes & Market Sts., B. & O. RR. Sta. 234 Vincennes St., Bus Depot. Toll Bridge to Louisville, Ky. Accoms.: Golf & other recr. facils.

New Albany, center of veneer industry, is another hist. rivertown on edge of Clark's Grant. Residential dists. lie among hills that rise (NW) into the ranging Knobs. Around marketplace & along Main St. are 19th cent. Hs. built by shipyard & steamboat owners. Platted by settlers from N.Y. (1813), New Albany became one of most important towns in Ind. From its shipyards came record-making "Robert E. Lee" & the "Eclipse," whose long-distance record was never beaten. Flood of 1937 destroyed property valued at $5,000,000. PTS. OF INT.: 600 E. Main St., **Sloan H.** (1853), square mansion on hilltop, with pilot's cabin. E. Main St. near State St. **Scribner H.** (O.1814.sm.fee). Market & Lafayette Sts., **Site of Anderson Seminary,** est. in 1841 by John B. Anderson, RR. magnate who gave Andrew Carnegie & other working boys the use of his lib. On Ekin Ave., **Nat. Soldiers' Cemetery,** ded. in 1862.

## Sec. 2: NEW ALBANY to IND.-ILL. LINE. 147. St.62, St.66, St.62

**0. NEW ALBANY.** J. with St.111, river Rd. **7.** J. with St.11 (parallels St.111 inland). St.62, the main tour, cuts across Harrison Cty. along ledge of rock. **19. CORYDON,** on steep hill in center of dairying reg.; several quarries in vic. Corydon was capital of Ind. Terr. (1813-16) & st. capital (1816-25); also scene of Civil War skirmish with Gen. Morgan. On steep slopes above crowded downtown sec. are residential streets lined with white-painted & brick Hs. On lower level are wagon works, lamp-chimney factory & other plants. Town was platted in 1808 & named by Gen. Harrison for shepherd in popular "Pastoral Elegy." PTS. OF INT.: Market St. bet. Beaver & Walnut Sts., **Old Corydon Capitol,** St. Mem. (1811-12.O.sm.fee.rest.1929), built of local blue limestone & handhewn timber. W. end of Cherry St., **Posey Mansion** (O. 1811), now D.A.R. Hall; **Pioneer Mus.** Col. Thos. L. Posey cared for many orphans here. Market & Chestnut Sts., **Kintner Hotel,** now business bldg.; Morgan's hqs. when he raided town in 1863. N. of Keller St., on Market St., **Cedar Glade,** where Confed. Gen. left Lady Morgan, ancestor of noted race horses.

**27. WHITE CLOUD** (trlr.camps.cabins). Near-by are **Wyandotte Caves** (hotels. cabins.guided tours.fee), among largest in the world, extending for 25 miles on 5 levels. **Monumental Mt.,** one of tallest underground formations. **Pillar of the Constitution,** biggest known stalagmite. **28.** J. with St.462, which leads (S) 3m to **Harrison Cty. St. For.** (camp.pic.shelterh.), more than 15,000 as. **34. LEAVENWORTH,** rebuilt town on relocated hy., looking down on old site wrecked by 1937 flood. Founded in 1818 in bowl-shaped valley, it was busy port for many yrs. Here St.62 unites with St.66.

SIDE TRIP: On St.66 (N) 12m to **Marengo,** resort center in reg. of limestone caves & mineral springs. **Marengo Cave** (fee.guided tours).

**42. SULPHUR.** St.66 turns (S) here, running close to R. to Evansville.

SIDE TRIP: On St.66 (S) 1.5m to **White Sulphur Springs** (f.h.cabins), popular resort.

St.62 unites with St.37 as far as **ST. CROIX, 49.** Here St.37 turns (S) through the Lincoln country in Ind. (see below). Main tour cont. (W) over St.62, some distance from R.

SIDE TRIP: On St.37 (S) through **Perry Cty.,** heavily forested hill country, with a few old-fashioned villages. 27m **Tell City** (ferry), sett. 1857 by Swiss colony. Among street names are Steuben, Schiller, Pestalozzi & Mozart.

On St.66 (S) 3m from Tell City to **Cannelton.** 5m **Lafayette Springs,** near which Lafayette camped in 1825, when his steamer struck a rock & sank. Lincoln's family made 1st stop in Ind. near same spot in 1816.

**64.** On St.62, **ST. MEINRAD** (1854), German Cath. town. Among craggy hills above it is **Benedictine Abbey,** built of local sandstone by Benedictines. **Abbey Ch.**

(Romanes.) has several chapels with fine stained-glass & Ital. altars. On forest Rd. is **Monte Cassino Chapel** (1868). **68.** J. with St.162.

SIDE TRIP: On St.162 (N) 4m to **Ferdinand,** another German Cath. community; seat of Convent of the Immaculate Conception. **Ch.** (Romanes.), with campanile & dome. On St.284 (E) 6m from Ferdinand to **Ferdinand St. For.** (f.h.boat.pic.) & **Fish Hatchery** (O).

**75. DALE.** St.62 unites (S) with St.45. **79. GENTRYVILLE,** where Lincoln was clerk in store of James Gentry. St.162 leads (E) 2m to **Lincoln City,** on part of the Lincoln farm. **Lincoln St. Pk.** (sm.fee.pic.camp.recr.area); trls. to **Nancy Hanks Lincoln Mem.,** at grave of Lincoln's mother; & to **Site of Lincoln Cabin.** Near **Pigeon Creek Bapt. Ch.** (O) is grave of Lincoln's sister, Sarah. On St.162 (E) 5m from Lincoln City is **Santa Claus,** where Christmas mail is postmarked by the ton. **Santa Claus Pk.**

**83.** St.45 turns (S). Tour cont. on St.62.

SIDE TRIP: On St.45 (S) 12m to **Rockport,** sett. in 1807. Here Lincoln attended court & found a wider world than Pigeon Creek afforded. **Lincoln Pioneer Village** (sm.fee) has reprods. of Pigeon Cr. Bapt. Ch., Schoolh., Lincoln Cabin, Brown's Inn & pioneer Hs. **L. Alda** (pic.boats). Ferry to Maceo, Ky.

**97. BOONVILLE,** platted in 1818. **Ratliff Boon H.** At NE. edge of town is **Scales L. St. For.** (f.boat.pic.).

**110. EVANSVILLE**

Fulton Ave. & Ohio St., Union Sta.; Division St. & Elsis Ave., Southern RR. Sta.; Franklin St. & 6th Ave., Ill. Cent. RR. Sta. Sycamore & 3rd Sts., Bus Terminal. Airport, (N) 5m on US41 (new port, 1949, planned). Good accoms.; many pks. & playgrounds. Dade Pk. Race Track (Aug.-Sept.). Symphony; theaters, stage & screen & Little Theater. Info.: C. of C., 410 3rd & Main Bldg.

Evansville, seat of Evansville College, has fine harbor on narrow loop of Ohio R. It is 5th largest city in st. & only metropolitan center within radius of 100 miles. Main St. runs (NE) from Dress Plaza, city's front on R., & Evansville-Henderson Bridge (free) links the states. Pop. is almost wholly native born. A small village grew up here around Col. Hugh McGary's log cabin (1812) & ferry. In 1818, Gen. Rbt. Evans bought a section, & Evans' Town was platted. River traffic grew enormously, & soon shipyards, foundries, sawmills, flour mills & other industries came. Successive floods, cholera epidemics & financial panics brought death & disaster, but city struggled through bad periods & rebuilt. Gov.-sponsored levee has lessened danger from R., & city ranks high in pub. health. Besides being nat. refrigeration center, Evansville has some 200 industries, incl. metal-working, plastics, food & textiles.

PTS. OF INT.: (1) **Dress Plaza & Sunset Pk.,** along river front. (2) Joseph & Ohio Sts., **Mead Johnson River-Rail-Truck Terminal.** (3) Mesker Pk. Dr. & Bement Ave., **Mesker Mun. Pk.** (f.pic.playfields.amusements). **Mun. Zoo,** one of finest in U.S.; African Veldt & Monkeys' Ship, replica of "Santa Maria." (4) Ingle & Carpenter Sts., **Willard Carpenter H.** (1848.Georg.), home of Amer. Legion post. (5) 216 W. 2nd St., **Mus. of Fine Arts & Hist.** (O). (6) Court St. bet. 1st & 2nd Sts., **Soldiers & Sailors Mem. Coliseum** (O.Gr.Rev.). (7) Morton Ave. bet. Franklin & Division Sts., **Servel, Inc.** (O), org. in Evansville in 1926, pioneer in commercial refrigeration & air-conditioning. Other plants are **Seeger Refrigerator Co., Internat. Harvester, & Schnake, Inc.,** (8) Penn. St. bet. S. Lemke & St. Joseph Ave., **Mead Johnson & Co.** (O), makers of infant & dietary foods. (9) Another large food industry is **Igleheart Bros.** (O.appl.); flour mills. (10) Rotherwood & Lincoln Aves., **Evansville College** (Meth.), coed.; founded at Moores Hill, Ind., in 1854; degrees in liberal arts, nursing, medical & industrial technology. "Urban pattern" of education is stressed, with cooperation of local organizations. **Adm. Hall** (O); pioneer, Ind., geol. & biol. colls. J. with US41 (see) & St.66.

**132. MOUNT VERNON,** on another bend of R., resembles Southern town in many ways; seat of Posey Cty., agric. & oil-producing reg. Near Cth. is **Soldiers' & Sailors' Mon.,** by Rudolph Schwartz, sculptor of similar mon. in Indianapolis (see). J. with St.69, on which main tour cont. (N).

SIDE TRIP: St.69 (S) to **Hovey L. Game Preserve,** bet. Wabash & Ohio Rs. Heron, duck & other wild fowl congregate in spring, & flora incl. N. & S. species.

**146.5. NEW HARMONY,** changeless town on Wabash, famous for 2 communal experiments: Rappite (1815-25) & Owen Community (1925-27). Hundreds of golden rain trees, planted more than cent. ago, fill the air in June with drifting yellow petals. In 1815, followers of George Rapp came from Pa. & built "Harmonie" on 30,000 as. The Rappites, who came from Germany in 1805, believed in celibacy & communal ownership. They cleared fors., drained swamps & planted fields & vineyards. In 1825, their leaders sold Harmonie to Rbt. Owen (1771-1858), Welsh humanitarian, author of "A New View of Society" (1816). Harmonie seemed ideal place for a "New Moral World" (title of his journal), based on cooperative effort & advanced educational facils. One of most influential of the early teachers was Wm. Maclure, later 1st pres. of Phila. Academy of Natural Science & "father of American geology." The colony failed (1827), but New Harmony became cultural center, & many liberal colonies derived from it.

PTS. OF INT.: Main St. bet. Church & Granary Sts., **Community H.** (1816-22), typical Rappite bldg., in Pa. Dutch style. Another is **Tavern** on Church St. bet. Main & Brewery Sts. West St. bet. Church & Granary Sts., **Old Fauntleroy H.** (O. 1815), home of Owen & other leaders. Here Minerva Club, 1st org. women's club in Amer., was founded in 1859 by granddaughter of Rbt. Owen. Main & Church Sts., **Rapp-Maclure H.** (O.1814), surrounded by golden rain trees; built for Father Rapp & remod. by Maclure. Tavern & West Sts., **Workingmen's Inst.** (O); Lib. & Mus. org. in 1838. Dr. Edw. Murphy built and endowed lib. & several similar institutions benefited under his will. Next door is **Murphy Auditorium.** J. with St.66, alt. route. **147.** Bridge crosses Wabash R., **IND.-ILL. LINE.**

# CITIES OF THE CALUMET—INDIANA

The Calumet (Gary, Hammond, East Chicago & Whiting), a physical & industrial unit massed against L. Mich., is most concentrated industrial development in the world. This "smoke-blinded, taut, metalllc jungle" (Gunther in "Inside U.S.A.") is crowded with factories, forges, mills, refineries, steel towers & bridges, docks & RR. tracks. It is considered part of Greater Chicago, & city planning is done in cooperation with that city's Planning Commission. The name derives from Fr. word for "reed," & pipes made by Potawatomi from reeds growing along R. were later called "calumets."

## GARY

RR. Stas.: Broadway & 3rd Ave., Union Depot; Chase St. & W. 5th Ave., Pa. RR.; 1045 Broadway, M.C. RR.; 901 Broadway, Wabash RR.; 4100 Adams St., Nickel Plate Rd. 470 Broadway, Union Bus Depot. Chicago Airport is 1 hr. drive from Gary; book passage at Travel Bur., 470 Broadway. Accoms. Sports facils. in Marquette & other pks.; bath. beach. Info.: C. of C., in Gary Hotel, Broadway & 6th Ave.

Gary, 3rd among Ind. cities, home of main plant of U.S. Steel, has grown in less than 50 yrs. from group of tar-papered shacks to metropolis with planned residential dists. & school system of nat. note. Business sec. around J. of Broadway & 5th Ave. has been built up largely since 1921. Along 9th Ave., S. of Wabash RR. tracks, are neighborhood centers of many foreign-born groups & large Negro pop. Larger industrial plants are separated from rest of city by Calumet R. In 1905, Judge Elbert H. Gary chose duneland site for U.S. Steel plant, & soon sand mts. were being levelled, river rechanneled, & site for plant raised 15 feet. A city of bleak shacks on narrow, sandy streets housed thousands of workers. In 1921 even the more substantial bldgs. were razed & a planned city created. Labor relations also have developed from early paternalism to union contract; outstanding events were A.F. of L. steel strike in 1919 & reorganization under C.I.O. in 1937. Work-study-play school system was begun by the late Dr. Wm. Wirt.

PTS. OF INT.: (1) N. Broadway, **Gary (U.S.) Steel Works** (tours). In coke plants, 1,000 ovens & 12 blast furnaces are grouped beyond huge ore & limestone yards. Spectacular features are ore-loading docks, open-hearth furnaces, & rolling & wheel mills. On N. Buchanan St. are **Sheet & Tin Mills** (tours). (2) In Buffington, on L. Mich., **Universal Atlas Cement Co.** (tours on appl.), U.S. Steel subsidiary. (3) 2700 E. 5th Ave., **Union Drawn Steel Co.,** Republic Steel Corp. (4) 716 E. 5th Ave., **Sun Motor Co.,** builders of airplane engines. (5) Grand Blvd., on L. Mich., **Marquette Pk.** (pic.beaches.recr.facils.), beginning of dunes. **Statue of Pere Marquette.** (6) 220 W. 5th Ave., **Pub. Lib.;** outstanding metallurgical coll.

**HAMMOND**

RR. Stas.: 423 Sibley St., for C. & O. & other lines; 475 Plummer St., M.C. RR.; 5310 Oakley Ave., Nickel Plate RR.; 4601 Hohman Ave., Wabash Ry. 4919 Hohman Ave., Greyhound Bus Sta.; 5036 Hohman Ave., Union Bus Depot. Accoms. Recr. facils., Wolf & other Ls. (swim.). Cook Cty. For. Preserve, at W. limits. Info.: 423 Fayette St., C. of C.

Hammond, next in size to Gary, is a strange-looking town, cut (E-W) by Calumet R. & its downtown crossed by network of RR. tracks. It was the big town in 1900 & a leading meat-packing center. In 1869, Geo. H. Hammond came from Mich. to est. a slaughter house in the settlement, bringing with him the idea of a refrigerator car invented in Detroit for shipment of fish. A few mos. later, an iced car packed with dressed beef arrived in Boston, the beginning of present-day shipping methods. With development of Calumet dist., other industries were est. here, incl. printing & bookbinding & manufacture of corn syrup, RR. equipment, surgical supplies & steel products. PTS. OF INT.: (1) 601 Conkey Ave., **Conkey Printing Plant** (O.appl.). (2) 1271 Indianapolis Blvd., **Lever Bros. Plant** (O), makers of soap flakes. (3) 113th Ave. & Roby Sts., **Amer. Maize Products Plant** (O). Other big plants are **Pullman Standard Car Mfg. Co. & Amer. Steel Foundries.** (4) Hohman St. & Michigan Ave. **Pub. Lib.;** special chemistry, steel & petroleum colls.

**EAST CHICAGO**

RRs.: Mich. Ave. & Guthrie St., Pa. RR.; Watling & Regent Sts., N.Y.C. RR. & B.&O. RR. 3448 Guthrie, Harbor Bus Depot. Accoms. Recr. facils. in several pks. Info.: 4618 Magoun Ave., C. of C.

East Chicago, incl. Indiana Harbor, is almost wholly given over to industry, the sky being blood-red at night & the air in the daytime gray with smoke & strong with smell of gas & oil. Steel works, rolling mills, refineries, RR. car shops, blast furnaces, packing plants & plate mills reach down from the L. & line Calumet R. Pop. is about 75% native-born, incl. thousands of Negroes. City has good sch. & lib. system, many churches & theaters, & some 350 clubs. E. Chicago was inc. in 1889, when Standard Oil Co. built world's largest oil refinery in adj. Whiting, extended later into E. Chicago. 1st steel mill was built in 1901, & work began almost immediately on Indiana Harbor & Ship Canal, which receives both ocean & L. vessels at 5m stretch of wharves. PTS. OF INT.: (1) 3210 Watling St., **Inland Steel Co.** (O.appl.), 1st in Calumet. (2) 3301 Indianapolis Blvd., **Sinclair Refinery** (O. appl.). (3) 4343 Kennedy Ave., **Harbison-Walker Refractories** (O), makers of silica firebrick. (4) Cline Ave., **Cudahy Packing Co.** (tours). (5) Grand Blvd. bet 42nd & 44th Sts., **Washington Pk.;** only zoo in Calumet; Stadium.

**WHITING,** (Through RR. & bus conns. Accoms. & recr. facils. Concert halls), although home of Standard Oil of Ind. refineries, is much smaller than other Calumet cities & is unlike them in other respects. Originally a German settlement, it has present pop. 90% foreign born or of foreign descent (1940). Civic life is colored by these varied racial groups, their love of cleanliness & sociability &, notably, of music. **Lake Front Pk.** has excellent recr. facils. **Wolf L.** (f.). Standard Ave. & Front St., **Standard Oil Co.** (tours on appl.).

## FORT WAYNE—INDIANA

**FORT WAYNE**

RR. Stas.: Harrison & Baker Sts., Pa. RR.: Grand St. bet. Harrison & Calhoun Sts., Wabash RR.; 912 Cass St., N.Y.C. RR.; Superior & Calhoun Sts., L. Erie & Ft. Wayne, Nickel Plate & other lines. Jefferson St., bet. Harrison & Webster Sts., Bus Sta. Airport; 7.5m (SW), Baer Field. Hotels & tourist accoms. Numerous pks. & playgrounds, St. Joseph R. beach & L. dist. easily accessible. Civic Theatre. Art Mus. Lincoln Mus. (see below). Info.: 826 Ewing St., C. of C.

Fort Wayne (inc. 1829), st.'s 2nd city, is on site of capital city of the Miami & of 1st ft. in Ind., an active factor in development of Northwest. City's importance derives from strategic position at meeting of St. Joseph & St. Mary's Rs. to form the Maumee. A 7m portage at this pt. once linked Great Ls. & Miss. R. Also it is center of a rich agric. & industrial area, a few hrs. from Indianapolis, Chicago, Detroit & Toledo. Downtown dist., with Calhoun its main st., is just (S) of confluence of Rs. Clinton St. (US27-US33) runs N-S through city, & Washington St. (US30-US21) is main E-W artery. On the 3 waterways, bridged at many pts., are pub. pks. & residential secs.; Foster Pk. Dr., along St. Mary's R., broadening into Foster Pk., is one of most attractive roads. Pop. is predominantly native-born. City has country's largest gasoline pump & tank plants; other products are electrical equipment, wire coils & truck bodies. Ft. Wayne is known as one of most solidly unionized cities in Ind.

Probably La Salle portaged here in 1669. Ft. Miami, est. on St. Mary's R. in late 17th cent., was a principal trading post for 100 yrs. Ft. was surrendered to Brit. in 1760, taken by Pontiac but soon retaken by Brit. After Rev., Gen. Jos. Harmar est. another post at Miami Town, but the forces of Little Turtle were too strong for him &, later, for Gen. St. Clair. Then, in 1794, Anthony Wayne built a stockade across R. & made a treaty with Inds. Capt. Wm. Wells, Ind. agent, & the intelligent Little Turtle kept Miami out of Tecumseh's confederacy. Ft. was evacuated in 1819, & shortly afterward Judge Sam. Hanna & Jas. Barnett set up post & gristmill. Settlement was rapid. Tanneries, mills, distilleries & boatyards flourished. The Miami were removed to Kansas in 1846, but their leader, Fr.-Ind. Jean Baptiste Richardville, who had persuaded them to cede lands, remained in brick house given him by Gov. Chief Francis La Fontaine (see), his son-in-law, led his tribesmen out of the valley. Ft. Wayne was important Underground Sta.

PTS. OF INT. DOWNTOWN: (1) 1026 Berry St. **Art Sch. & Mus.** (O), founded in 1888. J. Otis Adams & other prominent Indiana artists were assoc. with sch. (2) 1301 S. Harrison St., **Lincoln Mus.** (O.wks.), at Lincoln Nat. Life Co. Hqs.; lifework of Dr. L. A. Warren, curator since 1928 under Lincoln Nat. Life Foundation. Coll. is said to be one of largest in world about any person, incl. more than 12,000 books & thousands of photographs, paintings, sculptures, letters. In plaza is **Statue of Lincoln** (by Paul Manship), as a Hoosier boy. (3) 301 W. Wayne St., **Pub Lib.** (also Cty.); special colls. of music, costume & local hist. (4) Calhoun St., bet. Lewis & Jefferson Sts., **Cathedral of the Immaculate Conception** (Cath.Goth.). (5) 601 W. Berry St., **Trinity Ch.** (Episc.) with notable altar. (6) 116 E. Berry St., **Lincoln Bank Bldg.** (mod.observ.tower), tallest in city. (7) Main & Clay Sts., **Old Ft. Pk.**, site of 2nd Amer. ft. (1815-57). **Soldiers' Mon.** (8) Clay & Berry Sts., **Site of 1st Amer. Ft.** (1794).

PTS. OF INT. on ST. MARY'S R.: (9) In Swinney Pk., Jefferson & Garden Sts., **Allen Cty.-Ft. Wayne Hist. Mus.** (O.exc.Mon.), in **Swinney Homestead** (1844). In Pk., N. of St.24, is **Site of Portage. Johnny Appleseed Mem.** (10) N. of W. Main St., **Aqueduct** (ruins) of W. & E. Canal. (11) Beyond Aqueduct, **Site of Ft. Miami**, abandoned for site on St. Joseph R. (see below). (12) 616 W. Superior St., **McCulloch H.** (1838.Col.remod.), built for Hugh McCulloch, Sec. of Treas. in Lincoln's cabinet.

OTHER PTS. OF INT.: (13) E. bank of St. Joseph R., at Delaware Ave., **Site of Post Miami**, Fr. ft. surrendered to Brit. in 1760. (14) E. of Parnell Ave., in Archer Cemetery, **Grave of Johnny Appleseed** (see). (15) Harmar St. & Maumee Ave., in Hayden Pk., **Statue of Gen. Wayne** (1918.by C.E.Mulligan). (16) Lewis & Gay Sts., **Samuel Hanna H.** (O), former home of city founder; now Children's Mus. & crippled children's school. (17) Washington & Anthony Blvd., **Concordia College** (Jr.) & **Theological Seminary** (Luth.). (18) Wayne Trace at New Haven Ave., **Marker** on route of armies. (19) On US30 at E. edge of city, **Mem. Pk.** Among Industrial Plants (O) are: (20) **General Electric Co.**, plants on Broadway, Winter & Taylor Sts. Along Bueter Ave.: (21) 3$^{m}$ (SE) from downtown, **Internat. Harvester Co.**, city's 2nd largest industry. (22) **Magnavox Co., Home Plant.** (23) **Zollner Machine Works**, makers of aluminum pistons. (24) 3700 E. Pontiac St., **Farnsworth Television & Radio Corp.**

TRIPS OUT OF FORT WAYNE. I. US27 (N) 44$^{m}$ to **Angola.** Via: Garrett, Auburn, Waterloo, Pleasant L. US27 (Clinton St.) runs past **Ft. Wayne Speedway**, a half-mile beyond limits; race tracks. **Exposition Pk.** 19$^{m}$ **Garrett**, small industrial center. 24$^{m}$ **Auburn**, oldest town in DeKalb Cty. **Warner Automotive Plant.** 29.5$^{m}$ **Waterloo**, tourist center at edge of L. reg. 44$^{m}$ **Angola**, popular with fishermen, vacationists & tourists (all kinds of accoms. in vic.).

Trip cont. to **Pokagon St. Pk.** (Potawatomi Inn), **L. James** & other large Ls. (see US20) & to Ind.-Mich. Line, 52.5$^{m}$.

II. US27 (S) 38$^{m}$ to **Geneva.** Via: Middletown, Decatur, Berne. Hy. parallels **Wayne Trace** for more than 20$^{m}$, route of Gen. Wayne after Battle of Fallen Timbers (see)

& of Gen. Harrison when he came to defense of Ft. Wayne in 1812. 11.5$^m$ **Middletown.** Reminder of stagecoach era is **Ruch Tavern** (1851). 18$^m$ **Monmouth,** sugar-beet center. 21$^m$ **Decatur,** once home of Gene Stratton Porter. 27$^m$ J. with St.124.

SIDE TRIP: On St.124 (W) 9$^m$ to J. with St.201, which leads (S) short distance to J. with Rd. (SE) into **Wells Cty. St. For.** (pic.facils.shelterh.); preserve for wildfowl, deer, bear, raccoon. **Wildlife Display.**

33$^m$ **Berne,** founded by Swiss Mennonites; publishing house & bookstore for Mennonite General Conference. Near **Geneva,** 38$^m$, is **Limberlost St. Mem.** (sm.fee), incl. cabin in which Gene Stratton Porter lived 1886-1913 (see also Rome City on US20). The swamp, now drained, was setting for "Song of the Cardinal" & other books that have been read by millions.

III. US24 (W) 26$^m$ to **Huntington.** Via: Roanoke.

US24 follows Washington Blvd. across St. Mary's R., then (SW) along Little Wabash R. in heart of Miami country, 11.5$^m$ **Vermilyea Tavern,** most popular inn in canal days. 26$^m$ Huntington (see US24), seat of Huntington College. **Mem. Pk.**

IV. US33 50$^m$ (NW) to **Benton.** Via: Churubusco, Merriam, Wolflake, Kimmell, Ligonier. US33 is pleasant route through Eel R. valley where Little Turtle was born, then crosses reg. of st.'s largest Ls. to Amish & Mennonite communities around Goshen (see). 15$^m$ **Churubusco,** named for battle in Mex. War. 20$^m$ J. with St.102, which runs (W & S) to **Tri-Lakes St. Fish Hatchery** (pic.camp.cottages.f.swim). 23$^m$ **Merriam.** J. with St.9., the route (N) through Noble Cty. lake reg. 28$^m$ **Wolflake,** named when wolves howled around cabins in for. 33$^m$ **Kimmell,** in marshy onion-producing area. 39$^m$ **Ligonier,** on Elkhart R. Many townspeople are descended from early Jewish settlers. **Grave of Nath. Prentice,** who was with Washington at Valley Forge. 50$^m$ **Benton,** surrounded by large dairy, wheat & general farms of Amish & Mennonites.

## INDIANAPOLIS—INDIANA

S. Illinois St. & McCrea Pl., Union (RR.) Sta. N. Illinois & W. Market Sts., Terminal Bus Sta. Off US40 (SW) 6$^m$ Weir Cook Airport. Ample accoms. Sports events at Motor Speedway, St. Fairgrounds, Victory Field & Butler Stadium. Golf & other recr. facils. in numerous pks., incl. Broad Ripple (amusement). Theaters (stage & screen), Symphony Orchestra. Summer opera. Internat. Automobile Race (Mem. Day). 777 N. Meridian St., Nat. Hqs. of Amer. Legion. Info.: 320 N. Meridian St., C. of C.

Indianapolis is country's largest city not on navigable water & 2nd-largest St. capital city (Boston 1st). It is also St.'s RR., hy. & banking center & leading market for corn, grain & livestock; hqs. of Bobbs-Merrill Co., publishers. Atmosphere & tempo, however, are much the same as in other Hoosier towns, partly because it has expanded gradually over level plain, its industrial plants are scattered & labor supply comes from rural communities. Less than 3% of pop. is foreign born. Cultural institutions are Butler Univ., Ind. Cent. College, 4 Schs. of Ind. Univ., Arthur Jordan Conserv. of Music, John Herron Art Sch., Symphony Orchestra & Civic Theater. When capital site was chosen in 1821, a few cabins & Ind. villages made up the Fall Cr. settlement. Alex. Ralston, assistant to L'Enfant in planning Washington, D. C., plotted orig. "mile square" around Governor's Circle (now Mon. Circle), with main aves. radiating from it. Washington St. (E-W) is business thoroughfare. Meridian St. (S-N), with slum dist. at lower end, broadens into residential ave. Only a few tall structures stand out among downtown gov. & business bldgs. To (N) are Butler Univ., Fall Cr. Pky. & numerous pks., playgrounds & residential areas. Indiana Ave. leads (W) to crowded Negro sec. (more than 11% of pop.). In 1830 the Nat. Rd. crossed Indianapolis, & in 1853 the 1st union RR. sta. in U.S. was built. The rustic capital boomed with the Civil War & sank with the 1873 depression, but industrialization had begun. 1st convention of Greenback party was held here in 1874. It was leading automotive center until giant corporations developed on natural waterways. During 20th cent., city became important meat-packing & market center & seat of some 900 industrial plants. It was an "open shop" town until late in 1930's. Probably greatest "Konklave" of Ku Klux Klan was held in Indianapolis on July 4, 1923. In 1928, "Indianapolis Times" received Pulitzer Prize for exposure of corruption in St.

PTS. OF INT. DOWNTOWN: (1) Center of Mon. Circle, **Soldiers' Mon.** (1867-1901. O.sm.fee), 285′ shaft surmounted by 38′ "Victory" (observ.platform). Bronze statues (by Geo.T.Brewster) of Clark & Govs. Harrison, Whitcomb & Morton; granite sculptures (by Rudolph Schwartz) symbolic of war & peace. (2) On Circle (NE), **Christ Episc. Ch.** (1858.spire 1869.Eng.Goth.). (3) W. of Circle, **Ind. State H.** (1878. O.wks.), in 9-a. pk.; limestone bldg. with Corinthian colonnades, topped by copper dome. **St. Mus.** (O.wks.) has Tarleton Coll. of swords & knives. (4) On Ohio St. N. of Circle, **U.S. Cth. & P.O.** (Class.). (5) 140 N. Senate St., **State Lib.** (1934.O.wks.); coll. has many books in Braille. Ind. Hist. Bureau (6) **World War Mem. Plaza,** extending 5 blocks (N) from New York St., bet. Meridian & Pennsylvania Sts.: **Univ. Pk.,** set aside for univ. in 1827; **Depew Mem. Fountain** (by A. Sterling Calder). **Shrine Bldg.** (1927.O.wks.); on S. stairway is bronze "Pro Patria," by Hering; on top floor. **Shrine of the Flag.** Altar top is mosaic of colored enamels showing eagle, shield & other emblems. **Obelisk Sq.,** paved court around black-granite obelisk. **Cenotaph,** black-granite mem. to dead of World War I. (7) N. of Cenotaph Sq., **Amer. Legion Nat. Hqs.** (1925.neo-Class.). (8) Meridian & North Sts., **Scottish Rite Cathedral** (1929.Tudor Goth.O.Sat.aft.). In 212′ tower is fine carillon of 63 bells. (9) 40 E. St. Clair St. **Pub. Lib.** (1917. Doric.by Paul Cret). (10) 1150 N. Meridian St., **Children's Mus.** (O); exhibits in natural science, hist. & art. (11) 528 Lockerbie St. **Jas. Whitcomb Riley H.** (O.Vict.), where some of most popular poems were written; period furnishings. (12) Pennsylvania & 15th Sts., **John Herron Art Mus.** (1906.mod.Ren.) & Art School. Paintings by Hassam & other Amer. artists; Cézanne, Seurat, Van Gogh, Hobbema, Cuyp.

OTHER PTS. OF INT.: (13) Bet. Mich. & 10th Sts., E. of White R., **Ind. Univ. Medical Center,** incl. Riley Hospital for Crippled Children, Univ. Medical & Dental Schools. (14) 4001 Ottervein Ave., **Ind. Central College** (United Brethren), coed.; opened in 1905; incl. Liberal Arts & Teachers Colleges, Conservatory & Bible Institute. (15) Garfield Dr. & Shelby St., **Garfield Pk.;** L. Sullivan, sunken gardens, lagoon, open-air theater. (16) S. of 38th St. near Riverside Dr. **Riverside Pk.,** city's largest. **St. Fish Hatchery.** (17) 1230 N. Delaware St., **Benj. Harrison H.** (O.sm.fee. 1872.Regency); period furnishings. (18) Sunset Ave. & W. 46th St., 5$^{m}$ N. from downtown, **Butler Univ.** (coed.) has 246-a. campus in former Fairfield Pk.; founded by Ovid Butler & Henry W. Beecher as Northwestern Christ. Univ. in 1855. Incl. Univ. College, Colleges of Liberal Arts, Education, Business Admin. & Pharmacy, School of Religion & Graduate Division. (19) W. 34th St., **Crown Hill Cemetery.** Graves of Pres. Benj. Harrison, J. W. Riley, Kin Hubbard, & Vice Presidents Chas. Fairbanks & Thos. Marshall. (20) 2402 Cold Spring Rd., **Carmelite Monastery** (lobby O.1832.Med.). (21) 2400 W. 16th St., **Motor Speedway** (1909.O.wks.); Mem. Day races. (22) 38th St. off Fall Cr. Pky., **Fairgrounds,** scene of one of largest st. fairs. **Coliseum.** (23) 1500 Kentucky Ave., **Stockyard** (O.wks.), one of largest in U.S.; opened in 1877. (24) Georgia & Blackford Sts., **Kingen & Co. Meat Packing Plant.** (25) S. Alabama St., **Eli Lilly Co. Plant,** large pharmaceutical manufacturer. (26) 611 Park Ave., **Real Silk Hosiery Mills.** (27) **Beach Grove Shops** of Big Four-N.Y.C. RR.

TRIPS OUT OF INDIANAPOLIS: I. US36 (W) 20$^{m}$ to **Danville** (sett.1824), seat of **Canterbury College,** only coed. Episc. college in U.S. Until May, 1946, it was known as Cent. Normal College (est. 1878). **Seminary Bldg.** (1829), of early Danville Academy.

II. US36, St.67, St.9 (NE) 35$^{m}$ to **Anderson.** Via: Ft. Benj. Harrison & Fortville. Follow Mass. Ave. to J. with US36-St.67. 11.5$^{m}$ J. with Post Rd. (N) to **Ft. Benj. Harrison** (est. 1903), large Army post; modern air field. 20$^{m}$ **Fortville.** 26$^{m}$ **Ind. St. Reformatory.** Just (S) of **Huntsville,** 29$^{m}$, US36 turns (E), & trip cont. (N) on St.67 to J. with St.9, which leads (N). 35$^{m}$ **Anderson** (through RR. & bus conns. accoms.), large industrial center; seat of Anderson College & Theological Seminary; platted in 1823 & named for "Capt. Anderson," Delaware chief of village that occupied site. After several false starts, discovery of natural gas in 1880's brought a real boom to the town. One of most publicized sit-down strikes occurred in Anderson's G. M. plants in 1936. PTS. OF INT.: Arrow Ave. & 25th St., **Guide Lamp Co.** (O), G. M. subsidiary. 25th St. & Columbus Ave., **Delco-Remy Division** of G. M. (O). Orig. factory was est. in 1895 by Remy brothers. Union Ave. & 5th St., **Gospel Trumpet Co.,** probably largest publisher of religious material in U.S. Union Ave. & 5th St., **Anderson College & Theological Seminary** (Ch. of God), coed. liberal arts college, est. in 1917. From Anderson, on St.32 (E) 4$^{m}$, is **Mounds St. Pk.** (f.camp.pic.

recr.facils.refreshments), along White R.; some of country's most unusual prehist. mounds, incl. one 1,200′ around & 9′ high. **Wildlife Sanctuary.**

III. US40 (E) 21$^{m}$ to **Greenfield.** Via: Cumberland & Philadelphia. Tourist camps. Trip to birthpl. of Jas. Whitcomb Riley is through country such as he described in his poetry. **Riley Mem. Pk.** (see US40 for description of trip).

IV. US40 (W) & St.43 (N) 44$^{m}$ to **Greencastle.** Via: Plainfield, Stilesville. Trip to De Pauw Univ. passes numerous small trade centers. 14$^{m}$ **Plainfield,** reg. hqs. & yrly. meeting place (Aug.) of Soc. of Friends. **Indiana Boys' School,** est. in 1867 as reform sch. **Mus.** 18.5$^{m}$ **Belleville,** popular tourist stop. 28$^{m}$ **Stilesville.** 39$^{m}$ J. with St.43, on which trip cont. (N). 44$^{m}$ **Greencastle,** seat of **De Pauw Univ.,** est. in 1837 by Meth. Episc. Ch.; degrees in liberal arts & music. Alumni incl. Chas. A. Beard, historian; Albert J. Beveridge, U.S. Sen.; & Wm. Wirt, creator of work-play-study school system in Gary (see).

V. St.29 (SE) 28$^{m}$ to **Shelbyville.** Via: New Bethel & Pleasant View. Route follows path of Mich. Rd. (Ohio R. to Gt. Ls.) through mostly unspoiled rural scenery. Old-fashioned customs linger among scattered pop. 9$^{m}$ **New Bethel.** Big event is Marion Cty. Fair. Hy. crosses Brandywine Cr. to **Shelbyville,** 28$^{m}$, on Big Blue R.; home of Thos. A. Hendricks, Gov. & U.S. Sen., & of Chas. Major (1856-1913), author of "When Knighthood Was in Flower." Shelbyville is seat of st.'s richest corn cty. **RR. Marker,** (S) 1$^{m}$ from town, comm. 2nd RR. W. of Alleghenies (1834.erroneously marked "1st"), which traveled over iron straps nailed to wooden tracks.

VI. On St.135 (S) 34$^{m}$ to **Nashville** (see St.46), artists' colony near Brown Cty. St. Pk. US31 & other good Rds. run from Indianapolis into scenic Brown & Monroe counties & Hoosier Nat. For. Purchase Unit (accoms. of all kinds in st. pks. & villages.

VII. US31 (S) 22$^{m}$ to **Franklin.** Via: Greenwood & Whiteland. Route crosses center of tomato-growing belt. 10$^{m}$ **Greenwood,** canning center. 22$^{m}$ **Franklin,** canning & trade center & college town. In late summer, workers flood into town to pick & pack tomatoes, living in all kinds of shacks & shelters. In Cth.; **Johnson Cty. Mus.** (O). **Franklin College** was founded by Indiana Bapt. Education Soc. & opened in 1837; became st.'s 1st coed. college in 1842. **Main Bldg.** (1843).

VIII. St.37 (SW) 30$^{m}$ to **Martinsville.** St.37 follows White R. for part of route. 17$^{m}$ **Waverly** (sett.1837). 28$^{m}$ **Grassyfork Fisheries** (O), where millions of goldfish are bred in 1,000 pools; also lilies & other aquatic plants. 30$^{m}$ **Martinsville,** widely known spa; large modern sanatoria. Birthpl. of Paul V. McNutt, Gov. & Commissioner of Philippines.

## US 20—ILLINOIS

**ILL.-IND. LINE** (Whiting, Ind.) **(W) to ILL.-IOWA LINE** (Dubuque, Iowa). **199. US20**

Via: Chicago, La Grange, Elgin, Marengo, Belvidere, Rockford, Freeport, Stockton, Galena, E. Dubuque. Hotels in cities; cabins & camp sites.

US20 enters on Dunes Hy. from Calumet dist. in Ind. & follows stagecoach route across low NE. sec. & then through Fox, Rock & Apple R. valleys. In unglaciated NW., lead-mining center in 19th cent., are picturesque limestone cliffs & wooded gorges. **0. IND. LINE.** (Chi. limits), tour turns (W) on 95th St. Pkwy. **4.** J. with Stony I. Ave. Here hy. forks. [City 20 cont. (N) to Grant Pk., then (W). See Chi. Trip IV.] Beyond J., the C. & N.W. RR. yards offer dramatic spectacle of streamlined trains distributed over some 60 tracks by electrically operated system. **18.** US20 turns (N), united with US45 across Sanitary & Ship Canal & Des Plaines R. (see Ill. Waterway Tour). **26.5. LA GRANGE. 32.** J. with City 20. Tour turns (NW).

**54. ELGIN**

W. Chi. & State Sts., Chi., Milwaukee RR. Sta.; 156 Douglas Ave., Chi. & N.W. RR. Sta.; 3 E. Chi. St., Chi., Aurora & Elgin RR. Sta. 9 N. Grove St., Union Motor Coach Sta. Good accoms. Recr. facils. & amusements in large pks. Fox R. (f.boat.). Annual Agric. Fair (Aug.). Info.: Assoc. of Com., 178 E. Chi. St.

Elgin, home of world's largest jeweled-watch factory, is in center of richest dairy reg. in U.S. Fox R. crosses center of town, with attractive pks. along banks. Upriver is Chain O' Lakes winter & summer resort area. In 1835 Jas. & Hezekiah Gif-

ford built cabins here & cut post Rd. to Belvidere (see below). When city was inc. in 1854, it was already an important dairy center, & Gail Borden made it nationally known. Besides watches, milk & milk products, Elgin is known for toasters, paper cartons, auto parts, street sweepers, windmills & religious publications.
PTS. OF INT.: (1) 107 National St., **Elgin National Watch Co.** (O); founded in 1854. Clock Tower. At 267 S. Grove St. is **Elgin Watchmakers College** (est. 1920). Watch & Raymond Sts., **Observatory** (O.appl.), where master clocks are checked to thousandth of second. (2) Pk. & College Sts., **Elgin Academy,** jr. college. **Main Hall** (1855.Gr.Rev.). (3) Pk. St. & Academy Pl., **Laura Davidson Sears Academy of Fine Arts** (O.Doric). Coll. incl. Peale, Whistler & other early Amer. paintings; Barbizon & early Ital. (4) Pk. St., **Lord's Pk.,** along Poplar Cr. **Zoo. Audubon Mus.** (O.exc. holidays May-Oct.); good nat. hist., Ind. & pioneer colls. (5) 853 Dundee Ave., **Ill. Watch Case Co.** (O.appl.). (6) Grove & Lincoln Aves., **Cook Publishing Co.,** one of largest publishers of Sunday School material. (7) 16 N. State St., **Borden Co.** (O. appl.). Other plants are McGraw Electric Co., makers of Toastmaster; Elgin Mfg. Co. (O); Shedd-Bartush Foods, Inc.; Elgin Sweeper Co. & Haeger Potteries (O), in Dundee (N).
In country (W), farmhouses & well-painted barns & silos stand among great cattle pastures & fields of corn. **92. BELVIDERE,** market town & mfg. center; stagecoach stop in 1830's.

**106. ROCKFORD**

RR. Stas.: 815 S. Main St., Ill. Cent. RR.; 515 S. Main St., Chi. & NW. RR.; 609 S. Main St., Milwaukee Rd. & C.B. & Q. RR. 330 Elm St., Union Bus Depot. Ample accoms. Recr. facils. in extensive pk. system. Art Gallery, Civic Symphony, college events & concerts by many groups. Theaters (stage & screen, incl. Swedish films) & Little Theater. Info.: C. of C., in Hotel Faust, W. Jefferson St.

Rockford, 3rd largest city in Ill., seat of Rockford College, is highly industrial community & cultural & trade center for large area. Rock R. winds through center, past pks., for. preserves & private estates. Large dam supplies water power to many industrial plants producing machine tools, textiles, hardware, automobile & airplane parts & furniture. Rockford was founded in 1834 & sett. by New Englanders. In early 1850's, J. H. Manny began to manufacture his reaper & mowing machine, & Chi. & Galena Union RR. was completed. Swedish immigrants arrived in large numbers & est. co-op. furniture factory. Present pop. is approx. 40% Scand.

PTS. OF INT.: (1) S. Main & Green Sts., **Federal Bldg.** (1933). (2) Overlooking Kent Cr., **Tinker Chalet** (O.certain afts.& on appl.sm.fee.1869); period furniture & curios. (3) 737 N. Main St., **Burpee Art Gallery** (O), in mansion of Civil War period. Annual Jury Show (Jan.-Feb.). (4) 813 N. Main St., **Natural Hist. Mus.** (O.exc.Sun.). (5) N. Main St., in Beattie Pk., **Turtle Mound,** effigy 150′ long. (6) N. 2nd St., **Sinnissippi Pk.,** on Rock R., **Sunken Gardens.** (7) College Ave. & Seminary St., **Rockford College,** ranking liberal arts college for women, one of oldest in U.S. It was chartered in 1847 & took present name in 1892. Jane Addams, founder of Hull H., received 1st degree conferred. **Middle** (1852) & **Linden** (1854) **Halls** & **Chapel** (1866.now Talcott) are in midst of some 30 modern bldgs.

SIDE TRIP: On St.2 (SW) 42$^{m}$ over **Black Hawk Trl.** along Rock. R. to Dixon. Markedly beautiful valley was home of Sauk & Fox Inds. Black Hawk refused to leave Ill. under terms of treaty made in 1804 (some historians agree with his interpretation), but in 1831 he was induced to sign treaty permitting removal. The following spring, his followers began to harry border settlements. He says in his autobiography, "My reason tells me that land cannot be sold." His forces were gradually destroyed, & he himself was captured in Wis. by the Winnebago, who turned him over to Gov. He died in Iowa in 1838. At 15$^{m}$ **Byron,** sett. by New Englanders in 1830's. Near Stillman Valley, (E) 5$^{m}$ on St.72, is **Ill. Soldiers' Mon.** comm. 1st battle in Black Hawk War. At c.23$^{m}$ **Black Hawk Mon.** (1911.by Lorado Taft), gift of sculptor; on high bluff on E. bank in **Lowden Hist. Pk.** (f.pic.camp.refreshments.). 26$^{m}$ **Oregon.** In **Pub. Lib.** are sculptures & paintings of Eagle Nest Art Colony, founded by Taft & other artists in 1898. **White Pines For. St. Pk.** (f.pic.camp.lodge.cabins), 8$^{m}$ (W) from Oregon. 36$^{m}$ **Grand Detour,** old village on deep bow of R. John Deere opened plow factory here in 1841. Trl. crosses R. to **Dixon** (see US30), 42$^{m}$.

US20 cont. (W) in valley of Pecatonica R. Stephenson & Jo Daviess counties were untouched by glaciers, & here primeval rock has been eroded into irregular bluffs, terraces & canyons. Many settlements along route were begun by returning prospectors after rush to Galena (see below) lead mines in 1820's. Tourist accoms. at frequent intervals. **134. FREEPORT** (through RR. & bus conns. accoms.), fair-sized farm center, known nationally for Structo & Arcade toy-making factories, also has large Kraft-Phoenix Cheese Corp. plant. Among early settlers were many Pa. Germans attracted to lead mines. Notable gardens (O.appl.). N. State Ave. & E. Douglas St., **Site of 2nd Lincoln-Douglas Debate,** 1858, during which Douglas formulated "Freeport doctrine" that a territory had right to exclude slavery.

SIDE TRIPS: (A) On St.26 (N) 5m to **Cedarville.** (NW) 6m from here to **Birthpl. of Jane Addams;** grave in burial plot on grounds.
(B) On St.26 (S) 14m to **Forreston,** scene of annual Sauerkraut Festival (Sept.free).

**155. STOCKTON. 157.** J. with Rd. that leads (N) 5m to **Apple R. Canyon St. Pk.** (f.pic.camp.). From bluffs along R. is view (W) of **Charles Mound** (1,241'), highest pt. in Ill. **169.** Hy. crosses Apple R. J. with St.80 (see Miss. R. Tour).

**184. GALENA** (through RR. & bus conns.hotels & tourist accoms.recr.facils.). City lies in valley against semicircle of bluffs cut by Galena R. It was 1st important lead-mining center in Old N.W. Along sts. & stairways climbing the hills are Gr. Rev. mansions built in 1840's & 50's when Galena was big town of booming area extending into Wis. When Gov. took over the lands, & steamboats began to come up Miss. R., thousands of prospectors rushed to Middle Border. At its peak, Galena dist. produced 85 per cent of lead mined in U.S., then world's leading producer. Taverns were busy, circus & traveling players entertained, whiskey flowed, & wolf & cock fights were popular. Lead industry began to decline when Ill. Cent. RR. made Dubuque its terminus. Also, the shallower diggings were exhausted. In Ap. 1860, U. S. Grant came to clerk in his father's store, & a yr. later he departed quietly for Springfield to be made colonel in Union Army. In Aug., 1865, he returned in triumph.

PTS. OF INT.: (1) Hill & Prospect St., **Grace Episc. Ch.** (1847.Tudor). (2) Bouthillier St., **U. S. Grant H.** (O.1857), gift from city, was showplace of Galena. Completely furnished, incl. china used in White House. (3) 121 High St., **First Grant H.,** contrasting in its simplicity with mansion across R. (4) Main & Diagonal Sts., **Dowling H.** (1828), oldest bldg. (5) Bench & South Sts., **Gen. Smith H.** (1848.Gr.Rev.), considered finest in city. (6) S. Bench St., **Galena Mus.** (O). (7) 512 Park Ave., **Jos. Hoge H.** (1845.Gr.Rev.), Southern style.
In wild, rugged country (NW) of Galena are prehist. mounds, sites of battles in Ind. wars, abandoned mines. US20 runs down into Miss. bottomlands. **199. E. DUBUQUE.** Bridge (toll) **at ILL.-IA. LINE.**

## US 30—ILLINOIS

**ILL.-IND. LINE** (Dyer, Ind.) **(W) to ILL.-IOWA LINE** (Clinton, Iowa). **152. US30**
Via: Chicago Hts., Joliet, Plainfield, Aurora, Hinckley, (Dixon), Sterling, Morrison, Fulton.

US30, the Lincoln Hy., runs along W. edge of Greater Chicago, turns (N) to Aurora & then directly (W) to Miss. R. gorge. A short distance from Ind. Line, hy. forks. US30 Alt. leads (N) to Grant Pk., then (W) through suburbs & across state to J. with main tour at Sterling (see Alt. Tour below).

**6. CHICAGO HTS. 17. FRANKFORT. 23. NEW LENOX.** These suburban communities developed on former marshlands left by prehist. sea.

**30. JOLIET**

Union & Scott Sts., Union (RR.) Depot. 301 N. Ottawa St., Greyhound Bus Sta.; 32 E. Jefferson St., Union Bus Depot. Mun. Airport. Accoms. & recr. facils. Info.: Assoc. of Com., 436 Clinton St.

Joliet, named for explorer, is notable for its fine homes, schs. & chs., modern bus. dist. & beautiful pk. system. It is one of leading industrial cities of Ill., a RR. & trade center, crossed by Gt. Ls.-Gulf Waterway (see). From time of settlement in 1833, rich natural resources & potential water power have made it a key city. Among its 150 or more plants are 8 mills producing more than half nation's supply of wall paper. Other products are steel rods & tanks, wire, furnaces, chemicals & fire brick.
PTS. OF INT.: **Wall Paper Mills** (O.appl.). Chicago St. & Doris Ave., **Amer. Institute of Laundering** (guides), technical & research institute. 303 Taylor St., **College of St. Francis** (Cath.), accredited women's college. Ottawa & Clinton Sts., **Pub. Lib.,** of local limestone. On US30, **Pilcher Pk. Arboretum.** J. with US6 (see Ill. Waterway Tour) & US66 Alt.

US30 swings (NW) through open country. **39. PLAINFIELD,** where post was est. in 1790 on site of Ind. village. **Halfway H.** (1834.Gr.Rev.). J. with US66. **48.** J. with US34 (see).

**52. AURORA**

175 S. Broadway, C.B. & Q. RR. Depot; 51 S. Broadway, C.A. & E. RR. Depot & Bus Sta. Airport (privately operated). Hotels; motor court. Golf, f., boat. & other recr. facils. at Exposition Pk. (amusements) & other pks. Info.: C. of C., 17 Island Ave.; Chicago Motor Club, 48 Galena Blvd.

Fox R., dividing line bet. metropolitan area & prairies, runs through heart of Aurora. On largest of many Is. is city center, incl. City Hall, Lib. & P.O. Several bridges carry (E-W) aves. over R., & at N. end is **Mem. Bridge** (1931.by E.P.Seidel). After Black Hawk War, Jos. McCarty, from N.Y., chose site occupied by Potawatomi village, & town was platted in 1836. Two communities developed along R., & even after city was inc. in 1857, bitter battles were fought. City center, on Stolp I. in middle of R., was the happy solution. Name "Aurora" honors local Ind. chief, Wabonsie ("morning light"). Burlington RR. shops gave Aurora its biggest impetus to industrialization. Cultural institutions incl. Aurora College, Toenniges Conservatory of Music, & Marmion Military Academy.

PTS. OF INT.: Oak Ave. & Cedar St., **Hist. H.** (1837.O.Wed.Fri.Sun.aft.). On exhibit is 9'-high Blanford Clock, completed around 1913 by Wm. Blanford; shows time of day, phases of moon & calendar day, month & yr. Oak Ave. & Cedar St., **Hist. Soc. Bldg.** (O.1857); pioneer furniture. Gladstone Ave., **Aurora College,** founded by Advent Christian Ch. in 1893 in Mendota; evening courses in labor management & other fields. Along US30 from Parker Ave., **Phillips Pk.** Mus. & Zoo. **Burlington Shops** (O.appl.).

Beyond Aurora begin the grasslands that gave Ill. name of Prairie State, "as green & as wild & as wide as the sea," according to pioneer poet. At harvest time, modern machinery reaps the harvest from great acreages of corn & grain; many large dairy farms. **75.** J. with St.23.

SIDE TRIP: On St.23 (N) 10m to **De Kalb,** center of barbed-wire industry. Inventor, Jos. Glidden, & Jacob Haish, holder of patent for mfg. process, had long legal battle over rights. At 1719 S. 1st St. is **Glidden Hospital,** & on Oak & N. 3rd Sts., **Haish Mem. Lib.** On wooded campus along Kishewaukee R. are bldgs. of **N. Ill. St. Teachers College** (1895). The turreted "Castle on the Hill" is **Adm. Bldg.**

**92.** J. with US51 (see). **112.** J. with St.26.

SIDE TRIP: On St.26 (N) 6m to **Dixon,** on Rock R. at end of Black Hawk Trl. (see US20); center of cement industry. In pk. on Site of Ft. Dixon is **Lincoln Mon.** (by Leonard Crenelle); at base of bronze statue is plaque comm. John Dixon, "proprietor of the ferry & tavern here during the Black Hawk War." **J.** with US30 Alt.

**124.** J. with St.88, which links US30 & US30 Alt. across Rock R. **STERLING,** on US30 Alt., & **ROCK FALLS,** on US30, are linked by dam built in 1857. Pk. on I. (pic.swim.). **128.** J. with St.2, Rock R. Rd. **139. MORRISON** (tourist camps & cottages in vic.). **Unionville Mill** (O.1858). **150. FULTON.** J. with St.80 (see Miss. R. Tour). Many greenhouses. **152.** Bridge (toll) across Miss. R., **ILL.-IOWA LINE.**

## US 34—ILLINOIS

**CHICAGO (W) to ILL.-IOWA LINE** (Burlington, Ia.). **231. US34**

Via: La Grange, Oswego, Sandwich, Mendota, La Moille, Princeton, Sheffield, Kewanee, Galva, Galesburg, Monmouth, Biggsville.

**0. CHICAGO** (see). US34 crosses metropolitan area & zigzags diagonally across dairy country & prodigious fields of corn & grain. Along route are several college towns but few industrial centers. **29.** Hy. by-passes **NAPERVILLE** (see Chicago Trip III). **38.** J. with US30, (S) 4m from **AURORA** (see US30). **53. PLANO.** Grain elevators along C.B. & Q. RR. tower above strikingly level fields. Town was sett. in 1830's by Quakers from Norway. **77. EARLVILLE.** J. with Rd. which leads (SE) 6m to **Shabbona Statue Mon.** (pic.camp.), comm. friendly Ind. chief. **89. MENDOTA.** J. with US51 (see) & US52. **113. PRINCETON,** in center of orchard & farm country. In E. part of town is former **Home of Owen Lovejoy** (1811-64), abolitionist leader & brother of Elijah Lovejoy (see E. St. Louis Trip IV). At 1518 S. Main St., **Bryant H.** (1850's), where John Bryant, brother of poet, lived; friend of Lincoln &

one of founders of Republican party. J. with US6, with which US34 unites for a few miles. **120. WYANET,** on Ill. & Miss. Canal. **St. Fish Hatchery. 128. SHEFFIELD.** US34 turns (S) here.

**143. KEWANEE,** on W. Fork of Spoon R.; one of largest industrial towns on route. Kewanee steam boilers & workmen's gloves are known throughout country, & **Walworth Mfg. Plant,** pioneer industry, is one of country's largest makers of fittings & valves. Wethersfield, older part of town & wholly residential, was sett. by Conn. (Prot.) Assoc. in 1836. Forerunner of **Kewanee Boiler Co.** was founded in 1850's. **155. GALVA,** Swedish settlement (1854) that grew out of Bishop Hill colony. **159.** J. with Rd.

SIDE TRIP: On Rd. (N) 2.5m to **Bishop Hill St. Pk.,** site of Swedish communal religious colony est. by Eric Janson in 1846; acquired by st. in 1945. Hist. of colony follows classic pattern of many attempts at the good life. Janson was a man of extraordinary fascination & vitality. After denouncing corruption of Luth. Ch. of Sweden, he was forced to find refuge from persecution, & he escaped from Sweden on skiis & disguised as a woman. With his followers, he crossed the ocean & came by Gt. Ls. & canal to Henry Cty., Ill., where community lived in dugouts the 1st winter. Nearly 100 died of Asiatic cholera & are buried in **Bishop Hill Cemetery.** Janson lived a life of fleshly comfort & later, as dictator, became reckless in his demands. Whatever the cause, he was shot in 1850. Settlement had become prosperous but, after loss of their leader, it was disrupted by factionalism, religious differences & financial mismanagement. State is restoring Bishop Hill as example of pioneer life. **Old Colony Ch.** (1848) has coll. of paintings of scenes at Bishop Hill, done by Olof Krans, blacksmith. Other bldgs. are Schoolh., Storeh., Hospital, Cheese Factory & Bakery.

**182. GALESBURG,** birthpl. of Carl Sandburg & seat of Knox College. Town was planned as religious & educational center by its founder, Geo. Washington Gale, Presb. minister, before he left Mohawk Valley parish (see New York) in 1835. A group of Oneida families came to selected site in 1836-37, & city was laid out in orderly fashion. Knox Manual Labor College was opened in 1838 in town meetingh., & scholarships were given with farm lots. The RRs. in 1854 were resented by the settlers but brought new life to the college. Galesburg was important sta. on Underground Railroad. City is now one of largest divisional hqs. of C.B. & Q. RR. & important livestock market. **Knox College** is coed. (since 1849) liberal arts college, with roster of noted alumni, incl. Carl Sandburg, Don Marquis & Eugene Field (of Lombard College, united with Knox in 1930). **Old Main** was scene of **5th Lincoln-Douglas Debate.** E. of Galesburg is **Rice L.,** resort center. **198. MONMOUTH,** named (1831) for Rev. War battle in N.J., is seat of cty. named for Maj. Gen. Jos. Warren, hero of Bunker Hill. On E. Broadway is shady 30-a. campus of **Monmouth College,** founded by Presb. Ch. in 1853. **Wallace Hall,** named for 1st pres., & **Science Hall** (1910). **Lib.** (1907) has art coll., gift of Carnegie Foundation.
Monmouth is center of level corn belt where cattle are fattened for the stockyards. US34 tends steadily (S), paralleling roughly C.B. & Q. RR. **212. BIGGSVILLE. 217.** J. with St.164.

SIDE TRIP: On St.164 (N) 1.5m to **Gladstone.** On R. (NW) is **Lock & Dam No. 18.** At 3m is **Henderson Cr.** & near-by **Covered Bridge** (pic.), more than 100 yrs. old. 6m **Oquawka,** once a trading post, keeps busy getting button pearls from mussels. Good sand beaches (camp.cabins) along Miss. R.

**230.5. GULFPORT.** US34 crosses Burlington (toll) Bridge, to Burlington, Ia. **231.** Miss. R. here is **ILL.-IA. LINE.**

## ILLINOIS WATERWAY TOUR

**CHICAGO (W) & (S) to MISS. R.** (at Grafton, Ill.). **339. ST.4A, US6, ST.29, US24, St.100**

Via: Summit, Lockport, Joliet, Morris, Ottawa, La Salle, Peru, Spring Valley, Henry, Chillicothe, Peoria, Orchard Mines, (Pekin), Beardstown, Bluffs, Milton, Kampsville, Hardin. Tour by boat would follow Chicago R., Sanitary Ship Canal (or Ill. & Mich. Canal by canoe), Des Plaines R. & Ill. R. No charge for use of waterway or locks. Knowledge of rules & regulations is of special importance, as channel draught varies bet. 9′ & 20′, & locks & numerous bridges of varying clearance are along route. Info. & strip maps avail. from U.S. Engineer's Office, Room 520, Merchandise Mart, Chicago.

Tour follows part of Great Ls. to Gulf Waterway along commercially important, hist. int. & naturally beautiful route (well-developed st. pks.; good h. & f. grounds). Steep bluffs, marshy bottomlands & lush valleys, rivertowns & industrial centers give extraordinary variety. **Chicago Harbor Controlling Locks** (N. of Loop) stand where Chicago R. once sluggishly entered L. Mich. Michigan Ave. Link Bridge over main channel extends from **Site of Ft. Dearborn** (S) to **Site of 1st Settlement** (N). Near Locks are **Navy Pier** (amusement) & **N. Terminal Pier.** Originally the S. Branch crept (N) out of Mud L. & united with N. Branch to form main channel. Outlet was often choked with sand, but during spring freshets Mud L. spread over area, draining into both S. Branch & across continental divide into Des Plaines R. Pere Marquette noted "River of the Portage" in 1673, & Jolliet saw feasibility of canal to link Niagara R. & Gulf of Mex. The Chicago Portage was key pt. in exploration, trade & settlement. Since completion of Drainage Canal (1892-1900), R. flows backward, & blue L. waters pour into its channel. Survey for canal was made in 1830, & squatter settlement was inc. 3 yrs. later. In 1835 a shockingly high death rate called attention to need for sewerage, & pipes were laid to carry waste into L. & R., which became a stream of filth. In 1871 R. was diverted into S. Branch, with no better result. Finally in 1900 the Drainage Canal was completed, & R. flow was reversed so that its load emptied into Ill. R. across old portage. Subsidiary canals relieved Chicago of sewage problem, but downriver cities were wrathful. Proposal to sluice away impurities by inflow from L. Mich. was accepted after yrs. of nat. & internat. argument. Later the Drainage Canal was taken over by Fed. Gov., improved & renamed Sanitary & Ship Canal. Amount of diversion, est. by U.S. Supreme Court, is controlled by Army engineers.

### Sec. 1: CHICAGO to PEORIA. 169. St.4A, US6 & St.29

From Loop, tour follows Cermak Rd. (W) to J. with St.4A (Archer Ave.), which roughly parallels waterway (US66 parallels route on N. side). Hy. crosses S. Branch, a few blocks N. of Union Stockyards, to J. with Ashland Ave. Beyond J. is mouth of abandoned **Ill. & Mich. Canal** (1848-1933), & a half-mile farther on, waterway enters Sanitary & Ship Canal. At c.**13. SUMMIT,** on crest of continental divide. **LYONS,** across waterway, stands on edge of Chicago Portage. Just W. of Summit, the Des Plaines R. swerves into valley & parallels canal to **LOCKPORT, 34.**, where it becomes a link in the waterway. **Lockport Dam & Lock,** where intake is measured & controlled. St.4A & US66 enter **JOLIET** (see) at **39.** J. with US30 (see). **Brandon Rd. Lock & Dam.** The 2,000′-long retaining wall around Brandon Rd. Pool incl. moss-covered lock of I. & M. Canal. J. with US6, on which tour cont. along best-developed areas of **Ill. & Mich. Canal Pky.** (pic.boat docks.good auto rd.). **50. CHANNAHON,** where Du Page R. joins the Des Plaines. A few miles W., the Kankakee enters from the S., & then, as the Ill. R., the united waters flow W. through rocky gorge cut by glaciers. Along Kankakee R. is **McKinley Woods Cty. Pk. 62. MORRIS.** Adj. is small **Gebhard Woods St. Pk.** (pic.camp.f.& game preserve). **81. MARSEILLES.** On S. riverbank is **Illini St. Pk.** (pic.camp.dining room.f.recr.facils.). Near-by **Marseilles Lock** lifts traffic over the rapids. **85.** J. with St.71, scenic route (W) through St. Pks. (see below).

SIDE TRIP: On St.71 (NE) to **Norwegian Settlers' Mon.,** at **Norway,** small village on site of 1st permanent Norweg. colony in Amer. Bronze plaque (1934) comm. Cleng Peerson, who est. at least 30 settlements in Miss. valley.

**87. OTTAWA,** on wooded terraces overlooking R., was laid out as canal town in 1830 & sett. largely by New Englanders. Largest industry is **Libby-Owens-Ford Glass Plant,** but making of agric. implements & colored marbles & other toys is important. PTS. OF INT.: In Washington Pk., **Site of 1st Lincoln-Douglas Debate.** Columbus & Lafayette Sts., **Appellate Cth.** (Gr.Rev.). Gaton Hill Rd., **Gen. W. H. L. Wallace H.** (1860), St. mem. to Union officer killed at Shiloh; coll. of furniture, paintings & flags. On N. bank of R. (W) 4$^{m}$ is **Buffalo Rock St. Pk.** (f.pic.camp).

SIDE TRIP: On St.71 (S) & (W) 6$^{m}$ to **Starved Rock St. Pk.** (camp.pic.lodge.cabins.play fields.f.), st.'s oldest & one of best-developed recr. areas. Boat trips daily. Trls. to Skeleton Cave, Tonti Canyon, Eagle Cliff, Lost L., Hennepin Canyon. **Starved Rock** (125′) is circular mass of sandstone with flat summit. Across R. was Kaskaskia, Ind. village where Marquette & Jolliet, in 1673, were received by the charming, unreliable Illini. Marquette est. mission in 1675, & 1st Mass was celebrated on open prairie for more than 2,000 Inds. In 1679, La Salle & Tonti, his lieutenant with the iron hand, & the boastful Father Hennepin came to same spot. Ft. St. Louis du Rocher was erected on Starved Rock as part of La Salle's dream of colonizing Miss. valley. Ft. Crève Coeur, near site of Peoria (see US24), was left in charge of Tonti when La Salle went back to Frontenaç for equipment. Deserted by his rebellious followers, Tonti came to Starved Rock with a few faithful missionaries &

men to await La Salle. Then the Iroquois came down upon the village & a confused slaughter began. Only 1 Frenchman was killed, but the Iroquois ruthlessly pursued the Illinois, wrecked the town & even dragged dead bodies from their graves. Tonti's party escaped & made their way to Green Bay. When La Salle returned in high hope, he found only the dead around the ruined village & fortress. At Crève Coeur also he found the ruins of his ft. & an unfinished boat on which 1 of his men had written "Nous sommes tous sauvages." In 1682 he returned to est. fort on Starved Rock, which Tonti maintained for some yrs. after La Salle's death in 1687 (at hands of his own men). It was abandoned in 1702 & burned by Inds. in 1721.

**97.** On US6, J. with St.178 (S. 1m on St.178 is **Utica,** a supply center). **103. LA SALLE,** canal town founded in 1827. Coal deposits & water power attracted several industries, chief of which now are the zinc works. Locks, towpath & old warehouses near hy. J. with US51 (see). **105. PERU,** home of Big Ben Clocks, made by **Western Clock Factory** (O.appl.). Peru was 1st terminus of Canal, but La Salle built steamboat basin & outstripped the other town. Spanning R. is **Wooden Bridge** (1869). **109. SPRING VALLEY.** J. with St.29, over which tour cont. around Gt. Bend & close to riverbanks through primitive country where landings & scattered cottages are outposts of half-hidden hamlets. Below Gt. Bend is entrance to **Ill. & Miss. Canal** (good f.), opened in 1907.
Character of valley changes remarkably downstream. Instead of relatively strong current, R. is much shallower & flows lazily through marshland (f.h.) & around innumerable islets. Valley is broad instead of gorgelike, extending sometimes over several miles bet. steep walls of rock. **134. HENRY,** at mouth of **Senachwine L.,** in old riverbed paralleling main channel for 5m. **Henry Lock** (unused). J. with St.18, which crosses R. to J. with Rd. that follows E. shore to **Sparland F. & H. Grounds.**

**142.** Village of **SPARLAND** (f.& h.info.). Near **CHILLICOTHE, 150.,** on an island, are **Woodford Cty. H. & F. Grounds.** Peoria & Goose Pond Ls. are (S). Lights & other navigation aids are numerous in this part of R. because of sandbars & stumps. **169. PEORIA** (see US24). J. with US24 & US150.

### Sec. 2: PEORIA to GRAFTON. 170. US24, St.78, St.10, St.100

**0. PEORIA.** Tour cont. along W. side of R. on US24. St.29 crosses R. here (E) to **E. Peoria & Crève Coeur St. Pk.** (see US24).

SIDE TRIP: On St.29 (S) from E. Peoria. At 10m **Pekin,** favorite stopping place for Lincoln & others on 8th Circuit. 14m J. with St.122; (E) 5m on St.122 to **Delavan** (RR. conns.), charming town on "High Prairie" in fertile cornbelt; Delavan Assoc. was org. to promote temperance colony, & 50 R.I. & Mass. families arrived in May, 1837. **Daniel Cheever H.,** depot on Underground Railroad. **Straut's Store,** oldest bldg. **Prairie Rest,** orig. cemetery. **Civil War Mon.**

Innumerable small Ls. reach into marshlands E. of R., & Is. of varying size interrupt its easy flow. **33.** US24 unites with St.78. **36.** Tour turns S. with St.78. **42. W. HAVANA,** near mouth of Spoon R. (see). Rd. leads (NW) here to **Dickson Mounds St. Pk.** (see). Across Ill. R. is **Havana,** center of duckhunting area. Tour turns (W) on US24 to J. with St.100 at **45.,** then (S) on St.100, which winds back & forth across R. Downriver is **Grand I.,** splitting R. into narrow channels. **77.** St.100 crosses C.B. & Q. RR. Bridge (toll) to **BEARDSTOWN,** rural trade center lying low in the valley & washed by many floods. **91.** (W) J. with St.104.

SIDE TRIP: On St.104 (W) 3m to **Meredosia** (corruption of Fr., "marais d'osier"), where st.'s 1st RR. ended in 1837, a strap-iron Rd., 24m long, intended as part of Rd. to link Cairo & Gelena.

**92.** (E) J. with St.104.

SIDE TRIP: On St.104 (E) 17m to **Jacksonville** (Wabash, C.B.& Q., & Alton RRs.; Greyhound & other busses), one of prettiest Ill. cities & cultural center for 120 yrs. Founded as seat of Morgan Cty. in 1825 & sett. 1st by Southerners, it became within a few yrs. virtually a New England community, which it resembles today. It was important Underground RR. Sta. Stephen A. Douglas & Wm. J. Bryan both practiced law here. In Jacksonville are Ill. & MacMurray Colleges, St. Sch. for the Deaf, one of largest in U.S., St. Sch. for the Blind, noted for music dept., & St. Hospital for the Insane. PTS. OF INT.: (1) College & Webster Aves., **Site of Home of W. J. Bryan,** grad. of Ill. College. (2) 4 Duncan Pl., **Gov. Jos. H. Duncan H.** (1835.Georg.O.appl.), hqs. of D.A.R. (3) E. State St., **MacMurray College for Women,** privately endowed, nonsectarian college of high standing, conferring degrees of bachelor & master in arts & science & bachelor in music. Est. in 1846 by Ill. Meth. Conference as an academy, MacMurray became college in 1909. Among many fine bldgs.

on attractive campus are **Henry A. Pfeiffer Mem. Lib.** (1941), **MacMurray Hall** (1928) & **Ann Rutledge Hall** (1937). (4) 1101 W. College Ave., **Illinois College,** 1st Ill. school to graduate a college class (1835). John M. Ellis, Presb. minister, planned the college, & 1st teachers were of "Yale Band" of theological students who helped est. many early colleges. Edw. Beecher, brother of Harriet & Henry Ward Beecher, was 1st Pres. School was closely identified with cause of abolition. In 1903, the Jacksonville Female Academy (1835) was formally inc. with it. Today, Illinois is ranking liberal arts college, nonsectarian but assoc. with Cong. & Presb. churches. Notable among its red-brick bldgs. are: **Beecher Hall** (1829), oldest college bldg. in Ill.; **Sturtevant Hall** (1857); **Tanner Mem. Lib.** (1929), a model of functional architecture.

The broad lower valley has been compared to tranquil landscapes of early Ital. paintings. R. winds around small Is. & past Naples, Florence, Montezuma & Buckhorn Landings. **106.** J. with US36-US54, with which St.100 unites (W).

SIDE TRIP: On US36-US54 (E) 6m to **Winchester,** platted in 1830. **Stephen A. Douglas Mon.**

St.100 crosses R. & turns (S) again at **DETROIT, 112. 138. KAMPSVILLE,** center for hunters, fishermen & vacationers. **Bartholomew Beach** is one of best along R. Country around is increasingly primitive. **148. HARDIN,** shipping pt. for apples. Here St.100 crosses (E) R., which parallels Miss. for several miles. **164. PERE MARQUETTE ST. PK.** (f.h.pic.camp.refreshments.lodge), one of most scenic in Ill., looking down over both Rs. (see E. St. Louis Trip IV). Stone cross marks site where Pere Marquette & Jolliet made camp. **170. GRAFTON,** at pt. where relatively clear stream of the Ill. enters turbid R. that Lincoln called "Father of the Waters."

## US 24—ILLINOIS

**ILL.-IND. LINE** (4m from Kentland, Ind.) **(W) to ILL.-MO. LINE** (6m from Taylor, Mo.). **250. US24**

Via: Sheldon, Watseka, Gilman, Chatsworth, Chenoa, El Paso, Peoria, Lewistown, Astoria, Rushville, Mount Sterling, Quincy. Accoms.: Throughout route.

US24 is straight route across prairie to Peoria, where tour turns (S) along Ill. R., then crosses Spoon R. valley, made famous by Edgar Lee Masters.

### Sec. 1: IND. LINE to PEORIA. 116.

On E. half of tour are many fine farms & somewhat austere villages of Amish & Mennonite communities whose ancestors sett. here a hundred yrs. ago. Communal principle is still strong, & the various groups usually form self-dependent rural communities. **3. SHELDON,** shipping pt. for grain. **12. WATSEKA,** on bend of Iroquois R. Many large Hs. & bus. bldgs. remain from golden age after Civil War. Gurdon Hubbard, Amer. Fur Co. agent, 1st white settler in Iroquois Cty., married Watch-e-kee ("pretty woman"), daughter of Potawatomi chief, but after 2 yrs. he abandoned both fur trade & his opportunistic marriage. When village became cty. seat in 1865, it was named for the deserted wife. **20. CRESCENT CITY.** J. with St.49.

SIDE TRIP: On St.49 (S) 16m to **Cissna Pk.,** center of large New Amish community. The men & women dress simply in dark clothes, take no part in gov. or military action. US24 passes several villages with relatively large Amish pop.

**50. FORREST. 55.5. FAIRBURY. 75. GRIDLEY. 96.5. EUREKA,** seat of Eureka College & Mennonite Home for the Aged. Leading industry is **Libby, McNeill & Libby** (O.appl.), canning plant. **Eureka College,** founded in 1830's by Ky. pioneers, has been recognized by Disciples of Christ Ch. since 1852. It was 1st college in Ill. to admit women on equal basis with men. **Adm. Bldg.** (1858.remod.). J. with St.117.

SIDE TRIP: On St.117 & St.116 (NW) 10m to **Metamora.** In **Metamora Cth. St. Mem.** (1845.Gr.Rev.wings 1884), Judge David Davis, "best stump speaker in Ill.," held court in Lincoln's time: **Courtroom** (rest.), on 2nd fl.; Woodford Cty. **Hist. Soc. Mus.,** on 1st fl. Judge Davis, later Supreme Ct. Justice, was largely responsible for Lincoln's nomination in 1860.

**114. EAST PEORIA,** home of **Caterpillar Tractor Co.** (O.appl.). On St.29 (S) 2m is **Ft. Crève Coeur St. Hist. Pk.** (pic.) along the bluffs; game preserve. Mon. at probable **Site of La Salle's Ft.** (1680), wrecked by his own men while Tonti, who had been left in charge, was at Starved Rock (see Ill. Waterway Tour).

**116. PEORIA**

S. Adams St., near Franklin St. Bridge., Union Depot. Hamilton Blvd. & Jefferson Ave., Bus Stas. On St.9 (SW) 5m, Mun. Airport. Excursions on R. & boats for rent. All kinds of accoms. Recr. & pic. facils. in Bradley, Glen Oak (Zoo) & other pks. Players Theater. Bradley Inst. & Pub. Lib. art exhibits & other events. Civic orchestra. Info.: Assoc. of Com., Alliance Life Insurance Bldg., Main St. & Jefferson Ave.

Peoria, on site of 1st white settlement in Ill., is now st.'s 2nd city, cultural & trade center for wide area rich in coal, grain & livestock; one of greatest whiskey-producing cities in world. US24 enters over Cedar St. Bridge (1933, more than a mile long without lift or draw span) or by Franklin Bridge (E), which leads into downtown Peoria. On low R. plain are most of the many industries served by Mun. River & Rail Terminal. Business & residential secs. rise on higher & older riverbed. Grand View Dr. along R. passes great estates, Grand View & other pks. (long-span bridge under const.). Leading manufactures are alcoholic, dairy & food products, sheet metal & castings & farm implements. In 1673 Jolliet & Père Marquette crossed L. Peoria. Then, in 1680, La Salle est. Ft. Crève Coeur (see) on E. bank, & after his death, Tonti (see) returned to the wrecked ft. & est. a 2nd Ft. St. Louis (see Ill. Waterway Tour), to which came the Fr. & Inds. from abandoned post at Starved Rock. The Fr. village Au Pé ("among the Peoria"), or Peoria, begun in 1730 on W. bank, was abandoned in 1796. Meanwhile New Peoria had been est. in 1779 & flourished under Brit. protection. When Clark took Kaskaskia & Vincennes (see), Au Pé was left undisturbed, but, in War of 1812, the Amers. became suspicious of the Fr. villagers. Capt. T. E. Craig landed armed boats & allowed his men to pillage & burn the town. Fr. prisoners, followed by their families, were taken to site of Alton (see E. St. Louis) & left without food or proper clothing. Some claims against Gov. were sett. later, & Gov. Edwards formally condemned the pillaging. In 1813 a new stockade was built & named for Clark, & a new city began with influx of New England settlers. When cty. was created in 1825, the old name, Peoria, was restored. N. Reg. Research Lab. of U.S. Dept. of Agric. was built here in 1940.

PTS. OF INT.: (1) In Cth. Sq., bet. Jefferson Ave. & Adams St. & Hamilton Blvd. & Main St., is the domed **County Cth.** (1876.Ital.Ren.). **Site of Lincoln-Douglas Debate** is marked by Civil War Mon. (1899.by Fritz Treibel). (2) Jefferson Ave. & Hamilton Blvd., **Rbt. Ingersoll H.** (3) 209 Jackson Pl., **Peoria Players Theater,** fully equipped. (4) 111 Monroe St., **Pub. Lib.** (1897), est. in 1880, 1st lib. under 1872 Ill. law; Art Exhibit. (5) 1101 Hamilton Blvd., **First Presb. Ch.,** org. in 1834; hist. coll. (O). (6) Liberty & Water Sts., **Site of Ft. Clark** (1813). (7) **Hiram Walker & Sons Distillery** (O.appl.), subsidiary of Walkerville, Ont., plant (see Detroit, Mich.). Other distilleries & breweries (O.appl.). (8) S. Institute St., **Bradley Polytechnic Institute,** incl. College of Arts & Sciences, College of Music, Sch. of Fine & Applied Arts, Industrial & Trade Sch. & Sch. of Horology, with courses in watch-making. **Horology Hall & Bradley Hall** are oldest bldgs. on campus (1897). (9) Off Prospect Rd., **Glen Oak Pk.** (pic.playfields.zoo) notable Palm H. & gardens. Near Perry Ave. entrance, **Statue of Rbt. Ingersoll** (by Fritz Treibel), who practiced law in Ill. & nominated "the plumed knight," J. G. Blaine, for Presidency in 1878. J. with US150, St.29 (see Ill. Waterway Tour).

SIDE TRIP: On US150 (NW) 14m to **Jubilee College St. Pk.** (pic.), former campus of pioneer sch. Weathered golden-yellow bldgs. stand under tall elms along Kickapoo Cr. Here Philander Chase, 1st Episc. bishop in Ohio & founder of Kenyon College (see), founded Jubilee College in 1839. **Bishop Chase's Grave.**

## Sec. 2: PEORIA to MO. LINE. 134.

US24 follows Ill. R. out of Peoria, past small mining & R. towns. **9. ORCHARD MINES.** Across R., on St.9, is **PEKIN,** trade & transp. center. For many miles along both sides of R. are good f. & h. grounds. At c.**37.5.** J. with Rd.

SIDE TRIP: On Rd. (SW) 3.5m to **Dickson Mounds St. Pk.** (O.9-5.pic.). The mounds, acquired by st. in 1945, were explored by orig. owners of site, Dr. Don F. Dickson & his father, with help of archaeologists. More than 230 skeletons of prehist. men, women & children were discovered & left exactly as they were found, with arrowheads, pottery & ornaments around them. Exhibit, under permanent shelter, reveals much of life of agric. villages that were scattered over Ill. country 1,000 yrs. ago. The great number of burials, incl. several family groups, indicates that epidemic struck the village on river plain below.

**38. LEWISTOWN,** early home of Edgar Lee Masters, poet of Spoon R. valley. Maj. O. M. Ross founded town, in 1821, on land grant to soldiers of War of 1812. **Ross**

**Mansion,** at 409 E. Milton Ave., is "McNeely Mansion" of "Spoon River Anthology." At 1127 N. Main St., **Maj. Newton Walker H.** (1833), built for friend of Lincoln. **Oak Hill Cemetery. 44.** Hy. crosses Spoon R. **72. RUSHVILLE,** founded in 1825, center of coal-mining, orchard & grain-growing country. **Scripps Pk.** was once farm of E. W. Scripps, founder of newspaper chain. **81. RIPLEY,** on Le Moine Cr. From here, US24 winds (W) among ranging hills, past rural centers sett. largely by Germans. **132. QUINCY** (through RR. & bus conns. accoms.), spreading out along Miss. R. & extending up to the steep bluffs; important industrial town & seat of Adams Cty. In 1850's it was st.'s 2nd city & still keeps atmosphere of a big town. Quincy Bay, once harbor of a leading port from which were shipped millions of dollars worth of goods & thousands of hogs, is now recr. center (f.boat.swim.). Drills & pumps, farm machinery & supplies for chicken farms are important products. PTS. OF INT.: In Washington Pk., **Site of 6th Lincoln-Douglas Debate,** marked by bronze bas relief (by Lorado Taft). 425 S. 12th St., **John Wood H.** (1835), home of 1st settler; now **Hist. Soc. Mus.** (O). Main & 7th Sts., **St. Boniface Ch.** (1847). **U.S. Lock & Dam No. 2.**

US24 crosses **QUINCY MEM. BRIDGE** (toll) over Miss. R., **ILL.-MO. LINE,** at **134.**

## LINCOLN NAT. MEM. HY.

**ILL.-IND. LINE** (Vincennes, Ind.) **(W) to BEARDSTOWN, ILL. 246. St.181, St.1, Cty. Rd., St.16 & St.121**

Via: Russelville, Palestine, Marshall, Charleston, Campbell, Decatur, Springfield, Petersburg.

Lincoln Nat. Mem. Hy. follows (marked) route of Thos. Lincoln from Hodgenville, Ky., into Ind., & then, in Mar. 1830, from Vincennes across Ill. prairie. Along trl. in Ill. are mems. & statues, st. pks. & nat. shrines, incl. restored village of New Salem & Lincoln's Tomb.

### Sec. 1: IND. LINE to DECATUR. 154.

**0. LINCOLN MEM. BRIDGE** (1931) over Wabash R. In 30-a. pk. (camp.pic.), near Ill. approach, stands **Lincoln Trl. Mon.** (by Nellie Walker). Trl. parallels R. on St.181 (W).

SIDE TRIP: US50-US150 enters Ill. at bridge. 9m **Lawrenceville,** oil-refining center in richest oil & natural gas reg. 31.5m **Olney.** Near here is **Larchmond** (grounds O.), former estate of Dr. Rbt. Ridgway, noted ornithologist.

**12. RUSSELVILLE.** Ferry in operation more than 120 yrs. **26. PALESTINE,** thriving settlement in Lincoln's time with land office, taverns, mills & stores. From here the Lincolns headed (W) on what is now St.33 to J. with St.1 at **30.,** then across open prairie. **57. MARSHALL.** J. with US40, which crosses (W) **Stone Bridge** built for Cumberland Trl. in 1830's. Mem. Hy. follows Marked Rd. (NW) through sparsely settled reg. **85. CHARLESTON,** seat of Eastern Ill. St. Teachers College. In cty. fairgrounds are **Grave of Dennis Hanks,** Lincoln's spirited cousin & **Site of 4th Lincoln-Douglas Debate,** heard by 12,000. In Morton Pk. is **Sally Lincoln Chapter H. of D.A.R.,** named for Lincoln's stepmother, in log cabin (1832) where the young circuit rider visited. **Coles County Cth.** has Lincoln papers. **Eastern St. Teachers College,** housed in attractive stone bldgs. (Norman); founded in 1895. J. with St.130.

SIDE TRIP: On St.130 (S) 7m to **Fox Ridge St. Pk.** (f.boat.camp.pic.), 700 as., deeply wooded, near Embarrass R.

The Lincolns' covered wagon cont. (W) from Charleston, but Mem. Hy. follows marked route (S) to 3 later homes of Thos. Lincoln. It passes **Sarah Lincoln H.,** in **CAMPBELL, 92.5.,** where Lincoln's mother lived after her husband's death, 1851-69. **94. LOG CABIN ST. PK.** (pic.), 86 as. of Thos. Lincoln's 4th & last homestead in Ill. **Thos. Lincoln Log Cabin** (reconst.1935); period furnishings. **97.5.** (NW.) from st. pk. is **Thos. Lincoln Cemetery** (formerly Shiloh), where Sarah & Thos. Lincoln are buried. **101. Site of Lincoln's 3rd H.** in Ill. (1834-37). **104. Site of 2nd Lincoln H.,** to which family moved in 1831 after Abraham had set out to make his own way. **107.** J. with St.121, over which Mem. Hy. cont. (N). **110. MATTOON** (see). **Fish Hatchery.** J. with US45 (see).

Mem. Hy. follows St.121 (NW) across Kaskaskia R. valley. **146. SPITLER WOODS ST. PK.** (pic.camp.facils.). **154. DECATUR** (see US51), where the Lincolns came to end of wearisome journey. Down Sangamon R., John Hanks had found site on high bluff, & there they put up 3-sided cabin. The winter was discouraging. A blizzard stormed around the shelter in Dec. & cut off all communication. After the spring floods, Thos. Lincoln started back across the prairie to find another home (see above).

**Sec. 2: DECATUR to BEARDSTOWN. 92. US36, St.97 & Marked Rd.**

**0. DECATUR. 9.** on US36 **1st Lincoln Home Site Marker.** Along Sangamon R. (S) is **Lincoln Trl. Pky.,** past site of cabin (1830-31). **33.5. CAMP BUTLER NAT. CEMETERY,** on site of Civil War camp & prison.

**40. SPRINGFIELD**

Through RR. & bus conns. Capital Airport (NW) 3.8m. Hotels. Tourist camps. Theaters (stage & screen). Recr. facils. in several pks., L. Springfield & Sangamon R. (f.boat. swim.). Annual Beaux Arts Ball (Jan.); Ill. St. Fair (late Aug.). Info.: C. of C., 5th & Capitol Sts.

Mem. Hy. crosses S. side of the st. capital, which spreads out over rolling prairie. Ninth St. & Wabash RR. tracks divide W. sec., incl. gov. bldgs., bus. & residential areas, from E. half, where are industrial plants, RR. yards & homes of some 4,000 Negroes. Springfield is, above all else, the city of Abr. Lincoln. Here he lived for many yrs. & here stand his tomb, his home & other cherished mems. Carl Sandburg & the Springfield poet, Vachel Lindsay, have paid tribute to the man & the city. Elisha Kelly came here from N.C. in 1818, & by 1821 the little community became cty. seat. In 1832 the "Talisman" created a sensation as it came up the Sangamon from St. Louis, but the river fell, & the steamer had to back downriver, taking with it Springfield's hopes. With opening of Erie Canal, the rich prairies attracted thousands of settlers, & agitation began for more centrally located capital. Lincoln led Sangamon Cty.'s "Long Nine" (legislators whose total height was 54') in successful effort to remove capital from Vandalia (see) to Springfield. Prosperity came with the RRs., & coal mining began late in 1860's. Since then city has grown quietly with the state.

PTS. OF INT.: (1) S. 2nd St., Capitol Group (O): **The Capitol** (1868-87.Ren.by J.C. Cochrane), tallest bldg. in S. Ill. Above cross-shaped limestone structure rises a ribbed dome with Corinth. columns around base. Inter. frieze by E. Nicolai. **Statue of Lincoln** (by Andrew O'Connor). **Statue of Stephen A. Douglas** (by Gilbert Riswold). **Centennial Bldg.** (1918-23.neo-Class.), incl. **St. Lib.; Mus.,** with anthrop., biol. & geol. colls.; **Art Gallery, & St. Hist. Lib.,** in which is Lincoln Room. **Archives Bldg.** (1937.1st floor O.), **Supreme Ct. Bldg., & St. Armory & Office Bldg.** complete harmonious group, part of Springfield Plan. (2) 315 E. Adams St., **Site of Globe Tavern,** where Abr. & Mary Lincoln lived (1842-44). (3) Public Sq., **Sangamon County Cth.** (O.1837.Gr.Rev.), Capitol for 40 yrs. Orig. bldg. of age-darkened stone was lifted in 1899 & new 1st story erected beneath. The "House Divided" speech was made in **Circuit Ct. Room,** & here the President's body lay in state, May 3-4, 1865. (4) 101-3 S. 5th St., **Site of Speed's Store** & last Lincoln-Herndon Law Office (1844); (5) 109 N. 5th St., **Site of Lincoln-Stuart Law Office** (1837-41); (6) 203 S. 6th St., 3rd floor, **Logan Lincoln Law Office** (1841-44); (7) 7th St. & Capitol Ave., **First Presb. Ch.,** attended by Lincoln family (1850-61); (8) 8th & Jackson Sts., **Lincoln Home** (O.1839.Gr.Rev.), only house Lincoln ever owned; well preserved; inter. unchanged, with period furnishings. (9) 801 N. 5th St., **"Edwards Place"** (1833), housing Springfield Art Assoc. Gallery & mus. in wing (1937-38). The beautiful H., rest. & furnished with orig. & period pieces, was home of Judge Benj. S. Edwards, son of Gov. Ninian Edwards. (10) Enos Ave. & 12th St. **Concordia Theol. Seminary** (Luth.), offering 6-yr. course. Est. in Ft. Wayne, Ind. (see), it was moved to Springfield in 1874.

(12) In Oakridge Cemetery, Monument Ave., **Lincoln Tomb** (1874.by Larkin G. Mead). Erected in 1874, with contributions from all over country, the tomb was remodeled in 1901, & in 1930-31 the inter. was reconstructed & tomb rededicated. The 100' obelisk rises above simple sq. bldg. of white marble. At entrance is reprod. of Gutzon Borglum's "Head of Lincoln," & in registration room, bronze replica of D. C. French's "Seated Lincoln" (see Washington, D.C.). Sarcophagus, near N. wall, is marked simply "Abraham Lincoln 1809-1865." Mrs. Lincoln & 3 sons are buried

in crypts along S. wall. (Rbt. Todd Lincoln is buried in Arlington Cemetery). (13) (S) on Belt Hy. to 4,000-a. **L. Springfield.** Water impounded at Spaulding Dam supplies city Water & Light Plant (O). The 60-mile shore line is lined with cottages, private clubs & yr.-round residences. Pk. (on E. side), conn. with mainland by Vachel Lindsay Mem. Bridge, incl. **Lincoln Mem. Garden. Bridge View Beach (Negro).**

SIDE TRIP: On US66 (NE) 30$^{m}$ to **Lincoln,** only town in U.S. named for Abr. Lincoln during his early yrs. He gave legal assistance in its planning & incorporation. **Site of Postville Cth.** (now in American Village, Dearborn, Mich.). **Lincoln Jr. College** (Presb.).

On St.121 (SE) 11$^{m}$, near J. with US54, is **Mount Pulaski Cth.** (1847.Gr.Rev.inter.rest.), also assoc. with Lincoln.

Mem. Hy. leaves Springfield on St.97-St.125. At **48.** it turns (N) with St.97. **60. NEW SALEM ST. PK.** (f.pic.camp.restaurant), 200 as. on bluff overlooking Sangamon R. Here is authentic reprod. of village where Lincoln lived for 6 yrs. (1831-37), where he clerked, chopped wood, served as postmaster, surveyor & lawyer. Village began with gristmill built by Jas. Rutledge & John Cameron in 1828, & its brief prosperity declined when cty. seat was est. at Petersburg (see below) in 1839. In 1906, Wm. R. Hearst bought site for Old Salem Chautauqua Assoc., & in 1918 title was transferred to st. Only orig. bldg. is **Onstot Cooper Shop** (1835). **Rutledge Tavern,** where Lincoln stayed; 13 cabins, sch. & ch. cabin & 10 stores, shops & mills have been reprod. & furnished; also dam, sawmill & gristmill on R. **62. PETERSBURG.** In Oakwood Cemetery is **Grave of Ann Rutledge,** who died in 1835. Lincoln Trl. (not yet completed) winds (W) through Sangamon valley. **92. BEARDSTOWN,** on Ill. R. **City Hall** (1845) was scene of Duff Armstrong trial, in which Lincoln defended son of Hanna Armstrong, friend of New Salem days. His eloquence brought pioneer jury to tears. J. with US67 & St.100 (see Ill. Waterway Tour).

## ST. 1—ILLINOIS

**CHICAGO (S) to ILL.-KY. LINE** (11$^{m}$ from Marion, Ky.). **336. St.1**

Via: Harvey, Chicago Heights, Momence, St. Anne, Watseka, Danville, Georgetown, Paris, Marshall, Lawrenceville, Mount Carmel, Norris City & Cave-in-Rock.

St.1 is excellent hy. down E. border to J. of Wabash & Ohio Rs. & then some miles inland to Ky. Line. For much of route, hy. travels Hubbard Trl. from Vincennes to Ft. Dearborn. Gurdon Hubbard, Amer. Fur Co. agent, marked trl. with his Conestoga wagons from Danville to Chicago in 1833.

**27.5. CHICAGO HTS.** (see Chicago Trip I), J. with US30 (see). **52. MOMENCE,** industrial town on Kankakee R., was a stopping place on Hubbard Trl. J. with St.17, which leads (W) to Kankakee (see US45). **65. ST. ANNE. Replica of St. Anne de Beaupré Shrine** (Canada) in St. Anne's Ch. Route of St.1 through mining & farm country (S) is varied by pleasant R. valleys & ridges of glacial moraines. **132. DANVILLE** (through RR. & bus conns. Accoms.), coal-mining & industrial center with one of largest brick plants in U.S. Large dairy & stock farms in vic. After Kickapoo ceded Vermilion Cty. area in 1819, the site was developed as cty. seat. Gurdon Hubbard est. post in 1828 & was leading citizen until he moved to the "smaller town" of Chicago on the prairie. Another early settler was Ward Hill Lamon, law partner & trusted friend of Lincoln, though temperamentally his opposite. Lamon was a Va. man, convivial & full of robust good humor. Jos. G. Cannon was a later Danville resident. **Soldiers Mon.** (1922.by Lorado Taft). **Victory Mem. Bridge** (1922). J. with US150, with which St.1 unites (S).

SIDE TRIP: On US150 (W) 8$^{m}$ to **Kickapoo St. Pk.** (f.boat.camp.pic.), 1,500 as. along Middle Fork of Vermilion R. After salt & coal deposits were exhausted, the area was abandoned until acquired by st. in 1939. Meanwhile, the woodland & precipitous banks of larger Ls. & ravines had regained primeval beauty.

**167. PARIS,** mfg. & RR. center, with fine houses & wide streets around pub. sq. Here Lincoln began law practice in 1842. During Civil War, Edgar Cty. had many belligerent Copperheads whose attack on Paris, Feb. 1864, was prevented only by Fed. troops. Antislavery feeling also was strong, & both Lincoln & Owen Lovejoy (see) spoke to large audiences. **183. MARSHALL,** J. with US40 & with St.67, part of Lincoln Nat. Mem. Hy., with which St.1 unites as far as J. with St.33 at **210.** At **229.** is **LAWRENCEVILLE,** on Embarrass R. (E. 10$^{m}$ from Vincennes, Ind.). Org. in 1821, settlement was named for Jas. Lawrence, Comdr. of "USS Chesapeake" in War of 1812. It is center of richest oil-producing reg. in Ill. Also in vic. is large natural gas field. J. with US50. **252. MOUNT CARMEL,** center of good farming country. In rugged S. sec. of tour, hy. crosses numerous Rs. **286. CARMI,** crossed by Little Wabash R. which joins greater Wabash a few miles N. of confluence with the Ohio. **298. NORRIS CITY,** J. with US45 (see). **317.** St.1 crosses Saline R. at edge of E. sec. of **Shawnee Nat. For.** (see). **335.5. CAVE-IN-ROCK.** Near village is **Cave-In-Rock St. Pk.** (f.boat.pic.camp.). The great cave in bluff on Ohio R. was discovered by white man in 1744, known to Inds. as "Dwelling Place of the Great Spirit." After Rev. War, it was hiding place for robbers who preyed on riverboats. Entrance, 55′ wide, is halfway up bluff, & tunnel extends nearly 200′ into the rock. Ferry (auto & passenger) crosses Ohio R., **ILL.-KY. LINE,** at **336.**

## US 45—ILLINOIS

**ILL.-WIS. LINE** (5$^{m}$ from Bristol, Wis.) **(S) to ILL.-KY. LINE** (Paducah, Ky.). **430. US45**

Via: Milburn, Mundelein, Des Plaines, La Grange, Bradley, Kankakee, Gilman, Paxton, Rantoul, Champaign & Urbana, Mattoon, Effingham, Flora, Fairfield, Norris City, Harrisburg, Vienna, Metropolis, Brookport.

US45 traverses Ill. (N-S) from lake reg. near border, through suburban Chicago & across prairie & mining area; then over Ozarks to Ohio R.

### Sec. 1: WIS. LINE to MATTOON. 227.

Tour crosses Chain O' Lakes recr. area, among hilly glacial moraines. For nearly 100$^{m}$, route is in Greater Chicago. Then (S) are pastures & red barns of important dairy reg. **55.** Hy. enters valley of Des Plaines R., route utilized by Inds. & explorers. Ill. & Mich. Canal followed R. gorge, & Sanitary & Ship Canal takes same path.

**100. BOURBONNAIS,** an old settlement where Fr. is still the popular language. Noel La Vasseur, partner of Gurdon Hubbard (see), est. trading post in 1832 & encouraged Fr.-Can. settlement in Kankakee R. valley. Through the cty. are their stone fences & houses, chs. & convents, & many villages & towns have names such as L'Erable, St. Anne, Papineau, Momence.

**103. KANKAKEE,** on R. of same name, began as part of Bourbonnais but was inc. in 1855, when Ill. Cent. RR. made it a depot. In short time, it became cty. seat & important town. **Geo. Grey Barnard Coll.,** in Central Sch., was given by the sculptor, a former pupil. **Kankakee St. Hospital for the Insane,** est. in 1878, is one of largest in U.S.; cottage plan (O.appl.). Scenic R. drives on St.113. From Kankakee, US45 travels through one of world's richest corn & grain areas, where immense fields are broken only by separating hedges & woodlots. Along hy. are many sm. villages. **130. GILMAN** & **135. ONARGA,** are larger settlements with some sm. industries. **152. PAXTON,** sett. by Swedish people, many of them graduates of ancient Univs. of Lund & Upsala; seat of Augustana College (see Rock I.), 1863-75. **162. RANTOUL,** known for **Chanute Field,** important Army Air Force post & Technical Training Command, named for Octave Chanute, pioneer in gliding.

**180. URBANA & CHAMPAIGN**

Through RR. & bus conns. Airports (no scheduled serv.). Accoms. Golf at Kenwood Links (sm.fee). Mun. swim. pool & rink. Univ. tennis courts (O. to pub.). Dramatic, musical & other Univ. events. Info.: Champaign C. of C., 318 N. Neil St.; Urbana Assoc. of Com., 201 W. Main St.

The 2 municipalities, with Wright St. as dividing line, share one of st.'s leading univs. Urbana, older & smaller city, with most of Univ. bldgs., is much like other attractive college towns, while Champaign has large bus. dist., numerous factories & the RRs., as well as pleasant residential secs. College dormitories & houses, shops & eating places are about equally divided. Urbana, sett. in 1820's, boomed with laying of Ill. Cen. RR. tracks 2$^{m}$ N. in 1854, but Depot refused to be inc. with Old Town & became Champaign in 1860. The rival cities united in lobbying for new univ. est. in 1867 as Ill. Industrial College. Under Gov. John P. Altgeld (see) in 1890's, the sch. received sufficient aid to gain recognition as ranking st. univ. PTS. OF INT. IN CHAMPAIGN: (1) Neil St. & Univ. Ave., **City Bldg.** (1937.Mod.), simple & beautiful structure with 6-story tower. (2) Church & State Sts., in West Side Pk., **"Prayer for Rain,"** by Edw. Kemeys, sculptor of Chicago Art Institute lions. PTS. OF INT. IN URBANA: (3) Park St. & Broadway, **Crystal Lake Pk.** (swim.bridle paths.). **Univ. of Illinois** has 12 colleges & schools on Urbana-Champaign campus & 3 colleges in Chicago. South Campus is devoted largely to excellent College of Agric. **Old Campus** is N. of Green St., & main quadrangle with newer Georg. bldgs. is S. (4) On the Mall, **Lincoln Hall,** with Mus. of European Culture (O.wks.). (5) S. Campus, **Mem. Stadium** (1924), one of finest in U.S. (6) N. Campus, Mathews St., **Illini Union** (1938). (7) S. end of Mall, **Lib.,** one of ranking libs. in U.S. (8) S. of Mall, **Morrow Plots,** among oldest soil experiment plots (1876). Of special int. also are **Natural Resources Bldg., Home Research Center** (1940) & **Smith Mem. Music Hall.**

**194. PESOTUM,** like many prairie towns, is centered by towering grain elevator beside RR. tracks. **203. TUSCOLA & 212. ARCOLA** are centers of broom industry. Much fine-leaved broom corn is grown in vic.

SIDE TRIP: On St.133 (W) 9m from Arcola to **Arthur,** center of large Amish community; traditional crafts, customs & speech.

**227. MATTOON,** one of larger towns on US45; shipping & mfg. center for prosperous agric. reg. **Fish Hatchery,** on L. Mattoon (SW). J. with St.16 sec. of Lincoln Nat. Mem. Hy. (see).

## Sec. 2: MATTOON to KENTUCKY LINE. 203.

**SHELBYVILLE MORAINE,** (S) of Mattoon, marks farthest reach of Wis. Glacier. Corn, hay & wheat are important crops, but fields are broken by orchards & wooded valleys of numerous streams. **7.** Hy. rises over ridge of moraine. **28. EFFINGHAM,** largest center in Effingham Cty., which was sett. largely by Germans in 1860's. Near town (W) is **L. Kanaga** (bath.cottages). J. with US40 (see). At **60.** US45 unites (E) with US50 for a few miles. **61. FLORA,** the big town of Clay Cty. Around it are immense beet & clover fields. **63.** Tour turns (S) past some of Clay Cty. oil wells. **88. FAIRFIELD,** sett. in 1819, mingles modern industry with relics of the past. J. with St.15.

SIDE TRIP: On St.15 (E) 17m to **Albion,** 1st of Eng. colonies founded by Geo. Flower (1788-1862), who was enchanted by Ill. prairie. He brought colonists from England & founded Albion in 1818, was prominent in antislavery movement.

**109. ENFIELD** (sett.1813); mule sale on Homecoming Day (Oct.). **117. NORRIS CITY.** J. with St.1 (see). From here onward, country is quite different from rest of Ill., both in its rugged contours, & in hist. & social pattern. Scenery is strikingly beautiful, especially in Ozark Range. Tulip tree, sycamore, beech, butternut & other common trees reach greater height & size in the ravines & rich bottomlands. The people keep sense of hist. importance & family kinship to marked degree. **130. ELDORADO,** sm. mining town. **137. HARRISBURG,** on C.C.C. & St.L. RR., important coal-mining center. Hqs. of **Shawnee Nat. For.** (see below). **151. STONEFORT,** one of numerous prehist. structures in these hills. **155.** E. sec. of **Shawnee Nat. For.** borders hy. near **NEW BURNSIDE.** Almost directly E., in for., is **Williams Lookout** (pic.) on 2nd highest pt. in Ill. Shawnee Nat. For. (camp.pic. cabins.boat.f.), only one in Ill., incl. secs. along Ohio R. & on Miss. R.

**158.** J. with Eddyville Rd., which branches (E) to **Trigg Lookout** (pic.), honoring L. O. Trigg who spent yrs. in working for est. of for. [Rd. cont. to **Bell Smith Springs** (pic.), & (S) to **Dixon Springs Exper. Sta.** of Univ. of Ill.] US45 gradually descends into wooded country through which Clark marched to peaceful conquest of Kaskaskia (see). **170. VIENNA,** seat of Johnson Cty. since 1818. J. with St.146, which leads (E) 13m to **L. Glendale & Dixon Springs St. Pk.** (pic.group camp.), around one of st.'s oldest resorts. US45 follows embankment along **Cypress Swamp,** lumbered in 1880's. Cypress here grows from 80′ to 130′ high. **192. METROPOLIS** began with Ft. Massac (see below). Later, the "metropolis of the West" was platted a little N., in belief that Ohio R. would be bridged there. Metropolis (ferry) has charm of Southern city, with magnolia & gum trees on ample lawns. A mile (S) is **Ft. Massac St. Pk.** (f.camp.pic.refreshments.facils.game preserve). **Site of Ft. Massac** (to be reconstructed), built by Fr. in 1757. Gen. Clark & his Ky. Long Knives stopped here in 1778. In 1794 Gen. Wayne ordered site refortified under Capt. Zebulon Pike. **Statue of Clark** (by Leon Hermant). **202.5. BROOKPORT.** Near-by is **Lock & Dam No. 52,** constructed of movable wickets. US45 crosses Ohio R. (free bridge) to Paducah, Ky., **203.**

# US 51—ILLINOIS

**ILL.-WIS. LINE** (Beloit, Wis.) **(S) to KY. LINE** (5m from Wickliffe, Ky.). **417. US51**
Via: Rockford, Rochelle, Mendota, Peru, La Salle, Wenona, El Paso, Normal & Bloomington, Clinton, Decatur, Pana, Vandalia, Sandoval, Centralia, Ashley, Du Quoin, Carbondale, (Mound City), Cairo.

## Sec. 1: WIS. LINE to DECATUR. 197.

US51 sweeps (N-S) down middle of st., giving view of almost every type of scenery, & intersected by main (E-W) routes. From **S. BELOIT,** tour follows winding Rock R. known for beauty of valley; many waterpower sites & industrial centers. **19. ROCKFORD.** J. with US20 (see) & St.2, river Rd. **44. ROCHELLE,** attractive prairie town; was home of Chas. Butterfield, who wrote "When You & I Were Young, Maggie," & Francis Roe, composer of "Just Before the Battle, Mother." **Spring L.;** mun. bathh. (sm.fee). **56.** J. with US30 (see). Tree-capped ridges of merged Bloomington & Shelbyville moraines are silhouetted against sky (W) from here to Bloomington. US51 ascends slope of 1st ridge. **74. MENDOTA,** from which millions of cans of corn are shipped annually. J. with US34 (see) & US52, with which US51 unites. **79.** US52 turns E.

SIDE TRIP: On US52 (E) 2m to **Troy Grove,** birthpl. of Jas. Butler (Wild Bill) Hickok (see). **Wild Bill Hickok St. Mon.**

**86.** US51 forks, one branch (E) entering **Peru,** & main route **LA SALLE,** at **90.** (see Ill. Waterway Tour). J. with US6 & St.71, routes (E) through Starved Rock & Buffalo Rock St. Pks. (see). **94. OGLESBY,** center of cement industry, drawing upon limestone & slate deposits of Vermilion R. valley. At edge of town is **Matthiessen St. Pk.** (pic.guides.refreshments), nature preserve. **105.** J. with St.18.

SIDE TRIP: On St.18 (E) 12m to **Streator,** industrial town in midst of rich deposits; glass, tile, brick & foundry products are leading industries. In Riverview Cemetery is **Grave of Honey Boy Evans,** noted black-face minstrel & composer.

**111. WENONA.** Hy. is bordered with fields of soy beans, of which Ill. is a leading producer. **134. EL PASO.** J. with US24 (see). **140.** J. with Rd. (E) to **L. Bloomington** (f.boat.swim.), summer resort. **142. HUDSON** (E.of hy.). **Five Oaks** (1836), birthpl. of Melville E. Stone, gen. mgr. of Assoc. Press in its early yrs.

**152. BLOOMINGTON & NORMAL**

Through RR. & bus conns. Mun. Airport, on St.9 (E). Accoms. Golf & other recr. facils. College events. Miller Pk. (zoo & aquarium.boat.swim.). Amer. Passion Play (Palm Sun. & 10 Suns. following), at Scottish Rite Temple.

US51-US66 (Main St.) crosses W. edge of Normal, seat of Ill. St. Normal Univ., & cont. (S) through center of Bloomington, home of Ill. Wesleyan Univ. In early 1820's, settlers of Brit. stock came to trading post near grove at meeting of Ind. trls., & settlement came to be known as Blooming Grove. Jas. Allin, in 1830, took land N. of grove & offered McLean Cty. a cth. site. The new town, platted as Bloomington, prospered with est. of univ. in 1853 & laying of RR. tracks in 1854. Ill. St. Normal Univ., 2nd W. of Alleghenies, was awarded to N. Bloomington (now Normal) in 1857. Lincoln's crucial "Lost Speech" was made here at Anti-Nebraska Convention, 1856, when Ill. Republican party was org. Bloomington was home of Judge David Davis (see); Adlai Stevenson, U.S. Vice-Pres.; Govs. J. M. Hamilton & Jos. Fifer; Rachel Crothers, writer, & Margaret Illington, who honored town & state in her stage name. "Bloomington Daily Pantagraph," staunch supporter of Lincoln, has been published continuously since 1846. Spreading over wooded moraine, Bloomington looks much more a univ. town than the important mfg., commercial & RR. center which it also is. Residential & campus neighborhoods have many Vict. mansions on broad lawns, while bus. dist. was largely rebuilt after fire in 1900.

PTS. OF INT. IN BLOOMINGTON: (1) 901 N. McLean St., **Adlai H. Stevenson H.** (1850's.Tudor). Stevenson (1835-1914) came from Ky. in 1852, was elected Vice Pres. in 1893 & defeated with Wm. J. Bryan in 1900. (2) 1100 E. Jefferson St., **David Davis H.,** where Davis lived before becoming Judge of 8th Circuit (see US24). (3) 110 E. Mulberry St., **Scottish Rite Temple** (Ital.Ren.). (4) East & Grove Sts., **McLean Cty. Hist. Soc.** (O.wks.), in McBarnes Mem. Bldg.; Lincolniana & hist. coll. (5) Grove & S. Main Sts., **Site of Birthpl. of Elbert Hubbard,** author of 170 "Little Journeys" to homes of famous people. (6) East & Front Sts., Plaque comm.

**Lincoln's Lost Speech,** May 29, 1856. (7) On Chestnut St., **Alton RR. Shops,** town's largest industry. First Pullman car was built here & made 1st trip Sept. 1, 1859. (8) East St., bet. Graham & Emerson Sts., **Ill. Wesleyan Univ.** (opened in 1851), est. & supported by Meth. Episc. church. Hodding College, founded in Abingdon, Ill, was united with univ. in 1930. **Hodding Hall** (1871). **North Hall** (1850's). **Buck Mem. Lib. Presser Hall** (Mod.). PTS. OF INT. IN NORMAL: (1) Bet. Beaufort & Mulberry Sts., **Ill. St. Normal Univ.,** (est. in 1856), conn. with Wesleyan by Franklin Ave. **Old Main** (1857). **Milner Lib.** (1940.Georg.), notable for functional design. **Demonstration Farm.** (2) 202 W. Mulberry St., **Site of Hovey H.** Col. C. E. Hovey was 1st pres. of Ill. St. Normal Univ. & father of Rich. Hovey, poet. Beech & Lincoln Sts., **Ill. St. Soldiers' & Sailors' Children's Sch.,** on beautiful 160-a. campus. J. with US66 & St.9, which cont. (NW) 20$^{m}$ to **Dells of Mackinaw R.** (good f. & h.). S. of Bloomington, the union of modern machinery & agric. is evident on all sides but especially in the vast cornfields. **175. CLINTON.** Lincoln, riding the 8th Circuit, often stopped at **Barnett Hotel** (O.appl.). US51 crosses Salt Cr. & follows edge of Shelbyville Moraine.

**197. DECATUR**

Through RR. & bus conns. Mun. Airport, 2.5$^{m}$ (E) off US36. Good accoms. Recr. facils. in Nelson & other pks. L. Decatur (swim.boat.winter sports). Town & Gown Players & Little Theater. Midwinter Ice Carnival. Info.: Assoc. of Com., in Decatur Club Bldg.

Decatur, prairie town on Sangamon R., seat of Millikin College, is trade, cultural & recr. center for wide area; sometimes called Soybean Capital of Amer. The Sangamon, an early link bet. backwoods & Ill. & Miss. Rs., crosses town to L. Decatur, formed by dam (1923) at NE. limits. Gold dome of Staley Mfg. Co. Adm. Bldg. (14 stories) is visible for miles around. Staley Co., makers of corn & soybean products, is a leading industry, & Wabash RR. shops provide employment for thousands. Coal fields & more recently discovered oil in vic. make Decatur one of st.'s important industrial towns. It was laid out in 1829 & named for hero of Tripoli. Abr. Lincoln began to study law in Decatur County Cth. & was 1st mentioned for Presidency at Ill. Republican convention here in 1860. Lincoln went down the Sangamon in 1831, when he hired out with Denton Offut to take flatboat to New Orleans, his 1st experience of world beyond the prairies. PTS. OF INT.: (1) W. Main St., **Jas. Millikin Univ.,** accredited liberal arts & vocational univ., & **Millikin Conservatory of Music.** Pres. Theodore Roosevelt made dedicatory address when 4 of the attractive Elizabethan bldgs. were opened in Sept., 1903. (2) Adj. campus (NW) is **Fairview Pk.** (pic.recr.facils.). **Log Cabin Cth.** (1829), "chinked & daubed by John Hanks." (3) 457 N. Main St., **Pub. Lib.;** Lincoln Coll. (4) 200 E. Main St., **Site of Wigwam** where Lincoln was nominated. (5) N. 22nd & E. Eldorado Sts., **A. E. Staley Mfg. Co. Plant** (O.tours), incl. 40 or more bldgs. **Adm. Bldg.** (1929.by Aschauer & Waggoner). (6) **L. Decatur,** circled by 12$^{m}$ drive.
J. with US36 (see Lincoln Nat. Mem. Hy.), St.121 & St.105.

SIDE TRIPS: (A) On St.121 (SE) c.7$^{m}$ to **Spitler Woods St. Pk.,** considered one of loveliest; left largely in natural state.
(B) On St.105 (NE) 23$^{m}$ to **Bement.** Here **Bryant Cottage St. Mem.** was ded. in 1947. Here Lincoln & Douglas planned the 7 debates. F. E. Bryant, their host, was cousin of Wm. Cullen Bryant.

## Sec. 2: DECATUR to KY. LINE. 220.

US51 crosses Shelbyville Moraine & cont. (S) through coal country. **16. MOWEAQUA,** scene of mining disaster in 1932. **34. PANA,** rose-growing center. Hothouses utilize local coal supply. **Kitchel Pk.** (tourist camp.pic.swim.). **65. VANDALIA,** on Kaskaskia R. with wooded moraine in background, was 2nd capital of Ill. (1819-39). To inaugurate land boom, Congress was petitioned & granted land where capital should remain for 20 yrs. **Vandalia St. H.** (1836.Gr.Rev.), orig. furnishings. In this bldg. an act was passed incorporating the sm. prairie town of Chicago in far N. In front is **Madonna of the Trl. Mon.,** one of 12 erected by D.A.R. along Nat. Rd. (now US40), which terminated at Vandalia. **Pub. Lib.;** Lincolniana.
For next 100 miles, US51 crosses some of richest coal fields in U.S., a reg. also rich in oil. **76. VERNON,** surrounded by peach & pear orchards, in pleasant contrast to mining centers. **79. PATOKA,** in st.'s largest oil field. **90. SANDOVAL,** mining town. J. with US50.

SIDE TRIP: On US50 (E) 10m to **Salem,** oil center; birthpl. of Wm. Jennings Bryan (1860-1925), pacifist & defender of free silver & fundamentalism; Secy. of War under Pres. Wilson until World War I. **Bryan H.** (O.1852), now a Mus.

**97. CENTRALIA,** platted by Ill. Cent. RR. in 1853 & still very much a RR. town. Among 1st settlers were many Germans who gave it solid financial beginning, its "saengerfest," & prevailing architectural style. Coal miners, oil workers & RR. men mingle in stores, bars, banks & union halls. Scattered oil derricks rise in the fields while hillsides bloom with peach orchards. One of worst mining disasters occurred in Centralia Mine No. 5 on March 25, 1947, when 111 men were killed in explosion. Extensive underground workings of the mine, opened in 1907, made a trap for the miners. Dangerously dry & dusty state of mine had been recognized for several yrs. Centralia Coal Co. was indicted for "wilful negligence" & fined $1,000. Legislature passed resolution expressing "profound grief & sorrow" & purchased painting "The Coal Miner." Since 1938, oil in vic. has surpassed coal in importance. Strawberries are a leading product. **IRVINGTON,** at **106.,** was once strawberry capital, with migratory pickers arriving from all sides. Today its peach orchards are of greater value. **117. ASHLEY.** J. with St.15.

**139. DU QUOIN,** largest of string of mining towns on route to **CARBONDALE, 160.,** RR. & trade center at heart of coal-mining reg. **Southern Ill. Univ.,** founded in late 1860's, is coed. liberal arts univ., with colleges of Education, Liberal Arts & Sciences, & Vocations & Professions; master's degree in education. Child Guidance Clinic. Concerts by orchestra, chorus, band (O). **Mus. of Natural & Social Sciences** (O). J. with St.13, which leads (E) to **Crab Orchard L.** Across level prairies (S), the Ozarks range along horizon. Their highest peaks reach only 700', but their beauty lies in massive formations, densely forested slopes & ravines. At c.**165.,** hy. enters sec. of **SHAWNEE NAT. FOR.** (pic.camp.f.h.boat.), hqs. at Harrisburg (see US45). **172.** (E. of hy.) **GIANT CITY ST. PK.** (pic.camp.lodge.cabins.refreshments), in which are some most remarkable phenomena of these ancient folded hills. Rd. ascends to tableland (lodge O.yr.round) overlooking Ozarks. Near Lodge (W) is **Giant City,** created by erosion, which cut narrow "avenues" bet. towering walls of sandstone. Near N. entrance is **Old Stone Ft.** During Civil War, the caves of the Ozarks harbored deserters from both armies, & Knights of the Golden Circle held secret meetings here. **177.** Rd. angles (W) a mile or two to **Alto Pass;** best lookout in St. on **Bald Knob** (1,030'), in U.S. For. Serv. Tower. **181. ANNA.** On St.146 (W) 1m is **Jonesboro,** scene of 3rd Lincoln-Douglas Debate. **214. MOUNDS.** Bet. US51 & St.37 is **Mound City Nat. Cemetery** (est.1866), where are buried more than 5,600 soldiers & sailors of several wars. **Ill. Soldiers' Mon.** (1874). In **Mound City,** (E) 1m, are **Marine Ways,** on Ohio R., used in Civil War. **217.** Hy. unites with St.3. **220. CAIRO** (see Miss. R. Tour), at J. of Ohio & Miss. Rs. US51 crosses impressive cantilever bridge (toll), **ILL.-KY. LINE.**

## MISSISSIPPI RIVER TOUR

**ILL.-IOWA LINE** (Dubuque, Iowa) **(S) to ILL.-KY. & MO. LINE (Cairo, Ill.). 562. US20, St.80, US67, St.94, St.96, St.100, US67, St.3**

Via: E. Dubuque, Galena, Savanna, Fulton, Moline, Monmouth, Biggsville, Dallas City, Nauvoo, Quincy, Pittsfield, Kampsville, Grafton, Alton, E. St. Louis, Cahokia, Waterloo, Chester, Thebes. Through RR. & bus conns. Accoms., recr. facils. in cities; numerous St. & roadside pks., pic. & camp sites.

Miss. R. is followed by Fed. & St. hys. for greater part of course along W. border of Ill., through impressive scenery & past notable sites & hist. cities.

### Sec. 1: IOWA LINE to DALLAS CITY. 190

**0. E. DUBUQUE. 11.** J. with St.80, which unites with US20 to Apple R. **13. GALENA** (see US20). **26.** Tour swings (S) with St.80 through increasingly rugged country; many quarries. **45. MISS. PALISADES ST. PK.** (f.pic.camp.refreshments). Campgrounds are high above R. in old orchard; trls. to crest of Palisades, Twin Sisters, Ind. Head & other strange formations. **46. SAVANNA,** founded in 1828; RR. & trade center & livestock shipping pt. **Savanna-Sabula Bridge** (toll) crosses R. to J. with US67, in Iowa. Near Savanna (S) is **Fish Rescue Sta.** St.80 parallels C.B. & Q. RR. at some distance from bluffs, crossing prairie country given over to dairy

& fattening of cattle. The sandy soil is also good for melons. **55. THOMSON,** center for duck hunters. Annual Melon Day. **64. FULTON,** residential community & truck-gardening center. J. with US30, which crosses (toll bridge) to Clinton, Ia. From this point to Quad Cities (see Rock I. & Moline), St.80 is close to R. (fine camp sites & cabin groups). **100. MOLINE** (see). Here St.80 ends at J. with US6 (see). Adj. Moline is **ROCK ISLAND** (see), at **103. Black Hawk St. Pk.** (f.pic.camp.guides. refreshments). For 100 or more miles there is no main hy. along R. Tour cont. (S) on US67. At **148. MONMOUTH** (see US34). J. with US34, with which tour unites (W). **164.** J. with St.94, which becomes main tour (S) to **179.**, where it turns (W) again on St.96. **190. DALLAS CITY,** river town.

## Sec. 2: DALLAS CITY to EAST ST. LOUIS. 222

**16. NAUVOO,** mecca of thousands who wish to see annual Grape Festival in beautiful old town, site of Jos. Smith's Mormon community & of Cabet's Icarian village. Nauvoo extends from Flats up terraced hills & into level country beyond. Vineyards in vic. produce wines for which Nauvoo has been known since 1850's. In 1824, Capt. Jas. White traded 200 sacks of corn to Sac & Fox Inds. for their village, & by 1830 a p.o. was est. in Venus, as new settlement was called. Commerce, an older town, absorbed Venus in 1834 & was formally org. in 1837. When Jos. Smith (see) was driven from Mo., he brought his followers to Commerce City &, under special charter, renamed it Nauvoo (Hebrew for "pleasant land"). A city of 20,000 grew up, & bldg. of great temple was begun in 1841 (never completed). The Gentiles feared political strength of the Saints, & charges of polygamy (never openly practiced) & other offenses were made against them. When "Expositor" was published by faction of the church "striking a blow at tyranny & oppression," Smith had the press & copies of paper destroyed. The Laws, leaders of the faction, had Smith & his brother arrested & lodged in Carthage jail (see below). A mob broke in, June 27, 1844, & murdered the Prophet & his brother Hyrum. Brigham Young took the leadership, disposed of the rich properties & led the Saints to Salt L. City (see). In 1849, the Fr. Icarians, led by Etienne Cabet (1788-1856), took possession of the deserted town. In Cabet's "Voyage to Icaria," the ideas back of this experiment are developed, similar to contemporary communism in emphasis on st. control of social & economic affairs. Colony prospered until dissension & dissatisfaction destroyed its harmony. Cabet, with some 200, went to St. Louis, Mo., while others est. colony near Corning, Ia. (see). The Cath. pastor started grape-growing with vines from St. Louis settlement, & the remaining Icarians started making wines, aided by Irish & German immigrants. Before Civil War, Nauvoo wines were shipped from 40 arched cellars to all parts of country. The industry flourished until Prohibition, when the making of a blue cheese, similar to Roquefort, was begun in abandoned wine cellars. After repeal, Nauvoo returned to wine making &, at annual Grape Festival, celebrates "Wedding of the Wine & Cheese" as it is done in Roquefort, France. PTS. OF INT.: (1) **Jos. Smith Homestead** (O.1823), built by Ind. agent. Near-by are **Graves** of Jos., Emma & Hyrum Smith. (2) **Mansion H.** (O.1842-43.remod.), Smith's 2nd home; a 2-story, white-pine bldg. maintained by Mormon Ch., as Mus. In coll. are editions of "Book of Mormon" & other works of the Prophet. (3) **Nauvoo H.** (begun in 1841). (4) **Brigham Young H.** (O). (5) **Site of Temple,** which was burned by incendiaries in 1848. (6) **Icarian H.**

St.96 runs close to R. (numerous pic. sites). **Keokuk Lock & Dam,** near **HAMILTON, 28.,** farm trade center. J. with St.10, which crosses R. (toll bridge) to Keokuk, Ia.

SIDE TRIP: On St.10 (E) 11m to **Carthage,** substantial community est. in 1837. **Carthage Jail,** property of Mormon Ch., was scene of murder of Jos. Smith in 1844. **Carthage College** (Luth.), coed., was est. in 1870. 39m **Macomb,** seat of **Western Ill. St. Teachers' College,** opened in 1902.

St.96 unites with St.10 for 4m. [Here St.10 turns (W) to **Ft. Edwards Mon.,** at Warsaw.] St.96 runs inland in straight line. **62.** J. with US24 (see).

### 67. QUINCY

C.B. & Q. & Wabash RRs. Greyhound & other buses. Mun. Airport (E. 10m on St.104). Quincy Mem. Bridge (free). Accoms. Steamboat excursions to Hannibal, Mo., from Levee. Golf, swim. & other recr. facils. in Ind. Mound, South, & other pks. Annual powerboat regatta. Info.: C. of C.

Quincy, seat of Quincy College & Notre Dame Academy, has beautiful setting along bluffs in Mark Twain's country, a few miles N. of Hannibal, Mo. (see). Along waterfront are numerous large pks. & most of the industrial plants. Quincy is mfg. & trade center for large area in 3 states. In 1822, John Wood (later Civil War gen. & gov.) came to explore Military Bounty Tract. Soon soldiers & adventurers built up small settlement which they named for the new Pres., John Quincy Adams, seat of Adams Cty. For many yrs. it was st.'s 2nd city, trans. & commercial center.

PTS. OF INT.: (1) In Washington Pk., center of bus. dist., **Site of 6th Lincoln-Douglas Debate,** marked by bronze bas relief by Lorado Taft. **Statue of John Wood.** (2) 425 S. 12th St., **John Wood H.** (O.1835), now Hist. Soc. Mus. of Quincy & Adams Counties; fine example of plantation style. (3) Main & 16th Sts., **Lorenzo Bull H.,** now Women's City Club; charming H. of pioneer period. (4) In Riverview Pk., **Statue of Geo. Rogers Clark** (by Chas. Milligan). (5) NE. sect., **Ill. Soldiers & Sailors H.** (1887). (6) S. limits, **Ind. Mounds Pk.** (7) 18th St. & College Ave., **Quincy College,** coed., under Franciscan Fathers; founded in 1860. (8) 8th & Vermont Sts., **Notre Dame of Quincy,** Cath. school for girls; founded 1867. (9) E. 27$^m$ from Quincy, **Silcam Springs St. Pk.;** more than 2,000 as. around former resort.

St.96 cont. (S) through fertile bottomlands. **91. KINDERHOOK.** J. with US36, over which tour turns (E) inland. **113. PITTSFIELD,** sett. by Mass. pioneers & known as gathering place of brilliant & cultured of early Ill. **120. DETROIT.** J. with St.100, which becomes main tour (S) along Ill. R. (see Ill. Waterway Tour). **171. PERE MARQUETTE ST. PK.** (f.pic.boat.swim.winter sports.lodge.cabins. refreshments.boat dock.mus.). **178. GRAFTON. 196. ALTON. 222. E. ST. LOUIS** (see E. St. Louis Trip IV for this sec.).

**Sec. 3: E. ST. LOUIS to KY. LINE (Cairo). 150. St.3**

**0. E. ST. LOUIS.** Tour follows St.3, paralleling Miss. R. through Amer. Bottom, once heart of Fr. empire in Amer. **4. CAHOKIA,** oldest town in Ill., founded in 1699 by missionaries, guided here by Tonti, of the Iron Hand (see). **42. RUMA.** [From here St.155 leads 7$^m$ (W) to **Prairie Du Rocher,** founded in 1722 as part of Miss. Bubble lands, & to **Ft. Chartres St. Pk.**] **55.5.** Rd. leads a mile of so from hy. (W) to **Ft. Kaskaskia St. Pk.** (pic.comp.), near Kaskaskia, 1st capital in Ill. (see E. St. Louis Trip I). **62. CHESTER.** St.3 runs close to R. for some miles, then veers (E) through sec. of **Shawnee Nat. For.** (see). **85. MURPHYSBORO.** From here hy. edges the bluffs, then crosses rugged Ozark country (many pic. sites & spectacular views). People in reg. show Southern ancestry in speech & customs; here & there are patches of cotton. **80. FOUNTAIN BLUFF** (W), curious formation more than 5 sq. miles in area; narrow Rd. to **Fire Tower** (O.lookout). **94. GRAND TOWER.** Motorboat to **Tower Rock** in Miss. R. **103. WOLF L.** (scenic drive follows Ozarks for 5$^m$). **108. WARE.** J. with St.146.

SIDE TRIP: On St.146 (E) 3$^m$ to **site of Cherokee Encampment,** where thousands of Inds. from Ga. encamped for winter of 1839. Some 2,000 died of starvation & cold. At 5.5$^m$ is **Union Cty. St. For.** (pic.).

**125. ST. ROADSIDE PK. 132. OLIVE BRANCH** (f.h.boat info.). **Horseshoe L. Game Refuge,** on 1,400-a. I.

**149. CAIRO**

Through RR. & bus conns. Accoms. & recr. facils. Golf (daily fee) at Egyptian Country Club, (N) 10$^m$ on US51. Steamboat excursions from Ohio Levee. Info. at Assoc. of Comm., 216 7th St.

Cairo, where spring begins in Feb., has atmosphere of South, with gingko trees & magnolias, canebrakes, cotton patches & catfish. It is still a river town of importance, on levee-protected peninsula bet. Ohio & Miss. Rs. Long steel barges float into the terminals, replacing packets of the past when this was biggest city in S. Ill. Because of concrete wall along Ohio Levee (improved by Fed. Gov. in 1936), Cairo was only city on lower river to be untouched by flood of 1937. From the beginning, the city turned toward the Ohio, & Ohio St., now lined with deserted taverns, warehs. & stores, was once noisy with traders, steamboatmen, & travelers of all kinds. City is residential except for industrial N. sec. In S. end, houses stand close together on sm. lots sold by early promoters. In other areas, Vict. mansions on ampler estates are scattered among modern bungalows. In center of city are schs., chs., homes, bus. & professional offices of Negro residents, about a third of total pop. Principal industries are cottonseed processing, warehousing & transshipping, & lumber milling. In country around, long known as "Egypt," the fertile delta soil produces oats, corn & hay, vegetables, fruit & watermelons.

Père Marquette & other explorers noted the finger of land at meeting of Ohio & Miss. Rs. & in 1702 a Fr. colony under Charles Juchereau de St. Denys set up ft. & tannery. Juchereau & others died of a mysterious disease, & the rest joined the Fr. at Mobile. In 1817, Wm. & Thos. Bird & John Comegys, St. Louis merchant, took up land within present city limits. Comegys had city & Bank of Cairo inc. in Jan. 1818, so named because of resemblance to city on the Nile. In 1820 Comegys died & so did his plan for a diked city. A 2nd attempt was made in 1837 when the Boston Yankee, Darius B. Holbrook, helped organize Cairo City & Canal Co. Levee was built, pop. rose to 1,000 within yr. but the co. failed in 1840. Most inhabitants left, & the flood of 1842 rolled over "the breeding place of fever, ague & death" Chas. Dickens had visited that spring. When traffic began on Ill. Cent. RR. bet. Cairo & Chi., Cairo got its finally successful start, & was inc. in 1857. During Civil War, it was concentration pt. for Union Army. In postwar yrs., it was most important city in S. Ill., with superior schs. & chs., sewers & sidewalks. Both R. & RR. shipping prospered, but gradually the steel rails triumphed over the steamboat & period of growth was over, although Cairo remains an important port.

PTS. OF INT.: (1) In pk. bet. 9th & 10th Sts., **"The Hewer,"** by Geo. Grey Barnard. (2) 1609 Washington Ave., **Pub. Lib.** (1883). Mus. has colls. of Ind. & hist. materials, incl. file of Cairo newspapers. (3) 2723 Washington Ave., **Rendleman H.**, outstanding among early Hs. (4) **Ohio Levee Wall,** bet. 2nd & 8th Sts. (5) 609 Ohio St., **Ohio Bldg.** (1858); Gen. Grant's hqs. (6) **Ill. Central Bridge** (1889.by Geo.S.Morrison). (7) **Ohio R. Hy. Bridge** (1938.by Ray Williams & others); one of country's notably beautiful bridges. (8) 2nd & Ohio Sts., **Halliday Hotel** (fee to non-guests), opened in 1859 as St. Chas. Hotel. Room 215 has furnishings from time when Gen. Grant was a guest. **Site of Ft. Defiance** is S. of hotel. (9) **Miss. R. Hy. Bridge** (1929.by J.A.L.Waddell). Main channel span affords view of 3 states & confluence of Rs. (sightseer's toll). (10) 4210 Sycamore St., **Swift & Co. Oil Mill** (O.appl.). (11) On St.3 (NW) 2.4$^{m}$, **Roberts Bros. Cotton Gin** (O.appl.), st.'s largest. **150. ILL.-KY. LINE.**

# CHICAGO

RRs. (22 trunk & 17 belt lines): Maj. Stas.: LaSalle & Van Buren, LaSalle St. Sta.; S. Dearborn & Polk Sts., Dearborn Sta.; Wells & Harrison Sts., Grand Central Sta.; Roosevelt Rd. & Mich. Ave., Central Sta.; W. Madison & Canal Sts., Chi. & NW. Sta.; Canal St. & Jackson Blvd., Union Sta. Buses: E. Randolph St. bet. State St. & S. Wabash Ave., Trailways; 1157 S. Wabash Ave., Union Bus Depot, Greyhound. 6000 S. Cicero Ave., Mun. Airport (observ.sm.fee). End of Grand Ave., Navy Pier, for Georg. Bay & other steamship lines. Cruises from Mich. Ave. Bridge. Accoms.: All kinds. Recr. info. at 425 E. 14th Blvd., Chi. Pk. Dist. For. Preserve Dist. provides pic. & camp sites, summer & winter sports facils. Annual Events: Theodore Thomas Mem. Concert, Orchestra Hall (early Jan.); Golden Gloves Tournament, Stadium (Feb.-Mar.); Internat. Sportsmen's Show, Navy Pier (Feb.-Mar.); Easter Sunrise Serv., Soldier Field; Mem. Day Parade; Ravinia Music Festival, Ravinia Pk. (July-Aug.); Chi. Reg. Artists Exhibition, Art Institute (June-Aug.); Chi.-Mackinac Races (July); Chicagoland Music Festival, Soldier Field (Aug.); Internat. Live Stock Exposition, Internat. Amphitheater (Nov.); numerous other music festivals, art exhibits, concerts, nationality group celebrations, regattas & trade shows. Info.: 1 N. LaSalle St., Assoc. of Com.; 2400 S. Mich. Ave., Ill. Auto Club. Observ. Towers: Board of Trade Bldg., Tribune Tower & Wrigley Bldg.

Chi., stretching 28$^{m}$ along L. Mich., is 2nd city in size & importance in U.S., its greatest livestock & grain-shipping market & distribution pt. & world's leading meat-packing center. Water-borne traffic in harbor exceeds that of Panama Canal. From lake front, city rolls back across former swamplands over more than 200-sq.-mile area, a fabric of neighborhoods, sm. towns & industrial communities. Site was key pt. on portage bet. Gt. Ls. & Gulf of Mex., on edge of country's richest agric. belt & midway bet. great ore & coal fields. Thousands of pioneers & foreign born were drawn into Chi.'s expanding labor market. Present pop. is one-fourth foreign born, with Poles, Germans, Russians, Itals. & Irish among largest groups. Most concentrated Negro community in world lives within sm. area bounded by 22nd & 67th Sts. & Cottage Grove & Wentworth Aves.

The name, Chicago, comes from Ind. word for "strong, powerful," applied by Miami to the R. because of pungent garlic beds along its banks. The modern metropolis justifies orig. meaning in its vigor & bigness. It has world's largest hotel (Stevens), largest commercial bldg. (Merchandise Mart) & one of largest stockyards. It is a city of spectacular sports, mammoth conventions, fabulous fairs, mass demonstrations & riots. Chi. has been, in turn, the pride of capitalistic enterprise & capital of political corruption, gangsterism & market speculation. It has also been country's greatest melting pot, hotbed of muckraking & leader of social reform, literary capital during "Amer. Renaissance" & home of univ. of internat. repute. Columbian Exposition, 1893, celebrated Amer.'s position as world power & set architectural standards for the nation. Cent. of Progress, 1933-34, flaunted miracles of science & technology. In 1940's, Univ. of Chi. accepted responsibility for administration of atomic energy labs. at Oak Ridge.

Along lake front is series of beautiful pks. & famous Mich. Ave. & L. Shore Dr., lined with great estates. Wacker Dr. follows curve of R. around the Loop, a towering mass of stone, concrete, steel & glass encircled by elevated tracks. From Board of Trade Bldg., city's tallest structure, a gigantic aluminum "Ceres," goddess of grain, looks down LaSalle St. Branches of Chi. R. cut rest of city into so-called N., S. & W. sides.

Hist. begins with the R. (see Ill. Waterway Tour). In 1673 Joliet & Père Marquette portaged from Des Plaines to Chi. R. In 1676, Father Allouez was greeted by Ill. Inds. & sailed his canoe over the ice of frozen L. About 1690 a Miami Ind. band est. 2 villages in vic., & Count Frontenac stationed garrison & trading post. Father Francois Pinet's Mission lasted from 1696 to 1702, & then Fr.-Ind. settlement declined. Jean Baptiste Point Sable, Santo Domingo Negro, built trading post in 1790's, & here 1st permanent white settler, John Kinzie, made his home in 1804. Blockhs. & stockade were erected by soldiers under Capt. John Whistler, grandfather of painter, & ft. was named for Henry Dearborn, Pres. Jefferson's Secy. of War. During War of 1812, ft. was evacuated, & soldiers, women & children on their way to Detroit were set upon by Inds. & more than half of them massacred. The Inds. burned Ft. Dearborn. It was not until Chi. was proposed as terminal for Ill.-Mich. Canal that settlement really began.

City was platted in 1830 & inc. in 1833. Settlers crowded in after Black Hawk War, & feverish speculation in land ensued. Surviving panic of 1837, Chi. became greatest grain market in the world in 1840's & 50's & by time of Civil War was world's leading lumber market & RR. center. Union Stock Yards were built & McCormick & other factories rose. Most of the 300,000 residents were flimsily housed, & sewage filtered into water supply, but mansions were rising along the L., mills, factories & distilleries were busy, & saloons, race tracks & bawdy houses flourished. In July 1871, Main Chi. R. was diverted into S. Branch; & on Oct. 8 the great fire began in the O'Leary barn. Within little more than a day, 250 Chicagoans were dead & thousands homeless & destitute. Nearly 18,000 bldgs. had been destroyed. Aided by people all over Amer. & Europe, reconstruction began immediately, & in next few yrs. a new city emerged. In 1892 the Drainage Canal was begun.

During last yrs. of 19th cent. nation-wide labor unrest found a focus in Chi. After RR. strike of 1877 was broken by Fed. troops, the struggle became more intense & bitter. Haymarket bombing & riot occurred in 1886; Alfred Parsons & 3 other leaders were hanged. Gov. John P. Altgeld, one of great figures in Chi. hist., pardoned 3 men who had been imprisoned. During Pullman Strike in 1894, Gov. Altgeld protested Pres. Cleveland's action in sending in Fed. troops. Altgeld was not reelected in 1896. During these same yrs. Hull H. was created (1889), Pub. Lib. & Civic Federation founded, Louis Sullivan & other Chi. architects developed the skyscraper, Theodore Thomas org. Chi. Orchestral Assoc., & Univ. of Chi. was opened (1892). In 1893 the "White City" on built-up marshlands (present Jackson Pk.) housed World's Columbian Exposition, & in 1896 Wm. J. Bryan made "Cross of Gold" speech at Democratic Nat. Convention. City also had gained unrivaled reputation for political corruption, organized vice & hoodlumism. With 1900's, the country's 1st juvenile court was est. & D. H. Burnham, architect of White City, drew up plan for civic development. During World War I, Wm. Hale (Big Bill) Thompson, an isolationist, was mayor, but Chi. entered the war with gusto & came out with swollen profits. Thousands of Negroes had come to replace workers drawn into armed forces, & conflict arose in congested areas. In South Side riot (1919),

22 Negro & 16 white persons were killed. In 1920's Chi. was notorious for gangsterism & corruption. Then came stock market crash, fall of Insull's empire & other financial structures, repeal of prohibition & imprisonment of Al Capone. Chi. suffered in the depression, but bravely opened Progress Exposition. Chi. still has breezy, light-hearted air, but its schs., libs., & other civic institutions are convincing evidence of maturity.

PTS. OF INT. DOWNTOWN: In **Grant Pk.** are: (1) Roosevelt Rd. & L. Shore Dr., **Nat. Hist. Mus.** (O.tours exc.Sun.cafeteria.1893.Gr.Ionic.by D.H.Burnham), one of world's leading museums; formerly called Field Mus. In Stanley Field Hall are Carl Akeley's groups of African natives. Of special note also are Malvina Hoffman's "Races of Mankind," Hall of the Stone Age, Egyptian & meteorite colls. (2) NE. of mus., **John G. Shedd Aquarium** (O.1924.Gr.Doric.by Graham, Anderson, Probst & White), one of finest in U.S. (3) End of Congress St. concourse, **Buckingham Fountain** (1927.by Bennett, Parsons & Frost, & Jacques Lambert), cited by "Encyclopedia Britannica" as "magnificent example of modern monumental fountain." (4) Mich. Ave., at Adams St., **Art Institute** (O.guides), 2nd largest in U.S. Connected with it are Sch. of Art, Goodman Mem. & Children's Theaters; Ryerson, Burnham & other libs. Main bldg. (Ital.Ren.by Shepley, Rutan & Coolidge) was Parliament of Religions Bldg., Columbian Exposition. In Hutchinson Wing is McKinlock Mem. Ct. with Carl Milles' (see) **Triton Fountain.** Notable colls. of 19th & 20th cent. Fr., Flemish primitive & Sp. painting. S. of Grant Pk. is **Burnham Pk.** (yacht harbor. beaches.playfields.pic.f.), incl. site of Cent. of Progress. (5) **Soldier Field,** scene of Dempsey-Tunney fight in 1927, Eucharistic Congress in 1926, Easter Sunrise Serv. & Chicagoland Music Festival. Causeway on Northerly I. leads to (6) **Adler Planetarium** (O.shows.1930.by Ernest Grunsfeld, Jr.), gift of Max Adler; Astronomical Mus. Reprods. of Ft. Dearborn & Jean Point Sable's Cabin (N.O.).

(7) **Loop,** bounded by Wabash Ave., Van Buren & Wells & Lake Sts. State St. is shopping center. (8) 215 N. Mich. Ave., **Chi. Galleries Assoc.** (O.free); work of leading Midwestern & Western artists. (9) 86 E. Randolph St., **John Crerar Lib.** (O. wks.est.1894), internat. known for medical, histological & other scientific colls. Adj. is **Lib. of Internat. Relations** (O.wks.). (10) Bet. Mich. Ave. & Garland Ct. on Randolph St., **Pub. Lib.** (1897.by Shepley, Rutan & Coolidge). Coll. began in 1872, after the fire, with several thousand books sent from London under inspiration of Thos. Hughes, author, & donated by Queen Victoria, Tennyson & other notables. (11) 216 S. Mich. Ave., **Orchestra Hall** (1904.Fr.Ren.by Dan. Burnham), home of Symphony Orchestra & Sunday Evening Club. Half cost of bldg. was pub. contribution in honor of Theo. Thomas (1835-1905), orchestra founder. (12) Congress St. bet. Mich. & Wabash Aves., **Auditorium** (1887-89.by Louis Sullivan), once housed most famous theater & hotel in Amer. (13) Wabash Ave. & 9th St., **Old St. Mary's Ch.** (Cath.1865), survivor of great fire; home of Paulist Choir. (14) State & Madison Sts., **Carson Pirie Scott Store** (1899.by Adler & Sullivan). (15) State, Washington & Randolph Sts. & Wabash Ave., **Marshall Field Store** (tours), one of largest & best known in world. (16) State & Madison Sts., **Mendel Bros. Store** (tours). (17) Clark & Washington Sts., **Chicago Temple** (Meth.Episc.1923.Goth.by Holabird & Roche); org. in 1831. (18) 16 S. Clark St., **Chi. Loop Orthodox Synagogue** (symbolic murals by Raymond Katz). (19) S. La Salle & Monroe Sts., **Chi. Stock Exchange** (gallery). (20) Clark St., bet. Adams St. & Jackson Blvd., **Fed. Bldg.** (1905.Rom.Corinth.by H.I. Cobb), scene of Standard Oil Co., Al Capone & other noted trials. (21) Jackson Blvd. & La Salle St., **Board of Trade** (observ.tower.gallery), world's largest grain exchange (org. in 1846). (22) 141 W. Jackson Blvd., **Mercantile Exchange** (gallery), world's largest market for trading in eggs, butter, potatoes. (23) La Salle & Adams St., **Field Bldg.** (1924.by Graham, Anderson, Probst & White), on site of 1st steel skyscraper, the Home Life Insurance Bldg., designed by LeBaron Jenney in 1803. (24) Wacker Dr. & Madison St., **Civic Opera Bldg.** (1929.by Graham, Anderson, Probst & White), promoted by Sam. Insull.

(25) **Mich. Ave. Bridge** (1920) spans R. bet. **Site of Fort Dearborn** & **Site of Earliest Settlement,** on N. bank. (26) On W. Plaza, **Wrigley Bldg.** twin units, one with clock tower (observ.sm.fee). (27) On E. Plaza, **Tribune Tower** (observ.sm.fee.tours). (28) Several blocks E., **Outer Dr. Bridge** (1937), said to be largest bascule bridge in world. (29) (W) along R. at N. Wells St., **Merchandise Mart** (1930.by Graham, Anderson, Probst & White), a Marshall Field enterprise.

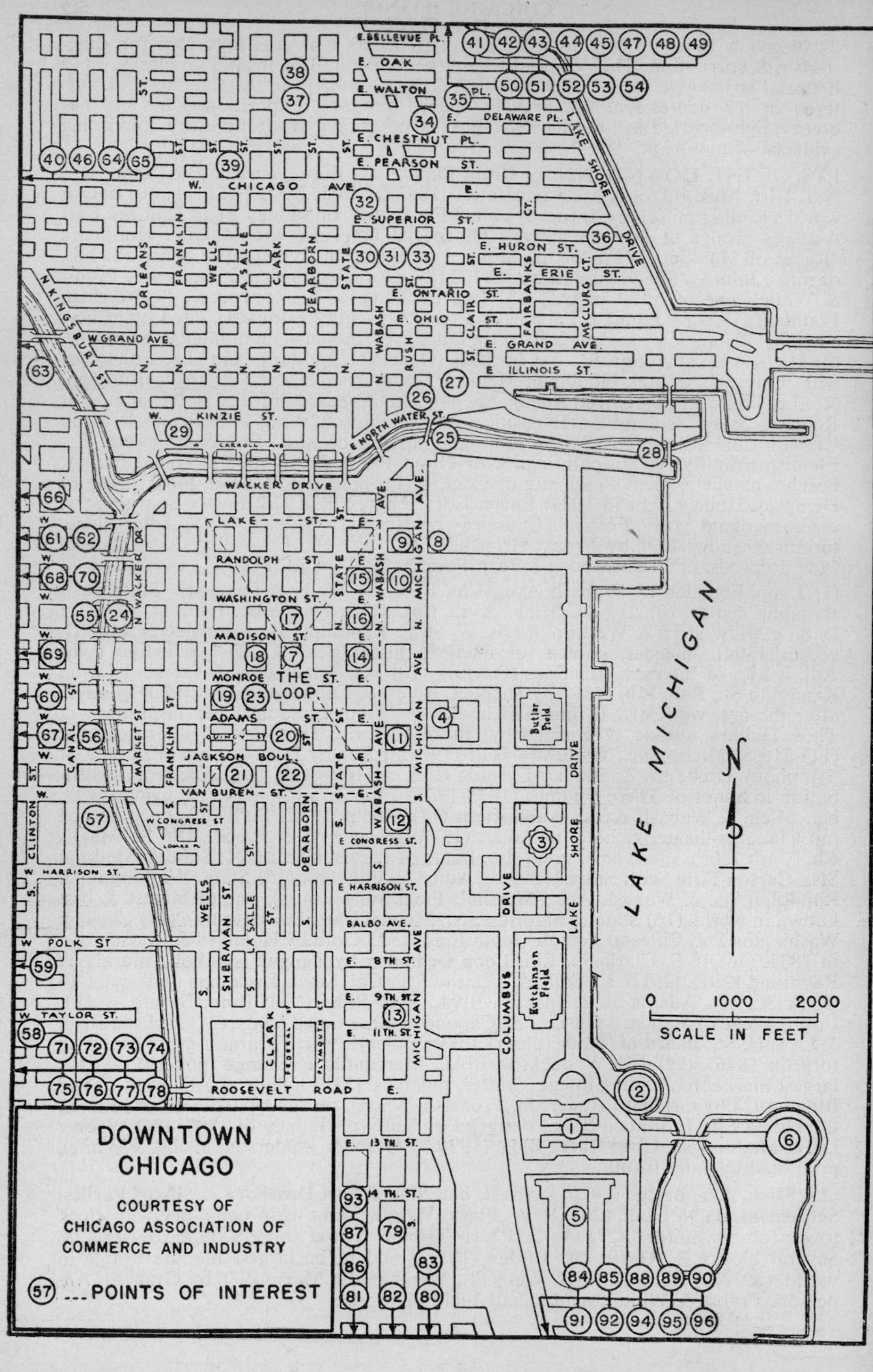
DOWNTOWN
CHICAGO
COURTESY OF
CHICAGO ASSOCIATION OF
COMMERCE AND INDUSTRY
57 --- POINTS OF INTEREST
SCALE IN FEET
0 1000 2000
LAKE MICHIGAN
THE LOOP

PTS. OF INT. NORTH SIDE: Here are Bughouse Sq. & remains of 19th cent. Gold Coast; modern towers & depressing tenements; an artist colony in outdated mansions; palatial cafes & cheap saloons. Along L. (N) is new Gold Coast. Rush St., paralleling Mich. Ave. through oldest part of city, has been called "combination of Manhattan's 52nd St. & Greenwich Village." Until its bridge was superseded by Mich. Ave. Bridge, this st. was sedately lined with mansions like **Cyrus Hall McCormick H.** at No.675. (30) 40 E. Erie St., **College of Surgeons** (O.wks.). (31) 50 E. Erie St., **John B. Murphy Mem. Auditorium.** (32) Superior & State Sts., **Holy Name Cathedral** (Cath.). (33) Wabash Ave. & Huron St., **St. James Ch.** (Episc.). **Chapel of St. Andrew** (1913.by Bertram Goodhue). (34) Mich. Ave. & Chestnut St., **Fourth Presb. Ch.** (Eng.Goth.by Ralph Adams Cram). (35) 919 N. Mich. Ave., **Palmolive Bldg.** (by Holabird & Root), topped by aluminum tower. (36) Along Lakeshore Dr. are: **Amer. Furniture Mart** (1924) & **Chi. Campus of Northwestern Univ.** (see Evanston below). **Montgomery Ward Mem. Bldg.** (Tudor Goth.by Jas.Gamble Rogers), houses oldest medical college in U.S.; Mus. (O) & Lib. (37) Walton Pl. & Clark St., **Bughouse Sq.,** near **Washington Sq. Pk.,** oldest pk. in city; dedicated by donor to free speech. (38) Across pk. on Clark St. is notable **Newberry Lib.** (O.wks. est.1887.Sp.Romanes.by Henry I. Cobb); rare items in humanities & genealogy, prints & maps.

(39) LaSalle St. & Chi. Ave., **Moody Bible Institute** (O), where several thousand students are trained for missionary serv. (interdenom.); founded in 1889 by Dwight L. Moody, evangelist. (40) 618 W. Chi. Ave., **Montgomery Ward & Co.** (O.tours on appl.), one of world's largest mail-order houses. (41) Along L. bet. North & Foster Aves., **Lincoln Pk.** (f.boat.pic.playfields), city's largest. Notable **Statue of Abr. Lincoln** (1887.by Saint-Gaudens). **La Salle Mon.** (1889.by Jacques de la Laing). **Garibaldi Mon.** (1901.by Gherardi). **U. S. Grant Mon.** (1891.by Rebisso). **Altgeld Mon.** (1915.by Borglum). (42) **Zoological Gardens** (O.yr.round). **Eugene Field Mem.** (1920.by Ed. McCartan). **Benj. Franklin Mon.** (1896.by Rich. Parks). (43) N. of Zoo, **Lincoln Pk. Conservatory** (O.free). **Bates Fountain** (1887.by Saint-Gaudens & MacMonnies). (44) 1600 North, **Chi. Hist. Soc. Mus.** (O.free.wks.Sun.sm.fee); series of 38 period rooms. (45) Clark St., bet. Ogden & Armitage Aves., **Chi. Acad. of Sciences Mus.** (O.free.1893.Ital.Ren.by Patton & Fisher). (46) 1121 N. Leavitt St., **Russian Holy Trinity Cathedral** (Gr.Orth.); noteworthy icons. (47) Sheffield Ave. & Melrose St., **Viking Temple,** serving Swedish neighborhood. (48) Webster & Sheffield Aves., **DePaul Univ.** (Cath.coed.founded 1898). **Adm. Bldg.** (Mod.Goth.). **St. Vincent's Ch.** (Romanes.). (49) Halsted St. & Belden Ave., **Presb. Theol. Seminary,** founded in 1829 & endowed by Cyrus McCormick. **Virginia Lib.;** exhibits from missions. (50) Broadway & Brompton Aves., **Wm. Booth Mem. College** (1914. Tudor Goth.by Holabird & Roche), Salvation Army sch. occupying Tilt mansion. On Clark St. (N) are (51) **Wrigley Field,** home of Chi.'s Cubs & (52) **Graceland Cemetery,** in which are **Getty & Ryerson Tombs** (by Louis Sullivan). N. of Lincoln Pk. on lakeshore are 2 outstanding Cath. schs. (53) **Mundelein College** (women) was founded at instigation of Cardinal Mundelein, 1930. **College Bldg.** (by J.W. McCarthy & Nairne Fisher). (54) **Loyola Univ.** (men), founded 1879 by Jesuit order, acquired beautiful lakeshore campus in 1922; recently purchased site for $12,000,000 medical & dental school. **Elizabeth M. Cudahy Mem. Lib.** (Mod.Romanes.by A.N.Rebori); incunabula & rare Jesuit items.

PTS. OF INT. NORTHWEST & WEST SIDE: N. Branch threads heavily industrialized sec., then flows (N) among pks., fors. & suburban villages; several colleges, large high schs., housing projects, hospitals & sanitoria in area. Sec. W. & S. of Loop was once great melting pot of Old World neighborhoods. Hull H. & other settlements are here. (55) 400 W. Madison St., **Daily News Bldg.** (1929.by Holabird & Roche). (56) Canal St. bet. Adams St. & Jackson Blvd., **Union Sta.** (1926.by Graham, Anderson, Probst & White). (57) Canal & Van Buren Sts., **Post Office** (1934.by Graham, Anderson, Probst & White), largest in world. (58) 538 De Koven St., **Site of O'Leary Barn,** where Fire of 1871 began. (59) 800 S. Halsted St., **Hull H.** (O), founded by Jane Addams in 1889, one of 1st in U.S. **Labor Mus. Benedict Art Gallery. Jane Addams Study.** (60) Adams & Des Plaines Sts., **St. Patrick's Ch.** (Cath.1896), oldest ch. edifice in Chi.; fine windows by Thos. O'Shaughnessy. (61) Des Plaines & Randolph Sts., **Site of Haymarket Bombing** (1886). (62) Randolph St. bet. Des Plaines & Sangamon Sts., **Farmers' Market;** to N., **Fulton St. Market.**

(63) Grand Ave. & Morgan St., **Chi. Commons** (est.1894), settlement where forerunner of "Survey" was published. (64) 1400 Augusta Blvd., **Northwestern Univ. Settlement** (O), in Polish neighborhood; founded in 1891. (65) Augusta Blvd. & Sacramento Ave., **Humboldt Pk.,** one of city's most beautiful; notable sculptures. (66) Central Pk. Ave. & Madison St., **Garfield Pk.** (summer & winter recr.facils.), with world-famous Conserv. (O.yr.round.4 maj.shows). (67) Central Ave. & Jackson Blvd., **Columbus Pk.,** landscaped in prairie style. (68) Ogden Ave. & Washington & Ashland Blvds., **Union Pk.,** where May Day parade traditionally starts; **Haymarket Riot Mon.** (69) Madison St. & Damen Ave., **Lewis Institute,** 4-yr. college founded in 1896; **Psychological Mus.** (O.est.1937). (70) Madison & Honore St., **Chi. Stadium,** where F. D. Roosevelt was 1st nominated for Presidency. (71) Bounded by Congress, Taylor & Wood Sts. & Wolcott Ave., **Medical Center** (O.appl.), incl. Cook Cty. Hospital & Sch. of Nursing; Loyola Univ. Sch. of Med., Univ. of Ill. College of Med. & Dept. of Pub. Welfare bldgs. (72) Bet. 14th & 16th Sts., Morgan St. & Racine Ave., **Old S. Water St. Market,** largest in U.S. (73) Homan Ave. & Arthington St., **Sears, Roebuck & Co.** (tours), hqs. of world's largest mail-order house. (74) Roosevelt Rd. & Sacramento Ave., **Douglas Pk.,** scene of Orthodox Jewish New Year ceremonial. (75) 3500 Douglas Blvd., **Jewish People's Institute** (O), social & educ. center. (76) 3448 Douglas Blvd., **Hebrew Theol. College** for Orthodox rabbis & leaders; noteworthy lib. (77) 26th St. & Western & Blue I. Aves., **Internat. Harvester Co.** (O.appl.), successor to Cyrus McCormick's works built in 1847. (78) E. end of Damen Ave. Bridge, **Marquette Mem.,** mahogany cross comm. place where Father Marquette made camp, 1674-75.

PTS. OF INT. SOUTH SIDE: Extending beyond Calumet R., this area cont. through interlocking communities to edge of Calumet cities of Indiana (see). Along lakeshore & in wooded suburbs are many of Chi.'s most beautiful Hs. Inland area is welter of industrial plants, stockyards & RR. yds. Black Belt, from 16th to 67th St., is a city in itself, where hundreds of thousands of Negroes live in area of about 6 sq. miles. In industrial area are Polish, Czechoslovak, & other communities, incl. Irish neighborhood described by J. T. Farrell. (79) 1463 S. Wabash Ave., **Coliseum,** in which Pres. candidates were nominated before 1932; **Wall of Libby Prison** is part of bldg. (80) Mich. Ave. & Cullerton St., in Gold Coast area, **Second Presb. Ch.** (1874.by Jas. Renwick); windows by Wm. Morris. (81) Around Cermak Rd. & Wentworth Ave., **Chinatown,** 3rd largest in U.S. **Chinese City Hall;** on 3rd fl. are Temple Shrine & Hall of Justice (O). (82) Wabash Ave. & 24th St., **Quinn Chapel** (org.1847), built by Negro congr. (83) 3300 Fed. St., **Armour Institute of Technology,** founded 1892. (84) End of 35th St., **Stephen A. Douglas Mon.** (1879.by Leonard Volk), near site of Camp Douglas (Civil War) & tracks of Ill. Cent. RR., which the "Little Giant" helped to est. Tomb is in base of shaft. (85) 700 Oakwood Blvd., **Abr. Lincoln Center** (O.by Frank Lloyd Wright), internat. inter-racial & inter-religious institution. (86) Halsted St. bet. Pershing Rd. & 47th St., **Union Stock Yards** (special train from Indiana Ave. makes loop tours over yards), where millions of animals are penned until removed to Wilson, Armour or Swift plants (tours) or shipped to feeders & outside packers. (87) 4630 McDowell Ave., **Univ. of Chi. Settlement,** founded 1894 by Wm. Rainey Harper, 1st pres. of Univ. (see below). (88) Cottage Grove Ave. & 49th St., **St. Xavier College** (Cath.women); founded 1912 as successor to academy opened in 1846. (89) Along 51st St. from South Pk. Way to Cottage Grove Ave., **Washington Pk.** (pic.swim.recr.facils.), well-equipped playground for Negro community. (90) On Midway Plaisance, **Fountain of Time** (by Lorado Taft). (91) Plaisance, Midway of Columbian Exposition, conns. pk. with wooded **Jackson Pk.** (f.boat.swim.pic.sports facils.boat harbor). At N. end is (92) **Mus. of Science & Industry** (O.restaurant), housed in reconstruction of Exposition's Fine Arts Bldg. (by Chas. Atwood). Exhibits incl. machinery of farming, bldg., mining (sm.fee), communication, travel, welding & other work; theater & lib. (93) 96th St. & Longwood Dr., in Ridge Pk. Fieldhouse, **Vanderpoel Mem. Art Gallery** (O.free). (94) E., around L. Calumet, is **Pullman,** model town built 1881 by Geo. M. Pullman for his employees. After epochal strike of 1894, Pullman Co. was denied by Ill. Supreme Ct. the right to lease to its workers, & town bldgs. were sold. (95) Along lake front at E. 89th St., **Carnegie-Ill. Steel Corp. Works** (O.appl.).

(96) **Univ. of Chicago.** Campus covers 100 as. along N. side of Midway, with 85 Goth. bldgs. in several quadrangles. City's 1st univ. was in operation 1857-86 on land donated by Stephen A. Douglas. In 1889 the Assoc. Bapt. Educ. Soc. took

action for est. of a new college, & $1,000,000 was pledged, $600,000 by John D. Rockefeller. Marshall Field donated land, & Univ. of Chi. was incorporated 1890. Wm. Rainey Harper, Yale Univ. Prof. of Hebrew, was 1st pres. & assembled notable faculty, & Rockefeller subscribed another $1,000,000 to implement his plans. Univ. is one of country's leading institutions in influence & scholarship, as well as one of its largest; adm. through 4 Divisions—Humanities, Biol., Phys. & Social Sciences; 6 professional schools; & Univ. College. On 59th St. at Dorchester Ave. is **Internat. H.** (1932.Holabird & Roche). Facing 59th St., Ida Noyes Hall (1916. Tudor Goth.by Shepley, Rutan & Coolidge), women's clubh. **Rockefeller Mem. Chapel** (nonsect.by Bertram Goodhue), striking adaptation of Goth. cathedral; **Laura Spelman Rockefeller Carillon.** In same block are **President's H., College Bldg., Lexington Hall** & **Breasted Hall** (1931. by Mayers, Murray & Phillip), named for the late Jas. H. Breasted (1865-1935), archaeologist, author & for many yrs. director of Oriental Institute, which has treasures of ancient civilizations. In block N., bet. 57th & 58th St., **Chi. Theol. Seminary** (coed.), affiliated with Univ.'s Divinity Sch.; founded by Congr. Ch. in 1855. Among seminary bldgs. (1928.by H.H.Riddle) are **Lawson Tower, Clarence Sidney Funk Cloisters, Thorndike Hilton Mem. Chapel** & **Graham Taylor Hall.** (E) is (affiliated) **Meadville Theol. Seminary**, founded in 1844. Main quadrangle occupies 4 blocks with entrance at **Mitchell Tower,** copied from Magdalen College, & **Hutchinson Hall.** Other bldgs. of Tower Group (1903. by Shepley, Rutan & Coolidge) line sunken garden of Hutchinson Ct. **Rosenwald Hall**; geol. & geographical mus. **Walker Mus.** (O.wks.), outstanding paleontological center. **Harper Mem. Lib.** (O.wks.), one of great libs. of world.

## TRIPS OUT OF CHICAGO

### I. CHICAGO (S) to MOMENCE. 52. St.1

Via: Calumet Pk., Harvey & Chicago Heights.

St.1 follows old Hubbard Trl. (see) through industrial centers, spreading suburbs & aborted subdivisions. **15.5. CALUMET PK.** At 13635 Western Ave. is main packing plant of **Libby, McNeil & Libby** (O.appl.). **16.5. RIVERDALE. 19. HARVEY,** industrial center promoted in 1890's by T. W. Harvey, lumberman. **20.5.,** J. with US6 (see). **23. WASHINGTON PK. RACE TRACK.** (Aug-Sept). Adj. pk. is **Homewood,** platted 1852. **23.5. GLENWOOD MANUAL TRAINING SCH.** (O), institutional farm & village for underprivileged boys, on edge of Valparaiso Moraine. On Moraine is **CHI. HEIGHTS 28.;** large steel, glass & other plants (O.appl.). J. with US30 (see). **Sauk Trl. For. Preserve** (pic.camp.) **33. CRETE. Lincoln Field Race Tracks** (Sept.). **40. BEECHER,** shipping pt. for farm area. **50.5. ST. JUDE'S SEMINARY** (Cath.O.Sun.& holidays). **52. MOMENCE,** old town on Kankakee R., once stopping place on Hubbard Trl.

### II. CHICAGO (SW) to JOLIET. 40. US66

Via: Cicero, Berwyn, (Brookfield Zoo), Lyons & Stateville.

US66 follows Jackson Blvd. to J. with Ogden Ave., on which it angles (SW) paralleling Des Plaines R. **7. CICERO,** independent industrial city of some 70,000 pop. Of 100 or more industrial plants, **Western Electric Co.,** Cermak Rd. & Cicero Ave., is largest. Al Capone had hqs. in Cicero & made town notorious until 1931. **Hawthorne Race Track** (Sept.-Oct.). **9. BERWYN,** large & almost wholly residential town. Just (W) is J. with Harlem Ave. on which US66 turns (S) for short distance, then (SW) on Joliet Rd. across watershed. **12.5., J.** with 1st Ave., on which, (N) $2^m$, is **Chi. Zoological Pk.** (pic.), one of largest in U.S. Ancient L. plain sweeps gradually (W) up to **Valparaiso Moraine,** which extends almost to Joliet. L. Chi., ancestor of L. Mich., was formed bet. this ridge & retreating ice sheet, & beautiful L. reg. was thus created. **36. STATEVILLE,** on US66A, modern penitentiary & prison farm.

**40. JOLIET** (see US30).

### III. Loop tour on US34 & St.65 (W) to AURORA & return on St.31 & US30 Alt. 85.

Via: Cicero, La Grange, (Downers Grove), Naperville, Batavia & Wheaton.

Trip runs through rolling country of Du Page Cty., sett. more than 100 yrs. ago & still delightfully rural, with Gr. Rev. farmhs., sm. wooden chs. in severely Goth. style, & only 4 mfg. centers. **0. CHICAGO.** US34 is united with US66 (see Trip II) as far as J. with St.42A. **11. LYONS,** near place of portage for Marquette & Jolliet.

**13.5. LA GRANGE.** J. with US45 (see). **21.5. DOWNERS GROVE** (1832), the pioneers' 1st "island in the midst of prairie." **Downer Mon.,** on grave of Pierce Downer, 1st settler. **23.5. LISLE.** J. with St.53.

SIDE TRIP: On St.53 (N) 1m to **Morton Arboretum** (O.free), est. by Jay Morton, son of founder of Arbor Day.

**29. NAPERVILLE,** oldest town in Du Page Cty. Most of pop. is native born, with many of German ancestry. **Kroehler Mfg. Co. Plant** (tours on appl.), est. in 1887; one of world's largest makers of upholstered furniture. **Evangelical Theological Seminary,** est. in 1873, affiliated with Northwestern Univ. (see). **North Central College,** founded as Plainfield College in 1861. **Old Main** (1870 & 1890). **New York H.** (1849). **Mrs. Bailey Hobson's H.** (O.appl.1830's), home of wife of town's 1st settler. Trip follows St.65 (W) to **AURORA** at **38.,** J. with US30 (see). Return trip turns (N) on St.31 (parallel to US30). **45. MOOSEHEART,** children's community maintained by L.O.O.M. (grounds O.guides), run by the young people; hospital, research labs., bank, auditorium. **47. BATAVIA,** one of earliest settlements after Black Hawk War; many Hs. of limestone that once made it the "Quarry City." City bldgs. are on island in Fox R. Near city are **Riverbank Labs.** (acoustical). **50. GENEVA,** attractive town spreading across Fox R.; many Gr. Rev. bldgs. J. with US30 Alt., over which trip cont.

SIDE TRIP: On St.31 (N) 2m from J. is **St. Charles,** long est. community in recr. area. **Potawatomie Pk.** (boat.swim.pic.f.& other facils.); amphitheater & scenic drives.

**61.** On US30 Alt. **WHEATON,** seat of Wheaton College & Theosophical Society center & birthpl. of Judge Elbert Gary (see). Town's 1st settlers were the Wheaton bros. in 1838. **Wheaton College** was org. as Ill. Institute in 1838 by Wesleyan Meth. ch.; reorg. in 1860 under Jonathan Blanchard; accredited, nonsect., liberal arts college, with high standards. **Blanchard Hall** (Vict.Goth.org.1854). **Theosophical Soc. Temple** (O.wks.by I.K.Pond); interpretative murals by R. B. Farley; notable lib. On Cty. Rd. (S) is **Warrenville** (sett.1832). **Col. Warren H.** (1834.Gr. Rev.). **Albright Gallery** (O.Sun.aft.1850's), in old ch. bought by A. E. Albright, painter, in 1920's. Adj. are studios of his artist sons: Ivan L., & Marvin M. (Zsissly). **63.5.** (N. of hy.) **GLEN ELLYN & LOMBARD. Lombard Ch.** (1869), typical "Amer. Goth." in wood, with vertical siding. **Lilacia Pk.;** annual festival. In Glen Ellyn are **Stacy's Tavern** (N.O.1837.Gr.Rev.) & **Meth. Meeting H.** (1839.Gr.Rev.). **68.** J. with St.83. Beyond J. is Rd leading (N) to **Elmhurst** (sett.1837), largest center in cty. (through RR. & bus conns. accoms.). **Elmhurst College,** coed. liberal arts sch. founded 1871. Orig. **Main Hall & Music Hall.** US30 Alt. cont. (E) on Roosevelt Rd. to lakeshore, at **85.**

## IV. CHICAGO (W) to ELGIN. 38. US20

Via: Oak Park, River Forest, Maywood & Melrose Park.

Trip follows City 20 from Michigan Blvd. (W) on Washington Blvd. to city limits. **10. OAK PK.,** world's largest village (pop.c.65,000). Some of Frank Lloyd Wright's most characteristic houses are here & in near-by River Forest. At 210 Forest Ave., **Thomas H.,** in prairie style. In **Blue Parrot Patio,** 1120 Westgate Ave., is Celebrity Room, with silhouettes of Wright's finest bldgs. Lake & Grove St., **Unity Temple** (1905.by Wright), spireless monolith in concrete. **First Congr. Ch.** (by Norman S. Patton); Biblical Mus. 621 Garfield Blvd., **Oak Pk. Conservatory** (O.free.chrysanthemum show, Nov.Dec.). **RIVER FOREST,** beautiful suburb developed around old Thatcher Sta., on Chi. & N.W. RR. At Chi. Ave. & Thatcher St., **Thatcher's Woods,** former lands of D. G. Thatcher. **Trailside Mus. of Nat. Hist.** (O.free) occupies Thatcher H. (1856). At Division & Bonnie Brae Sts. are yellow-brick bldgs. of **Concordia Teachers College** (Luth.); good lib. Forest Ave. & Division St., **Rosary College** (Cath.), liberal arts sch. for women, housed in fine Goth. bldgs. (by Ralph Adams Cram.). Division St. at Harlem Ave., **Dominican House of Studies,** seminary. **12. MAYWOOD,** good-sized industrial town. **14.5.** J. with US20 (see). Trip angles (NW) through dairy country. **20.5. ADDISON,** German Luth. center for more than 100 yrs. Near **ONTARIOVILLE, 30.,** is **Ill. Pet Cemetery. 36. ELGIN** (see), industrial center on Fox R.

## V. CHICAGO (W) & (N) to WIS. LINE. 65. City 12, US12.

Via: Park Ridge, Des Plaines, L. Zurich, Wauconda, Fox L., Chain O' Lakes St. Pk. & Richmond.

City 12 follows Mich. Blvd. & Lake Shore Dr. to J. with Foster Ave., then W. on Foster Ave. **17. PARK RIDGE,** large suburb among wooded hills. Trip cont. (NW) through great summer playground among glacial Ls. in Fox R. valley. **21.5.** City 12 unites with US12 just N. of **DES PLAINES** (sett. 1830's.). Annual Meth. summer camp (hotel & cotts.). **37.5. L. ZURICH.** Popular resort village is on E. shore. **54. FOX LAKE,** resort village (bathh.pic.grounds.dance halls.cottages.restaurants). **Chain-O'-Lakes St. Pk.** (f.boat.hunt.bathh.pic.camp.sports facils.), one of major recr. areas of Midwest. Among largest Ls. are Fox, Grass, Pistakee, Nippersink & L. Catherine. **59. SPRING GROVE FISH HATCHERY** (O). **64. RICHMOND,** resort village; sett. 1837. **65. WIS. LINE.**

## VI. CHI. (N) to WIS. LINE (Kenosha). 53. St.42

Via: Evanston, Wilmette, Kenilworth, Winnetka, Glencoe, Highland Park, Lake Forest, N. Chicago, Waukegan & Zion.

St.42 is lakeshore drive through beautiful suburbs & pks. & past Mundelein College & Loyola Univ. (see Chi. North Side above).

### 12. EVANSTON

901 Davis St., Chi. & N.W. Ry.; 909 Church St., Chi., Milwaukee RR.; 79 W. Monroe St., N. Shore Line. 1201 Central St., Evanston Bus Co. Community golf course & (daily fee) clubs. Northwestern Univ. & Children's theaters. Annual North Shore artists' exhibit at Art Center. Info.: 519 Davis St., C. of C.

Evanston is home of Northwestern Univ. & Nat. College of Education & the nat. hqs. of W.C.T.U. Adj. Chi., it has noticeably different character, distinguished by wide, shady, uniformly lighted sts. & lake frontage given over to pks., beaches & private estates. Industries are restricted to well-defined areas. In 1674 Father Marquette stopped in harbor at present Grosse Pt., & 1st settlement was made here in 1854. A yr. later, Northwestern Univ. was opened, & village named in honor of John Evans, a trustee.

PTS. OF INT.: (1) 1703 Orrington Ave., **Pub. Lib.** (1904); Hist. Soc. Mus. & Art Center. (2) 1730 Chi. Ave., **Frances E. Willard H.** (O.free), now a mus., was family home of famous Temperance leader. Hqs. of W.C.T.U. are in brick bldg. to rear. (3) **Grosse Point Lighth.** (N.O.1865). (4) 2770 Sheridan Rd., **Nat. College of Education** (est.1886), accredited 4-yr. college giving training for teaching & parenthood; cooperates with Chi. social agencies. **Harrison Hall** houses well-equipped Children's Sch. & 3 libs. incl. Lib. of Childhood. (5) Haven St., opp. Northwestern Univ., **Seabury-Western Theol. Seminary** (Episc.), created in 1933 as union of Seabury Divinity Sch. (Faribault, Minn.1858) & Western Theol. Seminary (Chi.1883). College bldgs. (1929.Goth.) incl. **Anderson Mem. Chapel. Hibbard Oriental** & **Gregory Mem. Libs.** Foot of Garrett Pl. bet. Willard Pl. & Tech. Institute (see below), **Garrett Biblical Institute,** graduate (Meth.Episc.) theological school, founded 1855. (6) L. Mich. shore, bet. Clark & Lincoln Sts., **Northwestern Univ.,** on campus of 75 as. with 84 bldgs.; one of leading institutions of higher education in U.S. It was est. 1851 as nonsectarian college, although its founders—Grant Goodrich, Dr. John Evans & Orrington Lunt—were of Meth. faith. Evanston College for Ladies, founded in 1871, with Frances E. Willard as pres., was absorbed by Univ. Northwestern incl. Technological Institute, Grad. Sch., College of Liberal Arts, Schs. of Commerce, Journalism, Speech, Education & Music, on Evanston campus; & in Chi., Medical & Dental Schs., Sch. of Law & Univ. College. On James A. Patten Campus (N): **Technological Institute** (tours. 1942), largest bldg. on campus; gift of W. P. Murphy. **Men's Quadrangle. Patten Gymnasium,** dedicated 1940. **Dyche Stadium** is (W) on Central St. **Dearborn Observatory** (O.Fri.night), on lakefront; has equipment (1863) from old Univ. of Chi. **Howes Mem. Chapel** (O. early Eng. Goth). On Milton H. Wilson Campus (S): **Lunt Bldg.** (1893), gift of a founder. **Deering Lib.** (by J.G.Rogers), beautiful limestone & marble bldg. in style of King's College; coll. of World War II underground publications of Denmark, Greece & Norway. **Univ. Hall** (1869), with clock tower (1879). **Annie May Swift Hall. Mineralogical Lab.** (O.). **Old College** (1855). **Fisk Hall** (Romanes.1898), former Evanston Acad. From S. campus (W) are **Women's Quadrangles, Scott Hall,** social center, & **Sch. of Music.**

Bordering Evanston (N) is **Wilmette,** largest N. shore community. Outstanding pt. of int. as **Bahá'í House of Worship** (by Louis Bourgeois); cornerstone laid in 1912, inter. to be completed by 1953. This graceful, 9-sided temple will be surrounded by college, hospital & other bldgs. Architecture & ornament (designed by Bourgeois) symbolize basic beliefs—unity of religion, cooperation with scientific & social organizations; world federal gov.; equal opportunity; destruction of divisive prejudices. First Bahá'í temple was built in Caucasus by Persian colony in 1890's. The Wilmette nat. temple is only one in America. **20. KENILWORTH. Graves of Eugene & Mrs. Field,** in churchyard of Holy Comforter Ch. (Episc.), 333 Warwick Rd. **22. WINNETKA,** large & attractive suburb, inc. 1869; became widely known for experiment in publ. schools designed to teach children self-gov. At 584 Lincoln St. is Hadley Correspondence Sch. for the Blind. Another village with progressive sch. system is **GLENCOE, 25.** Large residential suburb of **HIGHLAND PK., 29.,** began with stagecoach tavern (1834). **Ravinia Pk.** (S), once an amusement pk., is now scene of Ravinia Music Festival (July-Aug.). **32. FORT SHERIDAN,** used in Sp.-Amer. War; permanent unit of Fifth Army Area. **35. LAKE FOREST,** college town & wealthy residential suburb. Sheridan Rd. & Deerpath Ave., **Lake Forest College,** ranking coed., nonsect., liberal arts college; chartered in 1857 under Presb. auspices. **College Hall** (1878.remod.), orig. bldg.; **Reid Mem. Lib.** (1889) & **Chapel; Durand Commons & Plaza** (1907-08). Across Sheridan Rd. is **Presb. Ch.** (1871), org. in 1859. 360 Deerpath Ave., **Pub. Lib.;** won Craftsmanship Award in 1931. Westleigh & Sheridan Rds., **Barat College of the Sacred Heart** (Cath.), liberal arts college for women. Fine red-stone **College Bldg.** (1904) stands in midst of 45-a. wooded campus.

**40. GREAT LAKES NAVAL TRAINING STA.** (O.), one of largest in U.S. Beyond is industrial suburb of **N. CHICAGO.** Along L. is **Foss Pk.** (summer camp sites). **43. WAUKEGAN,** mfg. center with busy harbor; on site of Ind. village. N. is **Dunes Pk.** (playgrounds.pic.camp.sm.fee); on Chi. & N.W. RR. Flora of special int. **50. ZION,** founded in 1901 by John Alex. Dowie, organizer of Christian Cath. Apostolic Ch. Lace, cement & other factories were est. by W. G. Voliva, who succeeded Dowie. At first a typically theocratic community, Zion has been modernized but still enforces fairly strict blue laws. Annual Passion Play. **Zion H. & Zion Adm. Bldg.,** on Elijah Ave. St.42 crosses dairy. reg. of which Zion & **WINTHROP HARBOR, 52.,** are centers. **53. ILL.-WIS. LINE.**

## E. ST. LOUIS—ILLINOIS

14 Missouri Ave., Relay (RR). Depot. 505 Missouri Ave., Greyhound Bus Sta. Off St.3 (S) 2m from city, Curtiss Airport. (See also St. Louis, Mo.). Good accoms. & recr. facils. Info.: C. of C., Spivey Bldg.

East St. Louis, important meat-packing & mfg. center, is surrounded by smaller industrial suburbs of big city across R. Reg. is assoc. with Geo. Rogers Clark, who took possession of Northwest during Rev. Bet. Cahokia at outskirts & downriver Kaskaskia were trading post & fts., Fr. missions & settlements, taken by Brit. in 1763 & then conquered by Clark ("Washington of the West") in 1778, by tact instead of bloodshed.

### TRIPS OUT OF EAST ST. LOUIS

#### I. E. ST. LOUIS (S) to FT. KASKASKIA ST. PK. 57. St.38 Cty. Rd.

Via: Cahokia & Ft. Chartres St. Pk. St.3 crosses Amer. Bottom where Fr. colonists made 1st settlements in st. & created civilized life in the wilderness, making friends with Inds. & dealing prosperously in fur. **3.5. CAHOKIA POWER PLANT** (O.appl.). **4. CAHOKIA,** an islet in the industrial sea; oldest town in Ill., home of ultramodern Parks College. In 1698 Seminary of Foreign Missions est. mission here among Tamaroa Inds., & Cahokia remained only Miss. Valley settlement not under Jesuit jurisdiction. After ft. passed to Brit. in 1765, the Cahokians were undisturbed in their way of life. When 30 of Clark's Kentuckians & a multitude of Fr. who had taken oath of allegiance arrived at Cahokia one summer day in 1788, the ft. was surrendered without a shot being fired. When the Brit. & Ind. allies attacked Sp. city of St. Louis in 1780, Clark crossed R. from Cahokia to aid Don Fernande de Leyba. There is evidence that Terese de Leyba, the Gov.'s sister, was the 1 woman loved by the leader of the Big Knives. She went back to Spain, & entered a convent, where she died 2 yrs. after Clark's death (1818). In 1795, Cahokia became seat of cty. covering about three-quarters of what is now Ill. PTS. OF INT.: **Cahokia Cth. St. Mem.** (O.restaurant.1760.by Francois Saucier). It was used as cth., 1793-1814, &

then as saloon. From St. Louis World's Fair in 1904, it was moved to Jackson Pk., Chicago; then, in 1939, brought back to orig. site & faithfully rest., with vertical-log walls, falling eaves & veranda. At J. of St.3 & St.157, **Ch. of the Holy Family** (1799), oldest ch. in Ill. Near-by is handsome new ch. & **Old Cahokia Cemetery.** E. of Ch., **Jarrot Mansion** (O.c.1800.Col.), oldest brick H. in Ill. Across hy., **Parks College of Aeronautical Technology,** called "Harvard of the Air." Est. as private sch. in 1927, it is oldest Federally-approved aviation college in U.S. (1928) &, in 1946, it became college of St. Louis Univ. (see).

**8.5. DUPO** (Prairie du Pont). **15. COLUMBIA,** an attractive German settlement. **25. LEMENS.** J. with Rd.

SIDE TRIP: On Rd. (S) 11$^m$ to **Renault,** named for director of mining in John Law's Mississippi Bubble (1718-20) scheme, aimed to pay off Fr. nat. debt by exploiting La. Terr. Disappointed in dreams of gold & silver, the expedition became a colony with several hundred Santo Domingo Negroes, brought be Renault.

**42. RUMA.** J. with St.155.

SIDE TRIP: On St.155 (SW) 7$^m$ to **Prairie Du Rocher,** founded in 1720's by Law's Fr. colonists. 11$^m$ **Fort Chartres St. Pk.** (pic.facils.mus.), on Miss. R., on site of last ft. in N. Amer. to fly Fr. flag. The 1st Fort du Chartres was wooden stockade built in 1720 & rebuilt in 1727. In 1753-56, the famous engineer, Vauban, built great stone stronghold, pride of New France. In 1765 it became Ft. Cavendish, seat of Brit. gov. in Ill. country until 1772. **Gateway** & combined **Chapel** & **Guardh.** are reconstructed & orig. **Powder Magazine** restored.

**55.5.** J. with Rd. leading 1.5$^m$ (W) to **Ft. Kaskaskia St. Pk.** (pic.facils.). Kaskaskia, one of principal Fr. settlements & 1st capital of Ill., was destroyed when Miss. R. changed its course & overflowed neck of land bet. it & Kaskaskia R. Kaskaskia today lies bet. old & new channels, the only part of Ill. W. of the great R. **Earthworks** of ft. are on crest of the bluffs, **Garrison Hill Cemetery & Pierre Menard H.** (O.1802. Fr.Col.), at foot of the hill. Settlement, founded in 1703, petitioned for protection during Fr. & Ind. War, & palisaded ft. was built. In 1765 the Fr. destroyed it rather than turn ft. over to Brit.

Geo. Rogers Clark, born (1752) in Va., was 2nd of 10 children. Five of the brothers were Rev. officers, & Wm., the youngest, shared fame of Meriwether Lewis. At 19, the tall, red-haired, dark-eyed Virginian took up land in Ky. & gained a following. Ky. had always been neutral ground for all tribes, & the Inds. resented the white settlers. Clark saw necessity for defense of the frontier &, in 1776, influenced Va. Assembly to org. Kty Cty. & aid the frontier. Clark conceived daring plan of possessing Fr. key fts. in Miss. Valley—Cahokia, Kaskaskia & Vincennes (see Indiana) —& eventually, Detroit (see Mich.). In summer of 1778, he had 175 frontiersmen, scouts & Ind. fighters under ruthless discipline on Corn I. (see Ky.). The men set out on June 24, 1778, marching single file over wilderness trls., each man with hunting knife, hatchet & rifle. On evening of July 4th, they arrived at Kaskaskia, & within a few minutes the ft. was taken peacefully. The Fr. awoke to find the dreaded Big Knives in their village, but Clark's handling was notable for sagacity & tact, & he could announce that France was supporting the Rev. The Kaskaskians joined in the march on Cahokia (see above). Father Gibault carried the news to Vincennes, which was "captured without an American present." Clark's dealing with the Inds. in particular reveals his extraordinary flair for leadership. The Meadow Inds., a vagrant band, tried to surprise him in his Cahokia hqs. At the council, Clark ordered that the "silly" Inds. who had "tried to catch a bear asleep" should be treated like squaws. Then the Inds. pleaded with him to smoke the peace pipe. In Feb. 1799, Clark began arduous march to retake Vincennes, which Gen. Hamilton had recaptured. Clark's men crossed the Ill. R., wading for hours in icy water, the Little Wabash, Embarrass & Big Wabash Rs. to surprise Hamilton. Beyond Vincennes was Detroit, but "for want of a few men," due to bankruptcy of Va.'s treasury, Clark was denied that victory. Neither he nor his men had been paid, & his lands were mortgaged to finance expeditions. After the Kentuckians were defeated at Blue Licks, Gov. Benj. Harrison censured Clark & demanded vouchers so that accounts could be settled. The auditor could find no vouchers. Under Jas. Wilkinson (see), the adventurer-soldier who had been in Conway Cabel against Washington, an anti-Clark campaign labeled the great frontiersman a marauder, cheat & drunkard. Clark's career was at an end. The Va. Assembly, in 1812, presented him with annual pension of $400. Half-paralyzed & old at 56, Clark died at Locust Grove, in Feb.,

1818. Nearly 100 yrs. later, in 1913, more than 2,000 vouchers were found among old documents in Lib. of Congress. Clark's name was cleared of reproach & a mem. unveiled in Charlottesville (see Va.), where he was born. The noted Draper Coll. of Clark material is in lib. of Wis. St. Hist. Coll. (see Wis.).

**II. E. ST. LOUIS (E) to LEBANON. 22. US50.**

Via: Grand Marais St. Pk. & French Village. Trip follows W. end of Trace Rd., from Louisville, Ky., through Vincennes, Ind. to Cahokia. At E. edge of town is J. with Kings Hy. which runs (S) 1$^{m}$ to **Grand Marais St. Pk.** (pic.swim.), improved recr. area with several Ls., riding stables & trls. **6. FRENCH VILLAGE,** remains of old settlement. **11.** J. with St.159.

SIDE TRIP: On St.159 (S) 5$^{m}$ to **Belleville,** industrial center on bluffs at edge of Amer. Bottom. Town site was platted in 1814, but large German pop. dates from development of coal fields in 1830's. Has many brick Hs., built when town was brickmaking center 100 yrs. ago. In vic. is **Scott Field,** hqs. of Air Forces Tech. Sch.

**18. JOHN MASON PECK MEM.** (st. pic. ground), on site of Rock Spring Seminary, 1st institution of higher learning in Ill.; founded by Bapt. missionary in 1827, it is now Shurtleff College, in Alton (see below). **22. LEBANON,** early 19th cent. town; home of **McKendree College,** oldest Meth. college in Middle West, founded by pioneers in 1828 as Lebanon Seminary; on beautiful campus in highest part of town. **Old Main** (1850). **Mermaid Inn** (N.O.1830), where Lincoln, Dickens & other noted travelers stopped.

**III. E. ST. LOUIS (E) to GREENVILLE. 40. US40**

Via: Cahokia Mounds St. Pk. **4. FAIRMONT CITY,** industrial suburb; large Mexican pop. **6.5. CAHOKIA MOUNDS ST. PK.,** (mus.camp.pic.refreshments. facils.) around Great Cahokia Mound & 80 or more smaller earthworks. **Cahokia Mound,** usually called Monks Mound because of Trappist monastery that stood at base (1809-13), is largest orig. earthwork in U.S., covering more than 13-a. base of Great Pyramid of Cheops. In form of truncated pyramid, it rises by 4 terraces to 100'. The village, of which this was center, extended over site of E. St. Louis & as far as Collinsville Bluffs. In **Mus.** are exhibits of handiwork of these agricultural people. **L. Cahokia** fills pit from which clay & gumbo were taken to build mounds. **11.5. COLLINSVILLE,** coal-mining & mfg. center; founded in 1817 by 5 Collins bros. from Conn. **Collins H.** (1821). **Blum Mfg. Plant** (O), where cowbells have been made by hand since 1880. **Miners' Institute,** built in 1917 by local United Mine Workers, is labor center, with theater. **19.5. TROY,** small mining center. Farther E., US40 enters dairy reg. **31.5. HIGHLAND,** dairy center on Looking Glass Prairie; sett. in 1830's by Swiss. **Wicks Organ Co.** is noted for technical improvements. **50. GREENVILLE,** seat of Bond Cty. & home of Greenville College; also home of **Pet Milk Co.** (O.appl.) & other manufacturers. Rbt. Ingersoll, freethinker, lived in Greenville for several yrs. while his father occupied Congr. pulpit. **Greenville College,** liberal arts sch. under Free Meth. Ch., occupies site & orig. bldg. of earlier Almira College for Women. On St.140 is **Greenville City Pk.** (pic.camp.boat.f.), around L. Greenville.

**IV. E. ST. LOUIS (NW) to PERE MARQUETTE ST. PK. 50. US67 Alt. & St.100.**

Via: (Venice), Madison, Granite City, Hartford, E. Alton, Alton, Grafton. A little W. of hy. are industrial suburbs of **National City** & **Venice,** est. in 1804; conn. with St. Louis by McKinley Bridge (toll). Below bridge is **Kerr I.,** Negro community. Bet. Venice & National City is Brooklyn, another Negro community. **6.5. MADISON,** 2nd largest of group of industrial suburbs, is a steel town on banks of Miss. R. **8. GRANITE CITY,** largest of group, named for its chief product. **Granite City Steel Works** & **Commonwealth Steel Mills** (N.O.) are near center of town. Beyond this industrialized area lie acres of cornfields in black, fertile soil protected against flood. **19. HARTFORD,** sm. settlement around large tannery, at edge of another industrial belt where sm. communities cluster around Shell & Standard Oil refineries. **22.5. LATON. Western Cartridge Co.** (O.appl.).

SIDE TRIP: On St.159 (E) 8$^{m}$ to **Edwardsville,** named for Ninian Edwards, Terr. Gov. when town was platted, 1813. Jas. Gillham, 1st settler, came c.1800, & soon many S. Carolinians followed. Coal mining became chief industry, as it is now. **Cty. Hist. Soc. Mus.** (O.appl.), in Cth.; Ind. & pioneer relics.

**26.5. ALTON,** seat of Shurtleff College & an important industrial center in Miss. Valley. A few miles (NW) is confluence of Mo. & Miss. Rs. Bus. dist. spreads along

R. where steamboats collected freight at one of leading 19th cent. ports. Back among the hills are fine residential areas, with many Hs. capped by lookouts, from which merchants watched R. traffic. Close to R. are shacks & tiny gardens of many Negroes & foreign-born residents. The 1st white settler was a Frenchman in late 18th cent. In 1837, several early settlements were inc. as Alton. One of leading plants is **Owen-Illinois Glass Co.** Alton is famed as home of Elijah Lovejoy who fought lonely battle against slavery. Born at Albion, Me., in 1802, he went to St. Louis, Mo., as Congr. minister in 1827, became devoted to abolitionist cause & left pulpit to edit the "Times." In 1833, the "Observer" appeared, devoted to emancipation. In 1835, public sentiment forced Lovejoy to move to Alton, where "Observer" cont. until Aug., 1837. His native moderation changed to passionate denunciation of the "whip of the republican task master." Three times his presses were destroyed by mobs, & 3 times his friends rallied to his aid. Stubbornly he ordered a 4th press. An armed mob fired the wareh. & shot Lovejoy as he came from the bldg. On his grave in local cemetery is written (in Latin): "Here lies Lovejoy. Spare him now that he is buried." Last of Lincoln-Douglas debates was held in Alton.

PTS. OF INT.: (1) Broadway & Washington Sts., **Owen-Illinois Glass Co.** (O), one of largest of its kind in world. Power plant & various shops are housed in walls of translucent glass. (2) End of Monument Ave., at entrance to Cemetery, **Elijah Lovejoy Mon.** (1897). (3) Foot of Market St., **Site of Lincoln-Douglas Debate,** Oct. 15, 1858. (4) In N. Alton is **Confed. Soldiers' Cemetery,** where victims of 1863 smallpox epidemic are buried. (5) College & Seminary Aves., **Shurtleff College,** granting B.A. degrees in liberal arts & music & offering pre-professional courses. Dr. Benj. Shurtleff, of Boston, was a principal benefactor. **Academic Hall** (1832). (6) 2$^{m}$ (N) on St.111, **Monticello College,** liberal arts college & sch. for girls; founded in 1853 by Benj. Godfrey, Cape Cod seaman.

Trip cont. (W) from Alton on St.100. **38.5.** J. with dirt Rd. which runs (S) 4$^{m}$ to **Principia College,** liberal arts, coed. sch. for children of Christian Scientists. Bldgs. (Goth.) are arranged as in a village, with College Chapel spire (Wren style) rising among the trees. St.100 cont. (W) from J. to **GRAFTON,** meeting of Ill. & Miss. Rs. **52. PERE MARQUETTE ST. PK.** (lodge.guest houses.group camp.boat.dock.f. boat.swim.pic.), st.'s largest pk. **Trailside Mus. McAdams Peak** (lookout). **Quitt Peak,** highest in pk.

## ROCK ISLAND & MOLINE

Quad Cities area incl. Rock Island, Moline, East Moline & the larger city of Davenport, Iowa (see). The Ill. cities have developed largely on peninsula bet. Rock R. & the Miss. R., which flows (W) past their industrial & bus. dists. On the island of Rock I., in the Miss., is large U.S. Arsenal.

Through RR. & bus conns. in Rock I. & Moline. Moline Airport, 7$^{m}$ (SE) on US150. Good accoms. & recr. facils. incl. mun. swim. pool & pub. golf courses. Annual Pow Wow (Labor Day wk. end) in Black Hawk St. Pk. (see below). Info.: Moline Assoc. of Com., 5th Ave. Bldg.; Rock I. C. of C., Ft. Armstrong Hotel. Miss. R. Bridges: US6 crosses Rock R. into E. Moline & then Miss. R. over Iowa-Ill. Mem. Bridge (toll) to Bettendorf, Iowa, by-passing downtown Rock I. & Davenport. US67 crosses Rock R. & W. edge of Rock I., then Miss. R. over Centennial Bridge (toll) to J. with US61 in Davenport. Gov. Bridge (fee) conn. Rock I., U.S. Arsenal & Davenport. Some distance (S) & (W) of metrop. area, St.92 crosses Muscatine Bridge (toll).

Rock I. & Moline are in many ways indistinguishable, & their history & development have been much the same. Economy of both depends mainly on the Arsenal, one of largest in U.S., & on tremendous farm-implements industry. E. Moline, much smaller, is almost wholly industrial. Moline is generally known as "The Plow City" because of century-old Deere Plow works & plants of Minneapolis-Moline Implement & Internat. Harvester Companies; but Rock I. has Farmall Works of Internat. Harvester Co. & J. I. Case Co. plants. Augustana College & Black Hawk St. Pk. are within city limits of Rock I., while to Moline belong Prospect & Riverside Pks. & large airport. Ill. Inds. had villages on Rock R. (see US20), & it was to them that Father Marquette came in 1673; but about 1680 they were driven out by Fox & Sauk. In 1815, Col. Geo. Davenport came to Ft. Armstrong, & white settlers began to claim Ind. lands. Among early settlers was a doctor at the ft. & his Negro servant, Dred Scott, who was later to ask for freedom on ground that he had lived in free states of Ill. & Minn. Rock I. Cty. was org. in 1833 & present city named in 1841. Moline was inc. in 1848. Steamboat era was at its height, & hundreds of boats docked here. John Deere brought plow factory from Grand Detour in 1847, & in 1855, Rock I. RR. spanned Miss. R. with its 1st RR. bridge, declared a "mammoth nuisance" by steamboat interests. Abr. Lincoln helped defend the bridge in suit brought by steamboat companies after several boats had crashed against the piers. During Civil War, the Arsenal (1862) was used as prison for Confed. soldiers. In decline of R. traffic & lumbering industry, which had once jammed the Miss., the Quad cities built up other industries. Their importance as trade centers has grown rapidly, & Rock I. has also become insurance center, home of Modern Woodmen of Amer., Royal Neighbors of Amer. & Bituminous Casualty Corp.

PTS. OF INT. IN ROCK I.: (1) 5th Ave., **Augustana College** (coed.) & **Theological Seminary,** supported & controlled by Augustana Lutheran Ch.; founded in 1860 in Chicago, moved to Paxton in 1863 & present site in 1875. Sch. of Music is famous for Augustana Choir. Seminary, on hill to (S), is grad. sch. for Augustana Luth. Ch., which traces its ancestry back to Ch. of Sweden & its name to Confession at Augsburg (1530), for which "Augustana" is Latin name. **Swedish Bell Tower,** bell & timbers from orig. bldg. **Old Main** (1887). In marble **Denkmann Mem. Lib.** (1910) are Augustana Hist. Soc. Coll. & Swedish art treasures. (2) 200 13th Ave., **Villa de Chantal,** Cath. girls' sch. founded in 1864. (3) Bet. 40th & 44th Sts., on 3rd Ave., **Internat. Harvester Co.** (O.appl.), one of world's largest tractor plants. (4) At S. Limits, on US67 & St.2, **Black Hawk St. Pk.** (f.pic.inn.facils.playfields), on Rock R. At annual Pow Wow descendants of Sauk & Fox warriors gather for tribal dances. On Watch Tower Hill is **Hauberg Mus.,** gift of John H. Hauberg, authority on Ind. lore; unusual coll. PTS. OF INT. ON I. OF ROCK ISLAND: (5) NW. tip, **Ft. Armstrong Blockh.** (1816). (6) Near-by is **Pier of RR. Bridge** (1855). (7) **U.S. Arsenal** (grounds O.), where 19,000 men were employed during World War II. **War Mus.** (O). (8) **Confed. Prison Cemetery.** (9) At W. end, **Lock & Dam No. 15.** PTS. OF INT. IN MOLINE: (10) On 3rd Ave., **Deere & Co.** (O.appl.); largest plow factory in world, one of largest wagon factories, farm implements plant (others in Moline & E. Moline). (11) 7th Ave. & 18th St., **Scottish Rite Cathedral** (1929.Mod. Goth.). (12) 4th Ave., bet. 27th & 34th Sts., **Riverside Pk.** PTS. OF INT. IN E. MOLINE: (13) **Campbell's I. St. Pk.** (pic.). At SW. end, **Site of Battle of Campbell's I.,** in which Black Hawk was defeated. (14) **Internat. Harvester Co.** (O.appl.).

## US 25 & ST. 25—MICHIGAN

**MICH.-OHIO LINE (N) to BAY CITY. 267. US25 & St.25**

Via: Erie, Monroe, Detroit, Mount Clemens, Muttonville, Port Huron, Lexington, Harbor Beach, Port Austin, Sebewaing, Unionville. US23 (see), US24 & US25 enter Mich. from J. with US20 & US68 in Toledo, O. US24 by-passes Detroit & ends in Pontiac. On US24 (N) 6m from St. Line is St. Hy. Dept. Tourist Info. Lodge. Accoms. in towns; resorts, inns, cabins, camp sites along route. Airports & landing fields at intervals. Off US24A near St. line is Erie Marsh St. Game Area.

### Sec. 1: MICH.-OHIO LINE to PORT HURON. 108.

US25 runs close to L. Erie, last of Gt. Ls. to be seen by white men. Jolliet sailed out on long, narrow L. in summer of 1669, & in 1679 La Salle launched the square-sailed "Griffin." Countless disasters are recorded on this unpredictable water. Tour follows old military turnpike through Detroit & most thickly pop. sec. of Mich.

**15. MONROE** (sett.1780. Through RR. & bus conns.), the "Floral City" for 50 yrs.; only Mich. port on L. Erie. Midway bet. great metropolitan centers, it is unexpectedly tranquil & charming, with Raisin R. winding across town. Hy. is bordered by flowers from large nurseries. Hist. Trl. (marked) leads past sites assoc. with War of 1812, Toledo War, & Gen. Custer (see), who spent early life here. Monroe is nat. center of paperboard & paper-products industry. Col. Francis Navarre's cabin was built in 1780, & by 1796 an Amer. flag flew over blockh. at "Frenchtown," later renamed for Pres. Monroe's inaugural. In War of 1812, Brit. won victory at Battle of Raisin R., & their savage allies massacred Gen. Winchester's Ky. militia-men. PTS. OF INT. (sites marked): (1) **Massacre Victims Mon.,** at site of Battle of Raisin R. (2) **Custer Equest. Statue** (by C.A.Potter), comm. cavalry leader killed in battle with Sitting Bull (see Montana). (3) **Custer H.** (4) **St. Mary's Convent,** mother house of Servants of the Immaculate Heart of Mary, & **St. Mary's Academy.** (5) **First Presb. Ch.** (1846), oldest Presb. Ch. in St. Underground Railroad Sta. (6) **St. Mary's Ch.** (Cath.), founded in 1784. (7) **Ilgenfritz** (1847), **Greening** (1850) & **Monroe Big Tree** (nurseries). (8) On La Plaisance Bay, **Egyptian Lotus Beds.** (9) **Sterling Monroe St. Pk.**

**30. FLAT ROCK** (1824). US25 runs bet. **Lincoln Pk.** (E) & **Allen Pk.** (W) & crosses **Melvindale** on Dix Hy. **50. DETROIT** (see). **64. ROSEVILLE. 71. MOUNT CLEMENS** (see Detroit Trip VI), nat. known spa. **72.** J. with Joy Rd., which leads (E) 2.5$^m$ to **Selfridge Field,** U.S. Army Air Base. **74.** J. with St.29, Algonquian Trl.

SIDE TRIP: On St.29 (alt. route) (E) & (N) to Marysville & Port Huron. At 5$^m$, **New Baltimore,** largest of resort villages of early Fr. origin around Anchor Bay (f.ice-f.h.boat. resort & sports facils.). In winter, gaily-colored villages of f. shacks spread out on frozen L. & bay. 8$^m$ **Anchorville,** 10$^m$ **Fair Haven.** Hy. borders **St. Clair Flats,** marshy delta of Is. at mouth of St. Clair R. (resorts.h.f.). In late 19th cent., the "Venice of America" arose here, with summer homes built on piles & gaily decorated hotels. Something of Gallic wit & gaiety lingers along these shores, brightening boat & bait signs & wayside taverns. 18$^m$ **Algonac St. Pk.** (f.bath.pic.camp.facils.). 20$^m$ **Algonac,** marine town & shipbuilding center for 100 yrs. **Chris-Craft Plant** (O), said to be world's largest builder of speedboats. Ferry for **Harsen's I.** On Canadian **Walpole I.** is Ind. Reserv. (handicraft). Ind. men & women are often seen on hy., carrying sweet-grass baskets & boxes for sale. Many fine Vict. Hs. 28$^m$ **Marine City,** shipbuilding center in sailing-ship & early steamboat days. Midsummer Mardi Gras, with Outboard Regatta. 34$^m$ **St. Clair,** plotted in 1818; many beautiful Hs. **Diamond Crystal Salt Works.** 39$^m$, **Gar Wood Boat Works** (O.appl.). 40$^m$ **Marysville,** lumbering settlement which has become industrial village around boat works, Morton Salt, Chrysler Corp. & other factories. Adj. Marysville (N) is **Port Huron** (see below), 44$^m$.

**86. MUTTONVILLE** (lunchroom.Greyhound Bus stop). Route swings (NE) through farmlands broken by low hills & wooded ravines. **101.** at (N) edge of **Marysville** (see above), hy. comes in sight of vividly blue **St. Clair R.,** which it follows (N).

### 108. PORT HURON

Through RR. & bus conns. Ferry to Sarnia, Ont. Inns & cottages at beaches; cabin & trlr. camps in vic. Golf & yacht clubs; f.h.boat. facils. Info.: C. of C., Wall & Military Sts. Port Huron & Mackinac Yacht Races & Bluewater Festival (July).

Port Huron, resort town & trade center for industrial & farm area, is port of entry from Canada & on short route to Niagara Falls. It is an old lumber town, beautiful in midsummer with oak & elm trees. Here L. Huron flows into deeply channelled St. Clair R., one of best places to watch the long steamers. Lightship is stationed at mouth of R., a danger pt. 2nd only to Detour, on St. Mary's R. (see Sault Ste Marie). Eight ships were lost with all hands in storm on L. Huron, Nov. 9, 1913, worst storm in hist. of Gt. Ls. St. Joseph, 2nd ft. in Lower Peninsula, was built here in 1686, & pioneer community was est. on Black R. in 1790. Ft. Gratiot replaced old ft. in 1814, & a boom followed bldg. of Gratiot Turnpike (US25) in 1826. Four villages united in 1837 to form Port Huron. More than 180 vessels were built here bet. 1838 & 1908, about half of them sailing ships. In 1891, Port Huron-Sarnia Ry. Tunnel was opened, 1st electrified underwater tunnel ever built. PTS. OF INT.: (1) Pine Grove Ave. (S) of Elmwood St., **Blue Water Internat. Bridge** (1938.Modjeska & Masters). (2) Johnstone & 10th St., **St. Clair RR. Tunnel** (1891.electrified 1908). (3) Wall & 6th Sts., **Pub. Lib.** (1917) & **St. Clair Cty. Lib.,** 1st cty. lib. in St.; **Mus.** (O.appl.); **W. L. Jenks Room of Mich. Hist.** (O.appl.). (4) 518 Wall St., **J. L. Miller Homestead** (1836). (5) State St., near J. with Stone St., **Fort Gratiot Mon.** (6) In Pine Grove Pk., **Edison Boulder,** comm. inventor who spent boyhood yrs. here.

SIDE TRIP: to **Sarnia,** Ont., by ferry, or bus over Internat. Bridge (see "How to Enter Canada" in Detroit sec.). Sarnia is port of entry & industrial center in resort reg. Its waterfront at night is spectacular with flame stacks & glow of powerhouses of **Polymer Corp.,** synthetic rubber plant opened in 1943; **Imperial Oil Ltd.,** largest Brit. oil refinery; & **Dow Chemical Plant** (plastics).

## Sec. 2: PORT HURON to BAY CITY. 159.

US25 runs close to lakeshore around rim of Mich.'s "Thumb." At c.9., **FRANKLIN D. ROOSEVELT LABOR CENTER** & summer camp (C.I.O.). **10. LAKEPORT ST. PK.** (pic.bathh.facils.store.no camp). **12. ST. CLAIR ST. PK.** (camp.bathh.facils. store.boats). **22. LEXINGTON,** resort village, in Huron Shores dist. **38.5., SANILAC CTY. PK.** (pic.camp.bathh.). **63. HARBOR BEACH,** one of oldest f. & resort centers on L.; birthpl. of Frank Murphy, U.S. Supreme Ct. Justice & former Gov.

**71. PORT HOPE LIGHTH. 89. PORT AUSTIN,** another popular resort; J. with St.53 & St.25, on which tour turns (SW).

SIDE TRIP: On St.53 (S) 17m to **Bad Axe,** where packing chicory is main industry. (Outside of Mich., only Belgium & Holland produce chicory in quantity.)

St.25 is scenic hy. in view of white sand beaches & blue water. **101. ALBERT E. SLEEPER ST. PK.** (f.bathh.store.elec.group camp). **116.5., BAY PORT,** on Wild Fowl Bay, has one of largest f. fleets on Ls. **Wallace Stone Co. Quarry,** for Bay Port stone. St.25 crosses sugar-beet country, once an impassable swampland. **128.5. SEBEWAING** (f.h.trlr.camp).

**159. BAY CITY**

Water & 7th Sts., G.T. RR. Sta.; end of Jackson St., Mich. Central RR. Sta.; 501 Fifth Ave., P.M. RR. Sta. 1010 Saginaw St., Bus Sta. Tri-city Airport, at Freeland. Good accoms. Recr. facils. (f.summer & winter sports). Wenonah Beach, Bay City St. Pk., & Waterworks Pk. Info.: C. of C., in Wenonah Hotel Bldg.; 5th Ave. (E) of Adams St., E. Mich. Tourist Assoc. Log Office.

Bay City, on site of Chippewa campground, is one of the great & rough lumber towns on Saginaw Bay; now largest L. Huron port & industrial center. During World War II, Defoe Shipbuilding Co. (est. in early 1900's) built mine sweepers, rescue tugs, & PC's & then applied new methods in construction of destroyer escorts. Other large industries are Monitor Sugar Co., Industrial Brownhoist Corp., Chevrolet Motor Co., Wheeler Shipyard, which built 1st 600′ steel freighter; Electric Auto-Lite Co. & Dow Chemical Co. The 20m long Saginaw R. (canoe.trl.), with largest basin in St., has always been of major importance. In 1831, traders were attracted to site, & by 1860's, Lower Saginaw (later Bay City) & other villages had grown up. In 1870's & 1880's, the great R. cut through a roaring sawmill town bet. piles of logs, while rafts, tugs & barges jammed its channel. Then pine woods virtually vanished. The booming town, mecca of lumberjacks after spring drives, was threatened, but fishing, beet-sugar refining & coal-mining kept it alive. PTS. OF INT.: (1) Water St., **Defoe Shipbldg. Co.** (2) 700 Belinda St., **Aladdin Plant,** makers of ready-cut Hs. (3) SW. city limits, **Monitor Sugar Refinery,** largest in eastern U.S. (4) Center Ave. & Jackson St., **Pub. Lib.;** file (1872-84) of "Lumberman's Gazette." (5) 515 Center Ave., **Bay Cty. Bldg.;** Hist. Mus. (O.wks.). (6) Water & 24th Sts., **Tromble H.** (1836). (7) On Saginaw R. (N), **Wenonah Pk.,** one of finest in Mich. J. with US23 (see) & St.47, which leads (N) 5m to **Bay City St. Pk.**

## US 12—MICHIGAN

**DETROIT (W) to MICH.-IND. LINE. 220. US12**

Via: Plymouth, Ann Arbor, Jackson, Albion, Marshall, Battle Creek, Galesburg, Kalamazoo, Paw Paw, Hartford, St. Joseph-Benton Harbor, New Buffalo. US112 (see) parallels route (S).

US12 follows route of stagecoach through several large cities & educational centers, among farmlands, orchards & villages of long standing. At (W) end is important fruit belt.

### Sec. 1: DETROIT to BATTLE CREEK. 116.

**0. DETROIT** (see). **23. PLYMOUTH.** Sett. in 1820's by New Englanders. **World's Largest Air-Rifle Factory.**

**37. ANN ARBOR**

Foot of State St., Mich. Central RR. Sta. W. Huron St., off Main St., Bus Sta. Willow Run Airport (see Detroit Trip II). Accoms.; pic. & camp sites in vic.; resorts around many Ls. Lectures, plays, concerts & other events sponsored by Univ. & civic groups. May Festival (music), Dramatic Festival (May-June), Repertory Players (summer), Oratorical Lecture Series (Feb.-Mar.). Info.: C. of C. (see also Univ. of Mich. below).

Ann Arbor is delightful residential & college town in Huron R. valley, surrounded by gently sloping, forested hills. Univ. of Mich. campus occupies (E) half of town. Pub. Lib., sch. system & community affairs reflect tone set by one of oldest & largest of st. universities. In Feb. 1824, John & Ann Allen, Dan. Cross & Elisha & Mary Ann Rumsey built log cabins in "oak opening" on Huron R. In 1837, the village became seat of st. univ., & by 1870's it was a thriving city. At 1405 Pontiac Rd., **Beckley H.** (1842-1845.Gr.Rev.rest.), used by Underground RR. Bet. Cedar Dr. & Broadway, **Riverside Pk.** (pic.sports facils.golf course). **Univ. of Mich.** The "Catholepistemiad, or Univ. of Mich." was est. in Detroit by Terr. Legislature in 1817, largely due to Father Gabriel Richard (see Detroit). In 1837 the struggling academy was reorg. by St. legislature & given to Ann Arbor. Under Jas. Burrill Angell (father of J.R.Angell, of Yale Univ.), pres. 1871-1909, Ann Arbor took high rank among st. universities. Instruction is given in 14 schs. & colleges. Bet. 1909 & 1925, more than 20 major bldgs. were erected on & around the old campus. During World War II, Univ. carried out large Gov.-sponsored programs & shared in atomic energy & other research projects. Most recent is aeronautical research program at Willow Run (see Detroit Trip II). Info.: 221 Angell Hall; Business Office, Room 1, Univ. Hall. PTS. OF INT. OLD CAMPUS: (1) **Alumni Mem. Hall** (1909.Class.by Donaldson & Meier); art coll. (2) **Angell Hall** (1924.Albert Kahn), adm. bldg. (3) **Lib. Bldg.** (1918.Kahn); rare items in Drama, Ornithology, Economics & Hist. of Science colls. (4) **W. L. Clements Lib. of Amer. Hist.** (1923.Ital.Ren.by Kahn); noted coll. of books, mss. & maps. (5) **President's H.** (1841.Gr.Rev.), oldest bldg. (6) **Univ. Hall,** incl. Main Bldg.(1873.Fr.Ren.), Mason Hall 1841) & S. Wing (1849).(7) On W. side of State St. **Mich. Union** (1919.by Pond & Pond), men's clubh. (N) OF CAMPUS: (8) **Hill Auditorium** (1913.by Kahn & Ernest Wilby); Stearns Coll. of Musical Instruments (O.appl.). (9) **Burton Mem. Tower** (1937.Kahn); Chas. Baird Carillon (O.exc.Sat.). (10) **Rackham Bldg.** (O.guide.1937.mod.Class.by Smith,Hinchman & Grylls); Sch. of Grad. Studies. (11) **Mich. League** (1929.by Pond & Pond), women's clubh. & theater. (S) OF CAMPUS: (12) **Law Quadrangle** (1924-33.Coll.Goth.by York & Sawyer), notable group. (13) **Hospital Group,** in hilly (NE) sec. (14) Facing Hospital, **Observatory** (O.Mon.-Fri.& special nights); facils. for astronomical physics, in which Univ. ranks high.

**51.** J. with St.92.

SIDE TRIP: On St.92 (N) c.1m to **Chelsea,** sm. mfg. town. St.92 cont. (NW) bet. **Pinckney Recr. Area & Waterloo Recr. Area,** largest in St.

### 73. JACKSON

Through RR. & bus conns. Reynolds Airport. Fine city & cty. pks. (pic.camp.cottages. resorts). Rose Show (mid-June). Info.: New Center Bldg., C. of C.; in Hotel Otsego, Tourist & Convention Bureau.

Jackson, birthpl. of Republican party, is cut by Grand R. & is seat of lake-studded Jackson Cty. Industrial plants on E. side have drawn large & racially complex pop. City was inc. in Feb., 1854, & named for Pres. Jackson. On Franklin & 2nd Sts., **Republican Party Site,** where 5,000 citizens officially formed & named party on July 6, 1854. W. Michigan Ave. & Wildwood St., **Civil War Mem.** (1903.by Lorado Taft). On St.147 (N) 4m is **St. Prison of S. Mich.,** one of world's largest penal institutions. **93. ALBION,** home of **Albion College** (Meth.Episc.), coed., liberal arts; one of oldest denom. schs. in St. (1833). **Chapel & North Hall** (neo-Class.), orig. bldgs.; **Stockwell Mem. Lib. & Hall of Fine Arts** (1938.neo-Class.).

### 116. BATTLE CREEK

Main & Hall Sts., G.T. RR. Sta.; W. Van Buren St. at Capital Ave., Mich. Cent. RR. Sta. Arcade Bldg., 51 W. Jackson St., Union Bus Sta. W. K. Kellogg Airport. Good accoms. Recr. facils. in numerous pks. Horse Show (May or June). Dahlia Club Show (Sept.). Maneuvers at Ft. Custer. Info.: C. of C. & Auto Club of Mich., both on N. McCamly St.

US12 follows Mich. Ave. across "Health Food City," at confluence of Kalamazoo & Battle Creek Rs. Beyond R. (N) are fine residential areas; many Ls. & resorts in vic. Preeminent among many industries are world-famous Kellogg, Post & other cereal plants. Town (sett.1831) is named for very small battle (1824) bet. 2 members of surveying party & 2 Inds. who resented being pushed out of their sugar camps. In 1855, Battle Creek was made hqs. of Seventh Day Adventist Ch. Western Health Reform Institute (now Sanitarium), 1st of many est. by that ch., was founded in 1866, & in 1876 put in charge of Dr. John H. Kellogg, who perfected the flaked cereal. C. W. Post, inventor of Postum (1894), was another leading manufacturer. Characteristic of Battle Creek are the magnificent **Youth Bldg.,** hqs. of Civic Recr. Assoc., & the Ann J. Kellogg Sch., with facils. for handicapped children. PTS. OF INT.: (1) Washington Ave. & Champion St., **Battle Creek Sanitarium** (O.Mon.-Fri. 1927.mod.Ren.). (2) Near Sanitarium, **Percy Jones Gen. Hospital,** U.S. War Dept. (3) Michigan Ave. & 20th St., **Leila Arboretum. Kingman Mem. Mus. of Nat. History** (O) has 125,000 specimens from all over world. (4) Near-by on W. Michigan Ave., **Barney Tavern** (1848.N.O.). (5) W. Michigan Ave. & McCamly St., **Post**

**Tavern** (O); C. W. Post Art Coll. (6) W. Van Buren & McCamly Sts., **Kellogg Auditorium.** (7) In Oak Hill Cemetery, **Grave of Sojourner Truth** (1790-1883), famous Negro woman who crusaded against slavery. (8) Cliff & Academy Sts., **Post Products,** incl. orig. plant (1895). (9) **Kellogg Co. Plant** (O); 40-a. pk. & botanical garden. (10) $5^m$ (W), **Ft. Custer,** U.S. Army Post. **Kellogg Field,** Army Air Base. (11) (NW) $10^m$ is **Gull L.,** popular resort. (13) On Wintergreen L. (E), **Kellogg Bird Sanctuary** (O.daytime).

### Sec. 2: BATTLE CREEK to MICH.-IND. LINE. 104.

Route enters reg. of prosperous farms. **14. GALESBURG.** Many early bldgs. **19. COMSTOCK,** site of Fourierist colony in 1840's.

**23. KALAMAZOO**

Willard St. bet. Rose & Burdick Sts., Mich. Central RR. Sta.; Pitcher St. & Mich. Ave., Penn. RR. Sta. Portage St. & Mich. Ave., Greyhound Bus Sta.; N. Rose & Water Sts., for other lines. Mun. Airport (S) $3^m$. Good accoms.; tourist homes & resorts in vic. Recr. facils. in numerous pks. Symphony Orchestra. Civic Players. Pansy Festival (Ap.); Community Concert Series. Info.: C. of C., 316 Commerce Bldg.

Kalamazoo was founded as trading post on "the boiling river" in 1823. Besides being important trade & industrial center & one of great paper-making cities, it is also a rural market edged with celery fields & a college town with few skyscrapers & many trees, an exasperating downtown dist. of alley-streets & impressive suburbs. It has an active Institute of Arts, civic orchestra & theater & 3 colleges. Celery-growing was begun in 1850's by Jas. Taylor, from Scotland, & in late 19th cent., Kalamazoo Paper Co. was est., & several large stove companies, iron industries & pharmaceutical factories. PTS. OF INT.: (1) **Civic Center,** surrounding Bronson Pk. **Civic Auditorium** (1931.by Aymar Embury II), home of Civic Theater & Orchestra. **Site of Lincoln's Address** in Aug. 1856. On S. Rose St. are: (2) **Pub. Lib.;** (3) **Natural Hist. Mus.** (O.wks.), notable visual education exhibit; (4) **Institute of Arts** (O.wks.& some evenings). (5) Academy St. (W) of Oakland Dr., **Kalamazoo College,** one of oldest in St. (1833); Bapt. controlled but nondenom.; fine bldgs. in Georg. style. (6) **Western Mich. College of Education** (1903), on 200-a. campus along Davis St.; granting degree in arts, music & sciences; facils. for graduate study. **Kleinstueck Wildlife Preserve.** (7) **Nazareth College & Academy.** Kalamazoo is at J. with US131 & St.43, which leads (W) $7.5^m$ to **Wolf L. St. Fish Hatchery** (O). **39.5. PAW PAW,** center of leading grape & wine-producing reg. Grape Festival. **Wineries** (O). **Paw Paw Bait Co. Plant** (O). **Cth.** (1841). **62. COLOMA,** canning center & resort.

**73. BENTON HARBOR-ST. JOSEPH**

Through RR. & bus conns. Airport. Steamer to Chicago in season. Good hotels (mineral baths); tourist pks., cottages & resorts in vic. Riverview, Silver Beach (amusement), House of David & Waterworks Pks. Blossom Festival (May). Yacht Races. Info.: C. of C. in each city.

The 2 ports are surrounded by as. of orchards, traditionally descended from Johnny Appleseed's (see) trees. Missionaries & explorers knew the marshy site at R.'s mouth, & La Salle built Ft. Miami here in 17th cent. Another ft. & mission, built on site in 1700, was destroyed by Chief Pontiac in 1763. A settlement begun in 1831 soon moved back from sandy shore to site of St. Joseph, & later settlers crossed R. & built town which outstripped its neighbor. Benton Harbor became widely known after House of David colony was est. in 1903.

PTS. OF INT., ST. JOSEPH: In Lake Front Pk., **Site of Old Ft.** Here also is **Ben King Mon.** to poet who wrote "The Old St. Joe" in honor of his birthpl. **Old Lighth.** (1859) & **Mem. Hall.** BENTON HARBOR: Market & 9th Sts., **Mun. Fruit Market,** largest non-citrus fruit market in world. (2) At (E) limits, **House of David;** amusement pk. with miniature trains, pic. groves, handsome bldgs. & outdoor theater. Benj. Franklin Purnell brought his "Israelites" to Benton Harbor in 1903 & est. religious colony which became exceedingly prosperous. King Ben died in 1927 before he could learn that he had been acquitted in scandalous trial. After waiting some time for promised resurrection, his followers carried the King's embalmed body to **Diamond House.** E. of H. of David, Israelite **City of David,** founded by Queen Mary, Purnell's widow. At J. with US31 (see). **80. TOURIST CAMP** operated by H. of David. Rd. leads (E) to **Stevensville,** lakeshore resort center, in wildest dune country. **87. BRIDGMAN,** among flower-covered dunes. **Warren Dunes**

**St. Pk.** (no camp.good beaches). **93.5. HARBERT,** for many years home of Carl Sandburg. **100. NEW BUFFALO** (large group camps in vic.). **St. Line Rest Lodge & Info. Serv.** J. with St.60-US112 (see). **104. MICH.-IND. LINE.**

## US 112—MICHIGAN

**DETROIT to NEW BUFFALO. 210. US112**
Via: Dearborn, Inkster, Wayne, Ypsilanti, Saline, Clinton, Somerset, Jonesville, Quincy, Coldwater, Sturgis, White Pigeon & Niles.

US112 follows Great Sauk Trl. which in 1825 became Terr. Rd. Rich soil & smoothly flowing Rs. attracted the Algonquin long before white men came, but few sites remain & their famous garden beds have disappeared. Route is notable for pastoral charm of farmlands & lovely Irish Hills & L. reg. (pic.camp.cabins.resorts.f.h.swim. boat.).

**0. DETROIT** (see). US112 becomes loop expressway to Willow Run Airport. **9.5. DEARBORN. 17. WAYNE.** Hy. forks (S). Byp.112 becomes part of expressway, while US112 cont. (W). **29.5. YPSILANTI** (see Detroit Trip II for this sec.). **40. SALINE,** at edge of Irish Hills, which extend some 30$^m$ (W). **52. CLINTON. St. John's Ch.** (Episc.1835). J. with St.52 & cty. Rd.

SIDE TRIPS: (A) On Rd. (E) 5$^m$ to **Macon,** center of Ford's soybean acreage. **Pennington Sch.** (1851), bought by Henry Ford & rest. with old-fashioned furniture. Oil is pressed from soybeans in 19th cent. **Gristmill** on Saline R.
(B) On St.52 (S) 5$^m$ to **Tecumseh,** an "oak opening" sett. in 1830's. **St. Peter's Ch.** (Episc. 1832.Doric portico), oldest Episc. ch. (W) of Alleghenies continuously in use; built by Rev. Wm. Lyster with aid of Pres. Jackson, Dan. Webster & others.

**61. W. J. HAYES ST. PK.** (pic.camp.trl.store.community bldg.bathh.), 400 as. in **Irish Hills,** incl. 90-a. **Round L.** & **Wamplers L.** (resorts.f.winter sports.boats). **Two Observ. Towers** (sm.fee). Near pk. (W) is **St. Joseph's Ch.** (Cath.1854-63). On St.11 (N) is **Manchester,** supply center. **65. CAMBRIDGE JUNCTION.** At J. with St.50 is Mich.'s most famous inn, **Walker Tavern** (1832), where Dan. Webster, Jas. Fenimore Cooper, Harriet Martineau & "Priest" Lyster were guests. In **Walker Brick Tavern** (1856) are orig. taproom, barber shop & kitchen. **72.** J. with US127 & US223.

SIDE TRIPS: (A) On US223 (SW) to **Devil's L.,** resort center. 20$^m$ **Adrian,** prosperous trade center. **Adrian College,** liberal arts; under Meth. Conference; org. in 1845 as Mich. Union College from 2 older schs. & moved to "Maple City" in 1859. In **College Row** are older bldgs. **Civic Auditorium** (1939), property of city. **St. Joseph's Academy** & **Siena Heights College** (women), well-known (Cath.) schools.

US112 unites with US127 to **74. SOMERSET CENTER. 88. JONESVILLE,** at hist. ford on St. Joseph R. **Grace Ch.** (Episc.1844); orig. walnut furniture. **Munro H.** (1840.Class.Rev.). J. with St.99.

SIDE TRIP: On St.99 (SE) 5$^m$ to **Hillsdale,** in scenic area with many Ls. (f.h.swim.boat. winter sports). Campus of **Hillsdale College** covers 60 as. on St. Joseph R.; liberal arts; coed. sch. founded by Freewill Baptists in 1844. **Slayton Arboretum. B. A. Barber Amphitheater.**

**100. QUINCY,** at head of 14$^m$ chain of Ls. in great f. & sports reg. **106. COLDWATER,** named by Inds. for near-by R. & L., largest in chain (good f.camp.resorts. beaches). In early 1800's a trading post stood on site of **Oak Grove Cemetery.** Inc. in 1837, Coldwater grew rapidly; was active Underground RR. sta. **St. Home & Training Sch.** (Children's Village) is doing excellent work with subnormal children. **Branch County Cth.** (19th cent.); Pioneer Mus. J. with US27 (see) & St.86.

SIDE TRIP: On St.86 (W) to **Colon,** magicians' capital, where Percy Abbott makes & demonstrates magic apparatus; Magicians' Jamboree (late summer). **Sturgeon L.,** source of St. Joseph R. (canoe trl. resorts).

**118. BRONSON** has nat. known plant for making tackle. Jabez Bronson built tavern in 1828 & later used his taproom for court sessions. Liquor was removed to kitchen. **Old Opera H.** US112 dips (S) through fertile St. Joseph Cty., tilled 1st by Potawatomi who held 73,000-a. reservation until after Black Hawk War. **134. STURGIS,** ranking high in manufacture of furniture & decorative appliances. Flower Show. Pet Day Parade. J. with St.78.

SIDE TRIP: On St.78 (N) 8$^m$ to J. with St.86. On St.86 (W) 2$^m$ to **Nottawa,** Amish trading center; apple butter, sausage & other foods for sale.

**141.** US112 passes **KLINGER L.** (resort.cottages.beaches). **147. WHITE PIGEON,** named for Ind. chief who saved settlement from tribal uprising. US112 crosses S. edge of Cass Cty., known for trout streams, flower gardens, resorts & prehist. & hist. sites. **183. NILES** (see US31). **203. THREE OAKS,** in midst of former Ind. lands. **Chamberlain Mem. Mus.;** fine Ind. & pioneer colls. **Warren Woods,** 320-a. tract of virgin hardwood. **210. NEW BUFFALO,** on L. Mich. J. with US12 (see).

## US 16—MICHIGAN

**DETROIT (W) to MUSKEGON. 185. US16**

Via: New Hudson, Brighton, Howell, E. Lansing, Lansing, Portland, Cascade, Grand Rapids, Fruitport. Good accoms. at short intervals.

Route of US16 was made by Inds., & pioneer wagons followed the trl. Now broad lanes of heavy traffic cross center of Mich. through capital city & Grand Rapids, 2nd largest center.

**0. DETROIT** (see). US16, Grand R. Trl., runs (NW) through St. recr. & resort areas in lake dist. of Oakland & Livingston ctys. **16. BOTSFORD TAVERN** (O.1836). **19. FARMINGTON,** sett. in 1824 by Quakers. **25. NOVI. 32. NEW HUDSON.** (See Detroit Trip V for this sec.) **40. BRIGHTON,** pleasant village in midst of 50 or more Ls. **Greek Temple H.** (1840), at 314 Grand River Ave. Off hy. (SW) 3$^{m}$ is **Brighton Recr. Area. 50. HOWELL** (RR.& bus.accoms.), one of country's largest Holstein cattle markets, is restful town in fine setting on Thompson L., in vic. of Tyrone Hills & Ind. L. chain. On St.155 (SW) 3$^{m}$ is **St. Sanatorium** (tuberculosis).

**60. FOWLERVILLE** (sett.1835), tourist center.

**82. E. LANSING** & **86. LANSING.**

126 N. East St., Union Depot; 1223 S. Washington St., Grand Trunk Sta. 118 S. Grand Ave., Bus Sta. Airport (NW) 3$^{m}$ on US16. Hotels & other accoms.; tourist pk. Concerts, lectures & stage productions. Recr. facils. in numerous pks. Farmers' Week (Jan.-Feb.) at Mich. St. College. Info.: 202 S. Walnut St., C. of C.; Industrial Bank Bldg., Auto Club of Mich.

E. Lansing, seat of Mich. St. College, merges with Lansing, st. capital. The Capitol dome & 23-story Olds Tower rise above tree-shaded city, like symbols of its hist. from "capital of the woods" to prosperous industrial, as well as political, center. Valley is entered by Grand, Sycamore & Red Cedar Rs., & bridges here & there span the winding streams. E. Lansing has grown up around the college & is entirely residential. When legislature decided, in 1847, to move capital from Detroit, a border city, Lansing had a sawmill & a log house in dense for.; but it was given the honor, tentatively, to settle a long controversy. After coming of Ransom E. Olds (in 1900's), maker of one of 1st practical automobiles in U.S., the city's development was very rapid. Present output from more than 100 industries, with automotive in lead, gives Lansing high rank. Also it is commercial & financial center for St.'s richest farm country.

PTS. OF INT.—LANSING: (1) Capitol Ave., **Capitol** (1878.Class.Ren.by E.E. Myers); War Relics Mus. (O.wks.). (2) Washington & Genesee Sts., **St. Hist. Mus.** (O). (3) 124 W. Allegan St., **Olds Tower** (O.1931.by Hopkins & Dentz). (4) S. Pennsylvania Ave., on Red Cedar R., **Potter Pk.;** Zoo. (5) Among larger industrial plants are **Oldsmobile Division of G.M., Reo Motors, Inc.,** & **Motor Wheel Corp.** The new **Kettering Engine Plant** (1948) has been called "engineer's dream," embodying principle of progressive machining. Cost, exclusive of bldg., has been estimated at $15,000,000.

PTS. OF INT.—E. LANSING: (1) Harrison Rd. at Marigold Ave., **St. Police Hqs.** (O.tours). (2) E. Grand River & Michigan Aves., **People's Ch.** (1923.by W.E.N. Hunter), interdenom. social & religious center. (3) Grand River Ave. & Abbott St., **Mich. St. College,** oldest agric. college in U.S., (1855); under control of St. Bd. of Agric. Campus of 160 as. on Red Cedar R. is very attractive; athletic fields, housing facils. & College Farm on 3,000 as. (S) of R. Of special int. are: **Quonset Village** of more than 100 housing units; **Agric. & Dairy Bldgs.; Union Mem. Bldg.** (O.cafeteria.1923.wings 1936.adds.1946-47.by Pond,Pond & Martin); **College Lib.** (1920's. Coll.Goth.by Edwyn Bowd); **Beaumont Mem. Tower** (1928.Goth.by Donaldson & Meier); **R. E. Olds Hall of Engineering; Kedzie Chemical Lab.** (1927), a beautiful bldg. Lansing is at J. with US27 (see) & US127.

SIDE TRIP: On US127 (SE) 13m to **Mason. St. Game Farm** in vic.; ringneck pheasants, Hungarian partridge & other beautiful wildfowl.

US16 runs through agric. valley, rising gradually to rolling hills. **120.** J. with Rd. to **L. Odessa** (resort.).

**139. CASCADE,** residential suburb. Hy. forks. By-pass US16 runs (S) of Grand Rapids.

**148. GRAND RAPIDS**

60-63 Ionia Ave., Union Sta. 239 Michigan St., Grand Trunk RR. Sta. 55 Oakes St., (SW) Union Bus Terminal. Pennel Rd., (S) 4m, Grand Rapids Airport. Good accoms. Mun. Tourist Camp. Many city & cty. pks. Civic Players. Symphony Orchestra. Info.: Federal Sq. Bldg., C. of C.; Rowe Hotel, W. Mich. Tourist & Resort Assoc. Furniture Fair (Jan.& June); May Theater Festival; "The Messiah," Calvin College (2nd.wk.in Dec.).

Grand Rapids, "the Furniture City," is 2nd-largest & one of most attractive of Mich. cities, owing much to its 58 city pks. & 45,000 trees. Around it are hundreds of small Ls. & trout streams. Educational institutions incl. Calvin College & Seminary, Aquinas & Mount Mercy Colleges (Cath.), Jr. College & Univ. of Mich. Sch. of Business Adm. (1946). Besides furniture, Grand Rapids produces sticky fly paper, automatic musical instruments, auditorium seats, gypsum & paper products, carpet sweepers, food products & chemicals. It is also a ranking printing & lithographing center. In vic. are highly productive gas & oil wells. Bapt. mission was est. on W. bank of Grand R., 1824-26, & Louis Campau built fur-trading post. Steamboats began service from Grand Haven in 1837. Stewart Edw. White (1873-1946), who was born in Grand Rapids, described in "The Riverman" the heyday of lumbering on the Grand & Rogue Rs. Furniture industry began in 1858, & gained recognition at Philadelphia Centennial Exposition (1876). Grand Rapids has largest Dutch pop. of any city in U.S. & a large Polish settlement.

PTS. OF INT.: (1) 427 E. Fulton St. (US16), **Furniture Mus.** (O.1938). (2) 54 E. Jefferson Ave., **Pub. Mus.** (O.free.1940.by Roger Allen), severely functional, windowless bldg. (3) 230 Fulton St., **Art Gallery** (O.1844.Gr.Rev.). (4) Campau Ave. & Lyon St., (NW) **Civic Auditorium** (by Robinson, Campau & Crowe). (5) 24 Fountain St., **Fountain St. Bapt. Ch.** (Ital.Ren.by Coolidge & Hodgdon), fine group of ch., campanile, arcade & parish H. (6) Bostwick Ave. & Library St., **Ryerson Pub. Lib.** (mod.Ren.by Shepley, Rutan & Coolidge); country's finest coll. on furniture. (7) 109 Market Ave., **Mun. Wholesale Market,** one of largest open-air markets in U.S. (8) Along R. (N) & (S) are some 80 **Furniture Factories** (O.appl.). (9) Franklin St., bet. Benjamin & Giddings Aves., **Calvin College,** in red-brick Georg. bldgs.; liberal arts college under auspices of Christian Reformed Ch. **Hekman Mem. Lib.** (10) In Comstock Pk., **Dwight Lydell St. Fish Hatchery.**

**177. SPRING L.,** at end of Grand R.; mineral springs & resort developments.

**185. MUSKEGON**

586 Western Ave., Pere Marquette Depot; Peck & Laketon Sts., Penn. & G.T. RRs. 184 Western Ave., Bus Terminal. Muskegon Cty. Airport, Mun. Airport & Interstate Seaplane Base. Wis.-Mich. Steamship Co. & G.T.-Penn. Carferries (no autos) to Milwaukee, Wis. Concerts. Little Theatre. Resorts around White & Muskegon Ls. Info.: 970-3rd St., C. of C. Nat. Convention of Polish societies (spring). West Shore Music Festival (May). Harvest Festival. Winter carnivals.

From marshlands at mouth of Muskegon R., the port of Muskegon, largest on E. side of L. Mich., extends for more than 5m along shore. With natural harbor (5m-long L. Muskegon) & sheltering dunes, city has always been important port &, even in lumber era, a recr. center. Millions of tons of petroleum products, pig iron, coal, coke, stone & industrial products are shipped yrly.; regular sailings to N. European ports. Principal manufactures are automotive & foundry products, machine tools & dies, office furniture & billiard tables. Large oil companies operate marine terminals with capacity approx. 39,000,000 gals. Nicolet stopped here in 1634, & Father Marquette in 1675. Fur-trading began in 1810 & lasted until 1st sawmill was erected, 1837. From Civil War days until late 1880's, Muskegon was "Sawdust Metropolis." M. M. Quaife says (in "Lake Michigan"), "A single generation of furious destruction spanned the rise & fall of Muskegon . . ." Near end of cent., lumbering declined, & a fire destroyed much of the fabulously wealthy city, but mfg. plants succeeded the lumber mills.

PTS. OF INT.: (1) W. Clay Ave., **Hackley Pk.;** Soldiers' & Sailors' Mon. (2) Waterfront, **West Mich. Mart,** one of finest port terminals on L. Mich. (3) Morris St. bet. 1st & 2nd Sts., **Ind. Burial Ground** (1750); St. Supreme Ct. ruling prevents industrialization of site. (4) Clay Ave. & 3rd St., **St. Paul's Ch.** (Episc.1892.Goth.); figures carved by Alois Lang. (5) 296 Webster Ave., **Hackley Art Gallery** (O.free.Oct.-Je.); coll. begun by C. H. Hackley, lumberman, who also gave Pub. Lib., Hackley Pk., hospitals, & other large bequests. Paintings by Cranach, Burchfield, Inness, Picasso, Orozco, & other major artists; sculptures by Lachaise, Manship & others. (6) Adj. gallery, **Hackley Pub. Lib.** (1890.Romanes.by Patten & Fisher). (7) Webster Ave. bet. 3rd & 4th Sts., **McKinley Mem.** (by C.H.Niehaus). (8) Washington Ave. & Jefferson St., **Hackley Mem.** (by Lorado Taft). (9) In Evergreen Cemetery, **Grave of Jonathan Walker** & Mon. raised by Photius Fisk, abolitionist. Walker, who lived near Muskegon in later life, was Mass. sea captain who was imprisoned & branded for trying to run slaves to Bahamas. On Mon. is stanza from Whittier's "The Man with the Branded Hand." (11) On St.20, **Muskegon St. Pk.** Muskegon is at J. with US31 (see).

# US 10—MICHIGAN

**DETROIT (NW) & (W) to LUDINGTON. 237. US10**

Via: Ferndale, Birmingham, Bloomfield Hills, Pontiac, Flint, Saginaw, Midland, Clare, Reed City & Baldwin. Paralleled by Grand Trunk & P.M. RRs. Accoms. throughout. Car & Auto Ferry to Manitowoc, Wis., from Ludington.

US10 follows Woodward Superhy. through automotive centers, then (W) through former pine belt & central farm area to thinly settled but scenic country along L. Mich.

## Sec. 1: DETROIT to MIDLAND. 117.

**0. DETROIT** (see). In this sec. are some of Detroit's most attractive suburbs, incl. Huntington Woods, Birmingham, Cranbrook Foundation & Bloomfield Hills. **25. PONTIAC,** in noted L. dist. (see Detroit Trip III). Developed recr. areas, incl. **Bald Mt., Rochester-Utica, Pontiac L. & L. Orion** (resort).

SIDE TRIP: On St.218 (SW) to **Walled Lake. Cass L.,** at (SW) limits; at 3$^{m}$ **Orchard Lake,** resort & residential communities. 6$^{m}$ off hy. near **Commerce** is **Dodge Bros. St. Pk. No. 5** (pic.camp.store.facils.). 12$^{m}$ **Walled Lake,** on L. encircled by natural wall of tree-covered boulders. On (S) side are popular **Dodge Bros. St. Pks. No. 2 & No. 15;** good beaches.

**30. DRAYTON PLAINS. Large Fish Hatchery** (O). On Rd. (E) 2$^{m}$ is **L. Angelus,** on which is **McMath Hulbert Observ.,** of Univ. of Mich. **39. HOLLY ST. RECR. AREA.** Rd. leads (E) c.6$^{m}$ to **Ortonville St. Recr. Area** (tent.trlr.& group camps). **52. GRAND BLANC,** on site of early trading post. J. with cty. Rd.

SIDE TRIP: On Rd. (E) 14$^{m}$ to **Metamora St. Recr. Area. L. Minnewana.**

**54.** US10 forks. Branch-US10 enters downtown Flint, while US10 cuts across W. side.

**59. FLINT**

S. Saginaw & 15th Sts., Grand Trunk RR. Sta.; Beach & Union Sts., Pere Marquette RR. N. Saginaw & 3rd Ave., Bus Sta. Bishop Airport, (SW) 4.5$^{m}$. Good accoms. Golf & other recr. facils. Symphony orchestra; civic opera. Atwood Stadium. Emancipation Day (Jan.1) & other events at Negro Civic Center; Folk Festival (June) & other group festivals. Info.: C. of C. & Automobile Club.

Flint, on Flint R., is Mich.'s 3rd largest city & 2nd to Detroit as automotive center. Giant factories are spread throughout city around congested downtown area. Municipality owns waterworks, airport, fine hospital & lib., sch. & pk. systems. Community Music Assoc. offers yr.-round program, & Institute of Arts conducts series of exhibits & lectures & sch. of art. Mott Foundation has charge of Children's Health Center, Mott Camp for underprivileged boys & adult recr. & education programs. Many racial groups & large Negro pop. give rich diversity to civic life. The R., named for the flintstone, attracted Chippewa & Potawatomi, then fur traders (1819) & missionaries. Settlers ventured into the wilderness in 1830's, & tavern & ferry were est. With lumbering, village expanded & soon became "The Vehicle City," making carts & carriages. In 1900, David Buick org. in Detroit the Buick Auto-Vim & Power Co., which became Buick Mfg. Co., maker of 1st Buick automobile in 1902. A yr. later, co. merged with Flint Wagon Works, & Buick Motor Co. was est. in Flint. W. C. Durant, who shared ownership of several vehicle companies with Jos. Dallas Dort (see Detroit Trip II), bought out Buick with aid of other Flint citizens. General Motors Co. was org. by Durant in 1908, & in 1909, he almost gained control of Ford interests. In 1910, Durant lost control of G. M., partly because bankers feared his "dashing methods & hairbreadth adventures." From experiments of Louis Chevrolet, which he had backed, Durant built Chevrolet Motor Co. &, by 1913, had controlling interest in G. M. Durant was Pres. of G. M. until 1920. Other local leaders were C. S. Mott, C. W. Nash & W. P. Chrysler. Another event in city's automotive hist. was 1st large-scale sit-down strike, in 1937.

PTS. OF INT.—INDUSTRIAL (O.appl.): (1) Leith St., **Buick Motor Co., city's** largest plant. (2) Chevrolet Ave. & Bluff St., **Chevrolet Plants.** (3) 4300 S. Saginaw St. & 210 N. Chevrolet Ave., **Fisher Body Plants.** (4) Harriet St. & Industrial Ave. & at Davison Rd. & Dort Hy., **AC Spark Plug Plants.** When co. began in 1908, workers came at 6:30 a.m. on bicycles or in horse-drawn carriages to make spark plugs for 2-cylinder cars. (5) Industrial Ave., **Marvel-Schebler Carburetor Division** of Borg-Warner Corp. (6) Chevrolet & W. 3rd Ave., **G. M. Institute. Auditorium,** civic center, & **Atwood Stadium.** OTHER PTS. OF INT.: (7) 703 Beach St., **Old Vehicles Coll.** (O.appl.). (8) Crapo & Kearsley Sts., **Flint Jr. College** (est.1923). Amer. & Ind. colls. in Mus. (9) Kearsley & Clifford Sts., **Pub. Lib.** (1905.Ren.).

**92. SAGINAW**

W. Genessee Ave., near Mich. Ave., N.Y.C. RR. Sta.; Potter St., near Washington Ave., P.M. Ry. Sta. 217 Federal Ave., Eastern Mich. Bus Sta. Saginaw Airport, (NE) 2m. Tri-City Airport, at Freeland. Good accoms. & recr. facils. Tourist camp. Saginaw Cty. Fair (Sept.). Info.: Board of Commerce Bldg.

Saginaw, 4th-largest city & 3rd-largest wholesale market in Mich., is trade center of industrial & rural valley of Saginaw R., which flows through center of town. It is an attractive place, with a host of tall old trees, 19th cent. mansions, well-designed modern bldgs. & numerous bridges. Except for street-corner pumps, few mementoes of lumbering era remain in town once nationally known for roaring sawmills & R. choked with logs. In 1818, Louis Campau built a cabin & the council h. where Lewis Cass negotiated with Inds. Ft. Saginaw was built in 1822, & Saginaw City inc. in 1857. Along with booming lumber industry, Saginaw developed its large salt deposits, coal & graphite, & by 1900, when lumbering began to decline, 70 or more mfg. plants had been est.

PTS. OF INT.: (1) Genessee, Lapeer & Jefferson Aves., **Tower Bldg.** on which "Little Jake" Seligman in 1890's erected clock tower & statue of himself, once city's salient pt. of int. (Copper statue was blown down some yrs. ago). (2) 1315 S. Washington St., **City Hall** (1937.Mod.by Macomber & Merrill), of local Bay Port stone. (3) Jefferson Ave. & Janes St., **Hoyt Lib.** (1890.Romanes.by Van Brunt & Howe); notable hist. coll. (4) **Ezra Rust Pk.** along R.; in center is City Waterworks (Goth.). (5) Hamilton & Throop Sts., **Site of Ind. Treaty,** signed in 1819 by Gov. Cass. (6) 301 N. Hamilton St., **Ye Olde Musee** (O.free) in Schuch Hotel (1868), probably oldest continuously open tavern in St. John P. Schuch's remarkable coll. incl. 10,000 theater programs dating back to 1753 & some 200 Toby jugs. (7) **Chevrolet Grey-Iron Foundry,** largest in world. (8) **Bean & Grain Elevator,** largest in world. J. with US23 (see).

US10 crosses Sugar Bowl. **107. FREELAND.** Tri-City Airport. **117. MIDLAND** (accoms.RR.bus.airport). Functional bldgs. show influence of Dow Chemical Co., which was est. by the late Dr. H. H. Dow in 1890's, & changed the lumbering village into important research center & town of outstanding architectural int. Oil found during Dow drillings for salt brine has developed into central Mich.'s petroleum industry. Hs. & pub. bldgs. are striking in style & construction, many of them designed by Alden Dow, pupil of Frank Lloyd Wright. PTS. OF INT.: W. Main St., **Dow Gardens** (O), designed in 1899 by Dr. & Mrs. Dow. **Dow Chemical Co. Plant** maintains People's Univ. Main & Fitzhugh Sts., **Midland County Cth.** (mod. Tudor.by Bloodgood Tuttle); colored exter. murals (reg. & hist.) by Paul Honore. St. Andrew's Rd., **Midland Country Club** (by Alden Dow), used as hotel & civic center.

## Sec. 2: MIDLAND to LUDINGTON. 120.

Route cont. (NW) across low hills & through cut-over areas (good f.h.). At W. end of route is Manistee Nat. For., popular recr. area, drained by hist. Tittabawassee R., tributary of Saginaw R., & the Pere Marquette. **8.5.**, J. with St.30, which leads (N)

10$^{m}$ to **Edenville,** near which, in Tittabawassee R., is place (now covered by Wixom Dam) celebrated in "The Jam on Gerry's Rocks," best-known ballad of the North Woods, sung from Portland, Me., to Portland, Ore. **29. CLARE** (community pk. trlrs.good accoms.RR.& bus). Altitude & pine woods make it favored country for hay-fever & asthma patients; many streams & abundant wildlife. Near Clare are important oil & gas fields. J. with US27 (see). **69. REED CITY,** prosperous town with large maple-flooring mill; tourist center. Oil refinery in vic. & 4 of St.'s most productive oil wells. J. with US131, route to Straits. **77. CHASE,** edge of **Manistee Nat. For.** (pic.camp.areas.f.h.winter sports.ranger stas.at White Cloud, Baldwin, Manistee & Cadillac. hqs. at Muskegon). **Chittenden Nursery,** at Wellston, often ships 1,000,000 trees a day to for. crews. In Cadillac Dist. is **Mt. Caberfae Winter Sports Area** (see). **88. BALDWIN,** seat of Lake Cty., on P.M. RR.; popular resort center.

**120. LUDINGTON**

RR. & bus conns. Airport at J. of US10 & US31. P.M. RR. Car Ferry to Milwaukee, Manitowoc & Keewaunee, Wis. Accoms.: All kinds. Golf courses, stables, boat liveries, summer & winter sports facils. Info.: C. of C.

Ludington, important shipping pt. at mouth of Pere Marquette R. on L. Mich., is also one of St.'s hist. sites. Rustic cross marks **First Grave of Father Marquette** (see St. Ignace, on US2), in pk. bet. Ls. Mich. & Marquette. The long Pere Marquette R. (canoe trl.trout) flows into Marquette L. here. J. with US31 (see) & St.116.

SIDE TRIP: On St.116 (N) 8.5$^{m}$ to **Dunes Pk.** (f.boat.cottages) & **Ludington St. Pk.** Inland is **Hamlin L.** (pike,bass,muskellunge), center of resort colonies.

## US 23—MICHIGAN

**MICH.-OHIO LINE** (4$^{m}$ from Toledo, O.) **(N) to MACKINAW CITY. 370. US23**

Via: Temperance, Dundee, Milan, Ann Arbor, Brighton, Hartland, Flint, Saginaw, Bay City, Pinconning, Standish, Tawas City, Harrisville, Alpena, (Rogers City), Cheboygan. Accoms. throughout. Ferry to St. Ignace.

US23 passes comfortable farmsteads in long-settled SE. Mich. From Ann Arbor (N) are many recr. areas. Tour then follows L. Huron shore, rimming cut-over lands that have become vast woodland playground.

### Sec. 1: OHIO LINE to BAY CITY. 150.

Old-fashioned villages in this sec. suggest their New England origin—**21. DUNDEE, 31. MILAN,** & (W) of US23, **Deerfield, Blissfield** & **Adrian** (see). **40.** J. with US112 (see). **48. ANN ARBOR** (see). In rolling hills of terminal moraine are many Ls. & marshes. **65.** J. with US16 (see). **73.** J. with St.59. Both hys. lead into St. Recr. Areas. **74.5. HARTLAND,** center of **Hartland Foundation** projects, incl. sch., crafts shop, lib. & music hall. **86. FENTON,** prosperous resort town. J. with St.87.

SIDE TRIP: On St.87 (E) 5$^{m}$ to **Holly,** known locally for its flower gardens. 10$^{m}$ J. with US10 (see), which crosses **Holly St. Recr. Area,** in rugged country of great natural beauty.

**112.** J. with US10, with which US23 unites to **135. SAGINAW** (see US10). **150. BAY CITY** (see US25).

### Sec. 2: BAY CITY to MACKINAW CITY. 220.

US23 curves around Saginaw Bay, leaving industrial Mich. behind. L. Huron, 2nd largest of Gt. Ls., was the 1st discovered by white men. Champlain briefly recorded the great "Freshwater Sea." Saginaw, Au Sable, Thunder Bay & Cheboygan Rs. (canoe trls.), once lined with sawmills, drain upper half of Lower Peninsula, one of lumber kingdoms of the world until denuded of its towering pines in late 19th cent. Large areas lie in Huron Nat. For. & scattered st. fors. Along shore are huge estates, resort villages & camp sites; & inland are sports centers, tourist & trlr. camps, inns, cottage groups & hotels; bass, perch, pike, trout & muskellunge in hundreds of Ls. & streams; wild duck, heron, pheasant & grouse in marshlands, & rabbits, fox, deer, bear & coyote in wilder secs.

**20. PINCONNING & STANDISH, 29.,** trade centers for farm & dairy reg. & good stopping places (RR.& bus lines.accoms.camp sites). **44. AU GRES,** supply center for hunters, fishermen & summer colony at **Pte. Au Gres** (tourist pk.boats). **58. ALABASTER,** named for gypsum quarried in vic. since 1870. **64. TAWAS CITY**

**& 66. FORT TAWAS,** yr.-round sports centers on Tawas Bay; both were lumber towns. Tawas City originated Perch Festival, now held annually (Ap.) in many L. towns. **E. Tawas St. Pk.** (pic.camp.bathh.f.). **Beal Nursery** (SW), under U.S. For. Serv., produces 12,000,000 trees a yr. **Huron Nat. For.** (hqs. in E. Tawas.ranger stas. at Mack L. & Silver Creek.f.h.swim.boat.winter sports); 770,000 as. of burned & cut-over lands replanted with red, white & jack pine; 16 campgrounds. From Tawas (NW) 10$^{m}$ is **Silver Valley,** winter-sports area. Au Sable R. flows across for.; campgrounds (free) at dams in lower R. (pike,bass & bluegills). **80. AU SABLE,** destroyed by fire in 1911, & **81. OSCODA,** resort centers. Au Sable R. Dr. leads (W) c.15$^{m}$ from Oscoda to **Lumberman's Mon.** (Rbt.Aitken), on bluff overlooking R.; bronze figures of Landlooker, Lumberman & Riverman. **97. HARRISVILLE,** resort center with excellent beach (good f. & h.). **St. Fish Hatchery. Harrisville St. Pk. 112.** J. with Rd. to spring-fed **Hubbard L.** (ledges.inns.cottages.f.h.).

**128. ALPENA**

Through RR. & bus conns. Cty. Airport. Accoms. of all types; motor courts, beaches & camp sites. Boat harbor. Winter sports. Bobcat Hunt (late Jan.O.to pub.). Winter Carnival. Alpena St. For. (f.h.) along Thunder Bay. Info.: C. of C.

Alpena, largest town on L. Huron (N) of Bay City, is business & resort center of popular Thunder Bay reg. Town was swept by 4 for. fires in early yrs. From 1887, when Detroit & Mackinac RR. tracks were laid, until pine fors. were exhausted, the bay shore was lined with sawmills. Limestone quarrying began in 1869 & is still a leading industry. Thunder Bay R. flows through the city, & Long, Grand & Hubbard Ls. are in vic.; noted for white-tailed deer & native partridge. At (S) limits is **Michekewis Pk.** (bathh.boat livery.pavilion.trlr.camp), scene of Winter Carnival. Near (E) limits, Mich. Alkali Co.'s **Limestone Quarry** (O), largest in world.

Picturesque Presque Isle Cty. is considered ideal for relief of hay fever & asthma Hy. runs beside **Long L.** (pike.bass & bluegills). **139. LAKEWOOD.** J. with Cty.405.

SIDE TRIP: On Cty.405 (NE) 9$^{m}$ to **Grand L. Fire Tower** (O). **Presque Isle P.O.** (hotel. cottages) on NE. shore. **Presque Isle Lighth.** (O.1870) & **Tower of Old P. I. Lighth.** (1841. by Jeff.Davis).

Main tour follows W. shore of **Grand L.** (f.boats). **160.** J. with St.65.

SIDE TRIP: On St.65 (S) 12$^{m}$ (making 4 turns) to **Posen,** described in Konrad Bercovici's "On New Shores." On cty. Rd. (NE) are **Hawks & Metz.** These Polish & German communities were wiped out in for. fire in early 1900's. One rescue party was trapped in derailed train & burned to death.

Beyond J. US23 forks, Branch-US23 running (N) 3$^{m}$ to **Rogers City** (through RR. & bus conns. airport) & adj. **Calcite,** ranking port for limestone from near-by quarries. At **163.** on US23 is J. with St.68, alt. route to Rogers City.

SIDE TRIP: On St.68 (W) 24$^{m}$ to **Onaway,** resort center (hotels.summer homes.tourist camp.RR.& bus); Ls., waterfalls, sinkholes & lost Rs. in dense woods. St.211 leads (N) 6$^{m}$ to **Onaway St. Pk.**

**164.** US23 & Branch-US23 unite. **168. P. F. HOEFT ST. PK.** (pic.camp.facils. bathh.pavilion); trls. around **Huron Dune.** At c.**172., FORTY-MILE PT. LIGHTH.** (O.daytime.1896), 40$^{m}$ from Straits. Fog horn is heard for miles around. **178. COAST GUARD STA.** (O.1878), on Hammond Bay, shelter for many storm-driven ships.

**205. CHEBOYGAN**

Through RR. & bus conns. Boat serv. to St. Ignace, Mackinac I. & Les Cheneaux. Hotels, cottages, camp sites; winter & summer sports facils. Info.: C. of C.

Cheboygan ("place of entrance"), once a leading lumber town, is seat of cty. known for abundant wildlife & scenic beauty; f. port, trade center & hqs. for sportsmen. Short distance from town are Black, Burt & Douglas Ls. (whitefish, muskellunge & bass), & here begins Inland Water Route (canoe trl.) to Traverse Bay reg. Streets are lively in season with fishermen, deer hunters & woodsmen in bright-checked mackinaws & pegged trousers. Snow plows & paper & wood products are leading industries. **Sawdust Pile,** 1,000′ high, accumulated over 60 yrs. J. with US27 (see), with which US23 unites past **Hardwood St. For.** (f.h.trlr.camps.cottages).

**220. MACKINAW CITY**

Terminal of main RR. & bus lines & N-S hys. St. ferry to St. Ignace; cruiser to Mackinac I. Airport at Pellston, 20$^{m}$ (S) on US31. Hotels, cottages, camp sites; facils. for summer & winter sports.

The port city to the North Country is a lively place on the Straits, through which Nicolet paddled in 1634, bringing with him an embroidered robe to wear before Chinese court. Site was familiar to Inds., priests & voyageurs, & fur trader's canoe was called Mackinaw boat. Ft. Michilimackinac, est. at St. Ignace (1681), was re-est. on S. shore of Straits in 1715. After fall of New France, Brit. traders came. In 1780-81, Ft. was moved to Mackinac I. (see below). **Ft. Michilimackinac St. Pk.**

**Mackinac I. St. Pk.** (stores.hotels.cottages.no camp.no autos) is reached by ferry from Mackinaw City & St. Ignace; in winter over "ice bridge" by sleigh. Only motorized vehicle permitted is motor-bobsled (no org.winter sports), but rubber-tired carriages & basket buggies carry sightseers to hist. & scenic pts. Beyond Marquette Pk., beautiful terraces & gardens rise to Grand Hotel & the old fortress. The 17th-cent. missionaries were probably 1st white men to visit the rocky I. Brit. maintained Ft. Michilimackinac here from 1781 until Jay Treaty in 1798 & held possession again during War of 1812. John Jacob Astor est. Amer. Fur Co. post in 1817, & until 1830's a wild crowd of "coureurs des bois," adventurers & frontiersmen held forth in what is now Mich.'s show resort, enjoyed by Southern planters before Civil War. PTS. OF INT.: **Old St. Ann's Ch.** (1874.parish est.1695); **Ft. Mackinac** (reconst.); **Ft. Holmes** (1812), on highest pt.; **Astor Fur Post** (O.rest.); **Agent's H.** (O.1817), sometimes called Rbt. Stuart H.; **Arch Rock, Sugar Loaf,** & other formations.

# US 27—MICHIGAN

**MICH.-IND. LINE** (9m from Angola, Ind.) **(N) to CHEBOYGAN. 317. US27**

Via: Coldwater, Marshall, Olivet, Lansing, St. Johns, Alma, Mount Pleasant, Clare, Harrison, Houghton Lake, Roscommon, Grayling, Gaylord, Indian River. Accoms. throughout. Numerous resorts. Airport at (Battle Creek), Lansing & Pellston, near Cheboygan. US127 roughly parallels route, via Jackson, to Lansing.

## Sec. 1: MICH.-IND. LINE to CLARE. 165.

From J. with US20 in Ind., US27 enters reg. of Ls. **(5) COLDWATER L.;** resort colonies. **13. COLDWATER** (see US112). Near **GIRARD, 19.,** are traces of Ind. mounds & at **TEKONSHA, 24.,** is **Mon.** to Chief Tekonquasha. **36. MARSHALL;** fine Hs. of Col. & Civil War periods; one of earliest stops on Terr. Rd. (1812). **Brooks H.** (1830's.Gr.Rev.). J. with US12 (see). **49. OLIVET,** home of **Olivet College** (Congr.), coed., liberal arts sch. of high standing; founded 1844. Rev. John Shipherd, founder of Oberlin College (see Ohio), brought small colony by ox-cart to the hill he had named Olivet. Shipherd died within year. **Mather Hall; Mus.** (est. 1858). US27 winds among "sugar bushes" (groves of sugar maples) & rich pastures. **59. CHARLOTTE,** maple-syrup & sugar center. **Bennett Pk.** (trlr.camp.). **Mem. Grove & Mon.** J. with St.50 & St.78, with which US27 unites (NE).

SIDE TRIP: On St.50 (E) 10m to **Eaton,** the "Wool City"; mills (O). In vic. are **Veterans of Foreign Wars Nat. Home & Mich. Holiness Assoc. Camp.**

**66. POTTERVILLE.** Great flocks of sheep & herds of purebred cattle & Percheron horses in countryside. J. with Rd.

SIDE TRIP: On Rd. (W) 14m to **Vermontville,** founded by Vermonters in 1836; orig. ch. & academy (1843). Maple Sugar Festival (spring).

**79. LANSING** (see). US27 turns directly (N). **97. ST. JOHNS** (G.T. RR. & bus. accoms.), mfg. town & seat of Clinton Cty., noted pheasant country. In vic. are **Wolverine Stockyard** & **Clinton Mem. Hospital;** grain elevators, cider presses & creameries. J. with St.21.

SIDE TRIP: On St.21 (E) 19m to **Owosso** (accoms.airport.recr.facils.), former lumber town on Shiawawassee R.; easy access to pheasant & f. territory. Birthpl. of Jas. O. Curwood & Thos. E. Dewey. **Clubh.** of Cty. Conservation Assoc. **Curwood's Castle,** on riverbank. Off St.47 are **Dewey H.** & **Masonic Mem. Hospital.**

**120. ITHACA,** seat of oil-producing & agric. Gratiot Cty. **Ind. Trl. Mon.** in Tourist Pk. **126.** Hy. forks.

SIDE TRIP: On US27A (W) 3m to **Alma,** (RR.& bus.tourist pk. & usual accoms.), center of oil-producing reg.; mfg. of house-trlrs. is important industry. **Alma College** (Presb.1887), coed., liberal arts sch.; degree also in music. **Hood Mus.;** Mich. bird, Ind. & geological colls.

**128. ST. LOUIS** (sett.1853.RR.& bus conn.), "bugless" town on Pine R. Bottling of sparkling mineral waters in vic. & manufacture of D.D.T. caused considerable expansion of small industrial town & resort. **Mich. Chemical Co. (D.D.T.) Plant. 150. MOUNT PLEASANT,** pleasantly modern college town on Chippewa R.; hqs. of important oil companies. Good trout streams & hunting fields. **Mich. St. Home & Training Sch.** (O), originally an Ind. sch. On S. College Ave. are handsome bldgs. of **Central Mich. College of Education** (1895); good music dept. **165. CLARE** (RR.& bus), resort city named for Irish cty. because of hills & streams around.

### Sec. 2: CLARE to CHEBOYGAN. 152.

US27 runs (N) through pine, poplar & birch woods, past hidden Ls. where fish can be caught for pic. dinners; resorts & accoms. around tourist centers. **15. HARRISON,** on Budd L. **Wilson St. Pk.;** many Ls. & trls. to lumber camps (cabins.camp sites. boat liveries). Good h. for bear, deer, fox, rabbit & wildcat. J. with St.61.

SIDE TRIP: On St.61 (E) 17m to **Gladwin & Gladwin St. Pk.** (bus.airport.stores.facils.), on Cedar R. (canoe trl.). **Gladwin Game Refuge;** Grand Nat. Grouse Trials. Cty. has some of best f. & h.

**39. HOUGHTON L. VILLAGE** (RR.& bus.airport), at end of largest inland L. in St. (hotels.motor courts.cabins.restaurants.stores.golf). Other resort villages are **THE HEIGHTS & PRUDENVILLE, 44.** Good climate for hay fever. Excellent f. & game h. J. with St.55.

SIDE TRIP: On St.55 (E) 19m to **West Branch,** supply center for Rifle R. Area (f.h.bath. boat.winter sports). Annual Deer Hunters' Festival; wildcat hunts with trained dogs.

At c.**56.** (W) of hy., **Higgins L. St. Pk.** at (S) end of startlingly blue for. L. (cabins. hotels & summer homes). **St. For. Nursery,** said to be largest coniferous nursery in world. **59. ROSCOMMON,** important tourist center near **Huron Nat. For.** (see US23). **75. GRAYLING,** winter & summer sports capital; supply pt. for trips down Au Sable R. (trout f.canoeing); seat of Crawford Cty. (numerous resorts.). Grayling is named for native game fish that shared fate of passenger pigeon. **Grayling Winter Recr. Area** (snow trains), one of best-equipped in Mid-west.
Tour crosses Middle Branch of Au Sable R. **78.** J. with St.93 which turns (NE) 7m to celebrated **Hartwick Pines St. Pk.** (f.h.pic.camp.facils.stores), incl. 90 as. of virgin hemlock, white & red pine, last vestige of Lower Peninsula's primeval for. **95. OTSEGO L. VILLAGE** (cty.pk.). **Otsego L. St. Pk.** (f.camp.trlrs.bathh.boats.). **97. ARBUTUS BEACH,** named for exquisite woodlands flower. In spring, pails of the blossoms are sold along hy. Some of highest land in Lower Peninsula is in Otsego Cty., crest of long glacial moraine. **103. GAYLORD** (good accoms.stores), popular center for hunters & vacationers. Vic. ranks high in potato production. Admirable country for hik. & winter sports. **111. VANDERBILT.** (Rd. leads (E) to **Pigeon R. St. For.** where elk herds may be seen at dawn & twilight.). **122. WOLVERINE,** named for carnivorous weasel that gave Mich. its nickname but probably never lived here. **132. INDIAN RIVER,** at (S) end of lovely Burt L.; summer resort (good accoms.stores). Near-by are Ind. & Sturgeon Rs. (trout) & **Burt L. St. Pk. 138. TOPINABEE,** one of oldest resorts in Mich. (hotel.beaches.camp.bus), named for Potawatomi chief who signed treaty giving up site of Chicago. **149.** At (N) end of L., J. with St.33, which leads (S) 6m to **Aloha St. Pk. 152. CHEBOYGAN** (see US23). J. with US23 (see).

## US 31—MICHIGAN

**MICH.-IND. LINE** (6m from South Bend) **(N) to MACKINAW CITY. 356. US31**

Via: Niles, St. Joseph-Benton Harbor, South Haven, Saugatuck, Holland, Grand Haven, Muskegon, Montague-Whitehall, Hart, Ludington, Manistee, Beulah, Interlochen, Traverse City, Torch L., Charlevoix, Petoskey, Mackinaw City. Good accoms. Ferry across L. Mich. at several pts.

US31 follows shore of L. Mich. then cuts inland to tip of Lower Peninsula. Scenery shifts from orchards of fruit belt, past dunes & port cities, through Manistee Nat. For. & beautiful Traverse Bay Area, to "Holy Old Mackinaw" on the Straits.

## Sec. 1: MICH.-IND. LINE to J. with US10 E. of LUDINGTON. 166.

US31, united with US33, crosses St. line from J. with US20 in South Bend, Ind. **5. NILES** (good accoms.), old town in St. Joseph R. valley over which 4 flags have rippled: the "fleur-de-lis" in 1697, Brit. in 1761, Sp. in 1781 & U.S. in 1783. Along R. Rd. are **Site of Ft. St. Joseph** (1897) & **Father Allouez Mem. Cross,** near spot where missionary died in 1689. On Grant St. is **Site of Carey Mission,** founded in 1822 by Rev. Isaac McCoy (Bapt.). **Ring Lardner H.** In vic. **Beebe Mint Farm.** J. with US112 (see), St.60, & Red Bud Trl.

SIDE TRIPS: (A) On St.60 (NE) 15m to **Cassopolis,** famous junction on Underground RR.; seat of Cass Cty., known for its Ls. (good f.h.) & flower farms.

(B) On Red Bud Trl. (W) 5m to **Buchanan.** In Oak Ridge Cemetery **Jos. Coveney Mon.,** carved in England with atheistic sentiments. 9m **Bear Cave** (O.summer.sm.fee), one of few ancient tufa formations in Midwest.

**13. BERRIEN SPRINGS,** home of **Emmanuel Missionary College** (Seventh Day Adventist); liberal arts, nondenom. college, est. in 1873. **28. ST. JOSEPH-BENTON HARBOR** (see US12). US31 follows shore along edge of Van Buren Cty., which takes nat. rank in grapes & apples. **49.5. VAN BUREN ST. PK.** (beach.facils.group camp.store). **53. SOUTH HAVEN,** port & resort city with fine sand beach (good accoms.). Black R., which flows through town, was popular Ind. camp site, as was high ridge (E) marking ancient shoreline. Annual Peach Festival & Perch Run. Dunes give way to wilder scenery where steep clay banks are carved by wind & waves into strangely beautiful patterns. **71.** J. with St.89, which leads (E) across **Allegan St. For.** (f.h.pic.camp facils.), 58,000 as. along Kalamazoo R. (canoe trl.). **Swan Creek Wildlife Exper. Sta.; Archery Course** (nat.field trials).

SIDE TRIP: On St.89 (E) 25m to **Allegan,** lively resort center, known for 100-yr. old Cty. Fair.

**75. DOUGLAS & SAUGATUCK,** art colony & vacation center, at mouth of Kalamazoo R. (hotels.resorts.protected harbor). **Mt. Baldhead** (Old Baldy), across R., is highest dune on L. Mich. **Dune Desert** extends (N) for miles, a surrealist's dream of moving sandhills, towering trees without foliage, unusual flowers. **Ottawa Beach St. Pk.** (f.camp.facils.bathh.store).

**87. HOLLAND**

Through RR. & bus conns. Airport. Accoms. of all kinds. Recr. facils. Annual Tulip Festival. Info. at Warm Friend Tavern.

Holland is leading center of Dutch colony est. 100 yrs. ago. M. M. Quaife calls it "foremost center of Dutch cultural influence in America." Tulip Time (middle of May) draws hundreds of thousands to the Dutch hostelries to see wooden-shoe carvers, parades & dancing in costume in scrubbed streets. Shipping pt. for millions of baby chicks, ducks & geese. PTS. OF INT.: Central Ave. & 12th St., **Netherlands Mus.,** repository of Dutch records & folk material, incl. gifts from Netherlands Gov. **Hope College,** founded in 1855 as Rev. A. C. Van Raalte's "anchor of hope." **Mem. Chapel** (1929.mod.Goth.). **Western Theological Seminary,** for Dutch Reformed ministry. **Old First Ch.** (1856.Gr.Rev.), only bldg. to survive 1871 fire. **Little Netherlands** (O.sm.fee), miniature village.

**108. GRAND HAVEN,** f. port & resort center. **Grand Haven St. Pk.** (f.bathh.pic. camp.store.facils.). J. with US16 (see). **121. MUSKEGON** (see US16). J. with St.20.

SIDE TRIPS: (A) On St.20 (W) 4m to **Muskegon St. Pk.** (f.bathh.boat.livery.pic.group camp.store)

(B) On St.20 (NE) 64m to Big Rapids. At 26m **Fremont,** home of Gerber's Baby Food (tours); one of several sports centers in Newaygo Cty., noted f. & h. area.

On St.82 (S) & (E) 10m to **Newaygo** (trlr.pk.supplies.guides.boats), on Muskegon R., at edge of **Manistee Nat. For.** (see US10). **Newaygo Cty. Winter Sports Pk.**

St.20 conts. (NE) to **White Cloud,** 40m, ranger sta. of nat. for.; **White Cloud St. Pk.** 64m **Big Rapids,** home of **Ferris Institute,** coed., founded by W. N. Ferris (U.S. Senator & Gov.) as "school for the masses."

**36. WHITEHALL & MONTAGUE,** on White L. (f.pic.camp.boat.bathh.trlrs.stores), one of best yr.-round f. spots. In winter a few thousand f. shanties make gaily colored village on the L. At Little Point Sable is **Lighth.** said to be tallest on L. Mich. **146. HART,** among orchards & berry fields (fresh fruit, cider, pies & jellies for sale). **152. PENTWATER,** fruit-shipping port; also resort center noted for steelhead trout. **Chas. Mears St. Pk.** (pic.camp.facils.store). **166.** J. with US10, with which US31 unites. From J. (W) 2m is **Ludington** (see US10); ferry to Wis. cities.

**Sec. 2: J. with US10 to MACKINAW CITY. 190.**

**7. SCOTTVILLE;** large canning factories & grain elevators. Annual Cattle Show. US31 turns (N) across pioneer lumbering country, now resort area cut by the fast, crooked Pere Marquette R. (canoe trl. trout). **29. MANISTEE** (all kinds of accoms.). Manistee Nat. For. Festival (July 4). Along L. are plants of **Morton Salt Co. & Hardy Salt Co.,** largest in world (O.guides). **Century Boat Co. Plant** (O). On St.110 (N) is **Orchard Beach St. Pk.** J. with St.55.

SIDE TRIP: On St.55 (E) 43m to **Cadillac,** yr.-round resort. Info.: C. of C. Winter Carnival (late Jan.). City, named for founder of Detroit, was one of chief lumbering centers. **Mt. Caberfae Winter Sports Area** (accoms.bus from Cadillac & Wellston), one of best in Middle West; on highest land in Lower Peninsula (1,700′).

**35.** J. with St.22.

SIDE TRIP: On St.22 (N). (Tour of Leelanau Peninsula, on Grand Traverse Bay.) 7m **Onekama,** in Portage L. resort area. 18m **Arcadia,** Luth. summer resort. 31m **Elberta & Frankfort** (A.A. RR. Car Ferry to Menominee & Manistique, Mich., & Manitowoc, Wis.). One of largest commercial f. fleets on Gt.Ls. has hqs. at Frankfort (trips on appl.). Hy. curves around Crystal & Platte Ls. (f.resorts). 53m **Empire.** J. with St.72, route across peninsula through resort centers & miles of cherry orchards. 65m J. with St. 109, which makes loop tour of peninsula. 71m **Glen Arbor,** on lovely Glen L.; Dunesmobile trips. 89m **Leland,** summer artist's colony & f. village; boat to Manitou I. **Sugar Loaf Winter Sports Center.** 100m **Northport,** resort center. **Shady Trls. Camp.** for speech correction. **Northport Lighth.** (1839). St.22 turns (S) here to follow broken (E) side of peninsula. 121m **Bingham,** near L. Leelanau (resorts.camp sites). 132m **Traverse City.**

**47. BEAR LAKE VILLAGE,** resort. **61. BENZONIA & BEULAH** (f.boat.camp. cottages.hotels), on Crystal L. (annual smelt run.ice-f.). **70. INTERLOCHEN NAT. MUSIC CAMP,** of Univ. of Mich. (concerts in summer). On St.137 (S), **Interlochen St. Pk.** in Fife L. St. For.

**83. TRAVERSE CITY**

Through RR. & bus conns. Airport. Accoms. of all kinds. Trips on Leelanau Peninsula; to Sugar Loaf Winter Sports Club. Whole area is dotted with resorts. Info.: C. of C.

Traverse City, besides being health (hay fever & asthma) & vacation resort & sports center, is also leading U.S. market for cherries. It has one of most beautiful settings of any town in St. Traditional Blessing of Cherry Blossoms (mid-May) is event of nat. int. **Clinch Pk.** (yacht basin.beach). **Con Foster Mus.** J. with St.37.

SIDE TRIP: (N) On St.37 through **Old Mission Peninsula** (inn & other accoms.), a 15m tendril of land, white with cherry blossoms in spring. **Site of Presb. Mission,** 1st white settlement (1839) in bay area. **Old Mission Lighth.**

**85. TRAVERSE CITY ST. PK.** (f.bath.boat.pic.camp.facils.store). US31 runs (N) on narrow isthmus bet. bay & Torch L. **116. TORCH L. VILLAGE.** Dist. abounds in resorts; good country for deer & sm. game. Chippewa village sites, spears & arrowheads are frequently found. **135. CHARLEVOIX,** boating & deep-sea trolling center in wealthy community (cruises.canoe trls.beaches.tourist camp.steamship & plane to Beaver I. & Petoskey). J. with St.66.

SIDE TRIP: **Beaver I.** is largest in archipelago 30m or more (W) of Straits. **St. James** (hotel.cabins.info.at C.of C.). Chippewa & Ottawa Inds. were 1st inhabitants, & "coureurs de bois" roamed the woods before settlement was made on mainland. In 1847, the Mormons arrived from Voree, Wis. (see), under Jas. Jesse Strang. Homesteaders were admitted in 1848, but King Strang, crowned in 1850, was absolute monarch until prejudice & suspicion caused Gov. investigation. Strang was acquitted & served in Mich. Legislature. Rebellion later broke out against the tyrannical leader, & he was slain in 1856. Some 2,500 Mormons were driven away by mainlanders who took over the I. Irish fisherman est. colony around St. James, where pop. is still largely Irish. **Harbor Light,** erected during Mormon period.

**152. PETOSKSY** (RR. & bus conns. Accoms. & sports facils. guides). Thousands come by snow train to 10-day Winter Carnival (Feb.). Hiawatha Ind. Pageant (July-Aug.). On Little Traverse Bay is **Magnus St. Pk.** US31 unites with US131 through adj. **Bay View,** known for Bay View Assembly (Meth.) Summer & Music Sch. (concerts & lectures).

SIDE TRIPS: (A) On US131 from Petoskey (S) 9m to **Walloon Lake Village,** resort on one of lovliest inland Ls. (f.swim.h.hotels.resorts.cabins). 16m **Boyne Falls,** on fast Boyne R., great smelt stream.

(B) On St.131 from Bay View (N) & (W) 8m to **Harbor Springs,** resort on deep-water harbor. 29m **Cross Village,** Ind. town on high bluff. Autumn Pow-wow (may be photographed). **Father Weikamp's Tomb.**

**157. CONWAY,** on Crooked L., part of Inland Water Route (camp.f.& h.resorts). **170. PELLSTON** (airport.hotels & other accoms.). **190. MACKINAW CITY** (see US23). St. ferries to St. Ignace (see US2). J. with US23 (see) & Rd. along Cecil Bay.

SIDE TRIP: On Rd. (W) $8^m$ to **Wilderness St. Pk.** (f.h.), circled by truck trl.; serv. area (pic.camp.cabins.facils.no store). Much of inter. is impenetrable.

# US 2—MICHIGAN

## SAULT STE MARIE (W) to MICH.-WIS. LINE. 388. US2

Via: St. Ignace, Brevort, Naubinway, Manistique, Rapid River, Gladstone, Escanaba, Norway, Iron Mountain, Crystal Falls, Watersmeet, Wakefield, & Ironwood.

US2 is direct route bet. Soo & St. Ignace. From there, hy. follows L. Mich. (W) & then crosses cedar swamps & pine, balsam & spruce fors. to rugged iron country & land of Ls. Ottawa Nat. For. covers whole W. end of Upper Peninsula.

**Sec. 1: SAULT STE MARIE (S) to ST. IGNACE. 53.** (see Sault Ste Marie Trip II).

### Sec. 2: ST. IGNACE (W) to ESCANABA. 145.

**0. ST. IGNACE**

RR. & bus conns. Ferry to Mackinaw City & Mackinac I. Excursions to Les Cheneaux. Hotels, lodges, cabins. Info.: Bureau at City Hall.

St. Ignace, port of entry, 2nd oldest settlement in St.; commercial f. center, smoked whitefish a specialty. From across Straits, city is semicircle of bright-roofed houses, half-hidden by trees, against background of hills dark with cedar & pine. Scene in winter is a flashback to the past, with sailors & fishermen in dungarees, hunters & woodsmen in mackinaws, & horsedrawn sleighs in narrow, white roadways. Nicolet visited site in 1634, & fur traders followed. Père Marquette founded mission in 1670, & Ft. de Buade (later Michilimackinac) was erected by Fr., but after Cadillac left for Detroit (see), the outpost was abandoned. Near site of mission is **Grave of Père Marquette,** who died on return journey from Miss. R. exploration & was buried near Ludington (see US10), on L. Mich. Ind. friends brought his body back to St. Ignace by canoe, & grave was accidentally discovered in 1877. **Ind. Village;** baskets & souvenirs. **Ft. de Buade Ruins.** On St.122, **Straits St. Pk.** (pic.camp.).
US2 becomes scenic hy. (W) among dunes & hills (resort facils.cabins.pic. & camp sites). Jutting into L. are Pt. Aux Chenes, Pt. La Barbe, Gros Cap, Seul Choix Pt.

**15.** (E. of hy.) **Brevort L.,** resort center. **44. NAUBINWAY,** resort center (good f. & h.) in reg. of **Millecoquins L. 50.** J. with St.135, which leads (N) $8^m$ to **Curtis,** on edge of **Manistique L.** (best wall-eyed f. in St.resort facils.). **66. BLANEY PK.** (O.yr.round.sports facils.playh.); info. at New Camp 9, on hy.; trls. on logging Rds.; sleigh trains to deeryards & lumber camps. **Paul Bunyan's Camp,** on L. Louise; Lumberwoods Mus. **82. GULLIVER** (f.accoms.airport). On L. Mich. (SE) is **Port I.,** where Inland Lime & Stone Co. quarries millions of tons of limestone; loaded on freighters by conveyor system.

**90. MANISTIQUE**

Through RR. & bus conns. Ferries to Frankfort & Wis. cities. Airport. More than 30 sizable resorts in Cty. (f.h.swim.boat.).

Manistique is Upper Peninsula's only harbor clear the yr. round & is a leading resort center. Commercial f., shipping, & wood & paper mfg. are important. It was one of largest lumbermill towns. Bordering city are **Hiawatha Nat. For.** & **Cusino St. Game Refuge.** At N. edge is **Wyman Nursery,** probably largest in world. J. with for. Rd. & St.94, which leads (N) $11^m$ to **Hiawatha;** then (W) into **Hiawatha Nat. For.** (see St.28).

SIDE TRIP: On for. Rd. (W) c.$6^m$ to **Ind. L. St. Pk.** (f.bathh.electric.facils.camp.trlrs.). At N. end of L. is **Kitch-Iti-Kipi Spring,** a cold, clear pool in **Palms Book St. Pk.** (facils. store.no camp.). Resorts with good beaches & hotels.

**96. THOMPSON. St. Fish Hatchery** (O), said to be largest in world. US2 rounds head of **Big Bay de Noc** (bass.pike). **107.** J. with Rd. leading (S) into **Garden Peninsula** (harbors.cottages.resorts).
US2 runs (W) across top of **Stonington Peninsula,** Arcadian countryside (f.camp. boat.resorts). **115. NAHMA JCT.** Rd. leads (S) to **Nahma,** resort & sports center. **Bay de Noquet Lumber Camps** (O). **129. RAPID RIVER,** lumber & resort town in

good deer & small-game area. J. with US41 (see). **134. 5. KIPLING,** 2nd lumbering village named for poet (see Sault Ste Marie Trip II). **136. GLADSTONE** (through RR. & bus lines.accoms.tourist pk.), industrial town & sports center on Little Bay de Noc. Nat. Log Birling Tournament (July). Winter Festival (Feb.). **Sports Pk.** (O.yr.round). **Marble Arms Co.** (O), makers of hunting knives.

**145. ESCANABA**

Through RR. & bus conns. Mun. Airport. Accoms. Tourist Pk. Yacht harbor. Winter Carnival (Feb.); Smelt Jamboree (Ap.); Hiawathaland Festival (July 3-6); Venetian Night (Aug.); U. Peninsula St. Fair (Aug.). Info.: C. of C.

Escanaba (sett.1830) ships millions of tons of iron ore annually from lofty **Piers** extending nearly a half-mile into Green Bay. Named by Inds. "Land of the Red Buck," Escanaba is stopping place for deer hunters & fishermen & hqs. of Hiawatha & Marquette Nat. Fors. **Birdseye Veneer Co.** (O), largest in world.

### Sec. 3: ESCANABA to MICH.-WIS. LINE. 190.

US2 unites (W) with US41 (see) for 30$^{m}$ through iron ranges. **21. HARRIS,** named for M. B. Harris, who saved Potawatomi from starvation during smallpox epidemic. Rd. leads (S) to **Hannahville Settlement** (Ind.). **41. MENOMINEE CTY. PK.** (pic. camp.water). **48. LORETTO,** on rim of Menominee Iron Range. In vic. are **Hamilton Ls.** (camp.bath.). **53. NORWAY** (info.bureau.tourist serv.), prosperous resort village. Rd. leads (S) to **Old Town,** site of Norway before it caved into underground mine workings. **Ind. Head Fish Hatchery.** (US8 enters Norway from Wis.)

**60. IRON MOUNTAIN & KINGSFORD**

Through RR. & bus conns. Ford Airport. Hotels & resort & sports facils. Info. bureau at C. of C.

Iron Mountain is literally a mountain of ore; distributing pt. since 1878. Hillside village of Kingsford grew up around Ford Motor Co. plant. Good f. streams & dense fors. in vic. PTS. OF INT.: (1) **City Pk.** (pic.cabins.swim.). (2) **L. Antoine Pk.** (pic. bathh.). (3) **Cornish Mine Pump,** last in Upper Peninsula & one of largest in world; flywheel weighs 100 tons. (4) **Pewabic Mine Cave-in.** (5) **World's Largest Artificial Ski Slide.** (6) **Horserace Rapids,** in Menominee R. (canoe trl. through rugged country).

US2 unites with US141 & enters Wis. **79.** Hy. crosses Brule R. into Mich. again. Michegamme, Paint & Net Rs. unite with the Brule to form great Menominee R.

**90. CRYSTAL FALLS** (cottages.resorts), hqs. for canoe trls. & scenic trips. Bass Festival (July) on Paint R. **Peavey Falls Dam & L.;** record catches of bass, pike & perch. **94. BE-WA-BIC PK.** (pic.camp.bathh.sports facils.) **95.** Rd. (S) to **Pentoga Pk.** (camp.pic.group bldg.f.boats). **107. IRON RIVER & STAMBAUGH,** twin cities & latest of mining towns on Menominee Range; also lumbering & resort centers.

**109. OTTAWA NAT. FOR.** (hqs. at Ironwood.ranger stas.at Iron River, Bergland, Bessemer, Kenton, Ontanogan & Watersmeet.camp.f.h.), largest of St.'s 5 nat. fors.; incl. 1,743,000 wilderness as. broken by 400 Ls. & 1,200$^{m}$ of streams; major hys. & good for. & cty. Rds.; timber wolves, white-tailed deer, bear, beaver & porcupine.

**130.5.** US2 crosses **Lac Vieux Desert Trl.** Father René Menard, 1st recorded white man in reg., started out on trl. from L'Anse (see US41), on L. Superior, but went astray from party & was never seen again. Trl. leads (S) to Ind. village & Lac Vieux Desert, on Wis. border. **131. WATERSMEET,** where highlands divide Miss. R., L. Superior & L. Mich. drainage systems. For miles around are hotels, lodges, resorts, & cabin groups. J. with US45, route (S) through Land O'Ls. (see Wis.). **157. MARENISCO** has one of Upper Peninsula's largest lumber mills. Canoe trl. (for experts) on wild **Presque Isle R. 174. WAKEFIELD,** mining center on edge of Gogebic Iron Range, last to be explored. **Wakefield Mine,** one of largest open-pit mines on range. J. with St.28 (see). **181. BESSEMER,** beautiful valley town, once a mining camp. Rd. along **Black R.** (canoe trl.) to mouth on L. Superior; **Black R. Pk.** (pic.camp.).

**189.5. IRONWOOD** (through RR. & bus conns.airport;tourist & winter sports facils.), 3rd-largest town in Upper Peninsula; separated by Montreal R. from notorious Hurley, Wis. City began when Gogebic range was opened, 1884-85, & some of deepest mines are in vic. **Mount Zion Shelter Lodge** (skiing). **Eureka Mine. 190. MICH.-WIS. LINE.**

# ST. 28—MICHIGAN

**SAULT STE MARIE (W) to MICH.-WIS. LINE. 327. St.28**

Via: Eckerman Corner, McMillan, Seney, Shingleton, Munising, Marquette, Negaunee, Ishpeming, Michigamme, Sidnaw, Bruce Crossing, Bergland, Wakefield, Ironwood. Roughly paralleled by Soo Line RR. Hotels in larger centers; accoms. for summer tourists along hy.

St.28, occasionally blocked by snow, runs through timberlands where axe is heard on hy., still the territory of wild chickens & ducks, bear & deer.

## Sec. 1: SAULT STE MARIE to MARQUETTE. 165.

**0. SAULT STE MARIE** (see). J. with US2 (see). **8.** St.28 turns (W) across swamps & reforested areas. Piles of logs by roadside are reminders of lumbering days. Off hy. (S) are secs. of **Munoscong St. Game Area. 21.5. MARQUETTE NAT. FOR.** (hqs. at Escanaba, ranger stas. at Raco & Moran.f.h.pic.camp.). More than 500,000 people a yr. use this 500,000-a. playground of unbroken for.; countless Ls. & f. streams. In game refuges are wolf, bear, bobcat, fox & beaver. **38. ECKERMAN CORNER.** J. with St.123 to Whitefish Pt. (see Sault Ste Marie Trip IV). **43.5. HULBERT L. CLUB** (dining room), short distance off hy. **48.5.** J. with Rd. to **Soo Jct.** (parking), where little RR. takes passengers to Tahquemenon R. boat. (see Sault Ste Marie Trip IV). **55.** J. with St.48, with which St.28 unites (N) to **Newberry,** trade center; logging Rds. & wildflower trls. **Newberry St. Hospital** (mental). **86. SENEY,** serene town that was once the hell-hole of Upper Peninsula. **Hotel.** St.77 leads (S) into **Seney Migratory Waterfowl Refuge** (Fed.).

SIDE TRIP: On St.77 (N) 25m to **Grand Marais,** f. village, harbor & resort (good accoms.); known for whitefish & swirling sand dunes. Pau-Puk-Keewis "danced his Beggar's Dance on the beach at Grand Marais." Boats for **Pictured Rocks** (see below).

**110. SHINGLETON.** Hy. enters **Hiawatha Nat. For.** (hqs. at Escanaba.ranger stas. at Manistique, Munising & Rapid River.pic.camp.group camps.f.h.), 822,000 as. incl. some of St.'s most picturesque areas. In this for. Hiawatha & Nokomis had their wigwams, & from its N. rim Hiawatha departed "in the purple mists of evening . . . to the Islands of the Blessed." J. with St.84, which leads (N) to **Cusino St. Game Refuge. 121. MUNISING** (through RR.& bus conns.good accoms.sports facils.), in crescent-shaped valley, facing Munising Bay. Opp. is **Grand I.,** formerly 13,000-a. Ojibway camp. ground, now a resort (cabins.hotel). Munising began with iron furnaces in 1850's & grew with lumbering; still a woodworking center. Tours to Pictured Rocks & Grand I.

SIDE TRIP: **Pictured Rocks** are best seen from boat (July-Sept.& chartered serv.). Radisson's journal (1658) has 1st description by white man of the 27m wall of many-colored cliffs. Trip starts with **Grand I.** Near Sand Pt., the Pictured Rocks begin, red-sandstone formation carved by glaciers & wind, sun & rain of a thousand yrs. & painted by soluble oxide deposits. Impressive formations are **Colored & Rainbow Caves, Three Battleships, Ind. Drum Cave, Chapel Rock & Spray Cr. Cascade.** Beyond **Sullivan's Landing,** 30m, are **Grand Sable Banks,** dunes piled hundreds of feet high.

**114.** J. with dirt Rd. leading (N) through hardwood for. to **Laughing Whitefish Falls & Laughing Fish Pt. 160.** St.28 unites with US41 (see). **165. MARQUETTE** (see).

## Sec. 2: MARQUETTE (W) to MICH.-WIS. LINE. 162.

**12. NEGAUNEE. 15. ISHPEMING** (see US41). Iron country is wild & rugged, with sm. villages in midst of mine workings. Many lumbermen & miners went back to the land, & wherever possible, there are farms. **41. MICHIGAMME** (see US41). **73. COVINGTON,** popular with hunters. **Finnish Luth. Ch. 77.** Hy. crosses **LAC VIEUX DESERT TRL.** (see US2). Beyond is **Ottawa Nat. For.** (see US2). **82. NESBIT L. ORGANIZATION CAMP** (large group camps.electric.water plant. cabins.infirmary.pic.camp.sports facils.). **106. BRUCE CROSSING,** among dairy pastures. **127. BERGLAND,** at N. end of **L. Gogebic,** largest in Upper Peninsula; many resorts & tourist pks. Just (W) is J. with St.64.

SIDE TRIP: On St.64 (N) 18m to **Gull Pt. & Silver City,** village on site of silver boom in 1870's. J. with St.107, which leads (W) 10m to **Porcupine Mts. St. Pk.** (f.h.pic.camp.cabins. overnight shelters.trlr.pks.), Mich.'s newest (1943) & one of country's largest st. pks., covering 46,000 as. (6,600 under Fed.control). The Porcupines, highest range in Middle West, parallel lakeshore & reach highest pt. at **Gov. Peak** (2,023′). Trls. to **Mirror L.** (cabins. facils.trout), **Lily Pond, Carp R. Falls & Site of Copper Mine** (cabins).

St.28 unites with St.64 along N. end of L. Gogebic. **147. WAKEFIELD,** in heart of iron country. J. with Rd. to **Presque Isle Pk.** & Porcupine Mts. St.28 unites here with US2 (see). **153.5. BESSEMER. 161.5. IRONWOOD. 162.** Hy. crosses Montreal R., **MICH.-WIS. LINE.**

## US 41—MICHIGAN

**MICH.-WIS. LINE** (Marinette, Wis.) **(N) to COPPER HARBOR. 282. US41**

Via: Menominee, Stephenson, Escanaba, Gladstone, Trenary, Marquette, Negaunee, Ishpeming, L'Anse, Baraga, Houghton, Hancock, Calumet. Motor launch to Isle Royale from Copper Harbor. Resorts, tourist accoms.

US41 crosses broadest part of Upper Peninsula from Menominee Cty. farmlands & excellent f. grounds, (E & NW) to Marquette & (N) to Keweenaw Peninsula, the copper country.

### Sec. 1: MENOMINEE to MARQUETTE. 131.

Menominee Cty. is bordered (E) by Green Bay & (W) by Menominee R. (Wis. Line), celebrated in lumbering era for record log traffic. Stewart Edw. White (see Grand Rapids) was lumberjack here. Though only 15% cleared, cty. leads Upper Peninsula in farming.

**0. MENOMINEE**

Through RR. & bus conns. Menominee Cty. Airport, NW. limits. Interstate Bridge to Marinette, Wis. Ann Arbor RR. Car & Auto Ferry to Frankfort. Hotel, tourist accoms., cabins. Facils. for f., h., pic., camp., swim., boat., riding, & winter sports. Smelt Carnival (Ap.); Yacht Race (July). Info.: C. of C., First Nat. Bank Bldg.; St. Hy. Info. Lodge at bridge.

Power dams on Menominee R. (canoe trl.bass & walleyes) & dredged harbor on Green Bay make Menominee important industrial city, with f., cheese making, & shipping of Christmas trees & other wood & paper products in the lead. Thousands of deer hunters arrive in fall. Father Allouez (see) set up mission here, 1669, but trading post was not est. until 1797. Lumber era began with 1st steam sawmill, 1836, & Menominee became largest lumber-shipping port (1839-1910), filled with "sawmills, sawdust & saloons." **Yacht Basin** (free). **Henes Pk.** (pic.bath.). **Jordan College** (Cath.), on 100-a. campus. J. with St.35.

SIDE TRIP: St.35 is scenic hy. along Green Bay (camp sites). 16m **Menominee Cty. Mem. Pk.** (camp), near Airport. 20m **J. W. Wells St. Pk.** (pic.group camp.bath.).

**21. STEPHENSON.** J. with St.352, which runs (W) to **Menominee R. Game Area** (f.h.). **42. POWERS. Pinecrest Sanitorium** (tuberculosis). US41 unites with US2. **64. ESCANABA. 72.5. GLADSTONE. 79.5. RAPID RIVER** (see US2 for this sec.). US41 strikes (N) through fors. & swamplands. **116.5. SKANDIA.** J. with Rd.

SIDE TRIP: On Rd. (W) & (S) 11m to **Gwinn,** model village in **Escanaba R. St. Game Area;** many Ls. & fast-running Rs., large private estates & cabin colonies; deeryards (guides). Camera country.

**126.5.** J. with St.28 (see), with which US41 unites (N).

**131. MARQUETTE**

Through RR. & bus conns. Marquette Cty. Airport, 8m (W). Hotels, tourist rooms & cabins; tourist & St. pks. in vic. Facils. for f., h., swim., boat., golf & winter sports. Guides. Speedboat Races (July 4); Cty. Fair (Aug.). Info.: C. of C.; Upper Peninsula Development Bureau.

High among granite cliffs, the Upper Peninsula metropolis looks down on fine natural harbor picked out by Lighth. Pt., Presque Isle Pt. & Picnic Rocks; seat of Mich.'s largest cty., industrial center, college town, & summer & winter sports hqs. Père Marquette landed here in late 17th cent., & earliest Fr. maps show "Rivière des Morts," still the Dead R. although full of rapids. Settlement began as shipping pt. for Marquette lodes, discovered by white men in 1830's. Ore was carried inland by sleigh & mulecart over plank Rds., & freight was shipped by sail & portaged around falls until canal was opened (1855). Following peak in 1916, mines gradually became inactive, but various industries expanded, & city's great ore docks are busy. PTS. OF INT.: (1) Presque Isle & Kaye Ave., **Northern Mich. College of Education** (est.1899) has wooded campus on L.; cooperates with Univ. of Mich. in Grad. Sch. **Peter White Science Hall. Adm. Bldg. John D. Pierce Training Sch.** (2) **Presque Isle Pk.** (swim.recr.facils.pic.zoo) on rocky peninsula. **Granite Pt.**

(NW), view over "pathless woods & lonely shore." (3) Ridge & S. Front Sts., **Peter White Pub. Lib.** (1904.Ren.), gift of leading figure in mining boom. **Cty. Hist. Soc. Mus. & Lib.** (O.appl.). (4) Lakeside Pk., **Father Marquette Mon.** (1897.by Gaetano Trentanove); bronze figure on granite crag. (5) Bluff & N. Front Sts., **St. Peter's Cathedral** (1933.rebuilt 1936-37.mod.Romanes.by E.A.Schilling). Bishop Fred. Baraga (see), 1st bishop of diocese (1857), is buried in crypt. (6) **Ore Docks.** (7) **State H. of Correction & Branch Prison** (Romanes.). (8) **Superior Hills** (winter sports). J. with St.204.

SIDE TRIP: On St.204 (NW) 30m to Big Bay reg. around **L. Independence** (f.big game h.yr.-round hotel.cabins.store). Beyond (W) are **Huron Mts.,** roadless area of granite ridges & knobs; abundant wildlife.

## Sec. 2: MARQUETTE to BARAGA. 74.

**0. MARQUETTE. 12. NEGAUNEE** (sett.1846), underlain by mines of enormous richness; sports center. First large iron ore bodies in N. Amer. were found at Jackson Hill, in 1844, by Houghton's surveying party. **Jackson Mon.,** near site of discovery. **15. ISHPEMING** (sett.1856), hqs. for leading iron companies. Nat. Ski Assoc. meets held at Suicide Hill for more than 60 yrs. **Mather Mine,** one of world's deepest. **Tilden Mine,** open pit. **Barnes-Hecker Mine.** Abandoned **Ropes & Mich. Gold Mines. 28.** J. with St.95

SIDE TRIP: On St.95 (S) 7m to **Republic,** resort center on Michigamme R. (f.boat.camp. canoe trl.); seat of old Republic Mine.

**31. CHAMPION,** former mining center. **Van Riper Pk.,** on L. Michigamme (pic. camp.bathh.dance pavilion.recr.facils.restaurants). Above L. (W) is **St. Hy. Dept. Pk.** (pic.tower). **39. MICHIGAMME,** mining town & sports center. **59. ALBERTA,** all-white village built by Henry Ford around sawmill in midst of hardwoods. **69. L'ANSE,** center of resort area. Lac Vieux Desert Trl. (see US2) begins here.
US41 curves around Keweenaw Bay past **Baraga St. Pk.** (f.camp.electric.stores).

**74. BARAGA.** In vic. (W) are cheese centers, notably **Watton & Pelkie.** Cranberry bogs (N).

## Sec. 3: BARAGA to COPPER HARBOR (Isle Royale). 77.

Keweenaw Peninsula tour. Through RR. & bus conns. in larger centers. Airports at Baraga, Houghton, Laurium. Boats to Isle Royale from Copper Harbor; Great Ls. cruises; deep-sea trolling. Hotels, resorts, pub. pks., pic. & camp sites.

Keweenaw Peninsula, the copper country, extends like a horn into L. Superior; cut across by Portage L. & Portage Ship Canal. This highly scenic peninsula is settled mainly by descendants of miners, lumbermen & adventurers. Ind. copper workings are still visible. Nowhere else in world has massed copper been found in this pure form. Mining began in 1844, & since then millions of tons have been unearthed.

**2. ASSININS,** founded by Father Baraga in 1843. Across bay was Meth. mission of Rev. John Pitezel. **Baraga Mission,** Ind. sch. & farm.

**28. HOUGHTON & HANCOCK**

Through RR. & bus conns. Airport. Good accoms. & all kinds of sports facils. Tourist pk. Info.: C. of C.

Houghton, chief shipping pt. & college town, was born of copper industry & became political & financial center in early 1850's. Overlooking canal are bldgs. of **Mich. College of Mining & Technology,** one of country's leading tech. schs. **Engineering Bldg.;** Mus. College, founded by a few mining students, now has branch at Sault Ste Marie (see). **Hancock,** larger of twin cities, is conn. with Houghton by only bridge bet. 2 secs. of peninsula. Quincy Mine, oldest still-productive mine in St., was est. 1848 & became one of greatest on range. City was also lumber center. Almost every racial strain in Amer. is represented in pop.; large Finnish, Scand. & Cornish groups. Louis Adamic has written much about reg. US41 leads uphill to **Quincy Mine Tourist View & Quincy Mine** (surface plant O.); largest hoist in world. J. with St.203.

SIDE TRIP: On St.203 (W) c.11m to **F. J. McLain St. Pk.** (pic.facils.store), on **L.** Superior.

**39. LAURIUM** (airport), residential community. St.26 unites with US41. Adj. is **Calumet,** home of **Calumet & Hecla Mine** (N.O.), once queen of copper mines. **47.** Active **AHMEEK MINE. 57. PHOENIX.** St.26 here becomes Sand Dunes Dr.

SIDE TRIP: On St.26 (N) & (E) to **Copper Harbor.** 2m **Eagle River. Douglass Houghton Mon.,** to young geologist who was drowned near spot in 1845. **Eagle Harbor** (camp. cabins). **Agate Harbor.** Blueberry & blackberry country. 24m **Copper Harbor** (see below).

**70. L. MEDORA** (whitefish). On tableland above L. is **Keweenaw Pk.** (cottages. clubh.& golf course.tower). Beyond is turn-out to **Brockway Mt. Dr.** to **West Bluff** (1,380′). **77. COPPER HARBOR** (good accoms.airport.boats to Isle Royale), yr.-round resort. **80. FT. WILKINS ST. PK.** (f.swim.pic.camp.trlrs.store). **Ft. Wilkins (1844).**

**Isle Royale Nat. Pk.**

Boat Serv.: From Copper Harbor twice wkly. July 1-15; 3 times wkly. July 15-Sept. 6; by arrangement in June. From Grand Marais & Grand Portage, Minn., twice wkly. May 15-Nov. 15; & from Ft. William & Port Arthur, Ont., beginning June 30. Chartered airplane serv. Accoms.: Windigo Inn (July 1-Sept.1); Rock Harbor Lodge (June 15-Sept.7.guest H. & cottages); camp sites. Cars stored at ports; no hys. in pk. Registration & camp permits required. Guides, boats, tackle & supplies. Info.: Pk. Serv. Hqs., Rock Harbor. Supt., Houghton, Mich.

This 134,000-a. wilderness lies close to Can. boundary, some 50m (NW) from Mich. mainland. Shorelines are cut by numerous coves & bays, largest of which is **Siskiwit Bay.** Ojibway did not cede Is. until 1842. Amer. Fur Co. est. posts here in 1830's; & copper mining was carried on in late 19th cent. Prehist. tribes had worked the mines. The thin soil covers lava formation, & numerous peaks rise out of groves of ash, maple & oak, cedar, balsam & pine. Flora is unusually varied. Moose, coyote, mink, beaver & snowshoe rabbits are common; but bear, deer, porcupine & wolves either found Isle Royale unsuitable or never appeared there. PTS. OF INT. (directions at hqs.): **Mt. Lookout Louise,** highest pt.; **Mon. Rock, Mt. Franklin & Mt. Ojibway. Old Lighth.,** used until 1858. **Prehist. Mine Workings. Moose Wallows.**

# DETROIT

RR. stas.: 15th & Michigan Ave., Mich. Central; Fort St. & 3rd Ave., Union Depot; foot of Brush St., Grand Trunk Depot. Washington Blvd. & Grand River Ave., Bus Term. Airports: (W) c.25m on US212, Willow Run Airport; Conner & Gratiot Aves., City Airport; Seaplane Bases at Belle Isle & Grosse Pointe Pk. Great Ls. cruises; excursions to Cedar Pt. & Put-in-Bay, O.; Bob Lo I., Tashmoo I. & other pts. Good accoms.; recr. facils. Stage & motion picture theaters; dramatic, musical, & other events at Music Hall, Art Institute, Wayne Univ., Rackham Bldg., Pub. Lib. Resorts, st. pks. & recr. areas in vic. Info.: Opp. City Hall, Convention & Tourist Bureau; 139 Bagley Ave., Detroit Auto. Club; 320 W. Lafayette Ave., Board of Comm. Annual Events: Mich. Exposition (Jan.), Horse Racing (May-Sept.), St. Fair (Sept.), Mich. Artists' Show (Nov.); Auto, Dog, Flower & trade shows in Convention Hall. How to enter Canada: Detroit-Canada Tunnel (bus & auto), foot of Bates St.; Ambassador Bridge (toll), Porter & 22nd Sts. Info. Detroit: Customs Dept., Griswold & Larned Sts.; Immigration Dept., 3770 E. Jefferson Ave. No passports required of residents of U.S. or Canada, but identification, naturalization or proof-of-entry papers advised; car (for 6 mos. duty free) & vacation equipment.

Detroit, motor capital on world's busiest waterway, is 4th largest city in U.S., ranks 3rd as industrial center & 4th as exporting port. Metrop. area extends over 142-sq. miles, & Windsor, across R. in Essex Cty., Ont., is also an automotive center. Judge Augustus Woodward's city plan imitated L'Enfant's Washington, but geometric pattern covers orig. circular web. During phenomenal expansion in 20th cent., Detroit sprang into the air but failed, at first, to expand horizontally. Result is small & confusing downtown dist. running a few blocks (N) from R. & (E) & (W) of Woodward Ave. (US10). A block (W) of Ave. is Washington Blvd. where better shops, hotels & theaters cluster around Grand Circus Pk. Jefferson Ave. follows old shoreline (E) to wealthy Grosse Pointe communities & (W) to downriver industrial centers. The cities of Highland Park & Hamtramck (N) are completely surrounded by Detroit.

In absence of subway or elevated, traffic streams through congested sts. & over magnificent hys. Another stream of traffic pours night & day from immense functional factory bldgs. The nearly 3,000,000 residents of metrop. area (more than half of St.'s pop.) depend mainly on automotive power for their livelihood. This predominantly serious pop., from all parts of the world, gives aspect of grim automatism to city life, especially noticeable in ever-present, slowly moving lines waiting for buses. These same people give Detroit its tremendous, restless vitality. Of 20 sizable racial groups, the Polish is probably largest. Itals. form important element with considerable cultural influence, as do descendants of early Fr., German, Irish & Brit. settlers. Nearly 350,000 Negroes (1947) live in areas widely scattered from orig. nucleus around Hastings St. A few blocks (E) of City Hall are coffee shops of Arabic-speaking community. Leading the world in manufacture of automobiles, Detroit is also a growing steel center & ranks high in pharmaceuticals, adding machines, salt, varnishes, rubber goods & marine, aeronautical & television equipment. Wayne Univ., Univ. of Detroit, Marygrove College, Symphony Orchestra, Institute of Arts & other institutions give it increasing importance as cultural center. Founded by Antoine de la Mothe Cadillac for Louis XIV, Detroit began as fur-trading post, was taken by Brit. at close of Fr. & Ind. War & only relinquished after Battle of Fallen Timbers (see Ohio). Fire destroyed the settlement in 1805. During War of 1812, Detroit was again surrendered to Brit. by Terr. Gov. Wm. Hull & held until Perry's victory on L. Erie. After Civil War, the city began to develop industrially, & immigrants swarmed in from N.Y. & New England. Before the automobile, Detroit made RR. cars, carriages, & bicycles. With development of a practical motor car, expansion was fantastically rapid, & civic problems correspondingly more complex. With one of largest labor unions in the world, Detroit is important factor in nat. political & economic affairs.

PTS. OF INT. INDUSTRIAL: (1) **Automobile Plants:** Ford Motor Co. (see Trip II below). 1580 E. Grand Blvd., Packard Motor Car Co. (O). 12200 E. Jefferson Ave., Chrysler Corp. (usually O.); also Dodge, DeSoto & Plymouth Plants. Michigan & Clark Ave., Cadillac Motor Car Co. (O.8-4). W. Warren & Livernois Aves., Lincoln Plant, of Ford Motor Co. (O.appl.). (2) **Other Plants** (usually O.): 615 W. Lafayette Ave., "Detroit News" (tours); radio & television studios. 6600 E. Jefferson Ave., U.S. Rubber Co. 6900 E. Jefferson Ave., Detroit-Mich. Stove Co., 1 McDougall Ave., Parke-Davis Laboratories, world's largest producer of pharmaceuticals. 6008-75 Second Blvd., Burroughs Adding Machine Co. 2900 E. Grand Blvd., Jam Handy Motion Picture Studios.

PTS. OF INT. DOWNTOWN: (3) Woodward & Michigan Aves., **Cadillac Sq.,** on site of old City Hall & Market. On (W) side, **City Hall** (1871.Fr.Goth.by Jas.Anderson). On (E) side, **Wayne Cty. Bldg.** (1895-1902.Ital.Ren.by John Scott); bronze "Progress" groups above Corinthian portico by J. Massey Rhind. Opp. City Hall, **Soldiers' & Sailors' Mon.** (by Randolph Rogers); (E) of Mon. **Cadillac's Chair,** of age-darkened red sandstone, empty except for birds. (4) Woodward Ave. & Woodbridge St., **Mariners' Ch.** (1849.Eng.Goth), 2nd oldest in city; & **Mariners' Inn** (O), now Episc. City Mission Center. (5) Gratiot Ave., bet. Farmer & Library Sts., **Downtown Lib.** (1932.mod.Class.), on site of jail where Wayne tavernkeeper was hanged for murder of his wife, last legal execution in St., as popular reaction made Mich. the 1st St. to abolish capital punishment (1847). (6) 350 Madison Ave., **Music Hall,** home of Symphony Orchestra developed by late Ossip Gabrilowitsch. (7) Lafayette Blvd., 2 blocks (W) from Cad. Sq., **Federal Bldg.** (1934.mod.Class.); plaque at **Site of Ft. Shelby.** (8) Griswold & Fort Sts., **Penobscot Bldg.** (1928.by Smith, Hinchman & Grylls), city's tallest tower (O.telescope). (9) W. Fort & 3rd Sts., **Fort St. Presb. Ch.** (1855.Eng.Goth.by A.& O.Jordan); fine wooden spire (230'), richly decorated facade. (10) State & Griswold Sts., **Capitol Pk.,** site of 1st St. capitol (1828-47), burned in 1893. **Grave of Stevens T. Mason,** 1st Gov. (11) 1234 Washington Blvd., **St. Aloysius Ch.** (Cath.1930.Romanes.by Donaldson & Meier); unusual street-level balcony overlooking altar. (12) Head of Washington Blvd., (E) & (W) of Woodward Ave., **Grand Circus Pk. Edison Fountain** (1929). **Statue of Gov. Pingree** (by Rudolph Schwartz). **Alger Mem. Fountain** (1921.by Dan.C.French). (13) 2000 Witherell St., **Detroit Institute of Technology,** maintained by Y.M.C.A.

PTS. OF INT. (N) & (NE): (14) E. Vernor Hy. & Russell St., **Eastern Mun. Market.** At daybreak horse-drawn wagons mingle with hundreds of trucks; later the cross-shaped bldgs. are crowded with housewives of 50 nationalities. (15) 500 Temple Ave., **Masonic Temple** (1926.Goth.by G.D.Mason); concert hall. In Woodward & Kirby Aves. vic. is **Art Center,** with white-marble bldgs. under immense elms: (16) **Institute of Arts** (1927.mod.Ital.Ren.by Paul Cret & Zantzinger,Borie & Medary).

Arrangement in period rooms, by Dr. W. R. Valentiner, is especially notable. **Rivera Murals** of "Detroit Industry" in garden court. Mus. specializes in Ital. Goth. sculpture & N. European painting. (17) **Pub. Lib.** (1921.Ital.Ren.by Cass Gilbert); murals by F. J. Wiley, Edwin Blashfield & Gari Melchers; Clarence M. Burton Hist. Coll. (18) 441 Merrick Ave., **Detroit Hist. Mus.** (O.exc.Mon.free). (19) 5205 Cass Ave., **Children's Mus.** (O.exc.Sun.); hist. exhibits & dioramas. (20) Woodward & Putnam Aves., **Rackham Educational Mem.** (O.1942.mod.Class.by Harley, Ellington & Day), center for Univ. of Mich. Extension Serv. (see Ann Arbor on US12). (21) (W) of Art Center, **Wayne Univ.,** with hqs. in **Old Central High Sch.** (1896. Romanes.by Malcolmson & Higgenbotham); org. in Law Sch., Grad. Sch., Colleges of Education, Liberal Arts, Pharmacy, Engineering & Nursing & Schs. of Pub. Affairs, Social Studies, Medicine, Business Adm. & Gen. Studies (no degree). (22) 4800 Woodward Ave., **St. Paul's Episc. Cathedral** (1908-19.Goth.by Cram, Goodhue & Ferguson), for oldest Prot. Episc. parish in N.W. (est.1824). (23) W. Grand & 2nd Blvds. is **New Center Group** (1919-31.by Albert Kahn): **Gen. Motors Bldg.** (1919), 15-story structure begun by W. C. Durant (see) to cost $20,000,000. (24) Across Blvd., **Fisher Bldg.** (1928); exter. & inter. lavishly decorated with costly materials. (25) 2799 W. Grand Blvd. **Henry Ford Hospital** (1921.designed by company engineers). (26) 8801 Woodward Ave., **Temple Beth El** (Class.), Mich.'s oldest Jewish congregation (est.1859). (27) Woodward & Belmont Aves., **Blessed Sacrament Cathedral** (1938.Fr.Goth.by Henry A.Walsh) of Cath. Archdiocese. (28) McNichols Rd. & Livernois Ave., **Univ. of Detroit** (1927.Sp.Ren.by Malcolmson & Higgenbotham), under Jesuit Order; colleges of law, engineering, commerce, finance & dentistry. **Aerodynamical Lab. Mem. Tower.** (29) 8425 McNichols Rd., **Marygrove College,** st.'s oldest Cath. college for women; handsome white-stone bldgs. (Eng.Goth.). (30) **Hamtramck** & (31) **Highland Pk.** (see below).

PTS. OF INT. OFF E. JEFFERSON AVE.: (32) At. St. Antoine St., **SS. Peter & Paul's Ch.** (Cath.1844.Romanes.by Francis Letourno), oldest Ch. in city; (33) At E. Grand Blvd., **Belle Isle Bridge** (1923.cantilever). Near approach is **Gabriel Richard Pk.** (bus & ferry.pic.bathh.canoes.casino). (34) In **Belle I. Pk.** are: L. Takoma (skating pavilion), Barbour Mem. Fountain; Conservatory; Aquarium; Zoo; Livingstone Mem. Light; Scott Mem. Fountain; Boat & Yacht Clubhs.

PTS. OF INT. (SW): (35) Howard & 19th Sts., **Ste Anne's Shrine** (1886.Goth.), for 2nd-oldest continuously maintained Cath. parish in U.S., est. 2 days after Cadillac's landing in 1701. **Burial Place of Father Richard** (see) in crypt behind altar. **Ste Anne's Chapel** (O.appl.); 1828 altar & other relics of Father Richard, known as Mich.'s 1st educator; also served as Terr. Delegate. (36) Porter & 22nd Sts., **Ambassador Bridge** (1929.toll), beautiful $2^m$ link with Canada. (37) Foot of Livernois Ave., **Ft. Wayne** (c.1841.rest.& developed). (38) Fullerton & Warren Aves., Outer Dr. & Burt Rd., **River Rouge Pk.** (summer & winter sports.swim. pools of Olympics' standards).

## HAMTRAMCK

A city of c.50,000, Hamtramck is encircled by Detroit & practically indistinguishable from it. Hamtramck Township, named for Col. J. F. Hamtramck, Detroit's 1st Amer. military commdr., was rural community until Dodge Bros., in 1914, est. automobile plant. Present pop. is more than 50% Polish, & its closely org. social life keeps it a distinct & colorful entity. Negro community was also est. in early yrs. & 1st common council incl. a Negro member. Hamtramck gained nat. attention with its Pub. Sch. Code, developed by Dr. M. R. Keyworth to aid immigrants in adjusting to Amer. 3056 Hanley Ave., **Tau Beta Community H. & Pub. Lib.** Forian Ave., bet. Latham & Brombach Sts., **St. Florian's Ch.** (Cath.), oldest & largest parish.

## HIGHLAND PARK

Like Hamtramck, Highland Park is a city within a city, with Woodward Ave. as its main street. Building of Ford plant here before World War I brought thousands of workers, but since removal of plant to Dearborn (see) in 1920, Highland Park has become, again, a residential suburb. 12244 Woodward Ave., **McGregor Pub. Lib.** (1926.mod.Class.by E.L.Tilton & A.M.Githens). 13100 Woodward Ave., **Lawrence Institute of Technology;** coop. work-study plan.

DETROIT AND VICINITY
LEGEND
POINTS OF INTEREST
U.S. HIGHWAYS
STATE HIGHWAYS
0 1 2 3 4 5
SCALE OF MILES
BASE LINE ROAD
(EIGHT MILE ROAD)
Race Track
STATE FAIR GROUNDS
SEVEN MILE ROAD
OUTER DR.
McNICHOLS ROAD
FIVE MILE ROAD
OUTER
SCHOOLCRAFT AVE.
PLYMOUTH ROAD
ROUGE PARK
W. CHICAGO BLVD.
JOY ROAD
TIREMAN
WARREN ROAD
WARREN AVE.
FORD ROAD
MICHIGAN AVE.
McGRAW
MICHIGAN
ROTUNDA DR.
VILLAGE DR.
GREEN FIELD
TELEGRAPH ROAD
BEDFORD ROAD
COUZENS HWAY
GRAND RIVER
GRAND DR.
WYOMING AVE.
LIVERNOIS AVE.
DEXTER BLVD.
DAVISON
OAKMAN BLVD.
HAMILTON
JOHN R.
WEST
MEYERS
SCHAEFER
OAKMAN
MILLER
EVERGREEN
GREENFIELD
SOUTHFIELD
ESPER
BOSTON
BEECHWOOD
LINWOOD
12TH
CENTRAL
VERNOR
FORT ST.
JEFFERSON
ROUGE
RIVER
OUTER DR.

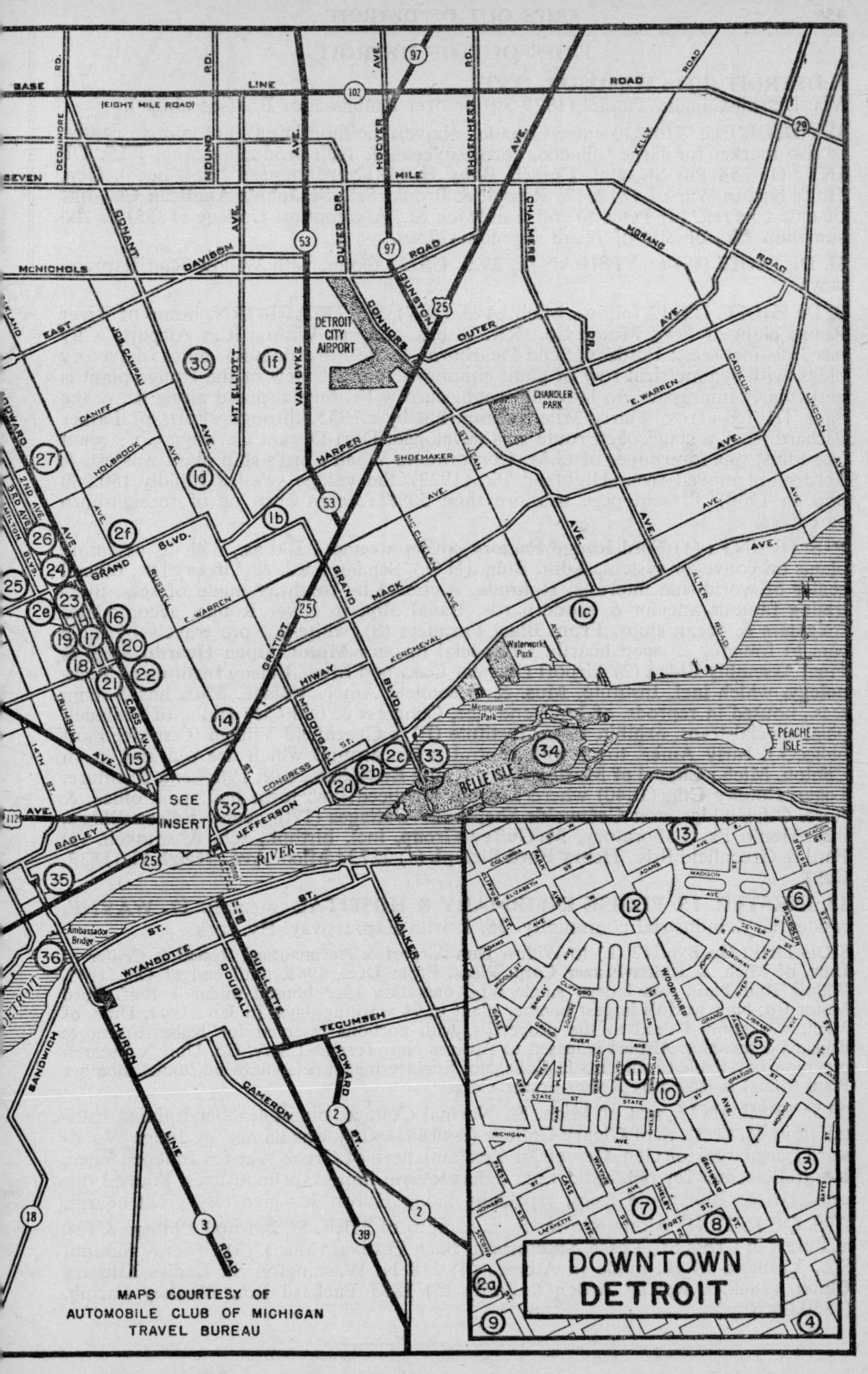
BASE LINE ROAD
(EIGHT MILE ROAD)
SEVEN MILE
McNICHOLS
DETROIT CITY AIRPORT
CHANDLER PARK
Waterworks Park
Memorial Park
BELLE ISLE
PEACHE ISLE
RIVER
DETROIT
Ambassador Bridge
SEE INSERT
DOWNTOWN DETROIT
MAPS COURTESY OF
AUTOMOBILE CLUB OF MICHIGAN
TRAVEL BUREAU

## TRIPS OUT OF DETROIT

### I. DETROIT (E) to WINDSOR, ONT.

Via: Detroit-Canada Tunnel (1929-30) or over Ambassador Br. (see above).

**WINDSOR** (see "How to enter Canada" above); the Dominion's automotive center, is also market for large tobacco, corn, soybean & fruit-producing area. PTS. OF INT.: (1) 254 Pitt St., **Col. Francis Baby H.** (1812.pronounced "Baw-bee"), Gen. Hull's hqs. in War of 1812. (2) Russell & Brooks Sts., **St. John's Anglican Ch.,** one of oldest in reg. (3) Peter St. off Sandwich St., **Assumption College** (1855) **& Assumption Ch.,** on site of Jesuit Mission (1750).

**II. DETROIT (W) to YPSILANTI. 29.5. US112** (conn. with Willow Run Expressway).

**0. DETROIT.** US112 follows Mich. Ave. (NW). **9.5. DEARBORN,** home of River Rouge plant of Ford Motor Co. (RR. & bus. accoms. Willow Run Airport). City has 3 distinct secs.: Fordson, "Old Dearborn" & the Ford domain, miles of factory bldgs. with symmetrical row of giant chimneys. A night view of the Rouge plant is particularly impressive. In late 18th cent., narrow Fr. farms spread along R., & the Sauk Trl. led across Thirty Mile Swamp, but by c.1835, through efforts of Father Richard (see), a stagecoach route was developed. Dort-Durant Carriage Co.'s plant (see Flint) was forerunner of G.M. Corporation. When Ford's ship plant was est. & Ford plant moved from Highland Pk. (1923), the village swelled rapidly (50,000 pop. in 1930). Present pop. is more than 50% foreign born or of foreign-born parentage.

PTS. OF INT.: (1) **Ford Rouge Factory** covers around 1,200 as., with its assembly plants on conveyor system. **Adm. Bldg.** (N.O.), Schaefer Rd. & Airport Dr., official center of worldwide interests. **Rotunda,** encircled by roadway made of secs. illustrating famous ancient & modern rds. **Canal Slip,** in River Rouge, accomodates freighters & ocean ships. From **Blast Furnaces** (S), white-hot ore travels by ladle cars to foundry & open hearth. Of special int. are **Motor, Open Hearth, Steel & Final Assembly Bldgs.** (2) Airport Dr. near Oakwood Blvd., **Edison Institute of Technology,** which incl. Institute, Mus. & Greenfield Amer. Village. **Mus.** has 5 main secs., housed in reprods. of Independence, Congress & Old City Halls, of Philadelphia; special trans. exhibit. From Institute (E) is **Greenfield Village** (O.sm.fee.most bldgs.O.), early Amer. town with central green around which are old **Inn,** from Clinton, Mich.; **Chapel of Martha-Mary** (Col.); **Brick Sch.,** with 19th-cent. furniture; **Logan County Cth.** (1840) where Lincoln practiced law; town hall, post office, & store. Other bldgs. are: **Cotswolds Shepherds' Cottages** (17th cent.); **Edison Bldgs.,** incl. Menlo Pk. Laboratory; **McGuffey Group,** incl. birthpl., sch. & smokeh. (3) Ford & Greenfield Rds., **Henry Ford Birthpl.** (4) 22734 Mich. Ave., **Haigh H.** (1833. Col.).

**13. INKSTER. 15. ELOISE INFIRMARY & HOSPITAL** (mental). **17. WAYNE,** residential & industrial community. **25.** J. with Expressway. Hy. forks.

SIDE TRIP: On Byp.112 (L) to **Willow Run Airport & Aeronautical Research Center** of Univ. of Mich. & **Kaiser-Frazer Corp. Plant.** From Dec., 1941, until end of Oct. 1945, Willow Run Plant was largest single mfg. operation ever housed under 1 roof. Ford Motor Co. built world's largest bomber plant in 94 working days. In Jan., 1947, Univ. of Mich. was granted deed to the properties, with portions reserved for Kaiser-Frazer & Packard companies. **Airport** is leased to Airlines Nat. Terminal Serv. Co. Univ.'s research program is available to students in College of Engineering; supersonic wind tunnel. **Bomber Plant** (tours) is leased by Kaiser-Frazer Corp.

**29.5. YPSILANTI,** seat of Mich. St. Normal College, oldest teacher-training institution in Midwest, & of Cleary College (est.1883). City was named by Judge Woodward (see above) for Gen. Demetrios Ypsilanti, hero of Greek War for Independence. It is trade center for rich agric. area & has several important industries. Many 19th-cent. Hs. & 100-yr.-old trees, especially along Huron R., give city great charm.

PTS. OF INT.: (1) Along Brower St. is campus of **Mich. St. Normal College** & (2), at Forest & Cross St., **Pease Auditorium;** Bach Festival (Mar.). (3) Cross & Summit Sts., **Ypsilanti Mon.,** made in Athens. (4) 218 N. Washington St. **Ladies Literary Clubh.** (1842.Gr.Rev.by Arden Ballard). (5) 1885 Packard Rd., **Breakey Farmh.** (1830.Gr.Rev.).

**III. DETROIT (NW) to PONTIAC. 25. US10.**
Via: Ferndale, Birmingham & Bloomfield Hills.

US10, the Saginaw Trl., follows Woodward Ave. (N) to **9. CITY LIMITS** (called Eight Mile Rd.). **10. FERNDALE,** attractive suburb. **10.5. PLEASANT RIDGE. 11.** J. with Ten Mile Rd., which leads (L) a short way to **Detroit Zoological Pk.** (pic.parking). Beyond J. is J. with Rd. (R) into **Royal Oak,** residential community. **11.5. HUNTINGTON WOODS,** highly restricted. **12. SHRINE OF THE LITTLE FLOWER** (1931-33.by Henry McGill), publicized by Rev. Chas. E. Coughlin. **17.5. BIRMINGHAM,** suburban city with many fine Hs. **19.** J. with Lone Pine Rd.

SIDE TRIP: On Lone Pine Rd. (W) 1.5m to **Cranbrook Foundation** (grounds O.), widely known for **Institute of Science** as well as for **Cranbrook Sch.** (boys) & **Kingswood Sch.** (girls). The 300-a. estate & large endowment are gifts of Ellen S. & Geo. G. Booth, formerly pres. of "Detroit News." Except for **Christ Ch.** (Episc.Fr.Goth.by Goodhue) & part of **Brookside Sch.,** all bldgs. were designed by Eliel Saarinen, eminent Finnish architect, now pres. of **Cranbrook Academy of Art** (O). **Orpheus Fountain** (by Carl Milles).

**20.5. BLOOMFIELD HILLS,** a city of half-acre or larger estates. Just beyond is J. with Opdyke Rd., which leads (E) half-mile to **St. Hugo of the Hills** (early Eng.1936. by Arthur Des Rosiers).

**25. PONTIAC**

Through RR. & bus. Mun. Airport. Good accoms. Many resorts, st. recr. areas & colonies on Ls. in vic.

Pontiac, named for Ind. chief, is Mich.'s 6th city & important automotive center. Settlement was begun in 1818, & by 1837 sawmills, flour mills & other industries were creating a prosperous town. Pontiac Spring Wagon Works was est. in 1880's, & in 1907, the Oakland Motor Car Co. ushered in automobile age. Among large plants are **Pontiac, Fisher Body, & G.M. Truck & Coach.** Oakland Cty. is famous for 400 Ls. (resorts.camp.summer & winter sports). In vic. are Bald Mt., Highland, Island L. & Proud L. Recr. Areas.

**IV. DETROIT (W. & S.) to GROSSE ILE c.18. W. Jefferson Ave. & Van Horn Rd.**
Via: River Rouge, Ecorse, Wyandotte, Trenton.

Downriver area is rich in hist., in geological deposits & industrial developments. It was once favored campground of Wyandotte (or Huron) Inds., & Cadillac explored reg. in 1701. Chief Pontiac held council on Grosse Ile. Stratified deposits of salt, dolomite, siliceous sand & other nonmetallic minerals are responsible for industrial developments.

W. Jefferson Ave. follows roughly the Detroit R. **5. RIVER ROUGE. Great Lakes Engineering Works.** Just beyond R. is **U.S. Gypsum Plant. 6.5. ECORSE,** known during Prohibition period as chief port of entry for liquor from Canada, a gangsters' capital on waterfront, with bullet-proof boatwells. **Great Lakes Steel Plant. 8.5. WYANDOTTE,** most important downriver city; nat. center for alkali & related products. First Bessemer steel in Amer. was manufactured in Wyandotte (1884).

**13. TRENTON** (plotted in 1827) shared industrial development of Detroit. **Elizabeth Pk.** (pic.recr.facils.). **Wayne Cty. Tourist Lodge** (trlrs.laundry.lunchroom). **17.** Tour turns (E) on Van Horn Rd. to **Grosse Ile,** largest I. in Detroit R.; independent township, exclusively residential. Its high, wooded shores attracted Inds., explorers & missionaries. Cadillac deeded it to his daughter, but in 1711 his lands were confiscated by Brit. Gov. PTS. OF INT.: **U.S. Naval Base & Grosse Ile Airport** (O.appl.).

**St. James Episc. Ch.** (Goth.in wood.by Gordon W. Lloyd). **Little Cote** (Vict.Goth. 1856).

**V. DETROIT (NW) to BRIGHTON. 40. US16.** Via: Farmington & New Hudson. US16 follows Grand River Ave., trl. of Inds., trappers, & 19th-cent. tourists. **16.** J. with Inkster Rd., which leads (R) 1m to **Ford Republic,** named for Emory L. Ford; similar to Children's Village, N.Y. Beyond J. is **Botsford Tavern** (O.meals.1836), white clapboarded farmh. bought & rest. by Henry Ford in 1924. In 1841 it was Sixteen Mile H. for stagecoach patrons. **18. MICH. CHILDREN'S HOSPITAL** (est. 1918), in beautiful setting. **18.5. LA SALLE WINERY** (O.wks.). **19. FARMINGTON,** sett. by Quakers in 1824. **Quaker Cemetery. Log Cabin** (1824). **Gov. Warner H.** (1860.Vict.). **25. NOVI.** J. with Novi Rd., which leads (N) 2m to **Walled L.,** popular resort; & (S) 4m to **Northville. Wm. Maybury Sanitarium** (tuberculosis). **32. NEW HUDSON. Hotel** (1831).

SIDE TRIP: On Milford Rd. (N) 6m to **Milford** in recr. area. Rd. leads (W) 11m to **G.M. Proving Grounds** (tours).

**38.5.** J. with US23 (see). US16 borders **Island L. Recr. Area. 40. BRIGHTON,** center of resort country.

**VI. DETROIT (NE) to MOUNT CLEMENS. 36.5. E. Jefferson Ave. & St.29.**
Via: Grosse Pointe & St. Clair Shores.

This beautiful route follows Detroit R. to limits at Alter Rd., where 5 Grosse Pte. & other lakeshore communities begin, the "Gold Coast" of Detroit. **10. GROSSE POINTE PARK,** largest of group; on site of battle bet. French & Ind. allies of Brit., in 1712. The French est. their mile-long ribbon farms extending down to L. St. Clair, which became a scene of carnival in winter, with sleigh parties over the ice to gala temporary taverns. In city of **GROSSE POINTE** is **Grosse Pointe Club** (N.O.), oldest in St. (1897). **13.5. GROSSE POINTE FARMS,** oldest shore settlement, has some of most impressive estates. **Dodge H.** (Tudor by Smith, Hinchman & Grylls), fabulous castle left unfinished in 1929. **32.** Lake Shore Rd., **Alger H. Branch of Detroit Institute of Arts** (tours & tea on appl.); reprod. of Florentine villa; Ital. Ren. & modern art colls. Foot of Vernier Rd., **Grosse Pointe Yacht Club** (1929. mod.Venetian.by Richmond & Morgan). **15.5. GROSSE POINTE SHORES;** no business sec. 1100 Lake Shore Dr., **Edsel Ford Estate.** The H. (1928.Eng.Cotswold. by Albert Kahn) is not visible from hy. **16. GROSSE POINTE WOODS.** Here tour follows Lake Shore Dr. **21.5. ST. CLAIR SHORES. 36.5. MOUNT CLEMENS** (bus.large hotels.bathhs.tourist accoms.), widely known health & summer resort on Clinton R. **G.T. RR. Sta.** where Thos. Edison worked as a boy. **Moravian Dr.**

# SAULT STE. MARIE

## SAULT STE MARIE

Portage Ave. & Magazine St., RR. Terminal Sta. Greyhound & other bus lines. On Ashmun Hill, Mun. Airport. Water St. piers for steamship lines; ferry to Sault Ste Marie, Ont., & Sugar I. Excursions through Locks. Hotels, rooms & camps. Yr.-round ice-skating at Pullman Stadium. Winter Sports Carnival & Herring-Choker Jamboree (Jan.or Feb.); Smelt Jamboree (May); Ice Revue (Aug.). Info.: C. of C., Hotel Ojibway Bldg.

Sault Ste Marie, gateway to Canada & tourist starting pt., was America's "No. 1 Military Target" in World War II, as nearly 90% of iron ore for ammunition passed through the Locks, greatest artery of marine commerce in world. Soo is also 1st permanent white settlement in Mich. & 3rd-oldest surviving in U.S. Important plants are Union Carbide & Carbon Corp., Mich. Northern Power Co., Northwestern Leather Co. & Cadillac Soo Lumber Co. Etienne Brulé (1618) & Jean Nicolet (1634) were probably 1st white men to see rush of L. Superior waters over sandstone & granite ledges in St. Mary's R. At falls, the Chippewa (or Ojibway) had one of most populous Ind. villages in U.S. area (2,000). In 1638, Radisson & Groseilliers brought fur trade to L. Superior, & in 1668 Père Marquette built 1st Christian Ch. in N.W. Terr. Louis XIV held possession from 1671 until Brit. raised Union Jack in 1761. It was 1820 before Gov. Lewis Cass hauled it down again. Ft. Brady was built in 1822. Soo was important post of Amer. Fur Co., & Fr.-Canadian voyageurs braved L. Superior in 40′ canoes. Grace L. Nute (in "Lake Superior") describes these debonair & haughty men in long bright sashes, singing their paddling songs. State, in 1855, built ship canal with aid of Congress. Weitzel Lock (destroyed in const. of MacArthur Lock) was built bet. 1870 & 1881. With the RRs. (middle 1880's) & building of modern locks, "the remotest settlement in the U.S., if not in the moon" rapidly became a brisk & colorful port. L. Superior whitefish, which Mrs. Jameson (1837) called "most delicious luxury that swims the waters," the muskellunge, trout & herring make reg. inviting to sportsmen & commercial fishermen.

PTS. OF INT.: (1) **Locks** at St. Mary's Rapids. **MacArthur Lock** (800′.1943). **Poe Lock** (800′.1896). **Davis** (1914) & **Sabin** (1919), twin locks. **Canadian Lock** (900′. 1895). (2) Head of Rapids, **Compensating Dam,** to regulate level of Gt. Ls. (3) **Internat. RR. Bridge** (1887), probably largest jack-knife bridge in world. (4) South St. & Ryan Ave., **Ft. Brady,** occupied by **Sault Tech.,** branch of Mich. College of Mining (see US41). Ft., reconst. in 1890's, was in continuous use 150 yrs.; enlarged during World War II. (5) **Gov. Pk.;** fine view. (6) **Brady Pk.,** landing place of early missionaries. **Repentigny Mon.** on site of Fr. ft. (1750) & orig. site of Ft. Brady (1822). (7) Armory Pl., bet. Kimball & Bingham Sts., **Pub. Lib.;** hist. mus. (8) Foot of Bingham Ave., **Site of Marquette's Mission.** (9) 413 Water St., **John Johnston H.** (1795), home of fur trader who married Chippewa woman; father-in-law of Henry R. Schoolcraft. (10) On Union Carbide Co. grounds, **Schoolcraft Ind. Agency** (1826-27.remod.). Schoolcraft was 1st Ind. agent at Soo, & his research into lore of Manabozho was basis of Longfellow's "Hiawatha." (11) **Sugar I.** (ferry.stores.guides. licenses.rooms.cabins.restaurant). (12) **Munuscong** (resort), (S) 23m on Munuscong L.

## TRIPS OUT OF SAULT STE MARIE

**I.** By ferry to **SAULT STE MARIE, ONT.** (see Detroit: How to enter Canada), larger of the twin cities; center of **Algoma Reg.** (f.h.resorts). **Hudson's Bay Co. Blockh.** & **Ft. St. Joseph Ruins.**

**II. SAULT STE MARIE (S) to ST. IGNACE. 53. US2**

**19. KINROSS** (airport). **24. RUDYARD,** one of Eng. poet's "sons in Mich." J. with St.48.

SIDE TRIP: On St.48 (W) 26m to **Trout L.** (f.h.hotels.good meals). **Carp L.** (hotels) is (W) in deer & bird country; Wildflower Festival.

**27.5. MARQUETTE NAT. FOR.** (see St.28). **48.** J. with Rd. to **Rabbit's Back;** view. **50. CASTLE ROCK** (sm.fee). **53. ST. IGNACE** (see US2). Ferry across Straits.

**III. SAULT STE MARIE (S) & (W) to DRUMMOND I. 60. St.129 & St.48**

Via: (Neebish I.), Pickford, (Cedarville & Les Cheneaux), De Tour. Trip describes routes to 3 important resorts. Drummond I. & Les Cheneaux are accessible also from St. Ignace.

**16.** J. with Rd. to Neebish I. ferry.

SIDE TRIP: On Rd. (E) 5m to **Barbeau** (cottage camps.restaurants.boats). 8m Ferry to **Neebish I.** (f.guides.boats.licenses.telephone.stores.cabins).

**27.** J. with St.48, on which trip turns (E).

SIDE TRIP: On St.129 (S) 37m to **Cedarville,** starting pt. for very popular **Les Cheneaux** (boat.serv.from near-by towns.regular schedules from Mackinaw City & St. Ignace). Narrow protected channels of gleaming water separate 35 wooded & romantically beautiful Is. (all kinds of accoms. & facils.in mod.resorts). Waters are famous for lake trout, black bass, pike & perch.

**55. CARIBOU L.** (f.beaches). **59. DE TOUR,** at turning pt. of Great Ls. commerce, where St. Mary's R. empties into L. Huron, one of most dangerous passages on Ls. (accoms.tourist serv.guides.boats.). Ferry to **DRUMMOND I.,** 1st of Is. along Canada's Algoma reg. (resorts.cottages.camp.boats.guide & other serv.). **Drummond,** only village, is on Potagannissing Bay, breeding ground for game fish.

**IV. SAULT STE MARIE (E) & (N) to WHITEFISH PT. 76.** On main hys., St.26, St.123 & other Rds. St.28 unites for a few miles with US2. **8.** St.28 branches (W). **16.** J. with St.221.

SIDE TRIP: On St.221 (N) 2m to **Brimley** (hotels.cabins.supplies.f.equipment) & **Brimley St. Pk.** Scenic hy. leads (N) 4m to **Bay Mills Ind. Mission** (visitors welcome) & village of **Bay Mills** (f.boats.guides.supplies).

St.28 runs through **Marquette St. For. 38.** J. with St.123, on which trip cont. (N).

SIDE TRIP: On St.28 (W) 11m to "Falls" sign: (N) 2m on Rd. to **Soo Junction,** where trolley conns. with boat (daily in season) on Tahquamenon R. (canoe trl.) to **Upper Falls.** Water tumbles 40′ down face of cliff into R. where Hiawatha sailed his birch canoe after Kwasind, the strong man, had cleared away the sandbars. **Tahquamenon Falls St. Pk.,** more than 2,000 as. of wilderness; trls. & logging Rds.

St.123 cont. (N) through Tahquamenon Swamp, once scene of large-scale lumbering, now resort & sportsman's country. **40. ECKERMAN** (f.h.cabins.supplies. licenses.winter sports.airplane landing). **57. EMERSON,** commercial f. village near mouth of R. on Whitefish Bay; sandy beach for many miles. Boat (daily in season) for 18m trip to lovely **Tahquamenon Lower Falls,** a drop of 40′ or more over 3 levels (lodge.tower.cabins.restaurant.pic.camp.swim.h.f.). **63. PARADISE** (cabins. cottages.restaurant.stores.f.h.swim.winter sports). Rd. runs (W) 11m to Lower Falls. **66. SHELLDRAKE** (hotel.store), blueberry country (late summer until frost). **74.5. WHITEFISH PT. P. O.** (est.1899). **76. WHITEFISH PT. LIGHTH.** (1900); deep-sea trolling.

# US 2—WISCONSIN

**WIS.-MICH. LINE** (at Ironwood, Mich.) **(W) to MINN. LINE** (at Duluth, Minn.) **106. US2**

Via: Ashland, (Bayfield), Superior. Chi. & N.W. RR. bet. Hurley & Ashland; N.P. RR. bet. Ashland & Superior. Accoms.: In cities; tourist camps & cabins en route.

US2, northernmost E.-W. hy., crosses from Mich. line to Superior, where it cont. on its transcontinental route to Seattle.

**0.** J. with US51. **1.5. HURLEY** (see US51). **The Penokee-Gogebic Iron Range** can be seen W. of the hy. **11. SAXON,** former lumbertown. Surrounding farms belong to the poorest of st. **13.5. LAKE VIEW CEMETERY** from which good view of **Oconto Bay** (S) & the **Apostle Is.** (N) in L. Superior. **18.** Hy. touches **BAD RIVER IND. RESERV.,** home for 1,375 Chippewa. Toward (N) are **Kakagan Sloughs,** one of largest natural game preserves in Wis. It is home of the wall-eyed pike. Wild rice gathered here provides food & income for the Inds.

**39. ASHLAND** (4 RR. terminals here). Its 1st settlement in 1665 consisted of crude ft. erected by 6 Frenchmen & bark chapel by Father Allouez, who labored among the Iroquois for 4 yrs. & then had to abandon mission to Father Marquette, who after 2 yrs. finally closed it. Two hundred yrs. later, town became an important shipping pt. for lumber, coal & iron ore. Geological surveys showed that entire Penokee-Gogebic Range had deposits of iron ore. By 1872 all of upper Wis. was caught in the mining fever. Boom lasted until 1887 when the crash brought down values & prices. Large paper mills ship their products to the E. & W. coasts, & millions of tons of iron ore are sent to lower lakes. Ashland is home of **Northland College.** In Ashland is J. with St.13.

SIDE TRIP: On this Rd. (N) hy. passes coal docks & skirts **Chequamegon Bay** on its way to tip of Wis. At 11m, **Washburn,** many of whose bldgs. are of reddish-brown stone, quarried near-by. Rd. soon touches Chequamegon Bay. 23m **Bayfield,** named for Adm. Henry Bayfield of Brit. Navy who surveyed Gt. Ls., 1823. Its commercial fisheries rank 1st among L. Superior's ports; it ships annually about 6 million lbs. of fish. City is best known for its lake-trout fishing in 150' deep water. Strong gear is needed for these gamey fish. The harbor is usually supplied with boats that can be rented by the day, & incl. licensed pilot. Excursion boats leave Bayfield daily in summer for **La Pointe** on **Madeleine I.,** largest of Apostle Is., lying off Bayfield. There are 22 Is. despite their name, ranging from Madeleine, the largest—14m long—to many small ones that are inhabited only by wild life. Intricate & grotesque carvings of the beach are striking examples of wave erosion. La Pointe, picturesque old town, once site of Fr. Fort & Cath. mission, was est. by Allouez, 1665. In 1832, oldest Wis. **Protestant Mission** was built here. St.13 cont. (N) 3m on gravel Rd. to **Red Cliff & Red Cliff Ind. Reserv.,** where 689 La Pointe Chippewa subsist, past fishing villages & Finnish settlements.

As US2 leaves Ashland the cities of **Washburn & Barksdale** can be seen across Chequamegon Bay. A natural breakwater is formed by **Long Island** about 10m out, making Ashland one of best L. Mich. harbors. At **55.** E. border of **CHEQUAMEGON NAT. FOR.,** northernmost div., is reached (hqs. at Park Falls). Here are hundreds of Ls., pine, spruce & balsam fors.; famous also for muskellunge, pike & bass fishing. This is blueberry country. The Inds. & transient pickers come from far & near. **65. IRON RIVER,** known to the Inds. as Medicine Springs because of mineral waters found here. First white settler arrived 1887, with fine lumber the attraction. W. of US2 Rd. passes through swampland & marshes & enters **Brule River St. For.** (7,750 as.; well known for its trout stream). This reg. was Pres. Coolidge's favorite fishing spot. Cleveland & Hoover also fished here & Eisenhower still does. The **Brule,** a famous fishing stream, is very popular for canoe trips through virgin fors. From its source one current can be seen going into the St. Croix on its way to the Miss. & another current flowing toward L. Superior, the St. Lawrence & the Atlantic Ocean. Country along shore of L. Superior was used by Longfellow as setting for his poem "Hiawatha." J. with Cty.H.

SIDE TRIPS: (A) On Cty. H. (L) is **Winneboujou country,** named for legendary Chippewa god & his grandmother Amik, who because of her disobedience to authority was changed into a beaver. Her descendants are still busy building dams here.

(B) On Cty. H. (R) 4m is J. with side Rd. On this Rd. (L) is **Wis. Co-Op. Pk.,** org. by Finnish people who sett. along L. Superior. It contains children's camps, community bldgs., kitchens, camp ground; also sport facils. & the "sauna," Finnish steam bath. (see Minn.)

**85. POPLAR.** J. with Cty.P.

SIDE TRIP: On this Rd. (L) $8^m$ is **L. Nebagamon** (excellent f.h.& boat.) on which is old **Weyerhaeuser estate,** now used as camp for Jewish boys.

**94. AMICON FALLS.**

**106. SUPERIOR**

Rail, plane & bus conns. Usual accoms.

Superior is Wis.' leading port of entry, situated on S. shore of L. Superior's western tip, & on **Bays of Allouez & St. Louis,** into which flow the Menadji & St. Louis Rs. It has $27^m$ of unexcelled harbor & though ice-locked for 4 months a yr., it, together with its twin city, Duluth, is next to N.Y. harbor in point of tonnage. It has the largest group of ore docks & grain elevators in world. Superior is also a RR. center with 9 RR. systems having terminals there. First white settlers arrived c.1661. During next 100 yrs., Hudson's Bay Co., Northwestern Fur Co. & J. J. Astor's Amer. Fur Co., in turn, est. trading posts here; but 1st permanent settlement was made only c.1853. After Minn. legislature made land grants for RR. construction, Superior was overrun with speculators; but after the panic of 1857, the town of 3,000 dropped to 1,000; & after the Ind. scare of 1862, only 500 people stayed on. At this stage, it remained for more than 20 yrs. Iron ore was discovered 1883 in Gogebic Range & a 2nd boom began. Superior's prosperity dates from then. At turn of cent., Superior became Wis.' 2nd largest city. It is the Consumer Co-op. Center of U.S. The **People's Co-op. Soc.,** begun by Finns & Scandinavians, was nucleus of what is now the full grown co-op. enterprise, incl. in its ranks not only working people, but professional & business men. Superior is internationally known for this & is considered by an Eng. Rochdale authority as "Principal center of consumer co-operatives in the world." There are 1,531,000 consumer co-op. members in U.S. doing a $260,000,000 volume of business.

PTS. OF INT.: (1) St. Louis Bay, **Great Northern Elevator,** rising 243′, highest grain elevator in world (1 of 8 in city). (2) 1901 Winter St., **Central Co-op. Wholesale** plant, where Finnish language daily is published. This outstanding Wholesale includes more than 100 companies & handles 3 to 4 million dollars worth of business. (3) 1115 Belknap St., **Cathedral of Christ the King** (Cath.1927 by Louis Preuss, replica of Santa Maria Maggiore, Rome). (4) 18th St. & Grand Ave., **Superior St. Teachers College.** (5) Foot of 35th Ave. (E), **Great Northern Ore-Docks,** largest group of ore-docks in world (shipments in 1947 were 25,800,000 tons). (6) **Knudson Shipbuilding & Dry-Dock Co.,** largest dry-dock on L. Superior. City also has horse-meat factory producing dog food. A 56-mile canoe trip can be started a short distance outside Superior on the Brule R.

SIDE TRIP: On St.35 (S) $13^m$ is **Manitou Falls** (165′) in **Pattison St. Pk.** (1,143 as.).

## US 8—WISCONSIN

**WIS.-MICH. LINE** (at Norway, Mich.) **(W) to WIS.-MINN. LINE** (at Taylors Falls, Minn.). **262. US8**

Via: Crandon, Rhinelander, Prentice, Ladysmith, St. Croix Falls. M., St. P. & S. S. M. RR. parallels route throughout. Accoms.: In resort reg.; in central part of St. limited to larger towns.

US8 beginning at Menominee R., natural Wis.-Mich. border, it passes through vast stretches of cut-over & abandoned land, as well as through resort territory amid the beautiful L. & for. country of the "North."

US8 & US141 travel as 1 route for **14.** to **PEMBINE.** Here US8 turns sharply (W) to cross the st. It passes deserted farms & lumber towns, & at **48.** begins its cut through **NICOLET NAT. FOR.** (see US45), emerging near Argonne (pronounced Ar-go′-ne by the villagers who named it thus because its 7 recruits for World War I died in Argonne For., France). Hy. turns (S) & at **70.** reaches **CRANDON** (see US45). It again turns (W), passing **MONICO JUNCTION** at **82.**, a RR. connecting sta. (A few miles in any direction from these towns brings one to fish-stocked lakes.) **96. RHINELANDER** (see US45). **149. PRENTICE,** both a recr. center & important dairy spot. Pastures become richer along the way. **FLAMBEAU R.** is crossed at **192.** Here Old Abe, the Wis. eagle, was captured. He became mascot for the 8th Wis. Infantry & went into Civil War battles with it, screaming & spreading his wings as soon as he heard the bugle. The reg.'s golden age of logging was in the 70's. Fred

Weyerhaeuser, German immigrant, who became greatest of lumber kings, began operations here in 1864. Town of **WEYERHAEUSER, 206.**, was named after him. In 1870 he org. the Miss. R. Logging Co., most important lumber syndicate of the time. He built & gradually owned the RRs. & everything connected with lumbering, & sawed his way through Wis. & Minn. In 1900 he bought a million acres of the richest timber lands in Ore. & Wash. After he left the Northwoods, activities slowed down & the lumberjacks gradually disappeared, leaving behind them a rich Paul Bunyan lore. Scandinavians who settled here gave the legendary Bunyan a logging crew of Norsemen—Big Ole, Criss Crosshaul, Axel Axelson, Hels Helson & Shot Gunderson—all were powerful & adept & became more so with each story. US8 at **215.** finds itself in very rich agric. land amid the blue & purple **BARRON HILLS** (600′). In vic. are important butter-producing farms. Rd. runs past **CAMERON** at **216.**, sm. town that came into prominence through exploits of John Dietz, "defender of Cameron Dam." In 1906 Dietz's crop had been ruined by flooding, for which Chippewa Log & Boom Co. was responsible. After appealing to them repeatedly for redress but to no avail he & his sons kept the company's workers off the premises with shotguns. A sm. band of 60 men & the sheriff surrounded the Dietz farm for 7 days & finally besieged the cabin. Dietz & his family kept them at bay for hrs. until several on both sides were wounded & 1 deputy killed. Dietz was sentenced to 20 yrs. After 15 yrs. he was pardoned by the Gov. but died 3 yrs. later. At Cameron is J. with US53.

SIDE TRIP: On this Rd. (N) 7m to **Rice Lake,** dairy & resort reg. (good boat. & f. Ls. near-by). 31m **Spooner,** shipping center for large but sparsely sett. L. country. **St. Fish Hatchery** in vic. Wis. Agric. Experiment Sta. here is working out methods of making the surrounding sandy, jack-pine land fertile. From 1843 to 1910 John Coit Spooner, RR. & lumber baron, lived here while he dominated Wis. politics & finance. Protegé of Philetus Sawyer, he fought against restoring the immense land grants to pub. domain, & won. Three yrs. after retiring he was made counsel of the collapsing N.P. RR. How he cut expenses by cutting workmen's wages & then invoking an injunction against the striking men was a great scandal. Despite it all, & the avowed enmity of Rbt. M. LaFollette, Spooner got back to U.S. Senate on an anti-Bryan wave.

US8 passes **TURTLE L.** at **237.** Surrounding territory is developed to the maximum, agriculturally & recreationally. At **258.5. CAMPING GROUND** (L) & at **262.** is **ST. CROIX FALLS,** lumber village, home of Ray Stannard Baker, who wrote under pen-name of David Grayson. His most famous work is biography of Woodrow Wilson. To the (L) is **Interstate Pk.** (780 as.;camp.pic.facils.bath.), oldest Wis. St. Pk. It contains int. geologic formations, such as **Devil's Chair** & the **Old Man of the Dalles,** thought by Chippewa to be their mythical giant hero, Winneboujou. Hy. here crosses Interstate Bridge (free) to Minn.

## US 12—WISCONSIN

**WIS.-ILL. LINE** (2m from Richmond, Ill.) **(NW) to WIS.-MINN. LINE** (14m from St. Paul, Minn.). **339. US12**

Via: Lake Geneva, Madison, Wisconsin Dells, Tomah, Eau Claire, Hudson. Cement Rd. Excellent accoms.

From SE. cor. of Wis. hy. makes an arc to Minn. line, incl. 2 of st.'s oldest resort areas: Lake Geneva & Wis. Dells. Hy. crosses Ill. line at **0.** & hits **LAKE GENEVA** (resort) at **9.** (see Milwaukee Trip VI). **18. ELKHORN** (resort town), founded 1837. Lack of water power & main-line communication kept it from becoming prosperous until c.1900. Many retired farmers live here now. It is home of **Holton Musical Instrument Co.,** N. Church St. Hymn, "Sweet Bye & Bye," was composed here by Jos. P. Webster & S. F. Bennett. At Elkhorn is J. with St.15.

SIDE TRIP: On this Rd. (SW) 6m to **Delavan,** named for the temperance leader (1793-1871) who planned it to be a temperance colony, but plan fell through. Around 1850 Ed. & Jerry Mabie of N.Y. had their circus here & most of the villagers were in some way connected with it.

**36. WHITEWATER** (see Madison Trip IV). **FT. ATKINSON** at **47.** In Riverside Pk. is **Panther Intaglio** (Ind. burial spot; excavated instead of mound shaped) (see Madison Trip IV). **82. MADISON** (see). **105. SAUK CITY & PRAIRIE DU SAC.** Here is J. with St.78.

SIDE TRIP: On this Rd. (NE) 10m to **Merrimac.** Here is free ferry across Wis. R. Near Merrimac on St.78, is **Durward's Glen** (closes at 8 p.m.). Here (L) is novitiate of Camillian

Fathers consisting of log cabin & chapel (1935.O.services daily); (R) trl. leads to home & studio of Bernard Isaac Durward & his son Chas., artists.

**119.** J. with St.159 leading to **Devil's L. St. Pk.** (see Madison). **122.** ($3^m$ to (R) **Baraboo,** see Madison Trip III). **131. WISCONSIN DELLS** (see Madison Trip III), one of most picturesque regs. in country. **164. CAMP DOUGLAS.** Here is J. with side Rd. (R) to entrance of **Camp Williams Military Reserv. Barracks.** Rifle range & target practice can be watched from Rd. **178. TOMAH,** named for Menominee chief. Fed. Gov.'s Ind. industrial school here. Beds of Amer. lotus near-by. **207. CASTLE MOUND PK.** (L) (camp.trlr.facils.water; 222 as.). Mound itself is of castellated rock formation. **209. BLACK R. FALLS.** One of 1st sawmills in Wis. was built here in 1819, & logging cont. throughout 19th cent. Among earliest settlers were Mormons from Nauvoo. An int. property theory was held by a Mormon deacon here. He told his "Saints" to clear land & when the owner, Spaulding, remonstrated, the deacon merely answered that the "wilderness belonged to the Lord." He urged his flock to go right on clearing & that they need not respect Gentile boundaries. Spaulding threatened to get military aid from Prairie du Chien. His strategy was successful & the Mormons finally left, but not without grumbling that their tormentors were "worse than Missourians."

**266. EAU CLAIRE**

Eau Claire at confluence of Eau Claire & Chippewa Rs., is a commercial & mfg. leader as well as a rich agric. & dairying center. From the tiny mills & logging operation of its lusty rivermen it became present & thriving city, with diversified industries. PTS. OF INT.: On Eau Claire R., **Gillett Tire Plant** of U.S. Rubber Co., whose bldgs. occupy more than 3 blocks, & whose capacity is 14,000 tires a day. **Carson Pk.** juts out into Half Moon L. In it is **Paul Bunyan Logging Camp Mus.** (O.free), fine replica of the old lumbering days of northern Wis. First caterpillar tractor to haul lumber was used in Eau Claire in 1861. Early models were steam propelled. City also has an excellent **St. Teachers College.** Here is J. with US53 leading (NE) $10^m$ to **Chippewa Falls** where Fr.-Canadians & Ind. lumberjacks began the 1st mill in 1836.

**294. MENOMONIE** is home of **Stout Institute,** only college in country devoted entirely to training of teachers in Home Economy, Industrial & Vocational Education. It was founded in 1893 by James H. Stout. In 1911 it was taken over by St. & made a college with right to grant degrees; in 1935 it granted the M.S. degree. At Menomonie is J. with St.29.

SIDE TRIP: On this Rd. (SW) $18^m$ is **Spring Valley.** Another mile (W) is **Crystal Cave** (O.all yr.guides.fee), Wis.'s only 3-level cave. Grotesque rock formations, petrified wood, volcanic ash, 22 rooms containing rare onyx & crystals; fossils of molluscs a million yrs. old; hundreds of living stalactites. ($5^m$ from the cave is modern motel with gas heat. & baths; good trout streams in vic.)

At **339.** US12 crosses **MINN. LINE.**

# US 41—WISCONSIN

**WIS.-ILL. LINE** ($49^m$ from Chicago) **(N) to WIS.-MICH. LINE** (at Menominee, Mich.). **224. US41**

Via: Milwaukee, Fond du Lac, Oshkosh, Appleton, Green Bay, Oconto, & Marinette. RRs. parallel route. Concrete Rd. Many camp sites & ample accoms.

US41 crosses Ill. Line at **0.** & heads for **MILWAUKEE** (see) at **37.** Hy. crosses city on S. 27th St. to W. Lisbon Ave. which it follows out of town. Then it runs through a reg. of rich farm land, settled mainly by Germans during 1st half of 19th cent., & reaches **MENOMONEE FALLS** at **48.** (For Menomonee Falls, Richfield, Slinger & towns up to Fond du Lac, see Milwaukee Trip IV.) Here is J. with St.55 which travels along E. side of L. Winnebago & conn. with Neenah-Menasha & Appleton. **100. FOND DU LAC.** South J. with US45, an alternate which travels along **L. Winnebago** for $21^m$ while US41 passes **N. FOND DU LAC** at **103.** & **VAN DYNE** at **109.** At **113.** North J. with US45. The 2 hys. follow 1 route along the L.

**119. OSHKOSH** (RR., plane & bus conns.).

Oshkosh on L. Winnebago is an important industrial center, & home of well-known Oshkosh B'Gosh Overalls, nationally-known trunks, & world famous axles. From being largest woodworking city of the reg. it developed into one of varied enterprises. It is also a resort city, noted for unexcelled fish., boat., hunt. & winter sports, especially ice-boat. & ice-fish. City has winding & irregular streets & 4 bridges that open for most tugs & freighters. Its pop. is a mixture of old-world descendants, but only German-Russians & Poles who arrived bet. 1890 & 1910 have remained closely-knit groups.

Father Jean Claude Allouez 1st landed here in 1670 to preach to Inds. Many yrs. passed until Augustin Grignon & Jacques Porlier set up trading post in 1818 near present-day Butte des Morts, which soon developed into town of Algoma. In 1837 after Inds. had given up the right to land N. of Fox R., a sm. group of Yankees started a community & called it Athens. While lumber industry was developing, Algoma & Athens were rivals. When Athens received a P.O., it was renamed Oshkosh, in honor of the Menominee Chief. Both towns grew & remained rivals until 1853 when Algoma was inc. into Oshkosh. Boat-building boomed & remained important industry. Revival of activity followed Civil War, but town was practically destroyed 4 times by fire & finally was rebuilt of brick & stone. Logging went on unabated, mfg. mills were set up, & Oshkosh became leading sash-&-door center of U.S. In 1898 a serious labor struggle took place when woodworkers struck against employment of women & children. Strike was broken by Nat. Guards from Milwaukee & leaders were arrested. Only the eloquence of Clarence Darrow got them acquitted. Oshkosh continued rough lumber mfg. long after Neenah & Menasha had to give it up for lack of timber. The Fox-Winnebago waterway, responsible for its early development, still contributes to its present-day industry & recr.

PTS. OF INT.: (1) Cor. Algoma Blvd. & Jackson Dr., **Winnebago County Cth.** (1938.mod.limestone.by Granger & Bollenbacher), with bas-reliefs by Alphonso Ianelli. (2) Algoma Blvd. bet. College & Forest Aves., **St. Teachers College** (Coll. Goth.1918), (3) Algoma Blvd. & W. Algoma St., **Pub. Mus.** (1908 by Wm.Waters, Eng.Goth.); contains hist. relics of reg. & fine art coll. (4) Algoma Blvd. & Congress St., **Nath. Paine H.** (Tudor Goth.). (5) W. Algoma St. & Fox R., **Paine Lumber Plant,** remnant of what once was largest sash & door factory in world. (6) Washington Blvd. & Lake Shore Dr., **Carl Schurz Mon.** by Karl Bitter. (7) Hazel St., bet. Merritt St. & New York Ave., **Menominee Pk.** (swim.boat.), where Allouez 1st said mass in 1670. In it is Statue of Chief Oshkosh, "who never lifted a hand against the white man."

Hy. leaves town by N. Main St., turns (L) at Murdock St. to J. with US45. As 1 route they head N. **127.** US41 branches (R) & at **130.** reaches **NEENAH & MENASHA,** twin cities on both sides of L. Winnebago channel. They are noted for their big paper mills. First sawmill was built 1849. By 1857 Menasha was known as hardwood market of this reg. while Neenah became a flour-milling city. When wheat growing declined, Neenah turned to paper making. It now has 11 mills, 2 large & several smaller plants connected with the paper-making industry; also more than 60 other industrial plants. Doty I., lying in the channel bet. 2 cities, was named for James D. Doty, speculator & 1st terr. Gov. of the island he had acquired in 1830. Nicolet Blvd. now divides the island. On Neenah's half is **Grand Loggery** (O), loghouse in which Doty entertained prominent Inds. & other notables. On Menasha side are 3 Ind. **Effigy Mounds.** In 1835 Gov. built a sawmill, gristmill & houses for the Inds. here. But Menominee tore up the dwellings & built lodges instead. The next yr. they ceded the land to U.S. Not only Menominee but also Winnebago & Fox occupied this sec. when Jon. Carver passed through in 1766 & stopped over as guest of Ho-po-ko-ekan, heroine of Wm. Ellery Leonard's "Glory in the Morning." From Neenah-Menasha hy. cont. N.

### 138. APPLETON

RR., plane & bus conns. Ample accoms.

Appleton on rapids of Fox R. is both an industrial city & college town. It is home of **Lawrence College,** founded 1848 as Meth. sch. of Grand Chute, then part of Appleton. From a sm. denominational sch., it has grown to a thriving coed. college with all advantages of a mod. Univ. Appleton owes its industrial growth mainly to hydroelectric power developed by Fox R. Falls, & boasts the 1st hydroelectric plant in world (replica of the orig. O.). City had one of 1st street-car lines in U.S. Appleton's 1st 2 industries are still its most important ones. When wheat production declined, flour milling was replaced by pulp & paper industry. The Institute of Paper

Chemistry (1929) is grad. sch. for scientific work in this fairly new field, & conducts important research. Appleton was birthpl. & home of Harry Houdini (1874-1926), famous magician. Edna Ferber spent many of her formative yrs. there & made it setting for some of her novels & short stories. PTS. OF INT.: At S. end of Mason St. is **Alicia Pk.** where is preserved century-old mansion of Hippolyte Grignon, 1st settler of Appleton.

## Sec. 2: APPLETON to MARINETTE 86.

**3.** N. of Appleton, US41 turns E. **8. LITTLE CHUTE,** in which are **Kimberley Clark Paper Mills. 10. KAUKAUNA,** former portage, used by early traders to avoid Fox R. Falls. In 1st legal transaction of the St., Dominique Ducharme bought this tract from Inds. for 2 bbls. of rum (1793). By 1875 farming was carried on extensively & now dairy products are chief income. From Tobanoir St. (R) is **Grignon H.** (1838.int.inter.) built by Augustin Grignon, grandson of Chas. de Langlade. **30. DE PERE,** site of St. Francis Xavier Mission, 1st Jesuit mission on Fox R., est. 1671, by Father Claude Allouez, whose hqs. it became. From here, Marquette & Joliet set out on their voyage of discovery. First Gov. dam was built in 1836 & tremendous land speculation followed; however, town had a serious setback, when in 1847 a storm swept the dam down the R. Present dam which furnishes power for DePere & near-by towns, was built in 1849 as part of a project designed to conn. L. Mich. & the Miss. R. DePere is home of **St. Norbert's College** (nonsectarian).

**31. GREEN BAY**

4 major RRs. serve city. Plane & bus conns. Usual accoms.

Green Bay, oldest settlement of Wis. at S. end of Green Bay, has one of best L. harbors. It is open from Ap. to Dec. making it a key link in Gt. Ls. traffic. Jean Nicolet was Gov. of New France c.1634, but not until Father Allouez founded the Jesuit mission in 1669 did reg. around the Fox become important. Marquette & Joliet crossed the portage on their way to the Miss. La Baye, as the post then was called, became a natural meeting ground for all interested in the abundant furs of this reg., which for 200 yrs. were the accepted currency. Nicholas Perrot, one of most brilliant men in NW. history, was Gov. in 1684. He made profitable alliances with Inds., thereby raising Fox-Wis. reg. to most important in New France. Then came Fox-Ind. wars & Perrot's diplomatic policy was followed by a military policy, but by 1740, the Fox were practically subdued, & permanent settlers arrived. Among them was Augustine de Langlade, whose gentle manners & understanding of the Inds., coupled with honesty & justice brought about complete cooperation with the Menominee & gave to him & his friends control of trade & commerce during Fr. & Bri. regime.

In 1783 the NW. was officially declared U.S. territory, but Fr. & Bri. traders made fur exchanges difficult for independent Amer. traders. In War of 1812 many Green Bayers became officers in Br. Army. However, J. J. Astor started Amer. Fur Co., & soon controlled greater portion of trade. He found it politic to form a trade assoc. with the early Fr. citizens. Ft. Howard at Green Bay was built at Astor's request for protection & until 1836 peltrying flourished. Black Hawk's defeat, & the "easy water-way" from the Gt. Ls. through the bay & Fox R. to the Miss. again made Green Bay important, this time as a trading center for flour & lumber. Around 1910 dairying & paper making, building materials, & iron & steel industries were principal sources of income. Cheese is leading product of this area & is 3/5 of nation's cheese output. Next to Milwaukee, Green Bay is largest jobbing & wholesale center in st.

PTS. OF INT.: (1) 1008 S. Monroe St., **Morgan L. Martin H.** (1837-39; Class.Rev.), known as "Hazelwood." Martin was member of 1st Wis. Constitutional Convention. (2) Inters. of E. Mason, S. Washington & Adams St., marks **Site of 1st Cath. Ch.** in Wis. (1823). (3) 120 S. Jefferson St., **Kellogg Publ. Lib.** (neo-classic), containing rich source material of pioneer days. **Neville Mus.** (O. 9-12 & 2-5) attached to it, contains some of most valuable & oldest relics of Fr. regime in Wis. such as Perrot's ostensorium (1686) & 22 self-portraits of Geo. Catlin, depicting psychological states of the Ind. painter. (4) Cherry St., bet. Monroe & Madison, **Moravian Ch.** (1850). (5) Walnut & Baird Sts., **Green Bay Packers Stadium** (games every Sun. from Sept.

to Jan.). The team, one of best professional football teams in U.S., won world's championship for many yrs. (6) Day & N. Madison Sts., **Northern Paper Mills,** one of largest tissue mills in country. (7) N. Chestnut & Kellogg Sts., **Ft. Howard Hospital & Surgeon's Quarters** (O. 10-5; fee; 1816; log & clapboard). (8) 10th Ave. & 5th St., **Tank Cottage** (O. 10-5; fee; 1776, adds.), oldest house in Wis., one of the few wattle & daub houses left in Mid-West; built by Francis Roi, Fr. trader. Eng. officers during War of 1812 gathered here. Mrs. Tank, Dutch wife of the 3rd & last owner, Nils Tank, a Norweg. Moravian, furnished the altered cottage & adds. with treasures from her Holland home, which are still to be seen. It now belongs to Green Bay Hist. Soc. (9) On W. bank of Fox R. 12$^{m}$ (S) is **Eleazer Williams H.** (c.1820; cabin 1½ stories of squared logs; rest.) built by the self-styled "lost dauphin."

Green Bay is starting pt. for a trip to **Door Peninsula** (see). Here also US41 unites with US141 to **54.**, then turns NE. & at **66.** reaches **OCONTO,** former Ind. village & Fr. mission. Later became lumber center. Ann Arbor Car & Auto Ferry operates bet. Marinette & Frankfort, Mich. On Chicago St., **Allouez Cross,** comm. founding of 1st Jesuit Mission in E. Wis. (1669). Main & Congress Sts., **Nich. Perrot Mon.,** honoring astute Fr. diplomat & trader of the period, who in 1669, took possession of all Upper Miss. R. for Louis XIV. He died in poverty in Canada. **81. PESHTIGO,** center of one of the worst fires in history (Oct. 8, 1871)—more than 1,200 known dead & 1,500 seriously burned. The raging fire began after 3 month's drought & swept through 8 counties, destroying more than 2 billion trees (over 1,280,000 as.). Death toll was 5 times that of Chicago Fire which happened the same night & the country was hardly aware of the great disaster. While the nation's newspapers shouted about the Chicago fire, the few existing telegraph lines in the North had been destroyed. It took 5 wks. for the news to get around. Town now is a hive of resort activity.

**88. MARINETTE,** on Mich. line, named for a Menominee chief's daughter, who became one of most noted fur traders of the NW., was founded (1795) as a trading post by Stanislaus Chappu, Amer. Fur Co. agent. Panic of 1857 & Civil War ruined lumber business that had grown up. It was begun again, but after 1900 the timber stands were depleted. Only 2 out of 27 mills survived. City got a fresh start & rebuilt with diversified industries. Annually when the smelts run, city declares a holiday. At night, the R. banks are ablaze with bonfires. The climax of the carnival takes place at Interstate bridge (bet. Wis. & Mich.), where the Smelt Queen is crowned. Winter sports are excellent on the bay, especially skate-sailing & ice-boating.

## DOOR PENINSULA LOOP TOUR—WISCONSIN

**GREEN BAY (NE) to Tip of PENINSULA & Return to MANITOWOC. 171. St.57 & St.42**

Via: Sturgeon Bay, Algoma, Kewaunee & Two Rivers.

Door Peninsula, a prolongation of Niagara Escarpment, juts into L. Mich. One of the great cherry-growing regs. of the world, it presents a magnificent sight when orchards are in bloom, & is summer resort & hayfever refuge. St.57 zigzags across peninsula up to Sister Bay. Here is J. with St.42 which goes (N) past Ellison Bay, to the very tip. St.42 is an alt. Rd. by which one can return via Sturgeon Bay, directly (S) to Manitowoc.

### Sec. 1: GREEN BAY to ELLISON BAY, 78. St.57

**0. GREEN BAY.** J. with US41. St.57 follows Main St. to **4.** where is J. with Cty. A leading (L) 7.5$^{m}$ to **Mon.** comm. site of Jean Nicolet's landing in 1634, the 1st time a white man set foot on Wis. soil. St.57 then turns inland & climbs to crest of **NIAGARA ESCARPMENT** (fine view of Green Bay), & reaches at **27. BRUSSELS,** a village sett. by Belgians in 1854. The natives retain many old Belgian customs & celebrations such as May Day & Kermiss. At c.32 is **TORNADO PK.** comm. conflagration that swept through 7 counties. **36.** J. with St.42. This Rd. can be taken (S) to **Algoma** c.13$^{m}$. At c.**40.5.** comes 1st glimpse of Door Cty.'s famous cherry orchards. Wis. ranks 6th in production of cherries. A Cherry Blossom Festival is held last week in May, & blossom time attracts thousands of tourists. Fruit is picked 1st wk. in July, by pickers from all parts of st. Many orchards permit visitors to pick their own fruit & pay for it later. **42.** J. with Rd. leading (L) c.0.5$^{m}$ to Entrance of **Potawatomi St. Pk.** (1,046 as.camp.trlr.facils.). At **42.5.** hy. crosses bay to heart of **Sturgeon Bay City,** (resort area) at head of narrow harbor running 1,000′ into the peninsula. Father Marquette landed here, 1673. Two centuries later, in 1878, a canal was blasted through the stone. Today it is center of "Cherry-land" & derives its income from handling & transhipping of fruit, & from tourists. In the drydocks are preserved once famous old ships, noted for their speed & luxury. St.57 travels (N) to J. with St.42 at **46.** Hy. cont. to the tip. At **51.5.** is a sign reading "Cave Point" & J. with gravel Rd.

SIDE TRIP: On latter (R) c.3.5$^{m}$ to a cave. Short walk leads to brink of 40′ cliffs overlooking **L. Mich.** whose waters have washed out wafer-like ledges pitted with holes.

**57. JACKSONPORT,** a fishing village where, after Civil War, ships from Gt. Ls. used to dock. **61.5. KANGAROO L.** (old resort). **63.5. BAILEY'S HARBOR,** discovered in 1848 & called Gibraltar by 1st fisherman. **Old Lighth.** (1868) is still in use. St.57 crosses to Green Bay side again to J. with St.42 & reaches **SISTER BAY** at **73. Sister Bluffs (190′)** & **Sister Is.** off shore are breeding ground for herring gulls & terns. St.42 picks up St.57 & follows the shore to fishing village at **ELLISON BAY 78. GILLS ROCK** at **83.** is at very tip of peninsula. Here are the 170′ **Death's Door Bluffs, Table Bluff** & **U.S. Preserve** for gulls & terns. The village's famous giant in the 1830's was "Old Bradley" who measured 4′ around the chest. He could lift fishing boats & huge rocks single-handed. **Landing Pier** for Washington I. Ferry is here on St.42. (Ferry leaves twice daily both from this pier to the Is. & from there for Gills Rock.) **Porte des Morts** (Death's Door) is half-mile strait bet. peninsula & the I. whose name derives from its treacherous undercurrent. Here La Salle's "Griffon" was wrecked in 1679. Earliest inhabitants of Washington I. were Potawatomi.

### Sec. 2: SISTER BAY (S) to MANITOWOC, 93., St.42

St.42, which can be used as an alt. in going to tip from Green Bay, returns via **SISTER BAY** at **0.** (see above). Here is J. with St.57. **EPHRAIM** on Eagle Harbor at **3.** is a colony settled by Moravian emigrants who had been brought over (1853) by a wealthy Norweg., Nils Tank (see US41). It is now 8th Ward of Green Bay (resort.boat.f.yacht.). Annual regatta held here for many yrs. Tank's dream of Christian Communism lasted for 1 yr. Then the colonists dispersed, some settling in Sturgeon Bay, while Tank stayed until his death. **Cottage of A.M. Iverson,** theological student who inspired Tank, & **First Moravian Church** (1857) are still standing. **Old Ch.** contains Iverson's journals and many old relics. To (SE) 1.5$^{m}$ is **Peninsula St. Pk.** (3,670 as.golf.pic.f.camp.horses).

**9. FISH CR.** (resort.boats to **Chambers & Strawberry Is.** for rent). St.42 climbs up the escarpment to **STURGEON BAY** at **31.** Here Ann Arbor RR. & Auto Ferry connects with Menominee, Mich. on its upper peninsula across Green Bay, & also with Frankfort, Mich. across L. Mich. St.42 unites with St.57 for 7$^{m}$ (S), then branches off (L) & runs along crest of ridge into **ALGOMA** at **51.** which, as its Ind. name indicates, is a long sandy beach (pic.camp.). At **63.** hy. reaches **KEWAUNEE,** sett. in 1795, although Nicolet passed through here in 1634. Land speculation soared after a rumored gold discovery in 1836. After the boom Kewaunee turned to lumbering & today its principal industry is manufacture of school & office furniture. **Coast Guard Sta.** is 1 block E. of Kewaunee R. Bridge. Adj. is terminus of the Pere Marquette Auto Ferries, operating bet. here & Ludington, Mich.; also Ann Arbor Ferry to Frankfort, Mich. (frequent schedules). **Decker Mus.** is at Cth. At **82.** is Side Rd. running (E) to **Point Beach St. For.** (846 as.). For. has 2$^{m}$ of sandy beach (recr.pic.camp.hik.riding). **87. TWO RIVERS,** home of large commercial fishing fleet (whitefish). The **Hamilton Mfg. Co.** & the **Aluminum Goods Mfg. Co.** (Mellon-controlled) are 2 largest industries. Snow (artificial) Festival in July.

**93. MANITOWOC** (see Milwaukee Trip III). Pere Marquette Auto Ferry across L. Mich. to Ludington, Mich. (frequent schedules). At Manitowoc is J. with US151 which turns (W) leading to **Valders,** Norweg. settlement, where parents of noted economist Thorstein Veblen sett. 1857. Veblen was born & lived here until family moved to Minn.

# US 45—WISCONSIN

**WIS.-ILL. LINE** (18$^{m}$ from Libertyville, Ill.) **(N) to WIS.-MICH. LINE** (at Land O'Lakes, Wis.). **304. US45**

Via: (Milwaukee), Fond du Lac, Oshkosh, Wittenberg, Antigo & Eagle River. RR.: Chi. & NW. Usual accoms.: In cities up to Antigo; N. of Antigo, at resorts.

## Sec. 1: ILL. LINE to FOND du LAC. 100.

US45 crosses **ILL. LINE** at **0.** & passes Bristol at **4.5.** where P. T. Barnum's circus appeared 10 yrs. before the Civil War. **36.** J. with side Rd. leading (R) c.3$^{m}$ to **Greendale,** a Resettlement Adm. Housing development for low-income group employees. Just before US45 reaches outskirts of Milwaukee, it passes **HALES CORNER,** then skirts **MILWAUKEE** at **37.** Hy. passes **CURRIE PK.** (pic.facils.) & in rapid succession, **GERMANTOWN, WEST BEND, KEWASKUM & EDEN,** all thriving little German towns. N. of **KEWASKUM** at **79., Kettle Moraine St. For.** begins (hqs. at Mauthe L. 25,000 as. in N. unit). **FOND du LAC** is reached at **100.** (see Milwaukee Trip IV).

## Sec. 2: FOND du LAC to WITTENBERG. 99.

US45 travels along L. Winnebago shore almost paralleling US41 & at **19.** reaches **OSHKOSH** (see US41). **43. HORTONVILLE,** where larger & more developed farms can be seen from the hy. **51. NEW LONDON** straddles Wolf R. at its J. with the Embarrass R. It is a lumber terminus at which steamboats, plying Wolf R. from Oshkosh, land. **67. CLINTONVILLE,** home of Chet Bennett, famous woodsman & explorer of the northern Ls. country. Clintonville is most highly industrialized city in reg. It has several cheese factories & Four Wheel Drive plants (O.appl.). **99. WITTENBERG,** sett. by Norweg. Lutherans toward end of 19th cent., was named for German Univ. town where Martin Luther began Reformation. A few Winnebago, subsisting on basket weaving & odd for. jobs, also live near-by. At Wittenberg is J. with St.29.

SIDE TRIPS: (A) On St.29 (W) 29$^{m}$ **Wausau** (see US51).

(B) On St.29 (E) 29$^{m}$ to **Shawano,** Menominee Ind. village before coming of white man. This tribe on its way (W) from Green Bay, in search of better f. & h. grounds, found L. Shawano & sett. on its shores. But early white pioneers realized almost immediately that the source of timber supply & power would be the Wolf R. & sett. there. From Shawano 2 good hys. (St.55 & St.47) run into the Ind. northwoods country.

St.55 traveling (N) as 1 Rd. with St.47 reaches dirt Rd. leading (L) across Wolf R. close to **Oshkosh Burial Plot,** where wife of Neopit Oshkosh & 1 daughter are buried. Graves are marked with animal representations. At 8$^{m}$ **Keshena** (see below). Here are hqs. of **Menominee Ind. Reserv.** (231,000 as.no overnight accoms.pic.), a wooded wilderness of virgin white pine & hemlock, through which Wolf R. flows. The quiet, shady, almost gloomy for. with its cool, musty smell is welcome relief, especially in summer, to preceding miles. Here c.2,300 Menominee Inds., wealthiest in Wis., live & work, more or less cooperatively. Each family has a subsistence farm; profits of sawmill, in which most of the men work, are paid into common fund held by U.S. Treasury, to be used for schools, hospitals, old age pensions & workmen's compensation. Older Inds. & those unconverted to Christianity, live by themselves, devoting most of their time to hunt. & fish. A secret spring festival is held here, with tribal ceremonies. In village of Keshena are Ind. agency bldgs.; school, hospital, & Cath. Mission. Most of the Menominee are Cath. Close by is **Keshena Falls,** trading post of Chief Oshkosh. Ceremonial lodge still stands near-by. St.55 now travels for c.22$^{m}$ without a cross Rd. through the beautiful Reserv. following, in the main, the old Military Rd. that ran from Ft. Howard, to Ft. Wilkins, Mich., passing en route at 10$^{m}$ **Spirit Rock** & at 15.5$^{m}$ **Beaupre Place,** old tavern, beyond which is a for. path to **Big Smoky Falls.** At 30$^{m}$ hy. reaches edge of **Nicolet Nat. For.,** crossing it from S. to N. (hqs. at Rhinelander). It encompasses a great part of northern Wis. Ls. reg., with pine, spruce & hardwood stands & has trout, muskellunge, pike & bass fishing as well as grouse & deer hunting (in season) except in wildlife refuges (clearly marked). There are 20 improved pub. camps & pic. grounds. Ranger Stas. at: Florence, Lakewood, Laona, Eagle River & Three Lakes.

## Sec. 3: WITTENBERG to MICHIGAN LINE. 105.

US45 at Wittenberg starts (N) again, climbing steadily from c.800′ past **Birnamwood** & **Aniwa** to J. with St.47 at **18.**

SIDE TRIP: On this Rd. (R) hy. turns back (SW) into Menominee Ind. Reserv., passes **Phlox** at 7$^{m}$ & **Neopit** at 19$^{m}$. Here in sm. unpainted houses live the Menominee who work in near-by sawmill, which in 1924 replaced old one & now is 1 of the best in Wis. U.S.

Dept. of Agric. supervises cutting of timber to assure constant supply of logs. **Pub. School** (R). There is no illiteracy among younger generation. Hy. runs diagonally through the reserv. & at 23m reaches **Keshena** (see above).

**25. ANTIGO** (1,496') is the "beginning of the Northland." Kraft-Phoenix, one of largest processed cheese factories of its kind, is located here. Antigo has flourishing co-ops, creamery, grocery, hatchery, food, & state-supervised maple syrup co-op. City is also distributing center for thousands of carloads of Wisconsin's best potatoes. **Deleglise H.** (1877) oldest bldg. & home of city's founder, stands on Pub. Lib. Grounds. It houses **Langlade Cty. Hist. Soc.** & contains pioneer documents, Ind. relics & old lumbering tools. At **41.** is beautiful **SUMMIT L.**, (1,723'), highest L. in Wis. & at **50. PELICAN L.** (1,605'), large, brooding & sometimes treacherous. Hy. cont. to **MONICO** at **55.** & J. with US8.

SIDE TRIPS: (A) On this Rd. (E) 12m to **Crandon**, near 4 Ls., a community retarded by depleted fors. & almost ruined by repeated fires. Settlers from Kentucky made "moon" here long before Prohibition. It now has the only legal distillery in Wis.

(B) On this Rd. (W) 14m is **Rhinelander**, "Capital of the Heart of the Lakes," one of most concentrated L. areas of the country. City is both winter & summer resort & from it most of L. reg. can easily be reached by hy., airway or RR. Though a lumbering town that began cutting timber as late as 1857 it exhausted most of the large timber in 60 yrs. & then turned to paper making. Now has some of largest paper-making plants in country, specializing in glassine, & wax paper. At 924 Davenport St. is **Logging Mus.** (O.daily.9-5 from May-Dec.) displaying logging implements, & relics of reg.'s early days, incl. a pair of enormous boots that only Paul Bunyan could have worn; also the "fabulous hodag beast" which, although known to be a hoax, is still a symbol of the North's old tradition. Here is J. with St.47.

NW. of Rhinelander 9m St.47 enters **Amer. Legion St. Pk.** (37,650 as.), a reg. of inland glacial Ls., streams & wooded country (pub.camp grounds; accoms. at resorts). At 16m is **L. Tomahawk St. Camp,** rehabilitation camp for tubercular patients; in operation 40 yrs. At 39m **Woodruff** (see US51). From Woodruff (W) 2m St.70 runs into **Lac du Flambeau Ind. Reserv.** On 70,000 as. of cut-over marginal land, c.700 Inds. eke out an existence, acting mainly as guides, & selling hand-made trinkets to tourists.

Back on the main hy. at Monico, US45 travels again as one Rd. with St.47, cont. N. & reaches **THREE LAKES** at **73.**, resort town surrounded by wild country (accoms., from rustic log cabins to the luxury resort, **Northernaire,** in vic.). Ranger hqs. for Nicolet Nat. For. are at **Virgin L.** 5m (E) on St.32.

US45 passes **CATFISH L.** at **82. 84. EAGLE RIVER,** recr. center for Northern Wis. wondrous lakeland, is located on the Eagle R., at start of Eagle Chain of Lakes, one of longest & finest lake groups of the Northwoods & completely navigable. There are 27 Ls. in chain & 65 for. fringed individual Ls. Muskellunge & wall-eyed pike f. is unexcelled. Eagle R. is Vilas Cty. seat, named after Wm. F. Vilas, who was nationally prominent as Postmaster Gen., Secy. of Interior & U.S. Sen., as well as timberlord of the Northwoods. His activities in timber were Federally investigated while he was Secy. of Interior. His bequest of $30,000,000, after death of his daughter, founded fellowships & scholarships (1/5 of which were to go to Negroes). Vilas Cty. is sett. largely by Scands. Finnish Co-ops have flourished here for many yrs. At Eagle R. is J. with St.70.

SIDE TRIP: On this Rd. (E) 0.5m are dist. hqs. for Nicolet For. At 7m **Anvil L. Campground** (spring-fed with excellent beach;facils.). **Anvil L. ski-trail** begins here. At 10m still in for. is **Franklin L. Camp** (facils.). Several Nat. For. camp & pic. grounds in vic.

(N) on US45 at **87.** is J. with St.17.

SIDE TRIP: On St.17 (R) c.5m hy. again enters **Nicolet Nat. For.** over gently rolling hills, deep into the pine woods. From high pt. in this vic. (1,800') **North Twin L.** can be seen (fine view). At c.13m Rd. cuts through a white birch stand & leads to **Phelps** at 18m on E. end of L., a lumber boomtown that dwindled into a ghost for yrs. & was kept alive by summer residents. Today, its sawmill & chemical plant are again busy at work. There are 40 Ls. & 100m of trout streams within 10m radius. At Phelps beyond mill (L) is Cty. E which touches S. shore of 10 mile sq. **Lac Vieux Desert** (resort.cabins.excellent pike & muskie f.), partly in Mich. Cty. E joins US45 c.2m outside **Land O'Lakes** (see below).

From Eagle R. US45 travels directly (N). At **95. CONOVER,** another lumber boomtown which in its heyday boasted 29 saloons on Main St. Now is a through-tourist place conn. by Rd. the numerous Ls. of vic. Hy. skims ahead through blueberry marshes & picturesque conifers into **LAND O'LAKES** on **MICH.-WIS. LINE** at **105.**, pt. of entry into one of the few "unspoiled areas in the U.S." **Northern Highland State For.** (126,700 as.camp.pic.Hqs. at Trout L. on US51) contains magnificent stands of stately pines, oak, birch & poplar. There are more than 150 Ls.

within boundaries of the For., many of them links of chains ideal for canoe trips. Land O'Lakes is also pt. of entry into Gogebic Cty., Mich., incl. **Porcupine Mts.** with **L. of Clouds, Agate & Bondwater Falls.** Headwaters of the **Wis., Brule & Ontanagon Rs.** are within a few miles. All winter sports facils. at **Kings Gateway,** (hotel & recr. center) on Wis.-Mich. Line.

## US 51—WISCONSIN

**WIS.-ILL. LINE** (19$^{m}$ from Rockford, Ill.) **(N) to WIS.-MICH. LINE** (at Ironwood, Mich.) **331. US51.**

Via: Janesville, Madison, Portage, Plainfield, Stevens Point, Wausau, Merrill, Tomahawk, Woodruff. Good Rd. Accoms.: In cities; cabins in Northern Lakes reg.

This is Wis.' main S-N tour which divides st. into 2 equal parts. From the rich farmland & highly industrialized cities of the south it skirts Madison & the Univ. center, & hurries through the poor, cut-over sec. of the Northwoods, where wolves are still hunted, to the Mich. Line.

**0. BELOIT,** (see Madison Trip I) on Wis.-Ill. Line. **12. JANESVILLE** (see). **55. MADISON** (see). Here is J. with St.23 leading (W) 21$^{m}$ to **Ripon,** disputed birthpl. of Rep. Party. **92. PORTAGE** (see Madison Trip II). **162.** J. with St.54 leading (R) 30$^{m}$ to **Waupaca,** named in honor of Potawatomi chief who died after making speech to his braves urging them not to massacre the whites. Waupaca is a potato market & recr. center. Chain of 23 Ls. begins here & offers excellent German brown trout. Long leisurely canoe or launch trips may also be taken from here. (NW) of Waupaca, Rd. again enters terminal morain country.

**169. STEVENS POINT.** J. with US10; located at strategic center of St. It has good mun. airport & is serviced by Wis. Central Air Line. City was 1st sett. in 1838 & since then has been a trade & transport center. At one time it was known as "Potato Capital of Wis." Among its industries, the 5 fishing-tackle plants rank high, but it has primarily service trades such as insurance, transportation & education & is seat of an important St. Teachers College. Town, even today, has large Polish-speaking pop. From Stevens Point hy. traverses sandy plain & farms look as poor as the jackpine fors. through which US51 passes. Here is J. with US10 leading (L) 35$^{m}$ to **Marshfield.** Town was completely destroyed by fire in 1887, but on its ashes a new city arose. Today it is a busy woodworking & casein center.

**202. WAUSAU,** an industrial city with more than 40 industries, is in the leading "Amer. cheese" producing reg. **Winter Sports Area of Rib. Mt.,** one of finest in Middle West, lies 7$^{m}$ (SW) of it, & is part of **Rib. Mt. Pk.** (1940′, highest in Wis.; 440 as. all ski facils). Annual Winter Frolic in March. Superb view from Lookout Rock. Rib. Mt. is scene of one of Paul Bunyan tales. The mythical giant of lumber camps climbed the mt. & saw beneath him the waters of the Wis. Impulsively he took a huge leap & landed in the R., creating such a splash that the sound could be heard miles away. When last drops of water had fallen, there were Wis.' beautiful Ls. From Wausau, Rd. runs down long, steep hill, past **Grandfather Falls** on Wis. R. (here 80 million ft. of timber were once piled up in greatest log jam in Wis. hist.), to **MERRILL** at **219.** J. with Cty. Rd. leading (W) 1$^{m}$ to **Council Grounds St. Pk.** (278 as. of white & Norway pines, also hardwoods; camp.pic.bath. at L. Alexander, upper end of for.). Hy. now passes through terminal moraine formed by Chippewa lobe of Wis. glacier—main northern dairy reg. & well-to-do farms. **241. TOMAHAWK,** at J. of Wis., Tomahawk & Somo Rs. As late as 1886, there was only 1 lonely tavern here. Four yrs. later, Tomahawk was a timber boomtown with pop. of c.2,000. After the collapse it turned to paper & pulp mfg. City is hqs. for st.'s for.-fire protection units. US51 now runs through undulating country, past blueberry marshes, stunted jackpines, & reaches **MINOCQUA** at **271.,** center of Northern Ls. Region. Town hibernates in winter but by 4th of July, literally booms. **272.** J. with St.70 running (L) through **Lac du Flambeau Ind. Reserv. 273. WOODRUFF,** consisting at one time mainly of saloons that catered to lumberjacks of surrounding woods; now a lively L. resort; **Ls. Minocqua, Sisshebogema, Sunday & Pike** are in vic. From Woodruff US51 & St.70 travel as 1 route for 2$^{m}$. Here St.70 turns (R) & leads directly into **Eagle R.** (see St.45).

US51 now crosses through NW. part of **NORTHERN HIGHLANDS ST. FOR.** (126,700 as. with 150 lakes, incl. bath.f.camp.& pic.) located in central part of Vilas

Cty. (c.1,600′), primarily a wilderness area of Ls., streams & pinewood country. Summer resorts & supervised campgrounds abound. For. hqs. at Trout L. **294. LITTLE BOHEMIA,** resort among the pines, where John Dillinger & his gang hid in April 1931, & from which all escaped after desperate fight with F.B.I. Personal belongings of Dillinger & fellow gangsters are on display at **Little Bohemia Lodge** (O). **302. MANITOWISH,** near Manitowish R., whose waters are famous for muskellunge fishing. **305. MERCER,** still displaying a relic of logging days, the **Go-Devil**—10′ wheels joined by an axis, which, until tractors were used, served to "snake out" timber from the woods. The Northern Ls. Reg., of which Mercer is N. entrance, has a ratio of water to land surface equalled only by 2 other places: one in Minn., the other, the Gulf of Bothnia. For. fires have gutted much of area N. of here. Blueberry swamps, deserted mine housing & dumps make next 23$^{m}$ a contrast to the for. just left behind. **331. HURLEY,** lumberjacks & miners town, with former reputation for bawdiness & crime. It & Bessemer, its twin across the st. line, came into existence in same yr., 1886, rivaling each other in lustiness. "The 4 toughest places in the world are Cumberland, Hayward, Hurley & Hell, but Hurley is toughest of all," the saying goes. Hurley is locale of Edna Ferber's novel "Come & Get It."

## US 61—WISCONSIN

**WIS.-IOWA LINE** (at Dubuque, Iowa) **(N) to WIS.-MINN. LINE** (at La Crescent, Wis.). **122. US61.**

Via: Lancaster, Fennimore, Boscobel, Readstown, Viroqua. Accoms.: In cities.

US61, together with St.35 & US151, crosses Miss. R. over Toll Bridge into Wis., heading (N) & reaching **POTOSI** at **19.,** a mining town with an old brewery, part of which was built in 1852 & is still running. Near it is **Potosi Station,** river port. Lead was struck here in 1829 & was shipped down the R. **30. LANCASTER.** J. with St.81 which unites with St.35 for 8$^{m}$ (St.35 travels S. & N. to **Prairie du Chien** & from there becomes River Hy. noted for its scenic beauty along steep banks of the Miss.).

SIDE TRIP: St.81 traveling (SW) for 11$^{m}$ reaches **Nelson Dewey Farmstead St. Pk.** (720 as.camp.& pic.facils.), estate of 1st Gov. of Wis., U.S. Sen., & leader of Wis. Progressivism. Orig. bldgs. of the farm home & many other old bldgs. are still standing; a few are restored. Pk. embraces some of the most attractive bluff scenery along upper Miss. R. (accoms. in **Cassville**).

US61 reaches at **42. FENNIMORE,** lying on a pt. of Military Ridge, which drains 4 ways: to the Blue, Green, Platte, & Grant Rs. Descending the 10$^{m}$ escarpment, Rd. reaches **BOSCOBEL** (Fr.-Ind. "beautiful woods") at **53.** When steamboats plied the Wis., this was an important shipping pt. Stage coaches brought travelers, ox carts, & produce from the inland. The Gideons, whose real name is Christian Commercial Travelers Assoc. of Amer., had their beginning here, when 2 traveling salesmen found themselves together in a hotel room reading the Bible as an evening's diversion. The 2 men, realizing how lonely most travelers are, thought it a good idea to supply hotels with Bibles. Hotels eagerly responded & now practically all rooms contain a Bible.

In the center of town is **Residence of John J. Blaine,** former Gov. of Wis. & U.S. Senator. From Boscobel 1$^{m}$ is J. with St.60 which follows Wis. R. (W) for c.25$^{m}$ to J. with St.35. The latter is a 100$^{m}$ **Miss. R. route** (For pts. of int. see US61). At **55.** a **NEW BRIDGE,** built in 1937 to supplant one of Wisconsin's last covered bridges, crosses Wis. R. This was once an important waterway, but because of its many islands & shifting channels large steamboats could not always ply it. In early yrs. of lead mining, it was thought that ore could be shipped from here up the Wis., across the portage to the Fox R. & thence through Gt. Ls. to N.Y. This did not prove feasible. Even before mining days, lumber was swept downstream & soon reg. had a class of rivermen who became experts in running the rapids & handling the difficult barges. In their stories, the mythical riverman, Whiskey Jack, who rivaled Paul Bunyan in prowess & strength, was created. Villagers still remember riotous paynights when rafters came to town. Sometimes 100 men would be fighting in the muddy streets while the city marshall sat, revolver in hand, "watching the affair with the enlightened eye of an expert & the enjoyment of a connoisseur."

**122. LA CROSSE.** (Served by 3 major RRs. Bus conns. Usual accoms.) La Crosse is at confluence of Black, La Crosse, & Miss. Rs., in a beautiful coulee country described by Hamlin Garland—a succession of high bony ridges, wooded glens & valleys, especially fine in fall & winter. The vista along the R., with its massive headlands, is impressive. The Hudson & the Rhine are the only Rs. that can compare with Upper Miss. Coulee Reg. From its highest bluff 3 sts., Wis., Minn., & Iowa, can be seen. It is the natural trading & shipping center of the rich agric. reg. around it. Town was 1st called Prairie La Crosse by the early Fr. travelers who named it for a game the Inds. played, which reminded them of the French game "la crosse." From its 1st settlement, 1842, until coming of the RRs., La Crosse was entirely dependent on Miss. R. transportation. River packets brought settlers & freight. In winter sleds took place of steamboats. Steamboat traffic averaged c.200 boats a month during 1856-57. Two-thirds of its pop. is of foreign descent. First settlers were from N.Y., Vermont & Ohio. Then came the artisans & craftsmen of Germany & Norway, who helped it grow economically & culturally. Around 1877, as the lumbering bus. grew & RRs. created new markets, La Crosse became the most important distribution pt. bet. St. Louis & St. Paul. In 1942, the Fed. Gov. created a 9' channel in the Miss., with locks & dams, assuring a deep waterway from Alton, Ill. to beyond the Falls of St. Anthony.

La Crosse had its 1st sawmill by 1852 & logging was dominant industry. By turn of the cent., the fors. were depleted & La Crosse quickly turned to diversified industries, today producing rubber articles, agric. implements, air conditioning equipment, beer, & photographic supplies. It is also a cultural center, known for its music, social & political clubs. During Civil War, followers of Mark "Brick" Pomeroy, editor of the "La Crosse Democrat," were Southern sympathizers & when Lincoln was assassinated, a near riot ensued among the opponents, charging that Pomeroy had instigated the murder. Geo. W. Peck, one of Wis.'s best-known humorists, was 1 of Pomeroy's editors. He was author of "Peck's Bad Boy" series & had his own newspaper, "The Sun," which was later published in Milwaukee. Here he became mayor, & eventually Gov. of the st. PTS. OF INT.: 501 N. 3rd St., **Allis Chalmers Farm Implement Plant;** 4 separate bldgs. with a $2,000,000 addition (tours appl.). 912 Market St., **St. Rose Chapel** (Cath.), a Romanesque basilica with exquisitely beautiful inter. of marble & inlaid mother-of-pearl. It is a chapel of Perpetual Adoration. La Crosse St., E. of 17th St., **Merrick St. Pk.** (with facils.) in which is only known Ind. Burial Mound in La Crosse, a "turtle" effigy, & a zoo. Cor. St. Andrew, Loomis & Harvey Sts., **La Crosse Rubber Mills** (O.9-12 Mon.-Thurs. guides.appl.). From La Crosse 12$^{m}$ (E) on US16 is **Hamlin Garland H.,** where author lived as a boy & about which he wrote in "A Son of the Middle Border."

## MILWAUKEE

RRs.: Milwaukee RR.; Chi. & NW.; Mil. & Chi. North Shore Line. Bus: Northland Greyhound Lines. Five accredited air lines. Wis. & Mich. (Auto Ferry) Co. to Muskegon, Mich. Ample accoms.

Milwaukee, located on the crescent curve of L. Mich., the most beautiful harbor on the Great Lakes, is at the confluence of Milwaukee & Kinnickinnic Rs. These Rs. quadrisect the city. Chief industrial sec. is in the Menomonee Valley. Along Wisconsin Ave., running (W) from the L., is main bus. sec., while other bus. areas are on the N., S. & W. sides of town in many neighborly centers. Homes, of which 50% are owned by the residents, spread all over town, with the more pretentious mansions along Lake Drive. Although 13th in pop. among American cities, Milwaukee ranks 10th in value of industrial production, which leads the world in manufacture of diesel & gas engines, outboard motors & motorcycles, tractors & wheel barrows. Four of the 7 largest breweries of U.S. are here. It also leads the country in the production of hosiery, leather gloves & mittens, work shoes, tin & enamelware, saw & flour mill equipment.

Annually, Milwaukee still receives national trophies. So far, it has had more than 25 nat. awards for fire-waste reduction, health conservation & traffic safety. The Wickersham Committee cited it as "a city free from crime or where a criminal is speedily detected, tried & convicted. No other city has such a record." Its alert police administers "24-hour justice." Milwaukeeans enjoy a fine cultural life. City has 7 colleges & a univ., art & music schs. & galleries, exceptionally good pub. libraries & museums. It has the largest vocational sch. in the world. Milwaukee's pop. now is 85% American born, although Germans form largest part of its foreign stock, while the Poles are steadily increasing. Most of them live on the South Side, where their cultural life is centered around the parish chs. They have 2 Polish dailies. Next come the Italians who are concentrated mainly in the 3rd Ward. Their frequent fiestas lend color to the life of the city. Negroes have sett. here only since World War I. In 1 generation, the city has assimilated people of many nationalities & done it so well that its representatives participate in all major activities & hold ranking positions, particularly in politics & sports.

The land of Milwaukee was surveyed as late as 1835 & was bought by 3 men, Solomon Juneau, Byron Kilbourn & Geo. H. Walker, who immediately set up rival towns. The quarrel centering around payment for the Milwaukee bridges, became so violent that at one point the bridges were partly destroyed & cannon trained on Kilbourn's house. Controversy was sett. in 1845 when legislature decided that the cost would have to be borne equally. A yr. later, the city received its charter & Juneau became its 1st mayor. From that time on there was a great influx of Germans. Most of them were professionals & skilled craftsmen, who advanced the city's progress immeasurably. Despite Ind. troubles, depressions & epidemics the pop. increased from 21,000 to 46,000 in 1 yr. Milwaukeeans were overwhelmingly abolitionists & freed many runaway slaves, thereby troubling the Fed. authorities. Culturally as well as economically, the German element began to take over the city. Shipbuilding raced forward & by 1856, the 1st transoceanic shipment was made in a Milwaukee-built schooner. The 2nd German opera to be performed in U.S. was put on here & 3 yrs. later, 1st German opera, "Mohega, die Blume des Waldes," based on Ind. legend, was composed & produced in Milwaukee. Particularly important in the music field were the Musikvereine & choral societies, & every Turnverein had its Saengerfest. The "Wiskonsin Banner," 1st German daily, was published in 1844; Byron Price had printed 1st Eng. paper in 1836. First German theatrical performance was given in 1850. Two tragedies hit the city—the sinking of the excursion steamer, "Lady Elgin," in 1860, in which 295 persons were drowned & the Newhall House hotel fire, 1880, in which 64 people died. Both events were comm. in ballad & verse. The ballads were still sung in 1892 when the famous 3rd Ward fire occurred, destroying 16 blocks of bus. & residential districts, causing millions of dollars of damage. Despite fire & panic of 1893, this was the real era of "Gemuetlichkeit." Cafés & beer gardens flourished; German theater & music were at their height. It was at this time that labor & the Socialist Party, under Victor L. Berger's leadership combined, gaining rewards for both. World War I changed a great deal of this domestic peace. German was no longer spoken on the streets, names were changed, & personal relations grew strained. Then came Prohibition which destroyed an industry & much of the city's conviviality; during the decade that followed, Milwaukee's industries became more diversified. From 1916 to 1940, Milwaukee had a Socialist mayor, Daniel W. Hoan, although its gov. was non-partisan. It was this system of checks & balances that helped to make the city solvent (it is largest debt-free city in U.S.) & to keep its civic record. World War II brought an "all-out" in production, bond buying & general participation. More than 100,000 women were working out during the war. Although there was great war-time expansion in industry, 99% of the factories were pre-war plants. Reconversion in Milwaukee, therefore, was primarily a switch to civilian goods.

PTS. OF INT.: (1) W. Wisconsin Ave. bet. N. 11th & N. 16th Sts., **Marquette Univ.** (nonsect.coed.operated by Jesuits;founded 1857) known for its schs. of Journalism, Medicine & Dentistry. Bldgs. are in different parts of city. (2) 900 W. Wis. Ave., **Wisconsin Club,** formerly known as "Deutscher Klub" (1870.tower;adds.later), & once the home of Alex. Mitchell, one of Milwaukee's wealthiest pioneers. (3) W. Wis. Ave. & N. 8th St., **Milwaukee Pub. Lib. & Mus. Bldg.** (1898.Ren.by Ferry & Clas). In front of mus. stands large **Totem Pole,** bought & brought from Haida Inds. in Br. Columbia, 1921. **Lib.** (O.daily & Sun.aft.). Readers charge & check their own books & practically all of its more than a million books are on the open shelves. **Mus.** (O.9-9.Nov.1-May 1;9-5:30 in summer;1:30-5 Sun.& holidays). It is largest mun. owned mus. in country. Notable are colls. of arms, Ind. artifacts, birds' eggs & stamps. In its typewriter coll. is 1st typewriter, as invented by 2 Milwaukeeans, Christopher L. Sholes & Carlos Glidden. (4) 901 N. 9th St., **County Cth.** (1931.neo-class.by A.R.Ross). Its great classic mass dominates proposed Civic Center. Near-by at 822 Kilbourn St., is **Pub. Safety Bldg.** (always O.1929 by Ross & Clas.mod.design).

The 2 bldgs. were built at a cost of more than $11,000,000. (5) 1004 N. 10th St., **St. Benedict the Moor Mission** (Cath.) for Negroes. Present Romanes. chapel built 1911. Capuchin Order is in charge of the mission which covers 2 city blocks, but Dominican nuns conduct sch. & Franciscan Sisters the hospital. Its patron saint was a descendant of African slaves. (6) 917 W. Juneau Ave., **Pabst Brewery** (tours hourly 9-4;guides), one of the largest in country. Founded 1842 by Jacob Best. Blue Ribbon Hall is its "guest center." (7) 1015 N. 6th St., **Milwaukee Vocational Sch.**, internationally recognized as world's largest. It has several hundred classrooms, 2 auditoriums, many workshops, more than 35,000 day & night students; training in 65 different trades. (8) 1034 N. 4th St., **West Side Turner Hall** (1892.Mod.German Romanes.), once cultural home of Germans who helped lay foundation for Socialism in Milwaukee. (9) 333 W. State St., **Milwaukee Journal Bldg.** (O.appl.mod.in design by Chase), home of st.'s largest, most influential daily newspaper & broadcasting sta. WTMJ. In the lunettes above the 3rd floor, are emblems of 20 famous printers of the world. Frieze represents history of printing. Lucius W. Nieman was the "Journal's" founder; his widow gave to Harvard Univ. $1,000,000 "to promote & elevate standards of Journalism in U.S." (10) 144 E. Wells St., **Pabst Theatre** (1895. German Ren.by Otto Straack), once home of German Repertory Theatre which for yrs. presented serious drama & musical comedies with some of the foremost actors of Germany. The classics as well as premieres of the latest operettas were staged. It now presents German movies, concerts & lectures. (11) 200 E. Wells St., **City Hall** (1894.Flemish Ren.by Koch & Esser), with 350' clock-tower & dome cupola. (12) 1120 N. Broadway, **Blatz Brewery** (tours hourly June-Sept.); founded by Johann Braun, 1844, taken over by his brewmaster, Valentine Blatz, 1851. (13) 802 Jackson St., **St. John's Cathedral** (1847.adds.in Ital.Ren;double tower by Ferry & Clas, 1892). (14) 772 N. Jefferson St., **Milwaukee Art Institute** (O.July & Aug.1910.Sp. Ren.by Harry Bogner). Valuable permanent coll. Free art training for children. (15) 758 N. Jefferson St., **Layton Art Gallery** (1888.Gr.Rev.by G.A.Audsley & E.T.Mix). (16) 419 N. Jackson St., **Madonna de Pompeii Ch.** (mod.Ital.Romanes.), center of "Little Italy's" many fiestas during which saints are carried around in procession, dollar bills pinned to their garments, through brilliantly lighted streets, decked in gay colors. National foods & trinkets are sold along sidewalks. (17) W. Lincoln Ave. & S. 6th St., **St. Josaphat's Basilica** (1898.Ital.Ren.by E. Brielmaier & Sons.copper dome 204' high). Some of its murals are copies of Polish originals. (18) N. end of Lennox St., **Jones Island,** once the colorful fishing colony, where in its heyday (1890-1915), 6,000,000 lbs. of fish were seined annually. It also was haunt of sea-food epicures. Now is city's **Sewage Disposal Plant** (tours hourly Mon.-Fri.), occupies 50 as. & is internat. known for its highly developed & profitable treatment of sewage. By using the activated sludge principle, artificial fertilizer was produced as a by-product, known as Milorganite, netting the Metropolitan Sewage District $600,000 annually, besides reducing lake & stream pollution. (19) S. end of 27th St. Viaduct, **Mitchell Pk.** on a 63-a. bluff overlooking the Menomonee Valley. Here Jacques Vieau, Milwaukee's 1st fur trader, had a trading post, 1795. A replica of his cabin stands in NE. part of pk. **Conservatory & Botanical Gardens** (O.summer.8-10;otherwise 8-5), especially notable for orchid & chrysanthemum shows. Near Mitchell Pk. is 27th St. Viaduct, beneath which is **Pigsville,** called so because of pigs raised there in former days. (20) W. National Ave. bet. S. 44th & S. 56th St., **National Soldiers' Home,** Vet. Adm., the 350-a. federally-operated medical & rest center for soldiers, sailors & marines, one of the oldest in U.S. Veterans were admitted as early as 1867. One of its founders was mother of Brig. Gen. Mitchell (see below). Now has 90 bldgs. incl. 3 hospitals & 10 barracks (3,000 beds in entire center). (21) Along L. Mich. from E. Wis. Ave., **Juneau Pk.** From upper level is magnificent view of harbor, spreading N. & S. from confluence of its 3 rivers. To the (S) is winter dock of the L. fleets; (N) Yacht Club & **Lake Pk.,** best loved for its natural ravines. **Lincoln Mem. Drive** extends practically from N. to S. city limits on "made land." E. of Drive is **Water Purification Plant** (O.2-5 daily); completed in 1938 at cost of $5,100,000. On L. shore (SE) **Seadrome,** used exclusively for seaplanes & amphibians. (22) 3203 N. Downer Ave., **St. Teachers College,** noted for its Division of exceptional children which trains teachers for the deaf & mentally handicapped. (23) 2512 E. Hartford, **Milwaukee Downer College** (Tudor Goth.) founded 1895, formed out of Milwaukee Female Seminary, 1848, & Wis. Female College, 1851. (24) 2033 E. Hartford Ave., **Milwaukee Univ. School,** founded 1851 as German-English Academy by Peter

Engelmann, German political refugee, is a private coed. sch., from nursery sch. to college.

(25) **Estabrook Pk.** off E. Capitol Dr., incl. small **Ben. Church H.** (1844.Gr.Rev.by Ben.Church), moved from N. 4th St., where it stood for more than a century. (26) 1631 N. 4th St., **Linus N. Dewey H.** (1855.porch added.octagonal house). (27) 235 W. Galena St., **Schlitz Brewery** (tours every half hour.Mon.-Fri;9-11 Sat.) founded in 1849 by Aug. Krug. His bookkeeper, Jos. Schlitz, married his widow & in 1874 org. present brewery known the world over by its slogan, "The Beer that made Milwaukee famous." (28) 3533 N. 27th St., **Research & Engineering Bldg.,** one of 60 bldgs. of A. O. Smith Corp., known as "the glass house" (1931.Holabird & Root), outer walls being of aluminum & glass. (29) 1324 N. Milwaukee St., **Notre Dame Convent,** the Amer. mother-house of School Sisters of Notre Dame. Of the 416 schs. conducted by the nuns in North America, 28 parochial schs. & Mount Mary College (see below) are in Milwaukee Cty. The convent was founded in 1850. Today is home for aged nuns. (30) 2900 N. Menomonee R. Dr., **Mount Mary College,** an accredited Cath. college for girls (bldgs.Col.Goth.by Herbst & Kuenzli). (31) 1629 N. Prospect Ave., **Peck H.** (1870) one-time home of Geo. W. Peck, author of "Peck's Bad Boy" stories (see Madison). (32) 2822 N. 5th St., **Nunn-Bush Shoe Co. Plant** (O.appl.). Company received national recognition for its "Yrly. Salary Plan," begun in 1935. Each employee is assured an annual income. A committee of workers & executives determines wages, based on gross income of Co. & type of work performed. (33) W. Atkinson Ave., **Garden Homes Subdivision,** 1st Amer. co-op housing venture bet. citizens & local gov. (34) **Mitchell Air Field,** named to honor posthumously Brig. Gen. Wm. (Billy) Mitchell, stormy petrel of American air power. He was grandson of Alex. Mitchell, RR. king & banker, & was made Brig. Gen. at St. Mihiel, France, 1918. His insistence on importance of air power in future wars & his scathing attacks on "the hidebound bureaucrats of the army" so infuriated his superiors that he was suspended in 1925. He continued his warnings until his death in 1936.

## TRIPS OUT OF MILWAUKEE

### I. MILWAUKEE (W) to MADISON. 82. US18

Heading (W) on Bluemound Rd., US18 leaves Milwaukee & reaches **WAUKESHA** at **18.5.** former Potawatomi Village & later a famous health resort, known as "Saratoga of the West" because of its health waters; now an industrial city with well-known limestone quarries. Home of **Carroll College** (Presb.1841). Waukesha was an abolitionist center in pre-Civil War days & an important Underground RR. Sta. The "American Freeman" was printed here (1844-48). After the health boom, factories replaced resorts & bottled spring water is still one of its principal products. Waukesha is home of White Rock Mineral Springs. Mud Baths & Spa are still famous. At Waukesha is J. with St.59 leading (SW) 8$^{m}$ to **Genesee Depot.** In vic. is estate of Alfred Lunt & Lynn Fontanne. At **26.5.** J. with St.83 which leads (L) 1.5$^{m}$ to **Wales,** a Welsh community that until recently celebrated Eisteddfod festival of harvest, & still observes St. David's Day. US18 now passes through kettle moraine country past **GOLDEN LAKE** at **36.** At **56.5.** a tobacco-growing area begins, beautiful in summer with flowers whose blooms are later hooded to prevent cross-fertilization, presenting strange looking as. of paper blossoms. At **80.5.** J. with US14 & then (R) on Park St. to University Ave., **MADISON** (see) at **82.**

### II. MILWAUKEE (W) to MADISON. 82. St.30.

This is an alternate Rd. to US18, narrower & less traveled, but especially good for hikers, cyclists & horseback riders. At **14.** St.30 branches (R) & at **25.** is **DELAFIELD.** Here is **St. John's Military Academy** (Episc.). Goth. bldgs. (dress parade Sun.4 p.m.). Near-by is **Nashotah House,** Anglo-Cath. mission founded 1841, now Episc. seminary. **27. UPPER & LOWER NEMAHBIN LS.** (swim.boat.f.). **50. AZTALAN MOUND PK.** 2.5$^{m}$ (E) of the present city of **LAKE MILLS** at **52.5.** In Pk. are ruins of an ancient city which stood on banks of **Crawfish R.,** inhabited by people very advanced in civilization & arts as evinced by plan of village itself, their burnt brick & mortar construction & pottery & posts cut by sharp-edged stone implements. Although discovered in 1836, it was not presented to Wis. Archeological Soc. until 1922. Alex. Humboldt's writings suggested the name. Although it is fairly certain that Aztecs were not ancestors of these peoples, still their crafts show Mexican influence. Truncated pyramids with their plastered walls & shells from the Gulf coast identify Aztalan with the culture of the Middle & Lower Miss. rather than with Upper Miss. Milwaukee Pub. Mus. has a very fine replica of one of the bodies found. At **76.5.** is J. with US51. **82. MADISON.**

**III. SHOREWOOD (Milwaukee) (NW) to WATERTOWN. 47.5. US16**

**0. SHOREWOOD,** suburb of Milwaukee on L. Michigan at J. with US141. From here, on W. Capitol Dr., US16 passes Estabrook Pk. to J. with US41 at **7. 21. PEWAUKEE** (resort), on whose lake sail & ice boats skim in season. **28. PINE L.** (now mainly summer homes) where 1st Swedish immigrants settled in Wis. & called it New Upsala. **31.** Resort village of **OKAUCHEE, & L. Okauchee** near-by (boat.f. cottages). **34. OCONOMOWOC,** bet. **Fowler & LaBelle Ls.** (resorts.watering place; popular during week-ends;summer & winter sports). U.S. & Canada Skating Meets & Central States Ski-jumping contests held here. Out of town 3m is **Devil's Hollow,** where ski-jumping takes place. At **39. ROCK R.** is crossed. **45.5. OCTAGON H.,** a 4-story bldg. with many mechanical devices, such as central heating & air conditioning, that were advanced ideas 100 yrs. ago. (O.daily.May 30 to Nov.1,1849-53). **47.5. WATERTOWN,** sett. c.1836 by New Englanders. Four yrs. later German professionals or political refugees began to arrive. Carl Schurz, famous political reformer, arrived in 1856, having fled the "1848 revolution" in Germany. Schurz who hated slavery joined Republican Party although most Germans in Wis. were Democrats. In 1857 he ran for Lt. Gov., but was defeated, & next yr. campaigned for Lincoln, who made him Minister to Spain, 1861. He became brigadier gen. (1862) & major gen. of U.S. Army (1863); later U.S. Senator from Mo. & Secy. of Interior under Hayes. Mrs. Schurz, a pupil of Froebel, est. in Watertown 1st kindergarten in America, 1856. Bldg. in which it began is still standing on N. 2nd St. Ralph Blumenfeld, another notable Watertowner, introduced journalistic methods into England & became editor of London "Daily Express." Watertown is nationally known for its geese & supplies N.Y. markets. It also produces cutlery, cash registers, locks, furnaces, auto linings & canned peas. It has 2 sm. colleges, **Northwestern** (Evang.Luth. 1865) modeled on a German Gymnasium, & **Sacred Heart College** (Cath.normal sch.for boys). At **70.** is **COLUMBUS.** Here an antiquated gristmill & hotel built 1840 still stand. Near-by on James St. & among many plain bldgs. is **Farmers' & Merchants' Union Bank,** designed by Louis Sullivan (teacher of Frank Lloyd Wright), & considered one of his finest pieces of work. On St.60 (W) of Columbus, hillsides are covered with pea vines. It is considered some of best pea-growing land in st.

**IV. MILWAUKEE (N) to MANITOWOC. 87. US141.** Via: Port Washington & Sheboygan.

Leaving Milwaukee by Lake Dr. along beautiful curve of the bay & heading (N), US141 passes **SHOREWOOD, WHITEFISH BAY & FOX PT.,** suburbs of Milwaukee, on wooded bluffs to **THIENSVILLE** at **5.5.** For many yrs. this was home of Victor L. Berger, Milwaukee's famous 1st Socialist Congressman. Because of his anti-war publications during World War I, he was accused of violating the Espionage Act. Congress repeatedly refused to seat him, while his case was being appealed, despite the fact that his Wis. constituents re-elected him. Finally in 1921, after being completely exonerated, he served 2 more terms in the House. As far back as the turn of the cent., Berger was editor of the "Social Democrat." In 1911, after Milwaukee's gov. became socialist, Victor Berger founded & edited the "Milwaukee Leader" which became the most important Socialist paper in the country. He served as chairman of nat. executive committee of Socialist Party, from 1927 until his death in 1929. At **19.** hy. crosses **SAUK CR.,** which divides city of **PORT WASHINGTON, 29.,** important lake fishing port with an artificial harbor in an int. L-shaped setting. A great bluff on (S) side of city marks site where Ozaukee Cty. farmers fought against being drafted for Civil War. A thousand rioters ransacked **Draft Commissioner Por's H.** (still standing at 405 Wisconsin St.), threw him down the stairs, loaded the sm. 4th of July cannon with the only cannon ball in town & took over the bluff, until Gov. troops captured 80 men & broke further resistance. Port Washington is an industrial city. Besides commercial fishing, it manufactures office equipment, rubber goods & machinery. PTS. OF INT.: **Old Pebble H.** (1848) built by Edw. Dodge & his wife with pebbles from shore. Now is gate of Wis. Electric Power Co. **Blong H.** at 317 Pier St. is a century old. Lincoln lived in it for a short time after the death of Ann Rutledge. At **43.** is **JOLIET & MARQUETTE**

**MARKER** comm. their travel along L. Mich.'s shore. **49. OOSTBURG,** sett. by Dutch immigrants. It was off shore here that the ill-fated "Phoenix" in 1847 burnt with its load of immigrants. More than **150** drowned. At c.**50.5.** J. with Cty.KK leading (R) to **Terry Andrae St. Pk.** 2m (camp sites.pic.); 120 as. of dunes, pines & sandy beach.

**57. SHEBOYGAN.** RR. & bus conns.

Sheboygan, on shore of L. Mich. at mouth of Sheboygan R., had 2 beginnings. One was in 1835 when lumber prospectors from the East built 20 frame bldgs. In the 1837 depression, real estate crashed & the bldgs. were torn down & moved to another town; only 1 remained. The settlement became wilderness again. Yankee traders returned next yr. to build once more, this time to take root. The town, in 1844, still known as "The Mouth," attracted, because of its good harbor, lighth. & pier, settlers who came by way of the Gt. Ls. Lake steamships, particularly from Chicago & Buffalo, made daily calls, carrying each time new settlers. Most of these were German immigrants. Many were Lutherans who objected to Prussia's attempt to unite Calvinists & Lutherans. By 1849 members of other sects settled here. The next yr., although the town had only a hotel, blacksmith shop, foundry & brewery, it boasted 3 wkly. papers. First Dutch language paper in U.S. was published in Sheboygan. The "Forty-eighters"—a generation of Germans who sought religious & political freedom in America—did much to establish a fine community spirit. They kept up religious practices & cultural activities of the homeland & org. the famous Turnvereine (1854) to provide for physical culture & at same time serve as a political meeting ground. By 1860 wheat raising was important enough to support 20 flour mills & dairying was being fostered. First cheese factory was built in 1864. Lumber from Wis.'s woodland & the skilled foreign cabinetmakers made Sheboygan famous for its furniture, particularly chairs. This industry, however, declined with Wis.'s forests. Sheboygan now manufactures enamel ware & plumbing fixtures.

PT. OF INT.: N. 6th St. & Center Ave., **Sheboygan County Cth.** (1933.mod.W.C. Weeks).

SIDE TRIP: W. of Sheboygan 4m is **Kohler Village** in which the **Kohler Plant** (O.tours 10 a.m. & 2 p.m.June-Sept.), nationally known manufacturers of bathroom fixtures. There are 450 cottages housing about 1/6 of its employees. To (S) of town is **Estate of Walter J. Kohler** who had been chairman of the company & one-time Gov. of Wis.

**87. MANITOWOC**

Served by Chi. & NW. RR. & Soo Line; also Orange Bus & Green Bay Stage. Carferry Lines: Ann Arbor & Pere Marquette, on L. shore.

A fair-sized city, Manitowoc sprawls along its harbor, whose shipyards once built the great lake steamers. When iron vessels replaced wooden ones, Manitowoc too declined; but only till World War I, when the yards again operated at full capacity. From then to World War II, the largest & most modern carferries, tug boats, tankers, dredges & pleasure craft were built. During last war, shipyards devoted themselves almost entirely to building submarines for U.S. Navy. Manitowoc has world's largest malting & evaporated milk plants. It is also the aluminum center of the world. First Wis. pea-canning factory was built here & Manitowoc still leads in canning. It has 60 different industries, among them the largest tinsel mfg. plant. At Manitowoc is J. with St.151.

SIDE TRIP: On latter (W) 12.5m to **Valders,** birthpl. of Thorstein Veblen. Beyond 3m is J. with Cty.A leading (L) 2.5m to **St. Nazainz,** Cath. community developed from Utopian dream of Father Oschwald's "experiment in Christian Communism." Land was held in common. Villagers raised their own food & manufactured all clothes & necessities. After Father Oschwald's death, 1873, complications arose & the Salvatorian Fathers & Sisters, who still operate the seminary & convent, took over.

**V. MILWAUKEE (N) to FOND DU LAC. 63. US41.** Via: Menomonee Falls.

US41 leaves Milwaukee by way of Lisbon Ave. going (NW) & at **13.** reaches **MENOMONEE FALLS,** practically a suburb of Milwaukee with most of its wage earners working in the metropolis. At **32.** just outside Richfield is J. with Cty.P.

SIDE TRIP: On this Rd. (R) 5m to where **Holy Hill** (1,361') can be seen (R); 2.5m beyond, Rd. reaches top of the hill on which pilgrimage ch. & **Monastery of Carmelite Fathers is.** In 1855 1st little ch. was built on this spot where miraculous cures were said to have taken place, & to this shrine of "Our Lady," even today the faithful make frequent visits & pilgrimages. Stations of the Cross are along the winding footpath, at which the devout stop to pray, on their way to the crest.

**43.5. THERESA,** lying in kettle moraine terrain, was named for daughter of Solomon Juneau, founder of Milwaukee (see).

**63. FOND DU LAC.**
Fond du Lac, on farther end of L. Winnebago, Wis.'s largest L., was a trading post as early as 1785. First permanent white settlers, Colwert & Pier, came in 1836. It remained a sm. town until 1850 when logs began coming down Wolf R. to L. Winnebago, & almost immediately sawmills flourished. In a little more than a decade, 11 mills cut 61 million feet of lumber. When logs no longer were plentiful, city concentrated on transportation. Plank Rds. were built bet. Fond du Lac & Sheboygan. By 1859, a RR. was completed to Chicago & other lines & hys. converged at tip of L., helping to make transition from lumbering to present day prosperity. It now has more than 70 large industrial plants incl. leather goods, burial caskets & refrigerators. PTS. OF INT.: **St. Paul's Cathedral** (Episc.Amer.Goth.). The inter. is especially int. for its Oberammergau wood carvings; contains effigy tomb & death masks.

**VI. MILWAUKEE (S) to KENOSHA. 36. St.42.** Via: Racine.

RRs.: Milwaukee RR.; Chi. & NW.; Mil. & N. Shore Line; T.M.E.R.& L.Co. (electric)
Beginning at E. State & Milwaukee Sts., St.42 runs (S) on Milwaukee & becomes the lakeshore route to Chicago.

**0. MILWAUKEE** (see). **4.5. SOUTH SHORE PK.** (bath.). A short distance beyond, **St. Mary's Academy** (Cath.girls). Near-by is **St. Francis Seminary** (1856) whose former director, Rev. Francis Haas, is now nationally recognized labor mediator; & **St. Aemilianus Orphan Asylum.** Milwaukee's 1st Cath. Ch., **St. Peter's** (1839) was removed to seminary grounds. **7.5. CUDAHY,** home of Patrick Cudahy's famous meat packing plants. John Cudahy, U.S. Ambassador, & Gilda Gray, of "shimmy" fame, lived here. **10. SOUTH MILWAUKEE,** one of Milwaukee's largest industrial suburbs and economically a part of it. Noted for heavy machinery & bldg. materials. Largest producer of excavating machinery in the world. **First Congr. & St. Mark's Chs.** (Episc.) are more than 100 yrs. old. **14.5. CARROLLVILLE,** well-known for glue & chemical plants of U.S. Glue Co.

**26. RACINE.** (RR. & bus conns. Usual accoms.)
Racine, port on L. Mich., is 2nd largest & most industrialized city in Wis., a big jump from 1841 when lots on Main St. sold for $2, now valued at $1,700 a ft. When founded by Gilbert Knapp (1834), it was known as Port Gilbert. After 1850 came influx of foreign-born Eng., Irish, Czechs, Germans & Scands., who founded chs., schs. & foreign language newspapers. Near turn of the cent., Racine became industrialized, freight lines crossed through it & harbor improvements were made. Case machinery & agric. implements, Nash auto-parts, Johnson's wax & Horlick's Malted Milk are internationally known & foremost among city's 129 industries. Labor is well recognized, with 90% of shops unionized. PTS. OF INT.: (1) 7th & Wisconsin Ave., **Cth.** (Mod.Holabird & Root.entrance reliefs by Carl Milles,Swedish sculptor). **First Cth.** was built 1842. (2) College Ave. & 7th St., **First Presb. Ch.** (1851.Gr.Rev. by Lucas Bradley). (3) 1135 Main St., **Taylor H.** (1853.Gr.Rev.). (4) 1235 Main St., **Knight H.** (1842), with steep gables & leaded windows; built by a bachelor who forgot to include closets & a pantry. (5) 1274 Main St., **Hunt H.** (1848.Gr.Rev.fine proportions). (6) 1319 S. Main St. & DeKoven Ave., **DeKoven Foundation,** formerly Racine College, now known as Cove Schs., one for crippled children, the other for children with brain injuries suffered at birth. (7) 16th St. bet. Howe & Franklin, **S. C. Johnson & Sons Office Bldg.,** usually referred to as "glass tower" (a streamlined wing-shaped penthouse by F. L. Wright). Wright also built Herbert Johnson's private residence, **"Wingspread"** (c.1938). (8) 1012 16th St., **Johnson Plant** (O.tours 10-11:30 & 2-3.Mon.-Fri.). (9) Packard Ave. S. of 17th St., **Nash Motor Plant** (O. 10-4.Mon.-Fri.). (10) 12th St. & Herrick Ave., **Co-op Corners,** entirely taken over by co-ops that began in 1934. Today have 2,500 people, owning a quarter million dollars in assets with sales approaching the $1,000,000 mark. It incl. service stas., supermarket, insurance agency, coal & fuel yard. It is one of largest city co-ops in U.S. (11) 941 Lake Ave., **H. of Olympia Brown Willis,** early suffrage leader; worked with Susan B. Anthony. (12) 2109 Northwestern Ave., **Horlick Malted Milk Plant** (N.O.; Tudor Goth.). (13) 700 State St., **J. I. Case Co. Plant** (O.appl.). (14) On Northwestern Ave., **Horlick Mill** (1836). Orig. dam still stands.

**36. KENOSHA.** (RR. & bus conns. Usual accoms.)
Kenosha, highly industrialized city, is situated along L. Mich., mfg. machinery, autos, beds & hosiery. Its pop. is largely of German, Ital. & Polish extraction. New England farmers of 3rd & 4th generation settled here as early as 1835 & brought with them ideas of a free press, free schs. & the authority to tax themselves. Kenosha was then known as Southport & its progressive newspaper, "The Telegraph," whose editor, C. L. Sholes, became the inventor of the typewriter, was wont to advocate, in particular, a free public school. First free sch. in Wis. was est. here 1849. As early as 1844, the "Wis. Phalanx," a Fourierist communal colony, was founded here by 20 men from Southport, who then went to Ripon to begin their experiment. The town's name was changed to Kenosha in 1850; not until 1884 did the Fed. Gov. appropriate $200,000 for harbor improvements. From then dates Kenosha's upward swing. By 1915, Simmons Bedding, Chicago & Rockford Hosiery, & Nash Auto Co. had joined other nat. manufacturers operating here. In 5 yrs. each employed bet. 4,000 to 5,000 workers. Its peaceful labor history was interrupted in 1928 with the Allen-A hosiery workers strike, which lasted 18 months. Strike was lost & Kenosha remained open shop. In 1933 Nash & Simmons workers struck & this time gained recognition of their unions. Since then, A.F. of L. & C.I.O. act together in the Trades & Labor Council, & support a weekly labor paper. City Manager System (1st in Wis.), under which Kenosha is governed, has lowered adm. costs & greatly improved conditions. PTS. OF INT.: 55th St. & 5th Ave., **Simmons Bedding Co.** (O.appl.), occupying 5 sq. blocks. Sheridan Rd. to 10th Ave., **Civic Center,** contains **Kenosha Hist. & Art Mus.** (O.Sun.1:30-5); also **Kenosha Cty. Hist. Mus.** (O.8-5 wks.). 1118 61st St., **Rev. R. H. Deming H.** was a sta. on Underground Railroad in the 1850's. 1420 63rd St., **Amer. Brass Co.** (O.appl.), now a subsidiary of Anaconda Copper Mining Co. 57th St. & 25th Ave., **Nash-Kelvinator Plant** (tours 10-2;Mon.-Fri.), largest factory in Kenosha.

**VII. MILWAUKEE (SW) to LAKE GENEVA. 47. St.36.** Via: Greendale & Burlington.
Hy. travels (SW) & at **11.** passes **GREENDALE** (see US45). **36. BURLINGTON,** sett. 1835 by Vermonters who named it for their capital city. To the W. 2$^{m}$ along riverbank is site of **Voree Strang Mormon Colony,** which in 1844 was known as Garden of Peace. Jas. J. Strang, its founder, was disciple of Jos. Smith until he broke with him & started his own colony at Voree. Colony was an economic failure & in 1849 abandoned Voree for Beaver I., Mich. (see). Strang's grave is in the Voree burial ground. St.36 reaches at **47. LAKE GENEVA,** known as the "Newport of Chicago society," & is frequented mainly by Chicagoans who have their homes & big estates there. The influx from Chicago became especially heavy after the Chicago fire in 1871, when wealthy Chicagoans moved their families here. **Town hotel,** near Fontana Williams Bay, was designed by Frank Lloyd Wright. Here on a hill, 190′ high, is famous **Yerkes Observatory** (O.free.June 1-Oct.1.Sat.1:30-3;Oct.1-June 1,10-12. 1897), operated by Univ. of Chicago. It houses world's largest refracting telescope (40″) set within a mammoth dome, gift of Chas. T. Yerkes. Reg. abounds in game fish & the famous cisco. In winter, fishermen set up a "town" of tar-paper shacks on the frozen L. & ice fish. Ciscos are caught at night, usually with flares & bright-colored bait. St.36 climbs a ridge & reaches **L. Como** (R) & **Cisco Bay** (L). Further 0.5$^{m}$ is **Williams Bay** (swim.boat.refresh.f.license & guides.speedboat trips). Winter sports & carnivals during season. At W. end of lake is **Fontana** (swim.boat.). Here, a century before, was camp of Potawatomi Chief, Big Toe. On S. shore of lake is **Northwestern Military & Naval Academy** & some Ind. mounds.

## MADISON

RR. Stas.: Milwaukee RR., 644 W. Washington Ave.; Chi. & NW., 201 S. Blair St. Bus Sta.: Union Bus Terminal, 122 W. Washington Ave. Airport: Municipal, on US51 6$^{m}$ (N), Northwest Airline. Accoms.: All types.

Madison is beautifully situated on an isthmus formed by Ls. Mendota & Monona, with Ls. Waubesa & Kegonsa to the (SE) joined by the Yahara R. The impressive Capitol rises 285′ above the heights of the isthmus, its granite dome crowned by the gilt statue of "Forward" visible for miles, from any approach to Madison. It is seat of St. Univ. which occupies the wooded shoreland of L. Mendota stretching to

the (S) & (NE). Fed. Judge John D. Doty saw its beauty & realized the possibilities of making this "four lakes region" the capital, when he 1st passed through in 1829. By 1836 he owned huge tracts of land on the isthmus & was able to persuade the legislature to choose it as the site of the capital & location of the Univ. From a "beautiful but uninhabitable" wilderness grew the present handsome city. In 1846 it was inc. as a village & was named after James Madison who had died 10 yrs. before. But development lagged until Jairus Fairchild from Milwaukee financed the enterprise. Soon after, although the isthmus was still a for., the town became populated, spurred on by arrival of the 1st RR. Business began, banks sprang up, mills operated continuously & public building went on furiously for a time.
The Univ. was slower in its growth. While Fairchild was mayor (1856), commercial & cultural interests vied with each other. Bayard Taylor, James R. Lowell & Horace Greeley visited the town & gave lectures. The financial panic of the next yr. slowed up business ventures & stopped the bringing in of Eastern labor. Civil War brought back the boom because Madison was a center of war activities. Camp Randall on St. Fair Grounds had 7,000-8,000 men. The Univ., however, suffered; hardly a student remained. In 1866, it was completely reorganized & from then began to expand. In 1904 Rbt. M. LaFollette was elected gov. & the Progressive movement, known as the "Wis. idea," was launched. It was backed by Prof. John R. Commons, famous political economist of the Univ. After 10 yrs. the adm. changed but the "Wis. idea" continued unaffected by alternating incumbents. In 1917, Univ. students, in a patriotic fever, burned LaFollette in effigy, because of his pacifist speeches. After the war, Madison again sett. down. In 1918, it had 35 chs. & 35 labor unions. Despite being known as a cultural center, it is also an industrialized city & ranks 4th in St. Town & Gown still form its 2 main sets of society but frequently these, too, meet on common ground.

PTS. OF INT.: (1) In Capitol Pk., **St. Capitol** (1906-17.by Geo.B.Post.Ital.Ren.). Its granite dome is the only one in the country & its height is 2nd only to the Capitol Dome in Washington. The gilt bronze statue of "Forward" is by Dan. C. French. (2) 2 W. Mifflin St., **City Hall** (1858.by Donnell & Kutzbock). Top fl. of bldg. was used as an opera house for many yrs. (3) 110 W. Washington Ave., **Grace Ch.** (1858. Episc.Congr.Goth.), oldest in Madison (org.1839). (4) 16 S. Carroll St., **Old Baptist Ch.** (1854), now hqs. of Wis. Tel. Co. Ole Bull & Adelina Patti appeared here in joint recital; Wendell Phillips & other notables lectured here. (5) 206 Monona Ave., **David Atwood H.** (1851), home of founder of "Wis. State Journal." (6) 22 N. Butler St., **Lamp H.** (1895.by Frank Lloyd Wright), a forerunner in style of his Oak Pk. houses. (7) 651 Williamson St., **Fauerbach Brewery** (O.appl.1848.Goth.& Romanes. by Fred Sprecher). (8) 130 E. Gilman St., **Executive Mansion** (1854), at one time home of Ole Bull & his wife, Sarah Thorp. They had the lawns terraced in Norweg. style. (9) 424 N. Pinckney St., **Pierce H.** (1858.by Donnell & Kutzbock). (10) 12 E. Gilman St., **College Women's Club** (1850.adds.1880), built for J. T. Clark & enlarged for U.S. Sen. Wm. F. Vilas. (11) 521 N. Henry St., **Vilas H.** (1851), home of Levi B. Vilas, 4th mayor of Madison & father of the U.S. Senator, now Stone Lodge. (12) 422 N. Henry St., **Braley H.** (1880); here Ella Wheeler Wilcox wrote "Laugh and the World Laughs with you." (13) 508 N. Frances St., **Dudley H.** (1855.completed after Civil War), with large low-set windows. Now known as the German H.; also home for women students. (14) 120 Ely Pl., **Airplane H.** (1906.by Frank Lloyd Wright), typical of "Illinois Prairie" style, designed for Prof. E. A. Gilmore. (15) At end of concrete drive bet. Allen St. & Highland Ave., **U.S. Forest Products Lab.** (1932.by Holabird & Root;mod.industrial style;5-story-U-shaped bldg.; tours 2:30 daily exc.Sun.). Lab. is operated by U.S. Forest Service & is equipped to do every possible research in wood products. About 3,000 samples of wood are identified annually for commercial use or in law court decision. Info. used in identifying the Lindbergh kidnapper was obtained through analysis here. (16) 3706 Nakoma Rd., **Old Spring Hotel** (1854), on main route, famous for its cookies & coffee. Rbt. La Follette, Sr., when a boy, frequented it. Prof. James Dickson, present owner, added a 2-story Georg.Col. porch. (17) 3402 Monroe St., **Plow Inn** (1836.post-Col. limestone) was overnight stopping place in stagecoach days; now a residence. Stucco hides orig. walls. (18) 451 W. Wilson St., **Giles H.** (middle of 19th cent.Vict.cream-colored brick). (19) 314 S. Broom St., **B. O. Webster H.** (yellow-frame), close to L. Monona. 1880-90 was residence of Rbt. M. LaFollette. Here he entertained many distinguished guests, among them Theodore Roosevelt. (20) 200 W. Main St., **St.**

**Raphael's Ch.** (1854.long & high with Georg.type steeple in Wren style), 2nd Cath. Ch. of Madison. (21) 214 W. Washington Ave., former **Synagogue** (1863.one of 1st synagogues in Wis.;Vict.Goth.), served later as a Unit. Social Hall, W.C.T.U. hqs., a chapel for 3 other denominations, funeral home & now the Ch. of Christ.

(22) **Univ. of Wis.** (bldgs.O.during sch.hours) spreads for a mile along crest of ridge bordering S. shore of L. Mendota. Univ. grounds are divided into 3 secs.: Upper Campus, Lower Campus, & Agric. Campus, with outlying centers. Bldgs. erected since 1900 are in mod. Ital. Ren. by Geo. B. Ferry & Alfred C. Clas, J. T. W. Jennings & recently Arthur Peabody. Some of the bldgs. on Lower Campus: **Men's Gym. & Armory** (1894.Norman fortress design); **Mem. Union** (1928.O.1st Sun.of month.Ren.); **Lib.** (O.during univ.sessions 8 a.m.-10 p.m.;summer 8-4), contains theater, club, 2 broadcasting stas., also a famous coll. of material on Geo. Rogers Clarke, built 1900 to house the Wis. Hist. Soc. Univ. shares bldg. with the soc. & Wis. Academy of Sciences, Arts & Letters. Upper Campus: **Science Hall** (1888. Romanes.by A.C.Koch)—Geology Mus. (O.8-5 wks.); **Radio Hall,** hqs. & studios for WHA, claimed to be oldest radio sta. in U.S.; **North Hall** (1851.oldest bldg. on campus) where John Muir lived as a student; **Bascom Hall,** on the hill (1857.mod. Roman Doric style), contains many of the general adm. offices. Agric. Campus: **Studio of the Artist in Residence** (1937.built for John Steuart Curry, 1st artist in residence appointed by the Univ.; **Univ. Farms** (841 as.) with labs., barns, & poultry bldgs.; also Animal Husbandry & Stock Pavillion (1908). **Camp Randall,** center of Civil War activities; later became St. Fair Grounds & now **Univ. Athletic Field. Univ. Stadium** (1918.with adds.), with seating capacity of 45,000.

## TRIPS OUT OF MADISON

### I. MADISON (S) to BELOIT. 55. US51. Via: Janesville, Edgerton, Stoughton.

At **19.** (S) on US51 is **STOUGHTON.** Dan. Webster bought land here in 1838. City's oldest enterprise was wagon-making, hence named "Wagon City." It now manufactures auto bodies. **30. EDGERTON.** Tobacco, introduced here in 1854, is grown in great quantity. **ALBION,** at **34.** was sett. in 1841, by Norweg. & Eng. An Academy & Normal Institute begun by Seventh Day Baptists dates back to 1854. Opp. is their ch. under which is the excavated sta. of Underground RR. **41. JANESVILLE,** an industrial town on Rock R., founded by Henry F. James in 1836. In 1837, he built a tavern & a ferry operating to E. bank. Soon the village grew into a trans. center. Stages passed through, boats came up the Rock R.; even steamships up from the Miss. In 1922, Gen. Motors set up Chevrolet & Fisher Body plants & city prospered, until the depression struck. The 2 plants were then shut down for 15 months & since have reached an all-time peak. Janesville is also home of Parker Pen Co. & manufactures cotton & woolen goods, shades, awnings & punch presses. The "Daily Gazette" under various names has had 102 yrs. of service. W. of the hy. $1^m$ is **Carrie Jacobs Bond H.,** now Clark's Filling Sta., & $3^m$ (S), **Frances E. Willard Home & Sch.** She was founder of W.C.T.U. Grounds are now Youth Hostel. On Cty.A, $7^m$ (E) Ella Wheeler Wilcox (1850-1919) lived as a child.

**55. BELOIT,** on Wis.-Ill. line, is seat of **Beloit College** (1847.Georg.Col.). It has a very important anthropological & archeological dept. Roy Chapman Andrews, famous explorer & naturalist, was born & received his training here. **Logan Mus.** on campus (O.1869) has more than a million aboriginal artifacts, many of which were fashioned by Cro-Magnon craftsmen 35,000 yrs. ago. **Theo. Lyman Wright Art Hall** (O) contains coll. of sculptures, paintings & prints; W. Grand Ave., **Hist. Soc.** (exhibs.). City has over 60 industrial plants & is one of the best winter-sport areas in Wis. Annually in Dec., a Winter Frolic is held. Beloit is one of the oldest settlements. Joseph Thibault, in 1824, est. here a trading post, & permanent settlers arrived in 1837.

### II. MADISON (N) to PORTAGE. 37. US51

At **5.** hy. passes **L. MENDOTA** (R). For about $16^m$ Rd. passes through rich agric. land with large farms, well developed through systematic crop rotation. **23. POYNETTE** (R. on dirt Rd. to **St. Experimental Game & Fur Farm).** From **26.** US51 follows old Military Rd. built in 1835 bet. Ft. Howard at Green Bay & Ft. Crawford at Prairie du Chien, into **PORTAGE** at **37.,** founded by travelers & traders of the Fox-Wis. waterway, a continuous natural water passage bet. the St. Lawrence &

Gulf of Mexico. Portage is birthpl. of Fred. J. Turner, noted historian, & of Zona Gale, a number of whose novels are based on Portage people. PTS. OF INT.: Wis. St. & Wauona Ave., **Joliet-Marquette Marker,** comm. 1st portage made here. Edgewater & Mac Sts., **Pawkette Marker,** site of 1st ferry across the Wis. Canal & Mac Sts., **Curling Rink,** where internat. matches are held, known here as Bonspiel, a combination of the German word "Bahn" or track & "Spiel" or game.

**III. MADISON (NW) to WISCONSIN RAPIDS. 109. US12 & St.13.** Via: Prairie du Sac & Wisconsin Dells. Leaving Madison, US12 & St.13 unite, going (NW). At **24.5.** they cross Wis. R. & reach **SAUK CITY & PRAIRIE DU SAC,** twin cities. Sauk City, founded 1842 by Count Agoston Haraszthy, colorful Hungarian nobleman, who brought with him the Freethinker philosophy, started the 1st "Freie Gemeinde" & gave to Sauk City the reputation, even abroad, of the "Freethinkers' Heaven." The 2 cities, built on site of Sauk villages, have a predominantly European flavor. Prairie du Sac is mainly Protestant while Sauk City is Cath. (German), & rivalry bet. the 2 still continues. August Derleth & Mark Schorer, Sauk City's well-known novelists, have recorded & interpreted the life of pioneer Wis.

US12 crosses the prairie & climbs **BARABOO RANGE at 34. 38.** J. with St.159 which in 1$^m$ joins St.123 into **Devil's L. St. Pk.** (1,313 as.camp.free for 1st 2 wks. thereafter sm.fee.hik.bath.pic.golf.), which lies in an area of great geological interest. After the glacial age Wis. R. carved its way through quartzite rock, leaving cleft to be filled up, thus forming the L. & many odd rock formations such as **Devil's Doorway, The Needle, Turk's Head, & Ancient Rock.** Bluffs are 600′ above sea level & densely forested. Only a hiking path around the L. Pk. is of interest not only to geologists, but also to biologists because it forms dividing line bet. Wis.'s N. & S. flora & fauna. Area has 3 Ind. mounds: **Eagle Mound** on S. shore; **Bear & Lynx mounds** on N. shore. At **40.** (R) 1.5$^m$ to **Baraboo,** resort city, named for Fr. trader, Jean Baribault. In 1837, the Winnebago who owned land at confluence of the Wis. & Baraboo ceded it to U.S. In center of town still stand bldgs. used by Ringling Bros. who began their circus here. In 1907 the Bros. sold their circus to Barnum & Bailey, which became "Greatest Show on Earth." Located near Baraboo are giant **Badger Ordnance Works,** built during World War II, $125,000,000; produced smokeless & rocket powder.

US12 again heads N. passing **L. DELTON** (airport & golf course) into city of **WISCONSIN DELLS** at **53.** Town, formerly known as Kilbourn, is starting pt. for water trips up & down the R. through magic rock formations of the Dells. There are miles of weird & richly colored bluffs, & rugged sandstone cliffs, washed out by the ancient R.'s force, into amazing shapes & forms, 30,000 yrs. old (excursion boats at frequent intervals;fee). Steamers follow serpentine route & pass such whimsically named pts. as **Chimney Rock, Hornet's Nest, Swallow's Nest, Turtle & Alligator Rocks, Inkstand, Sugar Bowl, Devil's Anvil** & **Witch's Gulch.** Hundreds of caves & grottos with vari-colored mosses & flowers line the shores; waterfalls & cascades are not far inland. (All types of accoms. in town;camp.& pic.). Winnebago Inds. hold annual ceremonials at **Stand Rock,** a natural bowl, so accoustically perfect that the slightest whisper can be heard. Season for visiting Dells—May 1 to Nov. 1. Just N. of the city is **Rocky Arbor Roadside Pk.** Int. rock formations in midst of heavily wooded area. (pic.camp.excellent for overnight tenting or with trlr.). At the Dells trip cont. on St.13 which runs (N) 56$^m$ to **Wisconsin Rapids** at **109.,** a large cranberry center. One company represents 90% of St.'s growers. Town now has modern industries of various kinds, but paper making predominates.

**IV. MADISON (SE) to LAKE GENEVA. 72. US12.** Via: Fort Atkinson, Whitewater & Elkhorn.

US12 joined with US18 travels (E), then (SE). **32. FORT ATKINSON.** Here in 1832 Gen. Henry Atkinson, while pursuing Black Hawk, set up a stockade & 2 blockhs. In 1873 Wm. Dempster Hoard, who perhaps contributed most toward making Wis. the dairyland of the country, set up the paper here which later became Hoard's "Dairyman," read today by most farmers. Hoard was Gov. of Wis. (1889-91) during which time he sponsored anti-oleomargarine legislation. Besides being a shipping & trading center for reg.'s dairy farmers, Ft. Atkinson is also a mfg. town producing among its various articles, musical saws of great perfection. It publishes the annual "Sawing News of the World." On Milwaukee Ave., in Pub. Lib. is **Ft. Atkinson Hist. Soc. Mus.** (O.Sat.10-12 & 2-5 p.m.). **44. WHITEWATER,** on whose shores stands an old **Mill** (1839). Whitewater is home of **St. Teachers College** & of **Morris Pratt Institute,** founded 1883, to prepare students for "the Spiritualist ministry or to develop psychic powers." **62. ELKHORN** (see US12). **71. LAKE GENEVA** (see Milwaukee Trip VII).

**V. MADISON (W) to MONROE. 36. US18 & St.69.** Via: Verona & New Glarus. On US18 (W) to **VERONA** at **9.** Here trip cont. on St.69 (S) to **NEW GLARUS** at **27.** New Glarus on Little Sugar R., is known as Little Switzerland because of its Swiss pop. whose parents came from Glarus, Switzerland. They lived in comparative poverty for 20 yrs., until they turned to dairying; then prosperity began. Their special type of Swiss cheese became known throughout U.S. & had a ready market everywhere. Annually on 2nd Sun. & Mon. of Sept. people of New Glarus celebrate Kilbi, a festival that originated in the old Canton. After the ch. festivities, parades, dancing & playing cont. for 2 days. S. of New Glarus, St.69 passes through a valley for 1$^{m}$ & reaches **New Glarus Roadside Pk.** (43 as.pic.facils.). Mon. here comm. the "Old Lead Trail," leading into lead mines of SW. Wis. In the woods are still traces of "badger holes," as the lead diggings were formerly called. At **45. MONROE,** known as "Swiss Cheese Center of the U.S." Annually a cheese festival is held with parades & pomp; even a cheese queen is selected.

**VI. MADISON (W) to PRAIRIE DU CHIEN. 98. US18.** Via: Platteville & Bridgeport.

On Monroe St. (W) US18 leaves Madison, runs past swamps, glacial hills & boulders (S) into the Swiss cheese area. **20. MT. HOREB,** Swiss & Norweg. village. At **23.5.** J. with dirt Rd. leading (R) to **Little Norway** (O.sm.fee), a village of sm. houses built by Norweg. craftsmen, & furnished in Scand. style to look like the Valley of Elves, with coll. of Norwegiana incl. Grieg Mss. & 2 canes of Ole Bull.

**24.** J. with gravel Rd. going (R) to **Cave of the Mounds,** odd rock formations & well preserved fossils. At **25.** US18 passes **BLUE MOUNDS** & joins Military Rd., a trl. used by Amer. soldiers (1835-38). **42. DODGEVILLE,** metropolis of the lead region (1827-29) named for Gov. Henry Dodge, colorful Wis. character. Before coming to Wis. he was implicated in Aaron Burr conspiracy & indicted by grand jury. Infuriated at their charge he "thrashed 9 jurors & the indictment was dropped." He is said to have mined Ind. land illegally & was deaf to protests; finally Inds. gave up title to the land. He was named 1st Terr. Gov. because of his handling of the Inds. during Black Hawk War. Later his old enemy, James Doty (see US45), replaced him. He also served as U.S. Sen. At Dodgeville is J. with US151.

SIDE TRIP: On US151 (L) hy. passes through Wis.'s oldest sett. reg.—its former mining country & only part of Wis. that is unglaciated. By 1828, the mining boom swept through here. Early miners came from Mo. & Ky., but after 1832, the Cornish arrived. While Milwaukee was still a trading post, this reg. had 10,000 people. Lead mining reached its peak bet. 1856-57 & then had quick decline. The miners turned to farming as soon as the land was for sale.

**92.** J. With Cty.C.

SIDE TRIP: On latter (L) to **Wyalusing St. Pk.** (facils.for camp.pic.no bath.), lying high on Miss. R. bluffs, with caves & water falls. Marquette & Joliet traveled along the upper Miss. Waterway bet. Green Bay & Prairie du Chien was for 150 yrs. main artery of travel in NW. On Sentinel Ridge (590′) is **Pt. Lookout** (fine view of Miss. R.) & **Signal Pt.,** boasting 3 bear effigy mounds among its Ind. earthworks, said to be almost intact.

US18 speeds (W) through hardwood areas & past old quarries. **98. PRAIRIE DU CHIEN,** named (1781) for Fox Chief, whom the Fr. called Le Chien ("the dog"), is a former Ind. & fur traders' stop-over & 2nd oldest city in st., now a leisurely R. town where the Miss. & Wis. meet. St. Friol, one of the Is. on which oldest part of city is built, is connected by bridges to other secs. of the city. PTS. OF INT.: On Bolvin & 1st Sts., **Amer. Fur Co. Post** was built by Rolette, 1835, & rented to John J. Astor, organizer of the fur post, 1842. (Now private residence & fur storage place.) Jos. Rollette, company's 1st agent, is buried in old **Fr. Cemetery** (N) of city. Hercules Dousman, Astor's most influential agent, made his fortune here. **Villa Louis** (O.May 1-Nov.1;fee.guides), his residence, is in **Dousman Pk.** (swim.pool & golf). Villa was built, 1843, on site of Ft. Shelby (remod.1872), a gracious "great house" of the North, true example of mid-19th cent. Wis. with int. furnishings. It was destroyed by Brit. at end of War of 1812 & was rebuilt by Amers. **St. Mary's College** (Cath.) is now on site of 1st Ft. Crawford. Jeff. Davis (see Miss.), then a young Lt. under Zachary Taylor, fell in love here with Sarah Knox, who later became his wife.

**Ft. Crawford** is now marked by a Military Hospital & near-by cemetery. On villa grounds is Mus. exhibiting articles found during excavation of Fts. Shelby, & Crawford (O.daily.adm.). Int. also are: **Diamond Jo Steamship Line Warehouse** on riverbank (1862); **Northwest Fur Co. Bldg.** on N. Beaumont Rd. (now a taxi office), & the former **Hqs. of Capt. W. Knowlton** (1842), comdr. in Mex. War (now occupied by League of Women Voters); **St. Gabriel's Ch.** (1839-40.Cath.), under direction of Father Mazzachellia, pioneer in Wis. religious work; **Egyptian Lotus Beds** in vic. are in bloom in Aug. US18 crosses **Upper Miss. R. Wildlife & Fish Refuge,** which extends 300$^m$ along Miss. R. with hqs. at Winona, Minn.

## VII. MADISON (NW) to RICHLAND CENTER. 64. US14.

US14 & US12 unite for 5.5$^m$ leaving Madison going (NW). Here is J. with side Rd. leading (R) to **Trailer Town,** on a 48-a. wooded tract overlooking L. Mendota (all facils.for trlr.camp.elec.laundry.store.gas sta.). **14. CROSS PLAINS.** Veterans of War of 1812 sett. here bet. 1832-50 but many left for Cal. during the gold rush. **Christina H.,** now residence, was a tavern in stagecoach days. **19. BLACK EARTH.** Here is Patrons' Mercantile Co., one of oldest farmer co-ops in state. **22. MAZOMANIE.** Brit. Temperance Emigration Soc. arrived here in 1843. Later German immigrants came whose bldgs. resembled Rhine castles with turrets & high gables. The **Salem Kirche** of handwrought stone & delicate lines is from this period. **36. TOWER HILL ST. PK.** (108 as.camp.pic.no overnight facils.). Here in 1828 stood old village of Helena & on banks of Wis. R. still stand the remains of old **Shot Tower,** where shot was manufactured & shipped down the R. Lead from the mines of SW. Wis. was hauled by ox team to smelter on the hill. Then it was dropped down the shot tower 200′ to solidify into balls in the cold water below. Industry cont. for over 30 yrs. until ore was exhausted. Here is J. with St.23.

SIDE TRIP: On this Rd. (L) 0.5$^m$ to **Taliesin** (no pic.but a conducted tour of grounds, fee), home of Frank Lloyd Wright, with roofs paralleling ridges of the hill around which it is built. Its name is Welsh, meaning "shining brow," & its history is tragic. Present structure is 3rd built on same spot. The 1st two were destroyed by fire & Taliesin III was almost lost in bankruptcy. Friends rescued it. A fellowship was est. in 1933 & c.30 young men or women serve apprenticeship in the arts & architecture here.

**40. SPRING GREEN.** Here side by side stand the Chs. & parsonages of Caths., Meths., & Congregationalists, on land given by A. C. Daley. In the village is a sawmill run by Miss Maurice Cavanaugh, "Lady Logger," who began her work in Minn. in 1926 & has since operated 11 sawmills in both sts. **64. RICHLAND CENTER** (1849). Woman's Suffrage was advocated here as early as 1882. Frank Lloyd Wright was born here (1869). He designed flat-roofed **Laurence Warehouse,** with Mayan ornamentation (1918).

## VIII. MADISON (SW) to PLATTEVILLE. 71. US151

US151 & US18 travel as 1 route to **DODGEVILLE** at **41.** (see Madison Trip VI). Then US151 turns (SW) 7$^m$ to **LEVI STERLING H.** (1828) at **48. 51. MINERAL POINT,** also known as Shake Rag town because at mealtime dishcloths were waved to call miners home from the mines. Mineral Point survived the depression of 1837, the Cal. Gold Rush, & a cholera epidemic. Alex. Hamilton's son, Wm., was 1 of its early settlers. After lead came zinc mining & when both declined, town turned to retailing & shipping. Most bldgs are more than 100 yrs. old. Among these are **Trinity Ch. & Parish H.; Meth. Ch.;** a row of **Cornish Hs.** on Shake Rag St.; best known is **Pendarvis H.** (now antique shop); also **Polperro H.** Cornish pasties are still served here upon request. At Pine & Davis Sts., **Gundry H.** (colonnaded porch & cupola). Although Jos. Gundry was a Cornishman, his mansion & estate recall Southern architecture. Here is housed the **Mineral Point Hist. Soc. & Mus.** Very fine mineral coll., old costumes & hist relics. Commerce St., **Walker Hotel** (1836). Opp. here one of the few Wis. hangings took place in 1842. Wis. was 2nd st. to abolish capital punishment (1851). First **Odd Fellows' Hall** (O) was converted into mus.; 1 block (E) of Front St., **Cothren H.** At **64.** is **BELMONT,** on a ridge. Here is J. with gravel Rd.

SIDE TRIP: To the (R) 3$^m$ is **First Capitol Bldg.** (1836); now a St. Pk.; 1st terr. legislature met here until capitol at Madison was erected.

**71. PLATTEVILLE,** surrounded by marginal mines. Here at 20 Elm St. is **Wis. Institute of Technology.** At 722 W. Pine St., oldest **Wis. St. Teachers College.** On 3rd St., 1 block (S), **Major John H. Rountree H.** (Georg.with Gr.pediment).

# US 2—MINNESOTA

**MINN.-WIS. LINE** (at Duluth, Minn.) **(W) to MINN.-N.D. LINE** (at Grand Forks, N.D.). **268. US2**

Via: Grand Rapids, Bemidji, Crookston, E. Grand Forks. RRs.: Gt. Northern RR.; N.P. RR. bet. Crookston & Grand Forks. Good Rds.: Bituminous & Paved. Accoms.: In larger towns.

US2 crosses through Duluth & Upper Minn., through the Arrowhead country & Chippewa Nat. For., into Paul Bunyan land to the Minn.-N.D. Line.

## Sec. 1: DULUTH to BEMIDJI. 155.

**0. DULUTH,** nestles high above L. Superior (600-800′). A beautiful 29-mile drive runs along outer edge of the bluffs. Its streets are often steep & winding & the air has the tang of the North country, which makes Duluthians buoyant & expansive in their undertakings. The harbor, a perfect landlocked basin bet. Minn. Pt.& Wis. Pt., admits the largest Gt. Ls. ships. City is considered one of the best Hay Fever refuges of the country.

In 1630 Fond du Lac, now a part of Duluth, was an Ojibway village. Except for visit of Sieur du Luth, who tried to make peace bet. the Ojibway & the Sioux in 1679, it was known only for fur trading until 18th cent. In 1826, Lewis Cass, Terr. Gov. of Mich., negotiated treaty of Fond du Lac, & 6 yrs. later Schoolcraft passed through on his way to discovering the real source of the Miss. R. Permanent settlement began in 1852 with Geo. P. Stuntz, who was wildly excited about the possibilities in this wilderness. Next 3 yrs. were boom yrs. because of the rumor of immense copper deposits along the N. shore & iron ore at L. Vermillion. In 1854 the Inds., by treaty, relinquished their rights to the mineral tracts & the boom went on until the national panic of 1857, which reduced the as yet unnamed but prosperous town to grass roots. On its heels followed the scarlet fever epidemic of 1859, leaving only 2 occupied houses in 1865. New reports of goldbearing quartz brought on a stampede for the bonanza, made even more alluring when financier Jay Cooke decided to make Duluth terminus of the Superior-Miss. RR. But after Cooke's failure in 1873, the city was again reduced to a village & for 10 yrs. not a new bldg. was erected on the shore of the L. Lumbering, wheat & development of RRs., elevators, docks & sawmills finally put the city back on its feet & gave it another boom.

Most important to Duluth are its harbor & docks. The Duluth-Superior Harbor ranks 2nd to N.Y. in yearly tonnage. There are 46 wharves handling freight other than ore, coal & grain, 21 coal docks, 7 iron ore docks, & 23 grain elevators. During World War II the Duluth-Superior shipyards landed 355 vessels incl. every type of craft. More than 60% of the ore produced in U.S. & 25% of world production derives from N. Minn. & is shipped through its port. The labor pop., of Scandinavian & Canadian descent, is very efficient. Duluth is a popular summer resort because of its invigorating climate, scenic beauty & unsurpassed fishing & hunting. It is hqs. for U.S. Forest Service, administering area of 3,727,540 as. There are sightseeing boat trips on L. Superior & St. Louis R. & through the harbor. Deep sea fishing boats & scheduled Gt. Ls. cruises are operated by the Georgian Bay & Northern Navigation lines.

PTS. OF INT.: (1) At foot of Lake Ave., **Aerial Lift Bridge,** connecting mainland with Minn. Pt. (1930). It is an elec. operated elevator bridge with an overall span of 510′. Huge freighters & passenger boats can pass through. Its lift is one of world's fastest. (2) 1st St. bet. 4th & 6th Aves., **Civic Center,** consisting of Cth., City Hall & Federal Bldg. (completed 1930.neo-class.). (3) 5th Ave.W & 1st St., **Soldiers & Sailors Mon.** (Cass Gilbert). (4) 7th Ave.W. & Superior St., **Incline Railway** (1891) making a 3,000′ ascent; excellent view from summit. (5) 932 E. 3rd St., **St. Paul's Evang. & Reformed Ch.** (belfry O.wks.exc.Sat.10-12.1872). Contains 900-℔. bell cast from cannon used in Franco-Prussian War & presented to the Ch. by Kaiser Wilhelm I of Germany. (6) 6 S. 12th Ave. E., **Little Theater,** est. 1914. one of 1st in U.S. (7) 1330 London Rd., **Duluth Curling & Skating Club Bldg.** (O.fee) among the best-equipped curling clubs in U.S. with the greatest number of indoor rinks. (8) 6008 London Rd., **U. S. Fish Hatchery,** (O.8-5) largest in State. (9) 3rd St. & 33rd Ave., **Iron Ore Docks** (O.appl.). (10) 1434 88th Ave. W., **American Steel & Wire**

**Co.** plant (O.appl.). (11) 1218 104th Ave.W., **St. George Serbian Orthodox Ch.** (1923.Byzantine). Liturgy in old Slavonic. (12) In **Spirit L.** is Spirit I. Here battle bet. Chippewa & Sioux is supposed to have been fought before arrival of white men. (13) Wrenshal St. in Chambers Grove., at St. Louis R., reproduction of a typical **Astor Trading Post** (O). (14) **Duluth Harbor.**

SIDE TRIPS: (A) On Minn. Point, reached by means of **Aerial Lift Bridge** (S) on Lake Ave., are following: (1) 10th & Minn. Ave., **Duluth Boat Club,** once private club (early 18th cent.Ital.Rococo), now pub. clubh. & dock. (2) 1225 Lake Ave. S., **U.S. Coast Guard Sta. & Watch Tower** (O). (3) 12th & Minn. Ave., **U.S. Naval Base** (training ship O.while in harbor). (4) 43rd St. & Minn. Ave., **Summer Playground** (200 as.swim.beach). (5) On tip of Minn. Pt., **First Lighth.** at head of the Ls. Only ruins remain, but site is still used as "Zero" for marine surveys.

(B) Skyline Pkwy. begins at NE. sec. of town in Amity Pk. & passes Chester Pk. At 7th Ave. W., **U.S. Weather Bureau Sta.** (O.exc.Sat.& Sun). 910 W. 3rd St., **Darling Observatory** (O.appl.), 13th-24th Sts., **Enger Pk.,** incl. Enger Peak with 40' octagonal tower (O). 65th & 68th Sts., **Oneota Cemetery.** Here are buried the Merritt Bros., known as the "Seven Iron Men" and discoverers of the Mesabi iron range, Geo. R. Stuntz, explorer, surveyor & discoverer of the Vermillion range, & many other pioneers of the Arrow Head country. Cont. on Skyline Pkwy. beyond J. with US61. At c.2m beyond this J. is **Snively Pk.** (R). At 3.5m **Bardon's Peak.** 4m **Magney Pk.,** uncommonly beautiful balsam & pines, although linden & maple predominate. In Spring, the blood-root is especially fine, & in fall maples color magnificently. At 6m **Ely's Peak,** one of highest pts. in reg. At 7.5m **Mission Cr. Pkwy.** branches off (L). At 8.5m **Jay Cooke St. Pk.** (8,176 as.pic.camp.f.). At 9.5m **Lookout Point,** 500' above river (excellent view.Tourist Camp site near). At 14.5m **Thomson,** & (L) **Thomson Dam.** At 16m **Carlton** & J. with US61 (see).

US2 leaves Duluth in a northwesterly direction & travels for **14.** to J. with St.94. At **22.** it enters **FOND DU LAC IND. RESERV.,** home of 1,417 Chippewa (see US61); at **28.** it crosses **ST. LOUIS R.** At **76.** Miss. R. passes near hy. **GRAND RAPIDS** is reached at **81.** surrounded by 4 Ls. & more than 100 resorts. Here is J. with US169 & St.38.

SIDE TRIP: On St.38 (R) 40m to Big Fork. At 6m (SE) is **Scenic St. Pk.** (2,121 as.) most primitive of all Minn. St. Pks. Large stands of Norway pine on Chase Pt. (camp.facils.).

At **86. COHASSET. DEER RIVER** at **99.** At **101.** is J. with St.46.

SIDE TRIP: On this Rd. (R) 16.5m to **Cut Foot Sioux L.** & **Turtle & Snake Ind. Mound.** Name of lake derives from the wounded Sioux warrior who was found by squaws of the victorious Chippewa the morning after a big battle.

US2 now enters **CHIPPEWA NAT. FOR.** (1,312,824 as.). For. is divided into 7 districts. There are 600 miles of forest trls. & 23 camps. Its stands of Norway & White Pine are magnificent. In spring, blossoming plum & cherry trees, as well as trailing arbutus make a trip through it unforgettable. More than 5,500 as. are reforested each yr.; fish & wild life are protected. Its thousands of Ls. vary in size from a few acres to 20m in length. Larger Ls. incl. Leech, Winnebigoshish, Cass, & Bowstring. Resettlement of land-owning farmers from isolated spots & from places where soil has been proved unfit for agric. to fertile land in a forest-farm community benefits both farmer & county. At **113. BENA,** touching L. Winnebigoshish (Ind., miserable, wretched, dirty water). A few miles (S) is **Leech L.,** site of last Ind. uprising in Minn. A **Federal Dam** is built here designed to control the flow of water on the lower Miss. At Bena, a Pow-Wow is held each July. **121. SCHLEY,** named for Rear Adm. Winfield Scott Schley of Sp-American War fame. At **132.** (L) **PUB. CAMP** (free). **CASS LAKE 136.** (sea-plane base). Here J. with US371 leading (R) 15m to **Leech L.;** 20m to **Walker** (see US71). **155. BEMIDJI,** J. with US71 (see). In 1895 tamaracks still grew in the streets but within 20 yrs. the surrounding fors. were almost denuded. There were more than a dozen sawmills in the neighborhood that among them cut a million feet daily.

## Sec. 2: BEMIDJI to N.D. LINE. 113.

At **7.** J. with St.89.

SIDE TRIP: On this Rd. (N) 27m to Agency of **Red L. Ind. Reserv.** Upper & Lower Red Ls. on which an Ind. village borders, are very shallow, though 30m in diam. (274,944 as.); largest fresh-water body within a state. At 33m is **Redby.** Here is **Co-op. Fishery** & a community-owned mill run by Chippewa. Gravel Rd. runs along shores of the 2 Ls. to 2 **Ind. Villages** at 25m & 30m from Redby.

**25. BAGLEY** & J. with St.92 leading (S) to **White Earth Ind. Reserv.** (see US10).

**42. FOSSTON.** Tourist Pk. at SE. end of town. Hy. passes along edge of **Fish & Game Refuge** & reaches **ERSKINE 60.**, at S. end of L. Badger, important shipping point for vic. At **74.** J. with St.32 running (R) to **Red L. Falls,** 9$^{m}$. Pop. is predominantly French, descendants of early trappers. US2 now runs along beach of ancient L. Agassiz. Colorful underbrush all the way. **86. CROOKSTON,** sett. 1872, is thriving trade center for the valley. **Northwest School & Experiment Sta.** is here; also **Mt. St. Benedict** (Cath.) school for girls. **88.** J. with US75 (see). **97. FISHER,** formerly called Fisher's Landing, at headwaters of Red R. After RR. was rebuilt through Warren to Winnepeg, village declined. In surrounding country are large sugar-beet fields of the American Crystal Sugar Co. These fields are worked by seasonal Mex. workers & their families, imported from Mexico to do the tedious weeding, for low wages. At **112. EAST GRAND FORKS,** once a trading post, now mainly center for the sugar-beet factory operating only in fall of yr. At **113.**, US2 crosses Red R. into **S.D.**

## US 10—MINNESOTA

**MINN.-WIS. LINE** (19$^{m}$ from Ellsworth, Wis.) **(NW) to N.D. LINE** (at Fargo, N.D.) **276. US10**

Via: St. Paul, St. Cloud, Little Falls, Staples, Detroit Ls., Moorhead. Served by Milwaukee RR., Chi., Burlington & Quincy RR., Gt.N. RR. & N.P. RR. Good Rd. Accoms.: All types.

US10 runs NW. from St. Paul through dairy & agric. reg. & through the Lake & Northwoods Country. From here it traverses Red R. Valley & potato & wheat fields to cross the Red R., W. boundary of Minn.

**0.** Hy. crosses **ST. CROIX R.** (toll bridge) at Prescott, Wis. At J. of Miss. & St. Croix Rs. is **POINT DOUGLAS.** At **3.** is J. with US61 which unites with US10, & enters **ST. PAUL** (see) at **20.** which is also at J. with US12. Hy. at **33.5.** reaches J. with US8 in a reg. of burning peat bogs. At **45. ANOKA.** One block (N) from Champlin-Anoka Bridge, **Woodbury H.** (1854.N.Eng. & Gr.Rev.). All early governors entertained in this house & during Sioux uprising (1862) more than 20 people took refuge here. A stone near mouth of Rum R. bears inscription of Fr. Louis Hennepin (1680), believed to have been carved by the missionary himself. Rum R. is one of Minn.'s most famous streams. From Anoka to East St. Cloud US52 joins with US10. At **50. DAYTON STATION,** Ind. trading post (1852). Crow R. flows into the Miss. near here. At c.**54. OLIVER KELLEY H.** (1896), home of founder & first Secy. of the Grange of Patrons of Husbandry. It is known as the Shrine of the Grangers, through whose annual picnics on the grounds the memory of Kelley is kept alive. **57. ELK RIVER,** named for herds of elk found here by Zebulon Pike. **67. BIG LAKE & 82. CLEAR LAKE,** towns that grew up with the coming of the RR. **94. EAST ST. CLOUD** in reg. of famous granite quarries. US10 parallels E. bank of Miss. R. At E. St. Germain Street US52 branches (L) crossing river to St. Cloud proper.

**95. ST. CLOUD,** a clean, thriving, industrial community which spreads out along W. side of Miss. R. Quarries lie beyond city's limits. Flanking the wide city streets are homes of Col. architecture, a style brought in by its early settlers. In the 1840's it was a fur trading post. Its fortunate geographical position on the Miss. kept it the leading outfitting post for the trade. It remained that until the RRs. took the steamboats' place, 1874. Then came the era of stone quarries. From a very small beginning in 1868, St. Cloud became one of leading building-stone & monument-producing centers of country. The stone of the reg. is fine-grained & ranges in color from black through red & pink to white. It is especially suitable for pub. bldgs., churches, bridges & memorials. Many structures in Washington, Philadelphia, Chicago & Detroit are built of it. PTS. OF INT.: (1) In Riverside Pk. is **Pine Log Cabin,** built 1855, used as a home, hotel, fort & jail. (2) Along the river, **St. Cloud St. Teachers' College,** founded 1869, 3rd largest Teachers' College in state. (3) 9th Ave.S. & 1st St., **St. Mary's Church** (Cath.Romanes.). Parish founded by Benedictines in 1856. Shortly after, they began a seminary, orphanage & a hospital. Latter is conducted by Benedictine Sisters. (4) St. Germain Street & Cooper Ave., a **Monument Factory** (O.appl.). (5) 4th Ave. & 3rd St.S., **St. Cloud Ch.** (Presb.), founded 1856. (6) NE. part of city, **Wilson Pk.** (33 as. tourist camp).

SIDE TRIP: On US52 (NW) is **St. Benedict's Convent & College for Girls.** Here also are hospital, 2 Ind. Schools & home for aged; latter has a very fine Ital. marble chapel (Ren.). At 11m just off hy. (L) is **St. John's Univ.** with exceptionally fine bldgs. College is especially known for its courses in architecture & Beuronese Art (founded in the Abbey School of Art, Beuron, Germany).

Main route cont. (N) on US10. At **97. SAUK RAPIDS,** once terminal of rail & ox-cart traffic, now a flour-milling town. Foundation of an **Old Sawmill** is all that remains of the early boom days. **103. SARTELL.** On banks of river is a paper mill manufacturing high-grade paper & operated by hydro-electricity. **129. LITTLE FALLS.** The rapids for which town is named were called "Painted Rocks" by early Fr. traders. In 1805, Zebulon Pike explored reg. Dam is built where river descends 11′ in ¼m. During flood of 1853 river carried steamboat "North Star" over the falls. On W. bank of river is **Lindbergh St. Pk.** (100 as.) surrounding home of Chas. A. Lindbergh (rest.1935). Lindbergh lived here until he was graduated from high school. His father, Chas. A. Lindbergh Sr., practiced law here & served as Progressive Republican in U.S. House of Rep. (1907-1917). He was known for his consistent denunciation of war propaganda & profiteering. A city-owned tourist camp is at N. city entrance on US371. At **140. RANDALL.** Here is J. with St.115.

SIDE TRIP: On this Rd. (R) 10m to **Camp Ripley Junction.** (W) of village is **Site of Ft. Ripley,** est.1849 as buffer against Inds. Used as shelter for 1862 uprising. Site is incl. in **Camp Ripley,** now Nat. Guard Camp (20,000 as.concerts.parade & guard mount). The Reserv. has 100 bldgs. (most Rds.O.exc.during maneuvers).

**145. CUSHING,** named for Caleb Cushing, Congressman & diplomat. **151. LINCOLN.** There are 4 Ls. (R) with numerous islands & wooded shores. Fish & waterfowl abound. At **160.** is J. with US210 which leads (R) 22m to **Brainerd** (see US61).

**178. VERNDALE. 185. WADENA.** These two towns fought bitterly over right to be cty. seat, as did so many other pioneer towns. They even hired "residents" until after the election. At **190.5.** US10 crosses Leaf R. **198. NEW YORK MILLS,** Finnish community retaining many of the old customs such as the use of the "sauna" (bathh.). To create steam water is thrown on heated rocks. Bathers loll in the steamy room & later beat their bodies with twigs to induce perspiration. Then they dash themselves with cold water & enjoy the invigorating effect. At **209. PERHAM,** entrance to vacation playground area. Otter Tail Cty. contains 1,000 of Minn.'s 10,000 Ls. Here is J. with St.78.

SIDE TRIP: On St.78 (L) 9m is **Otter Tail L.** (11m long) one of large Ls. of the reg. Along its shore, Red R. carts creaked on the Pembina-St. Paul cart route.

**221. FRAZEE,** summer resort (h.f.). **231. DETROIT LAKES,** capital of Minn.'s Park Region. Within a radius of 25m are 412 Ls. Town has summer & winter carnivals incl. logrolling & fly casting, as well as wood-chopping & sawing contests, & a dog derby. Here is J. with US59.

SIDE TRIPS: (A) On US59 (N) 21m to **Ogema** & J. with Side Rd. leading (R) 6m to **White Earth Ind. Reserv. Hqs.** (1,200 sq. miles). More than 9,300 Chippewa live on this reserv., once a magnificent pine forest, now largely cut-over land. Inds. sold many of their holdings because they needed money. Ind. Agency is now buying back some land there-by adding fertile ground to help Inds. make a living. This rehabilitation began 10 yrs. ago. Near-by, **St. Benedict's Mission** (Cath.) est. by Bishop Ireland (1868) is one of finest in Ind. Service. In adj. cemetery, Chief White Cloud is buried. The handiwork of the Chippewa is excellent, especially their buckskin products & birchbark canoes. Inds. hold an annual festival (O) in the village, comm. arrival of 1st group. Int. because at these pow-wows a sham battle, in formal costumes, bet. Chippewa & Sioux is staged.

(B) From Detroit Lakes (S), US59 passes a group of 28 **Ind. Mounds.** Near 21.5m was found, 1932, a pre-historic skeleton, estimated by anthropologists to be more than 20,000 yrs. old. Although known as "The Minn. Man," it is, in reality, the skeleton of a young Ind. girl of about 16 yrs. It was found during hy. construction, 20′ deep, in an ancient lake bed.

**238. AUDUBON,** named for the great ornithologist; at **244. LAKE PARK** & J. here with Cty. Rd.

SIDE TRIP: On Cty. Rd. (L) to **Big Cormorant L.** 10.5m. Here are 3 large **Anchor Stones,** each with a hole 9′ deep & 1′ wide. It is believed that they were used by Norse explorers, c.1362, to tie up their skiffs. These & the Kensington Runestone (see US71 Alexandria) are attributed to the same early Norsemen.

At **261.** just (S) off US10 is **Buffalo R. St. Pk.** (242 as.swim.pic.). River bottom is covered with elm, basswood, oak & poplar. Here was pre-historic Campbell Beach of L. Agassiz. **266. GLYNDON.** US10 here crosses S. branch of Buffalo R. At **275.** is **MOORHEAD,** on Red R., distributing center for rich agric. Red R. Valley. It has a million dollar creamery & many large wholesale grocer & fruit houses. Moorhead is seat of **Concordia College** (Luth.) & **State Teachers' College.** Here is J. with US52 & US75. At **276.,** US210 crosses Red R. into **Fargo, N.D.**

## US 12—MINNESOTA

**MINN.-WIS. LINE** (at Hudson, Wis.) **(W) to WIS.-S.D. LINE. 196. US12**

Via: St. Paul-Minneapolis, Delano, Litchfield, Wilmar, Benson, Ortonville.

US12 in Minn. passes from the St. Croix R. through the Twin Cities & a picturesque lake & farming country to S.D. Line at Big Stone Lake. For Twin City area see St. Paul-Minneapolis. For Wilmar area see US71. For Ortonville area see US75.

## US 14—MINNESOTA

**MINN.-WIS. LINE** (at La Crosse, Wis.) **(W) to S.D. LINE** (3m from Elkton, S.D.) **289. US14**

Via: La Crescent, Winona, Rochester, Owatonna, Mankato, New Ulm, Tracy, L. Benton. Chi. & N. Eastern RR. parallels route. Accoms.: In cities & tourist camps en route.

US14 crosses the state (E-W), beginning at Miss. R., & passes through beautiful lakeland reg. to the fertile farm areas of SW. Minn.

Bridge from La Crosse, Wis. crosses Miss. R. to **La CRESCENT 2.** (see US61). A species of apple imported from Russia thrives in orchards here. Reg. grows 50 different kinds of apples & 30 of plums. In La Crescent is J. with US16. Traveling (N) along river, US14 & US61 unite to **WINONA** at **26.** (see US61), home of **St. Teachers College, St. Mary's & St. Theresa** (Cath.) **Colleges.** It is hqs. for Upper Miss. Wildlife & Fish Refuge, incl. an area of 99,972 as. along Miss. R. Above Winona is **U.S. Dam & Lock #5A.** On US61 (E) is **Liers' Trained Otter Farm** (O.fee.) US14 now passes through a soil-erosion-control reg. to **STOCKTON** at **35.** At **42.,** just off hy., is **LEWISTON,** first stage-coach stop on Winona-Rochester Line. Ramer Tavern is relic of those days. At **51.5.** J. with St.74.

SIDE TRIP: On this Rd. (R) 6m to **Whitewater St. Pk.** (688 as.swim.f.camp.golf). Unusual escarpments of limestone, & dense growths of mature timber, red cedar & white pine.

**52. MUNICIPAL CAMP GROUND** (pic.facils.). Annually on County Day, youngsters trap as many gophers as they can & bring in the tails for prizes. At **75. ROCHESTER** (see St. Paul-Minneapolis). **90. Kasson.** Here is J. with St.57.

SIDE TRIP: On this Rd. (R) 3m to **Mantorville.** Most old bldgs. here, incl. the **Ch., Cth., Brewery,** & **Hubble H.,** were built in 1850's & are still standing. Frank B. Kellogg & Rear Adm. F. E. Beatty spent boyhood here.

**96. DODGE CENTER** & at **104. CLAREMONT.** US14 (W) of here runs in a straight line through dairy country to **OWATONNA, 115.** a health resort (mineral spring). Chief Wadena is said to have moved his entire village here so that his sickly daughter might drink the mineral spring waters, rich in iron & sulphur (Tourist Camp). County has 16 creamery co-ops. Carnegie Foundation & the Univ. of Minn. chose Owatonna as the typical American town. On Main St. is **National Farmers' Bank Bldg.** (1908.by Louis Sullivan), described by W.W.Norton & Museum of Modern Art as a bldg. of exceptional beauty principally because of its color scheme, both exter. & inter. Here is J. with US65. On S. Grove St., **Pillsbury Military Academy** (see US14).

SIDE TRIP: On this Rd. (N) 15m **Faribault,** where Alex. Faribault in 1826 had a trading post 25 yrs. before settlers arrived. **Faribault H.** was first frame bldg. in town; it cost $4,000 & still stands. Near it stood, until recent yrs., Episc. Bishop Whipple's home. It was Bishop Whipple who defended the Inds. & pleaded for clemency at the time of the mass execution in 1862 (see US71). His policy toward the Inds. later became that of **U.S. Gov.,** namely to consider them as wards of the Gov. Much acreage around Faribault is incl. in Fed. soil-conservation project.

**130. WASECA,** important wheat-shipping point. The Anti-Horse Thief Detective Society organized here in 1864, was abandoned only a few yrs. ago. **Tourist Camp** on W. shore of Clear L., also **Boy Scout Camp** (O). **156. MANKATO** (Sioux for Blue Earth). Here 400 Inds. of the Sioux Uprising in 1862, were tried & 300 were held at Mankato, to await Lincoln's verdict. He commuted sentences of all but 38. On Dec. 26, all 38 were hanged simultaneously. It was the largest legal mass execution in U.S. Mankato now is leading industrial & agric. center in SW. Minn. & parts of Iowa & S.D. It has a large hog market & produces brick, cement, flour & foods. On S. 5th St., **Mankato St. Teachers College,** founded 1868. **Bethany Luth. College** is in (S) part of town. Mankato is at J. of US169. At **182.** hy. passes **Old Redstone,** a 2 sq.-mile hill of pink quartzite & at **185.** is **NEW ULM,** sett. 1854, by Germans from Würtemburg, who named the new home after cathedral city Ulm. New Ulm in 1862 was site of an important Sioux uprising. By using zigzag & unfamiliar tactics they so surprised our soldiers that many lives were lost. The city was evacuated & refugees fled to Mankato. Town is known for its interest in music which was kept alive by German Turnvereine. At 25 N. Broadway, **New Ulm Lib. & Hist. Mus.** Along a hillside path to Loretto Hospital on N. 5th St. a **Way of the Cross** is kept up by the large Cath. pop. Here is J. with St.15 leading (L) to **Flandreau St. Pk.** 2$^{m}$ (837 as.swim.pic.facils.boat.) in the Valley of the Cottonwood R. **199. SLEEPY EYE,** named for friendly Ind. Chief. Near-by is **Sleepy Eye L. St. Pk.** (40 as. wayside pk.). Here is J. with St.4.

SIDE TRIP: From here (N) 10$^{m}$ to **Ft. Ridgely St. Pk.** (225 as.camp.pic.golf). Around this fort occurred some of the fiercest Sioux battles in 1862. Our soldiers held the fort against wild attacks, protecting 300 non-combatants & the settlements along the line.

**221. SPRINGFIELD.** Sauerkraut festival held each Sept. (eating contest & dancing). Here is J. with US71 (see), at **228. LAMBERTON** with **Kuhar Pk.** (23 as.pic.bath. beach & baseball). **245. TRACY.** At **252. BALATON,** named for a L. in Hungary (Tourist Camp). Here is J. with US59 leading (S) 4$^{m}$ to **L. Shetek** & other Ls. At **256.** J. with St.91 which leads 8$^{m}$ (R) to **Camden St. Pk.** (470 as.camp.hiking.swim). **266. TYLER,** founded 1870, by followers of Nikolai Frederik Severin Grundtvig, Danish theologian & poet, whose principal wish was to make an education available to the masses. **Danebod Folk School** (1888) is a typical folk high school founded by the Grundtvigeans. Tyler has co-op. creamery, buttery & stock produce plant. At **279. L. BENTON** on one of glacial Ls. now almost completely dry. Town & L. were named for Thos. Benton (see US75). Here is J. with US75. At **289.** US14 crosses **S.D. LINE.**

## US 16—MINNESOTA

**MINN.-WIS. LINE** (at La Crosse, Wis.) **(W) to S.D. LINE** (15$^{m}$ from Sioux Falls, S.D.). **286. US16**

Via: Preston, Austin, Albert Lea, Blue Earth, Fairmont, Worthington, Luverne. Served by Milwaukee RR. & Chi., St. P., Minneapolis & Omaha RR. Usual accoms.

US16, southernmost through-hy. in Minn. crosses **MISS. R.** at La Crosse, Wis. over a free bridge. Water lillies & water-hyacinths separate the islands in the river. Hy. cont. past many small waterways & a few Ls. through a rolling prairie & farm country.

**2. La CRESCENT** (see US61). **3. J.** with St.26.

SIDE TRIP: On this Rd. 7$^{m}$ (L) **Brownsville** on Miss. R., known as **Old Steamboat Landing** (1840). Trappers used to mount a stuffed wildcat on a pole to identify their landing.

**6. HOKAH,** dairying village, once site of 20 flour mills.

SIDE TRIP: From Hokah (L) on St.44 to **Caledonia,** 13$^{m}$, a Mormon Colony led by one of the Youngs who camped here for a while. Here the dandelion was introduced from Eng. by Jacob Webster, who hungered for greens. Minnesotans still blame him for the abundance of the beautiful weed flower on their lawns.

Hy. crosses through stoneless territory in which wild flowers thrive. Masses of them cover the countryside. At **21. HOUSTON,** once a steamboat landing of Root R., still has most of its early houses, many with ivy planted 60 yrs. ago. At **30.** Rd. travels into a valley, & at **32.** is **RUSHFORD,** where Root R. & Rush Cr. meet. Bluff which the hy. passes at **47.5.** is **BUFFALO BILL'S PEAK.** Near it one of Bill's Wild West Shows rehearsed. At **49.** in a charming valley is **LANESBORO.** Here the Norwegian naturalist, Hvoslef, carried on his ornithological work. At **51. PIC. GROUNDS.** Here Dawson Bros., inventors of special flour rollers, had a foundry. **55. PRESTON. Old Minn. Hotel** & **Tibbets H.** from stagecoach days are still standing, & the old **Courth.** (1863) is still in use. Here J. with US52 leading (N)

35$^m$ to **Rochester** (see St.P. & Mnpls. Trip IV.). **74. SPRING VALLEY.** J. with US63 leading (S) 13$^m$ to Iowa Line. Large Fed. Soil Conserv. Project in the reg. (Guides avail. at Project Office.) At **105. AUSTIN,** home of Hormel Packing & Food Products plant. The "Milwaukee Road's" roundhouse & shops are also here. Beginning at head of Main St. is **Horace Austin St. Pk.** (50 as.boat.bath.). Before 1841, U.S. soldiers had camped here, incl. a Ft. Snelling officer & Dred Scott, then a slave. American Fur Co. had a hunting shack here. One winter, their party shot 2,000 deer, 50 bear & some buffalo. Here is J. with US218. **119. HAYWARD,** with large co-op creamery, branch of the Land O'Lakes chain. At **125. ALBERT LEA,** named for Col. A. Lea, who surveyed reg. 1835. Today it is an industrial center with 4 RRs. Its dairy & oil co-ops do a million dollar business. Horse racing was & still is popular sport of the town. Its Main St. was once part of its race course. Sheriff Heath was once (c.1859) teased into running Old Tom, his shay horse for 13 yrs., against fleetest gelding of the surrounding country. Finally he did. To everyone's surprise, Old Tom won & for many yrs. was victor over such favorites as Crazy Frank, Sleepy Kate & even Itasca Fly ("fastest horse in the NW"). On **Albert Lea L.** is a State Game Refuge. At **137. ALDEN,** est.1869. Had one of earliest Grange organizations in the state (1873). **163. BLUE EARTH,** so named for the blue-green clay found on rocks of the river gorge by Inds. The municipally-owned light company uses a good part of its profit for lighting the streets with gay colored bulbs, making int. designs. One of largest pea- & corn-packing plants in U.S. is here; also an ice-cream factory & creamery co-op. Migratory Mexican workers help to weed, hoe & top sugar beets of the surrounding farms because wages are too low for local labor. At Blue Earth is J. with US169 leading (N) 37$^m$ to **Mankato** (see US14). **181. FAIRMONT,** 4th of a chain of 18 lakes (launch trip through 4 Ls.). **Cth.,** built (1862) on site of Sioux uprising, houses coll. of pioneer relics. In the 1870's, a 4-yr. locust plague almost ruined the community. A newly arrived colony of Eng. farmers, most of whom were Oxford & Cambridge grads., through their persistent efforts saved the community from complete devastation. Later this group, known as the Fairmont Sportsmen, introduced fox hunting into Minn. (S) of business sec. is **Tourist Camp** (free camping). **190. WELCOME, & 196. SHERBURN.** At **207.** J. with US71. Then US16 & US71 travel as one Rd. for 2$^m$. Here **US16 turns** (R) to **JACKSON** at **209.** where Ind. uprisings twice occurred. Town produces tow rope in great quantity from the flax of vic. **Tourist Camp** (cabins.mod.rates). At **240. WORTHINGTON,** with one of largest co-op. creameries in reg. Town has had highly rated polo players. In **City Pk.** is **Tourist Camp** (facils.). Bath.beaches on **L. Okabena.** At Worthington is J. with US59. At **271.** hy. crosses **ROCK R.** to enter **Luverne,** visited by Nicollet in 1839. Hostile Inds. & the 4-yr. grasshopper plague kept settlers away for 30 yrs. Now it has thriving creamery, grain, & livestock co-ops. At E. end of town, **Tourist Camp** (facils.). Also J. with US75 (see). At **286.** US16 crosses into **S.D.**

# US 61—MINNESOTA

**MINN.-WIS. LINE** (at La Crescent, Minn.) **(N) to CANADIAN BORDER** (42$^m$ from Ft. Williams, Ont.). **453. US61**

Via: Winona, Red Wing, St. Paul, Pine City, Duluth. Good Rds. Accoms.: N. of Duluth only in summer.

### Sec. 1: LA CRESCENT to ST. PAUL. 142.

US61 passes from La Crosse, Wis. over Miss. R. to La Crescent & follows it into St. Paul. From there hy. traverses flat farmlands, & cuts through evergreen fors. (N) to Duluth. Here beautiful L. Superior Dr. begins, running past rocky pts. & wooded shores of L. Superior to the Internat. Border.

At **0.** is **LA CRESCENT,** a town showing little of its early boom days. Rivalry with Wisconsin's **La Crosse,** on the other side of Miss. R., influenced settlers to name it La Crescent, after the Mohammedan emblem. The vic. lends itself to apple growing (see US14). From here US61 together with US14 head N. At **23.** (L) is **LIERS' TRAINED OTTER FARM** (O.fee). At **29. WINONA,** once a treeless prairie, now a beautifully landscaped city, on bluffs of the Miss. from which a panorama of

**Hiawatha Valley** can be seen for $15^m$ bet. L. Winona & the Miss. R. Winona, unlike other areas in this vic., was not affected by the Great Glacier. It was founded 1851 by Capt. Orren Smith of the steamboat "Nominee" at the same time that Chief Wabasha's Inds. were urged to withdraw to an island beneath the bluffs. The next yr. after ratification of the treaty, the Inds. gave up all claim to the reg. By 1855 the village boomed; by '56 it had 82 industries. Lumbering, saw mills, wheat growing, flour milling, followed each other in quick succession. Steamboats & the newly introduced RRs. helped to transport flour & lumber. Later the limestone of the vic. became recognized by country's leading architects. Brickmaking vied with the stone quarrying & as each declined, agric. products filled in. Winona is still the 2nd largest hay & clover seed market in the country. The city claims to be the wealthiest of its size in the U.S. It publishes newspapers, & magazines in Eng., German & Polish, evidence of its mixed pop. It is well known for its scenic beauty (Anthony Trollope described it in glowing colors) & for its educational institutions.

PTS. OF INT.: (1) J. of US61 & St.43 near center of city, **Sugar Loaf,** a limestone monolith rising 500′. Can be reached only by foot trl. (2) **Bay State Milling Plant** (O.appl.). (3) **J. R. Watkins Medical Plant** (O.appl.with a 10-story tower) is the home of the famous liniment "good for man & beast." (4) Johnson & Sanborn Sts., **State Teachers College,** founded the same yr. Minn. became a state, 1858. Its **Paul Watkins Art Coll.** (O.during school hrs.) contains 4,000 paintings, etchings, engravings & sculpture. (5) Wabasha & Gould Sts., **College of St. Theresa,** began in 1893 as Winona Seminary, conducted by Sisters of St. Francis. It is now an accredited college & also gives B.S. degree in nursing. (6) 102 E. Third St., **Merchants' Bank,** good example of Sullivan & Wright's "prairie style" (1910). (7) Rd. from Lake Blvd. to **Garvin Heights St. Pk.** (17 as.pic.facils.) good view of city & Miss. Valley. At Winona is J. with US14 (see).

At **34. MINNESOTA CITY,** a small village, where Rollingstone Colony was supposed to have been. It was a tragic tale in Minn. history. N.Y.C. group in 1852 had planned, on paper, a Utopian communal town & enticed city dwellers to share in this "well functioning community" which did not exist. Before the news of the disappointment reached N.Y. again, more than 400 persons had landed somewhere in the uncharted wilderness & because they were unequipped in talent or means for pioneer life they perished or eked out a sad existence. Some survivors sett. in Winona; others finally returned to the East. At **35.** J. with side Rd. leading (L) $3^m$ to **Rollingstone,** near which are 50 Ind. Mounds, many 100′ long. German colonists who came here 85 yrs. ago still cling to their native language & customs. At **43. JOHN LATSCH ST. PK.** (350 as.) on limestone bluffs, 450′ above Miss. R. **Whitman Dam & Locks** are near pk. A broad, panoramic view from one of the bluffs is reached by foot trl. Here Jonathan Carver came ashore in 1766, 1st white man to find the strange Ind. turf houses. **62. WABASHA,** in heart of Hiawatha Valley, nestles among bluffs. It was named after 3 successive Sioux Chiefs, who actively defended their "bountiful valley" against encroachment. The **Winneshiek Bottoms,** sloughs & bayous, extending hundreds of miles (S), begin at Wabasha. A toll bridge across Miss. R. into Wis. is E. of town. **63. READ'S LANDING,** important during Rev. when the father of Augustin Rocque was sent here to persuade Sioux from aiding Amers. In 1840 it became a trading post & in the 50's it had 17 hotels to accommodate Miss. R. travelers. At one time it also was one of the greatest wheat-shipping towns of the country.

**76. LAKE CITY,** on shore of beautiful L. Pepin, where it is particularly treacherous. Here the "Seawing" was wrecked in 1890 with a loss of 98 lives. Lake City was at one time a well known clamming port. **83. FRONTENAC** (L), named for Fr. Col. Gov. of Canada. Near-by (R) is **St. Hubert's Lodge,** built by Gen. Israel Garrard in pre-Civil War style, who lived on his large estate to hunt, fish & entertain like a feudal lord, but also produced food for hungry Sioux. Christopher La Farge & Geo. Heins, architects of St. John the Divine, N.Y.C., visited here in 1883-84 & later chose the limestone found in vic. for the cathedral. Other famous visitors were John La Farge, Joseph Jefferson, & Henry Ward Beecher. **Villa Maria,** Cath. School, was est. 1856 by Ursuline nuns from St. Louis on part of the Garrard estate. On L. Pepin's shore is **Frontenac Inn** (c.1871). **88. WACOUTA STA.** Here Miss. &

Chippewa Rs. rush together to form L. Pepin. Lac Qui Parle & L. St. Croix are the only other of Minn.'s 10,000 Ls. created in this way. **93. RED WING.** (For sec. bet. Red Wing & St. Paul at **142.** see St. Paul-Minneapolis Trip III.)

## Sec. 2: ST. PAUL to DULUTH. 157.

US61 follows Arcade Ave. (N) out of St. Paul (see) past **GOOSE & WHITE BEAR Ls.** at **11.5. BALD EAGLE** at **14.5.** At **24.** is J. with US8 (direct Rd. to Minneapolis). **25.5. FOREST LAKE,** popular summer resort, on L. of same name. From here to **WYOMING** at **27.5.** US61 & US8 are one route. Hy. passes through tamarack, birch & oak fors. to **NORTH BRANCH** at **42.** Here is J. with St.95.

SIDE TRIP: On this Rd. (E) 20m to **Taylors Falls** on Miss. R., area of special interest to geologists. **Dalles H.** (early 1850's), from which Stephen A. Douglas made one of his famous speeches against Lincoln, is in downtown sec. 54m **Rush City**. Here wooded secs. change to fenced fields. Hy. passes over undulating hills of sandy clay.

At **64. PINE CITY.** At **73.** J. with St.23.

SIDE TRIP: On this Rd. (L) 6m to **Brook Pk.** with mon. to those who lost their lives in forest fire of 1894.

**76.HINCKLEY,** center of terrible for. fire of 1894 in which 400 lives were lost. Jim Root, hero of this disaster, was engineer of N.P. RR. He backed his train through the flames over the burning creek all the way to Duluth, thereby saving 350 passengers. His hands were burned fast to the throttle when he reached Duluth. J. here with St.48.

SIDE TRIP: On this Rd. (R) **Mon. to the Fire Victims.** At 20m **St. Croix Recr. Area** (21,000 as.) under Fed. Gov. Rd. leads (S) to **Pub. Camp & Girls' Camp.** A leisurely downstream 30m canoe trip can be started here down St. Croix R. Canoeist can cont. 40m farther to **Taylor Falls.**

**86. SANDSTONE.** Orig. settlement, est. 1885 to quarry sandstone, was completely destroyed by 1894 fire. At **91.** is J. with St.23.

SIDE TRIP: On this Rd. (R) to **Askov** 3m, founded by Danish People's Soc., 1887, a working co-op. community with a folk-school. Known as the rutabago center of U.S. Town has never had or needed a jail.

**109. MOOSE L.** Was an overnight stagecoach stop in 1860. **115. BARNUM,** important egg-raising center of Minn. **134. CARLTON,** lying in an ancient glacial R. bed, surrounded by rich farms. **Jay Cook Tourist Camp,** near Otter & Crystal Crs. Here is J. with **Skyline Pkwy.** from Duluth (see). Also J. with US210.

SIDE TRIP: On this Rd. (W) 22m **Cromwell,** at SW. end of **Fond du Lac St. For.** (see below). **Tamarack** at 34m. Short distance (N) is entrance to **Savanna St. For.** which includes **L. Winnewawa** (Tourist Camp.free). At 47m **McGregor.** J. here with St.65 which passes (N) through Savanna St. For. 61m **Hassman.** The hy. turns (SW) to **Aitkin** at 69m, center of turkey-raising reg. Every fall Turkey Growers' Assoc. makes a tour to various farms feasting on turkey dinners & listening to speeches, often by Univ. of Minn. specialists. They also celebrate, June 24, Swedish Midsummer Festival, a day of food & fun. Hy. now passes through verdant fields of wildflowers, edible berries & mushrooms. Forty-six varieties of mushrooms have been found here. Rd. also touches the **Cuyuna Iron Range,** most recently developed range in Minn. Ore found here contains manganese, important steel-making ingredient. US210 reaches **Crosby** at 84m. Besides mining, the pulpwood industry is important. Town, like many others with wealthy mines & industries, has excellent schools. Good fishing is to be had in the 365 Ls. of the vic., especially in **Crow Wing St. For.** (NW).

(1) From Crosby (N) on country Rd. to one of the world's few **Sintering Plants** at 1.5m owned by **Evergreen Mine Co.** (O.guides).

(2) On St.6 (R) from Crosby to **Milford Mine** 6m. In 1924 this mine was flooded & 42 men lost their lives. Harley Harris, hero of this disaster, sounded warning siren before the water burst into the mine, then tied the rope around his body so that the weight would keep the siren shrieking. He died in this effort, & for yrs. miners believed they could still hear the siren & see Harris with the rope tied around him.

87m **Ironton,** also touches the Cuyuna Iron Range. On improved Rd. (R) 4m is **Riverton** with ore-drying plant of **Pick & Mather Co.** (O.), one of largest in country, drying more than 80 tons an hr. 95.7m **Brainerd,** Paul Bunyan's Capital. Annually, one wk. in July, Bunyan holds sway & fun & frolic take hold of everyone. Men of vic. wear beards to add realism to the occasion. Log-rolling, wood-chopping, & canoe tilting contests are famous. As many as 80,000 visitors have been attracted. Carnival in Feb. Town was platted, 1871, when N.P. RR. reached Duluth. Largest shops of this RR. are still here at cor. A & 3rd Aves. NE. Brainerd was named for the beautiful wife of a N.P. Pres., Ann Elizabeth Brainerd Smith. She received commission of Lt. Col. during the Civil War for her "gallant hospital service." At present it is a thriving city with especially fine grade & high schools. The Normal Dept. of **Franklin School** pioneered in pre-parental education. At 326 Laurel St., **Crow Wing Cty. Hist. Soc. Mus.,** in Cth., is considered one of most complete in Minn.; coll. Ind. relics & logging tools.

**134.5. CARLTON** & J. with Skyline Pkwy. (see Duluth). First spike of N.P. RR. was driven here. **138. SCANLON,** old lumber town. J. with St.45.

SIDE TRIP: On this Rd. (N) to **Cloquet** 2m, a modern city built on ruins of one which was completely destroyed by for. fire, 1918. Five large fires merged & c.8,000 sq. miles were involved, mainly around Duluth. More than 400 lives were lost, but only 5 in Cloquet, due to quick action of town officials. When city was rebuilt it concentrated on manufacturing of wood products. Arch St. & A Ave., **Wood Conversion Co.** East End Arch St., **Northwest Paper Co.** Cloquet has a very large co-op. retail association. At 1.5m (W) from Cloquet is **Fond du Lac Ind. Reserv.** (25,000 as.; 725 pop.) & Ind. hospital.

US61 crosses St. Louis R. **141. ESKO,** small Finnish community with co-op. creamery. Old Finnish customs are still observed, especially the taking of "sauna" or steam baths. **157. DULUTH** (see US2).

## Sec. 3: DULUTH to PIGEON R., ONT. 154.

At Duluth are Js. with US2 (see) & US53.

SIDE TRIP: US53 travels (NW) for c.20m then turns directly (N) & at 61m reaches **Eveleth,** range town whose importance dates from discovery of iron. Bet. 1900 & 1910 pop. increased from 2,700 to 7,036. Valuable ore was being turned up all through the city & early pioneers had difficulty in finding an ore-free spot for a cemetery. Open-pit mining is favored process & visitors can see enormous cavities from which millions of tons of iron ore have already been taken. Town & vic. have excellent schools, as do most range towns of Minn. Eveleth is known as "hockey capital of the nation" & has produced Ching John, Frank Brimsek, & Mike Karakas. At 70m is J. with St.169 which penetrates (S) part of **Superior Nat. For.,** incl. now 3,728,932 as. & more than 5,001 Ls. ranging in size from a few as. to 70 sq. miles. Its varied flora is fine at every season, but especially in fall when the gold & scarlet foliage of the hardwoods vies with the dark of the evergreens. Fish & wildlife abound. It is the natural habitat of the moose. For. contains hist. **Ind. Villages** & many **Painted Rocks,** most of whose scripts are still not deciphered. Matchless water hys. make this excellent canoeing country (facils.pic.& housekeeping accoms.). More than 170 resorts in vic. Pts. of scenic int. & special attractions incl.: **Cross R., Temperance R., Poplar R., & Cascade R. Falls,** all on N. shore of L. Superior; **Carlton Peak,** near Tofte, Minn., **Devils Cascade** (N) of Ely-Buyck Rd. **Rebecca, Curtain, Lower Basswood, & Upper Basswood Falls,** all on Internat. Boundary. US53 travels (N) past large **Pelican L., Cusson, Ray, Ericksburg** to **Internat. Falls** on the Canadian border at 158m (see US71).

From Duluth US61 begins famous scenic drive (N) along wooded shores of L. Superior to Port Arthur in Canada. At **11.** is **FRENCH R.** Rd. in this vic. in June is lined with arbutus, sarsaparilla & dogwood. **18. KNIFE R. 28. TWO HARBORS,** called by the Chippewa "Place-to-spear-by-moonlight." It is ore-shipping terminal of the Duluth, Iron Range RR., which later combined with the Duluth, Mesabi & Northern RR. City has 3 co-ops., a U.S. Coast Guard Serv., & excellent education facils. School busses sometimes bring in pupils from 35m away. **41. CASTLE DANGER** named for the wrecked boat "Castle." At **42.5.** hy. enters **GOOSEBERRY FALLS ST. PK.** (637 as.good f.camp.& pic.facils.;hay fever refuge). Shore is here covered with igneous volcanic rock. **Gooseberry R.** with 2 waterfalls, 300′ high, flows through pk. to L. Superior. At **46. SPLIT ROCK ST. WAYSIDE PK.** (35 as.pic. facils.). At **49. SPLIT ROCK LIGHTH.** (L) perched high on cliff. **54. BEAVER BAY,** only lake settlement bet. Duluth & Grand Portage that survived the 1857 panic. At **61.** J. with dirt Rd. leading (R) to **Palisade Head** (pic.80 as.) headland of volcanic rock. Beautiful view of **Apostle Is.** & the Wis. shore. **70. LITTLE MARAIS,** site of old Crystal Bay corundum mine, now resort village. From here for 10m hy. follows birch & aspen lined roads. At **73.** hy. crosses **CARIBOU R.,** famous trout stream. **90. LUTSEN,** small resort. **106.** Cascade R., within **CASCADE ST. PK.** (2,300 as.camp.). **114. GRAND MARAIS,** picturesque village on a natural harbor; center of tourist traffic. Amer. Fur Co. had fishing post here 1834, but abandoned it in 1842. In 1856 post office was opened but had to close 2 yrs. later. Finally in 1879 a lasting community was begun. Lumbering & fishing are still main industries. **Coast Guard Sta.** & **Forestry Office** are here. Grand Marais is E. gateway to **Superior Nat. For.** (see above). The well-known **Gunflint Trl.** begins here & leads through heart of the Nat. For. to famous chain of Ls. Excellent canoe trips from here on. Canoeists can begin at L. Superior & paddle to W. border of state. Moose, bear, deer, porcupine & other wild animals are found in great numbers. Camp. grounds & pic. spots are maintained by U.S. For. Serv. **134. HOVLAND** (resort;2 lakes,good trout f.). **138. RESERVATION R.,** northernmost of a series of trout streams. Hy. swings inward to **MINERAL CENTER** at **147.**

SIDE TRIP: From Mineral Center (R) 5m on country Rd. to **Grand Portage** in Grand Portage **Ind. Reserv.,** central depot of the Northwest Co. By 1792 it was the thriving "metropolis" of L. Superior, with shops, Fr. fashions, drinking places & police. The swaggering voyageurs lived in log bldgs. & Inds., with whom they traded, in wigwams. Canoe yard itself accommodated 150 canoes. Dashing Frenchmen in their gaudy red & blue capes & sashes, & Inds. in native attire, must have presented a gay assembly. Grand Portage now has only a few cabins, one of which has a **Hist. Mus.**

**154. INTERNAT. BORDER.** U.S. & Canadian customs officers have quarters on opp. sides of Pigeon R., which marks the border. A bridge spans the canyon. The whole reg. is one of striking beauty. Hy. crosses the **PIGEON R.** into Canada.

## US 71—MINNESOTA

**MINN.-IOWA LINE** (20m from Milford, Iowa) **(N) to CANADIAN BORDER** (at Fort Francis, Ont.). **432. US71**

Via: Jackson, Windom, Redwood Falls, Willmar, Sauk Center, Wadena, Bemidji.

US71 crosses W. Central portion of the state (S-N) passing through agric. & dairying fields of the SW. & Paul Bunyan lake reg. of the NW.

**8. JACKSON,** twice scene of Ind. uprisings in 1862. One yr. before, the 1st tow mill was opened here. (Tourist Camp.facils.) From Jackson hy. crosses over a high plateau covered with glacial drift that has made soil drought resistant & hence very fertile. At **31.WINDOM.** At **32.** is J. with St.60.

SIDE TRIPS: (A) On this Rd. 13m (SW) is **Heron Lake** on L. Heron, settled mainly by Germans, Irish & a mixture of Slavs & Scandinavians.
(B) On St.60 (NE) 10m to **Mountain,** a Mennonite Colony, that migrated here from Russia via Germany. Town has five churches, a hospital, & a home for aged. Many old customs still exist. Borscht & porzelchen are still served at New Year's.

**58. SANBORN,** on banks of Cottonwood R. (Tourist Camp). Here J. with US14. At **87. REDWOOD FALLS,** noted for granite found in its vic. At NW. end of town is beginning of **Alex. Ramsey St. Pk.** (185 as.pic.facils.playfields.foot trls.), named for first territorial Gov. of Minn. Redwood R. lies 140′ below. Near here J. with dirt Rd.

SIDE TRIP: On this Rd. (R) 0.5m to **Ind. Agency** (1,000 as.). Some Mdewakanton Sioux live here. Beyond 3m are remains of **Lower Agency,** famous for Ind. uprising of 1862, when within a few wks. more than 500 whites were killed. Inds., not completely understanding that they had signed over their land by treaty, continued to roam around where the white man had begun to settle. They were driven away & resented treatment. Added to this, their food supply was very low because of a bad harvest & fact that Gov. rations had been delayed by Civil War. A few "blanket" Inds. had been apprehended stealing & before argument was settled, 3 whites were killed. Fearing retaliation, the rest of the Inds., under Chief Little Crow, set out on the warpath & massacred all who got in their way. Settlers fled to Mankato for protection. Finally a punitive force under Gen. Sibley subdued them. Over 500 captured Inds. were tried; 300 found guilty & condemned to death. Lincoln pardoned all except those guilty of murder & rape, which left 38. These were hanged on Dec. 26, in the greatest legal mass execution of our Gov. Bishop Whipple, who pleaded for leniency in behalf of the Inds., was rebuked by Gov. officials & he, as well as Lincoln, suffered greatly in prestige as a result of his charitable intervention (see US14).

US71 turns (E) crossing **MINNESOTA R.** & at **93.** turns (N) again. Near-by (R) is **Birch Coulee St. Mem. Pk.** (82 as.pic.trls.), site of hardest-fought battle of the 1862 uprising. At **109.** is **OLIVIA** (Tourist Pk.camp.) & at **135. WILLMAR,** sett. 1869 & named for London RR. agent. It is center of farming & dairying reg. Here is J. with US12.

SIDE TRIPS: (A) US12 leads (W) directly into **Benson** at 32m. For several yrs. this was W. terminus of Hill's Gt.N. RR. Here (c.1838) party of Sioux women & children on hunting expedition with missionary, Gideon Pond from Lac Qui Parle, were attacked & scalped by Chippewa. Battle of Rum R. a few yrs. later was fought to avenge this deed. (Tourist Camp.) At 75$^{m}$, **Ortonville** at S.D. border, on shore of **Big Stone L.,** sett. 1872, as Sioux trading post (see US75).

(B) On US12 (E) hy. reaches **Litchfield** 25$^{m}$, from which practically every Rd. leads to a L.

At **149.** is **GREEN LAKE** (popular summer resort). Even early explorers accustomed to beautiful scenery were struck by its exceptionally vivid green setting & lingered on for some time. **151. NEW LONDON,** built around **Old Mill** which was begun before the 1862 uprising & was finished 1865. J. with St.23.

SIDE TRIP: On this Rd. (L) 5$^{m}$ **Sibley St. Pk.** (379 as.boat.f.swim.pic.camp.). Here are foot trils. up **Mt. Tom,** used by Inds. as a signal sta. Pk. is part of **Mongolia Game Refuge** & has 3 Ls.

**181. SAUK CENTER** at S. tip of Big Sauk L. (tourist camp.pic.golf.). Sinclair Lewis spent his boyhood here & used locale for many of his stories. J. with US52.

SIDE TRIP: On US52 (NE) **Osakis,** 13$^{m}$, popular fishing resort & site of fierce Ind. battles. 25$^{m}$ **Alexandria.** The much discussed Kensington Runestone, found 1898 on Olaf Ohman's Farm near-by, is supposed to have been placed there by visiting Goths (Swedes) & is dated 1362. Its authenticity was much disputed & is still under discussion. If it is a fake, the faker had a remarkable knowledge of runic writings. The stone has now been removed to Smithsonian Institution, Washington, D.C., for study & exhibit. Alexandria has many rather large lakes in its immediate vic. From Alexandria (S) on St.29 to **Glenwood,** 17$^{m}$ on beautiful L. Minnewaska. Here many **Ind. Mounds & Burial Grounds** of Chief White Bear & Princess Minnewaska.

**199. LONG PRAIRIE,** was a Gov. Agency, 1848, in charge of a tribe of Winnebagos put there to act as buffer bet. Chippewa & Sioux. (Tourist Pk.pic.cabins.) **207. BROWERVILLE. St. Joseph's Ch.** (Cath.early Romanes.) in center of town has 2 very fine pieces of sculpture by local artist, Jos. Kieselewski, who later received the Prix de Rome. **238. WADENA.** J. with US10 (see). **252. SEBEKA. 264. PARK RAPIDS,** founded 1880. In vic. are 300 Ls. reached by good Rds. J. with St.34.

SIDE TRIPS: (A) On this Rd. (L) 43$^{m}$ to **Detroit Lakes** (see US10).

(B) On St.34 (R) 28$^{m}$ to **Walker** on US371 & an inlet of **L. Leech** (1,298′). On shores of this large, beautifully wooded, inland L. the last Ind. battle in Minn. took place in 1898. Maj. Wilkinson & 6 privates were killed. Inds. were subdued but no lives were lost. From Park Rapids, hy. passes in vic. of a number of excellent fishing Ls.

**286.** J. with St.92. Here is **Itasca St. Pk.** (31,976 as.f.boat.pic.camp.swim.lodge.cabins. mus.zoo.lookout towers). In L. Itasca (1,475′), incl. in the area, is the source of Miss. R., objective of Henry Schoolcraft, 1832. It is 2,552$^{m}$ by stream from Gulf of Mexico. Univ. of Minn. operates a forestry school & biological sta. for summer students here. US71 turns (R) for 14$^{m}$ to J. with St.85 at **300. Leech L.** is on this Rd. 15$^{m}$ (R) (see above). At **318. BEMIDJI,** on L. Bemidji, named for Chippewa Ind. Chief, buried in Greenwood Cemetery near-by. At W. edge is **Chippewa Nat. For.** (see US2). It is the Paul Bunyan Playground, famous for more than 100 summer resorts. Equally famous for winter sports. In town is a giant statue of Paul Bunyan & his blue ox, Babe. A canoe Derby is held each July starting in L. Bemidji. From Bemidji (NE) 6$^{m}$ is **L. Bemidji St. Pk.** (205 as.pic.camp.shelters), within a splendid stand of Norway pine. **338. HINES.** Luth. Augustana Synod est. a colony here. There are 14 good fishing Ls. in vic. **343. BLACKDUCK,** home of thriving creamery co-op. Here J. with St.72.

SIDE TRIP: On this Rd. (N) past **Upper Red L.** (see US2) 76$^{m}$ to **Spooner,** at the Canadian border, town almost completely destroyed in 1910 by the flaring up of an old peat fire. More than 30 lives were lost.

**391. BIG FALLS** at J. of Big Fork R. (good f.& deer h.). **413. LITTLEFORK,** sett. 1905, surrounded by thousands of acres planted in clover for seed, a reliable yearly crop. At **421. PELLAND.** Here is J. with St.11 which runs (W) along the **CANADIAN BORDER** to **Baudette** & joins with US71 (E) for 11$^{m}$ to **INTERNAT. FALLS** at **432.** on S. shore of Rainy R. which forms the boundary bet. U.S. & Canada from Lake of the Woods to Rainy L., known as the "Queen of Lakes." Latter is 50$^{m}$ long & from 3$^{m}$ to 15$^{m}$ wide, containing 14,000 Is. (excellent f. at Black Bay). Internat. Falls is hqs. of the Border Patrol. The green, gray & blue uniforms of the various branches of the Patrol present a pleasant picture.

# US 75—MINNESOTA

**MINN.-IOWA LINE** (18$^{m}$ from Luverne, Iowa) **(N) to CANADIAN BORDER** (28$^{m}$ from Morris, Man.). **428. US75**

Via: Luverne, Pipestone, Ortonville, Breckenridge, Moorhead, Crookston, Noyes. Chi., Rock I. & P. RR. bet. Iowa Line & Pipestone; Milwaukee RR. bet. Ortonville & Moorhead; Gt.N. RR. bet. Breckenridge & Canadian Line. Good Rd. (bituminous or graveled). Accoms.: In larger towns.

Hy. runs through prosperous farming country in S., passes quarries dating back to Inds., & midway passes Ls. Traverse & Big Stone. In N. it runs through fertile Red R. Valley, bordering Detroit Lakes vacation area.

## Sec. 1: IOWA LINE to ORTONVILLE. 139.

**11. LUVERNE,** creamery & livestock center with a thriving grain co-op. For 30 yrs., after it was explored by the scientist J. N. Nicollet, reg. was ravaged by Inds. When settlers returned again a 4-yr. locust plague invaded vic. At E. end of town is tourist pk. with camp accoms. At **17.** J. with side Rd. leading (R) 1$^{m}$ to **Mound Springs St. Pk.** (195 as.pic.) with unusual geological rock formations of Sioux quartzite. At **36. PIPESTONE** on W. side of Coteau des Prairies. Many pub. bldgs. are of red quartzite mined in near-by hills. At **37.5.** J. with side Rd.

SIDE TRIP: On this Rd. (L) to **Pipestone Ind. Training Sch.** & **Pipestone Nat. Mon.** (116 as.). Part of the area has outcrop of quartzite ledges. **Winnewissa Falls** is formed where a stream crosses outcrops. Several quarry pits are open to secure the red pipestone or catlinite, as it was called, after Geo. Catlin, famous painter of N. Amer. Inds., who sent in 1st sample to Washington & who published first account of it. Phil. Prescott was here in 1831 but never published his findings. There are many Ind. legends as to orig. of this stone. One of most common is that red pipestone was formed by blood of warring tribes. The Great Spirit stopped the strife & ordered Inds. to regard area as a neutral ground & to use the red stone only as a symbol of peace. Hence the smoking of the peace pipe made from the stone. Longfellow in "Song of Hiawatha" immortalized the lore of these quarries. Trl. connects legendary & hist. points of int. incl. **Leaping Rock, Ind. Head Rock,** & the **Three Maidens.**

**56. LAKE BENTON,** on S. shore of a glacial L. now almost completely dry, named for Thos. H. Benton, son-in-law of John C. Frémont, who came here 1838, with Jos. Nicollet. Here is J. with US14. **71. IVANHOE,** highest land in SW. Minn. It was named for Walter Scott's hero; its streets bear names of leading characters in the novel. Here is J. with St.19, which leads (R) to **Marshall** at 24$^{m}$ on branch of Redwood R. in rich farming area. **90. CANBY** (Ind. "roots of yellow moonseed"), has well-run livestock co-ops., wool-shipping & creamery assocs. Tourist Pk., (N) of town (free camp.). At **106.** J. with US212.

SIDE TRIPS: (A) On this Rd. (W) 13$^{m}$ is S.D. Line.
(B) On US212 (E) 23$^{m}$ is **Camp Release,** St. Mem. Wayside (18 as.;granite mon.51′), 1st unit in St. Pk. System, comm. release of 269 prisoners to Gen. Sibley in 1862. Remnants of Sibley's entrenchment visible. Here also is site of Sioux village of Red Iron, friendly chief during the outbreak. Ind. breadroot, a plant with blue spikes & edible tubers used by early frontiersmen, still grows in reg. At 24$^{m}$ is **Montevideo,** named for capital of Uruguay. Here is J. wtih US59. In **Smith Pk.,** at W. edge of town, Tourist Camp (free facils.). Land is so level here that snow-sailing, similar to ice-sailing, used to be a favorite sport. Sometimes 100 miles a day could be covered. Sail-sleighing, as it is also called, is still enjoyed, but now only on shorter trips. US212 turns (SE) to **Granite Falls** at 33$^{m}$ on a granite bluff; the stones belong to oldest era of geological hist. Town was home of Andrew J. Volstead, author of "Volstead Act" for Federal prohibition.

At **111. MADISON,** founded by Jacob F. Jacobson, who led Iowa settlers here. Town has a thriving creamery co-op., a livestock-shipping assoc., several grain elevators, & greenhouse & nursery with **Log Hut** (O), a reprod. of owner's boyhood Norway home. At **139.** traveling NE. is **ORTONVILLE,** at S.D. Line. The town in 1873 a trading post for the Inds. is known for its granite-quarrying & canning industry. **Big Stone Canning Co.** has one of largest corn canneries in the country. It is originator of whole kernel canning. Every Aug. a Sweet Corn Festival is held, at which 20,000 persons eat a free corn dinner.

## Sec. 2: ORTONVILLE to MOORHEAD. 116.

At **19. TOQUA LS. ST. PK.** (40 as.camp.). **19.5. GRACEVILLE,** prosperous farming & dairying reg. Here is J. with St.28.

SIDE TRIPS: (A) On this Rd. (L) 22m to **Sam Brown St. Mon.** on E. shore of L. Traverse, named for head of Ind. scout patrol who, during a Sioux uprising, rode 120m one night warning settlers. Here bet. L. Traverse & Big Stone L. is **Brown's Valley,** where Brown's Valley Man was unearthed. His age was estimated at 12,000 yrs.; his jaw exceeds in width even the Heidelberg man. Buried with him were artifacts which belonged to an early Ind. race that made flint tools.
(B) On this Rd. (R) 26m to **Morris,** home of **W. Central Agric. College,** formerly Cath. Ind. Mission School, now under Fed. Gov. Near here is **Pomme de Terre Reserve** (363.5 as. recr.pic.facils.).

**36. WHEATON,** well-known for water fowl & pheasant hunting. City tourist camp (free). J. with St.27.

SIDE TRIP: On this Rd. (R) 17m to **Herman,** model Minn. town. Near it is margin of prehist. glacial L. Agassiz. In 1926 a mastodon tooth 10½" long was found in a pit near-by.

At **70. BRECKENRIDGE,** trade & shipping center of reg. Here is J. with St.3.

SIDE TRIP: On this Rd. (R) 26m to **Fergus Falls** on Otter Tail R., named for James Fergus, the Scot, who financed the Whitford exploratory & settling expedition 1857. Town is on W. side of large, hist. L. reg. Its first Postmaster was a German who couldn't read Eng. When mail arrived he emptied sack on cabin floor & allowed villagers to pick their own letters. June 1919 tornado almost destroyed the town. It now has 17 factories, 2 mills & a power company that furnishes 175 cities with electric power. Fergus Falls has largest co-op. creamery in NW. with 37 additional co-op. creameries in vic. It is one of largest poultry shipping pts. in the NW. Its **City Hall & Cth.** is a reprod. of Independence Hall, Philadelphia. **Otter Tail Hist. Soc. Mus.** in basement (O) contains pioneer utensils. At **L. Alice** summer & winter carnivals are held. At 44m is **Battle L.,** scene of fierce battle bet. Chippewa & Sioux.

US75 now follows N.D. Line N. for 46m to **MOORHEAD** at **116.** Here is J. with US10 (see) which leads to Detroit Lakes Reg. (see).

## Sec. 3: MOORHEAD to CANADIAN BORDER. 173.

**15. GEORGETOWN,** where 1st steamboat on Red R. was launched, & **HENDRUM** at **29.** Bet. these towns hy. still follows Pembina Trl. where less than 100 yrs. ago vast bison herds were hunted by Inds. Beyond town 1.5m, US75 turns sharply (E) to **ADA** at **43.,** dairy-products & potato-shipping center in large prairie reg. In Ada is J. with St.31 which leads (E) 28m to **White Earth Ind. Reserv.** (9,377 pop.). US75 turns (N) from Ada & cont. in straight line to Crookston at **79.** Here is J. with US2 (see). **110. WARREN,** surrounded by land that is so flat that from hy. one can see alfalfa fields for miles & miles, a view broken only by telephone posts & isolated silos. With the exception of Snake R. there are no Ls. or streams in vic. Rain water to feed stock is collected in large pits dug by the farmers. At Warren is J. with St.1.

SIDE TRIP: On this Rd. (R) 29m to **Thief River Falls,** formerly a camp of the Dakotas who were conquered by Chippewa. Name originally meant Secret Earth, then became Stealing Earth, then Thief Lake & finally Thief R. Old **Ind. Village Ruins** are near J. of Thief R. & Red L. In vic. large-scale land resettlements have successfully taken place.

At **138.** is **DONALDSON,** where the 65,000-a. "bonanza" farm of the Donaldson Ryan interests is located. Here is J. with St.11.

SIDE TRIP: Take latter (NE) 82m to **Warroad,** only port on **Lake of the Woods** (Perry Steamers, summer only; dogsled & plane in winter) to **Oak I., American Pt.** & the **Northwest Angle,** northernmost piece of land in U.S. entirely separated from mainland & favorite vacation resort (excellent h.salmon,trout & muskellunge f.). Lake of the Woods is 90m long & dotted with piney wooded islands.

**153. HALLOCK,** named for C. W. Hallock, sportsman & founder of "Forest & Stream" magazine. Hy. through this area follows Pembina Trl. Some scholars believe that trl. was used by the Norse-Gothic party, which as early as 1362 was supposed to have penetrated this territory (see Kensington Runestone). Along this trl. also traveled wooden ox-carts of Norman Kittson, who carried on successful business of transporting furs for Amer. Fur. Co. Rd. bet. here & **HUMBOLDT** at **166.** becomes more undulating. Humboldt is a J. J. Hill town, named by him for German naturalist, Baron Alex. Humboldt, as tribute to Germans who had invested heavily in his RR. bonds. Ground in vic. is very fertile & 45 bu. of wheat or 500 bu. of potatoes can be raised on 1 acre. Here is J. with terminus of US59. **173. NOYES** on the **CANADIAN BORDER.** Here is **U.S. Customs & Immigration Office.** Amer. & Canadian uniformed officials, of which there are a great number, bustling about transacting their boundary jobs, present a real contrast to the quiet of the northwoods country just traversed.

# ST. PAUL—MINNEAPOLIS

## ST. PAUL

RRs.: Union Sta., 4th & Sibley Sts. for 6 major RRs.—Northwestern, Northern Pacific, Gt. Northern, Burlington, Milwaukee, & Rock Island & Pacific. Holman Airport, 2m from loop, for Northwest & Mid Continent Airlines. Through bus conns.

St. Paul, on a great bend of the Miss. R., was settled by pioneers who lived in near-by Ft. Snelling & on the Winnebago Ind. Reserv. lying SW. Along the river's winding shore & high bluffs runs River Blvd. extending from Pelham Blvd. to the military fort. Elms & maples line most of the streets, many of which still zig-zag through the hilly town. Some downtown streets have been widened but only reluctantly because St. Paulites like their irregular & winding hys. They remind them of the paths that once lead from the river front to the hills beyond & give the city the appearance of being much older than its twin. The compactness of the business area, through 2m of which runs landscaped esplanade of Kellogg Blvd. overlooking Miss. R., makes St. Paul more like an eastern city than one of the Middle West. When St. Paul was only a fur-trading post, it had far more business dealing with N.Y. & the eastern sea-board than did Minneapolis, which at that time was primarily concerned with lumbering & agric. Railroading & banking were St. Paul's chief interest.

Father Galtier brought religion into the wilderness & gave the city its name by building a log chapel called St. Paul, 1841. In 1843 the settlement had 12 people. Six yrs. later when it became the capital of the new territory it had 642. Ideally situated at the head waters of the Miss., St. Paul received a flood of immigrants with each landing of a side-wheeler. The city itself was incorporated Mar. 4, 1854. Jas. J. Hill, RR. magnate of Canadian birth, arrived in 1856 & adopted St. Paul as "his city." His dream of making it the capital of the vast Northwest Empire almost became a reality. In 1873 he, with 2 partners, obtained control of St. Paul & Pacific RR. & from then dates his phenomenal RR. transportation saga. Archbishop Ireland shared with Hill the faith in the young Northwest & worked tirelessly to establish the Irish immigrants he had brought into the country. Through his ardent efforts one of the great Cath. dioceses in the U.S. was built up, incl. the erection of the magnificent Cathedral of St. Paul. The city is still predominantly Cath. & services are held in English & in at least 6 other foreign languages. There are about 50 other denominational churches in town. St. Paul has 7 accredited colleges & a univ. & is known as an educational center (see Minneapolis). The Univ. of Minn. School of Agric. is located here & comprises 465 as. & 72 bldgs., offering a full 4-yr. course in agric. economics & forestry.

Together with its twin, St. Paul is a great cultural metropolis. To the German element, which makes up the greater part of the city's pop., is due a fondness for music, evidenced by the enthusiastic support of the Minneapolis Symphony Orchestra & the Civic Opera Assoc., along with many choral societies & glee clubs. The Germans too are responsible for the rapid & highly scientific expansion of the medical profession; many of the early emigrants were skilled physicians. The numerous & good breweries are also a credit to the Germans. The Irish contributed greatly to the political development of the city & the Scandinavians, who came much later, added stability & hard work toward the building of the metropolis. St. Paul is a city of diversified industries & is recognized as a leader in transportation, wholesales & distribution. It is one of the largest rail centers in U.S. South St. Paul is 3rd among country's livestock centers & 1st as a commercial dairy cattle market. St. Paul is the gateway to an unequalled vacationland. Within a 50-mile radius are 583 Ls.; L. Como & L. Phalen are in the heart of the city. At the Winter Carnival (Feb. lasting 10 days), King Boreas & his Queen of the Snows reign in a series of torchlight parades & sports festivities, incl. Nat. ski-jumping, ice shows & ice-fishing contests in which more than 2,000 sportsmen compete, until Vulcan routs the forces of winter, the last evening.

PTS. OF INT.: (1) 15 W. Kellogg Blvd., **City Hall & County Cth.** (1932.excellent example of Mod.architecture by Ellerbe, St. Paul, & Holabird & Root, Chicago), has 19 stories & cost $4,000,000. Carvings around entrance are by Lee Lawrie, pupil of Saint-Gaudens; sculptoring on elevator doors by Albert Stewart; paneling of the various mun. & cty. offices is done in 28 different kinds of Amer. & imported woods; 4th St. Lobby is especially striking with its marble floor & blue

Belgian marble piers. The concealed lighting begins about 8′ from the floors, gradually growing dimmer toward the ceiling, where mirrors give impression of indeterminate height. In the concourse is white onyx **Peace Mem. Statue** by Swedish artist, Carl Milles. It harmonizes in color & texture with the walls & stands 36′ high representing an Ind. God of Peace with a group of Inds. crouching around his feet. (2) 5 W. Kellogg Blvd., **West Publishing Co. Plant** (O) is world's largest publisher of law books. (3) 145 W. 4th St., **Mun. Auditorium** (1932) one of largest & best equipped bldgs. of its type, seating in main area, 15,000; hockey arena, 8,444. (4) 5 W. 5th St., **Old Customs H.** (1867.mod.Roman.details) most pretentious of city's early bldgs. (5) 700 Wabasha St., **Minn. St. Capitol** (O. frequent tours.1896.by Cass Gilbert.Ital. High Ren.). All decorative elements were coordinated by a Board of Design consisting of famous artists & architects, & the results achieved are a harmony seldom found in public bldgs. Large dome is practically a copy of St. Peter's in Rome; the arcaded loggias & the Corinthian columns blend beautifully into the general design (very int.inter.). **State Office Bldg.,** 425 Park Ave. (O) & **Minn. Hist. Soc. Bldg.,** 651 Cedar St. (O) complete Capitol group. (6) 214 E. 4th St., **Union Depot** (1920.class.façade with Doric columns) with a block-long waiting room. All RRs. entering city use this sta. (7) Rose & Arkwright Sts., **St. Michael's Grotto,** miniature church 18′ x 12′ which Gabriel Pizzuti built in memory of his little daughter. (8) 966 Miss. R. Blvd., **Ford Motor Plant** (O.10-2). (9) Cherokee Blvd., **Cherokee Heights Pk. & Lookout** (nightview magnificent). Here Pierre "Pig's Eye" Parrant, St. Paul's 1st settler, had his cabin & cache of whiskey which he bootlegged to Inds. The caves along river front are of the proper temperature & humidity for the ripening of Roquefort cheese. Experiments with this type of cheese are being conducted by Univ. of Minn. (10) Marshall & Western Aves., **St. Joseph's Academy,** oldest Cath. prep. school for girls; founded 1851. (11) 9th & Franklin Sts., **Ch. of the Assumption** (1871.by Edw.Riedel of Munich), oldest Cath. Ch. in St. Paul & 1st ch. in which the German language was used. (12) Mounds Blvd. bet. Clermont St. & Johnson Pky., **Ind. Mounds Pk.** (77 as.on high bluff), permits a magnificent view of city & valley. Mounds still contain human bones, mainly of Sioux chieftains. (13) Phalen Pky. bet. Maryland St. & N. city limits incl. **L. Phalen** (excellent bath.beach & recr.facils.). (14) E. Como Blvd., **Como Pk.** with L. Como, which in winter becomes one of city's largest outdoor skating rinks. Other attractions incl. band pavilion, rifle range, conservatory & zoo. Near here is statue of St. Francis of Assisi, patron of animals, by Donald Shepard. (15) Snelling Ave. N., bet. Hewitt & Capital Aves., on the Midway, **Hamline Univ.,** named in honor of Bishop Leonidas Hamline (Meth.). This fully accredited college is an outgrowth of the school founded in Red Wing, 1854. (16) Summit Ave. bet. N. Cleveland & N. Cretin Aves., **St. Thomas College** (1885), founded by Archbishop Ireland, then Rev. John. Its secondary dept. is St. Thomas Military Academy. (17) Miss. R. Blvd. bet. Summit & Goodrich Aves., **St. Paul's Seminary** (Cath.), endowed by Jas. J. Hill in 1892, is hqs. for **Cath. Hist. Soc.** (18) Randolph St. bet. S. Cleveland & S. Fairview Aves., **College of St. Catherine** (fully accredited.1858), named for St. Catherine, the philosopher of Alexandria, is city's only women's college & is built within what was formerly Ft. Snelling Reserv. Overlooking landscaped terrace is **Chapel of Our Lady of Victory** (1924.by H.A.Sullwold,early Romanes.). Inter., in polychrome tile, has Byzantine features. (19) Snelling Ave. S. bet. St. Clair St. & Grand Ave., **Mac-Alester College** (Presb.), outgrowth of Rev. Edw. D. Neill's early schools, received its present name in 1874. The old 1850 bell which, when first rung, caused great consternation among Inds., is still hanging in belfry of Ch. (20) Summit Ave. at Lexington, **St. Luke's Ch.** (Romanes.by J.T.Comes.fine proportions); crypt (1919) has Byzantine inter. Baptistry & triptychs are especially noteworthy. (21) Summit Ave. & Avon St., **House of Hope Ch.** (Eng.Goth.by Ralph Adams Cram, & Goodhue & Ferguson, Boston). (22) 240 Summit Ave., **J. J. Hill H.** (1887) has 32 rooms & cost $200,000; occupied today by **Diocesan Teachers College.** (23) Summit Ave. bet. Selby & Dayton Aves., **Cathedral of St. Paul** (Cath.1906-15.by E.L.Masqueray), has a general resemblance to St. Peter's, Rome. Both exter. & inter. are especially fine. (24) NW. part of town, **Farm Campus of Univ. of Minn.,** 3rd largest in U.S. (465 as.;73 bldgs.). (25) L. from campus, **Minn. St. Fair Grounds.** First fair sponsored in 1854 (260 as.). The famous horse, "Dan Patch," made the mile track here in 1.55 (1906), a record that stood for 31 yrs.

(26) Take 7th St. (SW) to **Mendota** on (E) bank of the Miss., known until 1837 as St. Peter's & key point & meeting place of fur trappers & traders. J. B. Faribault moved his family to this site in 1822 when an ice jam threatened his cabin. At confluence of Miss. & Minn. Rs., on Main St., is **Sibley Tea H.** (O.1854.by H.DuPuis, Sibley's Secy.). From the hy. (L) is **Home of H. H. Sibley,** "Father of his State." (O. 1835.rest.1910), first stone house in Minn. Sibley used it as business hqs. of Amer. Fur Co., whose representative he was, & as a social gathering place for such distinguished guests as Frémont, Schoolcraft, Catlin & Nicollet. It has 6 rooms & an outside stairway to office, on 2nd floor, said to have been used by Inds. & trappers so as not to disturb the household. Adj. the Sibley estate is **Faribault H.** (1837.rest. 1935), similar in construction to Sibley H.

(27) At confluence of Minn. & Miss. Rs., just SE. of town & reached by W. 7th St. or Sibley Mem. Hy. is **Ft. Snelling** (O.appl.), earliest military post in NW. Father Hennepin in 1680 & Le Sueur in 1700 visited the site & in 1805 Zebulon Pike acquired the tract for U.S. Gov. In 1822 Col. Josiah Snelling began construction of Ft. St. Anthony, as it was then called. Three yrs. later it was officially named Ft. Snelling to honor his accomplishment. The **Round Tower** was built in 1822. In this tower, Dred Scott, then a servant of the medical Attaché, was married to a girl slave. He was in the service of Dr. Emerson at that time. In 1820 Pres. Monroe appointed Lt. Lawrence Taliaferro, as Ind. Agent for this reg. For 17 yrs. this young Virginian labored with the Inds. hoping to accomplish 2 things: prevention of the recurring conflicts bet. the tribes & his plan to establish the Inds. as self-supporting agriculturists. Traders, fur-company representatives & politicans soon found out that he could not be bribed, something that annoyed them not a little. When he left he wrote, "I have the sad consolation of leaving the public service as poor as when I first entered—the only evidence of my integrity." By 1857 the Ft. fell into disuse & all but 2 tracts of land were sold. During Civil War the Ft. was again used for assembling troops. In 1864 Count Zeppelin, then a young military attaché to U.S., tried out his lighter-than-air experiments here. His idea was laughed at, but he was not easily put off. A military tailor sewed a bag for him into which he put as much illuminating gas as the old St. Paul Gas Co. would let him have &, on a bright night in spring, made a 30 minute flight, 300′ above the tower. For a few yrs. more, Ft. Snelling was used to help protect settlers against Ind. uprisings especially c.1862. Like other frontier forts, its function was not solely military but extended into many phases of pioneer life. It was then a social & cultural center.

## MINNEAPOLIS

RR. Stas.: Gt. Northern Depot, foot of Hennepin & Nicollet Aves., for Burlington, Northwestern, Omaha, Gt. Northern, Northern Pacific, Gt. Western, & Minneapolis & St. Louis; Milwaukee Sta., 3rd Ave. S. & Washington Ave., for Milwaukee RR., Soo Line, & Rock Is.; Minneapolis, Northfield & Southern RR. Sta., 710 3rd Ave. N. also for Anoka Line. Bus Sta.: Union Bus Depot, 29 N. 7th St. for Greyhound, Jefferson Trans. Co., & Twin City Bus Lines; Sioux Ltd. Bus Depot, 706 1st Ave. N., for Sioux Ltd. Lines, Grey Goose, & Gt. Western Stages. Airport: Wold Chamberlain Field for 9 major certified airlines.

Minneapolis, a great metropolis that rose in a phenomenally short time; where wilderness was a century ago the thriving city now stands. Its first log cabin was built in 1847 in what was then St. Anthony Falls. In 1854 the village of Minneapolis was platted & a Post Office est.; 2 yrs. later it became a city. Its big industrial builders, however, arrived only in the '70's & '80's. They were Yankees, who in order to hurry the building process, invited workers from N. Europe to settle here. The town was born beside the river & near the falls which Father Hennepin loved & named St. Anthony & which later, because of its beauty, was the main attraction for settlers. The rivalry bet. Minneapolis & its twin, St. Paul, has been one of the more enduring in Amer. city history. Although coming into existence about the same time as St. Paul, Minneapolis soon outstripped its cultured neighbor in things ordinarily considered progress. Its beginning was rather slow, but it grew up rapidly with the influx of Scandinavians who arrived during 2nd half of 19th cent. After census of 1890, when Minneapolis boasted a far greater pop. than St. Paul, the latter demanded a recount. To the surprise of everyone both cities were found guilty of dishonest enrolment. St.Paul added thousands whose addresses were Union Depot, pool halls, etc., while Minneapolis "in the interest of civic pride" added graveyard residents, copying more than 18,000 names from tombstones. In the Fed. recount, however, Minneapolis won by a safe margin. Articulate Minneapolitans demanded that their city become the state's capital but nothing came of it.

Because of water power developed at St. Anthony's Falls & the rich wheat lands near-by, flour milling was 1st & basic industry of Minneapolis. City became one of largest flour-milling centers in the world & the largest cash grain market in U.S. Today it is also an industrial center & hub of important transportation in the Upper Midwest. It has become the largest distributing center for tractors & agric. implements in country. Its pk. system comprises 22 Ls. which offer fishing, boating, canoeing & sailing in summer & iceboating & skating in winter. Its winter carnival is famous, but outsiders consider the weather too brutal. Duck hunting is the favorite sport of the twins & the favorite topic of conversation at any time. City is home of the Univ. of Minn. which is 2nd largest state univ. in U.S. Univ. takes great pride in its high academic standing. It embraces 22 schools & colleges & the world-famous Mayo Clinic (see Rochester in St. Paul area). Its main campus is located above the Miss. R. near St. Anthony Falls, while farm campus is in St. Paul & Extension Div. in Duluth.

PTS. OF INT.: (1) 1001 Hennepin Ave., **Minneapolis Pub. Lib.** (O.wks.9-9;Sun.2-9), est. 1885. Contains notable coll. of Scandinavian literature. (2) Hennepin Ave. & 16th St., **Basilica of St. Mary** (Cath.1907-26.Ren.by Eugene L.Masqueray). Its broad nave, ending in semi-circular chapels & its imposing dome on 4 great piers give it the architectural characteristics of a basilica. It was designated such in 1926 & affiliated with St. Mary Major & St. John Lateran in Rome. (3) 816 Wayzata Blvd., **Dunwoody Institute,** one of country's largest endowed trade schools. (4) 1710 Lyndale Ave., **Walker Art Galleries** (O.Tues.-Sat.10-5;Sun.12:30-5;alts.1944. asymetric in stone & brick); fine jade & ceramics coll. (5) 15th St. & Hennepin Ave., **St. Marks Ch.** (Episc.1910.by Hewitt & Brown.Goth.int.inter.). Windows over entrances are Ren. style by Chas. Connick. (6) 821 Marquette Ave., **Foshay Tower** (O. daily.fee), built by Wilbur Foshay, public utilities magnate, who was ruined in the 1929 crash. Bldg. has resemblance to Washington Mon. & is 447′ high (32 stories). Contains an orig. Houdon bust of Washington. (7) 6th & Marquette Aves., **Rand Tower** (O.1928-29.by Holabird & Root), 27-story bldg. that was awarded Amer. Inst. of Architects' prize, 1930. (8) 224 S. 5th St., **Northwestern Bell Tel. Bldg.** (1932.by Rhodes Robertson.guides for tours), typical Amer. skyscraper, rises 346′ above pavement. (9) 4th St. bet. 3rd & 4th Aves., **City Hall & Hennepin County Cth.** (Romanes.with 400′ tower). In 4th St. rotunda is colossal statue by L. G. Mead, **Father of Waters,** in Carrara marble. (10) 201 E. 24th St., **Institute of Arts** (O.Tues.-Fri.;Sat.10-12.fee.1912.neo-Class.by McKim,Mead & White). In it are Amer., Fr. & Eng. period rooms & a fine coll. of prints & paintings, some 16th & 17th cent. prints, a Titian & a Rembrandt; also 3 fine Goth. tapestries & some bronzes by Paul Manship, a native of St. Paul. (11) 200 E. 25th St., **Minneapolis School of Fine Arts** (O. 9-11 a.m.Tues.& Thurs.) has classes in painting, inter. decorating & industrial art under well-known teachers. (12) 2600 Park Ave., **Institute of Swedish Arts, Literature & Science** (O.Thurs.2-4), center of Swedish culture with exhibits of glassware, textiles & inventions, incl. orig. drawing of the "Monitor" by the inventor, John Ericsson. (13) Main St. & 9th Ave., N.E., **St. Anthony of Padua,** oldest church in Minneapolis, founded 1849. Present bldg. 1861. When the Irish outnumbered the orig. Fr. founders the Fr. joined with Notre Dame de Lourdes. (14) 1625 5th St. (NE), **St. Mary's Ch.** (Russ.Ortho.), social & religious center for c.2,000 Carpatho-Russians. Of special int. are Christmas & Easter servs. (midnight & sunrise). (15) **Gt. Northern Stone Arch Bridge,** below Third Ave., 2nd bridge to span Miss. R. It is built like a Roman viaduct with 23 arches. (16) 3rd Ave. & Main St. (SE), **Pillsbury "A" Mill** (tours wks.9-12 & 1-3), world's largest flour mill, built 1880. Interesting feature is circular stairway of cast iron. (17) 6th Ave. S. at 1st & Canal Sts., **Washburn Crosby "C" Mill** (O.tours 9-11 & 1-3;Sat.9-11). Its "A" Mill was destroyed by fire, 1878. (18) 4th Ave. S. at 3rd St., **Chamber of Commerce Grain Exchange Gallery** (O.Mon.-Fri.9:30-12), largest wheat, rye, barley & flax market in country & 2nd largest grain exchange. (19) End of Prince St., **Notre Dame de Lourdes Ch.** (Cath.1857.Goth.adds.). Connected with this Fr. parish is convent & the only Fr. school in city. (20) At Minnehaha Ave., **Minnehaha Pk.,** in which is Falls of Minnehaha, made famous through Longfellow's poem, "Song of Hiawatha." A short distance above the falls is bronze group statue of Minnehaha & Hiawatha by Jacob

Fjelde, 1893. (21) At Minnehaha Cr., **Stevens H.** (1849), 1st frame bldg. on (W) side. In it 1st white child, Mary Stevens, was born. Near-by is a bronze of Col. John Stevens by Jacob Fjelde. (22) 3900 W. Riverside Dr., **Michael Dowling School for Crippled Children** (O.appl.), provides corrective training & treatment for handicapped youngster. It is a mem. to Michael Dowling, who in 1881 when 14 yrs. old, while herding sheep in a blizzard, froze his legs, one arm & two fingers, all of which had to be amputated. Despite it, he became school superintendent, editor & banker. (23) 1501 E. River Terrace, **St. Frances Cabrini Ch.** (1948.by Long & Thorshor), excellent example of modern style.

## TRIPS OUT OF ST. PAUL—MINNEAPOLIS

### I. ST. PAUL (NE) to STILLWATER. 19. US212

US212 travels (NE) to **STILLWATER** at **19.**, formerly center of a logging industry. First commercial sawmill was built on St. Croix R. above Stillwater. From here logs were floated to St. Louis. Raft pilots had to be so skilled that those who qualified received salaries from $300 to $500 a month. One of most famous raftsmen was Capt. Stephen Hanks, cousin of Lincoln, who became almost a legendary figure. The revelry & rioting of the lumbermen is recalled every fall when the Lumberjack Festival is held.

### II. ST. PAUL (E) to ST. CROIX (Wis. Line). 11. US12

US12 travels directly (E) to **ST. CROIX R.** at **11.** Here a toll bridge crosses over to Wis. side.

### III. ST. PAUL (SE) to WACOUTA. 47. US61 (Via: Red Wing)

US61 unites with US10 in St. Paul & follows Hastings Ave. to J. with Pt. Douglas Rd. leading (R) to **RED ROCK PK.** at **5.** Here in 1837 was founded an early Meth. mission. In 1905 it became center of a large camp where leading evangelists held forth. These meetings drew as many as 30,000 people on a Sun. The red granite rock for which place was named was venerated by the Inds. who painted designs on it. At **15.5.** US61 crosses Miss. R. & enters **HASTINGS,** named for Gen. H. Hastings Sibley, fur trader, governor & member of Congress, but was 1st known as Oliver's Grove because in 1819 Lt. Wm. G. Oliver & his troops camped here. At Vermillion R. is old **Ramsey Mill,** remains of oldest mill in Minn., built by territorial Gov. Ramsey. On Miss. R. is U.S. **Dam & Lock #2,** one of 26 dams built by U.S. bet. Minneapolis & St. Louis. From business district (S) 1$^{m}$ on US61 is **Mansion of Gen. Wm. G. LeDuc** (O.appl.Vict.Goth.1860) graceful & simple, built in an age when simplicity was not the fashion. It was copied from Downing's book "Architecture for Country Houses," whose designs inspired many Hudson River estates. In Hastings is **Interstate Bridge** (1895), "only spiral bridge in world," built to avoid viaducting town's main street & soon (1949) to be replaced by mod. structure. At Hastings is J. with St.55.

SIDE TRIP: On this Rd. (R) 3$^{m}$ to J. with marked Rd. leading (R) to **Nininger** 5$^{m}$, home of Ignatius Donnelly, reformer & crusader. He was known as the "apostle of protest." His brilliant polemics in favor of the oppressed & his books, incl. "Atlantis" & "The Great Cryptogram" (the latter tried to prove Lord Bacon the author of Shakespeare's plays) were powerful & made Nininger the center of gay parties & lengthy political discussions. Panic of 1857 practically wiped out town & with it Donnelly's holdings. His house still stands but in disrepair. In 1860 he was made Lt. Gov.

At **43. RED WING,** center of clay industry, also has diversified industries, among them marine motors for Gov. (most plants offer tours). In 1680 Father Hennipin found here an Ind. village, named for Chief Red Wing by Fr. explorers. Swiss Protestant missionaries erected a post here as early as 1836 & Luth. congregation was est. in 1855. On Miss. R. is **U.S. Dam & Lock #3.** Majestic bluffs overlooking R. offer magnificent views. Annual ski meet held here is largest in state. Red Wing has country's 2nd municipally owned theater. **47. WACOUTA,** village at head of **L. Pepin** (34$^{m}$ long & formed by Chippewa & Miss. Rs.). Father Hennepin & 2 other Franciscans called it Lac des Pleurs because their captors wept all night, hoping to persuade their chief to allow them to kill at least one of the padres. Present name dates back to Pepin family of Canada, 2 of whose members accompanied Du Lhut to the upper Miss. In vic. formerly stood Sevastopol, a river town, peopled by lumberjacks & raftsmen. When R. channel changed, c.1860, town disappeared completely.

**IV. ST. PAUL (S) to ROCHESTER. 82. US52** (Via: S. St. Paul, Zumbrota, Oronoco)

**4.5.** J. with St.100.

SIDE TRIP: On latter (L) 2.5m is **S. St. Paul,** not a part of St. Paul, 3rd largest stock market in country. Here are: **Union Stockyards** built by A. B. Stickney (1888) covering more than 250 as. with facils. for feeding, vaccinating & caring for livestock; **Armour Packing Co.** (tours Tues. to Sat.), 22 bldgs. & 4m of RR. tracks; **Swift & Co. Plant** (tours Mon. to Fri.; Sat. a.m.).

**38. CANNON FALLS. 59. ZUMBROTA.** 0.5m (N) of center of town is Minn.'s only **Covered Bridge** (1863). **61. PINE I.,** Cheese Center of Minn. **66. ORONOCO.**

**82. ROCHESTER.** (Plane, train & bus conns.)
Rochester is world famous because of the **Mayo Clinic.** From an insignificant little hamlet 80 yrs. ago, it has become one of greatest medical centers of the world. The development of this institution unfolded rapidly from the time of the big cyclone, 1883, which almost wiped out Rochester, after which "Dr. Mayo & his boys," with the aid of the Sisters of St. Francis, who built for them St. Mary's Hospital, began their life work here. In 1915 the Mayos affiliated with the Univ. of Minn. & est. Mayo Foundation for Medical Research. With endowments totaling up to $2,500,000, the foundation provides for graduate medical education & research, & supplies clinic with adequate operators. Due to the genius of the Mayos, who combined professional ability with vision & capacity for organization, this mecca for the world's ill has been created. Sufferers from all walks of life & from every corner of the country & the world can be seen in town & in the clinic. Rochester is, therefore, a most cosmopolitan city. PTS. OF INT.: 102-10 2nd Ave. SW., **Mayo Clinic Bldg.** (O.1914-29 by Ellerbe & Co. of St.Paul.tours). This stately 22-story bldg. is completely modern in equipment & combines under one roof every facility for diagnosis, dressings, laboratories, meeting rooms & lib. Carillons, made in Croydon, England, the gift of the Drs. Mayo, are installed in the tower & are played daily at twilight. In pk. opp., **Mayo Foundation Mus. of Hygiene & Medicine** (O.wks.10-12 & 2-4;Sat.10-12;Sun.2-5); exhibits of normal & pathological tissue & organs of the human body. 3rd Ave. & SE. 12th St., **Reid-Murdock Vegetable Canning Plant** (O.10-10 June 15-July 15 & Aug.15-Sept.15), one of world's largest pea canneries.

**V. MINNEAPOLIS (SW) to MANKATO. 76.5. US169**
Via: Shakopee, Mudbaden, Jordan, Belle Plaine, Le Sueur, Traverse des Sioux & St. Peter.

US169 & US212 leave Minneapolis at 50th St. &, united, travel (SW) until US169 at **19.** branches off (L). **20. SHAKOPEE,** where in 1850 last battle bet. Chippewa & Dakota Inds. took place. On 1st St., **Log Cabin** of O. Faribault (O.1844). Carl Schurz, in 1859, called this sec. of the Minn. R. as beautiful as the Rhine. His praise of the reg. encouraged heavy German immigration. **29.5. MUDBADEN,** health resort with mud baths. **39.5. BELLE PLAINE.** Here the "Fanny Harris," bringing troops to St. Paul (1861), was caught in a raging torrent because of spring floods. The captain piloted the boat 10m across the flooded plain into calmer waters before returning to channel. **55. LE SUEUR,** named for 17th cent. explorer. On Main St. (L) is **Mayo H.** (O), residence of the two famous surgeons & their doctor father. In vic. is a Mex. Village consisting of Mex. beet workers recruited from Texas. **62.5.** (R) **TRAVERSE DES SIOUX ST. PK.** (pic.facils.23 as.) comm. signing of treaty with Sioux (1851). **64.5. ST. PETER,** which by some pioneers was expected to be state capital. A "first" capital bldg. was erected here in 1857. St. Peter was home of 5 Minn. Governors. Here is **Gustavus Adolphus College** maintained by Conference of Augustana Synod of N. America (Swedish). **76.5. MANKATO** (see US14). 4m (W) is **Minneopa St. Pk.** (110 as.pic.facils.hik.).

**VI. MINNEAPOLIS (S) to FARIBAULT. 58. US65** (Via: Northfield & Bridgewater)
**7.** J. with St.35 leading (R) to J. with dirt Rd. On this Rd. 2.5m (L) is **Bush L. Ski Slide,** making a 200′ jump possible. **11.** US65 crosses the **MINN. R. 21.5. ANTLERS PK.** on L. Marion (resort.beach.pic.golf). **28. FARMINGTON,** has a milk co-op. with more than 8,000 members. **32. CASTLE ROCK.** At c.**41.** hy. follows bank of **CANNON R.** on both sides of which Carleton College has its **Arboretum** (300 as.). **42.5. NORTHFIELD,** home of **Carleton & St. Olaf Colleges.** Carleton was founded 1866 & functions in cooperation with various denominational churches. Thorstein

Veblen, famous economist & philosopher attended Carleton & lived in Northfield from time he was 8 yrs. old. He was author of "Theory of the Leisure Class" & translator of "Laxdela Saga." St. Olaf, fully accredited liberal arts college is supported by Luth. Chs. of U.S. & is home of well-known **St. Olaf Luth. Choir,** which gives concerts all over the country & even abroad. O. E. Rölvaag, author of "Giants in the Earth" taught here. **The School of the Air** has a broadcasting sta. & gives courses in making broadcasts & in stimulating thoughtful listening. Annual Music Festival, 3rd wk. in May. Northfield was scene of a Jesse James bank hold-up, Sept. 7, 1876. Clel Miller & Bill Stiles were killed & Bob Younger wounded. Jesse & Frank James escaped on stolen horses. On Sept. 21, after a manhunt with 1,000 pursuers, Charlie Pitts was killed & the 3 Younger Bros. were captured & imprisoned for life. US65 bet. Northfield & Faribault passes 16 abandoned mill sites of Civil War period.

**46.5. DUNDAS.** Here in the 1860's the Archibald Bros. pioneered in a new flour-milling method, secret process brought over by La Croix family. Collapse of the Cannon R. land boom of 1856 left a string of deserted villages in this vic. described in Edw. Eggleston's novel "Mystery of Metropolisville" 1873. **51.5. BRIDGE-WATER. 56.5.** J. with St.21 leading (R) here 8$^{m}$ to **French L.** (f.duck h.). **58. FARIBAULT,** called by its horticulturists the "Nation's Peony Capital," was a fur trading post in 1826. In center of town is **Alexander Faribault H.,** first frame house. For a long time it & the Whipple H. were the town's social meeting places. Latter, no longer standing, was home of Henry Ben. Whipple, Episc. Bishop, a real friend of the Inds., a "rational abolitionist," & a conservative Democrat & politician. His counsel was sought by Queen Victoria & the Presidents of the U.S. He lies buried in **Episc. Cathedral** (1st in U.S.). Faribault also has **St. James Military Academy & St. School for Blind, Deaf & Dumb.** Attached is **School for Feebleminded,** which pioneered in that field with great success.

## VII. MINNEAPOLIS (SW) to CHASKA. 31. US212

**1.5.** J. with St.7.

SIDE TRIP: Take latter (R) 4$^{m}$ to **Minnehaha Cr.** At 4.5$^{m}$ is side Rd. leading (L) 2$^{m}$ to **Hopkins,** famed for raspberries. Annual raspberry festival during picking season. St.7 passes through a reg. of lakes. At c.12$^{m}$ is **L. Minnetonka,** the most beautiful, as its Ind. name indicates. Luxury side-wheelers such as the "Belle of Minnetonka" & the "Phil Sheridan," carrying as many as 3,500 persons plied the Minnetonka's waters, c.1867. The lake has become known particularly through Cadman's "Land of the Sky Blue Water" & Lieurance's "By the Waters of Minnetonka." Along the 50$^{m}$ of St.7, dozens of other lakes abound.

**27.** on US12 are the **SHAKOPEE LIMESTONE LEDGES** & at **31. CHASKA,** a predominantly German village with 3 **Ind. Mounds** in City Pk. & a local **Mineral Springs** known for healing qualities.

## VII. MINNEAPOLIS (N) to TAYLOR FALLS (Wis. Line). 53.5. US8 (Via: Center City)

**7.** J. with Cty. D., leading (R) 2$^{m}$ to **Nazareth Hall,** a seminary on L. Johanna. The bldgs., except the Romanes. chapel (int.chapel inter.), are architecturally similar to those in Lombardy. At **9.** J. with US10 & at **26.5.** J. with US61, running through lake country. **32. WYOMING** & at **39. Chisago City** which, together with **LINDSTROM** at **42.** & **CENTER CITY** at **43.5.,** form nucleus of Swedish culture in Minn. in reg. sett. 1850-51 when many pioneers came from Sweden to establish here a colony & a conference of the Swedish Luth. Ch. (1854). Swedes still celebrate Mid-summer night June 24-25. US8 turns abruptly (E). **TAYLOR FALLS** (see US61) at **53.5.** is especially interesting to geologists. To (R) is **Interstate Pk.** (154 as.). Here is Turbulent R. in a gorge rising 200′ from water's edge. Near-by, **"Glacial Gardens"** (boat.f.pic.facils.). Here rock formations were created after the "Ice Age." Excellent area to study geology & Ind. petroglyphs. On both sides of river are the Dalles of the St. Croix. Int. geological **Pot Holes. Lookout Mt.** is legendary battleground of the Sioux & Chippewa. So bloody were the conflicts that the Inds. called it "Valley of Bones." Here still is **Wm. H. C. Folsom H.** (1854.Georg.), constructed of locally sawed lumber & built by Maine carpenters, & Ch. built by Folsom (1861). Taylor Falls is at S. edge of white pine stands. Along river are found wild orchids, the Minn. state flower, sometimes called Indian-shoe or ladyslipper.

# THE PLAINS STATES

## MISSOURI—IOWA—KANSAS
## NEBRASKA—NORTH DAKOTA
## SOUTH DAKOTA

### THE PLAINS STATES

Westward from the Mississippi River in an almost unbroken sweep of prairie, gradually rising toward the High Plains area beyond which the Rockies begin, extend the Plains States: Missouri, Iowa, Kansas, Nebraska, North & South Dakota. Until little more than a century ago, this expanse of open country—almost treeless, with little water, where the wind rippled seemingly endless acres of grass—was part of the "Great American Desert," a barrier to westward settlement. Across it roved huge herds of buffalo, hunted by bands of nomadic Indians, horsemen & wigwam dwellers. Life was harsh for the earliest white settlers here, building their log shanties, their sod huts & dugouts along the river valleys & then across the plains: they faced blizzards & sudden floods, long droughts & parching, hot winds. Harassed at first by raiding Indians, later they were beset by frontier desperadoes—Quantrill's "bushwhackers," train & bank robbers like Jesse & Frank James or the Dalton brothers, & other adventurers. Law & order were precariously maintained in their pioneer towns, unlovely settlements of weatherbeaten frame buildings, against a floating population of gunmen, gamblers, prostitutes. Nevertheless settlement was pushed forward, spurred by westward traffic: steamboats on the rivers, pack trains & wagon caravans along the trails to Santa Fe and Oregon, the overland stage companies & the Pony Express, the first transcontinental railroads. Gradually, after the Civil War & the end of hostilities with the Indians, the open ranges were crisscrossed with barbed-wire, as homesteaders succeeded cattlemen, planting wheat & other crops; & the region developed into what it is today: the nation's breadbasket. Grain elevators & stockyards became the symbols of its prosperity; & newly sprung-up cities, gathering in the harvest of the farmlands, grew to metropolitan centers, fringed with railroad yards & factories.

The level or easily rolling terrain of this trans-Mississippi region, sparsely timbered except along river bottoms & broken only by the rugged, forested Ozarks of southern Missouri & the Black Hills of western South Dakota, sweeps all the way, gently tilting, from the Mississippi to the eroded uplands of the High Plains along its western border, where the sand hills of northwestern Nebraska & the Badlands of the Dakotas appear. By far the greater part of the whole area is drained by the wide, muddy Missouri River & its tributaries, among them the James & Big Sioux in the Dakotas, the Platte in Nebraska, the Kansas in Kansas, & the Osage in Missouri. Eastern Iowa is drained by tributaries of the Mississippi, largest of which is the Des Moines; eastern North Dakota by the Red River of the North; southern Missouri, by the St. Francis, White & other Ozark streams; southern Kansas, by the Arkansas River.

This was the abode of various tribes of Indians: the agricultural, village-dwelling Arikara, Hidatsa, Iowa, Kansa, Mandan, Missouri, Omaha, Osage, Oto, Pawnee, Sac & Fox, Wichita, & others & the plains-wandering, usually more warlike Arapaho and Cheyenne, Assiniboin, Chippewa, Comanche, Kiowa & Sioux. Of these, the much-feared Sioux ranged a vast territory stretching from western Iowa through northern Nebraska, South Dakota, & southern North Dakota, to the north, south & southwest of which roved the other nomadic tribes & to the east, southeast & south of which dwelt the agricultural tribes.

The first white men known to have set foot within this region were Francisco

Vasquez de Coronado & his army of 300 Spaniards from the south, seeking fabled Quivira in 1541. They traveled north to a point somewhere near the center of Kansas or farther before they turned back, disappointed in their search for gold & silver. Other Spanish explorers ventured into the region in 1594 & 1601. In 1673, Louis Jolliet & Père Jacques Marquette, on their voyage down the Mississippi River, touched land on the Iowa & Missouri shores; & in 1682 La Salle, traveling the Mississippi to its mouth, claimed the whole valley for France. Before the end of the 17th century, French-Canadian fur traders & missionaries were exploring the region; & in 1700 Jesuits established a short-lived settlement on the site of St. Louis. By 1720, southeastern Missouri's lead deposits were being worked & French voyageurs, traveling up the Missouri & its tributaries, had penetrated into Kansas & Nebraska. Fort Orleans was established on the Missouri in 1723. In 1743 Pierre Gaultier de Varennes, Sieur de la Verendrye, visited the Dakotas, the first known white man to do so. The first permanent settlement in the region was made by some Creole families at Ste Genevieve (Mo.) about 1750, & in 1764 the New Orleans firm of Maxent, Laclede & Co., having received a monopoly of the fur trade, founded St. Louis for its headquarters. French claims west of the Mississippi had been ceded in 1762 to Spain, but Spanish officials exerted little more than nominal control over Upper Louisiana. In 1788 the first settlement in Iowa was made by Julien Dubuque, French-Canadian, who established a fort & prospered at lead mining & trading with the Indians. About 1792 Louis Lorimier established a trading post on the site of Cape Girardeau (Mo.). By this time American settlers, encouraged by liberal Spanish land grants, had begun to settle Missouri. The Louisiana Territory passed back in 1801 to the French, & in 1803, through the Louisiana Purchase, to the U.S. From St. Louis exploring expeditions were soon dispatched: one in 1804 led by Capt. Meriwether Lewis & Lieut. Wm. Clark up the Missouri River & down the Columbia to the Pacific Coast, & one in 1806 led by Capt. Zebulon M. Pike up the Osage River & across Kansas & Nebraska toward Colorado. Wilson Price Hunt led a party of fur traders up the Missouri & across Nebraska in 1810 and Robert Stewart led another party east from Astoria (Ore.) over the same route in 1812. Maj. Stephen H. Long headed a scientific expedition up the South Platte to its headwaters in 1819. Fur trading posts, missionary schools, & military forts were rapidly established along the Missouri River & in the Dakotas.

Missouri, made a Territory in 1812, was admitted to the Union as a slave state in 1821, following adoption by Congress of the famous Missouri Compromise, which forbade admission in the future of any more slave states north of 36° 30′. Rapidly settled, principally by Southerners, it prospered on steamboat traffic along the Missouri & overland trade with Mexico via the Santa Fe Trail, opened in 1821. Settlement of Iowa was spurred by the Black Hawk Purchase of 1833, opening lands of the Sac & Fox Indians: Dubuque, Burlington, Davenport, & Keokuk were quickly laid out; in 1845 the region around Des Moines was opened to settlers, and the year following, Iowa (since 1838 a Territory) was admitted to the Union. The Indian frontier had now been pushed west of the Missouri River.

By the early 1840's a growing procession of travelers had begun to follow what became by far the most important of the overland trails to the Far West, along the Missouri & Platte River Valleys across Missouri, eastern Kansas, & central Nebraska; & pioneer trading centers along the route sprang up: Independence, Westport (now Kansas City), Atchison, St. Joseph, Omaha. The first large organized group to take this trail were the Mormons, forced out of Missouri by Gentile hostility, who traveled toward their Promised Land in Utah along the north bank of the Platte in 1847. The Oregon Trail, following the south bank, was soon a heavily traveled route, pursued after 1848 for part of its length by thousands of California-bound gold seekers in covered wagons. Along it were dispatched the overland mail & freight wagons of the Russell, Waddell & Majors Freighting Co., with headquarters at Leavenworth, Kansas; it was this firm which established on April 3, 1860 the famous Pony Express, carrying mail from St. Joseph to Placerville, California, in ten and a half days. The Butterfield Overland Stage Company, at first traveling across southern Missouri on the southern route to California, transferred to the central route after the beginning of the Civil War. In 1862 the firm of Russell, Waddell & Majors, having gone bankrupt, was acquired by Ben Holladay, who expanded operations until by 1866 he had what was probably the country's biggest one-man business, with 5,000 miles of stage line.

# PLAINS STATES

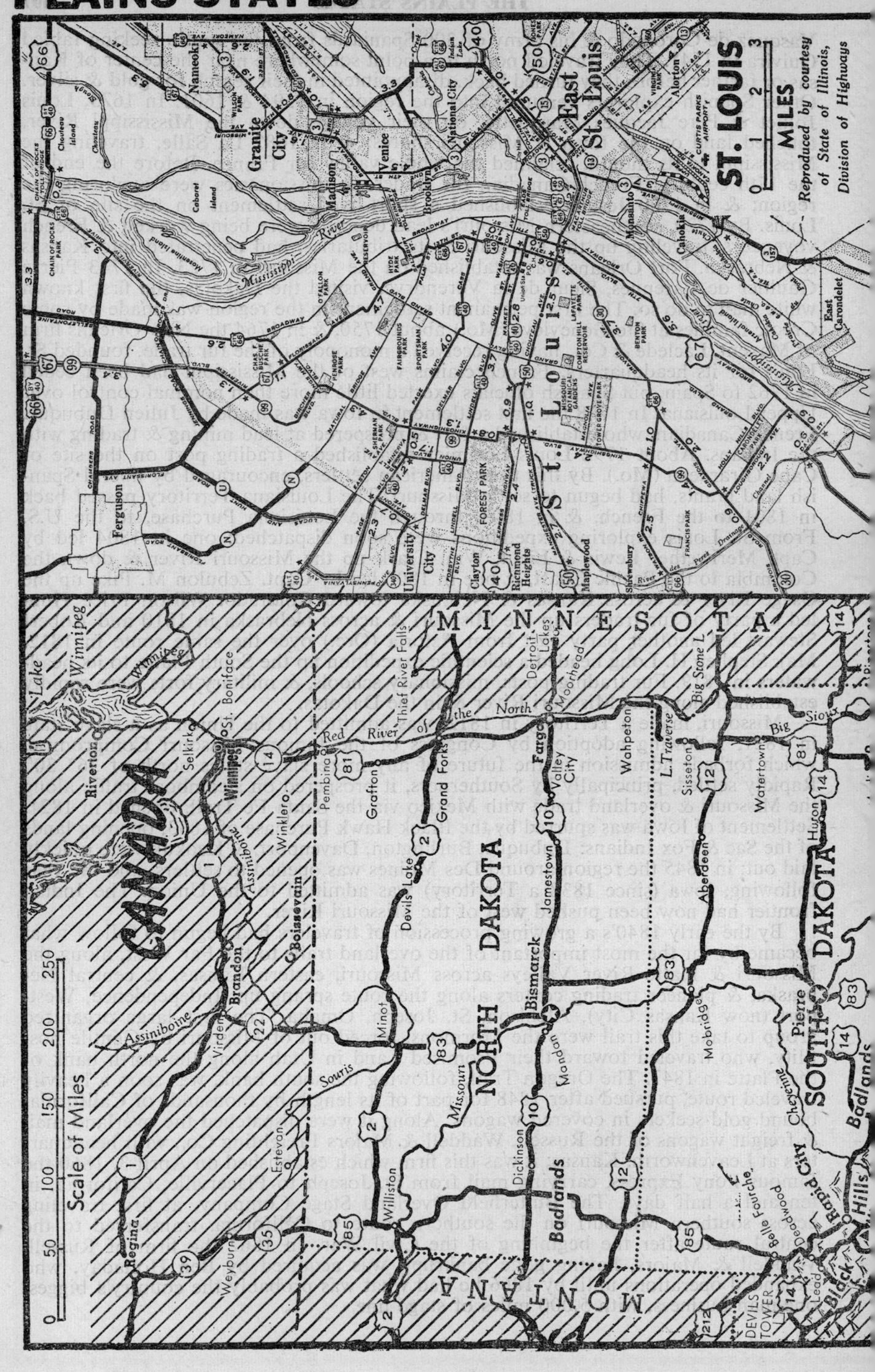

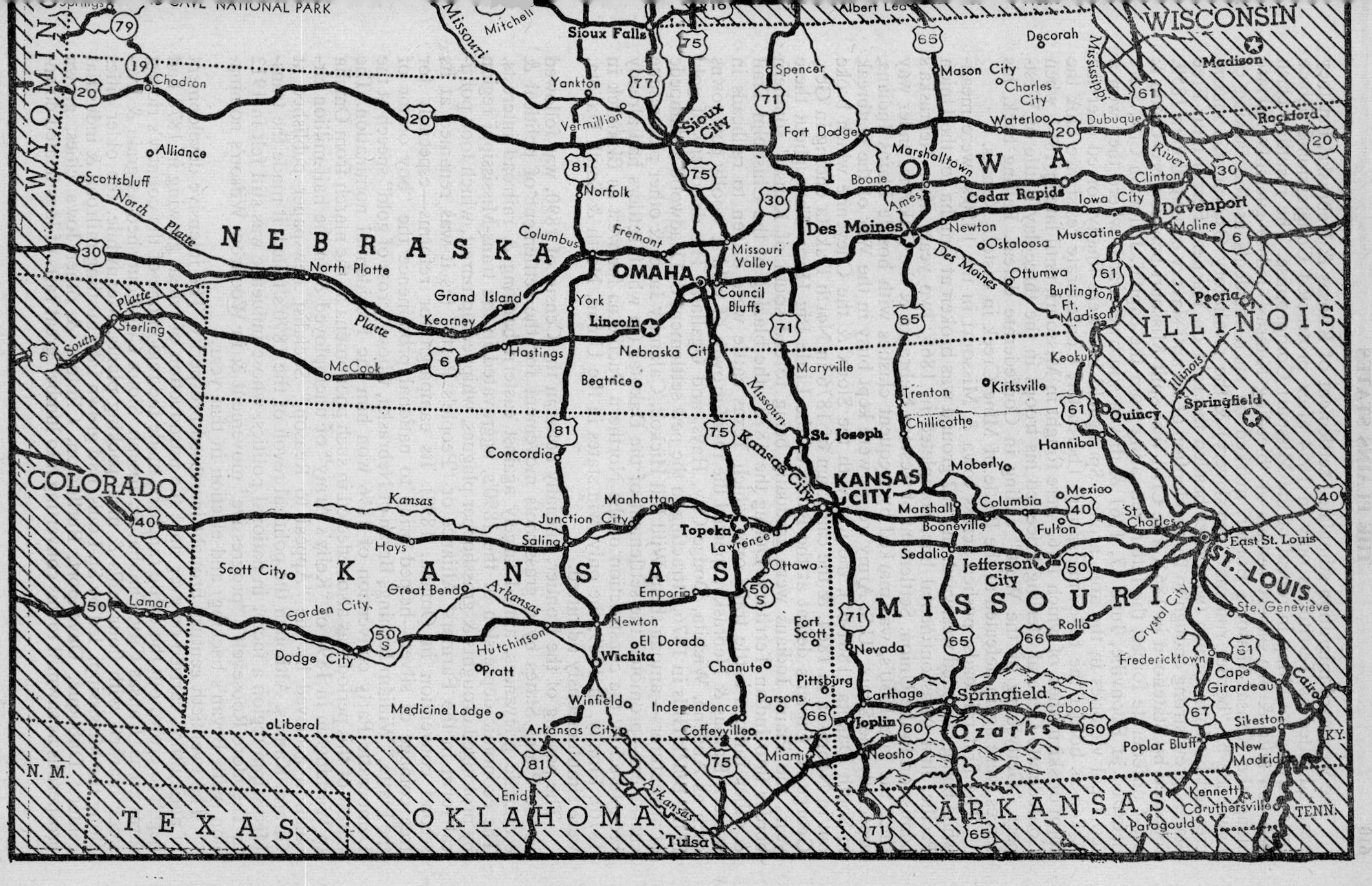
WISCONSIN
Madison
Rockford
ILLINOIS
Peoria
Springfield
Quincy
Illinois
Mississippi
River
Dubuque
Clinton
Davenport
Moline
IOWA
Decorah
Mason City
Charles City
Waterloo
Marshalltown
Cedar Rapids
Iowa City
Muscatine
Boone
Ames
Des Moines
Newton
Oskaloosa
Ottumwa
Burlington
Ft. Madison
Keokuk
Fort Dodge
Spencer
Albert Lea
Sioux City
Sioux Falls
Yankton
Vermillion
Mitchell
Missouri
NEBRASKA
Chadron
Alliance
Scottsbluff
North Platte
Platte
Columbus
Fremont
Norfolk
Missouri Valley
OMAHA
Council Bluffs
York
Lincoln
Grand Island
Kearney
Hastings
McCook
Nebraska City
Beatrice
Sterling
South Platte
WYOMING
COLORADO
KANSAS
Concordia
Manhattan
Junction City
Salina
Hays
Kansas
Topeka
Lawrence
Ottawa
Emporia
Scott City
Great Bend
Arkansas
Lamar
Garden City
Dodge City
Hutchinson
Pratt
Newton
El Dorado
Wichita
Winfield
Arkansas City
Medicine Lodge
Liberal
Chanute
Independence
Coffeyville
Parsons
Pittsburg
Fort Scott
KANSAS CITY
Kansas City
St. Joseph
Maryville
Trenton
Chillicothe
Kirksville
Hannibal
Moberly
Mexico
Columbia
Marshall
Booneville
Fulton
St. Charles
Sedalia
Jefferson City
MISSOURI
ST. LOUIS
East St. Louis
Ste. Genevieve
Crystal City
Rolla
Fredericktown
Cape Girardeau
Cairo
Nevada
Carthage
Joplin
Springfield
Cabool
Ozarks
Neosho
Miami
Poplar Bluff
Sikeston
New Madrid
Kennett
Caruthersville
Paragould
KY.
TENN.
ARKANSAS
OKLAHOMA
Enid
Tulsa
TEXAS
N. M.
79
19
20
30
6
81
75
77
71
65
61
40
50
50 S
66
60
67

The westward migration stimulated settlement of Kansas & Nebraska, but they were admitted as Territories only in 1854 after protracted Congressional debate over slavery, resulting in repeal of the Missouri Compromise. The resulting clash between anti- & pro-slavery settlers in "bleeding Kansas" led to guerrilla warfare along the Kansas-Missouri Border, marked by such incidents as the sacking of Lawrence by "border ruffians" (pro-slavery) & the retaliatory Osawatomie massacres led by John Brown (who later headed the raid on Harpers Ferry) until Free Staters grew strong enough to force adoption of an anti-slavery constitution in 1859, followed by Statehood in 1861. The Civil War split Missouri between pro-Union & pro-Confederate forces; the latter, retreating from the capital, Jefferson City, were defeated at Boonville, June 17, 1861 & driven southwestward, where they won a few local victories in the area around Springfield but were finally forced over the Arkansas border the following spring. Thereafter, Confederate resistance took the form of skirmishes, of which 1,162 were fought in Missouri, until late in 1864, when Confederate General Sterling Price led his troops in the three-day Battle of Westport, "Gettysburg of the West," ending in Confederate defeat. Falling back, his forces were again defeated at the Battle of Mine Creek in eastern Kansas.

The first railroads, pushed across Iowa & Missouri in the 1850's, were meanwhile being extended westward. In 1862 ground was broken at Omaha for the Union Pacific, first transcontinental line, completed in 1869, two years after Nebraska's admission to the Union. Settlement of western Nebraska & the Dakotas, under way since the late 1850's, was marked by frequent clashes with hostile Plains Indians, especially the Sioux. U.S. Army troops were kept busy in the War of the Outbreak in South Dakota (1861-65), the war with the Sioux & the Cheyenne which broke out in Nebraska in 1864, & the campaign of 1876 in North Dakota ending in Gen. George A. Custer's defeat at the Battle of the Little Big Horn. Throughout these years the Plains Indians were gradually being forced south of Kansas' southern border into Indian Territory. During the 1870's the blazing of the Chisholm Trail & other famous cattle trails over which Texas cattle were driven to railheads in western Kansas & Nebraska, spurred the rapid growth of wild & woolly cow towns such as Abilene, Wichita, Dodge City, Hays, and Ogallala. The discovery of gold in the Black Hills in 1876, attracting to the new settlement of Deadwood a stampede of adventurers—among them Wild Bill Hickok, Calamity Jane, & other picturesque characters—promoted the settlement of the Dakotas (to which settlers had already been lured by the construction of the Northern Pacific as far west as Bismarck in 1870). Finally, in 1889, the only twin states in the Union, North & South Dakota, were simultaneously admitted.

The passing of the frontier, officially noted in the Census of 1890, was followed in the Plains States by a grass-roots movement for the settlement of political & economic grievances, aimed largely against eastern banking & railroad interests. The economic depression of the 1890's, aggravated in the trans-Mississippi region by prolonged droughts & grasshopper plagues, whipped up unrest, which took political form in the Farmers' Alliance or "People's Party" (as it was renamed at its second convention in Omaha, 1892). Its campaign for reforms—especially for free coinage of silver—helped bring to national prominence the "boy orator of the Platte," William Jennings Bryan of Nebraska, whose "cross of gold" speech at the Democratic Party convention of 1896 won him the Presidential nomination. The unrest of this period was also reflected in such phenomena as the march from Omaha to Washington in 1894 of "Kelly's Army" of unemployed & in the half-million circulation achieved by the "Appeal to Reason," Socialist newspaper published at Girard, Kansas. Although the political revolt of the 1890's failed, it made the trans-Mississippi region a factor in national politics, whose influence was still felt in 1912 in Theodore Roosevelt's "progressive" movement & in Woodrow Wilson's nomination (with Bryan's backing) and election in that year.

The twentieth century brought increased prosperity. The intensive development of agriculture, carried on ever since the introduction of wheat growing in 1870 had begun to crowd out the cattle ranchers, made the region one of the country's richest farm areas. Kansas City, Omaha, St. Joseph, Sioux City flourished as grain & livestock markets with flour mills & meat-packing plants. Meanwhile, the older cities along the Mississippi, led by St. Louis, had grown into bustling railroad & industrial centers; Dubuque, Davenport, Burlington, Clinton, & other Iowa cities, grown prosperous as sawmill towns converting into lumber great rafts of logs floated downriver, acquired metalworking & other plants: Iowa tractors, farm machinery, & washing machines began to be produced, along with Iowa corn & hogs. Exploitation of mineral deposits—Iowa, Missouri & Kansas, coal; Iowa, gypsum; Missouri & Kansas, lead and zinc; Missouri, barite, clay, & silica; Kansas, oil & gas; Dakota, lignite & gold—brought new wealth. World War I spurred both agricultural & industrial expansion. The prosperous 1920's were reflected in the building booms & programs of civic improvement which transformed the region's urban centers; some of its smaller cities—Des Moines, Topeka, Lincoln, Wichita—grew rapidly bigger (especially Wichita, boomed to metropolitan importance by oil & aircraft manufacturing).

The economic depression of the 1930's, attended (like that of the 1890's) by disastrous droughts & crop failures, revived political unrest. The Farm Holiday Association, originating in Iowa, led farmers in struggles against foreclosures on farm mortgages & in picketing of market centers; the Farmer-Labor Party extended its political activities into the area. But gradually, after 1933, recovery began, aided by Federal & State legislation providing for mortgage moratoriums, agricultural subsidies & crop-control programs & by the growth of farmers' cooperatives. The introduction of long-needed conservation measures (whose best-known champion was Nebraska's Senator George W. Norris) began to put the region's agriculture on a sounder basis; irrigation projects, programs for erosion control, planting of shelter belts of trees (for wind protection) helped counteract the bad farming practices of the past. The building of dams, not only to impound water for irrigation but also to generate hydroelectric power, promoted industrial development. Support grew for the creation of a Missouri Valley Project, similar to the Tennessee Valley Project sponsored by Senator Norris, to aid the realization of the region's potentialities. However rich its harvest of farm & factory products—even after World War II, which boomed output to the highest level yet reached—these potentialities still remain to be fully exploited.

## US 40—MISSOURI

### ST. LOUIS, MO. (W) to KANSAS CITY, MO. 256. US40

Via: St. Charles, Warrenton, Columbia, Boonville & Concordia. RRs. parallel most of route. Accoms.: Tourist & trlr. camps at frequent intervals, hotels in cities.

US40 cuts across central Mo., roughly following main route taken by westward-moving settlers. It crosses Mo. R., NW. of St. Louis, & heads (W) over course of Boon's Lick Trl., once followed by stagecoaches & covered wagons. Crossing R. again at Boonville, it proceeds over rolling fertile prairie uplands.

For pts. of int. & towns on or near US40 bet. St. Louis & J. with US61 (see) at **WENTZVILLE, 40.**, see St. Louis II. **56. WARRENTON** is site of **Central Wesleyan College** (est.1852), E. end of Main St. **103.** J. with US54.

SIDE TRIPS: (A) Take latter (R) to **Mexico,** 17m, which calls itself "Fire Brick & Saddle Horse Center of the World," laid out in 1836. Its 1st inhabitants were horse lovers; by 1890's, town was site of many large stables. Huge deposit of fire clay was discovered beneath town site soon after 1900, leading to est. of clay refractories. **A. P. Green Fire Brick Co. Plant,** E. end of Breckenridge St., is one of largest plants of kind in world. Here also is **Mo. Military Academy.**

(B) Take US54 (L) to **Fulton,** 7m, seat of Calloway Cty., which since 1830 has been leading producer among Mo. counties of famed "Missouri mule." Fulton, founded in 1825, depends also on farm trade & its shoe-mfg. & clay refractories plants. **Capt. Jas. Calloway Mon.,** cth. square, comm. pioneer Mo. settler. E. 5th & State Sts., **St. Hospital No. 1** (opened 1849), was 1st institution for mental patients W. of Miss. R. Fulton is also site of **Mo. Sch. for the Deaf** (founded 1851), 5th & Vine Sts.; **William Woods College,** 12th & Nichols Sts., girls' jr. college directed by Christian Ch.; & **Westminster College** (opened 1853), Westminster Ave. bet. 4th & 7th Sts., 4-yr. institution supported by Presb. Ch. US54 cont. to **Jefferson City,** 32m (see US50) at J. with US50 (see).

**124. COLUMBIA** is university town of venerable lineage, garden-dotted, with well-stocked shops & department stores & farm produce wholesale houses & shoe & garment factories. It was laid out in 1821, around log cabin built earlier by Thos. Duley, & soon thrived as stopping place on Boon's Lick Trl. Its early settlers, largely from the Virginia & Kentucky reg. were strong for education: in 1829 was founded Bonne Femme Academy & in 1833, Columbia Female Academy; & when St. univ.

was projected, Columbia & Boone Cty. citizens began vigorous & successful campaign to have it located here. This, 1st St. univ. est. W. of Miss. R., was opened in 1841 in Columbia College (chartered 1835) bldg. Christian College & Stephens College, both girls' schools, were chartered later. PTS. OF INT.: At opp. ends of 8th St. stand (1) on N., **Columns of Old Cth.** (1848), left when bldg. which replaced 1st cth. (1824) was razed in 1908, & (2) on S., **The Columns,** in center of Francis Quadrangle of **Univ. of Mo.,** 6 ivy-covered Ionic pillars which are all that remains of 1st univ. bldg. (1840.burned 1892). Main entrance to campus is through gray-stone-pillared **Mem. Gateway,** Elm St. at 8th St. **Jesse Hall** contains, on 1st fl., orig. tombstone from Thos. Jefferson's grave at Monticello & on 3rd & 4th fls., art exhibits. **Jay H. Neff & Walter Williams Halls** house Sch. of Journalism, 1st in world to grant degree in journalism; former contains exhibit of objects dealing with history of printing. SE. of Francis Quadrangle is **Gen. Lib.,** Eng. Ren. style, which houses **St. Hist. Soc. of Mo.** coll. of more than 200,000 volumes & pamphlets; latter's 1st fl. reading room contains paintings by Geo. Caleb Bingham. Goth.-style 140′ **Mem. Tower,** NE. of Gen. Lib., stands at entrance to E., or White, Campus, whose white-limestone structures are more recent than red-brick ones of Main, or Red, Campus centering around Francis Quadrangle. Here also are experimental fields & livestock barns of College of Agric.; **Sanborn Field** (est.1888) is country's oldest experimental farm. Athletic facils., incl. **Rollins Field & Mem. Stadium,** are to (S). (3) Broadway Ave. bet. Waugh St. & College Ave., **Stephens College,** for women, grew out of Columbia Female, or Lucy Wales, Academy (1833-53), succeeded by Bapt. Female College (chartered 1856); latter, becoming St. institution in 1870, was renamed for Jas. L. Stephens, who gave it $20,000 endowment. Its bldgs., principally of modified Eng. Ren. style, are scattered over more than 200 as. (4) 1403 E. Broadway, **J. L. Stephens H.** (1843) was built by college's namesake. (5) 2001 E. Broadway, **Gordon Manor** (1823), now college property, was built by slave labor for pioneer settler Capt. David Gordon. (6) 100 Hitt St., **Presb. Student Center** occupies 2-story brick house built (1828) by Jas. Hickman. (7) Christian College & Rogers Aves., **Christian College,** women's jr. college housed in group of Romanes. & Eng. Ren. structures is on 20-a. campus.

Columbia is at J. with US63.

SIDE TRIP: Take latter (R) to **Moberly,** 36.5m, RR. division pt. & repair center with mfg. plants & near-by coal mines, dating from 1860's. N. Mo. RR. repair shops, built here in 1872, were 1st W. of Miss. R. Coal mining began in vic. in 1880's. Moberly Free Pub. Lib. has **Gen. Omar N. Bradley Trophy Room,** honoring World War II Comdr. who went to high sch. here. **Rothwell Pk.** (boat.swim.f.), W. edge of town, is 320-a. wooded area with large L. 59.5m **Macon,** known as "City of Maples" for many ancient maples, grew up with advent of Hannibal & St. Joseph RR. in late 1850's. Near-by coal mining area employs one of world's biggest strip mining machines. 94.5m **Kirksville,** center of grain & livestock raising area, with factories & wholesale houses, was founded in 1841. Here on Aug. 6, 1862, Feds. defeated Confeds. in Battle of Kirksville, whose site is incorporated in **Mem. Pk.,** Hickory St. bet. Mulaniz St. & Florence Ave. Pk. was also site of 1st normal school W. of Miss. R., opened in 1867; this institution, now **Mo. St. Teachers College,** occupies 20-a. campus on E. Normal Ave. bet. Marion & Mulaniz Sts. **Kirksville College of Osteopathy & Surgery,** W. Jefferson St. bet. 5th St. & Osteopathy Ave., country's 1st & largest of its kind, was founded in 1892 by Dr. Andrew Taylor Still, pioneer osteopath.

**148.** J. with St.5.

SIDE TRIP: Take latter (R) to **New Franklin,** 1.5m, laid out in 1828 along bluffs overlooking Mo. R. **Scott-Kingsbury H.** (1835), 3m, is surrounded by apple orchards. **Lilac Hill** (c.1832), 11.5m, is one of Mo.'s best examples of Fed. style. **Fayette,** 12.5m, was socially & politically important from time it became, in 1823, seat of Howard Cty., known as "Mother of Counties" since it included number of Mo. & Iowa counties later formed from it. N. end of Main St., **Central College,** 4-yr. coed. institution which began in 1844 as Howard High School. **Judge Abiel Leonard H.** (c.1835) was home of noted early politician. **Morrison Observ.,** Fayette City Pk., was largest observatory W. of Miss. R., when est. in 1874 in near-by Glasgow; it was moved here in 1935. **Claiborne Fox Jackson H.** (c.1847), 14m, was residence of Mo.'s governor at beginning of Civil War. **Glasgow,** 25.5m, spilling over steep Mo. R. bluffs, laid out in 1836, prospered until R. traffic declined. Long Chicago & Alton RR. Bridge built across R. here in 1878-79 was alleged 1st all-steel Ry. bridge; it served until 1922, when new one was erected. **Lewis Lib. Bldg.** (1866), built by Col. Benj. W. Lewis, Sr., is supposed to be Mo.'s oldest library bldg. Former **Lewis College Bldgs.** (1849-50 & 1852) have Gr. Rev. facades.

At **149.** are Js. with St.87 & unimproved dirt Rd.

SIDE TRIPS: (A) Take latter (L) short distance to **Rivercene** (1869), once home of steamboat owner Capt. Jos. Kinney, now mus. of early furnishings & paintings, incl. portraits by Geo. Caleb Bingham.

(B) Take St.87 (R) to **Site of Old Franklin,** 0.5m, designated by mon. erected by Mo. Press Assoc., comm. "Missouri Intelligencer & Boon's Lick Advertiser" (1819), 1st newspaper begun W. of Miss. R. Franklin became in 1821, 5yrs. after it had been laid out, head of Santa Fe Trl. Here Geo. Caleb Bingham, painter, & Kit Carson, trapper & trader, spent their early days. Its prosperity was short-lived, however; by mid-century, it had almost disappeared. At 2m is J. with an unmarked local Rd.; route cont. straight ahead on latter to J. at 9m with another unmarked local Rd.

(L) on this is **Site of Cooper's Ft.,** 1m, indicated by granite marker. Here, in biggest of fts. built in Boon's Lick reg., pioneer settlers, led by Col. Benj. A. Cooper, defended themselves against Ind. attack during War of 1812.

Route cont. straight ahead from J. at 9m to J. with cty. Rd., 9.1m, turns (L) on this to another unmarked gravel Rd., 11m, & (R) on this to farm at 12m on which is **Boon's Lick Spring.** Spring was probably named for Dan. Boone, who perhaps made salt here about year 1800, & whose sons, Nathan & Dan., with others, opened salt works on site in 1806.

US40 bridges Mo. R. to hill-fringed **BOONVILLE, 150.5.,** on bluffs, 1st sett. in 1810, which flourished as R. port & milling center & chief trading center for whole Ozark region of Missouri. Civil War's 1st conflict, ending in Confed. defeat, was fought 4m S. on June 17, 1861; 2nd Battle of Boonville was fought Sept. 13, 1861 on ridge of R. bluff. After Civil War, by-passed by RRs., Boonville suffered decline, but new industries & hy. trans. facils. have revived prosperity. **Kemper Military Sch.** (founded 1844), Center Ave. & 3rd St., one of whose alumni was humorist Will Rogers, is one of the first boys' schs. in the state, Goth. Rev. **Christ Episc. Ch.** (1846), Vine & 4th Sts., is oldest Episc. Ch. W. of Miss. R. Main & Vine Sts., **Lyric Theatre** (1855-57.Gr.Rev.), orig. Thespian Hall, is said to be first theatre of Western region. In Walnut Grove Cemetery, SE. part of town, is **Grave of David Barton,** pres. of Mo.'s Constitutional Convention & its 1st U.S. Senator. 745 Main St., **Sen. Geo. G. Vest H.** (remod.), was home of lawyer & politician whose "Eulogy of the Dog" was celebrated example of 19th cent. Amer. oratory. At **157.** is J. with St.41.

SIDE TRIP: Take latter (R) to **Arrow Rock,** 12.5m, pioneer Santa Fe Trl. town & Mo. R. port. Here, at R. crossing, fur trading post was est. Town was platted in 1829. **Old Tavern** (c.1834.enlarged & rest.fee.meals & overnight accoms.) contains authentic early Amer. furniture, incl. canopy bed in which Geo. Washington slept; its taproom is mus. of pioneer relics. Beyond is 34-a. **Arrow Rock St. Pk.** (pic.camp.), in which stand grim-visaged old stone **Arrow Rock Jail** (1871); **Arrow Rock Academy Bldg.,** of an early girls' sch. (est. 1842); & **Geo. Caleb Bingham H.** (c.1840.reconstructed), onetime residence of famed Mo. painter. (L) from Arrow Rock 0.7m, S. of Arrow Rock Cemetery, is **Wm. B. Sappington H.** (1844), one of St.'s more outstanding specimens of Gr. Rev.

**176.5.** J. with US65 (see). **196.5. CONCORDIA** is inhabited largely by descendants of orig. German settlers, who came soon after 1840 & laid out town in 1868. **St. Paul's College** (est.1884) is Luth. theological academy. **205.5.** J. with St.13.

SIDE TRIP: Take latter (R) to **Lexington,** 19.5m, with many ante bellum homes, which grew up around Mo. R. ferry est. here in 1819 & developed into prosperous R. port. PTS. OF INT.: (1) **Lafayette County Cth.** (1847-49.later adds.), center of town, is Mo.'s oldest still-used cth. & one of its best examples of Gr. Rev. architecture. (2) Also of Gr. Rev. design is **Pub. Lib. & Hist. Assoc. Bldg.** (main sec.1840.later adds.), 112 S. 13th St., orig. built as a ch. (3) Adj. **Christ Episc. Ch.** (main part 1848) is in Goth. style with octagonal tower. (4) **Wentworth Mil. Academy** (est.1880), 18th St. & Washington Ave., is high sch. & jr. college. (5) On R. bluffs, surrounded by **College Pk.,** N. end 16th St., is arcaded **Mem. Bldg.,** on site of world's 1st Masonic college (1848-1932), which it partly reproduces. (6) Near-by is the **Lexington Battlefield,** where in Sept. 1861 Confeds., after more than 48 hours' firing at earthen entrenchments (still visible) of Feds., advanced against furious fire of Union troops to win bloody victory. (7) **Wm. Oliver Anderson H.** (1853.fee) is now mus. of Civil War relics. Also overlooking R. at N. edge of town are (8) 18′ cast-stone **Pioneer Mother Mon.** (1928.Fred.C.Hibbard,sculptor) & (9) **World War Mem.** (1925), approached by long stairway. St.13, crossing Mo. R., cont. to **Richmond,** 27.5m, laid out in 1827, where is Gr. Rev. **Old Ray County Cth.** (ante bellum).

**217. ODESSA,** laid out in 1878, is farmers' trading & shipping center. **243.5.** J. with US Bypass 71 (Noland Rd.).

SIDE TRIP: Take latter (R) to **Independence,** 4.5m, today almost Kansas City suburb. It was laid out in 1827 as seat of Jackson Cty. & orig. log first **Jackson County Cth.,** 107 W. Kansas Ave., remains one of chief landmarks. Following arrival in 1831 of 5 Mormon elders sent by Jos. Smith from Ohio, it rapidly became populous Mormon settlement, until local resentment forced Mormons to leave in 1834. (Independence is today, however, world hqs. of Reorganized Church of Jesus Christ of Latter Day Saints, whose vast domed **Auditorium & Office Bldg.** (1927), Walnut St. bet. S. River Blvd. & S. Grand Ave., seats 10,000 people.) When Gold Rush to Cal. began, blacksmith shop & wagon factory opened by Sam. Weston in 1830 became starting point for covered-wagon trains. 1st RR. W. of Miss. R. was built 3.5$^{m}$ (N) to Wayne City landing on Mo. R. Modern Independence's most famous pt. of int. is **Pres. Harry S. Truman H.** (1865), 214 N. Delaware, frame Vict. mansion built by Mrs. Truman's grandfather, Geo. Porterfield Gates.

## 256. KANSAS CITY

Through RR., bus & plane conns. Accoms.: Plentiful & varied. Info.: C. of C., Hotel Continental, 11th St. & Baltimore Ave. Mun. Auditorium; Music Hall & Little Theater for concerts & plays; Arena for boxing & wrestling. Swim. at mun. pools in pub. pks. Mun. golf courses & tennis courts in Swope Pk. & other pks.

Mo.'s 2nd largest city, Kansas City nicknames itself "The Heart of America." Near geographical center of country, it spreads (S) from Mo. R. at its confluence with Kansas R. Its location has made it hub of vast network of transcontinental RRs., airlines & hys. It is one of Nation's chief markets for cattle, horses & mules, grain, fruits & vegetables, butter, eggs & poultry. In addition to its food processing & handling industries, it has steel, oil, aviation, automobile assembling & garment mfg. plants; & it is important wholesale & retail trading & banking center. It has skyscraper-dominated business dist. & impressive pub. bldgs.; imposing network of handsome blvds., pks. & landscaped residential areas; & variety of cultural & educational facils. In 1939, Kansas City had a major scandal when its corrupt political machine was exposed & Boss T. J. Pendergast was sent to jail for income tax evasion. The "machine" has not been able to make a comeback since.

Downtown Kansas City, centering around inters. of Main & 12th Sts., comprising largest stores, theaters & office bldgs. & Civic Center, lies in NW. sec. To W., along Mo.-Kans. Line skirting Kansas R. bottoms, lie RRs., stockyards & plants of Central Industrial Dist.; & other industrial areas extend in great semicircle along banks of Mo. R. (N) & city's outskirts (NE & E). Bet. downtown sec. & east-side industrial dist., long swathe of middle-class streets runs (S) toward planned, well-landscaped Country Club dist. in SE. Other handsome residential areas, crossed by broad blvds. & dotted with pks., lie on S. side. 1st settlement on site was est. in 1821 when Amer. Fur Co. agent, Francois Chouteau, opened trading post in Kansas R. bottoms, removed in 1830 to foot of what is now Grand Ave. Here supplies were unloaded from steamboats for hauling to town of Westport laid out in 1833 by storekeeper John Alvin McCoy at ford across Big Blue R. 4$^{m}$ SE.; Westport soon thrived as outfitting pt. for overland travelers until cholera epidemic in 1849 ended its prosperity. Westport Landing, as settlement around Chouteau's trading post had 1st been known, was by this time prospering, town site having been platted by Kansas Town Co., which renamed place Kansas; here products brought by steamboats & traders following Santa Fe Trl. were exchanged. Kansas too was hit by cholera epidemic, but recovered. Town site was graded & filled & streets laid out. Kansas City "Enterprise" was founded in 1854.

By middle 1850's Kansas City was already embroiled, however, in conflict bet. pro & antislavery forces over settlement of Kans. & Neb. territories. It increasingly became base for armed bands of Southerners who launched forays into Kans. to stuff ballot boxes & terrorize Free-State settlers. When conflict culminated in Civil War, town suffered abrupt business decline. Here in 1863 after Confed. guerrilla leader Quantrill's band had sacked Lawrence, Union Gen. Thos. Ewing, Jr., published famous Order No. 11, requiring all residents of Jackson, Bates & Cass Counties & part of Vernon Cty. who could not prove Union sympathies & did not live within mile of certain towns to vacate their lands. Following yr. Gen. Sterling Price's Confed. forces were defeated in 3-day Battle of Westport, which virtually ended rebellion in Mo. Only with end of war did Kansas City resume growth. Completion of 1st RR. from St. Louis, Mo. Pacific, in 1866 opened new era. RRs. soon were bringing grain & cattle to market. In 1870 Kansas City acquired its 1st stockyards & soon afterward, its 1st packing houses. It began doing thriving business milling flour, killing hogs & distributing agric. implements. In 1877, exchange bldg. for grain trade was erected. By this time, both Kans. & Mo. RRs. had been bridged. In 1878, Kansas City acquired a great new union RR. depot. In 1900, William Jennings Bryan was nominated by the Democrats in Kansas City.

It was in 1880 that city's greatest benefactor took over the local newspaper, the "Kansas City Star": he was Wm. Rockhill Nelson. "Star" quickly became powerful journal, & it campaigned continuously for civic improvements. Kansas City began to lay out broad, tree-lined blvds. & handsome, landscaped residential areas. It finally acquired philharmonic orchestra, university of its own, & one of country's foremost art galleries. Since 1928, when new water supply system, one of country's most modern, was completed, it has launched vast program of improvements in its public bldgs., its Mun. Airport, its streets & hys. & pks.

PTS. OF INT.: Kansas City's Civic Center bounded by 11th, Oak, 12th & Locust Sts., is dominated by (1) its $5,000,000 steel & Indiana limestone **City Hall** 425′ skyscraper (1937), richly decorated, on whose 30th floor is observ. balcony, & (2) adj. $4,000,000 Indiana limestone **Kansas City Div. Jackson County Cth.** (3) 13th & Wyandotte Sts., $6,500,000 10-story-high **Mun. Auditorium** (1936) contains arena seating 13,500, music hall seating 2,600, little theater seating 600. Other pub. bldgs. incl. (4) **$3,300,000 Fed. Courts Bldg.,** 8th, Grand, 9th & McGehee Sts. & (5) $4,500,000 **Post Office Bldg.,** 315 W. Pershing Rd. (6) 2400 Main St., **Union Sta.** (1914), 3rd largest in country & one of 5 largest in world, has imposing marble-inlaid lobby. (7) Facing it across plaza to S. are 217′ shaft, walled court & 2 flanking bldgs. of $2,000,000 **Liberty Mem.** (1926) comm. Kansas City's World War I soldiers, housing mus. of war relics. (8) E. of mem. is **Washington Sq.,** with equestrian statue of Geo. Washington. (9) SE. is 131-a. **Penn. Valley Pk.** (swim.tennis), 26th St. & Broadway. (10) At edge of Kansas R. Bluffs, **Lookout Pt.,** W. 10th & Summit Sts., with its broad stairway approach & terrace, affords far-reaching view of NW. industrial dist., Kans. & Mo. Rs. & Mun. Airport. (11) N. & S. of it extends **W. Terrace Pk.** (12) Below, to W., are **Kansas City Livestock Exchange & Stockyards,** 16th & Genesee Sts., with as. of cattle pens. (13) 23rd St. is **Amer. Royal Bldg.** (1925), in which is held annual Amer. Royal Livestock Show. (14) **N. Terrace Pk.,** extending more than 3^m^ along Mo. R. bluffs near city's N. edge, overlooks riverside industrial dist., traversed by scenic Cliff Drive; within pk. are colonnaded **Concourse,** Benton Blvd. & St. John Ave., with its **Thos. Hart Benton Mem.,** & **Ind. Mound,** Gladstone & N. Belmont Blvd. (15) At pk.'s edge is **Kansas City Mus.** (est.1939.O.wks.except Mon.;Sun.aft.2-6), 3218 Gladstone Blvd., housed in Fr. Ren. mansion built by lumber magnate R. A. Long, containing natural history, anthropological, hist. & other exhibits.

SW. sec. contains many of the city's best known cultural institutions, among them (16) **Kansas City Conservatory of Music,** 3500 Walnut, & (17) **Kansas City Art Institute,** 4415 Warwick Blvd., sch. of fine & industrial arts. (18) Rockhill Rd. & 45th St., **Wm. Rockhill Nelson Gallery of Art & Mary Atkins Mus. of Fine Arts** (O.wks.except Mon.;Sun.aft.), nationally famous, occupies modern Class. building on site of Wm. R. Nelson's home. Mus. has fine colls. of Oriental art & of bronze, pottery & sculpture from Egypt, Greece & Rome. It celebrated 15th anniversary in 1948 by opening 2 new exhibition galleries for class. art & medieval art & series of period rooms. Among painters represented are Bellini, Carpaccio, Titian, Tintoretto, Veronese, El Greco, Rembrandt, Velasquez, Gainsborough, Reynolds, Copley, Goya & Van Gogh. (19) Rockhill Rd. & 51st St., **Univ. of Kansas City,** est. in 1933 as 2-yr. liberal arts institution with enrollment of 264, had grown 15 yrs. later into full-fledged univ. serving more than 5,500 students. It is housed in a group of new bldgs., mostly of native stone in modified Fr. Ren. design, occupying 80-a., landscaped Wm. Volker Campus. Lib. contains Rbt. M. Snyder Western Americana coll. Adj. to campus is **Linda Hall Lib.,** Cherry St. S. of 51st St., containing notable coll. in field of science. (20) One of largest mun. playgrounds in America, **Swope Pk.** (pic.boat.bath.golf.tennis.f.zoo), Swope Pky. & 63rd St., spreads over rugged, forested hills & ravines. Scattered over grounds are pic. shelter houses, formally landscaped gardens, playgrounds & athletic fields, music pavilion & lagoons. The columned **Swope Mem.** is mausoleum of real estate magnate, Thos. Hunt Swope, who donated pk. site. (21) At Prospect Ave. & 75th St. is **Fairyland Amusement Pk.** (pic.swim.amusement zone). (22) At Wornall Rd. & 51st St. is **Jacob L. Loose Mem. Pk.** (pic.tennis.rose garden).

Near S. limits are Kansas City's chief hist. landmarks. (23) On mon.-designated **Site of Battle of Westport,** Meyer Blvd. at 63rd St., was fought Oct. 22-24, 1864, biggest Civil War engagement W. of Miss. R., involving c.9,000 Confeds. under Gen. Sterling Price & c.20,000 Feds. under Gen. Alfred S. Pleasanton. After desperate fighting, Confeds. were forced to retreat. The Battle ended organized Confed. resistance W. of Miss. R. (24) 8145 State Line, **Alex. Majors H.** (1855), home of organizer of firm shipping freight west before the RR.'s arrival; the firm operated wagon trains to Santa Fe, stagecoach line to Denver & Pony Express to Cal. (25) 4000 Baltimore Ave., **Harris Home** (1854), moved here in 1933 from orig. site, was built by Col. John Harris, who ran Westport's 1st hotel.

# US 50—MISSOURI

## ST. LOUIS, MO. (W) to KANSAS CITY, MO. 280. US50

Via: Union, Jefferson City, Sedalia, & Warrensburg. RR. parallels entire route. Accoms.: Plentiful.

In its course across central Mo., US50 bet. St. Louis & St. capital, Jefferson City, skirts N. edge of Ozark hill country & bet. Jefferson City & Kansas City cuts across grain- & livestock-raising prairie stretch.

### Sec. 1: ST. LOUIS to JEFFERSON CITY. 130.

For pts. of int. & towns on or near US50 bet. St. Louis & J. with St.100, **43.5.**, see St. Louis III. At **46.5.** is western J. with US66 (see). **52.5. UNION,** seat of Franklin Cty. since 1826, is small market town & manufactures shoes. **84.5.** J. with St.19.

SIDE TRIP: Take latter (R) to **Hermann,** 18.5m, overlooking Mo. R., German-Amer. settlement with characteristic appearance common to carefully laid-out German towns. Its 1st residents, sent out by German Settlement Soc. of Philadelphia, came here 1837. They planted vineyards, undertook wine-making & developed R. commerce, organized dramatic, choral & athletic societies & band. Among Hermann's chief landmarks are **Eagle Hall** (c.1852), E. 2nd St. near Market St.; **Concert Hall** (1878), Front St. near Schiller St.; **Strehly H.** (older part c.1845, addition came several years later), West 2nd St.; **Gentner H.** (c.1850), Market St. near Front St. W. edge of town, **Stone Hill Farms,** turreted, thick-walled former winery, is now devoted to growing mushrooms.

**118.5.** US50 bridges **OSAGE R. 130. JEFFERSON CITY,** capital of Mo., borders Mo. R., spreading over steep bluffs. Although St. gov. is its chief concern, it is also central Mo.'s largest city, with bustling bus. dist. & riverside fringe of factories & RR. shops. When site was chosen for St. capital in 1821, it was little more than R. landing, which its handful of settlers had named for Thos. Jefferson. 2-story brick Stateh. was completed in 1826, by which time community had acquired gristmill, distillery, tanneries. St. penitentiary was completed in 1836 & new & more lavish St. Capitol in 1842, replacing 1st, destroyed by fire. During 1840's pop. was swelled by German immigrants. When pro-Secessionist Gov. Claiborne F. Jackson defied decision to remain in Union of St. convention called in 1861 & led the militia away to Boonville to join Confed. cause, capital was occupied by Fed. troops. Industrial progress was resumed in 1880's, when printing & shoe manufacture became important.

PTS. OF INT.: (1) Rising from R. bluffs, N. High St. bet. Washington St. & Broadway, **St. Capitol** (1917) is Ital. Ren. marble structure some four stories high with retreating 5th story, adorned with Corinthian porticoes, from top of whose lantern-surmounted dome, 262′ above ground, rises bronze statue of Ceres. Flanking approach to main entrance are 2 fountains by Rbt. I. Aitken, & within, at base of grand stairway, same sculptor's symbolic figures of Mo. & Miss. Rs. Jas. E. Frazer's bronze Thos. Jefferson dominates stairway. Marble-finished rotunda, 68′ high, has murals at each floor. On main fl., at east end, is **Soldiers' & Sailors' Mus.,** containing battle flags & Govs.' portraits, & at W. end, **Mo. Resources Mus.** containing Ind. relics & agric., commercial & mineral exhibits. On 3rd fl., which has James E. Frazer's bronze statues of Meriwether Lewis & Wm. Clark, are chambers & lounges of Senate (R) & House of Representatives (L); lounge of latter contains murals by Thos. Hart Benton which provoked sharp controversy during mid-1930's. 5th fl. affords exit to gallery & dome. (2) Capitol & Madison Sts., **Executive Mansion** (1871.Fr.Ital.) is a handsome structure with portico & porte-cochère. Other official bldgs. incl. (3) **Supreme Ct. Bldg.** (1907), High & Washington Sts.; (4) **New St. Office Bldg.** (1938), Broadway & High St., & (5) **Mo. St. Penitentiary,** Lafayette & State Sts. (6) Lafayette, Chestnut, Dunklin & Franklin Sts., **Lincoln Univ.,** St.-supported institution for Negroes with landscaped 20-a. campus at city's highest elevation, was founded on initiative of soldiers of 62nd U.S. Colored Infantry, & opened in 1866.

SIDE TRIP: Take US54 (L) from Jefferson City into N. Ozark foothills. **Eldon,** 31.5m, laid out in 1882, depends on farm trade, RR. shops & sm. industries. US54 cont. to half-mile-long, 148′ high **Bagnell Dam,** crossed by hy. at 43.5m, impounding 673-billion-gallon, 129m-long **L. of the Ozarks.** Dam, built 1929-31, has 520′ spillway controlled by 12 flood-gates; it houses Mo.'s biggest hydroelectric plant. L.'s 1,300m shoreline is lined with resorts, offering boat., f., & other recr. facils. **Camdenton,** 64m, seat of Camden Cty., was founded in 1929. At 67m is J. with unimproved Rd.

Turn (L) on this 3.5m to 3,500-a. **Hahatonka Estate** of Kansas City's wealthy R. M. Snyder, surrounding his hill-top Eng. Ren. house, **Hahatonka Castle** (1905-22.fee. lodging). On grounds are natural bridge, one of Mo.'s larger springs, village, 5-story tower & carriage house.

At 93m is J. with US65 (see).

### Sec. 2: JEFFERSON CITY to KANSAS CITY. 150.

US50 heads into far-reaching prairie farming sec. **23. CALIFORNIA** dates from 1854. **Moniteau County Cth.** (1867.Gr.Rev.) is one of Mo.'s more notable early public bldgs. **62. SEDALIA** began as RR. center, 1857, & depends today on RR. repair shops. Its orig. promoter, Geo. R. Smith, one of Pac. RR.'s board of directors, coined name from his daughter Sarah's nickname, "Sed." Modern industries incl. shoe manufacture & food processing. **Mo. St. Fairgrounds,** with more than 50 permanent structures scattered over 300 as., is site annually (Aug.) of exhibit of Mo.'s products, harness races & other events. Sedalia is at J. with US65 (see). At **82.5.** is entrance to wooded **MONTSERRAT RECR. AREA** (3,441 as.pic.). **91. WARRENSBURG** was named for Kentucky Rev. War veteran Martin Warren, who sett. it, 1833. Its chief growth followed advent of Pac. RR. in 1864. **Central Mo. St. Teachers College** (est.1871), South & Taylor Sts., is housed in group of Eng. Ren. style handsome bldgs. Bronze plaque at entrance to **Old Cth.,** Main St. S. of W. Gay St., recalls that here on Sept. 23, 1870, George Graham Vest declaimed his "Eulogy of the Dog." **129.5. LEES SUMMIT,** platted in 1865 on one of highest pts. bet. St. Louis & Kansas City. First settlement was named Lees by railroad men when they set up station, in remembrance of Dr. Pleasant Lea, who fell afoul of unknown assassins here during Civil War. **132. UNITY FARM,** of Unity Sch. of Christianity, contains in addition to gardens, vineyards & orchards, a lofty bldg. in form of a tower & other bldgs. of Ital. Ren. type, swim. pool & L. amphitheater, & oil & gas wells. **150. KANSAS CITY** (see US40) is at Js. with US40 (see) & US50 (see).

## US 60—MISSOURI

**MO.-ILL. LINE** (3.5m from Cairo, Ill.) **(W) to MO.-OKLA. LINE** (41m from Vinita, Okla.). **367. US60**

Via: Charleston, Sikeston, Poplar Bluff, Springfield & Neosho. RRs. parallel entire route. Accoms.: Chiefly in larger towns, limited elsewhere.

US60 cuts across fertile Miss. R. alluvial plain, Mo.'s cotton belt, & then through forested, hilly Ozark country, thinly settled. In SW. sec. it traverses fruit-growing & dairying reg. around Springfield & Tri-State lead & zinc mining area.

### Sec. 1: MO.-ILL. LINE to SPRINGFIELD. 277.

**0.** US60 crosses Miss. R., which is **MO.-ILL. LINE,** on $3,100,000 bridge (toll). Route follows (SW) top of levee bordering **NEW MADRID FLOODWAY,** an overflow basin. **6.5. WYATT.** J. with Cty.E.

SIDE TRIP: Take latter (L) to J. with Cty.U, 11m, & turn (L) here to **Belmont Battlefield,** 17m, designated by mon. where on Nov. 6, 1861, 4,000 Feds. led by Gen. U. S. Grant, shipped downstream from Cairo, debarked to attack Confed. encampment.

**12.5. CHARLESTON,** laid out 1837, developed as trading & shipping pt. for cotton planters, which it remains, & more recently has become shoe mfg. center.

**26.5. SIKESTON** is prosperous cotton-reg. community, dating back to 1860, with cotton gins & compresses, RR. loading platforms & grain elevators, and ornate post-Civil War mansions of plantation owners. Sikeston is at J. with US61 (see). **50.5. DEXTER,** platted in 1873 on summit of Crowley's Ridge, is at inters. of 2 RRs.; among its products are flour & cotton, poultry & shirts. **77.5. POPLAR BLUFF,**

so named for poplar-shaded height overlooking Black R., on which it was laid out in 1850, is RR. division point with timberwork plants, shoe factories, produce houses & other industrial establishments. It was important lumber center until reg.'s timber supply fell off; discovery of near-by clay deposits contributed to later growth. Today it is chief trading center for 20 cities in SE. Mo. & NE. Ark. Poplar Bluff is at J. with US67 (see), with which US60 unites for 0.5$^{m}$.

US60 now enters forested, rolling Ozarks, where in clearings appear rude cabins & frame Chs. of descendants of 1st settlers, mostly of Scotch-Irish extraction from Kentucky. **120.5.** J. with St.21 (See US61). **128.5. VAN BUREN,** seat since 1859 of Carter Cty., is recr. center on Current R., at J. with St.103 leading (L) 3.5$^{m}$ to **Big Spring St. Pk.** (cabins.bathh.lodge.camp.pic.boat.riding), 4,582-a. forest tract surrounding what is said to be 1 of 2 largest springs in U.S. (more than 250,000,000 gallons daily). **149.5. WINONA,** at J. with St.19 (see US66), **BIRCH TREE, 158.5.** & **MOUNTAIN VIEW, 169.5.,** are mt. settlements, chiefly dependent on lumbering. **187.5. WILLOW SPRINGS** has, in addition to sawmills, produce houses handling eggs, poultry & dairy products. **188.** Hqs. for Rangers of **MARK TWAIN NAT. FOR., 210.5.** US60 now cuts through fruit orchards & pastures into one of most productive dairying regs. in U.S. It also grows more fruit, berries & tomatoes than any other part of Mo. **268.** J. with US65 (see) with which US60 unites to Springfield. **270. SEQUIOTA FISH HATCHERY** propagates bass & bluegill in its rearing ponds & spring-fed L., back of which is lighted cave through which boat trips may be made (sm.fee). **273. SPRINGFIELD NAT. CEMETERY** (est.1869) holds graves of Civil War dead, both Fed. & Confed., buried in separate plots with conn. gateway; to open gateway, bill had to be introduced in Congress.

### 277. SPRINGFIELD

Through RR. & bus conns. Info.: C. of C., Walnut St. & Jefferson Ave. Swim. at Grant Beach, Fassnight Pk., Silver Springs Pk., Doling L. Annual Rodeo, May; Ozark Empire Fair, Sept.

SW. Mo.'s chief city, one of state's largest, Springfield spreads over rolling plateau at N. gateway to Ozark Highlands. Its prosperity is based on its RR. shops, largest W. of Miss. R., & on industries processing dairy & poultry products, livestock & grain & lumber of vic.; it has U.S.' largest milk plant & plants mfg. harness, overalls, wagons & trlers. It has mun. owned public utilities & nationally known public sch. system.

All but 1 of 1st permanent white settlers on site, who began arriving in 1821, abandoned area when Delaware & Kickapoo Inds. were moved by Fed. Gov. to SW. Mo.; & only when Inds. were moved on farther W. did more white settlers come. Around claim staked near spring by John Polk Campbell grew settlement; & in 1833, Campbell's log cabin became cty. seat. After 1850, when livestock raising in vic. began to develop, Springfield, because of location at crossing of chief Rds. through SW. Mo., rose to commercial dominance. It became focal pt. in Civil War; Confed. forces took & stayed until expelled in 1862 by Fed. troops. Advent of Atlantic & Pac. (now Frisco) RR. in 1870 led to est. by land speculators of rival community, N. Springfield; in 1881, however, another RR. was run through older community, & in 1887 two towns were consolidated into one.

PTS. OF INT.: (1) City's oldest bldg., **John Polk Campbell H.** (1851), 975 Mary Ave., was built by its founder. (2) E. Benton Ave. bet. Calhoun & Central Sts., **Drury College** (est.1873), is coed. institution named for early benefactor, Sam. Fletcher Drury. (3) National Ave. bet. Grand & Madison Sts., **SW. Mo. St. Teachers' College** (est.1905) is 4-year coed. institution. (4) **Doling Pk.** (boat.bath. playgrounds) contains 1,000'-long limestone cavern & spring-fed L. (5) N. Grant St. & Norton Rd., **Central Bible Institute** is training sch. maintained by Assemblies of God. (6) In City Hall, is Springfield Art Mus. (O); coll. painting, prints & hist. matter. Springfield is at J. with US66 (see).

### Sec. 2: SPRINGFIELD to MO.-OKLA. LINE. 90.

**2. U.S. DEPT. OF JUSTICE MEDICAL CENTER** (1933), housed in U-shaped group of brick bldgs., is prison hospital for criminally insane. **13. REPUBLIC,** fruit- & vegetable-shipping pt., is at J. with local Rd.

SIDE TRIP: Take latter (L) 4$^{m}$ J. with Rd.; (L) on this & (L) again at 4.5$^{m}$ to dirt Rd. (private), 5$^{m}$, & (L) on this to **Wilson's Creek Battlefield,** 5.5$^{m}$, where on Aug. 10, 1861 was fought one of Mo.'s chief Civil War engagements, with nearly 2,500 casualties, after which Confeds. then took Springfield.

**33. AURORA,** laid out in 1872, experienced lead & zinc mining boom in 1880's & afterward turned to trade with farmers & sm. mfg. enterprises. **47.5. MONETT,** dating from advent of RR. in 1881, is RR. division pt. & chief shipping center in widespread strawberry-growing, dairying & poultry-raising, & diversified farming reg.

SIDE TRIP: Take St.37 (L) from Monett to **Cassville,** 18.5m, fishermen's outfitting pt. & farmers' shipping center. Here on Nov. 7, 1861, fleeing pro-Confed. members of Mo.'s general assembly signed ordinances of secession from U.S. Cassville & Exeter RR., 4.8m long, is shortest broad-gauge line in country; it freights farm produce. Route turns (L) from Cassville on St.112 to **Roaring R. St. Pk.** (hotel.lodge.cabins.camp.bridle trls. swim.boat.f. pic.), 7m, wooded 2,946-a. area in mt.-rimmed valley, whose chief feature is spring-fed Roaring R. (good trout f.).

**66. GRANBY,** SW. Mo.'s 1st lead & zinc mining center, now depends chiefly on farm trade. **75. NEOSHO,** christened with Osage Ind. name for clear water in reference to spring around which it grew, was laid out in 1839. It had become lead mining center by 1850. After Civil War, Neosho prospered as flour milling & dairy produce processing center. In vic., 2.5m away (L), is **Camp Crowder,** important U.S. Army training base during World War II. Neosho is at J. with US71 (see).**89.5. SENECA,** laid out in 1868, is dominated by its **Barnsdall Tripoli Grinding Mill Plant,** which processes U.S.' only important tripoli deposits. Tripoli is used as filter stone for water system & also in rubber manufacture. **90. MO.-OKLA. LINE.**

# US 66—MISSOURI

**ST. LOUIS, MO. (SW) to MO.-KANS. LINE** (1m from Galena, Kans.). **314. US66**

Via: Rolla, Lebanon, Springfield, Carthage & Joplin. RR. parallels route throughout. Usual accoms.; hotels in larger towns.

US66, cutting diagonally across S. Mo., traverses rolling, mostly wooded Ozark hill country. In SW. sec. it crosses important lead & zinc mining area.

## Sec. 1: ST. LOUIS to SPRINGFIELD. 233.

For pts. of int. & towns on or near US66 & J. with US50, at **38.,** see St. Louis Trip III. US66 unites with US50 for 6.5m & SW. of **ST. CLAIR, 53.,** sett. in 1843, US66 heads into Ozark foothills. **64., STANTON.** J. with local Rd., leading (L) 4m to **Meramec Caverns** (fee.guides) above Meramec R., 1st of whose chambers contains parking space for automobiles & dance fl. Among natural formations within are Natural Stage, Wine Table & Echo Room. **69.5.** J. with St.114, leading (L) 1m to 7,153-a. wooded **Meramec St. Pk.** (hotel.cabins.trlr. camp.pic.horses), Mo.'s largest St. pk., stretching along Meramec R. It has many springs & more than 20 large caves, nature mus. & St. nursery. **70. SULLIVAN,** rural center & shoe mfg. town, dates from 1856. **81.** J. with Cty.H.

SIDE TRIP: Take latter (L) 2.5m to **Cathedral Cave** (fee.guides), containing interesting formations. At 7m are **Mo. Caverns** (fee.guides), winding 200' to the underground Lost R. whose rock formations are colored in variety of hues. Entrance to **Onondaga Cave** (fee. guides), 7.5m, is by boat along Lost R.

**89. CUBA,** farmers' shipping pt., is at J. with St.19.

SIDE TRIP: Take latter (L) into rough, remote Ozark mt. area. **Steelville,** 9m, is trading center for farmers & outfitting pt. for fishermen, sett. 1833. **Ind. Trl. St. Pk.** (no accoms.), 31m, is game & for. preserve of more than 13,000 as. 44.5m **Salem,** est. in 1851, prospered following opening of iron deposits in vic. soon after Civil War. At 50m is J. with Cty.K.

Turn (R) on this to J. with Cty.E, 5m, & (R) on this to J. with St.119, 11m; (L) on St.119 to 758-a. wooded, mountainous **Montauk St. Pk.** (hotel.cottages.camp.pic.), 16m, surrounding spring with 40,000,000-gallon daily capacity.

St.19 bridges at 75.5m **Current R.,** fast-running stream (good f.). Short distance beyond is **Round Spring St. Pk.** (camp.pic.f.), 75-a. tract surrounding spring with tremendous daily flow. The spring rises in natural rock bowl & overflows beneath natural rock bridge. 88.5m, **Eminence** is starting place for fishermen's expeditions down Current R., at J. with St.106.

Take latter (R) to 407-a. **Alley Spring St. Pk.** (cabins. camp.pic.f.swim.),

St.19 cont. to J. with US60 (see) at 99.5m.

**102. ST. JAMES,** founded in 1859, ships farm products & lumber.

SIDE TRIP: Take latter (L) to **Stark Bros. Nursery,** 9.5m, one of nation's largest nurseries & probably its oldest, est. by Jas. Stark in 1816. 11.5m **Louisiana,** once an important shipping center, but now a market town, dates back to 1818.

**93. BOWLING GREEN,** laid out in 1826, is seat of Pike Cty.; in Gold Rush, Cal. term "Piker," orig. applying to Missourians from this cty., came finally to have present broader application. Near cth. is bronze **Champ Clark Statue** (by Fred. C. Hibbard), comm. Jas. Beauchamp Clark, long member from this dist. of H. of Representatives & for 8 yrs. speaker, whose white frame H., **Honey Shuck,** College St., remains. Opposite latter is **John Walter Bayse H.** (oldest part 1829).

**125.** J. with St.47, leading (L) 5.5m to 5,802-a. timbered **Cuivre R. St. Pk.** (pic.swim. boat.). **140.** J. with US40 (see), with which US61 unites for 29m. For towns & pts. of int. on or near US61 bet. this J. & **KIRKWOOD, 173.,** see St. Louis Trip **I.**

## Sec. 2: KIRKWOOD to MO.-ARK. LINE. 239.

For towns & pts. of int. on or near US61 bet. Kirkwood & **CRYSTAL CITY, 30.,** incl. latter, see St. Louis Trip IV.

SIDE TRIP: Take St.21A (R) from Crystal City short distance to **Festus,** laid out, 1878, providing trading facils. & residential areas which its factory-dominated neighbor, Crystal City, lacks. 12.5m **De Soto,** whose many artesian wells have inspired sobriquet "Fountain City," was est. in 1857 with advent of RR. & became center of lead reg. 22.5m is 1,101-a. hardwood-timbered **Washington St. Pk.** (cabins.lodge.pic.nature mus.), one of whose chief attractions is group of Ind. petroglyphs carved on stone hillside. St.21 cont. through area where Fr. settlers began to work lead deposits before 1750. At **Old Mines,** 31.5m, where lead and barite ore have been scraped from shallow pits since Fr. families sett. here in 1802, is **St. Joachim's Ch.** (c.1830). **St. Joachim's Cemetery** has hand-wrought iron crosses and unusual stone monuments. 38.5m **Potosi** began as Mine à Breton, so named for Francois Azor, nicknamed Breton, who discovered lead on site in 1773. Moses Austin acquired land here in 1797 & built more efficient furnaces, new in the region, along with other installations & a large mansion & a general country store, etc. Town was laid out in 1813 & named for Mexican silver-mining center, San Luis Potosi. Today most of Mo.'s output of barite, comprising from third to half of nat. production, comes from this vic. In Potosi's Presb. cemetery is **Grave of Moses Austin,** Mo.'s 1st industrialist & 1st promoter of Amer. colonization of Texas. St.21 cont. to J. with Cty.W, 63.5m.

(L) on this 4m is ghost mining town of **Iron Mt.,** near hump-shaped mt. orig. believed to be solid iron, where ore deposits were worked from 1836 until 1880's.

St.21 cont. to **Pilot Knob,** 66m, another ghost mining town at foot of another mountain believed to be solid iron. At 66.5m appear earthworks of ruined **Ft. Davidson,** built by Union forces to protect Iron Mt. & Pilot mines. 68.5m **Ironton,** founded in 1857, was U.S. Grant's hqs. in Aug. 1861. **Iron County Cth.** (1858.Class.Rev.) was occupied by Feds. retreating from Ft. Davidson. St.21 cont. into rugged Ozark mt. country. 77.5m **Hogan,** at J. with unpaved Rd.

(R) on this 6m to footpath leading to summit of **Tam Sauk Mt.** (1,772′), 12m, Mo.'s highest peak, which halfway up skirts 200′ **Mina Sauk Falls.**

At 133.5m is J. with US60 (see).

**31.** J. with St.25.

SIDE TRIP: Take latter (L). At 4.5m is J. with Rd.

(L) on this 0.5m to large, imposing **Selma Hall** (1854.N.O.), $125,000 mansion in Ital. Ren. style, Mo.'s finest of its period, built for steamboat operator Ferdinand Kennett.

S. of village of **Bloomsdale,** 20m, dominated by spire of Romanes. **St. Philomena Ch.,** lies hilly, pastoral reg. 1st sett. by Creole Fr. **Ste. Genevieve,** 31m, is Mo.'s oldest extant settlement. Today rural trading & marble-shipping & lime-producing center, it has outer ring of modern-looking avenues & bldgs.; but old town at its heart remains picturesquely Fr. First settlers, arriving probably in 1740's, to take up farming, fur trading, salt making & lead mining, were forced by floods to move c.1785 to higher land. As R. port, place early in 19th cent. rivalled St. Louis, but lost out with decline of fur, salt & lead industries.

PTS. OF INT.: (1) In center of Du Bourg Pl. is **Hist. Mus.** housing hist. & archaeological relics. (2) Du Bourg Pl. is dominated by **Ste. Genevieve Ch.** (1880.late 19th cent. Goth.), 3rd religious edifice on site; earliest surviving Missouri church. Also on Du Bourg Pl. are: (3) **Sisters of St. Joseph Convent** (1867) & (4) **John Price H.** (1800-04). (5) 4th & Merchant Sts., **Jacques Dubreuil Guibourd H.** (c.1800) is typical of Creole residences of its period: story-&-a-half structure of weatherboarded trimmed logs, the whole surmounted by a roof sloping to "galéries" at front & rear. Others of similar design are: (6) 20 S. Main St., **Vital de St. Gemme de Beauvais H.** (before 1791); (7) Main & Market Sts., **Jean Baptiste Vallé H.** (c.1785); (8) 123 S. Main St., **Bolduc H.** (c.late 18th cent.); (9) Old St. Mary's Rd., **Misplait H.** (before 1804); & (10) 244 Old St. Mary's Rd., **Green Tree Tavern** (1791). (11) Merchant St. W. of 2nd St., **Senator Lewis F. Linn H.** (1827) & (12) Merchant & 2nd Sts.,

**Dr. Benjamin Shaw H.** (probably before 1820) are frame dwellings showing Amer. influence in design. (13) Main St. bet. Market & Gabouri Sts., **Meilleur H.** (c.1815), is also frame dwelling of later type than Creole "maisons de poteaux sur sol." Of stone are (14) 2nd & Merchant Sts., **Philipson-Valle H.** (1811-14) & (15) 5th & Washington Sts., **Louisiana Academy Bldg.** (c.1810); latter housed sch. for poor white & Ind. children at which, after 1818, 1st Christian Brothers in U.S. were teachers. (16) 5th & 6th Sts., **Old Cemetery** contains many pioneer graves.

At 38.5m is J. with Ozora Rd. leading (R) short distance to **Salt Springs,** where Fr. residents of Kaskaskia were wont to come to make salt, earl 18th cent. Here developed 1st white settlement in Mo. 53.5m is J. with St.51.

Take latter (R) to **Perryville,** 0.5m, seat since 1822 of Perry Cty. At 1m is J. with Cty. T, leading (R) 0.5m to Cath. seminary of **St. Mary's-of-the-Barrens** (est.1818), on 640-a. wooded tract, with **Lib.** containing ancient mss. & illuminated books & log cabin known as **Bishop Rosati's Sacristy** (1818). **Ch. of the Assumption** (1827-37.alteration made 1913) reproduces on scale one-third that of orig. Ch. of Monte Citorio in Rome.

At 65m is J. of St.25 with Cty.A.

Take latter (L) to **Altenburg,** 9m, picturesque village of attractive houses & gardens, sett. as communal religious colony by Luth. emigrants from Saxony in 1839. Log **First Home of Concordia Seminary** (1839), which housed 1st educational institution conducted by Evangelical Luth. Synod of Mo., is now mus. of hist. relics.

St.25 cont. to J. with US61 at Jackson (see below), 85m.

S. of **BIG RIVER, 53.5.,** US61 cuts through world's biggest lead producing area.

**56.5.** J. with Cty.J, leading (R) 1m to **Bonne Terre** (Fr. "good earth"), oldest of reg.'s lead-mining towns, now up-to-date community surrounded by mine shafts. **St. Joseph Lead Co. Office Bldg.,** Main & Allen Sts., is hqs. of dist.'s biggest producer, which began operations in 1864. **62.** J. with St.32, leading (R) 3.5m to **Flat River,** rowdy lead miners' boom town in 1890's but now spruce, modern-looking community, dubbed "lead capital of the world." **69. FARMINGTON,** seat since 1821 of St. Francois Cty., is trading center of an area 1st known as Murphy Settlement for leading family, one of whom is said to have built **Tom V. Brown H.** (O.appl. c.1800), Murphy Ave. & Washington St. In Masonic Cemetery, Henry St., stone shaft marks former location of log church, **Site of First Sunday School** in the state, taught by Sarah Barton Murphy. W. Columbia & S. Franklin Sts., Farmington's **Community Mus.,** in Long Mem. Hall, has coll. of pioneer relics. Declining village of **Mine La Motte, 83.5.** was site of 1st lead diggings in Mo., opened by La.'s Gov. Gen., Sieur Antoine de la Mothe Cadillac, in 1715. At **86.5.** US67 (see), united with US61 from outskirts of St. Louis to this pt., diverges (S). **127. JACKSON,** platted in 1814, is rural trading & milling center. **128.** J. with McKendree Chapel Rd., leading (L) to weatherboarded log **McKendree Chapel** (c.1819.rest.), 2.5m, Mo.'s oldest existing Prot. church bldg.

**135.** J. with US61Alt., leading (L) to **CAPE GIRARDEAU,** 2m, spilling over bluffs by Miss. R. When Don Louis Lorimier came here c.1793 to est. Ind. trading post, place was already known by present name for Fr. army ensign, Girardot, who had settled early in 18th cent. on Cape Rock, jutting into R. near today's N. city limits. Lorimier encouraged Amer. immigration by offering free land; but after La. Purchase, rejection of his title to tract by U.S. Land Commission, which invalidated titles of other landholders, stopped growth of community. In 1836 his title was finally recognized & Cape Girardeau soon became thriving R. port, with lumber & grist mills & pork-packing houses. Civil War ended R. traffic, however, & Cape Girardeau's development was again delayed until RR. conns. were est. In recent yrs. revival of R. traffic, reclamation of new farm lands to S. & building of bridge across Miss. (1928) have spurred development.

PTS. OF INT.: (1) William & Spanish Sts., boulder inset with bronze plates designates **Site of Louis Lorimier's Red H.** (2) Fountain St. & Washington Ave., in Lorimier Cemetery is **Grave of Louis Lorimier.** (3) Spanish & Themis Sts., **Court of Common Pleas Bldg.** (Greek Rev. oldest part 1854, N. & S. wings 1889). (4) Main & Williams St., **St. Vincent's Ch.** (1851.Goth.Rev.). (5) 201 Morgan Oak St., **St. Vincent's College** (oldest part 1843.adds.1863 & 1871), founded as St. Vincent's Academy in 1838. Of Greek Rev. design are (6) **Wathen-Ranney H.** (1839), 501 N. Main St., & (7) 444 Washington Ave., **Sherwood-Minton H.** (1846). (8) Earthworks, moat & parade ground of **Ft. D,** Union fortified pt. during Civil War, are preserved in public park, Locust & Fort Sts. (9) Cape Rock Rd., **Cape Rock Pk.,** overlooking R., contains marker comm. Ensign Girardot's trading post. (10) Normal

Ave. bet. Pacific St. & Henderson St., **SE. Mo. St. Teachers College;** Adm. Bldg. contains Houck Coll. of statuary reprods. & Lib. Bldg. contains mus. with Ind. relics, fossils, firearms & other exhibits.

US61 now descends to low-lying Mississippi plain, where begins great cotton belt extending S. into Delta reg. **167.5. SIKESTON** (see US60) is at J. with US60 (see). **187.** J. with New Madrid Rd., leading (L) 1m to **New Madrid,** farmers' trading & shipping center, near which fur-trading post was est. c.1783 by Francois & Joseph Le Sieur. In 1789, Sp. authorities of La. territory granted Col. George Morgan 15,000,000 as. of land for Amer. colony here, & Morgan laid out straggling site by R. Violent earthquakes, beginning Dec. 16, 1811 & continuing 2 yrs., devastated site, & in later yrs. shifting of R.'s course required several removals of town to new site. Fortified by Confeds. in Civil War, New Madrid was besieged & captured by Gen. Albert A. Pope's Union forces in Mar. 1862.

US61 runs (S) along Miss. R. through rich, productive cotton acres of Mo.'s SE. sec., passing through such typical cotton towns as **PORTAGEVILLE, 203.,** & **HAYTI, 217.**

SIDE TRIPS: (A) Take St.84 (L) from Hayti to **Caruthersville,** 6m, levee-guarded town on Miss., which began as La Petite Prairie, fur trading post est. in 1794 by Francois Le Sieur. By 1808 there was settlement of 2 doz. log cabins. John Hardeman Walker in 1857 platted town on his plantation. It grew slowly until it became RR. terminus & in 1898, cty. seat.

(B) Take St.84 (R) to **Kennett,** 17m, on site of Ind. village ruled by Chief Chillecautaux, laid out in 1846. Cotton is king here, & Kennett is dominated by cotton gins, compress & oil mills; but soybeans have become important in recent yrs., & town is SE. Mo.'s soybean capital.

US61 cont. through several sm. cotton-growing communities to **MO.-ARK. LINE, 239.**

# US 67—MISSOURI

**ST. LOUIS, MO. (S) to MO.-ARK. LINE** (7m from Corning, Ark.). **177.5. US67**

Via: Fredericktown & Poplar Bluff. RRs. parallel route in parts. Accoms: Hotels in larger towns, cabins & camp. facils.

US67 traverses SE. Mo. skirting E. fringe of Ozarks.

**0. ST. LOUIS** (see). Bet. St. Louis & J. at **86.5.,** US67 is united with US61 (see).

**87.5. FREDERICKTOWN,** shipping center for farm, timber & mineral products, which began as Creole settlement in 1800. **118.** J. with St.34.

SIDE TRIP: Take latter (R) to J. with St.143, 4m; turn (R) on this to **Sam A. Baker St. Pk.** (7,138 as.dining lodge.cabins,boat.riding), 8m, rough, heavily timbered wilderness area through which flow Big Cr. & St. Francis R.

US67 cont., crossing at **124.5. L. WAPPAPPELLO,** through Ozark mt. country. **155.5. POPLAR BLUFF** (see US60) at J. with US60 (see). **177.5. MO.-ARK. LINE.**

# US 65—MISSOURI

**MO.-IOWA LINE** (75m from Des Moines, Iowa) **(S) to MO.-ARK. LINE** (24m from Harrison, Ark.). **339. US65**

Via: Trenton, Chillicothe, Carrollton, Marshall, Sedalia, Warsaw & Springfield. RRs. parallel most of route. Accoms.: Ample.

In NW. Mo. US65 cuts across vast prairie, intensively farmed. In S. sec. it winds into rugged Ozarks, emerges on fertile plateau surrounding Springfield, then winds again through Ozarks.

## Sec. 1: MO.-IOWA LINE to SEDALIA. 155.

**0. MO.-IOWA LINE. 14. PRINCETON,** dating from 1846, was the birthplace of Martha Canary ("Calamity Jane"), U.S. Army scout in Black Hills campaign against Sioux. **39. TRENTON,** sett. c.1834, serves large trade territory & supports sm. local industries & RR. yards.

SIDE TRIP: Take St.6 (R) from Trenton to 640-a. wooded **Crowder St. Pk.** (camp.pic.), 4.5m. At 25m is J. with St.13.

Turn (R) on this to Rd., 3m; (L) on this, across RR. tracks, & (R) to second local Rd., 5m; (L) on this, then (R) at 5.5m to cottage; (R) 200 yds. is **Site of Adam-ondi-Ahman** on

Grand R., Mormon settlement founded in 1838 by Prophet Joseph Smith but evacuated same yr. because of Gentile Missourians' opposition.

St.6 cont. to **Gallatin,** 27m, laid out, 1836, on S. side of Grand R., where antagonism bet. Mormons & Gentiles culminated in "Mormon War," 1838. At 35.5m is J. with US69, on which route cont. (L). **Cameron,** 48.5m, laid out, 1855, is farmers' trading & garment-mfg. center. At 52m is J. with St.121, leading (L) 1.5m to 160-a. wooded **Wallace St. Pk.** (cabins.camp.pic.). At 74m is J. with local Rd. leading (R) to narrow Rd., 1.5m, (L) on which is **Waltus Lockett Watkins Mill** (fee.1861), whose 1st fl. contains blacksmith shop & flour mill & its upper fls. woolen mill. Back of it is **Watkins H.** (1850.Class.Rev.); & to E. are **Franklin Sch. Bldg.** (1852) & **Mt. Vernon Missionary Baptist Ch.** (1870-71). At 74.5m is J. with St.92.

Turn (R) on this to J. with local Rd., 6m, (R) here to 2nd local Rd. at schoolh., 7.5m, & (R) here to **Rbt. James Farm** (oldest section 1822, the rest 1893.fee), 8m, birthpl. in 1847 of famous outlaw Jesse James & boyhood home of him & his brother, Frank.

Ringed with wooded hills, **Excelsior Springs,** 76.5m is Mo.'s chief spa, dating from discovery here in valley of Fishing R. in 1880 of Old Siloam Spring. Today there are several bathhs. Modern is the **Hall of Waters** (1938), Siloam Pk., houses baths & hydrotherapy & massage facils., swim. pool, Hall of Springs, & bottling plant. At 88.5m is J. with Liberty Cutoff.

Turn (L) on this to **Liberty,** 2.5m, laid out, 1822, which early became seat of merchant & plantation-owner aristocracy. Among its landmarks are: 307 N. Walter St., **Major Alvan Lightburne H.** (Greek Rev.); 124 N. Gallatin St., **Madison Miller H.** (1840.Greek Rev.); Gallatin & Mississippi Sts., **Bishop H.** (before 1840). Overlooking town from "Old Hill" is **Wm. Jewell College** (chartered 1849), coed. institution est. by Mo. Baptist Gen. Assoc. with financial aid from Dr. Wm. Jewell. **Wm. Jewell Hall** (1850-58) is one of Mo.'s best examples of Greek Rev. architecture. **Carnegie Lib.** houses important special colls.

At 101m is J. with US71 (see). At 106.5m US69 crosses Mo.-Kans. Line on Fairfax Bridge across Mo. R. to Kansas City, Kans.

**62.5. CHILLICOTHE,** which trades with farmers, processes agric. products & manufactures farm machinery & other articles, was laid out, 1837. Here during early 1870's Earl Sayer Sloan, then running livery business, invented famous "Sloan's Liniment." **Chillicothe Business College** (est.1890), 1220 Monroe St., has been said to be largest of its type in country. **95. CARROLLTON,** stands upon the heights above the Missouri River lowlands, was 1st sett. in 1819 & platted in 1834. Bronze **Gen. Jas. Shields Mon.,** near cth., comm. soldier & U.S. Senator who was Abraham Lincoln's friend; buried in St. Mary's Cemetery. Crossing wide lowlands, US65 bridges muddy Mo. R. to onetime R. port of **WAVERLY, 105.** & passes through orchard country along R. bluffs to J. with St.41, **124.5.**

SIDE TRIP: Take latter (L) to J. with Cty. 122, 7.5m & turn (L) on this to rugged, densely wooded 546-a. **Van Meter St. Pk.** (camp.), 12m, on Mo. R. bluffs, containing 2,700′ long earthworks of prehist. Ind. origin known as **Old Ft.**

**125. MARSHALL,** sett. in 1839, is supported by farm trade, processing of agric. products & shoe manufacture, & income from several charitable & educational institutions. Among latter is **Mo. Valley College** (est. 1888), Redman St. & College Ave., coed. institution supervised by Presb. Ch. **137.** J. with US40 (see). **SEDALIA, 155.** (see US50), is at J. with US50 (see).

## Sec. 2: SEDALIA to MO.-ARK. LINE. 184.

US65 heads (S) into Ozark hill country. **34.** J. with St.35, leading (R) 1.5m to **Warsaw,** seat since 1837 of Benton Cty. & until 1870's important shipping point for travel by boat on Osage R. Survivals of its early days are **Warsaw Disciples of Christ Ch.** (1840) & **Old Union H.** (ante bellum), Main St. opp. cth. Since Bagnell Dam was built impounding waters of Osage to form L. of the Ozarks, Warsaw has become tourist & fishing center. **36.5.** US65 bridges **L. OF THE OZARKS** (see US50) & plunges through rugged, thickly wooded country, then emerges on fruit, vegetable, & cattle raising plateau area. **108. CRYSTAL CAVE** (sm.fee) has fantastic stalactite & stalagmite formations. **113. SPRINGFIELD** (see US60). Js. with US66 (see) & US60 (see); with latter, US65 unites for 9m. S. of **OZARK, 130.** center of tomato-growing area, hy. winds bet. wooded slopes. **151.5.** J. with local Rd. leading (L) short distance to **Old Spanish Cave** (fee,guides), containing 6 caverns extending 1,600′ into hillside. **159.** J. with St.76.

SIDE TRIP: Take latter (L) to J. with St.76A, 7.5m.

(R) 2.5m on St.76A is **Rockaway Beach** (hotels.cabins.boat.f.riding.tennis.golf), resort on shores of 24m long **L. Taneycomo.**

From St.76, curving around L., other side Rds. lead to resorts on shore offering recr. & lodging facils. At 14m is J. with Cty. V.

(R) on this **Powersite Dam,** 1,700′ long & 52′ high, impounding White R. to form L. Taneycomo; near dam are several resorts.

**Forsyth,** 15m is recr. center.

**170.** Resort town of **BRANSON** with camps & hotels, boat docks, & restaurants & shops, faces L. Taneycomo.

SIDE TRIP: Take St.80 (R) from Branson through picturesque region figuring in Harold Bell Wright's romances, among whose landmarks are 1,341′ peak, **Dewey Bald,** 7m; log, gray, weathered, oldtime **Matt's Cabin** near-by; & **Inspirational Pt.,** 7.5m. One of Mo.'s finest limestone caverns, with 10m of corridors, containing fantastic rock formation, is **Marvel Cave** (fee), 10m. **Uncle Ike's Post Office,** near-by, is typical back-country p.o.

US65 bridges L. Taneycomo to another waterfront resort, **HOLLISTER, 172.,** notable for planned architecture & landscaping. **173.5.** J. with Cty. P. leading (R) short distance to **Sch. of the Ozarks,** housed in group of stone, brick & frame bldgs. on plateau overlooking White R. Valley. Presb. Ch.-sponsored high sch. with vocational training courses, this institution dates back to 1907; students work for part of their tuition, rest being paid by patrons. **184. MO.-ARK. LINE.**

# US 71—MISSOURI

**MO.-IOWA LINE** (28m from Villisca, Iowa) **(S) to MO.-ARK. LINE** (50.5m from Fayetteville, Ark.). **329. US71**

Via: Maryville, St. Joseph, Kansas City, Nevada, Carthage, Neosho. RRs. parallel route.

US71 roughly parallels Mo.'s W. border, orig. settled largely by slaveowners from South, who came into conflict during 1850's with antislavery settlers of E. Kans. Rich farming & livestock-raising reg.

## Sec. 1: MO.-IOWA LINE to KANSAS CITY. 117.

**0. MO.-IOWA LINE. 24. MARYVILLE,** center of famed hog-raising reg., named for 1st white woman settler, Mrs. Mary Graham, & site of **NW. Mo. St. Teachers College** (est.1905). **52. SAVANNAH** was laid out, 1841.

**65. ST. JOSEPH**

Through RR., bus & plane conns. Info.: C. of C., 209 N. 5th St. Swim.: Mun. pool, 22nd & Messanie Sts., & Hyde Pk. Pony Express Comm., Ap.; Apple Blossom Festival, early May; Baby Beef & Pig Show, 1st wk. Oct.

Although it still calls itself "Home of the Pony Express," St. Joseph is Mo.'s 3rd largest city, an important grain & livestock center with stockyards, packing plants, horse & mule markets, & flour mills, mfg. center with many industrial plants, & wholesale distributing center. It is brisk, modern town with a number of imposing public bldgs. Here on E. bank of Mo. R., Jos. Robidoux est. in 1826 fur trading post in what was then Ind. country. After Platte Purchase in 1836 opened surrounding area to settlement, many Southerners owning slaves took up land & began raising hog & cattle & hemp. Robidoux had town laid out, 1843. Steamboats freighted cargoes of staples upstream to be exchanged here for furs & buffalo hides. When Gold Rush to Cal. began, St. Joseph boomed as chief supply depot for wagon trains following N. route. Stockyards & slaughtering houses were est. On Feb. 14, 1859 1st passenger train arrived over Hannibal & St. Joseph Ry.; & on Ap. 3, 1860 1st rider on Pony Express left on mail run to Sacramento, Cal. During Civil War, St. Joseph became pt. for Confed. guerrilla operations until it was occupied by Union forces. Afterward it quickly recovered its prosperity, becoming important livestock center. Mo. R. was bridged in 1873 & by 1890 more RRs. had arrived. St. Joseph boasted more wealth per capita than any other city in country in latter year. It has grown steadily since.

PTS. OF INT.: Facing Civic Center Pk.'s broad lawn are (1) **St. Joseph City Hall,** Francis & 11th Sts., & (2) **Pony Express Mon.,** Francis & 10th Sts. (3) 11th & Charles Sts., **St. Joseph Mus.** houses Ind. & pioneer relics. (4) Poulin & 3rd Sts., **Robidoux Row** (early 1840's), is house in which founder of St. Joseph died in 1868. (5) Michel & 2nd Sts., **Beauvais Home** (early 1840's) was built by Joseph Robidoux for his daughter, Sylvanie. (6) 912 Penn St., **Pony Express Stable** is associated with pioneer organization whose riders carried mail 1,975m to Cal. (7) 36th St. N. of Seneca St., **Jesse James H.** is cottage in which famous outlaw, then living incognito, was killed in 1882 by former friend, Bob Ford, who wanted $10,000 reward. (8) **Krug Pk.** (168 as.pic.scenic drives.children's circus) contains lagoon & lily pond & large natural bowl & amphitheater. Among St. Joseph's chief industrial plants are (9) **Quaker Oats Co. Plant,** 2811 S. 11th St., largest of its kind in country, & (10) **Swift & Armour Packing Plants,** Packers Ave., W. end of Illinois Ave., with extensive livestock pens. (11) At N. 6th & Albemarle Sts., **Goetz Brewery** (O).

At **85.** is J. with Cty. H.

SIDE TRIP: Take latter (R) to **Weston,** 11m, old town in valley bet. Mo. R. bluffs, notable for ante bellum architecture, 1st sett. in 1837. Shift in R.'s course in 1857 suddenly cut it off from R. traffic: later it became tobacco-growing center & today is biggest loose-leaf tobacco market W. of Miss. R. Tobacco auctions are held each winter in its **Tobacco Warehouses,** Main St.

US71 cuts through tobacco-growing Platte Cty. to Cty. seat, **PLATTE CITY, 94.,** which grew up around ferry crossing Platte R. here, est. 1828. **110.** J. with US69 (see US65). **NORTH KANSAS CITY, 114.,** planned industrial community, was created by N. Kansas City Development Co. beginning in 1912. US71 bridges Mo. R. to **KANSAS CITY, 117.** at J. with US40 (see) & US50 (see).

### Sec. 2: KANSAS CITY to MO.-ARK. LINE. 212.

**16.5.** J. with Cty.10S.

SIDE TRIP: Take latter (L) to 1,700-a. **Longview Farms** (guides), 12m, showplace developed by Kansas City lumberman R. A. Long, producing flowers, dairy products, horses & hogs, with private racetrack.

**21.5. BELTON,** rural trading center laid out, 1871, is site of **Carry Nation Mon.,** Belton Cemetery, marking grave of hatchet-wielding prohibitionist. **39. HARRISONVILLE,** bus. center of fertile farming area. **66. BUTLER,** laid out in 1854, stages horse show each Aug. **78. RICH HILL** was booming coal miners' settlement during 1880's. Vic. is dotted with abandoned coal mines. **97. NEVADA,** laid out, 1855, was sett. by Kentuckians & Tennesseeans. As Confed. troop base during Civil War it became center of military activities & was burned to ground May 26, 1863 by Capt. Anderson Norton's Fed. militia from Kans. Its recovery dates from its est. as Mo.-Kans.-Tex. RR. division pt. in 1870. Today it ships livestock, feed, grain & poultry. W. Austin & S. Chestnut Sts., **Cottey College** (est.1884) is girls' jr. college. **123.** J. with US160, leading (L) to **Lamar,** 1m, dating back to 1856, whose Lamar "Democrat," founded before Civil War, is one of Mo.'s best-known small-town newspapers. Town's chief landmark is **Pres. Harry S. Truman Birthpl. 145. CARTHAGE** (see US66) at J. with US66, with which US71 unites to **JOPLIN, 162.** (see US66). **181.5. NEOSHO** (see US60) at J. with US60 (see). US71 winds into rugged, forested Ozarks, passing several sm. towns & resorts. **212. MO.-ARK. LINE.**

## ST. LOUIS

Through RR., bus & plane conns. Steamboat Landings: foot of Washington Ave. for Miss. sightseeing excursions. Accoms.: All types plentiful; more than 180 hotels. Info.: "Visit St. Louis" Info. Bureau, 607 C. of C. Bldg., 511 Locust St.; St. Louis Convention Publicity & Tourist Bureau, 911 Locust St. Recr. facils.: Henry W. Kiel Mun. Auditorium, Market & 14th Sts., for opera & concerts; Mun. Theatre (open-air) in Forest Pk. for summer light opera. Golf at mun. course in Forest Pk. & many private country clubs. Swim. at Fairgrounds Pk. (Grand Blvd. & Natural Bridge Ave.), Marquette (Osage St. & Minnesota Ave.) & other mun. pools. Annual events: Floral displays, Mo. Botanical Gardens, Jan., May, Nov., Dec.; Flower Show, The Arena, late Mar.; Mun. Opera, Forest Pk., June to Aug.; Nat. Horse Show, The Arena, 1st wk. in Oct.; Veiled Prophet Parade, 1st Tues. after 1st Mon. in Oct., & Veiled Prophet Ball night following; St. Louis Nat. Home Show, late Oct.; St. Louis Symphony Orchestra Season, Mun. Auditorium, end of Oct. to end of Mar.; Nat. Auto Show, late Nov.

St. Louis, country's 8th biggest city & biggest bet. Chicago & Pac. Coast, spreads (W) from great bend in Miss.; but its riverside location is no longer primary basis of prosperity, as in pioneer days; today RRs., rather than river craft, make it nation's 2nd most important transportation center. Furs were first articles of commerce and are important today; St. Louis is world's 2nd largest fur distributing & processing center. But it has evolved remarkable diversity of other

Episc. Diocese of Mo., **Christ Ch. Cathedral** (1859-67; adds. 1894 & 1911) is in the Eng. Goth. style. (16) Olive, Locust, 13th & 14th Sts., **St. Louis Cent. Pub. Lib.** (1912) has coll. of more than 1,000,000 volumes. (17) 15th & Locust Sts., **Campbell H.** (ante bellum.fee), last surviving mansion of Lucas Pl. residential area, fashionable in 1850's, contains orig. furnishings. (18) **Union Sta.** (1893-96), Market St. bet. 18th & 20th Sts., dominated by its peak-roofed 230′ clock tower, is part Romanes., part Fr. neo-classic in style. (19) Mem. to Louis P. Aloe, **Aloe Plaza,** facing Union Sta. is dominated by sculptor Carl Milles' fountain, "The Meeting of the Waters."

West Side: Forest Pk. & Environs: (20) Oldest Univ. W. of Miss. R., **St. Louis Univ.,** Adm. Bldg. at 221 N. Grand Blvd., is housed in scattered group of bldgs. concentrated around 2 centers on Grand Blvd., one at Olive St. & other 1$^{m}$ (S) at Caroline St. Founded by Louis Wm. Du Bourg, Bishop of La. & Floridas, in 1818, it became Jesuit institution in 1827 & was chartered as St. Louis Univ. in 1832. It operates world's foremost Cath. medical center. **Du Bourg Hall,** in whose corridors hang coll. of rare old paintings begun by Bishop Du Bourg, contains Univ. Central Lib. & mem. room honoring early grad. & faculty member Peter De Smet, S.J., renowned Ind. missionary. (21) Grand & Lindell Blvds., **St. Francis Xavier's Ch.** (1898), is Eng. Goth. edifice. Altar in S. transept was used by Jesuits of Kaskaskia Mission in Ill. (1705-1768); altar stone, brought by canoe from Quebec, in Jesuit mission near Chicago (1663-1700) & in Jesuit mission on site of St. Louis (1700-1705). (22) Newstead Ave. & Lindell Blvd., seat of St. Louis Cath. Archdiocese is $3,750,000 granite Byzantine-style **Cathedral of St. Louis** (begun 1907), of cruciform design with two 157′ towers & 227′ central dome.

**Forest Pk.,** Lindell & Kingshighway Blvds., Oakland Ave. & Skinker Blvd., covering 1,380 as., is country's 2nd largest mun. pk. Opened in 1876, it was site of La. Purchase Exposition (1904). (23) Theater & Government Drives, **St. Louis Mun. Opera Theater,** 10,000-seat open-air amphitheater. (24) Lindell & DeBaliviere Blvds., **Jefferson Mem.** (1913), with its huge marble Thos. Jefferson (by Karl Bitter) dominating loggia flanked by 2 wings, houses in E. wing **Hqs. of Mo. Hist. Soc.,** containing mus. of Ind. & pioneer relics & lib.; in W. wing **Lindbergh Trophies,** comprising gifts received by Chas. A. Lindbergh following pioneer transatlantic flight of 1927 in "Spirit of St. Louis." (25) Illuminated after dark, waters of **Polychrome Electric Fountain,** Government Dr. at Post-Dispatch L., fall over terraced limestone. (26) Wells & McKinley Drives, steel & glass **Jewel Box** is conservatory which houses spectacular displays of flowers & plants. (27) Concourse, Government, Washington & Wells Drives, **St. Louis Zoological Garden** (77 as.), housing more than 2,000 animals, birds & reptiles, pioneered in development of natural settings. (28) Roman-style **City Art Mus.** (1904.O.daily except Christmas & New Year's 10-5;Mon.2-9 May-Oct.), Art Hill, before which stands bronze equestrian **Statue of St. Louis the Crusader** (by Chas. H. Niehaus), has one of nation's foremost colls. of painting, sculpture, drawing, architecture & applied arts. Coll. of Chinese bronzes, ceramics & paintings is one of finest of its kind. Noteworthy are Medieval Rooms, Romanes. chapel & gallery, & Goth. & Hispano-Moorish Courts. There is notable coll. of paintings by Mo. artist Geo. Caleb Bingham. (29) Lindell Blvd. & Skinker Rd., **Washington Univ.,** housed in handsome group of modern bldgs. spreading over tree-dotted campus of 160 as. Twin-towered **Brookings Hall,** adm. bldg., crowns hill slope. Medical center with affiliated hospitals occupies separate campus at Kingshighway Blvd. & Euclid Ave. Univ.'s hist. goes back to Eliot Seminary, chartered in 1853, whose chancellor was Rev. Wm. Greenleaf Eliot, grandfather of famous poet & Nobel Prize winner, T. S. Eliot (born in St. Louis, 1888). (30) 801 DeMun Ave., country's largest Prot. seminary, **Concordia Seminary,** housed in 18 Goth.-style buildings on campus of more than 70 as., was est. in 1839 by Luths. from Saxony at Altenburg (see US61). **Adm. Bldg.** has the Concordia Hist. Institute coll. of relics, documents & books associated with pioneer Luth. immigrants.

South Side: (31) 5600 Oakland Ave., **Forest Pk. Highlands** is one of Midwest's biggest amusement centers. (32) 5700 Oakland Ave., **The Arena,** is $2,500,000 stadium seating 21,000, in which are held ice hockey & basketball games, skating shows, rodeos, flower & auto shows & other events. (33) Tower Grove Ave. & Flora Pl., Mo. Botanical Garden, popularly known as **Shaw's Garden** (O.8 to sunset, wks.10 to sunset, Sun.free) covering 75 as., contains largest coll. of plant life in W. hemisphere, with more than 12,000 species. Annual orchid & chrysanthemum shows are nationally known. **Lily Ponds** contain 17 hybrid varieties; **Plant Curiosities H.** exhibits botanical freaks. Garden was founded in 1858 by cutlery magnate, real estate operator & philanthropist Henry Shaw. Its older structures incl. **Adm. Bldg.** (1851), Shaw's town house; **Tower Grove** (1849), his country house; octagonal, sculpture-surmounted **Shaw's Mausoleum; Mus. & Lib. Bldg.** (1858-59); & **Linnean H.,** typical of mid-19th cent. greenhouse design.

(34) Tower Grove & Magnolia Aves., **Tower Grove Pk.,** covering highly-landscaped 277-a. area, comprises part of country estate of Henry Shaw. (35) Lafayette, Mississippi, Missouri & Park Aves., **Lafayette Pk.,** St. Louis' oldest, is 30-a. landscaped area set aside in 1836. (36) Broadway & Pestalozzi St., **Anheuser-Busch Brewery** (conducted tours), world's largest, occupies almost 140 large structures covering more than 140 as.; firm was begun in 1857. (37) Of walled-in cluster of brick & stone structures comprising **Old Arsenal,** 2nd & Arsenal Sts., est. in 1827, 8 were built in 1830 & 3 more in 1856. (38) Foot of Grand Blvd., **Carondelet Pk.,** a rolling, thickly wooded tract.

North Side: (39) 3015 Cass Ave., extensive Goth.-style **Amer. Wine Co. Plant** (1859.guides) is built over maze of stone cellars opened in 1832. (40) Fair, Grand, Kossuth & Natural Bridge Aves., **Fairgrounds Pk.** (athletic fields.tennis.swim.) occupies former site of annual St. Louis Fair & of aviation field on which 1st air mail ever flown was landed in Oct. 1911; it has one of world's largest outdoor swim. pools. (41) Bet. Florissant Ave. & Broadway at Taylor Ave., **O'Fallon Pk.** (boat.) is 159-a. tract cut by deep ravines overlooking Miss. R., with observatory. (42) 4947 W. Florissant Ave., **Bellefontaine Cemetery,** opened in 1850, contains graves of many notable early St. Louisans (maps showing location avail. at office at main entrance). Here is gray limestone, domed **Wainwright Tomb** (1892), resting place of Ellis & Charlotte Dickson Wainwright, considered one of the chief works of architect Louis Sullivan. (43) 5239 W. Florissant Ave., St. Louis' largest cemetery, 476-a. **Calvary Cemetery,** opened in 1864, contains graves of Auguste Chouteau, one of St. Louis' founders, & Gen. Wm. Tecumseh Sherman of Civil War fame. Within grounds is to be seen **Old Orchard,** house built by Henry Clay in 1845. (44) 11000 N. Riverview Dr., **Chain of Rocks Pk.,** overlooking Miss. from river heights, commands fine view.

## TRIPS OUT OF ST. LOUIS

### I. US40Alt. (NW) to J. with US61. 41.5.

**0.** From downtown St. Louis (12th & Olive Sts.) follow US40Alt. **17.** J. with combined US66 & US Bypass 67 (Lindbergh Blvd.).

SIDE TRIP: Take latter (R) 2m to **Lambert-St. Louis Mun. Airport,** one of country's biggest & best-equipped, est. in 1920 through efforts of Maj. Albert Bond Lambert. At 3.5m is J. with combined US Bypass 67 & St.140; turn (L) on this to J. with Charbonier Rd., 4m.

(1) Turn (R) on Charbonier Rd. to garden & orchard-surrounded old frame & brick houses of **Florissant,** 0.5m, sett. c.1785 by Fr. **Ch. of St. Ferdinand** (1821.extension & new facade 1870), facing Francis St., contains old paintings & tabernacles. Adj. are **Rectory** (1819) & **Convent of the Sisters of Loreto** (1821), built to house Mother Duchesne & Sisters of U.S.' 1st branch of Society of Sacred Heart. St. Louis St. at N. end of Pierre St., log, clap-boarded **Casa Alvarez,** typical of Mo. Fr. architecture, was home of Augustine Alvarez in 1790's.

(2) Turn (L) on Charbonier Rd. to J. with Howdershell Rd., 1.5m & (L) on this to **St. Stanislaus Seminary,** 2m, Jesuit novitiate est. in 1831. Central bldg. (1840-49) dominates quadrangle of other structures, incl. lib. with rare early books & paintings & chapel with altar brought from France. Cemetery contains **Grave of Father Peter John de Smet,** Ind. missionary, peacemaker & writer, ordained at Florissant in 1827.

US40Alt. cont. to J. at **19.** with US Bypass 40, on which it cont. (straight ahead) across Mo. R. at **22.** to **ST. CHARLES, 22.5.,** Mo.'s 1st capital (1821-26), climbing steep R. bluffs, sett. by Fr.-Canadians from 1769 on. After Lewis & Clark expedition of 1804-06, town was soon swamped by Amer. settlers. When Mo. became a territory, it was made seat of one of orig. 5 counties & 9 yrs. later, in 1821, was designated St. capital. German immigrants began arriving in early 1830's. In 1849, St. Charles was inc., but St. Louis soon surpassed it as commercial & industrial center. Second-floor rooms of 3 adj. brick bldgs. comprising **Old St. Capitol** (1814), 206-212-214 S. Main St., housed general assembly 1821-1826. **Ludwell-Powell H.** (1840. altered), 6th & Jefferson Sts., was built by 1st mayor. **St. Charles College Bldg.,** 117 N. 3rd St., housed college est. in 1835. **Lindenwood College** (chartered 1853) for women, Kingshighway at Madison St., founded in 1827, has grown from single log cabin to imposing group of Tudor Goth. brick bldgs. on wooded, 150-a. campus. Red brick bldgs. of **Academy of the Sacred Heart,** Decatur, Franklin, 2nd & 3rd Sts., 1st seat of this order to be opened in W. hemisphere, center around orig. bldg. (1838), which contains room occupied by convent's founder, Mother Duchesne, furnished with relics; she is buried in vault of shrine (completed 1853). **St. Charles Borromeo Cemetery,** W. of Blanchette Pk., contains graves of many pioneers.

**40. FT. ZUMWALT ST. PK.** contains stone-chimneyed log **Jacob Zumwalt Cabin** (1798), thought to be oldest surviving hewn timber cabin W. of Miss., which was inc. in Ft. Zumwalt, built for defense against Ind. attack during War of 1812. **41.5.** J. with US61 (see) & US40 (see).

**II. US40, St.94, St.47 (W) to WARRENTON, 71.**

**0.** From downtown St. Louis (12th & Market Sts.) follow US40 (Market St.). **11.** J. with US61 (see), with which US40 unites (W). **21.** J. with Cty.CC.

SIDE TRIP: Turn (L) on this 6m to J. with St.109 & (R) on St.109 to rolling wooded, 1,837-a. **Edmund A. Babler St. Pk.** (pic.hik.riding), 7m.

**30.** J. with St.94; route turns (L) on this to J. with local Rd. at **DEFIANCE, 35.**

SIDE TRIP: Turn (R) on this to J. with 2nd local Rd., .08m; (L) on this to J. at 1m; (R) to J. at 1.5m; (L) to J. at 2m & (L) to old **Nathan Boone H.** (before 1820), 3m, built by youngest son of Dan. Boone, who sett. here c.1799. Dan. Boone himself is said to have carved woodwork; he died here on visit to his son Sept. 26, 1820.

**37. MATSON,** at J. with poor Rd., leading (R) short distance to **Dan. Boone Farm.** South of farmhouse is **Site of Dan. Boone Cabin,** where famous frontiersman, having lost his Ky. property, came to settle in 1799 at age of 65 on Sp. land grant. **51.** J. with St.47; route turns (R) on this. **52.5.** J. with local Rd. leading (R) 1m to **Bryan-Boone Cemetery,** in which Dan. Boone & his wife were orig. buried; their remains were later moved to Ky. **54. FLANDERS CALLAWAY H.** (c.1800), home of Dan. Boone's daughter, Jemima, & son-in-law, was often visited by Boone. **71.** J. with US40 at **WARRENTON** (see US40).

**III. US50 & St.100 (W) to WASHINGTON. 54.5.**

**0.** From 12th & Market Sts., in downtown St. Louis, follow US50 (Market St.). **8.5. MAPLEWOOD,** one of St. Louis' many suburbs, dates from 1890's when Maplewood Realty Co. opened subdivision here. **10. BRENTWOOD,** another suburb, was inc. c.1900, uniting 3 adj. subdivisions.

SIDE TRIP: Take North & South Rd. (L) from Brentwood to **Webster Groves,** 3m. Post office was opened in 1884 & town inc. in 1896. **Webster College** (est.1916), 470 E. Lockwood Ave., is 4-yr. Cath. women's college which maintains **Locksley Observ.** (observation booth & 12" telescope.O.Tues.Thurs.8-10 p.m.). **Eden Theological Seminary** (est.1848), 475 E. Lockwood Ave., is grad. school maintained by Evangelical & Reformed Ch.

**13. KIRKWOOD,** laid out by St. Louis businessmen as suburban center following construction of Mo. Pac. RR. in 1853, was inc. in 1865 & named for RR. engineer Jas. P. Kirkwood. Kirkwood is at J. with US61 (see). **41. GRAY SUMMIT,** one of the highest pts. on RR. bet. St. Louis & Kansas City, was named for early settler Dan. Gray. Local Rd. leads (R) from Gray Summit 1m to **Ralston Co. Experimental Farm** (guides), world's largest private experimental farm, which tests commercial animal & poultry feeds. **41.5.** J. with US66 (see) with which US50 unites for 6.5m. US50-66 is bordered by **Henry Shaw Garden-Way,** extending along US66 30m (W) from St. Louis city limits, planted with native trees. **42. MO. BOTANICAL GARDEN ARBORETUM** (1,600 as.) on Meramec R., part of whose tract has been set aside to show the natural vegetation of Ozark meadow & woodland, has one of world's biggest colls. of orchids, grown in greenhouses. **43.5.** J. with St.100, on which route turns (R) to **WASHINGTON, 54.5.,** one of chief settlements of Mo.'s pioneer German émigrés; handsome, garden-bordered old red-brick dwellings, many distinctively German, line streets that slope steeply to Mo. R. Here, at ferry crossing, several German families settled 1833. Other Germans followed & Washington, soon thriving R. port, developed active social & cultural life centering around their theatrical & athletic societies. Processing of corncobs into pipes may be witnessed at **Mo. Meerschaum Plant,** Front & Cedar Sts.; **Franz Schwarzer Zither Factory,** 207 E. Main St., is said to be only one of its kind in U.S.

**IV. St.30, US61 (S) to CRYSTAL CITY. 40.**

**0.** From downtown St. Louis (12th & Market Sts.), take St.30 (12th St., Gravois Ave., Gravois Rd.). **11. GRANT'S CABIN,** Grant Rd. & Gravois Cr., 2-story log cabin built by Ulysses S. Grant in 1854, moved from orig. site, stands at entrance to wealthy St. Louisan's country place, Grant's Farm. **13.** J. with US61; route turns (L) on this. **17.** J. with US67 (Lemay Ferry Rd.), with which US61 unites (S).

SIDE TRIP: Turn (L) from J. with US67 on macadam Rd. 2m to **Jefferson Barracks** (O.Sun.only), U.S. Army post of more than 1,700 as. with many bldgs. surrounding the parade grounds, dating back to 1826. Among famous officers stationed here have been Jefferson Davis, Rbt. E. Lee, U.S. Grant, W. T. Sherman, J. C. Frémont. W. of parade grounds is **U.S. Nat. Cemetery.**

**22. MERAMEC R.** draws many St. Louisans for recr. jaunts (boat.swim.f.). **26.5.** Log **"OLD HOUSE"** (pre-1831) was at one time tavern where stagecoaches stopped. **28.5.** J. with Cty.K, leading (L) to **Kimmswick,** 1m, once Miss. R. port & after 1857 an iron-smelting & shipping pt. **Franz A. Hermann H.** (1859), built over deep broad beer cellar, is good example of Mo.-German half-timber construction. **36.** J. with Herculaneum Rd. leading (L) to **Herculaneum,** 0.5m, laid out by Moses Austin & Sam. Hammond in 1808 as Miss. shipping pt. for lead mines to S. **St. Joseph Lead Co. Smelter** was country's largest when it was built in 1890's. **40. CRYSTAL CITY,** built near world's largest known deposit of pure glass sand (discovered 1843), which has been supplying raw material for plate glass production since 1872, is dominated by huge modern brick & steel structures of highly mechanized **Pittsburgh Plate Glass Co. Plant.** Crystal City is planned industrial town.

## US 18—IOWA

**MARQUETTE, IOWA** (3m from Prairie du Chien, Wis.) **(W) to IOWA-S. DAK. LINE** (4m from Canton, S. Dak.). **317. US18**

Via: West Union, Charles City, Mason City, Algona & Spencer. RR. & bus lines parallel parts of route. Accoms.: Chiefly in cities.

US18 traverses scenic reg. of N. Iowa, dotted by Ls. & cut by Rs., with many St. pks. & recr. areas. W. of Mason City for 100m it crosses prairie.

### Sec. 1: MARQUETTE to MASON CITY. 127.

US18 crosses Miss. R., which is Iowa-Wis. Line, **0.,** on Marquette Toll Bridge. **MARQUETTE, 1.,** named for Père Marquette, who with Louis Joliet first saw Iowa territory in 1673, is Milwaukee RR. division pt. US18 follows R. bluffs to **McGREGOR, 3.,** in ravine edged by high cliffs, which in 1836 became terminus of ferry line from Prairie du Chien est. by Alex. McGregor. On McGregor Heights, Amer. School of Wild Life Protection, whose faculty includes naturalists & scientists from all over country, holds annual sessions in Aug. Within radius of 15m are hundreds of Ind. village sites, cave shelters & effigy mounds, fortifications & earthworks. **POSTVILLE, 29.,** named for Joel Post, who built house here in 1841, is cheese-producing center. At **30.** is J. with US52.

SIDE TRIP: Take latter (R) to **Calmar,** 17m, Czech settlement & farm shipping pt. at J. with St.24.

(1) Take St.24 (L) to **Ft. Atkinson,** 5m, whose residents also are chiefly of Czech descent, at ft. of bluff on which is 5-a. **Ft. Atkinson St. Pk.,** containing part of 2-story barracks, officers' quarters, blockh. & magazine from **Old Ft. Atkinson,** built in 1840 to protect Winnebago from Sac & Fox & Sioux, along with 2nd blockh. restored to orig. appearance after demolition.

(2) Take St.150 (L) from Calmar to J. with improved Rd., 5m, & turn (R) on this 2.5m to **St. Anthony's Chapel** (1885), 12' x 16', with 4 pews seating 2 each, built by John Gartner & Frank Huber. St.150 cont. to **W. Union** (see below), 17m, at J. with US18.

From Calmar, US52 cont. (N) to J. with St.325, 19m.

Turn (L) on this to **Spillville,** 5m, containing 2-story brick & stone **Dvorak H.,** where Bohemian composer Antonin Dvorak lived with his family in 1893 & worked on his "String Quartette in F Major, Opus 96" & last movement of his "New World Symphony," & handsome **St. Wenceslaus Ch.,** reprod. of cathedral at Kuttenberg, where Dvorak played organ.

US52 cont. (N) to **Decorah,** 28m, on Upper Iowa R., named for Chief Waucon Decorah, who aided whites during Black Hawk War. Decorah was sett. largely by Norwegians, who made it their chief center W. of Miss. R.; here is published most widely circulated Norweg.

language newspaper in country. **Luther College** (opened 1861), coed. Evangelical Luth. Ch. of America institution, occupies 40-a. natural pk., whose landmarks incl. **Pioneer Mem.,** built of honeycombed limestone, & **Koren Lib.,** rich in Norweg.-Amer. materials. Maintained by college, **Norweg.-Amer. Hist. Mus.** is repository of articles illustrative of Norweg. settlement in America, housed in 3-story bldg. & group of pioneer log structures with early furnishings; among exhibits are household articles, tools & costumes from Norway, fish. boats & 4-rm. Norweg. house & such pioneer relics as ox yokes & grain cradles. Picturesquely scenic reg. around Decorah is known as "Little Switzerland" of Iowa.

US18 cont. (SW) to **W. UNION, 45.,** seat of Fayette Cty., at J. with St.150.

SIDE TRIPS: (A) Take St.150 (L) from W. Union to **Fayette,** 9m, seat of nonsectarian Christian **Upper Iowa Univ.** (org.1857), which has mus. containing zoological, geological, ethnological, & hist. exhibits. Here also is Goth. cruciform **Meth. Ch.** (1876), beneath which, excavated from rock, are series of rooms, reproducing Franciscan cell under Cathedral at Assisi in Italy, cell in which Wm. Tyndale was imprisoned for translating Bible & Wittenberg room in which Martin Luther made his translation. At 14m is J. with St.154.

Take latter (L) 9m to 217-a. **Brush Cr. Canyon St. Pk.** (shelter.pic.trls.).

**Oelwein,** 26m, celebrated its diamond jubilee in 1948. Named for German who gave part of his property for RR. sta. & right-of-way, Oelwein is C.G.W. RR.'s central Midwest division pt., with roundhouse & shops & converging pt. for 6 RRs. Highly unionized industrial town, it has concrete, chemical & packing plants. At 27.5m is **L. Oelwein** (boats.swim.f. cottages). **Independence,** 42m (see US20 Tour) is at J. with US20 (see).

(B) Take St.56 (L) from W. Union to J. with dirt Rd., 1m; turn (L) on this to 101-a. **Echo Valley St. Pk.** (shelter.pic.boat.f.), 2m, so named because sounds echo & re-echo 3 times bet. its honeysuckle-covered cliffs, which overlook cedar-fringed L.

**78. NEW HAMPTON,** seat of Chickasaw Cty., dates back to 1850's. **96. CHARLES CITY** was 1st sett. in 1850 by Joseph Kelly, in honor of whose son Charles it was named. When Chas. W. Hart & his college classmate, Chas. H. Parr, began building stationary gasoline engines here in 1896, they also started series of experiments with machines to be used in farming; because they built traction motors, their advertising manager, W. H. Williams, coined new name "tractor." Today **Hart-Parr Works** ships tractors throughout country & all over world. Charles City is at J. with US218 (see).

**127. MASON CITY** is trading center for wide area, focal pt. for large system of bus & truck trans., & RR. & mfg. town with smokestacks pouring black smoke over corn & oat fields. Its pioneer settlers were mostly Masons, whose first name for place was Shibboleth. John B. Long & John L. McMillan staked 1st claims in 1853. Ind. uprising next yr. stampeded most of settlers into flight, but gradually they returned. 1st mill & lime kiln were erected in 1855 by Elisha Randall, who patented in 1872 what was known as Randall's Perpetual Lime Kiln, adopted in many parts of country. Development of clay tile industry began in 1880's when much of N. Iowa had to be drained. Until about 1934, Iowa used more drain tile than any other area of equal size in world & Mason City is said to have produced enough yearly to reach half-way around world. Manufacture of brick, tile & Portland cement is still leading industry. Other industrial giants are beet-sugar refinery, beef & pork packing plant, sand & gravel plant & creamery; smaller enterprises produce variety of articles. City's prosperity has brought many civic improvements, incl. modern airport & fine pks.; Iowa's 1st jr. college & many handsome schools; & other recr. & cultural facils.

PTS. OF INT.: Architecturally outstanding is Mason City's new $300,000 **Pub. Lib.,** on 7-a. wooded tract in heart of city. Severely modern in design is **Wagner-Mozart Music Hall,** one of few public school bldgs. in U.S. devoted exclusively to music. 15 W. State St., **Park Inn,** low bldg. with horizontal lines, is work of distinguished modern architect Frank Lloyd Wright, whose "prairie style" was radical innovation. E. State St. W. of Willow Cr. Bridge, **Rock Glen** is group of gray stone residences fitting naturally into limestone-bluff & creekbed environment, designed by Wright's disciple, Walter Burleigh Griffith. Mason City is at J. with US65 (see).

## Sec. 2: MASON CITY to IOWA-S. DAK. LINE. 190.

**CLEAR L., 10.,** named for 6m-long, 3,643-a. L. on whose shore it stands, is popular Iowa summer resort. St.106 follows shore (L) to 70-a. **Clear L. St. L. Preserve** (lodge. camp.pic.boat.f.bath.), 3m. **14.5. McINTOSH WOODS ST. L. PRESERVE** (f.boat. pic.), wooded 60-a. tract on N. shore of Clear L. **23. GARNER** is seat of Hancock Cty. At **24.5.** is J. with US69.

SIDE TRIP: Take latter (R) to **Forest City,** 11.5m, seat of Winnebago Cty., platted in 1856. Turn (R) from Forest City 4m to St.332 & (R) 2m on this to 369-a. **Pilot Knob St. Pk.**

(camp.pic.), named for glacial formation rising to one of highest elevations (300′) in Iowa, on which is 40′ stone lookout. Around **Dead Man's L.** are rugged slopes heavily wooded.

**30.** J. with gravel Rd. leading (R) $2^m$ to 27-a. **Eagle L. St. Pk.** (boat.f.pic.). **57. ALGONA,** on E. Fork of Des Moines R., was sett. in 1854 by Asa C. & Ambrose A. Call; former's wife suggested name, derived from word Algonquin. One of 5 bldgs. designed in Iowa bet. 1911 & 1914 by pioneer modern architect Louis Sullivan is **Druggist Mutual Insurance Co. Office Bldg.,** of which Sullivan's biographer, Hugh Morrison, said: "Few buildings of that period . . . match it in quality."

SIDE TRIP: Turn (L) from Algona on gravel Rd. intersecting Main St. $1.5^m$ to 130-a. **Ambrose A. Call St. Scenic Preserve** (lodge.camp.pic.), with rolling slopes shaded by magnificent trees.

**67.** J. with St.44.

SIDE TRIP: Take latter (L) to **W. BEND,** $9^m$, site of Grotto of the Redemption, religious structure whose construction was begun by Fr. Paul M. Dobberstein in 1928. Incorporated in it are rocks from every St. in Union; shells & coral from waters bordering America; & thousands of precious & semi-precious stones, ores, fossils, & bits of petrified wood. Near-by **St. Peter & St. Paul Ch.** contains Christmas Chapel with huge amethyst adorning its creche & Stations of Cross in mosaic.

**81. EMMETSBURG,** in valley of Des Moines R., was founded by Irish colony in 1856. Cty. Rd. leads (R) $2^m$ to 945-a. **Kearny St. Pk.** (pic.golf.boat.f.) near $5^m$-long **Five I. L.,** containing 5 wooded Is. **93. RUTHVEN.** J. with gravel Rd. leading (R) $3^m$ to 32-a. **Lost I. St. Pk.** (camp.pic.boat.f.), adj. 1,200-a. L. **106.** J. with US71 (see) with which US18 unites for $3^m$. **107. SPENCER** was founded in 1859 & named for U.S. Sen. Geo. E. Spencer. Its modern appearance is due to rebuilding after fire which razed most of business sec. in 1931. **HARTLEY, 127., SANBORN, 135.,** & **SHELDON, 146.,** are all small trading centers named for RR. officials. **161. HULL,** org. in 1882, was sett. largely by Dutch immigrants. **163.** J. with US75 (see). **170. ROCK VALLEY** has pop. predominantly of Dutch descent. US18 crosses Big Sioux R., which is Iowa-S. Dak. Line, **190.,** on free bridge.

# US 20—IOWA

**DUBUQUE, IOWA** ($63^m$ from Freeport, Ill.) **(W) to SIOUX CITY, IOWA. 323. US20**

Via: Manchester, Independence, Waterloo, Iowa Falls, & Ft. Dodge. RRs. parallel most of route, bus lines follow it. Accoms.: Chiefly in cities.

US20 skirts S. edge of rough, rocky reg., cut by gorges & patched by fors., to Iowa Falls, then traverses flat prairie checkered with grainfields.

## Sec. 1: DUBUQUE to IOWA FALLS. 147.

**0.** Dubuque Bridge (toll) carries US20 over Miss. R., which is Ill.-Iowa Line.

**1. DUBUQUE**

Through RR. & bus conns. Info.: A.A.A., Union Bus Depot. Swim.: Mun. Pool, NE. city limits near end of Thomberg Ave.

One of Iowa's oldest cities, Dubuque fronts Miss. R., its business & industrial dists. wedged in narrow riverside strip dominated by abruptly jutting bluffs. Dubuque prospers on farm trade; among its many industrial plants are sash & door mills (one of them said to be world's largest), tractor works, chemical fertilizer & sulphuric acid plants, metalworking establishments, & shipyard. 1st white man known to have sett. permanently in what is now Iowa, Julien Dubuque, Fr. Canadian, made his home just S. of city's site in 1788 & began mining lead ore in R. bluffs. He acquired great influence among Fox Inds. & when he died was given honors befitting chief. On June 1, 1833, under terms of treaty with Chief Black Hawk, territory was thrown open to white settlers; before Dubuque was yr. old, stores, saloons & cabins bordered muddy main street of rough-and-ready mining settlement. Here in 1834 Meths. erected 1st Ch. in Iowa; 1st bank was chartered & 1st newspaper est. in 1836. Although it lost to Burlington its rank as Iowa's largest city after 1840, it became site of 3 colleges & greeted arrival of Ill. Cent. RR. on opp. shore by forming Dubuque & Pacific RR. Co. to extend line across Iowa. By 1860 it was again Iowa's biggest city, doing thriving trade with many immigrants to vic. & converting huge rafts of logs into lumber & RR. ties. Lumber industry, though twice wiped out by fire, in 1894 and in 1911, flourished until 1915, & out of it grew today's woodworking factories. Salient features of economic picture today are Dubuque's curbstone City Market, where farmers bring wagonloads of garden truck, & its barge lines terminal & harbor, where towboats & barges on Minneapolis-St. Louis run tie up. Near-by is one of country's few inland shipbuilding yards.

PTS. OF INT.: (1) River & Tower Sts., picturesque reminder of the once-important lead-mining industry is **Shot Tower** erected in 1855 for moulding lead shot. (2) $20,000,000 **John Deere Tractor Co. Plant** is biggest & newest addition to industrial scene. (3) 2050 Delhi St., **Univ. of Dubuque,** founded in 1852 as German Theological School, passed later into control of Presb. Ch. It occupies group of brick bldgs., chiefly Goth. in style, on 50-a. hilltop campus. (4) End of Wartburg Pl., **Wartburg Theological Seminary** (founded 1854). Amer. Luth. Ch. institution occupies massive Romanes. bldgs. of design based on that of Wartburg Castle in Germany. On exhibition are special Reformation coll. of rare books & documents & coll. of ethnological specimens from New Guinea. (5) Seminary & W. Locust Sts., **Clarke College** (founded 1843), 1st Midwest liberal arts college for women, is Cath. institution conducted by Sisters of Charity of the Blessed Virgin Mary; among structures on 60-a. campus are **Chapel of the Sacred Heart** & **Grotto of Our Lady of Lourdes.** (6) Loras Blvd. & Alta Vista S., **Loras College,** Cath. men's college, traces its history back to St. Raphael's Seminary, founded in 1839 by Most Rev. Mathias Loras. Among bldgs. on hilltop campus are Romanes. **Chapel of Christ the King,** its int. richly marble-embellished, & **Keane Hall,** containing Lib. of over 100,000 volumes, including Bishop Mathias Loras' rare book coll. **Mus.** contains Ind. artifacts, pioneer relics, icons & religious carvings, paintings & hist. material. (7) 2419 Central Ave., **Herrmann Mus. of Nat. Hist.** is private mus. of Richard Herrmann, containing Ind. artifacts, pioneer relics, fossils, mineral & zoological specimens. (8) W. 11th & Bluff Sts., **Carnegie Stout Free Pub. Lib.** houses Mary E. Lull Coll. of Paintings, including canvasses by Iowa artist Grant Wood. (9) W. 2nd & Bluff Sts., **St. Raphael's Cathedral** (cornerstone laid 1857), is successor to Iowa's 1st Cath. Ch., built in 1835. In crypt lies body of Most Rev. Mathias Loras, who came to Dubuque in 1839 as 1st bishop of new diocese of the West. Beneath one of altars are remains of St. Cessianus, 2nd cent. Roman martyr, whose bones constitute Patronal Relic of St. of Iowa. (10) **Kelly's Bluff,** rising behind cathedral, was named for Thomas Kelly, eccentric recluse who, when he died in 1859, buried his fortune in ground; sums of as much as $10,000 have been excavated. (11) On Bluff is **St. Raphael's Cemetery,** 1st Cath. burial ground in St., with many ancient mons. (12) 1095 W. 3rd St., **Edward Langworthy H.** (1847), octagonal structure with octagonal cupola, still equipped with original ornate furnishings, was designed by John Francis Rague, architect of Old Capitol at Iowa City. (13) **Grave of Julien Dubuque,** 0.5$^m$ from end of R. fork of Rowan St., is marked by circular tower of Galena limestone (1897) in medieval design. (14) At N. end of Dubuque is 133-a. **Eagle Pt. Pk.,** overlooking Miss. R. Along natural ledges of limestone extends 790′ **Ledge Garden,** built with 7,000 tons of native stone, near which are 3 **Ind. Council Rings.** In center is **Log Cabin,** oldest house in Dubuque & said to be oldest in Iowa. (15) Bluffs afford view of **U.S. Dam & Lock No. 11,** one of 26 bet. Minneapolis & St. Louis.

Dubuque is at J. with US61 (see).

SIDE TRIP: Take US52 (R) from Dubuque to J. at 27.5$^m$ with an unimproved Rd.

Turn (L) here 3.5$^m$ to **White Pine Hollow St. Pk.,** 650-a. tract with unusual rock formations & last remaining stand of white pine in Iowa. Among attractions are **Balanced & Steamboat Rocks, Devil's Punch Bowl,** & **millhouse & dam** built in 1850.

At 34.5$^m$ is **Turkey R. Mounds St. Mon.,** where Turkey R. empties into Miss., containing Ind. mounds of the effigy type. **Guttenberg,** 39$^m$, 1st known as Prairie la Porte, was later named for inventor of printing press, Johann Gutenberg (his name being misspelled) when German immigrants sett. here in 1834; many of its older structures are of German design. Opposite Guttenberg **U.S. Dam & Lock No. 10** extends across Miss. At 45$^m$ is **Pioneer Rock Ch.** (1858), built by 1st members of St. Peter's German United Evangelical Luth. Congr. At 60$^m$ is J. with US18 (see).

**15. EPWORTH,** named for Epworth, England, John Wesley's birthpl., is site of **St. Paul's Mission H.** (1857), which has underground **Grotto** of native rock containing carved figures depicting scenes from life of Christ. **26. DYERSVILLE,** sett. in 1837-38 by Eng. families, is dominated by huge twin-spired **St. Francis Xavier Ch.**

(1888). **39.5.** J. with St.116, leading (L) 2m to **U.S. Fish Hatchery** (pic.). **43. MANCHESTER** is dairying center, whose 1st settler built cabin here in 1850.

SIDE TRIP: Take St.13 (R) from Manchester to J. with St.3 at 12m.

Turn (R) here to **Edgewood,** 3m, & (L) from Edgewood on gravel Rd. 2m to **Bixby St. Mon.** (shelter.pic.trls.), 69-a. tract with waterfall, several springs, ice cave, & pioneer log cabin.

At 15.5m is J. with St.19.

Turn (L) on this 4m to 1,412-a. **Backbone St. Pk.** (bath.boat.camp.pic.auditorium.f. winter sports), Iowa's 1st & largest St. pk. Rugged limestone bluffs rising 90′ to 140′ above Maquoketa R. form backbone which gives area its name. Among features are L., observ., deer range, trout hatchery.

On Wapsinicon R. is **INDEPENDENCE, 66.,** founded in 1837 at J. with St.150 (see US18).

## 90. WATERLOO

Through RR. & bus conns. Info.: C. of C., Russell-Lamson Hotel, W. 5th & Commercial Sts. Swim.: At Cedar R. Pk. Nat. Dairy Cattle Congress & Nat. Belgian Horse & Stallion Shows, late Sept. & early Oct.

Waterloo, metropolis of NE. Iowa, through whose business center winds Cedar R. bet. pk.-terraced banks, is leading industrial center. Foremost among its industries are meat packing & farm machinery manufacture: it has one of country's largest independent meat packing plants & world's largest wheel tractor company. There are 3 radio stations, $100,000 baseball stadium, one of Midwest's biggest mun. airports, nearly 500 as. of pub. pks. & variety of other recr. facils. Place was 1st named Prairie Rapids by Geo. W. Hanna, who sett. on W. bank of Cedar R. in 1845; by 1848 there were settlers on both banks. It acquired its present name when Chas. Mullan in 1851, filing petition for a p.o. on which name had not been filled in, saw Waterloo listed in p.o. directory & wrote it down because he thought it had "right ring to it." Despite disastrous flood in 1858, Waterloo by 1860 was booming town of 1,800. In next decade RR. arrived, brick schoolh. & wheat elevators were built, new dam was thrown across R., & 1st pk. areas were planned. In 1892, after John Froelich of Elkader, Iowa, had harvested crop of grain with his newly invented gasoline engine, Waterloo Gasoline Traction Engine Co. was est., & from then on history of city is closely paralleled by history of tractor industry. PTS. OF INT.: (1) Eastern R. bank bet. 5th & 11th Sts., **Pioneer Pk.** with rock-walled pools & flower beds, contains reprod. of pioneer cabin, cyclone cellar, & old German Ft. (2) Y.M.C.A. Bldg., 152 W. 4th St., **Henry W. Grout Exhibit,** contains minerals & crystals; fossils; Ind. artifacts & clothing; books, coins, & domestic articles of pioneer days. (3) Rainbow Dr. at NW. edge of town, **Dairy Cattle Congress Exposition Grounds,** contains Hippodrome, seating 8,200, in which are held Waterloo's cattle & horse shows. (4) **Rath Packing Plant,** Sycamore & Elm Sts., & (5) **John Deere Tractor Plant,** Black Hawk Cr. & Cedar R., both employ as many as 5,000 workers; latter is successor to pioneer Waterloo Gasoline Tractor Engine Co. US20 follows Cedar R., bordered by 173-a. **JOSH HIGGINS ST. PKWY.** (bridle trls.pic.), to **98. CEDAR FALLS,** city of wide, tree-shaded streets, lawn-surrounded homes, & pks. 1st settlers came in 1845; town was platted in 1851. From 1861 to 1869 it was W. terminus of what is now Ill. Cent. RR. & boomed as grain & livestock shipping pt. & gristmill & sawmill center. Milling declined toward end of cent. & was supplanted by industries producing farm equipment, cement block machines, seed-processing machinery, stock feed, serums, & other products. On R. banks are **Island Pk.** (pic.), 104-a. tract with recr. facils., & **Riverview Pk.,** whose landscaped campgrounds provide shelter for annual Cedar Falls Bible Conference & other groups. College St. bet. 23rd & 27th St., **Iowa St. Teachers' College,** opened in 1876 in former home for Civil War orphans, now occupies over 2 dozen bldgs. on 244-a. campus, at center of which rises 100′ campanile. **Lib.** houses art coll. & mus. of natural history.

SIDE TRIP: Take US218 (R) from Cedar Falls to **Waverly,** 14m, which owes its name to slip of tongue made by chief speaker at its christening, who substituted Waverly for name agreed upon, Harmon, honoring town's founder, W. P. Harmon, because he had spent morning reading one of Scott's Waverly novels. Waverly is site of **Wartburg Normal College,** a 4-yr. Amer. Luth. Ch. institution, whose **Waverly Mus.** contains artifacts from New Guinea, ornithological specimens, & Roman coins.

Turn (L) from Waverly on St.3 to J. with St.53, 12m & (R) on this to 380-a. **Heery Woods St. Recr. Reserve** (lodge.pic.f.), 14m, heavily wooded, with L.

**Nashua,** 32m, at confluence of Cedar & Little Cedar Rs., was named by E. P. Greeley for his home town in N.H.

(R) From Nashua on gravel Rd. 2m is **Little Brown Ch. in the Vale,** known through popular hymn of same name, built in 1860's.

**Charles City,** 43m (see US18) is at J. with US18.

**115.** 74-a. **BEAVER MEADOW ST. WAYSIDE** (pic.f.), heavily wooded. **PARKERSBURG, 117. & ACKLEY, 133.** are both rural trading centers; latter is known for annual Sauerkraut Day. **141.** J. with US65 (see), which unites with US20 to **IOWA FALLS, 147,** inc. in 1856, bordering deep limestone gorge of Iowa R. Cliff pigeons which nest on cedar & shrub-dotted canyon walls are found in only one other place in country. **Iowa Falls Mus.** (sm.fee) has among its large coll. of pioneer & Ind. relics & ornithological specimens one of country's largest exhibits of guns. **Ira Nichols Bird & Flower Refuge,** NW. edge of town, contains specimens of prairie flora now disappearing from reg.

## Sec. 2: IOWA FALLS to SIOUX CITY. 176.

**31. WEBSTER CITY** was sett. in 1850 by Wilson C. Brewer & named for early stage line owner. **Wilson Brewer Mem. Pk.,** SE. part of town, contains **Pioneer Bonebright Mus.** displaying pioneer relics in adj. cabins, one built in 1850, other in 1856. **Kendall Young Pk.** is 70-a. tract of rolling woodland along Boone R.

**52. FORT DODGE,** bordering both sides of Des Moines R., is center of agric. & mining dist., with one of nation's biggest gypsum deposits at its SE. edge. It has hatcheries, serum & packing plants, tile factory & gypsum mills. Here bet. 1850 & 1853 Fed. Gov. maintained Ft. named for Wis.'s U.S. Sen. Henry Dodge, on whose abandoned site Wm. Williams laid out town in 1854. Through efforts of pioneer settler John F. Dunscombe, Ft. Dodge succeeded in wrestling cty. seat from then-thriving town of Homer in election contest which culminated in hour's pub. wrestling match bet. Dunscombe & Homer's chief advocate, John D. Maxwell. Clay resources of vic. began to be exploited in 1858. Visit here in 1869—yr. in which 1st gypsum quarries were opened—of Geo. Hull & H. B. Martin resulted in famous Cardiff Giant hoax. Out of slab of gypsum which they had carted to Chicago, German stonecutters carved 10′ tall stone man who was shipped to Mr. Hull's brother-in-law. Latter, having buried giant near Cardiff, N.Y., "discovered" him. Pronounced by sculptors, geologists, & writers to be "prehist. man," giant was exhibited by P. T. Barnum to millions of people. Meanwhile gypsum bed in vic. covering nearly 30 sq. miles, was rapidly exploited. By 1890 there were 4 mills quarrying it from hillsides. When Cardiff Mill, named for Cardiff Giant, sank shaft in open prairie, new era in industry began. Concurrently city developed as agric. center. PTS. OF INT.: 1st Ave. N. & N. 4th Sts., **Site of Ft. Dodge,** is marked by boulder with bronze tablet. **Log Cabin,** built about 1850, which was originally Adjutant's office, is now in **Oleson Pk.,** 1100 12th Ave., SW.; it contains articles of hist. int. **Webster Cty. Hist. Mus.** in basement of Pub. Lib., 605 1st Ave. N., exhibits Ind. artifacts & pioneer relics. 3rd Ave. S. & S. 10th St., **Blanden Art Gallery** houses pictures & art objects. At **54.5.** is J. with US169.

SIDE TRIP: Take US169 (L) from Ft. Dodge to J. with St.50, 11m; turn (L) on this to St.121, 5m & (L) here to 498-a. **Dolliver Mem. St. Pk.** (cabins.camp.lodge.pic.f.), 6m, named for U.S. Sen. Jonathan P. Dolliver, advocate of conservation, with pool & mem. shaft designed by Lorado Taft in his honor. Heavily wooded tract incl. Ind. mounds, deep ravines, & limestone bluffs. Adj. is **Woodman Hollow St. Mon.** (hik.), comprising deep gorge cut in sandstone by Des Moines R.

**78. ROCKWELL CITY** has been called "golden buckle on the Corn Belt." **80.** J. with St.17.

SIDE TRIP: Take latter (R) to J. with St.124, 5m & turn (R) here to 15-a. **Twin Ls. St. Reserve** (pic.bath.f.).

**98. SAC CITY** is trading & corn-canning center on Raccoon R. **106.** J. with US71 (see), with which US20 unites for 4m.

**176. SIOUX CITY**

Through RR. & bus conns. Info.: C. of C., 520 Nebraska St. Swim.: Riverside, Lewis, & Carlin Pks. Monahan Post Band Concerts beginning in June; Swedish Midsummer Festival, June.

Iowa's 2nd largest city, Sioux City spreads over bluffs & flats where Big Sioux & Floyd Rs. empty into Mo. R. opp. Neb.-S. Dak. boundary. From lowlands rise smokestacks & tall bldgs., on bluffs are homes among trees. City is spacious. Center of rich agric. sec., it is important grain & livestock market & meat-packing center, with stockyards, creameries, & produce houses; it even has poultry & dairy farms, livestock feeding lots, & hay & grain fields within its limits, & it swarms with farmers' & stockraisers' trucks bringing in produce. Site lies on ancient buffalo trl. followed by Omaha, Oto, & Sioux Inds. & later by Fr. traders. Here in 1848 Wm. Thompson platted town of Thompsonville & during following yr. other settlers arrived: Rbt. Perry, & Fr.-Canadian trader Theophile Bruguier, with his wives, their father, Chief War Eagle, & other Sioux Inds. Joe Leonais, trapper, in 1852 bought Bruguier's claim & in 1855 sold it to Dr. John K. Cook, who platted it as Sioux City, E. Addition. Sioux City was inc. in 1857. Soon steamboats were tying up regularly at levee. Arrival of RRs. in 1868 & 1870 made place important shipping pt. By middle 1880's floating pop. of traders, miners, adventurers, steamboat crews, R. travelers, had given town of 20,000 an unsavory reputation. Rev. Geo. Channing Haddock, arriving in 1885, undertook campaign against saloons, brothels, gambling houses which led to his assassination; after that Sioux City reformed. Sinking of boatload of wheat in Mo. R. was accident that started meat-packing industry which changed Sioux City into industrial city. J. E. Booge recovered & bought waterlogged wheat & began feeding hogs with it; since there was no market for live hogs, he slaughtered them & sold meat. He built small plant & hired butchers. Others followed his lead. From this activity came Live Stock Exchange, org. in 1887. In same yr. Sioux City promoted festival whose principal attraction was world's 1st Corn Palace, domed & adorned with sheaves of grain & corn. Sioux City's evolution into industrial city gave rise, in time, to labor movement. Agitation by I.W.W., otherwise known as Wobblies, in 1915, interrupted but not defeated by arrest & jailing of agitators, was followed by election as mayor of local minister Wallace M. Short on pro-labor platform. Strikes broke out in packing plants in 1921 & 1922. And in 1932 & 1933 striking farmers & their sympathizers halted trucks & trains bringing produce to city under leadership of Farmers' Holiday Assoc. Sioux City today is Nation's 6th largest livestock market & one of its largest primary grain markets. It has world's largest creamery, its largest popcorn processor & largest manufacturer of wind-propelled generators. Its products incl. flour, honey, livestock feeds & serums, batteries, tools & machinery, & many other articles. It is Iowa's biggest wholesale & jobbing center, serving 7-state trade territory, & one of its chief retail centers. It is served by 6 RRs. & large mun. airport & is head of navigation on Mo. R. It has symphony orchestra & civic art center, 3 colleges, 10 pub. libs. & 40 pks. Among institutions on which it prides itself are its Monahan Post. Amer. Legion Band & its Abu-Bekr White Horse Mounted Patrol.

PTS. OF INT.: Sioux City's pub. bldgs. incl. (1) **City Hall** (1891), 6th & Douglas Sts.; (2) **Woodbury County Cth.** (1918), 7th & Douglas Sts.; (3) **Old Fed. Bldg.** (1896-97), 6th & Douglas Sts., with 148′ clock tower housing "Old Ben"; (4) **New Fed. Bldg.** (1933), 6th & Douglas Sts.; & (5) **Pub. Lib.,** 6th & Jackson Sts., which houses **Mus.** containing paintings, natural history specimens, & Ind. & pioneer relics. (6) Foot of Chambers St., **Sioux City Stockyards & Packing Plants** cover 100 as. (7) 400-700 Riverside Blvd., **Riverside Pk.** (pic.swim.amusement) contains **Bruguier's Cabin,** 2nd dwelling built within city limits. (8) End of War Eagle Dr., **War Eagle Pk.,** on high bluff overlooking R., contains **Grave of Chief War Eagle,** marked by concrete block with bronze plaques. Among other pks. are (9) 32-a. **Grandview Pk.,** Grandview Blvd. & 24th St., with **Band Shell** (1934) & natural amphitheater seating 6,000 & (10) 801-a. **Stone Pk.** (pic.camp.hik.bridle paths), Sioux R. Rd., with high peaks & thickly wooded valleys. (11) Atop **Prospect Hill,** Bluff & W. 1st Sts., commanding impressive view of city & environs is gray granite **Mon.** in form of 15′ shaft, erected by Presb. Ch. to comm. prayer meeting held here in April 1869 by 3 ministers, among them Sheldon Jackson, one of greatest of Presb. missionaries. (12) Lewis Rd. & Glenn Ave., **Floyd Mon.,** is 100′ white sandstone shaft, marking burial place of Sgt. Chas. Floyd, member of Lewis & Clark expedition, who died in 1804. (13) 1601 Morningside Ave., **Morningside College,** is 4-yr. liberal arts college founded by Meth. Episc. Ch. in 1894, occupying 23-a. campus; its conservatory of music is notable. (14) 32nd & Rebecca Sts., **Briar Cliff College** (opened 1930), woman's college conducted by Sisters of St. Francis with 60-a. campus. (15) **Trinity College,** NE. edge of town.

Sioux City is at J. with US75 (see).

# US 30—IOWA

**ILL.-IOWA LINE** (33$^m$ from Sterling, Ill.) **(W) to IOWA-NEB. LINE** (26$^m$ from Fremont, Neb.). **343. US30**

Via: Clinton, Cedar Rapids, Ames, Denison & Missouri Valley. RR. & bus lines parallel or follow route throughout. Accoms.: Chiefly in cities.

US30 cuts through R. bluffs & rocky hills into rolling prairie country, with thick-growing trees, & cont. across fertile prairie to Mo. R.

## Sec. 1: ILL.-IOWA LINE to CEDAR RAPIDS. 87.

US30 crosses Miss. R., which is Iowa-Ill. Line, **0.**, on Lyons-Fulton Toll Bridge. **3. CLINTON,** industrial & RR. center stretching 7$^m$ along Miss. R., has long avenues overarched by ancient elms & late 19th cent. mansions dating from its heyday as lumbering center, which contrast with humming factories & RR. yards. 1st settler in vic., Elijah Buell, est. ferry across Miss. in 1835. 3 yrs. later Jos. M. Bartlett laid out town & named it New York, which in 1855 was acquired by Iowa Promotion Co., replatted & renamed for DeWitt Clinton, onetime Gov. of N.Y. On what had been swampland & slough city came into being, with brick plant, boatbuilding yards, wooden sidewalks & mule drawn street cars, luxurious Randall Hotel. It grew rapidly after est. of sawmills, which reached peak of production in 1880's, when Clinton was recognized as largest lumber-producing city in world, with 17 millionaires. Sloughs & streams were filled with immense quantities of sawdust, on which additions to city rapidly rose. But lumber boom ended with last log raft's arrival in 1906; lumber people transferred their interests to railroading, & Clinton as a whole turned to mfg., trading & retailing.

PTS. OF INT.: (1) Bet. S. 1st St. & Miss. R., **River Front Pk.**, stretching almost 1$^m$, contains stadium, swim. pool & athletic fields, & mem. fountain & artificial waterfall. (2) End of N. 3rd St. on R. bluffs, **Eagle Pt. Pk.** has enormous natural stone face on limestone cliff & 35′ stone observation tower. (3) Springdale Dr. & 4th Ave. N., **Mt. St. Clare Academy,** housed in Romanes. bldg. on handsome estate, is Cath. girls' school; its mus. houses coll. of orig. paintings. (4) 850 S. Bluff Blvd., **Old Stone H.** (1837), oldest in Clinton Cty., served successively as squatter's cabin, tavern & farmhouse. (5) 2517 N. 3rd St., **Elijah Buell H.** (1857), was erected by Clinton's 1st settler. (6) 240 5th Ave. S., **St. John's Episc. Ch.,** in style of Eng. Goth. parish church with open timbered roof, has back of its altar **Brewer Mem. Mosaic,** one of finest examples of its art in America.

**22. DEWITT,** named for DeWitt Clinton, Gov. of N.Y., 1817-22, is at J. with US61 (see). **70. MT. VERNON,** sett. largely by Bohemians, is site of **Cornell College** (opened 1853), housed in red brick bldgs. of early Amer. design on landscaped hilltop campus dominated by stone Goth. towers of **Wm. Fletcher King Mem. Chapel. Armstrong Hall of Fine Arts** contains coll. of prints, reproductions & textiles. Near campus is **Norton Tulip Garden.**

SIDE TRIP: Take St. 261 (L) 4.5$^m$ from Mt. Vernon to Cedar R. & turn (R) here to 648-a. **Palisades-Kepler St. Pk.** (cabins.lodge.camp.pic.boat.f.trls.), 6.5$^m$, heavily wooded, with scenic limestone bluffs.

### 87. CEDAR RAPIDS

Through RR. & bus conns. Info.: C. of C., Mem. Bldg., Municipal I. Swim.: Ellis & Thomas Pks.

E. Central Iowa's principal industrial center, Cedar Rapids is situated in rich agric. area on Cedar R., whose swift rapids at this point inspired city's name. Its business dist. has brisk, metropolitan air; (N) & (S) are mfg. plants & RR. yards & shops, & back into rolling hills on both sides of R. extend tree-arched residential districts. "Little Bohemia," SW. end, is center of Cedar Rapids' large Czech colony. 3 yrs. after Osgood Shepherd settled E. side of R., N. B. Brown, Geo. Greene & others who purchased his squatter rights surveyed town in 1841. Dam soon built across R. furnished power for grist & sawmills. In 1852 David W. King laid out town of Kingston on W. bank, later annexed. Advent of RR. in 1858 turned city's attention toward mfg. & marketing. During 1870's oatmeal mills were established, gas for illumination installed, & horse-drawn streetcars introduced. 1880's brought opera house & bus. college; 1890's, new churches & schools & new p. o., electric cars & union sta. Cedar Rapids today is leading industrial city, producing cereals, meat products & poultry & stock feed; road bldg., mining, & milk processing machinery; radio equipment, truck parts, metal castings, pharmaceuticals; & other articles. It has a network of pks. & other recr. facils. & many cultural institutions, incl. symphony orchestra.

PTS. OF INT.: Hub of Cedar Rapids' civic plan is **Municipal I.,** in main channel of Cedar R. (1) Here is limestone, neo-classic **Mem. Coliseum** (1928), 7 stories high, surmounted by cenotaph-topped, colonnaded observ. tower; it houses city offices & auditorium. (2) Facing it, across formally landscaped plaza, is **Linn County Cth.** (1926). (3) On E. bank, across from Municipal I., is **Fed. Bldg.** (1933), 1st St. bet. 1st & 2nd Aves. SE., containing murals on theme of "Law & Culture." (4) 428 3rd Ave. SE., **Pub. Lib.** (1906), contains **Cedar Rapids Art Assoc. Gallery,** exhibiting contemporary Amer. paintings & prints. (5) 813 1st Ave. SE., **Iowa Masonic Lib.** (est.1844), one of oldest & largest of its kind in U.S., has mus. containing Masonic articles, firearms & armor, Ind. relics, & other articles. (6) 1st Ave. bet. 12th & 13th Sts. NE., **Coe College,** which had its beginning in sch. opened in 1851 by Rev. Williston Jones, is liberal arts college, affiliated with Presb. Ch. **Bert Heald Bailey Mus.,** top fl. of Science Hall, is one of Iowa's largest, containing zoological, botanical, geological, & ethnological exhibits. Of architectural interest are 2 examples of work of pioneer modern architect Louis Sullivan: (7) 3rd Ave. & 1st St. SW., **Peoples' Savings Bank Bldg.** (1911) & (8) 3rd Ave. & 14th St. SE., **St. Paul's Meth. Ch.** (1913). (9) Bever Ave. at Mem. Dr. SE., **Bever Pk.,** thickly wooded area with pic. grounds & zoo, contains (10) what is said to be city's 1st frame house, **John Vardy H.** (1842). (11) Ellis Lane at NW. edge of town, **Ellis Pk.** (boat.bath.golf) has **Shakespeare Garden** containing species of flowers grown in Shakespeare's garden in England. (12) N. end 3rd St. NE., **Quaker Oats Plant** (guided tours), world's largest cereal mill.

SIDE TRIP: Take US218 (L) from Cedar Rapids to **N. Liberty,** 18$^{m}$, & turn (L) here 5$^{m}$ to 774-a. **L. MacBride St. Pk.** (pic.swim.boat.f.), with 138-a. lake & woodland preserve. US218 cont. to **Iowa City,** 27$^{m}$ (see US6), at J. with US6 (see).

## Sec. 2: CEDAR RAPIDS, IOWA to IOWA-NEB. LINE. 256.

**47. TAMA** was platted in 1862. **TAMA IND. RESERV.** (3,300 as.), at **50.,** is tract of farm & timber land held in common by Sac & Fox Inds., descendants of group who bought holdings here in 1857 (it is not Gov. reserv., despite its name). Annually in mid-Aug. 4-day powwow is held, resembling cty. fair, with ceremonial dances.

**67.** J. with St.14.

SIDE TRIP: Take latter (R) to **Marshalltown, 3$^{m}$,** retail shopping center, livestock & grain market, & factory city producing furnaces & heating equipment, power lawn mowers & automobile parts, tools & other metal articles, & food products. City was named for Marshall, Mich., by its 1st permanent settler, Henry Anson, who arrived in a covered wagon in 1851. In 1st yrs. after Civil War city's industrial development began. PTS. OF INT.: 22-28 W. State St., **Mem. Coliseum** (1929), contains auditorium which houses Tall Corn Festival & other civic events. State & N. Center Sts., **Pub. Lib.** (1903) has mus. with hist. & geological collections. End of N. 3rd Ave., **Riverview Pk.,** bordering Iowa R., contains **Log Cabin Mem.** (1936), with foundation & fireplace stones from surrounding farms, each of its 195 logs bearing brass plate comm. one of cty.'s pioneers. Summit & N. 9th St., **Iowa Soldiers' Home,** approached by vaulted elms, comprises group of red brick bldgs. in Eng. Romanes. style on 156-a. grounds.

At **COLO, 89.,** is J. with US65 (see). **96. NEVADA,** est. in 1853. **104. AMES,** college town on prairie, bisected by Skunk R., has air of cleanliness & charm, with well-kept homes & wide shaded streets, a mun. utilities system & airport & well-planned street system insuring notably good traffic safety record. Here John I. Blair built sta. for Cedar Rapids & Mo. (later North Western) RR. & laid out town, which he named for one of RR.'s proprietors, Oakes Ames. 1st home was built in 1864. Soon brisk small town evolved, its growth paralleling that of adj. College Farm of St. Agric. College. Advent of rail line from Des Moines spurred development. During 1890's Ames extended its limits to include college & acquired city waterworks, lib. assoc., & mun. lighting system. Its growth has since been steady. **Iowa St. College** (est.1858, opened 1869), bordering US30, one of nation's foremost land-grant colleges & institutions of science & technology, occupies $16,000,000 plant comprising some 70 bldgs. on 3,300 as. of land with 120-a. campus whose broad lawn is broken by trees & shrubbery. Its normal enrollment of more than 6,000 makes it one of country's 25 largest institutions of higher learning. Best-known campus bldg. is 110′ **Goth. Campanile,** with 36 bells. **Mem. Union** is social hub. **College Lib.** contains murals painted by Grant Wood & assistants. Other landmarks are **Hist. Old Farmh.,** once stagecoach stop & inn; **College Cemetery,** one of few college cemeteries in world; **Formal Garden; & L. Laverne.** College farms, arboretum, herbaceous garden, horticultural orchards, & soil conservation nursery are of interest, as is 450-a. recr. area (golf.pic.hik.riding.skiing.tobogganing).

**118. BOONE,** on crest of expansive prairies, is mining, RR., & industrial center, with C. & N.W. shops & division office & coal mines & clay & gravel pits. Boone was laid out in 1865 by Cedar Rapids & Missouri RR. Co. on wild tract of unimproved land after citizens of near-by Boonesboro, laid out in 1851, had failed to donate to co. $10,000 demanded of them along with 20 as. for depot grounds & RR. right-of-way. Boonesboro remained cty. seat until 1887, when it was annexed by Boone; it is said many of old settlers of orig. community would never "set foot" in upstart city that supplanted their town as industrial center.

SIDE TRIP: Take St.164 (L) from Boone to 896-a. **Ledges St. Pk.** (cabins.camp.pic.f.), 4m, rugged area with big trees, named for its huge sandstone ledges rising from tributary of Des Moines R. to heights of 25′ to 75′.

**126. OGDEN** was named for capitalist W. B. Ogden & **GRAND JUNCTION, 137.,** for J. here of C. & N.W. & M. & St.L. tracks. **145. JEFFERSON** is market town est. about 1854 by settlers who borrowed $200 to purchase town site. **SCRANTON, 155. & GLIDDEN, 167.** are farmers' market towns. **172. SWAN L. ST. PRESERVE** (pic.f.boat.) is wildfowl refuge. **174. CARROLL,** named for Charles Carroll of Carrollton, signer of Decl. of Ind., is shipping pt. for grain, flour, livestock & other farm produce & milling, packing & industrial center mfg. farm implements & equipment. **201. DENISON** was named for its founder, J. W. Denison, Bapt. minister & land co. agent, who arrived in 1855. **Washington Pk.** contains log cabin built in 1857 which houses pioneer relics. **218. DUNLAP** was named for RR. official Geo. L. Dunlap; **WOODBINE, 228.,** for vine which grew profusely on early resident's house; & **LOGAN, 237.,** for Civil War Gen. John A. Logan. **245. MISSOURI VALLEY,** below high bluffs overlooking Missouri R., 1st settled in 1854, is trading & shipping pt. for farm produce. It is at J. with US75 (see). **256.** US30 crosses Mo. R., which is Iowa-Neb. Line, on Abraham Lincoln Mem. Bridge (toll).

## US 6—IOWA

**ILL.-IOWA LINE** (1m from Moline, Ill.) **(W) to COUNCIL BLUFFS, IOWA. 312. US6**

Via: Davenport, Iowa City, Newton & Des Moines. Route paralleled by RRs. & followed by bus lines throughout. Accoms.: Plentiful at short intervals.

US6, Iowa's most heavily traveled hy., cuts (W) across S. part of state, following route of first RR.

### Sec. 1: ILL.-IOWA LINE to DES MOINES. 177.

From downtown Moline, Ill., US6 follows 19th St. to J. with 5th Ave. near Miss. R. shore.

SIDE TRIP: Take 5th Ave. (L) to 16th St.; turn (R) on 16th St. & across arsenal bridge to 900-a. **Rock I. Arsenal,** one of most important ordnance mfg. plants, research & development centers, & storage depots of U.S. Army. Here in 1816 was established Ft. Armstrong, known as "Guardian of the Mississippi." After Ft. Armstrong was decommissioned, Rock I. became permanent arsenal for Army in W. During Civil War it manufactured weapons for Union forces & had one of largest prisons for Confed. prisoners of war. It has played major role in every subsequent war. On Grounds today are military mus., Nat. & Confed. cemeteries, & arsenal bldgs. Near S. tip of I. are **Site of Ft. Armstrong,** built in 1816, marked by log blockh. duplicating 1 of 3 constituting orig. ft. & by 2-story frame **Home of Col. Geo. Davenport** (1833.rest.). Davenport was an Englishman who served in U.S. Army 10 yrs. before coming to Ft. Armstrong site as Gov. troop provisioner; later he entered fur trade with Inds. In this home on Feb. 23, 1836 met group of 6 men to execute articles founding city of Davenport. Here in 1845 Davenport was murdered by bandits.

At 2m main Rd. across arsenal grounds conn. with US67; turn (R) on this across Miss R., which is Ill.-Iowa Line, on **Gov. Bridge,** one of few toll-free bridges across R., which affords good view (L) of $9,000,000 **Gov. Dam & Locks No. 15,** largest of 8 dams of roller gate type in U.S., with two parallel 110′-wide locks, one 600′ in length. 2 blocks (R) from end of bridge is **Site of 1st Bridge across Miss.** (1856), marked by boulder, whose construction provoked bitter feud bet. rivermen & RR. men. 1st legal test bet. them grew out of an accident to "Effie Afton," which struck pier & caught fire; young Abr. Lincoln represented RR. Co. in case of Hurd et al. vs. RR. Bridge Co., blocking steamboat captain's charge that bridge was "a nuisance & an obstruction," but issue was not finally decided until U.S. Supreme Court refused to uphold lower court decision ordering removal of bridge & affirmed RRs.' legal right to bridge any navigable R. in their westward path. At 3m, in **Davenport** (see below), is J. with US6.

US6 crosses Miss. R., which is Ill.-Iowa Line, **0.,** on **IOWA-ILL. MEM. BRIDGE** (toll), $1,450,000 suspension structure 5,552′ long. **1. BETTENDORF,** industrial suburb of Davenport, flourished after completion here in 1910 of huge plant built by co. headed by inventor W. P. Bettendorf, mfg. all-steel under-frame & one-piece cast steel side frame which became standard on all Amer. RRs. This plant, purchased by Gov. during World War II, became Quad-City Tank Arsenal & in 1947 was converted, together with Ordnance Steel Foundry Plant, into gigantic **J. I. Case Co. Plant,** mfg. hay balers, elevators, corn pickers & other products. Other Bettendorf factories turn out variety of products.

SIDE TRIP: Turn (R) from Bettendorf on US67 to $30,000,000 **Aluminum Co. of America Sheet Aluminum Rolling Mill,** 3m, completed in 1948, with 43 as. of space under 1 roof & capacity of 10,000,000 lbs. of sheet aluminum plate per month.

### 3. DAVENPORT

Through RR., bus & plane conns. Info.: C. of C., 403-406 Main St. Swim.: Mun. Natatorium, 120 S. Main St. Miss. Valley Fair, Aug.; Chrysanthemum Show, Vander Veer Pk., Thanksgiving; Annual Quad-Cities Art Exhibit, Spring.

Davenport, Iowa's 3rd largest city & largest of quad-city group comprising also Rock I., Moline & E. Moline, stretches almost 5m along Miss. R. From its landscaped river front fans (W) business dist. with shops, hotels & office bldgs.—chief trading & commercial center of quad-city industrial reg., bordered on E. & SE. by riverside industrial areas. On higher ground, spreading over semi-circle of bluffs as much as 160′ high & beyond, are residential dists. Its economic prosperity has brought Davenport cultural facils., incl. symphony orchestra, pub. art gallery & mus., fine pk. system & many schools, churches & hospitals.

Davenport boasts many "firsts" in its history: 1st bridge across R. & 1st RR. running W. of it, country's 1st national bank & 1st broadcasting sta. W. of R. It was founded on land (now main business dist.) given Fr. halfbreed Antoine Le Claire by U.S. Gov. at request of Chiefs Keokuk & Wapello of Sac & Fox tribes, after he had served as interpreter in negotiation of Black Hawk Treaty in 1832. Near site on which treaty was made Le Claire built home. He later acquired land adj. his reserve on W., which he sold to Col. Geo. Davenport & 6 other men; & here, in 1836, Davenport was founded. Within yr. it had sawmill, store, p.o. By 1840 pop. was 600 & by 1850, 1,848; it shot up to 11,267 by 1860, largely because of heavy immigration of German refugees from revolutions of 1848. Miss. & Mo. RR. Co. began construction of line to Council Bluffs in 1853 & Miss. R. Bridge Co. erected bridge across R. yr. after. No longer solely dependent on steamboat trans., Davenport rapidly forged ahead. It became hqs. of Gov. Sam. J. Kirkwood & his military staff at beginning of Civil War, since it was then terminus of telegraph facils.; & here in 1863 was opened First Nat. Bank of Davenport, 1st in U.S. to open after passage of Nat. Banking Act.

During yrs. after Civil War, when great log rafts were floated down Miss., Davenport became sawmill center. Sawmill industry attracted woodworking plants, especially cooperage firms. In one of these worked woodcarver Wm. H. Voss, who invented crude washing machine & in 1877 set up his 1st washing machine factory; by 1890 Davenport was washing machine capital of country. Wheels, 1st made of wood & later of metal, likewise had become leading Davenport product before end of century. Meanwhile, development of limestone quarries in 1880's had made possible establishment of today's important cement industry.

PTS. OF INT.: (1) Facing R. at foot of Main St. is 7-a. **Antoine Le Claire Pk.,** which contains **Black Hawk Treaty Boulder** with bronze plaque, replica of pioneer settler Capt. John Litch's **Log Cabin Store** (1836), **Peterson Mem. Music Pavilion** &

**Mun. Stadium.** (2) Adj. is **Mun. Natatorium,** supplied with artesian water. (3) 4th & Main Sts., **St. Anthony's Ch.** (Cath.1853); brick **Parish School Bldg.,** (1837-38) at rear was city's 1st church. Davenport's pub. bldgs. incl. (4) 4th & Perry Sts., **P.O. & Fed. Bldg.** (1933); (5) 4th & Ripley Sts., **County Cth.** (1888); (6) 4th & Harrison Sts., **City Hall;** (7) 4th & Main Sts., **Pub. Lib.** (8) 704 Brady St., **Davenport Pub. Mus.** containing important moundbuilder coll.; Ind., Eskimo, Mex., Peruvian & Midwest pioneer colls.; exhibits from Egypt, Greece, Rome, Babylon, Japan & China; geological specimens; scientific lib. (9) On grounds is clapboarded log **Home of Antoine Le Claire** (1833.rest.) built by Davenport's founder, which became Iowa's 1st RR. sta. after he moved to larger house; from it started 1st train to W. in 1855. (10) 120 W. 5th St., **Davenport Mun. Art Gallery** has large coll. of orig. paintings & reprods., etchings, cameos & intaglios. (11) Brady St. bet. 8th & 11th Sts., **Palmer School of Chiropractic** & **B. J. Palmer Chiropractic Clinic** are housed in rambling group of miscellaneous structures dominated by steel towers of **Station WOC** (est. 1922). Founder was D. D. Palmer, who discovered chiropractic in 1895; school & clinic were developed by his son, B. J. Palmer. On grounds is **A Little Bit O' Heaven,** garden mus. of statues & mementoes collected by B. J. Palmer. (12) 518 W. Locust St. **St. Ambrose College** (est.1882), & (13) 1607 W. 12th St., **Marycrest College** (opened 1939) are Cath. institutions for men & women respectively. (14) 10th St. & Tremont Ave., **St. Katharine's School** (opened 1884), on 10-a. wooded campus overlooking Miss., is an Episc. Ch. girls' school.

(15) W. end of 12th St., **Fejervary Pk.,** on land donated by daughter of Hungarian immigrant & early settler Count Nicholas Fejervary, accoms. elk, deer, buffalo & ostriches & has Monkey I. (16) Lombard St. & Central Ave. bet. Harrison & Brady Sts., **Vander Veer Pk.,** has lagoons & flowerbeds, electric fountain & glass conservatory. (17) **Credit I.** (pic.golf.tennis.baseball) occupies battlefield on which 334 Amer. soldiers commanded by Maj. Zachary Taylor were defeated Sept. 4, 1815, by 30 to 60 Brit. with about 1,000 Sac, Fox, Sioux & Winnebago allies. (18) On E. outskirts is **Duck Cr. Pk.** (pic.golf.tennis.baseball), E. end of E. Locust St.

Davenport is at J. with US61 (see). US6 cuts (W) to **W. LIBERTY, 41.,** center of live-stock-raising & dairying reg.

SIDE TRIP: Turn (R) from W. Liberty on graded Rd. to **Springdale,** 7m, Quaker settlement whose antislavery residents twice welcomed John Brown & helped care for fugitive slaves he was guiding to freedom, in 1856 & in 1858, & near which Brown trained 11 men for raid on Harpers Ferry. Turn (L) from Springdale on St.1 to **W. Branch,** 10.5m, where in 1874 was born Herbert Hoover, Pres. of U.S. (1929-1933). **Hoover Birthpl.,** W. side of Downey St., 2-room cottage to which 2nd story & attic have been added, was purchased in 1935 for preservation as mem. in 25-a. hist. shrine.

**58. IOWA CITY,** Iowa's 1st capital & now home of St. Univ. of Iowa, lies along both sides of Iowa R. Iowa City was founded by 1st Leg. Assembly in 1839 as capital of Terr. of Iowa. Surveyors laid out wide streets around 12-a. capitol square, & with funds from land sale held in Aug., construction of capitol was started. Furrow was plowed from Dubuque to guide influx of immigrants who rapidly built log cabins & few frame houses. Pending completion of capitol, 4th Terr. Leg. Assembly met Dec. 6, 1841 in frame bldg. loaned for temporary use. However, it was soon found that new settlement was not near St.'s pop. center, & in 1847, Monroe City was selected as capital; but public opinion did not approve choice, & Iowa City remained capital until selection of Des Moines in 1857. First RR., Miss. & Mo., completed its track to this pt. at midnight of Dec. 31, 1856, with aid of prominent citizens, who helped lay last several hundred feet of track in zero weather with light & heat provided by bonfires. For several yrs., Iowa City was RR. terminus, with large transient pop. of westward-bound travelers—among them Mormon handcart expedition of European converts, 1,300 strong, who camped here in 1856 & built wooden-wheeled pushcarts for 1,000m trip to Utah. St. Univ. opened in 1855 & in 1857 took over capitol bldg. In 1870's Iowa City acquired one of St.'s largest breweries; in 1880's, grape sugar factory; in late 1890's & early 1900's, flint glass co. & packing plant; & later, hybrid corn processing plant & advertising calendar plant. But its modern growth has depended chiefly on growth of univ.

PTS. OF INT.: (1) 727 Switzer Ave., **Rbt. Lucas H.** (1844) was built by 1st Gov. of Terr. of Iowa. (2) 1028 Kirkwood Ave., **Home of Sam. J. Kirkwood** (remod.) was residence of Iowa's Civil War Gov. (3) Clinton St. at Iowa Ave., Iowa's most honored bldg., **Old Capitol** (1838-46;John F.Rague, supervising architect), now houses adm. offices of **St. Univ. of Iowa,** whose Bedford stone buildings, mostly in Ital. Ren. or early Eng. Goth. style, spread around it. Old Capitol is sturdy & graceful structure with Doric columns at entrance portico & cupola with octagonal base from which rise Corinthian columns supporting dome. To SE. is **Schaeffer Hall,** containing Leigh Hunt Coll. of rare books & mss. & **Lib. of St. Hist. Soc. of Iowa** (3rd fl.), with pictures, flags & relics. To NE. is **MacBride Hall,** containing auditorium & Gen. Lib. & **Mus. of Nat. Hist.** (3rd fl.), with Mammal Hall & Bird Hall. On W. side of campus, across Iowa R., are **Fine Arts Bldg.,** which has coll. of paintings, sculpture & other art works; **Dramatic Art Bldg.,** whose Univ. Theater, with revolving stage, is leader in western theater movement; **Medical Center,** one of country's largest, with 3 hospitals & laboratories; & **Field H.,** with country's 2nd largest indoor swim. pool. There are some 60 permanent bldgs. & grounds cover 425 as. N. of westside campus, off Newton Rd., is **Veterans Hospital,** of advanced modern design, on which construction was begun in 1947.

SIDE TRIP: Take US218 (R) from Iowa City to J. with improved Rd., 9m; turn (R) 5m on this to 774-a. **L. MacBride St. Pk.** (pic.swim.boat.f.), woodland wildlife preserve with 138-a. L.

US6 cuts (W) through farming country to **HOMESTEAD, 79.,** one of several villages of Amana Soc., or Community of True Inspiration, which grew out of Pietist movement in Germany in late 17th & early 18th cents. & in 1843 began planned emigration to America, 1st to N.Y. St. & then to Iowa. Bet. 1855 & 1862, emigrants purchased village of Homestead & est. 6 other villages. Until 1932, both spiritual & temporal affairs of communities were managed by board of 13 trustees; since then Amana Ch. Soc. has supervised spiritual affairs & Amana Soc., production & marketing cooperative, has handled economic matters. Colony flourished from beginning, since its members had practical skill to quarry stone, hew wood, build houses & mills & farm land; each member was assigned to job he did best, sharing in community profits on equal terms with least & most skilled. Homestead, like other villages, has leisurely old-fashioned atmosphere. Plain rectangular 2-story gabled houses, stores & church, built of hardwood, red brick or brown sandstone, show old German architectural influence. General store & meat market sell society's produce—woolen blankets, German bread, Westphalian-type hams.

SIDE TRIP: Take St.149 (R) from Homestead to **Amana,** 3m, oldest of villages, with **Furniture Shop, Woolen Mill, Bakery** & **Main Office** of Amana Soc. Turn (L) from Amana on St.220 to **Middle Amana,** 5m, with another **Woolen Mill, Printing Shop** & **School; High Amana,** 7.5m; & **West Amana,** 9m, whose red brick & hardwood **Flour Mill** still uses its old mill stones. St. 220 cont. (L) from W. Amana to **Lower South Amana,** 11m, at J. with US6.

**90. MARENGO,** named for place in Italy where Napoleon defeated Austrians in 1800, is largest of several rural trading centers through which hy. passes. **126. GRINNELL** was named for man to whom Horace Greeley made famous statement: "Go West, young man, go West & grow up with the country!" He was Josiah Bushnell Grinnell, Congr. minister of N.Y., & in 1854 he followed Greeley's advice, coming W. to found with Dr. Thos. Holyoke & Rev. Homer Hamlin, on treeless prairie, town whose articles of founding set aside land for a college campus & forbade sale of liquor. **Grinnell College,** product of merger in 1859 of Iowa College, founded in Davenport in 1846, & of Grinnell Univ., opened 1856, is oldest educational institution W. of Mississippi which has continuously existed as college with 4-yr. program leading to degree. It was 1st in U.S. to develop sciences as part of liberal arts curriculum, to begin Dept. of Political Science in undergrad. college of liberal arts & to adopt Eng. housing system without sororities. In recent yrs. it has operated under so-called Grinnell Plan for a Liberal Education stressing students' individual needs, broad cultural orientation & intensive study in a specialized field. Campus (90 as.) is planned with separate residence units for men & women.

**145. NEWTON,** mfg. city in agric. reg. with smokestacks rising above cornfields. Newton refers to itself as world's washing machine manufacturer; it also produces farm & hy. equipment, household appliances, advertising specialties, blue cheese & other goods. Inc. in 1857, it was named for Rev. soldier, Sgt. Newton. After 1898, local incubator firm undertook manufacture of ratchet-slat washers. Fred H. Bergman, co.'s owner, patented hand-power washer in 1904 & began mfg. it. Three yrs. later, Automatic Electric Washer Co. began producing electrically powered washing machines. Hand-power washer designed by Howard Snyder, inventor for Parsons

Bank Cutter & Self-Feeder Co., which F. L. Maytag introduced in same yr., was afterward equipped with electric motor; in 1917 Snyder developed for Maytag cabinet type of cylinder washer & in 1922 gyrafoam washer. By 1925 Newton was in midst of industrial boom. F. L. Maytag, "Washing Machine King," became city's benefactor, financing many improvements, among them 40-a. **Fred Maytag Pk.** (swim.tennis.pic.), which contains **Thos. Reese Log. H.** (1848). **Maytag Co. Plant,** 512 N. 4th Ave. W., with more than 13 as. of floor space & office bldg. of striking modern design, has one of world's largest aluminum moulding foundries. Adj. is **Automatic Washer Co. Plant. 155. COLFAX,** named for U.S. Vice Pres. Schuyler Colfax, passenger on 1st train passing through; it grew up as a spa with mineral springs. Coal beds in vic. are now chief source of income.

## 177. DES MOINES

Through RR., bus & plane conns. Info.: C. of C., Savery Hotel, 14th & Locust Sts. Iowa St. Fair, last wk. in Aug.

Des Moines, capital of Iowa, is an important commercial & industrial center in rich agric. sec., spreading from both banks of sluggish Des Moines R. At its heart are gray stone bldgs. of Civic Center, linked by arched bridges. E. Side bus. center pushes up to foot of park-clad Capitol Hill with its gold-domed Capitol & St. bldgs.; beyond spread bus. houses & homes with mfg. area to (S). (W) of Civic Center, skyscrapers of main bus. dist. rise from valley floor. Farther W. is once-fashionable residential dist.; to NW. are Drake Univ. campus & newer residential areas. City, covering 66 sq. miles, is spaciously planned, with wide streets, broad yards & large pk. areas. Name Des Moines is probably traceable to moundbuilders who long ago lived near R. banks; Inds. called stream "Moingona" (river of mounds). After explorations of site led by Col. Stephen W. Kearny in 1835 & John C. Frémont in 1841 at behest of War Dept., military garrison was est. here at confluence of Raccoon & Des Moines Rs. in May 1843. Wilson Alex. ("Aleck") Scott had preceded Capt. Jas. Allen & his company of First Dragoons; & when ft. was est., he obtained permit to settle near-by & raise corn & hay for garrison. At midnight Oct. 11, 1845, after Sac & Fox had relinquished their rights, terr. was thrown open to white settlers, who rushed in to stake their claims when ft. cannon boomed out zero hour; Capt. Allen & his men cont. to occupy ft. until Mar. of following yr. "Aleck" Scott, securing 500 as. on E. bank, est. ferry & built bridge.

Settlement which grew up soon prospered as stopping place for Cal.-bound gold seekers. Steamboats made their precarious way upriver to drop anchor here. In 1858, place became St. capital, when 10 yoke of oxen hauled into town two bobsleds of archives from Iowa City. News of Civil War aroused struggle bet. northern & southern sympathizers, but city made substantial contribution to war effort. In spring of 1894 "Kelly's Army" of nearly 1,000 men en route from Omaha to Washington to plead their cause before Congress descended upon city & refused to move on until provided with 150 flatboats to cont. journey down Des Moines R. During World War I, & again during World War II, pop. reached new peak as thousands of friends & relatives & war workers were attracted to city while soldiers were trained at near-by Camp Dodge & Ft. Des Moines.

Modern Des Moines is city of diversified activities in which mfg., jobbing, retailing, banking, insurance & publishing contribute economic support. Its mfg. plants turn out over 500 different products: airplane parts, automobile accessories & tires, tools, machinery, wearing apparel, chemicals, medicines, cosmetics, food products & others; among important big new plants added since World War II are tire & rubber, agric. implements, farm equipment & furnace factories. Rich coal fields in vic. have promoted industrial growth.

PTS. OF INT.: Des Moines' Civic Center occupies both river banks in center of city, comprising (1) **City Hall** (1910), E. Riverbank bet. E. Locust St. & E. Grand Ave.; (2) **New Fed. Bldg.** (1930), E. Riverbank at E. Walnut St.; (3) **Coliseum** (1910), W. Riverbank bet. Grand Ave. & Locust St., seating 8,500; (4) **Pub. Lib.** (1904), W. Riverbank bet. Walnut & Locust Sts. (5) From its 85-a. pk. site on eminence E. of R., **St. Capitol** (1871-84;A.Picquenard,designer), E. 12th St. bet. Grand Ave. & E. Walnut St., lifts 275′ gilded dome, resembling that of Hotel des Invalides in Paris. Bldg. is eclectic in style. At main entrances on 4 sides Corinthian columns support ornamental pediments. Principal feature of inter., finished in marble, granite & finely carved native woods, is grand rotunda, colonnaded, with statuary, mural by Edwin H. Blashfield & mosaics by Frederick Dielman. On

main floor are battle flags of Iowa. On 2nd fl. are Senate Chamber & House of Representatives Room. Steps lead up to dome. On Capitol grounds are several mons.: **Soldiers & Sailors Mon.** (1879;Harriet A.Ketchum,sculptor); **Allison Mem.** (1913;Evelyn B.Longman,sculptor), comm. Sen. Wm. B. Allison of Dubuque; & **The Pioneers** (1893;Carl Gerhardt,sculptor). **Grave of Wilson Alex. Scott,** SE. cor. Capitol grounds, is marked with tablet; Scott donated part of Capitol site. (6) E. 12th St. & Grand Ave., Ionic-columned, dome-topped, **St. Hist. Mem. & Art Bldg.** (1899-1900), houses some of St.'s most valuable colls. In W. wing of main floor are Hist. Lib., Aldrich Autograph Coll., Grenville M. Dodge Mem. Room & Emerson Hough Mem. Room. In E. wing on main fl., mezzanine & 2nd fl. is General Division of Iowa St. Lib. Portrait Gallery on 2nd fl. contains portraits of State's Govs. & prominent citizens; Mus., adj., contains pioneer relics & mounted animals. Third fl. Mus. is devoted to prehist. & early Ind. objects. Also on 3rd fl. are Archives Division & World War Room. In basement is Industrial Exhibit of carriages & automobiles & pioneer implements.
(7) University Ave. bet. 25th & 28th Sts., **Drake Univ.** (est.1881), named for one of its founders, Gen. Francis Marion Drake, is coed. institution occupying group of brick buildings on 3-block campus. **Cowles Lib.** houses valuable special colls. **Drake Stadium,** block N., seats 18,500. (8) Outstanding for its advanced modern design, **Des Moines Art Center,** Greenwood Pk. facing Polk Blvd., completed in 1948, was designed by Eliel Saarinen; it serves both as mus. with coll. of paintings & as art study center. (9) In Waveland Pk., 48th St. & University Ave., is **Drake Univ. Mun. Observ.** (O.on specified nights) with 8¼″ visual & photographic reflecting telescope. (10) Woodland Ave. at 15th St., **Hoyt Sherman Place** (1877), mansion built by Gen. Wm. T. Sherman's brother, Maj. Hoyt Sherman, & adj. modern annex, containing auditorium, recr. & lib. rooms, & art gallery, comprise home of Des Moines Women's Clubs. (11) 18th St. S. of Raccoon R. bridge, **Waterworks Pk.,** 1,500-a. tract with bird sanctuary, scenic roadways, horseback & hik. trls., greenhouses, fountains & lagoons. (12) 6th Ave., just N. of Des Moines R., **River View Pk.** (boat. dancing.amusements), is city's amusement center. (13) **Greenwood Pk.** & (14) **Ashworth Pk.,** adj. each other at Polk Blvd. & Grand Ave., have hundreds of acres of natural wooded grounds, sunken flower gardens, shelter houses & tennis courts. (15) E. 9th St. & Mattern Ave., **Union Pk.** (pic.), has flower gardens, green lawns & stately old trees. (16) E. end Grand Ave., **Iowa St. Fair Grounds** are setting during last wk. of Aug. of one of world's largest agric. expositions, attracting more than 500,000 visitors, with livestock, poultry, garden, dairy, cooking & canning, art, industrial & other exhibits. (17) Army Post Rd. & SW. 9th St., **Ft. Des Moines,** opened as cavalry post in 1903, was "Home of the WACs" during World War II, serving as 1st training center for Women's Army Corps. (18) 30th St. & Euclid Ave., **U.S. Veterans' Adm. Facility** occupies oak-wooded 48-a. hilltop site.
Des Moines is at J. with US65 (see).

SIDE TRIP: Take St.163 (L) from Des Moines to **Pella,** 43m, sometimes called cleanest city in Iowa, sett. by Dutch immigrants in 1847. Local products incl. bologna, cookies, flour, canned goods, wagons & overalls, Venetian blinds. Annually in May, when thousands of tulips bloom, inhabitants don Dutch costumes for festival. **Pella Hist. Mus.,** reprod. in architecture & furnishings of Dutch home, displays relics, documents & home wares. **Central College,** founded in 1853 as Bapt. Ch. institution, has been conducted since 1916 by (Dutch) Reformed Ch. of America; among bldgs. on 20-a. campus are Goth. **Douwstra Chapel & Ludwig Lib. Oskaloosa,** 60m, is quiet college town & farmers' marketing center, sett. in 1843 by Quakers & later by Welsh coal miners. It was named for wife of Chief Osceola, Oskaloosa ("Last of the Beautiful"). 1st coal mines in St. were developed near-by about 1870 & worked until about 1910. W. side Market St. at N. edge of town, **Wm. Penn College** (opened 1873) is 4-yr. coed. liberal arts college, conducted by Iowa Yearly Meeting of the Religious Soc. of Friends, notable for emphasis on democratic community living & student work program. Modern brick bldgs. on 30-a. campus incl. **Wm. Penn Hall,** containing lib., astronomical observ., mus. with coll. of African relics, Ind. artifacts, geological & natural hist. specimens & hist. materials & white-columned **Spencer Mem. Chapel** (Georg. Col.) Near campus is **Friends' Meeting H.** (1913.Gr.Rev.), 656 N. C. St. University Park at E. edge of town, **Kletzing College** (org.1905), coed. liberal arts institution, supported by members of various Protestant evangelical churches, with several brick bldgs. in wooded setting. **Edmundson Mem. Pk.** (pic.swim.) is 60-a. tract in S. part of city. Near E. entrance is log **Morgan Cabin** (sm.fee), 1221 S. F. St., built in 1840's & furnished in pioneer style. Cont. (R) from Oskaloosa on US63 to **Ottumwa,** 89m, spreading from both banks of Des Moines R., whose name is white man's version of Ind. word meaning "rippling waters." N. Ottumwa is hilly sec. of fine homes, churches, pub. bldgs. & schools, seemingly remote from bustling industrial dist. that covers R. bottoms. Ottumwa is site of world's largest independent pork processing plant & largest hay machinery plant; it has variety of other industries. Settlement here sprang up almost overnight when site was thrown open May 1, 1843 & hundreds of pioneers made midnight dash across country to stake out claims. It developed slowly until est. of John Morrell & Co. packing plant & opening of bituminous coal beds in 1870's & 1880's. In 1890 "Coal Palace"—medieval-looking structure, much turreted, veneered with glittering jet—was built above reprod. of coal mine; & visitors flocked to Mardi Gras & fair. Coal mining industry soon declined, however, & Ottumwa has since depended chiefly on meat-packing. Outstanding feature of **Wapello County Cth.,** 4th & Court Sts., is statue of Chief Wapello of Fox Tribe surmounting apex over entrance. 129 N. Court St., **Ottumwa Pub. Lib.** has coll. of Babylonian tablets dating as far back as 2350 B.C. End of Hayne St., **John Morrell & Co. Plant** has more than 100 bldgs. covering 100 as. At 102$^{m}$ is J. with St.273.

Turn (R) here 13$^{m}$ to 1,130-a. **L. Wapello St. Pk.** (cabins.pic.camp.bathh.swim.f.), with 287-a. L. among wooded hills.

## Sec. 2: DES MOINES to COUNCIL BLUFFS. 135.

US6 goes (W) from Des Moines through several small rural trading centers to J. with US71 (see) at **79. 83. ATLANTIC** was thought to be halfway bet. 2 oceans, & coin was flipped to decide whether its name should be Pacific or Atlantic; Pacific won, but when it was learned that other Midwest towns already had that name, decision was reversed. Among chief industries are meat packing plants, factory producing folding stoves & Army cots, & huge corn & pumpkin cannery.

### 135. COUNCIL BLUFFS

Through RR. & bus conns. Info.: C. of C., 4th Ave. S. & S. 1st St. Swim: River Front Pk.

Council Bluffs, stretching from high bluffs across lowlands to Mo. R. bank opp. Omaha, is converging pt. of 8 RR. lines & one of nation's largest mail transfer pts. It is important farm market with huge grain elevators, drawing trade from dist. checkered not only with corn & grain fields but also with vineyards of one of Midwest's chief grape-growing areas; & it is biggest flower-growing center W. of Miss., with more than 100 greenhouses. Its industries turn out variety of articles. But in residential dists., removed from bustling RR. yards, it has air of peace & quiet.

Inds. first met along R. bluffs here to sell furs to Fr. traders, & explorers Lewis & Clark camped near-by in 1804. Itinerant traders & trappers later designated whole bluff territory along this part of Mo. as Council Bluffs. Francis Guittar took up residence on site in 1827 as agent of Amer. Fur Co. In 1837, Potawatami Inds. were moved into reg. & Fed. troops were est. in temporary camp to protect them from other tribes; year following, Father Pierre Jean De Smet arrived & for 3 yrs. conducted mission, using camp blockh. as a church. Following arrival of Mormons led by Orson Hyde in 1846, settlement known as Kanesville in honor of Thos. L. Kane, friendly Army officer, grew up. It became stopping place for travelers during Cal. gold rush of 1849, attracting gamblers, traders, thieves & desperadoes. Departure of whole Mormon pop., numbering nearly 8,000 in this vic. by 1850, to Utah in 1852 left town without gov.; remaining 1,000 residents reorganized & renamed community Council Bluffs. In same yr. Grenville M. Dodge came to survey Platte R. Valley for RR.; it is said that conversation about RRs. held here in 1859 by Dodge & Abr. Lincoln influenced latter's choice in 1863, as Pres. of U.S., of Council Bluffs as E. terminus of U.P. By 1870, 5 RRs. had made conns. with U.P. here. Development of trading & mfg. followed.

PTS. OF INT.: Boulders with bronze tablets mark several of chief hist. sites—(1) E. Broadway & Union Sts., **Site of Blockh.,** built by Capt. D. B. Moore's troops in Aug. 1837; (2) E. Broadway & State St., **Site of Father De Smet's Mission,** est. May 1838; & (3) N. side Bayliss Park, 1st Ave. & Pearl St., **Mormon Trl.** (4) **Lewis & Clark Mon.** (1935;Harry Stinson, designer), 4$^{m}$ N. of business dist. on Scenic Rainbow Dr., comm. Lewis & Clark's council with Oto & Winnebago Inds. in 1804. (5) 1512 S. Main St., **Mem. for Grenville M. Dodge** is stone marker placed in 1922 on 70th anniversary of his mapping route for Rock I. RR. across Iowa. (6) 605 S. 3rd St., **Grenville Dodge Residence** (1870), maintained with orig. furnishings & art works, is Council Bluffs showplace. (7) Point Lookout, head of Oakland Dr. & Lafayette Ave., **Lincoln Mon.,** tall granite shaft comm. Abr. Lincoln's visit to city,

Aug. 12-14, 1859. (8) **Lincoln Pk.,** Military Ave. & Oakland Dr., contains **Log Cabin** (1934), serving as mus., which contains Ind. artifacts & hist. relics. (9) At E. portal of U.P. Bridge, W. end of 12th Ave., is 7′ tall **Bronze Buffalo Head** (1916; Capt.Edw.Kenny,sculptor), welcoming travelers to land of buffalo W. of Mo. R. (10) **Golden Spike Mon.,** concrete replica of RR. spike, 56′ high, marks E. terminus of U.P. (11) In Fairview Cemetery, E. end of Lafayette Dr. is outstanding mem. in vic., bronze **Angel of Death** (1918.Dan.Chester French,sculptor), comm. Anne B. (Mrs. Grenville M.) Dodge. Cemetery also contains **Grave of Amelia Jenks Bloomer,** pioneer in woman suffrage movement & advocate of dress reforms, one of which public dubbed "bloomers" for her; she died in Council Bluffs in 1894. (12) 1132 E. Pierce St., built into bluffs, with more than 121,000′ under glass, **J. F. Wilcox Greenhouses** are said to have 2 of world's biggest rose houses. (13) 1300 Canning St., **Lainson Greenhouses,** with 250,000′ of glass covering, specialize in flowers & tropical plants; more than 3,500,000 roses a yr. are grown.
Council Bluffs is at J. with US75 (see).

# US 61—IOWA

**DUBUQUE, IOWA** (13m from Dickeyville, Wis.) **(S) to IOWA-MO. LINE** (26m from Canton, Mo.). **200. US61**

Via: Maquoketa, Davenport, Muscatine, Burlington, Fairfield, Ft. Madison, & Keokuk. RRs. parallel most of route from Maquoketa (S) & bus lines throughout. Accoms.: Chiefly in cities.

US61 winds through hills & valleys of E. Iowa to Davenport, skirts Miss. R. shore (S) to Muscatine, cuts short distance inland & then approaches R. bank again in Iowa's SE. cor.

### Sec. 1: DUBUQUE to DAVENPORT. 76.

**0.** US61 crosses Wis.-Iowa Line on Eagle Pt. Bridge (toll) over Miss. R.
**1. DUBUQUE** (see US20) is at J. with US20. **4.** J. with US52-67.

SIDE TRIP: Take latter (L) to J. at 2m.
Turn (L) here 1m to **Crystal L. Cave** (fee.guides), with tunnel more than 3,000′ long, containing stalagmites & stalactites & underground L.

**St. Donatus,** 11m, is small village, sett. by immigrants from Luxembourg, with picturesque 2-story yellow stone, green-shuttered Hs. of French design. On steep hill is 4-story stone convent; & at top of bluff, reached by winding path past Stations of the Cross, is **reproduction of Chapel du Bilchen** in Luxembourg. **Bellevue,** 21m, river-front town, has pottery works & oil burner factory. **Bellevue St. Pk.** (lodge.camp.pic.f.golf), S. end of town, is 149-a. tract on rocky promontory overlooking Miss. R.

At **5.** is J. with US151.

SIDE TRIP: Turn (R) on latter 7m to J. with improved Rd. & (R) here 2m to gray stone Goth. **New Melleray Abbey** of Trappist order, whose members live strictly apart from outside world & maintain almost complete silence. Named for Mt. Melleray Monastery in Ireland, institution was founded in 1849; it is self-supporting.

**34. MAQUOKETA,** seat of Jackson Cty., is site of **Ellis Mus. of Archaeology & Anthropology** (fee), containing extensive coll. of fossils & relics.

SIDE TRIP: Take St.130 (R) from Maquoketa 9m to 111-a. **Maquoketa Caves St. Mon.** (camp.pic.), containing caverns, natural bridge, balanced rock, & other geological curiosities.

**54. DEWITT** (see US30), is at J. with US30. **76. DAVENPORT** (see US6), is at J. with US6.

### Sec. 2: DAVENPORT to IOWA-MO. LINE. 124.

At **18.** is J. with St.160, leading (R) 2m to 322-a. **Wild Cat Den St. Pk.** (camp.pic.), forested area with cavern & unusual rock formations, containing old **Grist Mill & Dam** (c.1848). On E. edge of **FAIRPORT, 21.,** fish-rearing ponds of **U.S. Fish Hatchery** stretch for half a mile bet. hy. & R.

**29. MUSCATINE,** mfg. & trading city, calls itself "The Port City of the Corn Belt." It spreads out from riverbank with old brick bldgs. lining narrow, brick-paved sts. that slope away to dip bet. hills. Name is derived from that of Mascoutin Ind. tribe, who camped near-by. Trading post was est. here in 1833. Jas. W. Casey staked claim in 1835 & began cutting timber to fuel steamboats. Site was surveyed & place named Bloomington in 1836; name Muscatine was adopted 13 yrs. later. New settlers, many of them German, flocked in. Muscatine soon became important steamboat landing. Sawmill & pork packing plant were set up in the 1840's. Muscatine has since gone through 3 eras of industrial development. First, beginning about 1860, was dominated by lumber industry & later by sash & door mfg. About 1890 began manufacture of pearl buttons from Miss. R. mussel shells; Muscatine soon claimed rank of "Pearl Button Capital of the World." Present era is one of diversified industry. Sash, door & other millwork products & pearl buttons still are important products: Muscatine produces more of last than any other city. But other industries produce pulley & pumps, saddles & harness, tools & toys, canned vegetables, meat & poultry products, & other articles. PTS. OF INT.: 304 Iowa Ave., **Pub. Lib.** houses coll. of hist. materials & early pictures & relics. 211 W. 8th St., oldest of city's surviving early bldgs. is **Old First Mathias Ch.** (1842), on grounds of present Mathias Ch. 109 Walnut St., **Mark Twain H.** was home during 1853-54 of Mark Twain, who lived with his widowed mother & brothers, Henry & Orion, latter part owner of Muscatine "Journal." Washington St. just off River Rd. at NE. edge of town, **Weed Pk.,** with natural amphitheater, 2 artificial Ls. & wildflower preserve, overlooks R. from a bluff. It affords good view of **U.S. Dam & Lock No. 16** across Miss.

**51. WAPELLO,** chartered in 1856, is peaceful town sprawling along Iowa R. **79. BURLINGTON** is scattered over 4 hills along Miss., its sts. climbing slopes from riverside docks & bus. dist. at irregular angles. Descendants of early German, Irish, & Swedish settlers still predominate, clustering in their own distinctive settlements: Dutchtown (German), West Hill (Swedish), & Hibernia (Irish). Burlington is important mfg. & distributing center; it turns out electric motors, auto trailers, bags, fertilizer, building materials, clothing, & other products. Its 23,000-a. Iowa Ordnance Plant, built in 1941, manufactures ammunition. Site was known as Sho-ko-kon (Flint Hills) to Inds., who valued it for flint found there; & Ind. village was est. here temporarily in 1820. After Black Hawk Treaty opened terr. to settlement in 1833, white families staked claims; in Aug. of that year Dr. Wm. R. Ross opened 1st store. John Gray, native of Vermont, arriving in 1834, was allowed to name place for his home town. Here, in temporary capitol bldg., 2nd legislature of Terr. of Wis. convened in Nov. 1837; & when Terr. of Iowa was created in 1838, 1st Legislative Assembly met & appointed commission to choose permanent capital. During next decade town grew rapidly as hundreds of steamers docked to discharge freight & load pork, lard, & farm produce. Burlington's 3 pork packing plants made it "Porkopolis of Iowa." Completion of 2nd continuous railroad from Chicago to Miss. R. opp. Burlington in 1855 & beginning of operations on Burlington & Mo. RR. in 1856 soon made town bustling rail center. Miss R. bridged in 1868. By 1871 Burlington had 7 RRs. During 1870's it throve as sawmill center & lumber shipping pt., handling logs rafted down Miss. As lumber industry declined toward end of cent., other mfg. enterprises were est.

PTS. OF INT.: S. end Main St., **Crapo Pk.** (camp.playground.swim.), overlooking Miss., has boulder memorial marking spot where Zebulon M. Pike is said to have landed Aug. 23, 1805, & unfurled Amer. flag, & bronze plaque near Black Hawk Spring, comm. Ind. chief, who hunted here. Bronze plaques mark **Site of Old Zion,** 1st Iowa Terr. Capitol, W. side of 3rd St. bet. Columbia & Washington Sts., & **Site of 1st Masonic Hall in Iowa,** SE. cor. Main & Columbia Sts. 311 Washington St., **Hawk-Eye Gazette Bldg.** houses St.'s oldest newspaper in continuous publication, with files running back to 1837 (avail.at pub.lib.). 2700 West Ave., weatherboarded **Log Cabin** (1833) at Hay homestead, built by Jeremiah Smith, Jr., is thought to be oldest house in Des Moines County.

SIDE TRIP: Take US34 (R) from Burlington to **West Burlington,** 3m, dominated by its C.B.& Q. RR. repair shops. Here in small pk. at W. edge of town is **Our Lady of Grace Grotto,** dome-shaped structure whose exter. walls contain stones from every St. in Union & almost every country in world. **Mount Pleasant,** 28m, was site of Iowa's 1st cth., built in 1839. **Iowa Wesleyan College,** 4-year coed. Meth. college occupying 25-a. wooded campus in heart of town, had its beginning here in 1844. At N. end of Main St. is imposing old **Harlan H.,** former residence of Jas. Harlan, pres. of Iowa Wesleyan, U.S. Sen., & Abr. Lincoln's Sec'y of the Interior, whose daughter Mary married President's son Robert.

Turn (L) from Mount Pleasant on St.133 to 110-a. **Oakland Mills St. Recr. Reserve** (camp.pic.f.), $4^m$, forested & rocky, with L.

At $45^m$ is 25-a. **Woodthrush St. Mon.** (pic.), abounding in bird life & wild flowers. **Fairfield,** $51^m$, is an agric. trading center with several small mfg. plants. **Pub. Lib. Mus.** contains archaeological, Ind., pioneer, & nat. hist. exhibits. **Old Settler's Pk.** surrounds **Bonifield Cabin** (1836). **Parsons College** (opened 1875), N. edge of town, on 65-a. rolling, wooded campus, is Presb. institution.

**97. FORT MADISON** covers flatlands near Miss., hemmed in by high hills & steep bluffs. It derives name from Ind. trading post est. here in 1808 just after inauguration of Pres. James Madison, which was abandoned in 1813 when Chief Black Hawk & his allies laid siege to it. Town grew up around lone chimney which remained standing. Here in 1833 John H. Knapp est. another trading post. By 1847 S. D. Morrison was making plows by hand for local trade, beginning farm tool industry that still flourishes. Later, flour & lumber mills were erected. Steamboating & lografting added boisterous notes to life of town. Another growing period followed Santa Fe's est. here of freight & passenger division pt., at W. end of its bridge across Miss. Paper mills were opened in 1879, & manufacture of plows was begun on large scale. In early 1900's pearl button & wax-paper bread-wrapper factories began production. W. A. Sheaffer Pen Plant, founded here in 1913, one of 1st to use bar & lever filling device in fountain pens, is today Fort Madison's largest industrial enterprise. PTS. OF INT.: Ave. H & 4th St., **Lone Chimney Mon.,** marks site of ruins of old ft. for which city was named. Design of **Lee County Cth.,** 7th Ave. & Ave. F, oldest in use in Iowa, is attributed to Father Samuel Mazzuchelli, pioneer priest & architect; it is distinguished by immense Tuscan columns. **Atchison, Topeka & Santa Fe RR. Drawbridge** across Miss. is largest drawbridge in world. At E. end of Ave. E is **Iowa St. Penitentiary.** At **100.5.** is J. with St.2.

SIDE TRIP: Take latter (R) to **Farmington,** $20^m$, platted in 1839, in fertile Des Moines R. Valley, with coal mines & stone quarries near-by.

(L) from Farmington $0.5^m$ on gravel Rd. is 127-a. **Farmington St. Pk.** (camp.pic.f.), with L.

St.2 cont. to J. with St.1, $33^m$.

Take latter (R) $3^m$; turn (L) here $1^m$ to 2,216-a. **Lacey-Keosauqua St. Pk.** (cabins.lodge. camp.swim.boat.f.golf), largest of St. pks., in great horseshoe bend of Des Moines R., heavily wooded, with 30-a. L. St.1 cont. to **Keosauqua,** $4^m$, whose Ind. name means "great bend." **Van Buren County Cth.** (1842-43) has solid oak timbers more than foot square & thick brick walls. **Bonneyview** (1839), overlooking R., is town's oldest H.

**110. MONTROSE,** close to Miss., is site of one of 1st permanent settlements made by white men in Iowa. Here, Louis Honore Tesson, Fr.-Canadian, est. in 1799, trading post & planted apple orchards—1st in St., comm. by plaque in Montrose schoolyard, 3 blocks (L) from US61. Around 1st Ft. Des Moines (its site marked by plaque half block from RR. sta. near tracks), est. here in 1834 & maintained until 1836, grew up settlement. In 1837 D. W. Kilbourne laid out town later called Mount of Roses, for wild roses growing on near-by hillsides, which was contracted to Montrose. Steam ferry connects Montrose with Nauvoo, Ill.

SIDE TRIP: Take Lake Shore Dr. (L) from Montrose to **Galland School St. Mon.** $3^m$, replica of Iowa's 1st schoolh., opened here by Dr. Isaac Galland in 1830.

**122. KEOKUK,** rich in hist. associations, lies at mouth of Des Moines R. on Miss. Keokuk trades with farmers, manufactures variety of goods, & exports hundreds of tons of fish. 1st white man to settle here was Dr. Samuel C. Muir, who erected log cabin in 1820 for his Ind. wife & family. Moses Stillwell & Mark Aldrich opened trading post in 1829 for Amer. Fur Co.; & that same year, at July 4th celebration, it was proposed that settlement be named for Chief Keokuk of Sac & Fox. In 1837 town was platted by Isaac Galland, agent of New York Land Co. During next decade Keokuk became mfg. & jobbing hqs. for pioneer Middle West. Its position at foot of Des Moines rapids on Miss. made it pt. at which all steamboat passengers & freight had to be unloaded & lightered or forwarded by land. This obstacle to navigation was bypassed after 1856 by RR. running $12^m$ upriver, & finally solved by Gov. canal opened in 1877. PTS. OF INT.: (1) 3rd & Main Sts., **Pub. Lib.** (1881) houses coll. of curios, incl. city's 1st directory (1856) & menu set in print by Mark Twain when he was working in Keokuk job-printing plant of his brother, Orion. (2) 2nd & Main Sts., **Old Ivins H.** (1850.now Hawkeye Hotel) was Twain's boarding house; here he made his 1st after-dinner speech. (3) S. 7th St. at city limits, **Rees Pk.** contains old **Rees Homestead,** weatherboarded log cabin built by Thomas Rees, who printed Mark Twain's 1st paid articles in Keokuk "Saturday Post." (4) 15th St. & Grand Ave., **Rand Pk.** contains mon. & statue marking **Grave of Chief Keokuk.** (5) At W. end of Cedar St. is Iowa's only **Nat. Cemetery,** est. in 1861. (6) Foot of Orleans & Franklin Sts., **Keokuk Dam** (1910-13), nearly mile long, is gravity type, containing approximately same amount of masonry as one of great pyramids of Egypt. It forms 100-square-mile lake extending 65$^{m}$ (N). **Gov. Drydock & Gov. Lock,** near Iowa shore, are among largest ever built. (7) **Hydroelectric Plant** (conducted trips hourly 9-11, 1-3), farther out in stream, was equipped with turbines which, at time of construction, were 4 times size of any previously built. **124.** US61 crosses Des Moines R., which is Iowa-Mo. Line.

# US 65—IOWA

**IOWA-MINN. LINE** (11$^{m}$ from Albert Lea, Minn.) **(S) to LINEVILLE, IOWA** (58$^{m}$ from Chillicothe, Mo.). **223. US65**

Via: Mason City, Iowa Falls, Des Moines, Indianola. RRs. parallel route bet. Iowa-Minn. Line & Indianola. Accoms.: Chiefly in cities.

US65 cuts through central Iowa, traversing typical prairie country, through which meander shallow rivers. S. of Des Moines it passes through reg. overgrown with virgin timber.

### Sec. 1: IOWA-MINN. LINE to DES MOINES. 147.

**4. NORTHWOOD,** on Shellrock R., was settled largely by Norwegians, beginning in 1853. **MASON CITY** (see US18), **25.,** is at J. with US18. **51.** J. with gravel Rd. leading (R) 3$^{m}$ to 259-a. **Beed's L. St. Pk.** (pic.swim.boat.f.), with 130-a. L. **53. HAMPTON,** seat of Franklin Cty., was founded in 1856. **66.** J. with US20 (see), with which US65 unites to **IOWA FALLS** at **72. 83.** J. with St.57.

SIDE TRIP: Take latter (L) to **Eldora,** 8$^{m}$, orig. named Eldorado when John Ellsworth thought he had discovered gold here in 1851; he was mistaken, & name was later shortened. At 9$^{m}$ is 548-a. **Pine L. St. Pk.** (cabins.lodge.camp.pic.swim.boat.f.golf), with 2 Ls. among wooded hills, several Ind. mounds, & fish hatchery.

Hy. passes through several small rural trading centers on its way to J. with US30 (see) at **109. 147. DES MOINES** (see US6) is at J. with US6.

### Sec. 2: DES MOINES to LINEVILLE. 76.

**17. INDIANOLA,** seat of Warren Cty. since 1849, is site of **Simpson College** (est. 1860), Meth. Episc. liberal arts college with 20-a. campus. **23.** 774-a. **L. AHQUABI ST. PK.** (cabins.lodge.camp.pic.swim.boat.f.), rough & wooded area with L. **43. J.** with US34.

SIDE TRIP: Take latter (L) to **Chariton,** 9$^{m}$, on Chariton R., farm trading & shipping center.

**63.** J. with St.2.

SIDE TRIP: Take latter (L) to **Centerville,** 34$^{m}$, seat of Appanoose Cty., platted in 1846, & center of dist. rich in coal & gypsum.

US65 cont. to **LINEVILLE, 76.** through which runs Iowa-Mo. Line. It grew up around store built in 1851 half in Iowa & half in Mo. by pioneer merchant who sold clothing & groceries on Iowa side & liquor on Mo. side.

# US 71—IOWA

**IOWA-MINN. LINE** (82$^{m}$ from Redwood Falls, Minn.) **(S) to IOWA-MO. LINE** (64$^{m}$ from St. Joseph, Mo.). **242. US71**

Via: Spirit L., Spencer, Carroll, Clarinda. RRs. & bus lines parallel route in parts. Accoms.: Chiefly in cities.

Prairie sec. of N. Iowa through which US71 passes is treeless & flat, except where hy. dips into timber-fringed R. valley. S. of Carroll, rolling hills appear like waves on prairie, & soft crumbling bluffs line R. & banks.

### Sec. 1: IOWA-MINN. LINE to CARROLL. 129.

**5.** J. with St.9.

SIDE TRIP: Take latter (L) 7m to J. with improved Rd.

Turn (R) here 1m to 181-a. **Ft. Defiance St. Hist. Preserve** (pic.) where Ft. Defiance was staffed with cavalry in 1862-63 to protect pioneer settlers against marauding Sioux. There is modern log-cabin shelter.

**Estherville,** 8m, on bank of W. Fork of Des Moines R. River was sett. in 1857 & named for Mrs. Esther Ridley, wife of one of men who helped plat town.

**11. SPIRIT L.** lies S. of 5,500-a. L. of same name, Iowa's largest glacier-created L. (f.swim.duck hunt.). Surrounding reg. is dotted with 19 Ls. US71 now skirts 3,788-a. **WEST OKOBOJI L.**, 2nd largest in reg., on which lies at **16.** summer resort & winter sports center of **ARNOLD'S PK.**, sett. in 1856. Almost all of orig. 46 settlers were killed in March, 1857 by band of Sioux led by Inkpadutah. They are comm. by **SPIRIT L. MASSACRE MON.**, at **17.**, marking several of their graves. Near-by **Gardner Cabin,** which conts. relics of event & Ind. articles, was home of 1st victims of uprising, Mr. & Mrs. Rowland Gardner & their children. **Pillsbury Pt. St. L. Preserve** (pic.) adjoins, commanding fine views of L. At **31.** is J. with US18, with which US71 unites to **Spencer** (see US18) at **34. 72. STORM L.** is site of **Buena Vista College** (founded 1884), removed here from Fort Dodge in 1891, liberal arts college under Presb. auspices. L. Shore Dr. leads (L) to J. with gravel Rd., 1.5m, (R) on which is 18-a. **Storm L. St. Reserve** (pic.swim.boat.f.), 2.5m, adj. 3,060-a. Storm L. **88. EARLY.** J. with US20 (see). **103. L. VIEW** is summer resort (cottages. amusement facils.golf) on shore of Black Hawk L. **105.** J. with gravel Rd. leading (R) 1.5m to 353-a. **Black Hawk L. St. Recr. Reserve** (camp.pic.swim.boat.f.), with Iowa's largest fish-rearing ponds. **129. CARROLL** (see US30). J. with US30.

### Sec. 2: CARROLL to IOWA-MISSOURI LINE. 113.

**27. AUDUBON** was platted in 1878 by Chicago, Rock I. & Peoria RR. Cth. square contains 1st **Log Cabin** in cty., moved here from orig. site, with old furnishings. **50.** J. with US6 (see). **79.** J. with US34.

SIDE TRIP: (A) Turn (R) on US 34 to **Red Oak,** 13m, seat of Montgomery Cty., which has large calendar-manufacturing plant.

(B) Take US34 (L) to **Corning,** 15m, seat of Adams Cty., platted in 1855. At 18m is J. with dirt Rd.

Turn (L) on this 1.5m to **Site of Icarian Community,** marked by several old wooden bldgs., where Icarians, group of Fr. colonists led to Amer. in 1848 by political theorist Etienne Cabet, est. themselves in late 1850's & for nearly 4 decades carried on experiment in collective living.

US34 cont. to **Creston,** 37m, in heart of Iowa's bluegrass country, which in 1889 became hqs. of Blue Grass League of SW. Iowa & site of turreted, bluegrass-thatched Blue Grass Palace. Since 1869 Creston has been division hqs. of C.B.& Q. RR., whose shops, yards, & roundh. make it busy place.

**85. VILLISCA,** whose residents are predominantly of Dutch & Irish descent, bears name of Ind. origin said to mean "pretty place." **101. CLARINDA,** was named for Clarinda Buck, girl popular among early settlers. First postmaster est. his office here in a dugout in 1856.

SIDE TRIP: (A) Take St.2 (R) from Clarinda to **Shenandoah,** 19m, founded in 1870 with advent of RR., which owes its name to resemblance early settlers saw between Nishnabotna R. Valley at this point & Shenandoah Valley of Va. Shenandoah has number of large nurseries & seed and mail-order houses.

(B) Take St.2 (L) from Clarinda to **Bedford,** 20m, seat of Taylor Cty., (L) 4m from which is 386-a. **L. of Three Fires St. Recr. Reserve** (cabins.pic.swim.boat.f.) with 125-a. L.

At **113.** is **IOWA-MO. LINE.**

## US 75—IOWA

**IOWA-MINN. LINE** (17m from Luverne, Minn.) **(S) to COUNCIL BLUFFS, IOWA. 177. US75**

Via: Le Mars, Sioux City, & Missouri Valley. RRs. parallel route bet. Le Mars & Council Bluffs bus line bet. Valley & Council Bluffs. Accoms.: Chiefly in cities.

US74 traverses E. Edge of Gt. Plains to Sioux City & follows Mo. R. (S) to Council Bluffs. **6. ROCK RAPIDS** takes name from rapids in near-by Rock R. **22.** J. with

US18 (see). **50. LE MARS,** named for 1st initials of 6 young women who visited settlement in early days. It began in early 1880's as colony of Brit. settlers. Brit. customs were preserved; colonists rode to hounds & went steeplechasing, played polo, dressed for dinner. Venture failed, & people of other nationalities took over. At S. edge of town is **Western Union College** (founded 1900), controlled by Evangelical Ch. **75. SIOUX CITY** (see US20). J. with US20 (see). US75 now traverses flat bottomlands, where Mo. R. (R) meanders through wide valley bordered by brown crumbling cliffs. **111. ONAWA** was platted in 1857. It is noted for its tree-lined streets, 150′ wide. St.165 leads (R) short distance to **Lewis & Clark St. Pk.** (315 as.lodge.pic.boat.f.) on sandy-shored Blue L. near which Lewis & Clark camped. **150. MISSOURI VALLEY** lies by Mo. R. just below high bluffs. 1st settler came in 1854. Town is trading & shipping pt. for farm produce, especially hogs. Mo. Valley is at J. with US30 (see). **173. COUNCIL BLUFFS** (see US6) is at J. with US6. US75 bridges Mo. R., which is **IOWA-NEB. LINE** at **177.**

## US 40—KANSAS

**KANSAS CITY, KANS. (W) to KANS.-COLO. LINE** (c.7$^{m}$ from Arapahoe, Colo.). **461.5. US40**

Via: Lawrence, Topeka, Manhattan, Salina, Hays, & Oakley. RR. parallels route throughout. Accoms.: At short intervals.

US40 follows Kansas R. through rolling country, traverses central Kans. wheat belt, & crosses High Plains area rising toward Rocky Mts.

### Sec. 1: KANSAS CITY, KANS. to HAYS. 300.5.

**0.** On intercity viaduct over Kansas R. from Kansas City, Mo., US40 crosses Kans.-Mo. Line.

**6. KANSAS CITY, Kans.**

Through RR. & bus conns. Info.: C. of C., 727 Minnesota Ave. Swim. at pub. pks. Amer. Royal Livestock & Horse Show, Oct. or 1st of Nov.

Kansas' 2nd largest city & Wyandotte Cty. seat, Kansas City, Kans., preserves its own identity from its Mo. neighbor, together with which it makes up Greater Kansas City. Spreading over hills & bluffs N. & S. of Kansas R., it has irregularly patterned network of sts., having grown out of merger of 8 independent towns; it has 5 "main" streets, each centered on its own business & industrial district. "Kaw Point," neck of land bet. Kansas & Mo. Rs., where Lewis & Clark camped in 1804, became in 1818 part of reserv. granted Delaware Inds., from whom in 1843 it was purchased by Wyandot tribe, emigrating from Sandusky, Ohio. In same year Wyandot, who were farmers, educated, & more white than Ind. through intermarriage, laid out Wyandot City, which within year had church, council house, communally-owned store, & 1st free school in Kans. When Cal. gold rush of 1849 brought white emigrants, Wyandot began to demand territorial status for Kans.-Neb. reg. They were granted in 1855 rights of citizens with their lands in severalty, & promptly disposed of their property. White settlers who succeeded them renamed place Wyandotte & est. p. o. & 2 banks in 1857. Rival town of Quindaro, founded a little to N. & W. on bank of Missouri R. in 1856, soon offered competition. Both towns built Rd. to Kansas R. & est. free ferry. In 1859 Wyandotte was inc. & erected on levee block of business bldgs., in one of which was written in July 1859 constitution of Kans., est. Wyandotte Cty. & making Wyandotte its seat.

Est. in R. bottoms of a slaughter house in 1860 & a packing house in 1868 laid basis for place's best-known industry. Charles F. Adams, descendant of Pres. John & John Quincy Adams, persuaded Plankington & Armour to remove in 1871 packing house they had set up in Mo. to site near his stockyards. Around what is now Armour packing plant grew up new town, Armourdale, inc. in 1871. Around other packing houses & RR., completed to Topeka in 1866, grew up other towns: Armstrong (1871); old Kansas City, Kans. (inc. 1872); Riverview (1879). In 1880 Wyandotte absorbed Riverview; in 1886, Armstrong, Armourdale & Kansas City. Name of latter was then adopted for consolidated city. Two other settlements est. across Kansas R. to S.—Rosedale (1872), which received impetus from rolling mill opened in 1875, & Argentine (1880), which grew up around Santa Fe Ry. shops & yards &

Consolidated Kansas City Smelting & Refining Co. plant—were later absorbed, latter in 1909, former in 1922. Quindaro, having rescinded its inc., was absorbed by natural expansion.

During last quarter of 19th cent., thousands of "Exodusters," freed Negroes from S., swelled population, settling along Jersey Creek in "Rattlebone Hollow" & in old Quindaro or along levee in scrapwood shanties of "Mississippi Town." During same period there was great influx of European immigrants of peasant stock—Croats, Czechs, Slovakians, Poles, Germans, Russians—who settled around packing houses. City developed into important industrial center. Today its stockyards & meat-packing houses are 2nd only to Chicago's; & not even Chicago has all of "Big Four"—Armour, Cudahy, Swift & Wilson—with complete processing plants, as Kansas City has. Hay market & grain storage facilities are world's largest; animal serum plants, largest in nation. Soap factories, fabricating steel mills, flour mills, oil refineries, RR. shops & yards, & other enterprises contribute to economic stability.

Public bldgs. include: (1) 7th St. bet. Ann & Barrett Aves., **Wyandotte County Cth.** (1927); (2) 7th St. bet. Barnett & Tauromee Aves., **Soldiers' & Sailors' Bldg.** (1924); & (3) Huron Pk., **Carnegie Lib.** (1920-24). (4) Minnesota Ave., bet. 6th & 7th Sts., **Huron Pk.,** contains **Mun. Rose Garden** & (5) **Wyandot Nat. Cemetery.** Latter, with graves of many Wyandot chiefs dating from 1844 on, was reserved by Wyandot in treaty of 1855; when business interests in 1906 pushed bill through Congress authorizing its sale, Wyandot descendants carried litigation to Supreme Court, where Lydia B. Conley of Wyandot Zane family pleaded case, being 1st woman to appear before court. Although Supreme Court upheld Congressional bill, Congress in 1913 was persuaded by aroused public sentiment to repeal its statute & convert cemetery into city pk., extending sepulchral rights to Wyandot. City's educational institutions incl.: (6) State Ave. bet. 11th & 12th Sts., **Kans. St. Sch. for Blind;** (7) 27th & Grant Sts., **Western Univ.** (est.c.1862), coed. Jr. college maintained by African Meth. Episc. Ch. (8) From end of Mo. Pacific Bridge, Minnesota Ave. & 2nd Sts., **Panoramic View,** overlooking confluence of Mo. & Kansas Rs.

**16.** J. with Corum Rd. leading (R) 2.5$^{m}$ to 1,500-a. **Wyandotte Recr. Pk.** (1,500 as.; swim.boat.pic.f.), surrounding 305-a. L. with 20$^{m}$ shore line drive. **20.** J. with US73.

SIDE TRIP: Take latter (R) to **Lansing,** 8$^{m}$, centering around **St. Penitentiary** & **Industrial Farm For Women. St. Mary's College** (est.1860), 10$^{m}$, is Cath. girls' high school & college, with wooded 160-a. campus. **U.S. Veterans Adm. Facility,** adj., housed in c.100 bldgs. on high bluffs above Mo. R., cares for disabled vets. of all wars.

14$^{m}$ **Leavenworth,** 1st inc. town in Kans., claims to be best known city of its size in U.S. because of its 2 famous gov. institutions, Ft. Leavenworth & Fed. Penitentiary. On W. bank of Mo. R., it spreads over high bluffs & rolling hills. Retail trading center of rich agric. area, it is also industrial center. Here in 1827 Col. Henry H. Leavenworth erected Cantonment Leavenworth, now Ft. Leavenworth, to protect traffic on Santa Fe Trl.; farmers & missionaries attached to post were Kansas' 1st white settlers. After passage of Kans.-Neb. Bill (May 30,1854), meeting of pro-slavers at Weston, Mo., projected settlement here; town company, 1st in Kans., platted 320-a. tract, which by end of June was covered by squatters' tents & shacks. In 1855 Leavenworth became Territory's 1st inc. town. Early elections were corrupt, marked by ballot-box-stuffing tactics of dominant pro-slavery element. Business prospered, however, as industrial enterprises were est. in 1856, among them Abernathy Furniture Co. plant, today Leavenworth's biggest; in same year Russell, Majors & Waddell made Leavenworth hqs. for their vast transportation system. By 1860 Leavenworth with population of 8,000 was metropolis of Kans. It remained until 1880 State's largest city—gay place, with theaters, baseball team, fine mansions—but ultimately fell behind when Kansas City was preferred to it as RR. terminus.

PTS. OF INT.: (1) Shawnee & Main Sts., former **Planters' H.** (1856), now apartment h., was famous hostelry. (2) 511 Shawnee St., **Cathedral of the Immaculate Conception** (1864-68;Romanes.) was one of most imposing churches W. of Mississippi in its time. (3) Metropolitan & Grant Aves., **Ft. Leavenworth,** occupying 7,000-a. reserv. crossed by paved hys. & tree-shaded drives, is community in itself, containing 700 bldgs. On this site 4 companies of Third Regiment under Col. Henry H. Leavenworth's command erected in 1827 log & bark huts of Cantonment Leavenworth. Post became outfitting pt. for Mex. War troops & later for Cal. gold seekers. It was designated by Congress as temporary capital of Territory in 1854 & for time served as Gov. Reeder's residence. In all subsequent wars it has played important role. (4) S. end Scott Ave., **Command & General Staff College,** housed in consolidated group of yellow brick bldgs. surmounted by a clock tower, ranks 1st among Army officers' training schools; it was est. in 1881 by order of Gen. Wm. T. Sherman. Other pts. of int. are: (5) 1 Scott Ave., **Residence of**

**Commandant** (c.1861); (6) Scott & Grant Aves., **Gen. U. S. Grant Mon.** (1889.by Lorado Taft); (7) 12-14 Sumner Place, **Former H. of Gov. Reeder** (1834.brick extension 1879); (8) 17 Sumner Place, **Col. Style Brick H.** (c.1840), formerly U.S. Military Prison & Disciplinary Barracks. (9) **Ft. Leavenworth Mus.,** McPherson Ave. W. of 17th Infantry Barracks, contains old wheeled vehicles, Ind. artifacts, & dioramas depicting Kans. hist. (10) Opp. entrance to golf course on Biddle Blvd., **Nat. Cemetery** contains graves of soldiers who have fought in all country's wars; here is buried Gen. Henry H. Leavenworth. (11) 13th & Metropolitan Sts., **Fed. Penitentiary** is towering city of gray stone & red brick on 1,000-a. grounds. Built in 1895, it houses about 3,000 inmates, who work in factories producing brooms, brushes, shoes, clothing & furniture or on 1 of the 2 prison farms.

38m. **Atchison** lies on bank of "Great Western Bend" of Mo. R. in hill-fringed glacial amphitheater. Important as retail trade & wholesale & jobbing center, it ranks 10th in U.S. in flour milling industry & has 3 big iron foundries, as well as RR. shops, feed mills, seed concerns, industrial alcohol plant & many other enterprises. Town was organized & platted July 27, 1854 by 18 men, all but 2 from Platte Cty., Mo., who named town for Mo.'s pro-slavery Senator David R. Atchison. Inc. in Aug. 1855. Atchison had active pro-Southern faction, who published vehement pro-slavery paper, "Squatter Sovereign," & were likely to tar & feather Free Staters. In 1859, 1st telegraph from W. to E. was dispatched here & city became 1st W. of Mississippi to secure direct connection with St. Louis & E. when it decided to issue bonds for RR. With good steamboat landing & best wagon road to W., Atchison leaped ahead when in 1862 Ben Holladay bought bankrupt Russell, Majors & Waddell Freighting Co. & moved its hqs. here from Leavenworth & in 1864 Butterfield's Overland Dispatch was est. here to do million-dollar business carrying mails W. Atchison, Topeka & Sante Fe Ry. was another local enterprise, outgrowth of mun. bond issue; its 1st unit, to Topeka & Wichita, was opened in 1872.

PTS. OF INT.: (1) N. 5th & Parallel Sts., **Atchison County Cth.** (1897); on lawn is marker designating spot upon which Abraham Lincoln delivered in 1859 same address he later gave at Cooper Union, N.Y.C. (2) 819 Commercial St., **Soldiers' & Sailors' Mem. Hall,** contains Amer. Legion Mus. in which are Ind. relics. (3) 1600 S. 6th St., **Jackson Pk.** (120 as.) is noted for iris-bordered drives. (4) 801 S. 8th St., **Mt. St. Scholastica Academy & College for Girls** (est.1863.Cath.), has Tudor Goth. Adm. Bldg. & Norman-style chapel. (5) 2nd & Division Sts., **St. Benedict's College** (est.1858.Cath.) on landscaped Mo. R. bluffs, has $1,000,000 Tudor Goth. Monastery, modeled after Benedictine Monasteries of N. Europe. (6) 1400 S. 10th St., **Maur Hill Prep. School** (est.1920.Cath.), for boys, has several Tudor Goth. bldgs. on spacious campus. (7) S. edge of town, **Gov. Natural Cooler** is former limestone mine with 16.5 as. of storage space, largest storage unit of its kind in world, used by U.S. Dept. of Agric. for surplus commodities.

**33. J. with St.16.**

SIDE TRIP: Take latter (R) short distance to **Tonganoxie,** rural trading center with elm-shaded residential district. **Leavenworth Cty. St. Pk.** (506 as.boat.swim.f.h.camp.pic.), 3m, has 175-a. L.

Dipping into valley bottom fields of grain & potatoes, US40 crosses Kansas R.

## 46. LAWRENCE

Through RR. & bus conns. Info.: C. of C., 746 Vermont St. Swim. at Jayhawk Plunge, 6th & Michigan Sts.

Kansas' chief education center, Lawrence, with many fine old houses on broad lawns on its hilly W. side, is for most part an average-looking prosperous Kans. town. Founded in 1854 by Charles H. Branscomb & Dr. Charles Robinson, agents of New England Emigrant Aid Co., & named for Amos A. Lawrence of Boston, prominent member of co., Lawrence by Mar., 1855, was center of Free State activities in Territory, with Free State newspaper, "Kansas Tribune." In May, 1856, pro-slavery force led by Sheriff Jones attacked Lawrence, plundering town's newspaper offices, stores & homes & burning Dr. Robinson's house. Incident precipitated 2 yrs. of open warfare, ended only when pro-slavery party was shorn of power with adoption of Wyandotte Constitution (1859) & election of Dr. Robinson as Gov. Lawrence was sacked & burned again Aug. 21, 1863 by pro-Confederate Wm. Clarke Quantrill's band of 450 mounted guerrillas, who left 150 dead. Advent of Kans. P. RR. in 1864 made Lawrence prosperous trading & shipping point & it later acquired various industries.

PTS. OF INT.: (1) 6th & Mass. Sts., in Robinson Pk., **Old Settlers' Mon.,** boulder with bronze plaque bearing names of 1st settlers. Other markers indicate (2) 724 Vermont St., **Site of 1st Methodist Ch.** (1857); (3) 935 New Hampshire St., **Site of Massacre of Recruits** by Quantrill's guerrillas; & (4) 1115 Louisiana St., **Site of Robinson H.** (5) 1009 Vermont St., former **Trinity Episc. Ch.** (1858), now parish house adj. later church (1871) of same congregation, is Kansas' oldest religious edi-

fice. (6) 923 Vermont St., **Plymouth Congr. Ch.** houses State's oldest church organization, organized Oct. 1854. (7) 23rd St. & Barker Ave., **Haskell Institute** (est.1884), largest Ind. school in U.S., occupies landscaped campus with a group of brick & stone buildings & stadium. It has produced many noted football players. (8) **Univ. of Kansas,** its bldgs. strung along crest of Mt. Oread, occupies 160-a. campus commanding scenic panorama. Organized in 1862, univ. opened in Sept., 1866. Among chief bldgs. are: 13th St. & Oread Ave., **Mem. Union Bldg.** (1927); 14th St. & Oread Ave., **Dyche Mus.,** with natural history coll. which incl. largest univ. coll. of fossil remains in country; 14th St. & Oread Ave., **Thayer Mus. of Art,** which contains Ind. artifacts, Eng. porcelain & glassware, textiles & coins, Japanese lacquer, silverware, & prints, Chinese tapestries & Amer. handicraft; Campus Dr., **Green Hall,** housing Sch. of Law; **Fraser Hall** (1872), oldest bldg. on campus, containing **Wilcox Mus.** of facsimile reproductions of Gr. & Rom. objects; **Watson Lib.** (1924.Goth.) W. of Fraser Hall; **Haworth Hall,** housing **Paleontology Mus. & Geolog. Mus; Adm. Bldg.** (Ital.Ren.); **Snow Hall** (Coll.Goth.), W. of Adm. Bldg., housing natural sci. depts. & **Francis Huntington Snow Entomological Mus.,** one of best of its kind in country; 11th & Alabama Sts., **Mem. Stadium** (1927), seating 38,000.
US40 cont. (W) from Lawrence to J. at **56.** with gravel Rd.

SIDE TRIP: Take latter (R) to **Lecompton,** 3m, hillside village overlooking Kansas R., founded in 1854 & named for Sam. D. Lecompte, 1st chief justice of Kansas Terr., which from 1855 to 1858 was territorial capital. In **Constitution Hall,** W. side Main St., was written in 1857 Lecompton Constitution, which would have admitted Kans. as slave State but was overwhelmingly repudiated by electorate.

US40 now follows winding route through hills.

### 74.5. TOPEKA

Through RR. & bus conns. Accoms.: Plentiful. Swim. at mun. pools in Gage, Garfield & Ripley Pks. Annual events: July, Mex. Fiesta; Sept., Kans. Free Fair.

Capital of Kans. & 3rd city in pop., Topeka straddles Kansas R. & spreads over R. bottoms & up slopes N. & S. Factories, flour mills, & meat-packing plants of industrial dist. extend along R. in oldest part of town. Along Kans. Ave., bisecting city from N. to S., lies retail business & professional dist. To S. & W. are chief residential sections, with tall shade trees. Topeka is important distribution & trade, insurance & printing industry center. Biggest single industry is Santa Fe Ry. with world's largest repair shops & car-building facils. Dominant in Topeka's economy are meat packing, flour milling, poultry & dairy products & other food-processing plants; new $12,500,000 Goodyear Tire & Rubber Co. plant, producing tractor & heavy-duty tires; & city's metal-working industries, which supply national markets. Nationally-known Menninger Foundation, U.S. Veterans Adm. Winter General Hospital (specializing in neuro-psychiatric cases) & St. Hospital for Insane make Topeka "Rochester" of psychiatric treatment & training. Also important are city's permanent army installations: Army Air Forces Supply Depot & Topeka Army Air Base.
First white settlers were 2 Fr.-Canadians, Joseph & Louis Pappan, latter an ancestor of late Vice Pres. Charles Curtis, who married Kaw Ind. half-breeds & sett. here in 1842; they est. 1st ferry across Kansas R. Col. Cyrus K. Holliday, young Pennsylvanian interested in RR. building, & partners bought land & org. town company. At meeting in log cabin Dec. 5, 1854, they chose name Topeka, Omaha Ind. word meaning "good place to dig edible roots." Heavy influx of New England immigrants followed. Here, in 1855, convention of Free Staters framed 1st Kans. constitution; but "Topeka Government" was speedily overthrown when U.S. troops arrested legislators. In 1857 city was inc. & in 1858 became cty. seat. Following adoption of Wyandotte constitution, it was selected as St. capital. Topeka grew to town of more than 5,000 in 1870. Holliday's RR., Atchison, Topeka & Santa Fe Ry., began building W. in 1869 & in 1878 est. its general offices & machine shops here. During 1880's Topeka passed through hectic real estate boom which ended abruptly with ruin of many investors in 1889; but it retained doubled pop. & was able to weather depression of 1890's. Introduction of bridges, parks, blvds., motor busses, hotels & office bldgs. early in 20th cent. made Topeka modern city.

PTS. OF INT.: (1) **Kansas State Capitol,** surrounded by 10-a. pk. extending from 8th St. to 10th St. & Jackson St. to Harrison St., is of cruciform design, modeled on plan of Capitol at Washington, D. C., with 4 wings & central 304′ rotunda. Con-

struction began in 1866 but was not finished until 1903. Opp. **Governor's Office,** 2nd fl., on walls of E. corridor, is John Steuart Curry's mural dealing with Kans. hist., "Tragic Prelude," & on walls of W. corridor is his "Kansas Pastoral," depicting contemp. scene. **Senate Chamber,** 3rd floor of E. wing, & **Representative Hall,** 3rd fl. of W. wing, are both richly finished. On 3rd fl. of N. wing is **St. Lib.** On grounds are **Abraham Lincoln Statue** (1918) & **Pioneer Women of Kans. Statue** (1937), both by Kans.-born sculptor Merrell Gage.
(2) 10th & Jackson Sts., **Kans. Mem. Bldg.** (1914.Fr.Ren.) houses offices of various veterans' organizations & **Hqs. of Kans. St. Hist. Soc.,** 1 of 2 or 3 largest St. hist. soc. in America, org. in 1875, which has largest newspaper coll. in country next to that of Lib. of Congress; art coll. of more than 20,000 pictures ranging from tintypes to oil paintings; St. Hist. Lib. of more than 350,000 vols. & about 1,500,000 mss.; & **Mus.** (4th fl.) of pictures & objects illustrating hist. of Kans. ranging in size from Mexican dressed fleas to Concord stage coach & in time from Coronado sword of 1541 to present. (3) 17th St. & College Ave., **Washburn Univ.,** housed in 15 bldgs. on 160-a. elm-shaded campus, has been since 1941 Topeka's mun. univ. It began as Congr. Ch. institution, opened in 1866, named for Ichabod Washburn of Worcester, Mass., who donated $25,000. **Rice Hall** (1870-74) contains small Mus. of Nat. Hist. **Mulvane Art Mus.** (1923.Ital.Ren.) houses permanent art coll., traveling exhibits, & painting studio, classrooms, lib., & little theater.
(4) Quincy St. bet. 7th St. & 8th Ave., Topeka's **Mun. Auditorium & City Bldg.** (1940) has auditorium seating 4,257. Among city's more architecturally notable structures are (5) **Topeka Central High Sch.** (1930.Coll.Goth.), 10th & Taylor Sts., & (6) **Grace Cathedral** (Prot.Episc.), 8th & Polk Sts. Also of interest are (7) **Arthur Capper Mansion,** Topeka Blvd. & 11th St., onetime residence of noted newspaper publisher & U.S. Senator, now radio station, & (8) **Charles Curtis Home,** Topeka Blvd. & 11th St., residence of grandson of Kaw Ind. chief who became Shawnee Cty. prosecutor, Congressman, Senator, & Vice Pres. (9) 6th Ave. & Gage Blvd., Topeka's largest recr. center, **Gage Pk.** (swim.sports facils.pic.zoo), contains nationally outstanding **Reinisch Mem. Rose & Rock Garden,** floodlit at night; **Old Settlers' Mem. Cabin,** removed here from farm near Topeka of Adam Bauer, pioneer structure of walnut logs with pioneer implements & furnishings; & **Munn Mem.** with frieze picturing pioneer family & ox-drawn wagon.
Topeka is at J. with US75 (see).

SIDE TRIP: Take 29th St. (L) from Topeka to **Shawnee L. & Pk.** (1,017 as.f.boat.swim.ft. & bridle trls.scenic dr.), 3$^{m}$, wooded area with 10$^{m}$ drive around 405-a. L.

US40 crosses Kans. R. & follows its N. bank (W) through several small towns. **99. ST. MARY'S,** outgrowth of Potawatomi Ind. mission founded by Jesuit missionaries in 1848, is site of **St. Mary's College** (Cath.), where many Kans. priests are ordained, & of **Ch. of the Immaculate Conception** (Goth.). **114. WAMEGO** is well-kept old town on R. bank, whose **City Pk.** contains Dutch Windmill transported stone by stone from near-by farm where it had been built by Hollander in 1873. At Wamego is J. with St.99.

SIDE TRIP: Take latter (L) to J. with St.29, 3.5$^{m}$, & turn (R) on latter 2.5$^{m}$ to **Wabaunsee,** crossroads village with some walnut-beamed stone houses built by its 1st settlers, Beecher Bible & Rifle Colony, who arrived here April 28, 1856. This company of abolitionist emigrants, organized in New Haven, Conn., carried rifles & Bibles supplied by eminent anti-slavery minister, Henry Ward Beecher. **Beecher Bible & Rifle Ch.** (1862), S. edge of town, is narrow-windowed stone bldg. with squat belfry.

**128.5. MANHATTAN,** lying in hill-encircled natural limestone bowl W. of confluence of Big Blue & Kans. Rs., is tree-shaded college & farm shipping & trading town. Two towns were founded here in 1854—Poleska, est. by Col. George S. Park of Mo., & Canton, sett. by New England Emigrant Aid Co.; they were soon consolidated under name of Boston. Party of colonists from Cincinnati, bringing boatload of freight incl. 10 portable houses by way of Ohio, Miss. & Kans. Rs. on steamer "Hartford," arrived in 1855 & concluded deal whereby they were given half of townsite; deal provided for renaming place Manhattan. In 1859 Bluemont College, forerunner of Kans. St. College, opened its doors. Following advent of Rock I. & U.P. RRs. in 70's & 80's, it became shipping pt. for farm produce & cattle. 11th St. bet. Poyntz Ave. & Fremont St., **City Pk.** (45 as. sports facils.), with band pavilion & rose & rock gardens, contains marble **Tatarrax Mon.,** comm. Harahey Ind. chief who visited with Coronado on latter's expedition into Kans.; **Log Cabin Mus-**

containing pioneer relics; & **Old Stagecoach** formerly used in Yellowstone Nat. Pk. 14th & Anderson Sts., **Kans. St. College of Agric. & Applied Science,** founded 1863, occupies more than 2 dozen bldgs., chiefly limestone in mod. Goth. design, on landscaped 155-a. campus. Its primary aim is technical instruction in agric., architecture & engineering, home economics, veterinary medicine, & phys. & biol. sciences. In **Anderson Hall** is mus. of antique furniture, pottery, & other articles; in **College Lib.,** art coll.; in **Fairchild Hall,** Mus. of Nat. Hist.

**138.** US40 crosses boundary of **FT. RILEY MILITARY RESERV.,** covering vast tract of virgin prairie. **138.5. MON. TO GEN. LEONARD A. WOOD** marks site of Camp Funston, 1 of largest U.S. training camps in World War I, where Gen. Wood trained famous 10th & 89th Divisions. **141.5.** On site of Pawnee, Kansas' first "permanent" Territorial capital, is two-story limestone **OLD CAPITOL,** used for 4 days in July, 1855, before proslavery majority unseated Free Staters & adjourned Shawnee Mission; it is maintained as pub. mus., furnished as it was in 1850's. **142. CAMP WHITESIDE** is used in summer by Nat. Guard & other reserve units. **143.5. FT. RILEY** today houses Mounted Serv. School, largest cavalry training center in country. It was est. as Camp Center in 1852 to protect trade of Santa Fe Trl., under command of Maj. E. A. Ogden, & renamed Ft. Riley in honor of Maj. Gen. Bennett Riley of Buffalo, N. Y. in 1853. Ind. uprisings after Civil War led to org. in 1866 of George A. Custer's famous 7th Cavalry, based here. At Ft. Riley is J. with camp's main drive, encircling grounds (L) past post & installations. Near center is **Wounded Knee Mon.,** comm. slain of 7th Cavalry, led against Sioux at Wounded Knee Cr., S. Dak., Dec. 29, 1890, by Col. James W. Forsyth. **OGDEN MON.,** short distance beyond Ft. Riley, erected in 1880 to comm. Maj. E. A. Ogden, who died at Ft. Riley in 1855 during cholera epidemic, stands near Nat. Cemetery, est. during epidemic.

**147. JUNCTION CITY** has developed as trading pt. for Ft. Riley soldiers. It was founded in 1858 & so named because it is at junction of Republican & Smoky Hill Rs. **160.5. CHAPMAN,** trading center of stockraising area, has **First Cty. High Sch. in U.S.** (1889), US40 at W. edge of town, built following enactment by legislature of bill est. State-wide system of cty. high schools as first conceived by Prof. J. H. Canfield of Univ. of Kans., father of novelist Dorothy Canfield Fisher.

Valley widens to vast sweep of wheat fields, broken at intervals by tracts of alfalfa, as hy. cont. (W). **172. ABILENE,** at heart of Kans. wheat belt. Today farm produce shipping pt. & agric. processing center. For nearly 5 yrs., beginning in 1866, Abilene's position as terminus of U.P. RR. made it objective of great Texas cattle drives over Chisholm Trl. Here great droves of Texas longhorns were herded into stock pens awaiting shipment, while as many as 5,000 cowboys, paid off simultaneously, thronged brothels, saloons & gambling houses. Abilene, said in 1871 to have more cutthroats & desperadoes than any other town, was tamed somewhat by James Butler ("Wild Bill") Hickok, who became marshal; credited with 43 killings before he came to Abilene, he increased his total here to 100. **193.5.** J. with gravel Rd. leading (L) 1$^{m}$ to **Ind. Burial Pit** (fee), in which are preserved 109 whole skeletons & other bones just as they were when unearthed in Oct. 1936 in one of Middle West's most remarkable archaeological finds.

**196. SALINA.**

Through RR. & bus conns. Info.: C. of C., Ash & 5th Sts. Accoms.: Plentiful.

Metropolis of central Kans., Salina lies in basin W. of confluence of Saline & Smoky Hill Rs., is trading & recr. center for thousands of farmers. Wheat is all-important hereabouts; Salina is dominated by grain elevators & flour mills. It also produces milling machinery, agric. implements, & other goods. Townsite was staked out in 1858. Settlement began to thrive in 1860 as "jumping off" place for gold-hunters traveling to Pike's Peak. Extension of U.P. RR. here in 1867 brought settlers. Great crops of wheat began to pour into Salina in 1870's. Meanwhile alfalfa, first introduced to Kans. by Dr. E. R. Switzer of Salina in 1874, also became important crop in reg. By 1880 Salina had 3 flour mills, 6 grain elevators, carriage & wagon factory, & agric. implement works; & during succeeding decade, 3 RRs. were built through community.

PTS. OF INT.: 8th St. & Iron Ave., **Salina Pub. Lib.** contains Hist. Mus. of pioneer memorabilia. Pks. incl. **Oakdale Pk.** (pic.swim.sports facils.open-air auditorium), N. entrance on Oakdale Dr., & **Kenwood Pk.,** E. end of Oakwood Dr. Claflin St. &

Santa Fe. Ave., **Kans. Wesleyan Univ.,** Meth. Episc. liberal arts college, founded 1886; **Carnegie Science Hall** houses lib. & mus. E. end of Iron Ave., **Marymount College,** Cath. women's college, est. by Sisters of St. Joseph in 1922.
Salina is at J. with US81 (see). **233. ELLSWORTH,** founded in 1869, had its day as wild & woolly cow town, but is now agric. community. **250. WILSON** is farm market & milling town. **273.5. RUSSELL,** est. in 1870s, is now center of oil dist., dotted with derricks. **290.5. VICTORIA,** built to resemble Russian village with wooden-shuttered peak-roofed houses flush with St., is center of scattered settlements in W. central Kans. est. in 1870's by Volga Germans of Cath. faith emigrating from Russia when religious privileges granted their ancestors by Catherine the Great were revoked. To them Kans. owes its ranking place as wheat-growing State, for they brought variety of hard wheat known as Turkey Red which they had grown on Russian steppes & which proved adaptable to Kans. climate & soil. Known as "Cathedral of the Prairies," **St. Fidelis Ch.** (Romanes.) rears its twin 141′ towers above town, an imposing structure seating 1,700 persons. Victoria was first settled, however, by English immigrants: shipload of sons of wealthy families who came bringing horses, sheep & cattle to settle townsite platted by Sir George Grant & named for Queen Victoria. Colonists lived with joyous abandon, galloping in red coats over prairie in pursuit of jack rabbits & coyotes & impounding waters of Big Cr. to float steamboat brought overland partly by oxcart. Colony was failure, & its site was taken over by German-Russians.

**300.5. HAYS,** gateway & chief trading & educational center of NW. Kans., is wheat-milling & oil-field center. Founded in 1867, soon after est. of Ft. Hays, frontier military post, it was in early years gathering place for scouts, cattlemen, soldiers, & desperadoes. W. F. ("Buffalo Bill") Cody during 1860's is said to have killed 4,280 buffalo near Ft. Hays within 18 months, whose meat he sold to RR. workers' camps & ft. commissary. Ft. Hays, directly S. of city, was abandoned in 1889 following end of Ind. wars & its 7,000 as. given to St. of Kans. Within this area today is **Ft. Hays Kans. St. College** (est.1902), 6th & Park Sts., occupying 80-a. wooded campus. **Forsyth Lib.** contains college mus., with nat. hist., geological & paleontological, botanical & hist. colls. Just S. are **Ft. Hays St. Pk.,** containing 2 of old Ft. Hays' stone bldgs., &, across Rd. from it, 3,600-a. **Ft. Hays Agric. Experiment Sta.,** conducted jointly by U.S. Dept. of Agric. & Kans. St. College. **St. Joseph's College & Military Academy** (est.1931.Cath.), W. edge of town, is boys' high sch. & jr. college.

## Sec. 2: HAYS to KANS.-COLO. LINE. 161.

**14.5. ELLIS,** est. in 1867 as RR. tank & pumping sta., was cowtown in days of Tex. cattle trade; it is now U.P. RR. division pt., with repair shops. At **15.5.** is boundary of Mt. Time zone; westbound travelers should set watches back 1 hr. **33. WAKEENEY,** est. in 1878. At **COLLYER, 46.,** is J. with gravel Rd.

SIDE TRIP: Take latter (L) here to dirt Rd., 10m, turn (R) on this to 2nd dirt Rd., 12m; turn (L) on this to pasture gate, 13m & (R) through gate to **Castle Rocks,** 13.5m, chalk remnants eroded by rain & wind into pillars & domes, once Ind. lookout pt. & hiding place.

At **QUINTER, 54.5.,** Dunkard social & trading center, is J. with graded Rd. leading (R) 7.5m to 436-a. **Sheridan Cty. St. Pk.** (camp.f.boat.) surrounding 124-a. L. **91.**

**OAKLEY,** market center & shipping pt. with mun. swimming pool & golf course, is at J. with US83.

SIDE TRIP: Take latter (L) to J. with Rd., 21.5m.
Turn (L) on this to 2nd improved Rd., 4m, & (R) on this to 3rd, 6m, turn (L) on this, then (R) at 7m to **Mon. Rocks,** 7.5m, sometimes called "Kans. Pyramids," group of chalk rocks rising with startling abruptness from vast flatness of High Plains. At N. end of group is **Kans. Sphinx,** one of most unusual rock formations in Kans., resembling Egyptian mon., with face like that of Franklin D. Roosevelt.
US83 cont. to **Scott Cty. St. Pk.** (1,280 as.cabins.f.boat.), 35m, rugged tract surrounding 115-a. L. McBride. Here are **mon.** to H. L. Steele & his wife, homesteaders on park site, & limestone **H. L. Steele Home,** now mus. exhibiting old furniture, curios, & Ind. flints. Near center of pk. is **Buffalo Sanctuary,** where small herd are pastured in area carpeted by native buffalo grass with many water holes. Also in pk. are **Ruins of El Quartelejo,** believed to have been first solid walls erected within what is now Kans. Adobe stronghold was built by Picurie Inds., fleeing from Sp. rule in Taos reg. of New Mexico, early in 17th cent. 45m **Scott City,** is comfortable-looking plains town with well-kept streets & homes, surrounded by irrigated farms. **Garden City,** 81m (see US50), is at J. with US50.

**144. SHARON SPRINGS,** founded 1886, is well-shaded market town in treeless plains country. **161.** Kans.-Colo. Line.

## US 50—KANSAS

**KANS.-MO. LINE** (0.5m from Kans. City, Mo.) **(W) to KANS.-COLO. LINE** (32m from Lamar, Colo.). **490. US50**

Via: Ottawa, Emporia, Newton, Hutchinson, Dodge City, & Garden City. RR. parallels route throughout. Accoms.: In larger towns.

Paralleling route of old Santa Fe Trl., US50 cuts through farm country of E. Kans., bluestem pastures of Flint Hills, & Gt. Bend wheat belt, traverses irrigated Arkansas R. bottom lands & then enters barren upland country near Colo. line.

### Sec. 1: KANS.-MO. LINE to HUTCHINSON. 234.

At **0.** is Kans.-Mo. Line.

**SHAWNEE CEMETERY, 1.,** one of Kans.' oldest white burial grounds, contains graves of Rev. Thos. Johnson & his wife (see below). Just beyond is J. with Mission Rd. leading (R) 0.3m to **Shawnee Meth. Mission,** twice territorial capital of Kans. In 1838 Mo. Conference of Meth. Episc. Ch. directed Rev. Thos. Johnson, missionary among Shawnee, to build manual training sch. for Ind. children. School opened in Oct., 1839. Two-story former **Dormitory and Boarding Sch.** (1845) on Nov. 24, 1854, was occupied by Territorial Gov. Andrew H. Reeder, who moved his executive offices here from Ft. Leavenworth. Later he selected Pawnee (see US40) as territorial capital & convened 1st territorial legislature there in 1855; but proslavery faction passed law transferring capital back to Shawnee Mission. Legislature occupied big barracks-like **Schoolh.** (1839), adopting statutes of Mo. virtually in their entirety & legalizing slavery in Kans. until Lecompton was chosen as capital Aug. 8, 1855. Chapel is now mus., containing hist. furnishings & documents. Afterwards, mission declined rapidly, as Inds. moved away; finally abandoned in 1864. 3rd of remaining bldgs. is former **Home of Superintendent** (1839).

**20. OLATHE** was founded in 1857 & named with its founders' inaccurate version of Shawnee Ind. word for "beautiful" (wes-see). Here is **Kans. School for the Deaf** (est. 1866). Just E. of bridge over Cedar Cr., **22.5.** is **SANTA FE & OREGON TRL. MARKER.** On site of **GARDNER, 29.5.,** founded by Free Staters in 1857, these two trls. diverged; signposts originally stood here, reading: "Road to Oregon" (R) and "Road to Santa Fe" (L). **45.5. BALDWIN CITY,** stands near grove of black jack oaks on Santa Fe Trl. where on June 2, 1856, Henry Clay Pate's Border Ruffians were defeated by John Brown & his Free Staters in Battle of Black Jack. Baldwin City is dominated by yellow limestone bldgs. of **Baker Univ.** (est.1858), Kans.' oldest Meth. college, whose **Old Castle Hall** was territory's 1st college bldg. **Case Lib.** houses Wm. A. Quayle Coll. of Bibles, one of world's finest.

**51.** J. with US50N, alternate route (W) bet. this pt. & Garden City.

SIDE TRIP: Take latter (R) through upland farming country. At 23m is J. with US75 (see). US50N traverses soft-coal mining reg., passing through **Burlingame,** 32.5m. At 39m is J. with St.31 leading (L) 2m to **Osage City,** market center of coal-mining & farming area. **Council Grove,** 76m, inc. in 1858, on edge of Flint Hills in fertile Neosho R. valley. It grew up about old campground in oak grove near ford, supposedly used by Coronado & his expedition in search of Quivira in 1541; here in 1825 Fed. commissioners signed treaty with chiefs of Kansa & Gt. & Little Osage tribes to permit surveying of trl. to Santa Fe. 1st large caravan, led by Josiah Gregg, forded R. here in 1826; & in 1827 Kit Carson is said to have carved his name on a tree. By early 1840's, campground was most important sta. bet. Westport, Mo. & Santa Fe. Later, town sett. down to slow growth as agric. center; with advent of RR. in 1883, it became livestock shipping pt. Union & Main Sts., **Madonna of the Trl. Mon.,** represents frontier mother with children. Treaty of Aug. 10, 1825 was signed under **Council Oak,** 210 E. Main St., opp. which is mon. containing hist. documents in metal box sealed in its cement foundation. 112 N. Main St., Former **Hays Tavern** (1847), successively home, saloon, supply house, cth., & hotel; it was built by Council Grove's 1st white settler. Main & Chautauqua Sts., **Last Chance Store** (1857) was in Santa Fe Trl. days last place to buy supplies for journey to Santa Fe. Huffaker & Mission Sts., **Kaw (Kansa) Mission** (1849), opened by Meth. missionary Thos. S. Huffaker, began as Ind. mission school, but attracted so few pupils it was closed until 1854 & then reopened as 1st school for white children in Kans. **Herington,** 102.5m, laid out in early 1880's on 40 as. of Monroe D. Herington's 2,000-a. ranch, is RR. division pt. & farm shipping & shopping center. **City Pk.** (swim.) contains shaft erected in 1904 as **Mon. to Father Juan de Padilla,** soldier-priest who explored this reg. with Coronado in 1541. **Marion,** 128m, sett. in 1860, is shipping pt. for produce of fertile Cottonwood R. valley. **Hillsboro,** 138.5m, at J. of Cottonwood R.'s N. & S. branches, is center of large Mennonite community extending into neighboring ctys. & site of **Tabor College,** 2-yr. coed. Mennonite institution. Hillsboro has Mennonite publishing plant. **McPherson,** 165.5m, is shipping & refining point for central Kans. oil fields & site of 2 colleges: **McPherson College** (O.1888), Dunkard (Ch. of Brethren) coed. liberal arts institution, & **Central College and Academy** (founded 1914), Free Meth. secondary school & jr. college. McPherson is at J. with US81 (see). **Lyons,** 196.5m, laid out in 1876 on land owned by Truman J. Lyons, is salt-mining & wheat-growing center. 1st salt mine in vic. was opened in 1890; in 1920's oil fields were also discovered near-by. **Rice County Cth.** houses coll. of relics believed to be of Coronado's Quivira expedition of 1541, plowed up on near-by farm.

Turn (L) from Lyons on St.14 to **Sterling,** 10m, founded 1872, site of **Sterling College** (est.1886), 4 yr. coed. institution conducted by United Presb. Ch.

Near Cow Cr., 205m, is **Santa Fe Trl. Marker. Ellinwood,** 218m, founded 1871, has become since 1930 center of one of leading Kans. oil fields. Take Rd. (R) from Ellinwood short distance to **Robl Birdbanding Sta.,** 16-a. private refuge where in 1928 Frank Robl began banding migratory birds so that their flights could be studied. **Gt. Bend,** 229m, named for sweeping curve of Ark. R. on which it lies, sett. in 1871, is shipping, wheat, & oil center. In 1874 it became railhead on Chisholm Trl. from Texas, crowded with saloons & dance halls. Later its chief industry was flour milling. During 1930's it went through an oil boom. At 242m is J. with improved Rd. leading (R) 0.5m to 5-a. **Pawnee Rock St. Pk.** (shelter H.pic.), formerly rendezvous for Plains Inds. & scene of many savage battles. Pawnee Rock, mass of Dakota sandstone about 80′ high, commands sweeping view. **Pawnee Rock Mon.** (1912) is 30′ shaft of Barre granite. **Larned,** 250m, at confluence of Pawnee Cr. & Ark. R., grew up following est. near-by of Ft. Larned (see below). At 255m is J. with dirt Rd. leading (L) 0.5m to **Site of Ft. Larned,** est. in 1859 to protect travellers on Santa Fe Trl. from Ind. attacks. Adobe structures built in 1860 were replaced bet. 1864 & 1868 by present ones of sandstone, facing parade ground. Ft. Larned was supply base & agency for Arapahoe & Cheyenne, who sometimes besieged it when supplies ran low. It was abandoned in 1878. **Jetmore,** 299m, was founded in 1879. At 322m is J. with dirt Rd. leading (R) 9m to 853-a. **Finney Cty. St. Pk.** (camp.boat.f.), surrounding 324-a. L. impounded by one of Kans.' largest dams. **Garden City,** 358m (see below), is at J. with US50S.

**63.5. OTTAWA,** lying in saucer-like valley around Marais des Cygnes (pronounced locally "merry deseen") R., is farm trade center with RR. shops & division hqs. & several mills & factories. It had its origin in 1832 when Ottawa Inds. ceded their Ohio lands to U.S. in return for 34,000 as. in Franklin Cty. Here in 1837 Rev. Jotham Meeker & his wife opened Ottawa Ind. Baptist Mission. They were aided by Gov. agent on reserv., John Tecumseh (Tauy) Jones, half-breed Potawatomi & staunch abolitionist, who welcomed Free State settlers, bldg. hotel. Town was laid out in 1864. After removal of Ottawa to Okla. in 1867, white settlers flocked in; in 1872 town acquired its RR. shops & in 1888 an electric plant. 9th & Cedar Sts., **Ottawa Univ.,** Bapt. Ch. 4-yr. coed. institution, occupying heavily wooded 33-a. campus, was inc. in 1865 as result of agreement bet. Kans. Bapts. & Ottawa Inds., under which Ottawa gave 20,000 as. of land & Bapts. provided teachers, bldg., & special dept. for education of Ind. children. Oldest of bldgs. is **Tauy Jones Hall** (1869), housing mus. of fossils, minerals, Ind. artifacts, & Kans. memorabilia. W. end Tecumseh St., **Forest Pk.** (180 as.sports facils.swim.).

SIDE TRIPS: (A) Take Wilson St. (L) from Ottawa to J. with Rd., 2m.

Turn (L) on latter 4.5m to stone, 14-room, two-and-a-half-story **Home of Tauy Jones** (c.1865), with 34-inch-thick walls, built entirely with pegs.

Wilson St. cont. to **Site of Ottawa Bapt. Mission,** 3m, est. in 1837 by Jotham Meeker, missionary & printer, who published here 1st book printed in Kans., a textbook for Inds. Near Rd. at this pt. is **Ottawa Ind. Burial Ground,** containing graves of Jotham Meeker & his wife, Tauy Jones & his wife, & Ottawa Chief Compehau, among others.

(B) Take 9th St. (L) from Ottawa to **Chippewa Burial Ground,** 6m, in cedar grove on grassy hill above Marais des Cygnes R. Most of graves are covered by thick slabs of red sandstone, many of them elaborately carved.

At **65.5.** is J. with US59.

SIDE TRIP: Take latter (L) to J. with Osawatomie Rd., 6.5m, & cont. (L) on this. At 15.5m is J. with gravel Rd.

Take latter (R) to J. with dirt Rd. & turn (R) on this to timbered pasture, 4.5m, in which c.20 rods (R) from Rd. are **Graves of James P. Doyle & His Sons,** Wm. & Drury, who, with Wm. Sherman & Allen Wilkinson, were victims of Potawatomie massacre conducted by John Brown & his followers on night of May 24-25, 1856, in retaliation for sacking of Lawrence by proslavery "Border Ruffians."

At 22.5m on Osawatomie Rd. is **Mon. to Frederick Brown,** son of John Brown, killed near-by at age of 26 on morning of Aug. 30, 1856 by Rev. Martin White, proslavery fanatic accompanying advance guard of force of Border Ruffians led by Brigadier-General John W. Reid who were on their way to attack Osawatomie. About 200′ NW. of mon. is **Foundation of John Brown Cabin** (so-called), built by Brown's brother-in-law, Rev. Samuel Lyle Adair; cabin has been removed to Osawatomie (see below). Just W. of homestead, following shooting of his son, John Brown rallied force of about 30 Free Staters in fringe of timber along Marais des Cygnes R. on morning of Aug. 30, 1856 in unsuccessful attempt to hold back Reid's 250 Border Ruffians. Osawatomie fell to attackers, who reduced it to ashes. **Osawatomie,** 23.5m, on Marais des Cygnes R., founded in 1855 & said to have been named for Osage & Potawatomi Inds. living in vic., derives its income from neighboring farmers, near-by oil & gas fields, its State Hospital for the Insane, & shops of Mo. Pacific RR. (on which it is division pt.). W. end of Main St., **John Brown Mem. St. Pk.** (pic.swim. sports facils.) contains life-size bronze **John Brown Statue** (by George Fite Waters) &, on its highest elevation, so-called **John Brown Cabin,** removed here from Adair homestead (see above): log structure furnished as it was in 1850s, with many John Brown relics, protected by glassed roofed enclosure. Also in pk. is **John Brown Mem.,** 9th & Main Sts., marble shaft above graves of Fred. Brown, David Garrison, Geo. Partridge, Theron Powers & Chas. Kaiser, all killed during raid at Osawatomie Aug. 30, 1856. Osawatomie is at J. with US169.

Take latter (L) to **Paola,** 9.5m, est. in 1855. Here in 1860 prospectors digging with pick & shovel found oil at depth of 275′; this was 1st oil well W. of Mississippi R. Oil in commercial quantities was 1st found in 1889, when well was sunk 6m E. Discovery of gas field near-by in 1884 had already led to Paola's becoming 1st gas-lit town in Kans.

Main side route turns (R) from Osawatomie on US169 to J. with St.7 26m, & (L) on this to J. with St.35, 39m, then (L) on this to J. with US69, 51m, & (R) on US69.

At 58.5m on US69 is **Marais des Cygnes Massacre Mon.,** comm. massacre on May 19, 1858 of 11 Free St. men taken prisoner by 50 Missourians led by Capt. Chas. Hamilton. Massacre inspired John G. Whittier's poem, "Le Marais du Cygne." **Trading Post,** 60m, where as early as 1839 Michael Gireau est. an Ind. trading post, was thriving town in days of border warfare. **Pleasanton,** 66m, founded in 1869, was named for General Pleasanton, whose Feds. defeated Gen. Sterling Price's Confeds. near-by in **Battle of Mine Creek,** only decisive engagement fought in Kans. during Civil War, Oct. 24, 1864, involving nearly 25,000 men.

US50 cont. (S. & SW.) from Ottawa. **82. SITE OF SILKVILLE,** marked by whitewashed limestone bldgs. in mulberry grove planted in 1870s by colony financed & led by Ernest Boissière, who brought manufacturing experts & cocoons from France to found silk industry. Colony, operated along communistic lines, proved unprofitable & was abandoned.

At **94.** is J. with US75 (see), which unites with US50S for 3m.

**121. EMPORIA.**

Through RR. & bus. conns. Info.: C. of C., 6th Ave. & Merchant St. Accoms.: Plentiful.

Trading & RR. center of farming & dairying reg., Emporia lies on low ridge bet. Neosho & Cottonwood Rs., shaded by elms & maples. At gateway to Kans. bluestem pasture reg. where half million head of cattle are fattened yearly, it becomes cattle town during grazing season, celebrating with Blue Stem Round Up Picnic. Its industries center mostly around processing of farm products; among them is 1st soy bean mill of Kans. Emporia was est. in 1857 by Emporia Town Co., on land bought from an Ind. for $1,800. It was named for an ancient city in N. Africa. First issue of "Kanzas News," June 5, 1857, published town charter, which forbade use & sale of "spirituous" liquor; thus Emporia was Middle West's 1st "dry town." After Civil War it attracted cattlemen, who brought gaunt Texas steers to graze on bluestem grass of vic. 1st train on Mo.-Kans.-Texas RR. arrived in 1869; 1st on Santa Fe, in 1870. Gaslights were installed in 1880; st. cars, in 1881; electricity, in 1885; stockyards, in 1887. "Emporia Gazette," bought by Wm. Allen White in 1895, became under his editorship perhaps nation's most famous small-town newspaper.

PTS. OF INT.: 927 Exchange St., **"Red Rocks"** was residence from 1900 until his death of "Sage of Emporia," Wm. Allen White. 517 Merchant St., **Emporia Gazette Bldg.** is home of his newspaper. Randolph & Rural Sts., **Peter Pan Pk.** (50 as. pic. natural amphitheater) was donated by Mr. & Mrs. Wm. Allen White as mem. to their daughter Mary, who died in 1921. W. end of 12th Ave., **College of Emporia** (founded 1882) is 4-yr. liberal arts college conducted by Presb. Ch. 12th Ave. & Commercial St., **Kans. St. Teachers College of Emporia** (O.1865) occupies tree-shaded 55-a. campus.

SIDE TRIP: Take St.99 (R) from Emporia to improved Rd., 13m, & turn (R) on this to 582-a. **Lyon Cty. St. Pk.** (camp.boat.f.), surrounding 135-a. L.

**169. FLORENCE,** platted in 1870, is near edge of central Kans. oil fields, in midst of which stands **PEABODY, 179.,** low & spacious plains towns. **198. NEWTON** is Santa Fe Ry. division pt. & wheat-growers' trading center. In July 1871, Santa Fe Ry. extended its line to settlement, which thereby succeeded Abilene as terminus of Chisholm Trl., & until 1873 was cowtown crowded with saloons, dancehalls & gambling houses. German Mennonites from Russia sett. in surrounding area & planted prairies with wheat, following lead of Bernard Warkentin, immigrant of 1872 who org. in 1885 Newton Milling & Elevator Co. 713½ Main St., **Harvey Cty. Hist. Soc. Mus.** contains pioneer relics. W. end of 1st St., **Athletic Pk.** has deer pk., outdoor stage, artificial L., baseball & football stadium & mun. swim. pool. Newton is at J. with US81 (see).

SIDE TRIP: Take St.15 (R) from Newton to **Bethel College** (chartered 1887), 0.5m, oldest & largest Mennonite educational institution in America. In front of Science Hall are two threshing stones brought from Russia by pioneer Mennonites, which were drawn by oxen over wheat strewn on ground to remove grain. **Kauffman Mus.** contains hist., nat. hist. & art exhibits. Mennonite Song Festival, held here annually, draws church choirs from Kans. & other Sts.

### 234. HUTCHINSON

Through RR. & bus conns. Info.: C. of C., 203 W. 1st Ave. Swim. at Carey Mun. Pk. Sept., Kans. St. Fair.

Kans.' 4th largest city, Hutchinson is nation's largest salt mining & processing center, city of mills & factories spreading over level valley land from N. bank of Ark. R. Known as "Salt City" for its mine & evaporating plants, which exploit rich beds underlying city & extending miles in all directions, it is also important wheat storage & shipping center & oil refining & shipping pt. Named for its founder, C. C. Hutchinson, city was platted in Nov. 1871. Lot offered builder of 1st house on townsite as prize was won by A. F. Horner, who had already won similar prizes offered in Brookville, Florence & Newton, moving his 20′ x 60′ house from place to place. Promoters plowed wide furrow around settlement to protect it from prairies fires & marked off streets with buffalo bones. Churches, schools & opera house were soon built. By 1885 Hutchinson had begun to thrive as shipping & trading pt. & milling center. Discovery of natural gas led in 1887 to drilling of well on near-by farm, in course of which city's underlying salt deposits were discovered. During 1920s, discovery of oil & gas in neighborhood added to prosperity.

PTS. OF INT.: (1) 1st Ave. & Adams St., **Reno County Cth.** (1930), half-million-dollar structure, is of interest for its modern architecture. (2) Main St. bet. Park Ave. & Ark. R., **Carey Mun. Pk.** (320 as.swim.pic.golf.) has lagoon, sunken gardens & scenic drive; contains electrically lit **Emerson Carey Mem. Fountain & Arch** (1935), comm. prominent Hutchinson salt manufacturer & philanthropist. (3) In 1st Ave. Pk., 1st Ave. & Walnut St., is **Soldiers' Mon.** (1919), comm. Civil War vets; & (4) in Sylvan Pk., Ave. B & Walnut St., is **Sun Dial Mon.,** comm. Pres. Warren Harding's visit to Hutchinson in 1923. (5) **Barton Salt Plant,** Cleveland & Campbell Sts., (6) **Carey Salt Plant,** Poplar St. & Ave. B & (7) **Morton Salt Plant,** N. end of Morton Salt Stabilized Hy., all refine salt by purifying & evaporating brine from deep wells. (8) E. end Carey Blvd., **Carey Rock Salt Mine** has maze of subterranean chambers & passages, 645′ deep, with electrically run ry. & elevator.

### Sec. 2: HUTCHINSON to KANS.-COLO. LINE. 256.

US50 cont. (S) across vast prairie. **44.5. STAFFORD,** sett. in 1870s, became oil boom town when gusher came in near-by in 1938. **54.5. ST. JOHN,** founded in 1879, is trading & shipping center for reg. producing corn, wheat, barley & oats. **94. KINSLEY** enjoys comfortable living from wheat, corn, alfalfa & poultry products.

**133.5. DODGE CITY,** metropolis of (SW) Kans., lies on Ark. R., its modern business & pub. bldgs. breaking monotony of Kans. short grass country. Dodge City has been called "the buckle on the Kans. wheat belt"; it is supply center for rich farming & cattle-raising area. Near site in 1864 was est. Ft. Dodge, named for Col. Henry

I. Dodge & commanded by his nephew, Grenville M. Dodge; it was one of most important of frontier posts & several Army officers of note—among them Miles, Custer, Hancock & Sheridan—served here. In 1871, sod house, first bldg. on townsite, was erected 5m W. of Ft., near ford across Ark. R., to serve as stopping place for freighters & buffalo hunters. Townsite was laid out in 1872 & in Sept. of that yr., 1st Santa Fe Ry. passenger train arrived, bringing advance influx of immigrants, buffalo hunters, card sharps, gamblers & adventurers. Buffalo hunting soon became important pursuit; before depot could be built, buffalo hides by thousands were awaiting shipment. Before end of 1875, great herds of shaggy animals, estimated to number 25,000,000 or more in Dodge City territory, were practically exterminated. For some yrs. afterward, buffalo bones were collected & shipped E. for fertilizer; it came to be said that in Dodge City buffalo bones were legal tender. Soon after, Tex. longhorns driven by hundreds of cowboys & trl. bosses began arriving over Tex. Trl.; in 1882, Dodge City took its turn as cowboy capital of SW. Shooting frays became frequent; long & colorful succession of marshalls & sheriffs were hired to keep peace. Gradually Dodge City became less important as cattle center, as other shipping terminals were est.; & in 1884, increase of cattle disease known as Tex. fever brought legislation forbidding importation of Tex. cattle. Dodge City brought cattle era to resounding close with 4th of July celebration which incl. bull fight—first & probably only one held in U.S.; advance announcement of it prompted St. & Fed. authorities to wire that show could not be given in U.S., but Mayor A. B. Webster merely wired in reply: "Dodge City is not in the U.S." Dodge City, thereafter, turned to agric. as surrounding land was sown to wheat & other crops.

PTS. OF INT.: (1) 2nd Ave. & Water St., **Old Lone Tree,** dead cottonwood trunk with mem. plate, marks site where town was founded in 1872. Bronze tablets mark (2) **Site of First Bldg.,** 305 2nd Ave.; (3) **Site of First School,** 1st Ave. & Walnut St.; & (4) **Site of Old Ft. Dodge Military Reserv.,** Central & Military Aves. (5) 2nd Ave. & Trail St., **Santa Fe Marker** is red granite boulder with tablet bearing dates when Santa Fe Trl. was in use, 1822-72. (6) 4th Ave. & Spruce St., **City Hall** (1929-30) stands on **Boot Hill,** promontory of gypsum & clay rising 100′ above Ark. R. Valley, where victims of shooting scrapes were buried bet. 1872 & 1878. Grave markers now on site—bearing names like "Shoot-em-up Ike," "One-Eyed Jake," "Toothless Nell" —are imitation, planted here as atmosphere for Rotarian convention in 1930 by local dentist Dr. O. H. Simpson, sculptor of **Cowboy Statue** & **Longhorn Statue,** both of concrete, near City Hall main entrance; also "planted" is old cottonwood tree with dangling noose. (7) Front St. & Central Ave., 2 **Sundials** stand in Santa Fe sta. pk., visible from passing trains, E. one telling Central Standard Time & W. one, Mt. Time; bet. them passes 100th meridian W., time zone boundary. (8) 2nd Ave. & Water St., **Wright Pk.** contains **Mem. Fountains,** honoring World War veterans; **Hoover Pavilion,** used for entertainments & pub. meetings; & **Gt. Southwest Free Fair Bldgs.**

SIDE TRIPS: (A) Take US283 (L) from Dodge City to Beeson Rd., 1m, & turn (R) here to **Beeson Mus.** (fee), 1.5m, which exhibits one of Kans.' largest colls. of Ind. & pioneer relics, assembled by Chalk Beeson, scout & cowboy band leader, who was official guide of "Royal Buffalo Hunt" org. by Gen. Geo. Custer to entertain Grand Duke Alexis of Russia on his tour of America in 1871-72.

(B) Take US154 (L) from Dodge City to **St. Soldiers' Home,** 5m, on **Site of Old Ft. Dodge,** two of whose adobe barracks built in 1864 still stand, now veneered with native stone.

**152. CIMARRON** became seat of Gray Cty. after bitter fight with **INGALLS, 158.5.,** whose promoters dreamed of it as capital of great irrigated empire. Embankments of abandoned canal still line hy. **185. GARDEN CITY** lies on Ark. R. in irrigated belt producing sugar beets as chief crop. Metropolis of W. Kans., Garden City was founded in 1878. Wild boom of land speculation sent pop. up to 6,000 in late 1880's. Surrounding area was plowed & planted to corn, & in 1886 great crop was raised—1st & last ever achieved in this reg., for droughts followed. During World War I, new settlers poured in to raise wheat, but post-war collapse of prices led to decline in wheat production; & reg. has since turned to cultivation of sugar beets, alfalfa seed & maize & to livestock raising. Today Garden City has Kans.' largest sugar beet refinery & one of its largest alfalfa mills & dehydrating plants; in 1948, Standard Oil Co. of La. picked it as site of revolutionary $80,000,000 synthetic gasoline plant, 1 of 2 in U.S. using Amer. adaptation of German chemical process for making gasoline from natural gas, oxygen & water. In SW. corner of city on Ark. R. is **Frederick Finnup Mem. Pk.** (250 as.pic.sports facils.racetrack), containing Kans.' largest zoo & swim. pool, 220 x 330', which is said to be world's largest free mun. pool. Garden City is at J. with US50N (see above) & US83 (see US40).

SIDE TRIP: Take US83 (L) from Garden City to 3,600-a. **St. Buffalo Pk.,** containing largest herd of buffalo in Kans. At 29m is J. with US160.

Take latter (R) to world's largest **Carbon Black Plant,** 20.5m, where carbon black, used in manufacture of paint, is produced by incomplete combustion of natural gas. US160 conts. (W) through center of what became Kans.' dust bowl in 1931-37 to **Ulysses,** 28m, founded in 1885. (L) 12m from Ulysses on US270 is **Jedediah Smith Mon.,** marking pt. where in 1831 one of most renowned of early explorers—1st to cross Sierra Nevada into Cal., 1st white man to lead expedition overland from Cal. into Ore., & 1st to lead party over S. Pass in Rockies—was scalped by Inds. after losing his way on Santa Fe Trl.

At 35m on US83 is J. with St.45.

Take latter (R) 37.5m to **Hugoton,** which has remained prosperous, although it lies in dust bowl, because it is center of world's largest natural gas field, developed since 1927. Pipe lines carry Hugoton gas to Denver & other Colo. cities & as far as Minneapolis & Detroit. Hugoton, founded in 1885 & named for Fr. poet, Victor Hugo, waged bitter fight with neighboring Woodsdale to be made cty. seat; it culminated in violence & several assassinations.

US83 cont. to **Liberal,** 67m, founded in 1886. It was long terminus of Rock I. Ry. & thus became freight distributing center for ranchers in Okla., Tex., New Mex. & Colo. Cowboys came with their herds, often to spend year's wages in wk.-end carousing. Today Liberal has flour mill, gasoline-extracting plant & factories manufacturing farm implements. It has well-paved streets & modern schools & houses, mun. landing field & city pk. with swim. pool.

US50 passes through several small rural shipping & trading towns on its way to **SYRACUSE, 238.5.,** one of most favored towns on High Plains because its plentiful trees make it green oasis. At **256.** is Kans.-Colo. Line.

## US 66—KANSAS

**KANS.-MO. LINE** (6m from Joplin, Mo.) **(SW) to KANS.-OKLA. LINE** (14.5m from Miami, Okla.). **11.5. US66**

Via: Galena & Baxter Springs.

US66 cuts across SE. cor. of Kans., passing through lead & zinc-mining reg.

At **0.** is Kans.-Mo. Line. **GALENA, 1.,** pioneer lead & zinc-mining town, is surrounded by smelters, mills & chat piles. **Galena Smelter,** E. of town, is one of world's largest. When lead was discovered here in 1877, rival mining camps sprang up on both sides of Short Cr. Two communities were merged in 1911. At **5.5.** are Js. with improved Rd. & with St.26.

SIDE TRIP: (A) Take former (L) 0.5m to **Power Dam** of Empire Dist. Electric Co., whose hydroelectric plant furnishes power to 80 communities in Kans., Mo., & Okla. Dam forms 400-a. **L. Powell** (boat.swim.f.cabins).

(B) Take St.26 (R) to J. with US69, 7m, & cont. straight ahead on US69. **Pittsburg,** 22.5m, coal metropolis of Kans., founded in 1870's as mining camp. Zinc smelter was est. here in 1878, & town became leading zinc-smelting center of U.S. Pittsburg dist. produces 50% of coal mined in Kans. Open pit method of mining, employing some of world's biggest electric shovels, is used. Pittsburg manufactures variety of industrial products, but confines its soot-producing industries to outskirts; it has long clean main st. & well-kept homes, variety of pks., golf courses & swim. pools, network of schools, churches, & civic organizations. 17th St. & S. Broadway, **Kansas St. Teachers' College** (est.1903) occupies 55-a. landscaped campus. On 3rd fl. of **Porter Lib.** is college mus., containing geological & paleontological specimens, Ind. artifacts, insects & stuffed animals. **Crawford Cty. St. Pk.** (f.boat. camp.pic.zoo), 26m, is 418-a. tract surrounding 60-a. L. Site, one of most attractive in Kans., is result of strip mining; rain filled the canyons dug by shovels, trees & other vegetation grew on mounds of dirt heaped beside them, & finally in 1926 St. landscaped area. At mining town of **Franklin,** 29m, is J. with St.57; turn (L) here 7.5m to **Girard,** where in 1890's J. A. Wayward founded "Appeal to Reason," Socialist weekly which achieved circulation of half million. When it ceased publication in 1922, its current editor & owner, E. Haldeman-Julius, began publishing abridged editions of classics at 5 cents per copy & achieved, through these "Little Blue Books," one of greatest outputs in Amer. publishing history.

**9.** Trees, grass & flowers of Spring R. Valley, entered here, are in sharp contrast to barren mining area.

**10. BAXTER SPRINGS,** surrounded by lead & zinc mines, has more attractive homes with lawns and gardens than most small Kans. towns. It was named for A. Baxter, first settler, who built sawmill & tavern here after arrival in 1850 & here on Oct. 6, 1863, Confed. guerrilla leader Wm. Clarke Quantrill's band attacked Fed. garrison & killed 96. In 1860's Tex. cattlemen began to drive their longhorns here to pasture; when RR. was built in 1870, Baxter Springs for more than decade was wide-open cow town—"the toughest town on earth." Expansion of industrial, agric. & resort possibilities came later.

**11.5.** Kans.-Okla. Line.

# US 75—KANSAS

**KANS.-NEB. LINE** (29$^m$ from Auburn, Neb.) **(S) to KANS.-OKLA. LINE** (8$^m$ from Copan, Okla.). **239.5. US75**

Via: Sabetha, Topeka, Yates Center, Neodesha, Independence & Caney. RRs. parallel route bet. Kans.-Neb. Line & Topeka & bet. Yates Center & Kans.-Okla. Line. Accoms.: Chiefly in larger towns.

US75 crosses two of Kans.' chief agric. areas &, near Okla. Line, its earliest developed oil & gas belt.

## Sec. 1: KANS.-NEB. LINE to TOPEKA. 75.

At **0.** is Kans.-Neb. Line. **SABETHA, 7.,** an agric. trading point, was allegedly so named by Cal.-bound Biblical student because one of his oxen died here on day he calculated to be Hebrew Sabbath. At **11.** is western J. with US36.

SIDE TRIP: Take US36 (R) to **Seneca,** 14$^m$, founded in 1857 as stopping place on Ore.-Cal. Trl. & later Pony Express & Overland stage routes.

St.63 leads (L) from Seneca to **Nemaha Cty. St. Pk.** (705 as.f.swim.boat.pic.camp.), 5.5$^m$, with 356-a. L. **Marysville,** 45$^m$, on Big Blue R., center of prosperous grain, stock-raising & dairying area, was named for Mrs. Mary Marshall, wife of early tavern-owner Frank J. Marshall, who sett. here in 1846. **City Pk.** (pic.sports facils.) at S. edge of town contains **Ore. Trl. Marker.**

At **15.** is eastern J. with US36.

SIDE TRIP: Take US36 (L) to **Hiawatha,** 11$^m$, one of Kans. prairie's most beautiful towns, dominated by **Brown County Cth.** (Gr.Rev.). Mt. Hope Cemetery at SE. edge of town contains unusual **Davis Mem.,** consisting of vault, pavilion & 11 life-size portrait statues, erected for retired farmer John M. Davis & his wife.

Take US73-159 (R) from Hiawatha past 170-a. **Mission L.** (boat.f.pic.) at 12.5$^m$ to **Horton,** 13$^m$, founded in 1886 after RR. came through.

US36 cont. (E) to **Highland,** 26$^m$, quiet town among green hills, whose **Highland Jr. College** is one of Kans.' oldest educational institutions, chartered in 1857. At 28$^m$ is J. with St.136 leading (L) 0.5$^m$ to one remaining bldg. of **Iowa & Sac & Fox Mission,** now mus. in St. hist. pk., east by Presb. Ch. in 1837. US36 cont. to **Troy,** 37$^m$, surrounded by 10,000 as. of apple orchards, which has annual Apple Blossom Festival in late Ap. & Apple Harvest Festival in early Sept.

At **27.** on US75 is J. with graded Rd. leading (L) 0.5$^m$ to **Kickapoo Reserv.,** tract originally comprising over 76,000 as., but now less than tenth as large, assigned by treaty in 1832 to Kickapoo Inds. Today's reserv. inhabitants participate in ancestral rituals—New Year's, Spring, Corn & Harvest Dances, held 1st wk. in Jan., Ap., July & Oct. respectively (visitors welcome). **42.5. HOLTON,** sett. by Free Staters from Milwaukee & during 1850's & 1860's sta. on Underground Railroad. **50.** J. with improved Rd. leading (R) 0.5$^m$ to 7,040-a. **Potawatomi Reserv.,** Kans.' largest Ind. reserv., inhabited by tribe called Potawatomi of the Prairie, who came here in 1837 but still, unlike other Kans. Inds., have not lost all their identity through assoc. with white men. At 5$^m$ on side Rd. is 70-a. **Ind. Fairgrounds,** site annually in July or Aug. of fair. At **72.** is J. with US40 (see) with which US75 unites to **TOPEKA, 75.** (see US40).

## Sec. 2: TOPEKA to KANS.-OKLA. LINE. 164.5.

US75 now traverses highland prairies of Osage Plains, so called because they were inhabited by Osage when white men came to Kans. At **18.5.** is J. with US50N (see

US50). **30.5. LYNDON,** seat of Osage Cty., was founded in 1869. At **46.** is J. with US50S (see US50), which unites with US75 for 2m. **61. BURLINGTON,** is prosperous-looking town centering around cth. & long main st. **Runt Pk.,** 1 block N. of Main St., contains unusual group of concrete statues depicting Runt, diabetic dog once locally famous; King Alcohol, skeleton with whiskey bottle; & Eve, being tempted by serpent. **83. YATES CENTER,** important hay-shipping pt., was laid out in 1875 on crest of divide bet. Neosho & Verdigris Rs.

SIDE TRIP: Take US54 (L) from Yates to **Iola,** 20m, built around spacious Allen County Cth. square, its broad sts. lined with elms. Following discovery of natural gas here in 1890's, zinc smelter, acid plant & several smaller concerns were built; diminution of gas supply forced shut-down of industries. Today Iola has foundries, brickyard & cement factory, dress & overall factory, & milk condensery. US54 cont. (E) to **Ft. Scott,** 62.5m, on S. bank of Marmaton R., city of "jogging" sts. & fine old trees, with bldgs. older than Kans. sandwiched bet. modern structures. At J. of 3 RRs., it serves SE. Kans. as shipping & distribution pt. & manufacturing center. Its creameries & ice cream factories make it best known as dairying center, & it holds annually Kans. Dairy Show; it also has foundries & RR. shops, overall factory, brick plants & hydraulic cement plants. Town grew up around Ft. Scott, founded 1842. Garrison was withdrawn in 1855. Ft. was abandoned in 1855, but surrounding settlement carried on, trading with soldiers, settlers & Inds. Ft.'s officers' quarters became Free St. Hotel, hqs. for Capt. Jas. Montgomery & other determined anti-slavery leaders; term "Jayhawker" is said to have originated here when Pat Devlin, one of Montgomery's band, returning from raid on proslavery farmers, reported that he had been "jayhawking" & went on to explain: "The jayhawk is a bird in Ireland that catches small birds & bullyrags the life out of them like cats do mice." Name "Jayhawkers" came finally to be applied to all Kansans. After outbreak of Civil War, Ft. Scott again became military post. By beginning of 20th cent., Ft. Scott turned to trading & manufacturing. **Carroll Plaza,** Marmaton, Blair, Fenton & Lincoln Aves., is grass-grown square, once old ft.'s parade ground; on square & facing it are remaining ft. structures. **Ft. Blair,** near SE. entrance, is Civil War blockh. of sawed slabs, spiked. 103 Blair St., **Ft. Scott Mus.** (O.9-5), occupying 1 of 3 remaining officers' quarters (1842), contains souvenirs of ft., Ind. relics, & other pioneer articles. E. Nat. Ave., **Ft. Scott Nat. Cemetery,** est. 1862, covers 10 as. enclosed by stone fence.

At **102.** on US75 is J. with St.39.

SIDE TRIP: Take latter (L) to **Chanute,** 12m, RR. center in rich agric. dist., named for Octave Chanute, RR. engineer & pioneer aviation authority. Town was formed in 1872. It has oil refineries, brick & cement plants, garment factories, hatcheries & poultry packing plant, & livestock sales pavilion.

**121.5. NEODESHA** (pronounced Nee-o-desh-ay'), at confluence of Verdigris & Fall Rs., is refining center for near-by oil fields opened in 1892. **136. INDEPENDENCE,** seat of Montgomery Cty. & pioneer city of S. Kans. oil fields. Here in 1869, on 640 as. of Osage Reserv. bought from Osage Chief, Chetopah, Independent Town Co. built cluster of huts. Opening of reserv. to settlement in 1870, when Osage agreed to move to Okla., brought new inhabitants. Independence boomed after discovery of natural gas in 1881 & opening of 1st oil fields in 1903. Today it manufactures cement, plastics, alfalfa meal, washing machines, prefabricated buildings & other products. **Riverside Pk.** (pic.swim.f.) is 113-a. tract in canyon-like Verdigris R. valley with zoo, shelter Hs., athletic fields & swim. pool.

SIDE TRIP: Take US160 (L) from Independence to **Cherryvale,** 10m, founded by Kans. City, Leavenworth & S. Kans. RR. in 1871 & for some yrs. its terminus. Discovery of natural gas here in 1889 led to establishment of zinc smelter, brick plant & other industries, which operated until gas supply diminished about 1912. US160 cont. to **Parsons,** 31m, Mo.-Kans.-Tex. RR. division pt. with shops & roundhouses, shipping & distribution pt. for grain & dairy farmers & stockyard center.

**164. CANEY** began as trading pt. for Ind. Territory (Okla.) & became oil boom town when Mid-Continent oil fields were opened in 1890's.

SIDE TRIP: Take US166 (L) from Caney to **Coffeyville,** 20m, in sandy basin bordered by low hills & Verdigris R., leading industrial city, producing flour, stockfeeds, oil & gasoline, chemical products & pigments, roofing tile & structural steel, tank cars & machinery. Here in 1869 Jas. A. Coffey built house & trading post, around which settlement grew up when RR. came through following yr. Saloons, dancehall & gambling joints multiplied to serve visiting cowboys; riots, brawls & shootings prevailed. Dalton family sett. near-by in 1882 & on Oct. 5, 1892 occurred Dalton raid, during which Bob & Grat Dalton, having killed 3 citizens & Marshall Chas. T. Connolly, were themselves killed, along with fellow bandits Jack Moore & Wm. Powers, & their brother Emmett was wounded in gunfight following attempted bank robberies. Coffeyville boomed in 1903 with development of gas & oil fields in Kans. & near-by Okla. so that by 1910, with pop. of about 20,000, it ranked 6th among Kans. cities, & by 1915 had acquired its present leading position as an industrial city. It has been since 1930 center of org. labor activities in Kans. 8th St. at (E) edge of town, **Forest Pk.** has fairgrounds, pic. & campgrounds, athletic fields & children's playgrounds. **Pfister Pk.** contains swim. pool & tennis courts, scenic drives & airport.

At **164.5.** is Kans.-Okla. Line.

## US 81—KANSAS

**KANS.-NEB. LINE** (13.5m from Hebron, Neb.) **(S) to KANS.-OKLA. LINE** (16m from Medford, Okla.). **237.5. US81**

Via: Concordia, Salina, Newton, Wichita, & Wellington. RRs. parallel route at intervals. Accoms.: In larger towns.

US81 in N. Kans. crosses Blue Hills uplands, gently rolling, sown to corn, wheat & alfalfa, & after winding through rough pasture land, emerges on Great Bend Prairie, center of vast wheat belt, which it crosses to Wichita, & from latter, follows old Chisholm Trl. (S) to Okla. Line.

### Sec. 1: KANS.-NEB. LINE to WICHITA. 175.

**0.** Kans.-Neb. Line. **5.5.** J. with dirt Rd.

SIDE TRIP: Take latter (R) 11m to **Pike-Pawnee St. Mon.** (16 as.swim.pic.) on mesa where on Sept. 29, 1806, Zebulon M. Pike is said to have persuaded Pawnee to raise U.S. flag (see US81, Neb. for site few miles away (NW) where same incident is said to have occurred).

**13. BELLEVILLE,** founded 1869 & named for settler's wife Arabelle Tutton.

SIDE TRIPS: (A) Take US36 (L) from Belleville to **Washington,** 30m, agric. shipping & trading center founded in 1860's. At 41m is J. with St.15E; take latter (L). **Hanover,** 45.5m, founded 1869. City Pk. contains **Pony Express Mon.** St.15E cont. to former **G. H. Hollenburg Ranch H.** (1857), 47m, which served as stagecoach depot & Pony Express sta. on Ore. Trl., preserved in 7½-a. St. pk.

(B) Take US36 (R) from Belleville to **Mankato,** 33.5m, market center of grain & livestock area. At 51m is J. with US281.

Take latter (R) to **Lebanon,** 1.5m, nearest town to **Geographical Center of U.S.,** designated by marker in pasture of Meade's Ranch in White Rock Township 2m NW.

US36 cont. to **Smith Center,** 63.5m. **Smith Center Lib.** houses hist. mus. of pioneer relics. On E. Beaver Cr. near-by stands cabin in which Dr. Brewster Higley wrote (1873) words of song, "Home on the Range." At 64m is J. with dirt Rd.

Take latter (R) 1.5m to **Site of Sitting Bull's Ft.,** where in 1867 Sitting Bull, having leagued many Midwestern Ind. tribes for last stand against whites, converted hollowed-out soapstone mound long used by Inds. as trading pt. into ft. On site now stands unfinished **Plaster's Castle,** built by Wm. A. Plaster, homesteader of 1872.

**Phillipsburg,** 93.5m, & **Norton,** 127m, were both platted in 1872. **Oberlin Cemetery,** 159.5m contains granite **Mon. Comm. Last Ind. Massacre** in Kans., which occurred in 1878. **Oberlin,** 161m, is a prosperous hillside cty. seat town.

Take US83 (R) from Oberlin to 92-a. **Decatur Cty. St. Pk.** (f.boat.camp.), 1m, with 47-a. L. & 481-a. **Oberlin Sappa St. Pk.** (f.boat.swim.camp.), 1.5m.

**32.5. CONCORDIA,** RR. J. on Republican R., is farming & dairying trade center with creameries & mills, sett. in 1860's. At **47.5.** is eastern J. with US24.

SIDE TRIP: Take US24 (L) to **Clay Center,** 32m, on Republican R., founded 1862, which ships hay, corn, wheat, dairy & poultry products.

At **49.5.** is western J. with US24.

SIDE TRIP: Take US24 (R) to **Beloit,** 28m, dating from 1868, with several small industries, of which flour milling is chief. At 44.5m is dirt Rd.; turn (L) here to health resort of **Waconda Springs** (hotel.hospital), 45.5m. Great Spirit Spring, largest of three, 50′ in diameter, brims to level surface of rock mound 42′ high separated by chasm from Solomon R.

**65.5. MINNEAPOLIS,** trading & shipping pt. for grain, livestock & poultry & dairy products.

SIDE TRIPS: (A) Take improved Rd. (R) from Minneapolis 3.5m to **Rock City,** grotesquely eroded area with more than 50 balanced rocks, toadstools, pyramids, spheres, castle-like structures & other formations, thought to be unique in world.

(B) Take improved Rd. (L) from Minneapolis 6.5m to 711-a. **Ottawa Cty. St. Pk.** (f.boat.swim.cabins) with 138-a. L.

US81 now crosses rolling prairies to **SALINA, 87.5.,** at J. with US40 (see). At **104.5.** is J. with improved Rd.

SIDE TRIP: Take latter (R) 2m to **Coronado Heights** (pic.shelter), southernmost of Smoky Hill (or Spanish) Buttes. Here Coronado is reputed to have camped during his search for Quivira in 1541; fragments of chain mail have been found near-by.

**108. LINDSBORG,** in valley of Smoky Hill R., its pop. composed almost entirely of persons of Swedish birth or descent, was sett. in 1868 by Chicago Swedish Co. & took its name from 1st syllable of surname of 3 members—S. P. Lindgren, S. A. Lindell, A. P. Linde—& from word "borg" (Swedish, castle). Its Bethany College Annual Messiah Festival has been drawing thousands of visitors during wk. from Palm Sunday to Easter since 1882. **Bethany College** (founded 1881), Swensson & 2nd Sts., is Swedish Luth. coed. institution occupying elm-shaded campus. **Presser Hall** (1927-30), whose auditorium, with pipe organ, seats 2,750, is scene of music festival. **Old Main** (1886), contains **Bethany College Mus.** of nat. hist., archaeology, ethnology & numismatic exhibits. **W. W. Thomas Pavilion,** designed in style of Swedish manor house, was Swedish pavilion at La. Purchase Exposition at St. Louis in 1904; it houses Sch. of Art, which holds annual art exhibition during festival wk. & coll. of paintings by Kans. artists. Steepled gray stone **Bethany Ch.,** org. 1868, was site of 1st "Messiah" concert.

SIDE TRIP: Take US4 (R) from Lindsborg 22m to **Kanapolis Dam & Reservoir** (boat.f. swim.). Dam, 131′ high & 15,810′ long, with spillway 700′ wide, impounds Smoky Hill R. to form L. 12m long.

**122. McPHERSON** (see US50) is at J. with US50N (see US50). **150. NEWTON** (see US50), is at J. with US50S (see US50). Southward are oil derricks & broad wheatfields.

## 175. WICHITA

Through RR., bus & plane conns. Info.: Kans. Motor Club, 153 N. Market St. Swim. at S. Riverside Pk. Nov., annual pageants & stock show.

Wichita, Kans.' largest city & chief manufacturing center, spreads over tablelands at confluence of Ark. & Little Ark. Rs. Its business dist., centering around Main St. & Douglas Ave. E. of Rs., more metropolitan than that of any other Kans. city, is dominated by 10-to-17-story office & department store bldgs. N. & S. extend tree-shaded residential avenues. To E. is low-income residential sec. of frame houses. NE. are stockyards, RR. tracks, flour mills & grain elevators, oil tanks & refineries. Farther E., beyond drainage canal which bisects city, are exclusive residential secs. interspersed with pks., cemeteries & college campuses. On tongue of land bet. Ark. & Little Ark. Rs. is Riverside dist., terminating in Sim & Central Riverside Pks., latter containing one of rare stands of virgin timber remaining in this part of Kans. W. of Ark. R., repeated pattern of lawns, houses & neighborhood shopping dists. is broken by more college campuses. Entire terrain is nearly flat, varying only few feet from bed of Ark. R. to summit of so-called College Hill; it was, until after 1920, almost devoid of shade, but has since, in course of vigorous campaign of tree-planting, become thickly forested. Despite its industrial concentration, Wichita is noticeably clean & smokefree city, because it uses gas for fuel.
City got its name from Wichita Inds. who, having been driven into Tex. by Osage's invasion of Kans. returned to their native reg. in 1863 & built village near mouth of Little Ark. Jas. R. Mead, aided by Jesse Chisholm, half-breed Cherokee, set up trading post near-by in 1864; Wm. Greiffenstein set up another. In 1865 Mead sent Chisholm into SW. with wagonload of goods to exchange for buffalo hides; returning, Chisholm encountered storm but pressed on, his heavily laden wagon cutting deep tracks, & thus blazed Chisholm Trl., up which herd of 2,400 Tex. longhorns was driven in 1867 on way to U.P. RR. at Abilene. Removal of Wichita Inds. to Okla. in this yr. cleared way for growth of white settlement around Mead's trading post. Munger H. & "First & Last Chance Saloon" were built to accommodate herd-driving cowboys from Tex. In 1870 Wichita was platted & inc. When in 1872 RR. was extended to Wichita, it boomed as new "cow capital." Shops, saloons, & dance-halls were hastily built; scouts, Inds., gamblers, cowboys, Mex. ranchers & homesteaders milled in sts. Rev. Luther Hart Platt, known as "fiddlin' preacher," strove to improve moral tone by singing hymns in saloons & then when crowd had gathered, preaching sermon. Property values soared as settlers flocked in; by 1880 Chisholm Trl. was virtually oversown with wheat. Shifting of cattle trl. farther W. to Dodge City brought period of decline; in 1886 land values crashed. Within few yrs., however, settlers who had fenced off prairie more than atoned for Wichita's loss of cattle

trade. Wichita took on new lease of life as trade & milling center; soon lines of wheat-laden wagons blocks long were drawn up before mills. Where cattle had built dance halls & gambling houses, wheat built churches & schools: 3 colleges were est. bet. 1888 & 1898 & Wichita began to foster art, music & literature.
By 1900 pop. exceeded 24,000; thereafter, it all but doubled in each succeeding decade. Discovery of oil in so-called "door-step pool" near city shortly after World War I brought flood of wealth which built huge business structures & palatial residences; there are now 5 major pools within 10 miles of city, & although Wichita's oil boom days ended in 1930's, petroleum & natural gas still yield steady income. During 1920's Jake Moellendick invested oil earnings in small plant & began building "Laird Swallow," one of best commercial planes of time; Wichita's business men built factory after factory until by middle 1920's, 15 had been erected, which in 1928 produced 25% of all country's output of planes. Depression of 1929 brought crash, but 4 companies survived. During World War II, aviation industry boomed again, rising to peak employment of 60,000; Wichita's aircraft plants together turned out 10% of nation's planes. Meanwhile, other industries expanded, especially flour-milling & meat-packing. Important industries today incl. manufacture of gasoline-burning household appliances & oil field equipment, farm machinery & implements, textiles & leather goods, food products & bldg. materials.

PTS. OF INT.: (1) 920 Back Bay Blvd., **Old Munger H.** (1868), believed to be Wichita's 1st house, built by E. S. Munger, justice of peace, postmaster & innkeeper, who made 1st plat of Wichita. (2) Douglas Ave. E. of Santa Fe St., **Carrie A. Nation Mem. Fountain,** comm. militant prohibitionist who raided Carey Hotel barroom with her hatchet in 1900. (3) **Hist. Mus. of Sedgwick Cty. Pioneer Soc.,** exhibiting early pictures, Ind. weapons & utensils & pioneer relics, is on 2nd fl. of **Mun. Forum,** Water & English Sts., whose auditorium, seating 4,800, houses conventions, political rallies & expositions. (4) Adj. is **Exposition Bldg.,** whose Arcadia Theatre is used for concerts & road shows. Other pub. bldgs. incl. (5) **Sedgwick County Cth.** (1890), Central Ave. & Market St.; (6) **U.S. P. O. & Cth.** (1932), Market & 3rd Sts.; (7) **Wichita Pub. Lib.** (1915), 220 S. Main St.
Among city's more notable churches are (8) **First Presb. Ch.** (1910.Goth.), Broadway & Elm St. & (9) **Cathedral of the Immaculate Conception** (Cath.1912.Romanes. Ital.Ren.), Broadway & Central Ave. (10) Architecturally notable as an example of "prairie" style is buff brick, tile-roofed **Wichita High School, North** (1929), 13th St. & Rochester Ave. (11) **Minisa Bridge** (1932), 13th St. & Little Ark. R., was designed to harmonize with it. (12) Also of architectural note is **Henry J. Allen H.** (1920.by Frank Lloyd Wright), Roosevelt Ave. & 2nd St. (13) 619 Stackman Dr., **Wichita Art Mus.** (O.wks.11-5;Sun.2-6), housing exhibits of sculpture & painting, stands at S. entrance to (14) **Sim Mem. Pk.** (183 as.), containing mun. golf course, archery grounds, pic. groves & scenic drive along Ark. R. (15) **Riverside Pk.,** in 3 divisions along Little Ark. R., contains **Riverside Pk. Zoo** (O.9-5), River Blvd. & Nims Ave. (16) 21st & Hillside Ave., **Mun. Univ. of Wichita,** overlooking city from 117-a. campus, is outgrowth of Fairmount College, founded by Congr. Ch. in 1895. It became mun. institution in 1926 by referendum vote. **Science Hall** houses natural science mus. & Ark. Valley Hist. Soc. colls. (17) Univ. & Hiram Aves., **Friends Univ.,** founded 1898 by Soc. of Friends, occupies 20-a. tree-shaded campus. **Adm. Bldg.** houses **Mus.** which contains mineral & fossil specimens, moundbuilder & Ind. artifact coll., Henry Wear & Chilson-Hoyt colls. of African relics & coll. of Aztec & Inca pottery & carving.

SIDE TRIPS: (A) Take St.15 (L) from Wichita to **Wichita Mun. Airport,** 3.5$^{m}$, one of country's best, from & to which B29's were flown in World War II & around which cluster many of Wichita's aircraft plants.
(B) Take US54 (L) from Wichita to J. with improved Rd., 18$^{m}$.
Turn (L) 1.5$^{m}$ on latter to **Santa Fe L.** (swim.boat.f.cabins.pic.), where sailing regattas are held.
**Augusta,** 20$^{m}$, surrounded by rich farm lands & productive oil fields, refines petroleum & manufactures automobile trlrs. **Eldorado,** 37$^{m}$, surrounded by for. of derricks, is in center of Kans.' largest oil fields. Its business dist. is mixture of sturdy plain limestone bldgs. of pioneer days & ornate structures built since oil boom. Founded in 1860's, it developed as trading point & cattle town. Oil was discovered near-by in 1915. Today 2 large & many small refineries operate here.
Take St.13 (L) 5$^{m}$ from Eldorado to **L. Eldorado** (pic.boat.f.).

**Eureka,** 69.5m, founded soon after Civil War, developed as stopping pt. on early cattle trls. &, with coming of RR., as shipping center. After 1915, it became busy oil distributing pt. US54 cuts across bluestem-grass Flint Hills reg., where great herds of cattle are pastured. At 92.5m is J. with improved Rd.

Take latter (L) 5m to **Woodson Cty. St. Pk.** (445 as.f.boat.camp.swim.) in so-called Kans. Ozarks, surrounding 179-a. L.

**Yates Center,** 104m (see US75) is at J. with US75 (see).

(C) Take US54 (R) from Wichita to **Kingman,** 43m, founded 1872, on Ninnescah R. in good farming country. At 52m is improved Rd. leading (R) 0.5m to 1,562-a. **Kingman Cty. St. Pk.** (1,562 as.f.boat.swim.camp.) with 80-a. L. At 74.5m is gravel Rd. leading (L) 1m to **St. Fish Hatchery,** with aquarium, & **St. Pheasant Farm,** with mus. coll. of mounted birds & animals. **Pratt,** 77m, farmers' town, has smart shops & hotels, though overalls are usual costume. Founded in 1884, it is wheat-shipping pt. & site of Rock I. RR. repair shops.

## Sec. 2: WICHITA, KANS. to KANS.-OKLA. LINE. 62.5.

At **21.** is J. with St.55, leading (L) to **Belle Plaine,** 3m, on outskirts of which is **Bartlett Arboretum** (16 as.), with more than 4,000 varieties of trees, shrubs & plants. Here in Ap. 200,000 tulips bloom. **32.5. WELLINGTON,** old-fashioned plains town gradually assuming modern aspect, was founded in 1871 at pt. where travellers on Chisholm Trl. often paused to rest their teams. It went through real estate boom in 1880's & in 1930's felt quickening effects of oil discoveries in vic.

SIDE TRIPS: (A) Take US160 (L) from Wellington to **Winfield,** 23m, founded by town company org. in 1870 on land leased from Chief Chetopah of Osage for $6. On site, Coronado & his band are believed to have camped during their Quivira expedition of 1541, as indicated by unearthing of rusty piece of sword & other Sp. implements. R. crossing was later used by travellers on Santa Fe Trl. Today Winfield is supported by agric., oil & manufacturing. 7th Ave. & College St., **St. John's College** (est.1893) is Luth. Ch. institution; Adm. Bldg. contains hist. mus. College St. & Warren Ave., **Southwestern College** (est.1885), Meth. Episc. Ch. coed. institution, occupies 35-a. campus. At 37m is St.15; take latter (R) here to **Dexter,** 44m, one-street village at whose S. limits is **Helium Plant,** built in 1927. Helium, noninflammable & less than a seventh as heavy as air, was discovered here for first time in natural gas in 1903.

(B) Take US160 (R) from Wellington through wheat fields & grazing lands. **Argonia,** 21.5m, inc. in 1885, claims to have had 1st woman mayor in U.S.—Mrs. Susanna Salter, elected 1887. **Harper,** 37.5m, wheat town, bustles with activity during harvest early in July. **Medicine Lodge,** 72.5m, trim little town overlooking timbered valley of Medicine R., laid out in 1873, is wheat & cattle country trading & shipping pt., & has gypsum mill for plaster. Once every 5 yrs. since 1927 it has presented Peace Treaty Pageant comm. Medicine Lodge Peace Treaty negotiated here by U.S. Gov. representatives & chiefs of 5 plains tribes in Oct. 1867. Site was believed by Inds. of reg. to be under protection of Gt. Spirit; & representatives of all SW. tribes met in peace at medicine lodge here, to fast, pray & bathe. Here Oct. 1867, 15,000 Inds. met with 600 Gov. representatives in what is said to be largest gathering of Inds. & whites in history of U.S. Council meetings were held in large tent on R. bank. After 2 wks.' negotiations treaty was signed, providing that area S. of Kans.' S. boundary should be Ind. Territory "as long as grass grows & waters run." Town founded shortly after by white settlers depended chiefly on cattle business. Robbery of Medicine Valley Bank & killing of its president & cashier in 1884 by gang led by John Henry Brown, former companion of "Billy the Kid," was followed by lynching of culprits. Here in 1890 "Sockless Jerry" Simpson, Populist leader, campaigned successfully for election to Congress against Jas. R. Hollowell, whom he attempted to discredit when they appeared on same platform with statement: "My opponent wears silk stockings," whereupon Hollowell stooped to pull up Simpson's trouser leg, revealing bare ankle, & retorted, "My opponent wears no socks at all."

N. end Main St., **Peace Treaty Mon.** (1929) is marble statue of frontiersman & Ind. clasping hands. E. side of town on US160, **Mem. Peace Pk.** is wooded area with recr. facils., network of foot trls. & natural amphitheatre in which Peace Treaty Pageant is held. Fowler Ave. & Oak St., **Home of Carrie Nation,** is marked by bronze plaque. Mrs. Nation's first pub. demonstration occurred in Medicine Lodge in 1899, when she attempted unsuccessfully to storm saloon, brandishing big black umbrella.

**60. CALDWELL,** on almost treeless plain, surrounded by scattered oilwells, draws trade from both Kans. & Okla. Building of branch line by Santa Fe from Wichita in 1880 made it cattle shipping pt. & Caldwell's saloons & gambling houses welcomed spurred & sombreroed cowboys. Early in Sept. 1893, following Pres. Cleveland's proclamation opening Cherokee Strip to homesteaders, thousands of covered wagons converged here, until 15,000 "boomers" were gathered, packing sts., until at noon of Sept. 16, with firing of gun, "Cherokee Run" across border into Okla. began. At **62.5.** is **OKLA. LINE.**

# US 20—NEBRASKA

**NEB.-IOWA LINE** (across Mo. R. from Sioux City, Ia.) **(W) to NEB.-WYO. LINE** (23m from Lusk, Wyo.). **439. US20**

Via: Winnebago, Blair, Valentine, Cody, Chadron, Harrison. RRs. parallel route bet. South Sioux City & O'Neill & bet. O'Neill & Harrison. Bus serv. bet. Page & Crawford. Accoms.: In larger towns.

US20 runs through undulating prairie farming reg. of E. Neb., across vast hay fields of central plateau, along edge of treeless sand hills reg. of NW. Neb. & into pine & butte-dotted mt. reg. extending into Wyo. & S.D.

## Sec. 1: NEB.-IOWA LINE to CHADRON. 378.

From (S) limits of Sioux City, Ia., toll bridge crosses Mo. R., which is **NEB.-IOWA LINE, 0.**

At **0.5. SOUTH SIOUX CITY,** overlooking Mo. R. from wooded bluffs, was inc. in 1889. At **2.5.** is J. with US73-77.

SIDE TRIP: (L) 4m to **Dakota City,** quiet country town platted in 1855-56. **Luth. Ch.** (1860) was first of this denomination in Neb. Around **Winnebago** at 17.5m extends 97,497-a. **Winnebago Ind. Reserv.;** permission to visit may be obtained at **Winnebago Ind. Agency,** 18.5m. Winnebago, originally from Wis., migrated here in 1864. At **Howard Pk.,** (R) 0.5m from Ind. Agency, is held annual Winnebago Ind. Powwow (early Aug.). S. of Winnebago, route cont. (L) on US73E. 28m **Macy** is trading post for 205,335-a. **Omaha Ind. Reserv.,** since 1854, home of tribe who lived originally in Ohio. Ritual dances are performed at annual Omaha Ind. Powwow here (late Aug.). 54m, **Tekamah,** modern country town with paved sts. & attractive shops, was founded in 1854. 71.5m at **Blair** (see US30) is J. with US30 (see).

At **13.5.** on US20 is J. with St.12.

SIDE TRIP: Take latter (R) 8m to **Ponca,** one of Neb.'s oldest towns, platted in 1856.
Turn (R) 3m from Ponca to **Ponca St. Pk.** (260 as.pic.camp.shelters;lookouts.foot & bridle trls.), for.-covered, overlooking Mo. R.
At 13m on St.12, J. with unimproved Rd.
Take latter (R) 8m to so-called **Ionia Volcano,** steep bluff by Mo. R., whose clays & shales contain iron sulphide, which produces heat & therefore smoky vapor when acted on by water.
60.5m **Crofton** (see US81) is at J. with US81 (see).

**40. LAUREL,** is at J. with St.15.

SIDE TRIP: Take latter (L) to **Wayne,** 17m, laid out in 1881, where in 1891 was est. **Neb. St. Teachers College,** occupying 51-a. campus.

**58.** J. with US81 (see). US20 passes through several small rural trading centers on way to **O'NEILL** at **123.,** named for Irish immigrant John J. O'Neill, who helped lead armed Fenian invasion of Canada & after imprisonment for infraction of neutrality laws, founded here the 1st of 3 Irish-Amer. colonies. O'Neill is shipping pt. for butter, livestock, hay & grain; it has pk., playgrounds, & fairgrounds.
US20 now traverses vast hay-producing reg. The towns—among them **ATKINSON** at **143.** & **BASSETT** at **175.**—are chiefly hay-shipping pts. Bassett's blood-red stucco **Whiton Hotel** was once hangout of fast-shooting, hard-riding, hard-drinking Pony Boys, outlaws led by David C. ("Doc") Middleton & Kid Wade; Wade was caught E. of Bassett & hanged by vigilantes in 1884. **183. LONG PINE** is at boundary bet. Central & Mt. Standard Time Zones. **192. AINSWORTH** has log cabin **mus.** of old relics on its cth. sq. Through level, sandy, treeless country, US20 cont. to J. with US83 at **232.5.**

SIDE TRIP: Take latter (L) to J. with dirt Rd. Turn (R) here past chain of Ls. in sand-hill reg. in most of which f. is permitted, but not h.; almost all are within Valentine Nat. Wildlife Refuge (see below). 10m **Pelican L.** & 12m **Beaver L.,** latter within **Rat & Beaver L. Recr. Grounds;** accoms. & supplies are avail. **Marsh L.** at 16m is largest in Neb. US83 cont. (S) into 66,448-a. **Valentine Nat. Wild Life Refuge,** abounding in bird & animal life.

Beyond crossing of pine-shaded steep-walled canyon of Niobrara R., **235.** lies **VALENTINE, 238.,** typical western town, sett. in 1882. **Valentine Natural City Pk.** (cabins.camp.) contains L. Near (N) edge of town is **L. Minnechaduza** (boat.f.swim.).

SIDE TRIP: Take St.7 (R) from Valentine 2m to **St. Fish Hatchery,** est. 1912. St.7 cont. to **Niobrara Game Reserve** (18,719 as.O.daily.8-2.guides), comprising picturesque site of

Niobrara Military Reserv., est. 1879 to control Sioux Inds. on Rosebud Reserv. in S.D., which was set aside after 1908 as nat. reserve to perpetuate Amer. bison & other wildlife incl. antelope, bobcat, beaver, civet cat, coyote, deer, elk, mink, muskrat, possum, raccoon, skunk, weasel & numerous birds. On site of old Ft. Niobrara, near main office bldg., is small **Mus.** of nat. hist. exhibits. Truck & horse trls. make most of refuge accessible. Niobrara R. flowing through N. sec. has carved out 100′ banks.

For nearly 100$^{m}$, US20 now runs through sand-hill country, treeless & sparsely sett.

**275. CODY,** resembling movie set for western thriller, is at J. with country Rd.

SIDE TRIP: Take latter (L) 10$^{m}$ to **Boiling Springs Ranch,** one of famous ranches of the early cattle era, whose Boiling Springs, E. of ranch bldgs., are one of reg.'s natural wonders.

**299.5.** J. with dirt Rd. leading (L) 0.5$^{m}$ to **Cottonwood L. Recr. Grounds** (160 as.f.), with 80-a. L. Just beyond (W) edge of sand-hills area lies **GORDON** at **329.5,** shipping & trading center.

SIDE TRIP: Take St.27 (L) from Gordon to **Home of "Old Jules" Sandoz,** 25$^{m}$, well-known because of Mari Sandoz's spirited biography of her father. Sandoz was pioneer horticulturist of sand-hills reg.

US20 runs (W) bet. wide valley of Niobrara R. (L) & broken, rocky, pine-dotted tableland (R).

**342.5. RUSHVILLE** & **355. HAY SPRINGS** are farmers' trading centers.

SIDE TRIP: Take gravel Rd. (L) 7$^{m}$ from Hay Springs to **Walgren L. Recr. Grounds** (130 as.camp.pic.f.swim.).

Country through which US20 passes now becomes semi-mountainous, with yellowish hills & buttes & occasional pine trees.

**376. CHADRON** is typical western college town at edge of White R. Valley, surrounded by buttes & canyons. It has RR. shops, warehouses, & storage yards; industries incl. flour milling, oil refining, & processing of dairy products. Chadron, named for Fr.-Ind. "squaw man" who lived & trapped in reg., was sett. in 1880's; in its early yrs., cowboys often came into town to shoot up the saloons. **Chadron St. Teachers College** (est.1911), (S) edge of town, occupies 213-a. campus.

SIDE TRIP: Take St.19 (L) from Chadron to **Chadron St. Pk.** (800 as.inn.cabins.pic.swim. f.boat.horses.), 8.5$^{m}$, Neb.'s first St. pk., an area rich in natural rock formations, towering pines, deep canyons & high bluffs. St.19 cont. (S) to 59$^{m}$ **Alliance** in reg. raising seed potatoes. Alliance was sett. in 1888. **City Pk.,** one block E. of 9th St., contains **Sod. H. Mus.,** copy of pioneer houses in vic., housing pioneer relics. Panhandle Stampede, held annually last wk. in June, is rodeo characteristic of Old West. At 97$^{m}$ is J. with US26 (see US30).

## Sec. 2: CHADRON to NEB.-WYO. LINE. 61.

US20 now heads into rough country dotted with pines. **3. TRUNK BUTTE** (L) is large natural formation whose shape suggested its name. **24. CROW BUTTE,** according to legend, once served as a retreat for a band of Crow Inds. hard pushed by a Sioux war party. **25.5. CRAWFORD,** on White R. bet. two ranges of Pine Ridge, trading center for stock ranches & irrigated farms of vic., was founded in 1885 & in early yrs., was frontier boom town, wide-open, with flourishing red-light dist. **City Pk.** (golf.swim.racetracks.pic.) was once part of Ft. Robinson Military Reserv. (see below).

SIDE TRIP: Take St.2 (R) from Crawford, winding into Neb. Badlands, 21$^{m}$ to **Toadstool Pk.,** field of gigantic stone mushrooms, produced by erosion of soft clay from under stratum of sandstone & gumbo soil.

**29. FT. ROBINSON,** unit of U.S. Army Remount Serv., raising horses & mules in its fenced pastures, lies in NE. cor. of 36,000-a. Ft. Robinson Military Reserv., est. in 1874, immediately before last great Ind. uprising. Ft. is cupped in deep valley of Pine Ridge; behind it rise 1,000′ cliffs. In old post **Cemetery** lie soldiers, civilians, & Inds. of Ind. war period.

US20 ascends Smiley Canyon to top of Pine Ridge, & then reaches **HARRISON** at **52.,** ranch center.

SIDE TRIP: Take St.29 (L) from Harrison 23$^{m}$ to **Agate Springs Fossil Beds** where Niobrara R. has eroded Box Butte Plateau to depth of 400′, exposing rich deposit of Miocene fossils. **Cook Mus. of Nat. Hist.** contains many of finds. Fossils of prehist. rhinoceros, dinohyus, moropus, camels, alligators, hawks & oreodonts have been found.

At **61.** is **NEB.-WYO. LINE.**

# US 30—NEBRASKA

**NEB.-IOWA LINE** (11$^{m}$ from Mo. Valley, Iowa) **(W) to NEB.-WYO. LINE** (0.8$^{m}$ from Pine Bluffs, Wyo.). **447.5. US30**

Via: Fremont, Columbus, Grand Island, Kearney, N. Platte, Ogallala, Sidney. RR. parallels route throughout, busses bet. Fremont & Neb.-Wyo. Line. Accoms.: At short intervals.

US30, chief E-W. hy. across Neb., closely follows Mormon Trl. for two-thirds of its way, roughly parallels Ore. Trl. for one-third. Former route, following N. bank of Platte R. (W) from Grand I., was first blazed in 1813 by fur traders traveling (E) from Ft. Astoria, Ore. Mormons on way (W) to Utah in 1847 were first large org. group to take it. Ore. Trl. along S. bank of Platte was most traveled route in major period of Ore. emigration, following 1841, & became route of Ben Holladay's stage line (1859), Pony Express (1860-61), & U.P. RR. (1868). Terrain is almost unbroken prairie with steady rise from E. to W.

## Sec. 1: NEB.-IOWA LINE to GRAND ISLAND. 136.

At **0.**, US30 crosses Mo. R., which is Neb.-Iowa Line, on Abraham Lincoln Mem. Bridge (toll). **BLAIR, 3.**, sett. beginning in 1869 by Scands., is trade center for rich agric. area. N. of town is **Dana College,** 0.5$^{m}$, outgrowth of Trinity Seminary, founded 1884 to train ministry of United Evangelical Luth. Ch. **FREMONT, 25.5.**, lies on N. bank of wide, muddy, bluff-fringed Platte R. RR. center & distributing pt. for rich Elkhorn Valley farmlands, it has agric. processing & other industries & is hybrid seed corn & soybean center & cattle market. First claim stake was driven on town site, named for western pathfinder, John C. Frémont, on Aug. 26, 1856. Frémont Town Assoc. offered 2 lots to anyone erecting hewn log house & offered to furnish timber. Pawnee, resenting settlers' inroads on their timber, demanded place be evacuated, but were intimidated with aid of soldiers from Omaha. Settlement's first yrs. were time of near-starvation, but gradually prosperity came from trade with travelers. In 1866, U.P. RR. came through. Beginning to thrive, Fremont acquired flour mills, canning factory, sand & gravel works. **Midland College,** 720 E. 9th St., moved here from Atchison, Kans., in 1919, was founded in 1887 & is conducted by United Luth. Ch.

SIDE TRIP: Take US77 (L) from Fremont to **Wahoo,** 21$^{m}$, whose name was derived from Ind. word for red berry bushes. Wahoo's chief industries process farm products & produce farm equipment. **Luther College,** N. end Washington St., is Luth. Ch. Jr. College. US77 cont. (S) to **Lincoln,** 51.5$^{m}$ (see US6) at J. with US6 (see).

**U. P. PITS RECR. GROUNDS, 29.5.**, & adj. **FREMONT RECR. GROUNDS** (SE), together comprise 307 as. with 15 sandpit Ls. (camp.pic.f.). **SCHUYLER, 55.,** was named for Schuyler Colfax, Vice-Pres. of U.S. in 1869, when town was platted. **COLUMBUS, 73.**, founded in 1856 by group from Columbus, Ohio, developed as supply pt. for wagon caravans on westward trl. It has several industrial plants & is hqs. for Loup R. Pub. Power Dist. Project, sometimes called "little TVA," extending 200$^{m}$ across central Neb. along lower valley of Loup R., with 35$^{m}$ canal tapped by two power houses. Columbus is at J. with US81 (see). At **DUNCAN, 81.,** is J. with gravel Rd. leading (L) to **Kuenzli Mus.** (sm.fee), 2.5$^{m}$, developed by Swiss immigrant & veterinarian Dr. Frank Kuenzli, which exhibits curious articles from all parts of world; reptiles, octopi, Australian birds & butterflies, pioneer & Ind. relics, military equipment. **114. CENTRAL CITY,** busy community served by two RRs., grew up around sta. of U.P. named Lone Tree, for lone giant cottonwood on bank of Platte R. which became travelers' landmark.

### 136. GRAND ISLAND

Through RR. & bus conns. Info.: C. of C., 315½ N. Locust St. Accoms.: Plentiful. Swim.: The Pier, 500 S. Pine St.

Spreading over Platte R. bottomlands, Grand I. is RR. distribution pt. & manufacturing center which owes its prosperity largely to its position near center of St. & Nation—especially its popularity as convention town & as horse & mule market. Grand I. was laid out by U.P. RR. in 1866, assuming name of earlier settlement founded in 1857 on R. bank (S) opp. island known to Fr.-Can. trappers as "La Grand Ile." Early settlers of latter place, mostly Germans, throve by selling farm products to west-bound travelers. When RR. came through, stores & houses were removed to new townsite by tracks. By 1880's Grand I. had become prosperous enough to boast horse-&-mule-power streetcar system. Toward end of same decade, when soil of vic. was found adaptable for sugar-beet culture, one of first beet-sugar factories in U.S. was est. here: **Amer. Crystal Sugar Co. Plant** (guided tours during season, late summer & early fall), end of W. Koenig St. **Livestock Commission Co. Market,** E. 4th St. bet. C.B.& Q. & U.P. tracks, is meeting place for mule buyers of Deep South & mule raisers of NW.

SIDE TRIPS: (A) Take US281 (L) from Grand I. to J. with St.70, 1.5m; turn (R) on this to **Stolley St. Pk.** (43 as.pic.no camp.), 2.5m, comprising grove set out by German immigrant Wm. Stolley, who arrived in 1857 & in 1860 planted here in sandy shallows of Platte R. 6,000 trees of more than 50 varieties. For protection from Inds., Stolley built log Ft. Independence, which stood 150 yards (S) from well-preserved **Farm Home of Stolley Family.** Other extant bldgs. incl. **Frame Schoolh.,** first in Hall Cty., & **Log H.** with orig. slough-grass roof.

(B) Take St.2 (R) from Grand I. to J. with gravelled Rd., 5m.

Take latter (R) to **U.S. Central Monitoring Sta.** of Fed. Communications Commission, est. here in 1930 near geographical center of U.S. to check frequency of both Nat. & foreign broadcasting stas. 60-a. grounds are dotted with antennae.

**Ravenna,** 30m, first called Beaver Cr., was later renamed for city in Italy, & some of its older streets have Ital. names; first settler took up residence in 1874. **Broken Bow,** 80m, platted in 1882, is shipping center for livestock, hay, & grain & has cigar & broom factories. At **Merna,** 89m, is J. with St.80.

Take latter (R) 10m to **Victoria Springs St. Pk.** (60 as.cabins.pic.playgrounds.boat.swim. f.), comprising mineral springs, groves, & L. No two of many springs, rising along Victoria Cr., are chemically alike; waters are impregnated with chemicals from different sandstones. Within pk. are two log cabins built in 1873.

At **Halsey,** 132m, is J. with gravel Rd. Take latter (L) 1m to **Bessey Div. of Neb. Nat. For.** (90,388 as.pic.swim.sports facils.), est. 1902 here in sand-hills reg. Bessey Div., with 115,638-a. Niobrara Div. (NW), comprises largest man-made for. in U.S., incl. some 27,000 as. of plantations of coniferous trees.

## Sec. 2: GRAND I. to NORTH PLATTE. 136.5.

US30 cont. (W) along N. bank of Platte R. through several small towns. **42. KEARNEY** (pronounced Kar-nee), named for famous frontier gov. outpost est. here in 1848 to guard travelers on Ore. Trl. Town was platted in 1871 at J. of Burlington & Mo. (now C.B.& Q.) & U.P. RRs. Efforts of promoters to have it made capital of Neb. &, afterwards, of U.S. came to nothing; & Kearney, after boom period in 80's & 90's, became agric. trading center with several small industrial plants. 3 blocks off US30 is **Harmon Pk.** (pic.rock gardens.swim.open-air theater). At W. end of town is **Neb. St. Teachers College.**

SIDE TRIP: Take St.10 (L) from Kearney to **Ft. Kearney St. Pk.** (80 as.camp.pic.), 7m, where still are rifle pits & other earthworks. Ft. was begun here in 1848 & by 1852 comprised two blockhs., powder & guard hs., lookout & officers' quarters. It was abandoned in 1871, when no longer needed to protect wagon trains from Ind. attacks.

**45.5.** J. with gravel Rd. leading (R) 0.5m to **Cotton Mill L. Recr. Grounds** (160 as. lodge.camp.trlrs.pic.f.), with 50-a. L. **77. LEXINGTON,** is offspring of trading post & Pony Express sta. on S. bank of Platte R. on Ore. Trl., whose settlers moved across R. here when RR. came through & named their new town for Battle of Lexington. **91. COZAD,** in sec. noted for alfalfa & hay fields, has several feed & alfalfa mills & ships quantities of hay. City pk. of **GOTHENBURG, 101.,** contains **Fur-Trading Post** erected in 1854 near Ft. McPherson (see below) on Ore. Trl. & used at various times as Pony Express sta., overland stage sta., & ranch bldg. (moved here in 1931). At **MAXWELL, 123.5.,** is J. with Ft. McPherson Nat. Cemetery Rd.

SIDE TRIP: Take latter (L) across Platte R. to **Ft. McPherson Nat. Cemetery,** 3.5m, where in 1863, Gov. ft. was built in reserv. 16m sq. on bluffs to guard overland stagecoach travelers from Ind. attacks. Burial ground became nat. cemetery in 1873, to which bodies were transferred from other frontier posts after Ind. wars. Ft. McPherson itself was abandoned in 1887.

US30 crosses N. Fork of Platte R. to **N. PLATTE, 136.5.,** RR. town & trading center on narrow delta at Fork of Plattes, on boundary of Central & Mt. Time Zones. Here, Nov. 9, 1866, Peniston & Andrew J. Miller opened trading post near U.P. RR. construction camp. First newspaper, "Pioneer on Wheels," was begun same yr., printed in box car. Within few months, there were more than 300 bldgs.

& pop. exceeded 2,000—consisting chiefly of RR. laborers, gamblers & "toughs." Removal westward of RR. construction camp in June 1867, reduced pop. to about 300 & number of bldgs. to 20; everything was moved that could be. But U.P. picked N. Platte as division pt. & built shops, roundh. & hotel. Law & order was est. by vigilante action in 1870, mun. gov. was formed in 1875. Its chief growth has followed settlement of W. Neb. sand-hills reg. after 1904. **Mem. Pk.,** Tabor Ave. bet. E. 2nd & E. 4th Sts., contains **Log Cabin Mus.,** housing pioneer relics. Other pioneer articles are exhibited in 2nd-fl. Relic Room of **Lincoln County Cth.,** Jeffers St. bet. E. 3rd & E. 4th Sts. **Cody Pk.** (pic.f.athletic facils.), N. Jeffers St., 4 blocks N. of 12th St., 120-a. landscape riverside area, was named for Wm. Frederick (Buffalo Bill) Cody, long town's most noted citizen, who came here with his family in 1870, when already nationally famous as scout, guide & buffalo hunter.

## Sec. 3: N. PLATTE to NEB.-WYO. LINE. 175.

At **2.** is J. with dirt Rd. leading (R) 0.5$^{m}$ to **Scouts' Rest Ranch,** former home of "Buffalo Bill" Cody. **OGALLALA, 50.5.,** was named for Oglalla (also spelled Ogallala), band of Teton Sioux. Ogallala developed as one of 1st cattle shipping pts. on U.P. RR. when Texas cowboys began arriving with their herds in 1867. For nearly 3 decades, its history was typical cowtown's, peppered with shooting frays.

SIDE TRIP: Take US26 (R) from Ogallala, following Mormon Trl. along N. bank of N. Platte R. & paralleling Ore. Trl., which ran along S. bank. At 2.5$^{m}$ is J. with St.61.

Take latter (R) 7$^{m}$ to **Kingsley Dam,** world's 2nd largest earth-filled dam, costing about $36,000,000, which impounds N. Platte to form **L. McConaughy,** 23$^{m}$ long, largest body of water in Neb.

**Oshkosh,** 43.5$^{m}$, seat of Garden Cty., first sett. in 1855. **Bridgeport,** 90.5$^{m}$, holds annual celebration known as Camp Clarke Days (1st wk. in Sept.), comm. Camp Clarke across N. Platte R. where soldiers were stationed to guard Camp Clarke Bridge used from 1876 to 1900. Bridgeport is at J. with St.19 (see US20).

Take St.88 (L) from Bridgeport to **Cth. Rock** & **Jail Rock,** 5$^{m}$, two weathered sandstone buttes of unusual formation.

US26 cont. (NW) from Bridgeport to **Chimney Rock,** 105$^{m}$, hist. landmark on Ore. Trl., described by almost all early explorers, conical mound of reddish sandstone rising to narrow 150′ pinnacle. Here is J. with St.86.

Take latter (L) to **Gering,** 20$^{m}$, RR. division pt. with beet-sugar refinery, packing plant & stockyards, dating back to 1887, which celebrates Ore. Trl. Days yearly in wk. in which July 17 falls; July 17, 1830 was date on which first wagon train to cross plains to Rockies camped here. St.29 leads (L) from Gering to **Wildcat Hills Recr. Grounds** (1,000 as.camp.pic.), 10$^{m}$, extremely rugged, wooded tract of cliffs & canyons, which is St. game reserve containing elk, deer, antelope & buffalo. From Gering, St.86 cont. to **Scott's Bluff Nat. Mon.** (2,292 as.no pic.or camp.), 22.5$^{m}$, comprising first butte of dominating height to greet plains-weary eyes of Ore. Trl. travelers, named for fur trader Hiram Scott, abandoned by his companions to die here in 1828. First white men known to have seen Scott's Bluff (4,662′), which rises 750′ above N. Platte R. plain, were Rbt. Stuart & companions, bearing dispatches to John Jacob Astor from Ft. Astoria, Ore., in 1812-13. Past it came first wagon train to follow Ore. Trl., in 1830; it subsequently became landmark for thousands of emigrants. After 1852, when **Mitchell Pass,** which divides bluff in half, was excavated for traffic, they passed through it, as did riders of Pony Express in 1860-61; & through it was strung first transcontinental telegraph line. To protect lines of communication, Ft. Mitchell was est. NW. of bluff in 1864. At base of bluff is **Ore. Trl. Mus.** containing relics, water-color drawings, dioramas & geological exhibits. Automobile rd. (toll) leads (R) from mus., passing through 3 tunnels, to summit, 1.5$^{m}$, where observation pt. serves to locate hist. landmarks & to trace route of Ore. Trl. St. 86 cont. to **Horse Cr. Treaty Mon.,** 41$^{m}$, on site where in Sept., 1851, gathered more than 10,000 Inds. of plains & foothill tribes from Arkansas R. to Canada, in council with Fed. Gov. representatives, to agree on reserv. boundaries & privileges of whites in crossing them.

From J. with St.86 (see above), US26 cont. (N) across N. Platte R. & then turns (E) to **Scottsbluff,** 132$^{m}$, whose site in 1899 was an irrigated alfalfa field, is now chief trading center for N. Platte Valley area of Panhandle Neb. & E. Wyo., locally known as "America's Valley of the Nile," which produces alfalfa, sugar beets, beans, certified potatoes, all grown with aid of irrigation from several storage reservoirs. Within 30$^{m}$ radius are 7 beet sugar refineries. Packing, canning, & dairying are leading industries. **Mitchell,** 141.5$^{m}$, which has sugar factory & markets honey, is site of **Scottsbluff Cty. Fairgrounds;** annual fair here is one of Neb.'s leading events. At 155.5$^{m}$ is Neb.-Wyo. Line (32$^{m}$ from Torrington, Wyo.).

**60.5. PONY EXPRESS MON. 64. ORE. TRL. MARKER. 90. CHAPPELL,** in Neb.'s largest wheat-raising area, was named for U.P. RR. official John Chappell, who laid out town. **Chappell Mem. Gallery** has coll. of etchings & Jap. prints. **117. SIDNEY,** named for U.P.'s N.Y. solicitor, Sidney Dillon, lies in Lodgepole Valley. Town developed around **Ft. Sidney,** est. here to protect RR. workers against Ind. attacks & maintained until 1894; surviving remains incl. **Ammunition Storeh.,** now part of residence, 2 blocks S. of J. of Burlington & U.P. tracks; two **Barracks,** now dwellings, one block S. of US30 on 6th Ave.; & adj. latter, large well-preserved **Officers' Quarters.** Sidney, being nearer Black Hills than any other RR. pt. of consequence when 1876-77 gold rush began, did roaring business in its stores, dance-halls & saloons. Shootings were so frequent that U.P. is said to have warned through passengers not to step off train if they wanted to leave Sidney alive. **131. PT. OF ROCKS,** once observation post for soldiers protecting RR. builders, affords broad view of craggy, pine-dotted country. Trade center of extensive potato-growing reg., **154. KIMBALL** is noted for quantities of wheat it ships. **175. NEB.-WYO. LINE.**

## US 6—NEBRASKA

**NEB.-IOWA LINE** (across Mo. R. from Council Bluffs, Iowa) **(W) to NEB.-COLO. LINE** ($15^{m}$ from Holyoke, Colo.). **381.5. US6**

Via: Omaha, (Boys Town), Lincoln, Hastings, McCook, Trenton, Imperial. RR. parallels route bet. Omaha & Milford & bet. Dorchester & Imperial. Bus lines follow it throughout. Accoms.: Limited except in larger towns.

Typical cross sec. of Neb. is traversed by this route, which in E. & central secs. runs through slightly hilly farming country & in W. through semi-arid reg.

### Sec. 1: NEB.-IOWA LINE to McCOOK. 294.

From Council Bluffs, Iowa, US6 crosses Mo. R., which is **Neb.-Iowa Line, 1.,** on Douglas St. Bridge (toll).

### 1.5. OMAHA

Through RR., bus & plane conns. Info.: C. of C., 14th & Farnam Sts., Accoms.: Plentiful. Swim. at pub. pks. Sept.; Ak-Sar-Ben Festival & Livestock Show.

Spread out along (W) bank of Mo. R. for $12^{m}$ & rising far up into hills (W), Omaha is industrial & commercial city, Neb.'s largest, in heart of farm belt. Beginning as river town, it became RR. center, country's 4th largest. Its RRs. bring Colo. lead to one of world's biggest smelters; hogs, sheep, & cattle to world's 2nd largest meat packing center & livestock market; wheat & corn to one of world's largest grain markets, equipped with elevators, flour & feed mills & world's biggest industrial alcohol plant of its kind. Omaha makes more butter than any other city in world & ranks high as poultry processing & egg drying center. It has not altogether lost sense of surprise at becoming big city: overalls & straw hats may still be seen on its sts., & it cont. to take small town's int. in local boys who have made good elsewhere. Life here has more variety than is usual in Neb.: dancehalls, community art mus., livestock shows & formal banquets, folk festivals of European tradition & annual coronation of King & Queen of Ak-Sar-Ben.

Omaha's chief sources of civic pride are its pks., nearly 50 of them covering 2,500 as., & its schools, incl. many fine high schools, mun. univ., & one of America's ranking Cath. univs. It is also proud of its cultural center, $4,000,000 Joslyn Mem.; its municipally owned pub. utilities system; its 900-a. airport. Its fine shops, its hotels & theaters, its exclusive residential districts all lend it metropolitan air. Along flats & bluffs of Mo., which forms Omaha's W. boundary, spread RR. tracks & factories; much of river-bottom area has been filled, & channel has been improved in recent yrs., with object of making Omaha once again R. port. Westward stretches downtown business dist., where grading & filling have levelled off mounds & ravines of once-rugged terrain. S. Omaha is working-class residential dist. To N. is Omaha's Negro quarter, extending along 24th St. Far to W., where Omaha's characteristic hills remain untouched, are city's "exclusive" secs.

As far back as 1820's, few canny fur-traders lived just N. of site of Omaha: Manuel Lisa, Spaniard; Jean Pierre Cabanne, Frenchman; & man named Roye or Royce. In 1852 land sharks, speculators, & settlers began to congregate across R. in Council Bluffs, Iowa, awaiting treaty bet. Gov. & Inds. that would open Neb. for settlement,

& a few impatient ones crossed over to stake claims on lands still belonging to Omaha Inds. Signing of treaty on June 23, 1854, launched Omaha's first boom. Council Bluffs & Neb. Ferry Co. had town platted, naming it for dispossessed Omaha; by end of yr., newspaper had been est. & about 20 bldgs. erected—1 of them brick, in which 1st Territorial Legislature convened Jan. 16, 1855, although no Territorial capital had been officially selected. First settlers, mostly sons of farmers or common laborers, were hardy lot who seized on money-making opportunities. They org. Claim Club to protect allowance of 320 as. per settler, as against Gov.'s 160, & to forestall Gov.'s requirement that each man improve his claim & live on it, they built house on wheels, which could be moved from one claim to another; Claim Club proceeded to deal in summary fashion with claim jumping & claim quarrels. Lawlessness flourished, & now & then there were lynchings. City council, holding its first meeting in 1857, considered regulation of bowling alleys, liquor sales & gambling. By this time, smithy, sawmill, & brickyard had been est. & by 1858, capitol erected. Emigrants & gold seekers made city their outfitting pt., & Omaha merchants carried on thriving trade; at times arrivals at Omaha levee averaged steamboat daily.

Then RR. came. Abraham Lincoln selected Council Bluffs as terminus of U.P., but engineers & Douglas Cty. bonds brought it across R. to Omaha; in 1863 construction formally began, & 2 yrs. later 20 leading citizens led by Gen. Wm. T. Sherman, riding on flat cars with nail kegs for seats, took first train to Salings' Grove. Omaha boomed, stealing business from Council Bluffs. From Mo. R. to Capitol Hill, streets were filled with pack-carrying men in frontier garb, loitering Inds., businessmen & gamblers, & all characters common to frontier towns. Omaha Horse Ry. Co. laid its first track & first gas works was built. By 1870, there were 100 street lamps. Shortly thereafter, U.P. shops opened & 1st meat-packing plant was est. New high school, pub. lib. & Creighton Univ. all appeared during 1870s, along with smelting plant, grain elevators, more meat-packing plants & RR. bridge across Mo. Most important development of 80's was establishment of Union Stockyards. With establishment of great packing houses, thousands of immigrants, majority S. Europeans, thronged city. This was heyday of Cudahys, Kountzes, Paxtons, John A. Creighton, J. L. Brandeis, & others who brought Omaha into limelight. Omaha's underworld grew: fortunes were made in gambling. On crest of real estate boom, city acquired opera house, 1st waterworks, 1st asphalt paving, electric light company, electric street ry., 1st skyscraper, & Univ. of Neb. Medical College. 1890s brought panic, grasshoppers & drought. Undaunted Omaha businessmen org. Trans-Miss. Exposition.

Omaha's modern development began in 1910. City rapidly attained distinctions which school children learned to count off on their fingers: "Omaha macaroni is sold in Italy! . . . Omaha pig lead is sold all over the world." Second crop of famous characters took limelight: Joslyns in their castle listened to music & debated endowing a concert hall; Tom Dennison, driven into politics to protect his gambling interests, became (& remained until 1934) city's political boss. 1929 depression, followed by yrs. of drought & frozen credit, hit Omaha hard. City tried to take it lightly: when farmers picketed Rds. into city, overturning milk trucks, during milk strike of 1933, city people were unsympathetic; but sentiment turned: streetcar strike of 1934 was backed by surprising pub. solidarity. World War II brought vast expansion as city responded to war needs for its food products & even turned to assembling & testing B-29 airplanes at $30,000,000 Glenn L. Martin-Neb. Co. plant.

PTS. OF INT.: (1) Omaha's **Fed. Bldg.** (1933), 15th & Dodge Sts., an 11-story structure of granite, limestone & brick in modern design, stands on site of its 1st U.S. Cth. & P.O. (1872). (2) Near-by is **Capitol Hill,** 20th & Dodge Sts., site of 2nd Territorial capitol bldg. (1857-58), now occupied by **Central H.S.,** at whose S. & E. entrances are comm. tablets. Among Omaha's other pub. bldgs. are (3) **Omaha P.O.** (1892-1906.Romanes.), 16th & Dodge Sts., with 190′ tower; (4) **Omaha Pub. Lib.** (1893.Ital.Ren.), 19th & Harney Sts., housing numismatic coll. & private lib. of lib.-site-donor B. Reed & colls. of Ind. curios, Babylonian tablets, & archeological discoveries in Neb.; (5) massive brick & Bedford Stone **Mun. Auditorium** (1904), 14th & Howard Sts., which houses conventions, trade exhibits, & boxing & wrestling matches; & (6) domed, Corinthian-column-adorned **Douglas County Cth.** (1812),

17th & Farnam Sts. (7) Omaha's cultural center, **Joslyn Mem.** (Mod.Class.O.wks. 10-5;Sun.2-9;tours 2 p.m.), 22nd & Dodge Sts., its rose marble walls rising above row of evergreens, was donated by Sarah Joslyn as a tribute to her husband, Geo. A. Joslyn, founder of Neb. Western Newspaper Union; it was opened in 1931. Colonnaded loggia flanked by heavy corner pylons leads to bronze doors of the main entrance. Focal point of inter. is Floral Ct. with its fountains & tropical plants. Bldg. contains art lib., concert hall & art galleries with coll. of paintings, drawings & prints, sculptures, ceramics, textiles, silver, porcelain, furniture, & other art objects. (8) Impressive for its modernity is **Union Passenger Terminal,** 10th & Marcy Sts., consisting of 2 units: 23-a. Union Sta. (1931) & Burlington Sta. (1930). At E. end of Union Sta. is bronze tablet comm. breaking of ground for U.P., laying of first rail, & driving of golden spike at Promontory, Utah. (9) **U.P. Hqs.,** 15th & Dodge Sts., contains first-floor **mus.** (O.9-5.guides) of Civil War souvenirs, Ind. & pioneer relics, & objects of int. in U.P. history; Lincoln corner contains letter & pictures, furniture from Pres.'s funeral car, & model of latter.

On Omaha's W. side lie its college & univ. campuses. (10) **Creighton Univ.,** 25th & California Sts., city's oldest, founded in 1878 with donations from fortunes amassed by pioneer settlers Edw. & John A. Creighton, is Jesuit-administered institution with 7 coed. professional schools & separate men's & women's liberal arts colleges. Among chief bldgs. on hill-top campus are **Faculty & Adm. Bldg.** (1930), **Univ. Chapel** (1887.enlarged 1923), & **Astronomical Observ.** (1885). (11) **Univ. of Omaha,** Dodge St. & Elmwood Pk. Dr., grew in less than 3 decades after its opening in 1909 from enrollment of 26 to one of more than 3,600. It became mun. univ. in 1930. First of bldgs. erected on its 52-a. campus adj. Elmwood Pk. is handsome Georg.-style **Liberal Arts Bldg.** (1938). (12) **Duchesne College,** 36th & Burt Sts., occupying group of Tudor Goth. bldgs. on 13.5-a. campus, is Cath. women's college, founded in 1881, named for Mother Duchesne, who est. in U.S. in 1818 Order of the Sacred Heart, of which faculty are members. (13) **Brownell Hall,** Underwood Ave. & 54th St., with 11-a. wooded campus, is an Episc. college-prep. school for girls, first institution of higher education for women est. in Neb. (14) **Univ. of Neb. College of Medicine,** 42nd St. & Dewey Ave., inc. as Omaha Medical College in 1881, became affiliated with St. Univ. in 1902; its facils. incl. main hospital & adm. bldg., 2 lab. bldgs., & nurse's home. (15) **Presb. Theological Seminary,** 21st & Wirt Sts., was est. in 1891; (16) **Neb. School for the Deaf,** 45th & Bedford Ave., in late 1860s. (17) Outstanding among Omaha's churches is **St. Cecilia's Cath.,** 40th St. bet. Webster & Burt Sts., begun in 1905 & still under construction, imposing edifice of Sp. Ren. design with twin towers.

Omaha's pks. are scattered in great semicircle round city. (18) Largest is **Levi Carter Pk.** (boat.f.swim.pic.), E. end of Ames Ave., adj. Mun. Airport inside big bend of Mo. at city's NE. edge, which surrounds horseshoe-shaped L. that serves as wildfowl refuge. Others are (19) **Kountze Pk.,** Florence Blvd. & Pinckney St., on site of Trans-Miss. Exposition of 1898; (20) **Miller Pk.** (lagoon.pavilion.sports facils.), 30th St. & Kansas Ave., whose birch drive & redbuds make it an Omaha showplace, near which is (21) **Ft. Omaha,** 30th & Fort Sts., est. in 1868; (22) **Fontenelle Pk.** (pic. sports facils.), Fontenelle Blvd. & Ames Ave., planted with evergreens; (23) **Elmwood Pk.** (pic.sports facils.), Dodge St. & Happy Hollow Blvd., 207-a. wooded tract with natural spring & Alaskan totem pole, near which is (24) 170-a. **Ak-Sar-Ben Field,** Center St. W. of 60th St., equipped with racetrack & grandstand, horse & cattle barns, polo field & baseball pk., & coliseum seating 10,000, which is scene each autumn of coronation of king & queen by Knights of Ak-Sar-Ben (Neb. spelled backwards); (25) **Hanscom Pk.,** 32nd St. & Woodworth Ave. (pavilion.pic.tennis cts.), containing two conservatories; (26) **Riverview Pk.** (zoo.lagoon.swim.), E. end Pk. Blvd., overlooking Mo. R.; (27) **Mandan Pk.** (pic.), 13th & Harrison Sts., whose high bluffs command fine view of R., on camp site of Lewis & Clark Expedition. (28) **Mt. Vernon Gardens,** 13th St. bet. W & Y Sts., landscaped in manner of Geo. Washington's Va. estate.

(29) **Hummel Pk.,** River Dr. at Omaha's far N. tip, commanding panoramic view of wooded Mo. R. bottoms, contains marker locating site of trading post of Amer. Fur. Co., est. by Jean Pierre Cabanne c.1824. Omaha's few other surviving hist. landmarks are mostly found near-by (S), where in 1846 Mormons est. their last outpost on long trek to Salt Lake, calling place Winter Quarters, at what later became independent community of Florence. (30) Small, grassy **Florence Pk.,** 30th

St. bet. Mormon & State Sts., contains large cottonwood wearing plaque that states it was planted by Brigham Young. (31) **Mormon Cemetery,** Northridge Dr. & State St., contains **mon.,** "Winter Quarters," two bronze figures on granite base (by Arvard T.Fairbanks), comm. 600 Mormon emigrants buried in vic. during winter of 1846-47. (32) **Mitchell H.** (1855), 8314 N. 31st St., is said to be oldest house in Neb. still in use. Omaha is at J. with US75 (see).

SIDE TRIPS: (A) Take US73 (R) from Omaha 8.5m to J. with Ponca Rd.

Turn (R) on this 2m to J. & (L) up steep hill to pt. at 4m from which may be seen (R) on riverfront probable **Site of Ft. Lisa,** est. in 1812 by Manuel Lisa, which became principal trading post of plains reg.

At 16m on US73 is **Ft. Calhoun,** rural trading center inc. in 1858, whose pk. contains mon. erected on 100th anniversary (1904) of Lewis & Clark expedition. Court St. leads (L) 0.5m to mon. on promontory now known as Council Bluff, marking **Site of Ft. Atkinson,** first mil. post in Neb., est. in 1819 near-by (N) & moved here in 1820 to Lewis & Clark camp site of Aug. 3, 1804. At **Blair,** 25m (see US30) is J. with US30.

(B) Take US30 Alt. (R) from Omaha to **Boys Town,** 11m, 1,000-a. city. (inc. 1936) with facils. for 1,000 formerly homeless boys, 10 to 18 yrs. old, from nearly every St. in Union, which has its own city council, p.o., chapel, schools, vocational education shops, field house, auditorium, & modern farm. Outgrowth of hotel for indigent male transients est. by Father Flanagan in Omaha in 1912. Boys Town was celebrated in film "Boys Town" (1938) starring Mickey Rooney & Spencer Tracy.

US6 heads (SW) from Omaha to J. with St.85 at **27.5.,** leading (L) 6m to **South Bend St. Fish Hatchery,** (pic.) Neb.'s oldest, on N. bank of Platte R. US6 crosses Platte R. to **ASHLAND, 36.,** named for Henry Clay's Ky. home.

### 60.5. LINCOLN

Through RR. & bus conns. Info.: C. of C., 208 N. 11th St. Accoms.: Plentiful. Swim. at Mun. Pool, 23rd & M Sts. Neb. St. Fair, Sept.

Lincoln, Neb.'s capital, lying in shallow, creek-traversed basin, is completely dominated by white stone shaft of St. Capitol, visible from hilltops on all approaching hys. Central business dist. has modern store fronts, office bldgs. & hotels. Civic beauty & cleanliness are major concern: Cornhusker capital, handsomely provided with pks., has been locally christened "The Lilac City" for one of its most popular species of decorative vegetation. It was at one time, when it had one church for every 700 people, known as "Holy City." It is largely occupied with ministering to large pop. of students & civil servants. Its schools & colleges & its gov. bureaus were its econ. mainstay, along with its farm trade & agricultural processing industries, which made— & still make—crops & weather perennial topics of conversation, until after World War II. Lincoln's only prewar industrial enterprise which approached 1,000-employe mark was its C.B. & Q. RR. car shops; but its new motor engines & "scooters," telephone equipment, rubber belting, & watch-making plants, alone now employing nearly 7,000, have converted it into industrial center of consequence.

Lincoln's history goes back to 1856, when Capt. W. T. Donovan sett. on site—then expanse of salt-crusted creek flats bordered by marsh & prairie—as representative of salt company; he was followed few yrs. later by two salt boilers, Cox & Peckham. Town had been laid out to serve as cty. seat, on paper at least, as early as 1859; but it acquired permanent residents only in 1864, when members of Elder J. M. Young's Meth. colony built cabins & female seminary. Still tiny settlement in 1867, it was raised to prominence by replacing Omaha as St. capital. Legislature's removal act changed its name from Lancaster to Lincoln. In Dec., 1868, St.-owned books, documents, & furnishings were brought here from Omaha by covered wagon in dead of night for fear their transfer would be resisted by armed Omahans. By end of 1868 pop. had increased from 30 to 500 & town had acquired bank, jail, newspaper, lumberyard, livery stable, barber shop, tailoring establishment, & drug, harness & clothing stores. Legislature, meeting in new capitol in 1869, authorized land grants for RR. construction & est. Univ. of Neb. By 1870, when first RR. reached Lincoln, pop. was 2,500.

Depression yrs. from 1871 to 1876 brought hard times, yet Lincoln grew. Its growth was more rapid in 1880's, during which its pop. increased from 14,000 to 40,000: sts. were paved & new RR. lines extended to city; small industries flourished; stockyards & 2 packing plants were built; telephone exchange, water & sewer systems, & street ry. were est. During 1890s, schools & colleges, churches, & temperance societies multiplied; & Lincoln took pride in most ornate Romanes.-style opera house W. of Chicago. Electric trolleys replaced horse-drawn streetcars; city boasted 11 banks, 70 factories, 80 wholesale houses. During this period, Lincoln acquired several of its most famous residents: Chas. G. Dawes, John J. Pershing, Wm. Jennings Bryan. Bryan, after 2 unsuccessful campaigns for U.S. Presidency, returned to city in 1900 to est. his weekly journal "The Commoner," & to speak often at local church gatherings, pics., & banquets. World War I's end ushered in prosperity period. Little touched by labor unrest of the time, Lincoln boomed, erecting new bldgs. & annexing suburbs. New blvds. & drives, pks. & playgrounds, restricted residential areas, tree-plantings & landscaping lent city new beauty. Tower of new Capitol & soaring office bldgs. altered sky-line. 1930s were disastrous interruption in city's progress, marked by unemployment & bus. failures & by workers' & farmers' demands for gov. assistance, & recovery was retarded by successive yrs. of drought; but Fed. relief & pub. works program helped tide Lincoln over crisis, & World War II brought revival of prosperity.

PTS. OF INT.: (1) Rising 432′, its height emphasized by vertical lines & massive corner pylons, & by 32′ bronze "Sower" (by Lee Lawrie), symbolizing Neb. agric., central tower of **Neb. St. Capitol** (1919-32 by Bertram Goodhue.O.8-5.guided tours 10,2 & 3:30), 14th & K Sts., is Lincoln's chief landmark. Fifth capitol erected, this bldg., radical departure in capitol design, is designed in form of vast square divided by cross into 4 inner courts. On W. lawn is **Lincoln Mon.** (by Dan. Chester French). Before main entrance pavilion bronze **Statue of Wm. Jennings Bryan** was provisionally placed in 1948, 60 yrs. after Bryan sett. in Lincoln, later to be removed to another site. Hist. Soc.'s **Mus. & Picture Gallery** on ground floor, contains one of Nation's largest & most important archaeological colls., Ind. & pioneer relics, & many early photographs, mss., newspapers, & documents. On 2nd floor, N. Vestibule leads from main entrance to arcaded foyer, which in turn leads to 95′ high domed central rotunda, with colonnaded promenade gallery. To E. is **Senate Chamber** & to W., **House Chamber.** Only 1 of these is now in use, however, for traditional 2-house legislature was replaced in 1937 by unique 43-member unicameral (1-house) body. To S. of rotunda is **Supreme Ct. Chamber.** Reached through rotunda gallery is **Neb. St. Lib.,** one of nation's leading law libs. On 14th floor, beneath dome of tower, is richly decorated **Mem. Hall.** Among Lincoln's other pub. bldgs. are: (2) **City Hall,** 930 O St.; (3) **Mun. Bldg.,** 323 N. 10th St.; (4) **Lincoln City Lib.,** 14th & N Sts.; & (5) **Lancaster County Cth.** (1888), 10th St. bet. J & K Sts.

(6) **Univ. of Neb.,** 11th & R Sts., occupies more than 45 bldgs., scattered over 14-a. campus. Chartered in 1869 & opened in 1871, univ. now ranks in size among nation's 25 largest institutions of higher learning. Morrill Hall houses **Neb. St. Mus.,** 1st floor & basement, which has fine coll. of fossils & nat. hist. exhibits (incl. skeleton of Lincoln Cty.mastodon,largest mammal found on this continent) & **Art Colls.,** 2nd & 3rd floors, representing cross sec. of Amer. art unexcelled in Midwest. Architecturally most distinguished bldg. on campus is **Heat & Power H.** (1930), 14th & W Sts., of brick in modern design. Among others are **Univ. Hall** (1869-71); **Love Mem. Lib.** (1945); **Coliseum,** seating 10,000; **Stadium,** seating nearly 50,000; & **Student Union.** (7) Univ.'s **College of Agric.,** 36th & Holdredge Sts., occupies 320-a. campus of its own with 16 major & many minor bldgs., among them **Agric. Engineering Bldg.,** housing mus. of antiquated farm machinery.

(8) **Neb. Wesleyan Univ.,** 50th & St. Paul Sts., founded by Meth. Episc. Ch. in 1887, occupies 44-a. campus with 11 bldgs. (9) **Union College,** 3800 S. 48th St., is Seventh Day Adventist institution whose outstanding feature is student work program; **School Mus.** in College Hall contains curios from Pitcairn I. donated by Adventist natives there. Among Lincoln's most architecturally notable bldgs. are several churches. (10) **First Plymouth Ch.** (Congr.1931), 20th & D Sts., has 171′, 20-sided Singing Tower & arcaded forecourt containing stone from Martin Luther's birthpl. at Eisleben, Germany, & Pilgrim Stone from Plymouth, Eng., doorstep across which Pilgrims & their descendants walked. Other churches incl. (11) **First Presb. Ch.** (1925.Goth.), 17th & F Sts.; (12) **Westminister Presb. Ch.** (1926.Goth.), 2210 Sheridan Blvd.; (13) **Holy Trinity Ch.** (Episc.1888.Goth.), 12th & J Sts., typical of best architecture of its period; (14) **St. Paul Ch.** (Meth.1901.Goth.), 12th & M Sts. (15) **Antelope Pk.** (swim.tennis), S. of O St., along Antelope Cr., incl. Va. sandstone **O Street Columns,** until 1907 part of old Fed. Treasury Bldg. in Washington, D. C.,

from which Lincoln reviewed Civil War troops; **Sunken Garden; City Zoo;** & **War Mem.** & **Pioneer Woman Mon.** (by Ellis Burman). (16) **Pioneer Pk.,** SW. edge of city on Van Dorn St., 600-a. tract with zoo, pic. grounds & Pinewood Bowl, contains herds of elk, deer & buffalo; several small Ls. which serve as wildfowl refuges; & two statues, bronze figure of buffalo (by Geo.Gaudet) & "Smoke Signal" (by Ellis Burman), mem. to Neb. Inds. **Neb. St. Fairgrounds,** 17th & Clinton Sts., comprise 287-a. tract with $4^m$ of streets & hundreds of bldgs., racetrack & grandstand, stock pavilions, auditorium & aquarium. **Robbers Cave** (sm.fee), 10th & High Sts., winding passage with many chambers in an outcrop of Dakota sandstone, has served at various times as site of Pawnee religious ceremonies, immigrants' camp site & settlers' refuge & stone quarry.

SIDE TRIP: Take US77 (L) from Lincoln to **Neb. St. Penitentiary** (1867), $3^m$. **Beatrice** (pronounced be-at′-ris), $40^m$, seat of Gage Cty., spread out in scattered, spacious fashion on either side of winding, sluggish Blue R., is both farm town & industrial city. Beatrice was named for girl who saw town only once or twice—daughter of Judge John Kinney, president of Neb. Assoc., which selected townsite; she came with her father from Neb. City to read some of her own verses at christening ceremony in 1857. In 1871, Burlington RR. extended line here. Pop. doubled in 1870's & doubled again in 1880's. Industries were attracted by availability of electric power & even electrically driven street cars appeared as early as 1890. Community's growth continued into 20th cent. **Gage County Cth.,** 6th & Lincoln Sts., houses on 3rd floor Beatrice Mus., which contains pioneer relics. Largest of city's pks. is 31-a. **Chautauqua Pk.,** S. bank of Blue R. from 6th St. E.; & 2nd largest is **Riverside Pk.** (baseball.swim.ice skating.dance pavilion).

(1) St.4 leads (R) from Beatrice to **Homestead Nat. Mon. of America,** $4.5^m$, comprising former Dan. Freeman farm, first claim entered in U.S. under Homestead Act of 1862. Freeman, Union soldier on furlough, had staked out his claim but on Dec. 31, 1862, day before act became effective, received orders to proceed to St. Louis next morning. He was enabled to file his claim shortly after midnight, however, by lucky accident of meeting land office assistant at New Year's dance. He & his wife are buried near E. boundary. Place was made Nat. mon. in 1936.

(2) St.3 leads (R) from Beatrice to **Fairbury,** $27^m$, seat of Jefferson Cty., platted in 1869 & spurred toward prosperity by advent of RR. in 1872 & sett. of large Russian-German colony on RR. land near-by in 1874. It has creamery & packing plant & manufactures windmills, pumps, pipes & other articles.

**81.** US6 crosses Blue R. & at **89.5.** passes St.-owned **BLUE R. RECR. GROUNDS** (camp.f.) on (S) bank of W. Blue R. Route cont. through series of small rural trading centers, dating back to 1870s, to **U.S. NAVAL AMMUNITION DEPOT, 159.5.,** one of largest installations of its kind in world, covering over 48,000 as. with more than 1,900 bldgs. devoted to loading, filling & storing all kinds of naval ammunition.

**162.5. HASTINGS,** Neb.'s 4th largest city, seat of Adams Cty., is situated in heart of Kans.-Neb. wheat belt & depends largely on agric. & stock raising for prosperity but also manufactures food products, brick & tile, farm implements, pumps, windmills, air conditioning equipment & many other articles. Its skyline is accented by huge smokestacks & grain elevators. Mun. power plant, auditorium & airport are sources of civic pride. First settlers in vic. were group of Englishmen, lured by propaganda of immigration societies. On homestead of one of them, Walter Micklen, town was laid out in 1872 & named for man who graded last sec. of St. Joseph & Denver RR., which ended here; it later became Burlington RR. division pt. After becoming cty. seat in 1877, it grew rapidly &, surviving periods of recession during drought & panic-ridden 1890s & 1930s, has kept on expanding.

Hastings' mun. mus., **House of Yesterday** (1938), NW. cor. Highland Pk., houses one of biggest colls. of plains reg. Among thousands of exhibits are fossils & mounted birds & animals in natural habitats; Ind. artifacts & Ind. ossuary; pioneer articles, incl. relics of Ore. Trl., women's apparel, glass & china, old vehicles & farm machinery; relics of Rev. & Civil, Sp.-Amer. & World Wars; & firearms, lamps & coins of ancient & modern times. **Highland Pk.** (pic.sports facils.), 12th St. bet. Burlington & St. Joseph Aves., Hastings' oldest, is 40-a. landscaped tract containing **Jacob Fisher Rainbow Fountain,** 1 of 2 electrically illuminated fountains in Midwest. **Prospect Pk.** (camp.pic.bathh.), 3rd St. bet. Laird & Woodland Aves., has rock garden & pavilion. **Hastings College,** Univ. & Turner Aves., coed. liberal arts institution founded in 1882 & still supported by Presb. Ch., occupies 85-a. campus. Lib. bldg. houses **Kent Mus. of Nat. Hist.**

US6 cont. (W) through **MINDEN, 198.,** founded in 1875; **HOLDREDGE, 221.5.,** seat of Phelps Cty., sett. in 1885; & other small rural trading centers. **294. McCOOK.**

RR. town & farmers' trading center with RR. roundh. & repair shops & meat-packing plant & livestock sales center, lying in Republican R. Valley, where dam & reservoir projects of U.S. Bur. of Reclamation & U.S. Corps of Engineers are creating 200,000-a. area of irrigated land. Orig. settlement, consisting of p.o. & few straggling bldgs., was called Fairview; during RR. boom in 1882, 100 bldgs. sprang up in month & town was renamed for Maj. Gen. Alex. McDowell Cook. It has enjoyed other booms subsequently, during 1920's & again during 1940's, when new irrigation projects brought econ. expansion & pop. growth. **Home of Geo. W. Norris,** Main St. opp. City Pk., was home of late U.S. Sen., who moved to Neb. from Ohio in 1885 & soon began political career lasting half century, in which he opposed U.S. entrance into World War I, wrote Constitutional Amendment abolishing lame-duck session of Congress, & fathered act establishing Tenn. Valley Authority. At E. limits of McCook is boundary of Central & Mt. Time Zones.

### Sec. 2: McCOOK, NEB. to NEB.-COLO. LINE. 87.5.

US6 soon climbs from Frenchman R. Valley & crossing short strip of sand-hill country, strikes into high tableland sec. **13.5.** J. with St.17.

SIDE TRIP: Take latter (R) to **Hayes Center,** 23$^{m}$, seat of Hayes Cty., & turn (R) from Hayes Center 10$^{m}$ to St.-owned **Duke Alexis Recr. Grounds** (boat.f.pic.cabins), with 80-a. L., comprising Red Willow Cr. camp site to which in 1872 Grand Duke Alexis of Russia, accompanied by "Buffalo Bill" Cody, Gen. Sheridan & Army officers from Ft. McPherson, came to hunt buffalo & to be entertained by Sioux war dance.

At **15.** on US6, is J. with US34.

SIDE TRIP: Take latter (L) to **Massacre Canyon Mon.,** 7.5$^{m}$, shaft of Miss. pink granite carved with 2 Ind. faces which comm. last battle bet. Pawnee & Sioux, traditional enemies, fought here in 1873. **Trenton,** 10$^{m}$, seat of Hitchcock Cty., is site in early Aug. of Massacre Canyon powwow, celebrated with Sioux tribal dances, carnival & rodeo. **Benkelman,** 39.5$^{m}$, is seat of Dundy Cty. At 51$^{m}$ is J. with a dirt Rd. leading (R) 4.5$^{m}$ to St.-owned **Rock Cr. Recr. Grounds** (boat.f.), with 50-a. L., one of Neb.'s largest springs, & one of Midwest's largest fish hatcheries.

At **56.** on US6 is J. with St.61, leading (L) 4$^{m}$ to **Enders Dam,** impounding Frenchman R., Neb.'s first Bur. of Reclamation irrigation project in 40 yrs., dedicated May 29, 1948, which was expected to begin new era for SW. Neb. **62.5. IMPERIAL,** seat of Chase Cty., is bright-looking country town.

SIDE TRIP: Take St.48 (L) from Imperial to St.-owned **Champion L. Recr. Grounds** (f.), 10$^{m}$.

**87.5.** Colo. Line.

## US 75—NEBRASKA

**NEB.-IOWA LINE** (across Mo. R. from Sioux City, Iowa) **(S) to NEB.-KANS. LINE** (c.7$^{m}$ from Sabetha, Kans.). **94. US75**

Via: Fort Crook, Arbor Lodge State Pk., Nebraska City, Auburn. RR. parallels route. Accoms.: At short intervals.

Never more than few miles from Mo. R., US75 cuts (S) through E. Neb.'s prairie farming reg. At **4.5.** at S. limits of Omaha, is J. with St.31 (Bellevue Blvd.).

SIDE TRIP: Take latter (L) to 1,800-a. **Fontenelle For. Reserve,** 1$^{m}$, largest tract of unbroken native for. in Neb., covering hills & hollows overlooking Mo. R. Reserve was named for Logan Fontenelle, Omaha chief, head of delegation sent by his tribe to Washington in 1854, who is buried near-by. **Bellevue,** 5.5$^{m}$, oldest existing town in Neb., was successively fur trading center, Ind. mission, steamboat landing, & territorial gov. seat. Fur trader Manuel Lisa is said to have named place in 1807 because of its pleasing view of R. Here in 1823 agency of Omaha, Oto, Mo., & Pawnee Inds. was moved from Ft. Atkinson (now Ft. Calhoun) by Maj. Joshua Pilcher; & 4 yrs. later Joseph Roubidou & Baptiste Roi were licensed to operate trading post at site by Gov. Clark in St. Louis. Andrew Drips of Mo. Fur Co. had opened post 1$^{m}$ (N) in 1823, which his partner, Lucian Fontenelle, sold to Gov. for Ind. agency hqs. in 1831. About same time Amer. Fur Co. est. new post under Peter Sarpy. In 1833 arrived first missionaries, Moses Merrill, his wife, & Miss Cynthia Brown, sent by Baptist Missionary Union to convert Oto; they were followed by John Dunbar of Presb. Ch. in 1834. Presb. mission was completed in 1848, where on Oct. 16, 1854, Francis Burt, first Territorial Gov. took oath of office; & in 1856-58 was built **Presb. Ch.,** 20th Ave. & Franklin St., now oldest religious structure in Neb. Burt had intended to convoke Territorial legislature here, but died two days after inauguration; & successor,

Thos. B. Cuming, favored Omaha. Bellevue became seat of Sarpy Cty. but lost even that distinction to Papillion in 1875, & today **Old Cth.** (c.1853), Mission Ave. & Main St., serves as town hall & lib. **Site of Presb. Ind. Mission** is indicated by marker on E. side of Warren St. bet. 19th & 20th Aves., & in Washington Sq. are **Astorian Mon.** & **Mon. to First Masonic Lodge in Neb.** (1854). Site of trading post cannot be fixed exactly, but logs of which it was built are preserved at Lincoln by Neb. St. Hist. Soc.

**9.5. FT. CROOK,** Army post named for Gen. Geo. Crook, who fought in Civil & Ind. Wars, its red-brick bldgs. surrounding large parade ground, is equipped with rifle ranges & variety of recr. facils. Sunday band concerts attract many visitors. **18. PLATTSMOUTH,** seat of Cass Cty. at mouth of Platte R., was est. by town company formed in 1854 & was inc. in 1855. River traffic brought boom period in 1860s, as steady flow of migration filled town with caravans. Later, soil in vic. was found fertile & emigrants began settling roundabout rather than farther W. Bluffs along Mo. & Platte Rs. in vic. yield stone, clay & sand. Plattsmouth has refrigerator car factory, vegetable packing plant, & roller mill.

SIDE TRIP: Turn (R) from Plattsmouth on gravel Rd. to **Louisville,** 14m, fishing center with pottery & cement plant, & adj. St.-operated 190-a. **Platte View Recr. Grounds** (boat. f.swim.camp.).

Reg. surrounding **UNIV. FRUIT FARM, 34.5.,** experimental sta. of Univ. of Neb. College of Agric., is at its best in spring, when Apple Blossom Day is celebrated with guided tour through SE. Neb.'s apple country. **42.5. IND. TREATY MON.,** comm. Table Cr. Treaty with Pawnee (Sept.24, 1857), by which they ceded all but one small tract of their lands N. of Platte R. to Fed. Gov. **43. ARBOR LODGE ST. PK.** (O.Ap.1 to Dec.1, 1:30-5:30 until Je.15, all day Je.15-Dec.1; guide service,no camp.), comprises 65-a. grounds & 52-room mansion overlooking Mo. R. of its creator, J. Sterling Morton. Here in 1855 Morton & his wife took up home site by squatter's right; he built a house & set out trees, shrubs, & flowers. As pres. of St. Board of Agric., he brought about proclamation of first Arbor Day (Ap.10,1874), afterward made legal holiday, celebrated on his birthday (Ap.22); he later became Pres. Cleveland's Secy. of Agric. Mansion was built over period of 47 yrs. ending in 1902; it houses various articles of hist. interest, grounds are divided into 2 parts, one of timber & meadow in native state, other elaborately landscaped. S. of central walk is **Log Cabin,** exemplifying pioneer construction; & NW. of lodge is **Morton Mem.,** a massive bronze statue of place's onetime owner.

**NEB. CITY, 44.5.,** seat of Otoe Cty., began as trading post in 1850's, est. at site of abandoned Ft. Kearney (1847-48). Here steamboats landed to discharge cargoes for overland freighters. Bustling sett. grew up, with stores, warehouses, saloons, dance-halls & gambling dens. Here in **John Brown's Cave,** S. 19th St. N. of old cemetery, cellar beneath old log cabin with tunnel running to Table Cr., future martyr of Harpers Ferry hid runaway slaves traveling Underground Railroad (N) from Mo. In 1864 Neb. City built first high school in Neb., probably first W. of Mo. R. Today its **Otoe County Cth.** is State's oldest pub. bldg. Center of SE. Neb. apple-raising district, it cans fruit & vegetables & manufactures garments & cigars. **60.** J. with St.67.

SIDE TRIP: Take latter (L) to **Peru,** 7m, inc. in 1860, college town on Mo. R. at base of steep-sloped **Neb.'s Pike's Peak,** NW. of which appear 4 **Ind. H. Sites** & S. of which is **Ind. Hill,** burial mound. At S. edge of town is **Neb. St. Teachers College** opened in 1867.

**65. AUBURN,** seat of Nemaha Cty., is trading center in heart of apple orchard country. At **81.5.** is J. with US73.

SIDE TRIP: Take latter (L) to **Falls City,** 19m, near falls of Gt. Nemaha R., an agric. town & Mo.P. RR. division point sett. in late 1850s.

US75 cont. S. to Neb.-Kans. Line at **94.**

## US 81—NEBRASKA

**NEB.-S.D. LINE** (1.5m from Yankton, S.D.) **(S) to NEB.-KANS. LINE** (13m from Belleville, Kans.). **235. US81**

Via: Norfolk, Columbus, York, Hebron, (Red Cloud). RRs. parallel route bet. Norfolk & Columbus & bet. Stromsburg & Neb.-Kans. Line. Bus. serv. throughout. Accoms.: Limited.

US81 cuts through E. farming sec. of Neb., hilly in N. part, level in central & S. parts.

### Sec. 1: NEB.-S.D. LINE to COLUMBUS, 117.

Toll bridge over Mo. R. carries US81 across **NEB.-S.D. LINE, 0. 14. CROFTON.** J. with St.12.

SIDE TRIP: Take St.12 (R) 24.5m to **Maiden's Leap,** 100′ chalk rock overlooking Mo. R., whose name is accounted for by usual story: Ind. girl in love with one brave but betrothed by her father to another, committed suicide by riding one of father's finest horses over cliff. 27m **Niobrara,** on site of Ponca Ind. village, was sett. in May, 1856. At 28.5m is 408-a. **Niobrara I. St. Pk.** (R) cabins.camp.pic.f.swim.golf), on heavily wooded I. in Niobrara R.

At **41.** on US81 is J. with US20 (see) with which US81 unites for 6m. **69. NORFOLK,** lying among low hills of Elkhorn R. Valley in one of State's best farming regs., is trading center, RR. division point, & site of several small industries. Here in 1866 group of pioneer German farmers from Wis. arrived in ox-drawn prairie schooners & surveyed land, apportioning 160 as. to each of 44 families. Surrounding dist. produces corn, hay & oats, milk cows & beef cattle, horses, sheep & poultry. **85. MADISON** was founded in 1866 by German colony of 24 families from Wis. **117. COLUMBUS** (see US30) is at J. with US30 (see).

### Sec. 2: COLUMBUS, NEB. to NEB.-KANS. LINE. 118.

Crossing Platte R., US81 proceeds through farming sec.

**26.5. OSCEOLA,** surveyed & platted in 1872 & named for famous Seminole chief, is in dist. producing much broomcorn & has large broom factory. **34. STROMSBURG,** on elevated plain in Blue R. Valley, was sett. by Swedes in 1872. At **34.5.** US81 crosses Big Blue R. **51.5. YORK,** seat of York Cty., platted in 1869, is trading center of wide agric. area, & much of its industry serves agric. Its modern-style **City Auditorium,** seating 2,500, accoms. conventions, concerts, basketball games & dances. **Central Pk.** has modern mun. swim. pool; **East Hill Pk.,** formal gardens, pic. grounds, & baseball field. **York College** (est.1890), NE. edge of town, is a 4-yr. liberal arts institution conducted by Evangelical United Brethren Ch. York is at J. with US34 (see US6). At **68. FAIRMOUNT,** rural trading & shipping center, is J. with US6 (see). **76.5. GENEVA** is site of **Girls' Industrial School** (est.1891) for juvenile delinquents. **105.5. HEBRON,** seat of Thayer Cty., founded & named in 1869 by settlers who were Disciples of Christ, is site of **Hebron Jr. College,** Luth. institution opened as Hebron Academy in 1911.

SIDE TRIP: Take St.3 (R) from Hebron 8.5m to **Deshler,** whose chief pursuit is manufacture of brooms & **Red Cloud,** 54m, seat of Webster Cty. & childhood residence of novelist Willa Cather. **Home of Willa Cather** stands next to Meth. Ch., half block W. of cth. Here future author, brought from her native Va. at the age of 9, whose "O Pioneers" (1913) would deal with early Neb., decided she needed an "office" & had lean-to built against barn. Turn (L) from **Red Cloud** on US281, across Republican R. to dirt Rd. 3m & (L) on this 4m to J., (R) here to **Site of Pike Pawnee Village,** 5.5m, where in 1806, Lt. Zebulon M. Pike & 21 men stopped on their way to Rockies & on Sept. 29 prevailed upon Pawnee Inds. to lower Sp. flag & raise the Amer., thus ending Sp. authority on plains of the Middle West. (It should be noted that Pike-Pawnee St. Mon. in Kans., 5.5m S. of Neb.-Kans. Line & 11m W. of US81, is also claimed to be site of this incident; according to Smithsonian Institution experts, Kansas' claim is of doubtful validity.)

At **118.** on US81 is **KANS. LINE.**

## US 2—NORTH DAKOTA

**N.D.-MINN. LINE** (at E. Grand Forks, Minn.) **(W) to N.D.-MONT. LINE** (23m from Culbertson, Mont.). **369. US2**

Via: Grand Forks, Devils Lake, Minot & Williston. Accoms.: In main towns.

This hy. begins at the East coast & crosses Red R. at Minn. boundary, then travels direct (W) to border of N.D., revealing fertile Red R. Valley, grazing lands of Missouri Plateau, & lignite coal area of the western part.

**0. GRAND FORKS**

Rail, plane & bus conns.

As its name indicates, this city is at confluence of Red R. of the North & Red Lake R., & is gateway to one of world's largest wheat-growing centers. Its $3,000,000 State Mill & Elevator (O) dominates the skyline. Along Univ. Ave. are its architecturally int. residences. City has a privately owned flour mill, a potato dehydrating plant & a good-sized candy factory. Capt. Alex. Griggs, sent by James J. Hill to explore the Red. R., & Geo. Winship, later publisher of the "Herald," were its first settlers. In 1871 Griggs built 1st frame house. River trans. was practically supplanted when the Gt.N. RR. reached town. In 1874 the "Plaindealer" was founded by Geo. Walsh, & 5 yrs. later Winship's "Herald" made its appearance. For the next 5 yrs. there was continual bickering bet. the 2 papers. In 1884 the "Herald's" plant burnt down & Walsh generously shared his with Winship, but the editorial attacks continued until the 2 papers finally merged.

There is a considerable Norweg. pop. in Grand Forks; sufficient to support a Norweg. paper. They live for the most part in sec. called Little Norway, & celebrate Norweg. Independence Day (May 17) with pomp & oratory. PTS. OF INT.: The city has 5 pks. On Red R. bank is **Central Pk.**, a beauty spot & playground. (No pic.but winter sports facils.) **Lincoln Pk.** on Belmont Rd. has famous Ski Slide. It is on (S) edge of town & in it is part of Old Red R. Oxcart Trl. On Univ. Ave. 2$^{m}$ from center of town to **Univ. of N.D.** which opened in 1884. It is fully accredited, & numbers among its alumni Maxwell Anderson, playwright, & Vilhjalmur Stefansson, the Arctic explorer. The Univ. has Schools of Liberal Arts & Sciences, Education, Engineering, Law, Medicine, Commerce, Mines & an Extension Div. Since 1910 the bldgs. are all mod. Coll. Goth. Affiliated is **Wesley College** (adj.Univ. campus). Courses are offered here in Religion, Music & Expression. All denominations participate. The State Univ. is a vital part of city's cultural life. Musicals & dramatic performances are the social events of the yr. enjoyed by most of the townsfolk. College athletics attract visitors from entire (NE) sec. of the state. In Jan. is the All-American Turkey Show. At Demers Ave. & 5th St. is **J.** with US81, (see), important nat. N-S hy.

**20.** J. with a cty. gravelled Rd.

SIDE TRIPS: (A) On this Rd. (N) 1$^{m}$ to **Turtle River St. Pk.** (475 as.good bath.pic.camp. overnight cabins) named so because of many turtles found at river.

(B) Beyond the entrance (W) are 15 Ind. mounds, plowed over, with only small humps visible. Wild life refuge is near-by.

**21.5. ARVILLA,** small town with private school of music, **Arvilla Academy & N.D. Conservatory of Music,** founded 1886. **24.** J. with St.18 leading (S) 3$^{m}$ to **Larimore** named for N.D. Larimore, stockholder & head of bonanza Elk R. Valley Farm, once world's largest farm under one management. **60. MAPES,** named for Emery Mapes, who worked out formula for Cream of Wheat. **67. LAKOTA,** a city of trees in the prairie, result of one pioneer's devotion. Here **Tofthagen Lib. & Mus.** (O.1927) contains books & curios of Nelson Cty. famous pioneers. J. here with St.1 (leading (S) 55$^{m}$ to Cooperstown, see US10).

**95. DEVILS LAKE.** On what was once the shore of Devils L., remnant of glacial sea, whose orig. depth was 56′, once 2nd largest saltwater lake in country. Shore line is receding steadily. It has dropped 26′ since 1883, the time of last U.S. survey. On the (S) shore is Ft. Totten; now **Ft. Totten Ind. Agency,** c. 1,000 Sioux & a small number of Chippewa are under its jurisdiction. The steady shrinking of Devils L. is one of arguments for the Mo.-Souris Diversion projects, & the $200,000,000 Garrison Dam on Mo. R. This project would again raise level of lake, & place more than a million as. of land under irrigation. Lakeshore is skirted by **Burtness Scenic Hy.,** through a reg. delightfully wooded, passing **Sully's Hill Pk.,** Fed. Game Refuge. Ft. Totten was est. 1867, & named for its Chief Engineer. Ft. Totten troops took part in Dakota & Montana campaigns & also acted as escorts for surveyors for the N.P. RR. & the Internat. Boundary Line Commission (see US281). On St.20 (N) of Devils L., is **Sweetwater L.** whose shore line has also receded. **114.** J. with US281.

SIDE TRIPS: (A) On this hy. 49$^{m}$ (N) to **Canadian Border** (customh. & immigration office).

(B) On US281 (S) 16$^{m}$ to W. shore of **Devils L.,** formerly head of steamboat navigation.

**125. LEEDS** (1884). Many of the Gt. N. RR. stockholders were Eng. Hence the name.

SIDE TRIP: (L) On country Rd. 2$^{m}$ **L. Ibsen,** named for Norweg. dramatist. Here c.1858 peace treaty was made bet. Sioux & Chippewa Inds. It was observed by both. In L. are Petites Isles Aux Mortes, where Inds., after a smallpox epidemic, carried their dead & placed them according to tribal custom on scaffolds, which could be seen from the shore.

**151. RUGBY** marks supposed geographic **Center of North America,** with stone cairn. Here is Mus. with Ind. & pioneer relics & J. with St.3.

SIDE TRIPS: (A) On this Rd. 33m (N) to **Dunseith** at (S) entrance to **Turtle Mt. Ind. Reserv.** The Inds. (7,586) are of mixed Chippewa & Fr. blood. Hqs. at Belcourt; there are children's vocational & academic schools. Sun Dance is held annually by Inds. in June & a fair in Oct. At Belcourt is shrine in honor of St. Ann, to which people of the mts. make pilgrimages. On St. Ann's feast day, July 26, an outdoor procession is held.

(1) The Rd. (W) to Dunseith has not a single curve for 50m.

(2) 12.5m (N) of Dunseith is world's first **Internat. Peace Garden** (accoms.pic.) (see US281).

(B) On St.3 (S) to **Harvey** 49m.

From here (L) 7m to **Butte De Morale.** Here in 1840 famous buffalo-hunting expeditions took place. On one occasion 1,390 people camped here; 250 buffaloes were slaughtered.

**216. MINOT**

(RR.: Gt.N. RR. & Soo Line. Accoms.: All types)

Minot, in the Souris R. Valley, was known as Magic City because of its mushroom growth. Erik Ramstad was its first settler in 1885. In its first yr. it numbered more than 5,000 people. It soon became trading center of (NW) N.D. & now is medical center surrounded with fine hospitals & has excellent transportation. Minot in its early days had a reputation for lawlessness & iniquity. A favorite call of one RR. conductor when he reached the town was "Minot, M-I-N-O-T, end of the line. Prepare to meet your God." The Souris R. overflowed many times before the dam & dykes were built, but worst flood was in 1904 which lasted 3 wks., & the town's only means of travel through streets was by boat. Minot has become a natural shipping point for lignite mined in vic. Truax-Traer Co., with hqs. here, is one of largest lignite strip mining companies in the country. PTS. OF INT.: **Roosevelt Pk.** (swim.pic.tennis.tourist camp.85 as.). Not to be confused with Nat. Pk. in the Badlands. Beautifully landscaped, with bronze equestrian statue of Theo. Roosevelt. **St. Teachers College** here is fully accredited & has liberal arts courses. Here is J. with US52.

SIDE TRIPS: (A) On this Rd. (NW) 67m to **Canadian Border** through treeless mining country.

(B) US52 (SW) passes **Burlington,** an underground lignite mine at 8m. Also has the state's 1st Subsistence Homestead Project. At 32m is **Velva Mine.** To (NE) c.10m at Verendrye is **David Thompson Hist. Site,** comm. pioneer geographer & fur trader who visited N.D. in 1797 & surveyed the Internat. Boundary. At c.100m on US52 is **Fessenden,** an alfalfa reg. Here in Mar. of every yr. a festival is held, ending with crowning of the Alfalfa Queen.

**274. STANLEY** in a wonderfully fertile reg. According to an old saying, soil is so fruitful that a nail put in the ground at night becomes a crowbar by morning. Here is J. with St.8.

SIDE TRIP: On this Rd. (S) 26m to J. with St.23. On this Rd. (W) 10m to **Sanish & Verendrye Nat. Mon.,** comm. the Verendrye explorations in N.D. & along Upper Mo. R. It incl. **Crow Flies High Butte.** (565'; named for Hidatsa Ind. Chief.) Verendrye & his son were first white men to go into this territory in search of a route to "The Great Sea of the West," 1738. Lewis & Clark camped here 60 yrs. later. **Ft. Berthold Ind. Reserv.** was est. with 2,000,000 as. in 1870; now has only 625,000. Its pop. is divided among 782 Arikara, 849 Gros Ventres & 389 Mandan. Latter 2 tribes were very friendly to the white men who lived at Ft. Berthold & were harassed by hostile Sioux. Graves of Arikara chiefs are marked by mon. Because of their lofty ideas of justice & gentleness they ranked high among both white & red men & their graves are still sacred to the Inds.

**282.** The little town of **ROSS,** where in 1902 a group of 20 Moslem families sett. After 1929 they became naturalized but still cling to their Syrian customs & food. Wedding celebrations are colorful & symbolic. Handshaking frequently, no matter how recently they have met, is an old custom among these people. **324. EPPING,** near which is **Epping-Springbrook Dam,** largest earth-fill dam in St.

**337.** J. with US85 (see).

**347. WILLISTON.** Named by **J. J. Hill** for his friend S. Willis James, lies on the Mo. lowlands, & is a RR. center in midst of a mining, farming, & stockraising reg. Until coming of the RR. it was only a tent colony but after 1887 homesteaders flocked in. Story is told about Geo. Grinnell, one of the early hunters, who lived here. Like many other pioneers he mistreated the Ind. women with whom he lived. On one occasion, in 1888, while drunk he wanted to strike Josephine Manuri, his half-breed woman, with the butt of his gun. A tussle followed. Onlookers were afraid to interfere because of his loaded gun when suddenly he fell back limp, having been strangled to death by a leather thong with a sliding knot which he wore around his neck & to which she had clung. The coroner's verdict was that Grinnell " . . . came to his death through an act of Almighty God, by the hand of His agent, Josephine Grinnell." The Gt. N. RR. has its roundh. & car repair shop in Williston. Millions of bu. of grain are handled annually in city. It is also an important turkey market. Two annual events of note: Old Fiddlers contest (Jan.) & Upper Mo. Band Tournament (1st wk. in June). **369.** Hy. crosses **MONT. LINE.**

## US 10—NORTH DAKOTA

**N.D.-MINN. LINE** (at Moorhead, Minn.) **(W) to N.D.-MONT. LINE** ($37^m$ E. of Glendive, Mont.). **364. US10**

Via: Fargo, Valley City, Jamestown, Bismarck, Mandan & Dickinson. N.P. RR. & Northwest Airlines parallel route across state. Rds.: Paved or bituminous. Accoms.: In larger towns.

US10, beginning at Detroit, travels (W) through Wis., Minn. & N.D., passing from the low Red R. Valley across the plains to the Mo. Plateau & the strangely beautiful Badlands.

### 0. FARGO

Fargo is N.D.'s largest city & also its largest distributing pt. for farm implements, autos & accessories, as well as an important shipping center for grain, potatoes, dairy & poultry products. It leads the nation in production of grain & ranks very high in production of poultry. Until 1927 it was world's 3rd largest farm-implement distribution pt. At present it is considered the largest wholesale distribution center for a reg. extending 900 miles (W) & 150 miles (E). Fargo is known as the transportation hub of the NW. Starting with a few huts along Red R. of the North in 1871, Fargo developed into a thriving metropolis of 10,000 homes & c.36,000 people. It is a sportsmen's heaven with h. & f. within an hour's drive in any direction. Two of N.D.'s 4 skyscrapers are in Fargo. City is named for Wm. G. Fargo, director of N.P. RR., & founder of Wells Fargo Express Co. Pioneers, in their eagerness to know where the RR. would build a bridge, patrolled the shore line in relays, so that at the first indication, they might turn over sod, build a hut & make a land claim. Naturally there were many claims & counter claims. During first winter settlement was divided into Fargo-on-the-Prairie, home of RR. workers & surveyors, & Fargo-in-the-Timber, occupied by rivermen, a hard-drinking, rough group, that continuously disturbed the other community. Fed. Troops dispersed most of them the next yr. & took many to jail at Pembina, not only for poaching on Ind.-claimed property but for selling them liquor. Eventually those not guilty of any other offense had their claims returned to them. From wild prairie land the country surrounding Fargo soon became a rich farming reg. Bonanza farms were responsible for the enormous acreage increase & with it came an influx of settlers from N. European countries, with great energies, ambitions & a real community spirit. In 1889, N.D. State Agric. College was opened, although private colleges had existed 2 yrs. before. By 1893 the city built an Opera House seating 1,000 people. It became a favorite stopover for leading theatrical companies. Fargo at turn of the century also became a divorce colony, granting divorces in 90 days, & many wealthy people traveled here to est. residence. Business was good. Adding to the color of city, even at the present day, are the Norweg. holiday-customs & foods introduced by its early settlers.

PTS. OF INT.: (1) At 13th St., immediately adj. city is 100-a. campus of **N.D. Agric. College** with 35 bldgs. College maintains an Extension Div. & an Agric. Experimental Div. & is fully accredited. (2) Cor. 8th St. & 2nd Ave. (N), **First Ch.** (Presb. Mod.Eng.Goth.by Magney & Tussler) contains hand-carved altar by Anton Lang of Oberammergau fame. (3) 705 1st Ave. (N), **U.S. Post Office & Cth.** (1929.Ital. Ren.); cost $600,000. (4) 119 4th St. (S), **Fargo's First H.** (1871.oak logs). (5) 708 1st Ave. (S), **Cass County's First Cth.,** now DeVolne Flats (1874). (6) **El Zagal Pk.** with a natural amphitheater. (7) 19th Ave. (N), $1.5^m$ on N. Broadway, **Dovre Ski Slide** (140'), one of highest artificial ski scaffolds in U.S. (8) B'way at 6th Ave. (N),

**St. Mary's Cathedral** (Class.& Goth.1891.with 190′ bell tower), completed in 1899. At Front & 13th Sts., J. with US81 leading (N) to Grand Forks, 74$^{m}$.

At **5.** on US10 is **WEST FARGO & S.W.FARGO,** centers of meat-packing industry. **Armour Co. plant** (O.tours). Included in **Union Stockyards** is exchange bldg. housing company offices, commission firms, dealers, St. & Fed. agencies supervising markets. **20.** J. with St.18.

SIDE TRIPS: (A) On this Rd. (R) 2$^{m}$ is **Casselton,** storm center in Nonpartisan League politics. The League is a farmers' organization (1915) to improve business conditions of farmers through legislation. It encountered strong opposition but has had permanent effect on legislation. Here also is a Ch. belonging to German Moravians. 18$^{m}$ **Houston Farms.** D. H. Houston, inventor of kodak, homesteaded here in 1869 & later became bonanza farmer, having acquired 6,000 as. In the 1880's he successfully produced famous blue-stem wheat. In 1881 he developed the principle of the roll-film camera & sold patent to Geo. Eastman who coined "Kodak" from Dakota.

Hy. passes at **40.5. BUFFALO CR. HIST. SITE,** where Gen. Sibley marched by in 1863 with 3,400 soldiers, after driving Inds. across the Mo. **43.5. TOWER CITY,** named for Charlemagne Tower, from Philadelphia. **58.5. VALLEY CITY,** whose first settlers came with N.P. RR. in 1872, but left after 1873 panic. From '78 on there was a steady increase. Present city is center for dairy products & flour milling. A mun. lighting plant supplies free street lighting & very cheap energy-supply rates. It is home of **State Teachers College** founded in 1890. In auditorium is copy of statue of A. Lincoln (by Paul Fjelde, alumnus, pupil of Lorado Taft) which N.D. gave to Norway in 1914. In **Barnes County Cth.** is coll. of Vernon Gale's Ind. relics. In **Charlemagne Pk.,** swim. pool. Here also is J. with St.1.

SIDE TRIP: On this Rd. (N) 47$^{m}$ to **Cooperstown,** founded 1882 by Cooper Bros., who shortly before, had become wealthy miners. They settled here to become bonanza farmers. Cooperstown is home of Gerald Nye, James H. Sinclair, Thos. R. Amlie & Ed. D. Stair. On Cth. grounds is **Opheim Log Cabin,** 1st permanent house in cty. (1879).

**70. SANBORN,** named for Fargo pioneer. Another settler at the time was I. W. Barnum, brother of P. T. **82.5. SPIRITWOOD.** At **93.5.** J. with St.20.

SIDE TRIP: On this Rd. (R) 10$^{m}$ to **Spiritwood L.,** where state breeds Mongolian pheasants (bath.f.golf.cottages). Near here, heart-shaped stones marked with a small cross were found. Archeologists believe they are artifacts of very early Inds.; on display in Mus. at Valley City.

**96. JAMESTOWN**

RR.: Gt.N. & its branches; hqs. for Midland Continental RR. Busses make conn. with Gt.N. & the Soo Lines. Airline: Northwest with daily serv.

Jamestown was named by Fr. trapper for himself, & lies in valley of the James R., "largest unnavigable river in the world." First settlement was made in 1871 by some early RR. engineers. Two yrs. later construction crews arrived & only a month after that the 1st strike occurred when workers, angry at nonpayment, pulled up the tracks. In 1889 the town became seat of Cath. diocese in N.D. Land was so fertile in James R. valley that many farmers paid for their land in 2 yrs. Often land would yield twice what it cost, during the 1st yr. Maxwell Anderson, Pulitzer Prize playwright, & Curtis D. Wilbur, Secy. of War in Coolidge Adm., went to school in Jamestown. On high bluffs stands **Jamestown College,** founded (1883) by Presb. Synod. Christian education & Liberal Arts & Sci. courses. Fully accredited. (107-a. campus). City has 3 pks. City Pk. has mun. tourist camp & Klaus Pk. has swim. Cor. 5th Ave. S. & Pacific St. W., **Alfred Dickey Lib.** (Byzantine). Here also is J. with US281.

SIDE TRIPS: (A) On this Rd. (N) 43$^{m}$ to **Carrington.** On Central Ave., **Mun. Lib.** with 10,000 volumes.
(B) On US281 (S) 64$^{m}$ to **Ellendale** (see US281), in heart of pheasant-hunting country.

Short distance (NE) of Jamestown is **Ft. Seward Hist. Site. 127. MEDINA,** small town with Russo-German pop. Also J. with St.30.

SIDE TRIP: On this Rd. 10$^{m}$ (N) to **L. George,** known as Salt L. (swim.) because of heavy salt water; excellent sand beach on (S) shore.

**135. CRYSTAL SPRINGS LAKES. 139. TAPPEN.**

SIDE TRIP: From here (R) on trl. to **McPhail's Butte Hist. Site,** from which Col. McPhail directed Minn. Rangers (1863) in Battle of Big Mound, against Sioux. During truce parley, which was proceeding amicably, a young Ind. shot Dr. Weiser, a white, in the back.

Immediately, the battle was resumed & Sioux had to retreat farther (W). Beyond 2m (NE) is **Burman Hist. Site** where Dr. Weiser is buried.

**145. DAWSON,** with a **U.S. Game Reserve,** being on the route for migratory birds. At Dawson is J. with St.3.

SIDE TRIP: On this Rd. (S) 5m **L. Isabel.** Here Lodge & Game Reserve of G. L. Slade, son-in-law of J. J. Hill. Maintains his own pheasant-breeding grounds & created his own lake. Large parties of Easterners are invited here to hunt. At 25m **Napoleon.** Two pigeon-holes in homestead office desk served as its 1st post office. At 40m **Burnstad,** 2m (L) out of town is **Beaver Lake St. Pk.** (45 as.recr.swim.pic.) developed by WPA. At 77m, **S.D. Line.**

**156. STEELE.** When incorporated in 1882 it was smallest city in U.S. Town was named for Col. W. P. Steel, who in 1889 sent a cheque for $100,000 to 1st legislature with his bid to locate the St. capitol at Steele. He also had his own half-mile spur RR. line which he advertised as a main line. Called before directors of other RRs. to explain his hoax, he said: "While my line is not as long as yours, I want it understood, that it is every bit as wide." **167. DRISCOLL.**

SIDE TRIP: From Driscoll (R) on country Rd. 3m to **Chaska Hist. Site** & grave of Chaska, Sioux scout with Sibley expedition, who died during the campaign. He is said to have warned missionaries at Yellow Medicine Agency (Minn.) & led many whites to safety, 1862.

**175. STERLING,** J. with US83. US10 & US83 are one Rd. to Menoken. **181. McKENZIE,** named for Alex. McKenzie, early N.D. political boss. **185.5.** J. with dirt Rd.

SIDE TRIP: On this Rd. (R) to **Menoken Village Hist. Site.** Bastion & most of old fort still visible, where Verendrye is supposed to have met the Mandan. Verendrye's route has not been definitely determined by historians.

**186. MENOKEN.** A town with several names. Two official ones still exist, Blaine & Burleigh. Bet. Menoken & Bismarck the hy. crosses & recrosses Apple Cr., once a rushing stream along which Sibley's army traveled. **197.** J. with gravel Rd.

SIDE TRIP: On this Rd. (L) 3m to **Ft. Lincoln,** only survivor of 12 military posts in N.D.; est. (1895) as mil. reserv., intermittently garrisoned since 1903. Land in vic. was battleground of Sioux & Sibley's men. The Inds. were forced to abandon large stores of supplies.

**199. BISMARCK** (see). At Main Ave. & 6th St. is J. with US83. Hy. crosses Mo. R. over Liberty Mem. Bridge. On opp. side, time changes from Central to Mountain Time. In next 6m there are a number of tourist camps. **204. MANDAN** (see Bismarck). **252. GLEN ULLIN,** Russo-German town. J. with St.9.

SIDE TRIP: On this Rd. (S) 15m to **Heart Butte.** From it countryside around can be seen for 20m. Here on Heart R. is **Heart Butte Dam Site.** Dam is being constructed by Bureau of Reclamation & is 1st flood control & irrigation project to be built in N.D.

**264. HEBRON. 272. ANTELOPE.** Rd. follows Custer's 7th Cavalry trail on its way to Montana, 1876, where it met disaster. **278. RICHARDTON.** Here Benedictine Order built **Assumption Abbey** (Romanes.& Goth.1910), presenting striking picture of old-world architecture in the prairie land. It incl. a monastery, church, high sch. & jr. college for boys. Town was named for steamship agent who brought Russo-Germans to the state. **299.5.** J. with gravel Rd.

SIDE TRIP: On this Rd. (L) to **Lehigh,** mining town named for Lehigh, Pa. **Briqueting Plant** (O) is only plant in U.S. producing lignite briquets from carbonized lignite coal with B.T.U. rating of 15,000. Creosote, chief by-product, is shipped in large quantities to eastern markets.

**298. DICKINSON,** in heart of central Mo. slope; agric. reg. Some of world's best flax, wheat, rye & barley are grown here. It is also famous grazing area. Several large ranch operators still run cattle as they did on the open range with twice-a-yr. round-ups, or rodeos. On (N) side of town, are **Country Club** (golf), **Whitney Swim. Pool** (fee) & **Rocky Butte Pk.** (pic.). On 10th Ave. is **St. Normal Sch.** (1918.Eng. Tudor). At **299.5.** (R) is sub-station of the **N.D. Agric. Experiment Sta. 316.** Country (S) here was traveled by Gen. Alfred Sully & his troops after Battle of Killdeer Mt. & 7m (S), is **Custer Hill,** where Gen. Custer camped on his way to Big Horn, Mont.

**318. BELFIELD.** Has N.D.'s only bentonite plant, **Dakota Colloidal Corp.** Here is J. with US85 (see). Hy. now leads at **326.** into the **BADLANDS,** a garish confusion of buttes, yellow, salmon, brown & gray in color, formed by yrs. of geological erosion. At **328.** the **PAINTED CANYON,** magnificent display of gorges & buttes varying in color & shadow with the light of day. Rd. is lined with brick-colored scoriae, mottled with green, giving illusion of verdigrised bronze. US10 travels through the beautiful Badlands to E. Entrance of **ROOSEVELT PK.** Both N. & S. Pks. have been made into **THEO. ROOSEVELT MEM. PK.**; est. thus by Act of Congress, Ap. 25, 1947. It is 1st national Mem. Pk. in U.S. Its area comprises c.35,000 as. & is known as Badlands of the Little Mo. R., a huge expanse of fantastic beauty incl. a petrified for. Sands, shales & clays are of grey buff, & yellow interspersed with black coal beds & thin red & brown bands of ironstained sand; red baked shale adding brilliance to the scenery. Pk. is ambitiously planned, but at present, although main hys. are good, secondary Rds. are still impassable after heavy rains. There are no overnight accoms. in pk. for visitors. **Cottonwood Camp. & Pic. Ground** on Little Mo. R. is W. of hqs. area, & is maintained for visitors. Nearly all of pk. is accessible to horseback or hik. parties. Adm. hqs. are located in **Peaceful Valley,** 7$^{m}$ beyond entrance on US10.

**338. MEDORA**

Medora, a little town on E. bank of Mo. R. 0.5$^{m}$ (S) of US10, was named for the beautiful red-haired Amer. wife of Marquis de Mores, dashing young Frenchman, who came here in 1883 to set up meat-packing plant at source of supply. By using refrigerated railroad cars, he hoped to cut cost of meat, thereby capturing eastern markets. The Badlands fascinated him & he chose this country as site for his plant, as well as for the town. He also built **De Mores Chateau,** an enormous ranch house of 28 rooms, 2 stories high, with red-plush interior. Here he & his charming wife with their staff of Fr. servants entertained distinguished visitors from the E., incl. Theo. Roosevelt, who had come to the Badlands for his health & built himself a cabin in vic. By 1884 de Mores was shearing 14,000 sheep & grazing many thousands of cattle. Hundreds of animals were slaughtered daily & shipped East. Within 3 or 4 yrs., however, the venture failed; partly because de Mores, on account of his lavish living & unfriendly acts had antagonized neighbors with whom he often got into violent quarrels, especially when he began fencing in his property, something not customary in these parts. In one encounter an outsider was killed & the marquis was held for murder although later acquitted. He decided to abandon his dramatic project & returned to Europe. In 1896, at age of 43, he was killed by native in N. Africa. The meat-packing project failed & nothing but a chimney remains of the plant, but the idea was a practical one & at present there are several similar plants in existence in W. Fargo & Grand Forks. The Chateau, still intact, was given over to N.D. Hist. Soc. in 1936, by son of de Mores. All bldgs. survive & are now incl. in St. Pk., known as **De Mores Hist. Site** (128 as.tours.fee). Tom Mix was married to Olive Stokes, in Medora, 1909. On Main St., **Athenais Chapel** (1884), built for the marquise by her husband. Here also is **Rough Riders Hotel,** built by de Mores; formerly hqs. for cattlemen. Teddy Roosevelt spent a good deal of time here, & doubtless took its name for his Spanish-Amer. War Regiment. **339.** J. with graveled Rd. On this (R) is W. Entrance to **Theo. Roosevelt Mem. Pk.** (see above). **344.5. FLAT TOP BUTTE** (L). On its slope occurred skirmish bet. Sitting Bull's men & Amer. soldiers. Inds. kept up constant firing during the night, but when morning came, they withdrew & went hunting. **352.** Rd. now passes through prairie land, with **Sentinel Butte** (3,350′) (L). **361.5. BEACH,** grain shipping pt. almost at Mont. Line. Cartoonist John M. Baer was Postmaster here (1913-15) & later became N.D. Congressman. At **364.** hy. crosses **MONT. LINE.**

## US 12—NORTH DAKOTA

**N.D.-S.D. LINE** (at White Butte, S.D.) **(NW) to N.D.-MONT. LINE** (10$^{m}$ from Baker, Mont.). **90. US12**

Via: Hettinger & Bowman.

Hy. cuts across extreme SW. cor. of N.D. through prairie land & mesa-topped buttes, touching S. part of the **N.D. Badlands.**

**0.** US12 crosses S.D. border into land where the Plains Inds. used to have their big buffalo hunts. Last big one was in 1882. After it Inds. returned to a dull life on Standing Rock Reserv. **15. HETTINGER. 24. BUCYRUS, 33. REEDER, 44. SCRANTON,** named for Penn. town because of its coal mines. **50. BUFFALO SPRINGS.** (E) of town is RR. Reservoir (swim.f.). Coll. of Ind. artifacts, curios, petrified woods may oe seen in Ed. Gorman's hardware store. **58. BOWMAN.** Here is J. with US85 (see). **78.** J. with a dirt Rd.

SIDE TRIP: On this Rd. (R) to **Ft. Dilts St. Pk.** $2^m$ in which are preserved ruins of a sod wall fort built in 1864 by a party of Mont. gold seekers who were besieged by a band of Hunkpapa Inds. until help came from Ft. Rice. Fort was named for Jefferson Dilts, a scout for the expedition; he was killed by the Inds. as he was returning from reconnoitering.

At **86. MARMARTH.** This town was flooded 5 times bet. 1907 and 1921. To prevent floods, a dam was built over **Little Beaver Cr.,** near town (W). Here Theo. Roosevelt shot his first Buffalo. Near Marmarth oil was discovered in 1936 which brought the town a boom. **90.** Hy. crosses **MONT. LINE.**

## US 81—NORTH DAKOTA

**N.D.-S.D. LINE** ($39^m$ from Sisseton, S.D.) **(N) to CANADIAN BORDER** ($64^m$ from Winnipeg, Man.). **254. US81**

Via: Wahpeton, Fargo, Grand Forks, Grafton & Pembina. RR.: Bet. S.D. & Fargo, Milwaukee RR. parallels the route; bet. Fargo & Hamilton, Gt.N. RR.; bet. Hamilton to border, N.P. RR. Northwest Airlines cover route from Fargo to border. Gravelled Rd. from border to Fargo; bituminous from Fargo to Canada. Accoms.: Larger centers.

US81 almost parallels Red R. from S.D. Line to Canada, upward through very flat countryside, & in sight of W. bank of the river.

**8. FAIRMOUNT**

In Cath. churchyard is an obelisk on which figures are patterned from stones of varied shapes & colors brought from all parts of world. It is known as the "Sermon in Stone." Father Bierens, its builder, used to operate the **U.S. Biological Bird Survey Sta.** He banded thousands of native & foreign birds. In F. P. Nelson's home is coll. of Ind. artifacts & fire arms; also Chinese gun made in 1526. **23. WAHPETON,** situated at confluence of 2 Rs. which form Red R. of the N. This was at one time summer camping ground of Sioux who dried buffalo meat & skins here. On (N) side of town is **St. School of Science** (1903.vocational-technical) & **U.S. Ind. School.** Near entrance is statue of Hendrik Ibsen by Jacob Fjelde. Ind. Sch. houses 300 Sioux & Chippewa. On (NE) side of town, bet. banks of the old bed of Red R. & present channel lies **Chahinkapa Pk.** (recr.center.all facils.). Hy. travels (W) $7^m$ & then turns sharply (N) again to **ABERCROMBIE** at **43.** on bank of Red R. Near it is site of **Ft. Abercrombie,** first Fed. fort in N.D. & gateway to the Dakotas. During the Minn. uprising of 1862 it was besieged 5 wks. by Sioux. Because of insufficient ammunition it was in very precarious position until relieved by detachment of 350 men from Ft. Snelling. The Sibley Expedition set forth from this enlarged post the next summer. In the 70's trls. led from here to Fts. Totten, Random, Wadsworth & Garry. Many a wagon load of pioneers or gold seekers spent a night or two here before setting out across the Dakotas. Here also in 1870 treaty bet. Sioux & Chippewa was made through good offices of Father Genin, a Cath. priest. **Ft. Abercrombie St. Pk.** on (E) side of town (22 as.recr.facils.). Coll. of early relics is in an old cabin & near-by stands a Red R. oxcart used before RRs. & hys. appeared. At **54.** is **CHRISTINE,** named for noted Swedish opera singer, Christine Nilsson, who sang in U.S., 1873. **68. WILD RICE,** French-Can. farming community. At Wild Rice R., $3^m$ beyond (1807), during a battle bet. Chippewa & Sioux, Tabashaw, Chippewa chieftain, was slain while avenging death of his eldest son. **77. FARGO** (see US10). Here is J. with US10.

**114.** Hy. reaches **HILLSBORO,** having passed small towns of Harwood, Argusville, Gardner, Grandin & Kelso en route. Hillsboro was named for J. J. Hill & is situated on charming Goose R. (1880). In vic. is **Woodland Pk.** (recr.tourist camp). Here is log cabin with pioneer relics incl. handloom used by early families. **155. GRAND FORKS** (see US2). **156.** (R) **N.D. St. Mill & Elevator** (O.wks.9-5;conducted tours). This state-owned enterprise is product of Nonpartisan League (1922) & plays important part in N.D. politics (see US10). The St. Industrial Comm. successfully governs mill & elevator, consisting of 6 steel & concrete bldgs. with capacity of 1,659,600 bu. On gravelled Rd., (L) **Northern Packing Co.** (O). Near here is marker showing sec. of **Red R. Oxcart Path** which extended from Ft. Gary, Winnipeg, to Ft. Snelling, St. Paul.

**168. MANVEL,** formerly Turtle R. Sta., one of six stops on Ft. Abercrombie-Ft. Gary trl., 1860. It consisted of a one-windowed log hut with fireplace. Crude though it was, to overland travelers who paid 50¢ for a meal & privilege of sleeping on the dirt floor it was a very cheery place. **180. ARDOCH,** completely Polish community.

**187. MINTO,** Czechoslovakian & Polish sett. where Feast of St. Wenceslaus, Sept. 28, & Czech Independence Day, Oct. 28, are celebrated with pomp. Near Forest R. is a pk. (recr.swim.pool). **198. GRAFTON,** proud possessor of 1st Pub. Lib. in St.; also 1st city in that part of NW. to have a mun. power plant. At Grafton is J. with St.17.

SIDE TRIP: On this Rd. (W) 21m is Park R. Here lived Wm. Avery Rockefeller, father of founder of Standard Oil Co. He was known as Dr. Levingston, no real physician, but a seller of patent medicines.

**226. HAMILTON,** settled by Canadians. Here is oldest St. Bank in N.D., est. 1886. Pembina Cty. Fair, started 1894, is held here annually, June or July. Here is J. with St.5.

SIDE TRIP: On this Rd. (W) 9m to **Cavalier,** 35m to **Langdon.** Became Cty. seat through efforts of a dozen bachelors, who by changing names & apparel often on election day, voted for all absent voters. Here is **Children's Haymow Theatre,** barn used for 30 yrs. to present plays for the young.

US81 now turns (R) 10m to unite with St.44 running directly (N) again for 13m.

**252. PEMBINA,** a town of rococo architecture at confluence of Red & Pembina Rs. Around 1800, first fur posts were built here, but 2 yrs. later disappeared. It was then that the rival Hudson's Bay & the XY Cos. set up their posts. First white child born here was illegitimate baby of "Orkney Lad," a woman, who for yrs. had been disguised as a man. Only at birth of child was her imposture generally known. After 1812 colonization began here by Selkirk Scots, who returned to Canada (1818) when internat. boundary was fixed. By '51 Pembina had become an important river port. Town was starting pt. for the famous Pembina buffalo hunts. Followers traveled in Red R. carts. **Pembina Hist. Site** is (R) here (camp.pic.) incl. site of 1st trading post of North West Co. In **Masonic Pk.** flag of U.S. & Canadian Union Jack fly together July 4, & July 1, Dominion Day. **254.** Hy. crosses **CANADIAN BORDER.**

## US 281—NORTH DAKOTA

**N.D.-S.D. LINE** (6m from Frederick, S.D.) **(N) to CANADIAN BORDER** (10m from Cartwright, Man.). **236. US281**

Via: Ellendale, Edgely, Jamestown, Minnewauken, Cando, Hansboro.

US281 crosses **S.D. LINE** at **0. 6. ELLENDALE,** in heart of pheasant country. Seat of St. Normal & Industrial School. When this school opened (1889), it was 1st in U.S. to offer free manual training. **18.** J. with Cty. Rd.

SIDE TRIP: On this Rd. (R) to **Whitestone Hill Battlefield, Hist. Site.** (66 as.mus.shelter & other facils.). Here in 1863 most severe battle bet. whites & Inds. in N.D. was fought. Gens. Sully & Sibley had been sent from Minn. on punitive expedition against the Inds. because it was believed they participated in the Minn. massacre of 1862. Sully's men, in a bloody 3-day battle, drove the Inds. across Mo. R.

**32. EDGELEY. 70. JAMESTOWN** (see US10). J. with US10. On outskirts of town is **Ft. Seward Hist. Site.** Beyond town (N) on St.20 near Kensall is **Arrowwood Natural Wildlife Refuge** (16,044 as.). Area incl. 3 Ls. & is breeding ground for ducks, pheasants, grouse, & a large number of shore & water birds. Hy. passes **BUCHANAN** at **83.** & **PINGREE** at **91.,** named for Hazen Senter Pingree, who in 1880 arrived here with a rack & wagon to start a potato plantation. He failed in this undertaking, went to Mich. (see) where he became a successful shoe manufacturer; also was mayor of Detroit, & twice Gov. of Mich. **97. EDMUNDS.** J. with gravel Rd.

SIDE TRIP: On this Rd. (R) 6m to Arrowwood L., largest of a chain of Ls. through which James R. flows. Inds. came here from great distances to pick Juneberry shoots for arrow shafts. It is also summer breeding place for pelicans.

**103. MELVILLE. 113. CARRINGTON (tourist camp). 129. NEW ROCKFORD. 140. SHEYENNE.** Here is beginning of **Ft. Totten Ind. Reserv.** (137,000 as.). About 10m (N) is J. with St.57 which turns (R) & touches Devils L. at Ft. Totten. Orig. bldg.

was a log cabin, still to be seen (S) a half mile. Next to Ft. Lincoln, Totten is best built fort in St. Reserv. was named for Gen. Gilbert Totten, then chief of U.S. Army Engineer Corps. Est. in 1867 by treaty, it now houses c.1,142 Sioux (see US2).

**161. MINNEWAUKAN,** former steamboat landing. Beyond (S) is dry bed of part of Devils L. **183.** J. with Cty. Rd.

SIDE TRIP: On this Rd. (R) 4.5m to **Lac Aux Mortes** (named thus by Fr. trappers). After a severe smallpox epidemic, surrounding trees were filled with dead bodies (a tribal burial custom). The trappers burnt entire woods to prevent spread of the disease.

**190. CANDO.** J. with St.17.

SIDE TRIP: On this Rd. (R) 8m to a **Dunker Colony** (German Bapt.). Sect was founded in Germany (1708) & this branch arrived in N.D. (1894) with Gt.N. RR. to help colonize the reg. In early Oct. is annual harvest feast.

**200.** J. with Cty. Rd. leading (R) 3m to **Snyder L.** (recr.swim.pic.). **214. ROCK L.,** lying on edge of Rock L. U.S. Biological Survey has migratory waterfowl sanctuary here. **219.** J. with St.5.

SIDE TRIP: On this Rd. (L) 17m to **Rolla.** Here lived John Burke, 3 times Gov. of N.D. & Chief Justice of Supreme Ct. Town is also hqs. for Internat. Peace Garden (see below). Directly beyond (W) is **Turtle Mt. Ind. Reserv.** lying in valley of these mts. It is home of mixed Chippewa Inds. (7,856) who hold here annual sun dance (June). St.5 passes **Belcourt** in the reserv. & at 40m reaches **Dunseith.** Here is J. with St.3.

On St.3 (N) 13m into **Internat. Peace Garden,** a tract of land (2,220 as.) astride the internat. boundary. Both Canada & U.S. contributed the land (880 as. in U.S. & 1,300 as. in Canada), part of which is already developed into a beautiful formal garden. Conceived in 1929, it was dedicated in July, 1932, as a "symbol of everlasting peace bet. the 2 countries." A simple cairn of stones gathered from both sides of the border has inscribed on it the lines:

"To God in His Glory
We two Nations do pledge ourselves
That so long as men shall live
We will not take up arms against one another."

Each July, site is rededicated & people flock from both countries to the peaceful spot in fertile Turtle Mt. Valley, in which are many small & one large L. Wild life is abundant. A spacious lodge is avail. for pub. use, & so are overnight cabins, amphitheatre & pic. areas.

**229. HANSBORO,** named for 1st Representative to U.S. Congress from N.D. who later became Sen. Here is U.S. port of entry & customh. **236.** Hy. crosses **CANADIAN BORDER.**

## US 83—NORTH DAKOTA

**N.D.-S.D. LINE** (34m from Selby, S.D.) (N) **to CANADIAN BORDER** (5m from Coulter, Man.). **271. US83**

Via: Linton, Bismarck, Washburn, Minot, Westhope.

US83 in northwesterly course bisects state, first through hilly uplands, then central Drift Prairie, & finally fertile fields around former L. Souris.

**0.** US83 crosses **S.D. LINE. 6. HULL,** Dutch community. **15. STRASBURG,** settlement of Russo-Germans, whose great annual celebration is feast of St. Peter & St. Paul (June 29). **27. LINTON.** Most of pub. bldgs. are of N.D. sandstone.

SIDE TRIP: From Linton (L) 0.5m to country Rd. (R) on this 1.5m to **Ind. Turtle Effigy Mound,** almost perfect example. Outlines of turtle can be clearly seen. Rd. passes over turtle's neck.

**43. HAZELTON. 57. MOFFIT,** U.S. migratory waterfowl refuge. **67. STERLING.** J. with US10 (see). As one Rd., the 2 hys. run into **BISMARCK** (see) at **91. 116. WILTON** (see Bismarck). **132. WASHBURN** (see Bismarck). **144.** US83 turns sharply (L) to **UNDERWOOD** at **149.** Beyond Underwood (N) at **157.** is J. with Riverdale Rd.

SIDE TRIP: On this Rd. (L) c.13m to **Garrison Dam & Reservoir** (see Bismarck). The town of **Riverdale** in 1948 was still prairie land & the bridge across Big Muddy was not passable.

**160. COLEHARBOR. 165.** J. with St.37, leading (L) 5m to **Garrison,** named for Garrison Cr. Lignite is mined in vic. **177. MAX,** another Russo-German community.

Hy. now climbs Plateau du Missouri & at **205.** reaches **MINOT** (see US2). At Minot is also J. with US52 which cuts diagonally across state from Fargo to **Portal,** Internat. Airport of Entry, at **Canadian border,** 68m. Much traffic to Canadian N.W. passes through this Custom & Immigration Office.
US83 runs directly (N) to J. with St.5 at **242.** The 2 hys. unite to **259.**

SIDE TRIP: On St.5 (R) 26m to **Bottineau,** named for one of most famous N.D. personalities, Pierre Bottineau. He was guide who walked with J. J. Hill from Winnipeg to St. Paul, the scout who headed Jay Cooke's first N.P. RR. survey, the gambler who staked Nicollet I. & lost. Inds. in this vic. were very hostile to the whites. After the Gt.N. RR. passed near orig. town, site gradually moved about a mile away. In 1886, huge prairie fire almost destroyed all bldgs. Today there is **St. School of Forestry** in the NE. part of town, & plantings from it supply all ctys. of state. **Dunseith** is 22m farther (E). Here is J. with St.3.

(1) On this Rd. (N) 13m to **Internat. Peace Garden** (see US281). Near Dunseith, at edge of Turtle Mts., a buried treasure may still be hid, for the loot of notorious bank robbery of 1893 was never found & bank was forced to close. St.5 leads directly (E) into **Turtle Mts. Ind. Reserv.** (72 sq.miles) into which 7,586 Inds. are crowded. These Chippewa have intermarried with Fr. settlers & the Algonquin tongue has practically died out, contrary to practices on other N.D. reservations. Gov. has recently built new school & hospital for Inds. near Belmont.

(2) St.3 leads (W) to **Bowbells** 45m named by Eng. stockholders of the Soo Line, for St. Mary-le-Bow. Its tall water tower is visible for miles across flat prairie land. **Crosby** at 111m (W) is strategic rail center & focal point for trade in NW. sec. of state. From Crosby 36m, St.5 reaches **Mont. border.**

**259.** US83 turns (N) again, passing **WESTHOPE** at **265.** & reaches **INTERNAT. BORDER** at **271.**

## US 85—NORTH DAKOTA

**N.D.-S.D. LINE** (23m from Buffalo, S.D.) **(N) to CANADIAN BORDER** (58m from Weyburn, Sask.). **258. US85**

Via: Bowman, Amidon, Belfield, Watford City & Fortuna.

US85 passes through the majestically beautiful Badlands, crosses Coteau du Plateau du Missouri & then heads directly (N) to Saskatchewan.

**0.** Rd. crosses S.D. line. **16. BOWMAN,** near sandstone-topped Twin Buttes. Here is J. with US12 (see). At **34.** is J. with country Rd. leading 1m (L) to **Black Butte** (3,468′), highest elev. in St. On (S) side of butte is Snow Cave where winter snows often remain till Aug. **35.5.** Hy. passes **Chalky Butte** (R) & **Black Butte** (L). **39.5.** J. with graded dirt Rd. (bad curves & choppy hills).

SIDE TRIP: On this Rd. (L) 2m, then (R) descending into the **Badlands** to J. with a trl. On this trl. (L) 1m to **Burning Coal Mine,** which toward evening gives off red glow, with coal gas becoming annoying. Inds. called this "burning ground." Although coal has burned for hundreds of yrs., it has spread only few hundred ft. in the last 50 yrs. Visitors can peer down crevices, but it is advisable to approach from downhill side lest earth crumble beneath. In valley below grow columnar cedars, bright green conical trees 15′ high.

**40. AMIDON.** Good view (SE) of Chalky Butte, outlines of the Badlands (N) & Black Butte (W). At **46. MIDWAY.** J. with dirt Rd. leading (R) 6m to **Chalky Butte.** Along its fossilized slopes teeth & bones of prehist. animals have been found, among them skull & bones of an oreodon (prehist. hoofed animal). At **49.** is J. with St.21.

SIDE TRIP: On this Rd. (R) 16m to **New England,** today predominantly Scand. although founded by New Englanders. At S. end of Main St. is **Shrine** to Virgin Mary made of slabs of petrified wood & rock formation from the Badlands.

**75. BELFIELD.** J. with US10 (see).

SIDE TRIP: On this Rd. (W) 19m, is **Medora** in heart of the Badlands; also **De Mores Hist. Site** & Entrance to **Roosevelt Pk.**

**107.** J. with St.25. **113.5.** US85 passes **GRASSY BUTTE** founded in 1913 by 10 Russian laborers. Little Russians or Ukrainians inhabit surrounding country. They have retained most of their old customs & are still Greek Cath. **127.5.** Hy. crosses Little Mo. R. & in distance (R) Killdeer Mts. can be seen. **131.** Main entrance to **N. Roosevelt Reg. St. Pk.** (see US10), also called N. Roosevelt Recr. Demonstration Area, incl. petrified forests & Grand Canyon of the Little Mo. On both sides of river are the **N.D. Badlands,** strangely beautiful stratas of earth piled into fantastic shapes

& fringed by brilliant green spruce & cedar trees growing on the hilltops. Hy. passes through wierdly colored buttes & suddenly dips into a grassy plateau at **134.** **146. WATFORD CITY,** called "Island Empire" because it is almost entirely surrounded by Mo., Little Mo. & Yellowstone Rs. Mus. is in W. A. Jacobson law office (O.wks. 9-5) containing exhibits of gems, fossils, Ind. artifacts & a Bible printed in 1535. In Watford City is J. with St.23.

SIDE TRIPS: (A) On this Rd. (L) is excellent tourist camp.
(B) On St.23 (R) 4m is **Schafer,** named for Geo. Schafer, whose son became Gov. of N.D. 1929-32. On his homestead are **Schafer Springs** (near-by are fine campgrounds) which have a flow of 6,000 gal. per hr. even in dry season. St.23 E. & N. of Watford City reaches **Ft. Berthold Ind. Reserv.** (see US83 & US2) in c.29m. At 10m (R) on an incompleted Rd. is **Sanish.** Near-by is **Verendrye Bridge** spanning Mo. It used to be called "Old Crossing" by Inds. because huge buffalo herds crossed here as they annually migrated (S). Beyond town (S) is **Verendrye Nat. Mon.** (see US2). Here is **Crow Flies High Butte,** named for Hidatsa chief. On it is mon. to the Verendryes, father & son, who are supposed to have visited the "agric. Ind." here in 1738 while on their exploratory trip. Ft. Berthold Ind. Reserv. at present has c.2,018 Inds. (Arikara, Mandan & Gros Ventres). Because Inds. on this reserv. belong to agrarian tribe their economic status is better than others. Years of training in the fields has made them better adjusted to life on reserv.

From Watford City US85 turns sharply (L), passing en route **ARNEGARD,** certified seed potato market, to **154.** J. with side Rd.

SIDE TRIPS: (A) From here (L) 14m to N. Entrance of Roosevelt Pk. (see).
(B) From here (R) 3m to L. Pescheck (summer recr. ground).

**166. ALEXANDER,** named for Alex. McKenzie, political boss of early N.D. (see). **168.** J. with St.23 leading (W) 13m to **Cartwright** & at 17m passing **Yellowstone R.** The irrigated land in vic. is now planted mainly with sugar beets. Mex. labor is used for cultivation. **185.** Hy. crosses Mo. R. over **Lewis & Clark Bridge** (1927). **189.** J. with US2 (see). **Montana border** is 23m (L) from here. **194. WILLISTON** (see US2). US85 cont. (N) from Williston for 34m to J. with St.50 past **Zahl,** small town named for a buffalo hunter of the 70's. **251.** J. with St.5.

SIDE TRIPS: (A) On this Rd. (L) 3m to **Fortuna,** Scand. community (sett.1913). It is an immigration office & port of entry to Canada.
(B) On this Rd. (R) 18m to **Crosby.** Its City Recr. Pk. has all facils.

**258.** Main hy. touches **CANADIAN BORDER.**

# BISMARCK

**BISMARCK**

RR. Stas.: N.P. RR., Main Ave. bet. 4th & 5th Sts.; Soo Line, 117—7th St. Bus Sta.: Greyhound Lines & Interstate Transp. Co., 618 Broadway. Airport: 2m (SE) of city, for Northwest Airlines.

Bismarck, on (E) bank of Mo. R. is the spacious capital city of N.D. Long before arrival of white men Mandan Inds. considered this spot most desirable for camps & homes. This thought was shared by most Dakotans when they moved the capital from Yankton to Bismarck. Present capitol grounds are surrounded by sites of Ind. villages. Originally Camp Greeley, later known as Camp Hancock, was situated here in 1872. About this time the N.P. RR. reached Bismarck, then known as Burleightown. Being a railroad terminus & head of navigation gave the town double advantage. In 1883 it became capital of Dakota Territory. Bismarck is in center of wheat-growing reg. & has become supply depot to surrounding grain-growing, stock-raising & diversified farms. From earliest days, however, it was hqs. of political parties, which still is true today. Among city's exciting political experiences were: exposé by the Gov., in 1889, of the lobbyists of Louisiana Lottery; maneuverings of Alex. McKenzie & his railroad connections; & the rapid succession of four Governors in five months.

Pop. of Bismarck is largely German & Russo-German. Its name was given to it by an overseas steamship agent, who hoped thereby to attract many German-speaking settlers.

PTS. OF INT.: (1) High on Capitol Hill, dominating both the city & the prairie as well, is the **State Capitol,** a modernistic skyscraper, designed by 2 N.D. architects, Jos. B. de Remer & Wm. F. Kurke, together with Holabird & Root of Chicago. The vast unused prairie lands around it hardly justify a skyscraper, but the dignity &

beauty of its lines have given N. Dakotans, even those who originally objected to it, a feeling of pride. Its outer walls are of Bedford limestone, & the base is trimmed with a broad band of Rosetta black granite. The Senate Chamber is considered one of the most beautiful in U.S. The 18th fl. of the tower is designed as observation spot from which panoramic view of entire Mandan-Bismarck area, incl. Ft. Abr. Lincoln St. Pk. & Ft. Lincoln, can be seen. (2) Near Capitol, (SE) **Liberty Mem. Bldg.** (O.wks.9-5;1921 by Keith & Kurke), 4-story structure of Class. design. It houses St. Hist. Soc. Lib. & Mus. Latter contains excellent coll. of N.D. material & Ind. artifacts, also Emil Krauth butterfly coll. Plaster model of equestrian statue of Theo. Roosevelt by A. Phimister Proctor, & a desk used by him during his stay in the Badlands are on 3d fl. On lawn outside is bronze statue of Sakakawea, the Shoshone Bird Woman, (1910) by Leonard Crunelle (see Bismarck); also prow of Battleship "North Dakota" stands near-by. (3) On (E) side of Memorial Bldg., **Roosevelt Cabin** (O.June 15-Sept.15,wks.10-5;Sun.2-5). It was his home from 1883-85, while rancher in N.D. The cabin contains a few orig. items belonging to "Teddy" & many copies. Cabin had been taken apart & displayed at St. Louis World's Fair for Lewis & Clark Exposition (1905) & later set up here on Capitol grounds. (4) Near cabin is replica of an ancient **Circular Lodge,** built under supervision of an old Mandan woman, Scattered Corn (Mrs. Holding Eagle), daughter of last Mandan corn priest, Moves Slowly, & her niece Mrs. Sitting Crow. Mandans learned how to build earth lodges from their tribal hero, Good Furred Robe. (5) 320 Ave. B., **Governor's Mansion** (1893) typical architecture of Territorial days. (6) 722 5th St., **Home of Alex. McKenzie** (1856), N.D.'s arch-politician & RR. magnate whose intrigues prompted Rex Beach to write his novel, "The Spoilers." (7) 300 Main St., **Marquis de Mores' Storage Plant,** dilapidated bldg. used by the marquis for his meat-packing industry. It has 14″ walls of planks & brick. (8) 101 Main St., **U.S. Weather Bureau** (O.1874) one of oldest bldgs. in Bismarck, formerly hqs. of Camp Hancock. (9) 700 Main St., **Bank of N.D.** (O.wks.8:30-4:30) created by special referendum in 1919. It is managed & controlled by St. Industrial Commission to promote agriculture, commerce, & industry of the state, & is only state-owned bank in U.S. It was an important accomplishment of the Nonpartisan League. St. Regulatory Dept. Lab. (O.) on 4th fl. inspects food, fertilizer, water & oils.

## TRIPS OUT OF BISMARCK

### I. (Loop Tour) BISMARCK (S) to FT. YATES c.150. US10, St.6, St.24 & Unmarked Rd.

Via: Mandan, St. Anthony & Selfridge.

At **0.** US10 crosses Missouri R. Here Central changes to Mountain Time. Bet. Bismarck & Mandan are a number of tourist camps & night clubs.

**4. MANDAN**

City was named for agric. Ind. tribe that occupied the ancient site. It grew so rapidly that some of its orig. bldgs. are still standing. In 1881 the RR. entered town & was chiefly responsible for its rapid growth. Early ranching soon gave way to grain raising, diversified farming & dairying. The N.P. RR. is town's chief economic support, because it maintains here a division point & railroad yards with up-to-date facils. for handling large locomotives, incl. a 126′ turntable. In SW. part of city is **Chautauqua Pk.** (pic.tourist camp.recr.). At Mandan is J. with gravel Rd. (continuation of 6th Ave.).

SIDE TRIP: On this Rd. (L) 4.5m to **Ft. Abraham Lincoln St. Pk.** (750 as.) incl. Mandan village & 2 old military posts. In Slant Village, as it was called, are 5 lodges (rest.). More than 68 have been found along river valley. Pk. is developed by St. Hist. Soc. in cooperation with Nat. Pk. Service. **Ft. McKeen,** opp. village entrance, has also been restored. Orig. was built in 1782. Site of old Ft. A. Lincoln is near here. Pk. also has mus. containing archeological material & Ind. relics.

At Mandan is J. with St.6 on which route continues. Just (S) on this Rd., high on the bluffs, is **U.S. Northern Great Plains Field Sta.** (guides avail.). At **8.** is **U.S. NORTHERN GREAT PLAINS DAIRY STA.** At these 2 Gov. experimental stas. methods of farming & breeds of cattle are tested for adaptability to the Missouri Slope. At **13. CZECH SOCIAL CENTER** where semi-annual folk dancing of "Sala Naninka De Zeli" (Annie Went to the Cabbage Patch) is especially interesting to watch. Around **19.** Rd. passes **ST. ANTHONY,** tiny German-Hungarian community (sett.1887 by Catholics). At **36.** is J. with **BREIEN.** Here Rd. reaches **Standing Rock Ind. Reserv.** Agency hqs. at Ft. Yates. Reached by following St.6 to **SELFRIDGE** at **59.** At **65.** is J. with St.24 on which tour cont. (E) & (N) to **FT. YATES** at **76.** Opp. Agency is famous **Standing Rock,** a metamorphic stone resembling a seated Ind. woman. It belonged originally to the Arikara but came into possession of the Sioux & was carried along with them on their travels. Legend has it that a chief's squaw became jealous of his second wife & refused to move with camp, remaining in front of the fire with her child. The chief missed her & sent her brother to look for her. They found her sitting before the old campfire, petrified. From that time on, the stone occupied a prominent place in Sioux camp. Just S. of Ft. Yates is **Grave of Sitting Bull,** prophet, medicine man & onetime chief of the Sioux, whose lifelong aim was to save his people from the invading white men. Accounts differ as to his actual greatness as a warrior, but as prophet & medicine man he held undisputed ground. His rival chieftains, Gall & Crazy Horse, tried to minimize the respect accorded him by white generals, especially after Battle of Little Big Horn; he then fled to Canada. For one year he traveled with Buffalo Bill's Show, & being a born showman, enjoyed it. In later yrs. he never made an appearance or told a story without demanding remuneration. In N.D. Constitutional Convention parade he appeared in a Prince Albert. In 1890 the Messiah craze took hold of the Sioux. They expected a Messiah to deliver them from white men. Sitting Bull heard of this in Canada & secretly returned to his people, whipping them into a frenzy. To forestall an uprising, Ind. police were sent to arrest him. A struggle followed during which Sitting Bull & several police were killed. The great Ind. leader was buried without ceremony in cemetery of Ft. Yates. His grave is marked, but neglected.

To return to Mandan cont. (N) on St.24 to **104.** & J. with gravel Rd. leading to **CANNON BALL** at **111.** Cont. (N) past **HIST. SITE OF FT. RICE** (est.by Gen. Alfred Sully.1864) at **c.119.** & several Ind. Villages at **c.136.** Ruins of houses & a large dry moat with bastions are still visible. Rd. now leads (SW) into **MANDAN c.150.**

## II. BISMARCK-MANDAN (NE) to STANTON. 47. US10 & St.25

**5.** from Mandan on US10 is J. with St.25.

SIDE TRIP: On this Rd. (N) over **Square Butte Cr.** to **Center** at 30.5m. Granite marker here comm. 16-yr. old Hazel Miner, who froze to death during blizzard in 1920, protecting her little brother & sister with her own body. The small children were still alive when found after storm. Rd. begins to follow Mo. R. at 40.5m where there is J. with dirt Rd. leading (R) 1m to **Ft. Clark St. Pk.,** site (1829) of American Fur Co. trading post (S) of Mandan village. Only burying-ground depressions are left.

At **46.** J. with gravel Rd.

SIDE TRIP: On this Rd. (R) 1.5m to **Stanton.** Straight ahead from here on country Rd. 2.5m to **Scattered Village.** Here Charbonneau, Frenchman, & his Shoshone wife, Sakakawea (Sacajawea) were living when Lewis & Clark engaged them as guides on their hazardous journey across the country. Sakakawea, known as the Bird Woman, was captured by the Gros Ventres (Hidatsa) c.1796. It was on her trip with them, as captive, that she learned about paths & trls., which later stood her in good stead. She became the squaw of trader Toussaint Charbonneau, who shortly after was employed by Lewis & Clark as guide, although it was really Sakakawea, & her practical knowledge of the countryside, her patience, & heroic bearing, who was their real help. The party reached Bismarck c.1804.

## III. BISMARCK to GARRISON DAM. (N) c.60. US83 & Riverdale Rd.

US83 travels (N) passing **WILTON,** Ukrainian village at **24.5.** Here are 2 Greek Cath. Chs., one Orthodox, the other United. **36.5. WASHBURN,** on (E) bank of Mo. R., one of earliest & most important trading posts & boat landings; also site of Sioux-Arikara Battle (1869). On E. Main St., **Log Cabin** (O.appl.at"Leader" office) moved here from Painted Woods. It was built (1870) by Joseph Henry Taylor, soldier, trapper, hunter, printer, editor & author. He arrived from the East in 1867, & est. in Yankton first Democratic newspaper. Because of disappointment in love he gave up his paper & withdrew to the Painted Woods near-by. Here he set up a woodyard, carried on his hunting & trapping & was made Postmaster. Trunk of a tree served as his Post Office. After many yrs. in comparative isolation he returned to Washburn, where he wrote 4 books on early upper Missouri River days. He not only wrote his own books, but edited & printed them. In 1908 he died in the "Leader" office, still bachelor. **42. UNDERWOOD.** Circulating Lib. of this little town was begun by 72-yr.-old Ed. Erickson, who bound newspapers & magazine stories into books. It now has over 8,000 volumes. **45.** J. with Riverdale Rd. leading (E) 13m to **Riverdale** at **58.** Here famous **Garrison Dam** is being built for the control & development of water resources of Mo. R. Basin. When completed, it will be largest earthfill dam in the world. Its crest length will be over 2 miles; height 210′; it will generate about 1½ billion kw. hrs. annually. A construction bridge & hy. were built over the Mo. R. Riverdale itself is a Gov. housing project for 5,000 workers. Dam is expected to be completed in 6 yrs. Garrison Reservoir will be located just below confluence of Yellowstone & Mo. Rs. Its strategic position will permit water to be diverted by canal & lifted into James R. system. Its purpose is primarily to effect Mo. R. regulation for flood control & to provide storage for water.

## US 12—SOUTH DAKOTA

**S.D.-MINN. LINE** (40m from Benson, Minn.) **(W) to S.D.-N.D. LINE** (16m from Hettinger, N.D.). **323. US12**

Via: Milbank, Webster, Aberdeen, Mobridge, Lemmon. Milwaukee RR. parallels hy. Hard-surfaced Rd. Accoms.: In larger towns.

US12 runs halfway across St. & then obliquely into N.D. passing through 4 diff. secs.: Lake reg., James R. valley, Mo. R. ranch country, & fringe of badlands.
At **0.** hy. crosses **MINN. LINE,** & passes (S) end of **Big Stone L.,** which extends 36m to the N. It is named for its granite rock outcroppings. L. is stocked with game fish; (boats & f.equip. can be rented). **0.5. BIG STONE CITY,** summer resort center. Also has a granite quarry, brick factory, & corn cannery. In fall, the man who can eat most corn on the cob is crowned Corn King.

SIDE TRIP: From Main St. (R) is **Chautauqua Pk.,** with cottages avail. At 9m is **Linden Beach** (hotel & cabins) at site of old trading post. At 11m is **Hartford Beach,** with large old-fashioned hotel (resort facils.). W. of resort are **Hartford Mounds** from which skeletons & artifacts have been removed.

US12 crosses Whetstone R. at **2.** At **8.** is J. with gravel Rd.

SIDE TRIP: On this Rd. (L) is **Dakota Granite Quarry,** looking like strange fortress. Here mahogany, royal purple, & Hunter granite for tombstones are quarried.

**14. MILLBANK,** named for director of the Milwaukee RR., which est. division hqs. here. This attracted Dutch & Irish laborers. In center of town is large windmill. Town is known for its granite. **28. MARVIN.** Hy. rises over the **Coteau des Prairie** range to **SUMMIT, 36.** Town is at crest (2,000′) of the hills & here splendid view can be had. To N. lies **Sisseton Ind. Reserv.** which has been open to settlement since 1892, but is still considered Ind. country. At **37.** is J. with US81 (see). At **49.** is **WAUBAY,** at head of chain of Ls. (NW). Sioux Ind. families reside in town & wear both native & "store clothes." They have intermarried, in great numbers, with white people. Although this town is comparatively old (1880), there are still many frame bldgs. **Blue Dog L.,** is beside the hy. & here is J. with gravel Rd.

SIDE TRIP: On this Rd. (R) is part of Lake Reg. At 8m is **Enemy Swim L.** which has several summer resorts & hunting lodges. L. is best known for its bass. At 11m is **Pickerel L.,** a deep-water body popular with fishermen. (Hotel at (S) end; pub.recr.facils.). There is **State Fish Hatchery** near-by.

At **54.** is J. with gravel Rd.

SIDE TRIP: On this Rd. (R) is another chain of Ls. At 1m is **L. Minnewaste.** At 3m is **Waubay L.,** duck & goose hunting area. At 9m is **U.S. Fish & Wild Life Serv. Refuge** covering several shallow Ls.

**59. WEBSTER,** progressive town in prosperous farming area. Town has facils. for all types of sports & is hunting & fishing center. **70. BRISTOL,** founded in 1881 but not incor. until 1921. Large flocks of geese can often be seen from hy. **92. GROTON,** home of Earle Sande, onetime premier jockey in U.S. Hy. passes through rich farming reg. of James R. valley & at **100.** crosses the R. This is good pheasant-hunting country. **110. ABERDEEN AIRPORT** (Northwest Airlines). **112. ABERDEEN,** a beautifully wooded Mid-western city built artificially on dry prairie land. It is a manufacturing & distrib. center. Its pop. is mixture of Amer. stock from Eastern States & Europeans attracted by free homestead lands. Russo-Germans, who form substantial part of pop., are descendants of Germans from Alsace-

Lorraine, who for 2 generations resided in Dniester R. valley. They have preserved language & customs brought over. Town was founded by a party surveying for the Milwaukee RR. in 1881 & named for Aberdeen, Scotland, native city of Alex. Mitchell, then Gen. Mgr. of the Milwaukee RR. Two men who spent their early yrs. in Aberdeen & made their mark in literary fields are Hamlin Garland, author of "Main Traveled Roads," & "A Son of the Middle Border," & L. Frank Baum, author of delightful Oz books for children. The "Wizard of Oz" as a musical play & movie had phenomenal success. Major annual event is Golden Pheasant Festival, a wk.-long entertainment held in mid-Sept. Aberdeen has a baseball team in Northern League (Class C), 2 golf courses & swim. beach at Wylie Pk. PTS. OF INT.: Lincoln St. & 6th Ave., **Alex. Mitchell Lib.** 12th Ave. & Jay St., **Northern St. Teachers College,** with open-air amphitheatre. On campus is mon. comm. Father Rbt. Haire, who founded St. Luke's hospital & helped to make initiative & referendum into State law. N. Main St. & 12th Ave., **copy of Longfellow's home,** Cambridge, Mass. State St. at (S) end of city, **Melgaard Pk.** (pic.facils.). At Aberdeen is J. with US281 (see US281). **114. MILWAUKEE RR. STOCKYDS. 124.** Hy. touches **MINA L.** made by damming Dry Run Cr.; stocked with game fish. **139. IPSWICH,** attractive town. **Beebe Mem. Lib.** has int. coll. of pioneer materials. **169. BOWDLE,** center of farming reg. sett. by Germans. At **188.** is J. with US83. **192. SELBY,** founded 1899. It is center of reg. devoted to horse & cattle raising. **213. MOBRIDGE,** major town on Mo. R., bet. Pierre & Bismarck. On grounds of RR. Sta. are **Conqueror's Stones,** said to be spot where defeated Ind. Chiefs knelt as a sign of submission to their captors. At **215.** is J. with gravel Rd.

SIDE TRIP: On this Rd. (R) is **Riverside Pk. & Fool Soldiers Band Mon.** 2$^{m}$. During War of the Outbreak (1862), party of young Inds. joined whites & effected release of several women & children held captive by Santees. At 3$^{m}$ is **site of Arikara Village.** Artifacts have been removed & are exhibited at Smithsonian Institution.

**216. LINCOLN PK.,** (with pub.swim.pool & recr.facils.). At **216.5.** hy. crosses Mo. R. From bridge (R) **Ashley I.** is visible, named for Gen. Wm. Ashley, partner in Rocky Mt. Fur Co., who in 1823 conducted bartering party to Arikara village near-by. They traded trinkets for horses, but at dawn the Inds. attacked the party, killing 12 whites. News of massacre reached Ft. Atkinson, Kans., which sent out punitive expedition with one howitzer & trained it on village. First shot beheaded the chief. Inds. sued for peace & promised to return goods they had stolen, but by morning entire band had fled. At (W) end of bridge, time changes from Central to Mountain. **217.** on top of hill (L) is **SAKAKAWEA (SACAJAWEA) MON.** (see N.D.). At **225.** hy. enters (S) portion of **STANDING ROCK IND. RESERV.** Agency hqs. are at Fort Yates, N.D. (see). This is an "open" reserv. & only restriction is that no liquor may be carried into or through it. There are 2,266 Inds. on reserv., with average per capita wealth of $20. A number of stock ranches are Indian-owned & in town several businesses are operated by Inds. Rodeos are popular & many Ind. cowboys travel with shows from Calif. to N.Y. At **239.** is J. with hard-surfaced side Rd.

SIDE TRIP: On this Rd. (L) is **Little Eagle** at 5$^{m}$. It has an all-Ind. Amer. Legion post. Near here is **Sitting Bull Pk.,** marking site where the Sioux chief was killed during Messiah War (1890). Famous medicine man's home & numerous relics are preserved here.

**245. McLAUGHLIN. 272. McINTOSH,** oldest town in cty. (1910). At **312.** is **LEMMON,** cattle & grain trading center for large part of S.D. & N.D. At edge of town is **Petrified Wood Pk.** A number of bldgs. are made entirely from petrified wood found in area. Agate & wood curios are made for sale. **323. WHITE BUTTE,** movie-type Western village. Here US12 crosses **STATE LINE.**

## US 212—SOUTH DAKOTA

**S.D.-MINN. LINE** (14$^{m}$ from Dawson, Minn.) **(W) to S.D.-WYO. LINE** (22$^{m}$ from Sundance, Wyo.). **427. US212**

Via: Watertown, Redfield, Gettysburg, Belle Fourche. E. of Mo. R., Rd. is hard surfaced; remainder mostly gravel. Mpls.-Black Hills bus lines use this route. Chi. & N.W. RR. bet. Watertown & Gettysburg.

US212 is direct route across north central S.D. Long stretches of prairie devoid of trees or towns (W) of Mo. R.

At **9.** is J. with US77 to **14.** (see US77). Along hy. on both sides are lakes, (f. & h.). From here to Mo. R. are natural haunts & feeding grounds of Chinese ringneck pheasants. **35. WATERTOWN,** one of the major cities in S.D. Here is J. with US81 (see). **37.5. WATERTOWN AIRPORT.** At **39.** is S. end of **L. KAMPESKA,** popular summer resort (f.swim.boat.golf). **67. CLARK,** trade center of diversified farming reg. **107. REDFIELD,** prosperous cty. seat in predominantly German territory. Here is J. with US281 (see). **122. ROCKHAM. 146. FAULKTON. 166. SENECA. 179. LEBANON. 192. GETTYSBURG,** so named by Civil War vets who settled here, is on fringe of vast grazing country. **198.** J. with US83 (see). **209.** hy. crosses Mo. R. bridge & enters Cheyenne R. Ind. Reserv. About 3,500 Sioux Inds. on Reserv. rolls, most of them living nomadic lives. Many log cabins in area. Cattle-raising major occupation. **210. CHEYENNE AGENCY,** gov. hqs. & trade center. School & hospital are maintained here. **230.** is **LA PLANT,** trading post. **262. EAGLE BUTTE** at W. edge of Reserv. but Ind. country lies both (N) & (S) of hy. for 40$^{m}$. This is an area of big cattle & horse ranches, such as famed Diamond A, largest in St. **282. DUPREE,** typical ranchers' town which has retained board sidewalks & hitching posts. **304. FAITH,** built during homestead era on semi-arid prairie. Fenceless open range (W) to **NEWELL, 387.** This heavily-wooded town looms like an oasis, for it is hqs. of Fed. reclamation & irrigation project. From here (S) on St.79 is Sturgis (see US14). **396. NISLAND,** center of alfalfa & sugar-beet raising area. **404. BELLE FOURCHE,** (N) gateway to Black Hills & J. with US85 (see). US212 runs NW. & crosses **WYO. LINE** at **427.**

## US 14—SOUTH DAKOTA

**S.D.-MINN. LINE** (8$^{m}$ from Lake Benton, Minn.) **(W) to S.D.-WYO. LINE** (at Beulah, Wyo.). **462. US14**

Via: Brookings, Huron, Pierre, Rapid City, Sturgis, Spearfish. Rd. is hard surface. Milwaukee RR. bet. St. Line & Rapid City. Accoms.: In larger towns.

US14 traverses a vast prairie where the westward scene changes from neat farmsteads & shaded towns to wide open spaces & towns to match. Toward its W. extremity Rd. passes through northern Black Hills.

### Sec. 1: S.D.-MINN. LINE to RAPID CITY. 395.

At **0.** hy. enters S.D. Off the Rd., (L) is **Elkton** where the local gov. went off the gold standard in 1896 & coined its own money from aluminum until Fed. authorities halted the practice. **20. BROOKINGS,** typical midwestern college town & farm center. Home of **S.D. State College of Agric. & Mech. Arts.** On campus are several bldgs. & test walls built of rammed earth by process developed here. **Coughlin Campanile** (165′ high) has electrically-operated chimes & 8 million candlepower beacon. Hobo Day, last Sat. in Sept., is major annual event. Brookings is a "dry" town surrounded by taverns. Here is J. with US77, which leads (S) to Sioux Falls. **24.** Hy. crosses **BIG SIOUX R. 28. VOLGA. 38.** J. with US81 (see) to **ARLINGTON, 40. 46. HETLAND,** named by settlers for their home in Norway. Lakes border the hy. to **LAKE PRESTON, 53.** At **62., DE SMET,** setting of several books by De Smet-born Rose Wilder Lane, incl. "Let the Hurricane Roar" & "Old Home Town." S. of town is **Lake Thompson,** popular during duck hunting season. **77. IROQUOIS. 95. HURON,** bustling hub of James R. Valley. During autumn, it teems as pheasant hunting hqs. & home of St. Fair. Town was started as a RR. division pt. in 1879. As agric. developed, it became a meat-packing & farm trade center. Drought & dust storms of 1933-35 hit hard here, but reg. bounced back under concentrated soil conservation programs. PTS. OF INT.: Illinois Ave., bet. 7th & 19th Sts., **Huron College,** a Presb. school. W. 3rd St., **St. Fair Grounds & Zoo.** Fair is 2nd wk. in Sept. Off N. Dakota Ave., **Mun. Airport,** terminal for both Western & Mid-Continent Airlines. The attractive bldgs. are of native field stone. **107.** J. with US281 (see). **110. WOLSEY.** In 1882 Rich. Sears was RR. agent here & began mail order business with unclaimed shipment of watches. Later he org. Sears, Roebuck & Co. **114.** is J. with US281. **139. MILLER,** trade center of territory divided bet. farming & livestock raising. To the S. loom **Ree Hills,** old-time cattle rustling country. **190.**

**BLUNT,** scene of Hyatt Downing's novel, "A Prayer For Tomorrow," which deals with homesteading days. **194.** J. with US83 (see). **210.** J. with gravel Rd.

SIDE TRIP: On this Rd. (R) is **Oahe Dam & Power Plant** Project, 12m, major phase of 1 billion dollar Mo. R. program in S.D. Near-by is **site of Fort Sully,** built in 1866 & boyhood home of Fiorello H. LaGuardia when his father was the post bandmaster.

**211. PIERRE,** capitol of S.D. & outpost for vast West-river range. It is sprawled out over gumbo buttes & Mo. R. flats, belying its status as 2nd smallest capital city in U.S. By trading a shotgun for a squatter's claim, the RR. secured a terminus & began land boom in 1880. When the St. was admitted to Union in 1889, Pierre won a bitter capital fight. Surrounding land is subject to both bumper crops & severe drought, so gov. payroll has stabilizing effect. City operates its own electric, gas, water & liquor businesses, & owns the entire river front. Major annual event is celebration in July of "The Days of '81." PTS. OF INT.: E. Capitol Ave., **State Capitol** follows the traditional design. In Governor's reception room is Edwin Blashfield's "Spirit of the West" mural. On Statehouse grounds is Capitol Lake. Opp. Statehouse, **Soldiers & Sailors Mem. Hall** houses St. Hist. Soc. Lib. & Mus. Featured exhibit is the **Verendrye Plate,** buried in 1743, claiming territory for France. It provided 1st record of white men in Dakota. Bldg. is made of sandstone from Hot Springs & granite from Milbank. E. edge of town, **Pierre Ind. School,** a Fed. institution for boys & girls from Ind. Reserv. From hy. bridge to Belleview St., **Riverside Pk.** (swim.pool.pic.facils.). Here is J. with Lewis & Clark Rd.

SIDE TRIP: On this Rd. (L) is **Farm Island,** 3m, a heavily-wooded city park & sports center. Lewis & Clark expedition stopped here in 1804 to hunt elk & deer.

US14 crosses Mo. R. bridge to **FT. PIERRE, 214.** In its heyday the mecca of voyageurs, soldiers, & bullwhackers, it is a sleepy village filled with memories. Fort for trappers built in 1817 began this oldest continuous settlement in the St. Military post, commanded by Gen. Harney, was est. in 1855. During Black Hills gold rush, ox-drawn freight wagons & stage coaches loaded here for pts. W. On Verendyre Hill is a mon. marking spot where historic plate was found (see Pierre). US14 follows old Deadwood Trl. for several miles. **250. HAYES.** At **252.5.** is **LITTLE BROWN CH. ON THE HILL,** popular wedding place of the prairie people. **303. PHILIP,** named for James "Scotty" Philip whose private herd of 1,000 buffaloes was country's largest. Town is meeting place for cowhands from miles around. **309.** J. with US16 & the 2 routes are united to **RAPID CITY, 395.** (see US16).

### Sec. 2: RAPID CITY to S.D.-WYO. LINE. 67.

US14 runs N. from city. At **0.5.** is **CAMP RAPID,** S.D. Nat. Guard hqs. & camp. **1. S.D. CEMENT PLANT** (R), state-owned enterprise that has turned millions of dollars into St. treasury. Along hy. small deposits of gypsum can be seen imbedded in the banks of red shale known as Spearfish formation. At **1.5.** J. with the Nemo Rd.

SIDE TRIP: Through cool, high-walled canyons (L) Rd. enters **Black Hills Nat. For.** at 9.5m & follows Custer Expedition Trl. along Bogus Jim Creek. At 16m huge formation called **Steamboat Rock,** at base of which is pub. camp grounds. 19m **Nemo,** old logging camp of Homestake Mine now used as hqs. for several recr. camps in vic.

US14 skirts mts. **7. BLACKHAWK. 12.5. SIDNEY STOCKADE,** reproduction of stage station on old Sidney (Neb.) Trl. Here is J. with graded Rd.

SIDE TRIP: **Stage Barn Caverns,** 2m (L) is one of several crystal caves in this area.

**14. PIEDMONT. 17.5.** J. with graded Rd.

SIDE TRIP: **Calcite** (L), a ghost village & abandoned lime plant of Homestake Mine, 1m. At 2m is **Elk Creek Pic. Grounds.** Here (R) are **Crystal Cave,** 3m & **Wonderland Cave,** (L) 3.5m.

**29. STURGIS,** seat of Meade Cty. which is larger than Sts. of Del. & R.I. combined. This town has had a long military background. It was called "Scooptown" when near-by Ft. Meade was est. in 1878. For many yrs. Poker Alice ran a "house" here for pleasure & profit. Town is trade center for broad ranching country (NE). Major annual events are Jack Pine Gypsy Tour (mid-Aug.) & Key City Rodeo (Sept.). Here is J. with St.24.

SIDE TRIP: On paved Rd. (R) is **Fort Meade,** 2m. Since World War II, it has been used as a Veterans Admin. facility for mentally ill. Previously it was hqs. for famed 4th Cavalry for many yrs.

At Sturgis is J. with St.79 & a gravel Rd.

SIDE TRIP: Take latter (R) to **Bear Butte,** 12m. This conspicuous landmark rises 1,200′ above surrounding prairie. Summit can be reached by donkey train.

US14 turns (W) from Sturgis. **30.** J. with St.24, a short-cut across prairie to Spearfish & Belle Fourche (see US85). At **32.** hy. enters **BLACK HILLS NAT. FOR.** Rd. winds up scenic **BOULDER CANYON,** lined with limestone cliffs & tall ponderosa pines. At **41.** J. with US85 at outskirts of Deadwood (see US85). US14 & 85 join to run N. At **42.5.** is **PINE CREST CAMP** & **CABIN OF DEADWOOD DICK. 43. PREACHER SMITH MON.,** marking spot where Rev. Henry W. Smith was killed by Inds. in 1876. **50. BLACK HILLS AIRPORT,** terminal of Western Airlines & scene of annual Black Hills Airfair (July). **55. SPEARFISH,** quiet college town & home of **Black Hills Passion Play.** When Luenen Passion Play cast was forced to flee from Germany during Hitler regime, this town was selected to carry on centuries-old tradition. The play is presented twice a wk., during the summer in large amphitheatre with 800′ stage. During winter, show goes on tour of major cities. **Black Hills Teachers College,** founded in 1883, features frequent art shows & summer clinics for athletic coaches. **U.S. Fish Hatchery** on Spearfish Cr. produces 2 million trout each yr. for Black Hills streams. Here is J. with Spearfish Canyon Hy., scenic Rd. (S) to US85 near Lead (see US85). At **57.** is J. with US85 (see) & US14 turns (W) to **WYO. LINE, 67.**

## US 16—SOUTH DAKOTA

**S.D.-MINN. LINE** (5m from Beaver Cr., Minn.) **(W) to S.D.-WYO. LINE** (8m from Newcastle, Wyo.). **465. US16**

Via: Sioux Falls, Mitchell, Chamberlain, Kadoka, Rapid City, Custer. Rd.: hard-surfaced. Milwaukee RR. bet. Mitchell & Rapid City. Good accoms.: In larger towns. Lodges & cabins along Rd. in Black Hills.

US16, most heavily-traveled route across S.D., passes through level farming country to Mo. R., then rolling ranching domain into & through southern Black Hills.

### Sec. 1: S.D.-MINN. LINE to RAPID CITY. 381.

**1. Valley Springs. 3.** J. with gravel Rd.

SIDE TRIP: On this Rd. (R) is **Garretson,** 10m. From town (R) is **Devil's Gulch,** a bizarre spot of red & purple rock formations, cedar trees, & deep pools (pic.facils.). In this reg. of palisades & caves, Jesse James is reputed to have had a hideout.

**16. SIOUX FALLS**

Annual events: Pari-mutuel horse races & horse show (July), Sioux Empire Fair (Aug.). Sports: swim. pools at Drake Springs & Terrace Pk.; baseball, Northern League (Class C) at Howard Wood Field; golf, 18-hole courses at Elmwood Pk. & Minnehaha Country Club.

Sioux Falls is largest city in S.D. & important processing center of farm products. Orig. falls in Big Sioux R. have been reduced to rapids by altering for power production. Especially noticeable in city is the wide & varied use made of locally-quarried pink quartzite. City was est. by an act of Minn. Territorial legislature of 1856-57 as rival town site companies manipulated for possession of the falls but combined their efforts against marauding Sioux Inds. Publication of newspaper, "The Democrat," was started in 1859. In 1862, hostile Sioux destroyed the hastily-vacated village, threw press into the river, & carried away the type to decorate themselves & their peace-pipes. Fort Dakota was est. at town site in 1865 & the village took on new life to such a degree that by 1890's it was best known as a divorce colony patronized by wealthy Easterners. An expanding farm market, coupled with revision of divorce laws, turned Sioux Falls into a merchandising, distributing, & processing center. It is also the cultural & medical center for a large territory. During World War II an Air Force technical school that almost doubled pop. greatly accelerated business & entertainment activity.

PTS. OF INT.: (1) Main Ave. & 5th St., **Coliseum** operated by city for rd. shows, athletic events, dances & conventions. (2) Duluth Ave. & 8th St., **Pettigrew Mus.** has excellent coll. of pioneer materials & Sioux Ind. relics. (3) Dakota Ave. & 10th St., **Pub. Lib.** features local & regional colls. (4) Main Ave. & 13th St., **Calvary Cathedral** (Episc.) built with funds donated by John Jacob Astor. A cross embedded in front of altar is made of stones taken from St. Augustine Abbey, oldest ch. in England. (5) Duluth Ave. & 5th St., **St. Joseph Cathedral** (Cath.). (6) Prairie Ave., & 22nd St., **Sioux Falls College,** a Bapt. school. (7) Summit Ave. & 29th St., **Augustana College,** which has a choir that tours the U.S. each yr. (8) Garfield Ave. & 22nd, **Royal C. Johnson Veterans' Hospital,** a 4 million dollar Fed. facility built since World War II. (9) Kiwanis Ave. & 18th St., **Sherman Pk.** has a zoo, pic. area & numerous Ind. burial mounds. (10) Weber Ave. & Rice St., **John Morrell & Co.** employs 4,000 persons in meat-packing plant. (11) E. 6th St., **Manchester Biscuit Co.** began here (1900) as one-man shop.

At **26.** is J. with gravel Rd. leading (L) to **Wall Lake,** 1.5m (pic.facils.swim.f.). **49.** J. at Stanley Corners with US81 (see). **54. BRIDGEWATER,** home of Amer. Legion Colony Band that appears at conventions throughout the country. **62. EMERY. 71. ALEXANDRIA** & J. with gravel Rd.

SIDE TRIP: On this Rd. (L) 2m is **Hanson L.** (recr.facils.) & at 6m **Rockport Mennonite Colony** with grist mill on James R. Members of this religious sect retain Old World customs & dress.

**86. MITCHELL,** market center of a productive agric. reg. specializing in corn, hogs, & watermelons. Townsite selected by the Milwaukee RR. in 1879 was barren prairie, but a settler's wife who brought two hackberry sprigs in her valise started a tree-planting program. Residential areas now have canopy of shade trees & in all directions from city are shelterbelt projects. PTS. OF INT.: Main St. & 6th Ave., is gaily decorated **Corn Palace,** scene of harvest festival staged annually since 1892 during last wk. of Sept. Tons of corn & grains are used each yr. to create large murals & decorative designs. S. Sanborn St., **Dakota Wesleyan Univ.** houses Friends of the Middle Border coll.—orig. works of many regional artists, writers, & musicians. E. Main & Lakeshore Dr., **Lake Mitchell,** a large artificial body along banks of which are a bathing beach, outdoor theatre, golf course, & reconstructed earthen lodges of Arikara Inds.

**99. MOUNT VERNON. 109. J.** with gravel Rd. leading (R) to **S.D. Training School,** 0.5m. At **110.** is **PLANKINTON** & J. with US281 (see) running (N). **122. WHITE LAKE,** named for near-by lake visited by George Catlin in 1832. **129.** J. with US281 (see) leading (S). **148. PUKWANA,** Sioux for "peace pipe smoke." **157. CHAMBERLAIN,** old ferrying pt. on Mo.R., is popular stopping place for tourists, truckers, ranchers & Inds. Here is J. with St.47.

SIDE TRIP: On this Rd. (R) 9m into **Crow Creek Ind. Reserv.** (O.), where about 1,070 Sioux live in cabins, tents, & crude shelters. At 15m is **Crow Creek L.,** artificial body 10m long. **Ft. Thompson,** 25m, on Mo. R. is reserv. hqs. & trading post. Excellent native arts & crafts shop is operated here.

**158. AMERICAN IS.,** pk. & recr. center (cabin accoms.), was site of Ft. Aux Cedras (1809). **162. OACOMA,** Sioux for "place between" because it lies bet. Mo. R. & a range of hills. As Rd. steepens, outcroppings of crude manganese can be seen along hilltops & cut banks. **165. PILOT PLANT** est. by U.S. Bur. of Mines to test deposits for commercial use. **197. PRESHO,** unpretentious trade center for surrounding large-scale wheat farmers & livestock growers. **210.** J. with US83 (see) just (S) of Vivian; US16 & US83 join to **MURDO, 232.,** N. end of famed Tex. Cattle Trl. during 1880's when thousands of longhorns were turned loose to feed on native buffalo grass. Town was named for Murdo McKenzie, pioneer cattle baron. **243. OKATON.** Rd. passes through unfenced grazing land & stray cattle on hy., especially at night, cause frequent accidents. From Rd. (S) are huge ranch "spreads," some covering 30,000-as. **279. KADOKA,** Sioux for "hole in the wall," is a cattlemen's town, S. & W. of which the grassland prairie drops off sharply. Beyond lie White River Badlands. At Kadoka is J. with St.73.

SIDE TRIP: On this Rd. (L) is the rim of the Badlands Wall, 10m. At 12m is **Kodak Pt.,** which overlooks a prehist. sea bottom & part of the present Pine Ridge Ind. Reservation (see US18).

**286.** J. with St.40 (see Badlands Nat. Mon. Hy., Alt. for US16 bet. this J. & Wall). **295.** J. with US14 (US14 & US16 join to Rapid City). **307. COTTONWOOD. 326. WALL,** old cowtown that caters to tourists. Enterprising local merchants & servicemen have placed Wall mileage signs at conspicuous pts. in U.S., Europe, & Pacific area. From Wall (S) is **Badlands Nat. Mon.** (see US16 Alt.). **360. NEW UNDERWOOD. 374.** J. with improved Rd.

SIDE TRIP: On this Rd. (R) 2m is **Rapid City Air Force Base,** one of largest strategic military airfields in U.S. & postwar base for VH (very heavy) Bombardment Wing. Adj. (W) is terminal of Western Airlines.

**381. RAPID CITY,** E. gateway to Black Hills & major city of the reg. During gold rush of 1876, this foothill town sprang up as a central supply pt. for booming mining camps. Dubbed "Hay Camp" by gold seekers, it was laid out with a pocket compass, so that present business sec. is on a bias with true north. Impetus to growth of the town built along banks of Rapid Creek came in 1907, when the rival Milwaukee RR. & the Chi. & N.W. RR. raced to extend their lines across S.D. to the Black Hills. Twenty years later the bustling city became tourist conscious when Pres. Coolidge est. his Summer White House in the local high school & Gutzon Borglum began monumental carvings on near-by Mt. Rushmore. Local industries, reflecting the economic pattern of the reg., produce flour, lumber, cement, gold jewelry & leather goods. In 1948 the city limits were extended toward Canyon L. to take in new subdivisions of fast-growing city which doubled its pop. in 10 yrs. Annual Events: Range Days (mid-July). Sports: trout fish., Rapid Creek; horseback riding, various stables. PTS. OF INT.: E. St. Joe St., **S.D. School of Mines & Technology** has mus. (free) featuring extensive paleontological & mineral exhibits. St. Joe St. & W. Blvd., **U.S. Ind. Mus.** (free) with excellent coll. of Sioux materials. W. Quincy St. & Skyline Dr., **Dinosaur Pk.** has five monster prehist. creatures modeled in cement. W. Canyon L. Dr., **U.S. Ind. Sanitarium.** W. end Canyon L. Dr., **Canyon L. Pk.** (mun. bathh., boats, pic. facils., & huge fish fry).

## Sec. 2: RAPID CITY to S.D.-WYO. LINE. 84.

US16 begins ascent immediately (S) of city & enters Harney Nat. For. at **11.5.** At **12.** J. with dirt Rd.

SIDE TRIP: On this steep, twisting Rd. (R) is **Stratosphere Bowl,** 1m from which record altitude flight of 72,395′ was made. Balloon & gondola carrying Capts. Orvil A. Anderson (now Maj. Gen.) & Albert W. Stevens took off on Armistice Day, 1935, to study stratosphere. Findings formed basis for planning high altitude operations during World War II.

**12.5. ROCKERVILLE,** a ghost town relic that once boasted a lively newspaper. At **18.** is J. with a tarvia Rd. which is a shortcut to US85A (see), (N) of Hill City. **KEYSTONE,** mining village, is at **22.** The **Feldspar Mill** here crushes rock finer than flour for use in making glass & porcelain. Back along the creek lies old town where fabulous Holy Terror Gold Mine which once produced $70,000 a wk. has resumed operations after yrs. of being flooded underground. Here also are **Etta & Ingersol Mines,** leading producers of lithium & beryl, respectively. **23.** Boundary of **CUSTER STATE PK.,** (128,000-as. wildlife sanctuary) in which herds of buffalo, elk, & deer roam. **24.** J. with Mt. Rushmore Mem. Hy.

SIDE TRIP: On this Rd. (R) is **Mt. Rushmore Nat. Mem.,** 2m. Faces of Geo. Washington, Thos. Jefferson, Abr. Lincoln & Theo. Roosevelt have been carved on mt. side by Gutzon Borglum as "America's Shrine of Democracy." Figures are fashioned to men 465′ tall. This world's largest sculpture was begun in 1927 & is unfinished. Behind the faces a **Hall of Records** has been started. A studio, in which scale models can be seen faces the mem.

**24.5.** begins a series of 3 Pigtail Bridges & 3 Tunnels focused on Mt. Rushmore. **27.5.** is **SUMMIT OF IRON MT.** (5,500′), from which is a remarkable view of mts. & prairie. **40. GRACE COOLIDGE CR.,** formerly called Squaw, is a popular trout fishing stream. **42. ZOO** (free) of native animals. **43. GAME LODGE,** state-owned pub. hotel & summer home of Pres. & Mrs. Coolidge in 1927. **43.5. CUSTER STATE PK.** Mus. (free) features int. historical, geological, & botanical exhibits. **49.** J. with Needles Hy.

SIDE TRIP: Along this Rd. (R) is **Center L.** 3m. L. is series of beaver dams. At 8.5m **Balanced Rock** (R). 11m **Skyscraper Rock & Tunnel.** 12m **Views of Cathedral Spires** (R) **& Needles,** core of the Black Hills. 12.5m **Needle's Eye.** 14m **Sylvan L.** with Harney Peak, highest pt. (E) of Rockies (7,242′) looming (R). Here is J. 6m N. of Custer with US85 Alt. (see).

**49.5. LEGION L.** (St.-owned inn & lodge, swim.f.horseback). In Black Hills Playhouse here, Univ. of S.D. dramatists give nightly productions during summer months. **50.** J. with St.87.

SIDE TRIP: Here (L) is **Mt. Coolidge,** 2m. Atop this is tower with commanding view into parts of 3 states. 4.5m **Blue Bell Lodge,** another st.-owned resort, on French Cr. (f.horseback).

**52.5. STOCKADE L.** (swim.camp facils.). **54.5.** stone **MON. TO ANNIE D. TALLENT,** 1st woman in Black Hills with Gordon Expedition in 1874. To (R) is reproduction of **Gordon Stockade. 55. MARKER OF FIRST GOLD CLAIM IN HILLS.** It was along French Cr. here that gold was discovered by prospectors with Gen. Geo. A. Custer's expedition in 1874 which led to gold rush. **57. CUSTER,** oldest town in the Hills, is more than a mile high (5,301'). It was staked out in 1875; a log cabin built by Gen. Crook's soldiers houses a mus. Town was depopulated when gold was discovered in Deadwood Gulch in '76. Early history of the reg. is reenacted in pageant form each yr. during Gold Discovery Days (4th wk. in July). **Amica fabricating plant** started during World War II prepares the isinglass mineral for use in electrical devices. There is also a **Feldspar Mill** & **Rose Quartz Quarry** here. At Custer is J. with US85A (see). Here also is J. with old Hill City Rd. (gravel).

SIDE TRIP: On this Rd. (R) is **Crazy Horse Sioux Mem.,** 5$^{m}$. 30-yr. sculpturing project on Thunderhead Mt. begun in 1948 by Korczak Ziolkowski. One of his works is marble statue of Noah Webster in W. Hartford, Conn.

At **71.** is **JEWEL CAVE NAT. MON.** which has several miles of underground passages lined with crystal formations effectively lighted. **72.** Rd. crosses **HELL'S CANYON,** bugaboo of early Cheyenne Trl. freighters. **84. WYO. LINE.**

## US 16 Alternate—SOUTH DAKOTA

**J. with US16** (W. of Kadoka) **(W) to J. with US16** (at Wall). **49. US16 Alt.**

This route follows St.40 & Badlands Nat. Mon. Hy. Accoms.: At Cedar Pass Lodge.

A scenic route through the most fantastically eroded portion of the 150,000-a. **Badlands Nat. Mon.** This region is best viewed in early morning or evening when shadows add to the eerie beauty, rather than during heat of day. It is especially effective under a full moon. Area was set aside by Pres. F. D. Roosevelt in 1939 & is supervised by Nat. Park Serv. It was described by Gen. Custer as "a part of Hell with the fires burned out."

At **13.** freak formations & jagged peaks loom on either side of Rd. From crest of the wall, Rd. begins a descent through **CEDAR PASS, 16.** Stunted cedar trees & yucca plants point up the soft hues. To the (L) is **Dante's Inferno,** huge natural bowl of chaotic desolation. At **16.5.** is **VAMPIRE PEAK,** capped by two teats. **18. CEDAR PASS LODGE,** spread out on the grassy floor of the Badlands. Here are exhibits of fossils of prehist. creatures & stones peculiar to the region. Bet. lodge & wall are patches of wild flowers, inc. prickly pear cactus with clusters of brilliant blooms & the Mariposa Lily. Rd. turns (R) from lodge & plunges into heart of the Badlands. Layers of delicate purple, white & olive are more pronounced. Some 40 million yrs. ago when the Black Hills were being formed, great Rs. gouged this area. Centuries of erosion left new deposits & carried away others. Bones & teeth of prehist. creatures lie exposed after heavy rains & scientists come here each yr. to explore. **28. BIG FOOT PASS,** through which Chief Big Foot & his band eluded Capt. John J. Pershing during the Messiah War in 1890. At **40. THE PINNACLE POINT** (refresh.). From here, atop the wall, is view again of the bewildering maze of grotesque formations. **49.** J. with US16 (see).

## US 18—SOUTH DAKOTA

**S.D.-IOWA LINE** (6$^{m}$ from Inwood, Iowa) **(W) to S.D.-WYO. LINE** (48$^{m}$ from Lusk, Wyo.). **460. US18**

Via: Canton, Lake Andes, Winner, Hot Springs. Rd. is hard surface ⅔ of way; rest is gravel. No. RR. parallels route. Accoms.: E. of Winner & in Black Hills.

US18 crosses Iowa Line & traverses S. part of St. through farm lands, ranch country, Ind. reservs. & southern Black Hills.

### Sec. 1: S.D.-IOWA LINE to HOT SPRINGS. 420.

At **1.** is J. with gravel Rd. leading (L) here to Sioux Valley Ski Slide, 0.5$^{m}$, scene of ski tournaments. In summer hills are used for motorcycle contests. At **3.** is **CANTON,** founded in 1860. It is setting for Rölvaag's "Giants in the Earth." In 10 yrs., this country was struck with series of disasters: blizzard of 1880, flood of '81, prairie fire in '85, another blizzard in '88. **Augustana Academy,** a Luth. sch., is housed in bldgs. made of Sioux Falls quartzite. **10.** J. with US77 which leads (N) into **Sioux Falls.** US18 & US77 are joined to **15.** Hy. passes through fertile Vermillion R. valley where livestock from range country is brought for fattening before being shipped to market. At **49.** is J. with US81 (see). **57. MENNO,** a village started by Mennonites. At **62.** is **OLIVET,** on listless James R., longest unnavigable R. in U.S.

**77. TRIPP,** with its Russo-German pop. A Cty. Fair climaxes harvest season. **88. DELMONT.** At **114.** hy. follows shore of **L. ANDES.** U.S. Fish & Wildlife Serv. maintains waterfowl refuge here. There is also a **St. Fish Hatchery** near. **116. LAKE ANDES,** trade center of reg. & gathering place for Sioux Inds., who live here (S) along Mo. R. In 1946 town experienced a boom as U.S. engineers moved in to begin work on **FT. RANDALL DAM** project. Here is J. with a gravel Rd.

SIDE TRIP: On this rd. (L) is **Pickstown,** 6m. This construction camp & town was built in 1948 by Fed. Gov. for workers at near-by **Ft. Randall dam.** Town was named for Maj. Gen. Lewis Pick of Burma Road fame & co-author of the Pick-Sloan plan for Mo.R. basin development. Site of old Ft. Randall, built in 1856 to protect emigrants, disappeared in bldg. of dam to provide electricity, irrigation, flood control, & recr.

At **133.** is **WHEELER** & J. with US281 (see). Here is bridge (free) over **Mo. R.,** the history of which is really history of S.D. The R. roughly bisects the St., & its traffic in the 1830's was principal means of trans. At one time as many as 40 steamers plied the R. Quite frequently R. overflowed, leaving destruction in its wake. Beyond the Mo. R. (N) is rolling country, sett. by homeseekers when the Rosebud Ind. Res. was opened. **146. BONESTEEL,** patronized by farmers, ranchers, & Inds. **167. BURKE,** named for Chas. Burke of Pierre, who once served as Commissioner of Ind. Affairs. **175. GREGORY,** a town that has preserved its Western flavor. **179. DALLAS. 189. COLOME** & J. with US183 to Springview, Neb. **200. WINNER,** trade center of the Rosebud Country. Each fall it attracts hundreds of pheasant hunters, particularly sports figures. Town is noted for its hospitality. Founded in 1908, it is important shipping pt. for turkeys, rabbit skins & cattle. The **Outlaw Trading Post,** which covers a block, is known throughout reg. **218. CARTER.** At **219.** the E. boundary of the Rosebud Ind. Reserv. begins. It covers Todd Cty. & has an Ind. pop. of 6,362. Tribal councils & Ind. police have jurisdiction over most affairs. Great part of land is unproductive. Log houses & tents provide most of housing. **227. OKREEK,** a trading post. **Haystack Butte,** habitat for rattlesnakes, is visible (R). At **240.** is **GOV. IND. BOARDING SCH.** for about 200 children. **243. MISSION,** with Luth., Episc., & Cath. schs. & chapels. **At 243.** is J. with US83 (see). At **245.** is J. with a hard-surf. Rd.

SIDE TRIP: On this Rd. (L) is **Rosebud Agency,** (7,221 pop.) 8m. Here are gov. offices & trading posts featuring brightly-colored beads & calico. **Grave of Spotted Tail** is atop hill (R). This chief was distrusted by his followers because of his friendliness with the whites. To decide who should kill him, lots were drawn.

At **274.** is W. boundary of Rosebud Reserv. **305. MARTIN,** the major town of this thinly-settled country. A real Western town, it at times takes on rough & tough character. During 4th of July & Cty. Fair celebrations, Inds. add color to festivities. Here is J. with St.73.

SIDE TRIP: On this Rd. (L) is **La Creek Teal & Migratory Waterfowl Refuge,** 12m.

At **326.** is village of **BATESLAND.** Here hy. enters **PINE RIDGE IND. RESERV.** in which 10,090 Inds. live; 85% use Sioux language. There are 33 separate Ind. communities. Tribal life is best studied in these spots, which are rather difficult to reach. At **332.** (R) is **PORCUPINE BUTTE.** At **345.** is J. with graded Rd.

SIDE TRIP: On this rd. (R) is **Wounded Knee Battle Ground,** 6m. A white church on the hill overlooks site where U.S. soldiers massacred 200 Inds., incl. women & children. On Dec. 29, 1890, last major stand of Inds. vs. whites occurred here. This ended the Messiah War, a craze that had taken hold of the Inds. in their last attempt to rid themselves of white men. They whipped themselves into a frenzy through a "Ghost Dance" & frenzy spread like wildfire. Sitting Bull had just been killed in northern S.D., & Yellow Bird took up the mission. When soldiers were sent to take him into custody & to disarm his followers, he feigned compliance while exhorting his braves to resist. The fire of the Inds. was returned by soldiers & then a Hotchkiss gun turned the affair into carnage. Dead Inds. were left along Wounded Knee Cr. for 2m. Frozen bodies of Inds. were later put into a common grave, indicated by large marker in churchyard.

**355. PINE RIDGE,** agency hqs. Gov. maintains a modern sch. plant designed to develop agric. & keep arts & crafts alive. Home of famous Chief Red Cloud was here. At **370.** is **OGLALA,** with Ind. boarding sch. Hy. passes through wasteland, with clumps of pine trees & frequent creeks along route. At **413.** hy. crosses **CHEYENNE R.** This is part of Augustura dam project, a phase of vast gov. reclamation program. In 1945 work was begun a few miles up the R. to form a reservoir that would hold back the spring watershed. At **414.** hy. enters **FALL R. CANYON** & passes the falls. **420. HOT SPRINGS** (see below).

### Sec. 2: HOT SPRINGS, S.D. to S.D.-WYO. LINE. 40.

**HOT SPRINGS** is health center & S. gateway to **Black Hills.** Inds. had long used hot mineral waters both externally & internally before 1st white settlers arrived in 1879. Within a few yrs., promoters were advertising a cure for rheumatism, & special trains were run from Chicago. As other spas were developed throughout the country, this one dropped into the background & became a peaceful center for hospitals & soldiers' homes. It is a picturesque town. Fall R. winds through center of business dist., with Main St. on one side & steep banks on other. The tepid waters of Fall R. do not vary in temperature & visitors are attracted by huge gold fish that inhabit the R., summer & winter. The **Evans Plunge,** fed by a hot spring that pours 5,000 gals. of water in swim. pool every hr., is open yr. around (fee). Other springs used for both health & recr. are **Hygeia, Mammoth, Minnekahta, & Hot. Battle Mt. Sanitarium,** a huge Vet. Admin. hosp., overlooks town. It is built of native pink sandstone. **St. Soldiers' Home** & 2 hospitals are maintained here, latter being polio centers for a 3-St. area. Quarrying of varicolored sandstone is major local industry, but shipping is problem as RR. lines have been abandoned, due to washout floods. Major annual event is Water Carnival held 2nd wk. in July. Pari-mutuel horse races & St. Beauty Contest are features. Race track has ideal setting with **Saw Tooth Range** for backdrop. Here is J. with US85A (see). US18 & US85A join (W) & pass **Parker Peak** (L) at **11.** At **12.** is hamlet of **MINNEKAHTA** & J. with dirt Rd.

SIDE TRIP: On this Rd. (R) is **Fossil Cycad Nat. Mon.** 1m. This area was set aside by Pres. proclamation in 1922, but has not been developed. It covers deposits of fossilized plants of Mesozoic period. Fossils resemble trunks of tropical trees & fruit similar to pineapple. Specimens are exhibited at Hot Springs C. of C., Sch. of Mines Mus. in Rapid City (see US16), Yale University, & Smithsonian Institution.

**27. EDGEMONT,** small RR. town. A well here produces hot sulphur water at 115° for a sanitarium. Town provides night life for military ammunition depot near-by. Here is J. with gravel Rd.

SIDE TRIP: On this Rd. (L) is **Black Hills Ordnance Depot,** 8m. This huge war-born ammunition storage area has a civilian village & P.O. called Igloo. To enter the area, pass is required.

At **40.** is the **WYO. LINE.**

## US 77—SOUTH DAKOTA

**S.D.-IOWA LINE** (at Sioux City, Iowa) **(N) to J. with US12 at MILBANK, S.D. 211. US77**

Via: Sioux Falls, Brookings, Clear Lake. Rd. hard surfaced. Bus lines follow most of route. Accoms.: In larger towns.

US77 parallels E. border of S.D. through rich, level farmland.

At **0.** hy. crosses Big Sioux R. bridge at outskirts of Sioux City. Here is **Stevens,** village of night spots. **7. JEFFERSON,** dating back to 1859. It retains some of French flavor of its early settlers. **15. ELK POINT.** Hunters with Lewis & Clark Expedition of 1804 shot their 1st deer in this vic. At **27.** is **JUNCTION CITY,** road house. Here is J. with St.50.

SIDE TRIP: On this Rd. (L) 9m to **Vermillion,** on the bluffs of the Vermillion R., trading post as early as 1835. In 1863 it was settled, but destroyed by flood of 1881. To avoid recurrence, present city was built on the bluff. Vermillion is seat of **Univ. of S.D.** It was est. by Territorial Legislature (1862) but no provision for funds was made. Twenty yrs. later $10,000 was provided & work began with 1 faculty member, Dr. Ephraim Epstein, Russian Jew who had become a Bapt. minister. From then until present, Univ. has been great influence & real help to the people of S.D. On S.Dakota St., is **Audubon Pk.** In it is replica of first schoolh. in S.D. On E.Main St. is **Prentiss Pk.** (O.daily,summer;large mun.swim.pool). W. end of Main St. is J. with St.19, leading (R) to **Spirit Mound.** Lewis & Clark stopped here (1804) to discover whether the Sioux story that the hill was inhabited by mysterious small folk who shot arrows at anyone approaching, was true. 10.5m Rd. crosses **Vermillion R.** 17m **Meckling,** home of one of largest consolidated schools in S.D. 23.5m **Gayville Cemetery.** At 31.5m hy. crosses **James R.** Here is **Wildwood** (resort). 35m **Yankton,** 1st capital of S.D. (see US81). At 51m **Tabor,** all-Bohemian settlement in which all business & social transactions are carried on in native language. Particularly int. are the Sokols, their "setting up exercises" & gymnastic competition, as well as weddings at which great quantities of excellent food are consumed. 98m **Wagner,** trading center for Inds. who live on **Yankton Ind. Reserv.** (2,170 pop.). Here is mod. **Gov. Ind. Hosp.** (1937) built with Ind. labor. Surrounding country has many fine Ind. homes & also some int. "squaw coolers" 4 posts with branches & leaves forming the roofs. 108.5m **Ravinia.** At 109.5m Rd. joins US18.

**48. BERESFORD,** busy town named for Brit. Adm., Lord Charles Beresford. **49. BETHESDA HOME,** Luth. welfare institution. **60.** J. with US18 (see) to **65.** At **82.** is **SIOUX FALLS,** largest city in St. & J. with US16 (see). **102. DELL RAPIDS,** picturesque town on Big Sioux R., with a popular pub. pk. along hy. (swim.facils.). At edge of town are the **Dells,** series of purple quartzite gorges featuring Pulpit Rock, used for outdoor religious service. **114.** J. with St.34.

SIDE TRIP: On this paved Rd. (R) is Flandreau, 11m. Here is Fed. **Flandreau Ind. Voc. high sch.** Native arts & crafts exhibit.

**134. MEDARY MON.** which marks site of 1st town in Dakota Territory. It was started in 1857. **141. BROOKINGS,** home of **St. College,** & J. with US14 (see). **176. CLEAR LAKE,** typical country town. The L. has recr. facils. Along hy. are numerous sloughs popular with duck hunters. **186.** J. with US212 to **191. 211. MILBANK,** thriving trade center & entrance to lake reg. (N). Here is J. with US12 (see).

## US 81—SOUTH DAKOTA

**S.D.-NEB. LINE** (16m from Crofton, Neb.) **(N) to S.D.-N.D. LINE** (8m from Fairmount, N.D.). **249. US81**

Via: Yankton, Madison, Watertown, Sisseton. Allweather Rd. Fair accoms.

At **0.** US81 crosses the **NEB. LINE** over Meridian Hy. Bridge (fee for car & passengers). **0.5. YANKTON,** oldest city & capital of Dakota territory. In 1858 1st fur trader pitched his tent here & next yr. site was opened to settlers after an agreement had been reached with Smutty Bear, Sioux Chief, who protested against having his band moved to a reserv. First tavern was opened on Dec. 25, 1859. The **Territorial Council Chamber** has been restored. The "Weekly Dakotan" appeared as early as June 1861. **Yankton College** (Congr.) is oldest institution of higher learning in S.D. Its **Conservatory of Music** ranks high in the Middle West. On attractive campus is an out-door theatre with balcony & arbor. On Capital & 4th Sts., **Carnegie Lib.** with a 900-vol. S.D. coll. At **27.** is J. with US18 (see). **49. STANLEY CORNERS** & J. with US 16. **61. SALEM** in the early 80's was an important RR. center & prosperous town. **91.** J. with graded Rd. leading (R) 1m to **Lake Herman** (popular resort. cabins.f.boat.).

**94. MADISON,** so named because it reminded its founders, in 1875, of the capital of Wis. It is seat of **Eastern St. Normal Sch.** (1881), situated near 2 Ls. (especially fine in summer). Town is built on former Ind. camping ground, refuge of Black Eagle, who fled here after being ostracized by his people for having killed his brother, a favorite of the tribe. (S) of Main St. is J. with St.19 leading (R) to **L. Madison** 2m (popular resort). **101.** J. with graded Rd. leading (L) here 1m to **Lake Badus,** Swiss settlement that lives & works on cooperative principle. **116. ARLINGTON.** Here J. with US14. **125.** J. with graded Rd. running (R) 4m to low & shallow **Tetonkaha L. 129.5. L. ALBERT** visible (L). Hy. skirts **L. POINSETT** at **131.** (pub. resort). Other Ls. are in vic.

**155. WATERTOWN,** on Big Sioux R., in beautiful lake country near L. Kampeska, which is vacation spot for Watertowners, both summer & winter. Duck & pheasant hunting is favorite fall sport. Instead of a long Main St., as most Middle-western towns have, the business area here is concentrated in one sec. Though treeless prairie land when founded in 1873, it now has scores of tree-shaded blocks. Town is industrial & commercial center, principally concerned with processing & distributing of agri. products & farm machinery. Great impetus for settlement in & near Watertown came in 1892 when Sisseton Reserv. was opened for homesteading. Pop. has since increased steadily to an estimated 14,000 (1948). PTS. OF INT.: 5th St. & 5th Ave., NW, **Mellette Home,** residence of 1st territorial Gov. (1889); rambling H. with block towers. On River St., along Gt. N. RR. tracks is **Swift & Co. plant.** 1st St. bet. Maple & Broadway, **Codington Cty. Cth.** (1928, 1st cth. in st. of modern design). On Kampeska Rd. & Lakeshore Dr., **Old State Capitol,** but was never used as such because Pierre became the capital. On Shore Line Dr. (R) from Kampeska Rd., **City Pk.,** 140 as. along L. Kampeska (boat.bath.f.pic.). On Dr. at outlet is **St. Pike Hatchery** (O.daily). **168.** J. with gravel Rd.

SIDE TRIP: On this rd. (R) 6m to **Punished Woman's Lake.** About 2m beyond is effigy of Ind. maiden who spurned the love of 60-yr. old chief Chemoki. Enraged by her resistance, he killed her lover & had her bound to a tree. While berating her, he was struck by lightning. Later his effigy was placed at the feet of the 2 lovers.

**180.** J. with US12 (see). For 2m US81 & US12 are one Rd. **189.5. HURRICANE L. 193.** J. with graded Rd. leading (R) here 2.5m to abandoned **Ind. Church of the Ascension. 198.** J. with gravel Rd.

SIDE TRIP: On this Rd. (R) 4m is **Renville Mon.** Gabriel Renville, chief of Sisseton Tribe from 1862-92, worked continuously for a closed reserv. for his tribe. Renville joined Gen. Sibley's troops during Minn. Massacre & was made chief of scouts in 1864. About 2m beyond is abandoned **Sisseton agency hqs.**

**210. SISSETON. Ind. Reserv. Hqs.** on top of hill E. of Main St. (reserv. O.; boundary not marked). Sisseton & Wahpeton who lived in this vic. were peaceful & welcomed most of the whites, but misunderstandings kept occurring. Friendly Inds. asked whites to dress in Ind. attire to keep from being massacred. After Minnesota Massacre troops from Ft. Snelling marched against Sisseton. These fled, but turned about-face often so they could see how the cannonballs, a new kind of weapon for them, worked. In 1863 Inds., who had fled to Canada, returned & made a treaty with the whites. At present, there are 2,658 Inds. on reserv.; only 775 full blooded. Each family has a tract of 160 as. of land for his own. There is no tribal property. Social life is carried on in their churches, Cath., Episc. & Presb. **Series of mounds** in vic. are burial grounds of the Mound Builders, but their artifacts have been removed. In **High Sch.,** one block E. of lower Main St., a coll. of Ind. relics are on display. A modern hospital was built for the Inds. (1936). One of the recent colorful Ind. characters was Asa Sweetcorn, football player with Jim Thorpe. He was giant sized & wore a 21 collar. Sisseton is at J. with St.10. **239. ROSHOLT,** small town founded as late as 1913. **243.5. TRAVERSE-BOIS DE SIOUX GOV. DAM,** controlling flow of water from **L. Traverse** 3m beyond. Hy. runs along N. end of L. Traverse which is 30m long, & crosses through the last 4.5m of **Sisseton Ind. Reserv.,** to **N.D. LINE** at **249.**

## US 281—SOUTH DAKOTA

**S.D.-NEB. LINE** (at Fairfax, S.D.) **(N) to S.D.-N.D. LINE** (6m from Ellendale, N.D.). **235. US281**

Via: Platte, Redfield, Aberdeen. Rd. in S. half of State, gravel; N., hard-surface. Accoms.: In larger towns.

US281 is a direct N.-S. route through Mo. R. valley being developed in a long-range Fed. reclamation & power program.

**2. FAIRFAX,** a village that has experienced severe dust storms. **6.** J. with US18 (see). The 2 routes are united to **WHEELER J.** at E. end of **MO. R. BRIDGE, 16.** US281 extends (N) to **PLATTE, 33.** This town was sett. by colony of Hollanders. Its Cty. Fair is one of best in St. At **57.** is J. with US16 & the 2 routes are joined to **PLANKINTON** at **76.** Here (N) through rolling country to J. at **99.** with St.34.

SIDE TRIP: On this Rd. (L) is **Wessington Springs,** 5m. Town was founded by group of Free Methodists, who maintain a jr. college here. **Woonsocket** (R) 11m, a neatly-kept town with artificial L. in center.

**123.** J. with US14 through village of **WOLSEY** to J. at **130.** (see US14). Here US281 cont. (N) through stubble country stocked with Chinese ringneck pheasants. **139.**

**BONILLA. 159. REDFIELD,** center of prosperous farming community & pheasant hunting hqs. The **Eastern Star Home of South Dakota** is located in what used to be Redfield College. Artificial L. provides recr. facils. Here is J. with US212 (see). **186.** J. with a gravel Rd.

SIDE TRIP: On this Rd. (R) is **Rondell Pk.** 8m. In this large grove of oak trees & wild grape vines along James R. is **site of Oakwood Trading Post,** est. 1835 by Maj. Jos. R. Brown (pic.facils.).

**201. ABERDEEN,** major city of reg. & J. with US12 (see). **221. BARNARD,** with a large consolidated school & teachers' cottages. **228. FREDERICK.** Town has int. pk. featuring 2 meteorites. Near here was the "protectorate" set up by Waanata, Sioux warrior who fought for Brit. in War of 1812. After winning Capt.'s commission & being presented to King of England, he returned to collect fees from weak tribes in return for his protection. At **235.** US281 crosses **N.D. LINE.**

## US 83—SOUTH DAKOTA

**S.D.-NEB. LINE** (10m from Valentine, Neb.) **(N) to S.D.-N.D. LINE** (6m from Hull, N.D.). **247. US83**

Via: Mission, Pierre, Selby. About half the route is hard surface; rest is gravel. No RR. parallels route. Limited accoms.

US83 bisects St. & traverses sparsely-settled prairie devoid of large towns. Upper half of route roughly parallels Mo. R.

**0.** Rd. enters **ROSEBUD IND. RESERV.,** a vast grazing area & Sioux homeland. **24. MISSION,** Ind. trading post & J. with US18 to **27.** (see US18). At **34.** is **N. BOUNDARY OF ROSEBUD RESERV. 47. WHITE RIVER,** real Western cowtown. **74. MURDO** & J. with US16 with which US83 combines (W) to **96.** (see US16). US83 turns (N) through **VIVIAN** to **96.5.** At **125.** is **FT. PIERRE** (see US14). Here is J. with US14 through **PIERRE,** St. capital, to J. at **145.** Here US83 begins long, straight stretch (N). **159. ONIDA,** center of homestead settlement begun by New Yorkers. At **180.** is J. with US212 (see). At **211.** is a J. with US12 (see). The 2 routes are united through **SELBY** to **218. 232. MOUND CITY,** cty. seat, where 1st term of court was held in a machine shed until a hayloft was provided.

**240. HERREID,** trade center in a strong Russo-German community. At **247.** is **N.D. LINE.**

## US 85—SOUTH DAKOTA

**S.D.-WYO. LINE** (2m from Buckhorn, Wyo.) **(NE) to S.D.-N.D. LINE** (18m from Bowman, N.D.). **164. US85**

Via: Lead, Deadwood, Spearfish, Belle Fourche, Buffalo. Rd. is hard surface in Black Hills; gravel in N. No RR. parallels route. Accoms.: In Black Hills.

US85 passes through part of N. Black Hills & then through vast, desolate prairie broken by ranges of buttes & occasional ranches.

**0.** Hy. enters Black Hills Nat. For. For several miles it crosses the Limestone Country, uninhabited wilderness that comes to life during deer hunting season. Crook's Tower (7,114') dominates the skyline (R). **18. CHEYENNE CROSSING,** where old Cheyenne Trl. crossed Spearfish Cr. Here is J. with Spearfish Canyon Hy.

SIDE TRIP: On this scenic Rd. (L) are numerous pools & rapids for trout fishing. At 5m **Latchstring Inn,** (summer resort & h.lodge). Canyon walls here are 1,000' high. Within easy walking distance is Roughlock Falls, beautiful cascade (pic.facils.). 7.5m **Maurice,** hydroelectric plant of Homestake Mine. At 8.5m is **Bridal Veil Falls** (R), Rim Rock Lodge & Community Hall. Rd. cont. to **Spearfish,** 20m (see US14).

At **21.** Rd. enters **ICE BOX CANYON** with Terry Peak (7,071') (L). **28. LEAD,** a mile-high city built around fabulous **Homestake Mine,** largest gold mine in western hemisphere. When gold-bearing quartz veins were discovered here in 1877, a Calif. syndicate headed by Geo. Hearst bought the mining claim for $77,000. It produced more than $500,000,000 in gold. The company owns or controls all property in town & operates a hospital, recr. center, & gen. store. Much of town is undermined & subject to cave-ins. Lower Main St. has been abandoned, causing town to move up **Gold Run Gulch.** (Tours through the Homestake's surface workings are avail.). Underground shafts go as deep as 5,200′. Unlike most mining towns, Lead has no night life. Winter sports are popular. Indoor ice skating rink is operated in an old cyanide plant. Here is a 4-mile ski run with tow facils. Town's maj. annual event is Labor Day celebration. At **29.5.** is **PLUMA** & J. with US85A (see).

**31. DEADWOOD,** historic mining town & playground. It was here that Calamity Jane, Wild Bill Hickok, & other frontier characters cavorted. Deadwood Gulch was center of gold rush of '76. Within a few wks. after John Pearson struck pay dirt, the gulch swarmed with 25,000 gold-seekers & adventurers. Boom lasted several yrs. until most of the gold was exhausted. For 70 yrs. Deadwood clung to its reputation of being "wide open." Since World War II, however, games of chance have been outlawed & only bars & brothels remain. "The Days of '76" are reenacted in a three-day celebration 1st wk. of Aug. each yr., incl. dramatic portrayal of the Trial of Jack McCall. PTS. OF INT.: Sherman & Deadwood Sts., **Adams Mem. Mus.** (free) houses excellent coll. of pioneer mining devices & mementoes. 620 Main St., the **No. 10 Saloon,** where Wild Bill was shot in the back while holding a poker hand of aces & eights, since known as "dead man's hand." Van Buren Ave. & White Rocks Rd., **Mt. Moriah Cemetery** where graves of Wild Bill, Calamity Jane, Seth Bullock & others are marked. Shine St., up Mt. Rd., **Roosevelt Mon.,** a tower dedicated to Theo. Roosevelt, whose Rough Riders were recruited here.

At **32.** is J. with US16. US85 & US16 are joined through Spearfish to J. at **48.** (see US16). US85 runs (N) through Spearfish Valley irrigated area of orchards & truck gardens. Roadside markets along route. **60. BELLE FOURCHE,** trade center of far-flung cattle & sheep empire extending into Wyo. & Mont. Here 10-gal. hats are the genuine thing. Stockyards & wool markets are primary shipping centers. A 75,000-a. irrigation project surrounding town produces sugar beets for **Black Hills Sugar Plant.** Bentonite, gelatin-like mineral, is mined here for shipment E. for use in steel foundries. There is also a brick plant. Black Hills Round-Up, annual rodeo, is always held July 3, 4, & 5. Summer event designed for vacationers is an 8-day horseback & chuckwagon round trip through the Bear Lodge Mts. US85 passes (N) through broad area known as The Gumbo. The soil sticks like gum when wet. Herds of cattle & bands of sheep & a few herders' wagons are likely to be only signs of life. **107. REDIG,** lonely p.o. **134. BUFFALO,** a typical prairie town 50m from nearest RR. Town was born during homestead days & has changed little since. At Buffalo is J. with St.8.

SIDE TRIP: On this Rd. (R) are **Slim Buttes** & **Custer Nat. For.,** 23m. Unusual & picturesque range of pine-crested limestone cliffs. Site of stalemate Battle of Slim Buttes fought in 1876 bet. troops of Gen. Crook & Crazy Horse's band. Area abounds with antelope.

US85 passes through fringe of the **Cave Hills** & parallels another portion of **Custer Nat. For.** (L) to **N.D. LINE, 164.**

## US 85 Alternate—SOUTH DAKOTA

**S.D.-WYO. LINE** (2m from Mule Creek, Wyo.) **(NE) to J. with US85 near Deadwood, S.D.). 116. US85 Alt.**

Via: Edgemont, Hot Springs, Wind Cave Nat. Pk., Hill City. Rd. is hard surface. C. B. & Q. RR. roughly parallels route from Edgemont to Deadwood. Accoms.: good in towns & lodges along Rd.

US85 Alt. is scenic route that cuts through heart of Black Hills. From **0.** at S.D.-Wyo. Line route is same as US18 to **HOT SPRINGS, 40.** (see US18). Here Rd. turns (N). **46.** High fence & gate of **WIND CAVE NAT. PK.** game preserve (no adm.). Herds of buffalo, elk, deer, & antelope roam at large. Buffalo often stop traffic on hy. **53.** Hqs. bldg. & cave entrance (tours every hr.). **Wind Cave** is a limestone cavern. Elevator takes visitors to floor of cave & from there several miles of lighted routes pass through galleries of fantastic formations. Temperature is a constant 47 degrees yr. around. US85 Alt. cont. (N) through buffalo pasture. Along Rd. are prairie dog towns where animals perch beside their holes. **55.** N. boundary of pk. Here hy. enters **Harney Nat. For. 60. PRINGLE,** bldgs. of which have provided artists with material to illustrate western stories. **67. SANATOR,** a St. sanitarium for treatment of tuberculosis. Altitude here is 5,340′. At **72. CUSTER** & J. with US16 (see). From Custer, Rd. begins gradual ascent into Harney Range. **79. SYLVAN LAKE HOTEL,** luxurious St.-owned lodge overlooking mountain L. The large, rambling bldg. blends with landscape of pine & granite atop a cliff (6,300′) facing Harvey Peak. On walls of dining room are Ind. murals painted by Erika Lohmann of New York. A flagstone terrace affords delightful view. Here is J. with Needles Hy., scenic Rd. to US16 (see). There are several hiking & horseback trls. from the L. & hotel. Most popular is 3-mile climb to summit of **Harvey Peak,** highest pt. E. of Rockies (7,242′). From ranger station is view of mt. reg. & frequently mt. sheep can be seen scrambling on near-by crags. US85 Alt. descends in series of hairpin turns to **HILL CITY, 87.** This town was developed by Eng. firms interested in mining tin; gold & tungsten are the main minerals mined here now. Sawmills provide much of locality's industry. Hy. follows Spring Cr. which has trout pools & fast water. **81.** J. with For. Serv. Rd., which is a cut-off to US16 & Rapid City (see US16). At **84. SHERIDAN L.,** also called L. of the Pines (recr.facils.). It is largest L. in the mt. region & is stocked with fish. Speedboat races are held here during summer. Beneath waters of this artificial lake lies hist. town of **Sheridan.** Old town was stage station on Denver-Deadwood line & the 1st term of Fed. Court W. of Mo. R. was held here in 1878. At **86.** is boundary bet. Harvey & Black Hills Nat. Fors. **90. PACTOLA,** recr. center. Here is J. with graded Rd.

SIDE TRIP: On this Rd. (L) is **Silver City,** 4m, old ghost town where a $300,000 offer for a silver mine was turned down because owners were unfamiliar with large figures. Surrounding area is called Unknown Land because it is so inaccessible. At 5m is **Camp Wanzer,** summer camp for children.

**96.** J. with a gravel Rd.

SIDE TRIP: On this Rd. (L) is **Rochford,** 12m, one of most picturesque villages in Black Hills, having changed little from gold rush days. It is an excellent f. & h. area (camp.facils.).

**108.** J. with gravel Rd. leading (R) to **Roubaix,** 2m, a ghost town that was revived briefly when the price of gold doubled in 1934. **109. TOMAHAWK GOLF COURSE,** tricky 9-hole layout built around a mt. At **112.** the hy. begins steep descent down **Strawberry Gulch** to J. with US85 at **PLUMA, 116.**

# THE SOUTH

## VIRGINIA — NORTH CAROLINA SOUTH CAROLINA — GEORGIA — FLORIDA ALABAMA — MISSISSIPPI — LOUISIANA KENTUCKY — TENNESSEE — ARKANSAS

The boundaries of the eleven states here considered are not to be taken too literally as the exact boundaries of what has come to be known as the South. Maryland & Delaware have much that is southern, just as Birmingham & Atlanta have much that is not "typical south." The Ozark section of Arkansas & some of the mountain regions of Kentucky & Tennessee, it might be argued, belong to another category. Texas is not here included, although it was a "rebel" state, & Miami, Florida is about as southern as the Bronx.

Also, it should be pointed out, there are many Souths: the eastern seaboard region—Virginia, North Carolina, South Carolina, & Georgia—settled by the English & part of the original thirteen colonies; Florida, settled by the Spanish, & now boasting a large floating population of tourists from all parts of the United States; the Gulf Coast region of Alabama & Mississippi & all the Louisiana territory, settled by the French & sold to the United States by Napoleon. And, from another point of view, there is the South of the large plantation owner, who once worked slaves & now employs sharecroppers, the South of the small independent farmer, whose ancestors were not slave-holding, & the South of the poor white & the Negro.

The states included in this region are bordered on the east by the Atlantic Ocean, on the south by the Gulf of Mexico. All of them lie east of the Mississippi River with the exception of Arkansas & Louisiana. The broad Atlantic Plain extends along the border of the states from Virginia south, including all of Florida, & its continuation, the Gulf Coastal Plain, extends through much of Alabama, Mississippi, & Louisiana & part of Arkansas. Beyond the plain, running southwest, from above Virginia into Alabama, is the Piedmont Plateau, part of the Appalachian Highlands & beyond the plateau, the mountains proper, including the Great Smokies, the Blue Ridge, the Cumberland, & the Black, reaching their highest point in eastern United States at Mt. Mitchell, N.C. In Kentucky & Tennessee are interior plains centering around Lexington & Nashville, & in northwest Arkansas are the Ozark Mountains. In western Kentucky & western Tennessee, eastern Arkansas, Mississippi & Louisiana is the Mississippi Alluvial Plain, drained by the Mississippi River & its branches, one of the great river systems of the world, with a drainage area of one & a quarter million square miles (about 5/12 of the United States). The Mississippi enters the Gulf of Mexico, some 100 miles south of New Orleans.

The total area covered is approximately 525,290 square miles & here live some 28,261,000 people. Yet, in spite of great diversity, these states have so much in common that they constitute perhaps the most homogeneous section of the United States:

(1) In the South, much more than any other region in the country, the white population is native born & primarily of English-Scotch-Irish stock. There are, to be sure, foreign-born groups in the seaports, Florida has Spanish cigar-makers & Greek sponge divers, & South Louisiana is Roman Catholic & French (though most of the French are of native-born parents). But the percentage of population with American born parents is as high as 98.7% (Arkansas) & it is 90% or more in all the states except Florida & Louisiana.

(2) This Ango-Saxon stock is also principally Protestant (mostly Baptist & Methodist) & sometimes militantly so. The cotton belt & the Bible belt are fre-

quently identical. At Dayton, Tennessee, in 1925, occurred the famous Scopes or "Monkey" Trial & Tennessee passed a law (still on the statute books) making it illegal to teach the theory of evolution in state schools. Mississippi & Arkansas followed suit. The South, though it consumes a great amount of alcoholic beverages, is also a stronghold of the W.C.T.U.

(3) In the South are concentrated between nine & ten millions of the country's thirteen million Negroes, constituting the United States' greatest minority group & one of its most pressing problems. Although intermarriage is illegal in all southern (& some northern) states, about six million of the thirteen million are mulattoes.

Early explorers took Indians as slaves but the first Negroes were brought by a Dutch ship to Virginia in 1619. And, although much of the early labor on the plantations was done by white indentured servants, by 1790 Virginia alone had some 200,000 slaves. There is ample evidence that many owners were kind to their slaves, but there is also ample evidence of great cruelty. Most advertisements for runaways indicated that the slave had been branded or otherwise physically marked; pregnant slaves who had annoyed their masters were made to lie down over a shallow hole so they could be lashed without injury to unborn property; & a dinner guest in South Carolina passed, on his way to the plantation house of his host, a slave suspended in a cage for buzzards to pick at. The Quakers early attacked slavery, the northern states freed their slaves in 1777, & importation became illegal in 1808, though an estimated 2,000,000 were imported illegally. Eventually a strong abolitionist movement (that included colonization in Liberia) grew up even in the South, though the latter was completely dependent on slaves to work the cotton plantations that constituted the basis of its economy. In 1831, Virginia failed to pass by one vote only, a bill encouraging private freeing of slaves.

When slavery was abolished in 1863, there were some 4,400,000 Negroes in the United States of whom an estimated 95% were illiterate. In 1930 the percentage of illiteracy was decreased to an estimated 16.3% & there has been considerable progress since in various directions, in spite of Jim Crow laws, revivals of Ku Klux Klan terrorism, control of the franchise by poll tax, etc. Yet, although the thumbs of lynched Negroes are no longer exhibited in butcher shops, as they were not too many years ago, the southern bloc in Congress has consistently (on the basis of state rights) prevented the passage of an anti-lynching bill. Among the most encouraging signs of better race relations in the South may be listed the work of the Southern Conference for Human Welfare in Nashville & the Southern Regional Council in Atlanta.

(4) The South alone among the United States has suffered a devastating war on its own ground within the memory of men still living & it has still to recover from an even more devastating peace. The basic cause of the Civil War (which the South calls the War between the States & whose official name is the War of the Rebellion) was the sectionalism that developed from two essentially different economic & social orders—the free, industrial & commercial North & the agricultural South with its large plantations & its slaves. Tariff questions & the doctrine of state rights were contributing factors.

There is no space here to describe the desolation wrought by the war. The destruction of Atlanta has been compared to the destruction of Warsaw & Sherman's terrible march to the sea, which brought the war home to the civilians, is well known. The Reconstruction that followed was a period of almost unparalleled corruption & misrule. The franchise was given to newly freed & completely untrained Negroes & taken away from those who served in the Confederate Army. "Carpetbaggers" from the North (so called because of the kind of bag in which they carried their belongings when they arrived in the South) & "Scalawags" (Southerners who aided them) shamelessly manipulated Negro votes, the Freedmen's Bureau degenerated into a Republican political machine & legislatures composed of Negroes & carpetbaggers helped complete the economic & social ruin of the South. Eventually vigilante committees, which were to become known as the Ku Klux Klan, restored white supremacy, made true citizenship for the Negro even more difficult, & created the Solid Democratic South.

(5) The South is, to a very great extent, rural. Approximately 43% of the farmers in America live in 10 of these 11 states. The lowest proportion of city

dwellers in the United States is in Mississippi, with Arkansas & South Carolina not far behind. The main crop for more than a century has been cotton, of which the South raises 40% of the world's supply. Much of the farming is done by tenant farmers (those who own tools & perhaps some livestock but no land) & sharecroppers (who have only their labor to sell). Both work on shares, however, usually paying the landowner ⅓ to ½ of the crop. Tobacco is the second crop in cash value. Corn, peanuts, sugar cane, rice, & citrus fruits are all important. But more & more the tendency has been toward diversification & away from one-crop economy, & the raising of livestock is becoming increasingly profitable in many sections. All this is to the good. For it has been estimated that the mechanical cotton picker alone will displace 1,000,000 families in the next ten years.

In the last decade the manufacture of paper from the rapidly growing slash pine has become of considerable importance. And the South has a surprising amount of other industry, though it suffers from absentee ownership & discriminatory freight rates.

(6) The South is the poorest section of the United States & has the lowest general standard of living. It is at the bottom of the list in public education, public health & housing. In 1942 it was estimated that some 11 million Southerners had annual cash incomes of $250 or below. The chief reasons for this poverty in so potentially rich an area are: the Civil War & the Reconstruction that followed, the impoverishment of the soil (through erosion, the careless cutting down of forests, & the one crop system), a large population (both white & black) unskilled in any trade other than farming, & the continuance of segregation that produces the necessity of two schools, two hospitals, two insane asylums where one might have sufficed. To these, perhaps, should be added a climate frequently conducive to lethargy rather than to activity.

Virginia, the northernmost of the southern states bordering the Atlantic, is made up of a tidewater section in the east, the Dismal Swamp in the southeast, a Piedmont Plateau region to the west & then the forested hills & valleys of the Blue Ridge. Named for Elizabeth, the Virgin Queen, it was here that the first permanent English settlement in North America was made at Jamestown (1607). Here, too, the first representative assembly in the English colonies met (1619) & the first Negro slaves were sold. Virginia was the scene of much fighting during the Revolution, & in the framing of the Constitution, played a leading rôle. More presidents (8) have come from Virginia than any other single state. It was the chief battleground of the Civil War, its capital, Richmond, became the capital of the Confederacy, & it was at Appomatox that Lee surrendered. John Rolfe, who later married Pocahontas, introduced the cultivation of tobacco (thereby becoming the savior of the colonists) & tobacco today is one of Virginia's chief sources of income. Richmond is the biggest cigarette manufacturing center in the world. Diversified agriculture (especially apples), fisheries & the shipbuilding & naval yards at Norfolk & Hampton Roads are also important, as is textile manufacturing (rayon & cotton). Immensely proud of its aristocratic tradition & comparatively wealthy, Virginia is also immensely conservative. It has not had a lynching (1949) in 20 years, but it has still not abolished the chain gang. It has enacted restrictive labor laws including anti-picketing & anti-closed shop statutes. It has such distinguished colleges as William & Mary, the University of Virginia (1693) & Hampton Institute, one of the leading Negro schools in the country. But the school system ranks forty-third among the states & its one-room school houses are as bad as any in the United States.

North Carolina lies south of Virginia & into its northeast corner extends the Great Dismal Swamp. Its shoreline is much broken by lagoons & lakes & the land rises in the west to the Great Smoky Mts. & the Black Mts., in the latter of which is the highest point (Mt. Mitchell) in eastern United States. As early as 1584 explorers, commissioned by Sir Walter Raleigh, landed at Roanoke Island, where in 1587 a small colony was set up. Here Virginia Dare was born, first child to be born of English parentage in America. But by 1591 the colony had mysteriously disappeared & later settlement was not made until 1656. The frontiersmen were early in conflict with their governors & North Carolina was the first to direct her representatives to vote for complete separation from England. There was a strong feeling in the state against the importation of slaves & North Carolina opposed secession until Lincoln's call for troops. Its casualties in the war were, however, greater than that of any other state. Since the 80's, with the aid of cheap labor (in average annual wage per wage earner in all manufactures, North Carolina, South Carolina & Georgia are the three lowest states) & water power, its industrial development has been more rapid than that of the rest of the South. There have been many labor troubles, however, notably the Gastonia strike of 1929. Today tobacco & cotton are among the chief sources of income. North Carolina is first in value of manufactured tobacco (notably the Duke interests) & cotton goods, & second in rayon. Furniture manufacturing & fisheries are of considerable importance & the state is a chief source of felspar & mica. North Carolina has become probably the most liberal state in the South. The State University at Chapel Hill is one of the best in the United States & near-by is the new & very rich Duke University. North Carolina is the only southern state where Negro schools are comparable to white & where Negro & white teachers receive the same pay.

South Carolina is almost evenly divided in geography & temperament between the "low" country of the coast with its beach resorts & historic plantations & the "up" country of the western part of the state with its mill towns. It was explored by the Spanish in the 1520's & the French Huguenots established a settlement at Port Royal in 1562, later destroyed by the Spanish. Charles II granted land that included both North & South Carolina to a group of his favorites, & in South Carolina the Lords Proprietors attempted to establish a feudal system with a constitution drawn up by John Locke. In spite of difficulties with the French, Spanish, Indians & pirates, Charleston was found by the traveler Crèvecoeur, just before the Revolution, to be one of the most sophisticated cities in the country, exhibiting "a display of riches & luxury far superior to what are to be seen in our northern towns." At Fort Moultrie the first victory of the Revolution was won & in that year (1776) South Carolina adopted the first independent constitution in the colonies. In the 19th century its wealth & the influence of its statesmen, especially Calhoun, made it the leading slave state. It became the first to secede & the firing on Fort Sumter was the first engagement of the Civil War. South Carolina was in the line of Sherman's march; the capital, Columbia, was partially fired. The state remained under the rule of carpetbaggers & Negroes until 1874, while the public debt was multiplied by three & taxes by six. With an early economy based first on naval stores, then indigo, & then rice, South Carolina became a cotton state in the early 19th century; cotton remains its chief crop & textiles its chief industry. Tobacco, fruit & vegetables, lumbering, & fishing are also important. But South Carolina remains one of the poorest of the states & one of the most stubborn. It has been called the white supremacy state, par excellence, though it is also the only state in which Negroes have attempted to form their own party (1944).

Georgia, separated from South Carolina by the Savannah River, has a sea coast that extends about a hundred miles & is edged by low sea islands. In the southeast is the 600 square-mile Okefenokee Swamp. From the coast the land rises to a plateau region broken by outcroppings such as Stone Mt., said to be largest exposed granite body in the world, to the impressive ridges & valleys with which the Appalachians come to an end. De Soto was through this region (1540), as was the French explorer Ribaut, & Spanish Franciscans established missions in 1566. But Georgia remained the last of the thirteen original colonies to be settled by the English. In 1732 a land grant, named in honor of George II, was made to a group seeking to find a haven for English debtors & European Protestants. The first colonists, headed by James Oglethorpe, arrived the following year. Among other restrictions, slaves & the sale of rum were not allowed. Georgia signed the Declaration of Independence, though it had less cause for grievance than the other States & Savannah was taken by the British during the Revolution. Later there was much trouble with the Creeks & the Cherokees until both tribes were expelled to the West in the 30's. During the Civil War, Georgia was the scene of much destructive fighting & on September 1, 1863, Sherman took Atlanta & began his devastating march to the sea, laying waste town after town. Today cotton remains the leading crop & textiles the leading industry. Peanuts & lumber are next in importance. Georgia has the largest timber acreage east of the Mississippi, & is second only to California in peach production. It also has a wide variety of clays & its mineral deposits include gold which is still mined on a small scale. Its capital, Atlanta, a financial & industrial center, comes, perhaps, closer to being the capital of the South, than any other city, though it has many characteristics that are more middlewest than southern. A leading industry is Coca-Cola. Atlanta has the only Negro daily in the country, but it was in Georgia that the new Ku Klux Klan movement, which has become nationwide, originated in 1915.

Florida, the southernmost of the states, is a peninsula with a coastline of 3,751 miles separating the Atlantic from the Gulf of Mexico. Key West, at the end of a series of keys or small limestone & coral islands, now connected by an overseas highway, is only 100 miles from Cuba & is the only town in the country that has never had a frost. The Atlantic Coast of Florida is fringed with long, narrow, barrier beaches & such world-famous resorts as Miami & Palm Beach. The coast bordering the gulf is indented by bays. Inland the highest points seldom rise above 300 feet & the estimated number of lakes is 30,000, including Lake Okeechobee (733 square miles). South of the lake are the Everglades, an immense sub-tropical swamp area of some 5,000 square miles where live Seminole Indians who have still to make formal treaty with the United States. Parts of the Everglades have been drained for farming & part is now a national park. Ponce de Leon, in search of gold & the Fountain of Youth discovered Florida in 1513 & was followed by other Spanish explorers & by the French. The colonists of the latter were massacred "not as Frenchmen but as Lutherans" by Menéndez de Avilés who established a fort, 1565, at St. Augustine, which thus became the first permanent white settlement in the United States. Florida remained in the hands of the Spanish until 1762, when England took over, but was reconquered by Galvez in 1783. Andrew Jackson twice invaded the region during the war of 1812 & in 1820 Spain sold Florida to the United States. Then followed the expensive war with the Seminoles. In 1845 Florida became the 27th state. During the Civil War, Tallahassee was the only southern capital not taken by the Federals. Florida's great growth started in the 80's through two rival railroad builders, Henry M. Flagler & Henry B. Plant & the state experienced a tremendous boom & an equally tremendous crash in the 1920's. Its principal sources of income today are citrus fruits, cattle, naval stores, fisheries, & tourists. Florida presents an interesting example of the deep South with a tremendous overlay of people from the East & Middle West. "In winter," says the Florida cracker, "we live on tourists; in summer on fish."

Alabama lies north of the western arm of Florida & only a small portion of it, in the vicinity of Mobile, its only port, touches the Gulf. The southern half of the state lies in the coastal plain, the northern part in the foothills of the Appalachians. Alabama has more miles of navigable rivers—including the Tennessee, the Tombigbee, the Alabama, & the Chattahoochee—than other Southern states. The Spanish were through this region first—Narváez, Cabeza de Vaca, & De Soto—& Trista de Luna made the first unsuccessful attempt at colonization (1559). A hundred years later the region was being claimed by the English but the French made the first permanent settlement at Dauphine Island in 1702, later moving up the Mobile River & in 1711 establishing a fort on the present site of Mobile. French, English & Spanish fought over the region. The English held Mobile during the revolution. The Spanish next seized it & held on until 1813 when the United States sent General Wilkinson to take over. Alabama became a state in 1819 & Montgomery was the first capital of the Confederacy. Here on February 18, 1861, Jefferson Davis was inaugurated President. After the war the Republican Party was in control until 1874 & bankrupted the state. Cotton, iron, & steel are the leading sources of income, though there are also cement & clay products, diversified farming, lumber, & fishing. The region around Birmingham, the leading iron & steel center of the South, is one of the few places in the world where the three essentials necessary in the production of steel—iron, coal & limestone are found in close proximity. But Birmingham steel workers average about 17 cents an hour less than northern workers & the state ranks 48th in retail sales & school property value per pupil. Alabama ranks high as a textile producing state. The most important development in the last decades in Alabama has been the Muscle Shoals development on the Tennessee River. The state is the home of Tuskegee Institute of which Booker T. Washington was the first principal & one of whose teachers was George Washington Carver.

Mississippi, lying west of Alabama, has as its own western boundary the Mississippi River & much of the state lies in the Mississippi flood plain. In the northeast are the Tennessee Hills & in the far south the lowlands of the coast, separated from the Gulf by long, narrow sand bars. De Soto is said to lie buried in the river near Natchez & in 1682 La Salle passed this way on his journey to the mouth of the Mississippi. The first permanent colony was established in 1699 at Ocean Springs (Old Biloxi) by Iberville. But it was only after 1763, when the region was ceded to England, that colonists (chiefly from the Carolinas, Virginia & Georgia) began to arrive in any number. The invention of the cotton gin (1793) & the improvement of the Natchez Trace brought more & more colonists through Alabama, Mississippi & Louisiana. Times were becoming prosperous & soon a Natchez planter was writing: "For a young man just commencing in life, the best stock in which he can invest is, I think, Negro stock. When cotton can command twenty to thirty cents per pound, Negroes will yield a much larger income than any bank dividend." Even after the Louisiana Purchase the Spanish held parts of what is now Mississippi on & off until 1813 when the United States finally took over. Mississippi became a state in 1817. Led by Jefferson Davis, who spent his childhood here, it took an active part in the events leading up to the Civil War & was the scene of important & devastating engagements. "When Vicksburg fell," said Grant, "the fate of the Confederacy was sealed." Reconstruction was particularly bitter in Mississippi & there were violent collisions through 1875.

The state has suffered several severe floods, the worst, in spite of expensive levees, occurring in 1927. Since then spillways & other methods of control have been adopted. The United States Waterways Experiment Station is located at Vicksburg. One half of the annual crop in Mississippi is cotton & Mississippi ranks as one of the chief lumber producing states. Other crops include tung oil & peanuts. Ninety percent of the population is rural & forty-nine percent, Negro. Mississippi has the worst statistics of any state in the U.S., being highest in illiteracy (& lynchings) & lowest in public health & per capita income.

Louisiana, bounded on the north by Arkansas & on the south by the Gulf of Mexico, is separated from Texas by the Sabine River & from Mississippi by the Mississippi River, the last 300 miles of which lie wholly within Louisiana. There are hills near the Arkansas border, but most of the state is low level land comprising the flood plains of the Mississippi, the Ouachita & the Red rivers. Swamps & marshlands border the coast & there are many lakes & sluggish streams known as bayous. Narváez & De Soto both crossed the Mississippi. La Salle in 1682 descended to its mouth claiming all the lands drained by it from Canada to the Gulf for Louis XIV & naming the entire region Louisiana. Jean Baptiste le Moyne, Sieur de Bienville (brother of d'Iberville who founded the first "capital" of Louisiana near Biloxi, Mississippi), founded New Orleans in 1718. In 1762 all of the Louisiana territory west of the Mississippi & "the island of New Orleans" was ceded to Spain. The present descendants of these original French & Spanish settlers constitute the oldest aristocracy of the state & are called "Creoles." The word does not in Louisiana indicate mixed blood, as it does in some other places, though there are Creole Negroes (i.e. usually mulatto descendants of slaves of French-speaking families). Many of the French Acadians expelled from Nova Scotia also settled in south Louisiana. Their descendants are popularly called Cajuns & there are "parishes" (the local word for county) in Louisiana today where French is still heard more often than English. In 1800-01 Spain ceded the Louisiana Territory back to France & in 1803 Napoleon sold it to the United States for 80,000,000 francs. Out of the territory were carved all or part of thirteen states, from Arkansas to Montana, & the Territory of Orleans became the State of Louisiana in 1812. In the War of 1812, Andrew Jackson defeated the British in the Battle of New Orleans. Farragut took New Orleans during the Civil War & after the fall of Vicksburg much of the state came under control of the Federals. Louisiana, today, is about evenly divided between a Protestant North, which raises cotton (the state's most valuable crop) & a Catholic South which produces sugar cane & rice, in both of which Louisiana leads the nation. It also has valuable salt, sulphur, & oil deposits. New Orleans, the South's largest city, is also the third ranking seaport in the United States, & has been noted for more than a century for its gaiety, its Mardi Gras—the most spectacular festival in the United States—& for the excellence of its food.

Arkansas is separated by the Mississippi River, which forms its eastern boundary, from Tennessee & Mississippi & on the south borders Louisiana. The eastern & southeastern parts of the state lie in the alluvial plains of the Mississippi & the Ouachita rivers, the land rising to the scenic Ozark highlands in the northwest. Bisecting the state & flowing southeast to the Mississippi is the Arkansas River whose valley separates the Boston Mountains of the Ozarks from the higher but less rugged Ouachita Mountains. The Spanish De Soto & the French Marquette & Joliet explored the region & De Tonti established in 1686 what became the Arkansas Post, first permanent white settlement in the lower Mississippi Valley. After the Louisiana Purchase, Arkansas became part of the Missouri Territory & in 1836 a state of the Union. A state convention first decided not to secede but changed its mind after Lincoln's call for troops. Several battles were fought on Arkansas soil & the capital, Little Rock, fell September 10, 1863. Today more than eighty percent of its population is rural & cotton & cottonseed account for more than half of the state's agricultural income. Petroleum & lumber & natural gas are also of importance. Arkansas ranks first in the production of bauxite & has titanium deposits containing both thorium & uranium, which may become of increasing importance in atomic energy development. Its mineral springs are famous, especially in Hot Springs National Park, it has the only diamond mines in the United States & at Hope raises the largest watermelons in the world. But Arkansas is one of the poorest states in the Union & near the bottom statistically in other categories. Some of its backwoods areas are unusually inaccessible & primitive.

Kentucky, the first state to be organized west of the Appalachian Mountains, is bounded on the east by Virginia, on the north by the Ohio River, on the west by the Mississippi & on the south by Tennessee. It divides into three principal sections: the scenic mountains of the east, the limestone region of the southwest, with its many holes & caverns, the most famous of which is Mammoth Cave, & the bluegrass region centering about Lexington, where in May the blue anthers of its blossoms give the grass a steel-blue tint. La Salle was probably the first white man to reach this area & explorers from Virginia, of which Kentucky was originally considered a part, were through here as early as 1671. But it was not until 1750 that Dr. Thomas Walker came through the Cumberland Gap & built the first cabin. Daniel Boone arrived in the 60's & in 1775 the first permanent settlements were made at Boonesboro & Harrodsburg. During the Revolution the frontiersmen were much harassed by Indians inspired, & frequently led, by the British. For a while, distrustful of the Federal Government, Kentucky considered becoming an independent nation & making an alliance with Spain. But in 1790 it was admitted into the Union. In the Battle of New Orleans one fourth of Jackson's men were Kentucky "dirty shirts," as the red-coated British called them. Henry Clay was the political leader of the state in the 40's & Kentucky was the birthplace of both Abraham Lincoln & Jefferson Davis. The state did not formally secede through its regularly elected governing body & its citizens fought bravely on both sides. This division on political issues has marked the state throughout its history. "If Jesus Christ were running for sheriff," said a recent political candidate, "he'd get opposition in Kentucky." Civil War was almost precipitated in the state in 1900 when two men claimed to have been elected governor, & again in 1906 when there were difficulties between tobacco buyers & producers. Today at Fort Knox a large part of the gold reserve of the United States is stored. Except for Louisville (which next to New Orleans is the strongest Catholic town in the South), Kentucky has no large industrial center. It is the second state in tobacco production & the fourth in coal. It manufactures 40% of the whiskey made in the United States & is world famous for its thoroughbred horses. The Kentucky Derby is one of the most popular sporting events in America. Kentucky is second only to Mississippi in the number of illiterates & the forty-sixth state in death rate from tuberculosis.

Tennessee is a long narrow state stretching westward 432 miles from North Carolina to the Mississippi River. It is bordered on the north by Virginia & Kentucky & on the south by Georgia, Alabama, & Mississippi. In east Tennessee are the Unaka & the Great Smoky Mountains, the latter so-called because of the veil-like mist which hovers over the blue peaks. West of the mountains lies the valley of the Tennessee River & beyond, the Cumberland Plateau, affording such notable viewpoints as the Cumberland Gap & Lookout Mountain. In middle Tennessee, centering around Nashville, is the Great Basin, constituting the bluegrass region of the state & along the Mississippi is a strip of alluvial cotton land. De Soto camped near Memphis in 1540, La Salle built Fort Proud'homme about 1682, & the English from Virginia established Fort Loudoun, 1756, claiming the re-

# THE SOUTH I

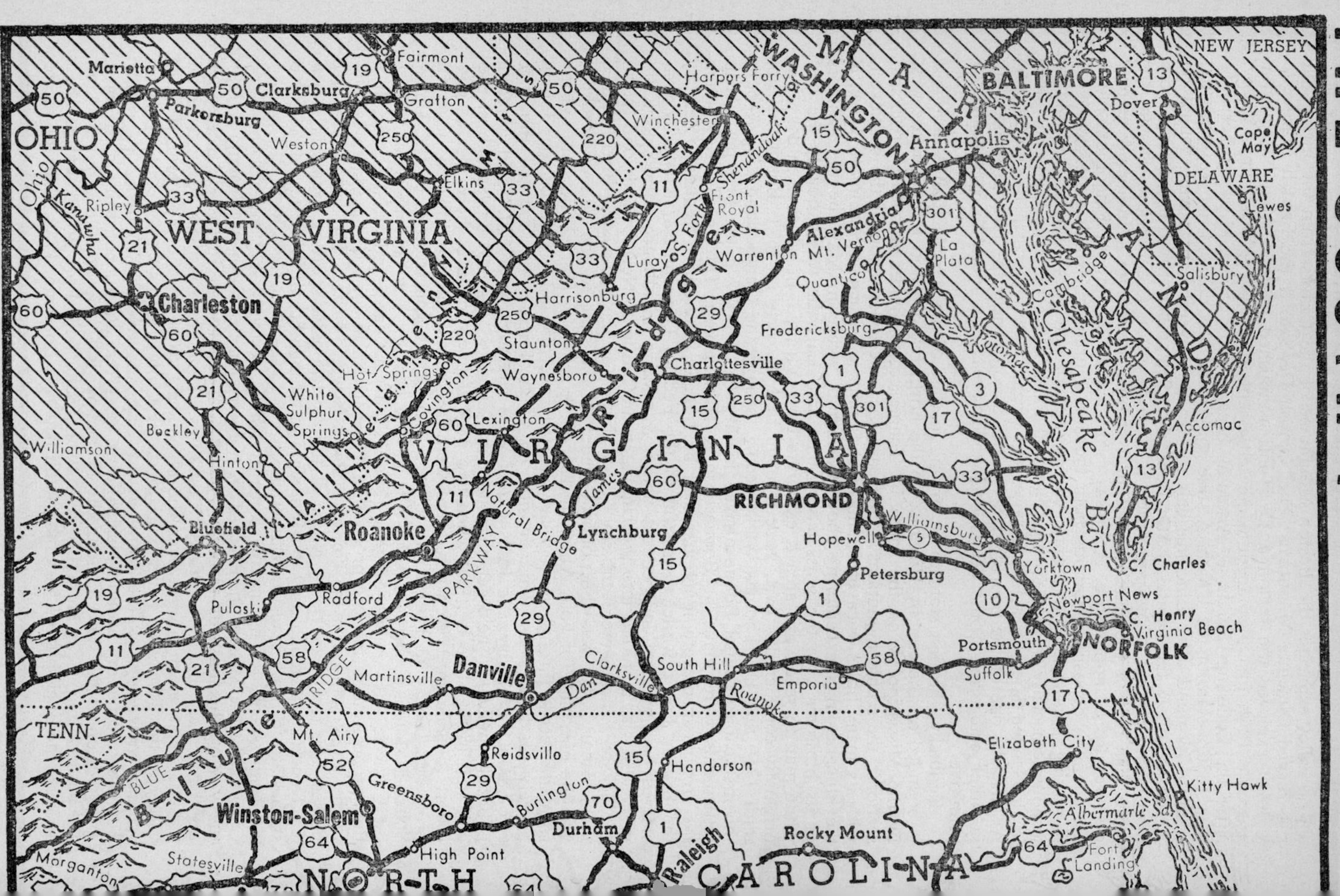
NEW JERSEY
Cape May
DELAWARE
Lewes
Dover
Salisbury
BALTIMORE
Annapolis
WASHINGTON
Alexandria
Mt. Vernon
La Plata
Cambridge
Accomac
Chesapeake
Bay
C. Charles
C. Henry
Virginia Beach
NORFOLK
Newport News
Yorktown
Portsmouth
Suffolk
Elizabeth City
Kitty Hawk
Albemarle Sd.
Fort Landing
Williamsburg
Petersburg
Hopewell
RICHMOND
Fredericksburg
Quantico
Warrenton
Front Royal
Harpers Ferry
Winchester
Luray
Charlottesville
Harrisonburg
Staunton
Waynesboro
Lexington
Natural Bridge
Lynchburg
Emporia
South Hill
Clarksville
Henderson
Rocky Mount
Raleigh
Durham
Burlington
Reidsvillo
Danville
Martinsville
Greensboro
High Point
Winston-Salem
Mt. Airy
Statesville
Morganton
Roanoke
Radford
Pulaski
Bluefield
Covington
Hot Springs
White Sulphur Springs
Hinton
Beckley
Williamson
Charleston
Ripley
Kanawha
Ohio
Marietta
Parkersburg
Clarksburg
Weston
Grafton
Fairmont
Elkins
WEST VIRGINIA
VIRGINIA
MARYLAND
NORTH CAROLINA
OHIO
TENN.
PARKWAY
RIDGE
BLUE
Shenandoah
S. Fork
James
Dan
Roanoke
Potomac
13
301
50
15
3
17
33
1
10
5
58
250
29
11
60
220
19
21
52
64
70

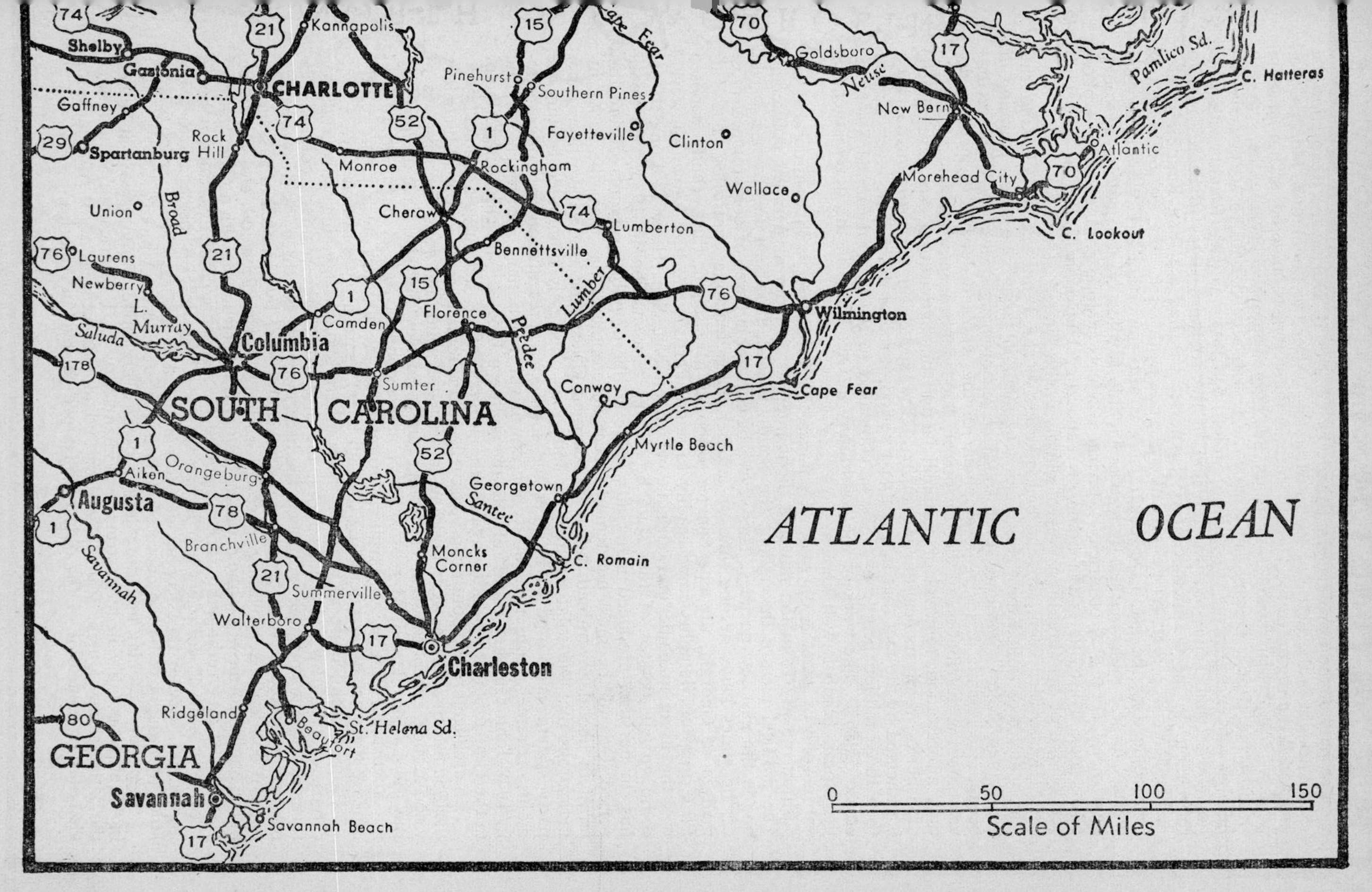

ATLANTIC OCEAN
SOUTH CAROLINA
GEORGIA
Shelby
Gastonia
Gaffney
Spartanburg
Kannapolis
CHARLOTTE
Rock Hill
Monroe
Union
Broad
Laurens
Newberry
L. Murray
Saluda
Columbia
Camden
Cheraw
Pinehurst
Southern Pines
Rockingham
Fayetteville
Cape Fear
Clinton
Wallace
Goldsboro
Neuse
New Bern
Pamlico Sd.
C. Hatteras
Atlantic
Morehead City
C. Lookout
Lumberton
Bennettsville
Lumber
Florence
Pedee
Sumter
Wilmington
Cape Fear
Conway
Myrtle Beach
Georgetown
Santee
C. Romain
Moncks Corner
Orangeburg
Aiken
Augusta
Branchville
Savannah
Summerville
Walterboro
Charleston
Ridgeland
Beaufort
St. Helena Sd.
Savannah
Savannah Beach
74
21
15
70
17
52
74
1
29
21
76
1
15
76
74
178
76
17
1
52
78
1
21
17
80
17
0
50
100
150
Scale of Miles

gion as part of the Carolina grant made by Charles II. During the Revolution the settlers fought in the Battle of Kings Mountain. After the Revolution, North Carolina ceded the region to the United States & the colonists, angered, set up an independent state which lasted four years. In 1796 Tennessee became the sixteenth state of the Union. During the Civil War it was second only to Virginia in the number of engagements (including Shiloh & Chickamauga) fought within its boundaries, but Tennessee was the first of the southern states to be restored to the Union. In the twentieth century Tennessee has had a strong Republican element. Tennessee remains an agricultural state with corn, hay, cotton, wheat & tobacco leading the list. Livestock raising is also important & Columbia has the world's largest mule market. Industries include textiles (rayon, cotton, & wool), light metal, lumber & electricity. Mineral products include coal, cement, & phosphate rock. Nashville is the home of Vanderbilt University & has in Fisk University one of the three best Negro schools in the United States.

At Knoxville, Tenn., are the headquarters of the Tennessee Valley Authority which has been called the "greatest development in large-scale social planning in the United States." Servicing seven southern & bordering states, TVA's object has been the economic & social development of the whole watershed & includes development & distribution of electric power, flood control, improvement of navigation, afforestation, removal of marginal lands from agricultural use, development of fisheries, & diversification of industry. How successful the program has been is indicated by the fact that in a ten-year period, it raised the income level of more than three million people by 75% as compared to the general United States increase of 56%. The work of the community at Oak Ridge in the development of the atomic bomb is well known.

In spite of great & obvious advantages, TVA has met with considerable opposition, mostly from the power & light interests & from disgruntled politicians. The political picture throughout the South, indeed, has been far from a bright one in the past few decades. There have been notable cases of corruption & most of the states have, at one time or another, been machine controlled. The Talmadges of Georgia, the late Senator Bilbo of Mississippi, the recently deposed Ed Crump of Memphis come readily to mind. Perhaps the best known, however, was the Long machine in Louisiana, which enabled Sen. Huey P. Long to become virtual dictator of that state before his assassination in 1935. The South has, to be sure, produced many admirable & liberal public servants during this period. One of the most heartening recent developments has been the active interest in liberal government taken by returned G.I.'s. And there have been other indications that the solid South is no longer as hopelessly dominated by the one party system as it used to be. Yet the southern representation in Congress remains extremely conservative, if not downright reactionary. So much so, that in 1948 John Gunther could refer to the southern bloc as "the chief single factor in the United States militating against the progress of the nation as a whole."

In architecture the South can boast true distinction. As early as the 17th century the Spanish in Florida were building in stone—& building well. The missions of wood & rock, except for some crumbling ruins near New Smyrna, have disappeared. But the Castillo de San Marcos, built of native coquina rock & begun in 1672 at St. Augustine, remains an excellent example of the military architecture of the time; & there are other interesting (though later) Spanish types in that city.

Pioneer architecture in most of the southern states, beginning with crude log cabins, evolved two indigenous types: the dog trot & the planter's cottage. The former, also known as the saddlebag, the breezeway, or the three P's (two pens & a passage) consisted of two separate units linked together by a roofed-in passage-way open at both ends & providing space for washing, storing firewood, etc. The latter, in its simplest form, was a one & one-half story frame structure with a wide "gallery" or porch & an overhanging roof supported by slender colonnettes. Such a house became a "raised" cottage when it was set on a high brick "basement" to avoid inundation, elevate the sleeping quarters above the miasmas rising from swamp lands (& thought to be the cause of malaria), & provide working quarters.

Georgian Colonial, including designs by Sir Christopher Wren, is seen at its best in Virginia, notably in reconstructed Williamsburg & in Charleston, S.C., though the latter shows Dutch, French & West Indian influences as well. In Charleston also may be seen some of the oldest landscaped gardens in America.

In the French Quarter of New Orleans a combination of French & Spanish influences, characterized by galleries ornamented with lacelike ironwork, the use of the courtyard or patio, etc., produced a distinctive "Creole" style, examples of which may also be seen in Mobile, Alabama & in Natchez, Mississippi.

Just before the Revolution, Jefferson, bored with the Georgian manner, ushered in the Federal Period with his Monticello, & his designs for the University of Virginia. Buildings in the Jeffersonian Palladian manner sprang up in many sections of the country & his architecture also helped pave the way for the Greek Revival. In the plantation houses of the South, the latter found a true functional expression. A plantation group often consisted of a "big house" flanked by two smaller houses (garçonnières) of similar design, for the bachelors of the family or for visitors, with these in turn flanked by ornamental dovecotes. Frequently there was also an outdoor kitchen &, down the road to the side of the big house, a row of slave quarters. In general the big house was set back from a river & a road, lined on both sides with overhanging trees, stretched from its front door to the levee. Many plantation homes have burned or fallen into the rivers they once faced, but excellent examples remain in every southern state & there are notable concentrations in Natchez, in the vicinity of Charleston, S.C. & Augusta, Ga., in the Feliciana country of Louisiana & along the river road between Baton Rouge & New Orleans. In the Garden District of the latter city may be seen examples of the Greek Revival as applied to the town house. Among the distinguished architects who worked in this style were Robert Mills of Charleston, designer of the Washington Monument, & Gideon Shryock of Kentucky. The latter was a pupil of Strickland, whose work in the South is well exemplified in the State Capitol at Nashville.

The Gothic Revival & what Mark Twain called the "Walter Scott disease" also affected the South. Interesting examples are the Old Richmond Academy in Augusta, Georgia, & the old State Capitol at Baton Rouge. But, because poverty after the Civil War prevented new building, many old towns escaped the worst excesses of the General Grant period, though "Steamboat Gothic" may be enjoyed in a number of river towns & there are some homes of retired captains of paddlewheelers that have the definite appearance of steamboats coming round the bend.

Henry Hobson Richardson was born in Louisiana, though most of his building was in the East & Middle West. The old Howard Memorial Library in New Orleans (now a radio station), built after his death from plans found among his papers, is in the Richardson Romanesque tradition. The promoters of Florida introduced Spanish Renaissance & Moorish motifs in the elaborate hotels they built in the 80's, & the Florida boom of the 20's produced a rash of Florida-Mediterranean architecture in stucco of every known color. Today the South has fewer skyscrapers & examples of "modern" architecture than some other sections of the country, but there are notable exceptions, such as Frank Lloyd Wright's chapel for Florida Southern College at Lakewood, Florida.

In many parts of the South, house & garden pilgrimages are held, usually in the spring, at which time private homes of architectural or historical significance are opened to the public.

The South has produced few native painters or sculptors of great distinction & today it has no art museums comparable to the great ones of the East, though there are numerous small collections of considerable interest.

Audubon traveled through much of the South, from Kentucky to Louisiana & Florida, making sketches for his "Birds of America," as did Catlin, painting his Indians. Gilbert Stuart & Charles Wilson Peale painted in Virginia. Sully, born in England, spent his youth in Charleston, & Washington Allston, later a teacher of Samuel F. B. Morse, was also born in South Carolina, a state that claims in Henrietta Johnson, who was painting pastels before 1708, America's "first woman artist." Rembrandt, Raphael, & Titian Peale, sons of Charles Wilson, worked in Georgia & Alabama, & George Inness & his son both had studios in Florida. Later, Winslow Homer was to spend much time in the vicinity of Key West. Frank Duveneck, painter & sculptor & typical exponent of the Munich School who became extremely influential as a teacher in late 19th century America, was born in Kentucky, as was Matthew H. Jouett (1787-1828) known in his day as "the best painter West of the Appalachians." Gari Melchers, portrait & landscape artist from Detroit, lived for many years in Falmouth, Va. & among the sculptors, Edward V. Valentine & Sir Moses Ezekiel were both from Virginia. Many artists have had studios in New Orleans, & Degas painted his relatives there in "Le Bureau de Coton à Nouvelle

# THE SOUTH II

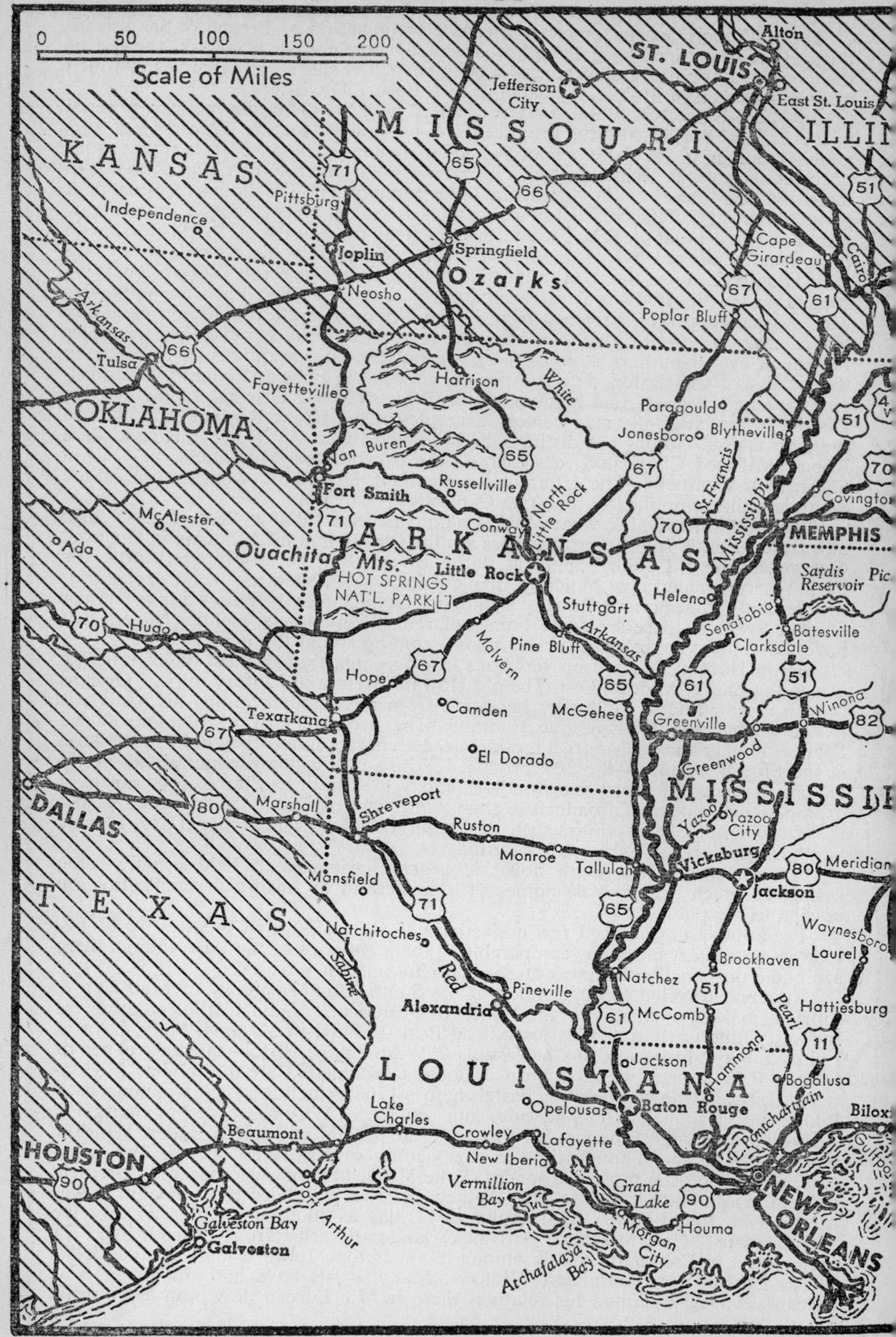

0 50 100 150 200
Scale of Miles
KANSAS
MISSOURI
ILLIN
OKLAHOMA
ARKANSAS
MISSISSI
TEXAS
LOUISIANA
ST. LOUIS
Alton
East St. Louis
Jefferson City
Independence
Pittsburg
Joplin
Springfield
Ozarks
Neosho
Cape Girardeau
Cairo
Poplar Bluff
Tulsa
Fayetteville
Harrison
White
Paragould
Jonesboro
Blytheville
Van Buren
Fort Smith
Russellville
North Little Rock
St. Francis
Mississippi
Covington
McAlester
Ada
Conway
MEMPHIS
Ouachita Mts.
HOT SPRINGS NAT'L. PARK
Little Rock
Stuttgart
Helena
Sardis Reservoir
Hugo
Malvern
Pine Bluff
Arkansas
Senatobia
Batesville
Clarksdale
Hope
Camden
McGehee
Greenville
Winona
Texarkana
El Dorado
Greenwood
DALLAS
Marshall
Shreveport
Ruston
Yazoo
Yazoo City
Monroe
Tallulah
Vicksburg
Jackson
Meridian
Mansfield
Natchitoches
Red
Sabine
Waynesboro
Laurel
Brookhaven
Natchez
Pineville
Alexandria
McComb
Pearl
Hattiesburg
Jackson
Hammond
Bogalusa
Opelousas
Baton Rouge
L. Pontchartrain
Biloxi
Gulfport
Lake Charles
Beaumont
Crowley
Lafayette
HOUSTON
New Iberia
Vermillion Bay
Grand Lake
Houma
NEW ORLEANS
Port Arthur
Galveston Bay
Galveston
Morgan City
Atchafalaya Bay
71
65
66
51
67
61
4
70
82
80
90
11

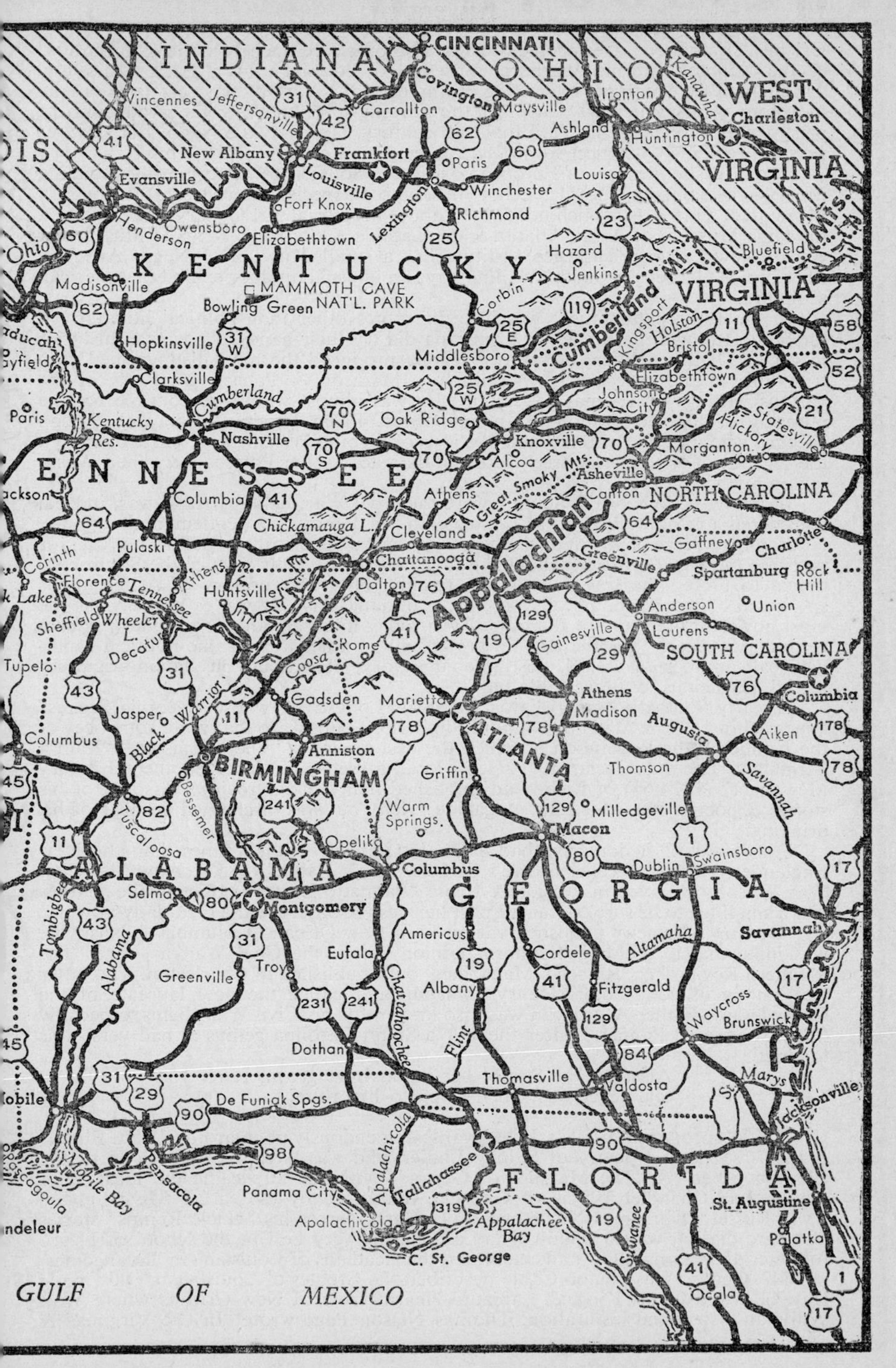

INDIANA
OHIO
WEST VIRGINIA
Charleston
CINCINNATI
Covington
Vincennes
Jeffersonville
Carrollton
Maysville
Ironton
Kanawha
Ashland
Huntington
New Albany
Frankfort
Paris
Louisville
Evansville
Fort Knox
Winchester
Lexington
Richmond
Louisa
Henderson
Owensboro
Elizabethtown
Ohio
KENTUCKY
Hazard
Jenkins
Bluefield
Madisonville
MAMMOTH CAVE NAT'L. PARK
Bowling Green
Corbin
Cumberland Mt.
VIRGINIA
Kingsport
Holston
Hopkinsville
Middlesboro
Bristol
Elizabethtown
Clarksville
Cumberland
Johnson City
Paris
Kentucky Res.
Oak Ridge
Knoxville
Nashville
Hickory
Statesville
Morganton
Alcoa
Great Smoky Mts.
Asheville
Columbia
Athens
Canton
NORTH CAROLINA
Chickamauga L.
Cleveland
Appalachian
Corinth
Pulaski
Chattanooga
Gaffney
Charlotte
Greenville
Spartanburg
Rock Hill
Florence
Tennessee
Athens
Huntsville
Dalton
Anderson
Union
Sheffield
Wheeler L.
Decatur
Rome
Gainesville
Laurens
SOUTH CAROLINA
Tupelo
Coosa
Athens
Columbia
Jasper
Black Warrior
Gadsden
Marietta
Madison
Augusta
Columbus
ATLANTA
Aiken
Anniston
BIRMINGHAM
Thomson
Bessemer
Griffin
Savannah
Warm Springs
Milledgeville
Tuscaloosa
Macon
Opelika
Swainsboro
Dublin
ALABAMA
Columbus
GEORGIA
Selma
Montgomery
Tombigbee
Americus
Savannah
Alabama
Eufala
Cordele
Altamaha
Chattahoochee
Greenville
Troy
Albany
Fitzgerald
Waycross
Brunswick
Flint
Dothan
Thomasville
Valdosta
Marys
Jacksonville
De Funiak Spgs.
Apalachicola
Pensacola
Mobile Bay
Pascagoula
Panama City
Tallahassee
FLORIDA
St. Augustine
Apalachicola
Appalachee Bay
Suwanee
Palatka
C. St. George
Ocala
GULF OF MEXICO

Orléans." In that city, free people of color also practiced the arts in the 19th century, & the sculptor Eugene Warburg represented Louisiana at a Paris exhibition. Throughout the South are interesting examples of the work of slave craftsmen many of whom were particularly adept at the carving of mantels & the production of ornamental wrought iron. Until the 20th century, however, the Negro, for obvious reasons, remained a subject for artists rather than a creative artist himself.

The largest collection of European art in the South is to be seen at the Ringling Museum in Sarasota, Florida. Other museums of special interest are the Virginia Museum of Fine Arts at Richmond, the Gibbes Memorial Art Gallery in Charleston, the High Museum of Art in Atlanta & the Cabildo & the Isaac Delgado Museum of Art in New Orleans. Tuskegee Institute has a small Museum of Negro Art. The Brookgreen Gardens in South Carolina have an unusual outdoor exhibit of American sculpture.

In the 18th century there was little literature other than political literature in the South (though the French of Louisiana did try their hands at poems & histories in verse). Of this political literature Virginia produced the most distinguished contributions in the speeches of Washington, Madison & Patrick Henry & in the various writings of Thomas Jefferson, who was almost wholly responsible for the phrasing of the Declaration of Independence. From Virginia also came Parson Weems, whose "Life & Memorable Actions of George Washington" (c.1800) started the legends of the "cherry tree" & the dollar across the Potomac & other Washington myths.

In many sections of the South before the Civil War, fiction writing was, indeed, considered a rather vulgar pursuit & beneath the dignity of a gentleman, though the latter might occasionally indite a verse or write historical or political prose for patriotic motives. And throughout the first half of the 19th century the South continued to prefer "hearing a book" to reading one. The oratory of such famous speakers as John Randolph of Roanoke, Calhoun, Clay, Hayne, & Yancey was the most powerful literature of the time. Even today many Southerners would prefer a second-rate speech to a first-rate library & will go miles to hear one political candidate call another "a willful, obstinate, unsavory, obnoxious, pusillanimous, pestilential, pernicious, & perversable liar."

An early Southern humorist was Augustus Longstreet, whose "Georgia Scenes" appeared in 1835, & William Gilmore Simms of South Carolina wrote romances of the frontier & the Revolution of which the best known is "The Yemassee." "I am a Virginian," Poe once declared. "At least I call myself one." The "Southern Literary Messenger" (1834-64) of Richmond published many of his reviews & some of his stories & poems. Poe edited the magazine briefly but was discharged because of his drinking.

Few books of fiction have had a greater impact on their times than the New Englander, Harriet Beecher Stowe's "Uncle Tom's Cabin" (1852). After the Civil War, Mrs. Stowe lived in Florida & wrote "Palmetto Leaves" (1873) while tourists (for a small fee to be sure) streamed past her desk & observed the great lady at work.

"De Bow's Review" published variously in New Orleans, Columbia & Nashville was influential in molding Southern opinion before the Civil War, as were "The Southern Review" & "Russell's Magazine," both published in Charleston. The latter had among its contributors Henry Timrod, later called the poet laureate of the Confederacy. Father A. J. Ryan was also known for his Civil War poems, especially "The Conquered Banner." After the war a South Carolina genius at bad verse was to sing:

> Alas, for the South! her books have grown fewer
> She never was much given to literature.

The 60's produced Augusta Jane Evans' tremendously popular novel, "St. Elmo," & the 70's, the first poetry of Sidney Lanier who was later to write "Song of the Chattahoochee" & "The Marshes of Glynn." With the 80's came the local color school. Joel Chandler Harris of Georgia, influenced by the earlier Mississippian, Irwin Russel ("Christmas Night in the Quarters") wrote his "Uncle Remus" stories in Negro dialect, which remain today among the very best in the school of Negro folk literature. Longfellow had celebrated the Acadians of Louisiana in "Evangeline" in 1847. George Washington Cable described the Creoles of Louisiana ("Old Creole Days"), as did Grace King, & Lafcadio Hearn wrote of New Orleans where Walt Whitman also found inspiration. Thomas Nelson Page wrote "In Ole Virginia" &

James Lane Allen, "A Kentucky Cardinal." Mark Twain also wrote of the deep South in "Life on the Mississippi" (1883) & "Huckleberry Finn" (1884). Thomas Dixon, born in North Carolina (as was O. Henry) was the author of "The Clansman" from which the famous motion picture "The Birth of a Nation" was made. Mary Johnston of Virginia wrote the romantic "To Have & to Hold" & Mrs. Mary Murfree (Charles Egbert Craddock) of Tennessee wrote historical novels.

After World War I the South witnessed a surprising renascence of literature aided by such "little" magazines as "The Fugitive" (Nashville) & "The Double Dealer" (New Orleans) & such quarterlies as the "Sewanee Review," now the oldest critical & literary quarterly in the U.S. Among the many Southern writers who have since appeared, the two most famous are the late Thomas Wolfe of North Carolina & William Faulkner of Mississippi. Others include—Virginia: Ellen Glasgow, James Branch Cabell, Francis Newman & Douglas Southall Freeman; North Carolina: James Boyd, Jonathan Daniels; South Carolina: Dubose Heyward, Julia Peterkin, Josephine Pinckney; Georgia: Erskine Caldwell, Caroline Miller, Margaret Mitchell & W. E. Woodward; Florida: Marjorie Kinnan Rawlings & George Dillon; Alabama: William March & Octavus Roy Cohen; Mississippi: William Alexander Percy, Stark Young & David Cohn; Louisiana: Lyle Saxon, Roark Bradford, Harnett Kane & Robert Tallant; Kentucky: Elizabeth Madox Roberts, Irvin S. Cobb, Jesse Stuart; Tennessee: T. S. Stribling, Caroline Gordon, Evelyn Scott, John Crowe Ransom, Allen Tate; Arkansas: John Gould Fletcher. More recent writers include Katherine Anne Porter, Robert Penn Warren, Eudora Welty, Carson McCullers, Lillian Smith & Truman Capote.

Of all the southern states it is probable that only in Louisiana did Negroes (& they were of the free colored group & French-speaking) express themselves in printed literature before the Civil War. Here they published a review as early as 1843 & two years later 17 poets contributed love songs to an anthology called "Les Cenelles" & dedicated "au beau sexe louisianais." Southern Negro writers have since included Booker T. Washington ("Up from Slavery") & James Weldon Johnson ("Autobiography of an Ex-colored Man") & such recent writers as Zora Neale Hurston of Florida & Richard Wright of Natchez, Mississippi.

Before 1600 religious brotherhoods presented plays to support Santa Barbara, the first hospital of St. Augustine, Florida, & there is record of strolling players in Virginia offering "Ye Bear & Ye Cub" in 1655. Williamsburg, Virginia, had a theater & actors from England as early as 1716 & here, in 1752, the citizens saw a performance of "Othello" also witnessed by "the Emperor of the Cherokee Nation, his Empress & their son, the Prince." Charleston had its first theatricals in 1730 (when one Tony Aston, shipwrecked near-by, turned player & wrote a play about the country) & in 1736 opened its Dock Street Theatre (since reconstructed) with Farquhar's "Recruiting Officer." Wilmington, North Carolina, claims first production of a tragedy written by an American & produced professionally on an American stage —Thomas Godfrey's "Prince of Parthia" (1767). New Orleans witnessed an amateur production of an amateur play "Le Père Indian" in 1753 & saw its first professional players, refugees from Santo Domingo, in 1791. By 1806 it had its first English drama & continued to have both French & English theaters throughout most of the 19th century.

The 19th century was the heyday of the American Theater throughout the South. Robert Edeson, Minnie Maddern Fiske & Edward Sothern were born in New Orleans; Adah Isaacs Menken, the "naked lady" of Mazeppa fame, at near-by Milneburg. Edgar Allan Poe's mother acted on the stage at Richmond & Junius Brutus Booth made his first appearance in America there. In 1818 Sam Houston was Secretary of the Thespian Society of Nashville.

The 1830's saw the beginnings of the "Negro Minstrel Show" (a native American form which soon became traditional & widely popular in Europe as well as in the U.S.) when T. D. Rice, a white comedian did a blackface performance in Pittsburgh, inspired by the "Jim Crow" song of a Negro stage driver. The minstrel show was important in the development of jazz & helped shape the theatrical conception of the Negro. Show boats, floating theaters that "made" the river-front towns & presented variety shows & melodramas, such as "Lena Rivers" & "St. Elmo," were also popular throughout the 19th & on into the 20th century.

Today the South like all of the U.S., other than New York & its immediate vicinity, has little professional theater & relies on an occasional road show & on the little theaters. Of the latter there have been some especially notable ones including

Le Petit Théâtre du Vieux Carré of New Orleans, the Barter Theater of Abingdon, Virginia, which has become the country's first state-subsidized theater, with an active professional repertory company that in 1949 went to Elsinore, Denmark to play "Hamlet," & the Carolina Playmakers at Chapel Hill, North Carolina. The latter, under the direction of Frederick H. Koch, produced many original folk plays & the early works of a number of successful playwrights, notably Paul Green. A southern playwright who has more recently achieved international fame is Tennessee Williams ("The Glass Menagerie," "A Streetcar Named Desire"). Possibly the best known southern actress of the 1940's is the flamboyant Tallulah Bankhead of Alabama; the best known Negro entertainer, Bill "Bojangles" Robinson of Richmond, Va.

Jefferson wrote of his slaves: "In music they are more generally gifted than the whites," & it is in music that the Negroes have made their greatest contribution to the cultural life of the nation. The origins of jazz have been carefully traced from the redlight district of New Orleans' Storyville to Beale Street in Memphis & beyond. (It is an interesting sidelight that W. C. Handy's "Memphis Blues" was composed as a campaign song for boss Ed. Crump & originally called "Mr. Crump."). In addition to Handy, a great many other jazz musicians & singers have come from the South, including such famous practitioners as Louis Armstrong (New Orleans) & the late Bessie Smith (Tennessee). The work songs, the "sinful" songs & the spirituals of the Negroes have been many times collected & the white people of Charleston have even organized a Society for the Preservation of Spirituals—specially those sung by the Gullahs of the sea island region. Famous Negro choirs such as the Fisk Jubilee Singers & that of Hampton Institute have built up their colleges by way of concert tours. The Fisk choir toured Europe as early as the 1870's & Roland Hayes was at one time a member. Dorothy Maynor comes from Virginia.

Among the whites of the Southern Appalachians many survivals of old English & Scottish popular ballads are to be found. Cecil J. Sharp, the English collector, wrote of a certain isolated mountain region: "I found myself for the first time in my life in a community in which singing was as common & almost as universal a practice as speaking." Ballad making here continues as a living folk art & along with "Barbara Allen" & "Lord Randal" are to be heard more modern compositions such as "The Death of Floyd Collins" &:

My name is William Edwards
I live down Cove Creek way
I'm working on the project
They call the T.V.A.

Variants of the songs have been popularized over the radio as "hillbilly" music, which since World War II has had such a vogue that in 1949 "Down Beat" magazine found it "just about pushing popular tunes, jazz, swing, bebop & everything else right out of the picture."

Throughout the South other country folk sing, especially hymns in the Wesleyan tradition, & "all day sings" or festivals are held during "lay by" seasons. The groups are sometimes called "fasola" or "shape note" singers because the songs are marked for reading with a triangle for "fa" & circle for "so" etc., or "sacred harp" singers after one of the most famous of the shape note song books. The tombstone of "Singing" Billy Walker in Spartanburg, S.C. reads: "In memory of William Walker, A.S.H. (i.e. Author Southern Harmony). . . . A consistent Baptist 47 yrs. Taught music 45 yrs. The Author of 4 Books of sacred music. He rests from his labors. He died in the triumphs of faith. Sing praises unto the Lord." More than one southern candidate has sung (with the aid of a mandolin or guitar) his way into public office. Jimmie H. Davis, elected Governor of Louisiana in 1945, was a crooner & the author of "I'm Gonna Write Myself a Letter."

The South's most popular song was "Dixie" written by Daniel Decatur Emmett, a member of a black-face minstrel troupe, in 1859 & sung by Confederate soldiers. The origin of the word "Dixie" is uncertain though it is possibly a corruption of Dixon, name of one of the two surveyors who surveyed the Mason & Dixon line which later separated slave & free states. Stephen Foster, author of "Old Folks at Home (Swanee River)," "Massa's in de Cold, Cold Ground," "Old Black Joe" & "My Old Kentucky Home," was born in Pittsburgh & wrote many of his famous songs before he ever visited the South.

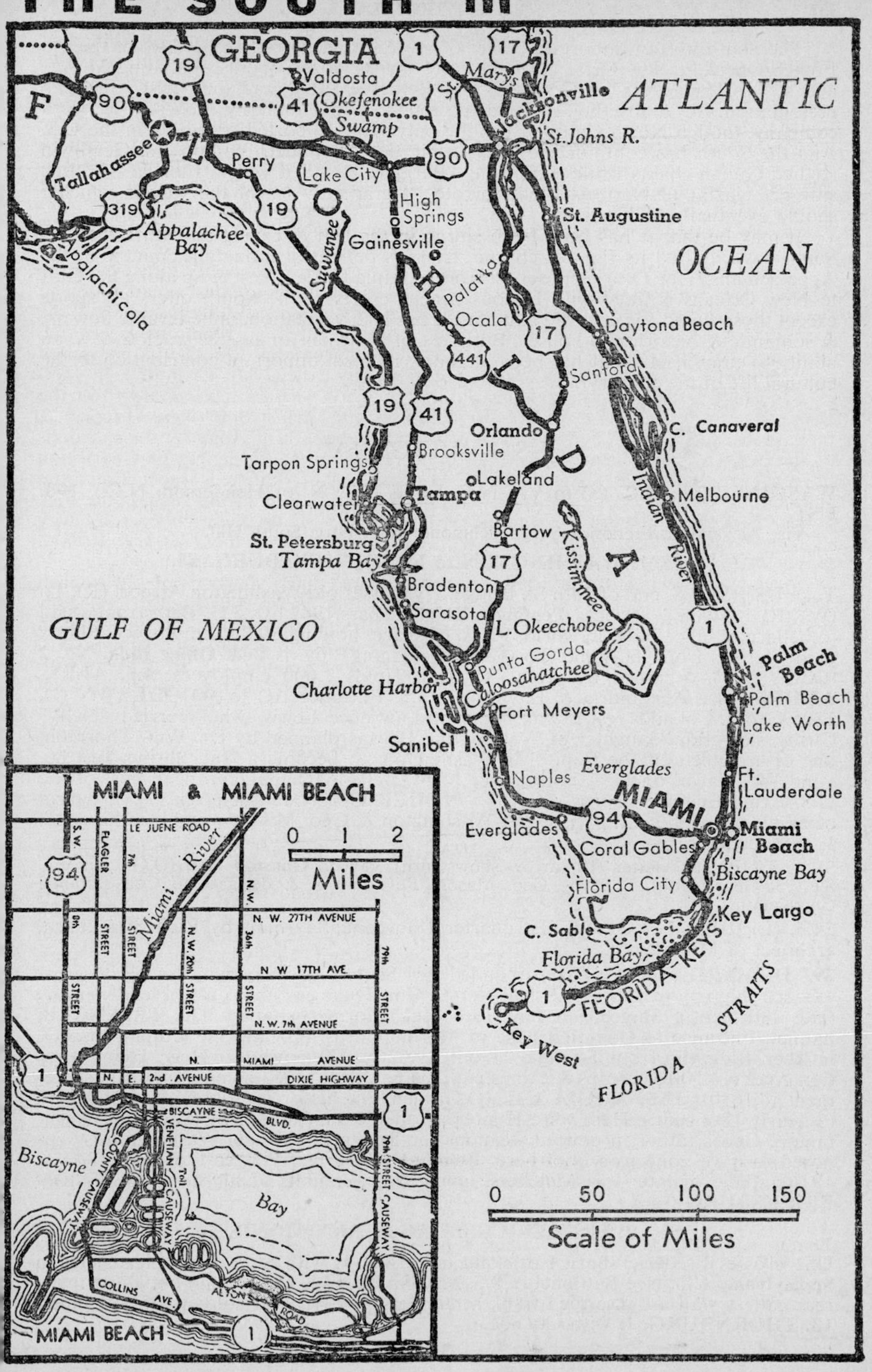
GEORGIA
ATLANTIC
OCEAN
GULF OF MEXICO
FLORIDA
Valdosta
Okefenokee
Swamp
St. Marys
Jacksonville
St. Johns R.
Tallahassee
Perry
Lake City
High
Springs
Gainesville
Appalachee
Bay
Apalachicola
Suwanee
St. Augustine
Palatka
Ocala
Daytona Beach
Sanford
Orlando
C. Canaveral
Brooksville
Tarpon Springs
Lakeland
Tampa
Clearwater
Melbourne
Indian River
Bartow
St. Petersburg
Tampa Bay
Kissimmee
Bradenton
Sarasota
L. Okeechobee
Punta Gorda
Caloosahatchee
Charlotte Harbor
W. Palm Beach
Palm Beach
Fort Meyers
Lake Worth
Sanibel I.
Naples
Everglades
Ft. Lauderdale
MIAMI
Everglades
Miami Beach
Coral Gables
Biscayne Bay
Florida City
Key Largo
C. Sable
Florida Bay
FLORIDA KEYS
STRAITS
Key West
FLORIDA
0 50 100 150
Scale of Miles
MIAMI & MIAMI BEACH
0 1 2
Miles
LE JUENE ROAD
S.W.
FLAGLER
7th
Miami River
N.W.
N.W. 27TH AVENUE
6th STREET
STREET
STREET
N.W. 20th STREET
36th STREET
29th STREET
N W 17TH AVE.
N.W. 7th AVENUE
N. MIAMI AVENUE
N. E. 2nd AVENUE
DIXIE HIGHWAY
BISCAYNE BLVD.
VENETIAN
COUNTY CAUSEWAY
Toll
CAUSEWAY
79th STREET CAUSEWAY
Biscayne
Bay
COLLINS AVE.
ALTON ROAD
MIAMI BEACH
1
17
19
90
41
90
319
19
17
441
19
41
17
1
94
1
94
1
1
1

The South was an important center of more formal music in the days of the old French Opera in New Orleans where more than a dozen operas, including Meyerbeer's "Les Huguenots" & Gounod's "La Reine de Saba" had their first American presentation. But today the South has no top-ranking symphony orchestra or opera company, though North Carolina has the only state-supported orchestra in the U.S. And the South has continued to offer inspiration to modern composers. Gershwin studied Gullah chants while composing "Porgy & Bess." It was in Florida "through sitting & gazing at Nature," Delius wrote, "I gradually learnt the way in which I should eventually find myself."

It may be that it has been from sitting in the sun & gazing at nature that the South has acquired its famous charm. There is delightful mountain country in the Appalachians & the Ozarks, the coast from Virginia to Key West & up along the Gulf to New Orleans is lined with famous beach resorts & the South offers all sports except those suited to very cold climates. It has lush vegetation, unbelievable flowers, & romantic & historic old houses. But most of all it has an ease & graciousness, an ability to enjoy itself, that has been, perhaps, its most important contribution to the cultural life of the country.

## US 1—VIRGINIA

**WASHINGTON, D.C. (S) to VA.-N.C. LINE** (15$^{m}$ N. of Henderson, N.C.). **198. US1**

Via: Alexandria, Fredericksburg, Richmond, Petersburg, South Hill.

### Sec. 1: WASHINGTON to FREDERICKSBURG. 50.

Take US1 (S) at S. end of 14th St. Bridge. Hy. passes old Washington Airport (R). To (W) (R) is Armed Services **Pentagon Bldg.** (O.pass.1942.by G.E. Bergstrom), said to be largest office bldg. in world, 93 as. of space, holding 30,000 employees. Bldg.'s name derives from its shape. To (W) of Pentagon Bldg. is **Fed. Office Bldg. No. 2** (O.wks.1941), occupied by armed services. Holds 7,000 employees. **4.5. ALEXANDRIA** (see Alexandria & Environs). **13.5.** Entrance (R) to **WOODLAWN** (O. 1805.Georg.-Col.adds.rest.); was home of Lawrence Lewis, who married "Nelly" Custis, step-grand-daughter of Washington. H. was planned by Dr. Wm. Thornton, one of architects of the Capitol in Washington; to become a Nat. Shrine. Just beyond Woodlawn, on US1, is Entrance to **Ft. Belvoir** (O.appl.entrance), post of the U.S. Army Engineer Corps. **16.5.** (L) **POHICK CH.** (O.Garden Wk.1774), typical of many sm. 18th cent. parish Chs. Washington & Geo. Mason worshiped here. **18.** J. with Cty.600.

SIDE TRIP: Take latter (L) (arrow shows turn) 3.5$^{m}$ to **Gunston Hall** (O.Garden Wk. fee.1758.Georg.-Col.), built by Geo. Mason, Rev. patriot & delegate to Constitutional Convention.

**24.5.** (L) **RIPPON LODGE** (1st quarter 18th cent.alts.) built by Rich. Blackburn, architect of Mt. Vernon.

**29. DUMFRIES** (sett.c.1707) founded by Scotch businessmen, formerly great tobacco shipping pt.; hoped to rival N.Y.C. Cor. Duke & Fairfax Sts., **Henderson H.** (late 18th cent.). **Stagecoach Inn** (18th cent.), formerly tavern. **30. TRIANGLE,** hamlet. Entrance to **Quantico Base** of Marine Corps. (O). **Marine Corps Mus.** (O) in Recr. Bldg. (R) from Triangle 2$^{m}$ on Cty.626 is **Chopawamsic Recr. Demonstration Area** (14,500 as.camps & cabins.pic.). **36.5. CRUCIFIX,** comm. 1st Cath. settlement (c.1650). **37.5. AQUIA CH.** (O.Garden Wk.1757.rest.). **48.5. FALMOUTH** (est.early 18th cent.). Here were Hunter's Iron Works, founded by Augustine Washington, Geo.'s father; produced weapons for Rev. armies. Geo. Washington is supposed to have gone to school here. **Belmont** (O.Garden Wk.fee.1761.adds.1843 & 1916); studio of late Gari Melchers, noted artist; exhibits of his work. **50. FREDERICKSBURG** (see).

### Sec. 2: FREDERICKSBURG to RICHMOND. 56.

US1 crosses Fredericksburg battlefield (see). **4.5.** J. with St.51 which leads (R) to **Spotsylvania Cth.** (see Battlefield). **8.5. MASSAPONAX CH.** (1859) on whose inter. rear gallery wall are inscribed frank sentiments by Civil War soldiers of both sides. **13. THORNBURG.** J. with Cty.606.

SIDE TRIP: Take latter (L). At 5.5m take country Rd. (L) short distance to **Stonewall Jackson Shrine** (O) where Confed. general, after being wounded at Chancellorsville, died; relics. Cty.606 cont. to J. with St.2-US301 (see).

**31. ELLINGTON** (R), (ante bellum), where Lee was shot at by Union troops. **40. ASHLAND.** Home of Randolph-Macon College (men.est.1830.by Meth.Episc. Conference), with branches: Randolph-Macon Women's College, Lynchburg, & Randolph-Macon Academy (boys) at Front Royal. City named for country estate of Henry Clay who was born about 4m (E), at **Clay Springs.** In College's **Hines Lib.** are hist. material of late Wm. E. Dodd, Ambassador to Germany (1933-37), & records & relics from Va. Chs.

SIDE TRIPS: (A) Take St.54 (L) (E) 1.5m to J. with Cty.662. Turn (L) on latter (arrow shows turn) 1.5m to entrance (R) of **Hickory Hill** (O.Garden Wk.fee.1734,rebuilt); notable boxwood walk. St.54 cont. to Hanover (see St.2-301).

(B) Take St.54 (R) (W) c.10m to **Negro Foot,** hamlet. J. with Cty.685. Take latter (R) to **Scotchtown** (L) at c.12.5m built in early 18th cent. by Scotch Col. Chas. Chiswell. H. was bought by Patrick Henry, & Dolly Madison lived in it as a girl. Cont. on Cty.685 to J. with St.51. At c.15m **Fork Ch.** (1735) where Patrick Henry & later Dolly Madison worshiped. Take St.51 (E) (R) back to J. with US1 at c.20m, N. of Ashland.

**51.** J. with St.301 (see St.2-301). **56. RICHMOND.**

## Sec. 3: RICHMOND to PETERSBURG. 23.

**6.5.** Huge **DUPONT PLANT.** Turn (R) here on Cty.638 (follow arrows) to **Meadowbrook Farm** (Gardens O.Garden Wk.fee). **11.5. OLD HALFWAY H.,** still an inn. **21. COLONIAL HEIGHTS.** On Arlington Place, **Violet Bank** (early 19th cent.), Lee hqs., summer of 1864; he heard explosion at The Crater here (see Petersburg). An ancient & curious cucumber tree attracts visitors' attention. On Archer's (Dunn's) Hill, at Carroll Ave., **Old Oak Hill,** from which Lafayette shelled Petersburg, 1781. **23. PETERSBURG** (see).

## Sec. 4: PETERSBURG to N.C. LINE. 69.

**3. CENTRAL STATE HOSPITAL** (L), 1st in U.S. exclusively for treatment of mental diseases of Negroes. On grounds, old **Mayfield H.,** somewhat in style of Wakefield (see). **9. HATCHER'S RUN,** where Grant's forces were defeated (Oct. 1864). **Beck's Beach** (bath.amusements). **9.5.** J. with Cty.613. (Take latter (R) 6.5m to **Five Forks** where was fought engagement, Ap.1, 1865, that led to evacuation of Petersburg.) **16. DINWIDDIE,** scene of conflict bet. Fed. Gen. Sheridan's & Confed. Gen. Pickett's forces, Mar. 29, 1865, in which Sheridan was repulsed. At Green, **Gen. Winfield Scott's Law Office,** before he embarked on military career. **22.5.** J. with Cty.646.

SIDE TRIP: Take latter c.5m (L) & then (L) again 0.5m to **Saponey Ch.** (O.1728), named for friendly Ind. Saponey tribe, which at instance of Gov. Spotswood, moved to Ft. Christiana, whose site is near Lawrenceville (see US58). Ft. was built by Gov. Spotswood in 1714.

**54. SOUTH HILL.** J. with US58 (see). **69. VA.-N.C. LINE.**

# US 13—VIRGINIA

**VA.-MD. LINE** (7m from Pocomoke City, Md.) **(S) to CAPE CHARLES. 62. US13**
Via: Accomac. RR. parallels route.

US13 traverses Delmarva Peninsula to Cape Charles, near S. tip, where ferry conn. with Norfolk & adj. pts.

**0. VA.-MD. LINE. 4.5.** J. with St.175.

SIDE TRIP: Take latter (L) to **Chincoteague I.,** 10m, fish. community at the wharves to unload oysters, clams, crabs & fish. I. noted for its so-called Chincoteague ponies, stunted descendants of horses that strayed away during Col. era. Yearly on Pony Penning Day (last Thurs.in July), they are rounded up & corraled.

**22. ACCOMAC,** business center for greater part of Va.'s Eastern Shore, seat of Accomac Cty. since late 17th cent., though town itself was not laid out until 1786. N. side of st. bet. US13 & Back St., **St. James Ch.** (Gr.Rev.). E. side of Back St., **Drummond H.** (1750).

**24.** J. with St.178.

SIDE TRIP: Take latter (R) 2m to **Onancock,** founded in 1680 as one of Va.'s orig. ports of entry, at site of Ind. village. From here Col. J. Cropper went to aid of Commodore Whaley in last naval action of Rev. (1782). **Kerr Place** (1779) is one of its most notable old houses.

**31.** J. with St.180.

SIDE TRIP: Take latter (R) through village of **Pungoteague,** 3.5m. Here Brit. Admiral Cockburn was defeated by state militia (1814). At J. with St.178, turn (R) c.0.5m to **St. George's Ch.** (early 18th cent.partly rebuilt), which contains communion service presented by Queen Anne.

**34.** J. with St.182.

SIDE TRIP: Take latter (L) to J. with Cty.605 c.4m; turn (R) on this to **Warwick,** 4.5m, interesting house (oldest part late 17th cent.extended & rest.).

**46.** J. with Cty.620.

SIDE TRIP: Take latter (R) to J. with Cty.618, 0.5m; (R) on this to Cty.619, 1.5m; (L) on this to **Hungar's Ch.,** 3m, rectangular ivy-covered edifice (1751.rest.) in pine & oak woods. At 3.5m is entrance to **Winona** (possibly c.1645.partially rest.). At 7.5m is **Vaucluse** (late 18th cent.adds.), birthpl. of A. Upshur, Sec. of State, killed in explosion of the "Princeton" at Washington, D.C. (1844).

**54. EASTVILLE** is built close around its **Northampton County Cth.,** in which records continuous from 1632 are preserved. Among old bldgs. in or near Cth. Sq. are ivy-clad brick bldg.; former **Clerk's Office** (c.1731), probably old Cth. moved here in 1677. From its door Decl. of Ind. was read (Aug.13,1776); small brick **Debtors' Prison,** with its whipping post; **Christ Ch.** (early 19th cent.); & **Taylor Tavern** (pre-Rev.now Eastville Inn); **Cessford** (early 19th cent.) has on its wall an order signed by Pres. Lincoln, instructing Union troops who occupied it during Civil War not to harm it. **59.** J. with St.186.

SIDE TRIP: Take latter (L) to Cty.645, 4.5m; (R) on this to Cty.644, 5m; continue to **Site of Arlington & Custis Family Graveyard,** 6.5m, on orig. estate for which better-known Arlington near Potomac R. was named by Geo. Washington Parke Custis. Here stood H. built by John Custis II before 1680, which sheltered Gov. Wm. Berkeley when he fled from Bacon's Rebellion (1676). Graveyard contains graves of many of Custis family, among them that of John Custis IV, whose tomb's inscription voices his bitterness over his life-time quarrel with his wife, the former Frances Parke, from whom he was finally separated.

**60.** J. with Cty.641. Take latter (L) short distance & then (L) again .05m to **Stratton Manor** (c.1657.reb.1764). **62. CAPE CHARLES** (passenger & automobile ferries to Old Point Comfort & Norfolk & to Little Creek, near Norfolk), faces break-water-protected harbor fringed with ferry slips & RR. barge terminals from behind its boardwalk & string of resort cottages. Southward stretches pine-fringed sandy beach to end of Delmarva Peninsula.

## ST. 2—VIRGINIA

**FREDERICKSBURG to RICHMOND. 59. US17, St.2, St.2-US301 & US1**

This is E. alt. to US1. For 6m St.2 & US17 are united (see US17). **8.5. GRACE CH.** (1st half 19th cent.) near J. with Cty.612. **11.** J. with Cty.606, which runs (R) to **Jackson Shrine** (see US1). **19. BOWLING GREEN** (est.c.1794). **Old Ch., Old Jail & Old Clerk's Office. Mon.** comm. persecution of Bapts. (1771). On S. outskirts is **Old Mansion** (late 17th cent.). J. with US301 with which St.2 unites (S). (US301 runs (N) to Baltimore, see Md. US301). **23.** J. with St.14.

SIDE TRIP: Take St.14 (L). Just beyond J. with St.2, on St.14, is **Hampton Manor** (O. summer.fee.1838). Garden by Salvador Dali. At 0.5m **Mulberry Place.** 7m **Sparta. Salem Ch.** (Bapt.1st quarter 19th cent.Gr.Rev.). 26.5m **St. Stephen's Ch.** J. with US360 (see US17 Alt. from Tappahannock).

**40. HANOVER. Cth.** (early 18th cent.); portraits of Va. notables. Here Patrick Henry opposed Maury suit, brought on behalf of clergy who wanted to recover back salaries. Maury was given verdict of a penny. Near Cth., **Old Clerk's Office. Hanover Tavern** (early 18th cent.) where Henry stayed. **45. HANOVER WAYSIDE PK.** (pic.camp.trlrs.). **45.5.** J. with Cty.643 leading (L) 2m to **Rural Plains** (R) (2nd half 17th cent.), where Patrick Henry married Sarah Shelton. **54.** J. with US1. Cont. on US1 to Richmond at **59.**

# US 29—VIRGINIA

**WASHINGTON, D.C. (S) to VA.-N.C. LINE** (2m from Pelham, N.C.). **251. US29**
Via: Cherrydale, Falls Church, Centerville, Gainesville, Buckland, Culpeper, Madison, Charlottesville, Lovingston, Amherst, Monroe, Madison Heights, Alta Vista, Lynchburg, Chatham & Danville.

US29 in Va., united with US211, crosses Manassas Battlefield Nat. Pk. to Warrenton where US211 branches off & US29 turns (S) & somewhat (SW) fairly close to the Blue Ridge, through fertile farm country. S. sec. crosses tobacco growing area.

### Sec. 1: WASHINGTON, D.C. to BUCKLAND. 37.

**6. FALLS CHURCH,** village. **Falls Ch.** (1767-69.rest.), larger, but somewhat on same plan as Pohick Ch. (see US1, Sec. 1). In Nat. Mem. Pk. Cemetery on Lee Hy. is being installed **Mon.** by Carl Milles, entitled by him, "The Meeting After Death." In Falls Ch. is J. with St.7. [5m (W) on St.7 & 2m W. of Tyson's Corners, is entrance of **Ash Grove** (O.Garden Wk.fee.18th cent.), built by Thomas, Lord Fairfax.]

**22. CENTERVILLE.** In this general vic. were fought the 2 battles of Bull Run (Manassas), 1861 & 1862.
**Manassas (Bull Run) Battlefield Nat. Military Pk.** (1,600 as.), incls. parts of the 2 battlefields. **Henry H.** on Henry Hill is Pk. hqs. & has Mus. of relics. **First Battle of Manassas,** July 21, 1861. Scarcely 3 mos. after Ft. Sumter's fall, Beauregard's & Fed. Gen. McDowell's forces clashed. Confeds. were driven across Warrenton Turnpike (US29). But Jackson's brigades captured Henry Hill where Jackson earned nickname of "Stonewall." Then Feds. were routed & driven toward Washington. **Second Battle of Manassas** (Aug. 29-30, 1862). After McClellan's failure to capture Richmond in his Peninsula campaign, Pope was put at head of Union armies. Jackson had captured Manassas, Union supply base, & moved to Warrenton Turnpike near Groveton. The converging forces of Jackson & Longstreet brought about Pope's defeat. Only desperate stand by Feds. on Henry Hill permitted Pope to escape. Feds. numbered c.100,000; losses 14,462. Confeds. c.55,000; losses 9,112.
Tour of Battlefield should begin at Henry House Hill & incl. Bald Hill & Groveton. Narrative markers have been erected on Battlefield.
At Centerville is J. with St.28.

SIDE TRIP: Take latter (L) 7m to Manassas.
(1) St.234 runs (R) from Manassas across **Battlefield Pk.** (see below).
(2) Take St.234 (L) from Manassas 9m to **Jackson L.** (cabins.pic.f.).

**25. STONE BRIDGE,** where 1st Battle of Manassas started. **26. STONE H.** (R) used as hospital during battle. Just beyond, on US29, is J. with St.234.

SIDE TRIP: This Rd. runs (L) across Battlefield Pk. to J. with St.28 in Manassas. Take this Rd. (L) 0.3m from J. with US29 & then (L) to **Henry Hill,** where Fed. troops made stand during 2nd Battle. H. on hill is reconstruction of former **Henry H.;** Mus. (O), relics & Pk. Hqs. Statue of "Stonewall" Jackson.

**28. GROVETON CEMETERY,** around which much of fighting in 2nd Battle centered. Just beyond Cemetery is **Dogan H.** (R) which saw fighting during 2nd Battle. **32. GAINESVILLE,** from which Longstreet, during 2nd Battle, advanced to Groveton. J. with US15 (see) & St.55 (see US15). **37. BUCKLAND. Moss H.,** where during Civil War, important Fairfax Cty. documents, incl. Geo. Washington's will, were hidden.

### Sec. 2: BUCKLAND to CHARLOTTESVILLE. 78.

**8. WARRENTON.** Here US211 branches off (W). J. with US15 with which US29 unites to Culpeper. (For Warrenton & this stretch see US15). **33. CULPEPER** (see US15). **50. MADISON** (est.1793). **Cth.** (1829), one of most beautiful in Va.; **Old Masonic Lodge** (1834); **Piedmont Ch.** (Episc.1834); **Harrison H.** (1823); **Old Washington Hotel** (now printer's shop & apartment). **62. RUCKERSVILLE.** J. with US33. (For stretch of US29 from Ruckersville to Charlottesville & US33, see Charlottesville Trips II, III & IV). **78. CHARLOTTESVILLE** (see).

### Sec. 3: CHARLOTTESVILLE to LOVINGSTON. 32. (see Charlottesville & Charlottesville Trips I & II).

### Sec. 4: LOVINGSTON to N.C. LINE. 104.

**0. LOVINGSTON. Cth.** (1808.adds.). **16. AMHERST** (for Amherst & stretch to Lynchburg see Lynchburg Trip IV). **56. AVOCA. Fauntleroy H.** (Mod.) on site of home of Chas. Lynch (see Lynchburg); walnut tree under which Chas. Lynch & friends administered "Lynch Law" during Rev. Marker on hy. **59.5. HURT.** J. with Cty.924 leading (R) short distance to **Clement Hill** (O.appl.1776), where lived Capt. Benj. Clement who manufactured powder for Rev. patriots. H. is within sight of US29.

**80. CHATHAM. Chatham Hall** (girls sch.O.Garden Wk.); gardens. Cont. (S) from Chatham on US29 to J. with Cty.703, leading (R) (arrow shows turn) to **Mountain View** (O.Garden Wk.fee); old boxwood. **98. DANVILLE.** J. with US58 (see). **104. VA.-N.C. LINE** (43$^{m}$ from Greensboro, N.C.).

## US 15—VIRGINIA

**VA.-MD. LINE** (15$^{m}$ from Frederick, Md.) **(N) to VA.-N.C. LINE** (18$^{m}$ from Oxford, N.C.). **235. US15**

Via: Leesburg, the Plains, Warrenton, Culpeper, Orange, Gordonsville, Sprouse's Corner, Farmville, Keysville, Clarksville.

After crossing Potomac R. from Maryland, US15 flanked by Blue Ridge (W), traverses farm country that specializes in horse-breeding, & in S. sec. tobacco-growing. Makes J. with practically all main cross-state routes.

### Sec. 1: MD. LINE to CULPEPER. 69.

**0.** Potomac R. **HEATER'S I.,** where Piscataways sought safety from attack by Ind. enemies (1697). **2. CHESTNUT HILL** (R) (c.1800), home of Sam. Clapham, whose iron foundry turned out weapons for Rev. armies. **8. ROCKLAND** (L) (1st quarter 19th cent.), home of Confed. Gen. Geo. Rust. **9.5. SPRINGWOOD** (R) (c.1st half 19th cent.add.). **11. MON.** comm. Battle of Ball's Bluff (Oct.1861) during which Oliver Wendell Holmes II, later Justice of U.S. Supreme Ct., was wounded. **Nat. Cemetery. 12. LEESBURG,** charming old town & center of fox-hunting reg. **18.5. OATLANDS** (L), home (early 19th cent.) of Geo. Carter, descendant of "King" Carter; garden; boxwoods. **22. OAK HILL** (R) (1st quarter 19th cent.), designed by Jas. Hoban, White House architect. Jas. Monroe lived here after his 2nd Pres. term. **24.** J. with US50. (W) 1$^{m}$ on US50 is **Aldie,** home of Chas. F. Mercer (1778-1858), advocate of manhood suffrage, free schools & colonization of free Negroes in Liberia. In Aldie lived John Champe who enlisted in Benedict Arnold's Brit. command (1780) in attempt, which failed, to capture the traitor. At **35.** J. with St.55 (see Shenandoah Nat. Pk.). **37.** J. with US29, near Gainesville. US15 unites with US29 to Culpeper. **45. WARRENTON,** charming old town, in horse breeding reg. of N. Va. **Fauquier County Cth.** (19th cent.); int. portraits. **Mon.** comm. Confed. guerilla chief, John S. Mosby. S. of Warrenton, c.0.5$^{m}$ is **Leeton Forest,** home of Chas. Lee, attorney gen. in Washington's & Adams' cabinets. **69. CULPEPER,** base for Confed. armies early in Civil War & later for Union armies. Betty Washington Lewis, Geo.'s sister, is buried c.3$^{m}$ (NE) of Culpeper on Western View Farm. Nat. cemetery on edge of town.

### Sec. 2: CULPEPER to SPROUSE'S CORNER. 81.

**1.5. GREENWOOD** (L) where Judge Wm. Green entertained Lafayette (1825). **19. ORANGE.** J. with St.20 (For vic., see Charlottesville Trip IV). **28. GORDONSVILLE** (see ditto). **32.** S. J. with US33 (see ditto). Near J. is **Boswell's Tavern,** where Lafayette stopped in 1781. **41. ZION CROSSROADS.** J. with US250 (see Charlottesville Trip II). **49. PALMYRA. Cth.** (1st half 19th cent.) & ancient jail.

**56. DIXIE.** N. J. with St.6, leading (E) 10$^{m}$ to J. with Cty.608, which take (R) 1.5$^{m}$ & then (L) on country Rd. to **Elk Hill,** once owned by Thos. Jefferson. From here his wife & children fled when Cornwallis' army drew near (1781). **58. FORK UNION.** S. J. with St.6. For pts. of int. on St.6 (W) & Rds. branching off it near Scottsville, Keene & Esmont, etc., see Charlottesville Trip I. **61.5.** Drive (R) (Hist. Marker) to **Bremo estate** (c.1720). **Bremo Recess** (O.Garden Wk.fee.1803.remod. 1890), adapted from Bacon's Castle (see) & Ambler H. at Jamestown (see); garden.

About 1.5m from Bremo Recess is **Lower Bremo** (L) (c.1843); **Old Stone H.**, adj., dates probably from 1725. At c.2m from Bremo Recess is **Bremo** (O.Ap.-Nov.fee. 1815-19.Jefferson Class.); built after plans by Jefferson & considered one of his most successful Hs.; old outbuildings. **81. SPROUSE'S CORNER.** J. with US60 (see).

**Sec. 3: SPROUSE'S CORNER to N.C. LINE. 83.**

**16.** W. J. with US460 leading (L) 24m to **Appomattox Cth.** (see US60). **19. FARMVILLE,** on Appomattox R., market center for "dark" tobacco. Here took place one of last battles of Civil War, during Lee's retreat to Appomattox. **St. Teachers College** (women.est.1835). **25. KINGSVILLE.** c.1m (W) is **Hampden-Sydney College** (men.est.1776), named for John Hampden, rebel against Charles I & Algernon Sydney, defender of religious liberty in reign of Charles II, 2nd oldest college in state. Noted grad. was Wm. Henry Harrison, 9th Pres. **26. WORSHAM.** Ruins of **jail** (1755) & **Clerk's Office** (early 19th cent.). Here Patrick Henry made speech (1788) against ratification of U.S. Constitution. **41. KEYSVILLE.** J. with St.40.

SIDE TRIP: Take St.40 (R). At 11m **Charlotte Cth.** (1823). Here, Mar. 1799, took place debate bet. John Randolph of Roanoke & Patrick Henry on States' Rights. Henry denied & Randolph unheld right of a state to nullify Fed. laws. This was Henry's last public speech & Randolph's first.

**56. WYLLIESBURG.**

SIDE TRIP: (W) 9m via Cty.607 is **Roanoke Plantation** of John Randolph of Roanoke, "âme damnèe" of the republic's early yrs. John Randolph, by Jane Bollings descendant of Pocahontas, belonged to the famous Randolph clan. Bachelor, noted for his excesses & eccentricities—in his later life bordering on insanity—he nevertheless occupied prominent place as member of House & Senate. A bitter hater of the Adamses, whom he dubbed the Amer. Stuarts, he eventually cut loose from his own associates, opposed Clay, with whom he fought a duel, & the Missouri Compromise, & became main exponent of State's Rights, preparing way for Calhoun. He often retired to the primitive log huts on this plantation.

**59. BARNES. 73. PRESTWOULD** (R) (1765.fine exter.& inter.) built by Sir Peyton Skipwith. **76. CLARKSVILLE,** J. with US58 (see). **83. VA.-N.C. LINE.**

## US 11—VIRGINIA

**VA.-W.VA. LINE** (12m from Martinsburg, W.Va.) **(S) to VA.-TENN. LINE** (at Bristol, Tenn.) **345. US11**

Via: Winchester, Strasburg, Woodstock, New Market, Harrisonburg, Staunton, Lexington, (Warm Springs), (Hot Springs), Buchanan, Cloverdale, Roanoke, Shawsville, Christianburg, Radford, Pulaski, Wytheville, Marion, Chilhowie, Abingdon, Bristol (Bristol, Tenn.).

US11 traverses the "great valley" bet. Blue Ridge & Alleghenies, which during Rev. saw considerable military activity. During Civil War, Valley became main thoroughfare of opposing armies. From it, "Stonewall" Jackson & Jubal Early successively threatened Washington & Lee made his 2 advances into the N. states, one checked at Antietam, the other at Gettysburg. Sheridan cleared reg. by his victories over Confed. Gen. Early. His policy of devastation deprived Confederacy of one of its main supply regs. Frequent Rds. branch from US11 (E) into Blue Ridge Reg. & (W) into ridges of Alleghenies.

**Sec. 1: VA.-W. VA. LINE to STAUNTON. 102.**

**3.** J. with Cty.672 leading (R) 1.5m to **Hopewell Meetingh.** (1788-89). **6.5.** J. with Cty.661. [Take latter (L) here 1m to **Hackwood Park** (1777), used as hospital by Feds. (1864).] **7.5. SITE OF STAR FT.** (1862), captured by Confeds. (June 1863), but recaptured by Sheridan (Sept.1864) during Third Battle of Winchester. **8. SITE OF FT. COLLIER,** Confed strong pt. during Third Battle.

**9. WINCHESTER** (est.1744).

Accoms.: All types. Info.: C. of C. Apple Blossom Festival in Spring. Blue Ridge Hunt Club Horse Show, June. Swim. & sports facils. in Rouse Pk.

Winchester, self-styled apple capital of world, is situated at N. end of Shenandoah Valley. Early pioneers in vic. were Germans from Pa. Washington org. defenses after Braddock's defeat. Gen. Dan. Morgan, Rev. hero, spent declining yrs. here. During Civil War, within radius of 25m, more than 100 engagements took place. Apple shipping, apple storage warehs. & processing plants constitute chief industries (O. appl.).

PTS. OF INT.: (1) Cameron & Boscawen Sts., **County Cth.** (O.wks.1840.Gr.Rev.). Around grounds was formerly wall within which were whipping post & pillory. (2) SE. cor. Loudoun & Cork Sts., **Red Lion Tavern** (O.appl.pre-1783), hostelry since late 18th cent. (3) On Loudoun & Peyton Sts., **Site of Ft. Loudoun** (1756-57), which Washington was authorized by Va. Assembly to build after Braddock's defeat. Its walls were made of logs with earthen core; 103′ well was sunk to assure water supply. One earthwork can still be seen. (4) 304 E. Piccadilly St., **First Ch.** (Presb.late 18th cent.), now armory. (5) NW. cor. Piccadilly & Braddock Sts., **Handley Lib.** (O.1908), presented to city by Judge John Handley; large painting by Burtis Baker depicting beginnings of Ft. Loudoun. (6) On opp. (SW) cor., **H.,** (Order of Elks), occupied in fall & winter of 1864-65, by Gen. Sheridan. From here he set out on his famous "ride" to Cedar Cr., celebrated in poem by Thos. Buchanan Read. (7) 415 N. Braddock St., **Stonewall Jackson Hqs.** (1861). (8) 226 W. Amherst St., **Home of Dan. Morgan** (late 18th cent.) where Rev. general died (1802); built by Hessians captured at Trenton & Saratoga. (9) Washington & Boscawen Sts., **Christ Ch.** (Episc. 1st half 19th cent.Goth.Rev.). In basement is buried Thomas, 6th Lord Fairfax (died 1781), proprietor of E. Panhandle of W. Va. (see). (10) Boscawen St., beyond East St., **Mt. Hebron Cemetery;** ruins of Luth. Ch. (2nd half 18th cent.). Grave of Gen. Dan. Morgan, hero of Rev. Battles of Saratoga & Cowpens. Near him are buried 6 of his famous bodyguards. (11) At Greenway Ave. & Cork St., **Stonewall Cemetery,** in which are buried 3,000 Confed. soldiers from 11 Confed. states & Md. & Ky. **Mon.** comm. unknown dead. (12) Opp., on Woodstock Lane, **Nat. Cemetery,** where are buried Union troops. (13) NE. cor. Braddock & Cork Sts., **Washington's Office** of logs & stone (1756-57), during building of Ft. Loudoun. Cannon & stone Mon. comm. Braddock's expedition. (14) NW. cor. Loudoun & Clifford Sts., **Cannon Ball H.** (O.Garden Wk.); spot painted on N. wall shows where Civil War cannon ball entered & then passed entirely through H. (15) On city's W. edge, off W. Amherst St. (US50) is **Glen Burnie** (1794) on site of H. of Jas. Wood, one of city's founders. (16) 1$^{m}$ (W) on US50 is J. with Merryman's Lane. (S) on latter c.0.5$^{m}$ to Spring Hill (O.Garden Wk.fee.pre-1768); view. (17) (S) 1$^{m}$ on US11, **Perkins H.** (pre-Rev.).

In Winchester are Js. with US340, US50 & US522-St.12. US522 runs NW. into E. Panhandle of W. Va. (see).

SIDE TRIPS: (A) Take US7-340 (E) to **Berryville** 11$^{m}$. **Clarke County Cth.** (1st half 19th cent.). Horse Show, Aug.

(1) S. on St.12, c.2.5$^{m}$ to J. with Cty.633; (R) on latter to **Annefield** (late 18th cent.), one of handsomest Hs. in reg., 4$^{m}$.

(2) Country Rd. (L) from Berryville, c.0.5$^{m}$ to **Soldier's Rest,** one of Gen. Dan. Morgan's homes (see above).

(3) Take St.7 (E) from Berryville, c.1$^{m}$ to **Audley** (O.Garden Wk.fee.1774), built by Warner Washington.

(4) Take US340 (N) from Berryville 4$^{m}$ to **Fairfield,** another Warner Washington H.

(5) Take St.7 from Berryville short distance, crossing RR. tracks & then turn (S) (R) on 1st Rd. 5$^{m}$ to **Springsbury** (O.Garden Wk.fee.1792.recently rest.), built by John Holker, 1st Fr. Consul-Gen.; Sta. of Underground RR. during Civil War. Plantation's stables are among most famous in Va.

Side trip cont. on St.12 (S) from Berryville, c.3.5$^{m}$ to **Old Chapel** (late 18th cent.). From Old Chapel, cont. c.4$^{m}$ via Cty.255 to **Millwood.**

(1) Short distance from village on Cty.255 (N) is impressive **Carter's Hall** (late 18th cent.).

(2) E. from Millwood on Cty.723 (old US50) c.0.5$^{m}$ is **Burwell's Mill,** built by Gen. Dan. Morgan.

Side trip cont. (W) (R) on Cty.723 (old US50) from Millwood. At 1.5$^{m}$ from Millwood, **Tuleyries** (1st half 19th cent.). At 2$^{m}$ **Saratoga,** built by Gen. Dan. Morgan & named for battle in which he played important role. Cont. on Cty.723 & new US50 to Winchester at 10$^{m}$ from Millwood.

(B) **Winchester to J. with US11 at Greenville, 111$^{m}$ US522-St.12 & St.12.** Via: Winchester, Front Royal, Luray, Elkton, Waynesboro. This route is an E. alt. to US11. Most pts. of int. on it are treated on US11 or other main tours. Take US522-St.12 (S). Chief pts. of int. not covered on other tours: (1) At 20$^{m}$ **Front Royal,** known as "Hell Town" in early days. Belle Boyd, Confed. sympathizer, lured Union officers to a ball here (May 1862); while they were asleep after celebration, she rode off to report to Jackson who attacked next day, defeating Feds. **Randolph-Macon Academy,** one of 3 Randolph-Macon Institutions (see). **Amer. Viscose Corp.** (sample rooms O.;Factory by appl.). (2) N. on US552 from Front Royal 2.5m & then 0.5m off US522 is **Front Royal Recr. Pk.** (entrance marked. sm.fee.swim.golf.sports facils.). (3) Near Front Royal is J. with **Skyline Dr.** (see Shenandoah Nat. Pk.). Near this J. are **Skyline Caverns** (O.fee.conducted tour). From Front Royal, side trip cont. on St.12 (S). (4) At 44m **Luray & Luray Caverns.** J. with US211 which connects (E) with Skyline Dr. (For Caverns & pts. on US211 see New Market, US11 below). (5) At 71m **Elkton.** J. with US33 (see). (6) 84.5m J. with Cty. Rd.

Take latter (L) 0.5m to **Grand Caverns** (O.fee.electrically lighted). Through ages, limestone drippings in solution with water have hardened on contact with air into extraordinary lace-like formations. These formations are typical of those in other Blue Ridge caverns.

97m **Waynesboro.** J. with US250 (see Staunton, US11). 111m J. with US11 near Greenville.

**12.5. KERNSTOWN,** near which, May, 1862, was fought Battle of Kernstown. **14.5. SPRINGDALE** (2nd half 18th cent.), built by John Hite, son of pioneer settler. Ruins of 1st H., known as **Hites Ft. 19.5.** J. with Cty.638 leading (R) 0.5m to **Vaucluse** (L) (2nd half 18th cent.). **21.5. MIDDLETOWN** (est.1766). (N) of here Sheridan ended his famous ride to rally wavering Fed. troops, Oct. 19, 1864. [(W) 5m to Marlboro & then short distance to **Old Stone Ft.** (c.1755).] **23.** J. with Cty.626.

SIDE TRIP: (R) here 0.5m to **Belle Grove** (late 18th cent.Class.alts.), built by Isaac Hite who married Jas. Madison's sister. Jas. & his wife, Dolly, honeymooned here.

**25.5. FT. BOWMAN** (Harmony Hall) (L) (c.1753), erected by Geo. Bowman, 2 of whose sons took part in Geo. Rogers Clark's Expedition to NW. territory. **26.5. CRYSTAL CAVERNS** (O.fee). **27.** Old **HUPP'S FT.** (R) (c.1755). **27.5. STRASBURG,** founded by Germans. Cor. Massanuten & King Sts., **Col. Inn** (early 19th cent.). J. with St.55 (see Shenandoah Nat.Pk.). **38. WOODSTOCK** (est.1761), sett. by Pa. Dutch. Here Rev. John P. G. Muehlenburg, author of the famous declaration anent rebellion against the King—"There is . . . a time for peace & a time to fight"—officiated as clergyman (see Pa.). **Shenandoah Cth.** (late 18th cent.). [About 7m from Woodstock, via mt. Rds., is **Little Ft. Pic. Area** (facils.) at Woodstock Tower atop Massanuten Mt., from which on clear days fine view of 7 bends of Shenandoah R.] **54.** J. with Cty.730; (R) on this to **Shenandoah Caverns** (O.fee). **57. BUSHONG H.** (R) around which swirled Battle of New Market, May 15, 1864, when cadets from Va. Military Institute earned fame by their desperate charge (see Lexington). **58. NEW MARKET** (sett.2nd half 18th cent.). J. with US211.

SIDE TRIP: Take latter (E) through **Geo. Washington Nat. For.** At 5m, For. Camp in **New Market Gap** (shelter.camp sites.pic.). 11m **Meeting H.** (Bapt.1770.orig.inter.). 13m **Belle Brown Mem. Tower,** whose 47 bells play recitals Mar.-Nov. Entrance to **Luray Caverns** (O.fee), considered among finest in U.S. 14m **Luray.** J. with St.12 (see above). On W. Main St., **Luray Mus.** (O.fee.in part 1818), alleged to be former home of Lewis Ramey, known as "Lew Ray" for whom town was named; coll. of amusing, hist. & other items. Mus.'s founder was Molly Zeiler, who nursed both Confed. & Union wounded during Battle of New Market. 26.5m **Bryan Ch.** (Bapt.1797.rebuilt), built by ancestor of Wm. Jennings Bryan; latter donated some of **Ch.'s** furnishings.

**61.5.** [(L) here 2m to **Endless Caverns** (O.fee)]. **62.5. COURT MANOR** (early 19th cent.Gr.Rev.), now noted stud farm. **69.5. MELROSE CAVERNS** (R) (O.fee). **77. HARRISONBURG.** On N. Court Sq., **Warren Hotel** (late 18th cent.alts.). NE. cor. Bruce & Madison Sts., **Old Stone H.** (1753), home of orig. settler, Thos. Harrison. On E. Market St., **Stoneleigh,** Civil War hqs. of Sheridan & boyhood home of Walter Reed, discoverer of cause of yellow fever. **Madison College** (est.1908). J. with US33 (see) & St.260.

SIDE TRIPS: (A) Take St.260 (R) from Harrisonburg through Edom & cont. on same Rd. to **Lincoln Homestead** (R) (O.fee.1760's) at 9m, built by 1st Abr. Lincoln. Here Thos. Lincoln, father of Abr. Lincoln, Pres., was born.

(B) Take US33 (E) to J. with St.276, leading (L) through Keezletown to **Massanuten Caves** (O.fee).

**93. AUGUSTA CH.** (1749.add.), oldest in Valley. Near it, remnants of stockade of old Ft. Defiance (1748). **100. MERRIFIELD** (remod.), one of oldest Hs. in Augusta Cty. **102. STAUNTON** (est.1761). (Info. C. of C. Accoms.: Various types. Swim. in City Pk. Staunton Fair end of summer); was briefly Va.'s Capital, when Assembly met here after fleeing from Tarleton's raid on Charlottesville. Located at crossroads of important hys., it was a lively commercial center, with usual complement of taverns, gambling & horse-racing. Here was born city-manager plan (1908). PTS. OF INT.: (1) 24 N. Coalter St., **The Manse,** Woodrow Wilson's birthpl. (O.Mon.-Fri.;Sat. a.m.sm.fee.1849). Woodrow's father, Jos., was Rector of First Presb. Ch. (2) 19 S.

Market St., **Kalorama Lib.** (1736). (3) 120 Church St., **Stuart H.** (1791), after designs by Jefferson for his friend, Archibald Stuart. (4) On Beverly St., **Old Trinity Ch.** (O. wks.Sun.servs.mid-19th cent.Goth.), on site of earlier Ch. where Va. Assembly met, 1781. When word came that Brit. were near, Assembly resumed its travels; Patrick Henry left in such haste that he mounted his horse with only one boot on. (5) On E. Beverly St., **City Hall;** hqs. of Stonewall Jackson Brigade Band (O.wks.), which was permitted by Grant to keep its instruments after Appomattox & in gratitude, played for him when he visited Staunton & later at unveiling of Mausoleum erected to him in N.Y.C. Orig. instruments & other items on display. (6) NE. cor. Johnson & Augusta Sts., **County Cth.** (Class.); coll. of portraits incl. one of John Marshall by Sully. (7) On Frederick St., **Mary Baldwin College** (est.1842.Class.women). Adm. Bldg. (1844) is oldest. (8) On Cty.732 (W) c.4.5$^m$ is **Mt. Pleasant Mansion,** where some members of the Assembly, escaping from Tarleton, found Asylum. (9) On St.254 (NE) 2$^m$ is **Bellefont** (log.adds.), former home of John Lewis (see Charlottesville), & his grave. (10) 4$^m$ (E) on mt.-top, **Swannanona** (O); sculptures. A 300′ statue of Christ is planned for this $2,000,000 estate. Staunton J. with US250.

SIDE TRIP: Take latter (E) from Staunton. At 7$^m$ **Fisherville.** Take Cty. Rd. (R) here 1$^m$ to **Tinkling Spring Ch.** (c.1790). At 12$^m$, **Waynesboro.** Near here, in one of final skirmishes of Civil War, Sheridan defeated Jubal Early. **Old Hotel Gen. Wayne** (Col.rest.). [About 14$^m$ (S) from Waynesboro, via Cty.664, is beautiful **Sherando L. Recr. Area,** in Geo. Washington Nat. For. (bath.pic.camp.). Info.: Geo. Washington Nat. For. Supervisor, Harrisonburg, Va.] At 16$^m$ on US250, **Rockfish Gap,** end of Skyline Dr. & J. with Blue Ridge Pky. & Shenandoah Nat. Pk. (see). (For pts. to E. on US250, see Charlottesville Trip III).

## Sec. 2: STAUNTON to WYTHEVILLE. 173.

**5. FOLLY** (R) (O.Garden Wk.fee.Class.), built by Jos. Smith, friend of Jefferson. Serpentine brick wall, similar to those at Univ. of Va. at Charlottesville; furnished in period. **18.5. MIDWAY VILLAGE** (Steele's Tavern). J. with Cty.606

SIDE TRIP: Turn (R) here 1$^m$ to **Walnut Grove** (L) (rest.), home of Cyrus McCormick, inventor of the mechanical reaper (1831). At 2$^m$, **Raphine Hall,** birthpl. (1829) of J. E. A. Gibbs, co-inventor of Wilcox & Gibbs sewing machine.

**25. CHERRY GROVE** (R) (log.clapboarded), birthpl. of Gov. Jas. McDowell, advocate of abolition. Just (S) of Cherry Grove on US11 is Cemetery (R) of McDowell family. Grave of Capt. John McDowell, killed with 7 companions by Inds. (1742). Near here was born Dr. Ephraim McDowell, pioneer in abdominal surgery. **29. TIMBER RIDGE CH.** (Presb.1756). Near-by is **Site of Birthpl.** (1793) of Tex. hero, Sam. Houston. **35. LEXINGTON** (see US60). Js. with US60, US501 & St.39. (For pts. of int. on US60, see US60 & for pts. on US501, see Lynchburg Trip I.)

SIDE TRIP: St.39 runs (N) from Lexington & then (W) through fine **Goshen Pass,** at 17.5$^m$, at whose entrance is **Maury Mon.** (See Richmond & Lexington). Maury greatly admired beauty of this pass through which in accordance with his wishes, his body was borne before burial. 44$^m$ **Warm Springs,** famous resort. Town's sulphur springs for a century have attracted visitors. All types of recr. facils. J. with US220. Take latter (S) c.5$^m$ to **Hot Springs,** another health resort, with ample recr. facils. (S) of Hot Springs on US220, 3$^m$ is **Healing Springs,** another resort. St.39 cont. to **Marlinton,** W. Va.

**49. NATURAL BRIDGE** (O.fee.electrically illuminated), 215′ high & 90′ across chasm of Cedar Cr., was once owned by Thos. Jefferson & said by John Marshall to be "God's greatest miracle in stone." J. with St.249.

SIDE TRIP: Take latter a few miles (E) to J. at Natural Bridge Sta. with Rd. leading (S) a few miles to **Cave Mt. Recr. Area** (pic.camp.trlrs.swim.L.). St.249 cont. (E) to Glasgow (see Lynchburg Trip I).

**51. FOREST TAVERN** (L) (18th cent.rest.). **58.5.** J. with Cty.611. [Take latter (R) here 1$^m$ to **Grey Ledge** (R). (O.Garden Wk.1850).] Last Ind. raid occurred near here, 1746. **80. HOLLINS COLLEGE** (est.1846.women).

**87. ROANOKE**

Rail & bus conns. Accoms.: All types. Info.: C. of C., 13 Church Ave., SW. Swim. in Gypsy Pk. Roanoke Cty. Fair (Sept.).

Roanoke, picturesquely located bet. Blue Ridge & Alleghenies, with Mill Mt. within city limits; has some 207 factories. Sett. in early 1830's, Roanoke was known as Big Lick which in 1882, having offered a bonus, became conn. pt. for Shenandoah Valley & Norfolk & Western RRs. That was the year they dropped "Big Lick" & adopted more appropriate name of Roanoke (Ind. "money") & town's boom began. PTS. OF INT.: (1) On E. 9th St., Amer. Viscose Plant (O.appl.). (2) On Norfolk St.,

**Norfolk & Western RR. Shops** (O.appl.). (3) SE. cor. Lynchburg Ave. & E. 4th St., **First Post Office** (1837) now home of Big Lick Garden Club (Negro). (4) Lynchburg Ave., bet. E. 2nd & E. 4th Sts., **Raleigh Tavern** (early 19th cent.); altered out of resemblance to orig. (5) In Elmwood Pk., on Jefferson St., **Pub. Lib.**, occupying old H. (O.1820); rare items & coll. of Va. material. (6) SW. cor. Franklin Rd. & 16th Ave., **Lone Oak**, built around an old log H. (18th cent.gardens.rest.). (7) **Mill Mt.** (2,183′) is reached by steep concrete toll Rd. At base of mt. is **Crystal Spring** which supplies a considerable part of the city's water. (8) Dale Ave., bet. 22nd & 23rd Sts., **Carr H.** (c.1800.log construction). Close by, **4 Negro Slave Cabins.** (9) On grounds of Monterey Golf Club is **Belmont** (log.1770's) former home of Dr. (Gen.) Wm. Fleming, Scotchman who took part in famous Andrew Lewis expedition down the Big Sandy (see W. Va.). (10) In Roanoke is **Booker T. Washington Mem. Trade Sch.** (est.1948.Negroes). School has branch at **Booker T. Washington's Birthpl.**, (Va. P.O.) 16ᵐ from Roanoke on St.122, where is log cabin in which Booker T. Washington, great Negro leader, was born as a slave. In Roanoke are Js. with US220, US460 & US221, latter running (S) to Adney Gap, J. for Blue Ridge Pkwy. (see).

**95. SALEM** (est.1802), formerly important stagecoach stop. **Roanoke College** (est. 1842). **Roanoke County Cth.** (1841). **East Hill Cemetery;** Grave of Gen. Andrew Lewis. About 7ᵐ to W. are **Dixie Caverns** (O.fee). **122. CHRISTIANSBURG,** named for Col. Wm. Christian, Patrick Henry's brother-in-law. **Christiansburg Industrial Institute** (est.1860.Negroes).

SIDE TRIP: Take US460 (R) (N) from Christiansburg. At 7ᵐ **Blacksburg,** which was raided by the Shawnee (1755). Settlers were either killed or kidnapped. **Va. Polytechnic Institute** (est.1872) incls. military training in curriculum. In 1944, the **St. Teachers College** (women) at Radford (see below) was absorbed by Institute. Institute has 4 branches: at Richmond, Norfolk, Danville & Bluefield. Also agric. extension service covering state. (W) of campus is **Smithfield** (1772-74), built by Col. Wm. Preston, of famous Preston family. **Solitude & Whitehorn Hs.** on campus, were built by Col. Preston's grandsons. 18ᵐ on US460 is J. with Cty.700. Take latter (R) to beautiful **Mountain L.** (3,500′;resort.f.).

**132. RADFORD** (1773) on New R. Gorge. Radford Branch (formerly St. Teachers College) of **Va. Polytechnic Institute** (see above). On campus, **Log H.** (O.c.1776); exhibits of Va. material. **163.5. SITE OF FT. CHISWELL** (L) (1760), built to protect the Austinville lead mines which Col. Chas. Chiswell operated during Rev. **164.** J. with US52, running (S) near the mines to J. with US58 (see). **173. WYTHEVILLE** (est.1792), named for Geo. Wythe, signer of Decl. of Ind. Union force was prevented from destroying RR. here by boys & over-military age men when Mary Tynes came on wild 40ᵐ ride to give warning of the attack. In **County Cth.** is bell, relic of Battle of L. Erie (see).

## Sec. 3: WYTHEVILLE to N.C. LINE. 70.

**26. MARION,** named for Rev. hero, Francis Marion; near here was fought Battle of Marion (1864).

SIDE TRIP: Take St.16 (N) here 3ᵐ to **Hungry Mother St. Pk.** (2,400 as.O.summer.f. camp.trlrs.swim.boat.restaurant.store.guest lodge.L.). Generally accepted legend is that Molly Marley & her child, having been kidnapped by Shawnee, escaped. Molly, when she reached what is known as **Molly's** (Marley's) **Knob,** could go no further. Youngster reached a settlement but could only say "Hungry-Mother." Molly was found dead on mt. top.

**36. CHILHOWIE** (Ind. "valley of many deer"). J. with St.79 (S) to **Konnarock School, White Top & Rogers Mts.** (see US58). **45.5.** J. with Cty.737 leading (R) 1ᵐ to **Emory & Henry College** (Meth.est.1836.coed.). **55. ABINGDON,** orig. known as Wolf Hills. **Black's Ft.** was built near here & though raided by Inds., was never taken. Town burnt by Union troops (1864). **Martha Washington Inn** (1830-32.adds. swim.golf.tennis), built by Gen. Francis Preston (see above). **Barter Colony** has theater that accepts commodities for admission. **70. BRISTOL** (sett.c.1771). (Through RR. & bus conns. Airport with through conns. Info.: C. of C.). Busy mfg. city, partly in Va. & partly in Tenn.; its c.60 plants (most of them O.appl.) are supplied with power from Wilbur Dam, located in a superb mt. setting to (N), & electric power from T.V.A. The S. Holston Dam on US421, a $36,000,000 project, forming L. with 200ᵐ shore front, will shortly make more power available. In 1771, Col. Evan Selby built Ft. Selby on site of present city, then known as Sapling Grove. Ft. successfully resisted Ind. attacks. Bristol figured as frontier trading post where Dan. Boone & other pioneers bartered skins for powder & lead. **King College** (Presb.coed. est.1867.bldgs.Georg.-Col.) is in Tenn. sec. of city. On city's outskirts is **Watauga**

**Pk.** (2,200 as.recr.boat.swim.f.). 5$^{m}$ from city is charming **Abram Falls.** Bristol is logical starting pt. for tours to Cherokee, Pisgah & Great Smokies Nat. Fors. (see Tenn.). In Bristol are Js. with US11, US11E, US11W, US19 & US421.

## SHENANDOAH NAT. PK. & BLUE RIDGE PKWY.

The Skyline Dr., through Shenandoah Nat. Pk. & Blue Ridge Pkwy. extends along the Blue Ridge for over 600$^{m}$, from just (E) of Front Royal, Va., to Smoky Mt. Nat. Pk., in N.C. Take St.12 (S) from Front Royal to J. with Skyline Dr. Appalachian Trl. generally parallels Skyline Dr. & Blue Ridge Pkwy. **SHENANDOAH NAT. PK.** comprises 183,111 as. along summits of Blue Ridge. Skyline Dr., beginning at pt. S. of Front Royal, runs to Rockfish Gap, W. of Charlottesville, c.106$^{m}$. From the Gap, Blue Ridge Pkwy. cont. (S).

Blue Ridge Mts. are covered mostly with hardwood; wildlife is plentiful, & there are more than 700 species of trees & plants. Succession of panoramic views from Dr. & pts. near it reached by trls., makes 106$^{m}$ pkwy. unique.

Seven pic. grounds. Camp. facils. at Big Meadows & Lewis Mt. Roadside lunchrooms & filling stas. at suitable intervals. (O.from late spring to Nov.1). Overnight facils. provided at various pts. F. in prescribed seasons; Va. license; artificial bait only. Permits to make fires must be procured from Pk. ranger, except for designated pic. & camp. areas. Info.: Supt. Shenandoah Nat. Pk., Luray, Va. RR. conns. at Luray, Front Royal, Waynesboro & Charlottesville. Numerous main hys. give access to Pk.: St.12 & St.55 at Front Royal; US211 at Thornton Gap; US33 at Swift Run Gap; US250 from Charlottesville at Rockfish Gap. Va. Trailways operates daily buses through Pk. from Front Royal & Charlottesville. 200$^{m}$ of trls. branch off Skyline Dr. to scenic pts. of int. For detailed info., cf. Gov. pamphlet "Shenandoah Nat. Pk."

**BLUE RIDGE PKWY.** extends from Rockfish Gap to Great Smokies, N.C., c.500$^{m}$. Not all of Pkwy. is completed (1949); some stretches have not yet been constructed & others have only a crushed stone surface. Completed is stretch from Adney Gap, (S) of Roanoke, to N.C. Line. St. license for f. Within Pkwy., special regulations as to h. Info.: Supt. of Blue Ridge Pkwy., Roanoke, Va.

Spring, best season. In mid-Ap., shadblow is in blossom; in May, wild azaleas &, somewhat later, rhododendron & mt. laurel. The galax is peculiar to reg. & covers ground with glorious color. Accoms. on Pkwy. have not as yet been provided, but are avail. at inters. hys. At Smart View & Rocky Knob, in Va., are camp sites (facils. trls.). At Cumberland Knob, near Va.-N.C. Line, are pic. facils. & a sm. restaurant, & at Bluff, N.C., are pic. & campgrounds. For detailed info., cf. Gov. pamphlet, "Blue Ridge Pkwy."

## US 33—VIRGINIA

**RICHMOND (W) to VA.-W. VA. LINE** (20$^{m}$ from Franklin, W. Va.). **144. US33**

Via: Louisa, Gordonsville, Barboursville, Standardsville, McGaheysville, Harrisonburg.

US33 after crossing central farming reg., climbs over Blue Ridge, into Shenandoah Valley, then through Geo. Washington Nat. For. into W. Va. Much of route has already been covered in regional treatments & on other tours. **43.5. SITE OF CUCKOO TAVERN,** from which proprietor's son, Jack Jouett, June 3, 1781, started out for Charlottesville to warn Jefferson & Va. Assembly of Tarleton's raid (see Charlottesville). **60. MON.** on Site of Battle of Trevilians, where Sheridan was repulsed by Confeds. **69. GORDONSVILLE.** Js. with US15 & St.231 (see US15 & Charlottesville Trip III). **75. BARBOURSVILLE.** Js. with St.20 & Cty.613 (see Charlottesville Trip IV). **97. SWIFT RUN GAP.** J. with Skyline Dr., Shenandoah Nat. Pk. (see). Here, it is said, Gov. Spotswood & his Knights of the Golden Horseshoe crossed mts. into the Shenandoah Valley, Sept. 5, 1716. **121. HARRISONBURG.** J. with US11 (see). (For Massanuten Caverns, see Harrisonburg US11.) **133. PAWLEY SPRINGS** (sm.resort.cabins.camp.). **144. VA.-W. VA. LINE.**

## US 60—VIRGINIA

**RICHMOND (W) to W. VA. LINE** (4.5$^{m}$ from White Sulphur Springs, W. Va.). **194. US60**

**31.** J. with St.13. [Turn (L) here 1$^{m}$ to **Powhatan. Cth. & Clerk's Office** (1817).] **49. CUMBERLAND. Cth. & Clerk's Office** (c.1818). Just off US60 is **Bear Creek L. Recr. Area** (pic.swim.May to Labor Day). **68. BUCKINGHAM. Maysville Hotel**

(mid-19th cent.) & opp., old **Buckingham Hotel** where Lee, after Appomattox, couldn't get a room. **71.** J. with St.24.

SIDE TRIP: Take latter (L) here, passing **Holliday L. Recr. Area** (pic.swim.May-Labor Day) to **Appomattox Cth. Nat. Mon.** (9,700 as.est.1940) at 20m; may also be reached by US460 from Lynchburg or Petersburg, or by US15 (see). Info.: Pk. office in village. Free guide serv. After Battle of Five Forks & abandonment of Petersburg & Richmond, Lee planned retreat to Danville from which he might have been able to join Johnson's army in N.C. But Grant encircled starved & ragged remnants of Confed. army who were forced to concentrate around Appomattox Cth. (Ap. 8, 1865). At daybreak, Palm Sun. (Ap. 9), Confeds. made last effort to break through, but failed. About 1:30 p.m., Lee & Grant met at McLean H., Lee carefully dressed in brand new uniform, Grant in mud-spattered outfit of a private, bearing merely shoulder straps of a Lt.-Gen. After reminiscenses of Mex. War & old army days, Grant wrote out his generous terms providing that only public property should be handed over. Later same day, both generals signed surrender agreement, by which more than 28,000 Confed. troops in vic. were paroled. Lee reviewed his troops for last time, riding bet. solid walls of soldiers who cried out that they would fight on if he wished them to & wept as he passed. There are various markers—on sites of Grant's & Lee's Hqs., respectively, & spot where Lee issued farewell order. Village is being restored. **McLean H.** is being reconstructed. **Patteson-Hix Inn** (1819), **Plunkett-Meeks H.**, an old store, **Peers H.**, & **Isbell-Bocock H.**, home of presiding officer of Confed. House of Reps. are being restored. **Old Cth.** to be reconstructed.
Joe Sweeney, famous banjo player, born at "The Surrender Grounds," was buried here. He was "Jeb" Stuart's unofficial court musician & traveled with him through the latter's cavalry campaigns. Other Confed. commanders complained that Sweeney's playing & singing lured their troops to desert & join Stuart's command.

**100. AMHERST.** J. with US29 (see Lynchburg Trip IV). US60 now climbs Blue Ridge. **118. LONG MT. WAYSIDE PK.** (camp.pic.). **123.** J. with Blue Ridge Pkwy. (see). **127. BUENA VISTA.** Ranger Sta. of Geo. Washington Nat. For., in Fed. Bldg. **Green Forest** (c.1790.rest.), former home of Arthur Glasgow, forefather of Ellen Glasgow, noted Va. novelist; here she spent her summers & wrote many of her books. J. with US501 (see Lynchburg Trip I). Just before reaching Lexington, hy. passes handsome **Col. Alto H.** (O.Garden Wk.fee.early 19th cent.), some orig. Randolph furniture; fine garden.

**134. LEXINGTON**, named for Battle of Lexington fought year before town's establishment, 1777. Earliest settlers were mostly Scotch-Irish, belonging to yeoman rather than cavalier class. What the Secy. of Province of Pa. said in 1724 of this alien influx, has a strangely familiar sound: "The common fear is that if they continue to come they will make themselves proprietors of the Province. It is strange that they thus crowd where they are not wanted." Before Rev., Shenandoah Valley's Scotch-Irish were devout & strait-laced—banning dancing, cards, horse racing, etc. But among less orthodox characters was Mary Greenlee, who offered to rescue a child kidnapped by Inds. on condition that she should be allowed to keep horse, bridle & saddle lent her for the undertaking. Mary had to go as far as Mammoth Cave, Ky., to make the rescue. After Rev., manners grew freer with accumulation of wealth. It was complained that intemperance increased (whiskey being only 37¢ a gallon), until in 1850's, people said no self-respecting woman would be seen abroad on court days. Nevertheless the little city had already become a considerable cultural center. Washington College (Washington & Lee Univ.), Va. Military Institute & an academy for young ladies had been established. The James & Kanawha Canal did not arrive until 1852. "Stonewall" Jackson's body was brought by canal boat in 1863 for interment. In 1864, Fed. Gen. D. Hunter attacked city & occupied it for 3 days. It is alleged that Hunter held some ladies of Lexington as hostages for good behavior of their men-folk. In environs were born Sam. Houston, Texas hero, Cyrus McCormick, inventor of mechanical reaper, & J. E. A. Gibbs, inventor of improved sewing machine.

PTS. OF INT.: (1) Behind Modern Cth. is **Old Jail** (oldest part 1779.rest.) in old Lawyers Row. (2) On Main St., **Cemetery,** where are Grave of "Stonewall" Jackson, Statue of Jackson by Valentine & Confed. Soldiers' graves. (3) 208 S. Jefferson St., **White H.** (O.Garden Wk.fee.early 1800's) with fine boxwood. (4) **Washington & Lee Univ.** had its origins in Augusta Academy (est.1749) whose name was changed, just before Decl. of Ind., to Liberty Hall. Later, when Washington gave endowment of 200 shares of James R. & Kanawha Canal Co., worth $50,000, name was again changed to Washington Academy. After Civil War, Rbt. E. Lee became College Pres., an office he held till his death, when name was again changed—to Washington & Lee. Bldgs. are classic in design, enhanced by columned porticos, reminiscent of Univ. of Va., at Charlottesville. Univ. has undergrad. school & schs. of law, commerce & administration, & journalism. The Washington Group of bldgs. (1824. rest.) has fine colonnaded porticos. Central bldg. of group is **Washington Hall** (O), in whose foyer are coll. of portraits; on 2nd fl. is Old **Washington Chapel** (rest.). **Lee Mem. Chapel** built by Rbt. E. Lee (1867). Recumbent Statue of Lee by Valentine. In crypt are buried Rbt. E. Lee, his wife, his father, "Light-horse Harry" Lee, his mother & other members of family. Beneath Chapel & near Mausoleum is room, preserved in orig. state, that served as Lee's office. Adj. is **Lee Mus.**; hist. relics & material & Lee coll. of Amer. portraits. In Chapel are portraits, incl. one of Washington by Rembrandt Peale & another by the same, of the young Lafayette. In **McCormick Lib.** is Bradford Coll. of oils, incl. examples of many European & Amer. masters. On campus is H. built for his own occupancy by Lee. The sec. that reaches Washington St. housed his horse, Traveller. Stall is still to be seen. Traveller's skeleton is preserved in Lee Mus.

(5) Adj. to Washington & Lee Univ. is campus of **Va. Military Institute** (est.1839), known as West Pt. of South. "Stonewall" Jackson & Comdr. Maury served as professors. Jackson is reported, because of his austerity, not to have been popular with students. School, closed for a time at Civil War's outbreak because its entire personnel & student body enlisted, was reopened in 1862 to train officers for Confed. armies. In June, 1864, Gen. Hunter's troops wrecked most of bldgs. At Battle of New Market, May 15, 1864, Institute cadets earned immortal fame when they charged Union lines. In front of **The Barracks** (dormitories.1850.adds.rest.) is Replica of Houdon's Geo. Washington (see Richmond Capitol). In Gen. F. H. Smith Room (O) of **Preston Lib.** is coll. of hist. relics & materials. In front of **Nichols Engineering Hall** is Seated Figure, by Sir Moses Ezekiel, mourning cadet dead of New Market. Ezekiel fought at New Market, as member of the corps. In Auditorium of **Jackson Mem. Bldg.** is large painting by Clinedinst depicting the famous charge. On N. side of Parade Ground, **H.** formerly occupied by Comdr. Maury. Across front of **Cooke Hall** is Mem. Garden with shrubs & mementos from famous gardens, battlefields & hist. places—marked by tablets. In Lexington are Js. with US501, St.39 & US11 (see Lynchburg Trip I & US11).

**136.5. MONMOUTH MILL** (mid-18th cent.), still functioning. **140. KERR'S CREEK MON.**, comm. massacre by Inds. (1763 & 1764) during Pontiac's War (see Pa. & Ohio secs.). **156.** J. with Rd. leading (L) to **Green Pastures Recr. Area** (for Negroes.bath.pic.parking), with L. in Jefferson Nat. Pk. Address: Dist. Ranger, Natural Bridge Sta. **164.5.** J. with Cty.629 leading (R) 5$^m$ to **Douthat St. Pk.** (5,000 as.bath.pic.accoms.restaurant.store.25 cabins.horses.trls.info.:Clifton Forge, Va.), with L. **178. COVINGTON,** located in a mt. enclosed valley, on Jackson R. **W. Va. Pulp & Paper Co.** (O.special appl.), one of country's most important paper-making plants. J. with US220 (see US11 Side Trip St.39). **182.** J. with US60 Alt. (R) shorter route, which Tour follows. **194. VA.-W. VA. LINE.**

# US 58—VIRGINIA

**VA. BEACH (W) to VA.-TENN. LINE** (1$^m$ from Cumberland Gap, Tenn.). **530. US58**

Via: Norfolk, Porstmouth, Suffolk, Franklin, Emporia, Lawrenceville, Clarksville, Danville, Martinsville, Stuart, Hillsville, Galax, Abingdon, Bristol, Gate City, Ewing, (Cumberland Gap, Tenn.).

US58, known as "Jeb" Stuart Hy., honoring famous Confed. cavalry leader, parallels Tenn. Line &, in W. sec., crosses picturesque Blue Ridge & Alleghenies to Cumberland Gap, Tenn.

### Sec. 1: VA. BEACH to SUFFOLK. 38.

(For this stretch, see Hampton Rds. Trip II & III.)

### Sec. 2: SUFFOLK to LAWRENCEVILLE. 78.

**32. COURTLAND. Clerk's Office,** now back part of Cth. (1st half 18th cent.) E. J. with St.35 leading (R) 7.5$^m$ to **Charlie's Hope** (1st half 19th cent.); old outbuildings, incl. slave quarters. In this vic. occurred 2-day slave revolt of 1831, led by Nat. Turner, who was hanged. **60. EMPORIA** (c.1717), just (S) of US58. Center of peanut-growing dist. & industrial town. **County Cth.** (1787). **Reese H.,** formerly an old tavern. US58 now traverses a tobacco-growing reg., where tobacco auctions are yr.'s chief events. J. with US301. **78. LAWRENCEVILLE,** famous for Brunswick stews. **St. Paul's Polytechnic Institute** (Negro.est.1888), founded in tiny shack, by S. Russell, ex-slave, grad. of Hampton Institute.

### Sec. 3: LAWRENCEVILLE to DANVILLE. 96.

**18. SOUTH HILL.** Tobacco auctions in winter. J. with US1 (see). **34. BOYDTON. St. James Ch.** (Episc.). **County Cth.** (both mid-19th cent.). **66.** J. with US501, just (S) of S. Boston.

SIDE TRIP: Take US501 (N) c.0.5m to **S. Boston** (est.1796), great tobacco market. Tobacco auctions from end of Sept. to Feb. First wk. of Sept., **Nat. Tobacco Festival,** attended by more than 150,000. A native, John L. Wade, claimed first to have granulated tobacco for pipes, calling it "Bull Doze." When he sold out to tobacco interests of Durham, N.C., name was changed to "Bull Durham." During Festival, many old Hs. are open, incl.: (1) (W) of S. Boston, c.4m on Cty.659, **Berry Hill,** show place of vic. (1828.Gr.Rev.), supposedly inspired by Parthenon; colonnade 200′ long. Builder, Jas. Bruce, was one of richest planters of America; owned 3,000 slaves; antiques, portraits (one of Jas. Marshall); relics. Near H., giant **Oak,** supposedly more than 400 yrs. old. (2) At 4m on US501 is J. with Cty.654, which leads (L) c.0.5m to **Green's Folly** (c.1789), so-called because of its size. Built by Capt. Berryman Green, Quartermaster at Valley Forge. (3) In vic. of Berry Hill, 6m from S. Boston, **"Tar Over"** (1790), so called because while waiting for roofing from England, workmen covered top of H. with tar. (4) At 6m (N) on US501 is **Halifax,** lovely old town, where in 1827, John Randolph of Roanoke made speech in defense of states' rights. Fine old **Cth.; St. John's Ch.** (early 19th cent.); **Meth. Ch.** (18th cent.); **Masonic Temple** (c.1830); & old Hs.: **Grand Oaks; Elm Hill; Woodburn** (fine gardens); **Magnolia Hill;** old **Leigh H.** In Halifax is J. with US360 which take (R) (E) c.7.5m & then Cty.725 (R) to **Staunton St. Pk.** (1,776 as.O.swim.pic.cabins.trls.restaurant where famous Brunswick stews are served. store), at c.11m. Pk. is at confluence of Dan & Staunton Rs.

**73.** Here, c.500 yards (S) of US58, on Dr. J. A. Owen's property, is old **Wiley's Tavern** (to be rest.) where Cornwallis stopped (1781) on his way to fight Gen. Greene at Guilford Cth., N.C. **75. TURBEVILLE. 96. DANVILLE,** industrial city on Dan R. & important dark tobacco market. Tobacco auctions, Sept.-Feb. Textile mills began to migrate from N. toward end of 19th cent. to Danville. Efforts to organize unions led to labor conflicts. On Main St., **Danville Pub. Lib.** (O), **H.** in which Davis' cabinet met for last time, Ap. 1865, just before Lee's surrender. Dan River Mills, allegedly largest single-unit textile mill in world. Its **Schoolfield Division** (O.guided tours) reached by US29. **Danville Knitting Mills** (stockings). (S) of Danville is **Danville Nat. Cemetery,** in which Union soldiers, who died during imprisonment at Danville, are buried. Js. with US29 (see) & US360.

### Sec. 3: DANVILLE to BRISTOL. 210.

At **4.** (W) of Danville, on US58, **DAN'S HILL H.** (R) (O.Garden Wk.fee.1833); orig. outbuildings & rest. garden. **9.** J. with Cty.863. (L. here 6m to **Oak Hill,** 1823; old garden & slave Hs.). **30. MARTINSVILLE** (sett.late 18th cent.), on Smith R., industrial town whose chief product is furniture. **Old Cth.** N. J. with US220. **61. STUART,** named for Confed. Gen. "Jeb" Stuart. Statue of Gen. at old Cth. **64.** N. J. with St.8.

SIDE TRIP: Take St.8 (R) c.4m to J. with Cty.625, which take (R) to lovely **Fairy Stone St. Pk.** (5,000 as.bath.boat.f.cabins.camp.trlrs.trls.L.horses.restaurant.store) at c.12m. Name derives from lucky or "fairy" stones found in reg.

**77.** J. with Cty.602 leading (L) & then Cty. Rds. 5m to **Pinnacles of Dan,** deep canyon of Dan R.; dam, reservoir & hydroelectric installations. Just beyond last J., on US58, is J. with Blue Ridge Pkwy. (see). **98. HILLSVILLE,** scene of raid by Allen Clan to free Floyd Allen (1912), in which judge & others were killed. J. with US52, running (NW) near hist. **Austin Lead Mines,** to Ft. Chiswell (see US11). **111. GALAX,** named for flowering mt. shrub, peculiar to vic. In summer, Fiddler's Convention, at which old-time musicians & ballad singers meet. **129. INDEPENDENCE.** J. with US21 leading (N) here c.15m to J. with Cty.57 which take (L) to **Comers Rock** (pic.) in **Jefferson Nat. For.** Fine view of Mt. Rogers. **144. VOLNEY.** J. with St.16 leading (NW) to Marion (see US11). From here to **Damascus,** 36m, US58 is not paved. **168.** J. with Cty.603.

SIDE TRIP: Take latter (R) short distance to **Luth. Mission & Konnarock Training Sch.** for mt. children. Serves isolated mt. communities by sending out preachers to them. (Accoms.: Summer). From school, Rd. runs to **White Top Mt.** (5,520′). Trl. up **Mt. Rogers** (5,719′), highest in st. (see Chilhowie US11).

**192.** J. with US11 with which US58 unites to **BRISTOL,** at **210.** (For Abingdon & this stretch, incl. Bristol, see US11.)

### Sec. 4: BRISTOL to TENN.-KY. LINE. 108.

**45.** Entrance to **NATURAL TUNNEL** (pic.trls.camp.fee) which Wm. Jennings Bryan called "8th Wonder of the World." Trl. runs to Lovers' Leap. **47.** W. J. with US23, near Duffield.

SIDE TRIP: Take US23 (N) 14m to **Big Stone Gap** where John Fox, Jr. lived, on Shawnee St.; author of "The Little Shepherd of Kingdom Come" & "The Trl. of the Lonesome Pine." **Janie Slemp Newman Mem. Mus.** (O); coll. relics of early Va. pioneer life. US23 cont. generally (N) & (NE) to Norton at 29m. From Norton, **High Knob** (4,162′), recr. area (pic. camp.L.), is accessible via St.73 (S). US23 cont. (N) past **Wise, Pound** & picturesque **Breaks of Big Sandy R.,** to **Jenkins,** Ky. (see) at 53m.

**59. STICKLEYVILLE.** Near here in 1785, Inds. led by notorious halfbreed, Chief Benge, massacred Scott family. **74.** J. with Cty.662. (Take trl. (L) here 2m down to very fine Natural Bridge. In vic. was born Dr. A. T. Still, founder of osteopathy. **80. METH. CAMP GROUND** (est.1810). **Auditorium** (1827-28) has int. hand-hewn oak columns. **94. EWING,** village. **99.** Near here, Oct. 10, 1773, Jas. Boone, son of Dan. Boone, & Henry Russell were killed by Inds. **108.** J. with US25 E. (see Tenn.), c.1m N. of Cumberland Gap (see Ky. & Tenn.).

## TIDEWATER TOURS—VIRGINIA

The Tidewater reg. consists of 5 peninsulas constituting the Md. & Va. E. Shore, extending down to Hampton Roads: 1 Md. peninsula extends (S) from Baltimore & Washington; Eastern Shore (Delmava) peninsula, running (S) from Pa. line to Cape Charles, incl. part of Md., nearly all Del. and 2 Va. counties; 3 peninsulas are wholly in Va.: Northern Neck, bet. the Potomac & the Rappahannock; Middle Peninsula, extending bet. the Rappahannock & York Rs.; S. Peninsula, extending from Richmond reg. bet. York & James Rs. The S. Peninsula, in particular, saw much Civil War fighting, although both the Middle & N. Neck Peninsulas were crisscrossed by opposing Union & Confed. armies as well. This Tidewater reg. is oldest part of st., where 1st settlements, beginning with Jamestown, were made & where during period when tobacco dominated Va. economy were built finest plantation Hs. For **E. SHORE PENINSULA,** see Maryland & US13 above.

## ST. 3—VIRGINIA

**FREDERICKSBURG to WESTLAND. 104. St.3.** Via: Montross, Warsaw, Lancaster, Kilmarnock, Irvington & White Stone.

### Sec. 1: FREDERICKSBURG to KING GEORGE. 18.

(For pts. of int. on this stretch of Rd., see Fredericksburg pts. of int. & Fredericksburg Trip I).

### Sec. 2: KING GEORGE to WARSAW. 39.

**2.5. OFFICE HALL. Rollins H.** (L) in which Booth stayed overnight on his flight. J. with US301, running (NE) to Baltimore (see US301 Md.) & (SW) via Jas. Madison Mem. Bridge, across the Rappahannock, to J. with St.2 (see St.2-US301). **13. OAK GROVE,** village, where Washington went to school, 1744-46. **16.** J. with St.204.

SIDE TRIP: Take latter (L) c.1.5m to **Geo. Washington National Monument.** (O.sm. fee). In 1718, Augustine Washington, Geo.'s father, bought tract on Pope's Cr., where he built his H., Wakefield, destroyed by fire, probably 1779. Geo. Washington was born there, Feb. 22, 1732. Mem. Mansion on the grounds is reconstruction of an early 18th cent. plantation H.; furnished in period; tip-top table in dining room only orig. piece; fine garden reproducing one typical of period; boxwood, brought from Sarah Tayloe Washington's home, more than 100 yrs. old. Near Mansion is reprod. of kitchen of period. About 1m (NW) of Mansion, near banks of Bridges Cr. are Sites of Col. John Washington's (Geo.'s great-grandfather) 1664 home & old Washington family burial plot. Here are buried members of the family; 32 burials in all.

**16.5. WASHINGTON'S MILL** (R) (early 18th cent.). Augustine Washington bought mill from 1st owner. **21.** J. with St.347, leading (L) 1.5$^{m}$ to Westmoreland St. Pk. (O.May 15-Nov.15.camp.sm.fee.cabins.boat.swim.Potomac R.). **21.5.** J. with St.214.

SIDE TRIP: Take latter (L) 1$^{m}$ to **Stratford Hall** (L) (O.fee.early Georg.c.1729.rest.) on Potomac R., notable plantation H. Built by Thos. Lee, great-great grandfather of Rbt. E. Lee, who was born here (1807). Home of 2 signers of Decl. of Ind., Francis Lightfoot Lee & Rich. Henry Lee. Furnished in period. Garden rest.

**26. MONTROSS. Westmoreland Cth.** (early 19th cent.add.); int. portraits by old Amer. masters. Here June 22, 1774, Rich. Henry Lee's resolutions were adopted, offering aid to Boston, whose port had been closed by Brit. **29.5. TEMPLEMANS CROSSROADS.** J. with St.202.

SIDE TRIP: **Templemans** to **Reedville.** 39$^{m}$ St.202 & US360. At 4.5$^{m}$ on St.202, J. with Cty.621 leading (L) 1.5$^{m}$ & then (L) again on country Rd. 1$^{m}$ to **Bushfield,** home of Bushrod Washington, Justice of U.S. Supreme Ct. 11$^{m}$ J. with Cty.604, which leads (L) 2$^{m}$ & then (L) once more on Cty.606, c.1$^{m}$ to **Yeocomico Church** (O.appl.1706). Mary Ball Washington, Geo.'s mother, attended services here. 17.5$^{m}$ **Callao.** J. with US360 which side trip follows (L). 26.5$^{m}$ J. with Cty.630.

Take latter (L) 1.5$^{m}$ to J. with Cty.629. Take latter (L) 1$^{m}$ & then country Rd. (R) 1.5$^{m}$ to **Mantua,** 18th cent. plantation H. overlooking Coan & Potomac Rs.

39$^{m}$ **Reedville,** menhaden fish. & processing center.

**30. NOMINI CH.** (Bapt.est.late 18th cent.). **39. WARSAW. County Cth.** & **Clerk's Office** (both mid-18th cent.).

SIDE TRIP: Take US360 (R) 1$^{m}$ to inters. with country Rd.

Take latter (L) 1$^{m}$ to **Sabine Hall** (O.fee.c.1730.adds.), another notable H.

At 1.5$^{m}$, US360 inters. country Rd. leading (R) 0.5$^{m}$ to **Mt. Airy** (O.Garden Wk.fee.c.1758), a Tayloe H.; old furnishings & coll. of portraits by early Amer. painters. US360 cont. crossing to Tappahannock at 6.5$^{m}$ (see US17).

### Sec. 3: WARSAW to WESTLAND. 47.

**10. FARNHAM. N. Farnham Ch.** (c.1737.rest.). Bullet holes in walls made by Brit. raiders in 1814. **21.5. LIVELY,** village. J. with St.201 leading (R) 3$^{m}$ to **St. Mary's White Chapel** (O.appl.at H.near-by.c.1650.rest.1740-41 & later restorations), where the Balls, maternal ancestors of Washington, worshiped; their tombs are in cemetery. **26. LANCASTER. Cth.** (early 19th cent.); int. portraits. **29. WHITE MARSH CH.** (Meth.est.1792.built 1848). Here was held 1st camp-meeting in this sec. **36.5.** J. with St.222. **Christ Ch.** (O.1732). John Carter, "King" Carter's father, his wives & children are buried in Ch. In cemetery are graves of "King" Carter & his wives.

**38. IRVINGTON** (resort). Ferry to Gray's Pt. across Rappahannock R., near beach resort. **47. WESTLAND,** S. end of Northern Neck, fish. & fish-packing town.

## US 17—VIRGINIA

**FREDERICKSBURG, VA. (SE) to VA.-N.C. LINE** (22$^{m}$ to Elizabeth City, N.C.). **170. US17**

Via: Tappahannock, Saluda, Glenns, Gloucester, Yorktown & Portsmouth

US17 parallels S. side of the Rappahannock R. to Newport News, then crosses James R. near Portsmouth & cont. (S) along Dismal Swamp to N.C. US17 from Fredericksburg unites with St.2 (see St.2-US301 for 6$^{m}$).

### Sec. 1: FREDERICKSBURG to GLOUCESTER. 94.

**18.5. GAY MONT** (O.Ap.-Nov.fee.1725.adds.). **21.** J. with US301 (see Md. US301).

SIDE TRIP: Take US301 (R) 2$^{m}$ to ruins of **Garrett H.,** where John Wilkes Booth, assassin of Lincoln, was shot resisting arrest. His co-conspirator, Herold, surrendered.

**30.5. VAUTER'S CH.** (c.1719) (1$^{m}$ from Vauter's Ch. is **Elmwood** (O.Garden Wk. fee.1773.rest.). Old garden. **38.5.** J. with Cty.631 leading (R) 2$^{m}$ to **Fonthill** (c.1835), home of Rbt. M. T. Hunter, Confed. Sen. & Secy. of St. **48. TAPPAHANNOCK** (est.1680), orig. known as Hobbs' His Hole, on Rappahannock R. Old **Hotel** near riverfront (part 18th cent.) is famous for its food. **County Cth.** (1848); **Old Cth.** (1728), incorporated in Ch.; **Old Clerk's Office** (pre-1750); **Old Debtors' Prison & Old Customh.** J. with US360, which runs (NE) to Warsaw (see St.3).

SIDE TRIP: (Alt. to US17.) From J. to Glenns. 55$^{m}$ US360 (SW), St.14 & St.33. Via: Stevensville, King & Queen, & Centerville. At 10$^{m}$ **St. Paul's Ch.** (1st half 19th cent.). 16$^{m}$

**St. Stevens Ch.,** hamlet. J. with St.14 on which tour cont. (SE). For pts. (NW) on St.14 see St.2-US301. 21m **Bruington Ch.** (est.1790.built 1851). 28.5m **Bel Air** (R) (early 18th cent.). 29.5m **Mattapony Ch.** (c.1720); tombs of family of Carter Braxton, signer of Decl. of Ind. 34m **King & Queen,** village, named for King William & Queen Mary. In charming **Little Cth.** (Mod.) are portraits of Va. notables. 42.5m **Old Stratton Major Parish Ch.** (1720.rest.). 47.5m **Centerville.** J. with St.33. St.33 runs (W) to Richmond, see Richmond Trip III. Tour cont. (E) on St.33. At 55m J. with US17 at Glenns.

**65. GLEBE LANDING CH.** (1839) founded by noted Bapt. preacher, John Waller.

**77. SALUDA.** North J. with St.33.

SIDE TRIP: Take St.33 (L). At 2m is J. with St.227.

Take latter (L) 1.5m to **Rosegill** (c.1650). In 1776, Ralph Wormeley, H.'s owner, was arrested as Tory.

At 3.5m on St.33 is **Christ Ch.** (1712.rest.1840). 10m **Lower Meth. Ch.** (1762). St.33 cont. to **Stingray Pt.,** so-called because Capt. John Smith was stung by a stingray here.

**80. GLENNS.** S. J. with St.33 (see above). **89.5.** J. with Cty.615, which leads (R) 0.5m & then (R) again on Cty.612, c.0.5m, & then (R) again 0.5m to **Marlfield** (1st half 18th cent.). Here lived John Buckner who had 1st printing press in Va., & because he printed laws of 1680 without license, was forbidden to print any more.

**94. GLOUCESTER,** charming old town. **Cth.** (1766). **Old Clerk's Office. Old Debtors' Prison.** Several other int. old bldgs. incl. **Long Bridge Ordinary** (O.1732. Info.for Garden Wk. Tour of 9 hist. bldgs.). **Bellamy Mus. of Gloucester Hist. Soc.** (O.special days & appl.caretaker in H.near-by); coll. hist. relics & other int. items.

SIDE TRIPS: (A) Take Cty.616 (R) 4m to tiny H. (R), **Birthpl. of Walter Reed,** discoverer of mosquito as yellow fever carrier.

(B) Take St.14 (L) from Gloucester. At 1m, **Ware Ch.** (O.Garden Wk.c.1690). At 3m **Elmington** (R) (O.Garden Wk.1848), where Thos. Dixon wrote "The Clansman." At 3.5m **Toddsbury** (R) (O.Garden Wk.fee.in part late 17th cent.). A short distance beyond Toddsbury is **Auburn** (O.Garden Wk.fee.early 19th cent.).

(C) To S. of Gloucester short distance is **Goshen** (O.Garden Wk.fee.pre-Rev.).

(D) To S. of Gloucester 4m via Cty.615 & then Cty.629 is **Warner Hall** (Estate O. Garden Wk.fee.1740.burnt 1840.rebuilt). Tomb of Mildred Warner, Geo. Washington's grandmother.

### Sec. 2: GLOUCESTER to VA.-N.C. LINE. 76.

**3.5. GLEBE H.** (early 18th cent.). **5.5. WHITE MARSH** (L) (Garden O.Garden Wk. fee); grove of more than 100 varieties of trees. **7. ABINGDON CH.** (L) (O.Garden Wk.1755), said to have been built after plans by Sir Christopher Wren. **10.** J. with Cty.639.

SIDE TRIP: Take latter (R) 0.5m to J.; here turn (L) & then (R) to **Powhatan's Chimney** (rebuilt), ruins of early H. on Site of Werowocomoco, chief town of Powhatan, where Capt. Smith, after his capture (1607) by Inds., was brought & rescued, according to legend, by Pocahontas.

**13. GLOUCESTER PT.** (sett.c.1677). Cornwallis planned to cross R. to Gloucester Pt. & so break through Yorktown blockade, but a storm interfered. A few miles (E) of Gloucester Pt. on Guinea Peninsula is **Little England** (O.Garden Wk.frame sec.pre-1690.brick sec.1716.rest.built supposedly after design by Sir Christopher Wren). US17 now crosses York R. by ferry (autos) to Yorktown (see Williamsburg Trip IV). **28.5. MORRISON.** J. with US60 (see). **34. JAMESTOWN BRIDGE** (toll) across James R. **56. PORTSMOUTH.** See Hampton Roads Reg. for Portsmouth & balance of US17 to **VA.-N.C. LINE** at **76.**

## ST. 5 & ST. 31—VIRGINIA

**RICHMOND (SE) to WILLIAMSBURG. 56. St.5 & St.31**

St.5 runs along N. side of James R. paralleling St.10 on S. side. In its 1st sec., it crosses Richmond Nat. Military Battlefield Pk., making J. with Rds. running into Pk. **19.5.** J. with Cty.608.

SIDE TRIP: Take latter (R) here (arrow shows turn) 1.5m to **Shirley** (O.Garden Wk.fee. c.1740.adds.1800), great Tidewater mansion & tallest house on James R. Birthpl. of Ann Hill Carter, Rbt. E. Lee's mother; coll. of portraits, incl. one of "King" Carter & orig. silver & furnishings.

**21.** J. with St.36, which turns off (R) to Hopewell-Charles City Ferry (see St.10).
**23.** J. with unimproved Rd.

SIDE TRIP: Take latter (R) short distance to **Berkeley Mansion** (R) (O.Garden Wk.fee. 1726), on James R., home of Benj. Harrison, signer of Decl. of Ind. & Gov. of Va. His son, Wm. Henry Harrison, born in this H., migrated to Ohio, became hero of Tippecanoe & 9th Pres. Wm.'s grandson, born in N. Bend, Ohio, became 23rd U.S. Pres. At 2.5m on Side Rd., **Westover** (O.Garden Wk.4 days.fee.c.1730.rest.), another famous James R. house built by Col. Wm. Byrd II, known as "Black Swan" because of his personal charm & great culture. His daughter, Evelyn, was a great beauty, & when presented at court, the King wisecracked that "his colonies could breed such beautiful 'Byrds'." Byrd's tomb is in garden, one of most beautiful in reg.

**25.** J. with country Rd. Take latter (R) short distance to **Westover Ch.** (O.1737. rest.). **31. CHARLES CITY. Cth.** (c.1730). On NE. outskirts of town is **Greenway** (L) (18th cent.), birthpl.(1790) of John Tyler, 10th Pres. of U.S. **34. SHERWOOD FOREST** (L) (Col.), home of Pres. John Tyler. He named mansion "Sherwood Forest" because he, like Robin Hood, was a political outlaw. Fine oak grove. **39.** J. with Cty.613 leading (R) to ferry to Claremont (see St.10). **54.** J. with St.31 (R) to Jamestown (see). Cont. on St.31 (L) to Williamsburg (see) at **56.**

## ST. 10—VIRGINIA

**VA.-RICHMOND to VA.-N.C. LINE** (9m N. of Sunbury, N.C.). **107. St.10**
Via: Chesterfield, Chester, Hopewell, Surry, Smithfield & Suffolk.

This route follows S. side of James R., through hist. plantation reg. with many fine old mansions.

**10.5. CHESTERFIELD.** Here Gen. Steuben's forces camped, 1780-81. **Old Clerk's Office** (1st quarter 19th cent.). On site of former jail, **Mon.** comm. victims of religious persecution (1776). **Castlewood** (2nd half 18th cent.). Take Cty.655 (R) 3m to **Pocahontas St. Pk.** (7,605 as.pic.swim.boat.f.3 group camps, one for Negroes. store Ls.). **26. HOPEWELL** (sett.c.1613) at confluence of Appomattox & James Rs. (Ferry to Charles City; Airport). Soon after settlement it was chosen as site of E. India School, whose scholars were to be graduated into univ. planned for Henricus across R. Ind. massacre of 1622 ended both projects. During Rev., Benedict Arnold bombarded town (1781) & during Civil War it was occupied by Feds. Modern city can be said to have been born in 1915, when E. I. du Pont de Nemours Co. built explosives plant, which greatly expanded during both World Wars. Hercules Powder Co., Tubize Artificial Silk Corp., & Hummel-Ross Fibre Co. are other large industries. The chief Hopewell Plants are open on appl. N. end of Cedar Lane, **Appomattox Manor** (oldest part mid-18th cent.rest.) was set afire during Rev. by raiding Brit. & shelled during Civil War by Fed. gunboats. Gen. Grant had hqs. & was visited here, Ap. 1863, by Lincoln, when news of fall of Petersburg was received. SE. cor. Cedar Lane & Maplewood Ave., **St. John's Ch.** (c.1840.adds.). N. end of Fourth St., on grounds of Randolph Hospital, **Site of Cawsons,** birthpl. of John Randolph. N. terminus Memorial Ave., beautiful **Nat. Cemetery.** In vic. of Hopewell are many fine old mansions. For info. on these, consult "A Guide to Hopewell & Prince George Cty." by Fed. Writers' Program (1939).
**32.** J. with Cty.641.

SIDE TRIPS: (A) Take latter (R) 0.5m to **Merchant's Hope Ch.** (c.1657), which derived its name from one of the ships, "The Merchant's Hope," owned by orig. planter.
(B) Take Cty.641 (L) c.0.5m & then (L) 0.5m on side Rd. to **Tar Bay H.** (R) (1st half 18th cent.). At 1m on this side Rd. is **Beechwood** (L) (pre-1843) built by Edmund Ruffin, who fired 1st gun on Ft. Sumter. Fed. gunboats took particular delight in using his H. as target.

**34. GARYSVILLE.** Ruins of ancient Garysville Mill. J. with St.106, running W. past many int. old Hs. to Prince George. At 2m (W) on this hy. is **Cummins' Store.** Just N. is Site of **Sycamore Ch.** where, 1864, Gen. Wade Hamilton's troops captured 2,486 head of cattle from Feds. When Union trooper ridiculed Confed. soldier for having a dirty face, latter replied: "I'm greasy from eating you all's meat, Yank." **35.** J. with Cty.639 leading (L) 4m to **Flowerdew Hundred** (late Col. rest.). **40. BURROWSVILLE. 40.5.** J. with Cty.611.

SIDE TRIP: Take latter (L) short distance to **Brandon Ch.** (L) (1850) near site of former Col. Ch. Cemetery (1700). At 5.5m on Cty.611 overlooking R. is **Brandon** (O.Tues.Wed. Thurs.Garden Wk.fee.18th cent.), one of notable Tidewater plantation Hs.; belonged to Harrison family which numbered govs. & 2 U.S. Pres. among its members. H. is 210' long; inter. has beautifully carved woodwork; old dependencies; magnificent old trees & box-hedged gardens; fine view.

Take Cty.600 (L) from Brandon, 1.5m to **Upper Brandon** (R) on R., surrounded by fine old trees & gardens, another Harrison H.; contains 2 portraits, one of Maria Byrd by Chas. Bridges & another of Martha Blount (Mrs. Tofts), believed to have been sweetheart of Eng. poet, Alexander Pope.

Some 3m from Brandon Ch. on Cty.600 & c.2m from Upper Brandon, is **Willow Hill** (O. Garden Wk.Tues.Wed.Thurs.fee.1823); old dependencies.

**48. SPRING GROVE,** village. J. with St.40.

SIDE TRIP: Take latter (L) (arrow shows turn) short distance to J. with Cty.610.

Take latter (L). At 4.5m **Eastover** (Garden O.Garden Wk.fee.late 18th cent.). Fine gardens & view.

At 5m on St.40, **Claremont,** village (sett.c.1632). **Mon.** marks site of landing by colonists, headed for Jamestown, May, 1607. **Claremont Manor** (Col.) is a handsome Tidewater mansion. Poe was frequent visitor & legend has it he wrote "Gold Bug" here. Rails from RR. here were used to armor Confed. Ram, "Merrimac." Ferry across James R. to J. with Cty. Rd. running to J. with St.5 (see).

**52. THE GLEBE** (pre-1724). **57. SURRY. Clerk's Office** (early 19th cent.). **Chanco Mon.,** comm. Ind. who warned Jamestown settlers of 1622 massacre by Inds.

SIDE TRIP: Take St.31 (L) here 2m to **Smith's Ft.** (Rolfe plantation) (O.sm.fee.1652.fine exter. & inter.), probably home of Thos. Rolfe, son of John Rolfe & Pocahontas, on land given by Powhatan to John Rolfe on his marriage to Ind. Princess. Remnants of orig. Ft. are near H. St.31 cont. (E) via Scotland Wharf & ferry to Jamestown (see).

**61.5.** J. with Cty.633, leading (L) (arrow shows turn) 3.5m to **Old Chippokes Mansion** (garden O.Garden Wk.fee). **63.5.** J. with Cty.617 leading (L) short distance to **Bacon's Castle** (O.sm.fee.1655) which was seized by some of Bacon's followers during his rebellion. **70.5.** J. with Cty.677, leading (R) 1m to Wrenn's Mill (1644), still turning out "water ground" meal. **75. SMITHFIELD,** famous for its Smithfield hams. **Masonic Hall** (1753) on E. Mason St. **Old Cth.** (18th cent.). Adj., **Old Clerk's Office** (now shop) & **Old Jail,** on Mason St. **Windsor Castle,** near Church St., former home of Arthur Smith, orig. owner of town's site. **79.** (Take Cty.659 (L) short distance to **Old Brick (St. Luke's) Ch.** (Goth.1632.rest.), supposed to be oldest Prot. Ch. in America. Among mem. windows are: one to Rev. A. Whitaker, who baptized Pocahontas & married her to John Rolfe, another to Pocahontas & another to Capt. John Smith. **94. SUFFOLK.** J. with US58 (see). **107. VA.-N.C. LINE** (near Sunbury, N.C.).

# CHARLOTTESVILLE

## CHARLOTTESVILLE

Through RR. & bus conns. Accoms.: All types. Swim.: Rivanna R., McIntire Pk. & Fry's Springs, & Albemarle L., 12m (W) of city. Riding to Hounds: Keswick Hunt Club. Sports: Univ. of Va. Stadium. Fish. in vic. In summer, Institute of Public Affairs at Univ. of Va. To (E) on US250, at Rockfish Gap, 25m, J. with Skyline Dr.

Charlottesville (est. 1762) is situated at foot of Blue Ridge, close to Rivanna (orig. Fluvanna) R. Among early 18th cent. patentees of land near city's site, were Nicholas Meriwether & Abr. Lewis, both forefathers of Meriwether Lewis, of Lewis & Clark Expedition fame, John Henry, father of Patrick Henry, & Peter Jefferson, Thos.' father; the latter bought Shadwell tract for price of bowl of Henry Wetherburn's famous Arrack punch (see Williamsburg). Thos. Jefferson was best-known citizen of Albemarle Cty., of which Charlottesville is seat. But cty. also claims Meriwether Lewis & Wm. Clark, of Lewis & Clark expedition, & Geo. Rogers Clark (see Ill.). Jas. Monroe est. his home at Ash Lawn, within sight of his friend Jefferson's at Monticello. Va. Assembly met in city after fleeing Richmond. Its stay was brief, because Brit. Col. Banastre Tarleton raided city, hoping to capture Jefferson & other Rev. leaders. Forewarned by Jack Jouett, son of host of the Cuckoo Tavern, where Tarleton paused en route, they all escaped. Today city is a Univ. town, & center of fine estates, fox hunts, great apple & peach orchards, dairy, cattle & stud farms.

PTS. OF INT.: (1) At 5th & Jefferson Sts., **Albemarle County Cth.** (O.wks.1803 & 1860.adds.1860 & 1870's.Jefferson Class.rest.enlarged 1938). Part of bldg., designed by Jefferson, was used as Ch. where Jefferson, Madison, Monroe & other notables worshiped. General Assembly held sessions in an earlier Cth. near site of this one (1781). Around the Sq. are some old bldgs. formerly used by lawyers & court officials. Pillory, stocks & whipping post were set up in front of older Cth. In Cty. Office Bldg. is Jefferson's will. (2) Opp. Cth., **Swan Tavern** (N.O.1773) which probably incorporates secs. of old inn owned by John Jouett, father of Jack who warned of Tarleton's approach. (3) E. end of Jefferson St., **The Farm** (part of Nicholas Meriwether's orig. plantation); main H. (c.1831), very similar to Edgehill (see Charlottesville Trip II); near-by is **Old H.** (pre-Rev.) where lived Col. Nicholas Lewis, descendant of orig. patentee. Here Tarleton stayed overnight, sleeping in his cloak on the floor. (4) At Lexington & E. High Sts., **Tarleton's Oak,** under which Tarleton is supposed to have pitched his tent. (5) **Mons.:** At 4th & Jefferson Sts., **Stonewall Jackson** (equestrian), by Chas. Keck; at 2nd & Market Sts., **Lee** on his famous horse "Traveller"; Ridge & W. Main Sts., **Lewis & Clark,** by Chas. Keck; W. Main St. & Jefferson Ave., **Geo. Rogers Clark,** by Rbt. Aiken. (6) On W. side of 9th St., (S) of Main St., **Oak Lawn** (c.1818.Jeff.Class.).

(7) Near last-named Mon. is **Univ. of Va.,** at W. end of town, occupying beautiful campus shaded by fine old trees which do not, however, hide the white, columned porticoes. Jefferson designed older structures grouped around The Lawn. The Rotunda closes in N. end of The Lawn & modern Cabell Hall by Stanford White, harmonizing with general classic style, closes in S. end. Univ. was founded by Thos. Jefferson, who, after years of agitating, finally, in 1816, saw his dream come true when legislature authorized founding of **Central College.** In 1819, Assembly authorized Central College to become a university. Jefferson was chosen director of board of visitors & remained dominating force in institution till death. "The institution," he said, "will be based on the illimitable freedom of the human mind. For here we are not afraid to follow the truth wherever it may lead, or tolerate error so long as reason is left free to combat it."

**Entrance Gate** (by H. Bacon, designer of Lincoln Mem., Wash., D.C.) at W. Main St., near its inters. with University Ave. To (L) are **Medical Sch. & Hospital Bldgs.** Among distinguished alumni was Walter Reed, discoverer of cause of yellow fever. Long Walk leads past **Brooks Mus.** (R) (O.Mon.-Fri.Sat.a.m.); geological & mineralogical colls. Facing Mus., **Washington Hall,** NE. cor. of Jefferson group & N. end of E. Range. Long Walk follows the Serpentine Wall, built in this wavy manner to add strength, since it is only one brick thick. At end of Long Walk is **The Lawn,** already referred to. E. & W. Lawns, enclosing it, are composed of pavilions with columned porticoes, connected by colonnades. Back of E. & W. Lawn are the E. & W. Ranges, respectively. In W. Range, No. 31, is room occupied by Woodrow Wilson (O.appl.) & No. 13, Poe's Room (O.appl.). In central section of W. Range, "Rowdy Row," is Jefferson Soc. Room. Madison & Monroe were members & Poe is supposed to have read an essay at a session, 1826; portrait of Jefferson by Trumbull. At N. end of Lawn is **The Rotunda** (1826.rest.1898.by Stanford White), Jeffersonian version of the Pantheon. In front of N. side of bldg. is **Liberty Bell Statue** of Jefferson, by Sir Moses Ezekiel, replica of Mon. in Louisville, Ky. In Rotunda, **Marble Statue of Jefferson,** by A. Galt. Closing in Lawn at S. end, is **Cabell Hall** with figures above portico by G. J. Zolnay. To (R) & (L), respectively, are **Mechanical Lab. & Rouss Physical Lab.,** all designed by Stanford White (1898). To (W) & (E) are **Statues of Jefferson,** copy of one by Karl Bitter, & of Washington, replica of Houdon's statue in Richmond. In front of Cabell Hall is **Statue of Homer,** by Sir Moses Ezekiel. To W. of the Commons is **Monroe H.,** home of Jas. Monroe for several years. Other notable bldgs. are: **Clark Mem. Hall** (Law Sch.) with murals by Allyn Cox; **Dawson** (1859), dormitories; **Alderman Mem. Lib.** (O.wks.Sun.p.m. 1939.Class.) behind which is McConnell statue, by Gutzon Borglum, in memory of J. R. McConnell, student killed while with Lafayette Escadrille, World War I; on Carr's Hill, **President's H.** (mod.Class., last bldg.designed by Stanford White before his death), & **Fayerweather Hall** (Class.1893.by Carpenter & Peebles) housing Sch. of Art & Architecture; fine arts Lib. (O.Mon.-Fri.). Behind Fayerweather Hall, **Bayly Art Mus.** (O.Tues.-Sat.Sun.aft.1935.by E.S.Campbell); 4 galleries devoted to permanent & 2 to loan exhibits. Among permanent exhibits are portraits of Jefferson by Sully & of Washington by Rembrandt Peale.

(8) (E) of city, 5$^m$ on US250, is **Site of Shadwell** (R), birthpl. of Thos. Jefferson (1743), marked by fenced-in enclosure (near present H.). When H. burned down, 1770, Negro reported to Thos. Jefferson that fortunately they had saved his fiddle. (9) Take St.53 (SE) from Charlottesville Cth. At 2.5$^m$, **Michie Tavern** (O.fee.c.1735. 18th cent.adds.reconstructed) removed here from orig. site. Supposedly oldest sec. was Patrick Henry's boyhood home; antiques. (10) At 3$^m$ on St.53 is **Entrance to Monticello** (L). Drive climbs to hilltop where, on plateau affording a magnificent

view, is **Monticello** (O.fee). This was favorite haunt in their boyhood of Jefferson & his friend, Dabney Carr. In 1770 Jefferson began bldg. Monticello, & in 1772, in middle of snow storm, which compelled them to finish journey on horseback, he & his young bride arrived at the half-completed H. Jefferson built Monticello in Graeco-Roman manner, inspired by Palladio; it is an outstanding example of class. style. The fine portico & the balustrade around the upper story are features that have been much copied. Circular windows in base of dome are unusual. H. has 35 rooms. Inter. is beautiful; woodwork, all designed by Jefferson, especially so. There are a number of amusing gadgets, invented by author of the Decl. of Ind.—narrow, hidden stairways, because Jefferson disliked the grand stairways of European palaces, specially devised dumbwaiters, a clock operated by cannonball weights & pulleys, recessed or disappearing beds, folding doors similar to those used today in streetcars & unusual lighting & ventilating arrangements. Old dependencies have been restored. Near H. is shaft on **Jefferson's Grave,** inscribed by his direction: "Here lies Thomas Jefferson, Author of the Declaration of Independence, of the Statute of Virginia for Religious Freedom & Father of the University of Virginia." (11) Cont. on St.53 to J. with Cty.795. Take latter (R) to J. with Cty.627, & then latter (R). At 5$^{m}$ Entrance (R) to **Ash Lawn** (O.fee.oldest sec.1796-98.rest.). Rear part was built by Jas. Monroe, who wanted to be near his friend, Jefferson. Monroe returned to Ash Lawn on & off till 1820. Statue of Monroe by Piccirilli. Fine view.

## NOTABLE BLDGS. IN VIC. OF CHARLOTTESVILLE

Below are listed some of more important bldgs. & their locations, as well as a few other pts. of int. in vic. of Charlottesville. For detailed info., see "Jefferson's Albemarle" compiled by Fed. Writers' Program, 1941.

I. (S) & (SE) OF CHARLOTTESVILLE: (1) **Tufton** (1790.adds.), part of which was built by Thos. Jefferson, c.0.5$^{m}$ off Cty.627, c.4.5$^{m}$ from city. (2) **Morven** (O.Garden Wk.fee.c.1820;influenced by Jefferson's style), old gardens, on Cty.627, c.1.5$^{m}$ (S) of Ash Lawn. (3) **Ellerslie** (c.1842), on Cty.627, c.8.5$^{m}$ from city. (4) **Blenheim** (mid-18th cent.), on Cty.727, c.9$^{m}$ from city. (5) **Christ Ch.** (1831-32) on Cty.713, c.1.5$^{m}$ from Keene village. (6) **Plain Dealing** (late 18th cent.built by Sam.Dyer, Rev.patriot), now stud farm owned by Prince Djerdjadze, on Cty.713, c.2$^{m}$ from Keene village. (7) **Glendower** (c.1808) & **Old H.** (1st half 18th cent.) 0.5$^{m}$ on Cty.713, c.18$^{m}$ from city. (8) **Cliffside** (1785) & **Chester** (c.1847) at Scottsville. (9) **Esmont** (mid-19th cent.), on Cty.719, c.2$^{m}$ from Esmont village. (10) **Tallwood** (c.1827. built by Tucker Coles, friend of Jefferson & Monroe); fine garden; on Cty.627, c.3$^{m}$ from Esmont village. (11) **Enniscorthy** (c.1770.rest.1850), built by John Coles II, Rev. officer. Here Jefferson took refuge from Tarleton's raid. On grounds, **Cabin** (pre-Rev.). H. is on Cty.627, c.4.5$^{m}$ from Esmont village. (12) **Estouteville,** probably finest H. in Albemarle Cty. Architect was Jas. Dinsmore, assistant to Jefferson; old Boxwood Garden. On Cty.712, c.1.5$^{m}$ from Keene village. (13) **Edgemont** (c.1806), possibly designed by Jefferson; very fine; on Cty.712, c.4.5$^{m}$ from Keene village. (14) **Piedmont** (1806) on US29, c.0.5$^{m}$ (S) of city; now owned by Univ. of Va. (15) **Bally-Les-Braden,** childhood home of famous Confed. guerrilla leader, Col. J. S. Mosby; on Cty.631, c.3.5$^{m}$ (S) of city. (16) **Montebello,** on US29, on outskirts of city.

II. (E) & (N) OF CHARLOTTESVILLE: (1) **Glenmore** (pre-Rev.& c.1845) on US250, 6$^{m}$ E. of city & 1$^{m}$ from Shadwell village. (2) **Keswick Hunt Club,** famous for its fox hunts, on St.22 near its J. with US250, 6.5$^{m}$ (E) of city. (3) **Edgehill** (1828. rest.probably after designs of Jefferson). Behind it, small brick H., home of Thos. M. Randolph & Martha Jefferson Randolph, daughter of Thos. Jefferson. On St.22, near its J. with US250. (4) **Cismont** (1st half 19th cent.), on St.22, c.8.5$^{m}$ from city. (5) **Merrie Mills** (rest.1939), formerly owned by J. A. Chandler. His sanity having been established by Va. Courts, he sent famous message to his brother "Bob" Chandler, painter & bon vivant, when latter had difficulties with his wife, Lina Cavalieri. Message read "Who's loony now?" On St.22, c.0.5$^{m}$ from its J. with Cty.600. (6) **Grace Ch.** (c.1848.Goth.rest.), on St.231, c.0.5$^{m}$ from Cismont village. (7) **Castle Hill** (1764. & c.1840.Jefferson Class.). Tarleton was delayed here in 1781 by the owners' calculated hospitality, & became so irritated that he ordered the servants whipped. But delay gave Jefferson & Va. Assembly time to escape from city. On St.231, c.2$^{m}$ from Cismont village.

III. (W), (NW) & (N) OF CHARLOTTESVILLE: (1) **Farmington Country Club** (pre-Rev.& 1850.adds.), begun on designs of Jefferson, c.4.5$^m$ (W) of city on US250. (2) **Seven Oaks** (1847-48.Gr.Rev.). Behind H. is ancient **Black's Tavern** where Geo. Rogers Clark (see Ohio) stopped over in 1777; c.17.5$^m$ (W) on US250. (3) **Mirador** (garden O.Garden Wk.fee.c.1830), where Mary Langhorn, later Lady Astor, & her sister, Irene, wife of Chas. Dana Gibson, for whose "Gibson Girls" she is said to have posed, spent their youth. On US250 (W) of city, c.18$^m$. (4) **Carrsbrook** (c.1794), built by Peter Carr, son of Dabney Carr, Jefferson's friend, & of Martha, Jefferson's sister. On US29 (N) of city a few miles. (5) **Bentivar** (c.1795), on Cty.643, c.2$^m$ from its J. with US29, (N) of city. (6) **Dunlora** (1828), built by Sam. Carr, brother of Peter, on Cty.631, c.2$^m$ from its J. with US29 & only c.2.5$^m$ (N) of city.

IV. FURTHER (N) OF CITY VIA CTY.613: (1) **Barboursville,** now in ruins, was designed by Jefferson for Gov. Jas. Barbour; fine boxwood. **Barboursville H.** (O. Garden Wk.fee.1790.designed by same). Both are in Barboursville at J. of Cty. 613, US33 & St.20. (2) **Monte Bello,** one of houses claiming to be birthpl. of Zachary Taylor, 12th Pres. 2$^m$ (E) of Barboursville on US33. (3) **Malbone** (garden O.Garden Wk.), on US33, (E) of Monte Bello. (4) **Gordonsville Inn** (1787), 6$^m$ (E) of Barboursville on US33. (5) **Frascatti** (O.Garden Wk.c.1830), after designs of Jefferson, notable H. (NE) from Barboursville on St.20 c.6$^m$ & then (R) on St.231, c.2$^m$ (arrow indicates turn). (6) **Madison Cemetery,** where are graves of Jas. Madison & his wife, marked by stones. On St.20, (NE) of Barboursville, 7.5$^m$ & then (R) 1$^m$ on Cty.639. (7) **Montpelier** (garden O.Garden Wk.fee.c.1741.adds.), Jas. Madison's home, in lovely grove. Built by Madison's father; Madison added columned portico (1793) at Jefferson's suggestion. Garden (rest.) is in form of amphitheater, allegedly after designs by Lafayette. Fine old boxwood. (NE) from Barboursville c.8.5$^m$ on St.20. (8) At 12.5$^m$ (NE) on St.20 from Barboursville is **Orange. St. Thomas Ch.** (1st half 19th cent.Gr.Rev.). (9) (E) from Orange, c.0.5$^m$ on St.20, is J. with Cty.612. (R) on latter to **Meadow Farm** (garden O.GardenWk.fee.1855) at c.2.5$^m$ from **Orange's Cth.;** on site of earlier H. built by Zachary Taylor, 12th President's grandfather. Pres. Taylor's great-grandfather, orig. patentee of the plantation, Jas. Taylor, was member of Gov. Spotswood's "Expedition of the Knights of the Golden Horseshoe" in 1716. (10) At 3.5$^m$ (E) from Orange on St.20 is **Bloomsbury** (1st quarter 18th cent.), once home of Jas. Taylor (see above). (11) c.5$^m$ (E) from Orange, on St.20, is **Chestnut Hill,** old tavern where Henry Clay often stopped. (12) (N) of Orange, c.1.5$^m$ on US15, is J. with Cty.633, which take (R) c.0.5$^m$ (arrow shows turn) & then (R) on Cty.632 short distance to **Montebello** (O.Garden Wk.fee.mid-18th cent.adds.), still in possession of descendants of orig. patentee (1728); old murals of Va. hist. scenes; old boxwood. (13) Return from Orange via US15 (S) & then US250 (W) to Charlottesville.

# FREDERICKSBURG

## FREDERICKSBURG

Through RR. & bus conns. Accoms.: All types. Info.: C. of C.

Fredericksburg, on Rappahannock R., & vic. are as crammed full of hist. landmarks as Williamsburg is of reconstructed history. First settlement was made c.1671. At head of navigation, city became important shipping pt. Interrupted temporarily by Rev., Fredericksburg's prosperity grew steadily, with influx of tobacco, grain, flax, etc., brought in by huge Conestoga wagons for shipment abroad, & of imports for wealthy planters. During Civil War, 4 bloody battles were fought for possession of city, which changed hands 7 times; but Union armies were halted & Grant switched to attack Richmond from (S), via Petersburg.

PTS. OF INT.: (1) On Princess Anne St., **County Cth.** (O.1852), hist. documents—among others, Will of Mary Washington, George's mother. (2) Opp., **Presb. Ch.** (1835.Gr.Rev.) which has 2 cannon balls imbedded in its portico column. Ch. was hospital for Union troops who were nursed there by Clara Barton, of Red Cross fame. (3) At George & Princess Anne Sts., **St. George's Ch.** (Episc.O.1849); in earlier Ch. on this site, members of Washington family & Jas. Monroe worshipped. In Cemetery are buried John Paul Jones' brother, Wm. Paul, & Martha Washington's father, John Dandridge. Under front steps is buried Col. Fielding Lewis (see below). (4) N. of Ch., on Princess Anne St., **City Hall** (O.1814). (5) (S) of Cth., at Princess Anne & Hanover Sts., **Masonic Lodge** (O.wks.Sat.p.m.sm.fee.1814), which initiated Washington; hist. relics & Gilbert Stuart portrait of Washington. (6) NW. cor. George & Charles Sts., **Masonic Cemetery,** supposedly oldest of order in U.S. (7) On Charles St., bet. Wm. & George Sts., **Jas. Monroe's Law Office,** 1786-91; furniture & furnishings used by Monroe in White House, incl. desk at which he signed Monroe Doctrine, hist. relics, documents, portraits by Peale & Trumbull. (8) NW. cor. Wm. & Charles Sts., **Slave Block.** (9) On Charlotte St., bet. Princess Anne & Prince Edward Sts., **H. of Comdr. Matthew F. Maury,** noted naval cartographer. (10) NE. cor. Caroline St. & Lafayette Blvd., **H. of John Paul Jones** & his brother, Wm. Paul, where latter had tailor shop. (11) On Caroline St., near terminus of Dixon St., is **Sentry Box** (pre-Rev.) owned by Gens. Geo. Weedon & Hugh Mercer, (see below). (12) On Gunnery Rd., branching off Dunmore St., **Gunnery Spring,** capped by brick & concrete, comm. women of Rev.; on site of 1st Rev. gun & ammunition factory. The tour returns to pt. near City Hall, at William & Princess Anne Sts.

(13) SW. cor. Caroline & Amelia Sts., **Hugh Mercer's Apothecary Shop** (O.wks.eves. appl.sm.fee.18th cent.rest.), where Dr. Hugh Mercer dispensed medicines. Mercer later became Rev. general & was killed at Battle of Princeton. (14) On Caroline St., bet. Hawke & Fauquier Sts., **Rising Sun Tavern** (O.wks.sm.fee.1780.rest.), built by Chas. Washington & kept by Gen. Geo. Weedon, German immigrant, actually named Gerhard von Wieden. Weedon was ardent patriot & tavern became a Rev. center; partially furnished in period. (15) NW. cor. Charles & Lewis Sts., **Mary Washington's H.** (O.wks.summer.& Sat.aft.sm.fee.18th cent.rest.), purchased by Geo. Washington for his mother (1772). She lived here from 1774 till her death, 1789. Orig. inter.; period furnishings; fine garden, with some of orig. boxwood. Mary Washington complained constantly of her financial straits when actually George provided for her generously. She never visited him at Mt. Vernon; indeed he asked her not to; but came to see her often—the last time in 1789 before his inauguration as Pres. in New York, shortly before her death.

(16) On Fauquier St., bet. Charles & Prince Edward Sts., is last surviving **Chestnut Tree,** of 13 planted by Washington symbolizing orig. states. (17) Princess Anne & Amelia Sts., **Doggett H.** (O.Garden.wk.fee.early 18th cent.); scenic wallpaper dating from 1813-17; furnished in period. (18) Washington Ave. & William St., **Confed. Cemetery.** (19) On Washington Ave. near Lewis St., **Mon. to Geo. Rogers Clark** (see Ill.). (20) On Washington Ave., bet. Fauquier & Lewis Sts., **Kenmore** (O.fee.1752.fine exter.& inter.), home of Betty Washington, Geo.'s sister. She married Fielding Lewis, maker of guns for Rev. army. Inter. of H. is almost entirely in orig. state & furnished in period; parlor has low-relief frieze, probably by Hessian prisoners, depicting Aesop's fable of "The Fox & the Crow"; portraits of Lewis & Betty, by Wollaston, in dining room; appanages reconstructed. (21) Washington Ave. & Fauquier St., **Statue,** by E. V. Valentine, of Gen. Hugh Mercer. (22) Washington Ave. & Pitt St., **Mon.** (23) near **Grave of Mary Washington.** (24) On Sunken Rd., around which centered much of Battle of Fredericksburg fighting at Marye's Heights (1862), just off US1, is **Brompton** (c.1837.Gr.Rev.). (25) Cor. Lafayette Blvd. & Sunken Rd., **Nat. Pk. Hqs. Mus.;** relics of Battle & other items. (26) Opp., **Nat. Cemetery** with graves of more than 15,000 soldiers. (27) At Sunken Rd. & Monroe St., **Mary Washington College** (women) of Univ. of Va. (28) Take St.3 (E) to J. with Cty.607 & then (L) on latter short distance to **Chatham** (c.1750), where Rbt. E. Lee came to court his wife. (29) At $1^m$ (E) on St.3 is Site of **Ferry Farm,** boyhood home of Geo. Washington, where he is supposed to have cut down cherry tree, thrown silver dollar across R. & while breaking a colt, to have killed it. His mother, Mary Washington, continued to direct farm, although Geo. wanted her to turn it over to an overseer. (30) Cont. on St.3 (E) passing **Stafford Heights** where Union forces were stationed during battle (1862). (31) At $12.5^m$ on St.3, J. with Cty.607 which leads (L) $0.5^m$ to **Lamb's Cr. Ch.** (pre-1750), badly damaged during Civil War.

## TRIPS OUT OF FREDERICKSBURG

### I. St.218 & St.206 (E) of FREDERICKSBURG.

Follow St.218 (E) out of Fredericksburg to J. with Cty.609.

SIDE TRIP: Take latter (R) here c.$0.5^m$ to **Marmion** (L) (O.fee.fine inter.pre-1701). Inter. woodwork of drawing room is now in N.Y. Metropolitan Mus. Much of inter. decoration was done by a Hessian soldier befriended by the then owners, the Fitzhughs.

St.218 cont. past or near some fine old Hs. to J. with St.206 & Cty.632.

SIDE TRIPS: (A) Take latter (R) short distance to **St. Paul's Ch.** (O.appl.at near-by dwelling.1766.rest.).

(B) Take St.206 (R) (S) c.1.5m to **Cleydale** (L) (1859), home of Dr. R. H. Stuart, to whom John Wilkes Booth, in flight after assassination of Lincoln, appealed for help—an appeal which he refused. Stuart later was accused of giving aid to the assassin, but proved his innocence. Just beyond Cleydale, on St.206, is **Dixon's Cabin,** hut of the Dixons, domestics at Cleydale, who helped Booth.

### II. St.3 (W) of FREDERICKSBURG to J. with St.20. 15.5.

Route crosses through N. sec. of Fredericksburg & Spotsylvania Nat. Military Pk. (see). **10. CHANCELLORSVILLE,** area where Battle of Chancellorsville was fought (see Nat. Pk.). **11. JACKSON MON.,** near spot where "Stonewall" Jackson was wounded. **14.5.** J. with St.210. In this vic. was fought Battle of the Wilderness.

SIDE TRIP: St.210 branches off (L) here past several pts. of int. of this Battle & Battle of Spotsylvania Cth., to **Spotsylvania** & there makes J. with St.51 back through Battlefield to J. with US1, (S) of Fredericksburg.

**15. SITE OF WILDERNESS TAVERN,** where, in a tent, "Stonewall" Jackson's arm was amputated. **15.5.** J. with St.20. Pts. on St.20 (L) from here are described on N-S tours it crosses & in Charlottesville Trip IV.

### III. FREDERICKSBURG & SPOTSYLVANIA CTY. NAT. MILITARY PK.

Approach Rd. for 1st battle of Fredericksburg: US1 from Lafayette Blvd. & Sunken Rd., at Nat. Pk. Hqs. For the other 3 battlefields: St.3 (W) from Fredericksburg to J. with St.210, then (L) on latter to J. with St.51, then (L) on latter to J. with US1, & then (L) on latter to Fredericksburg. Info.: Nat. Pk. Hqs. (O.sm.fee) which has Mus. containing battlefield dioramas, relief maps, coll. of firearms, wartime photos & hist. relics. Conducted tours of Fredericksburg Battlefield (free).

The Nat. Military Pk. (2,397 as.) takes in parts of all 4 battlefields: Fredericksburg, Chancellorsville, The Wilderness & Spotsylvania Cth., unsuccessful battles fought by Union armies to open up Rd. to Richmond. Miles of trench remains & gun pits are well preserved, & there are a number of mons. Pk. Rds. make pts. of int. accessible. Nat. Pk. Visitors Service Stas. furnish info.

**First Battle of Fredericksburg** (Dec.1862). Gen. A. E. Burnside made 2 unsuccessful attacks on Lee's forces at Spotsylvania Heights. Some of bitterest fighting took place along the stone wall of the Sunken Rd. Burnside withdrew Dec. 15-16, after losing 12,652 of his army of 142,000, as against Lee's losses of 5,309 out of 91,000.

**Battle of Chancellorsville** at Chancellorsville (on St.3) took place (May 1-3, 1863) when Lee decisively defeated Gen. Jos. Hooker. It was during this battle that Jackson was mortally wounded by his own men. Lee was forced to divert troops to support Jubal Early, who had been imperiled near Fredericksburg in the 2nd Battle of Fredericksburg, & Hooker escaped. Lee lost 12,821; Feds., 17,278.

**Battle of the Wilderness** (May 5-6, 1864), centered around area where St.3 & St.210 intersect. Grant had been put in command after Hooker's disastrous defeat at Chancellorsville. Battle of the Wilderness was 1st in which Grant opposed Lee. Feds., after bloody fighting, were unable to dislodge Confed. army from its positions on the Rapidan-Rappahannock line. Fed. losses were c.15,387 out of 118,000; Confed. losses, 11,400 out of 62,000.

**Battle of Spotsylvania Cth.** (on St.210) lasted 13 days, beginning May 8, 1864. Lee with his meager force of 51,000 successfully blocked Grant's army of about 110,000. It was here that Grant said he intended "to fight it out on this line if it takes all summer." Fed. losses were about 17,500; Confed. unknown.

## HAMPTON ROADS PORT AREA

**HAMPTON ROADS AREA:** Norfolk, Portsmouth, Newport News, Hampton & Environs.

Hampton Roads is chief artery through which commerce of SE. Atlantic coastal reg. flows. Cities located on it aggregate an import & export tonnage 2nd only to that of N.Y. The 4m strait connects Chesapeake Bay with James & Elizabeth Rs. by a deep channel, which in turn is conn. by a broad strait, bet. Cape Charles & Cape Henry, with the Atlantic Ocean. Newport News, on N. side of the Roads & Norfolk & Portsmouth on the S. side have harbors capable of berthing largest vessels. Huge Newport News Shipbuilding & Dry Dock Co.'s plant, & U.S. Navy Yard at Portsmouth, give reg. paramount importance as shipbuilding & reconditioning center. Great Naval Operational Base at Norfolk, Army's Langley Field, near Newport News, several fts. guarding the Strait's entrances, an army base & naval & marine hospitals, make it focal pt. for armed services. During both World Wars, reg. hummed with military activities, & the Roads cities experienced tremendous industrial & pop. expansion.

Ferries ply from Newport News & other pts. on the N. side to Norfolk, Portsmouth & pts. on the S. side of the Roads. A ferry connects Norfolk with Cape Charles on Delmava Peninsula & a bridge spans James R. from (W) of Portsmouth to a pt. near Newport News. James R. runs (NW) inland to Richmond from the Roads, & Elizabeth R. cuts in bet. Norfolk & Portsmouth. This R. has, since early times, been crowded with cargo vessels. It was said, formerly, you could cross from Norfolk to Portsmouth, from deck to deck, without getting your feet wet. Important export commodities are coal, scrap-iron, tobacco, grain, peanut products, fish & fish products. The metropolitan area, besides shipbuilding & reconditioning yards, has more than 243 industrial plants. Peanut products bulk large, due to fact that this is center of a great peanut-growing area; also sea food. Port cities are starting pts. for some of outstanding hist. shrines of the country & are located at heart of fine bay & ocean resort reg.

In 1607 the "Sarah Constant," the "Goodspeed" & the "Discovery" stopped over at Pt. Henry, (NE) of Norfolk, on way to Jamestown (see). In 1610, at Hampton, was made, it is claimed, 1st permanent Eng. settlement (Jamestown was eventually abandoned) on N. Amer. continent. Norfolk was est. 1682 on 50 as. whose purchase price was 10,000 lbs. of tobacco. Gosport, now part of Portsmouth, was sett. early, & almost from beginning, ships were careened for repairs on its beach where today sprawls great Navy Yard. Newport News, although sett. as early as 1621, remained mere crossroads until late in 19th cent. Collis P. Huntington made it tidewater terminal of Chesapeake & Ohio RR.; the great shipyard was built there soon after.

Commerce in early days was troubled by pirates, eventually eliminated when Teach, better known as Blackbeard, was caught & hanged, in 1718, by a native of Hampton. During Rev., War of 1812 & Civil War, the Roads reg. saw considerable fighting. Va. Gov., Lord Dunmore, established himself & a small horde of Tories at Gosport in 1775, but fled, after defeat at Great Bridge, to Brit. fleet which in 1776, bombarded Norfolk & reduced it to ruins; most of Hs. surviving Brit. guns were destroyed by patriots to "clean out the nest of Tories." After Rev., commerce had to face inroads of privateers during "undeclared" war with France. After that, Jefferson's Embargo Act & finally War of 1812 nearly wiped out what commerce was left. But full-scale attacks by Brit. were driven off; in 1813 a force of 4,000 from Brit. Adm. Cockburn's fleet was routed at Craney I. by 735 raw farmer lads & 150 sailors from USS "Constellation." After treaty of Ghent, Roads ports suffered equally from closing of W. Indies to America & Amer. retaliation by closing of Amer. ports to Brit. shipping. Va. commerce, in 1790 equal to N. Y.'s, by 1832 had dropped to $1,000,000 annually, as compared with N. Y.'s $57,000,000. But building of Dismal Swamp canal made the Roads ports natural outlet for N.C.'s agric. In 1855, yellow fever was imported from Danish W. Indies & killed off 2,000 in Norfolk & nearly as many in Portsmouth. Then came Civil War & destruction of Portsmouth Navy Yard which, however, was rehabilitated by Confeds. & turned out the armored ram, "Merrimac," that fought drawn battle with the "Monitor" off Norfolk on Mar. 9, 1862. Position of Confed. forces becoming increasingly precarious, Norfolk was evacuated, 1862, & Feds. moved in. But people of little Hampton, across the Straits, burnt down their homes rather than see them occupied by enemy.

After Civil War, with arrival of RRs., est. of great shipyard at Newport News & development of Portsmouth Navy Yard, Roads reg. recaptured importance & especially in last 4 decades, has developed as outlet for a great inland empire extending as far (W) as Ohio Valley.

## NORFOLK

Union Depot, on Main St., for chief RRs. in city. Union Bus Terminal on Tazewell St. Ferries conn. with RRs. in Newport News, Delmava Peninsula & to Old Pt. Comfort. Jamestown Bridge, via US17, from (W) of Portsmouth to pt. near Newport News. Accoms.: All types. Info.: C. of C., 107 W. Main St.; Tidewater Auto Assoc., Monticello Hotel. Swim.: Near-by beaches. Fish.: (saltwater) boats, tackle & bait avail. at various places on Ocean View Ave. & at Ocean View; (freshwater) f. in city-owned Ls., boats avail. Sm. fee for permits at Division of Water Supply, City Hall; non-residential f. licenses. F. also at L. Drummond (see Trip IV below); boats at Wallacetown; carry your own bait & tackles. Norfolk Fair, early Sept.

PTS. OF INT. DOWNTOWN NORFOLK: (1) E. City Hall Ave. & N. Bank St., **County Cth.** (Class.) & **Clerk's Office** (both 1847-50) stand near where once flowed Back Cr., navigable by large craft. (2) 201-33 Church St., **St. Paul's Ch. & Parish H.** (O.exc.Thurs.a.m.& Sun.1739.Col.Georg.) survived Brit. bombardment. Cannonball can still be seen in S. wall. Graveyard dates from 1673. Parish H.; coll. hist. documents, paintings, etc. (3) Main St. along which Lord Dunmore's ships lay when they bombarded Norfolk, & Commercial Sts.; **Confed. Mon.** (4) E. City Hall Ave. & Court St., **Police Mus.** (O). (5) N. Bank & E. Freemason Sts., **Myers H.** (O.sm.fee.1791.Georg.adds.c.1800) was home of Moses Myers, of Jewish derivation; portraits by Sully & Gilbert Stuart; period furniture. (6) Freemason & Cumberland Sts., **Christ Ch.** (now Gr.Orthodox;Gr.Rev.), where Lee attended services shortly before his death. (7) N. Bank St. near E. Charlotte St., **Norfolk Academy** (c.1840.Gr.Rev.) now occupied by a mun. court. (8) On or near W. Freemason St.: 227 W. Freemason St., **Whittle H.** (1791.Georg.Col.); 250 W. Bute St., **Milhado H.** (pre-Rev.), once home of Col. Gordon, Brit. Surgeon during Rev., who, after being captured, was brought to Norfolk; SE. cor. W. Freemason & Botetourt Sts., **Selden H.** (1807), hqs. of Feds. during Civil War. (9) At Granby St. & Brambleton Ave., imposing **Post Office & Fed. Bldg.** (Mod.). (10) Yarmouth St. & Lee Pk., **Mus. of Arts & Sciences** (O.aft.exc.Mon.); coll. of Ind. material, porcelain, pottery, etc.; loan exhibits; fine arts program. (11) On S. branch of Elizabeth R. at Front St., **Ft. Norfolk** (O.appl.War Dept.Office.,P.O.Bldg.;1791) which helped fight off Brit. during Craney I. battle. (12) Granby & Main Sts., **U.S. Customh.** (1857.Class.). (13) E. Main & N. Atlantic Ave., **Nat. Bank of Commerce**, in whose vaults (O.wks.Sat.a.m.) is kept Norfolk Mace presented to city, 1754, by Gov. Dinwiddie. During Rev. & Civil Wars, Mace was removed & hidden. **Craney I.** (see above) lies $2^m$ down & across Elizabeth River from Norfolk & Western RR. Piers (Old Dominion Wharf).

**PORTSMOUTH** (reached by Bridge & Ferry across Elizabeth R. from Norfolk).

RR. Stas.: Broad St., Atlantic Coast Line & Southern Ry. High St. for other RRs. Bus Terminal, High St. Accoms.: All types. Info.: C. of C. & Tidewater Auto Assoc. Swim.: Near-by bay & ocean resorts.

PTS. OF INT. PORTSMOUTH: (14) Cor. Court & High Sts., **Trinity Ch.** (O.1762. alts.). In cemetery (dating from 2nd half 18th cent.) among others is Grave of Commodore Jas. Barron, who, while in command of USS "Chesapeake," permitted Brit., without opposition, to take off alleged deserters, for which he was suspended. He attributed his misfortunes to Stephen Decatur, incl. failure to have his plans for an ironclad ram, plans later used for the "Merrimac," accepted by Navy. Challenged Decatur to a duel & killed him. (15) Opp. Ch., **Norfolk County Cth.** (O.wks.Sat.a.m.c.1844.by Wm.R.Singleton.alts.). (16) Among int. old Hs. are: Waterfront, at Crawford Place, **Dale H.**, credited with being Birthpl. of Rich. Dale, Lt. on Paul Jones' ship, "Bonhomme Richard," & later in command of fleet that brought Bey of Tunis to terms (1801); 213 Middle St., **Ball-Nivison H.**, used as barracks, 1812. Here Lafayette was entertained; NW. cor. Dinwiddie & North Sts., **Watts H.**, where Henry Clay & Chief Black Hawk were entertained. (17) At Queen & Dinwiddie Sts., **Monumental Meth. Ch.**, supposedly oldest Meth. Ch. org. in U.S. (18) On Elizabeth R., **U.S. Naval Hospital** (O.appl.1827), oldest still in use in U.S. **Boulder** & **Cannon** on site of Ft. Nelson, which was destroyed by Brit. (1779). In **cemetery** are buried yellow fever victims & dead of both Confed. & Union navies. **Mon.** comm. men lost on U.S. ships, "Cumberland" & "Congress," sunk by Merrimac. (19) 1st & 4th Sts., **U.S. Navy Yard** (O.453 as.), on Elizabeth R., oldest still in use in U.S. Old stone dry dock, built in Pres. Jackson's time, still in use. Yard has facils. for reconditioning largest naval craft. Here "Merrimac" was transformed into ironclad ram & rechristened "The Virginia."

PTS. OF INT. (N) & (E) OF NORFOLK DOWNTOWN DIST.: (20) 6225 Powhatan Ave., **Tazewell Manor** (1784), former home of Va. Gov. Tazewell. (21) Hampton Blvd. & Collins Ave., **Norfolk Div. of Wm. & Mary** & **Va. Polytechnic Institute.** (22) Church & Wood Sts., **Norfolk Div. of Va. State College** (Negro.coed.). (23) On Lafayette R. & E. Hampton Blvd., **U.S. Marine Hospital.** (24) On E. Hampton Blvd.,

**U.S. Naval Base** (850 as.O.) on whose grounds are Naval Air Sta., & near-by, Armed Forces Staff College whose courses for officers supplement those given at Washington's Naval War College. (25) On North Shore Rd., **Hermitage Foundation** (O.exc. Mon.fee.est.1937); fine garden; free art & cultural courses & exhibits; Mus., with art coll. (26) On 1400 Block of Westover Ave., **Mem. Oak,** allegedly largest live oak in Va. (27) Inters. St.170 & US60, **Ocean View,** famous amusement resort. (28) 35th & Granby Sts., on Lafayette R., **Lafayette Pk.** (pic.playground.sports), with zoo & biological gardens, reached by bus. (29) (E) on hy.13Y, **Mun. Airport.** Near it, **Azalea Gardens** (80 as.). Near here are a number of mun. Ls. (f.sm.fee.permits at Azalea Gardens Sta.). Off hy.13Y, c.$10^m$ from Norfolk (arrow shows turn), **Adam Thoroughgood H.** (O.wks.fee.1636-40), one of most int. old bldgs. in reg. Built by Adam Thoroughgood, who, with Duke of Norfolk, was granted tract on which Portsmouth & Norfolk stand; furnished in period. (30) Among larger mfg. plants (O.appl.) are: **Ford Assembly Plant,** Newton Park, Norfolk, Va.; **Aberfoyle Co.,** 40th St. & Killiam Ave., Norfolk, Va.; **Gary Steel Co.,** Hampton Blvd. & 25th St., Norfolk, Va.; **Lone Star Cement Co.,** South Norfolk, apply Bank of Commerce Bldg., Norfolk, Va.

**HAMPTON** (sett.1610) (on US60, see Williamsburg Trip III), on N. side of Hampton Roads, on site of orig. Ind. village of Kecoughtan, is oldest Eng. community in U.S. PTS. OF INT.: (1) On Queen St., **St. John's Ch.** (O.1728.rest.1827 & 1869), wrecked by Brit. during War of 1812 & again in 1861. Vestry has communion silver dating from 1622. This is probably oldest Ch. organization in U.S., having been est. 1610. In cemetery, graves of early settlers. (2) Victoria Ave., **Braddock Mon.,** on site of landing of Braddock's troops (1755). (3) **Hampton Institute** (est.1868.coed.) outstanding Negro educational institution. Geo. Washington Carver, noted Negro scientist, taught here. Booker T. Washington was graduate. Institute was aided by the Freedman's Bureau & N. philanthropists as well as other funds given primarily for education of Inds., who were sent to Hampton before special schs. were est. for them. College offers degrees in arts & sciences, but is primarily known for its vocational & professional training courses. Campus comprises 74 as. & 142 bldgs. Many of bldgs. were constructed by students. **Virginia Hall** was literally "sung up" by the Hampton Singers. **Adm. Bldg.** (O.wks.) contains ethnological & other exhibits. **Collis P. Huntington Lib.** has Carnegie coll. of architecture, sculpture & paintings & Peabody coll. of Negro material. In **Curry Hall,** exhibits of paintings & in Art Center, of sculpture & ceramics. **Armstrong Mem. Ch.** (Romanes.), constructed almost entirely by students, is one of finest bldgs. (4) **Nat. Cemetery** adj. campus. (5) Near E. entrance to Hampton town is **Mon. on Site of 1st Prot. Ch.** (est.1610) in U.S. (6) Take King St. from Hampton to **Langley Field** (5,000 as.) U.S. air base. Experimental & research div. of Nat. Advisory Council for aviation & Sta. of Tactical Air Command. Field was named for Dr. S. P. Langley, aviation pioneer.

**NEWPORT NEWS.** (On US60, see Williamsburg Trip III).

Chesapeake & Ohio RR. Sta. at 23rd St. Through bus conns. Accoms.: All types. F. boats at waterfront on Warwick Ave. Ferry to Norfolk.

Newport News (sett.1621) is located on N. side of Hampton Roads, at W. end of the Straits, opp. Norfolk; chief sources of income are the great shipyard, Chesapeake & Ohio RR. Terminal, & shipping. PTS. OF INT.: (1) **Newport News Shipbuilding & Dry Dock Co.** (O.appl.), one of largest in world. Here hundreds of vessels during both World Wars were laid down. (2) **Chesapeake & Ohio RR. Terminal,** alleged to be largest of its kind in world. (3) Pear Ave., **Va. St. Sch. for the Colored Deaf & Blind.** (4) 1915 Jefferson Ave. (19th St.), **Ch. of God,** formerly Solomon Lightfoot Michaux Temple, where Elder Michaux, Negro religious leader, who started out as fishmonger, had hqs. He held large meetings in a tabernacle, seating 5,000, on waterfront at end of Jefferson Ave. (5) A short distance (N) of James R. Bridge, on US60, is **War Mem. Mus.** (O). (6) On New Market Rd., **Newport News Homesteads,** Fed. Housing Project for Negroes.

## TRIPS OUT OF HAMPTON ROADS REG.

### I. PT. WILLOUGHBY to VIRGINIA BEACH. 24.5. US60

Skirts Atlantic Ocean from SE. side of the Roads. Reached from Norfolk by Granby St. & St.170 to Ocean View.

**0.** Pt. Willoughby, ferry to Old Pt. Comfort (see). **2. OCEAN VIEW** (bath.f.amusements.accoms.). Near-by is **Sarah Constant Shrine,** comm. anchoring offshore of one of the 3 ships headed for Jamestown (1607). **8.5.** [Take Rd. (L) here for Cape Charles Ferry to Northern Neck (see Md.-Va. US113).] **15. SEASHORE ST. PK.** (2,726 as. pic.cabins.restaurant.store.swim.f.trls.) faces Chesapeake Bay & salt water Ls. known as Lynnhaven Inlet; 2 freshwater ponds. Pk. has semi-tropical for. at its N. limit, notable for giant cypresses & pines draped with Sp. moss; many rare birds & flowering plants. **18. CAPE HENRY. Cape Henry Lighth. Old Lighth.** (1791). Stone Cross on site of landing, Ap. 26, 1607, by settlers from the 3 ships that subsequently carried them to Jamestown. **19. FT. STORY** (L), fortification guarding straits. **24.5. VIRGINIA BEACH** (resort), all types of accoms. & seashore recr. J. with US58 (see Trip II below).

**II. NORFOLK to VIRGINIA BEACH. 19. US58**

**8.5.** J. with Cty.647.

SIDE TRIP: Take latter (L) 2.5m to **Donation Ch.** (1736.rest.) so-called because in 1776, Thos. Dickson willed property to congregation. 3.5m, **Witch Duck Farm** (R) (late 18th cent.). In vic. occurred at beginning of 18th cent., "ducking test" administered to Grace Sherwood, accused of witchcraft, who, although her hands were tied, managed to swim, considered proof she had aid of the devil so that she was jailed.

**16.** J. with Cty.615.

SIDE TRIPS: (A) Take latter (L) 4.5m to **Broad Bay Manor Hs.** (O.Garden Wk.fee 1640-1770); old garden.
(B) Take Cty.615 (R). At 1m, **Eastern Shore Chapel** (1754) whose communion service (1759) was hidden in a hen-house during Civil War.

**19. VIRGINIA BEACH.**

**III. W. of NORFOLK to SUFFOLK. 20. US58**

At **20.** (W) of Norfolk, **SUFFOLK** (founded 1742) on Nansemond R., center of a peanut growing area. Burnt by Brit. (1779). Besieged by Confed. Gen. Longstreet (1863). Here is one of largest peanut products factories. **County Cth.** (1840.Gr.Rev.). **Constantia H.,** in Suffolk Cemetery, is reprod. of an ancient H. 510 N. Main St., **Withers H.** (1st half 19th cent.Gr.Rev.). J. in Suffolk with US460 & St.10 (see).

**IV. PORTSMOUTH (S) to VA.-N.C. LINE. 20. US17**

**7. DEEP CREEK,** on edge of Dismal Swamp (bear & deer h.f.). Hy. crosses **Dismal Swamp Canal,** & then parallels it. Canal was dug by Negro slaves (1790-1822). **17.5. ARBUCKLE'S LANDING** on branch of canal leading to Drummond L. (boats. f.guides).

SIDE TRIP: Take boat along branch canal to **Drummond L.** (f.:St.rules in some secs.& Fed.in others), in heart of swamp. L. named for Wm. Drummond, who took part in Bacon's Rebellion & was hanged by Gov. Berkeley. Swamp has been lumbered over & its peat bogs have often been set afire, destroying much of timber spared by axe. But there are still thick fors. of cypress, black gum & juniper. Many rare birds are found in reg. Also, water mocassins & other poisonous snakes. Washington helped survey swamp (1763) & foreseeing possibility of building canal to connect Chesapeake Bay & N.C. Rs., org. company to drain some 40,000 as.

**20. VA.-N.C. LINE** (c.20m (N) of Elizabeth City).

# LYNCHBURG

## LYNCHBURG

Through RR. & bus conns. Info.: C. of C. & Auto Club of Va. Accoms.: All types. Swim. (fee) in city pks. Community Market (int.on Sat.). Oct. Farm Show.

Lynchburg, located near st.'s geographical center, in foothills of Blue Ridge, straggles along bluffs above the James; its streets climb from R. bank, through shipping, factory & bus. secs., to residential districts. Quakers in 1750's, among earliest settlers, held 1st meeting, 1754, at Sara Lynch's farm, Chestnut Hill, & soon after built Meetingh. John Lynch, Sara's son, when only 17, est. ferry (1757) & it was on his "40 acres contiguous" to ferry that Va. Assembly est. the town in 1786. John's brother, Chas., during Rev. set up with his cronies a court at his home, Green Level, & imposed savage penalties, incl. flogging, on Tories & criminal elements alike, giving us the expression "Lynch Law". Lynchburg early became a shipping center, with upwards of 500 batteaux plying bet. it & Richmond on James R. After Rev., town was a lively social focus for neighboring plantations. Yet conditions were still primitive. Hogsheads of tobacco, rolling down the streets to the river, got stuck in mud, & little girls, to avoid being mired, hobbled to school on stilts. When St. Paul's Episc. Ch. introduced a pipe organ (1826), community was deeply shocked by such a popish innovation. Townsfolk for years tried to get James R. & Kanawha Canal through to Lynchburg. Abortive booms based on hopes deferred, drove price of certain Lynchburg real estate in 1818 as high as lots on Broadway, New York. Canal finally arrived, not much before 1st RR., & was used until after Civil War. Its noblest & most tragic freight was the body of "Stonewall" Jackson carried by canal boat from Lynchburg to Lexington (1863) for interment. During Civil War town became Confed. base; Union Gen. David Stone tried to take it but was thrown back by Jubal Early (June 1864).

Tobacco has always been backbone of city's economy. Today Lynchburg claims to be largest "dark" tobacco market in country. But its 75 plants turn out many articles, notably shoes, in addition to tobacco products. Theodore Presser who first brought out widely circulated periodical "The Music Etude," in Lynchburg, & Carter Glass, co-author of Fed. Reserve Act, U.S. Secy. of Treasury & Senator, were natives.

PTS. OF INT.: (1) Mon. Terrace, 9th & Court Sts., **Cth.** (O.Mon.-Fri.; Sat.a.m.1855. Class.), & **Confed. Mon.** at top of Terrace. At foot of Terrace, **World War I Mon.,** by Chas. Keck. (2) At end of 9th St., **Marker** on Site of Lynch's Ferry. (3) On Commerce St., (S) of 9th St. **old tobacco warehs.,** storing tobacco since 18th cent. (4) 9th & Floyd Sts., **Statue of John W. Daniel,** Confed. hero, by Sir Moses Ezekiel. (5) Garfield Ave. & Dewitt St., **Va. Theological Seminary & College** (Bapt.Negro.coed. est.1888). (6) On Fort Hill Ave., **Spring Hill Cemetery,** where several Confed. commdrs. & other notables are buried. (7) Vermont & Fort Aves., **Ft. Early & Mon.,** reconstructed breastworks where Early drove back Feds. (8) Mt. Vernon St., **Lynchburg College** (est.1903 by Disciples of Christ.co-ed.). (9) 112 Cabell St., **Point of Honor** (O.1806.Fed.fine inter.). (10) In Riverside Pk., **Miller-Claytor H.** (O.Garden Wk.fee.c.1793), in whose garden Jefferson made a respectable vegetable of the tomato which until then, called "love apple," had been considered poisonous; Jefferson publicly ate one. (11) On Rivermont Ave., **Randolph-Macon Women's College** (est.1833), 1 of 3 Randolph-Macon colleges (see Ashland, Va.). (12) (SW) of City, c.0.5$^{m}$ on Cty.676, just off St.128, is notable **Sandusky H.** (R) (1797), which its builder, Chas. Johnston, named for Ohio village whither he escaped after being kidnapped, when a youngster, by Inds. (13) On St.128, just beyond J. with Cty.676, is **Quaker Mem. Meeting H.** (now Presb.Ch.) (L) (1792-98), founded 1757, under leadership of Sarah Lynch. These early Quakers harbored strong abolitionist sentiments; in 1773 they adopted antislavery resolutions.

## TRIPS OUT OF LYNCHBURG.

### I. US501 (NW) of LYNCHBURG to BUENA VISTA, J. with US60. 40.

**22.** J. with Blue Ridge Pky. (Here unfinished, 1949). **29. BALCONY FALLS** in James R. gorge. (S) of this pt. on side Rd., c.0.5$^{m}$, in **Nat. For.** is **Snow Cr. Recr. Area.** (pic.facils.trlrs.). **31.** J. with St.249.

SIDE TRIP: Take latter (L) short distance to **Glasgow,** near which, 1743, Capt. John McDowell & settlers clashed with Inds. **Glasgow Manor** (1810), built by Jos. Glasgow (see Buena Vista). St.249 conts. (SW) to **Natural Bridge** (see US11).

**40.** US501 reaches Buena Vista, J. with US60 (see).

### II. US501 (SE) of LYNCHBURG to BROOKNEAL. 31.5.

**2.5.** J. with US460. [Take latter (L) c.21$^{m}$ to **Appomattox Cth.** (see US60).] **10. RUSTBURG,** named for Jeremiah Rust, orig. patentee. **Campbell Cth.** (1848). Opp., **Fountain Hotel** (1795) conducted as an inn by Finch family ever since. **Old Rustburg Inn. 19.5. GLADYS** [Take Cty.652 (L) here 1.5$^{m}$ & then (L) again on Cty.650 c.2$^{m}$ to **Shady Grove** (1814), built by Patrick Henry for his son, Spottswood Henry.] **31.5. BROOKNEAL.**

SIDE TRIPS: (A) 2.5$^{m}$ (E) of Brookneal is **Red Hill H.,** on site of Patrick Henry's home. Here is his **Grave,** on whose stone is inscribed: "His fame was his best epitaph." Members of his family are buried here as well.

(B) Take St.40 (L) from Brookneal 3$^{m}$ to J. with Cty.605. Turn (L) here 1$^{m}$ to J. with Cty.601 & then (R) c.4$^{m}$ on Cty.601 to **Hat Creek Ch.** (Presb.c.1742). In **Cemetery** are graves of Hanks family. Nancy Hanks, Lincoln's mother, is alleged to have been born in vic.

**III. US460 (SW) of LYNCHBURG to BEDFORD. 24.**

**7.5.** J. with Cty.661.

SIDE TRIP: (L) on latter 0.5$^{m}$ to Jefferson's **Poplar For.** (c.1809.rest.). Here he wrote "Notes on Virginia" & was pursued by Tarleton, 1781, who, as usual, arrived too late. Orig. boxwood borders lawn.

**24. BEDFORD,** from which **Peaks of Otter** (4,000′) can be seen. c.10$^{m}$ (N), 1$^{m}$ (W) of St.122, is **Bedford Cty. Pk.** (recr.boat.f.), with L. St.43 leads (NW) from Bedford, c.13$^{m}$ to **Peaks of Otter** & J. with Blue Ridge Pky. (see).

**IV. US29 (N) of LYNCHBURG to CLIFFORD. 17.**

**14. AMHERST,** named for Lord Amherst of Fr.-Ind. war fame. **Central Hotel** (18th cent.N.O.). **Sweet Briar College** (Women.Col.Georg.by Cram, Goodhue & Ferguson); oldest bldg., **President's H.** (c.1840) set in beautiful boxwood circle. (Garden O.Garden Wk.). At **16.** take St.151 (L) (N) c.1$^{m}$ to **CLIFFORD,** village. **Winston H.** where Sarah Winston Henry, Patrick's mother, died; grave on estate. **St. Marks Ch.** (Episc.c.1808). J. with Cty.610 leading (R) 1$^{m}$ to handsome **Tusculum** (1735), birthpl. of Wm. H. Crawford, prominent Va. politician & Pres. candidate, 1824.

# PETERSBURG

## PETERSBURG

Through RR. & bus conns. Accoms.: All types. Info.: C. of C.

Petersburg, the "Cockade City" situated at Falls of Appomattox R. spreads along S. side of river at pt. where a long peninsula, site of early Pocahontas settlement, splits stream. In 1646 Gov. Berkeley ordered building of Ft. Henry at the Falls &, near-by, Capt. Peter Jones built his trading post. River below city was constantly being improved; at one time as many as 125 batteaux plied up & down it. A canal built around the Falls enabled boats to navigate 100$^{m}$ up-river. In colonial era Petersburg had one of earliest theaters, succeeded by more pretentious ones in which Junius Booth, Poe's mother &, later, Edwin Booth & Tyrone Power (the 1st) played. There were numerous taverns, one of them, Haines', where Poe & Virginia Clemm, his 13-year-old bride, honeymooned. In 1781 city was occupied by Brit. Gen. Philips & shelled by Lafayette's troops from across R. In June, 1864, Union Gen. Kautz's cavalry was halted at city's entrances by a company of old men, boys & convalescent soldiers from the Confed. hospital, until arrival of Beauregard's regulars. But Grant soon concentrated all his forces here & then ensued bloody siege which wrecked more than 800 Hs. & ended in Lee's surrender at Appomattox. Today Petersburg is lively R. town, tobacco market & center of peanut growing reg. Its 57 factories turn out a variety of products. It claims to have world's largest luggage factory.

PTS. OF INT.: (1) At N. end of S. Market St., (W) of St., **Peter Jones Trading Post.** (2) From W. end of Grove Ave., fine view of **Falls of the Appomattox.** (3) Inters. N. South & McKenzie Sts., **McKenzie H.** supposedly on site of Ft. Henry. Near-by, is **Home of Capt. Flood,** Ind. interpreter, supposedly oldest H. in city. (4) N. end of N. West St., near RR. tracks, **Pride's Tavern** (O.pre-Rev.rest.) near which formerly was located famous Pride's Race Track of Col. era. (5) N. terminus of Battersea Lane, **Battersea** (pre-Rev.), home of Col. John Banister, who helped in defense of city against Brit. (1781) & was elected 1st Mayor. (6) 558 W. High St., **Beasley-Williamson H.** (O.appl.), 1 of 3 Hs. where Lee had hqs. during siege. (7) 320 High St., **Stirling Castle** (1735), country home of Peter Jones II, removed here. (8) 311 High St., **Dodson's Tavern** (Pegram H.) where Aaron Burr & his daughter Theodosia took refuge, 1805. (9) 224 N. Market St., **Trapezium H.** (O.appl.1818) which was built by eccentric Irishman, Chas. O'Hare, without any right angles because his E. Indian servant argued that in that way powers of darkness would be fended off. (10) On W. Washington St., bet. Lafayette & Davis Sts., **Folly Castle** (1763) so-called because its builder, Peter Jones II, had no children to house in its many rooms. (11) 204 S. Market St., **Seward-Wallace H.** (1855) where Grant & Lincoln met shortly before Lee's surrender. Grant considerately refused to use parlor, because he liked to smoke cigars.

(12) On N. Sycamore St., bet. E. Bank & E. Tabb Sts., **Cth.** (O.wks.1835.Gr.Rev.), supposedly reprod. of St. Mary Le Bow Ch. in London. (13) Bet. N. Adams & N. Jefferson St., facing Franklin St., reached by drive, is **Center Hill** (O.c.1825.remod. 1850); hqs. of Union Gen. Hartsuff. Will be Petersburg Nat. Military Pk. Hqs. When Lincoln visited here, he remarked on the subject of rent for the house, that "our batteries have made rents enough already." (14) On S. Sycamore St.: At Fillmore St., **Central Pk.,** where is Pocahontas Basin, a rock bowl in which the Princess is supposed to have bathed; 244 S. Sycamore St., **Geo. Bolling H.** (known as the Lawn) (c.1825); 220 S. Sycamore St., **St. Southern College** (O.appl.chartered 1863). (15) On Crater Rd., **Blandford Ch.** (O.appl.1735.wing added 1757.rest.). Ch. is Confed. Mem. Chapel; mem. tablets & windows. Adj., Blandford Cemetery. Thousands of Confed. dead buried here. Mon. to Gen. McRae & volunteers who took part in expedition against Canada during War of 1812, at dedication of which Madison referred to Petersburg as "Cockade City." (16) In S. sec. of city is **Lee Mem. Pk.** (864 as.bath.sports facils.).

(17) **Petersburg Nat. Military Pk.** (2,047 as.), reached by US1, US301, US460 & St.36. City buses every hour. Temporary Hqs. in P. O. Bldg., Petersburg. Permanent Hqs. will be in Center Hill Mansion (see above). Address Supt., Petersburg Nat. Military Pk., Petersburg, Va. Rds. give access to various pts. of int. Pic. at Battery 8. After battles waged for Richmond from North had ended in stalemate, Grant, June 1864, began campaign from South, via Petersburg. For nearly 10 months Lee's & Grant's armies were locked in desperate struggle. Opposing lines were constantly extended until, Mar. 1865, they were 35$^{m}$ long. Lee attempted break-through at Ft. Stedman, Mar. 25, 1865, which failed. Followed Union victory at Five Forks, Ap. 1, which forced evacuation of both Petersburg & Richmond. Visitors may follow Confed. & Union lines starting with St.36 (E) out of Petersburg, via Battery 5, Info. Sta. Most int. is **The Crater,** off Crater Rd., not far from Battery 5. Late in June & in July 1864, Pennsylvania miners dug 511′ tunnel & placed 4-ton charge of powder in it under Pegram's Confed. Battery. On July 30th mine blew up the battery killing c.300 men. However Confeds. rallied & halted Union onslaught. This failure cost Feds. 4,000 men. Here is **Mass. Mon.** & a **Mus.**

# RICHMOND

## RICHMOND

RR. Stas.: At Main St., for C.& O., & S.A.L.; at Broad St. for A.C.L., & N. & W.; at Hull St. for S. RR. Bus Stas.: 412 E. Broad St.; & Broad & 9th Sts. Mun. Airport, 4.5$^{m}$ (E) of city. Accoms.: All types. Info.: C. of C., 1304 State Planters Bank Bldg. Swim.: Byrd Pk.; Negro pool, Sledd & High Sts. Garden Wk. (late Ap.-early May). Va. St. Fair at Va. St. Fair Grounds, Sept. or Oct.

Perched on her 7 hills, overlooking island-strewn James R., where navigation ends just below the "Falls," Richmond at 1st glance appears to be completely modern city. But there is the older Richmond, of Col., Rev. & Civil War hist. landmarks; the city of literary & art shrines—of Poe, Thos. Nelson Page, Mary Johnston, Ellen Glasgow, Jas. Branch Cabell, John Powell, composer, & Edw. V. Valentine, sculptor. Bill Robinson, Negro tap dancer, earned his keep as a boy in Richmond tending horses & his nickname of "bojangles" by dancing for pennies in beer gardens. Another noteworthy Negro native was Maggie Walker, founder of St. Luke's Penny Bank, now Consolidated Banking & Trust Co., to help Negroes save & build their own homes. The 1st settlement, 1609, was made by Capt. Francis West, on land purchased from Powhatan. Richmond became hotbed of sedition at Rev.'s outbreak. In 1779, capital was removed from Williamsburg to Richmond, as safer from Brit. attack, but in 1781, St. gov. was forced to flee at approach of Brit. led by Benedict Arnold. With building of great canals (the James R. & Kanawha Canal in particular, westward to Buchanan), great Hys. & RRs., to link it to transmontaine reg., Richmond became center of st.'s bus. & social life in 19th cent. After shot fired on Ft. Sumter, Ap. 13, 1861, St. convention sitting in Richmond passed Ordinance of Secession. Richmond, as capital of the Confederacy, became focal point of bloody tug-of-war. For 4 yrs., Union armies tried in vain to batter their way into city, which was only evacuated when Lee's armies had become so depleted that he could no longer hold his extended lines against Grant's forces coming up from Petersburg. Before capital was abandoned, fire was set to a wareh., at Lee's orders, & spreading, reduced most of city to ashes. Today Richmond is important commercial & industrial city. By R. improvements, it has become a port for R. traffic. Its 325 plants produce $375,000,000 worth of goods per annum. It is one of chief tobacco markets & cigarette mfg. centers of the country.

PTS. OF INT.: Tour begins at (1) **Gamble's Hill Pk.,** 3rd St. & James R., (E) of Lee Bridge; fine view. (2) At NW. cor. E. Main & N. 5th Sts., curious **Octagonal H.** (pre-1814), home of Wm. Wirt, lawyer & author, & one of Aaron Burr's prosecutors at latter's treason trial. (3) At Foushee & Main Sts., noted novelist **Ellen Glasgow's H.** (O.Garden Wk.fee.c.1841.Gr.Rev.). (4) 707 E. Franklin St., **Gen. Rbt. E. Lee H.** (Va. Hist.Soc.) (O.wks.Sat.a.m.sm.fee.1844), home of Lee's family during latter yrs. of Civil War. In rear, fireproof add. containing documents, rare books & paintings, among them portrait of Lafayette by Peale, "Pocahontas," by Sully, & Death Mask of Lee. (5) SW. cor. Capitol Sq. (near 9th & Franklin Sts.), **Old Bell Tower** (1824), which replaced older wooden one whose bell used to summon citizens to Richmond's defense & tolled when city was evacuated in 1865. (6) 1916 E. Main St., **Poe Shrine** (O.sm.fee.c.1686.Jacobean), supposedly oldest H. in city. On front wall are letters "J.R.," allegedly for Jacobus Rex—James II, King of England; coll. of rare Poe items; lovely garden. (7) At SE. 20th & Cary Sts. formerly stood **Libby Prison,** where thousands of Union prisoners died of disease, cold & malnutrition. Old prison, orig. wareh., was torn down & rebuilt at Chicago World's Fair of 1893. Here is Richmond's famous "Tobacco Row." (8) 1805 E. Franklin St., **Old Masonic Hall** (O. appl.wks.Sat.a.m.1785), supposedly oldest in country. (9) NW. cor. N. 19th & E. Grace Sts., **Craig H.** (O.c.1790), birthpl. of Jane Craig Stanard, Poe's "Helen." (10) E. Broad St., bet. N. 24th & N. 25th Sts., **St. John's Ch.** (O.Sun.services.1741.adds.) where 2nd Va. convention met (1775) & Patrick Henry called for "Liberty or Death." Grave of Elizabeth Poe, actress-mother of the poet, is in cemetery; young Poe is said to have been found more than once sobbing on her grave. Grave of Geo. Wythe (see Williamsburg). (11) E. Broad St. at 32nd St., **Chimborazo Pk.,** affording fine outlook over city. (12) E. Broad St., near N. 12th St., **Monumental Ch.** (O.wks.Sun. services.1814.Gr.Rev.by Rbt.Mills), on site of theater in which Poe's mother had acted, & which was destroyed by fire, 1811, when 72 persons perished. Ch. was built as a memorial.

(13) At N. 12th & E. Marshall Sts., **Medical College of Va.** (est.1838). Egyptian Bldg. (1845) is reprod. of Egyptian temple. (14) SE. cor. N. 12th & E. Clay Sts., **Confed Mus.** (O.wks.Sat.a.m.sm.fee.1818.Class.), occupied by Jeff. Davis & known as White H. of Confederacy. Little Joe Davis died in this H. from injuries received falling off a balcony; coll. of Confed. hist. relics. (15) E. Clay & N. 11th Sts., **Valentine Mus.** (O.wks.1812.by Rbt.Mills.rest.), built by John Wickham, leading attorney for Aaron Burr at latter's treason trial. H. was later owned by sculptor, E. V. Valentine; coll. of his works, ethnological material & early 19th cent. & Vict. furnishings. (16) NW. cor. E. Marshall & N. 9th Sts., **John Marshall H.** (O.wks.Sat.a.m. sm.fee.c.1789), designed by Chief Justice of U.S. Supreme Ct. (17) N. end of 3rd St., **Shockoe Hill Cemetery,** where John Marshall & his family, Col. Crozet, engineer for Va. who designed many of her hys. & canals, Jane Craig Stanard, (Poe's "Helen"), & Elizabeth Van Lew, angel of Libby Prison, are buried. (18) In Capitol Sq., bounded by Capitol, Bank, Governor & N. 9th Sts., is fine equestrian **Washington Mon.** Around Mon.'s base are sculptured figures of famous Virginians. Mon., with exception of 2 figures which are by R. Rogers, is by Thos. Crawford; design by Rbt. Mills. John Marshall raised 1st funds for Mon. & his statue was added 1867. (19) **The Capitol** (O.wks.;Sat.a.m.completed 1793.adds.Romanes.Class.), designed by Thos. Jefferson, while minister in Paris, with aid of Fr. architect, Clarisseau, after Maison Carrée, ancient temple at Nîmes, France. Home of oldest representative legislature in America, it has witnessed many important events—trial of Aaron Burr, 1807; adoption of Secession Ordinance, 1861, & deliberations of Confed. Congress. In Hall, where his statue now stands, Lee accepted command of Va.'s forces, 1861. In 1870, balcony of Hall gave way, causing death of 63 persons. In Rotunda is Houdon's statue of Washington. In wall recesses are busts of Va.'s other sons who achieved presidency, & Houdon's bust of Lafayette.

(20) At Capitol Sq. are: **St. Office & Finance Bldgs.** Beautiful **Gov.'s Mansion** (O. Garden Wk.1813.Fed.), on site of earlier Gov.'s H., a ramshackle wooden structure ironically called "The Palace." (21) **St. Lib.** with valuable coll. of documents, rare books, portraits, etc. **The Archives Bldg.** is to rear of Lib. (22) At N. 9th & E. Grace

Sts., **St. Paul's Ch.** (Episc.O.wks.;Sat.a.m.;Sun.services.1845.Class.by Thos.Stewart). Jeff. Davis was attending services in Ch. when he received news of fall of Petersburg & word that Richmond would have to be evacuated. Lee & Davis pews marked by tablets. (23) Cherry & Albemarle Sts., beautiful **Hollywood Cemetery** (O.1849), above James R., has graves of John Randolph of Roanoke, Commodore Maury, Jeff. Davis, Monroe & Tyler. (24) 102 E. Franklin St., **Academy of Science & Fine Arts** (O.wks.summer.sm.fee), est. in 1786; exhibits & art classes. (25) 1500 N. Lombard St., **Va. Union Univ.** (Negro.coed.). (26) On Melrose Ave., **Union Theological Seminary** (Presb.est.1812). (27) Another education institution, but located further in town, at 901 W. Franklin St., is **Richmond Professional Institute,** of College of Wm. & Mary (est.1917); in 1946 it affiliated with Va. Polytechnic Institute. (28) At Lombardy St. begins Monument Ave., western continuation of Franklin St. Along this park-like residential thoroughfare are following **Mons.: Equestrian Statue of J. E. B. Stuart,** by Fred Maynihan; **Lee,** on his famous horse, Traveller, by Jean Antoine Mercié; **Jefferson Davis,** by E. V. Valentine; **"Stonewall" Jackson** on his horse, Little Sorrel, by F. W. Sievers; & **Commodore Maury.** (29) N. Boulevard & Kensington Ave., **The Battle Abbey** (O.wks.Sun.aft.sm.fee), Confed. Mem. Institute; coll. of portraits of southern patriots; murals depicting Civil War scenes by Chas. Hoffbauer, who had done much of preliminary work when he went back to fight for France, 1914. After returning he painted out what he already had done & depicted war scenes out of his own experience.

(30) At Boulevard & Grove Ave., **Va. Mus. of Fine Arts** (O.Tues.Sat.sm.fee.Sun. aft.1934.Fed.); colls. of paintings & prints; lecture program; symphony concerts. (31) S. of Cary St., at the Boulevard, is **Wm. Byrd Pk.,** with L. & sports facils. Columbus Mon. & World War I Mon., a carillon tower in which is Mus. (O); coll. of war relics. (32) At Windsor Farms, off Cary St., back from Rd. (R), old **Reveille;** lovely garden. (33) Via St.147 in Windsor Farms, on S. side of Sulgrave Rd., **Virginia H.** (O.Garden Wk.fee.1925), built of materials brought from Warwick Priory, Eng., & in part reprod. of Priory. Righthand sec. is exact reprod. of Sulgrave Manor, Eng., as it was when Lawrence Washington, Geo.'s ancestor, occupied it. (34) On S. side of Sulgrave Rd., just beyond Virginia H., **Agecroft Hall** (O.Garden Wk.fee), built, 1393, in Eng., & brought over stone by stone & reconstructed here. (35) S. terminus Ampthill Rd., near Cary St., **Ampthill** (pre-1723.adds.), at one time home of Archibald Cary, member of Continental Congress. (36) S. terminus of Wilton Rd., near Cary St., **Wilton** (O.Garden Wk.fee.1750.fine exter.& inter.rest.); furnished in period, former home of Wm. Randolph. (37) Still further (W) on St.147 (arrows shows turn) is **The Oaks** (O.Garden Wk.fee.pre-1750); period furnishings. (38) Off Three Chopt Rd., **Univ. of Richmond,** for men & **Westhampton College** for women.

## TRIPS OUT OF RICHMOND

### I. RICHMOND NAT. BATTLEFIELD PK.

700 as., covering main battle sites, in separate secs. Pk. Hqs. reached most directly by St.5 (S) from Richmond to J. with St.156 (Battlefield Route), then (R) to Ft. Harrison area. Pk. Hqs.: Info., maps, etc. Small Mus. & Lib. From (N) Pk. is reached by US360 to Mechanicsville, & then (R) on St.156. US60 makes J. with St.156 at Seven Pines, in Pk., (E) of Richmond. Info.: Superintendent, Richmond Nat. Battlefield Pk., R.F.D., Richmond, Va. Specially conducted tours, appl. in advance. St.156 (Battlefield Route) makes circuit of battlefields; 55$^{m}$. Markers identify main pts. which are reached by Pk. Rds. & trls. Horses avail.

Richmond Nat. Battlefield Pk. tells story of 4-yr. struggle for Richmond. First attempt to take Richmond (spring & summer of 1862) made by McClellan's peninsula campaign, brought Union armies within sight of city at Seven Pines, where they were checked by Gen. Jos. Johnston. Lee now took over Confed. command & in the series of clashes that followed culminating in "the Seven Days' Battles" McClellan was forced to end menace to Richmond by retreating across James R. Confeds. lost more than 28,000 men & Feds. more than 23,000.

Confeds. now set about building up system of defenses encircling city, which proved well-nigh impregnable.

After Battles of the Wilderness & Spotsylvania Cth., in which Lee blocked off Grant in Fredericksburg area, latter brought his army, by June 1, 1864, to vic. of Cold Harbor, only 8$^{m}$ NW. of Richmond. Here his 117,000 men, attacking Lee's 60,000, were repulsed with terrific losses. Within 30-min. period, killed & wounded mounted to 7,000. Grant said of Cold Harbor in his memoirs: "I have always regretted that the last assault at Cold Harbor was ever made." During period June 2-15 his losses were 12,737, while Lee's are said to have been less than 2,000.

**II. TRIPS ON ST.147**

(1) (W) on St.147 & straight ahead on it to **River Road Tavern** (arrow shows turn) to **Fairfield** (c.1750), built by half-brother of Patrick Henry; latter wrote many of his speeches here. (2) (W) on St.147 to **River Road Tavern.** Cross river, follow 1st arrow on (R) to **Bellona Arsenal** (O.Garden Wk.fee.1816) in which ammunition was stored during Civil War. (3) (W) on St.147. Turn (L) at **River Road Tavern.** Cross river to St.44, (W) 4.1$^{m}$ (follow arrows) to **Keswick** (O.Garden Wk.fee.1750) with old dependencies, incl. slave quarters. Across the R. is **Tuckahoe** (O.Garden Wk.fee. 1732), very similar in design. Thos. Jefferson, in his boyhood, stayed with family of Wm. Randolph & went to school here. (4) (W) on St.147. Turn (L) at **River Road Tavern.** Cross river to St.44, (W) (R) for 11.4$^{m}$ (follow arrows) to **Millwood** (O. Garden Wk.fee.1757), still owned by descendants of John Harris, builder of H.

**III. Loop Tour. US360 (NE) from RICHMOND to J. with ST.30 at CENTRAL GARAGE, ST.30 to J. with ST.33 at WEST PT. & ST.33 & US60 Back to RICHMOND. 88.**

**6.**, on US360, **MECHANICSVILLE.** J. with St.156 (R) (Battlefield Route. See Richmond Nat. Battlefield Pk.). **16. MARLBURNE,** home of Edmund Ruffin, who fired 1st shot at Ft. Sumter (Ap.1861). His grave is here. **23. CENTRAL GARAGE.** J. with St.30, on which Loop Tour cont. (SE). For pts. on US360 to (NE), see US17. Take St.30 (R). **29.5.** J. with Cty.629.

SIDE TRIP: Take latter (R) 2$^{m}$ to **Acquinton Ch.** (1st half 18th cent.). At 5.5$^{m}$ J. with Cty.600. Take latter (L) 1$^{m}$ & then Rd. (R) 1$^{m}$ to **Cheroke** (1767.rest.), home of Carter Braxton, signer of Decl. of Ind.

**31. KING WILLIAM,** town. C.9$^{m}$ (S) is **Pamunkey Ind. Reserv.,** all that remains of "empire" of the great Powhatan, who, when the Jamestown settlers arrived (1607), ruled all Ind. tribes of E. Md. & Va. **36.5.** J. with Cty.640, leading (L) 1$^{m}$ & then Cty. Rd. (L) to **Mattaponi Ind. Reserv.** Mattaponi were ruled by Powhatan. **38.5. ST. JOHN'S CH.** (1700-10 & 1734.rest.). **44.5.** J. with Cty.635 leading (L) c.1$^{m}$ to **Chelsea** (one sec.c.1710), where Gov. Spotswood made up his company for the Knights of the Golden Horseshoe expedition across the Blue Ridge. **47. WEST PT.,** at confluence of Pamunkey & Mattaponi Rs., site of Pamunkey, Powhatan's capital. J. with St.33, on which Loop Tour cont. (W). For St.33 (E), see US17 Side Trip Alt. **58.5. NEW KENT.** In Cth. are copies of Stuart portraits of Martha & Geo. Washington. **65. TALLYSVILLE.** J. with Cty.609.

SIDE TRIP: Take latter (R) (N) 1.5$^{m}$ to **St. Peter's Ch.** (R) (1703.steeple.1749); David Mossom, rector, married Geo. Washington & Martha Custis, & one story has it that wedding took place here. Cont. on Cty.609 to J. with Cty.608. Take latter (L) short distance to J. with unimproved Rd., which take (R) c.1$^{m}$ to **Poplar Grove** (c.1725), where Washington was introduced to Martha Custis (May,1758) as the "prettiest & richest Widow in Va." After this, he visited at her home, White H., whose site is c.1$^{m}$ (N).

**73. BOTTOM'S BRIDGE.** J. with US60, which Tour now follows (W) to Richmond. (For pts. to (SE) on US60, see Williamsburg Trip II.) **79. SEVEN PINES NAT. CEMETERY & SITE OF 2ND DAY OF BATTLE OF SEVEN PINES** (June 1862) (see Richmond Battlefield Nat. Pk.). **88. RICHMOND.**

# WILLIAMSBURG

**WILLIAMSBURG**

RR. Sta. on Boundary St.; Bus Sta., through bus conns., College Shop, Duke of Gloucester St. Reception Center, S. England St. Also at C. of C., Duke of Gloucester St. Christmas Celebration & unscheduled events at various restoration bldgs. Garden Wk., end of Ap. & beginning of May. Common Glory, hist. drama, beginning July 2, during summer, at Mataoka L. theater. Accoms.: Williamsburg Inn & Lodge & rest. or reconstructed inns. Six outstanding "exhibition" bldgs.—The Governor's Palace, The Capitol, Public Gaol, Raleigh Tavern, Geo. Wythe H. & Ludwell-Paradise H.—are open to public. Combination tickets for these bldgs. are avail. (fee). Tours of rest. gardens not otherwise open to public (fee). For special rates for groups, guides, inquire Reception Center. A number of restored or reconstructed bldgs. are open without adm. fee. Six old gardens are open free. Reprod. of some of furnishings in Exhibition bldgs. may be purchased at the Craft H. Swim. near Williamsburg Inn.

The orig. inspiration for restoration of Williamsburg came from the late Dr. W. A. R. Goodwin, rector of Bruton Ch., who suggested project to Mr. John D. Rockefeller, Jr. The old town offered an ideal location. Many 18th cent. Hs. were still standing & needed only to be restored. Williamsburg had been 18th cent. capital of colony & st., & center of Va.'s cultural & social life for almost 100 yrs. Restoration began in 1927. Houses erected since 1800, some 590, were torn down or removed. Patient research & excavation brought to light data concerning orig. plan of city & 18th cent. bldgs. which had disappeared. More than one hundred 18th cent. bldgs. still standing were restored & 231 completely reconstructed, among them the beautiful First Capitol, The Palace of the Governors, Raleigh Tavern, the Public Goal & Ludwell-Paradise Hs., all now maintained as "exhibition" bldgs.
Program contemplates restoration or reconstruction of more than 100 additional structures.
Williamsburg was est. as Middle Plantation (1633), located on stockade built across the peninsula for protection against Inds. "The Massacre" of 1644 by Inds. caused considerable havoc. Bacon's Rebellion brought a meeting of the rebels to the town in 1676 &, as aftermath, the hanging of Wm. Drummond of Jamestown for participation in the Rebellion, a reprisal ordered by bitterly hated Gov. Berkeley. When Jamestown was burnt down by Bacon's followers, capital was temporarily removed to Middle Plantation, which, after burning of stateh. at Jamestown, was renamed Williamsburg, in honor of William III, & became permanent seat of gov. (1699). A "noble great street," called Duke of Gloucester St., 6 poles (99′) wide, was laid out extending from the College at its W., to the Capitol, at its E. end. About half-way bet. was Palace Green, extending (N) to Gov.'s Palace. Old Bruton Parish Ch., which has survived vicissitudes of 250 yrs., stands at NW. cor. of Duke of Gloucester St. & Palace Green. Several streets paralleled Duke of Gloucester St., to the (N) & (S). Cross streets connected the E.-W. thoroughfares. Restoration has recreated the colonial city according to the orig. plan. Although never very large—pop. probably never exceeded 2,000—18th cent. Williamsburg became center of Va.'s political, social & cultural life. When House of Burgesses & courts were in session, pop. more than doubled. Taverns & public houses sprang up in great number. Shops exhibited latest London fashions. Balls, routs & banquets (at one of these, reported to have rivalled in elegance similar London functions, there were 400 guests), fairs, horse-races, gambling, slave auctions (auction block was in front of Raleigh Tavern), cock-fights, plays, kept little city humming.
From 1765 on Williamsburg became focal pt. of revolt against Britain. It was in that year that Patrick Henry rose in House of Burgesses & cried "Caesar had his Brutus, Charles the First his Cromwell—& George the Third"—here being interrupted by cries of "Treason," he continued—"& George the Third may profit by their example. If this be treason, make the most of it." In 1775 Lord Dunmore was forced to flee city. Authority now devolved on the Convention of Delegates which directed its representatives to declare for independence at Philadelphia. But even before Decl. of Ind., Williamsburg convention had adopted Geo. Mason's Decl. of Rights. In 1778 the capital was removed to Richmond, since Williamsburg was too open to attack. City suffered during Rev. from occupation by both Brit. & Amers. & after war ended, it cont. to shrink in importance. Some of its finest bldgs. either fell into decay or were destroyed by vandals or by fire. In 1781, Gov.'s Palace burnt down. By 1832 only the E. wing of the Capitol was left which was wiped out by a fire in that year. Civil War took further toll of town's distinguished architectural monuments.

PTS. OF INT.: Tour begins at Wm. & Mary College, at W. end of Duke of Gloucester St., & follows N. side of street. (1) **Wm. & Mary College** (chartered 1693.coed). Construction of its permanent bldgs. began 1695. College sided with patriots during Rev. & provided many leaders of that conflict & early years of the Republic: Thos. Jefferson, Rich. Bland, John Tyler, Sr., Benj. Harrison, Geo. Wythe, Jas. Monroe, John Marshall. Geo. Washington, although not a grad., received his surveyor's commission from college & served as its chancellor. In 1779, college est. the honor system. Bet. 1880 & 1888 college was forced to suspend for lack of funds; reopened with st. support & became st.-sponsored. College has branches at Norfolk & Richmond. **Wren Bldg.** (O.1695), facing Duke of Gloucester St., said to be oldest academic structure in U.S. & to have been designed by Sir Christopher Wren; destroyed by fire (1705), but rebuilt & thereafter repeatedly damaged by fire.

Restoration began under Rockefeller auspices, 1928, using orig. walls, on the basis of an old drawing of its ground plan & an old print, as well as other sources. **The Chapel** (1729) in the building has been rest. to its orig. state. Tombs of several notables, incl. tomb of Gov. Botetourt, are beneath the floor. In front of Wren bldg. is Statue of Gov. Botetourt, best-loved of Va.'s govs. (1768-70). Flanking Wren bldg. are: To (L) **Brafferton Hall** (O.academic season.1723.restored), built by funds left college by Rbt. Boyle, Irish-born scientist, & (R) **President's H.** (1732.allegedly by Henry Cary, Jr.) which was occupied for a time by Cornwallis, & during siege of Yorktown, by Fr. surgeon-general; it was at this time that it suffered serious damage by fire, which was made good by rest. whose costs were defrayed by Louis XVI. **The Lib.** (O.1908.early Col.); coll. of portraits, among them one by Lely & another by Wollaston, & rare portrait print of Washington. Among Lib.'s documents is the so-called Frenchman's Map which was one of chief sources for reconstruction of the Palace of the Govs. & other bldgs.

Tour now proceeds (E) along N. side of Duke of Gloucester St., both sides of which are lined with new shops in style of old Williamsburg. (2) **John Blair H.** (pre-1770. not rest.) & **Kitchen,** former home of John Blair, Jr., signer of the Constitution, near NW. cor. of Nassau St. (3) Opp. Blair H. is **Old Armistead H.,** also on Nassau St. (4) At NW. cor., Duke of Gloucester St. & Palace Green, **Bruton Parish Ch.** (O.1711.steeple 1769.rest.), venerable brick structure. Ch. has ancient communion service vessels & marble font brought from Jamestown. In octagonal steeple hangs **"Liberty Bell,"** so-called because it announced Decl. of Ind. Most of Va.'s great worshiped here: among them Washington, Jefferson & Monroe. Tour now follows (L) W. side of Palace Green. (5) **Geo. Wythe H.** & dependencies (O.fee.c.1755.fine exter.& inter.rest.) to (N) of Ch. on same side of street, said to have been built by Rich. Taliaferro for his daughter, Elizabeth, who married Wythe. Latter was prominent patriot, signer of Decl. of Ind.; became prof. of law at Wm. & Mary, probably 1st law prof. in America (see Litchfield, Conn.); died in 1806 after lingering illness due to poison administered by his ne'er-do-well grandnephew, whom he had the satisfaction of disinheriting before he died. H. furnished with antiques in period; fine garden. (6) Just N. of Wythe H., across Prince George St., **Deane H.** (reconstructed.frame), also facing Green, former home of Elkanah Deane, fashionable coach-maker; fine garden. Next door, on Prince George St., **Deane Blacksmith Shop & Forge,** one of Craft Shops of the Restoration. (7) At NW. cor. of Green, facing Palace, is **Carter-Saunders H.** (pre-1746.rest.) & lovely garden. The famous Va. planter, Rbt. "King" Carter, of Nomini, bought the H., 1761, & later sold it to Rbt. Saunders, Pres. of Wm. & Mary.

(8) **The Governor's Palace** (O.fee.1706-20.by Henry Cary.reconstructed 1930). Many splendid entertainments were given in the Palace & on these occasions "plenty of liquor was given the populace, & city was illuminated." In Dec. 1781, when the Palace was being used as hospital for wounded soldiers, it caught fire & burned down. In reconstruction of the bldg. perhaps most useful were an engraving found in the Bodleian Lib., of the structure, a floor plan of it drawn by Thos. Jefferson, & the Frenchman's Map already mentioned. Palace dependencies have been reconstructed & at least 10 gardens planted in 18th cent. manner. Inter. has been reproduced with fine paneling, lovely wall-coverings, & period furnishings. There are a number of old portraits, among them one by Lely & one by Van Dyke. (9) At NE. cor. of Palace Green, **Brush-Everard H.** (1717-19); fine garden (O), of John Brush, gunsmith & keeper of the Powder Magazine. (10) On E. side of Green, bet. Nicholson St. & the Palace, is site of **First Theater** (1716), to be reconstructed. (12) On Nicholson St. is **St. Geo. Tucker H.,** one of handsomest in town, whose owner became Prof. of Law at Wm. & Mary, as Wythe's successor. Tucker was also poet & dramatist.

(13) On Nicholson St., facing Market Sq., are **Archibald Blair H.** (c.1716-18) & **Randolph-Peyton H.** (pre-1723); home of Peyton Randolph, 1st Pres. of 1st Continental Congress. (14) At SE. end of Palace Green is **Geddy H.,** built by Jas. Geddy, gun & gold smith. Adj. is Geddy Garden (O). Tour now turns E. on Duke of Gloucester St. (15) Just (E) of Geddy H., on Market Sq., is **Norton H.,** acquired (1778) by John H. Norton, representing London firm from which the tea thrown overboard in Yorktown's tea-party was commissioned. (16) (E) of Norton H. is **Courth. of 1770** (rest.1932), at Market Sq.; Mus. of relics uncovered during restoration. (17) (E) of Old Cth., Market Sq., is **Chowning's Tavern** (O.reconstructed.

meals); furnished in period. (18) NE. cor. Duke of Gloucester & Queen Sts., is **Blair's Brick H.** (reconstructed), now antique shop. Behind it, Dr. Blair's Garden (O). (19) Next to Blair H. is **Ludwell-Paradise H.** (O.fee.c.1700-17.Georg.Col.rest. 1931), built by Philip Ludwell II. H. is among oldest in Williamsburg. Paradise part of H.'s name derives from John Paradise & his wife, Lucy Ludwell Paradise, who owned it in latter part of 18th & early 19th cents. Lucy was noted for eccentricities, such as pouring boiling water on gentlemen she disapproved of during a London tea-party. When she returned from abroad, 1805, as a widow, she had the habit of receiving her guests in her coach, while servants rolled it back & forth. Finally she was committed to an asylum. H. contains outstanding Mrs. John D. Rockefeller, Jr. coll. of Amer. Folklore Art, mostly 19th cent. items. Behind Ludwell-Paradise H. is fine garden. (20) On Nicholson St., facing garden of Ludwell-Paradise H., is **Tayloe H.** (18th cent.not rest.), very fine example. (21) Cont. (E) on Duke of Gloucester St., several old shops & houses are passed, incl. the **Wig-maker Shop,** on Colonial St., (E) of Ludwell-Paradise H., & **"The Sign of the Golden Ball,"** now the Pewterer's, formerly Dr. Geo. Gilmer's Apothecary Shop (both Restoration Craft Shops). (22) (E) of the Pewterer's is **Raleigh Tavern** (O.fee.pre-1742.reconstructed 1928), frequented by a host of notables (Geo. Washington was a frequent guest). Thousands of slaves were sold on block in front of Inn. One of tavern's proprietors, Henry Wetherburn, was famous for his hard liquor brews; Jefferson's father bought land on which he built Shadwell (see Çharlottesville) for the consideration of "Henry Wetherburn's biggest bowl of Arrack punch." Among its public rooms were the Apollo, the Daphne, the Bar, which was so arranged that the bartender could pull down wooden wicket while he went to the wine-cellar, & Gaming & Dining Rooms. During Rev., Tavern became center of "sedition," & the Assembly, dissolved by Governor, met in the Apollo Room, which also saw founding of Phi Beta Kappa Soc. (1776) by Wm. & Mary students. In Dec. 1859 the Raleigh was destroyed by fire. Inn is beautifully furnished with antiques & the famous rooms reproduced.

(23) (E) of Raleigh Tavern, on Duke of Gloucester St., are several fine col. Hs., incl. the **Nicholson Shop (Lee H.).** Tour now follows (N) through garden of Raleigh Tavern, passing **Public Records Office** (18th cent.), to Nicholson St. (24) The **Public Gaol** (O.fee.1704.adds.rest.1933) on Nicholson St., (NW) of the Capitol. In the old days rations were bad in the prison & during winter prisoners suffered intensely from cold. Some of Blackbeard's band were shut up here before being hung, & during Rev., gaol was crowded with traitors, Tories, deserters & spies. The foot-tour now circles around the Capitol, from Nicholson via Waller St. past **Waller H.** (middle 18th cent.) to Francis St. (25) Facing S. side of the Capitol, on S. side of Francis St., is handsome **Semple H.** (early Fed.), home of Judge Jas. Semple, prof. of law at Wm. & Mary's in early 19th cent. (26) Also on Francis St., near Capitol, **Robertson-Galt H.** (c.1709.not rest.), one of oldest in city. (27) To (SE) of Semple H., in fine grounds & gardens, is **Bassett Hall** (pre-1753.frame.rest.), occupied by John D. Rockefeller, Jr. (28) (S) of Capitol, facing Francis St., is **Ayscough H.,** built with funds given by Gov. Fauquier to his cook, Anne Ayscough, & husband; now The Cabinet-Makers, one of the Restoration's craft shops. (29) **The Capitol** (O.fee.1701-05.reconstructed 1934) is reproduction of 1st Capitol destroyed by fire in 1747. Second Capitol on same site was built 1753, in which, during Fr.-Ind. Wars, Washington received vote of thanks for his services, & stammered in embarrassment while attempting speech of thanks. He was told by the Speaker: "Sit down, Mr. Washington, your modesty is equal to your valour; & that surpasses the power of language that I possess." In the 2nd capitol developed the struggle of Va. against Brit. Crown, during course of which Patrick Henry made his famous "If this be treason" speech. After removal of seat of gov. to Richmond, 1780, bldg. fell into disrepair & its last remaining sec. was destroyed by fire, 1832. When restoration was being considered, the authorities decided to reconstruct 1st bldg. because of its great architectural distinction. Both exter. & inter. have been faithfully reproduced as well as orig. furnishings. Particularly noteworthy are: The **Council Chamber,** where the Gov. & his Council met; the **Office of the Clerk** of the H. of Burgesses, where hangs portrait of Washington by Chas. W. Peale; the **Court Chamber** & chamber of H. of Burgesses, in which is orig. chair used by the Speaker.

Tour now turns (W), along S. side of Duke of Gloucester St. (30) At E. end of this

St., at inters. with Blair St., is handsome **Kerr H.** (early 18th cent.adds.Gr.Rev.) & dependencies. (31) Next comes charming little **John Coke Office,** facing Raleigh Tavern. (32) Next, **Charlton H.** (rest.) Adj. is **Site of King's Arms Tavern,** due for reconstruction. (33) Next is **Bland-Wetherburn H.** (early 18th cent.not rest.), home of noted patriot, Rich. Bland, & bought by Henry Wetherburn (see above). (34) **Old Brick H. Tavern** (accoms.rest.), comes next; then (35) **Jas. Anderson H.** (pre-1770. reconstructed). (36) Charming **Mary Stith Shop** (reconst.). After passing other int. Hs., on S. side of Duke of Gloucester St., tour reaches (37) **Lightfoot H.,** int. for its unusual, projecting gambrel roof, (E) of Queen St. Tour now turns (S) on Colonial St. to Francis St., which parallels Duke of Gloucester St. (38) On this St. are a number of int. old **Hs.,** bet. Botetourt & Queen Sts. (39) Turning (S) on England St., from Francis St., tour passes handsome **Williamsburg Inn** (L) & **Lodge** (R) **Reception Center and Craft House** near Williamsburg Inn, containing reprods. of antiques. (40) Further (S) on England St., is **Old Tazewell Hall,** to (W), erected by Sir J. Randolph, father of Peyton Randolph and of John Randolph, the Tory.
Tour returns via England St. (N) crossing Francis St. (41) To (R) is **Powder Magazine** (O.fee.1716.rest.1935). At outbreak of Rev., Lord Dunmore roused popular resentment by removing powder from magazine to prevent its falling into patriot hands (1775). (42) The old **Guard H.,** where soldiers guarding the magazine were stationed, was recently reconst. (43) At SW. cor. of Duke of Gloucester & Queen Sts., is **Market Sq. Tavern** (O.accoms.c.1749.restored), fine garden (O). Tour now follows S. side of Duke of Gloucester St. (W) & passes, in succession: (44) **Greenhow-Repiton H.** (18th cent.), one of whose owners was John Greenhow, merchant who aroused considerable protest because of his outrageous prices, & next to it the **Boot & Shoemakers' Shop** of the Restoration. (45) **Travis H.** (accoms. restaurant.c.1765); Gardens (O). (46) **Jas. Galt H.,** adj. to 1st garden. (47) **Cole Shop** which today houses an interesting book & print store. (48) At inters. with Nassau St., **Taliaferro-Cole H.** (18th cent.), former home of Chas. Taliaferro, fashionable coach & sedan-chair maker. Tour ends at W. end of Duke of Gloucester St., opp. to Wm. & Mary College—where it began. (49) On the Jamestown Rd., just outside Williamsburg, is **The Common Glory Amphitheater** on Mataoka L. Here, in beginning of July & cont. through summer, is presented Paul Green's play, "The Common Glory," which carries the saga of America from 1775 through the Rev.

## TRIPS OUT OF WILLIAMSBURG

### I. WILLIAMSBURG (SW) to JAMESTOWN. 6.5. ST.31

Take St.31 (SW) to **JAMESTOWN I.** (O.sm.fee.c.1,559 as.) at **6.5.;** can also be reached by St.10 (see) from Richmond & by US17 (see). I. is owned in part by Fed. Gov. & in part by Assoc. for Preserv. of Va. Antiquities. Jamestown I. is site of 1st Eng. settlement in N. America. On May 13, 1607, 3 ships, the "Sarah Constant," "Goodspeed" & "Discovery," arrived offshore with company of 105 adventurers. In 1st yrs. settlement managed to survive under leadership of Capt. John Smith. The story of Pocahontas, who came with Powhatan's ambassador to Jamestown & amused settlers by turning cart-wheels in front of the ft., & Smith is known to every school-child—how she fell in love with Smith, rescued him from death at hands of her Ind. relatives, was induced to marry John Rolfe, went to England, was presented at court & died in England in 1617. She had 1 child, Thos., whose descendants became prosperous Va. planters. After Smith left for England, colony passed through terrible "starving time," due in part to ineptness of the "cavaliers" at planting corn, which therefore they had to procure from Inds., & disease, with malaria chief menace. John Rolfe worked out a method for curing native tobacco & this assured colony's prosperity. Indentured women servants were imported, from among whom settlers purchased wives at price of 150 lbs. of tobacco per wife. By 1619 Jamestown had become capital of colony. Burgesses met in the ch., 1st representative legislature of the New World. Jamestown suffered many vicissitudes—attacks by Inds., destruction by fire during Bacon's Rebellion, destruction of the last st. house, 1698. Finally capital was moved to Williamsburg, & Jamestown gradually declined, until today only ruins of ch. tower & Ambler H. remain. Extensive excavations have been conducted to uncover whatever remains there are underground.

PTS. OF INT.: Within grounds of Assoc. for Preserv. of Va. Antiquities: **Tower of Ch.,** 4th on this site. In 2nd Ch. Pocahontas was married to John Rolfe. In 3rd Ch., Burgesses met, and adj. is **Mem. Ch.** (1907). Gravestones of Rev. Jas. Blair & his wife, Sarah, are separated by a huge sycamore, fulfilling curse of Sarah's father, Col. Ben. Harrison, who tried to prevent marriage. Lady Berkeley, wife of Gov. Berkeley, against whose tyranny Bacon rebelled, also is comm. by tombstone. (W) of Ch. is **Relic H.;** objects uncovered in excavations. (W) of Relic H. are excavated foundations of several of town's former bldgs. Adj. is **Yeardley H.,** hqs. of Assoc. **Mons.:** House of Burgesses Mon.; Statue of Capt. John Smith by Wm. Couper; Mon. to Pocahontas, by Wm. O. Partridge; Hunt Mem. comm. Rbt. Hunt, who in June, 1607, administered 1st communion service in America.

PTS. OF INT. IN NAT. PK. SERVICE AREA: **Tercentenary Mon.** comm. founding of Jamestown, is bet. Assoc. grounds & Mus. **Mus. & Archeological Lab.;** material uncovered during excavations. Back of Mus., marle walk follows course of "Back Street" of the "New Towne" sec. of old Jamestown. "The High Way," another street of "New Towne," is similarly indicated. Here foundations of 1st st. H. have been uncovered. Along "Back Street" are **Ruins of Jacquelin-Ambler H.** (18th cent.).

## II. WILLIAMSBURG (NW) to HICKORY NECK CH. 11.5. US60

At **10.5. TOANO,** formerly known as Burnt Ordinary because of destruction by fire of local tavern. Here Lafayette camped, 1781. (E) 1$^m$ is **Olive Branch Ch.** (1835) one of oldest of Disciples of Christ Chs. **11.5. HICKORY NECK CH.** (1740 & late 18th cent.) where Rev. militia camped Ap. 1781.

## III. WILLIAMSBURG (SE) to OLD PT. COMFORT. 38. US60

**6.5. CARTER'S GROVE** (O.Mar.15-June 15.fee.1751.rest.) overlooks James R.; built by Carter Burwell, grandson of "King" Carter; antiques, coll of portraits. **10. LEE HALL,** village. **Lee Hall** (pre-Civil War) where Confed. Gen. J. B. Magruder had hqs., Ap. & May, 1862. **15. DENBIGH,** village. **Cty. Clerk's Office** (early 19th cent.). **21. JAMES R. GOLF CLUB.** (R) Golf Mus. (O); coll. of material pertaining to golf, of A. M. Huntington. **22.5.** N. J. with US17. For pts. on US17 to (S), see Hampton Roads. For pts. to (N), see US17. **23. MARINER'S MUS.** (O.wks. Sun.aft.); M. Huntington's coll. of more than 40,000 exhibits connected with seafaring, incl. a great variety of curious items—Japanese World War II suicide submarine, relics from famous ships, ship-models, figureheads, many of them by famous woodcarvers, Mark Twain's Pilot License, etc. **24. HILTON,** village. **25.** S. J. with US17. Near here, short distance (N) of James R. Bridge is **War Mem. Mus.** (O.aft. summer); coll. of arms & war material & aeronautical exhibits. **28. NEWPORT NEWS** (see Hampton Roads reg.). **34.5. HAMPTON** (see Hampton Roads Reg.).

**36. PHOEBUS.** Nat. cemetery. Not far from Phoebus, somewhat to (S), is **Roseland Manor** (Strawberry Hill) (O.fee), fine old H. with one of the most beautiful gardens in Va. **38. OLD PT. COMFORT,** famous resort. Here Jamestown settlers erected Ft. (1609). **Ft. Monroe** (c.1819-47) where Poe was stationed while in the army, & Chief Black Hawk was imprisoned (1832). Lincoln conferred with Confed. commissioners here (Feb. 1865) in futile attempt to negotiate peace. Jeff. Davis was jailed in ft. after Civil War. Ferry from Old Pt. Comfort to Pt. Willoughby. (For pts. on US60 from Pt. Willoughby to Va. Beach, see Hampton Roads Reg. Trip I.)

## IV. WILLIAMSBURG (NE) to YORKTOWN. 13. COL. NAT. PKWY.

Take Col. Nat. Pkwy. (NE) out of Williamsburg to **YORKTOWN NAT. MON.** on York R. at **13.** J. with US17 (see). Ferry to Gloucester Pt. Free guide serv. at Pk. Hqs. Near-by is York Beach (bath.sm.fee). Yorktown (est.1691, formerly thriving port, is today chiefly notable as site of the concluding act of Rev.

In summer of 1781, Brit. Gen. Cornwallis transferred his whole army to Yorktown, from Portsmouth, Va. Meanwhile De Grasse, Admiral of Fr. Fleet, moved up to cut Brit. off by sea. At end of Sept., Washington, with combined Amer. & Fr. armies (latter under Rochambeau's command), numbering 16,000, marched down peninsula to Yorktown. Allied armies soon silenced Cornwallis' guns & gradually narrowed encirclement of Brit. Cornwallis attempted to escape across York R. to Gloucester Pt. but was prevented by bad weather. On Oct. 17 he asked for a truce & in Moore H. (see below), terms of surrender were agreed upon. Brit. army laid down its arms, ending War for Independence.

PTS. OF INT.: (O.sm.fee): On Main St. are: **Customh.** (1706.rest.), where Edw. Ambler was collector of the port; he was member of the "tea party" (1774) which dumped the "Virginia's" tea-cargo into the R.; **York Hall** (Nelson H.) (1740.fine garden); during siege, Cornwallis lived here; house was home of Thos. Nelson, signer of Decl. of Ind.; a cannon ball, perhaps from a battery commanded by Nelson, himself, is in one wall; **Digges, Somerwell** (Pk.Hqs.), **Sessions & West Hs.** (all Col.). A block distant from Main St. is **Grace Ch.** (1697.rest.), used by Brit. to store powder. In cemetery are graves of Thos. Nelson, his son & grandson. Near Ch. are 2 other Col. bldgs.—**Smith H. & Pearl Hall. Swan Tavern** is reconstruction of orig. inn (1719) & dependencies on foundations of 1st structure; kitchen & stable contain coll. of hist. items. About $1^m$ out of Yorktown, on side Rd., is **Moore H.** (probably pre-1750.rest.) (see above), furnished in period. On the Battlefield, close around Yorktown, are remains of Brit. earthworks, & beyond them, reconstructed portions of Allied defenses which Washington ordered levelled after the siege. Guns, some of which were used at siege, have been set up. Throughout Battlefield & encampment areas are identifying markers. Near Yorktown is a Nat. Cemetery where Union troops are buried.

Note: For information concerning houses & gardens in Virginia, open during Garden Week (usually in last week of April), cf. pamphlet published by the Garden Club of Virginia. Further info.: Garden Club of Virginia, The Mayflower Hotel, Washington, D. C. & Jefferson & John Marshall hotels, Richmond, Va.

## US 64—NORTH CAROLINA

**FORT LANDING (W) to N.C.-TENN. LINE** ($4^m$ from Ducktown, Tenn.). **607. US64**

Via: Plymouth, Rocky Mount, Raleigh, Statesville, Morganton, Rutherfordton & Hayesville.

The route leads (W) through flat, swampy lowlands & the level Coastal Plain. In E., limited accoms.

### Sec. 1: FORT LANDING to STATESVILLE. 320.

**0. FORT LANDING,** fish. village on Little Alligator R. **15. COLUMBIA,** bank of Scuppernong R., (S) of Albemarle Sound. Streams & Ls. near-by abound in herring ("N.C. robin"), shad, perch & catfish. Game is plentiful. **26. CRESWELL.** J. with dirt Rd.

SIDE TRIP: (S) $7^m$ to **Pettigrew St. Pk.** incl. **L. Phelps** (c.16,600 as.), one of the St.'s most beautiful; black bass & other fish. The Pk. is located on portions of 2 ante bellum plantations, Somerset and Bonarva. **Somerset Manor H.** (1804) has been converted into sportsmen's hqs. The 4-story barn is unique.

**49. PLYMOUTH,** old port town. In yard of **Grace Ch.** (Episc.c.1850) 12 trees were planted and named for the Apostles. Lightning, in a bad storm, killed "Judas" without injuring any other. **110. PRINCEVILLE,** suburb of Tarboro, is one of few incorporated villages in the country politically controlled by Negroes; is an all-Negro administration. **102. TARBORO,** one of the older N.C. towns (1735), has spacious common. Claims to be only town in U.S. operating its own milk-pasteurizing plant. At one time the local hotel openly advertised itself as the worst hotel in N.C., but the picture has changed. **118. ROCKY MOUNT,** named for supposed Ind. mounds in reg. RR. tracks bisect town, halves being in different counties. In rich agric. area, it is mfg. town & one of largest bright leaf tobacco & cotton markets. Annual June German (O.2nd Fri.in June) given by Carolina Cotillion Club at Mangum's Tobacco Wareh. is one of N.C.'s outstanding social events. **174. RALEIGH** (see US1). **206. PITTSBORO,** an agric. market town, sett. (1771) by planters of Cape Fear reg., attracted by its summer climate. On Hillsboro St. is **Waddell H.** (N.O.), birthpl. of Capt. Jas. Iredell Waddell, comdr. of Confed. cruiser "Shenandoah," which carried the only Confed. flag that ever went round the world. Waddell was privateering in the Pacific when word came of demise of the Confederacy. He sailed around Cape Horn to Eng. where he remained until his crew was granted amnesty. Salisbury St., **St. Bartholomew's Ch.** (Episc.1833) has a slave gallery & communion service made of family silver given by communicants. **245. ASHEBORO.** Water power is furnished by the Deep & Uharie Rs. to c.40 industrial units. Sec. was once home of sm. tribes of Inds. Earliest white settlers are believed to have been Germans fleeing European wars (c.1740). Annual field trials of Fox Hunters Assoc. of N.C. (Sept.); fox hunts are held in Uharie Mts. (SW). **276. LEXINGTON** (see US52). **295. MOCKSVILLE.** In front of Cth. is **Marker** indicating that Dan. Boone "lived & learned woodcraft in Davie County"; his parents are buried near-by. **320. STATESVILLE,** industrial city surrounded by grain & dairy area of the Piedmont, stands on site of Ft. Dobbs (1755). Streets are tree & flower lined; by ordinance, city is bird sanctuary. On W. Meeting St., **Wallace Bros. Herbarium** (O) with large coll. of medicinal plants. W. Broad St., **Mitchell College** (Presb.1755.2-yr.).

SIDE TRIPS: (A) On St.90 (NE) 3m to **N.C. St. Experiment Farm** (O.appl.) has been important in agric. development of reg.
(B) On US21 (N) c.12m to **Allison's L.** (boat.swim.) with old water wheel at lower end of 2 sm. bodies of water which form L. 38m **Elkin; Chatham Mfg. Co. Plant** (O.appl.), producers of woolen blankets. 57m **Roaring Gap,** resort area (June-Oct.swim.boat. riding.hik.golf) on high plateau. Girl Scout Camp on L. Louise. On near-by Lake Dr., **Trout Hatchery** (O). 62m J. with Blue Ridge Pky. (see). US21 cont. to N.C.-Va. Line at 78m.
(C) From Statesville (S) on US21, 5m to **Barium Springs.** Discovered by Inds., springs in town contain salts of barium, sulfur & iron. 16m **Mooresville,** with Cotton Mills Plant (O), one of few that processes raw cotton to finished articles. 23m **Davidson.** (For Davidson at 23m & Charlotte at 44m & sec. (S) to N.C.-S.C. Line at 80m, see US74, trips out of Charlotte.)

## Sec. 2: STATESVILLE to N.C.-TENN. LINE. 287.

From Statesville to **MORGANTON** at **43.,** US64 unites with US70 (see). **77. RUTHERFORDTON** (see US74). Bet. this pt. & **102. BAT CAVE,** US64 unites with US74 (see). **117. HENDERSONVILLE** (see Trips out of Asheville). **135. DAVIDSON R.** (f.). **136. PISGAH FOREST.** J. with US276.

SIDE TRIP: (R) here c.1.5m to entrance of **Pisgah Nat. For.,** marked by concrete pillars. 5m **Davidson R. Campground** (water.fuel.facils.swim.pool). 9m is **Looking Glass Falls,** formed by Looking Glass Cr. tumbling 85′ from rocky precipice.
(R) on trl., along sm. cr. 1m to **Looking Glass Rock** (4,000′). When spring is rainy & water is frozen, this looks like a giant mirror. Wide view of peaks, valleys & streams from top.
14m **U.S. Fawn Rearing Plant** (O.appl.in season.June 1-Oct.1), only plant in U.S. whose chief purpose is rearing fawns. When 6 mos. old, they are shipped to other preserves. (L) here on For. Serv. Rd. to **Pink Beds For. Campground** (water.fuel.facils.); abundance of wild life seen here. **Wagon Rd. Gap** 17m affords good view of the Pink Beds, stretch of profuse Mt. laurel garden.

**138. BREVARD,** with its surrounding wealth of mt. attractions & numerous well-marked Rds. & trls., is summer resort. Here, before Civil War, high hat industry flourished. The town hatter offered hand-made wool, muskrat, & beaver hats. Owners of high hats once paid an annual st. tax of $4; those who carried gold-headed canes were similarly taxed. Annual Music Festival (Aug.) at Transylvania Music Camp on outskirts of town. **165. SAPPHIRE,** so named for precious stones found near-by & intense blue of sky & water. Sapphire reg. has long been favorite vacation area. At **c.170. FAIRFIELD INN** (accoms.swim.boat.horses avail.), overlooking Fairfield L. **171. CASHIERS** (summer resort), at J. with St.107 leading (L) to **High Hampton Inn & Country Club** (swim.boat.golf.f.tennis.riding.hik.). **183. HIGHLANDS,** summer resort that attracts many patrons, incl. naturalists who come to study its diversified flora; variety of plants & animal life from different zones make the area almost an encyclopedia of Carolina mts. Among rare plants found here is shortia, grown only in N.C. mts. & Japan. **Highlands Mus. & Biological Lab.** (O) preserves private colls. **Highland Golf Club** (swim.boat.f. tennis.skeet.riding.hik.). Trls. from Highlands lead to peaks of near-by mts.: Bearpen (N), Blackrock (E), Fodderstack (S). Leading (L) from Highlands is gravel Rd. up Satulah Mt. 1.5m to **Sloan Gardens** (O); unusual & common varieties of flowers. (NW) of town is a series of waterfalls. At **c.185. BRIDAL VEIL** falls over hy. Just beyond, **Dry Falls** (pic.) affords tourists opportunity to descend steps & stand behind falls where they may view the Cullasaja R. through a sheet of water. Low Falls are visible as route descends into Cullasaja Gorge. Hy. was literally carved out of perpendicular cliffs. **202. FRANKLIN** (see US23). **206.,** J. with gravel For. Serv. Rd.

SIDE TRIP: (R) on this Rd. (steep ascent & sharp curves) through thick fors. 3m to **Wayah St. Game Refuge.** 14,000-a. wildlife area in Nantahala Nat. For., containing deer, wild turkey, ruffed grouse, fox, gray squirrel, quail & wildcat. About 0.5m **Arrowood Glade** (pic.) are trout-rearing pools. 10m **Nantahala (Wayah) Gap Campground** (water.cook.facils.).

(R) from gap on For. Serv. Rd. 1m to **Wilson Lick Ranger Sta.** & up steep course 3m farther to summit of **Wayah Bald** (5,336′) reached by motor Rd. **John B. Byrne Tower** affords wide views.

**215. WALLACE GAP,** where route reaches crest of the Nantahala Range, is J. with For. Serv. Rd.

SIDE TRIP: (L) to **Deep Gap Campground** (water.facils.), adj. **Standing Ind. St. Game Refuge.** J. here with Appalachian Trl. leading (R) 0.5m on trl. (4′;graded) to **Standing Ind.,** bald peak called grandstand of the S. Appalachians.

In near-by Buck Cr. Valley at **c.225** is **BUCK CR. RANCH,** 1,000-a. pub. campground. **243. HAYESVILLE,** surrounded by mt. peaks. Mineral resources of sec. are rich but largely undeveloped. Mica occurs on higher ridges, & in valleys are kaolin, magnetic iron ore, corundum, etc. **256. BRASSTOWN** has general store with Cherokee relics coll. **John C. Campbell Folk Sch.** (O), non-profit venture in rural adult education is operated on 175-a. farm; course for young adults to supplement pub. sch. work patterned after Danish folk schs. & community program involving recr., cultural & economic as well as educational features. Handicrafts have been developed to supplement farm incomes. Display in Craft Room of main bldg.; folk mus. in old log cabin. There is also a creamery (O). **264. MURPHY** (see US74). At **c.274.** J. with St.294.

SIDE TRIP: (R) to Shoal Cr. at J. with T.V.A. access Rd. at 9m; then (R) here 5m to **Hiwassee Dam,** similar in design to Norris Dam (Tenn.), 300′ long with spillway in middle, 300′ high. It creates **Hiwassee L.** (f.boat.cottages.refreshments) whose 10 sq. miles extend to Murphy. It is a connecting link with interstate navigable streams, an aid in flood control; develops enormous electrical energy as a by-product. As hy. approaches the N.C.-Tenn. Line the landscape is barren, practically all vegetation having been killed by fumes from smelters at Copper Hill, Tenn.

US64 crosses the **N.C.-TENN. LINE** at **287.**

## US 70—NORTH CAROLINA

**ATLANTIC (W) to N.C.-TENN. LINE** (19m from Newport, Tenn.). **494. US70**
Via: New Bern, Goldsboro, Raleigh, Durham, Burlington, Greensboro, Salisbury, Morganton & Asheville.

US70, ascending from low Coastal Plains, to higher Piedmont & into mountainous reg. of western N.C., is a well-traveled & popular tourist route.

### Sec. 1: ATLANTIC to DURHAM. 208.

**0. ATLANTIC,** a fishing village on peninsula on Core Sound. Daily mail boats avail. for trips (no cars.fee) to Cedar I., Portsmouth & Ocracoke. At **30.,** J. with dirt Rd.

SIDE TRIP: (L) on this Rd. to log **Beaufort Community Center** (O.recr.facils.); 0.5m adj., **Marine Biological Lab.** of the Woman's College of the Univ. of N.C. (NE) from lab. is **Lennoxville Rookery,** a protectorate of the Audubon Soc., where thousands of heron, incl. egrets, propagate.

**32. BEAUFORT** (bō-fort, not bū-fort as in S.C.), has the atmosphere of an 18th cent. seacoast town, once known as Fishtown (sett.1709). Narrow streets are bordered with whitewashed oaks & elms. Houses have narrow front porches & no eaves. There was a ft. at Old Topsail Inlet built 1712. In 1747 Beaufort was captured by Sp. pirates, who were driven out a few days later. PTS. OF INT.: On Turner St., **Dr. Cramer H. & Odd Fellows Bldg.** (c.1830). On Front St., **Davis H.** (O), relics on display; **Thos. Duncan H.; Ernest Duncan H.; Otway Burns Mon.,** comm. the privateer Comdr. Otway Burns, now a semi-legendary figure. Andrew Jackson appointed him keeper of the Brant I. Shoal Light, "where he sank into his anecdotage, fond of his bright naval uniform, his cocked hat, good whiskey & a good fight." From Beaufort charter passenger boats are avail. for Cape Lookout, Portsmouth & Ocracoke.

SIDE TRIP: **Cape Lookout** 12m with **Lighth.** (O.160′;1859) notable for unusual alternate black & white markings; most outstanding headland (S) of Cape Hatteras. There are good

f. grounds off the Cape & natural harbor. "Buy boats" acquire hauls of local fishermen & resell them in Beaufort or Morehead City.

**35. MOREHEAD CITY** (always called Morehead) on the opp. side of Newport R. from Beaufort, is resort, f. center & ocean port. Summer cottages (W) are separated from the bus. dist. by the Promised Land, shacks & sm. cottages owned by boatmen & commercial fishermen. Fishing fleet seines for menhaden, used for oil & fertilizer. The **Ocean Shipping Port Terminal** (1935-37) with 1,000′ pier, is reached through a 11,000′ channel. Ships can enter, turn about & depart under their own power. Port is one of the best (S) of New York. Sizable fleet of charter boats avail. for sport & vacation fishing. In Morehead is J. with paved Rd.

SIDE TRIP: (R) on this Rd. 2.5m to **Atlantic Beach** (hotel.casino.bathh.pic.grounds), resort on Bogue I.

(L) from Atlantic Beach on paved Rd., winding its way bet. bare white sand dunes & thickly grown culverts 4m to **Ft. Macon St. Pk.**, at E. end of Bogue I. Steel lookout tower at **Coast Guard Sta.** (O). Ft. Macon (1828-35.rest.1936).

**61. CROATAN. For. Fire Tower** affords wide view of surrounding fors. & marsh. Town lies within **Croatan Nat. For.**, area of cutover timber acquired for use in for. conservation development. There are 5 shallow spring-fed Ls.: **Ellis** (For. Serv. campground), **Great, Long, Little** & **Catfish. 72. NEW BERN** (see US17). **107. KINSTON** (sett.1740), tobacco center on Neuse R. **134. GOLDSBORO,** mfg. & agric. town in approx. center of St.'s bright leaf tobacco belt. **157. SMITHFIELD. 185. RALEIGH** (see US1). **192. NANCY JONES H.** (1805), scene of the encounter bet. S.C.'s & N.C.'s Govs. & the classic: "It's a damn long time between drinks."

**208. DURHAM**

At Union Sta.: Southern; Norfolk & W.; D. & S.; Norfolk S.; Seaboard Air Line RRs. & other conns. Bus & air conns. Good accoms. Info.: C. of C. & Carolina Motor Club, 111 W. Parrish St. Annual Events: Kennel Club Show (Ap.), Flower Show (May), Horse Show (Sept.), Cty. Fair (3rd wk.Sept.) & Dahlia Show (Oct.).

Durham, "cigarette capital of the world," home of the Amer. Tobacco Co. monopoly formed in 1890 by Jas. Buchanan Duke, was broken into smaller companies in 1911 at behest of U.S. Supreme Ct. Home, too, of famous Bull of Durham, focus of earliest comprehensive advertising campaign launched at Amer. public. The Amer. Tobacco Co. covered the country with ads featuring Bull Durham (see Va. US58, Sec.3); likeness of Bull was painted by Rosa Bonheur, Fr. animal painter. "Buck" Duke also developed water power in Carolinas, forming Southern Power Co. (Duke Power Co. & its subsidiaries). Endowment to Duke Univ. ($80,000,000 at his death) is largest gift of S. origin. City is also largest medical center (S) of Baltimore. Durham has large progressive Negro pop. with its own college, business firms, banks, large insurance company, schs., newspapers, lib. & hospital. PTS. OF INT.: (1) Geer & North Sts., **Ephphatha Ch.** (Episc.for deaf mutes); (2) **Liggett & Myers Plant** (O.guides); (3) Pettigrew & Blackwell Sts., **Amer. Tobacco Co. Plant** (O). (4) 1911 S. Fayetteville St., **N. C. College for Negroes** (1910.coed.) on 50-a. campus. (5) (N) of Main St. on Morgan St., **Tobacco Warehouses** (O.mid-Sept.-Mar.), where uninitiated are bewildered by chant of auctioneer & buyers' signals. (6) Duke Univ. (1924) which had earlier been Union Institute & Trinity College (1838); moved to Durham (1892) on site now **Woman's College** (East) **Campus** (c.120 as.Georg.rebuilt 1925-27); 12 bldgs. added. Dormitories, domed auditorium, lib. (Fed.) & other bldgs., & Annie Roney fountain (one of oldest campus landmarks), on East Duke Lawn, are joined in quadrangle by lawns & walks. Conn. to East Campus by "faculty row" is **Univ.** (West) **Campus** (c.5,000 as.Tudor Goth.), incl. Trinity College (undergrad.men), Grad. Sch. of Arts & Sciences, Schs. of Divinity, Law, Medicine, Nursing, Forestry & College of Engineering. Chapel (1932.Goth.cruciform) with c.150 stained glass windows, ornate stone, iron & woodwork; tower (50 bell carillon) patterned after tower of Canterbury Cathedral. Duke Hospital (1930), $4,000,000 plant with pub. clinics. Stadium, natural hillside amphitheater, seats 40,000. Sarah Duke Garden with many varieties of trees, shrubs & flowers. In Durham are Js. with US15-501 (S) & US15 (N).

SIDE TRIPS: (A) On US15-501 (S) 12m to **Chapel Hill,** on granite rise above coastal plain, near center of St., where 2 main Rds. crossed; it was site of Episc. Chapel (late 18th cent.). Here is Univ. of N.C., oldest St. univ. in U.S., chartered in 1789. Chapel Hill, whose recent Pres., Frank Porter Graham, is a liberal leader in N.C. thought & legislation, now U.S. Senator (1949). Today univ. has branch in Greensboro (Woman's College) & in Raleigh

(St.College of Agric.& Engineering). Chapel Hill is fine example of small univ. town; dominated by ivy-covered bldgs. on campus of shaded walks, with houses of varying age & condition surrounded by abundant shrubbery & flowers. Univ.'s prestige is based on high standards of scholarship & research. Schs. of univ. incl.: Law, Commerce, Library Science, Medicine, Pharmacy, Pub. Health, Arts & Sciences, Fine Arts & grad. school. Institute for Research in Social Science (org.1924 by Howard W.Odum) has produced specialized studies of Southern life, with ultimate goal of cultural inventory of reg. Carolina Playmakers (org.1918 by Fred H.Koch) are notable for contribution to Amer. folk drama & famous alumni: Maxwell Anderson, Paul Green, Thomas Wolfe & others. The Univ. Press is active; emphasis is on social, economic & racial problems & technical journals. PTS. OF INT.: (1) Cameron Ave., **Old Well,** now a univ. "shrine," is no longer the only source of water for students. Opp., (2) **South** (Main) **Bldg.** (1798.1814.remod.1926). (3) **Old East** (1793.adds.1824.inter.remod.1924), oldest St. univ. structure in U.S. still in use. (4) **Person Hall** (1793-97.post-Col.), 1st chapel of univ., was laid in 3 secs. (5) Heart of "New" Campus is **Lib.** (1929); Hanes Coll. of Origin of the Book & colls. dealing with N.C. & the South. (6) Cameron & Hillsboro Sts., **Coker Arboretum** (5 as.), one of most complete botanical gardens of its kind. (7) 501 E. Franklin St., **Widow Puckett H.** (N.O. 1799), one of few remaining early Hs. (8) Franklin St., **Chapel of the Cross** (Episc.1842-46. Goth.Rev.) built by slave labor of pink Mt. Airy granite. (9) **Morehead Planetarium,** under construction (1949).

(B) On US15 (N) 3m to J. with paved Rd.

7m to **Fairntosh Plantation** (O.1802), home of Duncan Cameron who defended N.C. landowners when Lord Granville's heirs sued for recovery of property confiscated by St. at start of Rev. Old brick kitchen, Cameron's law office, schoolh., slave cabins, carriage H. & gray frame chapel with stained-glass windows & hand-made altar & pews.

At 4m on US15 is J. with unpaved Rd.

1m to **Duke Homestead** (O.Sun.1851.rest.), built by Washington Duke, founder of Duke dynasty. Walls & floors of hand-hewn pine, orig. furniture & pieces used in 1860's.

At 14m is **Quail Roost Farm** (O), 1,500-a. model Guernsey dairy farm. 30m **Oxford,** tobacco town with N.C.'s 1st wareh. specifically for aging cured leaf tobacco (1856). 40m **Stovall,** J. with unpaved Rd. leading 4m to **Site of John Penn H.,** N.C. signer of Decl. of Ind. US15 cont. to N.C.-Va. Line at 46m.

## Sec. 2: DURHAM to N.C.-TENN. LINE. 286.

**6. BENNETT MEM.,** inscribed: "Unity," site of Johnston's surrender to Sherman (Ap. 26, 1865). **13. HILLSBORO** (inc.1929) in lush valley of Eno R., (E) of Occoneechee Mts. Many Ind. relics & legends of Haw, Eno & Occoneechee Inds. who lived in vic. Manufactures incl. wood products, cloth & oil. Much of the stone used in bldgs. of Duke Univ. (see US15) was quarried near-by. Settled in Earl of Granville's territory, town was platted 1754, orig. called Orange. Later it was called Corbinton, then Childsboro, & in 1766 Gov. Tryon named it Hillsboro to honor Earl of Hillsborough, Secy. of State for the Colonies. Was summer capital of planters from low country, refugees from heat & mosquitoes. PTS. OF INT.: King & Churton Sts., **Orange County Cth.** (1845.Gr.Rev.by Capt. Berry) with records dating from 1755. Churton St., **Eagle Masonic Lodge** (c.1825.Gr.Rev.). Churton & Tryon Sts., **Confed. Mem. Lib.** (O.wks.). Adj. Lib. is **Presb. Ch.** (1815.Goth.Rev.), built with lottery funds. Behind Ch. is cemetery with orig. grave of N.C.'s signer of Decl. of Ind., Wm. Hooper. In front of Ch. is **Mon. of Archibald De Bow Murphey** (d.1832), social & educational reformer. City has Hs. pre-dating Rev. (many with adds. & remod.). **33. BURLINGTON,** large mill town; 1st hosiery mill est. 1896. At N. edge of town is J. with St.100.

SIDE TRIP: (N) 3m to **Elon College** (org.1889.mod.Georg.coed.), operated by Christian Ch.; town is also called Elon College.

Just beyond Burlington is Marker on site of **Alamance Battleground** where Amer. "Regulators" met Gov. Tryon's militia, May 16, 1771. **55. GREENSBORO** (see US29), J. with US421.

SIDE TRIP: (W) on US421 6m to **Guilford College.** School founded by Soc. of Friends is oldest Quaker college in South, an outgrowth of earlier New Garden Boarding Sch. (1837.coed.). In town is Friendly Rd. leading 0.5m to **Dolly Madison Well,** site of birthpl. of famous First Lady & hostess.

In Greensboro US29 unites with US70 to **LEXINGTON** at **91.** where US52 unites with hy. to **SALISBURY** at **108. 135. STATESVILLE** (see US64). Here US64 & US70 are united. Tour cont. on US64-70. **170. VALDESE,** sett. 1893 by Fr.-speaking colonists (called Vaudois or Waldenses) from Cottian Alps of Piedmont, Italy, followers of Peter Waldo, 12th Cent. reformer called heretic. Textile mills supplemented early wineries & bakeries which still operate. **Waldensian Presb. Ch.** conducts services in Fr. as well as Eng. In Ch. is **Mus.** with exhibit of orig. household goods & local hand-made products. **178. MORGANTON,** in Piedmont reg., is thriving cotton & lumber mill town. Sts. are named after those in Charleston, S.C. **St. Hospital for Insane** & adj., **N.C. Sch. for the Deaf.** Cont. (W) on US70. At c.**192.,** East J. with St.105.

SIDE TRIP: (N) c.5m to **L. James** (f.h.camp.), artificial L. with c.152m of hilly shore.

**199. MARION,** named for Gen. Francis Marion, Rev. figure known as "Swamp Fox." Here are hqs. for Mt. Mitchell ranger dist. of Pisgah Nat. For. **201. J.** with US221.

SIDE TRIP: On US221 (N) 23m to **Linville Falls.**

1m on St.105 (sm.fee) to falls dropping 90′ over boulders. St.105 leads to Linville Gorge & many spectacular views: sheer cliffs of Jonas Ridge with Hawksbill (4,030′) & Table Rock (3,090′) clearly defined; also views of Brown Mt. lights. In good weather it is possible to cont. on Rd. to L. James & on to J. with US70.

25m J. with Blue Ridge Pky. (see). At c.31m **Crossnore Sch.** (1911), self-help sch. founded by Drs. Eustace & Mary Sloop for mountain children as well as adults. It is largely supported by gifts & sales of donated second-hand clothing. 37m **Linville,** summer resort (swim.boat.f.golf). Bet. here & Blowing Rock, 57m, US221 is known as Yonahlosse (Cherokee, "black bear") Trl. which in June blazes with rhododendrons. Blowing Rock is only inc. town on Blue Ridge Pky., one of oldest S. Appalachian resorts (1880's). Fine accoms. & facils.; near-by Cone estate (O) has best bridle trl. system in N.C. 66m **Boone,** under Howard's Knob, named for Dan. Boone who lived in this reg. 1760-69. Site of Appalachian Teacher's Training Sch. (coed.). At 93m **Jefferson** (founded 1800), almost entirely surrounded by mts., rarely has full daylight. It is said of this reg. that "there are more cattle in Ashe Cty. than people, & more sheep than cattle." At 121m is N.C.-Va. Line.

**203.,** on US70 is J. with St.80.

SIDE TRIP: Entrance to **Mt. Mitchell Sec.** of **Pisgah Nat. For.** (f.h.recr.facils.swim.bridle & ft.trls.pic.cabins.resort). 2.5m **L. Tahoma.** 10m **Buck Cr. Gap. J.** with Blue Ridge Pky. (see). 12m **Busick,** J. with For. Serv. Rd.

(L) c.1.5m on this Rd. to J. with For. Serv. Trl., (R) 3m to **Summit of Mt. Mitchell** (6,684′), highest peak in Appalachian system. On N. side of Mt. is **St. Game Refuge & Fish Hatchery** (3 f.seasons per yr.). Near-by is **Carolina Hemlocks For. Serv. Campground** (water.facils.fuel.fireplaces).

**212. OLD FORT,** nestled in the Blue Ridge, site of Davidson's Ft. (1757), early outpost in settling of Blue Ridge reg. Near-by (c.3m) is **Old Ft. Pic. Ground.** US70, twisting almost constantly as it ascends the E. slope of the Blue Ridge, cont. (W) with many cutoffs with views of Royal Gorge & surrounding mts. **217. PT. LOOKOUT** (parking.refreshments). **219. RIDGECREST,** summer conference of Bapts. held here. Town is W. terminus of the S. RR.'s **Swannanoa Tunnel** (1879.1,800′) whose cutting marked completion of RR. **222.** J. with Mt. Mitchell Rd. (1-lane, rising more than 4,000′ in 18m), 20m to **Mt. Mitchell. 227. BLACK MOUNTAIN,** summer tourist center; golf, **L. Tomahawk** (boat.swim.recr.). Near-by is **Black Mt. College** (1933.coed.), experimental sch. where students & teachers govern, work, study & live communally. L. Eden is near sch. (boat.swim.). In Black Mountain is J. with St.9.

SIDE TRIP: On St.9 (N) c.2m to **Montreat,** 4,500 as. of for., streams & mts., owned by Southern Presb. Ch. 20,000 attend July & Aug. conferences (sm.fee).

**236. ASHEVILLE** (see). Bet. here & **N.C.-TENN. LINE** at **286.,** US70 is joined with US25 (see Asheville).

## US 74—NORTH CAROLINA

**WRIGHTSVILLE BEACH (W) to ASHEVILLE. 337. US74**

Via: Lumberton, Laurinburg, Charlotte, Rutherfordton & Forest City.

Hy. runs through low swamplands of Coastal Plain & up into the Piedmont, through sandhills, foothills & into rugged mt. country.

**0. WRIGHTSVILLE BEACH** (see Trips out of Wilmington, US17). **11. WILMINGTON** (see). **47. WANANISH,** tool plant for turpentine industry. J. with St.214.

SIDE TRIP: (L) here on St.214 which is 4m loop skirting shore of L. Waccamaw, 7m long & 5m wide, a summer resort (accoms.water sports).

**68. CHADBOURN,** strawberry-shipping pt. **94. LUMBERTON,** trade & lumber center of Coastal Plain reg. Town's theater has 3 entrances: one for Inds., Negroes & whites. **104. PEMBROKE,** center of Croatan Ind. settlement. These Inds. are supposed to be descendants from intermarriage with Raleigh's "Lost Colony," 1587 (see Roanoke I., US17). **Cherokee Ind. Normal Sch.** (coed.) trains teachers for Ind. schools, has high sch., 3-yr. college course & course for deaf Inds. **124. LAURINBURG** at J. with US15 (see). **133. OLD HUNDRED,** so named because of 100$^{m}$ post incorrectly set here when slave-built RR. was laid through here from Wilmington. **146. ROCKINGHAM** (see US1). **166. WADESBORO** (see US52). **193.5. LEE PK.** (swim pool.golf.ball pk.playground). **195. MONROE.**

**221. CHARLOTTE**

Southern, Seaboard Air Line, & Piedmont & N. RRs. Good air & bus conns. Info.: C. of C., 121 W. 4th St. & Carolina Motor Club, 701. S. Tryon St. Accoms.: All types. Annual events: Kennel Club Show (Ap.), Garden Club Show (May), Food Show (Sept.), Cty. Fair (Oct.), Golden Gloves Boxing Tourn. (Jan.or Feb.) & Textile Show (variable date in fall).

The largest city of the Carolinas, Charlotte's place as a commercial center is defined by its tall business bldgs., huge warehs. & numerous factories. City's residential secs. are intensively gardened & landscaped. Charlotte is surrounded by mill villages, except on SE. edge, each with endless rows of identical, boxlike houses. Known as greatest ch.-going city in U.S., it also has important place in Amer. hist., being home of Mecklenburg Decl. of Ind. (May 20, 1775), said to be Jefferson's basis for 1776 Decl. of Ind.

PTS. OF INT.: (1) Trade & Tryon Sts., **Independence Sq.,** site of 1st Cth. & site of Cornwallis' Hqs. (both marked). (2) 211 W. Trade St., **Capt. Jas. Jack Mon.,** to "Paul Revere of the South." (3) Trade St. near Poplar St., **First Presb. Ch.** (rebuilt 1894), orig. all denominational (1815); in rear, Old Cemetery has headstones & graves of Southern celebrities. (4) S. Mint & W. 4th Sts., **Shipp Mon.,** comm. military reinstatement of S. after Civil War. Lt. Wm. Ewen Shipp was 1st southerner graduated from West Pt. after Civil War. (5) 211 E. 9th St., **Little Theater** (O.appl.), presents several major & workshop productions annually. (6) 310 N. Tryon St., **Pub. Lib.** has Gen. Stonewall Jackson's lib. (7) Hampstead Pl. & Eastover Rd., **Mint Mus.** (1934.reprod.of U.S. Mint used 1837-61;1867-1913); coll. of handicrafts, hist. relics & art. (8) Queen Rd. & Radcliffe Ave., **Queens College** (Presb.women), founded 1857 as Charlotte Female Institute. (9) 400 Hermitage Rd., **Martin L. Cannon H.** (grounds O.appl.1915), bought in 1920 & remod. by Jas. B. Duke; landscaped 10-a. estate with azalea, dogwood & other shrubs blooming early spring to fall. (10) Beatties Ford Rd. near Martin St., **Johnson C. Smith Univ.** (Negro. 1867.Presb.), nonsectarian, coed. in senior division of Liberal Arts. Fine music coll. in Lib. (11) 1628 E. Morehead St., **J. B. Ivey Tulip Gardens,** over 20,000 plants of many varieties, labeled for visitors. In town is J. with US21.

SIDE TRIPS: (A) On US21 (N) 21$^{m}$ to Davidson. Here is **Davidson College** (Presb.1837. men) on beautiful 50-a. campus with near-by sports field & golf course. Woodrow Wilson was an alumnus. US21 cont. (N) to Mooresville (see Trip from Statesville, US64).

(B) On US21 (S) 11$^{m}$ to **Pineville** where Abr. Lincoln's mother, Nancy Hanks, is supposed to have gone to sch. US21 cont. (S) to N.C.-S.C. Line at c.13$^{m}$.

Bet. Charlotte & **KINGS MT.** at **250.,** US74 unites with US29 (see). **264. SHELBY,** named for Gen. Isaac Shelby of Kings Mt. fame, is seat of Cleveland Cty., also named for a Kings Mt. hero, Col. Benj. Cleveland. It was home of Gov. O. Max Gardner who died before he sailed for his post in England as Ambassador; of Clyde R. Hoey, Gov. & U.S. Senator (1944); & of playwright Hatcher Hughes, whose "Hell-Bent fer Heaven" won the 1924 Pulitzer prize. **290. FOREST CITY,** is well-planned textile town with business area built around a large pub. plaza; broad streets flank central pky. **297. RUTHERFORDTON,** at foot of Blue Ridge was one-time center of U.S. gold mining (1790-1840). Here 1st U.S. gold coin was minted (1834) by Christopher Bechtler. Bet. Rutherfordton & **ASHEVILLE** (see) at **337.,** US74 unites with US64 (see).

## US 17—NORTH CAROLINA

**N.C.-VA. LINE** (21$^{m}$ from Portsmouth, Va.) **(W) to N.C.-S.C. LINE** (23$^{m}$ from Myrtle Beach, S.C.). **284. US17**

Via: S. Mills, Elizabeth City, Hertford, Washington, New Bern, Jacksonville, Hampstead & Wilmington.

US17 runs through Albemarle reg. to S.C. border, paralleling Atlantic. The sec. from Deep Creek to S. Mills was surveyed by Geo. Washington (1763) & dug by Negro slaves (1790-1822); this sec. is called the Geo. Washington Hy.

**8. S. MILLS,** notorious Gretna Green, 120′ drawbridge crosses canal, link in the Intracoastal Waterway. **22. ELIZABETH CITY** (bus.plane.no RR.passenger serv.; yacht basin.shipyard;2 race tracks.h.f.boat.). Hub of the E. Albemarle, oldest settled sec. of St. & the 1 town on 40m Pasquotank R., it is fine inland harbor which is a port & wintering pt. for yachts as well as industrial shipping pt. & retail center. Shipbuilding was begun c.1665 by Bermudians. In 1862, at approach of Union ships, residents fired their homes. After Civil War, Elizabeth City was economically joined to near-by Va. cities until 1920's when a water & land trans. system reunited town with N.C. Nat. Moth Boat Regatta (Oct.). **Great Dismal Swamp** (big & sm. game h.f.). PTS. OF INT.: Colonial Ave., **Judge Small H.** (1800.inter.handcarvings), Union Hqs. & Fearing St., **Fearing H.** (1740.adds.), oldest H. in town. Church & McMorine Sts., **Christ Ch.** (Episc.1856.Goth.Rev.), on site of earlier Ch. **Shipyards** (O.appl.).

SIDE TRIPS: (A) **Elizabeth City** (SE) on St.170. 3m **Bayside** (N.O.1800.Class.Rev.), plantation H. The overseer's H. & 1 slave cabin still stand. At 4m are hangars, barracks & landing field of U.S. Coast Guard Air Sta. (free), huge wartime installation. 7m **Naval Air Facility** (O.1-5.wks.holidays), a blimp base. Both stas. do air-sea rescue work.

(B) NE. on US158 & St.34. (Tourist accoms.beach hotels.cottages at frequent intervals; guides.bath.boat.sound,inlet & deep-sea f.). The Virginia Dare Trl. branches from US17 at Elizabeth City over the Pasquotank R. drawbridge & traverses 1.5m of what is locally known at Floating Rd. It was an engineering headache for yrs., as it crosses swamp in which there is much quicksand & in which water is affected by tides. Route leads to upper banks, ocean beach & sport f. areas. 15m **Sligo.** (R) here on St.34 & thence through rich farm country 3m to Currituck Cth., picturesque cty. seat on Currituck Sound (h.f.). 12m **Barco,** where St.34 becomes US158 on which Side Trip cont. At 25m **Coinjock,** route crosses Va. sec. of Intracoastal Waterway. 52m **Point Harbor,** at Wright Mem. Bridge, 3m span at the confluence of 4 sounds—Albemarle, Currituck, Croatan & Roanoke. Rd. swings (R) & parallels beach. 60m J. with Rd. leading (R) to **Kitty Hawk** where Wilbur & Orville Wright flew 1st power-driven airplane, Dec. 17, 1903. At 63m is J. with Rd. leading to **Kill Devil Hill Nat. Mon.** (Wright Mem.1932). Kill Devil Hills are 2 dunes; one (c.90′) was artificially anchored & 60′ granite pylon with observ. gallery & beacon erected on it.

(R) 1m from Mon. are **Fresh Ponds,** largest covering 125 as. These ponds lie on narrow sand bar bet. salt waters of ocean & sound but are thick with waterlilies & offer excellent freshwater f.

68m **Nags Head,** has been a resort for more than a cent., from the days when it could only be reached by boat. Natives tell & sing of sporadic visits made by ghost of Virginia Dare. Vacation cottages & hotels line both ocean & sound shores. 75m J. with beach Rd. (unusable at certain times; inquire before proceeding).

Rd. parallels ocean, crossing **Oregon Inlet** (free ferry) & cont. over **Cape Hatteras Seashore Project,** 12,000-a. area to be developed by U.S. Gov. for scenic & hist. & recr. value. (S. terminus of Project is at Hatteras, 55m). At 82m **Cape Hatteras St. Pk.** (excellent surf casting, boats may be chartered at near-by villages for sound, ocean & inlet f.). Off E. Cape is treacherous **Diamond Shoals,** "the graveyard of the Atlantic," which extends 25m out to sea, guarded by Lightship.

US158 (on which trip cont.) branches (R) across 2.5m causeway & bridges over Roanoke Sound to reach **Roanoke I.** at 76m, 12m long & 3m wide. At 80m **Manteo** (guides.boats.h.f.). 83m **Ft. Raleigh Nat. Mon.** (O), site of the "Citie of Ralegh" in what was Va., 1st Eng. attempt to colonize in Amer. Bet. 1584 & 1591, 7 separate Eng. expeditions visited Is. Here was born on Aug. 18, 1587, Virginia Dare, 1st white child of Eng. parents born in America. Ananias & Ellinor Dare were among colonists sent by Sir Walter in attempt to est. a permanent settlement. By 1591, the only traces left of the colony were a fort-like palisade of trees & "Croatoan" carved on one. The story of the colony & its probable fate is told in Pulitzer Prizewinning Paul Green's symphonic drama, "The Lost Colony," presented annually July 4th to Labor Day in a waterside outdoor theater, which has no curtain, but uses main & side stages on different levels & unique lighting arrangement to change scenes. Actors are Carolina Playmakers (Univ. of N.C.), Westminster Choir students & natives of Is. Ft. Raleigh, reprod. of supposed structures of 1587; log palisade, cabins, chapel & mus. Mon. (1896) comm. Lost Colony. Birthday of Virginia Dare is annually celebrated here.

Main Tour cont. on US17. **38. HERTFORD,** in the bend of Perquimans R. with arching trees & comfortable river front homes. Main St., **Perquimans County Cth.** (1731.Georg.Col.adds.1818.remod.1890.rest.1932), records date from 1685. **51.**

**EDENTON** (f.h.boat.), one of oldest towns in N.C. (sett.c.1658). Fisheries, cotton mills & N.C.'s largest peanut-processing plant are the main commercial interest. Along the sound shore are many old plantation estates. PTS. OF INT.: Broad & Church Sts., **St. Paul's Ch.** (Episc.org.1701), cemetery has graves of Rev. patriots as well as royal govs. 408 S. Broad St., **Cupola H.** (O.sm.fee.1758) has mus. & lib. At head of Green & E. King St., **Chowan County Cth.** (1767.George.Col.), on site of earlier Cth. (1719), contains very fine wood paneling. On Colonial Ave., facing Edenton Green, is **Bronze Teapot,** marking site of Edenton Tea Party, Oct. 25, 1774; 1st women's "tea party" of Rev. **Jos. Hewes Mon.** (1932.by Rogers & Poor) honoring signer of Decl. of Ind. **72. WINDSOR. 85. WILLIAMSTON** had a pre-Rev. cth. built on stilts over the Roanoke R.; after court convened, the ladders were drawn up until end of session. **109. WASHINGTON,** 1st of 422 U.S. cities & towns to be named for Geo. Washington, is on bank of Tar-Pamlico R. (R.'s name changes at bridge). Two leveling fires (1864) left few old Hs. PTS. OF INT.: 2nd & Market Sts., **Beaufort County Cth.** (c.1800.adds.). Market St., **Johnston H.** (c.1810). Bonner & Main Sts., **St. Peter's Ch.** (Episc.1868.Goth.Rev.) has square tower. Water & Bonner Sts., **Telfair H.** (c.1818). Area has profusion of clematis in spring; Tulip Festival in Ap.

SIDE TRIP: (E) c.9$^{m}$ on St.92 to J. with St.32. (N) here 9$^{m}$ to **Acre,** where dirt Rd. (E) leads c.6$^{m}$ to **Terra Ceia.** Here is Bulb Farm with fields of tulips blooming in Apr.

**144. NEW BERN** (sett. 1710)

Union Sta., Hancock & Queen Sts. for Atlantic Coast Line, Norfolk S. & Atlantic & N.C. RRs. Bus conns. Info.: C. of C., Old City Hall, Craven St. Ranger Dist. Hqs. of Croatan Nat. For. in P.O. Bldg. Ample accoms.

Town was 1st sett. by Swiss Baron de Graffenried & his followers. In 1711 settlement was almost demolished by Tuscarora Inds. After 2 yrs. of Ind. wars & severe privation, de Graffenried & many of his small band returned to Switzerland. The colony was started anew under Col. Thos. Pollock. New Bern, seat of Colonial Assembly & later of royal gov., in 1774 became capital of Province of N.C. The same yr., delegates were sent to Continental Congress & in Ap. 1775 royal rule ended in N.C. Thriving social center in the post-Rev. period, New Bern was also a center of sea-trade with New England cities. Being captured in 1862 by Gen. Burnside, town escaped devastation of Civil War. N.C.'s 1st pub. sch. for Negroes was est. here (1862) by New Eng. soldiers who volunteered to teach.

PTS. OF INT.: (1) Front & S. Front Sts., **Union Point Pk.** at J. of R.'s, site of Ind. village, made into pub. pk. 1932. (2) Front & Broad Sts., **Marker** on site of 1st printing office in N.C. Here Jas. Davis set up press, 1749. (3) E. Front & Change Sts., **Louisiana H.** (N.O.c.1776.frame clapboard). La. style "is found convenient on account of the great Summer Heats here," said Wm. Attmore in 1787. (4) 95 E. Front St., **Smallwood-Ward H.** (N.O.c.1816), on grounds is **Cypress Tree,** overseer of Ind. treaties & Rev. meetings. (5) SE. cor. E. Front & Johnson Sts., **Jarvis-Hand H.** (N.O.1803.Georg.Col.), fine recessed doorway; Fed. hospital during Civil War. (6) SW. cor. E. Front & Johnson Sts., **Slover-Guion H.** (N.O.c.1835.early Repub.); hqs. of Gen. Burnside; modernized brick kitchen & slave quarters in rear. (7) SE. cor. Johnson & Craven Sts., **Richardson H.** (1828) with widow's walk used to sight ships. (8) SW. cor. Johnson & Craven Sts., **Jerkins-Duffy H.** (1790.by Alonzo T. Jerkins), on site of birthpl. of Judge Wm. Gaston. (9) Middle & Pollock Sts., **Christ Ch.** (Episc.1873.org.1715) on site of 2 earlier Chs.; has silver communion service & other items given by George II. On grounds is cannon taken from Brit. ship "Lady Blessington" during Rev. (10) Middle St. near Johnson St., 1st Cath. Ch. in N.C., **St. Paul's Ch.** (1841.org.1820). (11) New St. near Middle St., **Pub. Lib.,** formerly **John W. Stanly H.** (O.wks.c.1790.remod.1936 when moved to this site); coll. of items from Tryon Palace. Opp. is (12) **First Presb. Ch.** (1822.org.1817.designed by Christopher Wren.adds.1893); used as hospital by Feds. (13) Hancock & Johnson Sts., **Masonic Temple** (O.1808.Class.Rev.remod.1938), theater is one of oldest in U.S. Behind temple is site of hist. duel (1802). (14) End of National Ave., **Nat. Cemetery** with graves of 3,500 Union soldiers. (15) 24 George St., W. wing of **Tryon Palace** (N.O.1770), regarded as one of most beautiful bldgs. in colonial America; was early capitol & home of royal Gov. Wm. Tryon & of 1st constitutional Gov. Rich. Caswell & scene of Rev. activity (see items in pub. lib.). Tour cont. on US17.

**165. MAYSVILLE,** entrance to Croatan Nat. For. (f.h.boat.swim.). **182. JACKSONVILLE,** on bay-like New R., near Holly Shelter Swamp.

**233. WILMINGTON** (sett. 1730)

Seaboard Air Line RR., Brunswick St.; Atlantic Coast Line RR., Union Sta., Redcross & Front Sts. National Airlines & bus conns. Fine harbor with free yacht basin. Good accoms. Tourist campground (free), near-by beach resorts. Mun. golf course, tennis, hunt., fish., boat. & swim. Info.: C. of C., 4th & Princess Sts. (guides avail. for city tours). Annual garden tours (early spring); 209 N. 2nd St., Carolina Motor Club. Annual Cape Fear Horse Show.

Wilmington, 30$^{m}$ from mouth of Cape Fear R., is main deep-water port of N.C. Port handles oil & agric. products, fertilizer, cotton & lumber for foreign & domestic shipping; town conducts brisk retail trade. In contrast is yr.-round vacation & resort atmosphere (town is gateway to many popular play areas), enhanced by hist. ruins, bldgs. & elaborate gardens. Town is noted for beautiful central plaza with formal gardens & walks. Wilmington has a hist. of more than 2 centuries. Captured by Cornwallis, it was Brit. hqs. for one winter & was also seat of Rev. activity. In Civil War was main port of trade & communication with foreign govs. until 1865. PTS. OF INT.: (1) Entire Water St. block bet. Market & Princess Sts., **U.S. Custom H.** (1916.Class.) with garden esplanade & wide view of R. (2) Market & 3rd Sts., **Cornwallis H.** (1770's), Brit. hqs., 1781, basement used as dungeon. Opp. is (3) **St. James Ch.** (Episc.1839.Goth.Rev.adds.); in rear chancel hang 400-600-yr.-old painting of Christ captured from pirate ship, 1748. (4) 3rd & Princess Sts., **New Hanover County Cth.** (1892.add.1925.Georg.). **Mus.** (O) holds coll. of hist. int. (5) 4th & Market Sts., **Hebrew Temple** (1875), 1st in N.C. (6) Market St. near 4th St., **Wilmington Light Infantry Armory** (1852). Org. 1858, company was sponsored by Jeff. Davis. (7) Market & 5th Sts., **Bellamy H.** (N.O.1859.Gr.Rev.). U.S. Supreme Court Justice Sol. P. Chase spoke from here, 1865. (8) Market near 7th St., **Hugh McRae H.** (N.O.c.1850.Goth.Rev.remod.1902), was Fed. hospital. (9) 5th & Ann Sts., **St. Mary's Cathedral** (Cath.1913.Sp.Ren.by Rafael Guastavino) with tile mosaics of the saints & stained-glass windows by Franz Meyer, is said to be one of most beautiful Cath. chs. in S. (10) Market & 20th Sts., **Nat. Cemetery** with graves of c.2,500 Union soldiers & others of hist. int. (11) S. end of 3rd St., **Greenfield Lake Pk.,** with 5$^{m}$ drive around L. (recr.facils.bath.boat.beach). Here cypress, magnolias, camellias, azaleas, roses & other native plants grow in abundance.

SIDE TRIPS: (A) On US74-76 8$^{m}$ (E) to **Bradley Cr.** with view of Wrightsville Beach. 9$^{m}$ **Airlie** (O.some days in Ap.), landscaped gardens with almost every known variety of azalea as well as other rare plants. Cont. over Wrightsville Sound by bridge & causeway 10$^{m}$ to **Harbor I.** (pub.dance pavilion), summer hqs. of Carolina Yacht Club. 11$^{m}$ **Wrightsville Beach** (surf, sound & channel bath.yacht.boat.deep-sea f.dancing.amusements). Offshore are wrecks of blockade-runners scuttled during Civil War.

(B) On US421 15$^{m}$ (S) to **Carolina Beach** (Ap.-Nov.), mainland ocean resort with every type of accom. & seaside recr., called "N.C.'s Coney Island." 17$^{m}$ **Kures Beach** with 500′ f. pier. 20$^{m}$ **Ft. Fisher Beach** on site of Confed. stronghold. Only Mon. to soldiers of both sides & ruins of breastworks of old ft. remain. Tour cont. on US17.

**238.** J. with Old River Rd.

SIDE TRIP: (S) 14$^{m}$ to **Orton Plantation** (O.appl.1725.by "King" Roger Moore) with ruins of old Col. Ch. & town sites of Brunswick & Russellborough; scene of 1st resistance to Brit. Stamp Acts, Nov. 16, 1765. Beautiful gardens of azaleas & camellias still flourish. Old River Rd. cont. 24$^{m}$ to **Southport,** across harbor from Ft. Caswell; is on estuary of Cape Fear R. (bath.f.). Town was founded 1792 & called Smithville.

**269. SHALOTTE** (f.boat.guides). US17 crosses **N.C.-S.C. LINE** at **284.**

## US 1—NORTH CAROLINA

**N.C.-VA. LINE** (15$^{m}$ from South Hill, Va.) **(S) to N.C.-S.C. LINE** (10$^{m}$ from N. Cheraw, S.C.). **175. US1**

Via: Henderson, Raleigh, (Fayetteville), Southern Pines, Aberdeen & Rockingham.

Hy. traverses undulating plantation reg. of tobacco, cotton & corn, N.C.'s "black belt." **12. MANSON.** From here to Clarksville, Va., the Roanoke RR. (1850) was pried up by Gen. Longstreet's men & laid bet. Greensboro & Danville, Va., for moving Confed. supplies from western N.C. to Richmond, Va. **22. HENDERSON,** bright leaf tobacco town, is also industrial center. A grassed pky. with shrubs & dwarf magnolias marks entrance to **49. WAKE FOREST,** seat of **Wake Forest**

**College** (Bapt.1834.coed.). The old tree-shaded campus will be abandoned for a new site in Winston-Salem (see US52) where the college operates Bowman Gray School of Medicine.

**65. RALEIGH**

RR., bus & air conns. Accoms.: All types. Info.: C. of C., 17 W. Davie St.; St. Hy. Dept., 112 E. Morgan St. St. Fair (3rd wk. in Oct.) Southern Conference Basketball Tourn. (3 days in early Mar.).

Raleigh, capital city of N.C., is one of few planned capitals in country; 6-a. Capitol Square, shaded by great oaks & strewn with mons., has broad aves. which radiate from its 4 sides, & is surrounded by St. dept. bldgs. Two pks. survive of orig. 4 planned for new capital in 1792. When orig. Stateh. was completed (1794), so raw was this capital carved out of a wilderness that it was accused of being "a city of streets without houses." Raleigh's atmosphere, usually that of a settled community of tradition & charm, changes perceptibly during biennial sessions of the Legislature, though town is always aware of its numerous St. & Fed. workers. Raleigh is a publication & educational center. PTS. OF INT.: (1) On Capitol Sq., **Capitol** (1833-40.Doric.by David Patton & Ithiel Town) said to have no nails, iron pillars or rafters. Many mons. on grounds. (2) Salisbury & Edenton Sts., 1st fl. of Education Bldg., **Hall of Hist.** (St.Hist.Mus.); colls. of hist. material. (3) Halifax St., (N) of Capitol Sq., **St. Mus.,** colls. of nat. hist. (4) Edenton & Wilmington Sts., **Christ Ch.** (c.1845) replaced orig. wooden bldg. (1829). Adj. Rectory (1785) was St. Bank; oldest bank bldg. in N.C. (5) 210 N. Blount St., **Gov.'s Mansion** (O.appl.c.1890 by Gustavus Adolphus Bauer) in Queen Anne style, official residence during Gov.'s term of office; contains hist. relics. (6) Hillsboro St. (in W. Raleigh), State College of the Univ. of N.C. (1889), on 490-a. land-grant by R. Stanhope Pullen. On campus, in Pullen Pk., is **Andrew Johnson H.** (O.appl.), birthpl. of 17th Pres. moved here from orig. site near Capitol. (7) **Meredith College** (Bapt.org.1891) as N.C. Female Univ. on 170-a. campus 3$^{m}$ (W) of Capitol. (8) **Peace (Jr.) College** (Presb. women.org.1857); Civil War delayed opening until 1872. (9) **St. Augustine's College** (Negro.coed.Episc.1867). (10) 728 W. Hargett St., **Joel Lane H.** (O.c.1770.Dutch Col.), oldest H. in town.

**73. CARY,** farm community, is birthpl. of Walter Hines Page, Ambassador to Eng. (1913-18). Hy. crosses Haw R. at c.**100.** where hills seem more like small mts. & streams furnish power for sm. mills that handle locally-grown wheat. Deep R. at c.**104;** banks are c.100' high. **110. SANFORD,** is in pine belt on edge of Sandhill sec. In outlying country are descendants of Staffordshire potters, craftsmen for 200 yrs.; they use old-time kick-wheel & mule power for their grinding mills. In Sanford is J. with St.87.

SIDE TRIP: 25$^{m}$ to **Ft. Bragg,** one of largest military reservations in U.S. This site was hqs. of Gen. Francis Marion ("The Swamp Fox") & later of Lord Cornwallis. The post has a complete mun. system incl. schs., recr. facils. & chs. On old Yadkin Rd., **Long Street Ch.** (Presb.org.1758); near-by is site of Battle of Monroe's Crossing (Mar.1865).

38$^{m}$ **Fayetteville**

RR. & Bus conns.; mun. airport in progress.

Fayetteville, sett. 1739 on W. bank of Cape Fear R. by Scotsmen, was St. capital (1789-93) & here ratified Fed. Constitution (1789). City is trade center of tobacco & cotton area; port on Cape Fear R. is farthest inland in N.C. PTS. OF INT.: (1) Market Sq., **Market H.** (O.wks.1838), said to have orig. been a slave market, was Town Hall, now houses pub. lib. & Civil War relics. Curfew is still rung nightly at 9:00. (2) 242 Green St., **St. John's Ch.** (Episc.c.1832.Goth.Rev.) on site & with materials of orig. ch. (1817) burned 1831. (3) Murchison Rd. (NW), **Fayetteville St. Teacher's College** (1877.Negro), oldest normal sch. in N.C. (4) Bow & Ann Sts., **First Presb. Ch.** (org.1800.Class.Col.); fine details & ch. treasures. (5) Cool Spring St. & Cool Spring Lane, **MacKeithan H.** (N.O.1778) was ante bellum tavern. (6) Hay St. & Maple Ave., **Site of Confed. Arsenal** destroyed by Confeds. before Sherman's occupation, 1865.

**122. CAMERON,** one of largest dewberry markets in world. Reg. has a plentiful stock of fox, squirrel, rabbit, quail & dove. **136. SOUTHERN PINES,** Sandhills winter resort. During season its pop. doubles. Weekly golf tourns. (Dec.15-Ap.1); Women's Mid-South Championship (54 holes 3rd wk.in Mar.). Sandhills Steeplechase & Racing Assoc. Meet (3rd Sat.in Ap.). Gymkhanas (alt.Fri.), horse shows (Jan.& Ap.), hunter trials (Mar.). Spring tennis tourn. (2nd wk.in Mar.), Dogwood tennis tourn. (4th wk.in Ap.). In town is J. with St.2.

SIDE TRIP: $2^m$ to **Pinehurst,** off US1 at Aberdeen, winter resort that resembles a country village. Longleaf pines along winding Rds. & Drs. run past great estates, hotels, inns & smaller residences & cottages. There is harmony in the modified Georg. Col. style in which most of them are built; architectural style of colony was planned by Aymar Embury, II. The Pks., Drs., open spaces & all landscaping were planned by Frederick Law Olmsted, landscape architect of N.Y. Pinehurst is not an inc. town, but a private business enterprise operating under N.C. corporate laws. The owners exercise police powers & village regulations prohibit locomotives from operating at night, dogs from howling, & roosters from crowing. Envisioned first by the Tufts, founders, as a health resort, it has developed instead into a recr. & sports center. Golf Tourns.: Mid-South Prof. (mid-Nov.); Seniors, (2nd wk.in Mar.); United N. & S. Open Championship (3rd wk.in Mar.). N. & S. Championship for Women (last wk.Mar.& 1st wk.in Ap.); N. & S. Invitation Amateur Championship (2nd wk.in Ap.). Tennis: United N. & S. Tourn. (2nd & 3rd wks.in Ap.). Sandhills Steeplechase & Racing Assoc. Meet (3rd Sat.in Mar.). Horse Show: Pinehurst Jockey Club (Mar. 28-29); Field trials (late Nov.); Pointers Club of Amer. Open events (2nd wk.in Dec.); Pinehurst Jockey Club (2nd wk.in Jan.).

**140. ABERDEEN,** with near-by cemetery of Old Bethesda Ch. (Presb.) where is **Tomb of Walter Hines Page,** appointed Ambassador to Eng. by Pres. Wilson. **151. HOFFMAN,** center for Sandhills Utilization Project to demonstrate restoration of economic value to cut-over forests & submarginal farm lands by development into recr., forestry, & wildlife conservation areas. Within area are: Ind. Camp Recr. Pk. (cabins.trlr.camp.recr.pavilion) on an 80-a. lake (boat.bath.), hatchery, nursery & game farm. **166. ROCKINGHAM** (sett.1785) in a peach & cotton sec., is at J. with US74 (see). (S) of Rockingham, US1 parallels Pee Dee R. (f.) & crosses **N.C.-S.C. LINE** at **175.**

## US 29—NORTH CAROLINA

**N.C.-VA. LINE** ($5^m$ from Danville, Va.) **(S) to N.C.-S.C. LINE** ($16^m$ from Gaffney, S.C.). **176. US29**

Via: Reidsville, Greensboro, Salisbury, Charlotte & Gastonia.

This route runs directly through the Piedmont section. **19. REIDSVILLE** is an industrial town; one of N.C.'s 3 tobacco-mfg. centers, other factories produce cotton, silk, & rayon textiles; leather preservatives; concrete forms & foodstuffs. The **Amer. Tobacco Co. Plant** (O.Mon.-Thurs.9-4:15;Fri.9-12) covers an entire city block. The air-conditioned brick bldgs. have machinery capable of producing 100 million cigarettes a day. Because of the quantities of Turkish tobacco & cigarette paper imported, the town is a port of entry. **43. GREENSBORO** (RR.,bus & air conns. Info.: C. of C. in Giant Bureau Bldg.; Carolina Motor Club, King Cotton Hotel Bldg.). Garden Club Show (May 15), golf tourn. (spring & fall for women, championship for men in fall); Kennel Club Show (fall); Central N.C. Fair (fall). City is an educational center. Diversified industries produce structural steel, chemicals & terra cotta. The town was named in honor of Gen. Nathanael Greene, leader of Col. forces at Battle of Guilford Cth. Home offices of several large insurance co.'s are maintained here. PTS. OF INT.: (1) Market & Elm Sts., **Jefferson Standard Life Ins. Co. Bldg.** (O.1923.mod.Goth.), top fl. restaurant gives panoramic view of surrounding country. (2) 426 W. Market St., **Masonic Temple** (O.wks.1928), stands on site of O. Henry's birthpl. (3) Bet. S. Cedar St. & College Pl., **Greensboro College** (Meth.women.1846). (4) Tate & Spring Garden Sts., **Woman's College of Univ. of N.C.** (O.1892.joined Univ. of N.C.1931), one of largest women's colleges in U.S. (5) Independence Rd., **Idlewood** (rose garden O.May-June,day & night); 8,000 varieties of plants, incl. 1,500 varieties of roses. (6) Summit Ave. & Church St., **Community Center** (1938) housing pub. lib., art center & hist. mus. (7) **Agric. & Technical College of N.C.** (Negro.coed.1891). (8) E. Washington near Bennett St, **Bennett College** (Negro.women.est.1874 by Meth.Episc.Ch.). Greensboro is at J. with US220.

SIDE TRIP: Take latter (N) $11^m$ to **Guilford Cth. Nat. Military Pk.** (mus.O.), scene of Battle of Guilford Cth., Mar. 15, 1781. Here bet. Hunting & Horse Pen Crs., Cornwallis' troops defeated Amers. under Gen. Nathanael Greene, but at such crippling cost that encounter paved way to Brit. surrender.

Tour cont. on US29. At **48.** are offices of **Pilot Life Ins. Co.** (O.wks.), whose bldgs. stand on knoll in landscaped pk.; windows, made of N.C. quartz, permit maximum ultraviolet radiation. Across hy. is ent. to **Sedgefield,** resort where Sedgefield Inn, rambling Tudor-style bldg., stands in 3,600-a. wooded pk. **Valley Brook Golf Course**

(18 holes.sm.fee) is scene of open, amateur, & professional matches. The Sedgefield Hunt is widely known. **53. HIGH PT. CITY PK.** has 40-a. lake covering sites of pre-Rev. tannery, a Quaker hat factory & a woolen mill. The dam & spillway are illuminated at night. Pool (O.summer). Outdoor amphitheater seats 2,500. Near reservoir is old **Quaker Meetingh.** (c.1819), now mus., built of hand-made brick & hand-hewn timber. **60. HIGH POINT,** Piedmont industrial center, known mainly as production center of furniture & hosiery industries. Guilford Cty. was sett. by Quakers (1750) but town was not laid out until 1853 when St.-built N.C. & Midland RR. came through. Town was orig. laid out in exact $2^m$ sq. With completion (1854) of $130^m$ plank Rd. bet. Fayetteville & Salem, village became trading center. Orig. mileposts were placed along Rd. with figures not painted, but carved so that night travelers could feel their mileage. PTS. OF INT.: 415 N. Main St., **Giant Bureau** (O.wks.1925) houses C. of C. with front designed to simulate a bureau with drawers, knobs & mirror. 305 W. High St., **Tomlinson of High Pt. Plant** (O.appl.), one of largest furniture factories in S.; its **Williamsburg Gallery** (O.appl.) contains reprod. of early Amer. craftsmanship in Williamsburg, Va. Montlieu Ave. & College Dr., **High Pt. College** (coed.Meth.Prot.1920). S. Main St., **Blair Pk.** (clubh.tennis.mun. golf course.playgrounds).

SIDE TRIP: L. from High Pt. on Kivett Dr. c.$5^m$ to **Hayworth Springs Pic. Ground.** A footpath leads $0.5^m$ over hill to **Old Gold Mines,** where ruins, pumps & dam are obscured by dense stands of oak & pine. Three mines were opened here after discovery of gold in N.C. (1779), but the vein disappeared before it yielded any profit.

**67. THOMASVILLE,** advertises itself as producing more chairs than any other city, by displaying "largest chair in the world." The 1st chair factories began utilizing plentiful oak & hickory in 1870's. Bet. **79. LEXINGTON & 96. SALISBURY,** the route unites with US52 (see). At **98.** are **Rowan Cty. Fair Grounds,** & J. with Rd. leading (L) $1^m$ to **Salisbury Mun. Airport,** with 3,000′ runways & one of largest hangars in St. **105. CHINA GROVE.** Route to Concord via US29 is $2^m$ shorter, but branching (R) on US29A, at $112^m$ there is **Kannapolis,** largest unincorporated town in N.C., owned by Cannon Mills (N.O.), whose plants & warehs. line both sides of hy. for more than a mile. Org. 1877, towels were not produced until 1898. They are largest producers of household textiles in world; heaviest production is concentrated here, but other plants are scattered throughout South. **117. CONCORD,** so named because 2 factions at war over location for cty. seat finally agreed on this site. **First Presb. Ch.** is a replica of one in New Haven, Conn. Old cemetery in rear has been made into mem. garden; beyond back wall is a slave cemetery. **121. STONEWALL JACKSON TRAINING SCH.** (for boys), est. 1907 by St. & financed with pension funds declined by Mrs. Jackson. **138. CHARLOTTE** (see US74). **146.** entrance to **CHARLOTTE MUN. AIRPORT. 159. GASTONIA,** textile mfg. town in a rich agric. reg. Scene of sensational strike at Loray Mills, Ap. 1929. Chief of police was killed & 7 organizers were sentenced from 5 to 25 yrs., convicted of conspiring to murder him. Ella May Wiggins, strike sympathizer, was killed when a group of unarmed workers were fired upon. The Gastonia strike has been inspiration for several novels. There are several mill communities within city limits; its textile plants manufacture c.80% of fine combed yarn made in America. (Annual Cotton Festival, June). The **Cocker Machine & Foundry Co.** manufactures world's largest warp & dyeing machinery; **Firestone Textiles** has tire fabric plant. At c.**165. LINCOLN ACADEMY** (private.coed.Negro), conference center for Christian Assoc. of Negro Colleges. **167. KINGS MOUNTAIN,** textile mill town at foot of mt., bears name & is near scene of important Rev. battle; site is just over S.C. Line. US29 crosses the **N.C.-S.C. LINE** at **176.**

## US 52—NORTH CAROLINA

**N.C.-VA. LINE** (17$^m$ from Hillsville, Va.) **(S) to N.C.-S.C. LINE** (10$^m$ from Cheraw, S.C.). **153. US52**

Via: Winston-Salem, Salisbury, Albemarle & Wadesboro.

Known as the Fancy Gap Scenic Hy., this tour runs through the Blue Ridge Mts. & W. border of Piedmont Plateau.

**5. MT. AIRY.** Most of town's structures are beautiful local gray granite. Mt. Airy Granite Quarry (O) is one of world's largest open-face granite quarries. A single finished stone often takes up a whole flatcar. (SW) c.5$^m$ from Mt. Airy on US601 to White Plains, where are homes of orig. Siamese Twins (born Ap.15,1811 in Bangesau, Siam). **17. PILOT MT.** (motorists.hikers.sm.fee;camp.pic.). Curious rock formation rises 2,413′ from very low country to (E) & (S). **29.**, J. with St.66.

SIDE TRIP: (N) 12$^m$ on St.66 to **Gap,** entrance to **Hanging Rock State Pk.** (guides.f.swim. pic.camp.). This 3,865-a. recr. area is in heart of Sauratown Mts. Foot & bridle trls., motor Rds., 15-a. lake. Area lies wholly within 40,000-a. St. Game Preserve.

## 42. WINSTON-SALEM

RRs., bus & air conns. Accoms. & recr. of all types. 4 golf courses, 9 swim. pools, 26 pub. pks. & playgrounds. Info.: C. of C. Annual events: Moravian Easter Sunrise Service held annually for over 150 yrs. Easter Mon. German, Twin City Club; May Day pageant, Moravian Love Feast & Candle Service, Christmas Eve; Moravian Watch Night, New Year's Eve.

Winston-Salem is leading industrial city of N.C. & ranks 3rd in S. in value of manufactured products. It is one of world's largest bright leaf tobacco markets, the largest manufacturer of knit underwear in world & home of world's largest circular-knit hosiery mill. Furniture mfg. Winston-Salem sett. 1752 by Penn. Moravians on tract of land at 3 forks of Yadkin R. which they named "Wachovia" after Austrian estates of Count von Zinzendorf, an early patron. Soon 2 settlements were established: Bethabara (1754) & Bethania (1759). In 1766 a new town, Salem (Hebrew: "Shalom," peace), was laid out in center of the tract which by 1850 was prosperous center of religion, learning, agric. & industry. When Forsyth Cty. was formed (1849), the cty. seat was located 1$^m$ N. of Salem & named Winston which rapidly developed into industrial center & market. In 1913, by popular vote, the 2 were consolidated as Winston-Salem, the "Twin City." PTS. OF INT.: (1) S. Main & Academy Sts., **Moravian Brothers' H.** (1769.brick add.1786), now Moravian Ch. Home, is oldest bldg. in Salem. (2) 800 S. Main St., **Salem Tavern** (N.O.1784). (3) 529 S. Church St., **Home Moravian Ch.** (1800.inter.rebuilt), where famous Easter Sunrise Service is held. (4) Church St. opp. Salem Sq., **Salem College** (1772.women), run by Moravian Ch., is nonsect. (5) Main & Academy Sts., **Wachovia Hist. Soc. Mus.** (O.appl.1794.add.1937), exhibits of various early artifacts. (6) N. Main & 4th Sts., **R. J. Reynolds Office Bldg.** (1929) with Observ. Tower (O.wks.), N.C.'s tallest. Guided tours through **R. J. Reynolds Tobacco Co. Plant.** (7) **Tobacco Warehs.** (O. Sept.-Feb.) where baffling chant of auctioneer is heard. (8) N. Main & 6th Sts., **P. H. Hanes Knitting Co.** (O.appl.). (9) 1539 Waughtown St., **Nissen Wagon Plant** (O.wks.guides), successor of plant est. 1787 by Geo. E. Nissen. (10) **Bowman Gray Sch. of Med.** of Wake Forest College (see US1).

**63. LEXINGTON,** mfg. town, has cth. rebuilt on walls of an older structure, its Corinthian columns flanked by slave auction blocks. **80. SALISBURY,** one of oldest towns in Piedmont (1753.sett.by Moravians), is an industrial center with extensive granite-quarry industry. Near center of town the **Nat. Cemetery** (est.1863) contains c.12,000 unmarked graves; Union soldiers who died in "prison pen" maintained here, as well as veterans of Sp.-Amer. & World Wars. **Livingstone College** (coed.Negro) has 8 brick bldgs. on a 315-a. campus. **Catawba College** (Reformed Ch.1851) on edge of town. Frances Fisher Tiernan of Salisbury, who wrote more than 50 novels under pen name of Christian Reid, is said to have given Western N.C. its designation of "Land of the Sky." **94. GOLD HILL** with c.10 copper & gold lodes within 3.5 sq. miles. Pop. (1949) less than 200 but after gold was discovered (1842), pop. was 2,000. **98. MISENHEIMER,** seat of heavily endowed **Pfeiffer Jr. College** (1907.Meth.coed.), est. 1899 as missionary sch. in Lenoir, 2 yrs. college added 1928 & gradually lower grades were dropped; work in farm, dairy, gardens & orchards done on co-op. basis. **110. ALBEMARLE,** on crest of Uharie Mts. **Wiscasset Mills** (O.appl.), a Cannon unit. **111.** J. with St.740.

SIDE TRIP: (NE) 7$^m$ on St.740 to **Badin,** & one of world's largest aluminum plants, **Carolina Aluminum Co.** (O) which gets power from spillway dam (210′ high, 3,700′ long with max. 187′-water head, 20′ higher than Niagara) which forms **Badin L.** (water sports) at 10$^m$. J. with dirt Rd. (S) to **Morrow Mt. St. Pk.** (recr.facils.lodge.restaurant.pic.camp.trls. cabins), c.1,225-a. tract on Pee Dee R.

**140. WADESBORO,** seat of Anson Cty. formed in 1748 & named for Lord George Anson, English admiral who was sent to guard Carolina coast from pirates & Sp. raiders (1723-35). **153. N.C.-SC. LINE.**

# US 23—NORTH CAROLINA

**N.C.-TENN. LINE** (at Spivey Cr. Gap, N.C.) **(S) to N.C. LINE** (1m from Dillard, Ga.). **138. US23**

Via: Stocksville, Asheville, Waynesville & Franklin.

US23 winds bet. majestic peaks & deep valleys, through a sparsely settled for. reg. There are cliffs of bronze-streaked sandstone on one side & a rocky creekbed on the other, half-smothered in rhododendron & laurel. US19 & US23 are joined to Junaluska. **0. SPIVEY CR. GAP.** J. with Appalachian Trl.

SIDE TRIP: (R) on this trl. (4';cleared) to **Big Bald Mt.,** 6m, with views of **Little Bald** & **Flat Top** (N), **Ogle Meadows** (S) & **Mt. Mitchell** & **Celo** (E). Hy. follows curve of R. (bass.trout.perch) where mt. farms are connected with hy. by swinging foot-bridges.

At c.**15. HIGGINS; Markle Handicraft School** (O). At c.**38.,** J. with St.213.

SIDE TRIP: 2m to **Mars Hill College** (coed.Bapt.). On campus, **Mon. to Old Joe,** Negro slave who was jailed as security when founding fathers were short $1,000 in erecting 1st bldg. (1856).

**41. STOCKSVILLE.** J. with side Rd.

SIDE TRIP: (L) 6m to **Barnardsville;** (R) on marked Craggy Gardens Hy., 4m to **Dillingham,** at Ent. to Mt. Mitchell Division of **Pisgah Nat. For.** (pic.camp.springs.shelters). For. Serv. Rd. leading (L) 2m to **Big Ivy Campground** (water.fuel.fireplaces.facils.swim.pool). At 11m on Craggy Gardens Hy. is **Bear Pen Parking Ground:** (L) on easy trl. to **Craggy Flats,** to natural **Craggy Gardens** (bloom June), where is largest known stand of purple rhododendron, in places more than 1m wide, & extending 10m along 5,000' high crest of Great Craggy Mts. There are marked trls. to **Craggy Pinnacle** & **Craggy Dome.**

**43. WEAVERVILLE,** once home of Wm. Sydney Porter (O. Henry). **51. ASHEVILLE** (see). (SW) of Asheville, mountainous route gives access to Pisgah & Nantahala Nat. Fors. & Great Smoky Mts. Nat. Pk. (see). **54.** J. with St.191 (Brevard Rd.).

SIDE TRIP: (L) 6m to **Bent Cr.,** where is the **Appalachian Experiment Sta.,** one of 1st experimental fors. est. by U.S. Forest Serv. (R) on sand-clay Bent Cr. Rd. is ent. to Pisgah Division of Pisgah Nat. For. 3m **Bent Cr. Campground** (O.water.fuel.fireplaces.facils.swim. pool). From this pt., Rd. usually open in summer. 7m **Bent Cr. Gap,** J. with trl. leading to summit of Pisgah Mt. 13m **N. Mills R. Campground** (accoms.trlrs.tents.water.fuel.facils. swim.pool). 6m **Asheville Sch.** (prep.boys).

**58. AMER. ENKA CORP. PLANT** (O.appl.), one of largest factories in S., a subsidiary of Enka Corp. in Arnhem, Netherlands, manufactures rayon thread from spruce pulp. **61.** J. with St.112.

SIDE TRIP: At 4m on St.112, view of **Pisgah & the Rat,** twin peaks that from a distance resemble a rat with tail extended & head lowered bet. its front paws. 8m **Stony Fork,** colony of summer cabins. 9m **Ent. to Pisgah Nat. For. & Stony Fork Campground** (water. fuel.facils.). **Buck Spring Lodge** (closed), built by Geo. W. Vanderbilt on what was then his hunting preserve, is at J. with dirt Rd. leading (R) 2m to **Pisgah Parking Lot** (refresh. sold during summer). A 0.5m foot trl. leads to 1m stone stepped trl. to **Summit of Big Pisgah** from which N.C., S.C., & in clear weather, Ga., Tenn. & Va. are seen. 17m **Pisgah For. Inn** (accoms.) with views of Pink Beds & Looking Glass Rock from its verandahs. 19m **Frying Pan Gap** (water.facils.fuel), is highest campground (5,040') in For. 21m **Wagon Rd. Gap** is at J. with US276 (see US64).

**63. LUTHERS,** with Omar Khayyam Art Pottery (O), noted for unusual designs.

**70. CANTON,** home of **Champion Paper & Fibre Co.** (O.appl.), one of world's largest pulp, paper & extract mills. A continuous program of reforestation is maintained to insure against shortage of raw material. **78. LAKE JUNALUSKA** (Meth. Summer Assembly Grounds). Resort area with c.20m graded Rds., more than 200 summer homes, 20 public bldgs., incl. auditorium seating 4,000. Accoms. of various kinds. Annual water pageants & motorboat races & carnivals. Junaluska (Tsunu' lahosji), Ind. chief who saved Andrew Jackson's life at Battle of Horseshoe Bend (Mar.29,1814) bet. Creeks & Fed. troops. **83. WAYNESVILLE,** yr.-round vacation & health resort with varied accoms. surrounded by 5,000'-6,000' peaks of Balsam & Smoky Mts. **89. MORRISON ST. FISH HATCHERY** (O), for trout; sm. zoo has bear, deer, gophers & monkeys. Bet. near-by Balsam Gap, highest pt. of any standard-gage RR. (E) of Miss. R., where "pusher" locomotives are often used, & the Ga. Line, US23 runs through the Nantahala Nat. For. **124. FRANKLIN,** lying on a high ridge overlooking valley of the Little Tenn. R., which is surrounded by peaks of the Cowee, Fishhawk & Nantahala Mts. This was site of Cherokee settlement, Nikwasi, known as Sacred Town. Inds. & whites have mined sec. for gold & precious stones. Great holes in which grow huge trees are believed to be mines left by Sp. expedition (1560) which followed De Soto's trl. Experts believe that mineral resources of reg. have hardly been touched. Both precious & semi-precious stones occur, incl. garnet, sapphire, beryl, aquamarine & fine rubies. Offices of Ranger, Wayah District, Nantahala Nat. For., are in Fed. Bldg. (W) c.7$^{m}$ on For. Serv. Rd. is **Arrowood Glade Recr. Area** (bath.pic.) with rearing pools of trout used for restocking for. streams. **138.** US23 crosses **N.C.-GA. LINE.**

# ASHEVILLE

## ASHEVILLE

Southern RR. System; excellent air & bus conns. Accoms., recr. & sports facils. of all types; golf courses (O.yr.-round). Info.: C. of C., Booth on Pack Sq. or in City Hall. Annual events: Land of the Sky Open Golf Tourn. (Mar.or Ap.); Men's Invitation Golf Tourn. (2nd & 3rd wks.in Aug.); Women's Spring Golf Tourn. (3rd wk.in Ap.); Easter Sunrise Service; Rhododendron Festival (2nd or 3rd wk.in June); Negro Fair (Sept.); Mt. Folk & Dance Festival (Aug.); Kennel Club Show (Oct.); Big Game Hunts (Nov. & Dec.in Pisgah For.).

One of the South's cosmopolitan cities, it lies on a plateau ringed by ranges of the Blue Ridge, & is the economic & cultural center for 18 mt. counties. It is both tourist & health resort, as well as industrial center. Near the E. entrance to Great Smoky Mts. Nat. Pk. & close to Nat. For. lands, it gives access to recr. areas of more than million as. The site of Asheville was once Cherokee Ind. hunting ground. Traders were in the reg. as early as 1673, & there was a flourishing barter trade by 1700, but no settlers came across the Blue Ridge until after the Rev. Buncombe Cty. was formed in 1792, & named for a Col. Edw. Buncombe. The definition of "buncombe" (spelled also bunkum & bunk), as meaning anything spoken, written or done for mere show, derives from a speech made by Felix Walker in the 16th Congress. When the gentleman made a pointless long-winded speech & was asked by one of his colleagues what he meant, Walker replied, "I was just talking for Buncombe." With the opening of the Buncombe Turnpike in 1824, the reg. became more accessible to S.C., Ga. & other Southern states. Tourists & health seekers came in great numbers. With completion of 1st RR., more visitors came, & industrial plants increased. Textile mills were est. & other factories for mfg. wood & mica products, foodstuffs & other commodities. The coming of Geo. Vanderbilt, N.Y. capitalist, in 1889, & of E. W. Grove, St. Louis manufacturer, in 1900, greatly accelerated the city's growth & development. The spread of Fla. real estate boom to Asheville in the 1920's nearly wrecked the city's economy when it collapsed.

PTS. OF INT.: (1) Pack Sq., **Civic Center,** landscaped plaza dominated by Vance Mon. & cty. & city bldgs. (2) E. of Pack Sq., **City Hall** (1927.by D.Ellington) contains Sondley Reference Lib. (O.wks.), with fine coll. of early books, incl. vol. of St. Jerome's "Epistles" published in Parma, Italy. (3) Lodge St., **Biltmore** (O.wks. fee), Geo. Vanderbilt estate, with c.50 terraced as., wildlife reservation, model farms & for. lands. Spring gardens with fine coll. of Southern trees. Guides avail. for **Biltmore H.** (1895.Fr.Ren.by Rich.Morris Hunt), one of finest private Hs. in U.S. (4) Birch St., Riverside Cemetery with **Graves of O. Henry & Thos. Wolfe.** (5) On grounds of Grove Pk. Inn, **Biltmore Industries Plants** (O), producers of handloomed Biltmore homespun. (6) Valley St. & Biltmore Ave., **Tobacco Market** (O. Dec.15-Jan.15). (7) Home of Burnham S. Colburn, Greystone Ct., Biltmore Forest, **Colburn Mus.** (O.to mineralogists on appl.), one of most complete colls. of S. Appalachian minerals & Cherokee Ind. relics. (8) End of Macon Ave., **Sunset Mt.** (sm. toll), fine view of Asheville & surrounding mts.

## TRIPS OUT OF ASHEVILLE

### I. (W) on US19 to N.C.-GA. LINE. 120.

For sec. from Asheville to **L. JUNALUSKA** at **27.**, see US23. **35. MAGGIE,** near dude ranch. **49. CHEROKEE** (good accoms.), adj. Qualla Boundary (O), which comprises 50,000 as. in Swain & Jackson Counties & isolated tracts of 13,000 as.

in Graham & Cherokee Counties. Here lived the East. Band of Cherokee Inds., descendants of group who eluded Gen. Winfield Scott's soldiers in 1838 removal of Inds. to Okla.; they hid in the Smokies while defying capture. Scott agreed to let the fugitives remain if they would surrender Tsali & his kinsmen, who had slain a soldier. Tsali & all but his youngest son were shot when they surrendered, but remnant of the tribe remained. This is largest organized Ind. reserv. (E) of Wis. (guides avail.for reserv.tour). The women still carry their children slung on their backs. The Cherokee Ind. Fair (1st wk.in Oct.sm.fee) features archery, blowgun contests, primitive games, dances & Cherokee Ind. ball, similar to lacrosse. The Green-Corn Dance, ancient ceremonial celebrating coming of the harvest, is Ind. Thanksgiving. J. with St.107.

SIDE TRIP: 4m **Ravensford,** once thriving lumber village. Ranger Sta. hqs. for the Pk. (R) 3m on dirt Rd. to **Big Cove,** Ind. settlement that has more Ind. atmosphere & tribal solidarity than any other reserv. town. Here are preserved ancient folklore, songs, & legends; they occasionally dance the Dance of Friendship & the Beaver Dance, as well as Dance of Thanksgiving.

7m on St.107, **Smokemont.** Rd. leading (R) to campground & trlr. pk. maintained by Pk. Serv. Bears searching for food frequently awaken campers. (2 country stores & last gas serv. this side of Tenn.Line.). 17m **Newfound Gap** has turnouts which afford views from 5,048′ alt. Rd. has climbed 3,000′ in less than 20m.

The Skyline Dr., running from the Gap to Clingman's Dome, goes into Tenn. & back into N.C. It is c.1m high with easy grades & rounded curves & is regarded as masterpiece of engineering. From parking area at 8m, where Forney Ridge joins Clingman's Dome, a chain of mts. is visible in 3 directions with the final steep rise of Clingman's tree-covered peak (N). Here is 3m paved trl. to summit of **Clingman's Dome** (6,642′), loftiest pt. in the Smokies in Tenn. Observ. tower.

Trip cont. on US19 to **58. BRYSON CITY,** in bowl-like depression formed by the Tuckasegee R., at foot of Rich Mt.; once occupied by Cherokee. On lawn of the aluminum-painted cth. is **Marker to Tsali.** In town cemetery is the **Grave of Horace Kephart,** instrumental in est. the Great Smoky Mt. Nat. Pk. & author of books about the reg. **71. NANTAHALA GORGE** is the route's climax. The canyon is so deep that Inds. called it Land of the Middle Sun, thinking that only the mid-day sun could reach it. In the gorge on the (L) bank are caves said to have been occupied by a race anterior to the Cherokee. **72. WESSER.** Near-by is Gorge Dell Campgrounds (water.fireplaces.facils.). **83. TOPTON** in Red Marble Gap is J. with US129.

SIDE TRIP: (NW) 12m to **Robbinsville** in farm & pasture area, center for hunters & fishermen, is said to be closer to the capitals of 6 other Sts. than to its own. Just beyond town is Entrance to **Joyce Kilmer Mem. For.,** maintained by Nat. For. Serv. The route follows curve of L. Santeetlah for some miles. Good fishing & facils. of all kinds avail. This area has great stands of virgin hardwood trees of c.100 varieties. There are c.20m of winding foot trls. 16m **Cheoah L.,** created by Aluminum Co. of Amer. by damming northward-flowing Little Tenn. R. Lighted concrete walk leads across dam to power plant (O). Near-by is J. with Fontana Village Rd.

9m along L. Cheoah is **Fontana Village,** modern resort with all types of accoms. & sports facils. Beyond is **Fontana Dam** (guides avail.), largest in TVA system; highest (E) of the Rockies, & 4th largest in world.

35m **Deal's Gap** on N.C.-Tenn. Line has J. with Appalachian Trl. to Gregory Bald with views of Parsons Bald (W), Yellow Cr. Mts. & Cheoah Bald (S) & Rye Patch on Long Hungry Ridge (E). Tsistuyi (Ind.: "rabbit place") was Cherokee for Gregory Bald. Ind. lore marks this as the dwelling place of numerous rabbits whose chief, the Great Rabbit, was large as a deer.

**89. VALLEY R. DAHLIA FARM** (O), one of largest dahlia gardens in N.C. At **94.** are plant & quarries of Columbia Marble Co. (O), which produce high-grade marble (Regal Blue); white shades to grayish & mottled blue with occasional streaks of pink. **103. TOMOTLA.** In old mine shaft broken tools were found believed to have been used by De Soto & his Sp. expedition when they penetrated the reg. searching for gold (1540). **108. MURPHY,** one of the oldest settlements in western N.C. (est.c.1830 as Ind.trading post). US19 crosses the **N.C.-GA. LINE** at **120.**

**II. (S) on US25 to N.C.-S.C. LINE. 42.**

(S) of Asheville, following route of the old Buncombe Turnpike, hy. crosses the Blue Ridge; grade is easy & ridge low. **6. BILTMORE** is the entrance to Biltmore Estate (see Asheville). **10. ARDEN;** many old estates near-by not visible from hy. but notable for their boxwoods.

SIDE TRIP: (R) 2m on dirt Fanning Rd. to ante bellum **Rugby Grange** (N.O.), named for Eng. sch., one-time home of Geo. Westfeldt, Swedish diplomat. 2.5m **Buck Shoals** (N.O. 1891), once home of Bill Nye, humorist. While living at a cottage in near-by Skyland, Nye once remarked, "George Vanderbilt's extensive grounds command a fine view of my place."

**10.5.** J. with gravel Rd.

SIDE TRIP: (L) to **Christ Sch.** (Episc.boys.prep.) housed in granite bldgs. on terraced, landscaped campus. 4m **Struan** (N.O.1897), oldest mansion in vic., has lovely stairway. Raided by Union soldiers, H. shows marks left by their hobnailed boots.

**11.5. CALVARY CH.** (Episc.Goth.rebuilt.1937). Adj. churchyard contains grave of Bill Nye. Near-by is sand-clay Rd. to **Asheville-Hendersonville Airport. 12. FLETCHER.** (S) of here are fertile fields of Cane & Mud. Cr. Valleys. **21. HENDERSONVILLE** (all types accoms. incl.children's camps.golf.tennis.playground games.indoor sports.hik.h.f.mid-summer horse show), mt. resort that attracts yr.-round visitors from all over U.S. As many as 50,000 vacationers visit this 8,000-pop. town in a yr. Benches line the streets. There are 2 private prep. schs.—Fassifern (girls) & Blue Ridge (boys).

SIDE TRIPS: (A) From Main St. (R) 3m on 5th Ave. to **Laurel Pk. Estates** (O). Just beyond are **Rhododendron L.** (water sports) & **Hendersonville Country Club & Golf Course** (O). At 7m **Jumpoff Mt.** offers wide views. On summit, steel girders of Fleetwood Hotel stood for c.10 yrs. Planned as a skyscraper (a small fortune was invested in it) during the 1925-26 real estate boom, it was never more than a skeleton surrounded by rusting radiators & bathtubs.

(B) On Caswell St. 6m (R) to **Kanuga L.** (clubh.cottages.water sports.recr.pavilion), 400-a. summer assembly ground of the N. & S. Dioceses of the Episc. Ch.

**26. FLAT ROCK,** said to be oldest summer resort in western N.C., was developed by planters from S.C. & Ga. lowlands. Has many handsome estates. **St. Johns-in-the-Wilderness** (Episc.1836) was built by these planters; in churchyard are graves of the family of Count de Choiseul, Fr. consul at Savannah, Ga., whose son was killed fighting for Confed. **27. BONCLARKEN,** on Highland L. (water sports.9-hole golf course), is summer assembly grounds of Assoc. Reformed Presb. Ch. Christian & Luth. Chs. also hold annual conferences here. **30. L. SUMMIT** (f.swim.). **42.** US25 crosses **N.C.-S.C. LINE.**

**III. (NW) on US25 to N.C.-TENN. LINE. 50.**

**5. LAKE VIEW PK.,** with artificial **Beaver L. & Golf Course** (sports facils.). **17. MARSHALL,** built on French Broad R. gorge & named for Chief Justice John Marshall. Town's high sch. is built on Blannerhasset I. in the R., believed to be named for Blennerhasset I. (see Ohio R. Tour) where Aaron Burr planned his empire. In town is J. with St.213 which leads 6.5m to **Mars Hill** (accoms.) where is **Mars Hill** (Jr.) **College. 38. HOT SPRINGS** (known as Warm Springs), an early mt. resort. Hqs. for French Broad R. Ranger Dist. of Pisgah Nat. For. Here Appalachian Trl. crosses hy.

SIDE TRIPS: (A) On Trl. (L) 4.5m to **Rich Mt.,** fire tower for wide view in all directions.

(B) On Trl. (R) 1.5m to **Lookout Pt.** for view of French Broad R. gorge. Cont. on trl. for other exciting views.

(C) On For. Serv. Rd. (L) c.0.5m to **Silvermine Campground** (camp.water.facils.fireplaces) maintained by U.S. For. Serv.

Hy. cont., paralleling Southern RR. tracks on opp. river bank. Just this side of N.C. Line is J. with dirt Rd. leading 3m to **Paint Rock** (tinged red from iron oxidation), a sheer cliff above the French Broad R. which commands a fine view. **50. N.C.-TENN. LINE.**

## BLUE RIDGE PARKWAY

Grades, curves & roadbed (S) of Va. line are good although Rd. is not completed throughout. Accoms. can be found in towns on hys. which inters. Pky. Pic. & parking areas incl.: at **0.5.** (from Va.-N.C. Line) **CUMBERLAND KNOB** (comfort stas. water); **21. BLUFF** (pic.camp.trlr.facils.water) stretching more than 5m on hy. & incl. **Carolyn Brinegar Cabin & Wildcat Rocks** (1,500′) overlooking former homestead of Caudill family, typical isolated mt. dwelling; **54.5. CASCADES PARKING OVERLOOK** with woodland trl. along stream to cascades hundreds of ft. high; **90.5. BEACON HEIGHTS** (inquire for entrance to Daniel Boone Boy Scout Trl. over the 7 peaks of Grandfather Mt.); **124. CRABTREE MEADOWS** in **Pisgah Nat. For.** (pic.comfort stas.) near Crabtree Falls. **140.5. SWANNANOA**

**GAP,** J. with St.128 which leads 5$^{m}$ to Mt. Mitchell St. Pk. (see US70). At c.**163** Pky. skirts Asheville, largest city near Pky. & good info. center. At **253.,** J. with Great Smoky Nat. Pk. (see), planned (S) terminus of Blue Ridge Pky. See also Va. section, for Blue Ridge Pky.

## GREAT SMOKY MTS. NAT. PK.

Half in N.C. & half in Tenn., the Great Smoky Mts., greatest mt. mass (E) of the Black Hills of S. Dak., are among the oldest land areas on earth. They are a portion of the Appalachian Range, & are survivals of earliest geological times. The Great Smoky area is also celebrated as one of the richest sources of Eng. folklore & song found by Cecil Sharp when he toured the S. Appalachians for his famous coll. of Eng. ballads & folk songs. The Smokies, for 36 consecutive miles in the Pk., are more than 5,000′ high; 16 peaks are more than 6,000′ high. The Pk. is 54$^{m}$ long; greatest width is 19$^{m}$. It will eventually comprise 440,000 as. or 687.5 sq. miles. The Pk. offers unique opportunity for preserving frontier conditions of a cent. ago, & several mt. communities remain intact within its boundaries. There is in process of development a mus. of mt. culture, which should interest all tourists. The most extensive for. of virgin red spruce & unspoiled hardwoods to be found in the U.S. is in the Pk., with nearly half the area in its orig. forested condition. There are some 129 native tree species, 18 other varieties not native, & most trees as well as shrubs attain giant size. The variety of plants is amazing. More than 1,200 flowering plants, 1,000 fungi, 300 mosses, 200 lichens & 100 liverworts have been found. As in all Nat. Pks., wildlife is given complete protection & no hunting or trapping is permitted. More than 50 species of fur-bearing animals, some 200 birds, 34 reptiles, 36 amphibians, & 60 fishes have been identified. Feeding, touching or molesting of bears is prohibited. There is nothing to fear from unmolested bears, however. There are 56.5$^{m}$ of high standard Rds. in the Pk., 25$^{m}$ of secondary Rds., & 675$^{m}$ of bridle & foot trls. (O). All trls. are carefully marked. There are 8 trailside shelters along the 71$^{m}$ Appalachian Trl. which runs from Davenport Gap to Newfound Gap (31$^{m}$), & from Newfound Gap to Deal's Gap (40$^{m}$). These are nearly equally spaced for easy 1-day hik. trips. Shelters, Adirondack type, enclosed on 3 sides & provided with 6 bunks, always have both fireplace & spring near-by. Camp. is restricted to 1 day unless weather is inclement. There is also an organized Youth Hostel movement. (Inquire Asheville C. of C., Pisgah Nat. For. Serv., Asheville & Nantahala Nat. For. Serv., Franklin.)

## US 1—SOUTH CAROLINA

**S.C.-N.C. LINE** (36$^{m}$ from Aberdeen, N.C.) **(SW) to S.C.-GA. LINE** (1$^{m}$ from Augusta, Ga.). **171. US1**

Via: Cheraw, McBee, Camden, Columbia, Batesburg, Aiken. RR. parallels route bet. Cheraw & Columbia, & bet. Columbia & Batesburg. Accoms.: All kinds.

US1 runs diagonally (SW) across S.C., following fall line that divides level coastal plain, or "low country," from Piedmont Plateau or "up country," through a sandhill belt that produces peaches, grapes & berries. It cont. through several resort towns, incl. hist. Camden, a center for horse lovers, to Columbia, state capital, & then to Savannah R. reg. & Aiken, "polo capital of the South."

### Sec. 1: N.C. LINE to COLUMBIA. 97.

**10. CHERAW,** trading post in 1750's est. by pioneers of Welsh descent. Town formally laid out in 1768 with streets 100′ wide, some of which have 4 rows of trees. Cheraw became of increasing importance in 1820's as head of navigation on the Great Pee Dee R. PTS. OF INT.: (1) Main intersection of town, **Town Hall** (1858.Gr.Rev.) home of one of oldest Masonic Lodges in Amer. (2) **Old Market Hall,** directly opp., now police hqs. (3) "Scotchman's Route," near-by **Old Lyceum** (1810.1-story with columned portico), now lib. Well-known actors performed here in '80's. (4) 1st & Church Sts., **St. David's Ch.** (Episc.c.1768), frame structure with tiered tower. St. David est. many chs. in S. Wales. In graveyard lies Capt. Moses Rogers, who in the "Savannah," a full rigged sailing vessel fitted with steam engines & paddles, made 1st transatlantic crossing (1819) using steam power. (The engines were run for only 80 hrs.). (5) Kershaw & 3rd Sts., **Lafayette H.** (1820), where Fr. Gen. was entertained, 1824. (6) 143 McIver Ave., **Hartsell H.** (N.O.c.1780.frame,int. inter.) occupied by Gen. Sherman, 1865. (7) **Merchants Bank** (1835), one of last in S. to honor Confed. money. At Cheraw is J. with St.9.

SIDE TRIP: At 12m (W) is **Chesterfield,** honoring Lord Chesterfield & dating from 1798. It is 1 of 2 S.C. towns that claim 1st secession meeting (see Abbeville). Sherman burned pub. bldgs. during 1 of his final raids. In 1935 Chesterfield became a center of Fed. Gov.'s Sand Hills Development Project. **John Craig H.** (1798) is opp. Cth.

**14. CHERAW ST. PK.** on Eureka L. (hqs.Cheraw;7,360 as.beach. swim.f.boat.trls. pic.cabins.group camps.Negro areas). **27.** J. with side Rd.

SIDE TRIP: Take latter (R) 0.5m & (R) 1.5m to **Sugar Loaf Mt.** (excellent view) & beyond, **Horseshoe Mt.,** both part of f., game & for. reservs. of Sand Hills Development Project.

**37. McBEE,** center of grape-growing area. **52. WAYSIDE PK.**

**65. CAMDEN**

Through RR. & bus conns. No scheduled air serv. Accoms.: All types. Season: Oct.-May.

Camden, cty. seat in Piedmont sandhill & long leaf pine reg., at head of navigation of Wateree R., has long been popular as winter resort & is now favorite center for horse lovers. Large stables of hunting horses, steeplechasers, trotters, pacers & polo ponies are trained here. There are 200 miles of bridle paths; 3 polo fields (games Sun. Dec.-Ap.); the Springdale Course, one of finest steeplechase plants in country, with the Carolina Cup Classic (last Sat. in Mar.); the Marion Dupont Scott mile flat course; the Va. Horse Show (Feb.); & the Camden Horse Show (Mar.). Golf (by invitation), football, basketball, hunting & fishing avail.

Brit. pioneers were here as early as 1730's & were soon followed by Irish Quakers. Settlement was called Friends' Neck, then Pine Tree Hill, & then Camden, in honor of 1st Earl of Camden. Early industry was shipping local clay to Eng. potteries. Cornwallis est. garrison here (June 1780) & 14 Rev. battles were fought within 30m-radius, 2 within town limits: Battle of Camden (Aug. 16,1780) in which Amers. under Gates were routed & Baron DeKalb (see below) mortally wounded; & Battle of Hobkirk Hill (Ap. 19,1781) when Amers., under Nathanael Greene withdrew & Eng. under Lord Rawdon fired town (May.) After Rev. wealthy settlers est. estates. Because of fires & a malaria outbreak, residential district moved (N) to Hilly Kirkwood. Camden was birthplace of 6 Confed. gens. (see below) & was again burned by Sherman (Feb. 24,1865).

PTS. OF INT.: (1) DeKalb near Broad St., **Bethesda Ch.** (Presb.1820.by Rbt.Mills. rest.). Here is Mon. to Johann Kalb, adventurer who assumed title of Baron & became major-gen. in Rev. War but was bitter because his protege, Lafayette, was placed above him. He was with Washington at Valley Forge & died heroically of 11 wounds in battle of Camden. Lafayette dedicated Mon. (2) Broad & Rutledge Sts., **City Hall,** has weathervane (1826.by J.B.Mathieu) that is life-size likeness of Catawba Ind. Chief Haigler who sided with Amers. against Cherokee, 1759. (3) Mill near York St., **"Washington" H.** where Washington was entertained (1791). (4) Broad & King Sts., **Old Cth.** (1826.by Rbt.Mills.remod.1847), now Masonic Hall. (5) Mill near Meeting St., **Fair Grounds.** Near-by stood store & home of Joseph Kershaw. Latter became Brit. hqs. (1780-81) & Amers. were executed on premises. Later it was used by Confeds. & burned by Sherman's troops. (6) Meeting & Campbell Sts., **Old Quaker Cemetery,** est. 1759 on land rented to Quakers by Sam. Wyly for 999 yrs. (rental to be "one pepper corn in & upon 1st day of Aug. of every yr."); now enlarged to include other denominations. Epitaph of Sam. Mathis, said to be 1st white male born in Camden reads: "All is vanity which is not honest, & there is no solid wisdom but in early piety." (7) 1205 Broad St., **Ivy Lodge** (c.1815), birthpl. of Bernard Baruch, who gave so generously to local hospital that it is now said: "It seems he imbued the edifice with an invincibly masculine quality, for the record is that only sons are born here, & the very poultry on those premises never produce pullets." (8) 1307 Broad St., **Greenleaf Villa** (c.1807), possibly oldest h. in town & noted for old formal gardens, was home of Dr. Edward Lee, cousin of Gen. Lee. (9) Laurens & Mill Sts., **Court Inn** (1830.add.int.gardens). (10) Rectory Sq., **Pantheon,** comms. Camden's six Confed. generals: Jas. Cantey, Jas. Chestnut, Zack C. Deas, John D. Kennedy, Jos. B. Kershaw & John B. Villepigue. (11) Greene & Mill Sts., **Holly Hedge** (c.1842), with landscaped springs & lakes in rear. (12) Lyttleton

St. near Green Ct., **Goodie Castle,** inter. gardens. (13) Kirkwood Common, **Kamchatka** (1853.remod.) built by Gen. Jas. Chestnut. At Camden is J. with US521.

SIDE TRIPS: (A) Take latter 2m (N) from Camden to J. with St.97. (L) a short distance is **Springfield Race Track.** At 4.5m on US521 is J. with side Rd.

At 2.5m (L) here is **Site of Battle of Camden** (see above).

At 21m on US521 is **Kershaw,** J. with St.265.

At 2.5m (R) here is J. with side Rd. (R) here short distance to **Hailes Gold Mine** (O), worked intermittently since 1828.

At 26m on US521 (L) is **Ingram H.** used by Geo. Washington (1791), & Sherman's staff (1865).

(B) Take US521 (S) 2.5m from Camden to (R) **Mulberry Plantation H.** (1820.by Col.Jas. Chestnut after designs attributed to Mills).

**85.** (L) **SESQUI-CENTENNIAL ST. PK.** (1,500 as.beach.swim.boat.f.pic.trls.camp) centered about L. with unusually designed cascade spillway.

**97. COLUMBIA**

Through RR., bus & plane conns. Accoms.: All kinds. Info.: C. of C., De Soto Hotel. Usual sports facils.; h. & f. in vic. Recent sport development is training of thoroughbreds for flat racing. Convention city. S.C. Legislature (convenes Jan.); Music Festival, Ap.; 2 State Fairs (one for Negroes) Oct.

Dominated by dome of capital bldg., always called St. House, Columbia, political & convention center of S.C., is at head of navigation of Congaree R. c.3m from geographical center of St. It is agric. & industrial center with one of largest free farm markets in SE. Textile mfg., ceramics & clay products, lumbering, printing & quarrying are important. C. of C. emphasizes availability of labor that is almost 100% native born (1/3 Negroes) & comparative absence of labor disputes. Univ. of S.C. & 5 other colleges (2 for Negroes) are located here, as are many Fed. & St. agencies & institutions, incl. hqs. for Sumter & Francis Marion Nat. Fors. Ft. Jackson, on outskirts, est. during World War I, became in World War II largest infantry training post in U.S.

Area was settled as early as 1718 when Ft. Congaree was garrisoned just (S) of Columbia at Granby. In 1786 General Assembly decided to move capital from Charleston to site "near Friday's Ferry . . . including plain of hill whereon Thomas & James Taylor Esquires now reside," & an area 2 miles sq. was platted. Legislature met here 1st time in 1790. In 1805, S.C. College (now Univ.) opened its doors. A few yrs. later factories were started with slave labor. Soon steamboats were coming up river from Charleston & in 1842 1st engine-drawn train, "Robert Y. Hayne," arrived. Dec. 17, 1860 Secession Convention met here, voted unanimously to secede, & then adjourned to Charleston because of smallpox scare. During most of Civil War, Columbia acted as supply & refuge center. Feb. 16, 1865, Sherman began to shell city, whose pop. was almost entirely made up of women & children. Accepting surrender from mayor, Sherman promised no further damage. But following night fires destroyed much of city. Reconstruction was particularly difficult in this area. On one occasion prisons were almost opened because legislature had provided no money for their upkeep. White supremacy was restored with election of Gen. Wade Hampton, aided by white Democrats known as Red Shirts, to governorship (1876) in contest so disputed that President Rutherford B. Hayes proposed another election.

Columbia's metropolitan area, including suburbs, now covers c.75 sq. miles. Its wide streets, suggested by orig. planners, are well planted with oaks, elms, hackberries, magnolias, mimosa, & variety of shrubs. Hist. marker program has made it easy to identify hist. sites.

PTS. OF INT.: (1) Main & Gervais Sts., **St. House** (begun 1855.by J.R.Niernsee. completed 1907) is S.C.'s 3rd "St. House"; 1st was at Charleston, 2nd was burned by Sherman's troops, its flames crumbling basement cornice of present structure. Built of granite, quarried by slaves from near-by Granby Quarry, orig. design is somewhat marred by use of dome contrary to architect's plans. Metal stars mark strikes by Sherman's artillery on S. & W. walls. Mons. on grounds incl. Confederate Mem., a bronze cast of Houdon's Washington, grave of Capt. Lunsford of "Light Horse" Harry Lee's company (on what was once his own property), bronze palmetto tree honoring Palmetto Regiment of Mex. War, & Mon. to Dr. J. Marion Sims, S.C.'s internationally famous gynecologist. In inter. are many portraits & busts of S.C.'s great, Relic Room (O.wks.) & St. Lib. (O.wks.). Of interest also is pre-Rev. mace with arms of Gr. Brit., House of Hanover & Province of S.C. still in use by Senate; & sword, emblem of authority of H. of Representatives—a cavalry sword used in War of 1812 & Civil War & replacing orig. sword made by local smith in 1704 & used until its mysterious disappearance in 1941. (2) Gervais & Sumter Sts., **Trinity Ch.** (Episc.1846.adds.1861-62.Eng.Goth.) is modeled after York Minster, Eng. Baptismal font by Hiram Powers. Churchyard contains graves from Rev. times, incl. those of the 3 Wade Hamptons & poet Henry Timrod. (3) Sumter & Pendleton Sts., **World War I Mem.** houses S.C. Archives. On 2nd fl. is notable chapel. (4) Sumter bet. Pendleton & Divine Sts., **Univ. of South Carolina** (coed.chartered 1801, opened 1805) on 47-a. campus in heart of city. Older bldgs. are of gray-painted brick formally grouped about elm-quadrangle & enclosed by brick wall (1835). Early pres. was Thos. Cooper whom Jefferson called "the greatest man in America in the powers of his mind & in acquired information, & that without a single exception." He est. (1820) 2nd chair of mineralogy & geology in U.S. (only Yale had one at time) & what was probably 1st chair of political economy, under Francis Lieber, an ardent Unionist. But clergy opposed Cooper's "agnosticism," college was called "hotbed of Atheism," parents withdrew sons, & Cooper resigned. Augustus B. Longstreet, author of "Georgia Scenes," was a later pres. One Prof. Venable is credited with saying: "The teacher of mathematics at S.C. ought to know something about mathematics but he must be a gentleman." On campus are: **Old Lib.** (1840), now housing only S. Caroliniana (incl.portraits.busts.relics) & said to be "oldest separate library bldg." in U.S. **Maxcy Mon.,** honoring 1st pres. & designed by Rbt. Mills. **DeSaussure College** (1804). **McKissick Lib.** (by W.P.A.), with portraits of Jefferson & Madison & a Mus. (O.wks.Sun.aft.). **Rutledge College** (1805.by Rbt. Mills.rebuilt after burning 1855). **Melton Astronomical Observatory, Arboretum** of native S.C. plants.

(5) Senate & Barnwell Sts., last **Home of Wade Hampton III,** Comdr. of Hampton Legion (1861), Gov. of S.C. (1876-79). (6) Harden & Taylor Sts., **Allen Univ.** (Negro. coed.Meth.Episc.) on 10-a. campus, founded 1871 as Payne Inst. in Cokesbury & transferred here 1880. (7) Opp. Allen Univ. on Taylor St., **Benedict College** (Negro. coed. Bapt.1870) on 20-a. campus. (8) 1718 Hampton St., **Chestnut Cottage,** home of Gen. Jas. Chestnut, Jr., where Jeff. Davis & staff were entertained (1864). (9) 1705 Hampton St., **Woodrow Wilson Mus.** (O.wks.free), boyhood home (1871-75) of pres., built by parents when his father taught theology at old Columbia Theological (Presb.) Seminary (see below). (10) Blanding & Pickens St., a unit of **Columbia Bible College** (coed.1923). Bldg. facing Hampton St. designed by Rbt. Mills (1823) as home of Ainsley Hall, Columbia merchant. (11) Across from Columbia Bible, **Hampton-Preston H.** (c.1818 by Ainsley Hall.Class.Rev.); hqs. of Fed. Gen. Logan who was persuaded not to burn it by Ursulines. (12) 1601 Richland St., **Seibels H.** (1796). (13) Richland & Barnwell Sts., **Taylor Burying Ground,** where lies John Taylor, Columbia's 1st mayor, later Gov. of S.C. (14) Bull St. & Elmwood Ave., **S.C. St. Hospital,** authorized 1821. Mills Bldg. (1828.Gr.Rev.) is named for its architect. (15) Richland & Sumter Sts., **Ebenezer Ch.** (Luth.1931). The 1st Ch. dedicated in this square (1830) was burned by Feds., rebuilt 1870 & later used as Sunday School. (16) Gadsen & Richland Sts., **Cemetery of Columbia Hebrew Benevolent Society** contains graves of 2 of city's mayors. (17) 829 Richland St., **Boylston H.** (1822.Gr.Rev.).

(18) Richland & Lincoln Sts., **Governor's Mansion** (1855), once officers' quarters of Arsenal Academy. (19) E. Laurel & Sumter Sts., **Ladson Ch.** (Negro.Presb.1868. rebuilt.1896), congregation org. 1838. (20) Laurel & Marion Sts., **De Bruhl-Marshall H.** (1820.Class.Rev.possibly by Rbt.Mills). (21) Hampton near Sumter St., **First Bapt. Ch.** (1859.Gr.Rev.). Here Secession Convention 1st met. (22) Washington & Marion Sts., **Washington Street Meth. Ch.** (1875) on site of 3 earlier Chs. (23) NE. cor. Marion & Lady Sts., **First Presb. Ch.** (1853.Goth.Rev.). Woodrow Wilson's parents are buried in churchyard. (24) 1527 Senate St., **Horry-Guignard H.** (pre-1813). (25) Assembly St., bet. Lady & Pendleton Sts., **Curb Market,** a wholesale & retail distributing pt. for produce of S. Atlantic states. Here one can buy such S.C. specialties as water-ground meal, "fat lightwood," sugar cane & fresh figs. (26) Assembly & Hampton Sts., **St. Peter's Ch.** (Cath.1906); 1st ch., erected 1824; in churchyard, grave of architect John R. Niernsee. (27) Whaley St., (W) of Wayne St., center of **Pacific Mills Community,** Columbia's largest mill community. (28) Stadium Rd., **St. Fair Ground & Buxton Brothers' Stables** (O) where such famous horses as Cavalcade & Seabiscuit were trained.

SIDE TRIPS: (A) On US21 (N) through Eau Claire, separately inc. but often thought of as N. Columbia. On Main St., near Elmwood Ave. **Luth. Theological Southern Seminary** (est.1830) which moved to Columbia, 1911. At Main St. & Columbia College Dr., **Columbia College** (women.Meth.1854). Old campus now used by Columbia Bible College. When Sherman entered town from one direction (Feb.1865), carriages were departing with young ladies of the college from the other.

(B) On US76 (E) from Columbia 3m to J. with St.760. (L) here 3m to **Ft. Jackson,** army reservation est. 1917 & a center of military training for SE.

(C) On St.2 (S) 1m to **Cayce.** Here are **Ruins of Cayce H.** (1765). During Rev., Lord Rawdon, Gen. Sumter & "Light Horse" Harry Lee each took it & lost it. It was finally taken by Gen. Nathanael Greene.

(D) At 2m from Columbia (NW) US76 crosses Broad R. & Columbia Canal (1824), a link in the once-important inland waterway conn. Charleston to vic. of Ninety-Six. 9m J. with St.60.

(L) here 6m to **L. Murray** formed by the **Dreher Shoals Dam** (1929.211′ high, 1¼ miles long) & Saluda R. (swim.f.boats.regattas). L. is large enough (41m long, 14m wide at widest pt., c.50,000 as.) to attract sea gulls from coast.

At 18m on US76 is **White Rock,** so-named because of white flint outcroppings. In Luth. churchyard here is Mon., one of a series in vic., with names from graves covered by Lake Murray.

## Sec. 2: COLUMBIA to S.C.-GA. LINE. 74.

**12. LEXINGTON. 30. BATESBURG. 40.** (L) **AIKEN WAYSIDE PK.** (35 as.pic.).

**58. AIKEN,** J. with US78.

Through RR. & bus conns. Airport; no scheduled serv. Accoms.: All types. Tourist season Oct.-May.

Aiken, a famous center for polo players, has many large, beautiful estates, set along magnolia, oak & pineshaded Rds. frequently unpaved for comfort of horses & their riders. Town offers 15 polo fields, miles of scenic bridle paths, a mile trotting track, a flat racing track, 2 18-hole golf courses, field trials, kennel shows, foxhunts, drag hunts, trap shooting, & dove & quail hunting. Nation's outstanding polo players take part in Sun. aft. games during season, when Aiken becomes training center for some 2,000 polo, steeplechase, trotting & riding horses. In Mar. a pro-amateur golf tournament is held; a little later the gardens reach their brilliant best; & soon thereafter the wealthy & famous depart for other playgrounds. There were few settlers in this vic. before Rev., though Two Notch Rd. & Whiskey Rd. date from this time. Town was laid out, 1834, as terminal on Charleston-Hamburg line. In 1865, Gen. H. J. Kilpatrick, on his way to destroy mills at Graniteville (see below), was defeated by Confed. Gen. Joe Wheeler in skirmish on main street. During Reconstruction cty. was scene of 2 bloody riots. With introduction of polo in 1882, Aiken soon became famous as resort. Today tourist trade remains most important industry though many townspeople are employed in textile mills, kaolin mines, lumber mills, & granite quarries.

PTS. OF INT.: (1) SW. edge of town, **Hitchcock Woods,** 11,000 as. of beautiful woodland with bridle paths & carriage Rds. Automobiles not allowed. Woods are scene of drag hunts in which an aromatic drag is substituted for fox. (2) Vaucluse Rd. & Lancaster St., **Eustis Pk.** (sports.facils.recr.). (3) Vaucluse Rd. & Laurens St., **Rosebank,** with int. gardens. (4) Whitney Ave. & Chesterfield St., **Joy Cottage** (Georg.Col.). (5) Whiskey Rd. near Barnard Rd., **Converse H.** Front yard was scene of fighting during engagement of 1865. (6) Colleton Ave. & Fairfield St., **Elm Court,** town's 1st cth., remod. by Vanderbilts. (7) Colleton Ave. & Horry St., **"Let's Pretend,"** where author Gouverneur Morris entertained Kipling & Rich. Harding Davis. (8) Laurens St. & Edgefield Ave., **Henderson H.,** with marker comm. recording made by astronomers, sent by Germany, of passing of Venus bet. earth & sun, Dec. 6, 1882. (9) Richland Ave. & Fairfield St., **Baptist Ch.,** burned by Negroes (1876) & rebuilt. (10) 1m (S) of town on US1 & a short distance (W) is **Irvin Court** (ante bellum.Gr.Rev.adds.).

SIDE TRIP: Take St.215 (E) from Aiken 16m to **Aiken St. Pk.** (867.as.pic.swim.boat.f. cabins.camp.trls.refreshments), 1m (S) from hy. along S. Edisto R.

**59.5.** (R) **EDGEWOOD** (1831.frame) moved here from Edgefield in 1920's. Int. gardens. **62.** J. with side Rd.

SIDE TRIP: (R) 2m here to **Graniteville,** 1st southern mill town, where in 1845 Wm. Gregg (1800-67), "father of Southern cotton manufacture," erected a mill (of local granite) & homes for 300 workers. He est. an advanced factory welfare program & urged employment of "poor whites" rather than slaves. One of orig. granite mills & number of orig. workers' cottages are extant. In mill yard is **Mon.** to Gregg.

**68. BATH,** sm. textile center. In vic. is **Kaolin Mine,** producing clays from beds sometimes 45′ deep. Clay was shipped from S.C. to Europe as early as 1765 for making of fine china. Clays are now also used in automobile, paint & chalk industries. **74.** US1 crosses **SAVANNAH R.,** forming S.C.-Ga. Line, c.1$^{m}$ (NE) of Augusta, Ga. (see).

# US 76—SOUTH CAROLINA

**S.C.-N.C. LINE** (23$^{m}$ from Whiteville, N.C.) **(W) to S.C.-GA. LINE** (10$^{m}$ from Clayton, Ga.). **301. US76**

Via: Marion, Florence, Sumter, Columbia, Clinton, Laurens, Anderson, Clemson, Westminster. RR. parallels route bet. Nichols & Columbia & bet. Columbia & Laurens. Good accoms in towns.

US76 follows (E-W) route through center of S.C. & some of its best cotton, corn, & tobacco lands. It runs (S) from Low Country near coast through "High Hills of Santee," in reg. of Sumter, then swings upward through Columbia, state capital, to textile reg. near Anderson & into S.C.'s most mountainous area.

## Sec. 1: N.C. LINE to COLUMBIA. 129.

Crossing N.C. Line, US76 travels over bridges spanning Lumber R. & swamplands. **25. MARION** (see US52). **47. FLORENCE** (see US52). **58. TIMMONSVILLE,** a cotton & tobacco trading center. **86. SUMTER** (see US15). **97. STATEBURG** (see US15). **129. COLUMBIA** (see US1).

## Sec. 2: COLUMBIA to GA. LINE. 172.

**44. NEWBERRY,** seat of **Newberry College** (Luth.coed.1856) which moved to Walhalla in 1868 after depletion of endowment funds invested in Confed. currency but was brought back in 1877. Feds. occupied one of old campus bldgs. & stopped drains on top fl. to make a swimming pool. Caldwell St., **Old Cth.** (1850.Gr.Rev. remod.1880) with int. bas-relief on pediment. Osborne Wells, the designer, wrote: "Here in place of Blindfolded Justice, the eagle, representing the U.S., holds the uprooted palmetto tree, representing State of South Carolina. The gamecock, representing the people of the state, still game, on one side, balanced by the dove of peace on the other." Main & Calhoun Sts., **St. Luke's Ch.** (Episc.1855.Goth.). Newberry is also hqs. for Enoree Ranger Dist., **Sumter Nat. For.** (h.f.pic.campsites). **St. Fish Hatchery** in vic. & **Forest Reserve Pk.** (300 as.). At Newberry is J. with US176.

SIDE TRIP: Take latter (N) 17$^{m}$ to **Whitmire,** now a cotton mill town, 1st settled in early 1800's. **Drucilla Whitmire H.** (c.1801) was once a trading post. **Phoebe Hearst Garden** honors William Randolph Hearst's mother. Just (S) of town (R) is **Abrams (Epps) H.** (c.1855.remod.).

**66. CLINTON,** industrial town with cotton, ginning, hosiery, & fertilizer mills, an outgrowth of early Scotch-Irish settlement called "Five Points," was chartered 1890. First Presb. pastor was Rev. Wm. Plumer Jacobs, who battled against intemperance of early settlers, & founded a lib., Sunday School, orphanage & college. Latter two remain town's most noteworthy institutions: S. Broad St., **Thornwell Orphanage,** now one of largest Presb. orphanages in U.S. & a pioneer in "Cottage System" of housing orphan children. **Presb. College** (coed.), founded 1880 as Clinton College & changed to present name, 1890. Lib. has Caroliniana coll. At Clinton is J. with St.56.

SIDE TRIP: (N) 1$^{m}$ from Clinton on St.56 to J. with side Rd.

(R) 4.5$^{m}$, (L) 1$^{m}$ to **Duncan Creek Ch.** (Presb.1842.remod.1927) incorporating log walls of 1st Ch. (1763), scene in 1788 of a disagreement that led many of congregation to become Bapts. Ch. is said to have been used as ft. in Rev. In graveyard lie many Rev. soldiers.

Cont. (N) 10.5$^{m}$ on St.56 to **Musgrove's Mill Battlefield** with marker & mon. to Col. Sam. Inman, comm. skirmish fought Aug. 19, 1780 in which Amers. were victorious. At 13$^{m}$ is **Cross Anchor** & J. with St.92.

(E) or (R) 1.5$^{m}$ from Cross Anchor on St.92 to **Belmont** (1840.int.exter.inter). Brick used in construction was from near-by rural retreat of Judge Grimké, 2 of whose daughters, Sarah & Angelina, were ardent abolitionists & scandalized Charleston by claiming kinship with 2 mulatto boys whom they helped educate. One of latter, Archibald Henry Grimké (1849-1930), graduated from Harvard, became crusader for Negro privileges, was Amer. Consul to San Domingo (1894-98) & was awarded Spingarn Medal by Nat. Assoc. for Advancement of Colored People. At 3$^m$ on St.92 is J. with side Rd. (L) 1$^m$ to **Blackstock Battlefield** where Amers. under Sumter routed Brit. under Tarleton, Nov. 20, 1780.

**74. LAURENS,** J. with US221 & US276, mfg. center (cotton mills, glassworks). Seat of cty. in which many families are interrelated & descended from Irish-Scotch pioneers who settled here before Rev. **Laurens Cth.** (1838.remod.1911.gray stone.Gr. Rev.); records date to 1785. Church St., **Ch. of Epiphany** (1850). **Nat. Guard Armory,** scene of riot (1870) when Negroes, led by carpetbagger, tried to burn town.

**91. PRINCETON,** J. with US25. (For Pts. of Int. from here through Clemson see US29.) **136. CLEMSON. 138.5.** (R) marker comm. **Seneca Old Town,** Ind. town completely laid waste by Williamson (1776). **145. SENECA,** J. with St.28, a cotton print mill town (1874). Shape-note singing is popular in this mountainous reg.

SIDE TRIP: At 9$^m$ from Seneca (N) on St.28 is **Walhalla,** sett. 1850 by German Colonization Society of Charleston, now both a cotton mill town & a summer resort with hqs. for Gen. Pickens Dist. of **Sumter Nat. For.** The 3 divisions of for.—Long Cave, Enoree, & Gen. Pickens—comprise total of 319,375 as. & develop for., water, & soil resources in 11 counties. Pickens Division in itself incl. 53,691 as. of mountainous terrain with finest types of hardwood & typical mt. shrubs. At Walhalla is J. with St.271.

Take latter (N) 16$^m$ to **Tamassee Sch. for Mt. Children,** an industrial sch. conducted by D.A.R.

At 14$^m$ on St.28 (L) is **Yellow Branch Recr. Area** (pic. camp.) on mt. stream affording excellent view. At 17$^m$ is J. with St.107.

Take latter (R) c.2$^m$ to **Oconee St. Pk.** (pic.swim.boat.f.cabins.camp.trls.refreshments) with 20-a. L. & sand beach. At 11$^m$ is **Walhalla Fed. Fish Hatchery** (O.pic.) with annual capacity of more than a million trout.

**154. WESTMINSTER.** At **172.** US76 crosses **CHATTOOGA R. & GA. LINE.**

## US 17—SOUTH CAROLINA

**S.C.-N.C. LINE** (c.16$^m$ from Shallot, N.C.) **(S) to S.C.-GA. LINE** (10$^m$ from Savannah, Ga.). **229. US17**

Via: Myrtle Beach, Georgetown, Charleston, Walterboro, Ridgeland. RR. parallels route from Charleston to Savannah. Accoms.: All kinds, but only in season at some resorts.

US17, paralleling Atlantic as far (S) as Charleston, follows, in general, an Ind. trl. which later became King's Hy. Over this route journeyed many notables incl. Geo. Washington (1st presidential tour), who said he had never seen rice cultivation brought to such perfection as on plantations of reg. The rice plantations are no more (many are now winter homes of rich "Northerners"), but tour offers excellent beach resorts, some of most famous gardens of the South & S.C.'s largest & most hist. city, Charleston. Roughly paralleling hy. is Intracoastal Waterway.

### Sec. 1: S.C.-N.C. LINE to CHARLESTON. 117.

**2. LITTLE RIVER** (boats for fresh & salt water f. & Intracoastal Waterway tour. pic.). **5.** J. with St.90.

SIDE TRIP: At 24$^m$ (SW) on St.90 is **Conway** on Waccamaw R. (anchorage facils. boats for fresh & salt water f.;duck,quail,deer) seat of Horry (pronounced "O-ree") Cty. Crops incl. strawberries, melons, truck & tobacco. Lumber & naval stores are still important. Ante bellum structures incl. **City Hall** (Gr.Rev.from plans of Rbt.Mills) & **Presb. Ch.** (1858).

In next few miles, just off US17, are series of sm. beach resorts. **10.5.** J. with side Rd. leading to **Atlantic Beach,** Negro resort. **23. MYRTLE BEACH,** J. US501, yr.-round resort (excellent beach.surf.bath.boat.fresh & salt water f.boardwalk. seawall.piers.casinos.27-hole golf course.game courts. horse racing Wed.& Sat.June-Labor Day). Beach is so named because of luxuriant growth of evergreen myrtle from whose berries candle wax was once made. No through RR. or air conns. **26.5. MYRTLE BEACH ST. PK.** (323 as.surf.bath.f.trls.pic.camp.cabins). **33. MURRELL'S INLET** (excellent f.oysters.clams.mussels.crabs.shrimp.terrapin). There are Gullah Negroes in vic., described by Julia Peterkin in novel "Black April" (see Beaufort US21). **36.** (R) **BROOKGREEN GARDENS** (O.9-5:30.exc.Mon.& Xmas. free) founded by Mr. & Mrs. (Anna Hyatt) Archer M. Huntington, now owned by

St., ocuupy site of 4 rice plantations. Plan of gardens is butterfly with outstretched wings. There are some 580 species of trees, shrubs, flowers native to SE., a zoo & a 4,000-a. wildlife preserve. Unusual attraction is large coll. which reviews course of Amer. sculpture from mid-19th cent. to present. Some 272 works by 152 sculptors incl. St. Gaudens, Paul Manship, Anna Hyatt Huntington, & Gaetano Cecere are placed at vantage pts. or in open-air Mus. Original Brookgreen Plantation was birthpl. (1779) of Washington Allston, painter & author. Julia Peterkin used it as background in "Scarlet Sister Mary," Pulitzer Prize novel. Near-by is Allston family cemetery on what was Oaks Plantation, home of Gov. Jos. Allston & his wife Theodosia Burr. On his tombstone is engraved story of Theodosia, who set sail from Georgetown to visit her father, Aaron Burr, & was never heard from again. Parking space & wharf for Intracoastal Waterway craft avail. **45. PAWLEYS I.,** beach resort.

**57. GEORGETOWN,** on Winyah Bay, dates from 1730's & honored George III, then Prince of Wales. Indigo & rice soon made it prosperous. Rice has not been grown commercially since 1900 & with it went passing of tiny rice birds, once great delicacy of reg. Present day activities are centered about lumbering & large wood pulp mill. Many large plantations in area are now owned by Northerners whose yachts dock at town wharves. Duck, deer, turkey, quail, squirrel, rabbit & fox are avail. Fishing Rodeo Apr.-Dec. PTS. OF INT.: (1) Front & Screven Sts., **Market Bldg.** (1842) is said to have been used as slave market. Tablet comms. landing of Lafayette at North I. (1775). Feds. landed at dock in rear in attack on Georgetown. (2) Prince & Screven Sts., **Cth.,** cornerstone laid 1824 with Masonic honors, shows mannerisms of Rbt. Mills; claimed one of 1st "fireproof" bldgs. in U.S. (3) Prince & Screven Sts., opp. Cth., **Masonic Temple** (1735) of stucco bricks, once one of earliest Col. banks in Amer. (4) Prince & Cannon Sts., **Winyah Indigo Soc. Bldg.** (1857.Gr. Rev.). Society, originally the Convivial Club, dates from 1740 & obtained its charter under present name from King Charles of Eng. some yrs. later. Members paid fees in indigo & proceeds were contributed to educate children of dist. (5) Highmarket & Broad Sts., **Prince George Winyah Ch.** (Episc.1742-46.tower add.1820). Cemetery adj. contains grave of one John Cogdell who died of "influenza," 1807. (6) Front bet. Wood & King Sts., **Pyatt H.,** where Geo. Washington stayed. (7) Hawkins St. on US17 just (SE) of town, **S. Kraft Corp. Wood Pulp Mill.** (8) **Hotel Amphitrite,** floating hotel once USS Monitor "Amphitrite" that saw service in Boxer Rebellion, Sp.-Amer. War & World War I. At Georgetown is J. with US701.

SIDE TRIP: From Georgetown (N) on US701. At 9$^{m}$ is **Wayside Pk.** At 14$^{m}$ is **Plantersville,** summer resort of early planters. **Prince Frederick Chapel of Ease** (c.1767) is mother ch. of parish.

**62.** J. with side Rd.

SIDE TRIP: A short distance here (L) are **Belle Isle Gardens** (O.8-5 p.m.fee.height of season—Mar.& Ap.) on Winyah Bay, noted for their moss-hung oaks, magnolias, azaleas & japonicas. On grounds are ruins of Confed. Ft., **Battery White.** In the Bay is boiler of Fed. ship., "Harvest Moon," sunk by Confeds.

**70.5.** J. with side Rd.

SIDE TRIP: At 0.5$^{m}$ (R) is **Fairfield Plantation H.** (c.1730.remod.1766), once home of Thos. Pinckney who fought in both Rev. & War of 1812 & was 1st U.S. minister to Eng.

**71.5.** J. with side Rd.

SIDE TRIP: At 1$^{m}$ (L) is J. with another Rd. which leads (L) 1.5$^{m}$ to **Harrietta** (1797.remod. int. exter.inter.) with noteworthy gardens. At 2$^{m}$ on main side Rd. is **Hampton H.** (c.1735. add.after 1757).

(For pts. of int. bet. here & Charleston & Charleston & Walterboro, see Charleston.) **117. CHARLESTON** (see).

## Sec. 2: CHARLESTON to GA. LINE. 112.

**48. WALTERBORO,** J. with US15 (see), resort & stopover town for tourists along Atlantic Coast. hy., founded by 18th-cent. rice growers. (Good f. & h.—deer, duck, turkey, quail). Hampton & Jeffries Sts., **Colleton County Cth.,** made from ballast stone from Eng. & removed from orig. site, Jacksonboro, 15$^{m}$ away. Attributed to Rbt. Mills but considerably remod. First nullification meeting in S.C. held here (1828). 127 Wichman St., **Walterboro Lib.** (1820). 121 Washington St., **Klein's Drug Store,** est. 1845. **65.** J. with US21 which cont. (E) to Beaufort (see US21). **87. RIDGELAND. 88.5.** J. with side Rd.

SIDE TRIP: (L) here 1.5$^m$, (L) 4.5$^m$ & (R) short distance to **Tomb of Thos. Heyward,** signer of Decl. of Ind.

**107.** Hy. enters **Savannah R. Wildlife Refuge** where teal, wood ducks & other migratory birds live in abandoned rice fields. **112. Hy. crosses SAVANNAH R. & GA. LINE.**

## US 52—SOUTH CAROLINA

**S.C.-N.C. LINE** (4$^m$ from Morven, N.C.) **(S) to CHARLESTON. 160. US52**

Via: Cheraw, Florence, Lake City, Kingstree, Moncks Corner. RR. parallels route. Accoms.: In larger towns.

US52 journeys from piney hill country through a truck, tobacco & cotton area, passes swamplands that Gen. Francis Marion used to such advantage in Rev., crosses Santee & Cooper Rs., & descends to the Low Country & Charleston.

### Sec. 1: N.C. LINE to LAKE CITY. 72.

**10. CHERAW,** J. with US1 (see). **24. SOCIETY HILL,** J. with US15 (see). **40. DARLINGTON,** cty. seat, dates from 1798. In 1894 it was scene of "Darlington War" when citizens rebelled against liquor restrictions inaugurated by Gov. B. R. Tillman.

**50. FLORENCE**

Through RR. & bus conns. **Airport. Accoms.:** All kinds. Excellent h. & f. in vic. Pee Dee Fair, fall.

Florence is hy. hub & one of outstanding retail & wholesale distributing centers of S.C., with large RR. shops & re-icing plants that protect flow of fruits & vegetables from S. to N. & W. Industries incl. furniture, veneer & lumber mills, concrete, steel fabrication & fertilizer plants. A large number of St. & Fed. agencies have offices here. During Civil War Florence was in turn transportation center, hospital & finally prison camp where more than 8,000 Feds. were herded, many dying in typhoid epidemic. When Sherman's men came to free prisoners most of them were dead, escaped, or transported to N.C. PTS. OF INT.: (1) 319 S. Irby St., **Pub. Lib.,** has coll. of S. Caroliniana & Mus. with Ind. relics, big game heads & Chinese, Egyptian, Roman & Greek pieces. (2) City Pk. & Coit St., **Timrod Shrine** (O.free) 1-rm. school where Henry Timrod, Confed. poet & schoolteacher, taught. (3) E. Day St. at RR. freight yard, **Re-icing Plant** (O.day & night). (4) On US52 (NW) 2$^m$ is **Pee Dee Experimental Sta.** where experiments with boll weevil control & tobacco are conducted. (5) On Church St. (S) & then on Cemetery Rd. to **Nat. Cemetery** 2$^m$, for Feds. who died imprisoned in Florence. Florena Budwin (grave 2480) fought with Feds. wearing soldier's uniform & later served as nurse, in clothing furnished by scandalized women of Florence. Some of old earthworks of **Civil War Stockade** are still visible c.0.5$^m$ (E). At Florence is J. with US76 (see).

SIDE TRIP: At 6$^m$ (E) on US76 **Mars Bluff,** scene of Rev. skirmish (Aug.1768). 22$^m$ **Marion,** J. with US501, once an Ind. trading post on a Royal grant to Jas. Godbold in 1769. Cth. Sq. was laid out c.1800 & is now pride of the town. Industries incl. cotton, cottonseed & lumber mills. On Sq., **Cth.** (1853.Gr.Rev.) & **Pub. Lib.,** which has the orig. Royal grant. E. Godbold & Oak Sts., gardens of **Meth. Ch.** E. Godbold & Court Sts., **Masonic Lodge** (1810).

From Marion (N) 5$^m$ on US501 is **Site of Battle of Bowling Green** where Amers. under Gen. Francis Marion routed Brit. under Maj. Gainey, June 8, 1782.

**72. LAKE CITY,** auction center for truck crops & tobacco.

### Sec. 2: LAKE CITY to CHARLESTON. 88.

**16. KINGSTREE,** on Black R., had its origin in 1732 when Irish Calvinists sett. around pine marked for use as mast in the king's ships, & is oldest non-coastal town in S.C. **County Cth.** (1823.by Rbt.Mills). From near-by swamps, Gen. Francis Marion, "Swamp Fox" of Rev., harried Brit. **33.** US52 crosses Santee R. **39. ST. STEPHENS,** in a lumber reg. **St. Stephens Ch.** (Episc.1767-69). **54.** US52 crosses Cooper R. **56. MONCKS COR.** Hqs. for **Francis Marion Nat. For.,** 250,000 as. of pine-growing land (h.f.permitted outside game areas). Recr. areas near Huger (E) of Moncks Corner on St.11 (pic.camp.).

SIDE TRIP: Just (N) of Moncks Corner c.3$^m$ is **L. Moultrie & Pinopolis Dam** which, with L. Marion, is part of hydroelectric project begun 1939, conn. & harnessing Santee &

Cooper Rs. Old Santee Canal, completed 1800 but abandoned in 1840's after RRs. offered too much competition, was early attempt to unite Rs.

**88. CHARLESTON.** (For pts. of int. bet. here & Moncks Corner, see Charleston.)

## US 15—SOUTH CAROLINA

**S.C.-N.C. LINE** (8$^{m}$ from Laurinburg, N.C.) **(SW) to WALTERBORO, S.C. 161.** US15

Via: McColl, Bennettsville, Hartsville, Sumter, St. George. RR. parallels route bet. McColl & Bennettsville, & bet. Hartsville & Sumter. Accoms.: In towns.

US15 runs (SW) through a sec. of S.C. that is neither quite "Up Country" nor "Low Country." It crosses a series of river valleys—the great Pee Dee, the Lynches, the Santee, & the Edisto, in reg. primarily devoted to agric. & lumbering.

### Sec. 1: N.C. LINE to SUMTER. 80.

**11. BENNETTSVILLE,** chartered 1810 & seat of Cty. named for Duke of Marlborough, a rich cotton, corn, & tobacco raising area in which, in 1889, Capt. Zachariah A. Drake broke world's record for production of corn on 1 a.—254¾ bu. Industrial plants incl. cotton mill, lumber mill, furniture factory, & cannery. On banks of Crooked Cr., **Woodland Gardens.** (E) From Bennettsville 1$^{m}$ is J. with St.9.

SIDE TRIP: On St.9 (S) 26$^{m}$ is **Dillon** (sett.c.1887). In vic. live racial group known as Croatans whose claim to be descended from Lost Colony of Roanoke is doubtful. Most authorities believe them mixture of Ind., Negro, & pioneer whites.

**24. SOCIETY HILL,** center of Bapt. community which dates to 1736 on land granted Bapts. by George II. J. with US52 (see). **41. HARTSVILLE** has some 20 diversified industries including Sonoco Products Co., cotton, silk, & knitting mills, & pedigreed seed companies. PTS. OF INT.: **Lawton Pk.** on Prestwood Lake (swim. boat.pic.). **Coker College** for women (Bapt.1908). At 2.5$^{m}$ (W) on St.151, **Kalmia Gardens** (Sun.3-6 p.m.;wks.appl.free), with 65 as. & 3 sm. Ls. overlooking Black Cr. & planted with many species of trees & shrubs representing all parts of S.C.—mountain laurel, galax, rhododendron, camellias, swamp lilies. At 1$^{m}$ (E) on St.151, **Coker Pedigreed Seed Farms** (O.free) where improved varieties of cotton, tobacco, & small grain, are developed. **54.** J. with side Rd. At 2$^{m}$ (L) here is **Lee St. Pk.** on Lynches R. (swim.f.boat.pic.trls.f.-cabins).

**80. SUMTER**

Through RR. & bus conns. Good accoms.

Seat of Cty. named for Gen. Thos. Sumter, "Gamecock" of Amer. Rev., an agric. (especially cotton) & lumbering area, Sumter's industries incl. furniture mfg. & wood working. Settlers were here before 1785 & in 1800 town's limits were set as perfect circle at end of a 1-mile radius swinging out from present city hall. A lib. was est. in 1809. Sumter is one of few towns in st. to employ a landscape artist & 1st in U.S. to employ city manager under a commission form of gov. **Mem. Pk.** is dedicated "to the white soldiers of World War I." **Swan L. Gardens** on W. Liberty St. (O.during blooming season, last of May & early June.free) is planted with thousands of giant Japanese iris. **Morris College** (Bapt.Negro.coed.1908). At Sumter is J. with US521 & US76 (see).

SIDE TRIPS: (A) On US521 (N) 8$^{m}$ is **Dalzell.** In vic. live group of "Turks" who keep apart from both whites & Negroes & are said to be descended from a Turk. & a Fr. pirate who acted as scouts for Amers. during Rev.

(B) On US76 (E) 10$^{m}$ **Mayesville,** where was born Mary McLeod Bethune, Negro educator. 19$^{m}$ **Lynchburg** where Brit. were defeated by Gen. Marion's men (1781).

(C) On US76 (W) 2$^{m}$ is **Palmetto Pigeon Plant** from which thousands of squabs are shipped annually. At 12$^{m}$ is J. with St.261 & St.441.

(1) On St.261 (L) 8.5$^{m}$ to **Melrose H.** (c.1760). At 11$^{m}$ is **Poinsett St. Pk.** in the "High Hills of Santee" (hqs.Wedgefield; swim.boat.f.pic.trls.cabins.trlr.camps). Beds of coquina or shellrock, used in construction of pk. bldgs., are heritage of Eocene age when this sec. of S.C. was beneath Atlantic. At 15$^{m}$ (R) is **Milford H.** (c.1850.Gr.Rev.int.exter. inter.), built of Rhode I. granite & local bricks. House had running water & basement furnace in early 50's. Across hy. a short distance is **St. Mark's Ch.** (1856.Goth.).

(2) On St.441 (R) just off US76 is **Stateburg.** Here are **Borough H.** (1754), int. paintings, furnishings, gardens; **Ellison H.** (pre-1800), once home of free Negroes who themselves

owned slaves; & **Holy Cross Ch.** (Episc. 1850. Goth.). In graveyard are buried Joel Poinsett & wife.

### Sec. 2: SUMTER to WALTERBORO, S.C. 81.

**4. POCALLA SPRINGS** (swim.). **23. SUMMERTON.** J. with US301. (S) of Summerton US15 crosses L. Marion to **SANTEE, 34. 54. ROSINVILLE.** J. with US178. At **56.5.** J. with side Rd. (R) here 0.5m is **Ind. Fields Meth. Campgrounds** where camp meetings have been held since 1838 (now wk. of 1st Sun. in Oct.). **60. ST. GEORGE,** a trading post since 1788; J. with US78. **70. WAYSIDE PK. 81. WALTERBORO.** J. with US17 (see).

## US 21—SOUTH CAROLINA

**S.C.-N.C. LINE** (13m from Charlotte, N.C.) **(S) to PORT ROYAL, S.C. 225. US21**

Via: Rock Hill, Chester, Winnsboro, Columbia, St. Matthews, Orangeburg, Branchville, Yemassee, Pocotaligo. RR. parallels route bet. Charlotte & Columbia, St. Matthews & Branchville, & Yemassee & Beaufort. Accoms: All kinds in larger towns.

US21 runs (N-S) through central S.C. from textile mill towns to Columbia, St. capital, then through a rich agric. reg. to historic Beaufort & the Sea Islands.

### Sec. 1: N.C. LINE to COLUMBIA. 95.

**7. FT. MILL,** a textile mill village, has Mon. to Catawba Inds. & one to faithful slaves. **10.** Hy. crosses **CATAWBA R.**

**15. ROCK HILL**

Through RR. & bus conns. Good accoms. Mun. golf course (sm.fee).

Rock Hill, college & industrial town, was country crossroads & RR. stop as late as 1860's. Confeds. used it in transport of troops & supplies, & 1 townsman was killed when Fed. cavalry descended to destroy RR. Later town became a center for KKK operations. Today it has a cotton-printing plant, said to print 1/5 of all cotton goods manufactured in U.S., factories that produce denim, hosiery, rugs, & even coat-hangers, a hydroelectric power plant, & a $40,000,000 Celanese Corp. plant. **Winthrop College,** S.C. College for Women, came into existence in 1886 in sm. brick chapel of Columbia Theological Seminary (once carriage house built by Rbt. Mills for Ainsley Hall). Chapel was torn down in 1937, transported from Columbia, & rebuilt on present 440-a. campus. College itself moved to Rock Hill in 1895 when town floated bond issue as inducement. Bldgs. are of red brick & show Eng. influences. Yearly series of artists & lecturers open to public. Charlotte Ave. & Crest St., **Glencairn Azalea Gardens** (O.Ap.when in bloom.fee). White St., **White Plantation H.** (1838.remod.), once home of Geo. & Anne Hutchinson White & oldest house in town, incl. a "Prophets' Chamber," a room set aside for visiting ministers. **Confederate Pk.** (swim.golf.tennis.pic.). At Rock Hill is J. with St.5.

SIDE TRIP: Take latter (SE) 6m to **Leslie** & J. with side Rd. (L) here 3.5m, (R) 1m, (L) 0.5m to **Catawba Ind. Reserv.** where live S.C.'s only Ind. wards. Most are of mixed blood & few tribal customs remain. Throughout early Amer. hist. Catawba fought on Amer. side & even supplied soldiers to Confeds.

**35. CHESTER,** settled in 1750's, is textile mill town that also manufactures cotton seed products & farm implements. On Cth. (1850) grounds is **Mon. to Jack Simons.** At Chester is J. with US321, St.9, St.72, & St.97.

SIDE TRIPS: (A) On US321 (N) 9m to **Lowrys.** Here is **Erwin H.** (pre-Rev.add.int.exter. inter.) At 16m is **Guthriesville** & J. with side Rd.

(R) here 2m to **Brattonsville** with **Mon.** comm. defeat of Brit. troops & Tories by Whigs, July 12, 1780. Near-by is **Col. Bratton H.** (pre-Rev.).

Return to US321. 24m **York,** where 1st KKK in state is said to have been org. Among most active was Dr. Rufus Bratton, said to have served as model for Dr. Cameron in Thomas Dixon's "The Clansman" from which the movie, "The Birth of a Nation," was made. At 27m is J. with St.161.

Take latter (L) 9m to **Kings Mt. St. Pk.** (6,141 as.swim.boat.f.trls.pic.camp.2 group camps) which adj. **Kings Mt. Nat. Military Pk.** (pk.& mus.O.daily exc.winter holidays. free), 4,000 as. incl. 16m of Kings Mt. Range & Battlefield Ridge. Here on Oct. 7, 1780 the Amers., c.910 strong, under Col. Wm. Campbell surrounded Brit., c.1,100 strong under Maj. Patrick Ferguson & gained complete victory. Amer. loss was 28 killed & 62 wounded, while entire Brit. force was killed, wounded or captured. Ferguson was killed & buried on field; his mistress, so the story goes, along with him. Later, wolves found the shallow graves of those who died in battle & in 1815 scattered bones were gathered & a small marker erected. There are now a number of markers, the U.S. & Centennial Mons., & a Mus. displaying battle diorama & other exhibits.

(B) From Chester (E) 29m on St.9 to **Lancaster,** a mill-village center. Dunlap & Main Sts., **Lancaster Cth.** & adj., **Jail,** both designed by Rbt. Mills in 1823. W. Gray St., in Presb. churchyard is **Mon.** to Irvin Clinton erected by his slave Isom. Here is J. with US521.

Take latter (N) 6m to J. with side Rd. (L) here 1.5m & (L) again 1.5m to **Waxhaw Presb. Ch.** on site of original Ch. erected 1755. In cemetery are graves of Gen. Wm. R. Davie, Rev. soldier & delegate to Constitutional convention, & Andrew Jackson, Sr., whose corpse, it is said, was temporarily lost by members of his funeral procession who spent 2 days drowning their sorrow enroute from his home to cemetery. Cont. (N) 8m on US521 to J. with another side Rd. (R) 0.5m here to **Birthpl. of Andrew Jackson** (disputed. N.C. also claims him) with Mon. which quotes his letter saying he was born on the Jas. Crawford plantation "about 1 mile from the Carolina road-crossing of Waxhaw Creek."

(C) From Chester (SW) 3m on US72 (L) to **Chester St. Pk.** (523 as.pic.boat.f.camp.refreshments.trls.). Lake in 1949 unsuited for swimming but this is expected to be remedied in near future.

**62. WINNSBORO** (c.1755; inc. 30 yrs. later). Cornwallis occupied town, 1780 & Sherman fired part of it, 1865. **Fortune Pk.** has entrance honoring Negro slave who attended Lafayette. **Fairfield Inn,** said to have been Cornwallis' hqs. **Mill Village,** modern housing project. **72. RIDGEWAY. 95. COLUMBIA** (see US1).

## Sec. 2: COLUMBIA to BEAUFORT. 130.

**9.** (S) J. with St.5.

SIDE TRIP: From here St.5 cont. (SW), paralleled most of way to Hardeeville by RR. & dotted by sm. towns that serve as shipping & packing centers for reg. producing truck, tobacco, pecans, pasture & pine products as well as cotton. Accoms. limited. 29m (N) J. with US178 (see). 44m Hy. crosses **S. Edisto R.** 49m **Denmark.** J. with US78 (see). 70m **Sycamore,** J. with St.641.

(W) 8m on St.641 to **Rivers' Bridge St. Pk.** (400 as.pic.f.boat.camp.trl.) on Big Salkehatchie R. In vic., on Feb. 4, 1865, 1,200 Confeds. under Maj. Gen. McLaws held off 22,000 of Sherman's men to give scattered Confed. forces opportunity to unite, & families on Sherman's line of march chance to hide most valued possessions. In 1876 Confed. dead were buried in single grave. There is now a landscaped pk. & a small Mus. of relics. Annual mem. services are held.

107.5m **Robertville,** named for family of Henry Martyn Robert (1837-1923) who was born here but became a military engineer for Feds. He was author of celebrated "Robert's Rules of Order." 126m **Hardeeville.** J. with US17 (see) & St.46.

(E) 13m from Hardeeville to **Bluffton,** resort since before Civil War. Henry Timrod taught here. Town was shelled by Fed. gunboat. Episc. Ch. (Goth.Rev.) survived. In vic. is **Brighton Beach.**

**18. SANDY RUN. 29.** J. with St.6.

SIDE TRIP: Take latter (L) 4m to St. Matthews, sett. by Germans in 1730's & early center of flourishing sea island cotton plantations. Badly hit by boll weevil in 1920. Since then experiments have been conducted here with development of weevil-resistant strains. (Good h. deer, turkey, fox & f. in Wateree Swamp vic.).

From St. Matthews (L) 7.5m on St.26 to **J.** with side Rd. (L) here 2m to **Ft. Motte, a** village that was once a Rev. outpost.

**33.** J. with St.31, known as Old St. Rd. & 1st Rd. completed (early 19th cent.) from Charleston to Columbia & to N.C. **45. ORANGEBURG,** J. with US178, seat of one of leading agric. counties in U.S. (especially noted for cotton). Both are named for George II's son-in-law William, Prince of Orange, & date back to 1730's. PTS. OF INT.: (1) Russell & Broughton Sts., **Mem. Fountain** with number of mons. incl. 1 to volunteer firemen. (2) Banks of Edisto R., **Edisto Gardens** (O.best at end of Mar. free), a converted swamp area brilliant in the spring with wisteria, roses, azaleas. On one of turns of R. is Edisto Beach (swim.pic.). (3) **St. Agric. & Mech. College** (Negro.coed.1895). (4) College Ave. & E. Russell St., **Claflin Univ.** (Negro.coed. Meth.Episc.1869). (5) Amelia & Green Sts., **Lutheran Ch.,** used as hospital by Sherman. (6) Amelia & Windsor Sts., **Presb. Ch.** (1858.inter.remod.).

SIDE TRIPS: (A) From Orangeburg (E) 3.5m on St.4 to **Middlepen Plantation,** hqs. for Gov. John Rutledge as well as Lord Rawdon in Rev. & hqs. also for Feds. in Civil War. (B) From Orangeburg (SE) 1.5m on US178 to **J.** with side Rd. (R) here 0.5m to **Fed. Fish Hatchery** (O.wks.), producing bass, bream, etc.

(C) From Orangeburg (W) 1m on St.4 is J. with side Rd. (L) here 5.5m to **St. Fish Hatchery,** one of largest in St. & with 150 as. of ground used for recr. purposes.

**62. BRANCHVILLE,** point of junction of 1st branch RR. in S.C. (1842). Branch line connected Columbia to Charleston to Hamburg line. Here is J. with US78.

SIDE TRIP: Take latter (W) 10m on US78 to **Woodlands,** once home of S.C. author William Gilmore Simms ("The Yemassee," etc.), partly burned by Sherman's men. 15m **Bamberg,** seat of watermelon producing cty.

From Bamberg (L) 7.5m on St.36 to side Rd. (R) here 1m to **Clear Pond** (pic.f.). Here, local tradition says, Dr. F. F. Carroll built early submarine.

22m **Denmark,** J. with St.5 (see above). 30m **Blackville,** shipping center for melons & cucumbers, was destroyed by Sherman's army en route to Columbia. Here is J. with St.3.

Take latter (L) 3m to **Barnwell St. Pk.** (252 as.30-a.lake.beach.pic.swim.boat.f.,f.-cabins. camp.refreshments.trls.) Pk. has int. variety of native trees & flowers. At 10m on St.3 is Barnwell. Here Gen. Kilpatrick of Sherman's army invited ladies of the town to a dance. They accepted & went gallantly through entire evening though they knew their homes were being burned to the ground.

**68.** US21 crosses Edisto R. (good h. for water fowl in vic.). **102.** is J. with US17 (see). **106. YEMASSEE. 109. POCOTALIGO** S. J. with US17.

**115. GARDENS CORNER**

SIDE TRIP: (R) just (N) of here on marked side Rd. 2.5m to **Ruins of Sheldon Ch.** First Ch. (1745-57) was, along with Sheldon Hall, burned by Brit. in Rev.; 2nd on site burned by Sherman 1865. Churchyard has graves of Bull, Middleton & Drayton families. 3.5m **Tomotley Plantation,** ante bellum rice plantation with 200 yr.-old live oak avenue.

**130. BEAUFORT**

Through RR. & bus conns. On Intracoastal Waterway. Deep water harbor, sheltered yacht harbor, & yacht club. Round trips by boat to Savannah avail. Good accoms. Golf, tennis, beach, swim., boat. Fish: bass, cobia, sea trout, sheephead. Hunt.: deer, doves, quail. S. Atlantic Sailing regatta (July). St. Helena I. Fair (fall).

Beaufort, surrounded by network of rivers & inlets, situated on a deep natural harbor on Port Royal I., 1 of 65 Sea Is. of Beaufort Cty., is charming & hist. port town, 2nd oldest in S.C., that preserves to unusual extent atmosphere of another age. Old homes, deep in gardens, line winding oak-shaded streets with cabins of Negroes scattered among them. Negroes far outnumber whites in cty. as a whole.

Sp. were here as early as 1521, naming harbor "Punta de Santa Elena." Ribaut & his Fr. Huguenots attempted settlement on Parris I., 1562, & were responsible for name Port Royal. Brit. Lords Proprietors believing that here "would be the most proper place . . . to take in masts, pitch, tar, turpentine, & other naval stores" settled at Port Royal, 1670. Scotch followed in 1684 but were wiped out by Sp. & Inds. Beaufort proper was founded 1710 & almost destroyed by Yemassee Inds. in 1715. During Rev. post was est. here by Brit. to penetrate inland waterways, & in 1812 Brit. warships sailed into harbor but did not damage town. In next decades Beaufort became a fashionable summer home for neighboring planters. Bishop Asbury & John Wesley both visited here & Parson Weems, author of famous "Life of Washington," died here. When Feds. took possession in 1861, only 1 white man remained in town "and he had recently come from the North." Property of planters was confiscated & later sold to Northerners or divided among newly freed slaves. After the war persistent efforts were made by Northern groups to educate the freemen, some successful, some exceptionally visionary—as an attempt, in 1 case, at an all-classical curriculum. These efforts cont., notably in Penn Sch. But many of the educated Negroes move away. Others still cling to mores & customs that marked their life in ante bellum times. Doors are still painted blue to ward off evil spirits & graves are still covered with objects which deceased used just before death. Primitive methods of cultivation, induced by poverty as well as by custom, continue. Plows are drawn by oxen or marsh tackies (believed to be degenerate horses left over from Sp. occupation). Transportation is by the 2-wheeled cart. Of special interest are the Gullahs, whose largest concentration is on St. Helena I. Descended from W. African tribes, their dialect & the strange music of their spirituals have received much attention.

Cty. supplied Eng. with sea island (long staple) cotton for almost a century until crop was wiped out by boll weevil, 1918. Today principal sources of income of reg. are fishing (oysters & shrimp incl.), canning, & tourists. About ⅓ of cty. land is now taken up by private hunting preserves. There is also a large Naval Hospital & a Marine Training Sta.

PTS. OF INT.: (1) At entrance of US21 into town, **National Cemetery,** est. 1863, has some 12,000 graves of Feds. removed from Fla., Ga. & parts of S.C. & sm. number of Confed. graves. (2) Carteret & Boundary Sts., **Bellamy Inn,** an ante bellum frame structure. (3) Carteret & Green Sts., **Detreville H.** (early 1800's.Georg.). (4) Carteret & Washington Sts., **Barnwell H.** (1730's) constructed of "tabby" (half shells imbedded in & cemented by burnt oyster shell, lime & sand). (5) Carteret & Duke Sts., **Old Beaufort College Bldg.** (1852.Gr.Rev.adds.) now grammar sch., served as college (1st inc. 1795) & was once used by Freedman's Bureau. (6) Carteret & Craven Sts., **Beaufort Lib.** (1918). First lib. was organized 1802 & its books taken by U.S. Treasury Agents (1861) to N.Y. where part of them were auctioned off until Secy. of Treas. Chase stopped sale, saying: "The library was forwarded . . . with the intention of restoring it to the people of the town whenever the authority of the Union should be re-established in S.C. . . . We do not war on libraries." Remainder, forwarded to Smithsonian Inst., was burned in fire of 1865 & Beaufort remained without pub. lib. until Clover Club organized one, 1902. In 1940 U.S. Senate voted $10,000 to repay town for books. (7) Craven & Scott Sts., **Old Arsenal** (1795.rebuilt.1852.Sp.& Goth.influences) of brick & tabby construction, hqs. of Beaufort Volunteer Artillery (1776), 5th military co. recognized in U.S. (8) New St. near Port Republic St., **Gold Eagle Tavern** (1795.remod.add.). Land was owned by Henry Wm. De Saussure, director of U.S. Mint when 1st gold eagles were struck. (9) New & Port Republic Sts. (SW.cor.), **Oldest H.** has slots for muskets in brick basement. Legend has it that here one Peggy Johnson hid in a closet to eavesdrop on Masonic meeting. Unable to suppress her giggles, she was discovered. The men, now that their mysteries were known to a woman, immediately org. the Order of the Eastern Star with Peggy a charter member. (10) East St. near Craven St., **Porter Danner H.** (1850's), has something of the appearance of a medieval castle. (11) Short & King Sts., **The Oaks** (1856.Gr.Rev.). (12) Short St. near Prince St., **Crofut H.** (c.1850.Gr.Rev.) with tabby slave quarters in rear. (13) Opp. Crofut H., **Fripp H.** (c.1850). (14) Bay & Scott Sts., **Lafayette Bldg.** (late 1770's.inter.paneling, etc., in Adam manner brought from Eng.). Lafayette addressed citizens from gallery. (15) Bay & New Castle Sts., **Sea Is. Hotel** (1820.adds.) hqs. of Gen. Saxton in Civil War. (16) Bay & New Castle Sts., **The Anchorage** (pre-1778.remod.Gr.Rev.adds.). (17) Bay & Harrington Sts. (E. cor.), **Tabby Manse** (after 1786) is of stuccoed tabby with wooden portico. (18) Bay & Harrington Sts., (W.cor.), **Lee H.,** thought to be plantation house built before Rev. & moved here from St. Helena I. (19) Bay & Wilmington Sts., **McLeod H.** (early 1800's), during Civil War a U.S. Treas. Agent's hqs., Maj. Blair's hqs. & finally a hospital. (20) Church & North Sts., **St. Helena's Ch.** (Episc.1724.adds.), has communion silver given by Capt. John Bull (1734) in memory of Mrs. Bull who was carried away by Yemassee Inds. (1715). In churchyard is grave of John (Tuscarora Jack) Barnwell, Irishman who fought against Tuscarora Inds. & later represented Province of S.C. in Eng. during revolt of 1719. (21) Charles & King Sts., **Bapt. Ch.** (1844.Gr.Rev.). Congregation dates from 1780. In 1857 there were 182 white members & 3,317 slaves. (22) Church & Craven Sts., **Rhett H.,** remod. in Gr. Rev. manner (1861) from structure built soon after Rev. Other ante bellum structures incl.: (23) Bay & New Sts., **Wate H.** (24) Bay St., **Elliot H.** (25) Washington & New Sts., **Chaplin Court.**

SIDE TRIPS: (A) From Beaufort (NW) 2$^{m}$ on US21 is J. with St.280.

Take latter (S) here along moss-draped hy. (Jericho Rd.) to J. with side Rd., 2.5$^{m}$. (L) here 1$^{m}$ is **The Retreat,** pre-Rev. home of Frenchman, murdered by slaves. Head of 1 murderer was placed on pole & remained for 2 generations. Locality now known as Nigger Head. Return to St.280 & cont. (S) over causeway to **Parris I.,** 5.5$^{m}$ & **U.S. Marine Training Sta.** (O). At 8$^{m}$ on St.280 is J. with side Rd. (R) here 2$^{m}$ to **Charlesfort Mon.** Excavations (1917) revealed foundations thought by some to be those of Charlesfort erected by Fr. (1562), by others, Ft. San Marcos (Sp.1577). Island was explored by Sp. as early as 1520's & missionaries followed explorers. In 1562 Fr. navigator, Jean Ribaut, settled group of Huguenots here & erected fortification honoring Charles IX. Ribaut then returned to France for more colonists. Orig. settlers mutinied, killed their leader & set off for France in leaky boat with little food. They drew lots, ate 1 of their party, called La Chere, & were finally rescued by an Eng. vessel. Later, Sp. came back & est. post on island.

(B) From Beaufort (E) 2$^{m}$ on St.285 to J. with side Rd. (R) here 2$^{m}$ to **Beaufort Beach** (swim.pic.). At 7$^{m}$ on St.285 is **Frogmore** on St. Helena I., largest of cty.'s 65 Is. & home of the Gullahs (see above). At 14.5$^{m}$ is J. with side Rd. at sm. schoolh.

Take latter (L) to ferry (free) over Harbor R. & Johnson Cr. to **Hunting I. St. Pk.** (c.5,000 as.surf bath.pic.) with beach & a wildlife sanctuary. Separate areas are being developed for Whites & Negroes. **Coffin Pt. Egg Bank** (reached by water only, boats & guides avail.) is nesting place for thousands of sea birds.

At 19.5m is **Frogmore H.** (O.appl.) on plantation once property of Wm. J. Grayson, who wrote "The Hireling & the Slave," 1855. At 20.5m is **Fripp H.** (O.appl.Georg.int.exter. inter.). 25.5m **Ft. Fremont** (O) at Lands End, built in Sp.-Amer. War & now abandoned, though there are plans to convert it into mus. At 31.5m **Ruins of Old White Ch.,** pre-Rev. Chapel of Ease to Beaufort's St. Helena's Episc. Ch., of tabby construction, burned in for. fire. 32.5m **Penn Normal, Industrial & Agric. Sch.** (Negro.coed.1862) where "spiritual" singing (O) is conducted on Wed. afts. & 3rd Suns. At 33m hy. completes circle to Frogmore (see above). Other ante bellum houses incl.: **Coffins Pt. H.** (1809) & **Pope H.**

(C) From Beaufort (S) 1.5m on St.281, **Mather Sch.** (Negro.girls.industrial.1868). 2m is J. with side Rd. (L) here 0.5m to **Site of Stuart Town,** destroyed by Sp. 1686 & **Site of Ft. Lyttleton** erected by Eng., 1758. At 3.5m on St.281 is **Port Royal.** Near-by (L) is **Naval Hospital** (1949). On grounds are ruins of old **Ft. Frederick** (1731 by Eng.), said to have been largest tabby fort in U.S. Only foundations remain. Port Royal harbor here is deepest natural harbor (S) of Norfolk. Eng. under Wm. Sayle considered this location (1670) but then moved on to found Charleston (see).

# US 29—SOUTH CAROLINA

**S.C.-N.C. LINE** (9m from Kings Mt., N.C.) **(SW) to S.C.-GA. LINE** (19m from Royston, Ga.). **113. US29**

Via: Gaffney, Spartanburg, Lyman, Greenville, Williamston, Anderson. RR. parallels route bet. N.C. Line & Williamston. Accoms.: All kinds in cities.

US29 cuts across NW. tip of S.C. through a succession of mill towns & through 3 large textile mfg. centers: Spartanburg, Greenville & Anderson.

**5.5. BLACKSBURG,** once Stark's trading post, began to prosper with arrival of RR. (1886). Near-by fields have yielded Cherokee artifacts. At Blacksburg is J. with St.5.

SIDE TRIP: Take latter (S) 9m to **Smyrna.** In vic. both gold & tin have at 1 time been mined.

**14. GAFFNEY,** with 10 textile mills, 6 chenille plants & a glove factory, is market for surrounding farm area. Settlement dates from early 1800's & by 1830's town had been promoted into popular resort for wealthy planters who came to cure malaria at Limestone Springs. Several ante bellum residences are near old spring properties. **Limestone College** (Bapt.1845), oldest college for women in S.C., founded by Dr. Thos. Curtis & son, both of Oxford Univ., who took over former Limestone Hotel (built 1836), which remains as dormitory (remod.). On Pub. Lib. grounds, **Mon.** on grave of Col. Jas. Williams who died at Kings Mt. At Gaffney is J. with St.11.

SIDE TRIPS: (A) Take latter (N) 12m to J. with US221 & **Cowpens Nat. Battlefield Site.** Here Jan. 17, 1781, Dan. Morgan with a force of backwoodsmen & regulars, sent by Greene after Battle of Kings Mt. (see) to attack Brit. outposts, was met by Col. Tarleton sent by Cornwallis with a slightly larger force of c.1,000. Brit. loss: 100 killed, 229 wounded, 600 prisoners not wounded. Amer. loss: 12 killed, 60 wounded.

(B) From Gaffney (S) c.2m on St.11. In vic. of **Dogwood Spring** here, it is said, Col. Wm. Washington, in combat, sliced off Tarleton's fingers with his sword & was saved from a 2nd Brit. officer's attack by Negro slave. 19m **Jonesville,** mill town dating back to pre-Rev. blockh. **Wayside Inn** (early 1800's.adds.) built by Jas. Cooper. Near-by is **Mon.** to Prof. T. S. C. Lowe for whom Mt. Lowe Observatory in Los Angeles is named. In Ap. 1861 he landed in vic. in sand ballast balloon, having made trip from Cincinnati to conduct air current experiments. He was almost lynched by natives who thought him a Yankee spy but was rescued by a fellow Mason.

**20.** On US29, **THICKETTY,** so-named because of thick growth of shrubs & trees. On Thicketty Mt. (R) are abandoned iron mines. **25. COWPENS,** so-called because of pens maintained here for cattle owners driving herds to market in the Low Country. **27. CLIFTON,** textile mill town.

**35. SPARTANBURG**

Through RR., bus & plane conns. Accoms.: All kinds. Spartanburg Music Festival, usually in Ap.; Mid-Dixie Tennis Tournaments, July.

Spartanburg has 42 textile plants & claims to be "largest producer of cotton fabrics in world." There are usual supplies & service institutions—cotton brokers, machinery sales & maintenance companies—& town is also center of St.'s peach production. White pop. is primarily of Scotch-Irish descent, some of whose ancestors settled in reg. as early as 1761. Town & cty. take their name from the "Spartan Regiment" that fought throughout Rev. The 1st Cth. was erected 1787 on present Morgan Sq. & town was inc. 1831. An early industry was iron mfg. During Civil War, Spartanburg became a sort of supply station for clothes, food & arms for Confeds., & it suffered less during reconstruction than many S. towns. It was also a boom town in World War I when Camp Wadsworth, one of largest training camps of time was est. In World War II, Camp Croft, an Infantry Replacement Training Center, was located here.

PTS. OF INT.: (1) **Textile Mills.** Guided tours may be arranged in a number of mills by making appointments ahead of time. (2) Center of town, **Morgan Sq.,** has Statue of Gen. Dan. Morgan, hero of Battle of Cowpens (see above). (3) 429-509 N. Church St., **Wofford College,** for men (Meth.Episc.) had its origin when Rev. Benj. Wofford, Spartanburg's Meth. minister, willed $100,000 for founding of a college (1850). In **Main Bldg.** (1854), 1st classes were held. (4) E. Main & St. John Sts., **Converse College** (women.1890) has 45-a. campus that includes a golf course & a "Forest of Arden." Concert & lecture series & annual music festival (Ap.) are open to public. (5) Parks incl.: N. sec. of town, **Cleveland Pk.** (boat.swim.tennis.zoo); SW. sec., **Duncan Pk.;** (W) of town proper, **Wadsworth Pk.** on site of Camp Wadsworth; (S) of town 4$^{m}$, **Little Pk.** (pic.swim.ball.etc.) on Camp Croft site. (6) Magnolia St. near Union Sta., **Magnolia Cemetery,** grave of "Singing Billy" Walker who taught "shape note" singing throughout SE. & published the well-known "Southern Harmony" (1835). Inscription reads: "In Memory of William Walker, A. S. H. (author "Southern Hamony"). Died Sept. 24, 1875, in the 67th year of his age. He was a devoted Husband & kind Father. A consistent Baptist 47 yrs. Taught music 45 yrs. The author of 4 Books of sacred music. He rests from his labors. He died in the triumphs of faith. Sing praises unto the Lord." At Spartanburg are Js. with US176 & US221.

SIDE TRIPS: (A) On US176 (SE) 4.5$^{m}$ is **Foster's Tavern** (1812.add.1845), once stagecoach stop, with family cemetery. 11.5$^{m}$ **Glenn Springs,** sett. before 1765 & popular because of its medicinal waters as health resort from 1840's to c.1900. 17$^{m}$ **West Springs.** In vic. are abandoned gold mines.

(B) From Spartanburg (S) c.8$^{m}$ on US221 is (R) **Fredonia,** on land granted to Moore family in 1763. Present frame house contains parts of orig. log cabin.

Main tour cont. on US29 (SW) of Spartanburg. Hy. bet. here & Greenville is, possibly, busiest in S.C. **46. LYMAN,** a mill town. **46.5.** J. with Wood Ft. Rd.

SIDE TRIP: Take latter (R) 3$^{m}$ then (L) 0.5$^{m}$ to **Hampton Massacre Site** where Anthony Hampton (who tried to persuade Cherokee to aid Amers.), his wife, son, & grandson were killed by Cherokee Inds. urged on by a Brit. agent. Near-by is **Hampton Spring** (swim.pic.).

## 65. GREENVILLE

Through RR., bus, & plane conns. Accoms.: All kinds.

Bisected by Reedy R., broken up by 15 pks. (4 for Negroes), & with the Blue Ridge Mts. in the background, Greenville belies, at 1st glance, its essential character as an industrial center. There are 38 textile mills (incl.silk & worsted—the latter one of the few in the South) bleaching, printing, & dyeing plants, & factories mfg. textile machinery & peanut, tobacco, & wood products. The Southern Textile Exposition is held here every other year, usually early in Oct. Among 1st settlers in vic. was an Irishman named Rich. Pearis who married a Cherokee, acquired a large land grant from her tribe, juggled offers from both Amers. & Brit. during Rev., finally sided with Brit. &, after Rev. retired to the Bahamas. Lemuel Alston, brother-in-law of Theodosia Burr, laid out Pleasantburg, on part of Pearis' former plantation, in 1797, & town became Greenville, 1831. Cotton & iron mills, with power supplied by Reedy R. falls, were soon flourishing, & the RR. arrived in 1853. During Civil War town was supply & hospitalization center for Confeds. & near-by mountains a hideout for deserters.

PTS. OF INT.: (1) University Ridge on Main St., **Furman Univ.** (Bapt.coed.), founded 1825 at Edgefield, moved to vicinity of Sumter then (1836) to Winnsboro, & finally (1851) to Greenville. Furman Hall (oldest bldg.1854). Hall of Science houses Furman Mus. Arboretum adjoins campus. Artist & lecture series open to pub. (2) McBee Ave. & Richardson St., **First Bapt. Ch.** (1858). (3) 322 W. Washington St., **Textile Hall,** accommodates S. Textile Exposition, etc. (4) N. Church & E.

Coffee Sts., **Christ Episc. Ch.** (1852.Vict.Goth.). (5) College St., **Greenville Woman's College** (Bapt.1821) is now associated with Furman Univ. & its juniors & seniors are admitted to Furman classes. Bldgs. are in Georg. Col. manner; earliest (1851), now housing Mary C. Furman Lib., was once used by a boy's academy & later as hospital by Confeds. (6) College & Laurens Sts., **Pub. Lib.** has special coll. on textile industry. (7) N. Main St. & E. Park Ave., **McPherson Pk.** (recr.facils.zoo). (8) On N. limits of town, **Bob Jones Univ.** (coed.interdenominational), formerly of Tenn., occupies campus of modern bldgs. completed for 1947-48 term. It was founded by evangelist Bob Jones who insists on fundamentalist interpretation of scriptures. Of special interest are Rodeheaver Auditorium where many of Shakespeare's plays are offered by Univ. Classic Players & Bowen Biblical Mus. (O) which contains items from Holy Land. (9) **Shriners' Hospital for Crippled Children,** one of most modern of kind. At Greenville are Js. with US25, US123, & US276.

SIDE TRIPS: (A) From Greenville (N) 5m on US276 (which combines with US25 for 9m) to **Paris Mt. St. Pk.** (hqs.Greenville.1,275 as.pic.swim.boat.f.camp.trls.group camps) in a rugged thickly forested area that incls. Paris Mt. (2,054′), off hy. (R) c.3m, & 1 large & 2 smaller lakes. 9m **Travelers Rest,** once stagecoach stop on hy. that leads uphill into the "Blue Ridge." Here is N. J. with US25. Cont. on US276. At 25m is J. with St.183.

Take latter (S) a short distance to **Table Rock St. Pk.** (hqs.Pickens.2,860 as.pic.swim. boat.f.cabins.camp.trls.), heavily forested mt. area with lake, beach, streams, waterfalls & 3 enormous granite mounds: Table Rock (3,124′), Pinnacle Mt. (3,436′) & The Stool.

At 32m on US76 is **Caesar's Head,** resort since before Civil War. Caesar's Head Mt. (3,227′), with vertical cliffs of gneiss & granite outcroppings, overlooks Saluda R. Valley (called "The Dismal" here) with a sheer drop of 1,200′ from "head" to R. At 34.5m is N.C. Line.

(B) From Greenville (W) 18m on US123 to J. with US178. On US178 (N) 7m to **Pickens,** named for Gen. Andrew Pickens, partisan leader during Rev. & congressman (1793-95).

**76. PIEDMONT** has Mus. est. by mill (Ind.relics.coins).

**99. ANDERSON**

Through RR., plane & bus conns. Accoms.: All kinds.

Anderson has 26 textile mills & a wide variety of other industries in vic. It dates to 1826 when both cty. & cty. center were organized & named for Gen. Rbt. Anderson, partisan leader in S.C. & Ga. during Rev. War, who was a capt. of co. that fought at Ninety-Six (see). During Civil War ammunition was manufactured here.

PTS. OF INT.: (1) Main & Whitner Sts., **County Cth.** in front of which stands cannon used by Brit. & Amers. during Rev. War. (2) 765 E. Whitner St., **Arlington** (1859), once home of St. Gov. J. L. Orr, later (1872) minister to Russia. (3) Church St., **First Bapt. Ch.** (1853.remod.Romanes.). (4) (E) of White St. near Cemetery Rd., **Silverbrook Cemetery** was a pic. ground on which pic. was being held when Fed. raiders descended. (5) Boulevard & 4th St., **Anderson Jr. College** (Bapt.coed.) dates back to Johnson Female Seminary, 1848. It now accepts local boys as day students. At Anderson are Js. with US76 (see), US178 (see), St.80, 28, 81 & 24.

SIDE TRIPS: (A) From Anderson (S) 9m on St.81 to **Starr,** (S) of which hy. becomes St.82, on which cont., in general paralleling Savannah R. through series of sm. villages dating from 19th cent. boom in river traffic. 22m **Lowndesville,** inc. 1839, has several distinguished old Hs. 32m **Calhoun Falls.** 40m on St.82 is **Mt. Carmel** & J. with side Rd.

Take latter (L) 6m to **Calhoun Burial Ground** with mon. to parents erected by J. C. Calhoun.

47m J. with St.821.

(R) 2m here to **Bordeaux,** settled by Fr. Huguenots in 1764 who hoped to establish wine & silk industries. Granite cross near-by marks their ch. site.

48.5m, here (R) is **John de la Howe St. School,** oldest manual training foundation in Amer., founded by Dr. John de la Howe in 1797 & now St. controlled. School has operated almost continuously since foundation. On grounds are grave of Dr. & his faithful housekeeper, Miss Rebecca Woodin, surrounded by 8′ brick wall as requested in Dr.'s will.

(B) From Anderson (S) on St.28. At 17m **Antreville.** Hy. here passes through red clay hills. This reg., sett. by Protestant pioneers before Rev., produced such distinguished citizens as Calhoun, Jas. Petigru, Langdon Cheves, & Geo. McDuffie, men who made S.C. of great political importance in 1st half of 19th cent. 29m **Abbeville,** so-named by Fr. Huguenots who once attempted to establish vineyards & a winery here, has been called "the cradle & the grave of the Confederacy." Here, on Secession Hill, it is claimed, was held meeting (Nov.22,1860) that started Secession (disputed,however) & here, on Main & Greenville Sts., in **Burt H.,** Jeff. Davis held last Confed. cabinet meeting (May 2,1865). **Trinity Ch.** (Episc.Eng.Goth.); old cemetery in rear. 50m J. with St.10.

(L) $5^m$ on St.10 is **Troy** in vic. of which Negroes, probably because of some lack in their diet, are fond of eating a local clay.

(C) From Anderson (NW) $14^m$ on US76 is **Pendleton** (1790), once famous among Low Country planters for its skilled carriage makers & home of one of S.C.'s earliest newspapers: "Miller's Weekly Messenger" (c.1807), founded by John Miller who previously, in London, had been involved with publication of famous "Letters of Junius." Town Sq., **Pendleton Farmers' Soc. Hall** (1826), still housing a soc. org. 1815. Queen's St., **St. Paul's Ch.** (Episc.1822). In adj. graveyard are graves of Gen. B. E. Bee who 1st called Jackson "Stonewall," & Mrs. John C. Calhoun. Just beyond Pendleton off US76 (L) is **Old Stone Ch.** (Presb.1802).

$17^m$ **Clemson,** home of **Clemson Agric. College,** St. institution for men, which had its origin 1889, when Thos. G. Clemson left bulk of his estate for founding a technical college, & formally opened 1893. Grounds incl. c.1500 as. on Ft. Hill, homestead of John C. Calhoun incl. campus proper (200 as.), farm, & experimental sta. (there are 5 substas. in other parts of S.C.). **Mus.** in Lib. Bldg. contains paintings, Ind. & World War I & II relics & natural history specimens. Miniature ft., behind Adm. Bldg., marks **Site of Ft. Rutledge,** est. 1776 by Gen. Andrew Williamson to protect settlers from Cherokee who had been incited against them by Brit. **Ft. Hill** (O.1803.int.exter.& inter.add.), 2-story frame house with 2 porticos, was residence (1825-50) of John C. Calhoun, Secy. of War (1817), twice Vice-Pres. (1824,1828), & Secy. of State (1844) of U.S. H. contains some of orig. furniture & some reproductions incl. sideboard made of mahogany from the frigate "Constitution," presented to Henry Clay & in turn given by him to Calhoun. Trees on grounds incl. 1 presented by Stephen Decatur, 1 by Webster, & 1 by Clay.

**113.** US29 crosses **GA. LINE.**

## US 178, US 78, US 52—SOUTH CAROLINA

### N.C.-S.C. LINE ($6^m$ from Rosman, N.C.) (SE) to CHARLESTON, S.C. 269. US178, US78 & US52

Via: Pickens, Anderson, Greenwood, Saluda, Orangeburg, J. with US78, J. with US52. RR. parallels route bet. Anderson & Greenwood. Accoms.: All kinds.

US178 runs (SE) from mountainous regs. near N.C. through heart of industrial (primarily textile) reg. of Anderson & Greenwood on into an agric. sec. & J. with US78 which cont. through the Low Country to Charleston.

### Sec. 1: N.C. LINE to GREENWOOD. 93.

**4. ROCKY BOTTOM.** (L) here short distance to path to lookout tower on **Sassafras Mt.** (3,548′), highest in S.C. Sassafras tree is aromatic member of laurel family with brilliantly colored leaves & berries in fall. Tea made from bark & twigs has long been celebrated as a home "spring tonic." **10.** J. with St.288. (L) here to **Table Rock St. Pk.** (see US29). **20. PICKENS** (see US29). **50. ANDERSON** (see US29). Bet. Anderson & **HONEA PATH, 69.** US178 unites with US76 (see). **75. DONALDS.** J. with St.20.

SIDE TRIP: At $4^m$ (R) on St.20 is **Due West,** home of **Erskine College** (coed.Presb.1839). Due West has been known as the "Holy City" because of its strict observance of the Sabbath. In vic. on May 20, 1777 Cherokee signed over much S.C. land to whites following Gen. Pickens' attacks.

Just beyond Donalds (R) off main hy. is a **Wayside Pk. At 85.,** just beyond **HODGES** is J. with US25 which unites with US178 to Greenwood.

### 93. GREENWOOD

Through RR. & bus conns. Airport. Good accoms. Two golf courses (1 mun.). Usual sports facils.

Served by 5 RRs., 4 U.S. hys. & 12 St. hys., Greenwood lies in hilly reg. (S) of Saluda R. & is trading center for area producing cattle, dairy products, small grains, peaches & cotton. RR. tracks extend through heart of bus. district. Station is in center of main sq. near mons. to Confed. & World War dead. Greenwood boasts 11 major classifications of industry but particularly of the complete cycle of textile manufacture from "boll to bolt" & then to finished garment. Greenwood Mills have worked on a 3-shift basis since end of World War I & in 1948 were operating "the largest single unit manufacturing spun rayon cloth mill in the world." One of more unusual industries is a bell carillon foundry, a branch of the Dutch foundry that produced the Callie Self Carillon (see below). Greenwood had its beginnings in late 1820's when the plantation of Judge John McGehee was divided into lots. RR.

from Columbia reached town in 1852 & 20 yrs. later citizens, with the aid of convict labor, completed a line to Augusta, Ga. During Civil War Greenwood was supply center for Confeds. Cty.-owned Buzzard Roost Hydroelectric Power Plant (see below) built by PWA has been an outstanding development.

PTS. OF INT.: (1) Stanley & Durst Ave., **Lander College** (women.Meth.) was founded 1873 in Williamston & moved here 1904. Domestic science & commercial courses are offered beside usual degrees. (2) Maxwell Ave., W. edge of town, **Connie Maxwell Orphanage** (Bapt.1880) uses cottage system & is a village in itself. (3) S. Greenwood St., **Callie Self Mem. Ch.** (Bapt.Mod.brick with white trim) has carillon of 37 bells in scale of 30 octaves. Bells were part of Netherlands exhibit at N.Y. World's Fair. (4) Univ. & E. Cambridge Sts., **Brewer Normal Inst.** (Negro). (5) Spring St., **Park Seed Co.** has water lily ponds at their best in summer. (6) At foot of S. Main St., **Matthew Mill Village,** an int. residential development for mill workers. Cottages with tile baths, tile roofs, hardwood floors, garages, etc., on landscaped grounds rent for 50¢ per room per wk. (7) The various textile **Mills** are not normally open, but guided tours may be arranged on appl. At Greenwood is J. with St.22.

SIDE TRIP: Take latter (E) 9m to **Ninety Six** which moved to present site to meet RR. in 1855. Here is J. with side Rd.

(R) 2m here to **Site of Old Ninety Six,** a trading post est. c.1730. First Rev. bloodshed in S.C. occurred here Nov. 1775 when Amers. under Col. Andrew Williamson defeated Brit. under Col. Robinson. Cambridge Academy was chartered here 1785. Beginning May 12, 1781, Gen. Nathanael Greene, aided by Thaddeus Kosciusko, conducted unsuccessful siege of near-by Star Ft. held by Brit. Amers.' attempt to tunnel under ft. was discontinued with arrival of Brit. reinforcements. Through this area the legendary Emily Geiger is said to have carried a message from Greene to Gen. Sumter when no man could get through Tory lines.

At 11m on St.22 is **Greenwood St. Pk.** (1,114 as.pic.boat.f.camp.refreshments.trls.;Negro areas) on irregular shores of a 20m-long, 12,000-a. L. created by **Buzzard Roost Hydroelectric Project** on Saluda R. Dam is 2,400′ long, 82′ high & has installed capacity of 20,000 horsepower.

### Sec. 2: GREENWOOD to ORANGEBURG. 99.

**29. SALUDA,** cty. seat. In vic. are several ante bellum homes incl.: 2m (SW) of town, **Old Bonham H.;** Coleman Crossroads, **Coleman H.;** & **Mathews H.** near Mt. Willing. At Saluda is J. with St.43.

SIDE TRIP: On St.43 (W) 4.5m is J. with side Rd. (L) here 0.5m near **Lockhart Ch.** (Negro) is **Faith Cabin Lib.,** one of 21 libs. est. by white mill worker, Willie Lee Buffington, out of gratitude to his Negro teacher, Eury W. Simpkins.

**45. BATESBURY.** J. with US1 (see). **99. ORANGEBURG.** J. with US21 (see).

### Sec. 3: ORANGEBURG to CHARLESTON. 77.

**15. BOWMAN** in a pecan growing area. **39.** J. with US78. Main route now cont. (SE) on US78 to J. with US52 at **61.** US78 & US52 then unite to **Charleston, 77.** (see).

# CHARLESTON

## CHARLESTON

Atlantic Coast Line, Seaboard Air Line & Southern RRs. Through bus conns. Mun. Airport for Delta, Eastern & National Airlines. Seaplane base. S.S. lines to c.40 foreign, coastwise, & intercoastal ports. Accoms.: All kinds. Info.: C. of C. & A.A.A. Swim: Folly Beach, Sullivan's I. & I. of Palms. Golf: Mun. Course, Charleston Country Club (by card), Yeaman's Hall Course (by invitation). Overnight "Wildlife Tours" to Bull's I. near-by, part of Cape Romain Nat. Wildlife Refuge, during winter; write Nat. Audubon Society, 1000 5th Ave., N.Y. Hist. Houses Tour: Mar.-Ap.; write Hist. Charleston Foundation, 135 Church St., Charleston. Gardens at best Dec.-Mar. (especially japonicas) & Mar.-May (especially azaleas). Azalea Festival mid-Ap. Regattas by Charleston Yacht Club & Carolina Yacht Club.

In order "to avoid a too numerous democracy," the Lords Proprietors, who received a great land grant in this reg. from Charles II, had a charter drawn up for their 1st settlement by the later famous philosopher, John Locke (at the time, secy. to Lord Ashley Cooper). It provided for 3 orders of nobility: barons, caciques & landgraves. Even today an avoidance of a too numerous democracy is to be found among Charlestonians. Among some groups indeed, only those whose ancestors were here before 1720 (when the settlement ceased to be controlled by the Lords Proprietors & became a royal province) can be considered proper Charlestonians. Those who came bet. 1720 & the Rev. are new Charlestonians, those before 1865, green Charlestonians & all those thereafter merely visitors. The late Alex. Woollcott, commenting on this clannishness, said that at the end of the garden season in Charleston the tourists depart, leaving the natives "with no one to despise but themselves." Yet Charlestonians can be the most gracious of people (even their servants, as one Negro butler remarked, are "all broke out with behavior") & Charleston as much as any city in the U.S. retains the cardinal quality of grace.

Charleston is S.C.'s largest &, since the beginning, most important city. It is also the official St. port, situated on a narrow peninsula with an excellent landlocked harbor, "an untarnished jewel shining regally at that sacred spot where the Ashley & the Cooper join their majestic waters to form the Atlantic Ocean." It is one of Amer.'s most hist. & architecturally int. cities. The oldest & most fashionable sec. is that (S) of Broad St. especially in vic. of the Battery. Here twisting sts. & narrow alleyways retain their 18th cent. charm. Bldgs. are mostly Eng. Georg. of brick or stuccoed brick but showing Fr., West Ind. & Dutch influences. An unusual development is the Charleston "single" house which presents its side to the street, its front, lined with from 1 to 3 piazzas, to a brick-walled garden entered by elaborate wrought-iron gates. The gardens of Charleston & the outlying plantations have been world famous for more than a century & offer an unbelievable succession of wistaria, japonicas, azaleas, freesias, magnolias, banksia roses, crape myrtles, & oleanders. Charleston was the home of Dr. Alexander Garden (for whom the gardenia was named) & Joel R. Poinsett, Minister to Mexico (1825-29), who introduced the poinsettia to this country.

First settlement was made by Eng. under Wm. Sayle, 1670, at Albemarle Pt. & moved across Ashley R. to present location, 1680. Other groups of pioneers soon joined the colony—Scotch, Irish, Fr. Huguenots, Palatinate Germans, Fr. Acadians. Despite attack by combined fleet of Sp. & Fr., 1706, & usual troubles with Inds. & Lords Proprietors, settlement continued to prosper on an economy based successively on Ind. trade, naval stores, indigo, rice & cotton. Pirates preyed on this prosperity &, in 1718, 49 were executed in a single month (22 in one day). Charleston had the 1st public lib. in country, 1698, a free sch. in 1710, a theater in 1735. In 1740, Eliza Pinckney was teaching "a parcel of little Negroes to read," an act that was to become a felony 100 yrs. later. By 1775 Charleston was one of most important seaports in colonies & Crèvecœur found it to exhibit "a display of riches & luxury far superior to what are to be seen in our northern towns . . . its inhabitants . . . are the gayest in America." On his way to dinner at one plantation, however, he saw a slave, suspended in a cage in a tree, being picked to death by vultures.

Charleston withstood Brit. attacks of 1776 & 1779, but in 1780 was captured by Sir Henry Clinton from the landside & held for 2½ yrs. After Rev., prosperity again returned & 1st cotton shipped from an Amer. port went to England from here, 1784. In 1822 a Negro insurrection led by Denmark Vesey, a free West Indian mulatto, ended with 34 of the insurrectionists condemned to death & 44 to transportation. At Charleston was signed 1st Ordinance of Secession (Dec. 20, 1860); 1st hostile shot of Civil War was fired on Ft. Sumter & 1st submarine used effectively was Confed. "Hundley" which blew up USS "Housatonic." In spite of repeated attacks Confeds. did not evacuate until Feb. 17, 1865, burning pub. bldgs. & cotton & other supplies as they left. Charleston never recovered its pre-war importance. The earthquake of 1886 damaged 90 per cent of bldgs. many of them since strengthened with iron tie rods.

World War II brought Charleston the usual boom. In 1948 Charleston Cty. had some 229 ind. & mfg. concerns, incl. U.S. Naval Base & Naval Shipyard, which can be classified as major industry of area. Among others of importance were power, paper, pulp, asbestos, creosoting, lumber, tobacco & fertilizer plants. Situated in a prolific trucking reg., with annual crop-growing period of 280 days, & with waters that provide shrimp, crabs, oysters, & many varieties of salt-water fish, Charleston is also distribution & canning center for garden truck & seafood. Principal imports incl. petroleum, gasoline, & fertilizer materials; exports incl. coal, petroleum products, phosphates, cotton, tobacco, & lumber.

PTS. OF INT.: (1) 350 Meeting St., **Joseph Manigault H.** (O.wks.during season; Mon., Wed., Sat., thereafter, sm.fee.1790's by Gabriel Manigault), excellent example of Adam influence. (2) 342-348 Meeting St., **Second Presb. Ch.** (1811), known as Flinn's Ch. after 1st pastor. (3) Calhoun bet. Meeting & King Sts., **Marion Sq.** Facing (S) on Sq. are bldgs. erected (1822) as arsenal & later used as home of **Citadel Academy** (see below). Also on Sq. are **Citadel Sq. Bapt. Ch.** (1856) & **St. Matthew's Luth Ch.** (1867-72). In Sq. is part of colonial defense system, a sec. of old **Horn Wall.** (4) 160 Calhoun St., **Charleston Orphan H.** (1790-94), said to be oldest mun. orphanage & 1 of 3 oldest of any sort in U.S., & **Chapel** (O.wks.Sun.services.1802.by Gabriel Manigault.remod.1855.late Georg.). (5) George & St. Philip Sts., **College of Charleston** (coed.), on land set aside by General Assembly, 1770. Chartered 1785 & officially opened 1790 as private institution, it was reorganized as 1st mun. college in America, 1837. **Main Bldg.** (1828 by Wm.Strickland.Gr.Rev.portico & wings 1850 by Edward B.White). **Porters Lodge** (1850.by White). **Lib.** (1855). (6) 24 George St., **Central Y.M.C.A.,** (1914), org. 1854 & "2nd oldest 'Y' in U.S." (7) Wentworth near Glebe St., **Grace Ch.** (Episc.1847). (8) 6 Glebe St., **Glebe H.** (c.1770). (9) 74 Hasell St., **Beth Elohim Synagogue** (1840.Gr.Rev.); 1st congregation org. 1750 (probably 3rd oldest in U.S.); 1st synagogue on site 1792. Here Reformed Judaism got its start in U.S., 1824. (10) Hasell St. (E) of Meeting St., **Col. Wm. Rhett's H.** (c.1712), considered oldest H. in town. (11) Hasell & Anson Sts., **St. Johannes Ch.** (Luth.c. 1810). (12) 79 Hasell St., **St. Mary's Ch.** (1838), mother Ch. of Cath. Dioceses of Carolinas & Ga., org. 1789.

(13) 240 King St., **Washington Light Infantry Armory,** org. 1807, has coll. of war relics. (14) 198 Meeting St., **Charleston Hotel** (1839). Thackeray was among early guests. (15) Market St. from Meeting St. to E. Bay, **City Market** est. at end of 18th cent. **Market Hall** (1841) is now Confed. Mus. (16) Magazine near Logan St., **Old Cty. Jail** (18th cent.). (17) 10-12 Archdale St., **St. John's Ch.** (Luth.1818. remod.). Wrought iron gates & fences are noteworthy. (18) 6-8 Archdale St., **Unitarian Ch.** (1722.remod.1852.with "fan-tracery Goth." inter.). Harvard Room honors Rev. Sam. Gilman, pastor (1819-57), who wrote "Fair Harvard." (19) 184 King St., **Charleston Lib. Soc.** (O.wks.), in Mod. bldg., dates from 1748 (3rd oldest in U.S.), & has notable coll. of pre-Rev. newspapers. (20) 135 Meeting St., **Gibbes Mem. Art Gallery** (O.wks.except Aug.free) has following permanent colls.: S.C. portraits & prints, general coll. by Sully, Hoppner, West, Henri, Kollwitz, etc., miniature coll., & Japanese Prints coll. There are also local & national shows. (21) 23 Cumberland St., **Old Powder Magazine** (O.Nov.1-June 1.wks.Sat. a.m.sm.fee.1703). Now hist. mus. & hqs. of Colonial Dames. (22) 138-150 Meeting St., **Circular Congregational Ch.** (1891.Romanes.) is 3rd Ch. on site. Int. churchyard. (23) 144-146 Church St., **St. Philip's Ch.** (Episc.1835-38.Doric porticos.int.inter.add.1920). Congregation dates from 1670. It is said 1st pastor, in his cups, once christened a bear. Chimes of tall octagonal steeple were made into cannon by Confeds. & never replaced. Church St. divides graveyard where lie Edward Rutledge, signer of Decl. of Ind., Vice Pres. Calhoun, & Col. Wm. Rhett, who captured pirate Blackbeard. Gateway Walk leads through cemetery & past gardens & hist. spots.

(24) 145 Church St., **Pirate H.** (c.1750), reminiscent of Fr. village architecture & possibly erected by Fr. Huguenots. Doubtful if ever was pirate hqs. (25) Church & Queen Sts., **Huguenot Ch.** (Fr.Prot.1845.Goth.). Congregation dates to 1680. Until recently said to be only Huguenot Ch. in Amer. adhering exactly to liturgy of Fr. Prot. Ch. Services now in Eng. (26) Church & Queen Sts., **Dock Street Theater & Planters Hotel** reconstructed 1937 by F.E.R.A. Orig. theater (1736) was 1st playh. in country especially constructed for purpose. **Planters' Hotel** (1810), claimed to have invented Planters' Punch. It is now foyer & green room for theater which reopened with revival of its 1st performance of 2 centuries before, Georges Farquhar's "The Recruiting Officer." (27) 105 Meeting St., **Hibernian Hall** (O.1841.Gr. Rev.) home of Hibernian Soc. founded 1801 (nonsectarian) by Irishmen. Hall is scene of St. Cecilia Society Balls, most exclusive social events in S.C. St. Cecilia Society orig. org. (1762) to promote amateur musicals. (28) 87 Meeting St., **County Cth.** (c.1800) on site of old St. H. which burned 1788. (29) 2-4 Courthouse Sq., **Daniel Blake Tenements** (1760-72). (30) Meeting & Chalmers St., **Records Bldg.** (1821-26.by Rbt.Mills), said to be 1st fireproof bldg. in U.S. Now home of S.C.

Hist. Soc. (31) Meeting & Broad, **City Hall** (1801) was orig. U.S. Bank. Council Chamber (O.wks.9-6.Sat.a.m.) contains portrait gallery incl. John Trumbull's "Washington," without false teeth & wig (1791), S. F. B. Morse's "James Monroe," Vanderlyn's "Andrew Jackson," etc. **City Hall Pk.** (Washington Sq.) contains mons. to William Pitt, Gen. Beauregard & Henry Timrod, the S.C. poet.

(32) 50 Broad St., **C. of C.,** org. 1773 & said to be oldest city C. of C. organization in U.S. Bldg. dates from 1784 & was once Bank of S.C. (33) E. Bay & Broad Sts., **Old Exchange** (O.daily.sm.fee.1767-71.Georg.alts.) now houses D.A.R. Mus. incl. orig. Gilbert Stuart "Washington." In Court of Guards that formerly stood here, pirate Stede Bonnet was imprisoned (1718). In Exchange Bldg., Provincial Congress set up "1st independent govt. in America" (1774); 61 Amers. were imprisoned here by Brit., & here George Washington witnessed parade in his honor (1791). It was damaged during Civil War by Fed. fire & has since suffered many alts. (34) 78 Meeting St., **St. Michael's Ch.** (Episc.1752) designed in manner of St. Martin's-in-the-Fields, London, has a Doric portico with an octagonal clock tower rising 182′ from street. Chimes (1764) have crossed Atlantic 5 times & were wired for electricity 1946. Washington, Lafayette & Lee worshipped here. Graveyard incl. graves of Mary Layton, marked with a cypress bedstead, Rbt. Y. Hayne, & Jas. Louis Petigru, S.C. Unionist. (35) 88 Broad St., **Old Jewish Orphanage,** no longer used as such, est. by Hebrew Orphan Soc., founded 1801. (36) Meeting & Broad Sts., **County Cth.** (c.1800) on site of St. H. which burned 1788. (37) 138 King St., **Quaker Churchyard** (1694). (38) 125 King St., **"America's Oldest Drugstore"** (pre-1781). Much of orig. store equipment now at Charleston Mus. (39) 110 Broad St., **Izard H.** (before 1757), home of Ralph Izard, Rev. statesman who once had bitter controversy with Benj. Franklin in Paris. (40) 116 Broad St., **Rutledge H.** (c.1760.alts.) home of John Rutledge, gov. of S.C. & briefly (1795) Chief Justice of U.S.

(41) Broad & Legare Sts., **Cathedral of St. John the Baptist** (Cath.1888.neo-Goth.). (42) 72 Meeting St., **S.C. Society Hall** (O.1804.by Gabriel Manigault.adds.Gr.Rev.). Fr. Protestants founded society (1737) called the "Two Bit Club" because of amount assessed each member at gatherings. Bldg. served as charity school as well as meeting place. (43) 59 Meeting St., **Branford-Horry H.** (1751-67.typical brick "double house" of period.adds.). (44) 89-91 Church St., **Cabbage Row,** a group of conn. bldgs. surrounding a court, was original of Du Bose Heyward's "Catfish Row" in novel "Porgy" & operetta (by Gershwin) "Porgy & Bess." (45) 87 Church St., **Heyward-Washington H.** (O.daily.fee.3-story brick.Georg.1770.rest.) was home of Thos. Heyward, Jr., signer of Decl. of Ind., built for Dan. Heyward & inherited by son, whose wife twice defied Brit. orders to illuminate H. in celebration of Brit. victories. H. was turned over to Washington during latter's visit. Now furnished with mus. period pieces. (46) 78 E. Bay, **Vanderhorst Row** (c.1800.Georg.), built by Gov. Vanderhorst, said to be one of 1st apartment bldgs. in Amer. (47) 73 Church St., **Col. Miles Brewton H.** (c.1733), built by Col. for his daughter. (48) 71 Church St., **Col. Robert Brewton H.** (c.1733), early Charleston "single house." (49) 69 Church St., **Motte** or Smith H. (c.1745.alts.) was home of Jacob Motte, "Public Treasurer of Colony." (50) 61-65 Church St., **First Bapt. Ch.** (1820.by Rbt.Mills). Congregation dates from 1683. (51) 53 Meeting St., **First Scotch Presb. Ch.** (1814) has twin towers topped by copper cupolas. Congregation dates from 1731.

(52) 51 Meeting St., **Nathaniel Russell H.** (c.1811.inter.in Adam manner). (53) 32 Legare St., **Simonton H.** (N.wing c.1776. S.wing 1850-80) has noted wrought-iron entrance called the "Sword Gates" (1815-20). (54) 14 Legare St., **Smythe H.** (c.1770's); gates (1821), combine cypress & iron scrolls with marble pineapples (symbol of welcome) topping posts. (55) 106 Tradd St., **Stuart H.** (c.1772.add. miniature of 2nd fl. drawing room in Charleston Mus.). Gen. Francis Marion, it is said, jumped from a window here to get away from a wild drinking party. (56) 27 King St., **Pringle H.** (O.wks.fee.c.1769), built by Miles Brewton, good example of Charleston-Georg. double houses. Served as hqs. for Brit. (Cornwallis, Lord Rawdon), 1781-82 & for Feds., 1865. Int. furnishings, garden, carriage house. (57) 35 Meeting St., **Wm. Bull H.** (c.1760), once home of 1st Lt. Gov. of province. (58) 34 Meeting St., **Dan Elliot Huger H.** (c.1760.add.), home of Lord Campbell, last of Eng. governors. He escaped in H.M.S. "Tamar," 1775. (59) 7 Meeting St., **Josiah Smith H.** (c.1800.Gr.Rev.add.) (60) Battery Point, **Battery Pk.,** also known as White Pt. Gardens, at confluence of Ashley & Cooper Rs. has cannon & other relics of all Amer. wars & Ft. Moultrie & Ft. Sumter Mons. (61) 15 Meeting St., **John Edwards**

**H.** (c.1770), hqs. of Brit. Adm. Arbuthnot during Rev. (62) 64 S. Battery, **Gibbes H.** (c.1789.remod.1794 in Adam style.notable garden). (63) 68 S. Battery, **Middleton H.** (pre-1776) was home of Henry Augustus Middleton, pres. of Continental Congress (1774-75); wrought iron balcony, int. gardens. (64) 6 Gibbes St., **Manigault H.** (1820). (65) 4 Greenhill St., **Axson H.** (1805). (66) 172 Tradd St., **Alston H.** (1850-60.Gr. Rev.).

(67) 18 Bull St., **Wm. Blacklock H.** (c.1800), plantation type with out-buildings. (68) Calhoun & Pitt Sts., **Bethel M. E. Ch.** (1853) contains pulpit from which Wesley once preached. (69) Rutledge Ave. & Calhoun St., **Charleston Mus.** (O.wks.& Sun.aft. free), est. 1773 by Charles Town Lib. Soc., is "oldest city mus. in U.S." & is primarily concerned with arts, crafts, furniture & general culture of S.C. There are also art & natural history colls. (70) Lucas & Calhoun Sts., **Medical College of St. of S.C.** (coed.) had its origins in Med. College of S.C., 1st medical sch. in South, which opened its doors in 1824 & graduated its 1st class Ap. 1825. Present college was chartered 1832 & in 1840 est. hospital for express purpose of bedside teaching. Louis Agassiz taught here 1851-53. Among famous graduates was Dr. St. Julien Ravenel who invented Confed. torpedo boat, "Little David." (71) Moultrie & Cleveland Sts., **Hampton Pk.** incl. gardens, zoo & ballpk. (72) Murray Driveway, adj. Hampton Pk. on the Ashley R., **The Citadel,** the Military College of S.C. (1842. 200-a.campus with stuccoed bldgs.1922.Sp.-Moorish style), which had its origin when it was suggested that garrisons of 2 fortresses, Citadel in Charleston & Arsenal in Columbia, built in case of slave uprisings, be replaced by young men who, while serving as guards, would receive military training. Maj. P. F. Stevens, Supt., in command of Citadel cadets manning 24-pounders on Morris I. helped drive off steamer, "Star of the West," attempting relief of Ft. Sumter—thus firing what is claimed as 1st hostile shot of Civil War, Jan. 9, 1861 (disputed, see Ft. Johnson). (73) **Avery Institute** (Negro.coed.).

## TRIPS OUT OF CHARLESTON

**I. FT. SUMTER,** on artificial I. in Charleston Harbor (by boat only.regular trips from foot of King St.). Work begun 1827, but Ft. not completed when S.C. seceded & Feds. occupied it a few days later. When "Star of the West" tried to reach Sumter with provisions, Confeds. fired 1st shots of Civil War. After bombardment, Ap. 12-14, 1861 by Gen. Beauregard, Feds. evacuated. Confeds. held fort until Feb. 17, 1865.

**II. CASTLE PINCKNEY NAT. MON.,** on Schute's Folly I. in Charleston harbor (by boat only, no scheduled service), once a quarantine sta. for slaves & later land grant to a Quaker named Schute. Present Ft. erected 1810 to replace Rev. Ft. Confeds. surprised Union engineers who were fortifying it, 7 days after S.C.'s secession. It remained in Confed. hands until evacuation, Feb. 1865.

**III. US52 (N) to LEWISFIELD. 30.**

**4. FOUR MILE H.,** once stagecoach stop. At **6.5.** is J. with side Rd. (R) short distance is **U.S. Navy Yard** with The Marshlands (1810), now an officers' house. **17.** on US52, **GOOSE CREEK.**

SIDE TRIP: Take side Rd. here (R) 1.5m to **The Oaks** (O.fee.1897.Georg.) with old alley of oaks & int. sunken gardens. At 2m **Goose Creek Ch.** (1711-19), of stucco with the royal arms of Brit. still above chancel.

**23.** on US52, J. with St.520.

SIDE TRIP: Take latter (R) here 4m to **Cypress Gardens** (O.daily Thanksgiving-May.fee) notable for its plantings of azaleas & bulbs in a ghostly cypress swamp. Area once part of rice plantation of early 1700's. Boat trips through gardens avail.

**27.5.** On US52, J. with private Rd

SIDE TRIP: (R) here 1m to **Mulberry Castle** (O.in season.fee.1714.Jacobean), built by Gov. Thos. Broughton. It was fortified during Yemassee War & also used by Eng. cavalry. Formal gardens.

**29.** On US52, J. with side Rd. (R) here 1m to **Lewisfield** (1774) built by Keating Simmons & visited by Cornwallis.

**IV. US17 (NE) to MT. PLEASANT. 5.**

US17 crosses Cooper R. Bridge (toll) to **Mt. Pleasant 5.**, popular as summer resort for many yrs. S. edge of town, 1m from Ocean Hy., **Pierates Cruze Gardens** (O.9-6. fee). Camellias (100 varieties) bloom Jan.-Ap., azaleas & other flowers, mid.-Mar. to Mid.-Ap. Church & Hibben Sts., **Mt. Pleasant Presb. Ch.**, one of "Chapels of Ease," erected as convenience for planters who had to travel far & over bad roads to get to Parish Ch. Venning & Whilden Sts., **St. Andrew's Episc. Ch.** (1850's.). 111 Hibben St., **Hibben H.**, once hqs. for Gen. Moultrie. At Mt. Pleasant is J. with St.703.

SIDE TRIP: Take latter (R) to **Sullivan's I.**, 5m, beach resort since before Civil War. Center of I., **Ft. Moultrie** (1776.rebuilt), now free mus., was originally Ft. Sullivan but changed to honor 1st decisive victory of Rev., that of Maj. Gen. Wm. Moultrie over Sir Peter Parker, Brit. fleet commander (June 28, 1776, 6 days before signing of Decl. of Ind.). Ft. played prominent role in battle for Ft. Sumter. Osceola (see Fla.), Seminole Ind. chief, was imprisoned & buried (1838) here. Poe wrote "Israfel" here (1828) & used I. as background for "The Gold Bug." At 8m bridge conns. US703 with **Isle of Palms**, one of best ocean resorts in S.C. with 7m-long, 500′-wide beach.

### V. US17 & St.615 (SE) to FOLLY BEACH. 12.

Cross Ashley R. Bridge on US17 to J. at **3.** with St.615 (Folly Beach Rd.) on which cont. (L). At c.**5.** (L) is **McLeod H.**, used for wounded Confeds. & as Freedmen's Bureau. In neighborhood of Wappoo Creek, Elizabeth Lucas made 1st successful cultivation of indigo (1742) in S.C. **5.5.** J. with **Wappoo Hall Rd.**

SIDE TRIP: Take latter (R) 4m past mun. golf course (fee) to **Fenwick Hall** (1730.add. 1750). At 8m is **Angel Oak** (sm.fee) with circumference of 21′ & covering 14,560 sq. ft.

At **7.5.** on Folly Beach Rd. is J. with King's Hy.

SIDE TRIP: (L) here 5.5m to **Ft. Johnson**, oldest Charleston Harbor ft., built 1704 as protection against Fr., rebuilt 1759, taken by citizens, 1765, to seize tea stamps, again taken from Brit. Sept. 15, 1775 when Col. Moultrie raised blue & white S.C. flag, 1st "flag of liberty" raised in U.S. From Ft. Johnson, Confeds. fired "1st shot of Civil War" on Ft. Sumter (see Citadel above), Ap. 12, 1861.

At **12.** on Folly Beach Rd. (cross toll gate) is **FOLLY BEACH**, a 10-mile beach resort area (pier.bathh.amusements). At (E) end of I., ruins of an old Confed. Ft. may be seen.

**VI. St.700 (SW) to ROCKVILLE c.20.** where sailboat races are held in Jul. or Aug.

### VII. US17 (SW) to J. with St.174 at 22.

SIDE TRIP: Take St.174 (S) 27m to **Edisto I., Edisto Beach** & **Edisto St. Pk.** (1,255 as., 1.5m beach, surf bath.boat.pic.f.cabins). A rich bed of fossils here has yielded rare paleontological specimens, some of which are exhibited in temporary mus. Marine biological lab. is planned.

### VIII. St.61 (NW) to SUMMERVILLE. 26.5.

**12.5. MAGNOLIA GARDENS** (O.Jan.1-May 1.fee), on Ashley R. estate, property of Drayton family for more than 200 yrs. Gardens (25 as.) were begun c.1830 by Rev. John Grimké Drayton & contains magnolias, live oaks, cypress & other trees underplanted with possibly largest coll. of camellias in U.S., azaleas (incl. 1st plants of "Azalea Indica" imported in U.S., 1843), wistaria, roses. Of gardens John Galsworthy said: "Nothing so free & gracious, so lovely & wistful, nothing so richly colored yet so ghost-like exists, planted by the sons of men." **16. MIDDLETON GARDENS** (O.Dec.-May.fee), oldest landscaped gardens in U.S., begun 1741 by Henry Middleton, later Pres. of Continental Congress, who imported gardener & worked 100 slaves 10 yrs. on project. At Middleton, peace terms for departure of Brit. from Carolinas were arranged. Another Middleton, signer of Decl. of Ind., is buried here in family tomb. Present house is rest. right wing of orig. fired by Feds. Fr. botanist, André Michaux, planted here 1st camellia japonicas in U.S. Of 4 plants set out by him, more than 150 yrs. ago, 3 still thrive & bloom. **18. MATEEBA GARDENS** (O.Mar.1 to mid-Ap.fee.25 as.), part of old Ashley Barony, planted with azaleas, dogwood, etc. At **22.5.** is J. with St.65.

SIDE TRIP: Take latter (W) c.14m to **Givhans Ferry St. Pk.** (1,235 as.f.swim.pic.cabins).

At **23.** J. with side Rd. Short distance (R) here is **Old Ft. Dorchester** (O.free.c.1750). **Tower of Episc. Ch.** is all that remains of town of Dorchester.

**26.5. SUMMERVILLE**, winter resort (golf.f.h.horse racing meet in spring & fall) is famous for its flowers. **Mun. Azalea Garden** (28,000 azalea plants). **Pinehurst Gardens** started 1890 as experiment to grow tea commercially.

# US 76 & ST. 2—GEORGIA

**GA.-S.C. LINE** (18$^{m}$ from Westminster, S.C.) **(W) to GA.-TENN. LINE** (8$^{m}$ from Chattanooga, Tenn.). **153. US76 & ST.2.**

Via: Clayton, Hiawassee, Young Harris, Blairsville, Morganton, Blue Ridge, East Ellijay, Chatsworth, Dalton, Ringgold, Rossville. RR. & bus lines easily accessible from towns & resort centers. Numerous St. pks., resort & tourist areas. Nat. For. (see below) covers about three-fourths of N. Ga.

US76 crosses Chattooga R. into Chattahoochee Nat. For. (camp & pic.grounds. swim.boat.f.h.ranger stas. at Clayton, Woody Gap, Blue Ridge & LaFayette. hqs. in Gainesville), a prime recr. area with nearly 800$^{m}$ of for. Rds. & 170$^{m}$ more of trls. Blue Ridge & Cohutta ranges of the Appalachians roll across most of this narrow upper end of Ga. The Blue Ridge forms St.'s major watershed, & many swift Rs. rise here & descend in clear streams & waterfalls to the Piedmont Plateau. Appalachian Trl. (see) follows crest of ridge to Mt. Oglethorpe (see below). The extreme NW. corner lies within Appalachian Plateau, separated from rest of St. & until fairly recently, accessible only from Ala. & Tenn., via US11 (see end of tour), which cuts down steep-walled valley bet. Lookout & Sand (or Raccoon) Mts. Chickamauga & Chattanooga Nat. Military Pk. covers more than 5,500 as. near St. border, incl. c.3,000 as.in Tenn. (where Battle of Lookout Mt. was fought). Most common trees are the massive red oak, scrub pine, chestnut & hemlock; rhododendron, laurel, arbutus & other flowering shrubs & vines. Deer, bear & wildcats are scarce, but smaller animals & birds of many species are plentiful. Trout, bass & other fresh-water fish are found in mt. Ls. & Ls. formed in development of hydroelectric power. Before Calif. Gold Rush most of gold in U.S. came from Ga. (see Dahlonega below); coal, talc, marble & granite are also important. Back in the hills are the weathered, ramshackle homes of mountaineers, descendants of early settlers. Their Old English word forms & primitive customs are appealing, but isolation has also bred poverty, corruption & fanaticism. Today radio, chain stores & mass production are eliminating picturesque dilapidation along with misery & loneliness; paved hys. replace red-clay Rds.; & the Berry & other schs. are helping adults as well as children.

**10. CLAYTON,** resort center (good accoms.ranger sta.), was est. in 1823 on former Cherokee lands. Rabun Cty., of which it is seat, has pop. descended from New Englanders who came from Va. mts. Here & there are families with Cherokee ancestors. In vic. is Lillian Smith's **Laurel Falls Camp** (for girls); 1-week Institute for Labor Leaders each yr. (visitors). J. with US23 & Rd. to War Woman Dell.

SIDE TRIPS: (A) On US23 (N) 3$^{m}$ to **Mountain City. Black Rock Mt. St. Pk.** 7$^{m}$ **Rabun Gap.** Near-by is **Rabun-Gap-Nacoochee Sch.,** jr. agric. college, under Presb. Ch.; remarkable feature is farm-settlement sch. 8.5$^{m}$ J. with Rd. leading (E) 3$^{m}$ to **Estatoah Falls** & at 8.5$^{m}$ J. with Rd. to **Rabun Bald** (4,717′), 2nd highest peak in Ga.

(B) On US23 (S) 3$^{m}$ to **Tiger.** 8$^{m}$ **Lakemont,** supply centers for colony on **L. Rabun** (W). US23 follows Tallulah R. to **Tallulah Falls,** 13.5$^{m}$. Trl. to **Tallulah Gorge** (1,000′). **Tallulah Falls Sch.,** sponsored by Ga. Fed. of Women's Clubs (handicraft for sale). 14$^{m}$ **Tallulah Pt.** (2,000′); splendid view of gorge. J. with Rd. to **Tallulah Power Plant** (O. guides); inclined RR. along 600′ gorge. At 22$^{m}$, J. with St.17.

On St.17 (E) 11$^{m}$ to **Toccoa Falls** (recr.area & lookout). **Toccoa Falls Institute** (est. 1911), low-cost high sch.

27$^{m}$ **Clarksville,** in valley planted with orchards. 30$^{m}$ **Demorest. Piedmont College** (coed.), founded in 1897 by Rev. C. C. Spence (Meth.); now under Congr. Ch. 34$^{m}$ **Cornelia,** Ga.'s most important apple-packing center. **Big Red Apple Mon.** Apple Blossom Festival. 37$^{m}$ **Alto. Ga. Tuberculosis Sanitarium;** traveling clinic; most patients treated free.

**22.** J. with St.197, which runs (S) along shore of **L. Burton** (pic.cabins.swim.boat.f.), largest of 6 Ls. created on Tallulah R. **27.** US76 crosses Appalachian Trl. (see). **37.** J. with St.75.

SIDE TRIP: On St.75 (S) 19$^{m}$ to **Helen,** resort town in Nacoochee valley. **Nacoochee Ind. Mounds.**

US76 climbs (N). **39.5. HIAWASSEE. 47.5. YOUNG HARRIS,** seat of **Young L. G. Harris College,** est. in 1886, coed.; under Meth. Ch. Trl. to **Brasstown Bald** (4,784′), in Enota Glade; Ga.'s highest peak. **50.5 BLAIRSVILLE.** J. with US19 (see).

SIDE TRIPS: (A) On US19 (NW) 10m along L. Nottely to **Nottely Dam,** (W) 2m from hy.; this is a TVA storage project which forms 4,200-a. L.

(B) (S) 3m on US19 to **Mountain Experiment Sta.,** under Univ. System. 9.5m US19 crosses boundary of Chattahoochee Nat. For. 11.5m **Vogel St. Pk.** (O.Ap.-Dec.cottages.inn.store. pic.f.boat.swim.recr.facils.). At S. edge of Pk., at **Neel Gap,** US19 crosses Appalachian Trl., which leads (SW) to **Woody Gap** (f.h.camp.permits at ranger sta.recr.area.lookout). 2m (S) is **Blood Mt.,** highest peak on Ga. sec. of Trl. Just S. of Neel Gap is trl. (W.3m) to **De Soto Falls** (400′). 19.5m **Chestatee Knoll,** for. camp (free.huts.camp sites.water). 26.5m **Porter Springs,** summer resort since 1870's. J. with St.60, which runs (NW) to **Noontootly Nat. Game Refuge.** 35.5m **Dahlonega** (bus serv.hotel), where gold occasionally shines in streets after heavy rain; seat of North Ga. College. Dahlonega (Ind.: "yellow metal"), set among Blue Ridge foothills (1,500′), is known for pleasant climate. After gold was found in 1829, the Cherokee lands were invaded by prospectors, gamblers & swindlers. In 1830 the lands were acquired by the St. & eviction of the Cherokee began. Lumpkin Cty. was created & Dahlonega est. in 1833. A Gov. mint, opened in 1838, struck off gold coins valued at more than $6,000,000 before it was taken over by Confeds. in 1861. Fed. Gov. deeded land to Ga. in 1871. Numerous mines are active in vic. (O), & mountaineers still dig & pan among hills. Total output of Dahlonega fields has been est. at $40,000,000. **Lumpkin County Cth.** (1836). **North Ga. College,** unit of Univ. System; founded in 1871 as land-grant college. Emphasis is laid on military training for men students, leading to reserve commission. **Price Mem. Hall,** on site of Gov. Mint.

**70.5. MORGANTON.** From here, US76 follows crest of earthen dam on Toccoa R. which has created the bright-blue **L. Toccoa** (f.hunt.swim.boat). Wildfowl & white-tailed deer are common. **75.5 BLUE RIDGE** (ranger sta.), mining & lumbering center & resort. US76 unites with St.5, scenic hy. **91. ELLIJAY,** shipping pt. for fruit.

SIDE TRIP: On St.5 (S) 21m to **Jasper,** trade center, resting on bed of marble. Belt extends (S) for many miles, & even modest little Hs. are dressed with marble. J. with St.108, which runs (E) 8.5m to **Mt. Oglethorpe,** terminus of Appalachian Trl. On this spectacular peak is marble **Oglethorpe Mon.** 26m **Tate,** center of marble industry. Near Tate is solid vein of pure, beautifully colored marble nearly half a mile deep & 4 miles long, of which only top layers of some few as. have been cut. Ga. marble was used in Lincoln Mem. in Washington, Field Mus. in Chicago, & other important bldgs.

Bet. Ellijay & Chatsworth, US76-St.2, one of St.'s finest hys., traverses area of unusual beauty & int. **111.** J. with Rd. (R) leading up to **Fort Mt. St. Pk.** (O.Ap.-Dec.pic.f.lookout). **Old Stone Ft.,** a low wall, 12′ thick at bottom, encircling crest of steep mt. (2,832′); whether built by prehist. or hist. Inds., followers of De Soto, or the Brit. during Rev., is not known. **Mountain L.** (f.2,850′). **116. CHATSWORTH,** center of talc-mining reg. **119. SPRING PLACE** (see US41). Hy. rounds tip of W. sec. of **Chattahoochee Nat. For.** (ranger sta. at Lafayette), an area of lofty ridges & many streams cutting through densely wooded valleys. Route runs close to path of Sherman's men. **129. DALTON** (see US41). J. with US41 (see). At **138. TUNNEL HILL,** est. in 1851 after **Western & Atlantic RR. Tunnel** (R), one of 1st in South, had been cut through ridge (1848-50). **145. RINGGOLD** (see US41). J. with St.148.

SIDE TRIP: On St.148 & US27 (W) & (S) 20m to J. with St.2. Via Chickamauga Pk. 9m **Rossville,** near Tenn. Line. J. with US27 (see). At c.3m (S) on US27, **Chickamauga & Chattanooga Nat. Military Pk.** (see also Tenn.), largest in U.S., covering c.8,000 as. In Ga. (5,562 as.), are **Battle of Chickamauga Site** (rest.), marked with mons., tablets, & cannon; **Battle Line Rd.; Snodgrass Hill; Kelly Field;** & mons. of Confed. states. Mus. & hist. lib. in **Adm. Bldg.** 20m J. with St.2.

On St.2 (NW) 24m to J. with US11, route through extreme NW. Ga. 17m J. with St.157, which follows crest of ridge of long low **Lookout Mt.** Short distance (N) on St.157 is **Cloudland Canyon St. Pk.** (pic.camp.facils.). 24m J. with US11, main hy. (S-N) through isolated country of great beauty. Many rds. lead up hills & among sm. farms & pasturelands. Dade Cty. is rich in coal, but there is little industrialization.

From Ringgold, US76-US41 cont. (NW). **153. GA.-TENN. LINE.**

## US 78—GEORGIA

**GA.-S.C. LINE** (17m from Aiken, S.C.) **(W) to GA.-ALA. LINE** (18m from Heflin, Ala.). **240. US78**

Via: Augusta, Thomson, Washington, (Crawfordville), Lexington, Athens, Loganville, Stone Mountain, Atlanta, Douglasville, Bremen, Tallapoosa.

## Sec. 1: GA.-S.C. LINE to MONROE. 127.

**0. AUGUSTA** (see US1), on Savannah R. Beyond among red-clay hills are plantations, dark with oaks & magnolias, & unpainted Hs. of tenant farmers & sharecroppers. Many creeks & gullies run through bright, eroded fields. **36. THOMSON** (est.1820). **Hickory Hill,** estate of Thos. E. Watson (1856-1922), "Sage of McDuffie County"; Populist candidate for Vice Pres. with Wm. J. Bryan in 1896 & for Pres. in 1904. J. with St.12, which leads (W) through reg. of sm. farms once part of great cotton plantations. In the quiet towns are ante bellum homes, 18th-cent. gardens & burial grounds, stone chs. & cths.

SIDE TRIP: On St.12 (W & N) 29m to Crawfordville. 11m **Warrenton,** since 1797 the seat of Warren Cty., named for Rev. Gen. Jos. Warren. **Cty. Jail** (c.1800). **Walker H.** (1820), **McGregor H.; Pilcher H.,** scene of masked ball for LaFayette in 1825. 29m. **Crawfordville & Alex. Stephens St. Pk.** (pic.group camp.f.boat.swim.). **Liberty Hall** (rest.), home of "Little Alex," advocate of the Union & then beloved Confed. leader; orig. furniture; slave Hs. & other bldgs. (reconst.). J. with St.22.

On St.22 (S) 24m to Sparta. 9m **Powelton Bapt. Ch.,** org. in 1786 under Silas Mercer; slave cemetery. 18m Rd. (L) c.10m to **Camilla-Sack Center;** Negro farm group org. under Benj. F. Hubert (see Ga. Industrial College in US17). 24m **Sparta,** rural center & mill town on St.22. **Middlebrooks H.,** built c.1832 for Sparta Female Academy. **Sayre-Reese-Oliver H., Terrell H. & Wynn-Clinch H.** are good examples of Gr. Rev. style.

**47.** Short distance off hy. (R) are **Columbia Gold Mines,** worked since 1843. Discovery was made in 1823, & Ga.'s 1st stamp mill was set up in 1833. **59.** J. with St.47.

SIDE TRIP: On St.47 (R) 4m to **Smyrna Ch.** (Meth.) on site of Presb. Ch. (est.1793). 5m **Mt. Pleasant,** on former plantation of John Talbot, Ga. Gov. in 1819; grave in **Old Smyrna Churchyard.** Near H. is **Eli Whitney's Workshop,** & plantation Rd. leads to **Miller-Whitney Plantation** where the partners made gins for planters. St.'s 1st cotton mill was est. here in 1811.

**61. WASHINGTON,** enchanting town of many memories; tobacco market & leading city before Civil War; capital of Confed. during tragic last days. PTS. OF INT.: (1) **Wilkes County Cth.** (1904), on approx. **Site of Heard H.** where Jeff. Davis called last cabinet meeting, May 5, 1865. (2) Liberty & Jefferson Sts., **Mary Willis Lib.** (O.1887), 1st free lib. in Ga. (3) Rbt. Toombs Ave., **Toombs H.** (late 18th cent.), remod. in 1837 by Rbt. Toombs, opponent of Pres. Davis in bitter political battle that jeopardized Confed. Toombs refused allegiance to U.S. & fled to Europe but returned in 1867 to fight carpetbag rule. (4) W. Rbt. Toombs Ave., **Jesse Mercer H.,** on grounds of **St. Joseph's Home for Boys** (Cath.); former home of Bapt. minister, for whom Mercer Univ. (see US80) is named. (5) Rbt. Toombs Ave., **Presb. Ch.** (1826.Gr.Rev.). (6) On St.17, **Wingfield H.** (1790's), fine example of Gr. Rev. style; slave Hs. (7) **Kettle Cr. Marker,** comm. Amer. victory in Rev. War.

**83. LEXINGTON** (est.1806), seat of Oglethorpe Cty., home of Govs. Geo. Mathews, Wilson Lumpkin & Geo. R. Gilmer. **Lumpkin H. Presb. Ch.** (1875); org. in 1785. Rev. Thos. Goulding, father of Francis Goulding (see), org. Columbia Theol. Seminary here, 1828 (see Atlanta Trip I). **Gilmer H.** (1800.wings 1840.Gr.Rev.). **85. CRAWFORD,** named for Wm. H. Crawford (1772-1834), U.S. Senator, Minister to France, Secy. of War, & Secy. of Treas. **Crawford Mem.** (1933). **Grave of W. H. Crawford,** on former plantation (N).

### 103. ATHENS

RR. & bus conns. Airport. Accoms. & recr. facils. Info.: C. of C.

Athens has hillside setting in bend of Oconee R.; founded in 1801 as site for Univ. of Ga., 1st chartered st. univ. in Amer. Town has grown with college, sharing its traditions, prestige & social affairs. Many consider it most beautiful Ga. city, epitome of Deep South, with white Gr. Rev. Hs. behind magnolia trees & picket fences along its broad streets. Industries, of which textile is most important, are gathered mainly along R., & near the industrial plants in E. Athens are Hs. of most of the Negro citizens (c.30% of total). During Civil War, univ. bldgs. were used as hospitals & barracks for refugees. PTS. OF INT.: (1) 570 Prince Ave., **Home of Benj. H. Hill** (1855.Gr.Rev.), prominent Confed. & advocate of New South (see US27). (2) 248 Prince Ave., **J. H. Lumpkin H.** (1845.Gr.Rev.), home of St.'s 1st chief justice; now Woman's Club. (3) 973 Prince Ave., **E. K. Lumpkin H.** (1850). (4) 634 Prince Ave.,

**H. W. Grady H.** (1845.Gr.Rev.), portico has 13 Doric columns for orig. Colonies. Grady, born in Athens, delivered his famous speech, "The New South," in N. Y. in 1886. (5) 425 Hill St., **Howell Cobb H.** (1850.Gr.Rev.), home of pres. of Confed. Convention at Montgomery, Ala., in 1861. (6) 194 Prince Ave., **T. R. R. Cobb H.** (1830's.Gr.Rev.). Gen. Cobb was largely responsible for drafting Confed. Constitution. (7) On City Hall lawn, **Double-Barreled Cannon,** made in Athens during Civil War; believed to be only one of kind in world. (8) Prince & Oglethorpe Aves., **Coordinate College,** est. as St. Normal Sch. (1895). **Gilmer Hall** (1859-60), dormitory, was old Rock College. **Winnie Davis Hall.** (9) Cedar St. & College Dr., **St. College of Agric.,** campus & 1,500-a. farm. **Conner Hall.**

PTS. OF INT. IN UNIV. OF GA.: (10) College Ave. & Broad St., **Georgia Arch** (1856), designed after St. seal. (11) **Demosthenes Hall** (1824), home of literary society founded in 1803. (12) **Chapel** (1832), where commencement exercises were held for 100 yrs. (13) **Old College** (1805.post-Col.). Room occupied by Crawford W. Long (see) & Alex. H. Stephens (see), whose statues represent Ga. in Nat. Capitol. (14) **Harold Hirsch Hall** (1932.mod.Gr.Rev.), occupied by Lumpkin Law Sch. (15) **Lib.** Ga. hist. Coll. incl. **DeRenne Lib.** (see US17). (16) **Mem. Hall,** ded. to veterans of World War I. (17) **Lucy Cobb Dormitory,** orig. bldg. of Lucy Cobb Institute, est. in 1858. Athens is at J. with US29 & US129 (see).

SIDE TRIP: On US29 (NE) 18m to **Danielsville,** birthpl. of Dr. Crawford W. Long, who performed 1st operation using ether as anesthetic (1842). His claim was disputed by Dr. W. T. G. Morton, of Mass., because Long did not make known his discovery until after Morton's demonstration in 1846.

**127. MONROE** (founded 1821), sm. cotton-mill town. **Henry D. McDaniel H.,** home of Confed. officer & Gov. (1883-86). **Selman H.** (1800's.Gr.Rev.). J. with St.11.

SIDE TRIP: On St.11 (S) 15m to J. with St.12; (E) 8m on St.12 to **Rutledge. Hard Labor Creek St. Pk.** (group camp facils.), former Fed. recr. demonstration area.

### Sec. 2: MONROE to GA.-ALA. LINE. 113.

US78 enters reg. of Atlanta. **29. STONE MOUNTAIN. 39.5. DECATUR. 45. ATLANTA** (see Atlanta for this sec.). Across Chattahoochee R. are several industrial settlements. **63. AUSTELL.** On St.6 (N) 1.5m is **Clarksdale,** built around mills of **Clark Thread Co.** Numerous springs in this hill country were resort centers in early days. **65. LITHIA SPRINGS VILLAGE.** Near-by is **Lithia Springs** (cabins. pic.golf course). **83. VILLA RICA,** sett. c.1826 when gold was discovered. Tour cont. (W) on R. fork of US78. **98. BREMEN,** mill town & RR. center. J. with US27 (see). **107. TALLAPOOSA,** a boom city in 1890's when Northern capitalists began development of gold, copper & other deposits. **113.** US78 crosses **GA.-ALA. LINE.**

## US 80—GEORGIA

**SAVANNAH BEACH (W) to GA.-ALA. LINE** (21m from Marvyn, Ala.). **300. US80**

Via: Savannah, Statesboro, Swainsboro, Adrian, Dublin, Danville, Jeffersonville, Macon, Roberta, Talbotton, Geneva, Columbus. Good accoms. in cities.

US80 begins at the coast & crosses center of Ga., linking Savannah, its great seaport, Macon, in Middle Ga. & Columbus, important industrial town on Chattahoochee R.

### Sec. 1: SAVANNAH BEACH to DUBLIN. 145.

**0. SAVANNAH BEACH. 20. SAVANNAH** (see US17). **44.** US80 crosses Ogeechee R., which winds sluggishly through plantation belt & swampy pinelands, where fish, deer, quail & duck are plentiful (pic.camp sites.accoms.along route). **75. STATESBORO,** sportsmen's center & market for poultry, farm produce, cotton, tobacco & pecans. On US25 (S) 1.5m is **Ga. Teachers College,** unit of univ. system, one of orig. agric. & mechanical arts colleges est. under Act of 1862. US80 unites with US25 to **HOPEULIKIT** at **82.** Here route swings (W). **111. SWAINSBORO,** mill town & poultry-shipping center. J. with US1 (see). **127. ADRIAN.** Along hy. are woods that furnished slash pine for Dr. Chas. Herty's experiments with newsprint which revitalized St.'s economy (see US17). **145. DUBLIN,** on Oconee R.; prosperous center of large trade area. Lumber from oak, gum, hickory, & other trees is leading product.

SIDE TRIP: On US319 (S) 33m is **Little Ocmulgee St. Pk.** (pic.lodge.cabins.f.boat.bath.), popular area bet. Ocmulgee & Oconee Rs., which join to form the quiet Altamaha.

## Sec. 2: DUBLIN to GA.-ALA. LINE. 155.

Middle Ga.'s bright red earth is rich in clays & minerals. More than three-fourths of country's kaolin comes from this area. It also produces banner crops of cotton, peaches, peanuts, pecans & long watermelons. Reg. was sett. thousands of yrs. ago by moundbuilders, & here were many of the great plantations that produced cultural traditions of Deep South. **31. JEFFERSONVILLE. 45. DRY BRANCH.** Deposits of kaolin & white clay in vic., from which Bibb Cty. is developing ceramics industry. **50.** J. with St.87-US129 (see), which leads (S) 1.5m to **Lamar Area of Ocmulgee Nat. Mon.;** in 45-a. pk. are 2 mounds (with spiral ascent), built c.1500 by ancestors of Creek Inds., who held whole Macon Plateau sacred. **53. OCMULGEE NAT. MON.** (O.9-5.parking.guides), est. Dec. 23, 1936. **Mus.,** near Mound D, eventually will contain million objects excavated from 700-a. site. Rds. & trls. lead among remains of 4 successive cultures, incl. that of hist. Creek. On **Macon Plateau** are 3 large & 4 smaller mounds. **Mound D** (S) was once rectangular plateau more than 150′ long, built of sand & covered with red clay. **Council Chamber** (reconst.), sometimes compared to structures of Plains Inds. **Mound C** (W), partially excavated, was burial center. Archaeologists believe that, by 1250, the Swift Creek Inds. had settlement around Macon Plateau. They were driven out, c.1400, by the people who built the mounds & principal town, an agric. people with developed religious, artistic & social life.

### 55. MACON

Head of Cherry St., Terminal (RR). Sta. 320 Broadway, Greyhound Bus Terminal. Mun. Airport (SE) 6m. Good accoms. Mun. Golf Course (fee). Concerts at Mun. Auditorium. Lectures & concerts at univs. Bibb Flower & Bibb Cty. Camellia Shows (spring); St. Exposition (Oct.); Cattle Shows. Info.: C. of C., in Mun. Auditorium.

Macon, spreading out along muddy Ocmulgee R. in heart of Ga., is college town, textile-mill & market town, RR. & military training center. Pop. has increased to nearly 100,000 since 1940, & Macon stands high among cities likely to hold gains. Cherry St., main thoroughfare, is barren of shade, but side streets are arched by oaks, elms, & other fine old trees. Many Gr. Rev. Hs. are guarded by glossy-leaved magnolias, & all over city are pkys. & center plots of crape myrtle, palmettoes & roses. Across R. is **E. Macon,** a concentration of mills, factories & mill villages. Negro pop., about half the total, lives in back streets & hollows scattered about town & in well-kept suburbs of **Unionville** & **Pleasant Hill.** Wesleyan College for Women & Mercer Univ. are old & outstanding institutions; Ga. Academy for the Blind was est. in 1862; & Ga. Bapt. (jr.) College, Beda Etta (jr.) College & Memorial Trade Sch. are schs. of accepted standing for Negroes.

In 1703, Col. Jas. Moore came from S.C. to get help of Creek Inds. against the Sp.; & Oglethorpe, in 1739, passed through on way to conference with Inds. at Coweta Town (see Columbus below). Benj. Hawkins, in 1804, effected treaty in which Inds. deeded all lands bet. Oconee & Ocmulgee Rs. except 100 as. to be kept as trading grounds. Here Ft. Hawkins was built in 1806. After 1821 (Treaty of Ind. Springs), Newtown grew up around ft.; then Bibb Cty. was formed & Macon laid out & named for N.C. statesman, Nath. Macon. During Civil War, Gen. Howell Cobb had hqs. in Macon, & Pres. Davis & Gov. Brown aired their unhappy quarrel here. When Gen. J. H. Wilson advanced toward Macon in Ap., 1863, Gen. Cobb surrendered without resistance, having prudently destroyed all liquor in town. During Reconstruction, Macon Negroes held important offices & est. homes & business places. Camp Wheeler, est. in World War I, became great training ground during World War II, & U.S. Naval Ordnance Plant & Warner Robins Air Tech. Serv. Command were made permanent installations. Cochran Field trained thousands of Amer. & Brit. airmen. Today, with impetus of increased pop., new industries & diversified farming, Macon is 4th city in Ga.

PTS. OF INT.: (1) 450 Cherry St., **"Telegraph"** (1826) & **"Evening News"** (1884) **Bldg.** W. T. Anderson, who bought "Telegraph" in 1914, made nat. reputation with campaign against racial intolerance & by est. Negro edition. Harry Stillwell Edwards, author of "Aeneas Africanus," was well-known editor. (2) Cherry & 1st Sts.,

**Mun. Auditorium** (1924.by Egerton Swartout); large copper dome; art room. (3) Cherry & Spring Sts., **Temple Beth Israel** (est.1859); records from 1st temple. (4) College St., bet. Georgia & Washington Aves., **Wesleyan Conservatory** (1839), in rambling red-brick bldg., home of Wesleyan College (see below) until 1928. (5) College St. & Washington Ave., **Washington Mem. Lib.** (1919.neo-Class.); **Lanier Niche** (by Gutzon Borglum). (6) **Mercer Univ.,** on 65-a. campus facing Tatnall Sq. Pk.; endowed college, under S. Bapt. Assoc.; org. as College of Liberal Arts, incl. Roberts Sch. of Christianity & high-ranking Sch. of Law. Founded in 1831 & opened in 1833 at Penfield (see US129); named in honor of Rev. Jesse Mercer; chartered in 1837 & moved to Macon in 1871. Law Sch., est. at Macon in 1873, was inc. in 1920. **Adm. Bldg.** (1871), oldest bldg. **Willingham Chapel** (1890.tower in 1940). **Ryals Law Bldg.** (1930). **Hardman Lib.** (1907.adds.1936-37). **Shorter Hall** (1947). **Mary Erwin Porter Hall** (1941).

(7) Columbus & Orange Sts., **Mount de Sales Acad.** (1910.Cath.); org. in 1862. (8) 520 Orange St., **John Hill Lamar H.** (1839.Gr.Rev.), home of descendants of orig. owner. (9) 213 High St., **Lanier Cottage** (N.O.), birthpl. of Ga.'s best-known poet, Sidney Lanier (1842-81). (10) Poplar St. & Cotton Ave., **City Hall** (1836.remod. 1933-35.Class.), St. capitol in winter 1864-65, last session under Confed. (11) 523 Mulberry St., **Lanier Hotel** (1850.remod.); hqs. during Civil War for Jeff. Davis, Gov. Brown, Gen. Cobb & others. (12) Mulberry & 1st Sts., **First Presb. Ch.** (1858. Romanes.); org. in 1826. (13) Georgia Ave. & Bond St., **Marshall Johnston H.** (1883.Vict.Goth.). From veranda, Davis reviewed Confed. veterans in 1887. (14) 138 Bond St., **Cowles-Bond-O'Neal H.** (1836.Class.Rev.); 18 Doric columns. (15) 137 Jefferson Terrace, **Moultrie-Proudfit H.** (1842-43.Gr.Rev.); beautiful inter. (16) 304 Vineville, **Coleman-Speer-Birdsey H.** (1830's.Gr.Rev.), notable example of "H" plan. (17) 115 Rogers Ave., **Ralph Small H.** (1846.Gr.Rev.); a lovely white H., true to type. (18) End of Forest Ave., **Ballard Normal Sch.** (1865.Georg.Col.); 1st Negro sch. in Ga. on accredited list; org. in 1865 by Amer. Missionary Assoc. (19) **Cemeteries** along Ocmulgee R.: Riverside (1887); Oak Ridge (1840); William Wolfe (1879) & Rose Hill (1840), largest & most int.; graves of 500 Confed. soldiers. (20) 519 Walker St., **Cowles-Walker H.** (1830.Gr.Rev.); orig. woodwork. (21) 520 Walnut St., **Christ Ch.** (Episc.1852.neo-Goth.); est. 1825. (22) **Beaconsfield Pk.** (recr. facils.), along R. beyond **Stribling Mem. Bridge** (1935). (23) Maynard & Woolfolk Sts., **Site of Ft. Hawkins** (1806.being reconst.).

Macon is at J. with US41 & US129 (see).

SIDE TRIP: Take US41 (NW) 6m to Rivoli, **Wesleyan College,** 1st chartered college for women in world (1836) to confer regular degrees; under control of Meth. Conferences. On 170-a. wooded campus are 12 bldgs. (1928.Georg.Col.), trimmed in white Ga. marble. **Dining Hall;** marble colonnade. **Tate Hall,** adm. offices. **Candler Mem. Lib.,** gift of Judge J. S. Candler.

US80 cont. (W) through pleasant farm country. **81.5. ROBERTA. Mon. to Benj. Hawkins,** Ind. agent in 1796. **96.5.** Just (W) of Flint R. is J. with US19 (see). **116. TALBOTTON. Episc. Ch.** (1848.Tudor.Goth.). J. with St.41, which leads (N) 20m to **Warm Springs** (see US27).

## 154.5. COLUMBUS

12th St. & 6th Ave., Union Sta. 1300 Broadway, Union Bus Terminal. Mun. Airport (S) 2m. Good accoms. & recr. facils. Cotton Festival (May); Chattahoochee Valley Fair (Oct.). Info.: C. of C., Civic Bldg., 12th St. & 1st Ave.

Columbus, at foot of falls on Chattahoochee R., is St.'s 2nd city in industry & trade & runner-up with Greenville, S.C., as South's leading textile center. It is a planned city, with pkys. & flowering trees along main streets & residential areas that spread out into beautiful suburban developments. Class. Rev. influence shows throughout the town in older Hs. & bldgs. Along R. are most of textile mills & other plants that give Columbus nat. rank in industry; known also as iron & woodworking center & shipping pt. for dairy products, livestock & other produce. City is nat. known for Columbus Plan of sch. architecture & for Ga.-Ala. Sacred Harp Singing Society. In 1828 a town was laid out, & log cabins arose under giant pines. The "Steubenville" came up Chattahoochee R. that same yr., & RR. was extended from Macon in 1853. During Civil War, Columbus had large munitions works. After Reconstruction, textile industries, meat-packing & beverage plants spread out along R., & shipping & retail trade increased enormously. Ft. Benning had one of largest small-arms schs. in country during World War II.

PTS. OF INT.: (1) Broadway & 4th St., **Oglethorpe Marker,** near place where Gen. Oglethorpe crossed, 1739, to Coweta Town. (2) 908 Broadway, **Pease H.** (1854), similar to New Orleans raised cottages; iron grillwork. (3) **Bragg Smith Mon.,** in Porterdale Cemetery; raised by city to Negro who gave his life to save another man. (4) 2nd Ave. bet. 9th & 10th Sts., **Muscogee County Cth.** (1928). (5) 321 14th St., **Rutherford H.,** former home of Lizzie Rutherford Ellis; Southern Mem. Day (Ap.26) originated here in 1866. (6) 2810 St. Elmo Dr., **St. Elmo** (O.fee.1831.Gr. Rev.), built for Seaborn Jones; bricks made on plantation by slaves; 12 pillars 40′ high. Name changed from "El Dorado" after Columbus-born Augusta Evans Wilson described H. in her famous novel. (7) Wynnton Rd. & Wildwood Ave., **Wynnton Sch.,** one of 1st on Columbus Plan. (8) 19th Ave. & 13th St., **Farmers' Market** (co-op.). (9) Front Ave. at 13th St., **Eagle & Phoenix Mills,** part of Fairforest Co., oldest surviving in city; est. 1850. (10) Foot of 9th St., **Lummus Cotton Gin Plant** (O), one of largest manufacturers of gin machinery. (11) 10th Ave. & 8th St., **Tom Huston Peanut Co.** (O.guides). (12) 1000 9th Ave., **Nehi Bottling Co.** (O). (13) Front Ave. & Dillingham St., **Columbus Iron Works** (O), est. in 1853; arsenal during Civil War. (14) End of 35th St., Columbus Branch of **Bibb Mfg. Co.,** probably biggest textile mill in world. (15) Murray St. & 17th Ave., **Southern Foods Inc.** (meat-packing plant), opened in 1947. (16) (SE) 9m on US27, **Ft. Benning** (O.info. at Pub.Relations Office), country's largest infantry center (200,000 as.); est. 1918 & named for Confed. Gen. Henry L. Benning, of Columbus.

**155.** US80 crosses Chattahoochee R., **GA.-ALA. LINE.**

## US 17—GEORGIA

**GA.-S.C. LINE** (10m from Hardeeville, S.C.) **(S) to GA.-FLA. LINE** (31m from Jacksonville). **135. US17.**

Via: Savannah, Richmond Hill, Midway (St. Catherines I.), Darien, Brunswick (St. Simon & Jekyll Is.), Woodbine, Kingsland.

US17 runs close to broken, low-lying Atlantic shoreline through country of haunting natural beauty, where tantalizing evidences remain of human hist. before Oglethorpe's Utopia & less ambiguous relics of Brit. occupation & ante bellum plantation life. Here also, in millions of reforested as., in gigantic paper mills, & in steamships laden with naval stores, is proof of radically changing economy.

Ind. canoes flashed among the Golden Isles before De Soto came (N) from Fla. in 1540. In 1562, explorers under Jean Ribault named the Rs. "Somme" & "Seine" & "Gironde." Then after Menéndez massacred the Fr. settlers & founded St. Augustine (see Fla.), Sp. presidios & missions were est. in "Guale," the Ga. country. In 1606 (before Jamestown was founded), the Bishop of Cuba confirmed 1,000 Ind. Christians. When Sp. began settlement farther inland, Charles I of Eng. handed out to his Eight Lords Proprietors a strip of land that incl. the Sp. missions. Blackbeard & other pirates plundered the "Uninhabitated Land," & soon the missions were a heap of rubble & Spain had withdrawn to Fla. In 1732 the Colony of Ga. was founded by Gen. Oglethorpe at Savannah on land generously, but probably illegally, granted him by the King. At Battle of Bloody Marsh in 1742, the Sp. were defeated, & in 1763 they ceded Fla. to Brit. Large Negro pop. has contributed much to cultural development in the reg., especially around Savannah. It is believed that there were Negroes on the coast before Oglethorpe landed, to est. a colony in which slavery would be prohibited. With growth of cotton & rice plantations, however, slavery began (1749). More than 500 free Negroes were in Savannah in 1840, & more than half of these left for the "Promised Land" in Liberia. In 1864 a convention of Negro & white men in Savannah planned for Negro schs. in Ga. & by Dec. 1865, Savannah Negroes had opened several. Oldest hospital for Negroes in U.S. is Savannah's Ga. Infirmary (1832), & one of St.'s oldest Negro papers is "Savannah Tribune" (1875). In the political & economic picture, Savannah shows its remarkable flexibility, tranquilly preserving traditions, but granting city franchise to Negroes & replacing slums with model housing.

### Sec. 1: GA.-N.C. LINE to SAVANNAH. 10.5.

US17 crosses delta of Savannah R. over several concrete bridges. Delta Is. are incl. in **Savannah Nat. Wildlife Refuge. 2. PORT WENTWORTH,** a sm. community near **Savannah Sugar Refining Corp. Plant** (O), one of largest in South; makers of Dixie Crystals. J. with St.21.

SIDE TRIP: On St.21 (N) 13m to Rincon. 8.5m J. with Rice Hope Plantation Rd. which leads (R) to **Mulberry Grove Plantation,** formerly Lt. Gov. John Graham's silk plantation, confiscated & given to Rev. Gen. Nath. Greene (see). Here Eli Whitney, tutor of Greene children, invented cotton gin (1793); mansion was burned & groves destroyed by Union soldiers. 13m **Rincon,** in midst of turpentine area. On Ebenezer Rd. (E) is **Site of Ebenezer,** founded by Salzburgers in 1734. **Jerusalem Ch.** (rebuilt 1767-69).

**4.** Rd. to **Whitehall Plantation,** on land granted to Jos. Gibbons (1759); home of descendants of Thos. Gibbons (1757-1826), Loyalist in Rev. & later Mayor of Savannah. **5.5. INDUSTRIAL CITY GARDENS,** modern subdivision on site of Jonathan Bryan's Brampton Plantation, where a slave, Andrew Bryan, was ordained & preached to 1st Negro Bapt. congregation in Amer. **Union Bag & Paper Co.,** world's largest kraft-paper plant; on **Site of Hermitage Plantation.** In early 1800's, home of Henry McAlpin, maker of Savannah Grey brick. Henry Ford purchased mansion & used bricks for his home at Richmond Hill (see below).

**10.5. SAVANNAH**

RR. Stas.: 301 W. Broad St., Central of Ga.; Cohen & W. Boundary Sts., Savannah & Atlanta Ry.; 419 Broad St., Union Sta., for Southern Ry. 111 Bull St., Greyhound Bus Sta. Steamship lines to N. & S. Atlantic ports. Hunter Field (mun.) Airport, (SW) 5m on Emmett Wilson Blvd. & White Bluff Rd. Good hotels, tourist accoms. & recr. facils. in city & on Tybee & Wilmington I. Annual events: Emancipation Day Parade (Negro. Jan.1); Coastal Empire Paper Festival (Ap.); Dog Show (Ap.); Interstate Sailboat Regatta (July). Info.: C. of C., 137 Bull St.

Savannah, Ga.'s 2nd city & said to be 1st planned city in N. Amer., is outstandingly beautiful, fronting landlocked harbor & backed by live oaks & pine that made it the "Forest City." While expanding rapidly, the city keeps its Old World charm & cosmopolitan flavor of a port city, its Southern customs & individualistic ways. It is notably interested in art, music, literature, amusements & sports; its schs. & libs., incl. those for Negro children, maintain high standard. Aided by Col. Wm. Bull, Carolina engineer, Gen. Oglethorpe laid out Savannah on plan sketched in "Village of the Ancients," by his friend Rbt. Castell, who died in debtors' prison. At intervals along Bull St. & in other parts of city, are spacious squares planted with evergreens, magnolias, oleanders & azaleas. Bay St. runs length of the bluff overlooking Savannah R., & extending for miles along riverfront below are paper plants, sugar refineries, wharves & docks. Downtown Savannah crowds close to the Bay.

With Oglethorpe came 120 chosen colonists who were to produce silk, drugs & wine under the Trustees' direction. Rum, slavery & land ownership were prohibited. In May, 1734, Oglethorpe took his benefactor, Tomochichi, & other Ind. chiefs for visit to England, & John & Chas. Wesley & a group of Salzburgers & Moravians sailed with him on return. The "Father of Ga." provided for defense & followed conciliatory policy with Inds., but agitation against "our Perpetual Dictator" arose, & in 1743 Oglethorpe returned to England to stay. He died on June 30, 1785, at the age of 89. The colony that had failed to prosper became a Royal Province when charter expired in 1753. During Siege of Savannah in Rev., the Amers., aided by Count d'Estaing's Fr. forces, were repulsed in battle in which Count Pulaski (see below) & Sgt. Wm. Jasper were killed. After surrender of Cornwallis, Savannah again became seat of gov. in Ga. It was inc. in 1789 & had 1st disastrous fire in 1796 & a 2nd in 1804. City was not attacked during War of 1812 & development in transportation & commerce was rapid. In Dec., 1860, a secession flag was raised in Johnson Sq., & Gov. Brown ordered occupation of Ft. Pulaski, which fell to Fed. forces in Ap., 1862. News of Sherman's approach came Dec. 11, 1864. Ft. McAllister, which had withstood attacks in 1862 & 1863, was captured in spite of gallant defense under Gen. W. J. Hardee. Savannah was evacuated over pontoon bridge to Hutchinson I., & Sherman presented the city to Pres. Lincoln as Christmas gift. Gradually, the pinewoods were made basis of lumber & naval stores industries, & the gay 90's found Savannah prosperous. After 1900, other new industries were est., especially the making of paper & refining of sugar. Pres. Roosevelt visited Savannah at Bicentennial Celebration in 1933, & Internat. Monetary Conference was held at Gen. Oglethorpe Hotel in 1946. Growth since World War II has been record-breaking, but industrialization has not noticeably altered tempo or temper of Savannah, the world's leading port for naval stores & most important cotton port on S. Atlantic.

PTS. OF INT.—BULL ST.: (1) Bay St. at N. end of Bull St., **City Hall** (1905); tablet comm. sailing of "Savannah" in 1819, 1st steamship to cross Atlantic (model on 2nd fl.), & launching in 1834 of "John Randolph," 1st ironclad in Amer. waters. (2) SE. cor. Bay St., **U.S. Custom H.** (1850.Gr.Rev.by J.S.Norris), on **Site of Oglethorpe's Hqs.** Here John Wesley preached 1st sermon in Savannah. (3) Bet. Bryan & Congress Sts., **Johnson Sq.** (1733), 1st of orig. sqs. **Nath. Greene Mon.** (1825.by Wm. Strickland), above graves of the R. I. patriot & his son. (4) Facing Sq., **Christ Ch.** (Episc.1838.rest.1897.Gr.Rev.); 1st congregation in colony (1733) & served by John Wesley & Geo. Whitefield. (5) Broughton & Whitaker Sts., **Site of Tondee's Tavern,** meeting place for Sons of Liberty. First Provincial Congress met here, July 4, 1775. (6) SW. cor. Oglethorpe Ave., **Independent Presb. Ch.** (1889-90.Georg.Col.adds.by Ralph Adams Cram); org. in 1755 by Scottish Highlanders. In 1885, Ellen Axson was married to Woodrow Wilson in orig. manse. (7) At Perry St., **Chippewa Sq.** (1813). **Oglethorpe Mon.** (1910.by Dan.C.French.base by Henry Bacon). (8) 222 Bull St., **Savannah Theater** (1818. by Wm.Jay), oldest theater in continuous use in U.S. (9) Charlton & Harris Sts., **Madison Sq.** (1839). **Sgt. Wm. Jasper Mon.** (10) W. Macon St., **Green-Meldrim H.** (1856.Goth.Rev.), built by Chas. Green, grandfather of novelists Ann & Julian Green; hqs. for Gen. Sherman, 1864; now rectory of St. John's Episc. Ch. (11) Taylor & Gordon Sts., **Monterey Sq.** (1848). **Pulaski Mon.** to Polish Count Casimir Pulaski. (12) Gordon St. E., **Temple Mickve Israel** (mod.Goth.); congregation founded in 1733; orig. Scroll of Laws. (13) 501 Whitaker St., **Hodgson Hall** (1873); Ga. Hist. Soc. Coll. (14) Gaston St., bet. Whitaker & Drayton Sts., **Forsyth Pk.** (1851). **Confed. Mon. & Sp.-Amer. Mem.** (15) 2002 Bull St., **Pub. Lib.** (1916.Carnegie). Savannah Lib. Soc. was org. in 1809.

PTS. OF INT.—(E) OF BULL ST.: (16) River front, **Factors Wharf,** along 40′ bluff faced with ballast stones from Eng.; row of weatherworn bldgs. once occupied by cotton factors. On R. side, iron balconies overhang & iron bridges cross cobblestone ramp to River St. Some miles (W) are steamship terminals of Savannah Harbor, c.24$^{m}$ from deep water beyond the bar. (17) Cor. E. Bay & E. Broad Sts., **Ft. Wayne** (1762.walls 1812), on **Site of Trustees' Garden.** (18) 26 E. Broad St., **Flint H.,** Trustees' Garden Herb Shop; said to be city's oldest H. (19) 22 Habersham St., **Woodbridge H.** (1800.Georg.Col.). (20) 27-29 Lincoln St., **Dennis H.** (1800.Georg.Col.). (21) 27 Abercorn St., **Roberts H.** (1840). (22) 124 Abercorn St., **Richardson Owens H.** (1816-19.Regency.by Wm.Jay), praised as city's finest example of style. (23) 324 State St., **Davenport H.** (pre-1800.Georg.). (24) Abercorn & Harris Sts., **Cathedral of St. John the Bapt.** (1876.rebuilt 1900), one of handsomest Cath. edifices in SE.; shares seat of diocese with Atlanta's Co-Cathedral of Christ the King. (25) 328 Abercorn St., **Low H.** (1847.Class.Rev.), St. hqs. of Col. Dames; former home of Juliette Low, who org. Girl Scouts in drawingroom. **Girl Scout Hqs.** (26) 110 Oglethorpe Ave., **McIntosh H.** (c.1764), probably oldest brick H. in Ga. Ga. Legislature met in Long Room, 1782.

PTS. OF INT.—(W) OF BULL ST.: (27) On N. side of Bay St., **Marble Bench,** comm. Oglethorpe's 1st camp. (28) 510 River St., **Chas. H. Herty Pulp & Paper Lab.,** now conducted by Herty Foundation; est. by Dr. Herty (1867-1938) in 1932. (29) **Yamacraw,** W. side of W. Broad St., from Bay St. (S); on site of Ind. village. For more than 100 yrs. this has been Negro business & social center. At 111 W. Broad St., **Scarborough H.** (1818.Regency.said to be by Wm.Jay). In 1878, W. J. DeRenne (see Wormsloe below) gave bldg. for 1st Negro sch. in city. At 565 W. Bryan St., **First Bryan Bapt. Ch.,** outgrowth of Andrew Bryan's ministry on Brampton Plantation (see above). (30) 121 Barnard St., **Telfair Acad. of Arts & Sciences,** in **Telfair Mansion** (1820.Regency.probably by Wm.Jay), bequeathed with furniture to Ga. Hist. Soc. in 1875. Acad., opened in 1885, has one of South's leading sm. galleries. (31) 120 Oglethorpe Ave. W., **Giles Becu H.** (pre-1800); at one time home of Mrs. Montmollin, aunt of Aaron Burr. (32) 127 Oglethorpe Ave. W., **Waring H.** (c.1816. Georg.Col.). (33) 230 Barnard St., **McAlpin H.** (1835.Gr.Rev.), designed by Henry McAlpin & built of Savannah Grey brick. (34) 423 Oglethorpe Ave. W., **Wetter H.** (pre-1840), now Female Orphanage; one of most elaborate ante bellum Hs.; iron balconies with medallions of statesmen & poets.

## TRIPS OUT OF SAVANNAH

### I. SAVANNAH (SE) to SAVANNAH BEACH. 20. US80

Via: Thunderbolt (Bonaventure), Whitemarsh, Wilmington (Ft. Pulaski), Lazaretto, Ft. Screven.

On Bull St. (N) to Victory Dr. (US80), which crosses principal residential areas. At Waters St. is **Daffin Pk.,** leading amusement & recr. area. Mun. Stadium. **4. THUNDERBOLT,** fishing village around shrimp-canning factory. Shell Rd. leads c.1$^{m}$ (L) to **Bonaventure,** somberly beautiful burial ground on **Site of Tattnall Plantation,** on Wilmington R. About 1760, Col. John Mulryne, of Charleston, S.C., created Bonaventure in the wilderness, surrounding his big brick H. with terraced gardens & avenues of oaks. His daughter Mary married Josiah Tattnall, of Charleston, in 1761. Loyal to the King during Rev., the family went to Eng. & Bonaventure was confiscated. Josiah Tattnall II, at 18, came back to Ga. & served under Nath. Greene, & part of estate was restored to him. For 18 yrs. he lived at Bonaventure, became Ga. Congressman & Gov., & he & members of his family are buried here. In 1847 estate was bought by Capt. Peter Wiltberger &, in accord with his wish, made city cemetery in 1869.

SIDE TRIPS: (A) Along shell Rd. (S) 2$^{m}$ is **Greenwich,** one of most beautiful plantations. The wounded Count Pulaski was carried here, & his supposed grave is marked. It is also claimed he died at sea on Fr. warship.

(B) Paved Rd. leads (S) 1$^{m}$ to **GA. STATE COLLEGE** (Negro), part of Univ. System & an outstanding institution under Pres. B. F. Hubert.

**8. WHITEMARSH I.,** where several Civil War encounters took place. **10. WILMINGTON I.,** another battleground. Now has many estates & palatial **Gen. Oglethorpe Hotel. 16. LAZARETTO,** once a quarantine sta. incl. slave hospital where sick Negroes were taken from traders' boats. Those who lived were sent to Savannah for sale, & the dead were buried here. Negroes living here today support themselves largely by fishing & crabbing. Many are gifted in woodcarving & weaving. Boats leave Lazaretto for **FT. PULASKI NAT. MON.** (sm.fee), on McQueens I. & Cockspur I., at mouth of Savannah R.; reopened to pub. on Pulaski Day, Oct. 11, 1947, after use in World War II as Navy & Coast Guard sta. The fortress, built 1829-47 at cost of nearly $1,000,000, is 5-sided mass of fine masonry surrounded by 2 dry moats. It was believed impregnable, since nearest high ground was Tybee I., a mile away. Fed. batteries of rifled cannon were set up early in 1862 on Tybee I., &, on Ap. 11, after 30-hour bombardment, Col. C. H. Olmstead surrendered. This was 1st demonstration of superiority of rifled cannon to masonry. Ft. was made Nat. Mon., Oct. 15, 1924, in pageant ending with lowering of Stars & Bars. US80 crosses **Tybee I.,** to the ocean. **Ft. Screven** (1898), active Army Post. **Savannah Beach** (swim. boat.f.recr.facils.hotels.cottages.restaurants).

### II. Circle Tour (E. & S.) from SAVANNAH to COFFEE BLUFF. 43. Victory Dr. (US80), Moore & Ferguson Aves., & White Bluff Rd.

Via: Isle of Hope, Wormsloe, Bethesda, Beaulieu, Montgomery.

Victory Dr. runs (E) to J. with Moore Ave. **0.** on which trip turns (S). **10. ISLE OF HOPE,** village & resort on curving shell bluff. **Barbee's Diamondback Terrapin Farm** (O.sm.fee), started in 1893. From here shell Rd. takes sharp turn (S) to **WORMSLOE PLANTATION** (gardens O.fee), for more than 200 yrs. in continuous possession of family to whom orig. grant was made. Noble Jones leased 500 as. from Trustees in 1733 & est. mulberry plantation; in 1756 Crown confirmed grant & gave adj. tract to older son, Noble Wimberly Jones, & Long. I. to 2nd son, Inigo Jones. Capt. Noble Jones served Colony as soldier, surveyor, treas. & chief justice, & Noble Wimberly Jones was 1st pres. of Ga. Med. Soc. & one of founders of Sons of Liberty. Geo. Wymberly Jones, who added mother's family name "DeRenne," bequeathed lib. of Ga. hist. to St. (in Capitol). Wymberly Jones DeRenne followed tradition, & his coll. is in Lib. of Univ. of Ga. **Wormsloe H.,** rambling mansion with many wings & porches, was built before Civil War; famous gardens. Beyond Wormsloe, Rd. turns (W) at 1st cross Rd. **15. BETHESDA ORPHANS HOME** (boys), oldest existing orphanage in U.S. **Chapel** (1924), reprod. of Whitefield's chapel in Eng. Bethesda was Colony's most successful sch. until 1791; reorg. in 1801 as orphanage. Route turns (S) on Ferguson Ave. **17. BEAULIEU,** on bluff above Vernon R., where Count d'Estaing landed Fr. troops in 1779. Trip turns (W) again at 1st cross Rd. **21. MONTGOMERY,** waterside resort. Trip follows Montgomery Rd. (N) to Montgomery Cross Rd., then (S) on White Bluff Rd. **33. COFFEE BLUFF,** overlooking Forrest R. (ideal for pic.). Return to Savannah, (N) c.10$^m$, on White Bluff Rd., one of city's most beautiful drives.

## Sec. 2: SAVANNAH to DARIEN. 62.5.

**0. SAVANNAH. 6.** Subdivision on **Site of Silk Hope Plantation** (1756), noted before Civil War for mulberry fields & beautiful gardens; later a rice plantation. **11. LITTLE NECK PLANTATION,** now a farm known for Irish potatoes. Rd. leads (L) to **Wild Hern, Grove Hill** & **Vallambroso** plantations. **c.13 BAMBOO FOREST,** plant lab. where seedlings from all over world are tested for commercial & ornamental purposes. Dense grove of feathery bamboo has nearly 200 varieties; orig part of Chapman Plantation, it is now under U.S. Dept. of Agric. US17 crosses Ogeechee R. over **King's Ferry Bridge,** near site of Rev. engagement. **18. RICHMOND HILL,** community developed by Henry Ford. **St. Fish Hatchery** (R). Along Ogeechee R. is **Ford Estate,** made up of Old Cherry Hill & other plantations. H. built of Savannah Grey brick from the Hermitage. **31. MIDWAY,** village under towering oaks; sett. (1752) by Puritans who named it for Eng. Medway R. **Church** (1792). Abiel Holmes, father of O. W. Holmes, & Jedediah Morse, father of S. F. B. Morse, were early pastors. **J.** with St.38.

SIDE TRIP: On St.38 (SE) 14$^m$ to **Yellow Bluff, St. Catherines Sound** & **St. Catherines I.,** 1st of 6 Golden Isles of Guale claimed by Sp. in 16th cent. On **Sapelo I.,** (S) Thos. Spalding built tabby mansion on one of most extensive plantations along coast (rest.by Howard Coffin). Near center of I. is a sawmill village, & at either end are scattered settlements of Negroes who have always lived in isolation. The coastal Negroes, sometimes called Gullahs or Geechees (for Ogeechee R.), retain customs, beliefs & religious rites of their ancestors. Their dialect, intermingling African survivals & words & phrases of mixed origin, has a peculiar charm.

**34.5. SITE OF CEDAR HILL,** estate of Theo. Roosevelt's grandfather, Gen. Dan. Stewart. Hy. runs under arching live oaks to **EULONIA, 50.,** old-fashioned town in center of naval stores industry. **62.5. DARIEN,** village on bluff above Altamaha R. Sett. in 1735 by Scotch Highlanders, it became important lumber port. Below bluff are weatherbeaten docks, shipyard & canneries among old tabby bldgs. **Highlanders Mon.** (by R.Tait MacKenzie).

## Sec. 3: DARIEN to GA.-FLA. LINE. 62.

Altamaha R. channels through the delta lowlands. **2. BUTLER I.,** site of **Pierce Butler Plantation,** where Fanny Kemble Butler, Eng. actress, wrote with bitterness about plantation life. **St. Coastal Exper. Sta.** US17 enters Glynn Cty., famous for its marshes. **17. LANIER'S OAK,** where poet did finest work, inspired by the "limpid labyrinth of dreams."

### 18. BRUNSWICK

RR. & bus. Airports. Good accoms. Tourist Club. Info.: Bur. in C. of C. Bldg. Causeway to St. Simon & Sea Is.

Brunswick is busy seaport in midst of well-developed naval stores, lumber & cotton-producing reg.; also shrimp & crab-packing center. Since opening of Jekyll I. St. Pk. (see below), it has become important resort & tourist town. Brunswick was founded & named in honor of Royal House in 1771; evacuated in 1862 but reoccupied in 1863 by Confeds., who repulsed the only Fed. attack. By 1900, it had become leading port city. Large turpentine & resin & paper pulp plants. **Oglethorpe Hotel** (1885.remod.by Stanford White). **Oglethorpe Mem.** In Wright Sq., **Graves of Benj. & Nancy Hart** (see), Rev. patriots.

SIDE TRIPS TO SEA ISLANDS: (A) St. Simon Causeway (toll) runs (E) from J. with US17 near Brunswick Tourist Club & across Marshes of Glynn to J. with Sea I. Rd. & King's Way. **St. Simon I.,** summer resort for many yrs., is only one of Golden Isles accessible by motor; noted for beauty of moss-draped oaks, vivid flowers & smooth beaches. Timber for "Old Ironsides" was felled on St. Simon I. (1794). PTS. OF INT.: (1) On King's Way (L) **Sea I. Yacht Club** (reservations), on Frederica R., which is part of Inland Waterway from Chesapeake Bay to Key West. (2) J. of Sea I. Rd. with Retreat Ave. & Demere Rd., **Tabby Slave Cabin,** remnant of **Retreat Plantation** where sea-island cotton was developed. (3) **McKinnon Airport.** (4) At S. tip (following Retreat Ave.) are **Ruins of Slave Cemetery** near links of **Sea I. Golf Club.** (5) **St. Simon Village** (hotel.rooms.cottages. deep-sea f.boat trips). (6) Near Lighth. is **Site of Oglethorpe's Fort St. Simon.** (7) On Demere Rd. (N) 5$^m$ from village, **Bloody Marsh Battlefield,** where Sp. were decisively

defeated in July, 1742. Site became plantation where Mrs. Maxfield Parrish collected songs & lore of Sea Island Negroes. (8) **Sea I.** (hotel.f.h.swim.sports facils.). Eugene O'Neill & other writers made their homes on this isle of palms. **Sea I. Fish. Camp** (guides). (9) 1.5m (NW) from Battlefield (follow Frederica Rd.), **Ft. Frederica Nat. Mon.** (O). Ft. Frederica, strongest of Col. defenses, built on bend of R. in 1736; moat, cemetery, & portions of brick & tabby citadel & barracks remain. Near S. edge is **Christ Ch.** (Episc.1875), est. by John & Chas. Wesley in 1736; & **Site of Oglethorpe's H.,** his only Ga. home.
(B) **Jekyll I. St. Pk.** (O.yr.-round.f.swim.recr.facils.rms.restaurants.bicycles.no autos); "Robert E. Lee" makes 3 trips daily; accessible also by plane. Causeway will cross Jekyll R. to conn. with US17. This 11,000-a. I. was fabulously beautiful millionaires' retreat since 1895, with Sans Souci Clubh., palatial homes & 30-room "cottages." It was purchased by St. in 1947. The 9m beach is one of finest on coast.

US17 crosses Turtle R. Bridge from Brunswick; fine view of water front. **46. WOODBINE,** sm. community on Satilla R. **58. KINGSLAND.** J. with St.40.

SIDE TRIPS: (A) On St.40 (W) 19m to **Folkston,** at entrance to Okefenokee Swamp (see).
(B) On St.40 (E) 7m to **St. Marys,** fishing village on St. Marys R. Parish was org. in 1763. **Orange Hall** (c.1835.Gr.Rev.). **Presb. Ch.** (1808). **Clark H.** (1802). **St. Marys Cemetery.** Marble slabs mark **Graves of Acadians** banished from Grand Pré, 1755. Visible from town is **Cumberland I.** (N.O.), largest of Golden Isles; once popular watering place. **Dungeness** (1893), at S. end. Orig. bldg. was Oglethorpe's hunting lodge. Gen. Nath. Greene acquired property after Rev. & kept the name. "Lighthorse Harry" Lee (see) died here in 1818, & his grave was at Dungeness until 1913. Spur of St.40 runs (N) 5m to **Crooked R.** & **Santa Maria St. Pks.** Well-preserved **Tabby Ruins,** possibly remains of Santa Maria Sp. Mission (1570); others believe the 2-story bldg. was Sugar H. of plantation (1825). **Crooked R. St. Pk.** (by train or bus from Kingsland.f.h.swim.boat.pic.cottages.stores). Marsh-hen hunt. (Oct.1-Nov.30).

From Kingsland, US17 runs (S) to St. Marys R., **62. GA.-FLA. LINE.**

## US 1—GEORGIA

**GA.-S.C. LINE** (16m from Aiken, S.C.) **(S) to GA.-FLA. LINE.** (38m from Jacksonville, Fla.). **222. US1.**

Via: Augusta, Wrens, Louisville, Swainsboro, Lyons, Baxley, Alma, Waycross, Folkston. US25 is alternate route (E), ending at Brunswick. Accoms. in cities.

US1 crosses Savannah R. into old plantation belt. There are many graceful 18th & 19th cent. Hs. & modern farmsteads, but more numerous are the unpainted shacks of tenant farmers. In midsummer, the fields of cotton are alive with Negro pickers, trailing long burlap sacks.

**0. AUGUSTA**

800 block Walker St., Union RR. Sta. 700 block Broad St., Bus Terminal. Wheeless & Wrightsboro Rds., Daniel Field (airport). Info.: 712 Telfair St., & Municipal Aud., C. of C. Good accoms.; mun. golf course & polo field; beaches. Road shows in season. Masters Invitation Golf Tournament (early spring). Garden Club Tours (spring).

Augusta, a friendly city, has long been known for its gardens, pkys. & golf course, & as popular winter resort. It is also one of world's great cotton markets, center of textile mfg. & clay-products industries, leader in livestock business & inland port with assured future. The $45,000,000 Clark Hill project on Savannah R., 21m (N), 1st of 11 dams approved by Congress, will make Augusta a yr.-round port & protect it from dangerous floods. Augusta is seat of Univ. of Ga. Medical College, Richmond Acad., Haines Institute (Negro) & Paine College (Negro). Camp Gordon, Oliver General (Army) Hospital, Bush Field & U.S. Arsenal keep it a military center, as it was in Confed. when it had South's largest powder mill. Augusta has leisurely old-time charm even in downtown streets. In contrast are wharves & warehouses on 14m waterfront & some 100 mfg. plants. More than a 3rd of pop. lives in Negro "territory" in (SE) sec.
First white man to reach reg. was De Soto, 1540. In 1735, Gen. Oglethorpe ordered a town laid out across R. from Savannah Town (see S.C.), to be named Augusta, for mother of George III. Ft. Augusta was built in 1736, & Augusta soon became S.'s most important fur-trading post. Great Conference of Governors & Inds. was held here in Nov., 1763. In 1781, Augusta was delivered from Brit. occupation by "Lighthorse Harry" Lee, & Ft. Cornwallis (Ft. Augusta) was surrendered. Fed. Const. was ratified in 1788 while Augusta was capital (1786-96). When Pres. Washington came in 1791, it was a city of some elegance & a busy tobacco market,

but cotton gradually supplanted tobacco. Augusta suffered from floods in 1796 & 1840, earthquake in 1811, fire in 1829 & yellow fever epidemic in 1839-40. In 1862 the Arsenal was taken over by Confeds. Surviving war & reconstruction, Augusta grew rapidly. A disastrous fire in Nov., 1916, caused $2,500,000 damage & destroyed many fine Hs. & hist. bldgs., but whole new residential dists. were soon created. PTS. OF INT.: (1) (E) of US1, **Mun. Wharf.** (2) Greene St. bet. 5th & 6th Sts., **Signers' Mon.** (1848), comm. Lyman Hall & Geo. Walton, buried beneath shaft, & Button Gwinnett, signers of Decl. of Ind. (3) 519 Greene St., **Phinizy Place** (1841. Georg.). (4) 426 Greene St., **De L'Aigle H.** (1818.Tudor.later wings.fine inter. slave qtrs.). (5) 3rd & Walker Sts., **Thankful Bapt. Ch.** (O.1893), est. in 1840. Rev. Samuel Bell, 1st pastor, was 1st Negro missionary to Liberia, 1884. (6) 3rd St. bet. Watkins & Gwinnett Sts., **Magnolia Cemetery** (1818), incl. older graveyard. (7) Watkins St. bet. 2nd & E. Boundary, **Cedar Grove Cemetery** (Negro.1823). (8) 432 Telfair St., **Murphey H.** (1790.probably by Gabriel Manigault), built for "Government H." (9) 506 Telfair St., **Art Club,** "Ware's Folly" (O.appl.1818, said to be by Manigault); one of city's finest Georg. Hs. (10) 540 Telfair St., **Old Richmond Acad.** (O.1802.Tudor), now **Young Men's Lib.** (org.1848) & **Augusta Mus.** (1933); Acad. (see below) was est. in 1785. (11) 642 Telfair St., **First Presb. Ch.** (1809-12.by Rbt. Mills, designer of Washington Mon.), oldest ch. bldg. (12) In 600 block on Greene St. (N): No. 638, **Twiggs-Oertel H.** (1810). No. 619, **Eve H.** (1814) & **Mon.;** home of Dr. Paul F. Eve, founder of Ga. Med. College. No. 613, **Allen H.** (1859.Regency). (13) Greene St. bet. 7th & 8th Sts., **Poets' Mon.** to Lanier, J. R. Randall, P. H. Hayne, R. H. Wilde & Father Ryan. (14) Broad St. bet. 7th & 8th Sts., **Confed. Mon.** (1878.by Von Gunden & Young). (15) Nelson St. bet. 13th & 15th Sts., **Meadow Garden H.** (O.sm.fee.late 1700's), home of Geo. Walton. (16) Goodrich St. near Broad St., **Obelisk Chimney** (176'), relic of Confed. Powder Works (1862-65). (17) Harper St. bet. 15th St. & Railroad Ave., are **Univ. of Ga. Sch. of Medicine, Wilhenford Hospital** for Children, & **Univ. Hospital.** (18) Gwinnett & Harrison Sts., **Tabernacle Bapt. Ch.,** founded by Negro orator, Dr. C. T. Walker. (19) 1339 Gwinnett St., **Haines Institute** (Negro), supported in part by Presb. Ch.; founded in 1886 by Lucy Laney. (20) Gwinnett St. & Oglethorpe Ave., **Paine College** (Negro), coed. college est. in 1883 & controlled by Meth. Episc. Ch. Among graduates was John Hope, late pres. of Atlanta Univ. (see). **Haygood Hall Mus.,** African coll.

In **Sand Hills** area: (21) Baker Ave. bet. Walton Way & Hampton Ave., **Academy of Richmond Cty. & Jr. College** (1926.Goth.by Scroggs & Ewing); outgrowth of Richmond Acad. (1785). (22) 1014 Hickman Rd., **Mell Cottage** (late 1700's.adds.). (23) 2216 Wrightboro Rd., **Walton H.** (c.1795.Col.), built for Geo. Walton & still owned by descendants. **U.S. Arsenal** (grounds O.). Orig. bldgs. (1829). Along Walton Way are many Sand Hills cottages of early 19th cent. (24) 914 Milledge Rd., **Chafee Cottage** (pre-1784), good example of type. (25) 820 Milledge Rd., **High Gate** (pre-1800). (26) 2249 Cumming Rd., **Green Court** (gardens O.early 1800's. adds.). (27) On St.52 (W) 1.5$^m$, **Nat. Golf Course** (1934.by Bobby Jones & Dr. Alastair McKenzie). (28) On St.52 (SE), **Goodale Plantation** (1794).

Augusta is at J. with St.52, US25 (see) & US78 (see).

SIDE TRIP: On US25 & Old Savannah Rd. (S) c.8$^m$ to **Tobacco Road,** made famous by Erskine Caldwell's hit play; one of the rough trls. over which hogsheads of tobacco were drawn by oxen or mule to New Savannah or Augusta markets. Caldwell, son of a minister in near-by community, wrote of conditions he had seen in his childhood. New life came to Tobacco Rd. when **Lock & Dam** (at E. end) was opened in 1937 & Augusta became head of navigation on Savannah R.

Route of US1 cuts through cotton country, planted in some places with as. of pecan trees & large watermelon fields. Outstanding early Hs. in this sec. are: **35. OLIPHANT H.** (1820's). **42.5. WHIGHAM H.** (1790's). **46.5. GOBERT H.** (1790's). **48. LOUISVILLE,** founded in 1786, was Ga.'s 3rd capital (1796-1806). On site of old capitol is **Jefferson County Cth. Slave Market** (before 1800). J. with St.24.

SIDE TRIP: On St.24 (E) 25$^m$ to **Waynesboro,** named for Gen. Anthony Wayne (see), who lived in Ga. after Rev. Hqs. of Ga. Field Trial Assoc. (Jan.). J. with US25.

On US25 (S) 15$^m$ to **Magnolia Springs St. Pk.** (f.pic.bathh.restaurant). 20$^m$ **Millen. Jones H.** (1762.adds.1842.Gr.Rev.).

**78.5. SWAINSBORO,** livestock center & mill town. J. with US80 (see). Beyond are the piney woods that furnished material for Dr. Herty's experiments (see US17).

During reign of cotton, life was hard & poor in this reg. of independent farmers, but rural electrification & diversified farming are changing the countryside. **107.5. LYONS.** J. with St.30.

SIDE TRIP: On St.30 (SE) 14$^m$ to **Reidsville;** (S) 6$^m$ on St.147 to **Ga. St. Prison** (1936.by Tucker & Howell), model prison on 980 as.

**138.5. BAXLEY,** shipping & market center for tobacco (auctions), naval stores, lumber, syrup, & pecans; locale of Caroline Miller's "Lamb in His Bosom". J. with US341, direct route to Sea Is. (see US17). **156.5. ALMA.** J. with St.32, which runs (W) 22$^m$ to **Douglas,** seat of **South Ga. College** (Jr.). **183.5. WAYCROSS,** RR. center near entrance to Okefenokee Swamp St. Pk. (see below.hqs.at C. of C.) & Wildlife Refuge (hqs.in Fed.Bldg.). Town is commercial center for farm area, with important lumber, turpentine & naval stores industries. **190.5.** J. with Rd. leading (E) into **Laura S. Walker St. Pk.** (f.boat.swim.cabins.group camp), in midst of 48,000-a. **Coastal Flatwoods Utilization Project. 193.5.** J. with Vereen Bell Mem. Hy., comm. author of "Swamp Water" (killed in World War II). Hy. runs (W) 4$^m$ to **Okefenokee Swamp St. Pk.** (adm.children free.O.yr.-round to sunset.pic.). Elec. boat tours (fee) into flower-spangled inter.; trestle walks; alligator hunter's boat excursion (fee); Observ. Tower; Reptile H. (fee).

US1 cuts across (NE) edge of **Okefenokee Swamp,** drained by St. Mary's R. & the Suwannee, celebrated by Stephen Foster. Giant cypress & tupelo trees, hung with Sp. moss, rise out of morass. Area is broken by extensive "prairies," darkwater Ls. & Is. covered by impenetrable undergrowth & trees. Nearly 200 different birds & many species of fish, turtle & lizard live in the swamp, & alligator, deer, bear & sm. animals are abundant. Among the flowers are rare orchids & lilies, kitchen plants & floating hearts. Pres. Roosevelt, in 1937, designated boundary for some 480,000 as. in **Okefenokee Wildlife Refuge** (hqs.at Camp Cornelia, on E. boundary.permits & guides required.boats.f.no h.)

**222.** US1 crosses St. Mary's R., **GA.-FLA. LINE.**

## US 129—GEORGIA

**GA.-N.C. LINE** (11$^m$ from Murphy, N.C.) **(S) to GA.-FLA. LINE** (9$^m$ from Jasper & 38$^m$ from Lake City, Fla.). **375. US129.**

Via: Blairsville, Gainesville, Jefferson, Athens, Apalachee, Madison, Eatonton, Gray, Macon, Chester, Hawkinsville, Fitzgerald, Lakeland, Statenville.

US129 enters many middle Ga. cities & towns noted for ante bellum Hs., pleasant squares & pkys. From Macon, tour parallels US41 (see) through peach orchards, pecan groves & melon fields of the Piedmont & the semitropical landscapes near (S) border.

### Sec. 1: GA.-N.C. LINE to MACON. 197.

In **Chattahoochee Nat. For.** are some of highest peaks & most beautiful waterfalls in Ga. US129 is united with US19 through **Neel Gap** & across **Appalachian Trl.** (see). **32.** Route joins St.11 (see US76 for this sec.). **66. GAINESVILLE** (RR. & bus conns.), sett. 1821, on edge of Piedmont Plateau, is one of most prosperous cities in N. Ga. Leading industries are poultry-raising, textile, hosiery, & silk mills & furniture factories. Gold mining at Dahlonega brought many settlers, & by 1890's Gainesville was farm & poultry market. Tornado in 1903 destroyed lives & property, & in a 2nd & more serious one (1936) many were injured & 170 killed. Just off US23 on E. Washington St. are the 30 bldgs. of **Brenau College,** chartered in 1878 as Ga. Bapt. Seminary (for women). On US23 (S) 5$^m$ are factory & attractive workers' village of **Chicopee Mfg. Co.,** makers of Johnson & Johnson surgical supplies. **88. JEFFERSON. Mon. to Dr. Crawford W. Long** (see Danielsville on US78). **108. ATHENS** (see US78). **111.5. WATKINSVILLE. Eagle Hotel** (1789). **134. MADISON,** described in 1845 as "wealthiest & most aristocratic village . . . between Charleston & New Orleans." **Presb. Ch.** (1810). **Burney H.** (1845). **Snowhill** (1830's). **Travelers' Inn.** (1850). **Stokes-McHenry H.** (1830's). In Madison is **J.** with St.12.

SIDE TRIPS: (A) On St.12 (W) 8$^m$ to **Rutledge;** (N) 2$^m$ is **Hard Labor Cr. St. Pk.** (pic. bathh.shelters.trading post.boat.f.recr.facils.).

(B) On St.12 (E) 17m to **Greensboro,** cotton-mill town, laid out in 1786 as intended seat of Univ. of Ga.; became early cultural center. **Cobb-Dawson H.** (1810). 18.5m J. with Rd.; (N) 7.5m to **Penfield,** where Mercer Institute was opened in 1833 (see US80), aided by Adiel Sherwood & Jesse Mercer, Bapt. ministers; removed to Macon in 1871. In **Old Mercer Cemetery** are orig. **Chapel, Ciceronian Hall** & **Science Hall; Grave of Jesse Mercer.**

**149.5.** J. with Rd. which leads (W) 1m to **Eagle Mound,** called "most perfect effigy mound in North America." **155.5. EATONTON,** birthpl. of Joel Chandler Harris; a center of ante bellum cultural & social life. **J. C. Harris Mon.** Many beautiful white-columned Hs. **157.5.** J. with St.24.

SIDE TRIP: On St.24 (S) 18m to **Milledgeville,** seat of Ga. State College for Women; birthpl. of Dr. Chas. Holmes Herty (see US17). Capitol, Cemetery, Gov., & Penitentiary Squares, the 4 orig. 20-a. plots, form heart of town, where are most of the Hs. representing 50 yrs. of Gr. Rev. architecture. Milledgeville was seat of St. gov. (the 4th) from 1807 until 1868, when it was moved to Atlanta. Town is now center of pottery & clay industry & market town for cotton-growers. PTS. OF INT.: (1) **Old St. Capitol** (1807.adds.1828 & 1837.neo-Goth.), housing **Ga. Military College** (est.1879). Here Ga. passed Secession Act, 1861. (2) **Ga. St. College for Women,** opened in 1891 on Capitol & Cemetery Sqs.; became accredited unit of Univ. System in 1932. **Gov.'s Mansion** (1839.Gr.Rev.) has been President's H. since 1890; one of best-preserved Gr. Rev. Hs. in Ga. **Ina Dillard Russell Lib.;** excellent Ga. hist. coll. & newspaper file. Notable Hs.: (3) **Harris H.** (1832.Vict.porch added). (4) **Sanford-Powell-Binion H.** (c.1825.Gr.Rev.). (5) **William-Orme-Crawford H.** (1820.Gr.Rev.); early style with sm. balcony & massive chimneys. (6) **Old Masonic Hall** (1820). (7) In **Milledgeville Cemetery** are graves of Gov. D. B. Mitchell, Zachariah Lamar & his brother L. Q. C. Lamar, who drafted Miss. Secession Act.

**181.5. GRAY,** seat of Jones Cty., covered with peach bloom in spring; large canneries. **183.5. CLINTON,** once center of planters' society. **197. MACON** (see US80).

### Sec. 2: MACON to GA.-FLA. LINE. 178.

US129, most central route (S) from Macon, passes numerous rural villages & sm. industrial centers. Reg. around Macon is archeologically famous for mounds & villages in Ocmulgee Nat. Mon. (see US80). **5. BROWN'S MOUNT,** short distance off hy. (R); shelf-life cliff 180′ high & extending over 1,000 as. **40. COCHRAN.** A mile (S) on hill encircled by pines are red-brick bldgs. (1928.Georg.Col.) of **Middle Georgia (Jr.) College,** est. as New Ebenezer College in 1885. **49. HARTFORD.** US129 crosses Ocmulgee R. **50. HAWKINSVILLE** (see US1). J. with US341, route (SE) to Sea Is. (see US17). **73. ABBEVILLE. Poor Robin Springs,** (E) 1m, is tranquil pool in midst of pines; named for Ind. chief who was healed by the waters. **94. FITZGERALD,** one of largest centers along route. **St. Fish Hatchery. 103. OCILLA. 129. NASHVILLE.** US129 turns (E) from **RAY CITY, 138.,** to **LAKELAND, 148.,** across Alapaha R., then follows R. (S) through lake dist. & semitropical scenery. **156. STOCKTON.** J. with US84.

SIDE TRIP: On US84 (NE) 15m to **Homerville,** center of naval stores industry. Air is usually pungent with flowing sap, & in clean-floored fors., the pines run in slender rows.

US129 cont. (S) along Alapaha R. among pine fors. **178. GA.-FLA. LINE.**

## US 19—GEORGIA

**GA.-N.C. LINE** (1m from Murphy) **(S) to GA.-FLA. LINE** (8m from Monticello, Fla.) **365. US19.**

Via: Blairsville, Neel Gap, Dahlonega, Cumming, Boswell, Atlanta, Griffin, Thomaston, Butler, Americus (Andersonville), Smithville, Albany, Camilla, Thomasville. Good accoms. in cities.

### Sec. 1: GA.-S.C. LINE to GRIFFIN. 163.

US19, united with US129 (see), crosses spectacularly beautiful sec. of Appalachian Highlands. **11. BLAIRSVILLE.** J. with US76, route (E-W) across **Chattahoochee Nat. For. 22.5. VOGEL ST. PK.** (pic.inn.cottages.trl.post.bathh.f.h.boat). At N. border is J. with **Appalachian Trl.** (see), which follows crest of Blue Ridge Mts. Near (S) rim of for., US19 forks (R) from US129. **47. DAHLONEGA,** former goldmining town. Hy. swings (W), & crosses Etowah R. (see US76 for this sec.). **61.5. DAWSONVILLE,** neat market town of good farming area. **79. CUMMING. 100. ROSWELL,** residential town. In 1830's Roswell King bought land here & distributed it among friends from est. Southern towns, & Roswell had cotton-textile plant & handsome Hs. when Sherman's men made hqs. there. PTS. OF INT.: (1) **Colonial Place** (1857), built by Rev. Francis R. Goulding (see), author of "Young Marooners." (2) **Presb. Ch.** (1840.Gr.Rev.), used as hospital by Union soldiers. (3) Opp. is **Great Oaks** (Georg.Col.), built by Rev. Nath. Pratt, who designed the Ch. (4) **Barrington Hall** (1842), fine example of plantation H. (5) **Mimosa Hall** (1840's. Gr.Rev.). (6) **Bulloch Hall** (1842.Gr.Rev.), where Martha Bullock & Theo. Roosevelt were married in 1853, parents of Pres. Theo. & grandparents of Eleanor Roosevelt. Hy. crosses roiled, red Chattahoochee R. **121. ATLANTA** (see). US19 unites with US41. **163. GRIFFIN** (see Atlanta).

## Sec. 2: GRIFFIN to GA.-FLA. LINE. 202.

Beyond Griffin is peach & pecan country. **12. ZEBULON,** seat of Pike Cty., which has thousands of peach trees in new orchards, often lined with pecan trees. **27. SILVERTOWN,** not a peach city but an exceptionally pleasing mill town around **Martha Mills** (O.appl.), branch of B. F. Goodrich Co. **28. THOMASTON,** founded in 1825 & named for Gen. Jett Thomas, distinguished soldier in War of 1812; a leading peach center & textile town. **42.** Just (S) of Flint R., route unites with US80 (see) for short distance. **79. ELLAVILLE.** Along Sumter Cty.'s (World War I) Mem. Mile, **c.89.** to **90.** are marble slabs among evergreens & poppies. **91. AMERICUS,** seat of Sumter Cty., one of Ga.'s richest counties, with varied soils, kaolin & bauxite mines, hardwood & pine fors. **Ga. Southwestern (Jr.) College. Southern Field,** 5$^{m}$ (E), large aviation training field. J. with St.49.

SIDE TRIP: On St.49 (NE) 34$^{m}$ to **Marshallville.** Via Andersonville. 11$^{m}$ **Andersonville Prison Pk.** (Fed.), on site of Confed. prison camp (1864) where some 13,000 prisoners died in 13 months. Nearly 50,000 were admitted to stockade, an uncovered camp built for 10,000, & prisoners died of diseases brought on by shortage of food, polluted water, exposure & lack of medicine. In 1865, Henry Wirtz, prison supt., was taken to Washington, D.C., where he was sentenced to be hanged. In center of Andersonville is **Mon. to Capt. Wirtz.** Contributing causes for the mass deaths were unexpected flood of prisoners from N. Ga., shortage of food in the South, & delay in exchange of prisoners. **Andersonville Nat. Cemetery** (pic.outside walls), with 13,741 graves of Union soldiers. 19$^{m}$ on St.49, **Oglethorpe,** RR. town of 1850's with several int. Hs. Artesian wells in vic. 21$^{m}$ **Montezuma,** another RR. town which has become peach-shipping center; cottonseed-oil & other mills. 34$^{m}$ **Marshallville,** birthpl. of Georgia Belle & Elberta peaches.

**127.** Short distance (E) is **CHEHAW ST. FOR.** (pic.camp.recr.facils.O.yr.-round). The Chehaw (Chiha), a highly civilized tribe of Creek Inds., once roamed over whole Piedmont & Coastal Plains areas.

**129. ALBANY**

Through RR. & bus conns. Airport. Good accoms. Fat Cattle Show (Feb.8-9); SE. Field Trials (Jan.).

Albany, at head of Flint R., is papershell pecan & Spanish-peanut market of the world; also livestock center, with large packing plants in vic. On Front St., **Bridge H.** (1857), scene of early social life & later a theater; used as meat-packing plant in Civil War. **Cudahy Packing Co. Plant** (O); modern windowless bldgs. **Peanut-shelling Plants.** More than three-fourths of all Ga. peanuts are grown within 50$^{m}$ radius of Albany. Newer industries are wood & iron-working plants, **Clark Thread Co.** & **Dixie Leather Goods Co.** Ga. **Normal & Agric. College** (Negro), org. in 1903 & taken over by St. in 1917. US19 follows Flint R. for several miles. **134. RADIUM SPRINGS,** popular resort (f.h.hotel.cottages). **156. CAMILLA. Hawthorne Trl. Marker** (1818). **164. PELHAM,** sm. town with surprising number of mills, gins, peanut-shelling, canning & other plants. **187. THOMASVILLE,** the "city of roses among the pines," resort center since 1875. Wild turkeys, quail, doves, deer, raccoon, fox & opossum in the piney woods bring thousands of hunters, & salt-water fishing is available a few hrs. away in Gulf of Mex. In vic. are estates developed by Northern families, many in plantation style. Thomas Cty. is the watermelon kingdom & important sugar-cane & syrup-producing area. **Farm Market & Livestock Barn** (auctions weekly). Crawford & Monroe Sts., **Great Oak,** (250 yrs.old), with limb spread of 175′. N. Dawson St., **Mark Hanna H.** (1877). On Gordon St., **Archbold Mem. Hospital,** one of finest in reg. Notable plantations (mostly O.during Rose Show in Ap.): On US34 (W) 11$^{m}$, **Greenwood** (1844.Gr.Rev.by John Wind,Eng. architect). **Millpond Plantation** (Sp.Col.), off Pine Tree Blvd. **Melrose,** estate of H. M. Hanna, of Cleveland, O.; **White Garden. Pebble Hill,** with magnificent barn

(Class.Rev.); equipment incl. radio for milking time. **Winstead** (Gr.Rev.). Thomasville is at J. with US84, cross-state route (W-E) from Ala. Line.

SIDE TRIPS: (A) on US84 (E) 27m to **Quitman,** where roses bloom yr. round in downtown pks.; seat of Brooks Cty., known for home-smoked hams & sausage.
(B) On US84 (W) 13m to **Cairo,** famous for syrup & also center of tung oil & pickle industries. Camellias & other semitropical flowers bloom in gardens, & in spring, thousands of tung trees in vic. are groves of mauve & green. Beyond Cairo (W) are immense fields of sugar cane.

**202. GA.-FLA. LINE.**

## US 41—GEORGIA

**GA.-TENN. LINE** (11m from Chattanooga) **(S) to GA.-FLA. LINE** (45m from Lake City). **379. US41.**

Via: Ringgold, Dalton, Calhoun, Cartersville, Marietta, Atlanta, Griffin, Barnesville, Forsyth, Macon, Perry, Tifton, Adel, Valdosta. Accoms. in cities.

US41, Dixie Hy., winds through Appalachian Valley to Atlanta & then past farms, peach orchards, & tobacco fields of the rolling Piedmont.

### Sec. 1: GA.-TENN. LINE to GRIFFIN. 154.

Tour follows route of Gen. Sherman's advance on Atlanta in 1864. Most little towns along hy. were rebuilt after Civil War, as flour mills, stores, foundries &, in some cases all their Hs., were destroyed. Mts. & valleys of N.Ga. were home of the Cherokee until removal in 1838; home of Sequoyah (see).

**7. RINGGOLD,** scene (1862) of Confed. capture of "The General", woodburning locomotive (now in Union Sta., Chattanooga), from J. J. Andrews' raiders (see Atlanta). **Catoosa County Cth.** (1850's). **Bapt. Ch.** (1830's).

**14. TUNNEL HILL,** where Confed. forces repulsed Union men in Nov., 1863, but were defeated, 1864, in struggle for RR. **Old RR. Tunnel** (1848-50). **23. DALTON,** nat. known for candlewick-bedspread industry, begun a century ago. Rainbow lines of bedspreads are on display along hy. After Missionary Ridge, Gen. Braxton Bragg retreated to Dalton & resigned command to Gen. J. E. Johnston. **Johnston Mem.** J. with US76-St.2. (see).

SIDE TRIP: On St.2-US76 (E) 10m to **Spring Place;** site of Moravian mission est. in 1802 on land given by Jos. Vann, half-breed Cherokee chieftain. **Vann H.** (1799); beautiful detail. Marker records imprisonment in near-by cabin & trial (1835) of John Howard Payne, author of "Home, Sweet Home" & champion of the Cherokee. 13m **Chatsworth,** near **Ft. Mountain St. Pk.** (see US76).

US41 borders **Chattahoochee Nat. For. 38.5. SITE OF RESACA,** Civil War battleground. **First Confed. Cemetery.** Short distance off hy. (E), **Cherokee Capital Nat. Mem.** at site of **New Echota,** where "Cherokee Phoenix," 1st Ind. newspaper, was printed in 1828, using Sequoyah's (see) Cherokee alphabet. From hqs. here, Gen. Winfield Scott directed removal of some 13,000 Cherokee. **43.** US41 enters **Calhoun,** on Oostanaula R., through **Mem. Arch.** Beyond is **Statue of Sequoyah.** Calhoun is dairy & poultry center. **53. ADAIRSVILLE. c.64. CASSVILLE,** destroyed with its 2 colleges during Civil War; now a sm. market center. J. with US411.

SIDE TRIP: On US411 (W) 5m to **Kingston;** 7m **Barnsley Gardens.** The roofless mansion stands among ruins of magnificent gardens; said to be locale of "St. Elmo" by Augusta Evans Wilson (see US80).

**68. ATCO. Goodyear Tire & Rubber Co. Plant** (O.appl.) & workers' village. **70. CARTERSVILLE.** In vic. are limestone quarries, barite & other mines. **Roseland,** gabled H. where Sam Jones (1847-1906), "Mountain Evangelist", lived. **Sam Jones Tabernacle. Etowah Mounds,** among fields of cotton; largest is 2nd in size to Cahokia Mound (see Ill.). **Allatoona Dam.** Among plantations on Euharlee Rd. are **Valley View, Etowah Cliffs, & Malbone** (O.sm.fee). **"In the Valley"** (O.sm.fee), near **Rydall** (N), is former estate of Corra Harris, novelist. **Mem. Chapel** (1936.by Ralph Adams Cram). **77. ALLATOONA,** gold-mining village in 1840's & 1850's. **86. KENNESAW MT. NAT. BATTLEFIELD PK.** (O.to sundown.guides.mus.see US 761). **92. MARIETTA** (see Atlanta). **112. ATLANTA** (see). J. with US19, with which US41 unites (S) along Sherman's route to Griffin, where (E) march began. **128. FAIR OF 1850** (sm.fee), hist. mus. **129. JONESBORO.** In vic. occurred Aug.,

1864, last engagement in Battle of Atlanta. **150. UNIV. OF GA. EXPER. STA.,** where superior cotton & wheat have been developed. **154. GRIFFIN,** an attractive city, with important textile mills & pimento canneries. **Mun. Pk.**

### Sec. 2: GRIFFIN to GA.-FLA. LINE. 225.

**16. BARNESVILLE** (sett. 1826), one of many quiet country towns in middle Ga. **Gordon Military College** (Jr.). **29. FORSYTH** (sett.1822). Near Pub. Sq. are white-pillared, brick bldgs. of **Bessie Tift College** (women), founded in 1849 & adopted by Ga. Bapt. Convention (1898). On St.42 (S) 1$^{m}$ is **St. Teachers' & Agric. College** (Negro), high sch. & jr. college under Univ. System; began (1902) in class taught by Wm. M. Hubbard. Forsyth is at J. with St.42 & St.18, which leads (E) 11$^{m}$ to **Piedmont Nat. Wildlife Refuge.**

SIDE TRIP: On St.42 (N) 16$^{m}$ to **Ind. Springs St. Pk.** (O.Mar.-Dec.pic.recr.facils.hotels), health spa around mineral springs in reg. rich in Ind. lore. By Treaty of Ind. Springs in 1825, Creek Inds. ceded last of their Ga. lands (see US27).

Beyond Forsyth is campus of **WESLEYAN COLLEGE** (see US80). **52. MACON** (see US80). J. with US80 (see) & US129 (see). Macon is on fall line bet. Piedmont & Coastal Plain. **65.** J. with St.49.

SIDE TRIP: On St.49 (SW) 13$^{m}$ to **Fort Valley,** seat of Peach Cty. where are miles of orchards. **Fort Valley St. College** (Negro), coed. teachers' college; founded at Forsyth in 1902.

During harvest, thousands of pickers may be seen in orchards, & packing plants are scattered over countryside. **78. PERRY.** Century-old **Houston County Cth.,** where Negroes were sold at auction. J. with US341, the route (E) to St. Simon I. (see US17).

**107. VIENNA,** pecan-shelling center & market for pimentos & other produce. **116. CORDELE,** relatively new & industrialized town; large peanut-shelling plants; market for corn, watermelons & pecans. Important also are naval stores, lumbering & metal working, one of St.'s newest industries. J. with St.30.

SIDE TRIP: On St.30 (W) 10$^{m}$ to **Blackshear L. Mem. St. Pk.** (pic.f.boat.swim.), ded. in 1946 to vets. of World War II. **Power Dam.**

**136. ASHBURN,** center of livestock & farming area. **139. SYCAMORE.** J. with St.32.

SIDE TRIP: On St.32 (E) 12$^{m}$ to **Jeff. Davis Mem. St. Pk.** (pic.). At near-by **Irwinville,** bronze bust. comm. spot where Pres. of Confed. was captured, May 10, 1865. **Confed. Mus.**

South Ga. is land of slash & loblolly pine, turpentine & naval stores (Ga. supplies more than half nat. production), & the developing tung oil industry. Here are evident the effects of rural electrification & farmers' cooperatives, of Northern capital & local enterprise. Semitropical climate & beauty of setting make it resort country.

**154.5. ABRAHAM BALDWIN AGRIC. COLLEGE** (Jr.), part of Univ. System; assoc. with adj. **Coastal Plain Exper. Sta.** of Univ. of Ga. **157. TIFTON,** Ga.'s largest tobacco market & shipping center for millions of tomato & other plants. On St.50 (E) 1$^{m}$ is **Armour Meat-Packing Plant** (O.). **182. ADEL,** tobacco market. J. with St.37.

SIDE TRIP: On St.37 (W) 23$^{m}$ to **Moultrie** (RR. & bus conns. airport), trade center of Colquitt Cty., leading livestock & dairying area. Pure-bred cattle & hogs feed in rich pastures, & cotton, truck crops, pecans & some of St.'s finest watermelons flourish (average temp. 70° F.). Watermelon Festival. **Swift & Co. Plant** (O.), about 1$^{m}$ N.

**203. VALDOSTA** (good accoms.), in lake country; world's largest naval stores center, busy tobacco market (auctions in Aug.); trading & tourist town. **Livestock Auditorium. Emory-At-Valdosta,** Jr. College of Emory Univ. (see). **Ga. St. Woman's College,** on hillside campus. **225. GA.-FLA. LINE.**

## US 27—GEORGIA

**GA.-TENN. LINE** (Chattanooga, Tenn.) **(S) to GA.-FLA. LINE** (21$^{m}$ from Tallahassee, Fla.). **356. US27.**

Via: Rossville, Chickamauga Pk., LaFayette, Berry Schools, Rome, Cedartown, Bremen, Carrollton, La Grange (Warm Springs), Columbus, Lumpkin, Cuthbert, Blakely, Colquitt & Bainbridge

US27 crosses (NW) Ga. among sandstone cliffs of Lookout Range & darkly wooded Appalachian ridges, a reg. rich in iron, barite, bauxite & manganese, shales & clays. Route (S) of Columbus is through badly eroded lands bet. Chattahoochee & Flint Rs., where Little TVA Project will be completed in 1952.

## Sec. 1: GA.-TENN. LINE to LA GRANGE. 161.

**0. ROSSVILLE,** named for John Ross, Cherokee chieftain although only one-eighth Ind. Ross went with tribe in 1838 & spent his life helping educate the exiled Cherokee. **Ross H.** (O.c.1770), built by Ross' Scotch grandfather. Hy. cuts through **Ft. Oglethorpe,** est. in 1913. **5.5.** Ga. sec. of **Chickamauga & Chattanooga Nat. Military Pk.** (see US76). **20.** North J. with St.2, scenic hy. through mts. **22. LAFAYETTE,** scene of skirmishes during Sherman's campaign; hosiery & textile mills. **35. TRION,** textile center. **40. SUMMERVILLE. Rock Mus.** (O), privately owned coll. of stones incl. 7-ton chunk of Stone Mt. US27 swings (E) through **Chattahoochee Nat. For.**

**61. GATE OF OPPORTUNITY,** entrance to **Berry Schs. & College** (O.guides.overnight cottages). The 30,000-a. campus, with some 60 bldgs., farmlands & fors., extends for miles along hy. All students attend classes 4 days a wk. & work 2 days in some of school's many industries; only sm. number pay cash for expenses. Mr. & Mrs. Henry Ford were outstanding contributors to Berry fund. The founder, Martha Berry (1866-1942), opened 1st boarding schs. in 1902. **Mount Berry Chapel** (Georg. Col.). **Berry College,** fully accredited 4-yr. college, has many fine bldgs. on 150-a. landscaped campus. **College & High Sch. for Girls** (Goth.) was given by Mr. & Mrs. Ford. Rd. from here runs to **Laurel L.** & through woodlots & orchards to **High Sch. for Boys.** In **Possum Trot Rural Community** families are given formal education & training in farming. **Log Playh. & Hilltop Cottage. 64. ROME** (RR.& bus conns.airport.accoms.& recr.facils.), on 7 hills, is industrial & trade center at confluence of Etowah & Oostanaula Rs. (forming Coosa R.); seat of Shorter College; played important part in Civil War. Industrial plants incl. stove foundries, cotton mills, bedspread & clothing factories, rayon plant, lumber & flour mills, agric. implements factory & frozen-foods plant. **Coosa Valley Livestock Barn** (Wed.sales) has $1,000,000 sales record. PTS. OF INT.: Broad St. & 2nd Ave., **Forrest Statue,** comm. Confed. Gen. Nathan B. Forrest. On Neely Hill, **City Clock Tower,** part of waterworks system designed by Noble Bros. in 1871; bronze bell (1872) is now used in electric fire-alarm system. Broad St. & 2nd Ave., **Mun. Auditorium.** On lawn are **Capitoline Wolf,** gift of Benito Mussolini; **Battery Mon.,** comm. Rbt. Battery (1828-95), noted surgeon. On Shorter Hill, off Alabama Ave., are red-brick bldgs. (1911) of **Shorter College,** est. by Bapt. Ch. (1873); liberal arts college for women. In Myrtle Hill Cemetery, S. Broad St., **Grave of First Mrs. Woodrow Wilson,** born in Rome. Rome is at J. with US411, with which US27 unites for a few miles. **Agate Soil Conservation Project** (hqs. in Rome) covers 30,000 as. in Floyd & Polk counties.

**65. LINDALE,** mill town around **Pepperell Mfg. Co. Plant. 88. CEDARTOWN,** on site of Cherokee Village; large textile, tire & rubber plants & marble shops. **Big Springs,** with flow of 8,000,000 gals. **106. BREMEN,** another mill town. J. with US78 (see). Across Little Tallapoosa R. is **CARROLLTON, 118.,** prosperous textile town; seat of **W. Ga. (jr.) College,** part of Univ. System. On market days, it is lively place with mule-drawn wagons mingling with motor cars. On W. Ga.'s campus is **Stone Mounting Block** used by Gen. Wm. McIntosh, Scotch & Ind. chieftain who ceded Creek lands in Treaty of Ind. Springs. He was cousin of Gov. Geo. Troup, who militantly challenged Fed. Gov. to remove Creek Inds. For his signature McIntosh was given tract near **ROOPVILLE, 127.,** but he was put to death in Ap., 1825, by the Creek. **140. FRANKLIN.** Hy. crosses **Chattahoochee R.** in thickly wooded country. **161. LA GRANGE,** a notable blending of Old South & New, known both as Ga.'s largest textile center & for its ante bellum Hs. & gardens; seat of La Grange College, endowed by textile magnates. Town was named in 1828 after LaFayette's estate, to which the Marquis had compared rich planters' homes in W. Ga. PTS. OF INT.: (1) Vernon St., **Hills & Dales,** the Callaway estate, incl. extraordinary **Ferrell Gardens** (1827). The marble mansion (Ital.Ren.) overlooks older gardens where giant trees are overgrown with wisteria. **Church Garden** has harp of dwarf box with strings of golden amaranth. (2) In (SW) sec., **Gallaway Mills Community;** mill bldgs., employees' cottages, community Hs. **Callaway Mem. Clock**

**Tower** (1929). Besides liberal gifts to college & town, the Callaway family est. the "100 Ga. Better Farms." (3) 204 McLendon Ave., **Bellevue,** former plantation H. of Benj. H. Hill (1823-82), orator for the South during secession & Reconstruction, to both of which he was opposed & in both finally acquiesced. (4) 311 Vernon St., **Segrest H.** (1820's). (5) 1103 Vernon St., **The Oaks** (1845.Gr.Rev.). (6) Broad St., **La Grange College,** nonsect. liberal arts college for women; est. as academy in 1831 & bought by Meth. Conference in 1857. **Green Smith Hall;** ivy-covered pillars named for Matthew, Mark, Luke & John. **Pitts Hall,** built during World War II, is red-brick & white-columned like older halls. La Grange is at J. with US29.

SIDE TRIP: On US29 (SW) 11m to **West Pt.** on Chattahoochee R.; lumber & textile mills & ironworks; hqs. of **West Pt. Mfg. Co.,** org. in 1866 by LaFayette Lanier. **Griggs H.** (1857). **Ruins of Ft. Tyler.** Town was virtually destroyed during Civil War.

## Sec. 2: LA GRANGE to GA.-FLA. LINE. 195.

Tour cont. (S) through beautiful, primitive country with many reminders of Ind., pioneer & planter life. Here also are some of most seriously eroded lands.

**7. TROUP CTY. PRISON,** scene of Rbt. W. Burns' "I Am a Fugitive From a Georgia Chain Gang." **17. CHIPLEY,** in Pine Mt. valley, a starting pt. for Roosevelt Mem. St. Pk. (see below); served by train & bus from Atlanta & Columbus. **21.** J. with St.190, at entrance to **Roosevelt Mem. St. Pk.** (f.boat.swim.pic.cabins. tavern.group camps.recr.facils.), largest & best developed in Ga.; orig. Pine Mt. St. Pk., suggested by Pres. F. D. Roosevelt. **L. Delano** (pic.). **L. Franklin** (group camps). **Liberty Bell Swim. Pool** (sm.fee).

SIDE TRIP: On St.190 (E) 12m across pk. along crest of Pine Mt. to **Warm Springs Foundation & Roosevelt Mem.** Along slope are cottages for polio patients (N.O.). **Georgia Hall** (adm.center) was erected by contributions from thousands of Georgians; Thanksgiving Dinners were held in dining room (O). Beyond **Pub. Swim. Pool** (sm.fee) is **Solarium,** incl. patients' pool; gift of the late Edsel & Mrs. Ford. About a mile from Ga. Hall is **Little White H.** (O.sm.fee), ded. as nat. shrine, June 25, 1947, central pt. of int. of **Warm Springs Mem. Foundation,** which will incl. 3,500 as. devoted to recr. purposes. The simple, clapboarded, hilltop H. was planned by Pres. F. D. Roosevelt & built in 1932; & bldgs. & grounds are preserved as much as practicable in orig. state. Ship models, pictures, hangings, telephone & furniture remain in place. Pres. Roosevelt came to White Springs in 1924 & in winter of 1925 planned his 1st H., now called **McCarthy Cottage.** He bought 2,500 as. of farmland, which he later transferred to the Foundation created with his help in 1927 & developed under Dr. Michael Hoke, of Atlanta.

**50. COLUMBUS** (see US80). US27 unites with St.1 & crosses **FT. BENNING MILITARY RESERV. 88. LUMPKIN,** seat of Stewart Cty., in midst of Ga.'s "badlands." In thousands of as. devastated by erosion are vividly colored canyons & gullies, over which lean grotesquely misshapen pines. Stripped of their covering humus, the orange, red, white, yellow & lavender clays appear, & the gullies are lined with deeply worn limestone.

SIDE TRIP: On St.27 (E) 7.5m is enormous gully known as **Grand Canyon of Ga.;** 300′ deep, 200′ wide & covering several hundred as.

**108. CUTHBERT,** attractive town founded in 1834; popular with fishermen & hunters. **Andrew College** (Meth.), for girls; founded in 1854 & operated as 4-yr. college until 1917, when it became jr. college, part of Univ. System. **138. BLAKELY,** a good place to see peanuts in all stages from appearance on yellow-blossoming vine to shelled & processed nuts. In vic. (N) & only a few miles (W) of US27 is **Kolomoki Mounds St. Pk.** (pic.). **Kolomoki Mound** is truncated pyramid 57′ high, with level top 56′ x 66′. The 100,000-ton mass of earth was probably piled up as a burial mound by very early Inds. J. with St.62.

**156. COLQUITT,** a rural town with shaded cth. sq. as social center. **175. BAINBRIDGE,** on Flint R. Live & water oaks shade pleasant streets. Stagecoach stop in 18th cent. & prosperous lumber town during early 20th, Bainbridge still draws from the fors. for naval stores & lumber industries; also cotton & tobacco market. Along Flint R. are **De Soto Trl. Marker & Andrew Jackson Marker** (near bridge in W. Bainbridge), where troops rested during Seminole War, 1818. J. with US84.

**195.** US27 crosses **GA.-FLA. LINE.**

SIDE TRIP: On US84 (NW) 21m to **Donalsonville,** which has some of St.'s largest peanut-shelling plants. Deer, quail & sm. animals find excellent cover in surrounding area.

# ATLANTA

## ATLANTA

RR. Stas., Mitchell & Spring St., Terminal Sta.; 2 Forsyth St., Union Sta. (passenger). 81 Cain St., Union Bus Terminal. Mun. Airport (SW) 8m from Five Points. Good hotels & other accoms. Recr. facils. in numerous mun. pks. Theaters (stage & screen). Metropolitan Opera season. Annual events: McDowell Festival (Feb.). Flower Show, Grand Opera, Dogwood Festival, Irish Horse Traders' Reunion (Ap.). Uncle Remus Festival (May). Soap Box Derby (July). Sacred Harp Singers' Convention (Aug.). Southeastern Fair, DeKalb Cty. Harvest Festival (Oct.). Joel Chandler Harris Mem. Serv. (Dec.). Info.: C. of C., Pryor St. & Auburn Ave. 134 Peachtree St., Convention Bureau.

Atlanta, capital city, in Chattahoochee R. Valley among Blue Ridge foothills, is an almost aggressively modern metropolis; distribution & financial center of SE. & commercial center of nat. importance. Located here are U.S. military & naval training sta., Fed. hospitals, prison, Reserve Bank & more than 100 other Fed. agencies. Atlanta is also becoming a leading educational center. Despite strong ties with Eastern capital & atmosphere of commercialism & efficiency, it is still fundamentally a Southern city, & as in rural Ga., entertainment & sociability are largely home affairs. The Ku Klux Klan persists, but the city has registered official disapproval & leading chs. have denounced bigotry. Atlanta has world's largest educational center for Negroes, & "The World," one of the very few Negro dailies in U.S., is published here. Peachtree St. (US29) bisects the irregular downtown, where narrow streets, massive bldgs. & tall towers surround Five Points, hist. heart of financial dist. St. Capitol stands in what was fashionable sec. of 1880's. Many early chs. & Vict. Hs. survive, but this is now largely domain of Greek, Syrian, Ital. & other foreign-born groups. Markets, pushcarts, peanut & fruit vendors give color & animation. To (N) are Druid Hills, Ansley Pk., Buckhead & other luxurious suburbs. Along Auburn Ave. is quiet Negro business dist. & around Atlanta Univ. are more prosperous Negro neighborhoods.

First white settlement in area was a ft. erected, 1813, at The Standing Peachtree, an Ind. town on Chattahoochee R. When stake was driven in 1837 for J. of Western & Atlantic & Georgia RRs., Hardy Ivy was lone inhabitant of what is now downtown Atlanta. On Christmas Eve, 1841, the engine "Florida" arrived by mule-team at Five Points, where a few Hs. had been built. Settlement was chartered as Marthasville in 1843, in honor of Gov. Wilson Lumpkin's daughter, but 2 yrs. later the Ga. RR. was completed & town's name changed to Atlanta, for W. & A. RR. After Southern Agric. Fair, 1851, Atlanta's place as market town was assured. During Civil War city was placed under martial law & became hospitalization, supply mfg. & storage center. After battles of Lookout Mt. & Missionary Ridge (see Tenn.), Grant turned toward Lee in Va., & Wm. T. Sherman became principal general in the West. His admitted mistake was the attack on Kennesaw Mt. (see Trip III below), where Union troops were repulsed with heavy losses. Sherman recommenced flanking movements, & Confeds. retreated toward Atlanta. At this crucial time, Gen. Johnston was replaced by Gen. John B. Hood. Four major battles were fought around Atlanta. Thousands were killed & wounded on each side & of 3,800 bldgs., only 400 were left standing. By Sept. 7, some 80,000 Union men occupied the city. Before destroying stores, factories & pub. bldgs., Sherman asked that civilian pop. be evacuated, & his soldiers helped remove citizens & loyal slaves. On Nov. 15, torches were applied to Atlanta. A Fed. soldier's account ends thus: "All the pictures & verbal descriptions of hell I have ever seen never gave me half so vivid an idea of it, as did this flame-wrapped city tonight." On May 3, Ga. troops were surrendered to Maj. Gen. J. H. Wilson, & Gov. Brown & other principal leaders were arrested.

Almost immediately after Fed. troops departed, families began to come back to Atlanta, living in shanties, freight cars & ruined bldgs. In May, 1865, city was turned over to Fed. Gov. &, like the rest of Ga., submitted to conditions for readmission to Union. The St. Constitutional Convention met in Atlanta, Dec. 9, 1867, & Atlanta was made capital (the 5th). In Sept., 1868, Negro legislators were expelled & Gov. Bullock began movement for return of military rule. Ga. rejected 15th Amendment in 1869, & Fed. troops were once more in the city. In July, 1870, Ga. was again admitted to the Union, & Fed. troops were finally withdrawn in 1876. Atlanta became prosperous center of the "New South," of which Henry W. Grady was the brilliant prophet. In 1881, H. I. Kimball secured for the city the World's Fair & Great Internat. Cotton Exposition, attended by some 350,000. Pres. & Mrs. Cleveland attended Piedmont Exposition in 1887. At Cotton States & Internat. Exposition in 1895, Booker T. Washington was 1st Negro in S. to address white audience on important occasion. Training camp was est. in Atlanta during Sp.-Amer. War. In 1906 occurred a bitter race riot along Decatur St., in which mob of 5,000 participated. Racial tolerance group was org. & lasted until forming (in Atlanta) of Nat. Commission on Interracial Co-operation in 1919. Southern Commercial Congress met in the "Convention City" in 1911. In May, 1917, a fire caused some $5,000,000 damage. During World War I, Camp Gordon was est.; airport & hospital were built here in 1941.

Unlike the rest of Ga., early Atlanta had few slaves, & most of work was done by white settlers & freed Negroes, but after Civil War, thousands came into city. The leasing of convict labor also brought general lowering of wages. In early 1870's workers began to organize, growing more courageous with necessity during 1880's when about half the pop. lived below minimum standard. The Women's Industrial Union was formed in 1884, & internat. brotherhoods in various trades in 1888-89. Following campaign made by "Atlanta Constitution," a child labor law was enacted in 1906, & a much more advanced law in 1925. As in rest of country, many strikes occurred in 1930's. The 2nd Ku Klux Klan was org. on Stone Mt. (see Trip I below) in 1915, & the Black Shirts was founded in Atlanta in 1930, to drive Negroes out of industry. Rise of C.I.O. in 1930's & consequent rivalry among unions resulted in widespread labor organization. Atlanta began early to est. theaters, chs., schs. & other cultural facils. The recently organized University Center, aided by Rockefeller funds & millions of dollars raised by cooperating units, is designed to regain for Ga. its prestige in educational field. It is composed of Univ. of Ga. (Athens); Atlanta's Emory Univ. & Ga. Sch. of Tech. & High Mus. Sch. of Art; & near-by Decatur's Agnes Scott College & Columbia Theol. Seminary.

PTS. OF INT. DOWNTOWN: (1) Marietta & Forsyth Sts., **Henry Grady Mon.** (1891.Alex.Doyle). (2) 33 Pryor St., **Kimball House** (1885), hotel on site of Atlanta Hotel (1846) & 1st Kimball House (1870), political rendezvous for many yrs. (3) Capitol Ave. & Washington, Hunter & Mitchell Sts., **Capitol** (1889), gray Indiana limestone bldg. patterned after Nat. Capitol. On lawn is Borglum's equestrian statue of **Gen. J. B. Gordon,** 1st gov. in Capitol. **St. Lib.,** on 3rd fl.; **St. Mus.** Opp. Capitol is **St. Office Bldg.** (1939.by Augustus Constantine). (4) Mitchell & Washington Sts., **City Hall** (1929.by G. Lloyd Preacher), 14 stories, on setback principle. (5) Central Ave. & Hunter St., **Ch. of the Immaculate Conception** (Cath.1869-72. Goth.), oldest in city; on site of earlier ch. (1848). Irish Horse Traders hold funeral services here on Ap. 28 (see West View Cemetery below). Father O'Reilly, who saved 1st ch. by appealing to Catholics in Sherman's army, died before completion of new one & is buried beneath altar. (6) 126 Carnegie Way, **Carnegie Lib.** (1902. Class.by Akerman & Ross), development of Young Men's Lib. Assoc., org. in 1867. (7) Peachtree & Houston Sts., **Candler Bldg.** (1904-06.by G.E.Murphy), city's 1st skyscraper; 17-stories of white Ga. marble. (8) Butler St. & Auburn Ave., **Big Bethel** (Afr.Meth.Episc.1920), largest Negro ch.; nationally known for Choir & presentation of "Heaven Bound."

PTS. OF INT. NORTH: (9) North Ave., bet. Williams St. & Hemphill Ave., **Ga. Sch. of Technology,** engineering unit of Univ. System, member of Univ. Center. **St. Eng. Exper. Sta.,** on campus. **Adm. Bldg.** (1888.Richardson Romanes.). Cor. North Ave. & Cherry St., **Guggenheim Sch. of Aeronautics** (1930), gift of Guggenheim Fund. **Brittain Hall** (1928.Goth.by Julian Harris), beautiful bldg. ded. to M. L. Brittain, Pres. Emeritus. (10) 318 North Ave., **Coca Cola Co. Plant** (O), long, low modern factory. In 1886, J. S. Pemberton made "Coca-Cola," named for coca leaves & cola nuts used in formula. In Ap., 1888, Asa G. Candler purchased controlling interest & simplified formula, & in 1919 the Candlers sold their interest (see Emory Univ. below). (11) Marietta St. & Brady Ave., **Nat. Stockyards** (auctions Mon.), largest mule market in world. (12) Piedmont Ave. & 10th St., **Piedmont Pk.,** largest in city; incl. polo & playfields; scene of Piedmont Exposition, 1887, & Cotton States

& Internat. Exposition, 1895. (13) 1262 Peachtree St., **High Mus. of Art** (Tudor), in former home of Mrs. J. M. High; offices of Atlanta Art Assoc. Exhibition incl. Tiepolo, Salvatore Rosa, Reynolds, Raeburn, Sully, Duveneck, Hassam, Rembrandt & Whistler. **High Mus. Sch. of Art,** member of Univ. Center. (14) 1516 Peachtree St., **Rhodes Mem. Hall** (O.wks.1900), St. Dept. of Archives & Hist.; in former home of A. G. Rhodes, Confed. soldier. H. is modeled after Bavarian castle in Stone Mt. granite. (15) Peachtree Rd. at Peachtree Way, **Co-Cathedral of Christ the King** (Cath.Goth.by H.D.Dagit & Sons), sharing seat of diocese with Savannah's St. John the Baptist.

PTS. OF INT. EAST: (16) Fair St., bet. S. Blvd. & Oakland Ave., **Oakland Cemetery** (1850). **Grave of Martha Lumpkin Compton. Confed. Mem. "Lion of Atlanta"** honors unknown dead. (17) S. Blvd. & Cherokee Ave., **Grant Pk.,** city's oldest. **Candler Menagerie.** (18) In pk., **Cyclorama of Battle of Atlanta** (O.sm.fee), in white terra cotta bldg.; one of largest circular paintings in world.

PTS. OF INT. SOUTH: (19) McDonough Rd. & South Blvd., **Fed. Penitentiary** (1902.adds.), built of granite cut by prisoners. (20) Lakewood Ave., **Lakewood Pk.** (pic.); permanent midway & race track. Southeastern Fair Bldgs. (21) McDonough Rd. & Capitol Ave., **Gammon Theol. Seminary** (Negro.Meth.), founded in 1880 as part of Clark Univ. (see Atlanta Univ. below).

PTS. OF INT. WEST: (22) 1050 Gordon St., **Wren's Nest** (O.wks.sm.fee), home of Joel Chandler Harris (1848-1908), who created "Uncle Remus" while on "Constitution" staff. (23) Gordon Rd. & Mozley Dr., **West View Cemetery** (1884). Several lots are owned by Irish Horse Traders, descendants of 8 families who came to this country in 1850's. The Clan holds annual reunions in Atlanta & Nashville, Tenn., for burial of dead, betrothals & business affairs. (24) Hunter & C Sts., **Booker T. Washington Mon.,** replica of mon. by Chas. Keck, at Tuskegee Inst. (see Ala.). (25) Ella & Hunter Sts., **Atlanta Univ. System,** incl. Atlanta Univ., Morehouse College (men), Spelman College (women) & Atlanta Sch. of Social Work. Near-by are independent but cooperating Morris Brown & Clark Colleges. Sch. of Social Work, only Negro one in U.S., was affiliated in 1938. **Atlanta Univ.** was est. by Amer. Missionary Soc. in 1865. **Dormitories & Dining Room** (1933), $1,000,000 gift of anonymous donor. **Adm. Bldg.** (1932.Georg.Col.). **Univ. Lib.** (1932.Georg.Col.), model lib. erected by Rockefeller Foundation. **Morehouse College,** org. in Augusta in 1867 by Amer. Bapt. Home Mission Soc. & moved to Atlanta in 1879. The late Dr. John Hope (1868-1948), pres. of Morehouse, 1906-31, & 1st pres. of Atlanta Univ. System, 1929, was a teacher of internat. repute (see "The Story of John Hope," by Ridgely Torrence). **Spelman College,** on beautiful 25-a. campus, was opened in 1881 by New England women; named in honor of mother of Mrs. John D. Rockefeller. **Rockefeller Hall** (1886), 1st permanent bldg., was gift of J. D. Rockefeller family. At Tatnall & Hunter Sts., **Morris Brown College,** coed. liberal arts sch. under control of Afr. Meth. Episc. Ch. 240 Chestnut St., **Clark College,** opened in 1869. (26) In Druid Hills, **Emory Univ.,** which incl. colleges at Oxford (see) & Valdosta (see). On Druid Hills Campus (400 as.) are handsome Ga. marble bldgs. (since 1915.mod.Ital.Ren.) of one of largest & most richly endowed Southern schs., a leading member of Univ. Center; nonsect. but owned by Meth. Episc. Ch. In 1947, Emory received additional gift from Candler family worth bet. $5,000,000 & $7,000,000 & purchased Candler Co. stock amounting to $2,500,000. Incl. College of Arts & Sciences, Schs. of Business Adm., Nursing, Dentistry, Law, Med. & Theology, Grad. & Library Schs. Women are admitted in grad. & professional courses. Emory College was founded in 1836 at Oxford, Ga., & remained there until 1919. Under leadership of Bishop Warren A. Candler, Atlanta was chosen in 1914 as site for new church univ., & funds were provided by Asa G. Candler & others. Atlanta Med. College, a consolidation of several earlier schs., became Sch. of Med. in 1915. **Glen Mem. Ch.** (1931.Georg.by Hentz,Adler & Shutze). **Lamar Sch. of Law** (1916. by Henry Hornbostel). **Candler Sch. of Theol.** (1916); Univ. Mus. (basement) has Egyptian-Babylonian, Oriental, Ind. colls. **Wesleyan Mus.:** incl. John Wesley's prayer desk (1740). **Asa G. Candler Lib.** (1926.by E.L.Tilton); **Joel C. Harris Mem. Room. President's H.** Atlanta is at J. with US41 (see), US23, US78 (see), US19 (see) & US29, part of route (S) to Warm Springs (see US27).

# TRIPS OUT OF ATLANTA

## I. ATLANTA (E) to OXFORD. 35. US78 & St.12

Via: Avondale Estates (Stone Mountain), Decatur & Covington.

Decatur St. runs (E) to J. with US78. **6. DECATUR** (sett.1832), old town with oak-shaded streets but unusually modern Hs. & apartment bldgs.; seat of DeKalb Cty., rich agric. area, with some textile industries & granite quarries. Harvest Festival. **DeKalb County Cth.** On lawn is **Stephen Decatur Mon.** E. College Ave., **Agnes Scott College,** high-ranking college for women; occupies 31 main bldgs. on well-wooded campus. Org. in 1889 & chartered in 1906 to confer A.B. degrees under present name. Notable bldgs. (Coll. Goth.) are **Carnegie Lib.,** art exhibition, & **Presser Hall,** music bldg. Opp. RR. Sta. on College Ave., **Casa Allegra,** where Dr. Thos. Holley Chivers died in 1858. Chivers' poetry is believed to have influenced Poe. Grave in Decatur Cemetery. 701 Columbia Dr., **Columbia Theol. Seminary** (Presb.), est. in 1828 in Lexington, Ga., under Rev. Thos. Goulding (see); removed to Columbia, S.C. (1830), where it remained until 1927. **7. AVONDALE ESTATES,** residential suburb. J. with St.12.

SIDE TRIP: Cont. (E) 9$^m$ on US78 to **Stone Mountain,** largest exposed dome of granite in N. Amer., more than 7$^m$ around base. On sheer NE. side is unfinished **Confed. Mem.** Carving by Gutzon Borglum & his artists began in 1923, & head of Gen. R. E. Lee was unveiled on Jan. 19, 1924. A quarrel disrupted Stone Mt. Mon. Assoc., & Borglum destroyed his models except completed figure of Jeff. Davis. The next sculptor, Augustus Lukeman, had the Lee head blasted away. Work was suspended in 1930. Ku Klux Klan conclaves were held on summit in 1920's & later yrs.

Trip turns (SE) from Avondale Estates; on St.12 at **9.** granite gateposts indicate Rd. to **Lithonia.** Mile from town is **Pine Mountain,** quarried since 1883 (quarries O). **26.5. COVINGTON** (sett.1829), rural & cotton-trading center. Hs. of planter period are: **McCormick Neal H., Usher H.** (c.1840), **Gen. R. J. Henderson H.** & **Dixie Manor** (1859). J. with St.81, which leads (N) 1$^m$ to **Oxford,** seat of Emory (Jr.) College & birthpl. of Emory Univ. **Seney Hall** (1881.Vict.Goth.). **Chapel** (1873). **Phi Gamma Hall** (1851.Gr.Rev.). **Dixon H.** (1836). **Branham Hts.** (1840). **Old Emory Ch.** (1841.rest.).

## II. ATLANTA (N) to CHAMBLEE. 13. Peachtree Rd.

**10. OGLETHORPE UNIV.,** coed. sch., limited to (peacetime) enrollment of 300. The blue-granite bldgs. (Goth.), all built since 1912, stand on 600-a. campus, purchased largely through W. R. Hearst's donation. Est. as manual training sch. in 1823, it became Oglethorpe Univ. in 1835, with campus near Milledgeville, then St. capital. Sidney Lanier was grad. of Old Oglethorpe. Univ. was re-founded in 1913. **Crypt of Civilization,** beneath Adm. Bldg., was sealed May 26, 1940, to be opened in 8113 A.D., contains books on microfilm, radio, typewriter, phonograph & records, models of present-day artifacts & other exhibits. Description & location have been recorded in many languages & sent to libs. of the world. At **c.13.** are **N. ATLANTA & CHAMBLEE.** On Carroll Ave. (S) of Chamblee are **U.S. Naval Reserve Aviation Base** & **Lawson Gen. Hospital** (1940-41). Near Chamblee (NW) is **Flowerland** (O.free), spectacular rose garden on estate of Dr. L. C. Fischer.

## III. ATLANTA (N) to ACWORTH. 45. US19, St.120 & US41

Via: Sandy Springs, Rosswell, Marietta, Kennesaw Mt. & Kennesaw.

**13. SANDY SPRINGS.** In vic. are ruins of **Soap Cr. Paper Mills** (get directions in village.pic.). **Covered Bridge,** one of few in South. **21. ROSSWELL,** one of earliest cotton-mill towns; stretches along hy. for mile or more, edged by cotton & corn fields, timberland & orchards. **Barrington Hall,** home of Barrington King, son of town's founder. **Bulloch Hall,** scene of wedding of Pres. Theo. Roosevelt's father. **Presb. Ch.** & many Hs. were designed by Willis Ball, Conn. artist. Trip turns (W) on St.120. At **33. MARIETTA** (RR.& bus conns.interurban to Atlanta.hotels.tourist & trlr.camps). During World War II, this old & pretty town nearly tripled pop., & many employees of huge Ball Aircraft Plant (1941) have become permanent residents. Chief products are textiles, marble, furniture & prefabricated Hs. In 1850's Marietta was resort town, "most fashionable, most flourishing . . . and fastest town in Georgia." Sherman took possession in July, 1864, & in Nov., much of Marietta was burned. **St. James Episc. Ch.** (1842). **Nat. Cemetery,** where more than 10,000 Union soldiers are buried; several St. mons. **Confed. Cemetery,** in city cemetery.

Trip turns (NW) from Marietta on US41. At **35. KENNESAW MT. NAT. BATTLEFIELD PK.** (O.till sundown.tours on appl.). **45. ACWORTH,** where Sherman had hqs.

**IV. ATLANTA (S) to GRIFFIN. 42. US29 & US41**

Via: Hapeville, East Pt., College Park, Candler Field & Jonesboro.

Trip follows line of Sherman's march through plantation belt. **4. FT. McPHERSON** (N.O.), est. 1885 & named for Gen. J. B. McPherson, who was killed in Battle of Atlanta. **6. EAST PT.,** a leading industrial center; est. in 1887 as E. terminus of Atlanta & West Pt. RR. Ku Klux Klan brought town into nat. prominence in 1940 during series of floggings by night-riders. **8. COLLEGE PARK,** seat of **Ga. Military Academy,** one of country's honor military schools. [US29 cont. (S) to J. with St.41, route to Warm Springs.] Trip turns (E) from College Park on Virginia Ave. **9.5. ATLANTA MUN. AIRPORT.** A half-mile further (E) on Virginia Ave. is **Hapeville,** residential suburb, several mills & sm. industries (since 1929). J. with US41, on which trip turns (S). **19. THE FAIR OF 1850** (O.free), Col. John West's hist. mus. of furniture, clothing, vehicles, weapons, agric. tools & other articles. On **Site of Battle of Jonesboro,** last of engagements in Battle of Atlanta. **20. JONESBORO,** scene of action in "Gone with the Wind." **40. GA. EXPERIMENT STA.** (1889). **42. GRIFFIN** (RR.& bus conns.accoms.recr.facils.), leading textile center, is ambitious modern city. Residential secs., entirely separate from its 25 mills, are attractive with columned Hs. & flower-lined streets. Town began in 1840 on 800 as. given by Col. L. L. Griffin, & textile mills were est. in 1880's. PTS. OF INT.: (1) **Mun. Pk.** (clubh.golf.pic.dance pavilion.bathh.pool); planted with blue & white iris, for which Griffin is noted. (2) 210 S. 6th St., **Hawkes Lib.** (1916). (3) Poplar & 8th Sts., **Hunt H.** (O.appl.); coll. of Americana, esp. glass. (4) 126 W. College St., **Joiner H.** (1850.Class.Rev.). (5) **Dundee Mills, Inc.** (org.1888), world-famous makers of Turkish towels. (6) **Pomona Products Co. Plant.** (7) **Griffin Hosiery Mill.** (8) **Crompton-Highland Mill.**

## US 90—FLORIDA

**JACKSONVILLE, FLA. (W) to FLA.-ALA. LINE** (44.5$^{m}$ from Mobile, Ala.). **399. US90**

Via: Jacksonville, Lake City, Live Oak, Tallahasee, Marianna, DeFuniak Springs, Pensacola. RRs. parallel route bet. Jacksonville & River Junction & bet. River Junction & Pensacola. Accoms.: All kinds.

US90 traverses N. Fla. from Jacksonville (Fla.'s largest city) through swamp & pine lands to rolling red hills where cotton & tobacco plantations date from ante bellum times. It passes Tallahassee (st. capital) in a reg. of sm. Ls., proceeds (W) through area producing sugar cane, pecans & satsuma oranges & reaches Gulf of Mexico at Pensacola.

### Sec. 1: JACKSONVILLE to LIVE OAK. 84.

**0. JACKSONVILLE**

Through RR., plane & bus conns. Accoms.: All kinds. Info.: Tourist Bureau, Hemming Pk. Some 30$^{m}$ of bath. & motor beaches. Boat. Canoe trips to central Fla.'s lake route, Miami, & Okefenokee Swamp (see Seminole Canoe Club). Salt water (tarpon, sea trout, whiting) & fresh water (black bass) f. Quail, deer, dove, turkey & duck. 6 golf courses. Dog races.

Jacksonville, largest city in Fla. (Miami is runner-up & is larger in "greater area pop.") is also financial, commercial, & industrial center. A deep water world port, it is situated on the St. Johns R., which is navigable for most of its 200$^{m}$ & is only major R. in U.S. that runs from (S) to (N). R. separates Jacksonville from S. Jacksonville &, except for 8$^{m}$ devoted to docks, warehs. & piers, is bordered by pks. & residential sections. Jacksonville is largest naval stores market in U.S. (its naval stores yard is said to be 2nd largest in world) & largest lumber market on Atlantic coast. It has cigar factories, pulp & paper mills, glass, dry ice & fertilizer factories, shipyards, & large Naval Air Sta. Jacksonville is also yr.-round tourist resort & plays host (though in many cases only overnight) to more tourists, as they journey (S) at beginning of season & (N) at end, than any other Fla. city. But its atmosphere is much closer to that of a commercial town of Middle West than to that of a S. Fla. resort town. Jean Ribault & his Fr. Huguenots arrived in vic. in 1562 & René de Laudonnière followed 2 yrs. later. The Fr. were massacred by Sp. 1565, & avenged themselves 1568. But Sp. returned & in 1740 built Ft. St. Nicholas, which was burned by patriots defending St. Augustine, 1812. In 1822 land platted in area to which English had given name Cowford was called Jacksonville in honor of Andrew Jackson, Fla.'s military gov. Town suffered considerably during Seminole War & was taken on 4 different occasions by Feds., who left most of it in ruins when they departed in 1863. Before Sp.-Amer. War Cuban patriots sought refuge here & during war town was site of an Amer. encampment. In 1901 much of city was destroyed by fire which gutted 148 city blocks. Since then Jacksonville, because of diversified sources of income, has suffered less than many Fla. cities from depressions & seasonal changes.

PTS. OF INT.: (1) Hogan & Monroe Sts., **Hemming Pk.;** concerts in winter. (2) Main & Hubbard Sts., **Confed. Pk.,** on site of Confed. trenches; Mon. to Confed. women. (3) 459 E. 16th St., **King Edwards Cigar Factory** (O.wks.guides), "largest cigar factory in world under 1 roof." (4) (S) from 44th St. on Wigmore St. & then on Talleyrand Ave., **River Front;** oil terminals, mun. electric plant, pulp mill, mun. docks & terminals, naval stores terminal & Ford plant. (5) Bay & Liberty Sts., **Marker** comm. site of Cowford, where cows once swam across R. (6) Ocean & E. Adams Sts., **Pub. Lib.;** coll. of Floridiana. (7) Stuart & 19th Sts., **Ch. of God & Saints of Christ,** Negro "sanctified" ch.; white visitors welcome.

SIDE TRIPS: (A) From Jacksonville (N) on Main St. (US17) across Trout R. Beyond bridge c.1$^{m}$ is J. with Hecksher Dr. (R) on Hecksher Dr. c.400 yds. is grove (R) leading to **Mun. Zoo.** Cont. on Hecksher Dr., which becomes private toll Rd. winding 17$^{m}$ along N. bank of St. Johns R. to its mouth. At 1$^{m}$ beyond toll house is highest pt. on SE. coast, offering excellent view of R. & city docks. At 3.5$^{m}$ beyond 2nd toll house is **Observation Tower.** Beyond tower, 2$^{m}$, St. Johns Bluff across R. comes to view with ruins of ft. built during Sp.-Amer. War. Near-by is **Site of Ft. Caroline,** long since washed into R., est. 1564 by Laudonnière & Fr. Huguenots, who following yr. were massacred by Sp. Menèndez. Eng. est. settlement here in 1782, which disappeared some time after 1817. At Sisters Cr. (f.), 2$^{m}$ beyond, Intra-Coastal Waterway joins St. Johns R. At 15$^{m}$ is **Pilot Town** (f. boat.guides) where Ribault & his Fr. Huguenots are said to have knelt for 1st Prot. prayer in N. Amer., May 1, 1562. 17$^{m}$ **Ft. George I.** Here (1568) Fr. attacked Sp. outpost est. before 1567, mission of San Juan del Puerto flourished with many Ind. converts in 1600, & Jas. Oglethorpe (1736) & John McIntosh (1815) both encamped. **Ft. George Club** (N.O.) occupies plantation house of Zephaniah Kingsley, who brought back from Africa daughter of a Senegal chief he married in native ceremony.

(B) From Jacksonville (S) across Main St. Bridge. (L) on Miami Rd. which conn. with St.A1A, through S. Jacksonville. (L) at sign indicating Keystone for short drive to **Keystone Live Oak,** one of largest & oldest of kind. Return & cont. on St.A1A (Atlantic Blvd.) to **Atlantic Beach,** 18$^{m}$. If tide is low, driving on beach is excellent (use tide table in newspaper). (S) of Atlantic Beach 1$^{m}$ is **Neptune Beach;** 2$^{m}$ **Jacksonville Beach & Recr. Area;** 6$^{m}$ **Ponte Vedra Beach.** (N) of Atlantic Beach 4.5$^{m}$ is **Seminole Beach.** Entire area is famous recr. center. (NW) of Seminole Beach on Mayport Rd. 4.5$^{m}$ to **Mayport,** old fishing village (boats.guides). Here is **Ribault Mon.** comm. Huguenot arrival (1562).

(C) From Jacksonville (S) across St. Johns R. Bridge & along St.13 past fine riverfront homes. At 2$^{m}$ (S) of bus. dist., bet. San José Blvd. & St. Johns R., **Oriental Gardens** (O fee), with whole sections given over to iris, amaryllis, hydrangeas, gardenias & ornamented with arches, bridges & fountains. 4$^{m}$ **Epping Forest,** estate of late Alfred I. du Pont. 11$^{m}$ J. with side Rd. (R) here 2$^{m}$ to **Mandarin,** dating to Eng. occupation (1763-83) & so named after orange brought from China. As bustling little river port, it was shelled by Feds. There are orange, grapefruit & kumquat groves & an orchid farm. **Stowe Lodge** was (1867) winter home of Harriet Beecher Stowe who wrote "Palmetto Leaves," "Our Plantation" & other works here. R. steamers docked near-by & tourists, for a sm. fee, went through house & past her desk while she worked. The author of "Uncle Tom's Cabin" was one of most popular sights of trip. Chapel has Stowe mem. window. At 4$^{m}$ beyond Mandarin is **Julington Cr.** (f.boat.pic.).

(D) From Jacksonville (S) on Riverside Ave., which becomes US17 (see). At Post St. is the **Women's Club** & 1 block beyond, **Dickson H.** (int.antiques). At Margaret St. is **Mem. Pk.** with excellent view of R. Hy. next crosses Ortega R. to **U.S. Naval Air Sta.** At 13$^{m}$ is **Orange Pk.** with **Moosehaven,** home for aged maintained by Loyal Order of Moose. **Yerkes Labs. of Primate Biology** (O.only to qualified scientists with prior arrangement by mail) are conducted by Yale Univ. & Harvard Univ. Research covers problems in medicine & many biological sciences, working mainly with monkeys, apes & chimpanzees.

## 19. BALDWIN, J. with St.200.

SIDE TRIPS: (A) On St.200 (N) through cattle & hog-raising reg. where razorback hogs with notched ears instead of brands abound in piney woods. In 1937 legislature passed

law to make wild razorbacks "legally nonexistent," to prevent hog thieves pleading that they thought their stolen hogs were wild.
(B) On St.200 (S) to **Starke,** 27m, distributing center for strawberries, corn, peanuts, sugar cane & scuppernong grapes. Naval stores are also important. (Good f. & h.—quail & deer.) On St.16 here (L) 8m is **Kingsley L.** (cottages) & **Camp Albert H. Blanding,** military training center.

**31. GLEN ST. MARY** with large shrubbery, flower & citrus nursery (O). (R) here 12m on St.125 is **Burnsed Blockh.** (1837), on St. Mary's R. in **Taylor. 45.5. OLUSTEE ST. MON.,** on site of only major Civil War battle fought in Fla. Also known as Battle of Ocean Pond because near-by pond has a distinct current (f.swim.boat. lodge). Here Confeds. under Gen. Jos. Finnegan defeated Feds. under Truman Seymour (Feb.20,1864). **48. OLUSTEE,** naval stores center in **Osceola Nat. For.** (161,813 as.;hqs.Lake City), flatlands ranging from well-drained sand to swamp, producing pine, cypress & hardwood. Here is **Fla. For. Serv. Nursery.** (O). **60. LAKE CITY,** J. with US41 (see), surrounded by Ls. (f.swim.), has tobacco market active in Aug. Town, important in early Fla. hist., was called Alligator (corruption of Seminole Chief's name, Allapattah) until 1858.

SIDE TRIP: (N) from Lake City on St.47 through huge **Okefenokee Swamp,** most of which lies in Ga. (quail,deer,turkey,wildcat,bear).

**84. LIVE OAK,** largest "bright-leaf" tobacco market in Fla., takes on carnival atmosphere in Aug. when thousands arrive for auctions. Town also has cattle auction & is shipping pt. for watermelons, cotton, corn, pecans & peanuts.

### Sec. 2: LIVE OAK to TALLAHASSEE. 85.

**13.** Hy. crosses **SUWANNEE R. 14. ELLAVILLE,** named for a Negro servant. Just (N) is **Suwannee R. St. Pk.** (1,651 as.), as yet (1949) undeveloped. **29. MADISON,** est. 1830's by S.C. planters of sea-island cotton.

SIDE TRIP: (N) from Madison on St.53 is **Cherry Lake Farms,** 8m, planned community est. by Resettlement Adm. near **Cherry L.** (f.boat.swim.).

**49.5.** Hy. crosses **AUCILLA R. 59. MONTICELLO,** J. with US19 (see), sett. early 1800's. **Cth.** modeled on Thos. Jefferson's home. The Mahan pecan produced by nursery here is unusually large variety.

SIDE TRIP: (N) from Monticello on St.146, past a series of plantations that date from ante bellum times. On **Lynhurst Plantation,** 16m, is only large ante bellum house remaining in reg. (1850).

**68.** Hy. passes **LAKE MICCOSUKEE,** which Andrew Jackson crossed (1818) in spite of Ind. attackers & on opp. shore destroyed village where scalps of 50 whites were discovered.

**85. TALLAHASSEE**

Through RR., plane & bus conns. Accoms.: All kinds (difficult to secure when legislature is in session, Ap.-May of odd yrs.). Good f. & h.—quail, duck, deer, turkey. Swim. Golf. Tennis. Ga.-Fla. League professional baseball.

Tallahassee (Ind. "Old Town"), capital of Fla. since 1824, lies in a hilly country surrounded by Ls. & springs & by large plantations. Town is dominated by St. Capitol bldg., Florida St. Univ. & Agric. & Mech. College for Negroes, each situated on a hill. Main streets, noisily active when legislature is in session, the colleges celebrating, or farmers in for market day, are crossed by magnolia-shaded lanes. There is some Fla.-Mediterranean architecture but Tallahassee has more appearance of ante bellum Southern town than of Fla. boom town. Occupied by Apalachee (& later Seminole) Inds., region was visited by De Soto (1539). Franciscans (1633) set up mission & fertile lands supplied food for St. Augustine. In 1824 arrangements were made with Ind. chiefs who occupied lands, & town, 0.5m square, was laid out halfway bet. St. Augustine & Pensacola (then capitals of E. & W. Fla. respectively) to be terr. capital. Legislators arrived on horseback for assembly (Nov.8,1824). Soon planters were growing rich on cotton & giving town a reputation for hospitality & gaiety. Saved by defense of old men & cadets at Battle of Natural Bridge a month before Lee's surrender at Appomattox, the Capitol floated the Stars & Bars until last shot of Civil War.

PTS. OF INT.: (1) S. Monroe St. at Pensacola St., **Fla. St. Capitol** (oldest sec. completed 1845 though used 4 yrs. earlier & begun 1826; adds.), only St. capitol (E) of Miss. R. not seized during Civil War, stands on site of log cabin (marked by granite block on grounds) where 1st legislative council met, 1824. **St. Lib.,** 2nd floor.

(2) 209 E. Park Ave., **Walker Mem. Lib.** has portrait & mementoes of Prince Achille Murat, son of King of Naples & Napoleon's sister Caroline, who became postmaster (1826-38) of Tallahassee & married a great-niece of Geo. Washington. (3) E. Park Ave. & Gadsden St., **May Oak,** where May Day festivals have been held for more than cent. (4) N. Monroe & Call Sts., **St. John's Ch.** (Episc.1881.Eng. Goth.). (5) 700 N. Adams St., **Governor's Mansion** (1900). (6) N. Adams St. & 1st Ave., **The Grove** (N.O.1825.Gr.Rev.), built by Gov. R. K. Call for his bride (see "The Tallahassee Girl" by Maurice Thompson). (7) Boulevard & Call Sts., **Old Episc. Cemetery** contains graves of Prince Murat & wife. (8) N. Adams St. & W. Park Ave., **Presb. Ch.** (1832.remod.); slave gallery. (9) N. Adams St. & W. Park Ave., **The Columns** (1835). (10) W. Jefferson & Copeland Sts., **Fla. St. Univ.** (coed.) opened in 1857 as Fla. St. College, became Fla. St. College for Women in 1905 & assumed present status, 1947. General architectural theme is Tudor Goth. executed in red brick on 80-a. campus; off-campus facils. at Dale Mabry Field. Lib. has coll. Fla. maps, documents & relics assembled by Daughters of Confed. **Peruvian Mus.** (O.appl.) has one of best colls. of Peruvian artifacts in U.S. incl. ceramics, textiles, & objects of gold & silver, bone, etc. of Nasca, Chimu & Inca cultures. (11) Palmer Ave. & Perry St., **Fla. Agric. & Mech. College for Negroes** (coed.); 375-a. campus on highest of Tallahassee's hills. College began as St. Normal (1887) & became coed. 1905.

SIDE TRIPS: (A) From Tallahasee (NE) on US319 through red clay hill area. Part of hy. is lined with crape myrtles. 5.5m **Killearn Gardens** (O.Dec.-Ap.fee) feature camellia japonicas, azaleas & a variety of birds. 6m **Lake Hall** (swim.pic.).

(B) From Tallahassee (E) 3m on Miccosukee Rd. to **Goodwood** (1839.Georg.).

(C) From Tallahasee (S) on US319 to **Woodville,** 9m.

(W) here on St.59. At 4.5m **Rhodes Springs** (swim.dance).At 5m is **Natural Bridge** where St. Marks R. goes underground. Pk. here has Mon. on site of battle of Mar. 6, 1865, when Confeds., aided by cadets from W. Fla. Seminary, stopped march on Tallahassee.

Cont. (S) on US319 to **Wakulla,** 15m.

(L) here on side Rd. 6m to **St. Marks** (f.boats.tackle). **Ruins of Ft. St. Marks** (built of stone by Sp., 1739), 4th ft. on site, held at various times by Brit., Sp., Creek Inds., Amers. & Confeds.

Return to US319 & cont. (S). At 20m J. with side Rd. (R) here 2m to **Wakulla Springs,** largest spring from single source in Fla. (146,000 gal. per minute;depth 180′;hotel.swim.). Water is so clear that glass bottom boats permit good view of fish, vividly colored limestone formations & remains of mastodon (fee).

(D) From Tallahassee (W) 2m on Jackson Bluff Rd. to **Prince Murat H.**

(E) From Tallahassee (W) on St.20. At 2m **Site of Ft. San Luis** (Sp.1640) & also **Site of Mission of San Luis de Talimali** (est.by Franciscans.1633). 8m **Ochlockonee** on L. Talquin (f.boat.).

(F) From Tallahassee (SW) 7m on St.371 to **Apalachicola Nat. For.** (hqs.in Tallahassee), a low swampy area divided by Ochlockonee R. into 2 divisions, Wakulla (325,850 as.) & Wilma (306,395 as.). **Silver Lake Camp** (camp.pic.) is 7m (W) of Tallahassee on St.20. **Dog. L. Recr. Area** 10m (W) on For. Serv. Rds. 360 & 358 (f.deer, turkey, quail, duck, doves).

## Sec. 3: TALLAHASSEE to DEFUNIAK SPRINGS. 129.

**26. QUINCY,** in reg. producing Sumatra tobacco (used for cigar wrappers), has cigar factories & **Fla. Tobacco Experiment Sta.** In vic. is mined fuller's earth, clay with the property of absorbing basic colors & removing them from oils, is mined; now used chiefly in clarifying petroleum & refining edible oils. **47.5.** Hy. crosses **APALACHICOLA R. 71. MARIANNA,** business center of reg. producing peanuts, cotton, oranges, & pecans, has farmers' market & livestock auction. Town was scene of "Battle of Marianna" fought around **St. Luke's Episc. Ch.** on Wynn St. when Feds. attacked Home Guards, Sept. 1864. Cemetery contains graves of Confed. dead & of John Milton, Gov. of Fla. during Civil War. Among int. old houses are: Main St. & Campbellton Rd., **Ely H.;** N. side of Main St., **Merritt H.;** S. side of Main St., **Barnes H.;** Madison & Putnam Sts., **Davis H.;** N. Green St., **Nickles H.** (1830's); N. Jefferson St., **Edrihi H.;** opp. Cth., **Pittman H.**

SIDE TRIPS: (A) From Marianna (N) on St.167 to **Fla. Caverns St. Pk.** 3m (1,187 as.; hqs.Marianna;f.hik.golf.pic.), which has limestone escarpments, caverns (electrically lighted) with stalactites & stalagmites, an underground river, a natural bridge, & highly diversified flora & fauna. (Guides avail.). Fish hatchery adj. to Pk.

(B) From Marianna (S) on St.71 (which leads to Gulf Coast), to **Blountstown,** 28m, naval stores center named for Seminole chief, John Blount, who acted as Andrew Jackson's guide against Creeks.

(NE) from Blountstown c.13m on Apalachicola R. is **Torreya St. Pk.** (1,058 as.;f.pic. camp.).

Cont. (S) on St.71 through sparsely populated sec. At 45m **Chipola Pk.** on Dead Lakes (excellent f. guides).

**80. COTTONDALE** (excellent h.& f.—bream,trout, fox,squirrel,quail) at J. with US231.

SIDE TRIPS: (A) From Cottondale (N) on US231 through red soil hills, whose numerous caves once provided hide-outs for runaway slaves. & Confed. deserters. At 16m US231 crosses Ala. Line.

(B) From Cottondale (S) on US231 through sec. whose crops incl. pecans & satsuma oranges. At 15m **Compass L.** (f.swim.). Beyond **Fountain,** 23m, hy. traverses flat area of pine, black gum & swamp maple. In backwoods live many Fla. "crackers."

**88. FLA. NAT. EGG LAYING EXPERIMENT STA.** of Univ. of Fla. (O), has annual contest with entries from many sts. **117. PONCE DE LEON** on site of one of Fla.'s many "fountains of youth." **129. DEFUNIAK SPRINGS** has pool, formed by springs, 80′ deep & a mile in circum. (swim.). It was home of 2nd Chautauqua in U.S. & boasts Fla.'s 1st Confed. Mon. (1871).

## Sec. 4: DEFUNIAK SPRINGS to ALA. LINE. 101.

**27. CRESTVIEW,** whose crops incl. blueberries & pecans. **58. MILTON,** cotton ginning & sawmill center dating from 1820's. **71.** Hy. crosses causeway over **Escambia R.** (good f.in vic.camp.boats.tackle).

**84. PENSACOLA**

Through RR., plane, bus & SS. conns. Accoms.: All kinds. 3 beaches (2 mun.; swim. boat); 2 golf courses (1 mun.). Excellent fresh & salt water f. Yachting, sailing, motorboating.

Pensacola, port of entry on Pensacola Bay, natural land-locked harbor, is industrial & shipping center & yr.-round resort. City has had turbulent development under 6 flags; its government has changed 17 times. In history, architecture, & atmosphere, Pensacola is more closely related to Mobile & New Orleans than to most Fla. cities. The bay was entered by Maldonado, commander of De Soto's fleet (1540). Settlement was 1st made by Tristan de Luna (1559) with some 1,500 colonists, but was abandoned after bad storm 2 yrs. later. In 1698, Don Andres d'Arriola erected wooden ft. on site of present Ft. San Carlos. This was taken by Fr. (1719), retaken by Sp., then surrendered to Fr., & again to Sp. who took over in 1723 & est. new settlement on Santa Rosa I. Sp. moved on to Vera Cruz when Brit. took over (1763). Tories moved in during Rev. Sp. under Gálvez attacked & took over town (1781) & 2 yrs. later Fla. was ceded back to Sp. Brit. used harbor as base against U.S. in 1814 & Andrew Jackson, having attacked town in 1814 & again in 1818 (as hqs. of Brit. agents, Ind. raiders, runaway slaves), accepted transfer of W. Fla. to U.S. (1821). Abolitionist Jonathan Walker was tried & branded with letters "SS" (slave stealer) here in 1844 (see Muskegon, Mich.). The Confederate forces occupied town (although Ft. Pickens remained in hands of Feds.) until 1862. Pensacola was largest city in Fla. in 1860 & 2nd largest, 1900. Today, industries include Naval stores, wall board & furniture mfg.; mun. docks & terminals handle annual business in excess of $50,000,000. Pensacola is said to be world's largest red snapper fishing port.

PTS. OF INT.: (1) S. Palafox & E. Intendencia Sts., **Plaque** marking site of Gen. Andrew Jackson's house. (2) S. Palafox & E. Government Sts., **Plaza Ferdinand VII,** part of plaza of orig. Sp. settlement. Here Andrew Jackson accepted transfer of Fla. from Sp. (3) Below Main St., land has been built up of ballast brought from many countries. On (R) may be seen fishing fleets that go as far (S) as Mex. coast after red snapper. Mun. pier; benches. (4) W. Main St. bet. S. Barcelona & S. Baylen Sts., site of Panton-Leslie Co.'s **Ind. Trading Post.** Wm. Panton, said to have become one of U.S.' 1st millionaires, had wareh. & elaborate home here. Alex. McGillivray, Ind. chief, was buried in Panton's garden. (5) 137 W. Romana St., **Dorothy Walton H.** (O.sm.fee;1805), home of wife of Geo. Walton, signer of Decl. of Ind.; coll. of old maps, engravings, firearms, coins. (6) 210 W. Romana St., **Hulse H.** (1848), once home of surgeon distinguished for treating yellow fever. (7)

Barcelona & Brainard Sts., **Site of Sp. Ft. San Bernardo** (1781) used in siege of Ft. George. (8) N. Palafox & Jackson Sts., **Site of Ft. George** now occupied by K. of C. (9) N. Palafox & E. Wright Sts., **Perry H.** was home of Gov. E. A. Perry (1833-1889) & is now Scottish High Rite Temple. (10) N. Palafox & W. Chase Sts., **St. Michael's Ch.** (Cath.Goth.1888). (11) E. Chase & Alcaniz Sts., **St. Michael's Cemetery** (1781). Here lie Dorothy Walton & Stephen R. Mallory, Secy. Confed. Navy. (12) S. Alcaniz & E. Zarragossa Sts., **Seville Square,** once part of orig. plaza. (13) S. Adams & E. Zarragossa Sts., **Old Christ Ch.** (Episc.1834.Eng.Goth.), used as hospital & barracks by Feds. & now pub. lib.

SIDE TRIPS: (A) From Pensacola (N) on US29 which parallels Escambia R. through reg. producing oranges, pecans & grapes. 13m **Gonzalez,** named for Don Manuel González who refused Jackson's demands that he be guide in attacks on Pensacola. At 22m is J. with side Rd. (R) here 6m to **Chumuckla Mineral Springs.** At 44m is **Flomaton,** Ala., just on Fla. Line.

(B) From Pensacola (S) on US98 (see) across bay on Pensacola Bridge, then (R) on Beach Rd. across Sound Bridge (toll) 7m to **Pensacola Beach** (swim.boat.f.casino.city bus serv.) on 55m long Santa Rosa I. On W. end of I. is **Ft. Pickens** (1834.N.O.), pentagonal structure. Here (1886) were imprisoned Apache chief Geronimo & warriors. Across channel are ruins of **Ft. McRae** (1850), visible at low tide.

(C) On Government St. (W) past Sherril Oil Co., Owsley Lumber Co., etc. (S) on E St. to **Saunder's Beach** (swim.boat.). Cont. (W) on Barrancas Ave., past Newport Industries to **U.S. Naval Air Sta.** 6m (O), est. 1914. Many types of fighter planes may be seen. Visits arranged to Survival Mus. & aboard airplane carrier. Grounds were once part of Navy Yard est. 1825. Confeds. cut live oaks here & sank them in pond to prevent Feds. making use of them. In 1926 logs hard as iron were recovered & used in restoring USS "Constitution." **Ft. Barrancas,** now decommissioned, was scene of great activity during World War II, especially in protecting harbor from submarines. Adj. **Nat. Cemetery** dates from 1867. (NW) from Naval Sta. are **Old Ft. Barrancas** conn. by brick tunnel with **Ruins of Ft. San Carlos.** Old Ft. Barrancas, erected 1839-44 & held by Confeds., 1861-62, is U-shaped structure with moat & drawbridge. Ft. San Carlos (semi-circular.1780's), near site of wooden ft. erected 1698 by Sp. & destroyed by Fr. (1719). Brit. built a redoubt here (1771) & it in turn was destroyed by Sp., who erected present ft. In vic. is disputed site of Tristan De Luna's colony. (S) from Naval Sta. on St.295 to **Gulf Beach,** c.18m from Pensacola.

(D) From Pensacola (W) on St.298 c.10m to **Paradise Beach.**

**101.** US90 (W) of Pensacola crosses **ALA. LINE** on bridge over Perdido R.

## US 319 & US 98—FLORIDA

**FLA.-GA. LINE** (44m from Moultrie, Ga.) **(SW) to PENSACOLA, FLA. 266. US319, US98**

Via: Tallahassee, Crawfordville, Apalachicola, Port St. Joe, Panama City, Ft. Walton. RR. parallels route bet. Tallahassee & St. Marks, bet. Sopchoppy & Carrabelle & bet. Apalachicola & Port St. Joe. Accoms.: All kinds in cities.

Hy. journeys through Tallahassee, Fla.'s capital, to Gulf Coast & a sand dune reg. dotted with fishing villages & resorts.

### Sec. 1: FLA.-GA. LINE to PORT ST. JOE. 127.

**19. TALLAHASSEE. 34. WAKULLA** (for pts. of int. bet. Ga. Line & Wakulla, see Tallahassee Side Trips US90). **50.5.** J. with St.30.

SIDE TRIP: (S) here 4m to **Panacea,** so-called because of healing powers of springs (f.boats.guides).

**62.** Hy. crosses **OCHLOCKONEE R.** (f.). **78. CARRABELLE** (boats for deep-sea f.; guides & equipment for black bear h.). (L) on side Rd. short distance are Muskogean **Kitchen Middens. 100. APALACHICOLA,** on Apalachicola Bay at mouth of R. of same name (part of Intra-Coastal Waterway), prosperous cotton port in 1830's, is now canning & shipping center for fish, crab, shrimp & oysters—latter especially noted for copper content. (Boats for deep sea f.; annual bear hunt in Apalachicola Nat. For.) It is thought that on shores of Apalachicola Bay, Narváez & his men constructed several crude vessels in ill-fated attempt to reach Mexico (1528). Cabeza de Vaca, 1 of 4 survivors, wrote account published 1542 but narrative is vague & route not easy to ascertain. PTS. OF INT.: Gorrie Sq., with **Mon. to Dr. John Gorrie** who patented a machine for making artificial ice which he invented (1845) to help malaria-stricken patients. Statue of Gorrie also stands in Capitol at Washington. Gorrie Sq., **Trinity Ch.** (Episc.1838) has been called "1st pre-fabricated ch. in America" as lumber was cut, ready to be assembled, & shipped down from New England. **Cemetery** has cypress headstones that have weathered a century.

US319 ends at Apalachicola & US98 begins & cont. (W). At c.**122. SITE OF ST. JOSEPH,** a pine & palmetto thicket, but in 1830's boom town of some 6,000 inhabitants & largest in Fla. Yellow fever (1841) & succession of storms & tidal waves destroyed all evidence of town. **127. PORT ST. JOE,** fishing center, has fertilizer, lumber & kraft paper plants. In **Constitution Mem. Pk.** is Mon. to 1st constitutional convention in st. (1838), which met at St. Joseph (see above).

### Sec. 2: PORT ST. JOE to PENSACOLA. 139.

**36. PANAMA CITY,** J. with US231 (which extends (N) to Ala. Line at 67$^{m}$), incorporates old settlement of St. Andrew, est. by Tories as early as 1765. On St. Andrew's Bay, Panama City has oil terminal, shipyards, fish packing plants & a paper board mill. Southern Kraft Corp (O.guided tours). Excellent tarpon & other f.; regatta, May or June; golf tournament, Ap. Tyndall Field, near-by, is permanent Army base.

A series of fine beaches line Gulf coast bet. here & Pensacola (cottages.casinos. pic.facils.). In background are dunes covered with shrub magnolia & rosemary & interlaced by salt marshes. **98. FT. WALTON,** on Santa Rosa Sound, summer resort & yachting hqs., was est. during Seminole Wars. (Good f. from piers, bridges & charter boats.) Ind. mounds in vic. Cruise down Live Oak Creek offers view of Fla. jungle flora & fauna.

SIDE TRIP: (NE) from Ft. Walton on St.85 into **Choctawhatchee Nat. For.** (368,048 as., hqs. at Niceville, 13$^{m}$) with recr. area on Little Bayou, just (W) of Ft. Walton (boat. swim.pic.salt-water f.). For. supports large herd of deer & numerous sm. game, & has been under intensive management for nearly 30 yrs. Longleaf pine is principal tree. There is a large naval stores output (from 200,000 to 500,000 cups annually) & a sustained annual yield of 4,000,000′ of saw timber. It is said that 1st timber preserve est. by U.S. Gov. was inaugurated by Pres. John Quincy Adams in 1828 on Santa Rosa I. (see) just across Sound.

**139. PENSACOLA** (see US90).

## US 94—FLORIDA

### MIAMI, FLA. to NAPLES, FLA. 108. US94

Via: Coral Gables, Ochopee, Royal Palm Hammock. Through bus conns. Accoms. limited; camp sites.

US94 proceeds (W) from Miami over Tamiami Trl. (which conns. Miami with Tampa, Atlantic with Gulf) through Everglades (see US1). Canal, from which materials for Rd.-bed were dug, parallels much of hy. Reg. teems with wildlife. Small Seminole settlements, whose locations vary from time to time, are encountered along trl. **5. CORAL GABLES** (see Miami). **38.** Hy. enters **EVERGLADES NAT. PK.** (see US1). **72. OCHOPEE,** in tomato growing reg. **76. CARNESTOWN.** J. with St.29.

SIDE TRIP: (S) on St.29 to **Everglades,** 5$^{m}$, Gulf Coast resort (yacht.h.f.) & water gateway to Everglades Nat. Pk. & to Ten Thousand Is.

**92. ROYAL PALM HAMMOCK,** where grow towering pinnate-leaved royal palms ("Roystonea regia") with whitish trunks often enlarged or swelled out at base. J. with St.92.

SIDE TRIP: (S) on St.92 past **Collier-Seminole St. Pk.** (6,423 as.) as yet undeveloped, to **Collier City,** 10.5$^{m}$, on Marco I., one of the Ten Thousand Is. & trading center for native fishermen & for sportsmen who come for tarpon, shark, bear, deer, turkey & panther. Beach noted for variety of shells. Ind. mounds throughout reg. have attracted archeologists from Smithsonian & N.Y. Mus. of Natural Hist. Is. were for long time refuge for criminals & outlaws.

**108. NAPLES.** J. with US41 (see), est. as resort in 1880's (7$^{m}$ beach.f.charter boats.). Large Ind. mound is near Gordon's Pass.

# US 1—FLORIDA

**FLA.-GA. LINE** (5$^m$ from Folkston, Ga.) **to KEY WEST, FLA. 547. US1.**

Via: Jacksonville, St. Augustine, Bunnell, Daytona Beach, Melbourne, Vero Beach, Ft. Pierce, W. Palm Beach, Ft. Lauderdale, Miami, Key West. RRs. parallel route from Ga. Line to Florida City. Bus but no RR. conns. with Key West. Through air serv. Accoms.: All kinds.

US1 passes through largest city in Fla. (Jacksonville), oldest permanent white settlement in U.S. (St. Augustine), such fabulous beach resorts as Palm Beach & Miami & finally reaches southernmost city in U.S. (Key West). St. A1A hugs coastline for most of route & may be reached from many pts. on US1. Intracoastal Waterway extends some 400$^m$ from Fernandina to Key West. Channel has minimum depth of 8′ & a width of 100′ at low water.

## Sec. 1: FLA.-GA. LINE to DAYTONA BEACH. 132.

**0.** US1 crosses **FLA. LINE** on bridge over St. Marys R. At (R) is **Mon.** to Rbt. E. Lee. Hy. passes through pine lands, much of it cut over. Sedge that grows in ditches is used in mfg. brooms. Elaborate signs advertise Fla. resorts, products, tourist accoms.

**38. JACKSONVILLE** (see US90). At **c.63.** hy. crosses swamp where cypress & maples hung with Sp. moss tower above dank undergrowth. **76. ST. AUGUSTINE** (see). **108. BUNNELL,** ships palmetto for use on Palm Sunday. **118.5.** (L), **RUINS OF TISSIMI MISSION** (c.1696.by Franciscans). Burned by Brit. 1706 & rebuilt as sugar mill. At **123.5.** hy. crosses **TOMOKA R.** (f.). **124.5. IND. BURIAL MOUNDS. 126. ORMOND,** est. 1875 as health center for employees of Corbin Lock Co. of New Britain, Conn. Reached by bridge across Halifax R. is **Ormond Beach,** wealthy resort with large estates. **Casements Jr. College,** opp. Hotel Ormond, was winter home of J. D. Rockefeller during much of the latter part of his life. He played golf at Ormond Beach Golf Links (fee) & died at The Casements, May 23, 1937. Also opp. hotel, **Ormond Mem. Art Gallery** (O.daily 2-5) with 57 Biblical oil paintings by Malcolm Fraser; mem. garden.

SIDE TRIP: (W) from Ormond on Tomoka Ave. 4.5$^m$ to **Tomoka Jungle Pk.** where cruiser (fee) leaves daily (10 a.m. & 2 p.m.) down Tomoka R. through swamplands teeming with alligators & aquatic birds.

### 132. DAYTONA BEACH

Through RR., plane & bus conns. Accoms.: All kinds. Fish. excellent in R. & ocean. Town sponsors annual $12,000 Fish Tourney (Feb.1-Nov.30) with 26 eligible varieties: amberjack, barracuda, black bass, blue fish, bonito, channel bass, chobie, crevalle, cobia, dolphin, drum, flounder, king mackerel, lady fish, mangrove snapper, pompano, red snapper, sailfish, sea bass, sheepshead, snook, Spanish mackerel, speckled perch, tarpon, trout & whiting. City Dock (cruises on Halifax R. avail.) & Halifax Yacht Club provide docking facils. Pks. offer shuffleboard, bowling, tennis, skeet & trap shooting. 2 golf courses. Annual Nat. Motorcycle Races & 3 annual 150$^m$ stock car races. Islanders, farm team of St. Louis Cardinals, have worked out here.

Daytona Beach is consolidation (1926) of 3 towns: Daytona, Daytona Beach & Seabreeze. Area, once inhabited by Timucuan Inds., was explored by Franciscans (c.1587) who set up missions later (c.1702) destroyed by Eng. colonists from Ga. After 1765 Eng. est. plantations which by 1821 were taken over by the Amers. The town is divided by Halifax R., actually a salt water lagoon, spanned by 4 bridges, with "most famous beach in world" on E. Sts. are lined with oaks, magnolias, palms & especially oleanders. Since 1905 beach has attracted such automobile racing enthusiasts & drivers as J. J. Astor, W. K. Vanderbilt, Henry Flagler, Henry Ford, L. M. Dusenberg, Ralph De Palma & Barney Oldfield.

PTS. OF INT.: (1) **Daytona-Ormond Beach,** 23$^m$ long & 500′ wide at low tide, celebrated for speedway of hard-packed sand on which Sir Malcolm Campbell & others have est. a series of speed records for automobiles. Speedway 11$^m$ long; suitable for driving c.17$^m$ (end of safe driving marked). (2) **Boardwalk,** 1,866′ bordered by concessions incl. 1,208′ fishing pier (sm.fee) & casino. (3) **Oceanfront Pk.,** N. end of Boardwalk, landscaped area with large outdoor bandshell of coquina-rock. Clock tower with "Daytona Beach" on dial instead of numerals. (4) South Ridgewood Ave. & Big Tree Rd., **Daytona Beach Alligator Farm** (O). (5) Ridgewood & Volusia Aves., **Three-Trunked Palmetto Tree.** (6) 1m (S) of Silver Beach Ave., **Papaya Farm** (O). (7) 15 S. Wild Olive Ave., **Shorty Hoods' Marine Mus.** (free). (8) N. Beach & 2nd Sts., **Native Crafts Sch.,** st.-sponsored sch. at Holly Hill State Market. (9) 7 S. Ocean Ave., **Seashell Exhibit** at the Book Nook. (10) 2nd Ave. & McLeod St., **Bethune-Cookman College** (Negro.coed.with special emphasis on teaching), founded 1904 by Mary McLeod Bethune, "with 5 girls, a small cabin, $1.50, & a million dollars' worth of faith. We used charred splinters as pencils. For ink we mashed up elderberries." Merged with Cookman Institute (1922).

## Sec. 2: DAYTONA BEACH to FT. PIERCE. 135.

**5. PORT ORANGE,** dates from 1861. Shrimp & oyster fish. are chief sources of revenue though citrus culture is important. Halifax R. here was scene of Battle of Dunlawton, when Gen. Putnam & forces from near-by plantations were defeated & Seminoles under King Philip destroyed settlement. **Ruins of Old Sugar Mill,** in garden setting, are still to be seen just 1m (W) from town (O.daily 6-9.sm.fee). Mill is thought to be on site of Franciscan Mission dating from early 1600's. Sometime after 1763 Dr. Andrew Turnbull (see below) had a sugar & indigo plantation here. After destruction by Seminoles, mill was rebuilt & used as late as 1880. In Civil War sugar kettles were used to make salt for Confeds. **15. NEW SMYRNA BEACH,** resort (swim.boats.f.h.), where headwaters of Indian R. meet Atlantic, also derives income from citrus fruits & packing plants. Anglers' & Tourist Clubs are recr. centers for visitors. Bath. & auto-driving beach 1m from center of town. Sp. est. Mission of Atocuimi here in 1690's. In 1767 Dr. Andrew Turnbull, a Scot. physician backed by Eng. Gov., brought over large colony of indentured Minorcans, Greeks & Italians, drained lands by canals & raised indigo. Most of the surviving colonists moved on to St. Augustine after 1776. **Atocuimi Mission** (O.sm.fee), ruins owned by Fla. Hist. Soc. Est. 1696, mission was soon sacked by Jororo Inds. rebelling against priest's attempt to interfere with tribal ceremonies. Eng. used it as sugar mill; built of coquina rock, some of arches remain. **Foundations of Sp. Ft.,** said to date to 1565 & discovered when Ind. mound was excavated (1854). **Turnbull Canal,** constructed by early colonists & still used for drainage. **Anglers' Club** (O); coll. of Ind. relics.

SIDE TRIP: (L) from New Smyrna on Flagler Ave., lined with palms & pines, 1.5m to **Coronado Beach,** excellent bath. & auto beach. (R) on Turtle Mound Rd. to **Ind. Mound.**

**46. TITUSVILLE,** on Indian R. (actually a lagoon extending to Stuart), shipping center for Indian R. oranges, also has large fishing industry. **65. COCOA,** named for coco plum, sm. spreading tropical tree whose fruit, varying in color from white to black, is used for preserves. **Merritt I.,** across R., is noted for birds & other wildlife. **86. MELBOURNE** (fresh & salt water f.sm.game.bear & deer;guides) has golf course. Across R. are **Indiatlantic Beach,** 2.5m & **Melbourne Beach,** 4.5m.

SIDE TRIP: (W) from Melbourne, US192 traverses a thinly settled dist., much of it cut over & in some secs. often inundated. Brahman cattle have been imported from India to breed with local strains. 9.5m Hy. crosses St. Johns R. (boats.bait.tackle). 30m **Holopaw,** center of a cypress & pine lumbering dist. 40m **Alligator L.** (f.bath.camp.facils.). 47m **St. Cloud,** on shore of E. Tohopekaliga L. (bath.f.) dates from 1880's. 55m **Kissimmee** (see US17). J. with US92 which leads (W) to Tampa.

**107. SEBASTIAN.** Opp. is **Pelican I.,** gov. bird refuge (pelicans.terns). **118. GIFFORD. 120. VERO BEACH,** resort, partly on the mainland & partly on land across Indian R. extending to ocean. Spring training center for Brooklyn Dodgers. **Pocahontas Pk.** (bowling.tennis). **Mun. Pk.,** on excellent beach (casino.bathhs.f. facils.). In vic. remains of prehist. mammals have been found as well as those of once controversial "Vero Beach Man," later proven Algonquin Ind. **McKee Jungle Gardens** (fee.guides) has 85 as. of jungle planted with c.2,500 varieties of tropical & sub-tropical plants, native & imported from Africa, China, India, Asia, incl. int. orchid display & more than 100 varieties of hibiscus.

SIDE TRIP: (W) from Vero Beach, St.60 passes through a cattle, citrus & lumber reg. with few sizable settlements. At 30m **Yeehaw,** sm. trading center. 51m Hy. crosses Kissimmee R. near Kissimmee L. (f.bass.bream.catfish.perch.pickerel;boats.tackle). 70m **Hesperides,** in an orange-growing reg. Just beyond town (R) is **Shrine of Ste Anne des Lacs** (O.1920). 79m **L. Wales,** resort & residential community surrounded by 23 Ls. (f. boat.swim.) & 50,000 as. of citrus groves. **Crystal L. Pk.** has tourist clubh., beach, game facils. Chief attraction is **Bok Singing Tower & Mountain L. Sanctuary** (O.throughout yr. no pic.no dogs.parking 25¢: gentlemen requested to wear coats), c.3m (N) of town on summit of Iron Mt. (324′). Tower & Sanctuary are gift of Edw. Bok, editor of "Ladies' Home Journal" (1889-1919) & Pulitzer Prize-winner ("Americanization of Edward Bok"), who is buried here. Hexagonal tower, 230′ high, faced with pink & gray marble & ornamented with bas-reliefs, is work of Milton B. Medary of Phila. The 71 bells in carillon range from 11 tons to 12 lbs. & over 4½ octaves. Recitals are given on a number of occasions from Dec. through Ap. Anton Brees of Antwerp is carillonneur. Sanctuary, with view of some 30 Ls., is planted with large variety of trees & shrubs & is bird refuge. European nightingales have been imported & in contest with mocking bird (st. bird), it is said that mocking bird sang all of its own songs & then sang nightingale's song. At 96m **Bartow,** J. with US17 (see).

**135. FT. PIERCE,** shipping center of citrus, truck garden & f. reg.; has ship channel conn. Ind. R. with ocean. From its piers (incl. a super-refrigeration terminal), steamers leave daily for N.Y. Town, conn. by causeways to excellent beaches, also has 2 yacht basins & charter boats & golf course. More than 600 species of fish were catalogued for this sec. by St. Conservation Dept. Ft. Pierce was est. 1838 as military outpost against Inds. & named for Maj. B. K. Pierce. Wm. Tecumseh Sherman was assigned here when just out of West Pt. & distinguished himself by capturing Chief Wildcat in 2nd Seminole War. **St. Wayside Pk.** on St.A1A near-by is located on site of Ays Ind. village & 4-day camp site of Menéndez de Avilés' Sp. exploration party (1565).

At Fort Pierce is J. with St.70 which leads (W) across Fla. to Gulf of Mexico.

SIDE TRIP: (W) on St.70, St.675 & St.64 to **Bradenton** 153m. St.70 proceeds through Halpatiokee Swamp, once infested with cattle thieves, past desolate strip of cut-over land to **Okeechobee** 36m (Ind."big water"), just (N) of **L. Okeechobee** (see St.80), center of cattle, poultry & winter vegetable raising reg. Many of Fla.'s best Brahman herds are here. Catfish from L. & bullfrogs bred in fenced-in swampland are marketed. Col. (later Pres.) Zachary Taylor led forces (Christmas 1837) into swamps near-by against Seminoles. 46m Hy. crosses **Kissimmee R.** (good bass f.). 53m **Brighton.**

(S) here on side Rd. 8m to **Seminole Village** on reserv. of 35,000 as. Inds. here are of Muskogee or Cow Creek division.

69m **Childs** on L. Childs. 101m **Arcadia.** J. with US17 (see). 121m **Myakka City** in trucking & citrus reg., dates from just after Civil War. Cowboys from near-by ranges are often seen in town. 131m J. (R) with St.675 on which cont. 136m J. (L) with St.64 on which cont. 153m **Bradenton.** J. US41 (see).

## Sec. 3: FT. PIERCE to MIAMI. 123.

(S) of Ft. Pierce US1 passes through most widely advertised playground reg. of Fla. Near larger towns hy. is lined with signs advertising merits of various jungle gardens, Ind. villages, mineral springs, lion ranches & alligator farms. Roadside stores sell sub-tropical plants, honey, citrus fruits & souvenirs made of coconut shells, conch shells, cypress knees.

**18. STUART,** on St. Lucie R., E. end of S. Fla. Cross-State Canal (which extends through L. Okeechobee to Ft. Myers on W. Coast), important fishing center (boats. guides). Here is **Shark Industries. 31.5. HOBE SOUND. 39.5. JUPITER** (f.boats. guides.tackle). **Lighth.** is on site of Ft. Jupiter (1838) where Inds. & Negroes were held in Seminole War before removal to West. **Mon. to Celestial RR.** (S) of town, so-named because it once ran from Jupiter to near-by villages: Neptune, Mars, Venus & Juno.

**58. PALM BEACH & WEST PALM BEACH**

Through RR., plane & bus conns. Accoms.: All kinds. Fish: From beaches, piers, bridges, barges. Charter boats avail. Pks. incl.: Flagler, Howard, Bethesda, Phipps & Flamingo. Beach adj. Palm Beach Pier; Lido Pools near-by. Sailfish Derby (Jan.1-Feb.15); S. Fla. Golf & Tennis Matches (Feb.); Jaycee Rodeo (Mar.); Philadelphia Athletics (Mar.). Polo. Greyhound & harness races.

Palm Beach, one of most fashionable winter resorts in U.S., is a narrow island 18m long & never more than ¾m wide. Gulf Stream is 3m offshore. In 1873 there were few families in vic. Shipwrecked cargo of coconuts, 5 yrs. later, took root & gave place exotic flavor that has since been carefully cultivated. Harry M. Flagler began to build Royal Poinciana Hotel in 1893, & the wealthy (1st from Philadelphia) began to est. winter homes. Today Palm Beach is a place of fabulous estates (hidden behind gardens), elaborate hotels & clubs. Along Ocean Blvd. are private beaches & one public beach. Much of architecture is in "Fla.-Mediterranean" style introduced by Addison Mizner, with pastel stucco, courtyards, arcades & galleries. There are no tourist camps or public parking lots. The resort comes alive in Dec. when servants arrive to make ready. W. Palm Beach, separated by L. Worth from Palm Beach & conn. with it by 4 bridges, was est. by Flagler as commercial sec. of Palm Beach. It is now an important commercial & trading center & resort in its own right. Hibiscus, oleander & other exotic shrubs & 50,000 palms line its streets.

PTS. OF INT. IN PALM BEACH: (1) **Royal Poinciana Blvd.,** lined with royal poincianas, in late spring covered with flame-colored flowers. (2) N. County Rd. & Sunrise Ave., **St. Edward's Ch.** (Cath.Sp.Ren.). (3) Wells Rd. & N. County Rd., **El Mirasol** (N.O.), E. T. Stotesbury estate; bldgs. designed by Addison Mizner. Wells Rd. is bordered by trimmed Australian pines. (4) N. end of Palm Beach, **Palm Beach Inlet** (boat.f.bait.tackle). (5) Royal Poinciana Blvd. & Coconut Walk, **Gardens** of old Royal Poinciana Hotel (torn down 1936). (6) S. County Rd. & Barton Ave., **Bethesda-by-the-Sea** (Episc.Ch.Goth.1925); in rear, **Cluett Mem. Gardens** (O.daily). Earlier ch. with same name is on N. Lake Shore. (7) Royal Palm Way & Ceiba Ave., **Soc. of the Four Arts,** (O.wks.;Sun.aft.); art gallery, lib., demonstration garden & film theater. Flower Show in Feb. Royal Palm Way is lined with royal palms ("Roystonea regia"). (8) **Lake Trl.;** bicycle, wheel chair or "motorette" (no automobiles allowed). (9) Off Worth Ave. are int. lanes & patios (see esp. **Via Mizner & Via Parigi**). (10) Worth Ave. & Ocean Blvd., **Palm Beach Pier** (casino.swim.f.bait). (11) S. Ocean & Southern Blvds., **Bath & Tennis Club,** designed by Jos. Urban.

PTS. OF INT. IN W. PALM BEACH: (1) **Flagler Dr.** affords view of Palm Beach estates across L. Worth. (2) 5th St. & N. Flagler Dr., **W. Palm Beach Fishing Club** (O); coll. of marine specimens. (3) Lakeview & S. Olive St., **Banyan Tree,** measuring 65′ around base with spread of 155′. (4) Pioneer Pk., **Norton Gallery & Sch. of Art** (O.wks.Sun.aft.); permanent & loan exhibits; $1,000,000 coll. of Chinese jade. (5) Belvedere Rd., **Palm Beach Internat. Airport;** cargoes of rare animals are flown from S. America.

SIDE TRIPS: (A) On US1 just (N) from W. Palm Beach proper is **Riviera Beach,** seaport of Palm Beach area.

(B) On US1 (S) 4m is **L. Worth** (bath. casino. golf). On North B. St. & 10th Ave., **Baker's Aquarium** (O), tropical fish farm with 1/4 million fish of c.175 varieties. Just (S) of L. Worth on Military Trl. is **Pine Cr. Tropical Fish Hatchery.** At 6m on US1 is **Lantana** with **Lyman's Shell Coll.** (O.free.wks.Jan.-May) in roadside shop, & **Waites Bird & Animal Farm** (fee) on **Boynton Beach** (casino) in vic. At 9m is **Hypoluxo** with **Hydroponic Farms** (L) on Miner Rd. 12m **Boynton** with Boynton Beach reached by causeway over Intracoastal Waterway. In vic. are **Rainbow Tropical Gardens** (O.daily 8:30-dark.fee.refreshments).

(C) From Palm Beach (W) St.80 passes through Everglades & past S. border of L. Okeechobee to **Ft. Myers,** 126m (long intervals without service stas. Accoms.). (W) of W. Palm Beach hy. is paralleled by canal (f.), one of series which conn. L. Okeechobee with Atlantic & Gulf & part of project to drain Everglades, of which an important problem was to check overflow from L. Soil is extremely rich & 3 crops a yr. are frequently raised. Hy. passes through saw grass prairies broken by thickets of pine, cypress or palms. At 42m, **Everglades Experiment Sta.** (O) conducts dairying & agric. experiments incl. trials of great variety of tropical & subtropical plants. **Belle Glade,** 43m, est. 1925 & wrecked by hurricane in 1928, center of winter vegetable producing area. All along S. shore of **L. Okeechobee,** 2nd largest fresh water L. wholly within U.S. (40m long, c.25m wide & 15′ deep), camps & h. & f. equipment are avail. (black bass, catfish, perch; duck). A high levee hides water from view along most secs. of hy.

(N) from Belle Glade on St.15 to **Pahokee,** 11m, crowded from Dec. to Ap. with itinerant pickers come to harvest vegetable crops.

(W) of Belle Glade St.80 passes sugar cane fields where cane sometimes grows 20′ tall. At 47m **South Bay,** RR. terminus. In hurricane of 1928, 1,810 lives were lost, mostly in overflow from L. Okeechobee. Commercial fishing is important in vic. 63m **Clewiston,** est. 1921, has "largest raw sugar mill in continental U.S." (O.Nov.-Ap.free) with a daily grind of 6,000 tons of sugar cane. (W) of Clewiston, hy. passes through cattle country. Harvesting of buds of cabbage palm for eastern market (menus list it as hearts of palms) is carried on though it kills palm. Fronds are marketed for use on Palm Sunday. 95m **La Belle** has 4th of July rodeo with cowboys from neighboring ranches.

(S) from La Belle on St.29 to **Immokalee,** 25m, where, in 80's, Women's Nat. Ind. Assoc. est. sawmill, ch. & sch. but failed to entice Inds. who came to inspect but returned to swamps. At c.39m hy. enters **Big Cypress Swamp** sec. of Everglades, wilderness seldom explored except by hunters & Seminoles who have reservations in area.

(W) of La Belle hy. parallels Caloosahatchee R. through turkey & citrus-raising country. Trapping (otter, muskrat, wildcat, raccoon, opossum) is another source of income. 126$^{m}$ **Ft. Myers.** J. with US41 (see).

**74. DELRAY BEACH,** est. as resort 1901, is center of trucking area. (Excellent beach.f.sports facils.polo by well-known teams.) Annual winter season f. tournament had entries from 25 states (1948). There is also a gladiola festival. **82. BOCA RATON** (Sp., "rat's mouth"), home of Boca Raton Club, designed as hotel by Addison Mizner; good example of Sp. & Moorish architectural style he introduced to Fla. **90.** J. with side Rd.

SIDE TRIP: (R) here to **Pompano,** 1$^{m}$, once f. settlement. Moved after 1928 hurricane, it now has large Farmers' Vegetable Market (especially peppers & green beans) at height in Feb. & Mar. **Burry's Sea Shells** on Pompano Beach has int. coll.

**99. FT. LAUDERDALE**

Annual fish. contest & sailfish rodeo (Dec.1-Ap.15). Charter boats avail. In near-by Everglades, turkey, quail, duck, dove, deer & wildcat. Surf & pool bath., boat., golf, tennis, bowling, shuffleboard. Collegiate Aquatic Forum, with U.S. & foreign univs. competing, during Christmas. Boston Braves have spring training here. Sailing regattas. Midwinter horse show. Cty. fair (Feb.).

Ft. Lauderdale, on site of ft. est. 1838 during 2nd Seminole War, is resort & shipping center of citrus & vegetable-producing reg. It was not until drainage of Everglades was started in 1906 that town showed much growth; but during boom times of 20's it was scene of many fabulous promotions. One resident, who bought 2 lots for $6,000, was offered $110,000 before 6 months had elapsed & settled for $100 by end of yr. New R., with natural & artificial connecting canals, gives Ft. Lauderdale some 90$^{m}$ of navigable waterways (incl. Intracoastal Waterway) within city limits. One tenth of entire city is water surface. Tarpon, roballo & snapper have been taken in heart of bus. dist.

PTS. OF INT.: (1) Tarpon Bend (near 1st Presb. Ch.), **Colee Plaque** comm. massacre by Seminole of wife & children of one of 1st settlers. (2) Broward Blvd., **Hydroponic Gardens,** where crops are grown in chemicals circulated through gravel-filled troughs without aid of soil. (3) **Las Olas Beach,** former U.S. Coast Guard Base, now purchased by city for development, on site of one of Fed. refuge shelters constructed (1888) in vic. as protection against hurricanes. (4) S. border of city, **Port Everglades,** deepest harbor bet. Norfolk & New Orleans, was conceived in 1926 & now has bulk of its traffic with foreign ports. Here is N. terminus of F.E.C. Havana Car Ferry. From City Docks boats offer trips up New R. past elaborate homes, into Everglades where tropical flora & fauna, Seminole Inds. & alligator wrestlers may be seen. (5) **Pks.** incl.: Davis Pk., Andrews Ave. & 7th St.; **Birch St. Pk.** on beach; Pan American St. Pk. up New R. (6) at 3$^{m}$ (S) of Las Olas Blvd., proving ground for paint products of Pittsburgh Plate Glass Co. where c.10,000 test panels are exposed to sun. (7) At 3.8$^{m}$ on E. side of US1, **Wyldwood Tropical Nurseries** (O).

SIDE TRIP: (W) from Ft. Lauderdale 4$^{m}$ to St.7, (S) here 2$^{m}$ to St.84, (W) here 2$^{m}$ to side Rd. (S) here 3$^{m}$ to **Davie,** in Everglades, which has an Orange Festival (Feb.) & rodeo (spring).

(W) of Davie 5$^{m}$ on marked Rd. to **Flamingo Groves** (O.free.guides avail.) where grow c.400 varieties of tropical plants. Citrus experimental groves & lab. Among unusual fruits grown in quantity are the pummelo & shaddock in demand by Chinese for New Yr.'s festivities & citron or essric used in Jewish ceremonial rites.

**104. DANIA** has Annual Tomato Day Celebration. Hy. here is lined with royal palms. **Denis-Roosevelt Chimpanzee Farm** (O.sm.fee) on outskirts of town raises chimpanzees & monkeys for research work & motion pictures.

SIDE TRIP: (W) on Davie Rd., 4$^{m}$ is **Seminole Ind. Reserv.** (with vocational sch.) where Ind. affairs of Fla. are administered.

**106. HOLLYWOOD,** founded 1921 by group of Cal. business men during real-estate boom, widely advertised & ballyhooed, is now yr.-round resort with 6$^{m}$ of mun.-owned beach, 2 yacht basins, 2 golf courses & 5 pub. pks. Taylor St. & 18th Ave., **Tourist Club Pk.** offers shuffleboard & other recr. facils. Polk & 19th Aves., **Fireman Pk.,** has int. gardens. At Hollywood Blvd. & 19th St. is **Grove of Cajeput Trees** which produce a pungent greenish oil used in treatment of skin diseases. Town serves as winter quarters for Baltimore Orioles. F. Tournament (Jan.-Ap.); Tropical

Fiesta (win.). **108.** At **HALLANDALE** is **Gulfstream Pk.** race tracks. Infield has shallow L. on which fleet of sm. sailboats with vari-colored sails maneuver on racing days; pk. is landscaped with palms & tropical shrubs (O.except Sun.). **123. MIAMI** (see).

**Sec. 4: MIAMI to KEY WEST. 157.**

**22.** J. with side Rd.

SIDE TRIP: (R) here a short distance to **Monkey Jungle** (O.sm.fee) where visitors pass through caged-in walk while monkeys run wild in thicket of gumbo limbo trees (sm.tropical Amer.trees yielding aromatic resin called cachibou). Wild monkeys were orig. imported from Singapore & allowed to go native. There is caged coll. of other monkeys, apes & baboons.

**25.** J. with side Rd.

SIDE TRIP: (R) short distance to **Fennell Orchid Jungle** (O.fee) where orchids are grown outdoors, many in trees as in their native jungles.

**28. HOMESTEAD,** center of reg. producing winter vegetables, Persian limes, avocados & mangos. Sub-tropical Experimental Sta. of Univ. of Fla. does research work on such fruits as avocado, mango, papaya & guava. Sta. has more than 1,000 "economic" plant species. Avocado Rd. & Krome Ave., **Palm Lodge Tropical Groves** (O.free), has many varieties of tropical plants incl. Jack-fruit tree. **30. FLORIDA CITY.** J. with St.27.

SIDE TRIP: (R) on St.27 (no gasoline sta. beyond Florida City) to **Royal Palm St. Pk.,** 14m, a 4,000-a. wild life sanctuary, sec. of Everglades Nat. Pk. where magnificent royal palm is found in greatest numbers. On **Paradise Key,** 300-a. hammock overgrown with W. Ind. vegetation, is Royal Palm Lodge (meals & rms.;pic.free). Unimproved hy. cont. (SW) paralleled by drainage canal, through mangrove swamp to Cape Sable. There are occasional camp sites but no accoms. Food & water should be taken along. At c.49.5m (off hy. on Fla. Bay) is **Flamingo,** southernmost settlement on mainland, a sm. f. village named for W. Indies bird once plentiful here but now found only in captivity. Excellent beach at **Cape Sable,** 57.5m but Rd. conditions should be checked.

Everglades Nat. Pk. covers 500,000 as. which is to be increased to c.1,300,000 as.—8th largest Nat. Pk. in U.S. The Everglades themselves constitute c.5,000 sq. miles of swamp land covering most of Fla. (S) & (SW) of L. Okeechobee (see). A saucer-like reg., subject to heavy rainfall, its saw grass prairies & jungle-like hammocks are cut by endlessly intricate waterways. This is new land, much of it muck & marl still forming under the roots of mangroves (which here grow taller than any other place in world) & 89 other species of trees & 100 of shrubs, mostly of W. Indian types (cypress, 8 types of palms, gumbo limbos, strangler figs, cacti, c.37 varieties of fern & numerous airplants incl. c.30 species of orchids). Here are some of greatest concentrations of bird colonies in world incl. the white ibis, snowy & reddish egrets, green & small blue herons & the roseate spoonbill. There are 700 varieties of marine life, giant sea turtles, crocodiles as well as alligators, the manatee or sea-cow, & bear, panther, wild cat, & deer.

Much of area is accessible only by boat & known to few except Seminole Inds., who travel in dugout canoes. The Seminoles, a branch of the Creeks, migrated from Ga. in 18th cent. In 1817-18 Jackson invaded Fla. to punish them for assistance given Brit. in War of 1812 & in 1832 it was arranged for them to be moved to W. But group led by Osceola refused & thus began the Seminole Wars, the most costly of our Ind. Wars, which lasted until 1842 when most of Inds. consented to move. Of descendants of those who remained, Mikasuki branch live in the Big Cypress Swamp & (E) to Miami, the Muskogee in reg. (E) & (N) of L. Okeechobee. Seminoles live in villages of palm-thatched huts, some of which may be seen along Tamiami Trail (see US94). Other villages are near resort areas & cater to tourists. Traditional costumes are extremely colorful, the men wearing multicolored shirts, & the women blouses, long skirts, capes & many strings of beads with their hair gathered in a net in a kind of pompadour style.

(S) of Fla. City US1 passes through desolate mangrove swamps & at **c.43.** crosses **CARD SOUND BRIDGE** which conns. mainland with **KEY LARGO** at **51.** Key Largo (Sp., "long") is c.30m long & 1.5m wide & is 1st of a chain of reefs or narrow Is. that extend (SW) to Key West & separate Fla. Bay from Atlantic. Keys are divided into 2 groups: N. half coral reefs, S. half limestone. Few of them rise more than 6′ above sea level. Here grow such exotics as roseapples, eggfruit, Chinese dates, tamarinds, loquats & Surinam cherries but limes are main crop. There are some 27 varieties of hardwood, including mahogany, black ironwood & lignum vitae, & such oddities as torchwood tree & soapberry tree. Sponging & f. are important industries & keys are famous among sportsmen. Lodges, cabins, boats, supplies & guides avail. at frequent intervals. Sailfish, tarpon, barracuda, Sp. mackerel, bonito, bonefish, kingfish, tuna & many other varieties abound. US1 conn. entire chain by series of bridges (bus trips out of Miami). Hurricane-proof houses have been erected at various places on keys.

SIDE TRIP: (N) of Key Largo are a number of Is. (accessible only by boat) incl. **Black Caesar's Rock,** hqs. of Black Caesar, escaped slave turned pirate.

**59. ROCK HARBOR** has observation tower. **65. TAVERNIER,** named for member of pirate Jean LaFitte's crew who hid out in near-by creek. **70.5. WINDLEY I.** quarries produce coral limestone. **73. UPPER MATECUMBE KEY,** famous among anglers for bonefish. **74. ISLAMORADA** has **Fla. Keys Mem.** to World War I vets who were killed in 1935 hurricane while working on overseas hy.

SIDE TRIPS: (A) Reached (L) only by boat, are **Teatable Key,** naval base in Seminole War, & **Ind. Key.** On latter, Calusa Inds. once slaughtered shipwrecked mariners, notably some 400 Frenchmen c.1755.

(B) Reached (R) by boat, **Lignum Vitae Key,** with ruins thought to date from Sp. occupation.

**84. OVERSEAS RD. & BRIDGE TOLL STA.** for (S) traffic. **99.5. CRAWL KEYS,** so-called because of turtle pens called "crawls." **108. MARATHON,** only settlement of any size on Key Vaca. **111. PIGEON KEY,** named for white-crowned pigeon of W. Indies, painted here by Audubon; called "world's smallest inhabited I." (S) of here geology of keys changes from coral to oölitic limestone formations. Old Is. are held together by mangrove trees & new ones built up by deposits bet. their roots. Topsoil is thin but various crops thrive. Tarpon f. good in this reg. At times hordes of land crabs march across hy.; their shells can puncture tires.

**126. BIG PINE KEY** has groves of Caribbean pines & great variety of cacti. **Big Pine Key Toll Sta.** for (N) traffic on Overseas Hy. **133.5. LITTLE TORCH KEY & MIDDLE TORCH KEY** were named for torchwood tree whose wood burns twice as long as pine. (S) of here hy. passes through mangrove & buttonwood swamps, a reg. once haunt of bootleggers & smugglers of aliens.

### 157. KEY WEST

Through plane, bus (from Miami) & SS. conns. No RR. Accoms.: All kinds. F., swim. & sports facils. & 2 free beaches. Charter boats avail. Cock fights, Sun. afts.

Key West, southernmost & only frost-free city in U.S., 90$^{m}$ from Havana, lies on a coral I. c.1.5$^{m}$ wide & 4$^{m}$ long. Its deep water harbor is fringed with fisheries but most of its coast is lined with gov. property. Majority of homes are of wood, frequently unpainted, with broad sloping roofs designed to collect rainfall which furnishes drinking water. They show West Ind., Southern Col. & even New England influences; some were built by ship carpenters. Chimneys are rare. Vegetation is primarily tropical: Banyan tamarind, frangipani, coconut, & avocado trees, bougainvillea, coral, & bignonia vines, hibiscus, oleander & poinsettia. About ¼ of pop. is of Sp. or Cuban ancestry. Other elements incl. "Conchs," descended from Eng.-Cockney groups, & Negroes, originally from Bahamas. Latter's speech shows marked cockney influences. Cuban lottery is much in news & Duval St. frequently resembles a Sp. promenade. Afternoon siestas are respected. Coffee shops serve Cuban coffee with hot "bollos" (cakes of black-eye pea flour). Ice-cream parlors offer soursop, sugar apple & sapodilla ices along with green fried plantains. Some 600 varieties of fish, of which at least 100 are edible, abound (guides advertise "no fish, no pay"), & Key West is famous for green turtle soup, turtle steak, conch chowders. Industries incl. marketing of fish (4 million lbs. annually), crawfish, turtles, conchs, sponges & shells, as well as cigar-making & boat building.

Ponce de Leon (1513) & Menéndez (1566) may have visited I., but 1st evidences of white settlement date from c.1700. Name is said to be corruption of Cayo Hueso (Sp. "I. of bones"), so-called because Sp. found I. strewn with bleached bones of Ind. tribe pursued down keys by rival tribe & killed in last desperate battle. Don Juan de Estrada, Gov. of Fla., gave I. to a young officer, Juan Pablo Salas, "in consideration of several services" & Salas sold it to John W. Simonton of Mobile, Ala. U.S. took over (1819) & Commodore David Porter est. Naval depot (1822) in successful campaign to rid W. Indies of pirates. Frigate "Constitution" was sent to protect I. during Ind. massacre of 1835. In 1820's & 30's important industry was salvaging of wrecks, & fortunes are said to have been made by those who purposely led vessels astray. Parson Egan walked from pulpit to door of his ch. while preaching sermon on text, "Know ye not that they which run in a race run all, but one receiveth the prize?"; then, off to a head start, cried, "Wreck ashore! Now we will all run a race & see who receiveth the prize." Throughout Civil War,

I. remained in hands of Feds. Cuban pop. began to arrive with movement for Cuban independence & est. of cigar industry. Fire of 1886 drove industry to Ybor City (see). Henry M. Flagler brought 1st train to city in 1912, at a cost of $50,000,000 & 700 lives. During prohibition, town was center for rumrunners. Hurricane of 1936 destroyed miles of RR. & hy. was built on its foundations, opening 1938 as "longest overseas highway in world." Today Key West is center of submarine & anti-submarine development work.

PTS. OF INT.: (1) US1 & N. Beach Dr., **Bayview Pk.,** city's principal recr. center; Mon. in pk. to José Martí, Cuban national hero. (2) Margaret St. & Windsor Lane, **Key West Cemetery;** graves of many who died in Sp.-Amer. War, incl. most of crew of USS "Maine." (3) Margaret & Southard Sts., **Maine Mem.,** a turret of "Maine", sunk in Havana harbor Feb. 15, 1898. (4) Eaton & Williams Sts. (SW. cor.), **Old Bahama Hs.,** built by ship carpenters in Bahamas & brought to Key West on barges, 1865. (5) Caroline near Grinnell St., **Sport Fishing Docks,** where sportsmen return c.5 p.m. with day's catch. (6) Foot of Margaret St., **Turtle Crawls,** concrete posts spaced to allow sea water to circulate but prevent turtles escaping. Turtles that weigh up to 500 lbs. are brought from Cayman Islands off coast of Nicaragua, fed on ocean vegetation & their meat shipped to all parts of U.S. (7) N. end of Elizabeth St., **Fish Market** where buyer selects live fish; it is then dipped out of "fish car," killed, & dressed. (8) Gulf end of Whitehead St., **City Aquarium** (sm.fee) has more than 600 specimens in open air tanks, incl. giant jewfish, 300-lb. turtles, barracuda, sharks, & stingrays. (9) 322 Duval St., **Oldest H.** (O.sm.fee), built by Navy in 2 days in 1825 & held together entirely by wooden pegs. (10) Duval & Southard Sts., **San Carlos Institute** (O.9-5), hqs. of Cuban Gov. in Key West. (11) Southard & Thomas Sts., **U.S. Naval Submarine Base** (O.wks.4:30-6 p.m.Sat.& Sun.1-6;visitors in cars only). (12) SE. cor. Olivia & Whitehead Sts., **Ernest Hemingway H.** (N.O.c.1870). Hemingway's novel, "To Have & Have Not" has local background. (13) Whitehead & Division Sts., **Key West Lighth.** (O.wks. 2-4.1846). (14) 700 Division St., **Convent of Mary Immaculate** (1879.of native rock); Mus. (O.wks.) contains relics of Battleship "Maine," shell & marine life coll. & mementoes of Dr. Samuel A. Mudd (see below). (15) W. end of United St., **Ft. Taylor** (N.O.), begun in 1845 & occupied by Feds., though unfinished, at beginning of Civil War. (16) Atlantic end of Duval St., **Harris H.,** built 1899 by Judge J. V. Harris, long known as southernmost house in U.S. A smaller, modern house, a few feet further (S) now claims title. (17) Waterfront bet. Reynolds & White St., **W. Martello Tower** in center of new bath. beach is one of 2 sm. circular fts. built as coast defenses by Feds. (1861.E. Martello Tower is on S. Roosevelt Blvd. at Meacham Field.

SIDE TRIP: (W) from Key West by boat or plane (no scheduled serv.) 68ᵐ to **Dry Tortugas** (no accoms.), a group of 7 sm. keys or Is. that now comprise Ft. Jefferson Nat. Mon. (hqs. Key West). Is., so-called by Ponce de Leon (1513) because his crew caught 160 tortoises in one night (Sp. "tortugas," turtles), have long been famous for bird & marine life & have attracted such naturalists as Audubon (1832) & Louis Agassiz (1858). Tropical fish & huge sea turtles may easily be observed in the clear water. Noddy & sooty terns arrive every spring. On Bush Key alone some 130,000 terns nest annually. Keys were also hideout of pirates who descended on Sp. ships laden with treasure from Mexico. U.S. built lighth. on Garden Key (1825) & present one on Loggerhead Key (1856) &, believing that a military base at Tortugas "could control navigation of the Gulf," began construction of Ft. Jefferson in 1846. Construction cont. 30 yrs. Ft. is 6-sided, 0.5ᵐ in perimeter, with walls 8′ thick & 45′ high, & intended to garrison 1,500 men & 450 cannon. There are 3 gun tiers & a breakwater moat. One of largest brick fts. in U.S., invention of rifled cannon made it obsolete & it was never completed. Feds. held ft. throughout Civil War. Later it served as prison; most famous prisoner was Dr. Sam. A. Mudd, convicted of conspiracy because he set broken leg of John Wilkes Booth, Lincoln's assassinator. Mudd's heroism in a yellow fever epidemic that broke out in ft. eventually won him pardon. Battleship "Maine" sailed for Havana from Tortugas harbor. As early as 1903 Navy conducted wireless experiments at ft. & it was equipped as a seaplane base during World War I.

## US 17—FLORIDA

**FLA.-GA. LINE** (5ᵐ from Kingsland, Ga.) **(S) to PUNTA GORDA, FLA. 322. US17**

Via: Jacksonville, Palatka, De Land, Sanford, Orlando, Kissimmee, Winter Haven, Bartow, Arcadia, Punta Gorda. RRs. parallel route throughout. Accoms.: All kinds.

US17 descends from Jacksonville, Fla.'s largest city, through heart of citrus reg., a hilly area dotted with innumerable Ls., to Orlando, Fla.'s largest inland city, & then swings (W) to Gulf.

### Sec. 1: FLA.-GA. LINE to PALATKA. 82.

**0.** Hy. crosses **ST. MARYS R.,** est. as boundary bet. Ga. & Fla. when latter was ceded by Spain to England, 1763. Various encounters took place in vic. in Rev. Longleaf pine & thickets of saw palmetto (or palmetto scrub) line hy. **9. YULEE,** named for U.S. Sen. David Yulee, who had his name changed from Levy, pres. of Fla. RR. at outbreak of Civil War. After war he was imprisoned for assisting in Jeff. Davis' escape.

SIDE TRIP: (E) from Yulee 11$^{m}$ on St.200 to **Fernandina** on Amelia I., separated from mainland by St. Marys & Amelia Rs., fishing (shrimp,oysters,menhaden) & industrial (pulp. paper.rayon pulp.fertilizer) town. Sp. est. mission (Santa María) on I. in 1598 & ft. (San Carlos), 1686. Ft. was captured & mission destroyed by Gov. Jas. Moore of S. C. (1702). In 1736, Gen. Oglethorpe of Ga. built a sm. ft. & renamed I., honoring George II's sister. Amers. attacked in 1777. Tories flocked here after Rev. & pirates & smugglers in early 1800's. The LaFittes are said to have been here, & there are many tales of buried treasure (some of which has been found). John McIntosh took over ft. & org. "Republic of Fla." (1812) but Fernandina reverted to Sp. Various adventurers—the Scotchman, Gregor MacGregor, the Pennsylvanian, Jared Irwin, & the Fr. pirate, Luis Aury—took over until Amer. flag went up in 1817. PTS. OF INT.: (1) McClure's Hill, **Site of Battle of Amelia** (1817) where Irwin defeated Sp. (2) Bosquebello Dr., **Bosquebello Cemetery.** (3) Foot of White St., **Site of Ft. San Carlos;** footpath & crumbling wall remain. (4) Foot of San Fernando St., **Oldest Bldg.,** cottage with "tabby" foundation. (5) **Ladies St.,** so-called because of "unattached ladies" who lived here & entertained the soldiers. (6) N. end of I., **Ft. Clinch St. Pk.** (1,004 as.beach.swim.hik.f.camp.but limited facils.) with ruins of Ft. Clinch, pentagonal structure begun 1847, held by Confeds. & then by Feds., & garrisoned in Sp.-Amer. War. Mus. & special exhibits (sm.fee). (7) N. 6th & Alachua Sts., **Presb. Ch.,** 1850's, used as barracks by Feds. (8) **Amelia Beach,** 14$^{m}$ of surf bath. & driving, when tide is low (bathh.boats). (9) Amelia City, **Gerbing's Camellia & Azalea Gardens** (O.Dec.-Ap.;8:30-dusk.fee).

**31. JACKSONVILLE** (see US90). **54. BLACK CR.** (f.crab.boats). **55. MAGNOLIA SPRINGS,** popular spa as early as 1870's, is now sm. resort town whose Qui-Si-Sana Spring produces 3,000 gals. of warm sulphur water per minute & supplies swim. pool (fee).

SIDE TRIP: On side Rd. here (L) 3$^{m}$ to **Site of Ft. St. Francis de Pupa,** est. by Sp. 1737. Destroyed by Eng. 1740. Earthworks remain.

**57. GREEN COVE SPRINGS.**

SIDE TRIP: 7$^{m}$ (R) on St.16 to **Penney Farms Mem. Home Community,** built by J. C. Penney in memory of his father, Rev. Jas. Cash Penney, in 1927, as home for retired religious, educational & social workers & now maintained by "Christian Herald."

**82. PALATKA** (Ind.: "crossing over") outgrowth of post est. in 1820's & by 1870's important port on St. Johns R., 1$^{m}$ wide here; now center of cattle, lumbering & agric. reg. Palatka was a U.S. Army hqs. during Seminole Wars & was several times under fire from gun boats during Civil War. At one time, 5,000 Fed. troops occupied town. Madison & 1st Sts., **Mulholland Pk.,** with ante bellum **Bronson H.** Madison & 2nd St., **St. Mark's Ch.** (Episc.1852), designed by Rich. Upjohn, architect of N.Y.C.'s Trinity Ch. & used as barracks by Feds. **Ravine Gardens** (O.Jan.-June.sm.fee) 85 as. of woodland ravines planted with azaleas, magnolias, japonicas, palms, dogwood, flame vine, bougainvillea, crape myrtles, chrysanthemums. Azalea Festival (Feb.). Fishing cruises (especially black bass) on St. Johns avail.

### Sec. 2: PALATKA to ORLANDO. 98.

**2. E. PALATKA,** shipping center of potato & cabbage producing area; has a farmers' market. **5. SAN MATEO** has citrus groves that have borne for more than 50 yrs. **11. SATSUMA,** J. with St.309.

SIDE TRIP: (S) here to **Welaka,** 7$^{m}$. **Fla. St. Fish Hatchery & Game Farm** (O. 2,500 as.) incl. shad & black bass hatcheries, quail & deer farms, aviary & aquarium.

**33. SEVILLE,** where small Seville orange, said to have been brought over by Sp. & preferred for marmalades, grows wild. **49. DE LEON SPRINGS,** a village shaded by oaks & tall pines, is known for mineral springs, a flow of 90,000 gal. per min. into pool 250′ in diam. & then into St. Johns R. (swim.boat.). Near-by are **Ruins of**

**Sugar Mill,** said to have been built by Sp., added to by Eng., destroyed by Seminoles, rebuilt & again destroyed by Feds.

**56.** J. with US92 which unites here with US17 to Haines City. At **58. DELAND** (1876), resort & center of a citrus growing reg. (f.especially black bass.deer.bear. turkey.squirrel.duck.dove & quail). Among early settlers was Lue Gim Gong, Chinese creator of the Gim Gong grapefruit, the cherry currant, & an orange that won Wilder medal from U.S. Dept. of Agric. **John B. Stetson Univ.** (coed.1886) is named for hat king & outgrowth of DeLand Academy est. by town's founder, H. A. DeLand, baking powder manufacturer. On campus are **Hulley Mem. Tower,** an 80′ campanile, & **Elizabeth Hall,** housing Monroe Heath Mus. of Nat. Hist. (O), with special exhibits of skeletons, crystals, Fla. birds, & Ind. & Chaldean relics.

**64. ORANGE CITY.**

SIDE TRIP: (L) here on side Rd. to **Camp of the Cassadaga Spiritualist Assoc.,** 4m, which dates from 1893 & attracts mediums from all over U.S. during season (Nov.-Ap.).

**77. SANFORD,** center of Fla.'s celery raising dist., was (1837) trading post adj. Ft. Mellon. When, in 1871, Henry R. Sanford, once U.S. minister to Belgium, brought Negroes here to farm his land, local whites drove them off. Sanford next imported workers from Sweden. There were further protests, but most of Swedes stayed on. Sanford is at head of navigation on St. Johns R., which here has 12′ gov.-maintained channel, & barge conns. as far (N) as New Jersey. Good h. & f. in vic. Greyhound & quarter-horse races. Mellonville Ave. & 2nd St., Mon. marking **Site of Ft. Mellon.** Lake Shore Blvd., **Zoo, Mun. Pier** & **Band Shell** (winter concerts). In vic. are: **Big Tree,** a cypress 125′ high, 47′ in circumference at base, possibly 3,500 yrs. old; **Sanlando Springs, Rock Springs** & **Wekiwa Springs,** all offering excellent swim.; pic. **88. FERN PK.** has large fernery. **91. MAITLAND.**

**94. WINTER PARK** (through RR., plane & bus conns.; accoms.), built around 4 Ls., is college, residential & resort town est. as Lakeview (1858) but replanned in 1881 by group of New Englanders. PTS. OF INT.: (1) Park & Comstock Aves., **Scenic Dr.,** marked, starting at C. of C. & winding past citrus groves & avenues lined with live oaks & laurel oaks. (2) Foot of Morse Blvd., **Pleasure Boats** (fee) avail. for cruises along shores of Ls., past estates landscaped with tropical & subtropical plants. (3) Alabama Dr., **Kraft Azalea Gardens,** a city pk. (4) S. Pennsylvania & Fairfax Aves., **Mead Botanical Gardens** (55 as.fee); large orchid & bulb coll., many varieties of exotic trees & shrubs, individual gardens devoted to roses, camellias, azaleas, tulips, caladiums. (5) Holt & French Aves., **Rollins College** (coed.1885.with plant intentionally built to take care of not more than 500 students) is oldest institution of higher learning in Fla. The 45-a. campus, with bldgs. that show a strong Sp.-Mediterranean influence, has 0.5m frontage on L. Virginia. **Knowles Mem. Chapel** (designed by Ralph Adams Cram), **Annie Russell Theater** & **Morse Gallery of Art** are of special interest. **Beal-Maltbie Shell Mus.** (O.wks. Sun.aft.closed during summer.fee) houses internationally famous coll. of shells brought together by Dr. Jas. Hartley Beal. **Walk of Fame** has stones taken from homes of some 600 world celebrities. A Bach Festival, Economic Conference, Town Hall series, adult education course & an "Animated Magazine" program are on winter schedule.

**98. ORLANDO**

Through RR., plane & bus conns. Accoms.: All kinds. Excellent f. 4 golf courses. Swim. Boat. Dog racing (Sanford-Orlando Club). Seminole Driving Club is winter quarters for many race horses. Internat. Cock Fighting Tournament (Jan.). Central Fla. Exposition (Feb.). Tennis Tournaments, Horse Show (Mar.). Yacht Club Regatta (Ap.). F. Tournament (Dec.-Ap.). Casting Tournament (Mar.).

Orlando, largest city of inland Fla. & center of citrus & truck growing reg., lies on ridge in heart of Fla.'s L. district; 15,000 Ls. within radius of 50m, 31 within city limits. Architecture ranges from Vict. Goth. through chromium Mod., softened by luxurious vegetation which, with landscaped Ls., give much of city appearance of pk. After Seminole Wars pioneers from Ft. Gatlin (est.1837) set up stockade which achieved a post office (1850) under name of Jernigan, soon changed to Orlando.

PTS. OF INT.: (1) East Central Ave., **L. Eola Pk.,** which surrounds the L. on which wild ducks, sea gulls & swans are fed every afternoon. Wall of sweet peas, 200′ long, attains height of 14′. Mem. Marker to Orlando Reeves, runner bet. Ft. Gatlin & Mellonville, killed by Inds., for whom some claim town was named. Others say name came from hero of "As You Like It." (2) W. Livingston Ave., **Sunshine Pk.,** mun. recr. grounds & clubhs. of various tourist organizations. Near-by is **Exposition Pk.** with bldgs. of Central Fla. Exposition. (3) W. shore of L. Ivanhoe, **Gaston Edwards Pk.,** noted for azaleas. (4) L. Estelle, **Orlando Solarium;** swim., sun & oil baths. (5) E. Central Ave., **Dickson Azalea Pk.** (6) 718 Magnolia Ave., **The Orchidario** (O.Sat.& Sun.aft.sm.fee); some 400 species of orchids & 500 species of bromeliads. (7) W. Church St., **Tinker Field,** named for Joe Tinker of "Tinker to Evers to Chance" fame. Training camp for Amer. League Washington Senators, Joe Stripp School of Baseball & George Barr's Umpire School.

SIDE TRIPS: (A) From Orlando (E) on St.50 to **Christmas,** 24$^{m}$, to which many send mail during Yuletide holidays for postmark.

(B) From Orlando (S) on **Dixie Hy.** 7$^{m}$ to J. with marked Rd. (L) to **Daetwyler Azalea Gardens** (O.daily) with 200,000 azaleas & 10,000 palms & other plants.

(C) From Orlando (W) on St.50 to **Orlovista** 6$^{m}$, scene of Internat. Cock Fighting Tournament (Jan.); entries from U.S., Canada & Mexico. **Winter Garden** 14$^{m}$ on S. shore of L. Apopka, one of Fla.'s largest Ls., called "world's most dependable bass lake." L. is conn. by inland waterway with St. John's R. Complete Trailer City. Baseball spring training.

(D) From Orlando (NW) on US441 to **Apopka** 14$^{m}$, also on L. Apopka; shipping pt. for fern-growing area.

## Sec. 3: ORLANDO to PUNTA GORDA. 142.

**17. KISSIMMEE,** J. with US192, on L. Tohopekaliga, has one of largest livestock markets in Fla. As early as 1870's town boasted bar constructed so that customers could remain on horseback while drinking. Lakefront Pk. has **Mun. Zoo. Mon. of States** is composed of 1,100 stones from 48 states. Annual rodeo (July). Excellent f. (black bass) & h. (duck.snipe) in vic. **25. INTERCESSION CITY,** planned as boom town in 1924 & never completed, was later given to House of Faith, a non-denominational group. It now has Interdenominational Bible School. **40. HAINES CITY,** J. with US92 & St.17 (see), has **Mun. Beach** on shores of L. Eva. **51. WINTER HAVEN.** Principal industry is packing & canning of citrus fruit. Here are located Fed. & St. citrus bureaus, incl. an Inspection Bureau, an Experiment Sta. & a Products Lab. Annual Fla. Citrus Exhibition, with crowning of the Orange Queen, is held in Feb. Town is built around series of spring-fed Ls., 100 of which are within 5$^{m}$ radius. Ls. are well stocked with black bass & other game fish & 17 are conn. by canals forming 75$^{m}$ waterway. Many have women's names: Jessie, Maude, Fanny, Lulu. L. Silver has bath. beach; L. Howard has mun. pier. **Cypress Gardens,** 4$^{m}$ (SW) of town on L. Eloise, developed from cypress & oak swamp & planted with brilliant variety of native & exotic flowers (O.daily.fee); boat tours through flower-banked canals; daily water ski show (2:30); restaurant.

SIDE TRIP: (W) from Winter Haven 18$^{m}$ on US92 is **Lakeland** (f.swim.small game h.golf. boat.sports facils.), built around 14 palm-fringed, fresh-water Ls. Six million orange & grapefruit trees grow with 40$^{m}$ radius. Cattle, phospate & strawberries are also important. Town began when S. Fla. RR. reached here in 1884 & soon absorbed Acton, near-by settlement est. by Eng. historian, Lord Acton. Troops were stationed here during Sp.-Amer. War & Lt. John J. Pershing was quartermaster of a Negro cavalry unit. World's championship inboard & outboard regatta is held biennially on L. Hollingsworth. Detroit Tigers have winter training here. **L. Mirror;** Civic Center, surrounding L., offers many recr. facils. **L. Morton,** feeding place for wild fowl. E. shore of L. Hollingsworth, **Fla. Southern College** (Meth.coed), founded at Leesburg, 1885, & eventually moved to Lakeland, 1922, in citrus grove overlooking L. Western Campus, being built from designs by Frank Lloyd Wright, has number of int. modern structures completed incl. chapel, lib. & 3 seminar bldgs. Also on campus is Fisher Mem. Temple, exact replica of a small Hindu temple made of 239 pieces of hand-carved red sandstone & imported from Benares, holy city of Hinduism. Int. feature of summer program is summer sch. held in Antigua, Guatemala.

**63. BARTOW,** center of phosphate mining reg.—**Noralyn Mine** (O) is one of largest in U.S.—was sett. in 50's by slave-holding planters around site of Ft. Blount, est. during Seminole Wars. Civic Center (swim.tennis) & mun. golf course. **Schuck's Wonder H.,** (S) of town (O.daily.sm.fee), offers many curiosities, labor-saving devices, etc. **Kissengen Springs** is 3$^{m}$ (S) & 1$^{m}$ (E) of US17 (mineral waters.pic.camp.).

SIDE TRIP: (R) from Bartow on St.60 to **Mulberry,** 8$^{m}$, which in 80's, when phosphate mines were 1st opened, had traditional atmosphere of gold & silver camps of West. Fossils from mines may be seen in pavilion on (R) side of hy.

**87. WAUCHULA,** est. as Ft. Hartsuff during Seminole Wars. Frogs' legs are principal export. **91. ZOLFO SPRINGS,** so-called by Ital. laborers because of sulphur springs which now feed swim. pool in mun. pk. J. with St.64.

SIDE TRIP: (E) 21m on St.64 to **Avon Park** (swim.f.water skiing.golf.sm.game h.), with 16 fresh-water Ls. in or adj. to town. Mall through business dist. is planted with exotic shrubs, especially blue-flowered Jacaranda trees. Town is in citrus growing & cattle producing reg. Poultry, avacados & bulbs (especially gladioli) are also important. Avon Park was founded in 1886 by Oliver M. Crosby who went to Eng. to recruit settlers & named town for Stratford-on-Avon.

**116. ARCADIA,** in heart of cattle raising & citrus producing reg., has large livestock market & is scene of All-Fla. Championship Rodeo held July 4. Tin Can Tourists of the World, organization of tourists who live in trlrs., meets here to celebrate Christmas. **127. FT. OGDEN,** on site of ft. est. here in 1841 because of availability of cypress for canoes, only means of penetrating Everglades. **142. PUNTA GORDA,** J. with US41 (see).

## US 441—FLORIDA

### HIGH SPRINGS, FLA. (SE) to ORLANDO, FLA. 138. US441

Via: Alachua, Gainesville, Orange Lake, Ocala, Leesburg, Mount Dora, Zellwood. RRs. parallel route bet. High Springs & Mount Dora, Zellwood & Orlando. Accoms.: All kinds.

US441 runs through central Fla. in heart of rich citrus & truck growing reg. Numerous Ls. offer excellent fishing.

**0. HIGH SPRINGS,** J. with US41 (see). **22. GAINESVILLE** (swim.golf.f.sm.game h.collegiate sports) is college & resort town & shipping center for a reg. producing lumber, naval stores, cattle, & truck crops. It is also one of chief centers of tung oil industry in America, with oil extraction plants & experimental stas. Orig. settlement (1830's) was called Hog Town & renamed Gainesville in 1853 in honor of Seminole War Gen. E. P. Gaines. **Univ. of Florida** (1905.coed.). **Plaza of the Americas,** with a holly tree for each of the 21 Amer. Republics bisects campus. Lib. has special Florida room devoted to Fla. hist. **Chemistry Bldg.** houses Edmund Kirby-Smith Herbarium with coll. of 6,000 specimens. **Peabody Hall** offers art exhibitions. **P. K. Yonge Sch.** is model laboratory sch. from kindergarten through high sch. 522 W. Univ. Ave., John F. Seagle Bldg. houses **Fla. St. Mus.** (O.wks. 9-5.free); colls. pertaining to natural sciences, Inds. & hist. of Fla. Also on campus is **Fla. St. Radio Sta. WRUF. Fla. Agric. Experiment Sta.** uses part of 1,500-a. tract belonging to Univ. Sch. of Forestry, which controls Austin Cary Mem. For.

SIDE TRIP: (W) 3.5m from Gainesville on St.26 to J. with side Rd. (N) here 3m to **Devil's Millhopper,** a sink hole some 100′ deep into which a number of springs pour without raising level of pool.

**42. ORANGE L.** In vic. is an Audubon Soc. **Bird Sanctuary** (boats.guides avail.) where herons, egrets, ibises nest on islands of roots & grasses that float about in a strong breeze. **59. OCALA,** resort & trading center for a citrus, truck, phosphate & limestone area. De Soto (1539) discovered Ind. village of 600 huts near-by. Present town dates from trading post est. 1825. It was here that Seminole chief Osceola (1835) put his dagger through treaty (still preserved in Nat. Archives in Wash.) offered by Ind. agent Wiley Thompson. Ocala was scene of much activity when Gulf-Atlantic Ship Canal was begun by W.P.A. in 1935. SE. Brahman Breeders Assoc. has annual show here & there is a Petunia Festival (Ap.-May). Ocala is hqs. of **Ocala Nat. For.** (441,925 as.;f.h.especially deer) which contains largest existing area of sand pine ("Pinus Clausa") in world. Recr. areas incl.: **Salt Springs** on St.314 & **Juniper Springs & Fern Hammock,** 30m (E) of Ocala off St.40.

SIDE TRIP: (E) 6m from Ocala on St.40 to **Silver Springs,** one of largest in world, & one of most famous of Fla.'s natural wonders. A subterranean R. fed by some 150 springs, flows into a basin 300′ in diam. & 80′ deep, & hence into Silver & Oklawaha Rs. at rate that varies from 801 to 340 million gals. a day. Temperature is constant 72°, daily discharge of solids 1,902 tons, & water so clear a penny is visible at depth of 80′. Landscaped 80-a. pk., with free pic. grounds, bath. beach, & daily concerts, surrounds basin. Glass bottom boats (fee) afford views of 33 varieties of fish, 16 of turtles, hundreds of aquatic plants, such formations as the "Blue Grotto," "Devil's Kitchen," & prehist. bones of giant Ichthyosaurian. Fee incl. brief trip underwater in "Photo-sub." **Jungle Cruise** (fee) is 50-minute motorboat ride down Silver R. through territory used as background for such movies as the Johnny Weismuller "Tarzans" (orchids, strange aquatic plants, wild monkeys). Ross Allen's Reptile Institute (fee) has coll. of snakes, alligators, crocodiles & turtles, many for sale. Lecturer explains habits & characteristics & visitors may see snakes "milked" of venom hourly on Sundays (10-5 p.m.). Adj. **Everglades Exhibit** with Seminole Village & Fla. Wild Animal Ranch is incl. in fee. At 35m on St.40 is **Silver Glen Springs** (swim.f.h.cottages) in reg. where "The Yearling" was filmed.

**96. LEESBURG** (swim.boat.sports facils.avail.), in heart of L. dist., sponsors Nat. Fresh Water Bass Tournament (Nov.-Mar.). Indianapolis baseball club winters here. **Venetian Gardens,** a man-made area, is a 70-a. pk. with Is., drives, game courts, yacht basin, ball pk.

SIDE TRIP: (E) from Leesburg 14m on St.44 to **Eustis,** on E. shore of L. Eustis, in citrus & watermelon growing reg. (f.h.swim.boat.). Fla. Sportsmen's Exposition (Mar.). Eustis track is center of miniature auto racing & world's record of over 120 m.p.h. was made here.

**138. ORLANDO.** J. with US17 (see).

## US 41—FLORIDA

**FLA.-GA. LINE** (6m from Lake Park, Ga.) **to NAPLES, FLA. 384. US41**

Via: Jasper, Lake City, High Springs, Newberry, Inverness, Tampa, Bradenton, Sarasota, Punta Gorda, Fort Myers, Naples. RRs. parallel route bet. Ga. Line & Lake City, High Springs & Inverness, Bradenton & Sarasota, Fort Myers & Naples. Accoms.: All kinds.

US41 runs from N. Fla. to Tampa, leading industrial center on W. coast, then to Sarasota (circus winter quarters) on Gulf & finally along Gulf to Naples & J. with US94 which crosses Fla. to Miami on E. coast.

### Sec. 1: GA. LINE to NEWBERRY. 84.

**32. WHITE SPRINGS,** health resort. Mineral waters, effective in treatment of arthritis & rheumatism, were held sacred by Inds. Wounded warriors were free from attack while using springs. During Civil War many planters moved families here. On banks of Suwannee R., near-by, **Stephen Foster Mem. Pk.** is being developed & will have a carillon, an amphitheater & a statue of composer of "Old Folks at Home" (Swanee River). **45. LAKE CITY,** J. with US90 (see). **71. HIGH SPRINGS,** trading center for tobacco & peanut area, is J. with US441 (see).

SIDE TRIPS: (A) From High Springs (L) 6m on side Rd. to a **Natural Bridge** where Santa Fe R. disappears underground for 3.5m.

(B) From High Springs (R) 10m on St.20 to **Ft. White,** est. during Seminole War. Near-by are **Itchetucknee Springs** with flow of 300,000,000 gals. a day.

**84. NEWBERRY,** J. with St.26 which leads (E) 17m to Gainesville & Univ. of Fla. (see).

### Sec. 2: NEWBERRY to TAMPA. 130.

**45. DUNNELLON** (f.& h.in vic.) in heart of limestone & phosphate dist. In vic. Gen. Gaines & troops were attacked (1836) by Inds. under Osceola.

SIDE TRIP (N) 3.5m from Dunnellon to **Rainbow Springs** (swim.lodge.cabins). Submarine & glass bottom boats (fee) reveal fantastic underwater world. Brilliant prismatic colors are result of mineral deposits in solution.

**70. FLORAL CITY** (h.& f.center), J. with St.48.

SIDE TRIP: Take latter (L) 15m to **Bushnell.** In vic. is **Dade Mem. Pk.** (80 as.) with Mon. comm. massacre of Maj. Francis L. Dade & 108 of his men (only 1 escaped) by Seminoles, Dec. 28, 1835.

**80.5. CHINSEGUT HILL SANCTUARY** (O); botanical gardens, wildlife refuge & for. experiment sta. **85. BROOKSVILLE** in tangerine growing area that also has limestone quarries.

SIDE TRIP: (L) 3.5m on side Rd. to **Devil's Punch Bowl,** a sink hole covering entire acre.

**94. MASARYKTOWN,** founded by Czechs who still retain some old world customs.

**130. TAMPA**

Through RR., plane, bus & SS. conns. Accoms.: All kinds incl. large mun. trlr. camp. Tourist Recr. Center in Plant Pk. Swim. & sports facils. F. from bridges, piers & boats in Tampa & Hillsborough Bays. Greyhound Racing (Nov.-Feb.); horse racing (Jan.-Mar.). Cincinnati Reds spring training; Fla. St. Fair incl. Gasparilla Carnival (c.11 days in Feb.); Noche de Mantilla, Ybor City (Nov.); Davis I. yacht races & tennis tournaments (Jan.); Convention of Tin Can Tourists of World (Jan.-Feb.); Pistol Tournament (Mar.); Latin-Amer. Fiesta (Ap.).

Tampa, on excellent harbor at head of Tampa Bay & extending (S) on peninsula that separates Hillsborough Bay from Old Tampa Bay, is W. coast Fla.'s largest port & industrial center & a yr.-round resort noted for fishing. Hillsborough R. flows (N-S) through center. On (E) are principal business & industrial secs. incl. Ybor City, with its large Sp., Cuban & Ital. pop., its Sp. & Cuban restaurants & its hand-made clear Havana cigars in which Tampa leads U.S. Many Negroes speak patois of Eng., Sp., Cuban & other dialects & work in cigar factories. Tampa also produces canned citrus fruits, phosphates, lumber, cement, ships & packing cases. Narváez sailed into bay in 1528 & Juan Ortiz, one of his men captured by Inds., acted as interpreter for De Soto in 1539. For Sp., vic. remained primarily place to catch slaves. Bay was also used by pirates in 18th cent. Small settlement, Spanishtown, was here when Amers. arrived c.1820 & 3 yrs. after built Ft. Brooke. Feds. shelled city in 1863 & later occupied it to try to stop trade with Cuba. Cigar industry was est. 1886, & a million cigars manufactured 1st yr. Henry Plant built fabulous Tampa Bay Hotel (1889) in attempt to outdo Henry Flagler's enterprises on E. Coast. In Orange Grove Hotel, razed 1945, Sidney Lanier wrote "Tampa Robins" & J. A. Butterfield wrote music for "When You & I Were Young, Maggie." With sinking of the "Maine" thousands of troops were encamped here. Col. Teddy Roosevelt drilled his Rough Riders in backyard of the great hotel. Rich. Harding Davis came to report, & Frederic Remington to draw, the war. Clara Barton, founder of the Red Cross in U.S., est. hqs. in city. Gandy Bridge (1924) & Davis Causeway (1934) gave Tampa short cuts to St. Petersburg & Clearwater, respectively, & to Gulf beaches. Today Tampa is int. combination of southern background & politics, northern industrial enterprise & Latin gaiety, best illustrated, perhaps, in Fla. St. Fair with its Gasparilla Carnival when "pirates" yearly invade city & convert it into a place of parades, masked balls & other revels.

PTS. OF INT.: (1) W. bank of Hillsborough R., at Cass St., **Plant Pk.** (20 as.), with great variety of palms, night-blooming lilies. De Soto oak has limb spread of 117′. (2) Grand Central & Hyde Pk. Aves., **Univ. of Tampa** (coed.), founded 1931, now occupies immense Tampa Bay Hotel bldg. Classrooms, lib., dormitories are all in 1 bldg. which is over ¼ mile long & has a roof area of 6 as. Hotel was designed in Sp.-Moroccan manner & is topped by 13 golden minarets. (3) **Tampa Mun. Mus.** (O.Tues.-Sat.guides.free) in S. wing of Univ. Exhibits incl. Venetian & Florentine mirrors, Oriental rooms, antique furniture, paintings, sculpture. (4) Just (N) of Univ., Mun. Auditorium houses **Tampa Bay Mus.** (O.Mon.-Fri.aft.free) with natural hist. & archeological exhibits from Fla., the Orient, etc. Here also is **Tampa Art Institute** which has c.6 exhibitions a yr. (5) N. end of Plant Pk., **Tourist Recr. Center** (sports facils.). (6) (N) of Plant Pk., winter hqs. of **Royal Amer. Shows** (O), "largest Midway organization in the world," which furnishes amusement features for fairs throughout U.S. & Canada. (7) N. Boulevard & W. Sligh Ave., **Lowry Pk.** Moss H. here has 50,000 plants & shrubs incl. bamboo 60′ tall. (8) N. Rome Ave. & Spruce St., **Mun. Trlr. Pk.,** 12,000 trlr. parking lots constitute city in miniature. Site of annual convention of Tin Can Tourists of World. (9) N. side of Hillsborough R. & Nebraska Ave., **Sulphur Springs Pk.** (swim.greyhound racing). (10) Bay Shore Drive, following Hillsborough Bay (S) to **Ballast Pt. Pk.** offers excellent view of bay & skyline. Pk. has fishing pier. (11) Swan Ave. & W. Shore Blvd., **Beach Pk.,** residential dist. facing Old Tampa Bay. (12) Bridge, across Hillsborough Bay at Bayshore Drive, leads to **Davis Is.,** 800 as. of man-made islands cut by winding lagoons & canals; golf course, Dixie Tennis Tournament courts & elaborate residences in tropical gardens. (13) Across Hillsborough R. on Platt St. Bridge to Franklin St. (SW cor.) where Plaque marks **Site of Ft. Brooke.** (14) Nebraska Ave. & Broadway, center of **Ybor City;** Sp., Ital. & Cuban clubs, curio stores, fiestas & cigar factories (many O.wks.).

## Sec. 3: TAMPA to NAPLES. 170.

**44. ELLENTON,** center of truck & citrus area. **Gamble Mansion** (O.9-5.free.1840's. relics) was refuge for Judah P. Benjamin, Confed. Secy. of State when wanted by

U.S. Gov. Fed. gunboats came to Tampa Bay in pursuit but Benjamin got by disguised as Negro cook & escaped to England. **Atwood Grapefruit Grove** (O.free) dates from 1900 & is said to be world's oldest commercial grapefruit grove.

**49. BRADENTON** (boat.fresh & salt water f.sm.game), now combined with Manatee, is shipping pt. for winter vegetables. 9th Ave. & 14th St., **Recr. Pk.** In E. Bradenton, **Ruins of Braden Castle,** built 1840's by Dr. Jos. Braden & raided by Inds. Adj. **Palmetto** has large Cty. Farmers' Market.

SIDE TRIPS: (A) From Manatee (S) 3m on side Rd. to **Oneco & Royal Palm Nurseries** (O), one of largest in country.

(B) From Bradenton (W) 5m at Shaws' Pt. on S. bank of Manatee R., **De Soto Mon.** comm. landing of De Soto's expedition, 1539.

(C) From Bradenton (W) on St.684. At 6.5m **Cortez** (f.). At 7m **Anna Maria Key & Beach.**

(D) From Bradenton (NW) on St.45 & side Rd. to **Terra Ceia I.** c.6m with flower farms (gladioli, lilies, sweet peas, & Aloe vera).

**61. SARASOTA**

Through RR., plane & bus conns. Accoms.: All kinds. 40m of beaches. Good f. & h. in vic. Boat. Yacht. 2 golf courses. Recr. center with game courts. Dog races. Baseball. Internat. Tarpon Tournament (May 15-Aug.). Sara De Soto Pageant (a wk. in Feb. or Mar.) comm. Sara's (alleged daughter of De Soto) love for Ind. chief.

Sarasota, on Sarasota Bay, is modern resort town with pastel colored "Fla.-Mediterranean" stucco houses & elaborate hotels lining wide streets landscaped with palms & tropical shrubs. It is separated from Gulf of Mexico by series of sandy, landscaped keys (conn. to town by causeways) with excellent surf bathing. Wm. Whitaker arrived here in 50's & planted 1st orange grove. In 80's a Scotch syndicate est. holdings & Col. J. H. Gillespie, manager, built 1 of earliest golf courses (4 holes) in U.S. In 1911 Mrs. Potter Palmer, Chicago socialite, developed farm lands in vic. Principal income is from tourists (Sarasota has been winter quarters of circus since 1929), but town is also center of citrus & truck gardening area (especially celery). Dolomite is mined near-by.

PTS. OF INT.: (1) Inters. of Main, Central & S. Pineapple Aves., **Five Points** is center of town with City Hall, Mun. Auditorium & Civic Center, & Little Theater in vic. (2) (N) from Five Pts. c.2.5m just off US41, **Sarasota Jungle Gardens** (O.8:30-6.fee). Over 4,000 varieties of plants; large cactus coll.; 70-yr. banana grove; flamingoes & herons roam at liberty. (3) (N) from Five Points c.3.5m just off US41 (L) **John & Mable Ringling Mus. of Art** (O.9-4:30.fee.Mon.free). Cloistered wings, inspired by architecture of Ital. Ren., surround 3 sides of terraced court which contains a fountain, statues & 86 marble columns dating from 12th to 15th cents. Top balustrade surmounted by 76 statues. Mus. contains c.450 originals representing all W. European schools from 14th to 20th cents. incl. Rembrandt, Raphael, Titian, Tintoretto, Veronese, Van Dyck, Franz Hals, Andrea del Sarto, Murillo, Goya, Velasquez, El Greco. Especially noteworthy are Rubens coll. & 17th cent. Ital. coll. There are also sculpture & pottery colls. & a few Amer. paintings. **Ringling Sch. of Art,** 33rd St., founded by John Ringling, is now separate entity. (4) Bay Shore Drive, **"Ca d'Zan"** (O.daily conducted tours.fee) was home of Ringling, & inspired by Doges Palace, Venice. Fee incl. Mus. of the Amer. Circus with costumes, masks, posters, photographs, old circus wagons. (5) Foot of Main St., **Art Assoc. Gallery** (O.wks.except Mon.1-9,Sun.1-5p.m.free); contemporary paintings, sculpture, ceramics. (6) (E) of Five Pts. 1m **Ball Pk.;** Boston Red Sox spring training. Trlr. pk. adj. (7) (E) of Five Pts. 2m on Fruitville Rd., **Sarasota Reptile Farm** (O.daily.fee); large coll. of reptiles, animals & birds. Venom "milked" from rattlesnakes on Thurs. (8) E. end of 18th St., **Ringling Bros.-Barnum & Bailey Circus Winter Quarters** (O.c. Nov.15-Ap.1.daily.10-4:30.fee). Training & rehearsals daily. Special exhibitions on Sun. afts. (9) Across Ringling Causeway to **St. Armand's & Lido Keys.** Latter has mun. casino. (N) from here across bridge, **Longboat Key** with **Cheeri-Ho Beach.** (S) is **Siesta Key,** with **Mira-Mar & Sarasota Beaches.**

SIDE TRIP: (SE) of Sarasota c.16m on St.72 to **Myakka R. St. Pk.** (15,693 as.hqs.Sarasota. pic.hik.f.boat.cabins).

**109. PUNTA GORDA,** J. with US17 (see), commercial & sports fish. center (boats. guides avail.). Cattle & gladioli raising are also important in vic. Town has mun. docks & yacht basin, fishing pier & Tarpon Tournament (Ap.15-Aug.1). **Punta Gorda Beach** on I. conn. by bridge is c.26m away.

**133. FT. MYERS**

Through RR., plane & bus conns. Accoms.: All kinds. Fresh water & deep sea f. Boats & guides avail. at Fort Myers & vic. Mun. golf course. Edison Pageant of Light (Feb.). Tarpon Tournament (Ap.).

Ft. Myers, on Caloosahatchee R. & W. terminus of Fla. Cross-St. Canal linking Atlantic with Gulf, grew up around ft. est. 1841 during Seminole War & attacked by Confeds. during Civil War. It is now center of citrus & trucking area, one of nation's largest shippers of winter flowers, & a winter resort in one of Fla.'s most famous fishing grounds (especially tarpon). Streets are lined with some 70 varieties of palms incl. royal, coconut, traveler & fishtail. PTS. OF INT.: Main & Carson Sts., **Evans Pk.** Bay & Hendry Sts., **City Pk.** 2130 McGregor Blvd., **Edison H.** (O.daily; int.grounds,esp."Coconut Walk"), where Thos. Edison had his winter home from 1886 until death in 1931. Here he conducted experiments in electric lighting & manufacture of rubber from various plants incl. goldenrod. He urged citizens to plant exotic trees & shrubs & within city limits now grow a cannon ball tree, kapoks, banyans, strangling figs. His offer to supply city with electric lights was once, it is said, rejected on grounds it would keep cows awake. Henry Ford & Harvey Firestone were visitors. 2200 McGregor Blvd., **Ford Estate** (N.O.). Terry Ave. & E. 1st St., **Terry Pk.**

SIDE TRIPS: (A) From Ft. Myers 6m (SW) on St.867 to **Everglades Nursery** (O), noted for palms, tropical plants. Bougainvilleas, gardenias & hibiscus attract special attention (winter). At 10m is J. with side Rd.

(S) here 6m to **Ft. Myers Beach** on Estero I. (7m of beach for driving, surf swim. & f.; no undertow).

Cont. (S) on St.867 to **Punta Rassa** (f.village) at 16m.

(B) From Ft. Myers (W) lie group of Is. (famous for f.esp.tarpon;swim.boat.shell collecting) which may be reached by boats avail. at number of places. (1) **Pine Is.** may be reached by land: (N) across Caloosahatchee R. 3m on US41 to J. with St.78. (W) here 15m. Mango groves noteworthy. (2) **Sanibel I.,** reached by ferry from Ft. Myers, noted as shell gathering ground. Sea Shell Fair held in Mar. (3) **Captiva I.,** joined to Sanibel by bridge, so named because here pirates kept women captives. Burial ground of Caloosa Inds. is on tiny near-by I. (4) **Useppa I.** has inn & golf course. (5) **Gasparillo I.,** once hqs. of Sp. buccaneer José Gaspar (or Gasparillo) whose diary records 36 ships captured & sunk bet. 1784-95. In 1822, defeated by U.S. gunship disguised as merchantman, he threw himself overboard wrapped in anchor chain. On I. is **Boca Grande,** resort famous for its Tarpon Tournament, reached by train & ferry from Placida. Gasparillo has deep natural pass permitting access of ocean freighters to inland phosphates.

**148. ESTERO.** Religious group. Koreshan Unity, founded by Cyrus R. Teed, maintains tropical nursery (O), general store & Art Hall (O.aft.). **154. BONITA SPRINGS** (f.in Imperial R.). Near-by beach good hunt. ground for shell collectors. **170. NAPLES.** J. with US94 (see).

## US 19—FLORIDA

**FLA.-GA. LINE** (41m from Moultrie, Ga.) **(S) to ST. PETERSBURG, FLA. 255. US19**

Via: Monticello, Cross City, Old Town, Otter Creek, Weekiwachee Springs, Tarpon Springs, Clearwater. RR. parallels route bet. Ga. Line & Monticello, Lamont & Chiefland, Tarpon Springs & St. Petersburg. Accoms.: All kinds.

### Sec. 1: FLA.-GA. LINE to OTTER CREEK. 127.

**8. MONTICELLO.** J. with US90 (see). **11. DRIFTON,** near site of Ibitachuco, home of Ind. chief Vitachuco who in hand-to-hand battle personally fell upon De Soto (1539) & severely beat him. Franciscans est. mission in vic. which Gov. Moore of S.C. spared in his raids (1704). **31. ERIDU,** center of turpentine producing area, was once hqs. for Confed. deserters (geese,duck,turkeys,deer avail.). **47. PERRY,** forestry products center. **Lee Tidewater Cypress Co.** here is said to be "world's largest cypress sawmill."

SIDE TRIP: (W) from Perry on St.30 to **Hampton Springs** 5m, one of oldest health resorts in this sec.

**76.** Hy. crosses Steinhatchee R. (good.h.in vic.) which empties into Dead Man's Bay, once pirate retreat. **102. OLD TOWN,** on site of Ind. village where Andrew Jackson took prisoner Rbt. Ambrister, Brit. officer who had helped Inds. against

U.S. Jackson had Ambrister tried & executed & thereby created internat. incident. Sp. moss is dried & prepared for upholstering use in local factory. **105.** Hy. crosses Suwannee R. **106. FANNIN,** on site of Ft. Fannin (1838) of which there are still some traces. **Fannin Springs** have flow of 48,000 gals. per min. (S) of here hy. passes through good h. & f. country. **127. OTTER CREEK,** J. with St.24.

SIDE TRIP: (W) 21m on St.24 to **Cedar Key,** island fish. settlement. Burial mounds of pre-Columbian Timucuan Inds. have been excavated on neighboring keys, some of which are Gov. bird sanctuaries.

## Sec. 2: OTTER CREEK to ST. PETERSBURG. 128.

**42. HOMOSASSA SPRINGS,** has **Nature's Giant Fish Bowl** (O.fee), natural aquarium formed by springs (flow of 70,000 gals. per min.) that attracts thousands of fish of some 30 fresh & salt water varieties, many of which spawn in underground caves (swim.pic.jungle trls.boat cruises avail.). Near-by is **Yulee Sugar Mill Pk.** with ruins of sugar mill that once supplied Confeds. **62. WEEKIWACHEE SPRINGS** (f.swim.glass-bottom boats.zoo.fee) has flow of 100,000 gals. per min. Underwater Theater advertises "Underwater Babes' Ballet," an underwater show put on by girls at depths of 25′ to 100′.

**92. TARPON SPRINGS** with 23m of waterfront within its city limits incl. Ls., bayous, R. & Gulf (excellent fresh & salt water f.swim.boat.sports facils.dog races), is popular resort. Main income derives from $3,000,000 sponge fish. industry, largest in U.S. Sponge fleet consists of some 175 gaily painted boats manned by 600 men, mostly Greeks. Diving of soft suit variety has mostly supplanted naked diving & hooking from bottom by men working on surface. Principal commercial sponges found, in order of value are sheepswool, yellow, grass & wire or velvet. Sponge sold across counter is skeleton of the original animal, outer skin & interior cellular matter having been allowed to decay & then removed before skeleton is bleached or dyed. Cruises to sponge beds, with lectures & demonstrations, avail. (as are "Jungle" cruises up Anclote R.). Sponge auctions are held on certain Tues. & Fri. Greek Orthodox ceremonies, when fleet leaves & returns (about 4 times a yr.), are colorful & impressive, as are other ch. ceremonies, especially "Diving for the Cross" (Epiphany service symbolic of baptism of Christ, descent of Holy Spirit & recovery of Cross under Constantine) on Jan. 6 which attracts thousands. Of interest are **Greek Orthodox Ch.,** curio & coffee shops in the Gr. quarter, & religious paintings of Geo. Inness, Jr. in **Ch. of the Good Shepherd,** Grand Blvd. & Read St. (Geo. Inness, Sr., famous Amer. landscapist, built a studio here in 1877.) **103. DUNEDIN,** citrus & truck center, dates from 1850's. Town has yacht basin, golf course & waterfront pk. with visitors' clubh.

**106. CLEARWATER,** resort since 90's & residential town (f.fresh & salt water. swim.sail.golf), lies on highest coastal elevation in Fla. bet. 2 bays, Clearwater & Old Tampa, & is conn. to Clearwater I. by Mem. Causeway (free), landscaped with palms, marigolds & 30,000 petunias. I. has excellent beaches, yacht club, boats & guides for f. expeditions & trlr. pk. Town has citrus packing plants & is seat of Pinellas Cty. which also produces truck, flowers (especially gladioli bulbs), cattle & dairy products & honey. Philadelphia Phillies have spring training here; Professional Golfers' Assoc. has annual tournament (Jan.). PTS. OF INT.: Druid Ave. & Jasmine Way, **Site of Ft. Harrison,** marked by plaque in wall of Rbt. Brown Estate. Osceola Ave., **Pub. Lib.;** coll. of relics & documents on Clearwater & coll. of costume dolls. Coachman Sta. c.4m (E) of town, **Pioneer Log Cabin** (O). Haines Rd. & Bay Blvd., **Seville Grove** (O). Peafowl wander free here among prizewinning grapefruit trees. Birds may best be seen at feeding time, 5 p.m. N. Haines Rd., **Kapok Tree,** grown from seed brought from India (1877) & known for flame-red orchid-like blossoms. **108. BELLEAIR.** Just (S) of town are **Eagle's Nest Japanese Gardens** (O.Christmas-May.fee.refreshments), where hidden speaker produces music from tops of palms & pines.

**128. ST. PETERSBURG**

Through RR., plane & air conns. Accoms.: All kinds. Info.: C. of C. & Tourist Center. Excellent beaches & f. Cruises & f. trips. All sports facils. suitable for climate. Greyhound racing (Dec.-Mar.). Shuffleboard Tournament (Feb.). Trapshooting Tournament (Mar.). N.Y. Yankees & St. Louis Cardinals (spring training). Kingfish Derby (Mar. & Ap.). Festival of States (1 wk. Ap.). Regatta (Ap.). Tarpon Round-Up (May 15-July 31).

St. Petersburg, founded in 1880's "with climate its principal commodity," boasts 360 days of sunshine a yr. Its afternoon paper gives away entire edition whenever sun has not appeared before press time (3 p.m.) & has had to do so fewer than 5 times annually in 31 yrs. Climate is main attraction to annual ¼ million visitors, many of whom are beyond middle yrs. Streets are lined with thousands of green benches on which they sit, curbs are provided with ramps for convenience of wheelchairs, & there are such "athletic & social" clubs as Half-Century Club (membership limited to those bet. 50 & 75 & Three Quarter Century Club (75 or over). St. Petersburg, whose city limits include several inlets & fresh water Ls., is on S. end of Pinellas Peninsula. There are bridge conns. with Port Tampa & ferry conns. with pts. (S) on mainland. Narváez crossed peninsula in 1528 but 1st white settler is thought to be one Antonio Maximo (1843) whose fishing camp stood at Maximo Point. Feds. shelled village that sprang up & most settlers then moved to Tampa. In 1876 John C. Williams, of Detroit, bought land here & Russian Peter Demens Piotr Dementieff), who gave town its name, built RR. that reached here 1888. Today there is a variety of sm. industries but tourists remain only large industry. Next to sitting in the sun, fishing is most popular pastime. Every saltwater fish of Gulf of Mexico is plentiful at one season or another incl. speckled trout or weakfish (Jan.), mackerel (Feb.& Mar.), kingfish (Ap.), tarpon (Mar.-July), redfish (Aug.), shark (Sept.) & sheepshead (Nov.).

PTS. OF INT.: (1) Bayshore Drive, **Waterfront Pk.** (recr.facils.) looks out on palm-lined shore drive, North Yacht Basin, Central Yacht Basin, & Seaplane Basin. (2) 2nd Ave. N. & Beach Drive, **Art Club of St. Petersburg** (O.aft.free) exhibits members' work. (3) 2nd Ave. N. extends (E) to form Municipal Pier. Along this Ave. & Pier are: 335 2nd Ave. NE., **St. Petersburg Hist. Mus.** (O.aft.sm.fee); archeological, hist. & natural hist. exhibits. **Mun. Solarium** (sm.fee). **Mun. Spa. Pool & Beach** (sm.fee). **Mun. Pier** (free), extending 2,400′ into Tampa Bay, with driveways, streetcar line, fish. balconies & casino. (4) 1st Ave. S. & Bayshore Drive, **Lang Ball Pk.,** training center for St. Louis Cardinals. (5) 3513 2nd Ave. S., **Mus. of Shells & Minerals** (O.appl.). (6) Mirror Lake Dr. & 7th St. N., **Mirror Lake Pk.,** home of "largest shuffleboard club in world." (7) 2339 7th St. N., **Caswell Orchid Garden** (O.Sun.Wed.& Fri.sm.fee) has large variety of orchids & other rare tropical plants. (8) 12th Ave. N. at 5th St. N., **Huggins Field,** training grounds for N. Y. Yankees. Crescent L. adjs. field. (9) 305 18th Ave. N., **Turners' Sunken Gardens** (O.fee); camellias, azaleas, bougainvilleas, sausage trees, ginger trees. (10) 2221 4th St. N., **Wood Parade & Mus.** (O.wks.free); woods from many lands & hist. of wood. (11) 4th St. & 48th Ave. N., **Animal Ranch** (O.daily.sm.fee); native & foreign birds, animals & reptiles; extraction of venom from snakes. (12) 6th St. & 6th Ave. S., **Ind. Shell Mound.** (13) **U.S. Maritime Service Training Sta.,** largest on S. coast.

SIDE TRIP: From St. Petersburg (W) across 1 of 3 causeways to group of Is., united by landscaped hy., that fringe Gulf of Mexico across Boca Ciega Bay. (Excellent bath. from many points; f.,boats,recr.refreshments & other facils. avail. at intervals.) Free Corey Causeway reaches **Long Key,** largest of Is., with **St. Petersburg Beach & Pass-A-Grille Beach. Shell Key,** just (S) of Pass-A-Grille (reached by boat only); shell collecting ground. Treasure Island Causeway reaches **Treasure I. Beach.** Seminole Bridge & Free Walsh Causeway reach **Madeira Beach Ind. Rocks.**

# MIAMI

## MIAMI

Through RR., plane & bus conns. Accoms.: All kinds. Info.: C. of C., Shoreland Arcade. Horse & dog racing (3 tracks each, Dec.-Ap.). Jai-alai nightly (Dec.-Ap.). Winter (Jan.-Ap.) & Summer (July-Sept.) F. Tournaments. Miami-Nassau Yacht Race, Sir Thos. Lipton Cup Race, (winter); other sailing events in season. Open Golf Tournament (Dec.). All-Amer. Air Maneuvers (Jan.). Orange Bowl Football Game & Festival (Jan.1). "Fiesta de las Americas" (spring). Poinciana Festival (June). Nat. Audubon Soc., 311 E. Flagler St., conducts 2-day Everglades tours.

Greater Miami includes municipalities of Miami, Miami Beach, Coral Gables, Hialeah, Miami Shores, N. Miami, S. Miami, Miami Springs, Opa Locka, N. Miami Beach, Surfside, Biscayne Park, El Portal & Golden Beach. It is the commercial & tourist center of S. Fla. & one of the great resort areas of the world. In 50 yrs. it has grown from pop. of 260 to one of c.400,000 & it entertains some 2 million visitors annually. As an international airport it is 2nd only to N.Y. as U.S. port of entry & 1st as gateway to S. America. Its 1945 income from horse racing (Hialeah, Tropical Pk., Gulfstream) was c.$100,000,000, 5 million of which went for old age pensions. It has miles of ocean & bay beaches, a mun. yacht basin, 10 golf courses, 50 tennis courts, a full concert season & high-priced stars in high-priced nightclubs. The ocean & Biscayne Bay afford sailfish, marlin, tuna & hundreds of other varieties.

**MIAMI:** Menéndez de Avilés first visited site in 1567 & found large Ind. town. Ft. Dallas was est. 1836 but modern development of area did not begin until 1895 when Henry M. Flagler made it RR. terminus. Today Miami is city of "ultra-modern" hotels, clubs, cabanas & office bldgs., surrounded by fantastic estates & houses that make use of every known architectural variation & every color of rainbow. Extravagant skies, sands, waters & vegetation add to general carnival spirit. Streets are lined with shops & vendors selling everything from Paris gowns to baby alligators & it is possible to spend $15,000 for a single necktie. Much of the social life centers around (though not necessarily in) spectacular swim. pools. Each winter playboys, movie stars, labor leaders, heiresses, professional gamblers & whoever else happens to be in the money descend to acquire a sun-tan. For here, perhaps even more than in California, the sun shines every day. Winter remains important season but tourists are also now being attracted by reduced summer rates. At Miami is J. with US94 (see) which leads across Everglades to Gulf of Mexico.

PTS. OF INT.: (1) Biscayne Blvd., **Bayfront Pk.,** has amphitheater where Mayor Cermak of Chicago was killed (Feb.1939) when attempt was made to assassinate Pres. Roosevelt, clubh. for chess players & outdoor observatory of Southern Cross Astronomical Soc. At adj. Mun. Yacht Basin, f. & sightseeing trips (incl.glass-bottomed boats) avail. (2) 337 NE. 5th St., **Miami Aquarium** (O.8 to midnight,sm. fee), in beached Danish ship, "Prinz Valdemar" which at one time also served as hotel. (3) W. Flagler St. & NW. 1st Ave., **Dade County Cth.** (neo-Class.). (4) E. Flagler St. & SE. 3rd Ave., **1st Presb. Ch.** (1900.neo-Class.), Miami's oldest ch. (5) SW. 2nd Ave. & Miami R., **Curb Market.** (6) 1367 N. Miami Ave., **Pflueger's Marine Mus.** (O.in winter exc.Sun.). (7) NW. 4th St. & 3rd Ave., **Ft. Dallas** (O. free), built 1836 & recently moved to Lummus Pk. (8) 2790 NW. 17th Ave., **Exotic Gardens** (O.free). (9) NW. 7th St. & 19th Ave., **Coppinger's Pirate Cove** (O.fee) has Seminole Village, tropical gardens & alligator coll. (10) 815 NW. 22nd Ave., **Miami Tropical Garden** (O.free). (11) NW. 25th Ave. & NW. 16th St., **Musa Isle Ind. Village** (O.fee) where Seminoles live & work (mostly at making curios) in native thatched huts; zoo, natural hist. mus., alligator wrestling. (12) 1481 NW. 27th Ave., **Orchid Dell Gardens** (O.free). (13) 1525 NW. 27th Ave., **Tropical Hobbyland** (O.fee) has tropical garden, rare birds, monkey colony, Seminole village, alligator wrestling. (14) NW. 36th St., **Pan-Amer. Airways Field,** one of busiest internat. airfields in world. (15) 79th St. & Bougainville Ave., **Hialeah Pk. Race Track** (O. fee during season), landscaped with royal palms & Australian pines, has spectacular flock of salmon-pink flamingos on artificial lake. (16) 300 NE. 132nd St., **Miami Zoo** (O.fee).

**MIAMI BEACH,** a sandbar separated from mainland by Biscayne Bay & conn. to it by 3 causeways, was once mangrove swamp inhabited by Tequesta Inds. As early as 1567 Sp. tried to est. port of call here but place remained a wilderness until 1882 when Harry B. Lum of Ohio & associates attempted a coconut plantation. Rabbits ate young shoots & project failed. In 1907 J. S. Collins of N.J. had somewhat better luck with avocados. By 1913, with financial aid of C. G. Fisher, he built 1st bridge & town was inc. 2 yrs. later. Today it has no factories or industries but boasts ¼ of all hotel rooms in Fla. & an immense annual tourist trade. It has 12 mun. pks., $8^m$ of well-lifeguarded beach, 91 salt water pools, 5 golf courses (2 private), $20^m$ of winding inland waterways, polo grounds, kennel clubs & facils. for all diversions suitable for climate. PTS. OF INT.: (1) **Beach,** flanked by elaborate hotels, night clubs & colorful cabanas; 4 mun.-owned beaches. (2) Meridian & 13th St., **Flamingo Pk.,** city's main recr. center. Miami Beach Flamingos play such baseball teams as Philadelphia "A's" & Baltimore Orioles. (3) Collins Ave. & 22nd St., Collins Pk. with **Art Center** where paintings & ceramics are exhibited throughout yr., & **Astronomical Observ.** (O.Mon.7:30 a.m.-9:30 p.m.free). (4) Collins Ave. & 44th St., **Harvey Firestone Estate.** (5) Daily sight-seeing cruises leave from **Roney Plaza Docks,** 24th St. & Collins Ave., moonlight cruise from **C. of C.**

**Dock,** 5th St. & Alton Rd., & afford opportunity of viewing elaborate private estates incl. **Vanderbilt Estate** (Fisher I.), **Al Capone's H.** (Palm I.), **Herbert Hoover Estate.** (6) (N) of Miami Beach proper, across Baker's Haulover, is **Haulover Beach Pk.,** now being developed.

SIDE TRIP: (S) of Miami Beach is **Biscayne Key,** N. third of which, thickly planted with coconut palms, is being converted into **Crandon Pk.** Rickenbacker Causeway (4m long) conn. Biscayne Key to Virginia Key & hence to mainland. Biscayne Key has often been used by motion picture Cos. as South Sea I. locale. Pk. when completed will have accoms. for 20,000 autos, 2m of excellent beach protected from undertow by reef, many recr. facils. Lower sec. of Key is expected to develop into resort area similar to Miami Beach. An aquarium & beach for Negroes are planned for Virginia Key.

**CORAL GABLES,** adj. Miami on (SW), had its origin in 1921 when Geo. E. Merrick began selling lots in his father's orange grove. Entire town was planned on paper before construction started & during boom days busses traveled through N. bringing back buyers. Ital. gondolas & gondoliers were imported for fabulous Biltmore Hotel (now veterans' hospital). Wm. Jennings Bryan lectured on & Rex Beach wrote a book about Coral Gables. Many bldgs. incorporate Sp. or Mediterranean motifs, sts. are lined with royal & coconut palms & royal poinciana trees. A waterway (8′ channel) emptying into Biscayne Bay, runs through S. part of town. Residential & business areas are both rigidly zoned.

PTS. OF INT.: (1) Coral Way, from Douglas Rd. to City Hall, **"Miracle Mile,"** 4-block long exclusive shopping dist. (2) **City Hall** with tower inspired by that of town hall of Seville, Spain. (3) 907 Coral Way, old **Merrick Homestead,** of coral rock with gabled peak, hence name Coral Gables. (4) **War Mem. Youth Center,** incl. dance patio, game courts, hobby shops & lib. (5) **Salvadore Pk.,** in heart of residential sec. (6) **Univ. of Miami** (1926.coed.), having weathered worst hurricane to hit area (1926) & the bursting of real estate boom, is now in process of creating a new modern campus. Mem. Classroom Bldg. is of special int. for its Mod. functional design. (7) **Riddle Inter.-Amer. College,** is Jr. college dedicated to training Amers. for life in S. Amer. & vice versa. (8) Biscayne Bay, **Tahiti Beach** (sm.fee) has South Sea atmosphere. **Venetian Pool** (sm.fee) on Sevilla Ave., is fresh water swim. pool of unusual design in quarry that once furnished street paving. (9) Ingraham Hy. (S) of Tahiti Beach, **Matheson Hammock,** a cty. pk. (swim.boat.beach.pic.) incl. 5m of virgin for. with trls. along which gumbo limbo trees, strangler figs, air plants & orchids may be inspected. (10) Just (S) of Matheson Hammock, **Fairchild Tropical Garden,** 83 as. of trees, vines, shrubs from tropical areas throughout world. (11) **Tropical Pk. Race Track** (W) of Coral Gables on Bird Rd. (O.daily.fee during season).

## TRIPS OUT OF MIAMI

### I. MIAMI (S) to LOST LAKE. 15. Side Rds.

(S) on Red Rd. (57th Ave.). **11. PARROT JUNGLE** (O.fee), where parrots, macaws & cockatoos fly free. (R) from Red Rd., on Bird Rd. **15., LOST L. & CAVERNS** (O.fee), L. caverns & gardens in a rock pit, once hideout during Seminole Wars. Teakwood, rubber, banyan & other trees have been imported. A wild duck show, featuring mallards, is held several times daily.

### II. MIAMI (S) to KENDALL. 10. US1

On US1 is **KENDALL. 10.** with **MIAMI'S RARE BIRD FARM** (fee); flamingos, peacocks, ostriches, cranes, monkeys, alligators.

# ST. AUGUSTINE

### ST. AUGUSTINE

Through RR. & bus conns. Feeder air lines conn. with Jacksonville & Orlando. Accoms.: All kinds. Info.: C. of C., San Marco Ave. (N) of City Gates. Excellent beaches (swim. beach driving, f. boat.). Mun. Pier. 2 golf (1 mun.) courses, fee. Sp. Fiesta (Fri. & Sat. before Palm Sun.). Pilgrimage to Our Lady of the Milk (Sun. after Easter). Nat. Sea Trout Derby (Oct.-Feb.). Internat. Black Drum Rodeo (Mar.-May). St. John's Cty. F. Tournament (June-Oct.).

St. Augustine, oldest city in U.S. (1565) & yr.-round resort, offers many hist. & architectural pts. of int. & preserves to an unusual degree the flavor of its Sp. origins. Oldest sec. of town centers around Plaza de la Constitucion from which narrow sts. (one block is only 6′ wide) radiate, lined with overhanging balconies & walled gardens or patios, bright with scarlet hibiscus, oleander, pomegranate, golden allamanda, bignonia, bougainvillea & coral vines. Oldest remaining bldgs. are local adaptations of Sp. village types, usually 1½ to 2 stories high & employing coquina stone & wood construction. Brit. influenced later houses by introduction of fireplaces & steep roofs. St. Augustine occupies sandy peninsula bordered on (E) by North & Matanzas Rs. (parts of Intercoastal Waterway whose union forms Matanzas Bay) & by San Sebastian R. on (S) & (W). All 3 are really salt water lagoons. City is separated from ocean by Anastasia I. In addition to tourist trade there are RR. shops, boat yards, shrimp fishing, & cigar mfg.

In Mar. 1513, Juan Ponce de Leon, looking for gold & the fountain of youth, first sighted Fla. "And," wrote the royal Sp. historian, "believing this land was an island, they named it 'La Florida,' because it has a very beautiful view . . . & because, moreover, they discovered it in the time of the Feast of Flowers." On Apr. 3, he landed, a little (N) of present town. In 1565 Don Pedro Menéndez de Avilés, sent to destroy Fr. Ft. Caroline (see) some $40^{m}$ (N) est. here (Sept. 8) 1st permanent settlement in U.S. & named it St. Augustine after saint on whose day he first sighted land. St. Augustine became Sp. military & mission hqs. & was sacked by Eng. under Sir Francis Drake (1586) & under buccaneer, John Davis (1668). In 1672 construction of Castillo de San Marcos (see below) of coquina stone quarried in vic. was begun. (Coquina is a soft, whitish limestone formed of broken shells & coral cemented together.) Castillo has been called "finest example in U.S. of military architecture of its day." Runaway Eng. slaves were given refuge at near-by Ft. Moosa & in 1702 & 1728 Eng. from S. Carolina plundered town & took as slaves Inds. belonging to Sp. But Castillo withstood attacks, as it also did 27-day siege under Gov. Oglethorpe (1740) during "War of Jenkins' Ear," so-called after shipmaster Rbt. Jenkins exhibited before parliament his bottled ear, sliced off by a Sp. officer.

After Fla. was ceded to English (1763-83), large plantations were est., producing indigo, cotton, naval stores & citrus fruits. Slave-owning Royalists sett. here during Rev. & Sam. Adams & John Hancock were burned in effigy. Three signers of Decl. of Ind., Heyward, Middleton & Rutledge, were imprisoned in ft., & attacks on Savannah & the Bahamas (which won latter for Britain) were launched. In 1777, a large colony of Minorcans from New Smyrna (see) arrived. Again under Sp. rule large land grants were made avail. to Amers. On July 10, 1821, Amer. flag was raised. Six years later Ralph Waldo Emerson on a visit wrote: "What is done here? Nothing. It was reported in the morning that a man was at work in the public square, & all our family turned out to see him. What is grown here? Oranges, on which no cultivation seeks to be bestowed. . . . The Americans live on their offices; the Spaniards keep billiard tables, or, if not, they send their Negroes to the mud to bring oysters, or to the shore to bring fish, & the rest of the time, fiddle, mask & dance." Confeds. seized ft. (Jan. 7, 1861) but surrendered to Feds. March 11, 1862, after which women of town cut down flagpole. In 1880's Henry M. Flagler, a retired founder of Standard Oil, rediscovered St. Augustine & it became, & remains today, hqs. of Florida E. Coast RR. & Hotel System. As the oldest city in the U.S. St. Augustine has been more than generous with the superlative. It now boasts the "oldest" wooden sch. house (not true), the "oldest" orange grove (possible), the "oldest" alligator farm (probable) & "the most historical religious spot in the U.S." The Hist. Soc. tries hard, however, to correct some of the wilder exaggerations (there is considerable disagreement bet. its members & some local promoters) & the touring public is perhaps not quite, as Henry James once described it: "so placidly uncritical that the whitest thread of the deceptive stitch never makes it blink . . . it fairly goes upon it knees to be humbuggingly humbugged."

PTS. OF INT.: (1) San Marco Ave., **C. of C. & Civic Center,** incl. Tourist Club with card & game rooms. (2) San Marco Ave. & Orange St., **Old Prot. Cemetery** (sometimes called Huguenot though there are no records of Huguenot burials), est. just outside City Gates during yellow fever epidemic (1821). (3) St. George & Orange Sts., **City Gates** (1804), once guarded drawbridge & were part of defense system that incl. coquina-rock wall, a moat, & earth breastworks planted with thicket of Sp. dagger ("Yucca gloriosa"). They replaced earlier gates dating from 1745. (4) 14 St. George St., **Old Wooden Schoolh.** (O.9-6.sm.fee.rest.), a red cedar clapboard structure covered with vines, was built c.1778, probably by Juan Genoply as residence & probably used as sch. before Civil War. (5) 37 St. George St., **Casa Carrera,** used as chapel in 1770's. (6) 44 St. George St., **Casa Arrivas** (remod.), dates from 1st Sp. occupation. (7) 43 St. George St., **Spanish Inn** of coquina rock also dates from 1st Sp. occupation. (8) 54 St. George St., **Old Curiosity Shop** built by John Paredes bet. 1803 & 1813 (adds.) has coquina walls 2′ thick. (9) 105 St. George St., **Burt H.,** example of Sp. house of later period. (10) St. George & Treasury Sts., **Sp. Treasurer's H.** (O.wks.9-5.sm.fee.tea served in garden), lower story of coquina, upper of wood, erected bet. 1690 & 1695 on site of orig. wooden treasury bldg. (c.1600). Present structure damaged during siege (1702) & upper story added later; antiques & heirlooms. (11) Ft. Marion Circle & Bay St., **Zero Milestone** in Osceola Pk. marks E. terminus of Old Sp. Trl., 1st transcontinental hy. from St. Augustine to San Diego, Cal. (12) Matanzas Bay, N. end Bay St., **Castillo de San Marcos Nat. Mon.** (O.8:30-5:30.fee.free guided tours), built 1672-1756 & now also known as Ft. Marion, was Sp.'s northernmost military fortification on Atlantic Coast & is oldest masonry ft. existing in U.S. A symmetrical, 4-sided & bastioned structure with moat & drawbridge, it is built of coquina blocks cemented with oyster lime & contains guardrooms, dungeons, living quarters, storerooms, & chapel, almost all of which open on 100′ sq. court. Stairway, once gun ramp, leads to roof which provides excellent view. Hot shot oven was once used to heat cannon balls, effective missiles for firing wooden ships. Brit. unsuccessfully besieged ft. in 1702, 1728 & 1740 but secured Fla. in Treaty of Paris (1763) & renamed stronghold Ft. St. Marks. Amers. renamed it in honor of Gen. Francis Marion. Ft. served as prison for Seminole leaders (1835) & some of Geronimo's Apaches (1887). Confeds. held it 14 months during Civil War. It was last used to confine court-martialed soldiers during Sp.-Amer. War. (13) **Ponce de Leon Circle,** with replica of statue of Fla.'s discoverer erected in San Juan, Puerto Rico. It was cast from a cannon.

(14) Charlotte & Cathedral Sts., **Public Market** (1824, rest.1887). Now used by chess & checker enthusiasts. (15) Cathedral & Charlotte Sts., **Plaza de la Constitucion,** est. 1598 & oldest pub. sq. in U.S., received present name in 1813 when shaft was erected to comm. liberal constitution adopted in Spain. When, in following yr., Ferdinand VII repealed constitution, all such mons. were ordered destroyed, but this, somehow, remained. (16) N. side of Plaza, **Cathedral of St. Augustine** (Cath.), in Sp. Mission style, was built 1793-97 & partially destroyed by fire in 1887. In restoration, transepts & campanile were added. Smallest of 4 bells in old facade is inscribed "Sante Joseph, Ora Pro Nobis, 1682." Stained glass windows depict life of St. Augustine. A sun dial keeps Central Standard Time, having been installed before Fla. changed to E. Standard kept by town clocks. (17) Cathedral & St. George Sts., **Post Office,** erected in 1930's with 1764 drawing as model, embodies architectural details & much of stone used in construction of Gov.'s Mansion of 1690. (18) St. George & King Sts., **Trinity Ch.** (Episc.1825.Eng.Goth.remod.), oldest Episc. Ch. in Fla.

(19) 214 St. George St., **Lindsley H.,** dating to 1st Sp. occupation. (20) 224 St. George St., **MacMillen H.** appears on many old maps. (21) 241 St. George St., **St. Joseph Academy & Convent** (1858). (22) 250 St. George St., **Prince Murat H.** (bet.1790-1815), said to have been residence of Napoleon's nephew during his stay in city. (23) 279 St. George St., **Graham H.** (c.1791). (24) 31 St. Francis St., **Llambias H.** (before 1763), has int. old garden. (25) 14 St. Francis St., the **"Oldest H."** (O.9-6.fee), with low ceilings, huge fireplaces & crushed coquina fls., is thought to date to late 1500's & hence to be oldest H. in U.S. It is also believed that Franciscan Friars took refuge here after 1599 fire. From here one may enter modern bldg., housing St. Augustine Hist. Society's **Webb Lib. & Mus., & House of the Cannonball,** also a mus., walls of which held cannonball from Eng. siege of 1740. Among exhibits are Ind., whaling, armor & St. Augustine rooms. (26) 108 Marine St., **St. Francis Barracks** (State Arsenal). Orig. Franciscan Monastery dates to c.1580 & was burned by Gov. Moore of S. Carolina (1702) though some of Friars' cells remained. Restored as barracks it was used by Eng., U.S. (during Seminole Wars), & Fed. troops. It was almost entirely destroyed by fire again in 1915 but some of orig. walls were incorporated in present structure. (27) Marine St. & Cemetery Lane. **Nat. Cemetery** dates from beginning of Amer. occupation & contains graves of victims of Dade Massacre.

(28) Marine St. opp. Barracks, **King's Bakery** (remod.), where bread was baked for Brit. troops in 1780's. (29) 5 Aviles St., **Pub. Lib.;** bldg. erected 1780's; birthpl. of Edmund Kirby Smith, last Confed. gen. to surrender. (30) Aviles St. (S) of lib., **Fatio H.** (O.built bet. 1806-21), now property of Colonial Dames; slave quarters, patio, balconies. (31) Aviles St., within Convent walls, **O'Reilly H.,** left by Don Miguel O'Reilly, native of Ireland, for purposes of est. a "religious house under the plan of St. Francis de Sales." (32) 230 Charlotte St., **St. Augustine Arts Club Gallery.** (33) Aviles & Bridge Sts., **Don Toledo H.** (reconst.), example of houses of 2nd Sp. occupation. (34) King & Cordova Sts., **Ponce de Leon Hotel** (1888), 1st of Henry Flagler's E. coast chain, est. St. Augustine as fashionable resort. Flagler sent architects Carrère & Hastings abroad to study architecture of Spain, & domes, spires & arched gateways of hotel inc. many motifs they brought back. Hotel attracted, in words of Chauncey Depew, so many "newlyweds & almost-deads," that others were inclined to try resorts further South. (35) 83 King St., **Villa Zorayda** (O.9-6.fee.1885), designed by Franklin Smith who used motifs borrowed from Sp. Alhambra; coll. of carved & inlaid furniture & oriental rugs. (36) Valencia & Sevilla Sts., **Flagler Mem. Ch.** (Presb.1890), erected by Henry Flagler as mem. to daughter. Flagler Mausoleum adj. & next to Ch. property is Flagler's old home, Kirkside. (37) Cordova & Orange Sts., **Sp. Cemetery;** graves date 1794-1878. (38) San Marco & St. Louis Aves., **Orange Grove** (O.9-5.fee) is one of oldest budded orange groves in U.S. (39) Ocean St. E. of San Marco Ave., **Nuestra Señora de la Leche y del Buen Parto** (Our Lady of the Milk & Easy Childbirth; O.9-5.free), chapel in Sp. Mission style erected 1918 on site where 1st Holy Mass was celebrated (Sept.8,1565), marking spot where Menéndez landed (Aug.28,1565); 1st chapel was destroyed 1728; 2 others preceded present one. (40) Magnolia Ave. & Myrtle St., **Fountain of Youth Pk.** (21 as.O.7-7.fee), deep ancient well enclosed in mission-like grotto of coquina rock, is advertised as fountain Ponce de Leon may have visited in 1513. Modern "discoverer" was Louella Day McConnell, said to be orig. of Rbt. W. Service's "Lady whose name was Lou." Asked by authorities to stop fooling public with her "rejuvenating waters," she replied: "But there is iron in that spring! I know, because I threw an old cookstove in it." Near-by is excavated Ind. burial ground revealing skeletons in positions (crossed arms, etc.) that may indicate Christian interment.

## TRIPS OUT OF ST. AUGUSTINE

### I. ST. AUGUSTINE (N) to PONTE VEDRA BEACH. 25. St.A1A

From St. Augustine (E) on May St. Causeway across Kurth's I. & North R. (f. from bridge) to J. with St.A1A, **2.5.** on which turn (N). St.A1A parallels miles of good beach (for long stretches beach may be driven on in safety but check with filling stas.) & passes series of sm. resort areas, Vilano Beach, Surfside, Usina's Beach, etc. **25. PONTE VEDRA BEACH** (golf course.fee). Beach from here to Jacksonville is large resort area (see US90).

### II. ST. AUGUSTINE (S) to MARINELAND. 18. St.A1A

From St. Augustine (E) across Matanzas Bay on Bridge of Lions & then (S) on St.A1A which runs length of **ANASTASIA I.** At **1.** is J. with side Rd. Here (L) 0.5$^{m}$ along Davis Shores to **Oglethorpe Mon.,** site of battery from which Brit. bombarded town (1740). Return to St.A1A. At **1.5. LIGHTH. PK. & BEACH** (swim.f.pic.). Lighth. is near site of Sp. watchtower sighted by Sir Francis Drake when he sacked town (1586). **2.** (R) **OSTRICH & ALLIGATOR FARM** (O.8:30-6.fee) boasting "largest coll. of alligators in world," also has zoo & mus. of Fla. wildlife. **3.5. COQUINA QUARRY** from which came much of stone used in early St. Augustine bldgs. **ST. AUGUSTINE BEACH,** beginning **c.4.** from center of town, has 18$^{m}$ of sand on which cars may be driven at low tide (swim.f.pic.): **14. FT. MATANZAS NAT. MON.** (O.8:30-5:30.free.guide serv.). Adj., on **Rattlesnake I.** is sm. (c.40′ sq.) fortified watchtower of coquina blocks which Sp. erected (c.1742) to guard S. water approach to St. Augustine. Near-by, Menéndez, on Sept. & Oct., 1565, put to death some 300 Fr. Huguenots: "Not," he said, "as Frenchmen but as Lutherans." Hence Matanzas (Sp.,"slaughter"). **18. MARINELAND** (swim.boat.tourist court); Marine Studios (O.8:30 to sunset.fee) offer large display of marine life (sharks, giant rays, porpoises), viewed through some 200 portholes, in environment comparable to that of open sea.

**III. ST. AUGUSTINE (S) to MOULTRIE. 6. US1**

From St. Augustine (S) on US1 is **MOULTRIE, 6.** (R) here on side Rd. 1m to **Marker** (L) on site of what "N.Y. Herald" called "the perfidious capture of Osceola when the chieftain was engaged in an honest parley—which it is believed would have terminated the Seminole war" (1837). At 1.5m is **Site of Fort Peyton** for which Osceola was headed to confer with Gen. Hernandez.

**IV. ST. AUGUSTINE (W) & (S) to SITE OF IND. ATTACK. 13. St.16 & St.208**

From St. Augustine (W) **6.** on St.16 to J. with St.208 on which cont. (S). At **13.** is **Marker** comm. Ind. attack (1840) on company of traveling actors. When Inds. were overtaken they were found intoxicated & wearing the costumes of some of Shakespeare's best known characters.

# US 11—ALABAMA

**ALA.-GA. LINE** (c.13m from Trenton, Ga.) **(SW) to ALA.-MISS. LINE** (19m from **Meridian, Miss.). 266. US11**

Via: Ft. Payne, Attalla, Springville, Birmingham, Bessemer, Tuscaloosa, Eutaw, Livingston. Southern RR. parallels route. Accoms.: All kinds.

US11 enters Ala. in reg. near Lookout Mt. where streams, falls, caves, springs & forested ridges, covered with undergrowth of rhododendron, azalea, mountain laurel & dogwood, attract visitors. Mountaineers here retain ballads, old forms of speech & customs of their Elizabethan ancestors. Hy. next cuts across mineral belt of central Ala., whose rich deposits of coal, iron-ore & limestone have made Birmingham leading iron & steel producing center in South. It then cont. through series of mining towns to Tuscaloosa, home of Univ. of Ala., into fertile "Black Belt" lands of Warrior & Tombigbee Rs.

## Sec. 1: GA. LINE to BIRMINGHAM. 126.

**1. SULPHUR SPRINGS;** mineral springs once used by Inds. (tourist cabins). **10.** J. with St.58.

SIDE TRIP: (L) here through sec. of the Blue Ridge, known locally as "Little Alps." Hill folk, many of whom are descendants of abolitionists who during Civil War fought guerrilla warfare against the rich planters, follow a life in many ways similar to that of early settlers. At 1m is **Valley Head. Winston H.** (1836), built around a "dog trot" log cabin, is surrounded by mulberry trees planted in unsuccessful attempt to est. silkworm industry. It was hqs. for Union Col. Jefferson C. Davis, once asked by mountaineer: "Jeff, which pays you the most? Colonelin' the Bluecoats or Presidentin' the Confederates?" 5m **Mentone,** on mt. crest, a summer resort. Boat trips from here down **Little River** offer mountain scenery & bass & bream. Tour cont. on Mentone Pky. (R) from St.58. From **Sunset Rock,** c.6m, is view of Ga. & Tenn. At 10.5m J. with side Rd.

(L) here 9.5m to **River Pk.,** summer resort. Bass, bream & trout avail.

11m J. with side Rd.

(L) here 1m **De Soto St. Pk.** (4,650 as.f.hik.pic.golf.cabins.Ap.1-Oct.31.hqs.:Ft.Payne) offers 28m of rugged country incl. **Little R.** with its many cascades & falls. **May's Gulf,** one of largest gorges (E) of Rockies, **De Soto Falls** (120′ drop), old mills, Ind. caves & blossoms of laurel, azaleas, dogwood & jasmine are also to be enjoyed.

**22. FT. PAYNE,** trading center of reg. mostly inhabited by descendants of Anglo-Saxon pioneers. There are few Negroes. In vic. are deposits of clays, fuller's earth, coal & iron. Near-by is site of **Will's Town,** Ind. village where Sequoyah (George Guess, c.1770-1843), Ind. half-breed silversmith & trader, lived in early 1800's & later invented Cherokee syllabary, principal of which was later used in other Ind. languages. He was tried by tribe for witchcraft in 1821, but convinced them by sending messages to his daughter, aged 6, & soon whole tribe was learning to read & write. Lt. John Payne, who was in charge of removal of Cherokee to W. territory, had his hqs. here. **54.5.** J. with side Rd.

SIDE TRIP: (L) here 3m to **Noccalula Falls** (100′) which, depending on rain, varies from trickle to torrent.

**59. ATTALLA,** industrial & shipping center for coal, cast iron & steel products, is J. with US11 Alt. & US241 (see). **64. GADSDEN** (see US241). **85. ASHVILLE,** N. seat of St. Clair Cty. of which Pell City, 23m away, is S. seat. This arrangement, once necessary because there were no adequate Rds. over Beaver Cr. Mts., has been cont. although good Rds. now exist. Ante bellum **Cth.** (rest.1938) has int. records of Creek Inds. **96. ST. CLAIR SPRINGS,** whose 5 springs produce sulphur water, red sulphur, black sulphur, chalybeate & lithia. **98.** S. J. with US11 Alt. **100. SPRINGVILLE.** (For pts. of int. bet. here & Bessemer, see Birmingham.) **126. BIRMINGHAM** (see).

## Sec. 2: BIRMINGHAM to MISS. LINE. 140.

**13. BESSEMER** (see Birmingham Trip V). Bet. Bessemer & Tuscaloosa, US11 passes through wooded hills broken by a series of mining towns.

**60. TUSCALOOSA.** J. with US43 (see).

Through RR. & bus conns. Airport. Accoms.: All kinds.

Tuscaloosa, seat of Univ. of Ala., is a quiet old town with streets shaded by water oaks planted more than a century ago. It lies on banks of Black Warrior R. & both city & R. take names from Chief Tuscaloosa (Ind. "tusko," warrior & "loosa," black) who fell in battle with De Soto. Area was explored as early as 1781 & in 1809 Creek Chief Occechemolta received permission from U.S. to est. settlement at falls in R. In 1813, during Ind. uprising, Gen. John Coffee (aided by Davy Crockett) destroyed village & in 1816 whites started settlement c.2$^{m}$ (N). Town was inc. 1819 & became st. capital (1826-46). It also became a rich cotton center though it lost much of its other business when capital was transferred to Montgomery. On Ap. 4, 1865 Fed. Gen. Croxton took over town & burned Univ. Tuscaloosa remained under military control during reconstruction, many of old mansions being auctioned off & plantations divided up. Town cont. primarily as agric. center until turn of century. In 1948 there were some 40 industrial establishments incl. Gulf States Paper Corp. (O.appl.), Central Foundry Co. called "largest individual soil & sanitary pipe plant in world," & others producing cotton, lumber, brick, metal & rubber products.

PTS. OF INT.: (1) On E. edge of town, **Univ. of Alabama** (coed.1831). On campus are: **Gorgas H.** (1829), square 2-story brick house with curving iron-railed stairways rising to raised portico, 1 of 3 bldgs. spared by Feds. when they fired campus, 1865. Gen. Josiah Gorgas, Confed. Chief of Ordnance, was Pres. of Univ. in 1880's. **Little Round H.,** octagonal structure once used by students on guard duty. When Croxton's Raiders arrived, gunpowder was stored in it. Knowing this, faculty wives formed a bucket brigade & saved bldg. In rear is mound containing ashes of bldgs. destroyed by Feds. & boulder comm. cadets who resisted Union advance. **President's H.** (1840.Gr.Rev.designed by Chas.Nichols of Philadelphia) was fired by Feds., but after plea by president's wife, Mrs. L. C. Garland, Negro slaves were allowed to extinguish flames. Also on campus are: **Smith Hall Mus. of Nat. Hist.** (O.8-5.wks.), incl. coll. of artifacts from Moundville, Ala., (see) & special coll. of minerals, **Denny Chimes** in stone & brick tower 115′ high, **U.S. Bureau of Mines Labs.,** & **Amelia Gorgas Lib.** (2) 23rd Ave. & 18th St., **Drish Bldg.** (1822), built for local physician, housed Fed. prisoners during Battle of Shiloh & was later female college. (3) 2512 5th Ave., **Old French Tavern** (1830's); 1st legislative session, after Tuscaloosa became capital, said to have met here. Members used it as inn (1826-46). (4) 5th St. & 28th Ave., **Capitol Pk.,** site of st. capitol (1829-46), destroyed by fire, 1923. (5) Greenboro Ave. & 7th St., **County Cth.,** with Mon. to Chief Tuscaloosa. (6) 1925 8th St., **Moody H.** (c.1820). (7) 2414 8th St., **Snow H.** (1830.Gr.Rev.), built originally as "Academy for Young Ladies." (8) 1305 24th Ave., **Jemison H.** (late 1850's.Ital.influences). (9) 2114 14th Ave., **Swaim H.** (c.1838.Gr.Rev.).

(10) 421 18th Ave., **"Governor's Mansion"** (1829.Class.Rev.with Adam fanlight & Ionic columns). Francis Scott Key was visitor in 1833. Mrs. Gayle, wife of Gov., wrote in her diary: "He is a man of much intelligence, a lawyer of high standing, a man of honor, a poet & Christian. He wrote in my daughter's album today. The piece was beautiful." (11) 6th St. & 25th Ave., **Christ Ch.** (Episc.1830). (12) 9th St. & 25th Ave., **St. John's Ch.** (Cath.c.1840). (13) 15th St. & 36th Ave., **Stillman Institute** (Negro.coed.Presb.est.1876). On campus is former **Cochrane H.** (1830.Gr.Rev.), the capitols of whose Corinthian columns were imported from Italy. (14) 610 36th Ave., **Carson-Mayfield H.** (1838). (15) 1427 24th Ave., **Presb. Manse** (1820.possibly oldest in town. (16) 1217 24th Ave., **Wm. Battle H.** (1850's). (17) 1010 24th Ave., **Friedman H.** (1835), built by Alfred Battle, said to be wealthiest planter in Tuscaloosa. (18) 1011 24th Ave., **Nicholson H.** (1850's). (19) 919 24th Ave., **Rosenau H.** (c.1845). (20) 816 22nd Ave., **Marlowe H.** (1840), home of J. L. Martin, Gov. of Ala. (1845-47). (21) 905 21st Ave., **Collier H.** (c.1826.Gr.Rev.). (22) 1904 Broad St.

(1822), now a mortuary, was home of Dr. Lafayette Guild, chief surgeon on Lee's staff; said to be 1st brick residence in town. (23) 325 18th Ave., **Ormand-Little H.** (1835.Gr.Rev.). (24) **Stafford Sch.** (1820), oldest pub. sch. bldg. in use in Ala. (25) In Tuscaloosa also is **Bryce Hospital,** central unit of Ala.'s hospitals for insane, & **Partlow State School** for mental deficients.

SIDE TRIPS: (A) From Tuscaloosa on US82 (NW) through a number of lumbering towns 34m to **Reform.** When traveling preacher Lorenzo Dow was asked to name settlement, he cried: "Call it Reform! Brethren! Call it Reform!"

(S) from Reform on St.17 to **Carrollton,** 10m, whose Cth. has window in which appears "ghost face" of Negro, Henry Wells. Wells is said to have helped Feds. burn old Cth. & to have escaped townfolk's revenge until new Cth. was completed. At this time he was discovered, brought back to town, & locked upstairs in Cth. to protect him from mob because jail was not strong enough. A storm came up & eventually drove mob away. When sheriff went up, Wells was dead. Next morning his likeness was discovered engraved on window panel. In 1940, Carrollton Civic Club investigated & issued this statement: "While Wells was standing at the window, looking upon the mob below, the unusually bright flash of lightning struck. This was a case of lightning photography, for it stamped the prisoner's features indelibly on the window pane."

(B) From Tuscaloosa (S) 17m on St.13 to **Moundville.** (R) here a short distance to **Mound St. Mon.** (300 as.;34 sq. & oval Ind. mounds; mus.O.9 until dark, sm.fee.pic.) one of finest mound groups in South, marking site of prehist. city. Mus. exhibits artifacts from area & other displays explaining hist. of Inds. who built city.

(S) of Tuscaloosa US11 journeys through valley of Black Warrior R., whose swamps, along with those of the Tombigbee, offer good deer, turkey, squirrel & 'possum hunting. Quail is to be had not far from main hy. **95. EUTAW,** S. J. with US43 (see), est. 1818 as Mesopotamia, had its name changed in 1838 to comm. Battle of Eutaw Springs, S.C. (1781). It is typical southern town on N. edge of Black Belt reg. **Cth.** (Gr.Rev.reprod.of one burned in 1860's). **St. Stephen's Ch.** (Episc.1848). (W) of Cth. on Mesopotamia St., **Kirkwood.** 309 Main St., **Webb-Alexander H.** Prairie St., **Wilson H.** (1830's). **106. BOLIGEE, J.** with side Rd.

SIDE TRIP: (L) here to number of ante bellum houses described in Carl Carmer's "Stars Fell on Alabama." At 1m (R) **McKee-Gould H.,** "Hill of Howth"; orig. "dog trot" log cabin erected c.1812 by U.S. agent to Chickasaw nation, John McKee. 8m **Thornhill** (O. appl.1833.Gr.Rev.). Relics incl. field glass given by Geo. Washington to his cousin, the master of Thornhill. 10.5m **Rosemount** (O.fee.1830-35.rest.), one of most elaborate plantation houses in W. Ala., has 20 rooms each provided with bell-pull conn. with distinctive bell in slave quarters.

**112.** Bridge crosses Tombigbee R. **JONES BLUFF,** S. end of bridge, is Site of Ft. Tombigbee (R), est. 1735 by group sent out by Bienville. In 1736, Bienville passed ft. with fleet of some 60 boats on way to attack Chickasaw at Ackia, Miss. Defeated, he retreated to fort. In 1752 Marquis de Vaudreuil repeated Bienville's performance. Brit. (1763) renamed outpost Ft. York. Sp. (1783) rebuilt it as Ft. Confederation. In 1802, U.S. made treaty here to take over certain Choctaw land. **116.** J. with St.39.

SIDE TRIP: (R) here to J. with side Rd. 3m. (L) here 4.5m to **Sumterville.** Near-by is **Forked Lightning Ranch** (O). At 11m on St.39 is **Gainesville.** Here Gen. N. B. Forrest surrendered to Fed. Gen. Canby, 1865.

**122. LIVINGSTON.** Here US11 unites with US80 (see). **140.** US11 & US80 cross **MISS. LINE.**

## US 80—ALABAMA

**ALA.-GA. LINE** (at Columbus, Ga.) **(W) to ALA.-MISS.LINE** (17m from Meridian, Miss.). **227. US80**

Via: Crawford, Tuskegee, Montgomery, Lowndesboro, Selma, Demopolis, Livingston. RR. parallels route bet. Montgomery & Demopolis. Accoms.: All kinds.

US80 traverses (E-W) rich rolling farm lands of Black Belt, for more than a cent. identified with cotton but now producing livestock & dairy products as well, & passes through Montgomery, Ala.'s capital.

### Sec. 1: GA. LINE to MONTGOMERY. 80.

**0.** US80 crosses Chattahoochee R. Bridge to enter **PHENIX CITY,** J. with US241 (see), mfg. center—cotton, textile, brickmaking—of a reg. once home of the Kawita, prehist. Ind. tribe. On bridge is **tablet** stating, incorrectly, that here was fought (Ap.

16, 1865) "last" battle of Civil War. **Breastworks** are to be seen along R. In Phenix City is incorporated older town of Girard. Horace King, part Negro & part Ind. slave, who built many of 1st houses in Girard & Columbus, Ga., erected in Godwin Cemetery, over grave of his owner, **Mon.** inscribed "by Horace King in lasting remembrance of the love & gratitude he felt for his lost friend & former master."

SIDE TRIP: (S) from Phenix City on US241, 5m, is J. with graded Rd. (L) here 3.5m, (L) again 6m to U.S. military cemetery on **Site of Ft. Mitchell,** built 1811. Lafayette (1825) & Francis Scott Key (1835) were both entertained here. There are Ind. mounds (N) of site.

**11. CRAWFORD,** formerly Crockettsville, dates from 1814. **Masonic Hall** (1840). **35.** J. with US29.

SIDE TRIP: (N) on US29, 11m, to **Auburn,** home of **Ala. Polytechnic Institute,** early land grant college est. 1872 & 1st educational inst. in Ala. to admit women on equal basis with men (1892). State Agric. Experiment Sta. is adjunct of college. Town was sett. in 1830's & named from line of Goldsmith's "Deserted Village": "Name it Auburn, Sweet Auburn, loveliest village of the plain!" Among ante bellum structures are **Langdon Hall** (O.Gr.Rev.) on campus, once part of Masonic female college; Gay St., near US29, **Drake H.** (1830's); E. Drake Ave., **Simeon Perry H.;** College Ave., **Jones Hotel** (1840's); College & Thatch Sts., **Presb. Ch.** (1850) used as Confed. hospital.

(SE) from Auburn on dirt Rd. 4m is **Chewacla St. Pk.** (hqs. Auburn.875 as.;swim.dance. cabins).

**42. TUSKEGEE,** 1st sett. by Fr. traders in 18th cent., is home of famous **Tuskegee Normal & Industrial Institute for Negroes** (coed.), est. in 1881 in an old ch. with 30 students & a single teacher—Booker T. Washington—who remained head until his death in 1915. The late Geo. Washington Carver, ex-slave whose work with the peanut & sweet potato brought him international recognition, was one of institute's most distinguished teachers. On campus are: **Chapel,** whose stained-glass windows depict themes from Negro spirituals; **Booker T. Washington Mon.; Infantile Paralysis Center; Carver Mus.** (O) housing Carver exhibits & Mus. of Negro Art & culture with dioramas depicting Negro contributions to world civilization, part of famous Blondiau coll. of African art (W. African primarily), & coll. of contemporary Amer. Negro Art. In town proper are: Montgomery St., **Varner-Alexander H.** (1840), which escaped destruction when commdr. of Feds. recognized owner, Mr. Varner, as a Harvard classmate; Main St., **Woodward H.** (c.1830), built by Ind. fighter Gen. T. S. Woodward; 303 Main St., **Thompson H.** (Gr.Rev.); 511 Main St., **Drakeford-Curtwright H.** (c.1838).

**50. UNION CH.,** a white wooden structure. In vic. (L) Creek Inds., under half-breed chief High Head Jim, ambushed (Jan.26,1814) some 1,300 Georgia militia & Inds. under John Floyd. Creek losses were greater but they scored technical victory. **55. MON.** (in front of ch.) to Matthew Parham Sturdivant, 1st minister sent (1808-09) into Ala. territory by Meth. Episc. Ch. **56. POLE CAT SPRINGS** was Ind. agency as early as 1805. **59.** J. with dirt Rd.

SIDE TRIP: (R) Here 3m, (L) 4m, & (L) 5m to **Ft. Decatur,** overgrown with trees but with earthworks in good state of preservation. Built 1814 by Col. H. V. Milton.

**80. MONTGOMERY,** J. with US31 (see) & US231 (see).

Through RR., bus & plane conns. Accoms.: All kinds.

Montgomery, st. capital & 1st capital of the Confederacy, is Ala.'s 3rd largest city. De Soto passed through this reg. in 1540. Site was once occupied by 2 Ind. villages. When Ala. lands were put up for sale (1817) 2 groups started rival settlements which merged (1819). Village was then named in honor of Maj. Gen. Rich. Montgomery of Rev. In 1821 1st steamboats arrived & town that yr. boasted a dancing sch. as well as a day sch. In 1846 it was voted new st. capital & 1st legislature met following yr. Seceding sts. met here Jan. 6, 1861 & set up provisional gov. of Confederacy. Jefferson Davis was unanimously elected pres. & inaugurated Feb. 18. "The man & the hour have met," said the famous orator, Wm. L. Yancey, & a granddaughter of former Pres. Tyler raised Confed. flag. Capital was soon moved to Richmond, Va. In Ap. 1865 Gen. Jas. Wilson took Montgomery, finding 100,000 bales of cotton burned by Confeds. & burning, in turn, RR. stock, steamboats, & arms factory. During Reconstruction, Sidney Lanier wrote: "On our streets Monday is like Sunday. . . . Our whole world here yawns in a vast & sultry spell of laziness." In 1890's lumber, textile, & fertilizer mills were est. Today Montgomery is important cotton market handling hundreds of thousands of bales each yr. & one of largest livestock markets in SE. Hydroelectric power development has in recent yrs. brought added industries.

PTS. OF INT.: (1) E. end of Dexter Ave., **St. Capitol** (O.Mon.-Fri.8:30-4:30.Sat. 8:30-12.rotunda & halls only.1851.Gr.Rev. stuccoed brick with 97′ dome & Corinthian columns.designed by Geo.Nichols of Phila.& patterned after Nat.Capitol. adds.1885,1907 & 1912), was Confed. capitol at beginning of Civil War & appointments used by representatives of seceding sts. may be seen in senate. In rotunda are double spiral stairway & murals on Ala. history by Roderick MacKenzie. On W. portico brass star marks spot where Jeff. Davis took presidential oath. On grounds are number of Mons. incl. Confed. Mon. with cornerstone laid by Jeff. Davis & statue of Allen Wyth, Confed. surgeon, by Gutzon Borglum. (2) Adams Ave. & Bainbridge St., **World War Mem. Bldg.** (O.Mon.-Fri.9-4:30.1940.Gr.Rev.) houses colls. of St. Dept. of Archives & Hist., incl. Ind., Confed. & Fr. relics, documents & portraits. (3) 625 Washington St., **First White H. of Confederacy.** (O.Mon.-Fri. 9-4:30.c.1852.white-frame house with heavy cornice) became home of Pres. Davis & family, Mar. 4, 1861, & now displays relics & portraits. (4) 2 Dexter Ave., **Winter Bldg.** (O.wks.8:30-6.1841.Vict.remod.) from which Confed. Secy. of War, Leroy Pope Walker, sent message to Gen. Beauregard giving him power to open fire on Ft. Sumter. (5) 21 S. Perry St., **Hill Bldg.,** once infirmary of Dr. J. Marion Sims who achieved internat. reputation for a number of unprecedented operations. (6) 221 Court St., **Lomax H.** (O.1848.Gr.Rev.adds.), now insurance office. (7) 405 Adams St., **Seibels H.** (1845). (8) 203 S. Lawrence St., **St. Mary of Loretto's Academy** (O. appl.1851.Gr.Rev.), built by Perley Gerald who made fortune in Cal. gold rush of '49. (9) 440 S. Perry St., **Teague H.** (1850.Gr.Rev.) from porch of which Fed. Gen. J. H. Wilson read Emancipation Proclamation. (10) High & S. Lawrence Sts., **Mus. of Fine Arts** (O.wks.10-12 & 2:30-5.Sun.2:30-5:30.free), has Ind. rooms, period rooms, & colls. of firearms, silver & st. heirlooms. (11) 535 S. Hull St., **Evans H.** (1853), where 1st st. flag was cut out from design by J. W. A. Sanford, III (1895). (12) Fairview Ave. & Narrow Lane Rd., **Huntington College** (Meth.) for women; (13) art gallery & mus., **Houghton Mem. Lib.** (14) Madison Ave. & N. Perry St., **St. John's Ch.** (Episc.1855.Eng.Goth.), has tablet marking Jeff. Davis' pew. When Bishop Wilmer told congregation to pray for Confed. Pres. instead of Pres. of U.S., Feds. closed Ch. (16) 12 Bibb St., **Elks Club,** once private house (1840) was occupied by Feds. in Civil War. (17) 725 Jackson St. S., **St. Teachers College for Negroes.** (18) At NW. city limits is **Maxwell Field,** "Air War College."

SIDE TRIP: On St.9 (NE) from **Montgomery** 6m to J. with side Rd. Take latter (R) a short distance to **Lagoons St. Pk.** (240 as.pic.camp.). Cont. on St.9. At 9.5m hy. crosses Tallapoosa R. At 15m J. with side Rd.

(1) Take latter (L) 3m to **Site of Ft. Toulouse** indicated by marker; built by Fr. (1714), taken by Brit. (1763), rebuilt by Andrew Jackson (1814) to whom Wm. Weatherford, half-breed Ind. Chief, surrendered here after Battle of Horseshoe Bend. Boats & guides avail. for visiting Ind. mounds & townsite in vic.

(2) On same side Rd. (R) from St.9 a short distance to **Horrowgate Springs,** a resort in early 1800's. In cemetery is gravestone of Negro girl reading: "Henry Ritter, Emma Ritter, Demma Ritter, Sweet Potato, Creamatartar, Caroline Bostwick, Daughter of Bob & Sookey Catalan—Born at Social Circle 1843. Died at Wetumpka, 1852." It is said she ran errands for hotel guests & was called by all names listed.

At 16m on St.9 is **Wetumpka,** trading center, divided almost in half by Coosa R. Here are **Presb. Ch.** (1835.with slave balcony), **Bapt. Ch.** (1852.with basement for Negroes) & **Kelly Fitzpatrick H.** (1837.Gr.Rev.).

(1) From Wetumpka (N) 4m on St.11 to **Wallsburg.** (L) here along old turnpike 1.5m to Site of **Little Tallassee,** believed birthpl. of Alex. McGillivray, son of Scotch trader & Creek half-breed, who became Creek leader &, because of losses sustained during Revolution, hated the Amers. He accepted a colonelcy from Brit. & later another from Sp. Finally, after secret treaty with Pres. Washington, he became a Brig. Gen. in U.S. Army. But he cont. to be a foe to Amers. while pretending to be a friend. In vic. is **Jordan Dam** on Coosa R. which creates **Jordan Lake** (good f.).

(2) From Wetumpka (E) 21m on St.14 to **Tallassee & E. Tallassee,** divided by Tallapoosa R. Here excursions to Creek townsites along R. may be made (guides & boats avail.). Townsites incl. Tallassee, Tukabatchee (where Tecumseh urged Creeks to join other tribes against U.S.), Atasi, Huiliwahli, where De Soto stopped, Aug. 31, 1540, Fusihachee, Sawanogi, Muklasa & Kulumi. On a sm. island at Kialijee on L. Martin, is boulder with outline of large foot. Legend has it that Tecumseh stamped his foot in fury here when tribesmen refused to join his party.

## Sec. 2: MONTGOMERY to MISS. LINE. 147.

**22. LOWNDESBORO** (1818), long home of rich cotton planters. Main St. across from high sch., **Squire Thomas H.** Also on Main St., **Old Homestead** (1823), once home of U.S. Sen. D. H. Lewis who tipped scales at 500 lbs. & for whom special seat was built in Congress. A joke of the time was that Ala. had a larger representation than any other st. On **Negro Meth. Ch.** is dome (from Cahaba) of Ala.'s 1st capitol. **35. BENTON,** J. with side Rd.

SIDE TRIP: (R) 0.3m, (R) 7m, (L) 9m, (R) 10m & then (R) on lane to **Site of Holy Ground,** where Creek Inds., told by their prophet Josiah Francis that here they would be invincible, were nevertheless routed by whites & Inds. under Gen. Claiborne (Dec. 1813). In vic. are sites of ancient Ind. villages. Fine examples of urn-burials have been discovered.

**46.** J. with St.43.

SIDE TRIP: (L) on St.43 to **Sardis** 6m. Here is **King Plantation,** once property of Wm. Rufus King, U.S. Minister to France & Vice-pres.-elect before he died in 1853. In small area along Ala. R. near-by grows 80% of tree varieties native to Ala.

**50. SELMA,** shipping center of dairy products, cotton & livestock, is situated on high bluff on Ala. R. De Soto (1540) passed through this reg. & Bienville (1702) is said to have fought a minor engagement with a band of Inds. here. By 1809, Amer. settlers were calling the place High Soapstone Bluff (later Moore's Bluff) & in 1817 Wm. Rufus King org. a land co. & renamed settlement from Ossian's "The Song of Selma." Town soon became rich cotton center noted for its thoroughbred horses. (A mare named Letty Lee once captured 1st prizes in London, Paris & Berlin.) In 1848, group of skilled Germans arrived & introduced iron casting & gun making. During Civil War, Selma became supply depot (with arsenal, powder mill, shell foundry & navy yard) second only to Richmond, Va., in importance. After defeat of Gen. N. B. Forrest's men by those of Gen. Jas. H. Wilson on outskirts (Ap.2, 1865), much of town was burned by Fed. troops, drunk on a cache of Confed. gov. whiskey. Wilson ordered all horses & mules not needed by his men, killed, & stench remained long in the nostrils of Selma citizens, making task of reconstruction a difficult one.

PTS. OF INT.: (1) 232 Broad St., **Hotel Albert,** contracted for 1854, begun 1860, not completed due to war, until 1891, has details adapted from the Doge's Palace in Venice by its architect, J. E. Sweet of Albany, N.Y. (2) Water Ave., bronze **Marker** at end of bridge comm. Lafayette's visit in 1825. (3) 1200 Water Ave., **St. James Hotel Bldg.** (1837.remod.) has int. iron-work balconies & was once used as prison for Fed. soldiers. (4) Water Ave., & Sylvan St., **Naval Foundry Mon.** marks site of Confed. Navy Yard, where guns of type known as "Columbus 10, 11, & 12" were cast, & rams "Tennessee," "Gaines," "Morgan" & "Selma," built. (5) Water Ave. & Lauderdale St., **Ecor Bienville Boulder** marks site where Bienville fought Inds. 1702. (6) Water Ave. & Church St., **Arsenal Place,** site of Confed. Arsenal burned by Wilson's raiders. (7) 412 Lauderdale, **Burns-Bell H.** (1830.spiral stairway). (8) Lauderdale St. & Selma Ave., **Carnegie Lib.** with coll. documents & portraits pertaining to local hist. (9) 722 Ala. Ave., **Pettus H.** (1850), home of Confed. Brig.-Gen. E. W. Pettus. (10) Valley Cr., **Live Oak Cemetery** contains graves of many of Ala.'s famous, incl. Vice-pres. King. (11) 719 Tremont St., **Morgan H.** (1850's), where Gen. John T. Morgan was fired upon by Carpetbaggers. (12) 704 Tremont St., **Dawson H.** (1842), home of Col. Dawson & his 3rd wife, Elodie, who was a half-sister of Mrs. Lincoln. (see her int. mon. in cemetery.) (13) Ala. Ave. & Union St., **Vaughn Mem. Hospital** (1841.Gr.Rev.) was erected as Masonic sch. & 1st used as hospital in Civil War. Later it became cth. (14) 629 Tremont St., **Mabry H.** (1850. Gr.Rev.). (15) 603 Ala. Ave., **Philpot H.** (1830.raised cottage). (16) 713 Mabry St., **Gilman H.** (c.1852 Gr. Rev. Corinthian columns.cupola.int.inter.). (17) 623 Selma Ave., **Parke H.** (1854.Gr.Rev.) with japonica garden. (18) Lapsley St. & Minter Ave., **Selma Univ.** (Negro.coed.) founded 1878. (19) 307 Lapsley St., **Gen. Hardee H.** (20) 439 Lapsley St., **"Wash" Smith H.,** used as Fed. hospital after Battle of Selma. (21) Dallas & Union Sts., **Baker H.** (c.1850's). (22) 607 Union St., **Welch H.** (1858).

SIDE TRIPS: (A) From Selma (N) 17m on St.22 to **Valley Cr. St. Pk.** (1,080 as.;pic.swim. cabins). At 28m on St.22 is **J.** with St.6. (L) through Oakmulgee Dist. of Talladega Nat. For. (410,168 as.;f.swim.pic.turkey & squirrel h.) to **Centerville,** hqs. of For., 21m. **Payne L.** (in Hale Cty.) is favorite recr. area.

(B) From Selma (S) 4m on St.22 is J. with side Rd. (S) 6m on this Rd. to **Site of Cahaba** where st. capital was est. in 1820, but removed after disastrous floods to Tuscaloosa in 1826. Cahaba was prosperous until Civil War but little remains now except boulder marking site.

**71.** J. with St.5.

SIDE TRIP: (R) on St.5 to **Marion** 15m, once known as Muckle Ridge (after early settler, Michael Muckle), is one of oldest towns in st. (c.1817). In front of Perry County Cth. is **Mon.** to Nicola Marschall, Prussian artist & music teacher who taught at Judson College & designed Confed. flag. **Judson Female Institute** was founded (1839) by Milo P. Jewett, who was instrumental later in influencing Matthew Vassar to est. Vassar College. **Elmcrest** (1840), on Judson Campus, was home of John Trotwood Moore, author of local color stories & poems. Near cemetery is a **Mon. to Harry,** slave who died in fire after making sure all students had escaped burning dormitory of Howard College (since succeeded by Marion Military Inst.). 318 Green St., **Lea H.,** where Sam Houston (see Texas) married Margaret Lea (1840). Main St., **Capt. Porter King H.,** home of officer to whom Gen. Bee, at battle of Manassas, said of Gen. Thos. J. Jackson that he stood "like a stone wall"—hence "Stonewall" Jackson.

(1) From Marion (NE) 4.5m on St.5, is cross Rd. (L) here to **Fed. Fish Hatchery** (600 as.black bass.bream.crappie). Near hatchery on Cahaba R. is one of disputed sites of Chief Tuscaloosa's capital referred to by De Soto's chroniclers.

(2) From Marion (NW) 19m on St.41, to **Greensboro,** called Troy in 1816. Main St., **Magnolia Grove** (c.1830), later home of Rear Adm. R. P. Hobson, remembered for his gallant effort to sink Collier "Merrimac" so as to blockade Santiago harbor in Sp.-Amer. War. Church St., **John Erwin H.** (1830's). N. Main St., **Pickens H.** (moved here 1856), home of Israel Pickens, 3d Gov. of Ala. Main St., **Otts Place** (1856.Gr.Rev.). W. Main St., **Tunstall H.** (1850's.Gr.Rev.).

**81. UNIONTOWN,** sett. 1818. In center of town in paved area grows an old Chinaberry (Pride of India) tree which serves as cty. gathering place. Ante bellum houses incl.: (R) on old Cahaba Rd., **Pitt's Folly** (1849.Gr.Rev.) & (R) on St.61, **Westwood** (1840). **101. DEMOPOLIS,** sett. in 1818 by a group of Napoleonic exiles who arrived in Mobile previous winter on ship "MacDonough" & called themselves the "Assoc. of Fr. Immigrants for the Cultivation of the Vine & the Olive." They incl. Napoleon's "dear comrade," Count Chas. L. Desnouettes, who had ridden in the Emperor's carriage during invasion of Russia. Soon there were expensive carpets on the floors of log cabins; but the colonists knew nothing of farming & the project failed. Later, Amers. moved in & in flush times before Civil War built Gr.Rev. mansions, most elaborate of which, & one of outstanding homes in Ala., is **Gaineswood** (1842.rest.) built by Gen. Nathan Boyan Whitfield, which incl. Doric, Ionic & Corinthian details. Another is **Bluff Hall** (O.1832) at 407 N. Commissioner St. **The Lyon's H.** in heart of town, is about same age as Bluff Hall.

SIDE TRIP: (S) of Demopolis on US43 15m to **Linden.** (R) here on side Rd. to **Chickasaw St. Pk.** (640 as.;pic.).

**128. GRAMPIAN HILL** (O.appl.1867), replacing earlier structure, was meeting place for Confeds. during Reconstruction. Here, before Civil War, a "flying machine" operated with a hand & foot pedal was built but collapsed on 1st take-off. **129. LIVINGSTON,** home of a St. Teachers College (founded as Livingston Female Academy. 1840), was a hotbed during Reconstruction. Most legendary figure of time was Steve Renfroe, dashing leader of vigilantes, who became sheriff, was later arrested twice for thievery & was finally strung up by his "friends" on a Chinaberry tree. **139. YORK,** in agric. & lumbering reg. **147.** US80 crosses **MISS. LINE.**

## US 90—ALABAMA

**ALA.-FLA. LINE** (17m from Pensacola, Fla.) **(W) to ALA.-MISS. LINE** (11m from Moss Point, Miss.). **77. US90**

Via: Robertsdale, Mobile & St. Elmo. Louisville & Nashville RR. parallels route bet. Mobile & Miss. Line. Accoms.: All kinds at Mobile.

US90 passes through an area of sand dunes, with occasional clumps of palmettos & scrub pines, broken by lush swampy woodlands along waterways, then crosses Mobile Bay & cont. into La. Crops in reg. incl. Satsuma oranges, pecans, tobacco, potatoes, watermelons & tung oil. Good fresh-water fishing (bream & black bass), deep-sea fishing in Gulf & hunting (quail & dove).

**0. PERDIDO R.,** old boundary bet. Sp. Fla. & Fr. La. In Civil War, raiding Feds. strung up Henry Allen Nunez (who had grown rich operating ferry here since 1815) by his thumbs to make him reveal hiding place of fortune. He refused but his wife led them to cache of silver. Later they returned & suspended him by the neck over a deep well, threatening to cut the rope if he did not produce his gold. Again he refused & again his wife, unable to stand his torture, revealed hiding place. **16. ROBERTSDALE,** shipping center for Satsuma orange, pecans & vegetables. **22. LOXLEY,** in potato-growing area. **32.** J. with Bay Shore Rd. (see Mobile Trip III).

**33.** J. with US31 (see). **33.5.** Entrance to **COCHRANE BRIDGE,** a 10m causeway over Mobile Bay. **49. MOBILE** (see), reached also through Bankhead Tunnel (shorter route.toll), J. with US43 (see) & US45. **67. ST. ELMO,** named for enormously popular novel (1867) by Ala. author, Augusta Jane Evans. When hero, St. Elmo Murray, finally wins hand of Edna Earl she says: "Never was more implicit faith, more devoted affection, given any human being than I now give you, Mr. Murray; you are my first & last & my only love." **77.** US90 crosses **MISS. LINE.**

## US 241—ALABAMA

**ALA.-TENN. LINE** (13m from Fayatteville, Tenn.) **(S) to DOTHAN, ALA. 380.5. US241**

Via: Huntsville, Guntersville, Gadsden, Anniston, Talladega, Sylacauga, Alexander City, Opelika, Phenix City, Eufaula, Dothan. RRs. parallel route bet. Huntsville & Phenix City. Accoms.: All kinds.

US241 descends from Tenn. Valley through hilly reg. of E. central Ala. (S) of Anniston it cont. along E. edge of Coosa Valley with Talladega Mts. to (L). At Sylacauga, Hy. turns (SE) across Blue Ridge & Valley of Tallapoosa R. (S) of Phenix it roughly parallels Chattahoochee R. & enters a flat, wiregrass & piney woods sec. leading to Fla.

### Sec. 1: TENN. LINE to ANNISTON. 124.5.

**4. HAZEL GREEN.**

SIDE TRIP: (L) here on side Rd. 1.5m to **Jeffries H.,** once (1830-50) home of Mrs. Gibbons-Flannigan-Jeffries-High-Brown-Routt, who used place as a tavern & each of whose husbands died mysteriously. After it was charged that her "bridal chamber was a charnel house . . . around whose marriage couch six grinning skeletons were hung," Mrs. Routt moved to Miss.

**14.5. NORMAL,** home of **St. Agric. & Mech. Institute** (Negro), founded 1875 at Huntsville by Wm. Hooper Councill, ex-slave. **Student Center** is on site of Green Bottom Inn where Presidents Andrew Jackson, Jas. Monroe & Jas. E. Polk vacationed.

**18.5. HUNTSVILLE.** J. with US72.

Through RR., bus & plane conns. Accoms.: All kinds. Fish.: Guntersville, Wheeler & Wilson Ls. in vic. Hunt.: Quail, dove, duck.

Huntsville lies in beautiful hill reg. with Monte Sano (1800′) topped by Monte Sano St. Pk. (see) to (E). It is farm trade & textile center in reg. that produces cotton, corn, & dairy products, hardwoods & nursery stock. It has warehs. capable of storing 125,000 bales of cotton, is nation's largest producer of water cress &, during World War II, had one of world's largest chemical warfare arsenals. Orig. named Twickenham by Leroy Pope of Va., after home of poet Alex. Pope, it was renamed Huntsville (1811) to honor John Hunt, 1st settler, who built cabin here in 1804-05. Huntsville was meeting place of 1st st. constitutional convention, resulting in Ala.'s admission to Union, & 1st st. legislature was in session here Dec. 1819; but Cahaba became seat of gov. following yr. Town had a lib. in 1818, a cotton mill in same yr. that developed into Ala.'s 1st incorporated cloth factory (1832), & Ala.'s 1st newspaper that lasted more than a few yrs.—Huntsville "Advocate" (1815-1893). Feds. took over city (1862) & burned much of it. Huntsville has been home of 9 Ala. govs. & actress Tallulah Bankhead.

PTS. OF INT.: (1) Gallatin St. (W) of Cth. Sq., **Big Spring,** one of largest springs in U.S. has daily flow of 24,000,000 gals. & furnishes town's water supply. Spring & adjacent land is now Mun. Pk. with swim. pool. (2) Bank & Canal Sts., **First Nat. Bank** (1835-36.Gr.Rev.) has quarters in rear which served as detention cells for slaves held for their masters' debts. (3) Eustis & Green Sts., **Ch. of Nativity** (Episc.1858-59. Eng.Goth.) was only place of worship not confiscated for living quarters, hospitals, etc. by Feds. (4) 421 Adams Ave., **Moore H.** (1850) was once scene of party at which a cow (Lily Flagg who won 1st prize for butter production at Chicago Columbian Exposition in 1893) was guest of honor. Fed. Gen. John A. Logan used house as hqs. (5) Randolph & Green Sts., **First Meth. Ch.** (1867) stands on site of orig. Ch. (1821) destroyed by Feds. after they used it as stable. In 1916 Fed. Gov. compensated congregation. (6) Green & Gates Sts., **Weeden H.** (c.1819-1832) once occupied by Feds. (7) Adams Ave. & McClung St., **Pope-Walker H.** (c.1815), built by Leroy Pope & later home of Leroy Pope Walker, Confed. Secy. of War, who gave order to fire on Ft. Sumter, precipitating Civil War. (8) Gates & Lincoln Sts., **First Presb. Ch.** (1860) has congregation dating to 1818. (9) Williams & Green Sts., **Bibb-Newman H.** (1837.Gr.Rev.), built by Gov. Thos. Bibb. (10) Washington & Green Sts., **Madison County Cth.** (1836.remod.1915) has coll. of relics & hist. documents. (11) Franklin St., **Fearn H.** (c.1820.Gr.Rev.). Dr. Thos. Fearn made early experiments with quinine as treatment for malaria. (12) 558 Franklin St., **Neal H.** (c.1821). On site was birthpl. of Gen. John Hunt Morgan of famous Confed. raiders. (13) 517 Adams Ave., **Chase H.** (1848), once hqs. of Fed. Gen. Ormsby M. Mitchell. (14) Oak Ave., **St. Bartley Primitive Bapt. Ch.** (1872.Negro) has congregation dating to 1820's. (15) McCullough Ave., **Steele-Fowler H.** (1840.Gr.Rev.).

SIDE TRIP: (E) from Huntsville on US72. At $40^{m}$ is **Scottsboro,** scene of famous "Scottsboro Case" in which 9 Negro boys (1931) were charged with rape of 2 white girls. Case became "cause célèbre" among liberals, was twice brought to U.S. Supreme Court which in 1935 handed down decision that case must be retried on grounds that Negroes had been denied (by custom & practice, not by law) right to serve on juries in Ala. (R) from Scottsboro on side Rd. $8^{m}$ to **Saltpeter Cave,** one of no. of caverns along Tenn. R. in this area.

**21. MONTE SANO** ("mountain of health") **ST. PK.** (2,140 as.pic.hik.cabins.horses) affording excellent view of Tenn. Valley from summit of **Monte Sano** (1,800'). **Natural Well** here is great circular hole 40' in diameter & 200' deep. **59.5. GUNTERSVILLE,** once a flatboat landing &, with coming of steamboats, boom town on route down Tenn. R. to New Orleans. In vic. are no. of Ind. mounds. **Guntersville Dam,** impounding lake c.$82^{m}$ long, is c.$10^{m}$ (NW) on Tenn. R. (swim.f.boat.f.-camps).

**89.5. ATTALLA,** J. with US11 (see).

**94. GADSDEN,** J. with US11 (see) & US411.

Through RR. & bus conns. Mun. airport. Accoms.: All kinds.

Gadsden, Ala.'s 4th city in size & 2nd only to Birmingham in industrial employment & production, lies in a high level area bet. Red & Lookout Mts. Reg.'s natural resources incl. iron, coal, limestone, clay, manganese, bauxite, building stone & variety of timber (pine, ash, hickory, cedar, oak, gum & poplar). Among larger mfg. plants are those producing steel pipes & fittings, furnaces & stoves, rubber tires, tubes & heels, textiles, ribbons, furniture & aluminum utensils. Gadsden, seat of Etowah (Ind. "good tree") Cty. grew up around farm settlement orig. called Double Springs. In 1840 Gabriel Hughes of N.C. bought land here & planned city which was named for Jas. Gadsden, RR. promoter & diplomat, who negotiated Gadsden's Treaty—the purchase of lands from Mexico that incl. most practicable RR. route to Pacific. In 1863 Fed. Col. Streight & his cavalry raided town & John H. Wisdom made famous ride of $67^{m}$ to Rome, Ga. to warn Confeds. at munitions base there. Emma Sansom, aged 15, achieved fame by leading Confed. Gen. Forrest, who followed hard upon Streight, to ford over Black Cr. after Feds. had burned bridge. When a shot tore her dress she is said to have cried, "They've only wounded my dress," & gaily waved her sunbonnet to Feds. Streight's men discovering Rome had been forewarned, surrendered to Forrest. Gadsden was inc. 1871. In 1931 commission form of gov. was adopted.

PTS. OF INT.: (1) Broad & 14th Sts., **Etowah County Cth.** (1870.Romanes.), has oaks in rear grown from acorn from Magna Charta Oak at Runnymede, Eng. (2) 16th St. & Forrest Ave., **Etowah Curb Market** (O.Sat.& Wed.6:00 a.m.-2:00 a.m. Mon.& Thurs.3:15 p.m.), one of largest in Ala., is controlled by cty. farm & home demonstration agents. (3) 15th & Walnut Sts., **Forrest Cemetery** contains many Confed. graves & int. chapel built by W.P.A. & modeled after 12th cent. Eng. parish church. (4) Bay & 1st Sts., **Civic Center** (7 as.;auditorium.amphitheater.swim. pic.barbecue). (5) Broad & 1st Sts., **Emma Sansom Mon.** comm. 15-yr.-old heroine of Civil War (see above). (6) (NW) cor. 3rd St. & Tuscaloosa Ave., **Hughes H.** (1835. log cabin, later weather-boarded & remod.). (7) **Industrial Plants,** steel, textiles, rubber (O.appl.).

SIDE TRIP: From Gadsden (NE) on US411 to **Blount H.,** 12m, frame structure (R), site of skirmish bet. troops of Gen. Forrest & Col. Streight. At 19m is **Leesburg,** trading center for Lookout Mt. folk who retain certain Elizabethan characteristics in speech, music & customs. Just beyond Leesburg is J. with side Rd. (L) here 9m to **Yellow Cr. Falls.** At 24m on US411 is **Centre,** once home of John Jonathan Pratt, inventor of pterotype (c.1867), an early kind of typewriter. 30m **Cedar Bluff.** At 34m (L), on hill near hy., **Sam Lawrence H.** where Fed. Col. A. D. Streight surrendered to Gen. N. B. Forrest. 37m **Farill.**

(R) here 4m on Pool's Ferry Rd. to Coosa R. **Pool's I.** (boats.avail.), downriver a short way, is said to be location of **Chiaha** (much disputed) where De Soto's men in 1540 took many Ind. slaves.

Main tour cont. (S) from Gadsden on US241 to **BLUE MOUNTAIN, 122.5.**

SIDE TRIP: On St.11 (L) here is **Ft. McClellan,** 3m, U.S. military reserv. At 3.5m on St.11 is side Rd. & (L) short distance is **Weaver Cave** where saltpeter was mined by Confeds. A World War II munitions plant was est. here. Cont. (N) on St.11 to **Jacksonville,** 10m, home of a **St. Teachers College.** Town dates to 1822 & was damaged by Feds. in 1862. Following yr. it served as hqs. for Gens. Beauregard, Polk & Wheeler. Cemetery has **Mon.** to "gallant John Pelham," major of Confed. Army at age of 24. Ante bellum structures incl.: E. Clinton & Church Sts., **Presb. Ch.;** S. Pelham Rd., **C. W. Daugette H.** (O.appl.Gr.Rev.); **Rowan H.** (1857.int.inter.), once hqs. of Beauregard.

**124.5. ANNISTON,** J. with US78.

Through RR. & bus conns. Mun. airport. Accoms.: All kinds.

Anniston, "hub of the Coosa R. Valley," lies in foothills of Blue Ridge Mts. In 1860 it was still a cotton field. Confeds. est. camp & supply base at Blue Mt. just (N) in 1862 & iron works at Oxford just (S). In 1873 Woodstock Iron Co., with Sam. Noble as gen. manager & A. L. Tyler as pres., took over Oxford Co. holdings & planned town with aid of engineers, architects (incl. Stanford White) & workers from E. Orig. called Woodstock, it was renamed Anniston (Annie's Town) in honor of Mrs. Tyler & remained a private corporation until 1883, when it was chartered as municipality & opened to public. One of editors of its 1st newspaper, the "Hot Blast" (later "Anniston Star") was J. R. Randall, author of "Maryland, My Maryland." In World War I, Ft. McClellan, one of nation's largest ordnance & reclamation depots, was est. near-by. In 1949 Anniston had some 120 mfg. plants, incl. 23 textile mills, 11 soil pipe plants (it is said to be largest producer of cast iron soil pipe in world) & a large electro-chemical plant. PTS. OF INT.: (1) 10th St. & Wilmer Ave., **Carnegie Lib.** has special poetry coll., known as "Poet's Corner," & panoramic view of Anniston in 1882 painted by Pa. artist C. H. Shearer. (2) **Regar Mus. of Natural Hist.** (O.free) in wing of lib. contains Regar-Werner coll. incl. Werner habitat bird groups (900 specimens with nests & eggs, incl. 11 species now extinct), wild animals, fish, & reptiles & Egyptian, Roman, Ind. & other relics. (3) 13th & Gurnee Sts., **Zinn Pk.** Women's Civic Club bldg. incorporates part of inn, designed by Stanford White (1880's) & destroyed by fire. (4) 17th & Cobb Sts., **St. Michael & All Angels Ch.** (Episc.1888.Norman Goth.native stone.int.exter.& inter.) has 90′ bell tower. (5) **Oxford L.** just (S) of town (amusement pk.boat.swim). (6) **Monsanto Chemical Co.** (O.appl.) just (W) of town on St.78, one of largest electro-chemical plants in South, produces phosphoric acid, calcium carbide, diphenyl, phosphate, cleaners, plant food.

SIDE TRIP: (W) of Anniston on US78 9m to J. with side Rd. (R) here 1m to **St. Fish Hatchery** (35 as.bass & bream) & **Choccolocco Sportsmen's Club.**

## Sec. 2: ANNISTON to PHENIX CITY. 148.

**2.5. HOBSON CITY,** all-Negro town, inc. 1899 after Oxford changed its town limits, leaving inhabitants of Hobson City outside. **3. OXFORD** is closely related industrially to Anniston. At Oxford is S. J. with US78.

SIDE TRIP: (E) from Oxford US78 enters **Shoal Cr. Ranger District** of Talladega Nat. For. (hqs.at Anniston.212,795 as.), which incl. some of the most striking mt. scenery in Ala. & highest peak, **Cheaha Mt.** (see below). There is a Wildlife Management Area with pic. facils. at **Horseblock Tower.** In 1847 sec. was a gold-mining center, deserted when Cal. rush got under way. At 23m on US78 is **Edwardsville,** boom town of Ala.'s gold rush days. In 1937 some of old workings were reopened but grade of ore found was low. Reg. also has deposits of silver, zinc, iron, pyrites, kaolin, copper & mica. At 31m **Muscadine,** named from wild grape of reg. (good f.).

**14. MUNFORD,** where an outnumbered Confed. force was scattered by Gen. J. H. Croxton's men, Ap. 23, 1865.

SIDE TRIP: (L) here on side Rd. (marked) 12m to **Cheaha St. Pk.** (2,679 as.f.beach.swim. boat.hotel.cabins.pic.). Tower on **Cheaha Mt.** (2,407'), Ala.'s highest, affords magnificent view.

**25. TALLADEGA,** industrial & educational center for agric. & mineral reg., lies among foothills of Blue Ridge & is one of oldest settlements in inter. of Ala. Here, on boundary line bet. Creek & Cherokee lands, John Bruner, Ind. half-breed, who served as interpreter for U.S. Gov. built a ft. later called Leslie's Sta. Attacked by raiding Inds. after massacre at Ft. Mims, it is said that friendly Ind. disguised in hog skin, got through enemy lines to bring news to Andrew Jackson who, on Nov. 9, 1813 in Battle of Talladega, defeated c.1,000 Creeks in 1st of series of victories that destroyed Creek Confederacy's power. South St., **Talladega Mus.** (O.Wed.& Sat.afts.sm.fee) has Sp., Col., Ind., Civil War & other colls. On East St. are several old Hs. incl. **Aboyne Court** (1805), **Hamilton H.** & **La Tours** (int.inter.). On Ashland Hy., **Talladega College** (Negro.coed.), founded 1857 by 2 former slaves, centering about orig. bldg. (1852), once high sch. for white boys. **Ala. Institutes for Deaf & Blind** are also located at Talladega.

SIDE TRIPS: (A) From Talladega (N) on St.102 to **Shocco Springs,** 2m, mineral springs around which summer resort & religious conference center has sprung up.
(B) From Talladega (SE) 15m on St.48 to Talladega Ranger Dist. of Talladega Nat. For. (228,156 as.hqs.at Talladega), a mountainous dist. of mixed pine & hardwood fors. Here are **Sherman's Cliffs** on Horn Mt. 9m (S) of St.48 near Skyway Hy. (pic.shelters), **Robinson Cr. Falls** 14m (SE) off St.48 on Clairmont Springs Rd. & **L. Chinnabee** (boat.f.).

**30. JACKSON TRACE MARKER** indicates that hy. follows old Ind. trl. later improved by Andrew Jackson during Creek War. **32.** J. with side Rd. (R) here 1.5m to **Lawler Place** (O.appl.1839.Gr.Rev.), setting for Augustus Thomas' play "Alabama" (1891). **36. WINTERBORO.** (W) here 5m on side Rd. to **Kymulga Cave. 47. SYLACAUGA** (see Birmingham Trip III).

SIDE TRIP: (S) here on St.11 to J. at 11m with side Rd. (R) here 12m to **Weogufka St. For.** (hqs.Weogufka.400 as.;hik.pic.cabins), incl. crest of Weogufka Mt. St.11 cont. 21m to **Rockford** on site of ancient Ind. village, Unifulka.

**77. ALEXANDER CITY,** on site of Creek Ind. town, has one of largest knitting mills in South, one of world's largest mills producing tickings, & foundry which casts iron "lacework" from patterns more than a century old. J. with St.63.

SIDE TRIP: (R) here 19m on St.63 to J. with side Rd. (L) here to **L. Martin** (f.calico,bass, bream;h.rabbits,quail,turkey;boats.cabins). Formed by Martin Dam, L. has shore line of c.750m, much of it bordered by wild azaleas, dogwood & honeysuckle.

**93. DADEVILLE,** an Ind. trading post in 1832, now lumber town in reg. that also has deposits of tin, asbestos & gold. (N) of Cth. Sq., **Dennis Hotel** (1832. remod.1840).

SIDE TRIP: (L) from Dadeville on side Rd. to **Site of Battle of Horseshoe Bend,** 12m. Here, Mar. 29, 1814, Andrew Jackson (with help from Davy Crockett & Sam Houston) broke power of Creek Inds.

**121. OPELIKA,** cotton market & textile mfg. center, was 1st sett. in 1836 by pioneers from Ga. At Opelika is J. with US29.

SIDE TRIP: (NE) from Opelika on US29 to **Lanett** 21m. Here hy. crosses Ga. Line on a bridge over Chattahoochee R. conn. Lanett with West Pt., Ga. On W. bank of R. at Lanett is **Site of Ft. Tyler** (R) where sm. group of wounded Confeds. made (Ap.16,1865) unsuccessful attempt to hold bridge against Fed. Gen. Wilson's forces on way to attack West Pt.

**148. PHENIX CITY** (see US80).

## Sec. 3: PHENIX CITY to DOTHAN. 108.

**48. EUFAULA** (Ind. "beech tree"), home of large cotton mill & of mill settlement in which many of houses are owned by workers through financing sponsored by mill co. Eufaula was orig. called Irwinton & vic. was scene of various skirmishes with Inds. in 1820's & 30's. Fed. Commissioner Francis Scott Key finally settled difficulties. When Mass. "Free Soilers" org. to help abolitionists settle in Kans., at time control of that st. was political issue, Maj. Jefferson Bufford of Eufaula organized & financed 500 "Southern Rights Men" to oppose them. PTS. OF INT.: (1) Randolph St., **Thornton H.** (1845). (2) Randolph & Broad Sts., **Old Bank Bldg.** Here in 1865 conspiracy of former slaves to loot town (under direction of carpetbaggers) was betrayed by Negro named Alex. Hamilton. Whites presented to Hamilton, in appreciation, a watch & a lot on edge of town. (3) N. Broad St., **Kendall Manor** (1848. Gr.Rev.). (4) 325 N. Eufaula St., **Couric H.** (1860's). (5) 330 W. Barbour St., **Woods H.** (c.1840), (6) Livingston St., **Gen. Wm. Wellborn H.** (7) W. Barbour St., **Young H.** (1856) used as Confed. hospital. (8) On bluff, **Ferrell Gardens** (1836), probably oldest house in town.

SIDE TRIP: From Eufaula (W) on St.30 to **Clayton** 20m. In cemetery is **Whiskey Bottle Tombstone,** erected by a Mrs. Mullins, a teetotaler, to her husband Amos, a drinking man. Worn out with attempts to reform him she told him to drink himself to death. And he did.

**77. ABBEVILLE,** an agric. center, cty. seat since 1833. **108. DOTHAN.** J. with US84 & US231 (see).

# US 31—ALABAMA

**ALA.-TENN. LINE** (20m from Pulaski, Tenn.) **(S) to MOBILE, ALA. 431. US31**

Via: Athens, Decatur, Cullman, Birmingham, Greenville, Montgomery, Mobile. Louisville & Nashville RR. parallels route. Accoms.: All kinds.

US31 cuts (N-S) through center of Ala. & its 3 largest cities: Birmingham (largest), Montgomery (capital) & Mobile (Ala.'s only seaport). Hy. descends from Tenn. Valley, enters rugged mineral belt, then rich agric. land of Black Belt, & finally passes through pine woods & sub-tropical reg. near coast.

### Sec. 1: TENN. LINE to BIRMINGHAM. 125.

**0. ARDMORE,** trading center half in Tenn. & half in Ala. Hy. now passes through one of richest cotton regs. of Ala. **19. ATHENS** (1816) preserves, perhaps, more of flavor of old South than ony other town for next 200m. Yet is was also 1st Ala. town to buy electric current from T.V.A. Three of largest T.V.A. dams (Wilson, Wheeler & Guntersville) are within 50m (excellent f.boat.swim.camp.). Athens was under control of Russian-born Fed. Brig. Gen. Ivan Vasilivitch Turchinov during much of Civil War & number of ante bellum houses were burned. PTS. OF INT.: **Athens College** (Meth.coed.), just (N) of town, founded 1843, has been in operation without interruption (even by Civil War) ever since. Bricks of **Founders Hall** (1842. Gr.Rev.adds.) were made by slaves from local clay. N. Jefferson St., **Pryor H.** (c. 1850.Gr.Rev.cast-iron ornamentation). (W) of Court Sq., **Houston H.,** former home of Gov. of Ala. (1874-76), houses Mem. Lib. Washington St., **St. Timothy's Episc. Ch.** has int. old churchyard. 211 S. Beaty St., **Mason H.** (1826.remod.1845.int.inter.). **Trinity Sch.** (Negro) on Coleman Hill. In vic., in 1864, Gen. N. B. Forrest marched his men before entrenched Feds. (under Col. Campbell) first as cavalry & then (by having them dismount & fall behind rear guard) as infantry. Believing his troops outnumbered, Campbell surrendered.

SIDE TRIPS: (A) From Athens (NW) on side Rd. 12m to **U.S. Fish Hatchery** on Elk R., one of largest warm-water hatcheries in world.

(B) From Athens (W) on US72 is **Coxey,** 13m. On hill (R) is Site of Ft. Hampton, used in Ind. uprisings & by Confeds. At 25m is **Elgin** & J. with Wheeler Dam Rd.

(L) here 3m to **Wheeler Dam Reserv.,** named for Gen. "Fighting Joe" Wheeler, a T.V.A. project. At 6m is **Port LeMay** (boat.f.cabins).

**34. DECATUR**

Through RR. & bus conns. Good accoms. Morgan Cty. Fish Rodeo, May.

Decatur, whose industrial activities have been considerably stimulated by T.V.A., is center for cotton factors (dealers in actual staple) & mfg. center—textiles, fertilizer, steel barges. Town is situated on high plateau on S. bank of Tenn. R. & many plants parallel R. which is 2m wide here & has a 7′ channel where vessels from Cincinnati & other northern ports dock. Townsite was ordered reserved by Pres. Monroe in 1820 & named in honor of naval hero, Stephen Decatur. Later an adj. municipality, Albany, originally New Decatur, grew up but combined with old Decatur in 1927. During Civil War, after occupation by both armies, only 3 bldgs. remained intact. 120 Sycamore St., **Hinds-McEntire H.** (1835.Class.Rev.), used as hqs. by both Feds. & Confeds. It is said that here Gen. Albert Sidney Johnson planned battle of Shiloh. Bank St. & Wilson Ave., **Amer. Legion Home** (O.afts.1832. Class.Rev.), built to house a st. bank & designed in manner of old Federal Hall in N.Y. City. Pres. Van Buren attended dedication at which slaves, who built it, were granted freedom by their owner, Jas. Fennell, pres. of bank. It now houses small hist. mus.

SIDE TRIPS: (A) From Decatur (E) on St.20 to Mooresville 4m. (L) from Mooresville 1m to **Belle Mina** (1826.Gr.Rev.rest.), built by Thos. Bibb, Gov. of Ala. (1820-22).
(B) From Decatur (W) on St.20 to **Wheeler** 17m & **Wheeler H.** (O.E.wing 1818;W.1860's), home of Gen. Jos. Wheeler—lawyer, planter, author, member of Congress, Lt. Gen. in Confederacy, Maj. Gen. in Sp.-Amer. War. There are portraits & heirlooms. At 20m is **Courtland** where Dr. Shackelford organized Ala. Red Rovers, all of whom, except the doctor, were killed in Mex. War. **Sanderson Garage** here (O) has coll. of military relics. **Rocky Hill Castle,** 23.5m (1845), once scene of much entertaining, has tower apart from house in which valuables were hidden from Feds. 26m **Town Cr.,** scene of skirmish (Ap.27, 1863) when Confeds. under Gen. Roddy beat back Feds. under Gen. Dodge.

**38. CEDAR L.,** Negro farm project dating back to 1897.

SIDE TRIP: (L) here on St.67 c.3m to J. with side Rd. (L) here 4.5m to **Cave Springs,** a cave & brook popular as pic. spot. At 6m on St.67 is a natural rock formation called **Ft. Bluff** used by Inds. & later by scouts during Civil War. At 12m is **Somerville,** founded 1819, whose **Meth. Ch.** (1836) contains pews partitioned to separate men from women. At 14m is J. with St.33.
(E) here 9m to **Valhermoso Springs** whose 3 springs—white sulphur, black sulphur, & chalybeate—made it a popular resort in 1830's. In vic. is **King's Cave** also called Bat Cave since its bat droppings have been used commercially as fertilizer.

**70. CULLMAN,** sett. by Germans from Rhine valley under direction of John Cullman, is center of a strawberry reg. & scene of annual strawberry festival. On campus of **St. Bernard College** near-by is **Ave Maria Grotto** (O.sm.fee) with more than 50 shrines, mosques, chs., temples & ruins of Holy Land reprod. in miniature. **84. GARDEN CITY.**

SIDE TRIP: (L) here on side Rd. to **Blountsville** 10m where Col. Streight & his cavalry, pursued by Confeds., set fire to his supply wagons which fell into hands of Confeds. in time, however, for them to save supplies. Near-by Ind. mounds have yielded many artifacts.

Beyond Garden City US31 crosses Mulberry Fork of Black Warrior R. & leads through Rds. cut in solid rock overhung with dense growths of maples, beeches, gums & elms. **101. WARRIOR,** coal-mining town. Bet. here & Birmingham hy. passes mining villages usually consisting of general store, ch., shabby houses of miners, & filling station. **114. GARDENDALE.** In vic. (R) c.3m is **Mt. Olive Homesteads,** Fed. Gov. project with rammed-earth houses designed by Thos. Hibben.

**125. BIRMINGHAM** (see). J. with US11 (see) & US78.

## Sec. 2: BIRMINGHAM to MONTGOMERY. 100.

**33. CALERA** (Sp. "lime pit") is one of number of towns in this area that produce lime.

SIDE TRIP: (R) here on St.25 to **Montevallo,** 6m, seat of **Ala. College** (St. College for Women.1896). Artist & lecture series open to public. On campus are **Reynolds Hall** (1851. remod.), orig. home of Montevallo Male Institute where men in vic. were mustered into army in Civil War, & **King H.** (1823), said to be 1st brick house & 1st house with glass windows in this part of Ala.
(SW) 22m from Montevallo on St.25 to **Centerville,** hqs. of Oakmulgee Dist. (410,168 as.;pic.swim.f.h.turkey & squirrel) of Talladega Nat. For. 7m (S) on St.5 & then 17m (W) on St.92 is **Lake Payne Recr. Area** (beach.swim.pic.).

**49. THORSBY,** in farming area that produces watermelons, strawberries, peaches & pecans as well as cotton. 1st settlers were mostly Scand. **65.** J. with St.22; (L) here 7m is **Mitchell Dam** (f.). **66. VERBENA.** In vic. along Chestnut Cr., poet Sidney Lanier once camped in a tent in effort to recover from illness. **94.5.** A white stone (R) is inscribed: "This stone marks the site of the Ind. Town, Tawasa, visited by De Soto Sept. 13, 1540; also by Bienville, 1715." **100. MONTGOMERY** (see). J. with US80 (see) & US231 (see).

## Sec. 3: MONTGOMERY to MOBILE. 206.

**36. FORT DEPOSIT,** est. by Jackson during Ind. Wars. **50. GREENVILLE,** sett. 1819 by pioneers from Greenville, S.C. **66. GEORGIANA,** named by early Bapt. minister who came from Georgia (after 1824) & had daughter named Anna. **73. McKENZIE,** in a strawberry, bean & cucumber producing reg., is N. J. with US84 which unites with US31 to 3m (S) of Evergreen.

SIDE TRIP: (L) or (E) from McKenzie on US84 to **Andalusia,** $24^m$, hqs. for **Conecuh Nat. For.,** 83,867 as., much of it reforested with slash pine. There are also groves of live oaks, magnolias & virgin pine & black bear, deer, wildcat & alligators.

(SW) from Andalusia, $12^m$, on US29 to J. with St.88. (S) here c.$6^m$ to **Open Pond Recr. Area** (swim.pic.shelters.refreshments).

**93. EVERGREEN** ships smilax, holly, mistletoe & other evergreens. **96.** J. with US84.

SIDE TRIP: (W) on US84 to **Belleville,** $7^m$. Near-by, on Burnt Cork Cr., was 1st skirmish in Creek War. Amers. attacked & routed Inds., July 27, 1813, but were in turn routed. $31^m$ **Monroeville** & vic. suffered raids soon after Creek War by mixed-breed John Haigue, better known as "Savannah Jack," & his followers. Haigue was finally killed in Fla.

**105. CASTLEBERRY,** strawberry shipping center. **119. BREWTON,** N. J. with US29, had its origin in 1818, in what is now E. Brewton, as Ft. Crawford, U.S. stronghold against Inds. Murder Cr. separates Brewton from E. Brewton, & is so named because of traders killed on its banks by Inds. Here, after massacre at Ft. Mims (see below), a small band from Jackson's army annihilated group of Inds. by setting dummies in sleeping positions around campfire & thereby attracting enemy to close range. When **Pollard** ($10^m$ away) lost cty. seat to Brewton, its citizens sent latter a boxcar full of cats to become town pests. **135. FLOMATON.** S. J. with US29. Latter cont. to Pensacola, Fla. **150. ATMORE.** J. with St.11.

SIDE TRIP: (R) on St.11 to **Little River St. Pk.** $17.5^m$ (2,120 as.f.boat.bath.camp.trlr.pk. cabins). Near-by are Ind. village sites.

**171. BAY MINETTE,** declared county seat of Baldwin in 1900 by Ala. Supreme Ct. Daphne, former seat, twice refused to give up court records. Finally, citizens of Bay Minette, under ruse of bringing a Negro to Daphne jail, made sheriff a prisoner, tore jail apart & took records & judge home with them. Guides avail. for Tensaw R. & swamp area (excellent f.& h.—deer, squirrel, quail, ducks & turkey).

SIDE TRIP: (N) from Bay Minette on St.59 to **Tensaw** $23^m$.

(L) here $4^m$ to **Site of Ft. Mims,** marked by mon. Here, about noon, on Aug. 30, 1813, Creeks, under Peter MacQueen, Bill Weatherford & High Head Jim, half-white leaders, surprised & massacred inhabitants, incl. women & children, & burned ft. "Remember Ft. Mims" became rallying cry during rest of Creek War.

**183.** J. with side Rd.

SIDE TRIP: (R) here $9^m$ to Confed. earthworks of **Ft. Blakeley,** thrown up in 1865 & named for town that once was a rival to Mobile but was deserted after 2 yellow fever epidemics & a financial depression. On shore near townsite are shell mounds left from Ind. camps & (S) of townsite is **Site of Old Spanish Ft.** est. by Galvez in 1799.

**192.** J. with US90 (see), which unites with US31 to **MOBILE** (see) at **206.** J. with US43 (see), & US45.

## US 231—ALABAMA

**MONTGOMERY, ALA. (S) to ALA.-FLA. LINE** ($16^m$ from Cottondale, Fla.). **132. US231**

Via: Montgomery, Orion, Troy, Ozark, Newton & Dothan. Atlantic Coast Line RR. parallels route bet. Montgomery & Dothan. Accoms.: All types.

US231, "Bee Line Hy." to N.-central Fla., crosses level reg., broken by swamps & pine covered hills, that was once almost entirely devoted to cotton but now has dairy & cattle farms & apiaries & raises watermelons, pecans & especially peanuts.

**35. ORION,** once wealthy cotton town, sett. 1830's. **Siler H.** (1840-50.Gr.Rev.), home of Solomon Siler, who with Isaac Nall gave cty. one of its earliest schs.: Orion Institute (1848). **47. TROY** has cotton gins, cottonseed oil mills, fertilizer & veneer factories. It is in heart of reg. that had concentration of almost 75% of Ala.'s slaves before Civil War. Troy had its beginnings in 1824 when Three Notch Rd. was opened up as military hy. to Pensacola, & "Granny" Love & her 2 sons built a tavern. It is home of 1 of Ala.'s 4 St. Teachers Colleges. At Troy is J. with US29.

SIDE TRIP: US29 (L) bet. here & Banks at $10^m$, follows Three Notch Rd. over which Sam Dale rode his horse, Paddy, $600^m$ to New Orleans to report to Gen. Jackson that War of 1812 was officially over. He arrived in middle of Battle of New Orleans. Jackson is quoted as saying: "Too late! Too late! Washington is always too late!" At $42^m$ is **Union Springs.** On Main St., **Della Rosa,** ante bellum H. described in Augusta Evans Wilson's novel, "At the Mercy of Tiberius."

**88. OZARK,** trading center for a hog-raising reg. Here is **Claybank Ch.** (Meth.1830), a split-log structure. **98. NEWTON** was raided in 1865 by Joe Sanders & a band of whites who did not own slaves & who had organized against Confeds. & conscription when it became known that some of wealthy planters were hiring soldiers to take their own places in the lines. Sanders was murdered shortly after close of Civil War. **115. DOTHAN,** RR., trade & cotton mfg. center was, in 1880's, a tough sawmill settlement whose 1st mayor is said to have resigned after 24 hrs. & whose 1st town marshall called his salary "nothing but a few dollars toward burying me." Dothan is J. with US241 & US84.

SIDE TRIPS: (A) On US84 (E) to J. with side Rd. 22.5m. (S) here 9m to **Chattahoochee St. Pk.** (590 as.f.pic.). At 23m US84 crosses **Ga. Line.**
(B) On US84 (W) to **Choctawhatchee R.** 18m. At **Enterprise** 30m, which changed to raising peanuts after boll weevil destroyed cotton (1910), is **Mon. to Boll Weevil:** "In profound appreciation of the boll weevil, & what it has done to herald prosperity, this monument is erected by the citizens of Coffee County & Enterprise." Here also is large peanut butter plant.

**130.** J. with side Rd.

SIDE TRIP: Take latter (L) 4m. (R) on another side Rd. 8m & (R) again to **Sealy's Hot Salt Mineral Well,** health resort. Well has flow of 10,500 gals. an hr. Water is charged with natural gas & burns with blue flame when ignited. It also contains iron, lime, chloride & sodium & aluminum oxides. Pool (O.all yr.sm.fee) & private baths.

**132.** US231 crosses **FLA. LINE.**

# US 43—ALABAMA

**ALA.-TENN. LINE** (21m from Lawrenceburg, Tenn.) **(S) to MOBILE, ALA. 378. US43**

Via: Florence, Sheffield, Tuscumbia, Russellville, Hamilton, Tuscaloosa, Fayette, Demopolis, Jackson. Accoms.: All types in cities; tourist camps.

US43 journeys (N-S) through W. part of Ala. It crosses Tenn. Valley, passing T.V.A. "Tri-Cities," & cont. through wooded hills & sm. farms. At Tuscaloosa it skirts W. boundary of iron & coal mining reg. & passes to rich valleys of Warrior & Tombigbee Rs. & finally through flat sandy pinelands to Gulf Coast.

## Sec. 1: TENN. LINE to TUSCALOOSA. 167.

**19. FLORENCE**

Through RR. & bus conns. Adj. airport services Florence, Sheffield & Tuscumbia. Accoms.: All kinds. Fish.: In Wilson & Pickwick Ls. Hunt.: Duck, goose, snipe, quail, dove, rabbit & squirrels. Nat. Fox Hunters' Assoc. Field Trials have been held here. N. Ala. St. Fair, fall.

Florence, in a rolling plateau land backed by hills, lies on N. bank of Tenn. R. in heart of Muscle Shoals area of which it is largest of "Tri-Cities" that incl. Sheffield & Tuscumbia. It is immediately adj. to Wilson Dam, 15m (W) of Wheeler Dam & 38m (E) of Pickwick Dam, all part of Tenn. Valley Authority program that has turned Tenn. R. into a series of long lake-like reservoirs connected by locks for R. traffic over a 630m channel & has become one of nation's great regional experiments in navigation, flood control, power development & conservation. Florence is seat of Lauderdale Cty. that produces cotton, corn, hay, livestock & wide variety of timber. Some 41 minerals incl. coal, iron, bauxite, asphalt rock, nitrates, phosphates, kaolin & ochre are to be found within 50m radius. Area was fought over by Chickasaw & Cherokee Inds. & whites (c.1799) est. trading post which later became flatboat base called Muscle (or Mussel) Shoals, either because of mussels to be found in waters or because of muscles needed to navigate them. Before completion of Wilson Dam, Tenn. R., in 30m sec. above Florence, fell more than 130′ in series of practically unnavigable rapids. In 1818 Cypress Land Co. headed by Gen. John Coffee bought land & laid out town which was named by Italian surveyor, Ferdinand Sanona, for Florence, Italy. Investors incl. Presidents Jas. Madison, Jas. Monroe & Andrew Jackson, & a $30,000 tavern was erected. A canal around shoals was completed 1836, improved 1840 & again in 1876 but never used commercially. RR. bridge across Tenn. R. was wrecked & town invaded by Feds. (1865). In 1916 Pres. Wilson authorized construction of hydroelectric dam & 2 nitrate plants to mfg. supplies for World War I. After war it was thought U.S. would turn project over to private industry, principal bidder being Henry Ford (1922). Instead T.V.A. was created (1933) with David E. Lilienthal, director. Wilson Dam & T.V.A. both produced booms in Florence & it is said that here, perhaps more than any other part of Ala., Negroes have had cultural & financial advantages. Wm. C. Handy, composer of "Memphis Blues" & "St. Louis Blues," is a native of Florence.

PTS. OF INT.: (1) Head of Court St., highest pt. in town, **Courtview** (O.appl.1854. Gr.Rev.) built for Geo. Washington Foster who was so hospitable he opposed est. of tavern, believing citizens should entertain all guests within their own gates. (2) Morrison Ave. & Wesleyan Ave., **St. Teachers College** (1873), outgrowth of Florence Wesleyan Univ. (1855) & La Grange College (1830), is "oldest existing St. Teachers College in South." **Bibb Graves Hall**, houses Lib. & Mus. (O.during school session) with Ind., pioneer & other colls. (3) E. Mobile & N. Seminary Sts., **Florence Curb Market** (O.Tues.& Sat.). (4) 220 E. Mobile St., **First Presb. Ch.** (c.1824). (5) W. city limits along Cypress Cr., **Wildwood Pk.** (170 as.pic.). (6) 231 N. Court St., **Simpson-Irvine H.** (O.appl.1830.Class.Rev.), has int. furniture & documents. (7) Pine & Tuscaloosa Sts., **Perry H.** (c.1850), brick structure built by Rbt. Brahan. (8) S. Chestnut & Park Sts., **Monumental Pk.,** amusement pk. where breastworks were erected by Confeds. against Fed. Col. A. D. Streight. (9) On US43 within city limits, **Lambert H.,** once inn on Nashville-Natchez stagecoach route & used as hospital during Civil War. (10) Within city limits also is ceremonial **Ind. Mound,** one of largest in Ala.

SIDE TRIP: (NW) of Florence on Cypress Mill Rd. c.5$^{m}$ to **The Forks of Cypress** (1820), built by Gen. Jas. Jackson. Andrew Jackson & Jas. Madison both spent time here, being, along with the owner, much interested in horse racing. Estate was supplied with excellent track. Plaster on columns said to be made of mixture of sand & molasses.

At Florence is J. with US72, which unites (S) with US43 to Tuscumbia. US43 (S) of Florence crosses Tenn. R. on bridge from which **Wilson Dam** may be seen (L), to reach **SHEFFIELD** at **23.,** 2nd of the "Tri-Cities" & industrial & RR. center of this area. Industries incl. iron mfg. & coal by-products. Town has experienced succession of booms since its origin as trading post (1815) & the buying of land in this reg. by Andrew Jackson & John Coffee (1816). Pk. Blvd. offers good view of **Pickwick L.** (f.boat.), an extension of Tenn. R. **25. TUSCUMBIA,** 3rd of the "Tri-Cities" on site of Chickasaw town raided & burned 1787 by Col. Jas. Robertson of Nashville & band of Cumberland settlers & Cherokee Inds. New town was platted by Gen. John Coffee & est. 1817. Tuscumbia is still bordered on 4 sides by old commons. In 1830's, canal was built around Muscle Shoals, & mule drawn RR., 1st RR. (W) of Alleghenies, laid bet. town & landing on Tenn. R. Tuscumbia was scene of minor engagements bet. Forrest's "critter army" & Feds. Ante bellum structures incl.: N. Main St., **Minor H.** (1820's) & **Goodloe H.** (1820's); 6th St., **Locust Hill** (1823); E. 4th St., **Pierce H.** (1820); N. Commons, **Johnson H.** (1837), **Winston H.** (1830's), & **Violet Hall** (1830's). On Keller Lane, **Ivy Green** (O.appl.), birthpl. of Helen Keller, who at age of 2, after attack of scarlet fever, lost sight & hearing. Under guidance of Anne Sullivan (Mrs. Macy), who remained her teacher & companion 49 yrs., she learned to speak & became internationally celebrated as author, lecturer & promoter of many social causes. Broad & 4th Sts., **First Presb. Ch.** (1824). In Legion Pk., **Big Spring,** daily output 55,000,000 gals., forms L. with outlet into Tenn. R. At Tuscumbia is S. J. with US72.

SIDE TRIP: Take latter (W) through rolling country of farms & ranches, once center of activity for outlaws who terrorized travelers on lonely stretches of Natchez Trace (see). In vic. of **Cherokee,** 16$^{m}$, are magnesia & sulphur wells, marble quarries & asphalt mines. At 17$^{m}$ (L) **Ind. Mound** visible. Just (S) of hy. beyond is **Barton Hall** (Class.Rev.) with int. stairway. At 19.5$^{m}$ on either side of hy. a L. has been formed by backwaters of **Pickwick Dam.** 24$^{m}$ US72 crosses Miss. Line.

**44. RUSSELLVILLE,** trading center named for Maj. Wm. Russell, commdr. of co. of Tenn. scouts in War of 1812, who sett. here after Battle of New Orleans.

SIDE TRIP: Take St.24 from Russellville (R) 8$^{m}$ to **Belgreen.** (S) 8$^{m}$ here on side Rd. to **The Dismals** or Wonder Gulch (L) with walls more than 100′ high. Caves, springs, pools, a stream, & luxuriant growth of mt. laurel & other flowering shrubs make this one of outstanding beauty spots of Ala.

**48. ISBELL.** (R) c.2.5$^{m}$ on side Rd. are ruins of **Cedar Cr. Furnace,** where iron was 1st smelted in Ala. (1818). **56. PHIL CAMPBELL.** J. with St.5.

SIDE TRIP: Take latter (SE) to **Haleyville,** 12m, hqs. of **Wm. B. Bankhead Nat. For.,** 560,604 as. of mountainous country forested with pine & hardwoods. Public hunts for deer, turkey & squirrel held annually. Recr. areas incl.: **Brushy L.,** 4m (NE) of Moreland (f. swim.pic.); **Sipsey R.** on Sipsey where crossed by Cranal Rd. (pic.shelters); & **Nat. Bridge** on Cheatham Hy. (pic.shelters). Bridge is sandstone formation 80′ x 15′ with arch of 30′ over a gorge with walls some 70′ high. **Clear Cr. Falls,** just (N) of Falls City, also attracts tourists.

**66. HACKLEBURG.** (NW) from here are traces of old Jackson Military Rd. **80. HAMILTON.** J. with US78 which unites (S) with US43 to Winfield. **101. WINFIELD,** S. J. with US78.

SIDE TRIP: (L) here on US78 to **Texas,** 9m, a mining town. In vic., beside New R., is Ind. mound. At **Eldridge,** 13m, are Ind. Springs & Baptist Academy (coed.) with school farm worked by self-help students. 37m **Jasper,** est. as trading center, 1815, now has coal mines & cotton & lumber mills. Jasper once boasted gallows tree from which, in 1850's, Lot Franklin was hanged on evidence given by 12-yr.-old son. "Tell the truth, son," he had said, "even if they break your father's neck." At last minute Gov. sent stay of execution, but sheriff, spurred on by mob, announced: "You've come here to see a hangin' & I'm not goin' to disappoint you."

**120. FAYETTE,** inc. in 1821, changed its name at least 6 times in 77 yrs.—Frog Level, Latone, Fayette Cth., Lafayette, Fayette Depot Town &, finally, Fayette. **134.** J. with Side Rd.

SIDE TRIP: (Take latter (L) 28m to **Parrish.** Take side Rd. here (S) c.10m to **Gorgas** where Bureau of Mines conducts experiments in underground coal gasification.

**167. TUSCALOOSA.** J. with US11 (see) & US82.

### Sec. 2: TUSCALOOSA to MOBILE. 211.

(S) of Tuscaloosa, hy. crosses Black Belt, wealthy cotton country since ante bellum days. Crops are much more diversified now & there are large apiaries. Bet. Tuscaloosa & **EUTAW** at **35.** US43 unites with US11 (see). **61. DEMOPOLIS.** J. with US80 (see). **74.** (R) **CHICKASAW ST. PK.** (640 as.hik.pic.). **78. LINDEN,** sett. by Napoleonic exiles. **124. GROVE HILL,** on Choctaw Ind. boundary est. by Brit. 1765, was known as Ft. White in 1813 when it was protection for pioneer settlers. **125.** J. with US84, which unites (S) with US43 to Wagarville. **141. JACKSON.** (S) of here in Tombigbee Swamp area, wild turkey & squirrel abound, & deer & black bear may be had. **148. LEROY,** once a gay cotton center, honors Leroy Bowling, host to Lafayette on latter's visit in 1825. **154. WAGARVILLE,** S. J. with US84, which leads (W) through heavily forested reg. to J. with St.29 & eventually to Miss. Line. **McINTOSH** at **167.,** lumber town in "Cajun" country (see Mobile Trip II).

SIDE TRIP: (R) here on side Rd. to **Black Gum Tree** (marked) where Aaron Burr was arrested by Capt. Edmund P. Gaines, Feb. 1807.

**211. MOBILE** (see), J. with US90 (see), US31 (see) & US45. (For pts. of int. bet. McIntosh & Mobile, see Mobile Trip I.)

# BIRMINGHAM

## BIRMINGHAM

Through RR., plane & bus conns. Water transportation to Gulf of Mexico from Birmingport, 18m W. Info.: C. of C.; Ala. Motorists Assoc., 1723 N. 6th Ave. Accoms.: All kinds. 48 pks., 8 playgrounds, 3 mun. golf courses. Fresh water f. & duck & quail h. in vic. Civic Symphony. Little Theater. Dogwood trl. & garden pilgrimage (Ap.-May).

Birmingham, Ala.'s largest city & 1 of most important industrial centers of the S., has largest steel furnaces (S) of Pittsburgh, a city to which it is often compared. Here is the new industrialized S. with almost no "before the war" antecedents & a tempo decidedly different from that of Montgomery or Mobile. City extends c.15m along Jones Valley in 1 of few regions of world where the 3 essentials for mfg. steel—iron, coal, & limestone—are found in close proximity in commercial quantities. Some mills & furnaces are in city proper, others in adj. Ensley, Fairfield & Bessemer. Birmingham district boasted (1949) some 761 industries incl. steel & iron & their products, heavy machinery, stoves, cement, chemicals, castings, textiles & furniture. It is said to lead world in production of cast iron pipe.

Some of the most fashionable estates (with gardens esp. notable for roses & dogwood) are on Red Mt., a mt. of iron ore whose red rock furnished Inds. with face & weapon paint. There was once a Creek trading post, Mad Town, a short distance (SE) & in 1813 John Jones & a few settlers est. Ft. Jonesborough at Bessemer. Wm. Ely, who came to sell land in area given to a New England deaf & dumb asylum by U.S. Gov., est. Elyton (1820's), now incorporated in Birmingham. Red Mt. ore was 1st used commercially in 1860 & Confeds. later used it for munitions. In 1871 Elyton Land Co. sold lots at new RR. junction that was to be Birmingham, 1st lot bringing $100. A cholera epidemic & a national financial panic followed almost immediately. But in Dec. 1873, Chas. Linn, a seafaring Finn, helped break local depression with a "Calico Ball" at his new bank to which guests from all parts of Ala. were invited. Since then iron & coal industries have continued to boom, though Birmingham has been scene of several long strikes.

PTS. OF INT. DOWNTOWN DISTRICT: (1) 716 N. 21st St., **Jefferson County Cth.** (O.wks.Sat.a.m.1931.Mod.by Holabird & Root) of Indiana limestone trimmed with Minn. granite, has stone carvings by Leo Friedlander & murals by John Norton & incl. cty. jail & law lib. (2) 700 N. 21st St., **Pub. Lib.,** with murals by Ezra Winter. Art Mus. on 3rd fl. has permanent coll. & exhibits traveling shows. (3) 7th Ave. at 20th St., **Woodrow Wilson Pk.** (8 as.with number of mons.). (4) 1830 8th Ave., **Elks Club** (1887.Vict.) was once, as Lane H., a center for city's most fashionable society. (5) 8th Ave. N. & 5th St., **A. H. Parker High Sch.** (O.school hrs.Negro), founded by son of freed slaves, particularly noted for its singing groups; said to be "largest Industrial High Sch. for Negroes in world." (6) 600 N. 18th St., **Ala. Power Co. Bldg.** (O.wks.Mod.vertical set-back style.by Warren, Knight & Davis). (7) 17th & 18th Sts. bet. 3rd & 5th, **Negro Bus. District,** used by Octavus Roy Cohen for many of his Negro stories. The Frolic, Famous & Champion Theaters & Pythian Bldg. figure in stories. (8) 1st Ave. & 32nd St., **Sloss Furnace** (O.appl.) mfg. pig iron presents spectacular scene at night & may be viewed from 1st Ave. viaduct. SOUTH SIDE: (9) On top of Red Mt. (US31) **Vulcan,** "largest iron man in world" & 2nd largest statue in U.S. (Liberty is larger), is 53′ tall, weighs 120,000 lbs. & stands on 125′ tower. Circular staircase leads to foot of statue. Designed by Guiseppi Moretti & made of pig iron, Vulcan was Birmingham's display at St. Louis Exposition, 1904. One thumb is 3′ long & weighs 175 lbs. Statue is surrounded by landscaped pk. Red Mt., composed of red hematite, offers excellent view of Birmingham & Jones Valley, especially impressive at night when blast furnaces light area. (10) **Shades Valley,** bet. Red & Shades Mts., is city's finest residential district. Summit of Shades Mt. (c.1,000′) is some 15$^{m}$ from heart of Birmingham. WEST SIDE: (11) 8th Ave. & 8th St., **Birmingham-Southern College** (coed.) is result of merger (1918) of Southern Univ. (Greensboro 1856) & Birmingham College (1898). Bldgs. are in Georg. style on a rolling wooded area commanding view of entire Birmingham valley. **Phillips Lib.** has McGregor coll. of early Americana. (12) 300 S. Center St., **Smith H.,** ante bellum H. in what was old Elyton. (13) 331 Cotton Ave., **Arlington H.** (1842.Georg.), hqs. of Fed. Gen. Wilson (1865) while destroying ironworks & Confed. supplies. EAST SIDE: (14) 5th Ave. & 21st St., **Avondale Pk.** (tennis.rose garden). (15) 7725 2nd Ave., **Howard College** (coed.Bapt.) began in 1842 when a sch. was opened to "nine little boys" in Marion, Ala. It attained status as college in 1848 & moved to Birmingham 1887. (16) 1st Ave. N. bet. 81st & 84th Sts., **East Lake Pk.** (swim.f.boat.). Other pts. of int. incl.: **Mountain Brook Club, Birmingham Country Club, Birmingham Little Theater, Independent Presb. Ch., Temple Emanu-el, Old First Presb. Ch., Walker Mem. Meth. Ch., Ruhama Bapt. Ch.**

## TRIPS OUT OF BIRMINGHAM

### I. BIRMINGHAM (NE) to SPRINGVILLE. 28.5. US11 & Side Rd.

At **8.5.** on US11 is J. with side Rd. on which cont. (L). **11.5. SPRING LAKE FARMS,** fenced by climbing roses. Incl. as part of present house is log cabin built by "Silver Billy" Reed, land speculator who drove around in a wagon loaded with kegs seemingly full of silver dollars & would only do business with silver. **19.5. CRYSTAL CAVERNS** (O.sm.fee) with c.1$^{m}$ of electrically lighted caverns, with stalactites & stalagmites, discovered 1840 & used as source of saltpeter during Civil War. At **25.5.** side Rd. rejoins US11. **28.5. SPRINGVILLE.** In center of town is walled spring stocked with tame fish that eat from the hand.

**II. BIRMINGHAM (E) to ANNISTON. 65. US78**

**18. LEEDS,** founded 1881, has large cement mfg. co. **29. COOKS SPRINGS** offers inviting pic. places near its mineral springs. **37. PELL CITY,** a textile mill town. **65. ANNISTON** (see US241).

**III. BIRMINGHAM (SE) to SYLACAUGA. 51. St.91**

St.91 crosses 3 ridges—Red, Shades & Double Oaks Mts.—through a residential sec. of large estates & then to a truck & dairying reg. At **2.** beyond Red Mt. is **LANE PK.** (203 as.bridle paths.pic.fish hatchery). The steep roadside in the Shades Mt. area is bright with violets, daisies, wild azaleas & dogwood in season. At **11.** is J. with side Rd. (L) here 2$^m$ to **L. Purdy** (f.duck h.). At **39.** on St.91 is **CHILDERSBURG,** with Mon. marking De Soto's route. A short distance (L) is **Site of Coosa Town** described by De Soto's secy. Ranjel as capital of a large area. Ind. graves containing Sp. relics have been uncovered in vic. At **51.** on St.91 is **SYLACAUGA** (Ind. "Buzzard Roost") whose quarries have supplied marble for U.S. Supreme Court Bldg., Lincoln Mem. & Presidential Palace, Havana. Cotton States Tennis Tournament held here in June. Sylacauga is at S. end of Talladega St. Pk. (see US241) & its Skyway Hy. which offers almost 100$^m$ of some of most striking Mt. scenery in Ala.

**IV. BIRMINGHAM (S) to OAK MT. ST. PK. 23. US31 & Side Rd.**

On US31 (S) at **6.** is J. with Shades Crest Rd.

SIDE TRIP: Take latter (L) 1$^m$ to **Vestavia,** home of former mayor of Birmingham. A copy of Temple of Vesta in Rome in red sandstone, it is a 2-storied circular H. surrounded by pillared portico. Across Rd. is miniature of temple of the Sibyl in Tivoli.

**17.** J. with side Rd. (L) here at **23.** is **OAK MT. ST. PK.** (940 as.) & **OAK MT. RECR. AREA** (8,200 as.hik.swim.cabins.lake.streams.falls).

**V. BIRMINGHAM (SW) to BESSEMER. 13. US11**

On US11 (SW), on outskirts of Birmingham, mine tipples & miners' houses are red with dust of red ore mines. **4.5. FAIR PK.** & J. with side Rd.

SIDE TRIP: (R) here 2.5$^m$ to **Ensley Steel Works** (O.appl.), one of 7$^m$-long line of plants that incl. blast furnaces, soaking pits, Bessemer converters, a rail mill, wire & nail mills & tin-plate mill. The fiery furnaces, belching smoke stacks, massive machinery & streams of molten ore make it easy to understand the cotton planter's comment: "This looks like hell to me!"

At **13.** on US11, is **BESSEMER,** founded 1887 & named in honor of Sir Henry Bessemer, inventor of Bessemer process of steel-making, is industrial & trading center for surrounding coal & iron mining settlements. Among larger plants are **Pullman Car & Mfg. Corp.** (O.appl.) & **U.S. Pipe & Foundry Co.** (O.appl.). **West Lake** & **Pineview Beach** are near-by recr. centers.

**VI. BIRMINGHAM (NW) to JASPAR. 45. US78**

(NW) from Birmingham US78 passes through rugged coal reg. **15. GRAYSVILLE,** a mining town. (R) here 4$^m$ to **Brookside,** sett. by Russians (1902) & still preserving certain Russian customs, especially at Christmas. **45. JASPAR,** another coal mining town.

# MOBILE

**MOBILE**

Through RR., plane & bus conns. SS. lines conn. with most world ports. Intracoastal canal conns. with Fla. & Texas. Accoms.: All kinds. Info.: C. of C. & A.A.A. 15 pks.; 3 golf courses; beaches on E. & W. shores of Mobile Bay. Fresh & salt water f. Mardi Gras (Feb. or Mar.), 5 days ending with Shrove Tues. Azalea Festival (Feb. or Mar.); 18$^m$ Azalea trl. Ala. Deep Sea Rodeo (July or Aug.).

Mobile, on W. side of Mobile Bay, Ala.'s only seaport & 1st permanent white settlement in st., offers an int. combination of old & new. Early 19th cent. houses, some with iron lacework balconies, stand side by side with modern structures. A 5-day Mardi Gras, with balls, parades & other revels, that can be traced back to Bienville's institution of the "Masque de la St. Louis" in 1704, vies with azalea festival (org.1929) that boasts 18$^m$ azalea trl. beginning in heart of city. Fish. & boat. have made Mobile a popular winter resort. Ala. State Docks, 1st complete st.-owned & operated plant of its kind in U.S., services more than 40 regular & 20 other SS. lines to ports all over world & have given Mobile (1949) claim of being 4th port in vol. of imports, 14th in vol. of exports.

Mobile Bay appears on the Waldeseemüller Map of 1505 & on Pineda's map of explorations in 1519. Narvaez was here (1528) & De Luna est. short-lived Sp. settlement in reg. (1559). In 1702 Bienville est. Ft. Louis de la Mobile (honoring Louis XIV & Mobile Inds.) 27m up Mobile R. In 1711 settlement moved to present site, Ft. Condé was erected & Mobile became capital of Fr. colonial empire until 1719 when transfer was made to Biloxi. Fr. ceded Mobile to Brit. 1763, & ft. was renamed Ft. Charlotte. Sp. fleet under Galvez took it from Brit., 1780, & Sp. held on until Amers. under Gen. Wilkinson forced them out, 1813. Confeds. occupied Mobile 1861 & held it for 3 yrs. though Fed. blockade considerably reduced its importance. In Battle of Mobile Bay, Aug. 5, 1864, Adm. Farragut sank Confed. ram "Tennessee." Ft. Gaines & Ft. Morgan soon fell & Gens. E. R. S. Canby & F. Steel took Mobile Ap. 12, 1865, 3 days after Lee's surrender at Appomattox. In Reconstruction Mobile cont. as important cotton port & experienced less hardship than other secs. of Ala. World Wars I & II both brought large booms, especially in shipbuilding & repairing; 3 shipyards are still maintained & U.S. Maritime Commission has selected Tensas Basin near Bay Minette as anchorage for laid up fleet of 1,000 ships. Mobile is one of nation's most important producers of pulp, paper & paper products. Other industries incl. textiles, iron & steel, cement, timber products, naval stores, alumina & oil-refining. Commercial fishing is also important.

PTS. OF INT. BUS. SEC. & PORT: (1) Dauphin & Joseph Sts., **Bienville Sq.,** starting pt. of **Azalea Trl.** (turn (L) on Conception St.), has cannon from Fr. Ft. Condé (1717-63) & cannon from Brit. Ft. Charlotte (1763-79). (2) Royal & Government Sts., **County Cth.** (1874.Gr.Rev.). In rear is plaque marking site of **Ft. Condé,** later Ft. Charlotte. (3) Royal & Government Sts., **Statue** of Adm. Raphael Semmes. (4) Royal & Church Sts., **City Hall** (1852) was built as market & used by Confeds. as armory & soup kitchen. Hist. murals by J. Augustus Walker. (5) 104 Theater St., **Kirkbride H.** (rest.) was Mobile's 1st cth. & jail & now houses Hist. Soc. Foundations are thought to be part of Ft. Charlotte. (6) 56-58 S. Conception St., **Fr. H.** (c.1820) has cast-iron balconies & carriage drive through center. (7) St. Emanuel & Church Sts., **Christ Ch.** (1828-40.Gr.Rev.), on site of "the church" built in 1711 & used by all Protestant denominations. (8) St. Francis & Royal Sts., **Old Customh.** (1854), now housing C. of C., has handsome wrought-iron gates, & is hqs. for Azalea Trl. (9) Royal & St. Michael St., **Old Register Bldg.** (c.1804), once Inn where Lafayette was entertained, later housed Mobile "Register." (10) 308 Conti St., **Durand H.** (1796), probably oldest standing structure in Mobile. (11) 8-10 N. Jackson St., **H. of Two Cities,** erected 1820 in Blakeley, taken down & rowed across Mobile R. by slaves & then rebuilt in present location; 2-stories with ground fl. cut by carriage drive. (12) Government & Jackson Sts., **Presb. Ch.** (1836.by Jas.Dakin. Gr.Rev.) embodies Ionic, Gothic, & Corinthian motifs. (13) Claiborne bet. Conti & Dauphin Sts., **Cathedral of Immaculate Conception** (1839-50.Cath.Class.Rev.adds.). Across from Cathedral (SW.cor.) is **Portier H.,** built for Bishop of Mobile (1830). (14) Government & Lawrence Sts., **Barton Academy** (1836), used as Confed. hospital. (15) Waterfront at Beauregard St., **Ala. St. Docks,** mod. ocean terminal system costing $13,000,000. (16) Riverfront & Dauphin St., **Banana Wharf.** (17) Levee & Government St., **Fruit Wharf & Wareh.** (18) Beauregard & Commerce St., **Molasses** Terminal. (19) Pinto I. across Mobile R., **Ala. Dry Docks & Shipbuilding Plant.** (20) Foot of Eslava St., **Oyster Docks,** landing place for oyster & shrimp fishermen. RESIDENTIAL SEC.: (21) 701 Government St., **Pub. Lib.** has Hist. Mus. with special coll. of African, Ind., & Oriental weapons, a Fine Arts Dept. with monthly exhibits, & phonograph record coll. (22) Rear of Lib. bet. Bayou St. & Washington Ave., **Old Ch. St. Graveyard,** has graves of Napoleonic exiles incl. that of Marquis De Vaubercy, last of the Lords of Champagne. (23) 802 Government St., **Admiral Semmes H.** (1858.iron-work balcony) was bought by popular subscription in 1871 for Confed. naval hero Raphael Semmes, who commanded the "Alabama" &, with Eng. crew & flag, captured over 60 prizes before the "Alabama" was sunk. (24) Springhill Ave. & St. Francis St., **Father Ryan Statue,** mem. to poet-patriot of Confed. (25) St. Anthony & Broad Sts., **City Hospital** (1825.Gr.Rev.). (26) Head of George St., **Magnolia Cemetery** contains graves of Gen. Braxton Bragg, Joe Jefferson, the elder, & Wm. Petrie, star of the "Black Crook" & "St. Elmo." (27) Government & Houston Sts., **Soldiers & Sailors Mem. Pk.,** showplace of Azalea Trl. (28) 1906 Springhill Ave., **Gen. Braxton Bragg H.,** built by his brother John. (29) 1456 Government St., **Blacksher's Gardens.** (30) Springhill & Lanier Aves., **Convent of**

**the Visitation** (1832). (31) 1810 Springhill Ave., **Harry Hardy Smith Town Garden.** (32) Other int. old houses incl.: Conti & Jackson Sts., **Craft H.** (1855); 303 Conti St., **Jordan Place** (1843); 503 Government St., **Maury H.** (c.1840); 1664 Springhill Ave., **Walsh H.** (c.1830); 963 Springhill Ave., **Acker H.** (c.1840); St. Anthony & Franklin Sts., **Gliddon H.** (1840); 256 W. Joachim St., **Richards H.** (1845.rest.). (33) Just (W) of Mobile in a residential suburb on Old Shell Rd. is **Spring Hill College,** a Jesuit college for men, est. 1830 by Bishop Portier assisted by money from an uncle of Napoleon. Campus (700 as.) has some of oldest & largest azalea bushes on trl. (20′ high, 100′ circum.). On grounds are Gothic Chapel, a shrine of St. Joseph & a replica of shrine of Our Lady of Lourdes in France.

## TRIPS OUT OF MOBILE

### I. MOBILE (N) to MT. VERNON. 29. US43

**3. PRICHARD.**

SIDE TRIP: (L) from Prichard 1.5m is **Plateau,** home of **Southern Kraft Paper Mill** (O. appl.). Here also is "Afriky Town" whose inhabitants are descendants of shipload of slaves brought over from Guinea Coast long after importation had become illegal. Capt. Tim Meaher, slave smuggler, had difficulty in disposing of his cargo, burned his ship, the "Clothilde," & left most of Negroes to fend for themselves in the swamps.

**6. CHICKASAW,** excellent fishing. At **c.22.** (R) is **TWENTY-SEVEN-MILE BLUFF** on Mobile R., Site of Ft. Louis de la Mobile, est. by Bienville, 1702. In vic. in unmarked grave lies Henri de Tonti, adventurer & explorer (c.1650-1704), whose iron hook, substituted for a hand lost in battle, caused him to be called "the man with the iron hand." At **23.** is **ELLICOTT'S STONE,** (R) just across RR., marking 31° N. Lat., boundary bet. Sp. & U.S. territory in 1799. **29. MOUNT VERNON,** military post in 1811. (R) from here 2.5m to **Site of Ft. Stoddert** where Aaron Burr was imprisoned before being sent to Richmond, & where, in 1887, Chief Geronimo of the Apache was brought after capture in Mexico. Near-by is grave of Ephraim Kirby (d.1802), early prohibition agitator.

### II. MOBILE (NW) to MISS. LINE. 62. US45

(NW) of Mobile on US45, **TOULMINVILLE,** an early suburb, now part of the metropolitan area of Mobile, was birthpl. of Wm. Crawford Gorgas, sanitation expert who rid Canal Zone area of yellow fever. Here also on Wilson Ave., **Gen. Theophilus Lindsey Toulmin H.,** haunted by ghost of Gen. & scene of many midnight searches for buried treasure. **3. WHISTLER,** so-named because a train engineer always greeted 1st surveyors here with special blasts from locomotive whistle. Many stamp collectors have acquired its postmark on stamp that reproduces Jas. McNeil Whistler's "The Artist's Mother." At **31.5.** J. with dirt Rd. that leads (R) to old hy. (R) here to **Cedar Creek St. Pk.** (640 as.h.f.boat.cabins). **34. CITRONELLE,** center of tung oil district. In vic. are settlements of "Ala. Cajuns." Unlike Cajuns of La., they are not descendants from Acadians of Canada but from early Fr., Sp., & Eng. pioneers who married Ind. women. Some add Mex. buccaneers to ancestors; others have been said to have Negro blood. Arguments over social status have been bitter. "Cajuns" are not allowed in Ala.'s white colleges; special grade schs. have been provided for them. **48. VINEGAR BEND,** so-named because moonshiners, smuggling whiskey to lumber camps operated here by convict labor, when caught always claimed to be carrying jugs of vinegar. **62.** US45 crosses **MISS. LINE.**

### III. MOBILE (SE) to FT. MORGAN. 73.5. US90, Bay Shore Rd. & St.3

(E) from Mobile across Cochrane Bridge to J. with Bay Shore Rd. at **11.** (S) on this Rd. along E. shore of Mobile Bay to series of resort & fishing towns. **12. JACKSON OAK,** St. Mon. (R), under which Jackson's troops camped on way to Pensacola, 1814. Here backwoods soldiers wanted to return to their farms, but "Old Hickory" denounced them & threatened to shoot 1st who turned back. **15. DAPHNE** has had an Ital. colony that intended to cultivate vineyards but switched to citrus fruit with Prohibition, & a Greek colony run on cooperative lines. **20.5. FAIRHOPE,** sett. 1893-94 by group from Des Moines, Iowa, as single tax colony based on Henry George theory, is winter & summer resort (f.fresh & salt.h.swim. beach). There is **Ind. Mound** at Knoll Pk. **Sch. of Organic Education** (est.1907) made early experiments in progressive education. **26. POINT CLEAR,** sett. 1820, by pioneers from Mass., became popular resort soon after Civil War. **Gunnison H.**

has cannonball hole covered by brass plate inscribed "Compliments of Admiral Farragut, 1865." Route now turns (L) through a piney woods turpentine-producing sec. **35. McKENZIE'S FERRY** (sm.toll) crossing **Fish R.** (f.duck.h.accoms.). **39. MAGNOLIA SPRINGS,** fishing resort. **44.5. FOLEY,** J. with St.3 & St.89.

SIDE TRIP: (E) on St.89 11m to J. with dirt Rd. (R) here 6m to **Perdido Beach** (f.swim. boat.). At 15.5m on St.89 is **Lillian** where toll bridge crosses Perdido Bay to Fla. (f.boat. guides).

Return to Foley & cont. (S) on St.3. At **47.5.** is side Rd. (R) short distance to **Bon Secour,** resort & fish & oyster center (boats to Dauphin Is.). **54.5. GULF ST. PK.** (4,582 as.;mile-long beach.3 Ls.fresh & salt water f.boat.cabins.guides). Pk. is 27m long, extending from Cotton Bayou (the Pk. harbor) to Ft. Morgan, & never really closes as climatic conditions justify yr.-round vacations. At **73.5.** hy. ends at **FT. MORGAN,** a popular pic. spot. Ft. Bowyer was fortified here during War of 1812 & held off Brit. fleet, Sept. 15, 1814. Brit. later captured Ft. In 1837 it was regarrisoned & named Morgan in honor of hero of Mex. War. Confeds. seized it but lost it to Adm. Farragut during Battle of Mobile Bay. It was regarrisoned again during Sp.-Amer. War & World War I. From Ft. Morgan, **Dauphin I.** (reached by boat from Bon Secour & Mobile) is visible.

**IV. MOBILE (S) to BELLINGRATH GARDENS. 20. West Bay Shore Rd.**

(S) from Mobile along Rd. that borders W. shore of Mobile Bay [or (W) on US90 to Theodore & then (S)], to **BELLINGRATH GARDENS** at **20.** ($1.00 plus tax), a high point of Mobile Azalea Trl. On **ISLE-AUX-OIES (Fowl) R.,** some 100 as., of which more than 60 have been landscaped, offer century-old-moss-hung oaks under which, & frequently reflected in lagoons, have been planted azaleas (more than 100,000 specimens, 125 varieties), camellia-japonicas (2,000 specimens, 375 varieties) & many other brilliantly flowered shrubs & plants. Camellias start blooming in Oct. & last till Ap., azaleas are at best Feb. & Mar. & are followed by mountain laurel, dogwood, & spiraea, later by hydrangeas & gardenias. In summer there are crape myrtles, oleanders, magnolias & hibiscus.

**V. MOBILE (S) to DAUPHIN I. 25.**

From Mobile (S) by boat (no schedule) **25.** is **DAUPHIN I.,** orig. called Massacre I. by Fr. because of skeleton-strewn beach encountered when they arrived in 1699 & est. base for colonization of "Louisiana." Devastated by Eng. privateers (1711), & 2 bad storms (1717 & 1740), it became Sp. possession 1762, Eng. 1763, & Sp. again 1783. Sp. held it until Ap. 1813 when it was seized by Gen. Jas. Wilkinson, U.S.A. **Ft. Gaines** was erected here 1822 in E. point; later **Ft. Powell** was est. on mainland at other side of Grant's Pass at Cedar Pt. Latter's guns may be seen at low tide. Both important in Civil War. Deep Sea Fishing Rodeo held here July or Aug.

**VI. MOBILE (SW) to CODEN. 29. US90 & Side Rd.**

**14. THEODORE.** J. with side Rd. (S) on this Rd. to **Bellingrath Gardens** 20m (see above). **20. IRVINGTON.** J. with side Rd. on which cont. (S). At **27.5.** is **BAYOU LA BATRE,** picturesque oystering & shrimping village. La Fitte & his pirates often used Bayou & there are many tales of buried treasure. Rd. cont. to **CODEN** at **29.** (corrupt Fr. for "Coq d'Inde," turkey gobbler), resort & fishing village (tarpon, kingfish, mackerel, pompano).

## US 82—MISSISSIPPI

**MISS.-ALA. LINE** (18m from Reform, Ala.) **(W) to MISS.-ARK. LINE** (9m from Lake Village, Ark.). **178. US82**

Via: Columbus, Starkville, Winona, Greenwood & Greenville. Columbus & Greenville RR. parallels route throughout. Accoms.: In towns.

US82 journeys from Black Prairie reg. around Columbus, through pine lands & swampland to the bluff country beyond Winona, & finally, to the Delta flatlands.

### Sec. 1: MISS.-ALA. LINE to WINONA. 90.

**9. COLUMBUS**

Through RR. & bus conns. Good accoms. Spring Pilgrimage. Horse Show, July. Fox Hunts, Nov.

Columbus, trade & industrial center for cotton, hay, grass seed, lumber, cattle, & bee & honey producing area, is quiet town where mod. façades stand in close proximity to columns of ante bellum mansions. De Soto, in 1540, entered Miss. just N. of Columbus & 200 yrs. later Bienville passed through reg. Choctaw ceded land to U.S., 1816. In 1817 1st log cabin was built & soon after Spirus Roach opened a tavern near J. of the Tombigbee ("box maker") & Luxapalila ("floating turtle") Rs. Inds. called settlement "Possum Town" in reference to Roach's physical appearance. Aristocratic settlers from Va. & Carolinas renamed it Columbus. Town was inc. in 1821 & Franklin Academy est. A female college (1847) grew into present Miss. St. College for Women. Many citizens objected to coming of RR. & some cont. to plant cotton along tracks, thereby forcing company to fence in rails. Confed. arsenal was est. here & town served briefly as St. capital. Jefferson Davis, serenaded one night by citizens, got up & addressed them in his nightshirt. Miss. Foxhunter's Assoc. holds hunts in vic. Nat. Foxhunters Assoc. had its origin at Waverly (see below) in 1893.

PTS. OF INT.: (1) 6th St. & 2nd Ave. N., **Christian Ch.** (Goth.Rev.), seat of St. Legislature in 1863 after Sherman burned Jackson. (2) 5th St. & 3rd Ave. N., **Old Franklin Academy** (Gr.Rev.), founded 1821, was 1st free school in Miss. (3) 7th St. & 3rd Ave. N., **Lee H.** (1844.Georg.int.iron grillwork), now part of high school, was home of Gen. Stephen D. Lee, aide-de-camp to Gen. Beauregard, who gave order to fire on Ft. Sumter. (4) 824 N. 7th St., **Leigh Crest** (1841.Gr.Rev.). (5) 8th St. & 6th Ave. N., **Meek Place** (1854.Gr.Rev.int.exter.) built by Col. Cannon whose widow married Alex. B. Meek, author of "Songs of the South." (6) 9th St. & 6th Ave. N., **Temple Heights** (1843.Gr.Rev.). (7) 9th St. & 3rd Ave. N., **Snowdown** (c.1854), patterned after Jefferson's Monticello. (8) 11th St. & 2nd Ave. S., **Miss. St. College for Women** (1884), 1st st.-supported institute of higher learning exclusively for women in U.S. Seniors carry a "Magnolia" chain at commencement. (9) 514 S. 2nd St., **Riverview** (1844.Georg.). (10) 2nd St. & 5th Ave. S., **Woodward H.** (1833.raised cottage.rest.). (11) 4th St. & 13th Ave. S., **Friendship Cemetery.** Here Mem. Day had its origin, Ap. 26, 1866, when women of town decorated graves of both Confed. & Union soldiers, an act which led Francis M. Finch to write "The Blue & the Gray." "Official" Mem. Day was inaugurated 1868 by Fed. Gen. John A. Logan (12) 9th St. & 13th Ave., **Rosedale** (1855.Ital.influence). In vic. are (13) **Whitehall** & (14) **Camellia Place** (1843). At Columbus is J. with US45 (see), St.12 & St.69.

SIDE TRIPS: (A) On St.12 (N) 9m is **Belmont (1822-25). Near-by are** springs where De Soto is said to have camped in 1540.

(B) On old US45 (N), then (L) at every turn, **7.5m,** is **Waverley** (1856), elaborate mansion built on plan of an "H" with wings conn. by an octagonal central hall with dome. Below Waverley 2m (no Rds.) is J. of Tombigbee R., with Tibee Cr., **Site of Plymouth.** Bits of armor & Sp. military equipment have been found here. Place thought to have been camping ground for De Soto, base of Bienville's operations against Chickasaw, & Andrew Jackson's base against Creek Inds.

(C) On US45 (N) 28m is **Aberdeen,** ante bellum plantation town, now cotton & dairying center.

PTS. OF INT.: (1) **St. Johns Ch.** (Episc.1850) with slave loft. (2) **Old Homestead** (1852. adds.). (3) **Prewitt H.** (1850) built by wealthy "foot-washing" Bapt. minister. (4) **The Magnolias** (1849). (5) **Reuben Davis H.** (1847.Gr.Rev.adds.). Davis practiced both medicine & law & on one occasion, it is said, in a murder trial, used red pepper in his handkerchief to produce tears. (6) **Paine H.** (1847.Georg.rest.). (7) **The Oaks** (c.1840). (8) **Parson Mann H.** (c.1840) of logs. (9) **Acker H.** (1842); int. garden. (10) **Holliday Haven** (1850). (11) **Ten Acres** (1837) on orig. 10-a. block. (12) Near-by is **Mon.** to S. A. Jonas, local editor & author of "Lines on the Back of a Confederate Note." (13) **Magnolia Hill** (1850). (14) On Cemetery Rd., **Old Cemetery.** Among mons. is one of woman in flames in memory, it is said, of lady whose hoop skirts caught on fire.

(D) On US45 (S) 30m is **Macon,** briefly seat of gov. after fall of Jackson. Here is J. with St.14.

Take latter (E) 8m to **Bankhead H.,** where W. B. Bankhead, once speaker of H. of Rep. & father of actress Tallulah, was married. Take St.14 (W) 11m to **Mashulaville,** once large Choctaw town. Just beyond Mashulaville is J. with dirt Rd. (L) on this Rd. 8m to **Dancing Rabbit Treaty Marker.** Here in 1830, some 20,000 Choctaw gathered to consider treaty by which ⅓ of north-central Miss. was ceded to U.S. Half-breeds were for, full-blooded Inds. against, treaty; but Greenwood Leflore (see) achieved a compromise.

**23.** J. with St.45 (see). **32. STARKVILLE,** once home of landed aristocracy from coastal states, has a number of ante bellum Hs. in vic. & is seat of **Miss. St. College** (coed.1878) founded as land grant college. On 4,200-a. campus are schools of agric., science, engineering, education, business & pre-medicine, & Experiment Sta. that incl. farms, pastures & woodlands. On Louisville St., **Gillespie H.** (1850.Gr.Rev.). Just (N) of town on St.23, **Montgomery H.** (1843.Georg.remod.).

SIDE TRIP: From rear of St. college campus gravel Rd. ("beat 5") leads (L) 5m to **Dorsey Outlaw H.** (c.1840). At 6.5m **Rice H.** (c.1842). Mantels in both houses were carved by slave-convict in chains, named Cooper. 9m **Gibeon H.** (c.1820), log house that once served as an inn run by David Folsom, half-breed Choctaw chief who in 1821 became a charter member of the Masonic Lodge organized in Columbus. Cemetery near-by is said to contain victims of drunken fights.

**59. EUPORA,** scene of many violent 19th cent. feuds, one of which ended with murder of almost entire Gray family by the Edwards' faction at near-by Greensboro jail. **90. WINONA.** J. with US51 (see).

### Sec. 2: WINONA to ARK. LINE. 88.

**26. GREENWOOD** (see US51). **80. GREENVILLE** (see US61). **88.** Toll bridge to Ark.

## US 80—MISSISSIPPI

**MISS.-ALA. LINE** (19m from Livingston, Ala.) **(W) to MISS.-LA. LINE** (78m from Monroe, La.). **158. US80**

Via: Meridian, Jackson & Vicksburg. Ala. & Gt.S. RR. parallels route bet. Ala. Line & Meridian; Yazoo & Miss. Valley RR. bet. Meridian & Vicksburg. Accoms.: All kinds in cities.

US80 crosses center of Miss. through its 3 largest cities (incl. the capital) from red hills of E. to a central prairie sec. & then to the bluffs at Vicksburg.

### Sec. 1: MISS. LINE to FOREST. 69. US80

**2. KEWANEE,** once home of Pushmataha, Choctaw chief who out-maneuvered Tecumseh's attempt to unite Inds. in War of 1812.

**19. MERIDIAN**

Through RR., bus & plane (Delta Air Line) conns. Good accoms. Miss. Fair & Dairy Show, Oct.

Meridian is RR. & mfg. center for reg. producing cotton, tobacco, fruit, vegetables, poultry & lumber & has one of st.'s largest stockyards. City is situated in foothills of the Appalachians. Neighboring woodlands are broken by outcroppings of limestone. Rich. McLemore of S.C. est. plantation here in 1831 & in 1854 a junction of Vicksburg & Montgomery RR. & Mobile & Ohio Line was planned. The 1st train from Vicksburg arrived in 1861. Early settlers disputed violently over name Meridian (some wanted Sowashee—Ind., "mad river") & over the laying out of town. In 1863 st. records were moved here & for 1 month Meridian was st. capital. In 1864, Sherman came through. He wrote in his official report: "For five days, 10,000 men worked hard with a will in that work of destruction . . . Meridian . . . no longer exists." Today Meridian is 2nd largest city in Miss. It adopted city-manager form of gov. in 1949. 23rd Ave. & 11th St., **Scottish Rite Cathedral,** designed in manner of famous temple at Philae, Egypt. 1009 18th St., **McLemore H.,** built around log cabin (1837) of 1st settler. 7th St. & 40th Ave., **Rose Hill Cemetery** with graves of Emil Mitchell (1942) & his wife, Kelly (1915), king & queen of all gypsies in U.S. The queen was buried in Romany costume strung with gold coins dating back to 18th cent. 16th St. & 38th Ave., **Highland Pk.** (43 as.swim.pool.arboretum). At Meridian are Js. with US45 (see), US11 (see) & St.39.

SIDE TRIPS: (A) On US45 (N) at 2.5m is gravel Rd., which leads (R) to **U.S. Horticultural & Sugar Plant Stas.**

(B) On US45 (S) along Roebucks Dr. across scenic Appalachian foothills 23m is **Clarkco St. Pk.** (792 as.f.swim.boat.cabin).

(C) On US11 (S) 2m is **Meridian Air Base** (Key Field). At 15m is **W. Enterprise.** (R) here on narrow Rd. 3m is **Dunn's Falls** (swim.).

(D) On St.39 (N) 17m is gravel Rd. which leads (L) to **Grave of Sam Dale,** picturesque trader & frontiersman, who in 1831 was appointed by Secy. of War to move Choctaw to Ind. lands in West. At 34m on St.39 is **De Kalb,** scene of massacre of Carpetbag judge & family by K.K.K. that gave cty. the name of "Bloody Kemper."

US80 (S) of Meridian passes through a number of small sawmill towns. 35. **CHUNKY,** whose name is an Anglicized version of name of a Choctaw game. 41. **HICKORY,** named after "Old Hickory," Andrew Jackson, said to have camped just S. of town in 1815. **50. NEWTON,** home of **Clarke Mem. Jr. College,** has lumber & cottonseed oil mills. Here is J. with St.15.

SIDE TRIPS: (A) On St.15 (N) from Newton, 17$^{m}$, is **Union,** on site of Ind. village Chauki, settled in 1829 & burned by Sherman, 1863. 36$^{m}$ **Philadelphia,** heart of Miss.'s Ind. country. In vic. live greatest number of the c.2,000 Inds. remaining in st., descendants of Choctaw warriors who refused to part with their lands in 1830. Choctaw Ind. Agency, est. here 1918, incl. hospital & a no. of day schools. Income of Inds. derives mostly from farming, though men make splitoak-bottom chairs & women weave brightly-colored baskets. Neshoba Cty. Fair (sm.fee.July or Aug.), held at near-by fairgrounds, incl. evening of tribal games & dances.

(B) From Newton (S) St.15 enters a long-leaf pine sec. of the "Piney Woods," & at **Montrose** 18$^{m}$ passes through corner of Bienville Nat. For. Bet. **Bay Springs** 29$^{m}$, a sawmill town, & **Laurel** (see US11) 53$^{m}$ is stretch of cut-over land & abandoned sawmills, land robbed of its timber wealth in space of 25 yrs.

**60. LAKE.** J. with gravel Rd.

SIDE TRIP: Take latter (R) 2$^{m}$ to **Patrons' Union Campground** where Aug. sessions of the Granges of adj. ctys. are held on agric., education & other subjects. 9$^{m}$ **Conehatta,** home of an Ind. Day School.

**69. FOREST** (see) J. with St.35.

### Sec. 2: FOREST to LA. LINE. 89. US80

**11. MORTON.**

SIDE TRIP: At c.4$^{m}$ (S) of Morton on side Rd. is **Roosevelt St. Pk.** (562 as.pic.swim.boat. f.cabins.sports facils.refreshments) in a countryside brilliant in spring with redbud, dogwood & wild azaleas.

**45. JACKSON,** st. capital (see US51). **55. CLINTON** (see US61). **89. VICKSBURG** with hist. battlefield & ante bellum Hs. (see US61). At Vicksburg US80 crosses toll bridge over Miss. R. to La.

## US 90—MISSISSIPPI

**MISS.-ALA. LINE** (30$^{m}$ from Mobile, Ala.) **(W) to MISS.-LA. LINE** (41$^{m}$ from New Orleans, La.). **82. US90**

Via: Pascagoula, Biloxi, Gulfport, Bay St. Louis. Louisville & Nashville RR. parallels route throughout. 2-lane hy. hugs coastline. Through bus conns. Airport: Gulfport. Accoms.: All kinds. Bait, tackle, boats & guides avail. throughout. Gulf shallow in most places, beware of diving.

US90 follows Old Spanish Trl. along Miss. Gulf Coast, yr.-round resort area. Here are oldest settlements in Miss. R. Valley. Through this legendary country—1st sett. by Fr. 1699, taken over by Brit. 1763 & then by Sp. 1781—hy. passes almost continuous succession of fine houses & resort hotels which, set deep in gardens, look out upon Gulf of Mexico. Wooden piers, diving platforms, & boat landings jut out from sea wall which extends along most of coast. Live oaks hung with Sp. moss, magnolias, pines, palms. Sp. daggers, azaleas, crapemyrtles, camellias & poinsettias provide luxuriant foliage & brilliantly-colored blossoms throughout yr. Unlike the rest of Miss., which is almost entirely Anglo-Saxon Protestant, the Coast has a Latin, Cath. ancestry. A Latin gaiety is always evident. Fishing is principal industry & furnishes basis of gumbos, jambalayas, & "courts-bouillons" which, in some instances, rival fare to be had in New Orleans. In many ways "The Coast" has a greater affinity to that city than it has to the rest of Miss. The st. is dry; but all along the coast bars are open day & night & natives & tourists (whose amusements constitute 2nd industry of area) may drink &, in most places, enjoy slot machines, keno, & other games of chance as well. Gulf provides such game fish as silver tarpon, Sp. & king mackerel, & sea trout. Various fishing "rodeos" are held. Inland streams offer bass, striped bass, crappie, bream & perch all year round. Whole families indulge in "crabbing," using a combination of lines & dip-nets or baited drop-nets, & on summer evenings flounders are speared by torchlight in shallow water along sea wall. Bird hunting (quail,duck,geese) along coast is excellent. Wild turkey & deer are also to be had.

At **5.** J. with side Rd. (L) 2$^{m}$ on this Rd. is **Kreole,** pioneer town in mfg. kraft paper.

**11. MOSS POINT** at J. of Escatawpa & Pascagoula Rs.

**13. PASCAGOULA** (Ind. "bread people"), sett. soon after Pascagoula Bay granted to Duchess de Chaumont by Louis XIV. Brit. took over in 1763, Sp. in 1781, & settlement became part of St. of W. Florida, 1810. Zachary Taylor named some of streets after his battles in Mex. War. Practically untouched by wars from Rev. to Civil, it received 1st big boom in shipbuilding in World War I. Pascagoula luggers have become traditional. World War II saw pop. increase sixfold (5,900 to 37,836). Ingalls Shipbuilding Corp. Plant, 1st in U.S. built for exclusive use of all-welded method of constructing ocean-going vessels, has 10 ways & slips for 9 ocean-going liners in wet docks. Aircraft carriers, cargo vessels, are still being built for U.S., Brit. & S. Amer. U.S. Coast Guard has base here. Commercial fishing (deep-sea red snappers, shrimp, oysters) & paper-shell pecans are also important. **Singing R.** (the Pascagoula) produces mysterious music. Of hypothetical scientific explanations —fish, natural gas, hidden caves—none has been proved. Ind. legend is that Pascagoula Tribe, chanting song of death, drowned themselves rather than surrender to more powerful Biloxi. **Old Sp. Ft.** or **Krebs H.** (O.free.1717-18), built by Joseph Simon de la Pointe, a 1½ story, oyster shell & moss construction with shingled roof is, possibly, oldest bldg. in lower Miss. Valley. At E. end of Beach Blvd., **Bellevue** (1854.Gr.Rev.3-story frame) where Longfellow wrote "The Building of the Ship." Here Augusta J. Evans-Wilson lived while writing "St. Elmo." Just E. of Mun. Beach Pk. is **Chestant Plantation H.** Local tradition says Lafitte, the pirate, was born near-by. **18. GAUTIER** (guides for Pascagoula Lakes & bayous).

SIDE TRIP: Just outside of Gautier, unimproved Rd. (L) leads short distance to **Oldfields,** a 1,000-a. plantation fronting on Gulf. The "big house" (1849) is surrounded by smoke houses, mill houses, slave quarters. Cemetery contains graves of family slaves. There is even a room where a "governor hanged himself."

At **21.** is J. with gravel Rd.

SIDE TRIP: Take latter (R) $2.5^m$, then (R) $1.5^m$ & (R) $1^m$ to **Farragut L.** & site of childhood home of Adm. David Farragut.

**25. FONTAINEBLEAU.** J. with St.59.

SIDE TRIP: On St.59 (R) at $16^m$, J. with unimproved Rd. (R) $0.5^m$ is **Live Oak Pond School,** serving children of mixed Sp., Fr., Ind. & Negro bloods.

**29.** J. with St.80. (L) short distance is **Magnolia St. Pk.** on Gulf (250 as.boat.swim.f. cabins). **32. OCEAN SPRINGS.** Occupies site of old Biloxi (& Ft. Maurepas), 1st European settlement in lower Miss. R. Valley, est. by Iberville (1699) as 1st capital. Near-by L. & N. RR. bridge is probably **Site of Ft. Maurepas.** Cannons have been dug up here & in bay. Tablet, probably cornerstone of Ft., now in Calildo, New Orleans. Capital moved to Mobile (1702). Springs in vic. known since Ind. times for healing properties. In 1880's tourists began to arrive. Like Oak Tree, one of largest in state, is named for John Ruskin who is said to have visited here in 1885. **Shearwater Pottery,** on East Beach, sells locally designed products.

**35. BILOXI** (Ind. "first people"), 1st permanent settlement in Miss. R. Valley, lies on low ridge bet. Miss. Sound (S) & Bay of Biloxi (N). Narrow streets run from bay through tunnels of oaks draped in Sp. moss to Gulf, now lined by concrete sea wall, artificial beaches, hotel resorts, amusement pks., & summer cottages. Biloxi makes playing its business. Golf is principal winter sport (tournaments Feb. & Mar.), yacht race course one of most difficult in South; regatta in July rated 2nd only to Newport in events of its kind. Biloxi is largest shrimp & oyster packing pt. in U.S. Its foreign-born pop. (Poles, Austrians, Slavs, 3.3%), largest in Miss., lives on the "Point" at E. end of Howard Ave. Large Negro pop. is primarily Cath. Settlement on present site was made c.1712, though "old" Biloxi (see above) dates from 1699 & "new" Biloxi served as administrative center for Fr. Territory from 1719 until New Orleans became capital in 1723. Chevalier Henry de Tonti, Sauvolle, brother of Iberville, & other early explorers lie buried in vic. Area was ceded to Brit. (1763), then to Sp. (1799), & in 1811 Jacques L'Adner became 1st U.S. Justice of Peace. In 1840's Biloxi became popular resort. PTS. OF INT. (easily reached from sea wall, US90): (1) E. Beach Blvd., Shrimp & Oyster **Canning Plants** (O). (2) 947 Beach Blvd., **Red Brick H.** (c.1763) & (3) 523 E. Beach, a "raised cottage" (1852), main fl. of wood, held together by pegs, raised high over brick ground fl.; typical construction for this climate. (4) E. Beach & Bellman Sts., **Church of Redeemer** (O.Goth.1890) contains Jefferson Davis family pew removed from orig. chapel, now parish house. (5) Beach Blvd. & Nixon Sts., **Community H. & Pk.,** center for tourist entertainment. In yard are cannon dredged from Back Bay & alleged to be from one of Iberville's ships. (6) **Yacht Club,** annual regattas & Lipton Cup Fisher-Class Races. (7) 206 W. Water St., **Spanish H.** (c.1790). (8) 128 Magnolia St., **French H.** (pre-1800). (9) Magnolia St. & W. beach, **Magnolia Hotel** (1847). (10) Benachi Ave., **Cathedral of Live Oaks.** (11) Beach Blvd. & Porter St., **Lighth.** (O.1848), & painted black after Lincoln's assassination. It was operated for 53 yrs. by a mother & daughter. (12) 1428 W. Beach, **Father A. J. Ryan H.,** once home of poet-priest of Confederacy, now has palm growing through from steps, marking sport where cross formerly stood. (13) **Biloxi Cemetery,** Beach Blvd. (O). Unusual custom is shading graves with Sp. moss. (14) **Seashore Campgrounds,** Beach Blvd. beyond cemetery, summer camping grounds for Methodists. PTS. OF INT. on Back Bay, reached by turning (R) from US90 on any one of principal cross-sts.: (R) on Oak St., to J. with Howard Ave. which runs through bus. dist. Cont. on Oak to Bayview Ave. (R) on Bayview past **Sea Food Canneries** (O.appl.) & **Boatbuilding Plants** (O.appl.) to Iberville Bridge which crosses Back Bay. At opp. end (R) are **Iberville Cross & Boulder** comm. landing of Fr., 1699. Here ceremony of blessing the shrimp fleet takes place 2nd Sun. in Aug. Cont. on Bayview to **Keesler Field,** large Army Air Force training center. Field incl. what was once Naval Reserve Pk., orig. est. by gov. to preserve trees for making knees for wooden ships. Beyond Pk. is **U.S. Veterans' Facility.**

From Biloxi to Bay St. Louis, hy. traverses new $4,000,000 sea-wall pky. **40.5. BEAUVOIR** (R) home of Jeff. Davis, his wife & daughter, Winnie. Here he wrote "The Rise & Fall of the Confederate Government." **Beauvoir** (O.1852-54) was est. as home for Confed. veterans, but at present only wives are in residence. It is a 1½-story structure, set above raised basement with wide central hall & galleries from which square white wooden pillars, support a hip-roof. House is flanked by "guest cottages" of similar design & contains orig. furniture & many relics of Confed. & of Davis' family, incl. Winnie's skiff. Cypress in bldg. is said to have come from La. & carried to L. Pontchartrain by camels. **41.5. EDGEWATER PK.** surrounds hotel, skeet range & golf course. **44. GULF COAST MILITARY ACADEMY,** a War Dept. honor school. **45. ST. MARK'S CHAPEL** (1855), where Jeff. Davis was vestryman.

**47. GULFPORT,** conceived by Gulf & Ship I. Co. as railroad outlet for the Piney Woods, is a planned mod. town with a deep-water harbor. Shipping is most important of industries which incl. creosoted timber, naval stores, seafood products, milk of magnesia, tung oil & the tourist trade. PTS. OF INT.: Bet. 26th & 30th Aves., **Harbor & Ship Canal** offers a panorama of freighters from all over the world. 31st Ave. & 13th St., **Lutheran Ch.,** formerly Presb., with marked pew where Pres. Wilson sat at time of his visit (1913). 13th & 25th Sts., **Hardy Mon.,** bronze bust to Judge W. H. Hardy who planned town, is work of Leo Tolstoy II, son of Russian novelist. E. Beach Blvd. & 25th St., small craft harbor & the **Mun. Clubh. & Yacht Club.** E. Beach Blvd. at Oak St., **U.S. Veterans Facility.**

SIDE TRIP: From Gulfport excursion boats leave daily during summer to **Ship I.** 12m (surf bath.recr.facils.). Ship I. is one of number of low sand bars lying bet. Miss. Sound & Gulf of Mex. (others incl. Horn, Deer & Cat Is.). Natural harbor made it center, from 1699 to 1720's, of Fr. exploration & settlement of coast. Here came 1st "filles à la cassette," marriageable girls who carried their dowries from France in chests or "cassettes." In 1815, when Brit. Gen. Pakenham tried to take New Orleans, Ship I. served as base for Brit. Navy. Construction on Ft. on western tip was begun 1858. Ft. was "destroyed" by Union garrison isolated there, taken briefly by Confeds., & then by Gen. Butler, who named it **Ft. Massachusetts** & used it as prison for captured Confeds.

At Gulfport is J. with US49 which branches (N) through Biloxi Recr. Area of **De Soto Nat. For.** (a cut-over longleaf & slash pine area now being reforested) to Wiggins, Hattiesburg & Jackson.

**51. LONG BEACH,** home of **Gulf Pk. College,** jr. college for girls. Vachel Lindsay once taught here. **57. PASS CHRISTIAN,** named for Christian L'Adnier, member of Iberville's crew said to have discovered deep water pass from Gulf to L. Pontchartrain, has been a popular resort for more than a cent. & claims 1st yacht club in South (org.1849). Offshore are some 30-sq. miles of shell banks producing excellent oysters. PTS. OF INT.: Beechhurst facing E. Beach Blvd., **Ossian Hall** (O.9-5 p.m.fee.1848.Gr.Rev.). 767 E. Beach Blvd., **Dixie White H.** (1854) with twin-curving outside stairways & cast-iron railings, so-named because of Wilson's visit here in 1913. St. Louis & Pine Sts., **Middlegate Japanese Garden.** 551 E. Beach Blvd., **Ballymere H.** (1839), a 1-story cottage, 130′ long & 2-rooms deep, with slender white columnettes supporting overhanging shingled roof, camellia garden. Second & Church Sts., **Trinity Ch.** (Episc.1849.Vict.Goth.) & cemetery stand in beautiful live oak grove. 730 W. Beach Blvd., **Dorothy Dix H.** was summer home of writer of "Letters to the Lovelorn" (Mrs. Elizabeth M. Gilmer).

**60. HENDERSON POINT,** entrance to $2^m$-long bridge crossing **BAY ST. LOUIS** to town of same name at **62.** Bay was scene of "Battle of Pass Christian" (1814), last naval engagement against foreign foe in Amer. waters. Brit. Vice-Adm. Cochrane, pursuing Andrew Jackson with fleet of 60 vessels, was delayed by Lt. Thos. Catesby Jones with 5 Amer. gunboats, all of which Brit. captured or sunk. Main Street of town follows sea wall with stores & bars, built out over water on pilings. On Main St., facing Gulf, is **St. Stanislaus College,** boys' boarding school. In rear, **Shrine of Our Lady of the Woods.** Straight ahead from bridge, a short distance (R) on US90, **St. Augustine Seminary** (Cath.), which trains Negroes for priesthood.

SIDE TRIP: From Bay St. Louis (L) along sea wall drive is **Waveland,** $2.5^m$ where many New Orleans families have summer homes. At c.$3^m$ is **Pirate's H.** (O.appl.1802.typical raised "planters cottage" with square columns supporting dormered roof), said to have been erected by a New Orleans overlord of Gulf Coast pirates. Lafitte is said to have stayed here.

From Bay St. Louis US90 runs through flat, cut-over pine lands. At **82.** bridge crosses **PEARL R.,** boundary line bet. Miss. & La., so-named by Fr. because of large pearl oysters found on banks.

## US 11—MISSISSIPPI

**MISS.-ALA. LINE** ($18^m$ from Livingston, Ala.) **(SE) to MISS.-ALA. LINE** ($47^m$ from New Orleans, La.). **180. US11**

Via: Meridian, Laurel, Hattiesburg, Poplarville, Picayune. New Orleans & Northeastern RR. parallels route. Accoms.: In larger towns.

US11 crosses cut-over pine lands of SE. Miss., passes through industrial towns of Laurel & Hattiesburg & cont. to center of Miss.' tung oil industry at Picayune.

### Sec. 1: MISS.-ALA. LINE to HATTIESBURG. 106.

**19. MERIDIAN.** J. with US80 (see) & US45 (see).
**67. SANDERSVILLE** dates from 1820's. On gravel Rd. (R) $3^m$ is **Bogue Homo Ind. School & Reserv. 76. LAUREL** was a pine for. 50 yrs. ago. Lumber interests, from which town originated, while they were cutting down the pines, also cut down the laurel shrub (from which the name derived) because shrub was poisonous to cattle. Today one of largest industries is manufacture of masonite, a fibre board, by explosion process from chips of 2nd-growth timber. Laurel has, in recent yrs., also become an oil center. Among industrial plants (O) is one that manufactures starch from sweet potatoes. **City Pk.** has a mimosa-bordered lake. **Lauren Rogers Lib. & Mus. of Art,** has paintings by such artists as Constable, Inness, Millet, & Whistler; sculpture; furniture; exceptional coll. of Ind. & other baskets. **Laurel Lib. Assoc.** also has art mus. At Laurel is J. with US84 & St.15.

SIDE TRIP: Take St.15 (SE) from Laurel to Chickasawhay sec. of the **De Soto Nat. For.** with $10^m$ recr. area centering around Thompson Creek.

**84. ELLISVILLE,** where non-slaveholding farmers once selected a delegate to vote against secession ("the Planters' War," they called it). He betrayed their vote at the capital (Jackson) & they burned him in effigy. Then, under leadership of Newt Knight, they conducted guerrilla operations against Confeds. throughout war. **106. HATTIESBURG,** industrial center, with 67 mfg. plants incl. naval stores, clothing factories, fertilizer mill & shrubbery farm, dates from 1880's. It was originally railroading & lumbering town & is now home of **Miss. Southern College** (a St. Teachers' college) & **Miss. Woman's College** (Bapt.). At Hattiesburg is J. with US49 & St.24.

SIDE TRIPS: (A) On St.24 (SE) of Hattiesburg is **New Augusta,** $28^m$. Near-by, across Leaf R. on **Site of Old Augusta,** are ruins of jail that housed Jas. Copeland, leader of notorious Copeland clan, before his execution in 1857. Clan was typical of gangs that had their hqs. in this part of Piney Woods before Civil War & extended their operations to Tex., La. & Fla. The Copelands were finally defeated when citizens outshot the outlaws in the "Battle

of Harvey" on Black Cr. New Augusta is on N. boundary of Leaf R. sec. of **De Soto Nat. For.**, a cut-over area now being replanted.
(B) On St.24 (W) of Hattiesburg, 37m, is **Columbia** in center of a cut-over pineland district. S. **Naval Stores** here produce turpentine, rosin & pine oil from pine knots & stumps of area. Columbia was St. capital briefly in 1821.

**Sec. 2: HATTIESBURG to LA. LINE. 74.**

**15. PURVIS,** where hands of the cth. clock were stopped at 4 p.m., by cyclone of 1908, which was the doom, so people of reg. believed, prophesied by preachers & reformers because of town's wickedness. Later, Will Purvis, related to town's founder, was tried & convicted of murder. But the rope slipped from his neck & again there was prophesying. His sentence was changed to imprisonment. Years later, a man dying of the poison of a snake he had allowed to bite him to prove his own immortality, confessed to the crime. Purvis was released & awarded $5,000 "for his inconveniences." **38. POPLARVILLE,** home of late Sen. Bilbo. "The Man" Bilbo's "Dream House," is near-by, next to Juniper Grove Bapt. Ch. **61. PICAYUNE,** named for New Orleans newspaper once edited by "Pearl Rivers" (Eliza Jane Poitevent), pioneer newspaper woman, who lived here. Picayune is now center of st.'s tung oil industry. Thousands of as. of tung trees, with heart-shaped leaves & striking white, red-centered flowers (blooming Mar.-Ap.) produce nut from which a powerful drying oil used in mfg. of paints & varnishes is made. In blooming season tourists may visit Pearl R. Cty. Tung Oil Trl. Cty. boasts largest tung groves & mills in U.S., as well as U.S. **Tung Oil Experiment Sta.**
Bet. **SANTA ROSA, 69.** & Pearl R., hy. passes through part of **Honey I. Swamp,** once pirate hideout. (Good f. but dangerous without guide.) **74.** Hy. crosses **PEARL R.** (see) to enter La.

# US 45—MISSISSIPPI

**MISS.-TENN. LINE** (12m from Selmer, Tenn.) **(S) to MISS.-ALA. LINE** (60m from Mobile, Ala.) **282.5. US45**

Via: Corinth, Booneville, Tupelo, Shannon, Columbus, Macon, Meridian, Quitman, Waynesboro. Mobile & Ohio RR. parallels route bet. Corinth & Shannon, Macon & Meridian, Quitman & Waynesboro. St. Louis & S.F. RR. parallels route bet. Aberdeen & Columbus. Accoms.: All kinds in larger towns.

US45 descends from Tenn. R. foothills, passes through prairie reg. around Columbus, once one of wealthiest cotton areas of Miss., & enters Ala. in a district of red clay hills. Much of this area suffered greatly during Civil War & legend still has it that even the bitterweed, which ruins milk of cows, was introduced by Feds.

**Sec. 1: MISS.-TENN. LINE to COLUMBUS. 117.5.**

US45 follows march of Feds. under Halleck, on Corinth, after victory at Shiloh, Tenn. (see). Markers indicate positions of troops. **2.5.** Fed. earthworks (marked) parallel hy. **4.5. CORINTH,** RR. & mfg. center (hosiery, furniture, sawmills), is only Miss. town of any size in Tenn. R. reg. It claims to have set up 1st cooperative distribution system in TVA territory & made 60% of all portable sawmills used by our armed forces in World War II. Chosen as J. of Memphis & Charleston RR. & Mobile & Ohio RR. in 1855, Corinth was first known as Cross City &, with outbreak of Civil War, became strategic point. Beauregard retreated here after Shiloh & then evacuated town peacefully to Halleck. Feds. occupied place 5 months. In Oct., 1862, Confeds. under Van Dorn made unsuccessful attempt to retake town.

PTS. OF INT.: 709 Jackson St., **Curlee H.** (1857.iron grillwork), hqs. for both Fed. Gen. H. W. Halleck, & Confed. Gens. Braxton Bragg & J. B. Hood. 617 Jackson St., **Elgin H.,** hqs. of Gen. Grant, contains bed in which he slept. 808 Fillmore St., **Weaver H.,** occupied by Confed. Gen. Leonidas Polk & Fed. Gen. A. Pleasanton. 1m SW. of Cth., **Nat. Cemetery,** contains graves of 5,763 Union soldiers of 273 regiments from 15 states. Polk & Linden Sts., **Confed. Pk.** with site of old Ft. Robinett & Mon. to Col. Wm. Rogers, killed in attempt to retake Ft. (1862). At Corinth is J. with US72.

SIDE TRIPS: (A) From Corinth (W) on US72 to **Walnut** 22m & J. with St.15.
Take latter (S) 16m to **Ripley,** home of Col. Wm. Faulkner, grandfather of present-day novelist, who fought many duels & was shot & killed by a former friend whom he defeated in St. Legislature. Cemetery contains Mon. to the Col. He was author of "The

White Rose of Memphis," said to have upset his generation as much as "Sanctuary" upset his grandson's. (L) from Court Sq. 2 blocks, **Murray H.** (c.1858.rest.). Just S. of town, **Gaillard H.** (c.1837).

At 26m US72 enters **Holly Springs Nat. For.** (see).

(B) From Corinth (E) on US72, 22m to **Iuka,** in a gravel hill & lumber reg. On site of Chickasaw village. Iuka dates from 1857 when RR. came through & entire town of old East Port moved over. Three skirmishes & Battle of Iuka (Sept.19,1862), when Gen. Rosecrans attacked Confeds. under Price, were fought here. After battle almost all bldgs. were transformed into emergency hospitals. Pickwick Dam project (see below) of TVA has been most int. recent development. PTS. OF INT.: **Mineral Springs,** in landscaped pk., are of 6 varieties, each with special curative powers. **Meth. Ch.** (1857.remod.). Main & Quitman Sts., **Matthew H.** (c.1856) moved from East Port, once hqs. of Gen. Nathan B. Forrest. Here women & children gathered during Battle of Iuka. From this house Col. Dan Kelly, "the Fighting Parson," went forth to shell & sink 3 gunboats of Negro soldiers at Eastport. On Quitman St., **T. M. McDonald H.** (c.1857) successively hqs. of Gens. Price & Rosecrans. Here were hidden notes of spy who disguised as woman selling gingerbread, got through Fed. lines & obtained Grant's plan of battle. Eastport St., **Brinkley H.** (c.1856.Gr.Rev.remod.), Grant's hqs. On leaving, Grant wrote note saying he left place in same condition he found it, even to pincushion on dresser. **Pickwick L.** (f.swim. boat.pic.), formed by dam at Pickwick Landing, a TVA unit, lies NE. of Iuka.

From Iuka (S) on St.25, 1m is **Iuka Battlefield** just beyond which is **Woodalls Mt.,** highest pt. in St. (806'). At 14.5m is **Tishomingo** (Ind. "warrior chief") in center of reg. that produces many kinds of clays & sandstone, bauxite & phosphorous rock. At 17m just off hy. (L) is **Tishomingo St. Pk.** (1,400 as.swim.trls.cabins) in a rugged countryside that offers some of most spectacular scenery in Miss.

**11.5. CHIEF TUSCUMBIA MEM.** marks grave of last of Chickasaw leaders. **23.5. BOONEVILLE** (fox,possum & quail avail.in vic.). **35.5. BALDWYN,** J. with gravel Rd.

SIDE TRIP: Take latter (W) 6m to **Brice's Crossrds. Nat. Battlefield Site,** 1-a. tract marked by granite Mon. comm. Nathan Bedford Forrest's brilliant tactical victory over Fed. Gen. Sturgis in what has been called "the best planned & fought engagement of the Civil War" (June 10,1864). A grave defeat for the Feds., it prevented Forrest, however, from cutting Sherman's line of communication at a critical time. But Sherman ordered his subordinate at Memphis "to make up a force & go out to follow Forrest to the death, if it costs 10,000 lives & breaks the Treasury."

### 54.5. TUPELO

Through RR. & bus conns. Good accoms. Miss.-Ala. Fair & Dairy Show, fall.

Tupelo, trading & mfg. center of cattle, cotton, & dairying country, dates from 1859 when Harrisburg (founded soon after cession of lands in 1832) moved over to the newly laid tracks of Mobile & Ohio RR. Station stop was first called Gum Pond & later Tupelo after Tupelo gum trees of reg. Beauregard retreated here after Shiloh & town was scene of bloody engagement (July 14,1864) between Confeds. under Gen. Stephen D. Lee & Feds. under Gen. A. J. Smith. Here Nathan B. Forrest of the cavalry, wounded & unable to ride his horse, raced about battle lines in a carriage. Confeds. were beaten back but 2 days later Smith retreated. In the 90's a series of drainage canals made the bottom lands suitable for farming & one of St.'s 1st cotton mills was est. In 1933 Tupelo entered TVA's 1st contract for power from Wilson Dam & was advertised as the "1st TVA City." There is a large weekly cattle auction. Manufacturing companies (O.wks.) incl. the Cotton Mill, Reed Bros. (women's work dresses), Milam Mfg. Co. (children's wear), Carr-Myers Dairy Co. On Main & Church St., **Marker** celebrating De Soto's alleged visit to this sec. Elizabeth St., **U.S. Fish Hatchery** (tours.wks.pic.). At Tupelo are Js. with US78 & St.6.

SIDE TRIPS: (A) On US78 (E) 2m is J. with gravel Rd. Cont. (R) here 3m to **Tombigbee** (Ind. "coffin maker") **St. Pk.** (822 as.f.swim.boat.cabins).

(B) On US78 (NW) 3m is J. with gravel Rd. (L) here short distance to **Ackia Battleground Nat. Mon.,** a 49-a. tract, site of Chickasaw Ft. attacked by Bienville May 26, 1736. Chickasaw, allies of Eng., held strategic position bet. Fr. of La. & Fr. of Quebec. Fr. were defeated, thereby opening this sec. to Eng. Site has been excavated & outlines charted.

(C) On St.6 (W) 15m is **Rosalba L.** (f.boat.camp.sm.fee). At 18m on St.6 is **Pontotoc.** (Ind. "battle where the cat-tails stood"), est. as land office for Chickasaw Territory. Battle refers to D'Artaguiette's defeat (see below). At Pontotoc is J. with St.15.

On St.15 (S) 1.5m is J. with St.41. (L) on St.41, 4m to **D'Artaguiette Marker** which reads "Pierre D'Artaguiette, Fr. Commander, was defeated in battle with Chickasaw Ind. Sun., May 20, 1736. A wk. later D'Artaguiette, Francois-Marie Bissot De Vincennes, Father Antoine Senat, Jesuit Missionary—in all 20 Frenchmen captured—

were burned at the stake by their captors. Father Senat, scorning the offer to escape martyrdom, remained with his comrades &, intoning the Miserere, led them into the destroying flames." Cont. (S) from Pontotoc on St.15. At 25m is **Houston,** center of dairying reg. **Tabb H.** (1845.Gr.Rev.) used as Confed. hospital after Gen. Grierson's raid. N. of Cth., **Geology Hill,** int. geological formations. Near-by are **Ind. Mounds.**

**63.5. SHANNON,** J. with St.45W.

SIDE TRIP: Take latter (S). A hilly reg., with outcroppings of white limestone, soon gives way to rolling Black Prairie Belt. A dairying & alfalfa & cotton growing country. 8m **Okolona,** was raided several times during Civil War & in 1865 completely burned. 19m Hy. crosses N. boundary of **Natchez Trace Forestry & Fed. Game Preserve.** Hqs. in Okolona (above). 36m **West Point,** once a battleground in Civil War, has one of largest cheese plants in middle South. At 38.5m are 2 **Ind. Mounds** (marked), burial places, so legend goes, of Chickasaw & Choctaw braves who died in great tribal battle here. 47m J. with US82 (see). 49m **Artesia.** Bet. here & Macon (see below) land is often fenced by thorny hedges of Osage orange trees (fruit inedible) planted more than cent. ago. Tree named for Osage Inds. who used its flexible wood for bows & clubs. 63m **Brookville.** J. with US45.

**89.5. ABERDEEN** (see US82). **117.5. COLUMBUS.** J. with US82 (see).

### Sec. 2: COLUMBUS to ALA. LINE. 165.

**30. MACON** (see US82). **51. SCOOBA,** home of **E. Miss. Jr. College** (coed.). **90. MERIDIAN.** J. with US80 (see) & US11 (see). **96. CLARKCO ST. PK.** (792 as. f.swim.boat.cabins). **115. QUITMAN,** completely destroyed by Sherman (Feb.17, 1864), became a booming lumber town until the pine forests were depleted in 1930's. **128. SHUBUTA** & J. with gravel Rd. Take latter (L) to **Langsdale** at 8m. **Lang H.** (O.appl.) has ballroom on 3rd fl. (17½' x 50'). **143. WAYNESBORO,** J. with US84 which unites with US45 to Ala. Line.

SIDE TRIP: From Waynesboro (W) 2m US84, crosses **Chickasawhay R.** (R) from here a short distance is **Pitts Cave,** unexplored limestone formation with entrance on side of a hill.

**148. WINCHESTER,** near Site of old Winchester, once important political center. Ditches of Fort Patton, est. 1813 as protection against Creek Inds., can still be traced. **155. BUCATUNNA,** sett. by Scotch-Irish pioneers from Ga. & S.C. On bridge over Bucatunna Cr., bandits, headed by Rube Burrows, once stopped a train &, since no man could escape without diving, went about their business with deliberation. **165.** US45 crosses **ALA. LINE.**

## US 51—MISSISSIPPI

**MISS.-TENN. LINE** (13m from Memphis, Tenn.) **(S) to MISS.-LA. LINE** (20m from Amite, La.). **300. US51**

Via: Senatobia, Batesville, Grenada, Winona, Jackson, Brookhaven & McComb. Illinois Central RR. parallels route. Accoms.: All types in larger towns.

This is shortest N.-S. paved route through Miss., cutting through heart of state, incl. capital at Jackson. It lacks hist. & scenic int. of US61, but in a series of brief side tours, the tourist can recapture much of ante bellum South.

### Sec. 1: MISS.-TENN. LINE to GRENADA. 87.5.

**12. HERNANDO,** named for Hernando De Soto. At **Farrington H.** (1860), once home of Col. T. W. White, Civil War prisoners were exchanged. **27. SENATOBIA.** On campus of Northwest Jr. College is **Rowell H.,** one of few ante bellum homes to survive when town was burned by Feds. At Senatobia is J. with St.4.

SIDE TRIP: Take latter (E) 35m to **Holly Springs,** sett. by 2nd sons of Tidewater families after Chickasaw ceded land to U.S. in 1832. By 1838 town boasted 14 law offices, 6 doctors' offices, 2 banks & 5 chs. Cotton was main int. & has remained so, though its exploitation has impoverished much of the soil, & today diversified farming, dairy products, & clay deposits are of increasing importance. Holly Springs was scene of 61 raids during Civil War, worst being by Confed. Gen. Van Dorn who took town & wrecked Grant's winter supplies, thereby considerably delaying fall of Vicksburg. Soil erosion, which has produced ravines 75' deep & covering 50 as., is now being controlled by conservation unit whose hqs. for Holly Springs Nat. For. are located in town (see below). Spring pilgrimage to old houses is held annually.

PTS. OF INT.: (1) Van Dorn Ave. & Spring St., **Meth. Ch.** (1849.adds.) used as court after cth. was burned by Feds. (2) Van Dorn & Randolph St., **Christ Ch.** (Episc.1858.Goth.).

(3) 800 Van Dorn Ave. **Strickland H.** (1828), 1st 2-story house in cty.; furnishings incl. bed built, it is said, to accom. 9 persons. (4) 810 College Ave., **Freeman H.,** home of Gen. Edw. Cary Walthall (1831-98). (5) 871 E. College Ave., **Gray Gables** (1830). (6) 800 E. Falconer Ave., **Jones H.** (1857.Gr. Rev.). (7) 221 Salem Ave., **Clapp-Fant H.** (1840's.Gr. Rev.int.exter.). Judge Clapp once escaped Feds. by hiding in one of the hollow columns. Gen. A. M. West, twice nominated for Presidency of U.S. was later owner. (8) 222 Salem St., **Montrose** (Class.Rev.1858). (9) 330 Salem Ave., **Airliewood** (1859.in manner of Swiss chalet). Grant had hqs. here & on stairway 3 escaping Confeds. were shot. (10) 411 Salem Ave., **Cedarhurst** (1858.Goth.Rev.int.iron grillwork). (11) Rust Ave. & N. Memphis St., **Rust College** (Meth.Episc.Negro.coed.1868). (12) S. Memphis St. & Gholson Ave., **Presb. Ch.** (1858.Goth.Rev.).

(13) 140 Gholson Ave., **E. H. Crump H.** (1830.orig.furnishings). (14) 290 Craft St., **Featherstone Place** (1834.built by Gen. Winfield Scott Featherstone. (15) 300 Craft St., **Polk H.** (1830's.built by Gen. Thos. Polk). (16) 331 W. Chulahoma Ave., **Walter Place** (1854.Goth. & Class. Rev. influences). Here Mrs. U. S. Grant made her home during Fed. occupation of 1862 & won her appeal to raiding Gen. Van Dorn to protect her privacy. In this way she saved Grant's papers. In return Grant made house out of bounds for Feds. when he retook town & it became a hideout for Confeds. (17) Among other homes included on spring pilgrimage (1948) were **The Mimosas, The Magnolias, Cuffawa, Linden Terrace,** & the **Crump Place.** (18) **Miss. Industrial College** (Negro.coed.). (19) **Experimental Sta.** of Miss. Agric. & Mech. College. At Holly Springs is J. with US78 & St.7.

(1) On US78 (NW) 8$^{m}$ is **Red Banks,** sett. 1820's. Ante bellum Hs. incl.: **Gardner H.** (1830's), **Moore H.** (1840's), **Goodman H.** (1840) & **Summer Trees** (1820's).

(2) From Holly Springs (SE) US78 passes through **Holly Springs Nat. For.** (Hqs., Holly Springs;123,066 as.). Good quail shooting. Nat. Field Trials held annually in vic.

(3) From Holly Springs (S) 7$^{m}$ is **Spring Lake St. Pk.** (855 as.;pic.swim.boat.f.sport facils.cabins.refreshments).

**39. SARDIS,** hqs. for Sardis Dam Project. Ante bellum Hs. incl. **Heflin H.** & **Laird H.** (1846) said to have been rendezvous for K.K.K. leaders. **Sardis Dam,** c.6$^{m}$ (SE), "2nd largest earth work dam in world" is 3$^{m}$ long & creates 31$^{m}$ long reservoir on Tallahatchie R. (swim.boat.f.duck h.). It is planned to make area into a Pk. **48.5. BATESVILLE,** J. with St.6.

SIDE TRIP: Take latter (E) 26$^{m}$ to **Oxford,** a quiet ante bellum town in a cotton, cattle & corn reg. It is home of Univ. of Miss. ("Ole Miss.") & the "Jefferson" of Wm. Faulkner's novels. In 1836, 3 traders bought the land from a Chickasaw woman named Ho-Kah; village was inc. in 1837. In 1848 the Univ. opened & sons of neighboring planters brought their slaves & horses to college with them. Grant's army took possession of town in 1862. In 1864 Feds. under A. J. Smith burned the town, incl. cth. Oxford is subject of John McCrady's painting, "Town Square." PTS. OF INT.: (1) 900 Garfield St., **Wm. Faulkner H.** (1848.Gr.Rev.add.). (2) Garfield St. opp. Faulkner H., **Site of Jacob Thompson's H.,** of which carriage house, etc., escaped destruction by Feds. Thompson, Secy. of Inter. under Buchanan, had a wife, Kate, so beautiful that after marriage he sent her to school in France rather than expose her to the dangers of Washington society. 14th St., **Lamar H.,** home of Lucius Quintus Cincinnatus Lamar who drafted Miss. Ordinance of Secession. He later became U.S. Supreme Court Justice & noted for his work in reconciliation of North & South. (4) E. end of Jefferson Ave., **St. Peter's Cemetery,** graves of Lamar & of A. B. Longstreet whose "Georgia Scenes" was forerunner of works of many humorists incl. Mark Twain. (5) 108 S. Lamar St., **Old Opera House.** (6) Fillmore & 11th Sts., **Neilson H.** (1855.Gr.Rev.). (7) Foot of University Ave., **Univ. of Miss.** with **Lyceum Bldg.** (1848.Gr.Rev.) center of 640-a. campus. During Civil War students organized "University Grays" & faculty, "cancelling an order for the world's largest telescope," resigned. Bldgs. used alternately by Confeds. & Feds. &, after Battle of Shiloh, as Confed. hospitals. In Oxford also are **Buie Mus.,** founded by descendants of Gen. Nathanael Greene, & **Ammadelle** (1848) built by Thos. Peques. At Oxford is J. with St.7.

Take latter (S) 19$^{m}$ to **Water Valley,** shipping center of a watermelon growing area.

**87.5. GRENADA,** cotton & lumber center. Here Line Street marks division bet. old towns of Pittsburg & Tulahoma started by rival companies. Tired of feuding, towns united in 1836, celebrating marriage of a Pittsburg man & a Tulahoma maid as symbolic of their union. Grenada was Confed. Gen. Pemberton's hqs. during Grant's 2nd campaign against Vicksburg. Dog hunt & field trials are now held in Jan. Cuff's Hill, **Campbell H.** once Presb. Mission for Inds. 422 Doak St., **Rollin H.** (1830's; hand-hewn logs). 217 Margin St., **Newsome H.** (Gr.Rev.). 605 Margin St., **Golliday Lake H.,** once Jefferson Davis' Hqs.

## Sec. 2: GRENADA to JACKSON. 114.

**8. ELLIOTT** dates from 1818 & was 1st mission among Choctaw. **12. DUCK HILL,** where Choctaw leader "Duck" held councils. **23. WINONA** (Ind. "first-born daughter"), trading center. 316 Summit St., **Col. Moore H.**, remod. log structure said to be oldest in cty. At Winona is J. with US82.

SIDE TRIP: Take latter (W) 26m to **Greenwood.**

Through RR., bus & plane conns. Accoms.: All types. Winter Carnival in Dec. Greenwood advertised as world's largest inland long staple cotton market is cut by the Yazoo R., (S) of which lies business dist., (N) the residential sec. Cotton fields extend to the very boundaries of town. In 1834 John Williams built landing here to ship cotton down Yazoo to New Orleans. Quarreling with Williams, Greenwood Leflore built rival landing. By 1844, when Williams Landing was inc., it was called, ironically enough, Greenwood. Leflore, son of Louis LeFleur (see Jackson) & Rebecca Crevat, niece of Pushmataha, was elected last chief of the Choctaw (1824) & later condemned by tribe for sponsoring Dancing Rabbit Treaty (see). Still later he became a successful planter but was again ostracized, this time by whites, when he refused to support Confeds. His palatial home Malmaison, long a show place, burned, 1942. **Leflore County Cth.** has chimes tuned to imitate those of Westminster. At c.3m (W) on old US82 is **Site of Ft. Pemberton** on narrow neck of land bet. Yazoo & Tallahatchie Rs., which here flow in opp. directions. Fed. ship "Star of the West" lies near-by in Tallahatchie R., sunk by Confeds. to block Fed. passage to Vicksburg. Cotton compresses, & cottonseed oil mills here, are not usually open to public but visits to these & cotton plantations can be arranged. Winter carnival in Dec.

**34. VAIDEN.** J. with St.35.

SIDE TRIP: Take latter (SE) through land 1st opened up by lumbering industry & now occupied principally in dairying & vegetable farming. 24m **Kosciusko,** overnight sta. on Natchez Trace at which Andrew Jackson, among others, pitched camp, was 1st called Peking, then Peakedend, then Paris, then Parrish, then Perish, & finally changed to name of Polish hero of Amer. Rev. 49m **Carthage.** On St.16, near-by is **Pearl R. Ind. Day School.** 77m **Forest,** J. with US80 (see), hqs. for **Bienville Nat. For.** It incl. 200-a. tract of virgin loblolly pine, one of few orig. stands of this type in country. 102m **Raleigh,** a Cth. town. Cemetery thought to be haunted because of noises now explained by a cave that echoes sound of hy. traffic. (S) of Raleigh tour cont. on St.35W. 117m **Mize,** also called "No Nigger," & "Capital of Sullivans' Hollow" was scene of feuding & fighting that began in 1810 when 9 Sullivan brothers each marked out a homestead. Soon they were calling the place "Merry Hell" & such characters as "Hog" Tom Sullivan, Wild Bill, Small Jim & Runty Bill each had his legend which incl. leaving sheriff to starve with his head bet. rails of a fence & hitching a rival to a plow, plowing him all day along, & then bringing him to the barn & feeding him oats. At Mize is J. with St.20.

Take latter (E) 8m to **Taylorsville.** On **Ind. Battlefield** many arrowheads have been found. In schoolyard is **Grave of Gentle South Wind,** Ind. maid killed by drunken father. At Taylorsville is J. with St.35E on which (S) at 6m is **Hot Coffee** so-named because of hot, strong, New Orleans coffee served by trader **J. J.** Davis who came from Shiloh after Civil War. At 10m on St.35E is J. with US84.

**57.** J. with gravel Rd.

SIDE TRIP: Take latter (L) 3m to **Holmes Cty. St. Pk.** (444 as.f.swim.boat.cabins.refreshments).

**67.** J. with gravel Rd.

SIDE TRIP: Take latter (R) c.6m to **Old Red School** where idea of Order of the Eastern Star was conceived, it is said, by Rbt. Morris, Masonic schoolteacher, 1849.

**90. CANTON,** sett. 1830's. **County Cth.** (1852.Georg.). On Center St. E. of Cth., **W. J. Mosby H.** (1856.Gr.Rev.) where Gen. Sherman stayed on upper fl. while his mules were quartered on lower. Near-by, **Rucker H.,** (1822.Georg.details.adds.). E. Academy St., **Luckett H.,** hqs. of Confed. Gen. Albert S. Johnston.

Bet. Canton & Jackson is a fruit & truck farming area. **102.** J. with paved Rd.

SIDE TRIP: Take latter (R) 7m to **Ingleside** (Gr.Rev.) & near-by **Chapel of the Cross** (1853.Goth.). In churchyard is grave of Henry Crew Vick, son of founder of Vicksburg, killed in duel in which he himself shot into air because of promise to sweetheart never to kill a man.

**106. TOUGALOO COLLEGE** (Negro.1868.coed.) founded by Amer. Missionary Assoc. of N.Y. & now accredited by S. Assoc. as standard 4-yr. college, Class B.

**114. JACKSON**

Through RR., bus & plane conns. Accoms.: All types. Info.: C. of C., Lamar Bldg.; Dept. of Archives, War Mem. Bldg. Miss. St. Fair, Oct.

Jackson, on W. bank of Pearl R., is capital & largest city of Miss. In 1821 legislature, which previously met in Natchez & Washington, appointed commission to recommend site within 20m of geographical center of state in territory sold to U.S. by Choctaw at Treaty of Doak's Stand, 1820. Commission decided on Le Fleur's Bluffs (c.35m S. of center) where Fr. Canadian Louis Le Fleur (called "the flower" because of his dancing ability) had set up keel-boat business & trading post in 1792. Le Fleur was father of Greenwood Leflore (see Greenwood). New capital was named for Andrew Jackson, designed on checkerboard plan with alternate squares reserved as commons, & its streets laid out before 1st settlers arrived. In 1822 legislature met in newly erected capitol but same yr. Audubon referred to district as "a mean place, a rendezvous of gamblers & vagabonds." 1st RR. arrived in 1840. 1st bridge over Pearl R. was completed 1848 & sign posted: "For each & every person on foot 5 cents. For man or woman & horse 10 cents. For cattle, horses & mules in a drove 5 cents per head. For sheep, goats & hogs 2.5 cents per head." By 1850 Jackson had pop. of 1,881, exclusive of slaves.

Legislature passed Ordinance of Secession (following S. Carolina) in 1861. Miss Amanda Hilzheim produced a blue silk flag with a single star for the occasion, & an Irish actor named Harry McCarthy, who was playing in town, wrote & sang 3 verses of the "Bonnie Blue Flag." Jackson was occupied 4 times by Feds. & on July 9, 1863 Sherman began siege which lasted until July 16 when Confed. Gen. J. E. Johnston evacuated. "We have made fine progress today in the work of destruction," Sherman wrote. "Jackson will no longer be a point of danger. The land is devastated for thirty miles around." Upon appeal of Mayor he arranged for 200 barrels of flour & 100 barrels of mess pork to be distributed to "people in want living in & near Jackson." An aide-de-camp of Fed. Gen. Winslow has recorded that it was while watching his troops struggle across a pontoon bridge over Pearl R. near Jackson that Sherman said, "War is Hell."

Opening of near-by gas field in 1930's began to attract industries & city enjoyed large World War II boom. In 1948 it boasted some 174 plants processing 268 products incl. lumber, cotton, filtering materials from clays, glass containers & fluorescent lamps. It is also hqs. for oil companies. A Census Bureau report lists it high among cities likely to retain wartime industrial advantages & pop. gains.

PTS. OF INT.: (1) E. Pascagoula & S. Congress Sts., **Hinds County Cth.** (1930.by C.H.Lindsley) faces mun. flower garden. (2) E. Pascagoula & S. President Sts., **City Hall** (1854.Gr.Rev.); cupola which once crowned bldg. was used as Confed. lookout. (3) State St. facing Capitol St., **Old Capitol** (1833-42.Gr.Rev.). Here Miss. Ordinance of Secession was passed, & Jeff. Davis made his last public appearance (1884). Statue of Davis in rotunda. Confed. Mon. is just S. of bldg. (4) Amite & N. State Sts., **War Mem. Bldg.** (1939) houses St. Hall of Fame, Dept. of Archives. (5) 411 Amite St., **J. L. Power H.** (c.1840.remod.) Jeff. Davis was visitor here. (6) Miss. & N. President Sts., **New Capitol** (1903.by Theodore Link),contains Mus., State Lib. Many portraits, incl. some by Gilbert Stuart & Ben. West. (7) N. West & George Sts., **Greenwood Cemetery,** unusual in reg. in that it has graves of both whites & Negroes. (8) N. West & Fortification Sts., **Manship H.** (1857); on lawn is only bell in city not melted during Civil War. (9) N. West & Marshall Sts., **Millsaps College** (coed.Meth. Episc.). (10) Peachtree & Pinehurst Sts., **Belhaven College for Women** (Presb.). (11) 839 N. State St., **Mun. Clubh. Art Gallery** has small permanent coll. & offers loan exhibits. (12) End of Amite St., **St. Fairgrounds.** (13) Capitol & President Sts., **Governor's Mansion** (1842.Gr.Rev.add.) has served as hqs. for Grant & Sherman & 34 Miss. governors. (14) Farish St. is heart of Negro district. (15) Porter St. at S.W. edge of town, **Battlefield Pk.,** 53 as., scene of Civil War skirmish (1863). Breastworks & trenches are still preserved. (16) W. end of Lynch St., **Campbell College** (Negro. coed.), affiliated with African Meth. Episc. Ch. (17) 2918 Capitol St., **Livingston Pk.** (79 as.swim.golf.zoo). (18) N. State St. & Riverside Dr., **Bailey Jr. High,** int. mod. bldg.

At Jackson are Js. with US80 & US49.

SIDE TRIPS: (A) On US80 (E) 3m **Knox Glass Co.** (O.appl.). 4m **St. Hospital for Insane.** 12m **Brandon,** destroyed during Civil War & rebuilt. Ante bellum structures that survived incl., at W. end of town, **McLaurin H.,** house of 2 Miss. governors & **McCaskill H.** (1830) once an inn.

(B) On US80 (W) 8m is **Clinton,** once Ind. agency. Grant & Sherman both had hqs. here & bloody race riot occurred in 1875. **Miss. College for Men** (Bapt.1826), founded as Hampstead & 2nd oldest school for boys in Miss. College Chapel (1858.Gr.Rev.) is only ante bellum bldg. **Hillman College** (Bapt.women.1853) founded as Central Female Inst., oldest existing school for girls in Miss., held classes throughout Civil War.

(C) On US49 (N) 15m is **Pocahontas** with adj. Ind. mound. At 20m is J. with narrow Rd. (L) 2m here is **Petrified For.,** a gully with logs 3′ to 20′ long submerged during Pleistocene or end of Tertiary Period & probably brought down by prehist. streams.

(D) From Jackson (S) US49 runs past Pearl R. Swamp on edges of which is large gas field.

### Sec. 3: JACKSON to LA. LINE. 98.5.

**2.** J. with St.18.

SIDE TRIP: (R) here 11m to gravel Rd.

(L) 2m to **Cooper's Wells** on land bought by Rev. Preston Cooper (1837) because of persistent dream that there were curative waters here. First hotel burned by Feds.

14m **Raymond,** sett. before 1829, was once larger than Jackson. It was taken by Feds. in Vicksburg Campaign. Here are **County Cth.** (Gr.Rev.), **Episc. Ch.** (Goth.), **Peyton H.** (1830's) & **Ratcliff H.** (1853). 35.5m **Utica Normal & Industrial Institute for Negroes.** Utica singers of spirituals have traveled in U.S. & abroad. School sponsors annual Farmer's Conference.

**35. HAZELHURST,** shipping center of a fruit & vegetable growing area. J. with St.20.

SIDE TRIP: Take latter (R) 10m to **Browns Wells,** resort dating back to pre-Civil War days (mineral waters.swim.golf.cottages).

**46. WESSON,** seat of **Copiah-Lincoln Jr. College. 55. BROOKHAVEN,** shipping center of S. Miss. dairying country. S. end Jackson St., **Hardy H.** (1870's); antiques. Cherokee St. near Cth., **Brooks H.** (1858). **Whitworth College** (1858), now Meth. Jr. College for Girls; dormitories were used as Confed. hospital. **81. McCOMB** is a RR., mfg. & shipping center for agric. products that incl. gladiolus bulbs. **88. MAGNOLIA.** J. with St.48.

SIDE TRIP: Take latter (R) 4m to **Percy Quin St. Pk.** (2,221 as.f.swim.boat.cabins.rooms).

**98.5.** US51 crosses **LA. LINE.**

## US 61—MISSISSIPPI

**MISS.-TENN. LINE** (12m from Memphis, Tenn.) **(S)** to **MISS.-LA. LINE** (17m from St. Francisville, La.). **325. US61**

Via: Clarksdale, (Greenville), Rolling Fork, Vicksburg, Port Gibson & Natchez, Woodville. Yazoo & Miss. Valley RR. parallels route. Accoms.: All types.

US61, advertised as "Old Man River Road," enters that sec. of Miss. known as "The Delta." Here Miss. R., in endless meanderings & overflows, has created land reputedly richer than the Nile valley. It has been cotton land for 150 yrs. & the cotton grows tall as a man. Plantation villages line hy. Beyond Vicksburg, high on the bluffs that Miss. R. has cut into soil, the Delta proper gives way to a loamy hill reg. Vicksburg is 1st of a series of hist. towns that preserve the feeling of the deep South of ante bellum days. Natchez is a museum piece as is, on a smaller scale, Port Gibson. Annual spring "pilgrimages" are celebrated in these towns & eventually take the tourist on to St. Francisville reg. of La. & to New Orleans.

### Sec. 1: MISS.-TENN. LINE to CLARKSDALE. 63.

**3. WALLS,** plantation village near Ind. mounds. **8. LAKE CORMORANT,** long & narrow, typical of Ls. left behind by Miss. R. **15. ROBINSONVILLE.** J. with St.3.

SIDE TRIP: Take latter (R) to **Commerce** 5m, where 1st levees in this sec. were built to save town, which once rivalled Memphis & is now a plantation. At 8m **De Be Vois Ind. Mounds,** thought to be site of Chickasaw skirmish with De Soto.

**26. TUNICA.** Here R. bed has changed so that what was once Miss. is now Ark. **44.** J. with side Rd.

SIDE TRIP: Take latter (R) 2m to **Lula.** In vic. is **Grant's Pass,** dynamited by Gen. Grant in attempt to get gunboats to Vicksburg. **Moon Lake** (swim.boat.f.) extends (S) to **Friar Point.** Here, as well as at Grant's Pass, are ferries to Helena, Ark.

**48.** J. with gravelled Rd.

SIDE TRIP: On latter (L) 3.5m is **Jonestown.**

(1) From Jonestown (L) 1.5m on gravel Rd. is **Matagorda,** plantation home of Col. D. M. Russell, who was commissioned by Confeds. to trade with Eng. & who planned raid on the banks at St. Albans, Vt., most northerly "engagement" of Civil War. Matagorda is name of variety of long-staple cotton.

(2) From Jonestown (R) 2.5m is **Eagles' Nest Plantation,** home of Gen. Jas. L. Alcorn, Gov. of Miss. (1870-71) & champion of levee system. Mon. marks his grave on Ind. mound.

**63. CLARKSDALE,** ginning, compressing & trading center for a great cotton-growing area (lumber is next in importance), is typical Miss. Delta town, with bus.

dist. of stores, gins, warehs., & loading platforms & residential sec. of comfortable frame homes with wide galleries shaded by maples & water oaks. Sunflower R. runs through town & many streets end suddenly in cotton fields. Fr. Huguenots were said to have been here at an earlier date, but founding is credited to John Clark, who bought Gov. land here in 1848 & in 1869 platted town on site of Ind. fortification. Delta Staple Cotton Festival held here Aug. NW. of Cth., **Hopedale,** orig. John Clark home (1858-66.remod). **Carnegie Pub. Lib.,** coll. Ind. relics from near-by mounds.

SIDE TRIPS: (A) From Clarksdale (N) on side Rd. 10m is **Yazoo Pass** through which Grant attempted to get to Vicksburg. Sunken gunboats still are visible.
(B) On side Rd. (W) 14m is **Sunflower Landing** designated by U.S. De Soto Exposition Commission as place where Hernando de Soto discovered Miss. R., May, 1541. One of chroniclers of his party wrote that R. was "Of great depth & of very strong current . . . and if a man stood still upon the other side one could not tell whether he were a man or something else."
(C) At Clarksdale is J. with St.1 which provides int. alt. route more closely paralleling Miss. R. & rejoining US61 at Rolling Fork, 132m. It passes some of oldest Delta plantations & along a number of horseshoe-shaped Ls. (f.buffalo,crappie,perch). On St.1 (R) at 13m is **Greengrove,** once plantation of Confed. Gen. N. B. Forrest. 23m **Delta Cooperative Farm,** est. 1935 by Sherwood Eddy as social & economic experiment with both white & Negro sharecroppers. 31m **Pertshire,** J. with side Rd.

Take latter (R) to **Dennis Landing** 4.5m, fishing & shipping pt. for buffalo & spoonbill catfish particularly valuable for their roe.

35m **Gunnison.** Near-by is **Concordia Cemetery,** relic of a town once so wild that many headstones merely say: "Killed in Concordia." 45m **Rosedale,** largest town on R. bet. Memphis & Greenville. Near-by, at **Montgomery Pt.,** it is said that David Crockett crossed on way to Alamo. 66m **Scott,** hqs. of Delta & Pine Land Co. with cotton plantation, 38,000 as., said to be largest in world. It is owned by Eng. company & worked by Negro sharecroppers. Asphalt Rd. to RR. Sta. is experiment in use of cotton textile as base to control road expansion & contraction. 76m **Winterville Ind. Mounds.** 82m **Greenville,** largest town in Yazoo-Miss. area, is a cotton, lumbering, & shipping center. There are pulp, wall board & cotton oil mills, wkly. stockyard auctions, & mun.-owned terminal. Greenville is 3rd seat of Washington Cty. (1st was destroyed by R.; 2nd was fired by the Feds. & then fell into R.). Greenville itself suffered in 1927 flood. In 1935 R. was routed to a new course several miles (W) & L. Ferguson became boundary of town. SE. cor. Percy & Broadway Sts., **Percy H.,** home of late Wm. Alex. Percy, author of "Lanterns on the Levee," son of Sen. LeRoy Percy. **Greenway Cemetery;** grave of Sen. Percy with figure by Malvina Hoffman. **Pub. Lib.;** Starling Coll. of old & rare vols. in many languages.
106m Hy. runs along L. Washington (f.& duck h.excellent). Area is nesting place for variety of birds incl. great blue heron, snowy egret, & Amer. egret. Alligators are hunted in L. Jackson which lies bet. L. Washington & Miss. R. 112m **Glen Allan.** On side Rd. 1.5m (R) are **Ruins of St. John's Church** (1857.Eng.Goth.), 1st Episc. Ch. in Delta reg. & grave of Negro sexton, Jesse Crowell, who carved altar. 113.5m **Richland** (L), a raised cottage built by Jim Richardson, son of Edmund Richardson, "Cotton King of the World," who cleared swamps & fors. of central Delta with convict labor. 131m **Rolling Fork,** at J. with US61 (see below).

### Sec. 2: CLARKSDALE to VICKSBURG. 145.

**26. MOUND BAYOU,** est. 1887 by Isaiah T. Montgomery & Benj. T. Green, Negroes. Former, once slave of Jeff. Davis' brother Joseph, was only Negro delegate to Miss. Constitutional Convention of 1890. **36. CLEVELAND,** seat of **Delta St. Teachers' College** (1924). **63. LELAND,** J. with US82 (see), has tool mfg. companies & cottonseed oil mill. Reg. produces pecans & vegetables as well as cotton. Near-by **Delta Experiment Sta. & U.S. Gov. Cotton Ginning Labs.** (O) experiment with some 2,000 varieties of cotton. **Deer Cr.,** landscaped, especially with roses, part of garden pilgrimage (May). **80. HOLLANDALE,** J. with side Rd.

SIDE TRIP: Take latter (R) 4m to **LeRoy Percy St. Pk.** (2,442 as.pic.f.swim.boat.lodge. cabins). Hunting areas adj.

**96. ANGUILLA,** J. with St.14.

SIDE TRIP: Take latter (L) 15m to J. with US49. Take US49 (S) 18m to **Yazoo City,** cotton trade & mfg. center & scene of various skirmishes during Civil War.

**102. ROLLING FORK,** with 3 Ind. mounds in vic. Bet. here & Yazoo R. hy. traverses **Delta Purchase Unit,** only bottomland Nat. For. in U.S. (good f. & deer h.). At **134.** US61 crosses **YAZOO R.** (Ind. "river of death") which marks end of "the Delta." Across bridge is Mon. on **Site of Ft. St. Peter** (called Ft. Snyder in 1863); Confed. earthworks remain. Ft. orig. est. 1719 by Fr. as protection against Yazoo & Tunica Inds. At **135.** is J. with side Rd.

SIDE TRIP: Take latter (L) 2m to **Blakely.** Orig. log cabin (erected pre-1833), believed to have been hideout of highwayman Murrell. Frame structure, brought by flatboat from Cincinnati, added before 1838 (adds.1842.remod.1873). Jeff. Davis (& later Grant & Sherman) dined here. Shell in front is 1st fired from Adm. Farragut's flagship at Vicksburg.

In Battle of Chickasaw Bayou (1862) bet. here & Vicksburg, Sherman's brigades were attacked from entrenchments along old hy. **139.** J. with unimproved Rd. Across R. here is **Eagle L.** (f.h.boat.accoms.). **143. VICKSBURG NAT. CEMETERY.** Here lie some 17,000 Union soldiers (of which nearly 12,912 are unidentified) who fell during Siege of Vicksburg. There have been subsequent burials of other veterans & some civilians but no Confeds. They are buried at Cedar Hill in Vicksburg.

**145. VICKSBURG**

Through RR. & bus conns. Toll bridge across Miss. R. to La. Accoms.: All types. Info.: C. of C. & Vicksburg Hist. Soc. Spring Pilgrimage, Feb.-Ap. Nat. Assembly of Participants of Campaign of Vicksburg, Spring.

Vicksburg, on Miss. R. at mouth of Yazoo, is shipping center for cotton, cattle & various manufactures & is a leading hardwood market of the South. Built on bluffs that rise 350′ above sea level, architecture presents transition from ante bellum through Amer. Goth. to mod. concrete structures, mostly of 4 or 5 stories, erected on natural terraces that rise up from R., which is bordered by concrete sea wall. On the land side, the city is surrounded by Vicksburg Nat. Military Pk.

Fr. were here in 1719 (see Ft. St. Peter above) & Sp. in 1791 est. Ft. Nogales (Sp. "walnuts") which was taken over by U.S., 1798. About 1812 Meth. Rev. Newitt Vick arrived & he & his followers planned city that was inc. 1825. Vicksburg expanded rapidly in spite of usual river-town difficulties with gamblers, flatboatmen, & other tough characters. (The 1st 5 editors of "Tri-Weekly Sentinel," est. 1837, met violent deaths.) Strategic importance of city in control of Miss. R. made it important target in Civil War. In June 1862 Adm. Farragut bombarded Vicksburg. In Nov., Gens. Grant & Sherman made another unsuccessful attack. In Ap. 1863 Grant, aided by Adm. Porter, was more successful. Port Gibson, Raymond, & Jackson fell. Siege of Vicksburg (defended by Gen. John C. Pemberton) lasted 47 days—while mule meat sold for $12 a pound, flour $200 a barrel, rum $100 a gallon, & newspapers were printed on back of wall paper. During siege some 3,000 civilians lived in caves. Mark Twain quoted one of the survivors: "It got to be Sunday all the time. . . . Seven Sundays & all of them broken up at 1 time or another in the day or in the night, by a few hours of the awful storm of fire & thunder & iron. . . . Twice we had 16 in our cave. Pretty suffocating in there then. We always had 8. Eight belonged there. Hunger & misery & sickness & fright & sorrow; & I don't know what all got so loaded into them that none of them were ever rightly their old selves after the siege." "When Vicksburg fell," said Grant, "the fate of the Confederacy was sealed." The "Gibraltar of the Confederacy" went through usual Reconstruction difficulties. In 1876 Miss. R. changed its course, leaving city high & dry; but Gov. engineers later diverted waters of Yazoo R. into old R. bed. Today hqs. of Miss. R. Commission & U.S. Waterways Experiment Sta. (see below) are located at Vicksburg which is now 3rd largest city in Miss.

PTS. OF INT.: (1) Grove & Monroe Sts., **Warren County Cth.** (O.sm.fee.1859-61. Gr.Rev.), now a Mus. Cupola riddled by Farragut's cannon, replaced at later date. (2) NW. cor. Monroe & 1st East Sts., **Gov. McNutt H.** (c.1828), New England farmhouse style. In yard is grave of Confed. officer who died in Siege of Vicksburg. (3) 701 Adams St., **Marmaduke Shannon H.** (1830's), home of early newspaper editor. (4) Lover's Lane, **Hough Cave,** one of those used during siege. (5) **Bodley Mon.** to "Dr. Hugh Bodley, killed by the gamblers while defending the morals of Vicksburg, July 5, 1835." (6) 1200 Main St., **Constitution Fire Co. H.** (1835). (7) NW. cor. Locust & Main St., **Christ Ch.** (Episc.1839-45.Eng.Goth.), cornerstone laid by Bishop Leonidas Polk who became Confed. Maj. Gen. (8) SW. cor. Locust & 1st East Sts., **Duff Green H.** (1840's.brick with iron grillwork galleries). (9) 805 Locust St., **Plain Gables** (c.1835.Gr.Rev.,damaged by shellfire.rest.). (10) 1128 Grove St., **Marshall-Bryan H.** (1835.Gr.Rev.). (11) 1116 Crawford St., **Luckett H.** (1830.add.), used as barracks & stable by Feds. (12) 1018 Crawford St., **Willis-Cowan H.** (c.1840), Gen. Pemberton's hqs. during siege. (13) Crawford & Cherry Sts., **Mon.** to Rev. Tobias Gibson, Meth. preacher who arrived in this reg. in 1799. (14) 1520 Cherry St., **Willis Richardson H.** (1830's.Gr.Rev.), once home of Vick family. (15) 1104

Harrison St., **Cook-Allein H.** (c.1862). Feds. stamped U.S. insignia on living-room fl. (16) 2200 Oak St., **Klein H.** (c.1856.Gr.Rev.).
(17) **"The Sprague"** (O.sm.fee), "largest towboat ever built for inland waters." (18) E. end of Clay St., **Vicksburg Nat. Military Pk.** (1,323 as.), est. by Congress in 1899 "to comm. the Campaign, Siege & Defense of Vicksburg" & "to preserve the hist. of the battles & operations on the ground where they were fought," contains 1,598 mems., mons. & markers representing 28 states. It is one of world's best marked battlefields; 3 types of fts.—the redan (triangular with apex toward enemy), the lunette (crescent shaped) & the redoubt (various forms, mostly square)—are preserved, & 2 types of trenches—the parallel & the approach or sap. **Park Mus.** (O.wks. 9-4:30.sm.fee) has models & exhibits of fortifications, Vicksburg terrain, plantation life. (Lecture Tours daily. Special provisions for student groups & clubs.) **Shirley H.** (rest.), only ante bellum bldg. remaining in area was damaged by shellfire. (19) **U.S. Waterways Experiment Sta.** (free tours wks. 10:30 & 2:30) on Hall's Ferry Rd. c.4m SE. of Vicksburg, is concerned with solving river & harbor problems over entire country. Hydraulic lab. is largest & best equipped of its kind in world & soil mechanics lab. one of largest in U.S. There are some 250 model studies incl. scale models of many famous Amer. & foreign waterways & 2-a. model of lower Miss. R. At Vicksburg is J. with US80 (see).

SIDE TRIP: Take latter (E). At 15.5m is **Edwards,** seat of **S. Christian Inst.** (Negro.coed.). From Edwards (R) on gravel Rd. to **Champion's Hill,** 4.5m. Here on May 16, 1863 Grant defeated Confeds. under Gen. Pemberton, a decisive engagement in Vicksburg campaign.

34m **Clinton,** college town, named in 1828 in honor of DeWitt Clinton, Gov. of N. Y., missed by 1 vote becoming Miss. capital in 1829. It was orig. Mt. Dexter, an Ind. agency & was site of 1st land office & 1st P.O. in Miss. Clinton & Vicksburg RR. (inc. 1831) is 2nd oldest in st. Clinton early became known as health resort. Grant & Sherman had hqs. here. In 1875 town was scene of bloody race riot. **Miss. College,** chartered by St. legislature as Hampstead Academy in 1826, became later a Presb. institute & then was taken over by the Bapts. as men's college. **College Chapel** (1858.Gr.Rev.) is only ante bellum structure on campus. Closely connected is **Hillman College,** est. by Central Bapt. Assoc. in 1853 as **Central Female Institute** & now oldest extant girls' school in Miss. **U.S. Waterways Experiment Sub Sta.** has under construction giant model covering 220 as. of entire Miss. R. incl. tributaries & reservoirs. 43m **Jackson,** St. capital (see US51).

## Sec. 3: VICKSBURG to NATCHEZ. 74.

**24. JOHN TAYLOR MOORE H.,** frame structure with wide galleries. Moore was "Marse John" of Irwin Russell's verse (see below). **26.** J. with gravel Rd.

SIDE TRIP: Take latter (R) c.1m to **The Hermitage** (c.1800.planter's cottage type). Andrew Jackson, remembering a pleasant visit, is said to have given his own house its name.

**30. PORT GIBSON,** on Bayou Pierre, small cotton town retaining much ante bellum flavor. (Spring pilgrimage held annually.) Sam. Gibson, its founder, who arrived in 1788, lies buried in **Protestant Cemetery.** Another citizen was Harmon Blennerhassett, associate of Aaron Burr, who came here after acquital & named his plantation "La Cache." Confeds. under Bowen were defeated in Grant's Vicksburg campaign about 5m S. of Port Gibson, Ap. 30-May 1, 1863 (see below). College & Coffee Sts., **Irwin Russell Mem.** (O), now a community center, in brick bldg. once home of Sam. Gibson, later Confed. hospital & a female college. Russell, born in Port Gibson (1853), was one of 1st writers of Negro dialect & author of "Christmas Night in the Quarters." Mem. contains some of his mss. Chestnut & Walnut Sts., **L. P. Williams H.,** birthpl. of Constance Cary who later, in Alexandria, Va., made 1st Confed. flag. It was from gallery Grant said, "Port Gibson is too beautiful to burn." Coffee St., **Cath. Cemetery,** contains grave of Resin P. Bowie, inventor of bowie knife. Knife was 1st used by his brother James, of Alamo fame. Church & Walnut Sts., **Presb. Ch.** (1859) has steeple surmounted by iron hand of a laborer with forefinger pointing to heaven. Orig. of gold-leaf-covered wood was hand of scholar. S. end of town, **The Manse,** built by father of Confed. Gen. Earl Van Dorn. Latter's grave is on hill opposite.

SIDE TRIPS: (A) From Port Gibson on side Rd. c.4m (SW) is **Magnolia Ch. Battlefield,** scene of Battle of Port Gibson (see above).
(B) From Port Gibson (R) on side Rd. 10m are **Ruins of Windsor,** 22 huge stone Corinthian columns joined by wrought-iron railings. Built by S. C. Daniels (1861.5-stories & observatory), it was one of most extravagant gestures of the ante bellum Gr. Rev. in Miss. &, it is said, was used by Mark Twain, while river pilot, to chart his course. It burned in 1890.

15m **Alcorn Agric. & Mech. College** (Negro.coed.1871), land grant college, trains most of Negro teachers of Miss. A no. of bldgs. were once part of Oakland College (1830). Chapel dates to 1831.

**56. MON.** (L) marking a crossing of Natchez Trace (see below). **58.5.** (L) is **SPRINGFIELD** (1791), with wide galleries & Doric columns, where Andrew Jackson & Mrs. Rachel Donelson Robards were married, Oct. 1791. **66. SELMA.** Here is **Selma Plantation,** est. by Gerard Brandon I, Irish revolutionist who fought at King's Mt. House, 2nd on site, is early "planter type." Gerard Brandon II was 1st native-born Gov. of Miss. **68. WASHINGTON** became 2nd Territorial capital of Miss. (Natchez was 1st) in 1802, & later 1st state capital. On Main St., **Jefferson Military College** (1802). Members of faculty incl. Audubon & Jos. H. Ingraham, author of pirate stories. In vic. Jackson stopped before & after Battle of New Orleans. Here Lafayette reviewed cadet drills, & Jeff. Davis went to school. Under "Burr Oaks" Aaron Burr (1807) was given preliminary trial for treason. In Washington also are **Spanish H.** (pre-1800), **Meth. Ch.** (1825), **Cowles Mead H.** (c.1800), home of man who gave order for Burr's arrest, & **Clear Cr. Ch.,** one of oldest Bapt. Chs. in Miss. At Washington is J. with US84.

SIDE TRIPS: (A) From Washington (L) on gravel Rd. 1.5m to marker on **Site of Elizabeth Female Academy,** opened 1818, chartered Feb. 1819, closed c.1843, which has a claim to have been "1st chartered college in U.S. to confer degrees on women."

(B) From Washington (R) on gravel Rd. to **Pine Ridge Ch.** 5m. (R) from Ch. on 1st Rd. 0.5m to **Edgewood** (1824) built on Sp. land grant to Juan Bisland & once home of Elizabeth Bisland, reconstruction novelist.

(C) From Washington (E) on US84 to **Meadville** 29m, seat of Franklin Cty. A few miles SE. of Meadville is **Clear Springs L.** (f.) & Recr. Area of **Homochitto Nat. For.** The Homochitto (Ind. "shelter creek") provides very favorable set of conditions for growing loblolly, shortleaf & longleaf pine, & some hardwoods. Cases are on record of trees growing 24" in diameter in 25 yrs. Area consists mostly of small steep ridges cut by innumerable creeks.

**72.5. D'EVEREUX** (O.sm.fee.1840), one of best examples of Gr. Rev. in Miss., numbered Henry Clay among guests. **73.** J. with paved Rd. (R) is site of **Slave Block** from which slaves were auctioned. (L) are several Hs. incl. in Natchez pilgrimage (see below).

**74. NATCHEZ.**

Through bus conns. Airport: No scheduled service. For RR. passenger info. call Ill. Cent. RR. which makes bus conns. Toll bridge to Vidalia, La. Accoms.: All kinds incl. "period" rooms in ante bellum Hs. Info.: C. of C.; Natchez Garden Club, Connelly's Tavern; Pilgrimage Garden Club, Stanton Hall. Fish: In near-by lakes. Hunt: Quail, duck; Foxhunters Club. Spring Pilgrimage c.Mar.1-Ap.3. Guides avail. all year but many of famous Hs. are open only during pilgrimage when some 33 are divided into 6 tours which take 3 days to complete. There are also Confed. balls & tableaux & Negro spirituals.

Natchez, on bluffs that rise some 200′ above the Miss. R., won approval even from the acid Mrs. Trollope (1827): "Natchez is beautifully situated . . . The contrast that its bright green hill forms with the dismal line of black forest that stretches on every side, the abundant pawpaw, palmetto, & orange, the copious variety of sweet-scented flowers that flourish there makes it appear like an oasis in the desert." Natchez has remained an oasis (you still can't get there by RR.) & has become the most extraordinary museum of ante bellum houses & Miss. R. culture in the South. "Never have I seen a community like this," John Gunther said ("Inside USA"—1947) but added, of this center of a reg. where the Negro pop. is greater than 50 per cent, here, "more than anywhere else in the South or the Nation, I heard expressed in their most extreme form the basic issues of the white-black conflict."
Natchez is named for Natchez Inds., a tribe of Muskhogean linguistic stock who practiced head flattening & indulged in complicated form of sun-worshiping. La Salle visited area in 1682. In 1716 Bienville est. Ft. Rosalie, named for Duchess of Pontchartrain, & in 1729 the Natchez massacred entire settlement. Fr., with aid of Choctaw, drove Natchez from reg. following yr. At close of Fr. & Ind. War, area was taken over by Eng. (1763) & remained a kind of 14th colony, more or less neutral during Rev. In 1779 Galvez took settlement for Spain. Much of previous bldg. had been along R. banks & Sp. engineer, Collel, designed town on the bluffs, so that today the Sp. influence still remains in heart of city. In 1798 U.S. took over in accordance with Treaty of Madrid (1795).
Then, with opening of Miss. R. & the Natchez Trace (see below), the great days of Natchez began. Down the R. came flatboats & keelboats, their crews boasting of

being "half alligator & half horse," & in 1811, the 1st steamboat, Nicholas J. Roosevelt's "New Orleans," arrived (Mrs. Roosevelt making the trip). Down the Trace came pioneers hungry for the newly opened lands. With them all came the adventurers, gamblers, prostitutes, & bandits who were to make "Natchez-under-the-Hill" infamous. "For the size of it there is not, perhaps, in the world a more profligate place," wrote John Bradbury in 1810 & in 1836 Tyrone Power, the actor, spoke of establishments "more obscene in their appointments than the lowest of the itinerant hells found at our races." In the meantime, Natchez on the bluffs grew rich & elegant. Indigo & tobacco had failed but cotton was to make Natchez as great a concentration of wealth as existed in U.S. The famous houses began to go up & the great & the near great to pass through. Aaron Burr & Harmon Blennerhassett used town as a base. Here Lorenzo Dow preached on "the latest news from Hell," & both Andrew Jackson & Jeff. Davis got married. In War of 1812, Inds. threatened town on various occasions & "Natchez Rifles" fought in Battle of New Orleans. In July 1863 town was attacked by USS "Essex" & taken over by Feds. under Ransom. After the Civil War, steamboating continued to bring some prosperity to town. Capt. Tom Leathers had lived here at Myrtle Terrace & built a series of steamboats called "The Natchez," one of which was to run the famous race with "The Lee" (1870). Yet Natchez never regained its importance, its pop. hardly increased in 3 generations & it was saved from the depths of the depression by the ladies who organized its 1st pilgrimage to old houses. The pilgrimages became so popular & the "ante bellum" in such demand that a Natchez child, asked the breed of her dog, is said to have replied: "Oh just a little ole ante bellum dog." Just before World War II rival pilgrimage clubs were suing each other; now peace reigns. But the recent est. of large tire & roofing mfg. plants, the discovery of oil near-by, & the use of the flame cultivator & mechanical picker in the cotton fields would indicate great social & economic changes in store even for Natchez.

PTS. OF INT.: (1) State & Main Sts., **Adams County Cth.** (O.1818) in what was center of city as planned by Sp. & probably on site of Ch. of San Salvador. (2) 311 Market St., **Parish H. of San Salvador** (1786), now a rooming house. (3) S. Wall & State Sts., **Mercer H.** (1818.Georg.), now a funeral home, where Andrew Jackson stayed on way to unveiling of his equestrian statue in New Orleans. (4) S. Wall & State Sts., **Lawyers' Row** (pre-1796 by Sp.) probably 1st used as commissary, now a colored rooming house. S. S. Prentiss, Gov. Quitman, Gen. Walker all had offices here. (5) 207 S. Wall St., **Gov. Holmes H.,** also known as Conti H. (O.fee.c.1788.Sp. Provincial). Holmes was last territorial gov. & 1st state gov. of Miss. (6) S. Wall & Washington Sts., **Spanish H.,** example of average dwelling during Sp. regime, now apt. house. (7) S. Pearl & Washington Sts., **Britton H.** (O.appl.1858.Gr.Rev.), struck by shell in bombardment of 1863. (8) S. Pearl & State Sts., **First Presb. Ch.** (1829 by Levi Weeks of Boston.Gr.Rev.). (9) 111 S. Pearl St., **Mem. Hall** (O.1852. mod.-Sp.) houses Fisk Mem. Lib. (10) 206 Main St., **Christian Science Ch.,** formerly Planters Bank, chartered 1830 & 2nd bank in state (by John Hampton White of N.J.; Class.Rev.). (11) 107 S. Canal St., **Banker's H.** (1809), erected for pres. of bank. (12) S. Broadway & Washington Sts., **The Parsonage** (1840's), built by Peter Little. Little, it is said, growing tired of steady stream of Meth. preachers entertained by his wife, Eliza, a convert of Lorenzo Dow, in his own home, Rosalie, erected this one for church to do its own entertaining. Parsonage is on edge of bluffs on old parade grounds of Ft. Rosalie, & affords view of what remains of Natchez-under-the-Hill. (13) Foot of S. Broadway, **Rosalie** (O.fee.c.1820-23.Georg.), a sq. brick bldg. with white-columned portico, is maintained as shrine by D.A.R. Feds. used it as hqs. & Grant & his family later stayed here. (14) **Ft. Rosalie,** directly in rear of Rosalie, recently reconstructed, with Council Room, Guard H., Chapel.

(15) 107 S. Broadway St., **Bontura H.** (1832) with patio & iron-work galleries. (16) N. Wall & Franklin Sts., **Marschalk's Printing Office,** now colored rooming house, where Andrew Marschalk, Rev. officer, issued "The Mississippi Herald," July 26, 1802, 3rd newspaper in St. His press also printed the 1st 2, "The Gazette" (1800 by Ben. Stokes) & "The Intelligencer" (1801). (17) N. Canal & Jefferson Sts., **Connelly's Tavern** (O.fee.1795.rest.by Natchez Garden Club), a frame house with long double galleries & slender columns supporting an interrupted hip-roof, a notable example from Sp. Col. period. On hill beyond, in 1797, Andrew Ellicott raised Amer. flag for 1st time in Lower Miss. Valley a yr. before evacuation by Sp. Here Burr & Blennerhassett are said to have met to plan their defense. (18) High & Wall Sts.,

**Choctaw** (1830's.Gr.Rev.rest.), home of Alvarez Fisk, philanthropist who gave 1st school to Natchez, now Amer. Leg. Home. (19) N. Pearl & High Sts., **Stanton Hall** (O.fee.rms.for tourists;1850-57.Gr.Rev.rest.), built by Fred. Stanton, is one of most palatial in dist. & now home of Pilgrimage Garden Club. Huge Corinthian columns support portico, some of ceilings are 22′ high & there is a 72′ ballroom. A ship was chartered to bring its mantels, mirrors & chandeliers from Europe.

(20) Cor. of Clifton & Oak Sts. afford excellent view of Miss. R. Near La. shore is **Sandbar,** once a famous dueling spot. (21) Down bluff from foot of Madison St. to **Site of Magnolia Vale** (1831), famous for its gardens. (22) 307 Oak St., **The Wigwam** (pre-1819.add.). (23) 803 Myrtle Ave., **The Towers** (c.1818) described in Stark Young's "So Red the Rose." (24) 816 Myrtle Ave., **Cottage Gardens** (c.1793), noted for int. stairway, was once owned by Sp. Gov. Don José Vidal. (25) N. end of Myrtle Ave., **Airlie** (pre-1790.add.int.inter.), simple Sp. Col. cottage, was once H. of Don Estevan Minor, Civil Gov. under Sp. 1798. (26) N. Union & Oak Sts., **Protestant Orphanage** (1820). (27) N. Rankin & Oak Sts., **Melmont** (1854) was used as barracks by Feds. Breastworks were thrown up on grounds. (28) Jefferson & N. Rankin Sts., **Kings Tavern** (O.sm.fee), oldest house (c.1745) in Natchez, built of ship timbers on high brick foundation, was a blockh. & later an inn on Natchez Trace. Here 1st U.S. mail brought over Trace is said to have been delivered by Ind. runner. (29) Union & Main Sts., **St. Mary's Cathedral** (Cath.1843-51.Goth.Rev.), 1st cathedral in Miss. Adj. Cemetery is portion of old Sp. cemetery. (30) State & S. Commerce Sts., **St. Joseph's Academy,** est.1844. (31) S. Commerce & Washington Sts., **Trinity Ch.** (Episc.1822) contains a slave gallery. While it was under construction meetings were held in Cth. (32) 601 S. Union St., **Ravenna** (1836), built by Wm. Harris. Near-by bayous were used to smuggle food to Confeds. (33) Washington & Union Sts., **Green Leaves** (O.sm.fee.1812.Gr.Rev.) with furnishings of 1840 & china said to be painted by Audubon. (34) Washington & Pine Sts., **The Elms** (O.fee.c.1783); int. iron stairway; rooms once provided with bells, each of different tone, to summon house slaves. (35) E. end Main St., **Arlington** (O.fee.c.1816.Gr.Rev.by Jas.Hampton White); antiques, early glass, paintings. (36) S. end Arlington St., **Dunleigh** (O.fee.1847.Gr. Rev.), a sq. house completely surrounded by tall Doric columns on orig. Sp. land grant to Routh family. Orig. dwelling destroyed by lightning, 1845. Legend has it that songs of the ghost of a lady-in-waiting at court of Louis Phillipe who visited here can still be heard at twilight. (37) (L) on Homochitto St., **Routh Family Cemetery.** (38) Homochitto St. & Auburn Rd., **Hope Farm** (O.fee.rooms for tourists), consisting of 2 wings: 1st built 1775 & conn. by galleries to 2nd, built by Sp. Gov. Carlos de Grandpre, 1789. (39) Auburn Rd. at Park Ave., **Auburn** (O.free.c.1816.by Levi Weeks.red brick structure with white Ionic portico), in center of Duncan Mem. (swim.golf.etc.). Entrance doorway & spiral staircase of note. Edw. Everett Hale, Henry Clay & John Howard Payne were entertained here. (40) 42-44 St. Catherine St., **Don Estevan Minor H.,** now colored rooming house, stuccoed brick structure once home of Sp. commandant at Natchez. (41) W. end of Irvine Ave., **The Briers** (O.fee.c.1812-15.1½-story dormered cottage with wide front gallery), birthpl. of Varina Howell who married Jeff. Davis here in 1845. (42) From S. Canal St. (R) a short distance is **Richmond,** illustrating 3 different building stages: central portion, Sp. coll. c.1786; L. wing, Gr. Rev. 1832; R. wing, Eng. or modified Empire, 1860.

OTHER PTS. OF INT. within a few miles of Natchez: (1) S. Canal St., **Glenfield** (pre-1845.cottage-type) where Capt. Wirt Adams & cavalry had skirmish with Feds. (2) E. Franklin St., **Monmouth** (1818.Gr.Rev.) home of Gen. John A. Quitman, Gov. of Mex. City in occupation by Amers. (1847) & Gov. of Miss. (1850-51). (3) High St., **Cherokee** (O.Oct.-May.fee.1794.add.1810). (4) Linden Rd., **Melrose** (1845. Gr.Rev.), one of best preserved houses in area; furnishings remain almost as they were in 1840's & incl. punkah over dining-room table & Audubon's Natchez landscape. (5) Linden Rd., **Linden** (O.fee.1790.add.1825), home of Thos. Reed, 1st U.S. Sen. from Miss. (6) Liberty Rd., **Oakland** (1830's) contains relics from Concord, destroyed mansion of Sp. Govs. (7) Liberty Rd., **Monteigne** (1855.adaptation of Fr. chalet.remod.), home of Gen. Wm. T. Martin of Confederacy. It is said that Yankee horses were stabled in parlor & its rosewood furniture used to kindle fires. (8) **Windy Hill Manor** (pre-1807.Gr.Rev.add.). Here Aaron Burr visited while out on bail & fell in love with Madeline Price whom he unsuccessfuly tried to persuade to elope with him. (9) Pine Ridge Rd., **Landsdowne** (O.fee.1853.Gr.Rev.); orig. furnishings incl. pieces from Rbt. E. Lee's Stratford Hall & a portrait by Sully. (10) Lower

Woodville Rd., **Longwood** (O.fee), begun in 1850's, interrupted by Civil War & never completed, is also known as "Nutt's Folly." Planned by Sam. Sloan of Phila. for Dr. Haller Nutt, it is "Steamboat Gothic," 6 stories high, with 32 octagonal rooms, elaborate jigsaw ornamented galleries. Tools, paint pots & materials left behind by workmen remain. (11) Lower Woodville Rd., **Gloucester** (pre-1804.Gr. Rev.) was 1st "mansion" in Natchez district & home of Winthrop Sargent, 1st territorial gov. of Miss. (12) **Elgin** (O.fee.1812.adds.1840). Among other houses open during Pilgrimage are **Mistletoe** (1808), **Pleasant Hill** (1809), **Twin Oaks** (1813) & **The Burn** (1832).

**NATCHEZ TRACE PARKWAY,** extending from Natchez to Nashville, Tenn., memorializes series of Ind. trails that became a wilderness hy. binding the Old SW. to the Union. Perhaps paths were 1st beaten by buffalo in search of salt licks. Later they linked together the Natchez, Choctaw, Chickasaw &, possibly, Cherokee tribes. Fr., Sp. & Eng. explorers, traders & missionaries traveled the Trace, worn with time deep into the earth (25′ & more in some places) & overshadowed by ancient trees. In 1800 a post Rd. was est. between Natchez & Nashville & in 1801 Gen. James Wilkinson, commander of U.S. Army in the West & in charge of improving hy., wrote: "This road being completed I shall consider our Southern extremity secured, the Indians in that quarter at our feet, & the adjacent Province laid open to us." In 1st half of 19th cent., pioneers journeying to the rich lands of the S. & merchants & boatmen returning (N) were preyed upon by notorious bands of outlaws incl. the Harpes, the Murrell gang (whom Mark Twain called "a colossal combination of robbers, horse thieves, Negro stealers & counterfeiters"), Hare & Mason. More than one of the bandits ended with his head ornamenting a pole on the side of the Trace. Mason's own head was 1st "rolled in blue clay to prevent putrifaction" by former associates, including "Little" Harpe, who brought it to Natchez for the reward, were recognized & themselves beheaded. The Natchez Trace played an important rôle in the development of at least 4 states: Miss., La., Ala. & Tenn. Parkway will feature a hy. of advanced design some 450-500$^{m}$ long (commercial vehicles excluded), preserve & mark various hist. sites, & provide pic. & other facils. At present (1949) it is only open for short distances, including sec. entered from US61, 12$^{m}$ (N) of Natchez, & another entered from US51, 6$^{m}$ (N) of Jackson, Miss. Make local inquiries.

## Sec. 4: NATCHEZ to LA. STATE LINE. 43.

From Natchez (S), US61 runs bet. banks overhung with ancient live oaks. **3.** (R) **ELMSCOURT** (O.sm.fee.c.1810.remod.), known as "House of a Thousand Candles," has iron lacework reminiscent of New Orleans. Jenny Lind, Thackeray, Jackson & Lafayette were among the guests. **3.5.** (L) **GLENWOOD** (1830's), in a sad state of dilapidation, achieved national notoriety in 1932 as "Goat Castle" when its owner, Rich. Dava & his guardian, Miss Martha Dockery, were arrested (& later acquitted) after the murder of Miss Jennie Merrill. **14.** J. with gravel Rd.

SIDE TRIP: Take latter (L) bet. banks covered by Cherokee roses to a reg. that marked one of 1st Protestant settlements in st. (1772), when Capt. Amos Ogden claimed his grant of 25,000 as. from the Brit. Gov.

At **18.5.** US61 crosses Homochitto R. **36. WOODVILLE,** seat of Wilkinson Cty., holds annual spring pilgrimage. **Post Office** was once sta. of W. Feliciana RR. (chartered 1831), 1st RR. Co. in Miss., 2nd in Miss. Valley, & 5th in U.S. Rails were made of wood & financed by Judge Edward McGehee who figures in Stark Young's "So Red the Rose." **Meth. Episc. Ch. S.** (1824) has slave gallery. **Bapt. Ch.;** 1st meetings of congregation were held in secret because of Sp. est. of Cath. as state religion. **St. Paul's Ch.** (Episc.1824); bell was sent to Gen. Beauregard to be melted into cannon. Office of **"Woodville Republican,"** oldest extant newspaper in St. (1812). At Woodville is J. with Ft. Adams Rd. & St.24.

SIDE TRIPS: (A) Take Ft. Adams Rd. 15$^{m}$ (R) to J. with gravel Rd.

On this Rd. (L) 7$^{m}$ is **Pinckneyville,** once home of Oliver Pollock, witness in investigation of Wilkinson-Burr conspiracy, & hideout of Kemper brothers, leaders of Amers. when land claims were being challenged by Sp. Among int. Hs. are **Arcole** (after 1790), **Desert** (1800), & **Coldspring.**

At 21$^{m}$ is **Ft. Adams.** Father Davion conducted mission here in 1698 & Ft., afterwards named for Pres. John Adams, was erected in 1798. It was locale of Ed. Everett Hale's "The Man without a Country." Only traces of Ft. remain.

(B) Take St.24 (L) 1m to **Rosemont Plantation,** boyhood home of Jeff. Davis. Davis attended Wilkinson Cty. Academy near-by. House (1830) was built for his sister, Lucinda. Family cemetery contains graves of his mother & sisters. 15m **Centerville.** Near-by **Dickson H.** (1819) erected by Meth. circuit rider William Winans. 39m **Liberty,** dates from 1809. **Amite County Cth.** (1840). Opp. Cth. on Main St., **Gail Borden H.** where Gail Borden is said to have condensed his 1st can of milk. **Walsh Bldg.** (1840), Old Opera H. where Jenny Lind sang. **Presb. Ch.** (1853) had a slave as one of its charter members. Dr. Tichenor, who invented a well-known "antiseptic" began experiments in Liberty before Civil War. "I will use my antiseptic freely on southern soldiers," he said, "but want no damn Yankees to get it."

**40.5.** (L) **ASHWOOD,** once plantation of Geo. Poindexter, Gov. of Miss. (1819-21) & chiefly responsible for "The Revised Code of the Laws of Miss." **43.** US61 crosses **LA. LINE.**

## US 80—LOUISIANA

**LA.-MISS. LINE** (3m from Vicksburg, Miss.) **(W) to LA.-TEX. LINE** (21m from Marshall, Tex.). **205. US80**

Via: Tallulah, Delhi, Rayville, Girard, Monroe, Ruston, Arcadia, Gibsland, Minden, Bossier City, Shreveport, Greenwood. RRs. parallel route. Accoms.

### Sec. 1: LA.-MISS. LINE to RUSTON. 112.

US80 cuts through N. La.'s fertile cotton plantations, skirts some of its most productive oil & gas fields, & climbs from Miss. basin into hilly farmland on its way to the Red R. valley. Hy. crosses St. line in center of a steel bridge (toll) across Miss. R. **De Soto I.** (N) was created in 1876 when R. broke through De Soto Pt. In 1863, when Gen. U. S. Grant's forces were besieging Vicksburg, Union engineers tried unsuccessfully to dig a canal across the pt. so that gunboats could by-pass Vicksburg & escape fire of Confed. shore batteries. The R. later accomplished the feat in less than a day. Part of **Grant's Canal** remains on La. side, just (W) of **DELTA,** at **2.**

**19. TALLULAH** is typical Delta cotton town, lying on the banks of Roundaway Bayou in River Basin Swamp, often flooded by the Miss. Town grew up after 1870 around J. of the Iron-Mountain & the Vicksburg, Shreveport & Miss. RRs. & was named for the Georgia sweetheart of a V., S. & M. RR. engineer. Tallulah is at J. with US65 (see). Reg. (W) abounds in bayous & Ls. known for good fishing. **38.5. DELHI,** sett. before Civil War, was so named supposedly because its founder had just read Thos. Moore's poem, "Lalla Rookh," the story of a journey from Delhi to Cashmere. Sawmills & cotton gins are principal industries. **54. RAYVILLE** grew up after Civil War around J. of Vicksburg, Shreveport & Pacific (now Ill. Central) & New Orleans & Northwestern (now Mo. Pac.) RRs. Gas field (S). **57.** Hy. crosses **BOEUF R.** (good f.), near **GIRARD** (sett.1821). **62. CREW L.,** in **Bayou LaFourche** reg. (f.). **73. NE. CENTER OF LA. STATE UNIV.,** jr. college opened in 1931; modern bldgs., athletic fields & stadium. **76.** J. with US165, which is united with US80 to Monroe (see below).

SIDE TRIP: On US165 (N) & (E) 26m to Bastrop. 7m J. with Rd. leading 0.5m (W) to **Monroe Fish Hatchery.** 15m J. with St.815, which runs (NW) 2m to **Sterlington,** operating base for natural gas industry; its **Thermatomic Plant** utilizes recently developed process for breaking down superheated natural gas molecules into hydrogen & carbon. **Sterlington Lock & Dam** regulate flow of Ouachita R. US165 cont. through **Perryville,** 18m, site of gas-pumping stations & carbon plant, to **Bastrop,** 26m, an industrial town with plentiful supply of natural gas for paper, brick, lumber & carbon-black industries. Although laid out in 1846, the town has acquired an up-to-date urban air, reflecting its prosperity. In vic. (N) 10m on St.204 is 500-a. pine-forested **Chemin-a-Haut St. Pk.** (f.boat.pic.camp.), with bayous providing good fishing.

**79. MONROE**

RR. & bus conns. Airport. Good accoms. & recr. facils; f. & h. in vic. Info.: C. of C.

Monroe is on Ouachita R., which separates cotton-growing lowlands from the timber, small-farm & cattle-raising hill lands (W). It is La.'s 4th-largest city. In 1785, Don Juan Bautista Filhiol, appointed commandant of Poste des Washitas, founded a settlement here, soon afterward fortified against Ind. attack. Big land grants were made in vic., & arrival of 1st steamboat in 1819 opened prosperous era of cotton trading. The RR. came in 1860. Monroe in 1916 suddenly became an industrial center following discovery of gas fields near-by. PTS. OF INT.: (1) 301 S. Grand St., **Ouachita Parish Cth.,** a colonnaded stone bldg. In courtroom is the sword of Don Juan Filhiol. (2) End of Island Dr., **Upper Pargoud Plantation H.,** a gable-roofed frame mansion with Doric columns, built in early 19th cent. Beyond (N) is **Pargoud Ind. Mound.** (3) 1300 block S. Grand St., **Layton Castle** (1910), pink-brick structure with feudal tower, in garden setting. It incorporates part of H. built 100 yrs. earlier by Judge Henry Bry & contains many works of John J. Audubon, who was often a guest. (4) Forsythe Ave. & N. 6th St., **Forsythe Pk.;** well-equipped with recr. facils. (5) Thomas & Wilson Sts., **Bernstein Pk.,** Zoo.

SIDE TRIP: On US165 (S) through valley of Ouachita R. At 30.5m on US165, **Columbia,** seat of Caldwell Parish. Site was cleared in 1827, & it was a busy port for river packets until advent of the RRs. US165 enters rolling pine hills of central La., passing through series of small lumber towns. 53.5m **Urania,** center of **Urania For.** & home of **Urania Lumber Co.,** known for its reforestation work. To the (S) is **Urania Oil Field,** whose commercial centers are **Tullos,** 57.5m & **Georgetown,** 62.5m.

US80 crosses Ouachita R. to **WEST MONROE,** trading center of wide farming & stock-raising area & site of several wood & paper mills. On Coleman Ave. (S) of town is **Brown Paper Mill,** one of largest sulphate pulp board & paper mills in the world. The farmers in the reg. (W) grow sugar cane, sweet potatoes, tomatoes & watermelons, as well as cotton. The hilly country here is forested with pine, oak & gum. **112. RUSTON** (RR. & bus conns.accoms.& recr.facils.) is farming & dairying town, with wide, tree-lined streets & neat, well-ordered flower gardens & lawns. Although reg. was settled early in 19th cent.—chiefly by Prot. Anglo-Saxons from older Southern states—town itself was not founded until 1884, when Rbt. E. Russ gave 80 as. on main line of Shreveport, Vicksburg & Pacific RR. to be plotted as townsite. Ruston soon became trade center for surrounding area. Discovery of natural gas in 1935 gave impetus to new industrial activity. **La. Polytechnic Institute** (founded 1894), on W. outskirts, is housed in fine red-brick bldgs. on extensive campus. At 300 E. Georgia Ave. is **Amer. Legion Mem. Pk.** J. with US167.

SIDE TRIPS: (A) On US167 (N) 5m to **Vienna,** founded in early 19th cent. & eclipsed by Ruston in 1880's.

(B) On US167 (S) 20.5m to **Hodge,** small industrial town, & **Jonesboro,** at 22.5m. 46.5m **Winnfield** (inc. 1855), seat of Winn Parish, a reg. of pine fors., canebrakes & fertile creek bottoms among red-clay hills; depends chiefly on limestone quarrying, salt mining & lumbering. Town has produced many prominent attorneys, among them Huey P. Long, whose stormy political career as Gov. & U.S. Senator terminated in his assassination in 1935. At 1107 Maple St. is **Site of Huey Long's Birthpl.**

## Sec. 2: RUSTON to LA.-TEX. LINE. 93.

**18. ARCADIA,** seat & largest town of Bienville Parish, a cotton growing & processing area. **27. GIBSLAND** (founded 1884), at J. of Ill. Central & La. & N.W. RRs., is a shipping center. **Coleman College** (Negro), on S. outskirts, was founded (1888) by Oliver L. Coleman, Miss. Negro. J. with St.89.

SIDE TRIPS: (A) On St.89 (N) 9m, near **Athens,** is highest pt. of land in La.

(B) On St.89 (S) 3m is **Mount Lebanon** (founded 1836), one of 3 La. communities to issue its own postage stamps during Civil War; the Mount Lebanon stamp is exceedingly rare.

**43. MINDEN,** trading center of farming & oil- & gas-producing dist., is a comfortable-looking town with tree-shaded pks. & streets; founded in 1836 by Chas. H. Veeder, who named it for his parents' birthpl. in Germany. The fertility of the reg. & the shipping facils. provided by neighboring bayous assured its prosperity. It suffered serious disasters—a cyclone & a fire—in 1933, but its recovery was aided by discovery of oil & gas in vic. J. with US79, with which US80 unites (N).

SIDE TRIP: On US79 (NE) are **Homer** 20m, & **Haynesville** 33m. **Claiborne Parish Cth.** (1848.Gr.Rev.).

US80 cuts through broad Red R. valley, crossing **RED CHUTE BAYOU** at **c.63.5.,** in locality used by Roark Bradford for many Negro stories. **71. BOSSIER CITY,** named for La. politician, Pierre Evariste Bossier; an industrial town with fertilizer factories, oil refineries, grease plants, cotton-oil mills & RR. shops. **Ft. Smith Pk.;** ruins of Confed. breastworks. US80 crosses Red R. over Long-Allen Bridge.

**73. SHREVEPORT**

Lake & Louisiana Aves., Union RR. Sta.; 104 Market St., Tex. & Pac. RR. Sta. Fannin & Marshall Sts., Tri-state Bus Terminal. Market St. (N) 2m, Mun. Airport. Good accoms., incl. tourist & trlr. camps. Mun. golf & other recr. facils. Good f. & h. in vic. Little Theater season & concerts at Mun. Auditorium. Garden Tour (Mar.or Ap.). St. Fair of La. (Oct.). Info.: C. of C., 412 Milam St.

Shreveport, La.'s 2nd largest city, seat of Caddo Parish, is—unlike typical cities of the South—a practical, hard-driving town with broad, well-paved streets & new skyscrapers in its bustling business dist. It has reputation of being among wealthiest cities of its size in the country, a center of great tri-state oil-producing area. Sieur de Bienville & Louis Juchereau de St. Denis, in 1700, found Caddo Ind. village here along the bluffs overlooking the Red R. About 1803 Larkin Edwards, a Tennessean, settled on the site, acting as interpreter for the Inds., & his land, given him by the Inds. in 1835, became the nucleus of Shreveport. During 1830's a number of settlers built log cabins, a trading post & hotel. By this time, Henry Miller Shreve, assigned by U.S. Gov. (1833) the task of breaking through the Great Raft, a jam of drifted timber blocking the Red R. for 160$^{m}$, had succeeded in clearing an 80$^{m}$ stretch. Shreve was inventor of double-decked river steamer, the "Washington." Opening of navigation brought more settlers. In 1837, after the Inds. had surrendered their lands by treaty, Edwards sold his tract to Shreve & others, & town was incorporated in 1839.

Shreveport boomed, trading with hunters, trappers & covered-wagon travelers & shipping cotton & furs by barge & steamboat. It was so important by the time of the Civil War that it became, in 1863, the Confed. capital of La. & hqs. of Gen. Edmund Kirby-Smith's Trans-Miss. Dept. It was the last Confed. stronghold. To guard the city against attack by Fed. gunboats, 3 forts & an embankment were built along R. The city quickly recovered after the war & embarked on an era of prosperity that has cont. ever since. Steamboat traffic fell off toward end of the century in the face of RR. competition, but population increased. Discovery of oil in 1906 in near-by Caddo L.—afterwards in East Texas Field (1930) & Rodessa Field (1935)—gave city a major industry, attracting thousands of new residents. Cotton remained an important source of income, with such by-products as cottonseed oil & meal; & the plentiful supply led to establishment of garment industries. Lumbering & wood- & metal-working industries developed later. Shreveport became an important producer of sawmill, oil field & dehydrating machinery & of glass.

PTS. OF INT.: (1) McNeil, Milam, Marshall & Texas Sts., **Caddo Parish Cth.** (1926), an 8-story, gray-limestone bldg., is good example of modern monumental architecture. (2) Edwards & Travis Sts., **Shreve Mem. Lib.** (1923.Ital.Ren.). (3) Kings Hy. bet. Linwood Ave. & Mansfield Rd., **Shreveport Incinerator,** which has attracted internat. attention as example of functional architecture. (4) Head of Edgar St., **La. St. Fairgrounds,** covering 150 as.; racetrack, stock barns, exhibit halls & stadium. **St. Exhibit Bldg.** (1939).

(5) 2911 Centenary Blvd., **Centenary College,** whose Georg. bldgs. dot 40-a. rolling woodland campus, had its origin in College of La., chartered at Jackson in 1825 & later combined with Centenary College at Brandon, Miss. Shreveport campus was acquired in 1907. (6) St. Vincent Ave. bet. Fairfield & Southern Aves., **St. Vincent's College & Academy,** founded in 1866, occupies attractive 100-a. campus. (7) Foot of Stoner Ave., **Fort Humbug Confed. Mem. Pk.,** around site of Civil War Fort where, on one occasion, the Confeds. put up imitation cannon. Earthen breastworks have been restored. (8) Jewella Ave. & Woodford St., **Libby-Owens-Ford Glass Plant** (O.appl.). (9) On W. outskirts, **Cross L.,** city's reservoir & recr. center; redbud trees (Mar.or Ap.) along shore drive. (10) On US71 (S) 4$^{m}$, **Barksdale Field,** U.S. military airport (see US71). Shreveport is at J. with US79, US71 (see) & US171.

US80 cont. (W) united with US79 to **GREENWOOD,** at **87.,** where US79 forks (L) to Tex. Line (at Bethany). **93.** US80 crosses **LA.-TEX. LINE.**

## US 90—LOUISIANA

**LA.-MISS. LINE** (37$^{m}$ from Gulfport, Miss.) **(W) to LA.-TEX. LINE. 322. US90**

Via: New Orleans, Raceland, Houma, Morgan City, Patterson, Franklin, Jeanerette, New Iberia, Lafayette, Crowley, Jennings, Lake Charles & Vinton. L. & N. & So. Pac. RRs. parallel secs. of route. Good accoms.

### Sec. 1: LA.-MISS. LINE to NEW ORLEANS. 41.

US90 crosses Pearl R. Bridge & enters a vast marshland stretching all the way to New Orleans. **8.5. RIGOLETS BRIDGE,** spanning one of two passes conn. Ls.

PTS. OF INT.: (1) 400 S. Main St., **St. Martin Parish Cth.** (1853.Gr.Rev.), old Fr. & Sp. documents. (2) 214 Port St., **Convent of Mercy School,** occupying probably oldest bldg. in former Attakapas Dist., a much-remod. brick structure that once served as village hostel. (3) 100 S. Main St., **St. Martinville Ch.** (Cath.1832). In one wing is reprod. of Grotte de Lourdes. In cemetery is **Evangeline Mon.,** posed & donated by Dolores Del Rio, actress; marks **Grave of Emmeline Labiche,** "Evangeline" of Longfellow's poem according to local tradition.

(4) E. Port St. & Bayou Teche, **Evangeline Oak** marks landing place of Acadians, & tradition claims it also as meeting place of Emmeline & Louis Arceneaux, the "Gabriel" of Longfellow's work.

9.5m **Longfellow-Evangeline Mem. Pk.** (pic.restaurant), est. in 1934 as La.'s 1st St. Pk. Longfellow never saw La., but he received help on local color from his Harvard classmate, Edw. Simon, of St. Martinville; thus it is possible that Emmeline Labiche, whose story is almost identical with that of Evangeline, may actually have been the poet's inspiration. **Acadian Cottage** has coll. of records & Acadian relics.

(B) From New Iberia (S) 2m on St.25 to J. with St.445.

(S) 7m on St.445 to **Avery I.** (fee), most striking of the "Five Islands," is nearly round, c.2m across & surrounded by sea marsh & swampy thickets, with a cluster of hills at its center. There are areas of virgin woodland, abounding in wild life. The I., acquired toward close of 18th cent. by John C. Marsh, has remained in the hands of his descendants. **Jungle Gardens** (fee), around the home of Edw. Avery McIlhenny, have botanical specimens from all over the world. **Bird City,** est. in 1893 by Mr. McIlhenny when he discovered that the egret had become extinct even on Avery I., its last haunt, is the home of largest colony of egrets in U.S. **McIlhenny Tabasco Factory,** near Bird City, packs the sauce created by member of McIlhenny family & put on the market in 1868. **Avery I. Salt Mine,** end of main Rd., has been in operation since 1860's, when it produced salt for Confed. Army.

St.25 cont. to J. with St.1189, at 9.5m.

(R) here c.1m to 1,200-a. **Jefferson I.,** which was acquired by actor Jos. Jefferson in 1870's. **Bob Acres** is the home built by Jefferson on island's highest pt. **Jefferson I. Salt Mine,** one of country's biggest producers, began operation in 1921 & has produced an average of 200,000 tons a yr.

St.25 cont. through reg. sett. by Acadian refugees. Here barefoot Cajuns are encountered along the Rd. & a Fr.-Eng. patois is spoken in the remoter dists. Hs. are usually small frame dwellings with batten shutters, outside chimneys & stairways, always spotlessly clean. 12m **Delcambre** & 14.5m **Erath** are typical Acadian villages. 21m **Abbeville,** live-oak shaded, with narrow streets & unpretentious homes set in gardens, is center of a fertile rice-growing area. It grew up around St. Marie Madeleine's Chapel, built on a bluff overlooking the Vermilion R. in 1845 by Capuchin missionary Abbé A. D. Mégret. Abbé Mégret acquired a large tract of land, on which he laid out the town, patterning it after Provençal towns with winding streets & central square. The intro. of rice at end of 19th cent. brought influx of Anglo-Saxon Midwesterners, but the customs of the Latin community were preserved. **St. Marie Madeleine's Ch.** (1910), across from Madeleine Sq., occupies site of Mégret's chapel. From Abbeville, St.25 passes through rice & cattle country, whose trading centers are **Kaplan,** 30m, **Gueydan,** 45m & **Lake Arthur,** 56m. Here St.25 turns (N). 66m **Jennings.** J. with US90, the main tour (see below).

US90 emerges from the Sugar Bowl into undulating prairies of the Rice Belt. **159.** Here begins the Côte Gelée (Fr. frozen hills) extending through Lafayette Parish, so named because the Acadian exiles found firewood very scarce. Their descendants are a deeply religious folk. Their small wooden cottages, often unpainted, are kept scrupulously clean, & in some homes the women still spin & weave. In the gardens are medicinal herbs & plants. A visiting stranger is sure to be offered "café noir," & in the true Acadian home the coffeepot never goes dry or becomes cold by day. **167.5. LES JARDINS DE MOUTON** (fee), designed by Congressman Rbt. L. Mouton; rose gardens & cypress gardens, azalea-banked esplanade & mile-long Way of the Cross.

**169. LAFAYETTE,** seat of Lafayette Parish & commercial center for rich mineral & agric. dist. Its industries incl. sugar refining, cotton ginning, canning & syrup manufacturing & RR. repair shops. Probably 1st settlers were the families of Andrew Martin & the brothers Jean & Marin Mouton, about the time of Amer. Rev. The chief industry, cattle raising, was jeopardized in 1850's by a highly organized band of thieves, against whom the cattlemen organized a force of 4,000 vigilantes who put the rustlers to rout in 1859. Old customs remain. Afternoon coffee is served with ceremony. Buggies drawn by long-maned Creole ponies are driven into town on Sun., which begins with Mass but is also celebrated with fairs, bazaars, motion pictures & visiting. French is still the language of Lafayette among both whites & Negroes. The preservation of Acadian traditions is sponsored by Assoc.

of La. Acadians, organized by Dudley J. LeBlanc of Lafayette in 1930. Lafayette is also the home of the Live Oak Soc., whose members are 100-yr. old trees, more than 50 of them in La., Miss. & Texas. Annual dues are 25 acorns, to be planted in Live Oak Nursery of Southwestern La. Institute Farm in Lafayette. PTS. OF INT.: (1) Main St. bet. Lafayette & Buchanan Sts., **Lafayette Parish Cth.** (2) W. Main & St. John Sts., **St. John's Cathedral** (1916), richly ornamented within. In cemetery is **Grave of Jean Mouton** (d.1834). (3) College Ave. & Azalea St., **Carmelite Monastery of Mary, Mother of Grace.** (4) 338 Sterling Ave., **Chas. Mouton H.** (1848.rest.with adds.). (5) College Ave. & General Gardner St., **Southwestern La. Institute,** a St. college est. in 1901.

## Sec. 3: LAFAYETTE to LA.-TEX. LINE. 112.

**0. LAFAYETTE. 1.** J. with St.5.

SIDE TRIP: On St.5 (N) 24m to Opelousas. At 6m **Carencro,** whose name derives from Ind. belief that a monster died here & that the air long afterward was thick with carrion crows. 13m J. with St.245, which leads (E) 1.5m to rambling, oak-shaded village of **Grand Coteau.** The **Jesuit Seminary,** one of the South's better-known Cath. seminaries, began in 1838 & cont. until 1922 as St. Charles College for boys. From Grand Coteau (L) c.1m is **College & Academy of the Sacred Heart,** founded in 1821 to educate daughters of Southern planters. **Convent** (1831) is a 3-story brick bldg. with Corinthian columns & wide galleries. At 17.5m on St.5, J. with Rd. running (L) c.2m to **Chrétien Pt. Plantation H.** (1831.Class.Rev.). 24m **Opelousas,** founded as trading post in mid-18th cent., retains somewhat the atmosphere of a pioneer Fr. settlement, the streets centering at the cth. square & resounding still with hoofbeats & noise of buggy wheels. In 1769, when Sp. took control of La., it became the governing center of the whole SW. reg., officially known as El Poste de Opelousas. Later, from Opelousas, conn. by branches with the Old Spanish Trl., great herds of cattle were headed for New Orleans. As cotton & sugar-cane cultivation took the place of cattle raising, the town grew in prosperity as a shipping center. During Civil War, after Fed. occupation of Baton Rouge in 1863, it served for a time as Confed. capital of La., & St. Supreme Ct. cont. meeting here until 1898. Reconstruction period was marked by racial conflict & rioting. Today Opelousas is prosperous merchandising & shipping center, but still an easygoing & pleasure-loving town where French is spoken & Creole cooking is especially good. Among old Hs. are: 233 Main St., **Dietlein H.** (pre-Civil War); 304 Bellevue St., **Hebrard H.** (c.1830); & 413 Market St., **Estorge H.** (1840 or earlier). Main & Church Sts., **St. Landry's Ch.,** has records dating from 1777. 872 Main St., **Academy of the Immaculate Conception,** occupies probable site of the Sp. post.

Level prairie country stretches (W) from Lafayette to the Tex. Line, & rice fields blanket the land. **15.5. RAYNE,** a typical La.-Fr. town, has had important place in development of rice industry & is also center of frog industry. **La. Frog Co. Plant** is said to be largest shipper of edible frogs in the world. **23.5. CROWLEY,** seat of Acadia Parish, vies with Lake Charles for designation "Rice Capital of La." Nat. Rice Festival is held here in Oct. **24.5. RICE EXPERIMENT STA.,** conducted jointly by La. St. Univ. & U.S. Dept. of Agric. **42. JENNINGS** (sett.1884) has rice mills, machine shops & other industries. It was the site of 1st discovery of petroleum in La. (1901). J. with St.25 (see above). **52. WELSH,** one of the more rapidly growing Rice Belt communities, is often the scene of Cajun dances called "fais-dodos."

**72.** J. with US171 (see US71).

SIDE TRIP: On US171 (N) 46m to De Ridder. At 3m hy. crosses hyacinth-banked Calcasieu R. 5m **Moss Bluff,** J. with side Rd. on which (L) 2.5m is 1,057-a. **Sam. Houston St. Pk.** (cabins.pic.boat.swim.). 20m J. with US190, which unites (N) with US171.

On US190 (W) 13m is **De Quincy,** a fast-growing town which derives its income from surrounding truck, fruit & poultry farms & stock ranches, from the rapidly expanding tung-oil industry & from its modern RR. repair shops & turpentine, pine oil & resin extraction plant, one of largest of its kind.

46m **De Ridder,** seat of Beauregard Parish, in one of most diversified farming dists. in S.; also produces turpentine & resin & serves as reforestation base; market for wool.

**76. LAKE CHARLES.** (RR.& bus conns.Accoms.& recr.facils.Info.:Assoc.of Commerce). Nearest to the Gulf (S.37m) of La.'s 3 deep-water ports, Lake Charles almost encompasses the wide oval-shaped reach of the Calcasieu R., bordered with willows, water hyacinths & the moss-bearded cypress from which R. derives its name. Plans are under way for a magnificent bridge to cost more than $12,000,000. Town is modern in appearance, having been almost wholly rebuilt after a fire in 1910; its dwellings, mostly of recent construction, are set in luxuriantly landscaped grounds. Lake Charles is a combination of a La.-Fr. community & a Texas town, having been sett. by people of both Fr. & Anglo-Saxon stock. Ten-gallon hats appear on the streets, but the people cook good gumbo & drink strong black coffee. It is seat of John McNeese Jr. College. Its prosperity is founded on the oil fields in vic., on its deep-water port (opened in 1926) & a variety of modern industries. Among large plants are: **Cities Serv. Refining Corp., Continental Refinery, Firestone Tire & Rubber Co.'s Synthetic Rubber Plant, & Navy Berthing Base.** The 1st settlers (c.1780) were Martin Le Bleu & Carlos Salia, a Spaniard, who married Le Bleu's daughter & changed his name to Charles Sallier, Early travelers named "Charlie's" Lake in his honor. In 1830, the U.S. est. a military post, Cantonment Atkinson, because of the threat of conflict with Mexico over W. boundary of La. Purchase. A small wooden bldg. housing gov. records was floated by raft down Calcasieu R. from Marion, 6$^{m}$ upstream, under leadership of the parish sheriff, Jacob Ryan, who has since been called "Father of Lake Charles." Town became seat of Calcasieu Parish in 1852 & was inc. in 1867 with a pop. of only 400. By 1890, following completion of S.P. RR. from New Orleans to Houston, it had jumped to 3,200. Sawmills had been built & rice culture promoted; an aggressive advertising campaign attracted settlers. Growth has been continuous ever since.

PTS. OF INT.: (1) 2709 Shell Beach Dr., **Barbé H.** (c.1850), on probable site of Chas. Sallier's 1st home. Here, too, the pirate Lafitte is thought to have built a log hut &, as protection against gov. boats, the embankment (100′ long & 25′ high) which remains in front of the H. (2) Kirkman St. near Fournet St., **Bilbo Cemetery,** on site of Cantonment Atkinson. **Grave of Jacob Ryan,** the "Father of Lake Charles." (3) Shell Beach Dr., **Burton H.** (1925), in 40-a. pk. (O.spring) notable for its azalea coll., one of largest in S., & its camellia garden. (4) Foot of St. Andrew St., **La. St. Rice Milling Co. Plant,** which manufactures plastics from rice hulls. (5) W. end of Shell Beach Dr., **Port of Lake Charles,** with extensive docking & warehouse facils. At **Lake Charles Cotton Compress,** center of the port, baled cotton is compressed for overseas shipment.

US90 crosses Calcasieu R., on which log booms may sometimes be seen floating to sawmills downstream. **87. SULPHUR.** A sulphur dome (N.1$^{m}$) produced nearly 10,000,000 tons of sulphur bet. 1905 & 1926. **100. VINTON,** founded c.1888 by settlers from Midwest who named it for Vinton, Iowa; depends chiefly on the oil fields discovered in 1911. **112. LA.-TEX. LINE,** in middle of bridge spanning Sabine R. Spanish explorers named the "Rio Sabinas" for the juniper growing on its banks; but the Fr., retaining the name, attributed its origin to an incident involving abduction of some Ind. women by a party of Frenchmen, comparable to the "Rape of the Sabines" in Roman hist. The R. was W. boundary of the Neutral Ground bet. Fr. & Sp. territories. When Mexico revolted against Spain in 1821, it became the Mex. boundary; & when Texas revolted against Mexico in 1836, the boundary of the Republic of Texas.

## US 51—LOUISIANA

**LA.-MISS. LINE** (16$^{m}$ from McComb, Miss.) **(S) to NEW ORLEANS. 97. US51**

Via: Kentwood, Amite, Hammond, Springfield & Laplace. Route is paralleled by Ill. Central RR. Accoms. at frequent intervals.

US51 descends from hills forested with pine into one of country's best strawberry-growing regs. **4.5. KENTWOOD,** inc. in 1893, was a favored spot among New Orleans excursionists for picnics, barbecues & trap-shooting meets. **9.** J. with Rd. which leads (E) into **Camp Moore Confed. Cemetery,** where Mon. marks burial place of 400 unknown soldiers who died during measles epidemic in training camp on this site. **13. FLUKER.** J. with St.35 (see US61), which unites (S) with US51 to Amite. **18. ROSELAND,** founded in 1888 by Chicago firm that owned surrounding timber lands. Influence of Northern architecture & farming methods is still noticeable. **20. AMITE,** an older settlement, began with bldg. of the RR., which attracted plantation families from remote secs. Dairying, truck-farming & lumbering are main sources of income. Amite is at southern J. with St.35.

SIDE TRIP: On St.35 (E) 44$^{m}$ to Bogalusa. At 24$^{m}$ is **Franklinton,** seat of Washington Parish. Until turn of the century it was a backwoods village, dating from 1819, but is now distribution pt. for pine, farm & dairy country. Here & there are pecan orchards & tung groves. 44$^{m}$ **Bogalusa,** bustling industrial town supported by manufacture of paper, tung oil & lumber; seat of La. St. Univ. Forestry School. It is in heart of heavily wooded yellow-pine belt under planned program of conservation & reforestation. **Great Southern Lumber**

**Mill,** opened c.1906, is said to be world's largest sawmill. c.16$^m$ (SW) is **Goodyear Plantation** (O.appl.), where thousands of tung trees are grown.

**26. INDEPENDENCE,** often called "Little Italy," is surrounded by strawberry farms. In early 1900's, 2 Ital. families were brought here by local residents who had faith in ability of Itals. as truck gardeners & berry growers. The venture was so successful that many more Itals. came. US51 cuts (S) through center of the strawberry belt. **35. HAMMOND,** the "Strawberry Capital of America," has shady streets lined with well-kept homes in groves of pine & oak. Settlement progressed slowly until 1885, when Ill. Central RR. inaugurated a colonization program to encourage immigration from the North. At height of the strawberry season in spring the town seethes with activity, as each day's pick is auctioned off by growers' associations. Strawberry Festival (Mar.). **Southeastern La. College** (founded 1925) is housed in group of modern buildings on 375-a. campus in N. part of town. Hammond is at J. with US190.

SIDE TRIP: On US190 (E) 23$^m$ to **Covington,** seat of St. Tammany Parish since 1828, a yr.-round health & pleasure resort on banks of Bogue Falaya. Reg. was sett. as early as 1769 & town itself was inc. in 1813. **Bogue Falaya Wayside Pk.** (pic.beach).

**41. PONCHATOULA** derived its name from Choctaw words meaning "falling hair," the Ind. name for Sp. moss; important shipping pt. for berries & vegetables. On Tangipahoa R., (E) 6.5$^m$ on St.122, is **Ponchatoula Beach** (f.pic.camp.cottages. hotels.swim.boat.). US51 cuts through pine woods & swamp-rimmed prairie to **MANCHAC** (f.h.), at **52.5.,** a resort at the bridge spanning Pass Manchac, which conn. L. Maurepas & L. Pontchartrain. Route cont. (S) through swampland to J. with Rd. at **66.** Rd. leads (E) c.1$^m$ to **Frenier Beach,** on L. Pontchartrain (hotels. boat.f.h.), where cypress & palmetto grow to the water's edge. **70. LAPLACE.** J. with St.1 (see US61-65) & US61-65 (see), with which US51 unites. **97. NEW ORLEANS** (see).

# US 65—LOUISIANA

**LA.-ARK. LINE** (12$^m$ from Eudora, Ark.) **(S) to LA.-MISS. LINE** (2$^m$ from Natchez, Miss.). **131. US65**

Via: Millikin, Lake Providence, Tallulah, St. Joseph, Ferriday. Route is paralleled by Mo. Pac. RR. Good f. country. Accoms. in larger towns.

US65 runs (S) near W. shore of Miss. R. Along the way are many Ls. left behind by the R. in its changing course. **3. MILLIKIN.** Route crosses plantation area where pop. is largely Negro. **4.** J. with Rd., which leads (E) c.1$^m$ to J. with River Rd., on which a short distance (S) is **Gossypia Plantation H.** (1856), designed in combination of Goth., Sp. & Moorish styles; named for the cotton plant, "Gossypium." **11.** N. end of **L. Providence** (f.swim.boat.), more than 5$^m$ long. Gaunt, gnarled cypresses dot the L. & its shores. **11.5.** J. with St.11.

SIDE TRIP: On St.11 (W) 10$^m$ **Oak Grove,** seat & prosperous center of W. Carroll Parish; several cotton gins & lumber plant. Old plantation bell near Cth. summons the cty. court.

**16.5. LAKE PROVIDENCE,** a quaint & charming town which rose to prosperity during steamboat era. **Grant's Canal** (see US80). Gen. U. S. Grant's plan, never completed, was to extend a circuitous waterway to confluence of Miss. & Red Rs. by way of Bayous Baxter & Maçon & the Tensas, Black & Red Rs. Across canal a gravel Rd. leads (L) c.1$^m$ to **Arlington Plantation H.** (1841). **44.5. TALLULAH.** J. with US80 (see). **68.5.** Hy. parallels **L. ST. JOSEPH** for several miles & then, after another short stretch, comes in sight of blue **L. Bruin. 85. ST. JOSEPH,** seat & largest town of Tensas Parish. Among ante-bellum Hs. are **Farrar H.** (O), community center, & **Bondurant H.** (O). **95.** Hy. winds around **L. ST. PETER. 97.** J. with Rd.

SIDE TRIP: On Rd. (W) 2.5$^m$ to **Wavertree,** plantation H. of plastered brick with balustraded observatory crowning hipped roof; marble mantels & silver locks & hinges.

**100.** J. with dirt Rd. leading (E) 0.5$^m$ to **Burns** (1853); frescoed int., marble mantels & silver trimmings. **c.102.** Along levee here is **SOUDAN** (O), a 2-story frame house. **103. WATER PROOF,** a town that has been moved (W) 4 times to escape encroachments of the R. Orig. site is now in State of Miss. **109.** US65 skirts **L. ST. JOHN** (good f.) &, farther on, **L. CONCORDIA. 117.5. PECANIA,** a 2,000-a. plantation, with largest pecan orchard in La. **121. FERRIDAY,** at S. end of L.

Concordia, was founded in 1903, has RR. shops, cotton gins, warehouses & lumber yard. J. with US84, with which US65 unites & swings (E) to Miss. R.

SIDE TRIP: On US84 (W) 43.5m to Trout. 16m **Jonesville,** on Black R.; largest town of Catahoula Parish, laid out in 1871. Chief industries are commercial fishing & lumbering. Site is believed to be that of Ind. village referred to as "Anilco" by Hernando de Soto about 1541. Inds. had built several large mounds, one of which, 80′ high, was one of highest discovered in America. Today only a small mound (topped by cemetery) in the center of town & another on river front remain. 31m Short distance (S) on dirt Rd. is **Catahoula L.** (good f.). 40m **Jena** (sett.in 1808), seat of La Salle Parish. 43.5m **Trout,** lumber town. J. with St.19, which runs (S) 16m to **Catahoula Div. of Kisatchie Nat. For.** (pic. camp.hotels near-by). Beyond entrance is **Fishville,** popular fishing & summer resort. **Big Creek Camp** (shelters.fireplaces.bathh.) is maintained by U.S. For. Serv.

US65-84 follows Nolan's Trace, a former cattle trl. to Texas blazed in late 18th cent. by Philip Nolan, horsetrader whose name was immortalized by E. E. Hale as "The Man without a Country." **130.5. VIDALIA,** seat of Concordia Parish. Here in 1786 Sp. Gov. Antonio de Ulloa est. a post, & in 1801 Don José Vidal founded settlement which became shipping pt. for great herds of Texas longhorns. It was known in early 19th cent. as "one of the toughest little towns in the world." Near shore of the Miss. may be seen a shifting remnant of **Vidalia Sandbar,** once a famous dueling ground. During duel in 1827 bet. Dr. Thom. Maddox & Sam. L. Wells, Jas. Bowie 1st used his famous knife when the seconds & several spectators took advantage of the meeting to settle their own old scores.

**131.** US65-84 crosses **LA.-MISS. LINE** on Miss. R. toll bridge. [Route cont. 2m (E) to Natchez, Miss., at J. with US61 (see).]

## US 61-65—LOUISIANA

**LA.-MISS. LINE (S & E) to NEW ORLEANS. 130. US61-65**

Via: St. Francisville, Zachary, Baton Rouge, Laplace. Accoms. in cities.

US61 (see) unites with US65 in Natchez, Miss. & cont. (S) to **LA.-MISS. LINE, 0.** Here route enters the beautiful Feliciana country, one of richest dists. in S.; sett. late in 18th cent. by pioneers who were of Anglo-Saxon rather than Latin stock. Many plantation Hs. in area are owned by their descendants.

**3.5. LAUREL HILL** (1820-30), galleried & columned H. built of logs & clapboarded. **8.5. WAKEFIELD PLANTATION** (est.1833). Cottage with pillared porch is part of orig. mansion. **12. AFTON VILLA** (1849), a 40-room Vict. Goth. mansion at end of avenue of live oaks. It has towers with cannon, Moorish galleries & cathedral windows & is ornamented inside & out with intricately carved woodwork.

**13. WAVERLY** (1821.Georg.), white frame H. with columns & gallery; notable for inter. woodwork. Just beyond is J. with St.124.

SIDE TRIP: On St.124 (NW) 7.5m to **Rosebank Plantation H.** (c.1790.extensive alts.), a gabled mansion with long galleries supported by brick columns. At 8m is J. with St.855.

Turn (L) 1m here to J. with gravel Rd.; then (L) on this Rd. c.1m to private Rd. (L) to **Ellerslie Plantation H.** (1835). Audubon, at one time, was tutor to the owner's children. Main side Rd. cont. 3m to J. with another Rd., on which is **Greenwood** (sm. fee.overnight accoms.), a square H. (1830) with Doric columns, panelled cypress doors & silver hardware; one of La.'s best examples of Classic Col. architecture.

St.124 cont. past **Live Oak Plantation H.** (1808-16), 8.5m & **Retreat Plantation H.** (early 1850's), 11.5m. At 20m is **La. St. Penitentiary,** a self-supporting institution, which has more than 12,000 as. under cultivation.

**15.** US61-65 crosses tracks of Yazoo & Miss. Valley RR., one of oldest in country, inc. in 1831 & completed c.1841. Orig. gauge & right-of-way are still in use. Near here is **The Oaks** (late Vict.), hip-roofed frame mansion with dormers & turrets, on avenue of live oaks. The neighboring **Myrtles** has huge verandas & ornate iron grillwork. Both Hs. are notable for their garden settings. **16.5.** J. with St.35.

SIDE TRIP: On St.35 (L) 0.5m is J. with gravel Rd.; (L) here 0.5m to **Rosedown Plantation H.** (1835), a 2-story frame H. notable for orig. imported furnishings. It stands among gardens at end of avenue of moss-hung oaks with Carrara marble statues. 12m **Jackson,** seat of **East La. St. Hospital** (est.1847), largest institution in La. for mental disease. Town was called Bear Corners & then Buncombe until Gen. Andrew Jackson camped here with his victorious troops after Battle of New Orleans. Part of orig. Cth. (1816) is now known as the **Schwing H.,** in center of town. What is left of **Old Centenary College** stands 4 blocks

(N) of hy. The institution, long one of La.'s largest & best, operated here from 1825 until its removal to Shreveport in 1908. 24.5m **Clinton** is a sedate town of shaded sts. & fine bldgs. of Gr. Rev. period. **Cth.** (1841.rest.1936) is hip-roofed, 2-story, plastered-brick bldg. with Doric columns & topped by octagonal bell tower. Of similar architecture are **Mayor's Office** (1824), **Dist. Attorney's Office,** Bank St., & 5 small bldgs. in **Lawyers' Row** (1825-29) on Courthouse Sq. Of same period also are **Chase H.** (c.1830), St. Helena St. near Bank St.; **Wm. Bennett H.** (c.1825), Baton Rouge St.; **Hardcastle** (c.1836), Baton Rouge & St. Helena Sts.; **Marston H.** (1837), Bank St.; & **Stone H.** (1806.adds.), Baton Rouge St. On Bank St., in 10-a. grove of beeches & magnolias, are 3 brick bldgs. of **Silliman College,** inc. 1852 & operated until 1931. St.35 cont. (E) through **Greensburg** at 46.5m, seat of St. Helena Parish, to J. with US51 (see), at 56.5m.

**17. ST. FRANCISVILLE,** called "the town 2m long & 2 yards wide," strings along ridge sloping on both sides to wooded gullies. At foot of ridge, overlooking Miss. R., is former twin town of **Bayou Sara,** founded in 1790 & disfranchised in 1926. Here the Capuchin friars, in 1785, built a monastery named for St. Francis of Assisi, from which St. Francisville derived its name. Oldest bldg. is **Audubon Hall** (1819), in center of town, a long narrow frame structure with columned porch. **Grace Ch.** (1858.Eng.Goth.) stands in grove of moss-hung oaks. **Virginia** (1839. adds.1852), on Royal St., is a stately H. with orig. furnishings. **Warriner Products Co. Plant,** where sweet potato dehydrating & canning industry began, achieved note during World War II by supplying huge quantities of these potatoes to the armed forces. **19.** J. with St.323.

SIDE TRIP: On St.323 (L) 3.5m to **Audubon Mem. St. Pk.,** formerly Oakley Plantation; a 100-a. area surrounding 2-story frame mansion (rest.) where Audubon spent several months painting & teaching art to Eliza Pirrie, belle of the family.

**22.5. FAIRVIEW** (1845), hill-top mansion which served for a time as Gen. Grant's hqs. & as Union hospital. **27.** J. with St.74.

SIDE TRIP: On St.74 (L) 3.5m to J. with dirt Rd.; (L) here to **Asphodel** (c.1833), a plastered-brick H. with Doric columns supporting wide gallery & gabled roof; flanking wings are miniatures of central part.

**30.5. PLAINS,** J. with gravel Rd.

SIDE TRIP: On this Rd. (R) 5m to J. with 2nd gravel Rd.; (R) here 0.5m to **Port Hudson,** once an important shipping center. Village has moved inland because of successive encroachments by Miss. R., which has deposited mile-wide batture below the high, white-faced bluffs that once formed the shoreline. Here in 1863 Confed. forces were besieged by Union men from May until July, when they finally capitulated. Remains of gun emplacements & earthen breastworks still stand. The 1st gravel Rd. cont. to J. at 6.5m with Rd. (L) to **Port Hudson U.S. Nat. Cemetery** (1867). Among graves of some 4,000 soldiers, only c.500 are named.

**40.** J. with Rd. leading (R) 0.5m to **Old Cheatham Place** (1818.mod.) in magnificent stand of live oaks named for Confed. generals. **43. SCOTLANDVILLE,** largely populated by Negroes, is site of **Southern Univ. & Agric. College,** founded in 1880. About 75% of La.'s Negro high school principals, supervisors, teachers & farm-demonstration agents are graduates.

**44.** J. with US190 (see US71), which unites with US61-65 as far as Baton Rouge.

**46. STANDARD OIL CO. OF N. J. PLANT, LA. DIV.,** one of largest oil refineries in world.

## 48.5. BATON ROUGE

RR. & Bus Stas.: North Blvd. at river for Yazoo & Miss. Valley RR. & Mo. Pac. RR.; Government & S. 14th Sts., La. & Ark. RR. & Kansas City S. Lines; Port Allen (see below) for Tex. & Pac. RR.; Florida & Lafayette Sts., Greyhound Bus Sta. Airports: 4m (E) on Government St., E. Baton Rouge Parish Airport; 7m (N), Harding Field. River Front & North St., Port Allen ferry (toll. auto & pedestrian). Accoms. of various types. Recr. facils. in City Pk. Steamboat excursions to Cincinnati & St. Louis. Info.: 444 Florida St., C. of C.

Baton Rouge, capital & 3rd-largest city of La., overlooks the Miss. R. from 50' Istrouma Bluff. It is a modern city bordered by great industrial plants & by the tree-shaded reaches of the Capitol grounds & La. St. Univ. campus. Residential sts. are lined with oaks, elms & magnolias. Here in 1719 the Fr. built a fort to subdue the Ind. tribes & gave it the Ind. name ("Istrouma" meaning "red stick" or in Fr., "baton rouge") derived from the reddened post that stood here to indicate the boundary bet. lands of 2 different tribes. Settlement was transferred, in 1763, along with other La. territory ceded by Treaty of Paris, to Great Britain, which made the port a pt. of origin for contraband commerce with Sp. La. During Amer. Rev., the Brit. garrison was defeated & forced to withdraw by the forces of Don Bernardo de Galvez, Sp. Gov. of La., at First Battle of Baton Rouge, Sept. 21, 1779. Baton Rouge remained under Sp. rule until Amer.-born residents of the surrounding parishes rebelled & captured the fort—also the settlement that had grown up around it—at Second Battle of Baton Rouge, Sept. 23, 1810. They raised the "Bonnie Blue Flag" of the W. Fla. Republic, & 3 months later Gov. Claiborne annexed the new republic. In 1817 the town of Baton Rouge was inc., & in 1849 it became the capital city.

At outbreak of the Civil War, Baton Rouge had c.5,500 residents, its pop. having doubled after 1820 when the steamboats opened up a thriving commerce with upper Miss. & Mo. valleys. The town was a miscellaneous cluster of unpainted bldgs., a few handsome dwellings, the penitentiary & 3 churches, flanked by the U.S. Barracks & the Capitol & newly erected School for the Deaf. Confed. flag was raised Jan. 26, 1861, following peaceful surrender of the Barracks, where it flew for more than a yr., until Union troops pressing N. toward Vicksburg after fall of New Orleans occupied the town. Town remained in Union hands until end of the war without opposition—except for the Confed. attack in Third Battle of Baton Rouge, Aug. 5, 1862, when Maj. Gen. Breckinridge's men waged for several hours a fierce but unsuccessful hand-to-hand struggle, raked by fire from Union gunboats. The Capitol was used thereafter to quarter Union troops until it burned down in Dec., 1862; it was not rebuilt until 1880-82, when the seat of gov. was returned from Shreveport, the wartime capital.

As the war debt lightened, economic & commercial development was rapid. With coming of the RRs., the port of Baton Rouge was recognized as an excellent distributing center, & industry was quick to take advantage. The pop. grew rapidly, tripling in 30 yrs., as dozens of industrial plants—oil refineries, chemical works & metal-working industries—were built in or near the city. Baton Rouge's deep-water port, served by several rail lines, assured its importance as a shipping center. Today agric., as well as industry, contributes to its income, for the surrounding area supports stock raising, dairying & growing of strawberries, cotton & sugar cane. It is, in addition, the retail center for a wide territory.

PTS. OF INT.: (1) North Blvd. & St. Philip St., **Old St. Capitol** (1882.Tudor Goth.), overlooking R. from terraced bluff; a castellated structure of cement-covered brick, granite & stone, 4 stories high, with 4 battlemented towers. It was designed in same style as orig. bldg. (1847-50), which Mark Twain called "a whitewashed castle, with turrets & things—materials all ungenuine within & without, pretending to be what they are not." (2) 3rd St. & Boyd Ave., **Pentagon Bldgs.** (1819-20), 4 identical hip-roofed structures of gray-painted brick with Doric columns supporting long galleries; used to house U.S. troops until 1877. At SW. cor. of Bldg. D is marble slab marking **Site of Sp. Ft. San Carlos,** built in 1779 on or near site of Fr. ft. built in 1719. (3) E. of new Capitol near Univ. L., **Old Arsenal,** built by U.S. Gov. (4) Lafayette & Main Sts., **Louisiana Hotel** (1840's). (5) St. Ferdinand & America Sts., **Old City Market** (1859). (6) 741 North St., **Dougherty-Prescott H.** (1840). (7) At S. edge of town bet. Nicholson Dr. & Highland Rd., **Magnolia Mound** (pre-1800).

(8) N. end of Third St., **La. St. Capitol** (1931-32.mod.Class.), constructed of Ala. limestone at cost of more than $5,000,000, towers above lawns, flowerbeds & landscaped drives of 40-a. pk. (9) In center of the sunken garden which Capitol faces is **Grave of Huey P. Long,** surmounted by 12′ bronze statue (by Chas.Keck) with bas-reliefs on marble base portraying scenes from political life of the late Gov. & U.S. Senator. A flight of 48 broad granite steps, flanked by monumental sculptures, leads to the bronze doors, c.50′ high. In Mem. Hall, mural-framed bronze portals lead to Senate & House of Representatives. Other notable chambers are St. Supreme Court, Circuit Court of Appeals & Law Lib. Inter. is lavishly finished with panelling & rare marbles & ornamented with sculptures & paintings. (10) North Blvd. bet. Royal & St. Charles Sts., **Gov.'s Mansion** (1930.Georg.). (11) Florida & N. 7th Sts., **U.S. P. O. & Cth.** (neo-Class.). (12) St. Ferdinand & America Sts., **E. Baton Rouge Parish Cth.** (13) St. Ferdinand & Asia Sts., **St. School for the Deaf** (founded 1852.main bldg.1859). (14) Government St. bet. East Blvd. & 13th St., **St. School for the Blind** (founded 1852).

(15) 5m (S) of J. of South Blvd. & Nicholson Dr., **La. St. Univ. & Agric. & Mechanical College,** one of South's highest-ranking univs. The 4,725-a. campus extends for 2m along the Miss. Beside R. are athletic fields & horseshoe stadium & fields & pastures used for experimentation. On 35′ plateau farther inland rise the main bldgs., mostly of brick with red-tile roofs in N. Ital. style, dominated by **War Mem. Tower,** a 175′ campanile. La. St. Univ. opened its doors in 1860 at Alexandria, under presidency of Wm. Tecumseh Sherman. Moved to Baton Rouge after a fire in 1869, it was accommodated in School for the Deaf bldg. & then in U.S. Barracks. In 1877, it united with Agric. & Mechanical College, formerly in New Orleans, & was moved to present campus in 1925-26. Notable bldgs. are: **Hill Mem. Lib., Huey P. Long Field H., Music & Dramatic Arts Bldg., La Maison Française & Casa de las Americas, Law Bldg., Agric. Center & Greek Theater. Audubon Sugar Factory** is maintained for experimental work. Baton Rouge is at J. with St.63, alternate route following E. bank of Miss. R. to New Orleans, longer than US61-65 but with more pts. of int. Also at J. with US190 (see US71).

SIDE TRIPS: (A) By ferry across R. to **Port Allen,** at J. with St.168. Take latter (S) along W. side of R. At 13m **Plaquemine** (inc.1838), named for bayou that flows through **Plaquemine Locks** (1909), where 5 sets of massive steel gates (55′ lift) control water in channel extending (S) to Morgan City. St.168 passes several plantations on way to **Bayou Goula,** at 20m, oldest settlement in Iberville Parish & long the center of thriving sugar area. Settlers came in 1718, & 1st levees on Miss. R. are said to have been built here. 21.5m **Nottaway Plantation H.** (1857). 23m **White Castle,** named for early 19th cent. plantation, whose site is now in Miss. R. 25m **Belle Grove** (1857), now in ruins, was one of La.'s finest plantation homes, built at cost of $80,000. At Bayou Lafourche Bridge near N. edge of **Donaldsonville** (see US90), 33m, is J. with St.29 (see US90).

(B) On St.63 (S) from Baton Rouge, 7.5m **The Cottage** (1824.Gr.Rev.), in grove of oaks. 13.5m **Longwood,** built of cypress during Sp. occupation (back part added 1835). 22m **Evergreen Plantation H.** (c.1840). 25.5m **Carville.** J. with Rd. leading (W) 2m to **U.S. Leprosarium,** only hospital in country where leprosy exclusively is treated. On 400-a. site, a group of modern fireproof bldgs. surround former **Ind. Camp Plantation H.** (1857), which now houses adm. offices; extensive facils. for occupational & recr. therapy. The institution, founded here in 1890's, was taken over by Fed. Gov. in 1921. Here in 1899 the chaulmoogra oil treatment was introduced & used until introduction in 1941 of sulfone therapy. 30m J. with St.1, on which trip cont. 32.5m **Belle Hélène** (1841), 2-story mansion with square columns, built by Duncan F. Kenner, Confed. Minister Plenipotentiary to Europe & later member of U.S. Tariff Commission. 38.5m **Darrow.** (Toll ferry crosses R. to Donaldsonville—see US90.) Here Rd. leads (E) to **Hermitage Plantation H.** (1812.Class. remod.). 41.5m **Bocage Plantation H.** (c.1801.remod.c.1845), built by Christophe Colomb, a refuge from Fr. Rev. who traced his ancestry to Christopher Columbus. 44m **Houma H.** (1840), popularly known as **Burnside,** a mansion of plastered brick with galleries & columns, flanked by hexagonal domed "garconnières." In village of Burnside is J. with St.88, which runs (N) to f. area. 45.5m **Tezcuco Plantation H.** (1855-61) is a raised cottage with columns & gallery, also flanked by "garconnières." Trip cont. (S) from Burnside. 51.5m The little wooden **Colomb H.** (1834), was built here by Dr. Christophe Colomb, Jr., a dentist who experimented with bagasse, the pulpy, straw-like substance remaining after juice is ground from sugar cane. He succeeded in producing a hard, clinkerlike substance that could be used as bldg. material, a predecessor of Celotex. 55.5m **Convent.** The handsome bldgs. (Gr.Rev.) of former **Jefferson College** (1831-1927), in wooded pk. of more than 100 as., are now used as a retreat by Jesuit Order. 65.5m **Lutcher,** trading center for vegetable & tobacco farmers. (Toll ferry crosses R. to J. with St.30—see US90.) 71.5m **Garyville,** a lumber town. 75.5m **Reserve,** trading center for productive sugar-cane reg. & site of **Refinery of Godchaux Sugars, Inc.,** one of country's largest. 81m **Laplace** (see below), at J. with US61-65.

US61-65 cont. (SE) from Baton Rouge. **70.5. GONZALES,** center of rich cane & vegetable-growing area. Below **SORRENTO, 76.,** once an important lumber town, US61-65 cuts through heavily wooded swamp, where concrete roadbed was laid at great expense over high embankment that had been scooped up by huge bucket dredges & allowed to settle for several yrs. before final layer was poured. Roadside ditches are covered with water hyacinths. Near here a narrow strip of land is used almost exclusively for cultivation of perique tobacco, a black & strong variety, one of most expensive grown. Producers are descendants of Pierre Chanet, nicknamed "Perique," an Acadian exile who arrived in 1776 & found the Inds. growing the tobacco. Attempts to cultivate the variety elsewhere have all failed. **102.5. LAPLACE.** Js. with St.1 (see Side Trip above) & with US51 (see), which unites with US61-65 from here to New Orleans. **130. NEW ORLEANS** (see New Orleans for description of city & pts. of int. bet. it & Laplace).

# US 71—LOUISIANA

**LA.-ARK. LINE** (31.5m from Texarkana, Ark.) **(S) to BATON ROUGE. 280. US71**
Via: Hosston, Shreveport, Bossier City, Barksdale Field, Campti, Kisatchie Nat. For., Colfax, Tioga, Alexandria, Lecompte, Bunkie. RRs. parallel route.

## Sec. 1: LA.-ARK. LINE to ALEXANDRIA. 170.

**1. IDA** was a drowsy agric. community until discovery of oil at near-by Rodessa Oil Field, in 1925, turned it almost overnight into a bustling oil town. **9. HOSSTON** marks entrance into Red R. bottomlands, where cotton fields & truck gardens stretch away to the horizon. Cotton is big crop in this area, & each hamlet has its own cotton gin. **39. SHREVEPORT** (see US80). J. with US80 (see) & US171, route (S) to Lake Charles (see US90).

SIDE TRIP: From Shreveport on US171 (W & S). Hy. parallels W. border of La. through rolling pinelands, entering several farmers' trading towns. 13m **Keithville.** 17m **Stonewall.** 32m **Grand Cane.** 39m **Mansfield,** seat of De Soto Parish & its largest town & shipping center. Founded by ante-bellum planters, it has broad tree-shaded sts. lined with dignified mansions. Lumbering, farming & oil contributed to its growth. Off US171 (S) 3.5m is **Mansfield Battle Pk.,** where 12,000 Confeds. under Gens. Edmund Kirby-Smith & Dick Taylor, on Ap. 8, 1864, defeated 25,000 Feds. led by Gen. Nath. Banks, in last engagement of Civil War fought in La.

US71 swings (E) across Red R. & then (S) through alternating stretches of farmland & wilderness. **43. BARKSDALE FIELD,** a military airport named for the late Eugene Barksdale, of Miss., World War veteran & flyer. It is among largest airports in the world in area, with facils. for 7,000 men. **85.** J. with US84, which unites (SE) with US71. **102. CAMPTI,** named for Ind. chief. **110. CLARENCE.** US84 turns (E). Here is J. with St.6.

SIDE TRIP: On St.6 (W & S) 8m to Natchitoches.

**Natchitoches**

RR. & bus conns. Accoms., incl. tourist camp. Recr. facils. Swim. & f. in Ls. in vic. Pageant on Cane River L. (May). Garden tour (May). Info.: C. of C.

Natchitoches (pronounced "Nak-a-tosh"), oldest settlement in La. Purchase, is now seat of Natchitoches Parish, home of Northwestern St. College, a tree-shaded town on W. bank of Cane River L. Here the old & the new, the Anglo-Saxon & Latin characteristics are pleasantly blended. Reg. was explored by La Salle in 1687 & by Sieur de Bienville & Juchereau de St. Denis in 1700. St. Denis, commissioned by Gov. Cadillac (see Detroit, Mich.) in 1713 to est. trade relations with Spaniards of Texas & Mex., posted 10 men with merchandise at Ind. village on site of present town. A detachment of soldiers came in 1715 & built a fort, of which St. Denis later became commandant. The post was often attacked by Inds. but survived. Its location at convergence of important water & land routes gave it commercial importance until, in 1832, the Red R. suddenly changed its course, leaving Natchitoches on the banks of a quiet lake, bereft of its chief artery of transportation. Town suffered greatly during the Civil War through cutting off of the cotton market. Today it depends chiefly on production, processing & transportation of cotton & its by-products.

PTS. OF INT.: (1) At E. end of bridge, on site of trading post, **Williams H.** (1776.remod.). (2) 142 Jefferson St., **Dranguet H.** (early 19th cent.), said to be Natchitoches' 1st brick bldg. (3) 530 Jefferson St., **Jean Baptiste Prudhomme H.** (4) 531 Jefferson St., **St. Amant H.** (c.1835.remod.). (5) 522 Jefferson St., **Serdot Prudhomme H.** (c.1850). (6) 104 Amulet St., **Chamard H.** (7) 436 Jefferson St., **Leopold Levy H.** (early 19th cent.). (8) 391 Jefferson St., **Winbarg** (or **Metoyer) H.** (c.1840). (9) 308 Jefferson St., **Lemée H.** (c.1830). (10) 706 Second St., **H. of Brides** (c.1790.remod.). (11) 223 Washington St., **Jos. Tauzin** (or **Campbell) H.** (c.1840). (12) 202 Washington St., **Old Lauve H.** (13) 120 Washington St., **Balcony Bldg.** (c.1835). (14) 612-614 Front St., **Ducournau Bldg.** (15) 606-610 Front St., **Lacoste Bldg.** (1852), now Elks Club. (16) Front & Horn Sts., **Prudhomme Bldg.** (1853). (17) 2nd & Trudeau Sts., **Trinity Episc. Ch.** (1857), said to be oldest Prot. Ch. in N. La. (18) Church & 2nd Sts., **Ch. of the Immaculate Conception** (1838). (19) Opp. is **Natchitoches Parish Cth.;** old records.

(20) At S. limits, on 650-a. pine-studded tract, **Northwestern St. College** (formerly La.St. Normal College), founded in 1884; housed in more than 20 modern brick & frame bldgs., all but hidden by trees. Campus has athletic fields, open-air theater, bridle paths & lake for boating. In Science Hall is **Geo. Williamson Mus.** (O). (21) Washington & Lafayette Sts., **Good Darkey Mon.** (1927), in "Grateful Recognition of the Arduous & Faithful Service . . ." (22) In 200 block 2nd St., **Amer. Cemetery,** on Site of Ft. St. Jean Baptiste (1721). Natchitoches is at J. with St.20.

St.20 runs (S) along Cane River L. into area dotted with plantation Hs. Within a few miles of each other are: **Achille Prudhomme H.** (c.1840), **Sompayrac Plantation H.** (c.1855), **Narcisse Prudhomme H.** (c.1840), **Bermuda (Prudhomme) H.** (1821). Just beyond latter, at c.10.5m, J. with St.423, which leads (SE) c.5.5m to **Melrose** (1833. adds.), a 2-story H. of raised cottage type almost hidden among large & tangled gardens; well known to writers, artists & research workers in La. hist. At c.10m on St.423, **Magnolia Plantation H.** (c.1870). St.20 cont. (S) from J. with St.423 (above). 22.5m **Derry,** center of 6,000-a. Derry Plantation. 24.5m **Cloutierville** (sett.1822). **Kate Chopin H.,** former home of author of "Bayou Folk" & "Nights in Acadia."

St.6 cont. (W) from Natchitoches to J. with St.428 at 22.5m.

A half-mile (N) on St.428 is **Los Adals Hist. Pk.,** where tablet & flagpole mark site of frontier fort. est. by Spanish in 1721 & which served as capital of Province of Texas until 1773. In 1806 the Sp. were forced by Amers. to withdraw.

23m **Fort Jesup,** farm town on site of Cantonment Jesup, founded by Zachary Taylor in 1822 as focal pt. of expansionist movement in the SW. All that remains of ft. are a log bldg. & some stone pillars in **Sabine Parish Hist. Pk.** Reserv. covered 25 sq. miles. Troops were sent from Ft. Jesup during revolution in Texas & during Mexican War. 29m **Many** (sett.1843), seat of Sabine Parish.

To either side of US71 lie secs. of **Kisatchie Nat. For.** (hqs.at Alexandria.pic.camp. cabins.f.h.), only nat. for. in La. **124. MONTGOMERY,** laid out in 1850, trade center known for fine watermelons. **140. COLFAX,** seat of Grant Parish, once an important shipping pt. on Red R.; named for Schuyler Colfax, Vice-Pres. during U.S. Grant's administration. It has several industrial plants & in vic. are large pecan orchards. On Ap. 4, 1873, it was scene of bloodiest riot of Reconstruction period in La., in which 3 white men & c.120 Negroes were killed. **162.5. TIOGA,** formerly a lumber town, has become trade center because of proximity to **U.S. VETERANS ADM. FACILS., 164.5.,** opened in 1930; provided with best equipment & recr. facils. avail. **167.** At N. approach to Red R. Bridge is J. with Rd. on which a short distance (R) are **Sites of Forts Buhlow & Randolph.** Here are remains of earthen breastworks erected in 1864 by 1,500 Confed. soldiers & thousands of slaves under command of Brig. Gen. Allen Thomas, in defense against invasion of Red R. valley.

**170. ALEXANDRIA**

RR. & bus conns. On St.5 (S) 4m, Airport. Good accoms., incl. tourist camps. Recr. facils. Reg. Tennis Tournament (Sept.). Rapides Parish Agric. Fair (Oct.). Hqs. of Kisatchie Nat. For. Info.: C. of C., in Bentley Hotel.

Alexandria, seat of Rapides Parish & La.'s 5th largest city, is often called the Hub City because it is at St.'s geographic center. Both it & Pineville (see below) across the R. are modern cities, distinguished by luxuriant pks. & gardens where flowers bloom throughout the yr. Site on the Red R., known as "Les Rapides" by the Fr., was sett. during 18th cent. when a military post was est. to protect the portage. Here Acadian exiles, Fr. soldiers from Canada, Sp. officials & traders est. themselves; & after La. Purchase came Anglo-Saxon pioneers from eastern states. Town was formally laid out c.1810 by Alex. Fulton, landowner & merchant, who named it for his infant daughter. It soon became a busy shipping pt. as steamboat traffic increased, exporting lumber, cotton, sugar cane & other products. In 1819 the ambitiously named College of Rapides was opened, & in 1824 a bank. What is said to have been the 1st RR. (W) of the Miss., running 40m (S), was begun in 1837; & in 1849 a steam ferry crossed the R. to the smaller settlement of Pineville.

Alexandria, unable to offer resistance, was occupied by Gen. Banks' Fed. soldiers in spring of 1864. Balked by the rapids, the Union forces dammed the R. so that they might send their gunboats upstream, to continue their invasion of the valley. Falling back after their defeat at the Battle of Mansfield, they set fire to Alexandria, May 13, 1864; the conflagration swept almost the entire business & better residential secs. Industrial life of Alexandria, 1st based on shipping & then on large-scale lumbering, is founded today on agric. Cotton is mainstay of the surrounding country, though there is much diversified farming. The woodworking industry is important, producing among other things textile-mill spindles & hickory billets to be made into millions of skiis. Fresh-water fishing is also a big business. Several St. institutons are located here.

PTS. OF INT.: (1) Fifth St. bet. Washington & Murray Sts., **Fed. Cth. & P. O. Bldg.** (1933). (2) Fourth St. bet. Beauregard & Fisk Sts., **St. Francis Xavier Cathedral** (Cath.1898). (3) Fourth & Fisk Sts., **Gemiluth Chassodim Temple.** (4) Bolton Ave. bet. Albert & Murray Sts., **St. James Ch.** (Episc.1926); Eucharistic service saved from bldg. burned in Civil War. Alexandria is at J. with US165 (see US80) & St.5.

SIDE TRIPS: (A) On US165 across Red R. to **Pineville,** united in community spirit with the larger city, though it has its own gov. Few stores have developed, those in Alexandria sufficing. On the other hand, there are no cemeteries in Alexandria; all are in Pineville. Most of its residences were built or rebuilt after destructive cyclone in 1923. Sett. in 18th cent., Pineville's hist. has paralleled Alexandria's, but city was not incorporated until 1878. PTS. OF INT.: (1) **Huey P. Long Charity Hospital** (1939). (2) W. end of Shamrock Ave., **Central La. St. Hospital** (est.1902), up-to-date institution for treatment of mental disease. (3) Shamrock Ave., Sanders, Reagan & Main Sts., **Pineville Nat. Cemetery** (est. 1867). (4) End of College Blvd., **Louisiana College** (Bapt.), which traces origin to Mount Lebanon Univ. (founded 1852).

(B) On St.20 & St.107 (W) 61$^m$ to **Leesville,** seat of Vernon Parish; founded in 1871 & named for Gen. Rbt. E. Lee. Lumbering & stock-raising are chief industries. The boots & wide-brimmed hats of the Southwest are often seen hereabouts. St.21 is alt. route.

(C) From Alexandria (SE) 101$^m$ on St.5, St.30 & St.93. Trip follows W. bank of Red R. for several miles. 31$^m$ **Marksville,** seat of Avoyelles Parish. Paved Rds. lead (N) 4.5$^m$ to breastworks of **Ft. De Russey** (pic.), held alternately during Civil War by Confed. & Union forces. J. with St.30, on which trip cont. (SE). [St.5 turns (S) to J. with main tour (US71) at Bunkie (see below), at 17$^m$.] 37$^m$ **Mansura,** in sugar cane & cotton-growing reg. At c.43$^m$, St.30 crosses guide levee of **W. Atchafalaya Basin Floodway.** 46$^m$ **Hamburg.** 54.5$^m$ **Simmesport.** 76.5$^m$ **Morganza.** At 87$^m$ J. with Rd., which leads (L) 2.5$^m$ to **St. Francis Ferry Landing** opp. St. Francisville (see US61). 87.5$^m$ **New Roads** stretches along N. shore of False R., a horseshoe-shaped L. (boat.bath.f.) lined with fine homes, outlining sharp neck of land known as Pointe Coupée. In front of High Sch. is **Poydras Mon.,** beneath which is buried Julien Poydras de Lallande (1746-1824), planter, philanthropist & poet, who amassed great wealth as plantation owner &, dying unmarried, set aside a dowry fund for impoverished maidens of Pointe Coupée & W. Baton Rouge parishes, where dowries are still given out. At New Roads is J. with St.93, on which trip turns (S) along W. bank of False R.

90.5$^m$ **Randall Oak** marks site of Poydras College, destroyed by fire in 1881. St.93 enters area rich in tradition, with many hist. plantation Hs. 92.5$^m$ **Old Oliva Plantation H.,** a low, hip-roofed adobe H. Near-by is **New Oliva Plantation H.** (mid-19th cent.). 93.5$^m$ **Parlange** (1750), one of La.'s oldest & most charming Hs., a raised cottage of cypress & mud & moss construction, hip-roofed & gallery-encircled, with flanking "pigeonniers." 94.5$^m$ **Austerlitz** (1832) & 95.5$^m$ **Pleasant View** are frame Hs. with pillar-supported galleries. 97.5$^m$ J. with Rd. leading (L) c.2.5$^m$ to **Alma Plantation,** once the property of Julien Poydras & center of slave conspiracy known as "Black Rebellion" in Ap. 1795. Present H. incorporates part of orig. Poydras H. (1789). 101$^m$ J. with US190 (see below).

### Sec. 2: ALEXANDRIA to BATON ROUGE. 110.

US71 cont. (SE) across fertile valley. **5.5. INGLEWOOD PLANTATION** has 3 Hs., each with galleries & pillars, built during 19th cent. **9.5.** J. with gravel Rd.

SIDE TRIP: On Rd. (R) 3$^m$ is **State For.** (camp.pic.facils.), an 8,000-a. for. preserve & wildlife refuge.

**15.5. LECOMPTE** (sett.in early 1800's) is one of central La.'s oldest settlements. A famous resident in vic. was Jas. Bowie, inventor of the knife that bears his name. He speculated in land with money made in slave-smuggling with pirate Jean Lafitte. **18. MEEKER,** sugar-refining center for surrounding area. **20.** J. with gravel Rd.

SIDE TRIP. On this Rd. (L) 3$^m$ to **New Hope** (c.1816.remod.).

Just beyond is J. with another Rd. on which (R) 0.5$^m$ is **Lloyd's Hall** (rest.1940), a brick plantation H. built by slaves. **21.5.** J. with 3rd gravel Rd. leading (L) short distance to **Wytchwood** (early 19th cent.extensive alts.), built of handhewn cypress timbers held together with wooden pins. **24. CHENEYVILLE** (sett.c.1811), surrounded by cotton & truck farms. From Cheneyville (L) across Bayou Boeuf are **Crescent Plantation H.** (1856) & **Walnut Grove** (rest.). **32. BUNKIE,** agric. & cotton center founded in 1882. J. with St.5 (see above). **68.** J. with US190, with which US71 unites (E). **71.** J. with Rd. (R) to **Krotz Springs.** Bayous in vic. are among best spots in La. for fresh-water fishing. US71-190 crosses **ATCHAFALAYA R.** & at **77.** the levee of **MORGANZA FLOODWAY. 78. LOTTIE** & **83. LIVONIA** are small sugar-cane settlements. **102.** J. with St.168.

SIDE TRIP: On St.168 (S) c.1$^m$ is **Monte Vista** (c.1855.rest.) among lovely gardens. 4$^m$ **Port Allen,** on Miss. R., seat & industrial center of West Baton Rouge Parish; laid out in 1854 & named for Confed. Brig. Gen. Henry W. Allen. The parish is probably only place in Amer. where custom of pub. dowry purse survives. Any bride of La.-Col. ancestry & resident in parish for 5 yrs. may share in annual division of fund left by Julien Poydras (see above). Toll ferry crosses R. to **Baton Rouge** (see US61).

US71-190 crosses Miss. R. Bridge (1840). **104. PERMANENTE METALS CORP. PLANT,** built during World War II; has yearly capacity of a billion lbs. of alumina, the powdery white substance extracted from bauxite to be converted into pig aluminum. **105.** J. with US61-65 (see), with which US190 unites (S) to **BATON ROUGE** (see US61), at **110.**

# NEW ORLEANS

**NEW ORLEANS**

RR. Stas.: 1001 S. Rampart St., Union Sta.; 1125 Canal St., Terminal Sta.; 705 S. Rampart St., S. La.& Ark. RR.; foot of Canal St., L.& N. RR.; 1300 Annunciation St., Mo.Pac.& Tex.& Pac. RRs. Bus Stas.: 1520 Canal St. for Greyhound Lines; Richards Bldg., for Mo.Pac. Trailways; 1314 Tulane Ave., Southern Trailways. Airports: At Kenner, 7$^{m}$ (NW), Moisant Internat. Airport; L. Pontchartrain, New Orleans Airport, Ferries: Five crossing to W. bank (sm.fee). Accoms.: All types plentiful. Road shows, concerts, ballets & opera at Mun. Auditorium. Horse racing at Fair Grounds. Swim. in Audubon & City Pks. & along sea wall on L. Pontchartrain (secs. for Negroes); f. at Chef Menteur & Rigolets sec., (E) on US90, & in L. Pontchartrain. Harbor Boat Trip (fee). Annual Events: Sugar Bowl Football Classic (Jan.1); Twelfth Night—King's day & official beginning of Carnival (Jan.6); Jackson Day, Battle of New Orleans ceremonies (Jan.8); Mardis Gras, Shrove Tues.; St. Joseph's Day (Mar.19); Spring Fiesta (before Easter). Horse Show (Ap.); La. Livestock Show (Ap.30); McDonogh Day (1st Fri.in May); Confed. Mem. Day (June 3); Southern Yacht Club Regatta (Aug.); All Saints' Day (Nov.1); beginning of racing season, Thanksgiving; Mid-Winter Sports Carnival (last wk.Dec.). Info.: Assoc. of Com., 315 Camp St.

New Orleans (founded 1718), port of the Mississippi Valley & largest city S. of Mason-Dixon Line, was a Fr. & Sp. city almost a century old when it became part of the U.S. The early town (Vieux Carré), with narrow streets & old bldgs., is preserved as a mon. to the past, while the growing city around it (3rd largest in area in U.S.) keeps pace with changing times. Orig. site of the "Crescent City" was at a sharp bend in the R., 107$^{m}$ from the Gulf of Mexico. Present New Orleans, enclosed by levees, extends from Miss. R. to L. Pontchartrain—an urban oasis in a lush, semitropical reg. surrounded by swamps & low-lying delta lands. The Vieux Carré, or French Quarter, the orig. Nouvelle Orléans, lies bet. Canal St. & Esplanade Ave., & from Rampart St. to the R. Here Latin customs & culture are jealously maintained by the Creole inhabitants, descendants of French & Spanish settlers & still forming a large part of total population. The architecture shows Fr. & Sp. influence but is peculiar to New Orleans. The 2 & 3-story bldgs. are adorned by balconies with wrought- or cast-iron railings & little wooden "perrons" (stoops) jutting into the street. Through hallways & porte-cocheres appear magnificent courtyard gardens. In the heart of the Quarter is Jackson Square, the old Place d'Armes, surrounded by the Cabildo, St. Louis Cathedral, the Pontalba Apts. & other hist. bldgs. The Quarter invites leisurely wandering about, browsing in antique shops, watching artists painting scenes that have been portrayed countless times, listening to the cries of peddlers of pralines, snowballs & other confections or, after dark, the sounds of gaiety from the night spots. Tree-lined Esplanade Ave., the E. boundary, was the "Promenade Publique" in the 1830's, lined with aristocratic mansions. In the "Uptown" sec., the intermixture of Anglo-Saxon & Creole makes the Latin influence less readily apparent. The Garden Dist., bet. St. Charles Ave. & the R., was settled by Amers. who arrived after 1803 &, finding the Creoles antagonistic, developed a settlement of their own outside the old town's ramparts. Here the houses, set in deep gardens, are of Gr. Rev. period, with characteristic white-columned wide verandas, cast-iron railings & white doorways.

The R. front has unfailing interest. Here, on wharves extending for miles, the longshoremen trundle cotton & coffee or tote bananas on their shoulders. Down the coffee-colored Miss., ships from every part of the world carry off the produce of the Miss. Valley.

On the N. boundary, connected with the Miss. by the Industrial Canal, is L. Pontchartrain, with a 6$^{m}$-long sea wall, a popular swimming place throughout the summer. Pontchartrain Beach is the amusement center, & the long Lake Shore Pky. is becoming a show place of the city. From this L., as from the R. & near-by waterways, comes the sea food for which New Orleans is justly celebrated.

Algiers, the 5th of New Orleans' 5 dists. (annexed in 1870), lies across R. opp. French Quarter (ferry from Canal St.). It seems more like a bayou or upriver town than part of the city, with industrial plants & small farms cramping the settled area. Most probable explanation of its name is similarity of its position in relation to New Orleans to that of Algiers in relation to France. Metairie, Jefferson Parish suburb NW. of city, is a rapidly growing residential dist.

Good food (as well as good drink) is only one of many pleasures to be enjoyed at any number of noted restaurants & night clubs, for New Orleans is a gay city, a place in which to have a good time. The gayest of good times is, of course, Mardi Gras, the bacchanalia that ushers in the Lenten season. In the weeks beforehand, a series of splendid & exclusive balls gives impetus to the growing carnival spirit, which bursts forth unrestrained when the Krewe of Babylon swings down St. Charles Ave. on the Wednesday night preceding Mardi Gras. From then until Ash Wednesday, parade follows parade, & dancing & merrymaking spread throughout the city. Cars from every state jam the streets, hotels are crowded, restaurant & night-club space is at a premium. On Mardi Gras, the whole city, attired in every conceivable costume, turns out for one of the greatest shows in America, thronging to Canal St., where dancing & buffoonery prevail until midnight.

New Orleans was founded c.1718 by Jean Baptiste le Moyne, Sieur de Bienville, who plotted the city & named it in honor of the Duc d'Orléans, Regent of France. The new settlement superseded Biloxi in 1723 as capital of the colonial empire of La., although it was then a mere outpost housing officials & soldiers, merchants, slaves & river men. To provide wives for the settlers, the French Gov., in 1728, sent out young women known as "filles à la cassette," because of the small chests of clothes & linens allotted them. They were to be chaperoned by 6 Ursuline nuns who had arrived the yr. before. Under the Marquis de Vaudreuil (1743-53), New Orleans developed a gay social life, imitating that of Versailles as reproduced for the citizens in the elegant manners & lavish entertainments of the Marquis. For a long time thereafter, New Orleans was known both as a rowdy river town & as a socially exclusive cultural center.

Following partition of La. bet. Spain & England (1763), New Orleans was made the capital of Sp. La. Its citizens received the commissioner, Antonio de Ulloa, with hostility in 1766 & after 2 yrs. of simmering revolt, rose up to demand his expulsion. New Orleans became the 1st colonial capital to rebel against European rule when, on Oct. 27-28, a mob of 400 took over the city & forced Ulloa to flee to Cuba. Independence was short-lived. On Aug. 17, 1769, Count Alex. O'Reilly arrived with 24 ships & more than 2,000 men, & the next day the flag of Spain was raised to shouts of "Viva el Rey" & the thunder of cannon.

The Great Fire of 1788 destroyed more than 800 bldgs., incl. nearly all of any importance. Hardly had the city been rebuilt, when a 2nd fire in 1794 destroyed 212 bldgs.

In 1803, New Orleans witnessed, within 20 days, the transfer of La. to 2 nations. On the day of formal transfer to France, Nov. 30, the populace, gathered in the Place d'Armes for the flag-raising, learned that the colony had been sold to the U.S. The raising of the Amer. flag 20 days later was greeted with little enthusiasm. The pop., however, increased from about 10,000 in 1803 to 24,552 in 1810. Much of the increase was due to arrival of refugees from Santo Domingo, but there was also a great influx of Amers. interested in the port's commercial possibilities. After incorporation on Feb. 17, 1805, New Orleans exercised for the 1st time the right to choose its own officials. The College of La. opened in 1811, & in 1812 the "New Orleans," 1st steamboat to descend the Miss., began making the run to Natchez. New Orleans became the capital of La. when the latter was admitted to the Union, Ap. 30, 1812.

At the close of the War of 1812 the city was belatedly attacked by a Brit. force led by Gen. Sir Edw. Pakenham. After several preliminary engagements, Gen. Andrew Jackson & his hastily organized army decisively defeated the invaders Jan. 8, 1815 in the Battle of New Orleans. The period preceding the Civil War was one of tranquil prosperity. As river trade increased, the city boomed as a cotton & slave market. By 1840 it was the 4th largest city (pop.102,912) in the U.S. & rivalling New York for 1st place among Amer. ports. A new public school system was est. in 1847, & the Univ. of La. (now Tulane Univ.) absorbed the Medical College of La., founded in 1835. Operatic & dramatic performances rivaled anything offered in America at the time; many European & Amer. artists set up studios, & society reveled at magnificent balls & receptions, horse & steamboat races, cock- & dog-fights, dueling & gambling. Only recurrent yellow fever epidemics & constant fear of flood darkened the scene.

New Orleans took an active part in the Civil War because it, more than any other city in the South, depended upon slavery & the cotton crop for its prosperity. As chief port of the Confed., it became an early Fed. objective. In Ap., 1862, it was forced to surrender when Adm. David G. Farragut, with a fleet of wooden ships & mortar schooners, crippled Forts Jackson & St. Philip on the Miss. R. below the city. Gen. Benj. F. Butler began, in May, a dictatorial rule that lasted till the war's end. From 1865 to 1877 racial & political strife dominated the city. Riots bet. whites & Negroes broke out frequently, as each sought to control the city gov. Elections resembled military campaigns. White citizens formed the Crescent White League, which defeated the police in a street battle Sept. 14, 1874 & set up its own gov. Military law was quickly est. by the Fed. Gov. & the Reconstruction regime reinstated.

In 1877 home rule was restored & slowly New Orleans rebuilt itself. Most important to a commercial renaissance was the deepening of the channel at the river's mouth, accomplished in the 1870's by Capt. Jas. B. Eads. In 1883 the city was linked by RRs. with the North & West, becoming the hub of the St. network. Canal St. had electric lights in 1882, & horsecars were supplanted by trolleys in 1892. From then on, civic enterprises—the Public Belt Ry., Inner Harbor Navigation Canal, improved docking facils., Bonnet Carré Spillway, Huey P. Long Bridge, & 3 Airports —have made New Orleans a modern metropolis. Recent developments are the Internat. House, the Internat. Trade Mart, & the Foreign Trade Zone, the country's 2nd "free port." Another Miss. R. bridge or tunnel, a new RR. terminal & a new tidewater channel are planned.

New Orleans is the country's 2nd port in value of foreign commerce & is the air hub of the Americas. It produces half the country's industrial alcohol & more than three-fourths of its washable suits for men. Burlap, cotton textiles, paper bags, fertilizer, lumber, furniture, petroleum, cottonseed & sugar products are also important.

PTS. OF INT.—FRENCH QUARTER: (1) Bourbon & Bienville Sts., **Absinthe H.** (post-1806), tavern where adventurers, traders & Creole gentlemen gathered, & where, according to legend, Andrew Jackson & Jean Lafitte planned defense of New Orleans. (2) Royal & Conti Sts., **Mortgage Office** (1826), now Amer. Legion Home; one of Royal St.'s finest bldgs. & once city's financial center. (3) 401 Royal St., **Old Bank of La.** (1821); built from design by Benj. H. Latrobe. (4) 417 Royal St., **Patio Royal** (1801), built as residence but used as Bank of La. (5) Royal, Conti, Chartres & St. Louis Sts., **New Orleans Cth.** (1910). (6) 820 St. Louis St., **Grima H.** (c.1825), noted for lovely courtyard. (7) 520 Royal St., **Brulatour Residence,** home of Francois Seignouret & afterward of Pierre Brulatour, wine importers. (8) 710 Toulouse St., **Court of the Two Lions** (1798), purchased in 1819 by Vincent Nolte, whose "Fifty Years in Both Hemispheres" provided source material for "Anthony Adverse." (9) 613 Royal St., **Court of the Two Sisters** (pre-1840). (10) 631 Royal St., **Patti's Court,** once home of Adelina Patti.

(11) Royal & St. Peter Sts., **First Skyscraper** (1811), said to be 1st bldg. in Old Square more than 2 stories high. (12) 700 Royal St., **Labranche H.** (c.1835). (13) 712 Royal St., **Arts & Crafts Club** (1823), in former home of Dr. Pierre Thomas. (14) 717 Orleans St., **Orleans Ballroom,** believed to have been scene of "quadroon balls." In 1881 it was purchased by Negro philanthropist, Thomy Lafon, for a Negro convent. (15) 632 Dumaine St., **Madame John's Legacy** (early 18th cent.), believed to be oldest bldg. in Miss. Valley, was built by sea capt. Jean Pascal, who came to New Orleans in 1726. (16) 941 Bourbon St., **Lafitte's Blacksmith Shop,** where, according to legend, Jean & Pierre Lafitte posed as blacksmiths while dealing in "black ivory." (17) 1140 Royal St., **Haunted H.** (1832.Fr.Empire), now an apt. H. This beautiful mansion is said to be haunted by the brutally mistreated slaves of Madame Louis Lalaurie. (18) 420 Esplanade Ave., **Old U.S. Mint** (1835), scene of Jackson's review of troops & of hanging, in 1862, of Wm. Mumford, who had pulled down the Amer. flag. (19) Decatur & N. Peters Sts. from Barracks to St. Ann St., **French Market** (1791.remod.). (20) 1114 Chartres St., **Ursuline Convent** (soon after 1727), occupied by Ursuline Order for 90 yrs. (21) 113 Chartres St.,

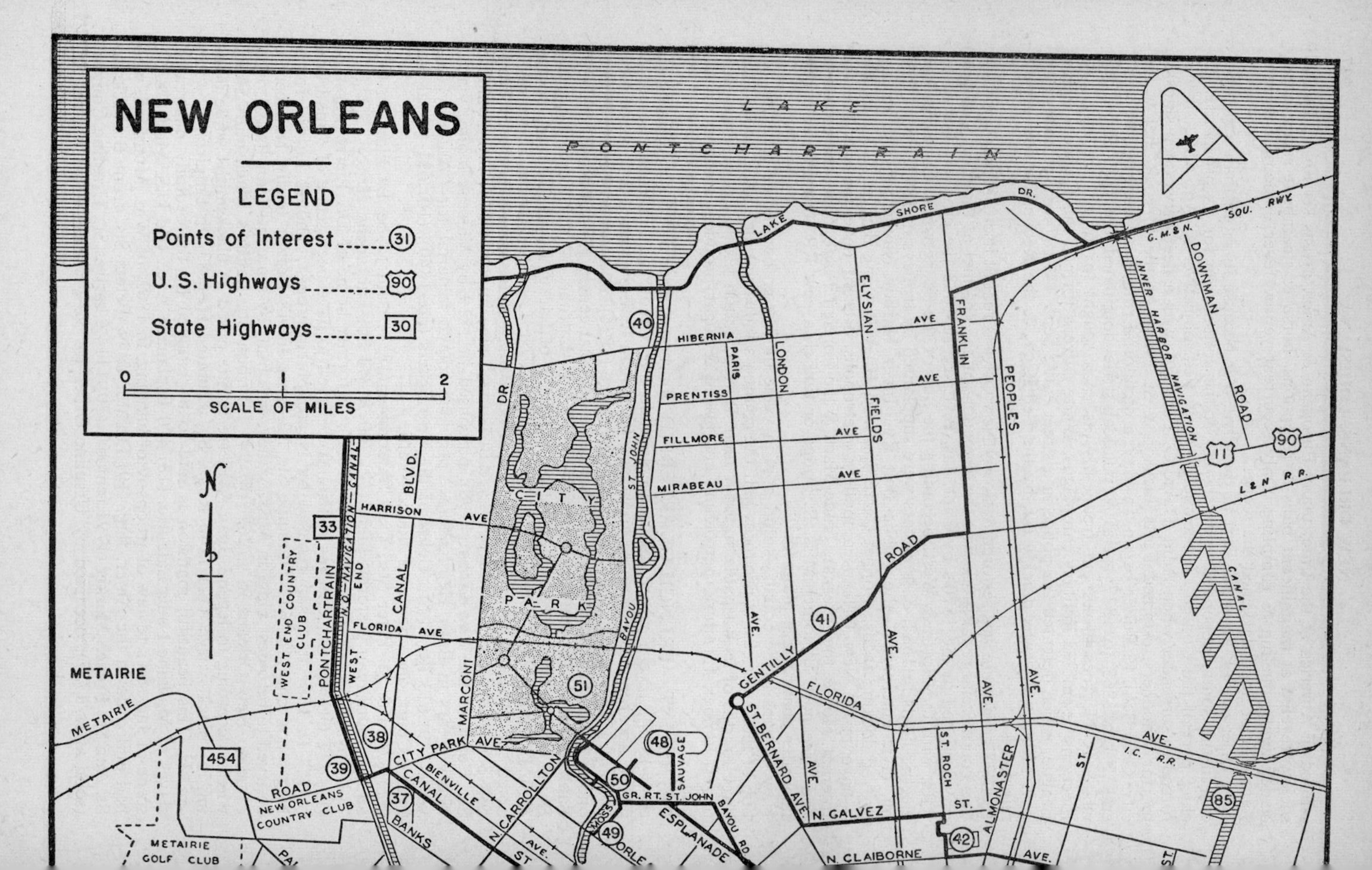
NEW ORLEANS
LEGEND
Points of Interest 31
U.S. Highways 90
State Highways 30
0
1
2
SCALE OF MILES
LAKE PONTCHARTRAIN
LAKE SHORE DR.
G. M. & N.
SOU. RWY
INNER HARBOR NAVIGATION CANAL
DOWNMAN ROAD
L & N R.R.
HIBERNIA AVE
PARIS AVE.
LONDON AVE.
ELYSIAN FIELDS AVE.
FRANKLIN AVE.
PEOPLES AVE.
PRENTISS AVE
FILLMORE AVE
MIRABEAU AVE
HARRISON AVE
CITY PARK
DR.
BAYOU ST JOHN
GENTILLY ROAD
FLORIDA AVE.
I.C. R.R.
ST. BERNARD AVE.
N. GALVEZ ST.
N. CLAIBORNE AVE.
ST. ROCH
ALMONASTER
ST
SAUVAGE
GR. RT. ST. JOHN
BAYOU RD
ESPLANADE
MOSS
ORLE
N. CARROLLTON AVE.
BIENVILLE
CANAL ST
BANKS
CITY PARK AVE.
MARCONI
CANAL BLVD.
WEST END
N-O-NAVIGATION-CANAL
PONTCHARTRAIN
FLORIDA AVE
WEST END COUNTRY CLUB
METAIRIE
ROAD
NEW ORLEANS COUNTRY CLUB
METAIRIE GOLF CLUB
40
41
42
48
49
50
51
37
38
39
33
454
85
11
90

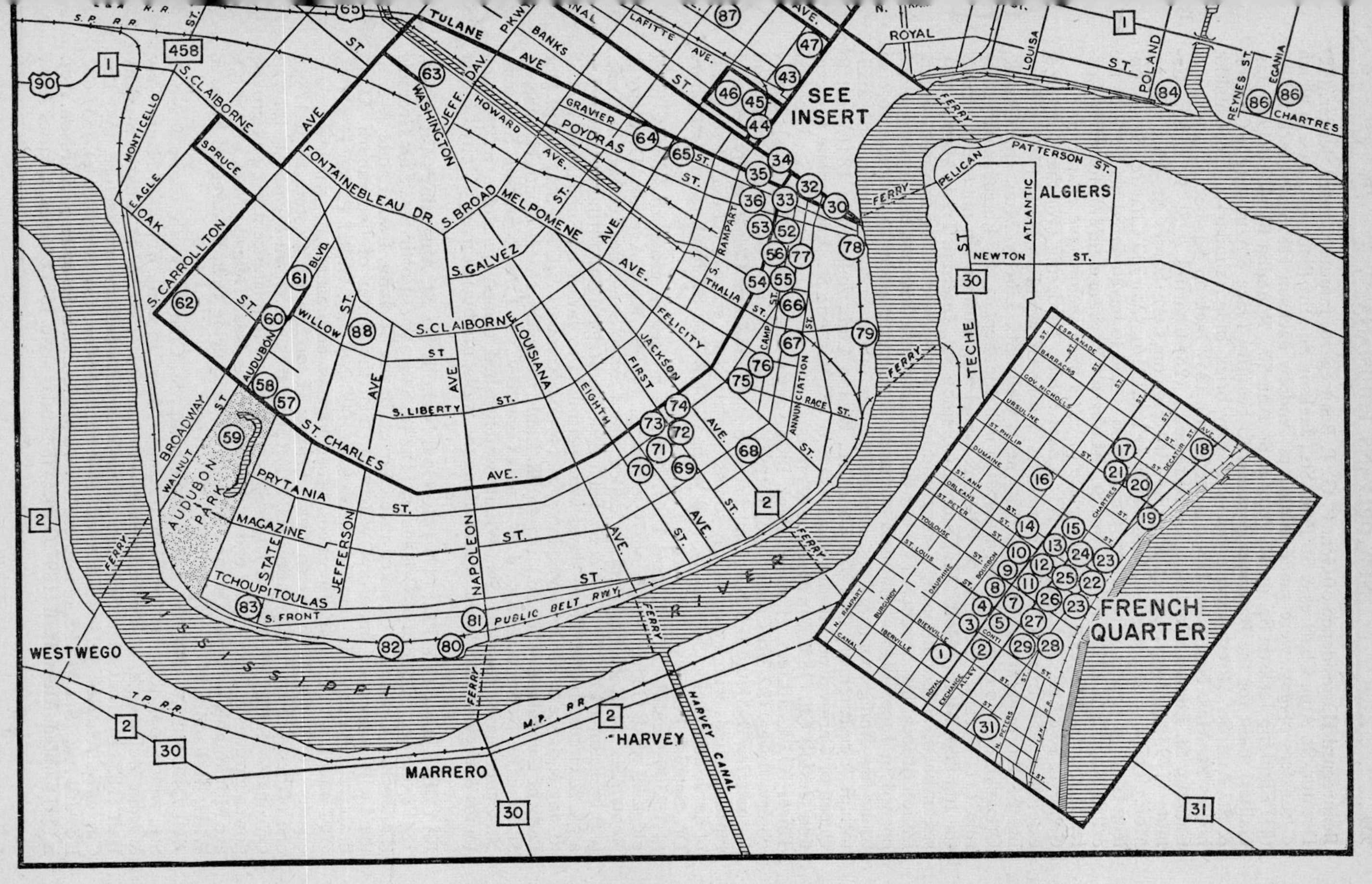
SEE INSERT
FRENCH QUARTER
ALGIERS
MISSISSIPPI RIVER
AUDUBON PARK
WESTWEGO
MARRERO
HARVEY
HARVEY CANAL
FERRY
PUBLIC BELT RWY.
S.P. R.R.
T.P. R.R.
M.P. R.R.
TULANE AVE.
BANKS ST.
LAFITTE AVE.
GRAVIER
POYDRAS
HOWARD AVE.
JEFF. DAV. PKWY.
WASHINGTON
S. CLAIBORNE AVE.
MONTICELLO
EAGLE
OAK
SPRUCE
S. CARROLLTON
FONTAINEBLEAU DR.
S. BROAD
MELPOMENE AVE.
S. GALVEZ
S. RAMPART
THALIA ST.
FELICITY
JACKSON AVE.
FIRST
EIGHTH
LOUISIANA AVE.
S. LIBERTY ST.
NAPOLEON AVE.
JEFFERSON AVE.
WILLOW ST.
BLVD.
AUDUBON
ST. CHARLES AVE.
PRYTANIA ST.
MAGAZINE ST.
STATE
TCHOUPITOULAS ST.
S. FRONT
BROADWAY
WALNUT ST.
CAMP ST.
ANNUNCIATION ST.
RACE ST.
ROYAL
LOUISA
POLAND ST.
REYNES ST.
EGANIA
CHARTRES
PATTERSON ST.
PELICAN
ATLANTIC
NEWTON ST.
TECHE ST.
ESPLANADE
BARRACKS
GOV. NICHOLLS
URSULINE
ST. PHILIP
DUMAINE
ST. ANN
ORLEANS
ST. PETER
TOULOUSE
ST. LOUIS
CONTI
BIENVILLE
IBERVILLE
CANAL
N. RAMPART
BURGUNDY
DAUPHINE
BOURBON
ROYAL
EXCHANGE ALLEY
N. PETERS
DECATUR
90
1
458
65
2
30
31
1 2 3 4 5 7 8 9 10 11 12 13 14 15 16 17 18 19 20 21 22 23 24 25 26 27 28 29 30 31 32 33 34 35 36 43 44 45 46 47 52 53 54 55 56 57 58 59 60 61 62 63 64 65 66 67 68 69 70 71 72 73 74 75 76 77 78 79 80 81 82 83 84 86 87 88

**Beauregard H.,** residence of Gen. P. G. T. Beauregard, famous Confed. leader. (22) Decatur, St. Ann, Chartres & St. Peter Sts., **Jackson Sq.,** the Place d'Armes, in which 4 transfers of gov. were made. **Statue of Andrew Jackson** (1856.by Clark Mills). (23) Flanking Jackson Sq. on St. Peter & St. Ann Sts., **Pontalba Bldgs.** (1849.by Jas. Gallier), built for the Baroness Pontalba to beautify Place d'Armes. (24) Chartres & St. Ann Sts., **Presbytère,** a heavy 2-story brick bldg., similar to the Cabildo; houses **St. Mus. Nat. Hist. Div.** (O.exc.Mon.). (25) Jackson Sq. bet. Presbytère & Cabildo, **St. Louis Cathedral** (1794.Sp.remod.). (26) Chartres & St. Peter Sts., **Cabildo** (1795), ancient seat of Sp. rule (3rd bldg.on site); houses **St. Mus.** (O.exc. Mon.). (27) 616 St. Peter St., **Little Theater** (est.1916). (28) 500 Chartres St., **Napoleon H.,** orig. residence of Mayor Girod, who is said to have offered his home to the exiled Napoleon. (29) 440 Chartres St., **Maspero's Exchange** (1788), formerly Coffee House Exchange, & gathering place of city's most picturesque characters.

CANAL STREET & LAKEFRONT: **Canal Street,** bordering (W) the Quarter & extending 3.5$^{m}$ from R. to the cemeteries, is one of world's widest (171′) & best-lighted thoroughfares. (30) Canal St. near Wells St., **Liberty Mon.** (by Chas.R. Orleans); ded. to citizens who participated in battle, Sept. 4, 1874, against carpetbag rule. (31) Decatur, Iberville, N. Peters & Canal Sts., **Custom H.,** notable especially for 2nd-floor **Marble Hall.** (32) Camp & Common Sts., **Internat. Trade Mart** (1948), streamlined, air-conditioned, 5-story trading center sponsored by nonprofit organization of local businessmen. (33) Gravier & Camp Sts., **Internat. H.,** 10-story bldg., opened in June, 1945 as business exchange & meeting place, to promote foreign trade; has dining rooms & bars, lounges, private offices & conference rooms, auditorium & research lib. (34) 824 Canal St., **Boston Club,** founded in 1841; host to Queen of Carnival on Mardi Gras Day. (35) 132 Baronne St., **Immaculate Conception** (Jesuit) **Ch.** (1857), in Hispano-Moresque style. (36) 812 Gravier St., **Hibernia Tower** (O.wks.aft.fee), Hibernia Bank Bldg., city's highest pt. (23 stories) & only observ. tower. (37-39) Canal St. & City Park Ave., **Cypress Grove & Greenwood Cemeteries,** & Metairie Rd. & Pontchartrain Blvd., **Metairie Cemetery** are beautiful burial grounds with many family tombs, preferred to graves because of sogginess of earth underlying the old city. (40) W. bank of Bayou St. John, (S) of Lakeshore Dr., **Spanish Fort** (early 18th cent.).

(41) 2300 Gentilly Rd., **Dillard Univ.** (Negro), housed in group of stone & brick bldgs. of mod. Georg. design, on 70-a. campus. (42) St. Roch Ave. bet. Derbigny & Roman Sts., **St. Roch Cemetery,** modelled after Campo Santo dei Tedeschi in Rome. (43) N. Rampart bet. St. Ann & St. Peter Sts., **Beauregard Sq.,** formerly Congo Sq., a pk. & circus ground where slaves were permitted to gather on Sunday afternoons to sing & dance & perform Voodoo rites. (44) N. Rampart & Conti Sts., **Ch. of Our Lady of Guadalupe** (1827.Sp.). (45-46) **St. Louis Cemetery** No. 1, Conti, N. Liberty, St. Louis, & N. Saratoga Sts., & **St. Louis Cemetery** No. 2, N. Robertson, St. Louis, N. Claiborne & Iberville Sts. Within whitewashed cement & stone, in crowded tombs & beehive-like "oven" vaults along the walls, are buried many of city's oldest families.

BAYOU RD.—CITY PK.: (47) 1210 Gov. Nicholls St., **St. Augustine's Ch.** (Cath. 1841), on site of College of Orleans (1811). (48) Sauvage & Fortin Sts., **Fair Grounds (La. Jockey Club),** last of noted race courses. **Bayou St. John,** from Lafitte Ave. to the L., was once an important waterway, then the center of fine suburb. Many beautiful 19th cent. Hs. stand along Moss St. (49) No. 924, **Walter Parker H.** (1798. O.12-4.fee), with columned porticos, broad loggias, embrasured Fr. windows; slave quarters. (50) No. 1300, **Helen Pitkin Schertz H.** or **Spanish Custom H.** (c.1784), one of best-preserved plantation Hs. (51) City Park Ave. from Bayou St. John to Orleans Ave., **City Pk.,** one of largest pks. in U.S., with magnificent live oak groves, flower gardens & lagoons. At end of Lelong Ave. is **Isaac Delgado Mus. of Art** (O. exc.Mon.& hols.). In pk. also are **Duelling Oaks, Suicide Oak, Beauregard Mon.** & **W. H. McFadden H.**

AUDUBON PK.—UNIVS.: (52) **Lafayette Sq.,** St. Charles, South, Camp & North Sts., which took the place of Place d'Armes. **Mons.** to Benj. Franklin, Henry Clay & John McDonogh, who gave fortune to free schools. (53) 543 St. Charles St., **City Hall** (1853.by Jas.Gallier,Sr.), fine example of ante-bellum architecture. (54) Lee Circle, St. Charles & Howard Aves., **Rbt. E. Lee Mon.** (by Alex.Doyle). (55) 601 Howard Ave., **Sta. WTPS,** in former Howard Mem. Lib. bldg. by H. Richardson. Adj. is (56) **Confed. Mem. Hall** (1897.O.wks.) in similar style. (57) 6363 St. Charles Ave.,

**Loyola Univ.** (est.1911. Jesuit), occupies group of Tudor-Goth. bldgs.; has New Orleans' only dental college & only seismological observ. & notable college of music. **Lib.,** in **Marquette Hall,** has fine coll. on La. & Ireland. Outstanding among bldgs. is **McDermott Mem. (Holy Name of Jesus) Ch.**
(58) 6823 St. Charles Ave., **Tulane Univ.,** whose bldgs., on a 93-a. campus, range in style from Romanes. to modern, was given present name in 1884 after bequest from Paul Tulane made expansion possible; facils. for instruction in virtually all branches, particularly noteworthy in art, engineering, law, medicine & social service. **Howard-Tilton Mem. Lib.,** Freret St. & Audubon Pl., has coll. of c.350,000 volumes, particularly rich in La. hist.; also book & mss. coll. of Middle Amer. Research Institute. **Mus. & Gallery of Middle Amer. Research Institute** (O.wks.) is in Dinwiddie Hall. **Tulane Nat. Hist. Mus.,** in Gibson Hall, is one of South's best from standpoint of representative material & scientific treatment. **Stadium,** scene of annual Sugar Bowl game. **Art Gallery** (O.wks.), in Art School Bldg. (59) **Audubon Pk.** (recr.facils.amusements.zoo), opp. Loyola & Tulane Univs. extending to R. **Statue of John Jas. Audubon.** (60) 1229 Broadway, **Newcomb College** (women), an integral part of Tulane Univ.; founded in 1886. (61) 14 Audubon Blvd., **Huey P. Long Mem. Residence.** (62) 719 S. Carrollton Ave., **Old Carrollton Cth.** (1855). (63) 7325 Washington Ave., **Xavier Univ.** (Eng.Goth.founded 1915), only Cath. univ. (exclusive of seminaries) in U.S. solely for Negroes. (64) 1802 Tulane Ave., **St. Joseph's Ch.** (Cath.1871-98.by P.C.Keeley), one of most notable churches. (65) Tulane Ave. bet. S. Claiborne Ave. & S. Liberty St., **Charity Hospital** (1938 main bldg.), very fine St. institution.
IRISH CHANNEL—GARDEN DISTRICT: (66) 534 Howard Ave., **Sarpy H.** (c.1764), among 1st bldgs. in Faubourg Ste. Marie; fine example of early plantation H., in heart of the city. (67) 1321 Annunciation St., **Mercy (Soniat Mem.) Hospital** (founded 1924). Main bldg. is **Saulet Plantation H.** (c.1816). (68) Constance St. from St. Andrew St. to Josephine St., **Redemptorist Chs. & Schools,** fine examples of (brick) Baroque architecture. The Garden District, from Jackson to Louisiana Ave. bet. St. Charles Ave. & Magazine St., was orig. residential sec. of Amer. colony. Many mansions, mostly of Gr. Rev. style, stand among palms, live oaks & magnolias. (69) 1134 First St., **Forsyth H.** (early 1850's), where Jefferson Davis, Pres. of Confederacy, died. (70) 1313 Eighth St., **Cable H.** (1874), home of writer, Geo. Washington Cable. (71) Prytania & Fourth Sts., **Britten H.** (1859), one of Dist.'s largest & most int. Hs. (72-75) Other ante bellum mansions are: 2340 Prytania St., **Westfeldt H.** (early 1820's), said to be oldest in sec.; 2405 Prytania St., **James H.;** 2221 Prytania St., **Miss Sarah Henderson's H.;** Race & Coliseum Sts., **Grace King's H.** (1830). (76) Race, Melpomene, Camp & Coliseum Sts., **Coliseum Sq.** (1830's). (77) 712 Camp St., **St. Patrick's Ch.** (1833); noteworthy frescoes, sanctuary & paintings.
WATER FRONT can be seen best from Eads Plaza at foot of Canal St. or from excursion boat. The 10$^m$ of wharves, concrete for the most part, rest on wooden piles. During high water, the R. is 10′ to 20′ higher than st. level. Above Eads Plaza are: (78) Poydras St. Wharf, **Coffee Unloading;** (79) Thalia St. Wharf, **Banana Unloading.** (80) Above Napoleon Ave., **Cotton Wareh.** (81) On Tchoupitoulas St., **Lane Cotton Mill.** (82) Foot of Bellecastle St., **Grain Elevator.** (83) Foot of State St., **U.S. Marine Hospital.** Below Eads Plaza: (84) Behind Poland St. Wharf, **U.S. Army Supply Base;** (85) **Inner Harbor Navigation Canal** & (86) 501 & 400 Egania St., **Doullut Hs.,** built to resemble steamboats.
METAIRIE: (87) Ursuline Ave. & N. Johnson St., **Nat. Shrine of St. Ann,** in miniature cave of pink artificial rock. (88) 2635 State St., **Ursuline College,** one of oldest educational institutions for girls in U.S. (founded 1727). In Ch. on the campus is **Shrine of Our Lady of Prompt Succor,** where annual novena, terminating on Jan. 8, is held in fulfillment of vow made before Battle of New Orleans in 1815.

## TRIPS OUT OF NEW ORLEANS

### I. NEW ORLEANS (E & N) to FT. PIKE. 31.5. US90

From Canal St. & Claiborne Ave., trip turns (NW) on Canal St., (NE) on N. Broad St., (N) on St. Bernard & then (NE) on Gentilly Rd. (US90). **6.5. INDUSTRIAL CANAL,** conn. L. Pontchartrain with Miss. R., was constructed at time of World War I as part of project (never completed) to open new outlet to the Gulf. **18.5.**

J. with US11 (see US90). **22.5. FT. MACOMB ST. MON.** Brick ft., built by Gen. Jackson in 1815 at cost of c.$360,000, is honeycombed with passageways. It guarded **Chef Menteur,** a deep tidegut conn. Ls. Pontchartrain & Borgne. **31.5. FT. PIKE ST. MON.,** on site of fortifications built in 1793. Present structure dates from 1818; abandoned in 1865.

**II. NEW ORLEANS (E & S) to POYDRAS. 15.5. St.1**

Trip turns (NE) on N. Claiborne Ave., (S) on Elysian Fields Ave. & (E) on St. Claude Ave. (St.1). **5. JACKSON BARRACKS,** built for Andrew Jackson; designed like Ind. fort, with high surrounding wall & 4 towers. Troops have embarked from these barracks in every major conflict engaged in by U.S. During World War II they served as hqs. for New Orleans Port of Embarkation. Just beyond is **ARABI,** a scattered suburb.

SIDE TRIP: From Arabi (R) on Angela Ave. & (L) on Peters St. c.1m to **Amer. Sugar Refinery** (O.guides), one of world's largest. On grounds is **Three Oaks Plantation H. Chalmette Slip,** 1.5m, is deep-water terminal with huge warehouses & special equipment for unloading copra from Philippine Is.

**6.5. CHALMETTE NAT. HIST. PK.,** incl. 2 secs. (c.30 as.) of Chalmette Battlefields, scene of Battle of New Orleans (Jan.8,1815). Part of Amer. Line where Jackson's 5,000 volunteers threw up breastworks, is still faintly visible near **Chalmette Mon.** (begun 1855.completed 1908), a 110′ marble obelisk (observ.). In **U.S. Nat. Cemetery** (1861) are graves of 14,000 Union soldiers. In Battle of New Orleans, fought more than 2 wks. after peace had been declared at Ghent, Jackson's army, incl. Choctaw Inds., Baratarian pirates & free Negroes, fought off a much larger Brit. force of Wellington's veterans led by Gen. Pakenham. **8. RUINS OF VERSAILLES** (1805), plantation H. built by Pierre Denis Delaronde, who planned to found a city that would outgrow New Orleans. From the ruins extends (R) a magnificent ave. of moss-festooned live oaks, popularly known as **Pakenham Oaks** in erroneous supposition that Gen. Pakenham died beneath them. **9. MARKER** c.100 yds. (L) designates pt. (now dry land because of shift in R.'s course) from which Amer. schooner "Carolina" poured a broadside into Brit. camp on Dec. 23, 1814. **15.5. POYDRAS.** J. with St.32.

SIDE TRIP: On St.32 (L) 1.5m is **St. Bernard,** named for Don Bernardo de Galvez, La. Gov. during Sp. regime & later Viceroy of Mexico. Surrounding dist. was sett. by many Canary Islanders, known as Isleños, who became fishermen & trappers. Their descendants retain many Sp. customs & speak Spanish more often than English. At 5m **Kenilworth** (1759.2nd story 1800), marked by wide galleries with massive brick columns. 9m **J.** with St.62.

On St.62 (R) 6m to **De La Croix I.,** supply center for rich fur-producing area & one of La.'s most popular fishing & duck-hunting grounds. Inhabitants are descendants of pioneer Isleños.

13.5m on St.32, **Yscloskey,** a trapping, hunting & fishing center. At 16m **Shell Beach** (bathh. restaurant.f.facils.), summer resort on L. Borgne.

**III. NEW ORLEANS (W) to LAPLACE. 36.5. US51**

From downtown (NW) on Tulane Ave. (US51-61-65). **10.5. KENNER,** shipping center for vegetable-growing community, with several small mfg. plants. Many inhabitants are Itals. & major celebrations are in honor of St. Joseph (Mar.19) & St. Rosalie (Sept.4).

SIDE TRIPS: (A) From Kenner (R) 1m to **Moisant Internat. Airport,** municipally financed, owned & operated; built during World War II & named for John Bevins Moisant, a pioneer aviator killed when his plane crashed while competing in New Orleans in 1910.

(B) From Kenner (L) 5.5m on St.1 to **St. Rose** & at 8.5m **Destréhan** (toll ferry), oil company towns. Destréhan occupies site of plantation owned by Jean Noel Destréhan, wealthy merchant, planter & politician whose Doric-columned mansion is now clubh. 10m **Ormond** (18th cent.), a 2-story mansion with brick pillars & cypress colonnettes; flanked by 2-story wings with open galleries. 13.5m **Norco,** another oil company town surrounding **Shell Petroleum Co. Refinery.** 17m J. with US51-61-65, main tour.

**33.** Bridge crosses **BONNET CARRÉ SPILLWAY** (1935), emergency floodway. Concrete dike is equipped with 350 bays, or weirs, opened & closed by electric crane on narrow-gauge track; earthen guide levees extend 7m (N) to L. **36.5. LAPLACE.** J. with US51 (see) & St.1 (see US61).

**IV. NEW ORLEANS (W) to LULING. 25.5. US90**

From downtown (SW) on S. Claiborne Ave., leading into Jefferson Hy. (US90). **6.5. CAMP PARAPET POWDER MAGAZINE.** Near-by (L) is remnant of

Confed. fortification. **7. AMER. FROG CANNING CO. PLANT,** surrounded by lily-decked pond. **8. HUEY P. LONG BRIDGE,** completed in 1935 at cost of $13,000,000; steel cantilever with truss spans supported by 6 caissons & 3 pile piers, 4.5$^{m}$ long; carrying hy. & RR. tracks. **10.** J. with St.30, which unites with US90 to Luling (see below).

SIDE TRIP: On St.30 (L) c.1$^{m}$ to **Seven Oaks** (1830). At 2$^{m}$ **Westwego** (toll ferry to Walnut St., New Orleans), an industrial town with one of country's biggest shrimp-packing plants & several large alcohol mfg. units. Town was a pt. of departure during Gold Rush. 3.5$^{m}$ **Celotex Co. Plant,** where "bagasse" (see above) is utilized in bldg. materials.

**25. ELLINGTON MANOR,** a big white plantation H., with square columns supporting hipped roof & curving outside stairways. **25.5. LULING** (accoms.), at western J. with St.30.

SIDE TRIP: From Luling (R) 3.5$^{m}$ on St.30 to **Hahnville,** seat of St. Charles Parish. At 4$^{m}$ is galleried **Keller H.** (1801) in grove of ancient pecan trees; notable handcarved woodwork. 8$^{m}$ **Locke Breaux Live Oak,** which has girth of 35′; "President" of Live Oak Soc., whose hqs. are at Lafayette (see US90). 12$^{m}$ **Glendale Plantation H.** (c.1800), cement-covered brick mansion, built with handhewn timbers & handforged hardware, flanked by "pigeonnières." 17.5$^{m}$ **Edgard,** once known as Caire's Landing for the store owned by E. J. Caire, the red-brick bldg. with iron doors facing hy. 22.5$^{m}$ **Evergreen Plantation H.** (c.1840.Gr.Rev.), with massive columns & wide galleries. All the numerous outbuildings are of brick & Gr. Rev. in design. 23.5$^{m}$ **Whitney Plantation H.,** a raised cottage with wide-pillared galleries; notable for handforged hardware & rear gallery & parlor painted in manner of Dresden china. 27$^{m}$ Ferry (toll) to Lutcher (see US61). 31$^{m}$ **Site of Valcour Aime Plantation,** called "The Little Versailles" during 30-yr. period of glory around 1845. Here Valcour Aime, the "Louis XIV of La.," lived like a feudal lord in mansion ornamented with rare marbles & richly furnished, standing amid magnificent gardens of exotic plants, with artificial R., L. & lagoon, a grotto & Chinese pagoda where peacocks strutted. 32$^{m}$ **Felicity & St. Joseph Plantation H.** were wedding presents to Aime's daughters. 32.5$^{m}$ **Oak Alley** (1836.Gr.Rev.fee), magnificent H. of pink-plastered brick, girdled by 28 Doric columns (8′ in circumference) & approached by long double line of oaks. Upper gallery has painted cypress railing of unusual beauty.

## V. NEW ORLEANS (S) to LAFITTE VILLAGE. 26.5. St.30

From downtown (SW) on S. Claiborne Ave., then (S) on Napoleon Ave. & across R. by ferry (toll). **5. MARRERO,** named for family of L. H. Marrero, a prominent politician of Jefferson Parish in late 19th cent. J. with St.30, on which tour proceeds (S). **5.5. MADONNA MANOR** (1932) & **HOPE HAVEN INSTITUTE** (1937), orphanages maintained by Assoc. Cath. Charities of New Orleans. **16.** J. with shell Rd. leading straight ahead 0.5$^{m}$ to **Crown Point** on Bayou Barataria (pic. f.boats for rent).

**20. LAFITTE P.O.,** starting pt. of major sports event of reg., the annual pirogue race (usually May) down Bayou Barataria, which parallels St.30. Pirogues are dugouts cut from cypress logs & require skill in handling.

**24.5.** At S. end of high-arched wooden bridge over Bayou des Oies is **LAFITTE CEMETERY** where, according to fantastic local tradition, Jean Lafitte lies buried bet. John Paul Jones & Napoleon Bonaparte. Story is that Napoleon was rescued from St. Helena by Lafitte in a fast sloop, but that he died on board & was buried here in secrecy. John Paul Jones, who had joined the pirates in smuggling operations, was buried later beside him.

**26.5. LAFITTE VILLAGE,** site of pirate settlement & rendezvous of Lafitte & his band. Today it is home port of many commercial fishing & shrimping boats, with several private fishing & hunting clubs. The many winding bayous, bays, inlets & treacherous marshes served as excellent screen for piratical & smuggling operations of the Lafittes during early 19th cent. Their apprehension was all but impossible. Descendants of the band are among the fishermen & trappers today.

## VI. NEW ORLEANS (SE) to VENICE. 72.5. St.31

Trip turns (SW) on S. Claiborne Ave., (SE) on Jackson Ave. & across Miss. R. ferry (toll). **4.5. GRETNA** sprawls along the R., dominated by industrial plants & shipping terminals, crisscrossed by RR. tracks. Products incl. commercial alcohol, cottonseed-oil, petroleum products, asbestos roofing, fertilizer & barrels. Town was founded early in 19th cent. by Nicholas Noel Destréhan, who settled some German immigrants on part of his land. In 1839 the St. Mary Market Ferry Co. laid out a much larger adjoining area; & a few yrs. later landowner John McDonogh est. McDonoghville a mile or so away (E). The settlements were incorporated as a town in 1913. The town came to be called Gretna, for Gretna Green in Scotland, because an early justice of the peace cheerfully performed marriage ceremonies at any hr. of the day or night. Since 1884, Gretna has been the seat of Jefferson Parish—sometimes called "Free State of Jefferson" because of its resistance to outside, & occasional inside, efforts to curb open gambling. **Mem. Arch,** foot of Huey P. Long Blvd., comm. the parish dead of all wars. **David Crockett Fire Co. Sta. No. 1,** 205 Lafayette St., houses one of nation's oldest volunteer companies still in existence (org.1841); & **McDonoghville Cemetery,** 500 Hancock St., once McDonogh's family burial place where, contrary to Southern custom, Caths. & Prots., whites & Negroes were buried side by side (until 1891). **McDonogh Cenotaph.**

SIDE TRIP: On St.2 (R) 1.5m from Gretna to **Harvey,** named for Capt. Jos. Hale Harvey, who married daughter of Nicholas Noel Destréhan, owner of extensive properties incl. Destréhan Canal (built 1835.enlarged 1853), later known by Harvey's name. In 1924 the U.S. Gov. bought the canal & built (1929-33) the **Harvey Locks,** linking Miss. R. & Intracoastal Waterway.

Trip cont. on Lafayette Ave. (SE) to J. with St.31, then (S) on this route. **11. BELLE-CHASSE** (early 19th cent.remod.1846), former home of Judah P. Benjamin, U.S. Senator, Secy. of State & War for the Confed. **12. ALVIN CALLENDER AIRPORT,** city's oldest, now used by cargo operators & charter companies. On R. bank opp. is huge steel crane which transfers loaded freight cars to the Seatrain, an ocean-going car ferry bet. New Orleans & New York. **35.5. MAGNOLIA PLANTATION H.** (c.1795), 10-room mansion built entirely by slave labor with handmade bricks, handhewn lumber & handcarved woodwork. **43.5. PORT SULPHUR,** town of Freeport Sulphur Co. employees.

SIDE TRIP: From Port Sulphur 10m by boat (free trip on appl. to Freeport Sulphur Co., New Orleans) to **L. Grande Écaille,** where sulphur is mined in a tidal marsh.

**57.5. BURAS,** La.'s orange-producing center; also fishing & hunting center. Inhabitants are of French, Spanish, Slavonian, Dalmatian, Chinese, Filipino & Negro descent, & virtually every other family is named Buras. Settlement was named for 7 brothers of the Buras family who arrived from France in 1840. Orange groves, developed chiefly since 1920, spread for miles around. **63.5. FT. JACKSON** (1815. 2nd unit 1861). The older & larger unit is bastioned, star-shaped embattlement with massive brick casements, heavy bombproofs & surrounding moat. **Fort St. Philip** (1795), directly across R., figured in very important Civil War engagement in which Adm. Farragut's Fed. fleet of 24 wooden gunboats & 19 mortar schooners attempted, in defiance of best military opinion, to move upriver under fire. After 5 days & nights of bombardment, Farragut ran past the forts with 17 war vessels in 3 divisions. Confed. gunboats & rams were put into action, & a wild melee followed, in which the Feds. were victorious. The bloodless capture of New Orleans & mastery of the Miss. R. were ultimate results of the engagement. **72.5. VENICE,** a village of trappers & fishermen at the end of St.31.

## OHIO RIVER TOUR—KENTUCKY

**KY.-OHIO LINE** (at Cincinnati, O.) **(SW) to KY.-MO. LINE** (16m from Charleston, Mo.). **394. US42-US60.**

Via: Covington, Carrollton, Louisville, Paducah, Wickliffe.

Route runs roughly parallel to Ohio R. from Cincinnati, Ohio, to its confluence with Miss. R., near Wickliffe. At times Rd. stretches for miles in view of the R. Other times it takes shortest way rather than follow R.'s meandering.

### Sec. 1: OHIO LINE to LOUISVILLE, 107. US42

US42 & US25 are united as they cross Ohio Line at **0.** on N. side of Ohio R. by way of suspension bridge from Cincinnati. This bridge was completed in 1881 at cost of $1,871,000. It was 1st of America's great suspension bridges—36′ wide, 2,252′ long, with 100′ towers. **COVINGTON, 0.5.,** 2nd largest city in Ky., is directly across Ohio R. from Cincinnati. It was sett. about 1800 with est. of a ferry & tavern near present approach to the bridge. Covington lies on a flood plain of Ohio R. at foot of suburban hills that reach back to a high plain of the Bluegrass. City does not have skyscrapers, large motion picture houses, big dept. stores, or huge hotels, for it has geared its economic & social life to that of Cincinnati. **Baker**

**Hunt Foundation & Williams Nat. Hist. Mus.** (O.1-3 wks.;1-6 Sun.) are at 620 Greenup St. Foundation offers after-school classes in arts & crafts for adults & children. Mus. has 20,000 insect specimens & 5,000 vols. on natural hist. **Linden Grove Cemetery,** Holman St. bet. 13th & 15th Sts., is one of Covington's oldest burial grounds. It contains graves of men who fought in Rev. War & all the nation's wars since. **Latonia Race Track,** S. end of Latonia Ave., is 2nd in Ky. only to Churchill Downs as a race course. Spring & fall racing seasons here follow those at Churchill Downs, home of Ky. Derby. Bet. Covington & **FLORENCE, 9.5.,** US42 is united with US25 (see). **20.5.** J. with gravel Rd.

SIDE TRIP: On this Rd. (R) 3m to **Big Bone Lick,** one of nation's outstanding prehist. boneyards, now depleted of relics because of expeditions in the past 100 yrs. to gather specimens for world's great museums. A deserted hotel is only relic today of what was once fashionable watering place in period just preceding Civil War.

**35.5. WARSAW,** on a level terrace overlooking Ohio R., was once prominent R. port, but town today depends upon its position as a trading center & as cty. seat. **45. GHENT** lies below rim of hills on a small plain looking down on R. **52. CARROLLTON** was inc. in 1794 under name of Fort Wm., later renamed in honor of Chas. Carroll of Maryland, signer of Decl. of Ind. Rd. crosses Ky. R. at **53.,** near confluence with the Ohio. (W) of Carrollton, Rd. breaks away from R. & winds through high hills, close to hy. **65. BEDFORD,** seat of Trimble Cty., is surrounded by valley farms producing tobacco, grain & livestock. Hy. makes sweeping curve & passes (L) **KY. TAVERN, 70.,** a long low structure that was an important stopping place in stagecoach days. US42 descends into **PROSPECT, 94.,** in Louisville metropolitan area. (For a description of pts. of int. from here to **LOUISVILLE, 107.,** see Louisville Trip IV).

## Sec. 2: LOUISVILLE to MO. LINE. 287. US60

(For description of pts. of int. from Louisville to Tip Top, see Louisville Trip II). At **TIP TOP, 30.5.,** is J. with US31W (see). West of Tip Top US60 crosses reg. of wooded knobs & extensive areas of farm lands. Ky.'s 1st natural gas was tapped in this area in 1858. **33. GRAHAMPTON** is on both banks of Otter Cr. Grahampton Textile Mills on W. bank of cr. have been operating since 1837. **42.** J. with gravel Rd.

SIDE TRIP: On this Rd. (R) 0.5m **Doe Run Hotel,** old water power mill, main part of which was built in 1821. Millstones were brought from France to New Orleans, thence by way of Miss. & Ohio Rs. to mouth of Otter Cr.

Route passes through **BRANDENBURG, 47., IRVINGTON, 57., & HARNED, 71. 75. HARDINSBURG,** seat of Breckinridge Cty., came into being as ft. built by Capt. Wm. Hardin in 1780. Bet. Hardinsburg & Cloverport US60 follows a devious course through hilly reg. **85.5. CLOVERPORT,** river town est. in 1808, is place where Lincoln family, consisting of Thos., his wife Nancy, their son & daughter, were ferried across Ohio R. in 1816 when they moved to Indiana. The water of **TAR SPRINGS, 88.5.** (R), has odor & taste of tar. This place was formerly a popular resort. **90. JEFFERY CLIFF** (R) has 40-a. table-like top shaped like a huge hand. From parking places (R) are exceptional views of broad valley of the Ohio. Cliff was once site of stockaded Ind. village. **93. HAWESVILLE,** seat of Hancock Cty., is important for shipping plants grown on farms in vic. Hawesville is conn. with Cannelton, Ind., by 24-hr. ferry serv. Here Lincoln Mem. Hy. will cross Ohio R. in following approximate course of Lincoln family when it moved from Hodgenville to Ind. **106. LEWISPORT.** J. with side Rd.

SIDE TRIP: From Lewisport (L) on side Rd. to old **Pate Farm H.,** 4m, where in 1827 Abr. Lincoln was brought before Magistrate Sam Pate on charge of infringement of ferry privileges. Local tradition says Lincoln, then employed in Ind., rowed a passenger to a boat in midstream. The 18-yr.-old Lincoln acted as his own counsel & exonerated himself.

**120. OWENSBORO,** 2nd largest city in W. Ky., is bustling oil town on bank of Ohio R. By 1850 it had already become an important R. port. Daviess Cty. is 2nd largest tobacco producing cty. in Ky. Owensboro has 8 tobacco factories, 2 distilleries, & other industries. **Planters Hotel,** 4th & Main Sts., was built in 1846. Among signatures on its register are those of Jenny Lind, singer, & Mary Anderson, Shakespearean actress. Hy. at **140.** crosses **GREEN R.,** widely known for the beauty of its water & for muskellunge. **150. HENDERSON,** seat of Henderson Cty., on high red bluffs facing mile-wide Ohio R. Town was founded in 1797 on 200,000 as. granted to Transylvania Co. by St. John Jas. Audubon, ornithologist, lived here 1810-1819. Henderson is at J. with US41 (see). **173. MORGANFIELD,** seat of Union Cty., whose farmers early pioneered in replacing "scrub" beef stock with purebred sires, & in growing soil-enriching Korean shrub, Lespedeza. **184. STURGIS,** is center of bituminous coal industry of Union Cty. **204, MARION,** seat of Crittenden Cty., is principal Ky. shipping center for fluorspar, mineral used in manufacture of steel products. **GRAVE OF LUCY JEFFERSON LEWIS** (R), **217.,** is marked by granite shaft. Lucy Jefferson was only sister of Thos. Jefferson. US60 crosses **LUCY JEFFERSON MEM. BRIDGE, 230.,** over Cumberland R. near pt. where stream ends its winding journey of 687m. **234. SMITHLAND** spreads along high bluff above confluence of Ohio & Cumberland. Quiet village was once looked upon as coming metropolis of entire reg. in days when both Rs. teemed with commerce. Boats from New Orleans & Pittsburgh kept Smithland's wharves busy as cargo transfer pt. At Smithland is J. with US62 (see). Two routes are united bet. this point & Paducah. US60 crosses **GEO. ROGERS CLARK MEM. BRIDGE** over Tenn. R. at **247.** At **248.** is J. with US68 (see).

**251. PADUCAH,** seat of McCracken Cty., is most important port & distribution center for extreme W. sect. of Ky. Town lies on flood plain of Ohio R. where Tenn. R., pours down from Southern Highlands & joins larger stream before it flows to Miss. R. Town was est. in 1827 by Wm. Clark, of famous Lewis & Clark expedition, upon land granted to his brother, Geo. Rogers Clark, for services in Rev. War. Founded about time extensive river shipping began, it throve as an ice-free port bet. Pittsburgh & New Orleans & as distribution center for cargoes bound up Tenn. & to some extent up the Cumberland. In latter half of 19th cent. when river shipping dropped off, it became an important railroad town. It attained new importance when river shipping was revived in 1920's. Still more growth came with building of great Ky. **Dam of T.V.A.** 20m upstream on Tenn. R. (see US68). Town was home of the late Irvin S. Cobb, American humorist. Paducah is at J. of US45 (see), US62 (see), & US68 (see). **BARLOW** at **276. WICKLIFFE, 283.,** seat of Ballard Cty., is at confluence of Ohio & Miss. Rs. **Ancient buried city** (O.daily), is here on a lofty bluff above the J. of 2 Rs. Some mounds made by a prehist. race are still intact, while others have been opened with such care that all remains are in their orig. position. Wickliffe is at J. with US62 (see) & US68 (see). Bet. Wickliffe & E. Cairo US60 & US51 are united. At **287.** US60 crosses **ILL. LINE** & a tip of Ill. to **MO. LINE,** by way of Ohio & Miss. Rs.

## US 60—KENTUCKY

**KY.-W. VA. LINE** (10m from Huntington, W. Va.) **(E) & (SE) to KY.-MO. LINE** 16m from Charleston, Mo.). **519. US60**

Via: Ashland, Lexington, Frankfort, Louisville, Paducah.

US60, longest single route in St., winds (E-W) through Ky., revealing all its varied topography.

### Sec. 1: W. VA. LINE to LEXINGTON. 138.

US60 crosses the **W. VA. LINE** at **0.** by way of bridge over Big Sandy R. **CATLETTSBURG, 0.5.,** seat of Boyd Cty., is at J. of Big Sandy & Ohio Rs. Bet. Catlettsburg & Ashland, US23 & this route are united. **ASHLAND, 6.,** largest & most important city in E. Kentucky, was sett. in 1815. E. Kentucky, especially in vic. of Ashland, is rich in non-plastic clays that possess unusual quality of resistance to temperatures up to 3,000° F. **Amer. Rolling Mill ("Armco") Plant** (O.appl.), Winchester Ave. W., was est. in 1920. Chiefly because of plant, pop. of city doubled in 5 yrs. **KILGORE, 22.5.,** is trading center of reg. of iron & coal country. **GRAYSON, 31.,** is largest trading center of active iron dist. & seat of Carter Cty. **41. J.** with St.182.

SIDE TRIP: On this Rd. (R) 5m to **Carter Caves & Natural Bridges.** Reg. contains several hist. caves & one of largest natural bridges in Ky. Bridge is 219′ long, 196′ high, & 12′ wide, & top is so level that hy. leading to Carter City crosses it.

**OLIVE HILL, 47.,** is a brickyard town in a narrow hollow bet. hills. This dist. is widely known for deposits of plastic clays of superior quality. **MOREHEAD, 68.,**

seat of Rowan Cty., was trading center for lumbermen working on extensive operations in South. Bldgs. of **Morehead St. Teachers College** (coed.) (R) are on 75-a. slope on E. edge of town. **FARMERS, 78.**, on Licking R., is trade center of clay reg. **89. OWINGSVILLE,** seat of Bath Cty., has many fine old Hs. **MOUNT STERLING, 103.**, is seat of Montgomery Cty. **WINCHESTER, 119.**, & **LEXINGTON, 138.** (For a description of pts. of int. in Winchester & from here to Lexington, see Lexington Trip I.)

**Sec. 2: LEXINGTON to LOUISVILLE. 82.**

(For a description of pts. on this entire sec., see Lexington Trip VII & Louisville Trip III.)

**Sec. 3: LOUISVILLE to MISSOURI LINE. 299.**

(For this sec. of Hy., see Ohio R. Tour.)

## US 62—KENTUCKY

**KY.-OHIO LINE** (at Aberdeen, Ohio) **(SW) to KY.-ILL. LINE** (at Paducah, Ky.). **359. US62.**

Via: Maysville, Georgetown, Versailles, Bardstown, Elizabethtown, Central City, Paducah.

This route, a pleasant alt. to more congested & commercialized hys. across St., traverses steep hills along Ohio R., rich bottom lands of Licking R. Valley, & rolling pasture lands of the Bluegrass. Bet. Springfield & Leitchfield it winds through the Knobs area; bet. Leitchfield & Cumberland R., it skirts undulating farm lands of the Pennyrile, local variant of pennyroyal, a pungent, aromatic plant of mint family that grows in abundance along banks of streams. Bet. Cumberland R. & Smithland, route passes through a semi-barren reg. that forms a watershed bet. Cumberland & Ohio Rs. These diverse physical features have produced a corresponding diversity of modes & conditions of life.

**Sec. 1: OHIO LINE to ELIZABETHTOWN. 170. US62**

US62 crosses Ohio Line at **0.** on N. bank of Ohio R., at Aberdeen, Ohio. **0.5. MAYSVILLE** is at J. with US68 (see). **4.5. WASHINGTON.** Bet. Maysville & Washington, US62 & US68 are one route (see US68). Route passes through **MOUNT OLIVET, 22., KENTONTOWN, 30. & CLAYSVILLE, 33. 46. CYNTHIANA,** lying in outer Bluegrass reg. on banks of S. Fork of Licking R., was scene of lively action during Civil War. It was captured by Confed. Gen. John H. Morgan in 1862 & again in 1864. **Cth.** (1851.fine Gr.Rev.). Behind it is **Old Log H.** (1790), used as residence, cth., law office & printing office. Here is J. with US27.

SIDE TRIP: On this Rd. (L) (S) 4m is **Peavine's Highland Chief Stud,** well-known saddle horse farm, typical of many in Bluegrass reg. **Old Covered Bridge,** 5m, over S. Fork of Licking R., is 275′ long. Erected c.1837, bridge has been in constant use ever since. It played important part in Gen. Morgan's raid on Cynthiana during Civil War. Opp. tiny settlement of **Lair** at 5.5m is **Lewis Hunter Distillery** (O), still producing grade of whisky it did in 1860's. 15m, **Paris** is at J. with US68 (see). (For description of pts. of int. from Paris to Lexington, see Lexington Trip II.) Bet. Paris & Lexington, US27 & US68 are united. 32m, **Lexington.** 67m, **Lancaster.** (For description of pts. of int. from Lexington to Lancaster, see Lexington Trip IV). 76m, **Stanford** is seat of Lincoln Cty., 1 of 3 orig. counties of Ky. Dist. of Va. formed in 1780. Through **Hall's Gap,** 83m, on dividing line bet. Bluegrass area & mts., an important Rd. has run since pioneer times. 96m, **Eubank** is an agric. reg. noted for quantity of buckwheat grown. 111m, **Somerset,** RR. town known as "Gateway to Mts." US27 crosses Cumberland R. 119m, **Burnside,** on banks of Cumberland R. at its confluence with its S. Fork. Route passes through **Parkers Lake,** 133m & **Stearns,** 145m, center of a thriving lumber industry & shipping pt. for both coal & timber of reg. 148m, **Pine Knot,** in foothills of Cumberland Mts. US27 crosses Tenn. Line at 151m.

**67. GEORGETOWN** (see Lexington Trip V) is at J. with US25 (see). **77. MIDWAY** is midway bet. Lexington & Frankfort. **87.5. NUGENT'S CROSSROADS,** named for members of Nugent family who operate general store (L) on cor. Opp. stands **Old Tavern** (R), in stagecoach days an important stopping place bet. Cincinnati & Louisville. **85. VERSAILLES** (see Lexington Trip VII). **97.5. JOE BLACKBURN BRIDGE,** spanning Ky. R., gives excellent view of R. & palisades. **95. LAW-**

**RENCEBURG,** seat of Anderson Cty., was named in honor of Capt. Jas. Lawrence, Commdr. of "Chesapeake," whose last words were "Don't give up the ship." **99. WALNUT GROVE FARM** (O.appl.), stock farm widely known for its saddle horses. **129. BLOOMFIELD,** founded in 1799. **144. BARDSTOWN** (see Louisville Trip I). (W) of Bardstown, US62 proceeds gradually into the Knobs belt, reg. of rounded hills. **169. ELIZABETHTOWN,** at J. with US31W (see) & with St.61.

SIDE TRIP: On this Rd. (L) $11^m$ to **Hodgensville,** seat of Larue Cty., $0.5^m$ below confluence of 3 branches of Nolin R. $13^m$, **Lincoln Mem. Nat. Pk.** on old **Sinking Spring Farm** (R), birthpl. of Abr. Lincoln. Lincoln Mem. incl. cabin believed to have been his birthpl. The water of Sinking Spring is still sweet & clear & is protected by stone walls & flagging at foot of knoll.

### Sec. 2: ELIZABETHTOWN to PADUCAH. 189.

US62 turns (R) at Cth. in **ELIZABETHTOWN, 0.,** & runs (SW) through the Knobs. **LEITCHFIELD, 31.,** was named for Maj. David Leitch, who owned land on which this cty. seat was sett. Leitch's land was adj. to 5,000-a. tract claimed by Geo. Washington. **9. BEAVER DAM,** an important mining center of W. Ky. coal fields. Ferry crosses **GREEN R.** at **77.** (good muskellunge fish.). **CENTRAL CITY, 88.,** a mining town in basin of hills. **GREENVILLE, 96.,** seat of Muhlenberg Cty. & center of the Black Belt, an area that produces most of St.'s output of dark tobacco & a large quantity of coal. On the bank of **POND R.** (R), **104.5.,** near hy. bridge is a ledge of rock bearing imprint of horses' hoofs. **112. NORTONVILLE,** a coal mining community, on site (R) of a prehist. village from which many artifacts have been recovered. Nortonville is at J. with US41 (see). **DAWSON SPRING** at **127.,** on W. edge of coal fields, has noted mineral springs & resort hotels. (W) of Dawson Springs US62 crosses Tradewater R. **139. PRINCETON,** an industrial & retail center & seat of Caldwell Cty., is widely known for its tree shaded streets & well kept old homes. **EDDYVILLE, 151.,** seat of Lyon Cty., is on bank of Cumberland R. **KUTTAWA,** at **153.,** is chiefly remembered for beautiful trees that border the hy. From Kuttawa (L) there is projected a Rd. to Tenn. Valley Authority's Ky. Dam across Tenn. R., $9^m$. The proposed Rd. would cross dam & join US68 (see) on other side of R. At **IUKA, 161.,** US62 crosses Cumberland R. by ferry & passes through narrow hilly strip of land that forms a watershed bet. Cumberland & Ohio Rs. Here tobacco & corn are chief products. At **SMITHLAND, 173.,** is J. with US60. The 2 hys. are united from this pt. to **PADUCAH, 190.** (For description of pts. of int. in this area, see Ohio R. Tour.)

## US 68—KENTUCKY

**KY.-OHIO LINE** (at Aberdeen, Ohio) **(SW) to KY.-ILL.** (at Paducah, Ky.). **367. US68**

Via: Maysville, Lexington, Bardstown, Cave City & Bowling Green

Bet. Ohio R. & Licking R., US68 follows old buffalo trl. used by early travelers. It was known as Smith's Wagon Rd. because in summer of 1783 a Lexington man named Smith took a wagon over it for 1st time. Route by 1816 was part of nat. post Rd. bet. Zanesville, Ohio, & Florence, Ala.

### Sec. 1: OHIO LINE to LOUISVILLE. 63.

US68 crosses Ohio Line at edge of Aberdeen, passing over Ohio R. on bridge. **0. MAYSVILLE,** as seen from Ohio side of R., resembles Italian hill town, built on steep slope of R. bank, terrace upon terrace, with gray walls & red roofs against green background. Town was est. 1787 & flourished as traffic center for merchandise floated down Ohio R. on barges & shipped from Maysville inland. As a boy, Ulysses S. Grant attended school here for 1 yr. Maysville is at J. with US62 (see). US68 & US62 are united bet. this pt. & Washington. (S) of Maysville hy. rises in curves from R. to rolling Bluegrass downs. **4. WASHINGTON,** once a "center of fashion & education," & 2nd largest town in St. It came into existence because the hill from Maysville was so long & difficult that it sometimes took wagons a whole day to get to top. Teamsters & travelers usually spent the night at top of hill, or at least paused there to take refreshment. **12. MAYS LICK,** named for a salt lick near-by. **23. BLUE LICKS BATTLEFIELD ST. PK.** (R), is site of bloody battle of Aug. 19, 1782, that ended the Rev. War in the West. Granite shaft bears names of those killed in battle. **Pioneer Mus.** houses many relics, incl. **Hunter Coll.** of prehist. remains unearthed at the licks. **37.5. MILLERSBURG** to (S) is heart of Bluegrass, with gently undulating surface & fertile soil. Hy. crosses **STONER CR., 45.5.**, tributary of Licking R., named in honor of Michael Stoner, companion of Dan. Boone. **46. PARIS. 63. LEXINGTON.** (For description of pts. of int. from Paris to Lexington, see Lexington Trip II.) Lexington is at J. with US60 (see), US25 (see) & US27 (see US60).

### Sec. 2: LEXINGTON to BOWLING GREEN. 160.

(For description of pts. of int. from Lexington to **HARRODSBURG, 32.**, see Lexington Trip III.) **42.5. PERRYVILLE,** whose name is connected chiefly with battle fought 2$^{m}$ from here in Civil War. Many bldgs. were used as hospitals or quarters during & after Battle of Perryville. Here is J. with Mackville Pike which leads (R) 2$^{m}$ to **Perryville Battlefield,** marked by mons. to Feds. & Confeds. At Perryville is J. with US150.

SIDE TRIP: On this Rd. (R) 27$^{m}$ to **Springfield,** founded in 1793. At Main & Cross Sts., **Washington County Cth.** (1814). Among its records, which date from 1792 are the marriage bond of Thos. Lincoln, father of Abraham; also the certificate of marriage of Thos. Lincoln & Nancy Hanks, & 1 of 2 known signatures of Lincoln's grandmother, Bersheba Lincoln.

At **52.5.** is **LEBANON,** home of **Loretto Jr. College & St. Mary's College for Boys.** (W) 1$^{m}$ is **Lebanon Nat. Cemetery,** est. 1862. **72.5. CAMPBELLSVILLE. 83. GREENSBURG,** named for Nath. Greene, Rev. War Gen. On Pub. Sq., **Cth.** (1799). **109. EDMONTON,** named for Edmond Rogers of Va. **128. GLASGOW,** lively, bustling town; trading center of a petroleum-producing field. Alex. Spotswood, Rev. Gen., grandson of Col. Gov. of Va. **160. BOWLING GREEN,** seat of Warren Cty., is on uplands along Barren R. Town was sett. in 1780. **Western Ky. St. Teachers' College,** 5th St., is on hill once occupied by a ft. built in 1861. Part of earthworks & equipment are preserved on campus.

### Sec. 3: BOWLING GREEN to PADUCAH. 144.

(S) of **BOWLING GREEN,** through the southern Knobs sec. of St., hy. passes a series of upland fors. & well cultivated farms. This fertile agric. area produces high grade of dark tobacco & many thoroughbred horses. **18. AUBURN,** on border bet. rolling fertile land & abrupt knobs. **28.5. RUSSELLVILLE,** founded in 1890, is in a valley among the knobs. **Old Southern Bank Bldg.,** SW. cor. 6th & Main Sts., was robbed by Jesse James & 4 companions March 20, 1868. **ELKTON, 44.,** is seat of Todd Cty. In **FAIRVIEW, 52.,** is **Jefferson Davis Mon.** in Davis Mem. Pk. (L), comm. birthpl. of man who became pres. of Confed. **63. HOPKINSVILLE.** J. with US41 (see). Town is one of leading dark-fired tobacco markets in country. First settlement was made in 1797. **84. CADIZ** is in center of large dark-leaf tobacco-growing area & is home of several wealthy planters. Town is well known for number & quality of hams it ships. **92.5. CANTON,** by Cumberland R., was once a busy landing place for river cargo boats. To (W) of Cumberland R. is Ky. **Woodlands Wildlife Refuge,** which is demonstrating methods of utilizing lands unsuitable for farming, by devoting them to forestry wildlife conservation. At **103.,** Rd. crosses **KY. L.** in Tenn. R. **BENTON, 118.,** seat of Marshall Cty., is in land ceded by the Chickasaw in 1818. At **123.5.** J. with TVA access Rd.

SIDE TRIP: On this Rd. (R) 6$^{m}$ to **Ky. Dam** (fish.boat.hunt.swim.) across Tenn. R., a maj. installation of TVA. This is largest of all TVA dams, 211′ high & 8,700′ long, built at cost of $115,000,000. Situated 20$^{m}$ upstream from mouth of Tenn. R., dam impounds water to form Ky. L., 85$^{m}$ long with shoreline of 2,200$^{m}$ covering more than 158,000 as.

**139.5.** J. with US60 (see) & US62 (see). **PADUCAH. 144.** (For description of pts. of int. from here to Paducah, see Ohio R. Tour.)

## US 23—KENTUCKY

**KY.-OHIO LINE** (at Portsmouth, Ohio) **(S) to KY.-VA. LINE** (at Jenkins, Ky.). **193. US23**

South Portsmouth, Ashland, Paintsville, Pikeville, Jenkins

Route follows low bluffs along curving Ohio R., Big Sandy Valley, & Levisa Fork, a tributary of Big Sandy R. Farther (S) it passes through mountain country rich in folk lore. It was last part of Ky. given up by the Inds. US23 crosses Ohio Line at Portsmouth by way of bridge over Ohio R. **SOUTH PORTSMOUTH 0.5.** is on **Site of Lower Town,** 1st white village in Ky., est. by Fr. traders some time before 1750. Bet. **FULLERTON** at **2.5.** & Greenup, Hy. parallels a long right-angle bend of the Ohio. Fruit growing is chief activity in this level reg. **GREENUP 19.** is seat of Greenup Cty. During his later years Dan. Boone is said to have made his home on Ky. side of Ohio R. near Greenup. (E) of Greenup US23 passes through some of best eastern Ky. bottom lands. There are occasionally fine views of sweeping Ohio R. **26. RACELAND** has a track that is center for horse racing in eastern Kentucky. **28. RUSSELL** lies directly opp. Ironton, Ohio, with which it is connected by hy. bridge. **34. ASHLAND** (see US60). Bet. Ashland & **CATLETTSBURG, 39.,** US23 & US60 are united (see US60). **75. LOUISA,** seat of Lawrence Cty., is at head of navigation on Big Sandy R. N. end of Louisa along US23 is Big Sandy Dam (L), 1st movable needle-type dam in U.S. Dam was built in 1896. **107. PAINTSVILLE,** seat of Johnson Cty., is on site of Paint Lick Sta., old trading post. **Rock H.,** natural rock formation, with circular opening cut by Inds. to provide shelter. It stands on hill facing the R. just (N) of **Concord Baptist Ch. 113. EAST POINT** lies directly across Levisa Fork of Big Sandy R. from Blockhouse Bottom, **Site of Harmon's Sta.,** 1st ft. in Big Sandy Valley, est. 1787. The Bottoms bet. East Pt. & Prestonsburg were used as camping grounds during Civil War by Union forces under Gen. Jas. A. Garfield.

**120. PRESTONBURG,** bet. the R. & the hills, was 1st settled in 1791. It was scene of a battle Jan. 10, 1862, giving Union forces control of eastern Ky. **151. PIKEVILLE** is a lumbering & coal mining center. **Hotel Jas. Hatcher,** Main St., has in lobby an odd assortment of relics. Pikeville is at J. with US119 (see). Bet. Pikeville & **JENKINS, 189.,** US23 & US119 are united (see US119). (S) of Jenkins route leads over series of continuous elevations to crest of **Pine Mt.,** thence through historic **POUND GAP, 193.,** a mt. pass. Kentucky, Cumberland, & Big Sandy Rs. rise near here. A marker on Ky. side of gap lists important dates in early history of St. & of this pass, through which Ind. trls. & pioneer roads ran. Pound Gap is on **VA. LINE.**

## US 25 & US 25W—KENTUCKY

**KY.-OHIO LINE** (at Cincinnati, Ohio) **(S) to KY.-TENN. LINE** (67$^{m}$ from Knoxville, Tenn.). **222. US25 & US25W**

This route crosses low wooded hills of Ohio R. & passes rolling orchard land & prosperous country estates with waving bluegrass meadows. Then from great gorge cut by Ky. R. to rugged foothills of Appalachians, it follows Dan. Boone's Wilderness Rd.

### Sec. 1: OHIO LINE to LEXINGTON. 83.

US25-US42 crosses **OHIO LINE,** at **0.,** on S. outskirts of Cincinnati, over **OHIO R. SUSPENSION BRIDGE,** built in 1867 & 1st of nation's great suspension bridges. **COVINGTON, 0.5.** (see Ohio R. Tour). Bet. Covington & Florence, US25 & US42 are one route, traversing hilly orchard land of Ohio R.'s N. bend, with a fine view of Cincinnati & the winding R. **4. FT. MITCHELL** is a residential suburb. During Civil War when Confed. forces were threatening invasion of the North, Gen. Lew Wallace, author of "Ben Hur" & commdr. of Union forces defending Cincinnati, led 15,000 men across the Ohio & erected series of earthworks here. **8. ERLANGER** is a residential town of Cincinnati-Covington metropolitan area. At **9. FLORENCE,** US42 turns (R) & leaves US25. In **CRITTENDEN, 26.,** is (R) **Lloyd Reserv.** founded in 1918 for preservation of native plant life. It covers more than 400 as. Route passes through **DRY RIDGE** at **34.** & **WILLIAMSTOWN** at **38. 71. GEORGETOWN. 83. LEXINGTON.** (For a description of pts. of int. in Georgetown & from Georgetown to Lexington, see Lexington Trip V.)

### Sec. 2: LEXINGTON to TENNESSEE LINE. 139.

At **0. LEXINGTON.** (For a description of pts. of int. from Lexington to Richmond see Lexington Tour VI.) **26. RICHMOND** (see). At **31.** Boone's Trace turned to follow Otter Cr. to S. bank of Ky. R., where Ft. Boonesboro was built. **BEREA** at **40.** in foothills of Southern Highlands, is seat of **Berea College,** founded 1853. This is oldest & largest of the mt. schools in Ky. It has 85 bldgs. on 300-a. campus.

**MOUNT VERNON, 58.,** is in foothills of Cumberland Mts. Immediately behind Cth. is old **Landford H.** (O), built in 1790 as a blockh. for defense against Inds. Route passes through **LIVINGSTON, 68.,** crosses **ROCKCASTLE R.,** & then passes through **LONDON, 91.** Entrance (L) to **LEVI JACKSON WILDERNESS RD. ST. PK.** is at **95.5.** Forty pioneers traveling over the Boone trl. in 1784 stopped here for a night on Little Laurel R. They were attacked by Inds., & all but 3 of co. were killed or taken captive. Grandchildren of Levi Jackson, Rev. War soldier who received land here for war services, gave to the St. more than 300 as. at this site to comm. the slain pioneers. At **105.** is **CORBIN.** Here US25 divides into US25W & US25E. Main route cont. on US25W.

SIDE TRIP: US25E branches (SE) from its J. with US25, passes bet. rugged cliffs & towering mts. & traverses an area in which coal mining is chief industry. At $37^{m}$ is entrance to 4,000-a. **Pine Mt. St. Pk.** (R), est. in 1928 (boat.swim.pic.facils.camp.), 1st St. Pk. in Ky. At $50^{m}$ is **Middlesboro,** trading center & largest town of SE. Ky., was named for the iron city of English Midlands. Town was built by Eng. co. that developed mineral resources, but bank failure in England later threw the co. into bankruptcy. Importance of coal in life of town is emphasized by **Coal H.** (O), on Cumberland Ave., office of Middlesboro C. of C., built of solid blocks of local coal. **Cumberland Gap** at $52^{m}$ on dividing line of Va. & Ky. to (N) & Tenn. to (S) is a trough bet. hills thickly covered with laurel & rhododendron. Through this gap many early settlers came into Ky. to travel on to the wilderness they had come to conquer. Because of its strategic importance, the gap was scene of considerable action in Civil War. In gap is J. with Skyland Hy.

On this hy. (L) $2^{m}$ to **Peak of Pinnacle Mt.** (2,860'). From here on clear days is a view extending $50^{m}$. Here also are **ruins of Ft. Lyon,** held in turn by both Union & Confed. forces.

At $53^{m}$ US25E crosses Tenn. Line.

Cont. on US25W. **105. CORBIN,** busy RR. center in level part of Cumberland Plateau, surrounded by a generally mountainous area with large tracts of timber. Coal mining is chief occupation. In 1775 when Dan. Boone cut his trace, which later became a part of the Wilderness Rd. into Ky., he turned (N) at this place. **127. WILLIAMSBURG.** In surrounding area are remains of prehist. occupation. Many artifacts have been found in old Ind. town sites near-by. The Ind.'s great southern trl. passed through here. **Cumberland College** (coed.) was founded here in 1889 by the Baptist Ch. On Cumberland R., 300 yds. from Cth., **King's Mill,** used for more than 100 yrs. Its dam is a popular fishing hole. (S) of Williamsburg US25W winds near towering **Jellico Mts.** (R). In Jellico at **139.** US25W crosses **TENN. LINE.**

## US 31W—KENTUCKY

**KY.-IND. LINE** ($8^{m}$ from Sellersburg, Ind.) **(S) to KY.-TENN. LINE** ($12^{m}$ from White House, Tenn.). **150. US31W**

Via: Louisville, Elizabethtown, Bowling Green, Franklin.

Taking a course through W. central Ky., US31W runs near Ohio R. for a time & then goes up Salt R. Valley. It enters the Knobs reg. where countryside is marked by small round hills streaked with ravines. Route follows general course of old Louisville-Nashville stagecoach Rd.

**0.** US31W crosses **IND. LINE,** $8^{m}$ (S) of Sellersburg, Ind., by way of bridge over Ohio R. **2. LOUISVILLE** (see). Louisville is at J. with US60, US31E (see) & US42 (see). **36. FT. KNOX.** (For description of pts. of int. from Louisville to Ft. Knox, see Louisville Trip II.) To (S) of Ft. Knox US31W passes among tall, ragged cliffs & gorges. At **41.** is J. with side Rd.

SIDE TRIP: On this Rd. (L) $7^{m}$ to **Mill Cr. Cemetery,** in which are **Lincoln Family Graves.** Here are buried Bersheba Lincoln, Abraham's paternal grandmother, & Mary Lincoln Crume & Nancy Lincoln Brumfield, his aunts.

**ELIZABETHTOWN, 48.,** is Cty. seat laid out in a wheel pattern. Town is trading center for a large rural area. Thos. Lincoln, father of Abr. Lincoln, lived here at different times. City has 2 outstanding colls. of Ind. artifacts found in Ky.: one on pub. sq. is owned by Bell Smoot & the other by Benn Ailes, of Poplar St. These colls. also have about 3,000 old firearms. In **Hardin County Cth.** is a room housing Lincolniana. **Brown-Pusey Community H.** (O), cor. N. Main & Poplar Sts., was a stagecoach inn built 1818. Gen. Geo. Custer lived next door to community house (1871-73) while writing "My Life on the Plains." Here is J. with US62 (see). **79.**

**MUNFORDVILLE,** seat of Hart Cty. **Old Fortifications** (R) are visible from hy. here. At **84.5.** is J. with St.335 leading (L) 3m to **Mammoth Onyx Cave** (fee), containing some of most beautiful formations in cave area. **87. HORSE CAVE.** It is said to have been so named because Cherokee used cave near-by as a corral for horses. Part of town is built over **Hidden R. Cave,** which has a continuously flowing underground R. with pearly white eyeless fish. Bet. Horse Cave & Bowling Green, US31W & US68 unite. **91. CAVE CITY,** at J. with St.70.

SIDE TRIP: On this Rd. (L) 9.5m to entrance of **Mammoth Cave Nat. Pk.** which has 49,000-a. area of forested hills, deep valleys & streams, with **Mammoth Cave** as chief attraction. With its 5 levels, Mammoth Cave covers an area of c.10m in circumference. Its explored passageways, of which about 325 have been mapped, extend to an estimated length of 150m. These passageways, of which about 325 have been mapped, extend to an estimated length of 150m. These passageways lead visitors to 3 Rs. & L., & many rooms & domes. Route is in heart of Cave Country. Mammoth Cave signs pt. (SW) to several caves, among them **Floyd Collins Crystal Cave** with unusual deposits of gypsum, crystal & onyx helictites. It was discovered by Collins while making a round of the traps on his father's farm. The cave contains the tomb of Floyd who lost his life (1925) in effort to discover a new entrance. While searchers were frantically trying to find the lost man, the whole nation waited for hourly bulletins.

**123. BOWLING GREEN** (see). **144. FRANKLIN,** a tobacco market. At **150.,** US31W crosses **TENN. LINE** 37m (N) of Nashville, Tenn.

## US 41 & US 41 ALT.—KENTUCKY

**KY.-IND. LINE** (2m from Evansville, Ind.) **(S) to KY.-TENN. LINE** (5m from Clarksville, Tenn.). **109. US41, US41 ALT.**

Via: Henderson, Madisonville, Hopkinsville.

Most of this route follows an old Ind. trl. that ran from Gt. Ls. to Gulf of Mexico. It was 1st made by buffalo in their seasonal migration from N. to S. Bet. Henderson & Nashville, (Tenn.), this route was long a post Rd., called Buttermilk Rd., because farmers along this route once set aside crocks of buttermilk & dippers from which travelers might drink freely.

US41 crosses Ind. Line at **0. Dade Pk.** (L) was built by Jas. Ellis in 1922, on N. part of Henderson Cty. that was cut off when Ohio R. changed its course. Races are held here for a period of 28 days, usually in Aug. Hy. crosses Ohio R. on **HENDERSON-EVANSVILLE** (Audubon Hy.) **BRIDGE** at **2. AUDUBON MEM. ST. PK.** (L) at 4. is a 400-a. tract donated by citizens of Henderson Cty. in mem. of John Jas. Audubon, ornithologist, who roamed Ky. hills from 1808 to 1826. At **5.** is J. with US60 (see), which is united bet. this pt. & Henderson with US41. **6.5. HENDERSON** (see Ohio R. Tour). Bet. Henderson & Dixon, Rd. passes through rolling lands covered with orchards & tobacco fields. At **29.5.** is J. with Harpe's Head Rd., so named because Big (Micajah) Harpe, a notorious outlaw, was killed here July 22, 1806, & his head placed on a pole by Rd. side. Bet. **DIXON** at **26.** & Madisonville, US41 passes through farming & mining country. **50. MADISONVILLE,** in center of plateau bet. Pond & Tradewater Rs. Town is one of principal loose-leaf tobacco markets in W. part of St. In this sec. a great many Ind. artifacts & relics have been found along Rs. & creeks. (S) of Madisonville US41 traverses coal fields. **54. EARLINGTON,** a RR. J. in heart of coal fields. **EARLINGTON L.** near-by offers excellent boat., swim. & fish. **58. MORTON'S GAP.** At **61. NORTONVILLE,** is J. with US62 (see). To (S) of coal fields of Hopkins Cty., hy. passes through stretches of level pasture & rugged picturesque hills. **86. HOPKINSVILLE.** J. with US68 (see) & J. with US41ALT.

SIDE TRIP: On this Rd. (R) 16m is entrance to **Camp Campbell,** est. by U.S. Army during World War II as training camp, especially for mechanized forces. In 1948 Dept. of War designated it a permanent post. Reserv. lies both in Ky. & Tenn. but hqs. are on Ky. side.

US41ALT crosses **TENN. LINE** at **109.** US41 cont. (SE) & at **112.** Rd. crosses **TENN. LINE.**

## US 51—KENTUCKY

**KY.-ILL. LINE** (1m from Cairo, Ill.) **(S) to KY.-TENN. LINE** (at Union City, Tenn.). **45. US51**

Via: Wickliffe, Bardwell, Clinton, Fulton.

US51, roughly parallel to the Miss. R., crosses westernmost tip of Ky. It passes through area rich in agric. products & replete with hist. assoc.

US51 crosses Ill. Line, **0.**, on W. bank of Ohio R., on a bridge over Ohio R. Bet. this pt. & Wickliffe, US51 & US60 are united. (See Ohio R. Tour.) **5. WICKLIFFE** (see Ohio R. Tour) is at J. with US60. **6. SITE OF OLD FT. JEFFERSON** (R) is on hill overlooking Miss. R. It was built by Gen. Geo. Rogers Clark in 1780. **15. BARDWELL,** seat of Carlisle Cty. Here is J. with St.123.

SIDE TRIP: From Bardwell (R) on St.123 to **Columbus,** 11.5m & **Columbus Belmont Mem. Pk.** (pic.grounds. shelters), 12m, on bank of Miss. R., old town site of Columbus. Town was moved to higher ground after disastrous flood in 1927. Site was scene of several important engagements during Civil War & St. Pk. comm. struggle that took place here bet. Fed. & Confed. forces. Fortifications & trenches have been reconstructed.

**30. CLINTON,** seat of Hickman Cty., is retail trade center for fertile agric. reg. At **41.** is J. with St.94.

SIDE TRIP: On this Rd. (R) to **Casey Jones Mon.** John Luther Jones, RR. engineer, known among other RR. men for his skill with a locomotive whistle, sacrificed his own life to save the passengers on his train in a wreck, Ap. 30, 1900. The incident became subject of a ballad that swept the nation. Jones' nickname, Casey, was derived from his boyhood home, **Cayce,** at 7m on this Rd. At 14m on St.94 is J. with a gravel Rd.

On this Rd. (R) 2m to J. with dirt Rd. beside an **Ancient Ind. Fortification** on high bluff. Called **O'Byam's Fort,** it is believed one of oldest mounds in Miss. Valley. Dirt Rd. leads (R) 4m to **Ft. Bayou de Chien Mounds,** known locally as **Roberts Mounds,** & believed to be very old. A short distance from this mound group is a prehist. canal, locally known as **L. Slough** which connects Bayou de Chien Cr. & Obion Cr. Canal (5m long) is believed to have been an entirely artificial waterway conn. 2 Ind. towns otherwise separated by an almost impenetrable jungle.

16m **Hickman,** on St.94, is built on 3 levels of high bluff overlooking Miss. R. Hickman is a shipping pt. for agric. reg. that surrounds it. In "Life on the Miss.," Mark Twain called it one of the most beautiful towns along the R.

**44.5. FULTON.** J. with US45 (see). At **45.** US51-US45 E. & W. cross **TENN.** LINE.

## US 119—KENTUCKY

**KY.-W. VA. LINE** (at Williamson, W. Va.) **(SW) to PINEVILLE, KY. 160. US119**
Via: Pikeville, Jenkins.

Route crosses a rugged & long-isolated reg. twisting around high mountain shoulders, where each turn in Rd. reveals range after range of dark green wooded slopes. US119 crosses at **0. W. VA. LINE,** at Williamson, W. Va., over Tug Fork of Big Sandy R. & follows Pond Cr. through drab coal-mining area. At this point the Rd. is artery of area once known as "billion dollar coal field," of which Williamson is the heart. **3.5. BELFRY,** typical of numerous half-abandoned mining towns of the area. **7.** US119 begins ascent from valley into the mts. One of most impressive views on US119 bet. Williamson, W. Va., & Pikesville is at **17.** From top of ridge, the surrounding ranges, deeply cut by narrow valleys & extending to horizon, form a scene of wild, rugged beauty. **31. PIKEVILLE.** J. with US23. Bet. this point & Jenkins US119 & US23 are united. **38. SHELBIANA,** small mountain hamlet. Bet. Shelbiana & Jenkins US119 winds through the valley, passing a few ragged mining settlements, almost lost among mountains. **69. JENKINS,** surrounded by impressive mountains whose vast coal deposits make it one of St.'s principal mining centers. Jenkins is at J. with US23 (see). To (SW) of Jenkins hy. passes through valleys & ascends uplifts of Cumberland Plateau, a reg. of much beauty & most extensively exploited coal area in St. Coal towns & camps are numerous. **Boone Creek** (R), **Boone Hill** (R), near headwaters of Ky. R., are reminders of Dan. Boone, who with several companions hunted in this country. Country pierced by this route is locale also of "The Little Shepherd of Kingdom Come" & "A Knight of the Cumberlands," by John Fox, Jr. **Pine Mt.** (2,600′) looms in distance. Over a part of the timbered craggy ridge extends Trl. of the Lonesome Pine. (SW) of crest of Pine Mt., US119 passes down great corridor formed by Pine (R) & Black Mts. (L). At **84.** is **WHITESBURG.** For 75m hy. parallels Cumberland R. **106. CUMBERLAND,** a mining town. At **BAXTER, 128.,** is mon. 12′ high made from blocks of coal from 45 mines in Harlan County. Here is J. with side Rd.

SIDE TRIP: From Baxter (L) on this Rd. 1m to **Harlan,** coal capital of the St. & seat of Harlan Cty. City & Cty. were scene of much strife bet. United Mine Workers Union &

mine operators during the 1930's. Mounds & rock shelters of this area have yielded many Ind. artifacts. Best known site is **Prehistoric Burial Ground** on Main St. opp. hotel. **Eversole Coll. Ind. Relics** (O.appl.), N. Main St., is unusually fine, incl. pottery, beads, arrowheads, & other articles.

Bet. Baxter & Pineville, US 119 is called Rhododendron Trl. because of profusion of shrub along the way. It blooms from May or early June to late July. **160. PINEVILLE,** & J. with US25E.

# LEXINGTON

**LEXINGTON**

Through rail & bus service. Ample accommodations. Info.: Bd. of Commerce, Main & Upper Sts.; Bluegrass Auto Club, Esplanade.

Lexington, 3rd largest city in Ky., lies on a rolling plateau in heart of the Bluegrass Country. City has few industries except those connected with tobacco & horses. It was named for Battle of Lexington by Rbt. Patterson, Simon Kenton, & others who in June 1775 were camped almost opp. present Lexington Cemetery, while on their way to build a ft. near the Kentucky R. Four years later town was founded when a blockh. was put up at Main & Mill Sts. In 1782 Gen. Assembly of Va. granted it a charter.

In 1784, Gen. Jas. A. Wilkinson, friend of Geo. Washington, opened 1st general store in town. Next yr. 1st tavern was opened. In 1787 Transylvania Seminary was removed here from Danville. By 1800 schs. of medicine & law had been added to Transylvania, making it one of the most important academic centers in W. Lexington was chief industrial city in St. until about 1820, when the paddlewheeler began industrializing Ohio Valley & attracting inland industrial plants to the R. banks. The nation-wide panic of 1837 stifled Lexington business. Then, as city was getting back on its feet, North & South came to blows. Civil War, however, est. the cigarette market. Before the war men were content to chew tobacco or smoke an occasional cigar, but soldiers began "rolling their own," and thus started one of America's largest industries. World War I also boomed cigarette business. Tobacco sales & prices went so high that Lexington did not suffer much when prohibition came & closed its distilleries. After Civil War, Lexington also concentrated on breeding, raising, & training fine horses. The number of well known horse farms & famous horses they have produced provide eloquent testimony of the success of this phase of Lexington industry. Univ. of Kentucky is one of the most important sources of business in the town.

PTS. OF INT.: (1) SE. cor. Sycamore & Richmond Rds., **Ashland** (grounds O), home of Henry Clay (1777-1852). Present house, reconstructed in 1857, follows plan of the orig. built for Clay in 1806. (2) SW. cor. High & Limestone Sts., **Ficklin H.** Here in 1820's lived Lexington's postmaster, Jos. Ficklin, & with him Jeff. Davis from 1821 to 1824 when he was a student at Transylvania Univ. (3) W. Main St. at city limits, **Lexington Cemetery,** is burial place of many of city's illustrious men, incl. Jas. Lane Allen, John C. Breckinridge, John Hunt Morgan, & Henry Clay. (4) 574 W. Main St., **Mary Todd Lincoln H.** (O.appl.), is Georg. Col. red brick home, where Mary Todd lived as a child & at the time she married Abr. Lincoln. (5) 193 N. Mill St., **Thos. Hart H.,** built in 1794 for Thos. Hart, whose daughter, Lucretia, married Henry Clay here. The young couple lived in the attached house on N. Hill St. until Ashland was ready for them. (6) 201. N. Mill St., **Hopemont** (O.10-5 wks.), the John Hunt Morgan home, built in 1811 by John Wesley Hunt, grandfather of John Hunt Morgan, is much the same as it was in 1861. An extensive Confed. Mus. has been installed, filled with treasures of 5 generations of Hunts & Morgans. (7) W. 3rd St. bet. Upper St. & Broadway, **Transylvania College,** maintained by Christian Ch. (Disciples of Christ), is oldest educational institution (W) of Alleghenies. (8) W. 2nd St. bet. Market & N. Mills Sts.,**Lexington Pub. Lib.** (O. 8:30-9 wks.; 2-6 Sun.), is oldest circulating lib. (W) of the Alleghenies, org. in 1795 as a pay lib. endowed by annual subscription. (9) W. Main St. bet. Upper St. & Cheapside, **Courthouse Sq.,** is in center of town. Within the park-like area stands **Fayette County Cth.** On E. Lawn of sq. is equestrian **Statue of John Hunt Morgan.** Among names on plaque of **Soldier's Mem.,** World War I Mon., before Main St. entrance, is that of Curry Desha Breckinridge, Red Cross Nurse. On W. side of sq. is **Breckinridge Statue,** erected by St. of Ky. in memory of John Cabell Breckinridge, (1821-

1875), Lexington lawyer, who at age of 30 was elected U.S. Representative, & at 35 was Vice-Pres. of U.S.

(10) **Tobacco Markets** (O. from 1st Mon. in Dec. until about Mar. 1), are held in SW. Lexington in heart of tobacco wareh. district. (11) (S) on Broadway, in rear of Tattersall's Sales Stables, **Trotting Track** (1873), is the mile oval of Ky. Trotting Horse Breeders' Assoc. Spring & fall meets on Grand Circuit are held here on what horsemen believe to be fastest trotting strip in world. More than 20 Amer. trotting & pacing records have been made on this track. (12) S. Limestone St. & Euclid Ave., **Univ. of Ky.** (Bldg. O. daily except Sun. & hols.), was est. in 1866 as land grant college. Plant incl. 48 bldgs. on 94-a. campus. Univ. is composed of 7 colleges, Experiment Sta., & Dept. of Univ. Extension. (13) **Sayre College** (O. appl. wks. during sch. yr.), a prep. sch. dating from 1854, was among 1st schs. in America to offer women a full college curriculum. In basement of Sayre is **Barlow Planetarium,** invented in 1844 by Thos. Hart Barlow of Lexington. Invention was so simple that 300 of them were made & sold to aid in teaching activity of solar system. Only a few are still in use. (14) 120 E. Main St., **Phoenix Hotel,** stands on Site of Postlethwait's Tavern, built in 1797. In lobby are pictures of great Ky. thoroughbred horses.

## TRIPS OUT OF LEXINGTON

### I. LEXINGTON (E) to WINCHESTER. 19. US60

At **5.** is **HAMBURG PLACE** (R), incl. **IROQUOIS HUNT & POLO CLUB & NANCY HANKS HORSE GRAVEYARD** (see Trip VIII). **11.5. DAVID PREWITT PLACE** (L), also known as Dunreath, typical of Ky. estates of early decades of 19th cent. **16.5. McCORMICK SEED HARVESTER WORKS** (O.), manufacturing machines for harvesting Bluegrass seeds. **17.** Marker on **SITE OF JOHN STRODE CABIN.** Strode founded in 1776 the sta. that later became town of Winchester. **19. WINCHESTER,** seat of Clark Cty., founded in 1793 & named for Winchester, Va. Primarily a residential town, it has several industries, incl. flour milling, lumbering, & assembly of farm machines. In old **Clark County Cth.,** on Main St., in center of bus. dist., Henry Clay made his last speech in Ky. His 1st Ky. speech was also made in Winchester on an oak stump on cor. of Main & Fairfax Sts., where Brown-Proctoria Hotel now stands. On College St., **Ky. Wesleyan College,** founded in 1866 by Meth. Episc. Church.

### II. LEXINGTON (NE) to PARIS. 18. US27-US68

At **4.2.** is **LEXINGTON COUNTRY CLUBHOUSE.** Opp. clubh. is entrance (through Swigert Lane) to **Haylands** (grounds O.), owned by Miss Elizabeth Daingerfield. Haylands is home of Morvich, winner of Kentucky Derby in 1922. At **5.5.** is (R) **LLANGOLLEN** (see Trip VIII) & J. with Johnson Rd.

SIDE TRIP: On this Rd. (L) 5$^{m}$ to **Bryan Station.** Here is mem., a stone wall, 4′ high, & octagonal in shape, around the spring that supplied water to defenders of the sta. when it was besieged in 1782 by Inds. under leadership of Capt. Wm. Caldwell & renegade Simon Girty. Sweeping (W) toward Lexington, invaders, on evening of Aug. 15, 1782, secretly surrounded Bryan Sta., anticipating easy victory when they should attack the next day. A story, the authenticity of which is disputed, is that the little company found itself with not enough water to withstand a long siege, & determined to risk sending women out in early morning for a supply; they were to act as if they did not know the enemy was in the canebrake around the spring. The women got water without undue haste, & without being attacked. A rescue party from Lexington & Boone Sta. arrived after 2 days & helped drive the enemy off.

At **6.5.** is **C. V. Whitney Farm** (see Trip VIII) 0.5$^{m}$ beyond is (L) **Elmendorf** (see Trip VIII). At **7.** is **GREENTREE** (see Trip VIII). **18. PARIS,** seat of Bourbon Cty. First court was held in May 1786 & in same yr. the combination cth. & jail was erected. Among old records are several suits against Daniel Boone, then resident of Maysfield, which then was part of Bourbon Cty. In 1790 one of St.'s earliest distilleries was erected here. Whisky made here was called Bourbon for the Cty. Later name was applied to any whisky made of corn according to the distillery's formula which produced a heavy-bodied, mellow liquor of deep amber color.

### III. LEXINGTON (SW) to HARRODSBURG. 32. US68

At **2.5.** is J. with Lane Allen Road leading (R) 1$^{m}$ to **Scarlet Gate,** now a stock farm but formerly home of Jas. Lane Allen (1849-1925). Allen was author of "Choir

Invisible," "Reign of Law," & other widely read novels. **3.5. BEAUMONT** (R), the 2,500-a. thoroughbred-horse farm of Hal Price Headley, is home of such noted runners as Supremus, Pharamond II, & Epinard. At **10.** is J. with Catnip Hill Pike.

SIDE TRIP: On this Rd. (L) 1m to **La Chaumiere du Prairie,** built in 1800 by Col. Davis Meade, officer of Rev. Army, on his 400-a. land grant. The dwelling became a series of rooms, some of log, others of stone, one of mud, & one—remaining today—of brick in octagonal form. Passageways of stone or brick connected rooms as they were built. Four men who were or had been Pres. of U.S., Thos. Jefferson, Jas. Monroe, Andrew Jackson, & Zachary Taylor, as well as Henry Clay, Aaron Burr, & Lafayette, were guests here at one time or another.

At **14.5.** is J. with St.29.

SIDE TRIP: On this Rd. (L) 2m is **Wilmore. Asbury College,** est. 1890, by Dr. J. W. Hughes of Meth. Episc. Ch., has 10 bldgs. & campus of 46 as. College offers both academic & religious courses & confers A. B. degree. Also on St.29 is **High Bridge St. Pk.** (camp.facils.), 7m, named for RR. bridge that rises 317′ above water & has 1,230′ span.

At **19.,** (S) of **Boone Tunnel,** cut through solid limestone in the great gorge of Ky. R., US68 crosses **BROOKLYN BRIDGE,** which offers a view of palisades & the R. **SHAKERTOWN, 24.,** locally called Pleasant Hill, was sett. in 1805 by Shakers, a religious cult that came into existence in England in 1747. People adhered to principles of communistic living, all "working for the good of all"; they believed in equality of the sexes. Shakers constructed 1 of 1st water systems in Ky. A horse provided power for a force pump that raised water from spring to the tank house, thence to a hydrant just outside the bldgs. Here is J. with side Rd.

SIDE TRIP: On this Rd. (L) 3m from Shakertown to **Dix Dam,** built in 1925 near confluence of Ky. & Dix Rs. **Herrington L.** formed by the dam, offers good bass fishing in season. In **Floating Bass Hatchery,** at Gwinn I. in Herrington L., large-mouth bass are propagated.

**HARRODSBURG, 32.,** 1st permanent white settlement in Ky., was sett. in 1778. In Harrodsburg, **Pioneer Mem. St. Pk.,** Lexington & Warwick Sts., is tract that occupies site of old Ft. Harrod & its immediate environs. In extreme SW. sec. of the city (Rd. marked), **Graham Springs** (O), a mineral spring in grove once occupied by famous resort.

### IV. LEXINGTON (S) to LANCASTER. 35.5. US27

At **2.5. ALLEGHAN HALL** (R), was built shortly before Civil War by William Pettit, who, during war, was driven out of St. & his house occupied by Union forces. There is a story that on outbreak of hostilities Pettit drove to Lexington, withdrew his money from the bank in gold, & buried it on his place. He died shortly after his return from wartime exile, & in his last hours is said to have made repeated but futile attempts to reveal hiding place of treasure.

**NICHOLASVILLE, 12.5.,** seat of Jessamine Cty., resembles Ky. town of earlier days. Many old houses border its quiet, shady streets. Here is Old Frankfort Pike.

SIDE TRIP: On this Rd. (R) 5m to **Jos. Drake H.,** which, according to legend, was built before 1770 by Joe Drake, described as a descendant & heir of Sir Francis Drake, Eng. admiral. In a primitive setting is **Glass's Mill** at 6m, erected in 1782, & said to have been 1st gristmill in Ky.

(S) of Nicholasville hy. descends gradually along banks of Hickman Cr. to Kentucky R. At **20., CAMP NELSON U.S. MILITARY CEMETERY** (L) contains graves of more than 500 soldiers who lost their lives at Battles of Perryville & Richmond during Civil War. **FORMER CAMP NELSON** (L), **21.,** is at mouth of Hickman Cr. This was one of leading concentration camps for Fed. troops & munitions during Civil War. At **25.** is J. with St.152.

SIDE TRIP: On this Rd. (R) 2.5m J. with an unmarked gravel Rd. leading to **Chimney Rock,** 5m, remarkable formation 125′ high, carved by slow erosion from limestone of Ky. R. cliffs. At 7m is **Herrington L.** (fish.boat.swim.camp.avail.in season).

In **BRYANTSVILLE, 26.** is (R) **Burnt Tavern** (O), a popular roadhouse in stagecoach days, so named because it was twice destroyed by fire. Tavern was birthpl. of Henry Smith, Provisional Gov. of Tex. (1824 & again 1827-38) who was son of orig. owner, Edward Smith of Va. **28.5. CAMP DICK ROBINSON,** est. 1861 over protests of Beriah Magoffin, then Gov. of Ky., was 1st Fed. Recruiting Sta. (S) of the Ohio. Here is J. with St.34.

SIDE TRIP: On this Rd. (R) 1m to **Camp Dick Robinson,** to J. with an unmarked Rd. leading (R) to **Birthpl. of Carrie Nation** (O) at 4m. The ardent temperance agitator was born here in 1846 at Pope's Landing on Herrington L.

**29. BURDETT'S KNOB** (L), a monadnock hill of resistant rock projecting from a plain that has been greatly reduced by erosion. It was used in pioneer times by settlers as a lookout. **35.5. LANCASTER,** seat of Garrard Cty., was settled in 1798 by pioneers from Lancaster, Pa., & was named for their native city.

## V. LEXINGTON (N) to GEORGETOWN. 13.5. US25

**2.5. EOTHAN H.** (R) was built in 1798 by Rev. Jas. Moore, later pres. of Transylvania Univ. This was home of music master described by Jas. Lane Allen is his story, "Flute and Violin." **7.5. HURRICANE HALL** (L), built before 1801. Its wallpaper in hall & parlor was hung in 1817. **13.5. GEORGETOWN** with many large trees & old houses. It is college town & seat of Scott Cty. Inc. in 1790 & named for Geo. Washington. Town (L) 1 block from hy. on Water St. grew up around **Royal Spring** & still gets its water supply from it. On College St. is **Georgetown College,** Bapt. institution est. in 1829. It has campus of 20 as. & grants A.B. degree. Charming **Showalter H.,** on W. Hamilton St., is on site of an old slave market, whose auction block still stands in yard.

## VI. LEXINGTON (SE) to RICHMOND. 27. US25

US25 passes through Ky. R. gorge (S) of Lexington, widely known for its scenic beauty, & crosses Ky. R. at Clay's Ferry. From parking space near top of bluff is splendid view of palisades & winding R. At **27. RICHMOND,** named for Richmond, Va., was 1st settled in 1784. **Madison County Cth.** (L), on Main St., was built in 1849. In Richmond is **Eastern Ky. St. Teachers' College,** which in 1906 took over bldgs. of old Central Univ., est. in 1874. Lancaster Ave., **Irvineton** (O), built in 1820, came into possession of Irvine family in 1829. Mrs. Elizabeth Susan Irvine, at her death in 1918, left house to Medical Society of Ky. which in conjunction with U.S. Public Health Serv. uses it as hospital for treatment of trachoma. Old paintings & heirlooms of Irvine family remain in bldg. Crowning a wooded hill at **28.** is **WOODLAWN** (R), built in 1822, by Gen. Green Clay for his daughter. John Fox, Jr., wrote a description of house in his novel, "Crittenden." Woodlawn was occupied by both Feds. & Confeds. during Civil War.

## VII. LEXINGTON (W) to FRANKFORT. 29.5. US60

US60 passes **CALUMET FARM** (R), at **4.5.** (see Trip VIII). At **6.** is **OLD KEENE PLACE** (R), built c.1790 on an 8,000-a. tract granted to Francis Keene by his kinsman, Patrick Henry, then Gov. of Va. Marquis de Lafayette was house guest here during his visit to Lexington in 1825. Adj. Keene estate, which now incl. but 20 as. of orig. tract, is new **KEENELAND RACE TRACK** (R), **6.5.** (see Trip VIII). Stables 800 horses. At **12.5.** is J. with Payne Mill Rd.

SIDE TRIP: On this Rd. (R) 1m to **Buck Pond.** House built in 1784 by Col. Thos. Marshall, father of John Marshall, Chief Justice of U.S., on land granted for services in Rev. War.

At **14.** is **VERSAILLES,** seat of Woodford Cty., named for Versailles, France, as tribute to Louis XVI for his aid in Rev. War. Town was est. in 1792. The town site is a circle whose radius is 600 yds. & whose center is the Cth. **29.5. FRANKFORT,** capital of Ky., was 1st sett. in 1773. It was made St. capital when Ky. became 15th St. in 1792, 1st St. (W) of Alleghenies. PTS. OF INT.: (1) The **New Capitol** (O.9-5 wks.), built in 1909 at S. end of Capitol Ave. Built of Bedford stone on a high granite base, it has high central dome raised on a graceful Ionic peristyle, crowned with a slender lantern cupola. (2) On capitol grounds & overlooking Ky. R. is **Executive Mansion,** residence of Ky.'s governors. (3) St. Clair St. & Broadway, **Old Capitol** (1827-30), houses St. Hist. Society (O.9-12; 1-4:30 wks.), custodian of a rich coll. of Kentuckiana incl. Aaron Burr's pistol with which he shot Alex. Hamilton. **Lib.** (O.9-12;1-4:30 wks.), a treasure house of Ky. history. (4) 218 Wilkinson St., **Liberty Hall** (excellent example of Georg.O.9-5 wks.adm.25¢), built in 1796, was home of John Brown, 1st U.S. Senator from Ky. Several Presidents & other important persons were entertained here. (5) E. Main St. **Frankfort Cemetery,** lies along edge of bluff that overlooks Frankfort. Near entrance (R) is **Goebel Mon.,** where the Gov.-elect is buried who, in 1900, was assassinated on steps of old Capitol. (6) At pt. where drive closely skirts edge of the bluff (R) is **Boone Mem.** A footpath winds down from drive to single grave where are buried Dan. & Rebecca

Boone. (7) E. Main St., **St. Arsenal** (N.O.), at ft. of hill, attracts attention by its commanding position, rather than by its size or style of architecture. It was erected in 1850 as storehouse for materials & equipment belonging to St. militia, & still serves that purpose. (8) **St. Industrial Institute** (Ky. Negro College). (9) E. Main St. & City Limits, **Teachers' Training Sch. for Negroes.** Sch., on 35-a. campus, has 6 bldgs. & dormitories for students & faculty. **Lib.** contains one of finest colls. of Negro literature in Ky. (10) In Frankfort are famous distilleries where Old Grandad, Old Crow, & Old Taylor (Bourbon) are distilled.

## VIII. HORSE FARM LOOP TOUR. 22.5. US60

Lexington to Lexington; Winchester Pike, Hume Rd., Bryan Sta. Pike, Johnson Rd., US27-US60 (Paris Pike), Ironworks Pike, Newtown Pike. Hard surfaced Rds. throughout. Horse farms on this route are O. to pub., but permission to visit stables must be obtained at farm offices. Visitors are required to refrain from smoking & to close all gates that they open.

E. on US60 from Zero Milestone, at cor. of Main St. & Union Sta. Viaduct on Walnut St., to Midland St.; (L) on Midland St. to 3rd St., here called Winchester Pike. **Entrance to PATCHEN WILKES STOCK FARM** (L) is at **3.** (O.9-4 appl.). This once busy horse place is now devoted to raising of cattle & sheep. Farm was owned more than a cent. ago by Capt. Benj. Warfield, on land granted the Warfield family by Colony of Va. before Rev. It was named for the blooded sire Patchen Wilkes. Peter the Great, purchased as a 9-yr.-old stallion, with a track record of 2:07½, that stood here for more than a decade, sold at the age of 21 for $50,000. At **3.5.** is **entrance to HAMBURG PLACE** (R), acquired 1897 by John E. Madden, & since owned & operated by his son, J. E. Madden, Jr. At Hamburg Pl. have been foaled & bred 6 Ky. Derby winners, largest number to come from any one nursery. These winners were: Plaudit (1898), Old Rosebud (1914), Sir Barton (1919), Paul Jones (1920), Zev (1923), & Flying Ebony (1925). Stables of Hamburg are now empty except in winter when polo ponies are quartered here. At **4.** (R) **NANCY HANKS HORSE GRAVEYARD** is burial ground of dozen horses that made John E. Madden famous as a breeder. Nancy Hanks, considered one of greatest trotters that ever lived, is buried in center of plot. Stone mon., topped with a miniature statue of the mare, stands over her grave. At **4.5.** is J. with Hume Rd. Main route of tour turns (L) here. On Hume Rd. (L) at **7.** is J. with Bryan Sta. Pike; (R) on Bryan Sta. Pike to J. with Johnson Rd., **9.;** (L) on Johnson Rd. Here is (L) **LLANGOLLEN** (Welsh, pronounced Thlangothlen), **10.5.,** whose color motif is white trimmed in black. Owned by John Hay Whitney, it is 1 of 3 Whitney farms in the Bluegrass. Johnson Rd. runs to dead end at its J., **11.** with US27-US68, which is here called the Paris Pike. Hy. turns (R) on US27-US68. **11.5. C. V. WHITNEY FARM,** (O. 11-4,Feb.-June, no specific hrs. at other times), has 11 barns, a 2-story frame cottage, a 2-story stone farm office, & a 1$^{m}$ training course. Bldgs. are painted yellow. About a mile from entrance, in a wooded area near one of the barns, is cemetery where famous horses of the farm are buried. These incl. Broomstick, Peter Pan, Whisk-broom II, Prudery, Regret, Pennant, & Equipoise.

At **11.5.** is also J. with Ironworks Pike. Main tour route later turns (L) on Iron-works Pike. Meanwhile straight ahead on US27-68, 0.5$^{m}$, to **Elmendorf** (L) (O.8-4 wks.), owned by Jos. E. Widener. Four Corinthian columns & 2 marble lions are all that remain of the marble palace built in 1897-1900 by Jas. B. Haggin, copper magnate, for his bride. House was razed in 1929 to avoid payment of taxes on so costly a bldg. Elmendorf stables produced many fine horses, among which were sire & dam of famous Man o' War. In **Elmendorf cemetery** is a large bronze statue of Fair Play, which, even as an aged stallion in 1919, brought $100,000. In front of statue are graves of Fair Play & Mahubah, sire & dam of Man o' War, with huge grave-stones bearing wreaths. Adj. Elmendorf is **Spendthrift Farm,** owned by Leslie Combs II. Since its est. in 1937, this farm has grown both in acreage & importance as a breeding center. Farm was begun on a 121-a. strip bought from Elmendorf, & it has now grown to 550-as. A recent stud acquisition of this farm is noted Australian Bernborough, winner of 15 stakes races in succession. Farm is named for one of Elmendorf's most famous horses. Paris Pike (US27-US68) cont. (R), another 0.5$^{m}$ to **Greentree,** a breeding farm owned by estate of late Mrs. Payne Whitney. The Whitney colors, white & black, are used on bldgs. & fences of the farm. Mrs. Whitney's Imp. St. Germans, Fr. horse, foaled in 1921, is sire of Twenty Grand, which set a record for the Ky. Derby in 1931 (2.01 4/5). St. Germans also sired

St. Brideaux, & Bold Venture, winner (1936) of Ky. Derby & the Preakness. Retracing our route back to J. of Ironworks Pike & Paris Pike, the main trip cont. on Ironworks Pike. At **13.5.** is J. with George Widener Farm Rd.

SIDE TRIP: On this Rd. (R) is back entrance (L) of **Dixiana Farm,** one of show-places of the Bluegrass, owned by Chas. T. Fisher, manufacturer of motor car "bodies by Fisher," who acquired farm in 1929. Land was once part of 13,000-a. estate owned by Jas. B. Haggin. At 1m is J. with Russell Cave Pike; (L) on this Rd. On Russell Cave Pike opp. J. is **Mt. Brilliant,** home of Louis Lee Haggin built in 1792. (L) 1m from Dixiana front entrance on Russell Cave Pike to J. with Huffman Mill Pike; on Huffman Mill Pike (R) 5m to **Faraway Farm** (O.7:30-4:00), owned by Samuel Riddle. This was home of Man o' War, greatest thoroughbred of his day & by some authorities ranked as greatest native performer of all times in this country. War Admiral was most famous of horses sired by Man o' War, having been one of the select group to win in succession the Ky. Derby, Preakness, & the Belmont. In winning the Belmont he shaded his sire's time. Russell Cave Pike cont. southward from its J. with Huffman Mill Rd. to J. with Ironworks Pike, 2.5m.

Ironworks Pike cont. (NW) (straight ahead) from J. with Widener Farm Rd., crossing Russell Cave Pike, at **13.5.,** J. with the side tour to home of Man o' War. To (NW) of J. with Russell Cave Pike, the Ironworks Pike passes the entrance (R) at **15.** to **Castleton** (1,132 as.), owned by David M. Look. This was once the estate of Castleman family & earlier was known as Cabell's Dale, home of John Breckinridge (1760-1806), sponsor of Ky. Resolutions of 1798-99, & U.S. Senator from Ky. 1801-05. Breckinridge left Senate to become Attorney Gen. of U.S. & died in office. The 2-story white brick house was built in 1806. The stables have housed many fine horses, among them Guy Castleton, Spencer, Rutherford, & Moran. Colin, foaled in 1905, was retired unbeaten after winning $181,610. At **16.** on Ironworks Pike is J. with Newtown Pike.

SIDE TRIP: On Newtown Pike (R) 1m to **Walnut Hall Stock Farm** (L). This estate of 3,500 as., having appearance of a well kept park, is one of the world's foremost trotting-horse nurseries. The farm was est. in 1892. Near the large Col.-style, yellow brick residence stands main barn. Peter Volo, who died in 1937 at the ripe age of 25, was at stud here. In cemetery is life-size statue of the horse Guy Axworthy. Walnut Hall Farm Rd. turns (L) & reaches J. with Ironworks Pike again at 3.5m. On this Rd. (L) 4.5m to **Spindle Top** (R), owned by Mrs. M. F. Yount, with 826 as. of almost treeless land. Palatial residence was built in 1936. Stables house some beautiful Amer. saddle horses. Among the best have been Beau Peavine & Chief of Spindletop. Latter was one of winners of $10,000 award annually offered by Ky. St. Fair for championship form in the three- & five-gaited class. Ironworks Pike reaches its J. with Newtown Pike 5m (SE) of the entrance to Spindletop, the point at which the loop to Walnut Hall Farm & Spindletop started.

Main route turns (L) from Ironworks Pike on Newtown Pike. On Newtown Pike is **COLDSTREAM STUD, 18.5.,** bordered by limestone wall 4m long. The 1,855-a. estate is owned by C. B. Shaffer. Main barn, remodeled from a dairy, contains 32 stalls for thoroughbreds. There is a legend that Price McGrath, 1st owner, hid a fortune in walls of the barn, but search has not revealed it. Newtown Pike cont. (S) to J. with Main St. in Lexington; (L) on Main St. to Zero Milestone, **22.5.**

## IX. HORSE FARM LOOP TOUR. 18. US60

Lexington to Lexington. Rice Pike, Elkchester Pike, Old Frankfort Pike.

(W) on US60 from Zero Milestone (Main & Walnut Sts. at Union Sta. Viaduct) on Main St. to Jefferson St.; (L) on Jefferson St. over viaduct to W. High St.; (R) on W. High St. which becomes Versailles Pike (US60).

On US60 (R) is **CALUMET FARM, 4.7.** (O.9-4), orig. known as Fairland when owned by Jos. W. Bailey, Senator from Tex. Calumet Farm was home of W. M. Wright, whose fortune was made in Calumet baking powder. It is now owned by his son, Warren Wright, of Chicago. It is also home of many great horses, incl. Whirlaway, triple crown winner in 1941 & selected in public poll after Man o' War's death as greatest living thoroughbred. More recent Calumet champion is Citation, 1948 winner of Derby, Preakness, & Belmont. Whirlaway also set new record for Derby in 1941 at 2:01 1/5. The 1,000-a. Calumet Farm was purchased by the senior Wright in hope of breeding a winner of the Hambletonian, the most desired stake in the harness horse field. At **6.5.** on US60, **KEENELAND RACE COURSE,** (R), held its inaugural meeting in 1936. This track, which supplants Lexington's century-old Assoc. Course, is considered one of fastest in America. In the 3-story clubh. are photographic murals by some of the best photographers in the Bluegrass; also offices & facilities incl. restaurant, bar, & private dining rooms. Keeneland Race Course occupies about 150 as. of old Keene Place, founded on tract of c.8,000 as. granted by Patrick Henry, then Gov. of Va., to his kinsman, Francis Keene. (W) of race course is J. with Rice Pike, **7.1.**; (R) from US60 on Rice Pike to J. with Van Meter Pike. **8.7.**; (L) on Van Meter Pike to J. with Elkchester Pike, **9.9.**; (R) on Elkchester Pike to J. with the old Frankfort Pike, **11.7.**; (R) on Old Frankfort Pike.

At **12.5.** is white fenced acreage that was **IDLE HOUR FARM,** owned by late Col. E. R. Bradley. It covered 1,300 as. on both sides of Old Frankfort Pike. Miles of white fence divided farm into paddocks & pastures. Underground passageway connected the paddocks on each side of the pike. Farm had a tiny chapel, a solarium for yearlings, a large brick residence, & many barns. Col. Bradley had 4 Ky. Derby winners: Behave Yourself (1921), Bubbling Over (1926), Burgoo King (1932), & Broker's Tip (1933). It is said of Col. Bradley, who purchased the estate in 1906, that name of an employee who died in his service was never removed from the payroll as long as there was a surviving dependant. Old Frankfort Pike returns (E) into Lexington over viaduct to Jefferson St. (L) on Jefferson St. to Main St. (R) on Main St. to Zero Milestone, **18.**

# LOUISVILLE

## LOUISVILLE

Through RR., bus, & air conns. Ample accoms. S.S. excursions up Ohio R. at least once daily in summer. Annual Events: Kentucky Derby, 1st or 2nd Sat. in May; Kentucky St. Fair, 2nd or 3rd week in Sept.

Louisville (Loo-i-vil) lies on a level plain that curves for 8$^{m}$ along Ohio R., somewhat more than 100$^{m}$ downstream from Cincinnati. Midway in the R. are Falls of the Ohio, which determined location of orig. settlement & gave it a name (Falls of the Ohio) until, as a gesture of gratitude for the aid given by Louis XVI & the Fr. nation to Amer. Rev., the name was changed to Louisville. It is largest & most important city in the St., commercially & industrially. Ohio R. played vital part in development of Louisville & surrounding country. Fr. were 1st to explore the R. During next 100 yrs. a long line of adventurers, explorers, traders, & surveyors saw the Falls of the Ohio, stopped for a time, & passed on. In 1773, after England had won the Ohio Valley from France, 1st permanent settlement was attempted at the Falls. In May 1778 young Geo. Rogers Clark, with 150 volunteer soldiers & about 20 families, came down the Ohio & camped on I. across from present site of Louisville. Island has long since been washed away by flood waters. After a summer in the N.W. Territory, Clark sent some of his men back to settlement to est. a ft. on mainland. Ft. was built during winter 1778-79 opp. Corn I. It became nucleus of settlement & hqs. of Gen. Clark until Ft. Nelson was completed in 1782. In 1781-82 Ft. Nelson was erected (N) of Main St., bet. 7th & 9th Sts., covering an a. of ground along Ohio shore.

Louisville was inc. 1828 & received its 1st city charter. Census of 1900 showed pop. of 204,731. Since 1920 city has spent millions of dollars in expansion & improvements. Downtown skyscrapers were all built after 1920, & in 1925 falls were harnessed for production of electricity. Great flood of 1937, the greatest recorded for this R., caused more than $52,000,000 damage. Louisville is a trading & mfg. center combining commerce & industry of a Northern city with a Southern city's enjoyment of living. Approximately one-fifth of nation's cigarettes are manufactured here. Old distilleries on Main St. have made city one of nation's top ranking distributing centers for whiskey.

PTS. OF INT.: (1) 435 S. 5th St., **Cathedral of the Assumption** (Cath.) was completed in 1852. Spire with 24′ cross rises to 287′. **Grayson H.,** 432 S. 6th St., 1st brick house built in city, was constructed some time before 1810. Outer walls are 17″ thick. (3) W. Chestnut St. bet. S. 8th & S. 9th Sts., **College Sq.** was set aside by city in 1837 as site for a college. Medical Institute, from which Univ. of Louisville ultimately developed, opened here in 1839. (4) NW. cor. N. 7th & W. Main Sts., **Ft. Nelson Mon.,** comm. ft. built in 1782, which extended from this pt. (W) approximately 2 blocks along what is now Main St. & (N) to R. (5) 320 W. Main St., **Old Bank of Louisville Bldg.,** (O.9-5 wks.), now occupied by Louisville Credit Men's Assoc., was built in 1837. It is popular with artists who come to sketch stately facade. (6) N. end of N. 3rd St., **Wharf & Water Front,** are closely associated with hist. of Louisville. Visible (L) along water's edge is upstream end of **Louisville & Portland Canal,** rebuilt in 1927. Orig. canal was built by slave labor in 1830 & opened new era of inland navigation. Canal was twice rebuilt before present locks & dam were completed. **U.S. Gov. Dam No. 41** floods rapids & eases a drop of 37′ in R. bed. Backwaters of dam flood Corn I., orig. site of Louisville. In immediate foreground is only inland **U.S. Coast Guard Sta.,** est. in 1881 to protect life at Falls of the Ohio. Directly across the R. is Jeffersonville, Ind., plant of Colgate Co., bearing a great illuminated clock that tells the time to the people of Louisville. Towhead I. (R), so named because, before the bldg. of the canal, it provided a harbor on the upper R. bet. it & Shippingport harbor below the falls. Goods were transported over land & boats were towed except when periods of high water permitted navigation of R. channel. (7) SW. cor. S. 4th & Walnut Sts., **Seelbach Hotel** has murals in the lobby depicting pioneer life in Ky. & NW. Territory. Work was completed in 1904 by Arthur Thomas.

(8) 419 S. 2nd St., **Christ Ch. Cathedral** (Episc.), oldest ch. in city, was built in 1822. (9) E. Jefferson St. bet. S. Brook & S. Floyd Sts., **Haymarket** (O. day & night throughout yr.), in the 1880's was an abandoned RR. yard where farmers congregated to sell produce. To protect their marketplace from intrusion by city bldgs., farmers formed a stock co. in 1891, which today owns & administers the property. No discrimination is made bet. near & distant producers so long as they can certify that produce offered for sale is of their own raising. (10) 200 E. Gray St., **Scottish Rite Temple** contains a room paneled with cedar of Lebanon. The cedar, pronounced genuine by Smithsonian Institution, was obtained from estate of Fr. officer, who had taken it from ruins of an ancient Syrian bldg. (11) 109 E. Broadway, **Presb. Theological Seminary,** (O.9-4 wks.), owns Palestinian Archeological Coll. of articles from Palestine. (12) W. York St. bet. 3rd & 4th Sts., **Louisville Free Pub. Lib.** (O.9-9 wks.2-6 Sun.), 1st opened to pub. in 1908. In basement is **Mun. Mus.,** containing coll. of unusual birds, butterflies, & fossils. (13) 118 W. Breckinridge St. **Wilson Club** (O.9-5 wks.), home of the hist. society which collects Kentuckiana. Club was founded in 1884 & named for 1st historian (1784) of Ky. Lib. contains large coll. of books & mss. pertaining to the St. In the mus. on 2nd fl., which exhibits pioneer relics, are mementos of Jas. D. (Jim) Porter, Ky. giant, incl. his rifle, 7′ 10″ long, & his boot, 14½″ long. Porter, 2nd tallest man in world at the time he lived, grew to be 7′ 9″ tall. (14) S. 4th St. & Magnolia Ave., **Central Pk.,** 17-a. tract containing several huge specimens of tulip poplar, survivors of virgin forest. Along RR. tracks extending (W) of Central Park is locale of Alice Hegan Rice's "Mrs. Wiggs of the Cabbage Patch." Land was orig. used as a cabbage field, then a sub-div. was laid out, but lots did not sell. Squatters came in & used scraps of material salvaged from city dump. Comfortable homes now fill area.

(15) 1839 Frankfort Ave., **Amer. Printing House for the Blind** (O.9-4:30 wks.), one of largest & oldest establishments of its kind, prints Braille books for the blind. It was est. 1858 & was supported by individual subscriptions until Congress made an annual appropriation of $10,000 in 1879 & increased the grant to $50,000 in 1919. (16) S. 3rd & Shipp Sts., **Confed. Mem.,** a large, tapering Georgia granite shaft erected by Ky. Women's Confed. Mon. Assoc., in honor of Confed. soldiers. (17) S. 3rd & Shipp Sts., running to Eastern Pky., **Univ. of Louisville,** claimed to be oldest mun.-owned univ. in Amer. To (L) of entrance, **Speed Mem. Mus.,** (O.10-5 Tues.-Sat.;2-5 Sun.). Bldg. contains coll. of pottery & porcelain by Eng., German, & Austrian artisans. Miniatures of past 3 centuries are on display, among paintings of more than 100 artists. (18) S. 7th St. & Central Ave., **Churchill Downs** (O), the 180-a. park-like tract of the Ky. Jockey Club, provides one of the fastest racing tracks in world for the 19-day Spring & 10-day Fall Racing meets, & for the Ky. Derby, usually run 1st or 2nd Sat. in May. (19) Eastern Pky. & Cherokee Rd., **Cherokee Pk.,** a rolling tract of 409 as. in E. sec. of city. Middle fork of Beargrass Cr., winding through the area, is fed by springs from limestone cliffs above. **Bird Observatory** houses large coll. of mounted native Ky. birds. In a wild spot is Enid Yandell's **Dan. Boone Statue,** placed so that Boone, clad in hunting garb, seems to be stepping out of a thicket. (20) at 2825 Lexington Rd., **Southern Bapt. Theological Seminary** (O.9-4:30 wks.) has a 55-a. campus. Opened in Greenville, S. C. in 1859, moved to Louisville in 1877. (21) At Baxter Ave. & E. Broadway, **Cave Hill Cemetery,** in which are graves of famous men & women, among them Gen. Geo. Rogers Clark & Geo. Keats, brother of Eng. poet.

## TRIPS OUT OF LOUISVILLE

### I. LOUISVILLE (SE) to BARDSTOWN. 40. US31E

At 5. is **FARMINGTON H.** (L), built in 1810 by John Speed, who came with his father over Wilderness Rd. from Va. to Ky. in 1782. Jas. Speed, one of sons of John Speed, was Attorney Gen. under Abr. Lincoln; & Joshua, another son, was Lincoln's intimate friend at Springfield, Ill. In 1841, Lincoln spent most of summer & fall here. **MOUNT WASHINGTON, 21.,** was a flourishing community on the turnpike from Louisville to Nashville as early as 1800. Settlement was 1st known as "The Crossroads," then as Mount Vernon, & finally, by order of postal authorities, as Mount Washington. The 2-story **Birdwell H.** (R), built in 1797 of rough hewn logs, has been little altered since its construction. In vic. of **SALT R., 26.** US31E suddenly comes alongside a great bottom land (L) far below the hy. Ornamental stone wall by roadside forms parking place (fine view). **COX'S CREEK, 32.5.,** was named for Col. Isaac Cox, who, with a sm. band of settlers, built a ft. here in 1775. At **37.** is J. with Rd. leading (R) to entrance of **Nazareth College & Academy,** Cath. sch. est. in 1814. Sch. has a mus. with an extensive coll. of geological specimens. **40. BARDSTOWN.** J. with US62 (see) & N. J. with US68 (see). Bardstown was inc. in 1778. In its youth it rivaled Louisville & Lexington as a center of social & educational activities. (NE) of Bardstown 0.5m is **Federal Hill** (see US68). **John Fitch Mon.** on Cth. Square, was erected by Congress to honor man now acknowledged to have invented the steamboat. John Fitch demonstrated a boat driven by steam on Delaware R. in 1787—20 yrs. before Rbt. Fulton launched the "Clermont" on the Hudson. The public was skeptical, & after repeated rebuffs, Fitch came to live here. Later, disillusioned with reception of his invention & with his domestic affairs, he is said to have taken his own life in 1798. **St. Joseph Proto-Cathedral,** begun in 1819, is notable example of ch. architecture of the period. Inside are many paintings, said to have been obtained from sacked churches of Belgium & France during Napoleonic era. Among them are works ascribed to Van Dyck, Van Eyck, & Murillo.

### II. LOUISVILLE (SW) to FORT KNOX. 36. US60-US31W

In **ST. HELEN'S** at **6.** is **Louisville & Jefferson Cty. Home** (L) for aged & infirm. **12. WAVERLY HILLS TUBERCULOSIS SANITORIUM** (L), on the heights overlooking the Ohio & the blue hills beyond the R., has accommodations for 515 patients, & is owned by municipality. **KOSMOSDALE, 18.5.,** is a company-owned town of the Kosmos Portland Cement Co. **22.5. WEST POINT,** was founded in 1800. In **Young's Inn,** on Main St., Jenny Lind sang in 1851. **29. MULDRAUGH** was at one time central P.O. for mail addressed to all towns along what is now US60 as far (W) as Hardinsburg. At **TIP TOP, 30.,** is S. J. with US60. US31W branches (SE) to **FT. KNOX, 36.,** a 33,000-a. military reserv. on both sides of US31W. Tract, incl. town of Smithton, was purchased by Gov. in 1917 for training camp. In 1932 War Dept. designated the camp a permanent military post. In 1936 Treasury Dept. built the **Gold Bullion Depository** (R) in which to store about 9,000,000 pounds of Fed. gold reserve. It was an important training center during World War II. During that time it also sheltered the orig. Constitution of the U.S.

### III. LOUISVILLE (E) to SHELBYVILLE. 31. US60

**4. SOUTHERN BAPT. THEOLOGICAL SEMINARY** (L), erected in 1926. **6. ST. MATTHEWS,** shipping pt. for a large quantity of Irish potatoes. Here is Westport Rd.

SIDE TRIP: On this Rd. (L) to **Ridgeway,** 0.5m, good example of Class. Rev. style of architecture built in 1804.

**12. DOUGLAS HOMESTEAD** (R), a spacious country house built before Civil War; once a stock & race horse breeding place & now a dairy farm. At 12. is J. with old US60.

SIDE TRIP: On this Rd. (R) 0.5m to **Middletown,** founded in 1797. In center of town is **Middletown Inn** (L), built more than a cent. ago with 24″ walls of brick & stone.

At **19.** is J. with an improved side Rd.

SIDE TRIP: On this Rd. (L) 2m to **Long Run Bapt. Ch.,** on Long Run Cr., so named because of long flight down its valley by those who escaped an Ind. attack. Two hundred yds. (N) of the ch. is site of **Cabin of Abr. Lincoln,** grandfather of Pres. of the U.S. Although some historians believe that the elder Lincoln died at Springfield, it is generally agreed that beneath wing of the old ch. is **Grave of Abr. Lincoln's Grandfather.**

At **22.** is **LINCOLN INSTITUTE** (R), at Lincoln Ridge, endowed vocational & agric. high sch. for Negro boys & girls; only one of its kind in Ky. **LINCRAFT FARM** (R), **22.5.**, is a 25-a. model farm. At **23.** is **SIMPSONVILLE,** hamlet dating from 1816. **OLD STONE INN** (L), **23.5.**, is a tavern in operation continuously since its est. more than 100 yrs. ago. Although local legend says it was erected before Ky. became a St., more reliable sources give date as 1794. **31. SHELBYVILLE,** seat of Shelby Cty., founded in 1792 & named, as was the Cty., for Isaac Shelby, Ky.'s 1st gov. First settlement was at **Painted Stone,** near-by. There, in 1799, Squire Boone, brother of Dan. Boone, built a ft. that for more than a yr. was only refuge on Rd. bet. Harrodsburg & Louisville. **Science Hill** (O.appl.), 6th & Washington Sts., is a sch. for girls, founded in 1825.

### IV. LOUISVILLE (NE) to TOMB OF ZACHARY TAYLOR. 7. US42

At **7.** is **TOMB OF ZACHARY TAYLOR,** in a park-like area (L), once part of Taylor Farm & now in custody of Federal Gov. Adj. pk. (L) is **Taylor H.** where the 12th Pres. of U.S. grew to manhood. The 2½ story house, built of brick, is on ample grounds, extending along (L) side of **Taylor Mem. Cemetery,** where members of Taylor family are buried. In 1785 Col. Rich. Taylor, native of Va. & soldier of the Rev., brought his family to this place, where he built a log house. Several yrs. later present house was begun, log house was moved to rear, to house slaves. Zachary Taylor (1784-1850), born in Va., was 9 mos. old when family moved here. He went to sch. in little log cabin near this house before entering Wm. & Mary College. Except when he was away on military duty & in the White House, the farm was always his home. Gen. Taylor's daughter, much against her father's wishes, became the wife of Jeff. Davis, later Pres. of the Confederacy.

## US 70—TENNESSEE

**N.C.-TENN. LINE** (40m from Asheville, N.C.) **(W) to ARK.-TENN. LINE** (at Memphis, Tenn.). **488. US70**

Via: Knoxville, Crossville, Cookeville, Nashville, Jackson, Memphis. Good accoms. RR., bus & airline conns. Pic. & camp sites along route.

### Sec. 1: N.C. LINE to KNOXVILLE. 66.

Bet. the N.C. Line & Newport the Rd. descends through rugged mountains into the valley of the French Broad R. which it twice crosses. US70 crosses **N.C. LINE, 0.,** & runs through the Cherokee Nat. For. At **3.** it crosses the French Broad R., then traverses a narrow valley. **14.** It crosses French Broad R. again. **19. NEWPORT,** seat of Cocke Cty. Church St., **Rhea-Mims Hotel** has large coll. of local stones of many varieties. On porch is coll. of millstones used by the Inds. 218 North St., **High Oak Tulip Gardens** (O) contains nearly every variety of tulip known. Full flowering season is last wk. in Ap. & 1st wk. in May. **John Sevier Preserve** (O), on S.W. edge of town, is 125,000 as. of virgin forest. Here is J. with US25E. **23. WILSON INN** (L) (c.1800) was built to accomodate travelers on the stage bet. Charlotte & Knoxville. **66. KNOXVILLE** (see).

### Sec. 2: KNOXVILLE to NASHVILLE. 196.

**0. KNOXVILLE. 46.** J. (R) with US27. **50. ROCKWOOD,** formerly an iron mining & smelting center. Near here are Ind. mounds, indicating long habitation. **59. MAMMY'S CR.** Tradition is that a family traveling by oxcart camped for the night by a cr. some miles away. The father concluded an argument by beating his wife, & to signalize his victory, he called the stream Daddy's Cr. The next night, camping by this stream, the mother & her children thrashed the head of the family & renamed the cr. for the new victor. **60. OZONE** was so named because of stimulating quality of the air here. **Ozone Falls** (60′ high), is visible from hy. (L). **65. CRAB ORCHARD** (R). **68. DADDY'S CR. 75. CROSSVILLE** is seat of Cumberland Cty. (Here is J. with US70S Alt. to Nashville.) **83. MAYLAND. 91. MONTEREY L.** (f.boat.swim.), a wild steepwalled gorge. The **Standing Stone** at E. end of town is said to have been used by Inds. for ceremonies. **108. COOKEVILLE,** seat of Putnam Cty. **Tenn. Polytechnic Institute** is a St. sch. with a 4-yr. technical curriculum leading to B.S. degree. **114. DOUBLE SPRINGS** has 5 mineral springs. **114.** J. with St.56.

SIDE TRIP: (S) on St.56 is **Center Hill Dam,** 14m, a flood control, navigation & hydroelectric power development by U.S. Army Engineers on the Caney Fork R., a tributary of the Cumberland R. Dam is 240′ high & 2,160′ long (swim.boat.f.camp.).

**145.** J. with St.25.

SIDE TRIP: (R) on St.25, after crossing the Cumberland R. on the Cordell Hull Bridge, is **Carthage,** 1m, home town of Cordell Hull, Secy. of State under Pres. Franklin D. Roosevelt.

**196. NASHVILLE** (see).

### Sec. 3: NASHVILLE to MEMPHIS. 226.

**40. DICKSON. 55. McEWEN. 64. WAVERLY,** seat of Humphreys Cty., is in peanut growing area.

SIDE TRIP: (L) 7m on St.13 to the Homing Fork of Duck R., near Hurricane Mills: here is the **Mound Group of Humphreys Cty.** on a village site of prehist. Inds. There are 2 groups, the Link site & the Slayden site, about 1m apart.

**73.** J. with a gravel Rd.

SIDE TRIP: (R) on this Rd. 1m to **Denver** where Jesse James in 1879 bought a farm in Big Bottom & lived as prosperous grain & livestock dealer under the name John Davis Howard.

**79.** US70 crosses a bridge over **KENTUCKY L.** (boat. & f. avail. at many pts.), formed by water impounded by TVA's Kentucky Dam near mouth of the Tenn. R. **84. CAMDEN. 94. BRUCETON. 105. HUNTINGDON. 141. JACKSON,** seat of Madison Cty., is a W. Tenn. RR. center, served by 5 RRs. Jackson was hqs. of Confed. Gen. Beauregard in 1862, & a supply depot for Gen. Grant's Fed. forces, June 1862 to Mar. 1863, when the city was captured by Gen. Nathan Bedford Forrest. Later that yr., it was recaptured by Feds. PTS. OF INT.: College St. bet. Irby St. & Hayes Ave., **Union Univ.** (coed.) has 4-yr. course with an av. enrollment of 400. Lambuth Blvd. bet. King & Maple Sts., **Lambuth College** (coed.), is a 4-yr. sch. with an av. enrollment of 225. NE. cor. Royal & Hardee Sts., **Catholic Cemetery** (O) is burial place of John Luther Jones, nicknamed "Casey." He was a RR. engineer famous among RR. men for his peculiar skill with a locomotive whistle. Substituting for a sick friend, he was killed in wreck of the "Cannon Ball Express," Ap. 30, 1900. The event was comm. in a popular ballad. Jackson is at J. with US45. **151. HUNTERSVILLE. 168. BROWNSVILLE,** seat of Haywood Cty., is one of the oldest towns in W. Tenn. **211.** J. with US54. **226. MEMPHIS** (see).

## US 64—TENNESSEE

**N.C.-TENN. LINE** (24m from Murphy, N.C.) **(W) to TENN.-ARK. LINE** (at Memphis, Tenn.). **397. US64**

Via: Cleveland, Chattanooga, Winchester, Pulaski, Selmer, Bolivar, Memphis. Good accoms. RR., bus & airline conns. Pic. & camp sites along route.

### Sec. 1: N.C. LINE to CHATTANOOGA. 72.

**2. ISABELLA,** 1 of 3 copper mining & smelting towns. Near the smelting towns are barren eroded hills where vegetation was killed by early smelting operations which filled the air with sulphur fumes. **11.** US64 crosses the E. boundary of the **CHEROKEE NAT. FOR.** & follows the Ocoee R. Ls. have been formed in the river by dams constructed by private interests & later bought by TVA. **14. OCOEE DAM No. 2.** The river is diverted through a wooden flume & returns to its bed 5m downstream by the power plant, which is 240′ lower than the upper end of the flume. **20.** Head of L. in the Ocoee R. **27. PARKSVILLE.** Here is **Ocoee Dam Hydroelectric Plant No. 1.** The dam is 130′ high & 110′ wide. **72. CHATTANOOGA** (see).

### Sec. 2: CHATTANOOGA to PULASKI. 134.

**0. CHATTANOOGA. 43.** Ascent of Cumberland Mts. begins. Route rises 1,200′ in next 6m. **50. MONTEAGLE,** at J. with US41, has been summer resort since ante bellum days. **57. SEWANEE,** seat of **Univ. of the South,** commonly called Sewanee.

Univ. owns 10,000 as. of which 1,000 as. are used as a campus. Bldgs. are of pink Sewanee sandstone quarried near-by. **63. COWAN** lies at foot of the W. escarpment of the Cumberland Plateau. **70. WINCHESTER,** seat of Franklin Cty. **80.** J. with gravel Rd. where granite marker gives directions to **grave of Polly Finley Crockett & well dug by David Crockett. 103. FAYETTEVILLE,** seat of Lincoln Cty. J. with US241. **134. PULASKI,** seat of Giles Cty. Ku Klux Klan was org. here on Christmas Eve, 1855, by Judge T. M. Jones & his son, Calvin.

**Sec. 3: PULASKI to SELMER. 100.**

**18. LAWRENCEBURG,** seat of Lawrence Cty. **47. WAYNESBORO,** seat of Wayne Cty. **59.** J. with St.114.

SIDE TRIP: (R) on St.114, is **Clifton,** 7m, home of T. S. Stribling, novelist, who was awarded Pulitzer prize in 1932 for "The Store." His novel "Teeftallow" is story of an attempt to build RR. in Wayne Cty.

**79. SAVANNAH,** seat of Hardin Cty. Just ahead is bridge over **Kentucky L.** in the Tenn. R. (boat.f.swim.). L. is formed by water impounded by Kentucky Dam near where Tenn. R. empties into Ohio R. **83.** J. with St.22.

SIDE TRIP: (L) on St.22 to entrance of **Shiloh Military Pk.** (guide serv.) 5m, & **Pittsburgh Landing,** 7m. At entrance is Adm. Bldg., which contains a lib. & coll. of prehist. artifacts taken from Ind. mounds in the pk. Battle of Shiloh, the 2nd great battle of War Bet. the States, took place in spring of 1862. It was costly to both sides but indecisive. (L) from Pittsburgh Landing on Park Rd. 2m to J. with St.57; (L) here 3m to (SE) entrance; (L) here 7m to **Counce** at J. with Pickwick Landing Rd. (L) on this Rd. 5m to **Pickwick Dam** (boat.swim.f.camp.). Dam forms L. backing up 53m to foot of Wilson Dam at Muscle Shoals, Ala. Dam is approx. 1.5m long & 101′ high.

**89. ADAMSVILLE. 100. SELMER,** seat of McNairy Cty. J. with US45.

**Sec. 4: SELMER to MEMPHIS. 91.**

**23. BOLIVAR,** seat of Hardeman Cty. **27. WESTERN ST. HOSPITAL FOR THE INSANE** (L). **48. SOMERVILLE.** Seat of Fayette Cty. was at one time heart of plantation area in W. Tenn. **76.** J. with US70. **91. MEMPHIS** (see).

## US 11 & US 11E—TENNESSEE

**VA.-TENN. LINE** (at Bristol, Va.-Tenn.) **(SW) to GA.-TENN. LINE** (at Chattanooga, Tenn.). **242. US11E, US11**

Via: Johnson City, Knoxville, Athens, Cleveland. Good accoms. RR., bus & airline conns. Pic. & camp sites along route.

**Sec. 1: BRISTOL to KNOXVILLE. 128. US11E**

US11E follows valley of upper E. Tenn., the route over which passed (W) moving wagon trains of the pioneers. They built blockhs. at strategic pts. & grouped their houses about them. They built so well that many bldgs. of the period are still standing. **0. BRISTOL** is 2 municipalities—Bristol, Tenn., & Bristol, Va. St. Line divides State St., the main thoroughfare. **17.** A marker (L) called attention to **Rocky Mount,** built in 1770 & one of oldest Hs. in Tenn. **19.** US11E crosses **HOLSTON R. 22.** J. with US23 which unites with US11E for 3m. On shaft of **Pioneer Mem.** are descriptions of hist. pts. of int. **25. JOHNSON CITY,** trade center & shipping pt. for farming & lumbering area. City is served by 3 RRs., which were influential in its industrial growth, incl. such businesses as box factories, tanneries & lumber mills. PTS. OF INT.: W. end of W. Maple St., **East Tenn. St. Teachers College** has 8 bldgs. (mod.Georg.) on 140-a. campus; it is standard 4-yr. college offering B.S. degree in education. Entrance to **U.S. Soldiers' H.** (O.for guide apply Adm.Bldg.), is on Lamont St., (W) of Harrison St. There are 57 bldgs. on 448 as. of landscaped grounds. It is home for permanently disabled soldiers; handicraft training is given; residents sell handicraft products to visitors. Johnson City is at J. with US23.

**32. JONESBORO,** seat of Washington Cty., is oldest town in Tenn. It was formally est. Nov. 4, 1779. Many of the Hs., Chs., & stores have changed little since pioneer days. Local people take pride in their picturesque town & discourage modernization on the main street. Washington Cty., which included all settlements in what is now Tenn., was political subdivision of N.C. & the 1st in the U.S. named for Geo. Washington. N.C. ceded terr. to Fed. Gov. in 1784. The settlers immediately formed the St. of Franklin & applied for admittance to the Union. John Sevier was elected gov. The constitutional convention & 1st legislative sessions of the St. of Franklin were held in Jonesboro until 1785, when capital was moved to Greeneville. N.C. objected to the new st. & repealed its act of cession. The Franklanders persisted & for next 4 yrs. there were many clashes bet. the dual govs. When Sevier's term was up, no successor was elected & the St. of Franklin ceased to exist. PTS. OF INT.: On Cth. lawn, at Main & Cherokee Sts., is marker in the shape of an arrowhead pointing the direction of the **Dan. Boone Trl.** that passed through here. Main & Cherokee Sts., **Chester Inn,** or Jonesboro Inn, has been a hotel since 1798. Presidents Andrew Jackson, Jas. K. Polk, & Andrew Johnson & other notables, incl. Chas. Dickens, stopped here. **41. WASHINGTON COLLEGE** (L), was chartered in 1795 as successor to Martin Academy, chartered in 1788. Sam Doak, frontier preacher, founded both schs. & brought the 1st books into the St. Building is now used for a cty. high sch. **43. LIMESTONE.** There are pic. spots near-by & waterfall at S. end of village. **Old Stone H.** (1792), where hy. goes under the bridge, was home of Geo. Gillespie, early settler, & served as fortress to protect settlers against Inds. It was often attacked by Inds. **53. TUSCULUM COLLEGE,** founded in 1818 as Tusculum Academy by Rev. Sam. Doak. **58. GREENEVILLE,** seat of Greene Cty., was capitol of the St. of Franklin during last 3 yrs. of its existence (1785-1787). When Tenn. legislature adopted the Ordinance of Secession in 1861, the loyalists of East Tenn. held a convention here & proposed that East Tenn. become separate St. Andrew Johnson (1808-75) moved here at age of 17 from N.C. with his mother & stepfather. He operated a tailor shop here until he entered politics. He was gov. of Tenn. (1853-57) & military gov. of Tenn. (1862-65) when he became vice-pres. of U.S. He became pres. upon death of Lincoln the next month. PTS. OF INT.: Depot & College Sts., behind the Cth., **Andrew Johnson Tailor Shop** (O). On W. Main St., **Andrew Johnson H.** (O.appl.1851), Johnson's home until his death in 1875. **73. BULLS GAP. 81. RUSSELLVILLE. 87. MORRISTOWN,** seat of Hamblen Cty., sett. in 1783. **Morristown Normal & Industrial College,** (E) of James St. at E. 6th Ave., is an experimental jr. college for Negroes. It has 10 bldgs. on 7-a. campus & a 320-a. farm. Av. enrollment is c.120. **128. KNOXVILLE** (see).

### Sec. 2: KNOXVILLE to CHATTANOOGA. 114. US11

**0. KNOXVILLE. 30.** US11 crosses Tenn. R. on the Loudon Bridge. **31. LOUDON,** seat of Loudon Cty. **41. TENN. MILITARY INSTITUTE** (R) is a college prep. sch. **43. SWEETWATER. 57. ATHENS,** seat of McMinn Cty., was scene of a "bullets & ballots" disturbance in 1946, when war vets just returned from service undertook to break up a political machine that had long dominated local politics. Several persons were killed & others injured in gun battles that took place. Further deaths occurred in election violence in 1948, & units of the Tenn. Nat. Guard again were called out to protect life & property. **Tenn. Wesleyan College,** in center of town, is a coed. jr. college. It has 8 bldgs. on 20-a. campus. **72. CALHOUN. 73. CHARLESTON. 114. CHATTANOOGA** (see).

## US 11W—TENNESSEE

**VA.-TENN. LINE** (at Bristol, Va.-Tenn.) **(SW) to KNOXVILLE, TENN. 121. US11W**

Via: Kingsport, Rogersville, Bean Station. Good accoms. RR., bus & airline conns. Pic. & camp sites along route.

US11W winds (SW) through reg. over which white men & Cherokee fought bitterly. It was part of the Cherokee Overhill country, with fertile bottom lands, & held several Cherokee towns.

**0. BRISTOL** (see US11E). **8. BLOUNTVILLE,** seat of Sullivan Cty. **23.** J. with US23. **24. KINGSPORT** is mountain-circled modern industrial city on the Holston R. Prominent among products manufactured here are books, paper, bookbinding cloth, photographic film, plastics of several types, cement, & ceramic products. PTS. OF INT.: **Boone Trl.** or **Wilderness Rd.** is marked by bronze plate at the Circle, between Sullivan & Watauga Sts. Arrowhead-shaped mon. points way Boone took in exploring Holston Valley in 1769. Roller & Reedy Sts., **Kingsport Press** (O), one of the largest plants in the world mfg. books exclusively. Plant turns out more than 2,000,000 vols. a month. 2144 Lee Highway, **Netherland Inn** (N.O.1811), was center of gay social life in upper E. Tenn. during early 19th cent. Andrew Jackson often stopped here on trips bet. Nashville & Washington. Presidents Andrew Johnson & Jas. K. Polk stopped here too. The **Long Island of the Holston** divides the R. for $4^m$ (SW) of Kingsport. On the I., in July 1777, the warring Cherokee, after 2 yrs. of fighting, met representatives of Va. & N.C. & ceded to those states additional territory in E. Tenn. **27.** By the E. end of the bridge over N. fork of the Holston, is stone mon. (L) marking **Site of Ft. Robinson & Ft. Patrick Henry.** Ft. Robinson was 1st structure built by white men at site of Kingsport. (R) along N. fork of the R. 600 yds. is the **Old Rotherwood Elm,** plainly visible from bridge. It has spread of 150′ & trunk has 22′ circumference. Dr. Thos. Walker, who mentioned it in the "Journal," kept on exploring the valley in 1748 & Dan. Boone is said to have camped under it. **54. ROGERSVILLE** is one of oldest towns in Tenn. Sett. in 1772. The Knoxville "Gazette," 1st newspaper in Tenn., began publication here in 1791 before plant moved to Knoxville. **74. BEAN STATION** is at J. of the Lee Hy. & US25E. The Dan. Boone Trl. & the Great Ind. Warpath also met here. The crossroads were named for 4 bros. who built a ft. here in 1787. **121. KNOXVILLE** (see).

## US 23—TENNESSEE

**VA.-TENN. LINE** ($47^m$ from Appalachia, Va.) **(S) to TENN.-N.C. LINE** ($58^m$ from Asheville, N.C.). **58. US23**

Via: Kingsport, Johnson City, Erwin. Good accoms. RR., bus & airline conns. Pic. & camp sites along route.

US23 traverses reg. of the Watauga Settlement, est. in 1770. These 1st settlers, feeling isolated from & ignored by N.C., from which they came, decided to org. their own Gov. In 1772 they created the Watauga Assoc., adopted a constitution, & est. an independent Gov., the 1st constitutional Gov. in the New World. When Rev. War began, they joined with the colonies in the fight for freedom.

**3. KINGSPORT** (see US11W). **5.** US23 leaves US11W. **8. HOLSTON R.,** which offers good bass f. **21.** J. with US11E-19W with which US23 is united for $3^m$. **24. JOHNSON CITY** (see US11E). **34. UNICOI. 36. FED. FISH HATCHERY** (R) covers 72 as. **39. ERWIN,** seat of Unicoi Cty. **Southern Potteries Plant** (O.wks.) turns out daily 30,000 pieces of painted & underglazed pottery. **58. N.C. LINE.**

## US 25E—TENNESSEE

**KY.-TENN. LINE** ($3^m$ from Middlesboro, Ky.) **(SE) to J. with US70. 65. US25E.**

Via: Cumberland Gap, Tazewell & Morristown. Usual sm. town accoms. RR. & bus conns. Pic. & camp sites along route.

US25E follows old Wilderness Rd. bet. Cumberland Gap to Bean Sta. This was a trl. across the mts. blazed by Dan. Boone in 1775 for benefit of immigrants. This route became main artery for settlement of much of the Terr. (S) of Ohio R. **0.** US25E crosses **KY.-VA. LINE.** It passes through **Cumberland Gap** (1,304′), & cuts across a tiny cor. of Va. & then crosses into Tenn. again. **1. CUMBERLAND GAP,** named for the pass in the mts., is in that cor. of Tenn. that was 1st explored by white men. It was the scene of much activity during the Civil War. **3. HARROGATE,** formerly a summer resort. Harrogate Univ., now **Lincoln Mem. Univ.,** was founded in 1897 as mem. to Abr. Lincoln. It has liberal arts course, Ind. relic mus. & coll. of Lincolniana. **13. TAZEWELL,** seat of Claiborne Cty. **21. OLD SPRINGDALE CH.,** erected by Bapts. soon after they had org. a congregation in 1796. Ahead, hy. crosses Clinch R., which with Powell R. forms Norris L. & then ascends W. slope of Clinch Mt. **34. MINERAL SPRINGS HOTEL,** summer resort.

**35. BEAN STA.,** J. with US11W (see). **46. MORRISTOWN.** J. with US11E (see). (S) of Morristown is the fertile New Market Valley. English Mt. is (R), the Unaka range ahead. In this valley, US25E crosses French Broad R. **65.** J. with US70, $1.5^m$ (W) of Newport.

## US 25W—TENNESSEE

**KY.-TENN. LINE** (16m from Williamsburg, Ky.) **(SE) to TENN.-N.C. LINE** (85m from Asheville, N.C.). **122. US25W, St.71**

Via: Jellico, La Follette, Clinton, Knoxville, Sevierville. Good accoms. RR., bus & airline conns. Pic., camp sites & resorts along route.

This route passes through area rich in natural resources, historic int., modern developments, & rare scenic beauty. N. part of the route runs through one of Tenn.'s coal producing secs. & near major installations of TVA & the Oak Ridge Area of the Atomic Energy Commission. The S. sec. ascends Great Smoky Mts. to Clingman's Dome on N.C. Line, offering many scenes of lofty grandeur.

**0. KY. LINE.** 600 yds. beyond is **JELLICO,** at (N) end of 24m ravine that US25 follows. **8. MORLEY. 24.** Rows of abandoned coke ovens are (R). **24. LA FOLLETTE** is in the Powell Valley at E. base of the Cumberland Mts. **29. JACKSBORO,** seat of Campbell Cty. **36. VASPER. 39.** J. (L) with the Norris Freeway.

SIDE TRIP: (L) on Norris Freeway 5m to **Norris Dam,** a major installation of the TVA. (see Knoxville Trip IX).

**40. COAL CR. 49. CLINTON** (850'). For description of pts. of int. in & near Clinton, incl. the **Oak Ridge Area** of the Atomic Energy Commission, & from Clinton to **67. KNOXVILLE** (see), see Knoxville Trip IV. **122. N.C. LINE.**

## US 27—TENNESSEE

**KY.-TENN. LINE** (46m from Somerset, Ky.). **(SW) to GA.-TENN. LINE** (at Chattanooga, Tenn.). **147. US27**

Via: Oneida, Harriman, Rockwood, Spring City, Dayton. Good accoms. RR., bus & airline conns. Pic. & camp sites along route.

### Sec. 1: KY.-TENN. LINE to J. with US70. 77.

For c.60m, US27 runs through beautiful mt. area broken by ragged gulches, through which swift streams & rivers flow. **9. ONEIDA. 19. NEW RIVER. 24. ROBBINS.** Shortly before reaching **SUNBRIGHT, 34.,** hy. crosses ridge that divides the watersheds of the Cumberland & Tenn. Rs. Sunbright is shipping pt. for an oil & gas field discovered in 1916. **46. WARTBURG,** seat of Morgan Cty. (S) of Wartburg, the route descends circuitously through the valley of the Emory R. into that of the Tenn. Bet. Harriman & Chattanooga it passes along the foot of the Cumberland Escarpment, known locally as Walden's Ridge, rising 1,000' above the valley to form the W. rim of the East Tenn. Valley. **62. HARRIMAN,** a farm trade center & has large hosiery & woolen mills. At Harriman is J. with St.61.

SIDE TRIP: On St.61 (L) is the **Oak Ridge Area** of the Atomic Energy Commission (see Knoxville).

**67.** J. with US70. Here to **77.,** US27 & US70 unite.

### Sec. 2: J. with US70 to GA.-TENN. LINE. 70.

At **0.,** 2m (S) of Rockwood, US27 leaves US70. **14. SPRING CITY.**

SIDE TRIP: From Spring City (L) on St.68 is **Rhea Springs,** 2m, valued by Inds. for its supposed medicinal qualities. Just before à sale, slave owners would bring work-worn slaves here to rejuvenate them & increase their value. **Hampton Group** of Ind. mounds is on the bank of the R. There are about 20 earthen mounds of prehist. origin. Some have been excavated.

**68. CHATTANOOGA** (see). **70.** US27 crosses the **GA.-TENN. LINE** in Chattanooga.

## US 31E & 31—TENNESSEE

**KY.-TENN. LINE** (36m from Glasgow, Ky.) **(SW) to ALA.-TENN. LINE** (18m from Ardmore, Ala.). **145. US31E, US31.**

Via: Nashville, Columbia, Pulaski. Good accoms. RR., bus & airline conns. Pic. & camp sites along route.

US31E passes over the Highland Rim & traverses the bluegrass basin of Middle Tenn. This area has been famous since pioneer days for its fertility & for quality of livestock. **1. SUGAR GROVE. 13. BETHPAGE** is barely within the bluegrass basin. **51. NASHVILLE** (see).

On US31 to **71. BATTLEGROUND ACADEMY** (R), a boys' prep. sch. **73. BREEZY HILL** (L) is densely covered with a natural for. of cedars. It is said that 7,500 Confed. soldiers died bet. Franklin & Breezy Hill. **83. SPRING HILL. 85. CHEAIRS H.** (L) (N.O.), built in early 1850's. The day before the battle of Franklin, advance units met in a spirited skirmish in front of the home. **95. COLUMBIA,** seat of Maury Cty., is in reg. of fertile farmlands. Columbia is considered the mule capital of world. On 1st Mon. in Apr., the largest street mule market in the world is held. PTS. OF INT.: 301 W. 7th St., **Sam. Polk H.** (O.sm.fee), was home of Sam. K. Polk, father of Jas. Knox Polk, 11th Pres. of the U.S. It contains coll. of Polk relics. 318 W. 7th St., **Jas. K. Polk H.** (N.O.), built by Jas. K. Polk in 1820's. Here he entertained Andrew Jackson & Martin Van Buren during campaign of 1844, in which he was elected pres.

SIDE TRIP: Take St.20 (W) 30m to **Meriwether Lewis Nat. Mon.,** est. 1925 to comm. leader of Lewis & Clark Expedition (300 as.pic.). Mon. contains **Grave** of Meriwether Lewis, site of **Grinder's Inn** where Lewis died, & remains of part of the **Natchez Trace. Mus.** with exhibits of Lewis hist. material.

**98. BEECHLAWN** (1852) was used as temporary hqs. by Fed. Gen. John M. Schofield & then by Confed. Gen. John B. Hood. In the front room here Gen. Hood & Gen. Nathan Bedford Forrest disagreed on most effective method of cutting off Fed. troops on their retreat to Nashville. **117.** Entrance (R) to **Milky Way Farms.** This estate, developed by the late Frank C. Mars, candy manufacturer, covers 2,705 as. Among the horses raised here were several winners of Ky. Derby. The farm is no longer owned by the Mars family. **126. PULASKI.** J. with US64 (see). As US31 proceeds (S), the bluegrass country becomes more rolling & less fertile. **145. ALA.-TENN. LINE.**

## US 31W—TENNESSEE

**KY.-TENN. LINE** (6m from Franklin, Ky.) **(SW) to NASHVILLE. 37. US31W**

Via: Mitchellville, White House, Goodlettsville. Good accoms. in Nashville. RR., bus, airline conns.; pic. & camp sites along route.

**1. MITCHELLVILLE. 3.** J. with St.52. **MARKER** honors Jenny Lind, who sang here in 1852. When it became known that the Swedish prima donna would pass along this stage route on her way from Nashville to Louisville, the country folk gathered at a spring, & when the coach stopped, asked her to sing. **12. WHITE HOUSE. 23.** J. with US41E. **37. NASHVILLE** (see).

## US 41W & US 41—TENNESSEE

**KY.-TENN. LINE** (16m from Hopkinsville, Ky.) **(SE) to J. with US64** (at Monteagle, Tenn.) **145. US41W, US41**

Via: Clarksville, Nashville, Murfreesboro, Manchester, Monteagle, Jasper. Good accoms. RR., bus & airline conns. Pic., camp sites & resorts along route.

### Sec. 1: KY. LINE to NASHVILLE. 54. US41W

**8. NEW PROVIDENCE.** At S. end of town, near the end of the Red R. bridge (R), is J. with a marked gravel Rd.

SIDE TRIP: (R) on this Rd. 200 yds. to an old stone **Blockh.,** built in 1788-89 by Col. Valentine Sevier. Col. Sevier repulsed a costly Ind. attack here, Nov. 11, 1794. After the attack, he wrote the following letter to his brother, John Sevier: "Dear Brother: The news from this place is desperate with me. On Tuesday, 11th Nov. last, about 12 o'clock, my station was attacked by about 40 Inds. On so sudden a surprise they were in almost every house before they were discovered. All the men belonging to the station were out save only Snyder & myself. William Snyder, Betsy, his wife, his son John, & my son Joseph were killed in Snyder's house. They also killed Ann King & her son Jas., and scalped my daughter Rebecca. I hope she will still recover. The Inds. have killed whole families about here this fall. You may hear the cries of some persons for their friends daily. The engagement commenced at my house continued for about an hour, as the neighbors say. Such a scene no man ever witnessed before. Nothing but screams & the roaring of guns, & no man to assist me for some time." During the War Bet. the States, the Confeds. called the blockh. Ft. Defiance.

**54. NASHVILLE** (see).

### Sec. 2: NASHVILLE to J. with US64. 91. US41

**0. NASHVILLE. 32.** J. with US241. (SE) of Murfreesboro, hy. follows a former Ind. trl. **61. Cumberland Mts.** are in view. **63.** Route reaches top of the **HIGHLAND RIM. 64.** US41 crosses Duck R. The Duck R. cascades are 600 yds. downstream. **65.** J. with an unmarked dirt Rd.

SIDE TRIP: (R) on this Rd. 6m to an **Old Stone Ft.**, an unusually fine example of ancient defense works. On a highly strategic position, its walls of earth & stone are 20′ thick & enclose 32 as. Its intricate inner defenses are obviously the work of skilled engineers. The builders are unknown, but authorities say a tree was growing on its ruins 78 yrs. before De Soto penetrated this area in 1541.

**66. MANCHESTER,** seat of Coffee Cty. At (NE) corner of the public sq. is large **Mound** of earth & stone, believed to have been built by ancient tribesmen as a signal pt. **87.** The route begins 3m ascent to top of Cumberland Mts. **91. MONTEAGLE** is at J. with US64 (see).

## US 241—TENNESSEE

**MURFREESBORO (S) to ALA.-TENN. LINE** (16m from Huntsville, Ala.) **68. US241**

Via: Shelbyville, Fayetteville. Good accoms. RR., bus & airline conns. Pic. & camp sites along route.

**26. SHELBYVILLE,** seat of Bedford Cty., is leading business shipping center of Duck R. Valley. **53. FAYETTEVILLE** is at J. with US64 (see). **68.** US241 crosses **ALA. LINE.**

## US 45E & US 45—TENNESSEE

**KY.-TENN. LINE** (24m from Mayfield, Ky.) **(S) to MISS.-TENN. LINE** (5m from Corinth, Miss.) **115. US45E & US45**

Via: Martin, Jackson, Henderson. Good accoms. RR., bus & airlines conns. Pic. & camp sites along route.

**11. MARTIN** is home of **Univ. of Tenn. Jr. College.** Institution is controlled by extension department of univ. & its curriculum is designed to meet needs of rural students, emphasizing agric., domestic, industrial sciences. Besides an ample campus, there is 285-a. experimental & demonstration farm. Sch. is coed. **19. SHARON. 25. GREENFIELD. 30. BRADFORD. 42. MILAN. 50. MEDINA. 55.** At **3 WAYS JUNCTION** route meets US45W. **66. JACKSON.** J. with US70 (see). **68. BEMIS** (R) is company town where bags are manufactured. **72. The NURSERY** (O), operated by State Div. of Forestry, produces more than 1,000,000 seedlings yearly. **77. PINSON.**

SIDE TRIP: (L) from Pinson on gravel country Rd. to **Ozier's Mound,** 3m (R), 1st in mound group of **Cisco Ind. Village.** In immediate area there is entire system of mounds, highest 73′ & more than 300′ in diameter, remaining from ancient walled city.

**83. HENDERSON,** seat of Chester Cty., home of **Freed-Hardeman Jr. College** (coed). **102. SELMER.** J. with US64 (see). **104.** J. with St.57.

SIDE TRIP: (L) on St.57 to J., 16m, with St.22; (L) here 12m to **Shiloh Nat. Military Pk.** & **Pickwick Dam** (see US64).

**115. MISS.-TENN. LINE.**

## US 51—TENNESSEE

**KY.-TENN. LINE** (in Fulton, Ky.) **(SW) to MISS.-TENN. LINE** (35m from Senatobia, Miss.). **136. US51**

Via: Union City, Dyersburg, Ripley, Memphis. Good accoms. RR., bus & airline conns. Pic. & camp sites along route.

US51 roughly parallels Miss. R. in crossing Tenn., running through St.'s chief cotton-growing area. **11. UNION CITY** (328′), seat of Obion Cty., is principal town in L. dist. Bet. Union City & Troy is one of 1st stretches of concrete roadbed built in St. **21. TROY,** one of oldest towns in W. Tenn., laid out in 1823 with help of David Crockett.

SIDE TRIP: (R) from Troy on St.21 to J. (L) with dirt Rd. 10m. (R) on this Rd. 3m to **Edgewater Beach & Blue Bank,** 4m; **Samburg,** 15m, & **Walnut Log,** 21m. These are villages on **Reelfoot L.** & outfitting pts. for sportsmen. At 14m from Troy on St.21 is Spillway of Reelfoot L. At 17m is **Tiptonville,** center of Reelfoot L. recr. area. There are sports supply stores, a hotel, tourist courts & other facils. Reelfoot L. Fish & Game Preserve was est. in 1925. (F.h.swim.guides with boats avail.) Lake 18m long & 2.5m wide, only 2′-9′ deep. The 6,000 as. of st.-owned land around it are almost entirely covered with dense fors. matted with vines. Within preserve are many varieties of fresh water fish. People of area make their living by hunting & fishing. More than 25 species of birds stop here on annual migrations. Before formation of L., reg. was luxuriant for. coursed by sm. streams. This area was near center of great New Madrid, Mo., earthquake movement that occurred bet. Dec. 16, 1811, & Mar. 15, 1812, when W. sec. of Tenn. was still land of Chickasaw. Ground sank & the Miss. R., reversing its current, rushed in mountainous waves to fill depression. Earth waves swelled low across surface, tilting trees & interlocking their limbs. Landslides swept down steep bluffs of R. Banks caved in & whole Is. vanished. Shocks were accompanied by semi-darkness, deafening noise & sulphurous odor. People feared Day of Judgment had come. The torn & twisted reg. was not long deserted. Fr. trappers & Amer. hunters came in considerable numbers. Among them was David Crockett, who settled on Rutherford Fork of Obion R. in 1821, & from his cabin often went on hunting expeditions into the "shakes country" around L.

**27. OBION. 38. NEWBERN. 46. DYERSBURG,** seat of Dyer Cty., is chief town in cotton-growing bottom land. It is scene of annual cotton carnival in May. **51. FOWLKES. 58. HALLS. 61. GATES. 65. CURVE. 71. RIPLEY,** seat of Lauderdale Cty. In its charter, corporate limits were outlined: ". . . thence north 85 degrees, east to a black gum marked with a cross & with mistletoe in the top, and with a blue bird sitting on a limb, which is a short distance east of Ed Johnson's horse lot . . ." **77. HENNING. 86. COVINGTON.**

SIDE TRIP: (R) from Covington on St.59, **Randolph,** 19m, on Miss. R. It is only a village, but in early days was rival of Memphis. In 1830 it was most important shipping pt. in W. Tenn. & was mentioned several times in Mark Twain's "Life on the Mississippi."

**125. MEMPHIS** (see). US51 turns (SW) in Memphis on Miss. Blvd. **136. MISS.-TENN. LINE.**

# CHATTANOOGA

**CHATTANOOGA**

RR., bus & air conns. Good accoms. & recr. facils. Tennis, swimming, golf, football, polo, theatre, concerts. Info.: C. of C., 819 Broad St.; Chattanooga Automobile Club, Patten Hotel. Music Festival, May; Chattanooga Flower Show, early spring; Nat. Pigeon Assoc. Races, June; Chattanooga Tri-State Fair, Sept.; Ft. Oglethorpe Horse Show, Sept.

Chattanooga lies near border of Ga. on sharp Moccasin Bend of Tenn. R. in valley walled by Missionary Ridge on (E), Signal Mt. on (NW) & Lookout Mt. to (SW). First white settlement at what is now Chattanooga was Ross' Landing, about 1815. Muskhogean Inds. were known to occupy valley before 1540. In fall of 1838, town was laid out & Ross' Landing became Chattanooga. In 1849, Western & Atlantic RR. conn. city with S. Atlantic seaboard. On eve of Civil War, Chattanooga was town of 5,545. It soon became one of most important military centers, since Fed. strategy was to capture Chattanooga & drive wedge bet. eastern & western armies of Confed. Several bitter battles took place here & on Nov. 25, 1863, Fed. troops took city. From then to Mar., 1866, Chattanooga was Fed. military camp & base of Gen. Sherman's Atlanta campaign. Abundance of raw materials & good trans. by rail & water aided in campaign during reconstruction to attract mfg. enterprises. 1920 pop. was 57,896 & more than doubled in next decade. Influx of money during World War I, when thousands of soldiers were stationed at Chickamauga Pk. & Ft. Oglethorpe, was factor in furthering commerce & industry. Later expansion was stimulated by activities of TVA & war industries during World War II. PTS. OF INT.: (1) W. 9th St., bet. Broad & Chestnut Sts., **Union Sta.,** owned by St. of Ga. & leased to N.C. & St. L. RR. Under shed bet. waiting room & platform is "The General," old woodburning locomotive whose spectacular run, Ap. 12, 1862, was part of scheme to cut Confed. communications bet. Atlanta & Chattanooga. (2) 603 Pine St., **The Kennedy-Rathburn-Nottingham H.** (N.O.1840), served in turn as hqs. for Col. D. B. Hill, Col. J. B. McPherson, & Col. J. M. Palmer during Civil War. (3) At top of Cameron Hill, end of Pk. Dr., **Boynton Pk.,** rising abruptly at edge of downtown Chattanooga, used by Signal Corps of both sides during Civil War. (4) 110 E. 1st St. **Grant's Hqs.** (N.O.); Gen. Grant arrived in Chattanooga Oct. 23, 1863 & took possession of house that had been vacated by its owners. (5) McCallie Ave. bet. Douglas & Baldwin Sts., **Univ. of Chattanooga,** est. 1886. Coed. with enrollment of c.500. (6) E. 3rd to E. 5th, bet. Lansing & Palmetto Sts., **Confed. Cemetery.** (7) **Nat. Cemetery,** main ent. at S. end of National Ave. Has dead from every war & foreign expedition in hist. of U.S. (8) Bet. Ivy & E. 5th Sts., **Orchard Knob,** unit of Military Pk. purchased by Fed. Gov. in 1894. From this pt. Gen. Grant & Gen. Thomas directed Fed. forces in battles of Missionary Ridge & Lookout Mt. (Nov.25-26, 1863).

## TRIPS OUT OF CHATTANOOGA

### I. LOOP TOUR to LOOKOUT MOUNTAIN. 18.5.

Lookout Mt. rises at SW. city limits. From its peak, Pt. Lookout, 1,400′ above Tenn. R., signals were displayed to warn early settlers against Inds. Mt. was a favorite Cherokee hunting ground. After Battle of Chickamauga, Confed. troops occupied Lookout Mt. besieging the Feds. in Chattanooga. The "Battle Above the Clouds" was fought here Nov. 24, 1863, as preliminary to storming of Missionary Ridge. A great deal of Mt. is now part of Nat. Military Pk. Two hys., Lookout Mt. Blvd. & Adolph Ochs Hy., pass through pk. A part of Mt. also forms residential area, **Lookout Mt. Township.** From 11th & Market Sts., in Chattanooga (N) 1 block on 11th St. & then (S) on Broad St. (US41) to J. with St. Elmo St., (L) on St. Elmo St. to Tenn. Ave. **Lookout Mt. Incline RR.** operates bet. street level & summit of Mt. **3. LOOKOUT MT. BRIDGE** forms ledge 1,060′ long, almost flush against palisades. At J. with Lookout Mt. Blvd. (L) up Mt. to **4. MEMORY PLACE** (R), abandoned rock quarry transformed into garden during building of Pk. **Caverns Castle** (R) is entrance & Adm. Bldg. to Lookout Mt. Caves. **5.** J. with Cravens Rd., leading (R) to site of most of the **"Battle Above the Clouds." 6.** (R) on E. Brow Rd. to **7. POINT PK.** (O.no autos.U.S. guide.free), terminates at Lookout Pt. Pk. has area of 17.5 as. In foreground is **Moccasin Bend** of Tenn. R. (R) is Chattanooga. Beyond are rolling hills of E. Tenn. (W) is **Raccoon Mt.** & (N) **Signal Mt.** & **Walden's Ridge.** At **10.** J. with Fleetwood Dr. At **11., FAIRYLAND,** suburban residential sec. named for weird shapes of massive boulders in vic. **Tom Thumb Golf Course** built & patented here in 1927 started craze that swept country. **12. ROCK CITY** (R) (fee) is natural city of rocks & caves covering 10 as. Past Rock City turn (R) on Ochs Hy. down Mt. From Rd. are many fine views of valley below. **13.** (L) is **mem. marker to Adolph S. Ochs. 16.** South Broad St. returns to Chattanooga at **18.5.**

### II. Loop Tour to CHICKAMAUGA & CHATTANOOGA NAT. MILITARY PK. 19.5.

From 11th & Market Sts., take US27 to Rossville, Ga., an industrial suburb of Chattanooga. **5. JOHN ROSS H.** (N.O.) (R), home of noted Cherokee chief (1770). In town, **Iowa Mon.** (L) is 50′ high. **7. FT. OGLETHORPE** became an army post in 1904 & was important training center in both World Wars. **8.** (R) is police information booth. **9. CHICKAMAUGA & CHATTANOOGA NAT. MILITARY PK.** (adm.bldg.free U.S.guide). Largest unit of pk. is site of Battle of Chickamauga. Organizations have erected hundreds of mons., & pk. commission with 2 exceptions has duplicated Rds. of 1863. **Kelly H.** (N.O.) is reconstruction of one that stood on Kelly Farm, scene of severest fighting of Sept. 20, until battle shifted to Snodgrass Hill. **Ga. Mon.** is on Poe Field near N. edge of gap in Fed. line through which Longstreet rushed Stewart's division. Across Rd. (R) is marker designating **Site of Poe H.,** another scene of bitter fighting. **Brotherton H.** (N.O.). US27 & Brotherton Rd., a reconstruction, marks site of disastrous break in Fed. lines. **Viniard Field** was scene of severest fighting, Sept. 19, 1863. **Wilder Tower** (Glenn-Kelly Rd.) on Wilder Hill, is **Site of Widow Glenn's Cabin,** Gen. Rosecrans' hqs., which burned Sept. 20, 1863. **Mon. to 1st Wisconsin Cavalry** across Rd., is a riderless horse. Reconstructed **Blacksmith Shop** was scene of severe fighting. **Snodgrass Hill,** scene of Battle of the Horseshoe, has a tower offering widest view of battlefield. From this pt., Gen. Thomas directed his attack after Rosecrans' retreat. Retrace on US27 from Pk. Office to Crest Rd., which traverses

**Missionary Ridge** to its termination at Chickamauga Dam. **15. BRAGG RESERV.** (L), is sm. circular plot, site of Gen. Bragg's hqs. Here in Oct. 1863 Jeff. Davis addressed Confed. troops. **Ill. Mon.** here. **16.** Shallowford Rd. branches (L) from Crest Rd. down Missionary Ridge to McCallie Ave. **McCallie Sch.** (L) is private military sch. for boys. (R) on McCallie Ave. to Chattanooga at c.**19.5.**

## III. CHATTANOOGA (NE) to DAYTON. 37. US27

**17. DAISY,** coal shipping pt., with large tile & brick ovens as supporting industries. **21. SODDY,** coal mining town at foot of Walden's Ridge. **22. SALE CR.,** site of Ind. mission sch. est. in 1806. **37. DAYTON,** seat of Rhea Cty. At **County Cth.** the "evolution trial" of John T. Scopes was held in summer of 1925. This case, known as the "Monkey Trial," grew out of alleged violation of a Tenn. statute, passed that yr., making it "unlawful for any teacher . . . to teach any theory that denies story of divine creation of man as taught in Bible . . ." As test of law, Scopes, a science teacher, admitted teaching evolution. The Amer. Civil Liberties Union offered to finance trial & lend its attorney, Arthur Garfield Hays. When Wm. Jennings Bryan volunteered as prosecutor, Clarence Darrow & Dudley Field Malone joined Hays in defense. The town swarmed with newspaper men, itinerant preachers, & thousands of curious. By time trial ended, there was a personal feud bet. Bryan & Darrow. Scopes was found guilty & fined $100. Bryan died here July 27, 1925, 5 days after trial ended. As mem. to him, Wm. Jennings Bryan Univ. was est.

SIDE TRIP: (R) on St.30 to **Cumberland Springs,** 2m, an artesian spring, by which is a **Geological Field Sta. of Ohio St. Univ.**

## IV. CHATTANOOOGA (NE) to CLEVELAND. 30. US64, US11

**7. CHICKAMAUGA CR.,** site of prehist. villages. Ind. mounds still stand. **7.** Marker (R) shows **SITE OF BRAINERD MISSION** for the Inds., est. 1817. A short distance (E) of 2 giant Sp. oaks is 1 of 1st wells dug in this sec. **9. FRANKSTONE INN** (R), formerly the Shepherd H., during Civil War, was occupied in turn by Confed. & Fed. officers, incl. Maj. Jas. A. Garfield, later Pres. of U.S.

At **12.** (L) is J. with E. Chattanooga Rd.

SIDE TRIP: (L) on this Rd. to **Chickamauga Dam,** 7m, which rises 60′ from bed of Tenn. R. The project, started in 1935, cost $31,000,000 & was 5th major TVA project. The concrete dam is 5,685′ long & creates L. with shoreline of 502m.

**12. SILVERDALE CONFED. CEMETERY** (R). Gen. Braxton Bragg stationed some men near here in summer of 1862. The 150 men who died at post were buried on this 1-a. plot. Their wooden markers have decayed. **17. OOLTEWAH,** former seat of James Cty., which in 1919 was combined with Hamilton Cty. **30. CLEVELAND,** seat of Bradley Cty., is on last area evacuated by Cherokee in 1858. PTS. OF INT.: **Central Ave. Tabernacle,** Central Ave., houses annual assembly of Tomlinson Ch. of God. Ch. is strictly fundamentalist, practicing faith healing, foot washing, & speaking in unknown tongues.

## V. CHATTANOOGA (W) to JASPER. 31. US64 & US41

US64 (11th St.) to J. with Broad St. (L) to J. at 5m with paved Rd.

SIDE TRIP: (R) on this Rd. 3m to **John Brown's Tavern** (1803). **Brown's Grave** is behind house. Many traders stayed here. Legend says Brown, an Ind., often appraised value of trader's stocks & then killed & robbed him when he returned from his rounds. To support his story that they had moved on, he is said to have broken up their wagons & thrown them in river. Story was given new credence some yrs. ago when dredging operations brought up several rotting wagon hubs.

At **6.** is J. with US11, leading (L) on US11 2m to **Wauhatchie Valley,** site of Civil War Battle of Wauhatchie. **8.** J. with gravel Rd.

SIDE TRIP: (L) 0.5m to **Tenn. Cave** (fee), which contains large stalactites & stalagmites, many of them delicately colored; yr.-round temperature of 54 degrees.

**9. WALDEN'S RIDGE,** which rises abruptly from bank of R., was named for Elijah Walden, who explored reg. in 1761. The rugged **Cumberland Escarpment** (L) is visible for several miles. At **19.** is J. with gravel Rd.

SIDE TRIP: (R) on this Rd. 0.5m to **Hale's Bar Dam & Powerhouse,** purchased from private interests by TVA. Completed in 1913, it was 1st major hydroelectric development in Tenn.

**31.** In **JASPER,** seat of Marion Cty., is **Sam Houston Academy,** 1824, 1 block (E) of town square. Houston taught here.

# KNOXVILLE

## KNOXVILLE

RR., bus & air conns. Excellent accoms. & recr. facils., horseback riding, golf, swim., tennis, etc. Info.: C. of C., 621 Gay St.; East Tenn. Auto Club, 920 Gay St.; Tourist Bureau, 811 Broadway; TVA Info. Office, New Sprankle Bldg., 508 Union St. SE. Basketball Tournament, last wk. Feb.; Tenn. Valley A. & I. Fair, last wk. Sept.; Burley Tobacco Market opens 1st wk. Dec.

Knoxville, seat of Knox Cty., is on the Tenn. R., which is formed 4$^{m}$ (E) by confluence of Holston & French Broad Rs. The city extends fanwise from the R. into the surrounding hills with the Chilhowee & Great Smoky Mts. in the background. The business dist. is crowded upon a plateau of 240 as. approached by narrow steep sts. In 1786, 25 yrs. after 1st white man traveled through the reg., Capt. Jas. White built a log cabin near the present Farragut Hotel & became the 1st white man to settle in the reg. Because the majority of E. Tennesseeans were loyal to the Union in the War Bet. the Sts., a Confed. army of occupation was sent into E. Tenn. in 1861, but all Confed. troops were withdrawn from Knoxville area during Aug. 1863 to be mobilized in Chattanooga. About the same time a Fed. force under Maj. Gen. A. E. Burnside arrived at Knoxville. During Nov. 1863 a Confed. army of 15,000 men under Gen. Jas. A. Longstreet successfully besieged Knoxville till Fed. troops were reduced to rations of a cracker a day. Reports that Gen. W. T. Sherman was on the way with 25,000 men to relieve Burnside prompted Longstreet to try to capture the city quickly by direct assault. The attack against Ft. Sanders was repulsed with heavy losses, & Longstreet's army withdrew to winter quarters near Morristown. When peace came, restoration was rapid. Many Fed. soldiers returned to make Knoxville their home & est. some of the leading business houses. The city has grown consistently. Other than its industries, mainly cotton textiles, marble, & hardwood furniture, Knoxville is a farm market, especially for tobacco. The city is also the uppermost terminal of the navigable portion of the Tenn. R. & has many hqs. of TVA.

PTS. OF INT.: (1) SE. cor. S. Gay St. & W. Clinch Ave., **Site of Blount College,** marked by bronze plaque on Gay St. side of the Burwell Bldg. College was inc. by the Territorial Assembly in 1794 as the 3rd institution of higher learning (W) of the Alleghenies. It was coed. from the first. Later, it became the Univ. of Tenn. (2) 620 State St., **First Presb. Ch.,** org. in 1793. Churchyard contains graves of early settlers, incl. Wm. Blount, 1st gov. of the Terr., & Jas. White, the city's founder. (3) SW. cor. W. State St. & W. Hill Ave., **Blount Mansion** (1792.Georg.Col.O.wks.), was 1st frame house (W) of Alleghenies, built by Gov. Wm. Blount. It contains relics from pioneer families of Tenn. (4) 217 Front Ave., **Chisholm's Tavern** (1792. O.appl.), offered accoms. to early travelers. Doors are made with double cross panels to repel witches. (5) West Main Ave., bet. S. Gay & Market Sts., **Knox County Cth.;** 2 mons. near the entrance mark the graves of John Sevier & his wife. A stone marker 100′ (S) of the Sevier mon., comm. the Treaty of the Holston, signed on July 2, 1791. (6) 217 Market St., **Lawson McGhee Lib.,** contains the C. M. McClung Hist. Coll., 6,000 volumes of hist. & genealogy of the S. (7) W. Vine Ave. bet. Market & Walnut Sts., **Summit Hill** was occupied by a battery of Confed. artillery in defending the city against a Fed. cavalry raid, June 21, 1863. (8) 422 W. Cumberland Ave., **Park H.** (O) is typical of the large dwellings erected by wealthy builders in pioneer days. It was begun by John Sevier in 1798 & completed by Jas. Park, later mayor of Knoxville; now used as an infirmary. (9) W. Cumberland Ave. bet. Hunter & 15th Sts., **Univ. of Tenn.,** est. in 1794. Bldgs. erected after 1917 conform to the Coll. Goth. style, but earlier bldgs. reflect the period of their construction. It has 40-a. campus. The univ. has schs. of liberal arts, engineering, education, law, home economics, & agric. Schs. of medicine, nursing & pharmacy are in Memphis. (10) 2600 Kingston Pike, **Univ. of Tenn. Experimental Farm** (O.wks.), contains 1,200 as. on both sides of the Tenn. R.

(11) 2800 Kingston Pike, **Bleak H.** (N.O.), was named for the novel by Chas. Dickens. Gen. Jas. A. Longstreet made house his hqs. during the siege of Knoxville. (12) 2890 Kingston Pike, **Sanford Arboretum** (O.wks.). At rear of the A. F. Sanford home is a non-commercial coll. of more than 2,200 varieties of dwarf trees & shrubs. (13) 1400 College St., **Knoxville College,** is one of oldest institutions for Negro instruction in the S., est. 1875. There are 28 bldgs. on campus of 20

as. It confers bachelor degrees in academic subjects & music. (14) Broadway bet. Tyson & Cooper Sts., **Nat. & Old Gray Cemeteries** adj. each other. Nat. Cemetery was est. by Fed. Gov. in 1863 for Fed. soldiers killed in E. Tenn. It also contains graves of Sp.-Amer. & 1st World War veterans. In Old Gray Cemetery are graves of Gov. W. G. (Parson) Brownlow & other noted persons.

## TRIPS OUT OF KNOXVILLE

Pts. of int. in vic. of Knoxville group themselves roughly into 3 distinct types: hist., scenic & modern pub. developments. Scenic attractions are largely concerned with the Great Smoky Mts. & nat. pks. & fors. Trips V, VI & VII cover such pts. Mod. pub. developments near Knoxville incl. the various major installations of TVA & the Oak Ridge Area of the Atomic Energy Commission. The Oak Ridge development is reached by following Trip IV. Major TVA dams will be found on Tours I, III, V & IX. Many hist. pts. are covered on virtually all the tours.

### I. KNOXVILLE (E) to JEFFERSON CITY. 27. US70, US11E

From Knoxville, **0.**, take US70 to the J. with US11E at **12.** Follow US11E. At **15.** is J. with paved Mascot Rd.

SIDE TRIP: On this Rd. (R) 3m is **Mascot,** with mines & reduction plant of the Amer. Zinc Co.

**15. STRAWBERRY PLAINS,** a trading pt. for farmers. At **21.** (L) is the scene of the **GREAT NEW MARKET WRECK,** subject of a hill ballad. On Sept. 4, 1904, 2 crack passenger trains of the Southern RR. collided, killed 70 & injuring 150. **22. SITE OF TUCKER'S TAVERN** (L), marked by chimney standing in a field. The inn was built in 1819 on the stage Rd. bet. Knoxville & Abingdon, Va. **23. NEW MARKET,** sett. in 1788. **27. JEFFERSON CITY.** In the center of town is **Carson Newman College.** The beautifully landscaped campus has 9 bldgs. The sch. grants the bachelor degree in arts, science, & science in commerce.

SIDE TRIP: From Jefferson City (L) on St.92 to the J. 3m with paved TVA access Rd. (R) on this Rd. to **Cherokee Dam.** Cherokee Dam is a storage dam across the Holston R., which with the French Broad R. forms the Tenn. R. by their confluence at Knoxville. The dam is 175′ high & 6,760′ long. It began impounding water Dec. 5, 1941, forming in Jefferson & Grainger counties a lake covering 30,700 as. with a shoreline of 463m. Cost of construction was c.$32,000,000.

### II. KNOXVILLE to RUTLEDGE. 35. US11W

At **8.** are the **JOHN SEVIER YARDS** of the Southern RR. (R) with 50m of track in a classification yard that can handle 3,500 cars. At **20.** is J. with gravel Rd.

SIDE TRIP: On this Rd. (L) to **Ind. Cave** (fee), 7m, with thousands of stalactites & stalagmites. Tradition says Cherokee used cave as hiding place after defeat at hands of an Iroquois war party.

**25. RED H. TAVERN** (L), erected in 1796, is in good condition today. At **29.** is J. with paved Jefferson City Rd.

SIDE TRIP: On this Rd. (L) to J. with dirt Rd. 3m. (L) here to **Buffalo Springs Game Farm,** 5m. The farm is 350 as. incl. a quail hatchery with an incubator & brooder having capacity of 100,000 birds.

**35. RUTLEDGE,** seat of Grainger Cty. is a trade center. The cty. was est. in 1796 before Tenn. was admitted to the Union.

### III. KNOXVILLE (W & S) to LENOIR CITY. 25. US11, US70

**25. LENOIR CITY** is on Tenn. R. near mouth of Little Tenn. R. Lenoir City is a farm market & an industrial town.

SIDE TRIPS: (A) From Lenoir City (R) on Eaton's Crossroad to a large **Ginseng Garden,** 2m, which has more than 2 million plants in a two-&-a-half a. plot. The plant is highly prized in China for its medicinal properties.
(B) From Lenoir City (L) on TVA access Rd. to **Ft. Loudon Dam,** 2m, across Tenn. R., a major installation of TVA. The dam was closed in Dec. 1943. It is 122′ high & 4,190′ long. It forms L. covering 14,600 as. in Loudon Cty. (f.boat.swim.etc.).

### IV. KNOXVILLE (NW) to CLINTON. 18. US25W

**18. CLINTON,** seat of Anderson Cty., has prospered considerably during recent yrs. because of TVA's Norris Dam development a few miles on one side of it & the Oak Ridge atomic energy development on the other.

SIDE TRIP: From Clinton (L) on the Oak Ridge Turnpike (St.61) 10m to **Oak Ridge Area of the Atomic Energy Commission,** & city of **Oak Ridge.** Oak Ridge Area of the Atomic Energy Commission is a 59,000-a. Gov. reservation approximately 90 sq. miles in which are situated 3 main operating units concerned with atomic energy work (2 plants for production of & research on uranium 235 & a 3rd that serves as a nuclear research center) & the community of Oak Ridge. The 3 main units at Oak Ridge are operated for the Atomic Energy Commission by the Carbide & Carbon Chemicals Corp. The Oak Ridge Area is also hqs. for the Research Project for the Application of Nuclear Energy to the Propulsion of Aircraft (the NEPA project) & the Oak Ridge Institute of Nuclear Studies, Inc. The NEPA project is a combined operation of 10 aviation companies & the Nat. Advisory Committee on Aeronautics working with the Fairchild Engine & Airplane Corp. as prime contractor under the AAF, a program in which the Atomic Energy Commission is co-operating. The Oak Ridge Institute of Nuclear Studies, Inc., is an organization of 14 member univs. in the S. & SW., which has as its objective a program of assistance to univs. in developing strong grad. & research programs in nuclear energy & to be available to the Commission in advisory capacities. The site of the Oak Ridge Area (formerly known as the Clinton Engineer Works) was selected on Sept. 19, 1942, by representatives of the Manhattan Dist., which was est. Aug. 13, 1942. The cost of the 59,000 as. was $2,600,000 & for the operating units & the town of Oak Ridge it was approx. $1 106,393,000. Preliminary site preparation began Nov. 2, 1942, & 1st production of U-235 on mass basis was begun Jan. 27, 1944. When the site was selected in 1942 & the site preparation begun, approximately 3,000 residents were removed from about 1,000 homes in the area. The Atomic Energy Commission took over the jurisdiction of Oak Ridge Area from the Manhattan Dist. Jan. 1, 1947. The Manhattan Dist. was abolished by the Corps of Engineers of the War Dept. Aug. 15, 1947.

If a loop tour is desired, cont. on St.61 to its J. with US27; (L) on that Rd. 4m to its J. with US70; & take US70 back to Knoxville following Trip XI backward.

## V. KNOXVILLE (E) to NEWFOUND GAP. 55.5. St.71

This route, from Knoxville to the N.C. Line, forms part of a circle tour locally called the Knoxville Scenic Loop. It gives magnificent view of the mt. ranges, enters the Great Smoky Mts. Nat. Pk., & ascends the mts. to their highest pt. The trip offers insight into folk life, markets for mt. handicraft, mt. climbing & other recr. At **3.** is J. with St.33 (Trip VII). At **6.** is a gap in **BROWN'S MT.,** from which on clear days there is a view of the Great Smoky Mts. **Thunderhead** (5,530′) & **Gregory's Bald** (4,948′) are visible (R) in the distance. **10. SHOOK'S GAP** notches a ridge that divides Knox & Sevier Counties. Several gun battles have occurred here bet. officers & liquor runners. At **13., Mt. Chapman** (6,430′), a 3-pointed peak, is visible & (L) is **Mt. Guyot** (6,621′), 2nd highest peak in Great Smoky Mts. Nat. Pk. **Mount Le Conte** (6,595′) is visible (R) at **19. 26. SEVIERVILLE,** seat of Sevier Cty., was est. Mar. 1785 as part of the short-lived St. of Franklin. The log house at Main St. & Park Rd. was built in 1806 and housed **Nancy Academy,** named for Nancy Rogers, probably 1st white child born in this sec.

SIDE TRIP: St.66 (N) to **Douglas Dam,** 6m (f.swim.boat.). Douglas Dam is an important installation of TVA. It is a storage dam across the French Broad R., which with the Holston R. forms the Tenn. R. by their confluence at Knoxville. The dam is 202′ high & 1,705′ long. It began impounding water Feb. 19, 1943, forming in Sevier Cty. a lake covering 30,600 as. with shoreline of 556m. Cost of construction was c.$41,600,000.

St.71 turns (S) & passes through a valley overshadowed by mts. **28.** An old-fashioned **SWINGING BRIDGE. 33. PIGEON FORGE.** From E. end of the town is good view of the Smokies. **39. GATLINBURG,** mt. resort at head of a cove through which the Pigeon R. runs (good accoms.). Shops in the town display handmade items that the mt. people produce. By the hy. (L) just (W) of center of town is store called **Great Smoky Mt. Mus.,** containing large number of pitchers, toby jugs, & specimens of Tiplet & Ridgway wares. **Mountaineer Mus.** (lectures. sm.fee) along hy. (L) (W) of the center, contains large & authentic coll. of old domestic & agric. implements, furniture, guns, bear traps & other articles long used by mt. folk of this reg. The **Barnes Cherokee Ind. Mus.** (sm.fee), opp. the Mountaineer Mus., has fine coll. of Cherokee Ind. artifacts. (SW) of Gatlinburg the Rd. follows the long valley of the Little Pigeon R. At **40.** is **MARKER** announcing boundary of the Great Smoky Mts. Nat. Pk. **Nat. Pk. Checking Sta.** is at the J. (R) with St.73 (Trip VI). There is a view of **Bullhead** (L) & of **Rock Spur** beyond. Both are on spurs of the massive Mt. Le Conte. **The Chimney Tops** (R), ragged twin peaks, are visible at **44.** At **47.** is site of the old **Ind. Gap Hotel.**

SIDE TRIP: From this pt. (R) a steep trl. leads to **Chimney Tops** (4,740′), 1m from which is view of the valley of the Sugarlands & the peaks on the divide.

At **48.** is **BEAR PEN GAP.**

SIDE TRIP: (L) from gap on a Class A trl. to **Mt. Le Conte,** 4m. From a sm. pk. the trl. ascends through dense conifers, beds of ferns & wild flowers. Bear pens, heavy deadfall traps, were once a hazard along the trl.

By **ALUM CAVE CR., 52.** & Walter Camp Prong of the Little Pigeon R. is J. with Alum Cave Trl., the steepest & shortest route to Mt. Le Conte.

SIDE TRIP: (L) on this trl., which follows Alum Cr. & goes up a steep half-mile to **Alum Cave,** 1m. Just below Alum Cave Bluff is (L) **Hide-in Rock Ridge.** In Alum Cave, under the immense overhanging bluff are deposits of Epsom salt & alum. The cave mouth is a good observation pt.

A stand of black birches, a species usually found in the latitudes of Canada, is at **55. 55.5 NEWFOUND GAP** (5,045′), where the Rd. crosses the St. Line, 85m (W) of Asheville, N.C. The Appalachian Trl. crosses hy. here.

SIDE TRIP: (R) on macadam Skyline Rd. paralleling the Appalachian Trl. bet. Newfound Gap & Clingmans Dome. At 2m Skyline Rd. crosses **Ind. Gap** (5,265′). The Appalachian Trl. crosses hy. here. **Clingmans Dome,** with fire tower, appears (R) at 5m. **Cove & Rich Mts.** are visible (R) & **Siler's Bald** & **Thunderhead Mt.** (L). At 7m is a good view of **Oconaluftee Gorge** (L). The highest pt. on the Rd. (6,311′) is just ahead. The Rd. ends at a large parking plaza at 8m. A Class B trl. to the summit of **Clingmans Dome** (6,641′) c.0.5m long, begins (R). From the plaza are fine views of the Blue Ridge Range, & the Nantahala Nat. For. & Andrew's Bald in N.C. From top of Clingmans Dome are visible some of the highest peaks in the Smokies; **Mt. Kephart, Siler's Bald** & **Mt. Collins.**

If returning to Knoxville, the Scenic Loop may be completed by following Trip VI to Maryville & St.33 from Maryville to Knoxville, following Trip VII backward bet. these two pts.

## VI. KNOXVILLE (W) to MARYVILLE. 39. St.73

At **0.5** is J. with a trl.

SIDE TRIP: (L) on this trl. 3m to **Holy Butt** (2,910′). The trl. cont. to **Mt. Harrison** (3,000′) with views of Mt. LeConte, the Chimneys & Siler's Bald.

**2.** An **OBSERVATION PT.** (2,089′) (L). At **3.,** where St.73 cuts through **Fighting Cr. Gap** (2,300′) is J. with trl.

SIDE TRIP: (R) 1m on this trl. to **Laurel Cr. Falls,** frequently visited because of their accessibility. **Devil's Chute,** 2m, is one of picturesque spots in the pk. At 3m is **Chinquapin Ridge** (3,500′). At 4m is a J. with trl. that leads (L) to **Cove Mt.** (4,091′), which offers broad view overlooking Wear Cove.

**4.** J. with macadam Rd.

SIDE TRIP: (L) on this Rd. to **Elkmont,** 1m, a resort (hotels.cabins), from which are scenic trls.

**10.** J. with gravel Rd.

SIDE TRIP: (R) on this Rd. 1m to **J.** with trl.; (L) on this trl. 1m to **Round Top** (3,080′).

At **SINK'S BRIDGE, 12.** is J. with trl.

SIDE TRIP: (R) here following a cr. 2m to **Curry He Mt.** & **Curry She Mt.** (3,014′). Curry He was mountaineer's version of an unknown Ind. word approximating it in sound, & having thus arrived at the name of one mountain they logically called a neighboring peak Curry She.

**21. TOWNSEND,** in Tuckaleechee Cove. **25. KINZEL SPRINGS,** summer resort, lies below 4 mts., Matthew, Mark, Luke & John. **29. WALLAND,** with mineral spring, is in a gap of the Chilhowee Mts. **39. MARYVILLE,** is at J. with St.33 & US129. To complete the Knoxville Scenic Loop, take US129 & St.33 from Maryville to Knoxville following that portion of Trip VII backward bet. those 2 pts.

## VII. KNOXVILLE (S) to MADISONVILLE. 44. US129

At **1.** is J. (R) with St. 71 (Trip VI). At **10.** is J. with Mentor Rd.

SIDE TRIP: (R) on this Rd. to **Remains of Gillespie's Ft.,** 0.5m, which was captured & burned by the Inds. who killed 30 white men, women & children here. The place was henceforth called Burnt Sta.

**13.** J. with paved Rd.

SIDE TRIP: (R) on this Rd. is **Alcoa,** 1m, founded by the Aluminum Co. of Amer. in 1913. The large aluminum plant was greatly expanded during World War II.

**15. MARYVILLE,** seat of Blount Cty. In 1807, Sam Houston, later the Tex. hero, came from Va. with his widowed mother & 8 bros. & est. a store in the town. The **Barclay McGhee H.** (O.1790), 306 Broadway, is characteristic of the more luxurious homes of the period. **Maryville College,** on College St., has 320-a. campus commanding view of distant Smokies. Degrees in the arts & sciences are granted. At Maryville is J. with St.73 (Trip VI). At **22.** is J. with US411 on which cont. to **33.** Hy. crosses **Little Tenn. R.** At S. end of the bridge is J. with Ft. Loudoun Rd.

SIDE TRIP: (L) on this dirt Rd. to J. with another Rd.; (R) here & across a bridge over Tellico R. to J. with another Rd.; (L) on this Rd. to the **Site of Ft. Loudoun,** 1m. Ft. Loudoun was constructed in 1756 by Brit. as friendly gesture to the Overhill Cherokee, who were allied with the Brit. War broke out with the Cherokee who laid siege to the ft. in Feb., 1760. The little band inside withstood the attack for 5 months, though they had to eat their dogs & horses. The ft. surrendered to the Inds. with the understanding that they could evacuate to Ft. Prince George or to Va. They evacuated Aug. 8, 1760, & the next morning they were attacked by a large number of Inds. who killed 30 of them & captured the rest. The survivors were later ransomed & delivered to Ft. Prince George. The old ft. was partially reconstructed by the WPA in 1937.

**44. MADISONVILLE,** seat of Monroe Cty. **Hiwassee Jr. College,** est. 1847, is a self-help institution where most of the students work part time.

SIDE TRIP: (L) on St.68 is **Tellico Plains,** 14m, at edge of the Cherokee Nat. For. (camp. h.& carrying firearms permitted only in specified areas; inquire at office of the pk.ranger in village.) Tellico Plains is operations base of the annual wild boar hunt. Wild boar run wild over 80,000 as., now the Tellico Game & Fish Management Area.

## VIII. KNOXVILLE (N) to MAYNARDVILLE. 25. St.33

**3. SCOTT H.** (O.1833). Wall paper of the living room was imported from France in 1833. Colors are still bright, though the room was used as hospital during the War Bet. the States. Because of a habit of the 2nd owner, a Col. Ledgerwood, there is a grove with 26 kinds of trees. When driving through the country, the Col. would cut a branch from some tree, use it as a buggy whip & on his return, stick it in this ground. At **5.,** marked site (L) of log blockh., **Adair's Sta.** It was built in 1788 by John Adair who financed expedition led by Isaac Shelby & John Sevier that defeated Brit. in Battle of King's Mountain. **16.** J. with gravel Rd.

SIDE TRIP: (L) & (L) again to **Big Ridge Pk.** (swim.pic.boat.f.& furnished cabins). The pk. covers 3,500 as. on S. shore of Norris L. Approx. 100 as. have been developed as recr. area.

**25. MAYNARDVILLE,** seat of Union Cty.

## IX. KNOXVILLE (NW) to NORRIS DAM. 25. St.33 & Norris Freeway

**10.** on St.33, J. with Norris Freeway. (L) on Norris Freeway to **18., MT. CABIN,** constructed of logs chinked with clay; preserved by TVA. **21. NORRIS,** built as gov.-owned residential town during construction of Norris Dam to house workers. After completion of dam, houses were rented principally by TVA personnel who worked in Knoxville. Town was sold in 1948 to private interests which in turn offered homes for sale to residents. **24.** J. with paved Rd.

SIDE TRIP: (L) on this Rd. to the **TVA Forest Nurseries** & **TVA Fish Hatchery Pools** & to the **Power House,** 1m (guide serv.), where there is exhibit showing construction of dam & its operation.

**25. NORRIS DAM** was 1st major project completed by TVA & began impounding waters of Clinch R., Mar. 4, 1936. Work had begun in 1933. Total cost was approx. $36,000,000. Norris Dam is 1,860′ long, approx. 208′ thick at the base & 265′ high. Norris Dam has created a reservoir, **Norris L.,** which has shoreline of approx. 705m & is 50 sq. miles in area.

SIDE TRIP: (R) from the Freeway at the traffic circle to entrance of **Norris Pk.** (all types recr.facils.furnished cabins). A water mill built in 1797 has been carefully rest. on bank of Clear Cr., 100 yds. (E) of the freeway.

At the traffic circle is a **Handicraft Shop** that sells handmade products of the mt. people.

## X. KNOXVILLE (E) to BEAVER DAM GARDEN. 37. US70

At **14.** is J. with US11E. **30. DANDRIDGE,** named for Martha Dandridge Custis, wife of Geo. Washington. The 1st white settlement in this sec. was made in 1783.

SIDE TRIPS: (A) On St.92 (R) to the 6′ **Dumplin Treaty Marker,** 4m, comm. treaty with the Cherokee that threw open the country (S) of French Broad R. to white settlers in 1785.

(B) On an improved Rd. (L) 3m to **Island Mound,** in the French Broad R. At lower end, c.300′ from water's edge, is site of a ceremonial bldg. used by Inds.

**32. GEN. LONGSTREET'S HQS.** (L) is a 2-story frame structure occupied briefly by the Confed. Gen. in Jan. 1864. **37.** (R) **BEAVER DAM GARDEN** (O). Stone walls support wistaria, japonica, alba & long-erecamosa; rambling roses bloom throughout the summer.

**XI. KNOXVILLE (W) to FARRAGUT. 39. US70 & US11**

**5. BEARDEN,** residential suburb of Knoxville. Just ahead is **J.** with Weisbarger Rd., paved.

SIDE TRIP: (R) on this Rd. to Middlebrook Pike; (L) to **Lonas H.,** frontier mus.

At **9.** is J. with gravel Gallaher View Rd.

SIDE TRIP: On this Rd. (R) 0.5m to J. with dirt Rd.; (R) here to **Site of Cavett's Sta.,** 1m, beside graves of the Cavetts killed here by an Ind. attack.

**15. FARRAGUT,** named in honor of David Glasgow Farragut, the 1st Admiral in U.S. Navy. **16.** A stone marks site of **CAMPBELL'S STA.,** a frontier ft. erected in 1787. At **20.** is J. with US11 (Trip I). Cont. on US70. **39. KINGSTON,** seat of Roane Cty., was the E. terminal of the pioneer Walton Rd. which ran to Nashville.

SIDE TRIP: On St.56 (L) 1m to **South Westport Ft.,** est. in 1792 on S. bank of the Tenn. R.

# MEMPHIS

## MEMPHIS

RR., bus & air conns. Excellent accoms. & recr. facils., baseball, swim., golf, plays, concerts. Info.: Dixie Motor Club, Hotel Peabody. Cotton Carnival, May; Mid-South Fair, Sept.

Memphis, largest city in Tenn., seat of Shelby Cty., is a metropolis for Tenn., Miss., & Ark. It is situated on the 4th or lower Chickasaw Bluff on the E. bank of the Miss. R. Now an industrial center, the city still has some of the glamour of early river days. For the first 100 yrs., hist. of Memphis was simply that of a boom town on the border line of the W. Only in the last 3 decades have restricted residential areas been laid out. The Chickasaw lived on the bluffs long before they were visited by the 1st white men in 1541, when De Soto & his gold seeking expedition stopped here. The bluff was not again visited by white men until 1673, when Joliet & Marquette stopped to trade with the Inds. La Salle followed in 1682, & built Ft. Prudhomme on the First Chickasaw Bluff, above the mouth of the Hatchie. Then Fr., Sp., & Eng. began the long struggle for control of the bluffs commanding the Miss. R. Neither intrigue nor force succeeded in winning the Chickasaw as Fr. allies. In 1763, the Fr. ceded to the Eng. the E. part of the Miss. Valley incl. the site of Memphis.

During the next 2 decades the Sp. influence grew strong among the Chickasaw. The Sp. planned to use the Chickasaw as a buffer against the growing Cumberland Settlement in Middle Tenn. In 1782 Gen. Jas. Robertson led a force to the bluff & est. a depot where the Chickasaw could be given supplies to offset Sp. bribes. John Overton, temporary agent for Ind. affairs, est. a trading post at the bluff in 1794. As late as 1795 Gayoso, Sp. Gov. of La., led troops to the bluffs to prevent the Cumberland settlers from building fts. A detachment of U.S. army forced their withdrawal. The bluff remained in Chickasaw control until 1818, when the western territory was ceded to the U.S. In 1783-86, N.C. granted John Rice & John Ramsey 5,000 as. on the site of Memphis; the grant was later sold to John Overton & Andrew Jackson. Immediately after the Ind. treaty (1818), they laid out the town. It was inc. Dec. 9, 1826, after Jackson had sold his claims.

With outbreak of the War Bet. the States in 1861, Memphis became a Confed. military center under Gen. Leonidas Polk. Early in 1862 Memphis became the temporary St. Capitol because Nashville lay unprotected before the advancing Feds. On June 6, 1862, the city was seized by Fed. forces under Commodore C. H. Davis. It remained in Fed. control until after the war, though there was a brief & spectacular Confed. raid led by Gen. Nathan Bedford Forrest in Aug. 1864. The 1st RR. bridge across the Miss. R., (S) of St. Louis, was built at Memphis in 1892, followed by the Harahan Bridge in 1909. The bridges brought increased traffic with the SW., & Memphis became the greatest inland cotton market & hardwood lumber center in the world. The port of Memphis exports merchandise valued at $250,000,000 annually, & the value of imports is only slightly less. More than 100,-000 visitors come in May to see the parades, street dancing, fireworks and lavish balls of the annual Cotton Carnival. As much a part of the city as the cotton market or the City Hall, is E. H. Crump, nationally known political leader & the head of the Shelby Cty. political organization, formerly a dominant influence in the political affairs of the St.

PTS. OF INT.: (1) SW. cor. Madison Ave. & S. 3rd St., **Goodwyn Institute** (O.8-10. wks.), where a series of lectures & concerts by leading personalities are given annually. (2) NE. cor. Madison Ave. & N. 3rd St., **Sterrick Bldg.**, a 29-story bldg. erected in 1929-30 by Ross Sterling, former Gov. of Texas & designed by Wyatt C. Hedrick. (3) N. Main St. bet. Jefferson & Court Aves., **Court Square** is the most noted of the 4 squares laid out by the proprietors of Memphis for public use in 1819. A **Fountain,** a copy of Canova's celebrated statue of Hebe, in the art gallery at Leningrad, is in the center of the square. (4) Adams Ave. bet. N. 2nd & N. 3rd Sts., **Shelby County Cth.** (O) has group of sculptures by J. Massey Rhind. (5) SE. cor. Auction Ave. & N. Main St., **Auction Square** is where slaves were auctioned. Bronze marker records the fact that in 1797 Capt. Isaac Guion took possession of the site for the U.S. (6) N. Front St. & Auction Ave., **Union Compress Plant** (O) is one of the largest cotton compresses in Memphis. (7) Riverside Dr. & Jefferson Ave., **Jeff. Davis Pk.** comm. the pres. of the Confed., who lived in Memphis, 1867-75. The pk. is **Site of De Soto's Shipyard,** where the Sp. explorer is supposed to have built barges to transport his men across the Miss. in 1541. (8) N. Front St. & W. Court Ave., **Confed. Pk.** comm. Battle of Memphis in the War Bet. the States & provides excellent view of the R. (9) S. Front St. at foot of Monroe Ave., **Cossitt Lib.,** contains 240,000 vols., incl. a special 1,500 vol. coll. on Memphis & Tenn. & 1,200 vols. of music. (10) SE. cor. Union Ave. & S. Front St., **Cotton Exchange** (O) is the official organization of the Memphis cotton trade, & the economic heart of the city. (11) 139 S. Main St., **Gayoso Hotel** (1844) was used as hqs. by both Confed. & Fed. Armies during Civil War. (12) Beale St. & S. 3rd St., **Handy Pk.** is scene of the Negro Cotton Fiesta during the Memphis Cotton Carnival.

(13) Beginning at the De Soto Fish Dock & running 1$^m$ to East St., **Beale Street,** noted in song & story as the center of Negro life in Memphis. (14) 533 Beale St., **Hunt-Phelan H.** (N.O.1835) was occupied in 1861 by Leonidas Polk, Confed. Gen., while organizing the Provisional Army of Tenn. It was seized by Fed. troops during their occupancy of Memphis & used by Gen. Grant in 1862, & as a Fed. hospital in 1863. (15) NE. cor. Union Ave. & S. Manassas St., **Forrest Pk.** contains equestrian statue of Gen. Nathan Bedford Forrest, Confed. cavalry leader, who, with his wife, is buried in front of the statue. (16) 874 Union Ave., **Univ. of Tenn. Health Division** comprises medical, dental, nursing & pharmacy schs. of the Univ. of Tenn. (17) N. Parkway, bet. N. McLean Blvd. & E. Parkway, extending to Poplar Ave., **Overton Pk.** which contains 355 as., of which 100 as. are of virgin timber, interlaced with drives and recr. areas. At the S. entrance are **Zoological & Botanical Gardens & Free Circus** (O. daily summer; Sun. yr. round). Zoo covers 47 as. Circus has 18 acts performed by zoo attendants, former circus trainers. Near the Poplar Ave. entrance, **Brooks Mem. Art Gallery** (O) features monthly circulating exhibits.

(18) N. Parkway at Univ. Blvd., **Southwestern, The College of the Miss. Valley,** is a sm. Presb. College (coed.) with a 100-a. campus & 7 bldgs. (19) 275 Tilton Rd., **Mus. of Nat. Hist. & Industrial Arts** contains exhibits of animals, firearms, marine life, Confed. Army & other relics. (20) NE. cor. Southern Ave. & Patterson St., **West Tenn. St. Teachers College** has 13 bldgs. on a campus of 82 as. It is coed. with av. enrollment of 600. (21) 807 Walker Ave., **Le Moyne College** (coed.) is one of the oldest Negro colleges in the S. It was est. in 1871 by the Amer. Missionary Assoc. & confers B.A. & B.S. degrees. (22) NE. cor. Walker Ave. & Neptune St., **Elmwood Cemetery** is the oldest cemetery in Memphis still in use; official burial ground for the Confed. dead. (23) Riverside Blvd. & S. Parkway, **Riverside Pk.** is a natural wooded pk. of 427 as. bordering the Miss. R. for 1.5$^m$ along high grassy bluffs, with golf course, pic. grounds, an artificial L. & pavilions. (24) Reached by boat from the foot of Wisconsin Ave., **President's I.** is the largest I. in the 2,500$^m$

course of the Miss. R. It is 12$^m$ long with an area of 32,000 as., mostly farm land. (25) W. end of Colorado Ave., **De Soto Pk.,** where Hernando de Soto & his followers are believed to have discovered the Miss. R., May 21, 1541. (26) Spanning the Miss. R. at W. end of Virginia Ave., **Harahan Bridge** (1909), the 1st vehicle & RR. bridge across the Miss. R. (S) of Cairo, Ill. (27) Beginning at the inters. of Virginia Ave., & Delaware St., **Riverside Dr.** offers good view of the R. (28) Reached by wharf boats at the foot of Madison, Union or Monroe Sts., **City I.,** formerly Mud I. It was formed by mud & gravel deposits washed up by an eddy current against the stern of the "Aphrodite," a gunboat used in the Sp.-Amer. War, which had to anchor at Memphis for 6 or 8 mos. in 1910 because of low water farther up the Miss. In 1919 the Supreme Court placed title to the land in the City of Memphis. (29) Chelsea Ave. & N. 6th St., the 2nd fl. of **Chelsea Ave. Presb. Ch.** (1860) was a hospital for the Union soldiers, & the 1st fl. a storage place & stable for Army mules & horses during the War Bet. the States. (30) 697 Vance St., tents pitched on the campus of **St. Agnes College** in 1862 served as Gen. Sherman's hqs. It is the only women's college in Memphis & the only Cath. college in Tenn. (31) S. end of Lauderdale St., **Fed. Compress,** one of the largest cotton compressing plants in the world. Cotton bales intended for export are compressed to 32 lbs. per cubic foot.

## TRIPS OUT OF MEMPHIS

### I. MEMPHIS (NE) to J. of US70 & US64. 16. US70

At **12.** the route crosses Wolfe R. near the former **NASHOBA,** a plantation est. in 1827 by Frances Wright, wealthy Scottish orphan, who wanted to perfect a democratic Utopia. Her purpose was execution of a plan by which Negro slaves would be "educated & upraised to a level with the whites, & thus prepared for freedom." In less than 3 yrs. Miss Wright abandoned the plantation & made arrangements to ship her slaves to the W. Indies.

At **16.** is the J. of US70 & US64.

### II. MEMPHIS (N) to LOCKE. 12. US51

At **MILLINGTON, 8.,** is the J. with Shelby Dr. (L) on Shelby Dr. to **LOCKE, 12. Shelby Forest Pk.** lies bet. Locke & Island 39 in the Miss. The pk. was created as part of a program of erosion control, reforestation, & game preservation. Woodland covers 12,000 as. In a developed recr. sec. are 2 lakes (boat.swim.camp.pic.hik.). The adm. bldg. has an auditorium, a recr. hall, commercial amusement devices & a cafeteria.

# NASHVILLE

### NASHVILLE

RR., bus & air conns. Info.: C. of C., 315 4th Ave., N.; A.A.A., Hermitage Hotel, 6th & Union Sts. Excellent accoms. & recr. facils.; swim., golf, baseball, community playhouse & civic symphony. Iris Festival, Ap.; State Fair, Sept.; Horse Show, Sept.; Iroquois Mem. Steeplechase, May.

Nashville is the capital, 2nd largest city in Tenn. & seat of Davidson Cty. It is situated on both banks of the Cumberland R. in a bowl-like valley formed by a ring of wooded hills. The capstone of the city is the St. Capitol atop a high hill overlooking Victory Pk. Although an industrial city, Nashville generally retains the easy-going quality of the Old S. Nashville's 1st permanent residents were a party led by Jas. Robertson who sett. in 1779 near French Lick, now Sulphur Dell baseball pk. About a yr. later other settlers, their women & children, arrived by river boat. They est. 7 forts, called stations, along the Cumberland, with a pop. of c.300. The French Lick Sta. was named Ft. Nashborough in honor of Rev. War veteran Gen. Francis Nash. In 1784, legislature of N.C. set aside as a municipality a 250-a. tract on the W. side of the Cumberland R., incl. Ft. Nashborough. It was named Nashville because of prejudice against the English sounding Nashborough. By 1790 the town was a trade & mfg. center with mills, foundries, & smithies. The town was chartered as a city in 1806 with a mayor & six aldermen. Nashville became capital of the St., Oct. 6, 1843.

The steamboat brought river trade in 1818. The Nashville, Chattanooga, & St. Louis RR. was completed in 1854. During the War Bet. the States, most able-bodied men enlisted in the Confed. Army, & their families left behind suffered great privation. The city was surrendered to Feds. in Feb., 1862. Andrew Johnson, then U.S. Senator, was appointed military gov. of Tenn. in Mar., 1862, & city was placed under martial law. When Gen. Thos. Hood succeeded Gen. Jos. E. Johnston as commander of the Confed. Army facing Gen. Sherman in Ga. in 1864, he was ordered to move northward into Tenn. & to capture Nashville & thus cut Sherman's supply line. Hood encountered Fed. forces under Gen. John Schofield at Franklin & forced him to retreat to Nashville. Then in the Battle of Nashville, Dec. 15 & 16, the Confed. line collapsed badly under Fed. might, & a general retreat began. Hood's Army, completely demoralized & depleted, was virtually destroyed as an effective fighting unit. Nashville, as st. capital, was seat of the Unionist st. gov., & political corruption throve in the city gov. dominated by carpetbaggers. Not until 1875-76, when a great business boom began, did Nashville begin to regain lost ground. On May 1, 1897, Pres. McKinley officially opened the Centennial Exposition celebrating Tenn.'s 100th anniversary as a St. There has been extensive expansion, industrial, commercial & residential, during & after World War II.

PTS. OF INT.: (1) Capitol Blvd. bet. Union & Cedar Sts., **War Mem. Bldg.,** mem. to 3,400 Tenn. dead of World War I, contains **World War Mus.** (O) & the **St. Hist. Mus.** (O). (2) SW. cor. 6th Ave. N. & Union Sts., **Hermitage Hotel.** Lobby contains 20 paintings of Confed. scenes by Gilbert Gaul. (3) Cedar St. bet. 6th & 7th Aves. N., on Capitol Hill, **St. Capitol,** highest pt. in the city, was completed in 1855. It was built of fossilized limestone quarried by slaves & prisoners. The bldg. & grounds contain statues of Tenn. notables & tomb of Pres. Jas. Knox Polk & Mrs. Polk. Wm. Strickland, architect of the capitol, is buried in the N. wall. The bldg. follows plan of an Ionic temple with long gable of the roof broken by a central tower. (4) Deadrick St. bet. 1st & 3rd Aves. N., **Pub. Square,** set aside by the Assembly of N.C. in 1784. **Davidson Cty. Pub. Bldg. & Cth.** in the center contains murals by Dean Cornwell. The bldg. houses city & cty. offices, courts & cty. jail. **City Market** contains market stalls, restaurants & rest rooms. (5) 1st Ave. N. & Church St., **Ft. Nashborough** (O), was built in 1930 as model of the ft. built by Jas. Robertson & party on the site in 1780. (6) NW. cor. 4th Ave. N. & Church St., **Maxwell H.** (1869), one of South's most famous hotels, for which a nationally-known brand of coffee is named. (7) SE. cor. Church St. & 5th Ave. N., **First Presb. Ch.** (O.mod. Egyptian by Wm. Strickland). During War Bet. the States, Fed. Army used it as a hospital. (8) 605 Church St., **Watkins Institute,** was built in 1885 & endowed by Sam. Watkins to furnish free instruction. (9) 2006 West End Ave., **Nashville Art Mus.** displays traveling local exhibits. (10) 900 Broadway, **Christ Ch.** (Episc.O.). SE. vestibule wall contains a sm. piece of stone from old York Minster & another from ruins of Pompeii. (11) 2011 West End Ave., **Cathedral of the Incarnation** (Cath.O), designed by Aristide Leonard of Rome. (12) West End Ave. bet. 25th & 28th Aves. N., **Centennial Pk.** contains reprod. of the Athenian "Parthenon" which houses reprods. of the Elgin Marbles & a sm. art coll. (13) West End Ave. facing Centennial Pk., **Natchez Trace Marker** is at J. of old Wilderness Rd. from Knoxville & the Natchez Trace to Natchez, Miss.

(14) Entrance at West End Ave. & 23rd Ave. S., **Vanderbilt Univ.** has schs. of Arts & Sciences, Law, Engineering, Religion, Medicine, Nursing. The bldgs. are grouped on a 76-a. campus. (15) 21st Ave. S. & Edgehill Ave., **Geo. Peabody College for Teachers,** coed. with an av. enrollment of 1,000. Its 12 principal bldgs. are on 50-a. campus. (16) 1008 19th Ave. S., **Scarritt College** consists of 4 units conn. by cloisters on 9-a. campus. It grants bachelor's degree. (17) 16th Ave. S. & Belcourt Ave., **Ward-Belmont College,** for young women, has for its main bldg., **Belmont** (1850), former home of Col. J. A. S. Acklen, one of finest private homes in South. Sch. has both high sch. & jr. college depts. (18) Chestnut St. & Ridley Blvd., **Ft. Negley** (O), erected by Fed. Gen. Jas. S. Negley in 1862, was rest. 1937 by W.P.A. During Reconstruction Period the ft. was used as a meeting place of the Ku Klux Klan. (19) Oak St. & 4th Ave. S., **City Cemetery,** opened in 1822, contains tombs of many notable early settlers of Tenn. (20) 6th Ave. S. & Ewing Ave., **Holy Trinity Ch.** (1852.Negro), resembles old English parish ch. (21) At $4^m$ on Granny White Pike, **David Lipscomb College** (coed.Mod.Gr.Rev.) offers elementary, high sch. & jr. college courses; 40-a. campus. (22) E. end Shelby Ave., **Shelby Pk.** (361 as.), mun. garden with more than 500 varieties of iris. (23) Jefferson St. & 17th Ave. N., **Fisk**

**Univ.** (Negro), 40-a. campus & 20 bldgs. It is one of the few Univs. for Negroes in the South & the home of the famous Fisk Jubilee Singers & the Fisk Choir. (24) 1005 18th Ave. N., **Meharry Med. College** (Negro) awards M.D. & D.D.S. degrees & offers 3-yr. courses in pharmacy & nursing. It is the S.'s only medical college for Negroes. (25) 3300 Centennial Blvd., **Tenn. Agric. & Industrial St. Teachers College** (Negro), 80 as. overlooking Cumberland R.; accredited st. college granting B.A., B.S. & M.A. degrees. (26) 62nd Ave. N. & La. Ave., **Treaty Oak,** under which in June 1783 white settlers & Inds. made peace, is estimated to be at least 360 yrs. old. Around the Treaty Oak were campgrounds where Tenn.'s soldiers were mustered for every war from Jackson's Cr. campaign in 1813 to the Sp.-Amer. War in 1898.

## TRIPS OUT OF NASHVILLE

### I. NASHVILLE (NE) to GALLATIN. 27.5. US51

**7. SPRING HILL CEMETERY** (R) is on site of Ft. Union, built in 1780. Settlement became town of Haysboro where the First Presb. Ch. & 1st educational institution in middle Tenn. (Craighead Academy) were est. in 1785. (L) are buried 16,000 Fed. soldiers killed in battles of Nashville & Franklin. At **17.** is J. with narrow gravel Rd.

SIDE TRIP: (L) on this Rd. 2m to the entrance gate, from which a lane leads 0.5m to **Rock Castle** (O.appl.), one of 1st houses erected (W) of the southern Alleghenies & today still stands firm. The foundation was laid in 1784 but because of Ind. raids 7 yrs. were required to complete it.

**25. GRASSLANDS** is an estate of 15,000 as. purchased & developed by a group of N. sportsmen as a private sporting club. Plans to est. an internat. steeplechase were abandoned after market crash of 1929. At **27.5.** is **GALLATIN** (521′), seat of Sumner Cty. Town is agric. & livestock market center for city & central Burley tobacco market for Middle Tenn.

### II. NASHVILLE (NW) to SPRINGFIELD. 29. US41E

**12. GOODLETSVILLE. 18. RIDGETOP,** on edge of Highland Rim. **21. GREEN BRIER,** former home of the Green Brier Distillery. **26. PERRY PK.** (sm.fee) with swim. pool, dance pavilion & pic. grounds. **29. SPRINGFIELD,** seat of Robertson Cty., is a large tobacco market. Some 25,000,000 lbs. of tobacco are sold in an av. season. **Springfield Woolen Mills,** locally owned, receive wool as it comes from the sheep & perform all processes in the mfg. of fine blankets. Tenn. Fox Hunter's Assoc. sponsors an annual st. meet here the 1st week in Oct.

### III. NASHVILLE (NW) to CLARKSVILLE. 46. US41W

**5.** J. with White's Creek Rd.

SIDE TRIP: (R) 0.5m is **E. B. Smith H.,** one of several occupied by Frank & Jesse James & their wives during their last period in hiding.

At **12.** is J. with gravel Bernard Rd.

SIDE TRIP: (L) 2m is 87-a. **Marrowbone L.,** constructed by W.P.A. & administered by the St. Dept. of Conservation as a recr. area. (1,110 as.f.boat.swim.pic.facils.).

**46. CLARKSVILLE,** seat of Montgomery Cty., is on a peninsula at confluence of the Cumberland & Red Rs. Settlement was made in 1784, & town was named for Gen. Geo. Rogers Clark. Clarksville is now one of the leading dark-fired tobacco markets in U.S. **Clarksville Foundry & Machine Works,** Commerce & Spring Sts., molded cannon & cannonballs for Confed. Army. In the **Old Castle Bldg.,** College St. & Univ. Ave., is the **Austin Peay Normal Sch. Wilson H.,** S. 2nd St. & Munford Ave., was occupied for several yrs. by Dr. & Mrs. Jos. R. Wilson, parents of Pres. Woodrow Wilson, while Dr. Wilson taught at Southwestern Presb. Univ., formerly situated here.

### IV. NASHVILLE (W) to WHITE BLUFF. 30. US70

**6. LEAKE AVE.** (L) on Leake Ave. is entrance to **Belle Meade H.** (N.O.), on site of Dunham Sta., or Ft. Dunham, built in 1783. John Harding, who came to Nashville from Va., built 2 log cabins conn. by a dog trot. They still stand near the big house (1853). **9.** Summit of **NINE MILE HILL,** which offers a panorama of Nashville & surrounding countryside. **22.5.** J. of Dog Cr. Rd., unimproved.

SIDE TRIPS: (A) (R) on this Rd. [bear (L) all the way] to the Narrows of the Harpeth R., 4m, where R. makes hairpin curve around a ridge 0.8m long & 300′ high. A tunnel that runs through the base was chiseled out by slaves of one of the earlier settlers, Montgomery Bell. Water flowed through this tunnel to furnish power for an iron foundry.
(B) Near the confluence of Dog Cr. & the Harpeth R. lies the **Great Mound Group,** on both sides of US70. These belonged to a group of prehist. stone-grave Inds. The Great Mound, 50′ high, was topped by a ceremonial bldg. & surrounded by a palisaded town with clay-plastered circular houses. The city was probably a densely populated trading center, for it was on trls. that led to ancient towns in the Cumberland & Miss. Valleys & to others near Mobile Bay.

**30. WHITE BLUFF.** There is a coll. of 2,500 Ind. relics, the Reeder Coll., at the general store by the hy.

## V. NASHVILLE (S) to FRANKLIN. 18. US31

In 1862-63 this route was the chief military hy. in Middle Tenn. The Battle of Nashville was fought in the hills along the Rd. from Nashville to Franklin. At **3.** is the **PEACE MON.,** work of Ital. sculptor, G. Maretti, comm. Battle of Nashville. **4.** On grounds of **LONGVIEW** (R), some of the hardest fighting of Battle of Nashville took place. **Glen Leven** (N.O.1857) (L) was bet. the lines of 1st & 2nd days of the Battle of Nashville. After Confed. retreat, it was used as Fed. hospital. At **8.** is J. with a surfaced Rd.

SIDE TRIP: (L) 1m to J. with Kelly Rd.; (L) here 0.5m to **Gordon Site** at the end of the Rd. This is site of prehist. Ind. village that was surrounded by a palisaded stockade.

US31 cuts through a narrow gap, **14.,** known locally as **HOLLY TREE GAP.** Steep hills on both sides made the spot favorite resort of robbers in stagecoach days. **18. FRANKLIN,** seat of Williamson Cty. On Nov. 30, 1864, one of bloodiest battles of the War Bet. the States was fought in & around town. More high staff officers were killed in this battle than any other battle of the war. The Confeds. alone lost six generals: Adams, Carter, Cleburne, Gist, Granbury & Strahl. Five others were wounded, & one was captured. About 8,500 men fell in 55 minutes.

SIDE TRIPS: (A) (L) on St.96 1m is **Willow Plunge** (swim.pool.sm.fee).
(B) At 1m on St.96 is J. with good gravel Rd.; (R) to **Carnton H.** (O), used as a hospital after the Battle of Franklin; 1,500 Confed. dead are buried here.
(C) At 3m on St.96 is the **De Graffenried Works,** a group of Ind. mounds named for the farm on which they stand. The prehist. earthworks spread over 32 as. along the bluffs of the Harpeth R.

## VI. NASHVILLE (SE) to MURFREESBORO. 32. US41

**8. BERRY FIELD,** Nashville mun. airport. **29. NAT. CEMETERY** (L), est. in 1867 for burial of soldiers killed near Murfreesboro. Of 6,177 graves, 2,360 hold unknown men. **31. STONE'S R. NAT. MILITARY PK.** (R), est. in 1927 to preserve relics of the Battle of Stone's R. 10,000 Confed. & 13,000 Fed. troops were lost in the battle. A pyramid of cannon balls (L), at the inters. of N., C. & St.L. RR. & hy., is the site of **TEMPORARY HQS. OF GEN. BRAXTON BRAGG,** commander of the Confed. Army of Tenn. (R) **REDOUBT BRANNAN,** built by Fed. troops in 1863 to protect Murfreesboro from invasion by Confeds. **32. MURFREESBORO,** seat of Rutherford Cty., was capital of the St. from 1819 to 1825. Noted for purebred Jersey cattle it is also an important shipping pt. for cotton & dairy products. A red cedar bucket factory makes churns, ice pails, etc. **Tenn. College** (Bapt.), on Main St., is the only senior college exclusively for women in the st. **Middle Tenn. Teachers College** has av. enrollment of 2,100.

SIDE TRIP: (L) from Murfreesboro on St.96 is a **Huge Flat Rock,** 2m, covering 3 as. This is the geographical center of the St.

## VII. NASHVILLE (E) to LEBANON. 31. US70

At **5.** is J. with Pumping Sta. Rd.

SIDE TRIP: (R) on this Rd. to **Demonbreun Cave** (guide), 1m, for several yrs. the home of Timothe Demonbreun, Fr.-Canadian trader who came to the place c.1766 to trap & trade with the Inds. He moved to French Lick (Nashville) after other settlers came.

**7. DONELSON,** named for John Donelson, father-in-law of Andrew Jackson. US70 crosses Stone's R. at **BURR'S LANDING,** so named because Aaron Burr embarked here for New Orleans, Dec. 27, 1806, after failing to obtain Jackson's backing for his expedition. Where the hy. crosses Stone's R. is **CLOVER BOTTOM,**

site of an early 19th cent. racing club where Andrew Jackson & others from surrounding plantations raced their horses. At **13.** is J. with Old Hickory Blvd.

SIDE TRIP: (R) on this Rd. to the short avenue leading to the **Hermitage** (O.wks.8:30-6; Sun.2:30-6.sm.fee), former home of Andrew Jackson. It is now owned & maintained by the Ladies Hermitage Assoc. The house was built in 1819 & expanded in 1831. It has been kept as mem. to Jackson since a few yrs. after his death. The furnishings for the most part are his. Those that were not Jackson's are of his period. The H. is a fine example of Amer. Col. design. Graves of Jackson & his wife, Rachel, are in the formal garden.

**13. TULIP GROVE,** home of Andrew Jackson Donelson, nephew of Mrs. Andrew Jackson. The H. (1832) is architecturally as int. as the Hermitage. **31. LEBANON,** seat of Wilson Cty., noted for its tall cedars. Lebanon life revolves around little **Cumberland Univ.,** founded in 1842. Cordell Hull, Secy. of State under Pres. Franklin D. Roosevelt, & many other distinguished men in public life, were graduated here. Site of **Sam Houston's Law Office** is on N. side of E. Main St. Here in 1818 Houston began his legal practice. **Castle Hts. Military Academy,** at the edge of town, is an elementary & prep. sch. for boys.

## US 70—ARKANSAS

**ARK.-TENN. LINE** (across Miss. R. from Memphis, Tenn.) **(SW) to ARK.-OKLA. LINE** (73$^{m}$ from Hugo, Okla.). **297. US70**

Via: Forrest City, Brinkley, Little Rock, Hot Springs Nat. Pk. & De Queen. RRs. parallel route from Ark.-Tenn. Line to Hot Springs Nat. Pk. Accoms.: In larger towns, many tourist camps.

One of Ark.'s most heavily travelled routes, US70 cuts through middle of St., passing through cotton country W. of Miss., climbing wooded hills of Crowley Ridge, & descending to level farmlands of Ark. R. Valley & Little Rock, where it turns (SW) through rugged country, traversing pasture, orchard, & timberlands, whose hills are rich in bauxite, cinnabar, clay & other mineral products.

### Sec. 1: ARK.-TENN. LINE to LITTLE ROCK. 136.

**0.** US70 crosses **ARK.-TENN. LINE** on Harahan Bridge over Miss. **1.5.** J. with private Rd., leading (L) 0.5$^{m}$ to **Corps of Engineers Dist. Office & Maintenance & Repair Depot,** hqs. for War Dept.'s flood control work & channel & harbor maintenance in 27,000 sq. mile area incl. Miss. R. & tributaries. Facils. incl. 500-ton floating drydock, 1,800-ton marine ways & various shops & warehouses. In **W. MEMPHIS 6.** cafés & stores, garages, serv. stas. & tourist courts stretch for more than 3$^{m}$ along hy. Behind neon signs & modern facades are town's varied industrial plants. Founded about 1910, W. Memphis was known as Bragg's Spur until 1927. Its pop. almost quadrupled in 1930's & more than doubled in the 1940's. In W. Memphis is J. with US61 (see). **12.5.** J. with US79.

SIDE TRIP: Take latter (L) 20$^{m}$ to **Hughes,** started in 1913 with advent of Iron Mt. (now Mo. Pac.) RR., in reg. where cotton fields stretch to horizon & cotton gins rise by RR. tracks every few miles. 42$^{m}$ **Marianna,** named for an early settler's wife, is cotton town atop Crowley's Ridge.

(L) From Marianna on St.1 to J. with St.20, 15$^{m}$, & (L) here to **W. Helena,** 23$^{m}$, founded in 1909, an industrial town built around several large mills which produce boxes & crates, wood parts for automobiles, & veneer hoops. 26.5$^{m}$ **Helena,** locally promoted as "Arkansas' Only Seaport," is only Ark. city to which Miss. R. is still important as traffic artery. Hemmed bet. Crowley's Ridge on W. & levee on E., it has what Mark Twain called "one of the prettiest situations on the Miss." Helena, named about 1820 for an early settler's daughter, in antebellum days was center of culture on Delta, lively with R. commerce. Of strategic value during Civil War, it was occupied by Feds. in 1862 & vainly attacked by Confeds. in 1863. Processing of timber & cotton is Helena's chief occupation today. **Phillips Cty. Mus.,** Pecan & Perry Sts., has Ind. & pre-Columbian relics, pioneer & war mementoes & documents, & art gallery.

76$^{m}$ **Clarendon** at confluence of Cache & White Rs., whose post office was est. in 1819, is an old R. town still supported by R. traffic & products. Latter incl., besides fish, pearl buttons made from mussel shells. US79 now enters Grand Prairie, vast level tract, cultivated for more than a cent., where rice supplanted cotton as staple crop soon after Wm. H. Fuller produced Ark.'s 1st successful stand in 1904. 98.5$^{m}$ **Stuttgart,** "rice capital" of Ark., is town of clean bldgs., wide sts. & busy stores, in which most local industry centers around rice—mills, elevators, pump & storage-tank works, well-drilling companies, implement houses & machine shops.

From Stuttgart take St.30 (L) 27m to **De Witt,** rice-milling & cotton-ginning center & shipping pt. for timber & livestock.

(1) Take St.1 (L) from De Witt to White R. commercial fishing center, **St. Charles,** 16m, & St.17 (R) from St. Charles to hqs. of **White R. Nat. Wildlife Refuge** 16.5m (camp.f.no hunt.), sanctuary for wild ducks & geese of 117,000 as. extending 65m along White R. (2) Take St.1 (R) from De Witt to **Gillett,** 14m, rice & lumber-milling center. At 20m is J. with St.169, (L) on which is **Arkansas Post** at 23m, Ark.'s oldest white settlement & 1st capital. Here in 1686 Henri de Tonti placed garrison of Fr. soldiers. John Law, whose La. colonization scheme came to be known as "Miss. Bubble," chose post as seat of his intended duchy; he sent 500 Negroes here in 1717 & 800 white settlers, mostly Alsatians, in following yr. When "Miss. Bubble" burst in 1720, most of colonists, half-starved, abandoned settlement; only handful remained, living in cabins around ft. stockade. When Sp. acquired La. in 1763, they took possession of Ark. Post but failed to carry out plans for strengthening it. Post was occupied by Amer. troops in 1804 after Napoleon sold territory to U.S. Ark.'s Amer. settlers, however, passed it by, pushing up Arkansas R. to higher land; & although P.O. was est. in 1817 & newspaper in 1819, territorial capital, est. here in latter yr., was removed 2 yrs. later to Little Rock. Steamboat commerce on R. later turned Ark. Post into thriving port, with peak pop. of 3,000. Fortified by Confeds. in Civil War, it was attacked Jan. 10, 1863 & captured after 2-day battle by 30,000 Feds. under Gen. John A. McClelland. But after war, as R. commerce dwindled, Ark. Post lost its pop. Adj. town is **Ark. Post St. Pk.** (swim. cabins), created in 1930, 62-a. grove surrounding L. that covers Conf. trenches; only remnants of the past are handmade brick cistern & well probably dug by 18th cent. Sp. garrison.

SW. of Stuttgart, US79 cont. through rice & cotton fields to J. with US65 (see) at **Pine Bluff,** 140m (see US65).

**20. BLACK FISH L.** has reputation for its fishing. **43.5. FORREST CITY,** on W. slope of Crowley's Ridge, is surrounded by peach-growing dist. It grew out of RR. construction camp & was named for Confed. Gen. Nathan Bedford Forrest who had contracted to put RR. through Ridge. **68. BRINKLEY,** cotton, rice & lumber center, began as RR. camp during construction of Memphis & Little Rock RR., whose 1st train arrived here in 1871; it was named for RR. pres. R. C. Brinkley.

SIDE TRIP: Take St.17 (R) from Brinkley to **Cotton Plant** 11.5m, laid out in 1840 by cotton planter Wm. D. Lynch. Near-by occurred on July 7, 1862, Battle of the Cache (sometimes called Battle of Cotton Plant), in which Gen. Sam. R. Curtis' invading Feds. forced Gen. Albert Rust's Confeds. to retreat W. across Cache R.

**111.5. LONOKE,** named for a solitary oak that stood here in pioneer days, at J. with Rds. from rice fields to (E), strawberry patches to (N), & cotton plantations to (W & S) is shipping pt. for all three crops. It was home of Jos. T. Robinson, U.S. Senator, known to all Arkansas as "Joe T." At **113.5.** is **ARK. ST. FISH HATCHERY,** which stocks waters of every cty. with at least 1 truckload of fish annually. **134.5. NORTH LITTLE ROCK,** spreading along N. bank of Ark. R., is an industrial community marked by factories, oil tanks & water towers, whose large Mo. Pac. RR. repair shops serve as financial backlog. Town was laid out here in 1839, year after steam ferry began crossing R. here, by U.S. Army officer who named it De Cantillon for himself; but his venture was unsuccessful, probably because cypress bog covered much of the town site. Slowly settled, place came to be known as Huntersville, for good hunting in the vic., & later as Argenta, for hotel by that name built by Frenchman at ferry landing. In 1872 Cairo & Fulton RR. est. its north-shore terminal, & in 1873, RR. & vehicular bridge was built, named Baring Cross Bridge for Alex. Baring, English banker who invested funds in its construction. Around RR. shops built near bridgehead, grew up village of Baring Cross, later joined to Argenta. In 1890 Little Rock annexed part of Argenta, designating it as 8th Ward, which came to be known as N. Little Rock; but by legislative action, Argenta recovered its lost territory in 1903, & in 1917 officially adopted new name, N. Little Rock. 3m long **Seawall** along Arkansas R. was built in 1936 under supervision of U.S. Engineers to protect city from floods. **Mo. Pac. RR. Shops,** 8th St. & Pike Ave., covering 160 as., form N. Little Rock's most important industry. Other industrial establishments incl. **Greater Little Rock Stockyards,** 200 E. 11th St., opened in 1938 & **Temple Cotton Oil Mill,** 9th & Maple Sts., opened in 1880, 1st of its kind in city. N. Little Rock is at Js. with US65 (see) & US67 (see).

**136. LITTLE ROCK**

Through RR., bus & plane conns. Info.: C. of C., 231 Louisiana St. Accoms.: Numerous hotels & tourist camps. Swim. at Y.M.C.A., 6th St., & Broadway. Ark. Livestock Show & Rodeo (N. Little Rock), Oct.

Capital & leading city of Ark., Little Rock lies on S. bank of Ark. R., conn. by 5 bridges with N. Little Rock at pt. near center of St. Chromium-trimmed store fronts, air-conditioned bldgs. & sleek buses give city modern metropolitan aspect, but it still stays close to earth, its residential dists. luxuriant with hedges, trees & flowers; air is clear & smokeless, lawns are green yr. round & mockingbirds can be heard on downtown sts. Main St., chief commercial artery, running N. & S., is lined with brick bldgs. with modern store fronts. To W., Capitol Ave. leads to Capitol, rising from elevation at foot of hilly Pulaski Heights, one of newer residential sections, with curved drives, terraced lawns, hedges & evergreens. W. 9th St. is Little Rock's Harlem, business & amusement center for its Negro residents. Chief industrial dist., site of woodworking & furniture plants, cottonseed oil factories, flour & feed & chemical works & other industrial establishments, extends along R. from E. Markham St., chief commercial artery during steamboat era.

City derives its name from moss-grown rock jutting out from Ark. R.'s S. bank. It was this pt. that Bénard de la Harpe on an expedition from New Orleans in 1722 called "Little Rock" to distinguish it from huge sandstone bluff up-river on N. bank which came to be known as "Big Rock." White settlers found the former rock at crossing of 2 main avenues of travel, Arkansas R. & Great Southwest Trail, & marked ford across R. Here in 1812, Wm. Lewis built rough clapboard hut & took up claim to surrounding land, which in 1819 he sold to Wm. Russell, land speculator from St. Louis. Russell laid out in 1820 town site which he named Arkopolis, only to face competition from rival claimants, Jas. Bryan & Wm. O'Hara, who laid out town of their own on same site; rivalry was resolved only by court decision favoring Russell's claim in June, 1821. In same month new town became 2nd capital of Arkansas Terr. & was named Little Rock. Dense forest gave way to sts., market places, & cultivated fields; but for some years Little Rock remained boisterous frontier village. Steamboat traffic on upper Ark. R. began with visit of "Eagle" on March 16, 1822; in June, 1838 1st steam ferry across R. went into service. By mid-century, wharf at foot of Commerce St. was scene of lively traffic, as steamboats took on bales of cotton grown on rich R. bottomlands. Little Rock's pop. was still in 1850, however, only 2,167. City in 1863 became hqs. for Gen. Frederick Steele's Northern invaders, when Gen. Sterling Price's Confeds. retreated to Arkadelphia, having set fire to 8 gunboats; capital had already been removed to Washington, Hempstead Cty. Postwar recovery was slow, marked by political chaos culminating in "Brooks-Baxter War" of 1874, when armed forces of rival claimants for the governorship faced each other across Main St.

Last 3 decades of 19th cent. brought rapid development of commerce & industry. Mule-drawn cars appeared on Little Rock's streets in 1876 (& electric trolleys in 1888); telephones were installed in 1879, waterworks system in 1884, & electric street lights in 1888. Expansion of RRs. in St. during 1880's brought an upsurge in city's pop. from 13,138 in 1880 to 25,874 in 1890. Suburban real estate developments were opened as Little Rock entered automobile age in 20th century. World War I brought boom times as near-by Camp Pike (which during World War II was renamed Camp Jos. T. Robinson) was built to train soldiers. Throughout 1920's, bldg. boom continued, giving Little Rock new gov. & office bldgs., hotels & schs. Today Little Rock divides its interests among industry, commerce & gov.

PTS. OF INT.: (1) Outstanding among Little Rock's historic landmarks is **War Mem. Bldg.,** Markham St. facing Center St., generally considered Ark.'s most beautiful bldg. & one of South's best examples of Gr. Rev. architecture. Construction began in 1833, following plans drawn by designer of Kentucky Stateh., Gideon Shryock; for three-quarters of century it served as St. Capitol. (2) 3rd & Cumberland Sts., **Old Henderliter Place** (rest.1939), boarded-over log structure, was meeting place of last territorial legislature in Oct. 1835. Among Little Rock's most imposing ante bellum residences are (3) **Albert Pike H.** (1840), 411 E. 7th St., pillared 2-story brick mansion in park-like setting, former home of Albert Pike, explorer, attorney & author; (4) **Trapnall Hall** (1843), 423 E. Capitol Ave., red-brick mansion with pillared portico & vine-hung shutters; & (5) **St. Andrew's Sch.** (1840), white plastered brick Georgian mansion now occupied by Cath. parochial sch. (6) Wood Lane facing Capitol Ave., **Ark. St. Capitol** (1899-1916), set on knoll & framed by wide landscaped grounds, has long wings extending from a classic portico & tall dome encircled by Ionic columns (Cass Gilbert, architect). From marble-finished rotunda,

N. wing leads to Gov.'s reception room, S. wing to supreme court & its library, stairways to chambers of Senate & House of Representatives. On 3rd floor is **Ark. St. Hist. Mus.,** displaying aboriginal pottery, pioneer relics, portraits, & battle flags.
Little Rock's public bldgs. incl.: (7) **Little Rock City Hall,** Markham St. & Broadway; (8) **Pulaski County Cth.,** Markham & Spring Sts.; (9) **Fed. Bldg.,** W. Capitol Ave. & Arch St.; (10) **Pub. Lib.** (1910), 700 Louisiana St.; (11) **Jos. Taylor Robinson Mem. Auditorium** (1940), Markham St. & Broadway. (12) W. Markham & Van Buren Sts., **Fair Pk.,** Little Rock's largest, covering 200 as., has zoo. (13) E. 9th & Commerce Sts., adj. 36-a. **MacArthur Pk.,** on land which was U.S. Army post from 1836 to 1893, are: (14) **Ark. Mus. of Natural Hist. & Antiquities,** occupying Old Arsenal, only remaining post bldg. (rest.1940), & (15) **Little Rock Mus. of Fine Arts** (1937), housing St.'s most important coll. of paintings & art objects. City's educational institutions incl. (16) **Ark. Sch. for the Deaf,** Markham St. & Park Ave., adj. (17) **Ark. Sch. for the Blind;** (18) **St. Mary's Academy,** 3224 Kavanaugh Blvd., girls' school & (19) **St. John's Seminary,** foot of N. Taylor St., training school for priesthood, both Cath.; (20) **Univ. of Ark. Sch. of Medicine,** 12th & McAlmont Sts.; & (21) **Philander Smith College,** 11th & Izard Sts., Meth. Negro college. Among more notable churches are (22) **St. Andrew's Cathedral** (Cath.1882), 7th & Louisiana Sts.; (23) **Temple B'nai Israel** (1896), Capitol Ave. & Broadway; (24) **Immanuel Baptist Ch.** (1929), 14th St. & Park Ave.; (25) **Trinity Cathedral** (Episc.1884-88), 17th & Spring Sts.; & (26) **First Presb. Ch.** (1920), 8th & Scott Sts.

## Sec. 2: LITTLE ROCK to ARK.-OKLA. LINE. 161.

**8.5.** Cedar-shaded, 2-story brick **Stagecoach H.** (1836), designed by Gideon Shryock, architect of Little Rock's Old Capitol (War Mem. Bldg.), was stopping pt. on old Southwest Trail. **17.** J. with St.183.

SIDE TRIP: Take latter (L) to **Bauxite,** 6m, largely owned by Alcoa Mining Co. & inhabited chiefly by its employes. **Alumina Plant** here, built for U.S. Gov. beginning in 1941, is largest of kind in country. Few minutes' drive in any direction leads to one of mines which yield large proportion of bauxite dug in U.S. Ore is used to make aluminum, abrasives, & aluminum chemicals. Deposits were discovered in 1887 & have been mined since 1896.

**23.5. BENTON,** on site subdivided in 1836, is timber-processing & pottery-making center. In Benton is western J. with US67. **58.5. HOT SPRINGS NAT. PK.,** Ark.'s 3rd largest city & best-known resort, is wedged bet. 3 forested hills of Ouachita Mts. From Central Ave. chief business thoroughfare, curving through an almost gorge-like valley, streets dart at odd angles, up canyons & hillsides. Bathhouse Row, series of elaborate stone, brick & terra cotta bldgs. set among magnolias, elms & hedges, is site of unceasing procession of vacationers. Restaurants & hotels, refreshment stands, curio shops & shooting galleries, an alligator & an ostrich farm, & race-track all compete for tourist business. City is commercial center of wide area as well, with department stores, used-car lots, woodworking plants & other commercial & industrial establishments. Behind Bathhouse Row is **Hot Springs Mt.,** from depths of which rise 47 springs yielding daily flow of c.1,000,000 gallons with constant temp. of c.143 degrees, delivered from central reservoirs through insulated conduits to bathhouses. Of various theories advanced to account for presence of springs, most favored is meteoric theory, which supposes that rain water sinking underground is heated by mass of hot rock.
Probably 1st white men to visit springs were De Soto & his followers, believed to have explored reg. in 1541. Wm. Dunbar & Dr. George Hunter reached springs in Dec. 1804 & found log cabin & several board huts erected by early white visitors. In 1807 came 1st permanent settlers, in 1820 Joseph Millard opened hotel in dog-trot cabin, & in 1830 Asa Thompson built 1st bathhouses. U.S. Gov. set aside 4 sections of land around springs as reserv. in 1832. Accoms. remained primitive until after completion in 1875 of "Diamond Jo" narrow-gauge RR. from Malvern built by Chicago capitalist "Diamond Jo" Reynolds & passage by Congress in 1877 of act separating Hot Springs Reserv. from town & opening part of reserved territory to private development. By 1882, 10 bathhouses were in operation, & during same year Congress established Army & Navy Gen. Hospital. Fire levelled 50 blocks of stores & residences in 1913, but city was soon rebuilt. In 1921 Hot Springs Reserv. became Hot Springs Nat. Pk.; since that time, Rds., trls. & pic. grounds have been laid out in overhanging mts.

PTS. OF INT.: Of 8 bathhs. along magnolia-bordered Bathhouse Row on Central Ave., (1) **Quapaw Bathh.** is known for its grotto, where hot spring flows at rate of 180,000 gallons daily, & (2) **Fordyce Bathh.** for its top-floor Mus. containing coll. of Ind. artifacts. (3) **Display Hot Spring,** approached by promenade bet. Fordyce & Maurice Bathhs., gives an impression of flow of waters as they probably appeared to early visitors before they were enclosed & sealed. (4) Towering above city from SW. tip of Hot Springs Mt. is **Army & Navy Gen. Hospital** (1941), its two 5-story wings forming V which converges on 7-story central portion with 10-story tower. (5) Central Ave. & Oaklawn Blvd., **Oaklawn Jockey Club** has glass-enclosed, steam-heated grandstand facing 1m track; it is scene of annual 30-day racing meets in spring. (6) **Hot Springs Nat. Pk.** covers more than 1,000 as. ranging over Hot Springs, North, West, Sugar Loaf, & Ind. Mts. around city. **Pk. Adm. Bldg.,** Reserve & Central Aves., contains mus. with exhibits illustrating natural & ethnological history of reg. Trls., bridle paths & automobile Rds. lead to clearings overlooking city below. At summit of Hot Springs Mt. is 165′ steel **Observ. Tower,** reached by elevator, which commands fine view.

SIDE TRIP: Take US270 (L) from Hot Springs 3.6m to J. with gravel Rd.

(R) on this 2.5m to **Carpenter Hydroelectric Dam** on Ouachita R., whose turbines have capacity of 80,000 H.P.

At 13m is J. with dirt Rd.

(R) on this 3m to **Remmel Hydroelectric Dam,** which forms L. Catherine. **L. Catherine St. Pk.,** 2,048-a. tract of rolling woodland along L.'s W. shore, is popular among fishermen; Rds. & trls. run through pine forest.

**Magnet Cove,** 14m, valley among low hills, which may be ancient volcano crater or prehist. L. basin, comprises one of country's most remarkable assortments of minerals; geologists have counted 42 kinds, incl. lodestone, barite & titanium. 22.5m **Malvern** (see US67) is at J. with US67 (see).

From Hot Springs, US70 curves past tourist camps & roadside restaurants to (W) J. at **60.** with US270.

SIDE TRIP: Take US270 (R) across Ouachita R., 6m, into Ouachita Mts. At 12.5m is E. boundary of **Ouachita Nat. Forest,** created in 1907, tract of more than 1,300,000 as. extending (W) into Okla. where shortleaf pine predominates. At 18m is **Charlton Pic. Area. Mt. Ida,** 36m, grew up around general store opened here in 1836 by Granville Whittington; its livestock yards handle cattle from surrounding mt. pastures.

(L) from Mt. Ida on St.27 is lumber town of **Norman,** 9m, on Caddo R. at J. with St.8. (R) on St.8 to J. at 18m with gravel Rd. & (L) on this to **Camp Albert Pike,** 35m, tree-shaded camping area (f.swim.) where Little Mo. R. cascades over boulders into clear pools, named for Albert Pike, explorer, newspaperman, poet, Confed. general & authority on Freemasonry, who retired here in 1862 after resigning his military command with the Confed. & built house at this wild & beautiful spot.

US270 cont. to J. at 47m with gravel St.88.

(L) on this is **Pine Ridge,** 12m, which was a backwoods village named Waters until radio comedians Lum & Abner (who had vacationed here as boys), using its inhabitants & background for a hillbilly program, made it so self-conscious that it even adopted their new name for it at elaborate ceremonies held on steps of St. Capitol in Little Rock & broadcast over national hook-up. St.88 cont. (W) to J. with US71 (see) at 31m.

From Mt. Ida US270 cont. (W) through sparsely settled Ouachita Nat. Forest to its J. with US71 (see) at 71m.

US70 bridges 9,000-a. **L. Hamilton,** created by Carpenter Dam (see above) on Ouachita R. in 1931. Its shores are dotted by cabins, lodges & boat landings. **99. KIRBY,** at J. with St.27.

SIDE TRIP: Take St.27 (L) to **Murfreesboro,** 15m, whose products incl. peaches, grown in vast orchards extending (S), & cinnabar, ruby-red ore from which mercury is produced.

(L) from Murfreesboro on dirt Rd. at 3.5m is closed **Diamond Mine,** only one ever discovered & exploited in U.S., on site where in 1906 farmer John M. Huddleston picked up 2 diamonds. Mine operated bet. 1908 & 1925; although a few valuable stones were found, most were small & imperfect.

29.5m **Nashville** is brisk, modern little city, center of reg. in which modern farming methods & diversification of crops are practiced.

US70 now cuts through pine-forested country whose widely scattered farmers live almost completely self-sufficient lives. **127. DIERKS** has sch., row of stores, & cluster of hip-roofed company houses surrounding loading shed & noisy main plant of huge **Dierks Lumber & Coal Co. Mill,** whose specialty is pine vegetable crates. At **143.** is (E) J. with US71 (see), with which US70 unites (W) to **DE QUEEN, 152.** (see US71). **161. ARK.-OKLA. LINE.**

## US 61—ARKANSAS

**ARK.-MO. LINE** (22$^{m}$ from Hayti, Mo.) **(S) to ARK.-TENN. LINE** (adj. Memphis, Tenn.). **78. US61**

Via: Blytheville, Osceola & W. Memphis. RR. parallels route. Accoms.: Limited, except in larger towns.

US61, paralleling Miss. R., traverses rich black-loamed cotton country.

**0. ARK.-MO. LINE. 6. BLYTHEVILLE,** cotton growers' center with gin, compress & cotton oil mill, cannery & garment factory, was named for Rev. Henry T. Blythe, who sett. here in 1853. Cotton gin was est. here in 1888, & village slowly grew up. Thick stands of timber in vic. attracted RRs. & lumber companies after 1900. Drainage of land stimulated cotton-growing; & when World War I raised prices, cotton became boom crop. **24. OSCEOLA,** on site of Ind. village, dates back to 1830's. **35. WILSON** is cotton town, creation of cotton magnate Robert E. Lee Wilson; plantations owned by co. bearing his name stretch for miles (S). **72. WEST MEMPHIS** (see US70), is at J. with US70 (see), with which US61 unites (E) to **ARK.-TENN. LINE, 78.**

## US 65—ARKANSAS

**ARK.-MO. LINE** (74$^{m}$ from Springfield, Mo.) **(S) to ARK.-LA. LINE** (44.5$^{m}$ from Tallulah, La.). **327. US65**

Via: Harrison, Conway, Little Rock, Pine Bluff & McGehee. RRs. parallel parts of route. Accoms.: Only in larger towns.

US65 curves (SE) through rolling, wooded Ozarks to Ark. R. Valley & Little Rock, then follows cotton-growing Ark. R. Valley (SE) to Miss. R.

### Sec. 1: ARK.-MO. LINE to LITTLE ROCK. 167.

**0. ARK.-MO. LINE. 24.5. HARRISON,** metropolis of N. Ozarks, in valley of Crooked Cr., is shipping pt. for red cedar & hardwood; it has cheese factory, flour mill & grain elevator, & produce houses for poultry & eggs. Inc. in 1876, it grew rapidly after turn of cent., when Mo. & N. Ark. Ry. made it hqs. for its offices & shops.

SIDE TRIP: St.7 (R) from Harrison to J. with gravel Rd., 20.5$^{m}$, & (R) on this to **Diamond Cave** (guides.fee) at 24.5$^{m}$, discovered in 1832; explorers have penetrated it 21$^{m}$ without reaching end. Cave is noted for its stalactites & stalagmites.

**29.5.** J. with US62.

SIDE TRIP: Take US62 (L) to **Yellville** 25.5$^{m}$, named for Col. Archibald Yell, romantic figure in early Ark. politics.

(L) from Yellville on St.14 is **Buffalo R. St. Pk.** 17$^{m}$, 1,735-a. woodland tract overlooking Buffalo R. from sheer cliffs.

53$^{m}$ **Mountain Home,** seat & largest town of Baxter Cty. on high plateau bet. North Fork & White Rs., is outfitting pt. for vacation trips.

(R) from Mt. Home on gravel St.5 is **Norfolk,** 13.5$^{m}$ at confluence of N. Fork & White Rs., booming R. port at head of navigation during early 19th cent., whose **Wolf H.** (1809), "saddlebag" cabin overlooking R., now mus., was once unofficial gov. center for N. Ark. St.5 cont. to **Calico Rock,** 26.5$^{m}$, on White R.'s N. bank, so steep that Main St. is built in 3 decks; town is named for limestone bluff across R. vividly patterned with strange designs in color.

US62 cont. (E) across rolling, thinly sett. Ozark back country to **Pocahontas,** 158$^{m}$ (see US67), at J. with US67 (see).

US65 cont. (SE), passing through several small mt. towns, among them **WESTERN GROVE** at **38.5.** & **ST. JOE** at **50.5.** Store bldgs. of **MARSHALL** at **66.** have tin marquees, small windows & narrow double doors that indicate an old Ozark settlement. **74. LESLIE,** whose surrounding hills were once covered with stands of white oak, grew up around mills turning out barrel staves & heads. **94.5. CLINTON,** seat of Van Buren Cty., has quietly grown up around Cth. Sq. US65 glides down from Ozarks into cotton-growing country, to J. at **133.** with US64 (see US71). **135. CONWAY,** founded in 1871, was named for pioneer family which had 7 sons, 1 of whom became Terr. Delegate to Congress & 2 others, Govs. of Ark. It has shoe factory, bus-body works, several plants for processing agric. products. Bruce St. & Donaghey Ave., **Ark. St. Teachers' College,** 4-yr. coed. institution. 1400 Front St.,

**Hendrix College** whose history goes back to 1876. **162.** J. with St.176, leading (L) $3^m$ to **Camp Jos. T. Robinson,** military reserv. est. during World War I as Camp Pike, which housed in 1918 as many as 100,000 men. Reopened in 1940 to accommodate World War II soldiers, it was enlarged in area & hundreds of new barracks were erected. **165.5. NORTH LITTLE ROCK** (see US70) is at Js. with US70 (see) & US67( see). **167. LITTLE ROCK** (see US70).

**Sec. 2: LITTLE ROCK to ARK.-LA. LINE. 160.**

**44.5. PINE BLUFF** lies at edge of far-reaching cotton fields along deep bend of Ark. R., bisected by two parallel RRs. along which are strung leading industries—lumber mills, cotton compresses & seed-oil mills, stockyards & repair shops. Here in 1819 came Jos. Bonne to start trading post on pine-covered bluff by R.; settlement grew up around it. Pop., only 460 in 1850, more than tripled in next decade as more & more steamboats stopped to take on cargoes of cotton; & plantation owners began bldg. ornate town houses. Here was fired what is locally claimed to have been 1st shot in Civil War in Ap. 1861 when several Fed. boats steaming upriver with military supplies were stopped & their cargoes seized for Confed. Army. Later, on Oct. 25, 1863, Col. Powell Clayton's Fed. troops, barricaded with cotton bales, successfully resisted Confed. attack on city. During Reconstruction period, Pine Bluff became Ark.'s leading cotton port. Following advent of RRs. in 1870's & 1880's, it became important RR. repair & lumber mill center as well. Of recent importance has been large-scale trading in livestock, begun in 1936. Barraque & Main Sts., **Jefferson County Cth.** (1858.mod.Georg.remod.adds.) dominates business sec. with its dome-capped clock tower. N. Cedar St., **Ark. Agric., Mechanical & Normal College** is St. institution for Negroes, opened in 1881. Among Pine Bluff's ante bellum mansions are **Portis H.** (1844), 216 E. 2nd Ave., & **Thompson H.** (c.1860), 519 W. Barraque St. 1115 W. 4th Ave., **Bocage H.** (1866) is architecturally interesting. US65 now crosses endless cotton fields, passing sharecroppers' cabins & plantation houses. Most of towns are small, clustering around RR. cotton-loading platforms & gins. Among larger ones are **GOULD** at **78.5.** & **DUMAS** at **87. 99.5.** J. with St.138.

SIDE TRIP: (R) on latter to J. with St.4 $6.5^m$, & cont. (straight ahead) on St.4 to **Monticello,** $22^m$, tree-shaded town among timbered hills, center of tomato-growing reg., (L) from which $3.5^m$ on St.13 is **Ark. Agric. & Mechanical College,** 4-yr. St. institution, housed in group of mostly Mod. bldgs. on landscaped campus.

**106. McGEHEE,** principal commercial center of SE. Ark., named for plantation owner Col. Abner McGehee, was spurred into industrial prominence by est. here in 1905 of Iron Mt. Ry. (now Mo. Pac.) repair shops. **130.5. LAKE VILLAGE,** est. in 1850's on curving shore of L. Chicot, has long been resort (f.boat.hunt.). Cotton gins, stave mills & commercial fishing provide income. Horseshoe-shaped **L. Chicot,** Ark.'s largest natural L., is abandoned channel of Miss. R., $15^m$ long & $0.5^m$ wide. **148. EUDORA** is cotton-ginning & sawmill town with usual red-brick stores & offices. **160. ARK.-LA. LINE.**

## US 67—ARKANSAS

**ARK.-MO. LINE** ($23.5^m$ from Poplar Bluff, Mo.) **(SW) to TEXARKANA, ARK. 337. US67**

Via: Pocahontas, Newport, Searcy, Little Rock, Malvern, Arkadelphia & Hope. Mo. Pac. RR. parallels route throughout. Accoms.: In larger towns.

Cutting diagonally across Ark. from NE. to SW., US67 divides St. into 2 triangles—to S., level, fertile Miss. delta; to N., rocky, forested region of Ozark & Ouachita Mts.

**Sec. 1: ARK.-MO. LINE to LITTLE ROCK. 182.**

**0. ARK.-MO. LINE. 7. CORNING** has 19th cent. air, its sts. lined with trees & its sidewalks shaded by tin marquees. **34.5. POCAHONTAS,** booming Black R. port in 1870's, climbs irregular valley wall, its narrow sts. hemmed by brick bldgs. Pocahontas is at J. with US62 (see US71). **49. WALNUT RIDGE** & **51. HOXIE,** conn. by an unbroken line of houses, are surrounded by flat lands where diversified crops & mechanized farming are in evidence.

SIDE TRIPS: (A) Take St.25 (L) from Walnut Ridge to J. with gravel Rd., 13m.

(R) on this 3.5m to **Crowley's Ridge St. Pk.** (swim.boat.camp.cabins), 347-a. tract on W. slope of rugged eminence named for early settler Ben. Crowley, whose home site & burial place pk. covers.

St.25 cont. to **Paragould** 29m, orig. lumber town named for 2 RR. men, J. W. Paramore & Jay Gould, which now has cotton gins, cold storage plants, canneries & shirt factory besides RR. shops & woodworking plants.

(B) Take US63 (L) from Hoxie to **Jonesboro** 23.5m, comfortable, conservative community spread on level expanse of Crowley's Ridge in diversified-farming area. It came into being around cth. built here in 1859 in clearing in underbrush to house gov. of newly created cty. named for St. Sen. Thos. B. Craighead who had opposed its formation; town was named for St. Sen. Wm. Jones who had advocated it. Inc. in 1883, it became by turn of cent. thriving sawmill town & afterward agric. trading center.

**87.5. NEWPORT** derives its commercial importance from its position on White R. & as RR. intersection. Gathering & shipping of pecans, picked from trees that grow wild in R. bottoms, is 1 of its chief activities. US67 now passes through Ark.'s chief strawberry-growing area, where fruit is picked in late spring & early summer. At **123.** is J. with US67W, leading (R) 7m to **Searcy,** 1st known as Sulphur Springs for now-vanished medicinal springs which made it popular 19th cent. health resort and now site of **Harding College** (opened 1889), Grand Ave. & E. Center St., coed. institution conducted by Christian Ch.; US67W rejoins US67 at 11m. Long storage & shipping sheds near RR. sta. at **144. BEEBE,** stand unused except during strawberry season. **180.5. NORTH LITTLE ROCK** (see US70) is at Js. with US70 (see) & US65 (see). **182. LITTLE ROCK** (see US70).

SIDE TRIP: Take US167 (L) from Little Rock to **Sheridan** 34m, lumber town & farmers' trading center. 68.5m **Fordyce** has cotton gins, lumber mill & woodworking plants, casket factory & service industries. 74m **Thornton.** J. with US79.

Take latter (R) to **Camden** 25m whose 3 RRs. & Ouachita R. traffic make it important shipping & distributing pt. By 1844 it was prosperous steamboat port. Schs., newspaper & woolen mill appeared before Civil War. When steamboat traffic waned, it retained its commerce as RR. center. Improvement of navigation on Ouachita by series of locks & dams (1915-26) reawakened int. in R. transportation, & Camden is now head of barge-line serv. to New Orleans. Among chief industrial establishments are the $130,-000,000 **Naval Ordnance Plant** on E. edge of town & **Camark Pottery Plant** on S. Edge; it has also woodworking, paper, roofing & beverage plants. Camden is at J. with St.7. Turn (L) on this to **Southern Kraft Corp. Pulp Plant** at 28m, larger of Ark.'s 2 pulp mills, which uses more electricity, gas & water than entire residential sec. of Little Rock. St.7 cont. to **Smackover** 44.5m which turned overnight from backwoods village into frenzied boom town when 1 of country's major oil fields was discovered here in 1922. Name "Smackover" is corruption of designation "Sumac-couvert" given place by early Fr. hunters who found dense sumac thickets here. At 57.5m is **El Dorado** (see below) at J. of St.7 with **US167.**

US167 cont. (S) from Thornton to **Hampton** 91m, once thriving sawmill center, & **Calion** at 106.5m, once prosperous steamboat port on Ouachita R. which revived with construction of RR. bridge & sawmills in early 1900's & of hy. bridge & barge terminal in 1930's. 118.5m **El Dorado,** "oil capital" of Ark., is prosperous city of imposing public & bus. bldgs. & comfortable residences, important not only for petroleum production & refining, but also as distribution center for lumber & agric. communities throughout S. Ark.-N. La. timber belt. It grew up around log cth. & hotel erected here in 1844 on land donated by 1st settler Matthew F. Rainey. It was still sm. village when 1st RR. came in 1891. Timber boom of early 1900's brought brief interval of prosperity but not until 1921, when oil began to flow from Busey Well 1m to W., did El Dorado become important. Within few weeks it was swamped by a pop. of more than 20,000. By end of 1921 c.460 wells had been drilled in vic. Recovering from 1st impact of boom, El Dorado soon transformed itself into city with an elaborate program of schs., chs., civic bldgs., streets & sewers. Today its chief industrial est., **Lion Oil Refinery,** S. end of Marsh Ave., largest of city's 4, is 1 of Ark.'s biggest industrial plants. El Dorado is at J. with St.7 (see above).

## Sec. 2: LITTLE ROCK to TEXARKANA. 155.

US67 unites with US70 (see) from Little Rock to **BENTON** at **23.5.** (see US70). **44.5.** Continuous-process **PERLA PLANT,** of Acme Brick Co., consists of series of corrugated-iron bldgs. & turret-roofed kilns, each on different level, conn. by winding narrow-gauge track. **45.5. MALVERN,** inc. in 1874, has, like many other Ark. cities, brick bus. bldgs. & frame residences. Vic. furnishes steady supply of timber for several lumber mills & tool-handle factory; in addition, city has ceramic, mineral, chemical & textile industries. US67 descends into valley of Ouachita R., where **ARKADELPHIA 72.,** is built along bluffs of valley wall. Founded in 1836, it became important steamboat landing, & maintained its commercial importance after advent of RR. Ouachita Ave. & 5th St., **Ouachita College,** Baptist coed. institution. 11th St. at Henderson Ave., **Henderson St. Teachers College,** former Meth. institution (est. 1890) taken over by St. in 1929. **88. GURDON,** RR. junction pt., was birthpl. in 1892, at height of Ark. timber boom, of Concatenated Order of Hoo Hoo, conceived in horseplay spirit by bored lumbermen, which spread throughout S. lumber country & later into NW. & Canada. **105.5. PRESCOTT,** lumber town in 1873, became trading center & cotton-shipping pt., as land was cleared. Marketing of produce from fruit- & vegetable-raising area stretching SE. is now leading activity. **121. HOPE,** leading fruit-shipping point, is Ark.'s "watermelon capital." Melons big as hogsheads are grown. It also has cotton compress & gins, furniture factory, basket & crate factory, handle plant & brick kiln.

SIDE TRIP: Take St.4 (R) to **Washington** 9m, St. capital in 1863-65 & Hempstead Cty. seat until 1938, now living mus. of old houses, old trees & old memories. Growing up around tavern built by Elijah Stuart in 1824 as stopping pt. on Southwest Trl., it acquired pop. of 2,000 before Civil War, when it became gathering place for Southern refugees (among them Gov. Flanagin & his staff) & its "Washington Telegraph" became 1 of few papers left W. of Miss. to publish war news from Confed. standpoint. Ark. legend claims it was place where Jas. Bowie's famous knife, reputedly hammered out here in Jas. Black's smithy, was invented; communities in Miss., La. & Tex. make same claim. **Old Hempstead County Cth. & St. Capitol** (1833.rest.1930), center of town, 2-story edifice with classic portico, was cty.'s legal hqs. until 1875 & St.'s in 1863-65. **Washington Tavern** or Travelers' Inn (1830), Franklin Ave. & St.4, was built mostly of hand-hewn timber & later weather-boarded. **Old Baptist Ch.** (c.1830) is sm. frame bldg. with pediment supported by columns.

**134.5.** Beside Red R., **FULTON,** founded in 1813 as frontier trading post, was jumping-off place at end of Amer. sec. of SW. Trl. for expeditions into Mex. territory. **155. TEXARKANA,** astride Ark.-Tex. boundary, is, formally, 2 cities in 2 Sts., separated only by imaginary line down middle of St. Line Ave. which bisects combined bus. sec. Legally 2 towns, each with its own mun. gov., sch. system & fire & police depts., it is socially & economically a unit. Although it has wood-working, clay products, vegetable canning, cotton compress & cottonseed oil plants among others, it is chiefly marketing & distribution pt., with 4 major RRs. City grew, beginning in 1873, out of RR. construction camps at W. terminus of Cairo & Fulton (now Mo. Pac.) RR. & E. terminus of Tex. & Pac. An untamed locality teeming with adventurers & gamblers in its early years, it gradually settled down to pursuit of prosperity. Among landmarks is **Fed. Bldg.,** middle of St. Line Ave. bet. 5th & 6th Sts., housing 2 Fed. courts, whose E. entrance is in Ark., its W. in Tex. & its center on boundary line.

## US 71—ARKANSAS

**ARK.-MO. LINE** (32m from Neosho, Mo.) **(S) to ARK.-LA. LINE** (39m from Shreveport, La.). **335. US71**

Via: Fayetteville, Ft. Smith, Mena & Texarkana. RRs. parallel parts of route bet. Ft. Smith & Texarkana. Accoms.: In larger towns, tourist camps in Ozarks.

US71 crosses fertile plateau in Ark.'s NW. cor., then plunges over Ozarks to Ft. Smith in Ark. R. Valley. It cuts (S) through timbered country, skirting Ouachita Mts., & emerges into wide flat lands, descending to fertile Red R. Valley.

### Sec. 1: ARK.-MO. LINE to FT. SMITH. 113.

**0. ARK.-MO. LINE. 2. SULPHUR SPRINGS** is spa with bathhouses & tourist camps. Hy. now crosses fertile country where apple orchards alternate with grain fields. **24. BENTONVILLE** handles poultry & dairy products as well as apples. Founded in 1837.

SIDE TRIP: Take St.100 (L) from Bentonville 5m to **Bella Vista,** well-patronized resort (golf.tennis.riding.swim.dancing), (R) 1m from which is **Wonderland Cavern,** huge underground cavern used as ch., night club & convention hall.

**31.5. ROGERS,** besides shipping poultry & apples, produces vinegar, canned milk & lumber products. J. with US62.

SIDE TRIP: Take US62 (L) to J. with St.72, 12m.

Turn (L) on this. At 14m **Site of Battle of Pea Ridge,** Ark.'s most important battle in Civil War. Here on March 6, 1862, Confed. force of Missourians, Texans & Okla. Cherokee commanded by Gen. Earl Van Dorn tried unsuccessfully to wipe out Fed. troops under Gen. Sam. R. Curtis advancing (S) from Mo.

US62 now passes (E) through rugged country, skirting deep canyons & rearing over high summits. It climbs from **White R.** at 26.5$^m$ to **Inspiration Pt.** at 29$^m$, affording impressive view. 36.5$^m$ **Eureka Springs,** climbing steep slopes from single winding st., has been catering to health-seekers for half century. Within city limits, 63 springs have been counted; caves also abound. 49$^m$ **Berryville** where on Sat. evenings in summer, fruit & dairy farmers & families from near-by hills & valleys join workers from sawmill & woodworking plant in crowded stores. At 73$^m$ is J. with US65 (see).

**42.5. SPRINGDALE,** another apple-shipping center, is at J. with St.68.

SIDE TRIP: Take latter (R) to **Siloam Springs,** 25$^m$, poultry & apple-shipping center which grew up around several iron & sulphur springs. (R) from Siloam Springs 1$^m$ is **John Brown Univ.** on 800-a. campus; interdenominational institution emphasizing vocational training & Bible study.

**50.5. FAYETTEVILLE** has been NW. Ark.'s leading town since 1st lots were sold in 1828. It became home of several sm. colleges in 1840's & 1850's. During Civil War its position halfway bet. Fed. base at Springfield, Mo. & Confed. positions on Ark. R. made it strategic goal for both armies; it changed hands many times, & colleges, stores & most of houses went up in smoke. In 1871 it became home of Ark. Industrial Univ., later renamed Univ. of Ark., whose presence, as well as healthful climate & town's nearness to Mts., has attracted professional men, writers, artists & retired farmers. Industries incl. fruit & vegetable canneries, woodworking plants, garment & wagon-mfg. mills. Arkansas Ave. & W. Dickson St., **Univ. of Ark.** with its various classroom bldgs., athletic stadium & Greek theater, centers around **Adm. Bldg.** (1875), stones for whose foundation were hauled by ox-wagon 70$^m$ over rough Mt. Rds. Univ. comprises schs. of lib. arts, education, engineering, agric., bus. adm., law, extension & grad. work, & has sch. of medicine at Little Rock. Among Fayetteville's ante bellum residences are **Waxhaws** (c.1835), S. College Ave.; **George Reed H.** (c.1835), W. Dickson St.; **Quesenbury H.** (1854), S. Duncan St.; & **Tibbetts H.** (late 1840's) 118 E. Dickson St. US71 climbs (S) into Ozarks, to **WINSLOW, 73.** on divide bet. watersheds of White & Ark. Rs. with highest altitude of any inc. town in Ark.

SIDE TRIP: Take St.74 (R) from Winslow to **Devil's Den St. Pk.** at 8$^m$, 4,320-a. tract of heavily wooded Mt. country (cabins.camp.trls.bridle paths.f.swim.).

Through rugged country, hy. climbs to summit of **MT. GAYLOR, 77.,** affording far-reaching vista. **79. ALBERT PIKE MUS.** (sm.fee) is log schoolroom in which explorer, soldier & writer for whom it was named taught in 1832; moved here from orig. site near Van Buren; houses hist. relics & early Amer. glassware. From Mt. top at **84.5.** appears 1st view of 640-a. **Lake Ft. Smith,** impounded by dam across Clear Cr. to provide Ft. Smith's water supply. **100. ALMA** is at J. with US64.

SIDE TRIP: Take latter (L) following Ark. R. valley (E) to **Clarksville** 48$^m$ which celebrates peach harvest in surrounding orchards with festival in July. N. end of College Ave., **College of the Ozarks** is 4-yr. coed. institution maintained by Presb. Ch. 74$^m$ **Russellville,** center of wide trade territory, depends on coal mines in vic., lumber mill & woodworking plants, cotton compress & gins. Named for Brit.-born Dr. J. T. Russell, settler in 1830's; inc. in 1870. 313 W. 8th St., **George Black H.** contains most famed Ark. painting, **"The Arkansas Traveler,"** done in 1858 by Ed. Payson Washburn, reprods. of which hung in drawing rooms all over Amer. in Vict. era. 100.5$^m$ **Morrilton** dates from advent of RR. in 1870's; has textile factory & oil mill, livestock yards & meat packing plant, cheese factory, bottling plants, lumber mills & woodworking plants.

Take St.9 (R) from Morrilton to J. with St.154, 4$^m$, & turn (R) on this to **Petit Jean Mt.** 9$^m$, named for Fr. aristocrat Jean la Caze, who fled Rev. & came here from New Orleans, where he went mad after death of his wife & child & was found by early Amer. settlers living on berries & playing his flute on Mt. 14.5$^m$ **Petit Jean St. Pk.** (lodge. cabins.bridle trls.pic.boat.f.swim.) is 2,999-a. tract of pine-covered plateau. St.154 cont. from **L. Bailey,** near entrance, past some of pk.'s chief features: 15.5$^m$ **Pioneer Cabin,** 16$^m$ **Cedar Falls** & (just beyond) **Mather Lodge,** 17$^m$ **Bear Cave** & 17.5$^m$ **Palisades.**

At 119$^m$ is J. of US64 with US65 (see).

**108. VAN BUREN** would be known primarily as once-important frontier post & stagecoach stop which eventually became subordinated to adj. city of Ft. Smith, had it not been given nat. publicity by Bob Burns, radio humorist. **Bob Burns H.,** 9th & Jefferson Sts., is local landmark. 1st settlers came as early as 1818; town was laid out 20 yrs. later. It became important outfitting place for expeditions into Ind. country & Tex., distributing pt. for goods shipped by steamboat up Ark. R. & main stop on Butterfield stagecoach route to W. Coast. US71 crosses **ARK. R.** at **109.**

**113. FT. SMITH,** 2nd largest, & most industrialized city in Ark., spreading (E) from Okla. Line at pt. where Ark. R. enters St., has, for economic support, factories that make furniture & brick, scissors, cans & glass; farms that raise corn, livestock & truck crops; & Sebastian Cty.'s coal mines. Along its unusually wide main bus. thoroughfare is concentration of hotels, restaurants & dept. stores surprising for city of its size; throughout tree-shaded residential dists. are gardens & pkwys. Military post for which city was named was est. here in 1817 to keep peace bet. Osage & Cherokee. Around 2 log blockhs. & several barracks on oak-shaded R. bluff, village took form. Stronger fortifications were built beginning in 1838. Almost overnight in 1849 town became supply depot & pt. of departure for Gold Rush emigrants to Cal. After Civil War it became seat of Fed. Dist. Ct. charged with jurisdiction over 74,000 sq. miles of Ind. Terr. to W. from which white offenders—train robbers, murderers, bank bandits—roaming in outlaw bands were brought in by hard-riding force of deputy marshalls for trial. Ft. Smith's transition from frontier post to city dates from 1871, when Ft.'s garrison was withdrawn. 1st RR. arrived in 1879; 2nd, 3 yrs. later. Opening of coal mines in vic. stimulated city's growth; drilling of natural gas wells near-by after 1900 attracted industries. Today, although it is trading center of wide agric. area, Ft. Smith derives its principal income from its factories & smelters. Highly unionized, it is Ark.'s most labor conscious city. It still celebrates its past with Wild West festival (May).

PTS. OF INT.: Of orig. military post, all that remains is (1) **Old Fort,** SW. cor. 3rd St. & Rogers Ave., intended orig. as barracks but remod. into courtroom & jail about 1843 & afterwards seat of Fed. Dist. Ct. & (2) **Old Commissary** (1839), S. side Garrison Ave. near Mo.-Pac. tracks, an iron-barred stone bldg. guarded by 2 cannons, now mus. of frontier relics. (3) S. end of 6th St., **Nat. Cemetery** was set aside in 1832 as burial ground for soldiers at Ft. & in 1867, was given national status. Other landmarks incl. (4) **Old Brewery** (c.1858), N. 3rd & E Sts.; (5) gabled, gambrel-roofed **Weaver H.** (1848.adds.), N. 4th & A Sts.; & (6) **B. L. E. Bonneville H.,** 3215 N. O St., former residence of soldier-explorer who was thrice commander of Ft. Smith & whose exploits were presented by Washington Irving in "The Adventures of Captain Bonneville." Ft. Smith is at J. with St.22.

SIDE TRIP: Take latter (L) 40.5m to **Paris,** center of St.'s chief coal mining area, which yrs. of activity by United Mine Workers have made into one of Ark.'s few strong union towns, & 46.5m **Subiaco,** dominated by twin medieval-style towers of **Subiaco College & Abbey,** self-sustaining Benedictine institution, which began as mission founded by 3 monks in 1878. 77.5m **Dardanelle** is 1 of Ark. R. Valley's oldest settlements, platted in 1843 but sett. earlier. Beyond N. end of Front St. is **Dardanelle Rock,** landmark for early explorers, jutting into Ark. R.; it commands impressive view.

(L) from Dardanelle on St.155 at 7m is **Mount Nebo St. Pk.** (pic.pavilion.cabins.baseball.bridle paths), 3,375-a. pine-covered area on slopes of Mt. (1,750′) offering fine view.

At Dardanelle is J. with St.7; (L) on St.7 is **Russellville** 82.5m (see above), at J. with US64 (see).

## Sec. 2: FT. SMITH to ARK.-LA. LINE. 222.

**17.5. GREENWOOD** is Sebastian Cty.'s chief coal-shipping pt. **29.5. MANSFIELD** & **49.5. WALDRON** are farmers' trading communities. At **63.5.** is J. with US270 (see US70). **85. MENA** was founded in 1896 when Kansas City S. RR. came through. Name Mena, contraction of Wilhelmina, was tribute to Queen of Netherlands by RR.'s Dutch investors. Its city hall until 1939 was log cabin built in 1851 on town site, which RR. engineers used as hqs. & left standing; cabin remains, little changed, in **Janssen Pk.** Mena is sportsmen's center, seat of Polk Cty.'s Possum Club, founded 1913, which annually in Dec. stages celebration during which persimmon trees are set up & festooned with live opossums, while hounds bay frantically. It is center of wide trade area; its industrial plants incl. gins, flour & feed mills, & woodworking plants & lumber mills. US71 passes through timberland, dotted with occasional farmed clearings & several small towns, to **DE QUEEN** at **134.,** orig. known as Calamity. It was renamed by Dutch capitalist, DeGeoijen, who bestowed his own surname on it when Kansas City S. RR. gave him privilege of christening several towns along right-of-way. DeGeoijen was soon anglicized to De Queen. De Queen is at (W) J. with US70 (see), with which US71 unites (E) for 9m. Beyond **RED R. 177.5.,** US71 crosses briefly into Texas, then rides St. boundary Line to **TEXARKANA** at **190.5.** J. with US67 (see). At **222.** is **ARK.-LA. LINE.**

# THE SOUTHWEST

## OKLAHOMA — TEXAS
## NEW MEXICO — ARIZONA

The far-flung Southwest, comprising Oklahoma, Texas, New Mexico & Arizona—a sun-baked stretch of plain & river valley, desert & mountain range, canyon & mesa extending west from the Sabine River to the Colorado & bordered on the south by the Rio Grande & Mexico—is in some ways the most ancient & in others the most modern part of the U.S. Oklahoma, New Mexico, & Arizona were the last of the 48 states to be admitted to the Union; & much of New Mexico & Arizona, along with much of western Texas, remains a still somewhat thinly settled region, where the sombreroed Spanish-Americans & booted cowboys of frontier days are yet to be found in real life.

All over Arizona & New Mexico are remnants of the advanced civilization achieved by prehistoric cliff-dwellers, & throughout the Southwest, the culture of its aboriginal inhabitants—whose descendants are far more numerous in Oklahoma, New Mexico & Arizona than anywhere else in the nation—has left a vivid impress. Texas, New Mexico & Arizona are dotted with the presidios & missions of the Spanish conquerors, dating back as far as the seventeenth century; more than three centuries of Spanish & Mexican rule have left a heritage of Spanish place names, architecture & cuisine—as well as a large Spanish-speaking population, since swelled by emigration from across the border. But, throughout the Southwest, side by side with the relics of the past, have appeared in the last half century signs of the present: skyscraper-dotted cities, super-highways & vast airports, oil fields & chemical plants, huge dams & irrigation projects & seaports—all with an air of challenging newness. Civilization has come late, perhaps, but largely, just for this reason, the Southwest has on the whole been spared the blighting effects of 19th-century industrialism: its young cities, mostly smoke-free because fueled with gas or electricity rather than coal, tend to be spacious & modern-looking & its industrial areas trim & efficiently planned. Its mineral resources & its plentiful supply of petroleum & natural gas have pushed it well on the way to becoming the center for the world's chemical industries.

This is a land of magnificent distances: Texas is the largest of the 48 states—as large as New England, New York, New Jersey, Pennsylvania, Ohio & Illinois combined—& New Mexico & Arizona are, respectively, the fourth & fifth largest. Space is the keynote of the land—vast, almost limitless stretches of plain, semi-desert & lofty mountains, buttes & mesas. Topographically, the Southwest comprises parts of several of the broad continental divisions within its area: the Coastal Plain, along the Gulf of Mexico in Texas; the Central Plains, extending through central Texas & Oklahoma; the Western High Plains, sweeping across western Texas & Oklahoma; the Rocky Mountains, extending into New Mexico & Texas, west of the Pecos River. Most of New Mexico is a rolling plateau, dotted with mountain ranges, averaging over 5,700′ in altitude, very dry & sunny. The Mexican Cordilleras, running diagonally across Arizona, divide it into a desertlike southwestern plains section & a northeastern mountain & plateau region; most of the state is criss-crossed by mountain ranges & canyons. The Southwest is a land of little water—except in the lush plain along Texas' Gulf Coast & in the irrigated river valleys—& of relatively few trees—except in the timber regions of eastern Oklahoma & northeastern Texas & Arizona's ponderosa pine belt; its vast semi-arid stretches are largely covered with "chaparral" (Mex., thick brush), where mesquite & cactus mingle, its arid parts with creosote bush & yucca. The rivers are normally sluggish, yellow streams, often dry or almost so, in summer; they change into furious torrents abruptly flooding their banks after heavy rains. Oklahoma is drained by the Arkansas & its tributaries: the Cimarron, Canadian, Grand & others & by the Red River, which divides it from Texas. The chief Texas streams, draining into the Gulf of Mexico, are the Sabine, which forms the Texas-Louisiana border; the Trinity, Brazos & Colorado, in the central part; & the Rio Grande, ninth longest river in the Western Hemisphere, bordering Mexico & extending into New Mexico. New Mexico is traversed by the Rio Grande & its tributary, the Pecos. Within Arizona lies the more than 200-mile course of the Grand Canyon of the Colorado River (not to be confused with the river of the same name in Texas); the Colorado forms Arizona's western border, running southward through Mexico to empty into the Gulf of Lower California. Across southern Arizona runs the Gila River.

The conservation of water resources has long been one of the Southwest's chief problems, on the solution of which has depended much of its development; the building of dams to impound reservoirs & the construction of canal systems has reclaimed vast areas for agriculture, especially in Texas & western Arizona. Natural lakes in the Southwest are few, but irrigation & hydroelectric power dams have created great artificial ones; among others, Lake of the Cherokees in northeastern Oklahoma, Lake Texhoma on the Texas-Oklahoma border in the Red River Valley & Lake Mead on the Colorado in northwestern Arizona. Wherever water is supplied, either by rainfall or irrigation, the land yields rich harvests: wheat, cotton, & field crops of all kinds on the vast Oklahoma & Texas Plains, rice on the Gulf Coast, fruits & vegetables in the irrigated river valleys. Livestock remains, as in pioneer days, one of the chief sources of wealth throughout the Southwest. The products for which Oklahoma & Texas are most famous, oil (now being intensively drilled for also in southeastern New Mexico) & natural gas, are by far the most spectacular of the region's abundant mineral riches, but not the only ones: others include coal & zinc in Oklahoma; helium, sulphur, salt, silver & mercury in Texas; copper, coal & potash in New Mexico. Mining is the chief industry of Arizona, which leads the nation in output of copper & asbestos & ranks high in production of gold, silver & lead. By no means the least of the Southwest's resources are its impressive scenic attractions—some of the chief of which are included in National Parks: Platt (Oklahoma), Big Bend (Texas), Carlsbad Caverns (New Mexico), Grand Canyon (Arizona); these, along with numerous historic shrines & monuments recalling the richly varied past, Indian, Spanish, Mexican & American, draw a steady stream of visitors.

Throughout the Southwest—except in Texas, where early white settlement all but obliterated Indian culture—the aboriginal inhabitants have left their marks most impressively in the great cities of the prehistoric Basket Makers whose ruins dot Arizona & New Mexico & in the artifacts of the Cave Dwellers. The first white explorers found most of central & eastern Texas inhabited by the Caddo, whose culture was similar to that of the Mississippi Valley Mound Builders; farther westward, the plains-roving Apache & Comanche tribes were numerous. The Comanche continued to harass pioneer settlers until the late 1870's, by which time the States had been virtually cleared of Indian inhabitants. The Apache kept up a bitter struggle with white settlers in Arizona, raiding ranches & settlements, until 1886, when Geronimo surrendered. The other, more peaceful agricultural tribes of Arizona & New Mexico—the Pueblo, Pima, Papago, Navaho, Hopi, Zuni, & Yuma—had long previously submitted to foreign conquest. Today numerous reservations, usually in less productive land, in both Arizona & New Mexico contain a large segregated Indian population. Oklahoma, where Indians from the rest of the country were herded from 1817 until late in the 19th century, retains, of course, the strongest Indian influence of any state, with more than a third of the Indian population of the entire U.S.

The lower Rio Grande, into which in 1519 Alonso Alvarez de Piñeda sailed his ship in the course of an expedition dispatched by the Governor of Jamaica to map the Gulf Coast, was the second place within the present limits of the U.S. to be visited by Europeans. Other expeditions soon followed. Shipwrecked on Galveston Island (Texas) in 1528, Cabeza de Vaca escaped from his Indian captors 7 years later & made his way on foot to the gulf of California. His account, published in 1542, was the first description of the interior of the region claimed as New Spain, to which 92 expeditions in all were dispatched within a little more than two centuries after Piñeda's voyage. The Franciscan friar Marcos de Niza, sent in search of the fabled "Seven Cities of Cibola," crossed Arizona & New Mexico in 1539, & coming upon the mud & stone cities of the Zuni sparkling in the sun, returned hastily to Mexico City in the belief he had seen their walls studded with gold & jewels. Led by Francisco Vasquez de Coronado, a great procession of cavalry, foot soldiers & Indians set out in 1540 & searched for treasure eastward & northward as far as Kansas for two years, returning finally in disappointment, empty-handed. At about the same time, survivors of the expedition of Hernando de Soto wandered, lost, below the lonely banks of the Red River. In 1598 Don Juan Oñate took formal possession of New Spain & established the first Spanish settlement & capital near the present San Juan, New Mexico. Santa Fé was founded as the new capital in 1610, & missions were established by the Franciscans. In 1680 the Pueblo Indians revolted against oppression & drove out the Spanish, who maintained their capital at El Paso on the Rio Grande for 13 years until they had repossessed the lost province. Settlement of Texas began only when the French established Fort St. Louis at the head of Lavaca Bay after the shipwreck in 1685 of the well-supplied fleet of Robert Cavelier, Sieur de La Salle. The plan of the Franciscan monks for a chain of missions was then quickly adopted: the easternmost Spanish outpost was founded May 25, 1690, near the Neches River, & by 1731 a dozen missions had been established.

Meanwhile, Padre Eusebio Francisco Kino, a Jesuit, had begun setting up a chain of missions to Christianize the Pima & Papago in Arizona; he also instructed them in the art of cattle herding. Padre Francisco Garcés, of the Franciscan order, founded more missions along the Colorado River among the Yuma; but the Yuma in 1781 killed him & many of his followers. After the Mexicans won their independence from Spanish rule (1821), Arizona, New Mexico & Texas became provinces of the Republic of Mexico.

Oklahoma, acquired by the U.S. as part of the Louisiana Purchase (1803), remained an unsettled region until the U.S. began moving Indian tribes from east of the Mississippi to new homes here & established military outposts to protect them—Fort Smith in 1817 & Forts Gibson & Towson in 1824. In 1834 a large part of Oklahoma was set aside as Indian Territory, which was divided up among the so-called "Five Civilized Tribes"—Cherokee, Choctaw, Chickasaw, Creek & Seminole—each with its own government.

Anglo-Americans began to infiltrate into Texas early in the 19th century. In 1800 Philip Nolan had let a party into the province, ostensibly to look for wild horses; Nolan was killed by Spanish soldiers. Filibustering expeditions of Americans campaigning for Texas independence from Spanish rule were led by Bernardo Gutierrez de Lara & Augustus W. Magee in 1812-13 & by Dr. James Long in 1819-21. In 1820, Moses Austin of Missouri secured authority from Spain to settle 300 families along the Brazos River. After 1821, the Mexican officials continued to grant colonization contracts to settlers from the U.S.; by 1829, nearly 7,000 families had been admitted. But the colonists' discontent with Mexican rule & desire for Texas' independence, culminating in an abortive rebellion in 1825-26, led by Hayden Edwards, who proclaimed the Republic of Fredonia but failed to win support, alarmed the Mexicans. In 1830 they forbade further emigration from the U.S. The American colonists continued to demand self-government. "Liberty & Texas" became the cry. When in 1835 the Mexican dictator, Santa Anna, dissolved the provincial legislature & sent troops northward, William Barret Travis went to Anahuac & drove out the Mexican garrison. The colonists organized Committees of Safety & on October 2, 1835, a group of farmers defeated a Mexican force at Gonzales; a volunteer army was mobilized, & a week later it captured the fort at Goliad, appointed Stephen F. Austin commander in chief & marched on San Antonio, which it took after a long siege on December 9, 1835.

Santa Anna, with a large force, arrived at San Antonio February 23, 1836 & on March 6 unleashed nearly 3,000 troops on the Alamo there, the defenders of which —among them Travis, James Bowie & Davy Crockett—they slaughtered to the last man. Meanwhile a Declaration of Independence had been adopted by the colonists; but the ad interim government, along with its constituents, was soon forced into flight before Santa Anna's swift advance. Col. James W. Fannin, Jr.'s force of about 330 were taken & massacred by the Mexicans at Goliad. Gen. Sam Houston, commanding the Texas army, retreated for 40 days eastward to the vicinity of Houston, there to take his stand & then, in 30 minutes of fighting on April 21, so soundly defeated Santa Anna's forces in the Battle of San Jacinto as to compel withdrawal of all Mexican armies & secure establishment of the Republic of Texas.

For 10 years thereafter, Texas was an independent nation, with a Navy of 4 vessels & the hard-riding Texas Rangers patrolling her frontiers; in 1845 it was annexed as a state of the Union. The annexation, regarded by Mexico as a declaration of hostilities, was followed swiftly by the Mexican War, whose first battle was fought near Brownsville, Texas, on May 8, 1846. Within three months, Gen. Kearney had occupied Santa Fe, New Mexico, without the firing of a shot. On February 2, 1848, defeated Mexico gave up to the U.S. Texas, New Mexico, Arizona north of the Gila River, part of Colorado & upper California; by the Gadsden Purchase (1853), the U.S. acquired from Mexico the rest of Arizona, between the Gila & the present boundary. Arizona remained a part of the Territory of New Mexico until established as a separate territory in 1863.

The outbreak of the Civil War found Texas, largely dominated by Southern planters, on the side of the Confederacy, despite the bitter opposition of Gov. Sam Houston, who refused to take an oath supporting the Confederacy & was deposed from office. The Texans, staving off Federal attempts at invasion in the Battles of Galveston & Sabine Pass (1863), furnished huge amounts of supplies to the Confederate armies up until the end of the war, the last battle of which was fought on Palmito Hill near Brownsville, May 12- 13, 1865. Under military government until 1869, Texas saw race riots, Ku Klux Klan riders & growing lawlessness during the Reconstruction period; it was readmitted to the Union in 1870. The Confederacy was likewise supported by most of the Indians of the Five Civilized Tribes in Oklahoma—each of whom had organized governments, farmed & traded, supported schools & held slaves. At the end of the Civil War they were forced to sign new treaties with the United States by which they relinquished their lands in the western part of Oklahoma. In the latter region, Fort Sill was established & reservations were set up on which plains Indians from the north were settled.

The great Texas cattle drives, in which millions of longhorn steers were herded overland by way of the Chisholm Trail & other routes to railheads at rip-roaring Kansas towns like Abilene or Dodge City, were well underway by 1870; & with the cessation of the Indian danger, vast cattle ranches soon spread over Texas' western & northern plains. But the steady penetration westward through Oklahoma & Texas itself of the railroads brought the trail-driving era to a close; by 1880 the barbed-wire fences of homesteaders, crisscrossing the ranges, were beginning to provoke bloody feuds between farmers & cattle men. A rapid & large influx of people & of capital swept into Texas. Then on April 22, 1889, central Oklahoma—a buffer region between territories in eastern & western Oklahoma reserved for Indian settlement—was opened to white settlement with the famous "run" which brought thousands of homesteaders; in 1890 the Territory of Oklahoma was created, incorporating the portion of the state opened to white settlement, & in the next decade & a half, the governments of the Five Civilized Tribes were gradually taken over by the U.S. with additional areas opened to white settlers. Finally Congress in 1906 united Indian Territory & the Territory of Oklahoma so that in the following year Oklahoma might be admitted to the Union as a state. Arizona & New Mexico, where Indian raids & scanty water resources delayed settlement, were finally admitted as states in 1912.

Until after the beginning of the twentieth century, agriculture & livestock raising—in which Texas, due to its early settlement, took the lead—were the Southwest's economic mainstays. But the discovery of oil—found in commercial quantities at Bartlesville, Oklahoma, in 1897, & Beaumont, Texas, in 1901—swiftly transformed the economic scene, creating fabulous wealth, as wells by the thousands were drilled, pipe lines laid, tank farms & refineries constructed. Tiny villages turned overnight into bonanza cities, swarming with adventurers. The Oklahoma Indians grew famously rich from the sale of oil leases. Tulsa, Oklahoma City, Dallas, Houston, San Antonio, springing to sudden affluence, were transformed into metropolitan centers. By 1940 Texas alone was producing a quarter of the world's oil supply. The oil industry has brought not only the wealth needed for irrigation projects to make fertile the Southwest's agriculture areas & expansion of transportation & marketing facilities; it has also brought other industries to balance what was once a predominantly agricultural economy. Nevertheless, with abundant resources still to be developed & plenty of space for a growing population, the Southwest has remained into the middle of the twentieth century a frontier wide open to new possibilities.

The evolution of cultural & educational facilities has taken place largely since

# THE SOUTHWEST

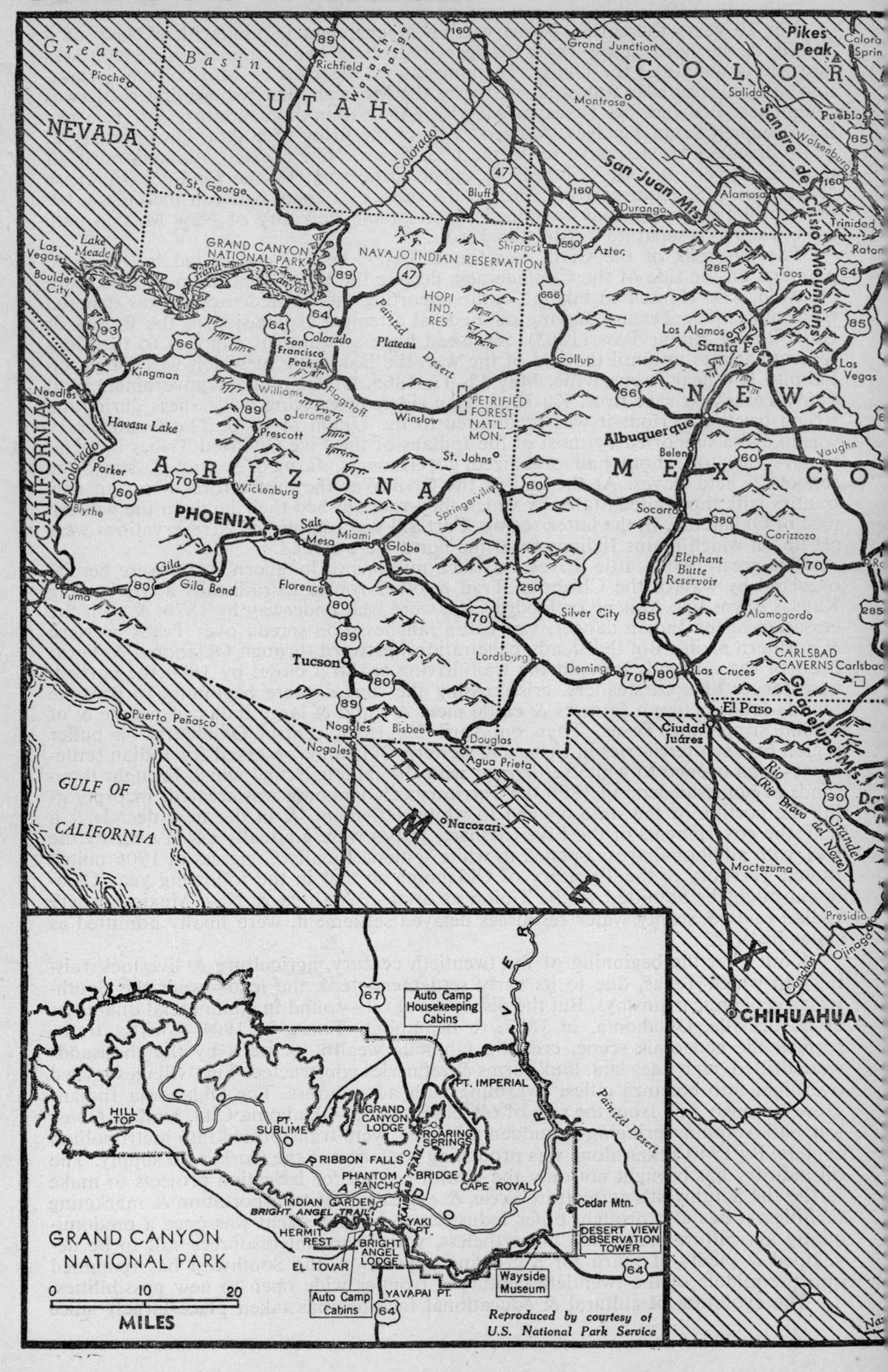

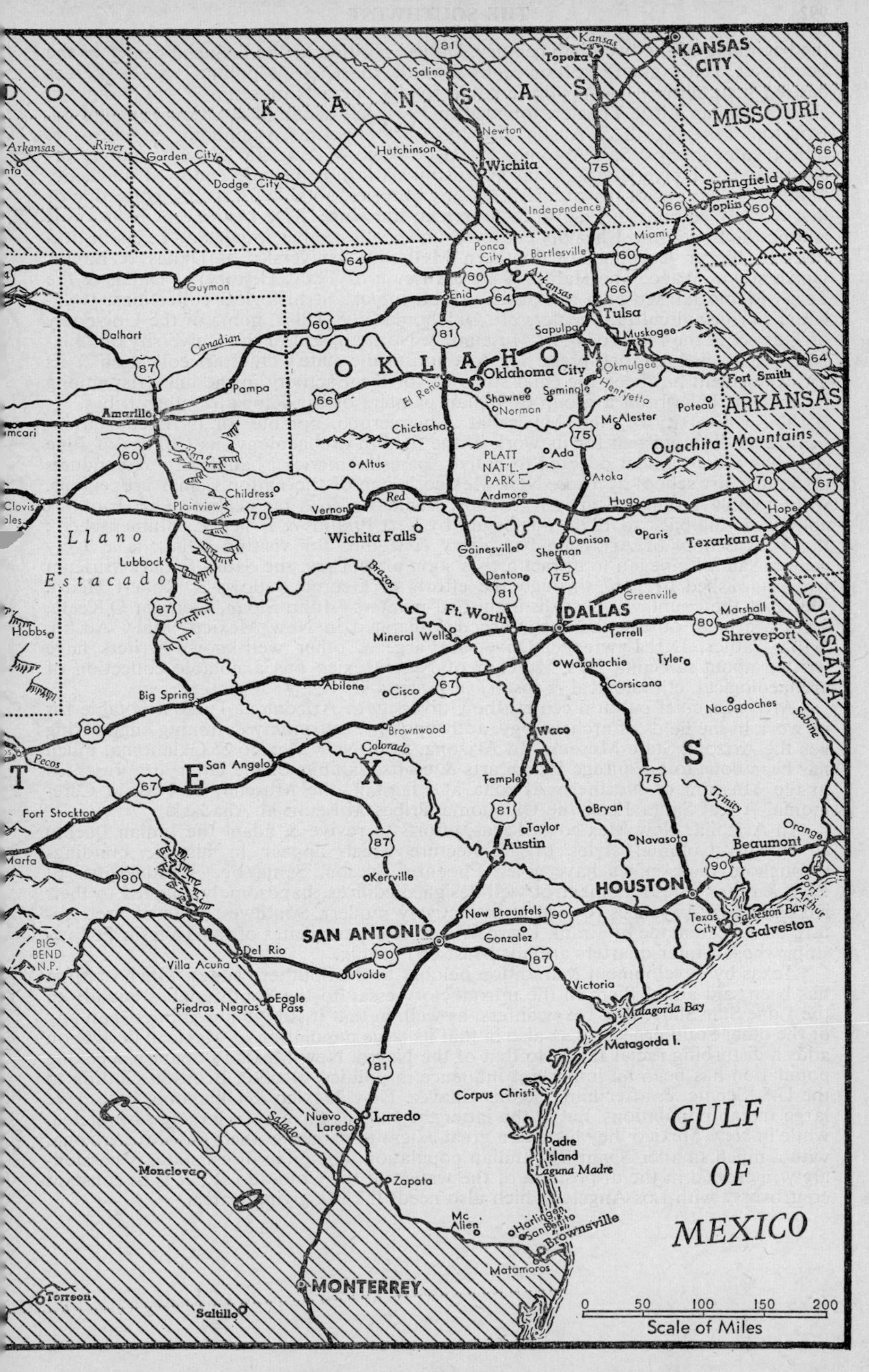

KANSAS
KANSAS CITY
Topeka
Kansas
Salina
Newton
Hutchinson
Wichita
Arkansas River
Garden City
Dodge City
Independence
MISSOURI
Springfield
Joplin
Miami
Ponca City
Bartlesville
Guymon
Enid
Arkansas
Tulsa
Sapulpa
Muskogee
Dalhart
Canadian
OKLAHOMA
Oklahoma City
Okmulgee
Fort Smith
ARKANSAS
Pampa
El Reno
Shawnee
Norman
Seminole
Henryetta
Poteau
Amarillo
Chickasha
McAlester
Ouachita Mountains
Altus
PLATT NAT'L. PARK
Ada
Atoka
Childress
Ardmore
Clovis
Plainview
Vernon
Red
Hugo
Hope
Wichita Falls
Paris
Denison
Texarkana
Llano Estacado
Lubbock
Gainesville
Sherman
Brazos
Denton
Greenville
LOUISIANA
Ft. Worth
DALLAS
Marshall
Hobbs
Mineral Wells
Terrell
Shreveport
Waxahachie
Tyler
Abilene
Corsicana
Big Spring
Cisco
Nacogdoches
Brownwood
Sabine
Waco
Colorado
Pecos
San Angelo
TEXAS
Temple
Trinity
Fort Stockton
Bryan
Taylor
Austin
Navasota
Orange
Beaumont
Marfa
Kerrville
HOUSTON
Port Arthur
New Braunfels
Texas City
Galveston Bay
Galveston
BIG BEND N.P.
SAN ANTONIO
Gonzalez
Del Rio
Villa Acuña
Uvalde
Victoria
Piedras Negras
Eagle Pass
Matagorda Bay
Matagorda I.
Corpus Christi
GULF OF MEXICO
Nuevo Laredo
Laredo
Salado
Padre Island
Laguna Madre
Monclova
Zapata
Mc Allen
Harlingen
San Benito
Brownsville
Matamoros
MONTERREY
Torreon
Saltillo
81
75
66
60
64
87
70
67
80
90
0
50
100
150
200
Scale of Miles

the beginning of the twentieth century. Dallas' position as the financial center of the Southwest, as a women's fashion center & as the most "cosmopolitan" of Texas cities has led it to cultural leadership, notable for its fine arts museum & symphony orchestra. Dallas' Little Theater, founded in 1921, has acquired a national reputation. Houston, Fort Worth & Austin also have art museums, symphony orchestras & little theater groups; San Antonio, El Paso, Waco & Amarillo have symphony orchestras. The University of Texas at Austin, sixth most heavily endowed university in the U.S., has one of the country's leading libraries, notable for its fine collection of first & early editions in English & American literature. Rice Institute at Houston is among the fifteen most heavily endowed universities; other important Texas institutions of higher learning are Southern Methodist University at Dallas & Baylor University at Waco. The Hall of State (Museum of Texas History) at Dallas & the Texas Memorial Museum at Austin exhibit important historical collections. Oklahoma's principal cultural centers are Oklahoma City; Tulsa, home of the University of Tulsa & of the Philbrook Art Museum; & Norman, seat of the University of Oklahoma & its distinguished press. The last houses the state's chief art collection & its art department has been the chief stimulus for local activity in the fine arts; among its students have been a group of Indian painters of the Kiowa & other tribes.

The University of New Mexico at Albuquerque, notable for its Pueblo architecture, is distinguished for its work in the field of archaeology; its College of Fine Arts has a department devoted to native Spanish-American handicrafts & conducts a summer art school at Taos. New Mexico is one of the nation's chief art regions, with notable groups of artists at Taos, Santa Fe & Albuquerque. The Taos art colony, dating back to 1898, was begun by Bert Phillips & Ernest L. Blumenschein; the Taos School of Art, with its gallery & studios for visiting artists, is a lively center. Santa Fe began to attract artists soon after Taos; the Santa Fe Art Museum was established in 1917 through the efforts of George Bellows & Robert Henri. Many of the country's most distinguished painters—John Sloan, Georgia O'Keefe, John Marin & others—have sojourned & painted in New Mexico. Mary Austin, Willa Cather, D.H.Lawrence, Oliver LaFarge & other well-known writers have written about it. Santa Fe's Museum of New Mexico has a notable collection of archaeological, ethnological & historical materials.

Arizona's chief cultural center, the University of Arizona at Tucson, notable for its work in the fields of archaeology, anthropology, astronomy & mining engineering has the Arizona State Museum. In Arizona, as in New Mexico & Oklahoma, much has been done to encourage Indian arts & crafts; exhibits of the latter are presented in the Museum of Northern Arizona at Flagstaff, the Museum of Navajo Ceremonial Art at Santa Fe & the Oklahoma Tribes Museum at Anadarko.

In Arizona, New Mexico & Texas, efforts to revive & adapt the Indian Pueblo & Spanish Colonial styles of architecture which appear in historic buildings throughout these states have given Phoenix, Tucson, Santa Fe, Albuquerque, El Paso & other cities a number of well-designed edifices, handsomely adapted to their backgrounds. Advances toward a distinctively modern Southwest style of architecture have been made by Frank Lloyd Wright & his associates of the Taliesin Fellowship, whose winter quarters are northeast of Phoenix.

Texas by development & tradition belongs to the Southern states. Much of what has been said about them in the introductory essay to the South applies equally to the Lone Star State. But Texas differs, as well, in that it is by far wealthier than any of the other Southern states, & also in that its large population of Mexican derivation adds a disturbing racial factor to that of the Negro. New Mexico's Spanish-speaking population has been an important influence in politics, electing Bronson Cutting to the U.S. Senate, & after him, Dennis Chavez. New Mexico & Oklahoma both have large Indian populations, but in the latter the Indians have been largely assimilated, while in New Mexico they have to a great extent remained in their pueblos. Arizona, with a much smaller Spanish & Indian population, being the driest state, is passionately interested in the disposition of the waters of the Colorado R., & is in constant controversy with Los Angeles which also needs the life-giving waters.

# US 60—OKLAHOMA

**OKLA.-MO. LINE** (0.5$^m$ from Seneca, Mo.) **(W) to OKLA.-TEX. LINE** (27$^m$ from Canadian, Tex.) **360. US60**

Via: Bartlesville, Ponca City, & Enid. RRs. parallel parts of route. Accoms.: Good bet. Mo. Line & Enid, more limited (W) of Enid.

US60 traverses rolling hills & canyon-cut plateaus of Okla. Ozarks, crosses grazing lands & oil fields of former Cherokee Nation & of Osage Ind. Reserv., cuts through Okla.'s beet agricultural region in vic. of Enid, then enters dry, dusty high plains area.

## Sec. 1: OKLA.-MO. LINE to ENID. 224.

**0.** From **OKLA.-MO. LINE,** US60 runs through Ozarks to **WYANDOTTE, 7.5.,** chiefly populated by Inds., at J. with country Rd. leading (R) 0.5$^m$ to Gov.-supervised **Seneca Ind. School,** est. 1869 by Quakers. **16. FAIRLAND** depends on a cattle-country vic. At **20.** is J. with US66-69 (see US66), with which US60 unites (SW) for 25$^m$ (see US66 for towns & pts. of int. in this sec.); at **43.5.** US69 (see US66) branches (S). At **45.** US66 (see) branches (SW) from US60, which cont. (W), traversing at c.**62.5.** world's largest shallow oil field, incl. more than 20,000 wells. **68. NOWATA,** whose name is taken from Delaware Ind. word meaning "welcome," grew up around trading post est. after 1868 when Kans. Delaware bought land here from Cherokee.

SIDE TRIP: Take US169 (L) from Nowata to J. at 18$^m$ with gravel Rd. leading (L) 2.5$^m$ to **Will Rogers' Birthpl.,** 2-story ranch dwelling built by pioneer cattleman Clem V. Rogers, where cowboy humorist was born in 1879.

**89. BARTLESVILLE,** spreading (W) from loop of Caney R., owes its name to Jacob Bartles, who bought mill nearby in 1875 from 1st settler, Nelson F. Carr, & opened trading post. Drilling of Okla.'s 1st commercial oil well here (1897) & advent of Santa Fe RR. (1899) spurred growth of town. With discovery of oil came discovery of gas, which provided cheap fuel for zinc smelters, cement plant, & other industries. At N. side of city, **Johnstone Pk.,** through which flows Caney R., contains **Discovery Well,** where oil was tapped April 15, 1897. Jennings Ave. at 6th St., **Phillips Petroleum Co. Research Lab.** is windowless glass brick building. Virginia & Cudahy Aves., **Petroleum Experiment Sta.,** largest of kind in U.S., was opened jointly by U.S. Bureau of Mines & St. of Okla. in 1918.

SIDE TRIP: Take St.23 (L) from Bartlesville 12$^m$ to 3,400-a. **Frank Phillips Ranch** (tours Tues.,Thurs.,Sun.2 p.m.free), where is native-stone **Woolaroc Mus.,** containing fine colls. of Western paintings & bronzes, Ind. artifacts, Navajo blankets, fossils & other articles. Ranch (swim.pic.f.) contains Ls., springs, Haunted Grove, Outlaw Gulch, game preserve, Ind. tepee, prairie schooner, & lodge.

US60 cont. (W) along borders of Osage Nation, tract of c.1,500,000 as. bought from Cherokee, to which Osage Inds. were removed from Kans. in 1872. Development of vast oil & gas fields here made them wealthiest of tribes. **OSAGE HILLS ST. PK.** (cabins.pic.swim.f.), **101.,** is 740-a. area of very picturesque scenery. At **112.5.** is J. with Cty. Rd. No. 7, leading (L) 1$^m$ to **Pawhuska Ind. Village. 114. PAWHUSKA,** named for famous Osage chief, Paw-Hue-Ska ("White Hair"), is tribal capital, with traditional Ind. atmosphere. Here bet. 1916 & 1928 were held oil lease auctions which netted millions, each member of tribe receiving equal share. At foot of Agency Hill is former **Osage Council H.,** Main & Grandview Sts., now City Hall; atop hill are bldgs. of **Osage Agency,** where tribal business is conducted. Among them, on site of 1st agency bldg., is **Osage Tribal Mus. & Aud.** (O.afts.free), housing extensive colls. of Ind. costumes, paintings, bead & feather work, treaties & documents. At **159.5.** is J. with US77.

SIDE TRIP: Take US77 (R) to J. with Rd., 0.5$^m$.

Take latter (R) 4$^m$ to 800-a. **L. Ponca** (f.boat.pic.).

At 3.5$^m$ is J. with asphalt Rd.

Take latter (R) to **Kaw City,** 12.5$^m$, whose Clubb Hotel contains **Laura A. Clubb Art Coll.** (O.free) of paintings, old laces, & rare books; among its more than 200 paintings are canvases by Titian, Gainsborough, Reynolds, Constable, Corot, Gilbert Stuart, Winslow Homer, & Geo. Inness.

US77 cont. (N) to J. at 21.5$^m$ with a good Rd. leading (L) 1.5$^m$ to **Chilocco Ind. Sch.,** est. 1882 by act of Congress, now outstanding vocational training institution with elaborate facils. & experimental farm.

**158. PONCA CITY,** a sprawling city with Okla.'s 3rd largest industrial payroll, came into existence afternoon of Sept. 13, 1893, when Cherokee Outlet was opened to settlers: group headed by B. S. Barnes settled here & secured RR. sta. & order to halt trains at site. Growth followed exploitation of oil fields (S) & (E), under lead of E. W. Marland, whose company not only drilled wells but also acquired pipe lines & filling stations; Marland developed Ponca City as a model town. Pop. trebled bet. 1920 & 1930. Today Ponca City prospers on oil refining, airplane mfg., flour milling, dairy products processing & other industries. E. edge of city, bronze **Pioneer Woman St. Mon.** (1930.by Bryant Baker). **Conoco Refinery,** SW. edge of town, orig. opened by Marland Refining Co. but acquired in 1929 by Continental Oil Co., is Okla.'s largest; on grounds are **Club** (O) & **Recr. Bldg.,** golf course & tennis courts, swim. pool & baseball grounds. Grand Ave. at 5th St., **Ponca City Lib.** (modified Sp.) is community center, containing **Ernest Emmett Thompson Mus.** of Ind. relics. Opp. lib., **Mun. Bldg.** (Sp.-Moorish), on landscaped grounds, has mission-type tower. Brookfield Ave. & 5th St., 10-a. **Blaine Pk.** contains **Ponca City Stadium.**

At **173.** is J. with US177.

SIDE TRIP: Take latter (R) 11m to **Blackwell,** market center, founded on day of Cherokee Run, Sept. 16, 1893, by group headed by A. J. Blackwell, self-ordained Bapt. preacher who maintained control for some years. Town prospered as a wheat market, meat packing, & zinc smelting center. Products now incl. oil, glass, bricks, cabinetwork, cheese & other dairy products.

**171. TONKAWA,** named for Tonkawa Inds. who were given this reg. for their reserv. in 1868, was laid out after the Cherokee Run & today is bustling oil city. Here is **N. Okla. Jr. College,** est. 1901. At **POND CREEK, 201.,** is J. with US81 (see), which unites (S) with US60 for 22m. At **205.5.** is (N) J. with US64, which unites (S) with US60-81 to Enid.

SIDE TRIP: Take US64 (R) to J. at 15.5m with Rd.

Take latter (R), turn (R) at 1m, (L) at 2m, & (L) again at 6m to **Great Salt Plains Dam,** impounding Salt Fork of Ark. R. to form 19,453-a. reservoir in flat, salt-encrusted plains area, glistening white, which has been set aside as wildfowl refuge.

**Cherokee,** 33m, is center of rich farm and livestock area. At 53m is **Northwestern St. College,** est. in 1897, at J. with College Ave., leading (R) 0.5m to **Alva,** a land-office town assigned at opening of the Cherokee Strip (1893), named for Santa Fe Ry. attorney Alva Adams. At 79.5m is J. with St.50.

Take latter (L) 5m to J. with poor Rd. leading (L) to **Cedar Canyon Pk.** (clubh.meals), in which are **Natural Bridge,** 150′ high, & **Alabaster Caverns** with many chambers containing fantastic formations, inhabited by millions of bats.

110.5m, **Buffalo,** founded in 1907, with mun. swim. pool.

Take US183 (L) from Buffalo to **Supply,** 19m, on site of Ft. Supply, est. 1868 by Gen. Philip H. Sheridan, later hqs. of Gen. Geo. A. Custer in his operations against Plains Inds. **Woodward,** 33m, market town within a farming & cattle-ranching area, was sett. at opening of Cherokee Strip (1893). From Woodward, take good Rd. (L) 1.5m, then turn (R) to **Boiling Springs St. Pk.** (cabins.pic.swim.bathh.), 6m, 820-a. hilly, wooded tract on N. Canadian R. with L. & springs. At **Seiling,** 69m, is J. with US60 (see below).

(W) of **Gate,** 136m, US64 traverses windblown "dust bowl" area of Okla. Panhandle, where tumbleweeds flourish, was orig. known as No Man's Land. At 162.5m is J. with US270.

Take latter (L) 6.5m to **Beaver,** named capital of "territory of Cimarron" at convention held here in 1887 by settlers trying to bring law & order to No Man's Land. Beaver became cty. seat when Beaver Cty. was added to Okla. Terr. in 1890. It is now a market town for agric. reg.

224m, **Guymon,** trading center for fertile wheat-growing reg., holds Pioneer Day Celebration (May 2), comm. Organic Act of 1890 which inc. Panhandle into Okla. Terr.

Take US54 (L) from Guymon to **Goodwell,** 11m, site of **Panhandle Agric. & Mechanical College,** est. 1909, with **Mus.** (in Hughes-Strong Hall) of colls. relating to Panhandle, agric. experiment sta. & livestock farm.

**Boise City,** 285.5m, is Cimarron Cty. seat. At 300.5m is J. with improved Rd.

Turn (L) on this 1m, then (R) on 2nd improved Rd. to **Wheeless P.O.,** 6m, then (R) on 3rd Rd. at 8m to **Site of Ft. Nichols,** 10m, est. by Kit Carson (famous Army scout) in 1865 to protect Santa Fe Trl. Stone fls. of barracks & hqs. bldgs. & part of rampart wall remain. Near-by, location of Santa Fe Trl. is marked by 3 sets of parallel ruts, 10′ deep & 20′ wide.

At 312m is J. with poor Rd.

Take latter (R) 8m to **Hallock Pk.** (cabins.pic.swim.), 10-a. area of rugged country with many springs, containing **Ind. Pictographs** on sandstone bluff.

At 312.5m is **Dinosaur Quarry,** from which most complete dinosaur coll. in U.S., incl. 3,600 bones weighing more than 18 tons, has been excavated. At **Kenton,** 321.5m, is J. with poor Rd. leading (R) 2m to fork, then (L) to **Black Mesa,** 4m, lava-capped plateau on which is highest pt. (4,978′) in Okla. At 324m is **Okla.-New Mex. Line.**

**224. ENID,** which is 4th in size & 3rd in industry among Okla. cities, is wheat & flour-milling, oil-refining & supply center. Once campsite on Chisholm Cattle Trl. because of large springs here, it was sett. following advent of Rock I. RR. in 1889. Rival settlement was located 3m (S) at opening of Cherokee Strip (1893), & lively competition ensued, from which S. Enid emerged victor. Advent of 2 more RRs. helped make Enid NW. Okla.'s chief wheat shipping & milling center. Oil fields in vic. were exploited in 1920's. City today also has poultry & dairy produce houses, packing plants, & stockyards. Broadway & Market Sts., **Gov. Springs Pk.** (pic.swim. bathh.) comprises old campsite & drinking hole on Chisholm Trl. 515 E. Spruce St., **Pillsbury Four Mill** (O.10-11:30.guides), Okla.'s largest. On city outskirts, **Phillips Univ.,** chartered 1906, is coed. Christian Ch. institution; in Main Bldg., 3rd floor, are Ind., zoological, & botanical colls. Enid is at J. with US64, conn. with US66 (see).

### Sec. 2: ENID to OKLA.-TEX. LINE. 136.

(W) of **ENID, 0.,** US60 cuts through high, dry wheat-growing & grazing land. **18. MENO** is Okla.'s largest Mennonite settlement. US60 crosses **CIMARRON R., 34.5.,** & passes fantastically shaped, gypsum-covered **GLASS MTS.** (R), sparkling with crystals. **FAIRVIEW, 43., & SEILING, 75.,** are farmers' trading towns; latter was home for several years of temperance crusader Carry Nation. Seiling is at J. with US270, conn. with US64 (see above) & US66 (see). **96. VICI,** agricultural center, lies at E. edge of "dust bowl," in which improved farming methods & planting of shelter belt of trees are helping reduce erosion by wind. **123. ARNETT** is trading center for stock & small grain area. **136. OKLA.-TEX. LINE.**

## US 66—OKLAHOMA

**OKLA.-KANS. LINE** (4m from Baxter Springs, Kans.) **(SW) to OKLA.-TEX. LINE** (14m from Shamrock, Tex.). **385. US66**

Via: Miami, Vinita, Claremore, Tulsa, Oklahoma City, El Reno & Sayre. RRs. parallel entire route. Accoms.: At short intervals.

Okla.'s most heavily travelled route, US66, known as "Will Rogers Hy.," cuts (SW) through mining districts & oil fields to Oklahoma City, then (W) through stock & farming country to high plains.

### Sec. 1: OKLA.-KANS. LINE to OKLAHOMA CITY. 229.

**0.** From **OKLA.-KANS. LINE,** US66 cuts through lead- & zinc-mining area to **QUAPAW, 4.5.,** formerly occupied by Quapaw Inds., where mining began before 1900. **COMMERCE, 10.,** town around which are mine debris dumps. **14.5. MIAMI,** chief center of mining reg., was laid out in 1891 in vic. of trading post called Jimtown for four "Jims" of vic., & named for wife of one of them, half-breed Miami Indian. Finding of lead & zinc in 1905 boomed the population. Miami today is also cattle-raising & dairy center. It operates Okla.'s largest concrete swim. pool. E. edge of city, **NE. Okla. A. & M. College,** est. 1919, specializes in mining & agric. instruction. **25.** J. with US60 (see), which unites with US66 for 25m. At **40.5.** is J. with St.82.

SIDE TRIP: Take latter (L) 15.5m to **Pensacola Dam,** world's longest multiple-arch dam (6,565′), completed 1941 as hydroelectric power project, impounding 59,000-a. **L. o' The Cherokees,** with 1,300m shore line (resorts.f.).

**45. VINITA,** founded with advent of RRs. in 1871, was named by Col. Elias C. Boudinot, Cherokee Ind. & town promoter, for Vinnie Ream, sculptress of Abr. Lincoln Statue in National Capitol. Will Rogers Mem. Rodeo (1st wk. Sept.) comm. cowboy humorist, who attended high sch. here. At **48.5.** is J. with US69.

SIDE TRIP: Take US69 (L) following route of old Texas Rd. through what was until 1907 Ind. Terr. **Cabin Cr.,** 6m, was site in 1863 and 1864 of Civil War battles when Confeds. attacked Fed. supply trains bound (S) for Ft. Gibson. **Pryor,** 24m, named for Capt. Nathaniel Pryor of Lewis & Clark expedition who sett. here in 1806, is agric. center.

Take St.20 (L) from Pryor 11m to **Salina,** oldest sett. in Okla., est. 1796 as trading post by Maj. Jean Pierre Chouteau of St. Louis, who persuaded 3,000 Osage Inds. to move here from Kans. Chouteau's son built pretentious home; after his death property passed to Lewis Ross, brother of Cherokee Chief John Ross, who erected mansion near spring; **Springh.** constructed by his slaves remains in SE. cor. of schoolyard. Later, Cherokee Orphans' Home was est. & operated here until 1903. Main St., **Stone Marker** comm.

Chouteau trading post & Cherokee town & asylum. Okla. Historical Day is celebrated here on Chouteau's birth date, Oct. 10.

**Chouteau,** 33.5m, is farm town. At 38.5m is J. with gravel Rd.

Take latter (L) 1m, turn (R) 3.5m, then (L) 1.5m to stone marker on **Site of Union Mission,** 1st in Okla., est. in 1821 for Osage Inds. by Presb. missionary Rev. Epaphras Chapman, whose grave is in mission cemetery. Old **Fr. Cemetery,** near-by, contains graves of early Fr. traders. Mon. is on **Site of Okla.'s 1st Printing Press,** set up by Rev. Saml. Austin Worcester (1835) to print textbooks in Creek, Cherokee, & Choctaw languages. Short dist. (N) from mission site is **Salt Spring,** where salt was made as early as 1806.

**Wagoner,** 50m, est. at J. of M.-K.-T. & Ark. RRs. in 1887. It was named for RR. employee, "Bigfoot" Wagoner. Carnegie Lib. has **Mus.** of Ind. & Civil War relics. At 50.5m is J. with paved hy.

Take latter (L) 8.5m to **Okay,** a tiny hamlet which was moved (N) to present site with advent of RR. in 1871; it is one of Okla.'s oldest white settlements. At E. end of Verdigris R. Bridge, 10m, is **Three Forks Marker** comm. Texas Rd., which crossed R. here; trading post & boat landing est. by Brand & Barbour & sold to Col. A. P. Chouteau in 1822; arrival of Creek Inds. in 1828 & est. of Creek Agency. Hy. follows Verdigris R. to its confluence with **Ark. R.,** 15m. At 15.5m is J. with asphalt Rd. leading (L) 0.5m to **Bacone College,** Ind. jr. college (& world's only fully accredited Ind. college) est. as Bapt. Mission Sch. in 1879 & removed to present site in 1885. On campus are **Milly Francis Mon.,** comm. Creek woman awarded Congressional Medal of Honor; **Art Lodge,** containing Ind. handicrafts, relics & art objects; **Ind. Cottage;** & other bldgs. Near-by is **Site of Ft. Davis,** Confederate Civil War stronghold.

63m, **Muskogee,** Okla.'s 3rd largest city, SW. of confluence of Ark., Grand & Verdigris Rs., which in Oct. 1948 celebrated Indian Centennial, comm. recognition of Five Civilized Tribes in Oct. 1848. Muskogee is bustling RR. & mfg. center with glass & iron works, oil refineries, dairy & poultry products houses, & other industrial plants. It dates from advent of M.-K.-T. RR. in 1872. Est. here in 1875 of Union Agency for Five Civilized Tribes made this most important city in Ind. Terr.; for years thousands of Creek Inds. camped on Agency Hill awaiting payments, rations, or other tribal services. Dawes Commission had hqs. here (1894-1905) while negotiating for union of Ind. Terr. & Okla. Terr. preparatory to admission of Okla. to Union. After 1900 opening of 3 oil fields in vic., followed by rapid industrial development, spurred growth. 40th St. & Park Blvd., Agency Hill is now site of beautifully landscaped **Honor Heights Pk.,** in which stands stone **Union Agency Bldg.** (1875-76). 5th St. & Broadway, **Fed. Bldg.** now has offices of the U.S. Union Agency for Five Civilized Tribes. D St. & E. Broadway, **Muskogee Pub. Lib.** (O.9-9 wks.1909) has an art coll. & Mus. of Ind. Relics. 3rd St. & Okmulgee Ave., **Mun. Bldg.** has 1st-fl. **Mus.** of hist. relics, photographs & documents. (S) of Honor Heights Pk., **U.S. Veterans' Facility** (1923), with many bldgs., occupies landscaped grounds.

(1) Take US62 (L) from Muskogee, crossing Ark. R., 3.5m, near **Site of Steamboat Landing,** where from 1824 until after advent of RR. in 1872 steamboats docked. **Ft. Gibson,** 10m, now a farming sett., occupies site of military post est. by Col. Matthew Arbuckle in 1824 to become chief military center for whole Ind. Terr. It was abandoned in 1857 but re-occupied during Civil War & until 1890. Many of bldgs. have been rest., incl. **Log Stockade** & **Stone Barracks.** There is **Mus.** of early relics. At 12m is J. with poor Rd. leading (L) 1m to **Ft. Gibson Nat. Cemetery.** At 26.5m is Gov.-maintained **Sequoyah Vocational Training Sch.** of arts & crafts for Ind. orphans, orig. est. by Cherokee. At 28m is J. with gravel Rd. leading (R) to **Jane Ross Meigs H.,** 0.5m, more than a century old, home of a daughter of Cherokee Chief John Ross; at 1m on this Rd. is J. with another leading (L) 1m to **Site of Pk. Hill Mission,** est. 1836 by Presb. missionaries for Cherokee Inds.; just beyond this J. on former Rd. is dilapidated **Murrell Mansion** of Civil War era, built by Cherokee merchant Geo. Murrell; & at 2m on this Rd. is **Ross Family Cemetery** containing **John McDonald Ross Mon.** to Cherokee chief. US62 cont. to **Tahlequah,** 31m, chosen as capital of Cherokee Nation in 1839, where 3 log cabins were erected to house council, senate & treasury & in 1845 main Sts. were platted. In Public Sq., present Cherokee County Cth. is housed in former **Cherokee Capitol** (1869). Across St. from SE. cor. of Pub. Sq. is brick **Supreme Court Bldg.** (1845), in which "Cherokee Advocate," official newspaper of Cherokee Gov., was printed. **Northeastern St. College** is outgrowth of Cherokee Female Seminary, est. at Park Hill (see above) in 1851; on campus is **Northeastern Hist. Mus.,** with Ind. relics & documents.

(2) Take US64 (L) from Muskogee to **Warner,** 20m, where is **Conners St. Agric. College** (est. 1908), jr. college with experimental farm. Just beyond **Gore,** 32m, is J. with St.10, leading (L) to J. at **Braggs,** 13m, with dirt Rd. which turns (R) 3m to **Cookson Hills Playgrounds** (lodge.cabins.swim.boat.), 32,000-a. recr. area developed by Fed. Gov., surrounding 950-a. **Greenleaf L.** US64 cont. to **Sallisaw,** 53.5m, agric. center. At 60.5m is J. with poor Rd. leading (L) 7.5m to a squat building containing the log **Home of Sequoyah** (1830), built by Geo. Gist, half-blood Cherokee, tribal leader & educator, better known by his Indian name, who invented the Cherokee alphabet; his statue stands in Statuary Hall in National Capitol, & Sequoia trees of Cal. were named for him.

At **50.** US60 (see) branches (NW). **63.5. CHELSEA** was site of 1st oil discovery in Okla. c.1889, when Edw. Byrd drilled shallow well on lease secured from Cherokee Nation. **82.5. CLAREMORE** was est. as Cherokee trading post but took its name from Osage Chief who led his band in battle against Cherokee which was fought (1817) on Claremore Mound, (NW) of city. Here in 1903 drilling of an oil well tapped flow of artesian mineral water, said to be of medicinal value, now piped to several bathhs. whose location here makes Claremore Okla.'s chief health resort. **U.S. Ind. Hospital,** est. 1928, cares for members of Five Civilized Tribes. Mason Hotel houses **J. M. Davis Gun Coll.,** said to be largest in U.S. W. edge of town, **Will Rogers Mem.** (O.8-5.free), on hillside site where Rogers had planned to build home, dedicated Nov. 4, 1938, has heroic-size bronze statue of humorist in foyer, Diorama Room with scenes from his life, 2 galleries displaying his personal effects, and Saddle Room; Rogers is buried in crypt on grounds. Adj. is St.-owned **Okla. Military Academy,** founded 1919, whose grads. may enter Annapolis or West Pt. without examinations. NE. edge of town, **L. Claremore Pk.** (640 as.pic.f.swim. boat.) has 60-a. L. Adj. is **Will Rogers Rodeo Pk.,** where rodeo is held (July).

**96.5.** J. with St.33.

SIDE TRIP: Take latter (R) to J. with Sheridan Rd., 8m, & turn (R) here to **Tulsa Mun. Airport, Spartan Sch. of Aeronautics & Factory, & U.S. Bomber Assembly Plant,** 10m; airport is one of nation's busiest.

## 109.5. TULSA

Through RR., bus & plane conns. Accoms.: Numerous hotels & roominghs., tourist camps & trlr. pks. on all hys. Info.: Tulsa C. of C., 5th & Cincinnati Sts. Recr. facils.: Convention Hall & Akdar Theatre for road shows & concerts, Tulsa Little Theatre; golf at 9 courses, mun. & pri.; tennis at numerous free mun. courts; swim. at Newblock Pool (mun.), Crystal City Pk., & YMCA; boat. & fish. at Mohawk Pk.; sports events at Skelly Stadium & The Coliseum. Annual events: Livestock Exposition, Mar.; Horse Show, May; Music Festival, May; State Fair, Sept. International Petroleum Exposition, May, biennially in even-numbered years.

Okla.'s 2nd largest city, Tulsa calls itself "Oil Capital of the World": over 500 oil drilling, producing, refining, marketing, pipe line, & equipment mfg. companies have hqs. here—more than in any other city—& Tulsa's biennial International Petroleum Exposition is largest regularly devoted to single industry; at hub of country's pipelines, Tulsa is chief center for petroleum technology, oil industry publications & associations. Almost entirely product of 20th century, it has increased its pop. from 1,390 in 1900 (year before drilling of Okla.'s 1st commercially important well at Red Fork, now within city limits) to over 190,000 in 1948. Its modern skyscraper-dominated bus. dist. & luxurious south-side residential quarter; its many pks., up-to-date schs. & chs.; its Tulsa Symphony Orchestra, Philbrook Art Mus., & Univ. of Tulsa—all give it metropolitan atmosphere untypical of oil-boom centers or other Okla. cities. Although petroleum & allied industries dominate, it has others: chemical, glass, & steel works; cotton mill & garment factories; furniture, automobile body, brick & tile, & oxygen-mfg. plants. Until 1882, when Atlantic & Pacific (now "Frisco") RR. est. terminus here, this was merely scattered Creek Ind. settlement on E. bank of Ark. R. named "Tulsey Town" for Inds.' former community, Tulsey (now Tallasee), Ala. Main St. was surveyed by RR. engineer. Soon bustling cow town, Tulsa became resort of gamblers & bad men; nevertheless Sunday Sch. was formed in 1883 & Presb. mission est. following year. When oil was discovered across R. at Red Fork, town began to grow; bridge was hastily built across R. By 1910 boom was underway: hotels & office bldgs. were erected, streets paved, banks est., as fortunes were made from Okla.'s 1st big oil field, 16m away (S). By 1920, population was 72,075. Influx of both white & Negro laborers after World War I was followed by violent race riot in June, 1921, during which Negro dist. was burned & 36 persons were killed. Continued growth soon brought social stability. World War II led to increased industrial expansion, followed by greatest construction boom in city's history.

PTS. OF INT.: (1) 3 S. Boston Ave., **Union Depot** (1931), Okla.'s 1st, is modern-style structure with imposing foyer. (2) Standing before a home at 1730 S. Cheyenne Ave., **Old Council Tree** marks ancient place of gatherings from 1836 to 1898 of heads of Creek families for their "busks" (town meetings). (3) Boulder Ave. & 18th St., **Boulder Pk.** occupies a former Ind. campsite. (4) Frisco & Elwood Aves., bronze plate marks **Ind. Boundary Site,** where borders of Osage, Cherokee, & Creek Nations joined before Okla. was a St. (5) W. Edison St. & Quannah Ave., **Owen Pk.,** handsomely landscaped, contains **Mon.** comm. treaties by which Cherokee, Creek, & Osage tribes were given their lands in Ind. Terr. (6) Boston Ave. bet. 13th St. & 13th Pl., **Boston Ave. Meth. Ch.** (1929), with soaring vertical lines, is notable for application of modern functional design to religious bldg. (7) 2727 S. Rockford Ave., **Philbrook Art Mus.** (O. except Mon. 10-6, Tues. & Sun.2-6), housed in former priv. residence, houses colls. of painting, sculpture, tapestry, & other art works, incl. notable examples of Ind. art. (8) Bet. 5th & 6th Sts., Delaware Ave. & Gary Pl., **Univ. of Tulsa,** founded 1894 as Presb. mission sch. in Muskogee & moved in 1907 to Tulsa, where in 1922 it took present name & in 1928 became nonsect., occupies group of brick & stone bldgs. on thickly wooded campus; its College of Petroleum Sciences & Engineering is one of 13 in world. (9) E. 11th St. & S. Florence Ave., **Skelly Stadium,** seating 15,000, is used by Univ. of Tulsa & city high schs. (10) E. end of 15th St., **Tulsa St. Fair Grounds** & **International Petroleum Exposition Grounds,** latter covering 25 as., with 27 permanent bldgs. (11) Peoria Ave. & 21st St., **Woodward Pk.,** notable for rose garden. (12) 17th St. & Union Ave., **Mid-Continent Petroleum Corp. Refinery** (O.daily.guides), Tulsa's biggest industrial plant, one of greatest refineries of its special type, operating with heavy crude oils. (13) NE. edge of city, **Mohawk Pk.** (pic.swim.boat.f.recr.facils.), 3rd largest mun.-owned pk. (2,400 as.) in country, contains 2 Ls., mun. golf course & polo field, & zoo with Monkey I. (14) 41st St. 1$^m$ (W) from US64, **Tulsa's 1st P.O.,** est. 1879 in former hqs. of Figure-4 Ranch. Tulsa is at Js. with US75 (see), US64, & St.33.

SIDE TRIPS: (A) Take US64 (R) from Tulsa to **Sand Springs, 7.5$^m$,** where Cherokee Inds. sett. in 1826 but were forced to move when Creek Inds. claimed area in 1831. At S. edge of city, near Ark. R., **Creek Burial Ground** is preserved. 3rd & Memorial Sts., **Page Mem. Lib.** comm. oil millionaire Chas. Page, who bought land here in 1907, built home for widows & orphans & conn. it by electric ry. with Tulsa. Industries followed, & in 1911 city was platted. 19.5$^m$, **Keystone,** at fork of Cimarron & Ark. Rs., once saloon-infested frontier center, is now simple rural sett. US64 follows Ark. R. to **Cleveland,** 37$^m$, called "Gate City" because for yrs. it had only bridge across R. bet. Tulsa & Kans. Line. It is supported by ranching, dairying, & oil production. **Pawnee,** 58$^m$, became site of Pawnee Agency in 1876; town developed when Pawnee lands became avail. for sett. in 1893. Ind. Schools, U.S. Ind. Hospital, & Pawnee Agency are located here today. St.18 leads (R) 1$^m$ to 305-a. **L. Pawnee** (swim.recr.facils.). At 59.5$^m$, on Blue Hawk Peak, is **Home of "Pawnee Bill"** (Maj. Gordon W. Lillie), Ind. interpreter & frontiersman & originator of Pawnee Bill's Wild West Circus, who built **"Old Town,"** 61.5$^m$, now somewhat in disrepair, illustrating a frontier settlement. At 73.5$^m$ is J. with St.40.

Take latter (L) 12$^m$ to **Stillwater,** 1st sett. by "Boomers" (illegal homesteaders), who were ousted in 1885 from their "Prairie Dog Town" of dugouts by U.S. troops. It was officially platted after opening of Okla. Terr. in 1889 & developed as college town & farm center with agric. processing industries. At NW. edge, **Okla. Agric. & Mechanical College,** est. by act of Terr. Assembly in 1890, occupies over 55 bldgs. on 200-a. campus & outlying farm holdings; it carries on notable agric. experiment program & operates nation's only firemanship training sch. St.51 leads (R) 5$^m$ from Stillwater to 3,360-a. **L. Carl Blackwell** (swim.pic.boat.h.).

**Perry,** 85.5$^m$, rural sett., designated a land-office town when Cherokee Strip was opened in 1893, began as mushroom town of tents & clapboards, soon overrun with saloons & gamblers. US64 cont. to **Enid** (see US60), 125.5$^m$, at Js. with US60 (see) & US81 (see).

(B) Take St.33 (R) from Tulsa, which unites with US64 (see above) for 19.5$^m$, then branches (SW) to **Drumright,** 49$^m$, oil-boom town laid out in 1913 among for. of derricks in Cushing Field, for several years after 1912 world's richest. **Cushing,** 58.5$^m$, settled in 1892, boomed overnight with discovery of rich field in vic., known by its name; 12 refineries, over 700 tanks, & vast network of pipe lines were soon built here. Since 1930 abundant supply of water & natural gas & mun. light & power plant have attracted other industries. 68$^m$, **Langston,** an all-Negro town est. in 1890 by E. P. McCabe & named for Negro educator & Congressman John M. Langston of Va., is site of **Langston Univ.,** chartered by Terr. legislature in 1897, which emphasizes teacher-training & vocational courses. **Guthrie,** 100$^m$, est. with construction of A.T. & S.F. RR. in 1887, was only name on RR. map until opening of Okla. Terr. to settlers in 1889, when 15,000 flocked to site & within 3 wks. prairie metropolis developed, soon equipped with newspapers, waterworks, electric lights. Designated seat of gov., it remained capital of Okla. until 1910, when Okla. City supplanted it after forced election. 304 W. Okla. Ave., early **City Hall** (1902) where Constitutional Convention convened during 1906-07. **Scottish Rite Temple,** built at cost c. $2,500,000, is said to be largest in world devoted exclusively to Masonic purposes. 402 E. Okla. Ave., **Carnegie Lib.** was 1st in Okla.; last Terr. gov. & 1st St. Gov. were inaugurated on steps, & here on Flag Day, 1908, 90 women from all parts of Okla. made 1st official flag. S. edge of city, **Mineral Wells Pk.** has several artesian mineral wells; at entrance is **Shakespeare Garden.** From Guthrie, St.33 cont. 1$^m$ (W) to **Benedictine Heights**

**College,** Cath. women's college, outgrowth of St. Joseph's Academy, opened 1897, conducted by Benedictine Sisters of the Sacred Heart. Guthrie is at J. with US77, leading (S) to J. at 116.5m with US66 (see below).

(S) of Tulsa, US60 & US75 (see) are united for 14.5m. **124. SAPULPA,** as terminus of "Frisco" RR. after 1886, developed as cattle-shipping pt., named for Creek "Chief" J. M. Sapulpa, early settler near site. With discovery of oil in vic., Sapulpa boomed, & many of Creek Inds. grew wealthy from oil leases. Sapulpa now has glass, brick, pottery & packing plants. At E. edge is **Euchee Ind. Boarding Sch.,** est. 1893 & acquired by Fed. Gov. in 1928. At Sapulpa US75 (see) branches (S). US66 cont. to **BRISTOW, 149.,** which began as trading post among Creeks in 1897 & was est. as town soon after when "Frisco" RR. extended line here. Oil & gas production in vic. dominate its economic life. **180.5. CHANDLER,** dating from 1891, is one of country's 1st pecan-distribution pts., with pecan-shelling plant. At **213.5.** is J. with US77 (see above). **217. EDMOND,** est. as a railroad stopover & cattle-shipping pt. on Santa Fe Ry. in 1887, grew into town overnight in homesteaders' "Run" of Ap., 1889. It depends chiefly on agric. & oil. On edge of town, **Central St. College,** est. 1891.

**229. OKLAHOMA CITY**

Through RR., bus & plane conns. Accoms.: All types, incl. many tourist camps. Info.: Okla. City C. of C.; Okla. Auto Club, Biltmore Hotel. Recr. facils.: Mun. Aud. & Shrine Aud. for concerts & road shows, numerous motion picture theatres; golf at 2 mun. courses, Lincoln Pk. & SW. 29th St. & May Ave., & at many priv. courses; tennis at many mun. courts; swim. at Lincoln Pk. & Rotary Pk.; boat. & fish. at L. Overholser. Annual events: Livestock Show, last wk. Mar.; State Fair, last wk. Sept.; Flower Show, 1st wk. Oct.

Capital & largest city of Okla., Oklahoma City spreads (N) & (S) of usually dry N. Canadian R., with skyscrapers rising at its center & oil derricks crowding in at edges. At heart of city is modern Civic Center. (NE) lie St. Capitol & other St. bldgs., overtopped (N) by steel oil derricks, with handsome residential sec. adj. On E. side, beyond RR. tracks, is chief Negro sec. To (SE), oil derricks crowd whole quarter of city, squeezing out residences. On S. side, modest homes set on wide aves. extend into suburbs & farmlands beyond. Stockyards, packing plants & other industrial establishments border bus. dist. on W. To (NW) spreads chief residential dist., with schs., hospitals, & pks. Okla. City's 5 Fed. hys., 5 major RRs., 3 mun. & 3 priv. airports make it important transportation center. Its high gravity oil field is world's 2nd largest in production; oil processing & mfg. of oil field equipment are important industries. Situated where cotton & wheat belts overlap, it has become grain milling & cotton processing center. Its stockyards & packing plants make it Okla.'s chief cattle market. Its prosperity has given it wide variety of recr. & cultural facils.: Okla. City Univ. & Univ. of Okla. Sch. of Medicine, Okla. City Symphony Orchestra & Okla. Art Center, 66 pub. pks. & 2 outdoor amphitheaters, country clubs & sports facils.

Site was nothing but bare prairie until "Run" of Ap. 22, 1889, when 10,000 homesteaders camped here on land set aside for townsite around freight car used as sta. by Santa Fe Ry. For 13 months community was ruled by provisional gov. It grew rapidly, pop. increasing from 10,000 to 66,000 bet. 1890 & 1910 as flour & cottonseed-oil mills & meat-packing plants were est. & 4 more RRs. extended lines here. Capital of Okla. was removed here from Guthrie in 1910. World War I spurred economic development. Iron & steel plants, furniture & clothing factories, & electrical equipment plants were added. In Dec. 1928 Okla. City oil field was discovered; within 2 yrs. world oil market was flooded, & derricks were crowding into SE. sec. of city; gushers & spectacular fires occurred often. Drilling cont. throughout 1930's; wells were sunk even within few yards of St. Capitol. By 1940 pop. had increased to 204,424. World War II, during which Okla. City's mun. airport became important Army Air Corps base, brought further expansion.

PTS. OF INT.: (1) Lincoln Blvd. bet. 21st & 23rd Sts., **St. Capitol** (1914-17.neo.-Class.by S.A.Layton) is a huge bldg. in the form of a cross with Corinthian porticoes on N. & S. facades; orig. design called for central dome, but this was not built for economy reasons. (2) Adj. on (S) & (W) is **Capitol Office Bldg.** (Mod.-Class.by J. Duncan Forsyth). (3) Adj. Capitol on S. & E. is **St. Hist. Soc. Bldg.** (O. except Sun. & Sat. aft. 1930. neo-Class. by Layton, Hicks, & Forsyth), housing **Mus. & Lib.** Mus. contains colls. of relics pertaining chiefly to SW., Okla., & Inds. (4) 700 E. 23rd St., **Governor's Mansion** (1928.Dutch Col.by Layton,Hicks & Forsyth). (5) 801 E.

13th St., **Univ. of Okla. Medical Sch., Univ. Hospital, & Crippled Children's Hospital.** (6) 120 N. Robinson St., **1st Nat. Bldg.,** Okla.'s tallest bank-office structure, built in int. modern style, with observ. platform on 32nd story. (7) Bet. Harvey & Shartel Aves. & 1st & 2nd Sts., **Civic Center** (1936-37) comprises **Cty. Bldg.** (mod. Class. by S.A.Layton & Geo. Forsyth), **Mun. Bldg.** (mod. Romanes.), & **Mun. Aud.** (mod. Class.by J.O.Parr). (8) 3d St. bet. Robinson & Harvey Aves., **Fed. Bldg.** (mod. Class. E.sec.1912,central & W. secs. 1934). (9) N. Blackwelder Ave. & 24th St., **Okla. City Univ.,** est. in 1904, is nonsectarian institution under Meth. Ch. jurisdiction, with notable Fine Arts Sch. (10) Exchange & Agnew Aves., **Stockyards & Packing Plants** (conducted tours 10:30-1:30 except Mon. & Sat.) form one of SW.'s chief livestock centers. (11) Eastern Ave. at NE. edge of city, **Lincoln Pk.** (pic.camp. hik. riding.golf.zoo) is Okla. City's largest pub. recr. center.

SIDE TRIPS: (A) Take US270 (L) from Okla. City. At 38m is J. with gravel Rd. leading (L) short distance to **St. Gregory's College for Young Men,** est. 1915 by Benedictine Fathers, whose **Gerrer Mus. & Art Gallery** (O.Sun.afts.) contains Ren. paintings & 4,500 curious objects gathered from all over world: Egyptian, Babylonian, Oriental, Greek, & others. **Shawnee,** 41.5m, on N. Canadian R., orig. Shawnee Ind. trading post, boomed to importance in 1920's with discovery of immensely rich oil fields. Laid out in 1892, it acquired 1st RR. in 1895 & 2nd in 1902. It was wrecked by cyclone in 1924 & by flood in 1928. Drilling of more than 10,000 wells in vic. in 1920's increased pop. to 35,000. Following oil boom, Shawnee began to depend on agric. processing industries: milling & cottonseed oil & cheese making & others. **Woodland Pk.** (swim.pic.tennis) contains **Beard Log Cabin,** 1st home in town. At NE. edge of city, **Okla. Bapt. Univ.,** opened 1911.

Take St.18 2.5m (R) from Shawnee to **Shawnee Ind. Agency, Sanatorium,** old **Quaker Mission, & Cemetery.** Mission was started by Society of Friends in 1885.

US270 cont. to **Seminole,** 60m, named for Seminole Inds. of vic., which was simple farming community until discovery in 1926 of Seminole oil pool, one of richest in history, brought pop. of 6,000 within a few days with attendant vice & crime problem of huge proportions. Oil is still main industry, but agric. is now also important. **Wewoka,** 72.5m, was est. as capital of Seminole Nation in 1866 on land bought from Creek Inds. RR. conn. was acquired in 1899 & white settlers began arriving in 1902. Development of Greater Seminole Oil Field in 1926 spurred rapid development. Immediate vic. is now famous for the corn it produces. **Holdenville,** 84m, laid out in 1895, also boomed with development of Greater Seminole Field. At 93m is J. with US75 (see).

(B) Take US77 (L) from Okla. City to **Norman,** 19m, sett. by homesteaders on day of "Run," Ap. 22, 1889. **Univ. of Okla.,** est. in 1890 & opened in 1892, occupies large group of Coll. Goth. bldgs. on shady, grassgrown campus; it is widely known for its Sch. of Geology & Sch. of Petroleum Engineering. In Art Bldg. is **Matzene Coll. of Oriental Art;** in basement of Monnett Hall, **Mus. of Ind. Relics;** in front of Geology Bldg., **Coll. of Fossilized Trees,** and inside, **Mus. of Paleontology** (O) with coll. of 100,000 invertebrate fossils; in Biological Sciences Bldg., **Mus. of Zoology.** Other bldgs. incl. **Lib.,** with valuable coll. of rare books & MSS., & **Mem. Stadium,** seating 32,000.

## Sec. 2: OKLA. CITY to OKLA.-TEX. LINE. 166.

**7. BETHANY,** sett. 1906 by members of Nazarene religious sect, is site of **Bethany-Peniel College,** est. in 1906 & moved here in 1909, specializing in training for Nazarene ministry. **9. L. OVERHOLSER** (1,700 as.f.boat.pic.), impounded by damming of N. Canadian R. to furnish Okla. City's water supply, is seaplane base. **14. YUKON,** in farm reg., is market town, platted in 1891. **27. EL RENO,** settled with advent of Rock I. RR. in 1889 near S. bank of N. Canadian R., attracted 1,500 settlers from across R. who had refused to pay bonus demanded by RR. for locating line on N. bank & moved here, carting all their belongings, even their homes. It is now marketing, flour milling & RR. repair shop center. El Reno is at J. with US81 (see). At **29.** is **U.S. SOUTHWESTERN REFORMATORY** (1934) for 1st offenders under 34 against Fed. law. Short distance beyond is J. with Rd. leading (R) 2m to **Ft. Reno,** est. 1874 to protect Darlington Ind. Agency against Cheyenne uprisings, & now U.S. Army's largest Remount Sta. with extensive stables. At **36.5.** is J. with US270.

SIDE TRIP: Take US270 (R) to **Geary,** 16m, est. 1898, farm trade center with flour mill & cheese factory. **Watonga,** 32.5m, named for Arapaho chief (name means "Black Coyote") & still inhabited by many Arapaho & Cheyenne, was est. in 1892; it has cotton gins & grain elevators.

Take St.8 (R) from Watonga 6m to **Roman Nose St. Pk.** (pic.trlrs.boat.swim.), comm. the last warrior chief of Cheyenne, Henry Roman Nose, who lived here in dugout; its 520 as. incl. springs, streams & L.

US270 cont. to **Seiling,** 72m (see US60), at J. with US60 (see).

**63. WEATHERFORD,** rural market village sett. in 1893, is site of **SW. INST. OF TECHNOLOGY,** founded 1901 as St. teachers' college, emphasizing vocational-training. **86.5. CLINTON,** laid out in 1903 with advent of "Frisco" RR., is cattle- & wheat-shipping center. Skirting the cotton-ginning center of **CANUTE, 108.,** Cath. Cemetery contains bronze **Crucifixion Group & Grotto** representing Sepulcher. At **114.** is J. with St.34.

SIDE TRIP: Take latter (R) 14.5m to **Hammon** & turn (R) here to **Cheyenne Ind. Settlement** on Cheyenne & Arapaho Ind. Reserv., where Cheyenne preserve old tribal customs.

**116.5. ELK CITY,** agric. trading & shipping center. At **133. SAYRE,** est. in 1901, is broomcorn market & livestock sales center, with oil refinery & carbon black plant, at J. with US283, which unites (S) with US66 to J. at **135.**

SIDE TRIP: Take US283 (L) 30.5m to **Mangum,** named for early landowner Capt. A. S. Mangum, now center of widespread agric. reg. At 43m is J. with St.44.

Take latter (L) 1.5m to J. with gravel Rd. & turn (L) on this to **Quartz Mt. St. Pk.** (3,300 as.f.swim.pic.cabins), with unusually colored granite hills, in which are **Lugert Dam,** 458' long, impounding **L. Altus** to feed 70,000 as. of W. C. Austin Irrigation Project, Okla.'s 1st.

**Altus,** 56.5m, oil & farm marketing center, founded in 1891, is seat of Jackson Cty., in 1920's world's biggest cotton-producing cty. & latterly one of Okla.'s chief wheat-producing cties.; W. C. Austin Irrigation Project (see above) is expected to boom population.

US66 cont. (W) to **ERICK, 148.5.,** est. in 1902, trade center for farms, cattle ranches, & natural gas field. Just (W) of **TEXOLA, 155.5.,** is **OKLA.-TEX. LINE, 156.**

## US 70—OKLAHOMA

**OKLA.-ARK. LINE** (8m from DeQueen, Ark.) **(W) to OKLA.-TEX. LINE** (16m from Vernon, Tex.). **313. US70**

Via: Hugo, Durant, & Ardmore. RRs. parallel most of route. Accoms.: In larger towns.

US70 is bordered (S) by cotton-growing area & (N) by once heavily timbered sec.; it follows trl. blazed by Choctaw Inds. who traveled westward from Miss. to new homes in Okla.

**0. OKLA.-ARK. LINE. 7.5. EAGLETOWN,** which became one of principal Choctaw settlements following their removal to Ind. Terr. (1831-33) & acquired Okla.'s 1st p.o., has old **Log Cth. & Whipping Tree** where lawbreakers were punished. At **8.5.** is J. with rural Rd. (R) leading shortly to a farmhouse where foot trl. cont. to **Cypress Tree,** 0.4m, one of largest known, 90' high, with circumference of 56'. **17.5. BROKEN BOW,** in heart of Okla.'s chief forest area, was named by Dierks Bros., pioneer lumbermen who built mill here, for their Neb. home.

SIDE TRIP: Take St.21 (R) from Broken Bow 9m to J. with improved Rd. & turn (R) on this to **Beavers Bend St. Pk.** (camp.pic.f.boat.), 1,300-a. rugged, wooded tract bisected by Mt. Fork R.

**29. IDABEL,** named for daughters, Ida & Belle, of Choctaw settler, depends on farming & lumbering. At **MILLERTON, 41.5.,** is J. with good Rd. leading (R) 2m to Gov.-supervised **Wheelock Academy,** est. 1832 for Ind. girls by missionary Alfred Wright, & **Wheelock Mission Ch.** (1842), oldest ch. in Okla., erected by Presb. missionaries. **VALLIANT, 46.5.,** is site of **Alice Lee Elliott Mem. School** for Negroes, begun in 1870 as industrial school for Choctaw freedmen. At **56.** is J. with poor Rd. leading (R) 0.5m to **Ruins of Orig. Ft. Towson,** est. in 1824 by Fed. Gov. to protect Choctaw Inds., twice abandoned & twice re-est., then occupied by Confeds. in Civil War; this was 2nd ft. est. in Okla. **72. HUGO,** which has pecan-cracking mill, peanut butter factory, & creosoting plant, was named by wife of townsite's surveyor for Victor Hugo, whom she admired. At **78.5.** is J. with US271.

SIDE TRIP: Take latter (R). **Antlers,** 14.5m, whose name is derived from Indian custom of marking site of near-by spring by fastening antlers to tree, is lumbering center. US271 winds through Kiamichi Mts. to **Tuskahoma,** 59m, whose name means "Red Warrior," dating from advent of "Frisco" RR. in 1888, from which dirt Rd. leads (L) 2m to red-brick **Choctaw Council H.** (1883), until 1906 political capital of Choctaw Nation, whose hqs. were est. in this vic. in 1838.

**BOSWELL, 94. & BENNINGTON, 105.** began as Choctaw settlements. At **BOKCHITO, 112.,** poor Rd. leads (R) 2.5m to ruins of **Armstrong Academy** (1844), est. by Choctaw Council. **126.5. DURANT** was sett. in 1870 by Choctaw Indian group which has cottonseed-oil mill, pecan cracking & picking plant, & peanut warehouses

& processing plants; surrounding reg. produces livestock, hay & grain, & potatoes, as well as peanuts & pecans. At N. edge, **SE. St. College,** opened 1909, is teacher-training sch. with stadium & amphitheatre on landscaped campus. On W. side, **Presb. College for Girls.** Durant is at J. with US75 (see). At **138.** US70 bridges arm of **L. Texoma** (f.boat.water sports), more than 100,000 as. in extent, formed in 1940's by damming of Red R. **154. MADILL** is center of livestock & farming area dotted with equipment of oil field opened in 1907 & still producing.

SIDE TRIP: Take St.99 (R) crossing arm of L. Texoma (see above), to **Tishomingo,** 12.5m, named for Chickasaw leader, which was capital of Chickasaw Nation, 1856-1907. Two-story granite Chickasaw capitol bldg. is now **Johnston County Cth.;** on grounds stands orig. **Log Council H.** At S. edge of town, **Murray St. Sch. of Agriculture,** authorized in 1908. At 14.5m is J. with a lane leading (L) 2m to **Devil's Den** (private.fee.f.camp.cabins), rocky area traversed by Pennington Cr. with grotesque caverns & formations.

**182.5. ARDMORE,** boasting itself "capital of S. central Okla.," est. in 1887 as cattle-loading pt. on A.T.& S.F. RR. & grew slowly as cotton market & farmers' trading pt. until development of Red Beds oil field after 1913 catapulted it to prominence. But unlike other oil-boom towns, Ardmore, though it still depends on oil, turned after 1920 to diversified agriculture & industrial development for support: it now has cotton gins, compresses & oil mills; dairy, livestock, & poultry products processing plants; flour milling & peanut oil plants; & other industries. At N. edge of city is **Carter Seminary,** Fed. Gov. sch. for Ind. girls, outgrowth of Bloomfield Academy founded near Durant (see above) in 1852.

SIDE TRIPS: (A) Take Washington St. (S) from Ardmore to 18,350-a. **L. Murray St. Pk.** (cabins.camp.pic.swim.boat.f.), largest St. pk. in Okla., surrounding 6,100-a. L. impounded by **L. Murray Dam;** one of chief attractions is **Tucker Tower,** jutting from rocky promontory over L.

(B) Take US77 (R) from Ardmore 17m to J. with country Rd. leading (L) short distance into **Turner Falls Pk.** (camp.pic.) in Arbuckle Mts., where Honey Cr. tumbles through rock gorge to clear pool. At 19.5m is J. with rural Rd. leading (R) 2.5m to **Price's Falls** (camp.cabins.pic.f.swim.). **Davis,** 24m, dating from 1887, is at J. with St.7, on which route turns (R) to **Sulphur,** 33m, pleasure & health resort with many swim. pools supplied by mineral water wells. At 33.5m is J. with St.18, leading (R) through **Platt Nat. Pk.** (camp. pic.swim.), well-wooded area (848 as.) of rolling hills traversed by Travertine & Rocks Crs. with springs & waterfalls. At 33.7m is J. with Perimeter Blvd., encircling pk. past chief pts. of int.: **Flower Pk.,** 33.8m; **Black Sulphur Springs,** 34m; **Bromide Springs & Campgrounds & Bromide Hill** 34.7m; **Buffalo Pasture,** 36.2m; **Buffalo Springs,** 39m; & **Antelope Springs,** 39.5m. At 41.5 is J. with St.18, on which route turns (L) past **Pavilion Springs & Adm. Bldg.,** 41.7m.

US70 cont. (W) to J. with US81 (see) at **231. WAURIKA, 232.5.,** farm & RR. center, dates from 1892. Turning (S) across Red R., hy. reaches **OKLA.-TEX.LINE, 313.**

## US 75—OKLAHOMA

**OKLA.-KANS. LINE** (2m from Caney, Kans.) **(S) to OKLA.-TEX. LINE** (5m from Denison, Tex.). **278. US75**

Via: Bartlesville, Tulsa, Okmulgee, Atoka, & Durant. RRs. parallel most of route. Accoms.: At convenient intervals.

US75, cutting (S) through E. Okla., traverses grazing lands & oil fields, farming & coal mining secs.

**0. OKLA.-KANS. LINE. 15. DEWEY,** est. 1898, has a large cement plant & holds annual rodeo. **18.5. BARTLESVILLE** (see US60) is at J. with US60. At **47.5.** is J. with poor Rd. leading (R) 6m to **Site of Hillside Mission,** est. 1884 by Society of Friends of Philadelphia for work among Inds.; in front of orig. bldg., still standing, is large elm grown from shoot from Wm. Penn Elm of Philadelphia. **75. TULSA** (see US66) is at J. with US66 (see), with which US75 unites (SW) to **SAPULPA** (see US66), **89.5.** It then branches (S) through Okla.'s 1st spectacularly productive oil field, known as Glenn Pool, developed 1905-06. **122. OKMULGEE,** whose Creek Ind. name means "Bubbling Water," was sett. in 1868 by Creek Inds., who built log Council H. to serve as capitol of Creek Nation. Here met not only Creek Council (comprising House of Kings & House of Warriors) but also Intertribal Council of head men of Five Civilized Tribes. After 1899, when Creek Lands were divided, came 1st white settlers. Rich oil field was opened in vic. in 1907. Today Okmulgee depends on oil, cotton & pecan crops, truck farming, poultry breeding & dairying. 6th & Morton Sts., **Creek Ind. Nat. Council H.** (O), 2-story stone structure with cupola, built following demolition of orig. log Council H. in 1878, is preserved by Creek Ind. Mem. Assoc.

SIDE TRIP: Take St.27 (R) from Okmulgee to **L. Okmulgee** (720 as.recr.facils.).

**137. HENRYETTA,** est. in 1900 with the advent of "Frisco" RR. & named for Hugh & Etta Henry, Inds., is industrial city with smelter, foundry, glass & glazing plants, & other industries. Country Rd. leads (L) 1.5$^m$ to **Jack Nichols Recr. Pk.** (640 as.swim.bathh.f.camp.pic.racetrack.rodeo & baseball grounds), incl. L. & 50-a. Creek Ind. nat. campground. **WELEETKA, 151.5.,** & **WETUMKA, 162.,** are farmer's trading centers with many Creek Ind. inhabitants. At **CALVIN, 182.,** is J. with US270.

SIDE TRIP: Take latter (L) to **McAlester,** 31$^m$, where James J. McAlester founded crossroads store in 1870 & with aid of Chickasaw & Choctaw friends opened rich coal deposits in vic. Town grew up later around inters. of Rock I. & M.-K.-T. RRs. McAlester is now Okla.'s chief coal mining center; other industries incl. meat packing, cotton-oil milling, lumbering, dry gas drilling.

Take Rainbow Hy. (L) from McAlester, past **Okla. St. Penitentiary** (O.Tues.& Fri. guides), 1$^m$, to **Rainbow Gardens** (O.on appl. at 319 E. Grand, McAlester), 8$^m$, summer encampment of international girls' organization, Order of the Rainbow. At 9$^m$ is **L. McAlester** (cabins.f.), with Rd.-encircled 35$^m$ shore.

US270 cont. (E) through several coal-mining towns, of which **Hartshorne,** 46.5$^m$, is largest, & past **E. Okla. Agric. & Mechanical College,** 61$^m$, St. jr. college est. in 1909, to **Wilburton,** 64$^m$, developed as coal mining center after 1890.

Take St.2 (L) from Wilburton 4$^m$ to **Robber's Cave St. Pk.** (cabins.camp.pic.swim.boat. f.hik.), 8,400 rugged as. with L. & streams, named for labyrinthine **Robber's Cave,** 100′ up side of limestone cliff.

At **211.** is J. with St.3.

SIDE TRIP: Take latter (R) to **Ada,** 33$^m$, named for daughter of 1st settler, Jeff Reed, who built log store & dwelling here in 1889. It acquired 1st RR. in 1900; its pop., over 4,000 in 1910, almost doubled by 1920 & almost doubled again by 1940. Rich oil fields in vic. have contributed to growth; Ada also has flour mills & cement plant. Main St. & Francis Ave., **E. Central St. College,** 1 of St.'s biggest, dating back to 1909; at entrance to campus is enormous fossilized stump of **Callixylon,** tree dating back to Devonian period. At S. edge of city, **Wintersmith Pk.** (137 as.swim.bathh.boat.f.hik.riding.) with large amphitheater.

US75 cont. (S) to **COALGATE, 215.,** where a mine was discovered in 1882. **228. ATOKA,** founded by Bapt. missionary Rev. J. S. Murrow in 1867 & named for famous Choctaw chief. At **229.** is J. with a country lane.

SIDE TRIP: Take latter (R) to J. with 2nd dirt Rd., 4.5$^m$, & turn (L) on this to **Site of Boggy Depot,** 9.5$^m$, est. 1838 to become flourishing Chickasaw-Choctaw trading center & (during Civil War) Confed. stronghold, with many big Hs., of which **Home of Chief Allen Wright** remains. Wright, who served 2 terms as Gov. of Choctaw Nation, gave Okla. its name (Choctaw phrase meaning "Red People").

At **255.5.** is **ST. FISH HATCHERY** on Blue R. At **256.** is J. with county Rd.

SIDE TRIP: Take latter (R) to J. with St.299, 1$^m$, turn (R) on this to J. at 9.5$^m$ with dirt Rd. & (L) here, then (R) at 10$^m$ & (R) again at 13.5$^m$ to **Site of Ft. Washita,** est. in 1842 by Gen. Zachary Taylor to protect Chickasaw & Choctaw Inds. from wild tribes of SW., marked by ruins of many bldgs. & old military cemetery.

**261. DURANT** (see US70) at J. with US70 (see). At **COLBERT, 275.5.,** is J. with county Rd. leading (R) 5$^m$ to earthen **Denison Dam,** 3$^m$ long & 140′ high, at confluence of Washita & Red Rs., impounding **L. Texoma** (see US70). US75 bridges Red R., **278.,** to **OKLA.-TEX. LINE.**

## US 81—OKLAHOMA

**OKLA.-KANS. LINE** (2.5$^m$ from Caldwell, Kans.) **(S) to OKLA.-TEX. LINE** (4$^m$ from Ringgold, Tex.). **233. US81**

Via: Enid, El Reno, Chickasha, Duncan, & Waurika. Rock I. RR. parallels route. Accoms.: At short intervals.

US81, roughly paralleling route of old Chisholm Trl., over which millions of Tex. longhorns were driven to RR. termini in Kans., traverses wheat-growing country in N. & cotton-growing & diversified farming area in S.

**0. OKLA.-KANS. LINE. 15. MEDFORD,** wheat-growing & farming center. At **POND CREEK** (see US60), **26.5.,** is J. with US60 (see), which unites with US81 to **ENID** (see US60), **49.5. HENNESSEY, 70.,** platted in 1889, was named for a pioneer on Chisholm Trl., tortured to death here by Cheyenne in 1874; **Grave of Patrick Hennessey,** surmounted by stone mem., lies 3 blocks (R) from hy. Cattlemen & stage line operator named King Fisher gave name to **KINGFISHER, 88.5.,** wheat-growers' center est. at time of Okla. "Run" in 1889. At **107.5.** is J. with improved Rd. leading (R) 2m to **Concho,** where large group of frame & brick bldgs. form **Cheyenne & Arapaho Agency,** administering 5,280-a. Cheyenne & Arapaho Ind. Reserv. Here on May Day & Labor Day c.5,000 Inds. assemble for festivities incl. tribal dances. Near-by is **Cheyenne & Arapaho Boarding Sch.** (SE) of agency (c.2.5m) is **St. Game Farm,** propagating quail & wild turkey, on site of Darlington Agency, est. 1869 by Brinton Darlington. US81 cont. (S) to **EL RENO** (see US66), **112.,** at J. with US66 (see). **146.** J. with US62.

SIDE TRIP: Take latter (R) to **Anadarko,** 19m, selected in 1858 as site of reserv. for Anadarko, Caddo, Delaware, Keechie, Shawnee, Tonkawa, Towakony, & Waco Inds. Agency was destroyed during Civil War & rebuilt in 1871. When Kiowa-Comanche & Wichita Reservs. were opened to sett. (1901), 20,000 people flocked here. Discovery of oil in 1920's spurred town's later growth. Annual Amer. Ind. Exposition (late Aug.) is attended by many Inds. in full tribal costume. **Ind. Agency,** housed in Fed. Bldg., 1st St. & Okla. Ave., serves members of Apache, Comanche, Kiowa & Wichita tribes; it has int. murals by Mopope, Kiowa artist. US281 leads (R) 1.5m to **Riverside Ind. Boarding School,** founded 1872. US62 cont. (W) to **St. Patrick's Mission Sch.** for Ind. children, 21m, est. 1892, whose **Mem. Chapel** has murals by Kiowa Ind. artists. At 52m is J. with St.49.

Take latter (R) into Wichita Mts. **Medicine Pk.,** 6.5m, is summer resort on edge of **L. Lawtonka** (f.swim.boat.). At 7.5m is E. Gate of 61,480-a. **Wichita Mts. Wildlife Refuge,** containing buffalo, elk, white-tailed deer, Tex. longhorns, wild turkeys, & birds. **Mt. Scott Campgrounds,** 8.5m, are near **L. Thomas** (swim.). At 9.5m is J. with Mt. Scott Scenic Rd. leading (R) 3m to summit of **Mt. Scott** (2,400'). At 12m is J. with Mears Hy., on which route turns (L) to J. with Rush L. Trl., 12.4m, leading (R) to **Easter Holy City,** 1m, with red sandstone bldgs. in natural amphitheater, site of Easter pageant, & to **L. Rush** (f.), 2m. Mears Hy. cont., past Js. with side Rds. at 12.5m & 15m to **L. Jed Johnson** & **Ind. Hill L.,** to J. at 15.5m with Scenic Hy., on which route turns R. At 16m is J. with Rd. leading (L) 1m to **Quanah Parker Dam** (70' high) & 68-a. L. At 16.5m is J. with trl. leading (L) 0.3m to **Quanah Parker Campgrounds** & **Seminole Beach** (bathh.) with attractive native-stone bldgs. At 19.5m is J. with Trl. leading (L) to **Lost L.,** 1m, & **Camp Boulder,** 2.5m. At 20.5m is **Prairie Dog Town,** with c.4,000 prairie dogs, & beyond are **Exhibition Pastures** with herds of elk, bison, deer, & Tex. longhorns. At 21.5m is J. with gravel Rd. leading short distance to **Refuge Hqs.** with **Coll. of Wildlife Specimens.** Route cont. to SW. Gate, 24.5m.

US62 cont. to J. at 55.5m with Ft. Sill Rd.

Take latter (R) into **Ft. Sill Military Reserv.,** comprising over 51,000 as., where in 1869 Gen. Philip H. Sheridan est. post to keep peace among Plains Inds. & since 1911 U.S. Army has maintained Field Artillery Sch. (now largest in country). Rd. passes **Old Corral** (1870), 0.3m; bldgs. of **Old Post,** 0.6m, incl. **Old Chapel** (1870), **Post Commandant's Quarters** & **Mus.** (O.wks. & Sun.afts.), housed in guardh. where Apache chief Geronimo spent last years; & **Adm. Bldg.** & adj. **Sta. Hospital** & **Officers Quarters,** 1.2m. It cont. around **New Post Parade Ground,** bordered by barracks & other post structures, to S. Gate at J. with US62, 6m.

59.5m, **Lawton** mushroomed up in 1901 after opening of the 3,000,000-a. Kiowa-Comanche lands to settlers, drawing overnight pop. of 10,000. It grew steadily until 1930, when expansion of Ft. Sill (see above) spurred more rapid development. It serves Ft. Sill & farmers of vic. as trading center & has several industries, incl. cottonseed-oil mill; vic. is rich in asphalt, granite & other bldg. materials. At W. edge, **Cameron St. Agric. College,** Okla.'s largest jr. college, founded 1909.

**147.5. CHICKASHA,** on Washita R., became favorite campsite on Chisholm Trl. Its growth dates from Rock I. RR.'s choice of its sta. here as division pt., with repair shops. Cattle-feeding pens & cotton gins, mills & compresses were soon est. Today neighboring oil & gas fields & broomcorn growing area (for which it is processing & marketing center) contribute to prosperity. At SW. edge are **Okla. College for Women,** founded 1908 & St.-supported, & **Shannoan Springs Pk.** (f.boat.), with L., zoo, & mus. of pioneer relics. **167. RUSH SPRINGS,** former Wichita Ind. village, is famous as watermelon marketing center. **176.5. MARLOW,** agric. center dating from RR.'s advent in 1892, was named for 5 Marlow Bros., cattle thieves. **188. DUNCAN,** laid out in 1892, has cotton gins & cottonseed oil mills & is one of Okla.'s chief primary markets for cream; it is central supply pt. for large oil field, & has plant serving oil industry throughout world with equipment for oil well cementing. At N. edge, **Fuqua Pk.** has mun. swim. pool. **197.5. COMANCHE** is sprawling town encircled by oil wells. At **212.5.** is J. with US70 (see). **233.** US81 crosses Red R. to **OKLA.-TEX. LINE.**

## US 60—TEXAS

**TEX.-OKLA. LINE** (15$^{m}$ from Arnett, Okla.) **(W) to FARWELL. 224. US60**

Via: Canadian, Pampa & Amarillo. RRs. parallel route. Accoms.: Ample.

US60 runs (SW) across Tex. Panhandle over High Plains, almost treeless, often dust-swept in summer. **27. CANADIAN,** on curve of Canadian R., 1st known as Hog-town, then as Desperado City, orig. sett. by RR. builders, buffalo hunters, freighters & soldiers. Surrounded by oil derricks, **PAMPA, 73.** lies on prairie resembling Argentine pampas. Long a cattle shipping pt., is now modern-looking oil town.

**101. PANHANDLE,** dominated by grain elevators. At **124.** is J. with US66 (see).

**129. AMARILLO** (see US66), at J. with US87 (see). **144.** J. with St.87 (see).

At **175.** is J. with Rd. leading (L) 1$^{m}$ to **Hereford St. Pk.** (540 as.pic.) in cottonwood-shaded Tierra Blanca Cr. canyon. **176. HEREFORD,** center of irrigated area. In vic. are slab-house ruins, erected by prehist. people of Stone Age. US60 crosses grain-growing sec. to **FARWELL, 224.,** agric. market center, named for Farwell Bros., builders of St. Capitol, who received land grant stretching into 10 counties.

## US 66—TEXAS

**TEX.-OKLA. LINE** (8$^{m}$ from Erick, Okla.) **(W) to TEX.-N.M. LINE. 178. US66**

Via: Shamrock & Amarillo. RR. parallels route. Accoms.: Ample.

US66 slices center of Tex. Panhandle, producing oil & gas, wheat & other grains, & cattle. **14. SHAMROCK,** with several carbon black & gasoline extraction plants, is in E. part of Panhandle; gas field, one of world's largest. J. with US83.

SIDE TRIP: Take latter (S) into hills known as **Rocking Chair Mts.,** so-called for Rocking Chair Ranch est. here in 1883 by group of Brit. noblemen, also known as "The Kingdom of Remittance Men." 25$^{m}$ **Wellington,** in center of rich cotton belt. 55$^{m}$ **Childress,** RR. division pt., with cotton compress, grain elevator & feed factory. US83 cont. to 86$^{m}$ **Paducah,** at J. with US70 (see).

**102.** J. with US60 (see), which unites with US66 to Amarillo.

**107. AMARILLO**

Through RR. & bus conns. Accoms.: Many hotels & tourist camps. Info.: C. of C., Amarillo Hotel. Golf at Wolflin & Thompson Pks.; swim. at Thompson Pk. Livestock Show, Mar.; Tri-State Music Festival, Mar. or Ap.; Tri-State Fair, Sept.

Metropolis of Panhandle, modern-looking city with shaded avenues & pks., ships cattle, wheat, oil & gas, & manufactured articles: clay & cottonseed products, boots & saddles, foundry items. Here is U.S. Helium Plant which processes much of world's supply. Town grew out of RR. construction camp of Ft. Worth & Denver City RR., built across Panhandle in 1887; town was known as "Ragtown," a coll. of huts—even a hotel—made of buffalo hide. After buffalo in vic. were slaughtered, bone gathering became profitable occupation as bones were shipped away to be made into fertilizer. Town was laid out by Henry B. Sanborn, who had it made cty. seat by offering cowboys of LX Ranch one lot each for their votes. New name, Amarillo (Sp., "yellow") suggested either by near-by yellow-banked Cr. or by yellow flowers that blanket prairie in spring, so pleased Sanborn he had all bldgs. in town painted bright yellow. For yrs. Amarillo was typical cow town. But in 1883, Sanborn himself fenced his property with barbed wire, J. F. Glidden's invention, which soon crisscrossed grazing lands of vic. PTS. OF INT.: (1) 8th Ave. & Hughes St., **Amarillo L.,** near which early settlement located. (2) Western Ave. & S. 4th Ave., **Early Drift Fence** (1882); range cattle shun cactus, giving rise to idea of barbs on wire. (3) **Ellwood Pk.** (25 as.playground) has **Mon.** to Fray Juan de Padilla, 1st churchman to enter reg. in Coronado expedition. At **116.** is **U.S. HELIUM PLANT** (O.appl.), which at one time processed more than half world's helium supply. **142. VEGA** is J. with dirt Rd.

SIDE TRIP: Take latter (R) 22$^{m}$ to **Old Tascosa,** on N. bank of Canadian R., queen of Tex. ghost towns, with old rock cth. & crumbling adobes, once "Cowboy Capital of Plains," with saloons, gambling halls, crowded boardwalks & frequent gunplay. Old cth. now houses **Maverick Boys' Ranch,** est. by Maverick Club of Amarillo, patterned after Boy's Town (Neb.).

**178. TEX.-OKLA. LINE.**

## US 70—TEXAS

**TEX.-OKLA. LINE** (2$^{m}$ from Davidson, Okla.) **(W) to FARWELL. 253. US70**
Via: Vernon, Paducah & Plainview. RRs. parallel parts of route. Accoms.: In larger towns.

US70 crosses N. Tex., where ranches & farms produce cattle, cotton, & wheat. Country flat & dusty; mirages common in summer.

**0.** Hy. bridges Red R. at **TEX.-OKLA. LINE. 6.** J. unites US287 for 8$^{m}$ with US70. **15. VERNON,** mill, meat packing plant & oil refineries. Began 1880 as supply pt. for cattle herders on Western Trl.

SIDE TRIPS: (A) Take US287 (SE) 23$^{m}$ to **Electra,** prosperous modern-looking town, named for daughter of W. T. Waggoner, who struck oil (1911) on his 600,000-a. ranch. Electra's oil wells have given rise to mfg. of drilling tools & oil-well machinery. 50$^{m}$ **Wichita Falls** (see US81).
(B) Take US287 (NW) from Vernon 16$^{m}$ to **Chillicothe,** grain & cotton center. At 24$^{m}$ is J. with Rd. leading (L) 1$^{m}$ to **L. Pauline** (boat.cabins), E. of which are 4 **Medicine Mounds,** once Comanche camp sites.
29$^{m}$ **Quanah,** named for Comanche war chief. In vic. are many plaster plants, utilizing near-by gypsum deposits.
On St.283 (S) 9$^{m}$ to ranch Rd. leading 1$^{m}$ (R) to C. T. Watkins Ranch, **Site of Tex.-Okla. Wolf Hunt** (last wk.Sept.).
US287 cont. 58$^{m}$ to **Childress,** J. with US83.
(C) Take US183-283 (S) from Vernon. 29$^{m}$ **L. Kemp** (boats.f.fee) with c. 100$^{m}$ of shore line, created by dam of Wichita Valley Irrigation Proj. 92$^{m}$, **Ft. Griffin,** military post est. 1867. **Ft. Griffin St. Pk.** preserves some crumbling bldgs. of old post. 140$^{m}$, **L. Cisco Dam** (f.swim.pic.fee). 143$^{m}$ **Cisco** is at J. with US80 (see).

US70 traverses cotton & grain-growing area whose chief market centers are **46. CROWELL, 82. PADUCAH,** & **114. MATADOR;** to (S) lies 466,000-a. **Matador Ranch.** US70 cont. through several small towns & past huge ranches to **253. FARWELL** & J. with US60 (see).

## US 67—TEXAS

**TEXARKANA (SW) to PRESIDIO. 784. US67**
Via: Sulphur Springs, Greenville, Dallas, Cleburne, Brownwood, San Angelo, Ft. Stockton & Marfa. RRs. parallel most of route. Accoms.: Ample.

US67 spans breadth of Tex., beginning in pine fors. of NE., crossing fertile Blacklands Belt & winding through hills at edge of Edwards Plateau & crossing arid plains of SW. to mt.-bordered Rio Grande.

### Sec. 1: TEXARKANA to DALLAS. 188.

**0. TEXARKANA** (sett.1873), divided by Tex.-Ark. Line, has twin city govs. **51.** J. with St.26 which leads (S) c.13$^{m}$ to **Daingerfield St. Pk.** (580 as.swim.boat.f.sports facils.camp.pic.accoms.dancing). **65. MT. PLEASANT. 104. SULPHUR SPRINGS. 135. GREENVILLE,** J. with St.24.

SIDE TRIP: (NE) 15$^{m}$ on St.24 to **Commerce.** RR. & industrial center & home of **E. Texas St. Teachers College** (est.1888).

US67 cuts across Blacklands (cotton) Belt to **188. DALLAS** (see US80).

### Sec. 2: DALLAS to SAN ANGELO. 273.

Cont. through fertile area to **51. CLEBURNE,** tree-shaded town on W. Buffalo Cr., shipping & trading center. **55.** J. with St.174, leading (SW) 1$^{m}$ to J. with gravel Rd. which turns (R) 3$^{m}$ to **Cleburne St. Pk.** (505 as.110-a. L.boat.bath.f.golf), in rolling woodlands along Brazos R. At c.**60. LOOKOUT PT.,** fine view of Brazos Valley. **76. GLEN ROSE** (f.swim.riding.resort), on Paluxy R. with many springs & mineral wells. **108. STEPHENVILLE** in farm & orchard reg. Here is **Tarleton Agric. College** (est.1917.coed.), branch of Tex. A. & M. **121. DUBLIN,** where pioneers built, for defense against Inds., double log cabin; "doublin' in" meant "retreat to cabin"; hence name. **142. COMANCHE,** once cowmen's supply town. **168. BROWNWOOD,** claimed as geographical center of Texas, has many tall bldgs.; is processing & shipping pt. for varied produce of rich area. Center Ave., **Howard Payne College** (Bapt.est.1889.coed.); bldgs. are in various styles. Austin Ave., **Baker College** (est. 1889.Presb.since 1903). In town is J. with St.279.

SIDE TRIP: (NW) on St.279 c.9m to **36th Div. St. Pk.** (swim.boat.f.pic.accoms.) on 7,500-a. L. Brownwood.

**189. SANTA ANNA,** near mt. of same name, has glass factory utilizing near-by silica deposit. **198. COLEMAN.** In City Pk. is **Reprod. of Old Camp Colorado** (U.S. military post abandoned at start of Civil War), mus. of pioneer relics. **236. BALLINGER,** on Colo. R. Annual songfest (Ap.). **273. SAN ANGELO,** one of largest primary wool markets in U.S. First known as Over-the-River, it subsisted on patronage from near-by U.S. Army's Camp Concho. It was later named "Santa Angela" by founders; in due time the masculine form, "San Angelo," was adopted. Its pioneer hist. is rich with stories of exploits of cowboys, soldiers, trail drivers & freighters. **Old Ft. Concho** (O), abandoned 1889, is still in good repair. In former officers' hqs. is **W. Tex. Mus.** (O); archeological coll. & pioneer relics.

### Sec. 3: SAN ANGELO to PRESIDIO. 323.

US67 now winds through wooded hills, then crosses far-reaching rangelands, dotted with oil fields, passing through infrequent small towns. **28. MERTZON. 71. BIG LAKE. 119. McCAMEY,** ringed with derricks & storage tanks; town boomed with discovery of oil (1925). **165. FT. STOCKTON,** fringed with adobe Hs. It grew up around **Old Ft. Stockton** (est.1859) whose ruins, incl. stone guardh. & several units of officers' quarters, remain in adj. **Jas. Rooney Pk.,** surrounding **Comanche** & **Government Springs.** Former flows at rate of 30,000,000 gals. daily; was important stopping place on "Camino Real," Cal. Trl. of 1849-50, & San Antonio-San Diego Stage Line route. **176.** is west J. with US290.

SIDE TRIP: (W) 45m on US290, near towering Davis Mts., is **Balmorhea St. Pk.** (boat.f. cottages.dancing), 950-a. tract around San Solomon Springs, with one of world's largest outdoor swim. pools. Hy. cont. (W) 65m to J. with US80 (see).

US67 cont. (SW) over rolling cattle ranges to J. at **234.** with US90 (see) with which it unites. **260.** At **MARFA** (see US90), hy. turns (S), climbing twisted course toward high-piled mt. ranges. **302. SHAFTER** is mine supply & shipping center. **323. PRESIDIO** (1st called "La Junta de los Rios" & then "Presidio del Norte") is cottonwood-shaded old town of adobe Hs. on Rio Grande in reg. 1st visited by Sp. explorers late in 16th cent. Missions were est. (1684) at behest of Inds. Here Chihuahua Trl. crossed Rio Grande into Mex. Non-Latin settlers began arriving in 1848. Today Presidio ships cotton, lettuce & cantaloupes from irrigated fields of Rio Grande Valley.

## US 80—TEXAS

**TEX.-LA. LINE** (17m from Shreveport, La.) **(W) to TEX.-N.M. LINE** (24m from Las Cruces, N.M.). **823. US80**

Via: Marshall, Dallas, Ft. Worth, Abilene, Big Spring, Pecos & El Paso. RRs. parallel route. Accoms.: All types.

US80 crosses width of Central Tex., contrasting people, customs & topography: from E. sec. where soil is red & modern appliances few, through middle reg. of urban & industrial influence molding progressive Western type, towards a rugged & colorful reg. whose sunbrowned people use phraseology rich in old tradition.

### Sec. 1: TEX.-LA. LINE to DALLAS. 169.

**20. MARSHALL** (est.1841), old-fashioned town little disturbed by oil & gas discoveries; named for Chief Justice Marshall. During Civil War, it was chosen as a Confed. capital. Here are 2 colleges for Negroes: **Wiley College,** 1m (S) on Grand Ave., oldest in Tex. (1873) & 900 block W. Grand Ave., **Bishop College** (Bapt.1881. coed.). Also 2 jr. colleges: 1200 block N. Grove St., **College of Marshall** (Bapt.coed.) & Railroad Ave. bet. E. Burleson & E. Grand Aves., **St. Mary's Academy** (Cath. coed.). Just (N) & (S) of town are Js. with St.43; in town is J. with US59.

SIDE TRIPS: (A) 16m (NE) on St.43 is entrance to **Caddo St. Pk.** (guides.boat.f.hunt. lodge) on shore of Big Cypress Bayou which flows into **Caddo L.** (fine f.duck hunt.), straddling Tex.-La. boundary, largest natural L. in South.

(B) On US59 (N) 17m to **Jefferson** (est.1836), on stagnant, hyacinth-choked Big Cypress Bayou, has many weathered 19th-cent. bldgs.

(C) 40m (SW) on St.43 to **Henderson** (est.1844), depended 1st on lumber, then on agric. & today is oil town. From Henderson, trip cont. (SW) on US79 to 73m **Jacksonville,** center of tomato-growing area. Although oil has brought it wealth, **Palestine** at 100m, retains old-fashioned charm; pioneer homes date from 1849. **Palestine Salt Dome,** 30,000′ in diam., one of largest in U.S.

(D) On US59 (S) 34m to **Carthage.** 48m **Tenaha,** J. with US96.

Take latter (S) 11m to **Center,** many fine old homes. 18m **Shelbyville,** in 1844 became center of internecine warfare provoked by outlaw & slave-stealing band of fugitives from U.S. known as Clan of Mystic Confederacy. Law-abiding citizens formed group known as Regulators to combat them; when Regulators were accused of joining with them, another group, Moderators, was formed to regulate Regulators. Open warfare broke out bet. them. Peace came only when Pres. Sam Houston ordered both parties to lay down arms.

US59 cont. to 85m **Nacogdoches,** named for Inds. of vic.; outgrowth of Mission est. 1716, to which settlers of Los Adaes near Sabine R. were removed in 1773. After La. Purchase, Sp. garrison maintained here. Destruction of plantation system during Civil War caused slump; advent of RR. revived town. Home of **Stephen F. Austin St. Teachers College** (1932). 105m **Lufkin,** one of biggest sawmill & oil well equipment plants in South; manufactures newsprint. 152m **Livingston,** J. with US190 leading (E) 18m to **Alabama-Cooshatti Ind. Reserv.,** home of only Inds. in Tex. 225m **Houston** (see US90).

Main tour cont. (W) on US80. **42. LONGVIEW. 47.5.,** 1st view of **E. Tex. Oil Field,** said to be world's largest. **55. GLADEWATER,** J. with US271.

SIDE TRIP: (SW) 26m on US271 to **Tyler,** center of so-called Rose Garden of the World, said to produce more than one-third U.S.'s rose bushes. At E. end of town is **Mun. Rose Garden,** formally patterned, with 10,000 bushes covering 3 as. In **Bergfield Pk.** is held Tex. Rose Festival (Oct.). In Tyler is J. with US69 on which side route cont. (S) 50.5m to **Love's Lookout St. Pk.** (swim.pic.), natural rock amphitheater.

At **67. JARVIS CHRISTIAN COLLEGE** (Disciples of Christ Ch.Negro.coed.). **106. GRAND SALINE,** where is **Morton Salt Co.'s Mine** (O.guides).

### 169. DALLAS

Through RR., bus & plane conns. Accoms.: All types. Info.: C. of C., 1101 Commerce St. Road shows at Fair Pk. Aud. & Dallas Little Theater, 3104 Maple Ave.; football & rodeos, Cotton Bowl & Ownby Stadiums; baseball, Dallas Baseball Stadium; golf at Tenison & Stevens Pks.; tennis; swim. at several mun. pools; White Rock L. Mun. Bath. Beach, 10m NE. on US67. Annual Events: SW. Style Shows, last wk. Jan. & 1st 2 wks. Feb.; St. Fair, 2 wks. in Oct.

Dallas, industrial & commercial city set in midst of vast cotton & oil fields, leads world in manufacture of cotton gin machinery & volume distribution of cottonseed products. It is fashion center of Southwest, 2nd in U.S. in production of wash dresses & women's hats. Lies at convergence of 3 forks of Trinity R. Has almost none of Wild West traditions of other Tex. cities, being more cosmopolitan than most of its sister cities. Town site platted in 1846, Judge Wm. Hord starting rival settlement on W. bank of Trinity R. Alex. Cockrell started bldg. campaign & est. ferry. Followers of socialist Victor Considerant est. cooperative community of La Reunion which failed & most of residents, trained & talented men, settled in Dallas. During Civil War, pop. swelled along with expansion of Ch. & school facils. From South flocked cotton growers to plant Blacklands; 1st RRs. arrived 1872 & Dallas rapidly became strangled, congested city. Flood of Trinity in 1908 brought demands for city planning which resulted in formulated program with new bldgs., handsome blvds. & industrial improvements. Channeling & building of levees on Trinity R. reclaimed 10,553 as. Such improvements aided industrial expansion & with this has brought city affluence & diversity of cultural facils.

PTS. OF INT.: (1) Commerce & Houston Sts., **John N. Bryan Cabin** (N.O.cedar logs.reconstr.) served as P.O. & Cth. (2) S. Ervay & Pocahontas Sts., **Sullivan Pk.,** city's oldest (1881). (3) St. Paul & San Jacinto Sts., **Dallas Cotton Exchange** (1926), hub of city's cotton industry. (4) 3104 Maple Ave., **Dallas Little Theater** (1928.Ital. Ren.) & sch. of theater. (5) Hall St. & Turtle Cr. Blvd., **Rbt. E. Lee Pk.** with **Community H.,** reprod. of Lee's Va. home; **Statue of Lee.** (6) Hillcrest Ave., in Univ. Pk., **Southern Meth. Univ.** (1910.Col.Georg.); **McCord Theater Mus.,** colls. on Continental, Chinese & Russian Theater; **Geological Mus.,** fossils, rare weapons & tools of prehist. man; **A. V. Lane Mus.,** pre-Aztec & pre-Inca, Babylonian, Egyptian, Oriental & Greco-Rom. articles. (7) Parry Ave., **Fair Pk.,** site of annual St. Fair. Also in Fair Pk. are: **Tex. Hall of St.** (O.wks.Sun.afts.), mon. to pioneers of Tex. independ.; life-size bronzes of Stephen F. Austin, Gen. Houston, David Crockett among others; **Dallas Hist. Soc. Mus.,** with Tex., Mex. & Ind. artifacts. **Mus. of Nat. Hist.** exhibits mammals & birds, wildflower paintings. **Mus. of Fine Arts,** repository for perm. coll. of sculpture & painting; loan exhibits. **Horticulture Mus., Aquarium**

**& Mus. of Nat. Resources.** (8) 13th at Crawford Sts., **Marsalis Pk.** with **Mun. Zoological Gardens,** one of country's 10 largest zoos. (9) **Hord H.** (1845.reconstr.1927), squared logs, limestone chimney. (10) Extreme NE. part of city, **White Rock L. Pk.** (clubh.camp.bath.f.hatchery.boath.), impounded by dam for city's water supply.

SIDE TRIPS: (A) On US77 (NW) 18$^{m}$ to J. with gravel Rd. leading (L) 2.5$^{m}$ to **Grapevine Springs St. Pk.** (no facils.), scene of attempt by Houston to keep N. Tex. Inds. from joining Mex. in war on Republic. 31$^{m}$ **L. Dallas** (resort.camp.boat.f.). From here St.24 leads 3.5$^{m}$ (R) to **Dam,** 11,000′ long, impounding Elm Fork of Trinity R. to form L. 40$^{m}$, **Denton,** quiet college town, home of **N. Tex. St. Teachers College** (1890) on wooded campus; **College Mus.** with large St. hist. coll., dolls & Amer. glassware. NE. sec. of town, **Tex. St. College for Women** (est.1903), one of largest women's colleges in U.S., combining industrial & vocational training with academic studies.

(B) On US77 (S) passing **U.S. Veterans Hospital** (1940) at 6.5$^{m}$, to 28$^{m}$ **Waxahatchie,** primary cotton market. **Trinity Univ.** (Presb.1869.coed.).

## Sec. 2: DALLAS to BIG SPRING. 295.

US80, now 4-lane hy., **19. ARLINGTON,** seat of **N. Tex. Agric. & Mech. College.**

### 33. FORT WORTH

Through RR., bus & plane conns. Accoms.: All types. Info.: C. of C., 114 E. 8th St. Road shows & concerts at Mun. Aud. & Will Rogers Mem. Coliseum; football & other sports at T.C.U. Stadium; tennis & swim. in pub. pks. Annual Events: SW. Exposition & Fat Stock Show, 9 days beginning 2nd Fri. in Mar.; Casa Mañana summer season, 10 wks. beginning July.

Ft. Worth, 4th largest city in Tex., "where the West begins," lies on Trinity R. at E. edge of (N) Central Plains. It is center for livestock industry with largest stockyards (S) of St. Louis & largest inland oil refining center in Tex., conn. by world's biggest network of pipe lines with oil fields; hqs. of more than 600 oil cos. here, as well as plants producing oil-drilling tools & rigs. This is the SW.'s terminal grain market & has variety of industrial plants. Irregularities of city's early growth have been corrected by smart city planning, giving town handsome blvds. cleanly lined by tall modern bldgs. Actually never a fort, was camp so named where in 1849 Brevet Maj. R. A. Arnold & troops kept watch on Inds. After 1870, Ft. Worth grew rapidly, with land values & pop. booming until "Panic of '73" hit. Population fell from 5,000 to 1,000 but those who stayed fought for completion of incoming Tex. & Pac. RR., halted by Panic, offering to grade remaining 26$^{m}$ of roadbed in exchange for lien against RR. This began desperate race with time to finish undertaking before land grant for right-of-way expired; every business house in town sent its employees to wield pick & shovel with women working in relays to feed men & water mules. On July 19, 1876, 1st train whistled into Ft. Worth with local newspaper editor fueling firebox, thus beginning city's present RR. network. Ft. Worth's location makes for most convenient base of operations for oil fields to (N) & (W); promotion companies sprang up in numbers making it "wildcat" center of world. An extensive bldg. program was carried on in 1930's with construction of city hall & pub. lib. & expansion of educational & charitable institutions. PTS. OF INT.: (1) N. Main St. & Exchange Ave., **Stockyards,** adj. to **Coliseum** (SW. Exposition & Fat Stock Show in Mar.). (2) **Armour Co. Plant** (O.Tues.-Fri.) & **Swift Co. Plant** (O.Mon.-Fri.), both offer frequent guided tours. (3) 2200 Block W. 7th St., **Trinity Pk. & Botanic Gardens** contains **Horticulture Bldg.** housing **Ft. Worth Garden Center,** with lib. for study of nat. sciences; **Albert Ruth Herbarium** is a leading coll. of classified dried plants. (4) 3100-3600 W. Lancaster Ave., **Tex. Frontier Centennial Pk.,** with **Pioneer Mem. Tower** (210′); **Mun. Aud.; Will Rogers Mem. Coliseum** (neo-Class.). At E. edge of pk., **Casa Mañana,** cafe theater (O.summer) & **Pioneer Palace,** café-bar, resembling pioneer saloon. (5) 1800 Forest Pk. Blvd., **Forest Pk.** (playgrounds.pic.tennis), best-equipped of city's pks.; **Mun. Zoo.** (6) Univ. Dr. bet. Canty & Tomlinson Sts., **Tex. Christian Univ.** (1873.Mod.Class.), with **Mary Couts Burnett Lib.** coll. of old & rare Bibles. (7) 1800 W. Gambrell St., **SW. Theological Seminary** (Bapt.1910.Mod.Georg.); **Missionary Mus.,** articles gathered by missionaries from world over. (8) Annis St. bet. Aves. B & F, **Tex. Wesleyan College** (Meth. Episc.coed.Mod.Georg.). (9) 4501 E. Lancaster Ave., **Amer. Rose Soc. Courtesy Garden** (O); roses tested for commercial purposes under SW. climatic condition.

SIDE TRIP: On St.199, 9$^{m}$ to **L. Worth,** adj. to **Fort Worth City Pk.** (casino.dancing.bath. beach.amusements). 14.5$^{m}$ **Eagle Mt. L.,** 10$^{m}$ long & 1.5$^{m}$ wide. Boat regattas from Spring-Oct.; waters stocked with fish.

US80 cont. (W) to **62. WEATHERFORD,** watermelon center, J. with US180.

SIDE TRIP: Take US180 (W) 16.5m to **Camp Wolters,** U.S. reserv. 19m **Mineral Wells,** health resort (accoms.). J. with US281.

On US281 leading 29.5m to J. with dirt Rd. (L) 0.5m to **Ft. Richardson,** elaborate frontier post before abandonment 1878; 40-a. pk.

**119. RANGER,** named for Tex. Rangers; in 1917, McCleskey Well came in, announcing discovery of great oil field; peak output in 1919 was 22,383,000 barrels. **128. EASTLAND,** with remains of horned toad found alive (1927) in cth. cornerstone where it had been for 31 yrs. **189. ABILENE** began as RR. workers' & buffalo hunters' settlement beside Tex. & Pac. RR. Has notable musical organization sponsored by schools & colleges, particularly Cowboy Band of **Hardin-Simmons Univ.** (Bapt.1890.coed.). College Dr., **Abilene Christian College** (1906.Mod.Class.). **McMurray College** (1923).

SIDE TRIPS: (A) On St.158 (SW) 22m to **Abilene St. Pk.** (swim.f.camp.) on shore of **L. Abilene.**

(B) On US277 (N) 24m to **Anson;** Cowboys' Christmas Ball. 39m **Stamford,** scene of Tex. Cowboy Reunion (c.July 4). **Hqs. of SMS Ranch;** coll. picturing cowboy life.

**229. SWEETWATER,** 2 oil refineries, gypsum deposits; Hereford cattle. **258. COLORADO CITY,** oil-processing plants. **295. BIG SPRING** (Cowboy's Reunion on Labor Day & Old Settlers' Reunion, last Fri.July). J. with US87 (see).

## Sec. 3: BIG SPRING to TEX.-N.M. LINE. 359.

**22. STANTON,** horse show 1st Mon. of ea. month. **41. MIDLAND,** oil center with huge reserve storage tanks. At **67.5.** is J. with dirt Rd. leading (L) to **Meteoric Crater,** 10 as. & 3rd largest in U.S. **96. MONAHANS,** flea-raising for circuses; **Hayes Mus.,** coll. from ruins of large wagon trains. **132. PECOS;** Red Bluff Irrigation Proj. on Pecos R. River was once considered W. boundary of civilization, giving rise to phrase "no law W. of the Pecos." **222. VAN HORN** surrounded by mts. rich in silver & minerals. US80 runs over Carrizo Range, descending to ranchers' supply center of **SIERRA BLANCA, 254.,** on sun-baked plains, then climbs low pass bet. Quitman Mts. (S) & Finlay Range & then dips down to irrigated Middle Valley of Rio Grande R. **326.** is J. with paved Rd. leading (L) 5.5m to **Socorro** where is **Misión de la Purisima Concepcion,** famed for painted wood statue of St. Michael, partly covered with etched gold leaf; 4 old paintings & hand-carved ivory crucifix. US80 now route of old El Camino Real to El Paso.

### 341. EL PASO

Through RR., bus & plane conns. Internat. bridges (toll) to Juarez, Mex.: Foot of Stanton & Santa Fe Sts. Accoms.: Ample. Info.: C. of C., 310 San Francisco St. Golf at Valdespino Course (mun.), 6m NE.; tennis & swim. at Mem. & Washington Pks. Annual Events: Sun Carnival, Dec.29-Jan.1; SW. Livestock Show, last wk. Mar.; Harvest Festival, Oct.; Pilgrimage to Sierra de Cristo Rey, 4th Sun. Oct. & Palm Sunday; "Los Pastores," nativity play, Dec. & Jan.

"City of the Pass" was port of entry to Mex. through which conquistadores trudged nearly 4 centuries ago seeking easiest route on expeditions through mts., leaving behind definite imprint of Sp. influence on area. City spreads fan-shaped at foot of Comanche peak & Sierra Madre Mts., forming effective background for El Paso's sister city, Juarez, across Rio Grande in Mex., which does tourist trade in pottery, leather goods, handicrafts & bull fights. Vic. of city's site visited in 1536 by de Vaca; in 1598 Juan de Oñate named city "El Paso del Norte." Mission settlements sprang up c.1680; not until 1827, however, was settlement made on present site, growing around ranchh. of Juan Maria Ponce de Leon, & remained Mex. town after est. of Republic of Tex. In 1846, Doniphan's regiment brought Mex. War to El Paso which surrendered amiably. City was inc. in 1873; residents saw turbulent times after arrival of RRs. brought stampede of lawless elements who found river a convenient crossing pt. to safety in another country. However, order was established by series of straight-shooting sheriffs & Tex. Rangers. Juarez took refuge here until Maximilian was executed, & Pancho Villa harried border until abdication of Porfirio Diaz. City presently embarking on huge conservation, flood control, power & irrigation project which will add progressively to city's beauty & wealth. PTS. OF INT.: N. Oregon & Mill Sts., **Site of Juan Maria Ponce de Leon Home,** 1st on site of city. W. Missouri & N. Santa Fe Sts., **McGinty Cannon** from Battle of Val Verde of Civil War, plowed up by farmer & brought to El Paso, used in sham battles &

torchlight parades by McGinty Club. W. Missouri & N. Santa Fe Sts., **Scottish Rite Cathedral** (reprod. of Pan-Amer. Bldg. in Washington, D.C.); pioneer Masonic relics. E. San Antonio & S. Kansas Sts., **El Paso County Cth.** (Class.) with murals by T. J. Kittelson which depict hist. of El Paso & Southwest. E. San Antonio & N. Kansas Sts., **Fed. District Cth.** (1926.Mod.Class.) with mural of El Paso pioneers by Tom Lea, Jr. W. end College Ave., **Tex. College of Mines & Metallurgy** (1917. Bhutanese architecture after Tibetan monastery). NE. end Pershing Dr., **Ft. Bliss,** largest cavalry post in U.S. (6,000 as.). Named in honor of Wm. Bliss, Chief of Staff to Gen. Zachary Taylor.

From El Paso, US80 turns sharply (N). Near-by is **Plant of Amer. Smelting & Refining Co.,** one of world's largest. Beyond towers **Sierra de Cristo Rey** (4,756'), on which are large sandstone **Cross & Statue of Christ the King** (by Urbici Soler).

**359. TEX.-N.M. LINE.**

## US 90—TEXAS

**TEX.-LA. LINE** (36$^{m}$ from Lake Charles, La.) **(W) to VAN HORN. 768. US90**

Via: Beaumont, Houston, Luling, San Antonio, Uvalde, Del Rio, Sanderson & Marfa. RR. parallels most of route. Accoms.: Ample.

US90 traverses S. Tex., running from humid, subtropical reg. of deep pine forests in E. to land of arid hills & limestone mts. in W.

### Sec. 1: TEX.-LA. LINE to HOUSTON. 112.

**0.5. ORANGE** was once frequented by Jean Lafitte's pirates.

SIDE TRIP: On St.87 (SW) 17$^{m}$ to **Port Arthur-Orange Bridge** (1938), highest bridge in South. 22$^{m}$ **Port Arthur,** shipping center for world's greatest oil refining district. PTS. OF INT.: Foot of Austin Ave., **Pleasure Pier** (recr.facils.pic.boat.f.), artificial island on N. shore of L. Sabine. 1500 Proctor St., **Port Arthur College,** coed. commercial & radio studies. W. city limits on St.87, **Gulf Oil Corp. Refinery** (O.appl.); & N. end Houston Ave., **Tex. Co. Refinery** (O.appl.); 2 of world's largest refineries.

**26. BEAUMONT**

Through RR. & bus conns. Accoms.: Varied. Info.: C. of C., 573 Pearl St. Sports facils. at pks. Annual Events: Wild Flower Show, spring; S. Tex. St. Fair, autumn.

Around cabin built by Noah & Nancy Tevis on Neches R. bank (c.1825) grew up community known as Tevis Bluff & R. Neches Settlement which became fur-trapping center. Town was laid out in 1835 by Henry Millard, who named it Beaumont. On Jan. 10, 1901, on prairie (S) of town, famous Spindletop oil well which inaugurated Tex. oil boom blew in as gusher; Beaumont turned into bonanza town. An Englishman, James Roche, obtained options on Spindletop's production & on 40-a. site for refinery; there began one of Tex.'s greatest oil corporations: Texas Co. New pool, "Spindletop," even more productive than old, tapped in 1925, brought new boom. PTS. OF INT.: (1) Riverside Dr. & Emmett Ave., **Pipkin Pk.,** good view of Turning Basin; **Temple to the Brave,** comm. Tex. heroes. (2) Main St. bet. Gilbert & College Sts., **Nancy Tevis Market** (mod.Sp.), colorful display of farmers' produce. (3) Entrance by Rd. from 800 block Pine St., **Pennsylvania Shipyards,** one of largest in South, builds oil barges & tankers & repairs all types of ships. (4) Gulf St. & Simmons Ave., **S. Texas St. Fairground,** hqs. S. Tex. St. Fair; at NE. cor. is **Beaumont Little Theater.** (5) Wiess Ave. bet. Gulf St. & Magnolia Ave., **Magnolia Pk.** (swim.tennis.playgrounds.pic.zoo).

**55. DEVERS,** at J. with St.61.

SIDE TRIP: On Rd. leading (S) 21$^{m}$ to **Anahuac.** Outlines of Mex. fort are still visible on bluff S. of town.

**112. HOUSTON**

Through RR., bus & plane conns. Steamship Passenger Pier on 75th St. Accoms.: All kinds. Info.: C. of C., 914 Main St. Annual Events: Livestock Show, spring; San Jacinto Day Celebration, Apr. 21; S. Tex. Exposition, Oct.

Largest city in Tex. & newest of country's major shipping centers, Houston is tidewater port 50$^{m}$ inland, conn. with Gulf by Houston Ship Channel; largest cotton-shipping port in U.S. & largest oil-shipping port in world. Dominating skyline soars above 73 sq. miles of surrounding prairie. First settlement on site was Harrisburg. Here in March 1836, Pres. "ad interim" Burnet of Republic of Tex. & his cabinet, taking refuge from approaching Mex. forces of Santa Anna, transferred seat of govt. from Washington on Brazos. Offered for sale as town site Aug. 30, 1836;

named for Sam Houston. Town was still so insignificant in Jan. 1837 that skipper of sternwheeler, "Laura M.," went past without noticing it, & had to back up. In May 1837, Tex. gov. occupied its new capital. It survived, though with indignation, removal of capital to Austin in 1839 & began to prosper as cotton-shipping pt.; by 1858 two RR. lines had been built, to Hempstead & Galveston. Deepening & widening of Buffalo Bayou ship channel was carried forward; improvements to accommodate modern steamships were made after 1900. Channel since widened to 200′ & turning basin with 1,100′ diam. created. Rapid growth of city's prosperity after 1915 was soon reflected in bldgs. & diversity of architectural styles.

PTS. OF INT.: (1) Plate near Main St. entrance of Rice Hotel marks **Site of Capitol of Tex.** (2) 712 Main St., **Gulf Bldg.** topped by **Observatory Tower** (O.sm.fee), highest pt. in Houston. (3) 601 Crawford St., **Ch. of the Annunciation** (Cath.1869-71. Romanes.), one of city's chief architectural attractions. (4) 1101-17 Tex. Ave., **Christ Ch.** (Episc.1893.Goth.), ivy brought from Westminster Abbey. (5) 810 Bagby St., **Sam Houston Coliseum,** 3 huge wings spreading from central stage, can be converted into single amphitheater. (6) 500 McKinney Ave., **Houston Pub. Lib.** (1926. Sp.Ren.) with special colls. of Texiana, rare books & curios, medieval illuminated mss. & incunabula. (7) Dallas Ave. bet. Bagby St. & Buffalo Dr., **Sam Houston Pk.,** with Shelter H. (bricks) built on Buffalo Bayou shortly after Battle of San Jacinto. (8) 1217 W. Dallas Ave., **Founders Mem. Pk.** (1936.rest.); many pioneer graves. (9) S. Main St. & Montrose Blvd., **Houston Mus. of Fine Arts** (O.wks.). (10) 6000 S. Main St., **Rice Institute,** endowed by Wm. Marsh Rice; bldgs. of mixed Byzantine, Moorish, Ital. & Sp. influence. (11) S. Main St. near Hermann Ave., **Hermann Pk.,** miles of scenic driveways, bronze **Statue of Gen. Sam Houston, Miller Mem. Theater** (plays & pageants), **Zoo & Mus. of Natural Hist.** (colls. include Ecuadorian handicrafts). (12) Wheeler Ave. bet. St. Bernard St. & McRae Ave., **Univ. of Houston** (1934) has large variety of evening classes.

SIDE TRIPS: (A) On St.225 (SE) from Houston 18m to J. with St.134, turn (L) 4m to **San Jacinto St. Pk.** (cafes.pic.), **San Jacinto Battlefield** where Texans led by Gen. Houston defeated Mex., terminating Tex. Rev. & assuring firm est. of Republic of Tex. Within pk. are **San Jacinto Mem. Mon.** (O.elevator.570′), whose base houses **San Jacinto Mus. of Hist.,** colls. depicting development of Tex. **Mem. Sundial** (12′), comm. Tex. soldiers.

(B) On St.35, known as Hug-the-Coast Hy., (L) 10m past **Howard Hughes Airport.** Cont. 52m to **W. Columbia,** capital of Republic of Tex. when its Congress met here Oct. 3, 1836. Here is J. with St.36.

Take St.36 (L) 18m to **Peach Pt. Plantation,** former home of Stephen F. Austin's sister, Mrs. Emily M. Perry. 25m **Freeport.** Across Brazos R. (L) is **Velasco** where in 1836 was signed treaty concluding Tex. Rev.

St.35 cont. (SW) 22m to **Bay City.** Hy. crosses Colo. R. on mile-long bridge & cont. to 114m **Palacios & Pier & Pleasure Pavilion** (dancing.bath.boat.f.).

(C) On US90 Alt. (L) from Houston 21m to **Sugarland,** around huge **Imperial Sugar Co. Refinery.** 29m **Richmond,** one of oldest towns in Tex. 32m **Rosenberg.** 64m **Eagle Lake,** founded by Austin colonists on site of old Ind. encampment. At 80m is J. with US90.

(D) On US290 (R) from Houston at 44m is J. with dirt Rd. leading (R) 1m to **Prairie View St. Normal & Industrial College for Negroes** (1876), largest Negro land grant college in U.S. At 48.5m is J. with dirt Rd. leading (R) 1m to **Liendo Plantation.** 50m **Hempstead,** J. with St.6.

On St.6 (N) 21m to **Navasota. La Salle Statue,** comm. Fr. explorer. Trip cont. (SW) 28m to **Washington,** where 1836 delegates assembled to draw up Tex. Decl. of Ind. Just S. cf town is **Washington St. Pk.,** with **Reprod. of early Capitol of Republic of Tex., Tex. Decl. of Ind. Mon.** (granite shaft) & **Home of Anson Jones** (clapboarded & timbered), last White House of the Republic. Amphitheater & rock auditorium. St.90 cont. (SW) to J. at 44m with dirt Rd. which leads (R) 8.5m to **Independence,** remains of **Baptist Ch.** (1839) which Gen. Sam Houston joined in 1854; **Houston Family Burial Plot,** across Rd. from Ch., with graves of Mrs. Sam Houston & her mother; old **Masonic Hall,** where pioneers of Tex. Masonry gathered.

From Hempstead US290 cont. (W) to **Chapel Hill** at 63m, with fine old homes incl. **Stagecoach H.** (1852), **Browning H.** (1856), **Sledge H.** (1850) & **Routt H.** (1846). 72m **Brenham.** W. 4th St., **Blinn College** (Meth.1833), now nonsectarian. Trip cont. on US290 to **Giddings** at 108m, sett. (1872) by Wendish immigrants. In Giddings is J. with US77.

(1) On US77 (S) from Giddings 21m to **La Grange** which contributed many fighters to Tex. Rev. At 24m is **Mon. Hill,** granite shelters. Mem. shaft overlooks tomb.

(2) On dirt Rd. (L) 6m from Giddings to **Serbin,** cultural center of Wends (Slavic stock) in Amer.

US290 cont. (W) from Giddings 135m to **Bastrop,** where in 1834 one of 1st Protestant churches in Tex. began holding services. J. with St.71 leading (L) 1m to **Buescher St. Pk.** (cabins.sports facils.).

## Sec. 2: HOUSTON to SAN ANTONIO. 199.

US90 heads (W) from Houston through intensely cultivated area where many stirring events of Tex. Rev. occurred. **46. SAN FELIPE,** est. 1823 as hqs. of Austin colony, was birthpl. of Anglo-Amer. settlement of Tex. & for yrs. unofficial capital of 1st tiny settlements of colonists from U.S. under leadership of Stephen F. Austin. Here was held in 1835 convention that led to open break with Mex. At entrance to **Stephen F. Austin Mem. Pk.** is **Stephen F. Austin Mem. Mon.** with heroic-size bronze figure (1938); reprod. of **Austin's Log Cabin & Austin's Well.** At **71.** is J. with US90 Alt. (see above). **95. SCHULENBERG,** founded by German & Bohemian colonists, is at J. with US77 (see above). At **138.** is J. with St.29.

SIDE TRIP: On Rd. leading (L) 5.5m to **Palmetto St. Pk.** (pic.supplies), bit of tropical jungle, with mud geysers & sulphur springs. At 14m is **Gonzales.** Here in Sept. 1835, when Tex. colonists refused to give up small brass cannon given them by Mex. gov. for defense against Inds., force of Mex. cavalry was sent to demand its delivery. Following the battle, Gonzales organized 1st Tex. Rev. army, which later captured San Antonio & then marched to join doomed garrison at Alamo. St.200 leads (R) from Gonzales 12m to **Gonzales St. Pk.,** with **Runaway Speech Oak,** where Houston made "Runaway Speech" advising colonists to flee before invading Mex. Army.

US90 cont. (W) **143.** to **LULING** & J. with Rd. leading (L) 0.5m to **Luling Foundation Farm,** demonstration farm. **165. SEQUIN,** founded in 1838 by Southern planters, has many residences dating from pre-1850.

### 199. SAN ANTONIO

Through RR., bus & plane conns. Accoms.: All types. Sports facils.: Varied & plentiful. Info.: Mun. Info. Bureau, Sp. Gov.'s Palace, 105 Military Plaza; C. of C. Tourist Bureau, Insurance Bldg., N. St. Mary's & Martin Sts. Annual Events: Fiesta de San Jacinto, Ap. 21; Feast of Christ the King, Misión Concepcion, last Sun. of Oct.; Ind. Summer Festival, Misión San José, Oct.; "Los Pastores," nativity play in Mex. Quarter, Dec. & Jan.

Third largest & most diversified in past hist. & present color of Tex. cities, San Antonio began as Sp. outpost, became Amer. frontier community & is now industrial center & tourist winter resort. Unlike most Amer. cities, it is laid out on radial principle, extending like a huge spider web from an irregular quadrilateral. Founded as military center, it remains one: within its limits is Ft. Sam Houston, largest Army post in U.S., & scattered in & around it are military aviation fields & varied military supply depots. San Antonio's ancient missions still stand; & its populous Mex. quarter perpetuates language & customs of earlier days. More than 30 nationalities are represented in cosmopolitan pop., 36 percent of which is of Mex. blood.

In 1691, Don Domingo Teran de los Rios, accompanied by Father Damian Massanet & 50 soldiers, found large Ind. village here; Father Massanet, having erected cross & arbor under which to say mass, christened place San Antonio in honor of St. Anthony of Padua. On May 1, Fray Olivares, who had come with 72 settlers from Mex. in 1718, founded Mission San Antonio de Valero (present-day Alamo). Gov. Alarcon 4 days later founded Villa de Bejar & within next 13 yrs., 4 more missions were founded along R. bank within distance of 7m. Fort, villa & settlement about Mission San Antonio were consolidated into San Antonio de Bexar, capital of Province of Tex. In 1835, many Mex. residents joined cause of independence from rule of Santa Anna, Pres. of Mex.; Tex. revolutionists stormed town & compelled surrender of Gen. Martin Perfecto de Cos; Santa Anna retaliated heavily & on Mar. 6 took the fortress of Alamo after every defender had died. Following victory of Tex. Rev., however, San Antonio became W. outpost of Republic & its non-Latin settlement increased. Beginning of cattle drives & advent of 1st RR. (1877) brought great changes, with San Antonio passing through lurid period typical of cow towns. Today, petroleum industry is city's biggest, with oil well operators, refineries & supply firms employing thousands.

PTS. OF INT.: (1) E. side Alamo Plaza, **Alamo** (O.wks.Sun.& hols.) comprises low gray chapel (c.1756,3rd on site) & crumbling courtyard walls, all that remain of mission fort where 187 men (incl. David Crockett) under Travis & Bowie died for Tex. independence; at time of siege (Feb.23-Mar.6,1836), mission was roofless ruin filled with debris, but high thick rock wall enclosing most of what is now Alamo Plaza shielded defenders, who made last stand in chapel. In 1849 building was repaired for use as quartermaster depot; chapel walls (rest.) & arched top added to present façade. Converted to pub. pk. in 1936. Adj. is **Alamo Mus.** (Sp.Col.), relics of Alamo & Repub. of Tex. **Heroes of the Alamo Cenotaph** (1939) occupies approximate center of former fortress area. (2) Bounded by Villita, S. Presa, Nacional & King Philip V Sts., **La Villita** ("little town") reconstructed 1939 by NYA provides cross sec. of building types 1722 & 1850; arts & crafts shops, restaurant & mus.; reconstruction & reprod. on site which is part of old Villita, sett. after founding of Mission San Antonio de Valero. (3) Villita & S. St. Mary's Sts., 31-story **Smith Young Tower** (sm.fee), best observation pt. in city. (4) Main Plaza bet. Trevino & Galan Sts., **San Fernando Cathedral** (1738.adds.1873) incorporates oldest parish ch. bldg. in Tex., from whose towers Santa Anna flew blood-red flag of "no quarter" during seige of Alamo in 1836. **Cathedral Mus.** (O.wks.); ch. relics & objects of hist. int. (5) S. Flores & W. Commerce Sts., **Military Plaza,** where soldiers of garrison resided. In center stands **City Hall** (1888.Ital.Ren.). (6) 105 Military Plaza, **Spanish Governor's Palace** (O.wks.Sun.afts.sm.fee), served in Sp. days as residence of capt. of presidio &, according to tradition, as site of gala balls, adm. hqs. & seat of judicial tribunals. Fell into decay until City of San Antonio purchased & rest. it in 1929. Bldg. contains Sp. Col. furniture & wrought iron. (7) W. Commerce & S. San Saba Sts., in heart of picturesque Mex. quarter, **Haymarket Plaza,** open-air produce mart by day, at night portable chili stands set up & wandering minstrels sing for coins. (8) N. Santa Rosa Ave. & W. Commerce St., **Mun. Market,** hub of activity in produce dist. (9) Buena Vista & S. Concho Sts., **Washington Sq.** is also produce market; Mex. handicraft shops of all types. (10) W. Commerce St. & N. Santa Rosa Ave., **Milam Sq.,** with granite mon. marking Grave of Ben Milam, killed during siege of Dec. 1835. On W. side is heroic-size bronze **Statue of Ben Milam.** (11) N. St. Mary's & Navarro Sts., **Ursuline Convent & Academy** was est. (1851) by nuns from New Orleans, who converted deserted mansion into 1st local boarding school for girls. (12) Auditorium Circle, **Mun. Auditorium** (1930), mem. to World War I dead, awarded gold medal (1930) in architectural competition for mun. bldgs. (13) Jefferson & Pecan Sts., **St. Mark's Ch.** (Episc.1859.Eng.Goth.) stands on ground which once belonged to Alamo property. (14) E. Houston & N. Alamo Sts., **U.S. Post Office & Cth.** (1935-37.mod.Sp.Col.) with murals (by Howard Cook) depicting Tex. history, industries & resources.

(15) Grayson St. & N. New Braunfels Ave., **Ft. Sam Houston.** Here in 1898 were organized Rough Riders, & here in 1910 Ben. D. Foulois made 1st flight in old Wright plane, which marked beginning of Army Air Corps. In 1926 bldg. program was launched at cost of $6,000,000 to make this one of most attractive & efficient posts in country. Adj. to Ft. on (S) are **Camp Cushing & Sam Houston Nat. Cemetery.** (16) Broadway at Pershing Ave., **Brackenridge Pk.** (320 as.tennis.golf.pic. swim.), city's largest; **Witte Mem. Mus.** (O.wks.Sun.afts.sm.fee); outstanding exhibits. Adj. (R) is **Pioneer Mem. Bldg.** (O.wks.& hols.Sun.afts.). **Reptile Garden,** snakes of many kinds, rattlesnakes predominating. **San Antonio Zoological Garden,** (L) of Witte Mem. Mus., provides barless quarters for most of its animals. **Japanese Garden,** NW. edge of pk., has Oriental lily pool & Japanese tea house. Adj. is **Sunken Garden Theater,** where civic operas are presented in summer. **Alamo Stadium** accommodates athletic events. **Mex. Village,** W. edge of pk., presents weavers & potters at work. (17) San Pedro Ave. bet. W. Washby Pl. & Myrtle St., **San Pedro Pk.** (swim.) with mun. **San Pedro Playh.** (18) S. Flores & Arsenal Sts., **U.S. Arsenal** (N.O.est.1858), oldest military institution in city. (19) Misión Rd. (S) of Mitchell St. near city limits, **Misión Concepcion** (O.wks.Sun.sm.fee), best preserved of Tex. missions (1731.adobe & tufa). Partly visible on façade & in rooms of inter. are orig. frescoes, very rare, painted by monks with vegetable & mineral dyes.

SIDE TRIPS: (A) On Mission Rd. (L) from San Antonio 5m to **Misión San José Nat. Hist. Site,** on which stands **Misión San José** (est.1720.adds.1930's), most beautiful, most prosperous & best fortified of Tex. missions, whose rich sculptural ornamentation has made it one of the most photographed bldgs. in Amer. Among its features are carved window, circular stairs to belfry, fine cloisters, old granary & mill, Ind. pueblo, outdoor oven & handmade-tile water system. 7m **Stinson Field,** San Antonio's mun. airport. At 7.5m is J. with Ashley Rd.

On Rd. leading (L) to J. at 7.5m with Espada Rd., (R) 2m to **Misión San Francisco de la Espada** (1720), with fortified tower, rough stone chapel with bell gable & Moorish doorway & barracks; said to be only complete ft. extant.

Mission Rd. crosses San Antonio R. to J. with San Juan Mission Rd. leading (R) 9.5m to **Misión San Juan Capistrano** (est.1731.rebuilt 1907). Unusual features are flat rather than round arches, pointed gables & pierced bell-tower in lieu of steeple.

(B) On St.16 (NW) from San Antonio 3.5m J. with Epworth St., leading (R) short distance to **Univ. of San Antonio** (Meth.1894). At 4m is J. with Cincinnati Ave. leading (L) 0.5m to **St. Mary's Univ.** (Cath.1852), primarily for men. At 28m is J. with toll Rd. leading (L) 11m to **Medina L.,** with 96m of shore line (lodges.camps.f.).
(C) On US181 (SE) from San Antonio, 30m **Floresville,** many houses of Sp. & Tex. colonial type. 60m **Kennedy** (1882), hot mineral wells attract health-seekers. 92m **Beeville,** modernized by oil wealth; Irish immigrants sett. 1830's. US181 cont. across one of most productive cotton belts in Tex. 130m **Taft,** often swept by hurricanes, named for Chas. P. Taft, half-brother of Pres. Taft, whose Ranch contained more than 1,000,000 as. before it was subdivided for settlement. US181 turns (R) along bluff overlooking Nueces & Corpus Christi Bays.

149m **Corpus Christi**

Through RR., bus & plane conns. Accoms.: All types. Info.: C. of C., City Hall, Mesquite St. bet. Peoples & Schatzel Sts. Annual Events: Corpus Christi Day, religious festival, 2nd Thurs. after Pentecost; Buccaneer Days, 1st wk. June.

Shipping center & all-year seaside playground, Corpus Christi overlooks bay of same name, sheltered from Gulf of Mex. by Mustang I. Half-moon shore is lined with piers, bathhs., tourist lodges & hotels, restaurants & trlr. camps. Both shore & deep-sea fish. & duck hunting in salt marshes attract sportsmen. Corpus Christi is one of 4 major ports of Tex. Sp. ranchers est. huge estates with fortified houses in vic. In 1839 came Col. Henry L. Kinney to est. trading post, inhabited largely by smugglers. Kinney began real estate promotion in 1848, advertising this as "the Italy of America." During Civil War, Fed. fleet est. land base on outlying islands & bombarded town into surrender. Bet. 1875 & 1885, cattle-raising took place of sheep-raising. Drilling of gas wells (W) of city in 1920's & of oil wells after 1930 spurred industrial growth. Port development, with Fed. aid, completed 1926. For beautification & protection of bay front, concrete sea wall nearly 2m erected (1940) according to plan of sculptor Gutzon Borglum after hurricane of 1919. PTS. OF INT.: 800 Chaparral St., **Artesian Pk.** with granite shaft marking site of Gen. Z. Taylor's Hqs. 411 N. Broadway, **Evans H.** of shell, concrete & brick was used as hospital during Civil War. N. end Lawrence Dr., **Southern Alkali Corp. Plant.** Beyond S. limits of Corpus Christi, extend flying fields of **U.S. Naval Air Sta.,** Corpus Christi's greatest enterprise. Erected at cost of over 100 million dollars, gave wings to over 40,000 Naval & Marine airmen who served in World War II.
(D) On US281 (N) 48m to **Blanco St. Pk.** (swim.f.pic.) on Blanco R. 85m is J. with Pk. Rd. 9m to **Inks L. St. Pk.** at head of L. of same name, created by dam impounding Colo. R.

Take Pk. Rd. No. 4 (L) 3m to **Longhorn St. Pk.** containing **Longhorn Cavern** (guided tours.fee), more than 11m long with many winding tunnels & spacious chambers containing weird limestone & crystal formations. Cavern was once hiding place of Inds. & outlaws, & powder was manufactured here during Civil War.

Short distance on St.29 (W) is **Buchanan Dam,** one of world's longest, extending more than 2m across Colo. R. to impound 62-sq. mile **Buchanan Reservoir.**
(E) On US281 (S) from San Antonio 33m **Pleasanton,** one of concentration pts. on old Western Trl. to Dodge City, Kans. At 69m is J. with St.9.
At 74m is **Three Rivers** (camp.boat.f.), J. of Frio, Atascosa & Nueces Rs. 138m J. with St.141.

On Rd. leading (E) 14m to **Kingsville,** home of **Tex. College of Arts & Industries,** which has Sp.-style bldgs., semitropical plants & trees, & experimental date & citrus groves, & hqs. of famous **King Ranch,** largest in Tex. (c.1,000,000 as.) acquired by one-time Rio Grande steamboat capt. Richard King. Besides supporting 120,000 head of cattle & 12,000 horses. King Ranch has date & olive groves & vegetable gardens & private game preserve. Fully 700 vaqueros ride ranges to round up cattle (Feb. & Aug.).

161m **Falfurrias.** 226m **Edinburg** has one of largest car-icing plants in SW. for handling perishable fruits & vegetables. Hy. cont. through irrigated area, bordered by citrus groves & green fields. 234m **Pharr.** US281 turns E. to follow course of Rio Grande.
294m **Brownsville,** southernmost tip of U.S., across Rio Grande from Matamoros, Mex.; winter resort. Center of rich delta reg. of citrus orchards, vegetable & cotton fields, irrigated by R. Here Gen. Taylor's troops built Ft. Taylor (1846), later renamed Ft. Brown for Maj. Jacob Brown, called upon to defend it when Mex. forced Taylor to retreat. Brown called for reinforcements; Taylor brought army & on May 8, 1846 fought 1st major engagement of Mex. War at **Palo Alto** 9m (NE). Advancing, Taylor's troops fought Battle of Resaca de la Palma on following day & arrived to find Maj. Brown & his men still in command of ft. After Mex. War, Chas. Stillman founded town of Brownsville. In 1849 & 1850 thousands of California-bound gold seekers converged here, waiting for R. steamers. During Civil War, it became one of chief ports of Confederacy, shipping cotton, wool & hides. In 1930 port development plan undertaken. Proximity of Mex. gives frequent occasion for fiestas, chief of which is Charro Days (pre-Lent). PTS. OF INT.: E. end SE. Elizabeth St., **Ft. Brown,** oldest Fed. garrison on Rio Grande, parts of orig. intact. 12th St. SE. bet. SE. Adams & SE. Washington Sts., **Market H.** (1850. Mex. hacienda period) food produce mart. 1309 SE. Elizabeth St., **Miller Hotel** (1850's.Class.Rev.) was early Brownsville's social center. SE. Levee St. at 13th St. SE., **Chamber of Commerce Pk.,** good view

of Rio Grande & Matamoros; contains many hist. relics. Ft. of 14th St. SE., **Gateway Bridge** (toll) across Rio Grande to Matamoros.

(1) On St.4 (L) from Brownsville 15m to **Site of the Battle of Palmito Hill** (R), last engagement of Civil War, fought May 12-13, 1865, more than month after Gen. Rbt. E. Lee's surrender. 24m **Boca Chica,** with shore line 7m (bath.f.), beach drive (R) to **Mouth of Rio Grande & L.;** 0.5m to resort of **Del Mar** (excellent f.).

(2) Take Paredes Line Rd. (L) from Brownsville 3m to **Site of the Battle of Resaca de la Palma,** 2nd engagement of Mex. War. (R) 8m to **Site of the Battle of Palo Alto,** 1st engagement of Mex. War. 12m **Los Fresnos,** J. with St.100, on which route turns (R) 17m to **Port Isabel** (extensive tourist facils.).

### Sec. 3: SAN ANTONIO to VAN HORN. 457.

**25. CASTROVILLE** retains remarkable resemblance to Alsatian village with its thick-walled, high-roofed houses, old ch. & cemetery. **62. SABINAL** raises Angora goats. **84. UVALDE,** in heart of goat ranching reg., ships mohair, as well as pecans, honey & asphalt. 333 N. Park St., **Home of John Nance Garner,** Vice-Pres. of U.S. during F. D. Roosevelt's first 2 terms. Kincaid Hotel, Getty St. & Cth. Plaza, **Garner Coll. of Gavels.**

SIDE TRIPS: (A) On US83 (N) 29m to **Garner St. Pk.** (lodges.riding.hik.swim.f.), with natural cave, 75′ deep.

(B) On US83 (S) 39m to **Crystal City,** self-advertised "spinach capital of the world," **Statue of Popeye** on town sq. 52m **Carrizo Springs,** J. with St.85.

On St.85 (R) from Carrizo Springs 44m to **Eagle Pass** (1850) tourist resort with Mex. border atmosphere. Upstream California-bound gold seekers crossed Rio Grande & est. tent town called Camp California. **Old Fort,** where Gen. Jos. Shelby with his unsurrendered div. of Missouri cavalry crossed Rio Grange, July 4, 1865, & cast their flag (last Confed. flag to fly over unsurrendered Confed. force) into R.

US83 cont. (S) to J. with US81 (see) at 116.5m.

**123. BRACKETVILLE** with **Ft. Clark** (1852), now military reserv. **154. DEL RIO.** At E. edge are **7 San Felipe Springs,** flowing at rate of nearly 50,000,000 gallons daily, which induced settlement & creation of irrigation system in 1868. **170. CASTLE CANYON. 192.5., SEMINOLE CANYON,** caves once inhabited by Cave Dwellers. At **197.** hy. dips into Pecos R. Canyon. At **202.5.** J. with gravel Rd. leading (L) short distance to **Hilltop Pk.,** commanding superb view; visible (E) is **Pecos High Bridge,** one of world's highest (331′) RR. bridges. **211. LANGTRY** is J. with dirt Rd. leading (L) 0.5m to **Old Langtry,** now much decayed, where stands frame **Saloon of Roy Bean** (rest.) with sign proclaiming that here once ruled "Judge Roy Bean, Law West of the Pecos." Bean, elected justice of the peace, filled position with one law book & six-shooter. Tradition says he renamed community, 1st known as Vinegaroon, for famous actress Lily Langtry, whom he wrote begging that she visit it; she did, but not till after Bean had died.. **272. SANDERSON** ships cattle, wool & mohair. **327. MARATHON,** J. with St.227.

SIDE TRIP: On St.227 leading (L) from Marathon into heart of Tex. Big Bend. Here are **Horse Mt.** (5,010′) with **L. & Santiago Peak** (6,521′). 41.5m to **Persimmon Gap** & entrance to **Big Bend Nat. Pk.** 46m **Dog Canyon.**

St.227 cont. (W) to J. with Pk. Rd. at 72m leading (L) into Chisos Mts., area of rare scenic beauty. To E. soars **Lost Mine Peak** (7,550′). 103m (SW) entrance of **Grand Canyon of Santa Helena,** through which Rio Grande passes.

Cont. (W) on US90 to J. at **349.** with US67 which unites with it for 34m. **357. ALPINE;** on heights (E) of town, **Sul Ross St. Teachers College** (1920) with **Big Bend Hist. Mus.**

SIDE TRIP: On St.118 leading (N) from Alpine 24m to **Ft. Davis** near **Ruins of Ft. Davis** (1854.abandoned 1891). Cont. (L) 5m to **Davis Mts. St. Pk.** (stopover facils.hik.swim. riding). At 46m on top of **Mt. Locke** (6,791′) is **McDonald Observatory** (O.1-1:30 p.m. wks.2-2:30 Sun.1939), world's 2nd largest (dome 62′ diam. atop 3-story structure housing 82″ telescope).

**383. MARFA,** large mt. ranches. **457. VAN HORN** at J. with US80 (see).

## US 75—TEXAS

**TEX.-OKLA. LINE** (15m from Durant, Okla.) **(S) to GALVESTON. 374. US75**

Via: Denison, Dallas, Corsicana & Huntsville. RRs. parallel parts of route. Accoms.: All types.

US75 traverses Blacklands Belt, richest agric. & industrial sec. of Tex., skirts W. edge of E. Tex. timber belt, & crosses coastal prairies to Gulf Coast.

**0.** Denison Bridge crosses Red R., which is **TEX.-OKLA. LINE. 5. DENISON,** dates to 1858 when Butterfield Stage Line passed town. One of principal shipping centers of Red R. Valley. **15.5. SHERMAN. Austin College** (1849) moved here 1876.

SIDE TRIPS: (A) Take US82 (E) 26m to **Bonham.** At NE. edge is **Reprod. of Old Fort Inglish** (1836.log.).

Take St.78 (R) from Bonham 2m to Gober Rd. Turn (L) here to **Bonham St. Pk.** (camp. bath.), with 60-a. L. 66m **Paris,** an agric. center of rich Blacklands Belt; processing factories. Here Frances Willard organized (1882) Woman's Christian Temperance Union.

(B) Take US82 (R) from Sherman 33m to **Gainesville,** frontier settlement, with California Street following route of 1849 gold seekers. Town became stop on Butterfield Stage Line & later base of supply for cowboys driving herds toward Dodge City, Kans.

**47. McKINNEY,** named for Collin McKinney, signer of Tex. Decl. of Ind. **79. DALLAS** (see US80). **114. ENNIS,** RR. town. **134. CORSICANA,** in 1894 1st commercial oil well in Tex. was drilled following discovery of oil in course of drilling for artesian water; 1st rotary drilling rig developed & manufactured here. **168. FAIRFIELD,** J. with US84.

SIDE TRIP: On Rd. leading (R) 23m to **Mexia,** encircled by oil tanks & derricks. 31m on St.14 to **Ft. Parker St. Pk.** Cynthia Ann Parker, captured by Comanche Inds., became mother of famous war chief, Quanah.

**225. MADISONVILLE,** J. with St.21.

SIDE TRIPS: (A) On St.21 (L) 39m to **Crockett,** founded in 1830's & named for Davy Crockett.

(B) On St.21 (R) 36m to **Bryan,** many big old plantations. On St.6 (L) 4m to **Agricultural & Mechanical College of Tex.** (est.c.1870.Mod.Class.), c.65 bldgs. on beautifully landscaped 400-a. campus. Orig. part of Univ. of Texas, now has 17 agric. substations & 3 branch colleges in St.; also conducts engineering research & forestry serv.

**253. HUNTSVILLE** was home of Sam Houston; **Houston H.** (clapboarded log), with rest. log kitchen & law office, stands on campus of **Sam Houston St. Teachers College** (1879). Also on campus is **Steamboat H.** (c.1860), where Houston came to live after his removal from office & where he died July 26, 1863. On St.219 (NW) is **Sam Houston's Grave. 324. HOUSTON** at J. with US90 (see). US75 cuts across level sweep of Coastal Plain, crossing Galveston Bay on causeway at **366.5.**

**374. GALVESTON**

Through RR. & bus conns. Accoms.: All kinds. Info.: C. of C., 2209 Market St. Concerts & athletic events at Mun. Auditorium; swim. at E. & W. Beaches, Lagoon Pool, E. end of Seawall, or anywhere on 32m shoreline; surf fish. on piers; deep-sea fish.; excursion boat trips around harbor from Pier 18. Annual Events: Mardi Gras, 5 days preceding Lent; Oleander Fete, spring; Fishing Rodeo, June or July.

Galveston lies at E. end of Galveston I., conn. to mainland by 2 vehicular causeways & RR. bridge. Harbor bustles with traffic from hundred ports; with extensive dock & warehouse facils. incl. drydock & ship repair plants. City protected against Gulf by formidable sea wall, would convey impression of powerful fortress but for masses of flowers, homes & fine pks., throngs of sea bathers.

On Galveston I., or near it, Cabeza de Vaca, 1st European to see inter. of Tex., was shipwrecked. Bay surveyed in 1785 or 1786, named for Count Bernardo de Galvez. Don Luis Aury, during Mex. Rev., est. settlement & fortifications, & used I. for base to prey on Sp. merchant vessels. Jean Lafitte sailed into Galveston Bay, took possession under flag of Mex. & named it Campeachy. Here he built a fortress home which he called Maison Rouge to which pirate expeditions brought spoils. Hurricane of 1820 left settlement in ruins, which was to be harassed by Karankawa Inds. Later, U.S. cutter gave ultimatum for Lafitte's evacuation; he left Campeachy in flames; finally reestab. when designated port of entry by Mex. Gov. of Tex. used Galveston as naval base operating against Mex. Navy. After est. of Republic came the tide of immigration; during Civil War after blockade, Fed. forces took city, 1862, recaptured by Confed. in 1863. Galveston made deep-water port, 1896. On Sept. 8, 1900 one of worst hurricane disasters hit town. Rehabilitation quickly undertaken to prevent recurrence; present seawall built & level of city raised on Gulf side; in hurricane of 1915, city spared serious damage as result of such planning. Galveston has developed in subsequent years until today it is one of country's leading ports & resort centers, its streets lined with oleanders.

PTS. OF INT.: (1) Church & Center Sts., **St. Mary's Cathedral** (1848.early Goth.), oldest in city, belfry surmounted by statue "Mary, Star of the Sea," placed there after hurricane of 1875 to become legendary: so long as statue remained standing, island would not be destroyed. (2) Tremont St. & Sealy Ave., **Rosenberg Lib.** (1904. Ital.Ren.), with large coll. of mss. (3) Broadway & 14th St., former **Walter Gresham H.** (1885-92.details.Romanes.Vict.). (4) 2328 Broadway, **El Mina Shrine Temple** (1859.La.Fr.Ren.) was home of Capt. J. M. Brown. (5) Ave. N bet. Rosenberg Ave. & 27th St., **Ursuline Convent** (1854.adds.1861.1892.Goth.Romanes.Moorish), in Civil War used as hospital for both armies. (6) Seawall Blvd. bet. 39th & 53rd Sts., **Ft. Crockett** (N.O.1899), Coast Artillery post. (7) E. end Galveston I., **Ft. San Jacinto,** coast defense.

SIDE TRIP: On St.46, 9m (N) to J. with St.6, then 4m (R) to **Texas City,** scene of tragic nitrate-ship disaster (1947) with multi-million dollar damages to town. Home of **Monsanto Chemical Co.,** rebuilt after blast of ship in harbor which destroyed industrial area & large part of residential area.

## US 81—TEXAS

**TEX.-OKLA. LINE** (14m from Ryan, Okla.) **(S) to LAREDO. 512.5. US81**

Via: Fort Worth, Waco, Austin & San Antonio. RRs. parallel secs. of route. Accoms.: Ample. (S. of San Antonio avail. only in larger towns.)

US81 cuts (S) through reg. traversed by Cal. Trl. & Butterfield Stage Line from Red R. Valley across Blackland reg. of central Tex. across rock-studded hills of Edwards Plateau, finally swinging SW. to Rio Grande.

### Sec. 1: TEX.-OKLA. LINE to FORT WORTH. 90.

**0.** US81 bridges Red R. at **TEX.-OKLA. LINE. 4. RINGGOLD,** J. with US82.

SIDE TRIP: (W) on US82. 34m to **Wichita Falls,** largest independent oil center in nation. **Shepperd Field,** 5m (N), Air Corps technical training school. (S) 4m to J. with St.79. leading (L) 7m to **L. Wichita** & **Lakeside Pk.** (dancing.swim.boat.f.pic.).

At **51. DECATUR,** agric.trading & shipping center, is J. with St.24 leading (R) 11m to **Bridgeport,** (L) 15m to **L. Bridgeport** (swim.f.camp.). **90. FORT WORTH,** at J. with US80 (see).

### Sec. 2: FORT WORTH to SAN ANTONIO. 267.

**56. HILLSBORO.** At N. edge is **Hillsboro L. Pk.** (swim.f.cabins.golf).

**89. WACO**

Through RR. & bus conns. Accoms.: All types. Info.: C. of C., 414 Franklin Ave. Concerts & road shows at Tex. Cotton Palace; golf at Waco Mun. Golf Course, S. 12th St.; tennis at Mun. courts in Cameron Pk.; swim. at Mun. pool, Cameron Pk. Brazos Valley Fair & Livestock Show, Tex. Cotton Palace, Fall.

Waco is thoroughly modern city, cultural & educational center of E. central Tex., & is leading inland cotton market. Name derives from Huaco Inds. of vic. Town site laid out in 1849. Waco Female College est. 1859; Waco Univ. (later absorbed by Baylor) in 1861. Waco loyal to Confederacy. Advent of RRs. converted it to modern city. PTS. OF INT.: (1) Bridge St., old **Suspension Bridge** (1870) was world's 2nd longest single-span (475′) on opening. (2) N. 3rd St. & Jefferson Ave., **Ch. of St. Francis on the Brazos** (1931.reprod.of Mission in San Antonio, incl.sacristy window). (3) Rotan Dr., **Cameron Pk.** (clubh.tennis.pic.playgrounds). (4) 1020 Elm St., **Paul Quinn College** (1881.maintained by African Meth.Ch.). (5) Dutton & S. 5th Sts., **Baylor Univ.,** Bapt. coed. chartered by Republic of Tex.; ivy-covered Vict. Goth. "Baylor Towers" date to 1880's. In **Carroll Lib.** is Browning Room, world's most complete coll. of 1st editions, drawings, letters & mementoes of Rbt. Browning. (6) S. 13th & Clay Sts., **Tex. Cotton Palace Pk.,** with **Cotton Palace Coliseum,** annual Brazos Valley Fair & Livestock Show.

**124. TEMPLE,** famous for large hospitals serving patients from all parts of U.S., Mex., Central & S. Amer. **133. BELTON,** site of **Mary Hardin-Baylor College** (1866.Bapt.women.Mod.Col.). **165. GEORGETOWN,** seat of **Southwestern Univ.** (Meth.coed.1873). **San Gabriel Pk.,** on San Gabriel L. (recr.facils.f.pic.). **174. ROUND ROCK,** J. with US79.

SIDE TRIP: On Rd. leading (L) 18m to **Taylor,** one of largest mattress factories in South. Nearly half pop. is Czech ancestry, remainder German.

**194. AUSTIN**

Through RR. & bus. conns. Accoms.: All types. Info.: C. of C., 803 Congress Ave. Hogg Mem. Aud., Univ. of Tex.; (concerts.roadshows) Mem. Stadium (sports events), Univ. of Tex.; Mun. Golf Course, N. of Dam Blvd.; Mun. Swim. Pools; Boat. L. Austin, 10$^m$ NW.

St. capital & seat of Univ. of Tex., est. 1839 by founders of Republic of Tex. as seat of govt.; is on curve of Colo. R. Many pks. & playgrounds, networked with scenic drives. First capitol, one-story frame structure, was enclosed with loopholed stockade. By 1840 Austin was incorporated with 856 residents. When San Antonio fell to Mex. army in 1842, seat of gov. was hastily removed to Houston, as consequence of which occurred "Archives War," when citizens of Austin stoutly resisted all attempts to evacuate St. records. When Mex. threat subsided, Austin became not only capital of Republic, but capital of St. During Civil War, percussion & cap factory & foundry for cannon & other weapons were set up to help supply Confed. In spite of strife of Reconstruction period, city prospered, acquiring 1st RR. in 1871 & 2nd in 1876. Completion of present Capitol was celebrated in 1888. PTS. OF INT.: (1) N. end Congress Ave., **Tex. St. Capitol** (1888.Class.) with National Capitol as its prototype, approximating Greek cross in plan. In rotunda are statues of Sam Houston & Stephen F. Austin (by Elizabet Ney); among documents are Tex. Decl. of Ind. & Ordinance of Secession. On walls are portraits of Presidents of Republic of Tex. & Govs. of St. On grounds are **Mons. to Confed. Dead, Volunteer Firemen, Tex. Cowboy, Terry's Tex. Rangers, & Alamo.** (2) SE. cor. Capitol grounds, **Old Land Office Bldg.** (1857.Medieval) with **Tex. Confed. Mus. & Mus. of Daughters of Repub. of Tex.** (3) Colorado St. bet. W. 10th & 11th Sts., **Governor's Mansion** (1855.Gr.Rev.) with furnishings incl. Sam Houston's bed, Stephen F. Austin's desk, crystal chandeliers & fine coll. of paintings. (4) East Ave. at E. 12th St., **Samuel Huston College** (coed.Negro.Meth.1900), named for Huston of Iowa. (5) E. 7th & San Jacinto Sts., **St. David's Ch.** (Episc.1855.Goth.) is 2nd oldest Protestant Ch. in Tex. (6) 409 E. 5th St., **O. Henry Mus.** occupies one-story frame cottage (removed from E. 4th St.), where author lived 1893-95. (7) 1100 block S. Congress Ave., **Tex. School for the Deaf.** (8) Navasota St. bet. E. 7th & E. 11th Sts., **Grave of Stephen F. Austin** & other distinguished Texans. (9) E. 11th & Chalmers Sts., **Tillotson College** (1877.Negro.Amer.Missionary Assoc.). (10) Ave. H & 44th St., **Elizabet Ney Mus.** was workshop & home of sculptress; coll. of her statuary here. (11) On W. 45th St., W. of Guadalupe St., **Tex. School for the Blind** (mod. Tudor Goth.). (12) On US81 3$^m$ S. of Capitol, **St. Edward's Univ.** (men.1885). (13) University Ave. & 21st St., **Univ. of Tex.** (1883.Sp.Ren.), which ranks today among 8 largest St. universities. **Adm. Bldg. & General Lib.** (1933) with 307′ clock & bell tower. Library's Rare Book Coll. contains 30,000 items; its Tex. Coll. is best in existence; notable Latin-Amer. & Southern Hist., Archives & Newspaper Colls. **Hogg Mem. Auditorium,** modern theater equipment. **Waggener Hall** contains **Anthropology Mus.** with large coll. of pre-hist. bone, flint & stone specimens; largest coll. of Ind. pottery in Tex.; **Mem. Stadium** seats 48,000. **Tex. Mem. Mus.** on heights has zoology, geology, botany, anthropology & history exhibits. (14) Bee Caves Rd. at SW. limits, **Zilker Pk.** (swim.sports facils.riding.polo.pic.), lily ponds, rock gardens. **Barton Springs,** popular bathing resort. (15) Just NW. of city limits, **Mt. Bonnell,** 775′ promontory for fine view.

SIDE TRIP: On Bull Cr. Rd. (R) 10$^m$ to **L. Austin Metropolitan Pk.** (camp.f.boat.swim. riding).

**224. SAN MARCOS,** popular pleasure resort, many caves, pks.; **St. Fish Hatchery & SW. Tex. St. Teachers College. 241.** J. with bypass route leading (R) 0.5$^m$ to **NEW BRAUNFELS,** where Prince Carl zu Solms-Braunfels est. German settlement 1845, but departed. New Braunfels has remained typically German (recr. facils.accoms.). **253.** is J. with St.218, leading (L) 3.5$^m$ to **Randolph Field,** termed West Point of the Air, one of world's largest military airdromes (1928-30). **267. SAN ANTONIO** at J. with US90 (see).

## Sec. 3: SAN ANTONIO to LAREDO. 155.5.

At **4.5.** is J. with Quintana Rd., leading (L) 0.5$^m$ to **Camp Normoyle,** landscaped military reserv. & with one of largest automobile repair shops in U.S. for U.S. Army equipment. **5.** Entrance (R) to **KELLY FIELD,** where cadets who finish primary flight instruction at Randolph Field (see above) are transferred for final training. Entrance (L) to **DUNCAN FIELD,** military aircraft repair depot. **55. PEARSALL,** home of annual Winter Garden Fair. **66. FRIO ST. PK. 88. COTULLA,** big hats, boots & cow ponies are familiar sights. **137.** is J. with US83. **155.5. LAREDO** is busy port of entry on Rio Grande, through which pass more than half the freight & tourists crossing International Border. Extensive irrigation from Rio Grande has created fertile area. On May 15, 1755, Sp. rancher Tomas Sanchez formally founded town, known as "Villa de Laredo." After Battle of San Jacinto (1836) disagreement over S. boundary of Republic of Tex. placed it in "no man's land." Finally occupied 1846 by Tex. Rangers, on their way to join Gen. Zachary Taylor at Brownsville. Advent of 2 RRs. in 1881 & 1882 & irrigation of R. valley stimulated development. World's largest antimony smelter here. Mex. limes are packed for U.S. distribution. W. end of Victoria St., **Ft. McIntosh** (renamed Camp Crawford,1849), Confed. garrison in Civil War. Foot of Convent Ave., **International Bridge** (toll) to Nuevo Laredo, Mex., with removable aluminum railings taken down when flood threatens; R. has been known to submerge bridge until only tops of lamp-posts are visible.

SIDE TRIP: On US83 (S) route runs through semi-arid plains into highly cultivated citrus fruit belt of Lower Rio Grande Valley between Mission and the Gulf. Warm pleasant valley through **Zapata** at 47m, one of oldest towns in Rio Grande Valley, to **Ft. Ringgold** at 102.5m, U.S. Military reserv., scene of skirmishes bet. Tex. Rangers & bands of Mex. outlaws under Juan Flores. At 137m J. with dirt Rd. leading (R) 4.5m to **Capilla de la Lomita** (chapel of the Little Hills), surrounded by great groves of orange, lemon, lime & grapefruit trees. Route runs on to **Harlingen,** 176m, site of Valley Mid-Winter Fair. 202m **Brownsville** (see US90).

## US 87—TEXAS

**TEX.-N.M. LINE** (8m from Clayton, N.M.) **(SE) to PORT LAVACA. 798. US87**

Via: Amarillo, Lubbock, Big Spring, San Angelo, San Antonio & Victoria. RRs. parallel parts of route. Accoms.: Ample.

Crossing Tex. diagonally from Panhandle to Gulf of Mex., US87 traverses High Plains & stony hill country & emerges on lush Coastal Plain to end at tidewater.

### Sec. 1: TEX.-N.M. LINE to BIG SPRING. 351.

**0. TEX.-N.M. LINE,** from which US87 heads (S) across vast wheat fields of Panhandle. **37. DALHART,** orig. cowtown, today is RR. center with grain elevators & cattle-shipping pens. **76. DUMAS,** oil town. **124. AMARILLO** (see US66). Here US87 unites with US60 (S) to **140. CANYON,** home of **W. Texas St. Teachers College.** On campus, **Panhandle Plains Hist. Soc. Mus.** (O); bldg. is engraved with brands of cattle barons; coll. of pioneer & Ind. relics. In town is J. with St.217.

SIDE TRIP: (E) 12m on St.217 to **Palo Duro Canyon St. Pk.** (15,100 as.sm.fee.foot & bridle trls.accoms.restaurant), great gash of many-colored walls exposing rock strata of 4 geologic ages explored by Coronado in 1541 while seeking Gran Quivira; traces of pre-Pueblo culture have been found here. After Civil War, Col. Chas. Goodnight led 1st herd of cattle on NW. Trl. from Tex. to Colo. & here est. 1st ranch in Panhandle, the **J A.**

**174. TULIA** (sett.1890), agric. town handling grain & dairy products. **199. PLAINVIEW. 245. LUBBOCK,** far-spreading industrial city, was founded in 1891 when 2 rival towns consolidated. Its 1st citizens were buffalo hunters, ranchers, bone-gatherers & trl. drivers. Unlike most cowtowns, however, it was "dry" except for brief interval when it had 1 saloon. At W. edge is **Tex. Technological College** (320 as.est.1823.coed.); courses incl. agric., engineering, liberal arts, etc. On handsome campus is **W. Tex. Mus.,** archaeological coll. **290. O'DONNELL** is cotton-ginning center. **307. LAMESA,** on the edge of Gap Rock, has an egg-dehydrating plant. **351. BIG SPRING** at J. with US80 (see).

### Sec. 2: BIG SPRING to SAN ANTONIO. 306.

**2. BIG SPRING ST. PK.** (363 as.pic.), with drive leading to top of mesa, **Scenic Mt.** (2,811'). US87 cont. through area of oil fields, sheep ranches, salt lakes & hill country. **70. TEX. ST. TUBERCULOSIS SANATORIUM,** against foothills of Carlsbad Mts. **88. SAN ANGELO** (see US67). US87 cont. through hill country sett. largely by people of German descent, raising sheep & goats, forage crops & grain. **133. EDEN,** trade center for ranchers & cotton farmers, at J. with US83.

SIDE TRIP: (S) 22m on US83 to **Menard,** wool & mohair shipping center.

(1) On dirt Rd. (L) from Menard 1m to **Mission San Saba** (also known as Santa Cruz) whose bldgs. (rest.) were erected by Sp. in 1757 but abandoned following yr. after Ind. attack.

(2) On dirt Rd. (R) from Menard 3m to **Presidio de San Luis de las Amarillas,** est. 1757 to protect Mission San Saba. Chapel & adj. rooms & bastion at NW. cor. have been rest.; chapel is used as mus.

**165. BRADY,** 1875 frontier trading post, is now one of State's chief shipping pts. for poultry, especially turkeys. **194. MASON** has many bldgs. constructed with stone taken from near-by old **Ft. Mason,** abandoned 1869, which once had more than 100 stone structures. **237. FREDERICKSBURG,** in hill-rimmed green valley, is trim German town preserving in architecture & customs an Old World air. Thick-walled old stone Hs. with high sloping roofs & outside stairways, bordered by neat flower beds, line its long, wide main street. It was sett. in 1846 by immigrants who named it for Frederick the Great of Prussia; surviving raids by Comanche Inds., it began to prosper on trade with soldiers of near-by Ft. Martin Scott. Settlers refused to enlist in Confed. cause; town remained isolated until it built its own RR. conn. in 1912 & thus became unusually self-sustaining, producing most necessities & some luxuries. Traditional festivals are still celebrated: most important is "Saengerfest" (May), when singing clubs of dist. gather for county-wide contest. Town's "Sunday houses" recall days when transportation from outlying farms was arduous & slow. Families which came to market Sat. & to ch. on Sun. built these homes as a convenient & inexpensive way of week-ending in town & Hs. are still used for this.

PTS. OF INT.: (1) E. Main St. bet. S. Washington & S. Elk Sts., **Kiehne H.** (O.sm. fee.1851), of stone & timber, was town's 1st 2-story H. (2) N. Washington & E. Main Sts., **Nimitz Hotel** displays coll. of hist. items in lobby. (3) Also on E. Main St., **Birthpl. of Adm. Chester W. Nimitz** in pioneer Henke H. (4) Main St. opp. cth., **Vereins Kirche** (O.1934) is exact reprod. of 1st ch., built 1847, resembling old-fashioned coffee mill: octagonal, with cupola; it is now mus. with coll. of hist. relics. (5) S. Crockett & W. Main Sts., **Old Cth. & P.O.** (1855). (6) W. San Antonio & S. Orange Sts., **Old St. Mary's Ch.** (Cath.1861.German Goth.). (7) W. Creek St. bet. S. Edison & S. Bowie Sts., **Staudt Sunday H.** (N.O.1847). (8) N. Bowie & W. Schubert Sts., **Tatsch H.** (O.appl.c.1852) has huge Dutch chimney. (9) N. edge of town, **Cross Mt.,** on which electrically lit concrete cross replaces old wooden cross found here when 1st settlers came. In town is J. with St.16.

SIDE TRIPS: (A) On NE. branch of St.16 at 4m is eroded red granite **Bear Mt.** (1,850′) whose chief attraction is **Balanced Rock.** 19m **Enchanted Rock** (1,815′), one of largest granite outcroppings in U.S. From top of rock (500′), view of other weird granite forms. At ft. of mt. is **Sand Cr. Pk.** (cabins.camp.).

(B) On (SW) branch of St.16 at 25m is **Kerrville** (resort.camp.accoms.), popular recr. & health center on banks of Guadalupe R. in area known as Heart of the Hills, near which are **Kerrville St. Pk.** (500 as.f.camp.pic.) & **Schreiner Game Preserve** (N.O.) with buffalo & antelope. St.16 cont. through scenic hill country to 66m **Bandera** (est.1850's), hemmed in by high hills, retains its frontier atmosphere with old rock Hs. & inhabitants who wear sunbonnets & homespun; N. of cth. is **Frontier Times Mus.** (sm.fee) with coll. of pioneer relics. St.16 cont. to 113m **San Antonio** (see US90).

**260. COMFORT,** recr. center (good h. & f.). **276. BOERNE** is health & recr. resort nestled in wooded hills, with winding sts. & old stone Hs.; sett. 1849 by German immigrants. It became home of Geo. Wilkins Kendall, who during Mex. War joined Amer. troops & with aid of chain of pony express riders, supplied "New Orleans Picayune" with 1st war correspondence of modern type. At c.10m NE. of Boerne is **Cave Without a Name** (O.fee.guides). **279.** J. with **Van Raub Rd.** leading 2m to **Cascade Caverns** (O.fee). **306. SAN ANTONIO** (see US90).

## Sec. 3: SAN ANTONIO to PORT LAVACA. 141.

US87 cont. (SE) across Coastal Plain. **50. NIXON,** peanut grading, poultry dressing & packing plants. **85. CUERO,** with many moss-draped shade trees lining wide sts., is cotton-shipping center & one of chief turkey-shipping pts. in Tex.; here is famous Turkey Trot (every 2nd Nov.), when thousands of turkeys are marched down main st. **113. VICTORIA** (sett.1824 by Sp.) has beautiful residences, gardens & pks. full of roses & pub. sq. with Old World atmosphere. In 1840's came German immigrants. Disastrous cholera epidemic occurred in 1846, but town survived. Today it is cotton, cattle & oil center. In town is J. with US59.

SIDE TRIP: On US59 (SW) 13m to **Fannin,** at J. with Rd.

Take latter (L) 1m to **Fannin Battlefield St. Pk.** where in Mar. 1836 Col. Jas. W. Fannin Jr.'s force of Texans were defeated by Gen. Jose Urrea's Mex. army.

23m **Goliad,** with oak-shaded streets & dignified old Hs., grew up around mission & presidio est. near-by by Sp. in 1749. Presidio was captured from Sp. by Augustus W. Magee's expedition in 1812 & again by Dr. Jas. Long's invading Mississippians in 1821. When Tex. Rev. was only 7 days old, in 1835, Ben Milam & Geo. M. Collinsworth drove Mex. garrison from Presidio & captured it; & in Dec. 1835, revolutionists issued 1st Tex. Decl. of Ind. here. After their defeat (see above), Col. Jas. W. Fannin Jr. & c.350 of his men were executed in Goliad.

(S) 2m on St.29 from Goliad to **Goliad St. Pk.,** in which are **Mission Nuestra Señora del Espiritu Santo de Zuñiga** (Our Lady of the Holy Spirit of Zuniga) (rest.) & well-preserved remains of **Presidio Nuestra Señora de Loreto de la Bahia** (Fort of Our Lady of Loreto of the Bay). Mission & presidio, founded at another site in 1722, were moved here in 1749. **Mission Mus.** contains relics. Chapel of Presidio contains **Shrine of Nuestra Señora de Loreto de la Bahia,** built 2 cents. ago.

US59 cont. (W) to **Ruins of Mission Nuestra Señora del Rosario de los Cujanes** (Our Lady of the Rosary of the Cujanes), founded 1754, eventually to be rest. At 55m is **Beeville** (see US90), at J. with US181, which conn. with US90 (see).

**141. PORT LAVACA,** founded by Sp. in 1815, is fishing port & fish packing center on bay of same name.

## US 66—NEW MEXICO

**N.M.-TEX. LINE** (73m from Amarillo, Tex.) **(W) to N.M.-ARIZ. LINE** (54m from Holbrook, Ariz.). **375. US66**

Via: Tucumcari, Santa Rosa, Moriarty, Albuquerque, Grants & Gallup. C.R.I. & P. RR. parallels route bet. Tex. Line & Tucumcari; S.P. RR. bet. Tucumcari & Santa Rosa; Santa Fe RR. bet. Correo & Ariz. Line.

US66 is one of main transcont. hys. At E. end in N.M. the land is flat & level, a continuation of Tex. Panhandle terrain & W. terminus of Llano Estacado ("Staked Plains"). There is a gradual rise to W. sec. where hills & Mts. predominate. Agric. areas are passed at different pts., mostly irrigated, though there is some dry farming in E. & central secs. & where cattle are numerous. There are more sheep in W. part, where also are Laguna & Acoma Pueblos; El Moro Nat. Mon.

**41. TUCUMCARI.** J. with US54 (see). (S.P. & Rock I. RRs.bus lines.info.:C. of C.). Seat of Quay Cty., Tucumcari was named for daughter of Apache Chief who lived on famed Tucumcari Mt. to (S). Tucumcari Irrigation Project, made possible by erection in 1939 of Conchas Dam (NW) of city. Cattle shipping pt.; tourist business is important source of income. **45. TUCUMCARI METROPOLITAN PK. AREA & ST. PK.** (swim.golf.pic.), extends over 300 as. within sight of hy. **74. NEWKIRK,** gateway to Conchas Dam.

SIDE TRIP: On St.129 (R) 25m to **Conchas Dam & St. Pk.** Project consists of concrete main dam in canyon of S. Canadian R. & contiguous earth wing dams. Main dam, 235′ above roadway; crest, 1,250′ in length. Reservoir has storage capacity of 600,000 acre-feet & extends up S. Canadian Valley c.14m & up Conchas Valley c.11m. Provides water for 100,000 people & for irrigating 45,000 as. Also reduces flood damage in Tex. & Okla.

**101. SANTA ROSA,** J. with US54 & US84 (accoms.tourist camp.), is on banks of Pecos R. Seat of Guadalupe Cty. Trading place for ranchers & shipping pt. for livestock & wool. First settlement called Agua Negra Chiquita ("little black water") developed here after 1865 when Don Celso Baca came from Mex. & became lord of reg. under old custom of range domain. **119.** J. with US84 (R) to Las Vegas & Santa Fe. **158. CLINES CORNERS** is at J. with US285 (R) to Santa Fe. **203. TIJERAS** ("scissors"), is within bounds of Cibola Nat. For. (W) of village where hy. emerges from canyon is fine view of Rio Grande Valley & Albuquerque in distance.

**219. ALBUQUERQUE.** J. with US85 (see). US66 (W) of Albuquerque passes fertile farms & orchards of Rio Grande Valley. The San Jose R. parallels hy. as it crosses E. boundary of **LAGUNA IND. RESERV., 251.,** a grazing area of over 125,000 as. set aside for Inds. of Laguna Pueblo. **264. LAGUNA PUEBLO,** named for near-by L., since disappeared. There was sm. sett. of Inds. here in 1697, but pueblo was not est. until 1699 when Sp. gov. ordered it done while on expedition to Zuni. This is only pueblo est. subsequent to Sp. invasion & is largest (E) of Continental Divide. Its people are mixture of 4 pueblo stocks: Tano, Keres, Shoshone, Zuni. It is "Mother Pueblo" of 7 summer farming villages scattered where there is irrigation. Hs. are mainly of stone plastered with adobe. Gov. schs. are here & most of people speak English. Trade center for Navajo, especially on Feast Day, Sept. 19, when Harvest Dance is given & Fair is held. San José de Laguna Ch. (1699), unlike many of N.M. mission chs., is of stone with plain, massive walls, having only 4 openings of any size —doorway & window in middle of front facade, 2 sm. belfry openings in false gable front, with glistening cross above. Inter. by Ind. craftsmen; finest examples of mural decorations in any N.M. mission. At **269.** is J. with St.23.

SIDE TRIP: (L) 14m on St.23, is **Acoma Pueblo,** known as the sky city, perched high on its rocky stronghold, where Inds. took refuge during nomadic invasion days. Farming is done in valley below mesa & drinking water is carried to summit from spring near base of stronghold. Materials for ch.—stone, soil for adobe, & water—had to be carried from valley to top of mesa. Mission is 150′ long, 40′ wide; its walls, 4′ to 6′ thick, rise to 60′. Roof beams, 14″ sq., were carried for 30m. Dwellings, 3-story, tiered structures extending 1,000′ across mesa, are of stone covered with white adobe plaster.

**295. GRANTS** is RR. town & trading center for large agric. & ranching terr., named for Grant Brothers who constructed Santa Fe RR. here in 1881. At **296.** is J. with St.53.

SIDE TRIP: On Rd. (L) leading 3m through **San Rafael.** 28m **Perpetual Ice Caves,** in volcanic sink hole, its crevices perpetually packed with solid ice, aquarmarine in color & banded with dark horizontal stripes. Ice bed is 50′ wide, 14′ high, depth underground unknown. 41m **El Morro Nat. Mon.,** tract of 240 as. est. in 1906 to preserve Inscription Rock, camping place on old Acoma-Zuni trl. Rock covers 12 as. Here, centuries ago, Sp. & others carved hist. "entries" by some means or other. Earliest now legible (1605) is that of Gov. Oñate, 1st colonizer of N.M.

**306. BLUEWATER,** RR. loading sta.

SIDE TRIP: On dirt Rd. (L) 9m from Bluewater to **Bluewater Reservoir** (cabins.f.boat. swim.); contains impounded waters from Zuni Mt. watershed & fills great depressions in high tablelands. Dam constructed here creates deep L. 1m wide, 7½m long. Rd. cont. 11m to **Thoreau;** or backtrack 9m to US66 & Bluewater.

**323. THOREAU** is J. with St.56.

SIDE TRIP: (N) on Rd. leading 64m to **Chaco Canyon Nat. Mon.;** has examples of prehist. Ind. architectural skill; the 18 major ruins here are without equal in U.S. Pueblo Bonito, largest of the ruins, covers more than 3 as. of ground & contains about 800 rooms & 32 kivas. Some of the walls are standing to the 4th story; it is estimated pueblo once housed 1,200 people. Chaco sett. was abandoned shortly after 1200 A.D.

**343. WINGATE STATION.** J. with Rd.

SIDE TRIP: (L) on this Rd. 3m to **Ft. Wingate,** integral part of **Ft. Wingate Military Reserv.,** comprising 64,000 as., est. 1812. Used during World War I by Army. Rd. cont. through fors. of pine, spruce, juniper & aspen. Cont. (S) to **McGaffey Winter Sports Area,** in Cibola Nat. For. Season Jan. 1-Feb. 15. Ski runs, Gentle slope for beginners. All accoms. Info. at Gallup & For. ranger at Bluewater, N.M.

**354. GALLUP.** J. with US666 (R), through Navajo Reserv. to Shiprock (see US85). (Santa Fe RR.bus lines.info.C. of C.). Seat of McKinley Cty., Gallup is RR. div. pt. & thriving industrial & trade center. Principal industries: coal mining, Ind. trading, railroading, tourist business. Its hist. is quite recent. Was inc. in 1891; became Cty. seat in 1901. Gallup is noted for annual Intertribal Ind. Ceremonials, held 4 days, middle of Aug. Here Navajo, Hopi, Apache & many other tribes take part in dances, ceremonials & rituals. Also contribute to arts & crafts displays.

SIDE TRIP: On St.32 leading (L) from Gallup 40m to **Zuni Pueblo,** on (N) side of Zuni R., whose waters are used for irrigation. Zuni Pueblo is village of red sandstone hs. Inds. are farmers & sheep-herders. Noted for dances & arts & crafts, particularly turquoise & silver jewelry.

**375. N.M.-ARIZ. LINE.**

## US 60—NEW MEXICO

**N.M.-TEX. LINE** (82m from Amarillo, Tex.) **(W) to N.M.-ARIZ. LINE** (17m from Springerville, Ariz.). **404. US60**

Via: Texico, Clovis, Ft. Sumner, Willard, Bernardo, Dátil, Quemado. Santa Fe RR. roughly parallels route bet. Tex. Line & Magdalena.

US60 runs (E-W) across center of N.M. from wide reaches of level Staked Plains, across extensive farming areas, over mt. ranges, through cattle & mining country. E. part is reg. of color, stillness & mirages. (W) of Socorro, Rd. winds through reg. of great nat. beauty, where Apache Inds. roamed & hunted. Rd. twists uphill &

down, through canyons & arroyos, through Cibola Nat. For. US60 & US70 unite at Clovis. Boundary bet. Central & Mt. Std. Time Zones. Westbound travelers set watches back an hour. **9. CLOVIS** is J. with US70 (see). **68.** J. with graded Rd.

SIDE TRIP: On this Rd. S. 2.5m to crumbled walls of **Old Ft. Sumner** & **Grave of Billy the Kid.** Old Ft. in Bosque Redondo (round grove of trees) on E. bank of Pecos R. is said to have been on trl. followed by Coronado in 1541 & Espéjo in 1583. Ft. was erected in 1862. Kit Carson, in 1864, rounded up 7,000 Navajo in Canyon de Chelly country during open warfare & moved them to Bosque Redondo where they were held for several yrs. but were returned to their native haunts after unsuccessful experiment of trying to make farmers of them. Near ruins of ft. is Ft. Sumner Cemetery containing **Grave of Billy the Kid,** Apache renegade, & terror of early N.M. & Ariz.

**71. FT. SUMNER,** at J. with US84, (N) is seat of De Baca Cty. Chief industries: cattle, sheep-raising, farming. Also shipping pt.

SIDE TRIP: On US84 (N) 16m to **Alamogordo Dam,** which impounds waters of Alamogordo Creek for irrigation of Carlsbad Irrigation Dist.

**128. VAUGHN** at J. with US54 & US285. Called "the oasis" for its shade trees, it is div. pt. on Santa Fe RR., roundh. being town's chief source of employment. **144. ENCINO.** J. with US285, (N) to Santa Fe. (W) of **WILLARD, 180.,** are raised most of pinto beans grown in U.S. **195. MOUNTAINAIR.** J. with St.10, (N) to Quari St. Mon. (see US85) & (S) to Gran Quivira Nat. Mon. (see US85), in heart of fertile Estancia Valley; shipping pt. for pinto bean industry. At **205.** is J. with unimproved Rd.

SIDE TRIP: On this Rd. leading (N) c.1m to **Abo St. Mon.,** ruins of important pueblo built on beautiful red sandstone, with kiva of unusual design & structure. **Ch. of Abo Mission,** built in 1646, has been excavated, repaired & preserved by Mus. of N.M. & is only bldg. with walls standing above surface, village & convent walls being level with ground.

**234. BERNARDO** unites with US85. **261. SOCORRO** (see US85). **288. MAGDALENA,** 2nd largest town in Socorro Cty., was named for Mary Magdalene. Trading & shipping pt. for cattle. No RR. sta. bet. Magdalena & Ariz. Founded in 1884 by miners who worked sm. claims, town began to flourish after coming of RR. short time later. When mining declined, town declined, until people turned to livestock, when town flourished again. **324. DÁTIL,** named by early Sp. for fruit resembling dates found in mts. Trade center for ranchers & supply pt. for hunters. U.S. Army built ft. here in 1888 to protect settlers from Apache raids.

SIDE TRIP: (L) from Dátil on St.12, an improved dirt Rd. leads past mts., ranches, springs & fors. where Apache roamed before subjugation. 26m **Horse Springs,** & springs near-by, named for wild horses that roamed here. At 40m, **Apache Nat. For.** is entered, which is two-thirds western yellow pine; remainder Douglas fir, white fir & spruce. Large herds of cattle, horses and sheep graze here under gov. permit. Continental Divide is crossed & Rd. goes through Tularosa Canyon at 46m, a winding gorge cut out by Tularosa R. which is dry most of year, swift & dangerous in rainy weather. 47m **Aragón** is trading center in narrow Tularosa Valley, with sm. irrigated farms, cattle & sheep raising for villagers. 68m **Reserve,** seat of Catron Cty., only cty. in N.M. without RR., on banks of San Francisco R., in heart of cattle country surrounded by fors. & mts. Farming & lumbering in area. Is starting pt. for pack trips & hunt. parties. At 75m is J. with US260 (see).

US60 runs through a narrowing valley & crosses boundary of **CÍBOLA NAT. FOR.** at **324.5.,** which it traverses for 20m. At **325.5.,** ranger sta. & cabins for tourists. US60 crosses **CONTINENTAL DIVIDE** at **343.,** & cont. through sec. of magnificent vistas. **347. PIE TOWN,** started with filling sta., whose owner had taken up mining claim on site. His 3rd occupation was baking pies, hence name. Marketing pt. for piñon nuts gathered in area by Inds., who sell to traders & wholesalers. **369. QUEMADO** ("burnt"), largest town in Catron Cty., is named for Apache Chief, whose hand, legend says, was burned in a campfire. Coronado's route in 1540 was through this reg. **404. N.M.-ARIZ. LINE.**

## US 70—NEW MEXICO

**N.M. LINE** (Texico, N.M.) **(W) to N.M.-ARIZ. LINE** (3m from Duncan, Ariz.). **455. US70**

Via: Clovis, Portales, Roswell, Hondo, Tularosa, Alamogordo, Las Cruces, Deming, Lordsburg.

Route traverses plains made productive by irrigation, & crosses Mescalero Ridge & Pecos Valley. Crossing through Lincoln Nat. For. & Mescalero Apache Ind. Reserv., hy. borders White Sands Nat. Mon. & over plains of Tularosa Valley, & mining area of SW. N.M.

**9. CLOVIS** is at J. with US60-84, (W). (Santa Fe RR.bus.info.C. of C.). Clovis named for 1st Christian King of France. Town began in 1907 as Riley's Switch, siding on Santa Fe, but grew rapidly after RR. brought shops & warehs. here from Melrose. Is 4-way div. pt. of Santa Fe RR., jobbing center, agric. & elevator storage pt., livestock shipping. Annual Pioneer Days & Mounted Patrol Rodeo in June; Lasso del Llano ("lariat of the plains"), Labor Day. Adj. S. city limit is **Hillcrest,** 140-a. mun. pk.; (18-hole golf.swim.zoo.f.-stocked L.baseball pk. & recr.). **28. PORTALES** is at J. with St.18 (S) to Hobbs & rich oil fields (see US85). (Santa Fe RR.bus.info.C. of C.), seat of Roosevelt Cty., in irrigated Portales Valley where over 700 irrigation wells furnish water for some 35,000 as. under cultivation, incl. 14,000 as. of peanuts, 1,000 as. of sweet potatoes. Cattle raising & dairying area. Home of **E. N.M. College,** founded 1934, on 90-a. campus (SW) of town. Youngest college in St., opened as 2-yr. jr. college. In 1940, became 4-yr. college of liberal arts. **Roosevelt Cty. Mus.** on campus, which houses coll. of archaeological & hist. nature. Sponsors & displays monthly traveling exhibits of paintings & crafts. **120. ROSWELL.** J. with US285 (see) & US380. US70-380 unite bet. Roswell & Hondo (Santa Fe RR.bus.info.C. of C.). Seat of Chaves Cty. Roswell is home of **N.M. Military Institute.** Industries incl. cotton gins, creameries, meat-packing plants & flour mill. Irrigation farming, with water from artesian wells, & livestock are main source of income. In 1869, Van C. Smith & partner constructed 2 adobe bldgs. that served as store, P.O. & sleeping quarters for guests. Town named for Van Smith's father, Roswell Smith. E. N.M. St. Fair, Rodeo & Old Timers' Celebration 1st wk. in Oct.

SIDE TRIPS: (A) 1m (N) of center of town, **N.M. Military Institute.** Campus consists of 75 landscaped as., with numerous bldgs. of handsome buff brick.

(B) On Rd. leading (E) 10m to Pk. J.; 3m (S) to **Bottomless L. St. Pk.**

**168. HONDO.** From here US70 traverses scenic Ruidoso Canyon, noted for its fors. of tall conifers, trout stream & recr. areas for campers in summer & skiers in winter. It crosses E. boundary of **LINCOLN NAT. FOR.** at **175.,** an area of 1½ million as. covered with large pines & crossed with canyons & ravines. Mt. sides stocked with game. Hy. crosses W. boundary of **MESCALERO APACHE IND. RESERV., 193.,** which is 35m long & 25m wide. **192. RUIDOSO,** gateway to Lincoln Nat. For. Winter Sports Area (Info.Hqs.Alamogordo). **Cedar Cr. Area,** 4m (NW) of Ruidoso (best season Jan.1-Feb.15.ski lift,run,trls.;shelter;equip.rented.food & lodging, Ruidoso). **208. MESCALERO,** agency hqs. Before 1872, Mescalero Apaches were quartered at Ft. Stanton with Navajo. In 1866 related groups quarreled & Mescalero Apaches resumed former nomadic life, murdering, pillaging & stealing. After army succeeded in returning 800 of them to Ft. Stanton agency, a reserv. there was set apart for them. Present boundaries est. in 1883. Of their 427,320 as., 2,000 are suitable for cultivation. Remainder are used for grazing. **225. TULAROSA** is at J. with US54, which unites with US70 to pt. 2m (S) of Alamogordo. Name derived from tule (Sp.: "reed" or "rush") & rosa (Sp.: "rose"). Founded in 1860 by Sp. & Mex. immigrants from Mesilla Valley, after Rio Grande at flood stage had wiped out their sm. farms, it prospered for a yr. but Apache raids caused abandonment. Colonized again (1862) when present townsite was plotted. Thriving community with large lumber mill & cotton gin. Loading pt. for cattle. **237. ALAMOGORDO** ("big cottonwood tree") is at J. with US54. (R.I. RR. & S.P. RR.bus line.info.C. of C.), seat of Otero Cty. & center of great lumbering industry. Two big projects located near Alamogordo are Holloman Air Force Base & White Sands Proving Grounds for testing guided missiles. In remote sec. of Alamogordo Air Base bombing range occurred 1st testing of atom bombing from the air. N.M. School for Blind situated here.

SIDE TRIP: On St.83 (E) 25m **Cloudcroft,** in Lincoln Nat. For. (Hqs.Alamogordo). Summer & winter resort at 9,000′. Ski runs & highest 9-hole golf course in world. Ski season Dec. 15-Mar. 15. Slopes for tobogganing & sledding. Equip. may be rented at Cloudcroft in area where meals & lodging may be obtained.

At **250.** is J. with dirt Rd.

SIDE TRIP: On this Rd. (R) 9m to **White Sands Nat. Mon.** & heart of Sands Loop Dr. One of world's strangest & most spectacular deserts, with huge gypsum dunes of purest white, some more than 50′ high. Fascinating tale of White Sands & its origin, told through use of photographs, paintings & models in mus. in Mon. Hqs.

**306. LAS CRUCES** is at J. with US80-85 (see US85). From Las Cruces to Ariz. Line US70-80 are same route. **365. DEMING** is at J. with US260, St.11-26. (Santa Fe & S.P. RRs.bus lines.info. C. of C.), seat of Luna Cty.; ranching, farming, mining center. Is in Mimbres Valley, which contains many thousand as. of fine farm land. Mining area.

SIDE TRIP: On US260 leading (N), route crosses through Mimbres Valley, named after tribe of Apache; skirts edge of **Gila Nat. For.** with Mts. on both sides; through **Apache Nat. For.,** crossing Gila R. near Cliff; & San Francisco R. above Alma. 38m **Hurley,** a company village owned by Chino Mine of Nev. Consolidated Copper Co.; is site of concentration mill for Santa Rita Mine. Village consists of over 100 company Hs., ore mill, steam plant, stores & mercantile establishments. 42m **Bayard** is at J. with St.180 (W) which unites with US260 to Silver City. 44m **Central,** because of proximity to old Ft. Bayard & present U.S. Veterans' Hospital, grew from sm. settlement to its present moderate size. 52m **Silver City** is J. with St.25-180. (Santa Fe RR.bus.info.:C. of C.), seat of Grant Cty.; occupies beautiful setting in foothills of Pinos Altos Range, an extension of Mogollón Mts. Shipping pt. for near-by Chino mines & livestock ranches, business center of SE. sec. of st. & home of N.M. St. Teachers' College. **County Cth.,** with murals by Theodore Van Soelen, W. Cooper St., & **St. Teachers' College,** W. College Ave. Silver City is gateway to Gila Nat. For. & Gila Wilderness Area, big game country—deer, antelope, elk, bear, turkey, mt. lion, lynx, etc. Trout f. (Inquire Silver City C. of C.h.f.camp.in for.area). For. incl. 4 major ranges—Mogollón, Pinos Altos, Black Range, & Big Burros. Covers nearly 2½ million as. of ponderosa pine, Douglas fir, white fir & spruce. (Hqs.Silver City).

(1) 78m **Gila Nat. For. Inner Loop Dr.** (N). Start City Hall, Silver City. Turns plainly indicated by "Turn," "Take," etc. Via: Pinos Altos or Santa Rita.

(2) 232.5m **Gila Nat. For. Outer Loop Dr.** Starts City Hall, Silver City. Inquire Silver City C. of C. regarding trips (S) into Gila Nat. For. & Wilderness Area, who will furnish logs of trips.

117m **Glenwood** is near J. of several deep canyons, almost hidden in grove of cottonwoods. In midst of h. & f. reg. Many trls. in these areas lead from Glenwood. US260 crosses **Ariz. Line** at 171m, 7m (E) of Alpine, Ariz., on Coronado Trl., scenic wonderland & recr. area.

Continental Divide is crossed at **395. 425. LORDSBURG** (S.P. RR.bus lines.info. C. of C.), seat of Hidalgo Cty., in mining area. Formerly named Lordsborough for construction engineer for S.P. RR. **455. N.M.-ARIZ. LINE.**

## US 54—NEW MEXICO

**N.M.-TEX. LINE** (41m from Dalhart, Tex.) **(S) to N.M.-TEX. LINE** (17m from El Paso, Tex.). **361. US54**

Via: Tucumcari, Santa Rosa, Vaughn, Carrizozo, Alamogordo & Newman.

Route running alternately through level plains & Mts. gives access to fors., f. & h. grounds as well as mines, pueblo ruins & grazing lands. **53. TUCUMCARI** is at J. with US66, which unites with US54 to Santa Rosa (see US66). **152. VAUGHN.** Here US54 joins US60; it branches (L) from US60 at **155.** (see US60). **187. CORONA** is thriving trading & shipping center, serving wide territory. Founded in 1899, cattle, sheep & goat ranching are leading industries, though considerable dry farming is carried on & beans are major crop. (W) of Corona lies part of Lincoln Nat. For., its E. boundary extending along hy. for 15m (N) & (S). **238. CARRIZOZO,** (Sp.: Carizzo, "Reed grass") is seat of Lincoln Cty., supply & shipping center. J. with US380.

SIDE TRIPS: (A) (W) of Carrizozo, US380 passes over lava beds & through open country, with beautiful Oscura ("dark") Mts. on both sides. There are few settlements along route in this vast, silent, barren country.

(B) On US380 leading (SE) 20m to **Capitán,** (h.f.), named for Capitán Mts. (L), center of mining, stock raising, farming areas. 32m **Lincoln,** in Lincoln Nat. For. (hqs.Alamogordo), 1st sett. in 1859, then called Las Placitas ("small settlements"), but after cty. was named for Pres. Lincoln, name of town changed. Was cty. seat until 1913, when seat was transferred to Carrizozo. **Lincoln St. Mon.** is Lincoln County Cth., rest. & administered by Lincoln Cty. Soc. of Art, Hist. & Archaeology, as branch of Mus. of N.M. Once held a store down stairs, with 2nd fl. containing courtroom, jail, & bedrooms. Courtroom is now auditorium; one of bedrooms is art gallery. Rooms of 1st fl. house hist. & archaeological material. Hist. room contains mementoes of mining & cattle-raising & of Lincoln Cty. War.

**283. TULAROSA** is at J. with US70 (see), which unites with US54 to Alamogordo.

**295. ALAMOGORDO** (see US70). **332. ORO GRANDE** ("much gold"), on plains SE. of Jarilla Mts., was 1st called Jarilla J.; grew from camp to town, then little city when gold rush occurred in 1905-06. Was lively community for few yrs. Two smelters were built. Occasional mining is done now. Area long noted for turquoise mined by Apache, then later by white men under both Sp. & Mex. regimes. At **361. NEWMAN,** border hamlet, US54 crosses **N.M.-TEX. LINE.**

## US 85—NEW MEXICO

**N.M.-COLO. LINE** (14m Trinidad, Colo.) **(SW) to N.M.-TEX. LINE** (El Paso, Tex.). **500. US85**

Via: Ratón, Las Vegas, Santa Fe, Albuquerque, Los Lunas, Socorro, Hot Springs, Las Cruces, Anthony (El Paso, Tex., & Juarez, Mex.). Santa Fe RR. roughly parallels entire route. Bus network throughout. Accoms.: in principal towns.

(N) & (E) of Santa Fe, US85 follows old Santa Fe Trl.; (S) of Santa Fe, it approximates "El Camino Real" ("the royal Rd."), both having played important parts in hist. of St. N. part of US85 goes through Ratón Pass & crosses alternating mts. & plains, conn. occasional villages. Below Santa Fe are mts., plains, farms, coal & turquoise mines, Ind. pueblos. Hy. borders Rio Grande R. which runs swiftly through land. US85 crosses over Ratón Pass, so named for many pack rats on mountainside. **7. RATÓN** (Santa Fe RR.bus lines.Info.: C. of C.) is J. with US64 (see), which unites with US85 bet. this pt. & Hoxie; seat of Colfax Cty., stock raising, agric., railroading & coal mining center.

SIDE TRIPS: (A) On US85 which unites with US64 bet. Ratón & Hoxie. (R) on US64, 41m to **Cimarrón,** divided into New Town & Old Town by Cimarrón R. Large stock ranches here produce excellent cattle & horses. Cimarrón was seat of Colfax Cty. from 1872 to 1882, but declined with transfer of cty. seat to Springer. PTS. OF INT.: **Old Cty. Jail & Cth.,** built in 1852; **Nat. Hotel,** 1858; **Swink's Gambling Hall** (1854.now garage); **Cimarrón Cemetery,** pioneer graves. 46m **Cimarrón Canyon,** narrow, twisting gorge whose stone walls seem to hang over hy. Scrub pine, juniper & aspen cover sides, coming down to edge of Rd. Fine camp. spots privately owned along hy. (fee). (W) of **Ute Park,** 54m, US64 follows twisting Cimarrón R. through reg. thick with pine & aspen fors. **Cimarrón Palisades** (R), formation of red sandstone rising 800′ above hy. extend for c.2m along RR. After 2 hairpin turns, hy. climbs over hills into Moreno Valley. At 62m, **Eagle Nest L.** (L) (boats & tackle for rent), considered by some best trout L. in St., annually visited by hundreds of fishermen. Hy. enters Taos Cty., cont. down into Taos Canyon in another series of hairpin turns, crosses sec. of Carson Nat. For. to **Taos Cr.** (pub.camp.facils.free camp). 98m **Taos** (bus lines.info.hotels & taverns.swim.f.pack trips.recr.). Taos (pronounced to rhyme with house) is in reality 3 towns: Sp. Town (Don Fernando de Taos), Ind. Pueblo (San Gerónimo de Taos), Ind. farm center (Ranchos de Taos)—all separate entities, yet always closely knit together in int. **Taos Cty. Project,** instituted 1943, sponsors comprehensive rehabilitation program for Sp.-speaking pop., by Univ. of N.M. through cooperative training & activities made possible by Carnegie grant. Aside from these are several smaller settlements near-by, members of community. Don Fernando de Taos is seat of Taos Cty., where 3 races, Ind., Sp. & Anglo-Amer. intermingle; is also home of Taos art colony. Village is trading center for surrounding ranches. San Gerónimo de Taos, familiarly called Taos Pueblo, oldest of 3 towns bearing name Taos, is 2.5m (N) of Don Fernando de Taos, reached by Pueblo Rd., leading from Plaza. Ruins of old mission, erected 1704, E. edge of pueblo. Standing walls 4′ thick, with remains of twin towers in ruined pile of adobe. Pueblo abounds in ancient ceremonialism. Dances performed at different seasons of yr. (Inq.events & dates). Fixed dates are San Gerónimo Fiesta, Sept. 30; Taos Corn Dance, Sept. 29; Deer Dance, Buffalo Dance, Matachines at Ind. Pueblo, Christmas-New Year's holiday.

(1) (S) on St.3 to 27m, **Carson Nat. For.,** improved winter sports area (Aqua Piedra) on Taos-Las Vegas hy. (hqs.Taos). Best season Dec.15-Mar.15 (ski lift.runs.trls.shelter. equip.for rent at near-by resorts;for sale at Taos). Food & lodging at **Lodge** 1m from area. (For.ranger,Penasco,N.M.;inquire Taos for all info.).

(2) (N) on St.3 to 43m, **Red River** winter sports area, in Carson Nat. For. (hqs.Taos). (N) of Taos via Questa. Best season Jan.1-Mar.1 (ski lift.runs.trls.shelters.equip.for sale at Taos & Ratón). Food & lodging at Red R. in area. (Inq.Taos for all info.).

(B) Route cutting across NE. cor. of N.M. traverses reg. strewn with masses of black lava rock. In old days this was cattle country & great herds roamed here until spring roundups. US87 skirts famed Capulin Mt. Nat. Mon., extinct volcanic cone, & passes through Raton Pass. Santa Fe RR. & C. & S. RR. roughly parallel route. Bus. Hotels in Raton, Clayton. Tourist camps & gas stas. at intervals. 29m **Capulin** (custodian Capulin Mt.Nat.Mon.for info.). **Capulin Mt. Nat. Mon.** is magnificent example of recently (c.2,000 yrs.) extinct volcano. Rising to alt. of 8,000′ above sea level, it stands 1,500′ above level of surrounding plain. Its steep sided, circular cinder cone, with well-marked crater at summit & broad platform at base, was built up through long period of time by successive lava flows. Autos may be driven from base to rim of crater, over cinder Rd. 38m **Des Moines,** named for Des Moines, Iowa, is trading & shipping pt. for extensive dry farming & ranching area. 83m **Clayton,** is seat & largest town in Union Cty.; on high plateau. Town is on 2 RRs. & serves as trading & shipping pt. for ranchers & farmers for E. part of country, which usually has enough snow in winter to provide moisture in spring for crops. Highlight in Clayton's hist. was wild career of "Black Jack" Ketchum, train robber & bandit, whose gang wrought havoc in this area in 1890's. Ketchum was tried & hanged here in 1901. At 93$^m$ is **N.M.-Tex. Line.**

**22. HOXIE.** J. with US64 (R) to Cimarrón & Taos (see above). **34. MAXWELL,** shipping center for cattle, sheep & farm produce. In late 80's Maxwell Land & Irrigation Co., an org. of Hollanders, began irrigation projects here. **47. SPRINGER.** J. with St.58 (E) to Clayton. Thriving crossroads town, trading center for cattle & sheep raising area, named for Springer Bros., owners of stock ranches. In 1882, it was seat of Colfax Cty., but in 1897, after protracted & bitter fight, seat moved to Raton. **New Mex. Industrial Sch. for Boys** here. **73. WAGON MOUND.** J. with St.120. Founded in 1850 by stockmen. First named Santa Clara for patron saint. Now flourishing trading center, wool & stock shipping pt. In early days, Inds. out foraging or passing by on buffalo hunts, met here & attacked overland traffic at this pt. **95. WATROUS,** at J. of Sapello & Mora R., is trading & shipping center serving farming & ranching community. **115. LAS VEGAS** ("the meadows"), at J. with St.3 & St.65., is cty. seat of Miguel Cty. Situated high in Sangre de Christo Mts., it is a principal trading, shipping & business center. Home of **N.M. Highlands Univ.,** est. 1893 as part of St. system of higher education. Was orig. est. as teachers' college; has expanded its bldgs. & facils. & now has full 4-yr. program of liberal arts & vocational work. Until coming of RR., Las Vegas was typical adobe town, stopover on Santa Fe Trl. In early yrs. of town, wealthy dons who were accustomed to take advantage of impoverished citizens, seized huge tracts of land & ran tenants off. Vigilante groups org. & through secret activities became so powerful that lands were again recovered for community. In **Old Plaza,** freighters on Santa Fe Trl. unloaded goods. Back of plaza is 1st Cth. & jail, oldest bldg. in town, where Billy the Kid spent a few anxious hours. **120. ROMEROVILLE.** J. with US84, which unites with US85 to Santa Fe. **130. BERNAL,** at J. with St.3, was first called Bernal Springs. Was 1st sta. on Las Vegas-Santa Fe sec. of old stage line. **155. ROWE.** J. with St.63.

SIDE TRIP: (N) on Rd. 6$^m$ to **Pecos,** named after Pecos Inds.; trading center for stock & dude ranches. Starting pt. for hunt. & fish. expeditions into Pecos Canyon. (Info., outfits & guides procured at Pecos.)

(N) from Pecos on St.63 to **Valley Ranch** (L) 1.7$^m$ (accoms.f.swim.golf.recr.facils.). Rd. winds along banks of Pecos R. crossing & recrossing it. Countryside is part of Santa Fe Nat. For. (hqs.Santa Fe). Heavy pine, aspen & fir clothe Mt. sides. Trout & other fish abundant; turkey, grouse, bear, deer & elk. Hy. enters broad R. canyon which after short distance narrows considerably; irrigated farms. 2$^m$ **Lisboa Springs Fish Hatchery,** principal unit of St.'s fish propagation system, featuring rainbow, Loch Leven, steelhead trout, crappie & Chinook salmon. Beginning at 7.5$^m$, Mts. crowd close to hy. & Pecos R. tumbles over rocky bed. 9.5$^m$ **Field's Pub. Campground,** For. Serv. maintained (facils.tourist camps avail.). Directly across R. is **Brush Ranch,** 11.5$^m$ (h.f.riding & pack trips). Ahead (L) in **Holy Ghost Canyon** are numerous private h. & f. lodges as well as pub. campgrounds on shore of **Spirit L.** at head of canyon. Hy. follows Pecos R. (N) to **Cowles,** 20$^m$ (camp.), hqs. to Catherine & Stewart Ls. area for f. & h.

**Pecos Nat. Mon.,** 3$^m$ (S) of Pecos, contains ruins of **Ch. of Our Lady of Angels** (1617).

At **173.** is J. with US285, which unites with US85-84 to Santa Fe.

**182. SANTA FE** (S.F. RR. & R.G.W. RR.;bus lines.Info.C. of C.;N.M.Tourist Bureau.) Santa Fe has been capital of N.M. for more than 300 yrs., & flags of 4 nations —Spain, Mex., Confed. & U.S.—have flown over its ancient Palace of Govs., which still stands along N. side of Plaza & whose hist. is hist. of Santa Fe & N.M. It is oldest capital within boundaries of U.S. Major industry is tourist & vacation trade. Santa Fe has seen much hist. in its narrow, crooked streets & venerable Plaza; it has seen wars & rebellions; Cath. feasts & devout processions; Sp. men-at-arms, soldiers of Mex., Confed. & the Union; the bullwhackers & caravans of the Santa Fe Trl.; Sp. women in black shawls, the Inds. from near-by pueblos wrapped in blankets; for here are blended, as nowhere else in U.S., the full rich patterns of 3 cultures—Ind., Sp. & Amer. Founded in 1609; independence from Sp. in 1821; province of U.S. in 1846; Statehood in 1912. Santa Fe became capital of 47th St. in Union.

PTS. OF INT.: (1) N. side of Plaza, **Palace of Govs.** (O.9-12 & 1-5 wks.2-4 Sun.) is adobe structure standing since 1609. Once it was most imposing & important part of royal presidio, an all-purpose fortress, which was surrounded by adobe wall. In Pueblo Revolt of 1680, presidio was besieged for 5 days by force of 3,000 Pueblo

Inds.; overpowering small force of citizenry, Inds. captured place & held it for 12 yrs. before being driven out by Sp. Palace during 18th cent. had 28 Sp. govs. Mex. regime, which lasted 25 yrs., housed its govs. here, as Sp. had. From 1806 until 1907, when present executive mansion was built, Palace was occupied by Amer. Terr. govs. By act of N.M. Legislature in 1909, Mus. of N.M. was est. & located in Palace. (2) NW. cor. Plaza, **Mus. of N.M. Art Gallery** (O.9-5.wks.2-4 Sun.), erected 1917 with funds by pub. subscription & donations, matched by St. Legislature. Owned by the people, Mus. offers any artist use of exhibition space, making it free to exhibitor & visitor. Design is architectural composite of 6 ancient Sp. missions. Built around patio with cloistered walls, mus. has gallery space for more than 200 pictures. Entrance hall had display of Ind. art in all its forms. Aside from monthly exhibits, Mus. has permanent coll., work of nationally known artists. (3) NE. cor. De Vargas & Don Gaspar Sts., **Supreme Court Bldg.** (Sp.Col.) houses Supreme Court, office of Attorney-Gen., St. Law Lib. & St. Treasurer. (4) On Galisteo St., at Montezuma, **St. Capitol Bldg.**, stands on site of 1st St. capitol (1884). Built 1900, it is composed of 2 wings & large central dome, described as neo-Eng. Ren. Houses most offices of St. gov., incl. legislature. (5) (E) of Mus. Navajo Ceremonial Art, **Lab. of Anthropology,** on 50-a. site (O.9-12.1-5 wks.except Sun.& holidays.free). Built in 1931 in early Sp.-Pueblo style, bldgs. incl. mus., lecture hall, lab., etc. Incl. great colls. of Pueblo pottery, Navajo & Pueblo textiles, silver, basketry, & arts & crafts of other tribes. (6) San Francisco & Shelby Sts., SE. cor. of Plaza, **La Fonda,** modern hotel on site of famous inn at end of Santa Fe Trail.

## TRIPS OUT OF SANTA FE

**I. Santa Fe to Taos (see Ratón above).**

**II. Santa Fe to Bandelier Nat. Mon. 44. US285, St.4**

From Santa Fe (N) on US285 to J. with St.4, 16$^{m}$ at **Pojoaque.** (L) on St.4 to **Los Alamos,** 34$^{m}$, where 1st atom bomb test was made. Town is located on mesa top set in scrub cedars & piñon pines at foot of tall mesas where sunset frames peaks of distant Sangre De Cristo (Blood of Christ) Mts., fitting portent for deceptively peaceful town, known as "Capital of the Atomic Age." Constantly patrolled by uniformed guards, its nearly 69,000 as. & outlying sites are surrounded by high wire fence enclosing test sites deep in wooded canyons or near-by mesas & "Tech. Area," the highly equipped research lab. (under contract with Univ. of Cal.), now working on atom bomb that will probably make obsolete the one used at Eniwetok. Los Alamos, composite of boom town, honky-tonk & metropolis, with over-all military flavor, plans for 100 million dollar modernization program, if Congress allows, which will increase present pop. to c.12,000. (L) on St.4, to **Monument,** 44$^{m}$. Most accessible features of Bandelier are ruins in Frijoles Çanyon. Cliff ruins extend along base of N. wall of canyon for 2$^{m}$. These Hs. of masonry, irregularly terraced, from 1 to 3 stories in height, had many cave rooms, gouged out of solid cliff. In front of caves is ruined pueblo of **Tryuonyi,** on floor of Frijoles Canyon, large structure of nearly circular plan, with 3 kivas in enclosed plaza. Area consists of 26,000 as. Mon. closed to pub. Dec. to Feb. yrly. Open to travel other months. Lodging & meals obtained May-Sept. (accoms.facils.at Frijoles Canyon Lodge. camp sites.trlr.facils.).

**III. Santa Fe to Santa Fe Nat. For. Winter Sports Area. 15.**

8$^{m}$ **Hyde Park** (NE) of Santa Fe. Best season Jan. 1-Mar. 1. (ski.runs,trls.shelter. equipment for sale or rent in Santa Fe.instruction.meals at shelter.lodging at Santa Fe). **Big Tesuque,** 15$^{m}$, (NE) of Santa Fe. Best season Dec. 15-Ap. 15. (ski runs, trls.shelters.equipment for sale or rent, Santa Fe.instruction.meals in area.lodging Santa Fe).

**IV. Santa Fe (SW) to Gran Quivira. 139. US85, St.10**

Via: Madrid, Paako St. Mon., Quarai St. Mon., Mountainair, Gran Quivira Nat. Mon. Carrizozo (US70-380).

Take US85 to J. with St.10, 9$^{m}$ (S) of Santa Fe. Route is through reg. of exceptionally fine vistas; also gold, coal & turquoise mining dists. 23$^{m}$ **Cerrillos** ("hills") (Santa Fe RR.bus) is center of mining dist. & RR. loading pt.; trade center. 26$^{m}$ **Madrid,** owned & operated by Albuquerque & Cerrillos Coal Co., where coal mining has record of steady production, both anthracite & bituminous, yielding 100,000 tons annually. Coal discovered here in 1835. Madrid's Christmas celebration has become well known. Thousands come from afar to see illumination. From Madrid is view of **Jémez Range** (R) & **Sandías,** ahead. 39m **Golden** has hist. of placer mining dating back to 16th cent., when Sp. worked deposits with Inds. as slaves. At 48m is **Paako** (Paw-aw-ka) **St. Mon.** (R), containing Ind. Pueblo ruins abandoned before 1670. Ruin, enclosed by barbed wire fence, is owned & has been partially excavated by Univ. of N.M. 50m **San Antonito,** typical N.M. Mt. village, with dry farming & sheep grazing; also considerable wool from near-by Sandía Mts. & foothills (R) is hauled to Albuquerque. At San Antonito is J. with graded Rd. (R) to Sandía Rim Dr. (see Albuquerque). Traversing Tijeras Canyon, main pass bet. Sandía & Manzano Mts., St.10 passes **Cedar Crest,** 54m, mt. resort where many residents of Albuquerque have summer homes. 56m **Tijeras** ("scissors") in Cíbola Nat. For. is at J. with US66 (see). 79m **Chililí,** on Arroyo de Chililí, one of Saline Pueblos, was 1st visited by Chamuscado in 1581 & by Oñate, 17 yrs. later. Site of pueblo was (S) of present town & is now extinct. 92m **Tajique** (Ta-hee-ke), village of farming mountaineers at foot of (E) slope of Manzano Range. 102m **Manzano** ("apple"), cluster of red adobes surrounded by verdant fields. Sett. c.1829 & still primitive. Supposedly named for early apple trees here. **Manzano Peak** (10,608′) towers (R) above town & at its base is **El Ojo Del Gigante** ("giant spring"), flow of cold water that forms L. around which are clustered adobe Hs. At S. extremity of L. is ancient tower built as defensive work & watch tower. At 109m is **Quarai St. Mon.** (R) 1m, containing ruins of **Immaculate Conception Monastery** & **Ch.,** 1629, built of red & brown sandstone. Was seat of Sp. mission. Some Ch. walls stand 20′ high, extending to former roof height, but thinner monastery walls have been razed to furnish bldg. stone. Ruins are in meadow near cottonwood grove, where a spring is walled & covered. In grove are camp accoms. 115m **Mountainair,** J. with US60 (see). At 133m is J. with St.41, which unites with St.10, to Claunch. (S) on St.10-41 to **Gran Quivira,** 139m, which is J. with Gran Quivira Rd.

SIDE TRIP: On this Rd. (R) 1m to **Gran Quivira Nat. Mon.** About the time Pilgrims were landing at Plymouth Rock, Sp. padres in N.M. were constructing Gran Quivira Mission to serve great Pueblo of Pira Inds. This small, older Ch., now in ruins, & newer Ch., begun in 1649, never completed, are contained within Mon. Gran Quivira is numbered among "The Cities that Died of Fear," because of depredations by East Plains Inds. (Custodian lives near camp sites).

Tour cont. on US85, **209.,** J. with dirt Rd.

SIDE TRIP: 4.5m (R) on this Rd. to **Pueblo of San Domingo,** inhabited by one of most rigidly integrated of all tribes; their dances are considered exceptionally fine. Aug. 4 is Fiesta & Corn Dance. These Inds. are sturdy, handsome tribe; are hospitable & welcome visitors.

**220. ALGODONES** ("cotton"), sm. farming center for ranches. Was named for cotton fields that supposedly existed here at one time. **227. BERNALILLO** ("little Bernal"), at J. with St.44 (R) is seat of Sandoval Cty. on (E) bank of Rio Grande. Sett. 1698 by descendants of Bernal Diaz del Castillo who was associated with Cortéz in his conquest of Mex. Town marks approximate site of Coronado's Hqs. (1540-42) & his departure for Quivira (Kansas) in 1541. Situated in rich part of Rio Grande Valley, town is now trading center for Inds. & white farmers, shipping pt. for cattle & lumber from Jémez country. **Coronado St. Mon.,** embracing ruins of Tiguex Pueblos where Coronado had headquarters in 1540-42.

SIDE TRIP: (NW) from Bernalillo, 206m to Shiprock, on St.44

Via: Bernalillo, Cuba, Aztec, Farmington, Shiprock, (Cortez, Colo.).

Route passes pueblo ruins, grazing lands, fossil beds, Apache & Navajo Reservs., fertile orchards & farms of San Juan Valley, & offers fine vistas & panoramas. At 8m is J. with dirt Rd.

On this Rd. (R) 3m to **Santa Ana Pueblo.** (Caution: crossing ford of Jémez R. to reach pueblo is dangerous & difficult. Inquire before crossing.)

At 16m is J. with dirt Rd.

On this Rd. (R) across wooden bridge 1m to **Zia Pueblo.**

At 23m is J. with St.4, 1m to **San Ysidro.**

From San Ysidro (R) on St.4 over Jémez R. & across RR. tracks 5m to **Jémez Pueblo.** At 20m is **Jémez St. Mon.,** containing ruins of mission of San José de Jémez. Tourist may proceed to J. with St.4 & St.126. (L) on St.126 to Cuba on St.44.

50m **La Ventana,** formerly coal mining town; no longer active. 65m **Cuba,** orig. named Nacimienta ("nativity"), center of ranching country. (W) from Cuba, hy. borders, then enters **Jicarilla** (hick-oh-re-ah) **Apache Ind. Reserv.,** beyond which are fossil beds, then oil fields. At 67$^{m}$ is J. with St.112. At 70.5$^{m}$ is W. boundary of **Santa Fe Nat. For.** At 77.5$^{m}$, **Continental Divide** is crossed. 156$^{m}$ **Bloomfield,** sett. 1881, was home of notorious Stockton Gang; its early hist. was one of cattle rustling, terrorism & violent death. Is now an agric. center, surrounding farms producing large crops of grain, beans & other products by irrigation farming with waters from San Juan R. A canal 30$^{m}$ long irrigates 4,000 as. From Bloomfield the route is (N) to Aztec & Aztec Ruins Nat. Mon, 9$^{m}$. 165$^{m}$ **Aztec,** at J. with US550, is seat of San Juan Cty. & principal trading center in prosperous fruit growing area.

(N) 1$^{m}$, **Aztec Ruins Nat. Mon.,** embracing a great E-shaped pueblo structure, built by architects & masons more than 800 yrs. ago. This 500-room pueblo with its 36 kivas could easily have accommodated 1,500 people. Walls of some of ruins are standing to 3 stories.

Tour cont. (R) on US550. 179$^{m}$ **Farmington,** at confluence of San Juan, Las Ánimas & La Plata Rs., is in heart of great agric. reg. First sett. by whites in 1876; town inc. in 1901; now is largest town in San Juan Cty. & flourishing commercial center. 209$^{m}$ **Shiprock.** J. with US666. Named for imposing rock mass (L), it was hqs. for N. Navajo Ind. Agency from 1903 till subagencies were consolidated at Window Rock, Ariz., 1938. Is now Navajo dist. office. In area (W) are **Rattlesnake Oil Fields,** containing some of highest grade oil in U.S., but flow is limited & lack of marketing facils. further reduces value. From these & 2 other fields on their Reserv., Navajo receive annually a total of c.$50,000 in royalties. Annual Navajo Fair held here early in Oct. From Shiprock (R) on US666 (N) to Cortez, Colo., & (S) to Gallup.

**230. SANDÍA PUEBLO** (L), village of Tewa (tay-wuh) speaking Inds.

**244. ALBUQUERQUE** (Al-buh-kur-key), at J. with US66 (see). (Santa Fe RR.bus lines.Info.C. of C.&A.A.A.) Seat of Bernalillo Cty. & largest city in N.M. Wholesale pt. & distribution center for large area. Is principal banking, industrial, RR. & airlines center. Rich timber, mineral & agric. resources in vic. At base of Sandía Range, city was founded in 1706. In 1790, pop. was 6,000. Was important military post during Sp. & Mex. regimes, 2nd in importance only to Santa Fe & El Paso del Norte. After Amer. occupation in 1846, it was important U.S. military outpost until 1870. Was still isolated frontier town during Civil War but decade following brought influx of E. & Midwestern farmers & livestock raisers. Santa Fe RR. came in 1881. PTS. OF INT.: (1) On E. Central Ave., **Univ. of N. M.,** c.1$^{m}$ from business sec. on landscaped campus of more than 400 as. Bldgs. are modified Pueblo Ind. style. Univ. was created by act of legislature, 1889, which provided 20 as. Opened in 1892 when 1st bldg. was erected; there are now 63 bldgs. & enrollment has grown from 1,000 to 5,000 students. Adm. Bldg. houses Mus. of Anthropology & Geology Mus. Continuous exhibition throughout sch. yr. in Gallery of Fine Arts. Bldgs. on campus of striking Pueblo design are Adm., Lib., Student Union, Inter-Amer. Affairs, Fine Arts; Hodgin, Hokona & Rodney Halls; Pres.'s home. (2) NW. cor. Plaza, **Ch. of San Felipe de Nerí,** except for remod. facade & other minor changes, stands exactly as in 1706, built to withstand firebrands & battering rams, such as were used during Ind. uprisings, with windows 20′ from ground & adobe walls more than 4′ thick. (3) **Rio Grande Pk. & Zoo** (free) on Laguna facing Tingley Dr. along Rio Grande, is on 80-a. landscaped area of beautiful trees, with playgrounds, recr. facils. Wild fowl ponds & coll. of animals & birds native to SW. (4) Laguna & Kit Carson Blvds., **Mun. Bath. Beach,** an artificial L. of constantly changing pure water, diverted underground from Rio Grande, along 3$^{m}$ of white sand beach. (5) Adj. Alvarado Hotel, **Harvey Ind. Mus.** (O.8:30-6.Cal.Mission architecture), fine examples of authentic early Ind. arts & crafts, with craftsmen demonstrating silversmithing & Navajo weaving. (6) End of Parkland Dr., **U. S. Veterans Hospital,** massive bldg., built to resemble Taos Ind. Pueblo, constitutes striking landmark on high mesa several miles (E) of city. (7) 1$^{m}$ (NE) on Dartmouth Ave., **U.S. Ind. Hospital,** imposing structure on landscaped area. (8) **Barelas Community Center** (Conquistador.1943) in heart of Mex. quarter, whose function is to guide community in adapting itself to its environment, by being used as training center for Sp.-speaking social workers; provides other forms of adult education, guidance & recr. for youth of Community.

## TRIPS OUT OF ALBUQUERQUE

### I. Sandía Loop & Rim Dr. Tijeras Canyon, Sandía Crest, Bernalillo & Albuquerque. 65.5. US66, Rim Dr., US85

Drive can be made in 5 hrs.; passes into rugged Sandía Mts. to observ. pt. (2$^{m}$ above sea level) where vast panorama of St. can be seen. Pic. & camp grounds along route. Crest Rd. open May-Nov. From Central Ave. & 1st St., proceed (E) on Central (US66), entering **Tijeras Canyon** at 10$^m$, cont. through **Tijeras Village,** 15$^m$. 18.5$^m$ **Forest Pk.,** (R), mt. resort (private), meals, cabins, saddle horses avail. At 22$^m$ is J. with St.10 (L), proceed over St.10 & Loop Dr. through Tejano Canyon past **Tree Springs,** 27.5$^m$, above which is winter sports reg. where ski & toboggan tournaments are held. At 29.5$^m$ is J. with Sandía Crest Rd. Upward over this Rd. through fors. of aspen to **Sandía Crest Observ. Pt.,** 34$^m$. Returning, retrace to J. (L) with Loop Dr., 42.5$^m$, descend into Las Huertas Canyon & proceed to **Bernalillo,** 51$^m$. Route cont. (SW) to Albuquerque & J. with US66 at 4th St. & Central, then (L) over Central to pt. of start, 65.5$^m$.

**II. Cíbola Nat. For. Winter Sports Area.**
(Info.Supervisor, Albuquerque) Sandía Mt. (La Madera), 29$^m$, (NE) of Albuquerque on US66. One of best developed winter sports areas in SW. (Dec. through mid-Mar.).

Cont. on US85 to **265., LOS LUNAS** (Info.C. of C.), seat of Valencia Cty.; founded early in Sp. Col. days. Los Lunas is trading & exchange center. Alfalfa, grains & sheep are raised here. **275. BELÉN,** 1st named Belem (Bethlehem), was settlement provided by Sp. authorities for captives ransomed by Sp. from Apache & Comanche Inds. & subsequently released from slavery. Modern Belén, in heart of fertile sec. of Rio Grande Valley, is RR. shipping & trading center for near-by agric. areas. **292. BERNARDO.** J. with US60 (see) which unites with US85 bet. this pt. & Socorro. Across Rio Grande (L) which cont. (S), gently rolling country gives way to Manzano & Pinos ranges. **319. SOCORRO,** seat of Socorro Cty., built on site of ancient Piro Pueblo, was focal pt. in events of Sp. occupation, Pueblo rebellion & re-conquest by De Vargas. It was not until 1817 that ancestors of present families sett. here, where agric. predominated. Freighting & storing of supplies here for Civil War campaign created activity that completely transformed town. Silver was discovered near-by in 1867, & during 1880's Socorro was largest city in N.M. As center of rich mining area it had 44 saloons & was supply & shipping pt. for 200 wagon trains that served mines. Mining activities waned in the middle 1890's when price of silver declined. **N.M. Sch. of Mines,** founded here by Terr. Legislature of 1889, has 32-a. campus on W. outskirts of city. **Ch. of San Miguel,** center of city, is one of oldest Chs. in N. Amer. Fine example of early Sp.-Ind. mission architecture, with massive 5′ walls, hand-hewn rafters, old paintings & sacred ornaments; remod. twice; one of present walls is the wall of 1st Franciscan mission built in 1598. **330. SAN ANTONIO,** J. with US380 (see), trading pt. for ranchers, on site of Piro settlement, Senecu. The Sp. San Antonio is a survival of name applied to mission here in 1629. Banks of Rio Grande are level on both sides here & water is avail. by gravity flow & pumping. Alfalfa most important crop. (W) of town is beautiful Nogal Canyon with perpendicular walls from 300′ to 1,000′. From **356.** to Hot Springs, US85 parallels **Elephant Butte Reservoir** (L), 45$^m$-long L. made by waters of Rio Grande impounded by **Elephant Butte Dam,** 5$^m$ (N) of Hot Springs. From L., thousands of as. of land in this area are irrigated.

**396. HOT SPRINGS** (h.f.accoms.info.C. of C.), largest town in Sierra Cty.; trading center for surrounding mines, stock raising & farming areas; also health resort. Town underlaid with hot rocks; at depth of 120′, temp. of 120° is encountered. Springs of Palomas, now called Hot Springs, furnish uninterrupted supply of hot mineral water highly alkaline & non-laxative. Hot mineralized mud & water baths, with competent attendants, avail. Elephant Butte Regatta held here annually (1st Sat.-Sun.in June). **Carrie Tingley Hospital** for crippled children (infantile paralysis cases) was erected here (1937) at cost of 1 million dollars. **410. CABALLO.** J. with St.180 (R) to Silver City (see US70). **477. LAS CRUCES** ("the crosses"). J. with US70 & US80, is seat of Doña Ana Cty.; farming & ranching center. In early days a caravan en route from Chihuahua was attacked by Inds. here & entirely destroyed. Later another freighting party from Doña Ana found the bodies, buried them & erected crosses over graves, naming site Las Cruces (sett.1848). Several trls. lead from Las Cruces to Mts. (E) & (W) & to Mesilla Valley, land of beauty, vast agric. & mineral resources. **Amador Hotel,** built 1853, was furnished with massive walnut pieces of period brought by oxcarts from E. **N.M. College of Agric. & Mech. Arts,** 2.5$^m$ from center of town, founded (1890) with 17 pupils, now has over 1,500.

At **478.** is J. with St.28.

SIDE TRIP: 3m (R) on St.28 to **Old Mesilla** whose plaza & surrounding flat-topped adobe houses reflect days when this was capital of vast new state that combined lower part of N.M. with all of Ariz., days when Emperor Maximilian, according to local tradition, sought sanctuary here; & the days of Billy the Kid & Lincoln Cty. War.

**500. ANTHONY,** where US85 crosses **N.M.-TEX. LINE.**

## US 285—NEW MEXICO

**N.M.-COLO. LINE** (6m from Antonito, Colo.) **(S) to N.M.-TEX. LINE** (52m from Pecos, Tex.). **411. US285**

Via: Ojo Caliente Hot Springs, Española, Santa Fe, Vaughn, Roswell, Carlsbad Caverns Nat. Mon. D. & R.G.W. RR. roughly parallels route to Santa Fe. Santa Fe RR. from Roswell to Pecos.

From Colo. Line, hy. crosses flat, grassy plateau lying bet. distant Mts. through Chama R. Valley, with cultivated fields past Ind. Pueblos to Santa Fe. **58. OJO CALIENTE** (facils.), little town of adobe hs. that have changed little in a century. Agric. community; in low hills near-by are number of Ind. pueblo ruins, & several mineral springs for which town is named. (R) from Ojo Caliente to **Ojo Caliente Hot Springs,** (bathhs.pools.cottages) at foot of Ojo Caliente Mt.; 5 springs contain arsenic, iron, sodium sulphate, lithia & soda, varying in temp. from 98° to 113°. Were valued by Inds. as medicinal springs before Sp. Conquest. **84. ESPAÑOLA.** J. with US64-84, which unite with US285 to Santa Fe. Town, on W. bank of Rio Grande, is shipping pt. for agric. products & stock. **109. SANTA FE** (see US85). Bet. Santa Fe & J. at **119.,** US285 unites with US84-85, then branches (R) over hilly pasture land with vistas of **Sangre de Christo Mts.** (L); **Manzano, Sandía & Jémez Mts.** (R). Rd. curves frequently as it descends into ravine of Apache Cr. Canyon. **161. CLINES CORNERS,** at J. with US66 (see).

**188. ENCINO** is at J. with US60 (see); they unite to **VAUGHN, 204. 300. ROSWELL** is at J. with US70 (see) & US380. (S) of Roswell, US285 parallels Pecos R., famed as boundary line of W. justice. "Law West of the Pecos" is W. idiom signifying justice summarily dealt. **318. DEXTER** is town of gardens & trading center for farmers, & is surrounded by fertile cotton & alfalfa fields. **343. ARTESIA,** sett. 1903, owes its rapid growth to oil discoveries in spring of 1923. Principal industries are farming, stock raising, oil refineries, gasoline storage & pipe lines. Many sheep & angora goats are raised in area. (L) of hy. below Artesia is **Carlsbad Reclamation Project,** which spreads waters of Pecos R., impounded in L. McMillan & L. Avalon, over land up & down valley. **379. CARLSBAD** (Santa Fe RR.bus.accoms.facils. swim.h.f.), seat of Eddy Cty. & gateway to Carlsbad Caverns Nat. Pk. Known as potash capital of Amer., it is also livestock, agric. & oil center, with tourist trade high on list.

SIDE TRIPS: (A) On US62-180 (S) 18m to **White City.** (R) on Caverns Rd., 8m to **Carlsbad Caverns Nat. Pk.** (fees). This wonderland each yr. draws one-half million visitors who come to marvel at its beauty. It embraces largest series of caves known in world. More than 37m have been explored at 3 distinct levels, & extent of caverns, which lie beneath foothills of Guadalupe Mts., is not yet known. Here a great cathedral has been created by nature; its symmetry & beauty surpasses man's limitations. Animate life, tropical verdure, stalactites, helictites & stalagmites, giant columns & massive curtains, all in stone, defy description. Cavern is equipped with artificial lighting, concealed from view, which illuminates 1,000′ of caves, adding to glory of sight. Caverns are openings made by water in massive Carlsbad limestone. (No facils.or accoms.at Pk., but are situated along route from Carlsbad to Caverns.)

(B) On US62-180 leading (E) to SE. cor. of N.M., which gushes oil; hy. crosses oil fields & potash mines through rolling terrain. 70m to **Hobbs** (T.& N.M. RR.bus.info.C. of C.). Town, only 21 yrs. old, was fastest growing town in U.S. bet. 1930-40, due to striking oil in area. First surveys begun in 1927. Within few days after 1st oil came in, tent city sprang up. In 1930, pop. was 600; 1940, over 10,000; then doubled during next 8 yrs. Lea Cty. now has thousands of producing oil wells, also 8 gasoline plants. Irrigation wells in area have brought great agric. development in raising of cotton, alfalfa, grains & vegetables. Cattle & sheep also high in production.

(S) from Hobbs, on St.18, 18m to **Eunice,** proclaimed a city by gov. in 1937. Named for daughter of J. N. Carson, who homesteaded site. Founded in 1909; in 1927 oil was discovered below here. 41m **Jal,** named for Jal Ranch (E). Town began to grow rapidly when Texas Production Co. brought in its No. 1 Rhoads Well.

**390. LOVING,** first named Vough, for Swiss settlers, then renamed Florence. Later named for John Loving, one of earliest cattle drivers up Pecos R. from Texas. **395. MALAGA,** trading pt. for farmers, named for abundance of sweet wine grapes grown near-by. **411. N.M.-TEX. LINE.**

## US 66—ARIZONA

**ARIZ.-N.M. LINE** (24m from Gallup, N.M.) **(W) to ARIZ.-CAL. LINE** (16m from Needles, Cal.). **384. US66**

Via: Holbrook, Winslow, Flagstaff, Williams & Kingman. Accoms.: All types. Bus conns., Santa Fe RR. parallels route.

US66 crosses high plateau of N. Arizona, incl. a cor. of the Navajo country, Hopi & Navajo Ind. Reserv., Painted Desert, Petrified For. & 2 Nat. Fors., high mesas of Hualpai Ind. reserv. & Mohave country bordering Mohave Desert.

**27. CHAMBERS.** J. with route to Canyon de Chelly Nat. Mon. & Ind. villages; to US89 & (S) to Flagstaff.

SIDE TRIP: Route (R) extends over improved Rds. (inquire Rd. conditions) into vast Navajo country of N. Ariz. Hopi villages are situated within Navajo Reserv. More than 25,000 Navajo roam far reaches of mesa, raise flock of sheep & goats, weave fine blankets, make magnificent silver & turquoise jewelry. They live in mound-shaped hogans (houses) but usually utilize near-by brush shelters during summer. Unlike other tribes they have no villages—their homes being widely spaced & locations changed from time to time dependent upon grazing needs. A deeply religious people, they have many legends, ceremonials & dances, held at unpredictable times throughout yr. 39m **Ganado,** at J. with St. Michaels-Moenkopi Rd. (limited accoms.). Trading post & home of famed Presb. Sage Mem. Hospital & Mission, headed by Dr. Clarence G. Salsbury, self-styled "Sage-Brush Physician" & known among tribesmen as "Dr. Big." On 200-a. tract are 50 bldgs. incl. ch., high sch., mission, mod. 150-bed hospital, shops, dormitories, residences, etc., a 1¼ million dollar investment dedicated to serving humanity & substituting white man's medical & surgical genius for the Navajo medicine man's "magic." (L) on St. Michaels-Moenkopi Rd., 6.5m, to J. with improved Rd. at 45.5m.

(R) to **Chinle,** 35m (limited accoms.), adm. hqs. & boarding sch. for Navajo children. Nat. Pk. Serv. Hqs. (L) 2m (accoms.guide serv. info.). Canyon de Chelly Nat. Mon. contains 3 separate canyons, de Chelly, del Muerto & Mon. canyons. Noted for many prehist. cliff dwellings, most notable being "White House Ruins." Rim Tour, from where White House Ruins can be viewed, may be taken in personally owned car any time of yr., but trips along floor of Canyon depend on weather conditions & are supervised by Pk. Serv. ranger in specially equipped car; also horseback trips.

Cont. (L) on St. Michaels-Moenkopi Rd. to **Steamboat Canyon,** 56m. Rd. follows floor of canyon for c.5m. At 58m (R) is large rock formation whose striking resemblance to a vessel is more apparent when viewed from (W). At 63m, Rd. crosses E. boundary of **Hopi** (Hoe-pea) **Ind. Reserv.** which is completely surrounded by Navajo Reserv. Hopi, numbering over 3,000, are agriculturalists & Ariz.'s only Pueblo Inds. All but 1 of 11 villages are on mesa-tops. Each village is autonomous, possessing its own lands, social & ceremonial organization. They all speak same language & have similar customs, although there is no feeling of unity among the villages. At 75.5m is J. with improved Rd. (L) to Holbrook (US66). **Keam's Canyon,** 81m, site of Hopi Agency. Coal is mined here for Reserv. use. At 94m is J. with improved Rd. (L) to Winslow (US66). **Polacca,** 96m, settlement developed around mesa, from which the 3 villages on 1st Mesa are visible.

(R) on dirt Rd. to summit: 1m **Hano,** composed of Tewa (Tay-wuh) speaking Inds. from Rio Grande who came to assist Walpi when attacked in 17th cent., then sett. here. 1.2m **Sichomivi,** little more than suburb of Walpi. 2m **Walpi,** perched precariously on narrow top of steep rock cliff; stone of angular houses merges so imperceptibly with stone of mesa that it suggests castle in sky. Walpi's houses, built 2-3 stories, are crowded on this narrow site, not wasting an inch.

On its winding ascent of the 2nd Mesa, Rd. passes villages of **Mishongnovi,** 99m (Snake Dance Aug.odd yrs.), & **Shipolovi,** 99.2m (Snake Dance Aug.even yrs.). 120m **Lower Oraibi** (Ore-eye-be), trading post. Coll. of Hopi hs. & peach orchards at foot of 3rd or westernmost Hopi mesa. At lower Oraibi is J. with improved Rd. to US66 (L) & Flagstaff. **Old Pueblo of Oraibi,** 121m, on top of mesa, visited by Padre Garces in 1776, once largest Hopi town of over 800; with less than 100 now, for in 1907 the conservative half of populace moved 7m (W) to found village of Hotevilla. Another group sett. Bakabi, following yr. 128m **Hotevilla,** most mod. & conservative of all Hopi towns. Rd. cont. & joins US89 at 188m, 60m (W) of Hotevilla. From J. with US89 (S) 61m to **Flagstaff** at 249m.

**35. NAVAJO,** sm. trading post.

SIDE TRIP: (L) on unimproved Rd. 3.5m to **Navajo Springs,** where terr. gov. of Ariz. was set up, Dec. 29, 1863.

At **47.** is most extensive view along hy. of **PAINTED DESERT** (R). Yellow, red, magenta, & mauve sands appear in terrace, mesa, & hill formations. **47.5.** J. with paved Rd.

SIDE TRIP: On loop drive (R) which skirts most brilliant section of Painted Desert, which extends for 300m along Little Colorado R. **Painted Desert Inn,** 1.9m, a pueblo-type structure containing Mus., trading post, ranger's quarters, naturalist's office & accoms. for tourists. At 4.5m is J. with US66.

At **50.** is J. with St.63.

SIDE TRIP: (L) on St.63, 5m to **Petrified For. Nat. Mon.** 85,000-a. tract contains greatest & most colorful concentration of petrified wood known in world. In pk. areas scenery & objects of prehist. & scientific int. are carefully preserved & displayed for pub. enjoyment. Within Mon. are 6 separate fors. where giant logs of agate lie prone, among them Blue, Black & Rainbow, the latter the most beautiful vari-colored specimens. At mus. here are many of finest stone specimens from all parts of reserve, many polished to display their brilliant hues. [Rd. through For. extends (S) to US260. (R) on US260 to Holbrook at J. with US66, the route.]

**76. HOLBROOK,** at J. with St.77, leading (L) to **Snowflake,** 31m; **Showlow,** 50m. Seat of Navajo Cty., Holbrook was sett. in 1879. Became important cow town & also site of notorious gun battle bet. Sheriff Commodore Owens & 4 members of Graham faction who had taken leading part in Pleasant Valley War bet. cattle & sheep men. **109. WINSLOW,** J. with St.65 leading (L) to Pine, Tonto Natural Br., Payson, Roosevelt Dam & Apache Trl.; sett. in 1882 as division of Santa Fe RR. Stock-raising center. Hotel La Posada, replica of Sp. hacienda, holds many pieces of furniture in use long before terr. of Ariz. was organized. **METEOR CRATER OBSERV., 128.,** where Crater can be viewed by telescope. At **129.** is J. with improved Rd.

SIDE TRIP: (L) 7m to **Meteor Crater,** a great pockmark c.1m in diam. & 600′ deep, in face of desert, caused by giant meteor which struck the earth c.50,000 yrs. ago, displacing some 5-6 million tons of earth, leaving huge ridge around rim.

**133. CANYON DIABLO** (Sp.: "Devil's Canyon"), colorful gorge in Kaibab sandstone, 225′ deep & 500′ wide. In 1889 an Atlantic & Pac. train was held up here by 4 bandits who fled with $1,000, but were captured 300m away in Utah after a running gun battle. At **149.,** enter **COCONINO NAT. FOR.** which contains western yellow pine, most valuable of st.'s timber. At **160.5.** is J. with dirt Rd.

SIDE TRIP: (L) 5m to **Walnut Canyon Nat. Mon.,** remains of some 300 cliff dwellings built c.900 to 1100 A.D., under sloping walls along both sides of Walnut Canyon, largest ruin containing but 6 to 8 rooms, some in fine state of preservation.

**163. TOWNSEND.** J. with US89 (see). US66-89 are one route between Townsend & J. with US89, c.0.5m (E) of Ashfork. **169. FLAGSTAFF** (see US89). US66 crosses E. boundary of **KAIBAB NAT. FOR.** at **179. San Francisco Peaks** (N), Arizona's highest (12,665′). **201.5. GRAND CANYON J.** J. with St.64 (R) 59m to S. rim, Grand Canyon (see Flagstaff, US89). **203. WILLIAMS,** RR., lumber & livestock center. **Bill Williams Mt.** (L) & town named for Old Bill Williams, pioneer mountain man, trapper & guide. At **219.** is J. with US89 (L) to Prescott, Phoenix & Tucson. **220. ASHFORK,** stock-raising center & division pt. on Santa Fe RR. **244. SELIGMAN,** shipping & trading center for miners & cattle ranchers. Located in heart of one of largest cattle-raising areas in SW. (change from Mt. to Pacific Stand. Time). Trade center of Hualpai (Wallapai) Inds. is **PEACH SPRINGS, 281.,** located on S. edge of million-a. reserv. These Inds. (c.500) have adopted many of white man's ways & have excellent horses & cattle. Never a warlike tribe, several of their braves worked with US Army as scouts, assisting in capture of Geronimo, Apache renegade, in 1886, after which soon came end of war bet. Apaches & whites in Ariz. **298. VALENTINE,** Truxton Canyon Ind. sub-agency & boarding sch. **331. KINGMAN** is seat of Mohave cty. & distributing pt. of vast area & trade center for cattle & sheep ranchers, one of few unincorporated cty. seats & one of largest unincorporated towns in U.S.; important mining center, producing gold, silver, zinc, lead & tungsten. Dig-N-Dogie Days Celebration, carnival, rodeo & mining contests, Labor Day week-end. To (S) is Hualpai Mt. Pk., recr. area (see Mohave Cty. C. of C. for info.).

SIDE TRIP: (R) on US93-466, St.62, 72m to **Boulder Dam.** This fine hy. to Boulder Dam & L. Mead Nat. Recr. Area, developed around L. Mead, crosses an almost uninhabited desert flanked by jagged ranges where colors change with the light from red to purple or blue. 3m **Castle Rocks** resemble a gigantic edifice. 5m **Coyote Hill** offers an excellent view of Kingman & mts. in area that have yielded fortunes in gold, silver & lead. 21m **Chloride,** sett. 1864 as a silver mining center, is distributing pt. for several mines. 26m **Joshua Forest,** sometimes called Yucca palms; they are 25′ to 30′ high, have dagger-shaped, olive-green leaves &, in spring, clusters of white flowers. At 65m, **Fortification Mt.,** on Ariz. side, is seen (R); from brilliant red at its base this fortlike Mt. rises in a mass of colors & is reflected in L. Mead. 72m **Boulder Dam,** world's highest dam (see Nev.). Visitors are taken by elevator to base of dam, equivalent to 40-story bldg. where inner workings are seen & described by guide. L. Mead, created by Boulder Dam, is world's largest man-made L., with shoreline of 550m. This L., one of finest for motor boat., sailing & canoeing, is under supervision of Nat. Pk. Serv. & is well-stocked with game fish. Resorts have been est. along shore & this is one of finest recr. areas in U.S. Hy. crosses Boulder Dam to Boulder City, Nev. & Las Vegas, Nev., 23m.

**359. OATMAN,** old-time mining camp in foothills of Black Mts. US66 is only street. Named for pioneer family attacked by Apaches near Gila Bend (Ariz.) in 1851; parents were killed, 2 girls taken into captivity & boy badly injured & left for dead. Boy recovered; 1 sister died in captivity, other released in 1856, joining brother at Fort Yuma. **384. TOPOCK** (Mohave: "bridge") at E. end of bridge over Colo. R. Half-way pt. on bridge is **ARIZ.-CAL. LINE.**

## US 60—ARIZONA

**N.M.-ARIZ. LINE** (36m from Quemado, N.M.) **(W) to ARIZ.-CAL. LINE** (4.5m from Blythe, Cal.). **404.5. US60**

NE. part of route, which cuts through 2 Apache Reservs., keeps within Apache, Sitgreaves & Tonto Nat. For., in area dense with pine & juniper. (S) of Black R. Canyon, where it winds to bottom of gorge, hy. crosses high juniper mesas & rolling hills covered with prickly pear cactus, yucca & greasewood, where thousands of range cattle & sheep forage.

Route joins US70 at Globe & cont. as same route to Phoenix where US89 unites with US60-70 to Wickenburg. At Wickenburg is J. with US60-70 & US89 (R) to Prescott, Flagstaff, Grand Canyon & Salt Lake City. (L) the route from Wickenburg to Blythe, Cal. (US60-70).

### Sec. 1: N.M.-ARIZ. LINE to GLOBE. 151.

**15. SPRINGERVILLE** (accoms.facils.info.C.of C.), is J. with US666 (Coronado Trl. see below). J. with US666 (R) to **St. Johns,** 30m, surrounded by extensive fors. of White Mts., 300m of trout streams & game lands on which bear, mt. lion, wild turkey & deer abound; caters to tourists & sportsmen who use town as focal pt. to extensive recr. area.

SIDE TRIP: (S) on Coronado Trl. (US66) 150m to Duncan. Tour reaches route believed to have been taken by Coronado in 1540, in search of "Seven Cities of Cibola." Crossing 2 Nat. Fors., dense with growth of aspen, Douglas fir & mt. fern, hy. winds & twists 135m through occasional clearings & vistas of cabins & lodges surrounded by green valleys & colorful distant mts. At 4m, enter **Apache Nat. For.** (camp.trout.f.h.). Though reserve abounds with big game, many thousand head of cattle, horses & sheep graze here. 28m **Alpine** (h.f.), summer resort valley. Near-by are several hunt. lodges & sawmills. 52m **Hannagan Meadow** (accoms.). From here Rd. descends from Mogollon (Moe-gay-own) Rim, natural barrier stretching across 200m in E. half of St. Rim is N. boundary of Crook Nat. For. (hqs.Safford.camp.). (S) of Mogollon Rim, hy. crosses Blue Range. 122m **Clifton,** center of copper mining dist., sett. by prospectors in 1872. Present copper smelter controlled by Phelps Dodge Corp. **Clifton Hot Springs** (swim.O.yr.-round) which bubble from San Francisco R. almost in center of town, have been privately developed. Water, with large salt content, comes from ground at 130° temp. **Clifton Cliff Jail,** built in 1881, was blasted from side of Mt. on edge of town.

On Rd. leading (R) 5m, **Morenci,** one of most precipitous towns in U.S. where tier on tier of houses cling to steep hillside. View from summit of **Longfellow Hill,** reached by path called Burro Alley is unforgettable. One of largest copper mines in U.S. was developed here; great open pit mine now owned by Phelps Dodge Corp.

At 125m is J. with US666. (Caution: Keep on St.75 (L) at J.). 150m **Duncan.** J. with US70. St. Hy. Checking Sta. (see US70).

**61. SHOWLOW.** J. with St.173 (S) to Lakeside, Pinetop, McNary, recr. areas. J. with St.77 (N) to Snowflake, Mormon town & Holbrook on US66, 50m. Towering pines border Rd. in dense stands to Carrizo Cr. in zigzag course through narrow red-walled gorge. **84. CARRIZO,** on Apache Ind. Reserv. (store.camp.). Apache farming camp (R) & wickiups in which Inds. live while tending fields. **90. BLACK**

**R. CANYON,** accessible only to pack outfits up to a few yrs. ago, now has fine hy. twisting along canyon walls to bottom of gorge. Immense peaks & caverns, spires with walls of rose & crimson changing with shifting light. **94. JIMANA INN** (accoms.facils.info.) on canyon floor where Black R. tumbles along over rock bed. Rd. descends gently toward Globe & reveals at **133.,** an extensive view of serried ranges that graduate from dark purple masses to faint blue outlines. **151. GLOBE.** J. with US70.

**Sec. 2: GLOBE to ARIZ.-CAL. LINE. 253.5.**

See US70.

## US 70—ARIZONA

**N.M.-ARIZ. LINE** ($25^m$ from Lordsburg, N.M.) **(W) to ARIZ.-CAL. LINE** ($4.5^m$ from Blythe, Cal.). **392. US70**

Via: Safford, Globe, Superior, Phoenix, Wickenburg & Blythe.

US70 traverses irrigated farming regs., copper mining towns, metropolis of Phoenix, dude ranch country of Wickenburg & W. semi-desert sec. of St. US60 & US70 unite, Globe to Phoenix; US60, US70 & US89 unite, Phoenix to Wickenburg; US60 & US70 unite, Wickenburg to Blythe.

**5.5. DUNCAN.** J. with St.75-US666 (Coronado Trl.—see US60). St. hy. checking sta. & marketing center for farming dist. irrigated by Gila (He-lah) R. Shipping pt. for cattle & ore. Was "tough town" in early days. Its citizens were obliged to contend not only with Apache, but also with notorious bad men incl. "Black Jack" Ketchem, stagecoach & express robber & gang. **Gila Mts.** (R); **Mt. Graham** (10,750′) from **22.** (W) on horizon. **Mt. Turnbull** rises in NW. **38.8. "GRIPE,"** inspection sta. maintained to prevent spread of insect pests & plant diseases in Ariz. Name bestowed by officers of Ariz. Commission of Agric. & Horticulture assigned to duty here. **41. SOLOMONSVILLE,** named for I. E. Solomon who sett. & est. a store here in 1876. His family on several occasions narrowly escaped Ind. attacks. In 1879 1st Mormon settlers arrived & their hist. is one of sacrifice, hardship & struggle. Was seat of Graham Cty. from 1883 to 1915, when it was removed to Safford. **46. SAFFORD.** J. with US666 (L) to Tucson (hqs.Crook Nat.For.info.camp.h.), seat of Graham Cty., founded in 1872, named for 3rd terr. gov., A. P. K. Safford. Montezuma canal constructed here by early settlers who later were joined by Mormons from N. part of terr. & a ft. was erected as protection against Inds. Farming is major occupation. **49. THATCHER,** named for Apostle Moses Thatcher of Mormon Ch. by 1st settlers who arrived here in 1881. Home of **Gila Jr. College,** founded in Safford in 1891 as St. Joseph Stake Academy, most of patrons & students being Mormons. Moved to Thatcher in 1892. In 1933, after 43 yrs. under Latter-Day Saints, sch. became a cty. jr. college & all courses of religious nature were eliminated. **51. CENTRAL; 54.5. PIMA; 64. ASHURST; 67. FT. THOMAS; 73. GERONIMO;** sm. Mormon settlements & trading pts.; cattle-raising communities. **SAN CARLOS IND. RESERV.** is crossed at **75.,** home of c.3,000 Apaches who live in native wickiups, generally discarding, for living purposes, gov.-built frame hs. Apaches are successful cattle raisers & have assimilated most of white man's ways, although they still perform certain rituals & ceremonials, incl. famed Devil Dance, when grotesque masks are worn to aid in "driving off evil spirits." **80. BYLAS,** trading pt. for farmers & Apaches, & **86. CALVA,** RR. pt., from which old Chiricahua Cattle Co. & Double Circle outfit have shipped many thousand head of cattle; is now shipping pt. for Apache cattle. **98. SAN CARLOS LAKE,** formed by Coolidge Dam across Gila R. Has capacity of 1¼ million acre-feet (excellent f.). **109. COOLIDGE DAM,** 1st, largest & highest multiple-dome type dam ever constructed. Named for Calvin Coolidge & dedicated by him in 1930. US70 crosses dam which is 259′ above bedrock; its domes are 21′ thick at base & 4′ thick at top. Dam cost 5½ million dollars; entire project, incl. power units, cost 10 million dollars. On W. horizon, visible from c.**121.,** are **Pinal Mts.** (L) & **Four Peaks** (R), landmark near Roosevelt Dam. **127. CUTTER** J. with San Carlos Rd.

SIDE TRIP: (R) on Rd. $13^m$ to **San Carlos,** founded as Rice, center for Apache Reserv., is agency & trading post. Sch. of native tufa stone, acres of lawns & shaded roadways.

**134.5. GLOBE** (S.P.RR.bus.info.C.ofC.), seat of Gila Cty., colorful old-fashioned mining & cow town. **Old Dominion Mine,** $1^m$ (N), producer of millions in copper, is a ghost now with nothing left but huge tailings dump. Broad St., town's main thoroughfare, follows Pinal Creek, which is dry most of time except after heavy rains. Apaches from near-by San Carlos, in colorful garb, old-time cowboys & miners mingle in daily life of old Broad St. Globe was sett. in 1876 as result of silver strike boom & was named Globe as result of discovery of huge ball of almost pure silver. Later prosperity was due to rich copper deposits found beneath the surface silver.

SIDE TRIP: On Rd. leading (S) $1^m$ to **Besh-Ba-Gowah Pueblo Ruins** (Apache: camp for metal), on high mesa overlooking Pinal Creek. Inhabited from 1225 to 1375 A.D. 1 & 2 story structure of rock & adobe; had 115 rooms, hallways & patios. Relics from site at Globe Mus. **Ferndale Recr.** Area at $17^m$ in Pinal Mts. (cabins.no h.), reg. of spruce, fir, aspen, pine, maple & oak, abounding in wild life, especially deer.

**139.5. CLAYPOOL.** J. with St.88 (R), (Apache Trl., Roosevelt Dam & Ls. reg. to Phoenix). **142.5. MIAMI** (S.P.RR.bus.info.C.of C.), home of Inspiration Consolidated & Miami Copper Cos. Before 1907, Miami dist. was almost uninhabited by white men. Up to that time its most exciting event was Bloody Tanks Massacre of 1864, when Col. King S. Woolsey & party, who had been sent in to "pacify" Inds., had attacked a band of Apaches, slaughtering many of them. With Miami Copper Co., begun in 1907, & construction by Inspiration of huge reduction works in 1909, camp began to boom, & in few yrs. had payroll of $750,000 monthly. During war yrs. "Concentrator City" lived up to its title, & since has had good yrs. & "lean" yrs., depending on price of copper. **161.5. SUPERIOR** (bus.info.C.of C.), began existence with discovery of rich Silver King mine in 1875 &, later, Silver Queen mine increased formed to take over Silver Queen properties & 14 yrs. later it constructed a large underlying deposits of copper were uncovered. In 1910 the Magma Copper Co. was formed to take over Silver Queen propeties & 14 yrs. later it constructed a large smelter here. Ore is very rich & operations cont. unabated when most others were shut down. **165.5. THOMPSON SW. ARBORETUM** (L), 160-a. tract containing great variety of rare & beautiful plants & flowers featuring SW. flora. **176.5. FLORENCE JUNCTION.** US60-70 unites with US80-89. **193.5. APACHE JUNCTION.** J. with St.88 (Apache Trl.) to Globe (R). **209. MESA** (see US89).

**225. PHOENIX** (see US89). J. with US60-70-89 & US80. (US80 to Gila Bend, Yuma & San Diego.) **278. WICKENBURG** (see US89). J. with US60-70 & US89. (US89 to Prescott, Flagstaff, Salt Lake City.) **332. SALOME** (accoms.facils.bus) was home of Dick Wick Hall, Ariz.'s widely-known humorist, who in turn made town of Salome known through "Saturday Evening Post" stories & syndicated articles as well as his local advertising at this desert hamlet. "Salome—Where She Danced," became a by-word. Hall's mimeographed sheet, "The Salome Sun," passed out to motorists, was devoted to humor, sketches & criticism, especially of the Rd. to Yuma which was then barely passable. Upon Hall's death in 1926, a **Mon.** was erected there to his memory, & some of the humorous old signs still hang where he placed them. **339. HOPE.** J. with St.72, leading (R) $50^m$ to Parker, trade center for Colo. R. Ind. Reserv.). **370. QUARTZSITE,** at J. with St.95 (L) ($87^m$ to Yuma), was formerly called Tyson's Well, important early stage stop. Site of old **Ft. Tyson** (L), built in 1856, prominent in Ind. warfare. **372. QUARTZSITE CEMETERY & HI JOLLY MON.** (R), grave and mon. to Hi Jolly, Syrian camel driver brought here by War Dept. for experiment (1858) with camels on Ariz. desert as beasts of burden. Project was soon abandoned as stony surface of terrain damaged animals' feet. Many legends have grown around Ariz.'s camels, some of which were turned loose, some sold to circuses. Hi Jolly remained to prospect for gold. **390. EHRENBERG,** named for pioneer Hermann Ehrenberg, German mining engineer who came to Ariz. 1854. **Boothill Cemetery** near-by, est. 1856, has countless unmarked graves containing bones of pioneers who died with their boots on, fitting end to Trl. of Graves. **Mon.** has embedded in concrete, guns, branding irons, burro shoes, spurs & other early day articles. At **392.** US60-70 crosses Colo. R. Bridge & **ARIZ.-CAL. LINE.**

## US 80—ARIZONA

**N.M.-ARIZ. LINE** ($46^m$ from Lordsburg, N.M.) **(W) to ARIZ.-CAL. LINE** (at Yuma, Ariz.). **415. US80**

US80 from N.M. Line to Douglas & Tucson; St.84 from Tucson to Gila Bend; US80 from Gila Bend to Yuma & El Centro, Cal. S.P. RR. & Greyhound bus parallel route. All types accoms. at Douglas, Bisbee, Tucson & Yuma; limited elsewhere

Route, continually surrounded by Mts., traverses S. semi-desert, which varies from 5,000′ to near sea level at Yuma (137′). Route incl. mining communities, metropolis of Tucson, & great irrigation farming areas.

**50. DOUGLAS,** on Mex. border, is smelter town in Sulphur Spring Valley, vast grazing & agric area. In 1900, Phelps Dodge Corp. of Bisbee, unable to expand smelter facilities at Bisbee due to unusual terrain, selected site of Douglas for new smelter, now **Calumet & Ariz. Smelter** (O). **Agua Prieta,** Mexico (across street from Douglas) is quaint Mex. town. Tourists cross freely; no visas or passports required. (Inquire C. of C. for pts. of int. & for conditions & best routes).

SIDE TRIP: On Rd. leading (N) 40$^{m}$ to **Rucker Canyon,** picturesque recr. area in **Coronado Nat. For.** (pub.campgrounds). **Chiricahua Nat. Mon.** (Wonderland of Rocks), 82$^{m}$, one of world's great natural wonders (camp sites). Here are giant rock formations, caused by centuries of erosion. Other rock formations, aside from giant boulders weighing many tons balancing on pin-point bases, resemble birds, beasts, human as well as fantastic forms. 95$^{m}$ **Rustler Pk.,** atop Chiricahua Mt. (8,500′), is an area of great beauty among pines & spruce (winter sports.pub.campground).

**73. BISBEE,** seat of Coachise Cty. & center of one of richest copper dists. in U.S. Principal town of Warren Mining Dist., comprised of Bisbee, Warren & Lowell. Built in Mule Pass Gulch, Bisbee houses cling to slopes of 2 long narrow canyons: Tombstone Canyon & Brewery Gulch. Bisbee is largest town in U.S. without home mail delivery serv., terrain being such that P.O. authorities decided it was too strenuous for postal carriers. Citizens trudge down hills to P.O. for mail. Phelps Dodge Corp. owns most of productive area of Warren Dist. as well as Bisbee's largest hotel, hospital, store, lib. & other enterprises, in addition to Copper Queen mining properties. **Sacramento Pit** (SE) of P.O. Plaza, is pit 435′ deep, cored out of Sacramento Hill, & covering 35 as. Yielded nearly 21 million tons of ore. A narrow-gauge RR., cut into pit walls, winds from highest shelf of man-made crater to its floor. **99. TOMBSTONE.** Ed Schieffelin, soldier-prospector in 1877, started out across Apache-infested country looking for gold. He was told instead of a mine he would find his tombstone. When he stumbled across some rich-looking ore, he was said to have remarked, "Here is my tombstone," & he gave that name to the place upon which arose the great Tombstone mining camp. Town was laid out in 1879; was inc. & made Cty. seat in 1881; Cty. seat later removed to Bisbee. As news of the strike spread, prospectors, miners, business men & gamblers came in by the hundreds. Tombstone, the "Town Too Tough To Die," is one of most colorful of Ariz.'s early boom towns—colorful because of its turbulent past, which reached its height in early 1880's with the Earp-Clanton Feud when a gunfight at O.K. Corral in center of town brought about the death of 3 men & several wounded in less than 1 minute of fierce exchange of gunfire. This & other early Tombstone escapades are re-enacted at annual Helldorado Days late in Oct. Camp had only 10 yrs. of highly active life, with an estimated 80 million dollars taken from its mines; then pop. dwindled. Today, Tombstone is again a lively town with health clinics & tourist business replacing the boom town mining days. Town is full of int. hist. pts. (all marked), incl. **Bird Cage Theater, Crystal Palace Saloon, Oriental Bar, Russ H., Million Dollar Stope, "Epitaph"** (newspaper) **Office, O.K. Corral,** world's largest **Rosebush** & others. **123. BENSON.** J. with US666, St.86. At **168.** is J. with US89. US80 & US89 unite through Tucson (see US89). At **174.5.** on US80-89 is J. with St.84 (L), which now becomes the route. At **219.** is J. with St.87 (R) to Coolidge, Casa Grande Nat. Mon. & Phoenix (see US89). **238. CASA GRANDE,** named for **Casa Grande** (Sp., "big house") **Ruins** near-by. Casa Grande Valley, in San Carlos Irrigation Project, utilizes water stored by Coolidge Dam, supplemented with pumping wells. Rich agric. area.

**297. GILA BEND** is J. with US80 (R), which now becomes the route (R).

SIDE TRIP: (S) on St.85 (L) 150$^{m}$ to **Rocky Pt.** on Gulf of Cal. Route is through desert country & mining community of Ajo (Ah-hoe). (No accoms.facils. or supplies bet. Ajo & Sonoyta, Mex. For Tourist Permit from Ariz. to Rocky Pt., inquire at Sonoyta, Ariz. at Border.) 42$^{m}$ **Ajo,** (Sp., "garlic", that grows wild in surrounding hills). **Ajo Copper Co.,** org. 1854, sent ore by pack mules to Yuma, 100$^{m}$ away, whence it was shipped down Colo. R. & around Cape Horn to Swansea, Wales, for smelting. New Cornelia Copper Co. was org. 1916 & town grew rapidly. In 1931, Co. became Phelps Dodge Corp., &, as in most mining towns, pop. fluctuates with price of copper. At 54$^{m}$ is boundary of **Organ Pipe Cactus Nat. Mon.** of more than 516 sq. miles of rolling hills, mt. ranges & alluvial plain to Mex. Border. Organ Pipe Cactus, with its dozens of tubular arms branching from main stem at the ground, grows straight up for 20′ or more, forming a cluster of perpendicular pipes that resemble an organ. It is as spectacular as it is rare, growing only in this relatively small area (mostly in S. part of Mont. & in Mex.). Saguaro, palo verde, ocotillo, cholla, & desert ironwood also grow profusely here. 85m **Sonoyta,** Mex., delightful border town of mud-colored huts & white plastered adobes, where customs of time of Sp. rule have little changed. 150m **Puerto Penasca** (Rocky Pt.) (accoms.camp.boat.f.facils. avail.) on Gulf of Cal. provides an abundance of deep sea fish in great variety, such as sea bass, red snapper, yellow tail, swordfish, jew fish, cabrilla. Town is quaint & its people quite primitive. Fishing is important industry. Boat-builders are usually busily engaged along shore constructing new boats for accom. of f. parties that can be arranged at hotel where Eng. is spoken.

**415. YUMA,** at confluence of Colo. & Gila Rs., is seat of Yuma Cty. & center of great irrigation dist. Rich alluvial soil supports extensive citrus, date & pecan orchards, cotton, alfalfa, wheat, barley & other rich crops. Much of flavor of Yuma is concentrated in shadowed recesses of covered sidewalks of Yuma's Main Street. Inds. from near-by Yuma & Cocopah Reserv. add color to scene. Sp. Missions est. here (1779) although there were earlier Sp. visitors. During war with Mexico in 1847, country became generally known to Amers. Steamer traffic on Colo. R. & ferries across R. cont. to operate until 1915, although S.P. RR. entered Yuma from Cal. in 1878. Yuma Cty.'s gold output amounted to many millions of dollars in early days. 1st terr. prison erected here (1876) & abandoned (1909) when new one was built at Florence. **Prison Ruins,** on ledge overlooking Colo. R. (O.9-5.wks.). Yuma is very close to **ARIZ.-CAL. LINE.**

## US 89—ARIZONA

**UTAH-ARIZ. LINE** (3m from Kanab, Utah) **(S) to MEX. BORDER** (Nogales, Sonora, Mexico). **607. US89**

Via: Jacob Lake, Cameron, Flagstaff, Oak Creek Canyon, Jerome, Prescott, Wickenburg, Phoenix, Apache Junction, Florence, Tucson & Nogales. Accoms. & facils.: All types. Bus & RR. conns.

US89 runs from colorful mesa country in N. Ariz. through great pine fors., over rolling hills & down into sun-drenched valleys of S. Ariz.; the scene is ever-changing & delightful. Skirting Grand Canyon in Navajoland, hy. passes through Kaibab & Prescott Nat. For., N. Ariz.'s all-yr. playground, & Oak Creek Canyon, 2nd only to Grand Canyon in sheer beauty & coloring. Great copper mining reg. of Jerome & Clarkdale is passed, & Prescott, mile-high city in pines, is reached. Hy. leaves pine-clad hills & drops to valley floor of S. Ariz.; beyond Phoenix climbs again through Tucson to Nogales on Mexican Border. From Utah Line to Mex. Border, from alt. of more than 7,000′ to 1,000′, with many nat. mons. & pts. of int. along way, diversity of climate & scenery makes route a most popular one.

### Sec. 1: UTAH-ARIZ. LINE to FLAGSTAFF. 205.

**3.5. FREDONIA,** most northerly town in Ariz., sett. 1885 by Mormons from Utah seeking freedom from religious persecution & fed. laws, is agric. & stock-raising community & one of prettiest sm. towns in St.

SIDE TRIP: On graded Rd. (W) 15m is **Pipe Spring Nat. Mon.,** group of hist. bldgs. on 40-a. tract, set aside as mem. to Mormon pioneers whose courage & faith in the country brought about development of this sec. of SW. One of group of early settlers, camping at spring & testing marksmanship, declared he could shoot bottom out of another's pipe placed at 50 paces; he did; hence the name, Pipe Spring. Small ft. against Ind. uprisings was est. first. Later present bldgs. were constructed. 1st telegraph sta. in Ariz. here (1871).

Within bounds of **KAIBAB NAT. FOR., 20.5.** (pic.camp site.hqs.at Williams), are magnificent trees—pine, spruce, fir, oak, aspen & juniper. Divided by Grand Canyon, for. has total of nearly 2 million as. Kaibab (Ky-bab, Ind.: "mountain lying down") is home of great herd of mule deer & other wild game. Favored hunt. ground. Beautiful white-tailed Kaibab squirrel (protected) found only in N. Kaibab. **33.5. JACOB LAKE** (accoms.camp.), in dense grove of western yellow pine, at J. of US89 & St.67.

SIDE TRIP: On St.67 (S) 44m to **North Rim, Grand Canyon** (season May 30-Sept. 30). Route traverses N. sec. of Kaibab for. abounding with wild life. Deer usually seen near hy. At 32m, boundary of Grand Canyon reserve, & checking sta. 44m, **Grand Canyon North Rim** (accoms.camp.facils.); some of most splendid views of Grand Canyon from here, over 1,000′ higher than **South Rim,** 14m distant. "The Grand Canyon of Arizona fills me with awe," wrote Theodore Roosevelt. "It is beyond comparison, beyond description; absolutely unparalleled throughout the wide world." (See Grand Canyon—Flagstaff sub-reg.)

**47.5. HOUSEROCK.** Here in Houserock Valley is home of Ariz.'s buffalo herd, numbering over 200 head, & seldom seen from hy. though they roam unfenced. Ariz. Game & Fish Commission purchased 100 buffalo in 1927 &, despite annual hunt, when certain number of persons selected by lot participate in supervised hunt, herd has increased substantially from year to year. **Vermilion Cliffs** are seen (E) of Houserock for 20$^m$, brilliantly colored walls rising majestically some 1,000′ from valley floor. **74. MARBLE CANYON** (accoms.). **Echo Cliffs** & **Kaibito Plateau** in Navajo reserv. visible (E). **75. NAVAJO BRIDGE,** triumph in hy. bridge construction, 834′ long with single arch span of 616′; 467′ bet. its floor & surface of Colo. R. Only hy. bridge crossing Colo. R. for distance of thousand miles—from Boulder Dam to Moab, Utah. **109. CEDAR RIDGE,** sm. trading post. Tourist camp built to resemble Navajo hogans (houses). **147. CAMERON** (accoms.), combined Ind. trading post & hotel on edge of Painted Desert. Suspension bridge here crosses Little Colo. R. At **149.,** J. with St.64 (R) to Grand Canyon South Rim.

SIDE TRIP: On Rd. leading (W) 56$^m$ to **Grand Canyon Village** (see Flagstaff below). Many scenic vantage points marked along way to Village & Hqs.

**169.** J. with unimproved Rd.

SIDE TRIP: On Rd. leading (L) to **Wupatki Nat. Mon.** At 5$^m$, **Citadel Group.** Of this group only **Nalakihu** (Hopi: "house alone") has been excavated & rest. On mesa top, **Teuwalanki** (Hopi: "citadel"), is partially excavated. 15$^m$, main **Wupatki** (Hopi: "Big House") **Ruins.** Unusual site interesting for manner in which builders utilized natural walls of red sandstone, constructing above & around them so that bldgs. seem to grow out of the earth. (Occupied bet. 11th & 12th cent.) Rd. cont. (S), joining US89 near Flagstaff.

**184. COCONINO NAT. FOR.** contains nearly 2 million as.; Amer. pine here is most valuable of st.'s timber; many fine recr. sites. **189.** J. with unimproved Rd.

SIDE TRIP: On Rd. leading (L) 4$^m$ to **Sunset Crater Nat. Mon.** (Hqs.Wupatki Nat.Mon.). Area preserved for scenic, educational & scientific values. Consists of large fields of cinders, lava & truncated cone of Sunset Mt. Around upper edge of mt. are vari-colored deposits of sulphur, ranging from black through red & yellow, giving rim appearance of sunset glow. Small caves in lava beds near Sunset Crater contain ice during warmest days. Area abounds with fossils of various marine animals, evidence of great sea that once covered reg.

**199. TOWNSEND.** J. with **US66** (see).

**205. FLAGSTAFF**

Santa Fe RR. & bus lines. Info.: C. of C. Annual events: All-Ind.Powwow, held during 1st wk. in July, features Ind. ceremonies by several SW. tribes, & All-Ind. Rodeo.

Flagstaff, Coconino Cty. seat, alt. 6,895′, with San Francisco Peaks rising over 12,600′ in background. In celebration of 4th of July, 1876, yr. of 1st white settlement here, a lofty pine was stripped of its branches & Amer. flag tied to its tip, from which town received its name. Lumbering is chief industry, though tourists are a main source of income since Flagstaff is a resort city & hub of vast recr. area. PTS. OF INT.: (1) W. city limit on US89, **Ariz. St. College,** founded 1899. College has numerous bldgs. of native red sandstone on 160-a. pine-clothed campus, & enrollment of more than 700. (2) 1.5$^m$ (W) of Flagstaff on Mars Hill, **Lowell Observ.** In 1894 Dr. Percival Lowell founded observ. & endowed it permanently. Planet Pluto discovered here. (3) 3$^m$ (R) from Flagstaff at sign, 9 blocks to Columbus Ave., (L) on Columbus to Country Club Rd., (R) on Country Club Rd. to **Mus. of Northern Ariz.,** constructed for promotion of archeological research & to preserve one of largest colls. of mammals, birds, reptiles & invertebrates in St. (4) 14.5$^m$ **Ariz. Snow Bowl** (season Dec.-May.Rd.kept O.ski facils.). Same route as to Mus. of Northern Ariz. & straight ahead on Country Club Rd. to San Francisco Peaks, Coconino Nat. For. & Snow Bowl Hqs. Elev. at Ski Shelter, 9,500′. Ski Runs extend 3,000′ higher. Ski tows in operation; beginners area near shelter. Though winter sports area, a trip during summer up mt. also attractive.

## TRIPS OUT OF FLAGSTAFF

### I. GRAND CANYON SOUTH RIM LOOP TOUR. 197.

(W) from Flagstaff on US66-89 to Grand Canyon J. with St.64, 30$^m$. (R) on St.64, 89$^m$ to **Grand Canyon Village** (accoms.camp facils.f.info.:El Tovar Hotel). Grand Canyon is nature's masterpiece, cut by Colo. R. over period of millions of yrs., with more than 200$^m$ course, wholly within Ariz., varying from 4 to 18$^m$ in width & c.1$^m$ deep. Geologic story of ages is here laid bare & from its depths rise a myriad of multi-colored spires, temples & buttes that defy description, the lights & shadows changing with the hrs. (Inquire El Tovar Hotel for muleback trip to Phantom Ranch at floor of Canyon, Havasupai Canyon, Rim Drives & other trips in area.) (R) via West Rim Dr. with vantage pts. at intervals to **Cameron,** J. with US89, 145$^{m}$. (R) at J. on US89 to **Flagstaff,** 197$^{m}$.

**II. FLAGSTAFF, MORMON LAKE, MONTEZUMA CASTLE & OAK CREEK CANYON LOOP TOUR. 130.**

From Flagstaff (L) on US89A at J. with US66-89, (L) to J. with US89, 2$^{m}$ on Mary & Mormon Lakes Rd. 9$^{m}$ (L) to **Lake Mary** (recr.area.boat.camp.h.f.). Fed partially by springs, L. was formed by earth dam, & is 5$^{m}$ long, covering about 1,200 as. 26$^{m}$ **Mormon Lake** (circle tour around L.). Natural body of water utilized by Mormons on trek (W). When full, L. covers 5,000 as. & attracts great numbers of people each summer (pic.camp.f.h.boat.recr.); cool pines fringe L. shores. 36.4$^{m}$ J. with gravel Rd. On this Rd. (R) 42.4$^{m}$ to **Stoneman L.** (h.f.), in midst of pine for., formed in a 200′ depression bet. precipitous rock walls. L. is 2$^{m}$ wide with no visible outlet. Site popular with summer vacationers. 62.2$^{m}$ **Montezuma Well,** part of Montezuma Castle Nat. Mon., is fed by underground springs; 470′ in diam. with water always at same level & temperature. About 2 million gals. of water flow from well daily through outlet into near-by Beaver Cr. Cliff dwellings in walls of well. 69.5$^{m}$ **Montezuma Castle Nat. Mon.,** one of most beautiful & best preserved cliff dwellings, 150′ up in recess in face of perpendicular cliff. Ash-pink adobe castle of 5 stories has numerous rooms, reached by series of ladders placed against walls of cliff. 2.5$^{m}$ back to entrance of **Montezuma Castle Nat. Mon.** & J. with Cornville Hy. at McGuireville. 82$^{m}$ **Cornville,** sm. settlement in Verde Valley. 86$^{m}$ J. with US89A to Oak Cr. Canyon & Flagstaff (R). 102$^{m}$ **Sedona,** gateway to Oak Cr. Canyon. 104$^{m}$ Oak Cr. Canyon (accoms.facils.throughout its several-mile course). Rugged & colorful spectacle of towering cliffs & verdant beauty that flanks trout-filled Oak Cr. 130$^{m}$ **Flagstaff.**

**III. FLAGSTAFF (N) to CAMERON, TUBA CITY, TONALEA, KAYENTA & MONUMENT VALLEY. 190. US66-89 & Improved Dirt Rd.**

US89 (paved) to J., 10$^{m}$, beyond Cameron. Graded shale roadbed to Utah Line. Passable except after heavy rain or snow. Water, gasoline & other emergency supplies should be carried. Route traverses colorful Ind. country via Klethla Valley Rd. Land is marked with broad valleys & poorly defined mesas which change in N. sec. to deep canyons & high cliffs. At 50$^{m}$ is J. with US89 & St.64. [(L) 56$^{m}$ on St.64 to **South Rim, Grand Canyon.**] At 52$^{m}$ on US89 is **Cameron,** combined Ind. trading post & hotel on edge of Painted Desert. Suspension Bridge across Little Colo. R. here. At 62$^{m}$ is J. with improved Rd. (R) on this to 78$^{m}$, **Tuba City,** J. with Klethla Valley Rd. & St. Michaels-Moenkopi Rd., Navajo trading post est. 1877 by Jacob Hamblin, Mormon missionary. Hq. W. Navajo jurisdiction; hospital & school. Route cont. (L) on Klethla Valley Rd. to 100$^{m}$, **Tonalea** (Navajo: "big lake"); near-by is Red L., so named from color of surrounding soil. Trading post. At 101$^{m}$ is **Elephant Legs,** gigantic columns of eroded tan sandstone resembling feet & legs of elephant. 107$^{m}$, J. (L) with dirt Rd. At 110$^{m}$ is J. with graded dirt Rd. (L).

SIDE TRIP: On this Rd. (L) to foot trl., 31$^{m}$. (L) on this trl. 1$^{m}$ to **Betatakin Ruin** (Navajo: "hillside house"), one of major cliff dwellings in Navajo Nat. Mon., & only one excavated & rest. Built in long cave, rooms are rectangular & few secs. are more than 2 stories, though different levels of their foundations give terraced effect. There were about 130 ground fl. rooms that extended approx. 450′ along cliff edge. Roofing beams found here were cut between 1242 & 1286 A.D. **Keet Seel** (Kitsil, Navajo: "broken pottery"), (R), (N), 8$^{m}$, is reached only on foot or horseback. Here are best preserved ruins in Mon., located in deep cave 350′ long. Hs. incl. over 250 rooms, arranged to form village with several courts & sts.

In **Marsh Pass,** 136$^{m}$, bet. Back Mesa (R) & Navajo Plateau, are great outcroppings of red & brown sandstone. From Boiling Springs, its source deep in Segi Canyon, Laguna Cr. flows through **Laguna Canyon** (L). At 140.5$^{m}$ walls of pass open into gradually widening valley & the unusual shapes in stone are forerunners of Mon. Valley formations. 152$^{m}$. **Kayenta** (limited accoms.supplies.trading post.tubercular hospital & day sch.). 161$^{m}$. **Agathla Peak,** volcanic neck with spire rising over 1,000′ above sloping base. At 186$^{m}$ **Utah Line** offers good view of the **Mittens** (L), one in Ariz., the other in Utah. Though larger part of Mon. Valley is in Ariz., some of best features are in Utah. At 186.5$^{m}$ is J. with dirt Rd.; 2$^{m}$ (L) to **Gouldings Post** (accoms.facils.), hqs. for Mon. Valley tourists; trips arranged through most secs. of Valley; special equipment necessary for sandy trls. 190$^{m}$ **Monument Valley,** with standstone formations, many over 1,000′, extends for several miles through a weird & beautiful land. Striking resemblance of some formations has evoked names like: Castle Rock, Emperor on Throne, Train Rock, The Mittens, The Camel, Elephant Herd, Yebitichi Dancers, Totem Pole, Rooster Rock. Numerous motion pictures have been filmed here.

## Sec. 2: FLAGSTAFF to TUCSON. 337.

US66-89 unites with US89A for 1$^{m}$. **14. OAK CR. CANYON** (accoms.facils.camp. pic.f.). Descent from Lookout to floor of canyon over 4 gradual switchbacks, drop of 2,000′. Rd. twists through 15$^{m}$ of broad red-walled gorges. Grandeur of these massive canyon walls is enhanced by orange-yellow ledges, saffron seams, fissures, towering russet buttes flanked with pines of Coconino Nat. For. Floor of canyon, through which flows Rainbow trout-stocked Oak Cr., is covered with ferns, flowers, oak, maple & other plant life. Sm. farms & orchards are seen. **30. SEDONA,** community center for stock & fruit ranchers. Has attraction, in its red & buff formations looming against deep blue sky, for artists & movie companies. **51. COTTONWOOD,** typical sm. Ariz. community serving rich agric., livestock & mining dist. **55. CLARKDALE,** considered model mining town, was built in 1911. Town named for Wm. A. Clark, Sen. from Montana & former owner of United Verde mines here, now owned by Phelps Dodge Corp. (smelter O.appl.at office).

SIDE TRIP: (R) 2.5$^{m}$ on dirt Rd. from Clarkdale, crossing Verde R., to **Tuzigoot Nat. Mon.,** ancient pueblo occupied c.1200 A.D., now partically rest. Housed several hundred persons. Articles found in ruin, now preserved in Mus. at site, indicate high degree of culture.

**59. JEROME,** copper mining town on side of Mingus Mt., houses a veritable jumble on stilts, with a 1,500′ variation in elevation bet. highest & lowest perches. Inhabitants must climb trls. & flights of steps in going about town. Pop. here as in all mining towns in Ariz. fluctuates with price of copper & activity at mines. In 1929, town boasted pop. of 15,000. Mines under control of Phelps Dodge Corp. At **85.** US89A (St.79) joins US89. (S) of J., hy. runs through **GRANITE DELLS,** recr. area amid beautiful granite formation, caused by erosion. Site of **Grand Canyon College** (Bapt.) (L) leaving Dells. **90. FT. WHIPPLE VETERANS' HOSPITAL,** formerly site of old Ft. Whipple, during early terr. days.

**91. PRESCOTT** (Santa Fe RR. Bus lines. camp.trlr.facils.in Prescott Nat. For. in area.). Info.: C. of C. & Yavapai Assoc. Prescott, seat of Yavapai Cty. in mountainous sec. of W. central Ariz., known as mile-high city; favorite summer resort & home of Smoki (Smoke-eye) People, group of business & professional non-Inds. who annually present Ind. dances & ceremonials, purpose being to pérpetuate rituals of SW. tribes; held 1st or 2nd Sun. in Aug. Climax of each performance is Smoki's interpretation of Hopi (Hoe-pea) Ind. Snake Dance, though the Prescott whites use non-poisonous reptiles, while Hopi use & prefer rattlesnakes. Prescott is home of 1st public rodeo, held annually since 1888, 4th of July wk. Cattle ranching, mining & tourist trade are Prescott's chief source of income. Terr. capital est. here in 1864 at **Pioneer Sq.,** 4 blocks (W) of Court House Plaza on Gurley St., housing mementoes of pioneer days, as does **Charlotte Hall Mus.** alongside. **HASSAYAMPA MT. CLUB, 95.** (accoms.facils.golf.swim.), one of st.'s foremost summer resorts in Prescott Nat. For. Most cabins privately owned. **128. SUMMIT YARNELL HILL.** From Lookout Pt., view incl. wide expanse of desert & mts. Hy. descends steeply 3,000′ in 7$^{m}$ toward Congress J. (Caution: keep cars to (R).) **135.5. CONGRESS JUNCTION,** once active cowboy & miner town; now important sheep-shipping center. Old town of **Congress** (R), place named for famed Congress gold mine (R) 3$^{m}$ which in early days produced millions of dollars in gold. **151. WICKENBURG** (Santa Fe RR.bus lines.info.:Roundup Club), at J. with US60-70 (see US70), known as the dude ranch capital, is also a trading post for mining, cattle-raising & farming; named for Henry Wickenburg, who came here before est. of terr. seeking gold. In 1863 he discovered famous Vulture gold-mine near-by. Hy. crosses legendary **HASSAYAMPA R.** where it is said: "He who drinks above the trail is ever truthful, while he who drinks below is lost to truth." Many dude ranches in area, some O. yr. around, combine rudeness of corrals & stables with modern hotel luxury. **162. MORRISTOWN** (orig. called Hot Springs Junction) is named for its 1st inhabitant, Geo. Morris, who discovered Mack Morris mine, well known early workings.

SIDE TRIP: On improved Rd. (L) $19^m$ to **Castle Hot Springs,** resort & sanatorium in beautiful valley bet. foothills of Bradshaw Mts. Mineral water flows from crevices in rocks at rate of 400,000 gals. every 24 hrs. & ranges in temp. from 115° to 122°. Bath. pools at various temps.

Bet. Wickenburg & Phoenix are several communities, **WITTMAN, MARINETTE, PEORIA & GLENDALE,** trade, farming & stock-raising centers in rich Salt R. valley irrigation dist.

**205. PHOENIX** (S.P.& S.F. RRs.buslines,airlines,info.:C.of C.all types accoms. facils.), capital city & seat of Maricopa Cty. Owes existence to magic of irrigation. Once semi-desert reg., today a veritable garden of green lawns, great palms, flowers & gardens yr. around. Climate is semi-tropical & in winter season thousands of visitors fill many resorts in area. On site of modern Phoenix an ancient people erected bldgs., dug canals, prospered at farming & at an unknown date, disappeared. Present city was founded & has developed within span of one lifetime. Was named for fabled Phoenix bird in mythology that was consumed by fire every 500 yrs. & arose anew from own ashes. Annual events: Dons' Superstition Mountain Lost Gold Trek, Feb.; Jaycee World's Championship Rodeo, April; Masque of Yellow Moon Pageant, May; State Fair, early Nov.; Salad Bowl Football Classic, Jan. 1; $10,000 Open Golf Champ., Jan. PTS. OF INT.: (1) W. Washington at 17th Ave., **St. Capitol,** in 10-a. pk. Bldg. neo-Class., 4 stories surmounted by dome topped with statue typifying liberty & justice. Orig. E. sec. completed 1900. In 1918, central wing added; W. wing completed 1938, which houses Dept. Lib., Archives & Mus. (2) Fronting capitol is **Frank Luke, Jr., Mem.,** erected to Ariz.'s heroic World War I ace aviator & balloon-buster. (3) E. Van Buren bet. 5th & 9th Sts., **Phoenix Union High Sch.,** 15-a. campus, one of nation's larger high schs. (4) 22 E. Monte Vista off N. Central, **Heard Mus.** (Nov.-June,O.10-4 except Mon.), contains large coll. of prehist. relics found in excavated ruins (La Ciudad) within city limits. Also Ind. & Sp. exhibits & artifacts from all over world. (5) **Encanto Pk.,** N. 15th Ave. & Encanto Blvd., 227-as. (recr.landscaped grounds.boat.golf.clubh.playground.pic.). (6) $7^m$ S. on Central Ave., **Phoenix S. Mountain Pk.** (pic.facils.) 15,000 as., largest municipal pk. in world, traversed by Rds. & trls. (7) **U. S. Ind. Sch.,** N. 3rd St. & Ind. Sch. Rd., comprised of 70 bldgs. on 40-a. campus, with 150-a. farm adj. Enrollment of 750 Ind. children, elementary through high sch. (8) 1002 W. Van Buren, **Ariz. Mus.** (O.2-5.except Mon.), relics of Ariz. pioneer days. (9) $5^m$ (E) on Washington St., **Pueblo Grande Ruins** (O.9-5 except Mon.), partially excavated mound of prehist. community. Many artifacts found are on display at site. (10) $8^m$ on E. Van Buren St., **Papago St. Pk.,** vast recr. area with cactus plants, f. hatcheries, red rocks, pic. grounds & Desert Botanical Garden of 300 as., with over 10,000 varieties of cactus plants from all over the world. (11) On Maricopa Mesa (S) of Phoenix, **Taliesin West,** winter camp of architect Frank Lloyd Wright; has tent-like superstructure set on massive rock & concrete base, made to blend with surrounding terrain.

**PHOENIX LOOP TOUR: APACHE JUNCTION, ROOSEVELT DAM & TONTO CLIFF DWELLINGS NAT. MON. 196. US60-70-80-89, APACHE TRL., US60-70**

From Phoenix (E) on US60-70-80-89, $32^m$ to **Apache Junction.** At J. is marker in front of famed **Superstition Mt.** where Jacob Walz's rich Lost Dutchman Mine is supposedly located. Several seeking to find this lost mine have perished in the mts. (L) on Apache Trl. $45.5^m$ to **Whirlpool Rock,** soft sandstone surface cut by erosion into patterns resembling swirling water. $48^m$ **Canyon L.** (swim.boat.f.), formed by Mormon Flat Dam. L., $10^m$ long, covers 1,000 as. $51^m$ **Tortilla Flat,** named for giant masses of rocks resembling platter of tortillas. $61^m$ **Fish Cr. Canyon,** whose vertical rock walls are called Walls of Bronze. $65^m$ **Apache L.,** formed by Horse Mesa Dam (boat.f.), covers 2,600 as. & is $17^m$ long. $78.5^m$ **Roosevelt Dam,** Reclamation Bureau's pioneer project. Completed 1911, dam was named for & was dedicated by Theo. Roosevelt; is world's highest rubble-masonry type dam, 284′ high, 184′ thick at base, 16′ thick at top. **Roosevelt L.** is $23^m$ long, covering 17,800 as. (boat.f.). Power plant has 24,000 h.p. capacity. At $82.5^m$ is J. with dirt Rd.

SIDE TRIP: (R) on Rd. 1m to Tonto Nat. Mon. cliff dwellings. **Tonto Nat. Mon.** contains 2 cliff dwellings built in 14th cent. by pueblo people. Lower house has 2 stories & 29 rooms. Upper house orig. was 3 stories with 60 to 75 rooms.

At 111m is J. with US60-70. [Globe (L) 5m (see US70)]. (R) on US60-70 to **Phoenix** at 196m.

**215. TEMPE** (accoms.facils.), home of **Ariz. St. College,** one of pioneer communities of St. Founded by father of Arizona's Sen. Carl Hayden, & called Hayden's Ferry, where he ran a boat across Salt R., town's name was changed to Tempe as it resembled Vale of Tempe in Greece. College borders U.S. hy. leaving Tempe, & was est. 1886 as Normal Sch. In 1925 became a standard Teachers College & in 1945 became Ariz. St. College. From single room with 31 students there has evolved a campus with 30 bldgs. on 120-as. with enrollment of 3,500 in 1948. **221. MESA** ("May-suh"), is Mormon town founded in 1878, center of rich irrigated area. **Ariz. Mormon Temple** (Class.), one of most beautiful edifices in nation, located at E. edge of town, was completed in 1927 at cost of $800,000, on 20-a. landscaped site for visitors (only members may enter Temple). **235. APACHE JUNCTION** is J. with St.88 (see Phoenix). Apache Junction Zoo contains many Ariz. wild animals, birds, reptiles. **Superstition Mt.** (E). **252. FLORENCE JUNCTION. 269. FLORENCE,** Pinal Cty. seat & one of oldest settlements in St.; has changed little through yrs., many old adobes still standing & in use.

SIDE TRIP: On Rd. leading (L) 1m to **Ariz. St. Prison** (O). A walled-in group of bldgs., the predominating structure, built almost entirely by convict labor, completed in 1909.

**319. Santa Catalina Mts.** (L) are in **Coronado Nat. For. Mt. Lemon** (9,180') is highest peak in range. Resort area among pines. **333.** J. with unmarked dirt Rd.

SIDE TRIP: On Rd. leading (R) 0.5m to **Pascua,** Yaqui Ind. village of 65 huts, larger of 2 villages in st. These Inds. are not wards of U.S., but migrated here 40 yrs. ago, exiles from their ancestral home in Mexico. Annual Yaqui Easter Ceremonials attract hundreds of visitors with weird rituals of several days duration, culminating on Easter Sunday.

**337. TUCSON** (S.P. RR. Bus lines. Info.: Climate Club, C. of C. facils. accoms.of all types). Known as the Old Pueblo, Tucson (Too-sahn) is seat of Pima Cty. & St. Univ. Is health & winter resort that has grown up around one of oldest Sp. towns in U.S. Once a walled fortress in Apache infested SW., it is now a modern city. In 1700 Padre Kino started to build **Mission San Xavier del Bac,** 9m (S) of Tucson. Gradually he was followed into valley by Sp. ranchers & mining men who fought Inds. for survival. After Civil War, town outgrew its adobe walls & began to spread out over valley. From its beginning, until outnumbered by Phoenix in 1920, Tucson was largest town in terr. or St. Distributing center for mineral, livestock & agric. reg., it has grown increasingly prominent as resort center. Annual events: La Fiesta de los Vaqueros (Festival of Cowboys) rodeo, late Feb.; Livestock Show, late Mar.; Yaqui Ind. Religious Festival, Easter. PTS. OF INT.: (1) N. Park Ave. bet. E. 2nd & E. 4th Sts., **Univ. of Arizona,** est. 1885. Campus comprises 85 as. incl. 40 bldgs. of mod. structure & design. Has faculty & staff of over 400 & student enrollment of more than 5,500. **Arizona St. Mus.** on campus contains artifacts from prehist. Ariz. ruins, nat. hist. & other colls. **Univ. Lib.** contains Ariz. coll. of 2,500 vols. **Steward Observatory** was made famous through research discoveries of Dr. A. E. Douglass, climatologist & originator of tree-ring method of determining climatic cycles, & by Dr. E. F. Carpenter, with his studies of stellar nebulae.

SIDE TRIPS: (A) Follow US80-89 from center of city (S) to Ajo Rd. Turn (R) & cont. to Mission Rd. (L) to **San Xavier del Bac Mission,** 9m, said to be finest example of pure mission architecture in U.S. Present bldgs. completed c.1797 & used continuously by Inds. to present. Called "White Dove of Desert," its great beauty is enhanced in desert-mt. setting.
(B) (E) on Broadway to end, follow signs to 14m, entrance of **Saguaro Nat. Mon.** Mon. incl. over 63,000 as. of arid desert, thickly covered with Giant (Saguaro, Suh-whar-oh) cactus, which sometimes reaches age of century with few to many arms extending from main trunk; its white-waxy blossom is St. flower.
(C) Drive to end of Speedway, (L) on Tanque Verde Rd. to Sabino Canyon Rd. to 16m, entrance of **Sabino Canyon,** popular Mt. recr. area of great beauty. 18m **Colossal Cave** (pic.facils.). (S) to J. with US80-89.
(D) (L) 18m on US80 to **Colossal Cave** sign. Partially explored cave's size unknown. Stalagmite & stalactites & grotesque rock formations. In early days bank robbers were supposed to have hidden their loot in cave, returning yrs. later to claim it.
(E) (S) on US80-89 to Ajo Rd. (L) to **Old Tucson** sign at 14m. Authentic replica of Old Tucson, constructed for motion picture "Arizona," & donated to community as pt. of int.

## Sec. 3: TUCSON to NOGALES, SONORA, MEX. 65.

(S) of Tucson on US80-89 is J. with US80 (L) to Lordsburg, N.M. Reg. bet. Tucson & Nogales is rich in hist. background. Early Sp. missions were located here incl. San Xavier del Bac & Tumacacori, both of which are still standing. First cattle were introduced into U.S. by Padre Kino here. Many Ind. fights & Apache raids left their scars upon this reg. At **7.** is J. with dirt Rd. [(R) 2.5$^{m}$ to **Mission San Xavier del Bac** (see above).] At **45.** is J. with dirt Rd.

SIDE TRIP: On Rd. leading 0.5$^{m}$ (L) to **Tubac,** cluster of mud-covered adobe hs. built around a white-plastered Cath. Ch. This quiet, farming, stock-raising & mining community in 1776 was assembly pt. of Anza's colonizing party before his epochal journey to San Francisco. Oldest town founded by white men in St., was garrisoned by Sp. in 1752 & became 1st Mormon settlement in Ariz. just 100 yrs. later. When "Weekly Arizonian," 1st newspaper published in terr., was started here in 1859, Tubac was area's most important settlement, but in 1861 it was virtually abandoned owing to continual bandit & Apache raids.

**48. TUMACACORI** (too-muh-cah-core-ee) **NAT. MON.** was proclaimed in 1908 to protect ruins of one of old Sp. mission sites, est. 1691 by Padre Kino. In early part of 19th cent., mission was attacked by Apache Inds., who drove priests away & disbanded peaceable Papago Inds. residing in vic. When found by Amers. c.1850, mission was in a state of ruin, consisting of the walls & tower of an old ch., walls of a mortuary chamber, churchyard & cemetery, surrounded by an adobe wall. **Mus.** (1937) has been fashioned in the style of Sonora missions. By means of various types of exhibits, mus. brings to life old days when mission was busy center. **65. NOGALES** (accoms.facils.info. C. of C. S.P. RR.Greyhound Bus), seat of Santa Cruz Cty. & largest Ariz. port of entry on Mex. border. Trading & banking pt. for rich reg. to (S). Town lies within rich mineral area & is focal pt. for shipment of cattle. International Ave. parallels wire fence bet. U.S. & Nogales, Sonora, Mexico (accoms.facils.). Free access across Internat. Line between 2 cities. (Regarding purchases & other info., inquire of U.S. Custom offices at Line.) Across street from Nogales, Ariz., is quaint & basically Sonoran community, vibrant with Mex. life. Most of its dwellings are compact plastered adobes, simple & colorful, suited to climate, society & customs. Some are built along the canyon floor which extends for several miles (W), others are built high on edges of cliffs. To add gaiety, groups of singers & musicians in colorful costumes serenade visitors in cantinas & night spots. Transition is complete as line is crossed to strange & colorful center, noted for wild game dinners; was orig. a gold mine, & in early 1880's was used as jail, being cut from solid rock for over 50′ into sloping hillside. **65. ARIZ.-MEX. LINE.**

# THE MOUNTAIN STATES

## COLORADO — UTAH — NEVADA
## WYOMING — MONTANA — IDAHO

Just where the West begins is hard to determine: the westbound traveler, having changed his watch from Central to Mountain Standard Time, still keeps on, as he crosses the eastern reaches of Montana, Wyoming or Colorado, through the same undulating High Plains area that stretches behind through the Dakotas, Nebraska or Kansas, drained by the same eastward-running rivers: the Yellowstone, the South & North Platte, the Arkansas. The rise toward the foothills of the Rockies is almost imperceptible. But certainly when he sees piling up far in the distance the rugged, snow-capped mass of the Continental Divide, he knows that the West is at hand. From Glacier International Peace Park on the Canadian border, the continent's backbone runs south through western Montana, diagonally across southwestern Wyoming, & south again in a twisting course across west-central Colorado into northeastern New Mexico. In western Montana the peaks of the Rockies soar to elevations of from 8,000 to 12,850 feet, & in Wyoming they reach up to 1,000 feet higher still; in Colorado, the "highest" state, are 50 of the country's 64 named mountains exceeding 14,000 feet in height. West of the Rockies lies an awesomely rugged terrain of timbered mountains & rocky gorges, high plateaus & deserts, threaded by the tortuous canyons cut by streams whose waters empty ultimately into the Pacific.

Along the Montana-Idaho border wriggle the crests of the Bitterroot & Beaverhead Ranges, & westward rise other ranges, of which the Sawtooth Mts. are the most spectacular; almost the only extensive level part of Idaho is the far-spreading lava plains of the Snake River basin in the southwest part, the chief agricultural area, largely dependent on irrigation, where most of the state's population lives. The Snake, twisting northward to its confluence with the Columbia, flows through Hell's Canyon, deepest gorge on the North American Continent. The western section of Wyoming, likewise, boasts impressive mountain scenery: Grand Teton National Park, with 11 major peaks; Jackson Hole National Monument; Yellowstone National Park, with its geysers & Grand Canyon of the Yellowstone; Devils Tower National Monument; the Bighorn & Medicine Bow Ranges.

Colorado, straddling the Continental Divide, has 1,064 peaks exceeding 10,000 feet, among them famous Pike's Peak & others even higher, including Mt. Elbert (14,431′) & Mt. Massive (14,418′); magnificent Rocky Mt. National Park, containing more than 400 square miles, is famed for its rugged gorges, spectacular peaks, scenic lakes & plunging streams. Colorado's largest stream is the Colorado River, which, with its tributaries—many of them coursing through deep canyons—drains the western part of the state; west of the Rockies are two other river basins, fertile & good for agriculture, besides that of the Colorado: the San Luis, in the south-central part, & the San Juan, in the southwest; but the irrigated South Platte & Arkansas River Valleys in eastern Colorado are its richest farming areas.

The Colorado River runs from Colorado across the high plateau-country of southeastern Utah, in which are Bryce Canyon & Zion National Parks—a land of rock, strangely eroded, brilliantly colored, carved by narrow canyons; & here it is joined by its tributary, the Green, flowing south from Utah's Uinta Basin at the foot of the east-&-west-running Uinta Mts. The high spine of the Wasatch Mountains, rising to heights of 12,000 feet, divides Utah in two, running north & south through the center of the State. Along the range's western base is a chain of fertile, well-watered valleys. Farther west, beyond the Great Salt Lake & the most irreclaimable of American deserts, the Great Salt Lake Desert, stretches an arid reach of salt flats & sun-baked mountain spurs, which takes in most of Nevada. Across the latter from north to south extend parallel ranges, dividing a series of long narrow valleys, where during the dry season the rivers lose themselves underground or evaporate, leaving hardened mudflats often caked with glistening white salts.

Perhaps 2,000 years before the discovery of America by Europeans, the Basket Makers of the Mesa Verde, Colorado's southwestern plateau, were building their habitations against cliff & canyon walls; they & their successors of later centuries, the Cliff Dwellers, achieved the highest level of civilization of its type yet discovered. Scouts dispatched by Coronado on his treasure-hunting expedition of 1540 penetrated the Utah region. But the remainder of the Rocky Mountain area went unvisited until the 18th century, although the section east of the Rockies was claimed for France by La Salle in 1682. The Spanish, who claimed southeastern Colorado in 1706, sent a military expedition headed by Valverde as far north as Pike's Peak in 1719. The two sons of the French Canadian explorer, the Sieur de la Verendrye, reached southeastern Montana in 1742; twenty years later, however, France ceded all territory west of the Mississippi to Spain. Francisco Escalante & another Franciscan friar explored parts of Utah & Colorado in 1776; but the whole Rocky Mountain area region was unsettled, & most of it unseen by white men, until after 1803, when the U.S. acquired the eastern part of it through the Louisiana Purchase.

In 1805-06 Lewis & Clark crossed & recrossed Montana & Idaho on their trip to & from the Oregon country (& a member of their expedition, John Colter, entered Wyoming in 1807); in 1806-07 Lt. Zebulon Pike (for whom Pike's Peak was later named) crossed Colorado. Fur traders, trappers & mountain men soon entered the area in large numbers, followed by missionaries; posts were established in the Arkansas & South Platte Valleys of Colorado & in Montana (where Jesuit missionary Father De Smet set up a mission in the Bitterroot Valley in 1841), at Fort Laramie (1834) & other points in Wyoming, & at several points in Idaho: Fort Hall near Pocatello (1834), the Spalding mission near Lewiston (1836), Old Fort Boise (1838) & the Coeur d'Alene Mission (1842). During the 1840's a growing throng of westward travelers crossed Wyoming & southern Idaho, following the Oregon Trail to Oregon or California; many California-bound travelers turned south from Fort Hall, Idaho, & followed the Humboldt River route through northwestern Nevada. The fertile valley of the Great Salt Lake in Utah (discovered by trapper James Bridger in 1824-25) in 1847 became the Promised Land of the Mormons, headed by Brigham Young, after a long trek overland; here they founded Salt Lake City & introduced irrigation (never previously practiced in America by other than the Indians).

The Treaty of Guadalupe Hidalgo in 1848 added Utah—& all the remaining part of the Rocky Mountain region not included in the Louisiana Purchase—to the U.S.; & in 1851 the Territory of Utah was set up, with Brigham Young as Governor. The Territory of Utah included most of Nevada, within which the Mormons had established the year before a trading post on the Humboldt Road to supply California-bound gold seekers. Colorado's first permanent white settlement was founded in the latter year in San Luis Valley, where irrigation was also begun; & here in 1852 Fort Massachusetts was established for protection against the Indians. During the next few years the Mormons founded other colonies in Utah, & in what is now Nevada as well, until in 1857 all Mormons were recalled to Salt Lake City when a gradually developing conflict with the Federal Government culminated in the dispatch of U.S. Army troops to "put down rebellion." (An Army occupation force remained until the Civil War, & conflict with the Federal Government, principally over the Mormon practice of polygamy, continued long afterward; only in 1896, after the Mormon Church had renounced polygamy, was Utah finally admitted to the Union.) The Mormons also established, in southern Idaho, that state's first agricultural settlements.

The real settlement of the Rocky Mountain States (except for Utah), however, began only when a backwash of prospectors from the California diggings began hunting for gold. Between 1858 & 1862, rich strikes were made in Nevada, Colorado, Idaho & Montana. The discovery in 1859 of Nevada's Comstock Lode, one of the most profitable gold & silver deposits ever found, brought a stampede of newcomers hoping to get rich quick; almost overnight Virginia City numbered 30,000 inhabitants. The opening of Colorado's first gold quartz mine near Central City in the same year brought a similar stampede, in the course of which Boulder, Denver & other settlements sprang up; the discovery of silver, soon after, swelled the fabulous stream of wealth from the mines. Gold was found in Idaho in 1860; lead-silver (in the Coeur d'Alene region) in 1864. From 1862 on, successive gold strikes were made in Montana, as a result of which Helena & other towns came into being. Gold was found in Wyoming's Sweetwater Valley. The mining camps which sprang up throughout the Rocky Mountain area swarmed with miners & merchants, with gamblers & bandits; rough-&-ready justice by Vigilantes soon became the rule.

Most of the camps were short-lived, but some of the survivors grew into cities. As a result of the sudden influx of population, Nevada was separated from Utah & became a Territory in 1861; it was admitted to the Union as a state in 1864, partly to insure loyalty among its inhabitants so that the Federal Government might depend on receiving its much-needed gold & silver. Colorado also became a Territory in 1861. Idaho Territory, organized in 1863, included all of Montana & much of Wyoming, as well as Idaho; but in 1864 Montana became a separate Territory & in in 1868, Wyoming did, too. Gold rushes occurred sporadically in the region during the rest of the 19th century. The rush to the Black Hills of 1876-77 brought settlers into the plains country of eastern Montana, which had remained an Indian hunting ground—with resultant warfare between whites & Indians culminating in the Battle of the Little Big Horn (1876), when Custer's troops were annihilated. When Montana was admitted to the Union in 1889 (a year before the admission of Idaho & Wyoming) its Great Seal carried the motto "gold & silver." In Colorado, admitted to the Union as the Centennial State in 1876, where wealth from the mines built thriving cities & railroads, the great gold field of Cripple Creek was discovered in 1891 & by 1900 was producing $20,000,000 annually. Colorado, second among the States in variety of mineral resources, still has an annual output of more than $12,500,000 in gold & $4,500,000 in silver. Even after 1900, new gold & silver strikes in Nevada brought the rip-roaring towns of Tonopah & Goldfield into being.

But although gold & silver are still mined in Montana, Idaho, Colorado, Utah & Nevada, other mineral resources have come to be more important in the region's economy. At Butte, Montana, whose Anaconda copper smelter is the world's biggest non-ferrous smelter, the "richest hill on earth" yields a third of the copper mined in the U.S.; nearly a third more comes from Utah, whose leading industry is still mining; & Nevada, also chiefly a mining state, produces an impressive amount. Idaho ranks first in production of lead, mined in the Coeur d'Alene district; lead is also mined in all the other states except Wyoming. Colorado ranks first in production of molybdenum, radium & tungsten; Nevada produces magnesite, manganese, platinum & uranium; Wyoming produces iron. Wyoming's coal resources are the greatest of any state's; coal is Colorado's most valuable mineral product; & coal beds underlie a fifth of Utah. Wyoming's oil fields (including the Salt Creek Field near Teapot Dome) are exceeded in importance only by its coal fields; western Colorado, where intensive drilling for petroleum was carried on during World War II, has become an important producing area; & petroleum refining is one of Montana's leading industries.

The salient influence of the mining camp in the Rocky Mountain region's history has helped shape a tradition of rugged individualism, often forcefully expressed during the last half century in struggles over economic & political issues. The proverbial distrust of Eastern financial interests which the mountain states still feel in common with the remainder of the West was vociferously expressed in the fight for free coinage of silver, that most conspicuous national issue of the 1890's, dramatized in William Jennings Bryan's "Cross of Gold" speech at the Democratic National Convention of 1896. Nevada even developed a Silver Party of its own, until Republicans & Democrats both accepted bimetallism. The tendency of Westerners toward impatience with legal restraints has appeared in such phenomena as Nevada's refusal to outlaw gambling or tighten up its divorce laws & the virtual defiance of Prohibition shown by Butte, Montana. Their urge to resort to direct action was given full play in Butte's "War of the Copper Kings"—William A. Clark, Marcus Daly & F. Augustus Heinze—in which Clark & Daly fought each other & both fought Heinze to obtain control of mining properties & to win political supremacy in the press, courts & legislature; Clark, elected U.S. Senator, resigned when charged with buying votes but was reelected. A half century later, the Anaconda Copper Mining Company, world's biggest nonferrous metal combine, remains a dominant factor in Montana politics. Yet, paradoxically, Montana was represented in Congress during the 1920's & 1930's by such nationally prominent progressives (at least in their earlier careers) as Senators Burton K. Wheeler & Thomas J. Walsh, who campaigned to expose the Teapot Dome scandal provoked by illegal leases of naval oil lands in Wyoming; the latter State's Senator Joseph C. O'Mahoney & Utah's Senator Elbert Thomas are other progressive leaders who have been contributed to national political scene by the Rocky Mountain area despite generally conservative bent in local politics.

Perhaps most forcefully in its labor history has appeared the Rocky Mountain region's somewhat rough-&-ready way of life. The power of Montana's copper magnates was challenged almost immediately by the Butte Miners' Union, organized in 1881 & soon the biggest & strongest miners' union in the West; under its leadership Butte eventually grew into "the strongest union town on earth." The lead miners of Idaho's Coeur d'Alene district, following the copper miners' example, were faced with State militia when they struck in 1892 (& again in 1899) & their leaders were imprisoned behind stockades (locally known as "bull pens"). The following year Idaho, along with Colorado, was represented at a meeting of miners' delegates in Butte to organize the Western Federation of Miners, of which William D. ("Big Bill") Haywood became secretary-treasurer. In Colorado, a State-wide strike of mine, mill & smelter hands in 1903 brought martial law at Cripple Creek & the forced deportation of hundreds of strikers. Leaders of the Western Federation of Miners, which had headquarters in Denver, met in Chicago with other organizations & individuals in 1905 to form the Industrial Workers of the World, which campaigned for industrial union organization with a vigorously anti-capitalist program. The I.W.W. soon began to organize lumbermen & agricultural workers as well as miners. The trial in 1907 of Haywood & two other Federation officers, Charles H. Moyer & George Pettibone, on charges of murdering ex-Governor of Idaho Frank Steunenberg (killed by a bomb in the course of a strike feud in the lead mining district), in which defense lawyer Clarence Darrow won their acquittal, brought to prominence William E. Borah, who acted as prosecutor; Borah, later Idaho's most noted political figure, eventually became dean of the U.S. Senate. Soon afterward, internal dissension in the Western Federation of Miners between radicals & conservatives (in the course of which the organization abandoned the I.W.W. for the A.F.L.) led to a split of the Butte local into rival factions; bombings of a union hall & mine employment office were followed by an employers' lockout & martial law. Butte became, & for 20 years remained, an open shop town. The United Mine Workers, sending organizers into the Colorado coal fields at this time, called a strike in the course of which occurred the famous Ludlow "massacre" of April, 1914, with 21 lives lost when the strikers' tent colony caught fire during an armed clash with militia. Violence broke out again at Butte in 1917, when strikers asked the Federal Government to take over the mines (supported by Congresswoman Jeannette Rankin, first woman in the U.S. to be elected to Congress, who had voted against entry into World War I); I.W.W. organizer Frank Little was shot by gunmen. Later strikes following the end of the war were broken, & suppressive measures against the I.W.W. (because of its opposition to U.S. participation in the war) were undertaken through the courts. By 1924 the power of the I.W.W. had been broken everywhere. Ten years later, the Butte local (No.1) of the reorganized International Mine, Mill & Smelter Workers struck & restored the closed shop in Butte, which soon became once again an almost 100% organized town. During the following years, labor organization developed in other centers throughout the Rocky Mountain area, as throughout the rest of the country.

Before the end of the nineteenth century, stock raising, lumbering & agriculture had begun to supplement mining as economic mainstays for the region. Western Montana became cow country soon after 1849, when cattlemen began pasturing herds in its grass valleys to supply travelers on the Oregon Trail; & after the cessation of the Indian wars in the 1870's, the vast buffalo range of eastern Montana soon filled up with cow herds. While the cattle-boom of the 1880's was short-lived, Montana is still an important stock-raising state; it ranks second in number of sheep. Wyoming has nearly as many cattle as during the 1880's, & even more sheep, although its open ranges were fenced long ago, after years of conflict between cattle barons & homesteaders, whom the cattlemen opposed as vigorously as they opposed the organized bands of cattle thieves, or "rustlers" who preyed on their herds—a conflict only less bitter than that between cattlemen & sheepmen which followed. Today cattle raising is a major industry; Wyoming ranks second in wool & mutton production. Utah is a leading sheep-raising state, & along with the other states of the region, pastures great herds of cattle as well as sheep.

The lumber industry is the largest in Idaho, which has the country's biggest tract of virgin pine; & lumbering is an important source of wealth in Montana as well. Throughout the Rocky Mountain region, timber resources have been protected by the setting aside of millians of acres in National Forests, which comprise 30% of Idaho's total land area & relatively high proportions in the other states.

Except in eastern Montana, Wyoming & Colorado, where dry farming is practiced, the progress of agriculture has been largely dependent on the development of irrigation. Wheat is Montana's leading crop, & an important one in Idaho & Colorado as well; corn, oats, hay & alfalfa & other field crops are also grown throughout the region. But the Rocky Mountain area's most distinctive agricultural products are potatoes & sugar beets. Idaho potatoes are nationally famous, & Colorado ranks fourth in production of seed potatoes. Sugar beets culture, widely practiced in irrigated areas throughout the region, has made beet-sugar refining a leading industry.

For the most part, the Rocky Mountain area's industrial development has been linked to mining or agriculture. The former has spurred establishment of its smelters, refineries, & brick, pottery & cement works; the latter, of its beet sugar refineries, flour mills, & meat-packing plants. Idaho, whose development of its hydroelectric power resources has been unusually intensive, was chosen in the late 1940's as the site of a huge new atomic reactor testing station, covering about 400,000 acres near Arco. In general, the relatively limited industrial development has limited population growth; Nevada & Wyoming are the least populous States of the Union, & even Colorado, the mostly thickly settled State in the Rocky Mountain region, ranks only 33rd in population among the 48 States, with Montana, Utah & Idaho ranking 39th, 40th & 42nd respectively. Boise, Billings, Butte, Denver, Cheyenne, Colorado Springs, Ogden, Pueblo, Reno & Salt Lake City are the only cities of more than 25,000 population; Denver & Salt Lake City are the only ones of more than 100,000.

Denver, the cultural capital of the region, as it is the financial, offers the amenities of a metropolis: a symphony orchestra & other active musical groups, concerts & a season of summer stock, a leading art museum, schools, libraries & parks. Colorado Springs, health resort & summer playground, has museums, Colorado College, & an art colony centering around its Fine Arts Center; Boulder is the seat of the University of Colorado, intellectual center of the whole mountain region; Central City, once a booming mining town, stages a nationally famous summer theater festival in its refurnished old opera house; Pueblo & other Colorado cities offer educational & cultural facilities. Utah's capital, Salt Lake City, whose chief points of interest are its architecturally interesting Mormon Temple & Tabernacle, is a religious & educational center, & its State Capitol houses the Utah State Art Collection. Utah has 10 institutions of higher learning in all, among them the University of Utah in Salt Lake City, Utah State Agricultural College at Logan, & Brigham Young University at Provo. Its chief collections of paintings, in addition to that at the State Capitol, are at Brigham Young & Utah Universities & at the art museum in the small town of Springville. Salt Lake City's Tabernacle Choir is its best-known musical organization. The sparsity of urban concentrations throughout the rest of the Rocky Mountain area has limited its cultural development. The University of Montana, at Missoula, is noted for its school of journalism; the University of Idaho, at Moscow, for its beautiful campus. The University of Wyoming, at Laramie, & the University of Nevada at Reno provide intellectual stimulus for their respective States. The tendency of many of the region's writers, artists & musicians—following the example of poet Ezra Pound, born in Idaho—to emigrate to the bigger cities in other parts of the country & Europe, has handicapped the growth of a healthy regional culture. Among writers native to the region who have achieved note have been Utah's Bernard De Voto & Wallace Stegner, Idaho's Vardis Fisher & Wyoming's Thurman Arnold, Nevada's Walter Van Tilburg Clark; among artists, Montana painter Charles M. Russell & Utah sculptors Cyrus E. Dallin & Mahonri Young.

The natural charms of the Rocky Mountain region, much of it unspoiled by civilization's inroads, make it one of the nation's chief playgrounds. In all these states huge tracts have been set aside in national parks, monument areas, & Indian

# THE MOUNTAIN STATES

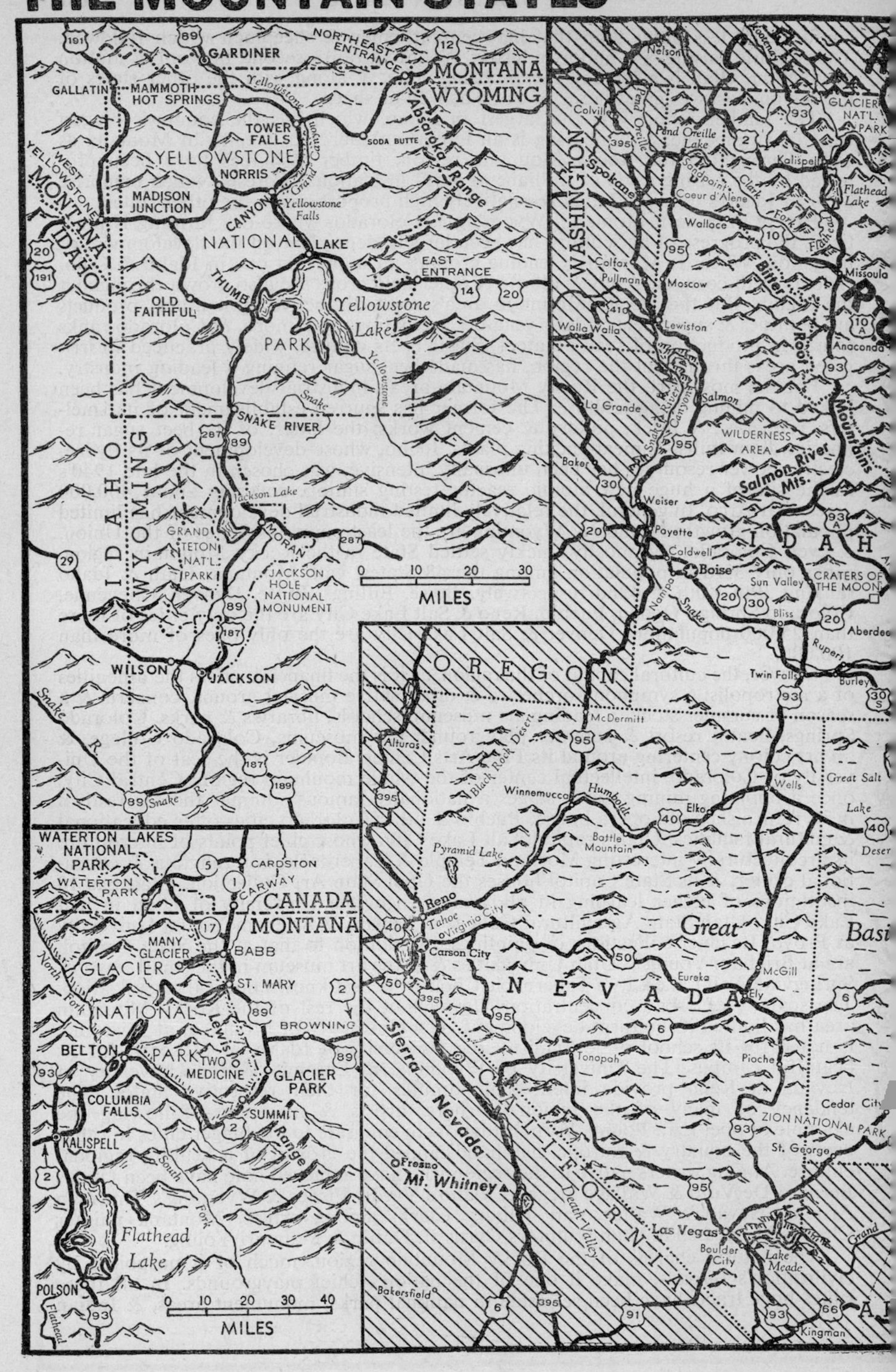

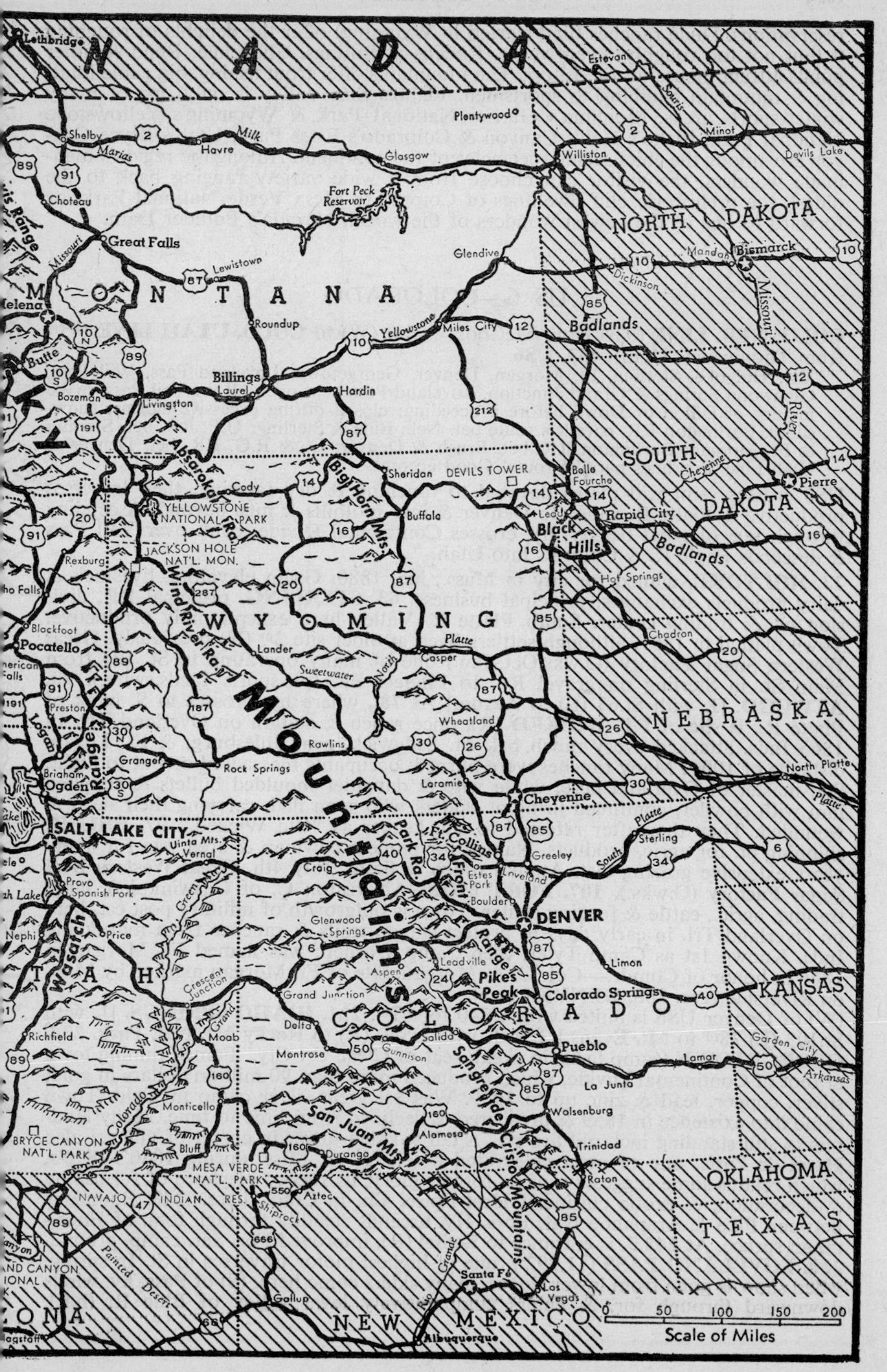

CANADA
Lethbridge
Estevan
Souris
Plentywood
Minot
Shelby
Havre
Milk
Marias
Glasgow
Williston
Devils Lake
Choteau
Fort Peck Reservoir
NORTH DAKOTA
Great Falls
Missouri
Glendive
Mandan
Bismarck
Lewistown
Dickinson
MONTANA
Helena
Roundup
Yellowstone
Miles City
Badlands
Butte
Billings
Laurel
Hardin
Bozeman
Livingston
Absaroka Ra.
SOUTH DAKOTA
Cheyenne
Pierre
Sheridan
DEVILS TOWER
Belle Fourche
Cody
YELLOWSTONE NATIONAL PARK
Big Horn Mts.
Buffalo
Lead
Rapid City
Black Hills
Badlands
JACKSON HOLE NAT'L. MON.
Rexburg
Hot Springs
Wind River Ra.
WYOMING
Blackfoot
Pocatello
Lander
Platte
Casper
Chadron
Sweetwater
North
Preston
Logan
Wheatland
NEBRASKA
Rawlins
Granger
Rock Springs
Brigham
Ogden
Range
Laramie
North Platte
Cheyenne
Platte
SALT LAKE CITY
Uinta Mts.
Vernal
Sterling
South
Park Ra.
Ft. Collins
Greeley
Craig
Estes Park
Loveland
Provo
Spanish Fork
Front
Boulder
Green
Glenwood Springs
DENVER
Nephi
Price
Wasatch
Leadville
Limon
Aspen
Pikes Peak
Crescent Junction
Grand Junction
Colorado Springs
KANSAS
UTAH
Grand
Delta
COLORADO
Richfield
Moab
Salida
Pueblo
Montrose
Gunnison
Garden City
Lamar
Sangre de Cristo Mountains
Arkansas
La Junta
Monticello
San Juan Mts.
Walsenburg
BRYCE CANYON NAT'L. PARK
Colorado
Bluff
Alamosa
Trinidad
MESA VERDE NAT'L. PARK
Durango
Raton
OKLAHOMA
NAVAJO INDIAN RES.
Aztec
Shiprock
TEXAS
Grande
Painted Desert
Santa Fé
Rio
Los Vegas
Gallup
NEW MEXICO
Albuquerque
Mountains
Rocky
0 50 100 150 200
Scale of Miles

reservations. Dude ranches (first started in Wyoming) offer the delights of roughing it (but not too roughly) everywhere. Rodeos at Billings, Cheyenne, Reno & other points attract thousands of visitors. The mountains offer trout fishing, big game hunting & mountain climbing to sportsmen. Idaho's Sun Valley is only one of many winter-sports areas. Montana's Glacier National Park & Wyoming's Yellowstone National Park, Idaho's Hell's Canyon & Colorado's Estes Park, Utah's Bryce Canyon are among the chief scenic spectacles of the continent. Among the region's man-made wonders, the visitor can choose from a wide variety ranging back to the oldest, the prehistoric cliff dwellings of Colorado's Mesa Verde National Park, or forward to one of the newest wonders of the world, Nevada's Boulder Dam.

## US 6—COLORADO

**COLO.-NEB. LINE** (93$^{m}$ from McCook, Neb.) **(W) to COLO.-UTAH LINE** (45$^{m}$ from Thompsons, Utah). **483. US6**

Via: Holyoke, Sterling, Ft. Morgan, Denver, Georgetown, Loveland Pass, Vail Pass, Glenwood Springs & Grand Junction. Loveland Pass kept open all yr. Vail Pass, make inquiry at Dillon or Dowd before proceeding; closed during excessive storms; snow-slides. Burlington RR. parallels route bet. Neb. Line & Sterling; U.P. RR. bet. Sterling & Ft. Morgan; Burlington RR. bet. Brush & Denver; D. & R.G. RR. bet. Denver & Utah Line. Bus lines parallel route. Good accoms.

US6 crosses semi-arid plains devoted to ranching & dry farming, then traverses productive S. Platte R. valley to Denver & into foothills & mts. beyond. Ascending through reg. of great beauty, hy. crosses Continental Divide, cont. over Vail Pass & descends Eagle R. & Colo. R. into Utah.

**13. HOLYOKE,** named for city in Mass., inc. 1880. Grain elevators, livestock & dairy products exchanges, principal business. **63. STERLING,** principal RR. division pt. & trading center. South Platte R. Valley here exceptionally productive. Town platted in 1881, although settlers lived at older site 3$^{m}$ (N) previously. **Great Western Sugar Factory** (O.wks.Oct.-Jan.) one of many operating in St. (R) from Main St. in Sterling on gravel Rd. to **Pioneer Pk.** (pic.sports facils.swim.). **70. ATWOOD.** [J. with St.63 (L) to **Akron.**] At **78.,** where hy. crosses to S. bank of Platte R., is site of **FT. WICKED** (R), once ranch & station on Overland Trl. In 1865 Inds. attacked every ranch bet. Ft. Sedgwick, near Julesburg, & Ft. Logan, distance of 100$^{m}$. Many ranches were burned; occupants massacred or put to flight. Sta. master of Overland here, while wife & daughter moulded bullets & supplied him with powder, continued firing at raiders who soon fled, carrying their dead & wounded. They thereafter referred to sta. keeper as "Old Wicked." **97. BRUSH,** shipping pt. for agric. products. Named for pioneer cowman & area was for many years extensive grazing dist. Annual rodeo & fiesta, July 4th. **Great Western Beet Sugar Factory** (O.wks.). **107. FORT MORGAN** (Info.: C. of C.;swim.pic.), large trading, agric., cattle & feeding center. Town is outgrowth of military post est. here on Overland Trl. in early days to protect wagon trails & ranches from marauding Inds. Known 1st as Camp Tyler, then Camp Wardell; was named Ft. Morgan in 1866 in honor of Comdr.—Col. C. A. Morgan. Site of Ft. Morgan marked by **Mon.** on Riverside Ave. **188. DENVER** (see).

(W) of Denver US6 is united with US40 for 41$^{m}$. **221. IDAHO SPRINGS.** [J. with St.103 (L) 28$^{m}$ to **Mt. Evans.**] **229.** J. with US40 (R) to **Rocky Mt. Nat. Park. 234. GEORGETOWN** (camp.facils.in area), seat of Clear Cr. Cty. Famed mining town at foot of Continental Divide, which produced more than 90 million dollars in gold, silver, copper, lead & zinc up to 1939. Was 1st great silver camp in Colo. Town came into existence in 1859 & prospered & declined from time to time. Many landmarks still standing incl. old fire sta., a tall wooden tower in center of village; also **Hotel de Paris,** one of most celebrated hotels W. of Miss. during 1880's-1890's, which retains some suggestion of its former glory, its rococo elegance of furnishing & decoration, & exotic cuisine. **Oldest Episc. Ch.** in Colo., here. **240.** Boundary between Pike & Arapahoe Nat. Fors. Hy. ascends steadily through fors. of Engelmann spruce. At **242.5.** is entrance to **Bethel** (R), improved For. Ser. camp. ground. **250. LOVELAND PASS** (11,992'), one of highest motor traverses in St. In spring, when snow is gone from lower slopes, many skiers come here. (S) of Pass, hy. winds downward through for. & enters comparatively level valley of Blue R. (h.f.).

**265. DILLON** (h.f.). Resort of frame hs. & log cabins on Blue R. in setting of jagged mts. Town formerly was sta. on Leadville-Breckenridge stage route. **275. WHEELER.** US6 crosses Continental Divide, follows Vail Pass hy. & descends to J. with US24. **300. DOWD.** J. with US24 (see) to **Leadville.** Bet. Dowd & Grand Junction US6 is united with US24. **449. GRAND JUNCTION.** J. with US50 (see). W. of Grand Junction US6 & US50 are same route to **COLO.-UTAH LINE 483.**

## US 34—COLORADO

**COLO.-NEB. LINE** (93$^m$ from McCook, Neb.) **(W) to GRANBY. 263. US34**

Via: Wray, Brush, Greeley, Estes Pk. Village, Rocky Mt. Nat. Park & Bear Lake. Burlington RR. parallels route between Neb. Line & Wiggins. Bus lines parallel route. Milner & Fall R. passes & Trail Ridge High Point, in Rocky Mt. Nat. Park, usually closed to winter travel. Inquire pk. ranger at Estes Pk. Village. Good accoms.

US34 traverses heart of plains country, once grazing land for buffalo herds & habitat of hostile Inds. Now devoted to dry farming & cattle-raising. Hy. crosses irrigation sec. before penetrating foothills to mt. gateway of Estes Pk. (For sec. traversing magnificent Rocky Mt. Nat. Pk. via Trail Ridge Rd. to Bear L. & Granby, see Denver Trip III.) **10. WRAY,** unlike many E. Colo. towns, lies in moist river land & is mass of verdure through spring & summer. SE. edge of town, reached by winding dr. from Main St., is **Flirtation Pt.,** limestone formation away from cliffs (L) that hem in valley.

**36. YUMA,** named for Ind. tribe, is in heart of dry farming district. **62. FED. GOV. EXPERIMENTAL STA.** (O), 160-as. in orchards & fields planted to 1,600 varieties of wheat, corn, oats & other crops, which are rotated in 20-yr. cycles. Experiments are important to reg. since they point to new methods in soil conservation. **64. AKRON** was only town site on new Burlington RR. at time of founding, 1882. Division pt. on RR. **87. BRUSH.** J. (R) with US6 (see). US34 & US6 are united for 24$^m$. **97. FT. MORGAN** (see US6). **150. GREELEY** (see US85). At **168.** is **EXPERIMENTAL FARM** (O.9-5), maintained by Colo. A. & M. College. Just 1$^m$ beyond is **Great Western Beet Sugar Factory** (O.9-4 wks.). **170. LOVELAND.** J. with US87. US34 cuts deeper through Big Thompson Canyon, one of most picturesque of all canyon drives; it grows more spectacular with every turn of the Rd., making abrupt entrance into highlands of Estes Pk. through portal of towering peaks. **184. LOVELAND MT. PK.** (pic.sports facils.) in Roosevelt Nat. For., 44-a. tract framed by sloping walls of natural bowl. Many winding trls. with fireplaces at selected pts. **187. DRAKE,** resort village. **200. ESTES VILLAGE.** (For this sec. of tour to **GRANBY** at **263.,** see Denver Trip III.)

## US 24—COLORADO

**COLO.-KANS. LINE** (19$^m$ from Goodland, Kans.) **(W) to GRAND JUNCTION. 474. US24**

Via: Burlington, Limon, Colorado Springs, Buena Vista, Leadville, Dowd, Eagle, Glenwood Springs, Rifle & Grand Junction. Rock I. RR. parallels route bet. Burlington & Colo. Springs; Midland Terminal RR. bet. Colo. Springs & Divide; D. & R.G. RR. bet. Buena Vista & Grand Junction. Bus lines parallel route. Good accoms.

US24 crosses vast cattle-raising & dry farming area & descends to base of mts. at Colo. Springs. W. of this great vacation area, hy. skirts Pikes Peak & traverses rugged reg. of great natural beauty & old mining towns. Tour winds through 4 of Colo.'s nat. fors. before entering fertile Grand Valley in W. of St.

**12. BURLINGTON,** seat of Kit Carson Cty., occupies site of ancient Ind. camp grounds, now center of rich grain area. **89. LIMON. 162. COLORADO SPRINGS** (see). **168. MANITOU SPRINGS** (Ind. "great spirit") (all accoms.facils.camp. Info.: Colo. Springs C. of C.). Resort lying in forested foothills that swell upward toward Pikes Peak. Great springs here long known to Inds. who had discovered health-giving waters. According to legend, their god, Manitou, dwelt at bottom of these healing springs. There are 50 developed mineral springs. Three are claimed to be orig. Manitou Springs: **Navajo Spring** (free) in front of Navajo Hotel; **Soda Spring** (N.O.) at rear of Manitou Mineral Water Co. plant; **Manitou Spring** (free) at Manitou Bathh. Twenty of the 50 springs, which produce radioactive waters, are open to public. Cog Rd. runs from Manitou to summit of Pikes Peak (fee).

SIDE TRIP: (R) from Canon Ave. into rugged Williams Canyon to **The Narrows** 1m where rugged cliff walls almost overhang hy. At 2m **Cave of the Winds** (fee), unusual geological phenomenon, its miles of passageways containing 17 compartments, hollowed out of W. limestone wall of Williams Canyon by underground waters, is a labyrinth of stalactites, stalagmites, crystal, calcite & flowering alabaster formations. Indirect lighting enhances beauty. Cave of the Winds Rd. cont. along Serpentine Dr. (R) to J. with US24, 4.5m at W. edge of Manitou Springs.

(W) of Manitou Springs US24 ascends by easy stages, crossing E. boundary of **PIKE NAT. FOR. 170.;** one of largest for. preserves in St., with c.1½ million as. **Rainbow Falls,** spanned by concrete bridge in for. of dense pine, just beyond for. entrance. **172. CASCADE.** J. with St.250 to **Pikes Peak** (L) 19m. (Inquire before proceeding to summit.)

SIDE TRIP: 8m **Half-way Campground** (camp.pic.facils.), 1st clear view of summit of Pikes Peak. 11.5m **Glen Cove** (rest home.food), where many visitors have photos taken in front of sign "Glen Cove, 11,300 alt." & receive prints on return from summit. **Log cabin** (O), owned by Pikes Peak Ski Club, is furnished with stoves, chairs. [0.5m (R) to Pikes Peak Ski Club Course (free).] From Glen Cove, hy. rises sharply to reach **Timberline** (11,400′) at 12.3m. Hy. ascends by series of switchbacks. (L) 14.8m **Bottomless Pit,** vast chasm c.1,000′ deep. From parking space giant pines in pit appear as matchsticks. 15.5m **Boulder Field;** red granite boulders strewn over summit of mt. **Hairpin Turn** 16.5m, impressive view of old gold mining dist. of Cripple Cr. 18m **Summit H.,** erected in 1882 as observ. tower for U.S. Signal Corps, surmounted by 25′ tower (sm.fee for use of telescope). **Pikes Peak** (14,110′), discovered in 1806 by Lt. Z. M. Pike, is most noted of Colorado's mts., principally because isolated from higher ranges & affords grand view. Peak early made accessible by Manitou & Pikes Peak RR., better known as Cog Rd.; 1st train of tilted cars reached summit in 1891. Auto races to summit, Labor Day, attended by thousands who line upper reaches to see stock cars in grueling grind.

**181. WOODLAND PK.** J. with St.67 (R) to f. area. **188. DIVIDE.** J. with St.67 (L) to old Cripple Cr. mining dist. Route crosses boundary of **PIKE NAT. FOR., 197.,** (h.f.camp.). **200. L. GEORGE.** J. with St.77 (L) on dirt Rd. 11m to **Eleven Mile Reservoir** (pic.f.). **227. HARTSEL,** resort near number of hot springs. **239.** J. with US285 (R) which unites with US24 for 13m. **254. BUENA VISTA** (h.f.swim.), center of mining country. Founded 1879 in valley formed by Ark. R. at foot of Collegiate Peaks. **Site of Colo. St. Reformatory.**

**289. LEADVILLE** (f. Info.: C. of C.), seat of Lake Cty., center of greatest mining dist. in world, in heart of Rockies. First a fabulous gold camp, then one of richest of silver camps, again a gold camp; has also mined great quantities of lead, zinc & manganese; gold & silver still mined. Town is c.2m above sea level (10,152′). **312.5. HOMESTAKE CAMPGROUND,** maintained by For. Serv. **313. MARKER** pointing to Mount of the Holy Cross. **323. MINTURN.** J. with For. Serv. Rd.

SIDE TRIP: (L) on this Rd. to **Mount of the Holy Cross Nat. Mon.** (13,996′). 9m **Camp Tigiwon.** From here trl. several miles long leads up **Notch Mt.** to an excellent view of Cross, which is 1,500′ in length; arms extend 750′ on either side. In spring, ravines forming Cross are filled with snowdrifts 50′ to 80′ deep.

**329. MT. EXPERIMENT STA.,** est. 1924 by Colo. A. & M. College. Here crops are grown to demonstrate efficient methods of farming at high alts. & to discover other crops that might be grown in such regs. **325. DOWD.** US6 here unites with US24 to Grand Junction. **351. EAGLE,** center of agric. & ranching district; hay & potatoes, principal crops. **358. GYPSUM.** Here rise high limestone cliffs for which community was named. Dirt Rd. leading (R) 8m to **Sweetwater L. Country** (camp. accoms.h.f.). **364. DOTSERO.** J. of Royal Gorge & Moffat Tunnel routes of D. & R.G. RR. At **370.,** route crosses E. boundary of **WHITE RIVER NAT. FOR.,** 1st nat. reserve in Colo. (1891) & 2nd in U.S. Recently White R. & Holy Cross Nat. Fors. were combined as White R., with 2 million as.

**372. HANGING L. PK.** (food.accoms.burros).

SIDE TRIP: (R) from pk. on trl. 1m to **Hanging L.,** where spring has formed its own natural cup in face of cliff. Spring pours directly from underground channel through hole in cliff & plunges downward into basin 500′ wide. Mineral content of extremely blue water is such that plant life touching it becomes petrified.

**382. GLENWOOD SPRINGS** (h.f.resort), at W. end of Glenwood Canyon; outfitting pt. for sportsmen. Also large ranching area. Community built around numerous hot mineral springs flowing from limestone formations. Town, orig. known as Defiance for a near-by fort, was laid out in 1883, later named for Glenwood, Iowa, birthpl. of one of its founders. An Eng. syndicate, interested in reg. as health resort, built the open-air swim. pool & bathh. in 1891. The 600′ swim. pool (O.fee) on N. edge of town is fed by hot & cold sulphur springs & used yr. around; the thermal springs, most copious in St., flow 3,000 gals. a minute. Adj. are several vapor caves (adm.). J. with St.82.

SIDE TRIP: (S) on St.82, many sharp turns bet. Independence Pass beyond Aspen & Twin Lakes. Pass closed to winter travel. Accoms.: Limited. 24m **Basalt** (f.h.), at J. of Frying Pan & Roaring Fork Rs. Important agric. center & rendezvous of sportsmen. 42m **Aspen** (f.h.winter sports.camp.accoms.facils.Info.:C. of C.). Borders White R. Nat. For. Founded by men who reached Leadville too late to stake claims. Soon rivaled older silver camps. Center of renowned ski area, with slopes terminating at edge of town. World's longest chair lift, in 2 secs., length 14,000′ (ski tows.ski school). **Roch Run,** on Monarch St., E. edge of town, spectacular 4m ski course, regarded as one of most spectacular & difficult in world. Aspen Ski Club & Rocky Mt. Ski Assoc. Slalom races in Jan. 61m, summit of **Independence Pass** (12,095′), highest & probably most impressive auto pass in St. **Stone Mon.** (L) & sm. lakes at summit. 76m **Twin Lakes** (camp.f.h.horses & burros avail.), popular resort. Ls. & streams offer splendid Mackinaw trout. In fall, good duck h. in season. At 82m is south J. with US24.

**409. RIFLE.** J. with St.13 (see US40). Center of sparsely-settled cattle-raising area. **U.S. Bureau of Mines Experimental Oil-Shale Development** (O.wks.no priv.cars; buses run by gov.guides.9 a.m.& 1 p.m.); formerly as "top secret" as atomic fission plants, unique mine & all phases to final production of synthetic oil may be seen. Tour, from Adm. Bldg., winds up 10,000′ cliff offering views of distant Aspen, Grand Mesa & Holy Cross Mt. Hy. parallels Colo. R., its banks fringed with cottonwoods & willows. **474. GRAND JUNCTION** (see).

## US 40—COLORADO

**COLO.-KANS. LINE** (16m from Sharon Springs, Kans.) **(W) to COLO.-UTAH LINE** (31m from Vernal, Utah). **495. US40**

Via: Cheyenne Wells, Limon, Denver, Idaho Springs, Berthoud Pass, Hot Sulphur Springs, Steamboat Springs & Craig. Route paralleled bet. Kans. Line & Denver by U.P. RR.; bet. Denver & Empire by C. & S. RR.; bet. W. Portal & Craig by Moffat RR. Passes kept open throughout yr. Bus lines parallels route. Good accoms.

US40, one of great transcontinental hys., traverses dry E. plains, ascends to uplands along foothills & penetrates mts. to reach vast NW. plateaus, crossing Continental Divide 3 times en route. **17. CHEYENNE WELLS,** farming town, in 1860's was sta. on Butterfield Overland Dispatch. **42. KIT CARSON,** named for western scout & began existence as trading sta. & military post in 1860. During construction of K.P. RR., settlement was busy outfitting pt. for traders whose wagon trains plodded on toward mt. pts. Skirmishes with Inds. were frequent. Burned to ground, town later rebuilt here, few miles (N) of orig. site. (Bet. here & Denver, US287 is united with US40.)

**88. HUGO,** supply town for surrounding farms, est. as trading post in 1880. **104. LIMON. 154. STRASBURG. 191. DENVER** (see). W. of Denver US40 & US6 are united for 41m, route proceeding through suburban dist. toward rolling foothills that obscure higher peaks beyond. **224. IDAHO SPRINGS** (accoms.facils.hqs.Arapahoe Nat. For. Info.: C. of C.), mining & resort town & gateway to mt. playground, is strung along narrow canyon. Before 1860, known as Sacramento City, Jackson Diggings, Idahoe, & finally Idaho Springs. City named for hot radioactive mineral springs. 5m **Argo Tunnel,** longest mining tunnel in world, is here, running from its mouth on S. Fork of Clear Cr. through mt. to Gregory Gulch where Central City is located. **Hot Springs** (bath.vapor baths.fee). J. with St.279.

SIDE TRIPS: (A) On St.279 (R) 7m to **Central City,** once known as "richest square mile on earth." Is on site of one of 1st gold discoveries in Colo., 1859, & Hs. cling precariously to steep slopes of gulch. **Old Opera H.** (rest.), Eureka St. (W) of Main St., erected after fire of 1874 had destroyed town's ramshackle playhouses. Four years later this stone building with its 4′ walls was complete. Many stars appeared here. Central City Opera & Play Festival held here 7 weeks in July & Aug. Town's history relived in Festival. Stars appear in operas & plays.

(B) On St.103 (L) 14m to **Echo L.** & at 28m Summit of **Mt. Evans** (14,260′) (inquire at Idaho Springs before proceeding in winter). Echo L. set in natural pk. Numerous trls. lead to surrounding slopes; at lower end of L. (pic.camp.). In series of hairpin turns, Rd. winds upward to summit of Mt. Evans, highest auto Rd. in U.S. On crest of Mt. Evans is **Cosmic**

**Ray Lab.,** of Univ. of Denver, highest lab. in world, built in 1936 for scientific study of cosmic ray, meteorological observation & experiments in biochemistry.

At **234.** US40 crosses E. boundary of **ARAPAHOE NAT. FOR.** (hqs.Idaho Springs, pic.camp.facils.accoms.). For. contains million as. & offers varied attractions to vacationists. Named for Plains Ind. tribe. **247. BERTHOUD PASS** (11,315') (camp. pic.), named for E. L. Berthoud, engineer who ran 1st survey over pass (1861). Now chief center for winter sports. Thousands use 2 ski runs & 800' ski tow maintained by For. Serv. Ski Meet in Feb. Descending pass, US40 crosses under tracks of Moffat RR., as they emerge from W. portal of Moffat Tunnel, driven under N. shoulder of James Peak for $6^m$, the 2nd longest RR. tunnel in U.S. Giant bore is realization of dreams of David H. Moffat, who began in 1902 to build RR. from Denver (W) through mts. Moffat Tunnel completed in 1927; cost 18 million dollars. **279. GRANBY.** J. with US34 (see) to Rocky Mt. Nat. Park (inquire at Granby or Grand Lake before entering pk. during winter). **289. HOT SULPHUR SPRINGS** (accoms. facils. Info.: C. of C.), resort with 12 hot radioactive springs at mouth of Byers Canyon. According to Ute legend, springs acquired medicinal properties in answer to prayers of old chief who had been left by his tribe to die. Chief built magic fires within springs & after drinking waters & bathing in them, was restored to health & rejoined his people. **Bathh. & Plunge** (fee) at N. edge of town. **305. KREMMLING,** market center of W. part of Middle Pk. & rich valleys of Troublesome & Muddy Crs. **332. MUDDY PASS** marks E. boundary of **Routt Nat. For.,** which occupies both slopes on Continental Divide, crossed here. For. contains over million as.; half lodgepole pine. At **336.,** hy. crosses **RABBIT EARS PASS** (9,680'), named for peculiar formation (R) at top of Rabbit Ears Peak (10,719'). (**Valley View Ski Run** is probably most popular run of area. Route from US40, $0.5^m$ W. of Rabbit Ears Pass Sta., is $3.5^m$ long & returns to US40 at Valley View Lodge.) Hy. descends into Yampa Valley, at **250.** crossing W. boundary of **ROUTT NAT. FOR.**

**360. STEAMBOAT SPRINGS** (accoms.f.camp.ski.recr.facils.). Hqs. Routt Nat. For. Info.: C. of C. Center of popular yr.-round recr. area. Within & adj. to town are 150 medicinal springs with combined flow of 2,000 gals. per minute, their temp. varying from 58° to 152°. Majority are public. Spring from which town was named, a fountain which emitted a chugging sound suggestive of river boat, was destroyed during construction of Moffat Rd. Steamboat Springs, in Routt Nat. For., is area of magnificent scenery, recr. areas, trout fish., hunt. & skiing. Ski Tourney on flood-lighted ski course at Howelsen Hill (S) of town, in Feb. **362.** J. with St.129 (R).

SIDE TRIP: (R) on St.129 through forested hill country, to **Hahns Peak Country,** $25^m$, one of best h. & f. areas in St. Deer, elk, sage hens are numerous; streams & Ls. well stocked with mt. & rainbow trout.

**386. HAYDEN,** shipping pt. for sheep grazed in Routt Nat. For. **403. CRAIG,** center of largest oil-producing area in St., also largest shipping pt. as terminus of Moffat RR. Large industrial, dry farming & stock-raising area. J. with St.13.

SIDE TRIPS: (A) $38^m$ (N) on St.13 to **Colo.-Wyo. Line** ($86^m$ from Green R., Wyo.) through country of large ranches, parallel to old wagon trl. to Laramie, Wyo.

(B) (S) on St.13 to $49^m$ **Meeker** (h.f.Info.: C. of C.), rich agric. & ranching area of White R. Valley; named for Nathan C. Meeker, Ind. agent, killed in Ute uprising at White R. Agency in 1879. In **Meeker Hotel,** Theo. Roosevelt's hqs. on 1 of his hunting trips, are specimens of animal life in White R. reg. $52^m$ **J.** with St.64, leading to **Meeker Mon.,** an uncut pink granite slab, marking approx. site of old White R. Agency & scene of Meeker massacre. $86^m$ J. with St.325.

(L) $15^m$ on St.325 to **Rifle Mountain Pk.** (camp.pic.f.). On beautiful stream & in box canyon here are **Glen Rulac Falls,** 2 cascades on E. Rifle Cr., the upper falls having drop of 150'; lower falls operate hydroelectric plant. Mineral springs here contain varying amounts of carbonate & sulphate of lime.

$90^m$ **Rifle** (see US24).

**434. MAYBELL.** J. with St.318.

SIDE TRIP: On St.318 (R) $7^m$ to **Sunbeam.** (Inquire Rd. conditions here before proceeding.) $52^m$ **Dinosaur Nat. Mon.** incl. 177,280 as. in Colo. & 26,605 in Utah. Only partly explored; rich fossil beds throughout Mon. are of great scientific int. $53^m$ **Lodore Canyon Camp** (limited summer accoms.boat.guides) situated near spring on E. side of Green R. at mouth of Lodore Canyon. $3^m$ boat trip to **Disaster Falls** & other scenic pts. through wild & impressive canyon.

**495.** US40 crosses **COLO.-UTAH LINE.**

# US 50—COLORADO

**COLO.-KANS. LINE** ($69^m$ from Garden City, Kans.) **(W) to COLO.-UTAH LINE** ($45^m$ from Thompsons, Utah). **478. US50**

Via: Holly, Lamar, La Junta, Pueblo, Canon City, Salida, Monarch Pass, Gunnison, Montrose, Delta, Grand Junction & Fruita. Santa Fe RR. parallels route between Garden City & Pueblo; D. & R.G. RR. between Pueblo & Utah Line. Bus lines parallel route. Good accoms.

US50 follows Ark. R. into irrigated valley lands, from plains into mts., ascends through wild & beautiful country to top of Continental Divide, descends into valley of Gunnison, famed trout stream, which it follows into high plateau country in W. part of St. Mons. along hy. in E. sec. marks part of old Santa Fe Trl.

**4. HOLLY,** lowest point in Colo. (3,385′), center of agric., stock-raising & feeding area. Earliest reservoir system in valley constructed here in 1890. **Santa Fe Trl. Marker** (L) in front of Santa Fe depot. **10.** Hy. crosses **ARK. R.,** greatest western affluent of Mo.-Miss. Rs. system. Named for Ark. Inds. who once lived along its lower reaches. **32. LAMAR,** named for L. Q. C. Lamar, Secy. of Interior under Pres. Cleveland. At Main St. & Santa Fe tracks (R), near RR. sta. is **Madonna of Trail Mon.,** dedicated to pioneer mothers of covered wagon days. **53. HASTY. J.** with surfaced Rd.

SIDE TRIP: (L) on this Rd. $2^m$ to **John Martin Reservoir** (boat.f.); impounded waters of Ark. R. This 17 million dollar project is flood control & water storage for irrigation.

**64.** J. with surfaced Rd.

SIDE TRIP: (L) on this Rd. $1.7^m$ to **Fort Lyon,** on site of historic old ft., formerly U.S. army post; later Naval tubercular hospital; now **Veterans Adm. Facility** (O). Landscaped grounds cover over 1,000 as. Brick hospital bldgs. have over 1,000 beds for treatment of psychopathic patients. In reserv. is **Kit Carson Mus.,** housed in cabin where noted scout died in 1868.

**70. LAS ANIMAS** lies in heart of fertile, irrigated Ark. R. valley. Is principal shipping pt.; named for Las Animas (or Purgatoire) R. which flows into the Ark. near-by. **89. LA JUNTA** (Sp. "junction"), orig. named Otero for Miguel Otero, Spanish settler. Today is important RR. center. City has brick & tile plant, flour mill & creameries. **Fort Bend Mus.** (O), in Court House Pk., exhibits fossils & relics of early days in Ark. Valley. **99. ROCKY FORD,** named for stony bed of Ark. R. here, which provided safe ford for freighting trains. Town noted for its melons, especially famed Rocky Ford cantaloupes. Melon Day celebrated during Ark. Valley Fair in Sept. **Amer. Crystal Sugar Beet Factory** (O.wks.) & **Canning Factory** (O.wks.). US50 crosses **ST. CHARLES R.** at **144.,** sm. tributary of Ark. R. **153. PUEBLO** (see US85). **193. CANON CITY,** divided into 3 municipalities at mouth of Grand Canyon of Ark. R., is noted for large beds of fine fire clay in area, used in manufacture of refractory tile, brick & flue lining. Marble quarries here & beautiful terrazza flooring made here. Other non-metallics mined in area. Once campground of Ute, town flourished with influx of gold-seekers in 1859-60. Joaquin Miller, poet, served as judge here. In 1868 choice between St. penitentiary & univ. resulted in favor of former. Apple Blossom Week in May. **Municipal Mus.** (O.wks.2-4 Sun.), 6th & River Sts. Archaeological & wildlife specimens & other exhibits. **Colo. St. Penitentiary,** on W. outskirts of city (O.9-11;1-4). **249. SALIDA** (Sp. "gateway"), on Ark. R. Founded by D. & R.G. RR. in 1880. Town's growth followed closely the extension of RR. to West. Is division pt. of main line & narrow gauge lines over Marshall Pass. Mining, agric. & cattle-raising in area. At S. end of I St., **Salida Hot Springs Pool & Bath** (O.exc.Mon.) with large indoor pool, sitz baths, cottages. In town is J. with St.291.

SIDE TRIP: $1^m$ W. on St.291 to **Frantzhurst Rocky Mt. Rainbow Trout Farm,** largest commercial trout farm in world.

**255. PONCHA SPRINGS,** built along mt. slope from which bubble mineral springs, water varying from 90° to 185°, & containing salts similar to those at Hot Springs, Ark. W. of town, route leaves valley & ascends Continental Divide through heavily timbered country, crossing at **260.** E. boundary of **COCHETOPA NAT. FOR.** (h.f. camp.pic.trlr.facils.ski). For. hqs. in Salida. This for. contains highest sec. of Rockies, highest elevation being **Mt. Elbert** (14,431′); many peaks 10,000′ to 14,000′. For. contains over million as. Engelmann spruce & lodgepole pine most important species of trees. **269. MONARCH,** at head of Monarch Pass. Early-day placer mining camp.

**271. NEW MONARCH PASS** (11,312';skiing); on crest of Continental Divide. From top of pass, one of highest in Rockies crossed by auto hy., is visible rough outline of Sangre de Cristo Range (L). Twelve peaks seen from this pt. exceed 14,000'; more than score rise above 13,000'. By series of switchbacks, Rd. descends W. slope into heavily timbered country. **314. GUNNISON.** Hqs. Gunnison Nat. For. Info.: C. of C. One of St.'s best recr. areas. Within easy driving range of town are more than 750m of trout streams. **Western St. College**, founded 1909, has **Archaeological Mus.** (O.wks.) in Central Hall, maintained by Southwestern Archaeological Society; contains exhibits of Cliff Dwellers & Basket Maker cultures, as well as Pueblo & Plains Ind. relics. In town is **La Veta Hotel,** one of oldest on Western Slope; 4-story bldg. in ornate eclectic design fashionable in late 1880's; built in 1884. **325.** J. with St.149.

SIDE TRIP: (S) on latter 1m to **Iola.** 16.4m is J. with dirt Rd. (L) here 1.5m to **Powderhorn,** trading center; medicinal **Cebolla Hot Springs & Carbonate Springs.** 46m on St.149 **Lake City,** one of 1st W. Colo. settlements, formerly shipping pt. for gold & silver ore from near-by mines. 48m J. with unimproved Rd. (L) on latter 1.5m to **L. San Cristobal** (h.f. cabins.inn), favored sportsmen's rendezvous; L. covers 3 sq. miles, has many sm. wooded islands. 54m **Gunnison Nat. For.;** 55m **Slumgullion Pass** (11,000'). 66m **Continental Divide** crossed at Spring Cr. Pass (10,901'), boundary bet. Gunnison & Rio Grande Nat. Fors. 72.5m **South Fork Cr.** (R) off hy. are **South Falls** (camp.rainbow trout), c.100' high, has 3 separate drops with numerous churning pools. (S) of falls is lofty forested mesa; resorts & dude ranches at intervals (exceptionally good h.& f.). 100m **Creede,** semi-ghost town. 109m **Wagon Wheel Gap,** wealthy resort town; mineral springs. Many camps and resorts in this reg. 120m hy. crosses boundary of **Rio Grande Nat. For.** & descends narrow canyon bet. evergreen-covered hills. 122m J. with US160, 1m S. of South Fork.

Tour cont. (SW) on US50. **340. SAPINERO** (f.), resort town beyond Blue Cr. Canyon. **363. CERRO SUMMIT,** overlooking Uncompahgre Valley, 40m long & 12m wide. **369.** J. with dirt Rd.

SIDE TRIP: (R) 7m to Black Canyon of **Gunnison Nat. Mon.** Markers set along Rd. at pts. where dark cavernous depths can be seen to advantage. Route follows canyon edge, covering 10m of most picturesque portion of 50m gorge, deepest in Colo. In places it narrows to 10'; walls rise 3,000' at highest pt. Wildest & most rugged sec. of canyon near center of Mon. (camp.pic.water). Towers, pinnacles, spires, fantastic rock forms create magnificent scene.

**381. MONTROSE,** trading center of irrigation agric. & stockraising area in heart of Uncompahgre Valley. **Buckley Pk.** (sports facils.). **Lion's Pk.** (pic.). In town is J. with US550

SIDE TRIP: (S) 3m on US550 is **Ouray-Chipeta Pk.,** honoring Chief Ouray, peacemaker, & his wife, Chipeta, who is buried here. 26m **Ridgway,** J. with St.62, a narrow surfaced Rd. with many sharp twists & steep grades; dangerous in wet weather; heavy snowfall. Lizard Head Pass closed in winter; inquire before proceeding. (Accoms.: Good at Telluride & Dolores.)

(W) on St.62 to **Leonard,** base for sportsmen; vic. is habitat of deer, elk & mountain lion. Rd. descends into valley of San Miguel R. (good fly f.). 23m **Placerville,** J. with St.145 on which this trip cont. 32m N. boundary of **Montezuma Nat. For.** At 36m J. with St.108. [3m (L) on St.108 to **Telluride,** mining camp in cup of gray granite mts. Living in past, perhaps more than any other Colo. town, Telluride was once great mining center; produced more than 60 million dollars in precious metals by 1909.] Cont. (S) on St.145. Hy. winds through yellow pine & Engelmann spruce into San Miguel Mts. 44m **Ophir Sta.;** below hy., half-way down mt. is **Ophir Loop,** remarkable engineering feat in construction of R.G.Southern RR. In order to route RR. past Ophir Sta. & eliminate excessive grades, tracks were laid in shape of great horseshoe, a sec. of which is supported on high wooden trestles; rails almost overlap themselves. 47m **Trout L.** (boat.f.camp.). 50m **Lizard Head Pass** on crest of San Miguel Mts. Top of pass is RR. covered for one-fourth mile by frame shed to prevent snow from blocking tracks. 62m **Rico,** string of false-front frame bldgs. along rutted st., one of last outposts of old West. S. of Rico, route follows old Ute Trl. along banks of Dolores R., flanked by low hills heavily wooded with aspen. 100m **Dolores,** in heart of rich grazing dist. 111m J. with US160 (see).

Side Trip cont. on US550. 36m **Radium Springs Pk.** (camp.swim.). Hy. cont. (S) through steep, twisting Uncompahgre Canyon. This stretch of hy. is known as Million Dollar Hy. because surfacing is of gold-bearing gravel whose value was not known until after completion of Rd. 49m **Red Mt. Pass** (11,018'), boundary bet. Uncompahgre & **San Juan Nat. For.,** largest of 14 national fors. in St. 59m **Silverton** (9,302';h.f.camp.recr.facils.summer resort), center of mining dist., frequently isolated for weeks during winter; sportsmen's hqs.

Rd. follows S. Fork of Las Animas R. which flows through 2,000′ deep gorge; many game animals in this reg. 65m **Molas L.** (f.). 83m **Columbine L.** (camp.), in beautiful pine groves. 98m **Pinkerton Springs** (accoms.facils.swim.summer resort). 111m **St. Fish Hatchery** (O.wks.). 112m **Durango.** J. with US160 (see). US550 crosses Florida R. at 128m & N.M. Line at 132m.

Main tour cont. on US50. **403. DELTA,** chief town in one of St.'s largest fruit-growing areas. **City Pk.** (swim.sports facils.). **Holly Corp. Beet Sugar Factory** (O. wks.). In Delta is J. with St.65 (Skyway Dr.).

SIDE TRIP: (R) on Skyway Dr. to **Grand Mesa Nat. For.** & **Mesa Lakes** (h.f.pic.camp. accoms.), winter sports area. Motorists may return to US50 via Lands End Scenic Hy.

**434. WHITEWATER.** (Land's End Hy. passes Grand Mesa (accoms.O.all winter), favorite winter sports area.)

**444. GRAND JUNCTION** (Hqs. Grand Mesa Nat. For. Airport through conns. Info.: C. of C.), in fertile Grande Valley at J. of Colo. & Gunnison Rs., also focal pt. at which 3 major lines of D. & R.G. RR. system converge. Largest town in St. W. of Continental Divide; chief trade & wholesaling center of large area. This reg. little known to white men until latter part of 19th cent. In 1881, townsite est. here & settlement of valley was rapid. **Lincoln Pk.,** 12th St. & Gunnison Ave. (sports facils. swim.pic.golf.zoo). 5th St. & Rood Ave., **Mesa St. Jr. College** (est.1925). J. with St.340.

SIDE TRIP: (L) from Grand Junction on St.340 to Rimrock Dr. 1m. (R) on Rimrock Dr. around Colo. Nat. Mon. 25m (conn. at Fruita on US50). **Colo Nat. Mon.** contains more than 18,000 as. of fantastically eroded highlands, sheer-walled canyons & towering monoliths, stratified ramparts & fluted columns, spectacle of imposing grandeur. Most impressive specimens of erosion found in Amer. Numerous caves & passageways honeycomb reg. Great walls & amphitheaters, petrified wood, dinosaur remains found in many places. Rimrock Dr., constructed by Nat. Pk. Serv., outstanding scenic trip over which visitors may view constantly changing panorama.

**458. FRUITA.** J. with St.340 (3m to Colo. Nat. Mon.) Trading center of lower Grand Valley irrigated area, raising sugar beets. Mesa Cty. Fair & Cowpunchers Reunion, Sept. US50 crosses **COLO.-UTAH LINE** at **478.**

# US 160—COLORADO

**WALSENBURG (W) to COLO.-UTAH LINE** (10m from Monticello, Utah). **316. US160**

Via: Alamosa, Del Norte, Pagosa Springs, Durango, Mesa Verde Nat. Park, Cortez & Dove Creek.

US160 crosses Sangre de Cristo Range & San Luis Valley, largest of 4 great mt. pks. in Colo. From Alamosa, route crosses agric. belt in mt. country, descending into reg. of plateaus broken by mesas & canyons, & reg. of prehist. cultures.

**0. WALSENBURG** (see US85). **20. OJO HOT SPRINGS** (accoms.facils.), beyond which hy. ascends by twists & loops. **28. LA VETA PASS,** low, heavily-timbered saddle between Sangre de Cristo & Culebra Ranges. Hy. descends through foothills into San Luis Valley, level prairie 125m long. (W) of La Veta Pass, route crosses sec. of 240,000-a. Trinchera Ranch, largest private estate in Colo. **49. FORT GARLAND,** named for Brig. Gen. John Garland. Ft. was built here in 1858 & maintained until 1883. Old Ft. Garland, on S. edge of town, series of long, low adobe bldgs. about central plaza. In **Central Hall** have been preserved journals in which comdrs., including Kit Carson, kept their records. Many early relics also on display here. J. with St.159.

SIDE TRIP: (L) from Ft. Garland on St.159 16m to **San Luis,** Sp.-Amer. & one of oldest communities in St. Stone **Ch. of Most Precious Blood,** erected in early 1860's, still stands. Chimayo weaving done here. **San Luis Institute of Arts & Crafts,** acquired by Adams St. College (Alamosa) in 1943. In center of San Luis the ground is part of old Sangre de Cristo grant from Mexican gov. & was set aside for public purposes. Bldg. of Sp. style contains auditorium & stage. Two yr. college program; also 4-yr. vocational program.

**74. ALAMOSA** (Info.: C. of C.; h.f.),shipping center; largest & most important town in San Luis Valley; hqs. for many potato brokerage concerns. Floor of valley is occupied by grain, vegetable farms & extensive grazing. **Adams St. College,** on W. edge of town, founded 1925, is 1 of 6 St. institutions of higher learning in Colo.

Campus is in 3 plots of over 60 as., with several bldgs. Mus. contains archaeological & hist. colls. Feature of every summer term is annual **"Top of the Nation" Coaching School,** featuring nation's top coaches in various sports. J. with St.17.

SIDE TRIP: (N) on St.17 to J. with St.150 at **Mosca** c.12m. (R) at J. on St.150 11m to **Great Sand Dunes Nat. Mon.** (camp.facils.), 80 sq. mile tract of highest-piled expanse of inland sand dunes in U.S., rising more than 1,500′ at base of snow-capped peaks of Sangre de Cristo Mts.

**90.** J. with oiled Rd.

SIDE TRIP: (R) on this Rd. 1.5m to **Colo. St. Soldiers & Sailors Home** (O). Red-roofed, white-tiled bldgs. house hospital & living quarters.

**91. MONTE VISTA** (h.f.camp.facils. Hqs. Rio Grande Nat. For., info.: Commercial Club), in heart of fertile agric. dist. Large potato-growing area & vegetable shipping pt. Once known as Lariat, then Henry, finally Monte Vista. **Ski-Hi Stampede,** 3-day rodeo in July. **104. DEL NORTE** (h.f.camp.facils.), founded 1860; early settlement built of stone & many business structures of that day still stand. **119. SOUTH FORK** is at confluence of Rio Grande & S. Fork Rs. At **120.** is J. with St.149.

SIDE TRIP: (R) 22m on St.149 to **Creede** (Inquire regarding Rd. conditions before proceeding.) (R) from Creede (proceed with guide.avail.here) on winding horseback trl. to **Wheeler Nat. Mon.,** named for George Wheeler, gov. surveyor. Its 300 as. incl. 60 of striking vari-colored sandstone formations. Monoliths carved by erosive forces stand in canyon, among them "The Temple," "The Cathedral," "Parade of Ghosts." Mon. is in Rio Grande Nat. For.

US160 crosses at **120.5.** (E) boundary of **RIO GRANDE NAT. FOR.** (camp.pic. h.f.in area), over 1 million as. of fed., st. & private land that almost entirely covers (E) slope of San Juan Mts. Hy. follows South Fork R. along canyon. Mts. are fine setting for yr.-round sports; slopes so smooth, construction of ski runs unnecessary. Route crosses Continental Divide through **WOLF CR. PASS, 139.,** climbing steep ascent. Pass marks boundary between Rio Grande & San Juan Nat. For. Descending sharply through Wolf Cr. Canyon, hy. follows San Juan R. (f.) to **147. WOLF CR. CAMPGROUND. 163. PAGOSA SPRINGS** (accoms.facils.f.in area. Info.: C. of C.), named for hot mineral spring, discovered in 1859 by U.S. Topographical Engineer Corps. Waters have av. temp. of 153°; heat many public & bus. bldgs. in town. Is favored recr. area with many fine trout streams in San Juan Nat. For. At **184.5.** hy. crosses Rio Piedra, clear stream believed named by Escalante expedition, 1776. In primitive area of San Juan Nat. For., Hy. winds up & down foothills that form divide between drainage basins of Rio Piedra & Los Pinos. Hills covered with rich stands of pine & aspen. **205. BAYFIELD,** in grove of cottonwoods & willows on Los Pinos R.; community resembles New England village. J. with St.284.

SIDE TRIP: (R) on St.284 to Vallecito Campgrounds & **Pine R. (Vallecito) Reservoir** 15m. Route from Bayfield parallels Los Pinos R. & crosses (W) boundary of San Juan Nat. For. Fine trout f. (Info.: Vallecito Ranger Sta.).

**226. DURANGO** (see US50). At **263.** is J. with Rd. (L).

SIDE TRIP: (L) on this Rd. 19m to **Mesa Verde Nat. Pk.** (auto permit $1. season May 15-Oct. 15. accoms.facils.camp.) Pk. contains 350 cliff dwellings, 400 mesa top pueblos, several Basket Maker pit dwellings. Motor trips, hikes, horseback trips offer close inspection of excavated cliff dwellings, mt. scenery, etc. Incl. over 50,000 as. of canyons & mesa lands. Mesa Verde (Sp. "green table"), so called because of its level top, offers 3 distinct pk. tours. (Info. Hqs.) Mesa Verde inhabited by Basket Makers about 700 A.D. Then Pueblo Inds. came & remained until about 1300 A.D., when drought struck area & abandonment began. **Spruce Tree H.,** one of most noted ruins, located in large cave across Spruce Tree Canyon from mus. H. is 216′ long; 89′ wide, with 122 rooms, of which 100 were dwellings. There were 8 kivas. Pop. of village was about 200. **Cliff Palace,** in Cliff Canyon, largest known cliff dwelling, in large cave over 300′ long, 100′ wide, with 200 dwelling rooms, 22 kivas. Pop. more than 400. **Balcony H.,** located in high cave in Soda Canyon, is very picturesque, with 20 rooms for dwelling, 2 kivas. Among best preserved ruins in pk. **Square Tower H.,** 138′ long, contained about 50 rooms, 8 kivas. **Fewkes Canyon Ruins** are 4 notable cliff dwellings, incl. **Fire Temple,** supposedly temple of fire cult. Many more outstanding ruins in pk. Also **Archaeological Mus.; Natural Hist. Mus.** (info. hqs.).

**273. CORTEZ,** trade center for sheep & cattle raisers. (Inquire at Cortez for info. concerning trips on US666 (L) to Yucca H. & Hovenweep Nat. Mons., outstanding archaeological sites). US160 crosses **COLO.-UTAH LINE** at **316.**

# US 85—COLORADO

**COLO.-WYO. LINE** (10$^{m}$ from Cheyenne, Wyo.) **(S) to COLO.-N.M. LINE** (7$^{m}$ from Raton, N.M.). **312. US85**

Via: Greeley, Brighton, Denver, Littleton, Castle Rock, Palmer Lake, Colorado Springs, Pueblo, Walsenburg & Trinidad. U.P. RR. parallels route between Wyo. Line & Denver; C. & S. RR. bet. Denver & Trinidad; Santa Fe RR. bet. Denver & Pueblo & bet. Trinidad & Raton, N.M.; D. & R.G. RR. bet. Denver & Pueblo. Bus lines parallel route. Good accoms.

US85 is most heavily traveled N. & S. hy. in Colo. & skirts Rockies entire distance, passing through most populous cities & traversing rich irrigated areas. (See US87, alt. route from Colo.-Wyo. Line to Denver.)

**30. AULT. 34. EATON,** in Cache la Poudre Valley, founded 1881 by Gov. B. H. Eaton who est. flour mill & grain elevator, still operating. Town's greatest development followed introduction of sugar beets. Diversified crops & livestock feeding in area. J. with St.5.

SIDE TRIP: (L) here 0.5$^{m}$ to **Great West. Beet Sugar Factory** (O). 7$^{m}$ **Galetown** (terminus of St.5. Rd. proceeds (E) to Cornish.) 16$^{m}$ **Cornish,** farming hamlet in Crow Cr. Valley. Here was homeland of prehist. people where arrowheads & artifacts have been uncovered & collected. First **Stone Age Fair,** held here in 1934; 25,000 artifacts of Yuma & Folsom man were displayed. Fair attracted 5,000 visitors; 20,000 attended in 1935, and again in 1936, when archaeologists throughout West contributed exhibits. Fair is annual event 1st week in Aug. Cornish coll. said to be one of largest of its kind in world.

**41. GREELEY** (Info.: C. of C.), center of rich agric. area, is outgrowth of Union Colony, cooperative enterprise conceived by & named for Horace Greeley, noted editor & publisher of N.Y. "Tribune"; was founded by his agric. editor, Nathan C. Meeker. Greeley, of "Go West, Young Man, Go West!" fame, visited reg. & was so impressed with possibilities an extensive campaign was conducted to create interest in est. colony in Colo. Territory. In 1870, 50 families, headed by Meeker, arrived here. Irrigation projects were begun; crops raised. With rapid development of irrigation, town grew rapidly & plants based on agric. were est., incl. beet sugar factory, vegetable canning plant, etc. Reg. noted for potato crops. Spud Rodeo, annually July 4th, is combination rodeo & agric. show. **Colo. St. College of Education** here closely parallels much of growth & development of Greeley Union Colony. Campus of 88 as. has 31 bldgs., incl. lib. with more than 125,000 vols. **Meeker Mus.** (1871.adds.), formerly home of Nathan C. Meeker; 4-room, 2-story bldg. of sod & adobe, with wooden framework. Mus. holds Meeker's furniture, saddles, trappings & papers; also plow that turned 1st sod in Union Colony & used in running furrows that marked out streets of town. **Lincoln Pk.** (sports facils.), landscaped square laid out during founding of city, centers around small artificial L. **Great West. Sugar Beet Factory** (O), town's largest industrial plant. (S) of Greeley hy. traverses valley of S. Platte, richest agric. sec. in E. Colo. Route crosses S. Platte R. **50. PECKHAM. 67. FORT LUPTON,** est. c.1872. Free lots were offered to home builders & 1 a. of ground to anyone putting up a business. Town is trading center for rich farm area. Beet sugar factory, vegetable cannery, condensed milk plant are main industrial enterprises. Tomato Day celebrated in Aug. **74. BRIGHTON,** one of largest sugar beet centers in St. First 4th of July celebration in Colo. held here when Maj. Stephen Long's expedition camped on site, 1820. **94. DENVER** (see). US85 proceeds S. via Santa Fe Dr. & is united with US87 to N.M. Line.

**102. LITTLETON** (accoms.facils.Info.: Civic & Commercial Assoc.), center of prosperous irrigated farm area, downstream from Denver. Is typical sm. town with advantages of rural life, yet is but 17 minutes from downtown Denver. **116. SEDALIA.** J. with St.67 (R), alt. gravel route to Colorado Springs via Jarre Canyon, Pine Creek, Snow Water Springs & Decker, summer resorts & recr. areas with accoms. facils.

**124. CASTLE ROCK,** named for high outcrop of salmon-colored stone (L) that served Inds., explorers & early settlers as landmark. Resembles medieval castle. Village is Gretna Green for Denver enamorati. (S) of **LARKSPUR, 135.,** route winds through pine-clad hills; approaches mts. (Area subject to sudden violent storms.) **143. PALMER LAKE,** built around spring-fed L. at top of divide. Was one of 1st resort towns in St. Many residents of larger cities still have summer Hs. here. When D. & R.G. RR. reached here (1872), town was known as Weisport, but in 1889 was renamed for General Wm. J. Palmer, builder of Rd. which did much to publicize resort. Annually, Sun. before Christmas, ancient ceremony of hunting & burning yule log is held here. **147. MONUMENT.**

**165. COLORADO SPRINGS.**

S. Sierra Madre Ave., between W. Pikes Peak Ave. & Antlers Pl., for S. bound D. & R.G. RR.; Santa Fe RR.; M.P. RR.; C. & S. RR.; Rock I. RR. Santa Fe Station, 509 E. Pikes Peak Ave., for all N. bound trains & for Midland Terminal RR. Bus Sta. at 113 E. Pikes Peak Ave. for Greyhound Lines. Union Bus Station, 2 East Pikes Peak Ave., for Cripple Cr., Victor & Colo. Springs Stage Co.; Denver-Colo. Springs-Pueblo Trailways; Rio Grande Trailways; Santa Fe Trailways. Airport: Through conns. All accoms. facils. Info.: C. of C.; A.A.A. Hqs. Pike Nat. For. All sports facils.ski.h.f.

Colorado Springs is resort city at foot of Pikes Peak. From early 1870's, city has been a summer playground & health resort. In little more than half cent. a dreary stretch of sagebrush & yucca has been transformed into garden spot of great beauty, enhanced by majestic grandeur of the forested foothills & lofty peaks in area. In summer, chartered cars, sightseeing buses & hundreds of touring cars roll in & out of city. The surrounding Mt. pks., Garden of the Gods, Cheyenne Canyon, Pikes Peak Dr. & many other scenic pts., are their goal. Flower festivals, rodeos, auto races, polo tourneys & other events are held during summer. On New Year's Eve, fireworks display is held on summit of Pikes Peak, site of Glen Cove, famed winter sports area. During 1st yrs. settlement was called Fountain Colony for its location on Fountain Cr.; later was renamed Colo. Springs for mineral springs at near-by village of Manitou. As fame of this resort city grew, pop. doubled & multiplied. Philanthropists contributed materially to its development; Pikes Peak Hy. was built; the Broadmoor Hotel arose at foot of Cheyenne Mt. The mt. pk. system, created in 1907, was increased when Garden of the Gods was bequeathed to city. Agric. development of E. Colo. made city trading & supply center, & together with mining & industries in area, coupled with great tourist traffic, Colo. Springs is one of St.'s most colorful playgrounds. City is seat of Colo. College & Colo. School for Deaf & Blind. PTS. OF INT.: (1) N. Nevada Ave., **Colo. College** (founded 1874.coed.privately endowed) has 50 brick & sandstone bldgs. on 50-a. campus blending into unified whole. Outstanding bldgs. incl: **Shrove Mem. Chapel** (O), limestone bldg. noted for Norman style. **Palmer Hall** (O.wks.Romanes.) contains Herbarium on 2nd fl. exhibiting 22,000 specimens, with coll. of 3,500 of flora from Pikes Peak reg. Mus. on 3rd fl. houses natural history coll. **Coburn Lib.** (O.wks.1894.2-story sandstone) contains fine coll. of Western hist. Oldest structure is **Cutler Hall** (1880). (2) 30 W. Dale St., **Fine Arts Center** (O.wks.Sun.aft.), opened 1936, is of plain concrete in mod. Sp.-Pueblo design; houses art sch., galleries, theater, mus., studios for resident & visiting artists. Is affiliated with Colo. College. (3) 25 W. Kiowa St., **Pioneers' Mus.** (O.wks.Sun.aft.) displays Western pioneer & Ind. relics, early Amer. pressed glass, New England coll. of antiques. (4) 26th & Cucharras Sts., **Colo. City Mus.** (O.early 1860's), orig. jail & firehouse; coll. of old guns, Ind. arms & relics of early Colo. (5) 1125 Glen Ave., **Van Briggle Art Pottery,** one of largest & most famous art potteries in U.S. Complete process shown, from clay to finished product. (6) **Mon. Valley Pk.** (160 as.sports facils.swim.pic.) extends along Monument Cr., largest convenient recr. area in city. Most extensive botanical gardens in St., presenting Colo. scenes in miniature. Bridle & foot trls. lead through secs. of pk.; adj. golf course. (7) S. Institute St., **Colo. School for Deaf & Blind** (O.wks.) was founded 1874 for deaf mutes, sch. for blind added in 1883. Courses from 1st grade through high sch.; also preparatory course for deaf mutes planning to enter college. (8) E. Colo. Ave., **Union Printers H.** (O), on 250-a. landscaped tract. Largest of 3 main bldgs., is imposing 5-story granite structure. First bldg. erected 1892. Home represents investment of 7 million dollars; cares for 400 men annually. Is maintained by Internat. Typographical Union as home & hospital for aged & sick members.

## TRIPS OUT OF COLORADO SPRINGS

### I. Broadmoor-Cheyenne Mt. Hy. to Zoo, Will Rogers Shrine & Lodge, 13m

Toll: adults $.50; children under 12, $.25, incl. admittance to Zoo, Shrine & Lodge. For Zoo only, when complete hy. trip is not taken, adm. to Zoo, $.25 per person. Cog Rd. operates during summer from Penrose Stadium, Broadmoor Hotel, to Cheyenne Mt. Zoo only, round trip, $.25 per person.

(S) on US85 to **Broadmoor Hotel,** c.2$^m$, built by late Spencer Penrose, Colo. Springs capitalist, & associates, opened 1918. Stucco brick & stone structure of Ital. Ren. design; has 2 4-story wings, which flank 8-story central sec. & tower. Elaborately landscaped grounds contain formal sunken gardens & terraces about a L. & numerous sport. facils. Around Hotel grounds & golf course (R) or (L) to entrance arch, 4$^m$. 6$^m$ **Zoo.** More than 300 species of wild animals from all over world, America's finest privately supported zoo. 9$^m$ **Will Rogers Shrine of the Sun.** Half way up Hy. (8,000′) stands memorial of dignified beauty. Floodlighted at night, gleaming in sun by day, it is a landmark of Pikes Peak reg. Perpetually lighted shrine dedicated to memory of humorist & philosopher. Shrine built to last as long as Mt. itself; from one huge pink granite boulder imbedded on slope of Mt. was taken 5,000 cubic yards of material to form the walls, banded together by immense steel beams. Chimes installed in tower. In shrine is pictorial record of Will Rogers' life. 13$^m$ **Cheyenne Lodge** (accoms.meals), on summit of Mt. (9,300′); terminal of Broadmoor-Cheyenne Mt. Hy. Architecture of Lodge is SW. Ind. style. Lodge offers commanding views in all directions.

**II. Colo. Springs to Summit of Pikes Peak, 32$^m$**

(W) on US24 to 9$^m$ **Manitou Springs.** 12$^m$ **Cascade** (see US24) where is J. with Pikes Peak Hy. (St.250) to **Summit** at 32$^m$.

**III. Rampart Range Rd. Loop Tour, 103$^m$**

For one of most gorgeous scenic routes in entire Pikes Peak reg., W. on US24 (Ridge Rd.) from Colo. Ave. to **Garden of the Gods** at c.5$^m$. 770-a. hilly area studded with variety of grotesque rock masses of red sandstone, with a few upthrusts of gypsum; has several pinnacled & grottoed ridges of impressive size, an area of great scenic beauty. Near-by is J. with Rampart Ridge Rd. Superb hy. climbs through heart of Front or Rampart Range of Rockies. 31$^m$ **Devil's Head** (pic.camp.facils.) On Rampart Range Rd. For. Serv. fire lookout sta. on top of Devil's Head Mt. offers easy but thrilling climb. 41$^m$ J. with St.67. (L) on St.67 to **Deckers** 57$^m$, at J. with St.126. (cabins.summer resort). (L) on St.67 to **West Cr.** 66$^m$. **Woodland Park** 82$^m$, at J. with US24. Pikes Peak (S); Front Range (E). (L) on US24 to **Green Mt. Falls** 87$^m$ (sports facils.boat.swim.riding.golf). Named for series of cascades (R). 91$^m$ **Cascade** (accoms.resort). 96$^m$ **Manitou Springs** (see US24). 103$^m$ **Colorado Springs.**

**IV. Colo. Springs to Seven Falls (South Cheyenne Canyon) 6$^m$**

(S) on US85-87 (Nevada Ave.) to J. with Cheyenne Rd. 2$^m$. (R) on Cheyenne Rd. through Cheyenne Canyon to **Seven Falls** 6$^m$. Seven distinct cascades of spraying water plunge almost perpendicularly down 300′ course. Stairway leads to top of falls from which pt. are spectacular views of surrounding country. Canyon & falls beautifully lighted in summer. Open yr. round.

**V. Beautiful High Drive, 17$^m$**

Thrilling feature of Colo. Springs Mt. Pks. System is High Drive, up North Cheyenne Canyon. (S) on US85, 87 (Nevada Ave.) to Cheyenne Blvd. 2$^m$. (R) on Cheyenne Blvd. to end of street to entrance N. Cheyenne Canyon. Through Canyon to **Bruin Inn & Helen Hunt Falls.** One-way Rd. over High Dr. gives spectacular view of **Bridal Veil Falls,** Cheyenne Mt., Broadmoor & Colorado Springs. On top of High Dr. is old log cabin of Capt. Jack, famous prospector. Here among pines & picturesque boulders High Dr. is through areas of great natural beauty. Return trip down **Bear Cr. Canyon** (follow marked Rds.) to Colo. Springs.

Leaving Colo. Springs, US85 proceeds (S) via Nevada Ave. **178. FOUNTAIN,** one of oldest settlements in central Colo. Important shipping pt. for alfalfa & sugar beets grown in irrigated sec. of valley.

**209. PUEBLO.**

B St. & Union Ave., for Santa Fe RR.; M. P. RR.; D. & R.G. RR.; C. & S. RR. 7th & Main Sts. for Greyhound Bus. Union Bus Sta., Court & 5th Sts. for Rio Grande Trailways; Santa Fe Trailways; Denver-Colo. Springs-Pueblo Trailways. Airport through conns. Hqs. San Isabel Nat. For. Info.: C. of C.; Rocky Mt. Motorists A.A.A.

Colorado's 2nd largest city. A mfg. & trade center. City lies at confluence of Fountain Cr. & Ark. R., in broad valley enclosed by low bluffs & rolling hills. History dates from Sp. occupation in late 17th cent. On his exploring expedition in 1806, Lt. Z. Pike camped on site & built 1st structure erected by Amers. in Colo. Settlement & naming of Pueblo credited to Jas. P. Beckwourth, mulatto trader, at one time a war chief of the Crow. He & his party reached the Ark. in 1842, erected a trading post. They were soon joined by 15 to 20 independent trappers & their families. Settlement grew & was largest in reg. until gold rush days, & served as rallying pt. for Mormon Battalion during Mex. War. After Mex. War, Pueblo declined & nothing remains of Mormon Pueblo. Party of prospectors from St. Louis in 1858 utilized material from walls of old pueblo in building 30 adobe & log houses in their new town, which they named Fountain City, now part of Pueblo. By 1870, when inc., Pueblo was quite a settlement of adobe houses, with pop. of 700. Industrial progress has been maintained in recent yrs. Colo. St. Fair late in Aug. PTS. OF INT.: Goodnight & Calla Aves., **City Pk.** (100 as. sports facils.pic.golf.) Stone Aviary exhibits native & tropical birds. Small zoo. 13th & Frisco Sts., **Colo St. Hospital for Insane** (O.est.1879) is group of red brick bldgs. on 500-a. tract. **Minnequa Steel Plant** (tours wks.10 & 2) Office, Bay St. & Abriendo Ave. Covers 600 as. at (SW) edge of city, being largest W. of Miss.

US85 proceeds (S) from Pueblo via Lake Ave., skirting L. Minnequa, mun. playground. **260. WALSENBURG** was orig. sm. Sp. village known as La Plaza de los Leones, named for prominent Sp. family. In 17th cent. Conquistadores visited reg. in search of gold. Later Sp.-Amer. farmers, Amer. traders & trappers settled along Cuchara R. & its tributary cr. Present city laid out 1873 by Walsen, pioneer German merchant. Vic. produces large crops of beans, wheat, hay, corn; cattle & sheep provide revenues to ranchers. **298. TRINIDAD** (Info.: C. of C.), named for Trinidad Baca, daughter of pioneer settler. First coal mine in dist. opened in 1867. As demand for coal increased, other mines were opened. Now important wholesale & distributing center; principal industries are coal-mining, agric., livestock raising, & mfg. plants. **Roundup Pk.** on US85 at N. edge of city is scene of annual Kit Carson Roundup in Aug. J. with St.12.

SIDE TRIP: (R) on St.12 31$^{m}$ to **Stonewall** (Camp Picketwire) (accoms.facils.h.f.) in Stonewall Valley at foot of snow-capped Culebra Mts. On mt. stream known as Middle Fork of Purgatoire R., which flows through center of camp. 36$^{m}$ **Monument L. Resort** (accoms.facils.h.f.boat.horses), owned by City of Trinidad & operated by Isaac Walton League, resort lies at foot of snow-crested Sangre de Cristo Mts. Large fish hatchery here.

**312.** US85 crosses **COLO.-N.M. LINE** (7$^{m}$ from Raton).

## US 87—COLORADO

**COLO.-WYO. LINE** (13$^{m}$ from Cheyenne, Wyo.) **(S) to DENVER. 100. US87**

Via: Ft. Collins, Loveland, Longmont & Lafayette. C. & S. RR. & bus lines parallel route. Good accoms.

Bet. Colo.-Wyo. Line & Denver, hy. skirts Front Range of Rockies, traversing dry range country, irrigated valleys & Cache la Poudre & South Platte Rs. & N. Colo. coal fields. This is an alternate tour to US85 (see) to Denver.

**22. WELLINGTON,** supply pt. for agric. territory. **31.** J. with US287 which unites with US87 to Denver. **33. FT. COLLINS** (Info.: C. of C.), chief wholesale & retail center of large agric. area & shipping pt. for extensive livestock feeding dist. Principal industrial unit is **Great Western Sugar Factory** (O.appl.). With W. entrance on Laurel & Howe Sts., **Colo. A. & M. College** (160 as.founded 1870.opened 1879), gray & red brick bldgs. grouped about oval landscaped drive. College also owns over 2,000 as. of adj., or near-by land, used for agric. experimental studies; owns or controls 7,600 as. of land at 8 sub-sta. experimental farms in St. **City Pk.** (sports facils.golf), landscaped area on W. edge of city, centers on natural L. In Ft. Collins is J. with US287.

SIDE TRIP: (NW) on US287 (alt. route to US87 & US85) hy. follows fertile irrigated farm area which soon gives way to stark, arid hill country broken by grotesque masses of sandstone, & then skirts Front Range of Rockies. Hy. follows routes of old Overland Stage & Ft. Collins-Ft. Laramie Stage Lines. 5$^{m}$ **La Porte,** rural supply center. Sett. c.1860 as permanent camp of band of Fr.-Canadian hunters & trappers. Hqs. of mt. division of Overland Stage Co., town flourished & aspired to be capital of Territory. 9$^{m}$ **Ted's Place,** log cabin built by forgotten pioneers. J. with St.14.

(L) on St.14 (gravel Rd.). Route enters canyon of Cache la Poudre R., noted for trout f. its entire length. Enters Roosevelt Nat. For., popular vacation area, to Continental Divide through dense stands of pine as hy. ascends by fairly easy grades into North Pk. 4$^{m}$ **Gateway** (accoms.), summer resort at edge of foothill country. Here hy. crosses E. boundary of **Roosevelt Nat. For.** (pic.camp.facils.) of over a million as. of pine &

spruce grandeur, named in honor of Theo. Roosevelt. Here are giant Rockies & ancient glaciers. 23m **Ft. Collins Mt. Pk.** (facils.camp.pic.recr.in Roosevelt Nat.For.here). Comprises several hundred as. of mun. owned land in broad wooded valley. **Nature Trl.,** constructed by Rocky Mt. Climbers Club, is so laid as to pass by at least 1 specimen of every variety of tree in for. Wild flowers & shrubs native to mts. are planted along trl., each variety labeled. 28m **Eggers** (accoms.f.), summer P.O. & resort in Poudre Canyon. 63m **Cameron Pass** (10,285′), named for its discoverer, Gen. Rbt. Cameron, pioneer RR. builder, is a narrow forested defile through which Rd. winds for 9m. (Pass closed to winter travel). Granite & bronze marker indicates highest pt. on pass. (W) of pass, hy. bordered with dense stands of logdepole pines as it descends by fairly easy grades into **North Pk.,** a level grassland, which leads St. in production of wild hay. 95m **Walden,** ranching supply center & only town of consequence in North Pk. Isolated from rest of St. during winter, village is closely knit community, living to itself. 130m **Muddy Pass.** J. with US40 to Steamboat Springs (R); Denver (L).

16m **Owl Canyon,** twisting bet. limestone cliffs that wall in narrow gorge. At E. mouth of canyon is **Owl Canyon Store.** 20m **The Forks,** also called Forks Hotel, built 1874 for workers in great lumbering operations, then major industry in this sec. 29m **Steamboat Rock,** landmark which resembles old fashioned steamer with 2 funnels. Formerly used by Inds. as lookout & pt. for signal fires. 34.5m **Virginia Dale Mon.,** bronze tablet pointing way 1m (L) on dirt Rd. to old **Virginia Dale Sta.** on Overland Stage route. Orig. Sta. H. (est. 1862) built of hand-hewn logs. Great rock chimney & orig. andirons are well-preserved. Logs have numerous bullet holes from Ind. days. 35m **Bishop Ranch,** founded 1873, log bldg., one of orig. structures, still standing. 39m **Colo.-Wyo. Line,** 27m from Laramie, Wyo.

At Ft. Collins US87 & US287 are united to Denver. **46. LOVELAND,** in heart of prosperous agric. dist. in Big Thompson Valley. City is at entrance of famed **Big Thompson Canyon,** chief gateway to Rocky Mountain Nat. Pk. Loveland is known as Sweetheart City & each yr. many thousand valentines are stamped with special valentine seal from here. Larimer Cty. Fair & Rodeo in Aug. **Pioneer Mus.** contains hist. relics. **64. LONGMONT** (Info.: C. of C.), named for discoverer of near-by **Long's Peak** (14,225′), Maj. Stephen H. Long. Community is center of prosperous sugar beet, vegetable & sm. grain area. Livestock raising & feeding, poultry & dairying, leading industries. **Great Western Beet Sugar Factory** (O). **Vegetable Canning Plant** (O). Boulder Cty. Fair & Livestock Show 3rd week in Aug. **Roosevelt Pk.** (sports facils.pic.), center of city's recr. program & 1 of 5 mun. recr. grounds. **Sunset Pk.** (trlr.facils.camp.accoms.swim.golf) is on rise of ground overlooking whole Front Range of Rockies. **75.** J. with St.7 to Boulder (see Denver Trip III). **77. LAFAYETTE. 100 DENVER** (see).

# DENVER

## DENVER

Union Sta., 17th & Wynkoop Sts. for A.T. & S.F. RR.; C.B. & Q. RR.; C. & S. RR.; D. & R.G.W. RR.; R.I. Lines; U.P. RR. Moffat Depot, 2101 15th St., for D. & S.L. RR. Union Bus Terminal, 1700 Glenarm Pl., for Colo. Motorways, Greyhound Lines, Union Pac. Stages. Bus Terminal, 501 17th St., for Burlington Trailways, Cardinal Stage Lines, Denver-Colo. Springs-Pueblo Trailways; Denver & Interurban; Denver-Salt Lake-Pacific Trailways; Rio Grande Trailways; Santa Fe Trailways. Airport through conns. Info.: C. of C.; Conoco Travel Bureau; Denver Convention & Visitors Bureau; Motor Club of Colo.; Rocky Mt. Motorists (A.A.A.); Texaco Tourist Serv.

Denver, vacation center of West, is St.'s capital & largest city. Located at foot of Rocky Mts., it is commercial, financial & tourist center for heavy summer trade. The mile-high metropolis is focal point of incomparable mountainous playground with system of Mt. Pks. Thousands of as. comprising many Denver Mt. Pks. are scattered over hundreds of sq. miles, with fine hys. connecting them. Denver is one of youngest of great Amer. cities, founded c.90 yrs. ago. In 1857, a trapper built a cabin where 2 streams came together: a good place for a home, plenty of wood, water, grass. Others arrived the following yr. & built cabins. When gold rush started to Pikes Peak Reg., still more settlers came. It was convenient base for mining operations. In 1860 settlement had become a bustling village, having been named 2 yrs. earlier after Terr. Gov. Jas. W. Denver of Kans. For yrs. Denver's fortunes rose & fell with those of gold camps in area. It remained for great silver discoveries to give substance to dream of early promoters who had envisioned a great metropolis at Cherry Cr. & the S. Platte. In 1861 Colo. Territory was est. & Denver chosen capital in 1867; St. capital in 1876 with advent of statehood. Growth of Denver in era of great silver camps was phenomenal. Bet. 1880 & 1890, pop. increased from 35,600 to 106,700. Construction went at unprecedented tempo. Growth of city since 1900 has been steady. Since decline of silver camps, subsequent growth largely along commercial & financial lines. Denver Union Stockyards, one of most important in country. Nat. Western Stock Show in Jan.; Folk Festival in May; Summer Outdoor Opera, in July; City Band Concerts, July-Aug.; Civic Symphony Concerts, Nov. through Ap.—are important annual events.

PTS. OF INT. (1) 16th St. bet. Court Pl. & Tremont St., **Old Court H. Plaza** is block-sq. area of terraced lawns, flower beds & lily ponds, in heart of downtown dist. & occupies site of former cth., demolished in 1934. (2) 19th & Stout Sts., **U.S. Custom H.** (1930.Ital.Ren.), 5-story Colo. marble structure. Is largest of Denver Fed. bldgs. (3) 18th & Stout Sts., **U.S. Post Office,** completed 1916 at cost of 2 million dollars, contains Fed. departments, including reg. offices of For. Serv. The 4-story bldg. of white Colo. marble has massive Ionic columns on Stout St. facade. (4) 16th & Arapahoe Sts., **Daniels & Fisher Tower** (O.9-6 wks.), modeled on Campanile of St. Mark's in Venice, is city's tallest structure, 375′. From tower is excellent view of city & surrounding country. (5) Bet. Curtis & Champa Sts.,**Mun. Auditorium** (O. 1908) By means of moveable walls, inter. can be changed within few hrs. from 12,000 seat auditorium to 3,000 seat theater. $80,000 organ is one of country's finest. (6) W. Colfax Ave., bet. Cherokee & Delaware Sts., **U.S. Mint** is massive 2-story granite bldg., one of 3 coinage plants in U.S.; also one of 2 chief Fed. gold repositories. (7) **City-County Bldg.** (1932), facing Capitol across Civic Center, represents joint design of 35 leading Denver architects. With simple class. lines the 4-story granite bldg., with concave facade of Doric columns, has large central portico surmounted with slender clock tower housing **Speer Mem. Chimes.** Corinthian caps on portico columns carved from 26-ton granite blocks, & bronze entrance doors are among largest ever cast. Inter. paneling & monolithic columns in lobby are of Colo. travertine. (8) **Denver Art Mus.** (O.wks.), on 4th fl. of City-County Bldg., with 12 galleries of permanent exhibits, incl. work of Corot, Millet, Jongkind, Sisley, Pissaro, Monet & Courbet; the Helen Dill Mem. Coll. of 19th & 20th cent. Amer. & Fr. works; & Junius Flagg Brown Mem. Coll. of 19th Cent. Amer., Fr. & Dutch paintings in manner of Barbizon School. Ind. coll. of several thousand examples of pottery, weaving, basketry, etc. Walter C. Mead Coll. incl. Chinese & Japanese porcelains & bronzes, Georg. furniture, paintings & prints; among other colls.

(9) W. Colfax Ave., between Bannock St. & Broadway, extending to W. 14th Ave., **Civic Center** is formal expanse of lawns, trees, walks & esplanades, flanked on either end by City-County Bldg. & St. Capitol. **Voorhies Mem.,** graceful arch of buff-colored limestone, with curved wings supported by Ionic columns, constructed from funds bequeathed by John H. P. Voorhies, pioneer mining man. **Colonnade of Civic Benefactors,** built in 1919, forms stage of open-air Greek theater.

**Denver Pub. Lib.** (O.9-9 wks.; 2-9 Sun.) NW. corner Civic Center is 2-story structure of Turkey Cr. sandstone, neo-class. design. Is main unit of city's lib. system of several branches. **St. Capitol** (O.1896.neo-Class.) facing Civic Center, dominates city from its commanding eminence. The $2,800,000 granite bldg., rising 3 stories above high basement, is dominated by high, gold-covered dome, floodlighted at night. Corinthian porticos front each of 4 entrances; on W., or main portico is statuary group symbolizing progress of St. & its resources. **Dome** (O.9-4) is reached by spiral stairs from 3rd fl., from balcony of which is fine view of city & Mt. ranges. (10) **St. Mus. Bldg.** (O.9-5 wks.;11-4 Sun.1915.neo-Class.) SE. Cor. Sherman St. & E. 14th Ave., Hqs. of St. Hist Soc, is 3-story granite structure. In East Room, main fl., is one of most complete colls. of artifacts of Pueblo culture in U.S. (11) E. 8th Ave., **Cheesman Pk.** is rolling 80-a. landscaped tract. Formerly a pioneer cemetery, it was acquired by city in 1890 & named Congress Pk.; renamed in honor of Walter Scott Cheesman, who played major part in development of Denver water supply system. **Cheesman Mem.** (neo-Class.), structure of Colo. marble, stands on eminence overlooking reflecting pool near E. side of pk. (12) E. 17th Ave., bet. York St. & Colo. Blvd., **City Pk.** (boat.) is largest pk. in city, covering 400 as. & has zoological gardens, containing 1,800 animals & birds of all kinds. Gardens are landscaped to simulate animals' natural habitat. **Electric Fountain,** in center of one of 2 large lakes, is reproduction of fountain in Mexico City; has 2,000 sprays discharging 4,400 gals. of water per minute; is lighted on summer nights in 125 combinations of 9

colors. Eighteen-hole golf course adjoins pk. **Colo. Mus. of Natural Hist.** (O.9-5 wks.Sun.aft.) in City Pk. at Colo. Blvd., contains thousands of specimens of mounted animals, birds, etc. **Phipps Mem. Auditorium** housed in wing of bldg., where lectures, plays & motion pictures are presented. (13) S. Marion Pkwy., **Washington Pk.** (boat.golf.polo.swim.skating in winter), has many beautiful flower gardens, among which are the **Colonial Gardens,** duplicates of the gardens planted and tended by Martha Washington at Mt. Vernon.
(14) **Univ. of Denver** (bldgs. open sch. hrs.), S. University Blvd. & E. Evans Ave., Colo.'s pioneer institution of higher learning, was chartered in 1864 as Colo. Seminary of M. E. Church. In 1880 the Univ. of Denver was organized as degree-conferring body of Seminary, & various schs. & colleges were added. S. Univ. Blvd. & E. Evans Ave., **Margery Reed Mayo Mem. Hall** (c.1929.Coll.Goth.) houses Univ. Civic Theater. (SW) of hall is **Margery Reed Mayo Mem. Chapel** (1910.Sp.Ren.). (SW) of chapel, **Student Union Bldg.** (1908), orig. Carnegie Lib., is social center of campus. Directly (S) of Student Union Bldg. is 4-story brick & limestone **Mary Reed Lib.** (1932.Coll.Goth.), impressive campus structure, surmounted by 100′ central tower. Dept. on Anthropology (O.wks.) in S. wing of basement has large coll. of bone & stone implements from America & Europe. (E) of Lib. is oldest Univ. bldg., **Univ. Hall** (1891). (15) E. 47th Ave. & Lafayette St., **Denver Union Stock Yards** (130 as.est.1886). E. 47th Ave. & Gilpin St., **Stockyards Stadium,** seating 4,400, is scene of **Annual Nat. Stock Show.**

## TRIPS OUT OF DENVER

### I. DENVER MOUNTAIN PKS. LOOP TOUR. 119.5. US40, St.68, St.119, St.279 & St.103

Facils. & accoms. along route. Info.: Denver Convention & Visitors Bureau, 519 17th St.

**0. ST. CAPITOL.** (W) on Colfax Ave. (US40). At **c.9.** is J. with St.68. (R) here to **GOLDEN** at **12.5.,** through Finlay L. MacFarland Gateway on way up Lookout Mt. **SUMMIT OF LOOKOUT MT. 17.5. Tomb of Buffalo Bill. Pahaska Tepee,** mus. filled with mementoes of Buffalo Bill & his times. **21.5.,** J. with US40 (R), passing Rd. to Genessee Mt. pic. grounds & buffalo preserve. At **33.** (R) is J. with St.119. Take St.119 to **BLACK HAWK** at **43.** At **44. CENTRAL CITY,** which, together with Black Hawk, was known as Gregory Diggings, "richest sq. mile on earth." **Opera H.** (annual drama-opera festival July-Aug. with "name" stars) & **Teller H.,** famed old hotel, early landmarks. (S) on St.279. **52.5. IDAHO SPRINGS.** J. with St.103 (L) to **66.5. ECHO LAKE** (10,600′), City of Denver & U. S. For. Ser. pic. & campgrounds. **Mun. Lodge** (accoms.facils.) (R) at Mun. Lodge 15$^m$ to **Summit of Mt. Evans** (14,260′), end of world's highest automobile hy. (R) from Echo Lake on St.68 to **BERGEN PK.** at **85.** Mun. playgrounds, shelter houses, refreshments. J. with St.74. (R) here to **90. EVERGREEN,** resort area. **101. MORRISON,** at mouth of **Bear Cr. Canyon** (sports facils.). Near-by is **Pk. of the Red Rocks** (pic.), great sandstone ledges form natural theater with perfect acoustics, seating 9,000 (Easter Sunrise Service & summer concerts). Route (St.74) enters Denver via Alameda Ave. **119.5. ST. CAPITOL.**

### II. GOLDEN & LOOKOUT MT. TOUR. 21.5. US6-40 & St.68

(W) from Denver on US6-40 (Colfax Ave.) to J. with St.68, **c.9.**
(R) on St.68 to **12.5. GOLDEN** (accoms.facils.Info.: C. of C.), which lies at foot of Lookout Mt. Founded in 1859 by the Boston Co. & named for Tom Golden, early miner. Town was capital of Colo. Terr. from 1862 to 1867 when Denver was made permanent seat of gov. Chief industries are Coors brewery & pottery plant. **Colo. Sch. of Mines** (1869), one of highest accredited schs. of its kind. Entrance at Illinois Ave. & 15th St., base of Lookout Mt. First courses offered in 1871; became St. institution in 1874. The 25-a. campus contains 15 bldgs., incl. **Berthoud Hall** 1940.Ital.Ren.), consisting of 4-story central unit with 2-story wing at either end. **Geologic Mus.** occupies W. wing, with collection of minerals, rocks, ores & fossils.
(L) on St.68, through **FINLEY L. MACFARLAND MEM. GATEWAY, 13.5.,** supported by salmon-colored sandstone towers. MacFarland was leader in development of Denver Mt. Pk. System. Rd. begins ascent of Lookout Mt. along series of hairpin curves; grade fairly easy; hy. wide. Golden & Clear Cr. Canyon drop away far below. **18. CREST OF LOOKOUT MT.** J. with short circular Dr. (R) on Dr. to **Buffalo Bill's Grave** on highest point of Mt. (7,375′). **Pahaska Tepee,** rustic

lodge built just below grave, houses coll. of relics of scouts & Inds. of Buffalo Bill Cody's day (see Trip I). At **c.21.5.** is J. with US40. (Return to Denver via US6-40, or (S) at J. with St.93 to Morrisson and Pk. of the Red Rocks, thence to Denver via US285.)

**III. DENVER (N) to ROCKY MT. NAT. PK. & GRANBY. 149. US87, St.7 & US34**

Via: Broomfield, Lafayette, Boulder, Lyons, Estes Pk. & Grand Lake.

This route, used chiefly to visit Univ. of Colo. at Boulder, & as short cut from Central Colo. to Estes Pk. & Rocky Mt. Nat. Pk., traverses rich farm lands in Boulder Valley to reach foothill country where ranching is chief occupation. Hy. ascends through colorful S. Saint Vrain Canyon & Trail Ridge Rd.

**0. DENVER.** N. on US87 to **16. BROOMFIELD. 22. LAFAYETTE. 24.** J. with St.7. L. here to **32. BOULDER** (Info.: C. of C., accoms.facils.fine trout f.), seat of Boulder Cty. & home of Univ. of Colo., lies in protected valley on face of precipitous foothills in which is Boulder's 5,000-a. Mt. Pk. Center of mining & agric. Prospect of obtaining RR. & univ. brought city to life in 1870's. Univ. increasingly became economic, social & cultural center of city's life. Univ. Artists Series, school yr. Powwow Days Rodeo, last wk. in July. **Univ. of Colo.,** main entrance Broadway & Pleasant St., is on 260-a. campus on S. edge of city, with more than 30 bldgs., athletic fields & stadium (Univ. Medical Center at Denver). Vine covered older bldgs. contrast with unique architecture of newer structures which are appropriate to Boulder locale, using a free adaptation of Ital. rural design; all bldgs. since 1922 have followed this design. Of native stone ranging in color from buff & pink to purplish red, bldgs. harmonize with picturesque setting. Among larger bldgs. are **Macky Auditorium,** which contains $65,000 organ; new **Lib.** which houses 2 million items incl. Music Room (used for chamber concerts & study hall) record coll. **Mus.** contains biological, zoological, botanical, mineral & other collections, together with fine arts gallery. Bet. Mus. & Arts & Sciences bldg., **Mary Rippon Mem. Outdoor Theater** of native "red rocks" has summer play festival featuring Shakespeare's & regional plays; outdoor spring & summer classes & lectures. (SW) of town is **Chautauqua Pk.** in **Bluebell Canyon** (hik.pic.bridle paths). (SE) of town c.5$^{m}$ on dirt Rd., **Eldorado Springs** (outdoor swim.recr.facils.sm.fee). (W) of town foot, auto & bridle trls. to **Flagstaff** & **Flatiron Mts.** N. of Boulder hy. follows rising grade lined with massive **Red Rocks** (pic.fireplaces). Near-by Boulder Canyon twists through pine & aspen covered mts. with many streams (pic.f.) from **Arapahoe Glacier,** area's water supply, & inns. **46.** J. with St.66 (alt. route to Rocky Mt. Nat. Pk.) which unites with St.7 for 2$^{m}$. **48. LYONS.** (L) here on St.7, hy. along canyon of S. Saint Vrain. At near-by Nederland, **Lazy VV Ranch,** world's highest Arabian horse breeding farm; summer rodeos (O.alt.Sun.sm.fee). **ROOSEVELT NAT. FOR.** at **51.,** which embraces Rocky Mt. Nat. Pk. on 3 sides & forms part of great Colo. St. Game Refuge. **63. RAYMOND.** J. with St.160 (L) to Nederland, resort area, & Boulder.

**86. ESTES PK. VILLAGE** (Info.: C. of C., Rocky Mt. Nat. Pk. Hqs.; accoms.facils. camp.golf) lies in W. neck of Estes Pk. & is principal entrance to & almost surrounded by Rocky Mt. Nat. Pk. Town is surrounded by forested hills, dude ranches, cabins, hotels, streams & a gay summer & winter tourist atmosphere. Pk. was named for Joel Estes, 1st settler (1860), & when 2 or 3 families followed, Estes moved his family, complaining of "too many people." Word of Pk. spread rapidly & many notable visitors came. Village & Estes Pk. are commonly confused with Rocky Mt. Nat. Pk. because so many visitors make village their hqs. J. with US34 on which trip cont. Between Estes Pk. Village & W. boundary of Rocky Mt. Nat. Pk., which it crosses, US34 is known & marked as Trail Ridge Rd., one of highest and most outstanding mt. hys. in America. **ROCKY MOUNTAIN NAT. PK. 90.** (O.to travel entire yr., but through traffic over Trail Ridge Rd. ends with closing of hy. by snow, usually in late Oct., through May. Hqs. Estes Park Village. Info. Ranger in Park or Hqs. for numerous pk. & trl. trips. Yearly auto permits $1 per car). Lying on both sides of Continental Divide, a 35$^{m}$ chain of giant peaks contains within its 400 sq. miles a remarkable grouping of mt. scenery & upland meadows, split & gouged by gulches & canyons, dotted with alpine Ls., altogether forming a bold, colorful scene. Many peaks ranging from 7,800′ to 14,255′ are in pk. Hundreds of streams are stocked with fish. Heavy fors. cover much of pk., which is wildlife sanctuary. Climate of pk. mild for such great altitudes, air light & dry. Summer nights always cool. Snowfall on ranges in winter ideal for winter sports. Long's Peak (14,255′) is highest in pk. Crossing Rocky Mt. Nat. Park, Trail Ridge Rd. (US34) is one of finest examples of mt. hy. engineering. Unlike other Rds. that ascend mt. ranges via valleys & canyons, trl. makes way upward to **Milner Pass** along ridge tops, much of route being above timberline, affording magnificent views of great mts., rivers, valleys, thousands of feet below. **91. HORSESHOE PK.,** high flat grassland where wild flowers bloom in profusion, named for shape of valley which was once thought to be bed of great lake which accounts for lack of forest here.

**92.** J. with Fall River Rd. (R), an attractive 1-way Dr. which rejoins US34 (W) after 11$^{m}$. From J. with Fall River Rd. speed limit of 35$^{m}$ strictly enforced. **95. DEER RIDGE,** J. with Moraine Pk. Rd., which traverses section of Big Thompson Valley, highly developed as summer resort. Substantial log cabins & cottages, perched on craggy slopes amid aspen & pines, border both sides of winding hy. This Rd. leads 11$^{m}$ to **Bear L. MANY PKS. CURVE, 99.** One of numerous parking spaces provided along Trail Ridge Rd., presenting broad view of scenery in E. sec. of pk.

Hy. climbs steadily, passing timberline several times within short distance, which varies considerably, being much lower on shaded than on sunlit slopes. **112. FALL R. PASS MUS.** (O.8-5.postoffice.lunch) with exhibits revealing geological evolution of pk. N. of Mus. parking area, hy. continues for some distance above timberline, then descends into timber. Continental Divide is crossed at **117. MILNER PASS** (10,759′). At top of pass are **Poudre Ls.** at J. with foot trl.; R. here on trl. through dense fors. to fork, 0.5$^{m}$, presenting view of **Cache La Poudre R.** (R) winding through open grassland. (W) of Poudre Lakes US34 winds down canyon between hills blanketed with heavy fors. Swings down in long horseshoe curve to campground. **128. WEST SIDE CAMPGROUND. 134. GRAND LAKE,** J. with improved rd.

SIDE TRIP: (L) 1$^{m}$ on this Rd. is **Grand L. Village** (accoms.facils.early June to mid-Sept.boat.swim.f.) Summer resort on L. shore. Lake is one of largest in St. & extremely deep, remaining a constant deep blue. Most of pine-fringed shore privately owned. Yacht races in Aug.

Grand L. is W. boundary of Rocky Mt. Nat. Park. US34 proceeds to J. with US40 at **149. GRANBY.** (Here is J. with US40 (see) to Hot Sulphur Springs (R), Idaho Springs, (L) Denver.)

**IV. DENVER (S) to COLO.-N.M. LINE** (9$^{m}$ from Chama, N.M.). **267. US285**

Via: Morrison, Kenosha Pass, Poncha Springs, Saguache, Monte Vista & Alamosa.

US285 leads through rugged country roughly paralleling Continental Divide, popular recr. area, with many trout streams. Hy. crosses South Pk. & San Luis Valley. S. portion of route traverses ranching & agric. areas, dotted with Sp.-Amer. settlements. **0. DENVER** proceed (S) on US285 to **13. MORRISON,** resort at mouth of Bear Cr. Canyon & site of famed **Pk. of Red Rocks** (see Denver Trip I). One of principal entrances to Denver Mt. Pk. System. **St. Fish Hatchery** (O.9-5). At **18.,** is Rd. (L) to **Tiny Town** 1$^{m}$, summer settlement, named for miniature city on bank of cr. Here, built to scale, 1″ to 1′, is complete town. **34. SHAFFERS CROSSING,** summer resort & supply town. **45. BAILEY** (camp.) at N. boundary of Pike Nat. For., reserve of over 1¼ million as., of which famed Pikes Peak (14,110′) is most prominent. (See US85). (W), hy. pursues winding course through dense for. of spruce & lodgepole pines. **50. SHAWNEE,** resort on wooded slope. **54. SANTA MARIA,** on hill across Platte R. (R) from Santa Maria Cassels (O) camp for girls, is 75-ton **Christ of the Rockies,** modeled in cream-white glazed porcelain, 52′ from base to top, floodlighted at night. Figure of Christ, guarded by 2 angels, reclines in crypt at base of statue. **64. KENOSHA PASS,** broad saddleback between 2 low mts.; divide bet. N. & S. forks of S. Platte. **68. JEFFERSON. 84. FAIRPLAY** is one of St.'s old mining towns. Near center of town is **Mon.** erected by citizens; it marks grave of "Prunes," burro said to have worked in every mine in dist. Sherwood, the miner who owned Prunes died in 1931 & was buried at rear of Mon. of Prunes as he had requested. **105. TROUT CR. PASS.** J. with US24 (L), which unites with US285 to J. at 14$^{m}$. **141. PONCHA SPRINGS** (Sp. "mild") (see US50). Route ascends through foothills to **152. PONCHA PASS,** chief N. entrance to San Luis Valley. **167.** J. with St.17 on which L. 2$^{m}$ to **Mineral Hot Springs,** resort with cottage camp & outdoor swim. pool. **181. SAGUACHE** (sa-wátch; Ind. "blue earth"), thriving but isolated community retaining some frontier spirit. Founded in 1866 when throngs of prospectors rushed into valley seeking gold. In early days was hqs. for Ute agency. J. with St.114.

SIDE TRIP: (R) on St.114 along Saguache R. is excellent trout fishing. St.114 crosses Continental Divide over **Cochetopa Pass,** continuing 61$^{m}$ to J. with US50.

**216. MONTE VISTA** (see US160). US285 unites with US160 for 17$^{m}$ to **ALAMOSA** at **233.** (see US160). US285 & St.17 are united to N.M. Line. **249. LA JARA** (Sp. "rock rose"), center of large truck-farming area; also livestock raising reg. **261. CONEJOS,** founded in 1854, one of oldest towns in Colo., though unincorporated. Retains old Sp. atmosphere. US285 crosses **COLO.-N.M. LINE** at **267.**

## US 30S—UTAH

**UTAH-WYO. LINE** (5$^{m}$ from Evanston, Wyo.) **(W) & (NW) to UTAH-IDAHO LINE** (59$^{m}$ from Burley, Idaho). **173. US30S**

Via: Echo, Morgan, Ogden, Brigham City, Tremonton, Snowville.

Route of US30S has always been chief means of entrance into Utah from (E); it was first an Ind. trl., later an immigrant trl., & eventually route of Pacific RR. After penetrating Wasatch Mt. wall, US30S follows another well-beaten trl. (N) around Great Salt L., known since 1849 as Salt Lake Cutoff to Cal. Trl.

### Sec. 1: UTAH-WYO. LINE to BRIGHAM CITY. 92.

US30S (W) of Evanston ascends rolling hills along Bear R. Valley to the divide bet. Bear & Weber Rs., **5.,** then descends to Echo Canyon. **OLD MORMON TRL. MARKER** (L), **10.5.,** marks pt. where pioneer trl. angles into Echo Canyon from (SE.). First traveled in 1846 by Cal.-bound wagons of Lansford W. Hastings & the Donner-Reed party, the trl. Mormons followed in 1847 crossed Bear R. 6$^{m}$ (S) of Evanston & climbed 2 low ridges to reach head of Echo. Brigham Young being ill with "mountain fever," Orson Pratt took an advance company down this canyon & then across mountains to Salt L. Valley (see Salt Lake City, Loop Tour II). **14. CASTLE ROCK** marks beginning of canyons' violently eroded rock formations which, in yrs. before the amazing character of S. Utah became known, aroused wondering comment from every Western traveler. At **THE NARROWS, 26.5.,** where the red walls are precipitous & canyon floor boulder-strewn, Mormons in 1857 planned to resist westward-moving troops of Utah Expedition. Breastworks were constructed along cliffs (R), & creek was dammed to constrict Rd. in canyon bottom. Onset of winter, however, forced Utah Expedition to set up winter quarters short of this pt., at Camp Scott, (S) of Ft. Bridger. By spring of 1858, Mormons had decided not to fight, & U.S. troops marched (W) through canyon. At mouth of **ECHO CANYON, 29.,** is W. J. with US189, with which US30S has been united (W) of Evanston. (For this hy. & balance of US30S to mouth of Weber Canyon, see Salt Lake City Loop Tour II.) At mouth of **WEBER CANYON, 65.,** is S. J. with US89 (see), & at **70.5.** in **OGDEN** is S. J. with US91, with which US30S is united to **BRIGHAM CITY, 92.** (see US91).

### Sec. 2: BRIGHAM CITY to UTAH-IDAHO LINE. 81.

(W) of Brigham City, US30S traverses desert country, sometimes drab, sometimes of reluctant beauty. **BEAR R.,** bridged at **6.,** is a tired, brackish stream. It has meandered for 350$^{m}$ through Utah, Wyo. & Idaho to empty into Great Salt Lake only 90$^{m}$ from its source. At intervals along its course, dams impound waters to irrigate more than 52,000 as. of fertile valley lands.

**7. CORINNE,** an easygoing farming village belying its uproarious past. No town unleashed more furious energies into Utah life than this quondam "Gentile Capital of Utah," & no tail ever came closer to wagging the dog. Founded early in 1869 at pt. where westward-building U.P. RR. crossed Bear R., Corinne envisioned itself as the future business metropolis of entire Terr., & a gentile wedge to split open the tight Mormon hegemony. From an alkali flat, Corinne changed overnight to veritable wilderness of frame bldgs., shanties, & tents in which dwelt a pop. of some 1,500, excluding 5,000 Chinese left behind by the Cent. Pac. All of Corinne's ambitions hinged on its being made the permanent junction pt. for 2 RRs., but when Ogden was selected as more suitable, Corinne made itself a base for freighting operations (N) into Idaho & Mont., put a steamboat on Great Salt Lake to connect it with Rush Valley Mines at its S. shore, memorialized Congress for aid in diverting waters of Bear R. for irrigation, & delayed not a moment in organizing a Liberal Political Party to combat Mormons at the polls. Economically Corinne was a luckless town; Mormon-built Utah N. RR. dried up freighting revenues; commercial navigation of Great Salt Lake was not a success; & Congress could not make up its mind to any affirmative action on reclamation proposals. But Liberal Party became vociferous organ of gentile minority in Utah, aroused powerful outside forces in its behalf, & was instrumental in finally bringing about Mormon submission on issues of marriage & political separation of Ch. & St. Altogether taken over by Mormon farmers after the Lucin Cutoff, in 1903, diverted rail traffic, Corinne will nevertheless stand for something intransigent in Utah life, as long as its name persists. Here is J. with St.83.

SIDE TRIP: On this Rd. (L) $26^m$ following old grade of the U.P., to **Promontory,** where pyramidal mon. marks site of the driving of the Golden Spike, May 10, 1869. Westward-building U.P. & eastward-building Central Pacific, racing for cash subsidies & land grants Congress awarded for each mile of track laid, had built grades as far (W) as Wells, Nev., & as far (E) as Ogden, but the C.P.'s "Jupiter" & the U.P.'s "No. 119" met here at windswept summit of Promontory Range. After Lucin Cutoff was built, $25^m$ (S), old Promontory route fell into disuse. In 1942, with U.S. at war, rails were taken up for scrap; with special ceremonies, the last spike was drawn where it had been driven 73 yrs. before.

**20. TREMONTON,** on W. bank of Malad R., is on line of hist. Salt Lake Cutoff from Bear R. to City of Rocks. Forty-niners crossed Bear R. $2^m$ (E) of here & then angled (NW) to intersect Cal. Trl. Route was first used by immigrants in 1848. Sam. Hensley, coming (W) with a sm. party in Aug., 1848, tried to follow Hastings Cutoff across Salt Desert (see US40). Finding the desert miry from recent rains, he turned back & found this way (N) around the lake. A few wks. later, far down Humboldt R., he encountered eastbound members of Mormon Battalion & gave them a waybill of his route. With their wagons, Battalion members marked out a trl. Thousands of Forty-niners adopted it next spring, & it saw heavy use until completion of Pacific RR. **56. SNOWVILLE,** center of farming area, interesting because irrigated & dry farm belts are so clearly distinguishable. Lower lands along Deep Cr. are irrigated; sloping benchlands are dryfarmed. (W) of Snowville US30S parallels **IDAHO LINE** for $18^m$ & then bends (NW.) to cross it at **81.**

## US 40—UTAH

**UTAH-COLO. LINE** ($92^m$ from Craig, Colo.) **(W) to UTAH-NEV. LINE** **($110^m$** from Elko, Nev.). **334. US40**

Via: Vernal, Duchesne, Heber, Salt Lake City, Grantsville, Wendover.

US40 in its eastern reaches closely approximates route by which Father Escalante entered Utah in 1776; it then crosses rugged Wasatch range to Salt Lake City. (W) of Salt Lake City, it is combined with US50 for crossing of most desolate portion of N. Amer., the glittering Salt Desert, a route made hist. by Cal.-bound immigrants who traveled it in 1846.

### Sec. 1: UTAH-COLO. LINE to SALT LAKE CITY. 207.

US40 makes dramatic entrance into Utah, under high pink & white escarpment of Cliff Ridge (R), S. wall of Yampa Plateau. At **6.5.** hy. surmounts low ridge to come into full view of wide sage basin (L) down which Father Escalante journeyed into Utah, 1776. For nearly $9^m$ hy. parallels route of Franciscan explorer, then turns sharply (W) across hills to dip down & cross **GREEN R.** at **17.** At **17.5. JENSEN,** surrounded by alfalfa & grain fields, its weathered log houses shaded by huge cottonwood trees, is farming community strung out widely along W. bank of Green R., named for ferryman who operated here in 70's. At Jensen is J. with St.149.

SIDE TRIP: On this Rd. (R) $4^m$ to boundary of **Dinosaur Nat. Mon.** The **Mon.** (R) notes place where Escalante forded Green R. St.149 cont. to Mon. hqs. $7^m$ & temporary mus. (free). From **Sandstone Quarry** here, reached by short foot trl., more than a million tons of rock have been removed to excavate dinosaur skeletons, many of them now on exhibit at Carnegie Mus. in Pittsburgh, Smithsonian Institution, Washington, D.C., Univ. of Utah in Salt Lake City, & Field House of Nat. Hist. in Vernal (see below). Quarry was opened in

1909 by Dr. Earl Douglass; since then 22 complete skeletons & thousands of individual bones have been removed incl. 5 species of dinosaurs, primitive mammals, crocodiles, invertebrate forms, & plants. No bones are now being removed from Mon.; gov. paleontologists will cut away rock to exhibit here bones of gigantic reptiles that roamed this country in Mesozoic times. Quarry is principal attraction, but short Rd. leads to gorge of **Split Mt.,** where Green R. bursts through Uinta Mts. Also comprised within Mon. are 247 sq. miles of wilderness in W. Colo., strung along canyons of Green & Yampa Rs.

**30. VERNAL** is set in middle of wide, green Ashley Valley. Formerly a trade center for cattle & sheep raisers, since end of World War II it has been caught in an oil boom which doubled pop. & physically transformed town. **Field House of Natural Hist.** (O.9-5 wks.) contains mounted dinosaur skeletons, paintings of prehist. scenes, geological displays, & displays of resources & activities of Utah counties. Bank of Vernal is famous for manner of its construction; it was built of brick sent from Salt Lake City by parcel post. Freight charges in 1919 exceeded parcel post rates, & enterprising builders flooded Salt Lake City, Price, & Vernal P.O. with packages of bricks. The idea quickly caught hold; tools, wagon parts, & canned goods were mailed in, & farm products mailed out. A shipment of corn required 10 4-ton trucks. Federal P.O. regulations finally were changed to forbid shipment of more than 200 pounds a day to any addressee. Here is J. with St.44.

SIDE TRIP: On this Rd. (R) across Uinta Mts. to Utah's most isolated cty., **Daggett,** on N. slope of Uintas. Rd. crosses **Diamond Mt. Plateau,** named for celebrated swindle of 1871 by which 2 prospectors who salted a claim here with South African "niggerheads" got away with $660,000 of a S. F. financier's bankroll. At 41.5m is J. with dirt Rd. leading (R) 1m past **Green L.** (f.), a 23-a. L. lying almost on rim of Red Canyon. Side Rd. cont. along canyon (R), with driveouts to rim at 2m & 3m where a spectacular view is had of Green R. (1,572') below. St.44 cont. to **Manila** at 74m, tiny seat of Daggett Cty., from which dirt Rds. branch (W) & (E) to Lyman & Green River, Wyo.

US40 climbs (SW) out of Ashley Valley to enter Uinta Basin, through which flow the Duchesne & its large tributaries, Uinta & Strawberry. This tremendous basin was set aside as a reserv. for Utes by Pres. Lincoln, Oct. 3, 1861, & was not opened for white settlement until 1905. Uinta Basin is walled in on (S) by Bad Lands Cliffs & Uinta Mts., Utah's highest & most difficult range. Except for St.44 (see above) near its E. end, no yr.-round Rd. crosses Uinta range along its entire 125m length, & only other Rd. of any description that crosses it is rough Mirror L. Rd. bet. Kamas & Evanston, Wyo. (see Salt Lake City Trip I). A 243,957-a. saddle across backbone of Uintas was set aside by U.S. Forest Serv. in 1931 as High Uintas Primitive Area, to be maintained substantially in "wild" state. A thousand glacial lakes are found in Uintas, with heavily forested mts., grassy pks., open meadows, & peaks (like 13,498' Kings Peak) which lift barren crowns high above timberline. Accoms. at Mirror L. on St.34; at Savage's Ranch, Hanna, & Defas Pk. on St.35; at Moon L. on St.134; & at N. end of Rock Cr. Rd. branching off from St.134; area may also be entered from (N), via Lonetree, Wyo. Info. at Adm. Office, Wasatch Nat. For., Salt Lake City. At **54.5.** on US40 is J. with St.88.

SIDE TRIP: On this Rd. (L) 1m to **Ft. Duchesne,** hqs. of Uinta & Ouray Ind. Reserv., occupied by Whiteriver, Uinta, & Uncompahgre bands of Ute Inds. Reserv. (1,680 pop.) covers c.384,000 as. situated along foothills of Uinta Mts. & on E. side of Green R., the 2 segments conn. by a narrow corridor along route of St.88. Inds. derive livelihood from farming & stock raising. Annual Ind. Fair is held at Duchesne in Sept., in conn. with 3-day Uinta Basin Industrial Convention. Bear Dance & Sun Dance (fee) are staged; Bear Dance (a spring festival) at Whiterocks, Ouray, & Myton in late Mar. or early Ap.; Sun Dance (to cure or avert physical infirmities) at Whiterocks in late July or early Aug. At 20m **Ouray,** above confluence of Green, White, & Duchesne Rs. is one of 3 bridges that cross Green-Colo. R. system in Utah. On E. side of Green R., above mouth of the White, are remains of old adobe ft., thought to have been built by Antoine Robidoux in winter of 1837-38, 1st yr.-round white dwelling in Utah. Site was favorite wintering ground for trappers, & some log huts had been raised here as early as 1834. "Fort Robidoux" was evidently occupied only a few months; its builder moved farther (N) & (W) to est. a new post on Whiterocks R.

At **56.5.** is J. with gravel Rd.

SIDE TRIP: On this Rd. (R) 13m to **Whiterocks,** site of annual Sun Dance, now Ind. settlement centered about Whiterocks Ind. sch. Three-quarters of a mile (E) & half mile (S) of sch. are remains of Ft. Wintey. Probably est. in 1838, trading post was abandoned by Antoine Robidoux in 1845 after Utes attacked his branch establishment, Ft. Uncompahgre, in Colo.

Beyond **ROOSEVELT, 60.,** trading center for farmers & ranchers, US40 crosses Duchesne R. & at **MYTON, 70.,** comes again into Father Escalante's trl. After crossing Green R., Escalante had come (W) up Duchesne Valley, parallel to route of US40. From this pt. Escalante cont. up river, crossing & recrossing it, to site of Duchesne, then after unavailing efforts to ascend Strawberry R., proceeded (W) up a wash (N) of US40. Crossing Strawberry R. just below Reservoir, he climbed to Strawberry Divide by way of Squaw Cr., & then descended Fifth Water Canyon & Diamond Fork to Spanish Fork Canyon (see US6-US50).

**89. DUCHESNE** is principal J. within Uinta Basin. At Duchesne St.33 goes (SW) up Ind. Canyon over 9,100′ summit to **Castlegate** at 45$^{m}$, on Denver & Rio Grande Western RR. (see US6-US50), while St.35 follows (NW) up Duchesne R. & over 9,480′ summit to rejoin US40 at **Hailstone,** 78$^{m}$ (see Salt Lake City Loop Tour I). A 3rd Rd. jounces up rugged canyon of the Strawberry to **Reservoir,** 40$^{m}$ (W), while mainline US40 goes almost directly (W) to cross Wasatch divide at head of Daniels Canyon.

(W) of Duchesne US40 runs through miles of sage & juniper country, & by way of Deep Cr. Canyon penetrates a great valley, in hollows of which lie blue waters of Strawberry Reservoir, completed 1915, Utah's 1st important Fed. Reclamation Project, & 1st project for diverting Colo. drainage waters into Great Basin. By a 19,000′ tunnel, waters impounded in Reservoir are released into Diamond Fork, & via Spanish Fork R. carried to Utah Valley. The Central Utah Reclamation Project envisions a vastly expanded diversion of waters from Green R. & its tributaries which by way of Strawberry Reservoir & 300$^{m}$ system of aqueducts shall water farmlands of central Utah as far (S) & (W) as Fillmore & Kanosh. By this means 300,000 as. of land now under irrigation would receive supplemental water, & 150,000 as. of new land would be brought under cultivation. At **130.** is J. with dirt Rd. which makes 15$^{m}$ loop around **Strawberry Reservoir** (trout f.boats.campgrounds), returning to US40 at **137.** Reservoir lies within boundaries of Strawberry Valley Bird Refuge. US40 climbs quickly to head of Daniels Canyon, then winds down this canyon past frequent For. Service campgrounds, until it opens out upon Provo Valley at **HEBER, 159.** (For balance of US40 to Salt Lake City, **207.,** see Salt Lake City).

## Sec. 2: SALT LAKE CITY to NEVADA LINE. 127.

At **36. GRANTSVILLE,** at W. verge of Salt Lake City, jumping-off place for crossing Salt Desert. One immigrant party in 1846 attempted to cross Stansbury Mts. by way of cleft in mts. immediately (W) of Grantsville, but even as a horse trl. this was hard going, & other early wayfarers, like mod. travelers, had to be content to circle N. slope of Stansbury range. Route across Salt Desert was pioneered by Frémont in 1845. Eastbound in 1846, Clyman-Hastings' party adopted it & later in summer, Hastings & Donner-Reed parties made a wagon Rd. of it. Their desperate experience in crossing Salt Desert thereafter discouraged use of "Hastings Cutoff" except by infrequent pack parties. Not until building of Western Pac. RR. in 1907 & modern hy. in 1925 was it possible for travelers to venture upon Salt Desert except at hazard of their lives. **51. TIMPIE JUNCTION.** As US40 rounds Stansbury Mts. there is J. with dirt Rd.

SIDE TRIP: On this Rd. (L) 15.5$^{m}$ to **Iosepa,** ghost town sett. 1889 by Hawaiian converts to Mormonism. In 1893 leprosy broke out among them, which resulted in Utah's only leper colony. Hawaiians were unable to adapt themselves to Utah climate, & after building of a temple at Laie, Hawaii, in 1916, most of colonists returned. The springs at Iosepa earlier had provided last supplies of good water & grass for those following Salt Desert trl.; after careful preparation here, immigrants crossed Skull Valley to low depression in Cedar Mts. ever since called Hastings Pass, & then struck out across desert for nearest water, at base of Pilot Peak, 75$^{m}$ away. Bet. Timpie Junction & Low Pass, US40 traverses N. end of Skull Valley, named from skulls found here by Mormon pioneers, custom of Gosiute Ind. having been to bury their dead in springs. US40 runs through Low Pass, bet. barren Lakeside Mts. (R) & Cedar Mts. (L).

**MON.** (R) at **75.** marks pt. where 1846 wagon trl. coming down out of Cedar Mts. crosses modern hy. **KNOLLS** at **87.** is a cluster of bldgs. at E. edge of salt beds. When Great Salt L. withdrew from this area, its waters had already become a concentrated salt solution & a billion tons of salt bestrew surface of desert. The concrete-like surface makes ideal course for auto racing. In 1914 Teddy Tetzlaff set unofficial world's record of 141$^{m}$ an hr. for a measured mile. Modern exploitation of salt flats began in 1926, when Utah's Ab Jenkins drove 24 hrs. without relief to shatter almost every world speed record; he drove 2,710$^{m}$ at average of 112$^{m}$ an hr. In 1935 Sir Malcolm Campbell, abandoning hazardous beach at Daytona, Fla., 1st broke 300$^{m}$ an hr. mark for measured mile & other Brit. drivers subsequently boosted record to 394.196$^{m}$ an hr., the mark of John Cobb in 1947. At **121.5.** motorists can leave hy. & drive as fast as they like across level surface of **Bonneville Salt Flats** (R), only place in Utah where there is no speed limit. **127. WENDOVER,** RR. town at W. edge of Salt Desert, lies two-thirds in Utah & one-third in Nev. In Nev. third of Wendover the thirsty traveler will find what he has nowhere seen in Utah, a cocktail lounge, since liquor is sold in Utah by package only, from St. liquor stores. At Wendover hy. crosses **UTAH-NEV. LINE.**

# US 6 & US 50—UTAH

**UTAH-COLO. LINE** (34$^{m}$ from Grand Junction, Colo.) **to NEVADA LINE** (60$^{m}$ from Ely, Nev.). **384. US6, US50**

Via: Green River, Price, Helper, Soldier Summit, Spanish Fork, Santaquin, Eureka & Delta.

Eastern half of this route, bet. Colo. Line & Utah Valley, is combined route of US6-US50 locally called US50, & is only hy. for travel to & from SE. Utah. It crosses a barren plateau reg., winds through canyons with rich coal deposits, & beyond Wasatch divide descends hist. Spanish Fork Canyon to fertile Utah Valley. US6 (W) of Spanish Fork, passes through an arid, semi-mountainous reg. of mining towns & irrigated valleys to rolling desert plains extending to Nev. Line.

## Sec. 1: UTAH-COLO. LINE to SPANISH FORK. 205.

US6-US50 enters Utah in midst of desolate wasteland, with only irrigated Book Cliffs (R) to lend variety to landscape. Across this red mesa, hy. undulates to **52., CRESCENT JUNCTION,** at J. with US160 (see). From this pt. (W) to Green R., hy. follows hist. route of Old Spanish Trl. making the only practicable all-yr. crossing of Green R. **72. GREEN RIVER** lies along W. bank of R. & is noted for its nationally-marketed watermelons & cantaloupes. It is starting pt. for many river-running expeditions. Maj. John Wesley Powell, in 1869, was 1st to descend canyons of Green & Colo. Rs. He repeated hazardous journey in 1871-72 to gain further information about this little-known area. In 1889 Brown-Stanton expedition, exploring a possible water-level RR. route to Cal. through canyons, lost 3 men by drowning. In Green R. is J. with St.24 (see US89). US6-US50 turns (W) & (N) from Green R. At **94.** is J. with Cty. Rd. leading (L) to **Castle Dale,** 43$^{m}$. This Rd. follows course of Spanish Trl. directly (W) to Castle Valley (see below). Main hy. cont. (N) toward Price R. Valley, following route 1st adopted for wagons in 1853, by Capt. J. W. Gunnison, who was exploring a central RR. route. US6-US50 crosses Price R. at **WOODSIDE, 98.,** & climbs steadily (SW). **136. PRICE,** business center for east-central Utah. Coal deposits opened up in Book Cliffs & in canyons of E. slope of Wasatch were exceptionally rich & gave name to Carbon Cty., soon org. with Price as its seat. During the 90's Butch Cassidy's Wild Bunch rode outlaw trl. from Hole in the Wall in Wyo., down through Browns Hole, to Robbers Roost (see below) & enlivened existence in Price. It gave name to annual Robbers Roost Roundup, held in Price 1st wk. in Sept. Intermountain Band Contest for high sch. bands held in Price each spring, annually attracts over 2,500 contestants & 20,000 visitors. Here is J. with St.10.

SIDE TRIP: On St.10 (L) through Castle Valley, named for its castellated walls. 31$^{m}$ **Castle Dale,** a solid farm town sett. 1875. To (SE) bet. Castle Valley & Green R., rises enormous San Rafael Swell. In its almost inaccessible recesses Robbers Roost gang took up residence during the 90's. St.10 cont. (S) through farmlands that give place to twisted red hills. At 73$^{m}$, **Fremont Junction,** is J. with St.72 (see US89). St.10, following route of Spanish Trl., climbs to head of Salina Canyon & descends it to **Salina,** 109$^{m}$ (see US89).

**144. HELPER,** clinging to steep walls on either side of Price Canyon, & thronged by RR. men & miners, was named in 1892 for extra engines, or "helpers," required to push trains up heavy grade to Soldier Summit. US50-US6 climbs on up canyon to **CASTLEGATE, 147.,** named for castellated rock formations at entrance to valley. In Castlegate, on Mar. 8, 1924, one of Utah's worst mine disasters occurred; 3 terrific explosions took lives of 173 men. At **192.** is E. J. in narrow Thistle

Valley with US89 (see). Below, at **195.** is confluence with Diamond Fork, down which Father Escalante came into Spanish Fork Canyon in 1776 (see US40). **201.** At mouth of **SPANISH FORK CANYON** is W. J. of US50 & US6. US50 angles down (NW) to J. with US91 6$^m$ below in Springville (see US91). US6 & US89 cont. down sloping benchland of Utah Valley to separate in **SPANISH FORK, 205.**

### Sec. 2: SPANISH FORK to UTAH-NEV. LINE. 179.

US6 (SW) of Spanish Fork runs concurrent with US91 to **SANTAQUIN, 14.**, at S. end of Utah Valley & then strikes off (W) into rolling, juniper-covered hills. **34. EUREKA** has been one of Utah's most productive mining towns since its inception in 1870, its gold, silver, copper, lead, & zinc valued in excess of $400,000,000. Mining here is deep-level mining, by perpendicular shafts 2,000′ or more. **52. JERICHO** has no pop. whatever except during shipping season, but thousands of sheep are sheared each spring in its large corrals, when it is one of leading wool shipping pts. in W. **85. DELTA,** with its clean wide streets, modern homes, & prosperous business sec., is a farming town & shipping center for sm. mines. Before 1900 this sec. of great Pahvan Valley was regarded as hopeless desert, but has been reclaimed by water from Delta Reservoir. In 1940, nearly one-fourth of alfalfa seed in U.S. was produced in Delta dist. US6 (W) of agric. area contiguous to Delta, hustles off into flat country covered with stunted sage & interspersed with patches of dark volcanic rock. **132.5. MARJUM PASS & 155. COWBOY PASS.** Hy. crosses Antelope Mts. & Confusion Range. Snake Valley opens out ahead; in it is **ROBINSONS RANCH, 174.,** hamlet with a few log houses surrounded by orchards & poplar trees. To (N) & (W) lift high, pine-darkened peaks of Snake Mts. **179.** US6 crosses **NEV. LINE.**

## US 160, ST. 47—UTAH

**CRESCENT JUNCTION** (on US6-US50) **(S) to UTAH-ARIZ. LINE** (93$^m$ from Tuba City, Ariz.). **186. US160, St.47**

Via: Moab, Monticello, Blanding, Bluff, Mexican Hat, (Monument Valley).

Route by US160 & St.47 (S) to Ariz. Line traverses San Juan country, one of least-known & most int. parts of Utah. Red permeates everything, plains, deserts, hills, cliffs, canyons—even homes & color of men's skin. Settlements are small & far apart; land is devoted almost exclusively to grazing of cattle & sheep.

Branching (S) from US6-US50 at Crescent Junction, US160 follows an almost straight course over broad, brush-covered plain. **Henry Mts.** (R) 80$^m$ to (SW), & **La Sal Mts.** (L), 35$^m$ to (SE), loom high above low, table-topped ridges of red, gray & yellow that hug the plain. At **14.** is J. with improved dirt Rd.

SIDE TRIP: On this Rd. (R) 35$^m$ to **Dead Horse Pt.,** where earth falls away in a 3,000′ chasm, Upper Grand Canyon of the Colo., perhaps the most sensational canyon spectacle in Utah.

US160 cont. (S) through eroded red hills to **J.** at **20.** with St.93.

SIDE TRIP: On this Rd. (L) 9$^m$ to **Arches Nat. Mon.** Here red canyon walls have been carved by wind & rain in wonderful & grotesque forms; there are arches & windows cut through solid stone, immense monoliths balanced perilously on disintegrating bases, chimneys, deep caves & high, sculptured walls of salmon-hued rock. Mon. has 5 secs., each different in geologic & scenic interest, the Windows in center, Cth. Towers in (S) & Klondike Bluffs, Devils Garden, & Delicate Arch, in (N). The Windows as yet is only sec. readily accessible by car.

Over a long steel bridge, US160 crosses Colo. R. at **30.** & arrives at J. with St.128.

SIDE TRIP: On this Rd. (L) 31.5$^m$ to **Dewey,** a spectacular drive up Colo. R. to its confluence with the Dolores; this is not, however, a Rd. for nervous drivers, or one to be driven in winter or during spring floods.

**32. MOAB,** beautifully green in its red valley. Seat of Grand Cty., it is main business center of SE. Utah. A Mormon Ind. mission attempted to est. a settlement here in 1855, but after 3 were killed, "Elk Mountain Mission" was abandoned. Remnants of their stone ft. may still be seen. Area was resettled 20 yrs. later by cattlemen who drifted (W) into Utah from Colo. Old Irrigation Canal Arroyo, 50 to 300 yds. (W) of US160 through Moab, is a channel carved by irrigation stream left running when Inds. drove missionaries from valley in 1855. Boats & guides are avail. at Moab for trips down Colo. R. to J. with Green R. & up that stream to town of Green River.

(S) of Moab, US160 crosses country vegetated with greasewood & prickly pear. To (E) rise La Sal Mts., 2nd highest in St. **48. CANE SPRINGS,** watering place for early travelers; a cave in a cliff opp. has been converted into ranch house by construction of a wall across its opening. **59. LOOKING GLASS ROCK** (L) is salmon-colored sandstone wall pierced by opening 25′ high & 50′ wide, so named because the view seems to be reflection of opp. wall. To (E), Sage Plain opens out, 1,200 sq. miles of monotonously level country extending to Dolores R. in Colo. US160 skirts its W. edge, flanked (R) by Abajo Mts., locally called Blue Mts., the 8 peaks of which rise abruptly from Sage Plain. **85. MONTICELLO,** lying at base of Abajo Mts., is seat of San Juan Cty. With abbreviated growing season, adj. country is devoted to raising of sheep & cattle. Here is J. with dirt Rd. At Monticello is J. with St.47 on which main tour cont. from here.

SIDE TRIPS: (A) On US160 (E) across Sage Plain to Colo. Line which is crossed at 10m (S) of Cortez, Colo. 51m.

(B) A dirt Rd. (R) 10m from Monticello leads into Abajo Mts. to **Cooley Pass** near summit (L) of **Abajo Peak** (11,357′). From top of that peak an unrivaled view of intricately carved & marvelously colored Colo. Plateau may be had.

Main tour now cont. on St.47. Branching from US160 at Monticello, St.47 runs (S) along green foothills of Abajo Mts. to **BLANDING** at **105.,** farming community on White Mesa. With less than 600 inhabitants in 1940, Blanding was most populous town in San Juan Cty., which has area equivalent to combined areas of Conn., Del. & R.I. Although Blanding dreams about a hy. (E) across Sage Plain to Colo., such a hy. would have to bridge 10 Sage Plain canyons within 15m.

SIDE TRIP: From Blanding on St.95 (R) 47m to **Natural Bridges Nat. Mon.** An area of spectacular erosive formations, Mon. is especially celebrated for 3 immense, water-carved bridges & number of prehist. cliff dwellings. Rd. to Mon. was formerly distinguished by strange formation called Goblet of Venus, a bowl of vermilion sandstone 6′ or 7′ in diam., weighing about 5 tons., which was delicately balanced atop a symmetrical stem 6′ long & about thickness of a man's leg; this formation, sad to record, was destroyed in 1948 by vandals. In Mon. itself 3 famous bridges are Owachomo, Kachina & Sipapu. St.95 cont. by rough Rd. down White Canyon to toll ferry at **Hite** on Colo. R. at 88m (see US89).

(S) of Blanding, St.47 runs along flat divide bet. Cottonwood Canyon (R) & Recapture Canyon (L); at one place canyons are less than 30′ apart. At **122.5.,** is J. with primitive dirt Rd.

SIDE TRIP: On this Rd. (L) to **Hovenweep Nat. Mon.;** Rd. is passable, but Mon. is more easily approached from Colo. Hovenweep preserves ruins of a remarkable prehist. civilization in 4 large & several tributary canyons cut in mesa bet. Montezuma & McElmo creeks. These Pueblo remains have been deserted at least 600 yrs.; time of their beginnings has not yet been established.

**132. BLUFF,** perched forlornly on red banks of San Juan R., has a history, heroic & heartbreaking. In 1879 Mormon Ch. dispatched one of its characteristic colonizing missions to settle narrow bottomlands of San Juan R. Mission elected to cut new Rd. (S) & (E) through heart of Colo. badlands to conn. new settlement with parent colonies in south-central Utah. Route adopted was (S) from Escalante to Colo. R., down to river-level by chute cut in solid rock of Hole-in-the-Rock, & thence across Slick Rocks & Clay Hills to site of Bluff. To carve a route across such country required entire winter of 1879-80; it was Ap., 1880, before journey came to its end. Floods eventually ripped out arable lands along the San Juan & San Juan missionaries had to migrate (N) to Blanding, Monticello & Moab. Bluff today is nearly deserted.

(S) from Bluff, St.47 is more primitive. (Travelers should carry water & should not stray from Rd. except with competent guide. In crossing the dozen unbridged washes bet. Bluff & Mexican Hat, care should be taken in times of torrential rain.) **139. COMB RIDGE** is climbed by succession of switchbacks & then Rd. winds down to **NAVAHO SPRINGS, 141.** (good water;reached by 100-yd.trl.to L.). Rd. weaves through Snake Canyon & climbs Lime Ridge to distant view of Mon. Valley. **156. MEXICAN HAT LODGE** takes its name from 400′ high, cone-shaped mound of red shale, resembling a gigantic Mexican sombrero balanced on its crown. Mexican Hat Lodge is owned & operated by Norman D. Nevills, "white water" boatman, with whom arrangements may be made for trips ranging from 4m to 200m on San Juan & Colo. Rs.

St.47 crosses San Juan R. at **156.5.** by suspension bridge. Normally one of largest streams in St., on occasion the San Juan has dried up entirely. It carries an enormous amount of silt—as much as 75% by vol.—which creates singular "sand waves" at flood stage. (S) of R., St.47 crosses Navaho Ind. Reserv., largest in Utah, which extends far (S) into Ariz. (Guides advised in this area.) From **MONUMENT PASS** at **178.** maroon buttes & pinnacles of Mon. Valley are seen to rise like skyscrapers out of red desert, towering 1,000′ above valley floor. "Stage Coach" was filmed here in 1939; other pictures which have used the strange valley as location incl. "Billy the Kid" (1941), "My Darling Clementine" (1946), & "The Harvey Girls" (1947). **184.** J. with dirt Rd.

SIDE TRIP: On this Rd. (R) 2m to **Goulding's Trading Post** (rooms.meals.guides.horses). From Goulding's Post pack-trips can be arranged to Navaho Mt. & Rainbow Natural Bridge, & to dozens of other natural bridges, canyons & cliff-dwellings. Rainbow Bridge Nat. Mon. cannot be reached by automobile, & must be approached by 2-day pack trip (NE) from Rainbow Lodge, Ariz., or by longer trips from Mexican Hat or Goulding's Post. This peerless natural bridge, beneath which the Capitol at Washingon could be placed with ample clearance, is a perfectly formed span of red & yellow sandstone, located c.6m (N) of Ariz. Line & 10m (SW) of J. of Colo. & San Juan Rs.

St.47 threads its way past red monoliths of Mon. Valley & at **186.** crosses **ARIZ. LINE.**

## US 89—UTAH

**UTAH-IDAHO LINE** (25m from Montpelier, Idaho) **(S) to UTAH-ARIZ. LINE** (4m from Fredonia, Ariz.). **458. US89**

Via: Logan, Brigham City, Ogden, Salt Lake City, Provo, Spanish Fork, Thistle, Manti, Richfield, Panguitch & Kanab.

US89 in N. part of St. provides occasional alt. routes bet. major pop. centers, then at Spanish Fork veers (E) to a chain of scenic interior valleys as direct route to Grand Canyon. A series of cross-roads conn. it with US91, while other Rds. branch off (E) & penetrate Utah's wild hinterland.

### Sec. 1: UTAH-IDAHO LINE to SALT LAKE CITY. 135.

US89 makes spectacular entrance into Utah along W. shore of Bear L. (f.boat. swim.), whose blue waters have delighted travelers from time of fur trade. Trappers held their trading fair or "rendezvous" at its S. shore in 1827 & 1828. Fights with Blackfeet long celebrated in mt. yarns were waged in narrow lowlands bet. L. shore & mts. After collapse of fur trade in 1840's, Bear L. was haunt only of Shoshoni Inds. until Mormon colonizers came (N) in the sixties. The Saints soon discovered in Bear L. a 1st-class monster, "not less than 90′ in length," with "ears or bunches on side of its head nearly as large as a pint cup," & able to cleave waters at a conservative mile-a-minute pace. **4. GARDEN CITY,** & J. with St.3.

SIDE TRIP: On St.3 (L) around S. shore of Bear L., over a low divide & (S) through rolling uplands to **Randolph,** 38m & **Woodruff,** 42m, which is at J. with St.39 (see US91). St.3 swings toward Evanston, Wyo., long blue rampart of the Wasatch beyond Saleratus Valley (R). At 52m, St.3 crosses Wyo. Line & cont. as Wyo. St.89 to **Evanston** at 69m.

From Garden City, US89 turns (W) to climb to head of Logan Canyon. At **10.5.** is enchanting view of Bear L. & distant mts. in Idaho & Wyo. Logan Canyon itself is one of Utah's most scenic gorges, with mile-high, almost perpendicular walls, forested slopes with numerous camp sites (all facils.) & sparkling Logan R., favorite f. stream. **30.** J. with dirt Rd.

SIDE TRIP: On this Rd. (R) 5m to **Old Juniper Camp.** (R) 1m from this camp on a steel foot trl. up a small lateral canyon through groves of aspen & pine to gnarled 44′ high, 15′ thick, 3,000 yrs. old **Juniper Jardine,** oldest tree in Utah, believed to be oldest juniper in world.

As hy. emerges from **LOGAN CANYON, 42.5.,** shorelines of prehist. L. Bonneville, which in Pleistocene times overspread most of W. Utah, are visible along mountainsides. **44. LOGAN.** J. with US91 (see). Bet. Logan & Brigham City, motorist has choice of routes; US91 is 10m shorter, but circuitous US89, having a lower elevation, is often preferred for winter driving. Through an open farming country along slope of Great Salt Lake valley, winding through small Mormon villages, hy. reaches at **79. BRIGHAM CITY,** & comes to J. with US30S (see), then with US91, & is united with them as far as Ogden (see US91). From **OGDEN, 100.,** US89 runs close under face of the mts. to mouth of **WEBER CANYON, 108.** (For rest of distance to **SALT LAKE CITY** at **135.,** see Salt Lake City Trip II.)

## Sec. 2: SALT LAKE CITY to RICHFIELD. 173.

Separating from US91 at **SPANISH FORK, 55.,** (S) of Salt Lake City, US89 is united with US6 and US50 through lower Spanish Fork Canyon to **THISTLE** at **68.** Here US89 turns (S) across brown hills to long Sanpete Valley. Sett. late in 1849, as 1st Mormon colonizing venture beyond limits of Great Salt Lake & Utah valleys, Sanpete Valley became a little Scandinavia after Mormon missionaries began to make headway in N. Europe. Climate was familiar to converts from that area, & they have made Sanpete Valley a showpiece in Utah agric. Especially in dairy farming & production of blooded stock, Sanpete Valley has made its influence felt. **113. PIGEON HOLLOW JUNCTION,** at J. with St.11, from Nephi (see US91). **118. EPHRAIM,** center of turkey & sheep raising area, is also home of **Snow College,** founded by Mormon Ch. in 1883 & taken over by St. as jr. college in 1932. **Central Utah Mus.** (O.2-4.wks.Sept.-June), with 11,000 specimens of Ind. pottery, arrowheads, sandals, moccasins & bone knives, reflects early Ute fondness for Sanpete Valley. The snow-white **Temple** on hill overlooking **MANTI** at **125.,** marks city from afar. Here in 1849 was made 1st settlement in Sanpete Valley. White limestone temple (O.only to Mormons) was begun by Brigham Young just before his death in 1877; it was completed 11 yrs. later. **140. GUNNISON,** at J. with St.28 coming up from Levan (see US91). Here Sanpitch R. flows into Sevier R., once Utah's mightiest interior stream, but now imprisoned by 4 large reservoirs along its course. **154. SALINA** takes its name from rock salt deposits in near-by hills. At mouth of Salina Canyon, J. with St.10 (see US6-US50) which follows hist. route across Wasatch used until early 80's for travel to & from Colo. plateau country. **165. SIGURD.** J. with St.24.

SIDE TRIP: St.24 is an adventure Rd. The 174m bet. Sigurd & Green River carry tourist across every kind of terrain. The 60m to Torrey are paved & succeeding 55m to Hanksville improved. The final 59m to Green River, however, is unimproved Rd. (1949) uphill & down, across numerous washes (carry water). From this through-route, Rds. branch off into even wilder country. From Sigurd St.24 climbs (SE) toward Fish L., Utah's most popular f. area. Beyond the **Rim of the Basin** at 29.5m is J. with St.25, leading (L) 7.5m to **Fish L.** (varied accoms.boats.guides.f.), a jeweled L. 5 ¼m long, ¾m wide, set in crater of ancient volcano. L. abounds with rainbow, brook, & mackinaw trout, & surrounding alpine fors. & meadows have deer, elk, snowshoe rabbits, & even a few mt. lions & coyotes. 43m **Loa** takes its name from Hawaiian volcano, reflecting worldwide labors of Mormon missionaries. St.24 cont. (SE) to J. at 56m with St.117 leading (R) 10.5m to **Grover,** where guides (absolutely necessary) & horses may be hired for climbing to 49-sq. mile **Aquarius Plateau,** with its numerous Ls., sage deserts, mesas, pinnacles, spires & vertical-walled canyons, all at elevations from 10,000′ to 12,500′. St.117 cont. (S) 32m to **Boulder,** at J. with St.23 (see below). Country becomes even wilder & more spectacularly colored, at 71.5m.

St.24 enters **Capitol Reef Nat. Mon.** The "reef," a great 20m-long ridge of rock upthrust high above surrounding terrain, takes it name from white Navaho sandstone domes. Capitol Reef formations combine fantasy of Bryce (see below) & grandeur of Zion Nat. Pks. with more color than either. Great temples & walls, huge arches & natural bridges are splashed & striated with every imaginable color. Petrified fors. are found & varied archeological remains, incl. carved petroglyphs & painted pictographs on cliff walls. 72.5m **Fruita,** within Mon., a green oasis founded in 1878 along red-walled Fremont or Dirty Devil R. Through **Grand Wash** at 73m & **Capitol Gorge** at 79m (dangerous during summer cloudbursts), St.24 crosses Mon., emerging upon a desert of pink, gray & yellow hills which roll away far to (E) & (SE). 115m **Hanksville** was a rendezvous in 90's for Robbers Roost gang which held sway throughout this country (see US6-US50).

From Hanksville (R) 52m on rugged desert Rd. to **Hite,** on Colo. R. Here is toll ferry. A rough Rd. (E) of Colo. up White Canyon climbs to **Natural Bridges Nat. Mon.** at 93m, then crosses broken red rock country to **Blanding** at 140m (see US160-St.47).

Bet. Hanksville & Green River, hy. fords series of streams & washes (dangerous to cross during heavy rains, when great walls of water may sweep down at any moment). 174m **Green River,** at J. with US6-US50 (see).

**173. RICHFIELD,** business center serving prosperous farming country of south-central Utah; has cheese factories, flour mills, a clay & metal mill, with coal & gypsum mines near-by. City is also widely known as base for deer hunt. in season & for lion hunt. in any season. Other Utah cities where packs of lion-hunting dogs are maintained incl. Kanab, Cedar City, Kanosh, Salina, Henrieville, Panguitch, Nephi, Goshen & Fruitland. (List of packs & guides obtainable from U.S. Biological Survey, Fed. Bldg., Salt Lake City.) Annual Black Hawk celebration in Richfield (mid-Aug.) comm. end of Black Hawk War with Utes, which bet. 1865 & 1868 forced evacuation of all Sevier Valley towns.

### Sec. 3: RICHFIELD to UTAH-ARIZ. LINE. 150.

(S) of Richfield spacious Sevier Valley narrows until at **SEVIER, 18.,** it is contracted into gorge of Marysvale Canyon. So formidable was this scenic canyon in pioneer times that both the Spanish Trl. to Cal. & later the Mormon wagon Rd. detoured it through the mts. to (E). At **25. BIG ROCK CANDY MT.** (R) is a rounded, lemon-colored hill sparsely grown with evergreens. No grass grows in the yellow, alum-tainted soil. Higher up the canyon a few small gold mines still operate, reminiscent of boom days of Bullionville & other ghost camps. Passing green, fresh valley of **MARYSVALE** at **30., PIUTE RESERVOIR** (L) at **41.** (f.h.), US89 comes to **JUNCTION, 45.,** seat of Piute Cty., at confluence of E. & S. Forks of Sevier R. At junction hy. joins St.22.

SIDE TRIP: On St.22 (L) to **Antimony,** 17m, isolated Mormon farm community & up E. Fork of Sevier to **Widtsoe Junction,** 42m.

Here St.23 leads (L) through brilliantly colored canyons to **Escalante,** 27m, remote Mormon community on Kaiparowits Plateau. Escalante is pt. of departure for trips to the badlands country along lower reaches of Escalante R. St.23 cont. down Escalante R. & then up Boulder Cr. to **Boulder,** 56m, along one of most isolated communities in U.S. & approachable only from (W) along a knife-edged ridge called Hells Backbone. St.23 now takes a more southern route 15m shorter. Boulder is at J. with St.117 (see above).

From Widtsoe Junction, St.22 cont. (S) to St.12, 56m, near the entrance to **Bryce Canyon Nat. Pk.** (see below).

On US89 at **79. is PANGUITCH,** seat of Garfield Cty., founded by settlers who penetrated valley of upper Sevier in 1864. Here is J. with side Rd.

SIDE TRIP: On this Rd. past great lava flows (R) 18.5m to **Panguitch L.** (f.h.camp.), favorite southern Utah recr. area. At 33m is J. with St.55 & St.143 at NE. cor. of **Cedar Breaks Nat. Mon.** (see US91).

At **86.,** on US89, is J. with St.12.

SIDE TRIP: On St.12 (L) 2.5m to mouth of **Red Canyon,** a scarlet gorge which at first glance rivals Bryce Canyon. After J. at 14m with St.22, however, St.12 turns (R) 3m to reveal true magnificence of **Bryce Canyon Nat. Pk.** (adm.jointly with Zion Canyon, $1). Ebenezer Bryce, who 1st began to range cattle here in 1875, described it as "a hell of a place to lose a cow." Rather than a canyon, Bryce is a series of "breaks" in 14 enormous amphitheaters extending 1,000′ down through pink & white limestones of **Paunsaugunt Plateau.** Domes, spires & temples predominate in Bryce, but the infinite variety & grace of all the erosive formations cannot be expressed in language. The 20m Rim Rd. affords many arresting vantage pts; most comprehensive & overwhelming is **Inspiration Pt.** At Pk. Hqs., 4.5m inside pk. boundary, are a pub. campground, cafeteria, cabins, store, mus., garage & Bryce Canyon Lodge. Trls. to floor of the canyon are numerous & safe; horses are avail., but trls. are readily followed afoot.

At **LONG VALLEY JUNCTION, 107.,** is J. with St.14 to **Cedar Breaks Nat. Mon.,** 25m (see US91). Winding down Long Valley, US89 at **124.** passes **ORDERVILLE,** where Mormons in 70's & 80's made valiant effort to live the "United Order," a venture in communal living. The Orderville "Order" was the most successful in Utah, & throve after most of the others had sunk in ruin. It provided complete security but insufficient reward for industry & ambition, & dissolved in 1886. **130. MT. CARMEL JUNCTION** at J. with St.15, the spectacular tunnel-&-window route to Zion Canyon (see US91). US89 here bends (SE) toward **KANAB, 147.,** center of vast farming, cattle-raising, & sheep-raising area which has also become in recent yrs. locale for many motion pictures & principal gateway to scenic regs. of S. Utah & N. Ariz. An annual "Forty-niners' Ball" (late autumn) is staged here each yr. US89 cont. (S) crossing **ARIZ. LINE** at **150.**

## US 91—UTAH

**UTAH-IDAHO LINE** (8m from Preston, Idaho) **(S) to ARIZ. LINE** (17m from Nev. Line). **458. US91**

Via: Logan, Brigham City, Ogden, Salt Lake City, Provo, Nephi, Fillmore, Beaver, Cedar City, St. George.

US91 is hist. (N-S) cross-state route traversing Utah's richest valleys & chief cities. Much of it was traveled in 1776 by Father Escalante; after Mormon occupation of Utah it became S. Rd. to Cal. & now is principal hy. bet. Yellowstone & S. Cal.

## Sec. 1: IDAHO LINE to SALT LAKE CITY. 102.

US91 winds it way (S) under E. rim of Great Basin, flanked by Wasatch Mts. & (R) by rich irrigated valleys. Scenically, historically, agriculturally & industrially, US91 affords best cross-sec. of Utah life. It enters Utah near N. end of Cache Valley amid prosperous dairy farming, sugar-beet & alfalfa-raising farmlands.

**19. LOGAN** is at J. with US89. Home of **Utah St. Agric. College,** Logan preeminently is Utah's college town. As Utah's 4th largest city, Logan has sugar beet factory, pea canneries, textile mills, candy factories & other agric. industries. (E) of city Wasatch Range rises abruptly to over 9,700′ & canyons in these mts. afford dozens of pic. & campgrounds. In city itself rise twin gray towers of Mormon Temple, the square gray belfry of Mormon Tabernacle, &, on mountainside campus, the bell tower of college's main bldg. Mormon herdsmen came into Cache Valley in 1855, & actual settlement began in 1859; in 1874 Utah N. RR., built from Ogden, gave town fresh vitality. Logan Temple, completed 1884, centered here Mormon religious activity of Salt Lake City. Four yrs. later, terr. legislature gave Logan its most important asset, the agric. college. The institution is internat. known for its studies in irrigation & drainage.

PTS. OF INT.: (1) 4th North & 7th East Sts., **Utah St. Agric. College.** Principal bldgs. are grouped around Quadrangle at SW. cor. of campus. (2) 1st North & 2nd East Sts., **Logan Temple,** a romanesque bldg. constructed of gray, rough-hewn limestone, set in landscaped grounds. Mormon temples are not O. to general pub., & are reserved for church members. (3) Main & Center Sts., **Mormon Tabernacle** (O. during services), cupola-crowned structure also of gray limestone, built 1866-79. (4) 1st West & 1st South Sts., Cache Cty. **Relic Hall** (O.appl.with Daughters of Utah Pioneers) is one-time stone stable & carriage house (1861), used since 1927 to display pioneer tools, farm implements, art & furniture.

(S) of Logan US91 climbs S. slope of Cache Valley, crosses divide, & drops down into rugged Box Elder Canyon. **34. BRIGHAM CITY,** situated on fan-shaped alluvial delta at canyon mouth, characteristic of towns all down frontal line of Wasatch. Brigham City is noted for its 2-day peach festival in early Sept. Brigham City is at N. junction with US89 & US30S, united with them for $21^m$.

SIDE TRIP: From Brigham City (W) $15^m$ on US30S is 64,200-a. **Bear R. Migratorial Bird Refuge** (O.9-5), on Great Salt Lake at mouth of Bear R. Here 2 continental waterfowl flyways join, & millions of birds fly through every yr. Hunt. in season is permitted on 40% of refuge.

Cont. (S) to Ogden, US91 winds through orchard lands above silvery Bear R. Bay & rounds shoulder of Ben Lomond (9,717′), one of Utah's most beautiful peaks; its summit affords a vast panorama of Valley of Great Salt Lake.

**65. OGDEN,** Utah's 2nd city & greatest rail center bet. Denver & Pac. coast. It takes its name from Hudson's Bay Co. fur trader, Peter Skene Ogden, who brought an expedition (S) from Ore. country in 1825. Miles Goodyear sett. on site of Ogden perhaps as early as winter of 1844-45, but Mormons bought him out in Nov., 1847. A sleepy country town, Ogden was transformed when U.P. RR. arrived in Mar., 1869. After golden spike ceremony at Promontory, May 10, 1869 (see US30S), Ogden was made J. city for U.P. & Central Pac. RRs. & grew rapidly. In Jan., 1870, the Mormon-built Utah Central was completed bet. Ogden & Salt Lake City. In 1903, spectacular Lucin Cutoff across Great Salt Lake, built by U.P. RR. to shorten route to San Francisco, permanently est. Ogden as Utah's chief rail center. With more than $110^m$ of trackage in city & some 140 trains routed in & out each day, Ogden's economic welfare is closely bound up with RRs. Numerous industries in & around "Junction City" have taken advantage of superior trans. facils. incl. livestock yards, packing plants, flour mills, canneries, sugar factories, creameries, breweries, box factories, brick & tile yards, concrete products & foundries. (See Salt Lake City.) Notables born in Ogden incl. John Moses Browning & Jon. Edmund Browning, inventors of improved automatic firearms, Bernard DeVoto & Phyllis McGinley, writers. Wasatch Mts., (E) of city, provide varied recr. opportunities, though Great Salt Lake beaches (W) of Ogden are too shallow & muddy for bathing. Chief annual events incl. Pioneer Day (wk.of July 24) & Ogden Livestock Show, one of 5 largest in U.S. (early **Nov.**).

PTS. OF INT.: (1) Washington Ave. bet. 25th & 26th Sts., **City Hall Park,** with 10-story mod. setback **City & Cty. Bldg.,** 1940, **Carnegie Free Lib.** & pioneer **Mons.** to Jedediah Smith, Capt. Jas. Brown, & Lorin Farr. (2) Wilson Lane (W) of viaduct ramp. **Ogden Livestock Coliseum,** scene of annual livestock show. (3) Washington Ave. bet. 21st & 22nd Sts., **Tabernacle Pk.,** on which stands Ogden **L. D. S.** (Mormon) **Tabernacle** (O. for services) & **Miles Goodyear Cabin,** oldest remaining white dwelling in Utah, several times removed from orig. location on Weber R. near 28th St. (4) 2445 Jefferson Ave., **Weber Jr. College,** founded by L. D. S. Ch. in 1889 & given to St. in 1933. (5) 507 25th St., **U.S. Forest Serv. Bldg.,** 4-story mod. structure which is hqs. for Reg. 4, administering fors. in Utah, Nev., Idaho, & Wyo. (6) 2554 Monroe Ave., **Rbt. Chapman H.,** pioneer adobe structure (c.1855), probably oldest bldg. in Ogden continuously used as home. (7) Harrison Ave. & 28th St., **Ogden Senior High Sch.,** a 4-story mod. bldg. designed like City & Cty. Bldg. & For. Service Bldg., by Leslie S. Hodgson, who has had largest single influence in mod. Ogden architecture. (8) Canyon Rd. & 16th St., **Ogden Stadium,** scene of annual Pioneer Days Rodeo. (9) 12th St. & Canyon Rd., **Old Mill,** now used as dance hall & restaurant, orig. gristmill 1849. (10) $7^{m}$ (E) on foot trl. up Taylor Canyon, (E) from 25th or 26th Sts., **Mt. Ogden,** highest pt. (9,575′) overlooking Ogden with views into 4 states. Here is J. with St.39.

SIDE TRIP: On this Rd. (R), a scenic hy. climbs up beautiful gorge of **Ogden Canyon.** At $8.5^{m}$ are Js. with St.162 & an improved Rd.

(1) On improved Rd. (R) up Wheeler Canyon to **Snow Basin,** $4^{m}$, a 6,000-a. winter sports area with 5,000′ ski lift, $2.5^{m}$-long Wild Cat Run, & mountainous terrain suited to all types of skiing & summer hiking.

(2) On St.162 (L) across **Pine View Dam** & along **Pine View Reservoir** (boat.bath.f.), a $4,000,000 Fed. reclamation project for watering 60,000 as. of land (W) & (N) of Ogden. With $20^{m}$ shoreline L. is favorite site for regattas. St.162 cont. (E) to **Eden** $4^{m}$ & then (N) to **Liberty** $8^{m}$ whence Rds. go (N) over mts. to **Cache Valley** & (W) up over high summit of N. Ogden Canyon back to Ogden. From Eden, on St.162, asphalt-paved Rd. regains St.39 at **Huntsville,** $5^{m}$.

St.39 circles S. shore of Pine View L. to **Huntsville,** $13.5^{m}$, characteristic Mormon farm village in bowl-like Ogden Valley. At $20^{m}$ is J. with dirt Rd.

On this Rd. (R) to **Monastery of the Holy Trinity** (Cath.), one of 5 Trappist Monasteries in U.S., & only one (W) of Mo. R., founded July, 1947. Monastery consists of 4 quonset huts arranged in 170′ square, with bell tower & cross 71′ high. This will eventually be replaced by a monastery of red sandstone. Monks belong to Cistercian order, 8½ centuries old, & follow a stringent discipline incl. religious exercises, much study, prolonged fasts, manual labor, restricted diet, & perpetual silence except with superiors & confessors or in choir. Women are permitted entry to chapel portion only.

St.39 cont. up S. Ogden Canyon past many pic. grounds & through groves of quaking aspen & fir to **Monte Cristo Recr. Area,** $43.5^{m}$, its 9,000′ height affording magnificent mt. views. St.39 then descends to **Woodruff,** $65.5^{m}$ from which motorists may drive (S) to US30S or (N) to US89, by either route looping back to Ogden.

US91 proceeds (S) to **SALT LAKE CITY,** at **102.** (see Salt Lake City Trip II).

## Sec. 2: SALT LAKE CITY to FILLMORE. 151.

**44. PROVO,** Utah's 3rd largest city, & center for Utah's burgeoning steel industry. Wide streets bordered by trees, lawns & flowing irrigation ditches have impress of Mormon culture. Old adobe houses, though interspersed with mod. dwellings, are everywhere. Ft. Utah, embryo Provo, was est. by Mormons, Ap., 1849. Later Brigham Young laid out townsite, which was named for trapper, Etienne Provost, who had given his name to Provo R. Provo became base of Mormon colonization southward; as frontier outpost, it picked up a salty reputation at variance with its modern reputation, which has been notably influenced by Brigham Young Univ., chief Mormon institution of higher learning. Utah's 2nd city until coming of RR., Provo retained vitality as commercial center of Utah's richest agric. district. In 1926 building of Columbia Steel plant at Ironton, just beyond S. city limits, promised industrial growth now beginning to be realized in operations of Geneva Steel plant, built in World War II on city's N. flank. Reed Smoot, who in 1903-07 won hist. fight for Senate seat & later became one of great powers of Senate, only to be ousted by Democratic landslide of 1932, was born in Provo. Dr. Harvey Fletcher, acoustical engineer, is also native of Provo & grad. of Brigham Young Univ. Annual events incl. Sunrise Services on Y Mountain, (E) of Provo, on Easter Sun.

PTS. OF INT.: (1) **Brigham Young Univ.** which is being removed from Lower Campus, University Ave. & 5th North St. to Upper Campus. (2) 8th East & Center Sts., **Soldiers Mem. Pk.** (3) 183 East 1st South St., **Reed Smoot H.** (Vict.), last Provo home of late Sen. & Mormon Ch. Apostle. (4) Homes of A. O. Smoot, father of Sen., built to house his 4 wives; they are located at 192 S. 1st East; 160 S. 1st St.; 65 E. 2nd South; & 136 W. 5th North Sts. In 3rd of these lived Anna K. Smith, 4th wife & mother of Reed Smoot. First has been remod. as hospital, 3rd as office bldg. (5) University Ave. bet. Center & 1st South Sts., **Provo St. Tabernacle** (O.for services.1883), unusual among Mormon ch. bldgs. because it is frankly conventional in Presb. tradition, "that the children of Saints might see in what kind of edifice many of their fathers worshiped before they heard the Gospel." (6) 5th West & 5th North Sts., **Sowiette Pk.,** named for friendly Ute chief, is site of 2nd Ft. Utah (1850). **Pioneer Mem. Bldg.** with adj. replica of Pioneer Cabin (O.9-5 wks.) has coll. of pioneer relics, incl. Amer. flag woven of Utah-produced silk which won a Chicago World's Fair award, 1893. (7) W. Center St., **Site of 1st Ft. Utah** (1849) marked by mon. (8) **Provo Lake Harbor** is a mun.-built harbor on Utah L., 2,550′ long across Provo R.

(S) of Provo, for c.100$^{m}$, US91 follows in footsteps of Father Escalante, who in 1776 rode this way in vain search for route to Monterey. In vic. of Holden he turned more westerly toward Sevier L. but had to abandon his purpose & turn back to Santa Fe; US91 comes again into this hist. trl. (S) of Cedar City. At **48.** blast furnace of orig. Columbia Steel Plant, now integrated with Geneva Steel Plant, stands cheek-by-jowl with the furnace which produces pig iron for Kaiser steel mills in S. Cal. **SPRINGVILLE, 51.,** is unique among Western cities. It has a nationally-known spring art salon & a fine permanent coll. maintained in Springville Art Gallery. In City Pk. are **Pioneer Mother Mon. & Mem. Fountain** by Cyrus E. Dallin, Springville-born sculptor. Springville is at S. J. with US50. In **SPANISH FORK** at **55.** is S. J. with US6; these hys. unite in Spanish Fork Canyon (see US6-US50). Beyond Spanish Fork terrain & patterns of settlement change. Green, close-set, intensively cultivated farms give way to rolling hay & grain fields & then to unfenced ranges. Towns are farther apart; & mts. on either hand are more arid, sometimes obscured by parched brown hills. Junipers make dark blotches along hillsides, & silver-green sagebrush appears in valley bottoms. Utah begins to take on desert aspect. At **64.,** beyond **PAYSON,** is J. (L) with unnumbered dirt "Nebo Loop" Rd., characteristic of many spectacular canyon drives down length of Utah. **89. NEPHI,** is one of half-dozen towns in Utah given Book of Mormon names. Sett. in 1851, it benefited from development of dryfarm techniques after 1900. At Nephi is J. with St.11 leading (E) up Salt Cr. Canyon, orig. trl. from Great Salt Lake City, to Sanpete settlements (see US89) & on to Colo. Plateau country (E) of Wasatch divide. **100. LEVAN,** in center of Utah's most prolific dryfarm area. Near **HOLDEN, 140.,** known in pre-settlement times as Cedar Springs, Father Escalante veered more westerly in his vain search for route to Monterey. **151., FILLMORE,** dryfarming & cattle town, intended by its founders to be capital of Utah. Seeking a central location for terr. capital, Brigham Young picked out site in 1851. By 1855 the 2-story S. wing of State H. had been completed; terr. legislature of 1855-56 convened there. Lack of facils., however, led to transfer of seat of gov. back to Great Salt Lake City. Existing wing is now used as a mus. for Ind. artifacts & pioneer relics.

### Sec. 3: FILLMORE to UTAH-ARIZ. LINE. 205.

**17.5** (R), **BLACK ROCK VOLCANO,** extinct, coneless crater, overgrown with sage. Cont. (S) through Baker Canyon, soil becomes more reddish. US91 reaches at **36., COVE FT.** (1867), most perfectly preserved of forts constructed in pioneer times during war with Black Hawk. Here is J. with St.13.

SIDE TRIP: From **Cove Ft.** (L) St.13 crosses a divide & in 20$^{m}$ descends organ-like rock walls confining Clear Cr. to US89, in Sevier Valley (see US89).

Bet. Cove Ft. & Beaver US91 crosses rolling sage & juniper country with infrequent weather-beaten ranchhs. along Rd. Crags of **Tushar Mts.** (L) & castellated ridges of **Mineral Mts.** (R) parallel hy. **68. BEAVER** is farming & stock-raising center sett. 1856. In 70's, Gentile miners opened rich claims in mts. (W), & Beaver became site of typical Mormon-Gentile political tug-of-war. It was here that John D. Lee was convicted in 1876 of participation in Mountain Meadows Massacre (see below). Here is J. with St.21.

SIDE TRIPS: (A) On St.21 (L) 19.5m through Beaver Canyon to **Fish L. Nat. For.** & up a series of switchbacks to **Puffer L.** (resort.accoms.boat.guides.horses) with fishing in Puffer L. & trls. to summits of Mts. Baldy (12,000'), Belnap (12,131'), & Delano (12,162'), highest peaks in SW. Utah.
(B) St.21 (R) leads (W) to **Nev. Line,** 115.5m, across broad desert valleys, over low mt. ranges. 31m, **Milford,** was sett. in 1870 as mine supply town; it has become a U.P. RR. division pt., a farming center, & an outfitting place for miners & cattlemen. 46m **Frisco** was born when Horn Silver Mine was accidentally discovered in 1875. In 10 yrs. it produced over $54,000,000. Frisco was reputed wildest camp in Utah, with 1 marshal so efficient, a "body mover" was hired to clean up after him. 110m **Garrison,** just short of Nev. Line, ranching community with windmills & tar-papered shacks, is area in which "The Covered Wagon" was filmed in 1922. US91 (S) of Beaver crosses sagebrush flats & foothills dark with junipers to drop down into hot, windswept valley.

**102. PAROWAN.** Sett. in winter of 1850-51 by colonizing mission under Geo. A. Smith, Parowan was designed to be agric. base for exploiting iron ores. Here is J. with St.143.

SIDE TRIP: From Parowan on this Rd. 4m through heavily timbered **Parowan Canyon** to J. with gravel Rd. (L) leading 1.5m to **Vermilion Castles,** with flaming pinnacles & battlements above gray conglomerate walls. St.143 climbs up through **Dixie Nat. For.** to arrive at 16m with J. (L) of improved Rd. to **Brian Head Pk.,** 2m, on crown of **Brian Head Peak** (11,315') with amazing view. St.143 cont. to J. with St.55 in **Cedar Breaks** 17.5m (see below).

**121. CEDAR CITY,** vigorous commercial center for all SW. Utah. Sett. in 1851 by "iron missionaries," it was mining & smelting town for which Parowan opened the way. Completion of branch line by U.P. RR. in 1923 began new era for Cedar City; mines awoke, farming boomed, & tourists began pouring in, attracted by publicity given Utah's new nat. pks. & mons. (E) & (SE) of city. Cedar City is most publicized mountain-lion hunting area of Utah, & also attracts many deer hunters. Among rolling sage plains & desert buttes (W) of city, numerous motion pictures have been filmed, incl. "Union Pacific," "Ramona," "The Good Earth," & "Green Grass of Wyoming." Branch Agric. College in Cedar City, founded in 1897, since 1913 has been a unit of Utah St. Agric College. Here is J. with St.14.

SIDE TRIP: From Cedar City (L) on this Rd. (impassable in winter) to **Cedar Breaks Nat. Mon.** Cedar Breaks is a half-mile-deep amphitheater 2m across. Walls, white or orange at top, dissolve into ridges & monoliths of deep rose & coral, eroded & broken in strange, wild shapes. An alpine country cool with spruce, fir, aspen, & mt. flowers, & with many singing birds, surrounds the "breaks."

Route over Rim of the Basin, surmounted at **131.,** & down Ash Cr. to Virgin R. was adopted by Father Escalante in 1776 & by Jedediah Smith in 1826, on his 1st overland journey to Cal. Spanish Trl. which later became wagon Rd. to S. Cal. instead veered westerly from Cedar City to climb Mountain Meadows & descend Santa Clara R.; present route of US91 came into general use only after colonization of Utah's "Dixie," warm country below Rim of Basin. **154. ANDERSON JUNCTION.** J. with St.15.

SIDE TRIP: On this Rd. (L) 6m down Ash Cr. to J. with St.17 (alt. route to St. George). From J. St.15 turns (E). At 22m is **Zion Nat. Pk.,** deep narrow, vertically-walled canyon entered along its floor (adm.jointly with Bryce Canyon). According to tradition, early Mormon settlers along Virgin R. were so impressed with its cathedral-like walls & vivid color that they called it Zion; when rebuked by Brigham Young, they renamed it Not Zion, but orig. name prevailed. Canyon itself is spectacular, but trls. to rim 3,000' above afford still more breathtaking views. 20m of improved Rds., 26m of trls., display Zion Canyon in all its multi-colored glory. St.15, cont. (E) 52m toward its J. with US89 at Mt. Carmel Junction, which winds over one of most spectacular pieces of hy. engineering in Amer., **Zion-Mount Carmel Hy.,** with its mile-long tunnel through solid rock & 6 great windows opening upon splendor of canyons.

**158.** gravel Rd. leads (W) 1.5m to **Silver Reef,** once-famous mining camp. Until horn silver was discovered at Silver Reef, geologists had maintained that silver could not be found in sandstone. Large development of area began in 1876, & by 1903 Silver Reef had produced $10,350,000 in silver. Despite intermittent mining since, Silver Reef has sunk into ruin. **165. HARRISBURG JUNCTION** is at J. with St.17, alt. route (E) to Zion Nat. Pk. (see above). **175. ST. GEORGE,** metropolis of Utah's Dixie, with rich history & fascinating character. When Civil War cut off southern cotton in 1861, Brigham Young organized a Cotton Mission to migrate to Virgin Valley. These pioneers founded St. George in Dec., 1861. Their struggles during yrs. that followed have been told in Maurine Whipple's "The Giant Joshua" (1941). Long after irrigation-raised cotton ceased to be profitable, members of mission cont. to grow it; it is still raised in a few St. George gardens. Although summers were furnace-hot, winters were mild, & in his last years Brigham Young maintained a winter home here, a 2-story buff adobe bldg. still in use (N.O.). Square-built **St. George Temple,** with its 3 tiers of tall, round-arched windows, was completed in 1877, 1st Mormon temple dedicated in Utah. Other bldgs. with notable pioneer flavor incl. sandstone **Mormon Tabernacle** (O.appl.) with square tower & white steeple; **Washington County Cth.,** square 2-story red brick bldg. of Col. design; **Jed Gates H.** (N.O.), 1-story adobe structure erected in 1863-65, representative of polygamous era with its door & window in each half of house. Fruit growing & facils. for tourists give St. George its mod. prosperity; it is also home of **Dixie Jr. College,** founded 1911 & given by Mormon Ch. to St. in 1933. Here is J. with St.18.

SIDE TRIP: On St.18 (R) 7.5m past vividly colored Snows Canyon (L) & 2 extinct volcanic craters (R) 13m up winding canyon of Santa Clara to **Mountain Meadows** at 29m. At S. end of Meadows a mon. (W) of 40′ wash comm. **Mountain Meadows Massacre.** Here an immigrant company from Ark. was attacked in Sept., 1857, an outgrowth of excitement over pending invasion of Utah by Fed. troops. After siege of several days, immigrants (140 men, women, & children) were decoyed from their rifle pits & slain. The sole survivors, 17 children, were later gathered up by Fed. Gov. & returned to Ark. On March 23, 1877, John D. Lee, a chief participant in massacre, was brought back to the Meadows & executed by firing squad.

**180. SANTA CLARA,** spread out along hy. as a succession of adobe, red sandstone, & mod. brick houses separated by green orchards, was sett. in 1854 by Jacob Hamblin & others of famous Southern Ind. Mission which attempted to convert tribes of the Mormon SW. Red stone **Jacob Hamblin H.** here, built 1862, is now a St. Pk. Hamblin is one of most memorable frontier figures Mormonism has produced; he died at Alpine, Ariz., 1886, in hiding from "polyg-hunting" U.S. marshals. US91 crosses at **188., SHIVWITS-SHEBIT IND. RESERV.,** where are gathered 80-odd survivors of numerous bands who once dwelt in S. Utah, N. Ariz., & E. Nev. **BEAVER DAM MTS.** are crossed at 4,600′ summit, & then US91 drops quickly down to 2,000′ elev. of **BEAVER DAM CR.,** lowest in St. Vegetation swiftly changes in character. Spanish bayonet appears, spiny cactus, suppliant Joshua trees, dense thickets known to SW. as chaparral. At **205.** US91 crosses **ARIZ. LINE** & cont. in Ariz. for 10m to Nev. Line.

# SALT LAKE CITY

## SALT LAKE CITY

Through RR., bus & airline conns. Info.: State Publicity Dept., 8 W. 2nd South; C. of C., 207 S. Main; Utah St. Auto Assoc., 30 E. 4th South. Accoms.: All types. Swim.: Wasatch Springs Plunge, city pks. & at Great Salt Lake beaches & Lagoon in environs.

Salt Lake City, in north-central part of St., is capital of Utah & world hqs. for Mormon Ch. (Ch. of Jesus Christ of Latter-Day Saints). As largest city bet. Denver & Pacific Coast, it powerfully influences social, political & economic life over a vast area extending (N) to Snake plain in Idaho, (W) to central Nev., (S) to Colo. R. in Ariz., & (E) to Colo. Line. Its primacy stems in part from its selection by Mormons in 1847 as their world capital, but strategic geographic situation & proximity to rich natural resources have equally contributed to its growth, vigor & power. On settlement in July, 1847, the name given was Great Salt Lake City, shortened by legislature in 1868. In pioneer times "the Valley" was Mormon mecca to which came converts from all over the world; from Salt Lake City they were dispatched in colonizing companies to still unsettled valleys. Semi-annual conference of Mormon Ch. in Ap. & Oct. brought yrly. gatherings from remote Utah settlements; & as Salt Lake City was ch. hqs., largest Mormon city, & principal Mormon showplace, it was for many yrs. considered synonymous with Utah & Mormonism, & attracted a constant stream of travelers curious to see "City of the Saints," "Utah Zion," or "The New Jesusalem."

A little less ingenuously, Salt Lake City has the same appeal still. A handsome metropolis with broad, tree-lined streets, it is situated on sloping plateau set in NE. segment of an arc of the Wasatch Mts. Immediately above city, the mts. are rounded hills but they rise to (SE) above Cottonwood canyons, to heights of alpine grandeur. Depending on angle of the sun, Great Salt Lake, 15$^m$ (W), is a ribbon of cobalt, or sliver of polished steel as seen from the city. In (SW) the long angular Oquirrh Mts. are visibly scarred by great open-cut copper mine at Bingham, & wreathed in smoke from Garfield smelters; the intervening valley is gold & green in neat rectangular patterns of its farms. The mts. hugging city on (E) are cleft by 8 canyons, in all of which except Red Butte (military reservation), cool camp sites & pic. grounds offer varied recr. Ecker Hill in Parleys Canyon, Brighton in Big Cottonwood, & Alta in Little Cottonwood, provide winter sports opportunities only a half hour's drive from center of city. Wasatch Blvd., which begins at St. Capitol & winds along benchlands (N) & (E) above city is favorite scenic drive.

PTS. OF INT.: (1) Main entrance, W. South Temple St. bet. Main & West Temple Sts., **Temple Square** (O.9-8:30.summer;8-5:30 winter.guides), is 10-a. city block enclosed by 15′ wall. Within landscaped grounds rise the majestic **Temple** (N.O.), which was 40 yrs. in building; turtle-domed **Tabernacle; Assembly Hall: Seagull Mon.,** comm. aid against cricket devastations in 1848; **Three Witnesses Mon.** & **Statues of Jos. & Hyrum Smith; Oldest H.** in Salt Lake City. (2) Inters. of Main & S Temple Sts., **Brigham Young Mon.** (3) 47 E. South Temple St., **L. D. S. Ch. Office Bldg.** (O.9-4 wks.guides), in which is Ch. Historian's Office & Lib. with rich coll. of source material on Utah & Mormons. (4) 63 E. South Temple, **Lion H.** (O.10-5.summer.10-10 winter), built by Brigham Young in 1856 to house his plural wives. (5) 67 E. South Temple St., **Brigham Young's Office** (O.9-4), entered from Lion H. (6) 75 E. South Temple St., **Beehive H.** (0.9-4.wks.guides), Brigham Young's Mansion built in 1855, most notable pioneer mansion in Utah. (7) Spanning N. State St. at E. South Temple St., **Eagle Gate,** formerly entrance to Brigham Young's estate. (8) 15 South State St., **Salt Lake Free Pub. Lib.,** with notable Utah & Mormon coll. (9) NW. cor. S. State & 1st South Sts., **Site of Salt Lake Theater.** (10) 4th South & S. State Sts., **City & Cty. Bldg.** (O.9-5.wks.;9-1 Sat.). (11) 225 E. 1st South St., **St. Mark's Cathedral** (Episc.O.9-9 wks.). (12) 145 S. 5th E. St., **Ambassador Hotel,** built orig. by Congressional grant to house women & children who would abandon polygamy (only 3 took refuge there). (13) 650 E. South Temple St., **Masonic Temple** (O.9-4 wks.). (14) 603 E. South Temple St., **Gov.'s Mansion** (N.O.), once Kearns Mansion, presented to St. in 1939. (15) NE. cor. E. South Temple & B Sts., **Cathedral of the Madeleine,** Cath. edifice. (16) 1st Ave. bet. N. State & A Sts., **Brigham Young Cemetery** (O.appl.), a green-lawned area where Young, 3 of his wives & several children are buried. (17) N. end of N. State St., **St. Capitol** (O.guide), classically styled 4-story structure overlooking city from N. Bench; it contains St. offices, art coll. & mus. displays. (18) **Memory Grove Pk.,** in City Cr. Canyon below Capitol, dedicated to Utah's war dead.

(19) Main entrance, NE. cor. 4th Ave. & N St., **City Cemetery,** a 267-a. hillside city of the dead; adj. the municipally-managed burial grounds are Cath., Jewish, & Japanese Buddhist cemeteries. (20) Ft. Douglas Blvd. & Gibbon St., (main entrance) **Ft. Douglas,** hist. post founded in 1862 & abandoned after World War II, when most of its 9,000 as. were given to Univ. of Utah & Salt Lake City. (21) Main entrance, Univ. & 2nd South Sts., **Univ. of Utah,** Utah's leading educational institution, lying immediately below old Ft. Douglas on benchland overlooking Salt Lake Valley; bldgs. were oriented around U-shaped campus at head of 2nd South St. until expansion (E) began. (22) 54 Finch Lane, **Art Barn** (O.10-10 daily), center for art & literary activities. (23) N. of mouth of Emigration Canyon, **This is the Place Mon.,** marking centennial of 1847 migration to Utah. (24) 2600 Sunnyside Ave. at mouth of Emigration Canyon, **Hogle Gardens Zoo** (O.free). (25) Head of 13th South St. on East Bench, **St. Mary of the Wasatch,** Cath. sch. for girls. (26) 1840 S. 13th East St., **Westminster College** (O.wks.), only Prot. coed. college in Utah. A 4-yr. Presb. jr. college, it incl. 2 yrs. of high sch., 2 of college. (27) Main entrance, 6th East & 9th South Sts., **Liberty Pk.,** mun. recr. area, once Brigham Young Farm, & now Salt Lake City's favorite pk. (28) 3rd South & 2nd West Sts., **Pioneer Pk.,** on which Mormon pioneers "forted up" for their 1st winter in the Valley. (29) NW. cor. 9th West & W. North Temple Sts., **St. Fairgrounds** (O.10-10 during fair wk.). (30) 2450 W. North Temple St., **Salt Lake City Mun. Airport,** one of nation's most important air terminals.

## TRIPS OUT OF SALT LAKE CITY

### I. LOOP TOUR. SALT LAKE CITY to PROVO & RETURN. 120. US91, US189, US40

Via: Utah Valley, Provo Canyon, Round Valley, Parkeys Canyon.

US91 heads straight (S) out of Salt Lake City via State St. At **7.5. MURRAY,** mixture of smelting town & rural trade center. Tall towers of Amer. Smelting & Refining Plant rise (S) of town. At **11.5.** is J. (R) with St.48, which crosses Salt Lake Valley (W) to great open-cut copper mine in **BINGHAM CANYON** at **16.** US91 cont. (S) into open farming country. In Wasatch Mts. (L) the stream-cut V of the mouth of Big Cottonwood Canyon contrasts with glacier-cut "U" of neighboring Little Cottonwood Canyon. At S. end of Salt Lake Valley, US91 swings up on benchland to surmount spur-range known as Pt. of the Mt. Jordan R., flowing from Utah L. to Great Salt L., so called by Mormon pioneers because of analogy with freshwater Sea of Galilee & saline Dead Sea of Palestine, has here cut a short canyon, Jordan Narrows (R). The silver sheen of Utah L. ahead gives green Utah Valley a misty unreality as US91 winds down slope & passes through prosperous sm. towns, chief among them **AMERICAN FORK, 30.** At **34.** is J. with St.114.

SIDE TRIP: On St.114 (R) 4m to **Geneva Steel Plant.** Gov.-built during World War II to provide planes, ship shapes & shell steel, it is regarded as finest & most modern plant in world. After the war, it was sold for $41,000,000 to U.S. Steel Co., which engaged to spend an additional $19,000,000 on a plate mill for rolling sheet & strip steel. Largest integrated plant in W., Geneva employs 5,000 workers & is now the largest single employer in Utah.

At **44.** in **PROVO** (see US91) is J. with US189. Loop tour now follows US189 up one of Utah's most pleasant gorges, Provo Canyon. **BRIDAL VEIL FALLS** (R), **54.5.,** is Utah's most beautiful waterfall. Hy. ascends past for. campgrounds & canyon resorts to J. with **TIMPANOGOS LOOP ROAD, 57.**

SIDE TRIP: On this Rd. (L) up through high alpine country around shoulder to Mt. Timpanogos (12,008′) & down Amer. Fork Canyon to **Timpanogos Cave Nat. Mon.** (adm.to Mon.free;to Cave,60¢), 17.5m. The cave is a series of 3 with curious limestone formations, reached by mile-long zigzag trl. up S. wall of Canyon. Timpanogos Loop Rd. cont. down Amer. Fork Canyon to **Amer. Fork** on US91, 25m.

Provo Canyon widens & US189 circles S. shore of **DEER CR. RESERVOIR** at **60.** (f.boat.), which impounds 150,000 acre-feet of water for Salt Lake City & for Valley farmlands. Above reservoir, at **72.,** is J. with US40 (see). Combined US40-US189 at **73.** reaches **HEBER,** seat of Wasatch Cty. & trading center for large ranching area. Here is J. with St.113 which leads (L) to near-by **Luke's Hot Pots** & **Schneitter's Hot Pots,** twin resorts centered above singular limestone craters formed by springs or geysers. **79. HAILSTONE,** lumber camp where Provo R. comes out of mts. to (E). US189, becoming a side Rd., turns up R.

SIDE TRIP: On US189 (R) to Kamas Prairie, bowl-like valley into which Provo & Weber Rs. flow, one turning (S), other (N) to pursue their separate ways to Utah & Great Salt Ls. Here is J. with St.35, which climbs up over Wolf Cr. Pass & down into Uinta Basin (see US40). US189 cont. (N) to **Kamas,** 9m, which is at J. with St.34, access route to scenic Mirror L. reg. located 31m (E). Crossing Kamas Prairie, US189 follows Weber R. down through its pleasant winding valley & at **Wanship,** 21m, arrives at J. with St.530, coming down Silver Cr. Canyon (see Loop Tour II).

Loop tour cont. (N) on US40 toward Salt Lake City & at **89.** comes to J. with St.6.

SIDE TRIP: On this Rd. (L) 1m to **Park City,** set in narrow opening where 3 canyons join. A famous silver mining camp since early 70's, Park City has maintained a gay, insouciant personality while producing over $350,000,000 in gold, silver, copper, lead & zinc.

Loop tour traverses lovely Round Valley to **KIMBALLS JUNCTION, 95.,** at J. with St.530 to Wanship (see Loop Tour II) & then climbs heavy grade to summit (7,035′) at head of Parleys Canyon, en route passing **ECKER SKI HILL** (L) **97.,** where many record ski jumps have been made. In Parleys Canyon, immediately above Mountain Dell Reservoir is J. (R) with St.65, **103.,** which winds back into hills to cross Little Mountain & descend Emigration Canyon to Salt Lake City (see Loop Tour II). Loop tour winds down bet. rugged walls of lower Parleys Canyon & emerges suddenly upon a spectacular view of Salt Lake City, outspread in valley below. Descending the benchland, loop tour returns to **SALT LAKE CITY** at **120.**

**II. LOOP TOUR, SALT LAKE CITY to HENEFER & RETURN. US40, St.530, US189, US91. 110.**

Via: Parleys Canyon, Silver Creek Canyon, Weber Canyon & Davis Valley.

Loop tour II follows US40 up Parleys Canyon (see Loop Tour I) to **KIMBALLS JUNCTION, 25.** & then veers (NE) by St.530 down barren Silver Cr. Canyon to **WANSHIP, 36.,** from which it follows US189 down Weber Valley. Bet. low mts. on either side, dairy & alfalfa farms along this valley have especial charm. **44. COALVILLE** takes its name from coal mines in Chalk Cr. Canyon (R), opened 1859, 1st in Utah to be commercially exploited, though production today is meager. US189 winds along E. shore of Echo Reservoir, Fed. Reclamation Project built 1930, which impounds 74,000 acre-feet of water for farm lands in lower Weber & Ogden Valleys. Below the dam, US189 comes to J. with US30S in the mouth of **ECHO CANYON, 50.** (see Trip III). Parting from US189, Loop Tour now follows US30S along hist. route down Weber Canyon. The upper canyon of the Weber, looming ahead, in 1846 had an ominous interest. Lansford W. Hastings, taking down the canyon the 1st wagon train ever to penetrate this area, had to avoid the narrows there by crossing low divide (N) into Croyden Valley. He crossed back into Weber Canyon at Devils Slide (see below) & then by infinite toil, sometimes in rocky bed of R., sometimes by windlasses which lifted wagons bodily, forced a way down the Weber to open valley of Great Salt Lake. The Donner-Reed party, coming along behind, was advised instead to try to cut a Rd. up over mts. Hy. crosses the Weber to **HENEFER, 55.** Here is J. with Pioneer Mem. Hy.

SIDE TRIP: From Henefer (L) to Salt Lake City by this hy. which follows in track of Donner trl. of 1846, adopted in 1847 by Mormon Pioneers. It climbs up over divide into **E. Canyon,** 8m & then turns up this stream, which pioneer wagons had to cross 13 times, to mouth of **Little Emigration Canyon,** 15m. The Mem. Hy. climbs this canyon to pass over **Big Mt.,** from which remarkable view across rolling pine-clad mts. discloses distant corner of Salt Lake Valley. Descending **Mountain Dell Canyon** at 26m, Mem. Hy. comes to J. with St.65 (see Loop Tour I) which here is looping back to cross Little Mountain divide, source of so many difficulties for pioneer ox teams & wagons. Hy. cont. down Emigration Canyon past **mon.** (R) at foot of Little Mt. & on down to **Salt Lake City,** 37m.

Loop tour follows US30S through Weber Narrows. At **58.5.** is J. (R) with St.158, dirt Rd. up **Lost Cr. Canyon** (f.); by this Rd., Hastings in 1846 crossed back into canyon of the Weber. **DEVILS SLIDE** (L), **59.,** is geologic formation consisting of 2 parallel vertical limestone reefs, 20′ apart, standing out 40′ from the canyonside. US30S cont. down narrow canyon of the Weber until at **MORGAN, 66.,** it opens out into wide meadows at its confluence with E. Canyon. Morgan is center of rich agric. dist., with canning its chief industry. Below Morgan, Weber Canyon narrows again & R. plunges through a difficult V-shaped gorge. **81. DEVILS GATE,** where gorge is walled up by vertical cliffs, was crucial barrier for Hastings' train in 1846, & principal reason the Donner party cut laborious new Rd. across mts. At **83.,** the mouth of **WEBER CANYON,** is J. with US89. Loop tour here turns (S) toward Salt Lake City, but alternatively the traveler may cont. on to **Ogden,** 8m (NW) & then drive (S) to Salt Lake City on US91, 45m in all. As Loop Tour traverses benchland (S), Great Salt Lake Valley opens out, foothills rolling down to green-swathed towns in valley bottom. **Hill Field,** one of several military installations which have since 1940 invigorated Davis Valley, is outspread below with its hangars & runways. On US89, Loop Tour angles down into valley & at **FARMINGTON JUNCTION, 92.,** unites with US91 for rest of way to Salt Lake City.

SIDE TRIP: From Farmington Junction (L) by US91 Alt. through **Farmington, Centerville** & **Bountiful,** pleasant sm. towns surrounded by orchards which have become a residential appendage to Salt Lake City, this alt. Rd. follows close under mts. & comes back to main route in 11m.

Loop Tour now following US91 at **98.** passes (L) entrance to **Lagoon** (O.Mem.Day to Labor Day), popular 50-a. resort with finest swim. pool in Utah, children's playground & carnival concessions. Straight through meadow lands of Davis Valley, US91 makes for S. J. with US91 Alt. (see above), **102.,** & then around scorched foothills (L) & past oil refining plants (R) into **SALT LAKE CITY, 110.**

**III. LOOP TOUR. SALT LAKE CITY to TOOELE & RETURN. US40, St.36, St.73, St.68. 109.**

Via: Great Salt Lake beaches, Tooele Valley, Rush Valley & Cedar Valley.

From Salt Lake City (W) US40 takes a straight course for Great Salt Lake, past mun. airport & high radio towers, across alkaline plains that slope toward the L. **ROYAL CRYSTAL SALT CO. PLANT** (O.appl.), **11.**, pumps water from L. into concentration ponds, & after precipitation by solar evaporation, refines & packs salt. At **14.5.** oiled Rd. (R) leads to **Saltair,** 1m. Most famous resort on Great Salt Lake (O.Mem.Day to Labor Day;bath.dancing.amusement concessions), it stands on a high platform supported by 10′ pilings driven into L. bottom.

US40 cont. along L. shore. **SALT LAKE MUN. BOAT HARBOR, 17.5.** has a rock-fill boat pier 860′ long from which launches, motorboats & sailboats gaily navigate the lake. At **18.** dirt Rd. (R) leads to **Sunset Beach** & **Black Rock Beach,** twin resorts with the L.'s best accessible beaches. As US40 rounds N. end of Oquirrh Mts., Tooele Valley opens out to (S). At **MILLS JUNCTION, 25.**, is J. with St.36. US40 continue (W) toward Nevada Line, while the Loop Tour proceeds (S) on St.36. **34. TOOELE.** (4,900′) is seat of Tooele Cty. & a mining & smelting center. (S) of town, St.36 climbs the Stockton Bar, an immense sandbar left by prehist. L. Bonneville, which separates Tooele Valley from Rush Valley. On this bar grows a rare variety of iris found nowhere else in Utah. St.36 descends far slope of Bar into Rush Valley, famous in 60's & 70's for "Rush Valley Mines," of which Ophir & Mercur, along W. slope of Oquirrh Mts., were richest & longest-lived. At **46.** is J. with St.73. Loop Tour turns (E) on St.73 to cross the mts. into Cedar Valley, & passes through still-not-dead **MERCUR, 57.** Reunion (1st wk.of Sept.) each yr. calls back old-timers. **67.** J. with St.191.

SIDE TRIP: On this Rd. (R) 3m to **Fairfield,** farming village. Immediately (S) of Fairfield the Utah Expedition est. Camp Floyd in 1858. Until Civil War broke out, army that had been sent to Utah to put down "rebellious Mormons" was quartered here. Ironically, their comdr. was Albert Sidney Johnston, who died fighting for S. at Shiloh. Nothing remains of famous army post today except fenced cemetery with its unmarked graves.

As Loop Tour turns back to Salt Lake City from Cedar Valley, it follows in reverse line of march of Johnston's army in 1858 by St.73 to the J. with St.68, **81.**, & then (N) along W. bank of the Jordan R. Route passes through Utah's Nat. Guard reservation, **CAMP WILLIAMS, 85.**, & then traverses succession of farming towns to return to **SALT LAKE CITY** via US40 at **109.**

# US 40—NEVADA

**NEV.-UTAH LINE** (107m from Salt Lake City, Utah) **(W) to NEV.-CALIF. LINE** (23m from Truckee, Cal.) **413. US40**

Via: Wells, Elko, Battle Mt., Winnemucca, Lovelock, Reno. Paved Rd. Accoms.: In larger towns. W.P. & S.P. RR. parallels the Rd.

## Sec. 1: WENDOVER to WINNEMUCCA. 237.

**0.** US40 (the Victory Hy.) together with US50 passes the Nev. line at **WENDOVER.** At **20.** it crosses through Silver Zone Pass (5,940′) into Goshute Valley to **33.5.** where a dirt Rd. leads (L) 12m to **Flowery L.,** spot at which Donner Party cached some of its travel load. The hy. now climbs to **PEQUOP SUMMIT** at **38.** (6,980′) & descends again into sage-covered valley. Gradually, snow-flecked Ruby Mts. (11,000′) come into view (L). **59. WELLS,** named for the Humboldt Wells near-by (deep springs), at one time an emigrant camp-site, now a supply center for the surrounding valleys. Good fishing in near-by mountain streams. For 20 yrs. (1870-90) cattlemen lavishly ran the town until great blizzard of '89 impoverished them. In **Humboldt Nat. For.** 13m (SW) is **Angel L. For. Camp.** At Wells is J. with US93 (see). Rd. turns (W) to **DEETH** at **79.** where it meets the Humboldt & a J. of Rs. It follows the Humboldt, named by Frémont for Alex. Humboldt, the German explorer, a hist. stream flowing (SW) to J. with St.11.

SIDE TRIP: On this Rd. (L) 1m to **Halleck** & past **Ranch 71** (100,000 as.) **Secret Canyon** at base of Ruby Mts. leads into Secret Valley, so called because in this verdant valley Inds. were wont to disappear. It was ideal hideout for man & beast. Rd. now ascends to cross **Secret Pass,** 23m into Ruby Valley.

US40 now crosses (N) fork of the Humboldt. At **105.** is **NEV. SCH. OF INDUSTRY,** for delinquent boys. **110. ELKO,** the most important cattle town of Nev. The name means "one woman" which was the cry of squaws when they saw the 1st whites enter bringing only 1 woman. It warned the other squaws to hide. Elko is the chief trade & service center bet. Salt Lake City & Reno, served by all major types of trans. At first, it looks like a cattle town of 1880's, with false front stores, but closer inspection reveals a modern city with chromium bars, cocktail lounges, & specialty shops. At one time it was the seat of Univ. of Nev., whose former home now is the **City Lib.** Across the R. is Mun. Swim. Pool (sm.fee), a popular recr. spot. Near-by is a hot mineral spring, used by early travelers to bathe in & wash their clothes. Now used by migratory workers. At Elko are supervisor's hqs. for **Humboldt Nat. For.,** starting pt. for many vacation trips into Rocky Mts., some of whose peaks are over 12,000′ high. In vic. are more than 2800 miles of trout streams. Elko Cty. Fair & Livestock Show in fall are famous. At Elko also is J. with St.11.

SIDE TRIPS: (A) On St.11 (N) Rd. passes **Dinner Station** at 23m & reaches **North Fork** at 50m (excellent f. & h.). Rd. cont. for more than 30m past **Wild Horse Reservoir,** man-made lake created by **Wild Horse Dam** on Owyhee R. (good f. & canoeing; camp grounds), to **Mountain City** in Humboldt Nat. For. (Humboldt Div., see above).

(B) On St.11 (S) Rd. runs 13m to **Lamoille,** small picturesque trading center. **Thomas Canyon Camp** (facils.) is c.5m (SE).

At **121.** S. Fork R. pours into the Humboldt & hy. skirts many large ranches. The R. passes through **Carlin Canyon,** an impassable gorge before Central Pac. RR. went through in 1867. The Mormon cricket is a pest in this vic.; it menaces not only farmers' crops but worries motorists, because layers of dead crickets make Rd. extremely slippery. **136. CARLIN,** where the S.P. RR. has repair shops. To the N. is **Emigrant Pass** (6,114′). Here are springs & fossil beds. In distance Shoshone Mts. rise, dominated by Twin Summits (5,703′). At **153.** J. with St.21.

SIDE TRIP: On latter 5.5m to **Beowawe.** Horseshoe Ranch near-by is remnant of vast ranch holding. To the (S) 2m is an **Emigrant Cemetery** (L). At 6.5m **Gravelly Ford,** where the Donner Party (see Cal.) experienced an early tragedy. James A. Reed's Palace Car (an elaborate cart drawn by 8 oxen) had to be abandoned in Utah, which left him in a bad mood. While quarreling with John Snyder, he killed him, whereupon the Party wanted to hang him, but because of his wife's pleading, suspended punishment, & sent him out alone & on foot to find his way to Cal. Strangely enough, he not only reached Cal. but was the 1st to send out a rescue force to aid the exhausted Donner Party (see Cal.). (SW) from Beowawe 7.5m is a colorful active geyser area, some mud pots & fumaroles; most pronounced in spring.

**184. BATTLE MOUNTAIN** (accoms.) in a mining dist. that now serves as trading center for ranchers. **Little Giant Mine,** discovered in 1867, yielded a million dollars worth of silver; veins near Galena yielded 5 million dollars worth of lead, silver, & gold; antimony deposits along Cottonwood Cr. amounted to 50 tons. **Copper Canyon,** which today has valuable copper, used to have good gold placers. Here is **Site of Ind. & Emigrant Battle,** 1857. At **196. VALMY** (cabins, gas.). To the (N) 2m **Treaty Hill,** on which a wall was built by the Inds. Land W. of it belonged to Paiute & E. to the Shoshone. At **215.** Golconda Summit comes into view (5,154′) & at **221.** Rd. passes **GOLCONDA,** a shipping point for ranchers. Near-by are **Golconda Summit & Golconda Hot Springs,** once valued for therapeutic qualities.

**237. WINNEMUCCA,** (accoms. hosp. swim. pool, golf), named for Chief Winnemucca. As early as 1850, a trading post had been est. here. Mining discoveries were made in this vic. long before the RRs. reached it in 1862. By 1869 it was a lively western spot. Freighting to outlying mines with mule teams became a profitable business & by 1874 there were enough teamsters to have the 1st strike, demanding 5¢ a ℔. on freight to Silver City. Cty. fairs became gala events & by 1900 the town even had a smooth-running Dramatic Society. Butch Cassidy's boys, part of famous Nev. outlaw band, robbed First Nat. Bank here of $32,000 & disappeared. Nev. Rodeo (usually 1st wk. in Sept.) attracts riders from distant parts. Neighborhood has a large Basque pop. that came originally as sheepherders. Their restaurants still have favorite Basque dishes & every meal is topped with café royal—black coffee with rum. The town has some impressive modern bldgs.: **Cty. Courth., St. Paul's Ch. (Cath.)** & the model **Grammar Sch.,** with excellent Lib. On Baud St., near US40, is **Chinese Joss-House** (1902) & on a hill on other side of US40 is a **Chinese Cemetery,** around which Inds. used to hover after a funeral in order to take the funeral meats later.

## Sec. 1: WINNEMUCCA to CAL. LINE. 176.

At Winnemucca is J. with US95 which, running (S), becomes one with US40. Going (N), it reaches Ore. border at McDermitt in 76m (see US95). US40, still following the Humboldt but now running (SW) reaches **MILL CITY** at **28.** Shipping pt. for tungsten. Here is J. with side Rd.

SIDE TRIP: From **Mill City** (R) 8.5m to **Tungsten Mine,** one of the important ones in country. Rd. passes **Rye Patch Reservoir & Dam** (R) 1.5m & (L) the Humboldt Range (9,835′).

**58. OREANA** with its Clear Cold Springs. **72. LOVELOCK** (accoms.), where emigrants prepared for crossing the desert. Here their trls. split—one (W) towards Reno, the other (SW) to Carson Valley. Whenever the Humboldt R. dried up, the plight of cattlemen became great. In 1908, reservoirs to irrigate surrounding country were constructed, & in 1934 U.S. Gov. built Rye Patch Dam (see above). Various types of irrigation are used depending on terrain. Lovelock today is a prosperous stock-growing center in which Basques are mainly responsible for the fine sheep raising. (f.h.good in vic.). Hy. cont. (SW) passing **Humboldt Sink,** with dreaded **Carson Sink** right beyond it (SE). **90.** J. with dirt Rd. marked: To Lovelock Caves.

SIDE TRIP: On this Rd. (L) 4.5m & then (L) again 2m across RR. tracks. Then (R) 4m & (L) 9m to a trl. leading into **Lovelock Cave.** From this cave Univ. of Cal. at request of Nev. St. Hist. Soc. has taken 10,000 artifacts, woven fabrics & skeletons c. 2,000 yrs. old. These are now exhibited at **St. Hist. Soc. Mus.** It is possible that this cave is the Horseshoe Cave about which early Nev. historians wrote. A story about the Paiute is that once, while at war with a cannibalistic tribe, said to have been short of stature, with red hair & freckles, the Paiute drove them all into a cave & tried to make them promise not to eat their neighbors. When the cannibals refused to promise, the Paiute covered up the cave's entrance with driftwood & set it afire, thus cremating entire tribe.

**113. HOT SPRINGS** (cabins, supplies). Popular old emigrant camp; early travelers called it Spring of False Hope & tarried there only a short time. Light here plays strange tricks, creating optical illusions. Rivers seem to flow up instead of down.

**130. FERNLEY,** a trading post for Ind. artifacts; terminal of S.P. RR. Branch. At Fernley, US95 branches off (S) to **Yerington,** supply center for agric. reg. US40 follows Truckee R. to Cal. Line. **133. WADSWORTH,** a scattered village even when Frémont camped here in 1844. Later when Central Pac. RR. arrived, 1869, shops were set up & Wadsworth became most important RR. town in Nev. They were again removed in 1905. At that time, shops, houses & stores were loaded on freight cars destined for Sparks, the new home. At Wadsworth is J. with St.34.

SIDE TRIP: On this Rd. (R) past **Pyramid L. Ind. Reserv.** (see Reno), to the L. itself at **Nixon** 16m. Here is Ind. Agency. About 560 Paiute & a few other Inds. still live here. In summer more Inds. come & bring their stock to graze. The Ind. cemetery is always decorated on Memorial Day with desert flowers, a custom adopted from the whites. St.34 cont. (N) & passes along the shore of Pyramid L. (excellent cutthroat bass f.; only with guide, but not expensive). In the L. is impressive **Pyramid I.** (475′ high), from which L. was named. Int. Ind. petroglyphs at **Court of Antiquity** are made with red ochre on the surrounding rocks.

**162. SPARKS,** est. by S.P. RR. in 1905; now is 3rd largest city in st. People from Reno commute here. Travelers on through trains often transfer here for a 20 min. stay in Reno, time enough to lose a little money on the slot machine, & then return to cont. their journey. Sparks is well known for its propagation of pheasants. The grace & beauty of the males with their flashing green, brown & purple feathers is a rewarding sight; to eat the stuffed bird served in orig. skin & feathers is a feast. There is a model pheasant farm at Pyramid & Prater. At Sparks is J. with St.32.

SIDE TRIP: On this Rd. (R) 2m to St.33. Take St.33 (R) 26m to **Pyramid L.** (see above, also Reno). More readily reached from Sparks than from Reno.

**165. RENO** (see). US40 now follows the Truckee R. To (R) are foothills of the Peavine Mts. & to (L) snow-capped **Mt. Rose** (see Reno). Hy. passes **Lawton's Hot Springs** at **172.5.** (pop. resort. swim.pool). Also training quarters for Reno prize fighters. **175. VERDI,** an old lumber camp. Near here are 2 petrified fors. believed to be from 1000-2000 yrs. old. Here the 1st train robbery took place, 1870. From here on Rd. runs through heavy evergreen stands. At **176.** it crosses **CAL. LINE,** running through hist. Donner Pass (see Cal.).

# US 50—NEVADA

**NEV.-UTAH LINE** (117$^{m}$ from Salt Lake City) **(W) to CAL. LINE** (112$^{m}$ E. of Sacramento) **469. US50**

Via: Ely, Eureka, Austin, Fallon, & Carson City. Paved Rd. Accoms.: In larger towns.

## Sec. 1: WENDOVER to AUSTIN. 268.

US50 is one of the state's most beautiful routes, over mountains, through valleys & meadows, colorful with sage & meadow blooms. The area is thinly populated. For many miles hy. follows emigrant & early mail trls.

US50 & US40 united cross Utah line at Wendover, hqs. & supply base for auto races on **Salt Flats** near-by. The hys. run together for 0.5$^{m}$, then US50 turns (SW) through deserts & rolling hills. **25. FERGUSON'S SPRINGS** (water), a hy. maintenance camp (5,800'). **36. WHITE HORSE PASS** (6,595'). **60. BECKY'S SPRINGS** is at J. with US93 (see). The Beckwith & Mormon Trl. crossed here, 1854. These 2 hys. travel as one to **75.** Here is J. with St.35.

SIDE TRIP: On this Rd. (W) 9$^{m}$ to **Cherry Cr.,** a former mining town with 6,000 people; now has only a few hundred. **Egan Canyon Pony Rd.** & the **Overland Mail** route ran (E) & (W) here.

**107. McGill,** a Nev. Consolidated Copper Co. town (smelter O.to mining specialists). Thousands of tons of copper are treated here daily; it is Nevada's largest single industry. Near-by is **Duck Cr. Area.** Fish hatchery & pub. camp grounds. **119. EAST ELY. 120. ELY,** chief maintenance depot of the Nev. Northern RR.; is company owned. Continuous mining operations since 1869 have been carried on here, except for 2 "depression yrs." John Ely for whom the town is named bought his mine for $3,500. Before he sold it, it netted him over 20 million dollars worth of metal. When he sold it, it brought only one-third of a million. At 614 High St., **Millard Mus.** (O. during bus. hrs.), contains large coll. of minerals. One gruesome item is a petrified foot & shoe of miner trapped in Eureka Mine. At Ely is J. with US6 & US93. Former runs (SW) to **Tonopah,** 168$^{m}$ & latter (S) to **Pioche,** 109$^{m}$, while US50 turns sharply (W) & cont. thus across the st. At **123.** is **RUTH** with its vast copper pit—more than a mile in diam. It is world's largest open cut copper pit, & is still being worked. At sunset pit is spectacular in coloring. US50 crosses **ROBINSON SUMMIT** (7,607') at c.**137.** At **157.,** hy. skirts N. boundary of White Pine Div. of **Nev. Nat. For.** (supervisor hqs. at Ely).

**153.5. MOORMAN RANCH** (water), hqs. for cattlemen. **157.** J. with Hamilton Rd. (gravel).

SIDE TRIP: On this Rd. (L) to **Hamilton,** famous community center for 15,000 miners in the old days; now deserted. Bldgs. that once housed roistering crowds are now only skeletons. In distance, **Hamilton Peak** (10,741') can be seen.

**163. LITTLE ANTELOPE SUMMIT** (7,432') (campsites. food & water). (1.5$^{m}$ (N), old **Antelope Springs,** st. sta.). **176. PANCAKE SUMMIT** (6,517'). **198. EUREKA.**

Eureka mine was discovered in 1864; 1st smelter built 5 yrs. later. Eureka had a typical mining boom-town history. As early as 1878 it was a lively place with 125 saloons, 25 gambling houses & 15 tent shows. In 1st 20 yrs. of its existence the mines produced a yield of $80,000,000 in silver, gold & lead. It also controlled at one time the world lead market. Now is experiencing a revival through diamond drilling, but lifestock raising has become principal industry. By 1883 it had a pop. of 10,000; now only 700. **Colonnade Hotel, Jackson House** (Hotel Brown), & the **Opera House** (Eureka Theater) are still standing. Countryside surrounding old mines is beautified by purple stinkweed, which despite its name presents a gorgeous sight. **229.** (L) **ANTELOPE PEAK** (10,207') begins to rise in Toiyabe Nat. For. (hqs. at Reno). **245. HICKERSON SUMMIT** (6,587') is crossed. Frémont passed near here, heading S. in 1845. **257. TOIYABE.** J. with St.8A.

SIDE TRIP: On this Rd. (S) in shadow of Toiyabe Range are hot springs, old placer camps & mining boom towns—all in **Toiyabe Nat. For.** (supervisor hqs. at Reno).

**263.** Hy. crosses **AUSTIN SUMMIT** (7,554'). Both sides of Rd. offer unobstructed view of seasonal flowers. White prickly poppies line roadside. **268. AUSTIN,** in Toiyabe Canyon (Ranger dist. hqs. for Toiyabe Nat. For.). In 1862 it was famous silver camp. Discovery of silver did not at first attract crowds because of Virginia City's boom; but late in 1863 "Reese River Reveille's" rumor & fact reporting brought in the masses. **International Hotel,** built that yr., still stands. 4 yrs. later town had 10,000 pop. with a pub. sch. & priv. schs. teaching French, vocal & instrumental music, dancing & calisthenics. It was in Austin (1864) that 9 camels were brought to carry salt for the quartz mills 100ᵐ to the S. It was these camels (1 was a gift from Sultan of Turkey to U.S. Gov.) that Jeff. Davis wanted to try out as beasts of burden in the S.W. desert. When Davis became Pres. of the Confederacy, the camels were sold to an Austin mining co. In 1875 a Nev. law prohibited camels on hys. & the animals were let loose. As late as 1901, prospectors claim they saw camels here & there. Austin was the girlhood home of Emma Wixon, who as Emma Nevada was one of the well-known sopranos of her day. Many early pub. bldgs. still survive, incl. 3 churches, the old hotel & the cty. courthouse; but the RR. was abandoned in 1938. Excellent hunt. in vic. At Austin is also J. with St.8A which leads (N) to **Battle Mountain** at 91ᵐ.

SIDE TRIP: From Austin (S) 1ᵐ on a dirt Rd. to **Stokes Castle** built 1879 by Stokes of Phila., who had heavy mining interests here. The bldg. is 50′ sq., has 3 stories, & a parapet.

## Sec. 2: AUSTIN to EDGEWOOD 201.

US50 now crosses (N) end of Shoshone Range past Emigrant Peak (8,059′) & Railroad Pass & ascends Carroll Summit (7,452′) to **EASTGATE** at **56.,** a former stage sta. **64. FRENCHMAN'S STA.** (supplies, meals). US50 passes vast salt deposit called **Twelve Mile Flat** & a point named **Sand Springs,** an old Pony Express Sta. **97. SALT WELL.** On both sides of Rd. are terraces of ancient L. Lahontan. Burial grounds & petroglyphs show that ancient Ind. tribes lived here. Aborigines are supposed to have inhabited this region from 600 to 2,000 yrs. ago. **113. FALLON,** home of "Hearts of Gold cantaloupes" & of famous Fallon turkeys. Town has a picturesque old **courth.** (portico & columns) & very mod. **Cty. High Sch.** Near-by is the Truckee-Carson or **Lahontan Dam** which impounds **L. Lahontan** to irrigate the surrounding ranches. Three-quarters of its cost have already been repaid to the Gov. Town is up-to-date in social & business enterprises. Near Fallon is excellent duck hunting. It is one of largest pub. hunting grounds in the W. Here also is Hist. Mon. for **Ragtown,** early emigrant trading post. At Fallon is J. with US95 (see) & at **139.** is J. with US Alt.95. This J. is also known as Lahontan J.

SIDE TRIP: On this hy. (S) 8ᵐ to **Ft. Churchill Garrison** (1860), adobe remains of military post est. to protect Pony Express, overland stages, & 1st settlements of Nev., opened during rush on Comstock Lode, but abandoned after RR. was completed.

**163. DAYTON,** at mouth of Gold Cr. Canyon, where gold was first found in 1849—placer gold mining. Known as Ponderers' Rest, because emigrants stopped over here while deciding whether to take the N. or the S. route.

SIDE TRIP: From Dayton a gravel Rd. runs (N) 7ᵐ to **Sutro Tunnel** (O), built by Adolph Sutro, a German-Amer. engineer whose greatest feat was this tunnel to the Comstock Lode. Equally as great was the method he used to finance the tremendous undertaking, since neither the Gov. nor the Big Four of the Comstock would aid him (see Cal.). The function of the tunnel was to drain from the mines along the Lode hot water & gaseous vapors which endangered lives of the miners & slowed up work. It took 13 yrs. to complete "Sutro's coyote hole," as the tunnel was called & by then the Great Comstock had passed its peak. **Geiger Grade,** one of the old shelf roads (drive carefully), is nearest & most scenic.

At **167.** J. with St.17.

SIDE TRIP: On this Rd. (N) 3ᵐ to **Silver City;** at 5.5ᵐ **Gold Hill** & at 7ᵐ **Virginia City** (Royal group of famous Comstock Lode) (see Reno).

**175. CARSON CITY,** capital of Nev. & smallest capital in U.S., lies 14ᵐ E. of L. Tahoe & 30ᵐ S. of Reno. It was founded in 1858 during silver stampede & was named for Kit Carson. By 1860 it was a Pony Express Sta. In 1861 the town already had an Opera House. Its most exciting event was the Fitzsimmons-Corbett fight for heavyweight championship, 1897, & here Gen. Tom Thumb, his wife & their little troupe appeared. Mrs. Thumb, as wife of Count Magri, had a return engagement. Stock-raising, mining, & agric. are chief industries now. Carson City is ranger dist. hqs. for Mono Div. of **Nat. For.** PTS. OF INT.: (1) N. Carson St., **State Capitol** (O. 9-4) by Peter Cavanaugh. N. & S. wings added 1915. On 2nd fl. is excellent portrait of Abraham Lincoln by Chas. Shean. (2) On Carson St., **Supreme Court &**

**St. Lib. Bldg.** (O. wks. 10-12; 1-5; 7-9). (3) NW cor. of Nev. & Telegraph Sts., **Abe Curry H.,** first "elegant" home in Carson City. (4) NW cor. of King & Curry Sts., **Matt Rinkel's H.,** another old structure. (5) Cor. Mussey & Curry Sts., **Warren Engine Co. Firehouse,** small stone bldg. with false front & bell tower. Dept. was org. by 20 leading young men in town. Membership in this co., as in so many other early Amer. Fire Cos., carried social prestige as well as responsibility. (6) NW cor. N. Carson & Robinson Sts., **Old Mint,** transformed into St. Mus. Gold & silver were minted here until 1893. (7) Division & Spear Sts., **Mark Twain H.** Legend inscribed in cement sidewalk states that this was once the home of Samuel Clemens (Mark Twain), although it really was the home of his brother, Orion Clemens, first Territorial Secretary. (8) Minn. & Robinson Sts., **H. M. Yerington H.** (Vict). (9) Elizabeth & Mountain Sts., **D. L. Bliss H.** (showplace of early days). (10) W. side of Mountain St., **Governor's Mansion** (1905) with broad verandas & white-columned portico. (11) S. Carson & 2nd Sts., **"Carson City Daily Appeal" Office.** The newspaper has been issued ever since 1865. (12) SW cor. 3rd & Minn. Sts., **Ormsby Home** (1860) from which Maj. Ormsby set out on punitive expedition against Inds. who had burned Williams' trading post in retaliation for kidnapping of 2 squaws. Ormsby was later killed at Battle of Pyramid L. (see Reno). (13) To the (E) of Carson City 2$^{m}$ is **State Penitentiary** (O). It has 1st lethal gas chamber in the country. Here also have been made important archeological finds; footprints of giant sloth & mastodon skeletons.

At Carson City US50 & US395 unite for a few miles. At **178.** is **STEWART.** Here (S) is Stewart-Carson Ind. Agency, est. 1890 (pop. 30). At **188. SPOONER STA.,** former stagecoach stop at L. Tahoe (now popular vacation resort, winter & summer. Many camps & trls., 6,300′). The L. is 23$^{m}$ long (lying partly in Nev. & partly in Cal.). Its waters are so transparent that objects are distinctly visible at a depth of 65′ on a clear day. High Sierra's peaks can be seen over treetops. Inds. used N. shore for summer camping grounds. At Spooner Sta. is J. with St.28.

SIDE TRIP: On this Rd. (N) around **L. Tahoe,** past **Crystal Bay** & over the Cal. Line.

US50 proceeds (S) along L., past Glenbrook (resort, riding, golf) to Cave Rock from which fine view of L. **197. ZEPHYR COVE** (hotels, horses). **201. LAKESIDE,** at **CAL. LINE.**

## US 6—NEVADA

**UTAH LINE** (92$^{m}$ W. of Delta) **(W) to CAL. LINE** (40$^{m}$ from Bishop). **310. US6**
Via: Ely, Tonopah & Coaldale. Mostly paved or good Rd. Accoms.: Good in Ely & Tonopah, limited elsewhere.

US6 crosses S. Central Nev. diagonally (SW) through mountain & desert country, copper regs. & 4 Nat. Fors. Brilliant rock outcroppings all along the route. From the Utah border hy. runs to (E) sec. of **Nev. Nat. For.** (hqs. at Ely). At **11.** is J. with gravel Rd.

SIDE TRIP: On this Rd. (L) 1.5$^{m}$ to **Baker** (camp.facils.) Dist. Range Sta. Near here is base of **Mt. Wheeler** (13,058′), 2nd highest peak in St.

To the W. of Baker on graded Rd. 6$^{m}$ is **Lehman Caves Nat. Mon.** (O). The caves of gray & white limestone are honeycombed by tunnels & galleries which rival the Carlsbad & Mammoth Caves in size & beauty. The stalactites & stalagmites are unsurpassed for delicacy of formation.

Main hy. cont. through the Nat. For., crossing **Sacramento Pass** (7,163′) & at c.**29.** touches another sec. of Nev. Nat. For. **67. EAST ELY** & J. with US93 (see).

**68. ELY** (see US50) & J. with US50. From here Rd. runs diagonally (SW) through 3d sec. of Nev. Nat. For. past sparsely settled region (gas stas. & facils. are rare). **72. MURRAY SUMMIT** (7,316′) winter sports area with ski lift, etc. Near **Ward Mt.** (10,929′) is **Ward Mt. Campground** (pic.trlrs.). At **106.** US6 crosses **GRANT RANGE.** Near here is **Currant Cr. Campground** (wood & water). **120. CURRANT** (6,999′; gas. supplies). **187. WARM SPRINGS** (bath., supplies, guides). **229. TONOPAH ARMY AIR BASE.**

**236. TONOPAH,** (all types accoms.) scene of one of Nev.'s greatest silver mining booms, though it got under way leisurely. Jim Butler, rancher, casually looked around for someone to assay a few rocks of ore he had picked up in Southern Klondyke while hunting for his lost burro (1900). No one was willing to assay them for a promised share in the findings except an old Austin sch. teacher. The ore yielded remarkable silver returns, but even then Butler placed little hope in the findings & delayed action until his wife went with him to stake his claims. Gradually the news spread; finally all of Nev. & the West were at Tonopah's doorstep. The 1st $4,000,000 of transactions, in leases & interest, were handled orally without any ensuing litigation. Tonopah, unlike other mining towns, was very orderly. Despite its name (Little Water), Tonopah could early discard signs that used to be found in saloons equipped with a bath or wash tub, "First chance $1, 2nd chance 50¢, 3rd chance 25¢," because the Crystal Water Co. soon supplied the town with the needed water. By 1906 the boom was in full swing. More than $135,000,000 of gold & silver have been taken out of this mine, & many predict still greater finds such as the Getchall mines. It was in Tonopah that the Wingfield dynasty began. Geo. Wingfield joined forces with Sen. Nixon, & by shrewd handling & consolidating of interests they created the **Goldfield Consolidated Mines Co.,** eventually producing 80 million dollars gross & paying more than 30 million in dividends. Wingfield not only opened mines but a dozen banks, & when the dynasty finally crashed, his personal property valued at $50,000,000 went with it. The fairly recent discovery of the **Getchall Mines,** N. of Reno, crowned Getchall the new "king." For "past favors received" Getchall made Wingfield an outright gift of one-third of his mining property. PTS. OF INT.: **Nye Cty. Courth.,** on a high bluff, containing valuable old records. **Tonopah Club** (R) still uses part of the old quarters, once the spectacular meeting place of both struggling miners & those who had become fabulously rich. **Kirchen Cairn.** Here John Kirchen predicted a rich find.

**276. COALDALE.** Here is J. with US95 leading (N) to **Walker L.** 64$^{m}$ (see US95). **Fish L. Valley** (S). Low grade coal discovered here. Turquoise & agate mines near Monte Cristo Range (N). **298. BASALT.** US6 crosses (SW) over Montgomery Pass (7,166'; service sta. & bar). **Boundary Peak** (L) (13,145') highest in Nev. At **310.** hy. reaches **CAL. LINE.**

## US 91—NEVADA

**NEV.-ARIZ. LINE** (38$^{m}$ from St. George, Utah) **(SW) to CAL. LINE** (50$^{m}$ from Baker, Cal.). **127. US91**

Via: Glendale, (Overton), Las Vegas & Jean. Paved Rd. U.P. RR. parallels route bet. Glendale & Cal. Line. Limited accoms. except in Las Vegas.

This hy. cuts (SW) across bottom of st. from Ariz. to Cal.

US91 (Arrowhead Trl.) crosses Ariz. border at **0. 1.5. MESQUITE,** ranchers' trade center, situated on E. side of Virgin R. On opp. side (along very wide main street), is **BUNKERVILLE** at **7.,** one of oldest ranching communities. Jedediah Smith, trapper & explorer, passed through here en route to Southern Cal. in 1826. At Bunkerville is a **Mormon colony** (sett. in the 90's) that helped bring irrigation to the community. At **33.** is J. with St.12.

SIDE TRIP: On this Rd. (L) 12$^{m}$ to **Overton,** another Mormon community, built on what used to be Patterson Ranch. Beyond 1$^{m}$ is **Overton Mus.,** an adobe, built by CCC under Nat. Pk. Serv. It preserves the archeological remains from Lost City (ancient Ind. village) now covered by L. Mead (see Las Vegas). Further on 5$^{m}$ is the strange & impressive **Valley of Fire St. Pk.,** (4 x 6 miles) on whose blood-red walls are well preserved Ind. petroglyphs. There are also fragments of a petrified for. near-by (see Las Vegas).

US91 here roughly parallels the old Spanish Tr., also called San Bernardino—Salt Lake Wagon Rd. Frémont crossed through here (1874). **35. GLENDALE.** J. with US93 (see). (W) is **Moapa R. Ind. Reserv.** (172 Paiute Inds.) & **50.** J. with St.40.

SIDE TRIP: On this Rd. 23$^{m}$ (E) to **Valley of Fire St. Pk.** (see above) & at 24$^{m}$ is **Overton Beach** on L. Mead (115$^{m}$ long; good f., boat. & bath.). All sorts of water sports have come to this desert country through man-made L. Mead (see Hoover-Boulder Dam), world's largest reservoir (campsites. shelters). Moapa Valley is noted for tomatoes which are shipped by air to Eastern markets.

To (L) of combined US91-93 hy. is J. with side Rd.

SIDE TRIP: On this Rd. (L) 7.5$^{m}$ to **Gypsum Cave** (300' deep with 6 rooms; entrance only 15' x 70'). In it are remains of prehist. sloth. Stone points for javelins & painted dart shafts were found here showing man existed, contemporaneously with the sloth. (Guides are advisable; carry water & candles).

**76. McCARRAN AIR FIELD** (bleached skulls of cattle border the field). **82. NORTH LAS VEGAS. 84. LAS VEGAS** (see). Hy. cont. through desert country past Blue Diamond Canyon (W) & Blue Diamond limestone mines. Near-by is a Wall Board Plant. Joshua trees line Rd. **114. JEAN,** a U.P. RR sta. US91 cont. its ascent toward Devil Peak (5,865′). At **127.** in sight of main power lines of Hoover Dam, it crosses **CAL. LINE.**

## US 93—NEVADA

**NEV.-IDAHO LINE** (47ᵐ from Twin Falls, Idaho) **(SW) to NEV.-ARIZ. LINE** (57ᵐ W. of Chloride, Ariz.) **537. US93**

Via: Wells, Ely, Pioche, Glendale, Las Vegas, Henderson, Boulder City. Paved Rd. Accoms.: In larger towns.

### Sec. 1: ARIZ. LINE to PIOCHE, NEV. 314.

US93 (Internat. 4 States Hy.) crosses Idaho line at **0.** It parallels Salmon R. to **CONTACT** at **16.,** then turns (N) to the Snake R. Contact was founded as a mining center in 1895. US93 now travels through a valley of luxuriant vegetation bet. 6,000′ mts. Fort Hall—Humboldt Emigrant Rd. crossed here in the 1840's. **68. WELLS.** J. with US40 (see). Near **88.** is where the Donner Party crossed in 1846 on their disastrous trek across the country. Hy. passes Snow Water L. (L) & travels through Clover Valley & its many large ranches. **131. CURRIE,** sheep & cattle shipping pt. In 1854 it was camp site of Beckwith U. S. Army Expedition & also was a Mormon shortcut to Carson Valley. **147.** J. with US50. The 2 hys. now proceed (S) as one Rd. **174.** To the E. 3ᵐ is **Site of Ft. Shelbourne,** Pony Mail Sta. **184. McGILL,** copper smelter (O. to mining specialists, see US50), Nev.'s largest single industry.

**206. EAST ELY** & adj. **ELY.** J. with US6 (see). These 2 hys. join for 27ᵐ passing bet. 2 divisions of **Nev. Nat. For.** (hqs.at Ely; h.camp.hik.saddle trips & winter sports. cabins, camps & dude ranches). Range & fors. intermingle. The **Lehman Caves** are in reg. (see US6). **232. CONNERS PASS** (7,732′). US6 branches E. 41ᵐ, to Lehman Caves. Snow-capped **Wheeler Peak** (13,058′) can be seen (E). US93 now heads directly (S), still in Nev. Nat. For. passing bet. Wilson Cr. (L) & Ely Range (R). The mts. here are flat-topped with deep canyons, while the cliffs become brighter colored & the Rd. is bordered with wild sunflowers. **314. PIOCHE,** still very active lead, silver & zinc mining town, that promises to be important in supplying the world with these metals for 25 yrs. From the beginning it was one of leading mining districts; produced $40,000,000 worth of ore. It was then known as a "wild & woolly" town in which 75 people were killed before 1 died of natural causes. Once was completely swept away by fire. Three yrs. later it again had 6,000 pop. Its mining activities have been continuous from the start. The old **County Courth.** (1870) costing $1,000,000 still stands. In 1933 it was condemned, 3 yrs. before it was paid for.

### Sec. 2: PIOCHE to ARIZ. LINE, 223.

**11. PANACA** (founded by Mormons, 1864), J. with gravel Rd.

SIDE TRIP: (W) 2ᵐ is **Cathedral Gorge St. Pk.** (1,578-as.). Peculiar rock formations, fluted spires & perpendicular walls of tan cemented sand give it its name. (pic.facils.)

**25. CALIENTE,** with attractive houses for RR. workers. Here is J. with side Rd. which leads c.15ᵐ (E) to **Beaver Dam St. Pk.** (719-as. campgrds. all facils.) **26.** J. with graveled Rd. leading (S) 3ᵐ to **Kershaw Canyon-Ryan St. Pk.** (240-as.; camping & pic. facils.) US93 leaves the canyon & climbs up Highland Range to a plateau filled with cacti, joshua trees & creosote bush. The Manly emigrant party, when it broke away from the experienced Jefferson Hunt route, followed this hy. to Death Valley. **80. ALAMO,** in Pahranagat Valley & near Pahranagat L.; once mecca of horsethieves & rustlers. The Bigler Party passed through here on their way to Cal.

**144. GLENDALE.** J. with US91 (see). To (W) is **Moapa Valley Ind. Reserv.** (172 pop). **184. McCARRAN AIRFIELD** (see Las Vegas). **190. N. LAS VEGAS. 192. LAS VEGAS.** J. with US95 (see Las Vegas). US93, US95, & US466 unite & reach **HENDERSON** (see Las Vegas) at **205., BOULDER CITY** at **215.** (see Las Vegas), **HOOVER DAM & ARIZ. ST. LINE** at **223.** (see Las Vegas). At Las Vegas there is also J. with US91 leading (S) 43ᵐ to **Cal. Line.** (see Las Vegas).

# US 95—NEVADA

**NEV.-ORE. LINE** (101$^{m}$ from Jordan Valley, Ore.) **(S) to CAL. LINE** (49$^{m}$ E. of Baker, Cal.) **685. US95**

Via: McDermitt, Winnemucca, Lovelock, Fernley, Fallon, Hawthorne, Tonopah, Goldfield, Las Vegas, Searchlight. Accoms.: In larger towns. Paved Rd.

US95, longest hy. in Nev. runs through regs. that give an excellent cross section of the St., its mountains, valleys, ranches, mines.

## Sec. 1: McDERMITT to TONOPAH, 403.

At **0.** US95 (the Bonanza Hy.) crosses Ore. Line & near-by **McDERMITT,** site of old Ft. McDermitt, est. to protect emigrants from Inds. But much earlier, in 1828, Peter Skene Ogden led his trappers through here to the Quinn & Humboldt Rs. The ft. was named for Col. Ch. McDermitt who was shot (1865) from ambush during skirmish with Inds. Bet. 1865-80 it was a sta. on old Stage Rd. to Idaho mines. J. here with side Rd.

SIDE TRIP: On this Rd. (L) 5$^{m}$ **McDermitt Ind. Reserv. Agency** (306 Paiute Inds.). Hqs. bldgs. are from reconstructed ft. bldgs.

**15.** J. with dirt Rd. leading (L) 11$^{m}$ to **Nat. Mine** (6,100′), rich mining dist. in **Toiyabe Nat. For.,** Santa Rosa Div. (trout stream in vic.). **30. OROVADA,** Red Cross 1st Aid Sta. Hy. has Quinn R. (R) & beautiful St. Rosa Mts. (E). **44.** J. with St.8A which leads to **Quinn R. Crossing,** & upwards to Ore. border again, through mining districts, wild life refuges, & ranches. **50.** J. with St.8B.

SIDE TRIP: On this Rd. (L) 18$^{m}$ to **Paradise Valley,** appropriately so called by the early prospectors & by everyone seeing it for 1st time. It is like an oasis bordered on 3 sides by mts. Flowers of varied hues abound.

**76. WINNEMUCCA.** J. with US40 (see). US95 & US40 travel as one Rd. to **FERNLEY** at **206.** (for intervening 130 miles see US40). **220.** J. with US50. These 2 Rds. unite for 9$^{m}$ to **FALLON** at **229.** (see US50). Here hy. turns abruptly (S) to **SCHURZ** at **268.** Agency Hqs. for **Walker R. Ind. Reserv.** (475 Inds.) mostly Paiute & some Shoshone who make their living by raising stock & making baskets & beadword. To the (L) 2$^{m}$ beyond is N. end of **Walker L.,** a beautiful remnant of ancient L. Lahontan, 30$^{m}$ long & 8$^{m}$ wide, amid steep rosy-hued mts. incl. **Mt. Grant** (11,303′); can be climbed by car. Frémont & Kit Carson on their 2d expedition (1845) into Nev. camped here while they awaited Jos. Walker, trapper guide for whom Frémont named this body of opaque blue water. **298. U.S. NAVAL AMMUNITION DEPOT** with all facils. of a military base. To find sailors & marines in this out-of-the-way mountainous region will seem unusual to the traveler (see Reno). **299. HAWTHORNE** (accoms.) with Mt. Grant (NW). Here Jos. Walker guided his 1st train of emigrants in 1843 through the area. Hawthorne now is a prosperous-looking trade center for ranchers & for prospectors & miners who were encouraged by discoveries of rich ore as late as 1939. From Hawthorne, US95 turns (E) through desert lands bordered with mts. **326. LUNING.** Here is J. with St.23 leading (N) 33$^{m}$ to **Brucite & magnesite mines. 334. MINA** (accoms. stores & service. sm. RR. shop). Rds. radiate from here in all directions. Frémont crossed here on his 2d expedition.

**363. COALDALE,** named for low grade coal found here. Also turquoise, agate & gem mines near-by. To (N) is brilliantly colored **Monte Cristo Range.** Here is J. with US6 (see). **403. TONOPAH** (see US6).

## Sec. 2: TONOPAH to CALIFORNIA LINE. 282.

**0. TONOPAH** (see US6). Vegetation changes **c14.** The sage is left behind & creosote bush begins. **26. GOLDFIELD** (tourist camp & gas near hy.). Goldfield is a hist. mining town of the 1900's, the child of Tonopah, without which it could not have achieved early recognition. Now it is only a reflection of its former importance & glory. On three score city blocks stand shells of impressive bldgs., once filled with business & excitement, now inhabited only by caretakers. Still a feeling of hope pervades, the feeling that this once fabulous gold & jewel ore reg. will again yield a treasure. Its production went to $105,000,000. During its heyday, the town outdid in elegance even Tonopah. A 200-rm. hotel was built with all modern conveniences. Here Tex Rickard staged the famous Gans-Nelson fight in 1906, & also brought Nat Goodwin & Edna Goodrich, the country's most popular comedy team, for the amusement of his patrons, while champagne flowed & his bar boasted 80 tenders. During World War II, Goldfield had spasmodic bursts of mining activity. US95 cont. (S) & for the next 4m sweeps through foothills of magnificent mt. ranges varying in color & shade with the season & time of day. Along the hy. at **c.40** a side Rd. branches (SW) & leads directly across the **Cal. Line** to **Scotty's Castle** (see Cal.) in Death Valley. **93. BEATTY,** charming sun-bleached village, E. gateway to **Death Valley Nat. Mon.,** on the Armogosa R. In 1906 it became shipping pt. for the surrounding **Bullfrog mines.** At Beatty is J. with St.58.

SIDE TRIP: On this Rd. (R) 5m to **Rhyolite,** ghost town. From 1905-08 it rivaled Goldfield in its ore production, but turned out to be only a superficial find. During the boom 2 RRs. entered town. Among the ruined bldgs. still standing is the once elaborate RR. sta. (now transformed into a gambling hall), & the Bottle House, whose walls are built of horizontally laid beer bottles. Recently, entire town was offered for sale incl. the 2 bldgs. above, a bar, & casino. St.58 cont. into Death Valley & at 13m crosses **Cal. Line.**

Hy. now runs over desert Rd. lined with cactus, yucca, & creosote bush. **123. LATHROP WELLS** J. with St.29, another Death Valley Rd. which crosses the Cal. Line at 16m. **166. IND. SPRINGS** (gas.sta.tourist camp). From here hy. turns (SE). **180.** J. with paved St.52 through Charleston Mt. sec. of Nev. Nat. For. (Ranger Office at Las Vegas, P.O. Bldg.). **Kyle & Lee Canyons** are the 2 most easily accessible beauty spots & lead to Charleston Peak (11,910′), an oasis of plant & animal life. Views toward twilight are spectacular. Within 30 min., one can get from desert to the snowfields. Winter sports very popular (all facils.).

SIDE TRIP: On St. 52 (R) 17m to **McWilliams Campgrd.** & **Camp Pittman** (L) in Lee Canyon. Here Rd. branches (L). At 24m is **Deer Creek Campgrd.** & at 47m in Kyle Canyon (campsites), another Rd. branches off, leading (L) to a 3m trl. that ascends Charleston Peak.

US95 cont. (S) through uninhabited **Charleston & Sheep Ranges,** one of last refuges of Nelson bighorn. **208. LAS VEGAS** (see). From here US93-95-466 are one route.

**222. HENDERSON** (see Las Vegas), southern Nev. industrial center. **227.** US93 branches off (E) to **Hoover Dam,** 12m (see). **263. SEARCHLIGHT** (Las Vegas). **282.** Hy. crosses **CAL. LINE.**

## US 395—NEVADA

**NEV.-CAL. LINE** (8m from Stoy J. with St.24) **(S) to CAL. LINE** (48m from Bridgeport, Cal.) **83. US395**

Via: Reno, Carson City, Minden, Gardnerville.

The major portion of US395 is in Cal. (see).

US395, after crossing into Nev., runs past Old Heinz Ranch across Peavine Summit & then to **RENO, 17.** (see) in beautiful Truckee Valley. Within 10m of Reno along the main hy. are the trio of mineral hot springs, **Steamboat, Lawton & Reno,** whose medicinal values rank with many of the better known spas of Europe. At **26.** is J. with St.17, **GEIGER GRADE** (see Reno) & with St.27 to Mt. Rose Rd.

SIDE TRIP: On St.27 (R) into **Toiyabe Nat. For., Mono Div.** (camp.,hik.) to **Mt. Rose Peak** (8,975′, wonderful walks up mt.). At 23m J. with St.28.; St.27 cont. around (N) shore of **L. Tahoe** with its exceptionally blue waters, to J. with Cal. St.89 at **Tahoe City** (see Cal.). From the Js. of St.28 & St.27 (above), cont. on latter along E. shore of L. Tahoe & around the L. Mark Twain considered this the best view bet. Rubicon Pt. & Echo L. At 38.5m J. with US50 (see).

At **37.** on US395 somewhat hidden from view is **home of WM. JENNINGS,** Mormon (brown ranchh. Vict.Goth.). At **39.** in a grove of trees is the **SANDY BOWERS MANSION,** associated with history of the Comstock era, 2-story sandstone bldg. reminiscent of a Mediterranean villa. Called by some an ugly relic, it was built by Bowers & his Scotch wife, Eilley Orrum, who had suddenly been raised from poverty to affluence by a rich strike in their adj. claims. No one knew their actual wealth. Some said their yearly income was from 1 to 3 million dollars. In a tiny hollow behind the house the Bowers & their adopted daughter, Persia, are buried. Ella Bowers, as Eilley signed her name in U.S.A., survived Sandy by many yrs. Soon after his death their gold vein stopped its yield. Ella, cheated by friends & enemies alike, & embroiled in litigation, soon lost everything; yrs. later (1903) died in poverty. She remained a fantastic woman to the end, interested in spiritualism & mesmerism & even resorting to crystal reading for fees, advising miners where the

ore finds were. She sincerely believed in her own powers & was convinced she had "seen" the Comstock Lode long before it was discovered.
US395, cont. past little **Washoe L.** to **CARSON CITY** on US50 (see) at **49.** US395 & US50 unite for $3^m$ to **STEWART** at **52.** Here is **Carson Ind. Agency** with 30 mod. bldgs. incl. school; trading post selling souvenirs. Pageant usually in June. **57. GENOA,** (1849) oldest settlement in Nev. Genoa, one of the most imp. stopovers during the Gold rush, was named by Mormon Bishop Hyde for birthpl. of Columbus. Its 1st ft. & stockade were built by Col. Reese, 1851. Both burned down in 1910, & were reconstructed in 1948 (O). To this stockade "Snowshoe" Thompson headed, when he started from Placerville "over the hill" carrying mail & medicine. In Genoa (1858) was started Nev.'s 1st newspaper, the "Territorial Enterprise" on which Mark Twain as "Josh" became a staff reporter, but after it was moved to Carson City. On Thompson's grave is a mon. topped by 2 skis. He now has become the patron of skiers, delayed late homage for his heroic deeds. For 20 yrs. he had covered the snows bet. Reno & Placerville on his homemade 10′ x 3″ 25℔. skis. **61. MINDEN,** trim-looking town, sett. by H. F. Dangberg, a German, not in quest of gold but of productive land. When he died in 1904 he had 36,000 as. in diversified farming. **77. TOPAZ L.** (f.camp.boats at Lodge.), formed by damming N. Walker R. for irrigation. **83. CAL. LINE.** The L. stretches across the border.

# RENO

## RENO

RR. stas.: 135 E. Commercial Row for S.P. RR. & for Virginia & Truckee RR.; 325 E. 4th St. for Western Pacif. RR. Accoms.: All types.

Reno, Nev.'s most talked-about city, lies in the beautiful Truckee Meadows bet. the slopes of the Sierra Mts. Truckee R. & Canyon were named by 1st emigrant train that passed through before the gold rush. In 1859 it was camp site of the unfortunate Donner party that rested here just 1 day too long & was trapped by the Sierra snows. Reno was founded in 1868 during the building of Central Pac. RR. & soon developed into a city of distinctive personality & cosmopolitan atmosphere. Present-day Reno is made up of different types of people. There are the out-of-staters, here to be married or divorced, the tax-weary who come to escape income, inheritance, or intangible property taxes. There are the new prospectors & the old F.F.V.'s, whose Virginia is the Comstock & who are not interested in displaying their wealth, but prefer to live as they did in the '80's. There are the Basque herdsmen with excellent reputations whose hqs. are Toscano Bar & whose gambling spot is the Northern Club. They own their own ranches & have their own dynasties. There are also the cattlemen, not to be mistaken for dude ranchers, who meet regularly at "The Roundup," their tavern hangout, to get tips on new jobs.
Mining & prospecting, however, still remain the principal challenge, a challenge newcomers, or those attracted by Reno's gambling & divorce fame may not recognize, although these two "things" have given Reno its modern fame. True, Reno has a hundred bars & almost a thousand slot machines, as well as countless roulette wheels, but "not to gamble in Nev. means not to be working for a living." For cattlemen, sheepmen, miners & certainly prospectors are gamblers in the broader sense. Even the name of Reno was chosen by lot. The city was platted in 1868 after the "Mormon Curse," pestilence & fire, had already visited Virginia & Carson Cities. After the gold & silver strikes at near-by Tonopah (1900) & Goldfield (1902) came Reno's 1st great boom, which lasted 10 yrs. Establishment of legal gambling & the publicity given to Nevada's easy divorce laws produced another great boom for the city, which is still going on, even though Las Vegas is becoming a close rival. The delightfully keen & bracing climate, a combination of desert dryness & mountain coolness, of "sunny Reno" (4,500′) makes visitors eager to return. Reno has city-manager type of mun. gov., while Sparks, its close neighbor, has the mayor-council system.
On the plateau, on N. edge of Reno, are the 86-a. grounds of Univ. of Nev. Campus was transformed from a desert to an oasis by lakes, trees & flowers. Reno is becoming more & more an all-yr. round sports center, offering fine fishing & hunting (some 30 streams in vic.); summer & winter sports on near-by Mount Rose ($17^m$ SW). On it are excellent ski slopes & here take place the Silver Dollar Derby & the Univ. of Nev. Winter Carnival. These ski meets attract skiers from Europe, Canada & the U.S. Reno Rodeo is held in July, with Nev. Inds. participating, but usually decked

out in headdress of other tribes or in Hollywood fashions. In & near city are 5 swim. pools. Reno is hqs. for Toiyabe & Mono Nat. Fors. City is surrounded with dude ranches.

PTS. OF INT.: (1) S. Center at Mill St., **Washoe Cty. Lib.** In basement is **Nev. St. Hist. Soc. Mus. & Lib.** (O. daily exc. Sun.), fine coll. of early Nev. articles. Among them is the sack of flour that dates from Civil War & netted a good sum for the Sanitary Fund (Civil War relief). An election bet was lost, & R. C. Gridley, the loser, had to carry this sack of flour from Clifton to Upper Austin. Afterwards it was auctioned off. Gridley himself started by offering $350. In a short time the gathered Nevadans, who love nothing better than a hot game, bid higher & higher. When bids passed the $2,000 mark, city lots were taken in lieu of money, until $10,000 was reached. After that the sack was re-auctioned many times throughout St. until it netted $275,000. It was another example of painless charity approved by Nevadans. (2) S. Virginia & Court Sts., **County Cth.,** where divorce cases are handled. Divorcees delighted with their freedom are said to kiss the front pillars of the bldg. Others toss their wedding rings into Truckee R. (both stories are denied by Renoites). (3) 631 Cal. Ave., **Nixon H.** (O. appl.) built right after the Goldfield boom, in a gracious style. (4) At W. limit of city, **Idlewild Pk.,** along beautiful Truckee R., incl. mun. pool. (5) SE. side of Reno, **Virginia L. & Pk.** (42-as. incl. 30-a. L. artificially created; summer & winter sports facils.). W. of the L. is **Washoe Cty. Golf Course,** one of the finest publicly owned courses in the W., created with W.P.A. aid. Houses built in this vic. are mostly conservative although some are of modern design. (6) Cor. 2nd & Chestnut Sts., **St. Thomas Aquinas Cathedral** (1908; Sp. Baroque). (7) 643 Ralston St., **Cutts H.** (O. appl.) contains coll. rare porcelain, paintings, old ivory, & embroideries. (8) 621 Washington St., **Smith H.,** with delicate wrought-iron balustrade, supposedly brought up from Cal. (9) 1309 Buena Vista St., **Ch. of Jesus Christ of the Latter Day Saints** (1940) with unusual clerestory & spire. Its white walls are broken by secs. of glass brick. The combination makes it one of town's most striking bldgs. (10) 9th & Univ. Ave., **Main Ent. to Univ. of Nev.** Most of newer bldgs. are of Coll. Ren. design. Univ. offers degrees in Arts & Sciences, Agric. & Engineering. Famous **Mackay Sch. of Mines,** founded by Mrs. John Mackay & her son Clarence, is recognized as one of nation's finest. (John Mackay was 1 of the 4 "bonanza kings" of the Comstock Lode). On campus is statue of John Mackay by Gutzon Borglum. To the (E) of Univ. is 60-a. **Agric. Experiment Sta.** of the Univ.

## TRIPS OUT OF RENO

### I. RENO (S) to CARSON CITY. 30. US395 & St. 17

Via: Virginia City, Gold Hill, Silver City.

On US395 (S) **9.** is **STEAMBOAT SPRINGS,** which provides hot water for small resorts. This is favorite place for geologists to study precious mineral deposits in rock. Here is J. with St.17, known as Geiger Grade, which has replaced the old Geiger Grade, a winding, dangerous shelf Rd. The new Geiger Grade runs (SW) to Geiger Lookout (gorgeous view; pic.facils.) at **14.** Old Geiger Grade over which Wells Fargo & Pioneer Stages raced, was built 1861-2, & over it the 1st locomotive was hauled by yoke of 14 oxen. At **18.** is **GEIGER SUMMIT.** Here the old grade & modern hy. join.

### 22.5. VIRGINIA CITY

Virginia City, on the Comstock Lode, now a "lively ghost town," once had a prominent place in history of silver-gold mining. It was 1st camp in which hard-rock mining was carried on successfully. Its fabulous production of silver & gold has left an indelible impression on all who ever heard of it, & played an important part in preserving the credit of the nation during Civil War. In 1859 while the land was still Utah, Peter O'Riley & Pat McLaughlin found a piece of strange-looking quartz & decided to stake a claim. That same day, H.P.T. Comstock, known as "Old Pancake," accidentally met these 2 men on the lode & immediately claimed an interest in their stake, saying he had staked it before. It was Comstock, who a short while before had found the secret of the Grosch Bros., who in their search for gold had discovered, being metallurgists, that the "blue dirt" was silver ore. Soon, thereafter, the brothers died tragic deaths, one through poisoning, the other through exposure, & Comstock alone knew their secret but was too unlearned to realize its real significance. Still he was haunted by the idea & that is why he lied when he said he had a claim on the lode. McLaughlin & O'Riley knew he was lying but rather than incur his enmity in this wild country, they gave him a quarter share. "Manny" Penrod, another old crony, also received a quarter share in the claim that soon assumed colossal significance. Prospectors were aroused to a high pitch of excitement. Methods of operation quickly changed & all scrambled to get the discarded "blue stuff" which turned out to be silver worth $1.29 an oz. Virginia City & the Comstock became part of Nev. St. in 1864. From a rough, rugged camp, Virginia City developed into a modern community with all conveniences of the day. The lode gradually extended & people believed the yield would last forever. Reports reached the Far East & the Far West, & names such as the Ophir, the Mexican, the Consolidated Virginia became synonymous with untold wealth. A new method of air-drilling speeded ore production & soon bullion came in such huge quantities from the Comstock that U.S. Treas. opened a branch mint at Carson City. Comstockers had a keen sense of quality of entertainment, relishing such stars as Emma Nevada, Modjeska, Patti, Ole Bull & Edwin Booth. Nothing was too good during their "flush" days; but periods of prosperity alternated with periods of depression, through a series of recurring cycles. In the big "bust," 1875, more than $100,000,000 was lost. Comstock's share shrank $42,000,000 in one week; but it weathered the storm & climbed to even greater financial heights. During the transition the "bonanza kings," Mackay, Fair, Flood, & O'Brien, arose & soon were in complete control. It was at Virginia City that the Hearst, Mackay & Mills fortunes were begun. Today the town with its broken streets & wooden sidewalks, still gives evidence of past glories, though most of its bldgs. are boarded up.

PTS. OF INT.: (1) On Taylor St., **St. Mary's in the Mountain** (Cath. 1877), one of most beautiful bldgs. in the st., with 2 delicate spires. Especially int. to artists & visitors alike is the fine interior—rosewood pillars & powder blue ceiling, similar to Sistine Chapel. (2) On Taylor St. & St.17 is **Crystal Bar,** relic of the champagne & squab days, with its gaudy gas chandelier & pictures of the Corbett-Fitzsimmons Fight; still serving. (3) On Union & B. Sts., **Piper's Opera House** (long,1-story, recessed porch; almost crumbling; O. key at the Bucket of Blood saloon), cherished shrine of the theatrical world, where all big names played behind its footlights. Here Adah I. Menken, idol of "the boys," the West & the world, had her long stand in "Mazeppa," tied naked to a mustang. The old bldg. is shaky & ready to fall apart or be razed by any stray spark. (4) C. & Union Sts., skeleton of **International Hotel,** the pride & boast of the Comstockers. Almost completely destroyed by fire. (5) **John W. Mackay mansion** (Vict.). (6) **Gould & Curry Office** (Vict.). (7) **"Territorial Enterprise" Office,** which had been moved from Genoa in 1860. Here Mark Twain worked as reporter & asst. editor, got his first experience as writer, & did exceedingly well; but by his outspoken writing got into difficulties & finally had to leave the st. Though Mark Twain did not treat Nevadans too kindly during his stay there, they now glory in his success & claim him as their own. (7) **Virginia City Fire H.** It was this brigade that made Julia Bullete, belle of the Comstock, an honorary member & fitted her out in a spectacular uniform. She went to all the fires. Men loved her as much as women hated her. Finally she was killed by John Millain, who wanted her diamonds. He was hanged for it, but the women of the town brought him flowers at the gallows, while the Fire Band played "The Girl He Left Behind Him." (8) **Grave & Marker of "Hank Monk,"** the notorious driver, who made Geiger Grade immortal by saying to his frightened passenger, Horace Greeley: "Keep your seat, Horace, & I'll get you there."

At **24.** on St.17 is **GOLDHILL,** remnant of the 1st prosperous camp. Here Mrs. Sandy Bowers had her boarding house & cooked for the disheartened prospectors during the bitter winter of 1860-61, which has been compared to Valley Forge, except that it was of their own choosing. Here also is another of the old fire-houses found in every mining community. Opp. it is **Bowers Mine,** by which Sandy & Eilley jumped from rags to riches. Rd. passes through **DEVIL'S GATE** & reaches at **25.5., SILVER CITY,** 3rd most important camp on the range. It has been the most consistent producer of silver ore in the last 85 yrs., though it has always been known as a "poor man's camp" because of its steady rather than spectacular production. Geyer's Brewery, though still standing, is no longer brewing & is only a reminder of the days when it took 8 brewery wagons to handle the daily delivery. Outside

Devil's Gate is **grave of Hosea Grosch,** one of 2 bros. who really discovered the Comstock Lode (see above). **30.** Hy. reaches Carson City & J. with US50 (see).

**II. RENO (NE) to PYRAMID L. 33. St.33**

From Reno St.33 leads directly (NE) to **L. Pyramid.** The approach to the desert lake is almost by surprise. A quick turn in the fine Rd. & there it lies, an inland sea 35$^{m}$ x 10$^{m}$ surrounded by rocky walls, the color of the Grand Canyon. In it are tufa (volcanic rock) islands, any one of which might have suggested the name to Frémont. One island N. of Anaho has a tufa pyramid 475′ high. Legends connected with the L. are numerous & you are likely to hear different ones. On **Anaho I.** is a Fed. Bird Refuge (284 as). On it is the West's largest rookery of pelicans. At S. end of L. is fishing ground. Landlocked salmon, also known as cutthroat salmon, grow here to unusual size. Fishing license must be obtained at Ind. Agency, at **Nixon** 10$^{m}$ (R) or at **Sutcliff** 3$^{m}$ (L), both Ind. towns on shore of the lake. Particularly beautiful are lighting effects at twilight & at full moon, when pic. & steak parties along the shore are favorite summer pastimes.

**III. RENO (S) to LAKE TAHOE. 32. US395 & St.27**

Take US395 (S) **9.** Here is J. with St.27. On this Rd. (W) at **32.** is **L. Tahoe,** famed "L. of the Sky" (6,200′), completely surrounded by for. covered mts. (yr.-round recr. center), (see US50). Endless stream of tourist cars drive up from Cal. & Nev. to see what Mark Twain considered best view bet. Rubicon Pt. & Echo L. Since the L. is not on an Ind. reserv. as Pyramid L. is, the shoreline is privately owned & filled with cabins & lodges. The **Cal.-Neva Lodge,** built on St. Line is int. because gambling is permitted only on Nev. side & often in the evenings when spirits are high, gamblers move onto the Cal. side. Now & then some prankster shouts "Jiggers, the Judge" & there is a mad scramble back to safety across the Nev. line. Here at Tahoe gambling for larger stakes than at Reno is carried on.

**IV. RENO (SE) to WALKER L. & HAWTHORNE AMMUNITION DEPOT. 140. US40 & US395 Alt.**

Take US40 to **37.** & J. with US395 Alt. On latter to **WALKER L.** at **119.,** another desert L. in a wonderful setting, coupled with the Navy's largest **AMMUNITION DEPOT** at **140.** on E. shore of the L. at **HAWTHORNE** (see US395). Here under the L.'s only trees stands "Baby Face" Nelson's cottage.

**V. RENO (SW) to MT. ROSE. 17. Mt. Rose Hy.**

Half way up mt. is **GALENA ST. PK.** (winter sports center). Beyond 3$^{m}$ is **Grass L. & Mt. Rose Bowl** (longest ski season in the West, 6 mos.). **MT. ROSE SUMMIT** (10,800′). Here famous Silver Dollar Derby & Univ. of Nev. Winter Carnival take place.

**VI. RENO (W) to DONNER & DONNER L. in Cal. 37. US40**

Take US40 for **15.** (SE) to **CAL. LINE.** At **33.** is **TRUCKEE** (see Cal.); at **37. DONNER PASS & ST. MON.** to heroic Donner emigrant Party (see Cal.).

**VII. RENO to CARSON IND. CEMETERY (S) 3.**

A short drive (S) of Reno near Carson Ind. Sch. in Ind. cemetery is the grave of Dat-So-La-Lee, the huge, cranky Washoe basket weaver. The fame of her baskets spread to both coasts & samples of her art are in the big museums of America. From her mother she inherited the right to make these ceremonial baskets on which are recorded the history & aspirations of her tribe. She died in 1925 at the age of 90, the last of the great Washoe basket weavers. "Migration" basket is her masterpiece, valued at $10,000. Every thread, fibre & color was home grown. She is said to be only weaver who had a perfect knowledge of perspective. She died in a medicine hut, wrapped in rabbit furs according to tribal custom, & was buried as she wished, with her last basket for which, unfinished, she had been offered $1,100.

## LAS VEGAS

**LAS VEGAS**

RR. sta.: U.P. RR. Busses: Burlington & Las Vegas-Needles Lines; also Las Vegas-Tonopah-Reno Stage Line. Mun. Airport for Western Air Express & T.W.A. Accoms.: All types.

Las Vegas, youngest of Nev. cities, lying in a reg. of great scenic beauty is only 24$^{m}$ from Hoover Dam Recr. Area (see) & is a distributing center for its ranching & mining countryside. Though still a "Frontier Town" (not quite 50 yrs. old), it **is** already rivalling Reno for its "place in the sun." Low-cost power, a rich mineralized hinterland & above all its dry desert air & sunshine throughout yr. augur well for its future. Since 1940 its pop. has almost trebled. The ultramodern pt. of view is emphasized by the fact that Hollywood & L.A. celebrities have made it a suburb to which they commute by air. At night the town is particularly lively. Bars, gambling & night clubs, & many restaurants are open until dawn on Fremont St. Here and in the swank hotels & casinos on "The Strip" mingle prospectors & miners, movie actors & cowhands, divorcees & maiden aunts. The homes & residences are modern & attractively set; beyond them & the suburbs is the desert. Annually in May the famous Heldorado, a typical western outdoor show, takes place. Winter sports fans have a wonderland to play in on Charleston Peak (see below) 30 minutes distant. Las Vegas has become almost unnoticed an all-yr. vacation spot.

## TRIPS OUT OF LAS VEGAS

**(I) LAS VEGAS to NEVADA NAT. PK. (Charleston Mt. Div.), 36. US95 & St.39.** On US95 (NW) to J. with St.39 at **15.** On this Rd. (W) to **36. NEV. NAT. FOR.** (Charleston Mt. Div.) at Kyle Canyon (camp.trlrs.). Trls. from canyon lead to summit of **Charleston Peak** (11,910′). From the tropical climate of Moapa Valley & L. Mead, the traveler can, within an hour's drive, reach these high altitudes. Lee Canyon is adj. to Kyle Canyon & the 2 provide a summer as well as winter playground (f.riding,skiing.toboggan.).

**II LAS VEGAS to GLENDALE & MOAPA IND. RESERVATION, 74. US91 & St.40**

Via: Valley of Fire St. Pk. & Overton

US91 runs (NE) from Las Vegas, past airport to J. with St.40 at **31.** On this Rd. (R) to **VALLEY OF FIRE ST. PK.** at **54.** (camp.facils.pic.shelters), passing en route **GYPSUM CAVE** (see US91). At St. Pk. are preserved archeological remains from **Lost City,** ancient Ind. village now covered by man-made L. Mead. The "Lost City" has been reconstructed near-by. The strange & impressive valley basin is 4 x 6 miles, on whose blood-red walls are well-preserved petroglyphs. The color & rock formations become more fantastic as Rd. reaches the pass. At twilight, when sun's rays strike the fiery pillars, the valley becomes aflame. There are also fragments of a petrified for. near-by. Here is J. with St.12. **62. OVERTON BEACH & OVERTON MUS.** (see US91).

At **74.** on the main hy. is **GLENDALE** & (W) of it, the **Moapa Ind. Reservation** (172 Paiute Inds.).

**III. LAS VEGAS to BOULDER CITY & BOULDER DAM, 23. US95**

US95 combined with US93 & US466 travels (SW) from Las Vegas & at **13.** reaches **HENDERSON,** southern Nev. Industrial center. **23. BOULDER CITY,** 8m from dam site, a town of c.4,000 people, designed & constructed by U.S. Reclamation Bur. (1931), yrs. before dam across Colorado R. was finished. It was built primarily to house the many thousands of workmen employed on the huge undertaking. Because of high temperature in Black Canyon vic. (130° in the shade), special care had to be given to the workmen. Air-cooled dormitories for single men & neat little homes for those with families were soon built. A complete modern city was ready to tackle the enormous job of constructing the dam. Rds. were built to & from the site & to Las Vegas. City also became terminus of a sec. of U.P. RR. & has an airfield. The community has a city manager who is directly responsible to Bur. of Reclamation, & now is hqs. for the administrative offices of the completed dam works.

Boulder City is the gateway for visits to Hoover (Boulder) Dam & the Grand Canyon of the Colo. (see) by air or by boat. A Rd. leads from it to shore of L. Mead. Visitors can view the dam from parking places on both sides of Black Canyon, & may cross the crest of the dam itself. At **Hemenway Wash,** 7m distant, boats leave on regular scheduled trips. (Hoover Dam Service Bur. in Boulder maintains guide serv. facils. through dam & power plant daily, 9-5). There are 4-hr. as well as 2-day trips to **L. Mead & Hoover (Boulder) Dam Nat. Recr. Area,** which beside the dam & Grand Canyon incl. L. Mead; **Pierce Ferry,** E. end of the lake, with a rustic camp; **& Overton,** on the Virgin R. arm of the lake. Boats & facils. are avail. both at Hemenway Wash & Overton Beach. Excellent bass fishing in L. Mead. Tackle & rowboats avail. Epecially int. are Boulder Dam & Grand Canyon Cruises.

**HOOVER (Boulder) DAM**

Hoover Dam, one of world's greatest engineering feats, was created to harness the mighty Colo. R., thereby achieving hydroelec. power, irrigation, flood control, city water, a recr. area, & wild-life preserve. To accomplish this a dam had to be erected which would stop the Colo.'s yearly floods & create a reservoir deep enough to trap millions of tons of silt which had swept down the river impairing any hitherto attempted control.

Since 7 SW. states were involved in the work, as well as the benefits of such an undertaking, it was extremely difficult to come to an agreement on the best site, type of admin., distribution of water & power benefits. Reclamation engineers studied the feasibility of the bold venture long before any agreement was reached. The Bur. of Reclamation recommended the construction of the dam in 1924, & 4 yrs. later the Engineer's Board reported its feasibility. 2 sites in the lower Colo. Basin were favored by the engineers: Boulder Canyon & Black Canyon, each with equal reservoir capacity & equal engineering difficulties. Final investigation showed that Black Canyon was the better site. In 1929 the Boulder Dam Proj. Act was declared effective, & by March 11, 1931 actual work began. This included construction of Gov. Rds. & RRs. to dam site & erecting Boulder City (see Las Vegas), the building of machine shops, warehouses, an air-compressor & huge cement mixing plants. The Gov. & contractors employed as many as 5,120 men, all of whom & their families had to be properly fed & housed.

The general plan of attack in building Hoover Dam was to drill tunnels through the canyon walls around the site, divert the Colo. through these tunnels, build cofferdams to block off the river, excavate the dam site, & build the dam & power plants. The vastness of the plan can only be comprehended when statistics are grasped. In May 1935, the last concrete was placed & in Sept. the dam was dedicated by Pres. Roosevelt. Not until April 1947 was the name officially changed to Hoover Dam. So far it is the world's highest dam—726′. L. Mead, which it impounded, is the world's largest artificial reservoir—115$^{m}$ long. As a result of the dam, surrounding desert has become the "Nation's newest playground" with unlimited facils. for water sports, scenic wanderings & camping. A wild-life refuge has been est. & the L. has been plentifully stocked with game fish.

**IV. LAS VEGAS to CAL. LINE** (via: Henderson & Searchlight), **74. US95**

Hy. travels directly (S) passing **HENDERSON** at **13.**, industrial center for S. Nev., in which is the huge magnesium plant which stimulated entire reg. during World War II. At **19.** US93 branches off (E) 12$^{m}$ to Hoover Dam. **29.** J. with St.60. **55. SEARCHLIGHT,** a mining camp that reached its climax in 1906. Millions of dollars worth of ore, mainly gold, was taken from its depth. Like Eldorado, it was one of the toughest mining towns with 38 saloons on its main street. Here is J. with unmarked Rd.

SIDE TRIP: On this Rd. (R) 7$^{m}$ to **ranch of Rex Bell,** cowboy movie actor, & his wife, Clara Bow. At 24$^{m}$ is **Crescent,** turquoise-mining district. In 1894 an Ind. discovered here not only turquoise but also ancient tools.

US95 travels through **Paiute Valley** & reaches **CAL. LINE. 74.**

**V. LAS VEGAS to CAL. LINE. 43. US91**

US91 runs (SW) through a stockraising & mining reg. past **Blue Diamond Canyon.** To the (W) is a Wall-Board Plant. Hy. skirts dried-out lake beds, former mining districts & passes amidst yucca trees into higher altitudes. Snow-capped **Charleston Peak** (11,910′) can be seen towering above the La Madre Mts. **43.** US91 crosses **CAL. LINE,** 50$^{m}$ (NE) of Baker, Cal.

## US 14—WYOMING

**WYO.-S.D. LINE** (14$^{m}$ from Spearfish, S.D.) **(W) to YELLOWSTONE NAT. PK. 410. US14**

Via: Sundance, Sheridan, Cody. C.B. & Q. RR. bet. Moorcroft & Ranchester. Accoms.: In larger towns & dude ranches along route.

US14 traverses N. Wyo. bet. Black Hills & Yellowstone Nat. Pk. Most of route is through open range country, but about mid-way hy. twists through rugged Big Horn Mts., noted for scenic & recr. features.

### Sec. 1: WYO. LINE to SHERIDAN. 205.

**1.** J. with graded Rd.

SIDE TRIP: On this Rd. (L) 2m is **Sand Cr.** where is some of best trout fishing in Black Hills. In vic., **Moses Annenberg Estate** built by Phila. publisher as mt. retreat.

**1.5. BEULAH. 20. SUNDANCE,** supply pt. for ranchers & loggers of **Bear Lodge Mts.** (N). Here is Dist. Ranger Sta. for Bear Lodge Div. of Black Hills Nat. For. (hqs.Deadwood,S.D.). Town bears name of Sundance Mt. (L), summer rendezvous of Sioux Inds. **Warren Peaks** (6,800′) loom (NW). **43.** J. with Devil's Tower Hy.

SIDE TRIP: On this oiled Rd. (R) 10m is **Devil's Tower Nat. Mon.** Unique geological formation & surrounding 1,153-a. area set aside by Pres. Theo. Roosevelt in 1906 as 1st nat. mon. in U.S. **Mus.** is maintained by Nat. Pk. Serv. at base of tower. This rock shaft of fluted lava rises 1,200′ above Belle Fourche R. here. Its thickness at base is estimated at 1,000′. Only skilled mt. climbers have scaled steep, fluted sides.

**68. MOORCROFT,** shipping pt. for ranchers. Here is J. with US16 which unites with US14 (W) to Ucross (see below). **70. TEXAS TRL. MON.** (R) marks route used in 1870's to bring Longhorn cattle to feed on buffalo grass. **91. WYO.-DAK. COAL MINE** (R) with thickest vein of lignite coal (90′) so far uncovered in U.S. More than 1 million tons of coal have been removed for use in gold mines in Black Hills. **95. UNIV. OF WYO. DRY LAND EXPERIMENT STA. 96. GILLETTE,** trade center for NE. Wyo.; cattle-shipping & oil refining pt. **149. POWDER R.,** famed among Westerners as being "a mile wide & an inch deep." **176. UCROSS,** town named for a local cattle brand. Here is J. with US16 (see). **190. WARPATH LOOKOUT** (R), observation pt. with view of Big Horn Mts. **203.** J. with US87 (see); the 2 routes are united through **SHERIDAN, 205.**

### Sec. 2: SHERIDAN to YELLOWSTONE NAT. PK. 205.

**0. SHERIDAN** (July Rodeo; hqs. Big Horn Nat. For.), major town of N. Wyo. & popular recr. area. Here dude wranglers, hunters, & tourists heading into Big Horns are feted & outfitted. Local industry incl. large sugar refinery, brewery, iron foundry, brick & tile kiln, & flour mill. Town was staked out along Big Goose Cr. in 1882 & named for Gen. Phil Sheridan, under whom some of settlers had served.

PTS. OF INT.: (1) Cor. Broadway & 5th St., **Sheridan Inn,** rambling pioneer structure where Buffalo Bill held sway during his heyday. (2) Badger St. & Clarendon Ave., **Kendrick Pk.** (80 as.swim.pool.tennis.playground). US14 & US87 run (N) from Sheridan. At **2.** is J. with improved Rd.

SIDE TRIP: On this Rd. (L) 1.5m is **Ft. MacKenzie Veterans Hospital.** Orig. fort & military reserv., est. in 1899.

At **17.** is **RANCHESTER** & J. with US87 (see). Here is J. with improved Rd.

SIDE TRIP: On this Rd. (L) 1m is **Connor Battlefield St. Pk.,** site of Battle of Tongue R. (1865). A band of Arapaho under Old David & Black Bear were engaged by Ft. Laramie troops under Gen. P. E. Connor.

**23. DAYTON,** center of dude ranching area. Ranger Sta. here. Near-by Eaton Ranch claims to be 1st Western dude ranch (est.1904). At **30.** hy. climbs to E. boundary of **Big Horn Nat. For.** (hqs.Sheridan). In this 1,121,534-a. for. are lodgepole, ponderosa, & limber pine, Engelmann spruce, & Douglas & alpine fir. Checking sta. maintained inside boundary for big game hunters. Average legal kill in for. each fall is 500 elk & 1,200 deer. At **36.** is **STEAMBOAT ROCK OBSERVATION PT.** (7,000′), from which is tremendous view as far as Black Hills (E). Tongue R. Canyon here is gorge of solid rock 2,000′ deep. From **CUTLER PASS** (8,550′) at **43.,** hy. traverses plateau of wild flowers. **44. SIBLEY L.** (recr. facils.). **50. BURGESS J.** & J. with St.14.

SIDE TRIP: On St.14 (R) through heavy for. around **Little Bald Mt.** (9,829′). 19m **Porcupine Ranger Sta.,** headwaters of several trout-stocked streams (campgrounds). 20m **Bald Mt.** (10,029′). 23m J. with For. Serv. Rd.

(R) here 3m to **Medicine Wheel** (parking area), prehist. relic in shape of wheel 70′ in diam. with hub & 28 spokes formed by placing stones side by side. Around wheel are 6 cairns, each built in form of chair.

US14 runs (S) through rugged country. **Cloud Peak** (13,165′), highest pt. in Big Horns, dominates skyline. **46. WOODROCK CAMPGROUND** (L). **58. GRANITE PASS** (8,200′) & **GRANITE CR. CAMPGROUND.** Rd. descends into Shell Canyon (f.in Cr.), with series of spectacular waterfalls & scenic vistas. **77.** W. Boundary of **Big Horn Nat. For. 83. SHELL,** with **Mus.** featuring fossilized shells found in vic. **98. GREYBULL,** seasonal hqs. for sportsmen. Dist. Ranger Sta. here. At Greybull US14 unites with US20 through Cody to E. Entrance of **Yellowstone Nat. Pk.** at **SYLVAN PASS, 205.** Pk. is W. terminus of US14.

## US 16—WYOMING

**WYO.-S.D. LINE** ($27^m$ from Custer, S.D.) **(W) to WORLAND, WYO. 282. US16**

Via: Newcastle, Gillette, Buffalo. C.B. & Q. RR. bet. Newcastle & Ucross; Wyo. RR. bet. Ucross & Buffalo. Accoms.: In larger towns; resorts in Big Horn.

US16 is popular route across N. Wyo. through S. portion of Big Horn Mts. Except for mt. reg., hy. crosses level ranch land & oil fields. At **8.** US16 unites with US85 (see) to **NEWCASTLE** at **10.** Town is important producer of bentonite, gelatin-like clay with varied uses, incl. mfg. of steel, cosmetics & cleansing agents. Named for Eng. coal port, town was started as shipping center for coal mines in vic. Major deposit was at near-by Cambria, now a ghost town (see US85). On Cth. lawn, old **Jenney's Stockade** (1875.rest.); built by Fed. expedition, headed by scientists W. P. Jenney & H. Newton, who evaluated mineral deposits in Black Hills with view of U.S. Gov. buying reg. from Sioux Inds. Here is J. with US85 (see). **25. OSAGE,** refinery center for surrounding oil fields. Nearly every store in town displays marine fossils found along ridge (S) of Osage. **39. UPTON,** bentonite milling pt. (N) looms **Devil's Tower. 59. MOORCROFT.** Here US16 & US14 (see) unite to **UCROSS, 167.** (see US14).

US16 winds (S) from Ucross through prosperous Clear Cr. Valley. **185. BUFFALO,** trade center for ranchers & gateway for visitors to Big Horns. Here is Dist. Ranger Sta. for Big Horn Nat. For. Few cty. seat towns have been scene of armed warfare such as raged at Buffalo during Johnson Cty. War (1892). Homesteading farmers contested water holes, grassland, & fences with large-scale, open-range cattlemen. Each side took law into own hands. Hangings were numerous. Cattlemen org. an armed expedition & marched on barricaded Buffalo, hqs. of settlers. Pitched battle was in progress at near-by T.A. Ranch (S) of town when U.S. Cavalry arrived from Ft. McKinney to halt fighting. At Buffalo is J. with US87 (see). **187. SITE OF FT. McKINNEY** (L), now Wyo. Soldiers & Sailors Home. The Ft. (est. 1877) has been St. institution since 1903, with 1,290-a. reserve. **198.** E. boundary of **Big Horn Nat. For.** (hqs.Sheridan). At **203.** is J. with graded Rd.

SIDE TRIP: On this Rd. (R) $1^m$ is **Hunter Ranger Sta.** (resort & h.camps). Trls. lead into beautiful **Cloud Peak Wilderness Area,** in which are scores of mt. lakes stocked with trout. **Cloud Peak** (13,165′) dominates area. For. Serv. campgrounds maintained at L. Solitude, L. Helen, & W. Tensleep L.

**207. S. FORK CAMPGROUND. 212. CRAZY WOMAN CAMPGROUND & MUDDY CR. FIRE GUARD STA.** Rd. becomes steeper as it traverses **Muddy Cr. Pass** (9,666′), headwaters of famous Powder R. **232. MEADOW L.,** 280-a. reservoir used for irrigation of Tensleep Valley. **236.** For. Serv. Rd. leading (R) $2^m$ to Tyrell Ranger Sta. **244. ST. FISH HATCHERY** (O), largest in Wyo. **247.** SW. boundary of **Big Horn Nat. For. 254. TENSLEEP,** outfitting pt. for vacationists. Nearly every man in town is an expert fly caster. Opening of fish. season is signal for stores to operate with skeleton crews. (W) of Tensleep hy. passes through area of badlands formations with livid red colorings. **282. WORLAND,** center of irrigated area specializing in sugar beets. Refinery is operated here. Important adjunct is feeding of beet by-products to fatten cattle. Wool shows are fall market feature (Sept.). Here is J. with US20 & W. terminus of US16.

## US 20—WYOMING

**WYO.-NEB. LINE** ($40^m$ from Crawford, Neb.) **(NW) to YELLOWSTONE NAT. PK. (E. Entrance). 440. US20**

Via: Lusk, Casper, Shoshoni, Thermopolis, Greybull, Cody. Chi. & N.W. RR. bet. Neb. line & Shoshoni; C.B. & Q. RR. bet. Orin & Greybull. Accoms: In larger towns; dude ranches & camps along route.

US20 takes zigzag course across Wyo., crossing broad prairie to mt. reg. & paralleling famous Mormon, Oregon, & Cal. Trls. along Platte R.

### Sec. 1: WYO.-NEB. LINE to CASPER. 129.

**2. VAN TASSELL.** (N) of here the marksmanship of Col. "Buffalo Bill" Cody saved his life in quick-trigger encounter (1877) with Yellow Hand, Sioux chieftain. **22. LUSK,** center of rich ranch trade & oil producing reg. Town was started as Runningwater Stage Sta. on well-marked Cheyenne-Black Hills Trl. (1876). In vic., **Grave of George Lathrop,** pioneer stage driver on this trl. **Lusk. Mus.** contains old Concord Stage Coach. Oil from Lance Cr. field (N) is piped to 2 Lusk refineries. J. with US85 (see). **32. MANVILLE.** J. with oiled Rd.

SIDE TRIP: On this Rd. (R) 18m is **Lance Creek,** sprawling community built around oil field operations. Continental has 3 million dollar plant here.

At **42.** is J. with dirt Rd.

SIDE TRIP: On this Rd. (L) 11m is area known as **Spanish Diggings.** Jasper, agate, & quartzite deposits found in 400 sq. mile area along Rawhide Buttes.

**52. SHAWNEE. 64. ORIN.** J. with US87 (see). (S) of US20 are **Laramie Mts.** & portion of **Medicine Bow Nat. For.** (hqs.Laramie). **77. DOUGLAS,** home of Wyo. St. Fair (Sept.). Town is wool market, cattle shipping, & seed pea packing center. J. with St.87.

SIDE TRIP: On this Rd. (R) is direct route to US14-16. At 22m is **Site of Lightning Cr. Battle** (1903) bet. band of Sioux antelope hunters & posse of peace officers.

At **79.** is J. with graded rd.

SIDE TRIP: On this Rd. (R) 7m is **Fort Fetterman Site,** est. on Bozeman Trl. during gold rush in Mont. & abandoned 1882. Two bldgs. are standing, one of which was constructed of packed earth.

At **95.** is J. with graded rd. which leads (L) 5m to **Ayres Pk.** (camp facils.) & **Natural Bridge,** spanning La Prele Cr. **104. GLENROCK,** with large oil refineries dominating town. Before town was started (1886), Mormons operated irrigated gardens in reg. to provide migrating Saints with fresh foodstuffs. **111. PARKERTON,** in heart of Big Muddy Oil Fields. **126. EVANSVILLE,** refining town. **129. CASPER** (see).

### Sec. 2: CASPER to CODY. 258.

US20 sweeps (W) through cattle & sheep grazing country. At **38.** is **POWDER R. 46.** (L) **DEVIL'S KITCHEN** (320 as.hik.), fantastically eroded formation in badlands reg. known as Hell's Half Acre. **78. MONETA,** wool-shipping pt. **98. SHOSHONI,** trade center at E. edge of Shoshone Ind. Reserv. (hqs.Ft. Washakie). Here is J. with St.320.

SIDE TRIP: Take latter (W) through irrigated reg. to **Riverton,** 23m. Oil prospecting & sugar beet raising new activities for Shoshone & Arapaho Inds. of region. At Riverton is J. with St.287, short-cut through reserv. which follows historic Wind R. (NW). Capt. Bonneville's 20-wagon train followed this route in 1832 on mission to investigate Brit. activities beyond Rockies.

US20 winds (N) through Wind R. Canyon. **132. THERMOPOLIS,** bustling town & health resort in Big Horn Basin. **Hot Springs St. Pk.** (640 as.). **Big Horn Hot Springs,** flowing 18,600,000 gals. daily, is one of largest in world. Night Herd Rodeo (Labor Day). At Thermopolis is J. with St.120.

SIDE TRIP: On this short-cut (L) to Cody is **Meeteetse,** 52m, in popular dude ranch country. Pack trls. lead into **Shoshone Nat. For.**

US20 parallels Big Horn R. through irrigated reg. & coal mining area. **166. WORLAND.** J. with US16 (see). **196. BASIN,** bean-raising center. Annual Bean Festival (Sept.). **203. GREYBULL.** Big Horn Mts. loom (E). Here US20 & US14 (see) unite (W) through plains country. At **209.** is J. with US310.

SIDE TRIP: US310 conn. US14-US20 in Wyo. & US10-US12 in Mont., traversing (N) alkaline desert to **Lovell,** 29m, a sugar beet factory town built by Mormon colonists. 33m **Cowley,** with pink & tan bldgs. of locally-mined sandstone. Church Sq. is social center for Mormon community. At 50m hy. crosses the Wyo.-Mont. Line (S. of Laurel, Mont.).

**258. CODY.**

### Sec. 3: CODY to SYLVAN PASS (E. Entrance Yellowstone Nat. Pk.). 53.

**0. CODY,** popular vacation center, sett. 1895 to capitalize on fame of Col. Wm. F. ("Buffalo Bill") Cody, pres. of townsite company. His boyhood home has been moved from Iowa to the RR. depot lawn here. **Cody Mus.,** housed in log cabin reprod. of Cody's TE Ranchh., contains int. coll. of personal effects & Wild West Show souvenirs. Main St., **Statue of Buffalo Bill** astride horse Smoky (by Mrs. Harry Payne Whitney). **Irma Hotel,** named by Col. Cody for his daughter, is prominent showplace. Annual Cody Stampede with rodeo & Ind. dances (July 4); Trappers' Ball (Mar.). In vic. are dude ranches & big game hunting camps. Here is J. with oiled Rd.

SIDE TRIP: On this Rd. (L) 6$^m$ to graded Rd. At 35$^m$ is **TE Ranch,** old Cody home. At 43$^m$ **Valley Ranch,** one of best known in Wyo. & private prep. sch. for boys.

(W) of Cody, US20 plunges into beautiful Shoshone Canyon. **4. SHOSHONE CAVERN NAT. MON.** (L), 210-a. area; several passages & galleries of crystal formations. US20 follows shelf along shores of **Shoshone L.** At **7.** is dam, built in 1910 to create reservoir for irrigation purposes. At **25.** is E. boundary of **SHOSHONE NAT. FOR.** (hqs.Cody). **Signal Peak** (R) & **Flag Mt.** (L) guard entrance. This is oldest nat. for. in U.S., est. as timber reserve in 1902. Open seasons for big game hunting (moose, elk, deer, bear, antelope, mt. sheep), subject to seasonal variations in regulations. For. Serv. campgrounds (individual camp stalls, fire grates, tables, water) are along hy.; resorts & dude ranches off the Rd. **27. HANGING ROCK CAMPGROUND. 29. HORSE CR. CAMPGROUND** (trlr.facils.). **30. BIG GAME CAMPGROUND.** At **31.** is **WAPITI RANGER STA.,** 1st in U.S. **37. REX HALE CAMPGROUND. 38. NEWTON CR. CAMPGROUND** (trlrs.). At **43.** (L) is **FISH HAWK GLACIER. 46. EAGLE CR. CAMPGROUND. 49. SLEEPING GIANT CAMPGROUND. 50. THREE MILE CAMPGROUND. 52. PAHASKA TEPEE,** hunt. lodge of Col. Cody. **53. SYLVAN PASS STA.** & E. Entrance of **Yellowstone Nat. Pk.** (US20 becomes part of Pk. hy. system.)

## US 26—WYOMING

**WYO.-NEB. LINE** (25$^m$ from Scottsbluff, Neb.) **(W) to J. with US87. 55. US26**

Via: Torrington, Ft. Laramie, Guernsey. C.B. & Q. RR. parallels route. Accoms: In larger towns.

**8. TORRINGTON,** center of prosperous reg. producing oil, coal, sugar beets, potatoes, turkeys & livestock. During summer, town is jammed with migrant beetfield workers. Here US85 (see) & US26 unite (W). At **13.** is J. with dirt Rd.

SIDE TRIP: On this Rd. (L) 2$^m$ is **Site of Rock Ranch Battle.** Blockh. with gun ports, still stands as reminder of Ind. attacks on early emigrants.

**18. LINGLE,** sugar beet loading sta. Bureau of Reclamation hydroelectric power plant operated here. Across R. (L) occurred the **Grattan Massacre** (1854). Lt. John Grattan, a newly-arrived West Pt. graduate, was sent from Ft. Laramie to investigate theft of a cow. When he rashly fired into tepee to arouse Inds., they returned fire. Grattan & 28 soldiers were killed on the spot. J. with US85 (see). **28.** Village of **FT. LARAMIE.** J. with graded Rd.

SIDE TRIP: On this Rd. (R) 2$^m$ over N. Platte R. bridge is **Old Ft. Laramie Nat. Mon.** (114 as.), hist. trading & military post administered by Nat. Pk. Serv. Several orig. bldgs. **Sutler's Store** (adobe.1834), considered oldest bldg. in Wyo. Here in 1868 the Sioux Treaty was signed by U.S. Peace Commission, ceding all land (N) of Platte R. bet. Big Horns & Black Hills to Inds. Hospital & barracks bldgs. have thick walls standing. **Old Bedlam,** officers' club, has staggered appearance, reminiscent of its reputation as gayest spot on old Oregon & Cal. Trls.

**41. GUERNSEY,** at mouth of Platte R. Canyon where huge Guernsey Reservoir is formed by damming R. (pic.). **Oregon Trl. Marker** has int. relics embedded. **Register Cliff** has names of early emigrants carved on walls. At Guernsey is J. with oiled Rd.

SIDE TRIP: On this Rd. (R) 6$^m$ is **Sunrise,** with some of largest iron mines (W) of Miss. R. Glory Hole is tremendous pit as deep as Washington Mon. is tall.

**55.** J. with US87 (see) & W. terminus of US26.

## US 30—WYOMING

**WYO.-NEB. LINE** (22$^m$ from Kimball, Neb.) **(W) to WYO.-IDAHO LINE** (22$^m$ from Montpelier, Idaho). **459. US30-US30N**

Via: Cheyenne, Laramie, Rawlins, Rock Springs, Kemmerer. U.P. RR. parallels route. Accoms.: In larger towns.

US30 passes through S. Wyo., following general route pioneered by Overland Stages & developed by 1st transcontinental RR. Because of gradual hy. grade over Continental Divide, this route is popular with motorists. In (W) Wyo., hy. is divided into US30N & US30S (see below).

### Sec. 1: WYO.-NEB. LINE to RAWLINS. 212.

**0.5. PINE BLUFFS. 33. ST. EXPERIMENT FARM,** at which crops suitable to semi-arid reg. are developed. At **35. WYO. HEREFORD RANCH** (L) spreads over 6,000-a. rangeland. **41. VETERANS' HOSPITAL** (R), est. 1933. **42. CHEYENNE** (see). Js. with US85 (see) & US87 (see). US30 cont. (W) into Laramie Mts. At **70.** (L) is **AMES MON.** (60';1881-82), a pyramid of stone honoring Oliver & Oakes Ames who helped finance construction of U.P. RR. US30 skirts S. & W. borders of Pole Mt. Div. of **Medicine Bow Nat. For.** (hqs.Laramie), 52,219-a. tract under joint jurisdiction of Depts. of War & Agric. Secs. are used for military maneuvers & artillery practice. Several For. Serv. Rds. lead to pic. grounds & scenic areas. Kaibab deer range in mts. Entire area is Fed. Game Refuge (no h.or f.). At **75.** is **FOR. SERV. SHELTER H.,** emergency storm sta. for motorists during winter blizzards. Here is J. with For. Serv. Rd. (R) 2m to **Vedauwoo Glen,** a natural 2-stage amphitheatre in solid granite (pic.facils.). At **78.** is Entrance to **Ft. Francis E. Warren Target & Maneuver Reserv.** (sentries on duty during use). Crest of **Sherman Hill** (8,835') at **81.** is highest pt. along route. Here is **Pole Mt. Ranger Sta.** (observ.tower). **SUMMIT WINTER SPORTS AREA** (R) covers 40 as. & incl. excellent ski run with motor-powered 850' tow (Dec.1-Mar.1). US30 descends steeply through **Telephone Canyon** toward broad plateau. At **84.** is J. with Happy Jack Rd.

SIDE TRIP: On this Rd. (R) 1m, **Happy Jack Pic. Grounds,** community camp. 2m **Happy Jack Winter Sports Area** (8,500'), with 1,400' toboggan run. Ski runs maintained for professionals & amateurs. At 16m is **Crystal L.,** popular with trout fishermen.

**92. LARAMIE** (see). J. with US287 (see). US30 & US287 run (N) from Laramie through **King Bros. Sheep Range** along Laramie R. to Rawlins. **Snowy Range** (L), capped by **Medicine Bow Mt.** (12,005'). **134. ROCK RIVER,** ranching center. In vic. (1865), Cheyenne Inds. attacked wagon train on Overland Trl. & carried away 2 young girls. One was ransomed, but other grew up with Arapaho on Wind R. Reserv. She was located 35 yrs. later but refused to leave tribe. **143. COMO BLUFF CREATION MUS.,** made of specimens from "dinosaur graveyard" near-by. Fossil beds (R) have provided complete dinosaur skeletons for paleontological exhibits. **153. MEDICINE BOW,** old-time cowtown that has changed little since description in Owen Wister's novel, "The Virginian." J. with dirt Rd. leading (R) 30m to **Petrified For.** (2,560 as.), remains of subtropical trees est. to be 50 million yrs. old. **173. HANNA,** coaling sta. for U.P. RR. Deposits orig. discovered by Lt. (later Gen.) John C. Frémont during 1843 expedition guided by Kit Carson. At **191.** is **WALCOTT** & J. with St.130.

SIDE TRIP: On St.130 (L) 22m is **Saratoga,** health & recr. center on N. Platte R. **Saratoga Hot Springs St. Pk.,** bathh. & pool (pub.). At 41m is old mining town of **Encampment,** supply pt. for hunters, fishermen, miners & campers going into Sierra Madre Mts. To (W) is **Hayden Div.** of Medicine Bow Nat. For. (see); several old ghost towns in vic., relics of copper boom.

**194. FT. FRED STEELE** (R), village on site of military post est. 1868, scene of early Ind. battles & kidnappings. (N) lies huge **Seminoe Reservoir,** part of U.S. Bureau of Reclamation vast irrigation & power project. **206. PARCO** (Sinclair on some maps), neatly-planned company town & Wyo. showplace. Sp.-style bldgs. are set around a plaza. Huge refinery here served by pipelines from **Lost Soldier Oil Fields** (N). **212. RAWLINS,** busy center for near-by reclamation projects, oil & gas fields, quarries, & ranching operations. Hatfield Dome is new oil field being developed. Red roofing paint, made from local pigments, is widely distributed. St. Penitentiary is massive structure here & noted for mfg. of wool blankets. Townsite was selected because of fresh spring, rarity in reg. discovered by Gen. John A. Rawlins during bldg. of U.P. RR. At Rawlins is J. with US287 (see).

### Sec. 2: RAWLINS to WYO.-IDAHO LINE. 247.

US30 makes gradual ascent (W) through barren, rolling country. **28. CONTINENTAL DIVIDE** (7,178'). To (W) lies broad **Red Desert,** inhabited by herds of sheep & solitary herders. US30 passes through level, monotonous sage brush & greasewood country. **63. TABLE ROCK** (6,840′) rises (L). Its **Diamond Mesa** was scene of excitement in 1870's when diamonds, rubies, emeralds, sapphires, & garnets were uncovered by 2 prospector-promoters. They enlisted Horace Greeley, the Tiffanys, & Eastern financiers in development company to tune of half-million dollars before it was discovered that prospectors had "planted" the gems. **83. PT. OF ROCKS,** quaint village at base of high, cave-marked cliff, once Wells-Fargo Stage Sta. Near-by stand stone cabins used by Overland Trl. stages before RR. was built. At **91.** is J. with oiled Rd.

SIDE TRIP: On this Rd. (R) 9m is **Superior.** Town is built around 2 huge coal mines that produce 2 million tons per yr. Bldgs. cling to sides of Horse Thief Canyon. In surrounding Leucite Hills are unique geological formations that attract many visitors.

**108. ROCK SPRINGS,** business hub of W. Wyo. & major western coal-producing community. In vic. is one of most extensive coal fields (W) of Miss. R. In recent yrs. town has gained importance as gateway to scenic & recr. areas to (N), incl. Jackson Hole, Wind R., the Tetons, & Yellowstone Nat. Pk. Miners of many nationalities live here, with Old World customs & cuisine maintained. At one time Chinatown here was larger than white settlement. On Sept. 2, 1885, striking white miners invaded Chinese area with guns & torches. Before peace was restored, 30 Chinese were dead & many homes burned. The so-called Chinese Riot led to est. of Camp Pilot Butte to maintain order; barracks of old military post still stand on Bridger Ave. opp. Washington sch. & Slovenski dome. Survey of extensive coal deposits made in area in 1852 by party of U.S. Topographical Engineers, with Jim Bridger as scout. Ruins of stockade built by Archie & Duncan Blair (1866) still stand (NW. edge of town). At Rock Springs is J. with US187 (see). **123. GREEN RIVER,** with **Castle Rock** towering (N) & **Profile Rock** (S). **Sweetwater County Cth.** (1876). On I. in Green R. is **City Pk.,** swim. pool, dance hall, & skating arena; starting pt. for thrilling, hazardous boat trips down Green R. & Colo. R. to Hoover Dam. Scenic **"The Firehole,"** (S). Green R. Valley (S) was trappers' & traders' rendezvous as early as 1824. US30 winds (W) over rolling, sandy country. **150. LITTLE AMERICA.** Here US30 divides into 2 routes, US30S going (SW) through Evanston (see US30S) & US30N (NW).

Tour cont. on US30N. **151. GRANGER,** stock-shipping pt. on U.P. RR. South Bend Stage Sta. (1850). At **177. OPAL,** wool-shipping center. At **191.** US189 (see) joins US30N through old mining village of **DIAMONDVILLE** to **KEMMERER, 193.** Business sec. of this mining, ranching, & outfitting center built around triangular pk. **Mun. Mus.** (log), exhibits petrified wood & fossils found in vic. Some of newest coal mines in Wyo. are being developed near-by. Hqs. of **Bridger Nat. For.** & offices of U.S. Bureau of Reclamation projects located here. Kemmerer is railhead (Oregon Short Line) for extensive cattle & sheep country to (N) where also lies excellent h. & f. country of Wyo. Div. of Bridger Nat. For. US30N runs (W) through desolate area that once was floor of inland sea. **204. FOSSIL. Mus.** displays unusual specimens of marine, bird, & plant life incl. tremendous palm leaves, from near-by Fossil Fish Beds. Fishing here is a quarrying operation into the cliffs of limestone & shale. **217.** J. with St.89 (SW. to Logan, Utah). US30N & St.89 join (N) through Bear R. Valley, paralleling branch of old Oregon Trl. **236. COKEVILLE. 247. BORDER,** on Wyo.-Idaho Line. St.89 cont. (N) to J. with US89 (see) at Montpelier, Idaho.

## US 30S—WYOMING

**J. With US30** (28m from Green River, Wyo.) **(SW) to WYO.-UTAH LINE** (29m from Echo, Utah). **74. US30S**

Via: Lyman, Evanston. U.P. RR. & United Airlines parallel route. Accoms.: Limited.

US30S is popular route conn. Utah & Wyo. Although sec. through Wyo. passes through arid plains, to (S) rise Unita Mts., only major E.-W. range in U.S. **1. LITTLE AMERICA,** one of most widely-advertised tourists stops in country. **Church Buttes** rise (L) at **13.,** oil & gas field development. On some of sandstone formations along Rd. are hand-carved names of early pioneers who followed Mormon, Oregon, Cal., & Overland Trls. At **27.** is **UNIV. OF WYO. EXPERIMENT STA. 28. LYMAN,** farm & ranch market for Mormon community. **Mus.** in high sch. (S) of Lyman in Cedar Mts., trappers from NW. gathered in 1825 to swap pelts, stories, & whiskey at call of Gen. Wm. Ashley's Rocky Mt. Fur Co. At **31.** is J. with oiled Rd.

SIDE TRIP: On this Rd. (L) 3m is **Mountainview.** Dirt Rd. (S) leads to **Site of Ft. Supply,** 13m, where Mormons from Utah began 1st agric. settlement in Wyo. (1853). In 1857 they burned ft. before fleeing from advance of Col. Albert Johnson's forces. To (S) **Ashley Nat. For.** extends into Utah.

**35. FT. BRIDGER ST. PK.,** preserved trading post of famous scout & frontiersman. Jim Bridger selected site in 1842 because it provided good fish. & hunt. Post Trader's Store now Mus. with many relics & trophies. Post became important stop on Oregon Trl. & once served as military post. Later Mormons took it over & built stone cabins, walls, & corrals. At **56.** is J. with US189 (see). **69. EVANSTON** (Cowboy Days in Sept.), market center for ranching, farming, brewing, & dairying area. Also, center for Church Buttes oil & gas fields development. Wyo. St. Hospital located here. At Evanston is J. with St.89. US30S crosses Bear R. Valley. At **74.** is **WYO.-UTAH LINE.**

## US 85—WYOMING

**WYO.-COLO. LINE** (87m from Denver) **(N) to WYO.-S.D. LINE** (27m from Lead, S.D.) **265. US85**

Via: Cheyenne, Torrington, Lusk, Newcastle. U.P. RR. bet. Cheyenne & Torrington. Western Airlines parallels route. Accoms.: in larger towns.

US85 follows roughly old Cheyenne-Black Hills stage coach route through rolling, sparsely-settled country.

### Sec. 1: COLO. LINE to LUSK. 150.

**4.** J. with US87 (see). **9. CHEYENNE** (see) & J. with US30 (see). US85 & US87 run (N) from Cheyenne to **17.** where US85 turns (E) through **Goshen Hole,** eroded reg. with large cattle & sheep ranches. **93. TORRINGTON.** Here US85 & US26 unite to parallel old Oregon Trl. to **LINGLE, 103. 108. INTERSTATE CANAL,** which carries irrigation waters for large area. **127. JAY EM,** a quarrying & stone cutting center for onyx, marble, jasper, agate & petrified rock. Its name is taken from the JM cattle brand. **150. LUSK** & J. with US20 (see).

### Sec. 2: LUSK to S.D. LINE. 115.

(N) of Lusk are large, producing oil fields. In distance loom Black Hills. Along US85 are occasional sandstone ridges where ruts left by gold-laden coaches & oxen-drawn freight wagons can be seen, reminiscent of Black Hills gold rush (1876-80). At **14.** is J. with gravel Rd. leading (R) 3m to **Site of Hat Cr. Stage Sta. Mon. & cemetery** mark scene of early holdups, horse-stealing forays, & murders. US85 passes along E. edge of **LANCE CR. OIL FIELD, 25.** This field has been operating since 1919, but new discoveries since 1939 are creating new boom. Maze of pipelines carry oil to distant refineries. Area is also known for fossil beds of "horned dinosaur" or Triceretops. At **46.** is J. with US85A & US18 (see S.D.). At **84.** US16 (see) joins US85 to **NEWCASTLE** at **86.** US85 courses (N) along W. slope of Black Hills. **94. FLYING V RANCH & MUS.** (O.swim.pools.golf). The stone ranch bldgs. & guest cottages resemble an Eng. estate. During World War II it was used as a camp for conscientious objectors. Here is J. with dirt Rd.

SIDE TRIP: On this narrow, twisting Rd. (L) 2m is deserted town of **Cambria.** It is comparatively modern ghost town, having been abandoned in 1928. For nearly 40 yrs. it was a major anthracite coal-mining pt. & produced 12 million tons of hard coal.

**97. MT. PISGAH** (6,000'). Path leads to tower. At **104.** is J. with St.585.

SIDE TRIP: On this oiled Rd. (L) 15m is **Inyan Kara Mt.** This prominent landmark was visited by several explorers into wild Sioux country. Sir George Gore camped here during summer of 1854, with 6 wagons, 110 horses & 40 servants. In 1857, Lt. G. K. Warren, topographical engineer, was turned back here by Inds. Gen. Custer carved name on summit (1874) during expedition into reg.

At **115.** hy. crosses S.D. Line & enters **BLACK HILLS NAT. FOR.** (hqs.Deadwood, S.D.).

## US 87—WYOMING

**WYO.-COLO. LINE** (35m from Ft. Collins, Colo.) **(N) to WYO.-MONT. LINE** (56m from Hardin, Mont.). **391. US87**

Via: Cheyenne, Douglas, Casper, Buffalo. Sheridan. Colo. & S. RR. bet. Colo. Line & Wendover J.; C.B. & Q. bet. Wendover J. & Casper; C. & N.W. bet. Orin & Casper. Accoms: In larger towns; dude ranches along route.

US87 winds through E.-Central Wyo. The S. portion skirts the Laramie Mts. & the N. sec. parallels the Big Horns. Bet. these ranges are vast, open stretches.

### Sec. 1: COLO. LINE to CASPER. 202.

**8.** J. with US85 (see) which unites (N) through **CHEYENNE** (see) at **13. 21.** US87 leaves US85 to follow old route of Cheyenne-Black Hills Stage Line to **CHUGWATER, 60.** Bet. 1883-1924 Brit.-owned firm operated huge Swan Land & Cattle Co. here. Hy. passes through irrigated lands devoted largely to raising sugar beets, a project begun in 1885 through efforts of Jos. M. Carey, later U.S. Senator. **88. WHEATLAND,** processing & shipping center for reg.; sugar beet refinery. Insulation products made at vermiculite processing plant. (W) of Wheatland is S. portion of Laramie Peak Div. of **Medicine Bow Nat. For.** (hqs.Laramie), est. 1935. Highest pt. is **Laramie Peak** (10,274′). Area is fingered by winding streams & fireguard Rds. **123. GLENDO** & J. with graded Rd.

SIDE TRIP: On this Rd. (L) 20m is **Esterbrook Ranger Sta.** & trls. into N. sec. of Medicine Bow Nat. For.

**137. ORIN.** J. with US20 (see); the 2 routes are united (W). **202. CASPER** (see).

### Sec. 2: CASPER to MONT. LINE. 189.

US87 runs (N) through long stretches of oil fields. **28. TEAPOT ROCK** (L), landmark of an oil field widely known as Teapot Dome. Area was naval reserve until 1922 when it was leased to Harry F. Sinclair by Secy. of Inter. Albert B. Fall. Following "Teapot Dome Scandal" & trial, both Sinclair & Fall received fines & prison sentences. Field is now part of U.S. Petroleum Reserve. **42. MIDWEST,** company town for oil operations. Salt Cr. Field here is one of world's largest light oil producing areas; 1st well drilled, 1888. Hy. passes through ranch country of Powder R. basin. **121. BUFFALO** & J. with US16 (see). Beyond (N) is dude ranch country, with trls. leading (L) into **Big Horn Nat. For.** (hqs.Sheridan). **126. FT. PHIL KEARNEY** (R). Stockade & several bldgs. reprod. During Red Cloud War, ft. was center of excitement. **140. STORY,** tourist center & outfitting pt. for pack trips into Big Horns. St. Fish Hatchery. Site of Wagon Box Fight (1867), where Red Cloud's warriors attacked detachment of 28 soldiers barricaded behind low wall of wagon boxes. Inds. were defeated by steady fire of new breech-loading Springfield rifles. **143. BANNER. Lodge Trl. Ridge** (R) was scene of hist. Fetterman Massacre (1866). Lt. Col. W. J. Fetterman & 81 men were killed when they set out from Ft. Phil Kearney to intercept band of Red Cloud & his Sioux believed to be threatening wagon train. At **153.** is J. with improved Rd.

SIDE TRIP: On this Rd. (L) 3m is colorful village of **Big Horn,** a real-life version of a cowboy movie set. Surrounding carefully preserved old cowtown are ranch-estates with all modern trappings, incl. swim. pools, tennis courts & polo fields.

**157.** J. with US14 (see), united (N) through **SHERIDAN, 159.,** to **RANCHESTER** at **176.** US87 winds (NW) to **WYO.-MONT. LINE at 189.**

## US 287—WYOMING

**COLO.-WYO. LINE** (35m from Ft. Collins, Colo.) **(NW) to YELLOWSTONE NAT. PK. (S. ENTRANCE). 442. US287**

Via: Laramie, Rawlins, Lander. U.P. RR. bet. Laramie & Rawlins. Accoms: In large towns; resorts along route.

US287 cuts catty-corner across Wyo. through diversified country. It passes through plains & forests, bustling towns & quiescent villages.

### Sec. 1: COLO. LINE to RAWLINS. 148.

**8. TIE SIDING,** logging camp for timber operations in Laramie Mts. **16. ST. FISH HATCHERY** (O). **29.** (R) **SITE OF OLD FT. SANDERS** (est.1866) to protect emigrants on Overland Trl. & workers building RR. Gens. Grant, Sherman & Sheridan once met here. Ft. fell into disrepair as town of Laramie sprang up near-by. **31. LARAMIE** (see). Here US287 unites with US30 to **RAWLINS** (see) at **148.**

### Sec. 2: RAWLINS to YELLOWSTONE NAT. PK. 294.

US287 runs (N) from Rawlins through alkaline desert dotted with sagebrush & greasewood. **34. LAMONT,** supply pt. for Lost Soldier Oil Field (L). **45. MUDDY GAP.** J. with St.220.

SIDE TRIP: On this Rd. (R) 10$^{m}$ is **Mon.** to Capt. Howard Martin, who led party of 576 Eng. followers of Brigham Young along this trl. in 1856. At 19$^{m}$ is famous **Independence Rock** on which thousands of names have been carved. Ruts of Oregon Trl. still visible. Markers here comm. 1st Masonic meeting in Wyo. (July 4, 1862); Mormon emigration; Father De Smet, missionary to Inds.; Ezra Meeker, founder of Oregon Trl., & others.

**55. SPLIT ROCK,** landmark & stage sta. on Oregon Trl. Shoshone Inds. once brought traffic to standstill (1862) by commandeering all horses along route, incl. those hitched to wagons & coaches. Also, along this trail, a youngster named Wm. Cody, Buffalo Bill, made record 322$^{m}$ ride for Pony Express. At **122. PERRIN.** J. with St.28, a cut-off to US187 (see).

SIDE TRIP: On St.28 (L) 16$^{m}$ is **Atlantic City,** depopulated gold mining camp of the 1870's. Gold fever revives occasionally as prospectors find new strikes in abandoned gulches. (E) of village is **Site of Ft. Stambaugh.** At 18$^{m}$ is For. Serv. Rd. leading (R) into **Shoshone Nat. For.** (Dist.hqs.Landers), with **Granite Peak** (10,418′) dominant. At 20$^{m}$ is **South Pass City,** ghost of fabulous gold mining city that was 2nd only to Cheyenne in pop. & roistering in 1870's. Dredges cont. to scoop Big Hermit Cr. & other streams for gold missing during boom period. At 32$^{m}$ is **South Pass,** broad valley across Continental Divide (7,550′). From pass discovery by Rbt. Stuart (1812) to U.P. RR. construction across Wyo. (1869), half-million persons crossed Divide here in prairie schooners, stage coaches, bull-whacker wagons, & on foot. Here is **Mon.** comm. visit of 1st white women into region (1836), members of Dr. Marcus Whitman's party of missionaries.

**130. LANDER,** gateway to Wind R. Mts. & Shoshone Ind. Reserv. As it is at W. terminus of C. & N.W. RR. branch across Wyo., town advertises itself as "where the rails end & the trails begin." Since 1946 the discovery of rich jade deposits has created a gem boom. Popo Agie R. winds through picturesque town which is outgrowth of 3 early fts.—McGraw, Augur & Brown. Pioneer Days (July) annually revive frontier life. **Popo Agie Primitive Area** in Shoshone Nat. For. lies (SW). At Lander are Js. with St.320 & unnumbered Sinks Canyon Rd.

SIDE TRIP: (A) On St.320 (R) 2$^{m}$ is **St. Training Sch.** At 10$^{m}$ is **Hudson** & boundary of Shoshone Ind. Reserv. 16$^{m}$ is **Arapaho,** sub-agency & Ind. trading post. Inds. in area raise livestock, farm, & a few are coal miners. Rd. cont. to Riverton.

(B) On Sinks Canyon Rd. (L) 10$^{m}$ is **The Sinks,** so-called because R. enters cave & flows underground 0.5$^{m}$ before reappearing in form of large springs. Univ. of Mo. maintains summer geology camp here. 13$^{m}$ is boundary of **Washakie Div.** of Shoshone Nat. For. 14$^{m}$ **Middle Fork Ranger Sta.** (campgrounds) with trls. leading into Popo Agie Primitive Area. **Wind R. Peak** (13,499′) is high pt. US287 runs (NW) through Shoshone Ind. Reserv., only one in Wyo. Shoshone & Arapaho live peacefully on same reserv. but there is little intermarriage. Thanks to lifelong efforts of Chief Washakie (1804-1900), it is one of most progressive reservs. in U.S. Inds. operate or lease irrigated tracts & have profitable livestock assocs. In 1938 they were awarded 4 million dollars in suit against Fed. Gov. in settlement of old claims.

At **142.** is J. with dirt Rd.

SIDE TRIP: On this Rd. (L) 1$^{m}$ is **Wind River,** with blockh. built in 1871 still standing. At 2$^{m}$ is **Shoshone Mission Sch.** (est.1889), built of home-made brick by Rev. John Roberts, Episc. missionary. Sacajawea, the Shoshone woman who guided Lewis & Clark Exped. (1804-05) through Rockies, is said to be buried in cemetery here.

**143. FORT WASHAKIE,** reserv. hqs. & trade center, popular summer gathering place where Inds. watch tourists for entertainment & amusement. Chief Washakie held the U.S. Gov. to promise to build & maintain ft. here for protection against Sioux Inds. It was not closed until 1909. In Military Cemetery is grave of Chief Washakie, only Ind. chief ever buried with full military honors by U.S. Army. **162.** J. with St.287.

SIDE TRIP: On this oiled Rd. (R) 1$^{m}$ is **U.S. Bureau of Reclamation Diversion Dam** (1923). It channels water through Wyo. canal to Pilot Butte power plant.

US287 follows Wind R. & crosses W. boundary of Shoshone Ind. Reserv. at **189.** In this area along hy. are numerous extinct geyser cones, caverns & pictographs. **204. DUBOIS,** supply pt. for parties of big game hunters, scientists & vacationers. (S) of Dubois is rugged, wild **Glacier Primitive Area** penetrated only by pack trls. In area are Dinwoody & Bull L. Glaciers, 2 of largest living glaciers in U.S. They cover area of 15 sq. miles. Dinwoody ice field is at foot of towering **Gannett Peak** (13,785′), highest in Wyo. (N) of Dubois is **Stratified Primitive Area,** noted for big game hunting. **219. SHOSHONE NAT. FOR.** E. boundary (hqs.Cody). **230.** W. boundary Shoshone Nat. For. & E. boundary **Teton Nat. For.** (hqs.Jackson). At **232.** hy crosses **CONTINENTAL DIVIDE** through Tog-wo-tee Pass (9,658′), named for Shoshone guide. **Teton Wilderness Area** lies (N). **250.** Blackrock Ranger Sta. on Buffalo Fork. Rd. leaves for. & enters fertile valley of **Jackson Hole,** since 1943 part of Jackson Hole Nat. Mon. (see US187). **267. JACKSON HOLE WILDLIFE PK.,** opened July 19, 1948. US287 parallels (N) boundary of 1,500-a. preserve dedicated to show wild animals in natural habitat & provide an "outdoors laboratory" for biological field studies. Pk. was created on land presented by Rockefeller family. **272. MORAN.** J. with US89 & US187 (see). US287 & US89 run (N), with **Jackson L.** & **Grand Teton Mts.** (L). Rd. crosses portion of for. area to **SNAKE CR. RANGER STA. & S. ENTRANCE, YELLOWSTONE NAT. PK., 294.**

## US 187—WYOMING

**ROCK SPRINGS, WYO. (J. With US30) (NW) to J. With US287** (in Jackson Hole). **211. US187**

Via: Pinedale, Jackson. Rd. hard-surfaced. Accoms: Guest ranches & resorts.

US187 is approach route to Jackson Hole Nat. Mon. & Grand Teton Nat. Pk. It passes through varied country, including sage brush flats (S) & mountainous forests (N).

### Sec. 1: ROCK SPRINGS to J. with US189. 111.

Hy. crosses alkaline desert (N) from Rock Springs. **37. EDEN,** center of irrigated reg. surrounded by barren flats. **41. FARSON,** trade center in Eden Valley irrigation project area operated by U.S. Bureau of Reclamation. **Mon.** marks site of Jim Bridger-Brigham Young Meeting where Mormon leader & frontiersman met June 28, 1847, to plan route into Great Salt L. valley. At Farson is J. with St.28, shortcut to US287 (see). **88. BOULDER. 100. PINEDALE,** outfitting center for campers & hunters. Here is Dist. Ranger Sta. for **Bridger Nat. For.** (hqs.Kemmerer), large area of which parallels hy. (E). Dude ranches & hunt. lodges in vic. (pack trips. guides). Within for. is 400,000-a. **Bridger Primitive Area.** At Pinedale is J. with For. Serv. Rd.

SIDE TRIP: On this Rd. (R) 4m is **Fremont L.** (pic.boat.f.swim.). At 14m is **Surveyor Pk.,** with trls. into Bridger Primitive Area of Alpine Ls., several mts. over 12,000′, & undisturbed wildlife.

**106.** is J. with oiled Rd. leading (R) to **Cora,** 4m, & **New Fork Ls.** area (campgrounds). **111.** is J. with US189 (see).

### Sec. 2: J. with US189 to J. with US287. 100.

At **0.5.** is J. with dirt Rd. leading (L) 3m to Site of Ft. Bonneville (log.1832), dubbed Ft. Nonsense by fur traders. At **1.** is **ST. FISH HATCHERY** (O). **20. TETON NAT. FOR.** boundary (hqs.Jackson). **32. BONDURANT,** dude ranch hq. At **37.** is marked **SITE OF 1ST PROT. SERMON IN WYO.** where Rev. Samuel Parker attended Green R. Rendezvous (Aug. 23, 1835) to preach to fur traders. At **42.** is J. with For. Serv. Rd.

SIDE TRIP: On this Rd. (R) 9m is **Granite Falls.** At 10m is **Hot Springs,** with warm water pool (free) maintained by For. Serv.

US187 twists through Hoback Canyon. **49. CAMP DAVIS** (L), summer sch. of engineering founded 1874. Near-by is Bryant Flat Ranger Sta. **54.** J. with US89 (see). Mt. hy. overlooks **Jackson Hole,** famous dude ranch & big game country.

**67. JACKSON,** colorful center for "Hole" recr. area (h.f.camp.winter sports;hqs. Teton Nat.For.). Town retains Old West influence of board sidewalks, hitching posts & log bldgs. Annual Days of '49 (rodeo); winter activities incl. ski tournaments, dogsled races, & fish. by ski-equipped airplanes. At Jackson are Js. with St.22 & Elk Refuge Rds.

SIDE TRIPS: (A) St.22 (L) conn. Jackson Hole & US20 in Idaho. Hy. rises steeply with corkscrew turns to **Teton Pass,** 12m & tremendous view of mts., for. & valleys. (W) lies **Targhee Nat. For.** At 18m is **Wyo.- Idaho Line** (5m from Victor, Idaho).

(B) On Rd. (R) 1m is **Nat. Elk Refuge** (see Jackson Hole Nat. Mon.). Flat Cr. here noted for good fly fishing.

US187 runs (N) through **Jackson Hole Nat. Mon.** (see). At **78.** is J. with graded Rd.

SIDE TRIP: On this Rd. (R) 5m is **Kelly,** village & Ranger Sta. on Gros Ventre R. Rd. leads deep into Teton Nat. For. At 23m is **Goosewing Ranger Sta.,** from which are mt. trls.

**80. MOOSE,** P.O. for Nat. Pk. Serv. hqs. Near-by is rustic **Ch. of the Transfiguration;** altar window frames beautiful view of Tetons. Rd. parallels (E) boundary of **Grand Teton Nat. Pk.** (see). At **82.** is J. with gravel Rd. which leads (L) 0.5$^{m}$ to **Park Hqs.** (Info.on h.f.camp.trls.& guide serv.). **85. JENNY L. STA.** (campground. boats.horses.guides). **Mus.** here features natural hist. of reg. Ranger lectures each evening during summer mos.; well-marked trls. lead into Grand Teton Nat. Pk. (see). Hy. winds along (E) shore of **Jenny L.,** beautiful 1,325-a. mt. L. with backdrop of for. & granite spires. At **87.** is J. with Pk. Dr.

SIDE TRIP: On this Rd. (L) 3$^{m}$ is **String L.** At 4$^{m}$ is **Leigh L.,** a triangular-shaped glacial L. with **Mt. Moran** (12,594') reflected in clear waters. Trls. finger this reg. (L) on **Indian Paintbrush Trl.** (footpath) is **L. Solitude,** 14$^{m}$.

**94. JACKSON L.** This large, deep L. covers 25,730 as. & has depth of 400' in places.

**99.** (R) is **JACKSON HOLE WILDLIFE PK.** (O). **100.** is J. with US287 (see). This is (N) terminus of US187.

## US 189—WYOMING

**UTAH-WYO. LINE** (29$^{m}$ from Echo City, Utah) **(N) to J. with US187** (11$^{m}$ from Pinedale, Wyo.). **157. US189-US30S**

Via: Evanston, Kemmerer, Big Piney. Accoms.: Limited.

US189 & US30S unite for 23$^{m}$ from Utah-Wyo. Line where US30S branches (NE) to J. with US30. **10. EVANSTON** (see US30S). At **23.** US189 turns (N), conn. route bet. SW. & NW. Wyo. (heavy traffic), traversing sage brush flats broken by occasional coal mines, many abandoned. At **60.** is J. with US30N (see), united to **KEMMERER** at **62.** Here US189 branches (N). **65.** Hy. crosses Slate Cr., route of pioneers seeking short-cut through desert, taking advantage of **Emigrant Springs** (R) & **Dodge Suspension Bridge** over Green R. **75. NAMES HILL,** so-called because early pathfinders carved their names in soft rock wall. **112. LA BARGE,** center of shallow-well oil field. Rd. parallels Green R., down which thousands of logs for RR. ties are floated each spring. Here sure-footed lumberjacks can be seen performing their log-rolling antics. To (W) **Salt Range** rises. This reg. is part of **Bridger Nat. For.** (hqs.Kemmerer). **132. BIG PINEY** (sett.1888;July Chuck Wagon Days), center of extensive ranching dist.; many log bldgs. J. with graded Rd.

SIDE TRIP: On this Rd. (L) into Bridger Nat. For. 25$^{m}$ is **Snider Basin Ranger Sta.** Fireguard Rds. & pack saddle trls. finger reg. To (S) are **Spring L. & Elk Cr. Campgrounds;** (W) is **Cottonwood Campground;** (N) is **Middle Piney L. Campground.**

At **153.** is J. with dirt Rd. leading (R) 2.5$^{m}$ to **La Prairie de la Messe. Mon.** marks site where Father Pierre Jean De Smet celebrated 1st High Mass in Wyo. (July 5, 1840); now annually (July 5). Near-by is **Mon.** marking Grave of Pinckney Sublette, member of fur trading family active in early Wyo. development. **132. DANIEL,** sm. supply pt. for ranchers & loggers. At **156.** hy. crosses Green R. To (L) is **Rendezvous Pk.,** scene of hist. Green R. gatherings of trappers & traders from Rocky Mt. reg. (1st in 1824). **Mon.** honors wives of Rev. Sam. Parker & Dr. Marcus Whitman, 1st white women to visit Wyo. (1835). At **157.** is J. with US187 (see).

## US 89—WYOMING

**IDAHO-WYO. LINE** (16$^{m}$ from Montpelier, Idaho) **(N) to YELLOWSTONE NAT. PK. (S. ENTRANCE). 159. US89**

Via: Afton, Alpine, Jackson. Rd. hard-surfaced except bet. Alpine & J. with US187. Accoms.: Dude ranches & resorts along route.

US89 is approach route into scenic & recr. areas of Grand Teton & Yellowstone Nat. Pks. & Jackson Hole Nat. Mon.

At **0.** is J. with St.89 (S) to US30 (see). **9. BRIDGER NAT. FOR.** (S) boundary (hqs.Kemmerer). **11. ALFRED FLAT CAMPGROUND** on Packstring Cr. At **19.** hy. enters Star Valley, reg. noted for Swiss cheese & Mormon communities. Following enactment of anti-polygamy laws, many Mormon men with plural wives took refuge in this remote valley. Wives & children developed signal system to warn of approaching Fed. authorities. Dairy farms & cheese factories form basic economy of prosperous reg. **26. SMOOT,** named for Reed Smoot, Mormon ch. apostle & U.S. Senator from Utah. In for. area (W) of town is Cottonwood Campground. At

**28.** is one of modern Swiss cheese factories of local coop. assocs. **34. AFTON,** business & religious center for Star Valley; Tabernacle dominant. **Univ. of Wyo. Experiment Sta.** here specializes in dairy research. J. with For. Serv. Rd.

SIDE TRIP: On this Rd. (R) 1m is **Swift Cr. Campground.** Trl. leads to Periodic Spring, at 6m, unique in that it flows several minutes, then stops for equal period.

Hy. traverses pass bet. Upper & Lower Star Valley known as The Narrows. For several miles Rd. parallels sec. (L) of Caribou Nat. For. in Idaho. **48. THAYNE.** At **49.** is J. with oiled Rd.

SIDE TRIP: On this Rd. (L) 2m is Freedom; Main St. is boundary bet. Idaho & Wyo. Different St. laws regulate affairs on each side of street, so citizens seek certain privileges simply by crossing over. This was particularly true when Mormon polygamists were safe in Wyo. but not in Idaho. Here is J. with St.34 (see Idaho).

**56. ETNA.** Dairy farms dot valley. Towering landmarks (E) are **Prater Mt.** (10,105′) & **Stewart Pk.** (10,080′). **64. ALPINE,** on the Snake R. Idaho-Wyo. line bisects village. Here is J. with St.29 (see Idaho). US89 runs (E) through Grand Canyon of Wyo., a scenic route, with heavily-wooded cliffs & gulches, herds of elk, mt. sheep, grizzly bear & moose. US89 joins US187 (see) in Hoback Canyon, uniting (N) through Jackson Hole to **MORAN J.** at **127.** Here US89 joins US287 (see) to **159.** at S. Entrance of **YELLOWSTONE NAT. PK.** (see).

## YELLOWSTONE NATIONAL PARK

**YELLOWSTONE NAT. PK.**

Hqs.: Mammoth Hot Springs, 5m (S) of N. Entrance. Season: May 1-Oct.15; official tourist season, June 20-Sept.12. RR. conns.: U.P., N.P., Milwaukee, & C.B.& Q. Bus tours within Pk. Entrances via: US12, US14, US20, US89, US191, US287. Within Pk. are 310m of hys. & 900m of trls. (horses & guides avail.). Accoms.: Hotels, lodges, cabins.

Yellowstone is oldest, largest, & best known of nat. pks. It is nature's fantasia—a land of water spouts, glass mts. & friendly bears. This popular vacationland has beautiful rambling hotels, scenic hys., & varied recr. facils. Pk. covers 3,472 sq. miles, overlapping borders of Mont. & Idaho.

It was created (1872) as 1st. Nat. Pk. during presidency of U.S. Grant & dedicated "for benefit & enjoyment of the people." Inds. considered this volcanic area as "bad medicine." First white man to wander into awesome reg. was John Colter, member of Lewis & Clark expedition who remained in W. to trap. Area became known as "Colter's Hell" from his stories. Jim Bridger, Capt. John Mullen, & other early frontiersmen visited reg., but it was not until 1870 that country was explored. In 1886 Army built ft. at Mammoth Hot Springs & began building Rds. By 1895 it was mecca for tourists who came by horseback & stagecoach. In 1915 it was opened to automobile traffic. U.S. Army relinquished jurisdiction of pk. in 1916. Entire area is wildlife sanctuary. Playful black bears beg for food near camps & rds. (be careful, bears are dangerous). Buffalo, moose, elk, deer, antelope, & mt. sheep inhabit area & can be seen from hys. & footpaths (no h.). Beavers may be seen at work along streams. More than 200 species of birds are in pk., incl. eagles, swans, & pelicans. Fish in lakes & streams incl. native brook, rainbow, Mackinaw, & Loch Leven trout & grayling (no license required; check on current limit regulations).

Pk. has large forested areas & wide variety of flowers (750 species). Most common trees are lodgepole & limber pine, alpine & Douglas fir, Engelmann spruce, & Rocky Mt. juniper. Familiar flowers incl. water lilies, violets, phlox, Ind. paintbrush (Wyo. St. flower), lungwort, magenta fireweed, wild geranium, harebell, night-blooming mentzelia, umbrella plant, windflower, shooting star, primrose, aster, & Pentstemon. Unique to Yellowstone is its geyser action. There are 3,000 geysers, hot springs, & pools. Greatest single attraction is Old Faithful Geyser (see below). Scenic features incl. Yellowstone R. Falls & Yellowstone L. (see below). Main hy. travel route is known as Grand Loop (see below).

### PARK TOURS

**I. E. ENTRANCE (US14-US20) to LAKE J.** (Grand Loop). **27.**

**0. SYLVAN PASS STA.,** 53m (W) of Cody. (N) is **Grant Peak** (11,015′); (S) is **Reservation Peak** (10,618′). At **7.** is crest of **Sylvan Pass** (8,557′). At **8.** is **L. Eleanor** in spruce setting. **12. TETON PT.** (parking area). **17. L. BUTTE** (R) with **Brimstone Basin** beyond. At **18.** Rd. swings along shore of **Yellowstone L.** Along sandy beaches may be found agates, cornelians, & pieces of petrified wood. L. covers 139 sq. miles. At **27.** is **FISHING BRIDGE & LAKE J.**—with Grand Loop Tour (see).

**II. S. ENTRANCE (US89-US287) to THUMB J.** (Grand Loop). **22.**

**0. SNAKE R. STA.** Rd. follows Lewis Canyon bet. **Pitchstone Plateau** (L) & **Red Mts.** (R). **12. LEWIS FALLS.** At **18.** Rd. climbs over **Continental Divide** (7,988′). Rd. opens onto W. Thumb Bay of Yellowstone L. Along shore is **Paint Pot** area, where small geysers spit & spew. At **22.** is **THUMB J.**—with Grand Loop Tour (see).

**III. W. ENTRANCE (US20-US191) to MADISON J.** (Grand Loop). **14.**

**0. W. YELLOWSTONE,** tourist center. At **2.** is **WYO.-MONT. LINE & CHRISTMAS TREE PK.** Rd. follows Madison R. (trout f.). **14. MADISON J.**—with Grand Loop Tour (see).

**IV. N. ENTRANCE (US89) to MAMMOTH HOT SPRINGS** (Grand Loop). **5.5.**

At Gardiner, Mont., is entrance arch dedicated by Theo. Roosevelt (1903). Rd. passes through valley & follows Gardiner R. (good f.). At **3.** is **MONT.-WYO. LINE** & 45th parallel, halfway pt. bet. N. Pole & Equator. **Mt. Everts** (7,000′) looms (L). **3.5. BOILING R.,** with steam rising from warm waters. At **5.5.** is **MAMMOTH HOT SPRINGS** & J. with Grand Loop Tour (see).

**V. NE. ENTRANCE (US12) to TOWER J.** (Grand Loop). **29.**

**0. SILVER GATE,** 4$^{m}$ (W) of Cooke, Mont. Rd. cuts through Absaroka Range. At **4.** Rd. crosses **MONT.-WYO. LINE.** At **15.** is **SODA BUTTE,** cone of extinct geyser. **18. BUFFALO RANCH,** feeding grounds for bison roaming area. **28. YELLOWSTONE R.** which flows (S) through "Grand Canyon of the Yellowstone."

**29. TOWER.** J. with Grand Loop Tour (see).

**VI. GRAND LOOP TOUR. 144. Grand Loop Rd.**

Via: Mammoth Hot Springs, Norris Geyser Basin, Madison J., Old Faithful Geyser & Inn, Thumb J., Yellowstone L., Lake Lodge & J., Canyon Hotel, Yellowstone Falls, Camp Roosevelt, Tower J., Mammoth Hot Springs. Rd. hard-surfaced. Howard Eaton Trl. (horseback) parallels.

**0. MAMMOTH HOT SPRINGS,** pk. hqs. & tourist center; steaming mineral waters flow over terraced hillsides. Algae & other microscopic plants cover terraces with multi-colored streaks & annual deposits of travertine are as deep as 1′. Offices of **Nat. Pk. Serv.** (info.); some of bldgs. are situated around former army parade ground of old Ft. Yellowstone. **Mammoth Mus.** (sandstone), coll. of natural & human hist. of reg. Opp. Mus., **House of Horns,** built entirely of antlers & horns. **Mammoth Springs Hotel,** oil paintings in lobby. At Mammoth Hot Springs is J. with N. Entrance Rd. (see). At **0.5.** is **LIBERTY CAP,** cone 38′ high. At **2.5.** is J. with Formation Loop Rd. leading (R) 1.5$^{m}$ to fantastic formations, highlighted by Angel Terrace which resembles fancy wedding cake. Rd. rejoins Grand Loop & at **5.** is 1-way Rd.

SIDE TRIP: On this Rd. (L) around base of **Bunsen Peak** (8,500′) is **Middle Gardiner Canyon,** 3$^{m}$. Here is basaltic rock of volcanic origin. At 3.5$^{m}$ is **Osprey Falls,** lovely ribbon of water. Rd. rejoins Grand Loop Rd. at 6.5$^{m}$.

Rd. traverses area of Ls., meadows, & moose swamps. **Electric Peak** (11,155′) looms (R). At **8.** is **SHEEPEATER CLIFF** (L), named for Ind. tribe that once lived in reg. **8.5. PUB. CAMPGROUND.** At **12.** is **APOLLINARIS SPRING** & campground. Near-by is **Lily Pad L. 13.** is **OBSIDIAN CLIFF** (L), fabulous mt. of glass, a pitch-black volcanic substance resembling glass. Geologic hist. of cliff contained in **Obsidian Cliff Exhibit** here. **17.** is **ROARING MT.** (7,575′), which rumbles as gas escapes from 100 vents. Near-by are **Twin Ls. 19.** is **NYMPH L.,** which appears to boil; field exhibit. **21. NORRIS RANGER STA. J.** with oiled Rd. leading (L) 11$^{m}$ on cut-off to Canyon J. (see below). Grand Loop Rd. follows Gibbon R. **22. NUPHAR L.** Along hy. is **Norris Basin Geyser Mus.** built of rhyolite & logs; pictorial explanation of thermal features of surrounding basin & volcanism in pk. From Mus. are Nature Trls. (foot paths, no guide necessary).

SIDE TRIPS: (A) Along path (L) are **Paint Pots,** in which earth bubbles. **New Crater** gushes water like a jug. **Fearless Geyser** is small mud spout that erupts periodically. **Veteran & Vixen Geysers** are irregular.

(B) From Mus. (R) to **Valentine Geyser,** which erupts every 18 hrs. to height of 75′. Other geysers in area are Arsenic, Whirligig, & Constant.

Grand Loop Rd. traverses feeding grounds for elk & deer. **25. GIBBON CASCADES. Mon. Geyser** (R). **30. GIBBON FALLS,** 84′ drop. **34. TUFF CLIFF,** mt. of volcanic ash; field exhibit. **36. MADISON.** J. with W. Entrance Rd. (see). **Mus.,** devoted to hist. events in pk. **37. FIREHOLE FALLS. 44. LOWER GEYSER BASIN.** In area are Leather Pool, Fountain Paint Pot, Fountain Geyser, Steady Geyser, Firehole L. & White Dome Geyser. Major attraction is **Great Fountain,** which reaches height of 100′ every 8 or 12 hrs. **45. MIDDLE GEYSER BASIN** (parking area); Grand Prismatic Spring & Turquoise Pool. **49. BISCUIT BASIN** (parking area); Sapphire Pool, Black Pearl Pool & Silver Glove Spring. **50.** Grand Loop Rd. enters **UPPER GEYSER BASIN.** Along Rd. are: **Artemisia Geyser,** spurts water 35′ for 10-min. periods every 24 hrs., unique granular sinter of sage-shade; **Morning Glory Pool** (photographic favorite); **Fan & Mortar Geysers,** named for type of eruptions each produces; **Riverside Geyser,** shoots water & steam over Firehole R., eruptions every 5-8 hrs.; **Grotto & Rocket Geysers,** often erupt at same time; **Giant Geyser,** irregular eruptions (3 mos.) but world's highest (250′) active geyser. At **51.** is J. with side Rd.

SIDE TRIP: On this loop Rd. (R) through **Black Sand Basin** are several pools & geysers of unusual beauty. **Daisy Geyser** erupts at an angle (every 90 mins.). At 0.5m is **Black Sand Pool,** which has deep blue water, black sand & creamy edges. **Sunset L.** is riot of color at 1m. Rd. rejoins Grand Loop Rd. at 2m.

**52. OLD FAITHFUL INN,** familiar Western landmark & popular 400-rm. hotel, built (1903) of native lumber and stone (chalet). The 6-story central portion is capped by observ. platform, from which powerful lights play on Old Faithful Geyser at night. Lobby features rough metal designs, rustic furniture & huge fireplace. Near-by is **Old Faithful Lodge,** rambling pk.-style structure used as recr. center; hqs. for cabin camp area. Hotel, lodge, & cabins served & entertained by college students known here as "savages." **Old Faithful Mus.,** operated by Rangers of Nat. Pk. Serv., has rustic, off-the-rd. setting; displays of geological specimens & pictorial explanations of hot water phenomena. **Amphitheatre** (adj.) used for evening lectures by naturalists. **Herbarium** contains growing specimens of rare & common plant life native to pk. **Old Faithful Geyser** which, like star of show, is center of natural stage. Its eruptions (average 65 mins.) are preceded by regurgitating roar from within cone, followed by cloud of steam that rises like smoke signal. Column of water rises slowly, bubbling over edge of cone & lifting gradually into air. When it reaches full height, stream is 120′ high. After approx. 4 mins., during which 15,000 gals. of water are discharged, column recedes & vapor clouds drift off. Near-by, **The Giantess,** unpredictable geyser that erupts about twice a yr., attaining height of 200′ & lasting more than 4 hrs. Eruption resembles billowing spout of Bikini atomic tests. In center of Upper Geyser Basin is **Geyser Swim. Pool,** largest of its kind in world (dressing rooms avail.).

From Old Faithful area, Grand Loop Rd. follows scenic route ascending to **ISA L.** on Continental Divide (8,262′), at **59.** Rd. winds through pine for. to another summit of Continental Divide (8,522′), at **67.,** then descends to Yellowstone L. At **69.** is **THUMB. J.** with S. Entrance Rd. (see); Ranger Sta. & Campground (boats & f.tackle avail.). Grand Loop Rd. follows shore of **YELLOWSTONE L.,** highest (7,731′) of larger Ls. in N. America, reaching depth of 300′. In L. are submerged geysers & hot pools, some of which spout boiling water into cold waters of L. **Fishing Cone** (R) protrudes above water, crater of hot bubbling water. There are several Is., largest of which is **Frank I.,** summer home of pelicans, swans, geese, & herons. At **88.** is **U.S. FISH HATCHERY** (display cases & rearing ponds). Fish native to Yellowstone L. are black spotted trout & suckers. **90. LAKE.** J. with E. Entrance Rd. Here is **Lake Lodge** (recr.center.cabins.campground). To (R) is **Fishing Bridge** which spans Yellowstone R. at outlet. Banks usually lined with fishermen. **Fishing Bridge Mus.** deals with biologic life of Pk., & hist. of Yellowstone L. Rd. runs (N) along Yellowstone R., past **CASCADES** at **94.** At **95.** is **MUD VOLCANO & DRAGON'S MOUTH;** latter is hot springs cavern. Hy. passes through Hayden Valley, named for Dr. F. V. Hayden, gov. geologist who mapped reg. (1871). At **102.** is **GRIZZLY BEAR FEEDING GROUNDS** (L). Bears gather here for evening feeding & spectators, caged in fenced pen, watch. Some of grizzlies weigh 1,000 lbs. At **103.** is J. with Artist Pt. Rd. leading (R) 0.5m to **Canyon Lodge** (cabins.recr.). Main lodge overlooks **Lower Yellowstone Falls,** 308′ waterfall (footpath & steps to canyon floor). At 1.5m is **Artist Pt.,** noted for scenic view. At **103.5.** is **CANYON RANGER STA. & CAMP-**

**GROUND. Upper Yellowstone Falls** (reached by footpath) has 112′ drop. **104. GRAND FALLS** of the Yellowstone (parking area), one of pk.'s major attractions. Broad Yellowstone R. plunges over cataract & falls more than 300′ into Grand Canyon of Yellowstone. Here also is J. with Cut-off Rd. to Norris Geyser Basin (see above). **104.5. CANYON HOTEL,** rambling structure with 400 rms. & show-place lobby. At **105.** is J. with Inspiration Pt. Rd. leading (R) 1$^{m}$ to observ. platform overlooking canyon. Grand Loop Rd. traverses forested mt. slopes through **DUNRAVEN PASS** (8,860′) at **111.** Here is J. with Mt. Washburn Rd.

SIDE TRIP: On this Rd. (R) 3.5$^{m}$ is summit of **Mt. Washburn** (10,317′). From **Lookout Tower** (telescope) is view of pk. & Teton Mts. (S).

At **122.** is **TOWER FALLS CAMPGROUND** (L). Near-by is **Tower Falls,** 132′; int. geologic formations in area. At **132.** is **OVERHANGING CLIFF,** a ledge that forms shelf over hy. **124.5.** J. with Camp Roosevelt Rd. leading (L) 1$^{m}$ to **Camp Roosevelt Lodge** in for. setting (recr.center.cabins).

At **125.** is **TOWER FALLS.** J. with NE. Entrance Rd. (see). Here is **Tower Falls Ranger** Sta. **126.5. PETRIFIED TREE** (L), part of what once was petrified for. Stump is fenced, other pieces having been carried off by souvenir hunters. Grand Loop Rd. traverses scenic Gallatin Mts. **140. UNDINE FALLS,** cascade over terraced lava formations (R). **144. MAMMOTH HOT SPRINGS** & J. with N. Entrance Rd. (see).

## GRAND TETON NAT. PK. & JACKSON HOLE NAT. MON.

Hqs. Moose, Wyo. No RR. conns. 4 hy. approaches: US89, US187, US287, St.22. US89 & US187 join through Jackson Hole & along (E) edge of Grand Teton Nat. Pk. (see). From route are trls. into Pk. Accoms.: Lodges, resorts, dude ranches, cabins, campgrounds.

These adj. areas form 1 unit geographically, biologically & recreationally. Together they dramatize scenic values of spectacular Tetons & fabulous basin of Jackson Hole. Areas lie (S) of Yellowstone Nat. Pk. Major town is Jackson (see US187).

**GRAND TETON NAT. PK.** embraces majestic Teton range for distance of 27$^{m}$ from (N) to (S), with width ranging from 3$^{m}$ to 9$^{m}$. Total area 150 sq. miles. So rugged is this range of 22 peaks, known as "The Alps of America," that only E.-W. Rd. across it is through Teton Pass (see St.22). Most striking is precipitous front, an almost sheer rise above Jackson Hole. Much of rugged area is above timberline accessible only by horseback & hik. trls. (see below & US187 for Pk. Drive; 90$^{m}$ supervised by Nat. Pk. Serv.). Highest peaks are **Grand Teton** (13,766′), **Mt. Owen** (12,922′), **Middle Teton** (12,798′), **Mt. Moran** (12,594′), **& South Teton** (12,505′). Name of reg. came from early French trappers who called 3 Teton peaks "les trois tetons"—the three breasts. Within Pk. are several glaciers, snowfields & Ls. Of special beauty are **Jenny** & **Leigh Ls.** (boat.f.swim.). Pk. was created in 1929.

PARK TRAILS: (A) From Pk. hqs. at **Moose** are trls. to **Taggart L.,** 163-a. body at mouth of Avalanche Canyon.

(B) **Cascade Canyon Trl.** From Jenny L. Sta. (see US187), on foot or horseback take Cascade Canyon Trl. (N) along (W) side of Jenny L. to **Hidden Falls,** 3$^{m}$. At 7$^{m}$ trl. joins **Skyline Trl.** & climbs to crest of Teton range, circling behind Mt. Owen, Grand Teton, & Cloudvel Dome, 14$^{m}$. Return trip is via **Garnet Canyon Trl.**

(C) **Teton Glacier Trl.** (S) from Sta. 6$^{m}$ to **Amphitheatre L.,** the trl. approaches **Teton Glacier** & snowfield, most accessible in Pk.

**JACKSON HOLE NAT. MON.** is an area of 222,929 as., set aside out of prospective oil fields by Pres. F. D. Roosevelt in 1943. Now noted for its dude ranches, big game hunting & fishing, Secy. of Inter. Harold Ickes, has described Jackson Hole as inhabited by "mail order cowboys." However, the isolated valley was known during the 1820's as a center of western fur trade. It was for one of the trappers & traders, David Jackson, who was assoc. with Gen. Wm. Ashley, for whom the hole was named. Earlier in 1807, John Colter of the Lewis & Clark Expedition visited the spot. In the 1900's the area was scene of bitter fights bet. cattlemen & sheepmen.

A geological & scenic unit with Grand Teton Nat. Pk. immediately (W), the valley lies bet. Teton & Gros Ventre Mts. Within area are beautiful **Jackson L.** (f.); **Nat. Elk Refuge** (23,950 as.), winter home & feeding ground for herd of 10,000 elk, mule deer, moose, sage grouse, wild ducks & geese; new (1948) **Jackson Hole Wildlife Pk.** (1,500 as. zoo); & rapidly developing winter sports area. Administered by Nat. Pk. Serv. (hqs. Moose).

## BIG HORN MTS. RECR. AREA

Hqs. of Big Horn Nat. For.: Sheridan. 5 hy. approaches: US14, US16, US20, US87, US310. C.B.& Q. RR. & Western Airlines make conns. Accoms.: Lodges, dude ranches, campgrounds.

**BIG HORN** mt. range & recr. area rises abruptly out of Great Plains to break prairie monotony bet. Black Hills & Rocky Mts. It is popular dude ranch (h.f.camp.), & scenic reg. About half of travelers who enter or leave Yellowstone Nat. Pk. E. Entrance pass through Big Horns. Heart of reg. covered by Big Horn Nat. For. (see US30). Within area about 80$^{m}$ long & 30$^{m}$ wide are 200 Ls., 1,200$^{m}$ of trout streams & wide variety of wildlife. Waters are stocked with native, rainbow, Loch Leven, eastern brook, & Mackinaw trout, & California golden trout & grayling are being introduced. Mt. sheep, elk, deer, & black & brown bear are native to reg. which is noted for big game hunt. There are 34 pub. campgrounds & 18 licensed resorts within for. area & at fringes of mts. are numerous dude ranches, from which pack-saddle trips can be made into inner recesses of reg. Trl. system of 150$^{m}$ has been developed which features 62$^{m}$ Solitude-Circle Trl. into Cloud Peak (13,165′) Wilderness Area.

## CASPER

**CASPER**

RR. stas.: N. Wolcott & E. C St. for C.B.& Q. RR.; RR. Ave. & Center St. for C.& N.W. RR. Bus Sta.: 152 N. Center St. Wardwell Field for Western Airlines. Accoms.: All types. Central Wyo. Fair & Stock Show (3rd wk. in Aug.).

Casper, 2nd largest city in Wyo., is oil, livestock, & power center for vast reg. Its situation at foot of Casper Mt. (8,500′) & its hist. background add color to city which advertises itself as "the gayest spot in Old Wyo." Early Mormon parties operated ferry near here during early Western migrations & Ft. Casper was est. in 1863. Probably 300,000 emigrants passed this way over Oregon Trl. Cattle ranchers & settlers followed to develop town. The bringing in (1917) of oil wells (N) & (E) turned quiet cow town into roaring mecca. Fabulous Tea Pot Dome & Salt Cr. fields (see US87) became country's major pub. land revenue producers. As Big Muddy & Cole Cr. fields were developed later, Casper boomed. Among oil companies that operate large refineries here are Standard, Texas & Socony-Vacuum. City cont. to be heart of range country & one of largest wool-shipping pts. in U.S. Kendrick reclamation & power project (see below) provides electrical current distributed over 3-St. grid. Casper Jr. College, 1st in Wyo., was opened 1945.

PTS. OF INT.: (1) Durbin & 2nd Sts., **Pub. Lib.;** colls. of Natrona Cty. Hist. Soc. (2) S. Center St. & Midwest Ave., **Pioneer Mon.** honors Oregon Trl. & early settlers. (3) Jefferson St. bet. E. 6th & 10th Sts., **Washington Mem. Pk.** (swim.tennis). (4) 13th St. to Carey Lane, **Old Ft. Caspar** (O.guides.reprod.log), pioneer furnishings, early-day vehicles & old telegraph room. Ferry across Platte R. operated by Mormons (1847) led to bldg. of adobe stage sta. (1858) to serve emigrants. Troops arrived next yr. & military post est. (1863) as Platte Bridge Sta. When Sioux & Cheyenne Inds. went on warpath to close Oregon Trl., ft. was scene of excitement. On July 26, 1865, Lt. Caspar Collins & 25 men set out to rescue wagon train threatened by Inds. Battle ensued in which Collins was killed while trying to hold off superior forces. War. Dept. renamed ft. in his honor & city later took on name with variation in spelling.

### TRIPS OUT OF CASPER

**I. CASPER (S) to CASPER MT. PK. 10. Casper Mt. Hy.**

Take Wolcott St. (S) on oiled Rd. to **BESSEMER TURN, 5.** Here Platte R. makes scenic bend. At **7.** is boundary of **ST. GAME PRESERVE.** Rd. passes **THUNDER BOLT SKI COURSE, 7.5.** Lodges & abandoned asbestos mines are along hy. At **8.** is **NURSERY SKI RUN,** scene of winter sports carnivals (no set dates). Rd. winds over the summit of **CASPER MT.** (8,500′) at **10.**

**II. CASPER (SW) to ALCOVA. 31. St.220**

Take St.220 along N. Platte R. Hy. roughly parallels old Mormon, Oregon, & Cal. Trls. & is short-cut to US287. At **10.** is J. with graded Rd.

SIDE TRIP: On this Rd. (R) 3m is **Goose Egg Ranch,** setting of humorous scene in Owen Wister's "The Virginian," in which 2 cowboys play trick at party by secretly exchanging sleeping togs of infants asleep in 1 room while parents are dancing in another. Not until each family is homeward bound in wagons & buggies is prank of baby sitters discovered & irate parents return to claim own children. Stone house (1877) stands in good condition. To (R) 12m is **Site of Battle of Red Buttes,** where Sgt. Amos Custard & 23 soldiers were ambushed by Inds. (1865) with only 3 soldiers escaping.

St.220 traverses Bessemer Bend valley. At mouth of Poison Spider Cr., Rbt. Stuart & his party of Astorians are believed to have built 1st cabin in Wyo. (1812). At **31.** is **ALCOVA,** gateway to huge reservoir area. Here is Alcova Dam, which backs up N. Platte R. for irrigation & power production. Thousands of as. of semi-arid land brought into cultivation.

SIDE TRIP: On Rd. (L) through Pathfinder Canyon is **Fiery Narrows,** a steep, colorful chasm. At 23m is **Kortes Dam** (1946) which provides power head for Seminoe Reservoir, largest body of water in Wyo. outside Yellowstone Pk.

## CHEYENNE

### CHEYENNE

RR. stas.: 15th St. & Central Ave. for U.P. RR.; Capitol Ave. bet. 15th & 16th Sts. for C.B.& Q. RR. Bus sta.: 1503 Capitol Ave. Mun. airport for United & Western Airlines. Accoms.: All types. Frontier Days (July).

Cheyenne is the capital & largest city of Wyo. It sprawls over a "high prairie" (6,060′) that slopes (W) toward Rocky Mts. Within its limits are old frontier bldgs., modern structures, & several pleasant Ls. (recr.facils.). It is widely known for its annual wild west celebration of Cheyenne Frontier Days (last wk. in July).

Cheyenne is important trans., military, political & stock growers center of long standing. Gen. Grenville Dodge, chief engineer for U.P. RR., selected site in 1867 & named it for Cheyenne Inds. With its selection as RR. division pt., U.S. Army est. Ft. D.A. Russell to provide protection for construction workers & townsmen from marauding Inds. Ft. later was redesignated Francis E. Warren, in honor of former U.S. Senator & father-in-law of Gen. John J. Pershing. Highlight in local history was Tom Horn hanging episode in 1903 following Johnson Cty. War (see US16). Horn was quick-trigger expert hired by cattlemen during their feud with rustlers & sheepmen. After several sudden deaths among sheepmen, a youth tending sheep in cattle country was killed. Horn was brought to trial & sentenced to hang. When his body was not exhibited publicly, it gave rise to persistent stories he may still be alive. While politics & gov. affairs add vitality to present-day life, Cheyenne's economic development evolves around its trans. hub. It is important pt. on 3 RRs., 2 airlines, & 3 Fed. hys. Its mun. airport is one of largest in W. Aviation tool mfg. plant & refinery producing 100-octane gas are new local industries.

PTS. OF INT.: (1) Capitol Ave. & 24th St., **Wyo. St. Capitol** (3-story.neo-Class.), lantern-type cupola atop 145′ dome; western murals within bldg. (2) Capitol Ave. bet. 23rd & 24th Sts., **Supreme Court Bldg.** (1937) of Bedford limestone. In it are **St. Hist. Mus.,** Ind. & pioneer relics; **St. Lib.,** 150,000 vols. & mss.; & **Judiciary.** (3) Capitol Ave. & 21st St., **St. Mary's Cathedral,** largest ch. in Wyo. (4) 1816 Carey Ave., **Wyo. Stock Growers Hqs.,** coll. of Old West relics. (5) N. end Frontier Ave., **Frontier Pk.,** scene of annual Frontier Days. During celebration, pk. has Ind. encampments, buffalo herds, wild horses, cowboys & concessions. Permanent exhibits incl. Jim Baker Blockh. built (1873) to accomodate noted frontiersman's Ind. wives; moved from Little Snake country (W). Adj. Frontier Pk. are several Ls. & recr. areas, incl. L. Makhplahlutah, L. Absarraca, & Terry L. Marker & wheel ruts (W) of Terry L. show where Old Ft. Laramie Trl. & Cheyenne-Black Hills Stage Line passed. (6) W. Randall Blvd., **Ft. Francis E. Warren,** one of country's largest military posts. During World Wars I & II thousands of men trained here. Maneuver & target practice areas maintained in Pole Mt. Div. of Medicine Bow Nat. For. (see US30).

## LARAMIE

### LARAMIE

RR. stas.: 1st & Kearny Sts. for U.P. RR.; W. end Fremont St. for N.Pk.& W. RR. Bus sta.: 3rd St. & Grand Ave. Mun. Airport for Challenger Airlines. Accoms.: All types. Swim., hockey & golf in mun. pks. Jubilee & Horse Races (July).

Laramie is the home of Univ. of Wyo. & gateway to beautiful Snowy Range & Medicine Bow Mts. (W). Although town appears to be a "plains" town, its altitude is 7,165′. Development of natural resources of area provides industrial activity. There are cement, gypsum, aluminum, natural gas, oil refining & for. products plants here. A sponge iron pilot mill to test local deposits of iron ores & coal for use in steel production is new project of U.S. Bureau of Mines. In 1866 Ft. Sanders was est. to protect emigrants along Cherokee Trl. & workers laying tracks of U.P. RR. In 1868 town was started & named for Jacques de la Ramie, early fur trader. Pioneer life in Laramie was stimulating. As early as 1870 women were serving on grand juries, incl. a manslaughter case. Periodicals throughout country sent correspondents. It was here, too, that Bill Nye, noted humorist & editor, organized his "den of 40 liars." Today Laramie is trade center for surrounding stock ranches & oil fields.

PTS. OF INT.: Ivinson Ave. bet. 9th & 19th Sts., **Univ. of Wyo.** (144 as.), only univ. in St.; incl. colleges of agric., commerce, education, engineering, law, & schs. of pharmacy & liberal arts. Summer sch., advertised as the "coolest in America," maintains a science camp in near-by Snowy Range (see below). **Univ. Hall** (Old Main), was 1st bldg. erected (1887). Native stone was used for most of structures. **Rocky Mt. Herbarium** (Engineer Bldg.) has 207,000 plant specimens & all flowering plants of reg. **Lib.** has 133,224 vols. & Wyo. Stock Growers Assoc. coll. of records & brand books dating back to 1873. **Wool Exhibit** (Agric. Hall) is a gift of King Bros. ranch. **Paleontological Mus.** (Science Hall) shows dinosaur skeletons taken from Wyo.'s fossil beds. Ivinson Ave. bet. 6th & 7th Sts., **St. Matthew's Cathedral** (Episc.); military sch. connected with it. Cor. 3rd & Garfield Sts., **Site of "The Boomerang,"** Bill Nye's newspaper, where his brand of humor attracted wide attention. He later joined Jas. Whitcomb Riley in lecture tours.

## TRIPS OUT OF LARAMIE

**I. LARAMIE (W) to W. BOUNDARY, MEDICINE BOW NAT. FOR. 62. St.130** (Via: Snowy Range).

From Laramie St.130 leads (W). At **1.** is **UNIV. OF WYO. EXPERIMENT STA.,** orig. Fed. Prison (1876-1900). **2.** J. with St.230 (see below). **Big Hollow,** a basin of oil wells (L). Hy. parallels (N) boundary of Sheep Mt. Fed. Game Refuge. **30. CENTENNIAL,** old gold mining camp. At **32.** is boundary (E) of **Medicine Bow Nat. For.** (see below & US30), created by Pres. Theo. Roosevelt (1902). More than 100 Ls. & many trout streams in area; most of timber is Lodgepole pine. **35. LIBBY CR. SKI AREA** (Nov.-Mar.), professional slalom runs & portable tow up slope. **36. SNOWY RANGE WINTER SPORTS AREA** (9,000′-11,500′), tobogganing, bobsledding & skiing; motor-powered tow (Nov.-Mar.). **37. NASH FORK PIC. GROUND.** At **38.** is **UNIV. OF WYO. SCIENCE CAMP** (June-July), provides field training & research experience in natural sciences. Adj. camp, **Snowy Range Natural Area,** 771-a. virgin spruce primitive reg. withdrawn for study. At **39.** is **BROOKLYN L. RANGER STA.** (R). In vic. are **Glacier, Lost & Telephone Ls.** (good f.). At **41.** is **LEWIS L. CAMPGROUND** (R) at foot of **Medicine Bow Peak** (12,005′). Hik. trl. leads to summit. At **42.** is **LIBBY FLATS OBSERV. PT.,** panoramic view of 100$^{m}$ on clear days. **43. MIRROR L. CAMPGROUND,** perpetual snowfields & Alpine flowers in vic. **44. L. MARIE PIC. GROUND. 47. SILVER L. CAMPGROUND. 61. BARRET RIDGE WINTER SPORTS AREA,** jumps & slopes for beginners & professionals. **62.** (W) boundary of **MEDICINE BOW NAT. FOR.** (hqs. Laramie), winter sports & playground area being developed in Snowy Range of Medicine Bow Mts. Area was snowbound & isolated during winter months until, recently, private groups & U.S. For. Serv. have developed large snowfields. Snow conditions ideal Dec.-Ap.; slalom runs & ski trls. for beginners & experts. During summer, 22 campgrounds for pub. use (hik.,mt. climbing,h.,f. & motoring). Rd. cont. (W) & (N) to join US30 at Walcott.

**II. LARAMIE (SW) to WYO.-COLO. LINE. 40. St.230**

From J. with St.130 (W) of Laramie, Rd. follows Laramie R. through ranching country. **25. WOODS LANDING,** old-time logging community. During spring seasons, logs for RR. ties floated down R. to creosoting plants in Laramie. **26.** (E) Boundary of **Medicine Bow Nat. For.** Through canyon to **LOWER WOODS CR. PIC. GROUND, 32.** At **34.** is **UPPER WOODS CR. PIC. GROUND;** large stand of lodgepole pine. Rd. passes through area known as Chimney Pk. because of shape of rock formations. At **36.** is Fox Pk. Rd. leading (R) to lumber camp & **Ranger Sta.** (resort & camp.area). **38. MT. HOME,** a rustic village. **40. WYO.-COLO. LINE.**

## US 2—MONTANA

**MONT.-N.D. LINE** (19$^m$ from Williston, N.D.) **(W) to MONT.-IDAHO LINE** (27$^m$ Bonners Ferry, Idaho). **690. US2**

Via: Glasgow, Havre, Shelby, Glacier Nat. Pk., Kalispell, Libby. Rd. hard-surfaced. Gt.N. RR. parallels route except bet. W. edge of Glacier Pk. & Libby. Accoms.: In larger towns; camps & resorts along route.

US2 sweeps across N. Mont.'s seemingly endless prairies, then plunges skyward among glacier-cached peaks of the Rockies. Montanans call this route "the Highline." Hy. follows at intervals weaving courses of 4 Rs.: The Mo., Milk, Marias, & Kootenai.

### Sec. 1: N.D. LINE to BROWNING J., GLACIER NAT. PK. 464.

**9. BAINVILLE. 24. CULBERTSON,** shipping pt. for surrounding wheat ranches.

**29.** Hy. enters **FT. PECK IND. RESERV.** It is natural home of Assiniboine & enforced home of Yankton Sioux who were moved here from S.D. Reserv. has been open to white settlement for many yrs. **44. BROCKTON. 57. POPLAR,** agency for reserv. Fed. hospital is maintained here for Inds. A modified Sun Dance is held annually (wk. of July 4). **79. WOLF POINT,** old-time cow town. Wolf Pt. Stampede (July) features local cowboys. **91. OSWEGO,** namesake of city in N.Y. with which it has little in common. At edge of town is **Ind. cemetery** with above-ground burials.

**115. NASHUA,** village that blossomed with building of Ft. Peck dam. It is at W. boundary of **Ft. Peck Ind. Reserv.** Here is J. with improved Rd.

SIDE TRIP: On this Rd. (L) 12$^m$ is **Fort Peck.** This Gov.-built town flourished during construction of dam (1933-World War II). Near-by **earthen dam** across Mo. R. has created reservoir 175$^m$ long, with 1,600$^m$ of shoreline. **Ft. Peck Game Refuge** covers surrounding area. Recr. facils. are being developed. The dam, built under supervision of U.S. Army Engineers, holds back spring flood waters & releases water as needed for navigation on lower Mo. Dam itself is 3.6$^m$ long. Original Ft. Peck trading post built (E) of here in 1867 by Col. Campbell K. Peck & Comdr. E. H. Durfee.

**129. GLASGOW,** oldest town in N.E. Mont. & twice the scene of hell-roaring booms. It began as saloon-lined camp in 1887 during building of James J. Hill's Gt.N. RR. After long yrs. of unspectacular existence, it found itself the center of attraction for thousands of Ft. Peck construction workers during the 1930's. Entertainment in all forms set the town aglow. Here is J. with St. 22 to Ft. Peck (see above). **172. SACO.** Hy. passes through irrigated area of Milk R. Valley; sugar beets & alfalfa main crops. **L. Bowdoin** (L). This area is habitat for ducks, pheasants, grouse, sage hens, deer, & antelope. At **184.** is J. with gravel Rd. leading (R) to **Amer. Legion Health Pool,** 4$^m$ (plunge). Here also is **Nelson Reservoir,** reclamation project. **200. MALTA,** a town that retains some of the Old West bldgs. & characters depicted by Chas. M. Russell, noted cowboy artist. In 1930's the "Malta Plan" was developed here to become 1st farm resettlement project in U.S. A pt. of int. is sacred **Assiniboine boulder** in City Pk. At **220.** hy. enters **FT. BELKNAP IND. RESERV.** (S). On this reserv. bands of Gros Ventre & Assiniboine live together harmoniously, raising cattle & sheep. **243. FT. BELKNAP,** agency hqs. A Sun Dance is held each yr. early in July. Here is J. with gravel Rd.

SIDE TRIP: On this Rd. (L) 5$^m$ through Ind. reserv. is **Snake Butte Quarry.** At 36$^m$ is **Hays,** scene of annual Ind. Fair (Sept.). 38$^m$ **St. Paul's Mission** (Cath.). At 42$^m$ Rd. enters Little Rocky Mt. portion of Lewis & Clark Nat. For. (hqs. Great Falls).

**259. ZURICH,** which has large sugar beet factory. **268. CHINOOK,** bearing Ind. name for warm, thawing winds of late winter. Here is **Pub. Lib.** which features Russell reproductions. Town has mun. swimming pool. Here is J. with graded Rd.

SIDE TRIP: On this Rd. (L) 16$^m$ is **Nez Perce Battleground.** A mon. marks site where Gen. Nelson A. Miles surprised Chief Joseph in 1877 & fought one of last major conflicts in U.S. After 4-day battle, Joseph surrendered in order to save women & children of his entourage.

Hy. passes through fields of natural gas wells. At **290.** is **HAVRE** (pronounced Hav-ver), home of **Northern Mont. College,** unit of Mont. Univ. The large new bldgs. are made of locally made brick. College was founded in 1929. Jas. J. Hill, the "Empire builder," was responsible for founding the town in 1887 when he est. RR. branch from here to Great Falls. Music Festival (May) & Fair (Aug.) are annual events. Here is J. with US87 to Great Falls (see). **309. KREMLIN,** village named by its Russian settlers. **330. RUDYARD. 368. GALATA.** At **393.** is **SHELBY,** a robust town that has gambled on land, oil, & prize fighting. In the 1890's townsmen hijacked a train carrying an opera troupe to provide local entertainment. In 1920's an oil boom was highlighted by a world's championship fight bet. Jack Dempsey & Tommy Gibbons (July 4, 1923). An **Absorption Plant** here extracts high test gasoline from natural gas. Here is J. with US91 (see). **417. CUT BANK,** center of large oil & gas field operations. Here is E. boundary of **Blackfeet Ind. Reserv.** Blackfeet have long tradition as fierce warriors & hunters. They were among 1st to adopt constitution for tribal self-gov. When U.S. acquired part of their lands for Glacier Nat. Pk., the money was invested in livestock & irrigation. Some receive royalties from oil wells. **448.** J. with US89 (see) & the 2 routes are united to **BROWNING, 452. 464. KIOWA,** or Browning J. Here US89 runs (N) along E. side of Glacier Nat. Pk. (see US89).

### Sec. 2: KIOWA to IDAHO LINE. 226.

US2 winds S. from Browning J. (Kiowa), **0.,** along E. edge of **GLACIER NAT. PK.** At **4.** is summit of **LOOKING GLASS HILL. 8.** J. with Two Medicine Rd.

SIDE TRIP: On this oiled Rd. (L) 3m along **Lower Two Medicine L.** is Pk. boundary. At 4m is **Entrance Checking Sta.** At 5.5m is **Trick Falls,** a waterfall with an outlet under lip of the main stream. At 7m **Two Medicine Chalets** (resort.boat.pack trips). **Rising Wolf Mt.** (9,505′) looms (W). Horseback & hik. trls. lead to scenic retreats.

**12. GLACIER PK. STA.** From June to Sept. thousands of visitors stop at this RR. pt.; in winter the village holes up under covering of snow. **Hotel** is major showplace. At **23.** is **SUMMIT** (5,212′), Marias Pass Way Sta. on Continental Divide. Here is E. boundary of **Flathead Nat. For.** (hqs.Kalispell). It is 2nd largest for. in U.S. (2,608,827 as.). At **69.** is **BELTON,** W. entrance to Glacier Nat. Pk. (O.yr.-round). Here is J. with Going-To-The-Sun Hy. (see Glacier Nat. Pk. & US89). **76. GORHAM** (Ranger Sta.). S. of here is **Hungry Horse Reclamation Project** (begun in 1948) & **S. Fork Wilderness Area** (pack trips from Gorham). At **94.** is J. (L) with oiled Rd. along **Flathead L.** (see US93). **102. KALISPELL,** prosperous town with broad Sts. & lovely pks. It is center of lumbering, agric. & recr. reg. (dude ranches, L. resorts & campgrounds). Here is J. with US93 (see). US2 winds (W) along several Ls.: **Foy, Smith, Little Bitterroot, McGregor, Thompson, Crystal** & **Loon.** At **160.** is **RAVEN RANGER STA.** in Kootenai Nat. For. (hqs. Libby). At **191.** is **LIBBY,** colorful sawmill town & supply pt. for surrounding logging camps. Lumberjacks give considerable life to the town, especially on paydays. **202. KOOTENAI FALLS,** series of cascades (For. Serv. campground). **209. TROY,** outfitting pt. for miners going into **Cabinet Mts.** (L). There are several silver mines in vic. (Mountain Time changes here to Pacific Time.) At **226.** Hy. crosses **IDAHO LINE.**

## US 10—MONTANA

**MONT.-N.D. LINE** (2m from Beach, N.D.) **(W) to MONT.-IDAHO LINE** (14m from Kellogg, Idaho). **736. US10**

Via: Glendive, Miles City, Billings, Bozeman, Three Forks, Butte, Garrison, Missoula. Rd. hard-surfaced. N.P. RR. parallels route throughout; Milwaukee RR. bet. Terry & Forsyth & bet. Bozeman & Idaho Line. Northwest Airlines stops at major cities. Accoms.: In larger towns; dude ranches, resorts, & camp sites along route.

US10 is divided bet. Three Forks & Garrison, US10S going via Butte (see US10) & US10N through Helena (see US10N).

US 10 passes through Mont.'s broad farm & ranch land, its mining belt, & its Rocky Mts. Much of route traverses hist. U.S. gov. land grant which gave the N.P. RR. every alternate sec. along its line, a total of 20 million as.

### Sec. 1: N.D. LINE to BILLINGS. 268.

**10. WIBAUX,** old cattle town. An Easterner known here as "Four Eyes" & named Theo. Roosevelt was frequent visitor when he operated his Maltese Ranch near Medora (see N.D.). Town's 1st sidewalk was made of cartridge shells. **39. GLENDIVE,** RR. town on Yellowstone R. Before arrival of N.P. RR. in 1881, a liquor spot known as Glenn's Dive was rendezvous for trappers & hunters. Old-timers

insist that it was from the saloon that town got its name. Major annual events are Rodeo (July 4) & E. Mont. Exposition (Labor Day). Here is J. with graded Rd. leading (L) 2m to **Maco Sico Pk.** It bears Ind. name for bad lands & comprises 56,000 as. of fantastically eroded formations.
At Glendive is J. with St.18.

SIDE TRIP: On this Rd. (L) hy. traverses sparsely-sett. E.-central Mont. At 23m is **Lindsay.** At 49m **Circle,** well known cattlemen's town. **Circle Home Ranch** still operates here. At 83m is **camp site** (pic.facils.rest rms.). N. of here is an arm of **Ft. Peck Reservoir.** This is largely sheep-raising country. At 115m is **Jordan,** trade center of the vast reg. 167m **Mosby** on Musselshell R. At 174m is J. with gravel Rd.

On this Rd. (L) 4m is **Cat Cr. Oil Field.** Since the discovery of oil here (1920), field has become a maze of wells & pumping plants.

At 190m is **Winnett,** with oil refinery & tremendous storage tanks.

**154. ROSEBUD.** J. with St.45.

SIDE TRIP: On this Rd. (L) 54m is **Tongue R. Ind. Reserv.** This is home of 1,560 Cheyenne. Reserv. was est. in 1884 & covers 442,840 as., half of which is tribal land. Much of it is leased to white farmers. The Cheyenne live in tents during summer. At 57m is **Lame Deer,** agency hqs. (See US212).

**192. HYSHAM.** Hy. passes through part of Mont. badlands. From eroded washes moss agates & fossils are frequently found. **207. BIG HORN,** a village of hist. background. It is site of trading post built in 1807 by Manuel Lisa. **Ft. Van Buren** was built in 1822 near here (S) by Col. Ashley. Here, too, Gen. Gibbon's troops hurriedly crossed Yellowstone R. in attempt to reinforce Gen. Custer in Battle of Little Big Horn (see US87). **213. CUSTER,** a quiescent ranchers' town. **235. POMPEY'S PILLAR,** named for prominent rock shaft that rises 200′ above banks of Yellowstone R.; it was named for Fr.-Ind. baby of Charbonneau & Sacajawea. When Capt. Clark climbed the pillar in 1806, he gave it the name of the child, Pomp. At **264.** is J. with US87 (see) & the 2 routes are united to **BILLINGS, 268.**

### Sec. 2: BILLINGS to J. with US10N & US10S near THREE FORKS. 174.

Billings is 3rd largest city in Mont. & distributing crossroads for an area larger than most Sts. Two colleges add to culture of community. Sugar beet processing, oil refining, meat packing, & flour milling are major industries. The N.P. RR. cuts through center of city on a bias. In SW. sec. is Mex. village of 50 white adobes. Town was est. in 1882 & named for Fred. Billings, pres. of N.P. RR. Experiments in irrigation resulted in building of sugar beet refinery in 1906; since then more than 600,000 as. surrounding town are irrigated. Int. craft enterprises here include cutting & polishing of semi-precious stones, woodworking, & leathercraft. Town has 3 golf courses, 3 ice rinks, 2 swim. pools, & 2 shooting clubs, in addition to college athletic events. Hqs. of Custer Nat. For. are located here. Annual events incl. Midland Empire Fair (Aug.), Mexican Fiesta (Sept.), & Turkey Shoot (Nov.). PTS. OF INT.: Mont. Ave. & 29th St., **Parmly Billings Mem. Lib.** features Western paintings & publications. **Fred. Billings, Jr., Mem. Wing** houses mus. of pioneer items & excellent gun collection. N. 30th St., Eastern Mont. **St. Normal Sch.,** a unit of Univ. of Mont. Sch. was est. in 1927 & enlarged in 1945 to provide both jr. college & 4-yr. teacher training dept. Main bldg. has 5-story tower & 2 large wings made of Mont. brick trimmed in Travertine, a rock mined at Gardiner (see US89). **Mus.** featuring Mont. flora & fauna exhibits is in this bldg. On Polytechnic Dr., **Rocky Mountain College,** founded in 1908. Until 1946 it was known as Billings Polytechnic Institute. Nine of the bldgs. on campus were designed, built, & equipped by student-operated industries. Students even quarried the native brown sandstone. In self-help plan, students get practical training by mfg. & marketing flour, cereals, publications, machinery, & electrical devices. Most attractive bldg. is **Losekamp Mem. Chapel.** N. Lindbergh Blvd., **Range Rider** of the Yellowstone, a bronze sculpture by Chas. Christadora. It was posed by Wm. S. Hart. At Billings is J. with US87 (see). US10 runs SW. along Yellowstone R. At **14.** is **LAUREL,** town in which life evolves around its RRs., as several branch lines join here. Here also are Js. with US12 & US310 (see) (short-cut to **Yellowstone Nat. Pk. N.** terminus). **41. COLUMBUS.** Here is J. with oiled Rd.

SIDE TRIP: On this Rd. (L) 14m into **Absaroka Range** & town of **Absarokee.** At 25m Rd. enters **Custer Nat. For.** (hqs. Billings). Here is **Beartooth Recr. Area** (resorts, dude ranches, trls., winter sports, trout fishing). Highest mt. in Mont.—Glacier Peak (12,850′)—is (S) of Mystic L.

**72. GREYCLIFF. Cayuse Hills** visible to N., **Crazy Mts.** to NW, & **Beartooth Mts.** (S). **81. BIG TIMBER,** a dude ranch hqs. First woolen mill in St. est. here in 1901. A **fish hatchery** here (O) produces millions of silver salmon & trout to stock crs. in area. Here is J. with St.19.

SIDE TRIP: On this Rd. (R) 22$^{m}$ paralleling Crazy Mts. (L) is **Melville.** In this reg. bucking horses & wild steers are raised for rodeos. Here is J. with For. Serv. Rd. leading (L) 12$^{m}$ to **Gallatin Nat. For.** (hqs. Bozeman). (Campgrounds, hunt., fish.). N. of Melville rd. passes through miles of Fossil Area. Fossilized remains of prehist. mammals, birds, & plants are object of frequent explorations. At 52$^{m}$ is **Harlowtown.** A large flour mill & 22 huge storage tanks dominate town.

**97. SPRINGDALE.** Here is J. with graded Rd. running (R) 1$^{m}$ to **Hunter's Hot Springs.** At **116.** is **LIVINGSTON,** bustling tourist center in summer & hunting hqs. in fall & winter. It is major gateway to Yellowstone Nat. Pk. Its Ranch Hand Rodeo (July 2, 3, 4) is annual wild west show. Nat. Trout Derby (2nd Sun. in Aug.) features $1,000 cash prize for largest trout caught that day. A restrained attempt is made to recapture some of gay night life of town's early yrs. There is **Bucket of Blood Saloon,** where Tex Rickard ran gambling games before turning fight promoter. The elephantine Madam Bulldog, who claimed she could outstrip any woman in her profession, lives only in the memories of a few old men. Calamity Jane once lived here in a pk. now known as the Plaza. At Livingston is J. with US89 (see) which leads (S) to Yellowstone Nat. Pk. & (N) toward Great Falls. US10 follows general route of old **Bozeman Trl.** blazed by John M. Bozeman in 1863 bet. Oregon Trl. & Mont. gold fields. Trl. opened way to W. Mont. settlement, but within a few yrs. Sioux forced its closing. From the hy., **Old Baldy** (8,640′), **Emigrant Peak** (10,950′) & **Mt. Cowan** (11,190′) loom (L). **Gallatin Nat. For.** (hqs. Bozeman) lies to each side of hy. US10 climbs to **Bozeman Pass** (6,003′) at **130.** To (R) lies Bridger range. At **142.** is **BOZEMAN,** prosperous Gallatin Valley center & home of **Mont. St. College.** Its streets are wide & tree-lined, the bldgs. are modern-styled, & gay life is restricted by rigid local ordinances. Peas & string beans are major crops; large cannery is operated here. In the 1890's Bozeman boasted an Opera H. that imported productions from N.Y. In 1893, **Mont. St. Coll.** was est. It has 95-a. campus & is noted for its research & experimentation in agric. Both indoor & outdoor museums have int. colls., latter featuring petrified trees. In **Sunset Hills Cemetery** are graves of John M. Bozeman, who was killed by Inds. in 1867; Henry T. P. Comstock (see Nev.). At Bozeman is J. with US191 to Yellowstone Pk. (see US91). Here also is J. with St.187.

SIDE TRIP: On this Rd. (R) 3$^{m}$ is **site of Ft. Ellis.** Fort was est. in 1867 & provided hqs. for explorations in what became Yellowstone Nat. Pk. At 5$^{m}$ Rd. enters **Bridger Canyon,** route used by Jim Bridger in competition with Bozeman Trl.

**161. MANHATTAN. 166. LOGAN.** At **172.** is **THREE FORKS,** so named for 3 Rs. that unite here. As early as 1810 it was site of lively trading post. At **174. US10** is divided (see US10N).

## Sec. 3: THREE FORKS to GARRISON. 113.

From J. with US10N, US10S runs SW. along Jefferson R. At **10.** is J. with St.1 which leads (S) to Yellowstone Nat. Pk.

SIDE TRIP: On this Rd. (L) 8$^{m}$ to **Harrison.** Rising to the (L) are **Tobacco Root Mts.** At 18$^{m}$ **Norris,** center of corundum mining dist. 28$^{m}$ **McAllister,** with hydroelectric plant on adj. L. 35$^{m}$ **Enis,** typical western village. Here is J. with St.34 which runs (R) through **Virginia City** & **Alder Gulch.** At 35$^{m}$ is J. with graded Rd. running (R) 4$^{m}$ to **Wall Cr. Ranger Sta.** At 69$^{m}$ is **Hutchins** (resort). To (R) is a portion of **Beaverhead Nat. For.** (hqs. Dillon). In this recr. area are moose, elk, deer, bear, & mt. goat. Creeks are noted for good trout. Here also is **Madison Bird Refuge** & largest colony of trumpeter swans in existence. Trls. bisect area. There are several improved For. Serv. campgrounds: **Bear Cr., West Fork, Cliff L. & Canyon.** Rd. now runs (E) along **Hebgen L.,** formed by damming the upper Madison R. At 98$^{m}$ is W. boundary of **Yellowstone Nat. Pk.** (see US191).

At **14.** is J. with improved Rd.

SIDE TRIP: On steep Rd. (R) 3.5$^{m}$ is **Lewis & Clark Cavern St. Pk.** It is 3rd largest cave in U.S. (guide serv.; adm. fee). It was discovered in 1902 by prospector named Don Morrison & closed in 1912 to prevent vandalism of rare formations. Reopened 1927. In 1935 cave & surrounding 2,770 as. became St. Pk. Formations incl. stalactites, stalagmites, helicites, boxwork, cascades, & clusterites.

At **15.** hy. enters **JEFFERSON CANYON,** scenic reg. **33.** J. with graded Rd. leading (R) 4$^{m}$ to **Pipestone Hot Springs** (vapor baths.plunge.accoms.). **38.** J. with St.41.

SIDE TRIP: On this oiled Rd. (L) is reg. famous in Mont. history. Route is modern counterpart of old Vigilantes Trl. to **Alder Gulch,** scene of one of richest placer gold discoveries ever made. At 13m is **Barkell Hot Springs** (plunge & campground). At 24m is **Twin Bridges & St. Orphans' Home.** Route turns (E) here on St.34. At 34m is **Sheridan,** mining & fishing center for **Tobacco Root Mts. & Beaverhead Nat. For. Recr. Area** (L). Ranger Sta. & 2 For. Serv. campgrounds maintained here. At 39m is **Robbers' Roost,** 2-story log bldg. which was hangout for road agents during gold rush. 47m is **Ruby,** old mining camp at mouth of Alder Gulch, from which 10 millions in gold was taken in 1 yr. following discovery in 1863. At 56m is **Virginia City,** oldest inc. town in Mont. & once Terr. Capital (1865). Wm. Boyce Thompson Mus. here has excellent coll. of relics.

At **44.5.** hy. enters **DEER LODGE NAT. FOR.** (hqs. at Butte). **Toll Mt.** looms (L). At **48.** Rd. crosses Continental Divide through **PIPESTONE PASS** (6,418′). The pass & 3,400 as. comprise **Thompson Pk.,** a mt. playground & winter sports area (ski jump, bobsled run, & toboggan slide). Pk. was gift to city of Butte from Wm. Boyce Thompson of N.Y. & Virginia City (see above). At **50.** is For. Serv. Rd. running (L) 21m to ghost town of **Highland City.** It once was larger than Butte.

**63. BUTTE,** largest city in Mont. & world famous mining center. It bears Fr. name for hillock & the butte upon which this city sprawls is popularly known as "the richest hill on earth." The Anaconda—largest copper mining, smelting, refining, & fabrication organization in the world—dominates the city & exerts tremendous influence on Mont. affairs. Company controls all mines in vic. incl.: Original Anaconda, Neversweat, Leonard, Mountain Con., Orphan Girl, Emma, Belmont, High Ore, St. Lawrence, Steward, Tramway, & Anselmo. Each is connected to the other by a series of tunnels. From these mines millions of tons of copper, zinc, manganese, & lead are extracted each yr.—sufficient to fill boxcars of a train 562m long. Only mine open to public is **Leonard** (see below). Butte wears the disfiguring scars of excavations & head-frames, but it no longer is the unkempt, smoke-blanketed town of a few yrs. ago. Smelting operations have been moved to near-by Anaconda (see US10A). Periodic anti-vice campaigns have dressed up Butte's liberal tendencies, but miners & visitors keep the more ornate saloons & gambling houses flourishing. Night club center is fairly well concentrated in Meaderville, at NE. edge of city (see US91). Butte started as a gold camp in 1864. Ten yrs. later a silver boom brought Marcus Daly, who represented the Hearst family & some Salt Lake City bankers. He struck a vein of unparalleled rich copper. Within 20 yrs. he was the most important man in the world copper market. Like most mining centers, Butte has a broad mixture of nationalities. There are more Sullivans in the Butte telephone book than Smiths. Cornish "Cousin Jack" meat pie is a part of local bills of fare. Chinese, Ital., & Finnish districts cling to old-world customs. A major annual event is the Mesopust, Balkan festival prior to Lent. Another annual affair is Miners' Union Day Celebration (June 13). PTS. OF INT.: (1) W. Park St., **Marcus Daly Statue,** last work of Augustus Saint-Gaudens, shows copper king holding his battered hat. (2) W. Park St., **Mont. St. Sch. of Mines,** a unit of Univ. of Mont. The 11½-a. campus overlooks city from terrace on Big Butte. Eight bldgs. of tapestry brick conform to long-range development program. At foot of terrace is huge natural bowl & athletic field. Sch. was opened in 1900 to train mining engineers & research specialists. The new Lib. & Mus. (1940) houses rare & representative mineral colls. (3) N. Mont. St., **Art Center.** (4) W. Broadway & Dak. St., **Pub. Lib.** with coll. of Montaniana. (5) E. Park St. at Noble St., **Leonard Mine** (O). This representative mine has electric hoists capable of moving 24,000 tons of ore each 24 hrs. from depth of 4,000′. (6) E. Park at City limits, **Columbia Gardens** (recr. facils.). At Butte is J. with US91 (see); the 2 routes are united to **69.** At **78.** is J. with US10A (see). At **84.** is **WARMSPRINGS,** home of **St. Hospital for Insane.** (S) of the Institute is **St. Game Farm** (O.), devoted to raising exotic game birds. At **99.** is **DEER LODGE,** colorful Western town with large mansions & tumble-down cabins dating back to 1860's. At **113.** is **GARRISON** & J. with US10N (see); the 2 routes cont. (W) as US10.

## Sec. 4: GARRISON to IDAHO LINE. 181.

US10 follows roughly wagon Rd. built by Lt. John Mullen 1858-62. At **9.** is historic village of **GOLD CREEK.** Francois Findlay, fur trapper, discovered gold flakes in cr. (1862) & when confirmed by Jas. & Granville Stuart, there began stampede of miners into Mont. In 1883 last spike in N.P. tracks was driven here by Henry Villard, RR. pres. At **22.** is **DRUMMOND** & J. with US10A (see). **32. BEARMOUTH,** ore shipping pt. for **Sapphire Mts.** (L) & **Garnet Range** (R). US10 follows Clark Fork (W) through long descent of **Hell Gate Canyon. 40. NIMROD HOT SPRINGS** (plunge.campground). At **68.** is **MILLTOWN;** Here is J. with St.20.

SIDE TRIP: On this Rd. (R) 0.5$^m$ is **Bonner. Bonner Sawmill,** largest in Mont., produces 130 million ft. of lumber yrly. for Anaconda Copper Mining Co. **Margaret Hotel** here is showplace of 1890 architecture.

**75. MISSOULA,** home of **Mont. St. Univ.** It is picturesque city on W. slope of Continental Divide, surrounded by 4 fertile valleys: Flathead, Bitterroot, Blackfoot, & Missoula. Fruit trees thrive because of mild climate & Pacific rains. U.S. For. Serv. Reg. hqs. here. Sugar refining, flour milling, meat packing, dairying, manufacture of finished wood products are basic industries. Area is being developed as vacation playground. Excellent fish. & hunt. for which W. Mont. is famous, augmented by hik. trls., dude ranches, winter sports. Annual event is W. Mont. Fair (Aug.). PTS. OF INT.: E. Univ. Ave., **Mont. St. Univ.,** major unit of Univ. of Mont. On campus is **Mt. Sentinel** which rises 2,000′ above sch. & city. In addition to college of arts & sciences, there are 7 professional schools. In **Natural Science Bldg.** is Edgar S. Paxson's painting of "Custer's Last Stand." School is widely known for its "Frontier & Midland" magazine. **Lib.,** largest in St., has 264,000 vols. Forestry sch. has nursery with 1 million trees & 2,000-a. for. lab. Univ. athletic teams compete in Pac. Coast Conference. W. Pine Sts. bet. Harris & McCormick Sts. group of Cath. Institutions. **St. Michael's Mission** was built in 1863. **St. Patrick's Hospital** (1873), 2 schools, & ch. complete the group.

At Missoula is J. with US93 (see); the 2 routes are united (W) past the sugar refinery to **82.** At **89.** is **FRENCHTOWN,** a Fr.-Canadian community built around its ch. **103. ALBERTON,** at E. edge of **Lolo Nat. For.** (hqs.Missoula). Rd. parallels the **Bitterroot Range** (L). Gorges along route are deep & colorful. **140. ST. REGIS.** Here is boundary bet. Lolo Nat. For. & Cabinet Nat. For. (hqs.Thompson Falls). **162. DEBORGIA.** Here is Savenac For. Nursery, claimed by U.S. For. Serv. to be largest reforestation project in country. **172. SALTESE,** named for Nez Percé chieftain. It is RR. town & supply pt. for miners in area. At **176.** is ghost town of **TAFT.** Lookout Pass Summit is on **IDAHO LINE. 181.**

## US 10N—MONTANA

**J. with US10 & US10S near THREE FORKS to GARRISON (US10). 110. US10N**

Via: Helena. Rd. hard-surfaced. Milwaukee RR. bet. Three Forks & J. near Tolson; N.P. RR. bet. Tolson J. & Garrison. Accoms.: In Helena; camps along route.

US10N is popular route & Alt. for US10S through capital of Mont. & over Continental Divide through McDonald Pass. From this Rd. are side routes to recr. & wilderness areas. From a pt. 2$^m$ (W) of Three Forks where US10 divides into N. & S. routes, US10N branches N. at **0.** into the broad valley of the Upper Mo. R. At **22.** is **TOSTON,** center of irrigated area. Here is J. with gravel Rd. leading (L) 8$^m$ to ghost town of **Parker.** At 13$^m$ is **Radersburg,** a revived mining camp with gold & silver lodes. **33. TOWNSEND.** To the (R) is rugged skyline of the Big Belt Mts., noted hunt. & fish. reg. The **Helena Nat. For.** (hqs. Helena) maintains fire guard Rds. in the area. To the (L) is **Deer Lodge Nat. For.** (hqs. Butte). At Townsend is J. with Confed. Gulch Rd.

SIDE TRIP: On this dirt Rd. (R) 23$^m$ is old **Diamond City.** Here at mouth of **Confed. Gulch** is relic of town that once had 10,000 gold-crazy inhabitants. One of richest placer diggings in America was discovered by novice miner. Called Mont. Bar, single pans yielded $1000. The gulch produced about 17 millions in gold before it was deserted.

**65. EAST HELENA,** dominated by high smelter smokestack. Zinc, lead, gold, & silver ores are shipped here from long distances for reduction in huge smelter (O. inquire at office).

**68. HELENA,** capital of Mont. & scene of historic Last Chance Gulch gold rush. The Capitol, with **Mts. Helena & Ascension** as backdrops, majestically overlooks the expanding city. **Last Chance Gulch** (now Main St.) still has many of the ornamental, slightly-sagging old mining camp bldgs. mixed with modern, streamlined ones. Little trace is left of the series of earthquakes that rocked the city in 1935 to cause millions of dollars damage. While Helena talks politics & patronizes its St. & Fed. office workers, it is an important trade & distributing center. Mining, cattle raising, farming, & power transmission operations make up for its lack of manu-

facturing. It is home of Carroll College, only Cath. men's college in Mont. Recr. areas are being developed in surrounding Helena Nat. For. In 1864, 4 discouraged prospectors wandered into the gulch & decided to take one last chance of finding "colors." They struck it rich. Last Chance Gulch was a by-word throughout the W. Within 3 yrs. Helena had 45 grocery stores, 5 banks, & 14 saloons. The town was inc. in 1881 & by 1888 claimed 50 millionaires. Florid & fantastic mansions were built by newly-rich. Major annual event is Vigilante Parade (May).
PTS. OF INT.: 6th Ave. bet. S. Mont. & Roberts Sts., **St. Capitol** (1899; 2 wings added 1911). Dominant feature is copper-covered dome, topped by reprod. of Statue of Liberty. Major painting is Chas. M. Russell's "Lewis and Clark Meeting the Indians." Other panels by Chas. A. Pedretti & E.S. Paxson. In E. wing is **St. Hist. Lib. & Mus.** Benton Ave. bet. Leslie & Peosta Sts., **Carroll College,** often confused by strangers with the Capitol because of its large buildings on Capitol Hill. College was founded in 1909 in presence of Bishop John P. Carroll & Pres. Wm. Howard Taft. Main bldg. on 50-a. campus is 5-story structure of native red porphyry trimmed in gray granite. The **convent of Sisters of St. Dominic** & observatory are also on campus. College has large lib., gym, athletic field, & science labs. Warren St. & E. Lawrence, **St. Helena Cath. Cathedral,** modeled after Cologne Cath. in Germany. Twin spires rise 218'. Park Ave. & Lawrence, **Helena Publ'c Lib.,** housed in converted church. Neill Ave. & Park Ave., **Algeria Shrine Temple** is of unique design with a high, slender minaret & large auditorium used for public entertainments. At Helena is J. with US91 (see).

**71. BROADWATER RESORT.** At **75.** is J. with gravel Rd. leading (L) 1$^{m}$ to **Rimini Recr. Area.** It is in **Helena Nat. For.** At 3$^{m}$ is **For. Serv. campground.** At 7$^{m}$ is village of **Rimini,** an old mining camp. **80.** hy. crosses **CONTINENTAL DIVIDE** at McDonald Pass (6,323'). A campground is maintained (L). On W. slope is ski run (R). **89. ELLISTON.** A lime quarry & mill are operated here. At **110.** is **GARRISON** & J. with US10S (see US10); the 2 routes unite to form US10 (see).

## US 10A—MONTANA

**J. with US10S** (7$^{m}$ W. of Butte, Mont.) **(NW) to MONT.-IDAHO LINE** (26$^{m}$ from Sandpoint, Idaho.). **281. US10A**

Via: Anaconda & Philipsburg. Rd. hard-surfaced. Butte, Anaconda, & Pac. RR. bet. Butte & Anaconda; N.P. RR. bet. Philipsburg & Drummond. Bus lines throughout. Accoms.: In above towns.

### Sec. 1: J. with US10S to DRUMMOND. 75.

US10A is alt. route bet. Butte & Drummond, & bet. Missoula & Idaho Line.
At **0.** hy. traverses 1st pavement in Mont. (1922). At **7.** is J. with oiled Rd. running (R) 2$^{m}$ to **Evans House** (O). It was built in 1870 & has pioneer furnishing. **10. ANACONDA,** mile high industrial city built around country's largest copper smelter. The 585' stack, larger than Washington Mon., is impressive landmark day or night. Town was platted by Marcus Daly in 1883 & developed by Anaconda Mining Co. At first it was known as Copperopolis. Sports play an important part in the life here. Major annual event is Winter Sports Carnival which features ski jumping, hockey, bob-sledding, & skating. Near-by **Anaconda-Pittler Wilderness Area,** comprising parts of 3 Nat. Fors. is popular in summer. There are also several pks., Ls., resorts, & dude ranches near city. PTS. OF INT.: E. 4th St., **Washoe Smelter** (O.wks.). Here the ore from Butte mines is smelted to produce copper, zinc, gold, silver, arsenic, & sulphuric acid. Main St. & Park Ave., **Mont. Hotel,** showplace built by Marcus Daly has ornate old-style bar. Main & 4th Sts., **Hearst Free Lib.**

At **19.** is **BOUNDARY** of portion of **Deer Lodge Nat. For.** (hqs. at Butte). **25. GOLD COIN MINE. 27. GEORGETOWN,** with L. & fish hatchery. **40. PHILIPSBURG,** silver & manganese mining center. Hope Mill here was 1st silver mill in Mont. & once was used as ft. for protection against Inds. **59. HALL.** At **75.** is J. with US10 at **DRUMMOND** (see US10).

### Sec. 2: From DRUMMOND to J. with US10 (7$^{m}$ W. of Missoula). 61. (see US10 for this Sec.).

### Sec. 3: From J. with US10 (7$^{m}$ W. of Missoula) to IDAHO LINE. 145.

Via: Ravalli, Plains, Thompson Falls. Rd. hard-surfaced. N.P. RR. parallels route. Accoms.: In above towns; camps along route.

US10A is an Alt. route bet. Missoula & Spokane. It follows Clark Fork of Columbia R. & passes through beautiful Cabinet Mt. reg. **0.** hy. branches N. off US10 at J. with US93. US10A & US93 are united to **RAVALLI, 28.** (see US93). Here US10A runs (W) along S. boundary of **Nat. Bison Range.** Herds of buffalo roam within 10,000-a. fenced area (guided tours Sat. & Sun.). Hy. passes through S. portion of **Flathead Ind. Reserv.** (see US93). **49. PERMA.** Here is J. with gravel Rd.

SIDE TRIP: On this Rd. (L) 10m is **Camas Prairie.** It is scene of annual Ind. Bitterroot & Camas Feasts (Spring). Inds. pitch tepees here in summer for ceremonial dances. At 22m is **Hot Springs** (accoms., bath. & fish facils.).

At **58.** is W. boundary of Flathead Ind. Reserv. **62. PARADISE,** orig. named Pair o' Dice for casino here. (Time change, from Mt. S.T. to Pacif. S.T.). **Cabinet Mts.** (R) & Coeur d'Alenes (L) parallel hy. At **68.** is **PLAINS,** village in area known as **Wild Horse Plains.** At **75.** is SW. boundary of **Cabinet Nat. For.** (hqs. at Thompson Falls). **94. THOMPSON FALLS,** pleasantly forested town built at site selected by David Thompson for his home in 1809. Thompson was 1st white man to explore Columbia R. from source to mouth. His **Salish House Site** is marked by Mon. Original falls have been dammed to produce hydroelectric power. **107. WHITE PINE.** At **145.** hy. crosses **IDAHO LINE.**

## US 12—MONTANA

**MONT.-N.D. LINE** (33m from Bowman, N.D.) **(W) to MONT.-WYO. LINE** (at Yellowstone Nat. Pk.) **374. US12**

Via: Baker, Miles City, Billings, Laurel, Red Lodge, Cooke. Rd. hard-surfaced. Milwaukee RR. bet. N.D. Line & Miles City; N.P. RR. bet. Miles City & Red Lodge. Bus lines throughout. Accoms.: In larger towns; dude ranches, tourist camps, & mt. resorts along route.

US12 traverses level E. Mont. to Red Lodge, then suddenly climbs along St.'s highest mts. to NE entrance of Yellowstone Nat. Pk. (W. terminus of hy.).

### Sec. 1: MONT.-N.D. LINE to LAUREL. 257.

At **0.** hy. enters Mont. 6m W. of Marmarth, N.D. Underlying this reg. are vast undeveloped deposits of lignite coal. Some is mined for local use. **13. BAKER,** center of natural gas field. In this area are specimens of petrified trees; exhibit on Cth. grounds. (S) of Baker are some of famous ranch spreads of Old West, incl. **101, Mill Iron, & Hash Knife. 26. PLEVNA,** RR. town colonized by Russian workers. At **92.** is J. with US10 near **Miles City** (see US10). From this pt. US10 & US12 are united to **LAUREL, 257.** (see US10).

### Sec. 2: LAUREL to COOKE. NE. ENTRANCE, YELLOWSTONE NAT. PK. 117.

US12 & US310 run (S) from Laurel, crossing Yellowstone R. at **0.5.** Here is Riverside Pk. (pic. facils.). At **9.** is **SILESIA,** with springs of siliceous water. **12. ROCKVALE.** US12 turns (W) into lofty Beartooth Mts. At **14.** is **MONT. AQUA HOT SPRINGS** (plunge & accoms.). **23. BOYD,** a Finnish community. **45. RED LODGE,** mile-high mining city & hqs. for numerous scientific expeditions. Paleontological explorations have uncovered skeletons of prehist. mammals & also human remains that support theory of early Asiatic migration. Specimens of frozen grasshoppers from **Grasshopper Glacier** (see below) are exhibited at "Carbon County News." Mun. tourist camp of Scand. architecture at S. edge of town. The **"See 'Em Alive" Zoo** near-by incl. animals, birds, & fish native to reg. (adm. fee). **47.** J. with graded Rd.

SIDE TRIP: On this Rd. (R) 1.5m is **Rock Springs Ranger Sta.** It is at E. boundary of **Custer Nat. For.** (hqs. Billings). At 3m is **Orthopedic Summer Camp for Children,** near Wild Bill L. At 4m is **Basin Campsite** (pic.facils.).

**50. PACKSADDLE GREENOUGH RANCH,** from which pack trips are conducted into Beartooth Mts. It is home of "Riding Greenoughs" of rodeo & trick riding fame. Here is E. boundary of **Beartooth Recr. Area** (Custer Nat. For.). To (L) is **Beartooth Geological Research Camp** at base of Mt. Maurice. Along hy. are several U.S. For. Serv. campgrounds: **SHERIDAN, 51.; RATINE, 53.; MILES, 54.; LIONS, 55.** At **56.** is **Richel Lodge** (accoms. & saddle horses). Pack trls. lead into **Beartooth Wilderness Area** (R). **Silver Run Peak** (12,610'), 2nd. highest mt. in Mont., looms (NW). **57. PARKSIDE CAMPGROUND. 59. TIN CAMP CAMPGROUND.** US12 over Beartooth range was built in 1930's at cost of $2,500,000.

First of a series of hairpin curves is **PRIMAL SWITCHBACK, 60.** (7,895′). At **63.** is **DEADWOOD SWITCHBACK** (8,625′) & at **66.** is **MAE WEST CURVE** (9,285′). **Granite Peak,** highest pt. in Mont. (12,850′), is (NW). Several glaciers can be seen in that direction. Near hy., is **Chrome Mt.,** so named because of its deposits & mines. At **68.** hy. dips into Wyo. **77. SUMMIT** (10,995′). At **78.** (R) is **FROZEN L.** At **82.** is **LONG L.** & For. Serv. campground. **83. LITTLE BEAR L. 84. ISLAND L.** & campground. **87. BEARTOOTH L.,** noted for fine trout fishing. On **Beartooth Butte** overlooking L. is sharp landmark known as **The Bear's Tooth,** for which the mt. range was named. At **89.** is **INSPIRATION PT.** (parking area). Hy. follows Clark Fork & recrosses **MONT. LINE** at **105. 108. SODA BUTTE CAMPGROUND. 109. COOKE,** colorful mining & tourist town. It was a booming gold camp when Chief Joseph & Nez Percé Inds. burned mills in 1877. Old cabins, saloons, & mine properties still stand behind brightly painted tourist shops. Here are several mt. trls. (horses & guides avail.).

SIDE TRIP: On trl. (R) 14m through Daisy Pass is **Grasshopper Glacier.** On face of glacier are black bands of frozen grasshoppers 60′ deep. When the ice melts during summer, hikers can get their bearings by smell.

**112. SILVER GATE,** a tourist center. At **114.** is official **NE ENTRANCE OF YELLOWSTONE NAT. PK.** From pk. boundary, hy. crosses **WYO. LINE** at **117.**

## US 87—MONTANA

**MONT.-WYO. LINE** (30m from Sheridan, Wyo.) **(NW) to HAVRE** (on US2) **451. US87**

Via: Hardin, Billings, Roundup, Lewistown, Great Falls, Fort Benton. Rd. hard-surfaced. C.B. & Q. RR. bet. Wyo. Line & Billings; Gt.N. RR. bet. Lewistown & Havre. Bus lines throughout. Accoms.: In larger towns.

### Sec. 1: MONT.-WYO. LINE to GREAT FALLS. 339.

US87 traverses cent. Mont. in zigzag course through Ind. reservs., cattle ranges, & wheatlands. It is known as the Custer Battlefield Hy.

At **0.** hy. enters Mont. This is also S. boundary of **Crow Ind. Reserv.** which covers 3,700 sq. miles. In this area are 2,488 Inds., many of whom raise livestock, alfalfa, & sugar beets. They live in unpainted houses for most part. During summer many move into tepees along shaded creeks. The Crow are native to this reg. & have kept alive their ceremonial dances & distinctive beadwork. They take particular pride in their horsemanship, with many following the cross-country rodeo circuits. **10. WYOLA,** cattle shipping pt. Hy. follows **Little Big Horn R.** bet. **Wolf Mts.** (R) & foothills of **Big Horn Mts.** (L). At **38.** is **GARRYOWEN,** named for the Irish battle song of Custer's 7th Cavalry. Here is **U.S. Dept of Agric. Experiment Range Revegetation Plot.** At **42.** is J. with gravel Rd.

SIDE TRIP: On this Rd. (R) 1m is **Custer Battlefield Nat. Cemetery.** Here on afternoon of June 25, 1876, occurred so-called Battle of Little Big Horn in which Gen. Geo. A. Custer & 265 cavalrymen were killed by Sioux & Cheyenne warriors. Names of soldiers are listed on sandstone mon. Marble slabs mark spots where the men are believed to have fallen. Also buried in this mile-sq. cemetery are men from Fts. Keogh, Smith, Phil Kearny, Abraham Lincoln, & Custer.

**43. CROW AGENCY,** adm. hqs. of reserv. It has trading post with Ind.-made crafts. Crow Agency Fair (Aug.) has Ind. horse races, trick riding, & dancing.

**56. HARDIN,** hqs. of huge Tom Campbell wheat ranch. The 45,000-a. tract produces the biggest yield of any 1 farm in U.S. Campbell started with 7,000 as. of land leased from Inds. & 2 million dollars lent by J.P. Morgan during World War I. It is completely mechanized, requiring only 14 man-minutes of labor per bushel of wheat. At Hardin is **Big Horn County Lib.** & **Mus.** which exhibits mementos of Gen. Custer. Here is J. with oiled Rd.

SIDE TRIP: On this Rd. (L) 23m is **St. Xavier.** This mission was founded by Father Prando in 1887 & Ursuline Sisters started the sch. It is popular meeting place for Inds. Rd. (graded) cont. to **Site of Fort C.F. Smith,** 38m. Only ruins remain of ft. est. in 1866 to protect travelers on Bozeman Trl. It was abandoned 2 yrs. later when the Sioux, under Red Cloud, made it uninhabitable.

At **92.** is J. with gravel Rd.

SIDE TRIP: On this Rd. (L) is **Pryor,** subagency. Here was home of famous Chief Plenty Coups, subject of Frank Bird Linderman's "American: Life Story of a Great Indian." At

35$^{m}$ is **Will James Ranch,** home of author-illustrator of "Smoky," "Lone Cowboy," & other books with Western settings.

**96.** (R) is **INSCRIPTION CAVE,** covered with hieroglyphics of uncertain origin. At **104.** is J. with US10 at **BILLINGS** (see US10). The 2 routes are united to **107.** US87 cont. N. through **Bull Mts.,** a stubby range with sandstone outcroppings & yellow pine trees. Good grouse & big game hunting (R). **151. KLEIN,** coal-mining community. At **201.** is J. with St.18 (see). US87 turns (W). At **215.** is J. with dirt Rd. leading (R) to a series of ghost towns in **Judith Mts.** At 6$^{m}$ is **Giltedge;** near here is **site of Ft. Maginnis,** est. on ranch of Granville Stuart in 1880. Mines in this vic. produced 18 millions in gold. At **232.** is **LEWISTOWN,** trade & distributing center of Judith Basin. It is well-planned & attractive town. Agric., mining, & oil activity combine to provide prosperity. To (S) loom the **Big Snowy Mts.** At **257.** is **HOBSON;** here is J. with gravel Rd.

SIDE TRIP: On this Rd. (L) 25$^{m}$ are **Yogo Sapphire Mines.** These mines, together with others in Siam & Australia, provide bulk of world's sapphire output. It is Brit. owned.

**261. MOCCASIN,** named for Mt. range. Here is hqs. for **Mont. St. College Agric. Experiment Sta.,** central branch (see US10). **313.** J. with US89 (see). From this pt. the 2 hys. unite to **GREAT FALLS, 339.** (see US91).

### Sec. 2: GREAT FALLS to HAVRE. 112.

US87 runs (NE) through Mo. R. valley to **FORT BENTON, 41.** This hist. town has preserved much flavor of the days when it was the head of navigation on the Mo. R. Some of older bldgs. are still furnished in 1870 style. Part of old trading post & blockh. are standing. **52. LOMA. Ft. Piegan** was est. here in 1831 but was destroyed by Inds. At **79.** is **BIG SANDY,** old cowtown popularized in "Chip of the Flying U" & other novels by B.M. Bower. **90. BOX ELDER.** Here is J. with gravel Rd.

SIDE TRIP: On this Rd. (R) 14$^{m}$ is **Rocky Boy Ind. Reserv.** agency. This int. reserv. in Bearpaw Mts. is home of 878 Cree & Chippewa Inds. They operate flour mill & sawmill, raise livestock & carry on profitable beadwork business. Tribal leader who brought the wandering bands here from Canada was Stone Child. White settlers promptly named the group "Rocky Boy's Renegades."

**100. LAREDO.** At **107.** is J. with dirt Rd.

SIDE TRIP: On this Rd. (R) 1$^{m}$ is **Ft. Assiniboine.** Some of bldgs. are still standing. The bricks were made on the spot. Ft. was built in 1879 as cavalry outpost to guard against Sioux under Sitting Bull.

At **112.** is **HAVRE** & J. with US2 (see).

## US 89—MONTANA

**MONT.-WYO. LINE in YELLOWSTONE NAT. PK.** (2$^{m}$ from Mammoth Hot Springs, Wyo.) **(N) to CANADIAN BORDER** (14$^{m}$ from Waterton, B. C.) **411. US89**

Via: Gardiner, Livingston, White Sulphur Springs, Great Falls, & Browning. Rd. hard-surfaced. N.P. RR. bet. Gardiner & Livingston; Milwaukee RR. bet. Great Falls & Choteau. Bus lines throughout. Accoms.: In larger towns; lodges, dude ranches, campgrounds along route.

US89 through Mont. is called Yellowstone-Glacier Beeline. It parallels the E. slope of the Rockies & passes through scenic fors. & mts.

### Sec. 1: WYO. LINE to LIVINGSTON. 60.

At **0.** hy. crosses **WYO. LINE.** At **3.** is **N. BOUNDARY OF YELLOWSTONE NAT. PK.,** marked by **Roosevelt Arch.** Rd. enters **Gallatin Nat. For.** here (hqs. Bozeman). **4. GARDINER,** yr.-round entrance to pk. (Info. at Ranger Sta.). Gardiner reg. is noted for good elk hunting; average of 3,000 elk killed here each fall. **11. CORWIN HOT SPRINGS,** (plunge, golf course, accoms.). Rd. follows **Yankee Jim Canyon** to boundary of Gallatin Nat. For. **19. Emigrant Peak** (10,960′) (R). At **35.** is J. with gravel Rd. leading (R) 1.5$^{m}$ to **Chico Hot Springs,** (plunge, pack trips, accoms.) There are several dude ranches in vic.; also good fish. & hunt. in **Absaroka range.** At **60.** is J. with US10 at **LIVINGSTON** (see US10).

### Sec. 2: LIVINGSTON to GREAT FALLS. 173.

US89 runs (N) from Livingston, following old Jim Bridger trl. **51. RINGLING,** named for circus family's horse ranches here. **71. WHITE SULPHUR SPRINGS** (summer resort). Excellent fish. & hunt. in **Big Belt Mts.** (L) & **Castle Mts.** (R). At **90.** is **S. BOUNDARY** of portion of **Lewis & Clark Nat. For.** (hqs. Great Falls). **105. PORPHY PK.** (L) & ski run. **108. KING'S HILL** (7,300′), a pass through Little Belts. Here is For. Serv. campground. **113. NEIHART,** mining center; silver, lead, gold, & zinc mined in this reg. Amethysts found here. At **120.** is **BELT CREEK RANGER STA. & ASPEN CAMPGROUNDS. 126. MONARCH,** recr. & mining center. **Block P** is major mine. There are several For. Serv. Rds. to campgrounds & waterfalls. At **130.** is **N. BOUNDARY OF LEWIS & CLARK NAT. FOR.** At **147.** is J. with US87 (see). The 2 routes unite to **GREAT FALLS, 173.** & J. with US91 (see).

### Sec. 3: GREAT FALLS to CANADIAN BORDER. 178.

US89 & US91 are joined to **VAUGHN, 11.** US89 turns (W) along Sun R. **52. CHOTEAU,** trade center on slope of Rockies. The **Continental Divide** looms (L). Rd. roughly parallels what historians call the Old North Trail. At **97.** is **S. BOUNDARY OF BLACKFEET IND. RESERV.** (see US2). Blackfeet operate irrigated lands & graze sheep in this area. At **123.** is J. with US2 (see); the 2 routes are united through **BROWNING, 127.** At **139.** is **KIOWA** & J. with US2 (see). Here US89 runs (N) along E. side of **Waterton-Glacier Internat. Peace Pk. 159. ST. MARY,** a village on boundary of Glacier Nat. Pk. Here is J. with Going-To-The-Sun Hy. (see Glacier Nat. Pk.). US89 parallels **Lower St. Mary L.** to **BABB.** Here is J. with Many Glacier Hotel Rd. into the Pk.

SIDE TRIP: On this Rd. (L) 7m along Swiftwater Cr. is **Entrance Sta.** Rd. follows N. shore of **L. Sherburne.** At 13m is **Many Glacier Hotel,** facing **Swiftcurrent L.** From here are numerous horseback & hik. trls.

At **172.** is J. with Chief Mt. Internat. Hy. (St.17 & Alberta 6).

SIDE TRIP: On this Rd. (L) is Chief Mt. (9,056′) at boundary of pk. At 14m is Canadian Border & entrance to Waterton Lakes Nat. Pk.

At **178.** is **PORT OF PIEGAN,** U.S. customs sta. at **CANADIAN BORDER.** Here is N. boundary of Blackfeet Ind. Reserv., the St. of Mont. & the U.S.

## US 91—MONTANA

**MONT.-IDAHO LINE** (at Monida, Mont.) **(N) to CANADIAN BORDER** (at Coutts, Alberta) **412. US91.**

Via: Dillon, Butte, Helena, Great Falls, Shelby, Sweetgrass. Rd. hard-surfaced. Oregon Short Line (U.P.) RR. bet. Idaho line & Butte; Gt. N. RR. bet. Butte & Sweetgrass. Bus lines throughout. Western Airlines to major cities. Accoms.: In larger towns.

US91 is a popular route that roughly parallels E. slope of Rocky Mts. Except for mountainous Butte-Helena reg., hy. traverses broad valleys & gently rolling foothills. Along this route are numerous hist. pts. & recr. areas.

### Sec. 1: IDAHO LINE to BUTTE. 130.

At **0.** is **MONIDA PASS** (6,823′) on the Continental Divide which forms boundary bet. Mont. & Idaho. Here is village of **Monida,** bearing contracted names of the 2 Sts. To the (L) rise **Beaverhead Mts.** & to (R) the **Centennials,** both noted for good fishing. **15. LIMA.** Hy. sweeps through Red Rock Valley, prosperous ranching country. **Beaverhead Nat. For.** (hqs. Dillon) is off Hy. (L). **42. ARMSTEAD.** Near here Lewis & Clark expedition witnessed dramatic meeting of their Ind. girl guide, Sacajawea, & Cameahwait, her brother. Upon entering the reg. in 1805, explorers sought out chief of Shoshone. He turned out to be Cameahwait, from whom Sacajawea had been separated since childhood abduction by enemy tribes. **56. MON.** to Lewis & Clark (L). **64. DILLON,** major wool-shipping pt. in Mont. & home of **Mont. St. Normal College.** The town was started when tracks of 1st RR. into Mont. were laid to this pt. The narrow gauge Utah & Northern RR. from Ogden reached here in 1880. Soon Dillon replaced near-by Bannack, 1st Capital of Mont., as major town of area. It is hqs. for Beaverhead Nat. For. During shearing season, Dillon is busy wool market. A huge wareh. can handle 3 million lbs. of wool. **St. Normal College** is a unit of Univ. of Mont. & has attractive 14-a. campus at S. edge of town. School opened in 1897 in **Main Hall. Lib.** has 27,000 vols. **Mus.** features Ind. items. At Dillon is J. with gravel Rd.

SIDE TRIP: On this Rd. (L) 13m is **Bannack.** This is Mont's oldest town & 1st capital. Discovery of gold along **Grasshopper Cr.** July 28, 1862, turned loose stampede of miners & adventurers. Soon the town, named for Bannack Inds., had pop. of 1,000; 1st Mont. Terr. legislature met here. Another gold strike in Alder Gulch depopulated Bannack & legislature moved to Virginia City (see US10). Several landmarks still stand, incl. bldgs. used as capitol, jail, & hotel. At 40m is **Elkhorn Hot Springs** (plunge & resort facils.f.& big game hunt.).

At **105.** is **DIVIDE,** cattle-shipping pt. At **115.** hy. crosses **CONTINENTAL DIVIDE** (5,915′) which is merely a hump of grassland here. At **124.** is J. with US10S & the 2 routes are joined to Butte, **130.** (see US10).

## Sec. 2: BUTTE to GREAT FALLS. 159.

From Butte, at **0.,** US91 runs NE. through the **Meaderville** night club sec. of city (see US10) & begins ascent to Continental Divide (6,354′) at **5.** At **15.** is **ELK PK.,** center of a dairy farm area. Here hy. enters **Deer Lodge Nat. For.** (hqs. Butte). **16.5. ELK PK. CAMPGROUND** (pic. facils.). **21. SHAMROCK CAMPGROUND.** At **24.** is J. with For. Serv. Rd.

SIDE TRIP: On this Rd. (L) along **Boulder R.** are 3 pub. campgrounds: Morman, Ladysmith, & Whitehouse. There are sm. gold & silver mines in reg.

At **27. is BASIN,** mining camp & For. Ranger Sta. Here is boundary of Deer Lodge Nat. For. **36. BOULDER,** mining & farming center. Here is J. with gravel Rd. leading (R) 3m to **Boulder Hot Springs** (plunge, resort facils.). At **48.** is **JEFFERSON CITY,** old mining town. **Mt. Washington Mine** here is still operating. **52. ALHAMBRA HOT SPRINGS. 54. CLANCEY.** In 1890's rich silver ores were freighted by wagon trains to Ft. Benton, shipped down Mo. R. to New Orleans, & reshipped to Wales for refining. **66. HELENA,** capital of Mont. & J. with US10N (see). From Helena, US91 runs (N) through **Prickly Pear Valley.** Chain of Ls. (R) are formed by damming the Mo. R. At **72.** is J. with gravel Rd. running (R) 5m to **L. Helena.** At **80.** the **Gates of the Mts.** are visible (R). Here is J. with gravel Rd.

SIDE TRIP: On this Rd. (R) 3m is the **Lewis & Clark Boat Landing** (launches make daily trips). The Gates of the Mts. is a deep gorge where the Mo. R. cuts through the Big Belt Mts. On an I. is **Meriwether Canyon Pic. Grounds.** In 1948, the U.S. For. Serv. dedicated 28,562 as. as the Gates of the Mts. Wild Area to remain in primitive state. Only horseback & hik. trls. traverse the area. Deer, elk, mt. sheep, & black bear inhabit the heavily-forested, rugged reg. that has 5 mts. over 8,000′.

US91 turns NE. past N. end of **Holter L.,** also formed by damming Mo. R. The L. backs up through Ox Bow Bend. At **134.** is **CASCADE** & J. with gravel Rd. leading (L) 17m to ruins of **St. Peter's Mission,** est. here in 1886. At **159.** is **GREAT FALLS** & Js. with US87 (see) & US89 (see).

## Sec. 3: GREAT FALLS to CANADIAN BORDER. 123.

Great Falls, 2nd largest city in Mont., is an industrial, agric., & trans. center. The city lies in bend of the Mo. R. a few miles from the falls for which it was named. Except for the broad valleyland (N), Mt. ranges rim the trade territory. A series of hydroelectric plants operated by Mont. Power Co., has created a variety of industries. The Anaconda Copper Mining Co. has a huge copper & zinc refinery & wire plant here. There are 2 large flour mills with a combined wheat storage capacity of 2 million bu., a meat packing plant, 2 breweries, & an oil refinery. Surrounding irrigated land & grazing country provide important market. "The Mont. Farmer-Stockman," published here, reaches most farm homes in the St. Air transport has been highly developed, with 3 major airlines: Northwest, Western, & Alaska. During World War II it was an important ferrying command base & thousands of aircraft & men passed through the city. Crews for Berlin airlift were given training here. Both Gore Mun. Airport & Great Falls Air Base are busy terminals. The well-planned town was laid out by a visionary Minneapolis man, Paris Gibson, in 1883. He became the 1st mayor; a city pk. & statue honor him. Hqs. of Lewis & Clark Nat. For. is here. Major annual event is the Northern Mont. St. Fair & NW. Internat. Hereford Show (Aug.). The Balkan Christmas Festival is colorful event (Jan. 6).

PTS. OF INT.: (1) 1217 4th Ave. N., **Chas. M. Russell Mem. Studio** (O) exhibits work of cowboy artist. (2) 1st Ave. & 3rd St., **Pub. Lib.** has notable coll. of NW. materials. (3) E. end of 1st Ave., **Mun. Pk.** with swim. pool. (4) 1st Ave. NW. (across bridge), **N. Mont. St. Fair Grounds & "Old Town."** Here is reproduced village of

1890's with barber shop, saddlery, blacksmith shop, general store & saloon. (5) Black Eagle Dist., (across bridge), **Anaconda Reduction Works** comprise electrolytic zinc plant, copper refineries & rod & wire mill (O.10-2). Plant employs 2,000 men. (6) (NE) on River Dr., **Giant Springs,** largest fresh water springs in world with flow of 388 million gals. every 24 hrs. Trout hatchery near-by. US91 from Great Falls is known as Alaskan Internat. Hy. This hy. & US89 unite to **VAUGHN, 11.** Here US89 branches (W) toward **Glacier Nat. Pk.** (see US89). **35. DUTTON,** wheat-shipping & milling pt. At **58.** is J. with gravel Rd.

SIDE TRIP: On this Rd. (L) 12m is **L. Francis,** a trout-stocked reservoir used to provide water for 100,000-a. irrigation district. On banks is village of **Valier,** Belgian settlement. Many native customs are maintained.

At **87.** is **SHELBY** & J. with US2 (see). **103. OILMONT,** oil field center. **Sweetgrass Arch,** a geological formation that embraces 5 natural gas & petroleum fields, has dome here. At near-by **Kervin** (L) 1st gusher was drilled in 1922. From here (N) are **Kervin-Sunburst Oil Fields** (L). **116. SUNBURST,** gusher town. **Sweetgrass Hills** rise (R). Highest pt. is cone-shaped **W. Butte** (7,000′). **123. SWEETGRASS,** quiet village on U.S. side of **CANADIAN BOUNDARY.** Here are custom & immigration offices. Only a sign separates it from Coutts, Alberta.

## US 93—MONTANA

**MONT.-IDAHO LINE** (47m from Salmon, Idaho) **(N) to CANADIAN BORDER** (30m from Elko, B. C.) **288. US93**

Via: Hamilton, Missoula, Kalispell, Eureka. Rd. hard-surfaced. N.P. RR. bet. Darby & Polson; Gt. N. RR. bet. Kalispell & Whitefish. Bus lines throughout. Accoms.: In larger towns.

US93 passes through mt. ranges, valleys, & fors. of the Rockies' W. slope. It is an int. & scenic route.

### Sec. 1: IDAHO LINE to MISSOULA. 94.

At **0.** hy. crosses Mont. Line & Continental Divide through Lost Trail Pass (6,951′). This is S. boundary of **Bitterroot Nat. For.** (hqs. Hamilton). At **9.** is J. with graded Rd.

SIDE TRIP: On this Rd. (R) 19m is **Big Hole Battlefield Nat. Mon.** It marks site of an engagement bet. U.S. troops under Gen. John Gibbon & a Nez Percé band under Chief Joseph in 1877.

**13. SULA.** At **15.** is J. with dirt Rd. running (L) 1m to **Medicine Hot Springs** (accoms. plunge). Hy. leaves **Bitterroot Nat. For.** which cont. to parallel hy. on each side & enters **Bitterroot Valley,** which is noted for its orchards, pastures, & peas. At **44.** is J. with St.38.

SIDE TRIP: On this Rd. (R) 13m into Bitterroot Nat. For. is **Black Bear Campground.** At 25m is **Skalkaho Pass** in Sapphire Range & beyond is wilderness area of Deer Lodge Nat. For. (hqs. Butte).

At **47.** is **HAMILTON,** town developed by Marcus Daly, copper titan & horse racing enthusiast (see Butte). Here is For. Serv. office & U.S. Pub. Health Service Lab. for Rocky Mt. spotted fever. Marcus Daly ranch is a showplace. At **67.** is site of **FT. OWEN,** trading post est. in 1850 to encourage settlement. **St. Mary's Mission,** built in 1867, stands near-by. **75. FLORENCE.** Near it (R) is **Red Rock gold mine** (O). At **84.** is **LOLO** & J. with gravel Rd.

SIDE TRIP: On this Rd. (L) 6m into **Lolo Nat. For.** (hqs. Missoula) to site of **Ft. Fizzle.** A barrier to detain Chief Joseph was built here in 1877. Its failure provided name. At 30m is **Lolo Hot Springs** (plunge, accoms.).

At **94.** is J. with US10 at **MISSOULA** (see US10).

### Sec. 2: MISSOULA to KALISPELL. 120.

From Missoula, US93 & US10 are united (NW) to J. at **7.** with US10 & US10A (see US10A). US93 & US10A run (N) together. At **14.** is **EVARO & S. BOUNDARY OF FLATHEAD IND. RESERV.** which covers 1,403,058 as. There are about 3,630 Inds. of Flathead Confederation of tribes which incl. Salish, Kootenai, & Kalispel. More than ¾ have white blood. Much of land is occupied by whites. The Flathead people are noted for their buckskin & beadwork handicraft. Dried bitterroot & camas are important food items. Ceremonial dances are held during summer.

At **35.** is **RAVALLI,** named for an Italian Jesuit missionary. Here is J. with US10A (see). US93 turns (NE) along the **Nat. Bison Range. 40. ST. IGNATIUS,** a sub-agency. Mission Range of mts. lie to (E) & there are numerous good fishing Ls. in vic. **55. RONAN,** trade center for irrigation district. **67. POLSON,** at S. end of Flathead L. Here is **Flathead Dam & Power Plant,** built at cost of 11 million dollars on tribal-owned lands. A 63-a. pk. faces the L. (boating, swim., golf). Major annual event is Cherry Regatta (Aug.). Here is J. with oiled Rd.

SIDE TRIP: On this Rd. (R) 8m along E. shore of **Flathead L.** is **Station Cr. Fish Hatchery** (O.). Along **Blue Bay** fishermen cast for landlocked salmon. At 17m is **Mont. St. Univ. Biological Experiment Sta. & Summer Lab.** 31m **Big Fork.** Rd. cont. (N) to US2 (see).

US93 runs along W. side of Flathead L. which is stocked with salmon, trout, whitefish, & bass. Av. depth 220′. At **80.** is **BIG ARM,** Ind. village. **90. DAYTON.** Powerboats operate to **Wild Horse Is.** (dude ranch). Hy. crosses N. boundary of Flathead Ind. Reserv. at **100.** At **120.** is J. with US2 at Kalispell (see US2).

### Sec. 3: KALISPELL to CANADIAN BORDER. 74.

US93 runs N. At **13.** is J. with oiled Rd. leading (R) 7m to **Columbia Falls** (see US2). **15. WHITEFISH,** attractive town at S. end of **Whitefish L.** It lies in valley bet. 2 portions of **Flathead Nat. For.** (hqs. Kalispell) & is important lumbering center. A pub. pk. & bath. beach are scene of annual 4th of July celebration. **32.** Hqs. of **STILLWATER ST. FOR. 41. SPRING CR. CAMPGROUND.** Hy. passes through long stretches of Douglas fir, tamarack, & huckleberries. **67. EUREKA,** a Christmas tree shipping center. **74. PORT OF ROOSVILLE,** U.S. customs & immigration sta. Here is **Canadian border.**

## US 191—MONTANA

**MONT.-IDAHO LINE** (55m from Ashton, Idaho) **(N) to BOZEMAN, MONT. 102. US191.**

Via: West Yellowstone, Gallatin Gateway. Rd. hard-surfaced. Milwaukee RR. bet. Gallatin Gateway & Bozeman. Bus lines throughout. Accoms.: In towns & lodges along route.

US191 is an approach Rd. to W. entrance of Yellowstone Nat. Pk. & a connecting route bet. US10 & US20 (see). Known as Gallatin Way, most of hy. in Mont. lies in valley bet. Gallatin & Madison Mts.

At **0.** US20 & US191 cross Mont. Line. Continental Divide crossing is made at **Targhee Pass** (7,078′), named for a Bannack chieftain. Here also is S. boundary of **Gallatin Nat. For.** (hqs. Bozeman). **10. WEST YELLOWSTONE,** popular tourist town at W. entrance to pk. Thousands pass through here each summer, but in winter it is deserted. Here is J. with US20 (see) which runs (W) 10m to Idaho Line. US191 runs (N) along boundary of the pk. Area is heavily forested with lodgepole pine. **13. BAKER'S HOLE CAMPGROUND** (camp. facils.). US191 crosses the pk. boundary & roughly parallels it (N). At **32.** is **GALLATIN RANGER STA.** Hy. follows Gallatin R. & crosses NW. boundary of pk. at **42.** At **44.** is J. with graded Rd. leading (L) 6m to **Taylor Ranger Sta.** & 7m **Wapiti Cr. Campground. 46. CINNAMON CR. RANGER STA. 60. SWAN CR. FOR. SERV. CAMPGROUND. 65. KARST'S CAMP** (accoms. & pack horses). **Spanish Peaks Wild Area** (L) comprises 50,000-as. of wilderness with 20 alpine Ls. Hiking & horseback trls. reach int. pts. **74. SQUAW CR. RANGER STA.** At **78.** is **N. BOUNDARY OF GALLATIN NAT. FOR. 88. GALLATIN GATEWAY,** tourist center. RR. operates a ranch-type hotel here. **97. BOZEMAN HOT SPRINGS** (health & recr. resort). The Night Rodeo (Aug.) is popular annual event. To (W) are vast holdings of **Flying D Ranch.** At **102.** is J. with US10 at **BOZEMAN** (see US10).

## US 212—MONTANA

**MONT.-WYO. LINE** (SE. corner of Mont.) **to MILES CITY. 141. US212**

Via: Alzada, Broadus. Rd. hard-surfaced. Limited Accoms.

US212 passes through open range country that has seen little change in 50 yrs. There are log houses, general stores, hitching posts, & genuine cowhands. From **WYO. LINE** hy. runs diagonally (NW) with hardly any towns along route. At **3.** is **ALZADA,** on Little Mo. R. This quiet village comes to life on Sat. nights when cow pokes take over. During Black Hills gold rush (see S.D.), this place was known as

Stonesville. It was scene of roaring gun battles bet. peace marshals & gang of outlaws who made Lou Stone's saloon their hqs. **38. BOYES. 61. BROADUS,** trade center for vast ranch area along Powder R. which flows through here. At **64.** is J. with St.8.

SIDE TRIP: On this Rd. (L) 20m is **Custer Nat. For.** (hqs. Billings). Here are 2 pub. campgrounds: **Whitetail** & **Holiday Springs.** At 41m is **Ashland,** on Tongue R. which forms E. boundary of **Tongue R. Ind. Reserv.** The Agency is at **Lame Deer,** 62m. Rd. cont. (W) into **Crow Ind. Reserv.** to Crow Agency & J. with US87 (see) at 104m.

**85. COALTOWN.** Hy. winds (N) through rolling country with outcroppings of red banks & buttes. At **141.** is **MILES CITY** & Js. with US10 & US12 (see).

# GLACIER NATIONAL PARK

## GLACIER NATIONAL PARK

Park Hqs. are at Belton (see US2 & Going-to-the-Sun Hy.). Official season is from June 15 to Sept. 15; O. to motorists May 1 to Oct. 15. Accoms.: 3 hotels at Glacier Pk. Sta., Many Glacier & L. McDonald. Chalets at Two Medicine, Cut Bank, Going-to-the-Sun, Granite Pk., Sperry, & Belton. High Mt. Camps at Red Eagle, L. Crossley, L. Goathaunt, & Fifty Mountain. Pub. campgrounds at Sprague Cr., Avalanche Cr., East Glacier, Many Glacier, Two Medicine, Kintla L., Bowman L., Polebridge, Quartz Cr., Logging Cr., Dutch Cr., Fish Cr., Walton Ranger Sta. & Cut Bank. There are several approach routes to the pk. US2 (Theo. Roosevelt Hy.) parallels S. boundary from Kiowa (Browning J.) to Belton (see US2). US89 skirts E. side of pk. from Kiowa J. with US2 to Canadian Border; from US89 are side tours to Many Glacier Hotel area & to Waterton Lakes Nat. Pk. via Chief Mt. Rd. (see US89). US93 is an approach route to W. entrance via Kalispell (see US93). Major route through pk. is Going-to-the-Sun Hy. bet. St. Mary (US89) & Belton (US2) (see Going-to-the-Sun Hy.). Pk. is on main line of Gt. N. RR. Airlines & bus lines make conns. to pk. entrances. Within pk., bus service conn. hotels & chalets, incl. Prince of Wales Hotel (Waterton Lakes Nat. Pk.). Sports: No fish.license necessary (check for seasonal regulations). Streams & Ls. are stocked with rainbow, cutthroat, brook, Dolly Varden, Mackinaw, grayling, pike, whitefish, black-spot. Hiking & horseback trips popular (guides, horses, & equipment avail.). Most glaciers & many Ls. accessible during summer months. No hunt. permitted.

Glacier Nat. Pk., with Canada's Waterton Ls. Nat. Pk., forms the Waterton-Glacier Internat. Peace Pk. Glacier is one of the most picturesque of all U.S. parks. Its 1,537 sq. mile area straddles the Continental Divide, backbone of the Rockies. Within its borders are more than 60 glaciers & 200 lakes. The pk., est. in 1910, is noted for beautiful scenery. Only one hy. (Going-to-the-Sun) crosses the pk., but area is fingered by 1,000m of horseback & hik. trls. Wildlife is plentiful. Mt. goats, Bighorn sheep, moose, elk, grizzly & black bear, deer, & bobcats frequent the area. Caribou are seen less often. Birds incl. ptarmigan, eagle, water ouzel, & osprey. There are 800 species of flowering plants in pk. Floral display at height in early July. Most profuse is beargrass, with showy heads of tiny white lilies. Others incl. blue columbine, carpet pink, heathers, glacier lily, scarlet mimulus, passion flower, shooting star, wild hollyhock, aster, & true forget-me-not.

**GOING-TO-THE-SUN HY. from J. with US89** (at St. Mary, Mont.) **to J. with US2** (at Belton, Mont.). **53.**

Via: St. Mary L., Going-to-the-Sun Chalets, L. McDonald Hotel, Pk. Hqs. Rd. hard-surfaced. Bus service. Accoms. along route. Route & accoms. O. bet. June 15-Oct. 1.

Going-to-the-Sun Hy. is the only Rd. across Glacier Nat. Pk. & was constructed to provide maximum scenic views. It was completed in 1933. It traverses a representative sec. of the pk. & off hy. are many hik. & horseback trls.

At **0.** hy. branches (W) from US89 at **ST. MARY** (see US89). Here is checking sta. At **0.5.** is **ST. MARY'S CHALET** (L). Rd. follows N. shore of beautiful **St. Mary L.** Across the L. peaks rise a mile above water line. High pts. (L. to R.) are: **Divide Mt.** (8,647′), **Red Eagle Mt.** (8,800′), & **Little Chief Mt.** (9,542′). At **7.** is **E. GLACIER CAMPGROUND** (cooking & facils. cabins. trlr.). Launch rides on St. Mary L. are popular. **10. GOING-TO-THE-SUN CHALETS** (L), called Sun Camp locally. This is largest group of chalets in pk. & follows Alpine style of architecture. Ranger naturalists conduct field trips daily & give illustrated lectures each evening. One of the scenic features in immediate area is **Sunrift Gorge,** a fantastic rainbow-tinted water course. From Sun Camp are several trls. which lead (S) to **Red Eagle L. Tent Camp;** to **Gunsight L., Blackfoot Glacier, & Sperry Chalets.** Trls. lead (N) to **Mt. Siyeh** (10,004′) & **Many Glacier Hotel;** to **Grinnell Glacier & Goathaunt Tent Camp.**

Hy. climbs around **Going-to-the-Sun Mt.** (9,594′) & passes through a long tunnel (408′). **18. LOGAN PASS** (6,654′) over Continental Divide. Rangers conduct short field trips from Logan Pass throughout summer months. Surrounding meadow area is known as **Hanging Gardens** because of profuse growth of timberline wildflowers such as glacier lily, heliotrope, gentian, & fringed parnassia. At **24.** is J. with Granite Pk. Trl.

SIDE TRIP: From parking area (R) 2$^{m}$ is trl. to **Granite Pk. Chalet.** This off-the-hy. native stone chalet is starting pt. for many horseback & hik. trips into high mts. Trls. lead (N) to **Iceberg L., Chaney Glacier, Fifty Mt. Tent Camp, Goathaunt Camp, & Waterton Ls. Nat. Pk. hqs.** in Canada. Other trls. parallel hy.

Going-to-the-Sun Hy. twists along a glacial wall with **Heaven's Peak** (8,994′) to (R). Burned over areas resulting from a for. fire in 1936 are noticeable. Hy. passes through tunnel at **27.** into **McDONALD VALLEY.** At **33.** is **AVALANCHE CR. CAMPGROUND** (cooking, shower, laundry, trlr. facils.). Gorge here is home of the water ouzel, a bird that seems to delight in walking under water. Rangers conduct entertainments each evening. **Avalanche L.,** on trl. (L), has soupy water, flavored with glacial debris. **37. LOGAN FALLS** (R). At **39.** is beautiful **L. McDONALD;** snow-capped peaks rise from & reflect in its waters. It seldom freezes. Fly fishing is popular here. **41. L. McDONALD HOTEL,** a large log bldg. overlooking the L. Cabin camp is operated in connection. Near-by is **Sprague Cr. Campground,** a pub. auto pk. & pic. area. From L. McDonald Hotel are trls. to **Sperry Chalets,** as well as to remote areas to (N). At **51.** is **APGAR,** a tourist center at S. end of L. McDonald. Here is J. with North Fork Rd. along W. edge of pk.

SIDE TRIP: On this narrow, unimproved Rd. (R) 1.5$^{m}$ is **Fish Cr. Ranger Sta. & Campground.** At 10$^{m}$ is **Dutch Cr. Campground. Logging Cr. Ranger Sta. & Campground** is at 18$^{m}$. At 22$^{m}$ is **Quartz Campground;** trl. leads (R) to **Quartz L.** At 26$^{m}$ is **Polebridge Ranger Sta.;** here is J. with dirt Rd. Rd. winds (N) to **Lower Kintla L. Campground** (R), a primitive area. At 50$^{m}$ is **Canadian Border** (1$^{m}$ S. of Flathead, B.C.).

At **51.** Going-to-the-Sun hy. widens at **GLACIER PK. HQS. 53. BELTON** & J. with US2 (see).

## US 10—IDAHO

**IDAHO-MONT. LINE** (110$^{m}$ from Missoula, Mont.) **(W) to IDAHO-WASH. LINE** (32$^{m}$ from Spokane, Wash.). **82. US10**

Via: Mullan, Wallace, Kellogg, Cataldo, Fourth of July Canyon, Coeur d'Alene, Post Falls. Paralleled by RRs. & bus lines. Accoms. of various kinds.

Coming into Idaho over **LOOKOUT PASS SUMMIT,** US10 traverses terrain, not notable for beauty, but full of hist. memories & one of richest areas of its size in the world—the great Coeur d'Alene mining area. Hy. passes through towns made nationally known by labor conflicts of the 1890's & among hills where ravages of tremendous for. fire of 1910 are still visible. **13. WALLACE,** financial & commercial capital of the reg., has no mines itself but is home of most of the wealthiest men & business leaders. Main portion of town is 8 blocks long by 4 wide. Residential dist. clings precariously to the S. hillside, & many of the finest homes are accessible only by long flights of wooden stairs. Cars are kept in garages at foot of hill. Below Wallace, the valley of the Coeur d'Alene R. is like something out of Dante's "Inferno." In the days before measures were taken against stream pollution, the R. overflowed every spring, carrying mine wastes into the bottoms & destroying all vegetation. **25. KELLOGG,** home of Bunker Hill-Sullivan Mine (guides), richest lead-silver mine in the world. Bunker Hill holdings skirt hy. for several miles; surface mine workings, & 2 large smelters. To (W) of Kellogg, the N. fork of the Coeur d'Alene joins the S. fork, & from here on, while the water still has an unwholesome gray color, the valley widens, & signs of devastation are not so apparent. **35. CATALDO MISSION** (restaurant), founded in 1840's by Cath. missionaries. It is int. architecturally, as well as historically, because it was built without a bit of metal. All joists, beams & joints are secured with wooden pegs carved out by Ind. hands at great effort.

For the next 20$^{m}$ the hy. runs through pleasant pasture lands, with grain fields & some truck farms. These serve the great mining dist. with milk, beef, pork, mutton & vegetables. At **50.** route turns (NW) & enters the woods of **FOURTH OF JULY CANYON.** Along roadside are giant cedars that escaped the fiery fate of many surrounding trees. The road at once begins to climb. About halfway to the summit stands the **MULLAN TREE.** In 1861 Capt. Mullan, U.S. Army, with a party of engineers, was laying out a trl. bet. Ft. Missoula, Mont., & infant village of Spokane Falls, Wash. On Independence Day they bivouacked in this shady spot & carved a record in the bark of the big cedar. The route cont. upward but, a few hundred feet from the top (3,070';magnificent view of L.Coeur d'Alene), it goes through a tunnel, designed to keep hy. open in snowy weather. From this pt., US10 winds along wooded & picturesque shores of L. Coeur d'Alene, which is bordered by summer homes of the well-to-do of N. Idaho & the Spokane country. **57. WOLF LODGE.** J. with US95 Alt., one of St.'s most scenic drives.

SIDE TRIP: On US95 Alt. (S) 47m to St. Maries. Hy. crosses bridge & follows E. shore of L. Coeur d'Alene past a series of bays. Trls. lead to higher Mt. peaks (E). The L. itself, among wooded hills, is exceptionally lovely, variable in color & mood. Before reaching the mouth of the Coeur d'Alene R., hy. enters a long canyon where the celebrated wildflowers of Idaho are at their best. Just beyond, at 39m, is **Harrison,** once a lumbermill town, now a small resort. 47m **St. Maries** (RR. lines), on St. Joe R., which flows into the L. Boat trips available. Hy. cont. (S) through beautiful **St. Joe Nat. For.** (hqs. at St. Maries.f.h.recr.area. pic.camp.cabins), rejoining main tour at Potlatch (see below).

**68. COEUR D'ALENE**

U.P., Milwaukee & N.P. RRs. Airport. Bus lines. Water Regatta (July). L. trips. Accoms. in city & vic. Inland Auto. Assoc. Tourist Bureau (O.wks.). Country Club Golf Course (O).

This lovely city, at head of L. & backed by high peaks, is a lumber town & growing commercial center in rich farm & dairying reg. It is known as the Gretna Green of the W., for hundreds of couples each yr., seeking to evade the stricter marriage laws of Wash., elope to Idaho. Also, because Idaho divorce laws are less stringent, many Washingtonians come to Coeur d'Alene to est. 6 wks.' residence & get a divorce. Hqs. of **Coeur d'Alene Nat. For.** (f.h.bath.boat.pic.camp.resorts). US10 from Coeur d'Alene to Wash. border, 4 lanes wide & paved with concrete, is regarded as the best in the St. & carries the heaviest traffic. **82. IDAHO-WASH. LINE.**

## US 30—IDAHO

**IDAHO-WYO. LINE** (55m from Kemmerer, Wyo.) **(W) to IDAHO-ORE. LINE** (23m from Huntington, Ore.). **472. US30N & US30**

Via: Pocatello, American Falls, Massacre Rock, Rupert, Burley, Hanson, Twin Falls, Buhl, Hagerman, Bliss, Glenns Ferry, Mountain Home, Boise, Meridian, Nampa, Caldwell, New Plymouth, Payette & Weiser.

Probably 75% of those who visit Idaho travel the route of the Old Oregon Trl. To many thousands of visitors, the trip along the Oregon Trl. is Idaho. Although perhaps the least scenic & spectacular of the main tours, it gives a better idea of workaday Idaho than any other route. It passes through the heart of the Old Mormon settlements (Mormons were the 1st permanent white settlers), along trl. followed by uncounted thousands to the "Oregon country" in pre-railroad days, & through some of most fertile & productive agric. areas in the world.

### Sec. 1: IDAHO-WYO. LINE to POCATELLO. 122. US30N

The trl. from the Wyo. Line lies through low hills covered with trees, through **MONTPELIER, 22.,** one of the larger Mormon towns, past **SODA SPRINGS, 52.,** where hot mineralized springs are extensively patronized by Idahoans in search of health, & on to **LAVA HOT SPRINGS, 85.,** where the St. owns & operates polio foundation for Idaho victims.

**122. POCATELLO**

At J. of N-S & E-W main lines of U.P. RR. Bus. Airport (NW) 6m. Two excellent hotels. Recr. areas in vic. Mun. golf course in Ross Pk.

Pocatello, is Idaho's 2nd largest city & is hqs. of Idaho Div. of U.P. RR. **Univ. of Idaho,** Southern Branch, one of 4 degree-granting institutions in st. J. with US91-US191 (see).

### Sec. 2: POCATELLO to BOISE. 268. US30N, US30

**0. POCATELLO. 25. AMERICAN FALLS.** Though it dates back some 50 yrs., the town is only c.23 yrs. old on its present site. The orig. town was purchased by the Gov. & its movable bldgs. transferred to higher ground in 1923-25, when the Reclamation Serv. built the giant **Amer. Falls Reservoir.** This impounds more than

Greater New York's annual supply of water. It serves to supplement irrigation needs of the middle & lower Snake R. valley & also generates an inconceivable amount of power. In the turbulent waters below the dam, rainbow trout sometimes reach a weight of 35 lbs. The Snake R. has 3 major canyons in its progress across Idaho: The 1st is at the pt. where the Snake cuts its way through mts. along Wyo.-Idaho boundary. The 2nd, generally called Snake R. Gorge, parallels US30 for nearly 200$^{m}$. The 3rd (see US95) is the fearsome chasm known as Hell's Canyon, or the Grand Canyon, the deepest on N. Amer. continent, extending from Huntington to Lewiston. The mid-canyon, or gorge, commences at American Falls, where it is of insignificant depth.

**35. MASSACRE ROCK.** Here the canyon widens & grows more shallow, so that hy. comes close to the R.—with ideal camping grounds on both sides. This was the undoing of a party of immigrants, who in Aug., 1862, outspanned their oxen & settled down for the night, close to water & good feed. Before morning they were all dead, massacred by Inds. On the flats around Massacre Rock can be seen the wheel marks of scores of immigrant wagons, some with sagebrush 3′ high growing in the ruts. (It is not generally appreciated that the Oregon Trl. was not just a wagon rut, but a wide band of ruts covering maybe a 100-yd.-width of sagebrush.) From Massacre Rock the trl. follows a rather monotonous sagebrush plain, with little to recommend it except that fishing in the near-by Snake is superlative. **73. RUPERT,** one of the principal towns of the Minidoka irrigation dist. & outpost of what Idahoans call the Magic Valley, one of the unbelievably fertile areas of farm land in the world. Rupert is shipping pt. for potatoes & sugar beets, with other smaller specialty crops. Crossing to the S. shore of Snake R., US30 enters **BURLEY** (hqs. of Minidoka Nat. For.), **79.**, a slightly larger town, but similar to other agric. centers of the tract. Large **Potato-flour Mill.** Rupert & Burley have distinction of being almost entirely lighted & heated by electricity from near-by **Minidoka Dam.** US30 leaves the lush irrigated farm lands, & plunges into another sagebrush desert. Along the Nev. border (S) rise the 10,000′ peaks of the Cache Valley range. **115. HANSEN,** in the midst of another rich agric. cty. At this pt. hy. swings close again to the middle gorge of Snake R. Two miles (N) of the village—shipping pt. for potatoes, dried beans, sugar beets, onion & celery—is what was once the highest suspension bridge in N. Amer. & still well worth seeing, though no longer used to any extent for trans-river traffic.

**124. TWIN FALLS**

U.P. RR. branch line. Bus. Airport (S) 5$^{m}$. Good hotels.

Twin Falls, economic capital of this vast irrigated empire, is one of the half-dozen largest towns of the st. & probably the wealthiest per capita. J. with US93. Four miles (N) is a sight worth a brief side excursion—but, like most side trips in Idaho, it calls for a driver with clear head, steady nerve, stout heart & iron grip on the wheel. At the rim of the Snake R. canyon, the Rd. passes a tollgate & descends a precarious & steep grade into the canyon's depths. About halfway down the steep dirt grade, it actually passes behind the cascading waters of Perrine Coulee Falls. At the foot is a bridge that leads to **Blue Lakes Ranch,** privately owned; a vast fruit orchard on the shores of 2 Ls. of an indescribable shade of blue. These Ls. are fed by underground springs & disappear into crevices in the lava rock, only to reappear lower as **Alpheus Cr.** ("where Alph the sacred river ran, through caverns measureless to man") & finally plunges in a tempestuous foaming dive called "The Devil's Washboard." In the Ls. & stream, large rainbow trout swim lazily around, apparently knowing that the owner of the land has strictly barred fishing. **Twin Falls —Jerome Bridge** (N) on US93 (see).

**142. BUHL,** another thriving agric. town. A few miles (W), the Rd. begins a slow descent into the Snake gorge, which is not quite so precipitous here as elsewhere. Along this stretch of R., for c.4$^{m}$ on the N. side, are the lovely **THOUSAND SPRINGS,** gushing out in small cascades down the face of the cliff. Crossing again to N. side of R., US30 enters **HAGERMAN VALLEY,** locale of the cowboy classic, "Chip of the Flying U." This, one of the older settlements—though not so old as the Mormon country—is dotted with groves of stately Lombardy poplars. Waters around **Upper & Lower Salmon Falls,** now harnessed for power, once provided the Shoshone Inds. with much of their food. Whole reg. is still a favorite rendezvous for trout fishermen, particularly when the season is closed (either by weather or by law) in the mt. streams. Shortly beyond **HAGERMAN, 164.,** is the **MALAD R.,** said to be shortest R. for its volume in the U.S. It is only 3ᵐ long but runs 3,000 cu. ft. per sec. R. is the same mysterious blue as are all the springs from Blue Ls. (W) & is extremely turbulent. It is much favored by more daring trout fishermen, some of whom have lost their lives in its violent currents. Hy. climbs out of the canyon to the hamlet of **BLISS, 173.,** where it rejoins the U.P. RR. main line. From here the trip is over a rough, rolling lava-rock desert, with scattered patches of irrigated lands of no great importance. **195. GLENNS FERRY** is an important RR. div. pt. Near town, in the sand bluffs (R), are peculiar lava formations that can be carved out & used as building blocks. At **Three Island Ford** (S), the Old Oregon Trl. abandoned the S. bank & crossed over the Snake. Relics of the pioneers are constantly being dug out of the river bottom or turned up by plowmen in the fields. Here begins the long trek across the Snake R. desert. Now it is broken by a few oases, & modern paved Rds. make it a matter of a few hrs. to Boise. But in the days of the Oregon Trl. it was more than a wk.'s trip from Glenns Ferry, & woe to the emigrant who failed to fill all his water barrels. The roadside is marked by numerous skeletons, mute testimony to thirst's ravages.

**224. MOUNTAIN HOME.** Here the venturesome tourist may turn (S) 40ᵐ on a side trip to **Bruneau Canyon,** off St.51, one of the most remarkable gashes in the earth's surface. It ranges in depth from 1,200′ to 2,000′, & at almost any pt. a man can throw a baseball across it, but in all its 100ᵐ there is only one place, it is said, where a man can cross it. A guide is needed, an old timer of the valley, for this wonder is not easily accessible. From Mountain Home, US30 stretches across a desert bounded (N) by the foothills of the Sawtooth Range & (S) by the 10,000′ peaks of the **Owyhee Mts.,** as barren as the desert. At the top of a low divide, the traveler sees in the distance the trees of Boise Valley, the trees, multiplied by 100 yrs.' growth, that led Capt. Bonneville's voyageurs to cry out in joy "les bois." The way now is downhill until the hy. crosses the "New York Canal" (which carries more water than all N.Y.'s aqueducts combined) & enters the irrigated fields of the valley. The Rd. still, however, is high above the R. bottom. Visible, about 10ᵐ away, is the commanding dome of the St. Capitol. Just before the Rd. dips into the valley, it passes the magnificent **U.P. RR. Sta.** (1912.wings 1919-20.by Tourlette & Hummel) with its notable gardens, called the most beautiful sta. in the U.S.

**286. BOISE**

U.P. RR. main line; transcont. & other bus lines. Airport. Good accoms. Winter sports. Hqs. of Boise Nat. For. Annual events: Music Wk. (May); Northwest Polo Tournament; W. Idaho Fair & Rodeo (Aug.). Info.: C. of C.

Boise (sett.1862), capital & largest city of Idaho, is also a great mining center & market for rich agric. & dairy reg. First Music Week in U.S. was observed in Boise (1919). US30 follows Capitol Blvd. past state bldgs., Mun. Art Gallery & beginnings of St. Hist. Mus. At the end is **Gov. Place,** which is flanked by the Capitol, City Hall, County Cth. & Fed. Bldg. PTS. OF INT.: (1) St. Capitol. **St. Hist. Soc. Mus.,** in basement; excellent coll. of Ind. artifacts. On main fl. are illuminated pictures of agric. & lumber industry, incl. cross sec. of a giant pine more than 300 yrs. old; a display of St.'s mineral ores; & an illuminated map of Idaho, showing development of irrigation & power resources. On 2nd fl. is **Wooden Statue of Geo. Washington,** carved in 1863 from native ponderosa pine by Chas. Ostner, one of earliest Idaho pioneers. It is gilded with Idaho gold dust. On 4th fl. are exhibits of Idaho game & song birds & birds of prey. (2) **Veterans' Hospital,** regarded as one of finest in U.S.; set in beautiful lawns & groves at base of the foothills. (3) **Julia Davis Pk.,** on Boise R. (4) **Sunset Pk.** (N) 9ᵐ, at 6,000′ alt. In vic. are caves, falls & placer mining grounds. J. with US20, St.15, St.44 & St.21.

SIDE TRIP: On St.21 (E) & up Boise R. 24ᵐ to **Arrowrock Dam,** one of largest irrigation dams, with splendid waterfall; 18ᵐ-long reservoir.

### Sec. 3: BOISE TO IDAHO-ORE. LINE. 82.

US20 & St.44 offer alternate routes (W), reuniting with US30 at 29ᵐ (W) of Boise. US20 has no particular elements of int., nor has St.44 except that it is orig. route of the Oregon Trl.

**10. MERIDIAN,** one of the greatest dairying centers in the St. **20. NAMPA,** important RR. center. **Lakeview Pk.**

SIDE TRIP: On St.45 (S) 31m to **Ind. Pictograph,** on N. shore of Snake R. just before reaching bridge. Pictograph, one of most remarkable ever found, has Rock Map of Snake R. valley & adj. areas.

**29. CALDWELL,** agric. processing center, seat of the **College of Idaho** & one of most devoted rose-growing centers. **Mun. Rose Garden** contains nearly 3,000 varieties, incl. a rose named for the late Dr. Wm. Judson Boone, Pres. of the College of Idaho & an enthusiastic rose-grower.

US30 unites here with US20 & St.44 coursing **BLACK CANYON DESERT** (now being irrigated). **54. NEW PLYMOUTH** (bus.accoms.), in the heart of great fruit belt. New Plymouth was founded by group of Congregationalists & is laid out in form of a vast wheel, with concentric avenues intersected by streets radiating from center. **58.** J. with US95, with which tour unites (N). **60. FRUITLAND.** US30 turns (W) here across Snake R. into Oregon; & tour cont. (N) on US30N-US95 through country of orchards & dairy farms. **73. PAYETTE,** fruit & dairy center; has Idaho's largest cannery, where peas, corn & beans are processed in great quantities. **82. WEISER** (see US95), on Snake R., the **IDAHO-ORE. LINE.**

## US 191—IDAHO

**IDAHO-MONT. LINE** (Targhee Pass, 8.5m from W. Yellowstone, Mont.) **(S) to IDAHO-UTAH LINE** (96m from Salt Lake City, Utah). **233. US191 & US191-US91**

Via: Trude, Ashton, St. Anthony, (Crystal Falls), Rexburg, Rigby, Idaho Falls, Shelley, Blackfoot, Pocatello, Downey, Franklin. Paralleled by RR., bus & airline routes. Accoms. of various types.

US91 is alternate route from Monida Pass, some miles (W), to Idaho Falls, where it unites with US191 as far as Downey (see below). It traverses highly uninteresting country, mostly desert. Bordering mts. are densely wooded, but there are few streams in the valley, ranches are far apart, & the towns little more than post office & store.

US191, united with US20, crosses beautiful country in the heart of **TARGHEE NAT. FOR.** (f.h.pic.&camp.cabins.ranches.protected moose herds.) & the **TETON MTS.,** a fine resort area. **13. MACKS INN** is favorite fishing & summer resort in the midst of the for. **15. TRUDE,** regular hqs. for Union Pacific officials who come to fish & hunt elk & deer. All the way along this stretch, the **Teton Mts.** are visible (E), towering up 14,000′. **39. LOWER MESA FALLS** of Snake R. may be approachable here, a beautiful cascade c.70′ high. **Upper Mesa Falls,** much higher, can be reached by dirt Rd. (E). **68. ST. ANTHONY.** Hqs. of Targhee Nat. For. In vic. are Idaho's **Sand Dunes & Crystal Falls Cave. 75.** J. with US20 Alt. which leads (E) & (S) through **Teton Pass** to **Grand Teton Nat. Pk.** (see Wyo.). **80. REXBURG,** in most famous potato belt in Idaho, though the tuber is grown in Twin Falls & Boise regions as well. Rexburg is seat of **Ricks College,** a Mormon Jr. college.

**109. IDAHO FALLS**

On main (N-S) line of U.P. RR. & through (N-S) airlines. Good accoms. War Bonnet Roundup (Aug.). Info.: C. of C.

Idaho Falls, one of largest towns in Idaho, is center of million-a. irrigated area & trade & cultural center of upper Snake R. valley. **Mormon Temple,** one of 5 in the W. Large **Potato Shipping Plant.** In **City Pk.** is one of St.'s fine golf courses; also Zoo. Here US91 (see above) unites with US191.

**136. BLACKFOOT.** Site of **Southern Idaho Mental Hospital.** J. with US20.

SIDE TRIP: On US20 (E & S) 84m to Craters of the Moon Nat. Mon. Hy. passes **Big Butte,** 2,300′ above valley, 7,000′ above sea level; & **Middle & East Buttes,** 700′ above valley floor. 62m **Arco.** J. with US93 Alt. (see), with which US20 unites (S) to **Craters of the Moon,** 84m, a vast burnt-out volcanic basin. It is believed the volcanoes were active as recently as 150 yrs. ago, & some imaginative souls say smoke & flame may still be observed at times in more secluded portions.

**149. FORT HALL IND. RESERV.** (1,970 pop.). Like all Idaho reservations save Duck Valley (off St.51 near Nevada line), it is now divided into ranches & is indistinguishable, except at the time of the Sun Dance (July), from any other settlement. **161. POCATELLO** (see US30). US91 joins US30 (E) & then (S) across rich farmlands of Bear R. & the Cache valley, the special home of the sugar-beet industry. **200. DOWNEY.** US91 forks (L) here.

SIDE TRIP: On US91 (S) $36^m$ to **Idaho-Utah Line,** at Franklin, oldest permanent white settlement in Idaho, founded by Mormons in 1860. **Franklin Hall;** hist. coll. US191 runs (S) from Downey through **Caribou Nat. For.** (f.h.pic.camp.cabins.hqs.at Pocatello).

**220. MALAD CITY. 233. IDAHO-UTAH LINE.**

## US 93—IDAHO

**IDAHO-MONT. LINE** ($47^m$ from Hamilton, Mont.) **(S) to IDAHO-NEV. LINE** ($65^m$ from Wells, Nev.). **365. US93**

Via: Gibbonsville, Salmon, Clayton, Stanley, Galena Summit, Ketchum, (Sun Valley), Hailey, Jerome & Twin Falls. One of St.'s most scenic routes. Accoms. limited except at resorts. Cabin camps in nat. fors.

**0. GIBBONS PASS** (6,995′), through which Lewis & Clark passed in 1805. Hy. crosses here the **CONTINENTAL DIVIDE,** whose majestic peaks watch over the old town of **SALMON, 48.,** on Salmon R., which flows (N) through steep gorges. Hqs. for **Salmon Nat. For.** (f.h.boat trips.pic.& camp grounds.cabins), incl. portion of **Primitive Area** (see). J. with St.28, which leads (SE) c.$20^m$ past **Birthpl. of Sacajawea** (see); **Fort Lemhi,** where Mormons before Civil War tried to est. settlement; & **Chief Tendoy Mon.** Route (S) lies through beautiful Salmon & Challis Nat. Fors. (see Primitive Area). **107.** Hy. forks here, & route follows R. fork (SW) along Salmon R.

SIDE TRIP: Take US93 Alt. (L. fork). Rd. goes down the valley through the Lost River range of the **Salmon River Mts.** Here are 5 of Idaho's loftiest peaks, incl. the highest, **Mt. Borah** (12,655′), & others of more spectacular beauty. In these mts. lives one of few surviving herds of pronghorns in U.S. $30^m$ **Dickey** (ranch Hs.). Rd. leads (SW) toward **Trail Creek Summit,** a breathtakingly beautiful route (calls for nerve & careful driving) to famed **Sun Valley** (see below), yr.-round resort, & $3^m$ beyond to J. with US93, considerable distance (N) of main J. (see below). $80^m$ **Arco.** Atomic Energy Commission plans (1949) to raise a great atomic reactor testing sta. on naval proving grounds here, to be built over period of yrs. Route swings (W) & enters the weird wonderland of **Craters of the Moon,** unlike any other area in U.S.; probably most recent volcanic eruptions in country. Among the 60 or more craters are some $1^m$ across. At $168^m$ is J. with US93, the main tour.

US93 follows Salmon R. (W) past peaks more than 10,000′ high. **166. STANLEY.** Near-by (N) is **Stanley Recr. Area,** in the heart of the **Sawtooth Mts.** On the (W), up the valley, the Sawtooth peaks march in all their grandeur, not so high but more impressive than the Lost River range (see above). In Primitive Area (E) are Salmon R. & White Cloud ranges. **199.** Rd. climbs over **GALENA SUMMIT** (9,000′). Ahead are the giants of the Wood R. range. Most prominent are **Galena, Boulder & Easley Mts.** (W), all above 11,000′ & huge in bulk. Boulder, at certain angles of the sun's rays, turns rose & green in color. **229. KETCHUM.** Near-by (E) is **Sun Valley,** one of most popular Western resorts (see Side Trip above). US93 cont. down Wood R. valley. **241. HAILEY.** Hqs. of **Sawtooth Nat. For.** (f.h.winter sports.pic.camp. cabins.dude ranches). **285. SHOSHONE,** important sheep & wool producing center. J. with US93 Alt. (see above). **304. JEROME.** Near here the Snake R. is arched by the **Jerome-Twin Falls Bridge** (476′ above water level), one of country's finest cantilever bridges. **317. TWIN FALLS.** J. with US30 (see). **365. IDAHO-NEV. LINE.**

## US 95—IDAHO

**CANADIAN BORDER** (Eastport, Idaho) **(S) to IDAHO-ORE. LINE.** (c.$20^m$ N. of Jordan Valley, Ore.) **591. US95**

Via: Bonners Ferry, Sandpoint, Athol, Coeur d'Alene, Plummer, Moscow, Lewiston, Winchester, Grangeville, Higgins, New Meadows, Cambridge & Weiser. Accoms. in towns. Camp sites. Bus lines along route.

US95, known to Idahoans as North & South Hy., has the distinction of being the longest &, with Oregon Trl., one of the most traveled Rds. in the st. (It extends from Canadian line (S) to Mexican border.)

### Sec. 1: CANADIAN BOUNDARY to LEWISTON. 241.

**0. EASTPORT.** Rd. lies along **Deep Creek Canyon,** in the heart of Cabinet Mts. & in **Kaniksu Nat. For.** (hqs. at Sandpoint.f.h.boat.swim.pack & saddle trls.pic.camp. cabins.resorts.). **30.** J. with US2 (transcont.route from Me.), with which US95 unites for $3^m$. **33. BONNERS FERRY,** noted chiefly as home of highest protein-content wheat in U.S. Along the lowlands of Kootenai R. are rich wheat fields, protected from high water by dikes. **67. SANDPOINT** (RR.& bus conns.), on the shores of **L. Pend Oreille,** one of the larger fresh-water Ls. in the U.S., with 125$^{m}$ shoreline. Across an arm of the L. is **Sandpoint Bridge,** built entirely of wood & 2$^{m}$ long. **93. ATHOL.** Many Ls. & beaches in vic. At S. end of L. Pend Oreille, (E) 3$^{m}$ from US95, is **Farragut College & Technical Sch.,** in bldgs. of Farragut Naval Training Sta., maintained during World War II (2nd in size to Gt.Ls.Sta.). **112.** J. with US10 (see US10 for description of US95 Alt.trip along W.side of L.). **114. COEUR D'ALENE** (see US10). **149. PLUMMER,** chief town of **Coeur d'Alene Ind. Reserv.,** which is mostly divided into private holdings. In vic. (E) 9$^{m}$ is **Heyburn St. Pk.** The land in the Pk. bordering on L. is largely given over to private cabins, but there are several smaller but beautiful Ls. in area (hotel.f.duck h.in season.boat.swim.). US95 enters the rolling, hilly Palouse country, noted for wheat, split peas, dried beans. **184.** J. with US95 Alt., which runs (E) 2$^{m}$ to the famed lumber town of **Potlatch,** drawing timber from the near-by **St. Joe Nat. For.** (hqs.in St. Maries.f.h.recr.area. pic.camp.cabins). **203. MOSCOW,** home of **Univ. of Idaho,** founded in 1892; beautiful campus. Hy. winds (S) across the Palouse Plateau to the brink of the **Clearwater Canyon,** where, if the traveler is fortunate enough to arrive just at dusk, is a view of Lewiston, 3rd largest of Idaho towns, stretching along the R. bottom 3,000′ below. Excellent Rd. leads 10$^{m}$ down to the bottom. (Nowhere is the grade greater than 5°.)

**241. LEWISTON**

RR. & bus conns. Airport. Accoms. Recr. facils. Excursions on Snake R. Cherry Blossom Festival (May). Lewiston Roundup (Sept.), one of largest in N.W. Info.: C. of C.

Lewiston, at an elevation of 700′, is the lowest city in Idaho, picturesquely situated at N. exit of **Hell's Canyon** of the Snake. It is the home of the **Northern Idaho College of Education,** on attractive campus, & of the great **Potlatch Forests, Inc., Lumber Mill,** which handles most of the cut from Clearwater & Nez Perce Nat. Fors. Town was founded in 1861, after discovery of gold, on the site of the campground of Lewis & Clark in 1805 & 1806.

## Sec. 2: LEWISTON to IDAHO-ORE. LINE. 350.

Here US95 gives access to the Blue & Wallowa Mts. reg. & Grand Canyon of the Snake R. The reg. incl. NE. cor. of Ore., SW. cor. of Wash. & Snake R. area along boundary bet. these states & Idaho. Main approaches are by US30 in Ore. (see Baker & La Grande, Ore.); US410 in Wash. (see); & US95 in Idaho. RR. & through bus lines roughly parallel routes. For. camps maintained by Nat. For. Serv. (see Nat. fors. below); few other accoms. except in towns on hy. Boat trips from Lewiston to within 20$^{m}$ of mouth of Canyon. Horses for pack trips available at Cuprum (see below).

Area has some of most spectacular scenery in the country: the Snake R. Canyon, which rivals the Grand Canyon of the Colo. in grandeur, the gorges of Grande Ronde, Tucannon, Powder & Imnaha Rs. & the Anthony Ls. Recr. & Idaho Eagle Cap Wilderness areas. Mts. rise on Oregon side to height of 10,000′, & on Idaho side to more than 9,000′. Incl. are parts of Payette & Oregon's Umatilla, Whitman & Wallowa Nat. Fors. (excellent h.f.for.camps.). Most sensational part of Snake R. lies (S) of Hat Pt., Ore., a part of the stretch variously known as Hell's Canyon, Seven Devils Gorge & Grand Canyon. It varies in width from 4$^{m}$ to 9$^{m}$. To the (E) are the Seven Devils Mts. (Idaho) & to (W.) are the Wallowa Mts. (Ore.). At one pt., near He Devil Peak (Idaho), Hell's Canyon is 7,900′ deep, about 2,350′ deeper than Grand Canyon of the Colorado. Most of the rock formations are vari-colored —yellow, red, orange & purple. The R. itself, in Hell's Canyon, is inaccessible to autos, but a number of viewpoints can be reached by road & short branching trls.

**0. LEWISTON. 11. SPALDING MEM. ST. PK.;** site of mission, 1st in Idaho, est. by Rev. Henry Spalding, in 1836. **14. LAPWAI,** hqs. of **Perce Ind. Reserv.** (1,525 pop.). **38. WINCHESTER,** in typical N. Idaho country of evergreen fors. & fields of wildflowers. **79. GRANGEVILLE,** in wheat country. Hqs. of **Nez Perce Nat. For.** (f.h.pic.& camp grounds.guides.cabins). **84. WHITE BIRD HILL** (5,430′). **132. RIGGINS.** Just beyond is J. with Rd. (L) to magnificent **Salmon R. Gorge.** (Mt. Time from here S.). **141. POLLOCK.**

SIDE TRIP: Rd. leads 6$^{m}$ (R) to trl. to **Dry Diggins Lookout;** fine view of Grand Canyon.

US95 cont. (S) along canyon of Little Salmon R. **167. NEW MEADOWS.** Here route is in **Payette Nat. For.** (f.h.bath.pic.& camp grounds.dude ranches); entrance to Primitive Area (see). On **L. Payette,** (E) c.12$^{m}$, are **Shore Lodge** & other resorts; summer & winter sports. **187. STARKEY,** resort. **197. COUNCIL.**

SIDE TRIP: On Rd. (NW) 39$^{m}$ to **Cuprum** (hotel.pack trip equipment). Rd. climbs to **Kinney Pt. & Sheep Rock,** among best viewpoints accessible from hy. for view of Grand Canyon.

**220. CAMBRIDGE.**

SIDE TRIP (hazardous): On improved Rd. (NW) 19$^{m}$ to **Heath.** Rd. runs bet. walls of stone approaching Canyon.

**253. WEISER.** J. with US30 (see). US95 cont. (S) & across Snake R. **350. IDAHO-ORE. LINE.**

## PRIMITIVE AREA—IDAHO

Can be entered by plane from McCall, by somewhat hazardous boat trip down Salmon R., or by pack trip from any outfitting pt. in season (July-Nov.). Info. at Salmon City, on the E.; Stanley or Boise, on the S.; Cascade or McCall, on the W.

The Primitive Area was set up in 1937. Most of Idaho's mt. reg. is, in reality, an impenetrable primitive area, but this sec. was est. by law to be kept free from the works of man, save those installations absolutely necessary to protect timber against fire or trespass. No road, not even a crude two-rut trl., penetrates the vast wilderness of pine & cedar. Aside from one or two isolated ranches, est. before the area was created, & the few necessary ranger stas., no human habitation is permitted. Supplies go into the rangers by pack train. Anyone desiring to view the wonders of the area must obtain permission & then make a long, toilsome & expensive pack-train trip. The area abounds in big game, & most of it is open to hunters.

The Primitive Area embraces large portions of the Boise, Sawtooth & Challis nat. fors. within its more than 1,500,000 as. Central feature is the awesome canyon of the Middle Fork of Salmon R., which, though not so deep as the parent canyon, is in many respects more terrifying. The Middle Fork starts as a peaceful little stream in Bear Valley, at N. end of the Sawtooth range; then, after chuckling through miles of mt. meadows, suddenly starts a series of wild cascades into the gorge. It has been navigated, but it is not a venture for the faint-hearted, particularly as some of the worst water of the main Salmon R. lies ahead, beyond the mouth of the fork. Another nat. wonder is **Rainbow Peak,** which, in certain lights, turns pink, emerald green, brilliant yellow & deep blue. The W. escarpment of **Castle Peak** (11,500′) is one of the most nearly sheer precipices (for 5,000′) known to alpinists. It is quite easily scaled on the E. side.

Deep within the area are the **Big Horn Crags,** regarded as among the spectacular mt. views of the U.S. They are almost a wk.'s pack-train journey from the nearest auto road, & the journey itself has many perilous spots. These stupendous granite monoliths rise to heights of 3,000′ & 4,000′ above the valley floor, & their valley sides are as sheer as the walls of the Washington Mon. They can, however, be attempted from the plateau side, where they are neither so lofty nor so formidable.

## NATIONAL FORESTS—IDAHO

There are 13 nat. fors. in Idaho. All are crossed by hys., but the visitor can see little of these areas because the Rds. are mostly dirt tracks designed purely for for. management purposes. To most travelers, these nat. fors. are great wooded hills, viewed from a distance of several miles across grassy savannahs. There are some delightful side trips to beauty spots in the heart of the hills, & the For. Serv. has done a great deal to make the camping spots attractive with stone fireplaces, rustic tables & benches, carefully rock-protected springs &, in some cases, a plentiful supply of firewood.

The Targhee, Sawtooth, Boise, Kaniksu, Coeur d'Alene & St. Joe fors. (hqs. respectively at St. Anthony, Hailey, Boise, Sandpoint, Coeur d'Alene & St. Maries) are perhaps the most intensively developed from a recr. standpoint. The Challis (Challis), Caribou (Pocatello), Minidoka (Burley), Payette (McCall) & Salmon (Salmon) fors. all fringe heavily traveled Rds. but, because of the rugged nature of the terrain, do not invite close inspection. The Nez Perce (Grangeville) & the Clearwater (Orofino) fors. are far off the beaten track. All these, however, have haunts attractive to native Idahoans with time & hill-knowledge to make use of their resources.

# THE WEST COAST

## CALIFORNIA — OREGON — WASHINGTON

### GEOGRAPHY OF THE WEST COAST STATES

The three states bordering on the Pacific have three topographic features more or less in common: their coastline, the coastal range which backs it & extends for more than 2,000 miles from Canada to Mexico, & a mighty inland mt. range extending with few breaks from Canada into S. Cal.

The common coastal range crowds the beach pretty much throughout its course, making for an extremely picturesque shore line. Its ridges seldom rise above 4,000′ except at its N. extremity where Wash.'s Olympic Mts. rise to altitudes of nearly 8,000′ & in its S. terminus in Cal., where it breaks into a jumble of peaks, attaining 10,000′ altitudes. The Columbia R.'s broad estuary makes a wide break at the Ore.-Wash. Line, & the rugged Siskiyous interrupt the mt. chain's continuity at the Cal.-Ore. Line, where they spread out in both states & connect the coastal range with the Cascades.

The mt. backbone, known as the Cascades in Ore. & Wash., & the High Sierra in Cal., is solidly continuous in the two N. states, where the only one real break is made by the Columbia R. But when the Cascades reach Mt. Shasta in N. Cal., there is a gap in the continuity until the High Sierra resumes the march S.

**WASHINGTON & OREGON:** These two states constitute a fairly complete topographic unit. The outstanding features are: Puget Sound in the N.; the seacoast & coastal range already referred to; an inland valley E. of the coastal range extending into S. Ore.; the mt. wall of the Cascades; the Columbia R. which cuts a deep swath from E. to W. & constitutes the boundary bet. the two states for some 400 miles; & the great inland plateau.

Puget Sound takes a big bite out of N. Wash. It is shaped like a "T" lying on its side. The stem of the "T" is San Juan de Fuca Strait, separating Wash. from Vancouver Island, Brit. Columbia. The "T's" crossbar is the Sound's E. arm which extends from Brit. Columbia in the N., to Olympia, Wash. in the S. It is along this E. arm that all of Wash.'s largest cities, with the exception of Spokane, are located.

E. of the coastal range lies a long broad valley which runs from S. Ore. right through to Olympia, Wash. where it is blocked off by Puget Sound. This valley, as well as the coastal range, has plenty of rainfall & consequently is extremely productive. In Ore. it is known as the Valley of the Willamette because Willamette R. winds through it to join the Columbia N. of Portland. Strung along through Willamette Valley are most of Ore.'s largest cities, reaching a N. climax in Portland's half-a-million.

E. of the valley rise the mighty Cascades, extending in a wide belt from Mt. Baker, just S. of Brit. Columbia to Mt. Shasta, to the S. of which the High Sierra carry on in Cal. There is only one real break in this mt. rampart, made by the Columbia's turbulent waters pouring through deep gorges on its way to the sea. The ridges of the Cascades, aside from this break, never drop below 3,000′, even in the mt. passes, & are punctuated by a series of high pks, many of them of volcanic origin: Extending N.-S. are: Mt. Baker (10,750′), Glacier Peak (10,436′), Mt. Rainier (14,408′) & Mt. Adams (12,307′), in Wash.; Mt. Hood (11,245′), Mt. Jefferson (10,495′), the Three Sisters (10,354′), the Crater Lake group (over 7,000′) & McLoughlin (9,493′), in Ore. The Cascades skirt Puget Sound in the N., then run within view of the valley region to the W., all the way to Cal. where they take a last, sensational spurt in Mt. Shasta's 14,161′. In N. Wash., the relatively low Okanogan Highlands link the Cascades with the mts. of Idaho to the E., & the Siskiyous in S. Ore. & N. Cal. connect the Cascades with the coastal range to the W.

To the E. of the Cascades rampart extends a vast inland plateau which lies at a considerable altitude, sometimes above 5,000′, & extends unbroken, except for a few mt. ranges, from the Okanogan Highlands through both states into the N. part of Cal. Because the Cascades' wall cuts off most of the moisture originating in the Pacific, the plateau is a fairly dry region, varying from the semi-aridity of S. Wash., to the 10-20″ annual rainfall in N. Ore., & the desert of S. Ore. In Wash. the plateau has a special character because of the deep coulees scoured out by prehistoric rivers. The best known of these is the Grand Coulee, part of which is being utilized for water storage by the Columbia R. Project. With completion of this great undertaking, some 1,200,000 acres (more than twice the area of Mass.) will be brought under cultivation. Even before the Columbia R. Project was initiated, the region's aridity had already been considerably relieved by large irrigation works. The Columbia R. Project will also, by generation of tremendous amounts of power, bring about an industrial transformation, not only of the "Big Bend" region of the Columbia R., but also of the cities lying W. along the Columbia R. Improvement of navigation on the Columbia & Snake Rs. will furthermore make much of the area accessible to shipping. This plateau region of Wash. has been variously known as the "Inland Empire," because of its vast productive potentialities, & as the "Big Bend."

The northern part of the plateau in Ore. is deeply scarred by canyons of the Deschutes & John Day Rs. & their tributaries. This area has a fairly good rainfall which, nevertheless, wherever possible, has been supplemented by irrigation. The southern section of the plateau in Ore. is the "Ore. Desert," also known as the Lakes District, because of many lakes which are more often dry than water-filled & frequently alkaline. However, large irrigation undertakings—the Owyhee-Vale project in the Ontario district, the Klamath Falls project to the SW. & others—have here too brought great areas under cultivation.

Pushing into the great plateau in the SE. corner of Wash. & the NE. corner of Ore. is the wedge of the scenically fine Blue-Wallowa Mts. area, bounded on the E. by the Grand Canyon of the Snake R. & cut through by the lateral canyons of the Grande Ronde & Powder Rs., & other streams emptying into the Snake. This is a region of high mts. c.10,000′ in alt., of fine forests, beautiful lakes, & sensational gorges, climaxing in the Grand Canyon of the Snake R. which rivals in magnificence the Grand Canyon of Colorado. The Walla Walla Valley which extends W. in this region to the Columbia R. is fertile & watered by many streams.

**RIVER SYSTEMS:** The Columbia is the main stream of the region & into it a great part of the watersheds of these two states drain. The Columbia runs S. from Brit. Columbia to the N. part of the great plateau, then turns abruptly W. to the edge of the Cascades, where it turns again in a southerly direction to a point near the Ore. Line. Here it again takes a W. course & is the boundary between Ore. & Wash., flowing through deep gorges & finally into the Pacific. The Columbia's chief tributary is the Snake which, at the Idaho Line, turns W. & flows through S. Wash. to join the Columbia near the city of Pasco. A less important tributary in E. Wash. is the Spokane, which takes off at the Idaho boundary, near Spokane, & twists westward to join the Columbia, not far from the Grand Coulee.

Much of the eastern watershed of the Cascades is also tributary to the Columbia. The streams in Wash. drain directly off the steep mt. slopes into the great R. or into the Okanogan, which itself is a tributary. In Ore., the Deschutes collects the waters that flow down the eastern slopes of the Cascades & delivers them into the Columbia. Only some of the smaller Rs. in the southern Ore. region of the Cascades take an independent course.

The western watershed of the Cascades belongs only in part to the Columbia system. In N. & central Wash., the drainage flows directly into Puget Sound. In S. Wash., the Cowlitz R. collects much of the water from the Cascades & delivers it into the Columbia near Kelso. In N. & central Ore. the Willamette delivers the drainage from the western side of the Cascades into the Columbia just N. of Portland. But in S. Ore., the Rogue, Umpqua & other smaller streams having their source in the Cascades, break through the coastal range & empty directly into the Pacific.

The coastal range has its own separate watershed, consisting, for the most part, of smaller streams finding their outlet in the Pacific.

Vast forests originally clothed all the mt. areas of the two states. Even considerable portions of the valley W. of the Cascades were heavily forested & pioneers found the job of land-clearing so arduous that they often left tree stumps standing in the streets, long after the first houses of their cities had been built. Frenzied lumbering operations have to a great extent depleted the originally available lumber. Both World Wars greatly speeded up this destructive process. It now is reliably stated that replacement by new growth is far below the annual cut. Unless more rational lumbering techniques are employed, the last great forest wealth of the country will soon be exhausted. During the final quarter of the 19th century & the first part of the 20th, considerable acreages of the best forest land, publicly owned, were acquired by private interests through political maneuvers & even by simple fraud. Some of these frauds finally were uncovered & became a nation-wide scandal. Fortunately, however, millions of acres have remained in the national forests, which are precluded from reckless private exploitation & so constitute a great timber reserve.

**CALIFORNIA,** second largest state in U.S., has a more or less longitudinal topography. It is about 780 miles long & its width varies from 150 to 350 miles. Its coastline, approximately 1,200 miles long, equals the combined Pacific frontage of Ore. & Wash. The state's S. coast has a pronounced eastward curve, so that San Diego lies farther E. than Reno, Nev., while its northernmost port of Eureka claims to be the most western city of the U.S.

The chief geographic divisions are the Coastal Range, the Great Central Valley, the High Sierra, the Mojave & Colorado Deserts & the Los Angeles Basin.

The Coastal Range extends along the entire coastline, except for a short distance in the extreme S., where it drops to the desert just N. of Mexico. The only considerable break in the range occurs at San Francisco. Here a gap gives access to the great Central Valley. Clustered around the mouth of this break-through are S.F. & the S.F. Bay cities, a metropolitan area in which live more than 2,000,000 Californians. In the SW. cor. of the state, the coastal range spreads out into a series of high ridges, turning somewhat eastward. Between these & the ocean lies the wedge-shaped coastal plain of the L.A. Basin, a metropolitan district whose more than 4,000,000 inhabitants live in an area scarcely 140 miles long & not half as wide.

The great Central Valley is shut in on the W. by the coastal range & on the E. by the tremendous, almost unbroken rampart of the High Sierra. The valley, which produces much of the agricultural wealth of the state, is dominated by Mt. Shasta at its N. end, & extends some 400 miles S. to the Tehachapi line, where the Sierra ridges turn westward toward the coast. It is watered by the Sacramento R. flowing S. from the vic. of Mt. Shasta, & the San Joaquin flowing N. Both Rs. debouch through a gap in the coastal range into Suisun Bay, of the S.F. area. Irrigation, on the one hand, & draining & ditching, on the other, have transformed the valley into a vast garden region.

The High Sierra, sometimes called a S. extension of the Cascades, interposes an almost unbroken mt. wall between the central valley & the arid mt. & desert region that extends E. into Nev. Toward its S. end, the Sierra drops to lower altitudes at Tehachapi Pass where it swings W. In its highest section, the Sierra is marked by lofty mts. towering above precipitous gorges & canyons. Forty-one peaks, between L. Tahoe & Mt. Whitney, exceed 10,000′, with Mt. Whitney, highest in the continental U.S., attaining 14,491′. Passes cutting through between the high peaks range from 9,000′ to more than 12,000′ in altitude. The Sierra region includes some of the finest scenery & recreation areas in the state: lovely L. Tahoe, Yosemite, Kings Canyon & Sequoia Nat. Pks., & the Kern R. Canyon. Within the Sierra region is the old mining district of the Mother Lode, extending N. & S. along the Sierra foothills; it yielded fabulous treasure & is still producing, although chiefly interesting today for its ghost towns.

Between the Sierra & the state of Nev. lies Owens Valley, enclosed by granite walls, & to the SE., ringed in by high ranges, is Death Valley, scooped out of the desert to a depth of some 270′ below sea level.

In S. & SE. Cal., are the Mojave & Colorado deserts, shut off from the L.A. Basin by high coastal ridges. The Mojave is an expanse of ancient dried lake beds, rugged ranges & widespreading sand valleys. Much of it lies at a considerable altitude. On the other hand, parts of the Colorado Desert lie below sea level, almost as much below it as the lowest parts of Death Valley. The Imperial Valley is a large oasis reclaimed by water supplied by the Colorado R. Salton Sea, created by a vagary of the R., spreads out in the bed of ancient Lake Coachella, which in prehistoric times covered a large part of what is now Colorado desert.

Aside from the watersheds of the San Joaquin & Sacramento Rs., which drain the W. watersheds of the Sierra into S.F. Bay, & are navigable respectively to Sacramento & Stockton, the chief watershed is that of the coastal range, flowing directly into the Pacific. In the south, the coastal streams are of less importance; many of them are intermittently dry, coming to life only during spring floods.

There are two groups of islands off the Cal. Coast: the Santa Barbara Islands extending from Santa Barbara almost to San Diego, of which the best known is Santa Catalina, off Long Beach, & the Farallones, a group of small, barren islands lying offshore from S.F.

## NOTES ON THE HISTORY OF THE WEST COAST STATES

The American frontier, which had been advancing slowly by land, traveling from the East Coast to the Mississippi Valley, in 1849 made a sudden leap across the Rockies. The tide of emigration, with the discovery of gold in California, circled the Horn & poured into San Francisco for the mad rush to the gold fields. Many other seekers for Eldorado threaded their weary way from St. Louis, across desert & through the snow-bound mountain fastness of the high Sierra, in which many of them lost their lives, into the valley of promise.

California's development has been largely colored by the gold & silver rush booms—first along the American River where John Marshall discovered the precious metal, then along the famous Mother Lode, & then in the Nevada Comstock area. The lawlessness & free-shooting mentality which ruled in the mining towns communicated itself to the financial & railroad interests & was injected into state & municipal politics; in these fields it assumed less free-shooting but equally extra-legal forms.

The emigration to Southern California, that little mountain & sea-locked oasis of metropolitan Los Angeles, came somewhat later, & was largely a land-boom phenomenon, not less sensational, however, in periodic booms & busts.

Settlement of Oregon & Washington likewise represented a jump of the frontier across the Rockies, but the attracting features were the rich agricultural land of the Willamette Valley to which the Easterners migrated over the Oregon Trail, the salmon fisheries of the Columbia, its tributaries & Puget Sound, & finally the seemingly inexhaustible lumber resources of the forests of the Western Cascade Mountains. The history of these two states is less punctuated with sensational booms & busts, less notable for lawlessness tamed periodically by vigilante committees, & less notable for political lawlessness.

Exploration of the Pacific Coast began in the 16th century. Juan Rodríguez Cabrillo, a Portuguese navigator, was sent in 1542 by Antonio Mendoza, Cortez' successor in Mexico, to explore the California Coast. Cabrillo sailed beyond the Golden Gate. He died before the voyage was ended & was buried on one of the Santa Barbara Islands. His successor in command, Ferrelo, sailed north, probably as far as Cape Mendocino. Francis Drake, in the "Golden Hinde," landed (1579) near San Francisco Bay & claimed that "faire" region for Queen Elizabeth. The Spanish voyages of discovery continued but, by some fatality, always missed the great bay where San Francisco crowds down to the ocean front.

Meanwhile, continued attempts had been made to find a northwest passage to the Atlantic. A Greek navigator, Juan de Fuca, is alleged to have discovered the entrance to Puget Sound as early as 1592. Bruno Heceta anchored between the capes of the Columbia in 1775 without, however, suspecting the existence of that great waterway. Before that date, a Dane, Vitus Behring, had begun exploration in 1734 of the Alaska coast for Catherine the Great. He also believed that there was a northwest passage to the Atlantic. His voyages established Russia's claim to Alaska & much of the coastal region to the south. There followed a number of Spanish and Portuguese expeditions.

By the end of the 18th century, the British began to take an interest in the Northwest. The renowned Captain Cook, discoverer of islands in the SW. Pacific, looked for Juan de Fuca Strait in 1776, but failed to find it. In 1788 another British sea-captain, Barkeley, found the strait & named it for Juan de Fuca. Americans arrived in 1789 & explored Puget Sound, circumnavigating Vancouver Island. The name Oregon was given the region by an American, Captain Carver, & immortalized in Bryant's "Thanatopsis" with the line: "Where rolls the Oregon and hears no sound." About the same time, the Britisher, Vancouver, & his lieutenant, Broughton, explored Puget Sound & the Columbia. On these early American & British explorations were later based conflicting claims to the Oregon region of Britain & the U.S.

The first Spanish settlement of California was delayed until 1769. In that year an expedition started out by sea & land from Loreto in lower California. It was accompanied by Franciscan Friars led by Fray Junípero Serra. Shortly a mission & presidio were established at San Diego. Gaspar de Portolá, one of the leaders of the expedition, continued northward in search of a good harbor, actually getting as far as San Francisco Bay, which some members of the party sighted; but he returned to San Diego & reported that his quest had failed. Soon after, however, a mission was established at Monterey. In the next years the Franciscans founded a string of missions in the coastal region all the way to the San Francisco peninsula & even beyond. To protect the missions, presidios were usually established with garrisons. These presidios were the kernels of future cities.

The padres devoted themselves to converting & civilizing the Indians. They had some 20,000 under their care when their work was at its height. But death from disease & flight from confining conditions in the missions constantly reduced the number of converts. On occasion the Indians revolted & destroyed the mission settlements. After Mexico gained independence, in 1821, hostility to the Franciscans became increasingly strong until, in 1833-34, the secularization laws were enacted, which brought about the rapid decline of the missions. But the Indians benefited little by the change. They were reduced to peonage by the Spanish & Mexicans, & when the Americans annexed California, in 1846, their lot did not improve. They were driven from their lands, exploited by various means—force, trickery & whiskey —in the labor market. In 1770 it is estimated there were 133,000 Indians in the state; by 1852 their number had decreased to 85,000. Several small-scale wars had to be fought to get most of the Indians to reservations. Today there are not more than 32,000 survivors.

After Mexico won independence, California was set up as a separate territory. Several attempts were made by the "Californios" to establish Alta California as an independent entity. Meanwhile "Yankees" began to infiltrate the region. Although the Spanish government had imposed an embargo, Yankee ships, even before 1821, had begun to trade along the coast. Under the Mexican regime, Americans were welcomed & many of them married Mexican & Spanish women, acquiring large ranches to which their wives fell heir.

As early as the 1830's the U.S. government became interested in the West Coast. President Andrew Jackson offered to buy California from Mexico but his proposition was turned down. By 1844 Captain Frémont had arrived in the southern part of the state, allegedly on a scientific & exploratory mission for the American government. The Mexicans eventually became suspicious of his activities & ordered him out of the region in 1846. But soon afterward, war was declared between the two countries & Frémont took an active part, together with Commodore Stockton, who arrived by sea, & Col. Kearney, who came overland, in winning California for the U.S.

The history of the white man in the Oregon-Washington region began somewhat later than in California. British trading companies, which eventually were all consolidated in the Hudson's Bay Co., began operations there in the late 18th & early 19th centuries. President Thomas Jefferson, foreseeing the great future of the Northwest, in 1804 sent out the Lewis & Clark expedition which reached the mouth of the Columbia River in 1805, thus establishing another source for American claims to the region. But the Hudson's Bay Co.'s control continued to grow. John Jacob Astor's expedition, which went by sea & land to Astoria in 1811, produced few results because the War of 1812 intervened & forced Astor to sell out to the British company. Under Dr. John McLoughlin's leadership, the Hudson's Bay Co. built forts along the north side of the Columbia which the British hoped would be the final boundary with the U.S. The Company was less interested in settling the land than in the fur trade, which at first they exploited through individual traders traveling into the back country, but eventually by regularly organized expeditions. When the inevitable tide of immigration set in from the U.S., the Company's restricted activities were swamped.

The vanguard of the American invasion was led by Protestant missionaries.

Strangely enough, the Indians who were to suffer most from the influx of settlers were instrumental in inducing the first missionaries to come in. In 1831 the Nez Percé & the Flatheads sent a delegation to St. Louis asking for missionaries to come & teach them the religion of the great white God. Jason Lee & a party of missionaries answered the call about 1834, & in company with a band of settlers, set out for the Oregon territory. They established a mission in the Willamette Valley, near present-day Salem. Soon afterwards, Dr. Marcus Whitman's party established itself at Waiilatpu, in the Wallowa R. valley, & shortly, Eells & Walker set up a mission at Tshimiakin in the Spokane region. None of the missions were very successful in converting the Indians. Lee's efforts soon turned to educational work for white settlers. The Tshimiakin mission was abandoned after the missionaries admitted that they had not succeeded in making a single Indian convert. The Whitman establishment, most ambitious of all the missions, was wiped out by the Cayuse Indians in 1847.

Meanwhile, however, the tide of migration from the East had been setting in. It was directed at first to the Willamette Valley & came along the old Oregon trail which followed the Columbia River, although some of the newcomers drifted in from California. As early as 1838 settlers began petitioning Congress to take action to establish American sovereignty over the Oregon region. In May 1843 a memorable meeting was called together at Champoeg, Oregon, which set up a provisional government in opposition to the Hudson's Bay Co. Finally, after much talk of a shooting war whose American slogan was "54-40 or fight," the U.S. boundary was fixed (1846).

Congress was slow to admit Oregon to the Union as a territory. This was due to the current antagonism of the slave states to admission of more "free" regions, although Calhoun was for admission, the South having been compensated by the annexation of Texas. Daniel Webster expressed the opinion during the course of the controversy that the Northwest would be an absolutely worthless acquisition. In 1848 the Oregon Territory was finally set up.

Meanwhile pioneers had moved north into what is today Washington, & settled in the western valley & at Puget Sound in the vicinity of present-day Olympia, Tacoma & Seattle. In 1851 a convention met at Cowlitz Landing to draft a constitution & demand that Washington be set up as a separate territory. The next year this demand was reiterated at the Monticello Convention. Congress acceded in 1853, creating the territory of Washington.

Oregon & Washington had at least six Indian wars, one of them with the coastal Indians, the others with the inland aborigines: the Cayuse War, to punish the Cayuse for the Whitman massacre, & the Yakima, Spokane, Modoc & Nez Percé conflicts. Treaties were made with the various Indian tribes, which Congress failed to ratify promptly or at all & which were really only notice to the Indians that the white man was going to drive them from their homes. Eventually, as in California, the Indians were removed to reservations.

The year 1848 proved a turning point in California history. That was the year that James Wilson Marshall, a carpenter employed by John Sutter (a Swiss immigrant who had carved out a little empire of his own in the central part of the state, which he called New Helvetia), discovered gold on the South Fork of the American River near Coloma. Although there already had been a considerable flood of immigration, following the Mexican War, this was nothing to the tide that set in when news of the discovery reached the East. By 1850 California's population had jumped from 15,000 to 92,000. Gold-rush towns sprang up overnight, fantastically named—Get-Up-&-Git, Red Dog, Lazy Man's Canyon, & so forth, with the inevitable complement of gambling, drinking, fandango dance-halls & lawlessness, eventually tempered by summary vigilante justice. San Francisco became the center of the gold-rush hysteria & boasted that it was the wickedest city in the world, a claim, however, disputed by other towns. Over a thousand murders were committed in the Bay City between 1849 & 1856. Gangs of lawbreakers ruled the roost, but were finally put down by vigilantes.

After 1859 the big boom collapsed & many miners turned to the land where they "squatted" & were protected against the rightful owners by the government. In the period preceding the Civil War there was a bitter struggle between the pro- & anti-slavery factions. But Lincoln carried the state, albeit by the narrow margin of a thousand votes.

After the Civil War another boom set in, connected with the Comstock Lode's rich mines in Nevada. This was an era of violent speculation which ended with the collapse of the Bank of California in 1875 & a severe panic. It was also the era of violent anti-Chinese agitation. Not only California but also Oregon & Washington staged riots against this element of the population. There was considerable unemployment & the flooding of the labor market by the Chinese, after the completion of the great transcontinental railroad lines on which they had worked, gave rise to anti-Chinese feeling. The passage of the Chinese Exclusion Acts of the 1880's ended this racial conflict.

The bitterest political fight in California developed out of the domination by the Southern Pacific RR. of the state's politics & economy. This fight was not ended until the first decade of the 20th century, when the opposition, led by Fremont Older, Hiram Johnson & others, introduced reforms curbing the power of the Southern Pacific & other great corporations. About the same time San Francisco's corrupt municipal government was cleaned up & a reform administration installed. Los Angeles had a somewhat similar reform wave.

World War I ushered in an era of dizzy expansion & boom. By 1930 the state's population had reached 5,677,251, a 65 percent increase in a decade. When the bubble burst, it brought in its train suicides of many of the most prominent speculators who had rated as millionaires only a short time before. Another phenomenon of the "bust" period were the radical movements which mushroomed up almost overnight (see Los Angeles). The drought, which during the 30's created the "dust-bowl" in the Plains States, brought a considerable migration of displaced farmers who were known as "Okies" because many of them came from Oklahoma. This added to the problems of a region already in the throes of depression & great unemployment.

Southern California, semi-urban in character, including the Los Angeles metropolitan area with its 4,000,000 inhabitants, had its own peculiar evolution: Irrigation made intensive cultivation, particularly of citrus fruits, possible; great oil deposits & cheap electric power brought a rapid industrial expansion; shipping & commerce were attracted by two excellent harbors—San Diego, one of the country's best natural ports, & San Pedro (L.A.), a great, man-made terminal; a sunny subtropical climate brought the movies to Hollywood &, together with recreational resources of the mountains, the sea shore &, more recently, of fashionable desert oases, accounted for the migration to S. California of hundreds of thousands of visitors as well as permanent residents. This L.A. metropolitan area was always a separate little world to itself, so much so indeed, that for many years it wished to break away from northern part of the state, alleging unfair discrimination. Today, the balance of population having shifted, the L.A. region is in a position to hold its own against the north.

Oregon & Washington developed more slowly than California. There were fewer "gold-rushes." The region's prosperity has been largely dependent on lumber, of which it still has the nation's greatest reserves, fisheries, & agriculture stimulated by great irrigation projects, of which the Columbia River project is the most recent & the greatest. Many of the region's industries are connected either with the processing of lumber, agricultural products, fish packing or mining. The two World Wars stimulated shipbuilding & industries connected with non-ferrous metals.

The tide of immigration continued along the old Oregon trail & the new road built by Sam Barlow through northern Oregon. Immigration into Washington from the south had to move up by boat on the Cowlitz River & then by swampy trail to Puget Sound. Finally a good highway over which stagecoaches drove was completed from the Columbia River to Olympia. In the 1870's the enterprising citizens of Seattle pushed a road across Stevens Pass in the Cascades. But the coming of the railroads, up from the south, to Tacoma, along the Columbia River, & last, over the Cascades, brought the greatest stream of immigrants. The population of the Willamette & Puget Sound cities doubled & trebled in a matter of decades. Discovery of gold in Alaska contributed to the expansion of the Puget Sound communities, especially Seattle, which has enjoyed a quasi-monopoly of the Alaska trade.

Both states have had local reform movements. Washington has experimented with radical legislation in various fields, a minimum wage law, the initiative & referendum, etc. Many of its cities have tried municipal ownership of public utilities, with considerable success. Seattle is at the present time engaged in the completion

# THE WEST COAST

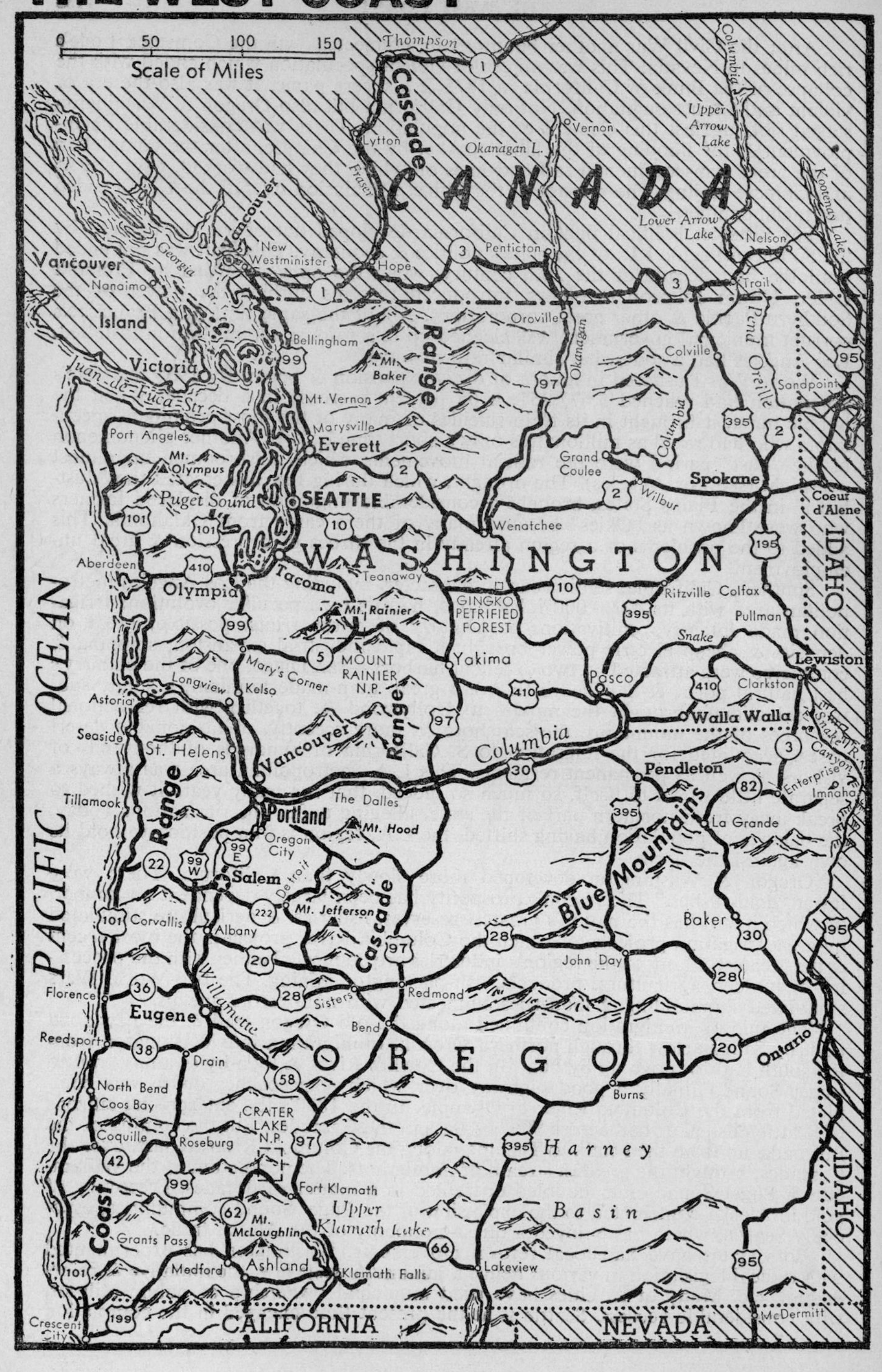

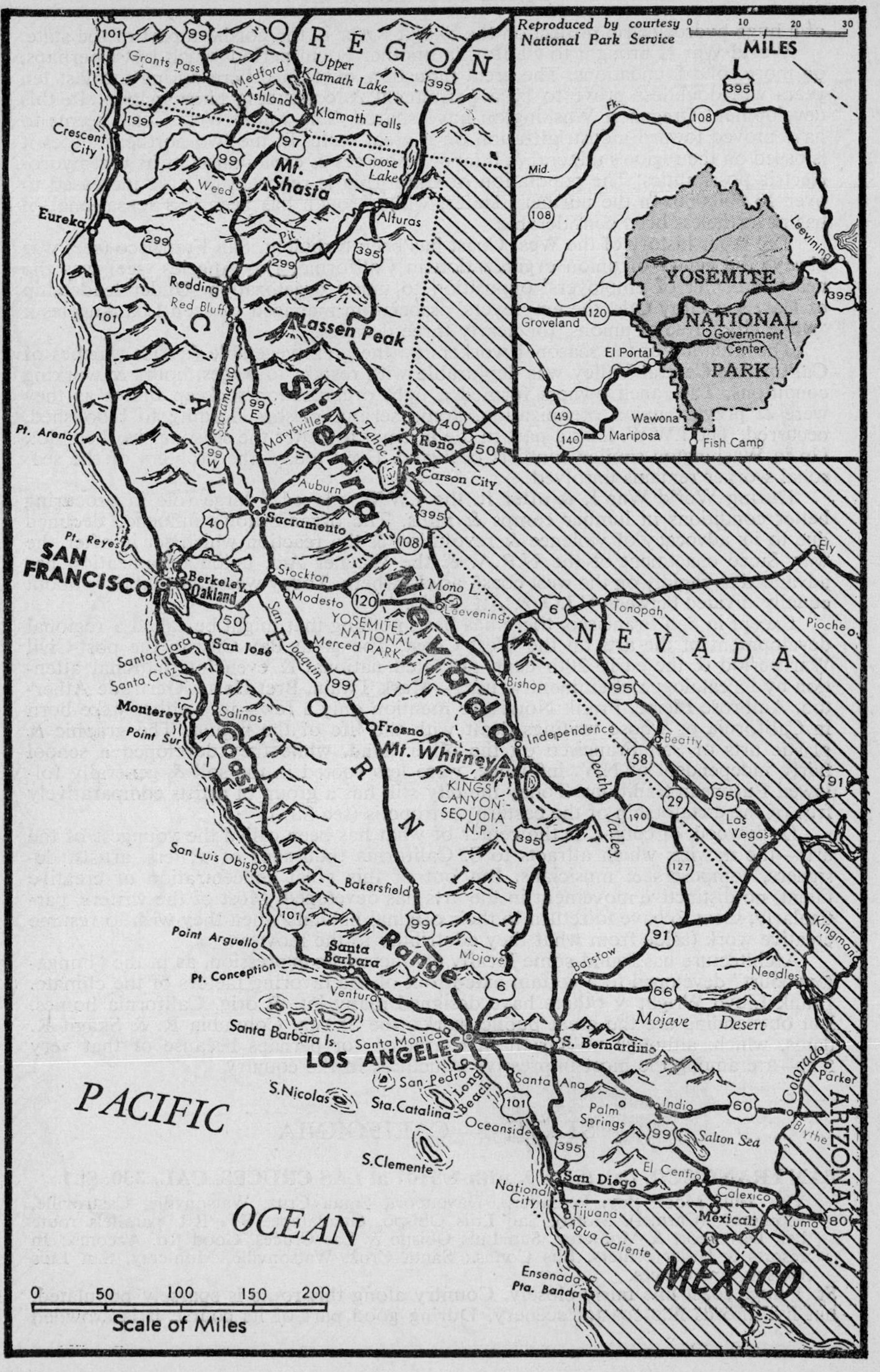

Reproduced by courtesy National Park Service
0 10 20 30
MILES
YOSEMITE NATIONAL PARK
Government Center
Groveland
El Portal
Wawona
Mariposa
Fish Camp
Leevining
Mid.
Fk.
OREGON
Grants Pass
Medford
Ashland
Upper Klamath Lake
Klamath Falls
Crescent City
Goose Lake
Mt. Shasta
Weed
Eureka
Alturas
Pit
Redding
Red Bluff
Lassen Peak
Sacramento
Marysville
L. Tahoe
Reno
Carson City
Auburn
Pt. Arena
Pt. Reyes
SAN FRANCISCO
Berkeley
Oakland
Stockton
Modesto
Mono L.
Leevening
YOSEMITE NATIONAL PARK
Merced
San Joaquin
Sierra Nevada
CALIFORNIA
San José
Santa Clara
Santa Cruz
Monterey
Point Sur
Salinas
Coast Range
Fresno
Mt. Whitney
Bishop
Independence
KINGS CANYON SEQUOIA N.P.
Tonopah
Ely
Pioche
NEVADA
Beatty
Death Valley
Las Vegas
San Luis Obispo
Bakersfield
Point Arguello
Pt. Conception
Santa Barbara
Ventura
Mojave
Barstow
Needles
Kingman
Mojave Desert
Santa Barbara Is.
Santa Monica
LOS ANGELES
S. Bernardino
San Pedro
Long Beach
Santa Ana
S. Nicolas
Sta. Catalina
Oceanside
Palm Springs
Indio
Salton Sea
Colorado
Parker
Blythe
ARIZONA
S. Clemente
San Diego
El Centro
National City
Calexico
Mexicali
Yuma
Tijuana
Agua Caliente
Ensenada
Pta. Banda
MEXICO
PACIFIC OCEAN
0 50 100 150 200
Scale of Miles
101
99
199
97
395
299
99 E
99 W
40
50
108
120
6
95
58
29
190
91
127
66
1
60
80
140
49

of a huge hydroelectric project on the Skagit River in the northern part of the state.

World War II brought to California another boom period which rests, perhaps, on more solid foundations. The great industries developed here during the last ten years will doubtless prove to be a permanent & continuing phenomenon. In this development Oregon & Washington have shared. The whole West Coast seems to have moved toward industrialization on a great scale. In the two northern states it is based on the region's mineral & lumber resources & exploitation of its vast hydro-electric possibilities. The population of California is reported to have increased to over 13,000,000. In the northern states, while growth has been less sensational, it has nevertheless been considerable.

The labor history of the West Coast has been turbulent. San Francisco (see) was always the center of union organization in California. Los Angeles (see) was the heart & center of employers' opposition to union organization. Under leadership of Harrison Gray Otis, the employers' association managed to keep Los Angeles a "white city," free of unions, for nearly three decades.

The situation of the seasonal workers on the great vegetable & fruit ranches of California's Central Valley was deplorable with respect to wages, hours & working conditions. The ranch owners formed a tight organization to keep things as they were & prevent union organization. Some serious clashes, leading to bloodshed, occurred. The I.W.W. took a part in the attempt to better the seasonal workers' lot. Up in Washington similar conflicts occurred. Even today, the problem of the seasonal worker remains unsolved.

During World War I, & after it, the I.W.W. played a large role in procuring better conditions in lumber camps & mills. The organization's influence declined due to its advocacy of violence & revolution & the reaction which set in after the war. Since enactment of the N.R.A. & the Wagner Act, union organization has advanced as rapidly on the west coast, as elsewhere. Today west coast labor is about equally divided between C.I.O. & A.F. of L.

Except in San Francisco, there has been nothing that might be called a regional development of the arts on the West Coast. The great Bay City in the post-Civil War period & the early 20th cent. attracted national & even international attention by its catalogue of eminent writers—Mark Twain, Bret Harte, Gertrude Atherton, Ambrose Bierce, Frank Norris, to mention only a few—who either were born in California or whose writings dealt with the life of the region. The graphic & plastic arts of San Francisco on the other hand, while they developed a school fairly independent of N.Y. influence, were less rooted in the soil & generally followed European traditions. Today the city still has a group of artists comparatively free of the dictatorship of the eastern metropolis (see S.F.).

Hollywood, of course, is the center of what has been called the youngest of the arts—the movies, which attracts to S. California thousands of writers, artists, designers, composers & musicians. But out of this great concentration of creative talent, no distinctive movement in the arts has developed. Most of the writers, particularly, seem to have to return to their original habitats when they wish to resume creative work (aside from what they contribute to the movies).

Architecture has found some locally characteristic expression, as in the "bungalow court" developed to a certain extent out of the favoring factors of the climate. Frank Lloyd Wright & others have designed many int. & orig. California homes. But outstanding are the great public works, the Shasta, Columbia R. & Skagit R. dams, which, although utilitarian in character—or perhaps because of that very fact—are among the most impressive structures in the country.

## STATE 1—CALIFORNIA

### SAN FRANCISCO, Cal. (S) to J. with US101 at LAS CRUCES, CAL. 350. St.1

Via: Half Moon Bay, Pescadero, Davenport, Santa Cruz, Watsonville, Castroville, Monterey, (Carmel), Morro, San Luis Obispo, Guadalupe. S.P. RR. parallels route bet. Davenport & Monterey, San Luis Obispo & Las Cruces. Good Rd. Accoms.: In resorts & larger centers. Bus Conns.: Santa Cruz, Watsonville, Monterey, San Luis Obispo, Las Cruces.

St. 1 hugs coast line fairly closely. Country along this route is sparsely populated, but hy. affords fine coastal scenery. During good part of its course it is crowded to edge of sea by mts. At times it climbs mt. heights, giving magnificent views of pounding surf below, & at times roadbed is literally hacked out of cliffs overhanging sea. This, in general, was route taken by Don Gaspar de Portolá in 1769 when he came up from San Diego searching for a good harbor. After almost 4 months of weary marching, members of his party discovered San Francisco Bay, but Portolá never saw it & returned to report that search had ended in failure.

**0. SAN FRANCISCO.** From Van Ness Ave. (W) on Hayes St. to Franklin St.; (R) to Fulton St.; (L) to Funston (13th) Ave.; (L) through Golden Gate Pk. into 19th Ave. & (S) into Junípero Serra Blvd. **10.** J. with St.5 (Skyline Blvd. see San Francisco VI). **18. SAN PEDRO CR.,** dominated by lofty **San Pedro Pt.** Chief crop of San Pedro Valley is artichoke. At San Pedro Cr. is J. with Rd. leading (L) 1.5$^{m}$ to int. **Sanchez Adobe** (1842). **22. MONTARA,** surrounded by fields of everlasting (straw) flowers, this region's special product. **23.5 MOSS BEACH,** beautifully situated on rock-bound shore. Marine gardens offshore are famous. **25.5.** Hy. circles beautiful **HALF MOON BAY,** with its rocky headland, **Pillar Pt. 56. PIGEON PT. LIGHTH.** (O.Tues.-Fri.& Sat.afts.), with fine views. Here in 1853 Boston Clipper "Carrier Pigeon" went ashore. Beyond **PUNTA DEL NUEVO, 63.5.,** also with lighth., St.1., after swerving inland, returns to shore & travels along roadway actually chopped out of cliffs. **65.5. WADDELL CR.,** where Portolá's expedition camped in Oct. 1769. Hy. now swings inland again, twisting up mt. spur (excellent views) & then descends through forested canyon & narrow valley to seaside.

**87. SANTA CRUZ,** facing Monterey Bay & backed up against Santa Cruz Mts. Here, Sept. 1791, Misión La Exaltacion de la Santa Cruz was founded. Colony of settlers sent from Mexico was est. here, 1797. This settlement, across R. from mission, was named Branciforte after Mex. Viceroy, Marquis de Branciforte. In 1818, Hippolyte de Bouchard, Buenos Aires privateersman, sacked Monterey, & padres fled to Misión Santa Clara. Santa Cruz Mission, secularized in 1834, soon fell into decay. But during Amer. regime, city around mission plaza developed as busy shipping center, while Branciforte remained much as it always was. It is recorded that as late as 1867, bullfights still took place in old village. Reproduction of **Misión de Santa Cruz** (O.fee), on Emmet St., was built in 1931, near site of old structure, destroyed by earthquake, 1857. It houses int. relics. On hill behind mission is ancient **Graveyard. Ch. of the Holy Cross,** facing Plaza, was built in 1858, rebuilt in 1889. Adobe **Neary H.,** on School St., was formerly hqs. of corporal of mission guard. Adobe **Rodriguez H.,** adjoining, dates from 1838. At ft. of Pacific Ave., on ocean, are **Santa Cruz Mun. Pier,** boardwalk with casino, bathing pavilion & amusement pk. Pacific Ave. leads (R) into West Cliff Dr., to **Santa Cruz Lighth. Sta.** (O.2-4 Tues.& Thurs.), **Mun. Laveaga Pk.,** & **Natural Bridges Beach St. Pk.** In Santa Cruz is J. with St.9 running (E) to J. with US101 (see).

**91. SOQUEL,** in Soquel Cr. Canyon, at J. with Rd. (R) to **Capitola** (resort), 1.5$^{m}$, & **New Brighton Beach St. Pk.** (surf f.). **94.** J. with paved Rd. leading (R) c.0.5$^{m}$ to **Sea Cliff St. Pk.** (surf f.) with fine beach. **106.5. WATSONVILLE,** straddling Pajaro R., ships annually 6½ million boxes of apples, as well as quantities of other fruits & vegetables, & has many food processing plants. Town's plaza was formerly scene of bullfights & bear baiting, as well as horse racing. Small cannon in square belonged to Pacific Mail Steamship "Oregon," & in 1850 fired salute announcing Cal.'s admission to Union. Beach Rd. leads (R) 5$^{m}$ to **Sunset Beach St. Pk.** (surf f.) on Monterey Bay. At **109.5.,** on edge of bluff stands, **H. of Glass** (c.1824), Casa Materna of Vallejo family, in state of disrepair. Its name is said to derive from its glassed-in veranda. Vallejo had received, by mistake, shipment of 12 dozen windows which he placed in upper veranda. From Vallejo Ranch in 1835, Juan Bautista Alvarado & José Castro led an expedition against Monterey (see below) in attempt to est. independent state of Alta California. **128. FORT ORD,** largest U.S. Army post on W. Coast. **132. U.S. NAVAL POST-GRADUATE ACADEMY** (formerly Hotel Del Monte). In surrounding fors. are bridle trls., race track, steeple-chase & cross country courses, swim. pools, golf course & ball fields.

## 133. MONTEREY

Accoms.: all types. Info.: C. of C., 585 Munras St.; Cal. St. Auto Assoc., 520 Fremont St. Swim.: Surf swim. at beaches in environs; Monterey High School pool, S. end of Larkin St. (free). Hunt.: Los Padres Nat. For.—deer, boar, rabbit, quail, doves &

pigeons; For. Service regulations. Fish.: Fresh water f. in near-by rivers; surf f. Monterey Bay, Pacific Grove, Carmel Bay & below Carmel. Deep sea f. boats at Fisherman's Wharf, N. end Main St. Annual Events: Birthday Party, pageants, June 3; Flower Show, June; County Fair, Sept.; Blessing of Fleet, Sept.

Monterey (1770) is located on peninsula at S. end of Monterey Bay, flanked (E) by Santa Lucia Mts. Indigenous Monterey cypress & Monterey pine grow along shoreline. City is center of famous resort & residential reg., with Pacific Grove & Carmel-by-the-Sea as its close neighbors. Bay was visited by Vizcaino in 1602. Gaspar de Portolá's expedition decided on site of Monterey as most desirable for presidio in Alta Cal. City was founded by Franciscan friars, who est. their Misión de San Carlos de Monterey, 2nd of Cal. chain, here, but later moved it to Carmel Valley (see below). In 1775, new settlement became capital of Alta Cal. In 1818 Hippolyte de Bouchard, Fr. pirate, pillaged town. In 1836, Juan Bautista Alvarado captured it after firing only one shot. Under Amer. rule, city became market center of rich agric. dist. & important port for fishing fleets. Leading industries today are fishing & fish packing. Although pop. consists largely of native-born Americans—some of them paisanos, descendants of original settlers (see Steinbeck's "Tortilla Flat")—Mexicans, Italians, Portuguese & orientals add color to street scene. Monterey, by beauty of its situation & charm of its old Sp. setting, has attracted many writers & artists to become residents. Rbt. Louis Stevenson was perhaps most famous visitor. Older bldgs. in city are adobe, built in fine old Mex.-Sp. style. Since Amer. occupation, distinctive type of architecture, known as "Monterey," blending of Sp. & Amer. features, has been developed.

PTS. OF INT.: (1) Church St. bet. Camino El Estero & Figueroa St., **Royal Presidio Chapel** (O.wks.Sun.1-5.guide.fee.1789.alts.& adds.), founded as mission by Father Junípero Serra, 1770. To keep his Ind. acolytes away from soldiers, Father Serra moved mission in 1771 to Carmel Valley (see below). This was 2nd of missions. Ch. is on site of earlier bldg., destroyed by fire. It is largely work of Ind. laborers & beautifully illustrates native primitive art. In upper gable of ornate façade is statue of Our Lady of Guadalupe. Stations of the Cross are originals, brought by Serra himself. Statue of Our Lady of Sorrows in sacristy is as old as Ch. Every Sept. Ital. fishermen celebrate Festival of Santa Rosalia here & then march to harbor for blessing of fishing fleet. (2) Main & Decatur Sts., **Old Customs H.** (O.1-5.adobe. early 19th cent.adds.rest.), now St. Hist. Landmark & oldest pub. bldg. on Pacific Coast, houses mus. of hist. relics. (3) 200-22 Main St., **Old Pacific Bldg.** (1847. adobe), one of biggest adobes in Monterey, has Memory Garden in patio (O). (4) Pacific St., bet. Jefferson & Madison Sts., **Friendly Plaza,** Monterey's civic center, with: **Colton Hall** (O.1847-49.by Rev. Walter Colton, Yankee mayor), where in 1848 Constitutional Convention was held; **Monterey Jail** (1854), where, in old days, were imprisoned some of bandits & road agents that infested hys.; **Few Mem. City Hall** (1934), in which is incorporated adobe H. built in 1843.

(5) 592 Abrego St., **Casa Abrego** (N.O.1830's.rest.), built by Don José Abrego. (6) Houston St. bet. Webster & Pearl St., **Rbt. Louis Stevenson H.,** now shop, where author lived in 1879, while working on "The Amateur Immigrant" & "Vendetta of the West." (7) Pearl & Tyler Sts., **Gen. José Castro's Hqs.** (N.O.). At rear are ruins of pit (visible from Tyler St.) in which bulls were matched with bears in old days. (8) 508 Munras St., **Cooper H.** (1829.adobe), built by Roger Cooper for his bride, daughter of Gen. Mariano Vallejo. (9) 516 Polk St., **Casa Amesti** (c.1830.adobe). (10) 500 Hartnell St., **Stokes H.** (N.O.late 1830's.adobe). (11) Main St., bet. Jefferson & Madison Sts., **H. of the Four Winds** (c.1830.adobe), named by Inds. for weather-vane on roof. (12) 464 Main St., **Sherman's Quarters,** occupied by Wm. T. Sherman, 1847-49. (13) 462 Main St., **Larkin H.** (1835), which served as U.S. consulate, 1844-46. Thomas O. Larkin was first & only Amer. consul in Cal. (14) 546 Dutra St., bet. Madison & Jefferson Sts., **Casa Vasquez** (adobe), said to have been birthpl. of bandit, Tiburcio Vasquez. (15) 510 Dutra St., **Casa Alvarado,** (adobe) home of Juan Bautista Alvarado, Gov. of Cal., 1836-42. (16) Pacific & Scott Sts., **First Amer. Theater** in Cal. (O.1-5 wks.adobe.1843). Candles & whale-oil lamps were used for footlights. Exhibits of early theatrical & hist. relics. (17) 200 Oliver St., **Casa de Oro** (O.pre-1846), used as barracks for Sp. & later for Amer. troops, now St. Hist. Mon. (18) 351 Decatur St., **First Brick H. in Cal.** (1847). (19) 391 Decatur

St., **Old Whaling Sta.** (adobe.1855), built for Portuguese whalers when 500 whaling vessels were in Pacific. Walk & patio are paved with whale vertebrae.

(20) Entrance Pacific St. beyond (N) Decatur St., **Presidio of Monterey** (360 as.), U.S. Army post. Near main gate, cross marking **Landing Pl. of Vizcaino.** On hill, **Statue of Father Serra,** who said mass here, 1770. Near ent., **Statue of John Drake Sloat,** who commanded forces that captured Monterey in Mex. War. (21) End of Main St., **Fishermen's Wharf.** Picturesque waterfront with fishing fleet, fish sheds, shops, & sea-food restaurants, is worth visiting. (22) **Cannery Row,** along which are sardine canneries & restaurants of half-dozen nationalities, is worth visit in eve. (23) On Tremont St., opp. Via Mirada, is **Cath. Cemetery** (1832). Here are buried Sp., Mex. & Amer. notables. Other int. old bldgs., mostly of adobe structure, are: (24) 599 Polk St., **Casa de La Torre** (c.1836); (25) 590 Main St., **Casas Gutiérrez** (1830's.adobe-frame); (26) 816 El Dorado St., **Casa de Soto** (c.1820); (27) 502 Pierce St., **De La Torre Adobe** (c.1852); (28) 460 Pierce St., **Casa Jesus de Soto** (c.1842); (29) 412 Pacific St., **Casa Serrano** (now restaurant.c.1834-40); (30) 414 Alvarado St., **Casa Sanchez** (c.1828.only S. part remains of orig. bldg.); (31) Pacific St. bet. Franklin & Soberanes Sts., **Merrit H.** (c.1860); (32) 314 Pacific St., **Casa Soberanes** (N.O.), hqs. of famous Vallejo family; (33) Oliver & Decatur Sts., **Casa Verde,** where Chas. Warren Stoddard, poet & writer, lived; (34) Franklin & El Estero Sts., former **French Consulate** (O.1840.adobe); (35) Boronda Lane, **Casa Boronda,** oldest residence in Monterey (1818.exter.preserved); (36) 602 Abrego St., **Casa Pacheco** (c.1840.rest.).

SIDE TRIP: Turn (R) from Monterey on Washington St., then (R) on Lighth. Ave., again (R) on 1st St. & then (L) on Ocean View Ave., to **Hopkins Marine Sta. of Stanford Univ.** on Cabrillo Pt., where studies of oceanic biology are carried on. Here also is coll. of marine life. 2.5m **Pacific Grove,** resort & residential community. On Forest Ave., **Mun. Museum** (O.exc.Mon.) containing coll. of Cal. butterflies, Monterey Bay marine life, etc. Salt water **Mun. Plunge** (fee) is near bath. beach, f. pier. Glass-bottom boats (May-Oct.), afford views of marine gardens. Follow Asilomar Blvd. (L) from Pacific Grove winding along fine coastline to J. at 3.5m with Rd. leading (L) 0.3m to **Pt. Pinos Lighth.** (O.1-4 Tues.-Thurs.). At 6.5m toll-gate to 17-mile Dr. (fee) which winds through fine forest of pines, skirting **Moss Beach** to **Pt. Joe** at 8.5m. Here fine views. 11.5m **Cypress Pt.,** overlooking Carmel Bay. Along cliffs grow Monterey Cypresses, which now are only to be found bet. Cypress Pt. & Pt. Lobos (see below). 14m. **Pebble Beach,** exclusive residential community at J. with Rd. leading (R) 0.3m to **Stillwater Cove** (resort.glass-bottom boats). At 16m turn (L) past lovely Carmel woods to J. with St.1 at 17.5m.

St.1 follows Washington St. in Monterey, turns (L) on Abrego St. & cuts across Monterey Peninsula to J. with 17-mile Dr. (see above) at **135.5. 136.** J. with Carmel Rd. leading (R) 1m to **Carmel,** famous art & literary colony. Here is center of art & literary settlement which supports open-air theater, art gallery, lecture forum & music society (presenting annual winter concerts & Bach festival). **Tor H.,** on Carmel Pt., is home of poet Robinson Jeffers, which he built with his own hands. **137.** J. with Rd.

SIDE TRIP: Take latter (L) along Carmel R. At 24m take dirt Rd. (R) climbing to **Tassajara Springs** (hot springs resort). Nearby is **China For. Camp** (4,500'; camp.facils.).

**137.5.** J. with Rd. leading (R) 0.5m to **Misión de San Carlos Borromeo de Rio Carmelo** overlooking Carmel Bay. Mission, 2nd in Cal., was est. 1770 at Monterey (see above) & moved to present site following yr. Ch. was founded in 1793 & served surrounding Ind. pop. After secularization, mission fell into ruin, but in 80's was restored. In Ch. are baptistry & font, carved by Ind. neophytes; modern mortuary chapel with reproductions of orig. murals; & **Mon.** to Fray Junípero Serra (by Jo Mora, sculptor), founder of mission. Serra, his co-worker, Padre Crespi, & his successors are buried in sanctuary. Serra Pageant, Aug. **140. PT. LOBOS ST. PK.** at entrance to Pt. Lobos Reserve (fee for cars.pic.no camp.) on scenically fine promontory. Sea lions congregate on pt. **155.** J. with Rd. leading (R) 0.5m to **Pt. Sur Lighth.** (O.1-4 Mon.Wed.& Fri.), high above surf. Off Pt. Sur, 1935, U.S. Navy dirigible "Macon" went down in dense fog. **163. PFEIFFER BIG SUR ST. PK.** (pic.swim.horses.cabins.restaurant.). **187. LUCIA** (hotel.restaurant), first place beyond Big Sur where gasoline is available. From here to **GORDA** at **200.** is one of most sensational stretches of route. Rd., in places, has been hewn out of solid rock. **213. SAN CARPOJO CR.,** where country becomes more open again. Here is 1st of 3 ranches that comprise W. R. Hearst's 270,000-a. ranch, which stretches for 50m.

**226.** J. with dirt Rd. leading (L) $6^{m}$ to **W. R. Hearst Castle** (N.O.), on summit of La Cuesta Encantada (enchanted hill), fabulous San Simeon home of the newspaper tycoon, resembling castle dominating fortified hilltop village. Estate has its own flying field, swim. pool, & zoo stocked with bison, giraffes & kangaroos. H. is furnished with paintings, statuary & other treasures of antiquity from all over the world. **232. SAN SIMEON CR. BEACH ST. PK. 249. CAYUCAS BEACH ST. PK. 255.5. MORRO,** named for **Morro Rock,** which rises 776′ above lagoon, at J. with Rd. leading (R) $1.5^{m}$ to **Morro Beach St. Pk.** (fee for car.camp.pic.recr.). St.1 now turns inland past volcanic cones, Cerro Alto, Cerro Romualdo, & Bishop's Peak. **269. SAN LUIS OBISPO** (on US101 (S). see) at J. with US101 with which St.1 unites to **PISMO BEACH, 281.,** where it branches off. **297. GUADALUPE.**

**328. LOMPOC,** center of great flower-seed growing region gay with blossoms in summer time. **329.** J. with paved Rd. leading (L) $2.5^{m}$ to **Misión La Purísima Concepción,** 11th of missions, founded in 1787. First Ch. was destroyed in 1812 by earthquake; thereafter present bldg. was erected. In 1824 Ind. neophytes seized mission, but month later were dispossessed by troops. La Purísima, after secularization, was sold, but in 1903 was donated to Santa Barbara Cty. Bldgs. restored. Residence bldg. has cloister with colonnade supporting low, red-tiled roof. Beneath floor in front of altar is grave of Padre Mariano Payeras, under whose direction Ch. was built. **350. LAS CRUCES.** J. with US101.

## US 101(S)—CALIFORNIA

**SAN FRANCISCO, CAL. (S) to MEXICAN BORDER** (at Tijuana, Mex.). **588. US101.**

Via: Burlingame, San Mateo, Redwood City, Palo Alto, Mountain View, Santa Clara, San Jose, Gilroy, Salinas, King City, San Miguel, Paso Robles, San Luis Obispo, Santa Maria, Santa Barbara, Montecito, Ventura, Los Angeles, Whittier, Anaheim, Santa Ana, San Juan Capistrano, Oceanside, Carlsbad, San Diego, San Ysidro. S.P. RR. parallels route to Los Angeles, A.T. & S.F. RR. to San Diego. Bus conns. throughout. Accoms.: Frequent & of all types.

US101, from S.F. (S), follows El Camino Real, which in days of Sp. rule linked Cal.'s 21 missions, its pueblos & presidios. It runs along tree-lined blvd. through "peninsula" suburbs, then through fruit-growing reg. of Santa Clara & fertile Salinas valleys, & crosses Santa Lucia Mts. to San Luis Obispo. It touches coast briefly, soon to swing back inland, only to return once more to shore front, which it then follows to Ventura. Here it again turns inland, through San Fernando Valley, to Los Angeles, from which it cont. through oil fields, gardens & orange groves to Doheny Pk. on ocean & from there follows barren coast line to San Diego & Mexico. Alt. routes, which hug coast more consistently, are St.1 bet. S.F. & San Luis Obispo (see) & US101 alt. bet. El Rio & Doheny Pk.

### Sec. 1: SAN FRANCISCO to SAN LUIS OBISPO. 243.5.

**0. SAN FRANCISCO.** For towns & pts. of int. bet. S.F. & J. with St.9, **40.5.,** see San Francisco VI. **42.5. ARMISTICE OAK,** scene of armistice, Jan. 8, 1847, ending Santa Clara Valley's revolt, led by Francisco Sanchez against Amers. **46. SANTA CLARA.** Here was founded Misión Santa Clara de Assisi (1777). All that remains of orig. bldgs. is remnant of adobe cloister. Ch. of comparatively recent date, reproducing one built in 1822, contains sacred mementos. Mission was transformed into college (chartered 1855), which became **Santa Clara Univ.** (Sp.type bldgs.). **Univ. Lib.** contains exhibits of precious relics & paintings.

**49.5. SAN JOSE**

Accoms.: All types. Info.: C. of C., Civic Auditorium, San Carlos & S. Market St.; A.A.A., 926 The Alameda; Cal. St. Auto Assoc., 1024 The Alameda.

San Jose (locally pronounced san-o-zay), is near S. end of S.F. Bay, in fertile Santa Clara Valley, bet. mt. ranges. Guadalupe & Coyote Rs. (dry great part of yr.) cut through city. Santa Clara (NW) is physically (although not administratively) part of San Jose. The Alameda, a broad ave., connects them. City was founded 1777, as San José de Guadalupe. In Mex. days, bull & bear fights were popular. San Jose's real expansion dates from tide of immigration in 1840's. In 1849 it became state capital, with accompanying celebrations & considerable conviviality, but kept this distinction only until 1851. After collapse of gold-rush boom, town developed as market center of valley's fruit farms. Today it is one of largest canning & dried-fruit packing cities of world.

PTS. OF INT.: (1) S. Market & San Carlos Sts., **Civic Auditorium** (1936), in which are Main & Little Theaters. (2) S. 4th & Antonio Sts., **San Jose St. College** (1862), oldest state-owned pub. educational institution in Cal. Bldgs. in Cal. Mission style. (3) 430 S. 8th St., **Edwin Markham H.,** now college infirmary. Here poet wrote "The Man with the Hoe." (4) 1342 Naglee Ave., **Rosicrucian Pk. & Hqs. for W. Hemisphere** (O.guides). Here is **Egyptian Temple & Oriental Mus.** whose inter. is lighted by artificial moonlight & whose walls are painted in ancient Egyptian manner & hung with tapestries said to be from temples in Cairo & Luxor. Mus. contains reproduction of ancient Egyptian rock tomb. Also worth visiting are **Planetarium** (O.lecture.Sun.aft.& eve.) & **Amenhotep Shrine.** (5) Naglee & Dana Aves., **San Jose Municipal Rose Garden** (O) with finest coll. of roses in U.S., at its best in May, when 100,000 roses are in bloom.

SIDE TRIPS: (A) Take E. Santa Clara St., which becomes Alum Rock Ave., (L) from San Jose to J. with Mt. Hamilton Rd., 6.5m.

(1) Turn (L) here on Alum Rock Ave. 2m to **Alum Rock Pk.** (629 as.pic.swim.recr. facils.). (2) Turn (R) from J. (above) on Mt. Hamilton Rd. (scenically very fine) to summit of **Mt. Hamilton** (4,029′) at 19m. On W. peak, **Lick Observatory** (O.guides. telescopes on specified nights), founded with a $700,000 endowment bestowed by James Lick, eccentric millionaire whose body is buried under one of bldg.'s supporting pillars. Observatory, costing $610,000, was completed 1888. Among other astronomical instruments, is observatory's 20″ astrographic telescope, gift of Carnegie Foundation. In 1892 scientists here discovered 5th satellite of Jupiter. Lick astronomers took 1st really successful photographs of comets & Milky Way & began modern study of nebulae.

(B) Take St.17 (San Carlos St.) (R) from San Jose 2m to J. with San Jose-Los Gatos Rd. Straight ahead here on Stevens Cr. Rd. 2m to **Winchester Mystery H.** (O.fee) in which are 160 rooms, formerly home of Mrs. Sara L. Winchester, widow of firearms manufacturer. Its many rooms were built because Mrs. Winchester, who had become spiritualist, was informed by message from beyond that as long as she kept adding to H., death would never overtake her. She died in 1922.

Cont. on St.17 from J. with Stevens Cr. Rd. (see above) to **J. with St.1** (see) **in Santa Cruz** at 33m.

**86.5.** J. with paved Rd.

SIDE TRIP: Take latter (L) 3.5m to **San Juan,** ranching community with int. adobe dwellings, at foot of Gabilan Range. Here is **Misión San Juan Bautista,** 15th & largest of Cal. missions. Annually, on St. John the Baptist's Day (June 25) week end, fiesta & pageant are held in open-air theater here to comm. founding in 1797. In mission Ch. are altar painted by Inds., old chairs, candelabra & figures of saints brought from Mexico. Reredos was carved by Thos. Doak, Cal.'s 1st Yankee settler, in return for board & lodging. Adj. room contains 2 baptismal fonts carved in 1797. Behind mission are buried some 4,000 Inds. Oldest bldg. in San Juan, **Plaza Hotel** (1792.enlarged 1856), was stagecoach stopover. Adj. is **Castro H.** (1825), built by Gen. José Castro, afterward Gov. of Cal. On S. side of plaza is **Zanetta H.,** center of social festivities in 60's & 70's. Various old structures in San Juan are now preserved as San Juan Bautista St. Mon. On Pagan Hill is large cross on site of original wooden one erected by mission fathers. Above it rises Gabilan Peak (3,169′), in **Fremont St. Pk.,** whither Lt. Col. John C. Frémont retreated, 1846, defying orders from Mex. authorities to leave country. Frémont finally withdrew in face of superior forces to Sutter's Fort. Main side route cont. to Hollister at J. with St.25 which take (R) to **Tres Pinos** at 19m. On neighboring ranch Frank Norris spent considerable time acquiring material about large-scale wheat farming for "The Octopus." 24m **Rancho Ciénega de los Paicines,** at Paicines, still intact. In this vic. bandit Tiburcio Vasquez was active. After robbery committed here, he was captured & hanged. 43.5m J. with Rd.

Take latter (R) 5m to entrance of **Pinnacles Nat. Mon.** (10,000 as.pics.camp.facils.), in magnificent mt. & for. reg. of caverns, ravines, cliffs & spire-like peaks.

St.25 cont. to J. with paved Rd. at 55m. Turn (R) here to **King City** at 70m, on US101 (see below).

US101 now runs into Salinas Valley, named for Salinas R. salt water pools. Valley is still cattle country, although bottom lands are cultivated. **104.5. SALINAS RODEO FIELD.** Rodeo is held in July. **105. SALINAS,** trading pt. for valley's ranches & big lettuce-packing center. Here in 1936 took place lettuce workers' strike which ended in violent clash bet. state police & strikers.

SIDE TRIPS: (A) Take Rd. (L) 5.5m from Salinas to **Natividad,** scene of Battle of Natividad, Nov.16,1846, bet. Mexs. & Amers. In Gabilan foothills near here is adobe **Casa de Joaquin Gomez.**
(B) From Salinas, Rd. branches off (W) to **Monterey,** (worth visit) on St.1 (see).

**132.5.** J. with paved Rd. leading (R) 1m to J. with 2nd paved Rd. leading (R) 2m to ruins of **Misión de Nuestra Senora de la Soledad** (O), founded 1791, 13th of missions. After its secularization in 1835 it became so impoverished that Padre Vicente Sarria, who refused to leave, died of starvation on altar steps before mass one Sun. morn. US101 cont. (S) to J. with Rd. at **150.5.**

SIDE TRIP: Take latter (R) here 17.5m to **Jolon.** Turn (R) here on dirt Rd. 6.5m to **Misión San Antonio de Padua,** 3rd of missions, founded 1771. Ch. (O.1810-21) & colonnade remain. Annually, St. Anthony's Day (June 13) is celebrated with masses & fiesta.

**198.5. SAN MIGUEL,** surrounded by almond orchards. Here is **Misión San Miguel Arcangel** (O), 16th of missions, fairly well preserved, founded 1797. Bldgs. surround court bordered by arched cloister. Ch. (1816-18) has wall designs painted by Inds. Ind. relics are displayed in adj. bldg. **207. PASO ROBLES.** Here are sulphur baths said to have medicinal value (mun.bath & hotels). **218.5. ATASCADERO. 226. SANTA MARGARITA,** where are remains of massive **Asistencia de Santa Margarita,** outpost of Misión San Luis Obispo. US101 now ascends Santa Lucia Mts. to **CUESTA PASS** (1,570'). In 1846, Frémont led his followers through this pass to attack San Luis Obispo. **243.5. SAN LUIS OBISPO,** at ft. of Santa Lucia Mts. Here, in 1772, Fray Junípero Serra est. **Misión San Luis Obispo de Tolosa,** 5th of chain. Ch. (1792) is surrounded by modern bldgs. & its exter. has been altered & disfigured. At San Luis Obispo is J. with St.1 (see).

## Sec. 2: SAN LUIS OBISPO to LOS ANGELES. 203.5.

**12. PISMO BEACH. 32.5. SANTA MARIA,** center for Santa Maria Valley ranches. **66.5. BUELLTON,** at J. with Rd. running (L) 4m to **Misión de Santa Ynez** (O), 19th of missions, est. 1804. **76. LAS CRUCES.** Here is J. with St.1 (see). Route now runs along narrow shelf above sea & then through farmland along Santa Ynez Mts., whose highest peak (L) is **La Cumbre** (3,985').

### 108.5. SANTA BARBARA

Accoms.: All types, incl. auto courts. Info.: C. of C., 11 E. De la Guerra St.: Recr. Center, Carillo & Anacapa Sts. Swim.: W. Beach, 320 W. Cabrillo Blvd., still water & surf. Fish.: Off breakwater & Stearns Wharf, S. end State St. Boats for deep-sea f. at Stearns Wharf. Annual Events: Garden Tours from Recr. Center, 100 E. Carillo St., spring & summer. Old Spanish Days, 3-day fiesta, during full moon in Aug. Semana Nautica, marine celebration, July 4.

Santa Barbara lies on slopes of Santa Ynez Mts. & is one of most charming of Cal.'s residential cities. Dominant architectural style is Sp. Its water front is largely devoted to bath. & recr. Present site of city was 1st visited in 1542 by navigator, Cabrillo. In 1603 Vizcaino named reg. Santa Barbara. City was founded by Capt. José Ortega in 1782, & Franciscan Fathers est. Misión de Santa Barbara soon after. In 1820's, after Mexico's liberation from Spain, exchange of ranch products for goods brought by Yankees developed on considerable scale. In 1846 Lt. Col. John C. Frémont occupied city. Three weeks later it was ceded, with rest of Cal., to U.S. From this time on, town prospered greatly as cattle raising center. But drought of 1864 killed off most cattle & ended this source of prosperity. In more recent times Santa Barbara has developed as tourist & wealthy residential community.

PTS. OF INT.: (1) Anapamu & Anacapa Sts., **Santa Barbara County Cth.** (Sp.style), with murals (2nd floor) by Dan Sayre Groesbeck. It houses **Mus. of Santa Barbara Hist. Soc.** (O.Mon.2-4) containing Ind., hist. & ranch relics. (2) 15 E. Carrillo St., old **Carrillo Adobe** (O.rest.& rebuilt) houses Santa Barbara Foundation. (3) 15 E. De la Guerra St., old **H. of Don José de la Guerra,** commandant of presidio. Court yards & passage ways called El Paseo de la Guerra surround house. (4) **Orena Adobe,** 29 E. de la Guerra St., & (5) **Covarrubias Adobe,** 715 Santa Barbara St., are also fine examples of early Sp. architecture. (6) Along W. Cabrillo Blvd., **Yacht Harbor & W. Beach** (bath.). (7) End of E. Cabrillo Blvd., **Andree Clark Bird Refuge.** (8) End E. Anapamu St., **Santa Barbara Cty. Bowl,** where hist. play is produced in Aug. as part of 3-day, annual celebration of "Old Spanish Days." (9) Cliff Dr., **Santa Barbara College of Univ. of Cal.** (10) Los Olivos St., bet. Garden

& Laguna Sts., **Misión de Santa Barbara** (O), founded 1786. It is best preserved of all missions. (Built 1815 to replace earlier bldg., destroyed by 1812 earthquake, & repaired after 1925 quake). Ch. was designed by Padre Riptoll. In Ch. is tomb of Father Francisco Garcia Diego y Moreno, 1st Bishop of Cal. The Stations of the Cross were brought from Mexico in 1797. Altar light has not been extinguished since mission's founding. Bodies of Franciscan friars are buried in crypts set in walls of bldg., & 4,000 Inds. are buried in trenches across garden. Art objects, relics of Canalino tribe & old paintings brought from Spain are displayed. (11) Puesta del Sol Rd. & Mission Creek, **Mus. of Natural Hist.** (O.Sp.Col.); nat. hist. & Ind. material. (12) 1289 Mission Canyon, **Santa Barbara Botanic Garden** (O); coll. of Cal. flora. (13) Offshore from Santa Barbara, c.20$^m$, separated from mainland by Channel, lie scenically int. **Santa Barbara Is.**, northernmost group of Channel Is. Largest are **Santa Cruz, Santa Rosa** & **San Miguel,** where deep-sea f. is good. Cabrillo. Sp. explorer, is said to be buried on last.

**112.5. MONTECITO,** millionaire colony (tours through many estates by Santa Barbara Garden Club). **118.5. CARPINTERIA.** Linden Ave. leads (R) to **Carpinteria State Beach Pk. 135. VENTURA,** oil well & lima bean farm center. Main & Figueroa Sts., **Misión San Buenaventura** (O.fee), 9th of missions & last of those founded by Father Serra, 1782. Mission has been rebuilt along authentic lines. Relics in small bldg. on patio. N. Cal. & Poli Sts. **Pioneer Mus.** (O) in Ventura County Cth., containing int. colls. In front of Cth., **Statue of Junípero Serra.** (First step toward canonization of Fray Serra—a plea by Diocesan Hist. Commission of Fresno—was taken Dec. 1948.)

**143. EL RIO** & J. with US101 Alt.

SIDE TRIP: Take latter, which strikes towards coast. 3$^m$ **Oxnard,** center of sugar beet reg. US101 Alt. now runs along coast. 37$^m$ **Malibu** (Ind.deer), resort of cinema celebrities. 42.5$^m$ J. with St.27.

Take latter (L) 7.5$^m$ through deep canyon to **Topanga Springs** (pic.). At 9.5$^m$, **Topanga Summit** (1,560′), with splendid view. At 13$^m$ J. with US101.

53$^m$ **Santa Monica** (see Los Angeles I) at J. with US66.

US101 cont. inland through cultivated & irrigated valleys.

**157.5.** J. with paved Rd. leading (R) to **Sherwood L.,** 9$^m$. This was location for several movies, notably "Robin Hood" & "Tarzan of the Apes." **162. THOUSAND OAKS** (accoms.). Here is **Goebel Lion Farm** (O.fee), supplying animals to movie studios. **175. LOS ANGELES PET CEMETERY. 181.** J. with St.1 (see Los Angeles V for pts. of int. bet. this J. & L.A.). **203.5. LOS ANGELES** (see).

## Sec. 3: LOS ANGELES to MEXICAN BORDER. 141.

**0. LOS ANGELES.** In L.A. follow Aliso St. from Civic Center, conn. with Boyle Ave., which leads into Whittier Blvd. For pts. of int. & towns to & incl. **Irvine** at 41$^m$, see Los Angeles III. **58. SAN JUAN CAPISTRANO,** which owes its existence to **Misión de San Juan Capistrano** (O.fee), is populated with descendants of early Mex. settlers. Mission suffered from earthquakes in 1812 & 1918. It was dedicated in 1776 by Fray Junípero Serra & bldgs. were completed, 1806. Ch. was finest of mission churches; cruciform, 180′ long & 90′ broad, with arched roof, 7 domes & tall belfry tower. Mission is noted for "Capistrano swallows" who build their nests in ruins. It is said that for nearly a century swallows have left their nests on St. John's Day, Oct. 23, & returned on St. Joseph's Day, Mar. 19. Once, it is reported, they were slightly delayed by storms. In 1947 they made up for their tardiness by arriving on Mar. 14. Opening on mission garden is **Mus.** with int. coll. of vestments, parchments & paintings. **60.5.** Massive adobe **CAPISTRANO MISSION TRADING POST** (1820). **61. DOHENY PK.** (resort) at J. with US101 Alt. **66.5. SAN CLEMENTE ST. PK.** (camp.pic.) on cliffs above ocean. **86.5.** J. with dirt Rd. leading (L) 9.5$^m$ to adobe hqs. of **Rancho Santa Margarita,** built in 1837 by Pio Pico, last of Mex. Govs. Ruined by his inveterate urge to gamble, Pio Pico was finally forced to sell his great ranch. **87.5. OCEANSIDE,** resort & farm shipping center.

SIDE TRIP: Take Second St. (L) here past Mt. Ecclesia, hqs. of Rosicrucian Fellowship. At 4.5$^m$, **Misión de San Luis Rey** (O), founded 1798 (Sp.Moorish & Mex.styles.; bldgs. completed 1802), is considered one of finest of Cal. missions. Ch. has been partly rest. & has int. murals. 10.5$^m$ J. with US395 (see).

**90.5. CARLSBAD,** near which (S) is **Carlsbad Beach St. Pk.** (bath.camp.). **106. DEL MAR** (resort), with **Del Mar Turf Club Track** (running races).

SIDE TRIP: Take paved Rd. (L) here 0.5$^{m}$ to **San Diego Cty. Fair Grounds** (fair usually in Aug.). At 5$^{m}$ is **Second Osuna Adobe,** built in 1830's, now portion of Bing Crosby's home. At 11.5$^{m}$ **Hodges Dam** & L., part of San Diego's water system. 18$^{m}$ **Escondido** at J. with US395 (see).

**109.5.** J. with several Rds.

SIDE TRIP: Take concrete Rd. (R) 1.5$^{m}$ to **Scripps Institution of Oceanography** (O) containing mus. & aquarium. At 4$^{m}$, **La Jolla,** on whose cliffs many lovely homes have been built. **La Jolla Caves** (O.fee) are accessible from Coast Blvd. From La Jolla side rd. passes through **Pacific, Mission & Ocean Beaches.** 13.5$^{m}$ J. with US101.

## 124. SAN DIEGO

Through RR., bus, & plane conns. Ferry: Coronado Ferry Slip, S. end Pacific Blvd. For bay tours covering harbor, Star & Crescent Pier, (W) end Broadway. Accoms.: Ample, all types. Info.: C. of C., 499 W. Broadway. Swim.: Municipal Pool, Texas & Upas Sts.; Mission Beach Pool; Pacific Beach, La Jolla, North & South Beaches, Coronado. Boat.: Sailboats & rowboats, Mission Bay; Coronado Yacht Club, Glorietta Bay. Fish.: Surf, pier, & barge; deep-sea & fresh-water lakes in back country.

San Diego, Cal.'s oldest Sp. settlement (1769) & today its 4th largest city, lies at the extreme SW. cor. of the U.S., spreading over seashore, canyon & mesa around fine landlocked harbor with bustling maritime traffic of yachts, fishing craft, Naval vessels & freight steamers. Its year-round equable climate & its pleasantly rolling seaside setting attract tourists & draw as permanent residents huge numbers of retired elderly people. But San Diego is also hqs. of U.S. 11th Naval Dist.; it is home port of huge fishing fleet, & cans 65 percent of Nation's tuna fish; & it has boomed in recent years as industrial center, particularly in aircraft manufacture. Since beginning of century, local struggle has gone on bet. those who want to keep it a residential city & those who want to promote its industrial development. During World War II, it expanded tremendously & war workers strained housing facilities. Nevertheless, San Diego retains much of its traditional leisurely, easygoing air.

City is bisected by Broadway, along which cluster skyscraper office bldgs., running (W) to piers & docks on bay shore. N. of Broadway spreads green stretch of Balboa Pk. (1,400 as.) bordered by handsome residential neighborhoods. Bet. Balboa Pk. & bay (W), along which are fish canneries & aircraft plants, is sec. known as Middletown; & NW. of latter lies Old Town, with adobe bldgs. around ancient Plaza where city's hist. began. Below Old Town, Point Loma, 7$^{m}$ long, extends (S) sheltering the bay. S. of Broadway are: Tenderloin area, patronized by sailors; wholesale & manufacturing sec.; & city's Mex. & Negro quarters in formerly exclusive, now run-down, Logan Heights & Golden Hill districts. In great semicircle on N. & E., spread out over brushy slopes, are various residential subdivisions: Mission Hills, North Park, East San Diego, Encanto.

First white man to enter harbor of San Diego was Juan Rodríguez Cabrillo, in 1542. Vizcaíno's three vessels dropped anchor here in 1602 & named bay for San Diego de Alcalá on Nov. 12, Saint's feast day. In 1769 sea & land parties sent from Mexico met here & est. 1st Sp. settlement in Cal. Fray Junípero Serra built small hut July 16, 1769, where he said mass; thus was est. Cal.'s 1st mission. Earthworks were thrown up & more huts built by Gov. Gaspar de Portolá's men; thus was founded 1st presidio. Mission was moved 6$^{m}$ up Mission Valley in 1774, but around presidio small settlement grew. Port was visited in 1793 by ship, "Discovery," commanded by Vancouver, & in 1800 by first Yankee vessel, "Betsy." Other ships began calling to take on cattle hides, & San Diego became center of coastal hide trade. In 1834 it was organized as pueblo, but afterwards lost pop. & from 1838 on was administered from Los Angeles. On July 29, 1846, Amer. sloop-of-war, "Cyane," entered harbor & Amer. flag was raised over plaza. Mex. forces rallied to capture town, but Amers. recaptured it soon after.

Old Town was incorporated as city in 1850. It was soon infested with rowdies, adventurers, & drifters. Numerous saloons plied Inds. with drink, & killings were frequent. Movement to found new city was launched by William Heath Davis, who bought land on present site & laid out settlement known as New Town, or "Davis' Folly"; but Davis' venture failed, & in 1860 only U.S. military base & barracks remained. Alonzo Erastus Horton, arriving in 1867, was more successful. He bought 1,000 as. on present site (at 21¢ per a.), built wharf, & plotted Horton's Addition; hectic real estate boom followed. In 1871 cty. seat was transferred from Old Town to New Town. Arrival of 1st RR. in 1885 launched another real estate boom, temporarily upping pop. to 40,000. City's later growth has been steadier, stimulated by Army & Navy bases during World War I, completion of San Diego & Ariz. Eastern RR. in 1919, expositions of 1915-16 & 1935-36, & expansion of fishing, canning & aircraft industries. Economic growth has promoted development of cultural & recr. facils.: parks, museums & libraries, symphony orchestra & other musical institutions. World War II brought greatest boom yet, during which pop. increased nearly 100 percent, lifting San Diego to metropolitan status.

PTS. OF INT.: (1) **Balboa Pk.**, entrance Laurel St. & 6th Ave. (1,400 as.). Laurel Ave. runs through pk., & along it are various public bldgs.: **Cal. Bldg.** (O.Sp. baroque.by Goodhue) incl. San Diego Mus. & Archaeological Institute, Hall of Anthropology, scientific lib., Chapel of St. Francis & Cal. Tower. **Alcazar Garden,** laid out for 1915 San Diego Fair, from which path leads across Palm Canyon to other exposition bldgs., in Sp. & Mayan styles. **Pacific Relations Group** (O.Sun.) contains furnishings & handicraft articles. **Ford Bldg.** (Mod.by Teague) contains mus. of mechanical development. **Federal Bldg.,** E. Palisades Dr., was built for city auditorium. **Spreckels Organ Pavilion** is open-air amphitheater with one of world's largest organs. **Fine Arts Gallery of San Diego** (O.wks.Sun.aft.Sp.Ren.) with fine coll. of art & art objects, incl. El Greco's "St Francis" & canvasses by Murillo, Goya, Rubens. **Zoo. Garden** (O.fee) on Avenida de Espana. **Mus. of Nat. Hist.** (O.Sp.Ren.). **Sp. Village Art Center** (art work for sale), with puppet show & café.

(2) Ft. of Second St., **Star of India,** (O) full-rigged ship built 1863, transformed into maritime mus. (3) Pacific Hy., bet. Ash & Grape Sts., **Civic Center** (O.wks.1938). (4) Pacific Hy. bet. Laurel & Sassafras Sts., **Lindbergh Field** (airport). (5) Calhoun & Walker Sts., **Old Town Plaza:** 4136 Wallace St., **Casa de Cabrillo** (O.c.1820); 2660 Calhoun St., **Casa de Bandini** (1829.enlarged 1869); Mason St., bet. Calhoun St. & San Diego Ave., **Casa de Estudillo** (O.sm.fee.1825.rest.1910), now mus. which figures in H. H. Jackson's novel, "Ramona"; San Diego Ave. & Harney St., **Whaley H.** (1856); Conde St., bet. San Diego Ave. & Congress St., **Adobe Chapel** (c.1850. rest.). (6) **Presidio Hill Pk.** In it is **Ft. Stockton,** named for Commodore Stockton, who fought in struggle against Mexs. for possession of Cal. (7) 2727 Presidio Dr., **Serra Mus.** (O.Tues.-Sat.10-5;Sun.2-5.Sp.Mission) contains hist. relics. Below hill, on river flats, stands **Serra Palm,** allegedly planted 1769.

SIDE TRIPS: (A) Take Pacific Hy. (US101) in San Diego (straight ahead) short distance to Coronado Ferry, which takes autoists across San Diego Bay to **Coronado** (residential resort). **Hotel Del Coronado.** From beach are visible uninhabited **Coronado Is.** (Mex.), named for Sp. explorer (good f.off shore). Below Coronado, (S) on St.75 is **Silver Strand St. Pk.** (camp.pic.) at $6^m$. **Imperial Beach** (resort) at $9.5^m$. J. with US101 at $13^m$.

(B) Turn (W) from Pacific Hy. on Barnett Ave., following N. bay shore, & cont. (S) down Pt. Loma via Lytton St., Chatsworth Blvd., & Catalina Blvd. to tip, where El Camino Cabrillo encircles **Cabrillo Nat. Mon.,** walled area commanding magnificent view of ocean, bay, islands, mts., valleys & plains, whose chief feature is **White Tower,** formerly Pt. Loma Lighth. (est. 1855). Mon. comm. discovery of Cal. by Cabrillo, who first sighted land here Sept. 28, 1542.

San Diego is at Js. with US395 (see) & US80 (see).

From San Diego, US101 cont. (S), through **CHULA VISTA, 134.,** flower & bulb raising center, to **SAN YSIDRO, 141.,** port of entry from Mexico at **MEXICAN BORDER.** Just beyond latter is **Tijuana,** much visited by Amers., & $80^m$ farther (S) is most int. old Mex. town of **Enseñada.**

## US 99(S)—CALIFORNIA

**SACRAMENTO, CAL. (SE) to MEXICAN BORDER** (at Mexicali, Mex.). **612.5. US99**

Via: Stockton, Manteca, Modesto, Merced, Fresno, Tulare, Bakersfield, San Fernando, Los Angeles, Pomona, Redlands, Beaumont, Banning, Indio, El Centro, Calexico. RR. parallels route bet. Sacramento & Bakersfield, Saugus & Banning & Mecca, Brawley & Calexico. Accoms.: In larger towns.

From Sacramento this tour runs through S. sec. of great "Central Valley" watered by Sacramento & San Joaquin Rs. Much of this reg. was once desert, brought to fertility by irrigation. Farms are not farms in eastern understanding of word, but veritable food factories, concentrated on few main crops. Migratory worker has posed difficult economic problem. Pay for his labor, except in boom years, is comparatively low. His annual income is further reduced by fact that his employment is largely seasonal. Steinbeck's novel, "In Dubious Battle," has vividly depicted his struggle with ranch owners for better pay. US99 in this sec. makes J. with Rds. giving access to much-visited Yosemite & Sequoia-Kings Canyon Nat. Pks. At Bakersfield, at S. end of valley, route cuts through cotton & oil-producing area, then climbs through canyon over Tehachapi Mts. & descends into Santa Clara Valley, climbs once more & then descends into San Fernando Valley, & proceeds to Los Angeles. From there it turns (E) through orange & grape growing San Bernardino reg. to Beaumont & then (SE) through irrigated Coachella Valley, cuts across stretch of desert near Salton Sea, traverses rich irrigated lands of Imperial Valley, whose ranches produce not only vegetables & fruits but cotton, & arrives finally at Mex. Border.

## Sec. 1: SACRAMENTO to LOS ANGELES. 375.

**0. SACRAMENTO,** at J. with US40 (see) & US50 (see). **30. LODI,** in San Joaquin Valley, celebrates Grape & Wine Festival in Sept.

**43. STOCKTON.**

RR. & bus conns. Accoms.: All types. Info.: Cal. St. Auto Assoc. (AAA), 929 N. Eldorado St.; C. of C., 234 N. Eldorado St. Swim.: Stockton Mun. Baths, S. end S. San Joaquin St. Concerts by Stockton Symphony Orchestra, winter; San Joaquin County Fair, last full wk. of Aug.

Stockton is situated on San Joaquin R. where 32′ channel permits ocean-going vessels to dock at city's wharves & load & carry off agric. products. City is also important industrial center. Large number of pks. afford ample recr. facils. Stockton was founded c.1847 by German named Weber who bought out his partner's interest in 50,000-a. tract, part of which is site of city, for $60. In 1849 gold rush swamped new settlement & swelled its pop. by thousands. Joaquin Murrieta, famous Mex. bandit of 1850's, once paid town visit. Noticing sign offering reward for his capture, he wrote underneath it: "I will give $10,000—Joaquin!" With irrigation introduced in 1860's, agric. became predominant industry. In order to meet need of ranchers, plants for manufacture of farm implements were est., producing first caterpillar tractors. Since then other important industries have developed.

PTS. OF INT.: (1) Main & Hunter Sts., **San Joaquin County Cth.** (1890.Class.by E. E. Myers & Son.). (2) 1930 S. Grant St., **Sikh Temple** (O), only one of this sect in U.S. (3) Main & El Dorado Sts., **Forty-Nine Drugstore,** in continuous existence since 1850. (4) Magnolia St. & Pershing Ave., **Haggin Mem. Gallery & Pioneer Hist. Mus.** (O.exc.Mon.), with large coll. of art & Cal. hist. relics. (5) Pacific Ave. & Stadium Dr., **College of the Pacific** (1851.Eng.Goth.) oldest incorporated educational institution in Cal. In Stockton is J. with US50 (see).

**56. MANTECA** (Sp., "butter"), a shipping center for dairy products.

SIDE TRIP: Take St.120 (L) 86m to **Yosemite Nat. Pk.** (see). St.120 cont. to J. with US395 at Leevining (see).

**63.** US99 crosses **STANISLAUS R.,** scene of great activity during gold rush era. R. figures in Bret Harte's "Down on the Stanislaus." **72. MODESTO,** canning, packing & dairying center, on Tuolumne R., which has been reduced to muddy trickle because its waters have been impounded behind 200′ dam to provide water for irrigation. **76. CERES.** Int. process of pollination of date palms in gardens surrounding town is done by hand (late March or Ap.) from platforms raised around trees. **84.5. TURLOCK,** trade center of fertile irrigated area. **108.5. MERCED,** in hay & cotton-growing area, with cement & pottery works. Rodeo takes place here, June; District Fair, Oct.

SIDE TRIP: Turn (L) from Merced on G Street, which becomes St.140, ascending foothills of Sierra 80m to **Mariposa** (Sp."butterfly") at S. end of Mother Lode mining reg. **Mariposa County Cth.** (1854) is oldest in Cal. In Mariposa is **J.** with St.49 (see US50). St.140 cont. to El Portal, entrance to **Yosemite Nat. Pk.** (see).

**161. FRESNO**

RR. and bus conns. Accoms.: All types. Info.: San Joaquin Valley Tourist & Travel Assoc., 1044 Fulton St.; Cal. St. Auto Assoc. (AAA), 666 Van Ness Ave., Fresno Cty. C. of C., 2345 Fresno St. For Kings Canyon & Sequoia Nat. Pks., Nat. Pk. Service, Fed. Bldg. Swim.: At numerous pub. pools. Raisin Day, 2nd Sat., May; Fresno District Fair, Sept.

Fresno is "world's raisin center." From city's limits vineyards radiate in seemingly endless rows. Pop. is mixed, incl. Spanish, Japanese & Armenian. Foreign sec. is of considerable int. Fresno, like so many other Cal. cities, dates its first real boom from gold rush, after which came great agric. development, when irrigation made cultivation of reg. possible. Finally, through efforts of Agoston Haraszthy, Hungarian immigrant, ranchers learned there was more profit in grapes than wheat. Since wine of this reg. proved of indifferent quality, vineyard owners abandoned wine-making & began turning grapes into raisins. Figs also are important crop. Industries followed in wake of agric. boom, & Fresno now ranks high among Cal. cities as industrial center.

PTS. OF INT.: (1) In front of **County Cth.** (neo-Class.), on Cth. Sq., are fountain, "Boy with a Leaking Boot," & statue of Dr. Chester Rowell, prominent citizen, by Haig Patigian. (2) 2435 Fresno St., **Fresno Mem. Auditorium** (1932.Mod.Class.), comm. war dead, contains Fresno Cty. Hist. Mus. (O.3-5 wks.), with coll. of early Cal. relics. (3) 1101 University Ave., **Fresno St. College** for training teachers (1921.Sp.Mission style). (4) Belmont & Thorne Aves., **Roeding Pk.**, in which are variety of int. botanical specimens & zoo. (5) 1340 Kern St., **Japanese Buddhist Temple** (O.1902.services Sun.8 p.m.), said to contain some ashes of Buddha, brought from India. (6) Butler Ave. & Hazelwood Blvd., **Sun Maid Raisin Plant** (O. wks.July-Jan.), largest raisin-packing plant in world. As by-products, seeds are bricked for fuel & stems sold for cattlefeed.

SIDE TRIPS: (A) Take Kearney Blvd. (L) from Fresno 7m to **Kearney Pk.**, 5,000 as., operated by Univ. of Cal. as experimental farm.
(B) Take St.41 (N) from Fresno 63m to S. Entrance of **Yosemite Nat. Pk.** (see).
(C) Take St.180 (Ventura Ave.) (L) from Fresno up fertile King's R. Valley through Sierra foothills, to Grant Grove sec. of **Sequoia-Kings Canyon Nat. Pk.** (see).
(D) Take St.168 (Fresno St.) (L) from Fresno to J. with Rd. at 5m.

Take latter (L) to **Pinedale,** 2m & turn (R) here to **Friant** 9m, near **Friant Dam,** world's 4th largest masonry dam (3,430′ long) impounding San Joaquin R., from which run 2 great canals irrigating San Joaquin Valley as part of Central Valley Project (see Shasta Dam, US99).

St.168 cont. to **Shaver L.** (5,200′;f.), 48m. At 70m **Huntington L.** (7,000′;resort.boat.guides for pack trips), impounded by 3 dams, each 1,000′ long. At 84m **Florence L.** both Ls. are part of huge hydro-electric proj. From Florence L., trl. runs into **Sequoia-Kings Canyon Nat. Pks.** (see).

From Fresno US99 cont. (S). **176.5. SELMA,** muscat grape-packing & wine-making center. **196.5. GOSHEN JUNCTION** at inters. with St.198.

SIDE TRIPS: (A) Take St.198 (R) 13m to **Hanford.** Mussell Slough feud, upon which Frank Norris based his novel "The Octopus," came to climax here. In 1880 ranchers fought sheriff's forces to prevent S.P. RR. from taking possession of certain secs. of land. Five ranchers & 2 deputies were killed; 17 ranchers were jailed. 46m **Priest Valley,** near crest of Coast Range. In this valley Joaquin Murrieta was killed, 1853. 71m **San Lucas** & J. with US101 (see).
(B) Take St.198 (L) from Goshen J. 6.5m to **Visalia.** Here also occurred conflicts bet. ranchers & settlers & S.P. RR.
St.198, at 37.5m, reaches Ash Mt. Entrance to **Sequoia-Kings Canyon Nat. Pks.** (see) & cont. to Grant Grove sec.

US99 cont. (S) past 7,000-a. **TAGUS RANCH, 199.5.** advertised as "world's largest apricot, peach & nectarine orchard." **205. TULARE,** agric. shipping center. In Hotel Tulare is **Whilton Mus.,** with coll. mounted native birds & mammals & extensive exhibit of Cal. wild flowers. US99 now passes through spreading cotton fields, into Kern Cty. oil field. **265.5. BAKERSFIELD,** at S. end of San Joaquin Valley, on Kern R., in heart of very large oil producing & refining reg. There are also extensive cotton, alfalfa, vineyard & fruit ranches. In 1885 gold was discovered along Kern R. & Bakersfield assumed appearance of tough mining town. With discovery of oil, rough-and-tumble era returned.

SIDE TRIP: Take St.178 (Nile St.) from Bakersfield (L) 7.5m to J. with Alfred Harrell Blvd.

Take latter (L) 6.5m to **Kern R. Cty. Pk.,** on high bluffs overlooking Kern R., with small zoo & pheasant & quail breeding farm.

At 11m on St.178, route enters **Kern R. Canyon,** deep gorge. 28m **Democrat Hot Springs** (sulphur), health resort. 30m **Hobo Hot Springs For. Camp** (2,000′;ample facils.) in Sequoia Nat. For. 38m **Bodfish,** ghost mining town. 43m **Isabella,** another ghost town. St.178 cont. through beautiful country along S. Fork of Kern R. 76.5m **Walker Pass** (1,548′), named for Joseph Walker who explored reg. in 1834. Rd. then descends to J. with US6 (see).

From Bakersfield US99 cont. (S) through cotton & oil producing reg., & then ascends Grapevine Canyon through Tehachapi Range, which runs (SW) to meet Coast Range, to **GRAPEVINE,** at **296.5.** (fuel.accoms.). Here is good view. **300.5. FT. TEJON ST. HIST. MON.,** comprising bldgs. of U.S. Army outpost est. 1854. **304. LEBEC** (3,575′). Fine view of alkaline **Castaic L. 306. CHANDLERS** (gas sta. garage). From here Rd. ascends **TEJON PASS** (4,182′). US99 now cont. along twisting course through Castaic Valley, into Santa Clara Valley. It crosses Francisquito Cr. at **339.5.** St. Francis Dam, which impounded this cr. in San Francisquito Canyon, broke on night of Mar. 13, 1928 & poured destructive flood into valley below. US99 soon begins to ascend again into foothills of Santa Susanna Mts. **344.** J. with Rd. leading (R) 2.5$^{m}$ to one-way private lane to **First Oil Well** in Cal., drilled 1875, at 4.5$^{m}$. Well is still producing. Hy. now crosses into San Fernando Valley. At **350. LOS ANGELES AQUEDUCT** is visible twisting down slope with open spillway near hy. (L). This 233-mile aqueduct coming from Owens R. has converted San Fernando Valley into "market basket of L.A." **353. SAN FERNANDO,** at J. with St.118 (see L.A. V for San Fernando & pts. (S) to L.A.) **375. LOS ANGELES** (see) at Js. with US60-70 (see) & US101 (see).

## Sec. 2: LOS ANGELES to CALEXICO. 237.5.

US99 unites with US60-70 (see) (E) to Pomona (for pts.of int.bet.L.A.& incl. Pomona, see L.A.IV). **30.5. POMONA.** US99-70 branches (S) from US60. **36.5. ONTARIO** is surrounded by orange groves. At **38.5.** is 5,000-a. **GUASTI VINEYARD,** with annual crop of c.20,000 tons of grapes. It produces dry & sweet wines & one of few Cal. "champagne wines." **57.5. COLTON,** near which US99-70 unite with US395 (E) short distance.

**63.5. REDLANDS,** packing & distributing point for citrus fruits & other farm products. At Cajon & Cypress Sts. is **Smiley Heights,** beautiful 400-a. garden in which grow great variety of plants & trees from all quarters of globe. At E. Colton Ave. & University St., **Univ. of Redlands,** founded by S. Cal. Baptist Convention in 1907. At 4th St., on grounds of Smiley Pub. Lib., **Watchorn Lincoln Mem.;** Lincoln relics & related exhibs.; murals by Dean Cornwell. Eureka Ave., in Smiley Pk., **Redlands Bowl,** outdoor theater where concerts are held. Barton Rd. & Mountain View Ave., **San Bernardino Asistencia,** reprod. of San Gabriel mission outpost. US99 winds through Reservoir Canyon & past orchards of nut trees, with views of San Bernardino Mts. (L). **90. BEAUMONT,** (2,559′), at J. with US60 (see), with which US99 unites again for 52$^{m}$. From here (E) hy. runs through cherry- & almond-growing region. **96. BANNING** (2,350′), from which good dirt Rd. leads (R) through Banning Canyon, 2$^{m}$, to **Highland Springs,** lovely mt. resort. On hotel grounds is pre-hist. Ind. grinding stone. At 2.5$^{m}$ **International Pk.,** resort area, where Spring Cherry Blossom festival is held. **Mozart Bowl** (pic.) is natural amphitheater. Main hy. runs through San Gorgonio Pass bet. **Mt. San Jacinto** & **Mt. San Gorgonio,** usually snow-capped. **138. INDIO,** RR. center & tourist center, as well as trading point for surrounding irrigated reg. **140.** US99 branches (S) from J. with US60-70 (see). **143.5. COACHELLA,** in valley of same name, which extends to N. shore of Salton Sea. Reg. produces dates, grapefruit, & cotton, & is irrigated by water from wells.

SIDE TRIP: Take St.111 (L) from Coachella, running below sea level, along Salton Sea (see below), through weird desert scenery & through grape- & date-producing region. In summer temperature often reaches 125°F. At 11$^{m}$ **Mecca** (197′) amidst date gardens.

Turn (L) from Mecca, on Shavers Canyon Rd. 3$^{m}$, to J. with Painted Canyon Rd., which leads (L) 3.5$^{m}$ through **Painted Canyon** (no water). At 3$^{m}$, on Shavers Canyon Rd. take foot trl. straight ahead 2$^{m}$ to **Painted Canyon Pic. Grounds,** where are int. multi-colored cliffs.

At 15.5$^{m}$ on St.111, Caleb's Siding, where St.111 veers (S) toward Orocopia Mts. & Salton Sea. 20$^{m}$ **Date Palm Beach.** 24$^{m}$ **Salton Beach** (—22′; resorts. camp.swim.boat.). At 29$^{m}$ (L) is visible **Cahuilla Ind. Rock Mound,** on which are petroglyphs & carved head of Ind. 36$^{m}$ **Bombay Beach** (resort). At 57$^{m}$ is J. with dirt Rd.

Turn (R) here 4$^{m}$ to **Dry Ice Plant,** where dry ice is manufactured from carbon monoxide from wells in near-by Mud Pots area. At 5$^{m}$ **Mud Pots,** 20 as. of boiling mud craters, geysers & mineral springs. In Mullet I., at N. end of this area, is **Davis Mus.** (O.fee), containing remains from L. Cahuilla, pre-hist. predecessor of Salton Sea, & old Ind. pottery. By foot trl. short distance (SW) from Mud Pots are **Ind. Paint Pots,** with weird colored incrustations caused by oxide springs.

60m **Calipatria** (—183′). Near-by good duck h. on S. shore of Salton Sea (blinds & boats avail.). 66m **New River.** Here Colorado R. broke through in 1905, creating Salton Sea. St.111 cont. to **Brawley** (see below), 74m, at J. with US99.

**152. SALTON SEA** (—244′ at surface), 30m long & 8-14m wide, created by overflow of Colorado R. when it broke out of bounds in 1905, is more or less on site of L. Cahuilla, created in pre-hist. times by Colorado R. Hy. now passes through date orchards. Ancient beach line of L. Cahuilla cuts an even whitish strip along sides of Santa Rosa Mts. (R). **161.5. TRAVERTINE ROCK,** on which are petroglyphs. **187. KANE SPRINGS** (—150′), oldest known water hole in Colo. Desert (service sta.restaurant). **209. BRAWLEY** (—115′), largest city in Imperial Valley. Considerable percentage of pop. is Mexican. **223. EL CENTRO** (—52′). Here is J. with US80 (see). Beyond El Centro route traverses alfalfa fields which yield 5 & 6 crops yearly. **234. CALEXICO** (5′) on **MEXICAN BORDER** opp. Mexicali. Here Mexican travel permits are avail. (No permits necessary to cross & return same day.) **Rockwood Hall** (rest.), on International boundary, is old adobe bldg. among date palms.

# US 40—CALIFORNIA

**CAL.-NEV. LINE** (13m from Reno, Nev.) **(SW) to SAN FRANCISCO, CAL. 216.5. US40.**

Via: Truckee, Auburn, Roseville, Sacramento, Dixon, Fairfield, Richmond, Berkeley, Oakland. S.P. RR. parallels Rd. bet. Nev. Line & Sacramento & at intervals bet. Sacramento & Carquinez Bridge. Bus lines follow route. Accoms.: All types.

In Cal. US40 follows generally route taken by early explorers, pioneers & settlers across rampart of Sierra Nevada. Leaving Nev., it follows crag-enclosed Truckee R., traverses Donner Pass, scene of Donner Party tragedy (see below), & the canyon of Yuba R., cont. past hist. Emigrant Gap, descends into Amer. R. gold-mining reg. to Auburn, follows Amer. R. to Sacramento & turns across fertile Sacramento Valley. It then runs along S. side of Carquinez Strait & W. side of San Francisco Bay to Oakland. Route crosses Tahoe & Mendocino Nat. Fors. Accessible for. camps are noted along route.

## Sec. 1: NEV. LINE to SACRAMENTO. 125.

US40, crossing Nev. Line 13m (SW) from Reno, follows Truckee R., crossing into **TAHOE NAT. FOR.** (c.600,000 as.), through which it runs for 50m. **20. TRUCKEE** (5,820′), still resembling frontier town, resort of lumberjacks & herders. Here is J. with St.89. Good skiing in vic.; toboggan slide with power pullback & ice rink. Short distance (N) from Truckee is **Truckee For. Camp** (trlrs.ample facils.). **22.5. DONNER STATE MON.** (L), small pk. comm. Donner Party of emigrants from Ill., who arrived here in Oct. 1846, & were caught in deep snows. Of 81 who had pitched camp in Nov., only 45 survived (see Nev.). In pk. is **Pioneer Mon.** Not far beyond (W) lies **Donner L.,** which US40 skirts, in view of **Cassel Peak** (R) (9,139′). Rd. now begins to climb steep wall of Sierra, beneath **Donner Peak** (8,315′) & **Lincoln Peak** (8,403′). **29. SUMMIT OF DONNER PASS** (7,135′), where is **U.S. Weather Bureau Observatory. 30.** (L) **VAN NORDEN L. & NORDEN** (6,880′;hotel), winter sports resort. **31.5. SODA SPRINGS** (6,748′;hotel & cabins). US40 now traverses canyon of S. Fork of Yuba R., passing vacation camps & inns &, at **37.** & **41.,** for. camps. **49.** J. with improved Rd. leading (L) 0.5m to **Emigrant Gap** (5,250′), f. & h. center for Tahoe Nat. For. (cabins,hotel). US40 runs along lofty ridge, through scenically int. region of gorges & fine forests, & drops down along gold-bearing Amer. R. **58.5** J. with improved Rd. leading (R) 3.5m to **Dutch Flat** (3,399′), sett. 1851 by gold miners of German origin. Spectacular hydraulic diggings in vic. **63.5. GOLD RUN TRADING POST,** now mus. for pioneer relics. This reg. was rich gold-mining area from whose streams more than $15,000,000 was taken by hydraulic operations in 1870's & 1880's. **90.5. AUBURN** (1,360′), on N. fork of Amer. R., was gold-rush town & some of its old bldgs. are still standing. It is now center of an orchard district. In Auburn is J. with St.49 running (S) through gold-mining reg. to conn. with US50 (see).

SIDE TRIP: Take St.49 (R) from Auburn. At 24m is **Grass Valley** (2,400′). On Gold Hill, near town, is **Mon. to Geo. Knight,** discoverer of gold-bearing quartz in Cal. Exploitation of this type of ore is still continuing in this vic. Most important of mines are Gold Hill, Empire, Golden Center, Idaho-Maryland. At cor. of Mill & Wall Sts., is **Lola Montez H.** (1852-54). The fabulous Lola acquired an internat. reputation as dancer, became mistress of Louis I. of Bavaria with title of Countess of Lansfeld, & was banished during Rev. of 1848. Her soirées, frequented chiefly by younger miners, were famous. Lola Montez finally married into respectability & is buried in a Brooklyn cemetery (see N.Y.). Near-by is childhood **Home of Lotta Crabtree,** pupil of Lola Montez. After making dancing tour through mining camps, Lotta scored success in S.F. & other Amer. cities. 28.5m **Nevada City** (2,450′). This town had gold rush, after gold was discovered at Deer Cr. in 1848. It engaged 1st in placer, next in hydraulic, & finally in deep quartz mining. On Broad St., **National Hotel** (R) was important stagecoach stopover at whose bar miners paid for drinks in gold dust. **Assayer's Office** (R) on Commercial St. has its original furniture & iron safe. Through this office, it is said, $27,000,000 in gold passed. 44m **North San Juan,** now almost ghost town, but once, when San Juan Ridge was still being exploited, boom-town of 10,000. Some of old bldgs. are still standing. 58.5m **Depot Hill,** where is **Joubert Hydraulic Mine,** which has produced more than $1,850,000 in gold. 75.2m **Downieville** (3,000′), surrounded by steep mts., once had pop. of 5,000 when fortunes in gold were being made. **Sierra County Cth.** (1855), in whose yard is old mill wheel used for gold crushing. Behind Cth. on Piety Hill is old **Town Gallows.** On Main St., **Meroux Mus.** (O.Sun.& Hols.;keys with storekeeper wks.), containing relics. Also on Main St. (L), **Costa Store** (1853), in which are scales formerly used to weigh gold. **St. Charles Hotel** (1853.well preserved). 88m **Sierra City** (4,100′) at foot of Sierra Buttes (8,600′), where gold was formerly panned from Yuba R. In Monumental Mine, in 1860's, 100-lb. gold nugget, valued at $25,000, was turned up. Some mines are still producing, & some bldgs. still survive from early days. 110m **Sierraville** (4,950′), at J. with St.89, formerly stage-coach crossroads. Turn (R) on St.89 to J. at 135m with US40 (see above).

From Auburn, US40 descends to floor of Sacramento Valley. **106.5. ROSEVILLE,** at J. with US99E (see), is in rich plum, berry, almond, & grape-growing reg. **121.5.** US40 crosses **AMERICAN R. 125. SACRAMENTO** (see US99) at Js. with US99W & US99E (see) & US50 (see).

### Sec. 2: SACRAMENTO to SAN FRANCISCO. 91.5.

From W. end of Sacramento route crosses Tower Br., vertical lift span over **SACRAMENTO R.,** Cal.'s largest R. US40 now crosses level, intensively cultivated Sacramento Valley. **14.** J. with paved Rd. leading (R) 1m to **Davis.** Just beyond Davis is entrance to **Davis Branch of College of Agri. of Univ. of Calif.,** with orchards, vineyards, poultry, pens, model dairy & pedigreed livestock. **23. DIXON,** rural trading center. **43. FAIRFIELD,** in whose plaza stands **Statue of Francisco Solano,** chief of all Ind. tribes (N) beyond Suisun & San Pablo Bays. He was baptized with Sp. name by fathers of Misión de San Francisco de Solano, aided Sp. in dealings with Inds., & was granted Rancho Suisun. US40 now climbs into American Canyon. As hy. leaves hills, there is panoramic view of Vallejo, Napa R. Valley & Mt. Tamalpais beyond San Pablo Bay. **59.** J. with paved Rd. leading (L) to **Benicia** at 5m. (For Benicia & pts. of int. bet. Benicia & San Francisco, see San Francisco IV). **91.5. SAN FRANCISCO.**

## US 50—CALIFORNIA

**CAL.-NEV. LINE** (27m from Carson City, Nev.) **(W) to SAN FRANCISCO, CAL. 239.5. US50.**

Via: Al Tahoe, Placerville, Folsom, Sacramento, Elk Grove, Lodi, Stockton, Tracy, San Leandro, Oakland. S.P. RR. parallels route bet. Placerville & Oakland; W.P. RR. bet. Sacramento & Stockton. Accoms.: All types.

From Nev. Line US50 skirts S. shore of L. Tahoe; crosses Sierra Nevada, cutting through El Dorado Nat. For., & follows S. Fork of American R. to Placerville & Sacramento. It then, in a wide arc taking in Stockton, cuts across fertile Sacramento Valley & over Mt. Diablo Range to S.F. Bay. This early became an important overland route into Cal. After discovery of Comstock Silver Lode in Washoe Valley, Nev., in 1859, it was heavily used toll-road. In 1860 it was first used by Pony Express, whose riders made trip from St. Joseph, Mo. to Sacramento in 8 days.

**0. LAKESIDE** (6,225′) is one of many resorts on **L. Tahoe** (R), largest in Cal. Walled in by snow-capped peaks, among which are **Monument Peak** (10,085′), **Mt. Freel** (10,900′) & **Job's Sister** (10,820′), L. is more than 21m long & 12m wide.

**2. EL DORADO CTY. PUB. CAMPGROUND** on L. shore (6,300′; camp.pic.no trlrs.) **2.5. AL TAHOE** (6,225′). **4.5.** J. with St.89.

SIDE TRIP: Take latter (R) along W. shore of L. through string of resorts, from which trls. radiate into Sierra. Overlooking Emerald Bay are **Bay View & Eagle Falls For. Camps** (no trlrs.) at, respectively, 7.5$^{m}$ & 8.5$^{m}$. At 41.5$^{m}$ is **Truckee** at J. with US40 (see).

**9.5. MEYERS** (6,400′), with For. Ranger Sta. (info.concerning El Dorado Nat.For.) & **Pony Express Mon. 12.5. ECHO SUMMIT** (7,365′) at top of Johnson's Pass. From Summit Lodge fine view. About 3$^{m}$ (S) from here is **Alpine For. Camp** (ample facils.no trlrs.). **13. FIRS FOR. CAMP** (7,000′; ample facils.no trlrs.) near J. with Rd. leading (R) 1$^{m}$ to **Echo L.** in whose vic. are many camps from which ft. trls. lead into **Desolation Valley Wilderness Area** (41,388 as.) of Ls. & high peaks. US50 now descends W. slope of Sierra, past for. camps & resorts. **13.5. AUDRAIN L. FOR. CAMP** (R) on Audrain L. Route now passes **Horse Tail Falls** (R), with **Pyramid Peak** (10,020′) at some distance (NW) & then follows S. fork of American R. **Lover's Leap** (6,985′), sheer 1,285′ (L) above R. **17.5. 45-MILE FOR. CAMP. 20.5. 42-MILE FOR. CAMP. 21.** J. with gravelled Rd. leading (L) 0.5$^{m}$ to **Strawberry H.**, formerly stage sta., now summer resort. **22.5. 39-MILE FOR. CAMP** (for trlrs.only). **23.5. PYRAMID RANGER STA.** (R) & **PYRAMID PUB. CAMP** (L). **25.5. ALDER CR. FOR. CAMP.**

**30. KYBURZ** (4,700′). **47.5. BULLION BEND MON.** where 2 stages were robbed same night in 1864. Bandit leader gave receipt for stolen cash, reading: "This is to certify that I have received from Wells Fargo & Co., the sum of $..... cash for the purpose of outfitting recruits enlisted in California for the Confederate States Army. R. Henry Ingrim, Captain Commd'g Co. C.S.A. June, 1864." **62.5. PLACERVILLE** (1,848′) at J. with St.49, strategically located on overland trail, was focal point of gold rush in 1848. Placerville was notorious for lawlessness & bandits who plundered miners. Lawbreakers were hanged from great oak that stood at cor. of Main & Coloma Sts. Town acquired unofficial name of Hangtown. Through Placerville passed Overland Mail & Pony Express; it became chief stopover point during rush to Comstock (silver) Lode in Nev. Mark Hopkins, later railway magnate, began his career here peddling groceries. Philip D. Armour, of meat-packing fame, had butcher shop in town, & John Studebaker here began his automotive activities by building wheelbarrows for miners. Many old bldgs. are still standing on Main St., along Hangtown Creek. At lower end of Main St., is **Old Hangtown Bell,** which was used to summon vigilantes.

SIDE TRIPS: (A) Take St.49 (R) from Placerville. This route runs through heart of gold country, the Mother Lode reg. Gold rush began Jan. 24, 1848 with discovery by James W. Marshall of gold (see below), followed by trek of thousands of prospectors into reg. & mushroom growth of mining towns where reckless spending of quickly earned riches, gambling, brawling & lawlessness, occasionally tempered by vigilante justice, held sway. When placer mining gave out, mining corporations moved in to exploit region's gold, first with hydraulic & then with stone-crushing machinery. All along St.49 are strung abandoned ghost towns & workings, although here & there some of early settlements have survived & considerable mining activity is still in evidence. 8$^{m}$ **Coloma,** near S. Fork of American R. Here is Mon. (L) marking **Site of Sutter's Saw Mill,** where Jas. W. Marshall first discovered gold in 1848. Marshall failed to profit by his find, as did his employer, John A. Sutter (see Sacramento, US99); he was ousted from his claims by prospectors.

Take uphill Rd. (L) from Coloma. 0.5$^{m}$ to **Marshall State Mon.,** in which are **Statue of Marshall** & **Marshall Cabin** (rest.), where he lived, 1848-68.

St.49 now runs bet. mt. ridges & through deep gorges. 24.5$^{m}$ J. with improved Rd.

Take latter (R) through former gold mining reg., via **Forest Hill** to **Michigan Bluff** (3,500′), 2,000′ above Middle Fork of American R. at 25.5$^{m}$. Here Leland Stanford, railway tycoon, kept store, 1853-5.

28$^{m}$ **Auburn** at J. with US40 (see).

(B) Take St.49 (L) from Placerville. At 5$^{m}$ is **El Dorado** (1,610′), first known as Mud Springs, because of near-by watering hole for cattle, which became mining camp. 20$^{m}$ **Plymouth.** Here are located **Plymouth Consolidated Mines** which produced about $15,000,000. 23$^{m}$ **Drytown,** whose surrounding gulches—Blood, Murderer's & Rattlesnake—produced fabulous amounts of placer gold. 28$^{m}$ **Sutter Creek,** still busy quartz mining center with a few int. old bldgs. 33$^{m}$ **Jackson,** in a deep quartz mining area. Jackson in early days was troubled by usual lawlessness which, during reform wave, led to stringing up of 10 men from great oak on Cth. Hill. **Amador County Cth.** (c.1850). 40$^{m}$ **Mokelumne Hill** (1,500′), on high ridge bet. Mokelumne & Calaveras Rs., was once one of Mother Lode's roughest towns. Legend has it that one man was killed each week end for 17 weeks running & 5 men in one week. St.49 passes **Golden Eagle Hotel** & **Sturges Store** (both 1854); old **Ledger Hotel** (1856) & former **Calaveras Cth.,** now hotel annex. Near-by is little **White Ch.,** built with contributions levied upon miners by a determined woman of religious convictions. Route runs (S) from Mokelumne Hill through Chile Gulch, where American & Chilean miners battled over claims in 1849. 50$^m$ **San Andreas.** In **Calaveras C. of C. Mus.** (L) is coll. of relics, incl. famous bandit Murrieta's red sash. 52$^m$ **Altaville,** (1,500'), in which are old **Inn** (L) & **Prinz Store** (R), both dating from 1850's. 55$^m$ **Angels Camp** (1,500'), where Mark Twain is said to have heard story of "Jumping Frog." Every May, Angels Camp has Jumping Frog Jubilee contest with prizes for winning frog. Some old bldgs. still standing. At S. end of town (L) is **Model of Undershot Water Wheel,** used for ore-crushing.

Take St.4 (L) from Angels Camp to **Murphys,** 9$^m$, with int. old **Mitchler Hotel** (1856). At 25$^m$ is **Calaveras Grove of Big Trees** (Sequoia Gigantea.). Destruction of this grove has been threatened by lumber companies, but recently there has been movement to set it aside as St. reserv.

60$^m$ **Carson Hill** (1,400'), another ghost town. $20,000,000 in gold was taken out of Mother Lode in this vic., mostly from Morgan Mine, in which was found, 1854, gold nugget weighing 195 lbs., largest ever turned up in U.S. 63.5$^m$ **Melones,** which took its name from gold nuggets shaped like melon seeds, found by Mex. miners in Stanislaus R. 65.5$^m$ J. with paved Rd. leading (L) to **Jackass Hill,** once, as Mark Twain noted, site of prosperous town of 3,000. On summit is **Mark Twain's Cabin** (rest.), where he met prototype of Dick Baker, of "Roughing It." 71$^m$ J. with paved Rd. leading (L) 2$^m$ to **Columbia** (2,200'), best preserved (now State Hist. Mon.) & once richest & roughest of Mother Lode camps. $87,000,000 have been taken out of this vic. In 1850 Dr. Thaddeus Hildreth & party were caught here in thunder shower; one member did some prospecting while waiting & struck gold. On town's S. edge is **St. Anne's Church** (1856), with altar murals by Jas. Fallon. On main St. are old **Fallon's Hotel, Wells Fargo Office** (O.fee), **"Stage Drivers' Retreat,"** old **Knapp Grocery Store,** old **Firehouse,** with antique engines & buffalo-hide hose, & **Pioneer Saloon.** 73.5$^m$ **Sonora** (1,850'). Largest pocket mine in Mother Lode is **Big Bonanza** on Piety Hill (R). Some old bldgs. have survived: **St. James' Ch.** (1860); **Bauman Brewery** on Washington St., which supplied town's 40 saloons; **Gunn Adobe** (1850 adds.), now Hotel Italia.

77.5$^m$ **Jamestown** (1,500'), which grew prosperous from rich Table Mt. mines where Humbug Mine produced more than $4,000,000. 87.5$^m$ **Chinese Camp** (1,400'), which figured in Bret Harte tales as "Salvado." Here at one time as many as 5,000 Chinese were mining gold & here in 1856 occurred tong war which resulted in 4 deaths. 93.5$^m$ J. with St.120, branching (SE) to Yosemite Nat. Pk. (see) & cont. to J. with US395 (see). 108$^m$ **Coulterville** (1,675'). Surrounding slopes yielded fortunes in gold. Some old adobe bldgs. survive. Still functioning is **Old Jeffrey Hotel** (L) & in Plaza stands oak tree from which "bad men" were hanged. St.49 now climbs to **Hell Hollow** at 123.5$^m$. Fine view. Near-by are **Pacific Mines,** where quartz veins are still being worked. 125$^m$ **Bear Valley** (2,100'), now ghost town, was built by Frémont as hqs. for his Mariposa mines. After years of litigation & then disappointing returns, Frémont exclaimed: "When I came to California I hadn't a cent. Now I owe $2,000,000!" 131.5$^m$ **Mt. Bullion** (2,100'), named for Frémont's father-in-law, Sen. Benton, nicknamed "Old Bullion" because of his many controversies concerning currency. **Marre Store** (L) supplied goods, at one time, to more than 2,000 miners.

Take Rd. (R) from Mt. Bullion 13$^m$ to **Hornitos** (1,000'), camp which was celebrated for its fiestas, fandango halls, gambling halls, & brawls. Facing Plaza (R) is **Fandango Hall.** On an upper street is **Hornitos Hotel** (1860). Here also is old **Jail** in which Chinese, who had shot miner was killed by mob.

137$^m$ **Mariposa,** at J. with St.140 (see US99), running (E) to Yosemite Nat. Pk. (see) & (W) to Merced on US99 (see).

From Placerville US50 follows old Carson Emigrant Trl. used by Forty-niners to Sacramento. **92. FOLSOM,** known in gold-rush days as Negro Bar on old Rio de los Americanos Ranch, which was owned by Wm. A. Leidesdorff, whose heirs sold it to Capt. Jos. L. Folsom in 1848 just before gold rush. Take Rd. (R) here to **Folsom State Penitentiary** on American R. in which J. N. McNamara, convicted of L.A. Times bombing, & Warren K. Billings of Mooney-Billings case were confined. Above the penitentiary are dam across Amer. R. & power plant. **110. SACRAMENTO** (see US99), at Js. with US99 (see) & US40 (see). Bet. Sacramento & Stockton US50 & US99 unite (see US99 for this sec.). **153. STOCKTON** (see US99). From Stockton US50 passes (S) through what was formerly Rancho Campo de los Franceses, granted in 1844 to Wm. Gulnac, who had married Mex. girl & become Mex. citizen. In 1845 he sold entire ranch for $60, amount of grocery bill he owed. **166.** Rd. crosses **SAN JOAQUIN R.** (boat.f.). **205.5 DUBLIN** at J. with St.21. For towns & pts. of int. bet. & incl. this pt. & **SAN FRANCISCO, 239.5.,** see San Francisco V.

## US 6—CALIFORNIA

**CAL.-NEV. LINE** (71$^{m}$ from Tonopah, Nev.) **(S) to LOS ANGELES, CAL. 330. US6**

Via: Bishop, Independence, Lone Pine, Brown Mojave, Lancaster, Palmdale. S.P. RR. parallels route bet. Nev. Line & Bishop. Accoms.: limited bet. Nev. Line & Bishop.

From. Nev. line this route passes (S) in shadow of 14,000′ White Mts. Then, united with US395, it runs bet. high Sierra (W) & Death Valley Nat. Mon. (E) to Brown, from which it crosses Mojave Desert & climbs through Mint Canyon to metropolitan Los Angeles area.

**0. NEV.-CAL. LINE. 7.5. BENTON STA.,** starting point for f. & pack trips into White Mts. (L). View of **Mt. Dubois** (13,545′). **17.** J. with dirt Rd. leading (R) 0.5$^{m}$ to **Ind. Track Carvings,** accessible by short climb (L). These are curious carvings of animals' tracks & those of a human infant. **25.** J. with dirt Rd. leading (R) 1$^{m}$ to **Ind. Picture Carving Labyrinth,** where are ancient rock carvings. **27. CHALFANT GROUP OF IND. WRITINGS,** visible (L) high on inaccessible wall. **34.5.** J. with dirt Rd. leading (R) 5$^{m}$ to **Paiute Ind. Reserv.** Paiutes once ranged through this entire reg. At 5.5$^{m}$ **Large Ind. Petroglyphs.** In addition, there is an "inscriptive wall" on which are carved designs, accessible only by ladder. **41.5. BISHOP** (see US395) at J. with US395 (see) with which US6 unites for 123.5$^{m}$ to **BROWN** (for this stretch see US395) at **165.** Beyond Brown (S), **Owens Peak** (8,475′) visible from US6. **185.5.** J. with Hartz Rd. leading (L) through Last Chance Canyon to **Roaring Ridge Petrified For.** (fee) at 7$^{m}$. US6 now traverses deep Red Rock Canyon. **223.5. MOJAVE.** Formerly 20-mule teams used to haul borax here from Death Valley. **227.** J. with dirt Rd. leading (R) 2$^{m}$ to rich **Golden Queen Mine,** discovered 1935, on slope of Soledad Mt. **237. ROSAMOND,** at J. with Rd.

SIDE TRIP: Take latter (L) past **Rosamond Dry L.** (alkaline) to **Muroc,** 20$^{m}$, on W. edge of vast, absolutely flat **Muroc Dry L.,** where is **U.S. Army Air Forces Base** for jet & rocket aircraft, world's largest, 70$^{m}$ sq.

Hy. now crosses Antelope Valley. **257.5. PALMDALE,** center of fruit & alfalfa growing area. **272.5. SUMMIT OF MINT CANYON GRADE** (3,429′). In canyon area is **Mint Canyon For. Camp. 289.5.** J. with Soledad Canyon Rd.

SIDE TRIP: Take latter (L) 6$^{m}$ to scenically fine **Soledad Gorge.** Here is **Soledad For. Camp** & in Ind. Canyon. 1.5$^{m}$ distant, is **Ind. Canyon For. Camp.** 8.5$^{m}$ J. with Agua Dulce Canyon Rd., which route now follows (L) through exceedingly int. rock formations to J. with dirt Rd., at 11$^{m}$. Take latter (R) to **Vasquez Caves** (fee) at 14.5$^{m}$ in Escondido Canyon, where notorious bandit Tiburcio Vasquez had his hideout. At 16.5$^{m}$ **Vasquez Rocks** (fee), also hideout of this bandit. Here are int. geological formations.

**295.5. SAUGUS,** RR. division point. **297.5.** J. with Placeritas Canyon Rd. leading (L) 0.5$^{m}$ to **Monogram Village,** outdoor location of Monogram Pictures Inc. At 3.5$^{m}$ **Oak of Golden Legend** (L), under which first discovery of gold, in Cal., was made in 1842 by Don Francisco Lopez. **298.** J. with dirt Rd. leading (R) 0.2$^{m}$ to second dirt Rd. Take this (L) to **Newhall Refinery,** 0.5$^{m}$, Cal.'s first, with old stills, retorts & oil vats, carefully restored. **298.5. NEWHALL,** trade center for ranchers & oil producers. **302.5.** J. with US99 (see), with which US6 unites to **LOS ANGELES,** at **330.**

## US 66—CALIFORNIA

**CAL.-ARIZ. LINE** (54$^{m}$ from Kingman, Ariz.) **(W) to LOS ANGELES, CAL. 298.5. US66**

Via: Needles, Barstow, Victorville, San Bernardino, Claremont, Monrovia, Arcadia, & Pasadena. RR. parallels route bet. Needles & Victorville. Accoms.: Scanty in desert secs.; gas, oil, water, & food available at desert hamlets en route, but extra supplies should be carried; sleeping accoms. limited to tourist camps, except in larger towns. Extremely high temperatures bet. Kingman & San Bernardino in midsummer.

US66, after leaving Colorado R., runs through Mojave Desert to Barstow. Here it branches (S) through desert, with stretch of irrigated reg. along Mojave R., & finally crosses San Bernardino Nat. For. & Sierra Madre Mts., descends to San Bernardino, & then follows along base of Sierra Madre through rich, citrus & fruit growing district, to L. A.

**0.** US66 crosses Ariz. Line on Topock Bridge over **COLORADO R. 15.5.**

NEEDLES, pleasant oasis among palms & pepper trees. US66 now climbs (W) into Mojave Desert. **43. MOUNTAIN SPRINGS** (2,720′), summit of pass through Paiute Range. Here is view of snow-covered **Mt. San Antonio. 55.5.** J. with dirt Rd.

SIDE TRIP: Take latter (R) 22.5m to extensive **Mitchell's Caverns** (camp.water & wood. guides.fee.), underground labyrinth of limestone caves.

US66 cont. through several desert hamlets, past salt-encrusted flats of **BRISTOL DRY LAKE. 87.** J. with dirt Rd. leading (L) 1.5m to **Amboy Crater.** Footpath leads to top of int. crater cone. **95.5. BAGDAD** (accoms.), once busy mining camp. Bagdad has less rain than any other place in or near Mojave desert—a mean annual average of 2.3″, & in 4 out of 20 yrs., no rainfall at all. **129.5. MT. PISGAH** (L), extinct volcano, looms from across old lava bed. US66 cont. past desert villages to **NEWBERRY** at **146.5.** where spring flows from beneath precipices of Newberry Mts., creating oasis. **167. BARSTOW** (2,106′), RR. division pt. & farmers' trading center, is desert's metropolis. US66 now turns (S) through desert past some hamlets, & fertile stretch along Mojave R. to **VICTORVILLE** at **202.5.** (2,716′). This town & back country have been used as settings for many "Western" movies. Old town across RR. track (L) has been carefully preserved. Rodeo held annually in arena here. **216.5.** J. with US395 (see), with which US66 unites to San Bernardino. At **220.** US66 enters **SAN BERNARDINO NAT. FOR.** (804,045 as.), in which are many streams & lakes (good trout f. & good hik. trls.). Hy. now climbs to **Cajon Pass** (Sp."box") through Sierra Madre Mts. **221. SUMMIT** (4,301′), with magnificent view. **226.** J. with St.2.

SIDE TRIP: Take St.2 (R) 8m to J. with St.138 & turn (L) on this. 14m **Wrightwood** (6,000′), conifer-sheltered mt. resort. 16m **Big Pines Recr. Pk.,** one of S. Cal. major winter sports areas & mt. playgrounds (camp.pic.).

**234. DEVORE** (2,025′), with view of **Mt. San Gorgonio** (11,485′). **242.** View of **Arrowhead Peak** on whose face nature has scoured out an arrowhead. **244. SAN BERNARDINO** (1,073′), named by party from San Gabriel Mission, who entered valley May, 1810, feast day of San Bernardino of Sienna. In 1851 party of Mormons from Salt Lake arrived here & bought Rancho San Bernardino, but later abandoned it & returned to Utah. City today is RR., food-packing & tourist center, in heart of citrus-growing reg. Chief annual event is citrus fruit exhibition held in **Nat. Orange Show Bldg.,** E. & Mill Sts., beginning 3rd Thurs. in Feb. (fee). In **Pioneer Pk.,** 6th & E. Sts., are **Mem. Auditorium,** comm. heroes of World War I, **Soldiers & Sailors Mon. & Pioneer Cabin** (O) containing Mormon relics. In San Bernardino is (S) J. with US395 (see).

SIDE TRIP: Take 3rd St. (L) from San Bernardino to Sierra Way (St.18 ) & follow latter (L), ascending Waterman Canyon in San Bernardino Nat. For. 8m J. with private Rd. leading (R) to **Arrowhead Hot Springs** (resort). From here fine views, especially of **Arrowhead Peak.** 17m St.18 becomes Rim of the World Dr. rising to 8,000′. Just beyond this pt. is J. with Crestline Rd. leading (R) 3m to **Camp Seeley** (accoms.resort). 20m **Arrowhead Highland Summit** (5,174′). Just beyond this last pt. is J. with unpaved Rd. leading (L) 3m to **Crestline Village** (4,850′;resort center) with magnificent views. Here is **Crestline Bowl,** used for plays, pageants. Near-by are ski-tracks & toboggan slides. 23.5m **Crest Summit** (5,756′) with fine view. 24.5m J. with Arrowhead L. Rd. leading (L) 2m to **Arrowhead Village** (5,109′) on **Arrowhead L.** (accoms.amusements.trls.). Rds. & trls. run from here to resorts on L. Arrowhead Rd. leads (R) from Arrowhead Village 3m to **Arrowhead Dam.** At 33.5m on Rim of the World Dr., J. with paved Rd. leading (R) 0.5m to **Arrowbear L.** (7,800′.camp.cabins.) 35m J. with Green Valley Rd. leading (L) 4.5m to mountain-enclosed **Green Valley L.** (resort). Rim of the World Dr. now descends gradually. At 45.5m it crosses **Big Bear Dam. Big Bear L.,** impounded by dam, 7m long, is popular yr.-round resort. 50m **Pine Knot Village,** regional center from which radiate Rds. & trls. 58.5m **Baldwin L.** (6,674′).

US66 runs from San Bernardino (W) through orange groves at ft. of Sierra Madre snow-capped peaks. **249. FONTANA** (1,242′), site of Henry J. Kaiser **Fontana Steel Plant,** among citrus groves. **258.5. CUCAMONGA,** named for Cucamonga Peak (8,911′). **259.5. OLDEST CAL. WINERY,** est. by rancho-owner Don Tiburcio Topin, in continuous operation since 1839. Old Adobe H. & original wine-making buildings are here. Also coll. of relics incl. press brought round Horn. **263.5. CLAREMONT** (1,555′), home of **Pomona College** (coed.), founded 1887, which is unit of Claremont Affiliated Colleges. **Scripps College for Women** is another unit. **267.5.** J. with San Dimas Canyon Rd. leading (R) 0.5m to **San Dimas Canyon Pk.** (pic.). Trls. from here lead into San Gabriel Mts. Motor Rd. winds through canyon to **Wolfskill Falls** at 11m. **268.5.** J. with St.71, branching (S) to **Pomona** (see L.A. IV). For towns & pts. of int. bet. here and L.A., see L.A. IV. **298.5. LOS ANGELES.**

# US 60-70—CALIFORNIA

**CAL.-ARIZ. LINE** (4.5m from Quartzsite, Ariz.) **(W) to LOS ANGELES, CAL. 229. US60-70**

Via: Blythe, Indio, (Palm Springs), Banning, Beaumont, Riverside, Pomona, & Monterey Pk. Route paralleled by S.P. RR. bet. Indio & L.A. Accoms.: Adequate; service stas. at infrequent intervals bet. Blythe & Indio; good auto courts.

US60-70 is desert route, although in its first few miles it runs along Colorado R.'s verdant banks. It cuts across Colorado desert to Indio & cont. through arid country until it climbs San Gorgonio Pass over San Jacinto range into fertile coast reg. At **3.** J. with US95.

SIDE TRIP: (R) on latter to **Indian Intaglios** at 18m, huge figures of men & animals cut into rock by pre-hist. Inds.

**49.5. COLORADO R. AQUEDUCT,** visible in distance (NW). It cost $220,000,000 & carries water to 13 S. Cal. cities. **101.** J. with US99, which unites with US60-70 to Beaumont. **103. INDIO,** RR. & tourist town as well as center for surrounding irrigated reg.

SIDE TRIP: Take St.111, Palm Springs Hy., (L) across Coachella Valley through date orchards & orange groves. **Mt. San Jacinto Peak** is constantly visible. 13m J. with St.74 (see US395). 25.5m J. with dirt Rd.

Take latter (L) 2.5m to mouth of Andreas Canyon (R) & past Murray Canyon (R), 2.5m, to **Palm Canyon Nat. Mon.** at 5m. Here is grove of 5,000 Cal. palms, only species native to Western U.S. At 12m is J. with canyon Rd. leading (L) 0.5m, past **Tahquitz Peak** (8,826'), to parking space. Trl. from here leads into Tahquitz Canyon. Here is **Tahquitz Bowl,** in which plays are given in summer. There are some fine rock gorges, a water fall, many trls., & good views.

27m **Palm Springs,** famous resort (hotels,golf courses & dude ranches in vic.airport) & desert oasis. Town sulphur springs lie just (E) beyond business dist., on Agua Caliente Reserv., where Ind. owners of property maintain bathh. Each year La Fiesta de los Monos, ancient Cahuilla rite, is held on reserv. Near Palm Springs (W) is **Tachevan** (dry rock) **Canyon;** short walk leads to mt. stream. St.111 cont. to J. with US60-70-99 (see below) at 37.5m.

From Indio, US60-70-99 cont. (N) to J. at **129.5.** with paved Rd.

SIDE TRIP: Take latter (R) to **Morongo Valley,** 12m, & **Twenty-Nine Palms,** 43m. Turn (R) from latter on dirt Rd., past **Twenty-Nine Palms Ind. Reserv.,** into **Joshua Tree Nat. Mon.,** at S. end of Mojave Desert, set aside to protect tree-like yuccas of lily family which grow almost exclusively in this area; beautiful blooms of Joshua tree give off fine scent.

US60-70-99 cont. (N) to J. with St.111 (see above), from which it rises through San Gorgonio Pass bet. **Mt. San Jacinto** (10,937') & **Mt. San Gorgonio** (11,485'), usually snow-capped. **147. BANNING** (2,559'), in rich fruit-producing area.

SIDE TRIPS: (A) Take dirt Rd. (R) from Banning to **Morongo Ind. Reserv.** at 5.5m.
(B) Take dirt Rd. (R) from Banning 2m to **Highland Springs,** mt. resort (hotel) among streams, canyons, pine woods. At **Internat. Pk.,** 2.5m, Jap. cherry blossom festival in spring.

**151. BEAUMONT,** surrounded in spring by acres of blossoming cherry, almond, & apple orchards. At Beaumont is J. where US99-70 branches (R). **175.5. RIVERSIDE,** situated on what was formerly Jurupa Rancho of Don Juan Bandini, mentioned by Dana in his "Two Years Before the Mast." Here is **GLENWOOD MISSION INN,** beautiful hostelry containing art objects & pioneer relics. Riverside is surrounded by citrus ranches. It was a Riverside woman who accidentally developed first seedless orange in 1873. Parent navel orange tree stands at cor. Magnolia & Arlington Aves. Near city limits (NE) is **Citrus Experimental Sta.** (O.wks.) of Univ. of Cal. In Riverside is J. with US395 (see).

SIDE TRIP: Take Magnolia Ave. (St.18) from Riverside (L) 5m to **Sherman Ind. Inst.** (coed.) for Ind. children more than 14 yrs. old.

Beyond Riverside, hy. passes **Mt. Rubidoux** (1,337'), on which is supposed to have been an Ind. altar for sun worship. Great **Cross** on peak comm. Fray Serra, founder of missions. On mountainside is **World Peace Tower** & at its ft., **St. Francis Shrine** with bird-fountain. **198.5. POMONA** at J. with St.71. For Pomona & other towns & pts. of int. from here to Los Angeles see L.A. IV **229. LOS ANGELES** (see).

## US 80—CALIFORNIA

**CAL.-ARIZ. LINE** (at Yuma, Ariz.) **(W) to SAN DIEGO, CAL. 177. US80**

Via: Holtville, El Centro, Jacumba, El Cajon, & La Mesa. (Caution: For side trips on sandy desert Rds., car & equipment should be checked carefully; extra food, fuel & water should be carried; also gunny sacks to provide traction in loose sand.) San Diego & Ariz. Eastern RR. roughly parallels route. Accoms.: Adequate, except on side Rds.

US80 is southernmost E.-W. route across Cal. & parallels Mex. border. It traverses great Colorado Desert & S. sec. of Imperial Valley. After passing Imperial Valley, it resumes its desert course, climbs Coast Range through Cleveland Nat. For. Juan Bautista de Anza was first to explore S. Colorado Desert in 1775. In 1858 stage line was established which followed this route, running from St. Louis to San Francisco. Travellers had to face menace of Comanche, Apache, Yuma & Mojave Inds., as well as highwaymen. Passengers were advised to provide themselves with rifles & ample ammunition. Trip was advertised to require no more than 24 days.

**0. COLORADO R.,** forming Ariz.-Cal. Line. Near W. bank of R. is **Yuma Ind. School & Ind. Agency** (R), on spot where Misión de la Puríssima Concepción was built in 1781, but destroyed by Inds. Statue of Father Garces stands in front of chapel. Just beyond school, on US80, is **Yuma Ind. Mission** (R) on Ft. Yuma Ind. Reservation. Just beyond (W) is J. with gravelled Rd.

SIDE TRIP: (R) on latter to **Yuma Ind. Reserv.** (8,350 as.). 6.5m **U.S. Experimental Farm** (L), which has developed disease-resistant alfalfa. 12m **Laguna Dam,** which diverts waters for irrigation purposes. 17.5m **Imperial Dam,** hqs. for All-American Canal (see below), part of Boulder Dam Project.

**6.5.** hy. crosses **ALL-AMERICAN CANAL,** 80m long, 200′ wide, which can deliver 15,000 cu. ft. of water per second to Imperial Valley. **40.5. ANCIENT BEACH LINE** of prehist. **Cahuilla L.,** predecessor of Salton Sea (see US99), is visible. **41. E. HIGHLAND CANAL,** one of canals supplying water to valley. **49. HOLTVILLE,** chief trading point for E. Imperial Valley. **52.5. MELOLAND.** Here is **Experimental Sta.** (O.to qualified persons) **of Univ. of Cal. College of Agric. 56.5. EL CENTRO,** important Imperial Valley town, heart of desert area reclaimed by irrigation, laid out 1905 by W. F. Holt. Imperial Valley produces melons, dates, alfalfa, grapefruit, strawberries, lettuce & other crops. In El Centro is J. with US99 (see). From El Centro US80 cont. (W) across desert, then climbs mts.

**88. SHEPARD'S BRIDGE** (2,784′). From here hy. ascends through Incopah Gorge. **104.5. JACUMBA** (2,800′;resort with mineral springs & baths), almost on Mex. Border. About 3m (N) from Jacumba is mouth of **Carrizo Gorge,** 11m long, one of most spectacular valleys of reg. **127.5. BUCKMAN SPRINGS** (3,225′) at J. with dirt Rd.

SIDE TRIP: (L) on latter 8.5m to **Morena L.** (resort.boats & tackle), part of San Diego's water system, with dam 171′ high.

**130.5. LAGUNA J.** (4,050′;serv.sta.restaurant) at J. with oiled Rd.

SIDE TRIP: Take latter (R) to **Mt. Laguna Recr. Area** in Cleveland Nat. For. (815,000 as. cabins.pub.camp.game refuge). Rd. winds high up over mts. with magnificent views of country below. At 10m, **Laguna P. O.,** hqs. for resort area. At 10.5m **For. Ranger Sta.** (info.).

**131. PINE VALLEY** (4,016′;hotel.cabins). **135.5. CUYAMACA** J. with St.79 (see US395). **147. ALPINE** (1,860′;resort.accoms.). **153.5. FLINN SPRINGS** (1,300′; resort.camp.pic.). **163.5.** J. with oiled Rd. leading (L) 1m to **Mt. Helix** (1,380′), topped by high cross. Here Easter sunrise services are held. **165.** J. with paved Rd. leading (R) 1m to **Murray Dam & Lake** (boat.), part of San Diego's water system. **169.** J. with College Ave. leading (R) 1m to **San Diego St. College. 177. SAN DIEGO** (see US101), at J. with US101 (see) & US395 (see).

## US 101(N)—CALIFORNIA

**SAN FRANCISCO, CAL. (N) to CAL.-ORE. LINE** (6.5m from Brookings, Ore.). **392.5. US101**

Via: Sausalito, San Rafael, Petaluma, Santa Rosa, Healdsburg, Ukiah, Willits, Laytonville, Eureka, Arcata, & Crescent City. RR. parallels route to Eureka. Bus lines parallel route throughout.

This route runs (N) inland from S.F. & is sometimes known as Redwood Hy. because of magnificent redwood groves through which it passes. In general it cont. in view of Coast Range (W) through fertile orchards, vineyards, & ranches to Laytonville. Beyond this point, country becomes more thickly forested. At Eureka US101 reaches coast, along which it cont. with magnificent views of cragbound shore.

**0. SAN FRANCISCO.** For towns & pts. of int. bet. S.F. & **COTATI, 46.** see San Francisco III. **54. SANTA ROSA,** market town for rich Santa Rosa Valley where Luther Burbank conducted his experiments in plant breeding. Santa Rosa Ave. & Tupper St., **Burbank Mem. Gardens,** comprising **Luther Burbank H.,** grounds & grave. **77.5. GEYSERVILLE. 83. ASTI,** where Ital. Swiss Colony wines are produced. Here is **Ch. of Our Lady of Mt. Carmel,** shaped like an enormous wine barrel. **90.** J. with graveled Rd.

SIDE TRIP: Take latter (R) 14.5m to **The Geysers,** supposed to have therapeutic value. One of them, Devil's Inkstand, emits black water which can be used as ink.

**102.** J. with paved Rd.

SIDE TRIP: Take latter (R) 18m to J. with St.29, & follow latter (L). 20m **Lakeport.** From here route skirts W. shore of beautiful **Clear L.** under shadow of Mt. Konochti (4,200'). Rd. then cont. to **Upper Lake** (resort village) at J. with St.20. Turn (L) on this, skirting twin mt.-enclosed **Blue Ls.** (resorts) to J. with US101 at 50m.

**116.5. UKIAH** (Ind.,deep valley), is situated in narrow valley of orchards, vineyards & hop farms. **Internat. Latitude Observatory** (O), one of 5 located at widely distributed points on same latitude (39° 8'N.), for special astronomical observations. From Ukiah, Rd. leads (R) 4m to **Vichy Springs** (resort). Another Rd. leads (R) 8m to **The Terraces,** where grows coll. of native Cal. & foreign botanical specimens. **127.5. BLACK BART ROCK** (R), named for famous bandit, who operated in this reg. 1875-83. He lived in S.F. as respectable mining engineer & was trapped there & jailed at San Quentin. **186. COOLIDGE REDWOOD PK.,** where arch has been cut through redwood big enough for an automobile to pass. US101 now cont. through gorge forested with redwoods, climbs to canyon rim & **LILLEY REDWOOD PK.** at **194.,** in which is **Quadruped Tree,** 250' high, 101' circum. **202. RICHARDSON GROVE ST. PK.** (cabins.camp.swim.pool). **227.5.** Rd. now skirts sheer bluffs of narrow gorge of S. Fork of Eel R. **240. FOUNDER'S GROVE,** in which is **World's Tallest Tree,** redwood, 364' high. US101 now passes **HUMBOLDT ST. PK. 256.5. SCOTIA,** so-called because its settlers, nicknamed "blue noses," came from Nova Scotia. Here is **Redwood Lumber Mill** (O) producing 1,500 kinds of wood articles & lumber, largely from Sequoia wood.

US101 now crosses Eel R. at **262.** to **CANYON PK.** (O.fee), noted for its many varieties of ferns & mosses, & cont. along Eel R., which it re-crosses, then turns (N) along Humboldt Bay. **287. EUREKA** was named by James Ryan when he drove his vessel onto mudflats, shouting "Eureka." Redwood mills are town's dominant industry. Overlooking bay, **Ft. Humboldt** where Pres. Grant was stationed in 1854; it is said he spent much of his time drinking in Ryan's Saloon. Hqs. of Commissary Dept. still stands & contains relics. On **Indian I.** in bay, Feb.25,1860, occurred massacre of Ind. women & children by white settlers. Ind. men had been away hunting. Bitter war of revenge followed. Bret Harte, who was editor of local paper, denounced outrage & was forced by threats to return to S.F. In 1885 anti-Chinese feeling in Eureka came to head & resulted in expulsion of Chinese from Humboldt Cty., of which Eureka is seat. **Stump H.,** on Broadway, is built of huge redwood logs & stumps, & contains coll. of redwood curios. In **Sequoia Pk.** (pic.recr.) are redwoods, lake & zoo. **292.5. ARCATA** (Ind., "where boats land"), formerly known as Union Town. Here Bret Harte worked as compositor & assistant to editor of "Northern Californian" & as agent for Wells Fargo & Co. On hill, **Humboldt St. Teachers' College.**

**297.** J. with US299, running (E) to J. with US99 (see). **306.5. LITTLE RIVER BEACH ST. PK. 309.5. TRINIDAD,** formerly mining town, at J. with Rd. leading (L) 1.5m to **Trinidad Head** on which is Cross, replacing one erected in 1775 by Sp. explorer, Heceta. **315. LAGOON PK.** (resort). **341.5. PRAIRIE CR. ST. PK.** (6,467 as.camp.recr.f.), located high above surf; fine views. Rd. now descends & crosses Douglas Mem. Bridge over Klamath R. to **KLAMATH at 349.5.** Klamath R. in summer is much frequented by sports fishermen. In Klamath is **Shaker Ch.** where

Inds. hold noisy services. This sect is not related to Shakers elsewhere. Hy. now cont. bet. ocean (L) & **DEL NORTE COAST PK.** (R) **368.5.** J. with narrow Rd. leading (R) $8^m$ to **Hiouchi Redwood St. Pk.,** containing Frank A. Stout Mem. Grove, distinguished by its variety of flowers & plants, especially giant Woodwardia fern. **370.5. CRESCENT CITY,** shipping center for lumber, dairy products & fish. **371.** J. with US199 (see US99, Ore.), leading (R) past Ore. Caves Nat. Mon. to J. with US99 (see) in Ore. **379. WEBBER GROVE,** northernmost for. of redwoods. **385. SMITH R.** (f.h. auto & trlr.camps). **392.5. ORE. LINE.**

# US 99(N)—CALIFORNIA

**SACRAMENTO, CAL. (N) to CAL.-ORE. LINE** ($22^m$ from Ashland, Ore.). **296. US99**

Via: Roseville, Marysville, Chico, Red Bluff, Redding, Dunsmuir, Mt. Shasta City, Weed, & Yreka. S.P. RR. parallels entire route. Accoms.: All types; camp. sites in N. counties.

US99 runs (N) from Sacramento through vast, fertile Central Valley, follows Sacramento R. & other gorges through mts., skirts Mt. Shasta & threads through wild canyons to ramparts of Siskiyou Mts. on Ore. border. Old Cal.-Ore. Trl., in its day, followed direction taken by this tour. It was first used by scouts & trappers & later by emigrants in their covered wagons. Still later, turnpike Rd. was built from Portland to Sacramento & stage coaches travelled it on regular schedules. Finally RR. was brought up from S., more or less paralleling route to Portland.

**0. SACRAMENTO**

Through RR. & Bus conns. Municipal Airport, $5^m$ (S) on Freeport Blvd. Info.: Cal. St. Automobile Assoc., 1700 L St.; C. of C., 917—7th St. Mem. Auditorium, symphony & choral concerts. Swim.: In mun. & other pools. Boat. & f. in Sacramento R. Rodeo, St. Fair Grounds, 5th Ave. & Stockton Blvd., in Ap.; Cal. St. Fair, 10 days in early Sept.

Sacramento, capital of Cal., is handsome residential city lying in loop of Sacramento R. near its J. with Amer. R. Although politics is chief industry, city is also very busy market town handling large percentage of all vegetables & fruits grown in Cal. Besides canneries, it has many other important industries. R. channel provides water transport to San Francisco Bay. Sacramento was founded in 1839 by Capt. John Augustus Sutter, Swiss ex-army officer, who obtained grant from Mex. Gov. of 50,000 as. He named settlement New Helvetia. It was Sutter's boss carpenter, James W. Marshall, who on Jan. 24, 1848, while building mill near Coloma (see US50) on S. Fork of Amer. R., discovered gold. Rush of prospectors swamped Sutter's baronial domain & ended in his ruin. Bet. 1849 & 1853 three disastrous floods & a fire wrecked town. In 1852 legislature met here, sitting on "hot ashes." In 1854 city was officially declared capital.

PTS. OF INT.: (1) Bet. 10th & 15th St., **Capitol Pk.,** with coll. of more than 1,000 varieties of trees & shrubs from all over world. (2) In pk. is **Cal. St. Capitol** (1860-73.Class.), topped by golden dome. Ball surmounting lantern of dome is 237′ above ground. On walls of rotunda are 12 murals depicting state hist. In rotunda's center is statue, "Columbus before Isabella," by Larkin G. Mead. Excellent view from 2nd balcony of dome. 10th St. bet. L & N Sts., (3) **St. Office Bldg.,** & (4) **St. Lib. & Courts Bldg.** Appellate Court Rm. is lavishly decorated. (5) 15th St. bet. J & I Sts., **Mem. Auditorium** (1927.Ital.Romanes.), comm. World War I veterans. (6) 9th & I Sts., **City Plaza,** with statue (by Albert Weiner) comm. A. J. Stevens, "friend of labor," & fountain (by Ralph Stackpole) comm. Wm. T. Coleman. (7) 4th & I Sts., **Southern Pacific RR. Sta.** In main entrance mon. to Theodore D. Judah, imbedded in which is old Central Pacific RR. tie; on E. wall of waiting room is mural by Arthur McQuarry. (8) 1015—2nd St., **Pony Express Mus.** (O) which was for some months, in 1860-61, office & relay sta. of Pony Express from Sacramento to St. Joseph, Mo. (9) 2nd & O Sts., **Crocker Art Gallery** (O.10-5 exc.Mon.summer 10-4); paintings, studies & drawings by many of world's great masters. (10) 26th & L Sts., **Sutter's Fort** (O.10-4 wks.), which is restoration on orig. site of Sutter's ranchh., workshops, home & fort (erected 1839). Bldg. contains colls. of early Cal. relics. Ind. Mus. contains 40,000 Ind. articles illustrating culture of Cal. Inds. (11) 2nd Ave. & Stockton Blvd., **St. Fair Grounds,** where Cal. St. Fair is held. At Sacramento is (E) J. with

US40 (see), (N) J. with US50 (see), & J. with St.24, conn. with US395 (see). From Sacramento (N), tourists may choose bet. US99E & US99W, paralleling each other (N) to Red Bluff. Present route follows 99E, longer but scenically & historically more int.

SIDE TRIP: Take US99W (L) from Sacramento to **Woodland,** 21m, trading center of rich area growing sugar beets & other crops. US99W cont. (N) through vast, flat grain and rice-growing area. 61.5m **Williams** is center of huge irrigated sec. One of West's biggest privately owned irrigation systems pumps water from Sacramento R. & distributes it over 60,000 as. in vic. 103m **Orland,** in irrigated grain-growing area. 118.5m **Corning,** center of olive-growing belt. 135m **Red Bluff,** at J. with US99E (see below).

Bet. Sacramento & **ROSEVILLE, 18.,** US99E is united with US40 (see). **28.5. LINCOLN,** grain & fruit-growing center, with big pottery works. **53. MARYSVILLE,** at confluence of Yuba & Feather Rs., is hist. Gold Rush town, in 1851 St.'s 3rd largest, now center of rich peach-orchard reg. & hydraulic gold-mining area. Hist. bldgs. incl. **Sisters of Notre Dame Convent** (1856), 7th & C Sts.; **Ramirez H.** (1850's), 220-222 5th St.; **Yuba County Cth.** (1855-56), 6th & D Sts.; & **Firehouse** (1855-56), 4th bet. B & C Sts. **54. YUBA CITY,** peach-growing center, laid out 1849. **64.5. SUTTER BUTTES** (L) juts from flat valley floor. **80.** J. with paved Hy.

SIDE TRIP: Take latter (R) 8m to **Oroville,** which sprang up 1849-50 as Ophir City when gold was discovered. It became Butte City, & was 5th largest in Cal. in 1856. During 1870's had State's largest Chinatown. N. Cal.'s first important orange grove planted near-by 1886. Cal. gold dredging began here 1898, with floating of 1st successful bucket elevator dredge. **Butte Cty. Pioneer Mem. Mus.** houses relics of gold days. Oroville is at J. with St.24, leading (NE) through picturesque Feather R. Canyon to J. with US395 (see). Turn (R) from Oroville on Berry Creek Rd. to **Bidwell's Bar,** 9.5m, on S. Fork of Feather R., where John Bidwell found gold July 4, 1848. Town of 2,000 sprang up but population stampeded away when diggings were exhausted. Cal.'s **First Suspension Br.** (1856) spans R. At its S. end is **Old Mother Orange Tree,** planted 1856, whose seeds started N. Cal.'s 1st citrus belt.

**100.5. CHICO,** chief trade center of N. Sacramento Valley, among grain fields & fruit & almond orchards, founded on pioneer horticulturist John Bidwell's Rancho Chico. Two-story stone **Bidwell Mansion** is now one of bldgs. of **Chico St. College.** At E. edge of town is 2,400-acre **Bidwell Pk.** (where "The Adventures of Robin Hood" was filmed, 1937), containing **Hooker Oak,** said to be world's largest, 1,000 yrs. old, 110′ high, with 28′ circum. & 147′ in diam. **141.5. RED BLUFF,** situated on heights overlooking Sacramento R. In 1850's paddle-wheel steamers travelled as far as this pt., but with introduction of irrigation, drawing large amounts of water from Sacramento R., water level fell too low for navigation. Pine & Washington Sts., in City Hall, is **Wm. B. Ide Mem. Mus.;** pioneer, Ind. & Chinese relics. 135 Main St., **John Brown Family H.,** built for John Brown's widow & three daughters who lived there until 1870. In Red Bluff is J. with US99W (see) & J. with St.36.

SIDE TRIP: Take latter (R) from Red Bluff, climbing into mts. 48.5m J. with St.89; on which route turns (L). 56.5m **Lassen Volcanic Nat. Pk.** (103,270 as. f.winter sports), at S. end of Cascade Range where it joins Sierra Nevada. 58.5m **Sulphur Works Checking Sta.** Rd. now skirts (L) **Black Butte Mt.** (8,288′), **Brokeoff Mt.** (9,232′), **Diamond Peak** (7,969′), **Diller Mt.** (9,086′), **Eagle Peak** (9,211′), all remnants of prehistoric Mt. Tehama Crater. At 59.5m **Sulphur Works,** with int. hot mud cauldrons & sulphur springs. 64m **Emerald L.** (no fish.). At 64.5m, just before reaching **Helen L., J.** with trl. leading (R) 1.5m to **Bumpass Hell,** impressive geyser, mud springs, & fumarole area. At 65m on St.89 is **Helen L.** (8,000′) surrounded by high peaks. 66m. **Summit** (8,512′) of Lassen Peak Loop (parking.). Trl. leads (L) here 2.5m to **Lassen Peak** (10,453′) with magnificent view. This mt. is still an active volcano whose last eruption occurred in 1917. 70.5m. **Kings Creek Meadows** (pub.camp.). Trl. leads (R) here 1.5m to **Kings Creek Falls.** 75.5m **Summit L.** (camp.recr.fish.). From here trls. run to Chain-of-Lakes district in E. sec. of Pk. Just beyond Summit L., on St.89, is **Summit L. Ranger Sta.** (info.). St.89 now traverses very int. volcanic area past **Chaos Crags** (8,458′) (R) & **Raker Peak** (7,466′) (L). 87m **Manzanita L.** (5,845′;recr.accoms.camp. f.). Here is **May Loomis Mem. Mus.** containing material concerning Mt. Lassen region. St.89 cont. bet. **Reflection & Manzanita Ls.** 88m J. with St.44, leading (L) 49.5m to **Redding** (see below) at J. with US99.

**142.5.** J. with paved Rd. leading (R) 1m to adobe **Gen. Wm. B. Ide H.** (1849). Ide was Pres. of shortlived Bear Flag Republic (see Sonoma), 1849. **167.5.** Clear Cr., at J. with dirt Rd.

SIDE TRIP: Take dirt Rd. (L) to **Reading's Bar,** 11m, where, in Mar. 1848, Pierson Reading found 1st gold in Shasta Cty. Reading's Bar became booming settlement of 1,000 inhabitants, known as One Horse Town, with 14 saloons; destroyed by fire in 1868.

**173. REDDING,** on Sacramento R., center of important agric. dist. & starting pt. for hunters & fishermen. Here is (S) J. with US299.

SIDE TRIP: Take US299 (L) from Redding, ascending into Trinity Mts. along old Trinity Trl. of 1840's. 6m **Shasta,** once center of roaring wide-open mining town through which mule pack trains from N. mining reg. passed. Here are **First Masonic Hall in Cal.** & Litsch General Store (1853), housing **Litsch's Free Mus. of Hist. Pioneer Relics.** Joaquin Miller lived among Inds. of reg., who were notorious for horse stealing, & was once lodged in town jail, from which, however, he managed to escape. At this time he had an Ind. wife & half-Ind. daughter. From Shasta US299 ascends (W) to summit of Shasta Divide (1,390'). 10.8m **Whiskey Town** (1,091'), so named because barrel of whiskey dropped into Rd. here from pack mule. In 1853 a bartender was lynched in town after shooting fray. 17m **Tower H.** (1852), former stagecoach sta. Rd. presently enters Trinity Mts. & then descends to **Buckhorn** (2,500'; auto camp), in fertile Grass Valley at 29.5m. 42m **Douglas City** (1,700') on Trinity R. 47.5m **Weaverville** (2,407'), once boisterous mining town whose hist. was punctuated by frequent shootings & summary hangings by vigilantes. **Weekly Trinity Journal Office** (1856) where "Weekly Trinity Journal," one of 4 oldest newspapers in state, is still published. In **St. Mem. Hall** is coll. of relics incl. Ind. scalp. **Chinese Joss H.** (O) is survival of time when there were 3,000 Chinese in town, who in 1854 amused white miners by staging lively tong battle. US299 cont. past a number of for. camps. At 147m **J.** with US101 (see).

**175.** (N) J. with US299, running (E) to J. with US395 (see). **180. CENTRAL VALLEY,** at J. with paved Rd. leading (L) 6m to **Shasta Dam,** impounding Sacramento, McCloud, & Pit Rs., chief unit of Central Valley Project, world's 2nd highest & 2nd biggest in mass content, 560' high & 3,500' long. Construction begun 1938. **187. PIT R. BR.,** world's highest double-decked bridge, carries hy. & RR. 560' above R. bed. US99 climbs mt. divide & then skirts 29,500-a. **SHASTA RESERVOIR,** Cal.'s 2nd largest lake, at **203.** (N). At **211.5. SHI-LO-AH MINERAL SPRINGS** (cabins. trlrs.camp.store). Hy. cont. along canyon to J. with dirt Rd. at **220.5.** leading (L) 3.5m to base of **Castle Crags** rising sheer 6,000' above fors. Here June 26, 1855, battle bet. Modoc Inds. & settlers took place. Settlers were victorious. Joaquin Miller has described battle. **222. CASTLE CRAGS ST. PK.,** 50-sq.-mile recr. region (camp.pic.f.). **226.5. DUNSMUIR,** RR. division pt. & sportsmen's supply center, in gorge of Sacramento R. **229.** J. with paved Rd. leading (L) short distance to **Shasta Springs** (2,556';resort), located above narrow canyon of Sacramento R. Here bubbling Shasta water is bottled. Near-by are beautiful **Moss Brae Falls. 237.5. MT. SHASTA CITY** (3,554') at base of Mt. Shasta (14,161'). Here is Shasta Nat. For. Hqs. for huge reserve of 1,656,477 as., stretching (E&W) along US99 for 60m.

SIDE TRIP: Take Alma St. (R) 3m to Shasta Trl., which runs to **Summit of Mt. Shasta.** Trip can be made on foot or, in part, on horseback. Season: July-Sept. Round trip from lodge (see below) requires 8-10 hrs. Climber should carry full mt.-climbing equipment. At 8m on trl. is **Shasta Alpine Lodge** (7,992'; firewood & blankets avail.). Summit is reached at 12m. Mt. Shasta, 6th highest mt. in Cal., but more impressive than highest, Mt. Whitney, because it rises alone, was discovered 1827 & first climbed 1854. It is an ancient volcano with five glaciers. Snow-covered in all seasons, it dominates landscape for 100m around. Descent of E. side of Mt. is feasible to J. with Pacific Crest Tr.

Leaving Mt. Shasta City, US99 skirts **Black Butte** (6,044') & cont. through cut-over forest land to **WEED** (3,466'), lumber town, at **244.** Here is J. with US97 (see). **273. YREKA** (prob. corruption of Ind., Wai-ri-ka, "mountain"). In 1851 gold was discovered at Black Gulch Camp by Abraham Thompson, which accounted for town's 1st boom. Early settlers narrowly escaped massacre by Inds., when pioneer woman, Klamath Peggy, travelled 20m across mts. to warn them of impending attack. From Yreka US99 twists (N) through narrow gorge of Shasta R., crossing it back & forth as it proceeds. **281.** US99 crosses **KLAMATH BR.** where Klamath R. joins Shasta R. US99 cont. (N) with views of Mt. Shasta (S) & **Black Mt.** (E) (5,270') in wild Siskiyou Range to **ORE. LINE, 296.**

## US 97—CALIFORNIA

**WEED, CAL. (N) to CAL.-ORE. LINE** (21m from Klamath Falls, Ore.). **57. US97**

Via: Macdoel, Dorris. S.P. RR. & bus lines parallel route from Weed to Klamath Falls, Ore. US97, most direct route to pts. of int. in Cascade Range in Ore., branches (R) from US99 (see) at Weed & runs (NE) over volcanic lava-encrusted plateau, overshadowed by Mt. Shasta (S).

**12.** J. with poor dirt Rd.

SIDE TRIP: Take latter (L) 3.5m to J. with dirt Rd.

Take latter (L) 0.5m to trl. (not well marked) leading 0.5m to entrance of **Pluto Cave,** series of impressive underground lava caverns.

**57. ORE. LINE.**

# US 395—CALIFORNIA

**CAL.-ORE. LINE** (14m from Lakeview, Ore.) **(S) to SAN DIEGO, CAL. 822.5. US395**

Via: Alturas, (Susanville), (Reno & Carson City), Bridgeport, Bishop, Independence, Inyokern, Brown, San Bernardino & Escondido. RR. parallels route from Ore. Line to Ravensdale, from Litchfield to Susanville, from Doyle to Carson City, Nev., & from Nev. Line & Inyokern. RR. conns. in San Bernardino, Riverside & San Diego. Accoms.: In larger towns; otherwise limited.

This route, in its N. sec., traverses semi-arid reg. walled in by high mt. ranges to Nev. Line. It dips into Nev., via Reno & Carson City, returns to Cal. at Topaz L. & cont. along E. side of High Sierra Ridge. US395 makes J. with only two hys. (St.108 & St.120), crossing latter to San Joaquin Valley, but gives access to stub Rds. & trls., to passes & peaks of High Sierra & to Yosemite & Sequoia-Kings Canyon Nat. Pks. (W). It also conn. with Rds. to Death Valley Nat. Mon. (E). Then it crosses Mojave desert to San Bernardino, whence it cont. through rich, citrus-growing area & finally across low barren ranges, with access to Mt. Jacinto reg., to San Diego, on coast.

### Sec. 1: CAL. LINE to NEV. LINE. 213.5.

US395 crosses from Ore. into Cal. at **PINE CREEK** (4,900') 14m (S) from Lakeview, Ore. Route skirts (R) **Goose L.,** usually dry, & (L) **Warner Mts.** (15,000'-10,000'). **14.5. SUGAR HILL** with fine view of Goose L. **43.5. ALTURAS** (4,446'), ranchers' trading center. There was considerable Ind. warfare in this reg. On Main St., hqs. of **Modoc Nat. For.** (1,500,000 as.camp.deer h.f.), extending (N) from Alturas.

SIDE TRIP: Take US299 (R) from Alturas. 18m **Canby,** named for Gen. E. S. Canby, of Modoc war fame. 18.5m J. with St.139.

Take St.139 (R). 25.5m J. with dirt Rd. Turn (L) on this (travel advised May-Oct. only; carry extra tire). At 31m is entrance to **Mammoth Cave** (R), short distance from Rd., marked by jumble of lava rocks. 32m J. with unpaved Rd.; turn (L) on this. At 36m turn (R) on another Rd. At 38m boundary of **Lava Beds Nat. Mon.,** rectangular area 10m long & 8m wide, dedicated 1925. It consists of labyrinth of caves & chasms, in which molten lava has hardened into strange shapes—arched bridges, fantastically sculptured rocks, some resembling animals. Caves, of which more than 100 have been explored, were formed when surface of lava hardened & still molten core drained away. In many of these underground galleries, delicate, lacelike traceries, & Ind. pictographs in red, green, or yellow-ochre decorate ceilings & walls; in some of deeper ones, frosted crystals, frozen waterfalls, or rivers of ice appear. This lava-covered reg. was formerly stronghold of warlike Modoc Inds. For 5 months in 1872-73, a band of warriors, never numbering more than 60, held off some 1,200 soldiers. During fighting 83 whites lost their lives, incl. Gen. E. R. S. Canby, commander, treacherously killed during truce parley, by Capt. Jack, Modoc chieftain (see Ft. Klamath, Ore.). 42m **Indian Well** (campground & adm. hqs. for Mon. info. available from ranger during summer) is starting pt. for exploration (gasoline lanterns for use in caves avail.; in larger caves, guide line of strong twine should be fastened at entrance & unwound as exploration progresses; stout hiking boots essential). Opp. Adm. Hqs., at entrance to **Labyrinth,** a two-mile maze of tunnels, is **Devil's Mush Pot,** huge kettle of rock from which molten lava once flowed. Opp. entrance to **Catacomb Cavern** is **Crystal Cave.** At 43.5m is J. with unpaved Rd., narrow & winding, pitted with sharp lava fragments, which loops around Mon. (advised only for experienced drivers, with good tires) to chief pts. of int.: **Big Painted Cave, Little Painted Cave, Skull Cave, Ship Cavern & White Lace Cave, Frozen R. Cave, Jack's Ice Cave, Fern Cave, Hospital Rock, Canby Cross, Gillem's Graveyard, Schonchin Butte, Bearpaw Cave.**

From J. with St.139, US299 follows Pitt R. & then swings (S) across it to **Canby Br. Camp** (For.Service) & then ascends into Adin Mts. 28m **For. Camp** (R) at **Adin Pass Summit** (5,196'). 33m **Indian Springs** (fuel.camp.). 40m **Adin.** Here is Big Valley Ranger Sta. Near-by are several For. Camps. 50m **Basset Hot Springs.** 61m Fine view of Bieber Ridge, snow-capped Mt. Shasta, Lassen Peak & Mt. Burney. 74m **Fall River Mills** (3,307'). Here, from diversion dam on Fall R., canal & tunnel direct the flow of water from Pitt & Fall Rs. to Pitt R. Canyon above Pitt Power H. No. 1 (see below). 78m J. with dirt Rd. leading (L) 1m to **Pitt Power H. No. 1,** in deep canyon, of Pacif. Gas & Elec. Co. From tunnel (see above) water is dropped through steel turbines 454'. Power is transmitted from here to Bay area. 83.5m J. with dirt Rd. leading (L) 3.5m to **Cassel** (2,050'.store). Near-by dwell members of

Hat Creek Tribe, whose baskets are on sale in store, which also displays **Ind.** relics & photographs. 89.5m **J.** with St.89.

Take latter (R) 7m to **McArthur Mem. (Burney Falls) St. Pk.** (335 as.camp.f.), surrounding 128′ Burney Falls, where Lost R. plunges into mossy, pine-shaded gorge on way to near-by L. Britton.

90m **Burney** (3,159′). 96m **Hatchet Mt. Lookout,** with splendid view (4,368′). 141m J. with US99 (see).

US395 cont. (S) from Alturas. **63. LIKELY** (4,500′). From here US395 climbs through pass bet. S. Fork Mt. & Tule Mt. (7,136′) & then along Tule L. Reservoir. **128. HONEY L. VALLEY,** walled in by lofty Sierra Nevada. **147.5.** J. with St.36.

SIDE TRIP: Take St.36 (R) along Susan R. 4.5m **Susanville** (4,195′;1853), lumber & cattle center. Isaac N. Roop & Peter Lassen discovered gold here, 1854, & settlement became typical mining camp. Settlers est. short-lived independent commonwealth here in 1856 which they called Nataqua & which they later attempted to have incorporated with Nev. Cal. set up claim to reg. & result was armed clash in 1863; finally settled peaceably. **Ft. Defiance,** Weatherlow St., is still standing. This was Roop's cabin, later occupied by embattled advocates of annexation to Nev. In Susanville are hqs. of Lassen Nat. For.

Take Weatherlow St. (L) to fork at 3m; turn (L) here to fork at 4m & (R) here to entrance, at 6m, to grove of pines in which are **Peter Lassen's Grave** & 2 mons. to his memory. Lassen was killed by Inds., 1859.

St.36 cont. (W) to J. at 43m with St.89, with which it unites to J. at 66m (see US99), where St.89 branches (N) into Lassen Volcanic Nat. Pk. (see US99).

**157. BUNTINGVILLE.** Beyond (S) stretches vast Honey L., usually dry. **205.5. STOY JUNCTION** at inters. with St.24.

SIDE TRIP: Take St.24 (R). At 2m **Beckwourth Pass** (5,220′), beyond which (S) lies **Mt. Ina Coolbrith** (8,311′). 17m **Beckwourth.** 34m **Blairsden** (4,500′), in winter sports area. Take Rd. (L) here 1.5m to **Mohawk** (all-yr.hotel, sulphur springs). 42m **Jackson Cr. For. Camp** (4,200′;trlrs.). 59m **Quincy,** hist. mt. town, sett.1854.

Take Rd. (L) here 8m to **Meadow Valley** (accoms.summer) & at 17m **Bucks** (accoms. summer) on **Bucks L.** (5,071′). Here is **Bucks For. Camp.** (trlrs.).

60m **Quincy For. Camp** (3,500′;trlrs.). St.24 soon traverses deep **Feather R. Canyon,** following N. Fork of R., magnificently picturesque. 73m **Twain.** 74m **Hallsted Flat For. Camp** (3,000′;no trlrs.). 87m **Belden,** where is **Belden For. Camp** (2,500′;trlrs.). 136m **Oroville** (see US99), at **J.** with paved hy. leading 7m to J. with US99 (see). St.24 turns (S), following Feather R. 165m **Marysville** at J. with US99E (see).

From J. with St.24 US395 skirts rocky heights of Sierra Nevada & crosses Nev. Line, **213.5.,** at **ALKALINE L.,** covered with white sheet of alkaline, 16m (W) from Reno.

### Sec. 2: NEV. LINE back to CAL. LINE. 83. For this sec. see US395 Nev.

### Sec. 3: CAL. LINE to SAN BERNARDINO, 391.

**0. TOPAZ L.** Hy. enters Antelope Valley, crossing at **4. WALKER R.,** named for Capt. Jos. Walker, its discoverer (1834), who was 1st to cross Sierra Nevada westward. **16.** Boundary of **TOIYABE NAT. FOR. 20.5. SHINGLE MILL PUB. CAMP. 24. CHRIS FLATS PUB. CAMP. 28.5.** J. with St.108.

SIDE TRIP: Take latter (R) across Sierra Nevada through scenically magnificent reg. by way of several resorts, for. camps & mining towns. At 15m is **Sonora Pass** (9,642′). At 53.5m **Strawberry** (resort), at J. with dirt Rd.

Take latter (L) 2m to **Pine Crest For. Camp** on **Strawberry L.,** near **Eleanor L.,** both dominated by lofty cliffs. Also near Strawberry L. is **Meadow View For. Camp** (ample accoms., trlrs.).

64m **Longbarn** (5,000′.hotel.summer & winter resort). 83m **Sonora** (1,924′), at J. with St.49, conn. with US50 (see).

**32. FALES HOT SPRINGS** (accoms.). **40.5. HUNTOON PUB. CAMP.** Route begins to climb again through fine country with views of snow-capped peaks. **45.5. BRIDGEPORT,** former mining town & tourist center. **59.5. VIRGINIA L. JUNCTION** (8,138′.gas sta.cabins). **69. MONO L.** (supplies), whose waters are salt & alkaline. Its 2 Is. are remnants of former volcanoes. On shore is **Monoville** (resort), formerly boom mining town. **72. LEEVINING.** Just (S) of village is J. with St.120 (see Yosemite Nat. Pk.), which crosses Tioga Pass into Yosemite Valley. (S) of Leevining are to be seen **Mono Craters** (L). **99.5.** J. with dirt Rd., at **CASA DIABLO HOT SPRINGS.**

SIDE TRIP: Take dirt Rd. (R) here 4m to **Mammoth P. O.** Just beyond is J. with another dirt Rd.

Turn (R) on latter 11.5m to **Devil's Post Pile Nat. Mon.** (ranger sta.camp.), in which are volcanic cliffs of unique formation. Near Mon. (N) are **Banner Peak** (12,933'), **Mt. Ritter** (13,153') & dark, granite pinnacles known as **Minarets** & (S) lofty **Rainbow Falls** of San Joaquin R.

At 8m on the main side Rd. is J. with another dirt Rd. Turn (R) or (L) here to **Mammoth Ls.** (8,931'.f.), in former gold rush reg., now resort area. There are several For. Camps in vic. of Ls.

**103.** J. with dirt Rd. leading (R) 2.5m to **Convict L.** (7,583'.resort.f.), dominated by **Mt. Morrison** (12,245'). On L. is **Convict L. & Cr. For. Camp** (7,600'.trlrs.). L.'s name derived from fact that some escaped convicts took refuge here, but were caught after gun battle. **111.** J. with Rd. leading (R) to **Rock Cr. L.** (lodge), where is **Rock Cr. For. Camp.** **131.5. BISHOP** (4,147') on Owen R., business center of valley & near-by mines (tungsten), also starting point for fish. & pack trips into Sierra.

SIDE TRIP: Take St.139 (R) from Bishop to J. with S. Fork Rd., 11m, leading (L) 7.5m to **South L.** (trout). St.139 cont. to **L. Sabrina** (trout) at 15m.

At Bishop is J. with US6 (see), with which US395 unites for 123m. US395 now traveses Owens Valley. **148. BIG PINE** (4,002'), outfitting pt. for mt. trips.

SIDE TRIP: Take Big Pine Cr. Rd. (R) from Big Pine to **Glacier Lodge,** 12m, & to trl. at 14m leading to **Palisades Glacier,** 20m.

**163. ABERDEEN,** starting point of $23,000,000 **L.A. Aqueduct,** extending 233m (S). **176.5. INDEPENDENCE** (3,925'). Here is **E. Cal. Mus.** (O.wks.), in basement of Cth., containing coll. of hist. documents, old newspapers, Ind. relics & natural hist. items. **192.5. LONE PINE** (3,728'), starting pt. for Mt. Whitney & trls. to numerous lakes of the reg. (trout f.).

SIDE TRIP: Take St.190 (R) from Lone Pine along Lone Pine Cr. through **Hunters Flat** (accoms.h.) at 10m. At 14m **Whitney Portal,** end of motor Rd., & beginning of pack trl. Near here is **Whitney Portal For. Camp** (8,300';trlrs.ample accoms.) At 18m **Outpost Camp** (10,300'), dominated by lofty cliffs. Trl. now passes waterfalls. At 19m **Mirror L.** From here trl. ascends through magnificent scenery & snowfields to **Summit of Mt. Whitney** (14,495') highest in U.S. (exclusive of Alaska), at 24m. Magnificent view. From summit High Sierra Trl. cont. (W) 62m to **Crescent Meadow** in **Sequoia-Kings Canyon Nat. Pks.** (see).

**195.** (S) J. with St.190, leading (L) to **Death Valley Nat. Mon.** (see). **201.5. BARTLETT** on Owens L., important borax mining center. **217. OLANCHA,** at J. with Rd. to Death Valley Nat. Mon. (see). **255.5.** US395 branches (L) from US6 (see). **256. BROWN** (2,400'). **265.5. INYOKERN** (2,442'), whose pop. increased from 29 to 10,000 during World War II, due to its having become center for U.S. Navy experiments with new weapons. Here is J. with Trona Rd. to Death Valley Nat. Mon. (see). **290.5.** J. with paved Rd. leading (R) 1m to **Randsburg,** gold-mining center. Ore in **Yellow Aster Mine,** now "glory hole" 1,200' deep, yields abundant tungsten, as well as gold. **293. RED MT.** (3,530'). Silver was discovered here in 1919, by a miner taking shelter from snow storm in a dugout. US395 soon crosses into Mojave Desert. At **363.5.** J. with US66 (see) with which US395 unites to **SAN BERNARDINO** at **391.** (For this stretch of Rd. & San Bernardino see US66.)

## Sec. 4: SAN BERNARDINO to SAN DIEGO. 135.

Route from San Bernardino runs through rich citrus producing reg. **10. RIVERSIDE** (see US60) at J. with US60, with which US395 unites for 5m. **26. PERRIS** (1,456') at J. with St.74.

SIDE TRIP: Take St.74 (L) to **Hemet** at 16m near which are int. aboriginal rock paintings.
(1) Take State St. (R) from Hemet 2m to **Ramona Bowl,** where is held annual pageant (Apr.&May), adapted from novel "Ramona."
(2) Take San Jacinto Ave. (L) from Hemet 2.5m to **San Jacinto,** near Lakeview Mts. & **Mt. Rudolph** (2,629'). At 7m is **Gilman Hot Springs** (resort). At 35m J. with paved Rd. Turn (L) here to **Idyllwild** (5,300';mt.resort.accoms.guides) at 39m. In Idyllwild is **For. Ranger Sta.** & near-by (W) is **Idyllwild For. Camp** (5,300'.trlrs.). Beyond Idyllwild (N) on Idyllwild Rd. are For. Camps at 46m, 54m, 59m, 63m respectively (no trlrs.). At 67m, Idyllwild Rd. makes J. near Banning with US60-70-99 (see).
St.74 cont. to J. at 70m with St.111, running (L) 12m to Palm Springs (see US60-70-99).

**38. ELSINORE** (resort). On **Elsinore L.,** which during dry season shrinks considerably. **51.** J. with Hawthorne St. leading (L) 3m to **Murrieta Hot Springs** (resort.accoms). **56.5. TEMECULA.** **58.** J. with St.71.

SIDE TRIP: Take St.71 (L) 14m to J. with St.79; turn (R) on latter. At 23.5m, **Old Grove Stage Coach Sta.** (adobe), now tavern. 24m **Oak Grove Pub. Camp** with fine oaks in Cleveland Nat. For. 29.5m **Warner's Ranch,** first stopover after crossing Colorado Desert in stagecoach days. It was owned by Juan José Warner, Connecticut Yankee, who acquired local Inds. after secularization of missions, with ranch; they worked for him, but not always of their own free will. 38.5m **Warner Hot Springs** (resort.accoms.). 42m J. with dirt Rd. leading (L) 1m to old **Hqs. of Warner's Ranch** & at 2m **Old Butterfield Stage-Coach Sta.** 52m **Santa Ysabel Chapel** on site of earlier one erected by Misión San Diego. 61m J. with good Rd. leading (R) 2.5m to **Pine Hills Resort** (accoms.). 61.5m **Julian,** once gold boom town, now center of resort area. 69.5m **Cuyamaca St. Pk. & Lake.** 82m J. with US80 (see).

**58.5.** J. with improved Rd.

SIDE TRIP: Take latter (L) through Pechanga Canyon to **Pala** (Ind. for water) at 9m, center for Pala Ind. Reserv. **La Asistencia de San Antonio de Pala** was est. here for Misión San Luis Rey. Ch. (O.fee.rest.) is still standing & has some int. Ind. murals & old statue of St. Anthony carved in wood. At 18m, **Rincon,** Ind. trading post, at J. with Rd. leading (R) 2m to **Rincon Ind. Reserv.,** where is held 3-day Fiesta Aug. 24. Main Rd. cont. (L). At 23m is J. with "Hy. to the Stars."

Take latter (L) 7m to **Crestline** (camp.), at J. with dirt Rd. leading (L) 3m to **Palomar St. Pk.** (camp.). N. of Crestline, Hy. to the Stars ascends steeply & reaches **Palomar Observatory,** on Palomar Mt. (6,126′). Observatory, 128′ high, contains famous 200″ telescope, world's largest, costing more than $6,000,000, given by Rockefeller Foundation, which will make it possible to photograph stars & nebulae hitherto unknown.

Rincon Rd. cont. to J. with St.79 (see above) at 39m.

US395 cont. to **OCEANSIDE,** J. at **80.5.** with Mission Rd., leading (R) to **Misión San Luis Rey,** c.5m & to J. with US101 (see). **85.** J. with St.78, leading (R) short distance & then (R) again to old **Couts Adobe H.** (1853) of Rancho Guajome, described in H. H. Jackson's, "Ramona." **98. ESCONDIDO** (hidden valley). Here in Sept. is held Grape Day celebration. In Escondido is J. with St.78.

SIDE TRIP: Take latter (L) 7.5m to **San Pasquale Battlefield Mon.,** where occurred battle in 1846 bet. Brig. Gen. Kearney's forces & those of Gen. Andres Pico. At 54.5m **Anza St. Pk.** (400,000 as.). At 60.5m J. with Borego Valley Rd.

Take latter (L) to **Palm Canyon Playground** (camp.). An hour's walk up Palm Canyon leads to groves of Cal.'s only native palm, said to date back to pre-historic times.

At 91.5m on St.78 is J. with US99 (see).

**103. HODGES L.** (boats.f.). **112. BIG STONE PK.** (pic.fee per auto), scenically int.; there are many Ind. rock paintings in vic. **126.** J. with dirt Rd. leading (L) c.0.5m to **Misión San Diego Del Alcala** (O.fee), founded 1769 by Fray Junípero Serra & removed here from Presidio Hill, San Diego, 1774. It was 1st of missions built by Franciscans in Cal.; destroyed by Inds. in 1775; rebuilt in 1780. Ch. was ruined by earthquake, 1803, but bldgs. were rest. & enlarged by 1818. With secularization after 1835, mission declined. Present bldg. is restoration dating from 1931. Mus. contains relics & int. records, incl. Mss. of Fray Serra. **135. SAN DIEGO** at J. with US101 (see).

# SAN FRANCISCO

## SAN FRANCISCO

Western terminal for through trains, planes & busses. S.F. Airport at Mills Field, 13m (S) on US101, for all lines. Accoms.: All types. Info.: Cal. St. C. of C., 340 Bush St.; Cal. Auto. Assoc., 150 Van Ness Ave.; C. of C., 33 Pine St.; U.S. For. Service, 630 Sansome St. Opera season, winter. Fish.: L. Merced; Mun. Pier at Aquatic Pk., N. end of Van Ness Ave.; water-front piers. Horse Racing: Tanforan Race Track, 11.5m (S) on US101, spring & fall races; Bay Meadows Race Track, 20.5m (S) on US101, spring and fall races. Swim.: Many mun. outdoor pools (O.Ap.1-Oct.31), incl. Fleishhacker Pool, Sloat Blvd. & Great Hy. Surf bath. at Aquatic Pk., ft. of Polk St.; Ocean Beach (undertow dangerous); Phelan Mem. Beach St. Pk.

Frank Norris, himself a San Franciscan, once wrote: "There are just three big cities in the U.S. that are story cities—New York, of course, New Orleans, & best of the three, San Francisco." What he probably meant was that S.F. had an undeniable & particular flavor of its own which derives less from unusual location & bigness than from picturesque history & has left its mark not only on the city, but also on the character of the people. Splendors of S.F. Bay, crowded with shipping from every quarter of globe, scenically rivalling Rio's harbor, have been described times without number. S.F. is center of vast communications system & financial heart of W. Coast, as New York is of E. Hundreds of factories line its metropolitan water front. Tall skyscrapers top its hills. Mighty bridges & tunnels link together municipalities of Bay reg., whose combined pop. exceeds 2,000,000, a pop. as cosmopolitan as that of N.Y. But what gives S.F. its peculiar quality &

has left an unmistakable mark on its people is amount & variety of hist. it has managed to crowd into its scant 100 yrs. of existence.

In 1841, 30 families comprised entire pop. of village of Yerba Buena, near end of peninsula on which city now stands. Not until discovery of gold on Amer. R. in 1848 did tiny settlement burst its dingy chrysalis & begin its march, through sensational booms & busts, toward cosmopolis. Since then S.F. has never had one dull decade; its life span, covering not much more than three generations, has been more exciting than that of E. seaboard towns three times as old. All phases of Western life have been kaleidoscoped into that short period: the pioneer gold-rush, with its accompaniment of gambling joints, brothels, fabulous saloons & deadly brawls; vigilantes restoring order among free-shooting pop.; upsurge of Comstock & RR. millionaires, breaking out into rash of gaudy mansions on city's hill-tops, & equally gaudy social functions; spectacular feuds bet. financial robber barons, followed by equally spectacular crashes; periods of extravagant corruption alternating with energetic reform waves, accompanied by considerable gunplay; bitter labor wars, incl. disastrous bomb-explosion & at least one general strike; an influx of immigrants from every part of country, of gold miners, of Chinese imported to build RRs., of Swedes, Germans, Italians, Jews, French flooding in to benefit by city's phenomenal expansion; a literary & journalistic flowering that for short time in late 19th cent. threatened cultural primacy of Boston & N.Y.; a succession of devastating fires culminating in holocaust of 1906, after earthquake; phoenix-like resurgence & more recent period of great public works.

San Franciscans, as result of this motley experience, have some of traits of people inhabiting much older communities. They do not suffer from that disease of youth, an almost irresistible urge to brag. They take their city for granted & assume that visitors will appreciate its good points without being "boosted" into admiration. They also, probably because of their inheritance from pioneer days, have a quiet belief in the right of individual to live as he pleases. S.F., even today, cherishes its eccentrics &, in old days, odd characters—"George Washington" Coombs, self-styled Father of his Country, "The Great Unknown," "Emperor Norton," & street beggars of special vintage, "Old Misery" & "Old Rosy", to name only two—were cordially tolerated. Nor has Puritanism ever taken root in this community that once proudly boasted itself "the Wickedest City in the World." Old Barbary Coast, famous "Red-light," gambling & hoodlum district, was finally suppressed & S.F. is probably as "clean" as any American town of comparable size. But crusades to regulate public's morals & censorship of literature & art are not encouraged. Social snobbery could scarcely develop, either, in town where today's millionaire might be tomorrow's roustabout. Comstock Lode & fortunes acquired & lost with meteorlike rapidity are scarcely foundation on which to build up an exclusive social set.

S.F. is city at world's cross-roads. You can hear every language spoken along its busy sts. It has country's most int. Chinatown & a teeming Italian quarter in N. Beach sec. Its eating places are just as famous & much more varied than those of New Orleans. In S.F. you can eat at reasonable prices practically any kind of food you care to try. Like other great cities, it is home of distinguished educational, scientific, & cultural institutions. Although heyday of its literary glory has passed, there is still considerable group of writers & artists working in comparative independence of N.Y.

Finally, S.F. has special climate of its own. There are no extremes of heat or cold. Temperatures vary from a mean of 50°F. in Jan. to mean of 61.5° in Sept. But climatic paradox is that summer frequently has cooler weather than winter. High fogs make it advisable to have topcoat handy in Aug. Despite rainy season, which occurs bet. Oct. & May, city has plenty of sunshiny days, about as many as N.Y. But it offers no rebates to tourists for rainy or foggy ones. If you must have more sunshine, you can get it in suburbs which lie beyond fog belt, a few miles (S) down S.F. peninsula.

S.F.'s geographic location somewhat resembles that of Manhattan I. It has been built at tip of finger-like peninsula into which its 750,000 inhabitants are crowded by surrounding bodies of water—Pacific Ocean (W), Golden Gate through which Pacific pours its waters (N), & S.F. Bay (E). Consequently, although like Manhattan it has spilled over in all directions onto mainland, it has also been pushed skyward. It is city of medium-sized skyscrapers, many of them built on survivors of

21 hills which originally punctuated rough terrain that was city's site. Today, serrated towers of San Francisco, seen from Bay approaches, give it skyline rivalling that of Manhattan.

Physical obstacles to expansion have been even greater than Manhattan's. In addition to imprisoning bodies of water on 3 sides of peninsula, high hills within it have presented serious barriers to spread of population. These hills had to be tunnelled to give elbow-room. The peninsula, itself, had to be linked with mainland. Ferries conn. with cities on E. shore, Richmond, Berkeley, Oakland, Alameda & San Leandro, soon proved inadequate to growing traffic. Bridges were flung across S. arm of Bay. Finally, in 1930's, world's longest bridge was built from downtown district to Oakland & longest single-span suspension bridge erected across Golden Gate, conn. Presidio with Marin peninsula (N), to break last links of chain that imprisoned S.F. Oakland, on its part, had to be joined to Alameda by tunnel under Oakland Estuary, which separated these two cities. And wall of mts. that borders metropolitan area (E) had to be pierced to give access to back country.

But with its islandlike conformation, S.F.'s similarity to Manhattan ends. S.F.'s natural setting far surpasses that of N.Y. Ranges of mts. are visible on three sides: N., E., & S. Bet. mts. & ocean sprawls metropolitan district with long, narrow finger of peninsula separating Bay from ocean. Along Bay's E. shore, facing peninsula, extends an almost unbroken series of cities. Yerba Buena I. serves as footstool for S.F.-Oakland Bay bridge. At N. tip of peninsula, heights of Presidio face those of Marin opp., & both are connected across deep 1.5$^{m}$ wide gap of Golden Gate by Golden Gate Br. Sinister Alcatraz & Angel I. lie beyond (E) where Golden Gate debouches into Bay. Along W. side of peninsula, Presidio heights are cont. (S), high above Pacific. Hys. running (S) from city along ridges of San Bruno Mts. afford panoramic views of surrounding country. Toward Bay (E), peninsula slopes down to low ground, once mud flats, today water-front district of piers & warehouses, edged by Embarcadero.

From city's hills—Telegraph Hill, which in pre-Morse era flashed semaphore signals to mainland, & which later became heart of Latin quarter; Russian Hill; Nob (short for Nabob) Hill, formerly covered with fantastic palaces of Comstock millionaires; Twin Peaks (S) & Mt. Davidson (SW)—views of metropolitan amphitheater are magnificent.

S.F. vic.'s first recorded discoverers were party of Gaspar de Portolá's expedition of 1769, which got as far as S.F. Bay. Portolá, himself, never saw it & reported that he could find no good harbor N. of Monterey. The Sp. royal standard was not raised on peninsula until 1776, when Juan Bautista de Anza arrived with group of 30 soldiers & their families. Presidio & mission were laid out, latter by Fray Junípero Serra. For 70 yrs., the little harbor settlement of Yerba Buena, at peninsula's tip, was all there was of today's great city. When new Republic of Mexico took over Alta Cal., Yankees began to drift into Bay reg. in considerable numbers. Due to growth of Russian threat from Ft. Ross, 100$^{m}$ away (N), Amer. Gov. became concerned for future of Mexican province which was already coveted by our expanding republic. Andrew Jackson offered $3,500,000 for it, but offer was spurned by Santa Ana. Shortly after outbreak of Mex. War, in July 1846, Amer. frigate, "Portsmouth," landed marines on peninsula itself, & hauled up Stars and Stripes over Yerba Buena, which was promptly re-christened San Francisco.

The future metropolis had at this time a pop. of about 50 or 60. Now, even before gold rush, began influx of immigrants from E. Sam Brannan brought in group of Mormons, founded newspaper, speculated & grew rich & became an influential citizen, although he ended, in true S.F. pioneer style, as roustabout & disreputable drunkard. Discovery of gold on Amer. R. in 1848, emptied city of every able-bodied male. Following that first frenzied migration, came flood of gold-seekers from all over nation. Village metamorphosed almost over night into frontier town, with usual trimmings—gambling, prostitution, brawling, gun-play & devastating fires. Portsmouth Sq. & Barbary Coast were centers of uncontrolled vice & hoodlumism, which flourished in partnership with corrupt politics.

In 1851, more conservative elements organized a vigilance committee, which hanged worst offenders & drove out rest. But like most Amer. reform waves, this one soon ebbed & had to be revived in 1856 to deal with new accumulation of lawlessness that culminated in shooting of U.S. Marshal & a courageous editor who demanded that assassin be brought to justice. Reforms were inaugurated & vice & corruption were somewhat toned down but by no means altogether suppressed. S.F., with its Barbary Coast, still remained a "wicked" city, with flourishing red-light traffic & scandalous misgovernment. Character of political corruption, however, gradually changed. With rise of great speculative figures who fought for control of rich Comstock mines, RRs., & other sources of wealth, politicians became tools of big business. Period of terrific speculation, known as "Golden Era," set in, followed, inevitably, by equally sensational deflation. Failure of Bank of Cal. in 1875, burst bubble, & boom finally petered out altogether by 1877. Succeeding years of unemployment & discontent gave birth to Workingmen's Party, which went all out for reform. This movement culminated, in true S.F. manner, with shooting of an editor, DeYoung, who opposed reform leader, Isaac S. Kalloch. But special interests, particularly S.P. RR., maintained their grip on city. Not until after earthquake & great fire of 1906 did crusaders succeed in prying them out of politics. Abe Ruef, head of corrupt political "system" which was in partnership with corporations, & his puppet mayor, were convicted & sentenced, & thereafter St. legislature finished clean-up job.

Most tremendous catastrophe S.F. ever experienced was, of course, earthquake & fire of 1906. There had been many devastating conflagrations before which destroyed sizable portions of town when it was still struggling out of its pioneer swaddling clothes, but at time of great fire, S.F. had reached maturity & was city of 450,000. Conflagration which followed earthquake destroyed some 497 blocks & 30,000 buildings. Not since Chicago holocaust had any Amer. city suffered misfortune of equal magnitude. But S.F. refused to be prostrated. Characteristic were placards on streets reading: "Don't talk earthquake. Talk business." Task of rebuilding began almost immediately. It was during years following fire that great public works, mighty bridges, tunnels & Hetch Hetchy development, to supply city with water & electric power, as well as most of skyscrapers were constructed. In 1917, by state law & city action, Barbary Coast was finally liquidated, & S.F. lost its most colorful, although least desirable, tourist attraction.

City's labor history has perhaps been almost as turbulent as its political. High point of early labor activities was movement, sometimes breaking out into violence, against cheap Chinese labor at time when Chinese comprised almost half S.F.'s factory workers. Process of organization continued vigorously from that time on, with early development of seamen's & water-front unions. Employers put up stiff opposition. Workers countered by entering politics, not always with fortunate results. In 1906, Union Labor Party succeeded in electing as mayor, Eugene Schmitz, member of Musicians' Union; but Schmitz became tool of Abe Ruef, corrupt political boss, & both were indicted during reform wave following fire. In 1916, longshoremen struck for higher wages. While strike was on, explosion of bomb during Preparedness Day parade occurred, killing a number of people. Two labor leaders, Mooney & Billings, were accused, convicted & jailed. After more than two decades of agitation, based on firm belief that these two had been "railroaded," they were finally pardoned by Gov. Culbert Olson.

However, labor had suffered serious setback. Employers, banded together in Industrial Assocs., succeeded in curbing growth of unions & breaking strikes. With enactment of Nat. Recovery Act, in 1934, labor movement revived. In same year, longshoremen's strike, led by Harry L. Bridges, ended by involving all workers in general work stoppage which completely paralyzed city. In 1938 labor once more demonstrated its political power, when Culbert Olson, backed by Unions as well as other elements, was elected Gov. World War II brought truce between employers & workers in S.F. as elsewhere; & since the war there have been perhaps fewer labor disturbances, aside from nation-wide strike of maritime workers, than in other great industrial regs.

Most of city's more important cultural institutions post-date 1850's. Univ. of S.F., founded under Catholic auspices, was est. in 1855, but was not chartered as univ. until 1859. Stanford Univ., founded & richly endowed by that Horatio Alger product of "Golden Era," Leland Stanford, was est. in 1885 at Palo Alto, one of city's southern neighbors; Univ. of Cal., growing out of an earlier local college, est. in 1855, was chartered in Berkeley across Bay, 1869. Several women's colleges, notable among which is Mills, in Oakland, had their beginnings in 1850's.

Literary upsurge was delayed until late 1860's & succeeding decades. Roster of writers of this era, native or adopted San Franciscans, is impressive: Bret Harte & Mark Twain; Joaquin Miller; Frank Norris, whose early novel, "McTeague," deals with local scene, & whose "The Octopus" is concerned with state-wide struggle of farmers against S.P. RR.; Jack London, who, while working in Oakland cannery or as an oyster pirate, developed special social philosophy that inspires his books; Gertrude Atherton, who wrote whole series of works about Cal. scene; Henry George, who migrated to Cal. in 1858, became editor of S.F. newspaper & wrote his epoch-making "Progess & Poverty," in S.F.; Ambrose Bierce, who wrote his bitter column, "The Wasp," in "The Argonaut" and "S.F. Examiner," & did most of his work in S.F., until his mysterious disappearance in Mexico; Wallace & Will Irwin, who celebrated S.F.'s Chinatown; Kate Douglas Wiggin, who was one of founders of city's 1st kindergarten; Rbt. Louis Stevenson, who spent some time in S.F. & haunted Merchants' Exchange, from whose exciting speculations he derived material for his "The Wreckers." Many of these were not native San Franciscans; others deserted city & state when they achieved fame. But their output was to great degree concerned with S.F. & Cal. backgrounds, & bore regional stamp & flavor.

S.F.'s achievements in graphic arts have been, perhaps, less exciting than her literary flowering. But from days of the Cal. School, which specialized in vast panoramic landscapes, to our own times, a great variety of work has been turned out, much of it, derivative, some of it distinguished by originality. Today S.F. has a group of honest & independent artists expressing themselves in original terms rather than those derived from foreign sources. City has produced several outstanding sculptors, among them, Douglas Tilden & his pupil Rbt. I. Aitken, who executed many public mons.; Ralph Stackpole, considered leader of contemporary school of sculpture; & Beniamino Buffano, S.F. art world's most controversial figure, whose stainless steel "Sun Yat-sen" stands in Chinatown. Cal. Institute of Fine Arts is principal art school. Various other institutions present exhibs. of classic & contemporary art. Civil Works Administration & Federal Art Project, 1934-42, furnished considerable stimulus to development of local art, & were responsible for fine mural decorations in a number of public bldgs., notably in Coit Tower & Aquatic Pk. Casino Lobby. Golden Gate Internat. Exposition of 1939, notable for its murals & sculpture, also provided stimulus.

S.F. has in its day had a rich theatrical history. David Belasco served his apprenticeship in old Baldwin Theater. Isadora Duncan was born in S.F. & did her first dancing here. But living drama, as elsewhere, has been killed by mass production of movies. There are several non-professional groups producing new plays. City has an excellent symphony orchestra, municipally subsidized, & a grand opera season, as well as frequent concerts & recitals.

PTS. OF INT.—DOWNTOWN, CIVIC CENTER, & NOB HILL DISTRICTS: (1) Ft. of Market St., **Ferry Bldg.** (1903.by A.P.Brown), with 240′ clock tower, modeled after Giralda in Seville, was city's gateway until completion of S.F.-Oakland Bay Bridge. On 2nd fl. is huge relief map of Cal. On mezzanine is **St. Mining Bureau Mus.** (O.Mon.-Fri.;Sat.a.m.). (2) On both sides of Ferry Bldg. extends **Embarcadero,** crescent-shaped blvd. lined with piers & wharves along water front. At Pier 14, Navy Landing from which boats take visitors to ships of fleet. (3) **S.F.-Oakland Bay Bridge,** whose lofty spans stretch from S.F. to Yerba Buena I. & from there to mainland. W. sec. of bridge consists of 2 spans, 216′ above water, supported midway bet. S.F. & Yerba Buena I. by steel & concrete anchorage, each 2,310′ long. E. sec. of bridge consists of main cantilever span of 1,400′ & smaller spans to mainland. Bridge proper is 4.5$^{m}$ long; with approaches more than 8$^{m}$ long. (4) **Yerba Buena I.** Midway bet. S.F. & Oakland, through which double-deck tunnel carries bridge traffic, is Gov. reserv. with various Gov. bldgs. (5) **Treasure I.** is connected by filled-in causeway with Yerba Buena. Here was held Golden Gate Internat. Exposition, 1939-40. Now one of U.S. Navy's important W. Coast bases. (6) 1st & Mission Sts., **Bay Bridge Transit Terminal** (1939), for interurban electric RR. system to E. Bay.

(7) Mission St. bet. 3rd & 4th Sts., **St. Patrick's Ch.** (est.1851.present bldg.c.1906) with fine stained-glass windows, & on floor, large mosaic, "The River of Life." (8) Market, Bush & Battery Sts., **Donahue Mon.** (by Douglas Tilden), comm. founder of city's first iron works. (9) Market & Montgomery Sts., **Nevada Bank Bldg.,** in

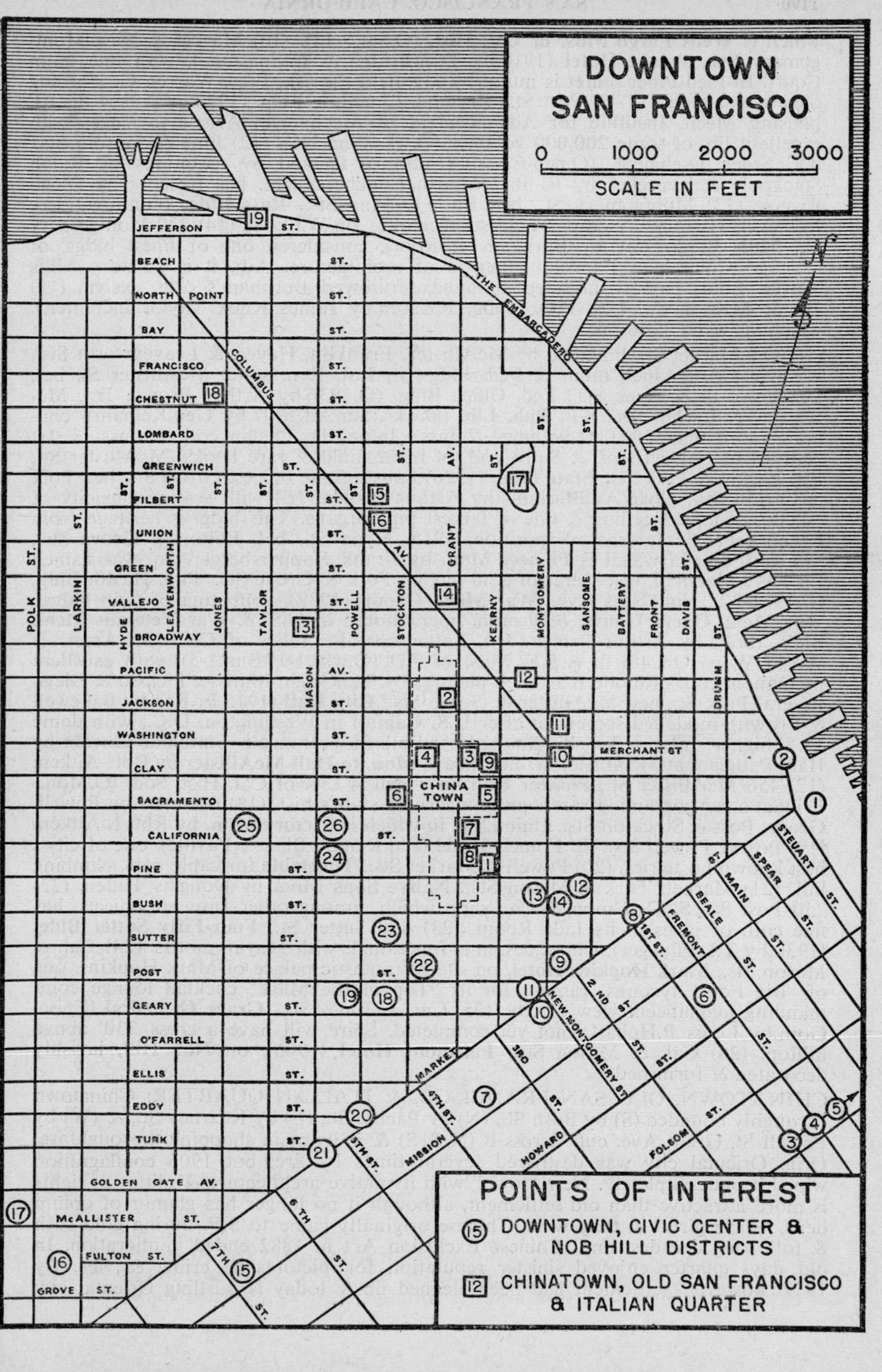
DOWNTOWN
SAN FRANCISCO
0 1000 2000 3000
SCALE IN FEET
POINTS OF INTEREST
DOWNTOWN, CIVIC CENTER & NOB HILL DISTRICTS
CHINATOWN, OLD SAN FRANCISCO & ITALIAN QUARTER
THE EMBARCADERO
COLUMBUS AV.
MARKET
MISSION
HOWARD
FOLSOM
JEFFERSON
BEACH
NORTH POINT
BAY
FRANCISCO
CHESTNUT
LOMBARD
GREENWICH
FILBERT
UNION
GREEN
VALLEJO
BROADWAY
PACIFIC
JACKSON
WASHINGTON
CLAY
SACRAMENTO
CALIFORNIA
PINE
BUSH
SUTTER
POST
GEARY
O'FARRELL
ELLIS
EDDY
TURK
GOLDEN GATE AV.
McALLISTER ST.
FULTON ST.
GROVE ST.
POLK ST.
LARKIN ST.
HYDE
LEAVENWORTH
JONES
TAYLOR
MASON
POWELL
STOCKTON
GRANT AV.
KEARNY
MONTGOMERY
SANSOME
BATTERY
FRONT
DAVIS
DRUMM
MERCHANT ST
CHINA TOWN
STEUART ST.
SPEAR ST.
MAIN ST.
BEALE ST.
FREMONT ST.
1ST ST.
2 ND ST.
NEW MONTGOMERY ST.
3RD ST.
4TH ST.
5TH ST.
6 TH ST.
7TH ST.
N

which is **Wells Fargo Mus. of Cal. Hist.** (O.Sat.9-12). (10) Market & New Montgomery Sts., **Palace Hotel** (1910.by Trowbridge & Livingstone), with fine Palm Court. In Pied Piper buffet is mural by Maxfield Parrish. Pres. Warren G. Harding died in this bldg. (11) 57 Post St., **Mechanics Institute Bldg.** (1910.by Albert Pissis), housing Mech. Institute for Advancement of Mechanical Arts & Sciences with excellent lib. of some 200,000 volumes (O.wks.;Sun.1-5). (12) Pine & Sansom Sts., **S.F. Stock Exchange.** (O.neo-Class.). Entrance flanked by sculptures by Ralph Stackpole & bas-relief by R. B. Howard; Luncheon Rm. has frescoes by Diego Rivera. (13) Montgomery St., bet. Bush & Pine Sts., **Russ Bldg.** (Goth.by Geo. Kelhem), 31-story skyscraper, biggest office bldg. on W.Coast. (14) 220 Montgomery St., **Mills Bldg.** (1891.by Burnham & Root), considered one of finest bldgs. of Chicago Columbian Exposition period of architecture. Adj. it is 22-story **Mills Tower.** Louis Hobart, architect of annex, followed Burnham's orig. design. (15) 7th & Mission St., **U.S. P.O.** (1905, Ital.Ren.by James Knox Taylor.fine inter.), which survived 1906 fire.

(16) Off Market St., bounded by McAllister, Franklin, Hayes, & Leavenworth Sts., is **Civic Center,** incl. mun. & Fed. bldgs. in Ital. Ren. style: McAllister St. bet. Leavenworth & Hyde Sts., **Fed. Office Bldg.** (O.1936.by Arthur Brown, Jr.). McAllister & Larkin Sts., **S.F. Pub. Lib.** (O.wks.;Sun.aft.1907.by Geo.Kelham), contains more than 500,000 volumes & mss., James D. Phelan coll. of mss. & 1st editions of Cal. writers, & Sutro coll. of incunabula & rare books. McAllister St., bet. Larkin & Polk Sts., **State Bldg.** (1926) houses State offices. Grove St., bet. Polk & Larkin Sts., **Civic Auditorium** (by Arthur Brown, Jr.) with seating capacity of 10,000, canopied ceiling & one of largest pipe-organs. This bldg. is heritage from Panama Pacific Internat. Exposition, 1915. Hyde St., bet. Fulton & Grove Sts., **Marshall Sq.,** in which is **Pioneer Mon.** by Frank Happersberger. Sq. was named for J.W. Marshall, discoverer of gold in Cal. Polk & Grove Sts., **Pub. Health Bldg.** (O.1931-32). Van Ness Ave., **War Mem. Group** (1932), consisting of twin bldgs., **War Mem. Opera House,** only mun. opera house in U.S. & **War Veterans Mem. Bldg.** (both by Arthur Brown, Jr.). Latter contains relics of Civil, Sp.-Amer. & World Wars. On 4th fl. is **S.F. Mus. of Art** (O.wks.1-10.Sun.1-5), with excellent permanent coll. of modern art incl. pictures by VanGogh, Matisse, Picasso & Diego Rivera. Polk St., bet. McAllister & Grove Sts., **City Hall** (1915.Fr.Ren.by Bakewell & Brown), modelled somewhat after U.S. Capitol in Washington, D.C., with dome 13.5′ higher. Inter. is lavishly finished. At Polk St. entrance is **Statue of Lincoln** by Haig Patigian; at McAllister St. entrance is **Mon. to Hall McAllister** by Rbt. Aitken. (17) 456 McAllister St., **Pioneer Hall,** in which is Lib. of Cal. Hist. Soc. (O.Mon.-Fri.;Sat.a.m.) containing rare items concerning state's hist. (18) Bounded by Powell, Geary, Post & Stockton Sts., **Union Sq.,** in which is **Victory Mon.** by Rbt. I. Aitken. (19) Post & Powell Sts., **St. Francis Hotel** (Ital.Ren.by Bliss & Faville), one of city's best known hostelries. (20) Powell & Market Sts., **Turntable** for cable cars, climbing hill. (21) Market, Turk & Mason Sts., **Native Sons Mon.** by Douglas Tilden. (22) 250 Post St., **S. G. Gump & Co.,** shop which, among other rare art objects, has fine coll. of jades in its Jade Room. (23) 450 Sutter St., **Four-Fifty Sutter Bldg.** (1930.by T.L.Pflueger), whose design is functional, with Mayan motifs. (24) Cal. & Mason Sts., **Mark Hopkins Hotel,** on site of fantastic palace of Mark Hopkins, one of "Big Four" tycoons, famous for its "Top of the Mark" cocktail lounge commanding magnificent view of city. (25) Cal. & Jones Sts., **Grace Cathedral** (Episc. Goth.by Louis P.Hobart), not yet completed. Spire will have a cross 230′ above hilltop. (26) Cal. & Mason Sts., **Fairmont Hotel** (1906), on Nob Hill, lavishly decorated & furnished.

CHINATOWN, OLD SAN FRANCISCO, & ITALIAN QUARTER: Chinatown is roughly bounded (S) by Bush St., (N) by Pacific St., (E) by Kearney St., & (W) by Powell St. Grant Ave. cuts across it (N & S) & is its main shopping thoroughfare. Orig. Oriental city was destroyed several times by fire, but 1906 conflagration wiped it out completely. New "town" with its native architecture & glitter of lights is more attractive than old settlement, although it no longer has glamor of opium dens, "slave girls" & tong wars. Chinese originally came to S.F. during gold rush & following decades, until Chinese Exclusion Act in 1882 ended immigration. In old days quarter enjoyed sinister reputation for picturesque crime & vice. By 1927, however, settlement had been cleaned up & today is bustling Oriental city of 16,000 comprised, in about equal numbers, of old Chinese clinging to ancient customs & young people of Amer. birth adapting themselves to Amer. ways. In this area of not much more than 12 square blocks are crowded shops with variety of Chinese goods, restaurants whose menus offer strange dishes, markets crammed with exotic food stuffs & "joss" houses, still centers of quarter's religious life. Chief festival, which lasts 17 days, is that of New Year. On 7th day takes place Dance of Dragon, spectacular parade along Grant Ave.

(1) 520 Pine St., **Kong Chow Temple** (O.eve.). Has very richly decorated inter.; well worth visit. (2) 1021 Grant Ave., **Mandarin Theater** (O.7:30 p.m.-12:30 a.m.), where native drama may be witnessed. (3) 743 Washington St., **Chinese Telephone Exchange,** richly decorated, only completely Chinese exchange outside of China. (4) 125 Waverly Place, **Tin How Temple** (c.1848.O.10 a.m.-1 a.m.), oldest Joss House in S.F. Tin How is worshipped as Queen of Heaven & Goddess of Seven Seas. (5) 730 Sacramento Ave., **Chinese C. of C.** (O.Mon.-Fri.;Sat.a.m.). (6) 843 Stockton St., **Chinese Consolidated Benevolent Assoc.** (O.1-5), best known as "Chinese 6 Companies," although it really represents 7. This organization has nationwide jurisdiction as a board of arbitration for settlement of disputes of various kinds. Inter. sumptuously furnished in Chinese manner. (7) Grant Ave. & Cal. St., **Old St. Mary's Ch.** (Cath.1854.Vict.Goth.). (8) **St. Mary's Sq.,** on which Ch. faces, & in center of which is stainless steel **Statue of Sun Yat-sen** by Beniamino Buffano. (9) Kearney St., bet. Washington & Clay Sts., **Portsmouth Sq.,** birthpl. of city and later Sp. & Mex. Plaza. At NW. cor. is plaque comm. raising of Amer. flag here, 1846. In sq., bronze **Stevenson Mon.,** comm. Rbt. Louis Stevenson who used to frequent this neighborhood. Modern replicas of S.F.'s old Mex. Customh. & First School were to be built here in 1949. (10) 628 Montgomery St., **Montgomery Block** (1853) which once housed Stock Exchange & now artists' studios. (11) 718-20 Montgomery St., **Golden Era Bldg.,** where popular weekly, "The Golden Era," was published. In it appeared Bret Harte's first poem (1857), "The Valentine."

(12) Inters. of Pacific St., Columbus Ave. & Kearney St. was formerly known as "Seven Points." On block running (E) from this pt., on Pacific Ave., is **Site of Barbary Coast.** (13) 908 Broadway, **Nuestra Señora de Guadalupe Ch.** (1912. Romanes.). Orig. church was destroyed by 1906 fire. Inter. is richly decorated & there are some fine stained-glass windows, int. fresco & murals. (14) 620 Vallejo St., **St. Francis Ch.** (1859.Goth.), 1st Roman Cath. parish church in city. Orig. church on this site was built by Fray Langlois, 1849, during Gold Rush. (15) 650 Filbert St., on Washington Sq., **Sts. Peter & Paul Ch.** (c.1924.by Charles Fantoni); int. mosaics & statuary. (16) **Washington Sq.** is heart of Italian Quarter. In sq. are **Volunteer Firemen's Mon.** (by Haig Patigian) & **Statue of Benj. Franklin.** (17) **Pioneer Pk.** on summit of Telegraph Hill, with **Coit Mem. Tower** (elevator 9-4.fee. by Arthur Brown, Jr.), mem. to firemen of 1850's & 1860's. Mon. has int. frescoes on walls of 1st & 2nd floors & stairway by various artists working co-operatively under Civil Works Administration. There is plaque at main entrance comm. old semaphore station & 1st western telegraph station here. Magnificent view of city & bay. (18) Chestnut & Jones Sts., **Cal. Sch. of Fine Arts** (Ital.Ren.), with campanile, on Russian Hill (fine views). (19) Ft. of Taylor St., **Fishermen's Wharf** (worth visiting for colorful fishing fleet moored here & many seafood restaurants).

ALONG GOLDEN GATE & THE OCEAN: (1) Ft. of Polk St. & Van Ness Ave., **Aquatic Pk.** (bathh.recr.), mun. recr. center with luxurious modern casino from which fine views. Casino is adorned with sculptures & murals by Fed. Art Project. (2) Van Ness Ave. & Bay St., **Fort Mason,** U.S. Military Reserv., in which are H. (1853) that formerly was home of John C. Frémont & Army Transport Docks. (3) Divisadero St. & Marina Blvd., **Municipal Yacht Harbor** & **Marina Pk.** (4) Baker St., bet. Jefferson & Bay Sts., **Palace of Fine Arts** (neo-Class.), survival of Panama Pacific Internat. Exposition of 1915. (5) Lincoln Blvd. & Lombard St., **Presidio of S.F.,** where once was housed garrison of Sp. soldiers; now U.S. military reserv. (1,480 as.). Within Presidio are Letterman & Station Hospitals, latter dating from 1854; **Nat. Cemetery,** next to Arlington largest U.S. soldiers' burial ground; & **Ft. Winfield Scott.** On shore line, below, is **Old Ft. Scott** (1860), on site of Sp. Castillo de San Joaquin (1794). In front of Officer's Club (adobe.c.1776), are old Sp. guns. (6) **Golden Gate Bridge,** conn. Presidio with Marine peninsula opp. Bridge has 2 towers, 746′ above water, height of 65-story bldg. Central span is 4,200′ in length, longest single suspension-type span in world. (7) Arguello Blvd., bet. Lake & Clay Sts., **Temple Emmanuel** (by Schnaittaker, Bakewell & Brown) with auditorium seating 1,700. Inter. richly decorated. (8) Ft. of Sea Cliff Ave., **James D. Phelan Mem. Beach St. Pk.** (pic.sanitary facils.safe ocean bathing).

(9) 33rd Ave. & Clement St., entrance to **Lincoln Pk.** (mun.golf links). In pk. is **Palace of the Legion of Honor.** (O.organ recital Sat.& Sun.3-4), mem. to Cal.'s dead in World War I, modelled on palace of same name in Paris. Bldg. contains 19 galleries with permanent & loan art exhibits & colls. Permanent colls. have outstanding works of various European & Amer. schools. In front of mus. are "The Shades" & "The Thinker" by Rodin. (10) By path (NE) from Lincoln Pk. to **Land's End,** precipitous promontory with fine views. (11) Seal Rock & 45th Aves., **U.S. Veterans Adm. Facilities,** handsome modern-style bldg. with Mayan temple pyramidal motifs. (12) Pt. Lobos & 48th Aves., **Sutro Heights,** pub. pk. with int. sculpture & landscaping, where formerly stood house of Adolph Sutro (see), Comstock Lode millionaire & mayor of S.F. (13) Pt. Lobos Ave. near Great Hy., **Sutro Baths & Ice Rink** (fee), much advertised swimming pool, ice rink & resort. (14) Great Hy., opp. Sutro Heights, **Cliff H.,** famous resort. From look-out platform there is fine view of **Seal Rocks,** on which hundreds of seals (Cal. sea lions) live, protected by St. law. On clear days, **Farallon Is.** can be seen. (15) Extending (S) from Cliff House to Golden Gate Pk. is **Ocean Beach** (dangerous undertow), bordered by esplanade. At (N) end is **Playland at the Beach,** small Coney I. (16) Ft. of Great Hy. at Sloat & Skyline Blvds., **Fleishhacker Playfield & Zoolog. Gardens,** with world's largest outdoor plunge, notable zoo with natural habitats, & extensive playfields with miniature RR. & other recr. facils.

WEST OF VAN NESS AVENUE: (1) 124 Buchanan St., **S.F. State College,** est. 1899; present bldgs. are modern. (2) Cor. of Duboce & Buchanan Sts., **U.S. Mint** (1937). (3) Dolores St. near Market St., **Sp. War Mon.** (by D. Tilden). (4) Fulton St., bet. Clayton & Parker Ave., **Univ. of San Francisco,** est. 1855 as St. Ignatius College by Jesuits. (5) Fulton St. & Parker Ave., **St. Ignatius Ch.** (1914,Ren.by Charles Devlin), with gilt dome, campanile, & two towers. (6) Turk St., bet. Parker & Masonic Aves., **S.F. College for Women** (Cath.Sp.Goth.) on Lone Mt., richly furnished with art objects, with fine lib. containing unique & rare items. (7) 1881 Pine St., **Hongwanji Buddhist Mission** of N. Amer., 1st Buddhist Ch. in America. Inter. is richly decorated in Oriental style. Contains relics, allegedly of portions of Buddha's body. (8) Gough & Bush Sts., **Trinity Ch.** (Episc.founded 1849.present bldg.Norman Goth.by Hobart,Cram & Ferguson). (9) O'Farrell St., bet. Gough & Franklin Sts., **St. Mark's Ch.** (Evang.Luth.1895.Romanes.); fine stained glass windows. (10) Van Ness & O'Farrell Sts., **St. Mary's Cathedral of the Assumption** (Cath.1891.Vict.Goth.fine inter.), seat of Roman Cath. diocese of S.F.; int. glass stained windows. (11) Van Ness Ave. & Green St., **Holy Trinity Russian Eastern Orthodox Cathedral** (Byzantine), first of this sect in U.S. There are no pews or seats; Congregation is obliged to stand. On first Sun. of Lent there is fine choir singing in Russian style. (12) Filbert & Webster Sts., **Hindu Temple** (strange mixture of architectural styles). Hqs. of Vedanta Society.

(13) **Golden Gate Pk.** (1,017 as.). This recr. area, a half-mile wide, extends more than $4^{m}$ (W) from Stanyan St. to Great Hy. at Ocean Beach. Among pk.'s many pts. of int. are: **Arboretum,** with conservatory of rare plants. **Kezar Stadium,** seating 60,000. **De Young Mem. Mus.** (O.wks.;Sun.1-5.Sp.Ren.). In front of W. wing, sculpture, "Vintage" designed by Paul Gustave Doré. Sculpture over main entrance by Haig Patigian. Other exter. sculpture by Leo Lentelli. Among sculptures near mus. are: Pool of Enchantment, Sun Dial & Statue of Burns by M. E. Cummings; Junípero Serra by Douglas Tilden & Cervantes Mon. by Jo Mora. Mus. has galleries containing comprehensive colls. of art, art objects, furniture, textiles, armor of all periods. Of int. are Aztec, Mayan, Incan & pre-Columbian Amer. Indian art colls. In Music Concourse is **Bandstand** (concerts Sun.afts.Ital.Ren.). **Oriental Tea Garden,** replica of one in Japan. **Cal. Academy of Sciences,** oldest scientific institution on W. Coast, comprises **N. Amer. Hall, Steinhart Aquarium & Simson African Hall;** extensive nat. hist. colls. **Shakespeare Garden** contains every flower mentioned in Shakespeare's plays. On Lloyd Lake is **Portal of the Past,** marble doorway from A. N. Towne home, destroyed in 1906 fire. **Dutch Windmills** are at NW. & SW. ends of pk. Also at NW. end is ship, **"Gjoa,"** in which Amundson navigated Northwest Passage.

VIC. OF MARKET STREET: (1) Dolores St., bet. 16th & 17th Sts., **Misión Dolores** (O.fine, authentic inter.), founded by Father Junípero Serra, 1776. Bldg. begun 1782. No nails used in construction; wooden beams of roof tied with leather thongs. Inter. walls painted 150 yrs. ago by Ind. artisans. Altar brought from Mexico, 1870. Behind mission is graveyard in which are buried many early notables, incl. Don Luis Argüello, 1st Mex. Gov. Graves of Casey & Cora, hanged by Vigilantes, 1856, also here. (2) On Buena Vista Heights, **Buena Vista Pk.**, from which are very fine views. (3) 17th & Clayton Sts., **Mt. Olympus**, on whose summit is copy of Liberty Mon. in Brussels by Antoine Wiertz. (4) Parnassus & 3rd Aves., **Univ. of Cal. Medical Center.** (5) On Twin Peaks Blvd., **Twin Peaks** (910′) called by Sp. Los Pechos de la Choca ("Breasts of the Ind. Maiden"). Dr. runs around peaks, affording fine views. (6) Off Portola Dr., **Mt. Davidson** (956′), in **Mt. Davidson Pk.** On summit is **Easter Cross** 103′ high, at which Easter services are held.

## TRIPS OUT OF SAN FRANCISCO

### I. Just across S.F. Bay (E) via S.F.-Oakland Bay Bridge to OAKLAND.

### OAKLAND

Through RR., bus & plane conns. Accoms.: All types. Info.: C. of C. & A.A.A. Municipal Auditorium, 12th & Fallon Sts., for concerts. Swim.: Lions Pool, Diamond Pk., Fruitvale Ave. & Lyman Rd. Boat.: L. Merritt, E. end 14th St.

Oakland, on E. side of S.F. Bay, is important port & industrial city, although many of its inhabitants commute to S.F. With Berkeley, San Leandro, Hayward, Emeryville, Piedmont & Alameda, it forms one solid city on Bay, backed by Berkeley Hills, along whose ridges runs Skyline Blvd., one of most int. scenic drives of vic. In city's heart lies L. Merritt (salt water) surrounded by Lakeside Pk. & Peralta Pk. City's pop. is of highly diverse origins, incl. Portuguese, Italians, Mexicans, Negroes, Chinese & Filipinos. Oakland stands on former Rancho San Antonio, granted Luis Maria Peralta in 1820. During gold rush many of immigrants from E. squatted on rancho lands. In early 1850's Horace W. Carpentier acquired considerable holdings within what are now city's limits, including entire water front; it was not till 1910 that, after extensive litigation, title to these properties reverted to city. During two World Wars, Oakland's industries developed greatly & today it is one of chief industrial centers & ports of Cal. City is connected by S.F.-Oakland Bay bridge with S.F. & by tunnel with Alameda (S).

PTS. OF INT.: (1) Washington St., bet. 14th & 15th Sts., **City Hall,** city's tallest bldg. (366′). (2) 274 19th St., **Snow Mus.,** containing nat. hist. exhibits, many from Africa. (3) On E. shore of L. Merritt, **Lakeside Pk.** (recr.band concerts.eves.Aug.-Oct.). (4) 1426 Oak St., **Oakland Pub. Mus.** (O.wks.Sun.1-5) containing natural hist. & hist. relics colls. (5) **Peralta Pk.,** on W. shore of L. Merritt. (6) 10th & Fallon Sts., **Mun. Auditorium,** with Arena, where sports events take place; Theater, in which operas, plays & lectures are presented; & Art Gallery with permanent art exhibits & annual exhibitions. (7) Fallon St., bet. 9th & 10 Sts., **Exposition Bldg.,** also used for athletics & civic events. (8) Fallon St., bet. 12th & 13th Sts., **Alameda County Cth.** (1936.neo-Class.). (9) 50 Webster St., **First & Last Chance Saloon** (int.inter.), where Jack London studied & wrote. (10) Oakland & Olive Aves., **Linda Vista Pk.,** in which are **Mun. Rose Gardens,** with many roses constantly in bloom. (11) 5212 Broadway, **Cal. College of Arts & Crafts** (1907), on whose grounds are two fine Sequoias. (12) On Joaquin Miller Rd. (NE), **The Hights** (so spelled by Joaquin Miller), now a pk. where poet & his friends planted 75,000 eucalyptus & other trees. **The Abbey** (O.appl.1886), where poet lived & wrote; he claimed he could not work without rain on roof & had pipes installed to sprinkle water on rainless days. Near-by, (N) on hill, he built foundation for his funeral pyre (never used), two towers dedicated respectively to Gen. J. C. Frémont & Rbt. Browning, & pyramid to Moses. (13) Adjoining The Hights (E) is **Sequoia Pk.,** in which is Zoo (O). (14) 4917 Mt. Blvd., **Chabot Observatory** (O.Tues.-Sat.). (15) Trenor St. & Seminary Ave., **Mills College for Women** (Sp.Col.), founded 1852, one of oldest in W. Among bldgs. are **El Campanil; Music Bldg.,** in style of Sp. Ren. Ch.; **Art Gallery** (O.Wed.& Sun.aft.) containing art exhibits & art lib.; **Lib.** (O) with notable coll. of early W. literature & books by Cal. writers.

### II. Just across S.F. Bay via S.F.-Oakland Bay Bridge to BERKELEY

**BERKELEY** . .

RR. Stas.: Univ. Ave. & 3rd St. for S.P. RR.; Univ. Ave. & West St., for A.T. & S.F. RR. Bus Sta.: Univ. & San Pablo Aves. for Pacific Greyhound Lines & Nat. Trailways. Accoms.: Ample, all types. Info.: C. of C., Amer. Trust Bldg., Shattuck Ave. & Center St. Swim.: Aquatic Pk., East Shore Hy., bet. Univ. & Ashby Aves. Boat.: Berkeley mun. yacht harbor, W. end Univ. Ave. Fish.: Yacht harbor wharf, bass & smelt; info. & licenses at sporting goods stores.

Berkeley is situated on E. shore of S.F. Bay. At E. end of city is campus of Univ. of Cal. Berkeley, although many of its citizens work in S.F., is also industrial center. City is located on former Rancho San Antonio, granted to Peralta family, 1820. In 1923, considerable portion of sec. lying N. of Univ. campus was destroyed by fire. Berkeley's council-manager form of government is regarded as model in mun. administration.

PTS. OF INT.: (1) **Univ. of Cal.** Campus of 530 as. extends from Oxford St. (E) to hills & from Hearst Ave. (S) to Bancroft Way. Campus affords fine views of Bay. Univ. had its beginnings in 1853 in Contra Costa Academy of Oakland, founded by Henry Durant, which in 1860 became College of Cal. In 1860, charter was granted & in 1869 Univ. was actually opened. It is coed. & has one of largest enrollments of Amer. univs. Newer bldgs. on campus are for most part neo-Class. Especially noteworthy among bldgs. on Lower Campus are: **Wheeler Hall** (arts & sciences); **Life Sciences Bldg.** (neo-Class.by Arthur Brown) containing, in addition to laboratories, **Mus. of Vertebrate Zoology & Herbarium; Agric. Group** (Ital.Ren.); **President's H.** (1911.Ital.Ren.); **Haviland Hall,** in which is housed School of Education & exhibit of photography, etchings, handicrafts; **Students' Observatory; Engineering Group,** in whose Engineering Lab. is one of world's largest testing machines, used to test materials for Boulder Dam; **Hearst Mem. Mining Bldg.** (Ital.Ren.), containing **Mus. of Paleontology; Anthropology Mus.; Bacon Hall** with int. geology exhibits; **Charles Franklin Doe Mem. Lib.** (O.8-10;neo-Class.), housing colls. relating to Sp.-Amer. & W. Amer. hist.; **Campanile** (397';elevator.sm.fee.1914.Ital.Ren.by J. G. Howard); **Stephens Union** (1923.Tudor Goth.), center of student activities; & **Univ. Art. Mus. & Gallery** (O.10-5), with Albert Bender Coll. of Chinese art & coll. of Russian icons. Among more noteworthy bldgs. on Upper Campus are: **Hearst Greek Theater,** in which take place musical & dramatic presentations & **Cal. Mem. Stadium,** seating 78,000, comm. students who fell in World War I. In Strawberry Canyon, above stadium, **Botanical Garden,** whose plant colls. incl. 5,000 rare rhododendrons & 2,000 cacti & similar plants. Top of Charter Hill, **Radiation Lab.** houses one of world's largest cyclotrons for atomic research.

(2) 1798 Scenic Ave., **Pacific School of Religion** (O.appl.guides), graduate theological school, interdenominational & coed. One of its three bldgs., **Holbrook Mem. Lib.,** houses book coll. which incl., among other rare items, 1560 "Breeches" Bible, Babylonian tablets, 4th cent. papyri, as well as archeol. exhibits of relics from 3500 B.C. (3) **Tilden Pk.** in Wildcat Canyon is part of 10,000-a. E. Bay Regional Pk. (4) At Regal Rd. & Hillside Ave., **Cragmont Pk.,** in which is lookout sta. with fine view. (5) On Bay shore are **Berkeley Aquatic Pk.** (recr.boat.) & **Yacht Harbor.**

**III. (Loop Tour) 155.5. US101. St.12. St.1**

Via: San Rafael, Petaluma, Sebastopol, Russian R., Ft. Ross, Tomales, Point Reyes Sta., Stinson Beach.

**0.** From Civic Center, follow US101 (N) on Van Ness Ave., (W) on Lombard St., across Golden Gate Bridge.

**11.5.** J. with paved Rd.

SIDE TRIP: Take latter (L) to **Mill Valley,** 2m, at base of **Mt. Tamalpais.** Cont. (L) from Throckmorton Ave. in Mill Valley, on Cascade Ave., to J. with Muir Woods Rd. at 4.5m. Take latter (L) 1.5m to **Muir Woods Nat. Mon.** (427 as.pic.), grove of redwoods in Redwood Canyon. Some of trees are 2,000 yrs. old & 250' high. In addition to redwoods, there is rich variety of other Cal. trees & plants. Pk. was named for John Muir, explorer of Cal. mts. & advocate of establishment of Nat. Pks.

At J. with Muir Woods Rd. (see above), main side trip swings sharply (R) along abandoned roadbed of Mt. Tamalpais & Muir Woods RR., known as crookedest in world. At 9.5m **Panorama Gate,** whence toll Rd. turns (R). At 10.5m, **Mountain Theater,** on slope of Mt. Tamalpais, in forest of redwoods. Fine view of S.F. Bay & Ocean. Plays are produced here on 3rd Sun. in May (fee). Toll Rd. cont. along slopes of Mt. Tamalpais' three crests to **Tamalpais Tavern** at 12.5m. Here magnificent view. Although mt. is less than 3,000'

SAN FRANCISCO BAY AREA
LEGEND
50 U. S. Highways
9 State Highways
0
10
20
30
SCALE OF MILES
SONOMA
NAPA
YOLO
SOLANO
MARIN
CONTRA COSTA
ALAMEDA
SAN MATEO
SANTA CLARA
SANTA CRUZ
PACIFIC OCEAN
SAN FRANCISCO BAY
SAN PABLO BAY
FARALLON ISLANDS
Ft. Ross
Rio Nido
Hilton
Guerneville
Fulton
Monte Rio
SEBASTOPOL
Bay
Valley Ford
Tomales
Inverness
Pt. Reyes Sta.
Pt. Reyes
Lagunitas
CALISTOGA
ST. HELENA
Rutherford
Oakville
Yountville
Kenwood
SANTA ROSA
Cotati
El Verano
SONOMA
PETALUMA
Shellville
NAPA
Monticello
WINTERS
VACAVILLE
Elmira
FAIRFIELD
SUISUN
Cordelia
VALLEJO
BENICIA
Novato
Ignacio
SAN RAFAEL
MARTINEZ
PITTSBURG
CONCORD
Clayton
RICHMOND
WALNUT CREEK
SAUSALITO
BERKELEY
OAKLAND
ALAMEDA
SAN FRANCISCO
Dublin
HAYWARD
BY PASS 101
SAN MATEO
Rockaway Beach
Moss Beach
Half Moon Bay
REDWOOD CITY
PALO ALTO
ALVISO
San Gregorio
Pescadero
SANTA CLARA
SAN JOSE
Saratoga
LOS GATOS
Big Basin
Boulder Cr.
Ben Lomond
Felton
Pt. Ano Nuevo
Davenport
SANTA CRUZ
Soquel
Capitola
1
101
12
29
40
37
48
21
4
24
50
17
5
9

high, it appears much higher because it rises directly from sea level. Entire mt. is game refuge; deer graze on its slopes.

**13.5. GREENBRAE**

SIDE TRIP: Take Rd. (R) here 2.5m to **San Quentin Prison** (O.9-2:30 wks.to persons entitled to visit prisoners.guided tours Thurs.). San Quentin's most famous prisoner was Tom Mooney, accused of & sentenced for 1917 Preparedness Day explosion in S.F., pardoned 1939.

**16. SAN RAFAEL,** S.F. suburb which owes its existence to Misión de San Rafael Arcangel, founded 1817, 20th of the missions. Present mission bldgs. are restorations. **38. PETALUMA** (Ind. "beautiful view") has sometimes been called Chickaluma because it is center of chicken & egg producing reg. In Petaluma's scientific chicken farms, eggs are hatched in mechanical incubators & chicks raised in heated brooders. Largest establishment has yearly output of 1,800,000 fledglings. On city's main st., **Chicken Pharmacy,** devoted to sale of poultry remedies.

SIDE TRIP: Take Rd. (R) from Petaluma 1.5m to J. with dirt Rd. & turn (L) on latter to **Casa Grande** (O.int.exter.& inter.) 2m, largest adobe structure in N. Cal., built by Gen. Mariano Vallejo, 1833-34, on his 75,000-a. ranch.

**46. COTATI,** at J. with paved Rd.; turn (L) on this. **54. SEBASTOPOL,** center of vineyard & orchard reg., J. with St.12, on which route cont. On outskirts, **Luther Burbank Experimental Garden.** St.12 cont. to **RUSSIAN R.** (good f.resort area) & then to **GUERNEVILLE** at **61.**

SIDE TRIP: Take paved Rd. (R) here 3m to **Armstrong Woods** (400 as.), grove of virgin redwoods. Here is **Armstrong For. Summer Theater,** presenting plays & festivals.

**66.** on St.12 is J. with paved Rd.

SIDE TRIP: Turn (L) on latter; short distance to **Monte Rio** (resort). Take Rd. (R) here 1m to **Bohemian Grove,** 2,437 as. of virgin redwoods along river. Here is outdoor theater of Bohemian Club of S.F. At annual two-week summer encampment of club celebrations called "High Jinks" have been presented since 1878.

St.12 cont. to J. with St.1 at **75.**

SIDE TRIP: (R) 1m on St.1 is **Jenner-by-the-Sea** (resort), at mouth of Russian R. St.1 cont. to **Ft. Ross** (St.Hist.Mon.), 13m. In 1812, Russians settled here & put up fort & other bldgs. Chief industry was sea-otter hunting. Despite Sp. opposition, they traded with S.F. Presidio & Mission & San Rafael & San Francisco de Solano Missions, founded to halt Russ. expansion. Czar in 1841 ordered withdrawal of settlement which had declined because of extermination of sea otters. Johann August Sutter, on whose land gold was discovered in 1848, bought Russ. property. He dismantled bldgs. & transferred material, as well as cattle, horses & other movables, to his town of New Helvetia (see Sacramento). **Old Gr. Orthodox Chapel** (O.rest.), containing some hist. relics, still survives as does Russ. commandant's hqs. St.1 cont. (N) along rugged coastline, sparsely settled, passing several small fishing & lumber settlements.

Main tour route turns (L) (S) on St.1 from J. with St.12. **76.** J. with Rd. leading short dist. (R) to **Bodega-Sonoma Coast St. Pk.,** stretching from mouth of Russian R. to Bodega Bay. **84.5. BAY,** on Bodega Bay, named for its discoverer, Juan Francisco de la Bodéga y Cuadra, who arrived here in his ship, 1775. In 1811, Russians est. themselves on bay, but were later pushed out by Amer. settlers. St.1 swings inland, & at **106.** runs along narrow firth-like **TOMALES BAY. 132.** J. with Rd.

SIDE TRIP: Take latter (R) along W. side of Tomales Bay & then across slopes of windswept **Point Reyes.** At 15m is dirt Rd.

Take latter (L) to **Coast Guard Life Saving Sta.,** facing **Drake's Bay,** circled by cliffs. Here Sir Francis Drake, on June 15, 1579, arrived in "Golden Hinde" to recondition his ships. Drake left brass plate with an inscription claiming country for Queen Elizabeth. Some years ago this plate was found near Drake's Bay. It is now at Univ. of Cal.

At 20m **Pt. Reyes Lighth.** (O) on cliff 294′ above sea. So many ships have piled up here that S.F. newspapers are said to always keep set up headline, "Ship Aground at Pt. Reyes."

**132. STINSON BEACH** (accoms.), resort on Bolinas Bay. **144.5.** J. with US101; route turns (R) on this. **155.5. SAN FRANCISCO**

**IV. (Loop Tour) 98. US101. St.37. St.29. US40**

Via: San Rafael, (Sonoma), Napa, Vallejo, (Benicia), Richmond, Berkeley.

**0.** From Civic Center, follow US101 (see III above for directions, towns & pts. of int. along route) (N) to J. with St.37 at **24.**; turn (R) on St.37. **40. SHELLVILLE,** at J. with St.12.

SIDE TRIP: Take St.12 (N) 3.5m to **Sonoma,** est. by Sp. as frontier protection against advance of Russ. colonization. Here in June 1823, Padre José Altamira chose site for Misión de San Francisco de Solano. Pueblo was built around plaza by Alferez Mariano Vallejo, 1835. On June 14, 1846, band of three dozen armed gringoes acting, probably, on orders from U.S. Capt. Frémont, broke into town & proclaimed Republic of Cal., raising hastily improvised homespun strip of red flannel on which was painted star & grizzly bear, emblem of new commonwealth. Insurgents were not aware of fact that war had already been declared on Mexico. On July 9, Amer. flag was raised in town. In 1856, Hungarian immigrant, Agoston Haraszthy, planted vineyards near town, which thereafter became wine-growing center. On plaza, besides modern Cth. & City Hall, is **Big Bear Flag Mon.,** by John MacQuarrie, sculptor. Adj., **Misión de San Francisco de Solano,** now St. Mon. (O.rest.1910-14.int.exter.& inter.), containing pioneer relics & specimens of Ind. handicraft. At 217 Spain St. E., **Blue Wing Inn,** built in early 1840's, reputedly oldest hotel (N) beyond S.F. Spain St. E. & 1st St. E., **Sonoma Barracks** (1836.adobe). Next door, **Vallejo H.** (adobe), home of Gov. Mariano Vallejo. At Spain St. W. & 1st St. W., **Hotel Eldorado** (1848-49.adobe.wooden 2nd story add.). SW. cor. of Plaza, **Fitch H.,** built by Vallejo's brother-in-law, Jacob P. Leese. Main St. W., frame & adobe **Ray H.,** in which U.S. army officers lived.

Turn (R) from Sonoma on 3rd St. W. 0.5m to **Vallejo H.** (O.St.Hist.Mon.), built by Vallejo, 1851. He called it Lachrymae Montis (tears of the mt.) because its water supply came from mt. spring. Near-by is **Vallejo Mus.** (O.1850) containing hist. relics.

St.12, known as Valley of the Moon Hy., cont. (N) through **Boyes Springs, Fetters Springs, & Agua Caliente** (resorts,hot mineral springs,swim.pools). 11m **Glen Ellen,** at J. with oiled Rd.

Take latter (L) 0.5m to entrance to **Jack London Ranch,** where author spent last years running experimental farm, now operated as dude ranch. Ranch H. is still standing & contains his lib. On "Little Hill" near ruins of "Wolf House" which he left unfinished, is boulder under which are his ashes.

St.12 cont. (N) through Sonoma Valley, to **Santa Rosa,** at J. with US101 (see), 25.5m.

St.37 cont. (E) from Shellville. **51. NAPA,** center of famous grape-growing & wine-making region, at J. with St.29.

SIDE TRIP: Take St.29 (L) from Napa. 18m **St. Helena,** largely populated by Swiss, Germans & Italians. Center of vineyard reg. **Beringer Bros. Winery** (O.int.).

Turn (R) here 7.5m to **Pacific Union College** (Seventh Day Adventist), located on crater of extinct volcano.

21.5m **Old Bale Mill** (1846.rest.). 26m **Calistoga,** resort founded by Sam. Brannan in 1859.

Turn (L) here 1m on St.28 to J.; then (L) 5m to **Petrified Forest** (very int.), consisting of redwood trees petrified by lava from Mt. St. Helena. St.28 cont. to J. with US101 (see), 23m.

Route now skirts **Mt. St. Helena** (4,343'). 35m **Robt. L. Stevenson Mon.** In cabin on this site he spent his honeymoon with Fanny Osbourne & wrote "The Silverado Squatters."

Main tour route turns (R) from Napa on St.29. **65.5. VALLEJO,** founded by Gen. Mariano G. Vallejo in late 1830's, & for short time (1852-53) St. capital. City is located at point where Napa R. enters San Pablo Bay, arm of S.F. Bay.

SIDE TRIP: Turn (R) from Vallejo 1m to **Mare I. Naval Shipyard,** (2,247 as.) largest facils. of kind in world. Name "Mare Island" derives from time when cattle ferry capsized in bay & Gen. Vallejo's favorite white mare managed to escape drowning by swimming to I.

**67.5.** J. with US40 (see), on which route cont. (R).

SIDE TRIP: Turn (L) 1.5m on US40 to J. with paved Rd. & follow (S) this (R) to **Benicia,** 5.5m, on N. shore of Carquinez Strait, founded by Gen. Mariano Vallejo on his Rancho Suscol. During gold rush, city boomed. PTS. OF INT.: (1) On W. J St., near 1st St., is Cal.'s oldest **Masonic Hall** (1851). Here St. Legislature met 1853, when Benicia was temporarily capital. (2) G & 1st Sts., **Old Capitol,** which housed legislature, 1853-4. It is now City Hall, lib. & mus. (3) 1st & E Sts., **Solano Hotel** (prior to 1850's). (4) Near 1st & D Sts., **Von Pfister Adobe Store** (1847), where Charles Bennett announced James Marshall's discovery of gold. (5) Ft. of M St., **U.S. Arsenal,** est. 1851; oldest bldg. dates from 1869. Off Carquinez Pt. was barge on which Jack London lived, 1882-83, as described in "John Barleycorn." (6) 5th & I Sts., **St. Dominic's Ch.,** founded 1854. (7) Turn (L) from 5th & M Sts., on St.21, to **St. Dominic's Cemetery,** c.0.5m, where Doña Maria Concepción Argüello is buried. She taught in St. Catherine's Seminary in Benicia from 1854 to her death in 1856 & figures in poetry of Bret Harte & in novel "Rezanov" by Gertrude Atherton. When not yet 16 she fell in love with Count Rezanov who visited her father, commandante of San Francisco Presidio. Rezanov reciprocated her love but had to obtain Czar's consent to marriage. He left for St. Petersburg & Concepción, after waiting for years, finally joined Dominican sisterhood. Much later word was received that Rezanov had died on journey home. (8) Short distance further on St.21 are old **Benicia Barracks** (1850) on **U.S. Military Reserv.**

**68. CARQUINEZ BRIDGE** (toll). This bridge is 4,288′ long & its towers rise 325′ above strait. It cost $8,000,000; its construction was expensive because of difficulties encountered in laying piers in Strait's swiftly running tides. Into Carquinez Strait flow Central Valley's Sacramento & San Joaquin Rs. **82.5. RICHMOND,** on headland reaching (W) into bay, important oil refining, shipping & mfg. center, &, during World War II, site of huge Henry J. Kaiser shipyards. At Ft. of Standard Ave. is **San Rafael-Richmond Ferry,** which crosses to San Rafael, J. with US101 (see). **83.5. EL CERRITO** (Sp. "little hill"). On San Pablo Ave., in eucalyptus grove, **Castro Adobe** (1831;add.1850). **87.5. BERKELEY** (see San Francisco II above). **90.5. OAKLAND** (see San Francisco I above). Hy. turns (R) at J. with US50 (see) at entrance to S.F.-Oakland Bay Bridge. **98. SAN FRANCISCO.**

**V. (Loop Tour) 74. US40. St.24. St.21. US50**

Via: Berkeley, Walnut Creek, Mt. Diablo, (Hayward), (Mission San Jose), Oakland.

**0.** From **CIVIC CENTER,** take US40-50 (E) on Fell St., (SE) on 10th St., (NE) on Harrison St., & across S.F.-Oakland Bay Bridge to J. with E. Shore Hy. at bridge approach. **8.** Turn (L) here on E. Shore Hy. to Ashby Ave. **11. BERKELEY** (see San Francisco II above). From Berkeley, follow St.24 (via Ashby Ave. & Tunnel Rd.) through 4-lane **BROADWAY TUNNEL,** 1.8$^{m}$ long. **25. WALNUT CREEK,** in midst of walnut groves, fruit orchards, & chicken ranches. J. with St.21.

SIDE TRIP: Take St.24 (L) from Walnut Cr. to **Pittsburg,** 36.5$^{m}$, Cal.'s best small-scale version of its Pennsylvania namesake, site of **Columbia Steel Co. Plant.**

Route turns (R) from Walnut Creek on St.21. **31.5. DANVILLE,** at J. with paved Rd.

SIDE TRIP: Take latter (L) 3.5$^{m}$ to entrance of **Mt. Diablo St. Pk.** (fee.pic.). Rd. winds through unusual rock formations to summit, 15$^{m}$, of **Mt. Diablo** (3,849′), commanding view of 80,000 sq. miles, one of broadest in N. Amer. Mt. Diablo was chosen as base point for all U.S. surveys of Cal., 1851.

**40.5. DUBLIN,** at J. with US50 (see).

SIDE TRIP: Continue (straight ahead) from Dublin 0.1$^{m}$ on St.21 to **St. Raymond's Ch.** (1859), & **Jeremiah Fallon H.** (1850), 1$^{m}$, built of redwood timber & lumber brought around the Horn. At 3$^{m}$, shaded by giant oak (L), **Alviso Adobe** (1845). At 3.5$^{m}$ **Bernal Adobe** (R) (1852), built by Augustín Bernal, one of grantees of Rancho del Valle de San Jose. St.21 cont. (SW) into Niles Canyon & to **Niles** at 16$^{m}$, where is J. with Foothill Blvd. (see below).

Route turns (R) on US50. **48.5.** J. with paved Rd.

SIDE TRIP: Take latter (L) 2$^{m}$ to **Hayward,** center of poultry-raising & truck-gardening reg. Turn (L) from Hayward, on Foothill Blvd. to **Niles,** 11.5$^{m}$. At 16$^{m}$ **Misión de San José,** 14th mission in order of time, founded by Padre Fermin Francisco Lasuen in 1797. Of orig. structures only sec. of living quarters remains (rest.1916). In belfry of modern parish chapel hang 2 bells of old mission. New Ch. contains some int. relics. Old mission grounds are lovely.

Turn (R) from Misión de San José on paved Rd. 1$^{m}$ to **Olhone Burial Ground.** Here 4,000 Olhone Inds. who helped build mission, are buried.

**53.5. SAN LEANDRO,** cannery & packing-house center, known as Cherry City of Cal. where is celebrated an annual Cherry Festival. Here is Cal.'s largest Portuguese colony, which holds annual religious festival. **55. OAKLAND** (see San Francisco I above).

SIDE TRIP: Turn (L) from 6th & Harrison Sts. in Oakland through Posey Tube 0.5$^{m}$ to **Alameda,** industrial & residential suburb on island in S.F. Bay. Along Alameda's SW. shore are several beach & amusement resorts. At W. end of I. is **U.S. Naval Air Sta.,** one of world's largest, accommodating land planes, seaplanes & aircraft carriers. Alameda's industries include shipbuilding & fish packing.

**66.** Approach to S.F.-Oakland Bay Bridge (toll). Here is J. with US40. **74. SAN FRANCISCO.**

**VI. (Loop Tour) 110. US101. St.9. St.5**

Via: Burlingame, San Mateo, Redwood City, Palo Alto, Saratoga, Skyline Dam.

**0.** From Civic Center, follow US101 (E) on Fell St., (SE) on 10th St., (S) on Potrero Ave. **11.5. TANFORAN RACE TRACK** (fall & spring running races), named for Torbirio Tanforan, Mexican rancher. **14.5. MILLBRAE.** Here is fabulous Victorian **Darius Ogden Mills Mansion** (1866), built by one of S.F.'s "bonanza kings." Mills had vast holdings in Comstock mines. His son, Ogden L. Mills, was Secy. of Treas. under Hoover. **17. BURLINGAME,** wealthy suburban community, had St.'s first country club. **19. SAN MATEO,** another suburban community. Here Sp. had hospice as way station bet. Misión Dolores & Misión de Santa Clara. At San Mateo Polo Club field polo matches take place. **20.5. BAY MEADOWS RACE TRACK** (running races). **23. BELMONT.** In this town Wm. Chapman Ralston, of Bank of Cal. & Comstock mines, built his lavish mansion in 1867. Extravagant festivities he inaugurated here, with often as many as 100 dinner guests, came to end when Bank of Cal. failed in 1875 & Ralston committed suicide. H. is now occupied by **College & Convent of Sisters of Notre Dame. 26. REDWOOD CITY,** seat & trading industrial center of San Mateo Cty. **28.5. ATHERTON.** Here Faxon Dean Atherton, Gertrude Atherton's father-in-law, & James L. Flood, former S.F. saloonkeeper, suddenly became rich through speculation in mines, built their luxurious mansions (no longer standing). **30. MENLO PK.,** where Milton S. Latham, Gov. & U.S. Senator, built his great mansion.

**30.5. The PALO ALTO** (Sp."tall tree"). By this tree Gaspar de Portolá pitched camp Nov. 1769. **31. PALO ALTO** is chiefly notable as home of Stanford Univ., formerly Palo Alto Stock Farm of Leland Stanford, one of S.F.'s financial "Big Four," Gov. & U.S. Senator. He & Mrs. Stanford founded Univ. as mem. to their only son who died at age of 16. Bldgs. were begun, 1887, & Univ. was opened, 1891. PTS. OF INT.: (1) **Stanford Mausoleum,** marble mon. to Henry J. Lathrop, Mrs. Stanford's brother. Beyond tomb are Cactus Gardens. (2) **Stadium** seating 89,000. (3) **Leland Stanford Junior Mus.** in which are art, anthrop., archeol., paleontol. & hist. exhibits. (4) **Lawrence Frost Amphitheater,** seating 8,000. Outer Quadrangle consisting of 14 bldgs. & Inner Quadrangle consisting of 12 bldgs. (Romanes.). (5) **Stanford Mem. Ch.** (Romanes.), built by Mrs. Stanford as mem. to her husband; mosaics on facade & in vestibule; above altar, mosaic reproduction of "Last Supper." (6) **T. W. Stanford Art Gallery;** paintings & statuary. (7) **Lib.,** adorned with stone figures by Edgar Walter; coll. of rare publications. (8) **Hoover Lib. on War, Revolution & Peace** (by Bakewell, Weihe & Brown) surmounted by 285′ tower; coll. of material dealing with World War I & its aftermath. (9) 623 Mirada Ave., **Residence of Univ. President,** formerly home of Herbert Hoover.

US101 now traverses fruit orchards of Santa Clara Valley, flanked by Mt. Hamilton Range (E) & Santa Cruz Mts. (W) From Feb. to Apr., orchards are mass of blossoms & in summer thousands of pickers come into valley to harvest fruit & almond crops. **40.5.** J. with St.9; route turns (R) on this. **47.5. SARATOGA,** where is held annual blossom festival. Here is great **Villa Montalvo** (1914.Sp.), built by Sen. James Duval Phelan. From Saratoga, St.9 winds into Santa Cruz Mts. to J. with St.5 at **55.,** on which route turns (R).

SIDE TRIP: Take St.9 (L) across Santa Cruz Mts. to J. at 5m with paved Rd.

Take latter (R) 7m to **Big Basin Redwoods St. Pk.** (10,028 as.lodge.camp). In Pk. is magnificent grove of primeval redwoods, many of them 300′ tall, incl. huge Animal Tree, Father of the Forest & Mother of the Forest.

St.9 cont. past **Ben Lomond,** at ft. of Ben Lomond Mt. to J. with dirt Rd. at 20m.

(L) on latter 0.5m to **Big Trees Cty. Pk.** in which is magnificent grove of redwoods.

St.9 cont. to J. with St.1 (see) at 25m in **Santa Cruz.**

Main route turns (R) to J. with dirt Rd. at **61.5.**

SIDE TRIP: Turn (L) on latter to J. at 4m & (L) here to **Islam Shrine Pk.,** 1,400-a. redwood grove.

**69.** J. with La Honda Canyon Rd.

SIDE TRIP: Take latter (L). At 7m is **La Honda,** mt. resort (cabins.camp.). Turn (L) from La Honda to J. at 1m & (R) here 5m to **San Mateo Cty. Mem. Redwood Pk.,** (310 as.)

**74. SKYLINE METHUSELAH REDWOOD,** more than 1,500 yrs. old, with 55′ circumference, dominates countryside. **84.5. SKYLINE DAM,** impounding **Crystal Springs L.** Hy. skirts W. shore of this & **SAN ANDREAS L., 89.5.** At **100.** J. with St.1 (see) at S. city limit of S.F. **110. SAN FRANCISCO** (Civic Center).

# LOS ANGELES

## LOS ANGELES

RR. Stas.: L.A. Union Passenger Terminal, N. Alameda Blvd. bet. Aliso & Macy Sts. Pacif. Elec. RR., 610 S. Main St. & 417 S. Hill St. (interurban). Bus Stas.: 6th & Los Angeles Sts., 6th & Main Sts. & immediate vic. for most bus lines. Airports: Union Air Terminal, & L.A. Mun. Airport. Piers: L.A. Harbor (San Pedro, Wilmington, &

Terminal I.). Boats for Santa Catalina I. leave Catalina Terminal (berths 184-5 ft. of Avalon Blvd.), Wilmington; boat train leaves Pacif. Elec. Sta., L.A. daily. Info.: All Year Club, 517 W. 6th St.; L.A. C. of C., Broadway at 12th St.; Auto. Club of S. Cal., 2601 S. Figueroa St.; Pacif. Elec. Co. Info. Bureau, 610 S. Main St.; Times Info. Bureau, 1st & Spring Sts. Fish.: Boats for deep-sea fishing may be chartered at L.A. Harbor, San Pedro. Swim.: Many mun. swim. pools; mun. bathhouses at San Pedro & Venice. Horse Racing: Santa Anita, Arcadia, 14m from downtown L.A.; Hollywood Pk., Inglewood, 11m from downtown L.A. Harness & running races at L.A. County Fair, Pomona (Sept.).

From a sleepy little Mexican village of 1,850, Los Angeles, in less than a century, has grown to be 3rd largest city in U.S. & one of nation's greatest ports & industrial centers. Metropolitan area of L.A. Cty. has total pop. of more than 3,000,000. Angelenos boast that city has doubled in size every decade. In its amoeba-like growth it has spread in all directions, until today it reaches from ocean to ft. of coastal ranges, incl. within its limits, 451 sq. miles. Adj. to it, in wide periphery, are a number of considerable municipalities which really constitute part of metropolitan complex.

Founded late in 18th cent. by Sp., it is one of oldest cities of W. Coast &, because of its meteoric expansion, also one of youngest. Out of 1,000 Angelenos you meet, probably not one has been born in L.A. Pop., although comprised of elements from all over globe, has been recruited for most part from various secs. of U.S. If New York is melting pot of Europe, L.A. is melting pot of U.S. During last 50 yrs., people from all over country have streamed into city. This immigration has, paradoxically, reversed usual Amer. pattern. First immigrants belonged to better-to-do classes, people who wanted to build themselves new homes in an all-year-round pleasant climate, invest in development of resources & speculate in real estate. They came, not in covered wagons, but in Pullmans. Next wave of immigrants consisted of businessmen & people in middle circumstances, to great extent retired farmers from Middle W. Only in later period came workers attracted by job opportunities in new industries. A large number of Negroes were part of this last migration, as well as many farm families evicted by drought in "dust bowl." Possibilities of jobs in factories & on great fruit & truck ranches also attracted flood of Mex. Today, L.A. has pop. derived from every St., incl. 150,000 Negroes. Mex. element, made up of a few descendants of orig. settlers but mostly more recent arrivals, numbers some 300,000. There is still a small Chinatown & Japanese, who were evicted during World War II, have recently returned.

L.A., probably because of heterogeneous character of its people, has always been famous as nursery of strange cults & fads, mushrooming overnight to nation-wide proportions & frequently withering as rapidly: Krotona, est. as home of Occultism in 1911, in heart of what is today Hollywood; "New Thought" movement; Aimee Semple MacPherson, who accumulated 30,000 followers, built $1,500,000 temple & maintained broadcasting station that cost $75,000; the great "I Am" movement, with nation-wide following of 300,000 in 1930's; & "Mankind United," founded in 1934. Social Utopias have flourished here as luxuriantly as region's flora under irrigation: Townsend Old Age Pension Plan which was to insure older people a large monthly income; "Ham & Eggs" movement, which was to give everybody a weekly $30 pay envelope—in "scrip"—a movement whose program narrowly escaped adoption by voters; & Upton Sinclair's EPIC movement, which was built more rationally on social ideology & almost elected its proponent to governorship in 1934.

Although general public still thinks of L.A. as setting for Hollywood, the film capital, actually L.A.'s host of other industries—oil exploitation, food processing, airplane & tire manufacturing, auto assembly plants, textile & furniture factories & shipping—are beginning to overshadow movies. City's industrial growth has been something of a miracle. Southern Cal. possessed no natural resources whatsoever—no lumber, no minerals, no coal. Hinterland was desert. It was not strange, therefore, that cinema should have been 1st industry, since it required nothing for its development exc. maximum of sunshine. The other orig. industry was conn. with exploitation of climate. Thousands of newcomers were attracted by intensive advertising campaigns extolling S. Cal.'s sunshine & scenery. However, two essentials to industrial & agricultural development were at hand. Early settlers made the desert in immediate vic. of city bloom by using water from L.A. River for irrigation. Later, artesian wells tapped underground sources, & diversion of streams has further contributed to irrigation of semi-arid lowlands. Today, city is center for one of richest agricultural regs. of country. Impounding of rivers by great dams, most recently by Boulder Dam, $400^m$ away, has supplied city not only with water but also with electric power. This power has been richly supplemented by oil discovered after 1st decade of century. When World War II broke out, L.A. had means at hand out of which was created tremendous industrial boom. Since 1940, pop. has almost doubled. Although city originally had no port, the Gov., in cooperation with municipality, has built one of finest harbors in country at San Pedro, which is becoming one of nation's most important shipping centers.

L.A. was founded in 1781 by Sp. Gov. Felipe de Neve & Fathers of San Gabriel Mission. They christened new settlement "El Pueblo de Nuestra Senora, la Reina de Los Angeles de Porciuncula," which is quite a mouthful in comparison with the current, "L.A." The new pueblo grew slowly, although surrounding lands were quickly distributed in great blocks to missions & a few favored individuals. Yankee traders began to filter in during early 19th cent. & their economic penetration continued on increasing scale, after Mex. revolution & right down to Amer. annexation. Secularization of missions in 1835, resulting in division of vast land holdings, probably stimulated city's growth. During Mex. War the "Californians" put up stiff resistance to Amers., capturing an Amer. garrison in the city & driving off attacking force of U.S. troops. It was not until several bloody battles had been fought that "Stars & Stripes" were permanently hauled up over the pueblo.

Like most pioneer towns of West, L.A., in era following Mex. War, developed reputation as "wide open" city, where gambling, prostitution & trigger vindication of private rights generally prevailed. Ind. workers, coming in from vineyards over weekends, were victims rather than instigators of lawlessness. Grog shops in San Gabriel, which they frequented, did smashing business. "By four o'clock on Sun. aft., L.A. streets would be crowded with a mass of drunken Inds., yelling & fighting . . ." Three or four revellers were murdered each wk. Finally, Inds. would be herded by marshall into a compound to sleep off their spree. Then they were sold for another week, into peonage, & their surplus earnings would be paid once more at the week-end, in aguardiente. Chinese also were victims of local persecution & violence, culminating, Oct. 24, 1871, in one of worst race riots of Amer. hist. Nineteen Orientals were lynched & Chinese shops & homes were thoroughly looted. This appears to have been last actual lynching in city. (L.A. Chinatown, during 1st decade of 20th cent., played important role in organization of Chinese Rev. Homer Lee, Lt. Gen. in Imperial Chinese Reform Army, was one of most picturesque figures in city of 1900-11 period, & was responsible for establishment of Western Military Academy which trained officers in U.S. for future Chinese Rev. Army. His hqs. were at Lankershim Hotel. Sun Yat-sen visited L.A. several times. Lee went with Sun to China after outbreak of 1911 Rev. He returned for visit in 1912 & died there same yr.)

Coming of RRs. in '70's & '80's precipitated 1st great boom. As result of rate war, Santa Fé reduced its passenger fares from Missouri to $1.00. Terrific land speculation followed, which ended in disaster, c.1888, when values nose-dived & lots that had sold for thousands reverted once more to desert sage brush. Said one ruined speculator: "I had half a million dollars wiped out &, what is worse, $500 of it was cash." Other minor booms succeeded. Campaign of advertisement of S. Cal. continued. Millions of pieces of literature were sent out to lure immigrants. The reg. was played up not only as summer, but also as winter, resort. Increase in irrigation turned desert into a garden. Oil was discovered & city sprouted derricks even in residential districts; finally derricks had to be excluded from grounds of public bldgs. by ordinance. Hollywood sprang up as movie capital of world. Next major boom occurred during 1920's. Most gaudy of oil speculators of period was Col. Chauncey C. Julian, whose fraudulent wildcat companies crashed in 1927, wiping out $150,000,000 contributed by 40,000 investors. The 1929 nation-wide depression merely climaxed "bust" of 1927. The suicide rate went up alarmingly. From bridge in Arroyo Seco, 79 people jumped to death, till finally structure had to be enclosed by barbed wire. Early 1930's were punctuated with scandals which sent former financial tycoons to San Quentin jail. Most recent boom has been that of World War II, which added more than 650,000 to city's pop. & has transformed it into an industrial beehive.

L.A. is situated on a semi-arid plain about $25^m$ from sea, flanked on E. by magnificent coastal ranges. Dry countryside has been transformed to fertility—anything will grow here—by irrigation. Problem of water has, of course, been perennial & large projects for making supplies available have been undertaken. Owens R., 250$^m$ away, has been tapped. This enriched owners of San Fernando Valley land but ruined farmers of Owens Valley, whose ranches were deprived of R.'s water, a loss for which they were never compensated. More recently, L.A. has gone 400$^m$ (E) to Boulder Dam for new water supply. Nevertheless, need for water will continue as major problem. Artesian wells have dangerously lowered level of sub-surface supplies. Destruction of plant coverings on mountainsides results in floods during rainy season & tends to lessen available water during dry season.

Unplanned expansion has been curse of L.A. as it has of many Amer. municipalities. Few steep hills that punctuate its more crowded sections have been preserved as parks; many of these hills have been horribly gashed by bulldozers gouging out streets & hys. These eminences might have afforded splendid vistas of city's magnificent mt. backdrop. But no amount of careless expansion could destroy L.A.'s lovely environment. A short drive will take autoist to Griffith Pk., N. of Hollywood, from whose heights are glorious panoramic views. Somewhat longer excursions will take him into San Gabriel Mts. & to Mt. Wilson (7,510'), or through San Gabriel & N. Fork Canyons to Crystal L. (5,700'). A somewhat more extended drive, through citrus groves of San Gabriel Valley, will transport him into San Bernardino Nat. For., past lofty peaks & lakes, to San Bernardino Mt. reg. (10,666'). With climate in direct competition with Miami's (Angelenos chuckle with delight when Florida frosts are reported, the 6-inch snow of Jan. 1949 is regarded as an irrelevant anomaly), out-of-doors life becomes a habit & tourism is one of important local sources of income.

L.A., like many Amer. cities, suffers from traffic congestion which is considerably enhanced by fact that there are no subways or other rapid transit facils. It is city of magnificent distances in which one must have an auto to get around easily. On the other hand, lack of these facils. has had beneficial effect. It has broken up city into a number of autonomous shopping centers. L.A. really consists of a group of cities—Hollywood, Wilmington & San Pedro, within municipal limits, & Long Beach, Pasadena, Glendale, Santa Monica & Beverly Hills crowding in from suburban periphery. L.A.'s unprecedentedly rapid growth has resulted in a considerable architectural hodgepodge—late Vict. & Grant period, before 1900, & universal rash of Sp. Missions in next decades, as well as demented aberrations of individual fantasy related to no style at all. More recently, however, trend toward modern functional has contributed a note of sanity. The bungalow & its off-shoot, the bungalow-court, are welcome & pleasant features of L.A.'s architectural scene. One would have expected that a municipality, largely product of 20th cent., would have suffered from conspicuous-waste disease of the skyscraper. But a sensible zoning law restricting bldg. heights to 150' has kept this source of congestion to minimum. There is only one real skyscraper, City Hall, 32 stories high.

L.A., because of its slow early development, but also because reg. at first depended on cheap labor of Inds., Chinese & Mexs., developed labor movement rather late in its hist. Continuous influx of immigrants was probably an additional reason for non-success of first attempts at union organization. Strikes occurred intermittently from 1890 on. But wages remained from 30 to 40 percent lower than in S.F. Merchants & Manufacturers Assoc., an amalgamation of two earlier employers' organizations, under leadership of Harrison Gray Otis, owner of L.A. Times, built up strong front against labor organizers. In 1909, city adopted drastic anti-picketing ordinance which led to serious clashes bet. workers & police. Then in Oct. 1910, during strike at L.A. Times, occurred disastrous bomb explosion. Sentiment, even after the explosion, was swinging toward strikers. In mun. election, socialist candidate, Job Harriman, received impressive vote. But when strike leaders, the McNamara brothers, confessed that they were responsible for bomb explosion, bitter reaction set in & till 1930's, Otis & Merchants & Manufacturers Assoc. could boast that L.A. was "white spot" of the country. From 1920-24, Merchants & Manufacturers Assoc. ruled despotically. State criminal syndicalist laws were invoked with crushing effect against radicals. Even as late as 1933-34, L.A. listed only 30,000 union members as against S.F.'s 200,000. Real strength of movement only developed after 1936, with creation of NRA. Since then, due in part to growth of industries that have already been well-unionized elsewhere, the picture has changed & union membership compares favorably with that in other great cities. Today even movie industry is organized, with membership of more than 12,000. Not unrelated to labor situation, & certainly somewhat in old pattern of city's behavior toward foreign racial elements, were anti-Mexican, so-called "Zoot-suit" riots in 1943, during which gangs, without interference from police, attacked Mexicans, Filipinos & Chinese. Riots lasted several days.

Mexs. pose a serious problem. They are, for most part, recent immigrants, unassimilated. They live in incredible slums; equal employment opportunities have at times been denied them; they benefit too little from city's social welfare organizations. Negroes, who are also discriminated against, & Mexs. combined add up to some 500,000.

Intelligentsia which migrates seasonally to Hollywood, tempted by inordinate salaries, has spread abroad the prevailing impression that L.A. is a dizzy metropolis composed of great movie studios run in weird confusion; sensational film "openings"; famous "hot night-spots," gaudy restaurants, & fabulous palaces of movie stars & magnates; "Bar-B-Q" open air eateries, crazy cults & equally fantastic architecture. But, by & large, this is a distorted picture. Bulk of city's pop. lives & works soberly, just as most Amers. do elsewhere. Nor are L.A. & cities that constitute its metropolitan area, by any means a cultural desert. There are several excellent orchestras; "Symphonies under the Stars" in huge Hollywood Bowl are famous. There are art museums with fine colls. & frequent exhibits of classic & contemporary art. Public school system is excellent; in city itself & in near-by centers are many outstanding institutions of higher learning. Notable among these are Univ. of Southern Cal., Univ. of Cal. at L.A. & Cal. Technological Institute, several of whose faculty members have been Nobel Prize winners. City has fine hospital & medical facils. & beautiful pks. & recr. areas.

In middle of 19th cent., Boston regarded N.Y. much as Easterners today regard L.A. Later it was N.Y. which sniffed at Chicago's uncouth manners. Today older communities E. of Miss. R., as well as San Francisco, display a certain annoying condescension toward their youngest rival. That is an attitude that L.A., prosperous & still expanding, can probably afford to ignore.

PTS. OF INT.—DOWNTOWN DISTRICT: (1) **Civic Center** (all bldgs.O.wks.), bounded by Main, 1st & Temple Sts. & Broadway, is eventually to be enlarged. **City Hall** (observ.tower.O.9-3.guides.by Perkins,Martin,Austin) has tower 464′ high. From its top rises Lindbergh Airplane Beacon. **Federal Bldg.** (by G.Stanley Underwood.fine inter.) is 18-story structure housing Fed. offices & courts. **L.A. Cty. Hall of Justice** (1925.Class.). **L.A. Cty. Hall of Records** (1909). **Cal. State Bldg.** (1933.by John C.Austin & Fred.M.Ashley.handsome inter.) houses State Gov. offices. In Assembly Hall are murals by Lucille Lloyd. (2) 202 W. 1st St., **L.A.Times Bldg.** (tours.wks.reserv.1935.by G.B.Kaufman). Eagle topping tower survived dynamiting of old bldg. in 1910. (3) 208 S. Main St., **Cathedral of St. Vibiana** (O.1876.designed in style of San Miguel del Puerto in Barcelona). Contains relic of St. Vibiana. (4) 430 N. Main St., **Old Pico H.,** built by last Mex. Gov. Will probably be demolished when Civic Center is extended. (5) N. Main St., **Plaza,** laid out in 1781, in which is bronze **Statue of Felipe de Neve,** founder of city, by Henry Lyon. (6) 100 Sunset Blvd., **Plaza Ch.** (O.founded 1784.present bldg.begun 1812.rebuilt). San Gabriel Mission Fathers donated several barrels of brandy to raise funds for its construction. One of bells in Campanario was donated by mission. (7) Inters. New High St., Bellevue Ave. & Sunset Blvd., **Statue of Fray Junípero Serra,** founder of Misión de San Gabriel & other missions (by E. Cadorin). (8) Facing Plaza, at 516-22 N. Los Angeles St., **Lugo H.** (O.1840.alts.), old adobe largely occupied by shops.

(9) **Olvera St.,** known as El Paseo de los Angeles, is named for Don Agustin Olvera, who fought against Frémont. At entrance is **Wooden Cross** comm. founding of L.A. Here in Dec. takes place ceremony of Los Posados (Sp."the lodgings"), comm. Mary's journey to Bethlehem, & Sat. before Ash Wednesday, "Blessing of Animals." (10) 14 Olvera St., **Avila Adobe** (O.sm.fee), home of early "Alcalde," now mus. (11) Near Marchessault St., opp. 35 Olvera St., is red brick strip that marks location of **La Zanja Madre** (Sp."mother ditch"), built 1782, which carried water from L.A. River to city. (12) 35 Olvera St., **Casa La Golondrina** (O.1850-68.int.inter.), formerly winery, now café. (13) Macey & Olvera Sts., **El Camino Watering Trough,** hand-hewn by Inds. of San Fernando Mission from which it was removed in 1930. (14) Bounded by Ord, Main, Macey & N. High Sts. is **China City,** Chinese-operated amusement center. (15) Broadway & College St., **New Chinatown.** In center is gar-

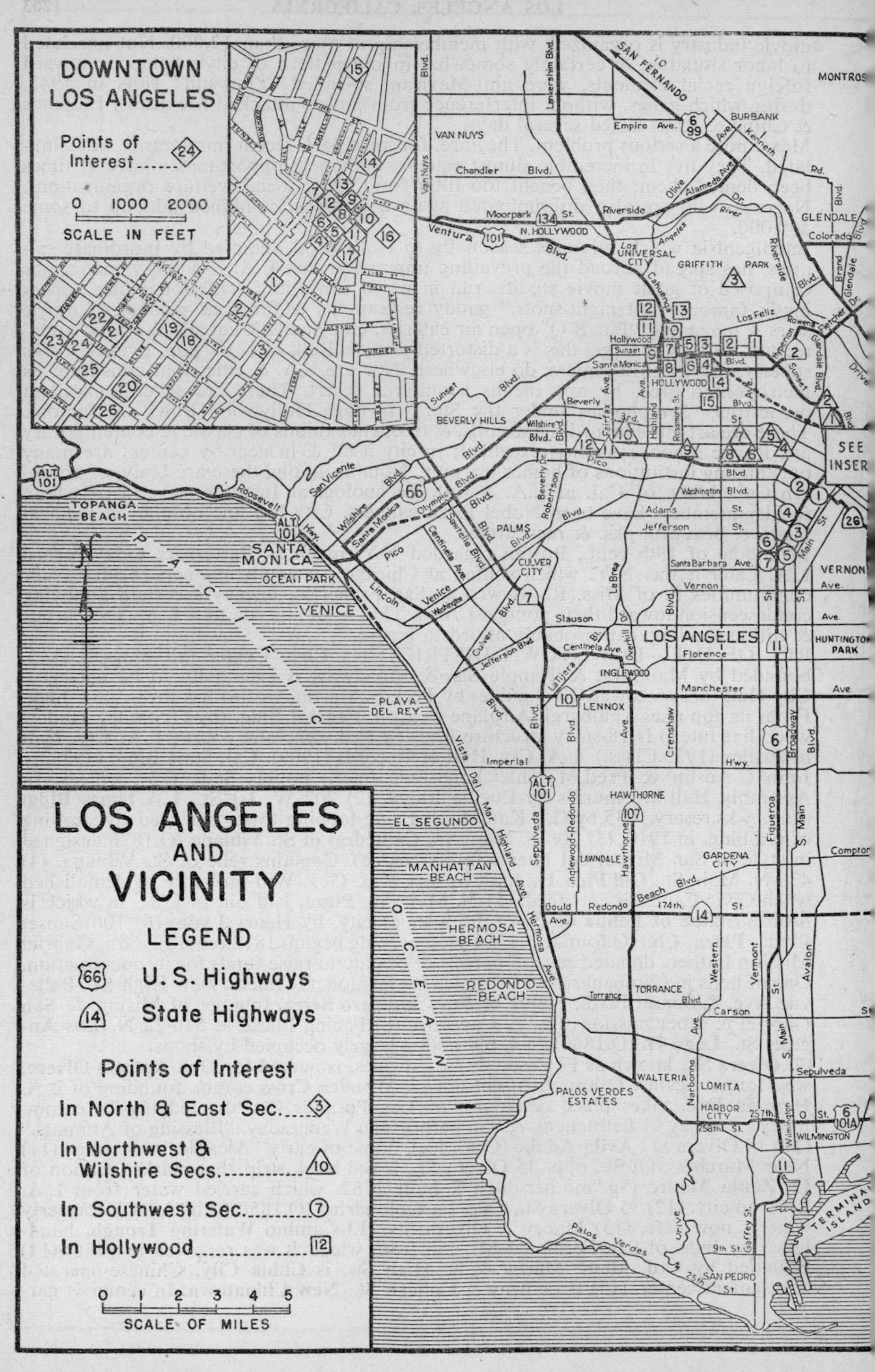
DOWNTOWN LOS ANGELES
Points of Interest
24
0 1000 2000
SCALE IN FEET
LOS ANGELES AND VICINITY
LEGEND
66 U. S. Highways
14 State Highways
Points of Interest
In North & East Sec.
In Northwest & Wilshire Secs.
In Southwest Sec.
In Hollywood
0 1 2 3 4 5
SCALE OF MILES
SAN FERNANDO
MONTROSE
BURBANK
VAN NUYS
GLENDALE
N. HOLLYWOOD
UNIVERSAL CITY
GRIFFITH PARK
HOLLYWOOD
BEVERLY HILLS
SEE INSERT
TOPANGA BEACH
SANTA MONICA
OCEAN PARK
VENICE
PALMS
CULVER CITY
LOS ANGELES
VERNON
HUNTINGTON PARK
INGLEWOOD
LENNOX
PLAYA DEL REY
EL SEGUNDO
HAWTHORNE
LAWNDALE
GARDENA CITY
MANHATTAN BEACH
HERMOSA BEACH
REDONDO BEACH
TORRANCE
WALTERIA
LOMITA
HARBOR CITY
WILMINGTON
PALOS VERDES ESTATES
SAN PEDRO
TERMINAL ISLAND
PACIFIC
OCEAN
Compton

LA CANADA
Haskell St.
Verdugo Blvd.
ALTADENA
FLINTRIDGE
Linda Vista
Arroyo
Lincoln Ave.
Montana
SIERRA MADRE
Central Ave.
MONROVIA
Blvd.
Foothill Blvd.
PASADENA
Colorado St.
California St.
Foothill
DUARTE
AZUSA
GLENDORA
San Gabriel Forest Hwy.
Shamrock Ave.
Huntington Dr.
Falling Leaf Ave.
ARCADIA
Foothill Blvd.
Alosta Ave.
SAN MARINO
Fair Oaks
Broadway
York Blvd.
Eagle Rock
Arroyo Seco Parkway
Huntington
Dr.
Duarte Rd.
Baldwin Ave.
Azusa Ave.
Bonita Ave.
S. PASADENA
SAN GABRIEL
Las Tunas Drive
TEMPLE CITY
Peck Rd.
Figueroa
Main St.
ALHAMBRA
Fremont Ave.
San Gabriel
Rosemead
BALDWIN PARK
COVINA
San Bernardino Rd.
EL MONTE
Valley Blvd.
Arroyo Ave.
TO POMONA
Garvey Ave.
Mission
Daly
Ramona Blvd.
MONTEREY PARK
Downey Road
Pomona Ave.
Puente Ave.
Blvd.
3rd St.
Mesa Dr.
Proctor Ave.
Road
Workman Mill
Valley Blvd.
Whittier Blvd.
MONTEBELLO
Olympic
BY PASS
Indiana St.
Soto St.
5th Ave.
PUENTE
WALNUT
Anaheim-Telegraph Rd.
Rio Hondo
Rosemead Blvd.
San Gabriel River
Norwalk Blvd.
Atlantic
MAYWOOD
Gage
BELL Ave.
WALNUT PARK
Firestone
SOUTHGATE
WHITTIER
Hacienda Blvd.
Fullerton Rd.
Brea Canyon Rd.
Santa Fe Springs Road
Whittier
Blvd.
SANTA FE SPRS.
Leffingwell Rd.
DOWNEY
Imperial Hwy.
LYNWOOD
Norwalk
Valley View Ave.
LaMirada Ave.
LA HABRA
Central Ave.
BREA
Hwy.
Imperial
NORWALK
Firestone Blvd.
LaMirada Rd.
FULLERTON
Pomona Ave.
COMPTON Blvd.
CLEARWATER
Michigan Ave.
HYNES Ave.
BELLFLOWER
Artesia
Artesia Ave.
NORTH LONG BEACH
ATWOOD
BUENA PARK
Orangethorpe
Ave.
Manchester Blvd.
ARTESIA
COUNTY LINE
Alameda St.
Long Beach
Los Angeles River
Carson
LAKEWOOD
St.
Bellflower
Lakewood
Lincoln
Ave.
OLIVE
ANAHEIM
Blvd.
American Ave.
Spring
St.
LOS ALAMITOS
STANTON
TO LAGUNA BEACH
Glassell St.
Tustin Ave.
Willow St.
Cherry
Highway
Pacific
Anaheim
Coast St.
Daisy
Pacific
Atlantic
Obispo
Ximeno
7th. St.
Ocean
Bl.
Garden Grove
Blvd.
ORANGE
LONG BEACH
17th
WESTMINSTER
Ave.
1st St.
Bolsa
SEAL BEACH
MIDWAY CITY
SANTA ANA
SUNSET BEACH
Huntington Beach
Stanton Blvd
Main
Los Alamitos
ALT. 101

den with fish pool, landscaped in Chinese manner & dotted with statues & shrines. (16) Alameda St., **L.A. Union Passenger Terminal** (by Don.B.Parkinson & others. impressive inter.); Observ. Tower (135'). (17) 215½ Ferguson Alley, 2nd fl., **Kong Chew Chinese Buddhist Temple** (O). (18) 317-23 S. Broadway, **Grand Central Market** (O.wks.worth visit), city's largest pub. market. (19) 3rd & Hill Sts., **Angel's Flight,** cable RR. taking passengers to top of Bunker Hill (315'). From Observ. tower, fine view.

(20) Bounded by 5th, 6th, Hill & Olive Sts., **Pershing Sq.,** in which are **Spanish War Mem.** (by S.Goddart), **World War I Mem.** (by Homberto Pedretti) & **Statue of Beethoven.** Among int. modern bldgs. in this vic. are: (21) 601 N. 5th St., **Edison Bldg.** (O.wks.by Allison & Allison). (22) 707 W. 5th St., **Sunkist Bldg.** (O.wks.Mod. by Walker & Eisen), in which are murals by Frank Bowers & Arthur Prunier; & (23) 558 S. Flower St., **Richfield Bldg.** (O.wks.by Morgan,Walls & Clements), with skeleton steel tower bringing it to height of c.300' & with sculptured figures by Haig Patigian over entrance. (24) 5th St. bet. Flower & Grand Aves., **L.A. Central Pub. Lib.** (O.wks.1926.by B.G.Goodhue & Winslow.sculpture by Lawrie), with tall tower. Within bldg. is pleasant patio with wall carvings illustrating Mother Goose & other subjects for children & frescoes by C. M. Kassler. In Ivanhoe Rm. are murals by Julia E. Garnsey & A. W. Parsons illustrating Scott's "Ivanhoe." On 2nd fl. are several sculptures; decorating rotunda, murals by Dean Cornwell. In Hist. Rm. are murals by Albert Herter. (25) 558 S. Hope St., adj. to Lib. is **Bible Institute of L.A.** (Mod.Ren.), coed. non-denominational evangelical training school. (26) 618 S. Olive St., **Clifton Cafeteria,** where patron pays what he thinks the food he has consumed is worth, although there are scheduled prices. (Merits visit because of several unusual features.)

NORTH & EAST SEC.: (1) 3772 E. 3rd St., **Church of Our Lady of Lourdes (Mod.** Sp.Mission.by L.G.Scherer), dominated by lofty tower. (2) 1200 N. State St., **L.A. Cty. Gen. Hospital,** comprising more than 120 bldgs. with extensive grounds. (3) Bet. Mission Rd. & Valley Blvd., **Lincoln Pk.,** in which are L. (boat.recr.) & conservatory containing large coll. of tropical plants. (4) 3609 Mission Rd., **L.A. Ostrich Farm** (O.sm.fee). (5) 3627 Mission Rd., **Cal. Alligator Farm** (O.sm.fee). (6) **Arroyo Seco Pk.** (276 as.) along Arroyo Seco, which is dry in summer & in rainy season carries run-off water into L.A. River. (7) 1600 Campus Rd., **Occidental College,** founded 1888 (bldgs.Ital.Ren.mod.), college of liberal arts & sciences, with outdoor theater seating 5,000. (8) Bounded by Figueroa St., Ave. 49, & Arroyo Seco, **Sycamore Grove Pk.** (recr.), favorite resort for picnickers. (9) 4605 N. Figueroa, **Casa de Adobe** (O.Wed.& Sun.aft.1916), replica of early 19th cent. Sp. H. of S. Cal.; antique furnishings & old paintings. (10) Cor. Marmion Way & Museum Dr., **Southwest Mus.** (O.aft.exc.Mon.;closed Aug.); relics & art of primitive peoples of W. Hemisphere. Mayan Portal at entrance to tunnel into hill on which mus. stands. In tunnel are dioramas of early Ind. cultures; from tunnel elevator takes visitors to mus. Another approach is by Hopi Trl., copied from stone trl. to Hopi "sky cities." **Torrance Tower** (O.appl.) contains lib. of works on primitive peoples of SW. & Sp. Amer. In auditorium, free lectures on Sun., Nov.-Mar. (11) (W) beyond Arroyo Seco, at crossing of Ave. 43, **El Alisal** (O.appl.at Southwest Mus.), former home of Chas. F. Lummis, who was largely responsible for mus. Contains part of Lummis coll. of Ind. & Sp. artifacts. (12) N. Broadway & L.A. River, **Elysian Pk.** (600 as. pic.), int. recr. area scarred by deep arroyos & canyons. At main entrance is Frémont Gate, comm. John C. Frémont, explorer & conqueror of Cal. Just beyond gate is **Portolá-Crespi Mon.,** marking spot where Gaspar de Portolá is supposed to have camped in 1769.

NORTHWEST & WILSHIRE SECS.: (1) Bounded by Glendale Blvd., Temple St. & Echo Pk. & Park Aves., **Echo Pk.** (boat.pic.). (2) 1100 Glendale Blvd., **Angelus Temple** (O.guides.contributions accepted). Huge circular concrete bldg. with low dome. Mother Ch. of 4-Square Gospel sect, founded by Aimee Semple McPherson. (3) Griffith Pk. & Riverside Dr., **Griffith Pk.** (3,761 as.recr.pic.), orig. part of Rancho Los Feliz, whose last owner was Col. Griffith T. Griffith. Hy. traverses pk., affording fine views; several canyons. Hiking & bridle trls. **Griffith Observ. & Planetarium** (O.demonstrations Fri.Sat.& Sun.sm.fee); exhibits illustrating various sciences—astronomy, electricity, optics—& 12-inch refractor-type telescope. At SW. end of pk. **Fern Dell** (pic.), heavily wooded ravine with int. ferns & other plants. **Zoo** (O). In Vermont Canyon is **Greek Theater.** (4) Bet. Alvarado & Parkview Sts., bisected by Wilshire Blvd., **Westlake Pk.** (boat.pic.), with statues of Prometheus & Gen. Harrison Gray Otis, editor & publisher of L.A. Times. (5) 2401 Wilshire Blvd., **Otis Art Institute** (O.guides.3-4 wks.), school of fine & applied art. (6) Wilshire Blvd. & S. Berendo St., **Immanuel Presb. Ch.** (O.appl.guides.Mod.Goth.), with lofty bell tower & fine stained-glass windows. (7) Wilshire Blvd. & S. Normandie Ave., **Christian Science Ch.** (by R.H.Orr) with lofty campanile & rose window copied from one in Rheims Cathedral. (8) Wilshire & Hobart Blvds., **Temple of B'nai B'rith** (O.during services), largest Jewish place of worship in L.A. Bldg. has low mosaic dome & inter. is richly decorated. Here are also Warner Mem. murals by Hugo Ballin. (9) Wilshire & Plymouth Blvds., **Wilshire Meth. Ch.** (O.exc.Tues.appl.) with façade modelled on that of Ch. of St. Francis, Brescia, Italy. (10) Wilshire Blvd. bet. W. 6th St., Curzon Ave. & Ogden Dr., **Hancock Pk.** (27 as.) in which are La Brea Tar Pits. These pockets are one of world's outstanding sources of prehistoric animal remains—chiefly skeletons, 20,000 to 50,000 yrs. old, preserved in asphalt. L.A. Cty. Pk. Dept. has attempted to recreate here, as nearly as possible, setting of Pleistocene Age by planting of appropriate flora & setting up modelled groups of prehistoric animals (by Herman T.Beck) among pits. (11) Along **Carthay Center Pky.** are various mons. (12) 6316 San Vicente Blvd., **Carthay Circle Theater,** which contains some int. paintings depicting early Cal. hist. Theater is used for presentation of important film premières.

SOUTHWEST SEC.: (1) 1111 S. Broadway, **L.A. Examiner Bldg.** (O.appl.), reprod. of Cal. Bldg. at 1893 World's Columbia Exposition, Chicago. (2) 1243 Trenton St., **L.A. Evening Herald & Express Bldg.** (1925.Sp.Ren.details.by Morgan,Wells & Clements), home of Hearst's aft. daily. (3) 514 W. Adams Blvd., **St. John's Ch.** (Episc.11th cent.Florentine) with main auditorium copied from Ch. of San Miniato in Florence. (4) 621 W. Adams Blvd., **St. Vincent de Paul Ch.** (Cath.1925.Sp. Baroque.by Albert C.Martin), with lofty dome & spire. Beneath altar is marble relief carving of Last Supper. (5) 3404 S. Figueroa St., **Figueroa Adobe** (O.appl. 1847.adds.) built by Ramon Figueroa, brother of Mex. Gov. (6) Univ. Ave. bet. 34th St. & Exposition Blvd., **Univ. of Southern Cal.,** founded 1876, one of largest & oldest in S. Cal. It has many handsome bldgs. Noteworthy is **Col. Seeley W. Mudd Mem. Hall of Philosophy** with Ital. Romanes. tower, in which is Mudd coll. of incunabula, mss. & lib. (7) Bounded by Figueroa St., Menlo Ave., Exposition Blvd., & S. Park Dr., **Exposition Pk.** (114 as.). In pk. are: **Mem. Gateway** comm. 10th Internat. Olympiad of 1932; sunken **Rose Garden; State Exposition Bldg.** (O.wks. 10-5.exc.Wed.aft.;Sun.& hols.aft.Sp.Mission.by Nathan Elery), housing permanent exhibit of resources & industries of Cal.; **L.A. Cty. Mus. of Hist., Science & Art.** (O.wks.Sun.& hols.aft.), containing various exhibits relating to art, nat. hist., science & hist., incl. coll. of Pleistocene remains from La Brea Pits in Hancock Pk. (see above), notable colls. of weapons & early L.A. relics, Rembrandt etchings, contemporary Amer. & Fr. paintings, & Oriental material; **L.A. Mem. Coliseum** (by John & Donald Parkinson), seating 105,000, here various sport events take place; in 1932, 10th Internat. Olympiad was held here.

HOLLYWOOD: District, N. of Wilshire Sec. (see above), is bounded (W) by Beverly Hills, (E) by L.A. proper & (N) by Santa Monica Mts. Hollywood Blvd., running E. & W., is main thoroughfare & midway along it, at Vine St., are shops, booking agencies, hotels, "hot spots," restaurants & theaters. Along W. Sunset Blvd. is what is known as "the strip" where there are more theater agencies, night clubs & expensive specialty shops. Although Hollywood is movie capital of world, most of large studios have migrated to near-by suburbs & many of film celebrities have their luxurious homes in Beverly Hills & elsewhere. Until 1911, city was just L.A. suburb. Then came the movie studios. Town boomed incredibly during 1920's. Today, Hollywood's pop. is largely dependent on film industry & broadcasting companies, which have established stations here. But city is also important music publishing center, making transcriptions of musical reviews for radio programs & millions of records. Recently, it has also become a leader in women's styles.

PTS. OF INT.: (1) Bounded by Vermont Ave., Edgemont St., Hollywood & Sunset Blvds., **Barnsdall Pk.** (pic.), given to city by Aline Barnsdall, oil heiress. In pk. is **Cal. Art Club,** former home of Miss Barnsdall, designed by Frank Lloyd Wright in style of Aztec temple. Bldg. houses coll. of Cal. relics & handicraft articles & presents occasional exhibits of contemporary art. (2) 5504 Hollywood Blvd., **Central**

**Casting Corp. Office,** where names of 4,500 movie "extras" & bit players are on file. (3) 6121 Sunset Blvd., **Columbia Sq.** (O.Mod.by Lescaze); contains 3 units: Columbia Sq. Playh. from which Columbia Broadcasting System broadcasts are sent, studio & office. (4) 1438 Gower St., **Columbia Pictures Corp. Studio** (N.O.). (5) Vine St. on Sunset Blvd., **Mutual-Don Lee Broadcasting System Studios,** world's largest, at time of completion, with 130,000 sq. ft. of office & studio space. (6) Sunset Blvd. & Vine St., **Nat. Broadcasting Co. Studios** (O.Mod.by Austin Co.). (7) Selma & Wilcox Aves., **Hollywood P.O.** (Mod.by Beelman), in whose main corridor is relief by G. Newell. (8) De Longpré & Cherokee Aves., **De Longpré Pk.,** in which is **Mem. to Rudolph Valentino** by R. Burnham. (9) 6661-81 Sunset Blvd., **Cross-Roads of the World,** shopping center built in picturesque styles; Atlas Tower over entrance. (10) 6712 Hollywood Blvd., **Egyptian Theater** (by Meyer & Haller), fantastic structure in Egyptian vein. Here film premières used to be presented amidst much publicity & ballyhoo. (11) 6925 Hollywood Blvd., **Grauman's Chinese Theater** (by Meyer & Haller), another architectural fantasy. On concrete slabs in forecourt are hand- & footprints of movie celebrities. Film premières are given here. (12) End of Bolton Rd., **Hollywood Bowl** (O.fee for performances), 60-a. natural amphitheater. Platform & shell designed by F. Lloyd Wright. Seats 20,000 people. Here are presented "Symphonies under the Stars" & Easter Sunrise Service. Heroic statues at main & inside entrances on Highland Ave. are by G. Stanley. (13) 2580 Highland Ave., **Pilgrimage Play Amphitheater** (O.during performance,fee) where, during July & Aug., play based on life of Christ is given. (14) 6076 Santa Monica Blvd., **Hollywood Cemetery,** in which are buried Hollywood & other celebrities. (15) 780 N. Gower St., R.K.O. **Pictures Corp. Studios** (N.O.).

Motion Picture Studios in addition to those already mentioned: 1416 N. LaBrea Ave., **Charles Chaplin Studios;** 1041 N. Formosa Ave., **United Artists Studio Corp.** In Universal City: **Universal-International Pictures Co., Inc.,** Lankershim Blvd. In Culver City: **Metro-Goldwyn-Mayer Studios,** 10202 Washington Blvd.; **Hal Roach Studios,** 8822 Washington Blvd.; **Vanguard Films Inc.,** 9336 Washington Blvd. In Burbank: **Warner Bros. First Nat. Studios,** 4000 S. Olive Ave.; **Walt Disney Studios,** 2400 S. Alameda St. In North Hollywood: **Republic Productions, Inc.,** 4024 Radford Ave.

## TRIPS OUT OF LOS ANGELES

**I. (Loop Tour) 67. US66, US101 Alt., St.15**

Via: Beverly Hills, Santa Monica, Redondo Beach, San Pedro, Long Beach.

**0.** from **CIVIC CENTER,** follow US66 (W) via Sunset Blvd., conn. with Santa Monica Blvd. at **3.**; turn (L) on latter. **11. BEVERLY HILLS,** independent city laid out 1907, almost surrounded by **L.A.** is noted as home of many cinema luminaries, whose splendid mansions nestle in slopes of foothills. **14. WESTWOOD,** suburb of Los Angeles. Westwood Blvd. & Le Conte Ave. (R), 344-a. hilly **Univ. of Cal. at L.A.** campus. This institution, S. branch of State Univ., grew out of old L.A. State Normal School, founded 1881. Among its bldgs., most imposing are **Josiah Royce Hall & Lib.,** latter with great arcaded octagonal tower (Ital.Romanes.by Geo. W. Kelham). **15. WILL ROGERS ST. PK.** (186 as.horses.golf.tennis,polo.), comprising former estate of humorist & actor. Ranch house is preserved with furnishings. **17. BERNHEIMER ORIENTAL GARDENS** (O.fee). **18. SANTA MONICA,** seaside resort city, at J. with US101 Alt. (see US101), on which route turns (L) **PALISADES PK.** stretches along bluffs overlooking yacht harbor. **21.5.** J. with Venice Blvd., leading (R) short distance to **Venice,** which originally was crisscrossed by canals & boomed as "new" Venice (Coney I. type of amusement resort). **24.** J. with 83rd St., leading (L) $1^m$ to **Loyola Univ.** (Jesuit) **24.5.** J. with Manchester Ave., leading (L) short distance on Manchester Ave. to **Inglewood,** where is old **Adobe del Aguaje de la Centinela** & where, in Aug., Sp. pageant takes place. **Hollywood Pk.** (running races) has one-mile track & grandstand seating 12,000. **29.5.** J. with Manhattan Beach Blvd. leading (R) short distance to **Manhattan Beach** (resort,f.) & **Manhattan Beach St. Pk. 30.5. HERMOSA BEACH** (resort). **32. REDONDO BEACH** (Coney I. type amusements). **40.** J. with Gaffey St.

SIDE TRIP: Take latter (R) $2.5^m$ to J. with Pacific Ave. (L) on latter to **San Pedro,** $3.5^m$, port of L.A. Rich. Henry Dana described his visit here in 1835 in his "Two Years Before the Mast." Originally San Pedro was an open roadstead. Present excellent harbor has been developed at cost of more than $60,000,000. There was great rivalry bet. San

Pedro & Santa Monica as to which should become port. S.P. RR. favored Santa Monica & L.A., San Pedro. L.A. won. Gov. breakwater extends into harbor for 2.5$^{m}$ **Harbor** is home base of Pacif. Fleet (O.Sun.& Hols.free transportation from E.Channel Landing). **Ft. MacArthur, Lower Reserv.** (O) is on Pacific Ave. At landward end of Gov. breakwater is **Cabrillo Beach Pk.** (bathh.boats). Here is **Cabrillo Beach Mus.** (O) containing aquarium & marine coll.

**42. WILMINGTON,** which has been incorporated with L.A. At E. M St. & Banning Blvd., **Banning Pk.** (O), in which is old **Banning H.**

SIDE TRIP: Turn (R) from Wilmington across drawbridge to **Terminal Island,** 2$^{m}$. Here is fishing village of Portuguese & Ital. &, before World War II, Japanese fishermen. Hundreds of fishing vessels put out from here daily. Also on Terminal I. are huge U.S. Navy installations: **Roosevelt Base, Terminal I. Naval Shipyard,** & **U.S. Fleet Air Sta.** At foot of Avalon Blvd. is **Santa Catalina I. Terminal,** pt. of embarkation by boat for Santa Catalina I. (automobile storage at pier) (see II below).

**47. LONG BEACH.**

Accoms.: All types. Info.: C. of C., 200 E. Ocean Blvd. Swim.: Surf at ocean beach; still-water in Alamitos Bay & E. end of American Ave.; still-water & salt-water plunge, Marine Stadium, Recreation Pk. Boat.: Rowboats & canoes, Alamitos Bay. Fish.: Boats leave beginning 5 a.m. from 1900 W. Seaside & 1520 W. 7th St.; surf & pier f.

Long Beach, on bluffs overlooking bay, is seaside resort, residential city & industrial & shipping center, to which home owners were 1st attracted in 1880's. Ocean Blvd. runs along heights from Long Beach Harbor to Alamitos Bay. With discovery of oil in 1921 at Signal Hill, Long Beach developed considerable boom, & oil is still important in its industrial life; it also has fish canneries, soap & vegetable oil plants & other factories. In 1933, earthquake demolished large part of city which, however, was quickly rebuilt.

PTS. OF INT.: (1) Broadway bet. Pacific & Cedar Aves., **Civic Center,** group of handsome pub. bldgs. (2) In Lincoln Pk., **Central Pub. Lib.** (O.wks.1936-37.Mod.) in which is mural by Suzanne Miller. (3) **Mun. Market** (O.7-12.Tues.Thurs.& Sat.), worth visit. (4) S. end Pacific Ave., **The Pike,** amusement zone (Coney I. type). (5) S. end American Ave., **Mun. Auditorium** (neo-Class.), with tile & mosaic mural on its façade, where Long Beach Mun. Band concerts (3:30 & 7:30.Tues.Sat.;2:30 Sun.). (6) Horseshoe-shaped **Rainbow Pier** (boat.bath.in lagoon). (7) Ocean Blvd. & Cherry Ave., **Bixby Pk.** (pic.). (8) Ft. of 2nd St., **Alamitos Bay** (still-water bath.boat.) popular resort. From bay, canals run into residential Naples sec. (9) Near-by is **Alamitos St. Pk.** (bath.pic.) on tip of peninsula. (10) 7th & West Blvd., **Recreation Pk.** (pic.recr.) with lagoon & pool & (11) **Marine Stadium** in which were held rowing races during 1932 Olympiad. (12) Panorama Dr. leads to **Signal Hill,** with its oil tanks & derricks. Fine view. (13) W. 7th St. leads to **Long Beach Harbor.** Boats leave here for cruise to L.A. Inner Harbor & return through Outer Harbor. Turn (L) from US101 Alt. at Long Beach, on St.15 (Atlantic Blvd.). **57. SOUTH GATE,** industrial suburb of L.A. **61.** J. with Anaheim-Telegraph Rd. in L.A., which route follows (L) to **L.A. CIVIC CENTER, 67.**

**II. WILMINGTON to AVALON, SANTA CATALINA I. 27. by Boat.**

Transportation to island from berths 184-5, Wilmington (boat train leaves Pacif. Elec. Sta., L.A., daily 8:20 & 8:50 a.m.) or by air. Santa Catalina I. is yr-round resort; summer months most popular; accoms. range from camps to luxury hotels.

**SANTA CATALINA I.,** 27$^{m}$ (SW) from L.A. in Pacif. Ocean, is 22$^{m}$ long and 8$^{m}$ wide (excellent swim f.h.); lovely scenery. It was first discovered by Juan Rodríguez Cabrillo in 1542 & visited, by Sebastian Vizcaíno in 1602, who named it for St. Catherine. In 1919 the I. was bought by Wm. Wrigley, Jr., who developed it as resort.

Take boat to Avalon, main center of island's resort & sports activities, with many hostelries, apartments & bungalow courts. On Avalon Promenade, **Avalon Casino,** with motion pictures, ballroom & lavishly decorated cocktail lounges. On Crescent Ave., **Greek Theatre,** used by various civic organizations. On Sumner Ave. & Fremont St., **Santa Catalina I. Visitors Country Club** with 18-hole golf course, tennis courts. On Fremont St. & Avalon Blvd., **Catalina Baseball Pk.** (exhibition games daily.Feb.25-Mar.15). In Avalon Canyon, reached by bus, **Avalon Bird Pk.** On hill near Avalon, **Glidden Ind. Mus.** (O.fee) containing Ind. relics.

Conducted Tours: (All boats leave from Avalon Pier; auto trips from Avalon Plaza). (1) **Glass Bottom Boat Trip** visits marine gardens that extend 17$^{m}$ along protected N. shore. (2) **Seal Rock Trip** skirts jagged lee shore to wave-lashed rocks just off Northeast Pt., where several hundred sea lions have habitat. (3) **Evening Flying-Fish Trip** (Apr.-Oct.) is 40-min. night ride behind 45-million-candlepower searchlight showing thousands of flying fish, their highly colored "wing" fins iridescent in glare. (4) **Starlight Drive** is 55-min., 7m eve. trip in open bus. (5) **Skyline Dr.** is 30-min. motor trip by daylight. (6) **Isthmus Boat Trip** is 3-hr., 28m round-trip cruise from Avalon Bay to Isthmus Cove along N. coast, with 1-hr. stop for lunch & sightseeing at Isthmus. (7) **'Round the Island Cruise.**

**III. (Loop Tour) 105. US101, St.185, US101 Alt., St.39, US Bypass 101**

Via: Montebello, Whittier, Fullerton, Anaheim, Santa Ana, Laguna Beach, Huntington Beach.

**0.** From **CIVIC CENTER,** follow US101 (Aliso St., conn. with Boyle Ave., which leads into Whittier Blvd.) **9. MONTEBELLO,** surrounded by flower gardens & oil fields. US101 shortly crosses San Gabriel R., passing at **12. PIO PICO MANSION,** adobe, built by Pio Pico, last Mex. Gov. of Cal., now State Mon. **12.5. WHITTIER,** home of **Whittier College. 28. ANAHEIM,** founded by Germans in 1857 as an experiment in communal living.

SIDE TRIP: Turn (L) from city on Center St. 9m to **Rancho Santa Ana Botanical Gardens,** with more than 40,000 Cal. Botanical specimens.

J. with Chapman Ave. **c.31.**

SIDE TRIP: Take latter (L) to **Orange** 2m, set among great orange groves. At 8m J. with Santiago Canyon Rd.

Take Rd. (L) here (straight ahead) 1m to **Irvine Pk.** (recr.camp.). At 3m **Santiago Reservoir & Dam** (160′ high & 1,400′ long).

Cont. on Santiago Canyon Rd. to J. at 14.5m with Silverado Canyon Rd.

Straight ahead (L) here to **Rome Shady Brook,** 3.5m (accoms.swim.pool). From here trls. run into **Cleveland Nat. For.** (518,000 as.), which has many for. camps with ample camp. facils.

Santiago Canyon Rd. cont. to **El Toro** at 28m. J. with US101 at 29m.

**35. SANTA ANA,** fruit & nut packing, sugar refining & mfg. center. N. Main & 20th Sts., **Bowers Mem. Mus.,** containing coll. of Cal. relics. **45. IRVINE,** J. with St.185. Route turns (R) on latter. **55. LAGUNA BEACH,** resort & art colony, beautifully situated on cragbound coast. Here is **Laguna Beach Art Assoc. Gallery.** Route turns (R) from Laguna Beach on US101 Alt. **64.5. NEWPORT BEACH,** resort town & yachting center on Newport Bay, in which are several islands. (Turn (L) here on St.55, c.1m to **Balboa** (resort) on I. in Newport Bay). **70. HUNTINGTON BEACH,** oil well center, with **Huntington Beach St. Pk.** Turn (R) from Huntington Beach on St.39 (Huntington Beach Blvd.). **85.** J. with US Bypass 101 (Firestone Blvd.); turn (L) on this. **105. L.A. CIVIC CENTER.**

**IV. (Loop Tour) 68. US66, St.71, US60-70-99.**

Via: Pasadena, Monrovia, Azusa, Pomona.

**0.** from **CIVIC CENTER,** follow US66 (N. Figureroa St.) (NE. & E.).

**10. PASADENA**

Through RR conns. 148 E. Colorado Blvd. for Pacific Elec. RR. (interurban). Accoms.: All types. Info.: C. of C., 65 Los Robles Ave. Theaters: Pasadena Playhouse, 39 El Molino Ave.: Civic Auditorium, Civic Center at Green St. Swim.: Huntington Hotel, all-yr. open-air plunges. Annual Events: Pasadena Tournament of Roses, Jan. 1; football game bet. E. & W. collegiate teams, Jan. 1, Rose Bowl; Pasadena Flower Show, Brookside Pk., 3 days in Ap. & Oct.

Pasadena is suburb of Los Angeles, located against impressive backdrop of Sierra Madre Mts., primarily residential, though recently it has acquired some light industries. It is richest city, per capita, in U.S., & home of Cal. Institute of Technology, known for work done by Dr. R. Millikan in his study of cosmic rays & nature of electron. Pasadena is famous for its giant deodars (grown from seedlings imported from the Himalayas) on Santa Rosa Ave. (Christmas Tree Lane) & its Tournament of Roses which takes place on New Year's Day.

PTS. OF INT.: (1) Garfield Ave., bet. Walnut & Green Sts., **Civic Center** (Sp.&Ital. Ren.); 100 N. Garfield St., **City Hall;** 285 E. Walnut St., **Pub. Lib.** (O.wks.) with beautiful inter.; 311 E. Green St., **Civic Auditorium** (O), seating 3,000. (2) **Brookside Pk.** (500 as.recr.& sports facils.). (3) On Arroyo Blvd., at Salvia Canyon, **Rose Bowl** (O), seating 85,000, in which football games & civic festivities are held. (4) 1201 E. Cal. Ave., **Cal. Institute of Technology,** famous research center, incl. Daniel Guggenheim Aeronautical Lab., Norman Bridge Lab. of Physics, W. K.

Kellogg Lab. of Radiation (cancer research), atom-smashing machine, wind tunnel & hydrodynamics lab. Its faculty has had, in addition to Dr. Millikan, several Nobel Prize winners. (5) Garfield Ave. & Foothill St., **Flores Adobe** (1839), built for Doña Eulalia Perez de Guillen, orig. owner of Rancho San Pasqual, part of which was site of Pasadena. (6) 39 El Molino Ave., **Pasadena Playh.** (O.9-4 exc.during Sat.matinees.1925.Sp.Col.) has School of the Theater & Lab. Theater, which serves to try out plays by new authors. This playh. is nationally famous for its productions.

SIDE TRIP: Take Linda Vista Ave. (L) from Colorado Ave., in Pasadena, leading into La Canada Rd., to Mich. Ave.; follow latter, which becomes Foothill Blvd. (L) to Haskell Ave., turn (R) on latter to Angeles Crest Hy. & follow (L) latter, which enters San Gabriel Mts. Hy. climbs through picturesque reg. of rocks, gorges & canyons to **Niño Canyon Lookout Sta.,** at 9m, from which fine view of **Brown Mt.** (4,485′), named for two sons of John Brown who settled near here. 15.5m **George's Gap** (3,750′), with view of **Mt. Josephine** (5,520′) & **Condor Peak** (5,430′) in distance. 20.5m **Red Box Divide** (4,666′), at crest of ridge. In distance is Mt. Wilson & beyond it, **Mt. Baldy** (10,080′). Turn (R) from Angeles Crest Hy. at Red Box Divide, on Mt. Wilson Rd. 25.5m **Mt. Wilson** (5,710′) (fee to grounds.accoms.). **Mt. Wilson Observatory** is located here. In it is famous 100″ telescope (shown 2-4p.m.wks.11-4:30p.m.Sat.Sun.& hols.), 2nd largest in world. There are also 60″ telescope, 12″ telescope (O.for cosmic observ. with accompanying lecture 7:30p.m.) & Sun Telescope (N.O.) in 150′ tower. Astronomical exhibit in hotel.

From Pasadena, US66 cont. (E). **13.** J. with St.19 (San Gabriel Blvd.)

SIDE TRIP: Take Blvd. (R) 4m to Mission Dr. Take latter (R) 5m to **San Gabriel,** suburb of L.A. At 314 Mission Dr., **Misión de San Gabriel Arcangel** (O.fee), now parish Ch. Mission was founded 1771 by order of Fray Junípero Serra. Present Ch. built 1800-06 & partly rebuilt after earthquake of 1812. Main altar of Ch. is one of its most int. features. Retablo & reredos antedate Ch. & were probably brought from Mexico. Painted & gilded figures of saints, elaborate scrolls & other ornaments were executed by Inds. On Mission Dr., near mission, is **Grapevine Adobe,** supposed to be birthpl. of "Ramona." In patio is huge grapevine bearing date 1771, but actually planted 1861. There are other int. old adobe houses in city.

**17. LYON PONY EXPRESS MUS.** (O.8-6.fee) contains hist. & Ind. relics. Here is J. with Huntington Dr.

SIDE TRIP: Take latter (R) 0.5m to entrance (R) of **Santa Anita Race Track** (racing during 2-month winter season beginning c.New Year's Day). 4.5m **San Marino,** wealthy residential suburb. Turn (R) here on Monterey Rd. At 5m **Huntington Lib. & Art Gallery** (O. 1:15-4:30 wks.exc.Mon.& 1st & 3rd Sun. each month. adm.by written appl.in advance only). In extensive pk., in which there are beautiful botanical gardens, are the 2 white marble bldgs.: (1) **Lib.** containing large coll. of books, incl. many rare items, incunabula, 4,000 mss. & more than 8,000 letters & documents dealing with Eng. & Amer. lit. & hist.; (2) **Art Gallery,** in which are famous coll. of 18th & 19th cent. Brit. as well as Flemish & Ital., paintings & coll. of porcelains & tapestries.

**34.5.** J. with St.71; route turns (R) on this. **37.5. POMONA,** located on what was formerly the Rancho San José. At head of Orange Grove Ave., **Casa de Palomares** (1853.rest.). 1569 N. Park Ave., older **Palomares Adobe** (c.1837). 1475 N. Park Ave., **Alvarado Adobe.** 548 S. Kenoak Dr., **Christian Oak,** under which, in 1837, Father Zalvidea of Misión de San Gabriel Arcangel said mass. Bet. Walnut & Val Vista Sts., **Ganesha Pk.** (recr.) in which is open-air **Greek Theater.** Lookout Pt., here, commands fine view. Adjoining pk., **L.A. County Fair Grounds,** where, what is alleged to be biggest county fair in America, is held in Sept. & frequented by 500,000 visitors.

SIDE TRIP: (R) from Pomona on Hamilton Ave. to J. with Valley Blvd. at 2.3m & follow latter (R) to Diamond Bar Ranch at 4.5m, where is **Vieja Adobe** (1850), one of best examples of adobe mansions in S. Cal.

Pomona is at J. with US60-70-99 (see), which route now follows (R). **41.5. W. K. KELLOGG ARABIAN HORSE RANCH** (O.exc.Mon.), with ring & grandstand where horse shows are given. **53.5. J.** with Rd. leading (R) 0.5m to **Gay's Lion Farm** (O.exc.Mon.10-5.fee). Here in 9 lion houses, more than 200 lions, many of which have appeared in movies, are raised for sale. **68. L.A. CIVIC CENTER.**

**V. (Loop Tour) 62. US66-6-99, St.2, St.118, St.7, US101**

Via: Glendale, La Cañada, San Fernando, North Hollywood, Universal City.

**0.** From **CIVIC CENTER,** follow US66-6-99 to pt. where US66 branches off from US6-99 (San Fernando Rd.) at **3.**; turn (L) here on US6-99 to J. with St.2 (Fletcher Dr.), **6.,** turn (R) on latter. **10. GLENDALE,** residential suburb of L.A. At Forest

& Glendale Aves., **Forest Lawn Mem. Pk.** (O), cemetery containing many unique mons. (but no headstones) & 2 churches. **Wee Kirk o' the Heather** is copy of Ch. in which Annie Laurie worshipped. At 1340 Dorothy Dr., **Casa Adobe de San Rafael** (1864-72), built by Tomás Sanchez, Sheriff of L.A. Cty., whose wife inherited part of great Rancho de San Rafael on which Glendale stands. From Glendale, follow St.2 (N) **18. LA CANADA,** foothill suburb, at J. with St.118. Take latter (L) skirting foothills at edge of San Fernando Valley, where olive & citrus orchards grow. **35.** St.118 turns (L). **36. SAN FERNANDO,** center of citrus orchards. **37.5. MISIÓN de SAN FERNANDO REY de ESPANA** (O.fee). Est. in 1797; by Dec. 1806 first chapel was completed. After secularization, 1835, mission bldgs. fell into decay. Convento has been restored & in it are relics & old paintings. Tower, also recently rest., has 3 of missions 4 orig. bells. Opp. Convento is **Memory Garden** in Brand Pk., one of few rest. mission gardens. **39.5.** J. with St.7 (Sepulveda Blvd.), which route now follows (L). **46.5.** J. with US101 (see). Cont. on US101 (L). **51.5.** J. with Lankershim Blvd.

SIDE TRIP: Take latter (L) 0.2m to **Universal City,** site since 1923 of huge **Universal-Internat. Motion Picture Studios** (N.O.), where office bldgs., sound stages, warehouses, & outdoor sets may be seen. 3913 Lankershim Blvd., **Campo de Cahuenga,** now L.A. city pk. with two adobes (recent), one containing hist. relics, was place where Treaty of Cahuenga was signed Jan. 13, 1847 bet. Amer. forces led by Lt. Col. Frémont & Mex. forces led by Gen. Andrés Pico & Gen. José Maria Flores. 1.5m **North Hollywood,** incl. in Los Angeles in 1923, is residential community in fruit-growing area.

Take St.134 (R) from N. Hollywood to **Burbank** 6m, at J. with US6-99, suburban residential & industrial center, with aircraft plants & motion picture studios.

From J. with Lankershim Blvd., US101 cont. to **L.A. CIVIC CENTER, 62.**

# YOSEMITE NATIONAL PARK

## YOSEMITE NATIONAL PARK

Summer season May 1-Oct. 1; winter sports Dec. 15-late Apr.; O. all yr. Info.: Pk. Hqs., Gov. Center, Yos. Nat. Pk. & Yos. Pk. & Curry Co., Gov. Center, Yos. Nat. Pk.; 39 Geary St., San Francisco; 514 S. Grand Ave., Los Angeles. Adm.: Free; yearly auto permit $2, issued at any entrance sta. Entrance Stas.: All-Year Hy. (St.140) at Arch Rock (O.5a.m.-12p.m.); Wawona Rd. (St.41) at S. Entrance Gate: (O.all yr.exc.during heavy snow 6a.m.-10p.m.); Big Oak Flat Rd. (conn. with St.140) at Crane Flat Entrance Sta. (O.c.May 1-Oct.15); Tioga Pass Rd. (St.120) at Tioga Pass (O.July 1-Oct. 1 6a.m.-12p.m.); & Rd. to O'Shaughnessy Dam (conn. with St.140) at Mather Entrance Sta. (O.6a.m.-12p.m.). Rd. Approaches: St.120 from Manteca (see US99), crossing pk. to Leevining (see US395); St.140 from Merced (see US99); St.41 from Fresno (see US99). Busses daily from Merced; daily from Fresno & L. Tahoe in summer. Daily bus serv. within pk. in summer. Saddle horses avail. near Happy Isles; guides (necessary for long trips only). Accoms.: 5 hotels (Yos. Valley, Glacier Pt., Mariposa Grove). Winter accoms.: Yos. Lodge & Ahwahnee Hotel. Badger Pass Ski House in skiing area (cafeteria.ski runs.ski school). Housekeeping tents & cabins (Yos. Valley, Tuolumne Meadows). Five High Sierra camps (O.July.Aug.) at Merced L., Vogelsang, Tuolumne Meadows, Glen Aulin, & May L. Six free pub. camp grounds in Valley; others at Glacier Pt., Mariposa Grove, Tuolumne Meadows & along main Rds. Camp. not permitted in winter. Campers must register at camp entrances. Special clothing & equipment can be rented or purchased at general store in Old Village. Special Regulations: Speed limit, 35m. Drive slowly at night, when bear & deer often cross Rds. Hunt.: Prohibited. Fish.: Licenses required. Closed waters posted. Entertainment: Regular summer schedule of entertainment, lectures and expeditions; programs posted on bulletin boards. Firefall nightly at 9 from tip of Glacier Pt. (best seen from meadows near Gov. Center or at Camp Curry). Dancing eves. at Camp Curry.

Yosemite Nat. Pk., spectacular scenic region, lies on W. slope of Sierra Nevada. Its E. boundary, 40m from Nev. Line, is on crest of Sierra; its W. edge is in dry foothills where mts. merge with San Joaquin Valley. Pk. incl. 760,951 as., in which are 429 lakes, chain of mt. peaks averaging 10,000′ & more, granite domes, monoliths, glaciers, high mt. meadows, many waterfalls & fine trout streams. Yos. Valley (3,985′), only fraction of pk's. area, but most visited, is U-shaped trough 7m long with average width of 1m. It lies 3,000′ below rim of pk. Merced R. flows through valley. Two main canyons bisect pk. (E & W): Yos. Valley in S. sec. & Grand Canyon of Tuolumne R. in N. sec. During Ice Age, glaciers jammed Yos. Valley & gouged out river canyons. Great Rs. of ice, 2,000′ thick, advanced through Little

Yos. Valley & Tenaya Canyon to form trunk glacier at head of valley, 3,000′ thick, that filled chasm with slowly grinding mass of ice reaching to El Portal. When Ice Age ended, glaciers melted & left deep L. 5m long in Yos. Valley, dammed by terminal moraine near El Capitan (see below). Streams & melting glaciers above it soon filled Valley with debris & sand, forming present valley floor. In 1864 Congress granted Yos. Valley & Mariposa Grove to Cal. as St. Pk. In 1890 it established Yos. Nat. Pk. & in 1906 Yos. St. Pk. was incorporated in it.

## YOSEMITE PK. TOURS

### I. ARCH ROCK ENTRANCE STA. to OLD VILLAGE; 16. All-Year Hy. & North Rd.

**0. ARCH ROCK ENTRANCE STA.** (2,855′), 72m (E) from Merced (see US99) via St.140. Just beyond Entrance Sta., on hy., is **ARCH ROCK,** formed by 2 granite boulders. **3. CASCADE FALLS** (L). **5. INSPIRATION PT.** (5,391′) & **PULPIT ROCK** (4,195′), across Merced R. (R). **6.** J. with South Rd.

SIDE TRIP: Take latter (R) across Merced R. to J. with Wawona Rd. (see Pk. Tour II), 1m, & cont. (L). At 1.5m **Bridal Veil Falls** (620′ drop). At 2.5m, **Cathedral Rocks** (R), rising 2,154′ above valley. Route cont. along S. rim of valley. At 4.5m starting pt. for trl. leading 4m to **Glacier Pt.** (7,214′). 5m **Old Village** (see below).

Main route, now known as North Rd., cont. (E) from J. (above) with South Rd. through **GATES OF THE VALLEY,** formed by precipitous **El Capitan** (L) & **Cathedral Rocks** (R). It passes **Ribbon Falls** (L) which drop 1,602′ in one leap. **Glacier Pt.** is across meadows, & behind it, **Half Dome** (8,852′). In distance (R) is **Cloud's Rest** (9,929′), highest pt. of Yos. walls. **7.** J. with Big Oak Flat Rd. (see Pk. Tour III.) **8. EL CAPITAN** (L), rising 3,604′ from valley, is world's largest monolith of exposed granite. **10. ROCKY PT.** with view of **Three Brothers Peaks. New Indian Village** (L), where live small number of Inds., who sell Ind. baskets & bead work. **10.5. YOS. LODGE** (cottages.cabins.swim.pool.cafeteria). Just beyond this pt. is J. with Rd. leading (L) short distance to view of **Yos. Falls,** which drop 2,425′. From end of this Rd., Lost Arrow Trl. leads 0.5m to ft. of lower Yos. Falls. **11. GOVERNMENT CENTER** (4,045′), Pk. Adm. Hqs. Here is **Yos. Mus.** (O.lib.& exhibs.concerning pk's. major features,incl.relief scale models showing trls.& Rds.). Behind Mus. are 2 Ind. bark huts, temescal (Ind."sweat house") & 2 Ind. grain storage stacks. Here local Inds. show visitors how ancestors worked & lived.

**11.5. AHWANEE HOTEL** (luxury accoms.). At **12.5.** are seen lofty **Royal Arches** & behind them, **North Dome** (7,531′). Here also is visible **Washington Column** (5,912′). **13. INDIAN CAVES** (L), which Inds. used for storage & shelter. Near entrance are mortar holes & bark huts. Just beyond Indian Caves is **J.** with Rd. leading (L) through Tenaya Canyon to beautiful **Mirror L.** at 0.5m, in whose surface are reflected lofty surrounding mts. (best time before 9 a.m.). **14. HAPPY ISLES** (parking space.pic.hik.). Here is **St. Fish Hatchery** (O) for trout. **15. CAMP FOURTEEN.** Just beyond, on hy., is **CAMP CURRY** (O.only in summer;lodge.cabins.tent houses;near-by skating rink & toboggan slide O.in winter.). **15.5. JOSEPH LECONTE MEM. LODGE** (L), comm. well known geologist. Lodge contains lib. on Yos. Nat. Pk. & Sierras & coll. of photographs. **16. OLD VILLAGE** (gen.store.cafe.chapel).

### II. S. ENTRANCE GATE to J. with SOUTH RD. 25. Wawona Rd.

**0. SOUTH ENTRANCE GATE,** 63m (N) from Fresno (see US99) via St.41.

SIDE TRIP: Take Rd. here (R) 2m to **Mariposa Grove of Big Trees** (lodge.mus.camp.), in which grow some 617 giant Sequoias. Oldest, **Grizzly Giant,** estimated to be 3,800 yrs. old with girth of 96.5′ & height of 209′. **Fallen Massachusetts Tree,** near mus., is 285′ long & 28′ in diam. **Fallen Monarch,** near-by, is 300′ long & 26′ in diam. **Telescope,** 175′ high & 18′ in diam., is still standing, although its heart was burned out by fire. Rd. through Grove traverses tunnel 8′ high, cut through base of **Wawona Tree** (231′ high). At end of loop Rd. through grove is **Wawona Pt.** (6,980′), affording magnificent view.

**4. WAWONA** (4,096′;hotel.store.camp.garage.swim.pool.saddle & pack animals). **16.** At **CHINQUAPIN JUNCTION** (6,050′) (gas.lunch.info.) is Ranger Sta.

SIDE TRIP: Take Glacier Pt. Rd. here (R) 5m to **Badger Pass Ski H.** (accoms.). Ski lift to **Ski Top** (7,950′), starting pt. for down hill runs. 16m **Glacier Pt.** (7,214′) (hotel.restaurant) with magnificent view of valley. From cliff top besides **Overhanging Rock** (L) Yos. Valley lies 3,254′ below.

**23. WAWONA TUNNEL,** 4,230′ long. **24. EAST PORTAL** (4,408′; parking). Here is fine view. **25.** J. with South Rd. (see Pk. Tour I).

**III. J. with Rd. to MATHER ENTRANCE STA. to J. with US395 at LEEVINING. 67. St.120 (Tioga Pass Rd. O.July 1-Oct.1).**

**0.** J. of St.120 with Rd. to Mather Entrance Sta., 101$^{m}$ (E) from Manteca (see US99).

SIDE TRIP: Take latter (L) 8$^{m}$ to **Mather Entrance Sta.** (O.6-9) of Yos. Nat. Pk. Rd. runs to **O'Shaughnessy Dam** at 14$^{m}$, which impounds reservoir supplying water & power to San Francisco. **Wapama Falls** is near N. side, below North Dome.

**0.5.** St.120 crosses Yos. Nat. Pk. boundary. **5.5. TUOLUMNE GROVE of BIG TREES.** Here are **Dead Giant,** through which side Rd. passes, & **Siamese Twins,** 2 trees, joined for c.20′ from the ground. Below Dead Giant, in small ravine, are remains of what was once huge tree supposed to be 4,000 yrs. old. **7.** J. with Big Oak Flat Rd.

SIDE TRIP: Take latter (R) to **Crane Flat Entrance Sta.** &, at 10$^{m}$, J. with St.140, All-Year Hy. (see Pk. Tour I).

Tioga Pass Rd. now passes **YOS. CR. CAMPGROUND** & skirts base of **Mt. Hoffman** (L) (10,836′) to **Tenaya L.** at **37.** Rd. then cont. (NE) along base of Polly Dome & Fairview Dome, to **TUOLUMNE MEADOWS** (8,594′) (gas.garage.stove.lodge. free camp.) at **46.** Nearby (N) is **Soda Springs** (camp.). Tuolumne Meadows is starting pt. for trips by ft. or horseback down Tuolumne R. gorge, by way of **Glen Aulin High Sierra Camp,** to **Waterwheel Falls, Muir Gorge,** & **Pate Valley** & from latter past beautiful **Rodgers L.** to **Smedly L.** Other trls. lead to **Mt. Conness;** glacier-covered **Mt. Lyell** (13,190′), highest peak in pk.; & **Gov. Center** in Yos. Valley. **53. TIOGA PASS** (9,541′), crest of Sierra. Here Rd. leaves Yos. Nat. Pk. at **Tioga Pass Entrance Sta.** (O.6 a.m.-12 p.m.). Visible (SW) is **Mt. Dana** (13,055′), on whose slopes is **Tioga L.** (R). Rd. descends very steeply to Leevining Canyon, passing **Ellery L.** (R). **67. J.** with US395 (see), at **LEEVINING.**

### YOSEMITE PARK TRAILS

Info. on trails, fish. & camp. & pk. camps available at Gov. Center & Ranger Sta. Hikers should avoid short cuts from designated trls., should start early on long hikes & return before dark & should register at chief ranger's office before starting on trips to isolated secs. Taxi service avail. to & from start of trls. in upper half of valley; phone avail. at base of all trails. Inquire at hotels or stables about daily saddle trips to trl. pts.

# SEQUOIA-KINGS CANYON NATIONAL PARKS

## SEQUOIA-KINGS CANYON NATIONAL PARKS

Both pks. open all yr. Entrances sometimes blocked by snow in winter. Pk. Hqs. at Ash Mt. Entrance. Info. pts. at Giant Forest, Grant Grove, Cedar Grove, Atwell Mill & outpost stas. Adm.: Free, yearly auto permit covering both pks. $1, except at Sequoia E. Fork Entrance, where no permit is required. Rd. Approaches: From Fresno (see US99) 53$^{m}$ (E) via St. 180 to Grant Grove Entrance (always O.) & Lost Grove Entrance (O.5a.m.-9p.m.;5a.m.-11p.m.Sat.& days preceding hols.), or from Goshen J. (see US99) 37.5$^{m}$ (E) via St.198 to Ash Mt. Entrance (O.5a.m.-9p.m.;5a.m.-11p.m.Sat.& days preceding hols.). Bet. June 10 & Sept. 10, busses leave Fresno (see US99) 2 p.m. daily for Giant Forest by way of Visalia & Ash Mt. Entrance & return at 8 a.m. daily through Grant Grove & Lost Grove Entrances. For bus service Sept. 10-June 9 make advance reservation. Saddle horses at Giant Forest & guide service for parties of 4 or more. Accoms.: In Sequoia sec. are Giant Forest Lodge, Camp Kaweah & Pinewood Shelter Camp (O.May 25-Sept.7); European, Amer. or housekeeping plan. Cabins & tent cottages, with separate dining rms., bath. & sanitary facils. Bearpaw Meadow Camp on High Sierra Trl. (overnight tents). Winter accoms. at Giant Forest Winter Lodge. More than 600 free camp sites for auto travelers (water.fireplaces.sanitary facils.). Largest campgrounds at Giant Forest, Lodgepole & Dorst Creek. In Grant Grove sec. are Grant Grove Lodge & Meadow Camp (O.May 15-Nov.15), European or housekeeping plan. Guide Service: Pk. naturalists at Giant Forest Adm. Bldg. in charge of guide service. Lectures daily & campfire programs nightly, in summer at Sequoia & two or three times weekly in summer at Grant Grove. Regulations: Camping, smoking & building of fires permitted only in designated areas. Fish.: Permitted only with license, available at Giant Forest. Hunt.: Forbidden. Swim.: In pools at Lodgepole Camp (fee), Bridge Camp, Hospital Rock Camp, & Heather L., (Sequoia) & in Sequoia L. near SW. boundary of Grant Grove.

Sequoia-Kings Canyon Nat. Pks. are notable for some of finest Cal. "big trees" (Sequoia gigantea). They have, in addition, fine scenic features, of which most sensational are Kings & Kern R. Canyons. They extend from Kings R. headwaters (N), encompassed in Kings R. Canyon sec. of pks., to Tule R. headwaters (S). Tallest peaks of High Sierra, barely dominated by Mt. Whitney (14,495′), highest pt. in continental U.S., bound them (E) & foothills of Sierra (W). Bisecting pks. (N.&S.) is jagged granite ridge, Great Western Divide, on W. side of which are pks.' major accoms. & most popular attractions, motor Rds., & shorter trls. Here, at 4,000-8,000′ elevations, are groves & forests of Cal. "big trees." Paralleling Great Western Divide for $25^m$, about half-way bet. it & crest of Sierra, is 3,000′ deep Kern R. Canyon. Even more spectacular is Kings R. Canyon, $10^m$ long, 2,500′-5,000′ deep, which, with Middle Fork, runs through N. sec. Latter has been preserved as wilderness area, reached only by trls. In E. sec. of Pks. are high mt. lakes of glacial origin & mountain sides of exposed rock & great, irregular granite ridges, cleared of earth & vegetation by ice thousands of years ago.

First official exploration of reg. began c. 1861, in N. sec. In 1873 Mt. Whitney was climbed for first time &, in 1885 an attempt was made by group which planned to found socialist community to stake out claims within what are now pks.' boundaries. Gov. suspended entire district from entry & in 1890 created Sequoia & Grant Nat. Pks. by act of Congress. For 15 yrs. both pks. were administered by military officers in face of considerable opposition from sheep & cattlemen who had been using reg. for grazing. In 1914 civilian administration took over. In 1926 Mt. Whitney-Kern district was added. In 1940 an act of Congress combined Sequoia & Grant Nat. Pks. under present name. One of chief attractions of pks. are groves of Sequoia gigantea, so named to distinguish this tree from related coast species, Sequoia sempervirens. Gigantea never exceeds c.330′ in height & its extreme diameter above root swellings averages c.27′. It is estimated that age of largest living specimens range from 1,500 to 3,000 yrs. Its foliage somewhat resembles that of incense cedar. On mature trees bark is from 1′ to 2′ thick, separated into long parallel ridges that give trunk appearance of immense fluted column. There are 32 "big tree" groves within pks.

## SEQUOIA-KINGS CANYON TOUR

### ASH MT. ENTRANCE to CEDAR GROVE. 70. Generals Hy. & St.180.

**0.** Pk. boundary ($37.5^m$ (E) from Goshen Junction at US99 via St.198). **1. ASH MT. PK. HQS. 3. CAMP POTWISHA,** former Ind. village, with mortar holes in which Inds. ground meal, visible in flat rocks below Rd., & well-preserved pictographs on cliffs above. Rd. now follows Middle Fork of Kaweah R. At **5. HOSPITAL ROCK CAMP** (all yr.cabins.camp.). Opp. camp is **Hospital Rock,** with cave beneath. **Castle Rock** (R) & **Morro Rock** (L) tower 4,000′ above camp. Take narrow dirt Rd. (R) from Hospital Rock to **Buckeye Flat Campground,** $0.5^m$. Rd. now climbs bet. Marble & Middle Forks of Kaweah R. At **10., AMPHITHEATER PT.** (4,450′, parking) with fine view. **16.5. GIANT FOREST VILLAGE** (6,412′). Trls. run from here into E. sec. of pks. **Giant Forest Lodge, Camp Kaweah, Pine Wood Camp** & several others are in immediate vic. Adm. Bldg. houses Mus. in which are some Ind. artifacts & relief map of pks., showing all major Rds. & trls. In front of main bldg. of Giant Forest Village is sec. of Sequoia tree, estimated to have been c.1,705 yrs. old.

SIDE TRIPS: (A) Take ft. path (L) from Village, short distance to **Beetle Rock,** from which fine view.

(B) Take Rd. (R) from Village. At short distance from latter is J. with another Rd.

Take latter (L) $0.5^m$ to **Bear Hill** (bears fed daily at 2:30 ranger nature talk at 3). This Rd. cont. past Hazelhurst Pic. Area (see below) to rejoin Generals Hy.

At $1^m$, **Auto Log,** huge fallen big tree onto which auto may be driven. Just beyond, on this Rd., **Trinity Cor.** Here main route goes (R) $1.5^m$ to **Morro Rock** (6,719′); magnificent view from summit, especially at sunset. At $2^m$ J. with paved Rd.

Take latter (R) $0.1^m$ to **Parker Group,** small grove of giant Sequoias.

Main side Rd. ends in parking area at S. end of **Crescent Meadow** at $3.5^m$, surrounded by Sequoias.

(1) Take trl. (R) from Crescent Meadow $0.5^m$ to **Tharp's Cabin** (1858), large hollow log converted into living quarters by Hale Tharp, who pastured cattle here.

(2) Take High Sierra Trl. $62^m$ from parking area to **Summit of Mt. Whitney.** This requires an average of 14 days as round-trip hike, leading through scenically spectacular

country to Sierra's highest peaks. Overnight camps are maintained during summer at c.10m intervals. Trl. cont. from summit to J. with Rd. conn. with US395 (see).
(C) Take Alta Trl. (foot & bridle) from Giant Forest Village (L) c.1.5m to **Keyhole,** big tree, fire-hollowed with openings resembling giant keyholes. Just beyond Keyhole on Alta Trl., at J. with Rim Rock Trl., stands **Lincoln Tree** (R), 259′ high & 31′ in diameter. At 1.5m on Alta Trl. is J. with trl. leading (R) short distance to Circle Meadow, where are **Founders Grove, Congress Group, & President Tree** (250′).

Generals Hy. cont. (E) from Giant Forest. At **17.** J. with graveled Rd. leading (R) short distance to **Lower Corral** (horses avail.) &, at 0.5m, **Hazelwood Pic. Area, 17.5.** J. with trl. leading (L) through **Sunset Rock Camp,** 0.5m, to **Sunset Rock** (fine view). **18.5.** J. with oiled Rd. leading (R) short distance to parking area. Here is **Gen. Sherman Tree,** largest living thing, 272.4′ high, bet. 3,000 & 4,000 yrs. old. At **21.** on Generals Hy. J. with graded Rd.

SIDE TRIP: Take latter (R) short distance to **Lodge Pole Campground.** (swim.trlrs.camp.).
(1) Take trl. (foot & horse) 2.5m (R) from Lodge Pole Camp to **Tokopah Falls,** scenically fine hike.
(2) Take Twin Ls. Trl. (foot & horse) 5m (L) from Lodge Pole Camp to Clover Creek. At 7m **Twin Ls.** (9,750′.trout f.), dominated by **Silliman Shoulder** (10,500′).

At **27.5.** on Generals Hy., Pic. Area. **31.5. DORST CR. CAMPGROUND** (L) on Dorst Cr. At **32.5., LOST GROVE RANGER STA.** Hy. cont. at an average of 6,500′ through magnificent forests & scenery to **S. ENTRANCE RANGER STA.** of Grant Grove sec. of Sequoia-Kings Canyon Nat. Pks. at **46.** Just beyond latter is J. with St.180, running (W) 53m to Fresno at J. with US99 (see). **47. ADM. HQS.** (cabins.camp.store.church.horses). Here is J. with Rocking Rock Rd. leading 2.5m (R) to **Rocking Rock** & near it, **Panorama Pt.** (7,500′), with magnificent views of Kings Canyon. **47.2.** J. with oiled Rd. leading (L) 0.1m, then (R) 1m to **Grant Grove,** largest of which is **Grant Tree,** 267′ high with diam. of 40.3′ at base. About 0.5m beyond Grant Grove is wonderful **North Grove** & beyond that at 4m on same Rd., **Sequoia L.** (5,300′.trout & bass f.).
Generals Hy. cont. (N) from Adm. Hqs. to **SEQUOIA-KINGS CANYON NAT. PKS. BOUNDARY** at **48.5.,** where it becomes St.180. At c. **53.5.** is J. with Rd. leading c. 2m (R) to **Hume L.** At **61.** hy. reaches **S. Fork of KINGS R. CANYON,** which it follows (E) to **CEDAR GROVE** at **70.** Near latter are 3 For. Camps., from which trls., radiating into Kings Canyon sec. of Sequoia-Kings Canyon Nat. Pks., a wilderness area of breath-taking scenic beatuy, lead to **Kanawyers,** on Copper Cr., 8m; **Paradise Valley,** 13m; **Vidette Meadows,** 20m; **Kearsarge Pass,** 28m; **Simpson Meadows,** on Middle Fork of Kings R., 28m. Other trls. through Kings Canyon area radiate from For. Camps at terminus of Rd. leading (E) from Shaver L. on St.168, which conn. with US99 (see) at Fresno.

# DEATH VALLEY NATIONAL MONUMENT

## DEATH VALLEY NATIONAL MONUMENT

Season: Oct.-May; main Rds. (O) all yr. Fall & spring, warm to hot days & cool nights; winter, cool days & chilly to cold nights; summer, extremely hot, daytime 100°-130° & nights 80°-100°. Low humidity at all times. Adm.: Free, registration at pk. entrances required. Rd. Approaches: Via US66 & US91 to Baker & (N) via St.190; via US6 to Olancha or Lone Pine & then (W) via St.190 or to Inyokern & then (W) via good desert-type Rd.; via Nev. St.5 to Death Valley Junction or to Beatty. By RR., U.P. RR. to Las Vegas with motor conns. to Death Valley. By airplane, chartered plane to Furnace Cr. Airport, or by United Airlines or W. Air Express to Las Vegas with limousine conns. to Death Valley. All-expense motor tours arranged by Riddle Scenic Tours, Las Vegas, Nev. Saddle horses at Furnace Cr. Camp. Private guide serv. at Furnace Cr. Camp & Inn. Accoms.: Furnace Cr. Camp (Sept.1-May 1;sleeping & housekeeping cabins.store.serv.sta.). Furnace Cr. Inn (Nov.1-May 1.Amer.plan). Stove Pipe Wells Hotel (Nov.20-May 1;emergency lodging & serv.sta.summer). Scotty's Castle (all-yr. Amer.plan.reserv.required). Texas Spring Campground (free.water.sanitary facils.). Warnings & Regulations: 45-mile speed limit. Register at Ranger Sta. Travel only on Rds. that are open & patrolled, or make inquiries at pk. hqs. Carry abundant water. Check gas & oil before all trips, & carry additional supplies, unless itinerary incl. serv. stas. Do not attempt to walk in valley during summer. Free Pk. Serv. lectures at Furnace Cr. Inn, Furnace Cr. Camp, & Stove Pipe Wells Hotel. Swim. pool at Furnace Cr. Inn.

Death Valley Nat. Mon., est. 1933, covers 2,981 sq. miles, 500 of which are below sea level. It is enclosed (W) by Panamint Range (6,000'-11,000') & (E) by Grapevine, Funeral & Black Mts. (4,000'-8,000'). Valley was once bed of ancient L.; at end of glacial period, water gradually evaporated. Badwater in valley's salt beds, —279.6' below sea level, is lowest spot in Amer. Mt. Whitney, highest in Continental U.S., is visible from Dante's Peak in Black Mts. In summer, valley is unbearably hot, with temperature as high as 134° in shade; but in winter, when mts. are lightly snow-clad, climate is sunny & delightful. Valley has minimal rainfall, in wet yr., 2" to 5". Barbaric colors of rocks & cliffs vary from hour to hour in changing light & mitigate harsh desert monotony. Death Valley, especially after rain, has considerable desert-type vegetation. Upper reaches of mts. have variety of trees. There is some animal life: bushy-tailed antelope, ground squirrels, lizard & birds. Rattlesnakes are rare. Death Valley, in pioneering days, took serious toll of prospectors & emigrants attempting to cross it. Its name derives from tragic experiences of emigrant train caught in its sandy wastes, 1849, some of whom perished.

## DEATH VALLEY TOURS

### I. W. ENTRANCE at Towne's Pass to E. ENTRANCE in Furnace Cr. Wash.; 56. St.190.

St.190, conn. with US395 at Lone Pine, descends E. slopes of Panamint Mts. to Death Valley, runs (S) bet. vividly colored high bordering ranges, then cont. (E) to Furnace Cr. Wash.

**0.** Mon. boundary (63ᵐ (E) from Lone Pine), at summit of **TOWNE'S PASS** (5,500'). St.190 crosses Panamint Range & descends Emigrant Wash **7.5.** to **RANGER STA.** at J. with Emigrant Canyon Rd. leading (R) through Emigrant Canyon 5ᵐ to **Emigrant Springs** (4,045'). 11.5ᵐ J. with Rd. leading (L) 6ᵐ to **Auguerreberry Pt.** (6,000'). From here fine view. In distance, **Charleston Peak** (11,910') in Nev. (see). From Ranger Sta. (above) St.190 descends, passing Grapevine Mts., banded in red & black (E). **17. STOVE PIPE WELLS HOTEL** (sea level). **25.** J. with Ubehebe Crater Rd.

SIDE TRIP: Take latter (R) paralleling Grapevine Mts. & climb gradually. 33.5ᵐ **J.** with dirt Rd.

Take latter (R) 3ᵐ through Grapevine Canyon to **Scotty's Castle** (O.adm.Sp.), which cost $2,000,000. Death Valley Scotty lived in valley more than 30 yrs. & achieved renown during his spectacular 45-hour trip in 1905 from L.A. to Chicago & for his spending sprees—without known resources.

At 36ᵐ on Ubehebe Crater Rd. is J. with short, one-way loop Rd. leading (L) through low mud cliffs & cinder hills to lip of **Ubehebe Crater** (2,900'). E. wall of this 800'-deep crater is striped in brilliant red & orange.

St.190 cont. (SE) to J. at **31.** with Daylight Pass Rd.

SIDE TRIP: Take latter (R) 10.5ᵐ to **Hell's Gate** (2,263') with fine view. Rd. cont. through canyon, circling **Corkscrew Peak** (5,000'), striped in gray & red bands. At 17ᵐ **Ranger Sta.** (4,317'). 17.5ᵐ Mon.'s boundary at Cal.-Nev. line, 13ᵐ from Beatty, Nev. (see) on US95.

At **38.5.** on St.190 is J. with oiled Rd. leading (L) 0.5ᵐ to **Death Valley Nat. Mon. Hqs. 40.5.** Visible (R) are ruins of **Harmony Borax Works,** from which borax was hauled by mule-team to Mojave, 160ᵐ distant. Works were closed because borax was more economically mined in Mojave Desert. **42. FURNACE CR. RANCH,** small oasis irrigated from Furnace Cr. Wash. Here is Death Valley Airport. Just beyond ranch is **Furnace Cr. Camp** (gas & service). **42.5.** J. with Rd. leading (L) 0.5ᵐ to **Texas Springs Pub. Campground** (water.fireplaces). **43.5.** J. with E. Hy. (see Pk. Tour II). Near here is **Furnace Cr. Inn** (sea level.garage.serv.sta.store). **46.5.** J. with oiled Rd. leading (R) 0.3ᵐ to **Zabriskie Pt.,** with fine view. **50.5.** J. with one-way loop Rd. leading (R) through **Twenty-Mule Team Canyon** to rejoin St.190 at 4.5ᵐ. St.190 cont. (E) past brightly colored Funeral Mts. with **Pyramid Peak** (6,725') at E. end of range. **54.5.** J. with Dante's View Rd.

SIDE TRIP: Take latter (R) through canyon with views of vari-colored Black Mts. to J. at 2.5ᵐ with oiled Rd.

Turn (L) here 2ᵐ to **Ryan** (2,500'). Sightseeing trains run to borax mines 7ᵐ distant. Dante's View Rd. cont. (R) to **Dante's View** (5,220';best in morning) at 14ᵐ, overlooking, from summit of Black Mts., Death Valley, Mt. Whitney (W) & nearer, Telescope Peak. White salt areas in valley below show up strikingly.

**55. RANGER STA.** registering incoming cars. **56.** St.190 crosses boundary, & cont. $17^m$ to Death Valley Junction, at J. with St.127, leading (N) $17^m$ to J. with US95 in Nev.

**II. FURNACE CREEK JUNCTION (see above) to SARATOGA SPRINGS. 63. East Hy.**

Oiled surface, bet. Furnace Cr. J. & Ashford J.; remainder graded dirt Rd. This route traverses E. side & extreme S. part of Death Valley Mon., passing Salt Beds & lowest pts. in N. Amer. W. Hy. is alt. to this route, paralleling it on somewhat higher ground; it branches (SW) from E. Hy. at pt. c.$6.5^m$ (S) from Furnace Cr. Junction, also crosses Salt Beds, & rejoins E. Hy. at Ashford J., $39^m$.

**0. FURNACE CR. JUNCTION** (see Pk. Tour I). From here E. Hy. runs (S) along foot of Black Mts. **5.** J. with unpaved, one-way Rd.

SIDE TRIP: Take latter (L) up through brightly colored hills & then down bet. steep walls. At $3.5^m$ it becomes Artist's Dr., & climbs again to **Lookout Pt.,** from which fine view of Death Valley. At $9^m$ it rejoins E. Hy.

**17. BADWATER** (—279.6′, lowest pt. in N. Amer.). **63.** J. with rough Rd. leading (L) $2^m$ to **Saratoga Springs.** Here, in pools, are tiny "Kill" fish, survivors of era when Death Valley was L. Near latter J. is Mon. boundary, from which E. Hy. cont. $27^m$ to meet St.127 at Death Valley J. (see Pk. Tour I above).

## US 101—OREGON

**ORE.-CAL. LINE** ($22^m$ from Crescent City, Cal.) **(N) to ASTORIA, ORE.** (across Columbia R. from Megler, Wash.). **394. US101**

Via: Brookings, Gold Beach, Port Orford, Bandon Coquille, Coos Bay, N. Bend, Reedsport, Florence, Yachats, Waldport, Newport, Ocean L., Tillamook, Seaside. S.P. RR. parallels route bet. Coquille & Florence, Tillamook & Mohler, Seaside & Astoria, & conn. with it at Yaquina. Accoms. in larger centers.

Route is extremely picturesque, often crowded to ocean's edge by cliffs & mts. In N. sec. it traverses lowlands leading to outlet of Columbia R. There are few cities of any considerable size, but many f. & resort villages & towns. Good f. along coast, streams, & Ls.

### Sec. 1: ORE. LINE to NEWPORT. 241.5.

**5. CHETCO R.** (f.). **6.5. BROOKINGS,** at J. with paved Rd. leading (R) $0.5^m$ to **Azalea St. Pk.** (pic.) with fine display of azalea blooms in spring. Some plants said to be 400 yrs. old. **8. HARRIS ST. PK.,** with smooth beach, rocky cliffs & azaleas in profusion. **21.** View (SE) of **Preston Peaks** & (NE), **Pistol R. Gorge. 22. CARPENTERVILLE** (1,715′). **36.** J. with improved Rd. leading (L) $1^m$ to **Cape Sebastian St. Pk.,** within which is promontory 700′ high. (Rds. & trls. here to good views.) **43.5. GOLD BEACH** (resort.accoms.) on Rogue R. & ocean, former placer-mining & present-day sport f. center. **44.5. ROGUE R.** (excellent steelhead & salmon f.). **48. ROGUE R. PK.** (accoms.supplies.boat trips to Agness in Rogue R. sec. of Siskiyou Nat. For. arranged). **50.5.** J. with Rd. leading (L) $0.5^m$ to **GEISEL MON.,** comm. John Geisel & 3 sons massacred by Inds., 1856. **69. HUMBUG MT. ST. PK.** (good for trls.), in which is Humbug Mt. jutting out into sea. **75. PORT ORFORD,** high above the sea, f. village & shipping pt. for cedar. Near-by is **Battle Rock St. Pk.,** where 1st white settlers held off Ind. attacks, 1851. **79.5.** J. with graveled Rd. leading (L) $5.5^m$ to **Cape Blanco Lighth.,** on most westerly pt. of Ore., named by Sp. navigator, D'Aguilar, in 1603. **103. BANDON,** resort town & cedar-shipping pt. **121. COQUILLE** (f.&h. in vic.) cty. seat & dairy center, inland on Coquille R. Here is J. with St.42, conn. with US99 (see). **139.5. COOS BAY** (sett.1853), on Coos Bay, is lumber, f.-handling & cheese-making center, largest city in S. Oregon. **City Pk.** (pic.) is on L. **Coos Bay Lumber Co. Plant** (O). Here is J. with paved Rd.

SIDE TRIP: Take latter (L) to J. with another paved Rd., $4^m$ & (L) on this to **Cape Arago St. Pk.** (pic.fine views.good f.off rocks) at $15^m$.

**142.5. NORTH BEND,** lumbering, f. & shipping center. US101 passes **Simpson St. Pk.** & crosses Coos Bay on bridge 5,340′ long with 130′ clearance. **157. LAKESIDE** J. with paved Rd. leading (R) $1^m$ to **Ten Mile L.** (boat.swim.f.) in fine for. reg. **158. EEL CR. RECR. AREA & FOR. CAMP** (L) (ample facils.). **163. CLEAR L. 165.** J. with paved Rd. leading (L) $1^m$ to **Umpqua Lighth. St. Pk.;** lighth. built 1857.

**166. WINCHESTER BAY** (resort.f.). **169. REEDSPORT,** at outlet of Umpqua R., lumber,f.& shipping center. Here is J. with St.38, conn. with US99 (see). US101 now crosses Umpqua R. Bridge; near here occurred massacre, by Inds., of party of fur trappers in 1828. At (N) end of bridge, is **Tideways St. Pk.** (pic.). US101 now skirts **SIUSLAW NAT. FOR.** (recr.hik.f.), passing **Elbow L.** (f.), **Tahkenitch L.** (f.) & **For. Camp** (ample facils.). **185. SILTCOOS FOR. CAMP** (facils.), at J. with Rd. leading (R) 0.5$^{m}$ to **Siltcoos L.** (f.boat.), largest on Ore. coast. US101 now passes **Woahink L.** (resort.f.). **187. JESSIE M. HONEYMAN MEM. PK.** (pic.boat.swim.f.). **191. FLORENCE** (resort.accoms.), on Siuslaw R., f. & farmers' market center. Florence has rhododendron festival last Sun. in May. Fine sand dunes on coast here. Just (N) beyond Florence is J. with St.36, conn. with US99 (see). US101 cont. (N) through Siuslaw Nat. For., passing **Munsell, Mercer, & Sutton Ls.** Near last-named are For. Camps. **201.5. SEA LION CAVES** (reached by footpath.guides.fee.restaurant). In these beautiful, multi-colored caves live a large herd of Stellar sea lions, named for their discoverer, Dr. Stellar. Some of the bulls attain weight of 2,000 lbs. They migrate to coast in fall from Alaska, to which they return in spring. **202.5. DEVIL'S ELBOW TUNNEL,** which passes through **Devil's Elbow St. Pk.** (fine view.pic.). **203. HECETA HEAD** (520′), discovered by Sp. navigator, Heceta, 1775. Lighth.; fine views. **205. SAND DUNE GARDENS,** colorful when rhododendron are in bloom. **206. OCEAN BEACH FOR. CAMP** (facils.no trlrs.). **210. TEN MILE CR.** (resort.f.). US101 cont., passing **Ponsler St. Pk.** (L) to J. at **214.** near **Cape Perpetua For. Camp** (ample facils.), with Rd. leading (R) 2$^{m}$ to **Cape Perpetua** (800′ observ. tower.pic.cabins), most impressive view on Ore. coast. Cape discovered 1778 by Capt. Cook, who named it for St. Perpetua. **217. YACHATS** (resort) on Yachats R. (pronounced Yahhots), famous for salmon f. US101 cont., close to sea, to **WALDPORT** (resort) at **225.5.** where is held Waldport Salmon Derby (Labor Day through Oct.). In Waldport is J. with St.34, conn. with US99W (see). Hy. cont. through luxurious rhododendron groves. **230. SEAL ROCKS ST. PK.** (pic.) where sea lions can be seen. US101 crosses Yaquina Bay on lofty bridge, at (N) end of which is **Yaquina St. Pk.** (pic.lighth.), to **NEWPORT** at **241.5.** (sett.c.1855.resort. accoms.f.swim.), situated on ocean & Yaquina Bay. Here f. fleet takes tourists on f. trips. On Ney Beach is lofty **Jump-Off-Joe Rock.** At Olsonville, part of Newport, Lt. Philip Sheridan built **Blockh.** (1856). Burial canoes which Inds. feared to remove to make way for fort were disposed of by Amer. troops, who sent them, with their ghostly freight, out to sea. At entrance to bay is **Yaquina Lighth.,** built over 70 yrs. ago. In Newport is J. with US20 (see).

### Sec. 2: NEWPORT to ASTORIA. 152.5.

**3. AGATE BEACH** (accoms.), where agates are found. Rd. here leads (L) 1$^{m}$ to **Yaquina Head Lighth.** on Yaquina Head (fine views). Near-by is int. **Marine Garden,** accessible at ebbtide. **9.** J. with improved Rd. leading (L) 0.5$^{m}$ to **Devil's Punch Bowl St. Pk.** (pic.). At ft. of bluff is Devil's Punch Bowl, cavern into which tides dash. **11. OTTER CREST ST. PK.** (pic.) located on lofty peninsula (fine view). **12.5 ROCKY CR. ST. PK.** (pic.). **14.5 DEPOE BAY** (resort.accoms.f.), starting pt. for deep-sea f. cruises (salmon,May-Oct.; tuna, July-Sept.). **Depoe Bay Aquarium** (O). Near-by is **Spouting Horn** through which tide sends water spouts. **Depoe Bay St. Pk.** affords fine view. Here is held "Fleet of Flowers" on Memorial Day in memory of lives lost at sea. Hy. cont. through **Boiler Bay St. Pk.** (no facils.). **22. KERNVILLE** (accoms.) on Siletz Bay & R. (f.). US101 now passes several seaside resorts. **33. OTIS.** J. with St.18, conn. with US99W (see). Just beyond Otis J., US101 crosses Salmon R. (trout f.). At **45. NESKOWIN** (resort.accoms.), with fine bath. beach. **58. Nestucca R.,** fine f. stream. Hy. again traverses Siuslaw Nat. For. **79. TILLAMOOK** (resort.accoms.) at head of Tillamook Bay, which is almost completely landlocked. Cheese & butter-making, commercial f., saw mills & woodworking are chief industries. There is sea-lion rookery off shore. In Tillamook is J. with St.6, conn. with US99 (see) at Portland.

SIDE TRIP: Take Rd. (L) from Tillamook 8$^{m}$ to **Netarts** (resort.accoms.). At (S) end of Netarts Bay is **Cape Lookout St. Pk.,** 400′ above sea with fine views & magnificent spruce forests. Off shore at **Oceanside,** 10$^{m}$, are bird & sea lion rookeries.

Leaving Tillamook, US101 crosses several good trout streams. **89.5. GARIBALDI,** in dairy reg. known as "Little Holland," because of dykes which protect it against floods. **91.5. BARVIEW,** at narrow upper end of Tillamook Bay. View of high Cape Mears, on which (S) is lighth. **95. ROCKAWAY** (resort.swim.bath.) affords view of Twin Rocks. **103. WHEELER** (accoms.f.), lumbering & f.-packing center. Hy. now skirts picturesque shoreline, through several resorts & past lofty promontories, affording fine views. **115. ARCH CAPE TUNNEL.** Here is **Short Sands Beach St. Pk.** Fine views from 700′ promontory above sea, on slopes of Neahkahnie Mt. which rises another 1,000′ from this pt. (fine for.trls.to beach.pic.facils.). **122. CANNON BEACH** (resort.accoms.f.). Just beyond town (N) is **Ecola St. Pk.** (pic.swim.fine view). **126.5. ECOLA** J. with St.2, conn. with US99 (see) at Portland. Hy. now passes Necanicum R. (f.) to **SEASIDE** at **131.** (large resort.extensive accoms.sports facils.fine beach), situated bet. Necanicum R. & beach, one of chief seashore resorts in Northwest. On Promenade, ft. of Main St., **End of the Trail Mon.,** comm. Lewis & Clark Expedition; at (S) end, remains of **Salt Cairn,** built by Lewis & Clark expedition, some of whose members had to boil down sea water to procure salt; & one block (N) beyond Turn-Around, **Seaside Aquarium** (O) with fine coll. of relics & minerals. Take foot path (L) from First St. 4m to **Tillamook Head** (1,260′) with view of Tillamook Lighth. off shore & fine panorama of ocean & coast. **133.5.** J. with Rd. leading (L) 0.5m to **Gearhart** (mod.resort. accoms.golf.). **145.** J. with Rd. leading (R) 2m to **Site of Ft. Clatsop,** marked by flagpole & plaque on Lewis & Clark R. Here Lewis & Clark Expedition camped, winter of 1805-6. **146.5.** Hy. crosses R. named for leaders of famous expedition. **147.5.** J. with Mile's Crossing Rd.

SIDE TRIP: (R) here 0.5m to **U.S. Naval Radio Sta.** 10m, **Young's River Falls.** 13m, J. with good Rd. leading (R) 12m to **Saddle Mt. St. Pk.** (hik.recr.pic.camp.h.f.). Ind. legend has it that Thunder Bird laid eggs on mt. summit & rolled them down into valley, & men were hatched out of them. Trl. to summit (3,266′), isolated rock formation commanding magnificent view.

**152.5. ASTORIA.**

Airport: 3m (SW) on US101. Piers: 14th St., ferry to Megler, Wash. (frequent daily trips); 11th St., steamers to Portland. Accoms.: all types incl. auto courts. Info.: C.of C., 14th & Exchange Sts. Swim.: in near-by beach resorts & Columbia R. Good f., salmon & trout, in Columbia & other streams & at ocean resorts. Guides & boats available. End of Aug. beginning of Sept. famous Annual Astoria Regatta & Salmon Derby.

Astoria, located near mouth of Columbia R., is an important shipping center & has many industries: sawmills, grain elevators, salmon canneries, agric. processing factories. It is also home port of large f. fleet.
In 1805, Lewis & Clark Expedition ended its long trek at pt. across bay. City was founded April, 1811, by John J. Astor's partners, Duncan MacDougal & David Stuart, who had come around Horn on "SS Tonquin." First settlers were reinforced in Feb. of next yr. by party coming overland from the E. Astoria, like many other Amer. settlements in the NW. was involved in struggle with Brit. Hudson's Bay Co. for trade & control of NW.reg. Astoria passed briefly into hands of Brit., who called it Ft. George. In 1824, however, Dr. John McLoughlin, chief factor of Hudson's Bay Co., moved his hqs. from Astoria to Vancouver, Wash. As immigration set in, coming both by ship & overland, Astoria began to boom. Its 1st industry was salmon f., since developed along with salmon canning to considerable proportions. Expansion was temporarily checked in 1922 by fire that wiped out many bldgs. Astoria also depends on farming in hinterland & on tourist traffic. Forty beaches in vic. & excellent salmon & trout f. attract vacationists.

PTS. OF INT.: (1) Exchange & 15th Sts., **Site of Old Ft. Astoria,** indicated by broad painted outline. (2) Exchange & 16th Sts., near City Hall, is boulder & plaque marking **Site of Original Settlement.** (3) Duane St. bet. 7th & 8th Sts., **Flavel Mansion** (O.wks.), built in 1880's of materials brought round the Horn. Fish-packing & processing plants are O. on appl. as is (4) **Pillsbury Astoria Flour Mill,** largest plant of its kind in Ore. (5) **Uniontown** (Bond St.) is foreign quarter (worth visit). Also Port of Astoria with mod. terminal facils. Waterfront is int. for seafaring activities. (6) **Shark Rock,** bet. 7th & 8th Sts. at Niagara Ave., is carved with initials of survivors from Amer. sloop of war "Shark," wrecked 1846. (7) **Shively Pub. Pk.,** end of 16th St.; fine view. (8) **Astor Column,** in Astor Pk., decorated by frieze illustrating discovery of Columbia R. & early hist. of Astoria; observ. platform (O.sm.fee) at top of column affords splendid view.

At Astoria is J. with US30 (see). From Astoria, ferry runs to Megler in Wash., from which US101 cont. (N).

## US 99—OREGON

**ORE.-CAL. LINE** (23m from Yreka, Cal.) **(N) to ORE.-WASH. LINE** (8m from Portland, Ore.). **344.5. US99**

Via: Ashland, Medford, Grants Pass, Roseburg, Cottage Grove, Eugene, Junction City, Albany, Salem, Woodburn, Oregon City & Portland. S.P. RR. accessible all along route; Ore. El. RR. bet. Junction City & Portland; interurban electric RR. bet. Portland & Ore. City. Accoms. all types.

This route runs through many of Oregon's larger cities & its most populous reg., especially Willamette Valley. In S. sec., US99 crosses, at considerable alt., magnificent Siskiyou range, after which it runs successively through Rogue, Umpqua & finally Willamette R. Valleys. It is flanked (E) almost continuously by Nat. Forests, accessible from various main cross-state tours branching off US99 & cutting (E) across recr. area of Cascade Range to conns. with US97 (see). US99 also passes Siskiyou & Siuslaw Nat. Fors. (W). Several hys. running across coastal range connect US99 with US101 (see), main coastal route. Much of reg. traversed by US99 was rich gold mining country; with exhaustion of mines, agric., & particularly fruit growing, displaced gold mining. Ore. sec. of this hy., like Cal. sec., roughly follows route of old stagecoach Rd. from Sacramento to Portland.

### Sec. 1: CAL. LINE to JUNCTION CITY. 230. US99.

US99 runs (N) from Cal. Line at considerable alt. to **SISKIYOU** (Ind.piebald horse) **PASS** (4,522′) at **5.5. 18. ASHLAND** (sett.1852) on Bear Cr. at S. end of Rogue R. Valley, lumbering, canning & farmers' market center. Town plaza has fountains spouting lithia water. There is an **Elizabethan Theater** (Shakespeare festival in summer) resembling old Globe Theater of Shakespeare's day. **Lithia Pk.** (recr.tourist camp) has zoo, grottoes, fountains & Elizabethan Garden. **S. Ore. College of Education** (est.1869) has rodeo grounds for horse shows.

SIDE TRIP: Take St.66 (R) from Ashland. At 15.5m, **Green Springs Mt. Summit** (4,551′). At 19m, **Tub Springs St. Pk.** (pic.). 63m **Klamath Falls** at J. with US97 (see).

LOOP TOUR: (S) from Ashland to **Mt. Ashland** (7,535′), with near-by **Highland Park For. Camp,** & return.

**26.5. PHOENIX** (sett.1850.accoms.). **Old Stage (Colver) H.** (1855), now apartments, used formerly as fort for defense against Inds. **30. MEDFORD** (sett.1883) on Bear Cr., in Rogue R. Valley. City's growth has been based on development of fruit packing, shipping & lumber industry. There are several plants (O) where large-scale fruit-processing may be observed. In Medford is J. with St.62 (Crater L. Nat. Pk. Hy.) running (E) to J. with US97 near Ft. Klamath (see US97).

SIDE TRIP: Take St.238 (L) from Medford to **Jacksonville,** 5m, former gold mining town. Here are old bldgs.: **Brunner H.,** in which is mus. of early mining relics; **U.S. Hotel,** in which are pioneer relics; **Meth. Ch.** (1854), which legend asserts was built with one night's income from gaming houses; **Beekman Bank** (1862), which shipped gold to Crescent City. St.238 cont. to J. with US99 near Grant's Pass (see below).

**44. GOLD HILL** (1,108′) in former gold mining district.

SIDE TRIP: Take St.234 (R) from Gold Hill 9m to J. & turn (R) here 2.5m to marked **Table Rock Treaty Site.** Here in 1853 Ind. conciliator Gen. Jos. Lane made treaty with Rogue R. Inds. In this reg. much of Ind. fighting took place. St.234 cont. to J. with St.62, Crater L. Nat. Pk. Hy. (see above) at 17m.

**52. ROGUE RIVER** (accoms.trlrs.camp.) on R. of same name (good f.). **56. SAVAGE RAPIDS DAM,** up which salmon & steel-head trout leap. **61.5.** J. with US199.

SIDE TRIP: Take US199 (L) through forested, picturesque mt. reg., crossing Applegate & Illinois R. Valleys, to Caves, J. with St.46 at 30m.

Take latter (L) 20m to **Ore. Caves Nat. Mon.** (O.May 29-Oct.15.lodge O.all-yr.cottages. no camp.pic.guides) in Ore. Caves Game Refuge in Siskiyou Nat. For. Bus from Berkeley, Cal., weekly; stop-over at Caves. Caves Chateau (accoms.). **Ore. Caves,** outstanding scenic pt. of int., were discovered in 1874. They are hollowed out of Elijah Mt. (7,000′), one of Siskiyou Range, & consist of series of chambers, conn. by corridors, fantastically carved out of marble. Searchlights play over weird formations. In one cave is **Niagara Falls,** great cataract in marble; in another, huge vaulted **Joaquin Miller's Chapel,** named in honor of poet's visit, 1907; & in another, **Dante's Inferno.**

US199 cont. to Cal. Line at 42m & (S) traverses redwood fors. & passes 5 for. camps. (ample facils.) on way to J. with US101 near Crescent City (see Cal.US101).

**62. GRANTS PASS** (accoms.), on Rogue R. & S. P. RR., is still mining & lumbering center; also market town for Grants Pass Irrigation District. It is starting pt. for h. & f. trips in Rogue R. reg. **Mineral coll.** in Grants Pass Assay Office. **City Pk.** (recr.) is on Rogue R. (f.bath.boat.). Siskiyou Nat. For. Hqs. are located in town. In vic. grows rare Ore. myrtle, found elsewhere only in Palestine. **67.** J. with Rd.

SIDE TRIP: Take Rd. (L) here along Rogue R. through old gold-mining reg. At 17m, **Galice,** former mining town. 21m **Alameda,** ghost mining town where is U.S. Ranger Sta. Alameda, which formerly figured in Rogue R. Ind. fighting, is in center of wild & picturesque Rogue R. district (good f.&h.) with fine gorges & canyons. 25m **Grave Cr. Bridge.** Here auto Rd. turns away from Rogue R., back to J. with US99. Travel down-river is by trl. Horses,guides available at Galice (above) & Illahee & Agness (below). Trl. leads from Grave Cr. Bridge, along Rogue R., passing several For. Guard Stas. & camps to **Illahee** at 55m where Rd. runs (N) past several for. camps to J. with St.42 (see below). Trl. cont. along Rogue R., passing **Waters Cr. For. Camp** (ample facils.), to **Agness** (resort) at 63m. From Agness boats conn. with Gold Beach on US101 (see).

US99 now ascends through **SEXTON MT. PASS** near Sexton Mt. (3,865′). **80. SUNNY VALLEY.** Here some Ore. men were killed in battle (1855) with Inds. **87. WOLFCREEK,** where is **Wolf Cr. Tavern** (c.1857). US99 cont. (N) along Canyon Cr., in Umpqua Nat. For., traversing Umpqua R. Valley. **111. CANYONVILLE,** on Canyon Cr., was formerly gold-mining center. **134. COOS.** J. with St.42.

SIDE TRIP: Take St.42 (L). At 15m, **Camas Mt. Pass.** Here is **Camas St. Pk.** Route now descends through fine stretch of country to Coquille R., 49.5m.

Take Rd. (L) 18.5m to **Powers,** then Rd. (S) into Siskiyou Nat. For., passing by or near 5 for. camps, around Bald Knob Mt. (3,614′), & through Illahee on Rogue R. (see above) to Agness, at 54.5m (see above).

62m **Coquille** at J. with US101 (see).

**140. ROSEBURG** (sett.1851) at J. of Umpqua R. & Deer Cr. in lumber & orchard reg. **176. DRAIN,** on Elk Cr. Here is J. with St.38.

SIDE TRIP: Take St.38 (L) along Elk Cr. & then Umpqua R. & across Elliot St. For. At 10.5m **Elk Cr. Tunnel Wayside For.** at J. of Elk Cr. & Umpqua R. on fine gorge (no facils.). At 37m **Mill Cr.,** at J. with Rd.

Take latter (L) 6m to **Loon L.** (f.boat.) in reg. of small Ls. accessible by trls.

50m **Reedsport** at J. with US101 (see).

US99 now crosses divide into Willamette Valley. **194. COTTAGE GROVE,** bisected by Coast Fork of Willamette R., center of fruit-growing, dairying, stock-raising & lumbering reg. **210. GOSHEN.** J. with St.58 running (SE) through Willamette Nat. For. across Cascade Range to J. with US97 (see). **213.** J. with US28, running (E) through Willamette Nat. For. via McKenzie Pass over Cascades to J. with US97 (see).

**216. EUGENE** (sett.1846).

RR. Sta.: 400 Willamette St., S. P. RR.; 5th & Oak Sts., Ore. Elec. RR. Through bus conns. Info.: C.of C. & A.A.A., 230 E. Broadway. Ore. Trl. Pageant (every 3 yrs. in July).

Eugene is situated on Willamette R. with view (E) of Cascade Range. It derives its name from Eugene F. Skinner, first settler. City is center of rich agric. district & has considerable industry connected with lumber-processing. Near-by, Chase Gardens produce flowers, incl. orchids, shipped by air to all parts of country.

PTS. OF INT.: (1) **Univ. of Ore.** (founded 1872). Its medical school is in Portland. Bldgs. especially worth visiting are: **Condon Hall,** in which is Mus. of Nat. Hist. (O.wks.); **Art Mus.** (O.appl.), in which is fine Murray Warner Coll. of Oriental Art; **Murray Warner Lib.** (1936), incl. Burgess Rare Book Coll. & Pauline Potter Homer coll. of beautiful books. **McArthur Court** for basketball games, seating 8,000; concerts are given during winter. **Hayward Stadium** (1931), seating 18,000. On campus are "The Pioneer Mother" & "The Pioneer Man," both by A. Phimister Proctor. (2) 364-2nd St., Mon. on **Site of First Cabin** in Eugene. (3) 6th & Willamette Sts., **Lane Cty. Pioneer Assoc. Mus.** with coll. of pioneer & Ind. relics. (4) E. 8th & Oak Sts., **Sp.-Amer. Mem. Fountain.** (5) **Skinner's Butte,** reached by driveway, is pk. affording fine views. (6) 11th & Aldey Sts., **N.W. Christian College,** est. 1895 as

Eugene Divinity School. In its **Fine Arts Bldg.** (1921) is Louis H. Turner Mus. (O.wks.appl.), containing material presented by missionaries & graduates.

**228.5.** J. with St.36.

SIDE TRIP: Take latter (L) toward coast. At 13m **Alderwood St. Pk.** (pic.) on Young Tom R. At 25m **Triangle L.** (resort), where is fine waterfall. At 67m **Florence** at J. with US101 (see).

**230. JUNCTION CITY.**

## Sec. 2: JUNCTION CITY to VANCOUVER, WASH. 114.5.

**0.5.** J. of US99E & US99W. Main tour cont. on US99E.

SIDE TRIP: Take US99W (L) along Willamette Valley. At 4.5m **Washburn St. Pk.** (pic.). 25m **Corvallis** (S.P. RR. Sta. Through buses. Accoms. all types). Corvallis (sett.1845), on Willamette & St. Mary's Rs., was formerly important stagecoach stop. For short period, St. legislature met here (1855). Today city is center of productive agricultural district & home of Ore. St. Agric. College.

PTS. OF INT.: (1) **Ore. St. Agric. College** (est.1868.coed.). This institution evolved out of Corvallis College (est.1852), became land-grant college & in 1885, St. Agric. College. Among its bldgs. (Mod.Class.for most part), noteworthy are: **Mus. Bldg.** (O.wks.Sun.aft.) with Horner Mus.; int. colls. **Armory,** great built-in stadium. **Forestry Bldg.,** with Mus. (O.wks.); coll. of N.Amer. woods. **Kidder Hall,** where loan art exhibs. are held. **Mem. Union Bldg.,** comm. war veterans; int. herbarium (O.wks.Sun.aft.). **Library** (O.wks.Sun. aft.); large book coll. incl. many rare items. **Mines Bldg.** (O.wks.); geolog. coll. **Education Hall;** Brawley coll. of mounted birds & animals. **Outdoor Stadium.** (2) 218 W. 3rd St., **H. Lewis H.** (1852.well-preserved). (3) 4th St. on Mary's R., **Corvallis City Pk.** (swim.recr.), in which are 2 mill stones brought around Horn (1856). In Corvallis is J. with US20 (see). 32m **Peavey Arboretum & McDonald For.** (1,600 as.), used as experimental area by Ore. St. Agric. College. 41.5m **Helmick St. Pk.** (ample pic. facils.) on Luckiamute R. 46m **Monmouth,** home of **Ore. College of Education** (teacher training sch.co-ed.). 52m **Rickreall,** at J. with St.22 (see below). At 71m, just before reaching McMinnville, J. with St.18.

Take St.18 (L). At 23m Valley J. with St.14 leading (R) 0.5m to **Site of Ft. Yamhill** (1856), where Lt. Phil. Sheridan was stationed. Old Blockh. was moved to Dayton (see below). 45m **Otis,** J. with US101 (see).

72m **McMinnville** (1,844'), which has been called "Walnut City," because vic. harvests nearly 2,000,000 lbs. of walnuts annually, as well as 1,000,000 lbs. of filberts. **Linfield College** (Bapt.) **Pioneer Hall** dates from 1857. 80m J. with St.221, leading (R) 1.5m to **Dayton,** here is log **Ft. Yamhill Blockh.** (see above) & several other int. early bldgs. 86m **Newburg** (sett.1869). **Pacific College** (est.1885.by Soc.of Friends), which former Pres. Herbert Hoover attended. 115 River St., **Hoover H.,** where Hoover lived with his uncle. H. has been acquired by College for Mus. 108m **Portland** (see), at J. with US99E.

From J. with US99W (see above), US99E cont. (N) through fairly flat country picturesquely broken by numerous volcanic buttes.

**31. ALBANY** (sett.1848) at confluence of Willamette R. & Calapooya Cr. City is now market town of agric. reg. whose products it ships or processes. Like many other W. Coast towns, Albany was depopulated by 1849 gold-rush. In 1850's, it turned violently anti-slavery & here Ore. Republican Party was born. Nevertheless, during Civil War, "Copperheads" (name given to Northerners who favored Southern cause) were numerous & vociferous. Albany is J. pt. for several RR's. & through bus lines & has airport. PTS. OF INT.: 518 W. 2nd St., **Montieth H.** (N.O.1848-50,remod.), built by city's first settlers, Montieth Bros. Water St., not far from Ellsworth St., **Old Steamboat Inn,** former steamboat & stagecoach stop. **Bryant Pk.** extends along Willamette & Clapooya Rs. & has auto camp & swim. pools. In Albany is J. with US20 (see).

**57. SALEM.**

RR. Sta.: 13th & Oak Sts. Bus Sta.: 228 High St. Accoms.: all types. Info.: C. of C., 147 N. Liberty St.; Ore. St. Motor Assoc., 515 Court St. Cherry Blossom Festival in Spring. St. Fair (Sept.).

From Salem, state capital (sett.1840) on Willamette R., Coast Range is seen (W) & at distance, lofty Cascade Mts. (E). Salem (Hebrew for Peace) was founded by Jason Lee. Lee came to Northwest in response to "Macedonian Call," by group of Ore. Inds. in 1828, who traveled to St. Louis to ask that missionaries be sent to instruct them about the Great White God. In 1834, Lee & some companions arrived & est. themselves among Flathead Inds. Finally, mission was moved to site of Salem, where missionaries founded Ore. Institute, later to become Willamette

Univ. Salem played part in struggle to obtain Ore. Territory for U.S. Like Albany, town lost large part of pop. to 1849 gold rush. In 1851 it became capital. In 1861, much of city was destroyed by floods of Willamette R. Since then, Salem has expanded, not only because it is state political hqs., but also because it is center of considerable agric. district & of industrial development.

PTS. OF INT.: (1) High St., **Marion County Cth.** (O.Mon.-Fri.8-5;Sat.8-1.1872). (2) Court St., **Fed. Bldg.** (O.Mon.-Fri.;Sat.8-12). (3) **State Capitol** (1937.Mod.Class. by Francis Kelly, Trowbridge & Livingston & Whitehouse & Church) replaced older bldg. destroyed by fire in 1935. On grounds, "The Circuit Rider," by A. P. Proctor, to comm. Rev. Rbt. Booth, early missionary. Bldg. is surmounted by truncated dome, on top of which is statue of "The Pioneer," by Ulric Ellerhusen. Main doors are flanked by sculptures by Leo Freedlander. Capitol's inter. is of marble & other rich materials. In rotunda are murals representing pioneer scenes by B. Faulkner & F. Swartz. Other smaller murals, on stairway walls, also by Faulkner & Swartz, depict industrial life of St. In lavishly decorated H. of Rep. Chambers is mural depicting Champoeg meeting (see below). In Senate Chamber, mural depicting Ore. admission to Statehood. Stairway leads to top of tower, whence fine view. (4) N. Winter & Court Sts., **State Lib.** (O.Mon.-Fri.;Sat.8-1.Mod.by Whitehouse & Church). Over entrance are sculptures depicting Ore. hist. events; in lobby is relief medallion; in Reference Rm. are wall sculptures, representing Ore. hist. events (all by Gabriel Lavare). Lib. contains, in Ore. Rm., important coll. of Oregonia. (5) 12th & Court Sts., **State Office Bldg.** (1914.Mod.Class.). (6) 12th & Court Sts., **Supreme Court Bldg.** (O.Mon.-Fri.;Sat.a.m.Mod.Class.). (7) Near-by is **State Agric. Bldg.**

(8) State St., **Willamette Univ.**, originally Ore. Institute, founded 1842. Among bldgs. are **Waller Hall** (1864-67); **Lib.** (O.Georg.), with int. coll. of hist. records; **Gymnasium,** in which is Univ. Mus. (O) with variety of int. colls. (9) 960 Broadway, **Home of Jason Lee** (c.1840). (10) Highland Ave. & Hazel St., **Herbert Hoover's Boyhood Home.** (11) 25th St., **Jason Lee Cemetery,** where Jason Lee & family are buried. (12) State & 24th Sts., **St. Forestry Bldg.** In inter., Amer. wood varieties are used in skillful & int. manner. (13) S. Commercial & Hoyt Sts., **Cemetery,** with pioneer graves.

Salem is at J. with St.222, crossing Cascades to J. with US97 (see).

SIDE TRIPS: (A) Take St.22 (L) from Salem. At 4$^m$, **Holman St. Pk.** (pic.) on pleasant stream. 14.5$^m$ **Dallas.**

(1) Take Ellendale Rd. (L) from Dallas 0.5$^m$ to old **Lyle H.** (1858).

(2) Take St.223 (L) from Dallas 11.5$^m$ to **Lewisville. Hart Cemetery** with grave of Jas. A. O'Neal, who played prominent part in fight to keep Ore. territory for U.S. At 22.5$^m$, **Chambers Grist Mill** (1853), driven by Luckiamute R. Some of orig. machinery still functioning.

29.5$^m$ J. of St.22 with St.18 (see above), leading to Otis J. with US101 (see).

(B) Take St.211 (R) from Salem to **Silverton,** 15$^m$, at J. with St.214.

Take St.214 (R) to **Silver Cr. Falls St. Pk.** (1,824 as.) on Silver Cr. (pic. concession bldg.) at 15.5$^m$. In pk. are some 10 waterfalls.

Cont. (NE) on St.211 to J. with St.215 at 29$^m$, on which route cont. (straight ahead).

Turn (R) on St.211 2$^m$ to **Molalla,** where July 3-4-5 is held widely attended rodeo. Turn (L) from J. (above) on St.215 to **Ore. City** (see below), 45$^m$, at J. with US99E.

From Salem US99E cont. to J. at **62.5** with Rd. leading (L) c. 1.5$^m$ to **Chemawa Ind. School,** where Ind. youths from various states receive education. **71.** J. with Champoeg St. Pk. Hy.

SIDE TRIP: Take latter (L) to **St. Louis** at 3$^m$. In cemetery is grave of Marie Dorion, wife of Ind. guide of Hunt's expedition, financed by Astor, which went overland to meet party that came by sea on "Tonquin" to Astoria (see US101). At 4$^m$ J. with St.219, which route follows (R). At 16.5$^m$ turn (R) on Rd. to Champoeg Mem. Pk. Lane, 18.5$^m$. Take latter short distance to entrance of **Champoeg Mem. St. Pk.** (1,106 as.), which incl. reg. of first settlement in valley by Jason Lee's Mission (see Salem above). Near entrance is small Mus. of hist. relics. Here also is stone **shaft** on spot where independent provisional regime for Ore. territory was set up 1843. Names of men who voted on this occasion to found new gov. are inscribed on shaft. New gov. was est. by Amers. in opposition to Hudson's Bay Co., which claimed entire Ore. territory for Britain.

**71.5 SAM BROWN H.** (c.1850), former stagecoach stop. **82.5. AURORA,** sett. mid. 19th cent. by Germans from Germany & Pa., under leadership of Dr. Wm. Keil, as communistic community, similar to many that sprang up in U.S. Everything was owned in common by settlers. With death of Dr. Keil (1877), colony disintegrated & land & homes fell into individual ownership. The village is in center of great hop-growing reg. & when hops are ripe, thousands of pickers flood valley. Still standing are 4 of orig. structures: **Will Kraus H.** (now occupied by Amer. Legion), **Emmanuel Keil H., Fred Keil H.** & **Geisey Store** (now butcher shop). In vic. are many of orig. farm houses & bldgs.

**95. OREGON CITY**

Through RR. & bus conns. Accoms. limited. **Info.:** C.of C., Hogg Bldg., 8th & Main Sts. & A.A.A.

Oregon City (sett.1829-30) on Willamette R., whose falls (42′ drop) here generate electric power, is near pt. where Clackamas R. flows into Willamette. Clackamas Inds. had Long House near mouth of Clackamas. First settlement was under jurisdiction of Hudson's Bay Co., of which Dr. John McLoughlin was redoubtable Chief Factor. As immigrants from E. arrived, there ensued sharp conflict bet. the Co. & Amers. In 1844, legislature of provisional gov. set up by Amers. met in hall over granary of Meth. Ch. In 1849, city was designated capital of Ore. Territory & cont. as seat of gov. till 1852. Edwin Markham, poet who won fame with his "The Man With the Hoe," was born in Ore. City (1852). Most of town's varied industries are powered by electricity generated at Falls.

PTS. OF INT.: (1) 10th & Water Sts., **St. John's Ch.** (Cath.), in which Dr. McLoughlin & his wife are buried. (2) 7th & Center Sts., **McLoughlin Pk.,** in which is (3) old **McLoughlin H.** (O.1845-46.rest.), removed here from orig. site. Also in pk. & also removed from orig. site is (4) **Barclay H.** (1846.Cape Cod style), built by Dr. Forbes Barclay, who was surgeon at Ft. Vancouver. Following sites marked by plaques: (5) 6th & Main Sts., **Site of First Capitol** of Ore. Territory. (6) Main & 7th Sts., **Site of First Prot. Ch.** (7) Bet. 2nd & 3rd Sts., on Main St., **Site of McLoughlin H.** (8) Near Water & 5th Sts., **Site of Old Mint** (1849), which handled gold brought in after Cal. gold rush. (9) On Willamette R., where Hawley Pulp & Paper Plant (O.appl.) now stands, **Site of First Home of Ore. Spectator** (est.1846), allegedly first paper in NW. (10) Bet. 5th & 6th Sts., on Water St., empty lot, is unmarked site of **Edwin Markham's Birthpl.** (11) 1115 Washington St., **Albion Post (Cochran) H.** (1852.Cape Cod style). (12) End of S. 2nd St., view of **Willamette Falls** (much depleted because of power installations); bet. Apr. & July, lamprey eels come up R. to this pt. (13) On Hilda St., **Mountain View Cemetery.** Here Dr. Barclay & Peter Skene Ogden, who led Hudson's Bay Co.'s fur-collecting expeditions, are buried.

SIDE TRIP: Alternate route from Ore. City to Portland on W. side of Willamette parallels US99E, which runs along E. bank. This route passes lovely **Oswego L.** at 6.5$^m$ from Ore. City.

**96.5. JOHN McLOUGHLIN BRIDGE,** named for famous Hudson's Bay Co. factor, which crosses Clackamas R. Just (N) beyond bridge is **GLADSTONE,** at J. with Clackamas R. Rd. leading (R) 3$^m$ to **Pow-Wow Tree,** giant maple already age-old when first settlers arrived. **101.5. MILWAUKIE,** known as "Cradle of West Coast Fruit Industry." Henderson Luelling brought first fruit trees from Iowa in 1874 & est. nursery here. He & associates developed some fine new varieties of cherries. **107. PORTLAND** (see). In Portland are Js. with St.50, Mt. Hood Hy. (see Mt. Hood Area); St.6 & St.2, conn. with US101 (see) on Pacific coast; & US30 (see), following Columbia R. Gorge.

US99 cont. (N) across Columbia R., **114.5.,** which forms Wash. Line, to **VANCOUVER, WASH.**

## US 97—OREGON

**ORE.-CAL. LINE** (57.5$^m$ from Weed, Cal.) **(N) to ORE.-WASH. LINE** (1$^m$ from Maryhill, Wash.). **305. US97**

Via: Klamath Falls, Bend, Biggs. S.P. RR. parallels route bet. Cal. Line & J. with St.58; Gt. No. RR. bet. Klamath Falls & Redmond; U.P. RR. bet. Bend & Biggs. Accoms. in towns, elsewhere limited

This route cuts (N) across Ore. along E. edge of snow-capped Cascade Range, with easy access to some of most int. scenery of state, incl. Crater L. Nat. Pk. & Mt. Hood. In its (S) sec. it traverses high, often semi-arid plateau, devoted for most part to sheep raising, although considerable areas are irrigated. In its S. middle sec., bet. J. with St.58 & Bend, it traverses region of craters & lava fields of great geologic & scenic int. In its N. sec. it passes through more fertile countryside of cattle ranches & wheatfields.

### Sec. 1: ORE. LINE to BEND. 161.

Almost immediately after it crosses Ore. Line, US97 cuts through **KLAMATH L. BIRD RESERV.**, in bed of what was formerly lower Klamath L., which dried up when its waters were shut off by Klamath Basin Irrig. Proj.

**17. KLAMATH FALLS** (sett.1866).

RR. Stas.: Park & Springs Sts. for S.P. RR.; 1340 S. 6th St. for Gt. No. RR. Info.: 323 Main St., C.of C. & Ore. St. Motor Assoc. Swim.: Hot Springs Natatorium & New Klamath Natatorium (fees). July 4th weekend, Buckaroo Days celebration, with rodeo.

Klamath Falls is located on Link R. & S. end of Upper Klamath & Ewauna Ls. Early development of Klamath Basin was retarded because of Ind. hostilities. First settler, Wendolin Nus, was killed during Modoc War. George Nus est. first ferry across Link R. (1867). As late as 1872, inhabitants of new settlement were terrorized by Inds. With ending of these troubles, city began its real growth. But boom did not come until construction of Klamath Irrigation Proj., which brought valley into rich production, & arrival of RR's. Main industry is processing of lumber, brought in from forested hinterland. Klamath Falls is also shipping center for agric. products of irrigated Klamath Basin. White pelicans & other birds, migrating by thousands in summer to near-by Ls. & Link R., are one of sights of town. Geese congregate here in great numbers. There is good bird h., as well as deer h., in vic. Some hot mineral springs in city feed 2 swimming pools & heat homes. In city are Weyerhaeuser Timber Co. & other large lumber & wood-processing plants (worth visiting).

SIDE TRIPS: (A) Take St.66 (R) from Klamath Falls. At 5m, J. with St.39.

(R) on latter to **Merrill,** at 14m. From here access to Ore. entrance of **Lava Beds Nat. Mon.** (see Cal.,US395).

St.66 cont. (E) to **Bly Mt.** (5,087′) at 30.5m. 40.5.m **Beatty.** 53.5m **Bly,** on Sprague R. St.66 now crosses tip of **Mule Deer Reserv.** & traverses Drew's Canyon. 85.5m **Booth St. Pk.** (pic.), in Antelope Cr. Canyon. 97m **Lakeview,** at J. with US395 (see).

(B) Take St.236 (L) from Klamath Falls along Upper Klamath L., to J. at 25.5m.

Take Rd. (R) here 3m, to **Rocky Pt.** (4,153′.resort) on Upper L. (accoms.recr.wild duck & goose h.). White pelicans numerous, but protected.

At 34m on St.236, entrance to **L. O' the Woods Recr. Area.** Here is J. with Dead Indian Rd.

Take Dead Indian Rd. (L) 1.5m to beautiful **L. O' the Woods,** on which are 5 for. camps. View of **Mt. McLoughlin** (8,493′), which can be climbed from this pt.

St.236 cont. to **Forest Guard Summer Hqs.** at 36m & beautiful **Fish L.,** within view of Mt. McLoughlin, at 42m (resort.recr.). Here is **Fish L. For. Camp** (4,670′). Beyond Fish L. Rd. turns (S) past **Dead Indian Soda Springs For. Camp** (trlers.community kitchen) to **J.** with St.62 (Crater L. Hy. see below), at Eagle Pt.

**46. AGENCY L.,** arm of upper Klamath L. In 1846 Capt. John C. Frémont's company was attacked here by Inds. His forces later wiped out Ind. village in retaliation.

**49. KLAMATH IND. AGENCY** for Klamath Ind. Reserv. (1,000,000 as.), set aside by treaty (1864) for Klamath, Modoc & Yahooskin Snake Inds. It is larger than R.I. & contains extensive grazing lands & great forests. From lumber cut, alone, each Ind. receives about $400 per annum. Inds. living on reserv. have their own tribal organization. Take Rd. (R) from Agency, 5m to **Chiloquin,** Ind. village.

**54. SITE OF OLD FT. KLAMATH** (L), where are buried 4 Inds., incl. Capt. Jack, who were hanged during Modoc War for killing Gen. Canby & two associates coming with flag of truce to negotiate peace. Just (N) beyond Ft. Klamath Site, on US97, is J. with St.62 (Crater L. Hy.).

SIDE TRIP: Take St.62 (L). At 1m **Ft. Klamath** (accoms.skiing). 6m **Ft. Klamath Pic. Grounds.** 7m **Wildcat For. Camp** at (S) boundary of **Crater L. Nat. Pk.** 18m **Annie Spring Camp** (registration for autos.fee $1.) at J. with St.209 (see Pk.Tour below).

**CRATER LAKE NATIONAL PARK.**

Best season: July 1 to Sept. 20. Bus, July 1 to Sept. 19, from Grants Pass (see US99) & Klamath Falls (see US99) to Rim Village. Accoms: Near Rim Village, Crater Lodge (European & Amer.plan & cabins.); in Rim Village are cafeteria & store facils.; 4 free camp grounds. Guide Service (free) by Pk. naturalists. Boat Trips daily to Crater L. Info. Bldg. (W) of Crater L. Lodge. Fishing: 12 fish per day per person; tackle can be purchased in village. No hunting. Tourists who intend to camp should bring camping outfits & blankets, since nights are cold even in summer. Pk. is also frequented by winter sports enthusiasts.

**Crater L.** 6m wide & 1996′ deep, is set in lofty crater of prehist. Mt. Mazama, which before its eruptions probably attained alt. of 14,000′. Basin, filled by L., resulted, scientists say, from mt.'s collapse & subsidence after eruptions. This strange body of water has no inlets & apparently no outlets. There are 2 Is., both of volcanic origin: Phantom Ship & Wizard. When first discovered by white men in 1853, there were no fish in L.; since then trout have been planted by Gov. Crater L., with its weird island craters, surrounded by precipitous, snow-capped peaks beautifully reflected in its brilliant blue waters, is one of Nation's scenic wonders, ranking with Grand Canyons of Colorado & Snake Rs. Pk. is full of game which, because hunting is forbidden, is fairly tame. Its valleys & slopes are clothed with magnificent forests & its meadows & marshes are rich in flowering plants. Inds. believe that Gods lived on mt. heights & in L.'s deep waters, which latter, they imagined to have special, purifying properties.

PARK TOUR: Take St.209 (R) from J. with St.62 (see above) 6m to **Rim Village** on L. Near-by are **Crater Lodge & Pub. Campground.** (1) Here take trl. (L) from Village to **Sinnott Mem.**, comm. Congressman Sinnott who devoted his energies to development of Pk. From here are to be seen **Wizard I.** (80′deep crater), rising 763′ above L.'s level, & **Phantom Ship I.** (2) From Rim Village take scenically impressive Crater Wall Trail. (R), narrow path above L., to shore, c.1.5m (3) Take trl. (R) from Rim Village 1.5m to **Garfield Peak** (8,000′) with magnificent view. (4) Take trl. (L) from Rim Village 0.5m to **Lady of the Woods,** sculptured image.

From Rim Village starts Rim Dr. (open all yr.), through magnificent scenery, returning to Rim Village at 39m. Along this route, ranger conducts daily excursion which automobile parties may join.

Take Dr. (S) from Village. 4.5m trl. leads (L) to **Wildflower Garden.** 7m **Vidoe Falls.** 12m **Lost Cr. Campground,** at J. with St.232, conn. with US97 (see below). At 20m J. with trl. leading 2.5m to **Mt. Scott** (8,938′) on which is lookout tower. 20.5m **Cloudcap Viewpoint** (8,070′), 1000′ above E. Rim. At 27.5m **Mazama Rock.** 29m **Pumice Pt.** (fine view). 33m J. with St.209 which runs (N) to J. at 9m with St.230, conn. with US97 (see below). 33.5m **Llao Rock** (8,046′), scene of legendary conflict bet. Ind. gods, Llao & Skele, which destroyed La-o-Yaina (Ind.name for prehist.Mt.Mazama). 34m J. with trl. leading (L) short distance to **Devil's Backbone.** 34.5m **The Watchman** (fine view), 2,020′ above L. 36.5m **Discovery Pt.,** first viewed in 1853. 38m fine outlook & view. 39m Rim Village.

From J. with St.209 (see above), St.62 cont. (W). 28m J. with Huckleberry For. Rd. leading (L) to **Huckleberry For. Camp.** (5,200′.trlers.). 34.5m **Farewell Bend For. Camp** (R) (trlers.) 35m Fine **Rogue R. Gorge.** 35.5m **Union Cr. For. Camp** (R) (trlers.community kitchen). 35.5m J. with Natural Bridge Rd. leading (R) to **Natural Bridge** (scenically int.). **Natural Bridge For. Camp** (trlrs.). 40.5m **Mammoth Sugar Pine,** 250′ high, said to be more than 500 yrs. old. 46.5m **Prospect.** 47.5m Beautiful **Miller Falls.** St.62 now follows Rogue R., through resort region. 50.5m **Wildwood For. Camp,** at Cascade Gorge. At 62m, **Casey's Camp.** Near here is **Casey St. Pk.** (caretaker,pic.) on Rogue R. At 92.5m **Medford** at J. with US99 (see).

**62.5. SUN PASS** at top of Sand Mt.

At **65.** on US97 J. with St.232 which runs (L) past **Pinnacles** of Sand Canyon to J. with Rim Drive in Crater L. Nat. Pk. (see above). **85.** J. with St.230.

SIDE TRIP: Take latter (L) to J. at 16m with St.209.

Turn (L) here on St.209 9m to J. with Rim Dr. in Crater L. Nat. Pk. (see above). Turn (R) from this J. on St.209 4m to **Diamond L.** (5,186′.resort.accoms.), one of most beautiful in Ore. Cascades. Mt. Bailey (8,363′) is seen (W) & Mt. Thielsen (9,173′) (E). St.209 skirts shore (E). Here are 10 for. camps (trlers., boat.bath.horses.Info.at For. Ranger Sta.).

US97 now crosses into Deschutes Nat. For. **95. CHEMULT,** dominated by **Walker Mt.** (7,000′), Chemult bears name of Ind. leader who signed 1864 treaty. Winter sports here; ski course (W) beyond town. **103.** J. with St.58.

SIDE TRIP: Take latter (L) to J. at 15.5m with unimproved Rd. leading (L) c.2m to **Crescent L.** (resort.accoms.), from which fine view of Diamond Peak (8,750′). Rds. circle L. There are 3 for. camps (trlrs.boat.bath.horses).

St.58 cont. to J. at 18.5m with side Rd. leading (R) 6m to **Davis L.** (4,389′) where is for. camp (trlers.boat.). Short distance beyond last J., St.58 makes J. with another Rd. leading (L) 0.5m to **Odell L.** (4,792′.accoms.). There are 4 for. camps on L. (Trlers.boat. horses.) On all sides rise mt. peaks. Trls. radiate to various pts. of scenic int.

At 24m on St.58 is E. boundary of Willamette Nat. For. At 41m **McCredie Springs** (resort. accoms.mineral springs.RR.conn.). 50.5m J. with improved Rd. leading (R) to **Oakridge,** supply pt. (accoms.). Dirt Rd. leads (N) to several for. camps. As St.58 cont. (NW), it passes several for. camps in Willamette Nat. For. 87m **Goshen** at J. with US99 (see).

At **132.5.** on US97 is J. with Century Dr.

SIDE TRIP: Take latter (L) into Deschutes Nat. For. Side Rds. lead at intervals to for. camps. At 26.5m is **Big Lava L.**, with for. camp. 31m **Elk L.** (resort.accoms.), with 3 for. camps (trlers.at 2 of these.boats & horses available near-by). Century Dr. now passes through broken lava terrain, one of whose features is great lava cliff. Obsidian rock from this reg. was sought by Inds. far & wide for arrowheads. At 37m **Devil's L.** (4,389′) & just beyond, **Devil's Chair,** on which are Ind. pictographs. Near-by, on main hy., **Devil's Garden,** with for. camp (trlrs.swim.). At 38m **Sparks L.,** whence trl. runs (N) to **Green Ls.** Century Dr. cont. to J. with US97 at **Bend** (see below).

At **136.5.** on US97 is J. with unimproved Rd.

SIDE TRIP: Take latter (R). At 11m, beautiful **Paulina Falls.** Short distance farther is **Paulina L.** (6,331′.accoms.boats.recr.) in **Newberry Crater,** created by eruption of prehist. mt. whose peak is believed to have risen to alt. of over 20,000′. There are hot & cold mineral springs in vic. Dominating skyline (S) is **Paulina Peak** (7,985′), named for Chief Paulina, who had his hideout here when fighting white men. At (W) end of Paulina L. is For. Camp (6,331′.trlrs.boat.). At 14.5m on side Rd., is tiny **Lost L.,** also in crater, but hidden (R) from Rd. At 16m **East L.** (accoms.camp.), with 2 for. camps (6,387′.trlers.). At 23m J. with unimproved Rd., on which route cont. (L) to second J. at 36m. Turn (L) here to J. at 5m with Rd. leading (L) 3m to **Arnold Ice Cave.** Main Side Rd. cont. to J. with US20 (see) at 40m.

At **146.5.** US97 makes J. with Rd. leading (R) 9m to **Lava Cast For.,** on slope of Newberry Crater, where is prehist. for. buried by lava flow. Across lava field is **Mus.** (O). **148.** (R) **LAVA R. CAVES ST. PK.** (O.summer.caretaker.), in which is one-mile tunnel gouged out by lava stream. **147.** J. with Rd. leading (R) 0.5m to **Lava Butte** (5,026′), deep crater. Skiing slope. **161. BEND,** on Deschutes R. with RR. conns., looks toward Cascade Range, whose most prominent features here are Three Sisters Peaks (W) & Pilot Butte (E). Town owes development to large irrigation proj., watering 300,000 as. of land, & to great timber resources of near-by mts. Mt. reg. around city is mecca for vacationists. 231 Franklin Ave., **Home of Klondike Kate,** legendary heroine of Alaska gold rush era. Both **Shevlin-Hixon & Brooks-Scanlon Lumber Mills** (O.wks.) afford opportunity to observe modern, large-scale lumber-handling operations. On (E) side of city is **Terrence H. Foley Pk.** In Bend is J. with US20 (see).

## Sec. 2: BEND to WASH. LINE. 144.

**16.5. REDMOND,** in irrigated farm & cattle region, at J. with US28, conn. with US395 (see).

SIDE TRIP: Take US28 (L) across Cascade Range. At 19.5m, J. with US20, with which US28 unites to **Sisters** (see US20) at 20m. At 32m **Windy Pt.,** from which trl. leads (L) to **Black Crater** (7260′.fine view). At 34.5m is J. with unimproved Rd., leading (L) 1m to **Lava Camp L. For. Camp.** At 15m **McKenzie Pass** (5,325′), in center of reg. of prehist. volcanic eruptions. To (N) is **Belknap Crater** (6,877′). Nat. For. Service maintains at this pt. **Dee Wright Observatory** (fine views).
37m J. with For. Rd. leading (L) 1m to **Huckleberry For. Camp** (trlers.) At 37.5m is **W. Lava For. Camp.** At 41m J. with dirt Rd. leading (R) 1m to beautiful **Scott L. & For. Camp** (trlers.boat.). US28 reaches at 47m **Alder Springs For. Camp** (trlers.shelter.pic.mt. trips). Trl. runs here (L) 1m to **Linton L.,** where are fine falls. 49m Scenic **White Branch Canyon.** At 50.5m, **White Branch Winter Sports Area** (shelter). At 53.5m **Lost Cr. Ranch** (supplies). 55.5m **Limberlost For. Camp** (trlrs.). 57.5m **Paradise For. Camp** (trlrs.). 62m **McKenzie Bridge,** resort in hiking & winter sports area (info.at Ranger Sta.hotel.store. cabins.guides.horses.), beside McKenzie R., famed f. stream. Several for. Camps in vic. Horse Creek Rd. leads (L) to **Horse Cr. For. Camp** (trlers.shelter.h.f.) at 1m & **Foley Hot Springs** (resort), at 4m. 65.5m J. with Box Canyon Rd.

Take latter (summer only) here (L) through int. scenery along S. Fork of McKenzie R. & then Roaring R., then through Box Canyon & then (SW), paralleling N. Middle Fork of McKenzie R., to **Oakridge** at J. with St.58 (see above) at 61m. Along this Rd. are 10 well-equipped for. camps.

72m **Blue R. Ranch** (accoms.guides.horses). 92m J. with US99 (see) at **Goshen.**

At **21.** on US97 is J. with good Rd.

SIDE TRIP: Take latter (W) here 6m to **Lower Bridge** & then (N) to beautiful **Steelhead Falls** of Deschutes R. at 11m.

At **25.5. OGDEN ST. PK.**, at pt. where US97 crosses bridge high over deep gorge of Crooked R. Pk. comm. Peter Skene Ogden, leader of Hudson's Bay Co.'s fur-trapping expeditions. At **29.5.** J. with Rd. leading (R) 1$^{m}$ **Opal Springs,** which lie at bottom of deep Crooked R. gorge, reached only by trl. Non-precious opals are found in vic. **35. CULVER,** at J. with unimproved Rd.

SIDE TRIP: Take latter (L) 5$^{m}$ to **The Cove,** at confluence of Deschutes & Crooked Rs., in **Cove Palisades Pk.** Canyon at this point is c.1000′ deep. In forks of these Rs. is **The Island,** mighty basalt rock, 2$^{m}$ long, rising 600′ above stream level. Beyond is **The Peninsula,** scenically fine volcanic formation. In pk. also is magnificent gorge near confluence of Metolius & Deschutes Rs. In (NE) part of pk. is **Round Butte** (3,290′). At (W) end of bridge over Deschutes R. are pic. & camp. facils. (info.caretaker) & from there trl. leads down stream.

**44. MADRAS,** in region rich in minerals, esp. agates. **72. COW CANYON J.** with St.50 (Mt. Hood Hy.), giving access to Mt. Hood Area (see). **84. SHANIKO,** today center for stock-raising & grain-growing area, in old days hub of conflict bet. cattle & sheep ranchers. US97 cont. (N) &, towards its terminus, begins descent through impressive Spanish Hollow Canyon to Columbia R. Gorge. **140. BIGGS.** on Columbia R. where US97 unites with US30 (see). At **144.** Ferry (day&night.autos), across Columbia R., which forms Wash. Line, to **Maryhill, Wash.**

## US 395—OREGON

**ORE.-WASH. LINE** (23$^{m}$ from Pasco, Wash.) **(S) to ORE.-CAL. LINE** (43$^{m}$ from Alturas, Cal.). **394. US395**

Via: Pendleton, Canyon City, Burns, Valley Falls, Lakeview. N.P. & U.P. RR. conns. at Pendleton; Nev. Cal. Ore. RR. conn. at Lakeview. Good Rd. most of way; not always passable in winter. Accoms. in cities; otherwise limited & at long intervals.

US395, running (S) through E. Central Ore., climbs from Columbia R. to more than 5,000′ bet. Blue & Wallowa Mts., through wheat-growing area & farther (S) through country of great cattle ranges, alternating with arid stretches. It skirts Umatilla Ind. Reserv. & Umatilla, Whitman, Ochoco & Frémont Nat. Fors.

### Sec. 1: WASH. LINE to BURNS. 240.

For 10$^{m}$ US395 follows S. Bank of Columbia R., then strikes (SE). **42. PENDLETON,** at J. with US30 (see). **46.5. MCKAY L. RESERVOIR,** impounded by dam, is used for irrig. (recr.bird refuge). **78. BATTLE MT. ST. PK.** (4,710′ recr.), comm. Battle of Wallowa Springs, 1878, in which Fed. troops defeated band of Paiute Inds. Near-by, Battle Mt. (5,080′). Hy. now skirts Blue Mts. (E). **103. WHITMAN NAT. FOR. CAMP** at N. Fork of John Day R. **139. BEACH CR. FOR. CAMP** (4,500′). **161. MT. VERNON,** ranchers' center, at J. with US28.

SIDE TRIP: Take US28 (R) 28.5$^{m}$ to beautiful **Picture Gorge** through which John Day R. flows. Pre-historic pictographs. 30$^{m}$ J. with St.19.

Take St.19 (R) along canyon of John Day R. past **Sheep Rock** (3,356′), rising 1,250′ above hy., & **Turtle Cove Mt.,** in which have been found many fossilized remains of pre-historic life. At 6$^{m}$ are **John Day Fossil Beds,** where extensive finds of fossils of pre-historic plants & animals have been made. 7.5$^{m}$ **Johnny Kirk Springs** (pic.), in one of richest fossil-bearing regs. in U.S. Canyon of John Day R. (N) is fantastically eroded. Hy. affords fine view of **Cathedral,** int. geologic formation. 12.5$^{m}$. View of **Pipe Organs,** int. stratified formation. 18.5$^{m}$ **Kimberly** (tourist facils.). 54$^{m}$ **Shelton St. Pk.** (pic.) near brook. 76$^{m}$ **Dyer St. Pk.** (pic.). 82.5$^{m}$ **Condon,** wheat growers' center. 124$^{m}$ J. with US30 (see).

US28 now runs along Rock Cr. & makes steep ascent through narrow canyon. 58.5$^{m}$ **Mon. to H. H. Wheeler,** wounded during attack by Inds. at Burnt Ranch, in this reg. 62.5$^{m}$ **Mitchel,** which was twice (1884 & 1904) wrecked by floods. US28 passes beautifully colored Painted Hills & shortly cliffs of **Courth. Rock** at 77$^{m}$. Hy. now enters Ochoco Nat. For. & passes several For. Camps. 105.5$^{m}$ J. with Rd. leading (R) 8$^{m}$ to Stein's Pillar (350′). 115$^{m}$ **Prineville** (2,865′) in center of agric. & ranching reg. In vic. occurred violent conflicts bet. sheep & cattle ranchers. US28 now crosses Crooked R. with views of deep canyon. 116.5$^{m}$ **Ochoco St. Pk.** (no facils.); fine view. 134$^{m}$ **Redmond** at J. with US97 (see).

At Mt. Vernon (see above) US395 turns (E).

**169. JOHN DAY,** at pt. where Canyon Cr. & John Day R. join, formerly was mining & cattle town, named for John Day of Astoria expedition. Town was once stopover for pony express riders bet. Canyon City & The Dalles, who made trip on one occasion in remarkable time of 28 hrs. Later, stagecoach lines followed same route. From John Day US395 cont. (S). **171. CANYON CITY,** once center of gold rush on near-by Whiskey Flat. In June, "Whiskey Gulch & Grand City Pioneer Assoc." celebration. In village is **Joaquin Miller Cabin** (O.appl.at Cth.), where poet's family settled, 1864. Above Canyon Cr. is **Cemetery** where disturbers of peace were buried in the old days. **175. CANYON CR. GAME REFUGE** (h. only with bow & arrow), one of few archers' preserves in U.S. **179. JOAQUIN MILLER RESORT** (accoms.). **186. STARR FOR. CAMP** (5,159′) at summit of this sec. of route. **220.5. JOAQUIN MILLER FOR. CAMP** (4,500′.trlrs.f.). **222.5. IDLEWILD FOR. CAMP** (5,000′.community kitchen). **224.** Scenically int. **DEVINE CANYON,** where is **Mon. to John Devine,** pioneer cattle-king. **238.** J. with US20 (see), with which US395 units for 29$^{m}$. **240. BURNS** (see US20).

**Sec. 2: BURNS to CAL. LINE. 154.**

**27.** J. with US20 (see), which branches off (W). **56.** Route passes **WAGONTIRE MT.** (6,500′). **102. ALBERT RIM** along Albert L. (some seasons completely dry). At times this strange rock formation rises sheer 2,000′ above valley. **123. CHANDLER ST. PK.** (pic.no overnight camp.), on Crooked R. at foot of Albert Rim. Cliffs here rise vertically 600-800′. **135.5.** J. with Warner Cr. Rd.

SIDE TRIP: Take latter (L) 28.5$^{m}$ to **Adel** & then (L) past Pelican & Crump Ls. to **Plush,** at 46.5$^{m}$. Take Rd. (R) from Plush past Flagstaff L., into **Hart Mt. Antelope Refuge** (200,000 as.several for.camps), at 67$^{m}$. Pronged antelope (limited h.season) abound, as well as mule deer & other game. **Hart Mt.** (8,020′) & other high peaks in vic.

**140. LAKEVIEW,** center of sheep & cattle range & farm country, at J. with St.66, conn. with US97 (see). Hqs. for Frémont Nat. For., 1st explored by Frémont, 1843. Beyond city (S) is **Goose L.** Three-day rodeo is held here over Labor Day. During Ind. fighting an Amer. force was ambushed in vic. of Lakeview. Later, range became battleground bet. cattle & sheep ranchers. Lakeview country affords good f. & h., incl. season for pronghorned antelope. Winter-sports area is being developed at head of Warner Canyon, 9$^{m}$ distant. Many ancient arrow-heads, of black obsidian & finest workmanship are found in dry L. bottoms; in Warner Valley are immense boulders on which are pre-historic pictographs. **154. CAL. LINE.**

## US 30—OREGON

**ORE.-IDAHO LINE (**64.5$^{m}$ from Boise, Idaho) **(NW) to ASTORIA, ORE. 512. US30**

Via: Ontario, Baker, Union, La Grande, Pendleton, Biggs, The Dalles, Hood River, Cascade Locks, Bonneville, Portland, St. Helens, Rainier. U.P. RR. parellels route to Portland; S.P. RR., bet. Portland & Astoria. Accoms. all types; camping facils. This route is known as Columbia R. Hy., because it follows course of Columbia R.

US30 follows, roughly, route of Lewis & Clark Expedition, which later became Ore. Trl., one of main hys. for settlers coming from East, although both these explorers & later travelers proceeded by boat when they reached Columbia R. itself. US30 is one of finest hys., scenically, of Pacific Coast region. From Ore. Line it runs (NW) through beautiful Whitman & Umatilla Nat. For. regions, making J. with Rds. that branch off to scenically magnificent Joseph Cr. Canyon, Wallowa L. & Grand Canyon of Snake R. (deeper than Grand Canyon of Colorado) & Blue & Wallowa Mts. regions.

Beyond Pendleton, US30 reaches Columbia R. & for c.300$^{m}$ follows R. gorge. Panoramic views of deep cleft carved out of Columbia plateau in prehist. times & lofty waterfalls plunging from canyons of tributary streams mark route at frequent intervals. As hy. proceeds (W), Mt. Adams & Mt. St. Helens loom into view (N), & Mt. Hood (S). To these natural wonders must be added man-made marvel of Bonneville Dam, which creates 40-mile L. in Columbia R., reaching from Bonneville (E) beyond The Dalles. This installation has made R. navigable for deep-draft vessels to The Dalles.

Tourists arriving at Portland who wish merely to follow Columbia R.'s course, may take US30 (E) from Portland & then cross R. at Biggs & return via US830 in Washington along (N) bank to Vancouver, Wash., whence bridge will take them back to Portland.

## Sec. 1: ORE. LINE to PENDLETON. 188.

US30 crosses Snake R., which forms Idaho Line, to **ONTARIO** (2,153′) at **1.5.** in heart of Owyhee & Malheur Projects, irrigating some 300,000 as. At **17.** J. with US30 (N).

**30.5. OLDS FERRY,** crossing of Snake R. on Old Ore. Trl. Here is marker. **35.5.** Boundary of Rocky Mt. & Pacific Standard Time Zones.

**82. BAKER** (sett.1863.alt.3,440′).

RR. & bus conns. Accoms. all types. Hqs. of Whitman Nat. For. Info.: C. of C., Baker Hotel on Main St.

This prosperous little city, on Powder R., now industrial center processing various products of farm regions & of ponderosa pine from near-by forests, was formerly typical boom mining town, with traditional gambling, brawling, easy gun-play, & "red light" adjuncts. Vic. of Baker is still rich in minerals (Baker Cty. produces 58% of Oregon's gold yield). Campbell & Grove Sts., Baker **Mun. Natatorium** (O.wks.fee.warm mineral springs). 2001 Main St., **Gold Exhibit** (O.wks.), in First Nat. Bank Bldg.

SIDE TRIP: Take St.86 (R), only direct Ore. approach to Grand Canyon of Snake R. (see Idaho). At 2m is J. with St.203.

Turn (L) 22m on St.203, to **Medical Springs.** Here is **Oxbow Guest Ranch** (natural hot springs.pool.pack trips into Wallowa Mt.region).

20.5m J. with dirt Rd.

Take latter (L) 12m to **Sparta,** old mining town. (N) of Sparta is **Eagle Cr. For. Camp.**

At 46m **Richland** (supplies for trips into Wallowa country). At 52.5m route turns (R) at fork on unnamed Rd.

Cont. on St.86 (L) & on unimproved Rds. to **Cornucopia** (4,800′) at 11m, near which is one of richest gold mines in Ore.

56.5m **Robinette,** on Snake R., which route now follows (N). At 82m **Homestead** (1,675′) on Snake R. near copper mines. At 85m hy. crosses **Snake R.** at (S) end of **"Hell's Canyon,"** becoming Idaho St.45.

Take Rd. here (N) along (E) side of Snake R. to **Eagle's Bar,** at (S) end of most spectacular part of Snake R. Canyon.

Idaho St.45 (see above), known as Kleinsmith Grade Rd. (very steep), runs (NE) to **Cuprum** (see Idaho) at 92m.

US30 cont. from Baker at high alt., passing Elkhorn Range whose peaks rise bet. 8,000′ & 9,000′. After crossing N. Powder R., hy. reaches **N. POWDER** (rodeo held here), **101.** at J. with Rd.

SIDE TRIP: Take Rd. (W) from US30 into Whitman Nat. For. & along Powder R., climbing into Blue Mts. At 21m **Anthony L.** (7,100′.accoms.all types.f.boat.for.ranger hqs. for.camps.playground.winter sports). Trls. lead to near-by Black, Mud, & Grande Ronde Ls.

Beyond N. Powder, US30 crosses divide into fertile Grande Ronde Valley. **117. UNION** (sett.1860). **E. Ore. St. Experimental Sta.** for agric. research. **122.5. HOT L.** (2,701′) whose waters, with boiling-pt. temperature, are supposed to have medicinal properties. **131.5. LA GRANDE** (2,744′) on Grande Ronde R., with Blue Mts. to (W) & Wallowa Range to (E).

Accoms. all types. RR. & bus conns. Info.: La Grande C.of C., New Foley Bldg.

City is center for considerable agric. & lumber district, & starting pt. for tourists who wish to explore scenically magnificent Wallowa Mt. region & (N) approach to Grand Canyon of Snake R. On hill, opp. B Ave., **Ore Trail Mon.;** fine view. On Hill Ave., **Eastern Ore. College of Education** (est.1929). On campus are handsome bldgs. (Ital.Ren.)

SIDE TRIP: Take St.82 (E) from La Grande across Grande Ronde Valley & into Wallowa Range reg. Wallowa Mts. reach altitudes of more than 10,000′ & are scarred by deep canyons through which flow picturesque streams. There are also some fine Ls. At 2.5m **Island City** (2,743′), at J. with Rd.

Turn (R) here 14m to **Cove** (2,892′). From here by Rd. to Moss Springs Guard Sta. & **Moss Springs For. Camp** (h.f.), where pack trl. leads to **"Red's Big" Minam Horse Ranch** ("dude" ranch.summer accoms.), on Minam R. at 15m. (Tel. ranch. Guides & horses will meet tourist at Cove; ranch can also be reached by plane from Baker or La Grande.)

20m **Elgin,** fruit-growing & lumbering center, at J. with St.204.

Take St.204 (L) to **Tollgate,** at 17.5m, near Blue Mt. Summit. Here is Langdon L., with two for. camps. Tollgate is winter sports center.

At c. 38m, **Wallowa Wayside For.** extending along cleft of Wallowa R. nearly 5m. At 48m **Wallowa** (2,940′). 56m **Lostine** (3,362′).

Turn (R) on Rd. following Lostine R. (S) into Eagle Cap Wilderness Area (223,000 as.), part of Wallowa Nat. For., to **Lostine Forks** at 18m. Along this Rd. are several well-equipped for. camps. From Lostine Forks trls. radiate to various mt. peaks & Ls.

66.5m **Enterprise** (3,755′), market town for Wallowa Valley. Here are hqs. for Wallowa Nat. For.(info.). In vic. are several for. camps.

Take St.3 (L) from Enterprise, along **Joseph Cr. Canyon,** an impressive gorge, 2,000′ in depth. St.3 cont. into Wash. to Clarkston (see US410).

70m J. with dirt Rd.

Turn on this (L) (via Midway & Zumwalt) to **Buckhorn Springs** (camp.pic.) 25m, & (R) here 1m to **Buckhorn Pt.,** overlooking **Snake R. Canyon.**

73m **Joseph** (4,400′), near (N) end of Wallowa L., named for elder & younger Chiefs Joseph, who led Nez Percé revolt against Americans. In Joseph reg. are many for. camps.

(1) Take unsurfaced Rd. (R) from Joseph 2m to its terminus. Then by trl. to **Hurricane Canyon,** affording wonderful views not only of canyon but of waterfalls & lofty peaks.

(2) Take Little Sheep Creek Rd. (L) from Joseph into Imnaha R. Canyon. At 30.5m **Imnaha** (1,850′), dist. hqs. for Wallowa Nat. For. From this pt. Rd. runs (R) along Grizzly Ridge 23m to **Hat Pt.** Here is For. Service Tower with magnificent view of **Grand Canyon of Snake R.** & surrounding mts. At & near Hat Pt. are for. camps.

St.82 cont., circling Wallowa L., passing **Grave (R) of Old Nez Percé Chief Joseph.** 79m **Wallowa L. Lodge** (hotel.cabins.golf.f.boat.horses.guides.). Dude ranch near-by. To (S) lies **Wallowa Mt. Sheep Refuge,** for few surviving bighorn sheep.

**160. EMIGRANT SPRINGS ST. PK.** (15 as.4,500′.good pic.facils.hiking), with marker to pioneers who made camp at springs. Good view. **162.5.** Hy. traverses reg. of int. views & crosses into **UMATILLA IND. RESERV.,** where still live more than 1,300 Inds. **174. EMIGRANT HILL VIEWPOINT ST. PK. 186.** J. with St.11.

SIDE TRIP: Take St.11 (R) to **Adams** at 12.5m.

Take Rd. here (R) 10m then (L) to **Bingham Springs** (resort), at 23m.

21.5m **Weston,** 36.5m **Wash. Line.** 43.5m **Walla Walla, Wash.,** at J. with US410 (see).

**188. PENDLETON** (1,070′).

RR. Sta.: Main & RR. Sts. Bus Sta.: 500 Main St. for through buses. Airport: through conns. Accoms.: all types. Info.: C. of C. in Elks Temple. Sports facils.: Round-Up Pk. (swim). Pendleton Round-Up. mid-Sept.

Pendleton is on Umatilla R. in wheat-growing reg. Important industry is flour milling. In addition, city has plants processing other agric. products & some lumber mills & wood-working establishments. Pendleton is on Old Ore. Trl. & was settled in early 60's. It escaped attacks by Chief Joseph of Nez Percé during his revolt of 1877. From rough, wide-open cattle-range town Pendleton gradually changed its character as surrounding region turned to wheat & other types of farming. City was named for Geo. W. Pendleton, Dem. Pres. candidate, 1868. World War II brought considerable boom, very nearly doubling pop.

PTS. OF INT.: **Taylor Pk.,** with equestrian statue by A. E. Proctor, comm. T. D. Taylor, former sheriff, killed while attempting arrest of several bandits. **Vert Mem. Bldg.** (O.wks.), civic center, houses coll. of Ind. & pioneer relics & little theater. On Jackson St., **Pioneer Pk.,** in which is burial ground of early pioneers. On W. Court St., **Round-Up Pk.,** with stadium seating 15,000. During mid-Sept., famous 4-day Round-Up Rodeo is held here in which participate not only cowboys from W. Coast ranches but also several thousand Inds. who celebrate, costumed, with dances & ceremonials. During Round-Up city transforms itself into frontier town & puts on series of pioneer day festivities, climaxing in special night show, entitled "Happy Canyon." Some 50,000 spectators attend. In pk. also is open-air theater where plays & concerts are put on.

## Sec. 2: PENDLETON to BIGGS. 108.

US30 now traverses wheat-growing area cultivated by mechanized farming methods. **74. ARLINGTON.** (sett.1880), in good duck-hunting reg. at J. with St.19 (see US395). US30 soon enters picturesque part of Columbia Gorge. **98. JOHN DAY R.,** named for John Day, one of members of Astoria Expedition. **103. RUFUS.** Across R., at this pt., is **Stonehenge Mem.** to World War I dead (see Wash.US830). **105.5.** Eastern J. with US97, which unites with US30. **108. BIGGS,** at Western J. with US97.

## Sec. 3: BIGGS to PORTLAND. 112.

**8. CELILO,** near Celilo Falls. Here Inds. had considerable settlement where they dried salmon. In 1860's, RR. portage was built around falls, & in 1905 Gov. constructed canal & locks to take R. traffic around them. **17. SEUFERT,** where there are Ind. writings & pictures on cliffs. J. with St.23 running (S) into Mt. Hood reg. & to J. with St.50 (see Mt. Hood).

**20. THE DALLES.**

RR. Sta.: Liberty St. Bus. Sta.: 311 E. 2nd St. Dalles Dock at Union St. for ocean & river steamers. Ferry to N. Dalles, Wash. Accoms. all types. Info.: C.of C., 2nd & Liberty Sts.

The Dalles, at narrows of Columbia R., was named by Fr. fur trappers, it is claimed because of imagined resemblance of local rock formation to flagstones ("dalles") of Fr. towns. City is picturesquely situated. Its bldgs. run from low-lying R. banks up very steep hillsides which reach at pts. an elevation of more than 1,000′. The Dalles was formerly mart for Inds. travelling Columbia R., coming from all directions to fish & buy from local tribes. Because of its location at rapids it became also focal pt. for fur traders who had to break their through trips here. In 1849 Ft. Lee was built on site. During 1860's, short-lived gold rush brought sudden boom which cont. afterwards due to growing stream of immigration. The Dalles was pt. of transshipment to avoid rapids. Building of Cascade Locks in 1896 &, more recently, of Bonneville Dam, below city, has greatly increased its importance as port, since deep-draft vessels can now come to its docks.

PTS. OF INT.: (1) 320 E. 3d St., **First Cth.** (1859.removed here from orig.site), now in private ownership. (2) Trevitt & 6th Sts., **The Dalles Mission Mon.,** comm. Meth. Mission founded here 1838. (3) (N) end Liberty St.: trl. leading to **Lewis & Clark St. Pk.** on **Fort Rock,** where Lewis & Clark Expedition camped 1805-6. (4) 12th & Union Sts., in pk., is **Ore. Trail Stone Tablet,** placed by Ezra Meeker, early pioneer. (5) 12th & Court Sts., **Pulpit Rock,** with fine views. Here are held Easter sunrise services. (6) At ft. of rock is **Amaton Spring,** used by Inds. & later by Meth. Mission. (7) Garrison & 15th Sts., **Old Fort Dalles Hist. Soc. Mus.** (O). This is last of structures of Old Fort Dalles. Contains Ind. relics & Americana. (8) On Scenic Dr., **Sorosis Pk.,** affording fine views. (9) On same Dr., **Pioneer Cemetery,** in which are gravestones of many first settlers. (10) E. 2d & Monroe Sts., old **U.S. Mint,** built to coin gold during gold-rush days.

US30 cont. from The Dalles along Columbia Gorge with views of Mt. Hood (S) & Mt. Adams (N). Route from here on is scenically spectacular. **31.5. MAYER ST. PK.** (260 as.) at Rowena Crest with magnificent views. **32.5. ROWENA DELL,** steep canyon. **35. MEMALOOSE OVERLOOK ST. PK.** with fine view of **Memaloose I.,** old Ind. burial place. On I. is mon. marking **Grave of Victor Trevitt,** pioneer, who wanted to be buried with Inds. he loved. Hy. cont. with magnificent views & then dives into Mosier Tunnels. **44.** J. with St.35, leading (S) to J. with St.50, Mt. Hood Hy. to Portland (see Mt.Hood Area). **45. HOOD RIVER,** situated above Columbia R. bet. Hood R. & Indian Creek Canyons. This small city, like The Dalles, climbs from R.'s banks up steep hillsides. From hilltops, fine views of Mt. Hood & Mt. Adams. Hood River is market town for fruit & strawberry-growing region, noted for Hood R. apple; also tourist center. At Columbia & 6th Sts. **Apple Growers Assoc. Cannery** (O.appl.), where fruit canning can be observed. At (N) end of May St., **Observation Promontory;** fine views. **Eliot Pk.,** in Ind. Creek Canyon. Toll bridge crosses from Hood R. to White Salmon, Wash., on US830 (see). **47. COLUMBIA GORGE HOTEL,** near beautiful **Waw-Guinguin Falls** (207′ high). Beyond this pt., hy. traverses **Mitchell Pt. Tunnel,** which affords fine views, through openings. **51. WYGANT ST. PK.** (pic.), on Perham Cr. Trl. runs to ridge (2,800′) with fine view of Columbia Gorge & Mt. Hood. **53. VIENTO ST. PK.** (pic.). **54. STARVATION CR. ST. PK.** (pic.) derives its name from train marooned by snow for fortnight, whose passengers had to go on short rations. Here is lovely waterfall, to top of which trl. runs. **62.5. COLUMBIA GORGE RANGER STA.,** Mt. Hood Nat. For. Hqs. (info.permits).

SIDE TRIP: Take Pacific Crest Trl. here (S) through magnificent forest scenery into Mt. Hood Nat. For. At 12.5m is **Wahtum L.** & beyond, **Lost L.** (see Mt.Hood Area, St.35).

**65. CASCADE LOCKS,** constructed by Gov. to permit R. navigation around Columbia rapids. In old days, rapids were sometimes negotiated by Inds. in canoes & French voyageurs in bateaux. Rd., built 1856, enabled traffic to trans-ship more easily at this pt. In salmon season Inds., who shy at being photographed, can be observed fishing. Just (W) of Locks, on US30, is **Bridge of the Gods** (toll) across R. to J. with US830 in Wash. (see). Name derives from Ind. tale to effect that God, in his wrath, destroyed natural bridge near this pt. **68.5. EAGLE CREEK PK.,** on beautiful Eagle Cr. with for. camp. (1,000′;trlrs.a community kitchen.swim.boat. hik.). Here is J. with trls. through fine Mt. country of Mt. Hood Nat. Forest (see Mt. Hood Area).

**70. BONNEVILLE,** named for Capt. Bonneville, explorer celebrated by Washington Irving in "The Adventures of Capt. Bonneville." Here is **Bonneville Dam,** 1,100′ long, with large locks sufficient to permit passage of ocean-going craft. This dam backs up L. 40 miles long. Dam includes int. fish ladders, up which salmon climb to spawning grounds. Proj. produces 4,500,000,000 kw. annually & has 10 generating units, each with capacity of 60,000 H. P. Total cost was $75,000,000. It is one of several projects to exploit resources of Columbia R. for power, irrigation & navigability. Take Rd. here down (R) to Gov. **Fish Hatchery,** one of world's largest trout & salmon breeding hatcheries. Near Bonneville Dam is **Sheridan Wayside Pk.** (fine view). **Marker** on spot where Lt. Sheridan (later Civil War General) crossed R. to relieve settlers besieged by Inds. on Bradford I. (1856).

**71.5. J. B. YEON ST. PK.** Near here, fine **Elowah Falls,** with drop of 300′. Just (W), on US30, is **WARRENDALE.** Ferry to Beacon Rock, across Columbia R., up which runs trl. (see US830). Hy. now passes **St. Peter's Dome** (2,000′), said never to have been scaled, & **Horse Tail Falls,** dropping over high cliff. **76.5. ONEONTA GORGE.** Take trl. (L) here short distance to lofty **Oneonta Falls. 78.5. MULTNOMAH FALLS** (upper falls have drop of 541′). Take trl. here across "Beacon Bridge" to **Larch Mt.,** 6.5$^{m}$. Here is **Larch Mt. For. Camp** (4,051′.ample facils.lookout tower).

**79. WAHKEENA FALLS,** among most beautiful in Columbia R. Gorge. Near-by is **Wahkeena For. Camp** (no overnight camp.ample facils.pic.boat.swim.). Hy. now passes **Mist, Coopey, Bridal Veil, Shepherd's Dell** & **Latourelle Falls** (latter has 249′ drop). **84. TALBOT ST. PK.** (caretaker) near Latourelle Falls. Fine view. **87. CROWN PT.** (725′ above R.). Fine view. **"Rooster Rock,"** 285′ high, near-by. **Vista H.** (O.Tudor) on summit of Crown Pt.; in H., mem. tablet comm. Lt. Broughton, member of Vancouver's expedition. **88.** Summit on Bluffs, 925′ above R., highest pt. on US30. **112. PORTLAND** (see) & J. with US99 (see).

### Sec. 4: PORTLAND to ASTORIA. 104.

**28. ST. HELENS,** on Columbia R. At 155 S. 4th St., **Knighton H.** (N.O.1847). **44.** Picturesque **LITTLE JACK FALLS. 48. RAINIER.** Here is bridge (toll) to Longview, Wash. **79.5. CLATSOP CREST,** 700′ above Columbia R. Here is **Bradley Mt. Pk.** (pic.). View of Puget Island. **92.5.** J. with paved Rd. leading (R) 0.5$^{m}$ to **Svenson,** center of several salmon fishing & packing settlements along Columbia R. **100.5. TONGUE PT. ST. PK.,** at J. with graveled Rd. leading (R) 0.5$^{m}$ to **Tongue Pt. Lighth. Service Base.** Not far from here, Lewis & Clark Expedition camped for few days in fall of 1805, but were driven out by high water. After several moves, they finally camped at Tongue Pt. **104. ASTORIA,** at J. with US101 (see).

## US 20—OREGON

**ORE.-IDAHO LINE** (53$^{m}$ from Boise, Idaho) **(W) to NEWPORT, ORE. 458.5. US20**

Via: Vale, Burns, Bend, Sisters, Lebanon, Albany, & Corvallis. Almost no service sta. for c.140$^{m}$ bet. Burns & Bend. On remainder of tour, accoms. in towns, limited elsewhere. Hy. occasionally blocked by snow in Cascade Mts. in winter. U.P. RR. parallels route from Vale to Burns; S.P. RR. from Corvallis to Newport.

This route presents extreme contrasts. Bet. Vale & Bend, it runs at high alt. across fairly barren plateau of sage brush & lofty buttes, broken occasionally by irrigated farmlands. From Vale, route runs (W) along Malheur R. for c.60$^{m}$ & then skirts secs. of Malheur & Ochoco Nat. Fors. From Bend, US20 climbs (W) into Cascade reg. through Deschutes & Willamette Nat. Fors., passing Ls. & high peaks to Santiam Pass (4,817′). On W. side of Cascades, US20 descends rapidly, following S. branch of Santiam R. into Willamette Valley. It then crosses Coast Range, through Siuslaw Nat. For. to Newport on Pac. Coast.

## Sec. 1: ORE. LINE to BEND. 267.

**20.5. VALE** (2,243′.accoms.), in center of Vale Irrigation Proj. bringing large area under cultivation. In Vale is natatorium fed by mineral springs. **43.5.** Hy. enters fine **MALHEUR CANYON. 77.5. JUNTURA** (2,953′). In old days cattle baron Henry Miller had his great ranch in this reg.

SIDE TRIPS: (A) Take Rd. (R) from Juntura 16m to **Beulah Reservoir,** impounded by Agency Dam, part of Vale Irrigation Project.
(B) Take Rd. (L) from Juntura 22m to Riverside, at **Warm Springs Reservoir** & Dam, also part of Vale Irrigation Project.

**133.** J. with US395 (see), which unites with US20 for 29m. **135. BURNS,** center for cattle ranches of reg. Within city limits is small **Paiute Village,** sett. after so-called Bannock War (1878).

SIDE TRIP: From Burns, St.205 which branches off St.78, c.1.5m (S) of Burns, runs (S) into Malheur & Harney Ls. reg. in which is **Malheur's Migratory Bird Refuge.**

**162.** J. with US395 (see) which branches (S). **175.5. SQUAW BUTTE LIVESTOCK EXPERIMENT STA.** of U.S. Dept. of Agric. Bet. **184.** & **195.** US20 passes **GLASS BUTTES** (6,385′), which rise abruptly several thousand feet above plateau. These buttes furnished Inds. of many tribes throughout country with obsidian arrow tips. **203.5. HAMPTON** (4,416′ accoms.), overshadowed by lofty Cougar Butte. View of Hampton Butte. **245. DRY RIVER.** On cliff walls here are great number of Ind. pictographs (accessible from hy. on foot only). **266. PILOT BUTTE ST. PK.** (3,400′) of volcanic origin, rising abruptly from plateau. Rd. runs to summit, from which fine view. **267. BEND** at J. with US97 (see).

## Sec. 2: BEND to ALBANY. 123.5.

**12.** At **TUMALO CR.** is **Skyliner's Winter Playground.** At **21.5.** is J. with US28 (see US97), which unites with US20 to **SISTERS** at **22.** Here is hqs. for Deschutes Nat. For. & for trips into mt. reg. At **29.5.,** US20 affords fine view of **Black Butte** (6,415′). At **31.5.** J. with Rd.

SIDE TRIP: Take latter (R) to **Camp Sherman** (resort) at 5m in **Metolius R. Recr. Area.** Metolius R. flows through deep gorge to J. with Deschutes R. Several for. camps in vic.

**35.5. SUTTLE L.** (resort.accoms.For.Ranger Sta.). Here is **Suttle L. Pic. & Link Cr. Camp** (trlrs.comm.kitchen.swim.bathh.boat.). **37. BLUE L.** at ft. of Mt. Washington (7,769′). **41.5. SANTIAM PASS** (4,817′). **46. LOST L.** (4,000′). **47.5. J.** with St.222.

SIDE TRIP: Take latter (R). Near J. with US20, **Little Nash Crater,** int. volcanic butte. 15.5m **Marion Forks Ranger Sta. & For. Camp** (trlrs.f.h.), starting pt. for trip into Mt. Jefferson Wilderness Area. Take Marion Forks Rd. (R) here 2.5m to **Gatch Falls** & at 3m, **Marion L.** 20m **Whitewater Cr. For. Camp.** 26m **Idanaha Winter Sports Area.** 32m **Detroit,** formerly good supply pt. for mt. trips. Town, however was wrecked by fire in 1947. Detroit is at J. with Breitenbush-Olallie L. Rd. (O.Aug.-Sept.).

Take latter (R). At 6m from Detroit is **Humbug For. Camp** (trlrs.ample facils.). 12m **Breitenbush Springs** (resort.accoms. hot min.springs). Near-by is **Breitenbush For. Camp** (3,200′.trlrs.). Main Rd. shortly passes Breitenbush Mt. (4,805′) & enters Mt. Hood Nat. For. 25m **Breitenbush L. & For. Camp** (5,500′.trlrs.ample facils.boat.f.). on L. surrounded by high peaks, with fine view of Mt. Jefferson. 30m **Olallie L.** (resort), with **Olallie For. Camp** (5,000′.trlrs.boat.swim.horses). 35m **Olallie Meadows For. Camp** (4,200′.trlrs.). Rd. now passes some fairly high mt. peaks & reaches **Clackamas L. & Clackamas L. Meadow For. Camp** (3,200′.trlrs.) at 57.5m. Here is For. Ranger Sta. Rd. now passes tiny **Clear L.** & ends at J. with St.50 (Portland-Mt.Hood Hy.) at **Blue Box J.,** 65.5m.

From J. with Breitenbush-Olallie L. Rd. (see above) St.222 cont. (W) to **Salem** at J. with US99E (see) at 87m.

**51.5.** J. of US20 with for. Rd.

SIDE TRIP: Take this Rd. (L) to **Fish L.,** where are For. Ranger Sta. (info.) & For. Camp. Rd. next passes at 4m to **Clear L.** with depth of 2,000′. Here is For. Camp. (trlrs.community kitchen.h.f.). Rd. cont. past beautiful Sahalie, Koosah & Tamolitch Falls to **Belknap**

**Springs Resort** (mineral springs) & to J. at 21m with US28 (see above), conn. with US97 (see).

**70.5.** US20 passes **HOUSE ROCK FOR. CAMP** (trlrs.f.h.boat.swim). **71. FERN-VIEW FOR. CAMP** (camp.shelters.swim.). **74. TROUT FOR. CAMP** (trlrs.camp. community kitchen.shelters.f.h.swim.). **81. CASCADIA** (resort.accoms.).

SIDE TRIP: Turn (R) here 0.5m to **Cascadia St. Pk.** (medicinal springs.pic.rest rooms. swim.) on S. Fork of Santiam R., from which lead (1) trl. (R) 1m to **Ind. Caves** in which are pre-hist. writings & (2) another trl. (R) 4m to **High Deck Mt. Lookout** (fine view).

US20 now descends foothills to Willamette Valley. **109. LEBANON** (sett.1851) has paper mill & is strawberry-growing center. **123.5. ALBANY** at J. with US99E (see).

### Sec. 3: ALBANY to NEWPORT. 68.

**17. PHILOMATH** J. with St.34.

SIDE TRIP: Take latter (L) over **Alsea Mt.** (1,400′), with fine view of coastal range, through Siuslaw Nat. For. 59m **WALDPORT** at J. with US101 (see).

**68. NEWPORT,** at J. with US101 (see).

# PORTLAND

## PORTLAND.

RR. Sta.: End NW. 6th Ave., Union Depot for all lines. Buses: SW. 5th Ave. & Taylor Sts., Union Stage Terminal for all major lines. SW. 5th Ave. & Salmon St., Portland Bus Terminal. W. Burnside St. & 5th Ave., Dollar Bus Line. For bus tours along Columbia R. Gorge to Mt. Hood reg. & "Seeing Portland Tours": Gray Line, 628 NW. 6th St., Rose City Tours Inc., 524 NW. 14th Ave. These last-named bus lines also offer round trips to Mt. Hood & Columbia R. Gorge. Airports: Portland-Columbia Airport on NE. 47th Ave. Portland Troutdale Airport near Troutdale, 15m from Portland. Info.: Portland C.of C., 824 SW. 5th Ave.; Ore. St. Motor Assoc. Club, 1200 SW. Morrison St.; Motor Club, 139 SW. Broadway & Multnomah & Benson Hotels. Concerts, drama & lectures in Mun. Aud., SW. 3rd St.; concerts & sports events in Multnomah Stadium. Accoms.: all types. Jantzen Beach (fee.amusement resort) near Interstate Bridge. Oaks Pk. (pic.bath.amusement.fee) near Sellwood Bridge. Many mun. swim. pools. Rose Festival, June; Portland Open Gold Tournament, autumn.

Portland, metropolis of Ore., known as City of Roses, is situated near pt. where Willamette R., which bisects city, flows into Columbia R. Across R. (N) lie high peaks of Cascades—Mt. St. Helens & Mt. Adams—& near-by (E) looms snow-capped Mt. Hood. Portland's business sec. lies along W. bank of Willamette R. Hills (W), along whose slopes have grown up residential districts, rise to height of 1,000′. However, majority of Portland's pop. still resides on E. side of R. Chief scenic landmarks of this sec. are Rocky Butte & Mt. Tabor. New industrial development is taking place along Willamette R. (NW.). Portland was sett. later than some other cities in Willamette Valley & therefore played no part in setting up of provisional gov. in 1843 at Champoeg. First white habitation on city's site was built before 1830, by member of Hunt's Overland Expedition of 1812, but was soon abandoned. Thereafter, several log cabins were erected, but these attempts at settlement achieved no permanence. It was not until 1844 that Asa Lawrence Lovejoy & Wm. Overton located 640-a. claim covering part of present city's site. Lovejoy transferred part of his claim to Overton & balance to Francis Pettygrove, who decided upon name for proposed town by toss of coin. Overton wanted to name it Boston, for his native city, & Pettygrove, who came from Portland, Me., favored Portland. Pettygrove won.

City's location at confluence of 2 navigable rivers early attracted commerce & immigration. Establishment of hqs. of Hudson's Bay Co. at Vancouver contributed to its rapid growth. Shipbuilding & lumbering were earliest industries. Then came Cal. gold rush, which emptied Portland of practically all its male pop., only 3 men remaining. Upon return of miners with gold in their knapsacks, short-lived boom ensued. In 1850, "Weekly Oregonian" was founded. It is said to be oldest surviving newspaper W. of Iowa & Mo., with exception of "Deseret News" in Salt Lake City. Not until quite some time later was Portland conn. by wire service with outside world. During 1860's, stagecoaches had to bring latest news from Yreka, Cal., nearest telegraph terminus, 400m, 4½ days away. Town cont. for some time in rather primitive stage of development with unpaved streets in which, during rainy season, mud was knee deep. Stumps of trees, which had been cleared away to make room for town site (orig. name of settlement was "Stump Town"), were painted white so that people would not bump into them. About time of Civil War, discovery of precious metals in E. Ore. & Idaho stimulated another gold rush & boom, & 3rd boom came with discovery of gold in Alaska during last decade of 19th cent. But Portland's growth depended upon more permanent factors: lumber, salmon fishing, shipping, RRs. & handling of wheat from fertile back country. Lewis & Clark Centennial Exposition of 1905 considerably spurred city's expansion, as did World Wars I & II.

Portland, only 110$^{m}$ from Columbia's mouth, with terminals capable of handling ocean-going steamers, has become one of principal seaports of Pacific coast. At same time, it is considerable inland port, since Columbia has been made navigable (E) to Umatilla. With completion of MacNary Dam at Umatilla, river will be made navigable to Pasco & ships will be able to use Snake R. from Pasco to Lewiston, Idaho. As result of these advantages, & its excellent rail conns., city is bound to become one of most imp. transportation & shipping centers of country.

Portland already has considerable industry. Abundant timber resources of Ore. have stimulated establishment of lumber & woodworking plants. Exploitation of rich agric. hinterland has led to establishment of flour mills & plants for processing of agric. products; vast cattle & sheep ranges, sending their products to Portland, have encouraged building of stock yards & slaughterhouses, & considerable annual export of wool. Fisheries of Columbia R. & W. Coast have created a large fishpacking, canning & freezing industry. Many shipyards have sprung up along river front. World War II brought Portland an enormous boom & considerable expansion of industry. Cosmopolitan character of city's pop. has been accentuated by influx of wartime jobseekers. Negro residents, alone, have increased from c.2,000 in 1940 to 12,000 in 1947 &, for first time in its hist., Portland has something of a race problem. In 1939, c.19,000 persons were employed in manufacturing while in 1944, number swelled to 159,000. Near-by Bonneville Dam has developed abundant cheap electric power. When Grand Coulee Proj. is completed, entire area E. of Portland will have at its disposal tremendous hydro-elec. power sources.

City is also important tourist center, since it is starting pt. for Columbia R. Gorge, Mt. Hood & coast resort regs., & has developed as cultural center, being seat of Univ. of Portland, Lewis & Clark College, Reed College, Univ. of Ore. Medical College & N. Pacific College of Ore. Jr. Symphony Orchestra is one of best of its kind on W. coast. There is an excellent civic theater. Although the old town is crowded, there are 55 pks. (1,600 as.) with fine recr. facils.

PTS. OF INT.: Portland's pub. bldgs. incl.: (1) NW. Davis St. & NW. 8th Ave., **U.S. Custom H.** (1901.Ital.Ren.). (2) SW. Morrison St. & 5th Ave., **Old P.O. Bldg.** (1875.by M.A.R.Mullet,architect of St.Dept.Bldg.in Wash.D.C.). (3) NW. Glisan St. & NW. 8th Ave., **U.S. P.O.** (1918.Ital.Ren.by Louis P.Hobart). (4) SW. 3rd Ave. & SW. Clay St., **Portland Civic Auditorium** (1917.Ital.Ren.by Freedlander & Seymour). In this bldg. is Ore. Hist. Coll. (O.wks.9-12 Sat.) of hist. & Ind. material. (5) SW. Salmon St. & SW. 4th Ave., **Multnomah County Cth.** (1913.Class.by Whidden & Lewis). (6) SW. 5th Ave. & SW. Madison St., **City Hall** (1895.Ital.Ren.by Whidden & Lewis). (7) SW. 10th Ave. & SW. Yamhill St., **Multnomah Pub. Lib.** (O.wks.Sun.3-9.1913.Ital.Ren.). (8) SW. Morrison St. & SW. 18th Ave., **Multnomah Civic Stadium** (by Whitehouse & Doyle), seating 30,000. Rose Queen crowned here. (9) NW. 28th Ave. & NW. Vaughan St., **Forestry Bldg.** (O), largest log cabin in world, with great inter. hall whose roof is supported by 52 log pillars, constructed entirely of fir; coll. of Oregon woods.

Some of hist. int. bldgs. are: (10) W. Burnside St. bet. NW. 2nd & 3rd Aves., **Erickson's,** which in old days boasted 640′ bar frequented by sailors, lumbermen, roustabouts & hoboes. (11) 49 SW. 1st Ave., **New Market Block & Theater,** where famous stars & lecturers (Henry Ward Beecher, Rbt. B. Ingersoll, etc.) appeared. (12) 536 SW. 1st Ave., **Greene Bldg.,** which in early days was famous as Emil Weber's gambling & drinking resort (owner, Weber, was killed, 1889, by rival gambler Sandy Olds). (13) 620 SW. Front Ave., **Esmond Hotel** (1881), fashionable hostelry of 1880's. (14) SW. Front Ave. & SW. Morrison St., **St. Charles Hotel** (1869-71), where Henry Villard & other RR. magnates were wont to put up. (15) SW. 6th Ave., **Hotel Port-**

**land.** Henry Villard undertook building of this hostelry in early 1870's, but when he became bankrupt, bldg. remained unfinished & was completed only in 1889; Stanford White was architect. (16) 57 Flanders St., **Boss Saloon,** dating from 1870's, another notorious hangout for sailors, dockhands & roustabouts. (17) SW. Park Ave., equestrian **Statue of Theo. Roosevelt** by A. Phimster Proctor. (18) SW. 9th Ave., **Portland Art Mus.** (O.10-5.wks.12-5 Mon.7-10 Sun.& hols.1932.by Pietro Beluschi.adds.1939). Mus. has colls. of Fr. & Amer. painting; Gr., Rom., Chinese, Persian & Egypt. art objects; & textiles & laces. Exhibits loan colls. & operates art school.

(19) SW. Marquam Hill Rd., **Portland Medical Center,** on whose grounds are **Univ. of Ore. Medical School, Multnomah Cty. Hospital, Doernbecher Hospital for Crippled Children.** Near-by **Veterans' Hospital & Admin. Bldg.** (20) W. of city center is **Council Crest Pk.** (1,073′) from which magnificent view of Columbia R. Gorge. (21) W. of business sec. of city is **Washington Pk.,** at whose entrance is shaft comm. Lewis & Clark. In pk. are statue of Sacajawea (by Alice Cooper), Ind. woman who guided Lewis & Clark Expedition across mts., & statue of two Inds., "The Coming of the White Man," by H. A. McNeil. Pk. also has zoo & rose gardens. (22) At NE. 57th Ave. & NE. Sandy Blvd. is **Statue of Geo. Washington** by Pompeii Copini. (23) SW. 2nd & 4th Aves., **Portland's Chinatown** (worth visit). (24) Also well worth visit is **Farmers' Market,** SW. Yamhill St. (25) 920 SW. 6th Ave., **Public Service Bldg.,** one of few skyscrapers. (26) In **Lownsdale Sq.** are Elk Fountain by Roland H. Perry & Mon. by Douglas Tilden comm. Ore. soldiers of Sp.-Amer. War. (27) In **South Pk.** blocks is statue of Lincoln by Geo. Fight Waters. (28) First & Ankeny Sts., **Skidmore Fountain** (sculptor,Olin H. Warner;architect,H.M.Wells). (29) **Statue of Thos. Jefferson,** in front of Jefferson High School. (30) **Centennial Plaque,** on boulder at SW. Front Ave. & Alder St., comm. Lovejoy & Pettygrove, city's founders. (31) On Sandy Blvd., **Sanctuary of Our Sorrowful Mother** (60 as.guide), maintained by Servite Fathers. Upper part of sanctuary is situated on cliff, 150′ high, & can only be reached by elevator (fee). In sanctuary are 34 shrines, with woodcarvings illustrating events in life of the Virgin, monastery of Servite Fathers & statue of Our Sorrowful Mother. (32) At end of Rd. running from N. Frémont St., **Joseph Wood Hill Pk.** in which is Rocky Butte (612′), volcanic cone. Here are aircraft beacon & outlook platform. From here can be seen Mts. St. Helens, Adams, Rainier & Hood. (33) 69th Ave. & SE. Yamhill St., entrance to **Mt. Tabor Pk.** Drive runs to summit (600′). This is also volcanic cone; & fine view. Here is statue of Harry W. Scott, well-known Ore. editor, by Gutzon Borglum. (34) On SE. Woodstock Blvd. is **Reed College** (1912 & 1930 Tudor Goth.coed.), liberal arts & sciences institution. (35) NE. 39th Ave. & NE. Glisan Ave., equestrian **statue of Jeanne d'Arc,** copy of Paris statue. (36) On N. Portland Blvd., **Peninsula Pk.** (pic.bath.sports facils.) in which are sunken gardens. (37) 5120 SE. 28th Ave., **Lambert Exhibition Gardens.** (38) Various **Shipyards** (O.appl.inq.C.of C.). (39) N. Denver Ave., **Vanport City,** created during World War II, was largest housing proj. in U.S. with 10,286 units. (40) On Willamette Blvd., **Univ. of Portland** (Cath.) with a number of handsome bldgs.

# MT. HOOD AREA

## MT. HOOD AREA

Season: Summer is best season, although Mt. Hood has recently also become winter sports center. Warm clothing for eves. & nights recommended, even in summer. Transportation: RR. conns. at Portland, Cascade Locks, Hood R., & Seuffert (US30) & at Cow Canyon J. where St.50 meets US97 (see). Sightseeing bus tours from Portland covering Mt. Hood loop (via St.50, St.35 & US830) by Gray Line, 628 NW. 6th St., & Rose City Tours, Inc., 524 NW. 14th St., Portland. Bus services conn. Portland, Mt. Hood & central Oregon. Accoms.: Hotel accoms. at Gov. Camp, Timberline Lodge, Cloud Cap Inn. For. camps & other accoms. at fairly frequent intervals. Service stas. at frequent intervals. Trl. trips: Horses available at Rhododendron, Timberline Lodge, Cloud Cap Inn. Pack trains start from Cascade Locks (US30). Guides available at Cascade Locks, Hood R. (US30) & Rhododendron. Ascent of Mt. Hood: 3 good trls. from Timberline Lodge, Cloud Cap Inn, & Tilly Jane For. Camp. In July, Amer. Legion organizes ascent from Tilly Jane For. Camp. Winter Sports: Skiing at Gov. Camp, Timberline Lodge (ski-lift) & Tilly Jane For. Camp. Several toboggan courses; winter sports carnival at Gov. Camp, 4 days in Jan. Forest Ranger Stas.: Zigzag R. (St.50), W. entrance to Mt. Hood Nat. For.; Parkdale (St.35), 17m. (S) from Hood R.; Bear Springs (St.50), 76.5m. (E) from Portland. Permits for camp fires required from local For. Rangers. Fish. licenses required, Info.: Mt. Hood Nat. For. Hqs., Terminal Sales Bldg., SW. Morrison St., Portland, & For. Ranger Sta., Zigzag R.; also at service stas. along hys.

**MT. HOOD** in Mt. Hood Nat. For. is perhaps most outstanding scenic feature of Ore. It lies some 65$^m$ (E) from Portland & some 25$^m$ (S) from Columbia R. Gorge. Its snow-capped peak, rising more than 11,245′, can be seen from Portland's hills & from Columbia R. Hy. (US30) & pts. (N) in Washington. Mt. is Ore. climax of Cascade Range, which drops sharply from Mt. Hood almost to sea level at Columbia R. From Mt. Hood reg. beautiful Olallie Ls. & Mt. Jefferson areas of Cascades (see US97) are easily accessible by Rd. from Mt. Hood Hy., St.50. Fine Clackamas R. reg. lies (SW) near Mt. Hood & is reached by Rd. branching off St.50 to Eagle Cr. Mt. Hood, scientists tell us, resulted from series of volcanic eruptions; indeed, mt. is still active. As recently as 1859 & 1868 volcanic activities were observed & even today there are vents from which gases & fumes are emitted. Following volcanic period, glaciers formed on mt. & in their slow, relentless descent scoured out deep R. & cr. canyons, which today stir wonder & admiration of visitors. Because of its volcanic origin, Mt. Hood has figured in Ind. legend, which variously attributed its creation to conflicts bet. gods for affections of mt. goddess, or bet. giants & demons hurling fire & brimstone at each other. Later, with white man's arrival, folklore invented tale that John Bunyan, piling rocks & debris on his campfire, after night's camping, was responsible for creation of mt. First recorded account of Mt. Hood was given by members of Lewis & Clark Expedition, in 1805. First hy. into area was Barlow Toll Rd., over which, for years, wagon trains from E. travelled "trail." First ascent of mt. was not made until July 11, 1857.

Several streams, some of which have gouged out their courses through deep gorges, have their sources in higher mt. area: Sandy R. (W); Zigzag & Little Zigzag Rs., flowing through deep canyons (SW); Salmon & White Rs. (S); Hood R., fed by precipitous creeks flowing (N). Many lovely lakes lie hidden in remote mt. valleys. Around Mt. Hood itself rise several lesser peaks to alts. of 5,000′ or more. Fors. of reg. are for most part evergreen, with Ponderosa pine most striking. However, there are many types of deciduous species as well: chinquapin, alder, aspen, & dogwood. Undergrowth is luxuriant & in spring & summer fors. & meadows are brilliant with blossoming plants. Rhododendron are especially fine, & colorful heather carpets mt. meadows. Flowers bloom nearly to snow line. Many varieties of birds populate forests, & deer, especially blacktail variety, bear & lesser mammals roam reg. in considerable numbers. Wolves & mt. lions are rare; coyote & special variety of NW. beaver, plentiful. Salmon, steelhead, cutthroat & other varieties of trout afford fine f. In spring smelt crowd up Sandy R. to spawn. Main Rd. approaches to Mt. Hood region are St.50, which runs (E) from Portland skirting S. side of Mt. Hood to Cow Canyon J. with US97 (see), & St.35, which runs (S) from near Hood R. on US30 (see) along E. side of Mt. Hood to J. with St.50 near Gov. Camp. Clackamas R. reg. is reached from St.50, via St.211.

## I. St.50 from PORTLAND to COW CANYON J. 123.

This hy. roughly follows old Barlow Toll Rd. built by Sam Barlow, over which passed immigrant stream into upper Willamette Valley. St.50 after leaving Portland runs through fertile farm reg. & then begins to climb Cascade Range into Mt. Hood Nat. For. St.50 skirts S. shoulder of Mt. Hood, then turns (S) through fine mt. scenery & then precipitously (SW) down to Deschutes R., & follows R. canyon (S) to J. with US97 at Cow Canyon J. This hy. & St.35, which it intersects on E. side of Mt. Hood, form what is known as Mt. Hood Loop Hy.

**26. SANDY,** at J. with St.211 & Bluff Rd.

SIDE TRIPS: (A) Take St.211 (R) to **Estacada,** 12$^m$ & from here turn (L) into Mt. Hood Nat. For. along gorge of picturesque Clackamas R., fine f. stream. At W. boundary of Mt. Hood Nat. For., is **N. Fork For. Camp** (2,500′trlers.).

(1) From this pt. Clackamas R. Rd., with for. camps at intervals, cont. (SE).

(2) Near N. Fork For. Camp, For. Rd. branches off (L), traversing fine mt. & stream country, with for. camps at intervals, to J. with Breitenbush-Olallie Ls. Rd.

(B) Take Bluff Rd. (L) along Sandy R. Canyon. At 3.5$^m$ J. with another Rd., leading (R) 2$^m$ to **Dodge Pk.** (pic.swim.camp.), where trls. radiate to lookout pts. affording fine views. Bluff Rd. cont. & rejoins St.50 at 7.5$^m$.

**43. ZIGZAG RANGER STA.** (permits.info.) at W. boundary of Mt. Hood Nat. For. Here is J. with Clear Cr. Rd. which leads (N) to **Clear Cr. For. Sta.** 4.5m.

**45.5. RHODODENDRON** (accoms.recr.horses). **46.** J. with Pioneer Bridle Trl.

SIDE TRIP: Take latter (R) past several for. camps & then, crossing under St.50 (N), & running over Laurel Hill to rejoin St.50 at Gov. Camp 11.5m.

**46.5. TOLL GATE FOR. CAMP** (ample facils.community kitchen). **48.5. CAMP CREEK FOR. CAMP** (2,100′;trlrs.community kitchen.swim.pool.f.). At **51. ORE. TRL. TAVERN** (resort). **51.5. TWIN BRIDGES FOR. CAMP** (trlers.) at J. with Paradise Pk. Trl.

SIDE TRIP: Take latter (L) up Zigzag Canyon to **Paradise Pk.** (shelter) at 6m in reg. of lovely meadows, beautiful with flowers in spring & summer. Here is **Stadter Buried For.** Trls. radiate here to many pts. of int. One of these is trl. up Mt. Hood (only for experts).

**52. BARLOW FOR. CAMP** (trlers.). **53.** Beautiful **YOKUM FALLS,** at Js. with Zigzag R. Canyon Trl. & Mirror L. Trl.

SIDE TRIPS: (A) Take former (L) to **Devil's Canyon** at 3.5m, with fine outlook & views of Devil's Cr. Falls & Mt. Hood. Trl. cont. along E. Zigzag Mt. (outlook) & along fine Zigzag R., with views, to **Paradise Pk.** (see above) at 10m. (B) Take latter (R) to **Mirror L.** at 2m, in whose sparkling surface Mt. Hood is beautifully reflected.

**56. GOVERNMENT CAMP** (3,870′ accoms.cabins.gas sta.), at W. terminus of Pioneer Bridle Trl. (see above). Trl. leads (S) from here 1m to **Multipor Mt. Ski Jump** (4,500′) & near-by **Ski Bowl.** Just (E) beyond Gov. Camp on St.50 is **Barlow Mon.** comm. Sam Barlow who built orig. toll Rd. **57.** J. with Sherar Burn Rd.

SIDE TRIP: Take latter (R) 0.5m to **SWIM** (resort) under shadow of **Multipor Mt.** (4,650′). Just beyond Swim is **Still Cr. For. Camp** (3,600′.trlers.swim.shelter.huckleberries. f.). At 1.5m **Summit Meadows.** Near-by is cemetery in which immigrants who succumbed to hardships of trek (W) are buried. At 4m, **Fir Tree For. Camp** (4,500′trlers.) on picturesque creek of same name. Trl. runs (R) from camp 1m to **Veda L.** (camp.). Rd. cont. along sharp ridge to **Kinzel L.** at 9m. Here is **For. Camp** (4,200′;shelter.cabins.huckleberries). **Devil's Peak** rises above L. Trl. runs c.1.5m to summit (5,054′).

**58.5.** J. with Timberline Lodge Rd.

SIDE TRIP: Take latter (L) 6m to **Timberline Lodge** (6,060′), on slope of Mt. Hood, hotel & center for Mt. Hood region. It was built by WPA & is int. example of results of collab. bet. architects, artists, handicraftsmen, & manual workers. Inter. is decorated with wood carvings & sketches by WPA artists. Furnishings are to great extent handmade. There are fine views of Mt. Hood (N) & of lofty Cascades (S). Near Lodge are ski runs & ski lift & from lodge radiate trls. to many pts. of int. Most popular trl. for ascent to summit, 3.5m long (time 8 hrs.), begins here. Another trl., Round the Mt. Trl., starts at Timberline Lodge & circles Mt. Hood. It is 36.5m long but scenically one of most int. It reaches **Paradise Pk.** (see above) at 4.5m. **Eden Pk.,** at 17m which after Paradise Pk. is most beautiful of high meadow valleys of region. Here is **Eden For. Camp.** From Eden Pk. trls. radiate to various pts. of int. incl. **Lost L.** (see below). At 23m, **Cloud Cap Inn.** There is much-used trl. to summit of Mt. Hood at this pt. (distance 3.5m; time 7 hrs.). At 24m **Tilly Jane For. Camp.** From this pt. starts another much-used ascent to summit. Trl. reaches Timberline Lodge once more at 36.5m.

**59.5. SALMON R. FOR. CAMP.** Short distance (E) beyond is J. with St.35 (see below), leading (N) along E. side of Mt. Hood to J. with US30 (see). **64. FROG L. & FROG L. FOR. CAMP** (3,700′;swim.f.). **64.5. BLUE BOX SUMMIT** (4,024′), highest pt. on St.50. **66.** J. with Breitenbush-Olallie Ls. Rd. running (S) to J. with St.222 (see US20). **76.5. BEAR SPRINGS FOR. CAMP** (3,200′;trlrs.ample facils. comm.kitchen), at J. with Rd. to Warm Spring Ind. Reserv.

SIDE TRIP: Take latter (R) to **Simnasho** at 12.5m in **Warm Springs Ind. Reserv.** Inds. in area hold various festivities, incl. Harvest Festival. At 33m **Warm Springs,** hqs. of reserv.

**101. MAUPIN,** in Deschutes R. Canyon. St.50 now follows Deschutes R. gorge to Criterion Summit, affording fine views, & finally descending to **COW CANYON J.** on US97 (see) at **123.**

## II. St.35 from J. with US50 to J. with US30 at Hood R. 45.

From J. with US50, St.35 runs (N) past several for. camps, all except one with trler. facils. At **3. BARLOW PASS** (4158′). **7.5. BENNETT PASS,** fine views of Mt. Hood. **8.5.** Beautiful **SAKHALI FALLS. 9. HOOD R. MEADOWS FOR. CAMP. 13. ROBIN HOOD FOR. CAMP** (trlers.facils.f.info.at service sta.), at J. with trl.

leading (E) 5.5$^m$ to **Badger L.,** where is another for. camp. **16. SHERWOOD FOR. CAMP** (trlers.facils.f.). At **21.** J. with Cooper Spur Rd.

SIDE TRIP: Take latter (L) 1$^m$ to **Homestead Inn** (accoms.). At 7$^m$ **Lookout Pt.** (fine view). At 9$^m$ J. with unimproved Rd. leading (L) 1.5$^m$ to **Tilly Jane For. Camp** (5,600'; trlers.), near trl. circling Mt. Hood (see above). From this camp starts one of best ascents of Mt. Hood. 10.5$^m$ **Cloud Cap Inn** (5,985';accoms.summer). From here also starts good ascent of Mt. Hood.

**29.** J. with improved Rd. leading (L) via Parkdale to **LAVA BEDS,** int. volcanic rock formations, at 1.5$^m$. **30. DIMICK ST. PK.** (camp.pic.). **34.** For. Ranger Sta. (info.permits) **38.** J. with paved Rd.

SIDE TRIP: Take latter (L) 24$^m$ to **Lost L.,** taboo to Inds. because of their belief in sinister legends concerning it. Lost L. is one of most beautiful in region; like Mirror L. (S), it perfectly reflects Mt. Hood in its depths. Here is For. Camp on (N) side of L. (trlers.ample facils.boat.swim.f.).

**45. HOOD R.** at J. with US30 (see).

## US 101—WASHINGTON

**MEGLER FERRY SLIP, WASH.** (across Columbia R. from Astoria, Ore.) **(N) to J. with US410** (5$^m$ from Olympia, Wash.). **367. US101**

Via: South Bend, Raymond, Cosmopolis, Aberdeen, Hoquiam, Port Angeles, (Port Townsend), (Port Ludlow) & Shelton. RR. conns. at Raymond, Aberdeen, Port Angeles & several other pts. en route. Bus. conns. throughout. Ferries to Victoria, B.C. & Seattle from Port Angeles & Port Townsend; to Seattle & other mainland pts. across Puget Sound from several pts. on Kitsap Peninsula. Fairly good Rd. throughout. Accoms.: All types in larger centers & resorts.

This route, known as Olympic Peninsula Hy., runs (N) from Columbia R., alternately following coast & dipping inland. At L. Quinault it begins to circle Olympic Nat. For. & Pk., turning (E) when it reaches Juan de Fuca Strait & (S) finally along Hood Canal to J. with US410 near Olympia. Olympic Nat. For. & Nat. Pk. (see) is primitive reg. of fors., mts., Ls. & streams teeming with wild life, dominated by Olympic Mts. Various stub Rds. & trls. branch off US101 into this huge reserv. US101, always close to picturesque seacoast, also gives access to shore resorts. Bus loop tour runs from Seattle, circling Olympic Peninsula & returning via Kitsap Peninsula.

### Sec. 1: MEGLER to ABERDEEN. 83.

**0. MEGLER** (regular ferry serv. to Astoria, Ore.). US101 runs along mouth of Columbia R. through **CHINOOK** to **ILWACO,** named for Ind. chief, on Willapa Bay, at **12.5.**

SIDE TRIP: Take Ft. Canby Rd. (L) here 1.5$^m$ to J. with second Rd.
Take latter (R) 0.5$^m$ to **Ocean View,** resort picturesquely situated on rockbound coast. Offshore are **Fishing Rocks** (excellent f.).
Ft. Canby Rd. cont. (L) past high **North Head** (Ilwaco) **St. Pk.,** in which is lighth., to old **Ft. Canby** (O.appl.1864). On grounds is **Cape Disappointment Lighth.**

**13.5.** J. with St.12A.

SIDE TRIP: Take latter (L) to N. Peninsula, narrow, 25$^m$-long strip of land on which are resorts. In **Long Beach** (ample accoms.) is multicolored stone **Lewis & Clark Mon.,** at end of wide hard-packed sandy beach more than 25$^m$ long, good for auto racing.

**29. JOHNSON'S LANDING,** at J. with US830 (see). **45.** J. with paved Rd. leading (L) 2$^m$ to **Bay Center,** with oyster cannery & shell-crushing plant, near which is **Bush Pacific Pioneer St. Pk.** (41 as.pic.camp.f.). US101 now runs along Willapa Bay, to **SOUTH BEND** at **55.,** wood products & oyster-packing center on Willapa Bay & R. **59. RAYMOND,** lumber & shipping town on Willapa R., which is navigable to this pt. Raymond has had labor conflicts, especially at time of World War I, when I.W.W. led labor agitation. Here is J. with St.12 running (E), via Rainbow Falls St. Pk., to Chehalis, J. with US99 (see).

**83. ABERDEEN** (sett.1867) at J. with US410 (see), & adj., **HOQUIAM** (sett.1859).
RR. Sta. in Aberdeen. Accoms.: All types. Info.: C. of C. in Aberdeen & Hoquiam. Bath. in Gray's Harbor & Aberdeen L. (3$^m$ E. on US410). Annual 4th of July Splash, with Ind. water festival.

Aberdeen & Hoquiam are today one continuous community on Gray's Harbor, discovered by Capt. Rbt. Gray (1792), at mouths of Chehalis & Hoquiam Rs. When Gray's ship arrived offshore, great numbers of canoes filled with Inds. came alongside to trade furs for blankets, etc. First settlement took place c.1860. In midst of its prosperity as a roaring lumber town, Aberdeen was swept by destructive fire, Oct. 16, 1903, but was quickly rebuilt. Besides lumber industry with its pulp, plywood & wood-working factories, there are oyster & salmon canneries. Large fishing fleet makes Gray's Harbor its base. During World War I, Gray's Harbor shipyards turned out wooden ships. Like most pioneer towns that depended on sailors & loggers for much of their business, Aberdeen had its "wide-open" period. It boasted of resorts with such names as "The Harvard," "The Yale" & "The Columbia." Loggers learned it was wise to "bunk" some of their bank rolls with trustworthy shop- & saloon-keepers before going on a "toot," but not all those trusted were worthy. Bentley Gohl, who had his establishment above Pioneer Saloon, seems to have "disposed" of many who left money with him; 43 corpses turned up in R. Gohl was convicted, sentenced & then committed to insane asylum.

PTS. OF INT.: (Aberdeen) **Samuel Benn Pk.** (pic.tennis). (Hoquiam) 28th & Cherry Sts., **Olympic Stadium & Recr. Field** seating 10,000. **Port of Gray's Harbor** is a large port development. Lumber, wood & fish-processing plants of both cities are well worth visit.

SIDE TRIP: Take St.13A (L) from Aberdeen skirting Gray's Harbor, passing fishing villages & cont. along ocean front. At 20m is **Twin Harbors Beach St. Pk.** (45 as.pic.camp. ocean swim.bath.facils.f.trlrs.community kitchen).

## Sec. 2: ABERDEEN to FORKS. 112.

**6. POLSON ST. PK.,** timbered area. **9.** J. with St.9C.

SIDE TRIP: Take latter (L) 9.5m to Copalis Crossing, where St.9C forks. Turn (L) to **Copalis Beach** (seaside resort), 15.5m, at J. with Rd. (L) 3m to **Ocean City** (resort). From Copalis Beach cont. on St.9C (N) (R) along picturesque shore to **Pacific Beach** (resort) at 23m. From Pacific Beach, Rd. runs (N) along coast with fine view, to **Taholah,** Ind. hamlet in **Quinault Ind. Reserv.** (110,000 as.1,822 Inds.) at 33.5m.

**46. L. QUINAULT,** at J. with paved Rd. leading (R) through resorts along S. shore (accoms.recr.horses.f.h.guides.pack-train trips), at edge of Olympic Nat. Pk. (see). (Bus conns. several times weekly with Hoquiam; info.: Quinault L. Hotel.) Inds. take tourists down Quinault R. from Quinault Hotel on exciting canoe trip to Taholah (see above). (Arrangements for return by motor can be made.) One day hiking or saddle trips to nearby peaks. On L. are 2 well-equipped for. camps. **47.** J. (R) with N. shore L. Quinault Rd. (Olympic Nat. Pk.). **64.** J. with Queets R. Rd. to **Kelly's Dude Ranch. 66.5.** J. with Rd. (R) along Clearwater R. to **Clearwater St. Pk.** (10 as.pic.camp.) at 3m, providing access to Olympic Nat. For., US101 now hugs rocky, broken shore line. **78.5. OCEAN VIEW ST. PK.** (pic.), with fine view of **Destruction I.** & rockbound coast. **98.** J. with Rd. (R) along Hoh R. into **Olympic Nat. Pk.** (see). **106. BOGACHIEL R.** & J. with Rd. leading (L) 1m to **Bogachiel St. Pk.** (pic.community kitchen.camp.) & another Rd. leading (R) along Bogachiel R. (see Olympic Nat. Pk.). **112. FORKS,** lumber industry center.

## Sec. 3: FORKS to PORT ANGELES. 56.

**11. BEAVER,** with **L. Tyee For. Camp** (f.) on L. shore (L). **13. SAPPHO,** lumber town, mountain enclosed, on Soleduck R. J. with St.9A.

SIDE TRIP: Take St.9A (L) to J. with Rd. at 9m.

Take latter (L) to **Clallam Bay** at 15m & cont. (W) along Strait of Juan de Fuca. At 18.5m J. with Rd. (1) Take latter (L) here 21m to **Ozette** on **Ozette L.** (recr.). (2) Cont. (R) from J. with Ozette Rd. along Strait of Juan de Fuca to **Neah Bay** at 33.5m, hqs. of **Makah Ind. Reserv.** (453 Inds.). From Neah Bay, trl. runs 5m to **Cape Flattery,** opp. which is **Tatoosh I.** with lighth. At Neah Bay in 1791, Sp. est. settlement, soon, however, deserted.

Cont. (R) from J. (above) on St.9A, along Strait of Juan de Fuca, with views, to Port Angeles & J. with US101 at c.55m.

US101 now turns (E) to J. with Rd. at **26.** running (R) along Soleduck R. 12m to **Soleduck Hot Springs** (see Olympic Nat. Pk.). Hy. from here runs to & along S. shore of beautiful **Crescent L.** (recr.accoms.f.), orig. habitat of Beardslee trout, named for Adm. Beardslee who rode to L. on "Cayuse" from which he was suddenly separated when settler fired shotgun salute in his honor. **STORM KING GUARD STA. & ST. FISH HATCHERY & ROSEMARY INN** at **36.5.** (For trls. see Olympic Nat. Pk.) **39.** J. with Rd. running (L) along N. side of Crescent L., 3m to **Piedmont** (resort). **43. SUTHERLAND L.** (accoms.f.), dominated by Mt. Storm King. **47.** J. with Hurricane Ridge Rd. into Olympic Nat. Pk.

**56. PORT ANGELES**

Through RR. & bus conns. to Olympia. Ferries to Victoria, B.C. & Seattle.

Port Angeles, was named Puerto de Nuestra Señora de los Angeles by Sp. explorer, Francisco Eliza, in 1791. City is an important port & has pulp, paper & lumber mills. **Klahane Mus. of Nat. Sciences** (O). Fine drive along Ediz Hook with views of harbor & Olympic Mts. At end of Hook is **Port Angeles Salmon Club,** which stages annual Puget Sound Salmon Derby. **Olympic Nat. Pk. Hqs.** are located in city.

**Sec. 4: PORT ANGELES to J. with St.9 at 35.**

At **1.** is J. with Rd.

SIDE TRIP: Take latter (R) here to **Heart o' the Hills** (resort) on **Dawn L.,** 6.5m, dominated by snow- & glacier-capped **Mt. Angeles** (6,039′). Here are beautiful **Webster Mem. Gardens.** Trl. runs to summit of Mt. Angeles; **Heart o' Hills For. Camp** (trlrs.ample facils.).

**5.** J. with Deer Pk. Rd.

SIDE TRIP: Take latter (R) to **Deer Pk.** (5,400′) at 17m, dominated by **Blue Mt.** (6,007′) in **Olympic Nat. Pk.** (see). In vic. are several ski runs. **Deer Pk. Lodge** (accoms.guests must bring own bedding).

**16. SEQUIM,** trading center for irrigated farming area. **21.** J. with Rd. leading (R) 2m to **Sequim Bay St. Pk.** (73 as.bath.facils.f.camp.pic.community kitchen). US101 now skirts Discovery Bay to J. with St.9 at **35.,** running (N) to Port Townsend (ferry to Whitby I.) & via 9E to Port Ludlow (ferry to Seattle).

**Sec. 5: J. with St.9 to J. with US410 at 81.**

**12. QUILCENE,** famous for its oysters. **15. RAINBOW FOR. CAMP** (ample facils. community kitchen.f.) on Quilcene R. From here trls. radiate into Olympic Nat. For. Take Rd. here (L) 1m to summit of **Mt. Walker** (3,018′). Near-by is **Mt. Walker For. Camp** (ample facils.). At **23.5.** is J. with Rd. running (R) along Dosewallips R. (see Olympic Nat. Pk.). US101 now skirts Hood Canal to **BRINNON, 25.,** at mouth of Dosewallips R. Ferry to Seabeck (see below). **29.5.** J. with Duckabush Rd. leading (R) into Olympic Nat. For. (see). **47. LILLIWAUP** on Lilliwaup Bay, at J. with trl. leading (R) 0.5m to **Lilliwaup Falls** (salmon run to foot of falls). **51.5. HOODSPORT,** shrimping & tourist center. J. with N. Fork Skokomish Rd. (see Olympic Nat. Pk.). US101 shortly crosses **Skokomish Ind. Reserv.** (232 pop.) to **POTLATCH** (auto court), hqs. of reserv., at **52.** Potlatch means "to give" & is festival at which gifts are presented to invited guests. At times these gifts have amounted in value to as much as $10,000. Members of Skokomish tribe have become Shakers & hold ceremonials. **57.5.** J. with St.14.

SIDE TRIP: Take latter (NE) up Kitsap Peninsula, farming, f. & resort reg. bounded (W) by Hood Canal & (E) by S. arm of Puget Sound. At 10m, **Twanoh St. Pk.** (210 as.camp. pic.community kitchen.bath.facils.boat.f.). 31.5m **Sinclair Inlet,** J. with St.21.

Take latter (N) here 3m to **Bremerton** (accoms.ferry to Seattle), site of great **U.S. Puget Sound Navy Yard** (O.wks.Sun.aft.).

St.14 at Sinclair Inlet turns (E). 35m **Port Orchard** (sett.1854), shipbuilding center before surrounding fors. were exhausted. At 37m is fork of St.14.

Cont. (S) on other branch of St.14 to **Gig Harbor,** 51m, fishing port & shipbuilding center. **Community Pk.** (pic.). St.14 cont. (S) to S. tip of Kitsap Peninsula, whence ferry runs to Tacoma (see US99).

**81.** J. with US410 (see), 5m (W) from Olympia, Wash.

# US 99—WASHINGTON

**WASH.-ORE. LINE** (at Vancouver, Wash. across Columbia R. from Portland, Ore.) **(N) to CANADIAN BORDER** (32.5m from Vancouver, B.C.). **295. US99**

Via: Kelso, Castle Rock, Chehalis, Centralia, Olympia, Tacoma, Seatle, Everett, Mt. Vernon, Bellingham & Blaine. RRs. parallel route throughout. Bus conns. Accoms.: Plentiful.

US99 runs along N. bank of Columbia R., travels N. along Cowlitz R. through sparsely populated reg., once heavily forested, & then traverses fertile agric. sec. At Olympia US99 reaches Puget Sound & follows its E. shore through some of chief pop. centers of Wash. to Canada. Route is paralleled (E) by lofty Cascade Range, to Brit. Columbia Line. As hy. swings (N) from Columbia in S. sec., Mt. St. Helens (9,671′) & Mt. Adams (12,307′) loom into view (E). Farther (N), as Rd. approaches Puget Sound, Mt. Rainier (14,408′) to (E) becomes outstanding landmark. Olympic Range (W), in which is Mt. Olympus (8,150′), can be seen across Puget Sound. Puget Sound Is. lie offshore. In extreme N. sec. of this route, Mt. Baker (10,827′) & Mt. Shuksan (9,038′), NW. outposts of Cascade Range, are to be seen (E).

## Sec. 1: VANCOUVER to OLYMPIA. 123.

This sec. of US99 roughly follows N. extension of old Ore. Trl. from Portland. Pioneers went by boat up Cowlitz R. from Columbia R. to Cowlitz Landing near present-day town of Toledo & then by trl. to Puget Sound. Trip was arduous & required more than 3 weeks. This route developed into a rough hy. Later San Francisco-Olympia stagecoach route roughly followed today's US99.

**0. VANCOUVER**

RR. & bus conns. Accoms.: All types. Info.: C. of C. & Auto Club of Wash. (A.A.A.), Evergreen Hotel, 604 Main St. Hunt. in vic.; fish. in Columbia R.

Vancouver (sett.1825), across Interstate Bridge from Portland on Columbia R., named for Capt. Geo. Vancouver, who explored Columbia R. in 1792, is important port & industrial town. In old days it was main outlet port for Ore. Trl. & during 1st half of 19th cent., young settlement figured in struggle bet. Brit. & U.S. for sovereignty of Ore. reg. Hudson's Bay Co., under aggressive leadership of Dr. John McLoughlin, est. at this pt., depot & fort to counterbalance John Jacob Astor's post at Astoria (see Ore.). David Douglas, famous botanist, sent out by London Royal Horticultural Soc., came to Vancouver in 1825 & here made his hqs. while engaged in botanical investigations.

City had development typical of NW.—several gold rush booms, lumber boom which brought lumber & paper mills to town & finally development as center for processing agric. products of hinterland & as port for deep-water shipping.

PTS. OF INT.: (1) **New Clark County Cth.** (1941). (2) In **Esther Short Pk.,** Pioneer Mother Statue (by Avard Fairbanks) & Mill Wheels brought around the Horn to grind grain. Port of Vancouver terminals & industries along water front are worth visit. (3) On 5th St., **U.S. Military Reserv.** in which are: **Vancouver Barracks** (est. 1848) & several bldgs. from period when Gen. Grant was stationed here 1852-53; **Grant Mem.;** E. 7th Ave. & T St., **Reserv. Mon.** & **Apple Tree** raised from seeds brought from England, 1826. City plans to build replica of old Hudson's Bay Trading Post here. (4) NE. of Reserv. bet. 10th & 13th Sts. is **Pioneer Cemetery.** (5) In front of Pub. Lib. on Main St., ancient **Cottonwood Tree,** at pt. where Lewis & Clark arrived in 1805. (6) 39th St., **Leverich Pk.,** in which are Obelisk comm. Geo. Washington, athletic field, grandstand & Covington H. (O. 2nd & 4th Tues.monthly. 1847), oldest in Wash. In Vancouver is (S) J. with US830 (see), which unites with US99 to Kelso (see below). At **20.** J. with St.1S.

SIDE TRIP: Take latter (R) along Lewis R. 10m to Ariel Dam at W. end of **L. Merwin** (resort.f.), 11m long. Tanks lift salmon & other fish up to L.'s spawning grounds. St.1S cont. (E) to **Lewis R. Guard Sta.** (permits for Columbia Nat. For.). Trl. runs (N) here to extensive **Lava Caves.**

**44. KELSO** near J. of Cowlitz & Columbia Rs., center for smelt fisheries (Jan.-Mar.). City was founded by P. W. Crawford, who was advised by Dr. Marcus Whitman that Cowlitz valley was good reg. in which to grow potatoes. In Kelso is (N) J. with US830 (see). **53. CASTLE ROCK,** named for near-by rock formation. **54.** J. with St.1R.

SIDE TRIP: Take latter (R) 9m to **Silver L.** (f.), 6m long. St.1R cont. to **Spirit L.** at 24.5m, also 6m long & of unknown depth. L. derives name from Ind. legend about young hunter who was drowned in it while pursuing phantom elk. Fine view of Mt. St. Helens (S). At Rd.'s terminus is **Spirit L. For. Camp** (ample facils.) on S. shore. On E. shore are 2 other for. camps.

Take Timberline For. Rd. (S) from Spirit L. For. Camp to **Timberline Mt. St. Helens For. Camp,** 3m, starting pt. for ascent, from N., of **Mt. St. Helens** (9,671'). Ascent is arduous & takes 8 hrs.

**67. TOLEDO,** originally known as Cowlitz Landing. Here travelers left boats & began difficult overland trek to Olympia. On Aug. 29, 1851, convention was held at Cowlitz Landing which issued memorial asking Congress to est. part of Ore. territory N. of Columbia R. as separate territory. **73.5. LEWIS & CLARK ST. PK.** (accoms.), noted for its virgin timber stand. **74. MARY'S CORNER.** Here is old **Jackson Prairie Cth.** (O.appl.1844.rest.) built of logs; formerly home of J. R. Jackson, 1st settler. Mary's Corner is at J. with St.5.

SIDE TRIP: Take St.5 (E) from Mary's Cor. At 24m is **Riffe,** at J. with St.5L. Main side route cont. (E) from Riffe on St.5. 47.5m **Randle.** In this reg. bark is peeled from cascara trees & cured to make drug.

(R) from Randle on Cispus R. Rd. At 14m is **N. Fork For. Camp** (trlrs.h.f.). At 19m J. with trl. leading (L) 3m to **Blue L.** (f). At 25m on Cispus R. Rd. is J. with For. Rd. Take latter (L) 14m to **Chambers L.** (f.) & **Chambers L. For. Camp** (h.f.). Main side Rd. cont. (S) to **Taklahk Pond** & **Taklahk Pond For. Camp** (h.f.). Near pond is **Chain-of-Lakes.**

At 49.5m on St.5 is **Silver Cr. For. Camp.** 65.5m **Packwood,** good starting pt. for Cascades trl. trips.

Trl. leads (R) from Packwood 6m to **Packwood L.** & **Packwood For. Camp** (2,867') (h.f. boat.).

St.5 cont., skirting lofty cliffs, to Ohanapecosh Entrance of **Mt. Rainier Nat. Pk.** (see) at 75m.

**85. CHEHALIS** (Ind. "shifting sand"), so named because of sand at Chehalis R.'s mouth (sett.1873). 1630 Chehalis Ave., **O.B. McFadden H.,** former home of chief justice of Wash. territory. In Chehalis is J. with St.12.

SIDE TRIP: Take latter (L) from Chehalis to J. with Riverside Rd.

Turn (L) 2m on latter to **Alexander Pk.** (pic.camp.community kitchen) on Chehalis R.

At 3.5m on St.12, **Old Claquato Ch.** (1856) & cemetery. At 16m **Rainbow Falls St. Pk.** (115 as.camp.recr.) on Chehalis R. 53m **Raymond** at J. with US101 (see).

US99 cont. (N). **85.5. LEWIS CTY. FAIR GROUNDS** (fair in autumn; Cty. Rose Show in June). **91. CENTRALIA** (sett.1852), at pt. where Chehalis & Skookumchuck Rs. join, is industrial town (lumber mills; processing of agric.products.). Sett. by Geo. Washington, a Negro slave who came to district with his master, J. B. Cochran. Latter freed Washington, who then built 1st house here. In Aug. occurs Pioneer Days celebration in **Borst Pk.** Here is: **Borst Blockh.** (O.1855.removed from orig. site), of log construction, formerly used as fort to repel Ind. attacks. In **Geo. Washington Pk.** (named for 1st settler) is statue comm. four legionnaires killed in clash with I.W.W. during celebration of World War I Armistice Day, after which an I.W.W. member was lynched.

**107. TENINO.** Near-by are quarries which have supplied stone for many important pub. bldgs. **City Pk.** (pic.). US99 cont. (N) across open countryside dotted by curious **Tenino Mounds,** whose origin is doubtful. Hy. has frequent stone markers designating course of old Ore. Trl. **117.** J. with St.1M, leading (L) 4m to **Millersylvania St. Pk.** (710 as.pic.camp.boat.f.community kitchen), on Deep L. **119. TUMWATER** (sett.1845), 1st Amer. settlement in Wash. territory, on Deschutes R. **Tumwater Founders Mon.,** comm. arrival of 1st settlers.

## 123. OLYMPIA

RR. Stas.: 4th & Adams Sts., U.P. RR.; Columbia St., N.P. RR. Bus Sta.: 107 7th Ave. E. Airport, with through conns. Accoms.: All types. Info.: C. of C., Auto Club of Wash. (A.A.A.), Olympian Hotel, Legion Way & Washington St. Thurston Cty. Fair, 2nd half of Aug.

Olympia (sett.c.1848), state capital, is situated on Budd Inlet at S. end of Puget Sound & mouth of Deschutes R. Looming beyond city are Mt. Rainier (SE), high Cascades (E & NE), & Mt. Olympus (NW). City is built on fairly flat land, although capitol stands on fine bluff overlooking Sound. First settlement of Olympia followed soon after that at Tumwater, now practically suburb. In 1845, E. Sylvester & L. L. Smith, young divinity student, filed for land covering part of present city's site. When Smith was drowned, Sylvester took over his claim. He put up cabin of cedar logs, midway bet. what are today State & Olympia Aves. Next year (1848), Oblate Fathers built St. Joseph's Mission on Priest's Pt. (now city pk.). Gold rush of 1849 emptied new settlement of most of its men; even Sylvester could not resist lure of gold. In 1850 town was formally founded, & following yr. U.S. Customh. (1st frame bldg.) was run up. In 1852 1st newspaper in Wash., "The Columbian," appeared. Meanwhile, tentative names of Smithfield & Smithster (latter combination of names of town founders) were discarded for more grandiose Olympia, inspired by snow-capped Mt. Olympus. In those days Squaxin Inds., probably branch of Duwamish, whose chief was famous Seattle (see Seattle), had winter settlement on Budd Inlet. They were described in contemporary diary as "a filthy, fish-eating, flat-headed lot!" Inds. worked for pioneers (not too enthusiastically) & received cotton handkerchief for day's labor & "hickory" shirt for week's toil. No Rds. connected new settlement with outside world in 1st yrs. Pioneers had to use canoes from Columbia R. up Cowlitz R. to Cowlitz Landing & then break trls. for their wagons & animals through swamps & virgin fors. Gradually trl. was developed as Rd. In 1853 Congress set up Wash. as separate territory. Olympia's early industrial development was based largely on lumber, & ever since, lumber & woodworking have dominated its economy, together with government & politics. Oysters from near-by Puget Sound waters are famous. Packing oysters & clams is considerable source of employment. Fine natural harbor, improved by dredging, & construction of excellent terminal facils. have attracted shipping.

PTS. OF INT.: (1) Capitol Way bet. 11th & 14th Aves., **Capitol Bldgs.** (1921-35. Mod.Class.by Wilder & White). Chief of this group are: **Legislative Bldg.** (O.wks. daily organ recitals), surmounted by dome (287') costing $7,000,000. Bronze entrance doors have reliefs showing aspects of pioneer life. **Temple of Justice** (O.wks. Sat.2-4) in which are offices of legal branches of St. Gov.; St. Lib. (O.Mon.-Fri.a.m.), containing rare items & hist. relics; & St. Law Lib. **War Mem. Mon.** (1938.by Victor Alonzo Lewis). **Governor's Mansion** (N.O.Mod.Georg.). (2) 7th Ave. bet. Wash. & Franklin Sts., **Old St. Capitol Bldg.** (O.wks.Sat.a.m.1893.by Willis A. Ritchie). (3) Marker in pavement on Capitol Way bet. State & Olympic Aves. marks **Site of First Legislative Meeting Place.** (4) 114 8th Ave., **Sylvester H.** (O.appl.1856), built by Edmund Sylvester, one of city's founders. (5) 502 4th St., **J. J. Bremer Oyster Packing Plant** (O.worth visit) where can be observed shucking, grading, and packing of oysters. (6) 1110 Capitol Way, **Thurston County Cth.** (O.wks.Mod.int.). (7) At Purdy, W. side of city, on Henderson Bay, is **Scientific Oyster Lab.** (O), in which experiments in oyster & clam culture are carried on. (8) At NE. end of city is **Priest's Pt. Pk.**, on E. Bay Dr., facing Budd Inlet.
In Olympia is J. with US410 (see), with which US99 unites to Tacoma.

## Sec. 2: OLYMPIA to SEATTLE. 61.

**13.5. FT. LEWIS,** U.S. Army Reserv. (110,000 as.O.appl.). Here is **World War I Mem. 16.5. CAMP MURRAY,** Nat. Guard camp, on Amer. L. **21.** J. with St.5G leading (R) short distance to **McChord Air Field** (U.S.Army), named for Col. W. C. McChord, killed while flying, 1937. **22. LAKEVIEW,** suburban residential center. **23.** J. with Rd.

SIDE TRIP: Take latter (L) to **Steilacoom L.** (resort), 1m. At 6m **Steilacoom** (1851) in which are several bldgs. of early 1850's. At near-by **Ft. Steilacoom** settlers from Puget Sound took refuge during Ind. troubles of 1855.

### 29. TACOMA

RR. Stas.: Union Sta., 1713 Pacific Ave., N.P., Gt.N., & U.P. RRs.; Milwaukee Sta., 102 E. 25th St., Chi., Mil., St.P.&P. RR. Bus Stas.: Central Terminal, 14th St. & Pacific Ave.; Mt. Rainier Nat. Pk. Bureau, 776 Commerce St., for Nat. Pk. Stages (round trip tours daily to Paradise Valley, Mt. Rainier Nat.Pk.). Ferries: Pt. Defiance Pk. for Gig Harbor & Vashon I.; 6th Ave. for Fox I. & Pt. Fosdick; Steilacoom for Anderson I. & Long Branch; 1105 Dock St. for Black Ball Line to Seattle; Tacoma Mun. Dock for Seattle, Quartermaster Harbor & Vashon I. Accoms.: All types. Info.: C. of C., S. 11th & A Sts.; Auto. Club of Wash. (A.A.A.), 772 Commerce St.; Mt. Rainier Nat. Pk. Bureau, 776 Commerce St. Swim.: Titlow Beach, 6th Ave. & Pt. Defiance Pk. Fish. in Puget Sound & in Ls. & streams of vic.

Tacoma is dominated by Olympic Range (NW) & Cascades (E), rising to Mt. Rainier. City is important RR. & industrial center, with pop. of mixed origins—native Amer., Irish, Scand., Greek, German, Swiss, Armenian, Polish, Filipino, Chinese. Its harbor is one of best on W. coast. Municipally-owned hydroelectric plants & near-by coal mines afford cheap power & fuel.

Water-front dist., with busy factories & docks, has been built largely on filled-in land. Business district, with several skyscrapers, lies behind it & better residential secs. climb the heights. Downtown area is laid out in grid pattern modified by exigencies of local topography. When this layout was adopted in 1873, city fathers rejected much more imaginative plotting submitted by Fred. Law Olmstead, famous N.Y. landscape architect, as being too picturesque & providing for too many pks. Nevertheless, city today is provided with ample pk. areas, 27 in number & 1,617 as. in extent. Largest, Pt. Defiance Pk., on Commencement Bay, has fine bath. facils. Shore front drives, on either side of bay, afford excellent views of city & vic. First settlement in reg. was by Hudson's Bay Co., which est. Ft. Nisqually c.17$^{m}$ (S) in 1833. It was not till 1852, however, that 1st settlers arrived—among them Nicholas De Lin, Swede, who built sawmill at Old Woman's Gulch, later filled in to afford site for present-day stadium. Next yr. came 1st wagon train from E., after experiencing terrible hardships in crossing Cascade Mts. In those early days Steilacoom rather overshadowed little hamlet of Chebaulip, as Tacoma was then known. U.S. Gov. built Ft. Steilacoom, around which grew up settlement, where inhabitants of Chebaulip took refuge during White R. Ind. raids of 1855. Puyallup Inds. had their village, which they called Ta-Ha-Do-Wa ("welcome") at head of Commencement Bay. Early pioneers used to tell of seasons when bay was covered with canoes of salmon-spearing aborigines & of gathering of 4,000-6,000 Inds. near Amer. L. in spring, who met to celebrate with gambling, horse-racing & religious rites. After White R. uprising, military executed some of Ind. leaders & attempted to prosecute white settlers married to Ind. women, who were accused of giving rebels aid.

Tacoma's real growth began with arrival from Portland (1868) of elderly M. M. McCarver, energetic town promoter, who vigorously boomed sale of lots. At same time name of Chebaulip was finally discarded & that of Tacoma, Ind. designation for Mt. Rainier, adopted. (Tacomans made great but unsuccessful efforts to have this name adopted for mt.) Tacoma's struggle against Seattle for rail conn. ended in 1873 when N.P. RR. built its line to Commencement Bay. Finally, in 1888, completion of same RR.'s tunnel through Stampede Pass across Cascade Mts. brought direct tie-up with E. In next decades other transcontinental lines entered city. Tide of immigration now set in & town grew by leaps & bounds from mere sawmill hamlet to city of 36,000 by 1900. Even after 1900 Tacoma preserved its general character of W. coast frontier town. Practically every saloon was a gambling joint. Says Hunt, Tacoma historian: "In passing along the streets even as late as 1905, one would hear the sing-song of the Keno dealer: 'Forty-four, sixty-eight, twenty-nine, thirty-six.' The winner shouts 'Keno' & from disappointed players comes the monotonous wail of 'O-o-h Hell!' " Drunks & loggers (even when not drunk) were regularly "rolled," & there were occasional murders. "Harry" Morgan was boss of vice district. To fight reformist press, he started newspaper of his own, "The Pierce County Globe," which, like his other ventures, proved a financial success. But eventually the vice district was closed down. Reform wave went to rather extravagant lengths when city fathers enacted an "anti-treat" ordinance that imposed penalty on man who sold liquor rather than man who was standing treat. Last lynching occurred in 1873. During 1880's, Chinese, some of whom had worked on building N.P. RR. & who competed in labor market with white man, were driven out of city when anti-Chinese movement swept entire W. coast. Labor became active in late eighties, & went into politics as Union Labor Party, which advocated, among other reforms, municipal ownership of public utilities. Coalition of conservatives defeated Union Labor Party in 1888, but public-ownership idea took hold & eventually resulted in acquisition or building of municipally owned power plants.

Tacoma's chief industries are still connected with wood products: lumber, plywood, pulp, furniture, barrels & kegs. But it also has important shipyards, large smelting plant, aluminum mfg. plant, electro-chemical works & coking plants which process coal from near-by coal fields, as well as many industries processing farm products.

PTS. OF INT.: (1) Division Ave., **Wright Pk.** (recr.), in which is arboretum & conservatory with coll. of exotic plants. (2) 11th & G Sts., **Pierce County Cth.** (1893.by Proctor & Dennis). (3) 10th & A Sts., **Totem Pole,** 105', perhaps tallest in the world, brought from Alaska, on which has been carved legend of Eagle Tribe. (4) S. 7th St., **City Hall** (Ital.Ren.by Heatherton & McIntosh) with campanile. (5) 9th St. & Broadway, **Tacoma Theater Bldg.** (1890.Stanford White) where many well-known theatrical stars appeared in old days. (6) N. E St., **Stadium** (seating 30,000). (7) N. Stadium Way, **Washington St. Hist. Soc. Mus.** (O.Mon.-Fri.;Sat.a.m.& Sun.& hol.afts.by Geo.W.Bullard), containing hist. relics, specimens of Alaska & Wash. Ind. handicrafts, pioneer equipment & other items. In bldg. are murals of early hist. scenes. In front of bldg. is cannon, brought from Alaska, from Russ. gunboat. To rear are parts of "The Beaver," 1st steam-propelled ship plying Wash. waters. (8) N. 26th & Carr Sts., **Chinese Mus.** (O.appl.fee) with oriental art & doll exhibits. (9) Adj. is **Sutter's Friendship Garden** with coll. of rocks from all parts of U.S. & many foreign lands. (10) Warner St., **College of Puget Sound** (Meth.coed.); in Jones Hall is coll. of S. Amer. Ind. cultural objects. (11) 45th & Pearl Sts., **Pt. Defiance Pk.** (640 as.pic.recr.f.restaurant), with zoo (O.fee) & aquarium (O.fee). Here also is (12) **Jacob Carr's Cabin** (O), log replica of 1st house built in Tacoma. (13) Near-by is **Ft. Nisqually** (O.1833) built by Archibald McDonald of Hudson's Bay Co. 17$^{m}$ from city & moved here. Ft. was attacked by Inds. in 1849. Stockades, bastions & other structures rebuilt on orig. plans. There is good pub. bath. beach in Pk. Excursion boats in summer. (14) Tacoma's **Water Front,** E. of business district, along 14$^{m}$ shore line, with 300 industrial establishments, is worth visit. (15) In Ruston, suburb of Tacoma, **Tacoma Smelter** of Amer. Smelting & Refining Co. (O.appl.) with tall stack, 565′. (16) 2002 E. 28th St., **Tacoma Sanatorium for Inds.** (O). Adj. is **Ind. Cemetery** where some famous Ind. chiefs are buried. (17) S. of city, near Parkland, is **Pacific Luth. College.** Trip through Tacoma's markets on Market St. is worth while because of variety of wares on display & cosmopolitan character of vendors.

SIDE TRIP: Take St.5 (S) from Tacoma. 8.5$^{m}$ **Spanaway Pk.** (recr.camp.) on Spanaway L. Cont. on St.5 to **Pack Demonstration For.** (2,000 as.guides), 31$^{m}$, operated by Forestry School of Univ. of Wash. Circuit of for. via Lathrop Dr. 32$^{m}$ **La Grande,** high above Nisqually R., on which is hydroelectric development, supplying Tacoma with power. St.5 now ascends through scenically fine country, paralleling Nisqually R. 55$^{m}$ Nisqually Entrance to **Mt. Rainier Nat. Pk.** (2,003′; camp.accoms.registration & permits to enter Pk.) (see Mt. Rainier Nat. Pk.).

From Tacoma US99 cont. (N) to J. at **45.5.** with St.1K, leading (L) through resort reg. via **Des Moines** 3$^{m}$ to **Salt Water St. Pk.** (86 as.camp.community kitchen.swim.f. pic.) on Puget Sound. US99 now crosses **Duwamish R.** to J. at **53.5.** with St.5M, leading (R) 4$^{m}$ to **Longacres Race Track** (season:July-Sept.pari-mutuel betting). US99 cont. through Duwamish R. Valley past **King Cty. Airport. 61. SEATTLE** (see), at J. with US10 (see).

SIDE TRIP: Take St.5 (SE) from Seattle 12$^{m}$ to **Renton.** Here is J. with St.2A, alternate to US99, along E. side of Washington L. to Everett. At 26.5$^{m}$ on St.5 is J. with St.5A leading (R) 3$^{m}$ to **Wilderness** & **Lucerne Ls.** (resorts). 32$^{m}$ J. with Rd. leading (R) 2$^{m}$ to **Flaming Geyser Pk.** (fee) where are natural gas vents. 37.5$^{m}$ J. with Rd. leading (L) 4$^{m}$ to fine **Green R. Gorge** (accoms.). 38$^{m}$ **Enumclaw,** at J. with US410 (see) from which St.5 cont. (S) (see US410) to Carbon R. Entrance to **Mt. Rainier Nat. Pk.** (see).

## Sec. 3: SEATTLE to CANADIAN BORDER. 111.

US99 cont. (N) from Seattle. **11.5.** J. with St.1W leading (L) 3$^{m}$ to **Edmonds,** on Puget Sound, terminal for ferries to Pt. Ludlow, Port Townsend & to Kingston on Kitsap Peninsula (see US101).

### 28.5. EVERETT

Through RR. & bus conns. Everett-Whidbey I. Ferry from near-by Mukilteo (see below). Accoms.: All types. Info.: C. of C. & Auto Club of Wash. (A.A.A.), Monte Cristo Hotel. Swim.: Mun. bath. beach. Fish. in Sound & near-by streams & Ls.; boats, motor & tackle avail. at most locations.

Everett is situated on landlocked Gardner's Bay, with fine views of Olympics (SW), Mt. Baker (NE) & Mt. Rainier (SE). In 1792 Vancouver took possession of Puget Sound reg. for Britain, landing at pt. near present-day Everett's site. Although 1st settlement dates back to 1862, no expansion occurred at Gardner's Bay until 1889 when Rucker Bros. (later Everett Land Co.) began exploiting for. wealth of Snohomish R. country. Gt.N. RR. arrived about this time, & Rockefellers invested in near-by Monte Cristo mines. Then boom set in. In 3 months the new town had 3,000 inhabitants. Everett had its stormy frontier days, with usual wave of robbery & murder. Among its dives was Bucket of Blood Saloon, built over Snohomish R., with convenient trapdoor in floor of its back room, through which, legend has it, loggers who had been robbed were dropped into R. Finally, true to frontier pattern,

Committee of Twenty-One summarily ended crime wave. Near-by Snohomish was eager to become cty. seat, & planned to send expedition to steal court records from Everett. Luckily, Snohomishites never came, for Everett people had planted dynamite under bridge over which invaders would have had to pass.

Town's early boom collapsed with closing down of various enterprises & 1893 depression. But with acquisition by Weyerhaeuser interests of great lumber tracts, it became lumber processing & shipping center. However, in recent yrs., due to exhaustion of timber resources, industrial emphasis has shifted to pulp wood, of which there is still plenty in fors. Everett's most sensational labor trouble resulted from I.W.W. agitation in 1916. Members of I.W.W. were generally known as "Wobblies," word said to be derived from lingual difficulties of Chinese storekeeper with name: Industrial Workers of the World. When Wobblies tried to speak on streets, they were arrested & jailed. Finally, new invaders were beaten brutally & in some cases forced to run gauntlet. In Nov., two ships loaded with Wobblies sailed from Seattle into Gardner's Bay, but were warned not to land. Shooting affray ensued in which several Wobblies & sheriff's men were killed & many wounded. Everett is excellent pt. for trips to Whidbey I. in Puget Sound, to beach resorts, & to high Cascades. In Snohomish Cty. are more than 140 Ls. & many streams affording fine recr. & f. Larger industrial plants of city may be visited.

PTS. OF INT.: (1) Hoyt & Everett Aves., **Everett Pub. Lib.** (O.wks.1934.Mod.by Webb & Gould); in bldg. are murals by John T. Jacobsen & some sculptured plaques by Dudley Pratt. (2) Hoyt Ave. & 23rd St., **Trinity Ch.** (O.wks.appl.Episc.; 1921.Goth.by E.T.Osborne), comm. victory of World War I; Ch. has high tower & fine stained glass window by Charles J. Connick of Boston, known for his windows in Cathedral of St. John the Divine, N.Y.C.; flanking altar are panels by Mary G. Allen. (3) On Federal St., **Forest Pk.** (120 as.recr.camp.) with zoo; Pigeon Cr., which flows through Pk., has been dammed at intervals, creating series of cascades. (4) 44th St. & Rucker Ave., **Totem Pole,** comm. Patkanim, one of 4 chiefs who signed Mukilteo Treaty with Gov. Isaac I. Stevens (1855). At foot of totem pole is tablet with relief portrait of Chieftain, by J. A. Wehn. Figures on pole were carved by Chief Wm. Shelton of Tulalip Inds. (5) At Pier 2, **SS. Black Prince** (O.wks.appl.), old sternwheel steamer (1901). (6) 9th St., **Everett Mem. Pk.** (187 as.pic.recr.), on Port Gardner Bay, site of former Snohomish Ind. village, comm. World War I soldiers. (7) Bet. 16th & 19th Sts., on Port Gardner Bay, **Grand Ave. Pk.** in which is marker on **Site of Vancouver's Landing.** (8) Bet. 24th & 25th Sts., **Clark Pk.** Here is great cedar tree stump, made into "tree house." In Everett is J. with US2 (see), crossing Cascades to J. with US97 (see).

SIDE TRIP: Take St.1-I (L) from Everett to **Mukilteo** 5m on Puget Sound. Ferries to Columbia Beach on Whidbey I. (see below). In Mukilteo, at school, is Mon. marking **Mukilteo Treaty Site,** where Gov. Stevens signed 1855 treaty with Inds., by terms of which they ceded considerable territory. At 11m, St.1-I rejoins US99.

US99 cont. (N) across series of bridges over Snohomish R. & marshlands. **33.5. MARYSVILLE** (sett.1877), fishing & lumber-mill town, resort & center of dairy & farming reg. reclaimed from Snohomish R. swamps. Strawberry Festival, June.

SIDE TRIP: Take Rd. (R) (SE) from Marysville 5.5m to J. with St.15A & follow latter (L) along N. shore of **Stevens L.** (resort.f.) to **Granite Falls** at 16m, beyond which (E) are falls of Stillaguamish R. 29m **Verlot** & **Verlot For. Camp** (trlrs.f.h.community kitchen). 31m **Gold Basin** (accoms.) & **Gold Basin For. Camp** (trlrs.f.community kitchen). 40m **Silverton.** 44m **Big Four Inn** (accoms.recr.horses.guides) at foot of **Big Four Mt.** (6,120′). 49m **Barlow Pass,** at J. with Sauk R. Rd. Turn (L) on latter. At 56m **Bedal.** At 62.5m **White Chuck For. Camp** (f.h.), where for. Rd. leads (E) to trl. to **Kennedy Hot Springs,** at foot of **Glacier Peak** (10,435′), extinct volcanic cone. 74.5m **Darrington,** tourist center. Here takes place annual Timber Bowl Celebration, typical backwoods festival. Winter sports in vic. Stub rds. & trls. radiate into High Cascades. Cont. (N) on Skagit Rd. along Sauk R. to **Faber Ferry,** at 96.5m. Cross Skagit R. by ferry to J. with St.17A.

Take latter (R) here 7m to **Rockport,** near which is **Rockport St. Pk.** (447 as.undeveloped), from which poor Rd. & City of Seattle RR. (electric) runs 23m up Skagit R. to **Newhalem,** hqs. for Seattle's Skagit R. Hydroelectric Project, comprising **Gorge Dam** (880′); **Diablo Dam** (398′), impounding **Diablo L.;** & **Ross Dam,** impounding **Ross L.,** 30m long. These artificial bodies of water are among most beautiful in NW, enclosed by towering, snow-capped, glacier-furrowed peaks whose lower slopes are magnificently forested. Power developed, when project is completed, will be upwards of 1,120,000 h.p. When completed, probably before 1950, guided tours of project & Ls. will be resumed.

Take St.17A (L) from J. (above) to **Concrete** at 98m.

From Concrete, improved Rd. runs (N) through magnificent area of Mt. Baker Nat. For., with access, en route, to **Shannon & Baker Ls.**. At 19.5m on this Rd. is J. with trl. to Austin Pass (see Mt. Baker Hy. below) from which ascent of **Mt. Baker** (see below) is made. At 22m **Baker L.**, on which is **Baker. L. For. Camp** (trlrs.f.community kitchen). Beyond (NW) towers **Mt. Baker** (10,750′) & (N) **Mt. Shuksan** (9,038′).

Cont. (W) on St.17A to **Sedro Woolley** at 122m, from which St.1F cont. (W) to J. with US99 at 127m.

**61. MT. VERNON,** on Skagit R., processing center of products of vic.'s low-lying farms, which are protected against R. floods by diking & draining. Mt. Vernon is another good starting pt. for trips into high Cascades of Mt. Baker Nat. For., as well as to San Juan Is. lying off-shore on Puget Sound. 9th & Section St., **Allen R. Moore Mus.** (O.appl.); coll. of Ind. relics, etc.

SIDE TRIP: Take St.1 (L) from Mt. Vernon. This route crosses to Fidalgo I., named for Sp. explorer, Salvador Fidalgo, & then turns S. & crosses to Whidbey I., named for Jos. Whidbey, who discovered it in 1792, & ends at Columbia Beach at I.'s S. extremity, where ferry runs to Mukilteo (see above). 7m J. with improved Rd.

Take latter (L). At 4m **Pioneer Mon.** At 4.5m **La Conner,** where is observ. tower (fine view). Cont. short distance to **Swinomish Ind. Reserv.** (336 Inds.) where is small Ind. settlement with carved totem pole, which has, among other ornaments, carved likeness of F.D. Roosevelt. (R) from here to **Long H.,** 2m, where is held, at end of Jan., festival comm. treaty bet. Gov. Isaac I. Stevens & Inds., 1855.

St.1 cont. to **Fidalgo I.** & J. at 12.5m with St.1D.

Turn (R) here on St.1, 4m to **Anacortes,** from which ferry runs to **San Juan Is.**

Main route cont. (S) on St.1D. 14.5m **Campbell L.** (camp.recr.f.). 17m **Deception Pass St. Pk.** (swim.recr.camp.f.community kitchen). 18m **Deception Pass Bridge,** spanning deep, tidal chasm which separates Fidalgo I. from Whidbey I. At 19m is J. with Rd. leading (R) 0.5m to **Cranberry L.** (camp.recr.fee for overnight parking), near which is **North Beach.** 33m **Old Cth.** (N.O.1855.remod.). 36m **Coupeville,** sett. by Thomas Coupe, 1852. **City Pk.** (camp.). **Alexander Blockh.** (1855.rest.) moved here from orig. site, contains small coll. of relics. Water festival is held here in Aug. by Inds., who come from great distance to take part in canoe races. During festival, ancient canoes are exhibited. On Front St., **Capt. Thomas Coupe H.** (1853). 37.5m **Prairie Center,** at J. with Rd.

Take latter (R) 0.5m to J. with 2nd Rd.; turn (L) on this to J. with Rd., 1m, & (R) on latter to **Sunnyside Cemetery,** 1.5m, where pioneer settlers are buried. Here is **David Blockh.** (1855.rest.). Cont. (L) from Cemetery to Frank J. Pratt, Jr. farm, with **Jacob Ebey Mon. & Jacob Ebey Blockh.** (1855.rest.O.appl.), comm. Col. Isaac N. Ebey who settled in vic. in 1850 & was killed & decapitated by Inds. in 1857.

38m J. with 2 Rds.

Take Rd. leading (R) 2.5m to J. with another Rd. Straight ahead a short distance is **Crockett Blockh.** (1855.rest.).

St.1D ends at **Columbia Beach** (resort), 66m Ferry to Mukilteo, near Everett (see above).

**64.5.** J. with US99 Alt.

SIDE TRIP: Take latter (L) to **Larrabee St. Pk.** (camp.swim.pic.community kitchen), at 15m, which gives fine views of Puget Sound Is. In pk. is amphitheater with excellent acoustics. US99 Alt. now circles up along cliffs of Chuckanut Mt. to **Bellingham** 24m.

**65.** J. with St.1F (see Loop Tour from Marysville above).

**87. BELLINGHAM**

Through RR. & bus conns. Accoms.: All types. Info.: C. of C., Herald Bldg.; Auto Club of Wash. (A.A.A.), Hotel Henry; Hqs. Mt. Baker Nat. For., P.O. Bldg. Swim.: Perfection Beach; Whatcom Falls Pk.; L. Samish. Good f. in Bellingham Bay & waters around San Juan Is. & in Ls. & streams in vic.

Bellingham is situated on Bellingham Bay, opp. Lummi I., with view of San Juan Is. Whatcom Cr. cuts through city. Bellingham is considerable port & industrial center with pulp & woodworking mills, canneries & salmon packing plants—some of world's largest. Coal & other minerals are mined in vic. Bellingham Bay was discovered by Sp. explorer, Eliza, 1791, & rediscovered by Whidbey, of Vancouver's expedition, next yr., but was not settled till after internat. boundary, some 18m (N), was fixed by treaty, 1846. Early settlers did not suffer from Ind. troubles of 1855-56, although, anticipating trouble, they built fort & stockade. Lummi & N. Coast Inds. were friendly. Nearest thing to Ind. trouble occurred somewhat later, when local sheriff arrested Lummi Chief & his son, who had killed another Ind. Band of Lummi came down to rescue their fellow tribesmen, but were driven off after fight on beach. In 1858 town was temporarily depopulated by short-lived Fraser R. gold rush.

Toward turn of cent. Bellingham finally came into existence as city when four orig. towns, Sehome, Fairhaven, Whatcom & New Whatcom, merged. Near-by coal mines were early source of prosperity; however, because quality of coal was poor, mines were temporarily abandoned. Exploitation of fors. in back country has been basis of city's prosperity, together with salmon fishing, vegetable & fruit-raising & dairying.

PTS. OF INT.: (1) W. Holly & E Sts., **Old Whatcom County Cth.** (O.appl.1858). (2) 910 Bancroft St., **Capt. Geo. Pickett H.** (O.aft.last Thurs.of month.1856-60), containing hist. relics, where lived Capt. Geo. Pickett, of Gettysburg fame, when he was stationed at Ft. Bellingham. (3) 1220 Central Ave., **Washington Co-op. Chick Assoc. Plant** (O.wks.Sat.a.m.) from which more than 1,500,000 chicks are shipped annually. (4) On High St., **Western Wash. College of Education** with several bldgs., incl. new gymnasium, added in recent years; in Lib. are int. bird coll., herbarium, & exhibits of Ind. material. (5) Near college campus, on Huntoon Dr., **Sehome Hill Pk.** (fine views). (6) In S. Bellingham, **Fairhaven Pk. & Rose Garden** (swim.tennis). (7) On Lakeway Dr., **Whatcom Falls Pk.**, in which are falls of Whatcom Cr. & Trout Hatching Sta. (O). (8) E. edge of city, **L. Whatcom** (resort facils.), skirted by Five Ls. Dr.

SIDE TRIP: Take St.1 (Mt. Baker Hy.) (E) from Bellingham. This route parallels Nooksack R. & near its terminus turns (S) to Shuksan Ridge. Reg. is scenically magnificent. There are many well-equipped for. camps along route or near it. 28m **Maple Falls,** at J. with Rd. leading (L) 1.5m to **Silver L.** (accoms.recr.f.). 36m **Glacier,** at J. with Coal Mine Rd.

Take latter (R) 2m. Then follow trl. (L) to **Kulshan Cabin** at 7m. From here starts ascent of **Mt. Baker** (10,750′), most popular route. However, guides should be employed & only experienced alpinists should undertake climb.

36.5m **Glacier Ranger Sta.** (info.permits). 40.5m **Nooksack For. Camp** (trlrs.f.) short distance (R) from hy. 41m take Church Mt. Trl. (L) here to **Mt. Lookout** (6,245′). 41.5m **Bridge Cr. For. Camp** (f.) across bridge (R). 42.5m Take Rd. short distance (R) to **Excelsior For. Camp.** (trlrs.f.). Rd. cont. to Nooksack Falls Power Plant. 45m **Nine Mile For. Camp** (f.). 49m **Shuksan Inn** (accoms.camp). Just beyond Inn, hy. intersects Twin Lakes Rd.

Take latter (L) 5m & then steep trl. 1m to **Twin Ls.**

50m **Silver Fir For. Camp** (trlrs.f.h.community kitchen) & Guard Sta. (info.permits). Hy. now climbs above deep Nooksack R. Canyon. 57.5m **Galena For. Camp** (trlrs.community kitchen). A little beyond are **Highwood L.** (4,012′) & **Picture L.** 58.5m **Mt. Baker Lodge** (4,177′;accoms.various types.skiing:Dec.-July.guides) located near Heather Meadows bet. shoulders of Mts. Baker & Shuksan. Fine views. Near Lodge is ski-tow. 59.5m **Austin Pass Pic. Grounds & Guard Sta.** Skiing area, with ski-runs from Panorama Dome. 60.5m **Austin Pass** (4,363′).

Take Austin Pass Trl. just above Guard Sta. (L) 0.5m to Swift Cr. (1) Take trl. (L) here 3m to **L. Ann,** below **Hanging Glacier** on W. wall of **Mt. Shuksan** (9,038′). (2) Take trl. (R) down Swift Cr. Canyon to J. at 10m with Baker L. Rd. conn. with St.17A (see above Loop Tour from Marysville).

61.5m **Kulshan Ridge** (5,000′). Views of Mts. Baker & Shuksan.

**Mt. Baker** ascent (difficult & hazardous & should not be attempted except by seasoned alpinists & with guides); take trl. (R) from Kulshan Ridge 1m to J. with Chain Ls. Trl. & cont. (L) from J. to **Camp Kizer** (overnight stopover) at 7m. From here climb begins, crossing or passing near spectacular glaciers & snow fields to summit, requiring 2 or 3 days. Climbers must register at Glacier Ranger Sta. or Austin Pk. Guard Sta.

US99 cont. (N) to **BLAINE,** last town before reaching Canada, at **110.5.** At **111. CANADIAN BORDER,** 32m from Vancouver B.C., **U.S. Customs Sta.** Here are **Sam. Hill Mem. Pk.,** landscaped, & concrete **Peace Arch.**

## US 97—WASHINGTON

**WASH.-ORE. LINE** (12m from Wasco, Ore.) **(N) to CANADIAN BORDER** (2m from Osoyoos, B.C.). **335. US97**

Via: Maryhill, Goldendale, Toppenish, Yakima, Ellensburg, Teanaway, Cashmere, Wenatchee, (Everett), Chelan, Okanogan, Omak & Oroville, N.P. RR. parallels route bet. Toppenish & Teanaway; Gt.N. RR. bet. Dryden & Oroville. Bus serv. throughout.

This route runs N. skirting E. slopes of Cascade Range. In its S. sec. it follows Yakima R.; in its N. sec., Columbia & Okanogan Rs. US97 passes successively Columbia, Snoqualmie, Wenatchee & Chelan Nat. Fors. (W) &, in extreme N., Colville Nat. For. (W). Known as Cascade Internat. Hy., it was formerly route by which traders brought furs to Hudson's Bay Co. at Vancouver. It was also route for several late 19th cent. gold rushes.

## Sec. 1: MARYHILL to TEANAWAY. 139.

**1.5. STONEHENGE,** group of concrete slabs, set up to resemble Druid remains at Stonehenge, Eng., comm. soldiers & sailors of Klickitat Cty. who died in U.S. wars. **2.5. MARYHILL** (see US830) at J. with US830, near which is Maryhill Castle Mus. (see US830). Hy. now climbs rapidly to **GOLDENDALE** (1,610′) at **13.** (E) 10$^{m}$ from Goldendale, **Brooks Mem. Pk.** (pic.f.camp.community kitchen.skiing). US97 cont. (N) through **Horse Heaven Hills,** where are said to be troops of wild horses.

**64. TOPPENISH,** center of fairly rich agric. district. 119 E. Toppenish Ave., **Mary L. Goodrich Lib.,** in what is hist. & Ind. coll. 201 S. Chestnut St., **Leyman's Home Mus.** (O.appl.in store), contains coll. of Ind. material. SE. part of town, **Long H.** (Ind. articles for sale), in which Yakima Inds. indulge in 3 wks. of Christmas celebration. **Utah-Idaho Sugar Beet Plant** (O) where process of beet sugar manufacture can be observed.

SIDE TRIP: Take St.3B (L) from Toppenish into **Yakima Ind. Reserv.** (3,229 Inds.). At 20$^{m}$, **White Swan,** Ind. village with **Cath. Mission** & **Truesdale Mus.** (N.O.) containing coll. of Ind. material. At 28$^{m}$ **Ft. Simcoe** (1856). One of orig. bldgs. survives; also old **Blockh.** (O).

From Toppenish, US97 runs along Yakima R. **67. BUENA,** at J. with US410 (see), which unites briefly with US97. **83. YAKIMA** (see US410), where US410 branches (NW). US97 cont. along E. bank of Yakima R. to **ELLENSBURG** (see US10). **119.,** at J. with US10 (see), which unites with US97 to **TEANAWAY, 139.** Here US10 branches (W). For sec. bet. & incl. Ellensburg & Teanaway, see US10.

## Sec. 2: TEANAWAY to CANADIAN BORDER. 196.

**0. TEANAWAY** (see US10). US97 strikes (NE) to Swauk R., which it follows (N), passing several for. camps. **19. MINERAL SPRINGS FOR. CAMP** (2,700′;supplies. f.h.). **21.** J. with Rd. (R) to **Swauk Cr. For. Camp** (no trlrs.), 1$^{m}$. **23. BLEWETT PASS** (4,071′;lodge.winter sports). **33.5. INGALLS CR. LODGE,** near waterfall & near-by **Ingalls Cr. For. Camp. 42.** West J. with US2, with which US97 unites (E) to Wenatchee (see below).

SIDE TRIP: Take US2 (L), through fine orchard reg., up Wenatchee R. Valley. 5.5$^{m}$ **Leavenworth. Leavenworth Ranger Sta.** (permits.info.), hqs. for Leavenworth Recr. Area. (N), winter sports area. At 6$^{m}$ is J. with unimproved Rd.

Take latter (L) through fine scenery & past for. camps to **Chatter Cr. For. Camp** (facils.) at 17$^{m}$. From this pt., trl. runs into high Cascades.

11$^{m}$ **Drury** (accoms.) near **Drury Falls.** 16$^{m}$ **Tumwater For. Camp** (trlrs.community kitchen. swim.f.h.) in Tumwater Recr. Area. 19$^{m}$ **Winton** (supplies). 20.5$^{m}$ J. with St.15C.

Take latter (R) 4.5$^{m}$ to **Wenatchee L.** (resort) where is **Wenatchee L. For. Camp** (trlrs. boat.swim.f.h.). There are other for. camps on L. Near here is **Wenatchee L. St. Pk.** (296 as.facils.). Rd. runs (W) from Wenatchee L. into high Cascades. Cont. on St.15C to Fish L. (f.) at 6.5$^{m}$. At 11$^{m}$, St.15C makes J. with For. Rd. which take (L) into high Cascades.

26.5$^{m}$ **Merritt & Merritt For. Camp** (2,000′;trlrs.ample facils.f.h.). 41$^{m}$ **Stevens Pass** (4,061′) & **Stevens Pass For. Camp** (4,065′;trlrs.f.h.). 49$^{m}$ **Scenic** (resort.winter sports). Near-by is **Scenic For. Camp** (f.h.).

At 71$^{m}$ **Eagle Falls.** 72.5$^{m}$. Take trl. here (L) to **Sunset Falls & Inn** (accoms.). 73$^{m}$ J. with N. Fork Skykomish Rd.

Take latter (R) 1$^{m}$ to **Index** & cont. along N. Fork of Skykomish R. through picturesque mt. country to **Galena Guard Sta.,** 9$^{m}$. At 9.5$^{m}$ Rd. forks. Take fork (R). At 12$^{m}$, **Troublesome Cr. For. Camp** (ample facils.f.h.). Side Rd. cont. past **Bear Falls** to **San Juan For. Camp** at 14$^{m}$ & **Garland Mineral Springs** (resort.accoms.supplies) at 15$^{m}$.

81$^{m}$ **Gold Bar,** at J. with Rd. leading (R) 4.5$^{m}$ to trls. to **Wallace Falls & Wallace L.,** latter dominated by **Mt. Stickney** (5,312′). 86.5$^{m}$ **Sultan,** at confluence of Skykomish & Sultan Rs., is lively lumbermen's town. Formerly, while hqs. for building of Gt.N. RR. down W. side of Cascades, RR. workers swarmed to its bars & it acquired reputation for brawling & disorder. 111$^{m}$ **Everett** (see US99), at J. with US99 (see).

US97 turns sharply (R) from J. (see above) with US2, with which it unites (E) for 15$^{m}$, & follows Wenatchee R. **44. DRYDEN. 49. CASHMERE,** in fruit-growing area. **57.** East J. with US2 (see US10) on N. outskirts of **WENATCHEE** (Ind. "place of the rainbow"). Center of town lies 4$^{m}$ away (SE) on US2.

RR. Sta: Columbia & Kittitas Sts. for Gt.N. RR. Airline serv. Accoms.: All types. Info.: C. of C., C. of C. Bldg.; Auto Club of Wenatchee, 106 Wenatchee Ave.; Wenatchee Nat. For. Hqs., P.O. Bldg.

Wenatchee, at J. of Wenatchee & Columbia Rs., is located in reg. formerly barren, rendered fertile by irrigation, which is noted for fine apples & other fruits. City is starting pt. for several recr. areas in Nat. Fors. covering Wenatchee Mts., & (N) in Mad R. & Entiat regs. of Cascades are fine Ls. & streams. Wenatchee celebrates Wash. St. Apple Blossom Festival (Ap.or May), lasting 3 days.

PTS. OF INT.: **Ohme Gardens,** with lookout tower (view). **Mem. Pk.,** in which is **N. Central Wash. Mus.** (O.exc.Mon.), containing archaeological, Ind. & pioneer exhibits. **Cedargreen's Frozen-Food Packing Plant** (O). Near city is **Wash. St. College Tree & Fruit Branch Experimental Sta.** (O).

SIDE TRIP: Take St.10 (R) 10m from Wenatchee to **Rock I. St. Pk.** on Columbia R. At 12m is **Rock I. Dam** (O.Sun.) on Columbia R., which develops maximum of 240,000 h.p. Dam has fish-ladders for fish to get above dam.

US97 cont. (N) from J. with US2 on outskirts of Wenatchee along Columbia R.

**62. LINCOLN ROCK,** supposed to bear resemblance to Great Emancipator. Near-by is **Replica of Lincoln Cabin. 70.** Ferry across Columbia R. to **Orondo** at J. with US2 (see US10). **74. ENTIAT,** at J. with Entiat R. Rd. which runs into high Cascades. **93. LAKESIDE,** at J. with Rd. leading (L) 12m to **Chelan St. Pk.** (140 as.).

**94. CHELAN** at S. end of **L. Chelan.** Rodeo July or Aug. L. Chelan is narrow body of water, crowded in on both sides by steeply rising mts. It is 40m long & is asserted to be one of deepest Ls. in world. At its upper end, mts. rise to heights of 8,000′ or more. Many trls. radiate from resorts on L. to pts. of scenic int. Rds. run from Chelan along SW. shore of L. for considerable distance & for shorter distance along NE. shore. On L. shore are for. camps. Boats ply bet. Chelan & Stehekin, at NE. end of L., stopping at resorts en route. From Stehekin, Rd. runs (NW) into high Cascades. **96.** J. with St.10D, leading (R) along Chelan R. Gorge to **Chelan Falls,** 4m, at Chelan R.'s J. with Columbia R. **113.** J. with St.16.

SIDE TRIP: Take latter (L) along Methow R. 11m **Methow.** 34m **Twisp,** at J. with Cascade Wagon Rd., leading (L) into Cascades on which are 5 for. camps. 43.5m **Winthrop,** at J. with several for. Rds. leading into mts., on which are for. camps. Cont. from Winthrop on St.16. 76.5m **Harts Pass** (6,157′). Near-by, **Harts Pass For. Camp.** This Rd. in future will be cont. across Cascades to J. with St.17A at Rockport (see US99).

**120. BREWSTER,** near confluence of Okanogan & Columbia Rs. Across Okanogan R. is **Site of Old Ft. Okanogan,** est. 1811 by John Jacob Astor, oldest settlement in Wash. **144. OKANOGAN,** in area irrigated from Concocully Reservoir.

SIDE TRIP: Take Rd. (L) from Okanogan through irrigated valley 16m to **Conconully,** bet. **Salmon L. & Conconully Reservoir.** Near-by is **Conconully St. Pk.** (pic.f.). Rd. cont. from Conconully (R) past several for. camps. At 10m **Salmon Meadows For. Camp** (5,000′; trlrs.f.h.community kitchen), with lodge & ski-run. Trls. radiate in various directions to near-by Ls. & streams. At 18m **Sinlahekin Cr.,** fine canyon decorated with Ind. paintings. View of **Tiffany Mt.** (8,275′).

**148.5. OMAK,** small lumber mill town. About 8m away (SE) is **Omak L.,** cliff-enclosed. In Aug., rodeo, known as Omak Stampede. **173.** J. with St.4.

SIDE TRIP: Take latter (R) across Okanogan R. via **Tonasket** to J. at 20.5m with Rd. & turn (L) here to **Bonaparte L.** at 5m, near which is **Bonaparte L. For. Camp** (h.f.boat.).

**191. OROVILLE,** at J. of Okanogan & Similkameen Rs., in heart of picturesque L. & mt. reg.

SIDE TRIP: Take Similkameen R. Rd. (L) through fine **Similkameen Gorge** to **Nighthawk** at 14m. At 17m **Palmer L.,** dominated by **Palmer Mt.** (4,267′).

US97 now passes **Osoyoos L.** (which extends into Canada) & reaches **Customh.** on **CANADIAN BORDER** at **196.**

## US 395—WASHINGTON

**CANADIAN BORDER** (at Cascade, B.C.) **(S) to WASH.-ORE. LINE** (42m from Pendleton, Ore.). **297. US395**

Via: Laurier, Colville, Chewelah, Deer Pk., Spokane, Cheney, Ritzville & Pasco. Gt.N. RR. parallels route bet. Laurier & Spokane; N.P. RR. bet. Spokane & Pasco. Bus line along route. Good Rd. Accoms.: In towns & cities; otherwise primitive.

This route traverses sparsely populated E. part of Wash. From Brit. Columbia it runs (S) along Columbia R. to Kettle Falls & then (SE) along Colville R., winding through mt. valleys bet. 2 secs. of Colville Nat. For., but emerges into more open country as it nears Spokane. From Spokane it runs (S) through fertile countryside & then through Big Bend plateau of Columbia R. Near Pasco, Snake R. joins Columbia. Completion of Grand Coulee Dam project on Columbia R. has backed up waters of Columbia R. in Roosevelt L. all the way to Canada & forced relocation of some towns & hys. This project will transform, by irrigation & power development, whole Big Bend reg.

**Sec. 1: CANADIAN BORDER** (at Cascade, B.C.) **to SPOKANE. 125.**

**10.5. ORIENT,** at J. with for. Rd. leading (L) 2m to **First Thought Mt. Lookout Sta.** (fine view). US395 crosses Columbia R. to **KETTLE FALLS, 34.,** formerly Meyers Falls, to which Kettle Falls was moved when flooded out by Roosevelt L. **43. COLVILLE,** formerly gold rush town & scene of usual gunplay of pioneer days, aggravated in this case by clashes bet. soldiers stationed in old Ft. Colville. Near-by **Mt. Colville** (3,667′) is accessible by Rd. At summit is **Summit H.** Vic. of Colville affords good h., f. & winter sports (info.: C. of C.). **67. CHEWELAH,** center of resort area of good f. in Ls. & streams; good h. & skiing. **MacPHERSON H.** (1860. log construction). **76. VALLEY,** at J. with Rd. leading (R) 3m to **Waits L.** (accoms. f.h.). **91. LOON L.** (resort.accoms.). Here Harry Tracy, noted bandit, had log cabin. It is locally reported that his behavior was exemplary. He earned his living by cutting wood at 50¢ per cord. **96.5.** J. with Rd. leading (L) 6m to **Deer L.** (O.accoms.).

**102. DEER PK.,** shipping pt. for clay, lumber & farm products. **119. J.** with US2-195.

SIDE TRIP: Take latter (L) to J. with Mt. Spokane Rd. at 5.5m.

Take latter (R) 16m to **Mt. Spokane St. Pk.** (5,808′;accoms.ski tows & lift.ski sch.), very popular winter skiing center, with St.-owned lodge 2m from summit, & stone **Vista H.** at summit (magnificent view).

US2-195 cont. (N) to **Pend Oreille St. Pk.** (393 as.camp.), tract of virgin for. at 27m. 43m **Newport,** farming, mining & lumbering community on Pend Oreille R., which forms Idaho Line.

US395 cont. (S) from J. with US2-195, which unites with it. **125. SPOKANE. J.** with US10 (see) & US195 (see US10).

**Sec. 2: SPOKANE to ORE. LINE. 172.**

US395 & US10 united from Spokane (SW) for 70m (for description of this sec., see US10). **85. LIND,** farmers' shipping pt. **113. CONNELL,** farm community. At **120.5** is J. with St.11B.

SIDE TRIP: Take latter (L) to **Kahlotus** 18m, on W. shore of **Washtucna L.,** 2m long & 0.5m wide. Near-by is lava dome, **Devil's Mon.,** in Devil's Canyon.

US395 cont. (SE) through sandy, rock-dotted desert area. **149. PASCO,** at J. with US410 (see), with which US395 unites, following bend of Columbia R. to J. at **166.,** where it branches (S), following R. to **ORE. LINE, 172.**

## US 10—WASHINGTON

**WASH.-IDAHO LINE** (14m from Coeur d'Alene, Idaho) **(W) to SEATTLE, WASH. 309. US10**

Via: Spokane, (Wenatchee), Cheney, Ritzville, Ellensburg, Teanawy, Cle Elum & North Bend. N.P. RR. parallels route bet. Spokane & Ritzville & bet. Cle Elum & Easton; Chi. Mil., St.P.&P. RR. bet. Cle Elum & N. Bend. Accoms.: All types; for. camps in mt. stretches.

US10 in Wash. cuts (SW) from Spokane across sparsely populated, high central plateau. This is country of deep coulees, scoured out by prehist. R. which once traversed reg. Lava outcroppings & uncultivated areas alternate with spreading wheat fields, rendered fertile by great irrigation works. Most sensational of these is recently completed Grand Coulee project on Columbia R. From Ellensburg, hy. ascends into Cascades, which it crosses by Snoqualmie Pass, into Snoqualmie R. Valley, finally reaching Seattle.

**Sec. 1: WASH.-IDAHO LINE to ELLENSBURG. 202.**

**1. EAST FARMS.** (R) here 7m to resort on **Newman L.**

**6.** J. with Rd. leading (L) 2m to **Liberty L.** (recr.f.).

## 19. SPOKANE

RR. Stas.: 416 W. Trent St., U.P. RR., Ore. Wash. RR.; 221 W. First Ave., N.P. RR.; Stephens St. & Havermale I., Gt.N. RR. & N.P. RR. Bus Sta.: Motor Bus Terminals, 229 N. Howard St. & Desert Hotel, 725 W. 1st Ave. Airport: Through conns. Accoms.: All types. Info.: C. of C. & Inland Auto Assoc., Civic Bldg. Fish. in near-by streams & lakes; hunt. in vic. Swim. in number of municipal pools. Skiing at Mt. Spokane (NE) where is held winter ski tournament.

Spokane (sett.c.1871) likes to refer to itself as capital of "Inland Empire." With completion of Grand Coulee project only 92$^{m}$ away, city hopes to become center of vast irrigated area of more than 1,000,000 as. & to have access to great new sources of cheap hydroelectric power. Even before building of Grand Coulee project, Spokane benefited from almost 300,000 h.p. produced by hydroelectric plants. Consequently, during World War II, there was considerable development of lighter metals industries, especially aluminum & magnesium. City is within short distance of some of greatest remaining lumber reserves of country, & lumber & woodworking mills play important part in its economy. It is also center of important mining reg. Rich surrounding land, much of it irrigated, produces quantities of agric. products, with trend away from wheat farming to more intensive cultivation. Spokane straddles Spokane R. at pt. where latter makes its impressive 150′ drop, known as Spokane Falls. Latah (Hangman's) Cr. circles city (W) & Coeur d'Alene Mts. make fine scenic backdrop (E). Spokane is hub of great recr. area. In vic. are more than 76 lakes & (N) Mt. Spokane (5,808′), mecca for winter sports enthusiasts. First settlement at Spokane was not made until 1871, despite its favorable location (salmon could not climb falls of Spokane R.). But in 1810, Northwest Fur Co., soon taken over by Hudson's Bay Co., had est. post 10$^{m}$ from site of present city. Spokane H., as this outpost was known, was famous throughout NW. for hospitality to trappers & Inds. Next year, Astor est. his Pacific Fur Co. at same pt., but was forced to sell out to his Brit. rival because of War of 1812. By 1838, mission was est. at Tshimakain. Missionaries admitted that, after 9 yrs. of effort, they had failed to make a single convert. It is recorded that one Ind. remarked: "Forget religion, have plenty tobacco." Nevertheless, these white men earned respect of the tribes. When they moved to Ft. Colville, Inds. went along to see them safely to their destination. Spokane Inds., under leadership of Chief Garry, converted to Christianity, turned friendly, which unfortunately for them did not prevent their being pushed off their lands by flood of settlers from E. It is recorded that in his later yrs., Chief Garry was reduced to begging for food in city streets. For short period in 1877, Nez Percé uprising created panic & many settlers came scurrying to take refuge on Havermale I. at Spokane. But now a stream of immigration set in. First newspaper, "The Times," was founded in 1879; its printing plant had to be laboriously hauled in from Portland. With arrival of N.P. RR. in 1883 & gold rush to Coeur d'Alene district in same yr., the boom was on.

Despite temporary set-back in 1889, when 32 sq. blocks were destroyed by fire, city's expansion continued pretty steadily. 1891-92 was memorable for strikes & resulting violence in Coeur d'Alene dist., when strike-breakers were employed by mine owners. Depression of 1893 led unemployed to organize contingents for Gen. Coxey's armies, which failed to reach their destination because of transportation difficulties. In later years I.W.W. invaded city. They were forbidden to speak on the streets by ordinance. Six hundred were sent to jail, which became so overcrowded that ordinance had to be repealed. Cheap "colonist rates" in 1902 brought additional floods of emigrants. It was around turn of the century that Lord Sholto Douglas, who was passing through Spokane, ordered city's bars to dispense free "booze" to all comers, which resulted in memorable Sun. celebration.

PTS. OF INT.: (1) Riverside Ave. & Lincoln St., **Federal Bldg.** (1909.Neo-Class.). (2) 1021 Riverside Ave., **Civic Bldg.** (1921.Ital.Ren.by Whitehouse & Price); entrance hall decorated by frieze & panels illustrating economic phases of NW. (3) 1115 W. Riverside Ave., **Our Lady of Lourdes Cathedral** (Cath.1908.Romanes.) is impressive bldg. with 2 lofty towers. (4) 18 S. Cedar St., **Pub. Lib.** (O.Class.by Preusse & Zittel); rare bibliophile items & hist. material concerning NW. (5) 2316 W. 1st Ave., **Spokane Pub. Mus.** (O.1-5 wks.2-5 Sun.Eng.Tudor.by Kirtland K.Cutter) contains nat. hist., anthropological & hist. relics. (6) **Monroe St. Bridge** (1911.by Cutter & Malgram) spans Spokane R. with beautiful concrete arch, 136′ high. (7) Broadway (across Spokane R.), **Spokane County Cth.** (1895.Fr.Ren.by W.A.Ritchie) has lofty tower. (8) Across upper end of Spokane Falls, 502 E. Boone Ave., **Gonzaga Univ.** for men (est.1887 by Jesuit Order). In Adm. Bldg., **Gonzaga Mus.** (O.appl.); coll. of hist. relics. Adj., **St. Aloysius Ch.** (Romanes.by Preusse & Zittel) with 2 tall spires. (9) In S. sec. of city, **Review Rock,** volcanic cone, in Cliff Pk. (10) 1125 S. Grand Blvd., **Cathedral of St. John** (Episc.Goth.by Whitehouse & Price), with 2 fine towers & beautiful rose & other stained glass windows by Boston's Charles J. Connick, who made windows of St. John's Cathedral in N.Y.C. (11) Grand Blvd., **Manito Pk.** with fine botanical gardens. (12) Down River Dr., near NW. city limit, **Down River Pk.** (recr.) on Spokane R. Canyon. (13) Across R., on Elliot Dr., **Ft. George E. Wright Military Reserv.,** comm. officer in command of Fed. troops that defeated Inds. at Spokane Plains. (14) Also across R. 3$^{m}$ (NW) from city, **Riverside St. Pk.** (5,380 as.pic.camp.trlrs.community kitchen) is on Spokane R. & has int. canyons & geological formations. (15) In Spokane also is **Whitworth College** (1883).

SIDE TRIPS: (A) Take US195 (S) from Spokane through vast spreading wheat fields of "Inland Empire." 33$^{m}$ **Rosalia,** farmers' community. 34.5$^{m}$, short distance (E) from hy. is **Steptoe Mem.,** comm. battle (May 17, 1858) in which Col. E. J. Steptoe was forced by Inds. to withdraw his troops. At 52$^{m}$ is J. with Rd. leading (R) 5$^{m}$ to **Steptoe Butte St. Pk.** 61$^{m}$ **Colfax** (sett.1870), wheat growers' trading center. 78$^{m}$ **Pullman,** grain storage & shipping pt. Here is **St. College of Wash.** (opened 1892), with notably large College Lib. & College Mus. with nat. hist., hist. & Ind. colls. It is 2nd largest educational institution in Wash. At 100$^{m}$ is **Idaho Line,** near **J.** with US95, 10$^{m}$ N. of Lewiston, Idaho at J. with US410 (see).

(B) Take Seven-Mile Rd. from Spokane 9$^{m}$ to impressive **Deep Cr. Canyon** &, at 10.5$^{m}$, **Nine-Mile Dam,** with Spokane power plant. Near here stood Spokane H.

(C) Take US2 branching (R) from US10 at W. city limit of Spokane. 12$^{m}$ **Spokane Battlefield St. Pk.,** with mon. where, in 1858, Amer. troops commanded by Col. Geo. Wright defeated band of Inds. & avenged Col. Steptoe's defeat (see above). 37$^{m}$ **Davenport,** center of considerable wheat growing & mining area. At Davenport is J. with St.22 running (N) along Roosevelt L. to J. with US395 near Kettle Falls.

At 66$^{m}$ on US2 is **Wilbur.** 66.5$^{m}$ J. with St.4.

Take latter (R) 3$^{m}$ to J. with St.4C & turn (L) on this to **Grand Coulee,** 25$^{m}$, near **Grand Coulee Dam,** boom town, which sprang up during construction of Grand Coulee Project. Near here is **U.S. Gov. West Conservation Pt.** with splendid view view of dam. In bldg. is large model of project. Dam is located at pt. where Columbia R. flows through deep & comparatively narrow gorge. Dam is one of the largest constructions ever created by man—550′ high, 4,137′ long, 500′ thick at its base, 3 times bigger than largest Egyptian pyramid. It backs up L. extending 151$^{m}$ into Canada. Elevated some 280′ above L., is **GRAND COULEE,** huge trough scoured out of surface of plateau by action of R. Grand Coulee is some 50$^{m}$ long, with average depth of 800′ & width varying 2$^{m}$ to 5$^{m}$. Gov. engineers have thrown earthen dams across this trough, enclosing sec. 27$^{m}$ long. Water is pumped up from L. below into basin thus created, which is filled during periods of high water when Columbia R. is at flood. Stored water is released from this reservoir as required for irrigation, & flows by gravity through main canal for distribution over formerly parched lands of plateau. Land to be irrigated, some 1,200,000 as., about equal to area of Delaware, lies for most part S. of Columbia R. Project also, by regulating water flow of Columbia R., permits increased power output at Bonneville & other pts. & provides greater navigation depths during low-water periods. Grand Coulee is but one of several projects planned for development of Columbia R.'s resources. Present dam's use only 27 percent of R.'s power capacity. Other dams, 10 altogether, will be built to utilize these resources up to 92 percent.

US2 cont. (W) to J. with St.7 at 99$^{m}$.

Take latter (L) 1.5$^{m}$ to **Dry Falls St. Pk.** (pic.camp.boat.f.no h.). Here is **Vista H.,** overlooking cliffs of canyon, 417′ deep & 3$^{m}$ wide, through which in prehist. times Columbia R. plunged into valley below. This canyon is extension of Grand Coulee. Cont. on St.7 through canyon past scenically fine **Park L., Blue L.** (recr.), **Lenore L.** & **Soap L.** to J. with US10 (see below) 53$^{m}$.

US2 cont. through impressive **Moses Coulee.** 150$^{m}$ **Orondo.** Ferry across Columbia R. to Entiat at J. with US97 (see). From Orondo, hy. runs (S) along E. bank of Columbia R., which it crosses, finally, to **Wenatchee,** 168$^{m}$, at J. with US97 (see).

At Spokane is J. with US395 (see), with which US10 unites (S) for 70$^{m}$. 32.5

**32.5. FOUR LAKES,** with mon. on **Site of Battle of Four Lakes** (1858) bet. c.5,000 Inds. & small U.S. Army force led by Col. Geo. Wright, resulting in U.S. victory. At Four Lakes is J. with Rd. leading (R) to **Silver L.** (f.) at 3.5$^{m}$ & **Medical L.** (resort) at 5$^{m}$. **38. CHENEY,** home of **E. Wash. College of Education.** Near **SPRAGUE, 63.,** is **Colville L.,** 6$^{m}$ long. **87. RITZVILLE,** wheat milling & shipping pt. At **89.,**

US395 (see) branches (S). US10 turns (W) across high plateau area. **133. MOSES L.,** 16m long. At **135. MOSES L. ST. PK.** (R) (pic.swim.boat.). **161.** J. with St.7 (see above). **174.** US10 bridges **COLUMBIA R.** which cuts rocky gorge deep through plateau. **176.5. GINKGO PETRIFIED FOR. ST. PK.** (5,979 as.) containing fossilized ginkgo trees & 75 other prehist. species, 10,000,000 yrs. or more old. **Adm. Bldg.** exhibits specimens & mineral coll. **202. ELLENSBURG** (sett.1867), dairying, farming & gold- & coal-mining center, with **Central Wash. College of Education** (est.1890), at J. with US97 (see), with which US10 unites to Teanaway.

### Sec. 2: ELLENSBURG to SEATTLE. 107.

US10-97 follows Yakima R. (NW), entering at **12.** picturesque gorge. **20. TEANAWAY.** Here US97 (see) branches (N). US10 cont. (NW) into Cascade Mts. **24. CLE ELUM.** At **25.** is J. with St.2E.

SIDE TRIP: Take latter (R) to **Roslyn,** 3m. Here is **Northwest Mine** (O). Utah & N. 2nd Sts., **Log Cabin** (1880). Rd. cont. through picturesque reg. to **Cle Elum L.** (resort) at 8m. L.'s waters are impounded by high dam & are used for irrigation.

US10 cont. (W) to **EASTON** with RR. Js., at **38.** At **39.5.** is J. with Rd. leading (R) 1m to **Kachess L.** (2,231′), on whose W. shore is **Kachess For. Camp** (2,250′;facils.f.).

**48. KEECHELUS L.** (resort), impounded by dam, is hemmed in by steep, forest-covered mts. Hy. now passes **ROCKY RUNS FOR. CAMP.** (2,530′;trlrs.boat.f.) at **52.** on L. shore. At **55.5.** is **HYAK** (resort). Take trl. 2m (L) here to **Snoqualmie Ski Bowl** (accoms.ski-lift). **57.5. SNOQUALMIE PASS SUMMIT** (3,004′). Near here is **Snoqualmie Pass For. Camp** (facils.). Short distance beyond is J. with trl. (L) to **Seattle Ski Club.** Short distance farther is trl. (L) to **Mun. Ski Lodge,** operated by City of Seattle (ski runs & lift).

US10 now begins downward course, along W. slopes of Cascades. **78. NORTH BEND** at J. with paved hy. leading (R) 3m to **Snoqualmie** & **Snoqualmie Falls,** 270′ high which is used for generation of electric power, at 4m. **90.5.** J. with US10 Alt. to Seattle via Renton. US10 cont. straight ahead (W), passing **L. Sammamish** (resort. recr.camp.f.) & crossing **L. Washington** by L. Washington Bridge (see Seattle) to reach **SEATTLE** (see), **107.** at J. with US99.

## US 410—WASHINGTON

**WASH.-IDAHO LINE** (1m from Lewiston, Idaho) **(W) to ABERDEEN, WASH. 450. US410**

Via: Clarkston, Pomeroy, Dayton, Walla Walla, Pasco, Kennewick, Prosser, Grandview, Sunnyside, Yakima, Enumclaw, Puyallup, Tacoma, Olympia, McCleary, Elma & Montesano. Rd. occasionally blocked by snow in Cascade Mts. RRs. parallel route bet. Clarkston & Yakima; Auburn & Aberdeen. Bus conns. throughout. Accoms.: All types in large centers. Camp. facils. in Cascades.

US410 is main cross-state hy. In its E. sec., it crosses high tableland of cattle & sheep ranges, then traverses fertile Walla Walla R. Valley & cont. into more arid reg. as it approaches Columbia R. This sec. gives access through side Rds. to Grand Canyon of Snake R. & Blue Mts. area. From Pasco, near confluence of Snake & Columbia Rs., hy. turns (NW) through orchard & farm reg. rendered fertile by great irrigation projects, following Yakima R., & then climbs along Naches R. into high Cascades, cuts across NE. sec. of Mt. Rainier Nat. Pk. & descends, along White R., into well-watered farmlands of Puget Sound reg. In its final sec., US410, circling (S) around Sound, runs (E) through Chehalis Valley to Aberdeen on coast.

### Sec. 1: WASH.-IDAHO LINE to YAKIMA. 229.

Bridge crosses Snake R. from Lewiston, Idaho, at J. with US195 (see US10) into Wash. **0.5. CLARKSTON** (accoms.), flanked (N) by high hills, is in fertile irrigated area at bend where Clearwater & Snake Rs. meet. Town was originally known as Jawbone Flats. From Spirit Hy., N. of city & 2,000′ above valley, there is magnificent view.

SIDE TRIP: Take St.3 (L) from Clarkston along Snake R. to **Asotin,** 6m, where picturesque Asotin Cr. debouches from canyon into Snake R.

Take unimproved Rd. (L) here 16.5m to **Buffalo Rock,** overhanging Grand Canyon of Snake R. On rocks of Wash. side are int. pictographs. Cont. on unimproved Rd. (S), paralleling Snake R., with magnificent views of peaks & canyon itself, to **Rogersburg,** at 22.5m, where Grande Ronde R. flows into Snake R.

Cont. on St.3 from Asotin to **Anatone,** 25m, encircled by Blue Mts., & to **Field's Springs St. Pk.** (23 as.camp.pic.community kitchen.skiing). At 38m **Grande Ronde R.** in beautiful mt. reg. Branch of St.3 cont. its picturesque course to Ore. Line 43m & (S) past scenically fine country, through **Paradise, Ore.,** to **Enterprise, Ore.,** at J. with Ore. St.82 (see Ore. US30).

**8.5. SILCOTT,** near which (NW) Snake R. drops into canyon 2,000′ deep. **27.5. PATAHA,** beyond which hy. runs through Pataha Cr. Canyon. **30.5. POMEROY,** once boom town on stage route to Lewiston, tough miners' & cattlemen's hangout.

SIDE TRIP: Take St.3K (L) from Pomeroy. At 7.5m turn (R) on fairly good Rd. into Umatilla Nat. For. At 18m J. with Rd. running (L) short distance to **Rose Springs** (resort). Cont. on main Rd. through scenically fine Blue Mts. At 43m is Ore. Line & at 50m, **Troy, Ore.,** from which various Rds. lead to Js. with Ore. St.82 (see Ore. US30), approaching Grand Canyon of Snake R.

**52.5. DELANEY**

SIDE TRIP: Take Rd. (R) from Delaney along Tucannon R. At 16.5m **Lyon's Ferry** across (R) Snake R. At 21m, J. with poor Rd., on which route turns (R) to J. at 22m with trl., short distance up which is **Palouse Falls,** where Palouse R. drops from great height & then flows through deep chasm to J. with Snake R. Near here is **Palouse Falls St. Pk.** (95 as.).

**67. DAYTON** (sett.1855), situated bet. Touchet R. & Patit Cr. Inds. camped here, as did Lewis & Clark & Bonneville expeditions. Dayton became important stage-coach stop & center from which prospectors started out on their hunt for gold in mts.

SIDE TRIP: Take Eckler Mt. Rd. (L) from Dayton. At 18m, Umatilla Nat. For. boundary. Cont. (S) on main route, now known as Blue Skyway Dr., through fine scenery, passing several for. camps, to **Table Rock** (6,370′) in Blue Mts., at 43m, whence fine views, especially of Grande Ronde Gorge. Blue Skyway Dr. reaches Ore. Line at 46m & cont. to **Tollgate, Ore.,** 73m (see US30,Ore.).

**71.5. LEWIS & CLARK TRL. ST. PK.** (35 as.camp.community kitchen) on Touchet R. where Lewis & Clark camped in 1806.

**97. WALLA WALLA**

RR. & bus conns. Airport. Accoms.: All types. Info.: Auto Club of Wash., Marcus Whitman Hotel, & C. of C., City Hall. In Sept., SE. Wash. Fair.

Walla Walla (Ind."many waters"), situated on R. of same name, in fertile valley threaded by numerous streams, is dominated to (SE) by Blue Mts. City is in hist. territory, just N. of Old Ore. Trl., travelled by Lewis & Clark. At near-by Wallula are ruins of Astor's Old Ft. Walla Walla. Only 6m from city is Whitman Nat. Mon., marking site of massacre of Waiilatpu missionaries by band of Cayuse in 1847 (see below). Gov. Stevens had his great powwow with 5,000 Inds. of E. Wash. at Walla Walla. He finally induced them to sign treaty. Stevens had an indestructible faith in utility of these pacts; but, as usual, soon after this one was signed, Inds. revolted again & War Dept. closed entire reg. as being too disturbed for settlement. It was not reopened until 1859, whereupon 3rd & last Ind. war promptly broke out. Meanwhile Walla Walla had been founded as Steptoeville. Col. Steptoe was commander of U.S. troops which narrowly escaped annihilation by Inds. (see US10). Building of Mullan Military Rd., at this time, from Ft. Benton, Mo., to Ft. Walla Walla, helped immigration, though its chief purpose was military. In 1861 discovery of gold at Orofino, Idaho, transformed little settlement into roaring mining town. Joaquin Miller is said to have become pony express rider bet. town & mines. Local lawlessness was tempered eventually by vigilante committees. In these early days when prospectors flooded into town, wooden frames were run up & covered with muslin. These were known as "muslin houses" & street on which they stood as "Muslin Row." In dance hall, where beside dancing, drinking & gambling went on, dance girls were organized in teams of four girls, presided over by "chaperons." Walla Walla's more recent growth has depended on agric. City ships out most of wheat grown on some 200,000 as. of surrounding countryside, & processes local vegetable & fruit crops, specializing in green peas of which 5 million cases are packed annually. When Columbia R. improvement projects are completed, vessels of fairly deep draft will be able to reach Pascoe, only short distance away. It is distinguished as birthpl. of Gen. Jonathan Wainwright, hero of Bataan.

PTS. OF INT.: Main & Colville Sts., plaque marking **Site of Second Ft. Walla Walla.** Isaacs Ave., **Whitman College** (1859.coed.), which has attendance of c.600 students. Here is **Whitman Mus.** (O.appl.) with colls. of NW. Americana, nat. hist. & anthropology. On campus is **Chief Lawyer Mon.,** comm. Nez Percé friend of Gov. Stevens. **103.5.** J. with Rd. leading (L) 0.5$^m$, then (R) 0.5$^m$ to **Whitman Nat. Mon.,** where stood bldgs. (to be rest.) of Waiilatpu Mission, est. 1836 by Marcus Whitman. Cayuse Inds. massacred Whitman, his wife & 12 others here in 1847. Stone marks burial place of missionaries. **126.** J. with US395 (see), with which US410 unites to Pasco. **127.** J. with unsurfaced Rd. leading (L) to **Wallula,** 0.5$^m$, & (L) here 1.5$^m$ to ruins of **Ft. Walla Walla** (1817-18) built by Northwest Fur Co. as strategic pt. near J. of Walla Walla & Columbia Rs.

US410-395 now runs N. along Columbia R. & at **139.** crosses Snake R. At **139.5.** is J. with Rd. leading (L) 2$^m$ to **Sacajawea St. Pk.,** comm. Ind. woman guide of Lewis & Clark Expedition. **143. PASCO,** on Columbia R. near its J. with Snake R., is small industrial center & market town for extensively irrigated reg. which will be considerably expanded with completion of Grand Coulee Project. Near site of Pasco, Lewis & Clark camped in Oct. 1805 & bought food & supplies—among other items, 40 dogs—from Inds. Later David Thompson of Northern Fur Co. put up sign at location pt. of Pasco, claiming reg. for Great Britain. City was officially born at completion of RR. bridge across Snake R., 1884. Construction hqs. were at near-by Ainsworth which developed reputation for gun play, vigilante justice, & quick hanging. But after job was finished, Ainsworth vanished almost over night. During World War II Pasco enjoyed its biggest boom. Population doubled, due largely to establishment of army depots & naval air sta. in neighborhood.

At Pasco, US395 (see) branches (N) & US410 crosses (L) Columbia R. **145. KENNEWICK.** Grapes are grown in vic., as well as cherries & other fruits. Rodeo held here around July 4 attracts many visitors. **149.5.** J. with Rd. leading (R) across R. 4$^m$ to **Richland,** before World War II, mere hamlet, now gov.-controlled city of 15,000, working on atomic projects, at S. edge of huge **Hanford Project, U.S. Military Reserv.** (N.O.). Community boasts it is crimeless, has empty jails, no one on relief rolls & no unemployment. US410 now follows (S) bank of Yakima R. past Horse Heaven Hills (see US97). **178. PROSSER,** on Yakima R. In **City Pk.** is **Petrified Sequoia** whose only habitat today is Cal. US410 crosses to N. Bank of Yakima R. from Prosser. **229. YAKIMA** (sett.c.1861), on Yakima R., center for irrigated reg. of c.500,000 as. In harvest time it is flooded with hundreds of seasonal workers who arrive to harvest crops.

PTS. OF INT.: 415 N. 2nd St., **Janeck H.** (O.appl.) containing large coll. of Ind. material. Adj., int. rock garden. 1408 W. Yakima Ave., **McWhorter H. Mus.** (O. appl.); coll. of Ind. material. Various plants which dehydrate & pack fruits may be visited on appl. (see C. of C.). In vic. is **Ft. Simcoe** (see US97). At Yakima US97 (see) branches (N).

## Sec. 2: YAKIMA to OLYMPIA. 174.

US410 follows Naches R. from Yakima ascending gradually into Cascades. At **5.** is J. with S. Naches R. Rd.

SIDE TRIP: Take latter (L) few hundred yds. to J. with trl. leading (R) few rods to cliff on which are **Prehist. Ind. Pictographs.** Cont. on S. Naches R. Rd. At 2.5$^m$ **Eschback Pk.** (fee.swim.pic.). Rd. cont. & at 12$^m$ rejoins US410.

US410 now enters impressive Naches R. canyon. **13.5. NACHES,** fruit-packing center. **18.5.** J. with St.5.

SIDE TRIP: Take latter (L) 20$^m$ through Tieton Gorge to **Tieton Dam,** impounding Tieton Reservoir, 21$^m$ in Tieton Recr. Area (Snoqualmie Nat. For.), reg. of high peaks, lovely Ls. & precipitous streams, incl. **Goat Rocks Wilderness Area,** whose outstanding feature is Goat Rocks (8,201′). Rd. cont. to **Clear Cr. Reservoir,** impounded by Clear Cr. Dam, 27$^m$, near which is **Clear L. For. Camp** (3,000′;ample facils.).

At **47.** on US410, **Indian Flat For. Camp** (ample facils.f.h.). **47.5.** J. with Amer. R. Rd.

SIDE TRIP: Take latter (L) along Amer. R. short distance to **Amer. R. Lodge** (accoms. winter sports.ski bowl). Take Rd. (L) here, passing several for. camps & **Goose Prairie** (small resort), dominated by **Goat Peak** (6,494′), to **Bumping L.** at 11.5$^m$, on which are tiny hamlet & **Bumping L. For. Camp** (f.h.boat.swim.).

US410 cont. (W) past **Fife's Peak** (6,954′) to **CHINOOK PASS** (5,400′) at **56.** (fine view of Mt. Rainier), named for mild winds that blow from Columbia R. reg. where Chinook Inds. used to live. These winds melt heavy snows in very short time. At **66. TIPSOO L.** (5,400′). **69.** J. with St.5 which runs (S) to **Ohanapecosh Entrance of Mt. Rainier Nat. Pk.** (see). **72.5.** J. with Rd. to **White R.** (Yakima Pk.) **Entrance** of Mt. Rainier Nat. Pk. (see). **79. SILVER CR. RANGER STA.** Near-by are **Fish Hatchery, Parkway P.O.** (cabins), & **Silver Springs For. Camp** (trlrs.ample facils.f.). US410 now parallels White R. **92.5. GREENWATER** (resort) & **GREENWATER FOR. CAMP** on White R. **105.** J. with Rd. leading (L) 2$^m$ to **Mud Mt. Dam,** allegedly highest earthen dam in world. Fish will be raised by ladders to spawning grounds in artificial L. created by project. US410 descending rapidly W. slopes of Cascades, reaches **ENUMCLAW** at **111.,** bet. White & Green Rs. 1453 Cole St., **Rochedale Cooperative Dept. Store,** run according to Rochedale system, one of few enterprises of its kind on West Coast.

SIDE TRIP: Take St.5 (S) here 4$^m$ to **Buckley,** at J. with branch of St.5.

Take latter (R) 2$^m$ to **Puget Sound Power & Light Co. Canal,** which runs from **L. Tapps Reservoir** near-by. Hydroelectric plant develops 82,600 h.p. Ladders permit fish to climb to spawning grounds. Ingenious rotary screens, largest in world, return fish that have wandered into power canal to White R.

At 23$^m$ on St.5 is **Carbon R. Entrance to Mt. Rainier Nat. Pk.** (see).

**120.5.** J. with Rd. Take latter (R) short distance, then (R) 1$^m$ & (R) again to **Ind. Graveyard,** in **Muckleshoot Ind. Reserv. 127. AUBURN,** important RR. division pt. & repair center. **132. DIERINGER,** where is **Puget Sound Power & Light Co. Plant** (O) which derives power from near-by L. Tapps Reservoir (see above). **135. SUMNER,** shipping & processing center for bulbs, berries & other agric. products of vic. **138. PUYALLUP.** One of attractive features of Puyallup countryside are hundreds of as. of daffodils whose cultivation is important industry. In Mar. is held daffodil festival. In **Pioneer Pk.,** statue by V. A. Lewis of Ezra Meeker, early pioneer & founder of the city. 321 E. Pioneer St., **Ezra Meeker H.** Puyallup celebrates "Days of Ezra Meeker" festival in Aug. & W. Washington Fair in Sept. City's various plants, mostly canneries (O). **145. TACOMA** at J. with US99 (see) with which US410 unites to **OLYMPIA** (see US99) at **174.**

### Sec. 3: OLYMPIA to WEST J. with US101. 47.

Leaving Olympia, US410 skirts Budd Inlet to E. J. at **5.** with US101 (see). **31.5. SATSOP,** at J. with Rd. leading (R) 8.5$^m$ to **Schaefer St. Pk.** (pic.recr.f.) on Satsop R. **37.5. MONTESANO** (sett.1854;good salmon f.), on Chehalis R., one of oldest towns in Wash. At 1st & Broad Sts., **Gray's Harbor County Cth.,** in which are murals depicting hist. events & typical Wash. scenery, by F. Rohrback & F. Bieberstein. There is plaque in bldg. comm. Collin McKenzie & A. V. Elmer, who were killed by John Turno, lawless character who for years infested reg. & finally killed these 2 men, who as sheriffs where hunting him after he had escaped from insane asylum. He was finally killed in fight with 2 other sheriffs. In cth. took place Centralia Massacre trials (see US99). Take 3rd St. (R) from Montesano 1.5$^m$ to **Sylvan L. St. Pk.** (pic.) on L. of same name. **47.** J. with US101 (see), 0.5$^m$ from **ABERDEEN** (see US101).

## US 830—WASHINGTON

**MARYHILL, WASH.** (at J. with US97) **(W) to JOHNSON'S LANDING, WASH. 212. US830**

Via: Bingen, North Bonneville, Camas, Vancouver & Longview. RRs. parallel route bet. Maryhill & Longview. Bus serv. throughout. Accoms.: All types. Good Rd.

This route runs along (N) side of magnificent Columbia R. Gorge & affords int. return trip to Portland for tourists who have traveled US30 along (S) side of R. Aside from gorge itself, chief features of this route are side trips, which branch off into Mt. Adams & Mt. St. Helens reg. of Columbia Nat. For.

### Sec. 1: MARYHILL to VANCOUVER. 104.

**0. MARYHILL,** at J. with US97 (see). Ferry crosses from Maryhill to Biggs, Ore., at J. with US30 (see) & US97 (see). Stonehenge Mon. (see US97) is 0.5$^m$ (W) from Maryhill. **4.** Take Rd. (L) here short distance to **Maryhill Castle** (O.pic.), built by Sam. Hill, son-in-law of RR. tycoon, Jas. J. Hill. Castle contains mus. in which are 50,000 items incl. Roumanian royal jewels; personal possessions of King Albert of

Belgium; relics of Napoleon & Queen Victoria; relics from the "Mayflower"; paintings & sculptures, incl. coll. of terra cotta & bronzes presented by Rodin; Ind. relics. **9.** Take Rd. (L) to **Wishram** & then trl. leading to **Celilo Falls** of Columbia R. **18.5.** Take Rd. (L) here 3m to **North Dalles,** where ferry runs to The Dalles, Ore. At this pt., R. plunges through very narrow gorge. E. of North Dalles c.2m at **Spearfish** are Ind. stone paintings. US830 now skirts lava formations of **Paha Cliffs. 26. LYLE. 27.** (R) on Rd. along **Klickitat R. Canyon,** 1,000′ deep, to **Klickitat Falls** 3m. **37.5. BINGEN,** J. with St.8D.

SIDE TRIP: Take latter (R) to **White Salmon** 1.5m.

Take Jewett St. (N) from White Salmon 3.5m to **Northwestern L.** (resort.swim.boat.f.). Cont. (N) on St.8D from White Salmon. At 22m **Trout Lake** (supplies).

(1) Take Rd. (L) from P.O. here 2m to **Guler,** where is Ranger Sta., & cont. to **Ice Caves,** 6m in which are int. ice formations. Here is **Ice Caves For. Camp.** Rd. cont. (W) & then (N), & passes number of for. camps to J. with Cispus R. Rd. to Randle (see Mary's Corner, US99).

(2) Take Rd. (R) from Trout Lake to **Bird Cr. Meadows For. Camp** (6,100′;facils.), starting pt. for ascent of **Mt. Adams** (12,307′). Multicolored cliffs & dazzling white glaciers accentuate peak's grandeur.

**39. WHITE SALMON-HOOD R. TOLL BR.** to Hood Rd., Ore., at J. with US30 (see). **56.5.** J. with St.8C.

SIDE TRIP: Take latter (R) via **Carson** at 1m & along Windy R. Valley, with view of Mt. Adams (NE) & Mt. St. Helens (NW) to J. at 10m.

Take Rd. here (R) around **Big Lava Bed** to **Race Track For. Guard Sta. & For. Camp** (3,900′) at 13m. Here is J. with Pacific Crest Trl. At 18m, **Goose L.,** along whose shores are lava formations bearing prints of human hands & feet. **Goose L. For. Camp** (3,250′; facils.). Rd. cont. to J. with Rd. from Trout L. (see above) at Peterson's For. Camp.

St.8C cont. to **Little Soda Springs For. Camp** (1,200′;f.h.) at 18m. At 19m, **Gov. Mineral Springs For. Camp** (trlrs.community kitchen.f.h.mineral springs).

**62.5. BRIDGE OF THE GODS** (toll) across Columbia R., at pt. near Cascade Locks, Ore., on US30 (see). US830 after circling cliffs of **TABLE MT.** (3,420′) reaches **N. BONNEVILLE** at **65.,** where is entrance to **Bonneville Dam** (O.guides. for description see US30,Ore.). **69. BEACON ROCK ST. PK.** with **Beacon Rock,** lava monolith whose walls drop sheer 900′ to R. & near-by **Little Beacon Rock,** where Lewis & Clark Expedition camped in 1805 & 1806. Hy. shortly skirts precipitous **Archer Mt.** & enters scenically fine stretch of Rd., passing **Mt. Zion** & craggy **Cape Horn,** where hy. runs far above R., to **CAMAS** at 90., on **Lackamas L.** (resort). Near site now occupied by town Lt. W. R. Broughton of Vancouver's expedition landed in 1792 & Lewis & Clark Expedition camped in 1806. In city is **Crown-Willamette Paper Co. Plant** (O.except Thurs.& Sat.appl.fee for guides), processing some 140 million board ft. of lumber annually & manufacturing various types of paper. 1600 Division St., **House Mus.,** containing coll. of Ind., pioneer & other relics. **95.** From this pt. Ind. carvings are visible on rocks along R. **98. ELLSWORTH.** Here are **St. Game Bldgs.** with fish-breeding pools. **104. VANCOUVER,** at J. with US99 (see). Bridge to Portland, Ore.

### Sec. 2: VANCOUVER to JOHNSON'S LANDING. 108.

From Vancouver US830 & US99 unite to pt. near Longview at **40.** (for this stretch of Rd. see US99). **42. LONGVIEW,** at confluence of Cowlitz & Columbia Rs., lumber mill & shipping town. Peninsula on which Longview is built was originally marshland but has been drained, leaving several charming Ls. in heart of city. Orig. settlement on site of Longview was known as Monticello & is famous as place where convention met in 1852, preparing way for setting up Washington as separate territory. Several large lumber mills in city may be visited to observe processes of making lumber, wood pulp, rayon, cellophane, fibreboard. Bridge crosses Columbia R. here to Rainier, Ore. on US30 (see). **108. JOHNSON'S LANDING** & J. with US101 (see).

## (Skeleton Tour) US 2—WASHINGTON

**WASH.-IDAHO LINE** (7m from Priest River, Idaho) **(W) to EVERETT, WASH. 246. US2**

Via: Newport, Spokane, Davenport, Wilbur, Orondo, Wenatchee, Cashmere, Skykomish, Snohomish.

This main cross-continental route is known in Wash. as the Stevens Pass Hy. because it crosses the Cascades through Stevens Pass. For secs. of US2 from Newport to Spokane & from Spokane to Wenatchee, see US10. Latter sec. incls. the Grand Coulee dam project. For sec. from J. with US97 (NW) of Wenatchee, to Everett, see US97.

# SEATTLE

## SEATTLE

RR. Stas.: King St. Sta., 3rd Ave. S. & Jackson St. for Gt.N. & N.P. RRs.; Union Sta., 4th Ave. S. & Jackson St., for U.P., S.P. & Chi., Mil., St.P. & P. RRs. Bus Stas.: Central Terminal, 8th Ave. & Stewart St., for major lines. Motor Tours: Gray Line, 1421-9th Ave., runs sightseeing land & water tours. Mt. Rainier Nat. Pk. Co., Olympic Hotel, provides daily bus serv. (June 27-Sept. 22) to Paradise & Yakima Pk. in Mt. Rainier Nat. Pk. Pan-Pacific Good Neighbor Tours, 107 C. of C. Bldg., 215 Columbia St., conducts combined steamer, RR. & bus tours from Seattle via Victoria, B.C. & other pts. of int. in Canada, & via Alcan Hy. to Anchorage, Alaska. Ferries: To Victoria, B.C., Port Angeles, Puget Sound Is. & pts. on Kitsap Peninsula. Airport: Through conns. at Boeing Field. Airline tours to Alaska. Accoms.: All types. Info.: C. of C., 215 Columbia St.; Wash. Auto. Club (A.A.A.), 1109 Pine St.; Mt. Rainier Nat. Pk. Bureau, 416 University St. Concerts at Meany Hall, Univ. of Wash. & at Civic Auditorium. Swim.: At 10 municipal beaches (salt- & fresh-water). Hunt.: In vic. Fish.: In Sound & near-by Ls. & streams; salmon derby in Mar. At Civic Stadium, amateur sports events; at Sick's Seattle Stadium, professional sports. Wash.-Cal. Univ. Crew Regatta. L. Wash., Ap. of alternate yrs. NW. Artists Annual Exhibit, Seattle Art Mus., Oct. Intercollegiate football games, Univ. of Wash., Fall.

Seattle, which boasts of having some 600,000 people within metropolitan area & of being one of great ports & industrial beehives of country, is youngest of Big Four of West Coast. 6 yrs. younger than Portland. First settlement was at Alki Pt., modestly called New York, in 1851. City was named for friendly Chief Seattle, who made noble but ineffective speech at powwow held in 1855 by Gov. Isaac I. Stevens. Finally, Inds. were induced to sign treaty, ceding millions of as. of land to whites. Nevertheless, white settlers had Ind. troubles. There was a massacre at White R. late in 1855, but due to lucky presence of U.S. sloop-of-war, whose guns barraged attackers, Seattle escaped with minimum damage in Jan. 1856.

Seattle is that exceptional Western phenomenon, a boom-town whose boom did not derive directly from gold rush—at least not till 1897. Lumber, still basic industry, provided boom stimulus. Henry Yesler put up sawmill in 1853 & his first order was for piles to be used in "Frisco", which was gold rush town. After that, fors., seemingly inexhaustible, accounted for Seattle's astounding growth, slow at first, & then increasing by geometric leaps & bounds—43,000 in 1890, 80,000 in 1900, 237,000 in 1910. Fish processing, which started with an unsuccessful venture about same time as Yesler's mill, & shipping were other 2 early industries. Alaska gold rush boom did not materialize until 1897. In 1909, town celebrated new Alaska era by putting on, with considerable pomp, Alaska-Yukon-Pacific Exposition. Seattleans have always been enterprising. In early days, bachelors of town far outnumbered eligible females—one account says, by ratio of nine to one. Live-wire entrepreneur of Frisco's Barbary Coast came up & built, in 1861, next to Yesler's, "house" whose occupants were mostly Ind. women. Asa S. Mercer, brother of Thos., who is notable for having brought 1st team of horses to town, undertook to protect local morals. He made two trips E., bringing back eligible spinsters each time. On last occasion, he was stuck in S.F., with his cargo & no money, but finally managed to ship through those girls that weren't snapped up locally, & most of these survivors were happily married to Seattle bachelors. Asa was made president of territorial univ. (which Seattle captured away from its rival, Tacoma), probably because he had worked clearing new campus & helped run up first bldg.; also probably, because he was an extremely moral young man & recent college graduate. His brother, Thos., meanwhile, had taken up claim on lake in N. part of city, which he called Union, because he foresaw that a canal would eventually be built to join Puget Sound, through this lake, with larger L. Wash.

Yesler's & Skid-Rd., as it was known (today, Yesler Way), became center to which gravitated loggers, buckers, roustabouts, sailors & other elements of floating pop. Hiring halls, cheap hotels, lodging houses & "joints," mushroomed to accommodate them. Although fire of 1889 levelled old bldgs., as it did almost entire business district, Yukon gold rush gave quarter new & gaudier lease on life. Fabulous saloons such as "Horseshoe," whose sign was solid silver horseshoe studded with gold nails & "Our House," which snobbishly made its patrons take calks off their shoes before entering & luxurious bawdy houses—one of them spent $200,000 on tapestries & plush fittings—appeared almost overnight. Today, after this short flare-up, Pioneer Sq. is still surrounded by cheap lodging houses, employment offices & "joints" & is center to which gravitate transient elements.

Seattle had advantages, fine harbor & magnificent for. resources at its back & salmon running in its Rs. But it needed conns. with outside world. Citizens didn't wait for gov. help. Surmounting considerable construction difficulties, they built Rd. across Snoqualmie Pass to E. They also needed RR. conns. Tacoma took N.P. RR. from them by making more attractive offer. Then Seattle began building its own line to Tacoma. Henry Villard, who about this time took over N.P., finished link for them & then went bankrupt. New owners of N.P. refused to give Seattle a break. Seattleans thereupon started another line, along Puget Sound's E. shore, to conn. with Canadian Pacific, which brought N.P. to terms. Subsequently three additional transcontinental lines came into city & bottleneck was burst wide open.

Seattle, partly because it was young, optimistic & radical, early tried mun. ownership. It built its own hydroelectric plant at Cedar R. & small steam-generating plant. Then it went in for mun.-owned electric power production in big way. City Light Dept. started great development on Skagit R. When completed, project will deliver some 1,120,000 h.p. Result: although privately-owned companies exist, local electricity rates are among lowest in country. There are also coal mines not far from city & these supply gas & fuel. Seattleans had good harbor, but they have made it better. They dug out channel of Duwamish R. in S. sec. of city to take freight steamers. Much of their industry is located there. They induced Fed. Gov. to realize Thos. Mercer's dream. In 1916, canal conn. Puget Sound & L. Wash. was completed, so that now they have huge inland harbor as well. Later they constructed great new terminal on Smith Cove, N. of city, & here are yards of their old foe, N.P. RR.

City was built on 7 hills, like Rome. But hills were nuisance & Seattleans levelled those most obnoxious to expansion, sluicing them out with hydraulic rams (an idea derived from Yukon) using resulting mud to fill in flats along water front.

Record would make it appear that city has had harmonious, peaceful development. But fact is that Seattle's hist. has been colorful with troubles & some violence. Last lynching, triple one, occurred in 1882. In 1886 there was an anti-Chinese riot in which at least 1 man was killed & several wounded. Thousands of coolies who had worked on Villard's RR. had, when that undertaking was done, become menace to white workers' jobs. Mob forced several hundred Orientals to ship for S.F. In 80's & 90's, Populism & socialism flourished & radical laws, such as recall & referendum, were adopted. Migratory character of lumber camp & sawmill workers & frequent ups & downs of lumber market produced bitter unrest. In late 19th cent., Knights of Labor made Seattle its hqs.; then, in early decades of 20th cent., revolutionary I.W.W.'s centered there. I.W.W.'s won better hrs. & working conditions in lumber camps, but their victory was temporary. In clash with armed deputies at Everett, number of Seattle I.W.W.'s were killed & wounded, & soon after, in Mar. 1918, 74 of them were indicted for murder; however, test case brought to trial resulted in acquittal & release of all accused. Early in 1919 occurred famous general strike which was successful for a few days, but collapsed because strikers didn't know where to go from there. During depression of 30's, A.F. of L., with its Central Labor Council, became powerful. Core of its strength was control of teamsters' unions. Later in decade, C.I.O., which had longshoremen, lumber & maritime workers' unions, became equally important. In 1938, occurred Newspaper Guild Strike which attracted nation-wide notice.

Seattle is beautifully situated. When you come in from the Sound, around Magnolia Bluff, with Alki Pt. closing in harbor (S), city lies before you, tiering up on hills against backdrop of high Cascades & snowcapped Mt. Rainier. When you are in city itself, on one of hills, you look (W) across island-studded Puget Sound & Kitsap Peninsula to snowy Olympics. Bordering Seattle (E) is $20^{m}$ long L. Wash. with high Mercer I. in its center, anchor for bridge which conn. city with mainland. Business district is crowded; residential areas have been pushed, for more elbow room, toward L. Wash. along which runs handsome blvd., & to heights above Sound. Poor live in flats of S. industrial district. Many people live on houseboats, mostly in vic. of Union & Wash. Ls.; some of these boats are luxurious, but many are slum tenements.

Klondike gold rush & two world wars boomed Seattle tremendously. Lumber & woodworking industries, shipbuilding, airplane manufacture, aluminum fabrication, f.-processing & processing of agric. products are among industries that have experienced great expansion. Seattle, because of convenient location, has become considerable tourist center.

PTS. OF INT.: (1) 3rd Ave., **City Light Bldg.** (O.wks.1935.by E.W.Morrison), housing City Light's offices. This is organization controlling mun.-owned power projects. In entrance is frieze presenting hist. of lighting by Albert G. Booth & John W. Elliott. In this bldg. are models of Diablo Dam (Skagit R.) Project. (2) 4th Ave., **Seattle Pub. Lib.** (O.wks.;Sun.& hols.2-9). (3) 5th Ave., **U.S. Cth. Bldg.,** in which are Fed. Courts & other Fed. offices. (4) Univ. St. & 3rd Ave., **Northern Life Tower Bldg.** (O.wks.;Sun.9-11.fee), with fine view from 27th story.

(5) 1st Ave. & Pike St., **Pike Pl. Pub. Market,** worth visit because of great variety of products displayed & cosmopolitan character of vendors. (6) Pier 3, end of Spring St., **Aquarium.** (7) Coleman Ferry Terminal, **Ye Old Curiosity Shop** (O.wks.), in which curiosities are exhibited, some for sale. (8) 1st Ave. & Yesler Way, **Pioneer Sq.** (9) 3rd Ave. & Jefferson St., **Cty.-City Bldg.** (O.wks.), housing various Gov. offices, courts & jail; at SW. cor. of bldg. is drinking fountain comm. Ind. attack (see above). (10) 2nd Ave. & Yesler Way, 42-story **L. C. Smith Tower Bldg.** (1914. by Gaggin & Gaggin). There is Chinese Rm. (O.fee) on 35th floor in which are art objects. Here also is observ. balcony, from which fine view. Upper stories of bldg. can be reached by staircase. (11) Denny Pl., in N. sec. of city, **Chief Seattle Mon.** (1912.by Jas.A.Wehn). (12) Mercer St. & 3rd Ave. N., **Civic Auditorium Group** (1928), incl. large auditorium for sports & other events, sports field & ice arena. (13) Phinney Ave., N. of Canal, **Woodland Pk.** (188 as.pic.tourist & sport facils. swim.) with **Zoo** (O) & **Mem. Comm. Pres. Harding.**

(14) On E. 45th St., bet. Union L. & L. Wash., **Univ. of Wash. Campus.** From campus, fine views of Mt. Rainier. Crowded out by growth of city, Univ. was moved to present site in 1894. Univ. curriculum covers undergraduate, graduate & professional courses. Unique, perhaps, is College of Fisheries; in one of its bldgs. are aquarium & coll. of preserved marine specimens. Also outstanding is instruction offered in aeronautics. Modern bldgs. are in Goth. & Tudor-Goth. styles. **Henry Suzzalo Mem. Lib.** (O.Mon.-Fri.Mod.Goth.) is most impressive. It contains excellent coll. of material concerning NW., Alaska & some rare Russian items; in NW. Rm. are murals by Paul M. Gustin & John T. Jacobsen depicting hist. events of NW. On Mem. Way are pillars comm. students killed in World War I. **Parrington Hall,** which houses Eng. Dept., was named for late Vernon L. Parrington, author of classic book on development of Amer. lit. Behind Meany Hall is **Geo. Washington Statue** by Lorado Taft, & near-by is **Edw. Grieg bust** by Finn H. Frohlich. Near-by is **Henry Art Gallery** (O.aft.); with coll. of mod. paintings. On lower campus near lib. is **Wash. St. Mus.** (O.wks.;Sun.aft.), which contains material concerning Inds. of NW., Alaska Rm., colls. of Australian, Melanesian, Malayan & Polynesian material & fine colls. of Chinese & Jap. art objects. Behind **Guggenheim Hall** (devoted to engineering sciences) is **Wind Tunnel** used for testing aircraft models. On campus are **Athletic Pavilion** for athletic activities & **Stadium,** topped by totem pole designed by C. Ken Weidner. Univ. crews practice on Union & Wash. Ls.

(15) Univ. Way & N. 31st St., **Repertory Playh.** in which repertory is presented Oct.-July. (16) Beyond Univ. Campus on L. Wash. Canal is **Univ. of Wash. Arboretum.** (17) NE. of Univ. on L. Wash. at Sand Pt. Way, is **Sand Pt. U.S. Naval Sta.,** with mon. comm. "Round-the-World Flight" of 1924. (18) E. Galer St., **Volunteer Pk.,** in which are **Conservatory** & **Seward Statue,** comm. purchase of Alaska in 1867. Here also is tower from which splendid view. (19) In N. sec. of pk. is **Lakeview Cemetery** in which Princess Angeline, daughter of Chief Seattle, is buried. (20) In Pk. is **Seattle Art Mus.** (O.wks.;Sun.2-6), with 2 marble rams at entrance from tomb of Ming prince (15th cent.A.D.). Mus. contains fine colls. of Oriental material & art objects as well as of European & Amer. art. During Oct., Mus. presents exhibit of work done by NW. artists. (21) 32nd Ave. NW., **L. Wash. Ship Canal Locks.** (22) Here is berthed clipper-ship, **St. Paul** (O.fee), which made trip from E. Coast around Horn. It contains marine exhibits & aquarium. (23) At Magnolia Bluff is

**Ft. Lawton** (640 as.), named for Maj. Gen. Henry W. Lawton, killed during Philippine Wars. Fine views. (24) W. Garfield St., **Smith Cove Piers,** mod. port terminal. (25) 14th Ave. S. & Judkin St., **U.S. Marine Hospital** (O.aft.Sun.Tues.& Thurs.by Beb & Gould, & John Graham); walls are decorated with murals by Kenneth Callahan. (26) Day St., **L. Wash. Bridge,** probably longest concrete pontoon-type bridge in existence; draw permits passage of large vessels. Structure from end to end is about 6.5$^{m}$ long. (27) Orcas St. & L. Wash. Dr., **Seward Pk.,** on peninsula projecting into L. Wash. Here are Gateway of Welcome presented by Seattle Japanese & large stone lantern presented by Yokohama in acknowledgement of help given after 1923 earthquake. (28) On Alki Ave. is **Alki Pt.,** site of first settlement (1851) with mon. comm. settlers. Fine view from Lth. (29) S. of Pt. on Beach Dr. is **Lincoln Pk.** (pic.). (30) Spokane St. & E. Marginal Way, **Frozen Fish Mus.** (O.wks.), which has coll. of rare frozen fish specimens at Port Terminal. (31) Boat tours from **Leschi Pk.** on **L. Wash.,** circling city to Madison St., on Elliott Bay, afford fine views of city & vic.

## OLYMPIC NATIONAL PARK

Season: Open all yr.; best season is summer. Equipment for climbing to high altitudes where there are glaciers & snowfields is necessary. Little rain during summer, but snow remains on higher trls. Rainy season in winter. Info.: Nat. Pk. Hqs., Port Angeles; also at hotels & For. Ranger Stas. Frequent informal talks on int. features of pk. given at campgrounds & lodges by pk. personnel. Regulations: Permit to make fires, except at designated camp sites, & registration at Ranger Stas. at Pk. entrances required. Hunt.: Prohibited. Fish.: License required. State License for residents, $3, for non-residents, $5; county license, non-residents, $3. Rd. Approaches: US101 (Olympic Hy.) circles Olympic Peninsula, on which pk. is situated & at Cresecent L., crosses N. sec. of pk. Stub Rds. & trls. branch from US101 at various pts. into Pk. Ferries run from Seattle & other pts. across Puget Sound & from Victoria, B.C. to conns. with US101. Wash. Motor Coach Co. serves Pk. direct, with transcontinental conns. at Seattle. Bus transportation is avail. from Seattle, Port Angeles & other Puget Sound pts. to hotels & camps along L. Crescent. Conns. may also be made at Olympia & Soleduck Hot Springs. Accoms.: Lodges & chalets, Gov. supervised, at Low Divide, Enchanted Valley & Graves Cr. on E. Fork Quinault Rd. Hotels in pk.: L. Crescent Tavern, Rosemary Inn, Storm King Inn & Ovington's. Housekeeping cabins at Waumilla Lodge, Olympic Hot Springs, L. Crescent Tavern, Rosemary Inn, Storm King Inn, L. Crescent Auto Park, Acadia, Bonnie Brae, Fairholme, Ovington's, Lenoir's Resort, La Poel Resort, Soleduck Hot Springs, Staircase Resort & L. Quinault. Shelters with open stone fireplaces found at convenient pts. along main trls. throughout pk. Info. on accoms. at Olympic Peninsula Resort & Hotel Assoc., Coleman Ferry Terminal, Seattle. Saddle & pack horses & guides: avail. at ends of spur rds., at Olympic Hot Springs, Whiskey Bend, Soleduck Hot Springs, N. & E. Forks of Quinault R. & Hoh, Bogachiel, Queets, Skokomish & Dosewallips Rs. Winter sports: Deer Pk. (accoms. but guests must provide own bedding).

Olympic Nat. Pk. in Olympic Nat. For. has an area of 835,411 as. Reg. was given its name by Capt. John Meares, who sighted Mt. Olympus in 1788. Reg. was set aside as Nat. Mon. by proclamation of Pres. Theodore Roosevelt in 1909. In 1938 Olympic Nat. Pk., containing 648,000 as., was est. by Act of Congress & in 1940 its area was increased to present size by Presidential order of Franklin D. Roosevelt. Olympic Mts., mass of high rugged peaks reaching their greatest altitude with Mt. Olympus (7,954′), are in heart of pk. Deep canyons, high mt. passes, glaciers, snowfields, lovely Ls., waterfalls, Rs., mt. meadows & valleys characterize reg. Since it lies in rain belt, W. of Cascades, pk.'s vegetation is varied &, at lower altitudes, of almost tropical luxuriance. Fors. are magnificent. Animal life, incl. rare Roosevelt elk, black-tailed deer, bear, smaller mammals & birds, is abundant. Rs. offer excellent trout f.

### ROAD & TRAIL APPROACHES

Rd. & trl. approaches branching from US101 (see), which skirts W., N. & E. sides of pk., are listed in succession, beginning at pk.'s SW. sec. & ending at SE. sec.

**I. EAST FORK QUINAULT RD.,** branching from US101 at Quinault along Quinault L. & following E. Fork of Quinault R. 20$^{m}$. Near Rd. terminus are **Campground** (trlrs.) & **Graves Cr. Inn.** At terminus (horses.guides) trl. cont. along Quinault R. to **Enchanted Valley Lodge,** 13$^{m}$.

**II. NORTH SHORE QUINAULT RD.,** branching from US101 $3^m$ (N) from Quinault & following N. Fork of Quinault R. $23^m$ to **N. Fork Ranger Sta.** (horses. guides). Here a trl. cont. $18^m$ to **Low Divide Chalet** (hotel.horses.guides) & across pk., with side trls. branching to various pts. of int., to J. with Hurricane Ridge Rd. (see below) at $43^m$.

**III. QUEETS RIVER RD.,** branching from US101 $18^m$ (N) from Quinault L., extending $12^m$ up Queets R. to **Kelly's Dude Ranch** (accoms.horses.guides) just outside pk. Here trl. leads up Queets R. to Quinault R. At $3^m$ on this trl. is largest known Douglas fir tree, over 17′ in diam.

**IV. HOH RIVER RD.,** branching from US101 $14^m$ (S) from Forks & following Hoh R. $18^m$ to **Jackson Ranger Sta.** in "rain forests." From Jackson Ranger Sta., Mt. Olympus Trl. leads to **Olympus Ranger Sta.,** $9^m$, & summit of **Mt. Olympus** (7,941′), $21^m$.

**V. BOGACHIEL RIVER RD.,** branching from US101 $6^m$ (S) from Forks & following Bogachiel R. short distance from which trl. leads to J. with trls. conn. with Soleduck & Hoh R. Rds.

**VI. SOLEDUCK HOT SPRINGS RD.,** branching from US101 $37^m$ (W) from Port Angeles & following Soleduck R. $12^m$ to **Soleduck Hot Springs** (cabins.supplies. swim.horses.guides). Deer Lake Trl., from end of Rd., leads $4^m$ to **Deer L.** & $8^m$ **Bogachiel Peak** (5,474′). Roosevelt elk occasionally are seen. From peak, magnificent panorama is spread—Pacific Ocean with hist. Destruction I. (W), Mt. Olympus from across mile-deep Hoh R. Canyon (S), Juan de Fuca Strait & Vancouver I. (N).

**VII. LAKE CRESCENT TRLS.** branching from S. shore of **Crescent L.** on US101: (1) Storm King Mt. Trl. leads from near Storm King Fish Hatchery & Rosemary Inn to **Storm King Mt.,** $2.5^m$. Mt. goats are occasionally seen along this trl. (2) Marymere Falls Trl. leads from near Rosemary Inn along Barnes Creek to **Marymere Falls,** $0.7^m$.

**VIII. HURRICANE RIDGE RD.,** branching from US101 $9^m$ (SW) from Port Angeles & extending $25^m$ to **Obstruction Pt.,** affording excellent panoramic view of Mt. Olympus, Bailey Ridge, Mt. Anderson, Juan de Fuca Strait, Vancouver I. & Port Angeles. At $9^m$ Elwha R. Trl. branches (R) to **Elkhorn Sta.** at $12^m$; **Hayes R. Ranger Sta.** at J. with Dosewallips—Hayden Pass Trl., $17^m$, & **Low Divide Chalet** (see above), $27^m$.

**IX. OLYMPIC HOT SPRINGS RD.,** branching (R) from Hurricane Ridge Rd. $4^m$ (S) from latter's J. with US101 & extending $8.5^m$ along Elwha Canyon to **Olympic Hot Springs** (hotel.cabins.swim.horses.guides). Here trls. run to various scenic pts. of int.

**X. DEER PK. RD.,** branching from US101 $5^m$ (E) from Port Angeles & extending $18^m$ to **Deer Pk.** (5,400′), winter sports area.

**XI. DOSEWALLIPS R. RD.,** branching near Brinnon from US101, $28^m$ (N) from Hoodsport & extending along Dosewallips R. $15^m$, ending in Douglas fir for. with wildflowers & plants of transitional zone. From end of Rd. extend trls. to various scenic pts. of int. One trl. runs (R) $4^m$ to **Constance L.** at foot of Mt. Constance (7,735′). Graves Cr. Trl. runs to J. with E. Fork Quinault Rd. (see above), $32^m$.

**XII. DUCKABUSH R. RD.,** branching from US101 $22^m$ (N) from Hoodsport & extending $6^m$ to trl. leading to **Duckabush Camp,** $17^m$, from which run trls. to various scenic pts. of int.

**XIII. N. FORK SKOKOMISH RD.,** branching from US101 near Hoodsport running to **L. Cushman,** at $5^m$. At $10.5^m$ J. with Trl. (R) to Mt. Elinor. Main Rd. cont. along Lake to **Staircase Resort** (cabins.supplies.horses.guides), near beautful **Staircase Rapids,** at $19^m$. Skokomish R. Trl. runs (N) here to **Enchanted Valley,** $30^m$. Another trl. branches off (W) to Graves Cr. (see Trail I. above) at c.$20^m$.

## MT. RAINIER NATIONAL PARK

Season: Summer (June-Oct.) is best season. Pk. entrances closed during winter, except Nisqually Entrance (O.all yr.). Skiing at Longmire & Paradise Valley (Dec.1-May 15), reached from Nisqually Entrance by Rd. maintained all yr. to Longmire & Paradise Valley, except after heavy snowfalls or slides, when it is kept open to Narada Falls,

1.5m from Paradise Valley. Info.: Nat. Pk. Serv., Fed. Office Bldg., Seattle; Nat. Pk. Serv. Hqs., Longmire; For. Ranger Stas. & lodges & hotels in Pk.; Rainier Nat. Pk. Co., Tacoma, with branch office at 418 University St., Seattle; A.A.A., Commercial Hotel, Yakima. Small exhibits in Community H. at Paradise; Campers' Shelter at Yakima Pk.; For. H. at Ohanapecosh & Pk. Mus. at Longmire, together with wayside exhibits along trls. help to explain features of importance. Trans.: RR. conns. nearest Pk.: Enumclaw (for White R., Carbon R. & Mowitch R. Entrances) & Ashford (for Nisqually Entrance). Bus serv. June 27-Sept. 2, daily from Seattle & Tacoma; departures at 8:20 a.m. from Seattle & 9:30 a.m. from Tacoma, 3:30 p.m. from Paradise (Ohanapecosh Entrance) & Yakima (Sunrise) Pk.; with arrival at Tacoma at 6:15 p.m. & at Seattle at 7:30 p.m. Annual auto permits $1 at Nisqually & White R. Entrances; permits not necessary at other entrances. Registration at all pk. entrances required if tourist wishes to use trls. Accoms.: At Paradise Valley (June 27-Sept. 2): Paradise Inn (Amer. plan) & Paradise Lodge (European plan.cafeteria.fountain.store). At Yakima Pk. (June 27-Sept. 2): Sunrise Lodge (cafeteria.store.fountain); no overnight accoms. At Longmire: Nat. Pk. Inn (O.all yr.) & cottage rms. (a la carte meals.fountain. store). At Ohanapecosh Entrance: (June 15-Oct. 31) Ohanapecosh Lodge (European & Amer.plan.stores); hot mineral springs (bath.facils.). Free pub. campgrounds well equipped at Longmire, Paradise Valley, Yakima Pk. & Ohanapecosh, White R., Tahoma Cr. & Carbon R. Guides & horses avail. in summer at Paradise Valley & Yakima Pk. Hik., riding, mt. climbing & fish. equipment may be rented at Paradise Valley. Regulations: Smoking while traveling on trls. not allowed. Permits must be obtained from pk. rangers for building fires at any pt. other than at auto campgrounds. Hunt.: Prohibited. Fish.: Trout in Ls. & streams (O.July 1-Sept. 30); no license required; Info. as to regulations at Ranger Stas.

Mt. Rainier Nat. Pk. is one of chief scenic features of NW. Pk. (241,524 as.) was created by Act of Congress in 1899. The creation of the pk. caused controversy since it consisted largely of land originally owned by RRs., land which they exchanged for some of the best for. tracts owned by U.S. Gov. Mt. Rainier (14,408′), one of highest peaks in Cascade range, covers c.one-fourth of pk's. area. Its snow-covered summit is visible from cities on S. arm of Puget Sound & is particularly impressive as seen from Seattle. Like Mt. Hood, Mt. Rainier was thrown up by volcanic disturbances & later glacial action gouged out pk.'s deep R. canyons. Today, only some hot springs & steam-emiting vents give evidence of volcanic origin. Summit of mt. was not conquered until 1870, although number of attempts had been made before that to achieve ascent. Mt. Rainier has 3 peaks, Liberty Cap (14,112′), Pt. Success (14,150′) & Columbia Crest (14,408′), of which 1st two form part of huge crater-like rim & Columbia Crest part of smaller but more perfect crater, some 1,200′ in diam.

Although Mt. Rainier is chief feature of pk., there are many other scenic attractions —rugged peaks, 26 glaciers, precipitous gorges, cliffs, lovely Ls. & equally lovely waterfalls. Trls. give access to most pts. of int. Valleys of pk. are crowded with great fors. & dense luxuriant undergrowth. Woods become more open on mt. slopes, gradually thinning until they disappear at timberline. Reg. is noted for variety of its flora & fauna. Great mt. cedars, often 11′ in diam., occur mostly in Ohanapecosh district. Mt. goats, seen only at high elevations during summer, descend to low ridges in winter & are often seen on Rd. bet. Nisqually Entrance & Glacier Bridge.

## PARK TOURS

### I. OHANAPECOSH ENTRANCE to J. with US410

Ohanapecosh Entrance is reached by branch of St.5 running (W) from US99 (see) at Mary's Corner. St.5 cont. (N) along E. side of pk., past **OHANAPECOSH HOT SPRINGS** on Ohanapecosh R., at which is **The Lodge** (accoms.). Forest H. has exhibits. Trls. radiate from here to various pts. of int. St.5 cont. to **SILVER FALLS** & then to **STAFFORD FALLS,** at **9.** At **11.5.** it reaches **Pk. Serv. Cabin.** Trl. here runs (L) to White R. Rd. (see below) at 6m.

St.5 cont. to J. with US410 (see & No. III below) at **13.**

### II. NISQUALLY ENTRANCE to PARADISE VALLEY.

Nisqually Entrance is reached by branch of St.5 running (SW) from Tacoma (see US99). At Entrance, annual auto permits ($1) are issued at Ranger Sta. Cont. on St.5 to J. with W. Side Hy. at **1.**

Take latter (L) through fine mt. & glacier scenery. At 7m is **Round Pass Lookout Sta.** (3,879′), from which Puyallup Glacier can be seen. Trl. here runs (L) to **George L.** (camp.f.) at 1m. At 11m, **St. Andrew's Cr.,** where trls. run (L) to fine waterfalls & (R) to **Klapatche Pk.** At $15^m$, **Puyallup R. Canyon** & views of Puyallup Glacier. Rd terminates here at J. with Wonderland Trl. (see below).

Cont. on main Rd. (R) to **LONGMIRE** at **6.5.** where are pk. hqs. Here are **Nat. Pk. Inn** (accoms.), **Pub. Campgrounds & Nat. Pk. Mus.** (O) containing coll. of flora & fauna of pk., maps, etc. In mus., info. about trls. is avail. Trips to various pts. of int. are organized by mus. staff. Longmire is starting pt. of Wonderland Trl., $95^m$ long, which makes complete circuit of Mt. Rainier, conn. with numerous side trls. to pts. of int. From Longmire, numerous other trls. radiate to various pts. of int. Main Rd. cont. from Longmire to **CHRISTINE FALLS** at **c.11.**, where trl. runs (L) past lofty waterfalls to **Van Trump Pk.**, $1^m$. At **c.12.** on main Rd., **NISQUALLY R. BRIDGE,** with fine view of **Nisqually Glacier,** to which short trl. runs (L). At **16.,** beautiful **NARADA FALLS.** At **17.5. INSPIRATION PT.;** fine view. At **20., PARADISE VALLEY** (5,400′) at foot of Mt. Rainier. Here are **Paradise Inn** (accoms.), **Paradise Lodge** (accoms.) & **Pub. Campgrounds.** Also **Community H.** (exhibits) where excursions are organized with guide serv. & info. about trls. is avail. From Paradise Valley starts trl. to **Summit of Mt. Rainier,** traversing magnificent scenery—crags, cliffs & glaciers. Two days are necessary for this trip—4-5 hrs. to **Camp Muir** (10,000′), where overnight stop is made; c.11 hrs. for balance of ascent, begun before dawn of 2nd day; & 4-8 hrs. for descent. Guides & Climbing equipment are essential. Climb is difficult & arduous. Numerous other trls. radiate from Paradise Valley to various pts. of int.

**III. WHITE R. ENTRANCE to YAKIMA (SUNRISE) PK.**

White R. Entrance is reached by Rd. branching (W) from US410 (see). At **1.5.** on this Rd. is Entrance Sta. where auto permits ($1) must be obtained. Rd. cont. past **FRYINGPAN GLACIER.** At **5.5. WHITE R.,** with fine views. At J. with Rd. leading (L) $1^m$ to **White R. Campgrounds,** whence trls. run to **Emmons Glacier & Yakima Pk.** (see below). At **c.13.** on main Rd., **SUNRISE PT.** (6,120′;fine views), where trls. radiate to various pts. of int. Main Rd. cont., ascending to **YAKIMA (SUNRISE) PK.** at **15.5.** Here is **Sunrise Lodge** (accoms.). At Camper's Shelter are exhibits. Fine view of Emmons, Fryingpan & Winthrop Glaciers. Numerous trls. radiate to scenic pts. of int.

**IV. CARBON R. ENTRANCE**

This entrance is reached by branch of St.5 running (S) from Enumclaw at J. with US410 (see). At **15.5.** on St.5, turn (L) **23.** to Entrance, at Ranger Sta. where tourists must register & obtain permits if they wish to use trls. & camps. No auto permits required. Visible (S) is **Tolmie Peak** (5,939′). Rd. cont. $5^m$ from Entrance to **Ipsut Cr.,** where trl. leads (R) to **Eunice & Mowitch Ls.** Main Rd. ends at $6^m$. From here trls. run to various pts. of int. & J. with Wonderland Trl. (see above).

## PUGET SOUND ISLANDS

**PUGET SOUND,** joined to the Pacific by the broad Strait of Juan de Fuca, is a great, island-studded inland sea which stretches N. into Brit. Columbia & S. to Olympia. Its S. extension is split into two arms by Kitsap Peninsula. The E. arm lies bet. peninsula & mainland along which are strung Olympia, Tacoma, Seattle & Everett. Its W. arm is known as Hood Canal & separates Kitsap from Olympic Peninsula. In the E. arm are **VASHON & BAINBRIDGE IS.,** lying roughly bet. Seattle & Kitsap Peninsula, & several smaller Is. in the S., the latter reachable from Olympia or Tacoma by boat. Vashon & Bainbridge Is. are most easily accessible from Seattle from which ferry makes round trip run, with busses to chief pts. on Is. These are really suburban summer resorts (excellent bath.,boat.& f.facils.). On Vashon I. is **Vashon St. Pk.** (pic.). On Bainbridge I., named for Wm. Bainbridge of "Constitution" (Old Ironsides) fame, is **Fay-Bainbridge St. Pk.** (pic.), recently est. **WHIDBEY,** largest of all Puget Sound Is., closes in E. arm on the N. & extends roughly from Everett to Mt. Vernon. Just N. of it lies **FIDALGO.** Both Is. have been described in US99 (see). Opposite the mainland, bet. Mt. Vernon & Bellingham, & for the most part W. of Fidalgo I. lie 172 **SAN JUAN IS.,** & still further W. lies huge **VANCOUVER I.** in Brit. Columbia.

The San Juan Is., belonging in part to U.S. & in part to Canada, are a picturesque group, mountainous, with rocky, jagged coastlines & separated from each other by narrow straits. Most Is. have a comparatively heavy rainfall & are thickly wooded.

There are trout in fresh-water Ls. & salmon offshore. The 3 largest of this group are Lopez, Orcas & San Juan, reached from Anacortes on Fidalgo I. by ferries (autos) of Black Ball Line, Colman Ferry Terminal, Seattle. Busses run regularly from Seattle to Anacortes. Smaller Is. are conn. with larger by boat. Passengers may cont. to Sydney, Victoria, B.C., from Friday Harbor, on San Juan I. Airline service conn. largest Is. with mainland. Bus service to pts. of int. on the Is. Accoms.: Summer. Island trip itself is picturesque, since steamer threads its way through narrow, rocky passages, past numerous Is., stopping en route at Lopez, Shaw & Orcas, finally reaching Friday Harbor on San Juan I.
**LOPEZ I.,** 1st stop, some $12^m$ long was named for Lopez de Haro, supposedly its discoverer. Landing is at rugged Upright Head. Info. at Lopez I. Commercial Club. **Odlin Pk. is near ferry** (pic.bath.facils.good h.& salmon f.community kitchen). **ORCAS I.,** 3rd stop, is $11.5^m$ long from E. to W., & $8.5^m$ from N. to S. Steamer lands at Obstruction Pass. Several impressive peaks punctuate I. contours—**Mt. Constitution** (2,450′), **Mt. Entrance** (1,200′) & **Turtleback** (1,497′). Ls. provide excellent trout. Salmon fishing offshore is exceptionally good. At $4.5^m$ from the landing is **Moran St. Pk.** (4,803 as.pic.community kitchen.camp.boat.bath.facils.f.skiing). Here is J. with Rd. leading (R) short distance to **Cascade Falls.** At $5^m$ J. with Rd.

SIDE TRIP: Take latter (R) $1.5^m$ to **Mountain L.** (camp.f.boat.), dominated by Mt. Pickett. At $5^m$ from J., summit of **Mt. Constitution.** Magnificent view from Observation Tower, of Cascades to NE., Olympics to S. & Puget Sound & Victoria I.

Cont. on main hy. At $6^m$, **Cascade L.** (pic.camp.f.).
Resorts on seacoast are at **Doebay, Lawrence Pt., Olga, North Beach, Eastsound** & **Deer Harbor.** At Eastsound is **W. R. Griffin House Mus.** (O) with coll. of fossils.
**SAN JUAN I.,** $15^m$ long & $9^m$ wide, is 4th stop. The boat lands at **Friday Harbor.** This town annually packs thousands of cases of salmon caught offshore on the famous Salmon Banks. Near town are **Univ. of Wash. Oceanographic Labs.** (grounds O.wks.). At $10^m$ from Friday Harbor is J. with Rd. leading (R) $0.5^m$ to **English Blockh.,** once occupied by Brit. Near-by, **Mon. & Davis House Mus.** with coll. of relics. At $21^m$ from Friday Harbor is J. with Rd. leading (R) $5^m$ to **Amer. Camp** which was Amer. center of opposition to Brit. claims in boundary dispute that resulted in the "pig war." An Amer. settler shot a pig belonging to Hudson's Bay Co. & Brit. insisted that the offender be sent to Victoria, B.C. for trial. U.S. troops under Capt. G. F. Pickett (later of Gettysburg fame) were sent to protect Amer. interests. Boundary dispute was settled (1872) by arbitration. At **Roche Harbor,** on N. end of Island, is **Roche Harbor Lime Plant,** of considerable proportions. Other pts. of int.: **Lime Kiln Lighth., San Juan Pk. & Sportsman's L.** (f.).

## THE PACIFIC CREST TRAIL

**THE PACIFIC CREST TRAIL** extends 2,156 miles from the Canadian to the Mexican border. It is for the W. Coast reg. what the Appalachian Trl., running from Mt. Katahdin, Me., to Ga., is for the E. However, the PCT is of more recent origin, begun only in 1932. It has incorporated several already existing trls., the Ore. Skyline Trl., the John Muir Trl., along the High Sierra in Cal., & others. Only 600 miles of new trls. had to be built. By 1937, the entire PCT had been rendered usable. Since then great stretches have been worked upon & improved, so that today it is in good shape throughout. The PCT System Conference, Hotel Green, Pasadena, Cal. has been largely responsible for stimulating the work of creating the trl., & has cooperated with the Nat. For. & Pk. Serv. in its management & operation. The conference has published a book, "The Pacific Crest Trailways," compiled by Clinton C. Clark, its President, which gives detailed descriptions & maps of the route throughout its entire length; in addition, the Conference publishes a series of bulletins giving detailed info. concerning various secs. of the trl. Most of the PCT demands high altitude climbing experience. Parts can be covered by horse pack-trains. Much of it can be negotiated only by "backpacking," the hiker carrying his own outfit. Except in the most N. sec. of the PCT, from the Canadian border to Glacier Peak, Wash., & in the sec. S. of L. Tahoe to Walker Pass in Cal., camp. facils. on the trl., or easily accessible from it, are reasonably frequent. The Wash. & Ore. secs. of the PCT are marked with PCT signs; the Californian sec. with local signs.
The PCT follows the upper ridges of the continental backbone through Wash., Ore. & Cal., to the end of the High Sierra in Cal. Then it crosses the Mojave Desert & ascends into the S. Coastal ranges, which it follows to its final descent to the Mexican border. Except for the desert sec. & when it crosses river canyons, it seldom drops below 3,000′ & for some 300 miles in the High Sierra, never descends below 8,500′. In its course it traverses

some of the country's finest scenic areas through an almost trackless wilderness of lofty mts., deep canyons, plunging rivers & beautiful Ls. It crosses a string of Nat. Fors., 5 great Nat. Pks.—Mt. Rainier, Mt. Hood, Crater L., Mt. Lassen Volcanic, Yosemite & Sequoia-Kings Canyon—& some 19 Wilderness & Wild areas, from which commercial exploitation has been excluded. It skirts the mightiest peaks of the W. To name only a few: Glacier Peak (10,436′), Mt. Rainier (14,408′), Mt. Adams (12,307′), in Wash.; Mt. Hood (11,245′), Mt. Jefferson (10,495′), The Three Sisters (10,354′), in Ore.; Mt. Shasta (14,161′) & Mt. Lassen (10,453′), N. of L. Tahoe, in Cal., & in the High Sierra, a whole series of peaks ranging bet. 13,000′ & 14,000′, climaxing in Mt. Whitney (14,495′), highest in the continental U.S. In the Coastal Range of S. Cal., it passes near Mts. San Antonio, San Bernardino, San Gorgonio & San Jacinto, all more than 10,000′ in altitude.

In Ore. & Wash., the PCT is paralleled fairly closely on the E. by US97, & at a greater distance, by US99 on the West. These 2 hys. are conn. by main E-W. Rds. crossing the Cascades Range. In the mt. passes traversed by these hys., occur Js. with the PCT. Stub Rds. off main hys. also give frequent access to the trl.

In Cal., US99 parallels the PCT at some distance to the W. & US395, in a general way, parallels it on the E. To N. of St.120, a number of E-W. main routes & Rds. branching off them, give access to the PCT. But bet. St.120, which crosses Yosemite Nat. Pk. from Manteca to Leevining, & St.178 which crosses the High Sierra reg. from Bakersfield to Freeman, there are no such E-W. hys. In other words, for a distance of about 185m, the PCT can be reached only by trls. branching off stub Rds. which in turn branch off of main N-S. hys. In the S. Cal. sec., the PCT makes numerous Js. with main & secondary hys.

# ABBREVIATIONS

*Note:* Plurals are formed by adding 's' as in a.—acre; as.—acres. Abbreviations refer to all forms of the word as in comm.—commemorate, commemorates, commemoration, etc. unless otherwise indicated as accoms.—accommodations—no singular or other form.

**a.** acre
**accoms.** accommodations
**add.** addition
**adj.** adjoining, adjacent
**adm.** administration
**aft.** afternoon
**agric.** agricultural
**Alt.** alternate route (as in US789 Alt.)
**alt.** alteration
**Amer.** American
**Ap.** April
**approx.** approximate
**assoc.** association
**avail.** available

**Bapt.** Baptist
**bath.** bathing
**bet.** between
**birthpl.** birthplace
**bldg.** building
**blvd.** boulevard
**boat.** boating
**br.** bridge
**Brit.** British
**bus.** business

**c.** circa, about
**C. of C.** Chamber of Commerce
**camp.** camping
**Can.** Canadian
**Cath.** Catholic
**cent.** century
**Ch.** Church
**Christ.** Christian
**circum.** circumference
**Class.** Classical
**Class. Rev.** Classical Revival
**co.** company
**Col.** Colonial
**coll.** collection
**Coll. Goth.** Collegiate Gothic
**Comdr.** Commander
**comm.** commemorate
**Confed.** Confederacy
**Congr.** Congregational
**conn.** connection
**cont.** continued
**cor.** corner
**Cr.** creek
**cth.** courthouse
**cty.** county

**Decl. of Ind.** Declaration of Independence
**diam.** diameter
**dist.** district
**Dr.** Drive

**(E) or E.** east
**econ.** economic
**Eng.** English
**Episc.** Episcopalian
**esp.** especially
**est.** established
**exc.** except
**exter.** exterior

**f. or fish.** fishing
**facils.** facilities
**Fed.** Federal
**fl.** floor
**for.** forest
**Fr.** French
**Ft. or ft.** fort
**ft. (occasionally)** foot

**gal.** gallon
**Gen.** General
**Georg.** Georgian
**Goth.** Gothic
**Gov. or gov.** Governor, government
**Gr. Rev.** Greek Revival

**H.** House
**. . . . h.** house, as in lighth.
**h. or hunt.** hunting
**hik.** hiking
**hist.** historic
**hols.** holidays
**hqs.** headquarters
**hy.** highway

**I.** island
**inc.** incorporated
**incl.** include
**Ind.** Indian
**info.** information
**int.** interesting
**inter.** interior
**internat.** international
**inters.** intersection
**Ital.** Italian

**J.** junction

**(L) or L.** left
**L.** lake
**lab.** laboratory
**lib.** library
**Luth.** Lutheran

**mech.** mechanical
**Med.** Medieval
**mem.** memorial
**Meth.** Methodist
**mfg.** manufacturing
**Mod.** Modern
**mod.** modernized, modified
**mon.** monument
**mun.** municipal
**mus.** museum

**(N) or N.** north
**N.O.** not open
**nat.** national
**nat. hist.** natural history
**nonsect.** nonsectarian

**(O)** open
**(O.appl.)** open on application
**observ.** observatory
**opp.** opposite
**org.** organized
**orig.** original

**pic.** picnicking
**Pk.** park
**pky.** parkway
**prehist.** prehistoric
**Pres.** President
**Presb.** Presbyterian
**Prot.** Protestant
**pop.** population
**pt.** point
**pub.** public

**(R) or R.** right
**R.** river
**Rd.** road
**reconst.** reconstructed
**recr.** recreation
**reg.** region
**remod.** remodelled
**Ren.** Renaissance
**reprod.** reproduction
**reserv.** reservation
**rest.** restored
**Rev.** Revolution
**rm.** room
**Romanes.** Romanesque
**RR.** railroad

**(S) or S.** south
**Scand.** Scandinavian
**Sch.** school
**sec.** section
**secy.** secretary
**serv.** service
**sett.** settled
**sm.** small
**soc.** society
**Sp.** Spanish
**Sq.** square
**SS.** steamship
**St.** State, Street, Saint
**st. (occasionally)** state
**sta.** station
**Ste** Saint (French)
**swim.** swimming

**terr.** territorial
**trans.** transportation
**trl.** trail
**trlr.** trailer

**Unit.** Unitarian
**Univ.** university

**vic.** vicinity
**Vict.** Victorian

**(W) or W.** west
**wks.** weekdays

**yacht.** yachting
**yds.** yards
**yr.** year

# BIBLIOGRAPHY

This brief reading list only suggests the wealth of available literature on life in the United States, past and present. An attempt is made, however, to include books of durable worth that will give the reader a comprehensive view of the country's historical, natural, social and cultural backgrounds. Fiction and biography, regrettably, are not included, although some of the most vivid and significant material on various localities and historic periods is found in regional novels and the lives of famous men and women. The Federal Government publishes many books of descriptive and informative nature, and state departments bring out bluebooks, historic marker books and other valuable material. For local detail, there are many attractive and authoritative books and pamphlets published by state historical societies, automobile and tourist associations, chambers of commerce and other organizations.

Of special note are the "Series" books, well illustrated and of high literary merit that are being issued by leading publishers. Foremost among these is *The American Guide Series,* compiled by the Federal Writers' Project. Among some 4,000 guides in the series are handsome volumes on each state and the larger cities, regional guides and other uncommon items. Other important "Series" are: *American Customs* (Vanguard), *American Folkways* (Duell, Sloan & Pearce), *American Lakes* (Bobbs-Merrill), *American Mountains* (Vanguard), *American Trails* (Bobbs-Merrill), *Look at America* (Houghton Mifflin), *Rivers of America* (Farrar & Rinehart), *Society in America* (Dutton), and *Visage of America* and *The American Landmarks* (Hastings House).

## GENERAL


ADAMS, JAMES T.: *Epic of America.* 1941.

AGAR, HERBERT S.: *The People's Choice.* 1933.

AMERICAN ASSOC. OF MUSEUMS: *Handbook of American Museums.* 1932.

ANDERSON, J.: *American Theater* & FULOP-MILLER, R.: *Motion Picture in America.* 1938.

ANDREWS, CHARLES M.: *The Colonial Period of American History.* 4 v. 1934-37.

BEARD, CHARLES & MARY: *Rise of American Civilization.* 1927-42.

BEMIS, S.F.: *Diplomatic History of the United States.* rev. 1942.

BENEDICT, RUTH: *Race: Science and Politics.* 1940.

BOTKIN, B.A.: *Treasury of American Folklore.* 1944.

BROGAN, D.W.: *The American Character.* 1944.

CAHILL, HOLGER & BARR, A.: *Art in America.* 1935.

CAMPBELL, WALLACE: *Here is Tomorrow; Consumer Cooperatives in the United States.* (Cooperative League of the U.S.A., N.Y.C.) 1947.

CHANNING, EDWARD: *History of the United States.* 6 v. 1905-25.

CHASE, STUART: *Economy of Abundance.* 1934.

CLARK, V.S.: *History of Manufactures in the United States, 1607-1806.* new ed. 1929.

COAN, OTIS W.: *America in Fiction* (listed by states & regions). 1945.

COCHRAN, T.C. & MILLER, W.: *The Age of Enterprise.* 1942.

COLLIER, JOHN: *The Indians of the Americas.* 1947.
COMMONS, J.R. et al.: *History of Labor in the United States.* 2 v. 1918.
CURTI, MERLE E.: *The Growth of American Thought.* 1943.

DE VOTO, BERNARD: *Year of Decision: 1846.* 1943.
DEWEY, JOHN: *Freedom and Culture.* 1939.
DULLES, F.R.: *America Learns to Play.* 1940.
———. *Labor in America: A History.* 1949.
DUNBAR, SEYMOUR: *History of Travel in America.* 4 v. 1915.

EMBREE, EDWIN R.: *American Negroes: A Handbook.* 1942.

FAULKNER, H.U.: *American Economic History.* 1943.
———. *American Political and Social History.* 1948.
FRAENKEL, O.K.: *Our Civil Liberties.* 1944.

GUNTHER, JOHN: *Inside U.S.A.* 1947.

HACKER, LOUIS: *Triumph of American Capitalism.* 1940.
HAMLIN, T.F.: *The American Spirit in Architecture.* 1926.
HOFSTADTER, RICHARD: *The American Political Tradition and the Men Who Made It.* 1948.
HORNBLOW, ARTHUR: *A History of the Theatre in America.* 2 v. 1919.
HINDS, W.A.: *American Communities and Cooperative Commonwealths.* 2nd ed. 1908.
HOWARD, J.T.: *Our American Music.* rev. ed. 1946.
———. *Our Contemporary Composers.* 1941.

JAMES, HENRY: *The American Scene.* 1907.
JENKINS, ELMER, ed.: *Guide to America.* (Public Affairs Press) 1947-48.

LILIENTHAL, DAVID: *T.V.A.: Democracy on the March.* 1944.
LORD, C.L. & E.H.: *Historical Atlas of the United States.* 1944.

MCMASTERS, JOHN B.: *History of the People of the United States from the Revolution to the Civil War.* 1913.
MCWILLIAMS, CAREY: *Brothers under the Skin.* 1945.
———. *Factories in the Field.* 1944.
MALBO, IRVING R.: *Our Country's National Parks.* 1941.
MENCKEN, H.L.: *The American Language & Supplements.* 1937-49.
MILLER, JOHN C.: *Origins of the American Revolution.* 1943.
MONROE, PAUL: *Founding of the American Public School System.* 1940.
MUMFORD, LEWIS: *Technics and Civilization.* 1934.
MYERS, GUSTAVUS: *History of the Great American Fortunes.* 1936.
MYRDAL, GUNNAR: *An American Dilemma.* 1944.

NEVINS, ALLAN & COMMAGER, H.S.: *Short History of the United States.* 1945.
NEW YORK CITY WPA: *Film Index: A Bibliography.* 1941.
NUTE, GRACE L.: *The Voyageur.* 1931.

OFFICE OF WAR INFORMATION: *A Handbook of the U.S.A.* 1944.

PARKMAN, FRANCIS: *LaSalle and the Discovery of the Great West.* 1869.
PARRINGTON, V.L.: *Main Currents in American Thought.* 1927, 1930.
PEATTIE, DONALD C., ed.: *Audubon's America.* 1940.
PERRY, RALPH BARTON: *Puritanism and Democracy.* 1944.

ROOSEVELT, THEODORE: *The Winning of the West.* 4 v. 1889-96.
ROURKE, CONSTANCE M.: *American Humor.* 1931.
———. *Roots of American Culture.* 1942.

SCHLESINGER, A.M. & FOX, D.R., eds.: *History of American Life.* 12 v. 1927-44.
SCHNIER, JACQUES: *Sculpture in Modern America.* 1948.
SHOOLMAN, R. & SLATKIN, C. E.: *Enjoyment of Art in America.* 1942.
SMITH, J.R. & PHILLIPS, M.O.: *North America* (geographic). 1940.
SPERRY, W.L.: *Religion in America.* 1946.
STEARNS, HAROLD E.: *Civilization in the United States.* 1922.

TAFT, LORADO: *History of American Sculpture. rev.* 1924.
TAYLOR, DEEMS & others: *Pictorial History of the Movies.* 1943.
TRAVEL GUIDE, INC.: *Travelguide* (Negro). Annual. 1674 Broadway, New York 19, N.Y.

TURNER, FREDERICK J.: *The Frontier in American History*. 1921.

———. *Rise of the New West*. 1906.

WISSLER, CLARK: *Indians of the U.S.* 1944.

WRIGHT, FRANK LLOYD: *When Democracy Builds*. 1945.

## REGIONAL

ADAMS, JAMES T.: *Founding of New England*. 1921.

———. *New England in the Republic*. 1926.

———. *Revolutionary New England*. 1926.

AIKEN, GEORGE D.: *Shaping of Vermont*. 1938.

AMORY, CLEVELAND: *The Proper Bostonians*. 1947.

APPALACHIAN TRAIL CONFERENCE: *Guides*. Washington, D.C.

ARENTS, GEORGE: *The Seed From Which Virginia Grew*. 1939.

ASBURY, HERBERT: *Barbary Coast*. 1933.

AUSTIN, H. RUSSELL: *The Wisconsin Story*. 1948. (Published by *Milwaukee Journal*).

AUSTIN, MARY: *The Land of Little Rain*. 1903.

BALDWIN, LELAND D.: *Pittsburgh: The Story of a City*. 1937.

BINGAY, MALCOLM: *Detroit Is My Own Home Town*. 1946.

BINNS, ARCHIE: *The Land Is Bright*. 1939.

———. *Northwest Gateway* (Seattle). 1941.

BOLEY, HENRY: *Lexington in Old Virginia*. 1936.

BOLTON, HERBERT E.: *Spanish Exploration in the Southwest, 1542-1706*. 1925.

BOSTON MUSEUM OF FINE ARTS: *New England Art Museums and Historic Houses*. 1948.

BRADLEY, GLEN D.: *The Story of the Pony Express*. 1920.

BRANCH, E.D.: *The Hunting of the Buffalo*. 1929.

———. *Travelways of Western Pennsylvania*. 1939.

BROOKS, VAN WYCK: *Flowering of New England*. 1936.

BURGHARDT, DUBOIS: *Black Reconstruction*. 1935.

BURT, STRUTHERS: *Powder River* (Wyoming). 1938.

CAPEN, LOUISE I. & MELCHIOR, D.M.: *Pennsylvania History*. 1944.

CARMER, CARL: *Stars Fell on Alabama*. 1934.

CARROLL, CHARLES: *Rhode Island, Three Centuries of Democracy*. 1932.

CHITTENDEN, H.M.: *The American Fur Trade of the Far West*. 3 v. 1935.

CLARK, G. L.: *History of Connecticut, Its People and Institutions*. 1914.

CLARK, PALMER: *George Rogers Clark*. 1930.

CLARK, T.D.: *A History of Kentucky*. 1937.

CLEMENS, SAMUEL L.: *Life on the Mississippi*. 1883.

COUCH, W.T.: *Culture in the South*. 1934.

CROSS, WILBUR L.: *Connecticut Yankee*. 1943.

DALE, E.E.: *The Range Cattle Industry*. 1930.

DANIELS, JONATHAN: *A Southerner Discovers New England*. 1940.

———. *A Southerner Discovers the South*. 1943.

DICKSON, HARRIS: *The Story of King Cotton*. 1937.

DODD, W.E.: *The Cotton Kingdom*. 1929.

DUFFUS, R.L.: *The Santa Fe Trail*. 1930.

DUNAWAY, W.F.: *A History of Pennsylvania*. 1935.

DUSENBERRY, GEORGE & JANE: *How to Retire to Florida*. 1947.

FEDERAL WRITERS' PROJECTS: *Berkshire Hills*. 1939.

———. *Cape Cod Pilot; by Jeremiah Digges*. 1937.

———. *Copper Camp*. 1943.

———. *Jefferson's Albemarle*. (Charlottesville, Va.). 1941.

———. *The Oregon Trail*. 1939.

———. *These Are Our Lives*. 1939.

FERGUSSON, HARVEY: *Rio Grande*. 1933.

FIRESTONE, CLARK B.: *Sycamore Shores*. 1935.

FLICK, ALEXANDER: *History of the State of New York*. 1937.

FORBES, ALLEN & CADMAN, P.F.: *Boston and Some Noted Emigres*. 1938. (One of publications of State Street Trust Co. of Boston.)

FORBES, GERALD: *Flush Production: The Epic of Oil in the Gulf-Southwest*. 1942.

FOREMAN, GRANT: *The Five Civilized Tribes.* 1934.
———. *A History of Oklahoma.* 1942.
FULLER, GEORGE W.: *A History of the Pacific Northwest.* 1931.

GHENT, W.J.: *The Road to Oregon.* 1929.
———. *The Early Far West.* 1931.

HART, A.B., ed.: *Commonwealth History of Massachusetts.* 5 vols. 1927-30.
HATCHER, HARLAN: *The Buckeye Country.* 1940.
HAVIGHURST, WALTER: *Land of Promise* (Old Northwest). 1946.
———. *Long Ships Passing.* 1942.
HAWTHORNE, DANIEL: *The Clipper Ship.* 1928.
HOBBS, SAMUEL H., JR.: *North Carolina, Economic and Social.* 1930.
HOLBROOK, STEWART H.: *Holy Old Mackinaw* (lumberjack history). 1938.
———. *Iron Brew* (history of iron industry). 1939.

JACKSON, JOSEPH H.: *Anybody's Gold.* 1941.
JEFFERSON, THOMAS: *Notes on the State of Virginia.* 1784.
JOHNSON, GUION G.: *Ante Bellum North Carolina; a Social History.* 1937.

KANE, HARNETT: *Natchez.* 1947.
KENNEDY, E.B.: *The Automobile Industry.* 1941.
KENNEDY, STETSON: *Southern Exposure.* 1946.
KULL, IRVING S., ed.: *New Jersey: A History.* 5 v. 1930. (American Historical Society.)

LAUT, AGNES C.: *Pathfinders of the West.* 1904.
LEIGHTON, GEORGE R.: *Five Cities.* 1939.
LEWIS, LLOYD & SMITH, HENRY J.: *Chicago: The History of its Reputation.* 1929.
LEWIS, OSCAR: *The Big Four (South Pacific Builders).* 1938.
LINCOLN, ANNA T.: *Wilmington, Delaware.* 1937.
LUMPKIN, KATHARINE: *The Making of a Southerner.* 1946.
LYMAN, GEORGE D.: *Saga of the Comstock Lode.* 1934.

MCWILLIAMS, CAREY: *Southern California Country.* 1946.
MASSIE, S.W. & CHRISTIAN, F.A.: *Homes and Gardens in Old Virginia.* 1931.
MILLER, MAX: *Reno.* 1941.
MOLLOY, ROBERT: *Charleston, a Gracious Heritage.* 1947.
MORGAN, DALE L.: *The Humboldt: Highroad of the West.* 1943.
MORISON, S.E.: *Maritime History of Massachusetts.* 1921.
MORTON, FREDERIC: *The Story of Winchester in Virginia.* 1925.
MUIR, JOHN: *The Mountains of California.* 1894.

NELSON, BRUCE: *Land of the Dakotahs.* 1946.
NEWMAN, C.W.: *Virginia, Economic & Civic.* 1933.
NICHOLSON, MEREDITH: *The Hoosiers.* 1900.

ODUM, HOWARD: *Race and Rumors of Race.* 1943.
———. *Southern Regions.* 1936.
OGG, FREDERIC A.: *The Old Northwest.* 1921.

PACIFIC COAST TRAILS CONFERENCE (Pasadena, Cal.): *Guides.*
PARKMAN, FRANCIS: *The Oregon Trail.* 1849.
PERCY, W.A.: *Lanterns on the Levee.* 1941.
PERRY, GEORGE S.: *Cities of America.* 1947.
PHILADELPHIA RAPID TRANSIT CO.: *The P.R. Traveler's Hiking Guide.* 1936.
PHILLIPS, U.B.: *Life and Labor in the South.* 1936.
POLLARD, LANCASTER: *A History of the State of Washington.* 1941.
PROVIDENCE JOURNAL CO.: *Almanac* (Rhode Island). Annual.

RANDOLPH, VANCE: *The Ozarks.* 1931.
ROBERTS, KENNETH: *Trending into Maine.* 1938.
ROTHERY, AGNES: *The New Dominion of Virginia.* 1940.
ROTHROCK, MARY U.: *Discovering Tennessee.* 1936.

SANBORN, FRANKLIN B.: *New Hampshire.* 1904.
SANCHEZ, GEORGE I.: *The Forgotten People, A Study of New Mexicans.* 1940.
SAXON, LYLE: *Fabulous New Orleans.* 1928.
———. *Old Louisiana.* 1929.
SCHAFER, JOSEPH: *A History of the Pacific Northwest.* 1942.

SCHARF, J.T.: *History of Delaware, 1609-1888*. 1888.

———. *History of Philadelphia, 1609-1884*. 1884.

SHEPPARD, MURIEL: *Cabins in the Laurel*. 1935.

SMITH, E.C. & THOMPSON, V.: *Traditionally Pennsylvania Dutch*. 1947.

SMITH, HENRY J.: *Chicago, a Portrait*. 1931.

STEED, HAL: *Georgia: Unfinished State*. 1942.

STEGNER, WALLACE: *Mormon Country*. 1942.

STEVENS, EILLIAM O.: *Charleston, Historic City of Gardens*. 1939.

STEWART, GEORGE: *Ordeal by Hunger (Donner Party)*. 1936.

STRUNSKY, SIMEON: *No Mean City (New York)*. 1944.

TALLANT, ROBERT: *Mardi Gras*. 1948.

THORNBOROUGH, LAURA: *The Great Smoky Mountains*. 1937.

VESTAL, STANLEY: *Mountain Men*. 1937.

WAINGER, B.M. & BAGLEY, E.B.: *Exploring New York State*. 1943.

WEBB, WALTER P.: *The Great Plains*. 1931.

———. *The Texas Rangers*. 1935.

WELLMAN, PAUL: *Story of the Cattle Range in America*. 1939.

WEYGANDT, CORNELIUS: *Philadelphia Folk*. 1938.

WHARTON, CLARENCE R.: *Texas Under Many Flags*. 1930.

WILLISON, GEORGE F.: *Here They Dug the Gold*. 1935.

WILSTACH, PAUL: *Tidewater Maryland*. 1931.

WYATT, EDWARD A.: *Along Petersburg Streets (Virginia)*. 1943.

# INDEX

Most points of interest in large cities have been listed in the index. For the less important points of interest, see each city. Points of interest belonging to definite categories—courthouses, churches, etc. —are listed alphabetically when they have a specific name—"Old South Church," or "Albemarle County Courthouse." When they have no specific name, they are listed by categories.

## — B —

## — C —

## — D —

## — E —

## — F —

## — G —

## —H—

## — I —

## — J —

## —K—

## — L —

## —M—

## — N —

## —O—

## — P —

## — Q —



## — R —

## — S —

## — U —

## —V—

## —W—

## — X —



## — Y —



## — Z —

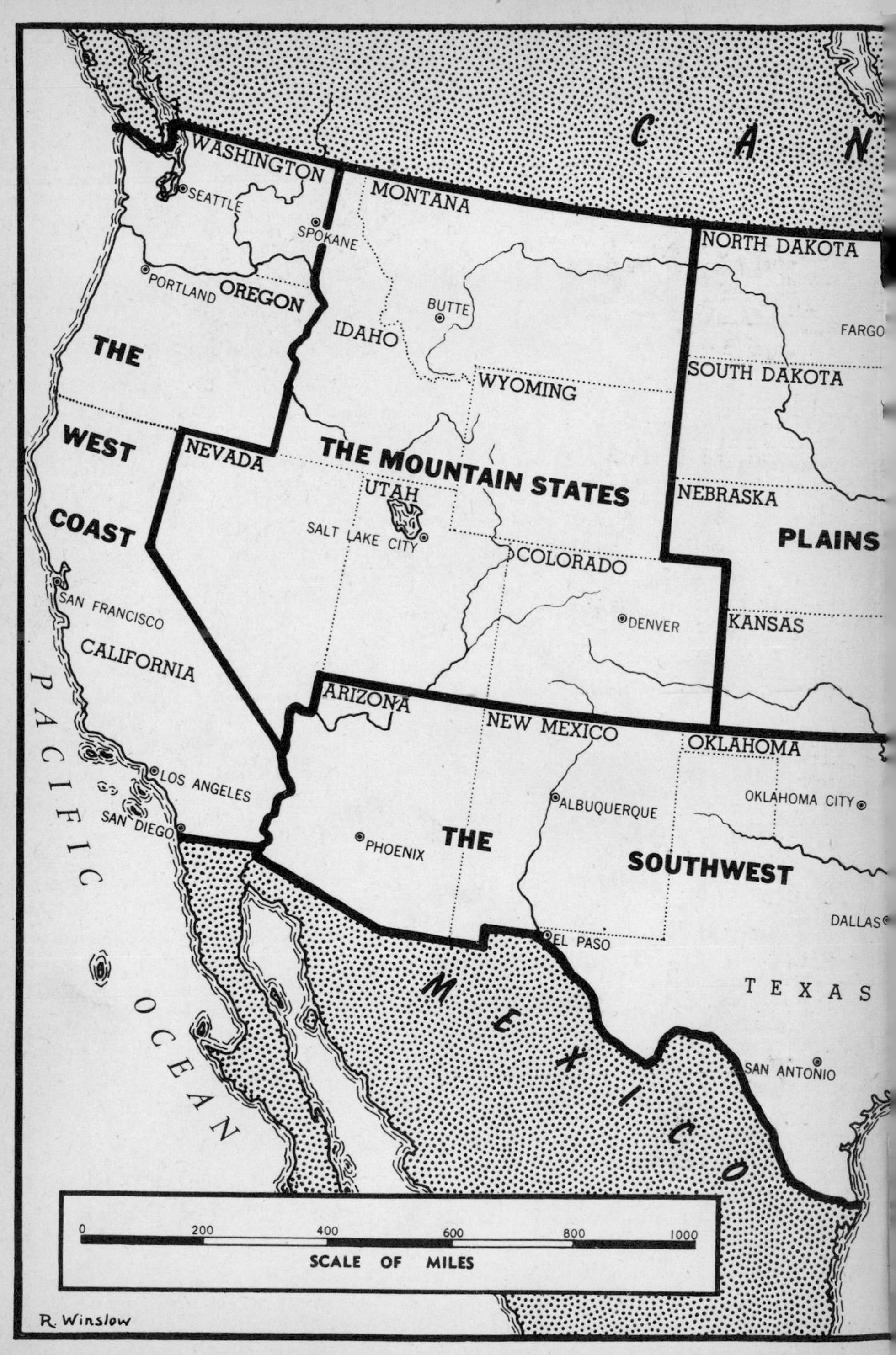
C A N
WASHINGTON
SEATTLE
SPOKANE
MONTANA
NORTH DAKOTA
PORTLAND
OREGON
BUTTE
IDAHO
FARGO
THE
SOUTH DAKOTA
WYOMING
WEST
NEVADA
THE MOUNTAIN STATES
UTAH
NEBRASKA
COAST
SALT LAKE CITY
COLORADO
PLAINS
SAN FRANCISCO
DENVER
KANSAS
CALIFORNIA
PACIFIC
ARIZONA
NEW MEXICO
OKLAHOMA
LOS ANGELES
ALBUQUERQUE
OKLAHOMA CITY
SAN DIEGO
PHOENIX
THE
SOUTHWEST
DALLAS
EL PASO
MEXICO
TEXAS
OCEAN
SAN ANTONIO
0
200
400
600
800
1000
SCALE OF MILES
R. Winslow